SUGGESTIONS FOR FAST, EFFECTIVE USE OF THE INDEX

1. PLEASE **READ THE FOREWORD** TO THE INDEX WHICH APPEARS IN THIS VOLUME.

2. STOP AND THINK ABOUT YOUR SUBJECT; TAKE A MOMENT TO **SELECT THE TERMS MOST DESCRIPTIVE OF YOUR RESEARCH SUBJECT.** IT HELPS TO SELECT THE PRINCIPAL SUBJECT RATHER THAN THE SECONDARY SUBJECT AND TO LOOK FOR NOUNS RATHER THAN ADJECTIVES.

3. IF YOUR SEARCH DOES NOT LEAD YOU TO THE CODE SECTION SOUGHT, OR IF YOU HAVE QUESTIONS ABOUT OR SUGGESTIONS FOR THE INDEX, PLEASE FEEL WELCOME TO **CONTACT THE INDEXERS.** THE INDEXERS MAY BE REACHED DIRECTLY BY THE FOLLOWING METHODS: **TOLL-FREE INDEX NUMBER, 1-800-897-7922,** BETWEEN 8:00 AM AND 4:30 PM, EASTERN TIME ZONE; **FAX NUMBER, 1-434-972-7686; INTERNET E-MAIL** ADDRESSED TO **lng-cho-indexing@lexisnexis.com.**

CODE OF VIRGINIA
1950

ANNOTATED

Prepared under the Supervision of

The Virginia Code Commission

BY

The Editorial Staff of the Publishers

Under the Direction of

SHARON BOWER AND JEAN KINDRICK

VOLUME 13

2013 REPLACEMENT VOLUME

LexisNexis®

701 E. Water St., Charlottesville, VA 22902

4922930

ISBN 978-0-7698-6324-5

www.lexisnexis.com

Customer Service: 1-800-833-9844

(Pub. 49005)

Foreword to the Index

This General Index, contained in two volumes (A-I and J-Z), cont legislation through the 2013 Special Session.

Included in the General Index is treatment of the laws compiled in the Code of Virginia, 1950, the constitutions of Virginia and the United States and the various rules of the state courts and state bar association, which are set out in Volume 11. Statutory provisions are referred to in the index by section number, e.g. §45.1-161.170.

The index is topical, meaning the main headings represent general concepts of law or specific statutory concepts. Additionally, certain main headings may be used where the material is known by a specific legal or common term, e.g. AMBER ALERT PROGRAM. Under this topical arrangement, each heading contains exhaustive treatment of the subject matter, using individual entries as well as cross references to related matters.

Below are a few general rules for use of this Index:

1) *Consult the principal and not the secondary subject.* For example, for information about motor vehicle registration, look under MOTOR VEHICLE REGISTRATION, and not under REGISTRATION.

2) *Consult related headings.* If your search for a heading or a sub-heading under a particular heading is to no avail, try a related topic. For example, if a search for "Inmates" under a particular heading proves fruitless, try looking for "Prisoners" or "Prisons and prisoners."

3) *Use cross references.* Cross references exist to direct you to the location where the subject matter you are seeking has been treated. Group section references (e.g. §§46.2-1500 to 46.2-1582) have been attached to many of our cross references as well as to many headings and sub-headings in the index. They provide the option of going directly to the statutes for the cited material, rather than delving deeper into the index.

4) *Use definitions to aid in your search.* Starting a search under the DEFINED TERMS heading presents a diverse sampling of statutory terminology which could suggest other headings to consult.

The index benefits from customer suggestions. Especially helpful are popular names or legal terms specific to your area of practice. We are grateful for your assistance in the ongoing improvement of the index. To contact the Indexing Department, you may use the following methods:

- Toll-free number, 1-800-897-7922, for assistance in locating material within the index, or to make comments or suggestions, or
- E-mail to lng-cho-indexing@lexisnexis.com.

For issues not directly related to the index, such as missing pages, ordering or other customer service information, you may contact Customer Service via a toll-free number, 1-800-833-9844, or by toll-free fax at 1-800-828-8341.

LexisNexis®

General Index

J

JACKASSES.
Animals generally.
See ANIMALS.
Liens on offspring, §§43-41, 43-42.

JACKPOT.
Charitable gaming.
General provisions, §§18.2-340.15 to 18.2-340.37.
See CHARITABLE GAMING.

JACKROCKS.
Manufacturing, distributing or possessing, §18.2-147.2.

JACKSON, GENERAL STONEWALL.
Lee-Jackson Day.
Legal holidays, §2.2-3300.

JAIL AUTHORITIES, §§53.1-95.2 to 53.1-95.24.
Article construction, §53.1-95.22.
Bonds.
Holder rights, §53.1-95.14.
Issuance of revenue bonds, §53.1-95.10.
Issuance of revenue refunding bonds, §53.1-95.16.
Sale proceeds, §53.1-95.13.
Trust agreements, §53.1-95.11.
Trustee rights, §53.1-95.14.
Charges for services, §53.1-95.12.
Conflict of laws, §53.1-95.24.
Construction of article, §53.1-95.22.
Creation, §53.1-95.2.
Required information, §53.1-95.4.
Defined terms, §53.1-95.3.
Design-build contracts, §53.1-95.18.
Director of finance.
Fiscal agent, §53.1-95.8:1.
Duties.
Rules and regulations, §53.1-95.20.
Exercise of power by governing body, §53.1-95.6.
Fiscal agents, §53.1-95.8:1.
Formation, §53.1-95.2.
Required information, §53.1-95.4.
Function, §53.1-95.17.
Funds, fiscal agents, §53.1-95.8:1.
Guards, §53.1-95.8.
Joinder of new subdivisions, §53.1-95.5.
Powers, §§53.1-95.7, 53.1-95.21.
Governing body to exercise, §53.1-95.6.
Purpose, §53.1-95.17.
Real property interests, §53.1-95.9.
Reimbursements by Commonwealth, §53.1-95.19.
Riverside regional jail authority, 1990 ch 726, 1993 ch 228, 1999 ch 642, 1999 ch 675.
Rules and regulations, §53.1-95.20.
Service charges, §53.1-95.12.
Severability, §53.1-95.23.
State reimbursements, §53.1-95.19.
Superintendents, §53.1-95.8.
Tax exemptions, §53.1-95.15.
Treasurer.
Fiscal agent, §53.1-95.8:1.

JAIL AUTHORITIES —Cont'd
Virginia retirement system.
Benefits provided to jail officers, §51.1-138.
Withdrawal from authority, §53.1-95.5.

JAIL INDUSTRY PROGRAMS, §§53.1-133.1 to 53.1-133.9.

JAIL OFFICERS.
Bonds, surety.
Blanket surety bond plan.
Risk management division, §2.2-1840.
Certification through training, §15.2-1706.
Criminal justice training academies, §§15.2-1747 to 15.2-1753.
See CRIMINAL JUSTICE TRAINING ACADEMIES.
Decertification, §15.2-1707.
Notice, §15.2-1708.
Immunity of employer for disclosure of information regarding former officers, §15.2-1709.
Jury service exemptions, §8.01-341.
Line of duty act, §§9.1-400 to 9.1-408.
Minimum qualifications for office, §15.2-1705.
Public safety medal of valor, §§9.1-800, 9.1-801.
Workers' compensation.
Employee defined, §65.2-101.

JAILS, §§53.1-68 to 53.1-133.9.
Alcoholic beverages, delivery to prisoners, §4.1-321.
Aliens, commitment, §§53.1-218 to 53.1-220.1.
Inquiries as to citizenship, §53.1-218.
Records pertaining to case, §53.1-219.
Transfers, §§53.1-220, 53.1-220.1.
Arrest warrants.
Execution of warrant by jail officer upon jail inmate, §§19.2-72, 19.2-76.
Authorities.
Generally, §§53.1-95.2 to 53.1-95.24.
See JAIL AUTHORITIES.
Riverside regional jail authority, 1990 ch 726, 1993 ch 228, 1999 ch 642, 1999 ch 675.
Burning or destroying occupied jail, §18.2-77.
Carnal knowledge of child detained in, §18.2-64.1.
Punishment upon conviction of certain subsequent felony sexual assault, §18.2-67.5:2.
Children taken into custody.
Carnal knowledge of detained child, §18.2-64.1.
Punishment upon conviction of certain subsequent felony sexual assault, §18.2-67.5:2.
Places of confinement for children, §16.1-249.
Placing child in jail, §16.1-247.
Violation of court orders, §16.1-292.
Child support.
Sentencing for failure to comply with obligation, §16.1-292.
Citizenship of inmate.
Jail officer to ascertain, §19.2-83.2.
City or town providing and operating, §15.2-1120.

JAILS —Cont'd
Civil commitment of mentally ill persons.
Persons with intellectual disability.
Jail confinement with criminals, prohibited, §37.2-832.
Transportation of admitted persons.
Detention in jail after order of admission, §37.2-831.
Clemency, §§53.1-229 to 53.1-231.
Commencement of term, §53.1-186.
Commitment of felons not placed in adult state correctional facility.
Compensation of local jails for costs of incarceration, §53.1-20.1.
Service of sentence in local correctional facilities, §53.1-20.
Communicable diseases.
Misdemeanants with, §53.1-22.
Prisoners with, §53.1-133.
Reports to transportation agencies, §32.1-116.3.
Communicable diseases of public health significance.
Isolation of certain persons, §§32.1-48.03, 32.1-48.04.
Communications by persons outside of jail with prisoners, §18.2-473.1.
Community corrections, §§9.1-173 to 9.1-183.
See COMMUNITY CORRECTIONS.
Community improvement projects.
Prisoners working on private property as part of.
Order, credit for working, §53.1-129.
Compensation from industry programs, §53.1-133.4.
Compensation of local jails for costs of incarceration of felons, §53.1-20.1.
Conduct records, §53.1-188.
Contagious diseases.
Isolation of certain persons, §§32.1-48.03, 32.1-48.04.
Misdemeanants with, §53.1-22.
Prisoners with, §53.1-133.
Reports to transportation agencies, §32.1-116.3.
Contraband.
Delivery of alcoholic beverages to prisoners, §4.1-321.
Delivery of articles to prisoners without authority, §18.2-474.
Delivery of drugs, firearms, etc., to prisoners, §18.2-474.1.
Corrections compact, interstate.
Director's authority, §53.1-217.
Form, §53.1-216.
Governor to execute, §53.1-216.
Costs of keeping prisoner, §53.1-131.3.
Contract for collection of fees owed, §53.1-127.5.
Installment or deferred payment agreements, §53.1-127.3.
Refusal to pay, suspension of privilege to operate motor vehicle, §§53.1-127.3, 53.1-127.4.
County and city jail farms, §§53.1-96 to 53.1-115.2.
See COUNTY AND CITY JAIL FARMS.
Court jails.
Utilization, §§53.1-72 to 53.1-79.1.
Credits.
Earned sentence credits.
Forfeiture and restoration, §53.1-189.
Time confined awaiting trial in addition to, §53.1-187.

JAILS —Cont'd
Credits —Cont'd
Good conduct, §53.1-116.
Felony offenses committed on or after January 1, 1995.
Inapplicability to sentence imposed upon conviction, §§53.1-197.1, 53.1-202.1.
Forfeiture, §53.1-189.
Persons confined on or after July 1, 1981, §§53.1-198 to 53.1-202.
Persons confined prior to July 1, 1981, §§53.1-192 to 53.1-197.
Restoration, §53.1-189.
Prisoners working on governmental property, certain private property or nonprofit organization property, §53.1-129.
Time confined awaiting trial, §53.1-187.
Youthful offender facilities, §53.1-67.
Crimes by prisoners, §§53.1-203 to 53.1-205.
Felonies, §§53.1-203, 53.1-204.
Foreign crimes, §53.1-208.
Trial, §53.1-205.
Damaged property.
Payment by inmate, §53.1-228.1.
Defendants, prisoners as.
Foreign prisoners, §53.1-209.
Surrender certification, §53.1-206.
Transportation costs, §53.1-207.
Defined terms, §53.1-1.
Appropriate court.
Agreement on detainers, §53.1-211.
Capital costs.
Reimbursements by Commonwealth, §53.1-82.2.
Financing costs.
Reimbursements by Commonwealth, §53.1-82.2.
Jail authorities, §53.1-95.3.
Jail industry program, §53.1-133.1.
Reasonable costs.
Pay for prisoners from other localities, §53.1-91.
Delivery of articles to prisoners without authority, §18.2-474.
Drugs, firearms, explosives, etc., §18.2-474.1.
Dental care.
Emergency medical, dental and psychiatric care for local prisoners.
Compact, authority of state to enter, §53.1-133.10.
Detainer agreement, §§53.1-210 to 53.1-215.
Appropriate court.
Defined, §53.1-211.
Central administrator.
Designation, §53.1-215.
Cooperation in enforcement, §53.1-212.
Enactment, §53.1-210.
Escape of detained person, §53.1-213.
Facility officers.
Powers and duties, §53.1-214.
Information agent.
Designation, §53.1-215.
Discharges.
Allowances, transportation and clothing, §53.1-190.
Crime victims notification, §53.1-133.02.
Identification card for those without government-issued identification, §53.1-116.1:02.
Drivers' licenses.
Suspension or nonrenewal of license for nonpayment of fees to local correctional facilities or jails, §46.2-320.2.
Drugs, delivery to prisoners, §18.2-474.1.

JAILS —Cont'd
Earned sentence credits.
Credit for time confined awaiting trial in addition to, §53.1-187.
Forfeiture and restoration, §53.1-189.
Eligibility of inmate for parole.
Persons sentenced for more than 12 months, §53.1-153.
Eligibility to participate in industry programs, §53.1-133.3.
Emergency medical, dental and psychiatric care for local prisoners.
Compact, authority of state to enter, §53.1-133.10.
Escape, §§18.2-473 to 18.2-480.1.
See ESCAPE.
Escape of convict, notice to state police, §53.1-116.1.
Establishment of industry programs, §53.1-133.2.
Executive clemency, §§53.1-229 to 53.1-231.
Explosives, delivery to prisoners, §18.2-474.1.
Extradition of criminals.
Confinement in jail when necessary, §19.2-97.
Farms, county and city, §§53.1-96 to 53.1-115.2.
See COUNTY AND CITY JAIL FARMS.
Fees for costs of keeping prisoner, §53.1-131.3.
Contract for collection of fees owed, §53.1-127.5.
Installment or deferred payment agreement for unpaid fees, §53.1-127.3.
Refusal to pay, suspension of privilege to operate motor vehicle, §§53.1-127.3, 53.1-127.4.
Felons not placed in adult state correctional facility.
Service of sentence in local correctional facilities, §53.1-20.
Compensation of local jails for costs of incarceration, §53.1-20.1.
Fine payments to jailers, §53.1-116.
Firearms, delivery to prisoners, §18.2-474.1.
Funding, §§53.1-80 to 53.1-95.1.
Approval of projects, §53.1-82.1.
Construction of local facilities, §53.1-80.
Budgeting schedule, §53.1-82.3.
Gubernatorial limitations on expenditures, §53.1-95.1.
Reimbursement methods, §53.1-82.2.
Construction of regional facilities, §53.1-81.
Budgeting schedule, §53.1-82.3.
Gubernatorial limitations on expenditures, §53.1-95.1.
Reimbursement methods, §53.1-82.2.
Establishment of program, §9.1-174.
Examination of books, §53.1-88.
Jail farms, §53.1-95.
Limitations on use of state appropriations for operating costs, §53.1-86.
Operating costs.
State appropriations.
Gubernatorial limitations, §53.1-95.1.
How determined, §53.1-83.1.
Payment times and manner, §53.1-85.
Use, §53.1-84.
Limitations, §53.1-86.
Pay for prisoners from other localities.
Disposition of money, §53.1-92.
Project approval, §53.1-82.1.
Regional jailing, §§53.1-81, 53.1-82.
Budgeting schedule, §53.1-82.3.
Gubernatorial limitations on expenditures, §53.1-95.1.
Maintenance costs, §53.1-87.

JAILS —Cont'd
Funding —Cont'd
Regional jailing —Cont'd
Pay for prisoners from other localities, §53.1-91.
Reimbursement methods, §53.1-82.2.
Temporary guards, §53.1-93.
Payment, §53.1-94.
United States prisoners, §53.1-90.
Disposition of money, §53.1-92.
Furloughs.
Work release, §53.1-132.
Good conduct allowances, §53.1-116.
Felony offenses committed on or after January 1, 1995.
Inapplicability to sentence imposed upon conviction, §§53.1-197.1, 53.1-202.1.
Forfeiture, §53.1-189.
Persons committed on or after July 1, 1981, §§53.1-198 to 53.1-202.
Application, §53.1-199.
Choice of system, §53.1-198.
Classification system, §53.1-201.
Conditions, §53.1-200.
Eligibility, §53.1-199.
Persons committed prior to July 1, 1981, §§53.1-192 to 53.1-197.
Article applicability, §53.1-192.
Career education, §53.1-197.
Credits earned prior to 1944, §53.1-195.
Educational training credits, §53.1-197.
Persons convicted after October 1, 1942, §53.1-196.
Persons convicted prior to October 1, 1942, §§53.1-193, 53.1-194.
Technical education, §53.1-197.
Restoration, §53.1-189.
Time confined awaiting trial, §53.1-187.
Youthful offender facilities, §53.1-67.
Governing body of county and city to provide, §15.2-1638.
Guards summoned or employed by jailer on order of court.
Payment of salaries and expenses, §19.2-328.
Health inspections, §53.1-68.
Home/electronic incarceration program, §53.1-131.2.
Immigration alien inquiry, §53.1-218.
Improper release of prisoners, §53.1-116.3.
Industry programs, §§53.1-133.1 to 53.1-133.9.
Artistic products, §53.1-133.7.
Charges, §53.1-133.9.
Collection of money, §53.1-133.5.
Compensation, §53.1-133.4.
Defined, §53.1-133.1.
Eligibility to participate, §53.1-133.3.
Established, §53.1-133.2.
Expenses, §53.1-133.5.
Marketing, §53.1-133.9.
Purchases by Commonwealth, localities and nonprofit organization, §53.1-133.8.
Sale restrictions on goods and services, §53.1-133.6.
Inmate payment for damaged property, §53.1-228.1.
Inspection of funding records, §53.1-88.
Intentional infliction of bodily injury by inmate.
Payment for injury by inmate, §53.1-133.01:1.
Interstate corrections compact.
Director's authority, §53.1-217.
Form, §53.1-216.

JAILS —Cont'd
Interstate corrections compact —Cont'd
Governor to execute, §53.1-216.
Jury service.
Exemption of superintendents and jail officers of regional jails, §8.01-341.
Juvenile detention and other care facilities generally, §§16.1-315 to 16.1-322.7.
See JUVENILE DETENTION AND OTHER CARE FACILITIES.
Juveniles taken into custody.
Carnal knowledge of child, §18.2-64.1.
Punishment upon conviction of certain subsequent felony sexual assault, §18.2-67.5:2.
Places of confinement, §16.1-249.
Placing child in jail, §16.1-247.
Violations of court orders, §16.1-292.
Magistrates.
Power to incarcerate persons, §19.2-45.
Marijuana, delivery to prisoners, §18.2-474.1.
Accommodation distribution to inmates, §18.2-248.1.
Medical and mental health information exchange, §53.1-133.03.
Medical treatment programs for prisoners, §53.1-133.01.
Emergency medical, dental and psychiatric care for local prisoners.
Compact, authority of state to enter, §53.1-133.10.
Payment for bodily injury.
Intentional infliction on any person by inmate, §53.1-133.01:1.
Mental health.
Emergency medical, dental and psychiatric care for local prisoners.
Compact, authority of state to enter, §53.1-133.10.
Psychiatric hospitalization of defendant prior to trial or sentencing, §19.2-169.6.
Military personnel.
Mental health and rehabilitation services support program, establishment, §2.2-2001.1.
Misdemeanants with contagious diseases, §53.1-22.
Misdemeanors, place of punishment, §18.2-15.
Name change by prisoner.
Crime victims notification, §53.1-133.02.
Nonconsecutive days in jail, §53.1-131.1.
Nonprofit organization property.
Prisoners working on.
Order, credit for working, §53.1-129.
Notice of intake of prisoners, §53.1-116.1:01.
Notice of release of prisoners, §53.1-116.1.
Officers.
See JAIL OFFICERS.
Overcrowding.
Compensation for incarceration in jails, §53.1-20.1.
Parole generally.
See PAROLE AND POSTRELEASE SUPERVISION.
Performance of institutional work assignments.
Granting additional good conduct credit allowance, §53.1-116.
Priority of receiving prisoners into state corrections system from local correctional facilities.
Determination by director of department of corrections, §53.1-20.

JAILS —Cont'd
Prisoner intake notice, §53.1-116.1:01.
Prisoner programs and treatment, §§53.1-128 to 53.1-133.
Contagious diseases, prisoners with, §53.1-133.
Defined terms, §53.1-131.
Home/electronic incarceration program, §53.1-131.2.
Medical programs, §53.1-133.01.
Payment for bodily injury.
Intentional infliction on any person by inmate, §53.1-133.01:1.
Nonconsecutive days in jail, §53.1-131.1.
Work forces, §§53.1-128, 53.1-129.
Interests in property by jailors, §53.1-130.
Work release, §53.1-131.
Furloughs, §53.1-132.
Prisoner release notice, §53.1-116.1.
Prisoners as defendants.
Foreign crimes, §53.1-208.
Foreign prisoners, §53.1-209.
Transportation costs, §53.1-207.
Prisoners as witnesses.
Civil action, §8.01-410.
Foreign prisoners, §53.1-209.
Surrender certification, §53.1-206.
Transportation costs, §53.1-207.
Prisoner transfers into and between correctional facilities, §53.1-21.
Probation officer arrests.
Warrantless arrest statements, §53.1-149.
Processing fee, §15.2-1613.1.
Property damage.
Inmate payments for intentionally damaged property, §53.1-228.1.
Psychiatric care for local prisoners.
Emergency medical, dental and psychiatric care for local prisoners.
Compact, authority of state to enter, §53.1-133.10.
Psychiatric hospitalization of defendant prior to trial or sentencing, §19.2-169.6.
Public building authority.
Jail projects, powers and duties, §2.2-2263.
Recordkeeping requirements of jailers, §53.1-116.
Records.
Exchange of medical and mental health information, §53.1-133.03.
Refusing to receive prisoners, §18.2-476.
Regional jails, §§53.1-105 to 53.1-115.2.
Construction.
Funding of construction of regional facilities, §53.1-81.
Budgeting schedule, §53.1-82.3.
Gubernatorial limitations on expenditures, §53.1-95.1.
Reimbursement methods, §53.1-82.2.
Established, §53.1-105.
Expenses, §53.1-112.
Prisoner transportation, §53.1-114.
Reimbursement, §53.1-114.
Fiscal agents, §53.1-109.1.
Funding, §§53.1-80 to 53.1-95.1.
Governance, §53.1-106.
Expenses of members, §53.1-108.
Organization of board, §53.1-107.
Reports, §53.1-107.
Jail officers.
Authority, §53.1-109.
Bonds, §53.1-110.

JAILS —Cont'd
Regional jails —Cont'd
Jail officers —Cont'd
Conflicts of interest, §53.1-109.2.
Oaths, §53.1-110.
Virginia retirement system benefits provided, §51.1-138.
Weapons.
Authority to carry, §53.1-109.01.
Location, §53.1-106.1.
Maintenance costs, §53.1-87.
Medical personnel.
Salaries, §53.1-115.
Prisoner work requirements, §53.1-111.
Private construction and operation, §§53.1-71.1 to 53.1-71.6.
Criminal laws.
Applicability, §53.1-71.3.
Limitations, §53.1-71.1.
Non-delegable powers and duties, §53.1-71.4.
Regulations.
Promulgation by board, §53.1-71.5.
Reimbursement by state to localities, §53.1-71.6.
Requirements, §53.1-71.1.
Security employees.
Authority, §53.1-71.2.
Processing fee, §15.2-1613.1.
Release of prisoners, §53.1-105.
Stores, §53.1-115.2.
Superintendents.
Authority, §53.1-109.
Bonds, §53.1-110.
Conflicts of interest, §53.1-109.2.
Oaths, §53.1-110.
Reports, §53.1-115.1.
Salaries, §53.1-115.
Transfer of prisoners, §53.1-105.
Virginia retirement system.
Benefits provided to jail officers, §51.1-138.
Release of prisoner.
Identification card for those without government-issued identification, §53.1-116.1:02.
Improper release, §53.1-116.3.
Notice, §53.1-116.1.
Crime victims, §53.1-133.02.
Sheriffs' duties, §§15.2-1609, 53.1-116 to 53.1-127.1.
Citizenship inquiry, §53.1-218.
Contract for collection of fees owed, §53.1-127.5.
Courthouse security, §§53.1-119, 53.1-120.
Crime victims notification, §53.1-133.02.
Failure to comply with requirements of board, §53.1-125.
Fine payments by prisoners, §53.1-116.
Fines imposed upon sheriffs, §53.1-118.
Good conduct credits, §53.1-116.
Home/electronic incarceration program, §53.1-131.2.
Improper release of prisoners, §53.1-116.3.
Industry programs, §§53.1-133.1 to 53.1-133.9.
Installment or deferred payment agreement for unpaid fees, §53.1-127.3.
Keeper of jails, §53.1-116.2.
Provisions for prisoners, §53.1-126.
Receipt of persons committed by court orders, §53.1-119.
Recordkeeping requirements, §§53.1-116, 53.1-123.
Daily tally of prisoners, §53.1-122.
Rules' violations, §53.1-117.

JAILS —Cont'd
Sheriffs' duties —Cont'd
Reports, §53.1-121.
Court requested, §53.1-124.
Stores, §53.1-127.1.
Telephone services.
Fees considered public funds, §53.1-127.1.
Urban county executive form of government, §15.2-836.
Visitors, §53.1-127.
Fees for electronic visitation or messaging, §53.1-127.2.
Work release, §53.1-131.
Spousal support.
Sentencing for failure to comply with obligation, §16.1-292.
Standards for facilities and personnel, §53.1-68.
Health inspections, §53.1-68.
State or local property.
Prisoners working on.
Order, credit for working, §53.1-129.
Substandard facilities.
Prisoner confinement limitations and transfers, §53.1-69.
Support of child or spouse.
Sentencing for failure to comply with obligation, §16.1-292.
Towns.
City or town providing and operating jails, §15.2-1120.
Town jail utilization, §53.1-73.
Transfer of prisoners into and between correctional facilities, §53.1-21.
Crime victims notification, §53.1-133.02.
Unemployment compensation.
Benefits.
Eligibility, §60.2-612.
Utilization, §§53.1-72 to 53.1-79.1.
Court jails, §53.1-72.
Adoption of another jail, §53.1-74.
Jurisdiction of judges or justices, §53.1-77.
Procedure after, §53.1-75.
Commitment to another jail, §53.1-76.
Jurisdiction of judges or justices, §53.1-77.
Use of another jail, §53.1-74.
Court of appeals jail, §53.1-78.
Supreme court jails, §53.1-78.
Town jails, §53.1-73.
Transfers, §53.1-79.1.
United States prisoners, §53.1-79.
Veterans services.
Mental health and rehabilitation services support program, establishment, §2.2-2001.1.
Visitation.
Fees for electronic visitation or messaging, §53.1-127.2.
Sheriffs' duties, §53.1-127.
Weapons.
Regional jails.
Officers.
Authority to carry weapons, §53.1-109.01.
Witnesses, inmates as.
Civil action, §8.01-410.
Foreign prisoners, §53.1-209.
Surrender certification, §53.1-206.
Transportation costs, §53.1-207.
Workers' compensation.
Reporting of imprisonment, §65.2-712.
Suspension of benefits, §65.2-510.1.
Work forces, §§53.1-128, 53.1-129.
Jailor interest in property, §53.1-130.

JAILS —Cont'd
Work release, §53.1-131.
Crime victims notification, §53.1-133.02.
Furloughs, §53.1-132.

JAMES CITY COUNTY.
Agricultural and forestal districts.
County executive form and certain other counties, §§15.2-4400 to 15.2-4407.
Circuit court, establishment, §17.1-500.
Keeping of docket books, §8.01-446.
Coastal primary sand dunes and beaches.
Zoning ordinances, §28.2-1403.
Cutting grass or lawn area of residential real property.
Requiring owner of occupied property, §15.2-1215.
Department of real estate assessment.
Establishment and agreement to establish joint department, §58.1-3274.
Former officers and employees.
Restrictions on activities, §15.2-1408.
Grand jury.
Selection of jurors from county and City of Williamsburg, §19.2-194.
Grass, weeds, other foreign growth on occupied or vacant property.
Cutting by property owners, ordinance prescribing, §15.2-901.
Joint court system with city of Williamsburg.
Removal, approval of electorate required.
Inapplicability of provisions, §15.2-1646.
Parking on secondary highways, §46.2-1222.
Port of Virginia economic and infrastructure development zone grant fund, §62.1-132.3:2.
Public service corporations, taxation of property.
Restriction of imposition of additional tax, §58.1-2606.
Real property taxes.
Special assessment for land preservation.
Additional provisions concerning zoning classification, §58.1-3237.1.
Retail sales and use tax.
Additional sales tax for Northern Virginia and Hampton Roads, §58.1-603.1.
Additional use tax for Northern Virginia and Hampton Roads, §58.1-604.01.
School board.
Salary of members, §22.1-32.
Transient occupancy tax.
Additional tax, rate, revenues, disposition, §58.1-3823.
Disposition of revenues, §58.1-3819.
Well abandonment ordinance.
Duty of owner to cap or close well.
Locality adopting ordinance, §32.1-176.5.
Well construction.
Standards, §32.1-176.4.
Testing requirements, §32.1-176.5.

JAMES MADISON UNIVERSITY, §§23-164.1 to 23-164.10.
Board of visitors, §§23-164.1 to 23-164.6.
Campus police departments, §§23-232 to 23-238.
Reporting campus crime, §23-9.1:1.
Coastal energy research consortium, §§67-600 to 67-604.
Conferring of degrees, §23-164.8.
Corporate name, §23-164.1.
Easements.
Granting easements over university property, §23-164.10.

JAMES MADISON UNIVERSITY —Cont'd
Payroll and other transactions.
Processing, §2.2-803.1.
Special license plates, §46.2-749.
Teacher curriculum, §23-164.9.
Transfer of property, §23-164.2.
Tuition, fees and other charges, §23-164.7.
Universities generally, §§23-1.01 to 23-9.2:8.
See COLLEGES AND UNIVERSITIES.

JAMES RIVER.
Basin.
Preparation of plans and programs for management, §62.1-44.38.
Crossings.
Newport News to Isle of Wight county, §28.2-555.
Dams.
Restrictions, §29.1-532.
Fences.
River as lawful fence restriction, §55-302.
Fish passage grant and revolving loan fund.
Requirement for fishways, §29.1-101.9.
Historic falls.
Scenic river, §10.1-412.
Historic lower James river, §10.1-419.
Declaration as state historic river, §10.1-419.
Hunting area.
Bosher dam to interstate 95 bridge, §29.1-610.
Oysters.
Dredging, §28.2-518.
Patent tongs.
Area prohibitions, §28.2-508.
Planting grounds.
Riparian oyster planting grounds.
Assignments, §28.2-602.
Seed oysters.
Permits to buy or carry, §28.2-535.
Rivers generally.
See RIVERS.
Scenic river, §10.1-413.
Waters of the state generally.
See WATERS OF THE STATE.

JAMES RIVER BASIN.
Preparation of plans and programs for management, §62.1-44.38.

JAMESTOWN.
400th anniversary of founding of Jamestown.
License plates commemorating anniversary, §46.2-749.2:13.
Tourism authority, duty to promote, §2.2-2318.

JAMESTOWN-YORKTOWN COMMISSION.
Secretary of education.
Agency responsibility, §2.2-208.

JAMESTOWN-YORKTOWN FOUNDATION, §§23-287 to 23-290.
Administration of historical museums, §23-287.
Adoption of regulations, §23-289.
Board of trustees, §23-287.
Closed meetings, §2.2-3711.
Continuation of foundation, §23-287.
Debts and obligations, authority to contract, §23-290.
Duties of foundation, §23-288.
Employees.
Personnel administration system, exemptions, §2.2-2905.
Payment of debts and obligations, §23-290.
Powers of foundation, §23-288.
Procurement.
Exceptions to competitive procurement, §2.2-4345.

JAMESTOWN-YORKTOWN FOUNDATION —Cont'd
Violation of foundation regulations.
Request of person to leave property.
Trespass for failure to leave, §23-289.

JAYCEES.
Special license plates for members, §46.2-746.7.

JAYWALKING, §46.2-923.

JEFFERSON NATIONAL FOREST.
ABC mixed beverage licenses.
Establishments on property, §4.1-126.

JEOPARDIZED COLLECTION OF LOTTERY MONEY OR PROCEEDS, §58.1-4021.

JEOPARDY ASSESSMENTS.
Forest products tax.
Absconding taxpayer, §58.1-1616.
Income tax, §58.1-313.
Lien of jeopardy assessment, §58.1-314.
Withholding, §58.1-473.
Retail sales and use tax, §58.1-631.

JET FUEL.
Fuel taxes, §§58.1-2200 to 58.1-2299.20.
See FUEL TAXES.

JETSAM, §§55-202 to 55-210.

JET SKIING UNDER THE INFLUENCE, §§29.1-738 to 29.1-738.6.

JET SKIS.
Instruction by rental agents of personal watercraft, §29.1-749.2.
Insurance on rented personal watercraft, §29.1-749.3.
Owner of personal watercraft permitting violations, §29.1-749.
Personal watercraft defined, §29.1-700.
Reckless operation of personal watercraft, §29.1-738.03.
Restrictions on operating.
Personal watercraft, §29.1-748.
Safety education course required prior to renting personal watercraft, §29.1-736.

JEWELRY.
Personal property taxes.
Classification, §58.1-3504.

JMU, §§23-164.1 to 23-164.10.
See JAMES MADISON UNIVERSITY.

JOB CREATION.
Governor's development opportunity fund.
New jobs, requirements, §2.2-115.
Green job creation tax credit.
Corporate income tax, §58.1-439.12:05.
Major business facility job tax credit, §58.1-439.
Small business new jobs and retraining programs, §2.2-1614.
Small business new jobs and retraining programs (eff until 1/1/2014), §2.2-904.01.
Virginia new jobs program, §2.2-1612.
Virginia new jobs program (eff until 1/1/2014), §2.2-903.2.

JOB TRAINING.
Community services for persons with disabilities.
Generally.
See DISABILITY OR HANDICAP.
Virginia jobs investment program, §2.2-1611.

JOB TRAINING —Cont'd
Virginia jobs investment program (eff until 1/1/2014), §2.2-903.1.
Vocational rehabilitation for persons with disabilities.
Generally.
See DISABILITY OR HANDICAP.
Worker retraining tax credit, §58.1-439.6.
Workforce retraining program, §2.2-1613.
Workforce retraining program (eff until 1/1/2014), §2.2-904.

JOCKEYS.
Bribery of jockeys, §59.1-399.
Crimes and offenses.
Transmitting jockey change information, §59.1-397.
Permits, §59.1-387.

JOHN DOE ACTIONS.
Owner or operator of vehicle causing injury or damage unknown, §38.2-2206.

JOHNSON GRASS.
Noxious weed control.
Counties, cities or towns, §15.2-902.

JOINDER.
Assignments.
Suit against joint assignors, §8.01-14.
Child custody proceeding.
Uniform child custody jurisdiction and enforcement act.
Laws of Commonwealth applicable, §20-146.16.
Circuit courts.
Joinder of parties.
Civil actions, VA SCt Rule 3:12.
Third party claims, VA SCt Rule 3:13.
Death or change of parties, §8.01-16.
Defendants, §19.2-262.1.
Insurance companies.
Limitation on joinder, §8.01-5.
John Doe owners or operators of motor vehicles, §38.2-2206.
Minors.
Joinder of action of tort to infant.
Action for recovery of expenses incurred, §8.01-36.
Multiple claimant litigation, §§8.01-267.1 to 8.01-267.9.
See PARTIES.
Ongoing litigation.
Later-filed actions.
Multiple claimant litigations, §8.01-267.7.
Parties.
Civil actions, VA SCt Rule 3:12.
Pleading tort and contract claims.
Separate trial in discretion of court, §8.01-272.
Tenants in common, §8.01-10.
Tort action to infant.
Action for recovery of expenses incurred, §8.01-36.
Venue improperly laid, §8.01-264.

JOINT ACCOUNTS.
Child support enforcement.
Service of lien or order to withhold on financial institution.
Support debtor's interest in account, §63.2-1931.
Multiple-party accounts.
Generally, §§6.2-604 to 6.2-620.
See MULTIPLE-PARTY ACCOUNTS.

JOINT AND SEVERAL LIABILITY.
Condominiums.
Declarant's obligation to complete and restore, §55-79.67.

JOINT AND SEVERAL LIABILITY —Cont'd
Condominiums —Cont'd
Special declarant rights.
Transfers, §55-79.74:3.
Subdivision of units, §55-79.70.
Credit union loans to credit committee members, §6.2-1373.
Delinquent local treasurers.
Treasurer and sureties, §58.1-3172.
Dental or optometric services plans, liability of participants, §38.2-4505.
Executions on joint judgments, §8.01-469.
Health services plans, liability of participants, §38.2-4210.
Income tax on corporations.
Affiliated corporations included in consolidated returns, §58.1-444.
Judicial sales.
Rule against special commissioner, purchaser, etc., for judgment for amounts due, §8.01-106.
Legal services plans, liability of participants, §38.2-4404.
Negotiable instruments, §8.3A-116.
Discharge of endorsers and accommodation parties, §8.3A-605.
Nonprofit corporation preincorporation transactions.
Persons acting as or on behalf of corporation, §13.1-821.
Real estate cooperatives.
Special declarant rights, transfers of, §55-461.
Security regulation violations, civil liability, §13.1-522.
Spousal liability for emergency medical care, §8.01-220.2.
Support of parents by children, §20-88.
Tobacco products manufacturers' responsibilities.
Nonparticipating manufacturers, §3.2-4208.1.

JOINT COMMISSION ON ADMINISTRATIVE RULES.
Definitions, §30-73.1.
Members, §30-73.2.
Powers and duties, §30-73.3.
Purpose, §30-73.1.
Staff assistance, §30-73.4.
Terms of office, §30-73.2.

JOINT COMMISSIONS.
Health care, §§30-168 to 30-170.
Legislative audit and review, §§30-56 to 30-63.
Transportation accountability, §§30-282 to 30-286.

JOINT CONTRACTORS.
Creditor compounding or compromising with and releasing from liability, §11-10.
Crediting contract, §11-11.
Right of contribution not affected, §11-13.

JOINT CUSTODY.
Court may order, §20-124.2.
Defined, §20-124.1.

JOINT EXERCISE OF POWERS BY POLITICAL SUBDIVISIONS, §§15.2-1300 to 15.2-1302.

JOINT GOVERNMENT PURCHASING.
Regional cooperation act, §15.2-4207.

JOINT GOVERNMENT SERVICE DELIVERY.
Regional cooperation act, §15.2-4207.

JOINT LEGISLATIVE AUDIT AND REVIEW COMMISSION, §§30-56 to 30-63.
Administrative process act.
Review of exemptions, §2.2-4005.
Advisory committees, §30-61.
Auditor of public accounts.
Assumption of duties by commission.
Failure of auditor to perform duties, §30-142.
Relationship to commission, §30-60.
Vacancy in office while general assembly not in session.
Appointment of successor, §30-130.
College savings plan oversight, §§30-330 to 30-335.
Creation, §30-56.
Director, §30-57.
Duties, §30-58.1.
Expense payments, §30-63.
Members, §30-56.
Office space, §30-56.
Powers, §30-58.1.
Quorum, §30-56.
Staff, §30-57.
State agencies.
Analysis of budget submissions, §30-58.4.
Defined, §30-59.1.
Furnishing information and assistance, §30-59.
State spending, report on, §30-58.3.
Supplemental studies and reports, §30-58.2.
Virginia college savings plan oversight, §§30-330 to 30-335.
Voting on recommendations, §30-56.

JOINT LOCAL PLANNING COMMISSION, §15.2-2219.

JOINTLY REGISTERED SECURITIES, §§13.1-434 to 13.1-436.

JOINT OBLIGORS.
Creditor compounding or compromising with and releasing from liability, §11-10.
Crediting contract, §11-11.
Right of contribution not affected, §11-13.

JOINT REINSURANCE ORGANIZATIONS, §38.2-1915.
Examination of, §38.2-1925.
Workers' compensation, automobile, home protection, etc., rates, §38.2-2002.

JOINT SCHOOLS, §22.1-26.

JOINT STOCK COMPANIES.
Fraudulent entries by officers or clerks, §18.2-113.
Unclaimed property, disposition of, §55-210.6:2.
Property of dissolved associations, §55-210.7.
Records, §§55-210.24 to 55-210.24:2.
Refunds, §55-210.6:2.

JOINT TENANTS.
Accounting in equity, §8.01-31.
Corporate securities registered in joint names with right of survivorship, §§13.1-434 to 13.1-436.
Disclaimer of property interests.
Disclaimer of rights of survivorship in jointly held property, §64.2-2605.
Divorce from bond of matrimony.
Extinguishment of tenancy, §20-111.
Ejectment.
General provisions, §§8.01-131 to 8.01-165.
See EJECTMENT.

JOINT TENANTS —Cont'd
Homestead exemption of householder.
Partition or sale, §34-8.
Multiple-party accounts, §§6.2-604 to 6.2-620.
See MULTIPLE-PARTY ACCOUNTS.
Murderers barred from claiming property rights of decedent, §64.2-2503.
Ownership of real or personal property as, §55-20.1.
Partition of land.
Generally, §§8.01-81 to 8.01-93.
See PARTITION OF LAND.
Partnerships.
Determining whether partnership established, §50-73.88.
Real property tax lien on jointly owned real estate, §58.1-3343.
Shares of corporations, voting entitlement, §13.1-662.
Survivorship, §55-20.
Disclaimer of rights of survivorship in jointly held property, §64.2-2605.
Exceptions, §55-21.
TOD security registration.
Multiple owners of security registered in beneficiary form, §64.2-613.
Waste, §55-212.

JOINT TORTFEASORS.
Contribution among tortfeasors.
When enforced, §8.01-34.
Effect of judgment against new parties, §8.01-444.
Effect of judgment against one, §8.01-443.

JOINT UNDERWRITING ASSOCIATIONS, §38.2-1915.
Basic property insurance, §§38.2-2700 to 38.2-2713.
Commercial liability insurance, §§38.2-2900 to 38.2-2913.
Examination of, §38.2-1925.
Medical malpractice, §§38.2-2800 to 38.2-2814.
Workers' compensation, automobiles, home protection, etc., rates, §38.2-2002.

JOINT VENTURES.
Banks.
Limitations on entering into, §13.1-627.
Nonprofit corporations.
Limitation on power to enter into, §13.1-826.
Corporations.
Powers to enter into, §13.1-627.
Credit unions.
Limitations on entering into, §13.1-627.
Nonprofit corporations.
Limitations on powers to enter into, §13.1-826.
Insurance companies.
Limitations on entering into, §13.1-627.
Nonprofit corporations.
Limitation on powers of entering into, §13.1-826.
Interest.
Usury.
Prohibited from pleading, §6.2-308.
Nonprofit corporations.
Powers to enter into, §13.1-826.
Public service companies.
Limitations on entering into, §13.1-627.
Railroad corporations.
Entering into, §13.1-627.

JOINT VENTURES —Cont'd
Savings and loan associations.
Limitations on entering into, §13.1-627.
Nonprofit corporations.
Limitations on powers to enter into, §13.1-826.
Usury.
Prohibited from pleading, §6.2-308.
Virginia Commonwealth University health system authority.
Authority to participate, §23-50.16:14.

JORDAN STATE SCENIC RIVER, §10.1-418.7.

JOURNAL BOXES OF RAILROADS.
Taking or removing waste or packing from, §18.2-156.

JOURNALS.
Congress, US Const Art I §§5, 7.
General assembly, VA Const Art IV §10.

JOYRIDING, §18.2-102.
Bona fide repossession under lien.
Inapplicability of provisions to, §18.2-148.

JUDGES.
Acknowledgments.
Recognition, §§55-118.1 to 55-118.9.
Allowances made for payments out of state treasury.
Listing, certifying to supreme court, §2.2-810.
Appearance of impropriety.
Avoidance, VA SCt Rule Pt 6 §III Canon 2.
Appointed person to run a corporation as judge's representative.
Attorney general, legal services provided for, §2.2-507.
Appointment to fill vacancy in local governmental elective office, VA Const Art VI §12.
Arbitration.
Prohibited to act as arbitrator or mediator, VA SCt Rule Pt 6 §III Canon 4.
Arrest under civil process.
Privileged from civil arrest, §§8.01-327.1, 8.01-327.2.
Arrest warrants.
Who may issue process of arrest, §19.2-71.
Assault and battery against, §18.2-57.
Assigning judges of courts of record to other court of record.
Chief justice, VA Const Art VI §4.
Assistance to judges.
Designation of judges to hold courts and assist other judges, §§17.1-105 to 17.1-107.
Attorney general.
Legal services provided in civil matters, §2.2-507.
Attorneys at law.
Rules of professional conduct.
False statement by lawyer concerning qualifications or integrity of judicial official, VA SCt Rule Pt 6 §II Rule 8.2.
Former judge or arbitrator, VA SCt Rule Pt 6 §II Rule 1.12.
Avocational activities, VA SCt Rule Pt 6 §III Canon 4.
Best evidence rule exceptions.
Issues of law or fact, VA SCt Rule 2:1008.
Bribery.
Public officers generally, §§18.2-438 to 18.2-450.
See BRIBERY.
Campaign conduct, VA SCt Rule Pt 6 §III Canon 5.

JUDGES —Cont'd
Canons of judicial conduct.
Adjudicative responsibilities, VA SCt Rule Pt 6 §III Canon 3.
Administrative responsibilities, VA SCt Rule Pt 6 §III Canon 3.
Appearance of impropriety.
Avoidance, VA SCt Rule Pt 6 §III Canon 2.
Arbitration.
Judges not to act as arbitrators or mediators, VA SCt Rule Pt 6 §III Canon 4.
Avocational activities, VA SCt Rule Pt 6 §III Canon 4.
Campaign conduct, VA SCt Rule Pt 6 §III Canon 5.
Civic and charitable activities, VA SCt Rule Pt 6 §III Canon 4.
Compliance with code, VA SCt Rule Pt 6 §III Canon 6.
Effective date, VA SCt Rule Pt 6 §III Canon 7.
Disqualification, VA SCt Rule Pt 6 §III Canon 3.
Remittal of disqualification, VA SCt Rule Pt 6 §III Canon 3.
Extrajudicial appointments, VA SCt Rule Pt 6 §III Canon 4.
Fiduciary activities, VA SCt Rule Pt 6 §III Canon 4.
Financial activities, VA SCt Rule Pt 6 §III Canon 4.
Impropriety.
Avoidance in all activities, VA SCt Rule Pt 6 §III Canon 2.
Integrity and independence of judiciary.
Duty to uphold, VA SCt Rule Pt 6 §III Canon 1.
Judges pro tempore.
Compliance with code, VA SCt Rule Pt 6 §III Canon 6.
Political activity, VA SCt Rule Pt 6 §III Canon 5.
Practice of law.
Prohibited, VA SCt Rule Pt 6 §III Canon 4.
Retired judges.
Compliance with code, VA SCt Rule Pt 6 §III Canon 6.
Censure.
Judges of courts of record, VA Const Art VI §10.
Supreme court jurisdiction in matters, VA Const Art VI §1.
Change of venue.
Judicial discretion, §8.01-267.
Circuit court judges.
Generally.
See CIRCUIT COURT JUDGES.
Civic and charitable activities, VA SCt Rule Pt 6 §III Canon 4.
Civil or criminal proceedings.
Competency to testify, §19.2-271, VA SCt Rule 2:605.
Commission of justices and judges of courts of record, VA Const Art VI §9.
Compelling attendance as witness.
Prior court permission required, §8.01-407.
Compensation and allowances for judges of courts of record.
General assembly to prescribe, VA Const Art VI §9.
Competency to testify.
Civil or criminal proceedings, §19.2-271, VA SCt Rule 2:605.
Conservator of the peace, §19.2-12.

JUDGES —Cont'd
Criminal history record information.
Dissemination to the committees for courts of justice.
Determining if person considered for judgeship convicted of crime, §19.2-389.
Criminal trial jurors.
Contact between judge and juror prohibited, §19.2-263.1.
Designation of judges to hold courts and assist other judges.
Courts of records, §§17.1-105 to 17.1-107.
Disqualification, VA SCt Rule Pt 6 §III Canon 3.
District court judges.
Generally.
See DISTRICT COURT JUDGES.
Evidence.
Best evidence rule exceptions.
Issues of law or fact, VA SCt Rule 2:1008.
Extra-judicial appointments, VA SCt Rule Pt 6 §III Canon 4.
Federal employees prohibited, exception, §2.2-2801.
Federal judges.
Compensation and tenure, US Const Art III §1.
Fiduciary activities, VA SCt Rule Pt 6 §III Canon 4.
Financial activities, VA SCt Rule Pt 6 §III Canon 4.
General district court judges.
See DISTRICT COURT JUDGES.
Homicide.
Capital murder, §18.2-31.
Impeachment, VA Const Art IV §17.
Impropriety.
Avoidance in all activities, VA SCt Rule Pt 6 §III Canon 2.
Incompatible activities of justices or judges of courts of record, VA Const Art VI §11.
Integrity and independence of judiciary.
Duty to uphold, VA SCt Rule Pt 6 §III Canon 1.
Judges pro tempore.
Circuit court judges, §§17.1-109 to 17.1-111.
Compliance with code, VA SCt Rule Pt 6 §III Canon 6.
Judicial conference of Virginia, §§17.1-706 to 17.1-709.
Judicial council, §§17.1-700 to 17.1-705.
Judicial inquiry and review commission, §§17.1-900 to 17.1-919.
See JUDICIAL INQUIRY AND REVIEW COMMISSION.
Jury service.
Automatic exemption, §8.01-341.
Juvenile and domestic relations district court judges.
See JUVENILE AND DOMESTIC RELATIONS DISTRICT COURTS.
Law library of state, use permitted, §42.1-64.
Magistrates, §§19.2-26 to 19.2-48.1.
See MAGISTRATES.
Military judges, §44-46.1.
Oath of office.
Persons administering oath to, §49-3.
Obstructing justice by threats or force, §18.2-460.
Performance evaluation program, §17.1-100.
Practice of law.
Prohibited, VA SCt Rule Pt 6 §III Canon 4.
Qualification.
Judges of courts of record, VA Const Art VI §7.
Revised constitution not to affect, VA Const Sched §4

JUDGES —Cont'd
Qualification —Cont'd
Judges of courts of record —Cont'd
Time for qualifying, §17.1-101.
Removal.
Judges of courts of record, VA Const Art VI §10.
Supreme court jurisdiction in matters, VA Const Art VI §1.
Retired judges.
Compliance with code, VA SCt Rule Pt 6 §III Canon 6.
Designation of judges to hold courts and assist other judges, §§17.1-105 to 17.1-107.
Recall to service.
Payment for services, §17.1-327.
Retirement.
Early retirement, §51.1-305.
General assembly to enact laws, VA Const Art VI §9.
Locality establishing system, §15.2-1510.
Mandatory retirement, §51.1-305.
Normal retirement, §51.1-305.
Notice, §51.1-305.
Retirement system generally, §§51.1-300 to 51.1-309.
See JUDICIAL RETIREMENT SYSTEM.
Supreme court jurisdiction in matters, VA Const Art VI §1.
Risk management plan for public liability, §2.2-1837.
Selection of judges of courts of record, VA Const Art VI §7.
Senior judge.
Compliance with code, VA SCt Rule Pt 6 §III Canon 6.
Court of appeals, §17.1-401.
Sickness and disability program.
Eligible employees.
Definition expanded to include judges, §51.1-1100.
Generally, §§51.1-1100 to 51.1-1140.
See SICKNESS AND DISABILITY PROGRAM.
Special justices.
Civil commitment of mentally ill persons.
Appointment by chief judge, §37.2-803.
Completion of training program, §37.2-803.
Fees and expenses, §§37.2-803, 37.2-804.
Compliance with code, VA SCt Rule Pt 6 §III Canon 6.
Substitute judges, courts of record.
Compliance with code, VA SCt Rule Pt 6 §III Canon 6.
Designation of judges to hold courts and assist other judges, §§17.1-105 to 17.1-107.
Supreme court.
See SUPREME COURT JUSTICES.
Terms of judges of courts of record, VA Const Art VI §7.
Time for qualification to office.
Judges of courts of record, §17.1-101.
United States courts, US Const Art III §1.
Vacancies in office of judge of courts of record, VA Const Art VI §7.
Failure of judge of court of record to timely qualify, §17.1-101.

JUDGES AT SPORTING CONTESTS.
Workers' compensation.
Employee not to include sports official, §65.2-101.

JUDGES PRO TEMPORE.
Appointment and powers, §17.1-110.

JUDGES PRO TEMPORE —Cont'd
Compensation, §17.1-111.
Qualifications to be appointed to hear case pending in circuit court, §17.1-109.

JUDGMENT BY CONFESSION, §§8.01-431 to 8.01-441.
See CONFESSION OF JUDGMENT.

JUDGMENT CREDITORS.
Defined, §8.01-427.
Domesticating foreign judgments, §§8.01-465.1 to 8.01-465.25.
Drivers' licenses.
Suspension of licenses for unsatisfied judgments generally, §§46.2-417 to 46.2-429.
See DRIVERS' LICENSES.
Fieri facias.
Interrogatories to judgment debtor, §8.01-506.
Foreign judgments.
Domesticating foreign judgments, §§8.01-465.1 to 8.01-465.5.
Judgment lien and enforcement, §§8.01-458 to 8.01-465.
Abstracts of judgments.
Granting to person interested, §8.01-461.
Alienees of different parts of estate.
Order of liability, §8.01-464.
Equity jurisdiction to enforce, §8.01-462.
Judgment not exceeding twenty dollars, §8.01-463.
Priority of judgments against same person, §8.01-459.
Recognizances and bonds having force of judgment, §8.01-465.
Recordation on judgment lien docket, §8.01-458.
Revived judgments, §8.01-458.
Sale of real estate, §8.01-462.
Support and maintenance decrees, §8.01-460.
Limited partnerships.
Assignment of partnership interests.
Partner's transferable interest subject to changing order, §50-73.46:1.
Sale of property.
Resale of property for purchaser noncompliance, §8.01-494.
Satisfaction of judgments.
Court entry of payment on judgment docket, §8.01-455.
Entry of payment or discharge on judgment docket, §8.01-456.
Notation of payment by creditor, §8.01-454.
Procedure when judgment creditor cannot be located, §8.01-456.
Secured transactions.
Sale of property subject to prior security interest, §8.01-480.
Subsequent executions, §8.01-475.

JUDGMENT DOCKET.
Documents recorded in, §17.1-232.
General index and daily index, §17.1-249.
Numbering, §17.1-249.

JUDGMENT FOR RECOVERY OF SPECIFIC PROPERTY.
Specific performance generally.
See SPECIFIC PERFORMANCE.
Writ of possession on judgment, §8.01-470.

JUDGMENT INTEREST.
Consumer finance companies.
Limitation after judgment, §6.2-1521.
Date at which interest begins, §8.01-382.

JUDGMENT INTEREST —Cont'd
Health insurance proceeds, action to recover, §38.2-3407.1.
Health maintenance organizations, actions to recover claim proceeds, §38.2-4306.1.
Life insurance or annuity proceeds, actions to recover, §38.2-3115.
Prejudgment interest, §8.01-382.
Rate of interest, §6.2-302.
State corporation commission, §12.1-36.
Support arrearage, §20-78.2.

JUDGMENT LIENS.
Consumer finance companies.
Persons presumed dead, §6.2-1524.
Delinquent local treasurers, §58.1-3172.
Homestead exemption of householder, §34-24.
Hospital or health center commission property exempt from, §15.2-5212.
Juvenile detention home, group home or residential care facility commissions.
Property exemption, §16.1-320.
Real estate trust, §55-17.1.
Recording, §8.01-458.
Southwest Virginia health facilities authority.
Exemption of property of, §15.2-5381.
State corporation commission, §12.1-37.
Support of child or spouse, §8.01-460.
Judgments created by operation of law, §16.1-278.15.
Taxes or assessments for local improvements, §15.2-2411.

JUDGMENTS AND DECREES, §§8.01-426 to 8.01-465.
Abstracts of judgments.
District court clerks, issuance, §16.1-69.40.
Divorce, affirmation of marriage or support, §16.1-278.18.
Issuance after papers returned to circuit court.
District court civil cases, §16.1-116.
Recording in judgment docket, §17.1-232.
Affirmation of marriage.
Money judgments arising out of suit, §16.1-278.18.
Amount less than twenty dollars.
Enforcement mechanism, §8.01-463.
Antitrust laws.
Effect of conviction in other proceedings, §59.1-9.13.
Assignment of judgment.
Entry of judgment lien docket, §8.01-452.
Fee for noting and filing, §17.1-275.
Attachment.
Judgment rendered on publication.
Rehearing permitted, §8.01-575.
Rendering judgment for defendant, §8.01-568.
Rendering judgment for plaintiff, §8.01-570.
Attorneys.
Drafts of orders and decrees.
Endorsement by counsel of record, VA SCt Rule 1:13.
Bankruptcy.
Recordation of documents, §§55-140 to 55-142.01.
Bill of review.
Injunction against decree subject to bill of review, §8.01-623.
Bond.
Motion on bond.
Court officers, §8.01-227.
Boundary line establishment.
Recordation and effect of judgment, §8.01-183

JUDGMENTS AND DECREES —Cont'd
Change in name of judgment debtors.
Fee for docketing and indexing, §17.1-275.
How judgments to be docketed and indexed, §8.01-451.
Child custody.
Uniform child custody jurisdiction and enforcement act, §§20-146.1 to 20-146.38.
See CHILD CUSTODY.
Claims against the state.
Recovery of claims.
Special appropriation required for payment of judgment, §8.01-195.
Clerical mistakes.
Correction, §8.01-428.
Collection of accounts receivable by Commonwealth.
Collection techniques, §2.2-4806.
Collection of state taxes, §58.1-1807.
Collection in foreign jurisdiction, §58.1-1808.
Memorandum of lien, effect of judgment in favor of Commonwealth, §58.1-1805.
Collection of taxes assessed by state corporation commission.
Memorandum of lien, §58.1-2021.
Collection of taxes by agencies other than tax department, §58.1-2023.
Enforcement in foreign jurisdiction, §58.1-2024.
Computation of time.
Prescribed amount of time to perform act after event or judgment, §1-210.
Confession of judgment.
General provisions, §§8.01-431 to 8.01-441.
See CONFESSION OF JUDGMENT.
Consumer finance companies.
Confession of judgments, §6.2-1524.
Lien upon real estate for security, §6.2-1524.
Limitation of interest and costs after judgment, §6.2-1521.
Contract actions.
When judgment to be given, §8.01-28.
Corporations, dissolution.
Judicial dissolution, §13.1-749.
Costs against Commonwealth, §17.1-629.
Costs and expenses of litigation generally.
See COURT COSTS AND FEES.
Costs on behalf of Commonwealth, §17.1-628.
Credit counseling.
Reports.
Judgment against licensee as grounds for licensee reporting, §6.2-2010.
Criminal forfeiture.
Judgment of condemnation and sale of property, §19.2-386.11.
Criminal trials.
See VERDICT.
Decedents' estates.
Executors and administrators powers, §64.2-519.
Declaratory judgments, §§8.01-184 to 8.01-191.
See DECLARATORY JUDGMENTS.
Decree embraces word judgment, §8.01-426.
Decrees pro confesso.
Correcting clerical errors.
When appellate court may grant relief, §8.01-429.
Fraud and deceit.
Setting aside decree, §8.01-428.
Setting aside decree, §8.01-428.
When appellate court may grant relief, §8.01-429.
Default judgments.
See DEFAULT JUDGMENTS.

JUDGMENTS AND DECREES —Cont'd
Detinue.
Final judgment, §8.01-121.
Discharge of judgment.
Entry, §8.01-455.
Dissolution of nonprofit corporations, §13.1-911.
Dissolution of stock corporation.
Judicial dissolution, §13.1-749.
District court civil cases.
Entry of judgment on warrant, motion for judgment, etc., §16.1-94.
Fieri facias or writ of possession on judgment, §16.1-98.
Forthcoming bonds, §§16.1-77.1, 16.1-91.1, 16.1-91.2.
Payment or discharge.
When and how entered on judgment, §16.1-94.01.
Divorce.
Consumer finance companies, §6.2-1524.
Money judgment arising out of suit for divorce, §16.1-278.18.
Docketing.
Assignment of judgment.
Entry on judgment lien docket, §8.01-452.
Change of name of judgment debtors, §8.01-451.
Clerks to keep judgment dockets, §8.01-446.
Executions issued on docketed judgments, §8.01-449.
Federal judgments and decrees, §8.01-447.
Fees charged by circuit court clerks, §17.1-275.
How indexed, §8.01-450.
Illegible abstracts of records, §8.01-446.
Indexing options, §8.01-450.
Judgments in favor of state, §8.01-448.
Keeping docket books, §8.01-446.
Executions issued on docketed judgments, §8.01-449.
Form of micrographic record, §8.01-446.1.
Use of micrographic process, §8.01-446.1.
Procedure, §8.01-449.
Recognizances and bonds having force of judgment, §8.01-465.
Revived judgment, §8.01-458.
Satisfaction of judgments.
Entry of payment or discharge on judgment docket, §§8.01-453, 8.01-455.
Marking satisfied judgments in favor of state, §8.01-457.
Social security number display on judgments provided via remote access, §8.01-449.
What judgments docketed, §8.01-446.
Domesticating foreign judgments generally, §§8.01-465.1 to 8.01-465.25.
See FOREIGN JUDGMENTS.
Draft of orders and decrees, VA SCt Rule 1:13.
Endorsement by counsel of record.
Electronic filing and service, VA SCt Rule 1:17.
Drivers' licenses.
Unsatisfied judgments.
Suspension of licenses for unsatisfied judgments, §§46.2-417 to 46.2-429.
See DRIVERS' LICENSES.
Endorsement.
Drafts by counsel of record.
Electronic filing and service, VA SCt Rule 1:17.
Enforcement of judgments.
Abstracts of judgments, §8.01-461.
Child support decrees, §8.01-460.
Lien on real estate, §8.01-460.

JUDGMENTS AND DECREES —Cont'd
Enforcement of judgments —Cont'd
Decreed sale of real estate, §8.01-462.
Decree for support and maintenance as lien on real estate, §8.01-460.
Docketing revived judgment, §8.01-458.
Foreign judgments, §8.01-465.23.
Judgments not in excess of twenty dollars, §8.01-463.
Lien on real estate upon recordation, §8.01-458.
Order of liability between alienees, §8.01-464.
Priority of judgments, §8.01-459.
Recognizances and bonds having force of judgment, §8.01-465.
Spousal support decree as lien on real estate, §8.01-460.
Support and maintenance decree as lien on real estate, §8.01-460.
Entry.
District court civil cases, §16.1-94.
Estates in land.
Action against several defendants, §8.01-143.
Evidentiary effect as to title or right of possession, §8.01-163.
Expiration of plaintiff's rights before trial, §8.01-154.
How judgment for plaintiff entered, §8.01-155.
Evictions, §§55-239 to 55-248.
Evidence.
Hearsay exceptions, VA SCt Rule 2:803.
Expiration of court term.
Power of court not affected, §8.01-445.
Federal judgments and decrees.
Docketing, §8.01-447.
Fees of circuit court clerks, §17.1-275.
Finality of judgments, orders and decrees, VA SCt Rule 1:1, US Const Art IV §1.
Failure to notify party or counsel of final order, §8.01-428.
Setting aside jury verdict.
When final judgment may be entered, §8.01-430.
Foreign judgments.
Child custody.
Uniform child custody jurisdiction and enforcement act, §§20-146.1 to 20-146.38.
See CHILD CUSTODY.
Generally, §§8.01-465.1 to 8.01-465.25.
See FOREIGN JUDGMENTS.
Foreign-money claims, §§8.01-465.14 to 8.01-465.25.
Foreign support orders.
Generally, §§20-88.66 to 20-88.77.
See INTERSTATE FAMILY SUPPORT ACT.
Forthcoming bonds.
District court giving judgment on, §16.1-77.1.
Costs to be included in judgment, §16.1-91.1.
Endorsement of judgment by judge, §16.1-91.2.
Judge to keep record of judgment, §16.1-91.2.
Full faith and credit clause, US Const Art IV §1.
General assembly.
Civil proceedings for or against members and clerks, §30-4.
Habeas corpus.
Conclusiveness of judgment, §8.01-663.
Hearsay exceptions, VA SCt Rule 2:803.
Homestead exemption of householder.
Lien of judgment or decree against householder, §34-24.
Waiver of exemption.
Judgment to state, §34-25.

JUDGMENTS AND DECREES —Cont'd
Husband and wife.
Responsibility for spouse's judgments, §55-37.
Indexing by circuit court clerks.
How indexed, §8.01-450.
Options, §8.01-450.
Injunction against decree.
Limitation of bill of review, §8.01-623.
Interest.
Consumer finance companies.
Limitation after judgment, §6.2-1521.
Date at which interest begins, §8.01-382.
Health insurance proceeds, action to recover, §38.2-3407.1.
Health maintenance organizations, actions to recover claim proceeds, §38.2-4306.1.
Life insurance or annuity proceeds, actions to recover, §38.2-3115.
State corporation commission judgments, §12.1-36.
Support arrearage, §20-78.2.
Joint wrongdoers.
Addition of new parties, §8.01-444.
Contract actions, §8.01-442.
Effect of judgment against new parties, §8.01-444.
Effect of judgment against one, §8.01-443.
Judgment creditors.
Defined, §8.01-427.
Judgment docket.
See JUDGMENT DOCKET.
Judicial sales.
Decree for sale, §8.01-96.
Rule against judgment for amounts due, §§8.01-105 to 8.01-108.
Hearing upon rule and judgment, §8.01-106.
Return of rule, §8.01-105.
Surety actions against rule, §8.01-108.
Trial by jury of issues, §8.01-107.
Juvenile and domestic relations district courts.
Money judgments, §16.1-278.18.
Landlord and tenant.
Residential landlords and tenants.
Money judgment, attorneys' fees, court costs.
Acceptance of payment with reservation, not waiver of right to evict, §55-248.34:1.
Post-termination remedies of landlord, §55-248.35.
Liens.
Consumer finance companies.
Persons presumed dead, §6.2-1524.
Delinquent local treasurers, §58.1-3172.
Homestead exemption of householder, §34-24.
Juvenile detention home, group home or residential care facility commission.
Property exemption, §16.1-320.
Persons presumed dead.
Consumer finance companies, §6.2-1524.
Real estate trust, §55-17.1.
Recordation, §8.01-458.
State corporation commission, §12.1-37.
Support of child or spouse, §8.01-460.
Judgments created by operation of law, §16.1-278.15.
Limitation of actions.
Defendants served by publication and not appearing.
Petition for rehearing, §8.01-322.
Enforcement, §8.01-251.
New action after arrest or reversal of judgment, §8.01-229.

JUDGMENTS AND DECREES —Cont'd
Limitations on enforcement, §8.01-251.
District court civil judgments, §16.1-94.1.
Local taxes, proceedings for collection, §58.1-3955.
Enforcement in foreign jurisdictions, §58.1-3956.
Lost records.
Establishing generally, §§8.01-392 to 8.01-395.
Lost shareholders, proceeding for determination, §13.1-777.
Married women's property rights.
Entry into land not barred by judgments, §55-38.
Responsibility for spouse's judgments, §55-37.
Money judgment.
Specific judgment for money to state specific amount, §8.01-446.
Motor carriers, passengers.
Execution of judgments.
Seizure of vehicles, §46.2-2011.19.
Motor carriers, property.
Execution of judgments.
Holding or seizing vehicles, §46.2-2128.
Motor fuels.
Enforcement of civil penalties, §59.1-167.2.
Motor vehicles.
Suspension of driver's license, §46.2-417.
Motor vehicle transaction recovery fund.
Effect of award of final judgment, §46.2-1527.3.
Satisfaction of unpaid judgments, §46.2-1527.1.
Nonprofit corporations, dissolution, §13.1-911.
Notice service generally, §43-64.
Nuisances.
Abating public nuisances, §48-5.
Obscene books, proceeding against, §18.2-384.
Oils, lubricating.
Enforcement of civil penalties, §59.1-167.2.
Partition of land.
Decree of partition to vest legal title, §8.01-88.
Partnerships.
Effect of judgments against partnership, §50-73.97.
Partners transferable interest subject to charging order, §50-73.108.
Paternity proceedings.
Determination of parentage, §20-49.8.
Persons with disability.
Rendition of judgment.
Error decree without guardian ad litem, §8.01-9.
Prejudgment interest, §8.01-382.
Property rights of married women.
Entry into land not barred by judgments, §55-38.
Responsibility for spouse's judgments, §55-37.
Quo warranto.
Defendant failure to appear, §8.01-640.
Defendant found guilty on merits, §8.01-643.
Real property.
Real estate trust, §55-17.1.
Recordation of judgments of United States courts affecting, §55-140.
Receivers.
Special receivers.
Effect of judgment against receiver, §8.01-598.
Reciprocal insurers, effect of judgment against, §38.2-1218.
Recordation.
Judgment docket, §17.1-232.
United States court judgments, §§55-140 to 55-142.01.
Rendition of a judgment.
Defined, §8.01-2.

JUDGMENTS AND DECREES —Cont'd
Safe deposit boxes.
Access denied except by court order, §6.2-2304.
Satisfaction of judgments, §§8.01-453 to 8.01-457.
Child support enforcement by department of social services.
Lien asserted by commissioner, §63.2-1934.
After foreclosure, §63.2-1935.
Docketing.
Entry of payment or discharge on judgment docket, §§8.01-453, 8.01-455.
Marking satisfied judgments in favor of state, §8.01-457.
Judgment creditor cannot be located, §8.01-456.
Notation of payment by judgment creditor, §8.01-454.
Payment by third parties releasing recognizances, §8.01-457.
Priority of judgments, §8.01-459.
Recognizances and bonds having force of judgment, §8.01-465.
Setting aside default judgment, §8.01-428.
Appellate court action, §8.01-429.
Default judgments generally.
See DEFAULT JUDGMENTS.
Shareholder determination proceedings, §13.1-777.
Sheriff or deputy receiving money by virtue of service of order, warrant or process.
Failure to make proper return, §15.2-1622.
Small claims courts, §16.1-122.6.
Social security number display on judgments provided via remote access, §8.01-449.
Specific judgment for money.
Statement that judgment for money in specific amount, §8.01-446.
Specific performance generally.
See SPECIFIC PERFORMANCE.
Specific property, recovery of.
Writ of possession on judgment, §8.01-470.
State.
Collection of money payable to state.
Force of judgment of bond for purchase money, §8.01-209.
Generally, §§8.01-196 to 8.01-216.
See STATE.
Nature of judgment, §8.01-199.
Correction of mistakes against state, §8.01-200.
Deceased obligors, §8.01-210.
Fraudulent claims against the state, §§8.01-216.1 to 8.01-216.19.
See FRAUDULENT CLAIMS AGAINST THE STATE.
State corporation commission.
Collection of taxes assessed by.
Memorandum of lien, §58.1-2021.
Docketing, §12.1-37.
Interests, §12.1-36.
Judgment to be in favor of Commonwealth, §12.1-35.
Liens, §12.1-37.
Time judgment takes effect, §12.1-36.
Statute of limitations.
Defendants served by publication and not appearing.
Petition for rehearing, §8.01-322.
Enforcement, §8.01-251.
New action after arrest or reversal of judgment, §8.01-229.
Summary jury trial, §8.01-576.3.
Summons, defined, §8.01-2.

JUDGMENTS AND DECREES —Cont'd
Support of child or spouse.
Interest on arrearage, §20-78.2.
Lien, §8.01-460.
Judgment created by operation of law, §16.1-278.18.
Money judgments for arrears, §16.1-278.18.
Supreme court.
Interlocutory judgments, §§8.01-670, 8.01-671.
Appeal by permission, §8.01-670.1.
Issuance of execution, §8.01-685.
Opinions and judgments, VA Const Art VI §6.
Setting aside judgment of trial court.
Criteria, §8.01-680.
Tax collection, agencies other than tax department, §58.1-2023.
Enforcement in foreign jurisdiction, §58.1-2024.
Term of court.
Distinction between term and vacation abolished, §8.01-445.
Terms interchangeable, §8.01-2.
Trover.
Effect of judgment in trover, §8.01-219.
Uniform foreign country money-judgments recognition act, §§8.01-465.6 to 8.01-465.13.
Uniform foreign money-claims act, §§8.01-465.14 to 8.01-465.25.
Unlawful entry and detainer.
Action for trespass or ejectment not barred, §8.01-130.
Damages, §8.01-128.
Unsatisfied judgments.
Driver's license suspended, §46.2-417.
Vacation of court.
Distinction between term and vacation abolished, §8.01-445.
Wills.
Probate, §§64.2-446, 64.2-448.
Words interchangeable, §8.01-2.

JUDGMENTS FOR COSTS.
Law of costs generally, §§17.1-600 to 17.1-629.
See COURT COSTS AND FEES.

JUDICIAL AUTHORIZATION OF TREATMENT.
Developmentally disabled persons.
See DEVELOPMENTALLY DISABLED PERSONS.
Mental health.
See MENTAL HEALTH.
Mental or physical disorders, §§37.2-1100 to 37.2-1109.

JUDICIAL CIRCUITS, §17.1-506.
New or changed circuits.
Election of judge, how court held until vacancy filled, §17.1-510.
Ratifying, validating and confirming certain actions, §17.1-508.
Number of judges in each circuit, §17.1-507.

JUDICIAL CONDUCT.
Canons of judicial conduct.
Rules part 6.
See JUDGES.

JUDICIAL CONFERENCE OF VIRGINIA, §§17.1-706 to 17.1-709.
Attendance at meetings mandatory, §17.1-708.
District courts, §§16.1-218 to 16.1-221.
Active members, §16.1-218.
Duties, §16.1-69.31.
Established, §16.1-218.

JUDICIAL CONFERENCE OF VIRGINIA —Cont'd
District courts —Cont'd
Executive committee, §16.1-219.
Expenses of members, §16.1-221.
Honorary members, §16.1-218.
Meetings, §16.1-220.
Motor vehicle and traffic laws.
Special session concerning, §16.1-220.
Notice of inability to attend meeting, §16.1-220.
President, §16.1-219.
Establish, §17.1-706.
Excused absences.
Attendance at meetings mandatory, §17.1-708.
Executive committee, §17.1-707.
Expenses, §17.1-709.
Meetings, §17.1-708.
Membership, §17.1-706.
President, §17.1-707.

JUDICIAL COUNCIL, §§17.1-700 to 17.1-705.
Additional circuit court judges, study, §17.1-507.
Appointment of members, §17.1-701.
Attendance at meetings, requirement, §17.1-702.
Civil immunity.
Investigations of commissioners of accounts, §17.1-705.1.
Commissioners of accounts.
Investigations, civil immunity, §17.1-705.1.
Committees, §17.1-700.
Meeting, §17.1-702.
Composition, §17.1-700.
Expense allowance, §17.1-704.
Investigations of commissioners of accounts.
Civil immunity, §17.1-705.1.
Meetings, §17.1-702.
Month council to meet, §17.1-702.
Presiding officer, §17.1-703.
Recommendations, §17.1-705.
Reports, §17.1-705.
Study of organization and rules and methods of procedure and practice of judicial system, §17.1-703.
Summoning council to meet, §17.1-702.
Terms, §17.1-701.
Travel expenses, §17.1-704.

JUDICIAL DISCRETION.
Change of venue, §8.01-267.
Commissioners in chancery.
Referral of accounts, §8.01-608.
New trial.
Power to grant new trial, §8.01-383.
Pleading several matters.
Separate trial in discretion of court, §8.01-272.

JUDICIAL EMERGENCY, §§17.1-330, 17.1-331.

JUDICIAL INQUIRY AND REVIEW COMMISSION, §§17.1-900 to 17.1-919, VA Const Art VI §10.
Assistance and information for, §17.1-917.
Compensation and expenses of members, §17.1-904.
Confidentiality of papers and proceedings, §17.1-913.
Costs, §17.1-916.
Creation, §17.1-901.
Definitions, §17.1-900.
Depositions, §17.1-910.
Duties, §17.1-902.

JUDICIAL INQUIRY AND REVIEW COMMISSION —Cont'd
Execution of orders, §17.1-919.
Freedom of information act.
Excluded records, §2.2-3705.7.
General assembly.
Transmission of certain information to, §17.1-918.
Investigations, §17.1-902.
Depositions, §17.1-910.
Powers in connection with, §17.1-907.
Suspension of judge, §17.1-911.
Legal counsel, §17.1-903.
Members, §17.1-901.
Compensation and expenses, §17.1-904.
Officers and employees, §17.1-903.
Physical or mental examination of judge, §17.1-912.
Powers, §17.1-902.
Investigations, §17.1-907.
Witnesses, §§17.1-903, 17.1-907.
Privileges.
Filing of papers with commission, §17.1-914.
Reports.
Annual report, §17.1-905.
Rules.
Answers, JIRC Rule 6.
Applicability of rules, JIRC Rule 1.
Charges.
Defined, JIRC Rule 2.
Disposition of charges, JIRC Rule 15.
Establishment of charges, JIRC Rule 3.
Termination of charges, JIRC Rule 3.
Complaints.
Defined, JIRC Rule 2.
Receipt of complaints, JIRC Rule 3.
Computation of time.
Extensions of time, JIRC Rule 10.
Holidays, JIRC Rule 10.
Definitions, JIRC Rule 2.
Disposition of charges, JIRC Rule 15.
Effective date of rules, JIRC Rule 17.
Evidence.
Defined, JIRC Rule 2.
Hearings, JIRC Rule 13.
Files.
Preservation, JIRC Rule 16.
Filing of documents.
Name of person filing, JIRC Rule 7.
Time for filing, JIRC Rule 9.
Where filed, JIRC Rule 7.
Hearings.
Evidence, JIRC Rule 13.
Exhibits, JIRC Rule 13.
Objections, JIRC Rule 13.
Order of presentation, JIRC Rule 13.
Transcripts, JIRC Rule 13.
Informal conferences, JIRC Rule 4.
Motions, JIRC Rule 11.
Pleadings.
Amendments, time for filing, JIRC Rule 8.
Answers, JIRC Rule 6.
Contents, JIRC Rule 6.
Facsimile transmission, JIRC Rule 5.
Number of copies, JIRC Rule 5.
Subscription, JIRC Rule 6.
Prehearing conference, JIRC Rule 11.
Preliminary matters, JIRC Rule 11.
Preservation of files, JIRC Rule 16.
Service of notice, process and other papers.
Persons to be served, JIRC Rule 8.
Proof of service, JIRC Rule 8.

JUDICIAL INQUIRY AND REVIEW COMMISSION —Cont'd
Rules —Cont'd
Service of notice, process and other papers —Cont'd
Subpoenas, JIRC Rule 12.
Where served, JIRC Rule 8.
Subpoenas.
Application for subpoena, JIRC Rule 12.
Issuance, JIRC Rule 12.
Service of subpoenas, JIRC Rule 12.
Transcripts.
Hearings, JIRC Rule 13.
Waiver of rules, JIRC Rules 1, 14.
Service of notice, process and other papers, §17.1-919.
Order compelling witness to attend and testify, §17.1-909.
Scope of process, §17.1-908.
State bar.
Transmission of certain information to, §17.1-918.
Supreme court.
Jurisdiction.
Complaints filed by commission, §17.1-906.
Suspension of judge, §17.1-911.
Witnesses.
Fees and mileage, §17.1-915.
Order compelling attendance and testimony, §17.1-909.
Powers as to, §§17.1-903, 17.1-907.

JUDICIAL NOTICE.
ABC board.
Regulations of board, §4.1-111.
Agency publications, §8.01-388.
Criminal cases, §19.2-265.2.
Definitions, §8.01-385.
Foreign law, §8.01-386.
Judicial documents.
Signatures of judges, §8.01-387.
Laws, §8.01-386.
Metropolitan Washington airports authority rules or regulations, §5.1-157.
Municipal ordinances, §8.01-386.
Official documents.
Signature of governor, §8.01-387.
Official publications, §8.01-388.
Ordinances, §8.01-386.
Signatures.
Judicial or official documents, §8.01-387.
Statutes, §8.01-386.
Table of speed and stopping distances, §46.2-880.
Tax rulings and administrative interpretations.
By tax commissioner and department of taxation, §58.1-205.

JUDICIAL RETIREMENT SYSTEM, §§51.1-300 to 51.1-309.
Administration, §51.1-300.
Allowance for disability retirement, §51.1-308.
Allowances for service retirement, §51.1-306.
Appearance as counsel, §51.1-309.
Beneficiary serving in covered position.
Cessation of retirement allowance while employed, §51.1-306.
Constituency, §51.1-302.
Continuation of previous system, §51.1-300.
Contributions by Commonwealth, §51.1-304.
Coordination of past and present plans.
Benefits continued, §51.1-402.

JUDICIAL RETIREMENT SYSTEM —Cont'd
Creditable service, §51.1-303.
Defined, §51.1-301.
Defined terms, §51.1-301.
Disability retirement.
Allowance, §51.1-308.
Notice of, §51.1-307.
Disclosure requirements, §§51.1-1000 to 51.1-1004.
Financial reports, §51.1-1003.
Scope, §51.1-1000.
Statement of benefits, §51.1-1002.
Summary plan description, §51.1-1001.
Use of electronic media, §51.1-1004.
Early retirement.
Service retirement allowance, §51.1-306.
General disability retirement guarantee, §51.1-308.
Health insurance credits, §51.1-1400.
Hybrid retirement program.
Participation, §51.1-302.
Membership, §51.1-302.
Normal retirement.
Service retirement allowance, §51.1-306.
Pooling of assets for investment, §51.1-124.31.
Reduction of allowance.
Disability retirement allowance, §51.1-308.
Retirement allowance.
Disability retirement allowance, §51.1-308.
Service retirement allowance, §51.1-306.
Service retirement, §51.1-305.
Allowance, §51.1-306.
Creditable service, §§51.1-301, 51.1-303.
Special retirement allowance guarantee.
Disability retirement allowance, §51.1-308.
State contributions, §51.1-304.
State retirement system generally, §§51.1-124.1 to 51.1-169.
See VIRGINIA RETIREMENT SYSTEM.
Workers' compensation guarantee.
Disability retirement allowance, §51.1-308.

JUDICIAL SALES, §§8.01-96 to 8.01-113.
Banks.
Holding and conveying property purchase, §6.2-872.
Receivers for banks.
Sale and execution of deeds, §6.2-917.
Bedding and upholstered furniture.
Exemption from provisions, §32.1-225.
Cemeteries.
Proceedings for removal of remains and sale of land vacated, §57-39.
Clerk of court.
Liability for false certificate or failure to give bond, §8.01-100.
Persons appointed to receive purchase money, etc.
Liability for failure to give notice of appointment, §8.01-103.
Misdemeanor, §18.2-209.2.
Collection of money payable to state.
Disposition of proceeds of sale, §8.01-207.
How sale made, §8.01-205.
Location of sale, §8.01-214.
Notice of sale, §8.01-204.
Return where sale not made because of prior encumbrance, §8.01-215.
Terms of sale, §8.01-206.
When sale to be made, §8.01-204.
Writ of fieri facias, §§8.01-201, 8.01-203.

JUDICIAL SALES —Cont'd
Collection of money payable to state —Cont'd
Writ of venditioni exponas, §§8.01-211 to 8.01-213.
Delivery of goods and chattels levied to sheriff, §8.01-212.
Issuance to sheriff of adjacent county, §8.01-211.
Sale of levied goods and chattels, §8.01-213.
Commission for services of commissioners or officers, §8.01-109.
Condominiums.
Special declarant rights.
Transfers, §55-79.74:3.
Dams for hydroelectric power.
Provision violations, §62.1-97.
Decree for sale, §8.01-96.
Distress.
Landlord and tenant, §§55-230 to 55-238.
Fraudulent conveyances.
Creditor's suits, §§55-82, 55-82.1.
Houses of prostitution, §§48-12, 48-13.
Hydroelectric power dams.
Provision violations, §62.1-97.
Landlord and tenant.
Distress, §§55-230 to 55-238.
Locality appointment as receiver to repair derelict and blighted buildings.
Enforcement of receiver's lien, §15.2-907.2.
Public service companies.
Holding of property, §56-12.
Purchase money.
Persons appointed to receive purchase money, etc.
Liability for failure to give notice of appointment, §8.01-103.
Misdemeanor, §18.2-209.2.
Purchasers relieved of liability for payment to commissioner, §8.01-101.
Purchases as holders in due course, §8.01-102.
Purchase price.
Sale of land insufficient to pay taxes, etc., §8.01-98.
Real estate cooperatives, §55-444.
Nonpayment of assessments, §55-472.
Special declarant rights, transfers of, §55-461.
Rule against judgment for amounts due, §§8.01-105 to 8.01-108.
Award against special commissioner, purchaser, etc., §8.01-105.
Hearing upon rule and judgment, §8.01-106.
Return of rule, §8.01-105.
Surety actions against rule, §8.01-108.
Trial by jury of issues, §8.01-107.
Sale of delinquent tax lands, §§58.1-3965 to 58.1-3975.
See SALE OF DELINQUENT TAX LANDS.
Sales commission, §8.01-109.
Special commissioners.
Appointment to execute deed, etc., §§8.01-110 to 8.01-112.
Deed specifications, §8.01-111.
Effect of deed, §8.01-110.
Reinstatement of cause to appoint commissioner to make deed, §8.01-112.
Bond required, §§8.01-96, 8.01-99.
Failure to give, §18.2-209.1.
Paid to give notice of appointment, §8.01-103.
Failure of clerk to give notice, §18.2-209.2.
Purchasers relieved of liability for purchase money paid to commissioner, §8.01-101.
Rule against judgment for amounts due, §§8.01-105 to 8.01-108.

JUDICIAL SALES —Cont'd
Taxes.
Ascertainment of delinquent taxes, §8.01-97.
Sale of land insufficient to pay taxes, etc., §8.01-98.
Timber.
Unclaimed timber, §59.1-106.
Title.
Setting aside sale, §8.01-113.

JULY 4TH.
Legal holidays, §2.2-3300.

JUMPING WAKE OF ANOTHER VESSEL.
Reckless operation of personal watercraft, §29.1-738.03.

JUNIOR ORDER OF UNITED AMERICAN MECHANICS.
Exemption from fraternal benefit society chapter provisions, §38.2-4135.

JUNK DEALERS.
City or town power to regulate, §15.2-1114.
County power to regulate, §15.2-1232.1.
Secondhand article sales generally, §§59.1-116.1 to 59.1-136.
See SECONDHAND ARTICLE SALES.

JUNK EMAIL.
Transmission of unsolicited commercial electronic mail, §18.2-152.3:1.

JUNK FAX.
Unsolicited facsimile transmissions of advertising, actions for, §8.01-40.2.
Consumer protection violations, §59.1-200.

JUNK VEHICLES.
Ordinance restricting the keeping of inoperable motor vehicle on residential or commercial property, §§15.2-904, 15.2-905.
County manager plan of government, §15.2-730.
Salvage vehicles generally, §§46.2-1600 to 46.2-1610.

JUNKYARDS.
Automobile junkyards, §33.1-348.
Locality taxing and regulating, §15.2-903.
Salvage vehicles.
Generally, §§46.2-1600 to 46.2-1610.
Ordinances restricting keeping of inoperable vehicles on property, §§15.2-730, 15.2-904, 15.2-905.

JURISDICTION.
Adoption, §63.2-1201.
Post-adoption contact and communication agreements.
Jurisdiction to approve, §63.2-1220.4.
Affirmation of marriage suits, §20-96.
Amount in controversy.
District court civil jurisdiction, §16.1-77.
Penal bonds.
How jurisdiction determined, §8.01-4.1.
Animals.
General district courts, §3.2-6590.
Animals running at large.
Unincorporated communities and villages.
Boundaries within which animals may not run at large.
Jurisdiction of circuit courts to designate, §55-323.
Annulment of marriage, §20-96.
Domicile and residency requirements, §20-97.

JURISDICTION —Cont'd
Antitrust actions, §59.1-9.8.
Investigations by attorney general, §59.1-9.10.
Venue, §59.1-9.9.
Appeals.
Errors insufficient to divest appellate court of jurisdiction, §§8.01-677 to 8.01-678.
Juvenile proceedings, §16.1-296.
Arbitration.
Circuit courts, §8.01-581.014.
Assignments of property for the benefit of creditors.
Challenges to claims of creditors, §55-158.
Attachment.
Circuit courts, §8.01-535.
District court civil jurisdiction, §16.1-77.
When retained and case tried, §8.01-569.
Attorney discipline.
Effect of rules, VA SCt Rule Pt 6 §IV Par 13-2.
Automatic vehicle identification system.
Toll roads and toll bridges, §§46.2-819.1, 46.2-819.3.
Autopsies, §32.1-285.
Bail bondsmen, investigation of.
Criminal justice services department, §9.1-185.3.
Bail enforcement agents, investigation of.
Criminal justice services department, §9.1-186.3.
Benevolent associations.
Trustee holding personal property, §57-21.
Big Sandy river.
Obstructing or dumping refuse into, §62.1-194.3.
Birth certificates.
Delayed birth certificate registration, §32.1-260.
Boat dealers licensing actions, §29.1-824.
Boating under the influence.
Persons participating in rehabilitation program, §29.1-738.5.
Boundaries.
Clearing watercourses between counties of obstructions, §62.1-6.
Bulkheads, §§62.1-164, 62.1-165.
Business opportunity sales.
Purchaser remedies, §59.1-268.
Capitol police, §30-34.2:1.
Cemeteries.
Disposition of property for maintenance and care.
Trusteeship for administering funds, §57-35.
Eminent domain, §57-25.
Improvement of abandoned and neglected cemeteries, §57-39.1.
Proceedings for removal of remains and sale of land vacated, §57-39.
Removal of remains from abandoned family graveyard, §§57-38.1, 57-38.2.
Trustees.
Appointment, §57-23.
Actions, appointment for, §57-24.1.
Removal, §57-23.
Certiorari.
Circuit courts, §17.1-513.
Child custody.
Issues, §16.1-244.
Uniform child custody jurisdiction and enforcement act, §§20-146.1 to 20-146.38.
See CHILD CUSTODY.
Church property.
Abandoned property actions, §57-11.
Appointment of trustees to effectuate purposes of conveyances, §57-8.
Determination of rights on division of church, §57-9.

JURISDICTION —Cont'd
Church property —Cont'd
Land held in adverse possession, §57-17.
Suits by members to have land sold or mortgaged, §§57-14, 57-15.
Suits by trustees to have land sold or mortgaged, §57-15.
Circuit courts, §17.1-513.
Adoption, §63.2-1201.
Corrected date of birth for foreign-born child, establishment by court, §63.2-1220.01.
Post-adoption contact and communication agreements.
Jurisdiction to approve, §63.2-1220.4.
Charitable corporations' assets, §17.1-513.01.
Family offenses, criminal jurisdiction, §16.1-278.14.
Formerly vested in county court, §17.1-515.
Voter registration cancellation.
Appeals from decisions of registrar, §24.2-430.
Voter registration denied.
Appeals, §24.2-422.
Voter registration objections.
Petitions concerning, §§24.2-431, 24.2-432.
Waters or bays lying between counties or cities, §17.1-516.
Civil commitment of mentally ill persons.
Involuntary admissions.
Transfer of jurisdiction over case following entry of mandatory outpatient treatment order, §37.2-817.
Claims against the state.
Tort claims act, §8.01-195.4.
Coal.
Port authority expediting shipments, §62.1-134.1.
Coal property seizures by Commonwealth.
Condemnation proceedings, §45.1-161.320.
Restoration of property to owner or operator, §45.1-161.322.
Coastal primary sand dunes and beaches.
Fines, §28.2-1420.
Injunctions, §28.2-1419.
College building authority.
Exclusive jurisdiction, §23-30.38.
Commissioners of accounts, §64.2-1200.
Assistant commissioners, §64.2-1201.
Deputy commissioners, §64.2-1202.
Commissioners of revenue, §58.1-3102.
Communicable diseases of public health significance.
Isolation of persons, §§32.1-48.03, 32.1-48.04.
Compulsory school attendance, §22.1-268.
Condominiums.
Real estate board, §§55-79.98, 55-79.99.
Conservation police officers, §29.1-203.
Conservatorship of estate of incapacitated persons, §64.2-2001.
Conservators of property of absentees.
Appointment, §64.2-2400.
Conservators of the peace.
Special conservators, §19.2-13.
Consolidation of localities.
Counties, cities and towns consolidating into single county or city.
Jurisdiction of courts, effect of consolidation, §15.2-3546.
Consumer protection.
Assurances of voluntary compliance, §59.1-202.
Investigative orders, §59.1-201.
Restraining prohibited acts, §59.1-203.

JURISDICTION —Cont'd
Contempt.
Court of appeals, §17.1-404.
Contracting to supply services or things.
Long-arm statute, §8.01-328.1.
Court of appeals.
Appellate jurisdiction, §17.1-405.
Original jurisdiction, VA SCt Rule 5A:5.
Original jurisdiction in matters of contempt and injunctions, writs of mandamus, prohibition and habeas corpus, §17.1-404.
Damage stamp program.
Claim filing and adjudication, §29.1-356.
Dams.
Applications for leave to build or rebuild, §62.1-116.
Hydroelectric power dams.
Provision violations, §62.1-97.
United States jurisdiction, §62.1-103.
Orders for construction or destruction, §29.1-532.
Department of agriculture and consumer services.
State control of charitable gaming, §18.2-340.18.
Descent and distribution, §§64.2-312, 64.2-313.
Desertion and nonsupport.
Effect of divorce proceedings, §20-79.
Exclusive original jurisdiction, §20-67.
Transfer of cases between courts, §20-83.1.
Devices on certain containers.
Provision violations.
Appeals, §§59.1-99, 59.1-100.
Discrimination against persons with disabilities, §51.5-46.
Disease prevention and control.
Public safety employee testing, §32.1-45.2.
District courts.
Civil cases, §16.1-77.
Partition of personal property, §16.1-77.2.
Criminal and traffic, §16.1-123.1.
Judges' powers, §§16.1-69.24 to 16.1-69.29.
Small claims courts, §16.1-122.2.
Divorce.
Domicile and residency requirements, §20-97.
Spousal support, §20-107.1.
Suits for divorce, §20-96.
Docks, §§62.1-164, 62.1-165.
Drainage projects.
Circuit courts, §21-292.
Driving while intoxicated.
Continuing jurisdiction of convicting court, §18.2-271.1.
Eminent domain.
Jurisdiction of proceedings, §25.1-201.
Employee liens.
Enforcement, §43-25.
Equal credit opportunities.
Provision violations, §6.2-505.
Escheats.
Duty failures by escheators, §§55-189, 55-190.
Ethics advisory panels, senate and house of general assembly, §30-119.
Exhumations, §32.1-286.
Farm products consigned to commission merchants.
Lien for, §43-62.
Fiduciaries.
Commissioners of accounts, §64.2-1200.
Assistant commissioners, §64.2-1201.
Deputy commissioners, §64.2-1202.
Conservators of property of absentees.
Appointment, §64.2-2400.

JURISDICTION —Cont'd
Fiduciaries —Cont'd
Property transfers to foreign fiduciaries, §64.2-1427.
Qualification, §64.2-1401.
Resignation, §64.2-1424.
Fire investigations.
Issuance of warrants, §27-32.2.
Property seizure.
Restitution, §27-34.1.
Fire marshals, local.
Entry to investigate releases of hazardous or regulated substances, §27-37.1.
Fishing, tidal waters.
Provision violations, §28.2-907.
Fishways.
Orders for construction or destruction, §29.1-532.
Freedom of information act proceedings.
District court civil jurisdiction, §16.1-77.
Grand juries.
Multi-jurisdiction grand juries.
Setting out jurisdiction, §19.2-215.8.
Guardians.
Appointment, §64.2-1702.
Incapacitated persons, §64.2-2001.
Transfers to minors, §64.2-1901.
Habeas corpus.
Court of appeals, §17.1-404.
Supreme court jurisdiction, §17.1-310.
Habitual motor vehicle offenders.
District court jurisdiction, §16.1-77.
Health.
Provision violations, §§32.1-27, 32.1-27.1.
Health care professional referrals.
Failure to disclose interest in referral facilities, §54.1-2964.
Health inspections.
Warrant issuance, §32.1-25.
Health spa investigations.
Orders to compel compliance, §59.1-308.2.
Heavy equipment dealers.
Provision violations, §59.1-358.
Home care organizations.
Injunctions to cease providing services, §32.1-162.13.
Hospitals.
Clinical privileges for podiatrists or midwives, §32.1-134.4.
Financial interest in out-patient service providers.
Disclosure violations, §32.1-125.2.
Staff membership or privileges.
Physician denial, expulsion or curtailment, §32.1-134.1.
Human research.
Compliance with federal policies and regulations, §32.1-162.20.
Hydroelectric power dams.
Provision violations, §62.1-97.
United States jurisdiction, §62.1-103.
Impoundment of surface waters.
Riparian owner rights.
Application for leave to store floodwaters, §62.1-107.
Income tax return preparer, action to enjoin, §58.1-348.2.
Indictments, presentments or informations.
Effect of defects in indictments, §19.2-226.
Industrial hygiene and safety profession.
Protection of use of job titles.
Enforcement, §40.1-141.

JURISDICTION —Cont'd
Injunctions.
Court of appeals, §17.1-404.
General jurisdiction of circuit courts, §8.01-620.
In personam jurisdiction, §§8.01-328 to 8.01-330.
In rem jurisdiction.
Basis authorized, §8.01-330.
Interpleader.
District court civil jurisdiction, §16.1-77.
Interstate family support act.
Continuing exclusive jurisdiction.
Duration of personal jurisdiction, §20-88.36.
Enforcement of child support order, §20-88.40.
Modification of child support order, §20-88.39.
Modification of spousal support order, §20-88.43:2.
Duration of personal jurisdiction, §20-88.36.
Modification of order of foreign country or political subdivision, §20-88.77:3.
Modification of support orders, §20-88.77:1.
Nonresidents, §20-88.35.
Applicability to nonresident subject to personal jurisdiction, §20-88.43:1.
Jail facilities substandard.
Prisoner confinement limitations and transfers, §§53.1-69, 53.1-70.
Jail farms, county and city.
Court jurisdiction over, §53.1-99.
Juvenile and domestic relations district courts, §16.1-241.
Appeals, §16.1-296.
Concurrent jurisdiction, §16.1-244.
Errors.
Time for raising claim of error, §16.1-272.1.
Family offenses, §16.1-278.14.
Retention during appeal involving children in foster care, §16.1-242.1.
Retention of jurisdiction until minor reaches majority, §16.1-242.
Subsequent offenses by juvenile, §16.1-271.
Transfer from other courts, §16.1-245.
Transfer to circuit court, §16.1-269.1.
Appeals by juvenile, §16.1-269.4.
Determinations by court, §16.1-269.6.
Placement of juvenile, §16.1-269.5.
Retention by juvenile court, §16.1-269.3.
Waiver in certain cases, §16.1-270.
Keeper liens.
Enforcement, §43-34.
Landings, §§62.1-164, 62.1-165.
Landlord and tenant.
Residential landlords and tenants.
Retaliatory actions, §55-248.40.
Legal separation.
Domicile and residency requirements, §20-97.
Spousal support, §20-107.1.
Suits for divorce, §20-96.
Local retirement systems.
Counties with urban county executive form of government, §51.1-823.
Long-arm jurisdiction, §8.01-328.1.
Magistrates.
Territorial jurisdiction, §19.2-44.
Mandamus.
Circuit courts, §17.1-513.
Court of appeals, §17.1-404.
Supreme court jurisdiction, §17.1-309.
Marks on certain containers.
Provision violations.
Appeals, §§59.1-99, 59.1-100.

JURISDICTION —Cont'd
Mechanics' and materialmen's liens.
Enforcement, §43-22.
Perfection.
Hearings on validity, §43-17.1.
Medicaid.
Benefits.
Fraudulently obtaining, §§32.1-312, 32.1-321.3.
Disclosure of information, §32.1-325.3.
Investigations, §32.1-320.
Payments.
Obtaining or attempting to obtain excess payments, §32.1-312.
Medical assistance services director.
Subpoena applications, §32.1-324.1.
Medical care facilities.
Certificates of public need.
Enjoining projects, §32.1-102.8.
Membership camping.
Investigations, §59.1-334.
Metropolitan Washington airports authority.
Courts of Commonwealth, §5.1-173.
Midwives.
Hospital privileges, §32.1-134.4.
Mills.
Applications for permission to build or rebuild, §62.1-116.
Mineral mine rescue crews, §45.1-161.292:43.
Minimum contacts.
Long-arm statute, §8.01-328.1.
Motorcycle dealers, §46.2-1993.3.
Names on certain containers.
Provision violations.
Appeals, §§59.1-99, 59.1-100.
Nonresidents.
Suits against state, US Const Amd 11.
Notaries.
Territorial jurisdiction, §47.1-13.
Nursing homes.
Provision violations.
Penalties, §32.1-27.1.
Ohio river valley water sanitation commission, §62.1-74.
Out-of-state defendants, §8.01-328.1.
Overhead high voltage line safety.
Enforcement of provisions, §59.1-412.
Oyster and clamming grounds, damages.
Improvement of stream navigability, §62.1-158.
Pari-mutuel wagering on horses.
Racing commission, §59.1-373.
Partition of personal property.
District courts, §16.1-77.2.
Party jurisdiction.
Traffic infractions.
Arrest of nonresidents, §§46.2-944 to 46.2-947.
Paternity proceedings.
Commencement of action, §20-49.2.
Pay-per-call services.
Orders to compel, §59.1-433.
Penal bonds.
How jurisdiction determined, §8.01-4.1.
Personal information privacy.
Provision violations, §59.1-444.
Personal jurisdiction.
Declaratory judgment actions, §8.01-184.1.
How acquired in certain actions, §§8.01-328 to 8.01-330.
Jurisdiction on other basis authorized, §8.01-330.
Person, defined, §8.01-328.
Recognizing foreign country money-judgments.
Effect of lack of personal jurisdiction, §8.01-465.11.

JURISDICTION —Cont'd
Personal jurisdiction —Cont'd
Service of process or notice on secretary of the Commonwealth, §8.01-329.
When personal jurisdiction may be exercised, §8.01-328.1.
Personal property taxes.
Personal jurisdiction for tax liabilities, §8.01-328.1.
Persons with disability.
Disposition of real estate, §8.01-68.
Petroleum products franchises.
Provision violation actions, §59.1-21.12.
Physicians.
Hospital staff membership or privileges.
Denial, expulsion or curtailment, §32.1-134.1.
Piers, §§62.1-164, 62.1-165.
Podiatrists.
Hospital privileges, §32.1-134.4.
Port authority.
Coal, expediting shipments, §62.1-134.1.
Provision violations, §62.1-132.12.
Port of Reedville.
Appointment of agent, §62.1-163.
Prison crimes, §53.1-205.
Prisoner releases improper.
Issuance of arrest warrants, §53.1-28.
Prisoners' health care.
Involuntary admission and treatment, §§53.1-40.1 to 53.1-40.10.
Professions and occupations licensure.
Enforcement of provisions, §54.1-111.
Prohibition.
Circuit courts, §17.1-513.
Court of appeals, §17.1-404.
Supreme court jurisdiction, §17.1-309.
Public building authority.
Actions against authority, §2.2-2277.
Public school authority.
Law suits against authority, §22.1-174.
Public service companies.
Remedies of persons aggrieved by, §56-6.
Wagonway construction, §56-16.
Public utilities, state operation.
Compensation to utilities, §56-522.
Injunctions against violation of provisions, §56-525.
Restoration of possession to utility, §56-521.
Quasi in rem jurisdiction.
Basis authorized, §8.01-330.
Quo warranto.
Circuit courts, §17.1-513.
Duty failures by water and sewerage companies, §56-264.
Racing commission.
Pari-mutuel wagering on horses, §59.1-373.
Railroad corporations.
Cattle guards, §§56-429, 56-430.
Appeals of decisions, §56-435.
Enclosed lands, §56-433.
Fences, §§56-429, 56-430.
Real estate board.
Condominiums, §§55-79.98, 55-79.99.
Reedville port.
Appointment of agent, §62.1-163.
Release of liens, §43-68.
Religious organizations.
Abandoned property actions, §57-11.
Appointment of trustees to effectuate purposes of conveyances, §57-8.

JURISDICTION —Cont'd
Religious organizations —Cont'd
Determination of property rights on division of church or society, §57-9.
Land held in adverse possession, §57-17.
Suits by members to have land sold or mortgaged, §§57-14, 57-15.
Suits by trustees to have land sold or mortgaged, §57-15.
Retail sales and use tax.
Collection of tax from dealers, §58.1-612.
Retaliatory discharges.
Workers' compensation.
Employee exercise of rights, §65.2-308.
Sales of purchaser information.
Provision violations, §59.1-444.
Sanitation districts law of 1938.
Court proceedings, §21-144.
Discharges into tidal waters, §21-221.
Sanitation districts law of 1946.
Discharges into nontidal waters, §21-289.
Separate maintenance.
Claims for, §20-96.
Service contracts, extended.
Orders to compel, §59.1-439.
Service of notice, process and other papers.
Generally, §§8.01-285 to 8.01-327.2.
See SERVICE OF NOTICE, PROCESS AND OTHER PAPERS.
Sewerage companies.
Failure to perform duties.
Quo warranto, §56-264.
Sexual sterilization, §§54.1-2975 to 54.1-2977.
Single act rule.
Long-arm statute, §8.01-328.1.
Small claims courts, §16.1-122.2.
Solicitation of charitable or civic contributions.
Contempt for obstruction of investigations, §57-59.
Local license appeals, §57-63.
Solid waste or recycling revolving fund.
Collection of money due fund, §62.1-241.5.
Spearfishing under the influence.
Persons participating in rehabilitation program, §29.1-738.5.
State.
Boundaries.
See STATE.
State corporation commission.
Concurrent jurisdiction of commission and court, §12.1-38.
Powers and duties generally, §12.1-12.
Remedies of persons aggrieved by public service corporations, §56-6.
Streams.
Improvement of navigability.
Claims for damages to oyster and clamming grounds, §62.1-158.
Submerged lands.
Fines, §28.2-1213.
Injunctions, §28.2-1211.
Supplier liens.
Enforcement, §43-25.
Supreme court.
Appeals, writs of error and supersedeas, §17.1-310.
Appellate jurisdiction, VA Const Art VI §1.
Habeas corpus, §17.1-310, VA Const Art VI §1.
Judicial censure, retirement and removal, VA Const Art VI §1.

JURISDICTION —Cont'd
Supreme court —Cont'd
Judicial inquiry and review commission.
Complaints filed by, §17.1-906.
Mandamus and prohibition, §17.1-309, VA Const Art VI §1.
Original jurisdiction, VA SCt Rule 5:7.
Surfboarding under the influence.
Persons participating in rehabilitation program, §29.1-738.5.
Surrogacy contracts.
Petition and hearing for court approval, §20-160.
Taxation.
Income tax return preparer, action to enjoin, §58.1-348.2.
Tax liens of Commonwealth.
Jurisdiction over Commonwealth for purposes of determining validity, amount and priority, §58.1-1809.
Tobacco product manufacturers' responsibilities.
Enforcement of requirements.
Submission to jurisdiction of Commonwealth, §3.2-4215.
Tobacco warehouses.
Establishment, §61.1-38.
Toll bridge photo-monitoring system.
Actions under, §§46.2-819.1, 46.2-819.3.
Tortious injury.
Long-arm statute, §8.01-328.1.
Traffic infractions.
Party jurisdiction.
Arrest of nonresidents, §§46.2-944 to 46.2-947.
Transacting business.
Long-arm statute, §8.01-328.1.
Transfers to minors, §64.2-1901.
Travel clubs.
Orders to compel, §59.1-451.
Trustees.
Appointment, §64.2-1412.
Removal, §64.2-1412.
Substituted trustees.
Appointment, §64.2-1405.
Surety bonds, §64.2-1412.
Testamentary trustees.
Qualification, §§64.2-1401, 64.2-1402.
Trusts.
Personal jurisdiction over trustee and beneficiaries, §64.2-711.
Unclaimed property, disposition of.
Claims to property of proceeds of sale, §55-210.22.
Unemployment compensation.
Claims adjudication, §60.2-625.
Appeals, §60.2-620.
Judicial review of board of review, §60.2-631.
Orders to compel, §60.2-627.
Criminal cases, §60.2-119.
Employer taxation.
Collection of taxes.
Injunctions, §60.2-522.
Evaluation of employing unit as employer, §60.2-500.
Uniform computer information transactions act.
Choice of forum, §59.1-501.10.
United States acquired lands.
Jurisdiction over lands acquired by United States, §§1-400 to 1-408.
Unlawful entry or detainer.
District court civil jurisdiction, §16.1-77.

JURISDICTION —Cont'd
Venereal diseases.
Compelling examinations, testing or treatment, §32.1-57.
Virginia Beach.
Territorial limits of city, concurrent jurisdiction with the Commonwealth, §15.2-1725.1.
Vital records.
Amendment petitions, §32.1-269.
Disclosure petitions, §32.1-271.
Volunteer firefighters relief.
Appeals of questions of fact, §27-48.
Wagonway construction, §56-16.
Waterskiing under the influence.
Persons participating in rehabilitation program, §29.1-738.5.
Waters of the state.
Big Sandy river.
Obstructing or dumping refuse into, §62.1-194.3.
Bulkheads, §§62.1-164, 62.1-165.
Clearing watercourses between counties of obstructions, §62.1-6.
Contaminating state waters, §62.1-194.1.
Docks, §§62.1-164, 62.1-165.
Landings, §§62.1-164, 62.1-165.
Obstructing state waters, §62.1-194.1.
Piers, §§62.1-164, 62.1-165.
Solid waste or recycling revolving fund.
Collection of money due fund, §62.1-241.5.
Streams.
Improvement of navigability.
Claims for damages to oyster and clamming grounds, §62.1-158.
Water supply revolving fund.
Collection of money, §62.1-237.
Wharves, §§62.1-164, 62.1-165.
Water supply companies.
Failure to perform duties.
Quo warranto, §56-264.
Forfeiture of surety bonds, §32.1-174.1.
Water supply revolving fund.
Collection of money, §62.1-237.
Wetlands.
Permit review, §28.2-1315.
Provision violations.
Fines, §28.2-1320.
Wharves, §§62.1-164, 62.1-165.
Wills, §§64.2-312, 64.2-313.
Grant of powers to personal representatives or trustees, §64.2-106.
Probate, §64.2-443.
Establishment bills, §64.2-448.
Filing, §64.2-448.
Final orders or decrees.
Effect, §64.2-448.
Impeachment bills, §64.2-448.
Filing, §64.2-448.
Workers' compensation.
Employee status.
Confirming jurisdiction.
Res judicata effect of judicial determination, §8.01-420.5.
False statements or representations, §65.2-312.
Payments.
Lump sum payments.
Appointment of trustees, §65.2-523.
Peer review of medical costs.
Discovery of communications, §65.2-1308.
Statewide coordinating committee.
Corrective actions, §65.2-1306.

JURISDICTION —Cont'd
Workers' compensation —Cont'd
Retaliatory discharges.
Employee exercise of rights, §65.2-308.
Workers' compensation commission, §65.2-700.
Workers' compensation insurance and self-insurance.
Policy clause requirements, §65.2-809.

JURY COMMISSIONERS.
Addition of names to jury list, §8.01-346.
Appointment, §8.01-343.
Delivery of jury lists to clerk for safekeeping, §8.01-346.
Electronic random selection techniques, §§8.01-345, 8.01-350.1.
Federal employees prohibited, exception, §2.2-2801.
Fee for drawing jury, §17.1-618.
Jury box.
Disposition of list of jurors drawn, §8.01-351.
How names of jurors drawn from box, §8.01-348.
How names put in jury box, §8.01-347.
Notations on ballots drawn, §8.01-349.
Preparation of list of jurors drawn, §8.01-351.
Redrawing of ballots returned to box, §8.01-349.
Return of ballots to box, §8.01-349.
Writ of venire facias, defined, §8.01-354.
Mechanical random selection process, §§8.01-345, 8.01-350.1.
Notification, §8.01-344.
Oath of office, §8.01-344.
Objections to irregularities in jury lists, §8.01-352.
Preparation of jury lists, §8.01-345.
Removal of names from jury list, §8.01-346.

JURY DELIBERATIONS.
Sound recordings, §18.2-468.
Summary jury trial, §8.01-576.3.

JURY DUTY.
See JURY SERVICE.

JURY FEES AND ALLOWANCES.
Additional allowance to juror summoned from other political subdivision, §17.1-618.
Amount juror entitled to, §17.1-618.
Board and lodging of jurors kept together overnight, §17.1-618.
Sheriff to present bill to governing body, §15.2-1614.1.
Entry on minutes stating amount due and by whom payable, §17.1-621.
Escheat inquests, §55-174.
Nonentitlement to compensation, §17.1-620.
Payment, §§17.1-619, 17.1-623.
Summary jury trial, §8.01-576.2.
Transmittal orders, §17.1-622.

JURY IN ESCHEAT INQUEST, §55-173.
Attendance, §55-174.
Compensation, §55-174.
Retrial, §55-177.
Verdicts, §55-175.

JURY INSTRUCTIONS.
Circuit courts.
Form, VA SCt Rules Part 1 Appx Form 2.
Local rules of court.
Compliance with prescribed forms, VA SCt Rule 1:15.
Criminal cases.
Nonconformity with model instructions, §19.2-263.2.

JURY INSTRUCTIONS —Cont'd
Form.
Circuit courts, VA SCt Rules Part 1 Appx Form 2.
Giving of instructions, VA SCt Rule 3A:16.
Local rules of court.
Compliance with prescribed forms, VA SCt Rule 1:15.
Model jury instructions.
Effect of nonconformity of proposed jury instructions, §8.01-379.2.
Objections.
Counsel's opportunity to object, VA SCt Rule 3A:16.
How made, VA SCt Rule 3A:16.
Proposed instructions, VA SCt Rule 3A:16.
Effect of nonconformity with model jury instructions, §8.01-379.2.

JURY SELECTION.
Appointment of jury commissioners, §8.01-343.
Notification, §8.01-344.
Oath of office, §8.01-344.
Challenge for cause, VA SCt Rules 1:22, 3A:14.
Confidentiality of juror information, VA SCt Rule 3A:14.1.
Corruptly procuring to be summoned, §18.2-466.
Criminal cases.
How jurors selected from panel, §19.2-262.
Deferral of jury service.
Occupational inconvenience, §8.01-341.2.
Disqualification from jury service, §8.01-338.
Electronic random selection techniques, §§8.01-345, 8.01-350.1.
Eligibility for jury service, §§8.01-337 to 8.01-340.
Eminent domain.
Just compensation proceedings, §§25.1-228, 25.1-229.
Employee service, penalizing for, §18.2-465.1.
Examination of jurors, VA SCt Rule 3A:14.
Exemption from jury service, §§8.01-341, 8.01-341.1.
Fraudulently drawing, §18.2-467.
Grand juror service as trial juror.
Case on which same grand jury returned indictment, §19.2-261.
Impartiality of officer summoning, §18.2-465.
Jury box.
Disposition of list of jurors drawn, §8.01-351.
How names of jurors drawn from box, §8.01-348.
How names put in jury box, §8.01-347.
Notation on ballots drawn, §8.01-349.
Preparation of list of jurors drawn, §8.01-351.
Redrawing of ballots returned to box, §8.01-349.
Return of ballots to box, §8.01-349.
Writ of venire facias, defined, §8.01-354.
Jury of vicinage, US Const Amd 6.
Jury panel selection, §8.01-357.
List of qualified persons.
Addition of names, §8.01-346.
Delivery to clerk of court, §8.01-346.
How names of jurors drawn from box, §8.01-348.
How names put in jury box, §8.01-347.
Objections to irregularities in jury lists, §8.01-352.
Preparation by jury commissioners, §8.01-345.
Removal of names, §8.01-346.
Safekeeping by clerk of court, §8.01-346.
Mechanical random selection techniques, §§8.01-345, 8.01-350.1.

JURY SELECTION —Cont'd
Number of jurors.
Civil cases, §8.01-359.
Criminal cases, §19.2-262.
Officer summoning to act impartially, §18.2-465.
Penalizing employee for service on jury panel, §18.2-465.1.
Peremptory strikes.
Criminal cases, §19.2-262.
Random selection process, §8.01-345.
Mechanical or electronic techniques for the term of court, §8.01-350.1.
Restrictions on jury service.
Number of times called, §8.01-342.
Striking from panel.
Criminal cases, §19.2-262.
Summary jury trial, §8.01-576.2.
Voter registration lists.
Courts may obtain for selection purposes, §24.2-405.

JURY SERVICE, §§8.01-337 to 8.01-342, 8.01-353 to 8.01-363.
Age limitation, §8.01-337.
Allowances to jurors for attendance and travel expenses, §§17.1-618 to 17.1-623.
Automatic exemptions from jury service, §8.01-341.
Blindness or partial blindness.
Persons not deemed incompetent, §8.01-337.
Boarding, §17.1-618.
Sheriff to present bill to governing body, §15.2-1614.1.
Bribery.
Giving or receiving bribe, §18.2-441.
Change of venire.
Impartial jury cannot be obtained locally, §8.01-363.
Deferral of jury service.
Occupational inconvenience, §8.01-341.2.
Discharge or dispensing with attendance of jurors, §8.01-355.
When court may discharge jury, §8.01-361.
Disqualification from service, §8.01-338.
Person to whom request not made, §8.01-339.
Person who has case during term, §8.01-340.
Drawing additional jurors, §8.01-355.
Protracted trial, §8.01-360.
Swearing in new juror in place of one disabled, §8.01-361.
Eligibility to serve, §8.01-337.
Employee service, penalizing, §18.2-465.1.
Exemption from jury service, §§8.01-341, 8.01-341.1.
National guard and naval militia, §44-94.
Voters during election, VA Const Art II §9.
Fees.
Additional allowance to juror summoned from other political subdivision, §17.1-618.
Allowances to jurors for attendance and travel expenses, §§17.1-618 to 17.1-623.
Amount juror entitled to, §17.1-618.
Board and lodging to jurors kept together overnight, §17.1-618.
Entry on minutes stating amount due and by whom payable, §17.1-621.
Nonentitlement to compensation, §17.1-620.
Payment, §§17.1-619, 17.1-623.
Summary jury trial, §8.01-576.2.
Transmittal orders, §17.1-622.
Identification of jurors, §8.01-353.1.

JURY SERVICE —Cont'd
Impartiality of jurors, §8.01-358.
When impartial jury cannot be obtained locally, §8.01-363.
Ineligibility, §§8.01-339, 8.01-340.
Jury list used for trial of cases during term, §8.01-355.
Jury panel.
How jurors selected from panel, §8.01-359.
Identification of jurors, §8.01-353.1.
Making copy available to counsel, §8.01-353.
Selection, §8.01-357.
Limitation of jury service.
Occupational inconvenience, §8.01-341.2.
Military personnel of U. S. armed forces.
Personnel not considered residents, §8.01-337.
National guard and naval militia active officers and members.
Exemption, §44-94.
Note-taking by jurors, VA SCt Rule 1:23.
Notice to jurors, §8.01-353.
Failure to appear, §8.01-356.
Objection, §8.01-353.
Number of jurors.
Civil cases, §8.01-359.
Criminal cases, §19.2-262.
Objection to notice to jurors, §8.01-353.
Occupational inconvenience.
Deferral or limitation of jury service, §8.01-341.2.
Permissive exemption from jury service, §8.01-341.1.
Petit jury, §8.01-359.
Protracted trial.
Additional jurors, §8.01-360.
Residency requirement, §8.01-337.
Restrictions on jury service.
Number of times called, §8.01-342.
Selection of jurors.
General provisions, §§8.01-343 to 8.01-352.
See JURY SELECTION.
Selection of jury panel, §8.01-357.
Service of summons, §8.01-298.
Special juries, §§8.01-359, 8.01-362.
Threats or force, obstructing justice by, §18.2-460.
Three-member jury, §8.01-359.
Travel expenses, allowances to jurors, §§17.1-618 to 17.1-623.
Verification of juror identity, §8.01-353.1.
Voir dire examination, §8.01-358.
Preliminary instructions, VA SCt Rule 1:21.
Voluntary exemption from jury service, §8.01-341.1.
Voters during election, privilege from, VA Const Art II §9.
Work shift.
Restrictions on beginning after day of jury duty, §18.2-465.1.
Writ of venire facias, defined, §8.01-354.

JURY TAMPERING, §18.2-467.

JURY TRIAL, VA Const Art I §8.
Allowances to jurors for attendance and travel expenses, §§17.1-618 to 17.1-623.
Additional allowance to juror summoned from other political subdivision, §17.1-618.
Amount juror entitled to, §17.1-618.
Board and lodging of jurors kept together overnight, §17.1-618.
Entry on minutes stating amount due and by whom payable, §17.1-621.

JURY TRIAL —Cont'd
Allowances to jurors for attendance and travel expenses —Cont'd
Fee to jury commissioner and commissioner in chancery, §17.1-618.
Nonentitlement to compensation, §17.1-620.
Payment of allowances, §§17.1-619, 17.1-623.
Transmittal orders making allowances to supreme court, treasurers and jurors, §17.1-622.
When juror not entitled to compensation, §17.1-620.
Alternative pleading.
Separate trial or motion of party, §8.01-281.
Appeals from general district courts in civil cases, §16.1-113.
Asbestos-related injuries.
Bifurcated trial, §8.01-374.1.
Consolidation of issues or claims, §8.01-374.1.
Attachment.
Suggestion that codefendant has not made full disclosure, §8.01-562.
Best evidence rule exceptions.
Issues of law or fact, VA SCt Rule 2:1008.
Bifurcated trial.
See BIFURCATED TRIAL.
Boarding and lodging jurors, §17.1-618.
Sheriff to present bill to governing body, §15.2-1614.1.
Bribery.
Giving or receiving bribe, §18.2-441.
Capital cases.
Sentencing, §§19.2-264.2 to 19.2-264.5.
Circuit courts.
Right to trial by jury, VA SCt Rule 3:21.
Trial by jury or by court, VA SCt Rule 3:22.
Voir dire of jury, VA SCt Rule 3:22A.
Civil cases, VA Const Art I §11.
Claims against the state.
Recovery of claims, §8.01-194.
Tort claims act, §8.01-195.4.
Clouds on title, §55-153.
Competency of jurors as witnesses, VA SCt Rule 2:606.
Constitutional right to trial by jury, §8.01-336, VA Const Art I §11.
Consumer protection, §59.1-206.
Contempt.
Fine and imprisonment limited unless jury impaneled, §18.2-457.
Imposed on juror in criminal case, procedure, §19.2-11.
Counsel's argument before jury.
Preservation of right, §8.01-379.
Court-ordered jury trial, §8.01-336.
Courtroom cameras.
Experimental program, §19.2-266.
Criminal cases, §§19.2-260 to 19.2-264.1, VA Const Art I §8.
Allowances to jurors for attendance and travel expenses, §§17.1-618 to 17.1-623.
Alternate forms of verdicts, VA SCt Rule 3A:16.
Applicability of Title 8.01, §19.2-260.
Bifurcated trial, VA SCt Rule 3A:17.1.
Capital cases.
Procedure for trial by jury, §19.2-264.3.
Sentencing proceeding, §19.2-264.4.
Sentencing proceeding after conviction, §19.2-295.1.
Persons twice previously convicted of violent felonies (three strikes), §19.2-297.1.

JURY TRIAL —Cont'd
Criminal cases —Cont'd
Bifurcated trial —Cont'd
Traffic offenses.
Jury consideration of prior traffic record before sentencing, §46.2-943.
Capital cases, §§19.2-264.2 to 19.2-264.5.
Charging grand jury in presence of person selected as trial juror, §19.2-261.
Confidentiality of jury information, §19.2-263.3, VA SCt Rule 3A:14.1.
Contact between judge and juror prohibited, §19.2-263.1.
Contempt of juror, procedure, §19.2-11.
Conviction of lesser offense, VA SCt Rule 3A:17.
Exclusion of persons from trial, §19.2-266.
Exclusion of witnesses, §19.2-265.1, VA SCt Rule 2:615.
Complaining witness.
Misdemeanor cases prosecuted without attorney, §19.2-265.5.
Victims and family members, §19.2-265.01.
How jurors selected from panel, §19.2-262.
Joinder of defendants, §19.2-262.1.
Jury instructions, §19.2-263.2.
Multiple defendants, VA SCt Rule 3A:17.
New trial as to some defendants, §19.2-287.
Number of jurors, §19.2-262.
Personal information of jurors.
Confidentiality, §19.2-263.3, VA SCt Rule 3A:14.1.
Poll of jury, VA SCt Rule 3A:17.
Return of verdict, VA SCt Rule 3A:17.
Separate verdicts, VA SCt Rule 3A:16.
Sequestration of jury in felony case, §19.2-264.
Striking from panel, §19.2-262.
Title 8.01, applicability, §19.2-260.
Unanimous consent of jury, VA Const Art I §8.
Venue.
Motion for change of venue, §19.2-244.
Views by juries, §19.2-264.1.
Waiver of jury trial, §19.2-262.
Criminal forfeiture, §19.2-386.10.
Damages.
Informing jury of amount sought, §8.01-379.1.
Death penalty.
Sentencing procedure for trial by jury, §§19.2-264.2 to 19.2-264.5.
Declaratory judgments, §8.01-188.
Defenses.
Motion raising defenses, VA SCt Rule 3A:9.
Deliberation of jury.
Sound recordings, §18.2-468.
Devices on certain containers.
Appeals, §59.1-100.
Directed verdicts.
Prohibited, §8.01-378.
Distress.
Landlord and tenant.
Rent payments not in money, §55-238.
Procedure for trial, §55-230.1.
Electronic media.
Judicial discretion to permit radio or television coverage, §19.2-266.
Publicity.
Attorneys at law, VA SCt Rule Pt 6 §II Rule 3.5.
Eminent domain.
Just compensation proceedings, §§25.1-228, 25.1-229.
Compensation of jury, §25.1-235.
Who determines just compensation, §25.1-220.

JURY TRIAL —Cont'd
Equity.
Issues tried before advisory jury, §8.01-336.
Plea in equity, §8.01-336.
Evidence.
Best evidence rule exceptions.
Issues of law or fact, VA SCt Rule 2:1008.
Formal exceptions to rulings, §8.01-384.
Variance between evidence and allegations.
Remedy, §8.01-377.
Exclusion of persons from trial.
Criminal cases, §19.2-266.
Exclusion of witnesses, VA SCt Rule 2:615.
Civil cases, §8.01-375.
Criminal cases, §19.2-265.1.
Complaining witness.
Misdemeanor cases prosecuted without attorney, §19.2-265.5.
Victims or family members, §19.2-265.01.
Exhibits.
What jury may carry from courtroom, §8.01-381.
Expert witnesses.
Exclusion of witnesses in civil cases, §8.01-375, VA SCt Rule 2:615.
Felony convictions.
How accused may be convicted of felony, §19.2-283.
Freedom of information act.
Exclusions from chapter, §2.2-3703.
Guilty pleas.
Waiver of jury trial in felony cases, §19.2-257.
Hung jury.
Motion to strike the evidence.
Renewal of motion, VA SCt Rule 1:11.
Instruction to jury.
See JURY INSTRUCTIONS.
Judicial sales.
Rule against judgment for amounts due.
Trial by jury of issues may upon rule, §8.01-107.
Jurors as witnesses.
Competency, VA SCt Rule 2:606.
Jury of vicinage, US Const Amd 6.
Jury selection.
See JURY SELECTION.
Jury service.
See JURY SERVICE.
Landlord and tenant.
Distress.
Rent payments not in money, §55-238.
Marks on certain containers.
Appeals, §59.1-100.
Media coverage.
Judicial discretion to permit radio or television coverage, §19.2-266.
Publicity.
Attorneys at law, VA SCt Rule Pt 6 §II Rule 3.5.
Multiple counsels.
Preservation of counsels' right to argue before jury, §8.01-379.
Names on certain containers.
Appeals, §59.1-100.
New trial.
Power to grant new trial, §8.01-383.
Note-taking by jurors, VA SCt Rule 1:23.
Objections.
Motion raising objections, VA SCt Rule 3A:9.
Occupational safety and health.
Evidence of civil penalties against employers, §40.1-51.3:2.
Petroleum products franchises.
Provision agreements concerning, §59.1-21.11.

JURY TRIAL —Cont'd
Photographs.
Judicial discretion to permit taking of photographs, §19.2-266.
Pleading in alternative.
Separate trial or motion of party, §8.01-281.
Pleadings.
What jury may not carry from courtroom, §8.01-381.
Presence of accused.
Felony trial, §19.2-259.
Prisoners' health care.
Involuntary admission and treatment.
Right to jury trial on appeal, §53.1-40.2.
Products liability.
Bifurcated trial, §8.01-374.1.
Consolidation of issues or claims, §8.01-374.1.
Publicity.
Attorneys at law.
Professional responsibility, VA SCt Rule Pt 6 §II Rule 3.5.
Public officers, removal from office, §24.2-237.
Public trial, US Const Amd 6.
Public utilities, state operation.
Compensation to utilities, §56-522.
Quo warranto, §8.01-643.
Radio broadcasting.
Judicial discretion, §19.2-266.
Publicity.
Attorneys at law, VA SCt Rule Pt 6 §II Rule 3.5.
Removal of public officer from office, §24.2-237.
Rule on witnesses, VA SCt Rule 2:615.
Civil trials, §8.01-375.
Criminal trials, §§19.2-265.01, 19.2-265.1, 19.2-265.5.
Preliminary hearings, §19.2-184.
Scheduling civil cases for trial, VA SCt Rule 1:20.
Selection of jury.
See JURY SELECTION.
Sentencing.
Ascertainment of punishment by jury, §19.2-295.
Modification of sentence by court.
Written explanation, §19.2-295.
Separate proceeding, §19.2-295.1.
Capital cases, §§19.2-264.2 to 19.2-264.5.
Separate trials.
Civil cases, §§8.01-272, 8.01-281.
Criminal cases, VA SCt Rules 3A:1, 7C:4.
Sequestration of jurors.
Criminal cases, §19.2-264.
Sexually violent predators, civil commitment.
Right to, §37.2-908.
Speedy trial, §19.2-243, VA Const Art I §8, US Const Amd 6.
Appeals by Commonwealth.
Dismissal because of speedy trial violation, §19.2-398.
Summary jury trial, §§8.01-576.1 to 8.01-576.3.
Television broadcasting.
Judicial discretion, §19.2-266.
Publicity.
Attorneys at law, VA SCt Rule Pt 6 §II Rule 3.5.
Threats or force, obstructing justice by, §18.2-460.
Title.
Clouds on title, §55-153.
Traffic infractions.
Appeal to circuit courts, §19.2-258.1.
Travel expenses, allowances to jurors, §§17.1-618 to 17.1-623.

JURY TRIAL —Cont'd
Trial de novo.
See DE NOVO TRIALS.
Unanimous consent of jury required for conviction, VA Const Art I §8.
Unlawful entry and detainer.
Application by either party, §8.01-125.
Variance between evidence and allegations.
Amendment of pleadings to conform to evidence, §8.01-377.
Venue.
Criminal cases.
Motion for change of venue, §19.2-244.
Verdicts.
Entering final judgment after verdict set aside, §8.01-430.
Unanimous consent of jury required for conviction, VA Const Art I §8.
Views by juries.
Civil cases, §8.01-376.
Criminal cases, §19.2-264.1.
Waiver of trial, §8.01-336.
Failure to appear in misdemeanor case, §19.2-258.
Wills.
Probate, §64.2-446.
Witnesses.
Exclusion of witnesses, VA SCt Rule 2:615.
Civil cases, §8.01-375.
Criminal trials, §§19.2-265.01, 19.2-265.1, 19.2-265.5.
Preliminary hearings, §19.2-184.
How summons for witness served, §8.01-298.
Jurors as witnesses.
Competency, VA SCt Rule 2:606.
Witness protection program, §52-35.

JURY VIEW OF SCENE.
Civil cases, §8.01-376.
Criminal cases, §19.2-264.1.

JUSTICES OF SUPREME COURT.
See SUPREME COURT JUSTICES.

JUSTICES OF THE PEACE.
Abolition of justice of the peace system, §§19.2-31, 19.2-32.
Acknowledgments.
Validating certain acts, §55-126.
Magistrates.
Generally, §§19.2-26 to 19.2-48.1.
See MAGISTRATES.

JUSTIFICATION.
Defamation, §8.01-46.

JUVENILE AND DOMESTIC RELATIONS DISTRICT COURTS, §§16.1-226 to 16.1-245.1.
Abortion.
Minor electing not to seek consent of authorized person.
Order authorizing physician to perform abortion, §16.1-241.
Admission of pleadings, VA SCt Rule 8:8.
Adoption.
Generally, §§63.2-1200 to 63.2-1248.
See ADOPTION.
Parental placement adoption.
See ADOPTION.
Advance sheets to Virginia reports.
Distribution to, §17.1-316.
Amended pleadings, VA SCt Rule 8:8.
Appeals, VA SCt Rule 8:20.
Juvenile proceedings generally, §§16.1-296 to 16.1-298.

JUVENILE AND DOMESTIC RELATIONS DISTRICT COURTS —Cont'd
Appeals —Cont'd
Representation of Commonwealth by Commonwealth's attorneys, §16.1-232.
Withdrawal of appeal of conviction, §16.1-133.
Appearances.
Child appearance before intake officers, §16.1-260.
Appointment of personnel, §16.1-69.39.
Arraignment.
Juvenile delinquency cases, VA SCt Rule 8:16.
Arrest warrants.
Who may issue process of arrest, §19.2-71.
Assistance to court, congestion in work.
Designation of judge to sit in district, §16.1-69.35.
Attorneys.
Role of counsel when representing children, VA SCt Rule 8:6.
Substitution of counsel, §16.1-69.32:1.
Attorneys' fees, §16.1-278.19.
Bail.
Generally, §§19.2-119 to 19.2-134.
See BAIL AND RECOGNIZANCE.
Bill of particulars, VA SCt Rule 8:8.
Bonds of officers and employees, §16.1-69.18.
Case records retention, §16.1-69.55.
Chapter controlling in event of conflict, §16.1-229.
Child abuse and neglect, §§63.2-1500 to 63.2-1527.
See CHILD ABUSE AND NEGLECT.
Child custody.
Generally.
See CHILD CUSTODY.
Transfer to for enforcement of orders, §20-79.
Child support.
Contents of petitions for support, VA SCt Rule 8:3.
Generally.
See CHILD SUPPORT.
Motion to reduce support arrearages to judgment.
Service of notice, process and other papers, VA SCt Rule 8:4.
Transfer to for enforcement of orders, §20-79.
Child visitation.
Generally.
See CHILD VISITATION.
Transfer to for enforcement of orders, §20-79.
Citizens advisory council, §16.1-240.
Clerks.
Bond, §16.1-69.18.
Continuance in office, §16.1-69.37.
Fees.
Services of clerks in certain civil cases, §16.1-69.48:5.
Generally.
See DISTRICT COURT CLERKS.
Oath of office, §16.1-69.17.
Protective order transfers, §16.1-253.1.
Emergency protective orders, §16.1-253.4.
Secure remote access to records, §§17.1-292 to 17.1-295.
Substitutes.
Authorization, §16.1-69.38.
Commonwealth's attorneys.
Prosecution of felony charges before court and representation of Commonwealth on appeal, §16.1-232.
Congestion in work of court.
Designation of judge to sit in district, §16.1-69.35.
Contempt powers, §16.1-292.
Continuance in office of personnel, §16.1-69.37.

JUVENILE AND DOMESTIC RELATIONS DISTRICT COURTS —Cont'd
Continuances, VA SCt Rule 8:14.
Court management.
Reporting requirements, VA SCt Rule 1:15.
Court-ordered reports, VA SCt Rule 8:5.
Court reporters, VA SCt Rules 8:10, 8:11.
Court services, §16.1-233.
Citizens advisory council, §16.1-240.
Compensation and expenses of court service staff, §16.1-238.
Directors of court services units, §16.1-236.1.
Duties of department, §16.1-234.
How probation, parole and related court services provided, §16.1-235.
Payment of travel expenses, §16.1-239.
Quarters, utilities and office equipment for service units, §16.1-234.
State-operated court services units.
Directors, §16.1-236.1.
Supervisory officers, §16.1-236.
Definitions, §§16.1-69.5, 16.1-228, VA SCt Rule 8:2.
Denial of pleadings, VA SCt Rule 8:8.
Destruction of records after transferring to electronic format, §16.1-69.55.
Discovery, VA SCt Rule 8:15.
Divorce proceedings, effect.
Transfer of matters to court, §20-79.
Dockets.
Trial de novo in circuit court, §19.2-240.
Electronic filing and service, VA SCt Rules 8:7, 8:8.
Electronic preservation of records, VA SCt Rule 8:12.
Emancipation of minors, §§16.1-331 to 16.1-334.1.
Emergency situations.
Judicial consent, VA SCt Rule 8:22.
Emergency surgical or medical treatment for juveniles.
Judicial consent proceedings.
Contents of petition, VA SCt Rule 8:3.
Endorsements of orders, VA SCt Rule 8:19.
Errors.
Time for raising claim of error, §16.1-272.1.
Establishment in county or city, §16.1-69.7.
Existing courts continued and redesignated, §16.1-69.8.
Family abuse.
Protection orders, §16.1-279.1.
Family offenses, criminal jurisdiction, §16.1-278.14.
Fees collected by judge, substitute judge, clerk or employees.
Payment to circuit court clerk, §16.1-69.48.
Services of judges and clerks in certain civil cases, §16.1-69.48:5.
Felony charges before court.
Prosecution by Commonwealth's attorneys, §16.1-232.
Felony prosecutions.
Jurisdiction limited to probable cause determination, §16.1-241.
Forum non conveniens, VA SCt Rule 8:10.
Guardians ad litem.
Role of guardian when representing child, VA SCt Rule 8:6.
Inanimate object sexual penetration.
Preliminary hearings, §19.2-218.2.
Intake officers, when court is closed, §16.1-235.1.

JUVENILE AND DOMESTIC RELATIONS DISTRICT COURTS —Cont'd
Interstate family support, §§20-88.32 to 20-88.82.
See INTERSTATE FAMILY SUPPORT ACT.
Judges.
Acting chief judge, §16.1-69.11:1.
Additional powers, §16.1-69.27.
Associate judge or assistant judge, inapplicability of terms, §16.1-69.11.
Bill of particulars, power to direct filing of, §16.1-69.25:1.
Bond, §16.1-69.18.
Canons of judicial conduct.
Rules part 6.
See JUDGES.
Chief judge, §16.1-69.11.
Acting chief judge, §16.1-69.11:1.
Administrative duties, §16.1-69.35.
Appointment and removal of personnel, §16.1-69.39.
Directing substitute to serve, §16.1-69.21.
Conservators of the peace, §§16.1-69.26, 16.1-241.
Contempt of court, powers and jurisdiction to punish summarily, §16.1-69.24.
Continuance in office of judges in office, §§16.1-69.9, 16.1-69.9:1.
Designated as juvenile and domestic relations district court judge, §16.1-69.11.
Designation to hear cases in general district courts, §16.1-69.35.
Detention orders, authorization to issue, §16.1-255.
Disqualification, grounds, §16.1-69.23.
Dual officeholding, §16.1-69.19.
Fees.
Services of clerks in certain civil cases, §16.1-69.48:5.
General assembly providing for judges of courts not of record, VA Const Art VI §8.
Inability to perform duties.
Substitute to serve, §16.1-69.21.
Incompatible offices, §16.1-69.19.
Number, §§16.1-69.6:1, 16.1-69.10.
Substitute judges, §16.1-69.14.
Oath of office, §16.1-69.17.
Practice of law limitations, §16.1-69.12.
Privileged from arrest under civil process, §§8.01-327.1, 8.01-327.2.
Qualifications, §16.1-69.15.
Removal, §16.1-69.22.
Residence requirements, §§16.1-69.6:1, 16.1-69.16.
Retired district court judges.
Temporary recall, §16.1-69.22:1.
Salaries, §16.1-69.44.
How payable, §16.1-69.46.
Substitute judges.
Appointment, §16.1-69.9:1.
Authorization for, §16.1-69.38.
Compensation, §16.1-69.44.
Designated as substitute judge, §16.1-69.11.
Number, §16.1-69.14.
Powers and duties, §16.1-69.21.
Practice of law limitations, §16.1-69.12.
Removal, §16.1-69.22.
When substitute to serve, §16.1-69.21.
Successor judges.
Appointment or election to fill vacancies, §§16.1-69.9:2 to 16.1-69.9:4.
Terms of office, §16.1-69.9.
Chief judge, §16.1-69.11.

JUVENILE AND DOMESTIC RELATIONS DISTRICT COURTS —Cont'd
Judges —Cont'd
Terms of office —Cont'd
Successors appointed or elected to fill vacancies, §§16.1-69.9:2, 16.1-69.9:4.
Time within which to qualify, §16.1-69.17:1.
Travel expenses, §16.1-69.47:1.
Vacancy in office.
Appointment while general assembly not in session, §16.1-69.9:2.
Election of successors by general assembly, §16.1-69.9:4.
Failure to qualify, §16.1-69.17:1.
Investigation and certification of necessity before vacancy filled, §16.1-69.9:3.
Pro tempore appointment, §16.1-69.9:2.
Terms of successors, §16.1-69.9:2.
Warrants, summons and subpoenas, issuance, §16.1-69.25.
Judicial consent.
Emergency situations, VA SCt Rule 8:22.
Emergency surgical or medical treatment for a juvenile.
Contents of petitions, VA SCt Rule 8:8.
Judicial emergency, §§17.1-330, 17.1-331.
Jurisdiction, §16.1-241.
Concurrent jurisdiction, §16.1-244.
Errors.
Time for raising claim of error, §16.1-272.1.
Family offenses, §16.1-278.14.
Retention during appeal involving children in foster care, §16.1-242.1.
Retention until child reaches majority, §16.1-242.
Subsequent offenses by juvenile, §16.1-271.
Transfer from other courts, §16.1-245.
Transfer to circuit courts, §16.1-269.1.
Appeals by juvenile, §16.1-269.4.
Criminal proceedings, §16.1-269.1.
Determinations by court, §16.1-269.6.
Placement of juvenile, §16.1-269.5.
Retention by juvenile court, §16.1-269.3.
Waiver in certain cases, §16.1-270.
Juvenile delinquency cases.
Arraignment, VA SCt Rule 8:16.
Juvenile justice information system, §§16.1-222 to 16.1-225.
Data submissions by court service units, §16.1-224.
Juvenile proceedings generally, §§16.1-246 to 16.1-309.1.
See JUVENILE PROCEEDINGS.
Local boards of social services.
Cooperation with court, §63.2-321.
Local court service units, §16.1-235.
Local rules of court.
Posting in clerk's office, VA SCt Rule 1:15.
Marital sexual abuse.
Preliminary hearings, §19.2-218.2.
Mediation program for alternative resolution of disputes.
Establishment of voluntary civil program by chief judge, §16.1-69.35.
Medical evidence admissible in courts, §16.1-245.1.
Mentally ill children.
Psychiatric treatment of minors, §§16.1-335 to 16.1-348.
See MENTAL HEALTH.
Motions to transfer venue, VA SCt Rule 8:10.

JUVENILE AND DOMESTIC RELATIONS DISTRICT COURTS —Cont'd
Newborn children substance abuse.
Proceedings regarding, §16.1-241.3.
Notice of withdrawal of appeal of conviction, §16.1-133.
Objections to felony jurisdiction, §16.1-241.
Objections to pleadings, VA SCt Rule 8:8.
Operation of courts, §16.1-230.
Orders.
Endorsements of orders, VA SCt Rule 8:19.
Organization of courts, §16.1-230.
Parents of undisciplined children.
Proceedings against, §16.1-241.2.
Parole officers.
How services provided, §16.1-235.
Powers, duties and functions, §16.1-237.
Replacement intake officers, §16.1-235.1.
Supervisory officers, §16.1-236.
Petitions.
Contents in certain proceedings, VA SCt Rule 8:3.
Matters alleged to be within jurisdiction.
Commenced by filing, §16.1-260.
Photographic preservation of records, VA SCt Rule 8:12.
Pleadings.
Filing requirements.
Judicial discretion, VA SCt Rule 8:9.
Format, VA SCt Rules 8:7, 8:8.
General rules as to pleadings, VA SCt Rule 8:8.
Judicial discretion, VA SCt Rule 8:9.
Motion or petition in certain proceedings.
Contents of pleadings, VA SCt Rule 8:3.
Pleas, VA SCt Rule 8:18.
Preliminary hearings.
Spousal sexual crimes, §19.2-218.2.
Preservation of records, VA SCt Rule 8:12.
Probation officers.
Compensation and expenses, §§16.1-238, 16.1-239.
Detention orders, authorization to issue, §16.1-255.
Filing of reports, §16.1-274.
How services provided, §16.1-235.
Intake duties and responsibilities, §16.1-260.
Interference with or obstruction of officer, §16.1-257.
Local court service units, §16.1-235.
Oath of office, §16.1-69.17.
Powers, duties and functions, §16.1-237.
Replacement intake officers, §16.1-235.1.
State court service units, §16.1-235.
Studying report prior to transfer hearing, §16.1-269.2.
Supervisory officers, §16.1-236.
Production of documents and things.
Requests for subpoenas for witnesses and records, VA SCt Rule 8:13.
Protective orders.
Child abuse or neglect, §16.1-253.
Emergency orders, §16.1-253.4.
Family abuse, §§16.1-253.1, 16.1-279.1.
Felony violations, §16.1-253.2.
Misdemeanor for violating, §16.1-253.2.
Psychiatric treatment of minors, §§16.1-335 to 16.1-348.
See MENTAL HEALTH.
Public school discipline of students.
Civil fine against parent for failure to comply with parental responsibility and involvement requirements.
Enforcement of civil penalty by court, §22.1-279.3.

JUVENILE AND DOMESTIC RELATIONS DISTRICT COURTS —Cont'd
Purposes and intent of chapter, §16.1-227.
Recognizances.
Generally, §§19.2-135 to 19.2-152.
See BAIL AND RECOGNIZANCE.
Records.
Case records retention, §16.1-69.55.
Destruction of records after transferring to electronic format, §16.1-69.55.
Expungement, §16.1-306.
Generally.
See DISTRICT COURTS.
Secure remote access to records, §§17.1-292 to 17.1-295.
Removal of personnel, §16.1-69.39.
Reopening case after conviction, §16.1-133.1.
Replacement intake officers, §16.1-235.1.
Reports.
Court-ordered reports, VA SCt Rule 8:5.
Retention of jurisdiction until child reaches majority, §16.1-242.
Retention of jurisdiction while appeal involving children in foster care, §16.1-242.1.
Rules of practice and procedure.
Authority to adopt, §16.1-231.
Construction and interpretation, §16.1-231.
Formulation by supreme court, §16.1-69.32.
Scope of rules, VA SCt Rule 8:1.
Criminal rules, VA SCt Rule 3A:1.
Scope of rules, VA SCt Rule 8:1.
Criminal rules, VA SCt Rule 3A:1.
Secure remote access to records, §§17.1-292 to 17.1-295.
Service of notice, process and other papers.
Electronic filing and service, VA SCt Rules 8:7, 8:8.
Juvenile proceedings.
Service of summons and waiver of service, §16.1-263.
Motion to reduce support arrearages to judgment, VA SCt Rule 8:4.
Services for courts, §16.1-233.
Citizens advisory council, §16.1-240.
Compensation and expenses of court service staff, §16.1-238.
Duties of department, §16.1-234.
How probation, parole and related court services provided, §16.1-235.
Payment of travel expenses, §16.1-239.
Quarters, utilities and office equipment for service units, §16.1-234.
Supervisory officers, §16.1-236.
Short title of statutes embraced in chapter, §16.1-226.
Spousal sexual crimes.
Preliminary hearings, §19.2-218.2.
Spousal support.
Contents of petitions for support, VA SCt Rule 8:3.
Motion to reduce support arrearages to judgment.
Service of notice, process and other papers, VA SCt Rule 8:4.
Standards for writings to be docketed, §55-108.
Use of copies admitted to record elsewhere, §55-109.
State court service units, §16.1-235.
Student disciplinary problems.
Proceedings against parents of undisciplined children, §16.1-241.2.

JUVENILE AND DOMESTIC RELATIONS DISTRICT COURTS —Cont'd
Subpoenas duces tecum.
Requests for subpoenas for witnesses and records, VA SCt Rule 8:13.
Substitution of counsel, §16.1-69.32:1.
Substitution of personnel.
Authorization, §16.1-69.38.
Supervisory officers.
Probation or other court services, §16.1-236.
Support and maintenance.
Contents of petitions for child or spousal support, VA SCt Rule 8:3.
Motion to reduce support arrearages to judgment.
Service of notice, process and other papers, VA SCt Rule 8:4.
Tape recording of proceedings by party or counsel, §16.1-69.35:2.
Termination of residual parental rights, §16.1-283.
Transcripts of proceedings, VA SCt Rule 8:11.
Transfer from other courts.
Exclusive jurisdiction lying within court, §16.1-245.
Transfer of child to circuit court for criminal proceedings, §16.1-269.1.
Appeals by juvenile, §16.1-269.4.
Determinations by court, §16.1-269.6.
Placement of juvenile, §16.1-269.5.
Retention by juvenile court, §16.1-269.3.
Transfer of venue, §16.1-243, VA SCt Rule 8:10.
Motion to transfer, VA SCt Rule 8:10.
Transition provisions.
Repealing clause, §16.1-69.1.
Travel expenses of court officers, §§16.1-238, 16.1-239.
Trial rights of parties.
Notification and waiver, VA SCt Rule 8:17.
Venue.
Motion to transfer venue, VA SCt Rule 8:10.
Original venue, §16.1-243.
Transfer of venue, §16.1-243.
Waiver of jury trial.
Trial de novo, §19.2-262.
Waiver of service in juvenile proceedings, §16.1-263.
Withdrawal of appeal of conviction, §16.1-133.
Witnesses.
Compelling attendance of witnesses, VA SCt Rule 8:13.

JUVENILE AND DOMESTIC RELATIONS DISTRICT COURTS LAW.
Generally, §§16.1-226 to 16.1-241.
See JUVENILE AND DOMESTIC RELATIONS DISTRICT COURTS.
Juvenile proceedings generally, §§16.1-245 to 16.1-309.1.
See JUVENILE PROCEEDINGS.

JUVENILE CARE FACILITIES.
Generally.
See JUVENILE DETENTION AND OTHER CARE FACILITIES.

JUVENILE COMMUNITY CRIME CONTROL, §§16.1-309.2 to 16.1-309.10.
Appropriations.
State appropriations for operating costs of programs.
How determined, §16.1-309.6.
Compliance review by department, §16.1-309.9.

JUVENILE COMMUNITY CRIME CONTROL —Cont'd
Costs.
Detention homes and other facilities.
Reimbursement in part by Commonwealth, §16.1-309.5.
Maintenance of juveniles in programs, §16.1-309.8.
Detention homes and other facilities.
Cost reimbursement in part by Commonwealth, §16.1-309.5.
Visitation and management, §16.1-309.10.
Establishment of community-based system of services, §16.1-309.3.
Financial assistance.
Payments, determination of amount, §16.1-309.7.
Legislative intent, §16.1-309.2.
Maintenance of juveniles in programs.
Costs, §16.1-309.8.
Payments of financial assistance.
Determination, §16.1-309.7.
Planning.
Biennial local plan, §16.1-309.3.
Statewide plan for juvenile services, §16.1-309.4.
Planning and budget system of state.
Appropriations for operating costs of programs.
How determined, §16.1-309.6.
Purpose of act, §16.1-309.2.
Reports.
Quarterly report, §16.1-309.3.
Superintendent, §16.1-309.10.
Standards.
State juvenile justice board to establish, §16.1-309.9.
Statewide plan for juvenile services, §16.1-309.4.

JUVENILE CORRECTIONAL FACILITIES.
See JUVENILE DETENTION AND OTHER CARE FACILITIES.

JUVENILE CORRECTIONAL OFFICERS.
Minimum standards, §9.1-102.

JUVENILE CORRECTIONS PRIVATE MANAGEMENT ACT, §§66-25.3 to 66-25.7.

JUVENILE DELINQUENCY.
Abduction by person confined to juvenile correctional center, §18.2-48.1.
Arraignment, VA SCt Rule 8:16.
Blood sample required for DNA analysis upon conviction or adjudication of felony, §16.1-299.1.
Carrying concealed weapons, persons ineligible.
Disqualification for concealed weapons permit, §18.2-308.09.
Commitment of children in secure local facilities, §16.1-284.1.
Duration of commitments, §16.1-285.
Commitment of delinquent child to juvenile justice department, §16.1-278.7.
Confidentiality of court records, §16.1-305.
Exception as to delinquent acts which would be felonies, §16.1-309.1.
Contributing to delinquency, §18.2-371.
Delinquent child defined, §16.1-228.
Disclosure of disposition in certain cases, §16.1-305.1.
Disposition of delinquent children for supervision, care and rehabilitation generally, §16.1-278.8.
First drug offense, §16.1-278.8:01.

JUVENILE DELINQUENCY —Cont'd
DNA analysis.
Blood sample required, §16.1-299.1.
Driving privileges of delinquent children.
Loss for alcohol, drug and handgun offenses, §16.1-278.9.
Drug offenses.
First drug offense, §16.1-278.8:01.
Evidence of juvenile's age, §16.1-274.1.
Fingerprinting or photographing children, §16.1-299.
Guilty finding, effect on status of child, §16.1-308.
Interstate compact relating to juveniles, §§16.1-323, 16.1-323.1.
Juvenile community crime control, §§16.1-309.2 to 16.1-309.10.
See JUVENILE COMMUNITY CRIME CONTROL.
Juvenile detention and other care facilities.
Generally, §§16.1-315 to 16.1-322.7.
See JUVENILE DETENTION AND OTHER CARE FACILITIES.
Placement in secure local facilities, §16.1-284.1.
Duration, §16.1-285.
Places of confinement, §16.1-249.
Proceedings in juvenile and domestic relations district courts generally, §§16.1-246 to 16.1-309.1.
See JUVENILE PROCEEDINGS.
Serious or habitual offender comprehensive action program, §§16.1-330.1, 16.1-330.2.
Sex offender and crimes against minors registry.
Generally.
See SEX OFFENDER REGISTRATION AND NOTIFICATION.
Registration procedures, §9.1-903.
Required registration, §9.1-901.
Nonresident offenders, §9.1-905.
Offenses requiring registration, §9.1-902.
Trespass after having been forbidden to do so, §§18.2-119, 18.2-120.
Venue of proceedings, §16.1-243.
Victims' right to be present at proceedings, §16.1-302.1.
Writ of actual innocence.
See WRIT OF ACTUAL INNOCENCE.

JUVENILE DETENTION AND OTHER CARE FACILITIES, §§16.1-315 to 16.1-322.7.
Abduction by detainee, §18.2-48.1.
Acquisition of property by commission, §§16.1-318, 16.1-319.
Aiding escape of child, §18.2-473.
Appropriation of funds to localities or commissions operating secure detention facilities, §16.1-322.
Apportionment of funds, §16.1-322.1.
Distribution and reallocation of reserve, §16.1-322.2.
Falsifying information, §16.1-322.3.
Political subdivisions, §16.1-321.
Quarterly payments, §16.1-322.2.
Reports monthly, §16.1-322.3.
Behavioral health and developmental services department.
Data collection on children and adolescents, §37.2-308.
Bond issues.
By commissions or political subdivisions, §§16.1-318, 16.1-321.

JUVENILE DETENTION AND OTHER CARE FACILITIES —Cont'd
Boot camps, §66-13.
Career training.
Academic and career training, §66-25.1:1.
Extension of limits of confinement and compensation, §66-25.1:3.
Technical education programs, §66-25.1:2.
Work release furlough to visit home or family, §66-25.1:4.
Carnal knowledge of child detained in, §18.2-64.1.
Punishment upon conviction of certain subsequent felony sexual assault, §18.2-67.5:2.
Cellular telephones.
Illegal conveyance to or possession by, §18.2-431.1.
Children from other counties or cities.
Secured detention facilities.
Payments for, §16.1-322.4.
Child taken into custody.
Criteria for detention or shelter care, §16.1-248.1.
Medical records, §16.1-248.3.
Mental health screening or assessment, §16.1-248.2.
Statements made at, §16.1-261.
Places of confinement for children, §16.1-249.
Placing child in detention home or in shelter care, §16.1-247.
Citizen detention commissions, §§16.1-315 to 16.1-322.
Acquisition of property by eminent domain, §16.1-319.
Admission of additional local governing bodies, §16.1-316.
Appropriations to commission by political subdivision, §16.1-321.
Bond issues, §§16.1-318, 16.1-321.
Chairman, §16.1-317.
Compensation and expenses, §16.1-317.
Exemption of property from execution and judgment lien, §16.1-320.
Joint or regional commissions authorized, §16.1-315.
Membership, §16.1-316.
Powers, §16.1-318.
Quorum, §16.1-317.
Record and reports of commission, §16.1-322.
Rules of procedure, §16.1-317.
Supervision by director of juvenile justice department, §16.1-318.
Commitment to secure local facility, §16.1-284.1.
Duration of commitments, §16.1-285.
Communications by persons outside of jail with prisoners, §18.2-473.1.
Community group homes or other residential care facilities.
Criminal background checks of employees or volunteers, §66-24.
Establishment and maintenance of system by department.
Authority of department, §66-24.
Conditions for initial licensure and renewal, §66-24.
Contractual agreements or staff expertise.
Proof, requiring, §66-24.
Criminal penalty.
Failure to comply with summary order of suspension, §66-24.

JUVENILE DETENTION AND OTHER CARE FACILITIES —Cont'd
Community group homes or other residential care facilities —Cont'd
Establishment and maintenance of system by department —Cont'd
Employment of personnel.
Authority of department, §66-24.
Human rights violations, notification, §66-24.
License or certification.
Homes or facilities contracted for rented by department, §66-24.
Regulations for license or certification.
Adoption by board, requirements, §66-24.
Self-reporting of lawsuits against.
Authority of department to require, §66-24.
Suspension of license or certification.
Summary order, §66-24.
Construction management contracts.
Fixed-price or not-to-exceed price design-build, §2.2-4307.
Contempt for violating court orders.
Commitment to facility, §16.1-292.
Contraband.
Delivery of articles to prisoners without authority, §18.2-474.
Delivery of drugs, firearms, etc., to prisoners, §18.2-474.1.
Credit for time confined awaiting trial, §53.1-187.
Crimes by detainees.
Abduction by detainee, §18.2-48.1.
Acts committed in facilities, §18.2-477.2.
Criteria for detention or shelter care of child taken into custody, §16.1-248.1.
Delivery of articles to prisoners without authority, §18.2-474.
Dental appointments for children under supervision.
Transportation responsibility and limitations, §16.1-254.
Department of juvenile justice.
Allowance to children, §66-22.
Appropriation of funds to localities or commissions operating secure detention facilities, §§16.1-322.1 to 16.1-322.3.
Authority to establish, staff and maintain, §66-13.
Boot camps, §66-13.
Care of children committed to department generally, §§66-13 to 66-25.2:1.
See JUVENILE JUSTICE DEPARTMENT.
Community group homes or other residential care facilities.
Establishment of system, licensure, regulation, §66-24.
Driver's license or employment applications.
Authority of superintendents, §66-23.
Education division, §66-13.1.
Powers of sheriffs, superintendents and agent, §66-21.
Religious preferences, collection of information, §66-25.
Supervision of citizen commissions by director, §16.1-318.
Detention homes.
Pre-trial and post-dispositional detention.
Mutual agreement between locality and department of juvenile justice, §66-14.
Reimbursement to locality for maintaining, §66-15.

JUVENILE DETENTION AND OTHER CARE FACILITIES —Cont'd
Detention homes —Cont'd
Schedule of per diem cost to locality for maintaining.
Department of juvenile justice to set, §66-15.
Drugs, delivery to detainees, §18.2-474.1.
Duration of commitments to, §16.1-285.
Eminent domain.
Powers of citizen detention commissions, §§16.1-318, 16.1-319.
Escape of child, §18.2-477.1.
Aiding escape, §18.2-473.
Officer allowing detainee charged with felony to escape, §18.2-475.
Officer allowing detainee charged with nonfelonious offense to escape, §18.2-476.
Establishment in locality without zoning ordinance.
Notice by person planning establishment, §15.2-2207.
Exemption of commission property from execution and judgment lien, §16.1-320.
Explosives, delivery to detainees, §18.2-474.1.
Failure to make monthly report, §16.1-322.3.
Falsifying information on monthly reports, §16.1-322.3.
Firearms, delivery to detainees, §18.2-474.1.
Fishing permits.
Special fishing permits, §29.1-317.
Hepatitis testing of employees, §32.1-45.2.
HIV testing of employees, §32.1-45.2.
Independent living services, provision of, §63.2-905.1.
Joint or regional citizen detention commissions authorized, §16.1-315.
Juvenile correctional officers.
Minimum standards, §9.1-102.
Juvenile justice board, §§16.1-322.5 to 16.1-322.7.
Local school boards not required to provide educational services, §66-25.6.
Post-project evaluation, records to be maintained, §66-25.7.
Powers and duties of director of department of juvenile justice not delegable, §66-25.5.
Private operation of detention facilities.
Authorization, §16.1-322.5.
Powers and duties not delegable to contractor, §16.1-322.6.
Promulgation of regulations, §16.1-322.7.
Regulations promulgated by board of juvenile justice, §66-25.6.
Term of contracts, §66-25.4.
Limitation on time for holding without adjudicatory or transfer hearing, §16.1-277.1.
Marijuana, delivery to detainees, §18.2-474.1.
Medical appointments for children under supervision.
Transportation responsibility and limitations, §16.1-254.
Mental health screenings and assessments, §16.1-248.2.
Statements made at, §16.1-261.
Misdemeanor.
Falsifying information on monthly reports, §16.1-322.3.
Notice by person planning to establish in locality without zoning ordinance, §15.2-2207.

JUVENILE DETENTION AND OTHER CARE FACILITIES —Cont'd
Placement in secure local facility, §16.1-284.1.
Duration of commitments, §16.1-285.
Places of confinement for children, §16.1-249.
Private facility to be established in locality.
Public notice and hearing by persons desiring to establish, §15.2-2207.
Private management of juvenile corrections, §§66-25.3 to 66-25.7.
Contracts for financing, site selection, design, etc., §66-25.4.
Definitions, §66-25.3.
Design-build-operate contracts authorized, §66-25.7.
Fixed-price or not-to-exceed basis contracts authorized, §66-25.7.
Juvenile justice board.
Authorization, §16.1-322.5.
Powers and duties not delegable to contractor, §16.1-322.6.
Promulgation of regulations, §16.1-322.7.
Psychological and psychiatric evaluations.
Transportation responsibility and limitations, §16.1-254.
Records and reports of citizen detention commission, §16.1-322.
Religious preferences, collection of information, §66-25.
Reports by localities or commissions eligible to receive state funds, §16.1-322.3.
Failure to make report, §16.1-322.3.
Falsifying information, §16.1-322.3.
School superintendent, notice prior to release of certain offenders, §66-25.2:1.
Secure facility or detention home.
Appropriation of funds to localities or commissions operating, §§16.1-322.1 to 16.1-322.3.
Children from other counties or cities.
Payments for, §16.1-322.4.
Defined, §16.1-228.
Serious offenders.
Notice prior to release, §66-25.2.
Smoke detectors, §§36-99.4, 36-99.5.
Stores in juvenile correctional facilities.
Establishment, §66-22.1.
Time limitation on holding without adjudicatory or transfer hearing, §16.1-277.1.
Transfer of information upon commitment to, §16.1-287.
Transportation of children, responsibility for and limitation on, §16.1-254.
Work program.
Children committed to department of juvenile justice, §66-25.1.
Academic and career training, §66-25.1:1.
Extension of limits of confinement and compensation, §66-25.1:3.
Technical education programs, §66-25.1:2.
Work release furlough to visit home or family, §66-25.1:4.

JUVENILE DIABETES RESEARCH FOUNDATION.
Special license plates, §46.2-749.115.

JUVENILE JUSTICE ADVISORY COMMITTEE.
Criminal justice services department, §9.1-111.

JUVENILE JUSTICE BOARD.
Civil actions against members or employees.
Attorney general or assistant representing, §2.2-507.

JUVENILE JUSTICE BOARD —Cont'd
Juvenile detention and other care facilities.
Generally, §§16.1-315 to 16.1-322.7.
See JUVENILE DETENTION AND OTHER CARE FACILITIES.
Juvenile justice department, §§66-4 to 66-10.
See JUVENILE JUSTICE DEPARTMENT.
State inspector general.
Powers and duties, §2.2-309.4.

JUVENILE JUSTICE DEPARTMENT.
Career training.
Academic and career training, §66-25.1:1.
Extension of limits of confinement and compensation, §66-25.1:3.
Technical education programs, §66-25.1:2.
Work release furlough to visit home or family, §66-25.1:4.
Care of children committed to department, §§66-13 to 66-25.2:1.
Acceptance and expenditure of funds, §66-16.
Allowance for maintenance of children in private homes or facilities not operated by department, §66-14.
Allowance to children in facilities established by department, §66-22.
Authority to receive children, §66-13.
Behavioral services unit, §66-19.
Boot camps for juveniles, §66-13.
Community group homes for juveniles pending permanent placement, §66-24.
Disposition of property left by child after release or escape, §66-17.
Driver's license application by child in department facility.
Authority of superintendents, §66-23.
Education division, §66-13.1.
Employment certificate by child in department facility.
Authority of superintendents, §66-23.
Examination and placing of children, §66-18.
Examination of child by behavior services unit, §66-19.
Facilities for rehabilitation, training and confinement.
Duties of department, §66-13.
Intellectual disabilities, children with.
Preference in placing, §66-18.
Treatment, §66-20.
Medical, technical and clinical personal, employment, §66-19.
Mentally ill children, treatment, §66-20.
Notice prior to release of serious offenders, §66-25.2.
School superintendent, §66-25.2:1.
Personal property left by child after release or escape.
Disposition, §66-17.
Placing of children, §§66-14, 66-18.
Pre-trial and post dispositional detention homes.
Mutual agreements with localities, §66-13.
Reimbursements to localities for maintaining detention homes, §66-15.
Religious preferences, collection of information by facilities, §66-25.
Schedule of costs to locality of maintaining child in detention home, §66-15.
School superintendent, notice prior to release of serious offenders, §66-25.2:1.
Serious offenders, notice prior to release, §§66-25.2, 66-25.2:1.

JUVENILE JUSTICE DEPARTMENT —Cont'd
Care of children committed to department —Cont'd
Sheriffs powers, superintendents or agents of facilities to have, §66-21.
Temporary care of children.
Agreements with institutions or agencies, or cities or counties, §66-13.
Transfer of mentally ill or intellectually disabled child to other facility for treatment, §66-20.
Work programs for child committed to department, §66-25.1.
Academic and career training, §66-25.1:1.
Extension of limits of confinement and compensation, §66-25.1:3.
Technical education programs, §66-25.1:2.
Work release furlough to visit home or family, §66-25.1:4.
Civil actions against members or employees.
Attorney general or assistant representing, §2.2-507.
Commitment of child to department, §16.1-278.7.
Carnal knowledge of juvenile committed to, §18.2-64.1.
Punishment upon conviction of certain subsequent felony sexual assault, §18.2-67.5:2.
Confidentiality of records and reports, §16.1-300.
Secure local facilities, §16.1-284.1.
Serious offenders, §16.1-285.1.
Release and review hearings, §16.1-285.2.
Transfer of information upon commitment, §16.1-287.
Community group homes or other residential care facilities, §66-24.
Confidentiality of records and reports of children committed to department, §16.1-300.
Court-appointed special advocate, §§9.1-151 to 9.1-157.
Creation, §66-1.
Criminal offenses.
Payroll reports.
Withholding or providing false or misleading information, §65.2-1006.
Delinquency prevention and youth development, §§66-26 to 66-35.
Demographic characteristics of juveniles incarcerated.
Collection of data pertaining to, §66-13.
Director, §66-1.
Gang members list forwarded to Commonwealth's Attorneys Council.
List of juveniles committed to department found guilty of predicate offense belonging to gang, §66-3.2.
Powers, §66-3.
Stores in juvenile correctional facilities.
Establishment, §66-22.1.
Supervision of department, §66-2.
United States department of justice state criminal alien assistance program.
Requests from for compensation for certain costs.
Duties as to, §66-3.2.
Employees.
Grievance procedure, §2.2-3007.
Escape cases.
Admissibility of records, §18.2-480.1.

JUVENILE JUSTICE DEPARTMENT —Cont'd
Gang members list forwarded to Commonwealth's Attorneys Council.
List of juveniles committed to department found guilty of predicate offense belonging to gang, §66-3.2.
Juvenile and domestic relations district courts generally, §§16.1-226 to 16.1-245.1.
See JUVENILE AND DOMESTIC RELATIONS DISTRICT COURTS.
Juvenile care facilities.
Generally, §§16.1-315 to 16.1-322.7.
See JUVENILE DETENTION AND OTHER CARE FACILITIES.
Smoke detectors, §§36-99.4, 36-99.5.
Juvenile corrections private management act, §§66-25.3 to 66-25.7.
Juvenile justice information system, §§16.1-222 to 16.1-225.
Juvenile proceedings generally, §§16.1-246 to 16.1-309.1.
See JUVENILE PROCEEDINGS.
Notice.
Initial notice by certified mail, subsequent notices by regular mail, §66-10.01.
Police powers of employees with internal investigation authority, §66-3.
Records.
Confidentiality of records of children committed to department, §16.1-300.
Escape cases.
Evidence, §18.2-480.1.
Release of serious offenders.
Notice to be given prior to, §66-25.2.
School superintendent, §66-25.2:1.
Reports.
Confidentiality of reports of children committed to department, §16.1-300.
Secretary of public safety.
Agency responsibility, §2.2-221.
Sex offender and crimes against minors registry.
Receipt of person for whom registration required.
Information to be forwarded to state police, §16.1-278.7:01.
Release or discharge of person for whom registration required.
Notice of registration requirements, §16.1-278.7:02.
Sexually violent predators, civil commitment.
Database of prisoners incarcerated for sexually violent offenses.
Access to records, §37.2-905.2.
Smoke detectors.
Juvenile care facilities, §§36-99.4, 36-99.5.
State board of juvenile justice, §66-4.
Definitions, §66-12.
Delinquency prevention and youth development, §66-28.
Human research regulations, §66-10.1.
Initial notice by certified mail, subsequent notices by regular mail, §66-10.01.
Meetings, §66-8.
Members, §66-5.
Compensation and expenses, §66-7.
Officers, §66-6.
Powers and duties generally, §66-10.
Quorum, §66-9.
State inspector general.
Powers and duties, §2.2-309.4.

JUVENILE JUSTICE DEPARTMENT —Cont'd
Stores in juvenile correctional facilities.
Director may provide for establishment and operation, §66-22.1.
Supervision, §66-2.
Term of office, §66-1.
Work programs, §66-25.1.
Career training.
Academic and career training, §66-25.1:1.
Extension of limits of confinement and compensation, §66-25.1:3.
Technical education programs, §66-25.1:2.
Work release furlough to visit home or family, §66-25.1:4.

JUVENILE JUSTICE INFORMATION SYSTEM, §§16.1-222 to 16.1-225.
Central criminal records exchange.
Dissemination of juvenile record information, §19.2-389.1.
Confidentiality of data stored in system, §16.1-223.
Misdemeanor for violation of confidentiality, §16.1-225.
Data submissions by court service units, §16.1-224.
Delinquent juveniles.
Data submissions by court service units, §16.1-224.
Dissemination of juvenile record information.
Central criminal records exchange, §19.2-389.1.
Established within juvenile justice department, §16.1-222.
Final disposition of cases.
Data submissions by court service units, §16.1-224.
Misdemeanor for violation of confidentiality of records, §16.1-225.
Powers of director of juvenile justice department, §16.1-222.
Receipt, classification and filing of data, §16.1-223.

JUVENILE JUSTICE, STATE BOARD, §§66-4 to 66-10.
See JUVENILE JUSTICE DEPARTMENT.

JUVENILE OFFENDER DEMOGRAPHICS REPORT.
Secretary of public safety to provide, §2.2-222.

JUVENILE PROCEEDINGS, §§16.1-246 to 16.1-309.1.
Abandoned children.
Adults charged with violations of criminal law, procedure, §16.1-259.
Disposition, §16.1-278.2.
Abduction by person confined to juvenile correctional center, §18.2-48.1.
Abuse or neglect of child.
Adults charged with violations of criminal law, procedure, §16.1-259.
Confidentiality of court records, §16.1-305.
Defined, §16.1-228.
Disposition, §16.1-278.2.
Emergency removal order, §16.1-251.
Generally.
See CHILD ABUSE AND NEGLECT.
Hearing on removal order, §16.1-252.
Dispositional hearing, §16.1-278.2.
Placement in secure local facilities, §16.1-284.1.
Duration of commitments, §16.1-285.
Preliminary removal order, §16.1-252.

JUVENILE PROCEEDINGS —Cont'd
Abuse or neglect of child —Cont'd
Protective orders.
Emergency protective orders authorized, §16.1-253.4.
Felony violations, §16.1-253.2.
Misdemeanor for violating, §16.1-253.2.
Preliminary order, §16.1-253.
Adjudicatory hearing time limitation, §16.1-277.1.
Adoption.
Voluntary post-adoption contact and communication agreement.
Authority to enter into, §16.1-283.1.
Adults charged with violations of criminal law.
Procedure, §16.1-259.
Adult sentencing of child, §16.1-284.
Adult taken into custody for delinquent act committed as a juvenile.
Release on bail, §16.1-247.
Appeals, §§16.1-296 to 16.1-298.
Effect of petition for or pendency of appeal, §16.1-298.
Final judgment, §16.1-297.
Review of court orders, §16.1-289.
Suspension of judgment, order or decree upon petition or pendency of appeal, §16.1-298.
Transfer of case, §§16.1-269.1, 16.1-269.4.
Retention by juvenile court, §16.1-269.3.
Withdrawal of appeal.
Effect, §16.1-298.
Appearances.
Child appearance before intake officers, §16.1-260.
Juvenile's appearance at detention hearing, §16.1-250.
Juvenile's appearance at review hearing on confinement, §16.1-284.1.
Appointment of counsel, §§16.1-266 to 16.1-268.
Compensation of appointed counsel, §16.1-267.
Emancipation of minor, §16.1-332.
Generally, §16.1-266.
List of qualified attorneys, §16.1-266.1.
Order of appointment, §16.1-268.
Pro bono counsel.
First and second judicial district, §16.1-266.2.
Psychiatric inpatient treatment of minors, §16.1-341.
Standards for attorneys appointed, §16.1-266.1.
Arrest of child.
Warrants issued by magistrates, limitations, §16.1-256.
When and how child may be taken into immediate custody, §16.1-246.
Attorney appointment, §§16.1-266 to 16.1-268.
Compensation, §16.1-267.
Emancipation of minor, §16.1-332.
Generally, §16.1-266.
List of qualified attorneys, §16.1-266.1.
Order, §16.1-268.
Pro bono counsel.
First and second judicial district, §16.1-266.2.
Psychiatric inpatient treatment of minors, §16.1-341.
Standards for attorneys appointed, §16.1-266.1.
Attorneys' fees, §16.1-278.19.
Attorneys for the Commonwealth.
Transfer of case to circuit court, §16.1-269.1.
Victim impact statements, motion for, §16.1-273.
Bail.
Forfeiture of bond taken, §16.1-258.

JUVENILE PROCEEDINGS —Cont'd
Bail —Cont'd
Generally, §§19.2-119 to 19.2-134.
See BAIL AND RECOGNIZANCE.
Right to bail of juvenile taken into custody, §19.2-120.
Suspension of judgment, order or decree pending appeal, §16.1-298.
Transfer of case to circuit court.
Setting bail after completion of hearing, §16.1-269.2.
Validity and enforceability of bonds taken, §16.1-258.
Blood sample required for DNA analysis upon conviction or adjudication of felony, §16.1-299.1.
Bonds and other undertakings or appearance of person or performance of duty.
Forfeiture, §16.1-258.
Validity and enforceability, §16.1-258.
Burden of rebutting presumption of competency to stand trial.
Transfer cases, §16.1-269.1.
Chapter controlling in event of conflict, §16.1-229.
Child custody.
Generally.
See CHILD CUSTODY.
Juvenile and domestic relations district court.
Transfer to for enforcement of orders, §20-79.
Child in need of services.
Compulsory school attendance.
Proceedings against children for noncompliance with law, §22.1-262.
Confidentiality of court records, §16.1-305.
Defined, §16.1-228.
Disposition, §16.1-278.4.
Placement in secure local facilities, §16.1-284.1.
Duration of commitments, §16.1-285.
Taking child into custody.
When and how child may be taken into immediate custody, §16.1-246.
Child in need of supervision.
Compulsory school attendance.
Proceedings against children for noncompliance with law, §22.1-262.
Defined, §16.1-228.
Disposition, §16.1-278.5.
Taking child into custody.
When and how child taken into immediate custody, §16.1-246.
Violation of disposition orders, §16.1-292.
Child support.
Generally.
See CHILD SUPPORT.
Juvenile and domestic relations district court.
Transfer to for enforcement of orders, §20-79.
Child visitation.
Generally.
See CHILD VISITATION.
Juvenile and domestic relations district court.
Transfer to for enforcement of orders, §20-79.
Child welfare agencies, placement with, §16.1-286.
Child without parental care.
Disposition, §16.1-278.2.
Commencement of matters within jurisdiction of court, §16.1-260.
Commitment of child with mental illness or intellectual disability, §16.1-280.

JUVENILE PROCEEDINGS —Cont'd
Commitment of serious offenders, §16.1-285.1.
Release and review hearings, §16.1-285.2.
Serving adult sentence, §16.1-285.2.
Commitment, review of orders, §16.1-289.
Commitment to detention home or other secure facility, §16.1-284.1.
Duration of commitments, §16.1-285.
Commitment to juvenile justice department, §16.1-278.7.
Placement in secure local facilities, §16.1-284.1.
Serious offenders, §16.1-285.1.
Release and review hearings, §16.1-285.2.
Transfer of information upon, §16.1-287.
Committed child, support of, §16.1-290.
Estate in hands of guardian or trustee, §16.1-290.
Competency to stand trial, §§16.1-356 to 16.1-361.
Disclosure by juvenile during evaluation or restoration.
Use at adjudication or disposition hearing prohibited, §16.1-360.
Disposition of unrestorably incompetent juvenile, §16.1-358.
Disposition when juvenile found incompetent, §16.1-357.
Evaluation and determination of competency, §16.1-356.
Compensation of experts, §16.1-361.
Disclosure by juvenile during evaluation or restoration.
Use at adjudication or disposition hearing prohibited, §16.1-360.
Litigating certain issues when juvenile found incompetent, §16.1-359.
Motion objecting to sufficiency of petition.
Adjudication not precluded by finding that juvenile is incompetent, §16.1-359.
Compulsory school attendance.
Proceedings against children absent from school, §22.1-262.
Concealment or removal of child, §16.1-257.
Confidentiality of information.
Court records, §16.1-305.
Circuit court, §16.1-307.
Exceptions, §16.1-309.1.
Reports of court officials and employees, §16.1-303.
Juvenile justice department records and reports, §16.1-300.
Law enforcement records, §16.1-301.
Reports of court officials and employees, §16.1-303.
Violations, §16.1-309.
Contempt.
Failure of responsible person to provide nursing or medical care, §16.1-275.
Violations of court orders, §16.1-292.
Continuing participation programs.
Motion to reconsider orders, §16.1-289.1.
Contributing to delinquency of minor, §18.2-371.
Cooperation of certain agencies, officials, institutions, etc., §16.1-278.
Costs of maintenance.
Placement with child welfare agencies, private or locally operated facilities or nonresidential programs, §16.1-286.
Counseling.
Court-ordered counseling or treatment.
Payment of costs, §16.1-290.1.

JUVENILE PROCEEDINGS —Cont'd
Court-appointed special advocate, §§9.1-151 to 9.1-157.
Reports by advocates, §16.1-274.
Court-ordered counseling or treatment.
Payment of costs, §16.1-290.1.
Credit for time confined awaiting trial, §53.1-187.
Criminal offenses.
Abduction by person confined to juvenile correctional center, §18.2-48.1.
Criminal offenses, child treated as adult.
Offenses committed while incarcerated in state correctional facility, §16.1-271.
Powers of circuit court over juvenile offenders, §16.1-272.
Transfer to circuit court, §16.1-269.1.
Appeals by juvenile, §16.1-269.4.
Determinations by circuit court, §16.1-269.6.
Placement of juvenile, §16.1-269.5.
Retention by juvenile court, §16.1-269.3.
Waiver of jurisdiction and transfer, §16.1-270.
Criteria for detention or shelter care, §16.1-248.1.
Custody of child, court taking into custody.
Bail, right to.
Generally, §§19.2-119 to 19.2-134.
See BAIL AND RECOGNIZANCE.
Commitment to juvenile justice department, §16.1-278.7.
Concealment or removal of child, §16.1-257.
Criteria for detention or shelter care, §16.1-248.1.
Detention hearing procedure, §16.1-250.
Detention orders, limitation on issuance, §16.1-255.
Duties of persons taking child into custody, §16.1-247.
Interference with or obstruction of officer, §16.1-257.
Mental illness or intellectual disability, commitment of children with, §16.1-280.
Places of confinement for children, §16.1-249.
Removal orders, abuse or neglect of child.
Dispositional hearing, §16.1-278.2.
Emergency removal order, §16.1-251.
Hearing, §16.1-252.
Preliminary removal order, §16.1-252.
Time limitation, §16.1-277.1.
Warrants for children, limitations on issuance by magistrates, §16.1-256.
When and how child taken into immediate custody, §16.1-246.
Custody, visitation or support.
Committed child, support of, §16.1-290.
Estate in hands of guardian or trustee, §16.1-290.
Disposition to protect welfare of child and family, §16.1-278.15.
Failure to comply with support, §16.1-278.16.
Pendente lite support, §16.1-278.17.
Formula for determination, §16.1-278.17:1.
Definitions, §16.1-228.
Disposition, §16.1-278.1.
Delinquency.
Blood sample required for DNA analysis upon conviction or adjudication of felony, §16.1-299.1.
Confidentiality exceptions.
Commission of delinquent act which would be felony if committed by adult, §16.1-309.1.
Confidentiality of court records, §16.1-305.

JUVENILE PROCEEDINGS —Cont'd
Delinquency —Cont'd
Defined, §16.1-228.
Disclosure of disposition, §16.1-305.1.
Disposition, §16.1-278.8.
Commitment to juvenile justice department, §16.1-278.7.
First drug offense, §16.1-278.8:01.
Loss of driving privileges, alcohol, drug and handgun offenses, §16.1-278.9.
Drug offenses.
First drug offense, §16.1-278.8:01.
Evidence of juvenile's age, §16.1-274.1.
Fingerprinting or photographing, §16.1-299.
Guilty finding, effect on status of child, §16.1-308.
Placement in secure local facilities, §16.1-284.1.
Duration of commitments, §16.1-285.
Places of confinement, §16.1-249.
Venue, §16.1-243.
Victims' right to be present at proceedings, §16.1-302.1.
Department of juvenile justice.
Care of children committed to department, §§66-13 to 66-25.2:1.
See JUVENILE JUSTICE DEPARTMENT.
Detention and other care facilities.
Duration of commitments, §16.1-285.
Generally, §§16.1-315 to 16.1-322.7.
See JUVENILE DETENTION AND OTHER CARE FACILITIES.
Placement in secure local facility, §16.1-284.1.
Private operation, §§16.1-322.5 to 16.1-322.7.
Detention hearings, §16.1-250.
Detention orders, limitation on issuance, §§16.1-255, 16.1-256.
Disclosure of disposition in certain delinquency cases, §16.1-305.1.
Disposition, §§16.1-278 to 16.1-290.
Abused, neglected or abandoned children or children without parental care, §16.1-278.2.
Attorneys' fees, §16.1-278.19.
Child in need of services, §16.1-278.4.
Child in need of supervision, §16.1-278.5.
Child sentenced as adult, §16.1-284.
Facilities for, §53.1-63.1.
Commitment, review of order, §16.1-289.
Commitment to child welfare agency or private or locally operated public facility, §16.1-286.
Commitment to juvenile justice department, §16.1-278.7.
Committed child, support of, §16.1-290.
Estate in hands of guardian or trustee, §16.1-290.
Continuing programs, motion to reconsider orders for participation, §16.1-289.1.
Custody, visitation or support, §16.1-278.15.
Committed child, support of, §16.1-290.
Failure to comply with support obligation, §16.1-278.16.
Pendente lite support, §16.1-278.17.
Formula for determination, §16.1-278.17:1.
Delinquent children, §16.1-278.8.
Commitment to department of youth and family services, §16.1-278.7.
Disclosure of disposition in certain cases, §16.1-305.1.
First drug offense, §16.1-278.8:01.
Loss of driving privileges, alcohol, drug and handgun offenses, §16.1-278.9.
Disclosure in certain delinquency cases, §16.1-305.1.

JUVENILE PROCEEDINGS —Cont'd
Disposition —Cont'd
Family abuse, protection orders, §16.1-279.1.
Family offenses, criminal jurisdiction, §16.1-278.14.
Foster care plans, §16.1-281.
Permanency planning hearing for children in foster care, §16.1-282.1.
Review of foster care, §16.1-282.
Information upon commitment.
Transfer of, §16.1-287.
Mentally ill or intellectually disabled, §16.1-278.11.
Money judgments, §16.1-278.18.
Motions to reconsider orders.
Participation in continuing programs, §16.1-289.1.
Nonresidential program, placement in, §16.1-286.
Other cases.
Generally, §16.1-278.2.
Parental consent.
Judicial consent in lieu of, when authorized, §16.1-278.12.
Parent defined, §16.1-278.1.
Petitions to obtain treatment, rehabilitation and other services, §16.1-278.13.
Public service project defined, §16.1-278.1.
Relief of care and custody of child, §16.1-278.3.
Religious affiliations protected upon placement of child, §16.1-288.
Revocation or modification of order.
Violation by juvenile, §16.1-291.
School boards.
Information to be furnished by and to upon commitment of child, §16.1-287.
Secure local facilities, placement in, §16.1-284.1.
Duration of commitment, §16.1-285.
Serious offenders, commitment, §16.1-285.1.
Release and review hearings, §16.1-285.2.
Sex offender and crimes against minors registry.
Receipt by department of person for whom registration required.
Information to be forwarded to state police, §16.1-278.7:01.
Release or discharge by department of person for whom registration required.
Notice of registration requirements, §16.1-278.7:02.
Status offenders, §16.1-278.6.
Violation of orders by child.
Revocation or modification of order, §16.1-291.
Violations of orders by any person, §16.1-292.
Work permits, judicial consent, §16.1-278.13.
Dispositional hearings on removal orders, §16.1-278.2.
Divorce.
Juvenile and domestic relations district court.
Transfer to for enforcement of orders, §20-79.
DNA analysis.
Blood sample upon conviction or adjudication of felony, §16.1-299.1.
Dockets, indices and other books, §16.1-302.
Separate docket of cases, §16.1-302.
Drivers' licenses.
Loss for alcohol, drug or handgun offense, §16.1-278.9.
Suspension for violation of court orders, §16.1-292.
Effect of adjudication on status of child, §16.1-308.
Electronic transmission of case files, §16.1-305.

JUVENILE PROCEEDINGS —Cont'd
Electronic video and audio communications.
Appearance of juvenile at detention hearing, §16.1-250.
Appearance of juvenile before intake officers, §16.1-260.
Juvenile appearance at review hearing on confinement, §16.1-284.1.
Electronic video and audio communication systems.
Use to conduct hearings, §16.1-276.3.
Emergency protective orders, §16.1-253.4.
Emergency removal order, §16.1-251.
Emergency surgical or medical treatment for child.
Judicial consent in lieu of parental consent, §16.1-278.12.
Entrustment agreements.
Approval, §16.1-277.01.
Estate of committed child in hands of guardian or trustee, education and maintenance, §16.1-290.
Evidence.
Age of juvenile and delinquency proceedings, §16.1-274.1.
Competency to stand trial.
Disclosure by juvenile during evaluation or restoration.
Use at adjudication or disposition hearing prohibited, §16.1-360.
Statements by child at intake, §16.1-261.
Transfer hearing statements made by child.
Admissibility in criminal proceedings following transfer, §16.1-269.1.
Exceptions as to confidentiality, §16.1-309.1.
Exclusion of general public from hearings, §16.1-302.
Ex parte preliminary protective orders, §16.1-253.
Expungement of court records, §16.1-306.
Fingerprints and photographs of children, §16.1-299.
Family abuse.
Adults charged with violations of criminal law, procedure, §16.1-259.
Defined, §16.1-228.
Protective orders, §16.1-279.1.
Emergency protective orders.
Authorized, §16.1-253.4.
Felony violations.
Misdemeanor for violating, §16.1-253.2.
Preliminary protective orders, §16.1-253.1.
Misdemeanor for violating, §16.1-253.2.
Family assessment and planning team, §16.1-286.
Family offenses, criminal jurisdiction, §16.1-278.14.
Family or household member.
Defined, §16.1-228.
Fees for investigations or mediation services, §16.1-274.
Fees of witnesses, §16.1-276.
Filing of reports, §16.1-274.
Fingerprinting or photographing child, §16.1-299.
Forfeiture of bond, §16.1-258.
Foster care.
Defined, §16.1-228.
Payments to department by parent or other legally obligated person, §16.1-290.

JUVENILE PROCEEDINGS —Cont'd
Foster care —Cont'd
Voluntary post-adoption contact and communication agreement.
Authority to enter into, §16.1-283.1.
Foster care plans, §16.1-281.
Annual review of care, §16.1-282.2.
Permanency planning hearing, §16.1-282.1.
Review of foster care, §16.1-282.
Foster homes, placing child on parole in, §16.1-294.
Guardian ad litem, appointment of attorney, §§16.1-266 to 16.1-268.
Compensation of appointed counsel, §16.1-267.
Generally, §16.1-266.
List of attorneys qualified, §16.1-266.1.
Order of appointment part of record, §16.1-268.
Relief of care and custody.
Petition for, §16.1-277.02.
Representation at hearing and all other stages of proceeding, §16.1-268.
Standards for attorneys appointed, §16.1-266.1.
Guardians.
Committed child's estate in hands of guardian, education and maintenance, §16.1-290.
Guilt finding on charge of delinquency.
Effect on status of child, §16.1-308.
Habitual or serious offenders.
Commitment, §16.1-285.1.
Release and review hearings, §16.1-285.2.
Comprehensive action program, §§16.1-330.1, 16.1-330.2.
Serving adult sentence, §16.1-285.2.
Halfway houses, placing in, §16.1-293.
Hearing on confinement in secure local facilities, §16.1-284.1.
Hearing on foster care placement review, §16.1-282.
Hearing on termination of residual parental rights, §16.1-283.
Hearings, exclusion of public, §16.1-302.
Home/electronic incarceration.
Release on unsecured bond or promise to appear, §19.2-123.
Immediate custody.
When and how child may be taken into, §16.1-246.
Independent living services on release from commitment, §16.1-293.
Information upon commitment, transfer of, §16.1-287.
Intake, §16.1-260.
Appearance by electronic audio and video communication, §§16.1-255, 16.1-260.
Statements made by child to intake officer, admissibility as evidence, §16.1-261.
Intake officer.
Defined, §16.1-228.
Intake responsibilities, §16.1-260.
Interference with officer, §16.1-257.
Investigation of complaints by intake officers, §16.1-260.
Investigation of social history prior to final disposition, §16.1-273.
Judgments for money, §16.1-278.18.
Judicial consent in lieu of parental consent.
When authorized, §16.1-278.12.
Judicial consent to work permits, §16.1-278.13.
Jurisdiction.
Subsequent offenses by juveniles, §16.1-271.

JUVENILE PROCEEDINGS —Cont'd
Jurisdiction —Cont'd
Transfer to other courts, §16.1-269.1.
Appeals by juvenile, §16.1-269.4.
Placement of juvenile, §16.1-269.5.
Retention by juvenile court, §16.1-269.3.
Waiver in certain cases, §16.1-270.
Juvenile and domestic relations district courts.
Generally, §§16.1-226 to 16.1-245.1.
See JUVENILE AND DOMESTIC RELATIONS DISTRICT COURTS.
Juvenile community crime control, §§16.1-309.2 to 16.1-309.10.
See JUVENILE COMMUNITY CRIME CONTROL.
Juvenile corrections private management act, §§66-25.3 to 66-25.7.
Kidnapping.
Abduction by person confined to juvenile correctional center, §18.2-48.1.
Limitation on time for adjudicatory or transfer hearing, §16.1-277.1.
Magistrate issuing detention orders and arrest warrants for child, §16.1-256.
Medical and nursing care.
Court-ordered counseling or treatment.
Payment of costs, §16.1-290.1.
Ordering person responsible for care and support to provide and pay for, §16.1-275.
Medical records.
Juvenile placed in secure facility or shelter care facility, §16.1-248.3.
Mental examinations, §16.1-275.
Child taken into custody, §16.1-248.2.
Statements made at, §16.1-261.
Mental health services transition plan, §16.1-293.1.
Mental hospitals or mental health centers.
Commitment of child with mental illness or intellectual disability, §16.1-280.
Court-ordered counseling or treatment.
Payment of costs, §16.1-290.1.
Psychiatric treatment, §§16.1-335 to 16.1-348.
See MENTAL HEALTH.
Sending child to for treatment, §16.1-275.
Mentally ill or intellectual disability disposition, §16.1-278.11.
Misdemeanor for disclosure violations, §16.1-309.
Money judgments, §16.1-278.18.
Motion for expungement of court records, §16.1-306.
Nonresidential programs, placement in, §16.1-286.
Notice of appeal of transfer, §16.1-269.1.
Notice of detention hearing, §16.1-250.
Notice of hearing on foster care placement review, §16.1-282.
Notice of hearing on termination of residual parental rights, §16.1-283.
Notice of petition alleging offense that would be felony if committed by adult.
Disclosure of notice of filing of petition and certain reports, §16.1-305.2.
Intake officer responsibilities, §16.1-260.
Notice of preliminary protective order hearing, §16.1-253.
Notice of preliminary removal hearing, §16.1-252.
Notice of transfer hearing, §16.1-269.1.

JUVENILE PROCEEDINGS —Cont'd
Obstruction of officer, §16.1-257.
Other case disposition, §16.1-278.2.
Parental consent.
Judicial consent in lieu of, when authorized, §16.1-278.12.
Parole, probation or protective supervision, §§16.1-291 to 16.1-295.
Bodily injuries caused by juvenile probationers, §18.2-55.
Child in need of services, §16.1-278.5.
Delinquent child, §16.1-278.8.
Foster home or institution.
Placing child on parole in, §16.1-294.
Halfway houses, placing juvenile in, §16.1-293.
Mental health services transition plan, §16.1-293.1.
Revocation or modification, §16.1-291.
Supervision of juvenile or person during commitment and on parole, §16.1-293.
Transfer of supervision from one county or city to another or to another state, §16.1-295.
Penalty for violating confidentiality.
Restrictions, §16.1-309.
Permanency planning hearing for children in foster care, §16.1-282.1.
Petitions.
Commencement of matters within jurisdiction of court, §16.1-260.
Cases in which filing of petition not necessary, §16.1-260.
Form and content, §16.1-262.
Custody, visitation, support, etc.
Filing by party with legitimate interest, §16.1-241.
Preliminary protective order, §16.1-253.
Review of foster care placement, §16.1-282.
Revoke or modify probation, parole, etc., §16.1-291.
Termination of parental rights, §16.1-283.
Treatment, rehabilitation or other services, §16.1-278.13.
Photographing child, §16.1-299.
Physical examinations, §16.1-275.
Places of confinement for children, §16.1-249.
Police.
Service of summons, §16.1-264.
Preliminary hearings.
Transfer of juvenile for proper criminal proceedings, §16.1-269.1.
Preliminary protective orders.
Family abuse, §16.1-253.1.
Felony violations, §16.1-253.2.
Misdemeanor for violating, §16.1-253.2.
Protection of child's life, health or normal development, §16.1-253.
Preliminary removal hearings, §16.1-252.
Preliminary removal order, §16.1-252.
Presence of child in court, §16.1-302.
Presumption.
Raising question, §16.1-356.
Transfer to circuit court, §16.1-269.1.
Unrestorably incompetent juvenile.
Disposition, §16.1-358.
Presumption of competency of child to stand trial.
Transfer of case to circuit court, §16.1-269.1.
Pretrial release on unsecured bond or promise to appear, §19.2-123.
Privacy of records, §16.1-302.

JUVENILE PROCEEDINGS —Cont'd
Private or locally operated public facility, placement in, §16.1-286.
Privilege of reports of court officials and employees, §16.1-303.
Protective orders.
Emergency protective orders.
Authorized, §16.1-253.4.
Family abuse, §16.1-279.1.
Felony violations, §16.1-253.2.
Hearings, §16.1-253.
Misdemeanor for violating, §16.1-253.2.
Preliminary orders in cases of family abuse, §16.1-253.1.
Preliminary order to protect child's life, health or development, §16.1-253.
Registry, §19.2-387.1.
State police department, duties, §52-45.
Psychiatric treatment of minors, §§16.1-335 to 16.1-348.
See MENTAL HEALTH.
Publication.
Service of summons, §16.1-264.
Public or private societies or organizations.
Cooperation with and use of services, §16.1-278.
Purposes and intent of chapter, §16.1-227.
Recognizance.
Forfeiture of bonds taken, §16.1-258.
Validity and enforceability of bonds taken, §16.1-258.
Records of proceedings.
Confidentiality of court records, §16.1-305.
Circuit courts, §16.1-307.
Confidentiality of juvenile justice department records, §16.1-300.
Confidentiality of law enforcement records, §16.1-301.
Delinquency cases, disclosure of disposition, §16.1-305.1.
Dockets, indices and other books, §16.1-302.
Exceptions as to confidentiality, §16.1-309.1.
Expungement of court records, §16.1-306.
Fingerprinting and photographing children, §16.1-299.
Juvenile records, §§16.1-222 to 16.1-225.
Penalty for violating confidentiality restriction, §16.1-309.
Privacy of records, §16.1-302.
School principal, disclosures to, §16.1-301.
Relief of care and custody, §16.1-278.3.
Petition for, §16.1-277.02.
Religious affiliations protected upon placement of child, §16.1-288.
Removal of case to circuit court, §16.1-269.1.
Determinations by circuit court, §16.1-269.6.
Retention by juvenile court, §16.1-269.3.
Removal orders, abuse or neglect of child.
Dispositional hearing, §16.1-278.2.
Emergency removal order, §16.1-251.
Hearing, §16.1-252.
Preliminary removal order, §16.1-252.
Reopening case.
Review of court order, §16.1-289.
Reports, filing, §16.1-274.
Review of court orders, §16.1-289.
School boards.
Information to be furnished by and to upon commitment of child, §16.1-287.
Sentencing child as adult, §16.1-284.
Serious or habitual offenders.
Commitment, §16.1-285.1.
Release and review hearings, §16.1-285.2.

JUVENILE PROCEEDINGS —Cont'd
Serious or habitual offenders —Cont'd
Comprehensive action program, §§16.1-330.1, 16.1-330.2.
Serving adult sentence, §16.1-285.2.
Service of notice, process and other papers.
Summons, §§16.1-263, 16.1-264.
Termination of residual parental rights, §16.1-283.
Waiver, §16.1-263.
Shelter care.
Defined, §16.1-228.
Sheriffs.
Service of summons, §16.1-264.
Short title of statutes embraced in chapter, §16.1-226.
Show cause orders.
Disposition order violations, §16.1-292.
Social history investigations prior to final disposition, §16.1-273.
Status of child, effect of adjudication, §16.1-308.
Status offender.
Defined, §16.1-228.
Disposition, §16.1-278.6.
Subpoena duces tecum, §16.1-265.
Subpoenas, §16.1-265.
Summons, §16.1-263.
Taking child into custody.
Appearance by electronic audio and video communication, §16.1-255.
Commitment to juvenile justice department, §16.1-278.7.
Concealment or removal of child, §16.1-257.
Criteria for detention or shelter care, §16.1-248.1.
Detention hearing procedure, §16.1-250.
Detention orders, limitation on issuance, §16.1-255.
Duty of persons, §16.1-247.
Interference with or obstruction of officer, §16.1-257.
Medical records, §16.1-248.3.
Mental health screening and assessment, §16.1-248.2.
Statements made at, §16.1-261.
Mental illness or intellectual disability, commitment of child with, §16.1-280.
Places of confinement for children, §16.1-249.
Removal orders, abuse or neglect of child.
Dispositional hearing, §16.1-278.2.
Emergency removal order, §16.1-251.
Hearing, §16.1-252.
Preliminary removal order, §16.1-252.
Time limitation, §16.1-277.1.
Warrants for children, limitations on issuance by magistrates, §16.1-256.
When and how child may be taken into immediate custody, §16.1-246.
Telephonic communication systems.
Use to conduct hearings, §16.1-276.3.
Termination of residual parental right, §16.1-283.
Time limitation, §16.1-277.1.
Transfer of child for criminal proceedings in circuit court, §16.1-269.1.
Determinations by court, §16.1-269.6.
Retention by juvenile court, §16.1-269.3.
Subsequent offenses by juvenile while incarcerated, §16.1-271.
Time limitation for transfer hearing, §16.1-277.1.
Waiver of jurisdiction and transfer to circuit courts, §16.1-270.

JUVENILE PROCEEDINGS —Cont'd
Transfer of information upon commitment, §16.1-287.
Transfer of supervision from one county or city to another or to another state, §16.1-295.
Transportation of children, responsibility for and limitations, §16.1-254.
Travel expenses of witnesses, §16.1-276.
Trespass after having been forbidden to do so, §§18.2-119, 18.2-120.
Trustees.
Committed child's estate in hands of trustee, education and maintenance, §16.1-290.
Two-way electronic video and audio communications.
Appearance of juvenile at detention hearing, §16.1-250.
Appearance of juvenile before intake officers, §16.1-260.
Juvenile appearance at review hearing on confinement, §16.1-284.1.
Venue, §16.1-243.
Victim impact statements.
Motion by attorney for the Commonwealth, §16.1-273.
Victims' right to be present at delinquency proceedings, §16.1-302.1.
Violations of orders by any person, §16.1-292.
Violations of orders by child.
Revocation or modification, §16.1-291.
Waiver of jurisdiction in certain cases, §16.1-270.
Waiver of service, §16.1-263.
Welfare boards, local.
Entrustment agreements.
Approval, §16.1-277.01.
Witnesses.
Fees and travel expenses, §16.1-276.
Prisoners.
Transportation orders, §16.1-276.2.
Summons requiring attendance in testimony, §16.1-265.
Work permits.
Judicial consent to apply for, §16.1-278.13.

JUVENILE RECORDS, §§16.1-222 to 16.1-225.
Confidentiality of court records, §16.1-305.
Circuit courts, §16.1-307.
Confidentiality of data in juvenile justice information system, §16.1-222.
Misdemeanor for violations, §16.1-225.
Confidentiality of juvenile justice department records and reports, §16.1-300.
Confidentiality of law enforcement records, §16.1-301.
Data submissions to juvenile justice information system, §16.1-224.
Dissemination by central criminal records exchange, §19.2-389.1.
Establishment of juvenile justice information system, §16.1-222.
Expungement, §16.1-306.
Fingerprints and photographs of children, §16.1-299.
Fingerprints and photographs of children, §16.1-299.
Powers of director of juvenile justice department, §16.1-222.
Privilege of court officials and employees, §16.1-303.

JUVENILE RECORDS —Cont'd
Receipt, classification and filing of data with juvenile justice information system, §16.1-223.
School principal, disclosures to, §16.1-301.

JUVENILE SERIOUS OR HABITUAL OFFENDERS.
Commitment, §16.1-285.1.
Release and review hearings, §16.1-285.2.
Comprehensive action program, §§16.1-330.1, 16.1-330.2.
Earned sentence credit.
Condition for earning, report by department of juvenile justice, §53.1-202.3.
Eligibility, §53.1-202.2.
Victim notice of release and review hearing, §16.1-285.2.

JUVENILES, INTERSTATE COMPACT, §§16.1-323, 16.1-323.1.

K

KEGS.
Sale of beer or wine in by licensee.
Permit to sell in, §4.1-212.

KENBRIDGE.
Water and sewage systems.
Lien for charges and taxes imposed, §15.2-2118.

KENMORE ASSOCIATION, INC.
Ferry Farm, George Washington's boyhood home.
Appropriation for restoration and maintenance, §10.1-2212.

KENNELS.
Lien of animal keepers, §§43-32 to 43-36.
Mistreatment of animals, §§3.2-6503, 18.2-403.3.
Sale of unclaimed animals, §3.2-6520.
Sales of dogs and cats by dealers, §§3.2-6512 to 3.2-6517.
Veterinary care requirements, §§3.2-6518, 3.2-6519.
Misdemeanors for violating, §18.2-403.1.

KENTUCKY.
Boundary with, §1-307.

KEROSENE.
Coal mines.
Underground coal mines.
Storage and use, §45.1-161.205.
Emergency petroleum products supplies, §§59.1-21.18:2 to 59.1-21.18:4.
Sale of liquid fuels, lubricating oils and similar products, §§18.2-226 to 18.2-232.
Taxes on fuel.
Fuel taxes, §§58.1-2200 to 58.1-2299.20.
See FUEL TAXES.

KEROSENE PUMPS.
Opening or carrying away, §18.2-151.

KETONES.
Inhaling drugs or other noxious chemical substances, §18.2-264.

KEYS.
Capitol building.
Division of engineering and buildings to keep, §2.2-1144.
Possession or duplication of keys to buildings owned by Commonwealth or localities, §18.2-503.

KEYS —Cont'd
Secondhand keys, buying or receiving with intent to defraud, §18.2-237.
Voting or counting equipment.
Custody of electoral board, §24.2-634.
Delivery to clerk of circuit court after election, §24.2-659.
Delivery to officers of election, §24.2-639.
Unauthorized possession, §24.2-1010.

KICKBACKS.
Practitioner self-referral act, §§54.1-2410 to 54.1-2414.
Procurement transactions, §2.2-4372.
Real estate settlement services, §55-525.12.
Title insurance, §38.2-4614.

KIDDIE PORN.
See CHILD PORNOGRAPHY.

KIDNAPPING AND RELATED OFFENSES, §§18.2-47 to 18.2-50.2.
Abduction and kidnapping defined, §18.2-47.
Abduction by parent, §18.2-49.1.
Punishable as contempt in any pending proceeding, §18.2-47.
Abduction by prisoner, §18.2-48.1.
Abduction of child for purposes of concubinage, prostitution or manufacturing of child pornography, §18.2-48.
Abduction with intent to defile, §18.2-48.
Punishment upon conviction of certain subsequent violent felony sexual assault, §18.2-67.5:3.
Suspension of sentence, placing on probation, §19.2-303.
Suspended sentence in addition to active sentence, §18.2-48.
Abduction with intent to extort money or pecuniary benefit, §18.2-48.
Suspension of sentence, placing on probation, §19.2-303.
Suspended sentence in addition to active sentence, §18.2-48.
Threatening, attempting or assisting, §18.2-49.
Abduction with intent to subject to forced labor or services, §18.2-47.
Amber Alert program.
Activation, §52-34.3.
Definitions, §52-34.1.
Established, §52-34.2.
Branch pilots, §54.1-920.
Capital murder, killing in commission of, §18.2-31.
Children.
Abduction by parent, §18.2-49.1.
Punishable as contempt in any pending proceeding, §18.2-47.
Amber Alert program.
Activation, §52-34.3.
Definitions, §52-34.1.
Established, §52-34.2.
Child victims' testimony.
Use of two-way closed-circuit television, §18.2-67.9.
Code Adam programs.
State buildings open to public, §2.2-1161.1.
Prostitution or concubinage purposes.
Threatening, attempting or assisting, §18.2-49.
Purposes of concubinage, prostitution or manufacturing of child pornography, §18.2-48.

KIDNAPPING AND RELATED OFFENSES —Cont'd
Child victims' testimony.
Use of two-way closed-circuit television, §18.2-67.9.
Code Adam alert programs.
State buildings open to general public, §2.2-1161.1.
Criminal forfeiture.
Seizure and forfeiture of property used in connection with abduction, §19.2-386.32.
Disclosure of information and assistance to law enforcement officers, §18.2-50.
Discretionary felony sentencing guidelines, §17.1-805.
Hostage or barricaded person situations, telephone service.
Emergency control, §18.2-50.2.
Mob crimes, §18.2-42.1.
Parental abduction, §18.2-49.1.
Punishable as contempt in any pending proceeding, §18.2-47.
Prostitution or concubinage purposes, §18.2-48.
Threatening, attempting or assisting, §18.2-49.
Punishment generally, §18.2-47.
Seizure and forfeiture of property used in connection with abduction, §19.2-386.32.
Sentence of persons twice previously convicted of certain violent felonies, §19.2-297.1.
Suspension of sentence, placing on probation.
Imposition of suspended sentence.
In addition to active sentence, §18.2-48.
Length of suspension, conditions of probation, §19.2-303.
Telephone service in hostage or barricaded person situation.
Emergency control of, §18.2-50.2.
Threatening, attempting or assisting in abduction, §18.2-49.
Wiretapping.
Court-ordered interception of communications.
When authorized by state police, §19.2-66.

KILLED IN ACTION.
Tuition and required fees for state supported colleges and universities.
Virginia military survivors and dependents education program.
Waiver for spouses and children of military personnel killed in action, §23-7.4:1.

KILLED IN LINE OF DUTY.
Allowances by governing body of locality, §15.2-1511.
Line of duty act, §§9.1-400 to 9.1-408.
See LINE OF DUTY ACT.
Tuition and required fees for state supported colleges and universities.
Waiver for spouses and children of certain military and public safety personnel, §23-7.4:1.

KILLING AT DIRECTION OF ANOTHER.
Capital murder, §18.2-31.

KILLING FOR HIRE.
Capital murder, §18.2-31.
Triggerman rule inapplicable, §18.2-18.

KINDERGARTENS.
Courses of public school instruction, §22.1-199.
Schools and education courses of instruction.
Optional education programs for kindergarten through grade five, §22.1-200.1.

KING AND QUEEN COUNTY.
Coastal primary sand dunes and beaches.
Zoning ordinances, §28.2-1403.
Middle Peninsula regional airport authority, 1997 ch 871.
Northern Neck-Middle Peninsula public education consortium.
Inclusion in region, §22.1-354.6.
School board.
Salary of members, §22.1-32.

KING GEORGE COUNTY.
Coastal primary sand dunes and beaches.
Zoning ordinances, §28.2-1403.
Fishing, inland waters.
Taking methods, restrictions, §29.1-531.
Public defenders office.
Established, §19.2-163.04.
School board.
Salary of members, §22.1-32.
Transient occupancy tax.
Disposition of revenues, §58.1-3819.
Water or waste authority providing street lights, §15.2-5118.

KING, MARTIN LUTHER, JR.
Dr. Martin Luther King, Jr. memorial commission, §§30-192 to 30-192.7.
Martin Luther King, Jr. Day.
Legal holidays, §2.2-3300.

KINGPINS.
Drug kingpins, §18.2-248.

KING WILLIAM COUNTY.
Coastal primary sand dunes and beaches.
Zoning ordinances, §28.2-1403.
Middle Peninsula regional airport authority, 1997 ch 871.
School board.
Salary of members, §22.1-32.

KINSHIP FOSTER CARE, §63.2-900.1.
Criminal history and central registry checks.
Approved kinship foster care parents, §63.2-901.1.

KISSING.
Penetration of mouth of child with lascivious intent, §18.2-370.6.

KITCHEN GREASE.
Waste kitchen grease.
Transportation, §§3.2-5508 to 3.2-5516.

KIWANIS.
Special license plates, §46.2-746.7.

KNIGHTS OF COLUMBUS.
Special license plates for members, §46.2-746.7.

KNIGHTS OF PYTHIAS.
Exemption from fraternal benefit society provisions, §38.2-4135.

KNOWLEDGE.
Trusts.
Notice or knowledge of fact, §64.2-702.

KOREA.
George Mason University.
Establishment of branch campus in Republic of Korea, §23-91.29:1.

KOREAN WAR VETERANS.
Appreciation week, §2.2-3309.1.
High school diplomas, §22.1-17.4.
Special license plates, §46.2-743.

KOSHER FOOD OR FOOD PRODUCTS.
Labeling food as, violations, penalty, §3.2-5124.

KRAFT PULPING PROCESSES.
Renewable electricity production program.
Grants, §§67-900 to 67-903.

KTW BULLETS.
Use or attempted use in commission or attempted commission of crime, §18.2-308.3.

KUWAIT.
Operation Desert Storm.
Special license plates for veterans, §46.2-743.

L

LABELS.
Agricultural liming materials, §3.2-3706.
Asbestos abatement in state and public school buildings.
Marks or labels where asbestos found, §§2.2-1163, 2.2-1166.
Batteries, storage, §59.1-189.
Rebuilt batteries, §59.1-190.
Cigarettes.
Fire-safe cigarettes.
Marking of cigarettes, §59.1-293.4.
Clams, §28.2-532.
Dairy milk cases or milk crates.
Defacing, obliterating, etc., §18.2-102.2.
Devices or marks on certain containers, §§59.1-93 to 59.1-102.
See MARKS ON CERTAIN CONTAINERS.
Feed, commercial, §3.2-4806.
Fertilizer, §3.2-3611.
Kosher or halal.
Labeling food as, violations, penalty, §3.2-5124.
Lubricating oil sales, §18.2-231.
Motor fuels, §59.1-167.1.
Oysters, §28.2-532.
Plastic containers, §10.1-1415.1.
Registration.
Agricultural liming materials, §3.2-3702.
Seeds.
Lawn and turf seed mixture.
Change in labeling or specifications, §3.2-4009.
Requirements as to labeling, §3.2-4008.
Exemptions, §3.2-4016.
Transgenetic seeds, §3.2-4008.
Tobacco.
Manufactured tobacco.
False labeling, §61.1-44.

LABOR.
Appearances in court.
Crime victims, leave given to attend criminal proceedings, §40.1-28.7:2.
Penalizing employee for, §18.2-465.1.
Apprenticeship, §§40.1-117 to 40.1-126.
See APPRENTICESHIP.
Asbestos NESHAP, §§40.1-51.23 to 40.1-51.41.
See ASBESTOS NESHAP.
Asbestos notification, §§40.1-51.20 to 40.1-51.22.
See ASBESTOS NOTIFICATION.
Blacklisting.
Anti-blacklisting act, §40.1-27.
Boiler and pressure vessel safety, §§40.1-51.5 to 40.1-51.19:5.
Career readiness certification, §2.2-2674.01.
Child labor, §§40.1-78 to 40.1-116.
See CHILD LABOR.

LABOR —Cont'd
Child support enforcement by department of social services.
Assignment of earnings honored by employer, §63.2-1945.
Discharge of employee voluntarily assigning earning prohibited, §63.2-1944.
Income withholding, §§63.2-1923 to 63.2-1926.
Virginia new hire reporting center.
Employing unit to report initial employment to, §63.2-1946.
Virginia state directory of new hires, §63.2-1946.
Conservators of the peace.
Liability of employers, §19.2-13.
Corruptly influencing or being influenced, employees or servants, §18.2-444.
Crime victims, employees given leave to attend criminal proceedings, §40.1-28.7:2.
Desertion and nonsupport.
Income deduction of support orders, §20-79.1.
Discrimination.
Human rights act, §§2.2-3900 to 2.2-3903.
Diseases of employees.
Reports to employers, §32.1-36.
Earned income tax credit.
Notice by employer to employee, §40.1-28.7:3.
Election officers.
Employer discriminating against person serving as officer.
Prohibition, §24.2-118.1.
Employee haulers.
Permits.
Application, §46.2-2069.
Required, §46.2-2068.
Restrictions on permit, §46.2-2070.
Employee protection and safety, §§40.1-22 to 40.1-28.6.
See EMPLOYEE PROTECTION AND SAFETY.
Employee theft.
Civil action for damages, §8.01-44.4.
Employment-related information disclosure.
Prospective or current employer disclosing.
Immunity, good faith presumption, §8.01-46.1.
Endangerment of children, §40.1-103.
Ethnic harassment, violence or vandalism.
Civil action for damages barred, §8.01-42.1.
E-Verify program for new hires.
State agencies to participate, §40.1-11.2.
Fair employment contracting act, §§2.2-4200, 2.2-4201.
Firearms and ammunition possessed by employee.
Storing at workplace in locked private motor vehicle, §15.2-915.
Forced labor.
Abduction with intent to subject to, §18.2-47.
General assembly power to regulate, VA Const Art IV §14.
Genetic testing as condition of employment, §40.1-28.7:1.
Human trafficking hotline.
Employers who must post notice regarding, §40.1-11.3.
Income tax.
Earned income tax credit.
Notice by employer to employee, §40.1-28.7:3.
Income withholding.
Child support enforcement by department of social services, §§63.2-1923 to 63.2-1926.
Industrial hygiene and safety profession.
Protection of job title, §§40.1-139 to 40.1-142.

LABOR —Cont'd
Jury panel service.
Penalizing employee for, §18.2-465.1.
Work shift.
Restrictions on beginning after day of jury duty, §18.2-465.1.
Labor and industry department, §§40.1-1 to 40.1-11.3.
See LABOR AND INDUSTRY DEPARTMENT.
Labor unions.
Generally, §§40.1-52 to 40.1-54.3.
See LABOR UNIONS.
Lie detector tests.
Prohibition of questions on tests for employment, §40.1-51.4:3.
Mediation and conciliation of labor disputes, §§40.1-70 to 40.1-75.
Minimum wage act, §§40.1-28.8 to 40.1-28.12.
Motor carriers, passengers.
Employee haulers.
Defined, §46.2-2000.
Permits.
Application, §46.2-2069.
Required, §46.2-2068.
Restrictions on permit, §46.2-2070.
National guard, state defense force or naval militia members.
Interference with employment of members, §44-98.
Notaries.
Civil liability of employer of notary, §47.1-27.
Criminal liability of employer of notary, §47.1-28.
Fee agreements with employer, §47.1-20.
Occupational safety and health, §§40.1-44.1 to 40.1-51.4:5.
See OCCUPATIONAL SAFETY AND HEALTH.
Personal identifying information of employee.
Employer prohibition from releasing, §40.1-28.7:4.
Prisoners.
Employment and training generally, §§53.1-41 to 53.1-62.
See PRISONS.
Public assistance.
Virginia initiative for employment not welfare, §§63.2-608 to 63.2-613.
Racial harassment, violence or vandalism.
Civil action for damages barred, §8.01-42.1.
Religious harassment, violence or vandalism.
Civil action for damages barred, §8.01-42.1.
Representatives of employees, designation, selection or authorization.
Right to vote by secret ballot, §40.1-54.3.
Residency status.
Grants by Commonwealth, requiring employer reports of certification of employees as condition, §2.2-621.
Ridesharing.
Liability of employer, §§46.2-1402, 46.2-1403.
Right to work, §§40.1-58 to 40.1-69.
See RIGHT TO WORK.
Sanitation districts law of 1938.
Agents and employees of commission, §21-177.
Sanitation districts law of 1946.
Employee hiring, §21-257.
Statute of limitations.
Free speech rights under federal labor law, §8.01-243.
Strikes at hospitals, §§40.1-54.1, 40.1-54.2.
Strikes by government employees, §§40.1-55 to 40.1-57.1.

LABOR —Cont'd
Temporary assistance for needy families.
Virginia initiative for employment not welfare, §§63.2-608 to 63.2-613.
Toxic substances.
Diagnosis of employee injuries and illnesses, §32.1-244.
Unemployment compensation, §§60.2-100 to 60.2-637.
See UNEMPLOYMENT COMPENSATION.
VIEW.
Virginia initiative for employment not welfare, §§63.2-608 to 63.2-613.
Virginia initiative for employment not welfare, §§63.2-608 to 63.2-613.
Wage assignments, §§40.1-29 to 40.1-33.
See WAGE ASSIGNMENTS.
Wages.
Minimum wage act, §§40.1-28.8 to 40.1-28.12.
Welfare.
Virginia initiative for employment not welfare, §§63.2-608 to 63.2-613.
Workers' compensation, §§65.2-100 to 65.2-1310.
See WORKERS' COMPENSATION.
Workforce training.
Workforce council, §§2.2-2669 to 2.2-2674.1.

LABOR AND INDUSTRY DEPARTMENT, §§40.1-1 to 40.1-11.3.
Administrative rulemaking procedure.
Regulations exempt, §2.2-4006.
Annual report, §40.1-4.1.
Application of provisions, §40.1-2.1.
Commissioner.
Appointment by governor, §40.1-5.
Other officers to furnish information, §40.1-8.
Overhead high voltage line safety.
Enforcement of provisions, §59.1-412.
Powers and duties, §40.1-6.
Prehospital patient care reports.
EMS agency to release to commissioner, protected health information, §40.1-8.
Request for prosecutions.
Attorney for Commonwealth, §40.1-7.
Commonwealth's attorneys.
Prosecution on request of commissioner, §40.1-7.
Confidential information, §40.1-11.
Definitions, §40.1-2.
Employment of illegal immigrants, §40.1-11.1.
E-Verify program for new hires.
State agencies to participate, §40.1-11.2.
Human trafficking hotline.
Employers who must post notice regarding, §40.1-11.3.
Interpretation of provisions.
Safety, health and welfare employees, §40.1-3.
Maintenance of department, §40.1-9.
Medical records released to commissioner.
Prehospital patient care reports.
EMS agency to release, protection, §40.1-8.
Notice.
Initial notice by certified mail, subsequent notices by regular mail, §40.1-2.01.
Offenses regarding examinations and inspections, §40.1-10.
Powers and duties, §40.1-1.
Secretary of commerce and trade.
Agency responsibility, §2.2-204.
Statistical information.
Annual report, §40.1-4.1.

LABOR AND INDUSTRY DEPARTMENT —Cont'd
Statistical information —Cont'd
State, county, town or city officers to furnish commissioner, §40.1-8.
Student internship programs.
Identification of programs eligible for exemption from federal and state laws, §22.1-17.3.

LABORATORIES.
Analysis evidence in criminal cases, §§19.2-187 to 19.2-187.2.
Certificate as evidence, §19.2-187.
Chain of custody, certificate as evidence of, §§19.2-187.01, 19.2-187.1.
Subpoena duces tecum, procedure, §19.2-187.2.
Analysis performed by forensic laboratory.
Fees charged by circuit court clerk in criminal prosecutions, §17.1-275.
Analytical function related to criminal investigations.
Division of consolidated laboratory services.
Providing law enforcement, §2.2-1104.
Division of consolidated laboratory services, §§2.2-1103 to 2.2-1108.
Created, §2.2-1103.
Disposal of personal property submitted to division but not reclaimed, §2.2-1108.
Environmental laboratory certification program, §2.2-1105.
Hazardous materials seized in criminal investigations.
Disposal by division, §2.2-1107.
Purposes, §2.2-1103.
Security and protection of evidence, official samples and other samples, §2.2-1104.
Taking in and absorbing laboratories operated by political subdivisions, §2.2-1106.
Testing and analytical functions, §2.2-1104.
Expert witnesses.
Right of accused to request testimony in lieu of certificate, §19.2-187.1.
Federal safe drinking water act mandated laboratories.
Inspection and certification program.
Division of consolidated laboratory services to establish, §2.2-1104.
Hazardous materials seized in criminal investigations.
Disposal by division of consolidated laboratory services, §2.2-1107.
Methamphetamine lab cleanup.
Liability of offender for costs, §15.2-1716.2.
State board of health.
Guidelines for cleanup of residential property used as clandestine methamphetamine laboratories, §32.1-11.7.
Patient provided copy of test results directly by laboratory.
Practitioner authorizing, §54.1-2409.4.
Security and protection of evidence, official samples and other samples.
Division of consolidated laboratory services, §2.2-1104.
Testing and analytical functions.
Division of consolidated laboratory services, §2.2-1104.
Tuberculosis.
Reports of active tuberculosis, §32.1-50.
Well construction.
Testing for oil contamination.
Department to maintain list of private laboratories, §32.1-176.5:1.

LABORATORY TEST RESULTS.
Health care practitioners.
Providing patient copy of result.
Request by patient, laboratory providing directly, practitioner authorizing, §54.1-2409.4.

LABOR DAY.
Legal holidays, §2.2-3300.
Opening of the school year, §22.1-79.1.

LABOR DEPARTMENT.
Commissioner of labor.
Federal employees prohibited, exception, §2.2-2801.

LABOR DISPUTES, §§40.1-70 to 40.1-75.
Agency designated to mediate, §40.1-70.
Collective bargaining contract.
Notice of proposed termination or modification, §40.1-71.
Designation of agency for mediation and conciliation, §40.1-70.
Governor.
Negotiation information, §40.1-73.
Notification of disputes, §40.1-72.
Labor unions generally, §§40.1-52 to 40.1-54.3.
See LABOR UNIONS.
Mediation and conciliation of labor disputes, §§40.1-70 to 40.1-75.
National railway labor act.
When article applicable, §40.1-75.
Negotiations.
Commissioner to keep governor informed, §40.1-73.
Notice.
Commissioner to notify governor of disputes, §40.1-72.
Proposed termination or modification of collective bargaining contract, §40.1-71.
Right of entry, §40.1-74.
Strikes by government employees, §§40.1-55 to 40.1-57.1.
Termination or modification of collective bargaining contract.
Notice of proposal, §40.1-71.

LABOR UNIONS, §§40.1-52 to 40.1-54.3.
Antitrust laws.
Applicability, §59.1-9.4.
Boycotts.
Right to work, §40.1-66.
Department of mines, minerals and energy personnel.
Affiliations with prohibited, §45.1-161.17.
Fees.
Payment of charges by carriers or shippers, §40.1-54.
Hospitals.
Strikes and work stoppages, §§40.1-54.1, 40.1-54.2.
Illegal picketing, §40.1-53.
Injunctions.
Picketing, §40.1-53.
Lockouts.
Right to work, §40.1-66.
Mediation and conciliation of labor disputes, §§40.1-70 to 40.1-75.
Mineral mine safety.
Conflicts of interest, §45.1-161.292:9.
Names or insignia, registration, alteration, cancellation, §§2.2-411 to 2.2-417, 18.2-177.
See REGISTRATION OF NAMES OR INSIGNIA OF ORGANIZATIONS.

LABOR UNIONS —Cont'd
Pickets.
Right to work, §40.1-66.
Preventing persons from pursuing lawful vocations, §40.1-53.
Public officers and employees.
Collective bargaining, §§40.1-57.2, 40.1-57.3.
Real property.
Authority to own, encumber and sell, §40.1-52.
Registration of name or insignia.
Illegal use of registered insignia, §18.2-177.
Representation of employees.
Right to vote by secret ballot regarding designation, selection or authorization, §40.1-54.3.
Right to work, §§40.1-58 to 40.1-69.
See RIGHT TO WORK.
Shippers or carriers.
Payment of charges to or for benefit of organization, §40.1-54.
Solicitation of charitable or civic contributions.
Provision exemptions, §57-60.
Strikes by government employees, §§40.1-55 to 40.1-57.1.
Unauthorized wearing or displaying on motor vehicles of button, insignia or emblem of, §18.2-176.
Work stoppages.
Right to work, §40.1-66.
Yellow dog contracts.
Abstention from membership in union, §40.1-61.

LACHES.
Premarital agreements.
Limitation of actions, §20-152.

LA CROSSE.
Mecklenburg-Brunswick airport commission, 1975 ch 211, 1982 ch 42.

LAKES.
Annexation.
Boundary line where territory fronts lake, §15.2-3210.
City or town powers, §15.2-1110.
Closing upon finding of toxic substances, §32.1-248.
Conservation police officers.
Daylight hours patrol of lakes from Memorial Day through Labor Day, §29.1-739.2.
Dredging sand and gravel, §§62.1-190 to 62.1-193.
Fish consumption advisories, §32.1-248.01.
Impoundment of surface waters generally, §§62.1-104 to 62.1-115.
See IMPOUNDMENT OF SURFACE WATERS.
Killing deer in lake, §29.1-516.
Surface water management areas, §§62.1-242 to 62.1-253.
See SURFACE WATER MANAGEMENT AREAS.
Waters of the state generally.
See WATERS OF THE STATE.

LAMBS.
Larceny, §18.2-97.

LAME DUCK AMENDMENT.
Congress.
Changing meeting of congress, US Const Amd 20.

LANCASTER COUNTY.
Coastal primary sand dunes and beaches.
Zoning ordinances, §28.2-1403.

LANCASTER COUNTY —Cont'd
Northern Neck Chesapeake Bay public access authority, §§15.2-6626 to 15.2-6651.
See NORTHERN NECK CHESAPEAKE BAY PUBLIC ACCESS AUTHORITY.
Northern Neck-Middle Peninsula public education consortium.
Inclusion in region, §22.1-354.6.
School board.
Salary of members, §22.1-32.
Small claims court designated, §16.1-122.1.

LAND.
Community property rights at death, §§64.2-315 to 64.2-324.
Conveyances generally.
See CONVEYANCES.
Deeds generally.
See DEEDS.
Descent and distribution generally, §§64.2-200 to 64.2-206.
See DESCENT AND DISTRIBUTION.
Disclaimer of property interests, §§64.2-2600 to 64.2-2614.
See DISCLAIMER OF PROPERTY INTERESTS.
Ejectment actions generally, §§8.01-131 to 8.01-165.
See EJECTMENT.
Escheat generally, §§55-168 to 55-201.1.
See ESCHEAT.
Estates in land generally, §§55-1 to 55-25.1.
See ESTATES IN LAND.
Fraudulent conveyances generally, §§55-80 to 55-105.
See FRAUDULENT CONVEYANCES.
Improvements to land generally, §§8.01-166 to 8.01-178.
See IMPROVEMENTS TO LAND.
Judicial sales generally, §§8.01-96 to 8.01-113.
See JUDICIAL SALES.
Land office, §§41.1-9 to 41.1-12.
Married women's property rights, §§55-35 to 55-47.1.
See MARRIED WOMEN'S PROPERTY RIGHTS.
Mortgages and deeds of trust.
Generally, §§6.2-406 to 6.2-423, 55-58 to 55-66.6.
See MORTGAGES AND DEEDS OF TRUST.
Open space lands generally, §§10.1-1700 to 10.1-1705.
Partition of land, §§8.01-81 to 8.01-93.
See PARTITION OF LAND.
Property owners' associations, §§55-508 to 55-516.2.
See PROPERTY OWNERS' ASSOCIATIONS.
Real estate investment trust.
See REAL ESTATE INVESTMENT TRUSTS.
Real property.
Generally.
See REAL PROPERTY.
Real property taxes, §§58.1-3200 to 58.1-3389.
See REAL PROPERTY TAXES.
Recordation of documents generally, §§55-106 to 55-142.9.
See RECORDATION OF DOCUMENTS.
Subdivision and development generally, §§15.2-2240 to 15.2-2279.
See SUBDIVISIONS.
Submerged lands, §§28.2-1200 to 28.2-1213.
Unclaimed property generally, §§55-210.1 to 55-210.30.
See UNCLAIMED PROPERTY.

LAND —Cont'd
Ungranted shores of the sea, marshes and meadowlands, §§28.2-1500 to 28.2-1514.
See UNGRANTED SHORES OF THE SEA.

LAND BOOK.
Alteration after delivery to local treasurer prohibited, §58.1-3311.
Changes noted in by commissioners of revenue, §58.1-3312.
Copies, disposition, §58.1-3310.
Entry of lands on lists to be transferred and charged, §58.1-3309.
Entry of tracts in counties, §58.1-3301.
Fees for entering and transferring lands on, §58.1-3314.
Collection of fees, §58.1-3315.
Form prescribed by department of taxation, §58.1-3301.
Mistakes corrected by commissioners of revenue, §58.1-3313.
Omitted lands, entry on, §58.1-3904.
Original retained by commissioners of revenue, §58.1-3310.
Use by boards of equalization, §58.1-3377.

LAND CONSERVATION BOARD OF TRUSTEES, §10.1-1018.

LAND CONSERVATION FOUNDATION, §§10.1-1017 to 10.1-1026.
Accounts, §10.1-1025.
Audits, §10.1-1025.
Board of trustees, §10.1-1018.
Conservation police officers.
Duties of department officers, §10.1-1019.
Creation, §10.1-1017.
Executive secretary, §10.1-1019.
Expenditures.
Natural area protection, §10.1-1022.1.
Prohibitions, §10.1-1023.
Restricted funds, §10.1-1022.
Use of interest income, §10.1-1020.
Farmland preservation office.
Cooperative development with, §3.2-201.
Fund, §10.1-1020.
Income.
Use of interest income, §10.1-1020.
Land management.
Duties of executive secretary, §10.1-1019.
Natural area protection.
Expenditures, §10.1-1022.1.
Powers, §10.1-1021.
Purposes, §10.1-1020.
Records, §10.1-1025.
Reports.
Executive summary, §10.1-1018.1.
Taxation.
Gifts and bequests, §10.1-1024.
Term limits.
Board of trustees, §10.1-1018.

LAND DEVELOPMENT.
Land subdivision and development generally, §§15.2-2240 to 15.2-2279.
See SUBDIVISIONS.

LAND EVALUATION AND SITE ASSESSMENT SYSTEM.
Agricultural and forestal districts.
Evaluating land for inclusion in district, §15.2-4306.
Withdrawal of land from district, §15.2-4314.

LANDFILL GAS.
Equipment used to generate electricity from.
Property exempt from taxation, §58.1-3660.

LANDFILL GAS PIPELINES.
Department of transportation permission to place within highway right-of-way.
Notice to counties through which pipeline passes, §33.1-223.2:11.

LANDFILLS.
Community service.
Recycling duties for probationers.
Civil immunity, §8.01-226.8.
Counties, cities or towns.
General powers as to waste and recycling, §§15.2-927 to 15.2-939.
Garbage generally.
See GARBAGE.
Leaves or grass clippings prohibited, §15.2-935.
Solid waste management generally, §§10.1-1408.1 to 10.1-1414.
See SOLID WASTE MANAGEMENT.
Tractor trailer semitrailer combination transporting solid waste.
Inspection by locality, §15.2-937.

LANDING OF SEAFOOD IN VIRGINIA.
License, §28.2-228.1.

LANDINGS, §§62.1-164, 62.1-165.
Franchise, privilege, lease or right to use city or town property, §§15.2-2100 to 15.2-2108.1:1.
Oyster planting grounds.
Riparian oyster planting grounds, §28.2-602.
Police powers over lands lying beyond localities, boundaries, §15.2-1725.
Sale of city or town property, §15.2-2100, VA Const Art VII §9.
Transportation board.
Acquisitions, conveyances and transfers of property.
Request to board for transfer to authority, §33.1-223.2:17.

LANDLORD AND TENANT, §§55-217 to 55-248.
Accounting for payments upon request.
Residential landlords and tenants, §55-248.7.
Affordable rental housing.
Property tax assessment.
Fair market value, determining, §58.1-3295.
Airports.
Military air installations, properties adjacent to.
Landlord obligations, disclosure, §55-248.12:1.
Appeal bond period for eviction cases, §8.01-129.
Attornment.
Unnecessary, §55-220.
When void, §55-221.
Bad checks for rent.
Checks drawn on accounts with insufficient funds, §55-248.31.
Amount recovered, §8.01-27.2.
Notice check return unpaid, §8.01-27.2.
Processing fee assessed, §55-248.4.
Billing for utility services.
Energy allocation and submetering equipment, ratio utility billing system used, §55-226.2.
Building code.
Compliance, landlord's duty, §55-225.3.
General provisions, §§36-97 to 36-119.1.
See BUILDING CODE.

LANDLORD AND TENANT —Cont'd
Building code —Cont'd
Obligations, compliance, tenant's duty, §55-225.4.
Building code compliance.
Residential rental dwelling units.
Rental inspections of units in rental inspection district, §36-105.1:1.
Burglar alarms.
Tenant installation, §55-248.18.
Charitable gaming.
Prohibited practices, §18.2-340.33.
Clean and safe conditions.
Tenant's duty, §55-225.4.
Community land trusts.
Defined, §55-221.1.
Not considered landlords, §55-221.1.
Condominiums.
Conversion condominiums.
Notice, §55-79.94.
Conduct of tenant and other on premises.
Duty of tenant, §55-225.4.
Consumer protection.
Application of provisions, §59.1-199.
County court leases validated, §55-55.
Crops.
Removal by tenant before rents and advances satisfied, §18.2-100.
Damage insurance.
Landlord may require as condition of tenancy, §55-248.7:2.
Payments for premium costs.
Deemed rent, §55-248.7:2.
Damages to unit at time of occupancy.
Defective drywall, remedy for nondisclosure, §55-225.11.
Move-in inspection report, §55-225.6.
Mold disclosure statement, §55-225.7.
Damaging, destroying premises.
Tenant, prohibition, §55-225.4.
Death.
Residential landlords and tenants.
Property of deceased tenant.
Disposal, §55-248.38:3.
Default in payment of rent.
Forfeiture of right of possession.
Failure to pay after 5 days' notice, §55-225.
Material noncompliance with rental agreement.
Breach of lease agreement, §55-225.13.
Payment of rent into court registry, §55-225.12.
Defective drywall.
Remedy for nondisclosure, §55-225.11.
Depriving tenant of possession.
Release of duties, §55-226.
Desertion by tenant, §55-224.
Destruction of leasehold.
Release of duties, §55-226.
Disabled tenants.
Reduced rent, rent reduction income tax credit, §58.1-339.9.
Discrimination.
Human rights act, §§2.2-3900 to 2.2-3903.
Distress.
Bond by plaintiff, §55-230.
By whom made, §55-230.
Entry by force to levy or attach, §55-235.
Execution returns, §55-237.
Goods that may be levied upon, §55-231.
Insufficiency as prerequisite to right of reentry, §55-239.
Irregularities not to void, §55-236.
Judicial review, §55-232.2.

LANDLORD AND TENANT —Cont'd
Distress —Cont'd
Limitation of act, §55-230.
Local taxes.
Tenant paying taxes or levies, credit out of rent, §58.1-3944.
Passing of power to grantee or devisee, §55-220.
Priorities between landlord and other lienors, §55-231.
Priority of creditors, §55-233.
Goods of undertenant, §55-234.
Recovery by owner of personal property removed from premises.
Residential premises, §55-248.38:2.
Recovery of possession by owner of personal property removed from premises, §55-237.1.
Rent payments not in money, §55-238.
Rent recovery, §55-227.
Storage and sale of personal property removed from premises, §55-237.1.
Residential premises, §55-248.38:2.
Tenant defenses, §55-232.
Trial procedure, §55-230.1.
Undertenant goods.
Removal terms, §55-234.
Warrant.
Issuance and service, §55-230.
When made, §55-230.
Domestic violence.
Termination of tenancies.
Early termination by victims of family abuse, sexual abuse or criminal sexual assault, §§55-225.16, 55-248.21.
Drugs.
Illegal drug transactions.
Closure of nuisance premises, §§48-16, 48-17.
Immediate possession.
Criminal or willful act, illegal drug activity, §55-248.31.
Residential landlords and tenants.
Landlord remedies.
Illegal drug activity by tenant or guests, procedure, §55-248.31.
Duties of landlord.
Defective drywall, required disclosure, §55-225.11.
Locks and security devices.
Landlord's obligations when one co-tenant is excluded from premises, §§55-225.5, 55-248.18:1.
Maintenance of dwelling unit, §55-225.3.
Methamphetamine.
Disclosures by landlord for property previously used to manufacture methamphetamine, §§55-225.17, 55-248.12:3.
Duties of tenant.
Maintenance of dwelling unit, §55-225.4.
Elderly.
Reduced rent, rent reduction income tax credit, §58.1-339.9.
Electricity, plumbing, heat, ventilation, air-conditioning.
Duty of landlord, §55-225.3.
Tenant's duty, §55-225.4.
Emblements, §§55-249 to 55-252.
Energy allocation equipment, §§55-226.2, 56-245.2, 56-245.3.
Evictions, §§55-239 to 55-248.
Bars to tenant relief, §55-240.
Fees, §55-246.
Limitation of suits against landlord, §55-248.

LANDLORD AND TENANT —Cont'd
Evictions —Cont'd
Money judgment, attorneys' fees, court costs.
Acceptance of payment with reservation, not waiver of right to evict, §55-248.34:1.
Prevention, §55-243.
Proceedings to establish right of reentry, §55-239.
Real estate cooperatives.
Remedies for nonpayment of assessments, §55-472.
Recordation, §55-245.
Recovery agents, §55-246.1.
Reentry time limitations, §55-244.
Residential landlords and tenants.
Defenses to actions, §55-248.25.
Retaliatory evictions, §§55-248.39, 55-248.40.
Tenant to surrender possession of dwelling unit, §55-248.20.
Unlawful evictions.
Tenant remedies, §55-248.26.
Retaliatory evictions, §§55-248.39, 55-248.40.
Tenant relief, §55-247.
Equity, §55-242.
Trustee relief from forfeiture, §55-241.
Failure of tenant to vacate at expiration.
Effect, §55-223.
Fair housing law, §§36-96.1 to 36-96.23.
See FAIR HOUSING.
Family abuse, tenant victim.
Termination of lease due solely to act of abuse against tenant prohibited, §55-248.31.
Foreclosure, protection of funds in event of.
Escrow accounts.
Prepaid rent, security deposit and application deposit placed in, §54.1-2108.1.
Forfeiture of possession.
Failure to pay rent, §55-225.
Limitations, §55-225.1.
Remedies for landlord's unlawful ouster, §55-225.2.
Garbage, rubbish, waste.
Removal.
Tenant's duty, §55-225.4.
Grantee rights, §55-217.
Habitable condition.
Duty of landlord, §55-225.3.
Hearing on action for immediate possession.
Criminal or willful act, illegal drug activity, §55-248.31.
Hearing on summons to terminate tenancy.
Tenement unlawfully detained.
Time for initial hearing on summons, §8.01-126.
Holdover tenants.
Evictions, §§55-239 to 55-248.
Landlord remedies, §55-248.37.
Time-share conversion projects, §55-374.
Homeless persons.
Reduced rent charged previously homeless tenants, rent reduction income tax credit, §58.1-339.9.
Horizontal property regimes generally, §§55-79.1 to 55-79.38.
See HORIZONTAL PROPERTY REGIMES.
Housing codes.
Compliance, landlord's duty, §55-225.3.
Obligations, compliance, tenant's duty, §55-225.4.
Husband and wife.
Property rights of married women.
Use of property, §55-35.
Illegal drug transactions.
Closure of nuisance premises, §§48-16, 48-17.

LANDLORD AND TENANT —Cont'd
Illegal drug transactions —Cont'd
Immediate possession.
Criminal or willful act, illegal drug activity, §55-248.31.
Residential landlords and tenants.
Landlord remedies.
Illegal drug activity by tenant or guests, procedure, §55-248.31.
Immediate possession.
Order of possession.
Criminal or willful act, illegal drug activity, §55-248.31.
Income tax credit for rent reductions, §58.1-339.9.
Insecticide or pesticide use.
Residential landlords and tenants.
Notice to tenants, §55-248.13:3.
Inspection of unit by landlord.
Damages to unit at time of occupancy.
Move-in inspection report, §55-225.6.
Mold disclosure statement, §55-225.7.
Insurance.
Requisite of lease, §55-248.7:2.
Lessee rights, §55-218.
Liability of possessor of real property for harm to trespasser, §8.01-219.1.
Maintenance of dwelling unit.
Duties of landlord, §55-225.3.
Locks and security devices.
Landlord's obligations when one co-tenant is excluded from premises, §§55-225.5, 55-248.18:1.
Duties of tenant, §55-225.4.
Manufactured home lot rental, §§55-248.41 to 55-248.52.
See MANUFACTURED HOME LOT RENTAL.
Married women's property rights.
Use of property, §55-35.
Methamphetamine.
Disclosures by landlord for property previously used to manufacture methamphetamine, §§55-225.17, 55-248.12:3.
Military air installations, properties adjacent to.
Landlord obligations, disclosure, §55-248.12:1.
Military personnel.
Early termination of rental agreement, §55-248.21:1.
Mold.
Residential dwellings and homes.
Definitions, §55-225.8.
Duty of landlord to prevent, §55-225.3.
Duty of tenant to prevent, §55-225.4.
Move-in inspection.
Mold disclosure statement, §55-225.7.
Tenant and guest, distinguished, §55-225.8.
Visible mold.
Relocation of tenants, remediation, §55-225.9.
Tenant's option.
Terminate tenancy or take possession, §55-225.7.
Residential landlords and tenants.
Definitions, §55-248.4.
Move-in inspection report.
Landlord disclosure requirements, §55-248.11:2.
Relocation of tenant, remediation, §55-248.18:2.
Tenant obligations, §55-248.16.
Visible mold.
Tenant's option to terminate or take possession, §55-248.11:2.

LANDLORD AND TENANT —Cont'd
Mold —Cont'd
Visible mold.
Duty of landlord and managing agent, §8.01-226.12.
Mold remediation.
Relocation of tenants, §55-225.9.
Residential landlords and tenants.
Defined, §55-248.4.
Relocation of tenant, §55-248.18:2.
Visible mold in unit, §55-248.11:2.
Visible evidence of mold within dwelling unit, §8.01-226.12.
Definitions, §55-225.8.
Tenant and guest, distinguished, §55-225.8.
Tenant taking or remaining in possession, §55-225.7.
Mortgagee relief from forfeiture, §55-241.
Move-in inspection.
Damages to unit at time of occupancy.
Report by landlord to tenant itemizing, §55-225.6.
Mold disclosure statement, §55-225.7.
Nonresident property owners.
Resident agent.
Required, agent for service of process, §55-218.1.
Notice.
Ejectment.
Writs of possession, §8.01-470.
Failure to pay rent after 5 days' notice.
Forfeiture of possession, §55-225.
Foreclosure, §55-225.10.
Insecticide or pesticide use, notice to tenant, §55-248.13:3.
Methamphetamine.
Disclosures by landlord for property previously used to manufacture methamphetamine, §§55-225.17, 55-248.12:3.
Residential landlords and tenants.
Acceptance of rent with reservation, §55-248.34:1.
Defective drywall, §55-225.11.
Ejectment.
Writs of possession, §8.01-470.
Locks and security devices.
Landlord's obligations when one co-tenant is excluded from premises, §§55-225.5, 55-248.18:1.
Methamphetamine.
Disclosures by landlord for property previously used to manufacture methamphetamine, §§55-225.17, 55-248.12:3.
Unlawful entry and detainer.
Writs of possession, §8.01-470.
Termination of rental agreement.
Landlord's breach, §55-225.13.
Tenant's breach not remedial by landlord, §55-248.31.
Termination of tenancy, §55-222.
Early termination by victims of family abuse, sexual abuse or criminal sexual assault, §§55-225.16, 55-248.21.
Peeping or spying on tenant.
Violation of occupant's reasonable expectation of privacy, §18.2-130.
Perfection of interest in leases, rents and profits, §55-220.1.
Periodic tenancy termination notice periods, §55-248.37.

LANDLORD AND TENANT —Cont'd
Personal property taxes.
Short-term rental property, §§58.1-3510.4 to 58.1-3510.7.
Possession.
Depriving tenant of possession.
Release of duties, §55-226.
Desertion by tenant, §55-224.
Evictions, §§55-239 to 55-248.
Forfeiture of possession.
Failure to pay rent, §55-225.
Limitations, §55-225.1.
Remedies for landlord's unlawful ouster, §55-225.2.
Holdover tenants.
Evictions, §§55-239 to 55-248.
Landlord remedies, §55-248.37.
Time-share conversion projects, §55-374.
Immediate possession.
Criminal or willful act, illegal drug activity, §55-248.31.
Locks and security devices.
Landlord's obligations when one co-tenant is excluded from premises, §§55-225.5, 55-248.18:1.
Writ of possession.
Execution, time for issuing, §§8.01-470, 8.01-471.
Principal and income.
Uniform principal and income act, §§64.2-1000 to 64.2-1032.
See PRINCIPAL AND INCOME.
Property rights of married women.
Use of property, §55-35.
Ratio utility billing system, §55-226.2.
Real estate brokers, salespersons and rental agents, §§54.1-2100 to 54.1-2145.
See REAL ESTATE BROKERS, SALESPERSONS AND RENTAL AGENTS.
Real estate cooperative.
Conversion buildings, §55-487.
Recordation of declaration, §55-443.
Termination of declarant lease, §55-462.
Real property taxation of leasehold interest, §58.1-3203.
Redemption tender.
Defined, §§55-243, 55-248.34:1.
Forfeiture prevention in unlawful detainer cases for nonpayment of rent.
Presentation to court, §§55-243, 55-248.34:1.
Reentry.
Passing of power to grantee or devisee, §55-220.
Remedies.
Breach of lease agreement, §55-225.13.
Landlord's unlawful ouster, §55-225.2.
Material noncompliance or danger, §55-225.12.
Rent.
Acceptance with reservation, §55-248.34:1.
Accounting for payments upon request.
Residential landlords and tenants, §55-248.7.
Actions, §55-227.
Apportionment on purchase of part of land by holder, §55-219.
Bad check for rent payment.
Checks drawn on accounts with insufficient funds, §55-248.31.
Amount recovered, §8.01-27.2.
Notice check return unpaid, §8.01-27.2.
Processing fee assessed, §55-248.4.
Cash or money order payments.
Receipt required, §55-225.15.

LANDLORD AND TENANT —Cont'd
Rent —Cont'd
Casualty damage to unit.
Termination or apportionment, §55-248.24.
Checks drawn on accounts with insufficient funds, §55-248.31.
Amount recovered, §8.01-27.2.
Notice check return unpaid, §8.01-27.2.
Processing fee for payment of rent with bad check, §55-248.4.
Damage insurance.
Payments for premium costs deemed, §55-248.7:2.
Defaults.
Forfeiture of right of possession, §55-225.
Defenses to landlord actions for rent, §55-248.25.
Depriving tenant of possession.
Release of duties, §55-226.
Destruction of leasehold.
Release of duties, §55-226.
Distress, §55-230.
Recovery by, §55-227.
Rent payments not in money, §55-238.
Escrow.
Material noncompliance with rental agreement, §55-225.12.
Essential services.
Abatement of rent for wrongful failure to supply, §55-248.23.
Failure by landlord to deliver possession.
Abatement of rent, §55-248.22.
Failure to pay after 5 days' notice.
Forfeiture of possession, §55-225.
Fire damage to unit.
Termination or apportionment of rent, §55-248.24.
Foreclosure, protection of funds in event of.
Prepaid rent, security deposit and application deposit placed in escrow accounts, §54.1-2108.1.
Landlord remedy for failure to pay, §55-248.31.
Maintenance failure charges.
Attachment to rent, §55-248.32.
Material noncompliance or danger.
Payment of rent into court registry, §55-225.12.
Termination or apportionment, §55-248.27.
Payment times and locations.
Residential landlords and tenants, §55-248.7.
Perfection of interest in rents, §55-220.1.
Prepaid rent, §55-248.7:1.
Recovery by distress or action, §55-227.
Redemption tender.
Defined, §§55-243, 55-248.34:1.
Forfeiture prevention in unlawful detainer cases for nonpayment of rent.
Presentation to court, §§55-243, 55-248.34:1.
Reentry for failure to pay, §55-239.
Rental agreement terms.
Residential landlords and tenants, §55-248.7.
Renter's insurance.
Payment for premium costs.
Deemed rent, §55-248.7:2.
Retaliatory conduct prohibitions.
Construction, §55-248.39.
Sale of tenant goods for rent, §§55-230 to 55-238.
Service of notice by sheriffs, §55-248.31:1.
Who liable for, §55-229.
Who may recover, §55-228.
Rental agents, §§54.1-2100 to 54.1-2145.
See REAL ESTATE BROKERS, SALESPERSONS AND RENTAL AGENTS.

LANDLORD AND TENANT —Cont'd
Rental agreements. See within this heading, "Residential landlords and tenants."
Rental inspections of units located in rental inspection district.
  Residential rental dwelling units.
    Building code compliance, §36-105.1:1.
Renter's insurance.
  Landlord may require as condition of tenancy, §55-248.7:2.
  Payment for premium costs.
    Deemed rent, §55-248.7:2.
Rent reduction income tax credit.
  Reduced rent charged previously homeless tenants, elderly, disabled, §58.1-339.9.
Repairs.
  Duty of landlord, §55-225.3.
Residential landlords and tenants, §§55-248.2 to 55-248.40.
  Abandoned unit rentals, §55-248.33.
  Abuse of access.
    Landlord and tenant remedies, §55-248.10:1.
  Access.
    Abuse of access.
      Landlord and tenant remedies, §55-248.10:1.
    Landlord's access, §55-248.18.
  Accounting for payments upon request, §55-248.7.
  Applicability of chapter, §55-248.3:1.
    Manufactured home lot rentals, §55-248.48.
  Application deposits.
    Defined, §55-248.4.
    Landlord may require, §55-248.6:1.
  Application fees, §55-248.6:1.
    Defined, §55-248.4.
  Application of security deposit, §55-248.15:1.
  Carbon monoxide detectors.
    Installation by tenant, §55-248.18.
    Removal by tenant, tampering with, §55-248.16.
  Cash or money order payments.
    Receipt required, §55-225.15.
  Casualty damage to unit.
    Termination of lease, §55-248.24.
  Chain latch devices.
    Installation by tenant, §55-248.18.
  Conditions, §55-248.7.
  Confidentiality of tenant records, §55-248.9:1.
  Consent to landlord to enter premises.
    Tenant not to unreasonably withhold, §55-248.18.
  Copies of lease for tenant, §55-248.7.
  Criminal or willful acts.
    Immediate termination of rental agreement, §55-248.31.
  Defective drywall.
    Remedy for nondisclosure, §55-225.11.
  Defined terms, §55-248.4.
  Denial of access.
    Landlord and tenant remedies, §55-248.10:1.
  Early termination by military personnel, §55-248.21:1.
  Electronic delivery of notice, §55-248.6.
  Emergencies.
    Entry of premises by landlord, §55-248.18.
  Entry of premises by landlord, §55-248.18.
  Escrow.
    Material noncompliance with rental agreement, §55-225.12.
    Prepaid rent, §55-248.7:1.
    Tenant remedies.
      Rent escrow required to continuance of tenant's case, §§55-225.14, 55-248.25:1.

LANDLORD AND TENANT —Cont'd
Residential landlords and tenants —Cont'd
  Exemption from provisions, §55-248.5.
  Failure by landlord to deliver possession.
    Termination of lease grounds, §55-248.22.
  Family abuse, tenant victim.
    Termination of lease due solely to act of abuse against tenant prohibited, §55-248.31.
  Fire damage to unit.
    Termination of lease, §55-248.24.
  Fire detection devices.
    Installation by tenant, §55-248.18.
  Guest or invitee.
    Barring from premises, §55-248.31:01.
    Defined, §55-248.4.
  Hearing on action for immediate possession.
    Criminal or willful act, illegal drug activity, §55-248.31.
  Illegal drug activity by tenant or guests, procedure, §55-248.31.
  Immediate possession.
    Order of possession.
      Criminal or willful act, illegal drug activity, §55-248.31.
  Insecticide or pesticide use.
    Notice to tenants, §55-248.13:3.
  Insurance, obtaining for tenant, §55-248.7:2.
  Judgment, attorneys' fees and court costs.
    Acceptance of payment with reservation and not waiver of right of eviction, §55-248.34:1.
  Landlord obligations, §§55-248.11:1 to 55-248.15.
    Cable television facility access, §55-248.13:2.
    Common area cleanliness and safety, §55-248.13.
    Defective drywall, §55-225.11.
    Disclosure, §55-248.12.
      Defective drywall, §55-248.12:2.
      Methamphetamine, previous use of property to manufacture, §55-248.12:3.
      Military air installations, properties adjacent to, §55-248.12:1.
    Electrical maintenance, §55-248.13.
    Elevator maintenance, §55-248.13.
    Fit premises, §55-248.13.
    Heating and cooling maintenance, §55-248.13.
    Insecticide or pesticide use, reasonable notice, §55-248.13:3.
    Inspections, §55-248.11:1.
    Limitation of liability, §55-248.14.
    Locks, §55-248.13:1.
    Locks and security devices.
      Landlord's obligations when one co-tenant is excluded from premises, §§55-225.5, 55-248.18:1.
    Mold in unit.
      Disclosure, remediation, §55-248.11:2.
    Peepholes, §55-248.13:1.
    Plumbing maintenance, §55-248.13.
    Sanitary maintenance, §55-248.13.
    Satellite television facility access, §55-248.13:2.
    Security deposits, §55-248.15:1.
    Television facility access, §55-248.13:2.
    Tenancy at will.
      Notice of change of provisions, effect, §55-248.15.
    Tenant assumption of duties, §55-248.13.
    Water supply, §55-248.13.
  Landlord remedies, §§55-248.31 to 55-248.38:3.
    Abandonment by tenant, §55-248.33.
    Absent tenants, §55-248.33.

LANDLORD AND TENANT —Cont'd
Residential landlords and tenants —Cont'd
Landlord remedies —Cont'd
Acceptance of rent with reservation, §55-248.34:1.
Barring guest or invitee of tenant, §55-248.31:01.
Deceased tenants.
Disposal of property of, §55-248.38:3.
Holdover tenants, §55-248.37.
Illegal drug activity by tenant or guests, procedure, §55-248.31.
Maintenance of unit failures, §55-248.32.
Monetary penalty for noncompliance with rental agreement, §55-248.31.
Noncompliance failures, §55-248.31.
Periodic tenancy termination notice, §55-248.37.
Personal property abandoned by tenant, §55-248.38:1.
Post-termination, §55-248.35.
Recovery by owner of personal property removed from premises, §55-248.38:2.
Recovery or possession limitations, §55-248.36.
Rent payment failures, §55-248.31.
Service of notice by sheriffs, §55-248.31:1.
Storage and sale of personal property removed from premises, §55-248.38:2.
Material noncompliance or danger.
Payment of rent into court registry, §55-225.12.
Termination of lease, §55-248.27.
Methamphetamine.
Disclosures by landlord for property previously used to manufacture methamphetamine, §§55-225.17, 55-248.12:3.
Military personnel.
Early termination of rental agreement, §55-248.21:1.
Mold in unit.
Move-in inspection report.
Landlord disclosure requirements, §55-248.11:2.
Relocation of tenant, remediation, §55-248.18:2.
Tenant obligations, §55-248.16.
Visible mold.
Defined, §55-248.4.
Duty of landlord and managing agent, §8.01-226.12.
Tenant's option to terminate or take possession, §55-248.11:2.
Mold remediation.
Defined, §55-248.4.
Relocation of tenant, §55-248.18:2.
Visible evidence of mold within dwelling unit, §8.01-226.12.
Visible mold in unit, §55-248.11:2.
Noncompliance by landlord, §55-248.21.
Nonemergency property condition.
Temporary vacation of property, §55-248.18.
Nonresident property owners.
Resident agent.
Required, agent for service of process, §55-218.1.
Notice, §55-248.6.
Acceptance of rent with reservation, §55-248.34:1.
Defined, §55-248.4.
Ejectment.
Writs of possession, §8.01-470.
Electronic delivery of notice, §55-248.6.
Intent of landlord to enter premises, §55-248.18.

LANDLORD AND TENANT —Cont'd
Residential landlords and tenants —Cont'd
Notice —Cont'd
Methamphetamine.
Disclosures by landlord for property previously used to manufacture methamphetamine, §§55-225.17, 55-248.12:3.
Temporary vacation of property.
Nonemergency property condition, §55-248.18.
Tenancy at will, change of provisions, §55-248.15.
Termination of rental agreement.
Landlord's breach, §55-225.13.
Tenant's breach not remedial by landlord, §55-248.31.
Unlawful entry and detainer.
Writs of possession, §8.01-470.
Order of possession.
Termination of tenancy for illegal drug activity, §55-248.31.
Possession.
Writ of possession.
Execution, time for issuing, §§8.01-470, 8.01-471.
Post-lease adoption of rules and regulations.
Effect, §55-248.17.
Post-termination remedies of landlord, §55-248.35.
Presumption of tenancy period, §55-248.7.
Prohibited provisions in leases, §55-248.9.
Purposes of chapter, §55-248.3.
Real estate cooperatives.
Conversion buildings, §55-487.
Declarant leases.
Termination, §55-462.
Recordation of declaration, §55-443.
Receipt required, payments in cash or money order, §55-225.15.
Refund.
Application fees and application deposits, §55-248.6:1.
Security deposit, §55-248.15:1.
Release of tenant information.
Consent of tenant required, §55-248.9:1.
Rental agreements.
Abandoned unit rentals, §55-248.33.
Casualty damage to unit.
Termination of agreement, §55-248.24.
Conditions, §55-248.7.
Copies for tenant, §55-248.7.
Early termination by military personnel, §55-248.21:1.
Failure by landlord to deliver possession.
Termination grounds, §55-248.22.
Fire damage to unit.
Termination of agreement, §55-248.24.
Landlord remedies for noncompliance, §55-248.31.
Material noncompliance or danger.
Payment of rent into court registry, §55-225.12.
Termination of agreement, §55-248.27.
Noncompliance by landlord, §55-248.21.
Post-agreement adoption of rules and regulations.
Enforceability, §55-248.17.
Post-termination remedies of landlords, §55-248.35.
Prepaid rent, §55-248.7:1.
Provisions prohibited, §55-248.9.

LANDLORD AND TENANT —Cont'd
Residential landlords and tenants —Cont'd
Rental agreements —Cont'd
Retaliatory actions by landlords, §§55-248.39, 55-248.40.
Service of notices required by, §8.01-296.
Termination.
Tenant's breach not remedial by landlord, §55-248.31.
Terms, §55-248.7.
Unilateral changes, §55-248.7.
Unlawful ouster, exclusion or diminution of services by landlord.
Tenant remedy of termination, §55-248.26.
Rent payments, §55-248.7.
Acceptance with reservation, §55-248.34:1.
Accounting for payments upon request, §55-248.7.
Cash or money order payments.
Receipt required, §55-225.15.
Checks drawn on accounts with insufficient funds, §55-248.31.
Amount recovered, §8.01-27.2.
Notice check returned unpaid, §8.01-27.2.
Processing fee for payment of rent with bad check, §55-248.4.
Failure to pay after 5 days' notice.
Termination of rental agreement, §55-248.31.
Temporary relocation, §55-248.18.
Retaliatory actions, §§55-248.39, 55-248.40.
Security deposits, §55-248.15:1.
Interest rates, §55-248.15:2.
Return upon landlord noncompliance, §55-248.21.
Security systems for commercial rental property, §55-226.1.
Service of notice, process and other papers.
Appointment of resident agent by nonresident property owner, §55-218.1.
Fee charged by circuit court clerk, §17.1-275.
Notice, §55-248.6.
Rental agreements.
Notices required by, §8.01-296.
Sheriff service of notice on tenant, §55-248.31:1.
Short title of act, §55-248.2.
Smoke detectors.
Removal by tenant, tampering with, §55-248.16.
Temporary vacation of property.
Nonemergency property condition, §55-248.18.
Tenancy at will.
Notice of change of provisions, effect, §55-248.15.
Tenancy period, §55-248.7.
Tenant obligations, §§55-248.16 to 55-248.20.
Access to unit by landlord, §55-248.18.
Assumption of landlord obligations, §55-248.13.
Building and housing codes.
Compliance, §55-248.16.
Carbon monoxide detector.
Removal, tampering with, §55-248.16.
Clean and safe premises, §55-248.16.
Conduct of self and guests, responsibility, §55-248.16.
Conduct of tenant and other on premises, §55-248.16.
Damage to premises, §55-248.16.
Garbage, rubbish, waste.
Removal, §55-248.16.
Maintenance of unit, §55-248.16.
Failures to maintain, §55-248.32.
Mold in unit, §55 248.16.

LANDLORD AND TENANT —Cont'd
Residential landlords and tenants —Cont'd
Tenant obligations —Cont'd
Occupancy of unit, §55-248.19.
Plumbing fixtures, §55-248.16.
Rules and regulations, §§55-248.16, 55-248.17.
Smoke detectors.
Removal, tampering with, prohibition, §55-248.16.
Surrendering possession of unit, §55-248.20.
Use of unit, §55-248.19.
Utilities, use, §55-248.16.
Utility payments, §55-248.16.
Tenant remedies.
Casualty damage, §55-248.24.
Continuances.
Rent escrow required for continuance of tenant's case, §§55-225.14, 55-248.25:1.
Defenses to landlord actions for possession or rent, §55-248.25.
Early termination by military personnel, §55-248.21:1.
Essential services.
Diminution of, §55-248.26.
Wrongful failure to supply, §55-248.23.
Failure to deliver possession, §55-248.22.
Fire damages, §55-248.24.
Material noncompliance or danger, §55-248.27.
Methamphetamine, previous use of property to manufacture.
Failure to disclose, §55-248.12:3.
Military air installations, properties adjacent to.
Failure to disclose, §55-248.12:1.
Noncompliance by landlord, §55-248.21.
Receipt required, payments in cash or money order, §55-225.15.
Unlawful ouster, §55-248.26.
Termination of rental agreement.
Tenant's breach not remedial by landlord, §55-248.31.
Termination of tenancy.
Application of security deposit, §55-248.15:1.
Terms of lease, §55-248.7.
Third parties to receive summons and notices.
Designation by tenant, §55-248.9:1.
Time-share conversion projects.
Termination of tenancies, §55-374.
Transfer disclosures for residential property.
Applicability of provisions, §55-517.
Undelivered leases, §55-248.8.
Unilateral changes to rental agreement, §55-248.7.
Unlawful ouster, exclusion or diminution of services by landlord.
Tenant remedy of termination, §55-248.26.
Unreasonable access or denial of access.
Landlord and tenant remedies, §55-248.10:1.
Unsigned leases, §55-248.8.
Utility payments by tenants, §55-248.16.
Writ of possession.
Execution, time for issuing, §§8.01-470, 8.01-471.
Rules and regulations imposed by landlord.
Duty of tenant to abide by, §55-225.4.
Satisfaction for use and occupation in lands, §55-227.
Security deposits.
Foreclosure, protection of funds in event of.
Prepaid rent, security deposit and application deposit placed in escrow accounts, §54.1-2108.1.

LANDLORD AND TENANT —Cont'd
Security deposits —Cont'd
Interest rates, §55-248.15:2.
Residential landlords and tenants, §55-248.15:1.
Transfers upon purchase, §55-507.
Security systems for commercial property, §55-226.1.
Self-service storage, §§55-416 to 55-423.
Service of notice, process and other papers.
Appointment of resident agent by nonresident property owners, §55-218.1.
Fee charged by circuit court clerk, §17.1-275.
Rental agreements.
Notices required by, §8.01-296.
Sexual abuse.
Termination of tenancies.
Early termination by victims of family abuse, sexual abuse or criminal sexual assault, §§55-225.16, 55-248.21.
Sexual assault.
Termination of tenancies.
Early termination by victims of family abuse, sexual abuse or criminal sexual assault, §§55-225.16, 55-248.21.
Smoke detectors.
Locality requiring in certain buildings, §15.2-922.
Tenant removing or tampering with, §55-225.4.
Smoke detectors in certain buildings.
Locality requiring, §15.2-922.
Submetering, §§56-245.2, 56-245.3.
Equipment use, §55-226.2.
Summons issued where tenement unlawfully detained.
Termination of tenancy pursuant to residential landlord and tenant act.
Initial hearing on summons, time for, §8.01-126.
Taxation of leasehold interest, §58.1-3203.
Termination of tenancies, §55-222.
Defective drywall, remedy for nondisclosure, §55-225.11.
Early termination by victims of family abuse, sexual abuse or criminal sexual assault, §§55-225.16, 55-248.21.
Locks and security devices.
Landlord's obligations when one co-tenant is excluded from premises, §§55-225.5, 55-248.18:1.
Security deposit.
Application by landlord, §55-248.15:1.
Time-share conversion projects.
Termination of tenancies, §55-374.
Trespassers.
Liability of possessor of real property for harm to trespasser, §8.01-219.1.
Unlawful entry and detainer.
General provisions, §§8.01-124 to 8.01-130.
See UNLAWFUL ENTRY AND DETAINER.
Utility payments by tenants, §55-248.16.
Billing for utilities.
Energy allocation and submetering equipment, ratio utility billing system used, §55-226.2.
Victims of crime.
Termination of tenancies.
Early termination by victims of family abuse, sexual abuse or criminal sexual assault, §§55-225.16, 55-248.21.
Waiver of rights or remedies, §55-248.9.
Waste, §§55-211 to 55-216.
Water supply.
Duty of landlord, §55-225.3.

LANDLORD AND TENANT —Cont'd
Writ of possession.
Execution, time for issuing, §§8.01-470, 8.01-471.

LANDMARKS.
Locality acquiring and preserving places and things of historical interest, §15.2-944.
Notification prior to transfer of ownership of certain historic properties, §15.2-944.1.
Procedure for designation, §10.1-2206.1.
Real property taxes.
Partial exemption for redevelopment or conservation areas or rehabilitation districts.
Demolition of registered Virginia landmark, inapplicability of exemption, §58.1-3219.4.
Separate class of property for local taxation, building listed on Virginia landmarks register, §58.1-3221.5.

LAND OFFICE, §§41.1-1 to 41.1-20.
Bills in equity.
Ownership establishment, §41.1-9.
Repeal of grants, §41.1-13.
Chain of title.
Denny Martin.
Change of name to Fairfax, §41.1-2.
Lost records and papers, §41.1-9.
Order of court for survey, §41.1-10.
Ownership certified by court, §41.1-12.
Testimony, §41.1-11.
Circuit courts.
Disposal of waste in unappropriated lands, §41.1-5.
Commonwealth's right extinguished.
Wasteland sales, §41.1-20.
Commonwealth's right relinquished.
Land settled on, §41.1-8.
Payment of taxes, §41.1-7.
Denny Martin.
Changing name to Fairfax.
Title to land, §41.1-2.
Evidence.
Copies of unsigned grants, §41.1-7.
Grants of certain lands to be void, §41.1-3.
Invalid grants, §41.1-8.
Librarian of Virginia in charge of, §41.1-1.
Lord Fairfax.
Title to land, §41.1-2.
Ownership of land.
Bills in equity, §41.1-9.
Previous land grants.
Ratification, §41.1-6.
Repeal of grants.
Bills in equity, §41.1-13.
Nature of proceedings, §41.1-14.
Recording decree of repeal, §41.1-15.
Taxation.
Payment of taxes.
Commonwealth's right relinquished, §41.1-7.
Unappropriated lands.
Disposal by circuit court, §41.1-5.
Void land grants, §41.1-3.
Wasteland disposal by circuit court, §41.1-5.
Wasteland sales, §41.1-16.
Distinguishing Commonwealth's title and interest, §41.1-20.
Motion for hearing.
Time and place, §41.1-17.
Proceedings by governing body, §41.1-19.
Subsequent proceedings, §41.1-18.

LANDOWNER'S LIABILITY.
Airport landing areas.
Limitation of liability of private landing area owner, §5.1-7.3.
Duty of care and liability for hunters, fishermen, sightseers, etc., §29.1-509.
Prescribed burning, §10.1-1150.5.
Southwest regional recreation authority.
Contracts to hold landowners harmless, §15.2-6020.
Limiting liability, §15.2-6024.
Trail system for ATVs and off-road motorcycles.
Locality providing.
No liability to locality or property owners, §15.2-1809.1.
Protection of persons property and interest and personal liability, §15.2-1806.
Trespassers.
Liability of possessor of real property for harm to trespasser, §8.01-219.1.

LAND PRESERVATION.
Budget bill, contents, §2.2-1509.4.
Farmland preservation, office of, §§3.2-200 to 3.2-203.
Tax credits, §58.1-512.

LAND PRESERVATION SPECIAL ASSESSMENT, §§58.1-3229 to 58.1-3244.
See REAL PROPERTY TAXES.

LAND PRESERVATION TAX CREDITS, §58.1-512.

LAND REGISTRATION ACT, §55-112.

LANDSCAPE ARCHITECTS, §§54.1-400 to 54.1-411.
Board for architects, professional engineers, land surveyors and landscape architects, §§54.1-403 to 54.1-405.
Building plans, §54.1-410.
Business license, requirements for obtaining, §54.1-410.1.
Continuing education, §54.1-404.2.
Defined terms, §54.1-400.
Emeritus designation for retirees, §54.1-405.
Examinations, §54.1-405.
Organization for practice, §54.1-411.
Practice of landscape architecture, §54.1-409.
Professional corporations.
Generally, §§13.1-542.1 to 13.1-556.
See PROFESSIONAL CORPORATIONS.
Shareholder qualifications, special provisions, §13.1-549.
Professional limited liability companies.
Generally, §§13.1-1100 to 13.1-1123.
See PROFESSIONAL LIMITED LIABILITY COMPANIES.
Special provisions, §13.1-1111.
Registration, §54.1-411.
Requirement of licensure, §54.1-406.
Exemptions, §§54.1-401 to 54.1-402.1.
Scope of licensure, §54.1-409.
Unlawful procurement of licensure, §54.1-102.
Unlawful use of licensure, §54.1-111.
Unlicensed practice, §54.1-409.

LANDSCAPE ARCHITECTURE WEEK, §2.2-3316.

LANDSCAPE IRRIGATION CONTRACTORS.
Licensing, §54.1-1103.

LANDSCAPING COMMUNITY SERVICE PROGRAM, §33.1-12.2.

LANDSCAPING VEHICLES.
Parking, ordinances prohibiting or limiting, §46.2-1224.

LAND SUBDIVISION AND DEVELOPMENT.
Generally, §§15.2-2240 to 15.2-2279.
See SUBDIVISIONS.

LAND SURVEYORS, §§54.1-400 to 54.1-411.
See SURVEYORS.

LAND TRUSTS.
Beneficiaries not specified by name and no duties laid to trustee.
Deemed personal property of beneficiary, §55-17.1.
Judgment liens, §55-17.1.
Power conferred on trustee to sale, lease, etc., §55-17.1.
Trust not to fail, §55-17.1.
Domestic insurers investment in real property.
Ownership through land trusts, §38.2-1441.

LAND USE PERMITS.
Department of transportation.
Issuance to company other than public service company, §2.2-1151.1.
Performance sureties.
Claims against company resolved before release, §2.2-1151.1.

LAND USE RESTRICTIONS.
Local planning, subdivision of land and zoning.
Capital improvement plans, §15.2-2239.
Comprehensive plans, §§15.2-2222.1 to 15.2-2232.
See PLANNING AND DEVELOPMENT.
Generally, §§15.2-2200 to 15.2-2209.2.
See PLANNING AND DEVELOPMENT.
Official map, §§15.2-2233 to 15.2-2238.
See PLANNING AND DEVELOPMENT.
Planning commissions, §§15.2-2210 to 15.2-2222.
See PLANNING COMMISSIONS.
Subdivisions, §§15.2-2240 to 15.2-2279.
See SUBDIVISIONS.
Zoning, §§15.2-2280 to 15.2-2316.2.
See ZONING.
Pet cemeteries, §§57-39.21, 57-39.24.

LAND USE TAX ASSESSMENT BOOK.
Applications for special assessment for land preservation.
Indexing of applicants by clerk, §58.1-3234.

LANE CHANGING WITHOUT FIRST ASCERTAINING SAFETY, §46.2-804.
Fine schedule, VA SCt Rule 3B:2.
Maximum fine for violating title 46.2, §46.2-113.
Prepayment of fine, §16.1-69.40:1.

LAPSE OF INSURANCE POLICIES.
Notice.
Life and health insurance policies, §38.2-232.

LAPTOP COMPUTER LOAN PROGRAMS.
Programs designed to promote educational opportunities, §22.1-199.1.

LARCENY, §§18.2-95 to 18.2-109.
Advances of money, merchandise or other thing.
Failure to perform promise for construction in return for, §18.2-200.1.
Failure to perform promise to deliver crop or other property in return for, §18.2-200.

LARCENY —Cont'd
Animals and poultry, §18.2-97.
Bad checks, issuance, §18.2-181.
Bailee's failure to return animal, aircraft, vehicle or boat, §18.2-117.
Ballot containers, voting or registration equipment, etc., §24.2-1009.
Bank directors, officers or employees.
Embezzlement, etc., §6.2-943.
Bank notes, checks or books of account, §18.2-98.
Buying stolen goods, §18.2-108.
Cargo theft, §18.2-147.1.
Charitable gaming funds.
Conversion to own use, §18.2-340.37.
Computer fraud, §18.2-152.3.
Computer services theft, §18.2-152.6.
Conspiracy, §18.2-23.
Construction promise.
Failure to perform in return for advances, §18.2-200.1.
Contractors.
Fund improprieties, §43-13.
Conviction of petty larceny.
Property worth more than $200, §19.2-290.
Prosecution for grand larceny, §19.2-289.
Crops.
Failure to perform promise to deliver in return for advances, §18.2-200.
Removal by tenant before rents and advances satisfied, §18.2-100.
Dairy milk cases or milk crates, unauthorized use, §18.2-102.2.
Uniform fine schedule, VA SCt Rules 3C:1, 3C:2.
Delivered for selection or approval goods.
Failure to pay for or return, §18.2-116.
Documents of title.
Stolen documents, §8.7-601.
Embezzlement, §18.2-111.
Bank directors, officers or employees, §6.2-943.
Employer embezzling payroll deduction, §18.2-111.2.
Entering bank armed with intent to commit, §18.2-93.
Entering dwelling with intent to commit, §18.2-91.
False pretenses, obtaining money or signature by, §18.2-178.
False statements to obtain property or credit, §18.2-186.
Financial exploitation of mentally incapacitated persons, §18.2-178.1.
Firearms, theft or receipt of stolen firearms, §18.2-108.1.
Fishing, tidal waters.
Arrests, §28.2-900.
Fraudulent conversion of leased personal property, §18.2-118.
Fraudulent conversion or removal of property subject to lien or title in another, §18.2-115.
General contractors.
Fund improprieties, §43-13.
Goods distrained or levied on, selling, pledging, etc., §18.2-101.
Grand larceny, §18.2-95.
Credit card theft, §18.2-192.
Insurers to report acts of agents or surplus lines brokers deemed larceny, §38.2-1810.
Joyriding, §18.2-102.
Jurisdiction for trial.
Conspiracy to commit, §18.2-23.

LARCENY —Cont'd
Mechanics' and materialmen's liens.
Fund improprieties, §43-13.
Medicaid.
Benefits, §32.1-321.4.
Payments, §32.1-314.
Mentally incapacitated persons.
Financial exploitation, §18.2-178.1.
Oysters, §28.2-560.
Parking meters, vending machines, pay telephones, etc.
Stealing from or tampering with, §18.2-152.
Personalty permanently marked.
Possession of personalty with removed, altered, etc., marks, §18.2-96.1.
Removing, altering, etc., mark, §18.2-96.1.
Petit larceny, §18.2-96.
Property worth more than $200, §19.2-290.
Prosecution for grand larceny, §19.2-289.
Statute of limitations, §19.2-8.
Photographs used as evidence, §19.2-270.1.
Possession of burglarious tools, prima facie evidence of intent to commit, §18.2-94.
Prima facie evidence.
Intent to sell or distribute, §18.2-108.01.
Proof of ownership to property, §19.2-284.
Public assistance fraud.
Unauthorized uses of food stamps, electronic transfer cards and energy assistance, §63.2-523.
Public records.
Theft or destruction by others than officers, §18.2-107.
Receiving stolen goods, §18.2-108.
Firearms, §18.2-108.1.
Vehicles, aircraft or boats, §18.2-109.
Sale of stolen property, §18.2-108.01.
Shoplifting, §§18.2-23, 18.2-103.
Agents of merchant defined, §18.2-106.
Civil liability to owner, §18.2-104.1.
Detention of suspected shoplifter, §§8.01-226.9, 18.2-105.1.
Electronic detection devices to shield against shoplifting.
Manufacture, sale, etc., §18.2-105.2.
Prima facie evidence.
Willful concealment of goods and merchandise while still on premises, §18.2-23.
Punishment, §18.2-104.
Willful concealment of goods and merchandise while still on premises, §18.2-23.
Shopping carts, removal from store premises, §18.2-102.1.
Special commissioner or receiver.
Collecting money and failing to account, §18.2-114.1.
Statute of limitations.
Petit larceny, §19.2-8.
Stolen vehicles, aircraft or boats, receipt or transfer of possession, §18.2-109.
Subcontractors.
Fund improprieties, §43-13.
Things fixed to freehold, §18.2-99.
Timber, §55-334.1.
Trust companies or subsidiary directors, officers or employees.
Embezzlement, etc., §§6.2-943, 6.2-1044.
Trust subsidiaries.
Embezzlement, etc., §6.2-1062.
Unauthorized use of animals, aircraft, vehicles or boats, §18.2-102.

LARCENY —Cont'd
Venue, §19.2-245.
Venue for trial.
Conspiracy to commit, §18.2-23.
With intent to sell or distribute, §18.2-108.01.

LARCENY AFTER BAILMENT, §18.2-117.

LASER GUN SIGHT.
Pointing at aircraft, §5.1-22.
Pointing at law enforcement officer, probation officer or parole officer, etc., §18.2-57.01.

LASERS.
Pointing at aircraft, §5.1-22.
Pointing at law enforcement officer, probation officer or parole officer, etc., §18.2-57.01.

LASER SPEED DETECTION DEVICES.
Determining speed of motor vehicles, §46.2-882.
Division of purchases and supply.
Determining proper equipment for monitoring, §2.2-1112.

LAST CAPITOL OF THE CONFEDERACY.
Danville.
Appropriations for preservation, §10.1-2212.

LATE CHARGES.
Consumer finance companies, §6.2-1520.

LATINO ADVISORY BOARD, §§2.2-2459 to 2.2-2461.
Assistance from other agencies, §2.2-2461.
Established, §2.2-2459.
Members, §2.2-2459.
Powers and duties, §2.2-2460.
Staff, §2.2-2461.

LAUNDRIES.
Intangible personal property tax, §§58.1-1100 to 58.1-1118.
See PERSONAL PROPERTY TAXES.
Liens on garments, §43-63.
Loss or injury to clothing, §8.01-42.
Machinery and tools tax, §§58.1-3507, 58.1-3508.
Names, marks and devices on certain articles.
Deposits, §59.1-101.
Prohibited acts, §59.1-96.
Procedure when violation charged, §59.1-98.

LAUREL LAKE.
Licensing exemptions.
Residents of Kentucky, §29.1-301.

LAW DEPARTMENT.
Debt collection recovery fund, §2.2-518.
Division of consumer council, §2.2-517.
Division of debt collection, §2.2-518.
Debt collection recovery fund, §2.2-518.
Prompt collection of accounts receivable, §2.2-518.
Division of human rights, §§2.2-520 to 2.2-524.
Generally, §§2.2-500 to 2.2-516.
See ATTORNEY GENERAL.

LAW ENFORCEMENT, DEPARTMENTS OF.
Campus police.
Mutual aid agreements with local or state law enforcement, §23-234.
County executive form of government, §§15.2-518, 15.2-528.
Urban county executive form of government, §15.2-836.

LAW ENFORCEMENT EMERGENCIES.
Sending police beyond territorial limits of locality, §15.2-1724.

LAW ENFORCEMENT EXPENDITURES.
Adjusted crime index.
Calculation and use, §9.1-167.
Amount of funds.
Counties and cities, §9.1-169.
Towns, §9.1-170.
Defined terms, §9.1-165.
Disbursement of funds, §9.1-166.
Discretionary fund, §9.1-171.
Local governments, §9.1-169.
Distribution of funds.
Discretionary fund, §9.1-171.
Towns, §9.1-170.
Variables.
Periodic review, §9.1-172.
Eligibility for funds, §9.1-168.
Local governments.
Receipt of state funds, §9.1-166.
Notice.
Minimum training standards, compliance, §9.1-168.
Receipt of funds, §9.1-168.
State funds, §9.1-166.
State assistance to local government, §§9.1-165 to 9.1-172.
Variables.
Periodic review, §9.1-172.

LAW ENFORCEMENT FIREARM SAFETY OR TRAINING COURSES.
Carrying concealed weapons permit application.
Demonstration of competence with handgun, §18.2-308.02.
Nonresidents, §18.2-308.06.

LAW ENFORCEMENT OFFICERS.
Abduction, disclosure of information and assistance to, §18.2-50.
Absence without leave from National Guard.
Power to take person into custody, §44-41.1.
Absentee voting, §24.2-700.
Accident reports.
Duty of investigating officer to file, §46.2-373.
Age requirement, §15.2-1705.
Agriculture.
Commodity boards.
Enforcement, law enforcement officers' duties, §3.2-1103.
AIDS.
Exposure.
Deemed consent to release of test results, §32.1-45.1.
Anatomical gifts.
Search of individual for document of gift, §32.1-291.12.
Animals.
Enforcement authority, §3.2-6567.
Killing or injuring law enforcement animal, §18.2-144.1.
Seizure and impoundment of animals, §3.2-6569.
Assault and battery against, §18.2-57.
Assistance to officer in execution of office, refusal, §18.2-463.
Bailiffs.
Compulsory minimum training standards, §9.1-102.
Barricades, lines, perimeters established.
Crossing, §18.2-414.2.
Blue Alert program.
Missing officers, §§52-34.7 to 52-34.9.

LAW ENFORCEMENT OFFICERS —Cont'd
Bribery of public officers generally, §§18.2-438 to 18.2-450.
See PUBLIC OFFICERS AND EMPLOYEES.
Capital murder, killing officer, §18.2-31.
Carnal knowledge of defendant or convicted person, §18.2-64.2.
Carrying concealed weapons.
Inapplicability of provisions, §18.2-308.
Central criminal records exchange, reports to, §19.2-390.
Virginia crime code references, required use, §19.2-390.01.
Certification through training required, §15.2-1706.
Chief of police.
See POLICE.
Child abuse or neglect reports.
Reason to suspect, required reports, fine for failure, §63.2-1509.
Children, psychiatric treatment.
Emergency custody orders, execution, §16.1-340.
Child taken into custody.
Duties of persons taking child into custody, §16.1-247.
When and how child taken into immediate custody, §16.1-246.
Civilian protection, police misconduct, §9.1-600.
Colleges and universities.
Campus police departments, §§23-232 to 23-238.
Payments to institutions for criminal justice courses, §23-9.2:4.
Tuition and required fees.
Waiver for child or spouse of officer killed in line of duty, §23-7.4:1.
Commodity boards.
Enforcement, law enforcement officers' duties, §3.2-1103.
Communicable disease reports, §32.1-116.3.
Conservation police officers.
Generally, §§29.1-200 to 29.1-218.
See CONSERVATION POLICE OFFICERS.
Conservators of the peace.
General provisions, §§19.2-12 to 19.2-18.
See CONSERVATORS OF THE PEACE.
Special conservators.
Order appointing designated conservators as, §19.2-13.
Special conservators of the peace, §§9.1-150.1 to 9.1-150.4.
Copies of documents requested from state agency.
Agency furnishing at no costs, §2.2-610.
Courts-martial processes and sentences, execution, §44-50.
Crime reporting program.
Cooperation with state police, §52-26.
Report duties of Commonwealth and local agencies, §52-28.
Criminal incident information.
Freedom of information act.
Records subject to disclosure, §2.2-3706.
Criminal justice services department.
Direct operational responsibilities not authorized, §9.1-103.
Crisis intervention teams.
Mental health or substance abuse, §§9.1-187 to 9.1-190.
Critical incident stress management team-EMS or public safety personnel privilege, §19.2-271.4.

LAW ENFORCEMENT OFFICERS —Cont'd
Death in line of duty.
Half mast display of state and local flags, §18.2-488.1.
Tuition and fees to state supported colleges and universities.
Waiver for surviving spouse or children, §23-7.4:1.
Decertification, §15.2-1707.
Notice, §15.2-1708.
Decibel level of sound.
Proper equipment to determine.
Standards established by division of purchases and supply, §2.2-1112.
Defined.
Assault and battery against, §18.2-57.
Emergency protective orders authorized in certain cases, §16.1-253.4.
Unlawful paramilitary activity, §18.2-433.1.
Workers' compensation coverage in off-duty capacity, §65.2-102.
Detoxification centers.
Transporting public inebriates to, §18.2-388.
Direction of traffic.
Authority to deputize persons, §46.2-1310.
Hand signals, §46.2-1309.
Disarming a law-enforcement or correctional officer, §18.2-57.02.
Dispatchers.
Compulsory minimum training standards, §9.1-102.
Emergency care and assistance immunity, §8.01-225.
Disregarding signal by officer to stop, §46.2-817.
Diversity and biased policing policy to be established, §9.1-102.
Dogs.
Dangerous dogs, authority, §3.2-6540.
Vicious dogs, authority, §3.2-6540.1.
Domestic violence policies and procedures for law enforcement agencies, §9.1-1300.
Driver information.
Commissioner of DMV.
Supplying upon request, §46.2-208.
Driving while intoxicated.
Preliminary analysis of breath.
Duties and responsibilities, §18.2-267.
Educational requirement, §15.2-1705.
Election abstracts of votes.
Law enforcement officers sent for abstracts not forwarded, §24.2-678.
Emergency calls, vehicle patrols responding to.
Training standards and model policy, §9.1-102.
Entrapment.
Compulsory minimum training standards, §9.1-102.
Ephedrine, sale of ephedrine or related compounds.
Access to data, records and reports, §18.2-265.12.
Evidence.
Compulsory minimum training standards, §9.1-102.
Exemptions from training, §9.1-116.
False alarms, §18.2-461.
False identity.
Giving to officer, §19.2-82.1.
False impersonation, §18.2-174.
False reports to police officers, §18.2-461.

LAW ENFORCEMENT OFFICERS —Cont'd
Family abuse.
Reliance upon foreign protective orders, §16.1-279.1.
Federal employees prohibited, exception, §2.2-2801.
Field training officers.
Compulsory minimum training standards.
Criminal justice services department, §9.1-102.
Firearm or object similar in appearance pointed, held or brandished.
Immunity from civil liability for making arrest under provision, §18.2-282.
Fleeing or eluding officer, §46.2-817.
Freedom of information act.
Limitations on disclosures, §2.2-3706.
Free tuition and fees to state supported colleges or universities.
Children or spouses of officers killed in line of duty, §23-7.4:1.
Funeral escort, wide-load escort, dignitary escort or other escort duty.
Certain traffic regulations, exemption, §46.2-920.
Furloughed prisoners.
Notice to locality, §53.1-37.
Giving false identity to, §19.2-82.1.
Heart disease.
Workers' compensation presumption, §65.2-402.
Hepatitis.
Exposure to body fluids.
Deemed consent to release of test results, §32.1-45.1.
Testing, §32.1-45.2.
Hepatitis C test, positive results.
Convicted prostitutes or injection drug users tested.
Limited disclosure to, §18.2-346.1.
Hepatitis, meningitis, tuberculosis and HIV.
Workers' compensation.
Presumption on death or disability from, §65.2-402.1.
Highway construction and maintenance by prisoners.
Notice to localities, §53.1-56.
HIV testing, §32.1-45.2.
Hostage or barricaded person situation.
Emergency control of telephone service, §18.2-50.2.
Hours of work.
Overtime compensation, §9.1-703.
Hunting incident reports.
Duty of law-enforcement agency or emergency medical service provider to report, §29.1-530.4.
Hunting while under influence of intoxicant or narcotic drug.
Enforcement of provision, §18.2-285.
Hypertension.
Workers' compensation presumption, §65.2-402.
Identification of operator of vehicle.
Exhibition of license, permit or registration card, signing name in presence of officer.
Right to request for identity purposes, §46.2-104.
Impersonating, §18.2-174.
In person and photo lineups.
Written policies and procedures for conducting.
Establishment, required, §19.2-390.02.
Training standards and model policy, §9.1-102.
Interjurisdictional law-enforcement authority and agreements, §§15.2-1724 to 15.2-1730.

LAW ENFORCEMENT OFFICERS —Cont'd
Internet publication of personal information of law enforcement officer, §18.2-186.4:1.
Itinerant merchants.
Examination of records or property, §54.1-4302.
Jurisdiction.
Public-private transportation act, §56-571.
Killed in line of duty.
Tuition and required fees to state supported colleges and universities.
Waiver for children or spouses, §23-7.4:1.
Laser, laser gun sight or device simulating laser.
Pointing at law enforcement officer, probation or parole officer, etc., §18.2-57.01.
Law enforcement expenditures.
State assistance to local government, §§9.1-165 to 9.1-172.
Law officers' retirement system, §§51.1-211 to 51.1-221.
See LAW OFFICERS' RETIREMENT SYSTEM.
Legal fees and expenses for prosecution of act committed in discharge of duties, §15.2-1711.
Licensing.
Special crossbow license, §29.1-306.1.
Line of duty act, §§9.1-400 to 9.1-408.
Lineups.
Policies and procedures for conducting in person and photo lineups.
Training standards and model policy, §9.1-102.
Written policies, establishment, required, §19.2-390.02.
Livestock.
Contagious and infectious diseases.
Authority to execute orders, §3.2-6013.
Machine gun manufacturer's and dealer's stock.
Inspection upon demand, §18.2-294.
Malicious bodily injury to, §18.2-51.1.
Firearm used or displayed, §18.2-53.1.
Medical records.
Disclosure by emergency medical services personnel.
Prehospital patient reports, §§32.1-116.1, 32.1-127.1:03.
Mental health.
Children, psychiatric treatment.
Emergency custody orders, execution, §16.1-340.
Minimum qualifications for office, §15.2-1705.
Misconduct.
Civilian protection, §9.1-600.
Missing children.
Amber Alert program.
Activation, §52-34.3.
Definitions, §52-34.1.
Established, §52-34.2.
Notice to clearinghouse upon location, §52-34.
Missing officers.
Blue Alert program, §§52-34.7 to 52-34.9.
Missing senior adult.
Senior alert program, §§52-34.4 to 52-34.6.
Motor vehicle accidents.
Reports.
Duty of investigating officer to file, §46.2-373.
Motor vehicle insurance.
Premium increases, §38.2-1905.
Motor vehicle titling.
Enforcement by uniformed officers, §46.2-102.
Mutual aid agreements between local or state law enforcement and campus police, §23-234.

LAW ENFORCEMENT OFFICERS —Cont'd
Noise levels.
Proper equipment to determine decibel level of sound.
Standards established by division of purchases and supply, §2.2-1112.
Obstructing justice by threats or force or false statements, §18.2-460.
Off-duty officers, employment, §15.2-1712.
Overtime compensation, §§9.1-700 to 9.1-706.
Compensation may exceed statute, §9.1-701.
Computation.
Hours of work, §9.1-703.
Work period, §9.1-702.
Defined terms, §9.1-700.
Employees' remedies, §9.1-704.
Enforcement.
Employees' remedies, §9.1-704.
Hours of work, §9.1-703.
Limitation of actions, §9.1-705.
Penalties, §9.1-704.
Rate of pay, §9.1-701.
Remedies.
Employees, §9.1-704.
Work period, §9.1-702.
Parking for disabled or handicapped.
Confiscation of parking placards, §46.2-1255.
Photo identification, §46.2-1254.
Personal identifying information.
Internet publication of personal information of law enforcement officer, §18.2-186.4:1.
Police generally, §§15.2-1700 to 15.2-1753.
See POLICE.
Political activities.
Coercion or discrimination of subordinates, §15.2-1512.2.
Polling places.
Preservation of order inside and outside, §24.2-606.
Poultry.
Contagious and infectious diseases.
Authority to execute orders, §3.2-6013.
Premises liability.
Duty of care to law enforcement officers, §8.01-226.
Prisoner furloughs.
Notice to locality, §53.1-37.
Prisoner work for localities, state agencies or nonprofit organizations.
Notice to chief law enforcement official of locality, §53.1-59.
Private security services businesses.
Exceptions, §9.1-140.
Privileged communications.
Critical incident stress management team-EMS or public safety personnel privilege, §19.2-271.4.
Protective orders.
Emergency protective orders.
When authorized, §§16.1-253.4, 19.2-81.3.
Psychiatric treatment of children.
Emergency custody orders, execution, §16.1-340.
Public inebriates.
Transporting to detoxification centers, §18.2-388.
Public officers and employees.
Grievance procedure.
Exemptions, §2.2-3002.
Public-private transportation act.
Jurisdiction, §56-571.
Public safety medal of valor, §§9.1-800, 9.1-801.
Racial profiling.
Diversity and biased policing policy to be established, §9.1-102.

LAW ENFORCEMENT OFFICERS —Cont'd
Radar.
Compulsory minimum training standards, §9.1-102.
Radio signal, message or transmission.
Use during commission of crime, §18.2-462.1.
Refusal to aid officer, §18.2-463.
Reports.
Writing reports.
Compulsory minimum training standards, §9.1-102.
Reports to central criminal records exchange, §19.2-390.
Retired law enforcement officers.
Carrying concealed weapon, §18.2-308.
Photo identification card, §9.1-1000.
Reward offers.
Apprehension of escaped inmates, §19.2-7.
Riot or unlawful assembly.
Dispersal, duty, §18.2-411.
Immunity of officers quelling, §18.2-412.
Salaries.
Enforcement of motor vehicles title.
Officers to paid fixed salaries, §46.2-102.
Overtime compensation, §§9.1-700 to 9.1-706.
Searches and seizures.
Compulsory minimum training standards, §9.1-102.
Search warrants, execution, §19.2-56.
Senior alert program.
Missing senior adult, §§52-34.4 to 52-34.6.
Sexual assault policies and procedures for law enforcement agencies, §9.1-1301.
Sexual battery of defendant or convicted person, §18.2-67.4.
Sheriffs.
See SHERIFFS.
Smoking in public places.
Enforcement of act by summons, §15.2-2822.
Special conservators of the peace, §§9.1-150.1 to 9.1-150.4.
Order appointing designating conservators as, §19.2-13.
Special policeman.
Federal employees prohibited, exception, §2.2-2801.
State police retirement system, §§51.1-200 to 51.1-210.
See STATE POLICE RETIREMENT SYSTEM.
Stingers.
Tire puncturing device authorized, §33.1-345.
Subpoenas.
Issuance, §19.2-73.2.
Summons.
Authority of law-enforcement officer to issue summons to witness, §19.2-267.1.
Termination.
Forfeiture of office for failing to meet training standards, §9.1-115.
Tire puncturing device use authorized, §33.1-345.
Training.
Certification through training required, §15.2-1706.
Compulsory minimum training standards.
Compliance, §§9.1-113, 9.1-114.
Criminal justice services department, §9.1-102.
Criminal justice training academies, §§15.2-1747 to 15.2-1753.
See CRIMINAL JUSTICE TRAINING ACADEMIES.

LAW ENFORCEMENT OFFICERS —Cont'd
Training —Cont'd
Exemptions, §9.1-116.
Forfeiture of office for failing to meet training standards, §9.1-115.
Line of duty act.
Training concerning benefits, §9.1-407.
Lineups, photographic and live, §9.1-102.
Vehicle patrols, responding to emergency calls, §9.1-102.
Trespass by hunters, fishers or trappers.
Enforcement of provisions, §18.2-136.1.
Tuition and required fees to state supported colleges or universities.
Waiver for child or spouse of officer killed in line of duty, §23-7.4:1.
Uniforms.
Unlawful wearing of officer's uniform, §18.2-175.
Unsafe vehicles.
Officers certified to perform vehicle safety inspections may remove from highways, §46.2-1001.
Vehicle patrols, responding to emergency calls.
Training standards and model policy, §9.1-102.
Vehicle safety inspections.
Certified officers authorized to remove unsafe vehicles from highway, §46.2-1001.
Workers' compensation.
Heart disease and hypertension.
Presumption, §65.2-402.
Hepatitis, meningitis, tuberculosis and HIV.
Presumption on death or disability from, §65.2-402.1.
Injury where weather constitutes particular risk of employment of public safety officer, §65.2-301.1.
Off-duty coverage, §65.2-102.

LAW ENFORCEMENT OFFICERS PROCEDURAL GUARANTEE ACT, §§9.1-500 to 9.1-507.
Defined terms, §9.1-500.
Hearing panel.
Recommendations, §9.1-504.
Hearing procedure, §9.1-504.
Immediate suspension without pay, §9.1-505.
Informal counseling, §9.1-506.
Investigations.
Conduct, §9.1-501.
Notice of charges, §9.1-502.
Personal assets, disclosure, §9.1-503.
Response to notice of charges, §9.1-502.
Rights not exclusive, §9.1-507.

LAW ENFORCEMENT VEHICLES.
Auxiliary lights, §46.2-1029.
Flashing blue or red and blue warning lights, §46.2-1022.
Flashing of headlights, §46.2-1029.1.
Warnings, sirens and whistles, §46.2-1061.

LAW FIRMS.
Attorneys generally.
See ATTORNEYS AT LAW.
Counsel of record.
Defined, VA SCt Rule 1:5.
Firm name.
Signatures, VA SCt Rule 1:5.
Professional corporations generally, §§13.1-542.1 to 13.1-556.
See PROFESSIONAL CORPORATIONS.

LAW FIRMS —Cont'd
Service of notice, process and other papers, VA SCt Rule 1:15.
Signatures, VA SCt Rule 1:5.
Warrant issued for search of attorney's office, §19.2-56.1.

LAW LIBRARIES, §§42.1-60 to 42.1-71.
Fees collected by circuit court clerks and designated for public law libraries, §17.1-275.
Local law libraries.
Circuit court clerks in charge of, §42.1-65.
Circuit court to enforce rules, §42.1-66.
Computer research services, §42.1-65.
Contributions from bar association, §42.1-70.
Cost in civil actions, assessments for, §42.1-70.
Voluntary contributions by members of bar, §42.1-65.
Property tax exemptions, §58.1-3606.
Regional law libraries.
Establishment by governing body, §42.1-71.
State law library.
Additions to, §42.1-62.
Books constituting, §42.1-61.
Managed by supreme court, §42.1-60.
Regulation and computer expenses, §42.1-63.
Use, persons permitted, §42.1-64.

LAW OF COSTS.
Generally, §§17.1-600 to 17.1-629.
See COURT COSTS AND FEES.

LAW OFFICERS' RETIREMENT SYSTEM, §§51.1-211 to 51.1-221.
Administration, §51.1-211.
Allowances.
Death before retirement, §51.1-218.
Disability benefit, §51.1-220.
Postretirement supplements, §51.1-219.
Service retirement allowance, §51.1-217.
Contributions by Commonwealth, §51.1-215.
Creation, §51.1-211.
Creditable service, §51.1-214.
Death before retirement, §51.1-218.
Deferred retirement.
Members terminating service, §51.1-216.
Definitions, §51.1-212.
Disability benefit, §51.1-220.
Early retirement, §51.1-216.
Allowance, §51.1-217.
Effective date of retirement, §51.1-216.
Election of benefits, §51.1-221.
Employees.
Creditable service, §51.1-214.
Defined, §51.1-212.
Membership compulsory for, §51.1-213.
Health insurance credits, §51.1-1400.
Irrevocable election of benefits, §51.1-221.
Membership, §51.1-213.
Normal retirement, §51.1-216.
Allowance, §51.1-217.
Postretirement supplements, §51.1-219.
Service retirement, §51.1-216.
Allowance, §51.1-217.
Surviving spouses.
Death before retirement, §51.1-218.
Virginia retirement system.
Applicability of provisions of, §51.1-211.

LAW SCHOOL STUDENTS PRACTICE OF LAW, §54.1-3900.
Supreme court power to promulgate procedures, §54.1-3909.

LAW SCHOOL STUDENTS PRACTICE OF LAW —Cont'd
Third year student practice rule, VA SCt Rule Pt 6 §IV Par 15.

LAWS OF THE STATE.
Bills of general assembly.
Generally.
See BILLS OF GENERAL ASSEMBLY.
Code of Virginia generally, §§1-1 to 1-9.
See CODE OF VIRGINIA.
Rules of statutory construction and interpretation generally.
See STATUTORY CONSTRUCTION.

LAW STUDENTS IN COURT PROGRAM, VA SCt Rule Pt 6 §IV Par 15.

LAWYERS.
See ATTORNEYS AT LAW.

LAWYERS HELPING LAWYERS.
Immunity, §8.01-226.1.

LAYAWAY AGREEMENTS.
Disclosure requirement, §59.1-200.

LEAD ACID BATTERIES, §§10.1-1425.1 to 10.1-1425.5.
Inspection of retailers, §10.1-1425.3.
Interpretation of provisions, §10.1-1425.5.
Land disposal, §10.1-1425.1.
Recycling, §10.1-1425.2.
Wholesalers, §10.1-1425.4.

LEAD AGENCY NONPOINT SOURCE POLLUTION.
Conservation and recreation department, §10.1-104.1.

LEAD-BASED PAINT.
Building code violation, punishment, failure to abate, §36-106.
Children with elevated blood-lead levels.
State board of health, duties, §§32.1-46.1, 32.1-46.2.
Virginia immunization information system (VIIS).
Linkages to other databases containing certain health records, §§32.1-46.1, 32.1-46.01.
Immunity.
Sale or lease of residential dwelling.
Agent immunity and disclosure requirements, §8.01-226.7.
Sale of residential structure with levels exceeding building code standards, §36-107.1.

LEAD CONTRACTORS AND WORKERS.
Board for asbestos, lead and home inspectors, §§54.1-500.1, 54.1-501.
Defined terms, §54.1-500.
Disciplinary actions, §§54.1-516, 54.1-516.1.
Duties, §40.1-51.20.
Inspections, §40.1-51.21.

LEADER DOGS.
See GUIDE DOGS.

LEAD POISONING.
Children with elevated blood-lead levels.
Protocol for identification, §32.1-46.1.
Testing, §32.1-46.2.
Virginia immunization information system (VIIS).
Linkages to other databases containing certain health records, §§32.1-46.01, 32.1-46.1.

LEARNERS' PERMITS, §46.2-335.
Application for driver's license, §46.2-323.

LEARNERS' PERMITS —Cont'd
Certification of Virginia residency, §46.2-323.1.
Citizenship or lawful presence requirement, §46.2-328.1.
Conditions for issuance, §46.2-335.
Departments recordkeeping requirements, §46.2-327.
Driving while privilege to drive suspended or revoked, §46.2-301.
Impoundment of motor vehicle, §46.2-301.1.
Driving while restoration of privilege contingent on proof of financial responsibility, §46.2-302.
Duplicate permit, §46.2-343.
Fake permits, §46.2-105.1.
Holding period.
Minimum holding period, §46.2-335.2.
Initial licensure.
Requirements for initial licensure of certain applicants, §46.2-324.1.
Knowledge test.
Waiting period prior to reexamination, §46.2-335.1.
Obtaining permit from department when not legally entitled, §46.2-105.2.
Persons 25 years of age or older with restrictions on driving privilege.
Issuance to, §46.2-335.
Proof of completion of driver education program, §46.2-323.
Reproduction without obtaining prior written consent, §46.2-346.
Required before driver's license, §46.2-335.2.
Unlawful procurement of permit, §46.2-105.1.

LEASE-PURCHASE AGREEMENTS, §§59.1-207.17 to 59.1-207.27.
Advertising, §59.1-207.26.
Application of provisions, §59.1-207.19.
Citation of chapter, §59.1-207.17.
Consumer protection, prohibited practices, §59.1-200.
Defined terms, §59.1-207.18.
Disclosures, §§59.1-207.20, 59.1-207.21.
Renegotiations, §59.1-207.25.
Enforcement of provisions, §59.1-207.27.
Prohibited practices, §59.1-207.22.
Provision violations.
Penalties, §59.1-207.27.
Receipts, §59.1-207.24.
Reinstatements, §59.1-207.23.
Renegotiations, §59.1-207.25.

LEASES.
ABC law.
Lease allowing person to operate licensed establishment.
Permit to continue operation, §4.1-212.
Air carriers.
Certificate, §5.1-114.
Airports.
Entity acquiring land, authority to lease, §5.1-40.
Privilege of using or improving facility, §5.1-2.14.
Armories, §44-136.
Temporary renting, §44-135.1.
Assets of nonprofit corporations, §§13.1-899, 13.1-900.
Banks.
Lease of personal property, §6.2-884.
Powers, §6.2-820.
Board of game and inland fisheries.
Land or buildings owned by board, §29.1-105.

LEASES —Cont'd
Building code compliance.
Rental inspections of units located in rental inspection districts.
Residential rental dwelling units, §36-105.1:1.
Clam planting grounds, §§28.2-631, 28.2-632.
Coal interests, trusts for.
Known owners, §45.1-161.311:8.
Missing owners, §§45.1-161.311:3 to 45.1-161.311:7.
Colleges and universities, §23-4.1.
Commercial code generally, §§8.2A-101 to 8.2A-532.
See LEASES, UCC.
Condominiums.
Conversion condominiums.
Notice requirements, §55-79.94.
Construction.
Reentries by lessor, §55-79.
That he will leave the premises in good repair, §55-77.
That he will not assign without leave, §55-77.
To pay the rent, §55-76.
To pay the taxes, §55-76.
County court leases validated, §55-55.
County manager plan of government.
Real property, §15.2-734.
Courthouses.
Other buildings acquired by governing body, §15.2-1641.
Vacant rooms, §15.2-1640.
Covenant not to assign without leave, §55-77.
Covenant of lessor reentry for default, §55-79.
Covenant to leave premises in good repair, §55-77.
Covenant to pay the rent, §55-76.
Covenant to pay the taxes, §55-76.
Deeds of release.
Execution effect, §55-18.
District courts.
Validation of county court leases, §55-55.
Escheats.
Provision for enjoyment, §55-194.
Use of land by escheators, §55-180.
Estates in property, §§8.01-94, 8.01-95.
Expiration.
Failure of tenant to vacate.
Effect, §55-223.
Form, §55-57.
Franchise, privilege, lease or right of use of city or town property, §§15.2-2100 to 15.2-2108.1:1.
Fraudulent conversion of leased personal property, §18.2-118.
Gas and oil exploration.
Duplicate leases, §45.1-361.10.
Extraction on state corrections board property, §53.1-31.
General services department.
Leases of public lands and buildings, §2.2-1146.
Highways and roads.
Authority to lease or convey airspace, §33.1-183.1.
Horizontal property regimes.
Establishment, §55-79.3.
Recordation, §55-79.7.
Ignition interlock systems, §18.2-270.2.
Insurance companies investments in obligations secured by, §38.2-1422.
Landlords and tenants.
Generally, §§55-219 to 55-248.
See LANDLORD AND TENANT.

LEASES —Cont'd
Landlords and tenants —Cont'd
Residential landlord and tenant, §§55-248.2 to 55-248.40.
See LANDLORD AND TENANT.
Local school boards.
Corporate powers, §22.1-71.
Manufactured home lots.
Automatic renewal, §55-248.42:1.
Copies to tenants, §55-248.42.
Period of tenancy, §55-248.42:1.
Retaliatory conduct prohibitions, §§55-248.50, 55-248.50:1.
Tenant provisions, §55-248.42.
Termination of tenancy, §55-248.46.
Waiver of landlord's right to terminate, §55-248.46:1.
Writing requirements, §55-248.42.
Memoranda of leases.
Recordation, §55-57.1.
Military personnel.
Execution for under defective powers, §55-56.
Mineral extraction on state corrections board property, §53.1-31.
Motor carriers, passengers.
Department regulation, §46.2-2001.
Motor vehicles, personal property taxes.
Payment of tax on leased vehicle by lessee, §58.1-3516.2.
Motor vehicles, unlawful sublease, §18.2-115.1.
Nonprofit corporation assets, §§13.1-899, 13.1-900.
Notice to terminate tenancy, §55-222.
Oyster planting grounds.
General oyster planting grounds, §§28.2-603 to 28.2-612.
See OYSTER PLANTING GROUNDS.
Riparian oyster planting grounds, §§28.2-600 to 28.2-602.
Partition of land.
Effect of partition or sale on lessee's rights, §8.01-91.
Perfection of interest in leases, §55-220.1.
Persons with disability.
Disposition of real estate, §§8.01-67 to 8.01-80.
See PERSONS WITH DISABILITY.
Port authority, §62.1-132.19.
Public building authority.
Authority to enter into, §2.2-2273.
Public buildings.
Leases of public lands and buildings, §2.2-1146.
Public lands.
Leases of public lands and buildings, §2.2-1146.
Public-private education facilities and infrastructure act, §56-575.4.
Comprehensive agreements, §§56-575.9, 56-575.11.
Public school funds.
Lands leased for flood control purposes.
Federal funds apportioned to school divisions, §22.1-109.
Real estate for collection of local taxes, §§58.1-3947, 58.1-3948.
Real property taxation of leasehold interest, §58.1-3203.
Recordation, §55-57.1.
Documents recorded in deed book, §§17.1-227, 17.1-229.
Memorandum of leases in lieu of lease, §55-57.1.
Recordation tax, state, §58.1-807.
Supplemental writings, when not taxable, §58.1-809.

LEASES —Cont'd
Reentries by lessor.
Effect of lease provision, §55-79.
Rental inspections of units located in rental inspection districts.
Residential rental dwelling units.
Building code compliance, §36-105.1:1.
Residential leases.
Abandoned unit rentals, §55-248.33.
Application fees, §55-248.6:1.
Building code compliance, §36-105.1:1.
Casualty damage to unit.
Termination of lease, §55-248.24.
Conditions, §55-248.7.
Confidentiality of tenant records, §55-248.9:1.
Copies for tenants, §55-248.7.
Early termination by military personnel, §55-248.21:1.
Failure of landlord to deliver possession.
Termination grounds, §55-248.22.
Fire damage to unit.
Termination of lease, §55-248.24.
Insurance as requisite of lease, §55-248.7:2.
Landlord remedies for noncompliance, §55-248.31.
Material noncompliance or danger.
Breach of lease agreement, §55-225.13.
Payment of rent into court registry, §55-225.12.
Termination of lease, §55-248.27.
Noncompliance by landlord, §55-248.21.
Post-lease adoption of rules and regulations.
Enforceability, §55-248.17.
Post-termination remedies of landlord, §55-248.35.
Prohibited provisions, §55-248.9.
Real estate cooperatives.
Conversion buildings, §55-487.
Declarant leases.
Termination, §55-462.
Recordation of declaration, §55-443.
Rental payments, §55-248.7.
Residential landlords and tenants generally, §§55-248.2 to 55-248.40.
See LANDLORD AND TENANT.
Retaliatory actions by landlords, §§55-248.39, 55-248.40.
Tenancy period, §55-248.7.
Terms, §55-248.7.
Transfer disclosures for residential property.
Applicability of provisions, §55-517.
Undelivered leases, §55-248.8.
Unlawful ouster, exclusion or diminution of services.
Tenant remedy of termination, §55-248.26.
Unsigned leases, §55-248.8.
Self-service storage, §§55-416 to 55-423.
State parks.
Capital improvement projects, §10.1-112.
State property.
Authority of division of engineering and buildings to lease, §2.2-1146.
Subdivided lands.
Restraints on leases, §55-343.
Submerged lands, §28.2-1208.
Taxation of leasehold interest, §58.1-3203.
Termination of tenancy, §55-222.
Tourism financing development authority.
Powers, §15.2-5519.
Trust companies.
Powers, §§6.2-820, 6.2-1002.
Trusts.
Power of trustee, §64.2-778.

LEASES —Cont'd
Unclaimed property.
Disposal of property in possession of police, §15.2-1719.
University of Virginia medical center, §23-77.4.
Virginia Commonwealth University.
MCV hospitals authority, §23-50.16:19.
Virginia Commonwealth University health system authority.
Hospital facilities, §§23-50.16:16, 23-50.16:19.
Wireless service authorities.
Powers as to property, §15.2-5431.35.

LEASES, UCC, §§8.2A-101 to 8.2A-532.
Acceleration of payment or performance.
Option to accelerate at will, §8.2A-109.
Accessions.
Rights of lessor and lessee when goods become accessions, §8.2A-310.
Alienability of interest, §8.2A-303.
Anticipatory repudiation, §8.2A-402.
Retraction, §8.2A-403.
Applicability of article, §8.2A-102.
Buyer in ordinary course of business.
Defined, §8.2A-103.
Cancellation.
Defined, §8.2A-103.
Effect of default, §8.2A-505.
Casualty to identified goods, §8.2A-221.
Citation of article, §8.2A-101.
Conflict of laws.
Certificate of title.
Territorial application of article to goods covered by, §8.2A-105.
Consumer lease.
Limitation on power of parties to choose applicable law and judicial forum, §8.2A-106.
Leases subject to other laws, §8.2A-104.
Consumer leases.
Acceleration of payment or performance.
Burden of establishing good faith, §8.2A-109.
Choice of law.
Limitation on power of parties to choose applicable law and judicial forum, §8.2A-106.
Defined, §8.2A-103.
Damages.
Default.
Lessee's default.
Lessor's remedies, §§8.2A-528 to 8.2A-530.
Lessor's default.
Lessee's remedies, §§8.2A-508, 8.2A-519, 8.2A-520.
Liquidation of damages, §§8.2A-503, 8.2A-504.
Market rent, §8.2A-507.
Proof of, §8.2A-507.
Remedies, §8.2A-503.
Default.
Cancellation.
Effect on rights and remedies, §8.2A-505.
Damages.
Lessee's default.
Lessor's remedies, §§8.2A-528 to 8.2A-530.
Lessor's default.
Lessee's remedies, §§8.2A-508, 8.2A-519, 8.2A-520.
Liquidation of damages, §§8.2A-503, 8.2A-504.
Market rent.
Proof of, §8.2A-507.
Remedies, §8.2A-503.

LEASES, UCC —Cont'd
Default —Cont'd
Fraud.
Effect on rights and remedies, §8.2A-505.
Generally, §8.2A-501.
Lessee.
Rights and remedies of lessor.
Damages, §§8.2A-528 to 8.2A-530.
Disposal of goods, §8.2A-517.
Identification of goods to lease agreement, §8.2A-524.
Incidental damages, §8.2A-530.
Possession of goods, §8.2A-525.
Rent, §8.2A-529.
Residual interest, §8.2A-532.
Third-party's injury to goods, §8.2A-531.
Lessor.
Acceptance of goods by lessee, §8.2A-515.
Burden of establishing default after acceptance, §8.2A-516.
Effect, §8.2A-516.
Notice of default after, §8.2A-516.
Cover.
Substitute goods, §8.2A-518.
Cure of improper tender or delivery, §8.2A-513.
Insolvency of lessor.
Lessee's right to goods, §8.2A-522.
Rejection of goods by lessee, §§8.2A-508 to 8.2A-510.
Cure by lessor of improper tender or delivery, §8.2A-513.
Duties as to rightfully rejected goods, §§8.2A-511, 8.2A-512.
Revocation of acceptance of goods by lessee, §8.2A-517.
Rights and remedies of lessee, §8.2A-508.
Damages, §§8.2A-519, 8.2A-520.
Duties as to rightfully rejected goods, §§8.2A-511, 8.2A-512.
Improper delivery by lessor, §8.2A-509.
Incidental and consequential damages, §§8.2A-519, 8.2A-520.
Insolvency of lessor, §8.2A-522.
Installment lease contracts, §8.2A-510.
Specific performance, §8.2A-521.
Substitute goods, §8.2A-518.
Waiver of lessee's objections, §8.2A-514.
Limitation of actions, §8.2A-506.
Notice.
After default, §8.2A-502.
Lessor's default, §8.2A-516.
Procedure, §8.2A-501.
Rescission.
Effect on rights and remedies, §8.2A-505.
Rights and remedies.
Effect of fraud, §8.2A-505.
Lease agreement may include, §8.2A-505.
Lessee's rights and remedies, §8.2A-508.
Damages, §§8.2A-519, 8.2A-520.
Duties as to rightfully rejected goods, §§8.2A-511, 8.2A-512.
Improper delivery by lessor, §8.2A-509.
Insolvency of lessor, §8.2A-522.
Installment lease contracts, §8.2A-510.
Specific performance, §8.2A-521.
Lessor's rights and remedies.
Damages, §§8.2A-528 to 8.2A-530.
Identification of goods to lease agreement, §8.2A-524.
Incidental damages, §8.2A-530.
Possession of goods, §8.2A-525.

LEASES, UCC —Cont'd
Default —Cont'd
Rights and remedies —Cont'd
Lessor's rights and remedies —Cont'd
Rent, §8.2A-529.
Residual interest, §8.2A-532.
Third-party's injury to goods, §8.2A-531.
Modification or impairment, §8.2A-503.
Risk of loss.
Effect of default, §8.2A-220.
Termination.
Effect on rights and remedies, §8.2A-505.
Waiver or renunciation of claim or right after, §8.2A-107.
Definitions, §8.2A-103.
Disposal of goods.
Lessee's default.
Right of lessor to disposal of goods, §8.2A-527.
Effect, §8.2A-301.
Enforceability, §8.2A-301.
Excused performance, §8.2A-405.
Procedure on, §8.2A-406.
Express warranty, §8.2A-210.
Third-party beneficiary, §8.2A-216.
Finance leases.
Defined, §8.2A-103.
Irrevocable promises, §8.2A-407.
Lessee under finance lease as beneficiary of supply contract, §8.2A-209.
Firm offers, §8.2A-205.
Fitness for particular purpose, implied warranty, §8.2A-213.
Exclusion or modification, §8.2A-214.
Fixtures.
Defined, §8.2A-309.
Right of lessor and lessee when goods become fixtures, §8.2A-309.
Formation, §8.2A-204.
Offer and acceptance, §8.2A-206.
Firm offers, §8.2A-205.
Fraud.
Rights and remedies for default.
Effect of fraud, §8.2A-505.
General provisions of commercial code, §§8.1A-101 to 8.1A-310.
See COMMERCIAL CODE.
Identification of goods, §8.2A-217.
Casualty to identified goods, §8.2A-221.
Default.
Lessee's default.
Right of lessor to identify goods to lease agreement, §8.2A-524.
Implied warranty.
Exclusion or modification, §8.2A-214.
Fitness for particular purpose, §8.2A-213.
Merchantability, §8.2A-212.
Installment lease contract.
Defined, §8.2A-103.
Insurable interest of lessee, §8.2A-218.
Irrevocable promises.
Finance leases, §8.2A-407.
Lease contract.
Defined, §8.2A-103.
Lessee.
Defined, §8.2A-103.
Insurable interest, §8.2A-218.
Sale or sublease of goods, §8.2A-305.
Lessee in ordinary course of business.
Defined, §8.2A-103.
Lessee's default, §§8.2A-523 to 8.2A-532.

LEASES, UCC —Cont'd
Lessor.
Alienability of residual interest in goods, §8.2A-303.
Creditors of lessor.
Special rights, §8.2A-308.
Defined, §8.2A-103.
Risk of loss.
Retention by lessor, §8.2A-219.
Subsequent lease of goods, §8.2A-304.
Liens.
Priority of certain liens arising by operation of law, §8.2A-306.
Priority of liens that attach before lease becomes enforceable, §8.2A-307.
Priority subject to subordination, §8.2A-311.
Limitation of actions.
Default, §8.2A-506.
Merchantability, implied warranty, §8.2A-212.
Exclusion or modification, §8.2A-214.
Modification, §8.2A-208.
Notice.
Default, §8.2A-502.
Lessor's default, §8.2A-516.
Offer and acceptance, §8.2A-206.
Firm offers, §8.2A-205.
Parol or extrinsic evidence, §8.2A-202.
Performance.
Adequate assurance of performance, §8.2A-401.
Excused performance, §8.2A-405.
Procedure on, §8.2A-406.
Insecurity as to adequate assurance of performance, §8.2A-401.
Substituted performance, §8.2A-404.
Possession of goods, §8.2A-302.
Creditors of lessor.
Special rights, §8.2A-308.
Lessee's default.
Right of lessor to possession of goods, §8.2A-525.
Rent.
Lessee's default.
Lessor's right to rent, §8.2A-529.
Repudiation.
Anticipatory repudiation, §8.2A-402.
Retraction, §8.2A-403.
Rescission, §8.2A-208.
Effect.
Rights and remedies for default, §8.2A-505.
Risk of loss, §8.2A-219.
Casualty to identified goods, §8.2A-221.
Default.
Effect, §8.2A-220.
Scope of article, §8.2A-102.
Seals inoperative, §8.2A-203.
Secured transactions.
Creation of security interest in party's interest under lease, §8.2A-303.
Priority of secured interest in goods, §8.2A-307.
Security interests arising under provisions, §8.9A-110.
Security interest.
Creation of, §8.2A-303.
Priority of goods, §8.2A-307.
Short title, §8.2A-101.
Specific performance.
Default.
Lessor's default.
Right of lessee to specific performance or similar remedies, §8.2A-521.
Statute of frauds, §8.2A-201.

LEASES, UCC —Cont'd
Stoppage of delivery.
Lessee's default.
Right of lessor to stoppage of delivery, §8.2A-526.
Sublease, §8.2A-305.
Defined, §8.2A-103.
Subordination.
Priority subject to, §8.2A-311.
Subsequent lease of goods by lessor, §8.2A-304.
Substituted performance, §8.2A-404.
Sufficiency of agreement, §8.2A-204.
Supply contract.
Defined, §8.2A-103.
Lessee under finance lease as beneficiary of, §8.2A-209.
Termination.
Defined, §8.2A-103.
Rights and remedies for default.
Effect, §8.2A-505.
Title of article, §8.2A-101.
Title to goods, §8.2A-302.
Transfer of rights, §8.2A-303.
Unconscionable agreements or conduct, §8.2A-108.
Waiver, §8.2A-208.
Warranties.
Construction of warranties, §8.2A-215.
Cumulative nature of warranties, §8.2A-215.
Exclusion or modification of warranties, §8.2A-214.
Express warranty, §8.2A-210.
Third-party beneficiaries, §8.2A-216.
Fitness for particular purpose.
Implied warranty, §8.2A-213.
Implied warranty.
Fitness for particular purpose, §8.2A-213.
Merchantability, §8.2A-212.
Exclusion or modification, §8.2A-214.
Interference or infringement.
Warranties against, §8.2A-211.
Exclusion or modification, §8.2A-214.
Merchantability.
Implied warranty, §8.2A-212.
Exclusion or modification, §8.2A-214.
Modification of warranties, §8.2A-214.
Third-party beneficiaries of warranties, §8.2A-216.

LEASH LAWS.
Referendum on city ordinance, §3.2-6539.
Violations, §3.2-6587.

LEAVES.
Prohibiting in landfills, §15.2-935.
Setting fire to, §18.2-86.
Carelessly damaging property by fire, §18.2-88.
Intentionally setting fire whereby another damaged or jeopardized, §18.2-87.

LEAVES OF ABSENCE.
Athletic leaves of absence for state employees, §2.2-124.
Bone marrow or organ donation.
State employees, §2.2-2821.1.
Military leaves for employees of Commonwealth or political subdivisions, §44-93.
Discrimination in hiring prohibited, §44-93.4.
Penalty for employer failure to comply, §44-93.5.
Reemployment rights, §44-93.3.
State employees ordered to active military duty.
Use of accrued annual leave, §2.2-2903.1.

LEAVES OF ABSENCE —Cont'd
Military leaves for employees of Commonwealth or political subdivisions —Cont'd
Supplement of military pay and additional life insurance benefits, §44-93.1.
Military leaves for nongovernmental employees, §44-93.2.
Discrimination in hiring prohibited, §44-93.4.
Penalty for employer failure to comply, §44-93.5.
Reemployment rights, §44-93.3.
State defense force or national defense executive reserve training, §44-204.
Volunteer fire and rescue services.
State employees, §2.2-2821.2.

LEAVING SCENE OF ACCIDENT, §§46.2-894, 46.2-896.
Arresting officer to request abstracts or transcripts of driver's conviction record, §46.2-384.
Duty to stop, §46.2-894.
One year revocation of driver's license, §46.2-389.
Pretrial payment of fine, §16.1-69.40:1.
When directed to do so by law-enforcement officer, §46.2-902.

LEE COUNTY.
Confederate cemeteries and graves.
Disbursement of funds appropriated for upkeep, §10.1-2211.
Cumberlands airport commission, 1958 ch 439.
Electric utility restructuring.
Transmission and distribution of electric energy.
Applicability of provisions suspended, §56-580.
Local licensing of motor vehicles, trailers or semitrailers.
Evidence of payment of all fees due county or solid waste authority.
Required prior to issuing license, §46.2-752.
School board.
Salary of members, §22.1-32.
Virginia coalfield economic development authority, §§15.2-6000 to 15.2-6015.

LEE-JACKSON DAY.
Legal holidays, §2.2-3300.

LEE MEMORIAL ASSOCIATION, §57-6.
Stratford, Westmoreland County.
Appropriations for development, §10.1-2212.

LEESBURG.
Personal property tax relief for elderly or handicapped.
Motor vehicles, alternative tax rates.
Ordinance to raise income and financial worth limitations, §58.1-3506.2.
Taxes and assessments on electricity customer.
Construction of electric transmission line, §15.2-2404.

LEGACIES.
Wills, §§64.2-400 to 64.2-458.
See WILLS.

LEGAL ADVERTISING.
Publication generally.
See PUBLICATION.

LEGAL AID PROGRAM UNDER VIRGINIA STATE BAR.
Fees charged by circuit court clerks, §17.1-275.
Additional fees, §§17.1-275, 17.1-278.

LEGAL AID SOCIETIES.
State bar governance, §54.1-3916.

LEGAL ENUMERATION OF POPULATION OF LOCALITY, §15.2-1414.

LEGAL ETHICS.
Opinions.
Promulgation of opinions, VA SCt Rule Pt 6 §IV Par 10.
Suspension of attorney for failure to complete course, VA SCt Rule Pt 6 §IV Par 13.1.

LEGAL INVESTMENTS.
Generally.
See INVESTMENTS.

LEGALLY INCOMPETENT.
Conservators.
See CONSERVATORS.
Generally.
See INCOMPETENCY.
Guardian and ward.
See GUARDIAN AND WARD.
Persons with disability generally.
See PERSONS WITH DISABILITY.

LEGAL RESERVE INSURERS, §38.2-3101.

LEGAL SEPARATION.
Abandonment.
Allegation or proof of offer of reconciliation, §20-102.
Grounds for divorce from bed and board, §20-95.
Absolute divorce.
Divorce a mensa et thoro no bar to absolute divorce, §20-117.
Amended pleadings.
No-fault divorce.
Decree of divorce without amended bill or amended cross-bill, §20-121.02.
Apprehension of bodily harm. See within this heading, "Cruelty and reasonable apprehension of bodily hurt."
Assessment of costs, §20-99.
Bail and recognizance.
Recognizance for compliance with order or decree, §20-114.
Confinement for noncompliance, §20-115.
Change of address.
Notice in proceeding involving custody or visitation, §20-124.5.
Child custody and visitation arrangements.
Best interest of the child, §20-124.3.
Court authority to decree, §20-107.2.
Court orders, §20-124.2.
Defined terms, §20-124.1.
Educational seminars.
Required attendance for parties seeking custody of children, §20-103.
Mediation, §20-124.4.
Modification of decrees, §20-108.
Records access, §20-124.6.
Relocation notice, §20-124.5.
Child support.
Court authority to decree, §20-107.2.
Modification of decrees, §20-108.
Commencement of suit, §20-99.
Commissioner's hearings, §20-97.
Contempt.
Recognizance for compliance with order or decree.
Failure or refusal to give recognizance, §20-115.
Conversion of divorce a mensa into divorce a vinculo, §20-121.

LEGAL SEPARATION —Cont'd
Corroboration of testimony, §20-99.
Cruelty and reasonable apprehension of bodily hurt.
Decree of divorce from bonds of matrimony without decree from bed and board, §§20-121.01, 20-121.2.
Grounds for divorce from bed and board, §20-95.
Protective order, §20-103.
Purchase or transportation of firearms by person subject, §18.2-308.1:4.
Default, defendant's failure to file answer, §20-99.
Desertion and nonsupport.
Allegation or proof of offer of reconciliation, §20-102.
Decree of divorce from bonds of matrimony without decree from bed and board, §§20-121.01, 20-121.2.
Grounds for divorce from bed and board, §20-95.
Divorce.
Divorce from bond of matrimony.
Divorce from bed and board no bar to absolute divorce, §20-117.
General provisions.
See DIVORCE.
Dockets.
Reinstatement of suit stricken from docket, §20-121.1.
Effect of decree on property rights, §20-116.
Evidence.
Sufficiency of evidence, §20-99.
Grounds, §20-95.
Decree of no-fault divorce without amended bill or amended cross-bill, §20-121.02.
Identifying information.
Petition, pleading, motion, order or decree.
Personal information not contained in, separate addendum if required, §20-121.03.
Jurisdiction.
Domicile and residency requirements, §20-97.
Spousal support, §20-107.1.
Suits for divorce, §20-96.
Merger of divorce a mensa into divorce a vinculo, §20-121.
Military.
Domicile of military personnel residing abroad, §20-97.
Ore tenus hearings, §20-99.
Pendente lite hearings, §20-103.
Personal identifying information.
Petition, pleading, motion, order or decree.
Information not contained in, separate addendum if required, §20-121.03.
Premarital agreements.
Disposal of property, §20-150.
Property settlement agreements.
Incorporation by reference, §20-109.1.
Protective orders.
Cruelty and reasonable apprehension of bodily hurt, §20-103.
Purchase or transportation of firearms by person subject, §18.2-308.1:4.
Registry, §19.2-387.1.
State police department, duties, §52-45.
Reinstatement of marriage, §20-120.
Relocation.
Notice in proceeding involving custody or visitation, §20-124.5.
Remarriage as bigamy, §20-116.
Revocation of decree, §20-120.

LEGAL SEPARATION —Cont'd
Sequestration of record, §20-124.
Service, acceptance by defendant, §20-99.1:1.
Service by publication, §§20-104 to 20-105.1.
Alternative procedures, §20-105.1.
Order of publication against nonresident defendant, §20-104.
Permissible form for orders of publication, §20-105.
Spousal support.
Court authority to decree, §20-107.1.
Transfer of venue, §20-107.3.
Validation of absolute divorce.
Decree of divorce granted where no decree from bed and board, §20-121.2.
Validation of certain divorces granted prior to April 23, 1962, §20-121.3.

LEGAL SERVICES FUND.
Additional fees collected by clerks, §17.1-278.

LEGAL SERVICES INSURANCE, §38.2-2300.
Defined, §38.2-127.
Rates generally, §§38.2-1900 to 38.2-1928.
See INSURANCE RATES.

LEGAL SERVICES INSURANCE AGENTS.
Licensing of insurance agents generally, §§38.2-1822 to 38.2-1836.1.

LEGAL SERVICES PLANS, §§38.2-4400 to 38.2-4418.
Applicability of certain general insurance law provisions, §38.2-4408.
Application.
Misleading, §38.2-4417.
Attorneys, board of directors plan created by, §38.2-4407.
Benefits of plan, subscriber to be advised, §38.2-4412.
Board of directors, §38.2-4406.
Plan created by attorney, §38.2-4407.
Change of participant, §38.2-4405.
Compensation to officers or directors for purchase or sale of property or obtaining loan, §§38.2-211, 38.2-213.
Contracts.
Definitions, §59.1-441.1.
Investigations, §59.1-441.4.
Misleading, §38.2-4417.
Not deemed plans, §38.2-4401.
Records available to inspection, §59.1-441.5.
Registration requirement, §59.1-441.2.
Rules to implement provisions, §59.1-441.3.
Violation of provisions, §59.1-441.6.
Controversies involving subscription contracts, §38.2-4418.
Corporate organization.
Required, §38.2-4402.1.
Definitions, §38.2-4400.
Directors, §38.2-4406.
Plan created by attorney, §38.2-4407.
Filing of policy forms with state corporation commission required, §38.2-316.
Free choice of attorneys available, §38.2-4411.
General insurance laws, applicability of provisions, §38.2-4408.
Information and privacy protection generally, §§38.2-600 to 38.2-620.
See INSURANCE INFORMATION AND PRIVACY PROTECTION.
Jurisdiction of state corporation commission to adjudicate controversies, §38.2-4418.

LEGAL SERVICES PLANS —Cont'd
Liability of participants, §38.2-4404.
Licensing, §38.2-4413.
Renewal, §38.2-4414.
Limitations on plan, subscriber to be advised, §38.2-4412.
Loans to officers or directors, §38.2-210.
Violations, §38.2-213.
Misleading applications or contracts, §38.2-4417.
Participants in plan.
Change, §38.2-4405.
Free choice of attorneys available, §38.2-3411.
Liability, §38.2-4404.
Payments under plan, §38.2-4409.
Plan payments, §38.2-4409.
Quarterly report, §38.2-4410.
Registration of contract, §59.1-441.2.
Rehabilitation, liquidation, conservation, §38.2-4408.1.
Reports.
Quarterly reports, §38.2-4410.
Retainer contracts not deemed plan, §38.2-4401.
Subscription contracts, §§59.1-441.1 to 59.1-441.6.
Taxes.
Application fees paid by organization in lieu of other taxes, §38.2-4416.
Unlicensed insurers process, §§38.2-800 to 38.2-807.
Virginia state bar may sponsor plan, §38.2-4403.

LEGISLATIVE AUTOMATED SYSTEMS DIVISION, §§30-34.11 to 30-34.15.
Creation, §30-34.11.
Director.
Appointment, §30-34.11.
Duties, §§30-34.12, 30-34.14.
Powers, §§30-34.12, 30-34.13.
Jury service.
Voluntary exemption, §8.01-341.1.
Reports to general assembly or other body within legislative branch.
Submission to division, executive summary included, §30-34.15.
Spokespersons or information officers for state agencies.
Publication of list, §30-34.14.

LEGISLATIVE DOCKET.
Lobbyists registration information recorded in, §2.2-425.

LEGISLATIVE PROGRAM REVIEW AND EVALUATION, §§30-65 to 30-72.
Construction of provisions, §30-72.
Criteria, §30-68.
Defined terms, §30-65.
Functional areas, §30-66.
Defined, §§30-65, 30-66.
Hearings, §30-70.
Construction of provisions, §30-72.
Criteria, §30-71.
Information, access to, §30-69.
Operation of provisions, §30-72.
Reports, §30-70.
Scheduling of study areas, §30-66.
Selection procedure, §30-67.
Joint legislative audit and review commission.
Supplementary studies and reports, §30-58.2.
Self-studies, §30-68.
Subcommittees, §30-72.

LEGISLATIVE SERVICES DIVISION, §§30-28.12 to 30-28.18.
Advance sheets to Virginia reports.
Distribution to, §17.1-317.
Bill drafting requests, §§30-28.16, 30-28.18.
Books, accessibility, §30-28.17.
Constitutional amendments.
Preparation of explanation of proposal, §30-19.9.
Continuance of actions for employees, §30-5.
Creation, §30-28.12.
Director.
Appointment, §30-28.12.
Duties, §30-28.16.
Freedom of information advisory council.
Membership of director or designee, §30-178.
Qualifications, §30-28.12.
Documents accessibility, §30-28.17.
Duties, §30-28.16.
Freedom of information act.
Exclusions from chapter.
Closed meetings, §2.2-3705.1.
Working papers and correspondence, §2.2-3705.7.
Freedom of information advisory council.
Membership of director or designee, §30-178.
Jury service.
Voluntary exemption, §8.01-341.1.
Library of Virginia.
Use, §30-28.15.
Local government expenditures, legislation affecting.
Preparation of estimates, §30-19.03.
Pleading extensions for employees, §30-5.
Report to general assembly, §30-28.16.
Resolution drafting requests, §§30-28.16, 30-28.18.
Small business commission.
Staff assistance, §30-182.
Supervisory control of, §30-19.5.
Virginia sesquicentennial of the American Civil War commission.
Staffing, §30-272.
Woodrow Wilson presidency centennial commission.
Staff support, §30-324.

LEGISLATIVE SUPPORT COMMISSION, §§30-34.1 to 30-34.10:3.
Acts of assembly.
Distribution of, §§30-34.4:1, 30-34.5.
Fees, §30-34.10.
Printing, §30-34.5.
Selection checklist, §30-34.4:1.
Bill copies.
Requisitioning, §§30-34.3, 30-34.4.
Calendar of houses.
Requisitioning copies, §30-34.4.
Capitol police.
Powers, duties and functions, §30-34.2:1.
Capitol tour guides, assistance to, §30-34.2.
Creation, §30-34.1.
Distribution of publications, §30-34.4:1.
Documents of senate and house.
Distribution, §30-34.4:1.
Fees, §30-34.10.
Selection checklist, §30-34.4:1.
Donations to law schools, §30-34.8.
Duties, §30-34.2.
Electronic information system, §30-34.10:1.
Access to code of Virginia, §30-34.10:2.
Fees, §30-34.10:3.

LEGISLATIVE SUPPORT COMMISSION —Cont'd
Housing document copies.
Requisitioning, §§30-34.3, 30-34.4.
Joint resolutions of the general assembly.
Distribution, §§30-34.4:1, 30-34.5.
Printing, §30-34.5.
Selection checklist, §30-34.4:1.
Journals of senate and house.
Distribution, §§30-34.4:1, 30-34.6.
Fees, §30-34.10.
Printing, §30-34.6.
Selection checklist, §30-34.4:1.
Law school book exchanges, §30-34.9.
Members, §30-34.1.
Powers, §30-34.2.
Resolution copies.
Requisitioning, §§30-34.3, 30-34.4.
Selection checklists, §30-34.4:1.
Senate document copies.
Requisitioning, §§30-34.3, 30-34.4.

LEGISLATURE.
See GENERAL ASSEMBLY.

LEGITIMATION OF CHILDREN.
Assisted conception, status of child, §§20-156 to 20-165.
Parentage of child, §20-158.
Relation of parent and child, §20-164.
Birth certificates.
New birth certificates established on proof of legitimation, §32.1-261.
Descent and distribution.
Delineation of parent-child relationship, §64.2-102.
Evidence of paternity, §64.2-103.
Marriage of parents, §20-31.1.
Paternity proceedings, §§20-49.1 to 20-49.10.
See PATERNITY PROCEEDINGS.
Surrogacy contracts, §§20-156 to 20-165.
Parentage of child, §20-158.
Relation of parent and child, §20-164.
Void marriages, §20-31.1.

LEGS.
Workers' compensation.
Medical attention to be furnished upon loss of use, §65.2-603.

LEMON LAW, §§59.1-207.9 to 59.1-207.16:1.
Actions, §59.1-207.14.
Limitations, §59.1-207.16.
Citation of chapter, §59.1-207.9.
Conformity to all warranties, §59.1-207.12.
Nonconforming motor vehicles, §59.1-207.13.
Defined terms, §59.1-207.11.
Disclosure of returned vehicles, §59.1-207.16:1.
Dog and cat sales by dealers.
Receipt by consumer of diseased animal, §§3.2-6514, 3.2-6515.
Nonconformity of motor vehicle, §59.1-207.13.
Presumption reasonable number of attempts undertaken to conform to warranty, §59.1-207.13.
Purpose, §59.1-207.10.
Return of motor vehicle or refund.
Nonconformity of motor vehicle within lemon law rights period, §59.1-207.13.

LENOWISCO PLANNING DISTRICT COMMISSION.
Coalfield economic development authority grants or loans.
Management, §15.2-6002.

LENOWISCO PLANNING DISTRICT COMMISSION —Cont'd
Southwest Virginia health facilities authority, §§15.2-5368 to 15.2-5386.
See SOUTHWEST VIRGINIA HEALTH FACILITIES AUTHORITY.
Tourism development authority, §§15.2-5500 to 15.2-5508.

LESA.
Agricultural and forestal districts.
Evaluating land for inclusion in district, §15.2-4306.
Withdrawal of land from district, §15.2-4314.

LESSEE IN ORDINARY COURSE OF BUSINESS.
Defined, §8.2A-103.

LESSER INCLUDED OFFENSES.
Acquittal of higher offense.
Conviction of lesser offense, §19.2-285.
Double jeopardy, §19.2-285.
Homicide cases, conviction of lesser offense, §19.2-266.1.
Malicious shooting, stabbing, cutting or wounding.
Conviction of lesser offense under certain indictments, §18.2-54.
Murder indictment, verdict of punishable homicide, §19.2-288.
Petit larceny conviction, grand larceny prosecution, §19.2-289.

LESS TOXIC GOODS AND PRODUCTS.
Procurement by public bodies, §2.2-4314.

LETTERS OF CREDIT, §§8.5A-101 to 8.5A-118.
Adviser.
Defined, §8.5A-102.
Rights and obligations, §8.5A-107.
Amendment, §8.5A-106.
Appeal bond.
Irrevocable letters of credit as security for appeal, §8.01-676.1.
Applicability of article, §8.5A-103.
Applicability of title, §8.5A-118.
Assignments, §8.5A-114.
Attorneys' fees, §8.5A-111.
Banks.
Acceptance, §6.2-883.
Beneficiary.
Change of name, §8.5A-113.
Defined, §8.5A-102.
Successor, §8.5A-113.
Breach of obligation, §8.5A-111.
Cancellation, §8.5A-106.
Captive insurers, §§38.2-1105, 38.2-1106.
Choice of forum, §8.5A-116.
Choice of law, §8.5A-116.
Citation, §8.5A-101.
Coal surface mining permits, §45.1-241.
Conditions.
Nondocumentary conditions, §8.5A-108.
Condominiums.
Irrevocable letter in lieu of escrowing deposits.
Condominiums of 50 or more units, §55-79.95.
Posting by declarants, §55-79.84:1.
Confirmer.
Defined, §8.5A-102.
Rights and obligations, §8.5A-107.
Conflict of laws, §8.5A-116.
Consideration, §8.5A-105.

LETTERS OF CREDIT —Cont'd
Contracts.
Sale of goods, §8.2-325.
Contracts or arrangements out of which letter of credit arises.
Rights and obligations, §8.5A-103.
Credit services businesses, §59.1-335.4.
Definitions, §8.5A-102.
Proceeds of a letter of credit, §8.5A-114.
Exchange facilitators.
Cash or irrevocable letters of credit.
Duty to deposit, amount, §55-225.4.
Expiration, §8.5A-106.
Extended service contracts, §59.1-437.
Failure to give timely notice of dishonor, §8.5A-108.
Forged or fraudulent documents, §8.5A-109.
Warranties against, §8.5A-110.
Formal requirements, §8.5A-104.
Fraud, §8.5A-109.
Warranties against, §8.5A-110.
General provisions of commercial code, §§8.1A-101 to 8.1A-310.
See COMMERCIAL CODE.
Health spas, §59.1-306.
Persons protected, §59.1-307.
Honor or dishonor, §8.5A-108.
Wrongful dishonor or repudiation, §8.5A-111.
Injunctions.
Forged or fraudulent documents, §8.5A-109.
Interest, §8.5A-111.
Issuance, §8.5A-106.
Issuer.
Obligations, §8.5A-113.
Rights and obligations, §8.5A-108.
Security interest of issuer, §8.5A-117.1.
Limitation of actions, §8.5A-115.
Liquidated damages, §8.5A-111.
Membership camping.
Nondisturbance provisions, §59.1-333.
Motor carriers, passengers.
Insurance requirements generally, §§46.2-2051 to 46.2-2058.
Licenses or certificates.
Bond or other security, §46.2-2011.9.
Motor carriers, property.
Certificate of fitness, applications, §46.2-2122.
Insurance requirements generally, §§46.2-2141 to 46.2-2146.
See MOTOR CARRIERS, PROPERTY.
Nominated person.
Defined, §8.5A-102.
Rights and obligations, §8.5A-107.
Security interest of nominated person, §8.5A-117.1.
Notice of dishonor.
Failure to give timely notice, §8.5A-108.
Notification to transferee beneficiary, §8.5A-107.
Perpetual, expiration of letter stating, §8.5A-106.
Persons notifying transferee beneficiary.
Rights and obligations of advisor, §8.5A-107.
Precious metals dealers, §§54.1-4106, 54.1-4107.
Presentation to issuer, §8.5A-108.
Proceeds, §8.5A-114.
Public-private education facilities and infrastructure act.
Comprehensive agreements, §§56-575.9, 56-575.11.
Remedies, §8.5A-111.

LETTERS OF CREDIT —Cont'd
Resources authority.
Powers to issue credit enhancements generally, §§62.1-197 to 62.1-223.
See RESOURCES AUTHORITY.
Return of dishonored documents, §8.5A-108.
Revocation, §8.5A-106.
Sales, UCC, §8.2-325.
Secured transactions.
Issuers.
Security interest, §8.5A-117.1.
Letter-of-credit right.
See SECURED TRANSACTIONS.
Nominated persons.
Security interest, §8.5A-117.1.
Service contracts, extended, §59.1-437.
Short title, §8.5A-101.
Signatures, §8.5A-104.
Specific performance.
Wrongful dishonor or repudiation, §8.5A-111.
Standard practices of financial institutions.
Issuer to observe, §8.5A-108.
Statement of rule.
Applicability to situation not provided or person not specified, §8.5A-103.
Statute of limitations, §8.5A-115.
Subrogation, §8.5A-117.
Successor of beneficiary.
Defined, §8.5A-102.
Powers, §8.5A-113.
Time limit, §8.5A-108.
Time-shares.
Developers' obligation to complete promised improvements, §55-386.
Transfers, §8.5A-112.
Operation of law, §8.5A-113.
Travel clubs, §59.1-447.
Varying provisions by agreement, §8.5A-103.
Venue, §8.5A-116.
Warranties, §8.5A-110.
Wrongful dishonor or repudiation, §8.5A-111.

LETTERS OF MARQUE AND REPRISAL, US
Const Art I §§8 to Art I §10.

LETTERS THREATENING DEATH OR BODILY INJURY, §18.2-60.

LEUKEMIA.
High-dose chemotherapy and bone marrow transplants.
Medical assistance service plans, §32.1-325.
Presumption as to death or disability.
Firefighters, §65.2-402.

LEVARI FACIAS, WRIT OF.
Abolishment, §8.01-467.

LEVEES.
Dams generally.
See DAMS.

LEWD AND LASCIVIOUS COMMUNICATION.
Harassment by computer, §18.2-152.7:1.

LEWDNESS.
Buildings or other structures harboring bawdy place.
Authority of locality to require removal, repair, etc., §15.2-908.1.

LEXINGTON.
Blue Ridge regional tourism council, §§2.2-2609, 2.2-2610.

LEXINGTON —Cont'd
Confederate cemeteries and graves.
Disbursement of funds appropriated for upkeep, §10.1-2211.
Maury service authority, 1972 ch 388.
Public defenders office.
Established, §19.2-163.04.
Revolutionary War cemeteries and graves.
Disbursement of funds appropriated for upkeep, §10.1-2211.1.
School board.
Salary of members, §22.1-32.
Transient occupancy tax.
Additional transient occupant tax, §58.1-3825.

LIABILITY INSURANCE, §§38.2-2200 to 38.2-2234.
Affiliated insurer willing to provide coverage at a lower premium than expiring policy.
Policy issued deemed renewal policy, §38.2-231.
Age of motor vehicle.
Failure to issue or renew motor vehicle insurance on basis of, §38.2-2215.
Aircraft insurance.
Defined, §38.2-125.
Antisubrogation statute.
Motor vehicle liability medical benefit insurer not to retain right of, §38.2-2209.
Assisted living facilities, §63.2-1805.
Right of residents to be informed of coverage, §63.2-1808.
Business trusts.
Trustees, §13.1-1230.
Cancellation, notice of, §38.2-231.
Cancellation of motor vehicle insurance.
Grounds and procedure, §38.2-2212.
Notice of cancellation.
Mailing or electronic delivery by insurer, requirements, §38.2-2208.
Reason for cancellation required on application, §38.2-2210.
Warning concerning cancellation to appear on application, §38.2-2210.
Carbon monoxide exclusions, §38.2-235.
Certified escort vehicle drivers.
Insurance required, §46.2-2902.
Chiropractors.
Policy providing for reimbursement for services, §38.2-2203.
Claims-made liability insurance policies, §38.2-2229.
Commercial liability insurance joint underwriting association, §§38.2-2900 to 38.2-2913.
Activation, §38.2-2901.
Annual statement, §38.2-2909.
Appointment of directors, §38.2-2903.
Cancellation of policy, §38.2-2905.
Commissions for placing and servicing risks, §38.2-2912.
Definitions, §38.2-2900.
Directors, §38.2-2903.
Administration of stabilization reserve fund, §38.2-2906.
Public officers or employees, §38.2-2911.
Review of actions or decisions, §38.2-2908.
Dissolution, §38.2-2902.
Examination into affairs of association, §38.2-2910.
Examination of business of association, §38.2-2905.

LIABILITY INSURANCE —Cont'd
Commercial liability insurance joint underwriting association —Cont'd
Group respective rating plans, §38.2-2905.
Immunity for actions in good faith, §38.2-2913.
Insurer's participation, §38.2-2907.
Market assistance plan, §38.2-2900.1.
Members, §38.2-2901.
Participation by insurers, §38.2-2907.
Placing and servicing risks, commissions for, §38.2-2912.
Plan of operation, §38.2-2904.
Policy form, §38.2-2905.
Powers, §38.2-2901.
Public officers or employees as directors, §38.2-2911.
Purposes, §38.2-2901.
Rates, §38.2-2905.
Review of actions or decisions of association, §38.2-2908.
Stabilization reserve fund, §38.2-2906.
Submission of plan of operation, §38.2-2904.
Voluntary market assistance plan, §38.2-2900.1.
Commercial multi-peril insurance.
Defined, §38.2-132.
Condominiums.
Condominium instrument may require, §55-79.81.
Construction contracts by public bodies.
Owner-controlled insurance program.
Purchase by public body in connection with, §2.2-4308.1.
Discrimination, §38.2-508.
Issuance of motor vehicle insurance, §38.2-2213.
Elderly, reduction in rates on motor vehicle insurance, §38.2-2217.
Employees, policies not to exclude coverage to, §38.2-2207.
Family day home.
Notice of coverage to parents or guardians, §63.2-1809.1.
Farmowners insurance.
Defined, §38.2-131.
Federal or civil regulations violations.
Aircraft liability policy not to deny coverage for, §38.2-2227.
Forms for motor vehicle insurance, standard forms, §§38.2-2218 to 38.2-2224.
Home care organizations.
Requirements, regulation establishing, §32.1-162.11.
Homeowners insurance.
Defined, §38.2-130.
Income loss benefits, provisions for, §38.2-2201.
Insolvency or bankruptcy of insurer.
Required provisions as to when action maintained against, §38.2-2200.
Installment payments, §38.2-2233.
Local government officers, employees and volunteers, §15.2-1518.
Departments and boards of welfare and social services, §15.2-1519.
Long-term care facilities, §32.1-127.
Marine insurance.
Defined, §38.2-126.
Medical benefit payment provisions, §38.2-2201.
Assignment of benefits, §38.2-2201.
Motor vehicle liability insurance.
Benefit offset against liability or uninsured motorist coverage prohibited, §38.2-2216.
Insurer not to receive credit for other medical expense insurance, §38.2-2211.

LIABILITY INSURANCE —Cont'd
Medical benefit payment provisions —Cont'd
Motor vehicle liability insurance —Cont'd
Medical benefit insurer not to retain right of subrogation to recover from third party, §38.2-2209.
Motor vehicle insurance.
Cancellation. See within this heading, "Cancellation of motor vehicle insurance."
Defined, §38.2-124.
Notice of cancellation, refusal to renew, reduction in coverage or increase in rate, §38.2-231.
Motor vehicle insurance.
Mailing or electronic delivery by insurer, §38.2-2208.
Notice of optional coverage available, §38.2-2202.
Omnibus clause.
Standard provisions, motor vehicles, aircraft and watercraft, §38.2-2204.
Payment in installments, §38.2-2233.
Personal injury liability insurance.
Defined, §38.2-117.
Policies and contracts generally, §§38.2-300 to 38.2-326.
See INSURANCE POLICIES AND CONTRACTS.
Private pleasure watercraft.
Optional coverage, §38.2-2232.
Rate classifications, motor vehicle insurance.
Statement provided insured, §38.2-2214.
Rate increase, notice of, §38.2-231.
Rate reductions for persons fifty-five years of age and older.
Motor vehicle insurance, §38.2-2217.
Rates generally, §§38.2-1900 to 38.2-1928.
See INSURANCE RATES.
Records, retention.
Cancellation, refusal to renew, reduction in coverage, §38.2-231.
Reduction in coverage, notice of, §38.2-231.
Refusal to renew.
Notice, §38.2-231.
Refusal to renew motor vehicle insurance.
Grounds and procedure, §38.2-2212.
Notice of refusal, mailing or electronic delivery requirements of insurer, §38.2-2208.
Reason for nonrenewal required on application, §38.2-2210.
Replacement policies, motor vehicle insurance, §38.2-2212.1.
Review of insurer action.
Cancellation, refusal to renew, reduction in coverage, §38.2-231.
Risk management plan for public liability, §2.2-1837.
Risk retention groups and purchasing groups, §§38.2-5100 to 38.2-5115.
See RISK RETENTION GROUPS AND PURCHASING GROUPS.
Sending copies of orders to companies affected, §38.2-2225.
Standard provisions.
Motor vehicles, aircraft and watercraft, §38.2-2204.
Applicability of other valid and collectible insurance, §38.2-2205.
Subrogation of motor vehicle liability medical benefit insurer.
Right of subrogation to recover from third party not retained, §38.2-2209.

LIABILITY INSURANCE —Cont'd
Surplus lines insurance law, §§38.2-4805.1 to 38.2-4816.
Suspension of coverage at insured's request, §38.2-2205.1.
Transportation district commissions.
Obtaining coverage, §15.2-4518.
Unfair insurance trade practices generally, §§38.2-500 to 38.2-518.
See INSURANCE, UNFAIR TRADE PRACTICES.
Uninsured motorist insurance coverage, §38.2-2206.
Vanpools, motor vehicle liability coverage.
Insurers required to renew, §38.2-2217.1.
Workers' compensation and employers' liability insurance.
Defined, §38.2-119.

LIBEL.
Attorneys.
Liability for words used in professional conduct proceedings, §54.1-3908.
Banks.
Derogatory statements affecting bank, §6.2-940.
Congress of US.
Privilege of members of Congress, US Const Art I §6.
Criminal offense, §18.2-417.
Damages.
Mitigation of damages, §8.01-46.
Newspaper or print media, §8.01-48.
Radio and television broadcast, §8.01-49.
Employment-related information disclosure.
Prospective or current employer disclosing.
Immunity, good faith presumption, §8.01-46.1.
False publications, §18.2-209.
General assembly members, speech or debate privilege, VA Const Art IV §9.
Insulting word, §8.01-45.
Insurance business, defamation with respect to, §38.2-504.
Internet defamatory material.
Liability of provider or user, §8.01-49.1.
Justification, §8.01-46.
Limitation of actions, §8.01-247.1.
Newspaper or print media.
Mitigation of damages, §8.01-48.
Radio and television broadcast.
Defamatory statements on air, §8.01-49.
Savings institutions.
Defamation of institutions and certain federal agencies prohibited, §6.2-1107.
School personnel reporting bomb threats, alcohol or drug use, etc.
Immunity of school personnel reporting, §8.01-47.
Shoplifting suspect arrest or detention, §8.01-226.9.
Statute of limitations, §8.01-247.1.
Trust companies.
Derogatory statements affecting trust company, §§6.2-940, 6.2-1042.

LIBRARIAN OF VIRGINIA, §§42.1-13 to 42.1-18.
Abstracts of grants of land.
Furnishing commissioners of revenue, §58.1-3306.
Appointment, §42.1-13.
Appropriations, request for, §42.1-13.
Assistants, appointment, §42.1-13.
Assistants, compensation, §42.1-14.
Bond, §42.1-16.
Charge of state library and archives, §42.1-15.

LIBRARIAN OF VIRGINIA —Cont'd
Collegial bodies.
State publications depository program, §2.2-609.
Compensation, §42.1-14.
Destruction of original records and documents by locality.
Notice to librarian of intention to destroy, §15.2-1412.
Duties, §§42.1-13, 42.1-15.
Exchange of Virginia publications with other states and institutions, record kept, §42.1-18.
Freedom of information advisory council.
Membership of librarian or designee, §30-178.
Library board.
Secretary of, §42.1-15.
Local treasurers.
Destruction of records, consent of librarian required, §58.1-3129.
Public records generally, §§42.1-76 to 42.1-90.1.
See STATE RECORDS MANAGEMENT.
Reproduction of records and documents by locality.
Notice of librarian of intention to destroy originals, §15.2-1412.
State archivists.
Librarian of Virginia to name, §42.1-79.
State departmental and agency publications.
State publications depository program, §2.2-609.
State publications depository program, §§42.1-92 to 42.1-97.
See LIBRARY OF VIRGINIA.
State records management.
Generally, §§42.1-76 to 42.1-90.1.
See STATE RECORDS MANAGEMENT.
Supervision of state library and archives, §42.1-13.
Terms of office, §42.1-13.
Virginia sesquicentennial of the American Civil War commission.
Advisory council member, §30-268.
World War II history relating to Virginians, §42.1-30.

LIBRARIANS.
Institutes for training.
Guidelines to be developed by state council of higher education, §23-9.13:1.
Librarian of Virginia, §§42.1-13 to 42.1-18.
See LIBRARIAN OF VIRGINIA.
Professional librarian positions, qualifications, §42.1-15.1.
Qualifications required to hold professional librarian position, §42.1-15.1.

LIBRARIES, §§42.1-1 to 42.1-32.6.
Arrest of suspected people, exemption from liability, §42.1-73.1.
Concealment of book or other property on premises, §42.1-73.
Damaging property located in, §18.2-138.
Damaging public buildings, §18.2-138.
Discarded library materials.
Donating to nonprofit supporting library functions, §15.2-953.
Disorderly conduct in public places, §18.2-415.
Drug sales on or near property, §18.2-255.2.
Electronic article surveillance devices, §42.1-73.1.
Establishment and development of public library service, policy of Commonwealth, §42.1-46.

LIBRARIES —Cont'd
Failure to return book or other library property, §42.1-74.
Freedom of information act.
Excluded records, §2.2-3705.7.
Free service available to all, §42.1-55.
Grant limitation, §42.1-50.
Grants for development of library system, §42.1-47.
Grants to improve standards, §42.1-48.
Grants to municipal library, §42.1-49.
Injuring or destroying books and other property, §42.1-72.
Internet use.
Local and regional libraries.
Acceptable Internet use policies.
Power and duty of library boards and certain governing bodies, §42.1-36.1.
Interstate library compact, §42.1-75.
Land office.
State librarian, §41.1-1.
Law libraries, §§42.1-60 to 42.1-71.
Local law libraries.
Circuit court clerks, charge of, §42.1-65.
Circuit courts, enforcement of rules for government of library, §42.1-66.
Computer research services, §42.1-65.
Contributions from bar association, §42.1-70.
Cost in civil actions, assessment for law library, §42.1-70.
Voluntary contributions by members of bar, §42.1-65.
Regional law libraries, establishment by governing body, §42.1-71.
State law library, §§42.1-60 to 42.1-64.
Additions to, §42.1-62.
Books constituting, §42.1-61.
Computer expenses, §42.1-63.
Legislative services division.
Use, §30-28.15.
Managed by supreme court, §42.1-60.
Regulation, §42.1-63.
Use, persons permitted, §42.1-64.
Librarian of Virginia, §§42.1-13 to 42.1-18.
See LIBRARIAN OF VIRGINIA.
Local and regional libraries, §§42.1-33 to 42.1-45.
Appropriations for free library or library service.
Conducted by company, society or organization, §42.1-43.
Boards, §42.1-35.
Not mandatory, §42.1-36.
Regional boards, §42.1-39.
Agreements to create, §42.1-38.
Powers, §42.1-40.
Contract for library services, powers of local government, §42.1-34.
Establishment and support, powers of local government, §42.1-33.
Internet use.
Acceptable Internet use policies.
Power and duty of library boards and certain governing bodies, §42.1-36.1.
Regional library system.
Establishment, §42.1-37.
Funds and expenses, §42.1-41.
Withdrawal, §42.1-42.
Transfer of properties of free public library to governing body of city, §42.1-45.
Networking, §§42.1-32.1 to 42.1-32.6.

LIBRARIES —Cont'd
Obligations of libraries and systems receiving federal and state aid, §42.1-51.
Offenses, §§42.1-72 to 42.1-74.1.
Policy of Commonwealth, §42.1-46.
Property exempt from taxation, §58.1-3606, VA Const Art X §6.
Public records generally, §§42.1-76 to 42.1-90.1.
See STATE RECORDS MANAGEMENT.
Purchase of books, materials, etc., using state funds.
Approval of state library and archives, §42.1-54.
Records.
State records management, §§42.1-76 to 42.1-90.1.
See STATE RECORDS MANAGEMENT.
Removal of book or other property from library, §42.1-73.
Reversion of city to town.
Continued state library aide, §15.2-4116.
School libraries.
Automation and provision of network capabilities, §22.1-199.1.
Standards of eligibility for state and federal aid, §42.1-52.
State and federal aid, §§42.1-46 to 42.1-58.
Books defined, §42.1-56.
Federal and matching funds, agreements providing for, §42.1-58.
Free service available to all, §42.1-55.
Grants for development of library service, §42.1-47.
Grants to improve standards, §42.1-48.
Grants to municipal library, §42.1-49.
Library board, authority to accept and distribute federal funds, §42.1-57.
Limitation of grant, §42.1-50.
Obligations of libraries and systems receiving aid, §42.1-51.
Payment on salary, §42.1-54.
Policy of Commonwealth, §42.1-46.
Procurement for purchase of books, materials, etc., §42.1-54.
Proration of funds, §42.1-50.
Reports on operation of library, §42.1-52.
Standards of eligibility, §42.1-52.
Supervision of services, §42.1-52.
State law library, §§42.1-60 to 42.1-64.
Additions to, §42.1-62.
Books constituting, §42.1-61.
Computer expenses, §42.1-63.
Legislative services division.
Use, §30-28.15.
Managed by supreme court, §42.1-60.
Regulation, §42.1-63.
Use, persons permitted, §§30-28.15, 42.1-64.
State library and archives, §§42.1-1 to 42.1-12.
See LIBRARY OF VIRGINIA.
Uniform computer information transactions act.
Construction and interpretation of contract.
Licenses to nonprofit libraries, archives or educational institutions, §59.1-503.10.

LIBRARY AND ARCHIVES OF STATE, §§42.1-1 to 42.1-12.
See LIBRARY OF VIRGINIA.

LIBRARY BOARD.
Federal funds, authority to accept and distribute, §42.1-57.
Public records generally, §§42.1-76 to 42.1-90.1.
See STATE RECORDS MANAGEMENT.

LIBRARY BOARDS, LOCAL AND REGIONAL, §§42.1-35, 42.1-38 to 42.1-40.

LIBRARY COMPACT, §42.1-75.

LIBRARY OF VIRGINIA.
Acquisition of books and other library matter, §42.1-10.
Archival agency of Commonwealth, §42.1-1.
Blind and visually impaired.
Library services, §51.5-74.
Business hours of library, §42.1-9.
Continued, §42.1-1.
Copies by library staff, fees for, §42.1-12.
Duplicate material, donation, exchange or sale, §42.1-18.
Duties, §42.1-1.
Educational institution and institution of learning, declared, §42.1-1.
Employees.
Personnel administration system.
Exemptions, §2.2-2905.
Exchanges of Virginia publications with other states and institutions, §42.1-18.
Fees for copies made by library staff, §42.1-12.
Governor to deliver official correspondence to, §2.2-126.
Historical books, pamphlets, manuscripts, procurement, §42.1-10.
Historical matter relating to Virginia, publication, §42.1-11.
Hours of business, §42.1-9.
Legislative services division.
Use, §30-28.15.
Library agency of Commonwealth, §42.1-1.
Library board, §§42.1-2 to 42.1-8.
Appointment of members by governor, §42.1-2.
Authority, §42.1-3.1.
Direction of state library and archives, §42.1-2.
Executive committee, §42.1-2.1.
Expenses of members, §42.1-5.
Federal funds, authority to accept and distribute, §42.1-57.
Minutes and records, §42.1-6.
Networking of public libraries, §§42.1-32.1 to 42.1-32.6.
Organization and officers, §42.1-2.
Public records generally, §§42.1-76 to 42.1-90.1.
See STATE RECORDS MANAGEMENT.
Rules and regulations, §42.1-8.
Secretary.
Librarian of Virginia, §42.1-15.
Terms of members, §42.1-3.
Vacancies, §42.1-3.
Powers, §42.1-1.
Publications by state agencies.
Commercial listings, §42.1-11.
Public records generally, §§42.1-76 to 42.1-90.1.
See STATE RECORDS MANAGEMENT.
Purchase of books, materials, etc., by public libraries using state funds.
Approval required, §42.1-54.
Reports by state agencies.
Editing and publishing, §42.1-11.
Seals of the Commonwealth.
Impressions displayed in library, §1-502.
Secretary of education.
Agency responsibility, §2.2-208.
State publications depository program, §§42.1-92 to 42.1-97.
Catalog of publications produced by state agencies.
Copies, distribution, costs, §42.1-96.

LIBRARY OF VIRGINIA —Cont'd
State publications depository program —Cont'd
Catalog of publications produced by state agencies —Cont'd
Duty of librarian to prepare and publish, requirements, §42.1-95.
Cooperation with library, §42.1-94.
Definitions, §42.1-93.
Duties, §42.1-94.
Establishment and administration, §42.1-94.
Furnishing copies to library, §2.2-609.
Local or regional agencies, duties, §42.1-94.
Report by librarian, failure of agency, §42.1-97.
Policy and purpose of chapter, §42.1-92.
Report by librarian, filing, time.
Agencies not furnishing or providing information, §42.1-97.
Short title, §42.1-92.
State agencies, duties.
Report by librarian, failure of agency, §42.1-97.

LIBRARY RECORDS.
State records management, §§42.1-76 to 42.1-90.1.
See STATE RECORDS MANAGEMENT.

LIBRARY SOCIETIES.
Disorderly conduct in public places, §18.2-415.

LICENSE AGENTS.
Department of motor vehicles, §46.2-205.
Hunting and fishing.
Delivery of licenses to, return of unsold licenses, §29.1-330.
Issuance, §29.1-323.
Payment of money received to department, §29.1-332.
Reports as to sales, §29.1-333.

LICENSE PLATES.
Disabled or handicapped persons.
Generally.
See PARKING FOR DISABLED OR HANDICAPPED.
Motor carriers, passengers.
Surrender of plates, markers, registration cards, etc., upon discipline, §46.2-2011.29.
Motorcycles.
Motorcycle dealers.
General provisions, §§46.2-1993.39 to 46.2-1993.63.
See MOTORCYCLE DEALERS.
Transfer of old license plates and registration number.
Owner selling or transferring registered motorcycle, §46.2-1993.36.
Motor vehicle dealers.
Generally, §§46.2-1546 to 46.2-1557.2.
See MOTOR VEHICLE DEALERS.
Temporary plates, §§46.2-1558 to 46.2-1565.
See MOTOR VEHICLE DEALERS.
Motor vehicles.
Generally, §§46.2-711 to 46.2-749.130.
See MOTOR VEHICLE LICENSE PLATES.
Parking for disabled or handicapped.
Generally.
See PARKING FOR DISABLED OR HANDICAPPED.
Temporary license plates.
Issuance by dealers.
Motorcycle dealers, §§46.2-1993.55 to 46.2-1993.63.
See MOTORCYCLE DEALERS.

LICENSE PLATES —Cont'd
Temporary license plates —Cont'd
Issuance by dealers —Cont'd
Trailer dealers, §§46.2-1992.56 to 46.2-1992.65.
See TRAILER DEALERS.
Trailers.
Trailer dealers, §§46.2-1992.39 to 46.2-1992.65.
See TRAILER DEALERS.
Transfer of license plates by owners selling or transferring registered trailers, §46.2-1992.36.
Watercraft trailers, §46.2-1992.55.

LICENSES.
See LICENSING.

LICENSE TAXES, §§58.1-3700 to 58.1-3735.
ABC licenses.
Local taxes, §4.1-233.
State fees, §§4.1-231, 4.1-232.
After-tax profit for taxable year.
Exemption of businesses not having, §58.1-3703.
Agricultural cooperative associations, §13.1-341.
Agricultural credit associations, §58.1-3730.1.
Amusement machines, §58.1-3720.
Amusement operators, §58.1-3720.
Exemption as to operators of weighing machines, automatic baggage or parcel checking machines, §58.1-3721.
Fine for failure to procure license, §58.1-3723.
Forfeiture of device or machine, failure to procure license, §58.1-3723.
Stickers to evidence payment, §58.1-3722.
Appeals and rulings.
Uniform ordinance provisions, §58.1-3703.1.
Apportionment of gross receipts.
Uniform ordinance provisions, §58.1-3703.1.
Arenas, §58.1-3729.
Artists exhibiting production of own art, §58.1-3728.
Auctioneers, §54.1-605.
Auditoriums, §58.1-3729.
Authority of counties, cities and towns, §§58.1-3702, 58.1-3703.
Automobile graveyards and junkyards.
Power of locality to tax and regulate, §15.2-903.
Bail bondsmen, §58.1-3724.
Basis for tax, uniformity, §58.1-3705.
Bondsmen, §58.1-3724.
Businesses, occupations, etc.
Situs for taxation, §58.1-3708.
Business license incentive program.
Qualifying businesses locating for first time in locality, §58.1-3703.
Business located in more than one jurisdiction, §58.1-3709.
Carnivals, §58.1-3728.
Circuses, §58.1-3728.
Clairvoyants, §58.1-3726.
Coal and gas severance tax, §58.1-3712.
Additional one percent tax on gas, §58.1-3713.4.
Delinquent taxes.
Exoneration from lien, etc., §58.1-3959.
Local coal and gas road improvement tax, §58.1-3713.
Distribution.
Water projects, §58.1-3713.01.
Local coal severance license taxes, §§58.1-3740 to 58.1-3745.
Coin machine operators, §58.1-3720.
Exemptions to operators of weighing machines, automatic baggage or parcel checking machines, §58.1-3721.

LICENSE TAXES —Cont'd
Coin machine operators —Cont'd
Fine for failure to procure license, §58.1-3723.
Forfeiture of device, failure to procure license, §58.1-3723.
Stickers to evidence payment, §58.1-3722.
Coin-operated amusement machines, §58.1-3720.
Coliseums, §58.1-3729.
Commission merchants, §58.1-3733.
Contractors.
Bond requirement, §58.1-3714.
Credit against county tax for payment of town tax, §58.1-3714.
License required where principal office located, §58.1-3715.
Principal office location, §58.1-3715.
Workers' compensation requirements, §58.1-3714.
County tax within boundary of town, limitation on, §58.1-3711.
Transient occupancy tax, §§58.1-3823 to 58.1-3826.
Credit unions, §58.1-3730.
Deductions from gross receipts, §58.1-3732.
Definitions, §58.1-3700.1.
Departments of license inspection, §58.1-3735.
Direct sellers, §58.1-3719.1.
Dog and cat licenses, §§3.2-6521 to 3.2-6536.
Due dates and rates.
Uniform ordinance provisions, §58.1-3703.1.
Electric authorities, §15.2-5423.
Evidence of payment of taxes before issuance of license, §58.1-3700.
Exclusions on gross receipts, §58.1-3732.
Exemptions, §58.1-3703.
Fee for issuing license.
Amount, limited by population of locality, §58.1-3703.
Fortunetellers, §58.1-3726.
Funeral services.
Gross receipts of providers of funeral services.
Limitations on, §58.1-3732.3.
Garbage and refuse pickup and disposal services, §15.2-930.
Gross receipts.
Deductions from, §58.1-3732.
Exclusions on, §58.1-3732.
Imposition of tax on by counties, cities and towns levying tax, §58.1-3702.
Limitation on, §58.1-3732.
Funeral services providers, §58.1-3732.3.
Pari-mutuel wagering, §58.1-3732.1.
Real estate brokers, §58.1-3732.2.
Security brokers and dealers, §58.1-3732.5.
Staffing firms, §58.1-3732.4.
Tax measured by volume, §58.1-3708.
Uniform ordinance provisions, §58.1-3703.1.
Health services plans, §38.2-4226.
Heat, light and power companies, §58.1-3731.
Industrial loan associations, §58.1-3730.1.
Insurance companies, §§58.1-2500 to 58.1-2533.
See INSURANCE COMPANIES LICENSE TAX.
Inventors exhibiting production of own invention, §58.1-3728.
Itinerant merchants, §58.1-3717.
Limitation of tax imposed on, §58.1-3719.
License requirement.
Uniform ordinance provisions, §58.1-3703.1.
Limitation on authority of counties, cities and towns, §58.1-3703.

LICENSE TAXES —Cont'd
Limitation on county tax within boundary of town, §58.1-3711.
Transient occupancy tax, §§58.1-3823 to 58.1-3826.
Limitation on gross receipts, §58.1-3732.
Funeral services providers, §58.1-3733.
Pari-mutuel wagering, §58.1-3732.1.
Real estate brokers, §58.1-3732.2.
Security brokers and dealers, §58.1-3732.5.
Staffing firms, §58.1-3732.4.
Limitation on rate of license taxes, §58.1-3706.
Advisory opinions by tax commissioner, §58.1-3701.
Direct sellers, §58.1-3719.1.
Guidelines promulgated by department of taxation, §58.1-3701.
Limitations and extensions.
Uniform ordinance provisions, §58.1-3703.1.
Local license tax on telegraph or telephone companies, §58.1-2690.
Local tax on public service corporations, §58.1-2690.
Local transportation services.
Exemption from license tax upon taxicabs.
Nonprofit serving elderly and disabled operating, §15.2-967.1.
Location of business in more than one jurisdiction, §58.1-3709.
Merchants' capital tax.
License tax in lieu of, §58.1-3704.
Military affairs.
Armed forces personnel returning from duty outside the United States.
Grace period for business credentialing, §46.2-221.2.
Motor carriers, property.
Licensees, permittees and certificate holders.
Licensing for payment of tax, §46.2-2108.5.
Motor fuel sales taxes.
Exclusion from professional license tax, §58.1-1724.4.
Motor vehicle dealers, §58.1-3734.
Trade-in sales, §58.1-3734.1.
Motor vehicle fuel sales tax.
Exclusion of tax collected from gross receipts for purposes of license tax, §58.1-1722.
Motor vehicle owners.
Alternative fuel vehicles, annual license tax, §58.1-2249.
Liability for tax, due date, §58.1-2251.
Ordinances imposing, §15.2-973.
Oil severance tax, §58.1-3712.1.
Ordinance levying license tax.
Uniform ordinance provisions, §58.1-3703.1.
Palmistry practitioners, §58.1-3726.
Pari-mutuel wagering, §§59.1-392, 59.1-393.
Gross receipts for license taxes not to include, §58.1-3732.1.
Peddlers, §58.1-3717.
Limitation of tax imposed on, §58.1-3719.
Peddlers at wholesale, §58.1-3718.
Limitation of tax imposed on, §58.1-3719.
Photographers.
No regular established place of business, §58.1-3727.
Professional bondsmen, §58.1-3724.
Proration of taxes, §58.1-3710.
Public service corporations, §58.1-3731.
Qualifying businesses locating for first time in locality.
Business license incentive program, §58.1-3703.

LICENSE TAXES —Cont'd
Rate of taxes.
Limitation on, §58.1-3706.
Advisory opinions by tax commissioner, §58.1-3701.
Direct sellers, §58.1-3719.1.
Guidelines promulgated by department of taxation, §58.1-3701.
Real estate brokers.
Gross receipts for license taxes.
Limitations on, §58.1-3732.2.
Refund upon succession of business, trade, etc., §58.1-3710.
Requirement of license to engage in business, employment or profession, §58.1-3700.
Savings and loan associations, §58.1-3730.
Security brokers and dealers.
Limitation on gross receipts, §58.1-3732.5.
Severance tax on coal and gas, §58.1-3712.
Additional one percent tax on gas, §58.1-3713.4.
Delinquent taxes.
Exoneration from lien, etc., §58.1-3959.
Distribution.
Water projects, §58.1-3713.01.
Local coal and gas road improvement tax, §58.1-3713.
Local coal severance license taxes, §§58.1-3740 to 58.1-3745.
Validation of ordinances.
Prior to 1985, §58.1-3713.3.
Severance tax on oil, §58.1-3712.1.
Situs for taxation of businesses, occupations, etc., §58.1-3708.
Situs of business located in more than one jurisdiction, §58.1-3709.
Sole authority of counties, cities and towns to levy, §58.1-3702.
Solicitation of charitable or civic contributions.
Local ordinance limitations, §57-63.
Speedways, §58.1-3728.
Staffing services.
Gross receipts for license taxes.
Limitations on, §58.1-3732.4.
Subjects of local taxation, §58.1-3000.
Succession of business, trade, etc.
Proration of taxes, §58.1-3710.
Surplus lines insurance.
Licensees to pay license taxes on insurers, §38.2-4809.
Telegraph, telephone, water, heat, light, power and pipeline companies.
Estimated tax, §§58.1-2640 to 58.1-2651.
See PUBLIC SERVICE CORPORATION TAXATION.
Generally, §§58.1-2620 to 58.1-2635.
See PUBLIC SERVICE CORPORATION TAXATION.
Telephone and telegraph companies, §58.1-3731.
Local tax, §58.1-2690.
Trade-in sales, §58.1-3734.1.
Traveling open air or tent shows, §58.1-3728.
Uniformity of tax, §58.1-3705.
Uniform ordinance provisions.
Ordinance levying license tax, §58.1-3703.1.
Virginia coalfield economic development authority tax, §58.1-3713.
Virginia taxable income.
Imposition of tax on by counties, cities and towns levying tax, calculation, §58.1-3702.
Volume, tax measured by, §58.1-3703.1.

LICENSE TAXES —Cont'd
Waiver of license requirement, §58.1-3703.1.
Water companies, §58.1-3731.
Wholesale merchants, §58.1-3716.
Wholesale peddlers, §58.1-3718.
Limitation of tax imposed on, §58.1-3719.

LICENSING.
ABC licenses.
Generally, §§4.1-200 to 4.1-240.
Accessibility mechanics.
Certification, §§54.1-1140 to 54.1-1143.
Accountants.
Public accountants.
Professional regulation generally, §§54.1-4400 to 54.1-4425.
See ACCOUNTANTS.
Administrative process act.
Suspension.
Exemptions from case decisions, §2.2-4018.
Adult day care center.
Generally, §§63.2-1700 to 63.2-1819.
See ADULT DAY CARE CENTERS.
Agricultural liming materials.
Manufacturers, §3.2-3703.
Agricultural produce dealers, §3.2-4750.
Agricultural products.
Agent certification, §3.2-3401.
Air carriers.
Brokers, §§5.1-108 to 5.1-112.
Contract carriers, §§5.1-9.2, 5.1-9.5.
Aircraft, §5.1-5.
Contract carriers, §5.1-9.2.
Operation of unlicensed aircraft, §§5.1-14, 5.1-24.
Airports, §5.1-7.
Misuse of licensed airports, §§5.1-16.1, 5.1-24.
Alcoholic beverage licenses.
See ALCOHOLIC BEVERAGE LICENSES.
Alcoholic beverages.
ABC law generally, §§4.1-200 to 4.1-240.
Architects generally, §§54.1-400 to 54.1-411.
Asbestos contractors and workers, §§54.1-500 to 54.1-517.
Asbestos or RFS contractors.
Duties, §40.1-51.20.
Assisted living facilities.
Generally, §§63.2-1700 to 63.2-1819.
See ASSISTED LIVING FACILITIES.
Licensing and regulating, residents rights and responsibilities.
See ASSISTED LIVING FACILITIES.
Attorneys, §§54.1-3900 to 54.1-3944.
See ATTORNEYS AT LAW.
Auctioneers, §§54.1-600 to 54.1-607.
Audiologists, §§54.1-2600 to 54.1-2604.
Automobile clubs, §§13.1-400.1 to 13.1-400.9.
Bail bondsmen, §58.1-3724.
Barbers, §§54.1-700 to 54.1-706.
Beaches, §28.2-633.
Bedding and upholstered furniture, §32.1-217.
Fees, §32.1-218.
Refusal to issue, §32.1-224.
Suspension, §32.1-224.
Verification, §32.1-224.
Behavior analysts, §§54.1-2957.16, 54.1-2957.17.
Bicycles, §15.2-1720.
Boat dealers, salesmen or demonstrators, §§29.1-808 to 29.1-825.
Bondsmen, §58.1-3724.
Boxing and wrestling events, §54.1-829.
Branch pilots, §§54.1-900 to 54.1-927.

LICENSING —Cont'd
Campgrounds, §§35.1-18, 35.1-20.
Advice and assistance to applicants, §35.1-24.
Display of license, §35.1-21.
Person deemed responsible for obtaining license, §35.1-19.
Captive insurers, §38.2-1102.
Casualty insurance agents.
Generally, §§38.2-1822 to 38.2-1836.1.
Casualty insurance consultants.
Generally, §§38.2-1837 to 38.2-1845.
Cats, §§3.2-6521 to 3.2-6536.
Rabies inoculation as prerequisite, §3.2-6521.
Cemetery operators, perpetual care trust funds and preneed burial contracts, §§54.1-2310 to 54.1-2342.
Certified substance abuse counselors, §§54.1-3500 to 54.1-3506.
Child-care facilities.
Ordinances regulating in certain counties and cities, §15.2-914.
Child support enforcement by department of social services.
Suspension, delinquency in payments, §63.2-1937.
Child welfare agencies.
Generally, §§63.2-1700 to 63.2-1819.
See CHILD WELFARE AGENCIES.
Chiropractors.
Generally, §§54.1-2929 to 54.1-2941.
See MEDICINE AND OTHER HEALING ARTS PROFESSIONS.
Cities or towns.
Requiring issuance of license in connection with enforcement of ordinance or regulation, §15.2-1125.
Clams, §§28.2-500 to 28.2-505.
Applications, §28.2-501.
Fees, §28.2-502.
Residency requirements, §28.2-500.
Revocation, §28.2-521.
Theft, §28.2-528.
Taking with tongs, §28.2-503.
Click-on licenses.
Uniform computer information transactions act, §§59.1-501.1 to 59.1-509.2.
Clinical psychologists.
Generally, §§54.1-2929 to 54.1-2941.
See MEDICINE AND OTHER HEALING ARTS PROFESSIONS.
Commercial dog breeders, §§3.2-6507.1 to 3.2-6507.6.
Commission merchants, §§3.2-4711 to 3.2-4715.
Common interest community managers, §§54.1-2345 to 54.1-2354.
Consumer finance companies, §§6.2-1505 to 6.2-1516.
Contractors, §§54.1-1100 to 54.1-1127.
Cotton gins, cotton warehouses and cotton merchants.
Licensure and regulation generally, §§3.2-4764 to 3.2-4775.
See COTTON HANDLERS.
Counselors, §§54.1-3500 to 54.1-3506.
Crabs.
Assistants, §28.2-703.
Extensions, §28.2-704.
Fees, §28.2-702.
Restrictions, §28.2-705.
Sale times, §28.2-704.
Dams for hydroelectric power.
Amendments, §62.1-102.

LICENSING —Cont'd
Dams for hydroelectric power —Cont'd
Applications, §62.1-85.
Granting, §62.1-89.
Hearings.
Proceedings, §62.1-87.
Investigations, §62.1-88.
Modifications.
Plans, §62.1-90.
Notice of hearings, §62.1-86.
Priority of location or appropriation, §62.1-92.
Rejection, §62.1-90.
Duration, §62.1-94.
Impoundment of surface waters.
Application of provisions, §62.1-114.
Intangible water-power value, §62.1-95.
Jurisdiction of United States, §62.1-103.
Navigation provisions, §62.1-91.
Notice to owners of existing developments, §62.1-92.
Prevention of unreasonable obstructions, §62.1-91.
Provision changes do not affect, §62.1-101.
Reports, §62.1-100.
Terms, §§62.1-91, 62.1-95.
Violations, §62.1-97.
Time limits, §62.1-93.
Transfers of license, §62.1-96.
Value of license, §62.1-95.
Dental plan organizations, §38.2-6102.
Agents, §38.2-6112.
Dental services plans, §38.2-4517.
Renewal, §38.2-4518.
Dentistry, §§54.1-2700 to 54.1-2729.
See DENTISTRY.
Disabilities, schools for students with.
Application for license, §22.1-324.
Commitments required in application, §22.1-325.
Supplementary application for additional categories of disability, §22.1-326.
Board may authorize superintendent to issue licenses, §22.1-321.
Categories of disability.
Limitation of license to, §22.1-326.
Conditional licenses, §22.1-323.1.
Denial of license, §22.1-329.
Investigations, §22.1-330.
Time to correct deficiency, §22.1-330.
Discipline of licensees, §22.1-329.
Investigations, §22.1-330.
Time to correct deficiency, §22.1-330.
Display of license, §22.1-325.
List of valid licensees, §22.1-332.
Operation without license, §22.1-331.
Provisional licenses, §22.1-323.1.
Renewal of license, §22.1-328.
Nonrenewal, §22.1-329.
Investigations, §22.1-330.
Time to correct deficiency, §22.1-330.
Requirement for license, §22.1-323.
Operation without license, §22.1-331.
Residential schools, §22.1-323.
Services delivered in group homes and residential facilities for children, §22.1-323.2.
Summary suspension of license, §22.1-329.
Doctors.
Generally, §§54.1-2929 to 54.1-2941.
See MEDICINE AND OTHER HEALING ARTS PROFESSIONS.
Dogs, §§3.2-6521 to 3.2-6536, 3.2-6534, 3.2-6535.
Commercial dog breeders, §§3.2-6507.1 to 3.2-6507.6.

LICENSING —Cont'd
Dogs —Cont'd
Rabies inoculation as prerequisite, §3.2-6521.
Drivers.
Commercial drivers' licenses, §§46.2-341.1 to 46.2-341.34.
See COMMERCIAL DRIVERS' LICENSES.
Generally.
See DRIVERS' LICENSES.
Electricians, HVAC contractors, plumbers, §§54.1-1128 to 54.1-1135.
Electric personal assistive mobility devices.
Licensing and disposition of unclaimed property, §15.2-1720.
Electric utility restructuring.
Aggregators, §56-588.
Retail electric energy suppliers, §56-587.
Elevator mechanics.
Certification, §§54.1-1140 to 54.1-1143.
Endangered plant and insect species.
Buying threatened species.
License required, §3.2-1006.
Wild ginseng, §3.2-1007.
Engineers generally, §§54.1-400 to 54.1-411.
Farm produce sales.
See FARM PRODUCE SALES.
Feed, commercial, §3.2-4803.
Cancellation, §3.2-4804.
Fees charged by circuit court clerks, §17.1-275.
Fertilizer.
Manufacture or distribution, §§3.2-3605 to 3.2-3608.
Cancellation of license, §3.2-3621.
Fidelity and surety insurers.
Required to transact business, §38.2-2402.
Firearm dealers, §§54.1-4200 to 54.1-4202.
Fishing, inland waters.
Altering, §29.1-337.1.
Borrowing or lending, §29.1-337.1.
Carrying licenses, §29.1-336.
Complimentary licenses, §29.1-339.
Credit cards.
Payment of license fees, §29.1-112.
Destroyed licenses, §29.1-334.
Disabled active duty military personnel, §29.1-302.01.
Disabled veterans, §29.1-302.
Displaying licenses, §29.1-337.
Exemptions, §29.1-301.
False statements, §29.1-337.1.
Fees, §§29.1-302.1, 29.1-310.
Daily use fees for specially stocked trout waters, §29.1-318.
Duplicate licenses, §17.1-275.
Fish and wildlife educational events.
Youth special permits, §29.1-315.1.
Guest fishing licenses, §29.1-302.3.
Issuance.
Accounting, §29.1-332.
Agents for sale, §29.1-327.
By whom, §29.1-323.
Delivery and return of licenses, §29.1-330.
Evidence of entitlement, §29.1-325.
Procedure, §29.1-331.
Reports, §29.1-333.
Telephone and online sales, §29.1-327.
Lifetime fishing licenses, §29.1-302.1.
Disabled persons, §29.1-302.1.
Lost licenses, §29.1-334.
Multiple-year licenses, §29.1-328.
Patients in state institutions, §29.1-313.

LICENSING —Cont'd
Fishing, inland waters —Cont'd
Permits for handicapped persons, §29.1-314.
Permits for youth camps, §29.1-316.
Persons entitled to resident licenses, §29.1-319.
Required, §§29.1-300, 29.1-335.
Nonresidents, §29.1-321.
Residents of juvenile learning centers, §29.1-317.
Revocation, §29.1-338.
School classes, §29.1-315.
Special permits for veterans, §29.1-312.
Sportsman's hunting and fishing license, §29.1-310.1.
Terms, §29.1-328.
Trip fishing licenses, §29.1-311.
Youth special permits.
Fish and wildlife educational events, §29.1-315.1.
Fishing, tidal waters.
Altering or changing.
Penalty, §28.2-230.
Authority of commission, §28.2-201.
Carrying, §28.2-231.
Commercial fishing piers, §28.2-302.
Saltwater recreational fishing, §28.2-302.9.
Credit cards.
Payment of license fees, §29.1-112.
Duration, §28.2-229.
Exemptions from requirements, §28.2-226.
False statements in application.
Penalty, §28.2-230.
Fees.
Collection, §28.2-224.
Gear licenses.
Commercial gear licenses.
Use for recreational purposes, §28.2-226.1.
Limitation on sales, §28.2-204.1.
Recreational gear licenses, §28.2-226.1.
Requirements, §28.2-226.2.
Harvesters' licenses.
Nonresidents, §28.2-227.
Nets, §28.2-300.
Commercial fishing piers, §28.2-302.
Fees, §28.2-301.
Purse nets.
Menhaden, taking, §§28.2-400 to 28.2-407.
Trawl nets, §28.2-315.
Nonresidents, fees, §28.2-201.
Oysters, §§28.2-500 to 28.2-505.
Presentation to officers, §28.2-231.
Purchases from catcher, §28.2-228.
Refunds, §28.2-229.
Required, §28.2-225.
Revocation, §28.2-232.
Health and sanitation provision violations, §28.2-822.
Saltwater recreational fishing, §§28.2-302.1 to 28.2-302.10:1.
Charter boats, §28.2-302.8.
Commercial fishing piers, §28.2-302.9.
Exemptions, §28.2-302.5.
Fees, §28.2-302.2.
Fisherman identification program, §28.2-302.1:1.
Free fishing days, §28.2-302.5.
Headboats, §28.2-302.8.
Lifetime license for residents and nonresidents, §28.2-302.10:1.
Recreational boats, §28.2-302.7.
Rental boats, §28.2-302.8.
Required, §28.2-302.1.

LICENSING —Cont'd
Fishing, tidal waters —Cont'd
Saltwater recreational fishing —Cont'd
Special lifetime licenses, §28.2-302.10.
Temporary licenses, §28.2-302.6.
Seafood landing licenses, §28.2-228.1.
Suspension.
Health and sanitation provision violations, §28.2-822.
Foxhound training preserves.
Nonresident hunting, §29.1-304.
Fraternal benefit societies.
Annual license, §38.2-4127.
Suspension, revocation or refusal of foreign or alien society licenses, §38.2-4131.
Freedom of information act.
Exclusions from chapter.
Disciplinary action against licensees, §2.2-3705.3.
Impaired practitioner program records, §2.2-3705.5.
Proprietary records and trade secrets, §2.2-3705.6.
Test and examination for license or certificate, §2.2-3705.1.
Funeral services, §§54.1-2800 to 54.1-2825.
Grain products dealers, §§3.2-4754, 3.2-4755.
Hair stylists.
Barbers, §§54.1-700 to 54.1-706.
Health maintenance organizations, §38.2-4301.
Fees, §38.2-4302.
Impairment of minimum net worth, §38.2-4302.
Issuance, §38.2-4302.
Minimum net worth, §38.2-4302.
Renewal, §38.2-4318.
Suspension or revocation, §38.2-4316.
Health professions department.
Regulatory boards.
Disciplinary proceedings.
Advisory boards, participation, §54.1-2409.3.
Mandatory suspension or revocation of licenses, certificates or registrations, §54.1-2409.
Procedures for licensing, §§54.1-2408.1, 54.1-2409.
Summary suspension of licenses, certificates, registrations or multistate licensure privilege, §54.1-2408.1.
Suspension of licenses, certificates, registrations or multistate licensure privilege, §§54.1-2408.1, 54.1-2409.
Health services plans, §38.2-4222.
Renewal, §38.2-4223.
Home care organizations, §§32.1-162.7 to 32.1-162.15.
Home protection companies.
Application fee, §38.2-2603.
Expiration and renewal, §38.2-2605.
Qualification, §38.2-2604.
Required, §38.2-2603.
Home service contract providers, §38.2-2619.
Horse racing, §§59.1-375 to 59.1-386.
See PARI-MUTUEL WAGERING.
Hospices, §§32.1-162.1 to 32.1-162.6.
Hospitals.
Alterations or additions to hospitals.
New licenses, §32.1-132.
Applications, §32.1-129.
Asbestos inspections, §32.1-126.1.
Commissioner duties, §32.1-126.
Defined terms, §32.1-123.
Denial of license, §32.1-126.

LICENSING —Cont'd
Hospitals —Cont'd
Display of license, §32.1-133.
Exemption from provisions, §32.1-124.
Expiration, §32.1-131.
Provision violations.
Penalties, §32.1-136.
Regulations, §32.1-127.
Renewals, §32.1-131.
Required, §32.1-125.
Service charges, §32.1-130.
Transferability of license, §32.1-125.
Hotels, §§35.1-18, 35.1-20.
Advice and assistance to applicants, §35.1-24.
Display of license, §35.1-21.
Human transporters.
Licensing and disposition of unclaimed property, §15.2-1720.
Hunting.
Altering, §29.1-337.1.
Apprentice hunting license, §29.1-300.4.
Archery licenses, §29.1-306.
Automated point-of-sale licensing system.
Sportsman's hunting and fishing license, §29.1-310.1.
Bear hunting, §29.1-305.
Borrowing or lending, §29.1-337.1.
Carrying licenses, §29.1-336.
Complimentary licenses, §29.1-339.
Deer hunting, §29.1-305.
Destroyed licenses, §29.1-334.
Disabled veterans, §29.1-302.
Partially disabled veterans, §29.1-302.02.
Displaying licenses, §29.1-337.
Exemptions, §29.1-301.
False statements, §29.1-337.1.
Fees, §§29.1-302.1, 29.1-303.
Duplicate licenses, §17.1-275.
Fish and wildlife educational events.
Youth special permits, §29.1-315.1.
Foxhound training preserves.
Nonresident licenses, §29.1-304.
Hunter education.
Certification, §29.1-300.1.
Program, §29.1-300.2.
Program fees, §29.1-300.3.
Issuance.
Accounting, §29.1-332.
Agents for sale, §29.1-327.
By whom, §29.1-323.
Delivery and return of licenses, §29.1-330.
Evidence of entitlement, §29.1-325.
Procedure, §29.1-331.
Reports, §29.1-333.
Telephone and online sales, §29.1-327.
Junior resident lifetime hunting license, §29.1-302.1.
Junior residents.
Fee, §29.1-303.2.
Lifetime hunting licenses, §29.1-302.1.
Lost licenses, §29.1-334.
Multiple-year licenses, §29.1-328.
Muzzleloading licenses, §29.1-307.
Nonresident trip hunting license, §29.1-303.1.
Persons entitled to resident licenses, §29.1-319.
Required, §§29.1-300, 29.1-335.
Nonresidents, §29.1-321.
Revocation, §29.1-338.
Shooting preserves.
Nonresident licenses, §29.1-304.

LICENSING —Cont'd
Hunting —Cont'd
Sportsman's hunting and fishing license, §29.1-310.1.
Terms, §29.1-328.
Turkey hunting, §29.1-305.
Veterans.
Special permits for veterans, §29.1-312.
Youth resident and nonresident combination hunting license, §29.1-303.3.
Youth special permits.
Fish and wildlife educational events, §29.1-315.1.
Hydroelectric power dams, §§62.1-80 to 62.1-103.
Instant ticket games or contests.
Promoting products, §58.1-4019.1.
Insurance adjusters, §§38.2-1845.1 to 38.2-1845.23.
See INSURANCE ADJUSTERS.
Insurance agents, §§38.2-1822 to 38.2-1836.1.
Dental plan organizations, §38.2-6112.
Insurance companies, §§38.2-1024 to 38.2-1039.1.
Captive insurers, §38.2-1102.
Dental plan organizations, §§38.2-6102, 38.2-6112.
Deposits required generally, §§38.2-1045 to 38.2-1058.
Reciprocals, §§38.2-1206 to 38.2-1208.
Refusal, suspension or revocation, §§38.2-1040 to 38.2-1044.
Insurance consultants, §§38.2-1837 to 38.2-1845.
Insurance for portable electronics, vendors, §38.2-1876.
Insurance premium finance companies.
Application and fee, §38.2-4701.
Disposition of license and other fees, §38.2-4709.
Engaging in business without, §38.2-4710.
Investigation of applicants, §38.2-4702.
Issuance of license, §38.2-4702.
Renewal, §38.2-4703.
Required, §38.2-4701.
Suspension, revocation or failure to renew, §38.2-4704.
Insurance producers license.
Business entity acting as insurance producer, §38.2-1820.
Interior designers generally, §§54.1-412 to 54.1-414.
Landing of seafood in Virginia, §28.2-228.1.
Landscape architects generally, §§54.1-400 to 54.1-411.
Legal services plans, §38.2-4413.
Renewal, §38.2-4414.
Lie detector test examiners, §§54.1-1800 to 54.1-1806.
Life-sharing communities.
Exemption for license requirements, §63.2-1808.1.
Liquefied petroleum gas fitters, §54.1-1129.
Application, §54.1-1130.
Expiration and renewal, §54.1-1132.
Grounds for denial or revocation, §54.1-1134.
Lottery sales agents, §§58.1-4009 to 58.1-4012, 58.1-4027.
Instant ticket games or contests, §58.1-4019.1.
Manufactured housing industry licensing, §§36-85.16 to 36-85.30.
See MANUFACTURED HOUSING.
Marriage and family therapists, §§54.1-3500 to 54.1-3506.
See COUNSELORS.
Marriage licenses.
See MARRIAGE.

LICENSING —Cont'd
Medicine and other healing arts professions, §§54.1-2900 to 54.1-2993.
See MEDICINE AND OTHER HEALING ARTS PROFESSIONS.
Mental health facilities, §§37.2-403 to 37.2-422.
See LICENSING OF MENTAL HEALTH FACILITIES.
Midwives, §§54.1-2957.7 to 54.1-2957.13.
Milk and milk products.
See MILK AND MILK PRODUCTS.
Mine licensing.
See MINE LICENSING.
Mineral mines, §§45.1-161.292:30 to 45.1-161.292:39.
See MINERAL MINE LICENSES.
Mopeds, §15.2-1720.
Mortgage lender and broker act.
Application, §6.2-1603.
Assignments.
Not assignable, §6.2-1607.
Bond, surety, §6.2-1604.
Contents.
Requirements, §6.2-1607.
Exemption from requirement, §6.2-1603.
Fees, §6.2-1603.
Investigation of applications, §6.2-1605.
Notice.
Suspension or revocation, §6.2-1623.
Qualifications, §6.2-1606.
Requirement, §6.2-1601.
Revocation.
Grounds, §6.2-1619.
Notice, §6.2-1623.
Suspension.
Grounds, §6.2-1619.
Notice, §6.2-1623.
Transferability.
Not transferable, §6.2-1607.
Mortgage loan originators.
Generally, §§6.2-1700 to 6.2-1721.
See MORTGAGE LOAN ORIGINATORS.
Motor carriers, passengers.
See MOTOR CARRIERS, PASSENGERS.
Motor carriers road tax, §58.1-2700.1.
Motorcycle dealers, §§46.2-1993.6 to 46.2-1993.19, 46.2-1993.75 to 46.2-1993.80.
See MOTORCYCLE DEALERS.
Motor vehicle dealers, §§46.2-1508 to 46.2-1521.
See MOTOR VEHICLE DEALERS.
Music licensing fees, §§59.1-460 to 59.1-466.
See MUSIC LICENSING FEES.
Mutual assessment property and casualty insurers, §38.2-2511.
Suspension or revocation, failure to maintain required memberships, §38.2-2515.
Nursing.
Generally, §§54.1-3000 to 54.1-3028.1.
See NURSING.
Interstate compact on nurse licensure, §§54.1-3030 to 54.1-3040.
Nursing home and assisted living facility administrators, §§54.1-3100 to 54.1-3103.1.
Nursing homes.
Alterations or additions to nursing homes.
New licenses, §32.1-132.
Applications, §32.1-129.
Commissioner duties, §32.1-126.
Defined terms, §32.1-123.
Denial of license, §32.1-126.
Display of license, §32.1-133.

LICENSING —Cont'd
Nursing homes —Cont'd
Exemption from provisions, §32.1-124.
Expiration, §32.1-131.
Fire suppression systems, §32.1-126.2.
Provision violations.
Penalties, §32.1-136.
Regulations, §32.1-127.
Authorization of sanctions and guidelines, §32.1-127.01.
Renewals, §32.1-131.
Required, §32.1-125.
Revocation, §32.1-135.
Service charges, §32.1-130.
Suspension, §32.1-135.
Transferability of licenses, §32.1-125.
Optometric services plans, §38.2-4517.
Renewal, §38.2-4518.
Optometrists, §§54.1-3212 to 54.1-3221.
Osteopathic medicine.
Generally, §§54.1-2929 to 54.1-2941.
See MEDICINE AND OTHER HEALING ARTS PROFESSIONS.
Oysters.
Applications, §28.2-501.
Dredging equipment on boat, §28.2-516.
Fees, §28.2-502.
Shucking or packing, §28.2-504.
Residency requirements, §28.2-500.
Revocation, §28.2-521.
Theft, §28.2-528.
Taking with tongs, §28.2-503.
Pari-mutuel wagering on horses, §§59.1-375 to 59.1-386.
See PARI-MUTUEL WAGERING.
Pawnbrokers, §§54.1-4000 to 54.1-4014.
Payday loans.
Persons engaged in business of making, §§6.2-1800 to 6.2-1829.
See PAYDAY LOANS.
Pesticide control, §§3.2-3924 to 3.2-3928.
Revocation or suspension, §§3.2-3939, 3.2-3940.
Summary suspension by commissioner, §3.2-3940.
Pharmacists, §§54.1-3310 to 54.1-3321.
Physical therapist assistants.
See PHYSICAL THERAPISTS.
Physical therapists.
See PHYSICAL THERAPISTS.
Physician assistants.
Generally, §§54.1-2950.1 to 54.1-2957.01.
See MEDICINE AND OTHER HEALING ARTS PROFESSIONS.
Physicians.
Generally, §§54.1-2929 to 54.1-2941.
See MEDICINE AND OTHER HEALING ARTS PROFESSIONS.
Pilots.
Branch pilots, §§54.1-900 to 54.1-927.
Plants and plant products inspection.
Nurserymen, dealers or agents to sell nursery stock, §3.2-3803.
Podiatrist assistants.
Generally, §§54.1-2950.1 to 54.1-2957.01.
See MEDICINE AND OTHER HEALING ARTS PROFESSIONS.
Podiatrists.
Generally, §§54.1-2929 to 54.1-2941.
See MEDICINE AND OTHER HEALING ARTS PROFESSIONS.
Polygraph examiners, §§54.1-1800 to 54.1-1806.

LICENSING —Cont'd
Polysomnographic technologists, §§54.1-2957.14, 54.1-2957.15.
Practical nurses, §§54.1-3019 to 54.1-3021.
Denial of license, §54.1-3007.
Fee, additional, §54.1-3011.1.
Lapsed licenses, §54.1-3011.
Qualifications, §54.1-3020.
Renewal of license, §54.1-3011.
Revocations, §54.1-3007.
Suspensions, §54.1-3007.
Precious metals dealers, §§54.1-4100 to 54.1-4111.
Principals, public schools, §22.1-293.
Standards of quality, §22.1-253.13:2.
Private security services businesses, §9.1-139.
Producer-controlled property and casualty insurers, §38.2-1346.
Professional and occupational regulation department.
Regulatory boards generally, §§54.1-100 to 54.1-114.
Temporary licenses and certifications.
Issuance to persons licensed in another state, §54.1-201.1.
Professional bondsmen, §58.1-3724.
Psychologists, §§54.1-3600 to 54.1-3606.1.
Public accountants.
Professional regulation generally, §§54.1-4400 to 54.1-4425.
See ACCOUNTANTS.
Public school employees.
Principals and assistant principals, §22.1-293.
Teachers, §§22.1-298.1 to 22.1-299.4.
Public weighmasters generally, §§3.2-5800 to 3.2-5820.
Radiation control, §32.1-231.
Rate service organizations, §38.2-1915.
Real estate appraisal management companies, §§54.1-2020 to 54.1-2023.
Real estate appraisers, §§54.1-2009 to 54.1-2019.
Real estate brokers, salespersons and rental agents, §§54.1-2100 to 54.1-2120.
Reciprocal insurers, §§38.2-1206 to 38.2-1208.
Registered nurses, §54.1-3018.
Denial of license, §54.1-3007.
Fee, additional, §54.1-3011.1.
Lapsed licenses, §54.1-3011.
Provisional license, §54.1-3017.1.
Qualifications, §54.1-3017.
Renewal of license, §54.1-3011.
Revocations, §54.1-3007.
Suspensions, §54.1-3007.
Reinsurance intermediaries, §§38.2-1347 to 38.2-1357.
Renovation contractors, §54.1-503.
Penalties for license violations, §54.1-517.
Rental location agents generally, §§54.1-2100 to 54.1-2120.
Residential building energy analysts, §§54.1-1144 to 54.1-1146.
Restaurants, §§35.1-18, 35.1-20.
Advice and assistance to applicants, §35.1-24.
Display of license, §35.1-21.
Risk retention groups, §38.2-1039.1.
Road tax of motor carriers, §58.1-2700.1.
Saltwater recreational fishing, §§28.2-302.1 to 28.2-302.10:1.
Seafood landing licenses, §28.2-228.1.
Seeds.
Sales or distribution, §3.2-4005.

LICENSING —Cont'd
Self storage insurance.
Lessors, §38.2-1882.
Shooting enclosures.
Destruction of certain diseased animals, §§3.2-6036 to 3.2-6038.
Shooting preserves, §29.1-600.
Nonresident hunting, §29.1-304.
Ownership or leasing prerequisite, §29.1-601.
Revocation, §29.1-609.
Shrink wrap licenses.
Uniform computer information transactions act, §§59.1-501.1 to 59.1-509.2.
Social security numbers, §54.1-116.
Applicants for renewal to provide, §63.2-1937.
License certificates not to display.
Government data collection and dissemination practices act, §2.2-3808.
Social workers, §§54.1-3700 to 54.1-3709.
Soil scientists, wetland professionals and geologists, §§54.1-2200 to 54.1-2208.4.
Solicitation of charitable or civic contributions, §§57-48 to 57-69.
See SOLICITATION OF CHARITABLE OR CIVIC CONTRIBUTIONS.
Speech pathologists, §§54.1-2600 to 54.1-2604.
Substance abuse counselors, §§54.1-3500 to 54.1-3506.
Substance abuse treatment practitioners, §§54.1-3507, 54.1-3508.
Summer camps, §§35.1-18, 35.1-20.
Advice and assistance to applicants, §35.1-24.
Display of license, §35.1-21.
Surveyors generally, §§54.1-400 to 54.1-411.
T&M vehicle dealers, §§46.2-1908 to 46.2-1921.
See T&M VEHICLE DEALERS.
Teachers, §§22.1-298.1 to 22.1-299.4.
Advisory board on teacher education and licensure, §22.1-305.2.
Telegraph or telephone companies.
Foreign companies, §56-484.
Tobacco products distributors, §58.1-1021.04:1.
Tour guides and tourist guides, §15.2-946.
Tradesman.
Electricians, HVAC contractors, plumbers, §§54.1-1128 to 54.1-1135.
Trailer dealers, §§46.2-1992.6 to 46.2-1992.19.
See TRAILER DEALERS.
Trapping.
Altering, §29.1-337.1.
Borrowing or lending, §29.1-337.1.
Carrying licenses, §29.1-336.
Destroyed licenses, §29.1-334.
Disabled persons and disabled veterans.
Lifetime license, §29.1-309.1.
Displaying licenses, §29.1-337.
Exemptions, §29.1-301.
False statements, §29.1-337.1.
Fees, §29.1-309.
Duplicate licenses, §17.1-275.
Issuance.
Accounting, §29.1-332.
Agents for sale, §29.1-327.
By whom, §29.1-323.
Delivery and return of licenses, §29.1-330.
Evidence of entitlement, §29.1-325.
Procedure, §29.1-331.
Reports, §29.1-333.
Telephone and online sales, §29.1-327.
Lost licenses, §29.1-334.
Multiple-year licenses, §29.1-328.

LICENSING —Cont'd
Trapping —Cont'd
Persons entitled to resident licenses, §29.1-319.
Required, §§29.1-300, 29.1-335.
Nonresidents, §29.1-321.
Revocation, §29.1-338.
Senior citizens.
Special lifetime license, §29.1-309.2.
Terms, §29.1-328.
Unemployment compensation.
Loss of or failure to renew license required as a condition of employment.
Disqualification for benefits, §60.2-618.
Veterinary medicine, §§54.1-3800 to 54.1-3813.
Viatical settlement brokers, §38.2-6001.
Generally, §§38.2-1865.1 to 38.2-1865.5.
Viatical settlement providers, §38.2-6002.
Watercraft dealers, salesmen or demonstrators, §§29.1-808 to 29.1-825.
Waterfowl blinds.
Application of provisions, §29.1-350.
Applications, §29.1-348.
Fees, §29.1-343.
Provision violations.
Penalty, §29.1-351.1.
Renewals, §29.1-347.
Riparian rights, §29.1-344.
Forfeiture, §29.1-345.
Stationary waterfowl blinds, §29.1-344.1.
Time for obtaining, §29.1-344.2.
Stationary waterfowl blinds.
Nonriparian, §29.1-345.
Time for obtaining, §29.1-345.1.
Riparian, §29.1-344.1.
Time for obtaining, §29.1-344.2.
Waterworks operators, §§54.1-2300 to 54.1-2302.
Weighmasters, public generally, §§3.2-5800 to 3.2-5820.
Wholesale distributors of prescription drugs, §§54.1-3435, 54.1-3435.1.
Exemptions, §54.1-3435.02.
Registration, §54.1-3435.01.
Workers' compensation insurance and self-insurance.
Group self-insurance associations, §65.2-802.

LICENSING OF MENTAL HEALTH FACILITIES, §§37.2-403 to 37.2-422.
Adult facilities licenses.
Summary suspension, §37.2-419.1.
Advertising, §37.2-421.
Authority of commissioner to grant licenses, §37.2-404.
Background checks.
Applicants for employment with providers, §37.2-416.
Children's residential facilities.
Background check on employees, §37.2-408.1.
Conditional licenses, §37.2-415.
Conditions for initial licensure.
Opiate addiction treatment providers, §37.2-406.
Definitions, §37.2-403.
Designation of licensing agency, §37.2-408.
Employees.
Background checks.
Applicants for employment with providers, §37.2-416.
Expiration of licenses, §37.2-410.
Fees for licenses, §37.2-410.
Group homes and residential facilities for children.
Suspension of license.
Summary orders, §§37.2-408, 37.2-418.

LICENSING OF MENTAL HEALTH FACILITIES —Cont'd
Human rights and licensing enforcement and sanctions, §37.2-419.
Human rights review.
Licensure contingent on compliance, §37.2-412.
Inspections, §37.2-411.
Interdepartmental cooperation, §37.2-408.
Intermediate care facilities for persons with intellectual disability.
Maximum number of individuals to be served.
Rulemaking authority, §37.2-409.
Internet posting of licensed providers by corporate, assumed or fictitious names, §37.2-405.1.
Offer or payment of remuneration in exchange for referrals, §37.2-420.
Opiate addiction treatment providers.
Conditions for initial licensure, §37.2-406.
Pregnant women with substance abuse.
Rulemaking authority, §37.2-407.
Proceedings to prevent unlawful operation of service, §37.2-417.
Provisional licenses, §37.2-415.
Referrals.
Offer or payment of remuneration in exchange for referral, §37.2-420.
Refusal of licenses, §37.2-418.
Renewal of licenses, §37.2-410.
Required, §37.2-405.
Revocation of licenses, §37.2-418.
Rules and regulations of board, §37.2-408.
Special orders.
Human rights and licensing enforcement and sanctions, §37.2-419.
Summary suspension of adult facility licenses, §37.2-419.1.
Suspension of licenses, §37.2-418.
Group homes and residential facilities for children.
Summary orders, §§37.2-408, 37.2-418.
Summary suspension of adult facility licenses, §37.2-419.1.
Transferability of license, §37.2-405.
Unlicensed institutions.
Proceedings to prevent unlawful operation, §37.2-417.

LIDOCAINE.
Physical therapists.
Administration of certain topical drugs, §54.1-3408.

LIE DETECTOR TEST EXAMINERS, §§54.1-1800 to 54.1-1806.
See POLYGRAPH EXAMINERS.

LIE DETECTOR TESTS.
Criminal procedure.
Written notice prior to examination, §19.2-9.1.
Employment polygraph tests.
Prohibited questions, §54.1-1806.
Occupational safety and health, §40.1-51.4:3.
Prohibition of use of polygraphs in certain employment situations, §40.1-51.4:4.
Teachers refusal to submit to.
Teacher not dismissed or placed on probation, §22.1-307.

LIENS.
Advances, §§43-27.1 to 43-30.
Clerk destruction of crop lien agreement and book, §43-27.1.

LIENS —Cont'd
Advances —Cont'd
Laborer advances, §43-29.
Remedies cumulative, §43-30.
Tenant advances, §43-29.
Agricultural stewardship, §3.2-407.
Aircraft keepers, §43-32.
Appeals, §43-36.
Enforcement, §43-34.
Validity, §43-35.
Animal keepers, §43-32.
Appeals, §43-36.
Enforcement, §43-34.
Validity, §43-35.
Animals.
Crossing lawful fences, §55-307.
Unclaimed animals left with veterinarian or boarding establishment.
Expenses incurred, §3.2-6520.
Assignments for the benefit of creditors.
Income assignments, §§55-161 to 55-167.
Property assignments, §55-156.
Attorneys' fees.
Lien for fees, §54.1-3932.
Priority over medical services lien, §8.01-66.3.
Baggage removed from hotel, motel, etc., while lien exists, §18.2-188.
Banks.
Bankruptcy and insolvency.
Liens on trust funds held by bank or trust company, §6.2-1005.
Fees for examination of bank, §6.2-909.
Bawdy place abatement by locality, §15.2-908.1.
Beacons.
Cost of repairing or replacing, §62.1-188.
Boat keepers, §43-32.
Appeals, §43-36.
Enforcement, §43-34.
Validity, §43-35.
Boats and other watercraft.
Security interests generally, §§29.1-723 to 29.1-732.
See BOATS AND OTHER WATERCRAFT.
Boat titling certificates.
Levy made by court order.
Priority of liens, §29.1-731.
Uniform certificate of title for watercraft, §29.1-733.14.
Buildings endangering public health or safety.
Cost of removal, repair or securing by locality, §15.2-906.
Bull offspring liens, §43-43.
Buoys.
Cost of repairing or replacing, §62.1-188.
Canal employee or supplier liens, §43-24.
Assignees' rights, §43-26.
Enforcement, §43-25.
Perfection, §43-25.
Carriers.
Bills of lading, §8.7-307.
Enforcement of liens, §8.7-308.
Certificate of satisfaction or partial satisfaction.
Release of lien, §55-66.3.
Child support enforcement by department of social services.
Claim by department for support debt, §63.2-1927.
Broker-dealers.
Service on, effect, §63.2-1931.
Civil liability for failure to comply, §63.2-1930.

LIENS —Cont'd
Child support enforcement by department of social services —Cont'd
Claim by department for support debt —Cont'd
Collection of support debt in jeopardy.
Demand for immediate payment, filing and serving lien, §63.2-1939.
Financial institutions.
Service on, effect, §63.2-1931.
Foreclosure, §63.2-1934.
Joint account holders.
Interest of support debtor in, determination, §63.2-1931.
Release by commissioner, §63.2-1938.
Satisfaction, §63.2-1934.
After foreclosure, §63.2-1935.
Service of lien, §63.2-1928.
Child support judgments created by operation of law, §16.1-278.15.
City lien against real estate, §15.2-105.
Clothing cleaning, dyeing, pressing or storing liens, §43-63.
Coal severance tax.
Local coal severance license taxes.
Lien on real and personal property of businesses severing coal, §58.1-3745.
Coal surface mining.
State lien for reclamation work, §§45.1-264 to 45.1-269.
Attachment, §45.1-264.
Hearing to determine amount, §45.1-268.
Notice, §45.1-266.
Perfection, §45.1-265.
Priority, §45.1-267.
Recordation and indexing, §45.1-266.
Satisfaction, §45.1-269.
Waiver, §45.1-265.
Collection of accounts receivable by Commonwealth.
Collection techniques, §2.2-4806.
Collection of state taxes.
Jurisdiction over Commonwealth for purposes of determining validity, amount and priority, §58.1-1809.
Memorandum of lien, §58.1-1805.
Collection of taxes assessed by state corporation commission.
Memorandum of lien, §58.1-2021.
Commercial real estate brokers' liens, §§55-526, 55-527.
Condominiums.
Assessments, §55-79.84.
Judgments for money, §55-79.80:1.
Release of liens, §55-79.46.
Termination of condominium, §55-79.72:1.
Confession of judgment.
Judgment confessed by attorney-in-fact, §8.01-434.
Consumer finance companies.
Lien upon real estate not to be taken as security except under judgment, §6.2-1524.
Cooperative association stock.
Rotating stocks, §13.1-310.
County lien against real estate, §15.2-104.
Credit line deed of trust, §55-58.2.
Creditor's suits.
Fraudulent conveyances, §§55-82, 55-82.1.
Credit unions.
Shares of members and dividends, §6.2-1359.
Crime victim compensation.
Lien for payment disbursed, against person alleged to have caused injuries, §19.2-368.15.

LIENS —Cont'd
Day marks.
Cost of repairing or replacing, §62.1-188.
Decedents' estates.
Debt payment order.
Affect upon, §64.2-530.
Real estate.
Liability to debts.
Liens acquired in lifetime of decedent, §64.2-538.
Deeds.
Reservation of vendor's lien, §55-53.
Definitions.
Release of deeds of trust or other liens, §55-66.3.
Delinquent local treasurers, judgment and execution, §58.1-3172.
Delinquent tax lands.
Lien for taxes paid, §58.1-3974.
Derelict buildings.
Locality authority to remove, demolish or renovate.
Costs constituting lien against property, §15.2-906.
Distress.
Landlord and tenant, §§55-230 to 55-238.
Documents of title.
Carrier's lien, §8.7-307.
Enforcement, §8.7-308.
Warehouseman's lien, §8.7-209.
Enforcement, §8.7-210.
Drainage projects.
Delinquent tax assessment constitutes lien, §21-374.
Drug blight on property.
Costs of corrective action by locality, §15.2-907.
Dry cleaner liens, §43-63.
Enforcement of judgments.
Generally, §§8.01-458 to 8.01-465.
See JUDGMENTS AND DECREES.
Equal credit opportunities.
Signature requirement not discriminatory, §6.2-504.
Estate tax.
Unpaid taxes, §58.1-908.
Fabric cleaning, dyeing, pressing or storing liens, §43-63.
False liens or encumbrances, filing, §18.2-213.2.
Farm products consigned to commission merchants.
Lien for, §43-62.
Federal lien registration, §§55-142.1 to 55-142.9.
Circuit court clerks fees, §17.1-275.
Electronic recordation of real property documents.
Uniform standards, §55-142.13.
Fences.
Animals crossing lawful fences, §55-307.
Forest products tax, §58.1-1603.
Form for extension of limitations.
Right to enforce deed of trust or mortgage, §8.01-241.1.
Forthcoming bonds.
Forfeiture constitutes lien, §§8.01-527 to 8.01-529.
Fraud.
False liens or encumbrances, filing, §18.2-213.2.
Fraudulent conversion of property subject to lien in another, §18.2-115.
Fraudulent conveyances.
Creditor's suits, §§55-82, 55-82.1.
Subsequent purchaser liens, §55-104.
Fuel taxes.
Memorandum of lien for collection of taxes, §58.1-2284.

LIENS —Cont'd
Fuel taxes —Cont'd
Sales tax in certain transportation districts.
Lien for collection of taxes, §58.1-2299.13.
Garage keepers, §46.2-644.01.
Appeals, §43-36.
Enforcement, §46.2-644.03.
Validity, §43-35.
Garnishment.
General provisions, §§8.01-511 to 8.01-525.
See GARNISHMENT.
Gas utilities charges and taxes imposed by localities, §15.2-2118.1.
Ground rent, §55-79.04.
Hangar keepers, §43-32.
Appeals, §43-36.
Chattel mortgages, subject to, §43-34.1.
Enforcement, §43-34.
Validity, §43-35.
Home solicitation sales.
Payments, tender of, §59.1-21.5.
Horizontal property regimes, §55-79.35.
Contributions by co-owners for expenses.
Defaults and payments, §55-79.13.
Recordation, §55-79.7.
Hospital, medical and nursing services lien.
General provisions, §§8.01-66.2 to 8.01-66.12.
See MEDICAL SERVICES LIEN.
Husband and wife.
Responsibility for spouse's contracts, §55-37.
Impoundment of animals, §3.2-6565.
Improvements to land.
After offsetting damages against improvements.
Balance as lien upon land, §8.01-172.
Income tax.
Jeopardy assessment, §58.1-314.
Memorandum of lien, §58.1-313.
Infant, personal injury to.
Lien for expenses in attempt to cure infant of injuries, §8.01-36.
Inoperable motor vehicle on residential or commercial property.
Ordinances restricting the keeping of, removal.
Cost of removal and disposal by locality, §§15.2-904, 15.2-905.
Insurance agents, §38.2-1806.
Insurance, cancellation of policies.
Notice to lienholders, §38.2-231.
Insurers deposits.
Policyholders and general creditors lien, §38.2-1046.
Investment securities.
Issuer's lien, §8.8A-209.
Jackass offspring liens, §§43-41, 43-42.
Jeopardy assessment.
Income tax, §58.1-314.
Memorandum of tax, §58.1-313.
Judgment liens.
See JUDGMENT LIENS.
Landlord and tenant.
Distress, §§55-230 to 55-238.
Perfection of lien of in leases, rents and profits, §55-220.1.
Laundry liens, §43-63.
Lease-purchase agreements.
Prohibited practices, §59.1-207.22.
Leases, UCC.
Priority of certain liens arising by operation of law, §8.2A-306.
Priority of liens that attach before lease contract becomes enforceable, §8.2A-307.

LIENS —Cont'd
Leases, UCC —Cont'd
Priority subject to subordination, §8.2A-311.
Limitation of actions.
Assessments for water, sewers or sidewalks, §8.01-240.
Unpaid purchase money, §8.01-241.
Extension of limitation form, §8.01-241.1.
Literary fund.
Locality indebtedness to fund, §22.1-161.
Livery stable keepers, §43-32.
Appeals, §43-36.
Defrauding person having, §18.2-188.1.
Enforcement, §43-34.
Validity, §43-35.
Livestock.
Advances to tenants and laborers, §§43-29, 43-30.
Crossing lawful fences, §55-307.
Localities lien against real estate, §15.2-104.
Appointment as receiver to repair derelict and blighted buildings.
Receiver's lien, §15.2-907.2.
Local treasurers, delinquent treasurers, §58.1-3172.
Lottery, state.
Attachability of prizes, §58.1-4013.
Manufactured home lot rental.
Abandoned homes, §55-248.44:1.
Home sales upon eviction.
Rent liability, §55-248.50:2.
Notice of changes to landlord, §55-248.42.
Rent liability, §55-248.44:1.
Manufacturing employee or supplier liens, §43-24.
Assignees' rights, §43-26.
Enforcement, §43-25.
Perfection, §43-25.
Marina keepers, §43-32.
Appeals, §43-36.
Enforcement, §43-34.
Validity, §43-35.
Married women's property rights.
Responsibility for other spouse's judgments, §55-37.
Mechanics' and materialmen's, §§43-1 to 43-23.2.
See MECHANICS' AND MATERIALMEN'S LIENS.
Mechanics' liens, §43-33.
Appeals, §43-36.
Enforcement, §43-34.
Repair of personal property, §46.2-644.02.
Enforcement, §46.2-644.03.
Validity, §43-35.
Medical services lien.
General provisions, §§8.01-66.2 to 8.01-66.12.
See MEDICAL SERVICES LIEN.
Membership camping.
Nondisturbance provisions, §59.1-333.
Memorandum of lien.
Collection of state taxes, §58.1-1805.
Collection of taxes assessed by state corporation commission, §58.1-2021.
Income tax.
Jeopardy assessment, §58.1-313.
Mining employee or supplier liens, §43-24.
Assignees' rights, §43-26.
Enforcement, §43-25.
Perfection, §43-25.
Mortgages and deeds of trust, §§6.2-406 to 6.2-423, 55-58 to 55-66.6.
See MORTGAGES AND DEEDS OF TRUST.

LIENS —Cont'd
Motor vehicle proof of financial responsibility.
Bond to constitute lien on real estate of surety, §46.2-447.
Order discharging lien of bond, §46.2-450.
Motor vehicles.
Enforcement of lien acquired, §46.2-644.03.
Impounded vehicles.
Repossession or removal by lienholder, §46.2-301.1.
Inoperable vehicles on residential or commercial property.
Costs of removal and disposal by locality, §§15.2-904, 15.2-905.
Keeper of garage or person keeping vehicle, §46.2-644.01.
Mechanics' liens for repairs or person authorized to request repairs, §46.2-644.02.
Sale of vehicle, §46.2-644.03.
Unlawful subleases, §18.2-115.1.
Mutual assurance society's liens, §43-66.
Notice service generally, §43-64.
Nuisances.
Lien for charge of costs, §15.2-1115.
Oil discharges.
Security for payment of damages, §62.1-44.34:20.
Partial satisfaction.
Release, §55-66.3.
Partition of land.
Application of proceeds of sale to payment of lien, §8.01-84.
Partnerships.
Charging order on partners transferable interest, §50-73.108.
Payment.
Release, §55-66.3.
Port authority.
Bond issues.
Trust agreement securing.
Limitations, §62.1-141.
Charges for use of facilities, §62.1-142.
Prizes of state lottery, §58.1-4013.
Property owners' associations, §§55-514, 55-516.
Property rights of married women.
Responsibility for spouse's judgments, §55-37.
Public assistance or social services.
No lien to attach to property of applicant or recipient, §63.2-409.
Public service corporation taxation, §58.1-2612.
Railway employees or supplier liens, §43-24.
Assignees' rights, §43-26.
Enforcement, §43-25.
Perfection, §43-25.
Real estate cooperatives, §§55-469, 55-473.
Judgments against the association, liens resulting from, §55-468.
Lender rights, §55-455.
Nonpayment of assessments, §55-472.
Release of liens, §55-486.
Special declarant rights, transfers of, §55-461.
Void without possessory interest, §55-444.
Real estate tax liens.
Service by publication, §8.01-321.
Real property taxes, §§58.1-3340 to 58.1-3345.
Accumulated amount of tax deferred and interest, §58.1-3219.1.
Deferral programs for elderly or handicapped, §58.1-3216.
Delinquent taxes.
Recording, §58.1-3930.

LIENS —Cont'd
Real property taxes —Cont'd
Release on portion of real estate upon payment of taxes, §58.1-3226.1.
Real property trusts.
Attachment, §55-17.1.
Recording.
Deed books, §§17.1-227, 17.1-229.
Reforestation of timberlands, §10.1-1173.
Registration.
Federal lien registration, §§55-142.1 to 55-142.9.
Electronic recordation of real property documents.
Uniform standards, §55-142.13.
Release, §§43-67 to 43-71, 55-66.3.
Affidavit by creditor filed or recorded with certificate, §55-66.3.
Certificate of satisfaction or partial satisfaction, §55-66.3.
Court releases, §43-68.
Definitions, §55-66.3.
Mechanic's liens.
Bond filings, §§43-70, 43-71.
Payment, §43-67.
Into court payments, §§43-70, 43-71.
Satisfaction, §43-67.
Vendor's liens, §55-66.3.
Reservations.
Vendor's lien reserved in deed, §55-53.
Residential ground rent, §55-79.04.
Resources authority.
Pledges, §62.1-210.
Retail sales and use tax delinquencies.
Memorandum of lien, §58.1-632.
Retention of ended case files by circuit court clerk, time, destruction, §17.1-213.
Rug cleaning, dyeing, pressing or storing liens, §43-63.
Safe deposit boxes.
Nonpayment of rent, §§6.2-2300 to 6.2-2314.
Sale of delinquent tax lands.
Nonjudicial sales properties of minimal size and value, §58.1-3975.
Taxes paid on real estate, §58.1-3974.
Satisfaction.
Release, §55-66.3.
Self-service storage, §55-418.
Enforcement, §55-419.
Other remedies not pre-empted, §55-419.1.
Service by publication.
Real estate tax liens, §8.01-321.
Severance tax on coal, gas or oil.
Local coal severance license taxes.
Lien on real and personal property of businesses severing coal, §58.1-3745.
Spousal support.
Judgments created by operation of law, §16.1-278.15.
Stallion offspring liens, §§43-41, 43-42.
State corporation commission.
Collection of taxes assessed by, §58.1-2021.
Judgments of commission, §12.1-37.
Statute of limitations.
Assessments for water, sewers or sidewalks, §8.01-240.
Unpaid purchase money, §8.01-241.
Extension of limitation form, §8.01-241.1.
Subdivided land sales, §55-342.
Property owners' associations.
Unpaid assessments, §55-344.
Support liens, §§63.2-1927 to 63.2-1935.

LIENS —Cont'd
Support of child or spouse.
Judgment created by operation of law, §16.1-278.15.
Tax collection, state corporation commission.
Memorandum of lien, §58.1-2021.
Tax collection, state taxes.
Jurisdiction over Commonwealth for purposes of determining validity, amount and priority, §58.1-1809.
Memorandum of lien, §58.1-1805.
Taxes or assessments for local improvements.
Lien of judgment of assessment, §15.2-2411.
Taxes paid on delinquent real estate, §58.1-3974.
Telephone solicitation sales.
Payments, tender of, §59.1-21.5.
Time-shares, §55-381.
Owners' association.
Lien for assessment, §55-370.
Protection of lienholder, §55-389.
Purchaser's rights under developer's foreclosure, §55-388.
Termination of certain time-shares, §55-373.
Torts.
Infant, personal injury to.
Lien for expenses in attempt to cure infant of injuries, §8.01-36.
Town's lien against real estate, §15.2-104.
Transient lodging place keepers, §43-31.
Appeals, §43-36.
Enforcement, §43-34.
Personal property sales, §43-37.
Distribution of proceeds, §43-39.
Subsequent payments of surplus proceeds, §43-40.
Withdrawal from sale upon payment of charges, §43-38.
Validity, §43-35.
Transportation company employee or supplier liens, §43-24.
Assignees' rights, §43-26.
Enforcement, §43-25.
Perfection, §43-25.
Trash or garbage removed from owners property.
Cost of removal by locality, §15.2-901.
Trust funds held by bank or trust company.
Securities set apart, §6.2-1005.
Trusts.
Advancement for protection of trust.
Lien to secure reimbursement, §64.2-762.
Trusts of real property.
Attachment, §55-17.1.
Unclaimed property.
Sales to extinguish, §55-210.18.
Unemployment compensation.
Employer taxation.
Collection, §60.2-523.
Unpaid purchase money.
Limitation of actions, §8.01-241.
Extension of limitation form, §8.01-241.1.
Unpaid rates, rents, fees or charges for use of revenue-producing undertaking, §15.2-2605.
Vehicle keepers.
Appeals, §43-36.
Validity, §43-35.
Vendor's liens.
Deed form, §55-48.
Equitable liens, §55-53.
Release, §55-66.3

LIENS —Cont'd
Vessels constituting obstruction or hazard to lawful use of water.
Cost of locality for removal, §15.2-909.
Warehouseman's lien, §8.7-209.
Enforcement, §8.7-210.
Water or sewer charges.
Certain counties, §15.2-2118.
Enforcement, §15.2-2120.
Fees and charges for sewer service, §§15.2-2119, 15.2-5139.
Waters of the state.
Oil discharges.
Security for payment of damages, §62.1-44.34:20.
Wharves, piers, etc., constituting obstruction or hazard to lawful use of water.
Cost of locality for removal, repair, etc., §15.2-909.
Wireless service authorities.
Rates and charges, §15.2-5431.27.
Workers' compensation.
Third party suit.
Settlement proceeds or verdict in, §65.2-309.
Uninsured or underinsured motorist benefits.
Lien of employer, §65.2-309.1.

LIEUTENANT GOVERNOR.
Age requirement, VA Const Art V §14.
Arrest.
Privilege from, §§30-4, 30-6.
Civil arrest, §§8.01-327.1, 8.01-327.2.
Qualifications of privilege, §30-7.
Compelling attendance as witness.
Prior court permission required, §8.01-407.
Compensation, VA Const Art V §14.
Discharge of duties when office vacant, §24.2-212.
Disclosure statement.
Filing, time, form, §§2.2-3114, 2.2-3117.
Duties, VA Const Art V §14.
Election, §24.2-210, VA Const Art V §13.
Absentee ballot applications.
Early absentee ballot, §24.2-702.
Abstract of votes, §24.2-675.
Certificate of election, §24.2-680.
Economic interest statement as requirement of candidate, §24.2-502.
Independent candidates' petition of candidacy.
Number of signatures required, §24.2-506.
Primary candidates' filings to be made, §24.2-522.
Primary candidates' payment of fees, §24.2-524.
Primary candidates' petition of candidacy.
Number of signatures required, §24.2-521.
Election contests, §24.2-804.
Primaries for statewide office, §24.2-805.
Freedom of information act.
Exclusions from chapter.
Closed meetings, §2.2-3705.1.
Working papers and correspondence, §2.2-3705.7.
Governor's office vacant or governor disabled.
Discharge of duties, §24.2-211.
Impeachment, VA Const Art IV §17.
Jury service.
Automatic exemption, §8.01-341.
Motor vehicles.
Special license plates, §46.2-736.1.
Oaths, US Const Art VI, Amd 14.
President of the senate, VA Const Art V §14.
Privilege.
Proceedings while general assembly is in session, §30-1.

LIEUTENANT GOVERNOR —Cont'd
Qualifications, VA Const Art V §13.
Succession to office of governor, §24.2-211, VA Const Art V §16.
Term, VA Const Art V §13.
Vacancy in office of lieutenant governor.
Discharge of duties, §24.2-212.
Witness duty.
Privilege from, §30-6.

LIFE, ACCIDENT AND SICKNESS INSURANCE GUARANTY ASSOCIATION, §§38.2-1700 to 38.2-1721.
Accounts, §38.2-1702.
Advertising funds, prohibition against, §38.2-1715.
Amendments to plan of operation, §38.2-1706.
Applicability of chapter, §38.2-1700.
Assessments, §38.2-1705.
Board of directors, §38.2-1703.
Certificates of contribution.
Issuance, §38.2-1705.
Tax write-offs, §38.2-1709.
Coverage provided, §38.2-1700.
Creation, §38.2-1702.
Creditor of impaired or insolvent insurer, association deemed, §38.2-1710.
Default judgments, reopening, §38.2-1714.
Definitions, §38.2-1701.
Detection and prevention of insolvencies, §38.2-1708.
Directors, §38.2-1703.
Disclosures to policy or contract owners, §38.2-1715.
Distribution and disbursement of assets, §38.2-1710.
Duties, §38.2-1704.
State corporation commission, §38.2-1707.
Examination of association, §38.2-1711.
Exemptions from coverage, §38.2-1700.
Exemptions from taxation, §38.2-1712.
Fines and penalties from violations of insurance title.
Credit to, §38.2-225.
Health insurance account, §38.2-1702.
Immunity, §38.2-1713.
Insolvencies, detection and prevention, §38.2-1708.
Instruction of chapter, §38.2-1710.
Investment and obligations by insurers, §38.2-1442.
Life insurance and annuity account, §38.2-1702.
Maximum amounts covered, §38.2-1700.
Member assessments, §38.2-1705.
Memberships, §38.2-1702.
Plan of operation, §38.2-1706.
Powers, §38.2-1704.
State corporation commission, §38.2-1707.
Purposes of chapter, §38.2-1700.
Records of negotiations and meetings, §38.2-1710.
Refund of assessments, §38.2-1705.
Report annually, §38.2-1711.
Safety fund, §§38.2-1716 to 38.2-1721.
State corporation commission duties and powers, §38.2-1707.
Stay of proceedings, §38.2-1714.
Summary document for distribution to policy owners, §38.2-1715.
Supervision, §38.2-1702.
Tax exemptions, §38.2-1712.

LIFE, ACCIDENT AND SICKNESS INSURANCE GUARANTY ASSOCIATION —Cont'd
Tax write-offs of certificates of contributions, §38.2-1709.

LIFE AND HEALTH INSURANCE AGENTS OR HEALTH AGENTS.
Continuing education, §§38.2-1866 to 38.2-1874.
Dental plan organizations.
Licensing, §38.2-6112.
License required to sell health insurance, §38.2-1828.
Licensing, examination required, §38.2-1815.
Licensing of insurance agents generally, §§38.2-1822 to 38.2-1836.1.
Resident life and annuities agent.
Licensing, examination required, §38.2-1815.
Temporary licenses and appointments, §38.2-1830.

LIFE AND HEALTH INSURANCE CONSULTANTS.
Licensing of consultants generally, §§38.2-1837 to 38.2-1845.

LIFE ESTATES.
Commutation in money of life estate.
Persons with disability, §55-276.
Decedents' estates, §64.2-527.
Default of tenant not to prejudice remainderman, §55-8.
Disposal power not to defeat remainder, §55-7.
Disposition of estates in property, §§8.01-94, 8.01-95.
Ejectment.
General provisions, §§8.01-131 to 8.01-165.
See EJECTMENT.
Emblements, §55-252.
Improvements to land.
General provisions, §§8.01-166 to 8.01-178.
See IMPROVEMENTS TO LAND.
Reimbursement of tenant for life for improvements, §8.01-173.
Interests on money or estates.
Annuity table, §55-269.1.
Calculation rules, §55-270.
Disabled persons, §55-276.
Example, §55-271.
Life estates, certain, §55-277.
Makehamized mortality table, §55-274.
Uniform seniority table, §55-272.1.
Calculations under, §55-273.
Real property tax on life tenant's interest.
Remainder held by United States, §58.1-3223.
Recovery at death of life tenant of taxes paid, §55-25.
Surrender of tenant not to prejudice remainderman, §55-8.
Valuation of decedent's property, §64.2-305.
Works on watercourses.
Forfeiture by tenant of works damaged or destroyed, §62.1-126.

LIFE EXPECTANCY TABLES, §8.01-419.

LIFE IMPRISONMENT.
Class 1 or class 2 felonies, punishment, §18.2-10.
Violent felony sexual assault.
Punishment upon conviction of subsequent assault, §18.2-67.5:3.

LIFE INSURANCE, §§38.2-3100 to 38.2-3144.
Abandonment of funds presumption, §55-210.4:01.
Demutualization proceeds, §55-210.4:2.
Access to benefits.
Retained asset accounts, §§38.2-3117.1 to 38.2-3117.4.
Age misstatement, §38.2-3108.
Group life insurance, §38.2-3329.
Individual life insurance, §38.2-3306.
Industrial life insurance, §38.2-3346.
Amount of proceeds limited in certain cases, §38.2-3123.
Annulment of marriage.
Revocation of death benefits by annulment, §20-111.1.
Application requirements, §38.2-302.
Assignees rights protected, §38.2-3125.
Assignment, §38.2-3111.
Group life insurance, §38.2-3337.
Backdating policies more than six months, §38.2-3104.
Beneficiaries.
Retained asset accounts, §§38.2-3117.1 to 38.2-3117.4.
Rights protected, §38.2-3125.
Testamentary trustees, designation as, §38.2-3112.
Change of beneficiary forms.
Required information, §55-210.4:01.
Child support determination.
Maintaining existing policy, designating children as beneficiaries, §20-108.1.
Claims against insured, proceeds payable to others free of, §38.2-3122.
Class of insurance companies may be licensed to write, §38.2-135.
Contestability period, §38.2-3107.
Excluded or restricted coverage, inapplicability, §38.2-3110.
Group life insurance, §38.2-3326.
Individual life policies, §38.2-3305.
Industrial life insurance, §38.2-3345.
Mutual assessment policies, §38.2-3912.
Reinstated policy, running of period not affected, §38.2-3109.
Conversion or exchange, backdating, §38.2-3104.
Cooperative nonprofit life benefit companies, §§38.2-3800 to 38.2-3818.
Credit insurance, §§38.2-3717 to 38.2-3738.
Defined, §38.2-103.
Creditor's claims.
Proceeds payable to other free of, §38.2-3122.
Protection of insurers from, §38.2-3124.
Death penalty, execution not grounds of defense, §38.2-3106.
Decedents' estates.
Slayer's act.
Proceeds of insurance, payment by insurance company or obligor, §64.2-2508.
Defined, §38.2-102.
Delivery of individual life insurance policies, §38.2-3301.1.
Discharge of claim upon payment, §38.2-321.
Disclosures, failure to make, §38.2-514.
Discrimination.
Prohibited, §38.2-508.2.
Unfair discrimination as to armed forces members, §38.2-508.1.
Unfair discrimination generally, §38.2-508.

LIFE INSURANCE —Cont'd
Divorce.
Revocation of death benefits by divorce from bond of matrimony, §20-111.1.
Educational loan provisions, §38.2-3113.3.
Excluded coverage.
Incontestability not applicable, §38.2-3110.
Filing of policy forms with state corporation commission required, §38.2-316.
Forms of insurance authorized, §38.2-3100.1.
Fraudulent procurement of policy, §38.2-3103.
Funding agreements, §38.2-3100.2.
Grace period.
Group life insurance.
Premium payment, §38.2-3325.
Individual life insurance.
Premium payments, §38.2-3303.
Industrial life insurance.
Premium payment, §38.2-3343.
Group insurance program for public officers and employees, §§51.1-500 to 51.1-514.
See PUBLIC OFFICERS AND EMPLOYEES.
Group life insurance, §§38.2-3318.1 to 38.2-3339.
Additional persons becoming eligible, §38.2-3335.
Age misstatement, §38.2-3329.
Assignment, §38.2-3337.
Benefits, payment of, §38.2-3330.
Certificates issued to policyholder, §38.2-3331.
Coverage.
Dependent children and children with disabilities, §38.2-3323.
Lives covered, §38.2-3322.2.
Minor dependent children, §38.2-3323.
Spouses, §38.2-3323.
Death after termination of group insurance and before issuance of individual policy, §38.2-3334.
Disabilities, dependent children with, §38.2-3323.
Eligibility of persons subsequently becoming member of group or class, §38.2-3335.
Entire contract included in policies, §38.2-3327.
Evidence of individual insurability, §38.2-3328.
Exemption from legal process, §38.2-3339.
Grace period.
Premium payment, §38.2-3325.
Incontestability provisions, §38.2-3326.
Individual certificates, §38.2-3331.
Individual insurability, evidence of, §38.2-3328.
Individual life insurance.
Death after termination of group insurance and before issuance of individual policy, §38.2-3334.
Right upon termination of employment or membership, §38.2-3332.
Right upon termination of group policy or termination of class of insured persons, §38.2-3333.
Legal process, exemption of policies from, §38.2-3339.
Limits, §38.2-3319.1.
Minor dependent children, coverages, §38.2-3323.
Misstatement of age, §38.2-3329.
Other jurisdictions, provisions required, §38.2-3336.
Out-of-state issuance of policies, §38.2-3320.1.
Payment of benefits, §38.2-3330.
Prohibited provisions, §38.2-3338.
Provisions required by other jurisdictions, §38.2-3336.
Record.
Review, §38.2-3319.2.

LIFE INSURANCE —Cont'd
Group life insurance —Cont'd
Regulations, §38.2-3322.1.
Representations, statements deemed, §38.2-3327.
Requirements, §38.2-3318.1.
Persons marketing group life insurance, §38.2-3321.1.
Standard provisions, §38.2-3324.
Requirements for those marketing group life insurance, §38.2-3321.1.
Spouses, coverages, §38.2-3323.
Standard provisions required, §38.2-3324.
Statements deemed representations, §38.2-3327.
Termination of employment or membership.
Right to individual policies, §38.2-3332.
Termination of policy or elimination of class of insured persons.
Death after termination of group insurance and before issuance of individual policy, §38.2-3334.
Right to individual policy, §38.2-3333.
Variable life insurance.
Certificates issued pursuant to, §38.2-3114.
Guaranty associations.
Virginia life, accident and sickness insurance guaranty association, §§38.2-1700 to 38.2-1721.
See LIFE, ACCIDENT AND SICKNESS INSURANCE GUARANTY ASSOCIATION.
Guardians.
Minor's estate.
Powers of guardian, §64.2-1805.
HIV testing.
Consent.
Application of provisions, §32.1-37.2.
Husband or wife effecting insurance contract upon each other, §38.2-302.
Group insurance coverages, §38.2-3323.
Hybrid retirement program.
Disability program for participants.
Life and accident insurance during disability absences, §51.1-1174.
Incontestability provisions, §38.2-3107.
Extended or restricted policy, inapplicability of provisions, §38.2-3110.
Group life insurance, §38.2-3326.
Individual life insurance, §38.2-3305.
Industrial life insurance, §38.2-3345.
Mutual assessment policies, §38.2-3912.
Reinstated policy, contestability, §38.2-3109.
Individual life insurance, §§38.2-3300 to 38.2-3317.
Age misstatement, §38.2-3306.
Cash surrender values, §38.2-3309.
Default in premium payment.
Reinstatement, §38.2-3311.
Defined, §38.2-3300.
Delivery of policies, §38.2-3301.1.
Entire contract, policy constitutes, §38.2-3304.
Examination of policy, ten-day right, §38.2-3301.
Exceptions to provisions, §38.2-3300.
Grace period, premium payments, §38.2-3303.
Group life insurance.
Death after termination of group insurance and before issuance of individual policy, §38.2-3334.
Right upon termination of employment or membership, §38.2-3332.
Right upon termination of group policy or termination of class of insured persons, §38.2-3333.

LIFE INSURANCE —Cont'd
Individual life insurance —Cont'd
How premiums payable, §38.2-3302.
Incontestability provisions, §38.2-3305.
Installment payment of proceeds, table of, §38.2-3313.
Interest rates.
Policy loans, §38.2-3308.
Loans, §38.2-3308.
Table of loan values, §38.2-3310.
Misstatement of age, §38.2-3306.
More favorable terms provided, §38.2-3315.
Nature and form of policy to be accurately and briefly described, §38.2-3314.
Nonforfeiture benefits, §38.2-3309.
Other jurisdictions, provisions required by, §38.2-3317.
Participation in surplus, §38.2-3307.
Policy constitutes entire contract, §38.2-3304.
Premium payments, §38.2-3302.
Grace period, §38.2-3303.
Prohibited provisions, §38.2-3316.
Provisions required by other jurisdictions, §38.2-3317.
Reinstatement, §38.2-3311.
Representations, statements deemed, §38.2-3304.
Requirements of policies, §38.2-3300.
Settlement, §38.2-3312.
Statements deemed representations, §38.2-3304.
Surplus, participation in, §38.2-3307.
Table of installment payments, §38.2-3313.
Table of values and options, §38.2-3310.
Ten-day right to examine policy, §38.2-3301.
Title, §38.2-3314.
Variations for certain forms of policies, §38.2-3315.
Industrial life insurance, §§38.2-3340 to 38.2-3354.
Age misstatement, §38.2-3346.
Cash surrender value, §38.2-3347.
Defined, §§38.2-104, 38.2-3340.
Entire contract in policy and application, §38.2-3344.
Examination of policy, ten-day right, §38.2-3342.
Grace period.
Premium payment, §38.2-3343.
Incontestability provisions, §38.2-3345.
Misstatement of age, §38.2-3346.
Nature and form of policy, description, §38.2-3351.
Nonforfeiture benefits, §38.2-3347.
Table of nonforfeiture options, §38.2-3349.
Other jurisdictions, provisions required, §38.2-3353.
Policies issued or granted in excess of nonforfeiture provisions.
Inapplicability of provisions to, §38.2-3352.
Prohibited provisions, §38.2-3354.
Provisions not required in certain policies, §38.2-3352.
Provisions required by other jurisdictions, §38.2-3353.
Reinstatement, §38.2-3348.
Representations, statements deemed, §38.2-3344.
Required standard provisions, §38.2-3341.
Settlement, §38.2-3350.
Standard nonforfeiture provisions.
Adjusted premiums, §38.2-3208.
Benefits and cash surrender values in policies issued prior to March 17, 1948, §38.2-3201.
Operative date for calculating adjusted premiums, §38.2-3216.
Standard provisions required, §38.2-3341.

LIFE INSURANCE —Cont'd
Industrial life insurance —Cont'd
Statements deemed representation, §38.2-3344.
Table of nonforfeiture options, §38.2-3349.
Ten-day right to examine policy, §38.2-3342.
Title, §38.2-3351.
Information and privacy protection.
Applicability of chapter, §38.2-601.
Generally, §§38.2-600 to 38.2-620.
See INSURANCE INFORMATION AND PRIVACY PROTECTION.
Insurable interest required, §38.2-301.
Insurance consultants.
License examination requirement.
Life and health insurance consultants, §38.2-1838.
Interest on judgment to recover proceeds, §38.2-3115.
Interest rates.
Individual life insurance policy loans, §38.2-3308.
Interstate insurance product regulation compact, §§38.2-6200, 38.2-6201.
Investments of insurers allocated to separate accounts.
Modified guaranteed life insurance, §38.2-1443.1.
Variable life insurance, §38.2-1443.
Judgment interest in action to recover proceeds, §38.2-3115.
Lapse or pending lapse of policy.
Notice, §38.2-232.
Legal reserve insurers, §38.2-3101.
Limits on proceeds in certain cases, §38.2-3123.
Loans, §38.2-1431.
Individual life insurance, §38.2-3308.
Table of loan values, §38.2-3310.
Loan value in policies.
Standard nonforfeiture provisions, §§38.2-3217, 38.2-3218.
Local government employees and retirees.
Locality providing group insurance program, §15.2-1517.
Local government group self-insurance pools, §§15.2-2700 to 15.2-2709.
Long-term care insurance.
Disclosure, life insurance policies, §38.2-5207.1.
Medicaid.
Consideration in making eligibility determinations, §32.1-325.01.
Minors.
Contract upon life or pertaining to minor, §38.2-302.
Group life insurance.
Dependent children and children with disabilities, §38.2-3323.
When contracts with respect to may be made, §38.2-3105.
Misstatement of age, §38.2-3108.
Group life insurance, §38.2-3329.
Individual life insurance, §38.2-3306.
Industrial life insurance, §38.2-3346.
Modified guaranteed life insurance.
Authority to issue, §38.2-3113.1.
Defined, §38.2-105.1.
Investments of insurers allocated to separate accounts, §38.2-1443.1.
Separate accounts, §38.2-3113.1.
Statements required, regulations issued, approval expenses, §38.2-3113.1.
Mutual assessment insurers, §§38.2-3900 to 38.2-3923.

LIFE INSURANCE —Cont'd
National Guard.
Rights and benefits on being called to active duty, §44-102.1.
Notice of lapse or pending lapse of policy, §38.2-232.
Payment discharges insurer, §38.2-321.
Payment in form of retained asset account, §§38.2-3117.1 to 38.2-3117.4.
Payment of proceeds to other free of claims against insured, §38.2-3122.
Persons not in insurable condition.
Fraudulent procurement of policy, §38.2-3103.
Policies and contracts of insurance generally, §§38.2-300 to 38.2-326.
See INSURANCE POLICIES AND CONTRACTS.
Policy loans by domestic insurers, §38.2-1431.
Preneed funeral contracts.
Life insurance or annuity contracts used to fund.
Requirements, §38.2-3100.3.
Proceed amount limited, §38.2-3123.
Proceeds payable to others free of claims against insured, §38.2-3122.
Prohibited provisions.
Individual life insurance, §38.2-3316.
State corporation commission to issue rules, §38.2-3117.
Protection of insurers from creditor's claims, §38.2-3124.
Public officers and employees.
Military duty leaves of absence.
Additional life insurance benefits, §44-93.1.
Public officers' and employees' group insurance program, §§51.1-500 to 51.1-514.
See PUBLIC OFFICERS AND EMPLOYEES.
Readability of policies, standards established by state corporation commission, §38.2-3116.
Rebates, §38.2-509.
Reciprocal states residence.
Domestic insurers prohibited from insuring lives and persons of, §38.2-3101.
Reinstatement.
Individual life insurance, §38.2-3311.
Industrial life insurance, §38.2-3348.
Reserves, §§38.2-3126 to 38.2-3144.
Acceptance of valuation of another state, §38.2-3127.
Actuarial analysis of reserves and assets.
Supporting reserves, §38.2-3127.1.
Actuarial opinion of reserves, §38.2-3127.1.
Annual valuation, §38.2-3126.
Assessment against insurers whose policies are valued, §38.2-3143.
Calendar year statutory valuation interest rates, §38.2-3133.
Weighting factors, §38.2-3134.
Decrease of valuation standards higher than minimum, §38.2-3128.
Foreign or alien insurers, valuation, §38.2-3127.
Fraternal benefit societies.
Inapplicability of article, §38.2-3144.
Industrial sick benefit insurance.
Inapplicability of article, §38.2-3144.
Interest rates.
Calendar year statutory valuation interest rates, §38.2-3133.
Weighting factors, §38.2-3134.
Reference interest rates, §38.2-3135.
Alternative method, §38.2-3136.
Legal reserve insurers, §38.2-3101.

LIFE INSURANCE —Cont'd
Reserves —Cont'd
Minimum reserve, §38.2-3139.
Minimum valuation standards, §§38.2-3129, 38.2-3130.
Computation, §38.2-3132.
Optional reserve calculation, §38.2-3140.
Reference interest rates, §38.2-3135.
Alternative method, §38.2-3136.
Reserve calculation, §38.2-3141.
Indeterminate premium plans, §38.2-3142.
Reserve valuation methods, §38.2-3137.
Valuation annually, §38.2-3126.
Valuation method.
Reserve method, §38.2-3137.
Valuation of another state, acceptance, §38.2-3127.
Valuation standards.
Decrease of standards higher than minimum, §38.2-3128.
Minimum standards, §§38.2-3129, 38.2-3130.
Computation, §38.2-3132.
Weighting factors.
Calendar year statutory valuation interest rates, §38.2-3134.
Restated policy.
Contestability period not affected, §38.2-3109.
Restricted coverage.
Incontestability not applicable, §38.2-3110.
Retained asset accounts, §§38.2-3117.1 to 38.2-3117.4.
Definitions, §38.2-3117.1.
Disclosures to beneficiary prior to selection of option, §38.2-3117.4.
Information to beneficiary describing settlement options, §38.2-3117.2.
Supplemental contract required, §38.2-3117.3.
Rights of beneficiaries and assignees protected, §38.2-3125.
Scope of chapter, §38.2-3100.
Separate accounts.
Modified guaranteed life insurance, §38.2-3113.1.
Variable life insurance, §38.2-3113.
Settlement.
Individual life insurance, §38.2-3312.
Industrial life insurance, §38.2-3350.
Simplification of policies, standards established by state corporation commission, §38.2-3116.
Slayer's act.
Proceeds of insurance, payment by company or obligor, §64.2-2508.
Spendthrift trust created under policies, §38.2-3118.
Limitation as to proportionate part of proceeds, §38.2-3119.
Segregation of proceeds not required, §38.2-3121.
Standard nonforfeiture provisions, §§38.2-3200 to 38.2-3229.
Additional benefits disregarded, §38.2-3228.
Adjusted premiums, calculation, §§38.2-3205, 38.2-3209.
Industrial policies, §38.2-3208.
Tables used, §38.2-3206.
Use of new mortality table, §38.2-3207.
Applicability of provisions, §38.2-3219.
Basis of minimum values, §38.2-3221.
Benefits and policies issued prior to March 17, 1948, §38.2-3200.
Calculation of adjusted premiums, §§38.2-3205, 38.2-3209.
Industrial policies, §38.2-3208.

LIFE INSURANCE —Cont'd
Standard nonforfeiture provisions —Cont'd
Calculation of adjusted premiums —Cont'd
New mortality table, use of, §38.2-3207.
Tables used, §38.2-3206.
Calculation of cash surrender value, §38.2-3223.
Maturity date, §38.2-3225.
Calculation of paid-up annuity benefits, §38.2-3224.
Maturity date, §38.2-3225.
Cash surrender value.
Calculation, §38.2-3223.
Maturity date, §38.2-3225.
Default in premium payments, §38.2-3203.
Individual life policies, §38.2-3309.
Industrial life insurance, §38.2-3347.
Insurance providing future premium determination, §38.2-3210.
Policies issued on or after January 1, 1986, §38.2-3212.
Policies issued prior to March 17, 1948, §38.2-3200.
Required provisions in policies, §38.2-3202.
Computation of present value, §38.2-3222.
Date provisions effective, §38.2-3229.
Date sections become operative, §38.2-3214.
Default in premium payments.
Cash surrender value, §38.2-3203.
Present value of paid-up nonforfeiture benefits, §38.2-3204.
Disclosure of limited death benefits, §38.2-3226.
Effective date of provisions, §38.2-3229.
Exemptions from application of certain sections, §38.2-3213.
Future premium determination, §38.2-3210.
Inapplicability of provisions, §38.2-3219.
Inclusion of lapse of time considerations, §38.2-3227.
Individual life insurance, §38.2-3309.
Industrial life insurance, §38.2-3347.
Adjusted premiums, §38.2-3208.
Benefits and cash surrender values in policies issued prior to March 17, 1948, §38.2-3201.
Operative date for calculating adjusted premiums, §38.2-3216.
Table of nonforfeiture provisions, §38.2-3349.
Lapse in time, factor in calculation, §38.2-3211.
Lapse of time, inclusion, §38.2-3227.
Limited death benefits disclosure, §38.2-3226.
Loan value in policies, §§38.2-3217, 38.2-3218.
Maturity date, §38.2-3225.
Minimum values, §38.2-3221.
Mortality table.
Operative date for use of new table, §38.2-3215.
Use of new table in adjusted premiums, §38.2-3207.
Operative date, §38.2-3214.
Industrial policies, calculation of adjusted premiums, §38.2-3216.
Use of new mortality table, §38.2-3215.
Other factors in calculations, §38.2-3211.
Paid up annuity benefits.
Calculation, §38.2-3224.
Calculation maturity date, §38.2-3225.
Paid-up nonforfeiture benefits.
Insurance providing future premium determination, §38.2-3210.
Present value under fault, §38.2-3204.
Required policy provisions, §38.2-3202.
Payment of fractional premiums, factors in calculations, §38.2-3211.

LIFE INSURANCE —Cont'd
Standard nonforfeiture provisions —Cont'd
Policies issued on or after January 1, 1986, §38.2-3212.
Present value, computation, §38.2-3222.
Proration of values, §38.2-3228.
Provisions required, §38.2-3202.
Required policy provisions, §38.2-3202.
Requirements for nonforfeiture, §38.2-3220.
Standards for policies issued by state corporation commission, §38.2-3117.
Suicide, grounds of defense, §38.2-3106.
Ten-day right to examine policy.
Individual life insurance, §38.2-3301.
Industrial life insurance, §38.2-3342.
Testamentary trustees, designation as beneficiary, §38.2-3112.
Title.
Individual life insurance, §38.2-3314.
Unclaimed property, disposition of, §55-210.4:01.
Demutualization proceeds, §55-210.4:2.
Unfair insurance trade practices generally, §§38.2-500 to 38.2-518.
See INSURANCE, UNFAIR TRADE PRACTICES.
University of Virginia.
Medical center employees.
Group life, accidental death and dismemberment, and disability policies, §2.2-2817.2.
Variable life insurance.
Authority to issue, §38.2-3113.
Defined, §38.2-105.
Group variable life insurance.
Certificates issued pursuant to, §38.2-3114.
Investments of insurers allocated to separate accounts, §38.2-1443.
Separate accounts, §38.2-3113.
Special voting rights and procedures for owners, §38.2-3113.
Statements required, §38.2-3114.
Viatical settlement broker licensing, §§38.2-1865.1 to 38.2-1865.5.
Viatical settlements generally, §§38.2-6000 to 38.2-6016.
See VIATICAL SETTLEMENTS.
Virginia retirement system group insurance program, §§51.1-500 to 51.1-514.
See PUBLIC OFFICERS AND EMPLOYEES.
Water and waste authorities.
Insurance for employees, §15.2-5117.
Wireless service authorities.
Insurance for employees, §15.2-5431.13.

LIFE PRESERVERS.
Personal watercraft, required to operate, §29.1-748.

LIFESAVING CREWS OR LIFESAVING ORGANIZATIONS.
Counties, cities or towns.
Gifts or donations to volunteer and nonprofit organizations, §15.2-953.
Emergency management, §§44-146.13 to 44-146.28.
See EMERGENCY MANAGEMENT.
Emergency medical services, §§32.1-111.1 to 32.1-111.16.
See EMERGENCY MEDICAL SERVICES.
Rescue squads.
See RESCUE SQUADS.

LIFESAVING CREWS OR LIFESAVING ORGANIZATIONS —Cont'd
Workers' compensation.
Average weekly wage of volunteer member, §65.2-101.
Coverage for first responders off duty during state of emergency, §65.2-104.
Employee defined as including volunteer member, §65.2-101.

LIFE-SHARING COMMUNITIES, §63.2-1808.1.

LIFE SUSTAINING PROCEDURES.
Anatomical gifts.
Advance health care directive, effect of gift, §32.1-291.21.
Living wills generally, §§54.1-2981 to 54.1-2993.
See LIVING WILLS.

LIFE TENANCIES.
See LIFE ESTATES.

LIFT BLOCKS TO MODIFY FRONT-END SUSPENSION, §46.2-1064.

LIFTING AND HAULING DEVICES.
Occupational safety and health.
Rules and regulations, §40.1-44.1.

LIGHT COMPANIES.
Articles of incorporation.
Conducting business as public service company, statement required, §13.1-620.
Consumer utility taxes, §§58.1-3814 to 58.1-3816.2.
Damage or trespass to, §18.2-162.
Diverting service, §§8.01-44.7, 18.2-163.
Estimated tax, §§58.1-2640 to 58.1-2651.
See PUBLIC SERVICE CORPORATION TAXATION.
License tax by county, city or town, §58.1-3731.
License tax generally, §§58.1-2620 to 58.1-2635.
See PUBLIC SERVICE CORPORATION TAXATION.
Metering service, tampering with, §§8.01-44.7, 18.2-163.
Meters.
Good working condition requirements, §56-245.1.
Pipelines, §§56-257 to 56-260.1.
Public service companies.
Generally, §§56-1 to 56-46.3.
See PUBLIC SERVICE COMPANIES.
Public utilities.
Generally, §§56-232 to 56-265.
See PUBLIC UTILITIES.
Special regulatory revenue tax, §§58.1-2660 to 58.1-2665.
Use of city or town property, consent required, VA Const Art VII §8.

LIGHT COMPANY LICENSE TAX.
Estimated tax, §§58.1-2640 to 58.1-2651.
See PUBLIC SERVICE CORPORATION TAXATION.
Generally, §§58.1-2620 to 58.1-2635.
See PUBLIC SERVICE CORPORATION TAXATION.

LIGHTHOUSE KEEPERS.
Militia duty exemption, §44-5.

LIGHTHOUSES.
Special license plates celebrating Virginia lighthouses, §46.2-749.31.

LIGHTING IN COAL MINES.
Underground coal mines, §§45.1-161.171 to 45.1-161.173.

LIGHTING NEAR CERTAIN FACILITIES.
Locality regulating outdoor lighting, §15.2-920.

LIGHTING OF BUILDINGS.
City or town powers, §15.2-1117.
County executive form of government.
Ordinances providing, §15.2-504.1.
County manager plan of government, §15.2-742.

LIGHTING OF PUBLIC RIGHTS-OF-WAY.
Counties, §15.2-2020.

LIGHT POLLUTION.
Outdoor lighting, locality regulating near certain facilities, §15.2-920.

LIGHTS AND TURN SIGNALS, MOTOR VEHICLES.
All-terrain vehicles, §46.2-1016.
Ambulances.
Animals caused to panic by lights or spotlights, §18.2-509.
Auxiliary lights, §46.2-1028.
Flashing amber warning lights, §46.2-1025.
Flashing red or red and white warning lights, §§46.2-1023, 46.2-1024.
Emergency vehicle exemption from traffic regulations.
When exemption applicable, §46.2-920.
Antique motor vehicles.
Acetylene lights, §46.2-1036.
Bicycles.
Headlights, §46.2-1015.
Boats, range lights.
Anchoring on range of, §62.1-189.
Contractors.
Flashing amber warning lights, §46.2-1025.
Emergency flashing lights.
Emergency, accident or mechanical breakdown on highway, §46.2-888.
Emergency vehicles.
Auxiliary lights, §46.2-1028.
Environmental quality department vehicles.
Flashing red or red and white warning lights, §46.2-1023.
Fine schedule, VA SCt Rule 3B:2.
Firefighting apparatus.
Auxiliary lights, §46.2-1028.
Flashing amber warning lights, §46.2-1025.
Flashing red or red and white warning lights, §46.2-1023.
Forest wardens vehicles.
Flashing red or red and white warning lights, §46.2-1023.
Funeral procession escort vehicles.
Flashing amber warning lights, §46.2-1025.
Generally, §§46.2-1010 to 46.2-1040.
See MOTOR VEHICLE EQUIPMENT.
Go-carts, §46.2-1016.
Maximum fine for violating Title 46.2, §46.2-113.
Minibikes, §46.2-1016.
Mopeds, §46.2-1015.
Motor vehicles equipment generally, §§46.2-1010 to 46.2-1040.
See MOTOR VEHICLE EQUIPMENT.
Municipal safety officers.
Flashing amber warning lights, §46.2-1025.
Neighborhood watch groups.
Patrol vehicles.
Flashing amber warning lights, §46.2-1025.
Public school transportation.
Warning lights, §46.2-1090.1.

LIGHTS AND TURN SIGNALS, MOTOR VEHICLES —Cont'd
Rescue squads.
Auxiliary lights, §46.2-1028.
Flashing amber warning lights, §46.2-1025.
Flashing red or red and white warning lights, §46.2-1023.
School buses.
Warning lights, §22.1-183.
Security services.
Flashing amber warning lights, §46.2-1025.
Snowmobiles, §46.2-1016.
Snow-removal vehicles.
Flashing amber warning lights, §46.2-1025.
Towing vehicles.
Flashing amber warning lights, §46.2-1025.
Flashing high-intensity amber warning lights, §46.2-1026.
Trail bikes, §46.2-1016.
Transportation department vehicles.
Auxiliary lights, §46.2-1028.
Winter sports area vehicles, §8.01-227.15.

LIMITATION OF ACTIONS.
Abatement, revival and survival.
Suspension or tolling of statute of limitations, §8.01-229.
Abortion.
Attempts, §19.2-8.
Abuse and neglect of child.
When cause of action deemed to accrue, §8.01-249.
Abuse of process.
When cause of action deemed to accrue, §8.01-249.
Abutting landowners taxed or assessed for improvement.
Appeals, §15.2-2410.
Accountants.
Complaints against CPAs or CPA firms, time for filing, §54.1-4425.
Accrual of right of action, §8.01-230.
Actual innocence.
Petition for writ of actual innocence, VA SCt Rule 5:7B.
Administrators. See within this heading, "Fiduciaries."
Adoption.
Attempts, §19.2-8.
Final order not subject to attack after six months, §63.2-1216.
Adverse possession, §8.01-236.
Affirmative defense.
Bar raised in responsive pleading, §8.01-235.
Agricultural equipment warranties, §59.1-207.8.
Amended tax returns, §58.1-1823.
Amercement, §19.2-8.
Antitrust laws, §59.1-9.14.
Appeals.
Appraisement of estates.
Appeal from proceeding before clerk, §64.2-445.
Bill of review, §8.01-623.
Refusal, §8.01-671.
Curators.
Appeal from proceeding before clerk, §64.2-445.
Rehearing by supreme court, §19.2-325.
Time within which petition must be presented, §8.01-671.
Workers' compensation commission, §65.2-706.
Appraisement of estates.
Appeal from proceeding before clerk, §64.2-445.
Asbestos.
Asbestos injuries, §8.01-243.

LIMITATION OF ACTIONS —Cont'd
Asbestos —Cont'd
Removal of asbestos, §8.01-250.1.
Rule of actions, §8.01-249.
Assessment of taxes, §58.1-104.
Income tax, §58.1-312.
Taxpayer problem resolution program, §58.1-1818.
Waiver of time limitation, §58.1-101.
Assessment of omitted or additional state taxes, §58.1-220.
Assignments.
Avoidance of assignments without consideration or upon consideration of marriage, §8.01-253.
Attachment and garnishment.
Rehearing when judgment rendered on publication, §8.01-575.
Attempts to commit crime.
Abortion, §19.2-8.
Obtaining public assistance by fraud, §19.2-8.
Attorneys at law.
Licensing, practicing without authority, §19.2-8.
Bail and recognizance.
Contracts.
Personal actions based on contracts, §8.01-246.
Bank deposits and collections, §8.4-111.
Unauthorized signature or alteration.
Claims against bank, §8.4-406.
Bank franchise tax.
Criminal prosecutions, §19.2-8.
Banking and finance.
Bankruptcy and insolvency.
Time claims against insolvent bank barred, §6.2-923.
Money on deposit.
Bank or personal corporation doing banking business, §8.01-249.
Bequests.
Enforcement, §8.01-254.
Bill of review, §8.01-623.
Appeals.
Refusal, §8.01-671.
Bills of lading.
Limitations in bill of lading or tariff, §8.7-309.
Birth-related neurological injury compensation claims, §38.2-5013.
Tolling of statute by filing of claim, §38.2-5005.
Bonds issued by locality.
Contesting validity of proposed issue, §15.2-2627.
Judicial determination of validity, contesting, §15.2-2653.
Bonds, surety.
Fiduciaries, §8.01-245.
Bond validation proceeding appeals, §15.2-2656.
Breach of fiduciary duty, §8.01-245.
Breach of implied warranties on new homes, §55-70.1.
Breast implants, §8.01-249.
Building code violations.
Criminal prosecution, §§19.2-8, 36-106.
Business opportunity sales, §59.1-269.
Criminal prosecutions, §59.1-269.
Campaign finance disclosure, §24.2-953.
Catch-all provision, §8.01-248.
Cemeteries.
Actions for damages, §57-26.
Damage done to adjacent land, §57-26.
Child abuse and neglect.
When cause of action deemed to accrue, §8.01-249.
Childhood sexual abuse.
When cause of action deemed to accrue, §8.01-249.

LIMITATION OF ACTIONS —Cont'd
Children or minors.
Abuse and neglect of children.
When cause of action deemed to accrue, §8.01-249.
Desertion and nonsupport.
Limitation inapplicable to prosecution for desertion or nonsupport of wife or child, §19.2-8.
Disabilities which toll statute, §8.01-229.
Parent or guardian action against tort feasor, §8.01-243.
Wills, suit to impeach or establish, §64.2-448.
Saving in favor of infants, §64.2-448.
Cigarette tax.
Criminal prosecutions, §19.2-8.
Circuit court dockets.
Reinstatement of cases struck from docket, §8.01-335.
Striking of certain cases from docket, §8.01-335.
Civil rights actions, §8.01-243.
Claims against counties.
Appeal from disallowance, §15.2-1246.
Illegal or improper allowance, §15.2-1245.
Claims against decedents' estates.
Time within which statute not to run, §64.2-552.
Claims against dissolved corporations, §13.1-746.1.
Corporations.
Known claim, §13.1-746.
Nonprofit corporations, §§13.1-908, 13.1-908.1.
Claims against the state.
Fraudulent claims, §8.01-216.9.
Presenting claim for payment.
Allowance made by court of record, §2.2-815.
Referral to governor.
Claim not presented within time limits, §2.2-816.
Tort claims act, §§8.01-195.6, 8.01-195.7.
Clerk's office closed.
Last day of limitation period falling on, §1-210.
Code of Virginia.
Repeal of statute.
Effect of repeal of general acts by code, §1-4.
Collection of local taxes, §58.1-3940.
Waiver of time limitation on assessment, §58.1-3903.1.
Collection of state taxes, §58.1-1802.1.
Assessment of omitted taxes, §58.1-1812.
Conversion of trust taxes prosecutions, §58.1-1816.
Commissioner of accounts.
Time within which statute does not run, §64.2-552.
Committee. See within this heading, "Fiduciaries."
Commonwealth.
State. See within this heading, "State."
Computation of period.
Last day falling on Saturday, Sunday, legal holiday, clerk's office closed, §1-210.
Computer crimes.
Civil actions, §§8.01-40.1, 18.2-152.12.
Tort liability for injury to person or property, §8.01-40.1.
Computer information transactions, §59.1-508.5.
Condominiums.
Instruments.
Challenges to validity of amendments, §55-79.71.
Lien for assessments, §55-79.84.

LIMITATION OF ACTIONS —Cont'd
Condominiums —Cont'd
Warranty against structural defects.
Actions for breach of warranty, §55-79.79.
Conflicts of interest.
Criminal prosecution, §30-128.
Public officers and employees, §2.2-3125.
Constitution of Virginia.
Effect of revision or amendment of constitution, §1-4.
Consumer credit.
Revolving credit open accounts.
When cause of action deemed to accrue, §8.01-249.
Consumer protection.
Suspension of statute, §59.1-204.1.
Violations of act.
When cause of action deemed to accrue, §8.01-249.
Contracts, §8.01-246.
Accrual of right of action, §8.01-230.
Actions based on contracts, §8.01-246.
Actions of contracts governed by law of another state or country barred in Virginia, §8.01-247.
Gaming contracts, §11-15.
Generally, §8.01-246.
Highway contracts, §33.1-192.
Executed after June 30, 1976, §33.1-192.1.
New promise in writing, §8.01-229.
Personal actions based on contracts, §8.01-246.
Rescission.
When cause of action deemed to accrue, §8.01-249.
Revolving credit open accounts.
When cause of action deemed to accrue, §8.01-249.
Sale of goods.
Breach of contract, §8.2-725.
Limitations by agreements may be reduced to less than one year, §8.2-725.
Contribution.
When cause of action deemed to accrue, §8.01-249.
Controlled substances.
Damages.
Minors, liability of drug dealers, §8.01-227.7.
Conversion of trust taxes prosecutions, §58.1-1816.
Correction of erroneous tax assessments.
Local taxes.
Appeal by locality of commissioner's correction, §58.1-3982.
Application to commissioner of revenue, §58.1-3980.
Waiver of time limitation on assessment, §58.1-3903.1.
Application to court to correct, §58.1-3984.
Refunds of taxes erroneously paid, §58.1-3990.
State corporation commission assessments, §58.1-2030.
State taxes.
Application to circuit court for correction, §58.1-1825.
Filing of amended return, §58.1-1823.
Protective claim for refund, §58.1-1824.
Costs.
Criminal procedure.
Limitation of actions for recovery of court costs, §19.2-341.
Counterclaims.
Tolling, commencement of plaintiff's action, §8.01-233.

LIMITATION OF ACTIONS —Cont'd
Counties.
Claims against counties.
Appeal from disallowance, §15.2-1246.
Illegal or improper allowance, §15.2-1245.
Credit line deed of trust.
Limitation on enforcement when no date fixed for maturity, §8.01-242.
Creditors' suits.
Debts proved in creditors' suits, §8.01-229.
Credit services businesses, §59.1-335.11.
Criminal cases, §§19.2-8, 19.2-243.
Attempts to commit crime.
Abortion, §19.2-8.
Building code violations, §§19.2-8, 36-106.
Business opportunity sales, §59.1-269.
Conflicts of interest, §30-128.
Court costs.
Limitation of actions for recovery of court costs, §19.2-341.
Income tax, §19.2-8.
Individual taxpayers.
Failure or refusal to file return or making false statement in return, §58.1-348.
Lapse of time after finding of probable cause.
Limitation on prosecution, §19.2-243.
Murder or manslaughter.
No limitation, §19.2-8.1.
Obtaining public assistance by fraud, §19.2-8.
Penalties other than fines, §19.2-341.
Retail franchise violations, §13.1-569.
Securities violations, §13.1-520.
Taxes, §19.2-8.
Cross-claims.
Tolling, commencement of plaintiff's action, §8.01-233.
Curators.
Appeal from proceeding before clerk, §64.2-445.
Generally. See within this heading, "Fiduciaries."
Custodial trusts.
Actions against trustee, §64.2-915.
Damages.
Accrual of right of action, §8.01-230.
Suspension of limitations during criminal proceedings, §8.01-229.
Death.
Effect of death, §8.01-229.
Death by wrongful act, §8.01-244.
Improvements to land.
Damages arising out of defective or unsafe improvement, §8.01-250.
No action when deceased has compromised claim, §8.01-51.
Debts.
Creditors' suits, §8.01-229.
Devise for payment of debts, §8.01-229.
Decedents' estates.
Claims against.
Time within which statute not to run, §64.2-552.
Enforcement of bequests and legacies, §8.01-254.
Decrees pro confesso.
Setting aside for fraud, §8.01-428.
Deeds.
Objections to irregularities in advertising sales made by trustees under deeds of trust, §55-24.
Defamation, §8.01-247.1.
Default judgments.
Setting aside for fraud, §8.01-428.

LIMITATION OF ACTIONS —Cont'd
Defenses.
Bar of expiration of limitation period.
Raised only as affirmative defense in responsive pleading, §8.01-235.
Delinquent tax lands.
Waiver of time limitation on assessment, §58.1-3903.1.
Delinquent tax lands sales, §58.1-3940.
Claims for surplus received from sale, §58.1-3967.
Descent and distribution.
Claims by illegitimate children, §64.2-102.
Elective share of surviving spouse.
When share may be claimed, §64.2-302.
Extension of time, §64.2-303.
Refunds of distributions, §64.2-556.
Settlement of accounts and distributions.
Claims, §64.2-552.
Desertion and nonsupport.
Limitation not applicable to prosecution for desertion or nonsupport of wife or child, §19.2-8.
Detinue.
Actions to recover personal property, §8.01-243.
Devisavit vel non, §64.2-448.
Directors of corporations.
Unlawful distributions, §13.1-692.
Disabilities.
Effect of disabilities upon right of entry, §8.01-237.
Discrimination against persons with disabilities, §51.5-46.
Dismissal, discontinuance and nonsuit.
Suspension or tolling of statute of limitations, §8.01-229.
Dispute resolution proceedings.
Vacating orders and agreements, §8.01-576.12.
Dissolution of stock corporations.
Claims against, §13.1-746.1.
Known claims, §13.1-746.
Distress.
Landlord and tenant, §55-230.
Rents, §55-230.
Time within which rent may be distrained, §55-230.
District court judgments.
Enforcement, §16.1-94.1.
Divorce.
Adultery.
Lapse of five years before instituting suit, §20-94.
Buggery.
Lapse of five years before instituting suit, §20-94.
Sodomy.
Lapse of five years before instituting suit, §20-94.
Drivers' licenses.
Suspension of licenses for unsatisfied judgments.
Custody and application of cash or securities deposited, §46.2-426.
Drug dealers liability, §8.01-227.7.
Effective date of chapter.
Rights and remedies existing when chapter takes effect, §8.01-256.
Ejectment.
Landlord and tenant, §§55-240 to 55-242, 55-247, 55-248.
Elective shares.
Claiming, §64.2-302.
Extension of time, §64.2-303.

LIMITATION OF ACTIONS —Cont'd
Email service providers.
Spam, civil relief for injury by, §18.2-152.12.
Eminent domain.
Title transfer by certificate.
Commencement of condemnation proceedings, §25.1-313.
Petition for determination of just compensation, §25.1-318.
Emotional distress, §8.01-243.
Enforcement of district court judgments, §16.1-94.1.
Entry on or action for land, §8.01-236.
Equal credit opportunities.
Remedies for provision violations, §6.2-505.
Tolling, §6.2-510.
Equity.
Suit to repeal grant, §8.01-238.
Equity security of domestic stock insurers.
Restrictions upon purchase and sale, action to recover profits, §38.2-214.
Escheat.
Recovery of money paid into state treasury, §55-200.
Estate tax.
Criminal prosecutions, §19.2-8.
Evictions.
Mortgagee relief from forfeiture, §55-241.
Relief against such forfeiture, §55-240.
Suits against landlord, §55-248.
Tenant relief, §55-247.
Trustee relief from forfeiture, §55-241.
Executions.
Enforcement of judgment, §8.01-251.
New execution after loss of property sold under indemnity bond.
Motion within five years, §§8.01-255.2, 8.01-476.
Executors, administrators or officers unable to receive service or defend suit.
Authority excludes defending actions or expiration of duties.
Filing tolls statute of limitations if suit names proper estate of deceased, §8.01-6.2.
Extension of time.
Suspension of statute. See within this heading, "Suspension of statute."
Fair housing.
Civil action by aggrieved person, §36-96.18.
Fee simple determinable.
Action for determination of determinable fee simple estate, §8.01-255.1.
Felony.
Within what time an indictment for felony must be tried or accused be forever discharged, §19.2-243.
Fiduciaries.
Annual settlement not required when statement filed within year in pending suit, §64.2-1217.
Bonds, §8.01-245.
Distribution of estate.
Suit for refund within five years, §64.2-556.
Exhibition of accounts every three years when sum does not exceed $10,000, §64.2-1313.
Inventories.
Filing with commissioners of accounts within four months, §64.2-1300.
Liability for failure to make defense, §64.2-1415.
Personal actions based on contracts, §8.01-246.
Fieri facias.
When writ may be destroyed, §8.01-484.

LIMITATION OF ACTIONS —Cont'd
Food and beverage tax.
Criminal prosecutions, §19.2-8.
Foreign countries.
Actions on contracts governed by law of another country barred in Virginia, §8.01-247.
Forest products tax.
Criminal prosecutions, §19.2-8.
Fraud and deceit.
Contract actions, §8.01-248.
Medical malpractice claims, §8.01-243.
Personal actions, §8.01-243.
When cause of action deemed to accrue, §8.01-249.
Frauds, statute of.
Agreement not to be performed within a year, §11-2.
Fraudulent and voluntary conveyances.
Loans of goods and chattels.
Recordation within five years, §55-87.
Pretend loans and reservations to be recorded, §55-87.
Freedom of information.
District court proceedings to enforce rights and privileges, §16.1-83.
Fuel taxes, §§58.1-2285, 58.1-2286.
Sales tax in certain transportation districts.
Limitations period for imposition of tax, §58.1-2299.16.
Waiver of time limit, §58.1-2299.17.
Fugitives from justice.
Limitation on prosecutions not applicable to fugitives, §19.2-8.
Funds in or under control of court.
Recovery of unclaimed money paid into state treasury, §8.01-605.
Gambling contracts or loss recovery, §11-15.
General assembly.
Conflicts of interest.
Prosecution of violations, §30-128.
Gifts.
Suits to avoid, §8.01-253.
Grants.
Suit to repeal grant, §8.01-238.
Ground rents.
Actions for recovery, §8.01-239.
Groundwater management.
Provision violations, §62.1-270.
Guardian and ward.
Fiduciaries. See within this heading, "Fiduciaries."
Liability for failure to make defense, §64.2-1415.
Health insurance, contestability period.
Group insurance policy provision, §38.2-3528.
Individual policies, §38.2-3503.
Highway construction contracts, §33.1-192.
Execution after June 30, 1976, §33.1-192.1.
Human rights, division of.
Filing of complaint deemed filing with any state agency in terms of compliance with time limits, §2.2-522.
Husband and wife.
Descent and distribution.
Elective share of surviving spouse.
When share may be claimed, §64.2-302.
Extension of time, §64.2-303.
Limitation not applicable to prosecution for desertion or nonsupport of wife or child, §19.2-8.
Renunciation of will, §64.2-303.
Implied warranties on new homes, breach, §55-70.1.

LIMITATION OF ACTIONS —Cont'd
Improvements to land.
Damages arising out of defective or unsafe improvements, §8.01-250.
Income tax.
Assessment of tax imposed, §58.1-312.
Criminal prosecutions, §19.2-8.
Individual taxpayers.
Failure or refusal to file return or making false statement in return.
Criminal prosecutions, §58.1-348.
Income tax withholding.
Refunds on overpayments, §58.1-479.
Indemnification.
When cause of action deemed to accrue, §8.01-249.
Injunctions.
Suspension of statute.
Actions stayed by injunctions, §8.01-229.
Insurance information and privacy protection, individual remedies, §38.2-617.
Insurance policy provisions, §38.2-314.
Life insurance, §38.2-3316.
Group life, §38.2-3338.
Industrial life, §38.2-3354.
Interest.
Usury, §6.2-305.
Interstate family support.
Arrearages, §20-88.69.
Invasion of privacy.
Unauthorized use of name or picture, §8.01-40.
Judgments and decrees.
Attachment and garnishment.
Rehearing when judgment rendered on publication, §8.01-575.
Defendants served by publication and not appearing.
Petition for rehearing, §8.01-322.
Enforcement, §8.01-251.
Liens.
Fieri facias.
When lien ceases, §8.01-505.
Limitations on enforcement of judgments, §8.01-251.
New action after arrest or reversal of judgment, §8.01-229.
Setting aside default judgments, §8.01-428.
Suit to enforce judgment lien.
When lien of fieri facias ceases, §8.01-505.
Judicial sales.
Disturbance of purchaser's title, §8.01-113.
Juvenile and domestic relations district courts.
Errors.
Time for raising claim of error, §16.1-272.1.
Juvenile proceedings, adjudicatory or transfer hearings, §16.1-277.1.
Labor and employee relations.
Free speech rights under federal labor law, §8.01-243.
Landlord and tenant.
Against person in possession by reentry, §55-248.
Distress, §55-230.
Ejectment, §§55-240 to 55-242, 55-247, 55-248.
Evictions.
Mortgagee relief from forfeiture, §55-241.
Relief against forfeiture, §55-240.
Suits against landlord, §55-248.
Tenant relief, §55-247.
Trustee relief from forfeiture, §55-241.
Reentry, §§55-240 to 55-242, 55-247, 55-248.
When defendant barred of relief, §55-240.

LIMITATION OF ACTIONS —Cont'd
Landlord and tenant —Cont'd
Relief from forfeiture for tenant's breach of covenant, §55-241.
Time in which tenant restored to possession, §55-247.
Time within which rent may be distrained, §55-230.
Larceny.
Petit larceny, §19.2-8.
Law-enforcement employees, firefighters and emergency medical technicians.
Overtime compensation, §9.1-705.
Leases, UCC.
Default, §8.2A-506.
Legacies.
Enforcement of legacies, §8.01-254.
Lemon law, §59.1-207.16.
Letters of credit, §8.5A-115.
Libel, §8.01-247.1.
Liens.
Assessments for water, sewers or sidewalks, §8.01-240.
Condominiums.
Assessment liens, §55-79.84.
Judgment liens.
Fieri facias.
When lien ceases, §8.01-505.
Mechanics' liens, §43-17.
Unpaid purchase money, §8.01-241.
Extension of limitation form, §8.01-241.1.
Water, sewer or sidewalk assessments, §8.01-240.
Life insurance, contestability period, §38.2-3107.
Excluded or restricted coverage, inapplicability, §38.2-3110.
Group life insurance, §38.2-3326.
Individual life insurance, §38.2-3305.
Industrial life insurance, §38.2-3345.
Reinstated policy, running of period not affected, §38.2-3109.
Life insurance, prohibited provisions, §38.2-3316.
Group life, §38.2-3338.
Industrial life, §38.2-3354.
Litter tax.
Criminal prosecutions, §19.2-8.
Local tax collection, §58.1-3940.
Waiver of time limitation on assessment, §58.1-3903.1.
Malfeasance in office, §19.2-8.
Malicious prosecution.
Accrual of actions, §8.01-249.
Malpractice.
Action against health care provider, §8.01-243.
Medical malpractice review panel.
Rendition of panel opinion, §8.01-581.7:1.
Minors, §8.01-243.1.
Mandamus.
Petition for mandamus, §8.01-644.1.
Manslaughter.
No limitation on prosecutions, §19.2-8.1.
Marriage.
Transfers upon consideration of marriage, §8.01-253.
Mechanics' and materialmen's liens.
Claims in memorandum, §43-4.
Enforcement, §43-17.
Perfection.
General contractors, §43-4.
Suit to enforce lien, §43-17

LIMITATION OF ACTIONS —Cont'd
Medicaid fraud.
Fraudulently obtaining benefits or payments, §32.1-312.
Unintentionally obtaining excess benefits, §32.1-313.
Medical malpractice, §8.01-243.
Minors, §8.01-243.1.
Review panels.
Joinder of additional parties or causes of action, §8.01-581.2:1.
Mentally ill.
Claims against the state.
Suit to impeach or establish will, §64.2-448.
Saving in favor of person of unsound mind, §64.2-448.
Suspension of statute.
Disabilities which toll statute of limitations, §8.01-229.
Military service.
Extension of time for filing pleading, §44-97.1.
Minors.
Abuse and neglect of children.
When cause of action deemed to accrue, §8.01-249.
Actions by parent or guardian against tort-feasor, §8.01-243.
Desertion and nonsupport.
Limitation not applicable to prosecution for desertion or nonsupport of wife or child, §19.2-8.
Disabilities which toll statute of limitations, §8.01-229.
Wills.
Suit to impeach or establish will, §64.2-448.
Saving in favor of infants, §64.2-448.
Misdemeanors.
Generally, §19.2-8.
Monopolies and corporate trusts.
Virginia antitrust act, §59.1-9.14.
Mortgages and deeds of trust.
Enforcement of lien.
Extension of limitation forms, §8.01-241.1.
Limitation of enforcement, §8.01-241.
No maturity date given, §8.01-242.
Objections to irregularities in advertising sales made by trustees under deeds of trust, §55-24.
Rent.
Relief from forfeiture for nonpayment, §55-241.
Motor fuel and special fuel tax.
Criminal prosecutions, §19.2-8.
Motor vehicle warranties.
Enforcement, §59.1-207.16.
Murder.
No limitation on prosecutions, §19.2-8.1.
Museums, property loaned to, §55-210.32.
Mutual assessment life, accident and sickness insurers.
Fraudulent misstatement defense, §38.2-3911.
Incontestability of policy, §38.2-3912.
Mutual holding companies conversion to stock holding companies, §38.2-1005.1:13.
Name or picture, unauthorized use, §8.01-40.
Negotiable instruments, §8.3A-118.
Deposit accounts and certificates of deposit, §8.3A-118.1.
New homes, breach of implied warranties, §55-70.1.
New promise in writing.
Effect, §8.01-229.

LIMITATION OF ACTIONS —Cont'd
Nonfelonious offenses.
Malfeasance in office, §19.2-8.
Nonprofit corporations, claims against dissolved corporations, §§13.1-908, 13.1-908.1.
Nonresidents.
Rehearing.
Parties served by publication and not appearing, §8.01-322.
Suit to impeach or establish will, §64.2-448.
Saving in favor of nonresident, §64.2-448.
Nonsuit.
Suspension or tolling of statute of limitations, §8.01-229.
Partnerships.
Action to settle accounts, §8.01-246.
Paternity.
Descent and distribution.
Claims of succession by illegitimate children, §64.2-102.
Payment bonds.
Public construction contracts, §2.2-4341.
Penalties, §19.2-8.
Landlord and tenant.
Relief from forfeiture for tenant's breach of covenant, §55-241.
Performance bonds, actions on.
Public construction contracts, §2.2-4340.
Perjury.
Special grand jury testimony, §19.2-212.
Personal actions.
Accrual in certain actions, §8.01-249.
Defined, §8.01-228.
Generally, §8.01-243.
No other limitation specified, §8.01-248.
Personal injuries, §8.01-243.
Accrual of right of action, §8.01-230.
Improvements to real property.
Actions for damages arising out of defective or unsafe condition of improvement, §8.01-250.
Wrongful death, §8.01-244.
Persons with disability, §8.01-237.
Wills.
Suit to impeach or establish will, §64.2-448.
Saving in favor of infant or person of unsound mind, §64.2-448.
Petroleum products franchises.
Provision violations, §59.1-21.12.
Pleading.
Manner of pleading statute of limitations.
Affirmative defense in responsive pleading, §8.01-235.
Promises not to plead statute, §8.01-232.
Premarital agreements, §20-152.
Prisoners.
Actions by confined persons.
Exhaustion of administrative remedies, §8.01-243.2.
Disabilities which toll statute of limitations, §8.01-229.
Health care.
Involuntary admission and treatment.
Appeal of order authorizing, §53.1-40.4.
Procurement by public bodies.
Denial of withdrawal of bid, appeal, §2.2-4358.
Ineligibility determination, appeal, §2.2-4357.
Nonresponsibility of low bidder, appeal, §2.2-4359.
Products liability, §8.01-243.
Personal actions based on contract, §8.01-246.
When cause of action deemed to accrue, §8.01-249.

LIMITATION OF ACTIONS —Cont'd
Professional occupational regulation department.
Complaints.
Time for filing, §54.1-307.1.
Professions and occupations.
Violations of local professional license requirements, §19.2-8.
Promise not to plead statute, §8.01-232.
Property owners' associations.
Liens for assessments, §55-516.
Property taxes.
Contesting real property assessments.
County manager plan of government, §15.2-717.
Criminal prosecutions, §19.2-8.
Publication.
Rehearing after judgment.
Attachment and garnishment, §8.01-575.
Petition by defendant served by publication and not appearing, §8.01-322.
Public officers and employees.
Conflicts of interest, §2.2-3125.
Public service corporation tax assessment review in circuit courts, §58.1-2670.1.
Real estate cooperatives.
Contract liability, §55-468.
Declaration amendments, §55-453.
Protection of cooperative purchasers.
Statute of limitations for warranties, §55-491.
Remedies for nonpayment of assessments, §55-472.
Tort liability, §55-468.
Warranties, §§55-490, 55-491.
Real estate time-share act, §55-383.
Real property.
Argument before jury, §8.01-379.
Bequests and legacies.
Enforcement, §8.01-254.
Breach of condition subsequent or termination of determinable fee simple estate, §8.01-255.1.
Death of person without heirs, §55-13.
Entry on land.
Disabilities.
Effect of disabilities upon right of entry, §8.01-237.
Limitation of entry, §8.01-236.
Ground rents.
Suits for recovery, §8.01-239.
Improvements to real property.
Damages arising out of defective or unsafe condition of improvement, §8.01-250.
Indemnifying bonds.
Motion for new execution after loss of property sold under indemnity bond, §8.01-255.2.
Personal actions for damages, §8.01-243.
Real property tax.
Contesting real estate assessments.
County manager plan of government, §15.2-717.
Criminal prosecutions, §19.2-8.
Real property transfer on death act.
Debts and obligations, property subject to.
Action to enforce liability, §64.2-634.
Recordation tax.
Criminal prosecutions, §19.2-8.
Reentry, §§55-240 to 55-242, 55-247, 55-248.
Against person in possession by reentry, §55-248.
Relief from forfeiture for tenant's breach of covenant, §55-241.
Relief of owner, etc., in equity, §55-242.
Time in which tenant restored to possession, §55-247.

LIMITATION OF ACTIONS —Cont'd
Reentry —Cont'd
When defendant barred of relief, §55-240.
Registered limited liability partnerships.
Disposal of claims, dissolved partnership.
Proceeding to enforce claims, §50-73.137:3.
Rehearing.
By supreme court, §19.2-325.
Parties served by publication and not appearing, §8.01-322.
Remedies.
Effective date of chapter.
Existing rights and remedies when chapter takes effect, §8.01-256.
Renewable energy.
Small renewable energy projects.
Criminal prosecutions, §10.1-1197.9.
Rents.
Distress, §55-230.
Mortgages and deeds of trust and deeds of trust.
Relief from forfeiture for nonpayment, §55-241.
Repeals.
Effect of repeal of general acts by code, §1-4.
Not to remove bar of statute, §8.01-234.
Repose, statute of, §8.01-250.
Residential property transfer disclosures, §55-524.
Retail franchise violations, civil remedies, §13.1-571.
Retail franchise violations, criminal prosecution, §13.1-569.
Retail sales and use tax.
Assessments, §58.1-634.
Criminal prosecutions, §19.2-8.
Revolving credit open account.
When cause deemed to accrue, §8.01-249.
Right of action.
Accrual, §8.01-230.
Rolling stock tax.
Criminal prosecutions, §19.2-8.
Sale of delinquent tax lands, §58.1-3940.
Claims for surplus received from sale, §58.1-3967.
Waiver of time limitation on assessment, §58.1-3903.1.
Sales and use tax.
Criminal prosecutions, §19.2-8.
Taxes imposed by chapter, §58.1-634.
Sales, UCC.
Breach of contract, §8.2-725.
Limitations by agreements may reduce to less than one year, §8.2-725.
Saturday, Sunday or legal holiday.
Last day of limitation period falling on, §1-210.
Scope of limitations, §8.01-228.
Securities violations, civil liabilities, §13.1-522.
Securities violations, criminal prosecutions, §13.1-520.
Service of notice, process and other papers.
Publication.
Rehearing of case on petition to correct injustice, §8.01-322.
Service of process prevented by defendant.
Suspension or tolling of statute, §8.01-229.
Sewers.
Assessments for sewers, §8.01-240.
Sidewalks.
Assessments for sidewalks.
Lien for assessment, §8.01-240.
Slander, §8.01-247.1.
Small renewable energy projects.
Criminal prosecutions, §10.1-1197.9.

LIMITATION OF ACTIONS —Cont'd
Soft drink tax.
Criminal prosecutions, §19.2-8.
Spam.
Injured email service providers, §18.2-152.12.
Stalking.
Civil actions against an individual, §8.01-42.3.
State.
Agencies of state incorporated for charitable or educational purposes.
Recovery of money paid into state treasury, §55-200.
Claims against the state.
Time for presenting claim against state, §8.01-255.
Tort claims against the Commonwealth, §§8.01-195.6, 8.01-195.7.
Proceedings to enforce judgment, §8.01-251.
State not within statute of limitations, §8.01-231.
Tort claims against the Commonwealth, §§8.01-195.6, 8.01-195.7.
State comptroller.
Claims against the state, §8.01-255.
State corporation commission.
Appeals, §12.1-39.
Supersedeas, petitions for writs of, §12.1-41.
Statute of frauds.
Agreement not to be performed within a year, §11-2.
Statute of repose, §8.01-250.
Stock corporation directors' unlawful distributions, §13.1-692.
Stock insurers conversion to mutual insurer.
Compelling completion of mutualization, §38.2-1012.
Striking cases from docket after certain periods, §8.01-335.
Subdivided land sales.
Enforcement of liens, §55-344.
Surrogate mother brokers.
Actions against persons acting as, §20-165.
Surrogate mother contracts.
Actions to test validity, §20-163.
Parentage of child resulting.
Husband's declaration of invalidity or annulment of marriage, §20-158.
Suspension of statute.
Actions for recovery of realty.
Effect of disabilities upon right of entry on or action for land, §8.01-237.
Consumer protection, §59.1-204.1.
Credit services businesses, §59.1-335.11.
Death of party, §8.01-229.
Disabilities which toll statute of limitations, §8.01-229.
Dismissal, nonsuit or abatement, §8.01-229.
Executors and administrators.
Filing of claims, §64.2-552.
Injunctions, §8.01-229.
Lemon law, §59.1-207.16.
Motor vehicle warranties.
Enforcement, §59.1-207.16.
Persons with disability, §8.01-229.
Real estate cooperatives.
Tort and contract liability, §55-468.
Service of notice, process and other papers.
Prevention of service by defendant, §8.01-229.
Wills.
Probate.
Bills to impeach or establish, §64.2-448.

LIMITATION OF ACTIONS —Cont'd
Suspension of statute —Cont'd
Workers' compensation.
Claims, §65.2-602.
Occupational diseases.
Claims, §65.2-405.
Persons with disability, §65.2-528.
Taxes.
Amended returns, filing, §58.1-1823.
Assessments, §58.1-104.
Income tax, §58.1-312.
Omitted taxes by the department of taxation, §58.1-1812.
Taxpayer problem resolution program, §58.1-1818.
Waiver of time limitation, §58.1-101.
Assessment of omitted or additional state taxes, §58.1-220.
Correction of erroneous tax assessments.
Local taxes.
Appeal by locality of commissioners for correction, §58.1-3982.
Application to commissioner of revenue, §58.1-3980.
Waiver of time limitation on assessment, §58.1-3903.1.
Application to court to correct, §58.1-3984.
Refund of taxes erroneously paid, §58.1-3990.
State corporation commission, §58.1-2030.
State taxes.
Application to circuit court, §58.1-1825.
Filing of amended return, §58.1-1823.
Protective claim for refund, §58.1-1824.
Criminal prosecutions, §19.2-8.
Delinquent taxes.
Period of limitations on collection, §58.1-1802.1.
Forest products tax.
Remedy of aggrieved taxpayer.
Limitation, §58.1-1622.
Fraudulent returns.
Commencement of prosecutions, §58.1-452.
Insurance companies.
Estimated taxes.
Refunds, §58.1-2526.
Local improvements.
Appeal by property owner, §15.2-2410.
Local taxes.
Limitation on collection, §58.1-3940.
Waiver of time limitation on assessment, §58.1-3903.1.
Refunds of local taxes erroneously paid, §58.1-3990.
Refunds, protective claim, §58.1-1824.
Release of liens for taxes delinquent twenty years or more, §58.1-3341.
Retail sales and use tax.
Period of limitations, §58.1-634.
Returns.
Filing amended returns, §58.1-1823.
Sales and use tax.
Imposition of tax by chapter, §58.1-634.
Third-party claims, §8.01-243.
Time-shares, §55-383.
Tire tax.
Criminal prosecutions, §19.2-8.
Tolling of statutes. See within this heading, "Suspension of statute."
Tort claims act, §§8.01-195.6, 8.01-195.7.
Torts.
Personal injuries, §8.01-243.

LIMITATION OF ACTIONS —Cont'd
Toxic substances.
Discharge, dumping or emission, §19.2-8.
Trade secrets, §59.1-340.
Trespass to land, §8.01-243.
Trusts.
Custodial trusts.
Limitation of actions against custodial trustees, §64.2-915.
Revocable trusts.
Contesting validity, §64.2-753.
Trustee, actions against, §64.2-796.
Unauthorized use of name or picture, §8.01-40.
Unclaimed property, disposition of.
Effect of expiration of action period, §55-210.17.
Enforcement of provisions, §55-210.25.
Judicial review of decision, §55-210.22.
Unemployment compensation, §60.2-514.
False statements to obtain or increase benefits, §19.2-8.
Taxation.
Proceeding to establish liability for taxes, §60.2-514.
Ungranted shores of sea, marsh and meadowlands.
Claim to lands designated in inventory, §28.2-1509.
Ungranted shores of the sea.
Claims to designated land, §28.2-1511.
Effect of legal disability, §28.2-1512.
Uniform computer information transactions act.
Remedies, §59.1-508.5.
Uniform statewide building code.
Criminal prosecutions for violations, §§19.2-8, 36-106.
Unlawful search and seizure, §8.01-243.
Unpaid purchase money.
Liens, §8.01-241.
Extension of limitation form, §8.01-241.1.
No maturity date given, §8.01-242.
Usury, §6.2-305.
Virginia workers' compensation commission.
Claim for occupational disease, §§65.2-405, 65.2-406.
Warehouse receipts.
Contractual limitation of warehouseman's liability, §8.7-204.
Warranties.
Real estate cooperatives, §§55-490, 55-491.
Warrants for payment of money drawn on local treasurers.
Presentation within two years required, §58.1-3134.
Waste management violations.
Commencing prosecutions, §10.1-1455.
Water and waste authority bonds.
Time for contesting validity, §15.2-5126.
Water companies and waterworks.
Assessment.
Liens for assessments, §8.01-240.
Waters of the state.
Groundwater management.
Provision violations, §62.1-270.
Pollution control offenses, §§62.1-44.31, 62.1-44.32.
Wills.
Bona fide purchasers.
Devises of real estate without notice, §64.2-456.
Intestacy, §64.2-458.
Later wills, §64.2-457.

LIMITATION OF ACTIONS —Cont'd
Wills —Cont'd
Elective shares.
Claiming, §64.2-302.
Extension of time, §64.2-303.
Probate.
Clerk orders.
Appeals, §64.2-445.
Establishment bills, §64.2-448.
Tolling, §64.2-448.
Impeachment bills, §64.2-448.
Tolling, §64.2-448.
Refunds of distributions, §64.2-556.
Settlement of accounts and distributions.
Claims, §64.2-552.
Witness fees and allowances.
Time limit on presenting claim for payment, §17.1-615.
Workers' compensation, §65.2-601.
Appeal from award, §65.2-706.
Claim for occupational disease, §§65.2-405, 65.2-406.
Filing claims, §§65.2-601, 65.2-602.
Incapacity after permanent loss, §65.2-501.
Occupational diseases.
Claims, §65.2-406.
Tolling, §65.2-405.
Persons with disability, §65.2-528.
Tolling of statute of limitations, §65.2-602.
Occupational disease claims, §65.2-405.
Workers' compensation award found void ab initio.
Tolling of limitations applicable to civil actions on claim, §8.01-229.
Writing.
New promise in writing.
Effect, §8.01-229.
Wrongful death, §8.01-244.
Improvements to real property.
Damages arising out of defective or unsafe condition of improvement, §8.01-250.
No action on compromised claim, §8.01-51.
Wrongful discharge, §8.01-243.
Zoning.
Appeals to board of zoning appeals, §15.2-2311.
Decision by local governing body.
Time for filing contest, §15.2-2285.

LIMITATION OF PROSECUTIONS, §§19.2-8, 19.2-243.
Murder or manslaughter.
No limitation, §19.2-8.1.

LIMITATION ON DEPOSITIONS.
Use in court proceedings, VA SCt Rule 4:7.

LIMITATIONS ON FREQUENCY OF HOLDING ELECTIONS.
Adopting or changing form of county government, §15.2-306.

LIMITED ACCESS HIGHWAYS, §§33.1-57 to 33.1-61.

LIMITED ACCESS STREET, §15.2-2026.

LIMITED LIABILITY COMPANIES, §§13.1-1000 to 13.1-1080.
Actions.
Derivative actions, §§13.1-1042 to 13.1-1045.
Registration fees.
Collection by lawsuit, §13.1-1066.
Right of action.
Derivative actions, §13.1-1042.

LIMITED LIABILITY COMPANIES —Cont'd
Actions —Cont'd
Third-party liability of members.
Parties to actions, §13.1-1020.
Admission of members.
Assignment of membership interest, §13.1-1038.1.
Agency role of members and managers, §13.1-1021.1.
Aliens.
Pattern or practice of employing unauthorized aliens.
Foreign limited liability companies.
Involuntary cancellation of certificate of registration, §13.1-1056.2.
Involuntary cancellation of existence, §13.1-1050.3.
Allocation of profits and losses, §13.1-1029.
Articles of organization.
Amendment, §13.1-1014.
Amendments.
Filing fees, §13.1-1005.
Cancellation of certificate for failure to pay fees, §13.1-1064.
Correction.
Certificate of correction, §13.1-1011.1.
Defined, §13.1-1002.
Filing fees, §13.1-1005.
Generally, §13.1-1011.
Name.
Generally, §13.1-1012.
Reserved name, §13.1-1013.
Filing fees, §13.1-1005.
Organizers, §13.1-1010.
Restatement, §13.1-1014.1.
Assignment of membership interest, §§13.1-1038 to 13.1-1041.1.
Admission of members, §13.1-1038.1.
Assignment of, §13.1-1039.
Certificate of interest, §13.1-1039.
Charging order.
Member's transferable interest subject to, §13.1-1041.1.
Defined, §13.1-1002.
Nature of, §13.1-1038.
Personal property.
Nature of interest, §13.1-1038.
Right of assignee to become member, §13.1-1040.
Transferable interests, §13.1-1038.
Attorney general.
Foreign limited liability companies.
Transaction of business without registration.
Actions by attorney general, §13.1-1058.
Automatic cancellation of existence, §13.1-1050.2.
Breach of operating agreement.
Remedies, §13.1-1023.1.
Cancellation of existence.
Automatic cancellation, §13.1-1050.2.
Citation of act.
Short title, §13.1-1000.
Clerical errors and filings by persons without authority.
Petition to correct, §13.1-1004.
Conflict of laws, §13.1-1001.1.
Domestication of foreign limited liability companies, §13.1-1074.
Foreign limited liability companies.
Law governing, §13.1-1051.
Mergers, §13.1-1060.
Construction and interpretation, §13.1-1001.1.

LIMITED LIABILITY COMPANIES —Cont'd
Contracts.
Third-party liability of members.
No personal liability, §13.1-1019.
Contributions.
Generally, §13.1-1027.
Information and records, §13.1-1028.
Statute of frauds.
Promise by member to make contribution, §13.1-1027.
Conversion of business trusts to new entity, §§13.1-1272 to 13.1-1277.
Conversion of corporation to limited liability company, §§13.1-944.1 to 13.1-944.7.
Abandonment of conversion, §13.1-944.7.
Action on plan, §13.1-944.4.
Articles of entity conversion, §13.1-944.5.
Definitions, §13.1-944.1.
Effect of entity conversion, §13.1-944.6.
Plan of entity conversion, §§13.1-944.2, 13.1-944.3.
Conversion to corporation.
Entity conversion, §§13.1-722.8 to 13.1-722.14.
Creditors.
Dissolution.
Distribution of assets, §13.1-1049.
Membership interest.
Assignment for benefit of creditor, §13.1-1039.
Rights of creditor, §13.1-1047.
Damages.
Third-party liability of members.
No personal liability, §13.1-1019.
Definitions, §13.1-1002.
Distribution, §13.1-1035.
Domestic limited liability company, §§13.1-603, 13.1-803.
Foreign limited liability company, §§13.1-603, 13.1-803.
Professional service, §§13.1-543, 13.1-1008.
Transacting business, §13.1-1059.
Dentistry, practice of, §54.1-2717.
Derivative actions, §§13.1-1042 to 13.1-1045.
Expenses, §13.1-1045.
Pleadings, §13.1-1044.
Proper plaintiff, §13.1-1043.
Right of action, §13.1-1042.
Dissociation of member.
Effect, §13.1-1040.2.
Events causing, §13.1-1040.1.
Dissolution, §§13.1-1046 to 13.1-1050.4.
Automatic cancellation of existence, §13.1-1050.2.
Certificate of cancellation.
Contents.
Required, §13.1-1050.
Filing fee, §13.1-1005.
Generally, §13.1-1050.
Claims.
Known claims against dissolved company, §13.1-1049.1.
Notice of dissolution and request for presentation of claims, §13.1-1049.2.
Court proceedings following notice, §13.1-1049.3.
Dissociation not to cause, §13.1-1040.2.
Distributions.
Assets upon distribution, §13.1-1049.
Events under which occur, §13.1-1046.
Involuntary cancellation of existence, §13.1-1050.3.
Judicial dissolution, §13.1-1047.
Entry of decree, §§13.1-1046, 13.1-1047.
Reinstatement, §13.1-1050.4.

LIMITED LIABILITY COMPANIES —Cont'd
Dissolution —Cont'd
Specified happening of events, §13.1-1046.
Waiver of right to wind up and cancel existence, §13.1-1047.1.
Winding up, §13.1-1048.
Distributions.
Defined, §13.1-1002.
Distribution in kind, §13.1-1034.
Interim distributions, §13.1-1031.
Liability upon wrongful distribution, §13.1-1036.
Restrictions, §13.1-1035.
Right to distribution, §13.1-1037.
Sharing of, §13.1-1030.
Wrongful distribution, §13.1-1036.
Domestication of foreign limited liability companies, §§13.1-1074 to 13.1-1080.
Abandonment, §13.1-1080.
Articles of domestication, §13.1-1077.
Articles of organization.
Surrender upon domestication, §13.1-1078.
Authorized, §13.1-1074.
Conflict of laws, §13.1-1074.
Effect, §13.1-1079.
Plan of domestication, §13.1-1075.
Action on plan by domestic limited liability company, §13.1-1076.
Surrender of articles of organization upon, §13.1-1078.
Domestication of non-United States entities, §13.1-1010.3.
Entity conversion, §§13.1-722.8 to 13.1-722.14.
Abandonment, §13.1-722.14.
Articles of entity conversion, §13.1-722.12.
Authorized, §§13.1-722.9, 13.1-1010.4.
Definitions, §13.1-722.8.
Effect, §13.1-722.13.
Plan of entity conversion, §13.1-722.10.
Action on, §13.1-722.11.
Evidence.
Issuance of certificate by commission.
Evidentiary effect, §13.1-1004.
Expulsion of member.
Events causing members dissociation, §13.1-1040.1.
Fees.
Articles of amendment, §13.1-1005.
Articles of entity conversion, §13.1-1005.
Articles of merger, §13.1-1005.
Articles of organization, §13.1-1005.
Certificate of cancellation, §13.1-1005.
Certificate of correction, §13.1-1005.
Certificate reciting change of name or conversion, §13.1-1005.
Foreign limited liability company merger instrument, §13.1-1005.
Foreign limited liability company registration, §13.1-1005.
Registration fees, §§13.1-1061 to 13.1-1066.
Failure to pay, §13.1-1050.2.
Reserved name, application, §13.1-1005.
Reserved name, notice of transfer, §13.1-1005.
Schedule of fees, §13.1-1005.
Filing requirements.
Clerical errors and filings by persons without authority.
Petition to correct, §13.1-1004.
Fees, §13.1-1005.
Generally, §13.1-1003.
Payment of registration fees.
Prerequisite to commission action, §13.1-1065.

LIMITED LIABILITY COMPANIES —Cont'd
Filing requirements —Cont'd
Recordation of documents, §13.1-1004.
Registration fees.
Prerequisite to commission action, §13.1-1065.
Signing false documents, §13.1-1006.
Fines.
Registration fees.
Failure to timely pay, §§13.1-1064, 13.1-1066.
Foreign entities.
Domestication of non-United States entities, §13.1-1010.3.
Foreign limited liability companies, §§13.1-1051 to 13.1-1060.1.
Agent for service.
Automatic cancellation of certificate of registration.
Clerk of commission appointed, §13.1-1056.1.
Aliens.
Pattern or practice of employing unauthorized aliens.
Involuntary cancellation of certificate of registration, §13.1-1056.2.
Conversion.
Entity conversion of foreign company registered to transact business in Commonwealth, §13.1-1060.1.
Defined, §§13.1-603, 13.1-803, 13.1-1002.
Domestication, §§13.1-1074 to 13.1-1080.
Entity conversion of foreign company registered to transact business in Commonwealth, §13.1-1060.1.
Laws governing, §13.1-1051.
Mergers, §13.1-1060.
Registered office and agent.
Agent for service of process and papers, §13.1-1018.
Change of registered office or agents, §13.1-1016.
Filing fees, §13.1-1016.
Principal office, §13.1-1018.1.
Designation of person to receive service, §13.1-1018.
Discontinuance of office, §13.1-1017.
Merger of agent into qualified entity, notice, §13.1-1016.
Name change, §13.1-1016.
Places of business, §13.1-1015.
Qualifications of registered agent, §13.1-1015.
Resignation of registered agent, §13.1-1017.
Failure to file statement of change after resignation, §13.1-1056.1.
Sole duty of registered agent, §13.1-1015.
Statement of resignation, §13.1-1017.
Termination of agency.
Resignation of agent, §13.1-1017.
Registration.
Certificate of registration.
Application for, §13.1-1052.
Amended applications, §13.1-1055.
Cancellation, §13.1-1056.
Automatic cancellation, §13.1-1056.1.
Failure to pay registration fees, §13.1-1064.
Filing fees, §13.1-1005.
Involuntary cancellation by commission, §13.1-1056.2.
Reinstatement, §13.1-1056.3.
Changes and amendments.
Filing fees, §13.1-1005.
Filing fee, §13.1 1005.

LIMITED LIABILITY COMPANIES —Cont'd
Foreign limited liability companies —Cont'd
Registration —Cont'd
Certificate of registration —Cont'd
Name, §13.1-1054.
Filing fees, §13.1-1005.
Required, §13.1-1051.
Registration fees, §§13.1-1061 to 13.1-1066.
Application of payment, §13.1-1061.
Assessment, §13.1-1061.
Collection, §13.1-1061.
Unpaid bills, §13.1-1066.
Failure to pay, §13.1-1056.1.
Payment, §13.1-1062.
Application of payment, §13.1-1061.
Failure to timely pay, §13.1-1064.
Filing requirements of commission prerequisite to commission action, §13.1-1065.
Penalty for failure to timely pay, §13.1-1064.
Service of notice, process and other papers.
Agent for service, §13.1-1018.
Automatic cancellation of certificate of registration.
Clerk of commission appointed, §13.1-1056.1.
Transaction of business without registration, §13.1-1057.
Actions by attorney general, §13.1-1058.
Conduct not constituting doing business, §13.1-1059.
Foreign stock corporation merging with, §13.1-766.1.
Formation, §§13.1-1008 to 13.1-1014.1.
Articles of organization.
Amendments, §13.1-1014.
Filing fees, §13.1-1005.
Contents, §13.1-1011.
Defined, §13.1-1002.
Filing fees, §13.1-1005.
Generally, §13.1-1011.
Name, §13.1-1012.
Generally, §13.1-1012.
Reserved name, §13.1-1013.
Filing fees, §13.1-1005.
Organizers, §13.1-1010.
Restatement, §13.1-1014.
Powers, §13.1-1009.
Purposes, §13.1-1008.
General assembly.
Reservation of power to amend or repeal, §13.1-1001.
Injunctions.
Operating agreements.
Enforcement, §13.1-1023.
Insurance agents.
Business entities acting as, §38.2-1822.
Insurance consultants.
Business entities acting as.
License required, §38.2-1838.
Interest.
Prohibited from pleading usury, §6.2-308.
Interim distributions, §13.1-1031.
Involuntary cancellation of existence, §13.1-1050.3.
Loans.
Managers.
Business transactions with limited liability company, §13.1-1026.
Major business facility job tax credit, §58.1-439.

LIMITED LIABILITY COMPANIES —Cont'd
Management, §§13.1-1022 to 13.1-1028.
Contributions of members.
Contribution, defined, §13.1-1002.
Generally, §13.1-1027.
Information and records, §13.1-1028.
Statute of frauds.
Promises to make contributions, §13.1-1027.
Information and records, §13.1-1028.
Managers.
Agency role of, §13.1-1021.1.
Breach of operating agreement by, remedies, §13.1-1023.1.
Business transactions with limited liability company, §13.1-1026.
Defined, §13.1-1002.
Duties, §13.1-1024.
Ethical standards, §13.1-1024.1.
Exception to liability limitations, §13.1-1025.
In whom management vested, §13.1-1022.
Limitation of liability, §13.1-1025.
Powers, §13.1-1024.
Qualifications, §13.1-1024.
Standards of conduct, §13.1-1024.1.
Operating agreements, §13.1-1023.
Breach of operating agreement, remedies, §13.1-1023.1.
Defined, §13.1-1002.
Records.
Generally, §13.1-1028.
Standard of conduct for managers, §13.1-1024.1.
Members as agents, §13.1-1021.1.
Membership interest.
Not effected by dissociation, §13.1-1040.2.
Merger, §§13.1-1070 to 13.1-1073.
Approval of merger, §13.1-1071.
Articles of merger, §13.1-1072.
Articles of organization or operating agreement.
Prohibition, §13.1-1070.
Certificate of merger, §13.1-1072.
Effect of merger, §13.1-1073.
Foreign limited liability companies.
Law governing mergers, §13.1-1060.
Foreign stock corporation merging with, §13.1-766.1.
Plan of merger, §13.1-1072.
Approval, §13.1-1071.
Contents, §13.1-1070.
Writing requirement, §13.1-1070.
Surviving business organization, §13.1-1073.
Motor vehicle sales and use tax exemption.
Transfers exempt, §58.1-2403.
Name, §13.1-1012.
Notice.
Dissolution of claims, notice and request for presentation of claims, §13.1-1049.2.
Court proceedings following notice, §13.1-1049.3.
Failure to pay registration fee, §13.1-1064.
Impending cancellation of existence, §13.1-1050.2.
Resignation of member, §13.1-1032.
Operating agreements, §13.1-1023.
Breach of operating agreement, remedies, §13.1-1023.1.
Defined, §13.1-1002.
Parties.
Derivative actions.
Proper plaintiff, §13.1-1043.
Partnerships.
Conversion of partnership to limited liability company, §13.1-1010.1.
Effect, §13.1-1010.2.

LIMITED LIABILITY COMPANIES —Cont'd
Person.
Defined, §13.1-1002.
Personal property.
Membership interest.
Nature of, §13.1-1038.
Person defined as including corporations and partnerships.
Limited liability companies also included, §1-231.
Pleadings.
Derivative actions, §13.1-1044.
Third-party liability of members.
Proper parties to actions, §13.1-1020.
Powers, §13.1-1009.
Principles of law and equity to supplement provisions, §13.1-1001.1.
Professional limited liability companies, §§13.1-1100 to 13.1-1123.
See PROFESSIONAL LIMITED LIABILITY COMPANIES.
Profits and losses.
Sharing of, §13.1-1029.
Property.
Third-party liability of members.
Estate or interest in property, §13.1-1021.
Title records, §13.1-1067.
Purposes, §13.1-1008.
Real property.
Third-party liability of members.
Estate or interest in property, §13.1-1021.
Real property taxes.
Land conservation incentives, §58.1-513.
Recordation tax, state.
Exemptions, §58.1-811.
Records.
Property title records, §13.1-1067.
Recordkeeping requirements, §13.1-1028.
Registered office and agent, §§13.1-1015 to 13.1-1018.1.
Change of office or agents, §13.1-1016.
Principal office, §13.1-1018.1.
Discontinuance of office, §13.1-1017.
Merger of agent into qualified entity, notice, §13.1-1016.
Name change, §13.1-1016.
Places of business, §13.1-1015.
Qualifications of registered agent, §13.1-1015.
Resignation of registered agent, §13.1-1017.
Failure to file statement of change after resignation, §13.1-1050.2.
Foreign companies.
Failure to file statement of change after resignation, §13.1-1056.1.
Service of notice, process and other papers, §13.1-1018.
Designation by agent of person to receive service, §13.1-1018.
Sole duty of registered agent, §13.1-1015.
Statement of resignation, §13.1-1017.
Termination of agency.
Resignation of agent, §13.1-1017.
Registration fees, §§13.1-1061 to 13.1-1066.
Application of payment, §13.1-1061.
Assessments, §13.1-1061.
Collection, §13.1-1061.
Unpaid bills, §13.1-1066.
Failure to pay, §13.1-1050.2.
Foreign companies, §13.1-1056.1.
Filing requirements.
Prerequisite to commission action, §13.1-1065.

LIMITED LIABILITY COMPANIES —Cont'd
Registration fees —Cont'd
Payment, §13.1-1062.
Application of payment, §13.1-1061.
Failure to timely pay, §13.1-1064.
Penalty for failure to timely pay, §13.1-1064.
Refunds, §13.1-1065.
Reinstatement, §13.1-1050.4.
Service of notice, process and other papers.
Attachment or garnishment proceedings, §8.01-513.
Foreign limited liability companies.
Agent for service.
Automatic cancellation of certificate of registration.
Clerk of commission appointed, §13.1-1056.1.
Registered agent as agent for service, §13.1-1018.
Short title.
Virginia limited liability company act, §13.1-1000.
Signing false documents, §13.1-1006.
Unlawful transaction of business, §13.1-1007.
State corporation commission generally, §§12.1-1 to 12.1-43.
See STATE CORPORATION COMMISSION.
Statute of frauds.
Contributions by members.
Promises to make contributions, §13.1-1027.
Filing requirements, §13.1-1003.
Resignation of member.
Written notification requirements, §13.1-1032.
Surplus lines insurance brokers.
License.
Business entities acting as, §38.2-1857.2.
Taxes.
Liability for failure to pay, §58.1-3906.
Payments.
Liability of member, manager or employee for failure to pay, §58.1-1813.
Third-party liability of members, §§13.1-1019 to 13.1-1021.
Parties to actions, §13.1-1020.
Personal liability.
No personal obligation in contract, tort or any other liabilities, §13.1-1019.
Property.
Estate or interest in property, §13.1-1021.
Title of act.
Short title, §13.1-1000.
Torts.
Third-party liability of members.
No personal liability, §13.1-1019.
Usury.
Prohibited from pleading usury, §6.2-308.
Viatical settlement broker license.
Business entity acting as broker, §38.2-1865.1.
Waiver of right to wind up and cancel existence, §13.1-1047.1.
Winding up.
Dissolution, §13.1-1048.
Worker retraining tax credit, §58.1-439.6.

LIMITED LIABILITY PARTNERSHIPS, §§50-73.132 to 50-73.143.
See REGISTERED LIMITED LIABILITY PARTNERSHIPS.

LIMITED PARTNERSHIPS, §§50-73.1 to 50-73.78.
Aliens.
Employment of unauthorized aliens.
Foreign limited partnerships.
Involuntary cancellation of certificate, §50-73.58:2.

LIMITED PARTNERSHIPS —Cont'd
Aliens —Cont'd
Employment of unauthorized aliens —Cont'd
Involuntary cancellation of existence, §50-73.52:6.
Amendment of certificate, §50-73.12.
Annual registration fees, §§50-73.66 to 50-73.71.
Applicability of act, §50-73.72.
Existing limited partnerships, §50-73.76.
Assignment of partnership interests, §§50-73.44 to 50-73.48.
Assignment, §50-73.45.
Nature of partnership interest, §50-73.44.
Partner's transferable interest subject to changing order, §50-73.46:1.
Power of estate of deceased or incompetent partner, §50-73.48.
Right of assignee to become limited partner, §50-73.47.
Assumed or fictitious names.
Certificate of limited partnership, §50-73.21.
Authorization to transact business in Commonwealth.
Required, §50-73.10:1.
Automatic cancellation of existence.
Grounds, §50-73.52:5.
Business transactions of partner with partnership, §50-73.10.
Cancellation of existence.
Automatic cancellation.
Grounds, §50-73.52:5.
Certificate.
Filing, contents, §50-73.52:4.
Involuntary cancellation, §50-73.52:6.
Judicial dissolution.
Completion of winding up of affairs, §50-73.50.
Registration fees.
Effect of certificate of cancellation on liability for fee, §50-73.67.
Reinstatement, §50-73.52:7.
Certificate of limited partnership.
Amendment of certificate, §50-73.12.
Certificate of amendment.
Filing, requirements, §50-73.12.
Events requiring amendment, §50-73.12.
Execution, signing, §50-73.15.
Filing fee, §50-73.17.
Assumed or fictitious names, §50-73.21.
Cancellation of certificate.
Filing fee, §50-73.17.
Contents, §50-73.11.
Defined, §50-73.1.
Delivery of certificates to limited partners, §50-73.20.
Execution of certificates, §50-73.16.
Fees, §50-73.17.
Filing requirements, §50-73.17.
Liability for false statement in certificate, §50-73.18.
Payment of registration fees as prerequisite to issuance of certificate, §50-73.70.
Reinstatement.
Partnership that has ceased to exist, §50-73.52:7.
Required to form, §50-73.11.
Restated certificate.
Filing, executing, §50-73.12.
Schedule of fees, §50-73.17.
Scope of notice, §50-73.19.
Signing certificates, §50-73.15.
Specifications, §50-73.11.

LIMITED PARTNERSHIPS —Cont'd
Certificate reciting change, correction, merger, conversion or domestication.
Request, admitted to record in deed books, continuity of title records, §50-73.76:1.
Change of registered agent, §50-73.5.
Citation of act, §50-73.73.
Construction of act, §50-73.72.
Application of existing limited partnership, §50-73.76.
Laws governing cases not provided for in act, §50-73.75.
Rules for cases not provided for in act, §50-73.75.
Savings provisions, §50-73.77.
Severability, §50-73.74.
Transition provisions, §50-73.77.
Contribution.
Defined, §50-73.1.
Form of contribution, §50-73.32.
General partner, §50-73.30.
Liability for contribution, §50-73.33.
Liability upon return of contribution, §50-73.43.
Person erroneously believing himself limited partner, §50-73.25.
Conversion.
Effect, §50-73.127.
General partnership to limited partnership, §§50-73.11:3, 50-73.11:4.
Limited partnership to general partnership, §50-73.126.
Correction of records.
Authority of commission, §50-73.17.
Date of formation, §50-73.11.
Deceased partner.
Power of assignment of partnership interest, §50-73.48.
Definitions, §50-73.1.
Domestic limited partnership, §§13.1-603, 13.1-803.
Foreign limited partnership, §§13.1-603, 13.1-803.
Delayed effective date.
Certificates filed under chapter, §50-73.17.
Derivative actions, §§50-73.62 to 50-73.65.
Expenses, §50-73.65.
Pleading, §50-73.64.
Proper plaintiff, §50-73.63.
Right of action, §50-73.62.
Designation of registered agent, §50-73.4.
Dissolution and winding up, §§50-73.49 to 50-73.52.
Cancellation of existence.
Certificate, filing, contents, §50-73.52:4.
Judicial dissolution, §50-73.50.
Disposal of known claims, §50-73.52:1.
Disposal of other claims, §50-73.52:2.
Application for court determination of security, §50-73.52:3.
Distribution of assets, §50-73.52.
Events causing, §50-73.49.
Judicial dissolution, §50-73.50.
Winding up, §50-73.51.
Distribution in kind, §50-73.40.
Distribution of assets.
Winding up, §50-73.52.
Distributions upon withdrawal.
Distribution in kind, §50-73.40.
Events of withdrawal on general partners, §50-73.28.
Interim distributions, §50-73.36.
Liability upon return of contribution, §50-73.43.
Limitations on distribution, §50-73.42.

LIMITED PARTNERSHIPS —Cont'd
Distributions upon withdrawal —Cont'd
No right to, §50-73.39:1.
Right to distribution, §50-73.41.
Sharing of distributions, §50-73.35.
Withdrawal of general partner, §§50-73.28, 50-73.38.
Dual status as registered limited liability partnership.
Criteria for establishing, §50-73.78.
Effective date of chapter, §50-73.77.
Effective time and date.
Certificates filed under chapter, §50-73.17.
Electronic filing of information required by chapter.
Commission may accept, §50-73.17.
Employment of unauthorized aliens.
Foreign limited partnerships.
Involuntary cancellation of certificate, §50-73.58:2.
Involuntary cancellation of existence, §50-73.52:6.
English language.
Documents to be in English, §50-73.17.
Execution of certificates, §§50-73.15, 50-73.16.
Execution of documents, §50-73.15.
Existence.
Cancellation.
Automatic cancellation.
Grounds, §50-73.52:5.
Certificate.
Filing, contents, §50-73.52:4.
Involuntary cancellation, §50-73.52:6.
Judicial dissolution.
Completion of winding up of affairs, §50-73.50.
Reinstatement, §50-73.52:7.
Facsimile signatures on documents filed under chapter, §50-73.17.
False information, signing document containing, §50-73.15.
Fees.
Reinstatement.
Partnership that has ceased to exist, §50-73.52:7.
Schedule of fees, §50-73.17.
Filing, §50-73.17.
Execution of documents to be filed, §50-73.15.
Failure to file required document.
Involuntary cancellation of existence, §50-73.52:6.
Finance.
Form of contribution, §50-73.32.
Liability for contribution, §50-73.33.
Sharing of distributions, §50-73.35.
Sharing of profits and losses, §50-73.34.
Foreign limited partnerships, §§50-73.53 to 50-73.61.
Aliens.
Employment of unauthorized aliens.
Involuntary cancellation of certificate, §50-73.58:2.
Conversion to other entity, §50-73.57:3.
Defined, §§13.1-603, 13.1-803, 50-73.1.
Employment of unauthorized aliens.
Involuntary cancellation of certificate, §50-73.58:2.
Failure to file documents.
Involuntary cancellation of certificate, §50-73.58:2.
Limited partnerships.
Merger filing fee, §50-73.17.

LIMITED PARTNERSHIPS —Cont'd
Foreign limited partnerships —Cont'd
Merger, §50-73.57:2.
Registered agent.
Failure to maintain.
Involuntary cancellation of certificate, §50-73.58:2.
Statement of change.
Failure to file, automatic cancellation of certificate, §50-73.58:1.
Registered office.
Failure to maintain.
Involuntary cancellation of certificate, §50-73.58:2.
Registration, §§50-73.53 to 50-73.61.
Amendment or correction, §50-73.57.
Application, §§50-73.54, 50-73.57, 50-73.57:1.
Filing fee, §50-73.17.
Automatic cancellation, §50-73.58:1.
Cancellation of certificate of registration, §50-73.58.
Automatic cancellation, §50-73.58:1.
Employment of unauthorized aliens, §50-73.58:2.
Involuntary cancellation, §50-73.58:2.
Reinstatement, §50-73.58:3.
Certificate of registration, §50-73.58.
Required to transact business, §50-73.53.
Employment of unauthorized aliens.
Involuntary cancellation of certificate, §50-73.58:2.
Failure to pay annual fee.
Automatic cancellation, §50-73.58:1.
Involuntary cancellation of certificate, §50-73.58:2.
Law governing, §50-73.53.
Liability for false statement in application, §50-73.57:1.
Name, §50-73.56.
Registration of business, §§50-73.59 to 50-73.61.
Reinstatement after cancellation of certificate, §50-73.58:3.
Requirements, §50-73.54.
Transaction of business without registration, §§50-73.59, 50-73.60.
Transactions not constituting transacting business, §50-73.61.
Service of process.
Cancellation of certificate of registration.
Clerk of commission appointed as agent for service upon automatic cancellation of certificate, §50-73.58:1.
Service on partnership whose registration has been canceled, §50-73.58.
Transaction of business without registration.
Initiating actions against foreign limited partnerships transacting without registration, §50-73.59.
Foreign stock corporation merging with, §13.1-766.1.
Formation generally, §§50-73.11 to 50-73.21.
General partners, §§50-73.27 to 50-73.31.
Admission of additional partners, §50-73.27.
Automatic cancellation of existence.
Duties as trustees in liquidation, §50-73.52:5.
Contributions, §50-73.30.
Events of withdrawal, §50-73.28.
General powers and liabilities, §50-73.29.
Involuntary cancellation of existence.
Duties as trustees in liquidation, §50-73.52:6.
Powers and liabilities, §50-73.29.

LIMITED PARTNERSHIPS —Cont'd
General partners —Cont'd
Right of derivative action, §50-73.62.
Right to vote, §50-73.31.
Voting, §50-73.31.
Withdrawal of general partner, §50-73.37.
Event of withdrawal, §50-73.1.
Insurance companies investments, §38.2-1427.1.
Interim distributions, §50-73.36.
Judicial dissolution, §50-73.50.
Limited partners, §§50-73.22:1 to 50-73.26.
Admission, §50-73.22:1.
Copies of partnership records, §50-73.26.
Delivery of certificates to limited partners, §50-73.20.
Inspection of partnership records, §50-73.26.
Liability to third parties, §50-73.24.
Membership, §50-73.22:1.
Person erroneously believing himself limited partner, §50-73.25.
Right of assignee to become limited partner, §50-73.47.
Right to information, §50-73.26.
Right to vote, §50-73.23.
Voting, §50-73.23.
Withdrawal of limited partner, §50-73.38.
Liquidation.
Automatic cancellation of existence, §50-73.52:5.
Involuntary cancellation of existence, §50-73.52:6.
Merger, §§50-73.48:1 to 50-73.48:4.
Approval of merger, §50-73.48:2.
Articles of merger, §50-73.48:3.
Execution, §50-73.15.
Filing, requirements, effective date, §50-73.17.
Signing, §50-73.15.
Compliance with statutory requirements, §50-73.48:1.
Contents of plan of merger, §50-73.48:1.
Corporations.
Foreign corporations, §13.1-766.1.
Effect of merger, §50-73.48:4.
Foreign limited partnerships.
Filing fee, §50-73.17.
Plan of merger, §§50-73.48:1 to 50-73.48:4.
Requirements, §50-73.48:1.
Name.
Assumed or fictitious names in certificate, §50-73.21.
Distinguishable upon records of commission, §50-73.2.
Requirements, §50-73.2.
Reservation of name, §50-73.3.
Fee, §50-73.17.
Words or abbreviation in certificate, §50-73.2.
Nature of business, §50-73.9.
Partnerships formed prior to January 1, 1987.
Continued existence not impaired, transition and savings provisions, §50-73.77.
Place of business.
Principal office and registered agent, §50-73.4.
Principal office.
Required to maintain, place of keeping records, §50-73.4.
Property title records.
Continuity upon change, correction, merger, conversion or domestication.
Certificate reciting, admitted to record in deed books, §50-73.76:1.
Recordkeeping requirements, §50-73.8.

LIMITED PARTNERSHIPS —Cont'd
Registered agent.
Change of registered agent, §50-73.5.
Failure to file statement.
Automatic cancellation of existence, §50-73.52:5.
Designation, §50-73.4.
Duty to forward process, notice or demand, §50-73.4.
Failure to maintain.
Involuntary cancellation of existence, §50-73.52:6.
Resignation, §50-73.6.
Service of notice, process and other papers, §50-73.7.
Designation by agent of person to receive, §50-73.7.
Registered limited liability partnerships, §§50-73.132 to 50-73.143.
See REGISTERED LIMITED LIABILITY PARTNERSHIPS.
Registered office.
Change.
Statement of change.
Requirements, filing, executing, §50-73.5.
Failure to maintain.
Involuntary cancellation of existence, §50-73.52:6.
Required to maintain, §50-73.4.
Registration fees, §§50-73.66 to 50-73.71.
Amount, special fund, paid into, use by commission, excess, general fund, paid into, §50-73.67.
Application of payment, §50-73.66.
Assessment, §50-73.67.
Cancellation of existence.
Effect of certificate of cancellation on liability for fee, §50-73.67.
Failure to make timely payment, §50-73.52:5.
Collection actions, §50-73.71.
Deadline for payment, §50-73.67.
Failure to make timely payment, §50-73.69.
Cancellation of existence, §50-73.52:5.
Imposition, §50-73.67.
Payment of fees as prerequisite to issuance of certificate, §50-73.70.
Penalty for failure to make timely payment, §50-73.69.
Refunds not permitted, §50-73.67.
Unpaid bills, §50-73.71.
Reinstatement.
Partnership that has ceased to exist, §50-73.52:7.
Reservation of name, §50-73.3.
Resignation of registered agent, §50-73.6.
Right to distribution, §50-73.41.
Scope of business, §50-73.9.
Service of notice, process and other papers.
Clerk of commission agent to receive.
Failure to appoint registered agent, agent not found, §50-73.7.
Designation by agent of person to receive, §50-73.7.
How process served, §8.01-304.
Office of registered agent, §50-73.7.
Severability, §50-73.74.
Short title, §50-73.73.
Signing document to be filed, §50-73.15.
State corporation commission generally, §§12.1-1 to 12.1-43.
See STATE CORPORATION COMMISSION.

LIMITED PARTNERSHIPS —Cont'd
Status as registered limited liability partnership.
Dual status, establishing, §50-73.78.
Title of act, §50-73.73.
Title records.
Continuity upon change, correction, merger, conversion or domestication.
Certificate reciting, admitted to record in deed books, §50-73.76:1.
Transacting business under assumed name, §50-73.21.
Certificate.
Failure to file.
Effect on right of action, §59.1-76.
Filing of copy with commission, §59.1-70.
Transactions of partner with partnership, §50-73.10.
Trustees in liquidation.
Automatic cancellation of existence.
Duties, §50-73.52:5.
Involuntary cancellation of existence.
Duties, §50-73.52:6.
Unauthorized partnership transacting business in Commonwealth.
Criminal penalty, §50-73.10:1.
Winding up, §§50-73.51, 50-73.52.
Withdrawal of registration as registered limited liability partnership, §50-73.78.

LIMOUSINES AND EXECUTIVE SEDAN CARRIERS.
Employee liens, §§43-24 to 43-26.
Motor carriers generally.
See MOTOR CARRIERS, PASSENGERS.
Public service companies generally, §§56-1 to 56-87.
See PUBLIC SERVICE COMPANIES.
Supplier liens, §§43-24 to 43-26.
Transportation companies generally, §§56-99.2 to 56-140.
See TRANSPORTATION COMPANIES.
Workers' compensation.
Drivers not included in definition of employee when excluded from taxation by federal unemployment tax act, §65.2-101.

LINE ITEM VETO.
Governor, VA Const Art V §6.

LINE OF DUTY ACT, §§9.1-400 to 9.1-408.
Allowances by governing body of locality, §15.2-1511.
Appeals.
Comptroller's decisions, §9.1-405.
Judgments, §9.1-406.
Burial expenses.
Payments for, §9.1-402.1.
Claims for payments, §9.1-403.
Comptroller.
Warrants for payment, §9.1-404.
Confidentiality of investigation records, §9.1-408.
Costs.
Investigations, §9.1-403.
Deceased persons.
Payments for burial expenses, §9.1-402.1.
Payments to beneficiaries, §9.1-402.
Defined terms, §9.1-400.
Disabled persons.
Claims for payments, §9.1-403.

LINE OF DUTY ACT —Cont'd
Disabled persons —Cont'd
Health insurance.
Continued coverage, §9.1-401.
Short-term disability benefit, §9.1-401.1.
Funeral expenses.
Payments for burial expenses, §9.1-402.1.
Health insurance.
Continued coverage, §9.1-401.
Investigations, §9.1-403.
Payments to beneficiaries.
Claims for payments, §9.1-403.
Comptroller.
Warrants for payment, §9.1-404.
Deceased persons, §9.1-402.
Short-term disability benefit, §9.1-401.1.
Surviving spouse.
Claims for payments, §9.1-403.
Health insurance.
Continued coverage, §9.1-401.
Title of chapter, §9.1-400.
Training concerning benefits, §9.1-407.
Tuition and required fees for state supported colleges and universities.
Waiver for spouses and children of certain military and public safety personnel, §23-7.4:1.

LINEUPS.
In person and photo lineups.
Written policies and procedures for conducting.
Establishment by law enforcement, required, §19.2-390.02.
Training standards and model policy, §9.1-102.

LIONS OF VIRGINIA.
Special license plates for members, §46.2-746.7.

LIQUEFIED PETROLEUM GAS CONTAINERS, §§18.2-493 to 18.2-498.
Definitions, §18.2-493.
Exempt containers, §18.2-498.
Fines and costs, §18.2-497.
5 gallon or less capacity containers.
Exempt containers, §18.2-498.
Presumptive evidence, §18.2-495.
Unlawful use of, filling or refilling or trafficking in, §18.2-496.
Presumption, §18.2-495.
Punishment, §18.2-496.

LIQUEFIED PETROLEUM GAS FITTERS, §§54.1-1128 to 54.1-1135.
Application for license, §54.1-1130.
Continuing education, §54.1-1133.
Defined, §54.1-1128.
Examinations, §54.1-1130.
Exemptions from provisions, §54.1-1131.
Expiration of license, §54.1-1132.
Grounds for denial or revocation of certification or license, §54.1-1134.
Licenses, §54.1-1129.
Applications, §54.1-1130.
Denial or revocation of certification or license.
Grounds, §54.1-1134.
Expiration and renewal, §54.1-1132.
Prohibited acts, §54.1-1135.
Renewal of license, §54.1-1132.
Reports.
Building officials and others, §54.1-1134.

LIQUIDATED DAMAGES.
Attorneys' fees.
Lien for fees, §54.1-3932.
Priority over medical services lien, §8.01-66.3.

LIQUIDATED DAMAGES —Cont'd
Employee theft, §8.01-44.4.
Fishing, inland waters.
Use prohibition violations, §29.1-533.
Leases.
Early termination by military personnel, §55-248.21:1.
Leases, UCC, §§8.2A-503, 8.2A-504.
Letters of credit, §8.5A-111.
Motor vehicle weight limit violations, §46.2-1135.
Petroleum products franchises.
Provision violations, §59.1-21.12.
Sales, UCC, §8.2-718.
Shoplifting, §8.01-44.4.
Uniform computer information transactions act.
Remedies, §59.1-508.4.
Wiretapping.
Unlawful interception, disclosure or use, §19.2-69.

LIQUIDATION OF ALIEN INSURERS, §38.2-1520.
When liquidation may be entered, §38.2-1521.

LIQUIDATION OF DENTAL OR OPTOMETRIC SERVICES PLANS, §38.2-4509.1.

LIQUIDATION OF FRATERNAL BENEFIT SOCIETIES, §38.2-4130.

LIQUIDATION OF HEALTH MAINTENANCE ORGANIZATIONS, §38.2-4317.

LIQUIDATION OF HEALTH SERVICES PLANS, §38.2-4214.1.

LIQUIDATION OF INSURERS.
Generally, §§38.2-1500 to 38.2-1522.

LIQUIDATION OF LEGAL SERVICES PLANS, §38.2-4408.1.

LIQUID FUELS SALES.
Assisting in violations, §18.2-230.
False trade name or mixing brand, §18.2-229.
Fraud and misrepresentation, §18.2-226.
Imitating indicia of other brand, §18.2-228.
Misdemeanor for violations, §18.2-232.
Sale from pump indicating other brand, §18.2-227.

LIQUOR CONTROL ACT, §§4.1-100 to 4.1-517.
See ALCOHOLIC BEVERAGES.

LIS PENDENS NOTICE, §§8.01-268, 8.01-269.
Decedents' estates.
Beneficiary liability, §64.2-536.
Derelict buildings.
Locality appointed as receiver to repair derelict and blighted buildings, §15.2-907.2.
Recording in deed books, §17.1-227.
Ungranted shores of the sea.
Filing of notice, §28.2-1513.

LIST OF HEIRS.
Decedents' estates, §64.2-509.
Fee on recording of list of heirs or affidavit.
Tax in lieu of probate tax, §§58.1-1717.1, 58.1-1718, 58.1-3805.

LIST PRICE.
Motorcycle dealers advertising, §46.2-1993.81.
Motor vehicle dealer advertising, §46.2-1581.
T&M vehicle dealer advertising, §46.2-1990.
Trailer dealer advertising, §46.2-1992.84.

LITERARY FUND, §§22.1-142 to 22.1-161, VA Const Art VIII §8.
Accountant for fund, §22.1-143.
Board of education to administer and hold, VA Const Art VIII §8.
Criminal fines and penalties.
Disposition of certain fines, §19.2-353.
Deposit of funds, §22.1-143.
Distribution of funds, §22.1-147.
Health regulatory boards.
Monetary penalties.
Disposition, §54.1-2401.
Insurance violations, disposition of fines and penalties, §38.2-225.
Investment of fund, §§22.1-142, 22.1-145.
Loans.
Additional funds for loans, §22.1-149.
Application for loan, §22.1-153.
Form, §22.1-153.
Disbursal of proceeds without approval prohibited, §22.1-153.
Distribution of funds, §22.1-147.
Evidence of loan, §22.1-151.
Form of application, §22.1-153.
Indebtedness of local governments, §22.1-161.
Levy of taxes for purpose of repaying school construction loans, §22.1-159.
Lien on locality's funds created, §22.1-161.
Payment of principal and interest, §§22.1-152, 22.1-159, 22.1-160.
Installment payments, §22.1-152.
Levy of taxes for purpose of repaying school construction loans, §22.1-159.
Provisions for governing bodies, §22.1-158.
School boards authorized to anticipate payment of loans, §22.1-160.
Power of board to make loans from fund, §22.1-146.
Provisions for payment by governing bodies, §22.1-158.
Rate of interest, §22.1-150.
Restrictions upon making loans, §22.1-148.
Retirement of previous loans, §22.1-148.
School boards authorized to anticipate payment of loans, §22.1-160.
School boards authorized to borrow from fund, §22.1-153.
Management, §22.1-142.
Money deposited into fund, VA Const Art VIII §8.
Motor vehicles.
Disposition of fines and forfeitures, §46.2-114.
Permanent and perpetual school fund, §22.1-142, VA Const Art VIII §8.
Prisoner estates.
Disposal of unclaimed personal property, §53.1-228.
Public school authority.
Management of funds transferred from literary fund, §§22.1-165, 22.1-175.
Repayments to literary fund, §22.1-170.
Transfers from literary fund to authority, §22.1-175.
Recovery of money due fund, §22.1-144.
School buildings.
Power of board to make loans for erection of school buildings, §22.1-146.
School buses.
Alternative fuel conversion.
Power of board to make loans, §22.1-146.

LITERARY GIFTS.
Generally.
See CHARITABLE GIFTS.

LITER TAX.
Wine, §§4.1-234, 4.1-235.

LITIGATION EXPENSES.
Attorneys' fees generally.
See ATTORNEYS' FEES.
Generally.
See COURT COSTS AND FEES.
Law of costs generally, §§17.1-600 to 17.1-629.
See COURT COSTS AND FEES.
Prisoner litigation reform, §8.01-691.

LITIGATION TAX, §§58.1-1727 to 58.1-1729.

LITTER.
Automotive engine maintenance, fluids for.
Management and recycling program, §10.1-1422.6.
Bags, §10.1-1420.
Beverage container.
Defined, §10.1-1415.2.
Cathode ray tubes recycling, §10.1-1425.26.
Civil penalties.
Improper disposal of solid waste, §10.1-1418.1.
Collection and survey, §10.1-1416.
Community service.
Roadway litter pick-up program for probationers.
Civil immunity, §8.01-226.8.
Container.
Defined, §10.1-1414.
Counties, cities or towns.
County manager plan of government.
Violations of litter control ordinances, §15.2-733.
General powers as to waste and recycling, §§15.2-901, 15.2-927 to 15.2-939.
Preemption, §10.1-1425.
Requiring property owners to remove from property, §§10.1-1421, 15.2-901.
Defined, §10.1-1414.
Degradable.
Defined, §10.1-1415.2.
Department of waste management.
Duties, §10.1-1422.
Disposable package.
Defined, §10.1-1414.
Enforcement of provisions, §10.1-1417.
Fully halogenated chlorofluorocarbons, §10.1-1424.1.
Funds.
Control and recycling fund, §10.1-1422.01.
Waste tire trust fund, §10.1-1422.3.
Grants.
Prevention of litter, §10.1-1422.04.
Hardwood floors.
Products containing trichloroethylene prohibited, §10.1-1424.2.
Highways.
Allowing escape of load material from vehicles, §10.1-1424.
Improper disposal of solid waste, §10.1-1418.1.
Tires, §10.1-1418.2.
Liability for large waste tire pile fires, §10.1-1418.3.
Lien for removal, §10.1-1418.5.
Removal of waste tire piles, §10.1-1418.4.
Labeling of plastic containers, §10.1-1415.1.
Litter bag, §10.1-1420.
Defined, §10.1-1414.
Litter control and recycling fund, §10.1-1422.01.
Advisory board, §10.1-1422.02.
Membership, §10.1-1422.03.
Littering.
Generally, §18.2-324.

LITTER —Cont'd
Litter receptacle.
Defined, §10.1-1414.
Placement, §10.1-1419.
Local ordinances.
Preemption, §10.1-1425.
Removal of litter, §10.1-1421.
Motor vehicles.
Allowing escape of load material, §10.1-1424.
Notice.
Public notice of provisions, §10.1-1423.
Oil.
Used motor oil.
Management and recycling program, §10.1-1422.6.
Oil filters.
Management and recycling program, §10.1-1422.6.
Person.
Defined, §10.1-1414.
Placement of litter receptacles, §10.1-1419.
Plastic container labels, §10.1-1415.1.
Plastic holding devices.
Beverage container connections, §10.1-1415.2.
Preemption of local ordinances, §10.1-1425.
Prevention.
Grants, §10.1-1422.04.
Program, §10.1-1415.
Public notice of provisions, §10.1-1423.
Public place.
Defined, §10.1-1414.
Recycling, §10.1-1422.2.
Defined, §10.1-1414.
Removing litter from receptacles.
Responsibility for removal, §10.1-1421.
Sales of the business within the Commonwealth.
Defined, §10.1-1414.
Six-pack rings.
Plastic holding devices, §10.1-1415.2.
Sold within the Commonwealth.
Defined, §10.1-1414.
Surveys, §10.1-1416.
Tires.
Disposal of waste tires, §10.1-1422.1.
Liability for large waste tire pile fires, §10.1-1418.3.
Lien for removal, §10.1-1418.5.
Partial reimbursement for waste tires, §10.1-1422.4.
Removal of waste tire piles, §10.1-1418.4.
Waste tire trust fund, §10.1-1422.3.
Trichloroethylene.
Products containing trichloroethylene prohibited, §10.1-1424.2.
Vehicle.
Defined, §10.1-1414.
Violations of provisions, §10.1-1418.
Waste tires.
Disposal, §10.1-1422.1.
Watercraft.
Defined, §10.1-1414.

LITTER CONTROL AND RECYCLING FUND ADVISORY BOARD, §10.1-1422.02.
Membership, §10.1-1422.03.

LITTERING.
Fines.
State parks.
Civil penalties, §10.1-200.2.

LITTER TAX, §§58.1-1706 to 58.1-1710.
Statute of limitations.
Criminal prosecutions, §19.2-8.

LITTLE LEAGUE BASEBALL CHALLENGER WEEK IN VIRGINIA, §2.2-3304.1.

LITTLE LEAGUE SPORTS.
Team physicians.
Immunity from liability, §8.01-225.1.

LITTORAL RIGHTS.
Submerged lands.
Rights of owners to extend to mean low-water mark, §28.2-1202.

LIVABLE HOME TAX CREDIT, §58.1-339.7.

LIVE-BIRD MARKETING SYSTEM.
Avian influenza prevention and control measures, §3.2-6023.

LIVE HORSE RACING COMPACT, §§59.1-394.1 to 59.1-394.4.
Compact committee.
Established, §59.1-394.1.
Members, §59.1-394.2.
Powers and duties, §59.1-394.1.
Terms of members, §59.1-394.2.
Cooperation of departments, agencies and officers, §59.1-394.3.
Racing commission.
Effect on powers, §59.1-394.4.
Terms of compact, §59.1-394.1.

LIVER TRANSPLANTS.
Medical assistance service plans, §32.1-325.

LIVERY OF SEISIN.
Estates to lie in grant as well as in livery, §55-5.

LIVERY STABLE KEEPER'S LIEN, §43-32.
Appeals, §43-36.
Defrauding person having, §18.2-188.1.
Enforcement, §43-34.
Validity, §43-35.

LIVESTOCK.
Agricultural and forestal districts, §§15.2-4300 to 15.2-4314.
County executive form and certain other counties, §§15.2-4400 to 15.2-4407.
Agricultural animals, care of by owner, §3.2-6503.1.
Agricultural cooperative associations, §§13.1-313 to 13.1-345.
See AGRICULTURAL COOPERATIVE ASSOCIATIONS.
Agriculture and consumer services board.
Diseases.
Laboratory for diagnosis, §3.2-5903.
Powers and duties as to, §§3.2-6001, 3.2-6002.
Law enforcement officers.
Duty to execute orders of board, §3.2-6013.
Animals generally.
See ANIMALS.
Beef industry council, §§3.2-1300 to 3.2-1308.
See BEEF INDUSTRY COUNCIL.
Bioterrorism.
Penalties, §18.2-46.7.
Breed of bull or cattle.
Fraudulent misrepresentation, §18.2-190.
Cattle.
See CATTLE.
Cattle guards, §§55-304, 55-305.
Lawful fence, §55-299.
Commercial feed, §§3.2-4800 to 3.2-4817.
See FEED.

LIVESTOCK —Cont'd
Damages.
Violations of certain provisions, §3.2-6019.
Definitions, §3.2-5900.
Diseases.
See LIVESTOCK AND ANIMAL DISEASES.
Dogs killing, injuring or chasing livestock, §§3.2-6552, 3.2-6553.
Hybrid canines, §3.2-6583.
Compensation for livestock and poultry killed, §3.2-6584.
Misdemeanor, §18.2-403.1.
Domestic animals generally, §§3.2-5900 to 3.2-5905.
Estrays, §§55-202 to 55-206.
Executions.
Sustenance provided for livestock, §8.01-490.
False pedigree, §18.2-205.
False pretenses in obtaining registration, §18.2-205.
Feed, commercial, §§3.2-4800 to 3.2-4817.
See FEED.
Fences.
Cattle guards and gates across rights-of-way, §§55-304, 55-305.
Crossing lawful fences, §§55-306 to 55-309.
Lawful fence, §55-299.
No-fence law, §§55-310 to 55-316.
Gates across rights-of-way, §§55-304, 55-305.
Hogs generally.
See PIGS.
Horses.
See HORSES.
Hunter injury.
Damage stamp program, §§29.1-352 to 29.1-358.
Intangible personal property tax.
Certain livestock producers, §58.1-1102.
Generally, §§58.1-1100 to 58.1-1118.
See PERSONAL PROPERTY TAXES.
Larceny, §18.2-97.
Liens.
Advances to tenants and laborers, §§43-29, 43-30.
Defrauding persons having, §18.2-188.1.
Maiming, killing or poisoning, §18.2-144.
Meat and poultry products inspection, §§3.2-5400 to 3.2-5418.
Motor carriers, property.
Exemptions from provisions, §46.2-2101.
No-fence law, §§55-310 to 55-316.
Personal property taxes.
Classification of tangible personal property, §§58.1-3503, 58.1-3505.
Pigs generally.
See PIGS.
Poultry.
See POULTRY.
Purchases from unknown persons, §§59.1-192 to 59.1-195.
Defined terms, §59.1-192.
Provision violations, §59.1-195.
Records.
Inspections, §59.1-194.
Livestock delivered by motor vehicle, §59.1-193.
Quarantine.
Contagious and infectious diseases, §§3.2-6003 to 3.2-6008.
No-fence law, §55-315.
Railroad corporations.
Appraisal of injured or killed stock.
Application of provisions, §56-439.
Board of appraisers' duties, §56-436.

LIVESTOCK —Cont'd
Railroad corporations —Cont'd
Appraisal of injured or killed stock —Cont'd
Costs, §56-437.
Fee of appraisers and clerks, §56-438.
Effect, §56-437.
Notice of injured or killed stock, §56-439.1.
Retail sales and use tax.
Agricultural exemptions, §58.1-609.2.
Running at large.
Permitting animals to run at large in county under quarantine, §18.2-121.1.
Unincorporated communities and villages, §§55-323 to 55-330.
See ANIMALS RUNNING AT LARGE.
Sale of unborn young, §8.2-105.
Slaughterhouses.
Sanitary requirements for food establishments, §§3.2-5105 to 3.2-5119.
Spotlight on agricultural land.
Trespass by, §18.2-121.2.
State institutions or agencies raising.
Selling instead of slaughtering, §2.2-614.
Stock feeds generally, §§3.2-4800 to 3.2-4817.
See FEED.
Swine.
See PIGS.
Trespass.
Permitting animals to run at large in county under quarantine, §18.2-121.
Spotlight on agricultural land, §18.2-121.2.
Unauthorized release of animals used for agriculture, §18.2-403.4.
Unborn young, sale of, §8.2-105.
Watering on riparian lands.
Conditions, §28.2-1203.
Weights and measures.
Generally, §§3.2-5600 to 3.2-5648.
See WEIGHTS AND MEASURES.
Sale of livestock.
Day and hour of livestock sale.
Announcement, §3.2-5639.
Determination of weight of livestock on date of sale, §3.2-5638.
Scale house in establishment where livestock bought from producers, §3.2-5636.
Type registering weighbeams or automatic weight recorders.
Required, §3.2-5637.

LIVESTOCK AND ANIMAL DISEASES, §§3.2-6000 to 3.2-6023.
Altering disease control identification, §3.2-6016.
Anthrax germs.
Unlawful acts as to, §3.2-6017.
Anthrax, possession.
Unlawful activities, §3.2-6017.
Appraisement of condemned cattle, §3.2-6020.
Bang's disease, §§3.2-6000 to 3.2-6023.
Biological residues.
Abatement, §3.2-6002.
Bringing infected animals into Commonwealth, §3.2-6011.
Compensation.
Euthanized or slaughtered animals, §3.2-6021.
Damages, §3.2-6019.
Enforcement of orders.
Circuit court judges, §3.2-6014.
Law enforcement officers, §3.2-6013.

LIVESTOCK AND ANIMAL DISEASES —Cont'd
Euthanasia or slaughter.
By owner, §3.2-6009.
Compensation, §3.2-6021.
Indemnity to owner, §3.2-6022.
Importation.
Certificate of veterinary inspection required for certain pet animals, §3.2-5902.
Prohibited acts, §3.2-6011.
Importation, proclamation prohibiting, §3.2-6010.
Violation, §3.2-6011.
Laboratory for diagnosis of diseases, §3.2-5903.
Law enforcement officers.
Authority to execute orders, §3.2-6013.
Pleuropneumonia.
Suppression, §3.2-6015.
Powers and duties of agriculture and consumer services board, §§3.2-6001, 3.2-6002.
Prevention and eradication, §3.2-6002.
Regulations, penalty for violations, §3.2-6023.
Protection of livestock and poultry, §3.2-6001.
Quarantine, §§3.2-6003 to 3.2-6008.
Contagious and infectious diseases, §§3.2-6003 to 3.2-6008.
Disposition of quarantined animals with potential to impact livestock or poultry, §3.2-6008.
Domestic animals not permitted to enter or leave quarantine, §3.2-6007.
Individuals exposed, §3.2-6006.
No-fence law, §55-315.
Notice of quarantine, §3.2-6005.
Regulations.
Prevention and eradication, §3.2-6002.
Separation and caring for diseased animals, §3.2-6004.
Right of entry, §3.2-6000.
Separation and caring for diseased animals.
Regulations, §3.2-6004.
State veterinarian.
Duty when animals suspected of having disease, §3.2-6003.
Stockyard operators, duties, §3.2-6012.
Stockyards.
Duties of operators, §3.2-6012.
Suppression of certain diseases among domestic animals, §3.2-6015.
Swine fever virus, possession on non-inactivated classical virus.
Unlawful activities, §3.2-6017.
Unlawful activities.
Altering disease control identification, §3.2-6016.
Anthrax, possession, §3.2-6017.
Swine fever virus, possession on non-inactivated classical virus, §3.2-6017.
USDA, cooperation with, §3.2-6015.
Vaccine, authority to test, §3.2-6017.
Violations.
Liability for damages, §3.2-6019.
Penalty, §3.2-6018.
Prevention and control measures, §3.2-6023.

LIVESTOCK WASTE RESOURCES.
Renewable electricity production program.
Grants, §§67-900 to 67-903.

LIVING HISTORICAL FARM MUSEUMS.
Locality operating and maintaining, §15.2-943.

LIVING INDIVIDUALS.
Trademark or service mark identifying particular living individual.
Written consent of individual for registration, §59.1-92.3.

LIVING SHORELINES.
Marine resources commission.
General permit, use for stabilizing tidal shorelines, §28.2-104.1.

LIVING WILLS, §§54.1-2981 to 54.1-2993.
Advance health care directive registry, §§54.1-2994 to 54.1-2996.
Confidentiality, §54.1-2995.
Declaration of anatomical gift.
Filing with registry, §54.1-2995.
Established, §54.1-2994.
Filing documents with, §54.1-2995.
Health care power of attorney.
Filing with registry, §54.1-2995.
Notarization of documents filed, §54.1-2995.
Online, §54.1-2994.
Regulations, promulgation, §54.1-2995.
Revocation of advance directive, §54.1-2985.
Submission of written advance directive, §54.1-2983.
Unregistered documents.
Validity, §54.1-2996.
Agent to make.
Advance directive may appoint, §54.1-2983.
Duties and authority of agent, §54.1-2986.1.
Anatomical gifts.
Advance health care directive, effect of gift, §32.1-291.21.
Assisted living facilities, §63.2-1807.
Brain death.
Criteria for determining, §54.1-2972.
Burden of proof, §54.1-2988.
Cancellation of advance directives, §54.1-2989.
Capacity to make informed decision, §54.1-2983.2.
Clinical studies.
Research, authorization for participation in, §54.1-2983.1.
Concealment of advance directives, §54.1-2989.
Defined terms, §54.1-2982.
Destruction of advance directives, §54.1-2989.
Documents not registered with registry.
Validity, §54.1-2996.
Do not resuscitate orders.
Durable do not resuscitate order, §54.1-2987.1.
Effective date of advance directives, §54.1-2991.
Emergency medical services personnel.
Procedures and forms authorizing personnel to follow, regulations to include, §32.1-111.4.
Euthanasia.
Construction of article, §54.1-2990.
Failure to deliver advance directive, §54.1-2989.1.
Form of advance directives, §54.1-2984.
Immunity, §54.1-2988.
Revocation of advance directive.
Failure to act upon without actual knowledge of revocation, §54.1-2985.
Incapable of making informed decision, §54.1-2983.2.
Incorporation by reference.
Wills, powers of attorney, trust instruments, §64.2-104.
Injunction of unauthorized activity, §54.1-2985.1.

LIVING WILLS —Cont'd
Insurance.
Effect of advance directive, §54.1-2991.
Medically unnecessary treatment.
Construction of article, §54.1-2990.
Mercy killings.
Construction of article, §54.1-2990.
Notice to physicians, §54.1-2983.
Oral advance directive, §54.1-2983.
Partial revocation of advance directives, §54.1-2985.
Physicians who refuse to comply with advance directives, §54.1-2990.
Patient transfers, §54.1-2987.
Preservation of existing rights, §54.1-2992.
Presumptions, §§54.1-2983.3, 54.1-2988.
Procedure for advanced directive without agent, §54.1-2986.
Procedure for making advance directives, §54.1-2983.
Procedure in absence of advance directives, §54.1-2986.
Protest of patient, procedures in case of, §54.1-2986.2.
Reciprocity, §54.1-2993.
Research, authorization for participation in, §54.1-2983.1.
Revocation of advance directives, §54.1-2985.
Scope of directive, §54.1-2983.3.
Short title of act, §54.1-2981.
Suicide.
Effect of advance directive, §54.1-2991.
Validity of documents not registered with registry, §54.1-2996.
Written advance directive, §54.1-2983.

LOAD COVERS.
Vehicles carrying gravel, sand, etc., §46.2-1156.
Fine for failure to prevent escape of contents, VA SCt Rule 3B:2.

LOADS.
Motor vehicle size and weight.
General provisions, §§46.2-1101 to 46.2-1156.
See MOTOR VEHICLE SIZE AND WEIGHT.
Vehicle load covers, §46.2-1156.
Fine for failure to prevent escape of contents, VA SCt Rule 3B:2.
Vehicle loading to prevent escape of contents, §10.1-1424.
Clean up of escaped objects constituting obstruction or endangering travel, §§10.1-1424, 46.2-1156.
Fine for failure to prevent, VA SCt Rule 3B:2.
Vehicles hauling logs, poles, lumber, etc.
Fastening loads, §46.2-1155.
Fine for failure to fasten, VA SCt Rule 3B:2.

LOAN OF OBSCENE MATERIALS TO JUVENILES, §§18.2-390 to 18.2-391.1.

LOANS.
Acceleration, §6.2-401.
Airports revolving fund.
Annual report on loans, §5.1-30.9.
Local government loans, §5.1-30.5.
Pledging loans to secure bonds, §5.1-30.6.
Sale of loans, §5.1-30.7.
Alternative fuels revolving fund.
State and municipal governments, §33.1-223.7.
Annuity contract loans, §38.2-3308.
Banks.
See BANKS.

LOANS —Cont'd
Behavioral health and developmental services department.
Substance abuse.
Review of agency applications for funds or services used in substance abuse programs, §37.2-311.
Boats and other watercraft.
Security interests generally, §§29.1-723 to 29.1-732.
See BOATS AND OTHER WATERCRAFT.
Brownfields restoration and land renewal, §10.1-1237.
Water facilities revolving fund.
Remediation of contaminated properties, §62.1-229.2.
Campaign finance disclosure.
Loans to campaign committees.
Interest payments prohibited, §24.2-947.4:1.
Clean energy improvements.
Localities financing, §15.2-958.3.
Colleges and universities.
Aid to nonpublic higher education, VA Const Art VIII §11.
Economic education and financial literacy courses and instruction, §23-9.2:3.5.
Commercial space flight authority.
Authority to receive, disperse and expend, §2.2-2211.
Construction loans.
Ordinary commercial loans, when considered, banks, investments in , limitation, §6.2-880.
Consumer finance act.
See CONSUMER FINANCE.
Consumer finance companies, §§6.2-1500 to 6.2-1543.
See CONSUMER FINANCE COMPANIES.
Consumer real estate settlement protection act.
See CONSUMER REAL ESTATE SETTLEMENT PROTECTION ACT.
Credit services businesses, §§59.1-335.1 to 59.1-335.12.
Credit unions, §§6.2-1300 to 6.2-1380.
See CREDIT UNIONS.
Dam safety, flood prevention and protection assistance fund, §§10.1-603.19 to 10.1-603.23.
Equal credit opportunities, §§6.2-500 to 6.2-513.
False statements to obtain, §18.2-186.
Farmer major drought, flood and hurricane disaster assistance, §3.2-504.
Fees.
Fee for purposes of influencing financial institution, §18.2-444.2.
Fiduciaries.
Court orders, §64.2-1500.
Reasonable diligence requirement, §64.2-1501.
Time limitations, §64.2-1501.
Fraternal benefit society certificate loans, §§38.2-3308, 38.2-4120.
Fraudulent transactions.
Pretend loans, §55-87.
Gift for purposes of influencing financial institution, §18.2-444.2.
Governor's development opportunity fund, §2.2-115.
Housing authorities.
Loans and donations to housing authority, §36-7.
Housing development authority.
Mortgage loans generally, §§36-55.31 to 36-55.36:1.

LOANS —Cont'd
Housing trust fund.
Authority to make loans, §36-146.
Income tax refunds.
Refund anticipation loans, §§6.2-2500 to 6.2-2505.
Industrial development corporation members, §13.1-989.
Industrial loan associations, §§6.2-1400 to 6.2-1421.
See INDUSTRIAL LOAN ASSOCIATIONS.
Innovation and entrepreneurship investment authority.
Authority to accept, receive, or disburse, §2.2-2228.
Installment loans.
Acceleration, §6.2-401.
Insurance companies.
Collateral loans, §38.2-1430.
Lending of securities, §38.2-1429.
Officers or directors, loans to, §38.2-210.
Policy loans, §38.2-1431.
Insurance policies.
Life insurance, §38.2-1431.
Individual policies, §38.2-3308.
Standard nonforfeiture provisions.
Loan values, §§38.2-3217, 38.2-3218.
Late charges.
Amount, §6.2-400.
Lending practices generally, §§6.2-400 to 6.2-437.
Life insurance policies, §38.2-1431.
Individual policies, §38.2-3308.
Table of values, §38.2-3310.
Standard nonforfeiture provisions.
Loan values, §§38.2-3217, 38.2-3218.
Limited liability companies.
Managers.
Business transactions with limited liability company, §13.1-1026.
Literary fund.
Additional funds for loans, §22.1-149.
Application for loan, §22.1-153.
Form, §22.1-153.
Disbursal of proceeds without approval prohibited, §22.1-153.
Distribution of funds, §22.1-147.
Evidence of loan, §22.1-151.
Form of application, §22.1-153.
Indebtedness of local governments, §22.1-161.
Levy of taxes for purpose of repaying school construction loans, §22.1-159.
Lien on locality's funds created, §22.1-161.
Payment of principal and interest, §§22.1-152, 22.1-159, 22.1-160.
Installment payments, §22.1-152.
Levy of taxes for purpose of repaying school construction loans, §22.1-159.
Provisions for governing bodies, §22.1-158.
School boards authorized to anticipate payment of loans, §22.1-160.
Power of board to make loans from fund, §22.1-146.
Provisions for payment by governing bodies, §22.1-158.
Rate of interest, §22.1-150.
Restrictions upon making loans, §22.1-148.
Retirement of previous loans, §22.1-148.
School boards authorized to anticipate payment of loans, §22.1-160.
School boards authorized to borrow from fund, §22.1 153.

LOANS —Cont'd
Local school boards.
Borrowing from Virginia retirement system, §§22.1-161.1 to 22.1-161.8.
See LOCAL SCHOOL BOARDS.
Lottery, state.
Assignment of prize as collateral for loan, §58.1-4020.1.
Mortgage lender and broker act, §§6.2-1600 to 6.2-1629.
See MORTGAGE LENDERS AND BROKERS.
Mortgage loan originators, §§6.2-1700 to 6.2-1721.
See MORTGAGE LOAN ORIGINATORS.
Mortgage loans.
Generally, §§6.2-406 to 6.2-423, 55-58 to 55-66.6.
See MORTGAGES AND DEEDS OF TRUST.
Housing development authority.
Generally, §§36-55.31 to 36-55.36:1.
Motor vehicle title loans, §§6.2-2200 to 6.2-2227.
Museums.
Property loaned to museums, §§55-210.31 to 55-210.38.
See MUSEUMS.
Partnerships.
Transactions between partner and partnership, §50-73.85.
Payday loan act, §§6.2-1800 to 6.2-1829.
See PAYDAY LOANS.
Port authority.
Federal loans, §62.1-132.15.
Prepayment.
Industrial loan associations.
Penalty for prepayment, §6.2-1409.
Rebates for unearned interest, §6.2-1409.
Rebates.
Unearned interest.
Applicability, §6.2-405.
Industrial loan associations, §6.2-1409.
Rule of 78, §§6.2-402 to 6.2-404.
Subordinate mortgage loans, §6.2-423.
Subordinate mortgage loans, §6.2-423.
Public building authority.
Authority to receive or disburse, §§2.2-2263, 2.2-2271.
Public-private education facilities and infrastructure act.
Comprehensive agreements, §§56-575.9, 56-575.11.
Government assistance, §56-575.10.
Public school authority.
Local school boards, §22.1-166.1.
Public school funds.
Temporary loans to school boards, §22.1-110.
Refund anticipation loans.
Loans in anticipation of income tax refund, §§6.2-2500 to 6.2-2505.
Resources authority.
Sale of loans, §62.1-240.1.
Rule of 78, §6.2-403.
Applicability, §6.2-405.
Notice on loan or sale on credit using method, §6.2-402.
Prohibition on use, §6.2-404.
Satisfaction by use of instrument.
Check tendered, when person not acting in good faith, §8.3A-311.
Savings and loan associations.
See SAVINGS INSTITUTIONS.
Savings banks.
Real estate loans, §6.2-1187.

LOANS —Cont'd
Savings banks —Cont'd
Repeal or amendment of statute or regulation.
Effect on existing loan or investment, §6.2-1188.
Septic tanks.
Betterment loans to repair or replace failing systems, §32.1-164.1:2.
Locality financing for repair of failed septic systems, §15.2-958.6.
Servicemen's readjustment act of 1944, eligibility of minor or widow for guaranty of credit.
Instruments executed to obtain benefits, §11-8.
Small business financing authority.
Authority to obtain, §2.2-2285.
Investment in, purchase or assignment, §2.2-2294.
Loans to lenders, §2.2-2293.
Powers and duties, §2.2-2287.
Solid waste or recycling revolving fund, §§62.1-241.6, 62.1-241.8.
Sale of loans, §62.1-241.9:1.
Student loans, §§23-38.10:2 to 23-38.10:7.
Teaching scholarship loans.
State board authorized to award, §22.1-290.
Tourism financing development authority.
Powers, §15.2-5519.
Trusts.
Power of trustee to borrow money or make loans, §64.2-778.
Truth-in-lending.
Consumer credit.
Compliance with federal law, §6.2-436.
Urban public-private partnership redevelopment fund, §15.2-2417.
Virginia broadband infrastructure loan fund.
Local governments, §15.2-2424.
Pledge of loans to secure bonds of Authority, §15.2-2426.
Prioritization of loans, §15.2-2425.
Sale of loans, §15.2-2427.
Virginia Commonwealth University health system authority.
Acceptance by authority, §23-50.16:11.
Virginia infrastructure loan fund.
Generally, §§15.2-2430 to 15.2-2440.
See VIRGINIA INFRASTRUCTURE PROJECT LOAN FUND.
Loans to local governments, §15.2-2435.
Wage purchases, §6.2-1525.
Water facilities revolving fund.
Agricultural best management practices, §62.1-229.1.
Brownfields restoration and land renewal.
Remediation of contaminated properties, §62.1-229.2.
Loans to local governments or other entities, §62.1-229.
Sale of loans, §62.1-231.1.
Open-space land.
Loans for land conservation, §62.1-229.3.
Remediation of contaminated properties, §62.1-229.2.
Stormwater runoff control best management practices, loans for, §62.1-229.4.
Water supply revolving fund, §§62.1-238, 62.1-239.1.

LOBBYING.
County officers and employees.
Restrictions on activities of former officers and employees.
County executive form of government, §15.2-515.

LOBBYING —Cont'd
County officers and employees —Cont'd
Restrictions on activities of former officers and employees —Cont'd
Urban county executive form of government, §15.2-810.
Public officers and employees.
Representing person or group before prior agency, restrictions, §2.2-3104.02.
Registration and reporting requirements of lobbyists, §§2.2-418 to 2.2-435.

LOBBYISTS.
Registration and reporting requirements, §§2.2-418 to 2.2-435.
Annual registration, §2.2-422.
Annual report of expenditures, §2.2-426.
Automated preparation and transmittal, §2.2-428.
Failure to file, civil penalty, §2.2-431.
Chairman of political party.
Employment prohibited, §2.2-435.
Change, modification or addition to status, §2.2-423.
Civil penalties, failure to file report, §2.2-431.
Contents of registration statement, §2.2-423.
Contingent compensation prohibited, §2.2-432.
Criminal acts, §2.2-433.
Definitions, §2.2-419.
Disclosure database, §2.2-428.
Disclosure statement, §2.2-426.
Automated preparation and transmittal, §2.2-428.
Failure to file, civil penalty, §2.2-431.
Employment by state agency, §2.2-434.
Engaging in lobbying entirely outside capital city, §2.2-422.
Exemptions, §2.2-420.
Expiration of registration, §2.2-422.
Fee, §2.2-424.
Filing, §2.2-427.
Electronic filing, §2.2-428.
Form of disclosure statement, §2.2-426.
Information recorded in legislative docket, §2.2-425.
Intent and purposes of article, §2.2-418.
List of registrants provided general assembly members, §2.2-425.
Local government employees acting as lobbyists, §2.2-422.
Political party chairman.
Employment prohibited, §2.2-435.
Public inspection of registration and reports, §2.2-427.
Registration prior to engaging in lobbying, §2.2-422.
Retention of records by lobbyist, time period, §2.2-429.
State agencies, §2.2-421.
Employment of lobbyist, §2.2-434.
Termination of registration, §2.2-430.

LOCAL AGENCIES.
Criminal justice information system.
Participation, §9.1-129.

LOCAL AND REGIONAL LIBRARIES, §§42.1-33 to 42.1-45.
Appropriations or service conducted by company, society or organization, §42.1-43.
Boards.
Generally, §42.1-35.

LOCAL AND REGIONAL LIBRARIES —Cont'd
Boards —Cont'd
Not mandatory, §42.1-36.
Contract for library services, power of local government, §42.1-34.
Establishment and support.
Powers of local government, §42.1-33.
Internet.
Acceptable Internet use policies.
Power and duty of library boards and certain governing bodies, §42.1-36.1.
Regional boards.
Agreements to create, §42.1-38.
Generally, §42.1-39.
Powers, §42.1-40.
Regional library system.
Establishment, §42.1-37.
Funds and expenses, §42.1-41.
Withdrawal, §42.1-42.
Transfer of properties to governing body of city, §42.1-45.

LOCAL AUTHORITY OVER HIGHWAYS, §§33.1-224 to 33.1-246.
See LOCAL ROAD AUTHORITIES.

LOCAL BOARDS OF EDUCATION.
See LOCAL SCHOOL BOARDS.

LOCAL BOARDS OF SOCIAL SERVICES.
Adoption.
Generally, §§63.2-1200 to 63.2-1248.
See ADOPTION.
Foster care generally, §§63.2-900 to 63.2-915.
See SOCIAL SERVICES.
Generally, §§63.2-300 to 63.2-323.
See SOCIAL SERVICES.
Public assistance.
Generally, §§63.2-500 to 63.2-805.
See PUBLIC AID AND ASSISTANCE.

LOCAL BUDGETS.
Public school funds.
Annual report of expenditures, §22.1-90.
Apportionment of funds, §22.1-99.
Approval of annual budget for school purposes, §22.1-93.
Classification of expenditures, §22.1-115.
Estimate of funds needed for public schools, §22.1-92.
Instructional costs, funds allocated for to be included in school performance report card, §22.1-90.1.
Limitation on expenditures, §22.1-91.
Local appropriations for public schools, §§22.1-94, 22.1-97.
Reduction in state aid.
Length of school term below 180 days or 990 hours, §22.1-98.
Statement of funds available, §22.1-115.
Unexpended school and educational funds, §22.1-100.

LOCAL CHILD FATALITY REVIEW TEAMS, §32.1-283.2.

LOCAL CONSTITUTIONAL OFFICERS, §§15.2-1600 to 15.2-1637.
Abolition of office.
Charters of localities, §§15.2-205, 15.2-206.
Accumulated vacation time.
Computing Commonwealth's financial obligations, §15.2-1605.

LOCAL CONSTITUTIONAL OFFICERS —Cont'd
Advanced payments based on actual expenditures incurred, §15.2-1636.13.
Advertisement of employment positions, §15.2-1604.
Annual audit of accounts and records, §15.2-2511.
Appeal of compensation board decisions, §15.2-1636.9.
Decisions affecting expenses of circuit court clerks, §15.2-1636.10.
Assignment of counsel for defense of constitutional officer, §15.2-1606.
Attorneys for the Commonwealth, §§15.2-1626 to 15.2-1633.
See COMMONWEALTH'S ATTORNEYS.
Bond, §15.2-1601.
Local officers generally, §§15.2-1527 to 15.2-1533.
See LOCAL OFFICERS AND EMPLOYEES.
City status granted town.
Continuance of commissioner of revenue in office, §15.2-3817.
Continuance of treasurer in office, appointment when no treasurer, §15.2-3816.
Elections, §15.2-3820.
Qualifications for office, §15.2-3821.
Sharing of offices, transfer of jurisdiction, §15.2-3822.
Terms of office, §15.2-3820.
Vacancies, §15.2-3821.
Civil penalty for unlawful employment practice, §15.2-1604.
Clerks of circuit courts.
Appointment of deputy, inability to perform duties, §15.2-1635.
Election, powers and duties, §15.2-1634.
Commissioner of revenue.
Election, powers and duties, §15.2-1636.
Salary of city commissioner, §15.2-1636.1.
Salary of county commissioner, §15.2-1636.2.
Compensatory time.
Working on legal holiday, §15.2-1605.
County board form of government, §15.2-408.
Defense of constitutional officer, §15.2-1606.
Deputies.
Appointment, powers, removal, §15.2-1603.
Discrimination with respect to compensation, terms, conditions or privileges, §15.2-1604.
Division of human rights.
Complaints regarding unlawful employment practices, §15.2-1604.
Dual office holding, §§15.2-1534, 15.2-1601.
Duties and compensation, §15.2-1600.
Election, §15.2-1600.
Sharing officers, §15.2-1602.
Expense allowances.
Duties of compensation board in fixing, §15.2-1636.8.
Time and manner of payment, §15.2-1636.13.
Expense of office request filed with compensation board, §15.2-1636.7.
Failure of county or city to make timely payment of salary or expenses, §15.2-1636.13.
Holidays, §15.2-1605.
Increase in salary in certain cases, §15.2-1636.12.
Joint officers and employees.
Exception to constitutional officers, §15.2-1516.
Legal fees and expenses.
Sheriffs and deputies prosecuted for acts committed in discharge of duties, §15.2-1607.

LOCAL CONSTITUTIONAL OFFICERS —Cont'd
Notice and advertisement of employment positions, §15.2-1604.
Petition to share officers, §15.2-1602.
Publication of advertisement for employment positions, §15.2-1604.
Qualification for office, §15.2-1601.
Residency requirements, §15.2-1601.
Salaries.
Based on population bracket of county and city.
Population determined by last preceding census, §15.2-1636.11.
Duty of compensation board in fixing, §15.2-1636.8.
Increase in certain cases, §15.2-1636.12.
Payments to counties not having certain officers, §15.2-1636.17.
Proportion borne by Commonwealth and locality, §15.2-1636.14.
Appropriations chargeable with Commonwealth's proportion, §15.2-1636.16.
Supplementation by county or city, §15.2-1605.1.
Time and manner of payment, §15.2-1636.13.
Segregation or classification of appointees, employees or applicants, §15.2-1604.
Sharing of officers by two or more units of government, §15.2-1602.
Transfer of jurisdiction, §15.2-1637.
Sheriffs, §§15.2-1609 to 15.2-1625.
See SHERIFFS.
Sick leaves, §15.2-1605.
Supplementation of salaries by county or city, §15.2-1605.1.
Transfer of jurisdiction.
Sharing of offices, §15.2-1637.
Treasurers.
Collection of license fees, §§15.2-1636.3, 15.2-1636.4.
Election, powers and duties, §15.2-1608.
Insurer's conversion to stock corporation.
Treatment of money received, §15.2-1608.1.
Salaries, §§15.2-1608.1, 15.2-1608.2.
Unlawful employment practices, §15.2-1604.
Vacancy in office, §15.2-1600.
Vacation leave, §15.2-1605.

LOCAL DEFENSE PRODUCTION ZONES.
Cities, counties, towns.
Authority to establish, grant incentives, regulatory flexibility, enterprise zone taxation, §58.1-3853.

LOCAL DEPARTMENTS AND DIRECTORS OF SOCIAL SERVICES.
Adult protective services, §§63.2-1603 to 63.2-1610.
Child abuse and neglect, §§63.2-1500 to 63.2-1527.
See CHILD ABUSE AND NEGLECT.
Child-protective services units, §63.2-1503.
Domestic violence prevention services, §§63.2-1611 to 63.2-1615.
Foster care generally, §§63.2-900 to 63.2-915.
See SOCIAL SERVICES.
Generally, §§63.2-324 to 63.2-336.
See SOCIAL SERVICES.
Public assistance.
Generally, §§63.2-500 to 63.2-805.
See PUBLIC AID AND ASSISTANCE.

LOCAL ELECTIONS.
Annexation.
Elections in city or town following, §15.2-3226.

LOCAL ELECTIONS —Cont'd
Annulment of town charters, §§15.2-3704, 15.2-3705.
Boards of county supervisors.
See COUNTY BOARDS OF SUPERVISORS.
Bonds issued by locality, §§15.2-2610, 15.2-2611.
Explanation of referendum questions, §24.2-687.
Change of city to town.
Town council and other elected officers, §15.2-4115.
City no longer qualifying for city status, §15.2-4005.
Cities.
See CITIES.
City status granted county.
Determination if voters desire transition, §15.2-3907.
City status granted town.
City officers, mayor and councilmen, §§15.2-3819, 15.2-3820.
Clerks of circuit courts, §15.2-1634.
Commissioners of revenue, §15.2-1636.
Commonwealth's attorneys, §§15.2-1626, 15.2-1630.
Consolidation of counties, cities or towns into single county or city, §§15.2-3538 to 15.2-3540.
Consolidation of like units of local government.
Election of county, city or town officers after consolidation approved, §§15.2-3508, 15.2-3509.
Election on question of consolidation, §§15.2-3505 to 15.2-3507.
Constitutional and local officers generally, §§24.2-214 to 24.2-224.
Contest of election, §§24.2-803 to 24.2-814.
Counties.
See COUNTIES.
Electoral boards, §§24.2-106 to 24.2-109.
Recreation and playground system, §15.2-1807.
Reversion of city to town.
Town council and other elected officers, §15.2-4115.
City no longer qualifying for city status, §15.2-4005.
Town granted city status, §15.2-3801.
City officers, mayor and councilmen, §§15.2-3819, 15.2-3820.
Towns incorporated by judicial proceeding.
First election, §15.2-3604.
Transition of county to city.
Determination if voters desire transition, §15.2-3907.
Treasurers, §15.2-1608.

LOCAL ELECTORAL BOARDS.
Generally, §§24.2-106 to 24.2-109.
See ELECTIONS.

LOCAL EMERGENCIES.
Declaration, §44-146.21.
Emergency management generally, §§44-146.13 to 44-146.28.
See EMERGENCY MANAGEMENT.

LOCAL ENTERPRISE ZONE DEVELOPMENT TAXATION PROGRAM, §§58.1-3245.6 to 58.1-3245.12.

LOCAL FIRE MARSHALS.
Generally, §§27-30 to 27-37.1.
See FIRE MARSHALS.

LOCAL GOVERNING BODIES.
Appropriating or borrowing money or imposing taxes.
Affirmative vote of majority, VA Const Art VII §7.
City councils generally.
See CITY COUNCILS.
Dual office holding, VA Const Art VII §6.
Election generally, VA Const Art VII §5.
Energy.
Policy of Commonwealth.
Role of local governments in achieving policy objectives, §67-103.
Town councils generally.
See TOWN COUNCILS.

LOCAL GOVERNMENT.
Admissions tax, §§58.1-3817, 58.1-3818, 58.1-3840.
Scott county.
Off-track horse race wagering facilities, §58.1-3818.01.
Stafford county, §58.1-3818.02.
Agricultural and forestal districts, §§15.2-4300 to 15.2-4314.
County executive form and certain other counties, §§15.2-4400 to 15.2-4407.
Air raid precautions, §§44-147 to 44-151.
Alleghany Highlands economic development authority, §§15.2-6200 to 15.2-6214.
Annexation.
Generally, §§15.2-3200 to 15.2-3235.
See ANNEXATION.
Immunity of counties from city-initiated annexation and city incorporation, §§15.2-3300 to 15.2-3308.
See IMMUNITY OF COUNTIES FROM CITY-INITIATED ANNEXATION AND CITY INCORPORATION.
Voluntary settlement, §§15.2-3400, 15.2-3401.
Annulment of town charters, §§15.2-3700 to 15.2-3712.
See TOWNS.
Associations of political subdivisions, §§15.2-1303 to 15.2-1305.
Blighted areas.
Tax increment financing, §§58.1-3245 to 58.1-3245.5.
Boards of equalization, §§58.1-3370 to 58.1-3389.
See REAL PROPERTY TAXES.
Boards of social services.
Local boards generally, §§63.2-300 to 63.2-323.
See SOCIAL SERVICES.
Bonds.
Generally, §§15.2-2600 to 15.2-2663.
See PUBLIC FINANCE ACT.
Local officers generally, §§15.2-1527 to 15.2-1533.
Boundaries.
Annexation.
Generally, §§15.2-3200 to 15.2-3235.
See ANNEXATION.
Immunity of counties from city-initiated annexation and city incorporation, §§15.2-3300 to 15.2-3308.
See IMMUNITY OF COUNTIES FROM CITY-INITIATED ANNEXATION AND CITY INCORPORATION.
Voluntary settlement, §§15.2-3400, 15.2-3401.
Contraction of corporate limits of cities or towns, §§15.2-3236 to 15.2-3245.
See BOUNDARIES.
Establishment of boundary lines by commissioners, §§15.2-3100 to 15.2-3105.
See BOUNDARIES.

LOCAL GOVERNMENT —Cont'd
Boundaries —Cont'd
Relocation or change by agreement, §§15.2-3106 to 15.2-3109.
See BOUNDARIES.
Buchanan county tourist train development authority, §§15.2-6700 to 15.2-6704.
Budgets, audits and reports, §§15.2-2500 to 15.2-2513.
Cable television systems.
Localities providing services, §§15.2-2108.2 to 15.2-2108.17.
See CABLE TELEVISION AND SERVICE.
Capital improvement programs, §15.2-2239.
Cash match plan for employees of Commonwealth, §§51.1-607 to 51.1-613.
Cat licensing, §§3.2-6521 to 3.2-6536.
Change of cities to towns.
City no longer qualifying for city status, §§15.2-4000 to 15.2-4005.
See REVERSION OF CITIES TO TOWNS.
Transition of city to town status generally, §§15.2-4100 to 15.2-4120.
See REVERSION OF CITIES TO TOWNS.
Charters.
Annulment of town charters, §§15.2-3700 to 15.2-3712.
See TOWNS.
Generally, §§15.2-200 to 15.2-209.
See LOCALITIES.
Cigarette tax, §§58.1-3830 to 58.1-3832.
Cities.
Generally.
See CITIES.
Uniform charter powers and other powers generally, §§15.2-1100 to 15.2-1133.
See CITIES.
City status granted county, §§15.2-3900 to 15.2-3919.
See TRANSITION OF COUNTIES TO CITIES.
City status granted to towns, §§15.2-3800 to 15.2-3834.
See TRANSITION OF TOWNS TO CITIES.
Claims against counties, §§15.2-1243 to 15.2-1249.
Clean energy improvements, financing, §15.2-958.3.
Commissioners of revenue.
Generally, §§58.1-3100 to 58.1-3122.2.
See COMMISSIONERS OF REVENUE.
Commission on local government, §§15.2-2900 to 15.2-2908.
See COMMISSION ON LOCAL GOVERNMENT.
Community development authorities.
Water and waste authorities generally, §§15.2-5152 to 15.2-5158.
Comprehensive plan, §§15.2-2222.1 to 15.2-2232.
Conditional zoning, §§15.2-2296 to 15.2-2303.
Consolidation.
Counties, cities or towns consolidating into single county or city, §§15.2-3520 to 15.2-3550.
See CONSOLIDATION OF LOCALITIES.
Like units of local government, §§15.2-3500 to 15.2-3519.
See CONSOLIDATION OF LOCALITIES.
Constitutional officers.
Generally, §§15.2-1600 to 15.2-1637.
See LOCAL CONSTITUTIONAL OFFICERS.
Consumer utility taxes, §§58.1-3814 to 58.1-3816.2.

LOCAL GOVERNMENT —Cont'd
Contraction of corporate limits of cities or towns, §§15.2-3236 to 15.2-3245.
See BOUNDARIES.
Counties.
Claims against counties, §§15.2-1243 to 15.2-1249.
Generally.
See COUNTIES.
Miscellaneous powers, §§15.2-1200 to 15.2-1232.
See COUNTIES.
County board form of government, §§15.2-400 to 15.2-418.
See COUNTY BOARD FORM OF GOVERNMENT.
County executive form of government, §§15.2-500 to 15.2-542.
See COUNTY EXECUTIVE FORM OF GOVERNMENT.
County manager form of government, §§15.2-600 to 15.2-642.
See COUNTY MANAGER FORM OF GOVERNMENT.
Courthouses, §§15.2-1638 to 15.2-1655.
See COURTHOUSES.
Criminal justice training academies, §§15.2-1747 to 15.2-1753.
See CRIMINAL JUSTICE TRAINING ACADEMIES.
Dams.
Construction for providing public water supply, §§15.2-2134 to 15.2-2142.
Disputes between jurisdictions involving dams, §§15.2-2135 to 15.2-2141.
Defense production zones.
Authority to establish, grant incentives, regulatory flexibility, enterprise zone taxation, §58.1-3853.
Departments and directors of social services.
Generally, §§63.2-324 to 63.2-336.
See SOCIAL SERVICES.
Dog and cat licensing, §§3.2-6521 to 3.2-6536.
Dual office holding, §§15.2-1534, 15.2-1535.
Electric authorities, §§15.2-5400 to 15.2-5431.
See ELECTRIC AUTHORITIES.
Emergency management and disasters.
Generally, §§44-146.13 to 44-146.23.
See EMERGENCY MANAGEMENT.
Eminent domain generally, §§15.2-1901 to 15.2-1906.
See LOCALITIES.
Energy conservation and costs savings.
Facilities owned by state and local governments.
Energy and operational efficiency performance-based contracting act, §§11-34.1 to 11-34.4.
Financing clean energy improvements, §15.2-958.3.
Enterprise zones.
Local enterprise zone development taxation program, §§58.1-3245.6 to 58.1-3245.12.
Excise taxes.
City or town, §58.1-3840.
Food and beverage tax, §§58.1-3833, 58.1-3834, 58.1-3840.
Former federal areas, authorities for development, §§15.2-6300 to 15.2-6322.
Forms of county government.
County board form of government, §§15.2-400 to 15.2-418.
See COUNTY BOARD FORM OF GOVERNMENT.

LOCAL GOVERNMENT —Cont'd
Forms of county government —Cont'd
County executive form of government, §§15.2-500 to 15.2-542.
See COUNTY EXECUTIVE FORM OF GOVERNMENT.
County manager form of government, §§15.2-600 to 15.2-642.
See COUNTY MANAGER FORM OF GOVERNMENT.
County manager plan of government, §§15.2-700 to 15.2-750.
See COUNTY MANAGER PLAN OF GOVERNMENT.
General provisions, §§15.2-300 to 15.2-307.
See COUNTIES.
Urban county executive form of government, §§15.2-800 to 15.2-858.
See URBAN COUNTY EXECUTIVE FORM OF GOVERNMENT.
Franchise, privilege, lease or right to use city or town property, §§15.2-2100 to 15.2-2108.1:1.
Freedom of information act.
Exclusions from chapter, §§2.2-3705.1 to 2.2-3705.8.
Garbage, refuse or trash removal and disposal.
General powers of localities, §§15.2-901, 15.2-927 to 15.2-939.
General powers, §§15.2-900 to 15.2-982.
See LOCALITIES.
General provisions as to localities, §§15.2-100 to 15.2-107.2.
See LOCALITIES.
Governing bodies of localities.
Generally, §§15.2-1400 to 15.2-1433.
See LOCALITIES.
Governmental fraud, §§18.2-498.1 to 18.2-498.5.
Group self-insurance pools, §§15.2-2700 to 15.2-2709.
Hampton Roads sports facility authority, §§15.2-5900 to 15.2-5916.
Hearings.
Public hearings generally.
See PUBLIC HEARINGS.
Hospital authorities, §§15.2-5300 to 15.2-5367.
See HOSPITAL AUTHORITIES.
Hospital or health center commissions, §§15.2-5200 to 15.2-5219.
See HOSPITAL OR HEALTH CENTER COMMISSIONS.
Housing revitalization zones, §§36-157 to 36-170.
See HOUSING REVITALIZATION ZONES.
Immunity of counties from city-initiated annexation and city incorporation.
Generally, §§15.2-3300 to 15.2-3308.
See IMMUNITY OF COUNTIES FROM CITY-INITIATED ANNEXATION AND CITY INCORPORATION.
Voluntary settlement, §§15.2-3400, 15.2-3401.
Impoundment of water.
Disputes between jurisdictions, §§15.2-2135 to 15.2-2141.
Income tax, §§58.1-540 to 58.1-549.
Incorporation of towns by judicial proceedings, §§15.2-3600 to 15.2-3605.
Indoor clean air act, §§15.2-2820 to 15.2-2833.
See SMOKING IN PUBLIC PLACES.
Industrial development authorities.
Generally, §§15.2-4900 to 15.2-4920.
See INDUSTRIAL DEVELOPMENT AUTHORITIES.

LOCAL GOVERNMENT —Cont'd
Industrial development authorities —Cont'd
Virginia regional industrial facilities authorities, §§15.2-6400 to 15.2-6416.
See VIRGINIA REGIONAL INDUSTRIAL FACILITIES AUTHORITIES.
Insurance.
Local government group self-insurance pools, §§15.2-2700 to 15.2-2709.
See LOCAL GOVERNMENT GROUP SELF-INSURANCE POOLS.
Joint activities.
Regional competitiveness act, §§15.2-1306 to 15.2-1310.
Joint exercise of powers, §§15.2-1300 to 15.2-1302.
Joint officers and employees, §§15.2-1513 to 15.2-1516.
Juvenile detention and other care facilities.
Operating and maintaining, §§16.1-315 to 16.1-322.7.
See JUVENILE DETENTION AND OTHER CARE FACILITIES.
Land preservation special assessment, §§58.1-3229 to 58.1-3244.
See REAL PROPERTY TAXES.
Land redevelopment in urban areas.
Urban public-private partnership redevelopment fund, §§15.2-2414 to 15.2-2418.
Laser speed detection devices.
Use by locality to measure speed of automobile prohibited, §46.2-882.
Libraries, local and regional, §§42.1-33 to 42.1-45.
License taxes, §§58.1-3700 to 58.1-3735.
See LICENSE TAXES.
Localities generally.
See LOCALITIES.
Machinery and tools tax, §§58.1-3507 to 58.1-3508.3.
Meals tax, §§58.1-3833, 58.1-3834, 58.1-3840.
Merchants' capital tax, §§58.1-3509, 58.1-3510.
Motor vehicle and traffic regulation powers, §§46.2-1300 to 46.2-1314.
Motor vehicle registration.
Local license taxes and fees, §§46.2-752 to 46.2-756.
Officers and employees.
Bond of local officers generally, §§15.2-1527 to 15.2-1533.
Cash match plan for employees of Commonwealth, §§51.1-607 to 51.1-613.
Commissioners of revenue, §§58.1-3100 to 58.1-3122.2.
See COMMISSIONERS OF REVENUE.
Constitutional officers.
Generally, §§15.2-1600 to 15.2-1637.
See LOCAL CONSTITUTIONAL OFFICERS.
Deferred compensation plans, §§51.1-600 to 51.1-605.
Dual office holding, §§15.2-1534, 15.2-1535.
Generally.
See LOCAL OFFICERS AND EMPLOYEES.
Group insurance programs, §§51.1-500 to 51.1-514.
Joint officers and employees, §§15.2-1513 to 15.2-1516.
Local government personnel generally, qualifications for office, bond, etc., §§15.2-1500 to 15.2-1543.
See LOCAL OFFICERS AND EMPLOYEES.

LOCAL GOVERNMENT —Cont'd
Officers and employees —Cont'd
Local trusts to fund postemployment benefits other than pensions, §§15.2-1544 to 15.2-1549.
Military duty leave, §§44-93.1 to 44-93.5.
Qualification of local officer for office, §§15.2-1522 to 15.2-1524.
Removal of public officers generally, §§24.2-230 to 24.2-238.
See REMOVAL OF PUBLIC OFFICERS FROM OFFICE.
Retirement systems generally, §§51.1-800 to 51.1-823.
See LOCAL RETIREMENT SYSTEMS.
Social security coverage generally, §§51.1-700 to 51.1-707.
Superintendents of public welfare generally.
See SUPERINTENDENTS OF PUBLIC WELFARE.
Treasurers generally, §§58.1-3123 to 58.1-3172.1.
See TREASURERS, LOCAL.
Official map, §§15.2-2233 to 15.2-2238.
Ordinances and other actions by local governing body.
Generally, §§15.2-1425 to 15.2-1433.
See ORDINANCES.
Park authorities, §§15.2-5700 to 15.2-5714.
See PARK AUTHORITIES.
Parks, recreational facilities and playgrounds, §§15.2-1806 to 15.2-1811.
See LOCALITIES.
Personal property taxes.
Exempt property generally, §§58.1-3600 to 58.1-3666.
See PROPERTY EXEMPT FROM TAXATION.
Generally, §§58.1-3500 to 58.1-3522.
See PERSONAL PROPERTY TAXES.
Machinery and tools tax, §§58.1-3507 to 58.1-3508.3.
Merchant's capital tax, §§58.1-3509, 58.1-3510.
Tax relief act of 1998, §§58.1-3523 to 58.1-3535.
See PERSONAL PROPERTY TAX RELIEF ACT OF 1998.
Personnel, qualifications for office, bond, etc., §§15.2-1500 to 15.2-1543.
See LOCAL OFFICERS AND EMPLOYEES.
Planning and development.
Generally, §§15.2-2200 to 15.2-2239.
See PLANNING AND DEVELOPMENT.
Road impact fees, §§15.2-2317 to 15.2-2329.
See ROAD IMPACT FEES.
Subdivision generally, §§15.2-2240 to 15.2-2279.
See SUBDIVISIONS.
Zoning generally, §§15.2-2280 to 15.2-2316.2.
See ZONING.
Planning commissions, §§15.2-2210 to 15.2-2212.
Planning district commissions, §§15.2-4200 to 15.2-4222.
See PLANNING DISTRICT COMMISSIONS.
Police.
Auxiliary police forces, §§15.2-1731 to 15.2-1736.
See POLICE.
Communications system, §§52-16 to 52-19.
Generally, §§15.2-1700 to 15.2-1753.
See POLICE.
Interjurisdictional law-enforcement authority and agreements, §§15.2-1724 to 15.2-1730.
See POLICE.
Special police officers in localities, §§15.2-1737 to 15.2-1746.
See POLICE.

LOCAL GOVERNMENT —Cont'd
Powers.
Cities.
Uniform charter powers and other powers generally, §§15.2-1100 to 15.2-1133.
See CITIES.
Counties.
Miscellaneous powers, §§15.2-1200 to 15.2-1232.
See COUNTIES.
General powers, §§15.2-900 to 15.2-982.
See LOCALITIES.
Joint exercise, §§15.2-1300 to 15.2-1302.
Towns.
Uniform charter powers and other powers generally, §§15.2-1100 to 15.2-1133.
See TOWNS.
Pretrial services program.
Assistance to judicial officers in carrying out bail and pretrial release duties, §§19.2-152.2 to 19.2-152.7:1.
See BAIL AND RECOGNIZANCE.
Probate tax, §§58.1-3805 to 58.1-3808.
Prompt payment of bills, §§2.2-4352, 2.2-4354.
Property taxes.
Exempt property generally, §§58.1-3600 to 58.1-3666.
See PROPERTY EXEMPT FROM TAXATION.
Machinery and tools tax, §§58.1-3507 to 58.1-3508.3.
Merchant's capital tax, §§58.1-3509, 58.1-3510.
Personal property generally, §§58.1-3500 to 58.1-3522.
See PERSONAL PROPERTY TAXES.
Real property generally, §§58.1-3200 to 58.1-3389.
See REAL PROPERTY TAXES.
Tax relief act of 1998, §§58.1-3523 to 58.1-3535.
See PERSONAL PROPERTY TAX RELIEF ACT OF 1998.
Public assistance.
Departments and directors of social services.
Generally, §§63.2-324 to 63.2-336.
See SOCIAL SERVICES.
Funding of public assistance and social services, §§63.2-400 to 63.2-412.
See SOCIAL SERVICES.
Generally, §§63.2-500 to 63.2-805.
See PUBLIC AID AND ASSISTANCE.
Local boards of social services, §§63.2-300 to 63.2-323.
See SOCIAL SERVICES.
Temporary assistance for needy families, §§63.2-600 to 63.2-621.
See PUBLIC AID AND ASSISTANCE.
Public hearings.
Generally.
See PUBLIC HEARINGS.
Public utilities.
Generally, §§15.2-2109 to 15.2-2121.
See LOCALITIES.
Sewage disposal systems, §§15.2-2122 to 15.2-2133.
See SEWAGE DISPOSAL SYSTEMS.
Water supply systems, §§15.2-2134 to 15.2-2148.
See WATER SUPPLY SYSTEMS.
Qualification of local officer for office, §§15.2-1522 to 15.2-1524.
Radar.
City council members, §§15.2-1414.5, 15.2-1414.6.
Use by locality to measure speed of automobile, §46.2-882.

LOCAL GOVERNMENT —Cont'd
Real property taxes.
Exempt property generally, §§58.1-3200 to 58.1-3389.
See REAL PROPERTY TAXES.
Rechargeable battery disposal and recycling, §10.1-1425.39.
Recordation tax, §§58.1-3800 to 58.1-3804.
Recreational facilities authorities, §§15.2-5600 to 15.2-5616.
See RECREATIONAL FACILITIES AUTHORITY.
Redevelopment projects.
See REDEVELOPMENT PROJECTS.
Refunding bonds, §§15.2-2643 to 15.2-2649.
Refuse collection and disposal authorities, §§15.2-5100 to 15.2-5159.
See WATER AND WASTE AUTHORITIES.
Regional cooperation act, §§15.2-4200 to 15.2-4222.
See PLANNING DISTRICT COMMISSIONS.
Regional partnerships.
Regional competitiveness act, §§15.2-1306 to 15.2-1310.
Removal of public officers from office, §§24.2-230 to 24.2-238.
See REMOVAL OF PUBLIC OFFICERS FROM OFFICE.
Renewable energy co-location of distribution facilities.
Public property, use of, §67-1102.
Use and occupation of public rights-of-way, §67-1101.
Fee, §67-1103.
Rental inspections of units located in rental inspection districts.
Residential rental dwelling units.
Building code compliance, §36-105.1:1.
Road impact fees, §§15.2-2317 to 15.2-2329.
See ROAD IMPACT FEES.
Roads, streets and public rights of way.
Generally, §§15.2-2000 to 15.2-2030.
See ROADS, STREETS AND PUBLIC RIGHTS OF WAY.
Salaries.
County boards of supervisors, §§15.2-1414.1 to 15.2-1414.3.
Town council members and mayors, §15.2-1414.7.
Sales tax, §58.1-605.
Scenic rivers.
Powers, §10.1-406.1.
Self insurance.
Local government group self-insurance pools, §§15.2-2700 to 15.2-2709.
See LOCAL GOVERNMENT GROUP SELF-INSURANCE POOLS.
Service districts, §§15.2-2400 to 15.2-2403.3.
Setoff debt collection, income tax, §§58.1-520 to 58.1-535.
Sewage disposal authorities, §§15.2-5100 to 15.2-5159.
See WATER AND WASTE AUTHORITIES.
Sewage disposal systems.
Generally, §§15.2-2122 to 15.2-2133.
See SEWAGE DISPOSAL SYSTEMS.
Sewer authorities, §§15.2-5100 to 15.2-5159.
See WATER AND WASTE AUTHORITIES.
Sheriffs.
Generally, §§15.2-1609 to 15.2-1625.
See SHERIFFS.
Signs.
Loitering on bridges or highway rights-of-way, §46.2-930.

LOCAL GOVERNMENT —Cont'd
Smoking in public places.
Virginia indoor clean air act, §§15.2-2820 to 15.2-2833.
See SMOKING IN PUBLIC PLACES.
Social services.
Adoption.
Generally, §§63.2-1200 to 63.2-1248.
See ADOPTION.
Adult protective services, §§63.2-1603 to 63.2-1610.
Child abuse and neglect, §§63.2-1500 to 63.2-1527.
See CHILD ABUSE AND NEGLECT.
Departments and directors of social services.
Generally, §§63.2-324 to 63.2-336.
See SOCIAL SERVICES.
Foster care generally, §§63.2-900 to 63.2-915.
See SOCIAL SERVICES.
Funding of public assistance and social services, §§63.2-400 to 63.2-412.
See SOCIAL SERVICES.
Local boards of social services, §§63.2-300 to 63.2-323.
See SOCIAL SERVICES.
Public assistance.
Generally, §§63.2-500 to 63.2-805.
See PUBLIC AID AND ASSISTANCE.
Solid waste management.
General powers of locality as to waste and recycling, §§15.2-901, 15.2-927 to 15.2-939.
Special police officers in localities, §§15.2-1737 to 15.2-1746.
See POLICE.
Subdivision and development.
Generally, §§15.2-2240 to 15.2-2279.
See SUBDIVISIONS.
Superintendent of public welfare.
See SUPERINTENDENTS OF PUBLIC WELFARE.
Taxes.
Admission tax, §§58.1-3817, 58.1-3818.
Scott county.
Off-track horse race wagering facilities, §58.1-3818.01.
Stafford county, §58.1-3818.02.
Cigarette tax, §§58.1-3830 to 58.1-3832.
Collection of local taxes generally, §§58.1-3910 to 58.1-3961.
See TAX COLLECTION.
Consumer utility taxes, §§58.1-3814 to 58.1-3816.2.
License taxes, §§58.1-3700 to 58.1-3735.
See LICENSE TAXES.
Local improvements, §§15.2-2404 to 15.2-2413.
See TAXES OR ASSESSMENTS FOR LOCAL IMPROVEMENTS.
Machinery and tools taxes, §§58.1-3507 to 58.1-3508.3.
Merchant's capital tax, §§58.1-3509, 58.1-3510.
Personal property taxes.
Car tax relief, §§58.1-3523 to 58.1-3535.
See PERSONAL PROPERTY TAX RELIEF ACT OF 1998.
Generally, §§58.1-3500 to 58.1-3522.
See PERSONAL PROPERTY TAXES.
Probate tax, §§58.1-3805 to 58.1-3808.
Public school special tax, §§22.1-102 to 22.1-106.
Real property taxes, §§58.1-3200 to 58.1-3389.
See REAL PROPERTY TAXES.
Recordation tax, §§58.1-3800 to 58.1-3804.

LOCAL GOVERNMENT —Cont'd
Taxes —Cont'd
Tax relief act of 1998, §§58.1-3523 to 58.1-3535.
See PERSONAL PROPERTY TAX RELIEF ACT OF 1998.
Transient occupancy tax, §§58.1-3819 to 58.1-3826.
Tax increment financing, §§58.1-3245 to 58.1-3245.5.
Temporary assistance for needy families, §§63.2-600 to 63.2-621.
See PUBLIC AID AND ASSISTANCE.
Towns.
Generally.
See TOWNS.
Uniform charter powers and other powers generally, §§15.2-1100 to 15.2-1133.
See TOWNS.
Traffic regulation powers generally, §§15.2-2028, 46.2-1300 to 46.2-1314.
Transient occupancy tax, §§58.1-3819 to 58.1-3826.
Transition of city to town status.
City no longer qualifying for city status, §§15.2-4000 to 15.2-4005.
See REVERSION OF CITIES TO TOWNS.
Transition of city to town status generally, §§15.2-4100 to 15.2-4120.
See REVERSION OF CITIES TO TOWNS.
Transition of counties to cities, §§15.2-3900 to 15.2-3919.
See TRANSITION OF COUNTIES TO CITIES.
Transition of towns to cities, §§15.2-3800 to 15.2-3834.
See TRANSITION OF TOWNS TO CITIES.
Transportation districts.
Generally, §§15.2-4500 to 15.2-4534.
See TRANSPORTATION DISTRICTS.
Multicounty transportation improvement districts.
See TRANSPORTATION DISTRICTS.
Transportation improvement district for individual locality.
See TRANSPORTATION DISTRICTS.
Transportation service districts.
See TRANSPORTATION DISTRICTS.
Travel expenses for persons on business of locality, §§15.2-1508.1 to 15.2-1508.4.
Treasurers, §§58.1-3123 to 58.1-3172.1.
See TREASURERS, LOCAL.
Virginia Beach arena, §§15.2-5921 to 15.2-5927.
See VIRGINIA BEACH ARENA.
Voluntary settlement of annexation, transition or immunity issues, §§15.2-3400, 15.2-3401.
Waste and recycling.
General powers, §§15.2-901, 15.2-927 to 15.2-939.
Water authorities, §§15.2-5100 to 15.2-5159.
See WATER AND WASTE AUTHORITIES.
Water supply systems.
Generally, §§15.2-2134 to 15.2-2156.
See WATER SUPPLY SYSTEMS.
Welfare.
Departments and directors of social services.
Generally, §§63.2-324 to 63.2-336.
See SOCIAL SERVICES.
Funding of public assistance and social services, §§63.2-400 to 63.2-412.
See SOCIAL SERVICES.
Generally, §§63.2-500 to 63.2-805.
See PUBLIC AID AND ASSISTANCE.
Local boards of social services, §§63.2-300 to 63.2-323.
See SOCIAL SERVICES.

LOCAL GOVERNMENT —Cont'd
Welfare —Cont'd
Temporary assistance for needy families, §§63.2-600 to 63.2-621.
See PUBLIC AID AND ASSISTANCE.
Zoning generally, §§15.2-2280 to 15.2-2316.2.
See ZONING.

LOCAL GOVERNMENT ASSOCIATIONS, §§15.2-1303 to 15.2-1305.

LOCAL GOVERNMENT BONDS.
Blighted areas.
Tax increment financing, §§58.1-3245 to 58.1-3245.5.
Committee to witness destruction of bonds and bond coupons paid, §58.1-3130.
Counties, VA Const Art VII §10.
Debt limitation, cities or towns, VA Const Art VII §10.
Destruction of bond and bond coupons paid.
Procedure, §58.1-3130.
Generally, §§15.2-2600 to 15.2-2663.
See PUBLIC FINANCE ACT.
Limitation on debt, city or town bonds, VA Const Art VII §10.
Petition by treasurer to destroy bonds and bond coupons paid, §58.1-3130.

LOCAL GOVERNMENT CHARTERS, §§15.2-200 to 15.2-209.
See LOCALITIES.

LOCAL GOVERNMENT DEBT, VA Const Art VII §10.

LOCAL GOVERNMENT GROUP SELF-INSURANCE POOLS, §§15.2-2700 to 15.2-2709.
Bond of officer satisfied with surety or fidelity insurance coverage, §15.2-2704.
Contract provisions required, §15.2-2705.
Declaration of policy, findings and purpose, §15.2-2700.
Deficit correction financial plan, §15.2-2707.
Definitions, §15.2-2701.
Election by pool members of governing authority, §15.2-2705.
Exemption from disclosure under freedom of information act, §15.2-2708.
Exercise of powers under provisions.
Authorization to Commonwealth or agency of Commonwealth, §15.2-2702.
Financial plan, §15.2-2705.
Financial statements, filing, §15.2-2707.
Intergovernmental contracts, required provisions, §15.2-2705.
Management plan, §15.2-2705.
Motor vehicle sales and use tax exemption, §58.1-2403.
Motor vehicle security.
Self-insurer for, §15.2-2704.
Not insurance company or insurer under laws of Commonwealth, §15.2-2709.
Pools authorized, §15.2-2703.
Powers of pools, §15.2-2704.
Reporting format for preparation of pool-audited financial statements, §15.2-2707.
State corporation commission approval, §15.2-2706.

LOCAL GOVERNMENT INVESTMENT POOL ACT.
Freedom of information act.
Records excluded, §2.2-3705.7.

LOCAL GOVERNMENT INVESTMENT POOL ACT —Cont'd
Generally, §§2.2-4600 to 2.2-4606.
See INVESTMENT OF PUBLIC FUNDS.
Treasury board.
Powers and duties, §2.2-2416.

LOCAL HEALTH DEPARTMENTS AND DIRECTORS, §§32.1-30 to 32.1-34.
Birth defects.
Folic acid's role in prevention.
Distribution of information, §32.1-69.1:1.
Board performance of duties, §§32.1-31, 32.1-33.
Center for health statistics, §32.1-276.1.
Contract with board, §32.1-31.
Department for the aging, services provided.
Commissioner of health to ensure clinical sites provided information, §32.1-23.1.
Donations, power to seek and receive, §32.1-34.1.
Establishment, §32.1-30.
Genetic disease control program, §§32.1-68, 32.1-69.
HIV.
Physician reports, §32.1-36.
Immunizations.
Certificates, §32.1-46.
Virginia immunization information system (VIIS), §32.1-46.01.
Independent departments and directors, §32.1-32.
Local health services advisory boards.
Appointments, §32.1-31.
Metabolic disease control program, §§32.1-68, 32.1-69.
Ordinances.
Scope, §32.1-34.
Qualifications of directors, §32.1-30.
Regulations.
Scope, §32.1-34.
Tuberculosis.
Examinations, §32.1-50.
Venereal diseases.
Examinations, §32.1-57.
Vital record duties, §§32.1-254, 32.1-255.

LOCAL IMPROVEMENTS.
Taxes or assessments, §§15.2-2404 to 15.2-2413.
See TAXES OR ASSESSMENTS FOR LOCAL IMPROVEMENTS.

LOCAL INCOME TAX, §§58.1-540 to 58.1-549.
Administration of tax, §58.1-545.
Apportionment of income, §58.1-543.
Certificate of residency, §58.1-547.
Collections of local income taxes.
Fund, §58.1-548.
Costs of administration, §58.1-548.
Credits against tax, §58.1-546.
Disposition of revenue, §58.1-548.
Effective date of tax, §58.1-544.
Estimated tax, §58.1-545.
Forms.
Balance used in referendum, §58.1-540.
Incomes not subject to local taxation, §58.1-300.
Levy, §58.1-540.
Notice.
Referendum, §58.1-540.
Referendum, §58.1-540.
Refund of overpayment, §58.1-546.
Reparations.
Subject to tax, §58.1-542.

LOCAL INCOME TAX —Cont'd
Repeal of tax, §58.1-544.
Residency, §58.1-541.
Certificate, §58.1-547.
Withholding, §58.1-545.

LOCALITIES.
Abandoned graveyards.
Acquiring title by eminent domain, §57-36.
Abandoned vessels constituting obstruction or hazard to use of waters.
Requiring owners to remove, repair, etc., §15.2-909.
Abatement of public nuisance, §15.2-900.
Account due pursuant to ordinance.
Penalty and interest for failure to pay, §15.2-105.
Acquisition of real property, §15.2-1800.
Acquisitions authorized for public use, §15.2-1814.
Approval of deeds, acceptance by locality, §15.2-1803.
Development of business or industry, §15.2-1802.
Near parks or other public property, §15.2-1801.
Notice of public hearing, §15.2-1813.
Actions by or against locality.
Sue or be sued in own name, §15.2-1404.
Administrative office, §§15.2-1540, 15.2-1541.
Administrators.
Administrative head of government, §15.2-1541.
Appointing chief administrative officer, §15.2-1540.
General duties, §15.2-1541.
Admission tax, §§58.1-3817, 58.1-3818.
City or town having general taxing powers, §58.1-3840.
Scott county.
Off-track horse race wagering facilities, §58.1-3818.01.
Stafford county, §58.1-3818.02.
Advertisement of levies and fees imposed or increased by locality.
Certain fees and levies, §15.2-107.
Advisory boards, committees and commissions.
Appointment, compensation, §15.2-1411.
Affordable housing.
Blighted structures and delinquent tax lands.
Nominal sales in Richmond, §15.2-958.1.
Building permit fees.
Wavier for permit fees, §15.2-958.4.
Community reinvestment in contracts for investment of funds.
Consideration of affordable housing, §2.2-4327.
County manager plan of government, §15.2-735.
Density of affordable housing units.
Permitting certain densities in comprehensive plan, §15.2-735.1.
Rental housing.
Assessment for property tax purposes.
Fair market value, determining, §58.1-3295.
Agricultural agents.
Urban county executive form of government, §15.2-841.
Agricultural and forestal districts, §§15.2-4300 to 15.2-4314.
County executive form and certain other counties, §§15.2-4400 to 15.2-4407.
Air cannons, carbide cannons or other loud explosive devices designed to repel birds.
Prohibiting use, §15.2-918.
Aircraft.
Locality acquiring through forfeiture.
List published by secretary of public safety, §2.2-224.

LOCALITIES —Cont'd
Airports revolving fund.
Annual report on loans, §5.1-30.9.
Local government loans, §5.1-30.5.
Pledging loans to secure bonds, §5.1-30.6.
Sale of loans, §5.1-30.7.
Air raid precautions, §§44-147 to 44-151.
Air space.
Selling, exchanging, leasing, etc., §15.2-1800.
Public streets, public rights-of-way, etc., §15.2-2030.
Alarm company operators, regulations, §15.2-911.
Alcoholic beverage sales at licensed establishment.
Temporary injunction.
Meeting place for persons committing serious criminal violations, §48-17.1.
Alleghany Highlands economic development authority, §§15.2-6200 to 15.2-6214.
All-terrain vehicles or off-road motorcycles.
Trail systems for, §15.2-1806.
No liability to locality or property owners, §15.2-1809.1.
Alteration or vacation of public rights of way, §§15.2-2006 to 15.2-2008.
Amateur radio antennas.
Height restrictions, §15.2-2293.1.
Animals.
County or city pounds, §3.2-6546.
Sales of animals, §3.2-6545.
Ordinances, §3.2-6543.
Dangerous dogs, control, §3.2-6540.
Dog and cat licensing, §§3.2-6521 to 3.2-6536.
Dogs running at large.
Prohibiting, §3.2-6538.
Permits for pet shops and dealers in companion animals, §3.2-6537.
Pounds.
Sale of animals, §3.2-6545.
Rabid animals, §3.2-6522.
Rabies control, §3.2-6525.
Running at large animals, §3.2-6544.
Vicious dogs, control, §3.2-6540.1.
Annexation.
Agreements between towns and counties defining town's annexation rights, §§15.2-3231 to 15.2-3235.
See ANNEXATION.
Generally, §§15.2-3200 to 15.2-3235.
See ANNEXATION.
Immunity of counties from city-initiated annexation and city incorporation, §§15.2-3300 to 15.2-3308.
See IMMUNITY OF COUNTIES FROM CITY-INITIATED ANNEXATION AND CITY INCORPORATION.
Voluntary settlement of annexation or immunity issues, §§15.2-3400, 15.2-3401.
Annual audit, §15.2-2511.
Annual statement of revenues, expenditures and fund balances, audited financial report.
Filing with auditor of public accounts, §15.2-2510.
Appropriating money, borrowing of money, imposing taxes.
Affirmative vote of majority of governing body required, VA Const Art VII §7.
Appropriations to certain regions, §15.2-1305.
Appropriations to regional organizations, §15.2-1304.

LOCALITIES —Cont'd
Arbitration of controversy, §15.2-1404.
Archery.
Arrow from bow landing upon property of another without permission, §15.2-916.
Arenas.
Providing and operating, §15.2-1808.
Armories.
Conveyance of public grounds for armory building purposes, §44-130.
Financial assistance by city and county, §44-137.
Joint use of public buildings for, §44-129.
Assessment of mandates imposed on localities.
State agencies to assess, §2.2-613.
Assistance by officers or employees beyond jurisdictional limits, §15.2-1724.
Associations of political subdivisions, §§15.2-1303 to 15.2-1305.
Attorney.
Authorized, appointment, salary and duties, §15.2-1542.
Attorneys for the Commonwealth.
Generally, §§15.2-1626 to 15.2-1633.
See COMMONWEALTH'S ATTORNEYS.
Audit of accounts and records, §15.2-2511.
Audit of officers handling public funds.
County board form of government, §15.2-417.
County executive form of government, §15.2-538.
Urban county executive form of government, §15.2-844.
Auditor of public accounts establishing system of bookkeeping, §30-137.
Auditors.
Duties of local government auditors, §15.2-2511.2.
Automobile graveyards.
Taxing and regulating, §15.2-903.
Auxiliary police forces, §§15.2-1731 to 15.2-1736.
See POLICE.
Bad checks to localities.
Ordinances providing for fee for passing, §15.2-106.
Bawdy places.
Removal, repair, etc., of buildings and other structures harboring, §15.2-908.1.
Bicycle paths.
Converting sidewalks to, §15.2-2001.
Bicycles.
Licensing, disposition of unclaimed bicycles, §15.2-1720.
Prohibiting on sidewalks or crosswalks, §46.2-904.
Unclaimed property disposition, §15.2-1720.
Biking trails, §15.2-1806.
Birds.
Air cannons, carbide cannons or other loud explosive devices designed to repel birds, §15.2-918.
Blighted areas.
Tax increment financing, §§58.1-3245 to 58.1-3245.5.
Blighted structures.
Nominal sales in Richmond, §15.2-958.1.
Blind persons operating stand for sale of newspapers, periodicals, confections, etc., in courthouse, §15.2-1805.
Blue Cross and Blue Shield of Virginia.
Conversion to stock corporation.
Disposition of property received by locality on conversion, §15.2-1512.1.
Board of health.
County manager form of government, §15.2-629.

LOCALITIES —Cont'd
Board of health —Cont'd
Urban county executive form of government, §15.2-839.
Board of welfare or social services.
Adoption.
Agency adoption.
See ADOPTION.
General provisions.
See ADOPTION.
County manager form of government, §15.2-626.
Legal representation, §15.2-1519.
Liability insurance for employees, §15.2-1519.
Urban county executive form of government, §15.2-835.
Boards of county supervisors.
See COUNTY BOARDS OF SUPERVISORS.
Boards of equalization, §§58.1-3370 to 58.1-3389.
See REAL PROPERTY TAXES.
Boat traffic congesting water way.
Pass-through zones.
Authority to adopt ordinance, §29.1-744.4.
Body-piercing salons and tattoo parlors, regulation, §15.2-912.
Body politic of Commonwealth, §15.2-1402.
Boiler and pressure vessel operator certification, §15.2-910.
Bonds.
Generally, §§15.2-2600 to 15.2-2663.
See PUBLIC FINANCE ACT.
Officers, §§15.2-1527 to 15.2-1533.
See LOCAL OFFICERS AND EMPLOYEES.
Bookkeeping and accounting system for use by local government.
Auditor of public accounts to devise, §15.2-2509.
Centralized system of accounting for counties, §15.2-1541.1.
Boundaries.
Annexation.
Agreements between towns and counties defining town's annexation rights, §§15.2-3231 to 15.2-3235.
See ANNEXATION.
Generally, §§15.2-3200 to 15.2-3235.
See ANNEXATION.
Immunity of counties from city-initiated annexation and city incorporation, §§15.2-3300 to 15.2-3308.
See IMMUNITY OF COUNTIES FROM CITY-INITIATED ANNEXATION AND CITY INCORPORATION.
Voluntary settlement of annexation or immunity issues, §§15.2-3400, 15.2-3401.
Charters.
County boundaries not included in charter, §15.2-208.
Municipal boundaries incorporated by reference, §15.2-207.
Consolidation.
Counties, cities or towns consolidating into single county or city, §§15.2-3520 to 15.2-3550.
See CONSOLIDATION OF LOCALITIES.
Like units of local government, §§15.2-3500 to 15.2-3519.
See CONSOLIDATION OF LOCALITIES.
Contraction of corporate limits of cities or towns, §§15.2-3236 to 15.2-3245.
See BOUNDARIES.
Establishment of boundary lines by commissioners, §§15.2-3100 to 15.2-3105.
See BOUNDARIES.

LOCALITIES —Cont'd
Boundaries —Cont'd
Relocation or change by agreement, §§15.2-3106 to 15.2-3109.
See BOUNDARIES.
Bow shooting prohibition, §15.2-916.
Buchanan county tourist train development authority, §§15.2-6700 to 15.2-6704.
Budgets.
Amendment, §15.2-2507.
Approved budget.
Publication, §15.2-2503.
Contents, §15.2-2504.
County board form of government.
Preparation by county administrator, §15.2-407.
County executive form of government, §15.2-539.
County manager form of government, §15.2-638.
Powers and duties of county manager, §15.2-614.
County manager plan of government, §15.2-710.
Discretionary funds to be included in itemized expenditures, §15.2-2503.
Establishment of funds for accounting and budgeting, §15.2-2501.
Estimated amount of money needed for ensuing fiscal year.
Submission by officers and heads of agencies, time, §15.2-2503.
Estimated amount of state money to be received and other information.
Notification by compensation board and department of taxation, §15.2-2502.
Information furnished by departments, offices, divisions, etc., §15.2-2508.
Preparation and approval for informative and fiscal planning, §15.2-2503.
Publication and notice, §15.2-2506.
Public hearing, §15.2-2506.
Reserve for contingencies and capital improvements, §15.2-2505.
Special budget provisions, §15.2-2513.
Tax rate for budget year.
Fixing, time, §15.2-2503.
Time for preparation, §15.2-2503.
Urban county executive form of government, §15.2-847.
County executives.
Submission of proposed annual budget, §15.2-811.
Building facilities on real property owned by locality in another locality's jurisdiction, §15.2-1804.
Buildings.
Harboring bawdy place.
Requiring removal, repair, etc., §15.2-908.1.
Persons with physical disabilities.
Access to public buildings, §§2.2-1159 to 2.2-1161.
Statewide building code generally, §§36-97 to 36-119.1.
See BUILDING CODE.
Buildings or other structures endangering public health or safety.
Authority to remove, demolish or renovate, §§15.2-906, 15.2-907.1.
Locality appointed as receiver to repair derelict and blighted buildings, §15.2-907.2.
Requiring removal, repair or securing, §15.2-906.
Burial.
Cemeteries on private property.
Official local register of places of burial, §15.2-978.

LOCALITIES —Cont'd
Burial —Cont'd
Cemeteries on private property —Cont'd
Property exempt belonging to memorial or monumental association, §15.2-978.
Bus fleet.
Sale with intent to lease back.
Approval of governing body required, notice, public hearing, §15.2-951.
Business and industry development.
Acquiring, leasing or selling land for, §15.2-1802.
Cable television systems.
Franchises, §§15.2-2108.19 to 15.2-2108.32.
See CABLE TELEVISION AND SERVICE.
Capital construction projects by state.
Availability of preliminary plans to locality upon request, §15.2-2202.
Capital improvement programs, §15.2-2239.
Local government facilities private capital lending, §§15.2-1815 to 15.2-1817.
Cash match plan for employees of Commonwealth, §§51.1-607 to 51.1-613.
Establishment of local plans, §51.1-610.
Cash proffers, use of, §15.2-975.
Cat licensing, §§3.2-6521 to 3.2-6536.
Cemeteries.
Abandoned graveyards.
Acquiring title by eminent domain, §57-36.
Conveyance of land to governing body for cemetery use, §57-22.
Private property.
Official local register of places of burial, §15.2-978.
Property exempt belonging to memorial or monumental association, §15.2-978.
Proper ownership prior to interment.
Good faith effort to ensure, §57-35.36.
Records, requirements, §57-35.36.
Centralized system of accounting for counties, §15.2-1541.1.
Change of city to town.
City no longer qualifying for city status, §§15.2-4000 to 15.2-4005.
See REVERSION OF CITIES TO TOWNS.
City status granted county.
Determination if voters desire transition, §15.2-3907.
City status granted town.
City officers, mayor and councilmen, §§15.2-3819, 15.2-3820.
Clerks of circuit courts, §15.2-1634.
Commissioners of revenue, §15.2-1636.
Commonwealth's attorneys, §§15.2-1626, 15.2-1630.
Consolidation of counties, cities or towns into single county or city, §§15.2-3538 to 15.2-3540.
Consolidation of like units of local government.
Election of county, city or town officers after consolidation approved, §§15.2-3508, 15.2-3509.
Election on question of consolidation, §§15.2-3505 to 15.2-3507.
Constitutional officers.
Abolition of office.
Charter enactment or amendment, §15.2-206.
Recreation and playground system, §15.2-1807.
Reversion of city to town.
City no longer qualifying for city status.
Town council and other elected officers, §15.2-4005.

LOCALITIES —Cont'd
Change of city to town —Cont'd
Reversion of city to town —Cont'd
Town council and other elected officers, §15.2-4115.
Sheriffs, §15.2-1609.
Town granted city status, §15.2-3801.
City officers, mayor and councilmen, §§15.2-3819, 15.2-3820.
Towns incorporated by judicial proceeding first election, §15.2-3604.
Transition of city to town status generally, §§15.2-4100 to 15.2-4120.
See REVERSION OF CITIES TO TOWNS.
Transition of county to city.
Determination if voters desire transition, §15.2-3907.
Treasurers, §15.2-1608.
Charitable gaming.
Proceeds exempt from local taxation, §15.2-912.2.
Charters, §§15.2-200 to 15.2-209.
Abolition of local constitutional offices.
Charter provisions not authorized to be used for, §15.2-205.
Special elections, §15.2-206.
Annulment of town charters, §§15.2-3700 to 15.2-3712.
See TOWNS.
Bill not introduced or failing to pass in general assembly, §§15.2-201, 15.2-202.
Change of city to town.
Resulting town charters, §15.2-4112.
County boundaries not contained in charter, §15.2-208.
Election on new charter or amendment, §15.2-201.
Evidence of compliance with requirements of provisions.
Legislation granting or amending charter, §15.2-203.
Municipal boundaries incorporated by reference, §15.2-207.
Notice of public hearing, §15.2-202.
Powers not affected by provisions of a title, §15.2-100.
Procedure for obtaining new charter or amendment, §15.2-200.
Publication of text of new charter or amendment.
Prior to election, §15.2-201.
Prior to public hearing, §15.2-202.
Public hearing in lieu of election on new charter or amendment, §15.2-202.
Reversion of city to town.
Resulting town charters, §15.2-4112.
Tort claims for damages.
Notice to be given counties, cities and towns, §15.2-209.
Transition of counties to cities, §§15.2-3910 to 15.2-3914.
Uniform charter powers, §15.2-204.
Chesapeake Bay preservation areas.
Designation by localities in Tidewater Virginia, §62.1-44.15:74.
Enforcement of provisions, authority of local governments, §62.1-44.15:73.
Outside Tidewater area, adoption of provisions, §62.1-44.15:75.
Water quality protection requirements, §62.1-44.15:76.
Chief administrative officer, §§15.2-1540, 15.2-1541.

LOCALITIES —Cont'd
Child-care services and facilities.
Regulation in certain counties and cities, §15.2-914.
Child welfare agencies.
Appropriations to, contracts with, §63.2-1816.
Churches and other places of worship.
Donations by locality prohibited, §15.2-953.
Local fees, restrictions on charging, §15.2-108.1.
Cigarette tax, §§58.1-3830 to 58.1-3832.
Corporate or partnership officer willful failure to collect and account for, §58.1-3907.
Excise tax, city or town having general taxing powers, §58.1-3840.
Cities.
City status granted by county, §§15.2-3900 to 15.2-3919.
See TRANSITION OF COUNTIES TO CITIES.
City status granted to towns, §§15.2-3800 to 15.2-3834.
See TRANSITION OF TOWNS TO CITIES.
Generally.
See CITIES.
Civil commotion or disturbance in nature of riot.
Regulation of assemblies or movement of persons in vehicles under certain circumstances, §15.2-925.
Civil service commission.
County manager plan of government, §15.2-721.
Claims against counties, §§15.2-1243 to 15.2-1249.
Clerks.
Appointing or designating, §§15.2-1536, 15.2-1538.
General duties, §15.2-1539.
Clerks of circuit court.
See CIRCUIT COURT CLERKS.
Closing temporarily public rights of way, §§15.2-2013, 15.2-2014.
Collection of rates, rents, fees or charges for use of revenue-producing undertaking, §15.2-2605.
Collection of state funds locally by financial officers.
Disposition, §15.2-1537.1.
Colleges and universities.
Conveyances and appropriations to Commonwealth for certain educational purposes, §23-3.1.
Commissioners of revenue.
Generally, §§58.1-3100 to 58.1-3122.2.
See COMMISSIONERS OF REVENUE.
Commission on human rights.
County manager plan of government, §15.2-725.
Urban county executive form of government, §15.2-853.
Investigations, §15.2-854.
Commission on local government, §§15.2-2900 to 15.2-2908.
See COMMISSION ON LOCAL GOVERNMENT.
Commonwealth's attorneys.
Generally, §§15.2-1626 to 15.2-1633.
See COMMONWEALTH'S ATTORNEYS.
Community development authorities.
Water and waste authorities generally, §§15.2-5152 to 15.2-5158.
Community revitalization.
Local funding.
Richmond, §15.2-958.5.
Comprehensive plans, §§15.2-2222.1 to 15.2-2232.

LOCALITIES —Cont'd
Computer services.
Power of certain localities to acquire or obtain control of, §15.2-2109.
Condemnation, §§15.2-1901 to 15.2-1906.
Conditional zoning, §§15.2-2296 to 15.2-2303.
Condominiums.
Conversion condominiums.
Ordinances, enactment, authority, §55-79.94.
Conduit entities.
Local government facilities private capital lending, §§15.2-1815 to 15.2-1817.
Consent to use streets, roads, alleys, etc., §§15.2-2015 to 15.2-2018.
Conservation or rehabilitation districts.
Individuals rehabilitating or purchasing owner-occupied residences.
Loans and grants to, §15.2-958.
Consolidation.
Counties, cities or towns consolidating into single county or city, §§15.2-3520 to 15.2-3550.
See CONSOLIDATION OF LOCALITIES.
Like units of local government, §§15.2-3500 to 15.2-3519.
See CONSOLIDATION OF LOCALITIES.
Constitutional officers.
Generally, §§15.2-1600 to 15.2-1637.
See LOCAL CONSTITUTIONAL OFFICERS.
Consumer utility taxes, §§58.1-3814 to 58.1-3816.2.
Continuity of government in case of enemy attack or other disaster, §15.2-1413.
Contraction of corporate limits of cities or towns, §§15.2-3236 to 15.2-3245.
See BOUNDARIES.
Counties.
Claims against counties, §§15.2-1243 to 15.2-1249.
Generally.
See COUNTIES.
Miscellaneous powers, §§15.2-1200 to 15.2-1232.
See COUNTIES.
Procurement by county purchasing agent, §§15.2-1233 to 15.2-1240.
Counties/cities school construction, renovation, maintenance, capital outlay and debt service fund.
Treatment of money received as result of insurer's conversion to stock corporation, §15.2-1608.1.
Counties/cities schools health insurance premium fund.
Treatment of money received as result of insurer's conversion to stock corporation, §15.2-1608.1.
County administrators.
Chief administrative officer, §§15.2-1540, 15.2-1541.
County board form of government.
Acting as purchasing agent, §15.2-414.
Appointment, compensation and removal, §15.2-406.
Powers and duties, §15.2-407.
County attorneys.
Authorized, appointment, salary and duties, §15.2-1542.
Claims against counties.
Representation before board, §15.2-1245.
County executive form of government.
Appointment, §15.2-529.
County manager form of government, §15.2-633.
Defense of localities and political subdivisions, governing bodies, officers or employees, §15.2-1520.
Departments or boards of welfare and social services, §15.2-1519.

LOCALITIES —Cont'd
County attorneys —Cont'd
Urban county executive form of government, §15.2-836.
County board form of government, §§15.2-400 to 15.2-418.
See COUNTY BOARD FORM OF GOVERNMENT.
County boards of supervisors.
See COUNTY BOARDS OF SUPERVISORS.
County clerks.
Appointing or designating, §§15.2-1536, 15.2-1538.
County executive form of government.
Selection, terms and vacancies, §15.2-536.
General powers and duties, §15.2-1539.
Urban county executive form of government, §15.2-838.
County engineer.
County manager form of government.
Head of department of public works, §15.2-625.
County executive form of government.
Generally, §§15.2-500 to 15.2-542.
See COUNTY EXECUTIVE FORM OF GOVERNMENT.
Urban county executive form of government, §§15.2-800 to 15.2-858.
See URBAN COUNTY EXECUTIVE FORM OF GOVERNMENT.
County executives.
County executive form of government, §§15.2-509 to 15.2-517.
Urban county executive form of government, §§15.2-804 to 15.2-814.
County manager form of government, §§15.2-600 to 15.2-642.
See COUNTY MANAGER FORM OF GOVERNMENT.
County manager plan of government, §§15.2-700 to 15.2-750.
See COUNTY MANAGER PLAN OF GOVERNMENT.
County purchasing agents.
County board form of government, §15.2-414.
County executive form of government.
Director of finance to act as, §15.2-524.
County manager form of government.
Director of finance to act as, §15.2-622.
Employment and duties, §15.2-1543.
Procurement by, §§15.2-1233 to 15.2-1240.
Urban county executive form of government.
Director of finance to act as, §15.2-831.
County treasurers.
See COUNTY TREASURERS.
Courthouses, §§15.2-1638 to 15.2-1655.
See COURTHOUSES.
Coyotes.
Bounties for coyotes, §15.2-926.1.
Crimestoppers information, confidentiality of information, §15.2-1713.1.
Criminal justice training academies, §§15.2-1747 to 15.2-1753.
See CRIMINAL JUSTICE TRAINING ACADEMIES.
Crosswalks.
Prohibiting bicycles, roller skates or skateboards, §46.2-904.
Curb ramps, specifications, §15.2-2021.
Curfew for minors, §15.2-926.
Cutting of grass and weeds.
Vacant property, §15.2-901.

LOCALITIES —Cont'd
Dairies and dairy products.
Local regulation, restrictions, §3.2-5202.
Damage to or defacement of public or private facilities.
Authority to enact ordinance making willful and malicious damage or defacement unlawful, §15.2-1812.2.
Clean-up, beautification, landscaping.
Community service may include, §15.2-1812.2.
Criminal penalty, mandatory minimum fine, §15.2-1812.2.
Deferring proceedings, placing defendant on probation, community service, §15.2-1812.2.
Locality cleaning or covering defacement at owner's expense, §15.2-1812.2.
Restitution, required for probation or suspension of sentence, §15.2-1812.2.
Dams.
Construction for purposes of providing public water supply, §15.2-2134.
Constructing across navigable stream, §15.2-2142.
Disputes between jurisdictions involving dams.
Special court proceedings, §§15.2-2135 to 15.2-2141.
Dance halls.
Ordinances regulating, §15.2-912.3.
Deannexation.
Contraction of corporate limits of cities or towns, §§15.2-3236 to 15.2-3245.
See BOUNDARIES.
Deeds conveying real estate.
Form, acceptance by governing body, execution, §15.2-1803.
Defacement of buildings, walls, fences and other structures.
Removal or repair, §15.2-908.
Defense production zones.
Authority to establish, grant incentives, regulatory flexibility, enterprise zone taxation, §58.1-3853.
Definitions, §15.2-102, VA Const Art VII §1.
Delinquency prevention and youth development programs, §§66-26 to 66-35.
Delinquent tax lands.
Nominal sales in Richmond, §15.2-958.1.
Department of assessments.
County executive form of government, §§15.2-518, 15.2-535.
Department of education.
Urban county executive form of government, §15.2-837.
Department of finance.
County executive form of government, §§15.2-518 to 15.2-525.
County manager form of government, §§15.2-617 to 15.2-624.
Urban county executive form of government, §§15.2-826 to 15.2-833.
Department of health, §§32.1-30 to 32.1-34.
County executive form of government, §15.2-534.
County manager form of government, §15.2-629.
Urban county executive form of government, §15.2-839.
Department of law enforcement.
County executive form of government, §§15.2-518, 15.2-528.
Urban county executive form of government, §15.2-836.

LOCALITIES —Cont'd
Department of public safety.
Urban county executive form of government, §15.2-842.
Department of public utilities.
Urban county executive form of government, §15.2-843.
Department of public works.
County executive form of government, §§15.2-518, 15.2-526.
County manager form of government, §15.2-625.
Department of records.
Urban county executive form of government, §15.2-838.
Department of welfare or social services.
County executive form of government, §§15.2-518, 15.2-527.
County manager form of government, §15.2-626.
Legal representation of employees, §15.2-1519.
Liability insurance for employees, §15.2-1519.
Urban county executive form of government, §15.2-835.
Departments and directors of social services.
Generally, §§63.2-324 to 63.2-336.
See SOCIAL SERVICES.
Derelict structures, removal or rehabilitation.
Grants, §36-155.
Destruction of original records and documents, §15.2-1412.
Director of finance.
County executive form of government, §§15.2-518 to 15.2-525.
County manager form of government, §§15.2-617 to 15.2-624.
Supplementing salary, §15.2-1605.1.
Urban county executive form of government, §§15.2-826 to 15.2-833.
Directors of emergency management, §44-146.19.
Disabled or handicapped persons.
Access to public buildings, §§2.2-1159 to 2.2-1161.
Public transportation system.
Access to, §51.5-44.
Disasters.
Continuity of government, §15.2-1413.
Sending officers, agents or employees beyond jurisdictional limits to assist, §15.2-1724.
Discontinuance of service by state agency to locality.
Notification, §2.2-612.
Discrimination.
Commission on human rights.
County manager plan of government, §15.2-725.
Urban county executive form of government, §§15.2-853, 15.2-854.
Disorderly conduct in public places.
Authority to adopt ordinance prohibiting, §18.2-415.
Dispute resolution proceedings.
Administrative dispute resolution, §§2.2-4115 to 2.2-4119.
Dog and cat licensing, §§3.2-6521 to 3.2-6536.
Dog ordinances.
Dangerous dogs, §3.2-6540.
Licensing, §§3.2-6521 to 3.2-6536.
Rabid animal, §3.2-6522.
Running at large, §§3.2-6522, 3.2-6537, 3.2-6538.
Vicious dogs, §3.2-6540.1.
Dogs trained for police work.
Sale, authority, §15.2-981.

LOCALITIES —Cont'd
Donations, powers.
Charitable, volunteer and nonprofit associations, chambers of commerce, §15.2-953.
Door-to-door vendors.
Ordinances regulating, §15.2-913.
Driving under the influence reimbursement, §15.2-1716.
Drug blight existing on property.
Requiring owner to undertake corrective action to abate, §15.2-907.
Drug trafficking problems.
Intensified drug enforcement jurisdictions, §15.2-1715.
Dual office holding, §§15.2-1534, 15.2-1535.
Ejectment proceeding against owner of property encroaching or obstructing right of way, §15.2-2009.
Elections.
Boards of county supervisors.
See COUNTY BOARDS OF SUPERVISORS.
City election generally.
See CITIES.
Constitutional and local officers, §§24.2-214 to 24.2-224.
Contest of election generally, §§24.2-803 to 24.2-814.
County elections generally.
See COUNTIES.
Electoral boards, §§24.2-106 to 24.2-109.
Expenses of general registrars.
Payment by locality, §24.2-111.
Generally.
See LOCAL ELECTIONS.
Governing bodies generally, VA Const Art VII §5.
Town elections generally.
See TOWNS.
Electrical energy requirements.
Aggregating for purposes of negotiating purchase of electricity, §56-589.
Electric authorities, §§15.2-5400 to 15.2-5431.
See ELECTRIC AUTHORITIES.
Electric personal assistive mobility devices.
Licensing and disposition of unclaimed property, §15.2-1720.
Electric power-assisted bicycles.
Licensing and disposition of unclaimed property, §15.2-1720.
Electronic communications meetings.
Governing bodies, school boards, agencies, §2.2-3708.
Emergency management and disasters.
Declaration of local emergency, §44-146.21.
Directors, §44-146.19.
Federal emergency management agency special flood hazard area map.
Changes.
Notification, §15.2-976.
Generally, §§44-146.13 to 44-146.28.
See EMERGENCY MANAGEMENT.
Immunity from liability, §44-146.23.
Joint action by political subdivisions, §44-146.20.
Powers and duties, §44-146.19.
Emergency medical services.
Entire locality, services maintained throughout.
Duty of locality, §15.2-955.
Establishment of organization.
Approval of locality required, §15.2-955.
Fire/EMS departments.
Ordinances relating to powers and duties of fire/EMS departments, §27 14.

LOCALITIES —Cont'd
Emergency medical services —Cont'd
Powers of counties, cities and towns, §32.1-111.14.
Eminent domain, §§15.2-1901 to 15.2-1906.
Abandoned graveyards.
Acquiring title by eminent domain, §57-36.
Acquiring property or property interest outside boundaries, §15.2-1901.
Authority, §§15.2-1901, 15.2-1901.1.
Certificate in lieu of payment when entering in property prior to condemnation, §15.2-1904.
Counties, special provisions, §15.2-1905.
Delaying tactics prohibited, §15.2-1901.
Entry and possession before conclusion of proceedings, §15.2-1904.
Special provisions for county, §15.2-1905.
Existing water or sewage disposal systems, §15.2-1906.
Initiating condemnation, §15.2-1903.
Payment into court of sum estimated to be fair value of property.
Possession prior to condemnation, §15.2-1904.
Petition, filing, §15.2-1903.
Possession prior to condemnation, §15.2-1904.
Special provisions for county, §15.2-1905.
Proceedings generally, §15.2-1902.
Reimbursement for pro rata portion of taxes paid, §15.2-1904.
Resolution or ordinance prior to initiating proceedings, §15.2-1903.
Special provisions for counties, §15.2-1905.
Spot blight abatement procedure, §36-49.1:1.
Water supplies and water lines, §15.2-1907.
Wetlands.
Condemnation for compensatory mitigation of wetlands, §15.2-1907.1.
Encroachment or obstruction of rights of way, §15.2-2009.
Enemy attack.
Continuity of government, §15.2-1413.
Energy conservation and costs savings.
Facilities owned by state and local governments.
Energy and operational efficiency performance-based contracting act, §§11-34.1 to 11-34.4.
Enterprise zones.
Local enterprise zone development taxation program, §§58.1-3245.6 to 58.1-3245.12.
Enumeration of population of locality, §15.2-1414.
Environmental impact report for major state project.
Duty of department of environmental quality to submit to locality, §15.2-2202.
Estimated amount of state money to be received during fiscal year and other information.
Notification by compensation board and department of taxation, §15.2-2502.
Evidentiary status of reproduced records and documents, §15.2-1412.
Excise taxes.
City or town having general taxing powers, §58.1-3840.
Executives.
Administrative head of government, §15.2-1541.
Appointing chief administrative officer, §15.2-1540.
General duties, §15.2-1541.
Exotic or poisonous animal running at large.
Fee by owner to cover cost in locating and capturing, §3.2-6544.

LOCALITIES —Cont'd
Failure to pay accounts when due.
Penalty and interest, §15.2-105.
Farmer major drought, flood and hurricane disaster assistance.
Grant programs for emergency financial assistance, authority, §3.2-505.
Farmers markets.
Establishing local retail markets, §3.2-3502.
Farmlands, designation of important farmlands, §3.2-205.
Fee for passing bad checks.
Ordinance providing, §15.2-106.
Fee system abolished.
County executive form of government, §15.2-540.
County manager form of government, §15.2-639.
Urban county executive form of government, §15.2-848.
Fences.
Swimming pools, §15.2-921.
Fertilizer.
Local government regulation, restrictions, §3.2-3602.
Financial reports.
Filing audited report with auditor of public accounts, §15.2-2510.
Firearms control, §15.2-915.
Lawsuits against manufacturers, distributors, etc.
Limitation on localities to bring suit, §15.2-915.1.
Ordinances governing transportation of loaded rifle or shotgun, §15.2-915.2.
Firearms, unclaimed property disposition, §15.2-1721.
Fire/EMS departments.
Ordinances, powers and duties, §27-14.
Fire fighters.
County manager form of government, §15.2-632.
Urban county executive form of government.
Department of public safety, §15.2-842.
Fire programs fund, allocation to, §38.2-401.
Fireworks permits, §15.2-974.
Fiscal year.
Uniform fiscal year, §15.2-2500.
Fish passage grant and revolving loan fund, §29.1-101.5.
Flood control.
Federal emergency management agency special flood hazard area map.
Changes.
Notification, §15.2-976.
Food and beverage tax.
Counties, §§58.1-3833, 58.1-3834.
Excise tax on meals.
City or town having general taxing powers, §58.1-3840.
Situs for taxation, §58.1-3841.
Foot-scooters.
Prohibiting on sidewalks or crosswalks, §46.2-904.
Forest products tax.
Allocation to counties or cities, §58.1-1611.
Former federal areas, authorities for development, §§15.2-6300 to 15.2-6322.
Forms of county government.
County board form of government, §§15.2-400 to 15.2-418.
See COUNTY BOARD FORM OF GOVERNMENT.
County executive form of government, §§15.2-500 to 15.2-542.
See COUNTY EXECUTIVE FORM OF GOVERNMENT.

LOCALITIES —Cont'd
Forms of county government —Cont'd
County management form of government, §§15.2-600 to 15.2-642.
See COUNTY MANAGER FORM OF GOVERNMENT.
County manager plan of government, §§15.2-700 to 15.2-750.
See COUNTY MANAGER PLAN OF GOVERNMENT.
General provision, §§15.2-300 to 15.2-307.
See COUNTIES.
Urban county executive form of government, §§15.2-800 to 15.2-858.
See URBAN COUNTY EXECUTIVE FORM OF GOVERNMENT.
Foster care generally.
See SOCIAL SERVICES.
Franchise, privilege, lease or right to use city or town property, §§15.2-2100 to 15.2-2108.1:1.
Levies and fees imposed or increased by locality.
Advertisement and enactment of ordinances, §15.2-107.
Funds established for accounting and budgeting, §15.2-2501.
Gambling devices, illegal possession.
Failure to enforce, enforcement by governor and attorney general, §18.2-338.
Garbage, refuse and trash, §§15.2-901, 15.2-927 to 15.2-939.
Charging and collecting compensation for services, §15.2-928.
Collection and disposal generally, §15.2-927.
Contracting for pickup and disposal services, §§15.2-928, 15.2-930, 15.2-932.
Requiring delivery to waste disposal facility located within or without county, §15.2-931.
Delivery required to certain disposal facility, §§15.2-931, 15.2-933.
Displacement of private waste company, §§15.2-930, 15.2-934.
Fee exemption for garbage and refuse disposal, §15.2-936.
General power as to recycling and waste disposal, §15.2-928.
Incinerators, dumps and other places and facilities for disposal, §15.2-927.
Leaves or grass clippings in landfills, §15.2-935.
License taxes upon and regulation of pickup and disposal services, §15.2-930.
Penalties for contracting with unlicensed collector or collectors, §15.2-930.
Penalties for unauthorized use or failure to use facility, §15.2-928.
Prohibiting disposal at place other than that provided, §15.2-928.
Requiring property owners to remove from property, §15.2-901.
Separation of solid waste, §15.2-937.
Solid waste management facilities.
Providing and operating, §15.2-928.
Siting approval, §15.2-929.
Unlawful disposal of garbage or trash, §15.2-931.
Unlicensed operations by solid waste collectors, §15.2-930.
General assembly power to provide for organization and government, VA Const Art VII §2.
General powers of local government, §§15.2-900 to 15.2-982.

LOCALITIES —Cont'd
Gifts, powers.
Donations to charitable, volunteer and nonprofit associations, chambers of commerce, §15.2-953.
Going out of business special sale permits.
Issuance, inspections, etc., §18.2-224.
Golf carts and utility vehicles.
Designation of public highways for operation, §46.2-916.2.
Governing bodies of localities, §§15.2-1400 to 15.2-1433.
Actions by or against localities.
Locality to sue or be sued in own name, §15.2-1404.
Administrative leave of elected member, §15.2-1407.
Advisory board, committees and commissions.
Appointment and compensation and expense reimbursement, §15.2-1411.
Arbitration of controversy, §15.2-1404.
Body politic of Commonwealth, §15.2-1402.
Chairman.
Generally, §§15.2-1422 to 15.2-1424.
Clerk.
Appointing or designating, §§15.2-1536, 15.2-1538.
General duties, §15.2-1539.
Compensation of governing bodies, §15.2-1406.
Continuing body, §15.2-1403.
Defense of governing bodies in certain proceedings, §15.2-1520.
Destruction of records and papers.
Preservation of records on photographs or microphotographs, §15.2-1412.
Disorderly behavior, punishment or fine, §15.2-1400.
Dual office holding, §15.2-1400, VA Const Art VII §6.
Election, §15.2-1400, VA Const Art VII §5.
Enemy attack or other disaster.
Continuity of government in case of, §15.2-1413.
Enumeration of population of locality, §15.2-1414.
Evidentiary status of reproductions of records and documents, §15.2-1412.
Expiration of term not to abate or discontinue matters, §15.2-1403.
Immunity of members of local governmental entities, §15.2-1405.
Insurer's conversion to stock corporation.
Treatment of money received, §15.2-1608.1.
Investigations relating to governmental affairs, §15.2-1409.
Legal enumeration of population of locality, §15.2-1414.
Mayor.
Electing as presiding officer, §15.2-1422.
Generally, §§15.2-1422 to 15.2-1424.
Vice-chairman, §15.2-1424.
Meetings, §§15.2-1415 to 15.2-1421.
Annual or organizational meeting, §15.2-1416.
Authorities, boards and commissions, §15.2-1419.
Calling, §15.2-1418.
Call or request for special meeting, §15.2-1417.
Electronic communication meetings, §2.2-3708.
Exercise of powers conferred, §15.2-1415.
First amendment right of freedom of speech.
Expressions by members and public prior to convening consistent with, §15.2-1416.1.
How questions determine, §15.2-1420.

LOCALITIES —Cont'd
Governing bodies of localities —Cont'd
Meetings —Cont'd
Majority of members voting to determine question, §15.2-1420.
Notice of special meeting, §15.2-1417.
Quorum, §15.2-1415.
Regular meetings, §15.2-1416.
Authorities, boards and commissions, §15.2-1419.
Special meetings, §15.2-1417.
Calling, §15.2-1418.
Tie breakers.
Counties have designated tie breakers, §§15.2-1420, 15.2-1421.
Virginia freedom of information act, applicability, §15.2-1415.
Numbers of members, §15.2-1400.
Oaths.
Power of chairman and mayor to administer, §15.2-1410.
Ordinances and other actions, §§15.2-1425 to 15.2-1433.
Adoption in performance of duties, obligations and functions, §15.2-1423.
Adoption of ordinances generally, §15.2-1427.
Amending generally, §15.2-1427.
Appeals from fine or imprisonment as in misdemeanor cases, §15.2-1431.
Appropriation, imposition of tax or authorization to borrow money.
Procedures, §15.2-1428.
Bonds of persons convicted for violations, §15.2-1430.
Codification and recodification of ordinances, §15.2-1433.
Emergency ordinances and counties, §15.2-1427.
Form generally, §15.2-1426.
Injunctive relief against continuing violations, §15.2-1432.
Majority of vote adopting, §15.2-1427.
Nonpayment of fines, proceedings, §15.2-1431.
Notice of intention to propose ordinance for passage.
Publication in counties, §15.2-1427.
Object clearly expressed in title, §15.2-1426.
Penalties for violations, §15.2-1429.
Publication of notice of intention to propose ordinance for passage.
Counties generally, §15.2-1427.
Recording final vote, §15.2-1427.
Repealing generally, §15.2-1427.
Repeals or amendments to identify title, §15.2-1426.
Tax imposed by town, two-thirds vote of members required, §15.2-1427.
Validity of adoptions, §15.2-1427.
Veto of appropriation, tax imposition or authorization to borrow money, §15.2-1428.
Pending matters not to abate or be discontinued by expiration of term or removal from office, §15.2-1403.
Personnel generally, qualification for office, bond, etc., §§15.2-1500 to 15.2-1543.
See LOCAL OFFICERS AND EMPLOYEES.
Powers granted localities vested in governing body, §15.2-1401.
Presiding officer.
Electing, §15.2-1422.
Power, §15.2-1423.
Vacancies, §15.2-1424.

LOCALITIES —Cont'd
Governing bodies of localities —Cont'd
Prohibitions, §15.2-1400.
Qualification for office, §15.2-1400.
Regular meetings, §15.2-1416.
Removal.
Pending measures not to abate or be discontinued, §15.2-1403.
Reproduction of records and documents, §15.2-1412.
Seal, §15.2-1402.
Service of process instituting suit against locality, §15.2-1404.
Subpoenas or subpoenas duces tecum.
Investigations relating to governmental affairs, §15.2-1409.
Tie breakers.
Counties designating, §§15.2-1420, 15.2-1421.
Vacancies in office, §15.2-1424.
Veto not given to presiding officer, §15.2-1423.
Vice-chairman.
Electing, §15.2-1422.
Vacancy, §15.2-1424.
Vice-mayor.
Electing, §15.2-1422.
Governmental fraud, §§18.2-498.1 to 18.2-498.5.
Grants for home ownership, §15.2-958.2.
Grass.
Clippings prohibited in landfills, §15.2-935.
Vacant property.
Requiring owners to cut, §15.2-901.
Grievance procedure.
County manager plan of government.
Police officers, §15.2-723.
Presence of equal employment opportunity officer, §15.2-738.
Local government officers generally, §§15.2-1506 to 15.2-1507.1.
Group insurance.
Local government group self-insurance pools, §§15.2-2700 to 15.2-2709.
See LOCAL GOVERNMENT GROUP SELF-INSURANCE POOLS.
Hampton Roads area refuse collection and disposal system authority, §15.2-5102.1.
Hampton Roads sports facility authority, §§15.2-5900 to 15.2-5916.
Handbills, leaflets, bulletins, literature, advertisements.
Distribution on highways, public roadways and medians.
Prohibition or regulation, §46.2-931.
Hazardous materials emergency response.
Coordinator of emergency management to enter into agreements with, §44-146.36.
Hazardous materials coordinator, appointment, §44-146.38.
Health director, §§32.1-30 to 32.1-34.
County executive form of government, §15.2-534.
County manager form of government, §15.2-629.
Health insurance program for officers, employees, teachers.
Long-term care insurance.
Board of trustees, Virginia Retirement System.
Assumption of responsibility, §51.1-513.3.
Establishment by department of human resource management, §2.2-1207.
Trust fund, §51.1-513.4.
Participation, §2.2-1204.
Health officer, §§32.1-30 to 32.1-34.
County board form of government, §15.2-411.

LOCALITIES —Cont'd
Health officer —Cont'd
Urban county executive form of government, §15.2-839.
Hearings.
Public hearings generally.
See PUBLIC HEARINGS.
Height restrictions on amateur radio antennas, §15.2-2293.1.
Helicopter landings.
Zoning ordinances, §15.2-2293.2.
High-occupancy lanes, authority to designate, §33.1-46.2.
Hiking trails, §15.2-1806.
Historical or cultural events, recreating or portraying, §15.2-942.
Historical places and things.
Authority to acquire and preserve, §15.2-944.
Notification prior to transfer of ownership of certain historic properties, §15.2-944.1.
Historic areas, landmarks, buildings or structures.
Acquiring and preserving, §15.2-2306.
Historic buildings.
Wrongful demolition, razing or removing.
County manager plan of government, §15.2-744.
Holding more than one office, §§15.2-1534, 15.2-1535.
Home demonstration agents.
Urban county executive form of government, §15.2-841.
Horseback riding trails, §15.2-1806.
Hospital authorities.
Generally, §§15.2-5300 to 15.2-5367.
See HOSPITAL AUTHORITIES.
Hospital or health center commissions, §§15.2-5200 to 15.2-5219.
See HOSPITAL OR HEALTH CENTER COMMISSIONS.
HOV lanes, authority to designate, §33.1-46.2.
Human rights ordinance.
Urban county executive form of government, §15.2-853.
Human services delivery pilot programs, §§15.2-2811 to 15.2-2817.
Adoption of regulations, §15.2-2814.
Altering regulations of state agencies, §15.2-2813.
Authorization from governor, §15.2-2812.
Cooperation of state agencies, §15.2-2816.
Costs of administration, §15.2-2817.
Definition of human services, §15.2-2811.
Resolution of local governing body required, §15.2-2815.
Immunity of counties from city-initiated annexation and city incorporation.
Generally, §§15.2-3300 to 15.2-3308.
See IMMUNITY OF COUNTIES FROM CITY-INITIATED ANNEXATION AND CITY INCORPORATION.
Voluntary settlement of immunity issues, §§15.2-3400, 15.2-3401.
Immunity of members of local governmental entities, §15.2-1405.
Impoundment of water.
Disputes between jurisdictions involving dams or water impoundment.
Special court proceedings, §§15.2-2135 to 15.2-2141.
Providing public water supply, §15.2-2134.
Improvements.
Taxes or assessments, §§15.2-2404 to 15.2-2413.
See TAXES OR ASSESSMENTS FOR LOCAL IMPROVEMENTS.

LOCALITIES —Cont'd
Income tax, §§58.1-540 to 58.1-549.
Incorporation of towns by judicial proceedings, §§15.2-3600 to 15.2-3605.
Indoor clean air act, §§15.2-2820 to 15.2-2833.
See SMOKING IN PUBLIC PLACES.
Industrial development authorities.
General provisions, §§15.2-4900 to 15.2-4920.
See INDUSTRIAL DEVELOPMENT AUTHORITIES.
Virginia regional industrial facilities authorities, §§15.2-6400 to 15.2-6416.
See VIRGINIA REGIONAL INDUSTRIAL FACILITIES AUTHORITIES.
Inoperable motor vehicles on residential or commercial property.
Authority to restrict keeping, removal, §§15.2-904, 15.2-905.
Inquiry into official conduct of office or officer.
County executive form of government, §15.2-506.
County manager form of government, §15.2-606.
County manager plan of government, §15.2-709.
Urban county executive form of government, §15.2-814.
Insurance.
Insurer's conversion to stock corporation.
Treatment of money received, §15.2-1608.1.
Liability insurance for officers, employees and volunteers, §15.2-1518.
Local government group self-insurance pools, §§15.2-2700 to 15.2-2709.
See LOCAL GOVERNMENT GROUP SELF-INSURANCE POOLS.
Interference with pupils at schools, preventing, §15.2-1717.
Internet access to local agency information.
Authorizing circuit court clerk to provide, §17.1-226.
Internet use by library employees and patrons.
Acceptable Internet use policies, establishment.
Local governments without library boards, §42.1-36.1.
Investigation by local governing bodies, §15.2-1409.
Itinerant merchants.
County manager plan of government, §15.2-732.
Johnson grass, multiflora rose.
Authority to control, §15.2-902.
Joint activities.
Regional competitiveness act, §§15.2-1306 to 15.2-1310.
Joint aid agreements by localities, §15.2-1300.1.
Joint exercise of powers, §§15.2-1300 to 15.2-1302.
Agreements generally, §15.2-1300.
Distributions to localities by Commonwealth, §15.2-1302.
Generally, §15.2-1300.
Voluntary economic growth-sharing agreements, §15.2-1301.
Joint officers and employees, §§15.2-1513 to 15.2-1516.
Junkyards.
Taxing and regulating, §15.2-903.
Juvenile detention and other care facilities.
Operating and maintaining.
Generally, §§16.1-315 to 16.1-322.7.
See JUVENILE DETENTION AND OTHER CARE FACILITIES.
Keys to buildings of political subdivisions.
Possession or duplication, §18.2-503.

LOCALITIES —Cont'd
Land in urban areas.
Urban public-private partnership redevelopment fund, §§15.2-2414 to 15.2-2418.
Land preservation special assessment.
Real property taxes, §§58.1-3229 to 58.1-3244.
See REAL PROPERTY TAXES.
Law enforcement.
Generally, §§15.2-1700 to 15.2-1753.
See POLICE.
Law libraries.
Assessment as part of cost in civil actions, §42.1-70.
Local law libraries, §§42.1-65 to 42.1-71.
Regional law libraries, establishment by county or city, §42.1-71.
Leaves prohibited in landfills, §15.2-935.
Legal enumeration of population of locality, §15.2-1414.
Legal notices.
Mail, alternative method for notice, §15.2-107.2.
Publication.
Website may be used as well as newspaper, §15.2-107.1.
Lending of credit, VA Const Art X §10.
Liability insurance for officers, employees and volunteers, §15.2-1518.
Libraries, local and regional, §§42.1-33 to 42.1-45.
License fees and taxes on motor vehicles, trailers and semitrailers, §46.2-752.
License taxes.
Generally, §§58.1-3700 to 58.1-3735.
See LICENSE TAXES.
Lien for bawdy place abatement, §15.2-908.1.
Lien for cost of correcting drug blight, §15.2-907.
Lien for cost of removal of inoperable motor vehicle, §§15.2-904, 15.2-905.
Lien for cost of removal of trash from property, §15.2-901.
Lien for cost of removal, repair or securing building or other structure.
Endangerment to public health or safety, §15.2-906.
Lien for removal of vessel constituting obstruction or hazardous waters, §15.2-909.
Lien for removal, repair, etc., of wharves, pier, etc., constituting hazardous use of waters, §15.2-909.
Liens against real estate, §15.2-104.
Unpaid rates, rents, fees or charges for use of revenue-producing undertaking, §15.2-2605.
Life gifts and donations by, §15.2-953.
Lighting near planetariums, astronomical observatories and meteorological laboratories.
Regulating outdoor lighting, §15.2-920.
Lighting of exterior of buildings and property.
County executive form of government.
Ordinances providing, §15.2-504.1.
County manager plan of government, §15.2-742.
Limited access streets, §15.2-2026.
Litter control ordinances.
County manager plan of government, §15.2-733.
Living historical farm museums.
Operation and maintenance, §15.2-943.
Loans for repair of failed septic systems, §15.2-958.6

LOCALITIES —Cont'd
Lobbying.
Former officers and employees in certain counties.
Restrictions on activities.
County executive form of government, §15.2-515.
Urban county executive form of government, §15.2-810.
Local government employees.
Registration and reporting requirements, §2.2-422.
Local government facilities private capital lending, §§15.2-1815 to 15.2-1817.
Defined terms, §15.2-1815.
Financing agreements, power to enter into, §15.2-1816.
Real estate taxes, §15.2-1817.
Local transportation services exempted from license tax upon taxicabs.
Nonprofit serving elderly and disabled operating, §15.2-967.1.
Loitering, §15.2-926.
Long-term care insurance.
Employees of local governments, local officers, teachers.
Board of trustees, Virginia Retirement System.
Assumption of responsibility, §51.1-513.3.
Establishment by department of human resource management, §2.2-1207.
Trust fund, §51.1-513.4.
Low and moderate income housing.
Building permit fees.
Wavier for permit fees, §15.2-958.4.
County manager plan of government, §15.2-735.
Density of affordable housing units.
Permitting certain densities in comprehensive plan, §15.2-735.1.
Machinery and tools tax, §§58.1-3507, 58.1-3508.
Mail notice.
Initial notice by certified mail, subsequent notices by regular mail, §15.2-107.2.
Major employment and investment projects.
Major employment and investment project site planning grant fund, §2.2-2240.2.
Managers.
Administrative head of government, §15.2-1541.
Appointing chief administrative officer, §15.2-1540.
General duties, §15.2-1541.
Mandates.
Assessment and catalog by commission on local government, §15.2-2903.
Imposed on localities, assessment, §2.2-613.
Prescribed by state government.
Application for temporary suspension, §2.2-113.
Maps.
Official map, §§15.2-2233 to 15.2-2238.
Mass transit.
Designation of source of revenue for, §15.2-948.
Locality not member of transportation district, §15.2-947.
Master plan of state agency affecting locality's comprehensive plan.
Duty of state agency to furnish on request, §15.2-2202.
Mayors.
Oaths.
Powers to administer, §15.2-1410.
Powers, §15.2-1423.
Presiding officer, §15.2-1422.

LOCALITIES —Cont'd
Mayors —Cont'd
Salaries, setting.
City mayors, §15.2-1414.6.
Town mayors, §15.2-1414.7.
Vacancy, §15.2-1424.
Meals tax.
County food and beverage tax, §§58.1-3833, 58.1-3834.
Excise tax, city or town having general taxing powers, §58.1-3840.
Situs for taxation, §§58.1-3840, 58.1-3841.
Meetings of governmental bodies, §§15.2-1415 to 15.2-1421.
Annual or organizational meetings, §15.2-1416.
Authorities, boards and commissions.
Regular meeting times, §15.2-1415.
Call or request for special meeting, §15.2-1417.
Exercise of powers conferred, §15.2-1415.
First amendment right of freedom of speech.
Expressions by members and public prior to convening meeting consistent with, §15.2-1416.1.
Majority vote upon question, §15.2-1420.
Notice of special meeting, §15.2-1417.
Questions determined, §15.2-1420.
Quorum, §15.2-1415.
Regular meetings, §15.2-1416.
Authorities, boards and commissions, §15.2-1415.
Special meetings, §§15.2-1417, 15.2-1418.
Tie breaker.
Counties designating, §§15.2-1420, 15.2-1421.
Virginia freedom of information act.
Applicability, §15.2-1415.
MEI projects.
Major employment and investment project site planning grant fund, §2.2-2240.2.
Merchants' capital tax, §§58.1-3509, 58.1-3510.
Methamphetamine lab cleanup costs.
Liability of offender in separate civil action, §15.2-1716.2.
Methane or other combustible gas.
Building or facility to collect and use for electric power.
Loans to local governments, §§15.2-2430 to 15.2-2440.
See VIRGINIA INFRASTRUCTURE PROJECT LOAN FUND.
Militia, appropriations, §44-113.
Militia, requests for assistance by localities, §44-78.1.
Monuments.
Acquiring real property near land used for monument, §15.2-1801.
War veterans, §15.2-1812.
Actions for damages to memorials, §15.2-1812.1.
Mopeds.
Licensing, disposition of unclaimed mopeds, §15.2-1720.
Motor carriers, passengers.
Common carriers.
Terminals.
Local licensing, §46.2-2095.
Government vehicles.
Exclusions, §46.2-2000.1.
Taxicabs.
Licensing and license taxation, §46.2-2063.
Restrictions on imposition, §46.2-2064.
Number of cabs, §46.2-2067.
Operator qualifications, §46.2-2065.

LOCALITIES —Cont'd
Motor carriers, passengers —Cont'd
Taxicabs —Cont'd
Regulation by localities, §46.2-2062.
Stand regulation, §46.2-2065.
Motor carriers, property.
Government vehicles.
Exemptions from provisions, §46.2-2101.
Motorcycle, moped and motorized skateboard or foot-scooter noise, regulating, §15.2-919.
Motorcycles, use of transportation facilities or projects.
Discrimination as to use of facilities or projects prohibited.
State or federal funds used by locality, §33.1-13.1.
Motor vehicle and traffic regulation, §§46.2-1300 to 46.2-1314.
Applicability of county ordinances within towns, §46.2-1311.
Authority to deputize persons to direct traffic, §46.2-1310.
Automobile graveyards and junkyards.
Taxing and regulating, §15.2-903.
Certain laws and ordinances not affected by repeal of Title 15.1, §15.2-101.
Construction or repair work within right-of-way lines of public roadways, §46.2-1303.
Designation of play areas, §46.2-1302.
Designation of private roads for law-enforcement purposes, §46.2-1301.
Designation of stop and yield right-of-way intersections, §46.2-1301.
Disposition of traffic fines, §46.2-1308.
Erection of signs and markers, §§46.2-1300, 46.2-1312.
Inoperable motor vehicles on residential or commercial property.
Authority to restrict keeping, removal, §§15.2-904, 15.2-905.
Law-enforcement direction of traffic, §46.2-1309.
Local regulation of trucks and carriers, §46.2-1304.
Off-road recreational vehicles.
Southwest regional recreation authority.
Operation in localities embraced by authority, §46.2-800.2.
Photo-monitoring systems to enforce traffic light signals, §15.2-968.1.
Powers generally, §15.2-2028.
Prohibiting parking near certain fire hydrants, §46.2-1306.
Regulation of DWI ordinances, §46.2-1313.
Regulation of parking, §§46.2-1306, 46.2-1306.1.
Regulation of vehicular and pedestrian traffic, §46.2-1305.
Traffic schools, §46.2-1314.
War, traffic regulation during, §44-205.
Weather conditions or emergencies, §46.2-1302.
Motor vehicle license plates.
Commemorative license plates for counties, cities and towns, §46.2-749.4:4.
Special license plates bearing seal, symbol or emblem, §46.2-749.4.
Motor vehicle registration.
Local license taxes and fees, §§46.2-752 to 46.2-756.
Personal property taxes, §46.2-752.
Motor vehicles.
Solid waste management.
Local regulation of vehicle construction, parking, etc., §46.2-1304.1.

LOCALITIES —Cont'd
Motor vehicle sales and use tax.
Local tax prohibited, §58.1-2418.
Revenue disposition, §58.1-2425.
Mount Vernon name reserved for home and tomb of late General George Washington, §15.2-103.
Museums.
Acquisition and housing of relics, paintings, carvings, etc., §15.2-945.
Musk thistle, curled thistle.
Authority to control, §15.2-902.
Naming roads, streets and alleys, §15.2-2019.
Natural gas consumption tax.
Imposition when gas service becomes available, §58.1-2905.
Noise control.
Applicability to sports shooting ranges, §15.2-917.
Civil penalties for noise ordinance violations.
Adoption of uniform schedule, §15.2-980.
Motorcycle, moped, and motorized skateboard or foot-scooter noise, §15.2-919.
Noxious weed control, §15.2-902.
Nuisances.
Abatement or removal, §15.2-900.
Numbers displayed on buildings fronting public right of way, §15.2-2024.
Obscenity.
Adoption of ordinances prohibiting, §15.2-926.2.
Officers and employees.
Administrative leave for elected member of local governing body.
Member also employees of locality, §15.2-1407.
Agricultural agents.
Urban county executive form of government, §15.2-841.
Attorneys for the Commonwealth.
Generally, §§15.2-1626 to 15.2-1633.
See COMMONWEALTH'S ATTORNEYS.
Audit of officers handling public funds.
County board form of government, §15.2-417.
County executive form of government, §15.2-538.
Petition filed in circuit court, §15.2-2512.
Urban county executive form of government, §15.2-844.
Auxiliary police forces, §§15.2-1731 to 15.2-1736.
See POLICE.
Bond of officers, §§15.2-1527 to 15.2-1533.
See LOCAL OFFICERS AND EMPLOYEES.
Cash match plan for employees of Commonwealth, §§51.1-607 to 51.1-613.
City status granted to town.
Generally, §§15.2-3800 to 15.2-3834.
See TRANSITION OF TOWNS TO CITIES.
Civil service commission.
County manager plan of government, §15.2-721.
Clerk of circuit court.
See CIRCUIT COURT CLERKS.
Clerks.
Appointing or designating, §§15.2-1536, 15.2-1538.
General duties, §15.2-1539.
Commissioners of revenue generally, §§58.1-3100 to 58.1-3122.2.
See COMMISSIONERS OF REVENUE.
Commonwealth's attorneys.
Generally, §§15.2-1626 to 15.2-1633.
See COMMONWEALTH'S ATTORNEYS.
Constitutional officers.
Generally, §§15.2-1600 to 15.2-1637.
See LOCAL CONSTITUTIONAL OFFICERS.

LOCALITIES —Cont'd
Officers and employees —Cont'd
County attorneys.
County executive form of government, §15.2-529.
County manager form of government, §15.2-633.
Defense of localities and political subdivisions, governing bodies, officers or employees, §15.2-1520.
Departments or boards of welfare and social services, §15.2-1519.
Urban county executive form of government, §15.2-836.
County board form of government.
Generally, §§15.2-400 to 15.2-418.
See COUNTY BOARD FORM OF GOVERNMENT.
County boards of supervisors.
See COUNTY BOARDS OF SUPERVISORS.
County clerks.
Appointing or designating, §§15.2-1536, 15.2-1538.
County executive form of government.
Selection, terms and vacancies, §15.2-536.
Powers and duties, §15.2-1539.
Urban county executive form of government, §15.2-838.
County engineer.
County manager form of government, §15.2-625.
County executive form of government.
Generally, §§15.2-500 to 15.2-542.
See COUNTY EXECUTIVE FORM OF GOVERNMENT.
Urban county executive form of government.
Generally, §§15.2-800 to 15.2-858.
See URBAN COUNTY EXECUTIVE FORM OF GOVERNMENT.
County executives.
County executive form of government, §§15.2-509 to 15.2-517.
Urban county executive form of government, §§15.2-804 to 15.2-814.
County manager form of government.
Generally, §§15.2-600 to 15.2-642.
See COUNTY MANAGER FORM OF GOVERNMENT.
County manager plan of government.
Generally, §§15.2-700 to 15.2-750.
See COUNTY MANAGER PLAN OF GOVERNMENT.
County managers.
County manager form of government, §§15.2-609 to 15.2-615.
County manager plan of government, §§15.2-706, 15.2-708, 15.2-710.
County purchasing agents.
County board form of government, §15.2-414.
County executive form of government.
Director of finance to act as, §15.2-524.
County manager form of government.
Director of finance to act as, §15.2-622.
Procurement by, §§15.2-1233 to 15.2-1240.
Urban county executive form of government.
Director of finance to act as, §15.2-831.
County treasurers.
See COUNTY TREASURERS.
Criminal background investigations, §§15.2-1503.1, 15.2-1505.1.
Deferred compensation plans generally, §§51.1-600 to 51.1-605.

LOCALITIES —Cont'd
Officers and employees —Cont'd
Director of finance.
County executive form of government, §§15.2-518 to 15.2-525.
County manager form of government, §§15.2-617 to 15.2-624.
Supplementing salary, §15.2-1605.1.
Urban county executive form of government, §§15.2-826 to 15.2-833.
Fee system abolished.
County executive form of government, §15.2-540.
County manager form of government, §15.2-639.
Urban county executive form of government, §15.2-848.
Financial officer, §15.2-1537.
Financial reports by county officers, §15.2-1230.
Firefighters.
County manager form of government, §15.2-632.
Urban county executive form of government.
Department of public safety, §15.2-842.
Former employees, prohibition from certain activities, §15.2-1408.
Generally, §§15.2-1500 to 15.2-1543.
See LOCAL OFFICERS AND EMPLOYEES.
Governing bodies generally, §§15.2-1400 to 15.2-1433.
Grievance procedure.
County manager plan of government.
Police officers, §15.2-723.
Presence of equal employment opportunity officer, §15.2-738.
Local government personnel generally, §§15.2-1506 to 15.2-1507.1.
Group insurance programs generally, §§51.1-500 to 51.1-514.
See PUBLIC OFFICERS AND EMPLOYEES.
Health director.
County executive form of government, §15.2-534.
County manager form of government, §15.2-629.
Health officer.
County board form of government, §15.2-411.
Urban county executive form of government, §15.2-839.
Home demonstration agents.
Urban county executive form of government, §15.2-841.
Homesite of county officer becoming part of city tenure and reelection, §15.2-3823.
Immunity of members of local governmental entities, §15.2-1405.
Inquiry into official conduct of office or officer.
County executive form of government, §15.2-506.
County manager form of government, §15.2-606.
County manager plan of government, §15.2-709.
Urban county executive form of government, §15.2-814.
Joint officers and employees, §§15.2-1513 to 15.2-1516.
Agreement between or among employing localities, §15.2-1515.
Employment permitted, §15.2-1513.
Exception as to constitutional officers, §15.2-1516.
Exception to officers elected by voters, §15.2-1515.
Exercise of powers and duties, §15.2-1514.

LOCALITIES —Cont'd
Officers and employees —Cont'd
Joint officers and employees —Cont'd
Salary, retirement, and other benefits, §15.2-1515.
Lobbying restriction on former county officers and employees.
County executive form of government, §15.2-515.
Urban county executive form of government, §15.2-810.
Local government personnel generally, §§15.2-1500 to 15.2-1543.
See LOCAL OFFICERS AND EMPLOYEES.
Local trusts to fund postemployment benefits other than pensions, §§15.2-1544 to 15.2-1549.
Mayors.
Oaths.
Powers to administer, §15.2-1410.
Powers, §15.2-1423.
Presiding officer, §15.2-1422.
Salaries, setting.
City mayors, §15.2-1414.6.
Town mayors, §15.2-1414.7.
Vacancy, §15.2-1424.
Meetings of governmental bodies, §§15.2-1415 to 15.2-1421.
Military duty leave, §§44-93.1 to 44-93.5.
Personnel system in certain cities, §15.2-1131.
Police.
Auxiliary police forces, §§15.2-1731 to 15.2-1736.
See POLICE.
County manager form of government, §15.2-632.
County manager plan of government.
Grievances, §15.2-723.
General provisions as to police and public order, §§15.2-1700 to 15.2-1753.
See POLICE.
Special police officers, §§15.2-1737 to 15.2-1746.
See POLICE.
Urban county executive form of government.
Department of law enforcement, §15.2-836.
Department of public safety, §15.2-842.
Preemployment information, §15.2-1505.1.
Purchasing agents.
County executive form of government.
Director of finance to act as, §15.2-524.
County manager form of government.
Director of finance to act as, §15.2-622.
Procurement by county purchasing agent, §§15.2-1233 to 15.2-1240.
Urban county executive form of government.
Director of finance to act as, §15.2-831.
Qualification of local officer for office, §§15.2-1522 to 15.2-1524.
Removal of public officers generally, §§24.2-230 to 24.2-238.
See REMOVAL OF PUBLIC OFFICERS FROM OFFICE.
Residency, §§15.2-1505, 15.2-1525.
Residency of local officers.
Removal of residence from jurisdiction officer required to reside, §15.2-1526.
Retirement system generally, §§51.1-800 to 51.1-823.
See LOCAL RETIREMENT SYSTEMS.
Salaries.
Council members, §§15.2-1414.5, 15.2-1414.6.

LOCALITIES —Cont'd
Officers and employees —Cont'd
Salaries —Cont'd
County boards of supervisors, §§15.2-1414.1 to 15.2-1414.3.
Town council members and mayors, §15.2-1414.7.
Sheriffs.
Generally, §§15.2-1609 to 15.2-1625.
See SHERIFFS.
Social security coverage generally, §§51.1-700 to 51.1-707.
Special police officers, §§15.2-1737 to 15.2-1746.
See POLICE.
Superintendent of public welfare.
County board form of government, §15.2-412.
Generally.
See SUPERINTENDENTS OF PUBLIC WELFARE.
Superintendent of schools.
Urban county executive form of government, §15.2-837.
Superintendent of social services.
Urban county executive form of government, §15.2-835.
Telecommuting, §15.2-1512.3.
Travel expenses for persons on business of locality, §§15.2-1508.1 to 15.2-1508.4.
Treasurers.
Election, power and duties, §15.2-1608.
Generally, §§58.1-3123 to 58.1-3172.1.
See TREASURERS, LOCAL.
General provisions as to local constitutional officers, §§15.2-1600 to 15.2-1607.
See LOCAL CONSTITUTIONAL OFFICERS.
Insurer's conversion to stock corporation.
Treatment of money received, §15.2-1608.1.
Salary of city treasurer, §15.2-1608.1.
Salary of county treasurer, §15.2-1608.2.
Terms, §15.2-1608.
Urban county executive form of government.
Generally, §§15.2-800 to 15.2-858.
See URBAN COUNTY EXECUTIVE FORM OF GOVERNMENT.
Official map, §§15.2-2233 to 15.2-2238.
Ordinances.
Bad checks passed to locality.
Fee provided by ordinance, §15.2-106.
Generally, §§15.2-1425 to 15.2-1433.
See ORDINANCES.
Joint aid agreements by localities, §15.2-1300.1.
Levies and fees imposed or increased by locality.
Advertisement and enactment of ordinances for certain fees and levies, §15.2-107.
Organization of local government, §15.2-1500.
Outdoor lighting near planetariums, astronomical observatories and meteorological laboratories.
Regulating, §15.2-920.
Pari-mutuel wagering on horses.
Local referendum, §59.1-391.
Park authorities, §§15.2-5700 to 15.2-5714.
See PARK AUTHORITIES.
Parks, recreational facilities and playgrounds, §§15.2-1806 to 15.2-1811.
Acquiring real property near parks, §15.2-1801.
Acquisitions authorized for public use, §15.2-1814.
All-terrain vehicles or off-road motorcycles.
Trail systems for, §15.2-1806.
No liability to locality or property owners, §15.2-1806.1.

LOCALITIES —Cont'd
Parks, recreational facilities and playgrounds —Cont'd
City or town immunity for operating, §15.2-1809.
Collection of fees, §15.2-1806.
Department or bureau of recreation.
Operation through, §15.2-1806.
Election on establishing system of public recreation and playground, §15.2-1807.
Establishing, §15.2-1806.
Hiking, biking and horse back riding trails, §15.2-1806.
Immunity of city or town operating, §15.2-1809.
Notice of public hearings, §15.2-1813.
Participation in, §15.2-942.
Powers, §15.2-1806.
Property tax for maintenance and operation, §15.2-1806.
Protection of persons property interest or personal liability.
Trail systems for ATVs and off-road motorcycles, §15.2-1806.
Public hearings.
Notice, §15.2-1813.
Recreation board or school board.
Operation through, §15.2-1806.
Sanitary districts, operating in sanitary districts, §15.2-1811.
Sport facilities, providing and operating, §15.2-1808.
Swimming pools.
Leasing lands owned or held by locality, §15.2-1810.
System of public recreation and playgrounds, establishing, §15.2-1807.
Peddlers.
County manager plan of government, §15.2-732.
Penalty and interest for failure to pay accounts when due, §15.2-105.
Personal property, acquisition, disposition, use, powers, §15.2-951.
Personal property taxes.
Exempt property generally, §§58.1-3600 to 58.1-3666.
See PROPERTY EXEMPT FROM TAXATION.
Generally, §§58.1-3500 to 58.1-3522.
See PERSONAL PROPERTY TAXES.
Machinery and tools tax, §§58.1-3507, 58.1-3508.
Merchants' capital tax, §§58.1-3509, 58.1-3510.
Tax relief act of 1998, §§58.1-3523 to 58.1-3535.
See PERSONAL PROPERTY TAX RELIEF ACT OF 1998.
Personal property tax relief act of 1998.
Reimbursement for administrative costs, §15.2-1636.20.
Personnel generally, qualifications for office, bond, etc., §§15.2-1500 to 15.2-1543.
See LOCAL OFFICERS AND EMPLOYEES.
Persons with physical disabilities.
Access to public buildings, §§2.2-1159 to 2.2-1161.
Photo-monitoring systems to enforce traffic light signals, §15.2-968.1.
Planning and development.
Generally, §§15.2-2200 to 15.2-2239.
See PLANNING AND DEVELOPMENT.
Levies and fees imposed or increased by locality.
Advertisement and enactment of ordinances, §15.2-107.
Road impact fees, §§15.2-2317 to 15.2-2329.
See ROAD IMPACT FEES.

LOCALITIES —Cont'd
Planning and development —Cont'd
Subdivisions generally, §§15.2-2240 to 15.2-2279.
See SUBDIVISIONS.
Zoning generally, §§15.2-2280 to 15.2-2316.2.
See ZONING.
Planning commissions, §§15.2-2210 to 15.2-2222.
Planning district commissions, §§15.2-4200 to 15.2-4222.
See PLANNING DISTRICT COMMISSIONS.
Police.
Auxiliary police forces, §§15.2-1731 to 15.2-1736.
See POLICE.
Communications system, §§52-16 to 52-19.
County manager form of government, §15.2-632.
County manager plan of government.
Grievances, §15.2-723.
Dogs trained for police work.
Sale, authority, §15.2-981.
Generally, §§15.2-1700 to 15.2-1753.
See POLICE.
Interjurisdictional law-enforcement authority and agreements, §§15.2-1724 to 15.2-1730.
See POLICE.
Special police officers in localities, §§15.2-1737 to 15.2-1746.
See POLICE.
Urban county executive form of government.
Department of law enforcement, §15.2-836.
Department of public safety, §15.2-842.
Police dogs.
Sale of dogs trained for police work, §15.2-981.
Political campaign signs, regulation of, §15.2-109.
Population of locality.
Constitutional officers' salaries based upon.
Determined by preceding census, §15.2-1636.11.
Legal enumeration, §15.2-1414.
Pounds, §3.2-6546.
Abandoned, animal past holding period deemed, §3.2-6546.
Confinement and disposition of animals, §3.2-6546.
Destruction of animals, §3.2-6546.
Fees.
Owners, fees for confinement or repeated confinement of companion animal, §3.2-6546.
Feral dog or cat, destruction, §3.2-6546.
Foster care providers.
Affiliation with, §3.2-6546.
Holding period, §3.2-6546.
Identification, duty of operator to ascertain, §3.2-6546.
Limit on delivery of animals to one person, §3.2-6546.
Maintenance by county or city, §3.2-6546.
Owners readily identifiable, notification, §3.2-6546.
Sale or gift of animals.
Animals past holding period, §3.2-6546.
Time period for keeping animals, §3.2-6546.
Powers of local government, §§15.2-900 to 15.2-982.
Abandoned vessels or vessels constituting obstruction or hazard to lawful use of waters, §15.2-909.
Abating, razing or removing nuisance, §§15.2-900, 15.2-907.1.
Affordable housing, funding, §15.2-958.

LOCALITIES —Cont'd
Powers of local government —Cont'd
Air cannons, carbide cannons or other explosives used for purposes of killing birds, §15.2-918.
Alarm company operator regulations, §15.2-911.
Appropriations, §15.2-950.
Cemetery upkeep, §15.2-972.
Charitable institutions and associations, volunteer and nonprofit organizations, etc., §15.2-953.
Armories, §15.2-971.
Automobile graveyards, taxing and regulating, §15.2-903.
Blighted structures.
Nominal sales in Richmond, §15.2-958.1.
Boiler and pressure vessel operators certifications, §15.2-910.
Buildings or other structures endangering public health or safety, §§15.2-906, 15.2-907.1.
Locality appointed as receiver to repair derelict and blighted buildings, §15.2-907.2.
Buildings or other structures harboring bawdy place, §15.2-908.1.
Buildings or other structures harboring illegal drug use, §15.2-907.
Cemeteries in which free burial space provided.
Appropriations for upkeep, §15.2-972.
Charitable institutions and associations.
Appropriations, gifts and donations, §15.2-953.
Child-care services and facilities, §15.2-914.
Cities.
Uniform charter powers and additional powers generally, §§15.2-1100 to 15.2-1133.
See CITIES.
Civil commotion or disturbance in nature of riot.
Regulating assembly or movement of persons or vehicles, §15.2-925.
Commissions on human rights, §15.2-965.
Compound bows, crossbows, longbow and recurve bows, §15.2-916.
Conservation of trees during development process.
Locality located in Planning District 8 classified as nonattainment area for air quality standards, §15.2-961.1.
Consumer affairs offices, §15.2-963.
Counties.
Miscellaneous powers, §§15.2-1200 to 15.2-1232.
See COUNTIES.
Coyotes.
Bounties for coyotes, §15.2-926.1.
Curfew of minors, §15.2-926.
Cutting of grass, weeds and other foreign growth.
Vacant developed or undeveloped property, §15.2-901.
Dams, levees, seawalls, etc., construction, §15.2-970.
Dangerous or unhealthy substances.
Abatement or removal of nuisance, §15.2-900.
Defacement of public building, wall, fence or other structure.
Removing or repairing, §15.2-908.
Delinquent tax lands.
Nominal sales in Richmond, §15.2-958.1.
Dogs trained for police work.
Sale, authority, §15.2-981.
Door-to-door vendors, §15.2-913.
Educational television stations, §15.2-966.
Emergency medical service organizations.
Approval for establishment of volunteer organization, §15.2-955.

LOCALITIES —Cont'd
Powers of local government —Cont'd
Emergency medical service organizations —Cont'd
Tuition reimbursement for personnel, §15.2-954.1.
Federal development program participation, §15.2-956.
Federal leasing program participation, §15.2-957.
Fencing of swimming pools, §15.2-921.
Firearms, §15.2-915.
Firefighting organizations.
Approval of volunteer organization, §15.2-955.
Loans to volunteer organization, §15.2-954.
Tuition reimbursement for personnel, §15.2-954.1.
Fires.
Regulating or prohibiting making of fires, §15.2-922.1.
Fireworks permits, §15.2-974.
Garbage removal and disposal, §15.2-901.
Collection and disposal of garbage by locality, §15.2-927.
Contracts, §§15.2-930 to 15.2-932.
Delivery of garbage to certain facilities, §15.2-933.
Fee exemption, §15.2-936.
Leaves or grass clippings in landfills, §15.2-935.
Private waste companies, displacement, §15.2-934.
Separation of solid waste for collection and recycling, §15.2-937.
Solid waste management facilities, §15.2-928.
Siting approval, §15.2-929.
Geographic information, mapping, surveying or land information.
Unified or centralized systems, §15.2-962.
Grass.
Clippings in landfills, §15.2-935.
Cutting of grass on vacant developed or undeveloped property, §15.2-901.
Historical or cultural events, participation in re-creation and portrayal, §15.2-942.
Historic places and things, acquiring and preserving, §15.2-944.
Housing research by locality not having redevelopment and housing authority, §15.2-959.
Human resources agencies, reorganization, §15.2-964.
Human rights ordinances, §15.2-965.
Inoperable motor vehicles on residential or commercial property, §§15.2-904, 15.2-905.
Itinerant merchants.
Door-to-door vendors, §15.2-913.
Joint exercise, §§15.2-1300 to 15.2-1302.
Agreements generally, §15.2-1300.
Distributions to localities by Commonwealth, §15.2-1302.
Generally, §15.2-1300.
Voluntary economic growth-sharing agreements, §15.2-1301.
Junkyards, taxing and regulating, §15.2-903.
Leasing program participation, §15.2-957.
Leaves in landfills, §15.2-935.
License taxes on owners of certain motor vehicles, §15.2-973.
Litter removal and disposal, §15.2-901.
Living historical farm museums, §15.2-943.
Loitering, §15.2-926.
Low and moderate income housing, funding, §15.2-958.

LOCALITIES —Cont'd
Powers of local government —Cont'd
Markets, providing and operating, §15.2-971.
Mass transit.
Designation of revenue to pay, §15.2-948.
Motorcycle, moped, and motorized skateboard or foot-scooter noise, §15.2-919.
Motor vehicles.
Inoperable motor vehicles on residential or commercial property, §§15.2-904, 15.2-905.
License taxes on owners of certain vehicles, §15.2-973.
Motorcycle, moped, and motorized skateboard or foot-scooter noise, §15.2-919.
Parking facilities, §15.2-967.
Parking regulations within boundaries of state-supported institutions, §15.2-968.
Regulating and taxing automobile graveyards and junkyards, §15.2-903.
Traffic light signals.
Photo-monitoring systems to enforce, §15.2-968.1.
Museums.
Acquisition and housing of relics, paintings and other works of art, §15.2-945.
Noise control ordinances.
Applicability to sport shooting ranges, §15.2-917.
Civil penalties, uniform schedule adoption, §15.2-980.
Motorcycle, moped, and motorized skateboard or foot-scooter noise, §15.2-919.
Noxious weeds, controlling, §15.2-902.
Nuisances, abatement or removal, §15.2-900.
Outdoor lighting near planetariums, astronomical observatories and meteorological laboratories, §15.2-920.
Parking facilities, §15.2-967.
Parking of vehicles within boundaries of state-supported institutions, regulating, §15.2-968.
Peddlers.
Door-to-door vendors, §15.2-913.
Personal property, acquisition, disposition and use, §15.2-951.
Planting and replacement of trees during development process, §15.2-961.
Planting of trees destroyed during construction, §15.2-960.
Property.
Blighted structures and delinquent tax lands.
Nominal sales in Richmond, §15.2-958.1.
Public transportation system by county or city not member of transportation district, §15.2-947.
Real property, §15.2-1800.
Receiver to repair derelict and blighted buildings, locality appointed as, §15.2-907.2.
Recycling, §15.2-928.
Paper and paper products.
Preference for purchase, §15.2-938.
Reports.
Nonresidential solid waste generators, §15.2-939.
Separation of solid waste, §15.2-937.
Refuse removal and disposal, §15.2-901.
Collection and disposal of garbage by locality, §15.2-927.
Contracting for services, §§15.2-930 to 15.2-932.
Delivery of refuse to waste disposal facilities, §15.2-933.
Fee exemption, §15.2-936.

LOCALITIES —Cont'd
Powers of local government —Cont'd
Refuse removal and disposal —Cont'd
Leaves or grass clippings in landfills, §15.2-935.
Private waste companies, displacement, §15.2-934.
Separation of solid waste for collection and recycling, §15.2-937.
Solid waste management facilities, §15.2-928.
Solid waste management facility siting approval, §15.2-929.
Relics, paintings, carvings, etc.
Acquisition and housing, §15.2-945.
Rescue organizations.
Approval for establishment of volunteer rescue squad, §15.2-955.
Loans to volunteer organization, §15.2-954.
Residential rental property owners, grants or loans.
Funding for low and moderate income housing, §15.2-958.
Resources and advances of locality.
Expenditures for promoting, §15.2-940.
Riots.
Regulating assembly or movement of persons or vehicles, §15.2-925.
Scalping of tickets, §15.2-969.
Shared ride taxi systems, §15.2-949.
Smoke detectors, §15.2-922.
Solid waste companies, displacement, §15.2-934.
Solid waste management facilities, §15.2-928.
Leaves or grass clippings in landfills, §15.2-935.
Requiring delivery of garbage, trash and refuse to waste disposal facilities, §15.2-933.
Siting approval, §15.2-929.
Spills or releases of dangerous or unhealthy substances.
Abatement or removal, §15.2-900.
Sport shooting ranges.
Applicability of noise control ordinances, §15.2-917.
State-supported institutions.
Parking regulations within boundaries, §15.2-968.
Swimming pools, fencing, §15.2-921.
Ticket resales to certain public events, §15.2-969.
Ticket scalping, §15.2-969.
Tour guides and tourist guides, regulation, §15.2-946.
Towns.
Uniform charter powers and additional powers generally, §§15.2-1100 to 15.2-1133.
See TOWNS.
Traffic light signals.
Photo-monitoring systems to enforce, §15.2-968.1.
Trash removal and disposal, §15.2-901.
Contracting for services, §§15.2-930 to 15.2-932.
Delivery of trash to waste disposal facilities, §15.2-933.
Fee exemption, §15.2-936.
Leaves or grass clippings in landfills, §15.2-935.
Private waste companies, displacement, §15.2-934.
Separation of solid waste for collection and recycling, §15.2-937.
Solid waste management facilities, §15.2-928.
Solid waste management facility siting approval, §15.2-929.
Tree planting and replacement during development process, §15.2-961.

LOCALITIES —Cont'd
Powers of local government —Cont'd
Trees destroyed during construction, planting, §15.2-960.
Unified geographic information system, §15.2-962.
United States property, acquiring, §15.2-952.
Vacant developed or undeveloped property.
Blighted structures and delinquent tax lands.
Nominal sales in Richmond, §15.2-958.1.
Cutting grass, weeds and other foreign growth, §15.2-901.
Vessel abandoned or constituting obstruction or hazard to lawful use of waters, §15.2-909.
Virginia shell building initiative, participation, §15.2-941.
Volunteer and nonprofit organizations.
Appropriations, donations and gifts to, §15.2-953.
Approval for establishment of rescue squad, emergency medical service organization or firefighting organization, §15.2-955.
Loans to volunteer firefighting and rescue organizations, §15.2-954.
Water conservation devices, installation, §15.2-923.
Water shortages or water emergencies, §§15.2-923, 15.2-924.
Weeds.
Cutting of weeds on vacant developed or undeveloped property, §15.2-901.
Noxious weed control, §15.2-902.
Wharves, piers, pilings, etc., constituting obstruction or hazard to lawful use of waters, §15.2-909.
Works of art.
Acquisition and housing, §15.2-945.
Preemployment requirements for Arlington County, §15.2-709.1.
Preservation of peace and good order, §15.2-1700.
Pretrial services programs.
Assistance to judicial officers in carrying out bail and pretrial release duties, §§19.2-152.2 to 19.2-152.7:1.
See BAIL AND RECOGNIZANCE.
Probate tax, §§58.1-3805 to 58.1-3808.
Procurement by county purchasing agent, §§15.2-1233 to 15.2-1240.
Procurement for public bodies.
Tie bids.
Preference for local products and firms, §2.2-4328.
Professions and occupations.
Violations of professional license requirements, statute of limitations, §19.2-8.
Proffered cash payments and expenditures.
Accepting as part of rezoning application.
Alternative improvements.
Utilization of proffered cash payments for, §15.2-2303.2.
Amount of proffered cash payments received during fiscal year.
Inclusion in capital improvement program, §15.2-2303.2.
Cash payments not accepted during fiscal year.
Notification to commission on local government, §15.2-2303.2.
Collecting or accepting after final inspection, §15.2-2303.1:1.
Commission on local government, report by, §15.2-2303.2.

LOCALITIES —Cont'd
Proffered cash payments and expenditures —Cont'd
Accepting as part of rezoning application —Cont'd
Forfeiture by locality of cash payments.
Failure to timely begin work on improvements for which cash payments proffered, §15.2-2303.2.
Reports to commission on local government, §15.2-2303.2.
Voluntary agreement to earlier payment date, §15.2-2303.3.
Waiver of future rights as part of proffer, severable and void, §15.2-2303.3.
When locality may require payment, §15.2-2303.3.
Conditional zoning, §15.2-2303.
Promoting resources and advantages of localities, §15.2-940.
Prompt payment of bills, §§2.2-4352, 2.2-4354.
Property sales.
Blighted structures and delinquent tax lands.
Nominal sales in Richmond, §15.2-958.1.
Property taxes.
Exempt property generally, §§58.1-3600 to 58.1-3666.
See PROPERTY EXEMPT FROM TAXATION.
Machinery and tools tax, §§58.1-3507, 58.1-3508.
Merchants' capital tax, §§58.1-3509, 58.1-3510.
Personal property generally, §§58.1-3500 to 58.1-3522.
See PERSONAL PROPERTY TAXES.
Real property taxes generally, §§58.1-3200 to 58.1-3389.
See REAL PROPERTY TAXES.
Tax rate for budget year.
Fixing, time, §15.2-2503.
Tax relief act of 1998, §§58.1-3523 to 58.1-3535.
See PERSONAL PROPERTY TAX RELIEF ACT OF 1998.
Public assistance.
Departments and directors of social services.
Generally, §§63.2-324 to 63.2-336.
See SOCIAL SERVICES.
Funding of public assistance and social services, §§63.2-400 to 63.2-412.
See SOCIAL SERVICES.
Generally, §§63.2-500 to 63.2-805.
See PUBLIC AID AND ASSISTANCE.
Local boards of social services.
Generally, §§63.2-300 to 63.2-323.
See SOCIAL SERVICES.
Temporary assistance for needy families, §§63.2-600 to 63.2-621.
See PUBLIC AID AND ASSISTANCE.
Publication of legal notices.
Mail, alternative method for notice, §15.2-107.2.
Website may be used as well as newspaper, §15.2-107.1.
Publications.
State publications depository program.
Duties of local agencies generally, §42.1-94.
Generally, §§42.1-92 to 42.1-97.
See STATE PUBLICATIONS DEPOSITORY PROGRAM.
Public finance act.
Bonds generally, §§15.2-2600 to 15.2-2663.
See PUBLIC FINANCE ACT.
Public hearings.
Generally.
See PUBLIC HEARINGS.

LOCALITIES —Cont'd
Public nuisances.
Abatement or removal, §§15.2-900, 15.2-907.1.
Public-private education facilities and infrastructure act, §§56-575.1 to 56-575.18.
See PUBLIC BUILDINGS.
Public-private transportation act, §§56-556 to 56-574.
See TRANSPORTATION.
Public procurement.
Contracts for investment of funds.
Consideration of affordable housing, §2.2-4327.
Public records generally, §§42.1-76 to 42.1-90.1.
See STATE RECORDS MANAGEMENT.
Public school property and buildings.
Property acquisition for educational purposes by counties, cities and towns, §22.1-126.1.
Public-private education facilities and infrastructure act, §§56-575.1 to 56-575.18.
See PUBLIC BUILDINGS.
Public service corporation assessments against property.
Review by governing bodies, §58.1-2602.
Public service corporations, taxation of property, §58.1-2606.
Railroads, §58.1-2607.
Public transportation system for localities not member of transportation district, §15.2-947.
Persons with disabilities.
Access to, §51.5-44.
Public utilities, §§15.2-2109 to 15.2-2121.
Acquiring utility facilities or providing services to customer of utility, §15.2-2109.
Acquisition of water supply or sewage system from sanitary district, §15.2-2116.
Agreements by political subdivisions for sewage or water service, §15.2-2112.
Computer services.
Power of certain localities to acquire or obtain control of, §15.2-2109.
Connection of water and sewage systems in certain counties.
Mandatory connection, §15.2-2110.
Connections of fire suppression systems, §15.2-2113.
Contiguous territory.
Purchase of gas, electric and water plants operating in, §15.2-2115.
Contracts for sewerage or water purification company, §15.2-2117.
Development plans.
Regulations as to water, sewer and other facilities in subdivisions, §15.2-2121.
Discounted fees and charges for low-income and disabled customers, §15.2-2119.
Easement for provision of water and sewer services.
Prescriptive easements, §15.2-2109.1.
Electric authorities, §§15.2-5400 to 15.2-5431.
See ELECTRIC AUTHORITIES.
Electric plants in contiguous territory, purchase, §15.2-2115.
Fees and charges for sewer services, §§15.2-2119, 15.2-5139.
Fire suppression systems.
Connections, §15.2-2113.
Gas plants operating in contiguous territory, purchase, §15.2-2115.
General powers, §15.2-2109.

LOCALITIES —Cont'd
Public utilities —Cont'd
Joint agreements for sewage or water service, §15.2-2112.
Lien for gas utilities charges and taxes, §15.2-2118.1.
Lien for water and sewer charges, §15.2-2118.
Enforcement, §15.2-2120.
Lighting of streets, fee for, §15.2-2158.
Loan program for repair of failed septic systems, §15.2-958.6.
Mandatory connections, §15.2-2110.
Mutual aid agreements for power and natural gas, §15.2-2109.2.
Natural gas distribution service within any underserved area or county, §15.2-2109.3.
Prescriptive easements for provision of water and sewer services, §15.2-2109.1.
Prevention of water pollution, §15.2-2109.
Purchase of gas, electric and water plants operating in contiguous territory, §15.2-2115.
Referendum on acquisition of gas or electric facilities, §15.2-2109.
Regulation of storm water, §15.2-2114.
Restrictions on powers, §15.2-2109.
Sanitary districts.
Acquisition of water supply or sewage system from, §15.2-2116.
Septic tank installation permit in Augusta county, §15.2-2157.1.
Septic tanks when sewers not available, §15.2-2157.
Enforcement, §15.2-2120.
Mandatory connection in certain counties, §15.2-2110.
Regulation of sewage disposal generally, §15.2-2111.
Sewage disposal systems.
Generally, §§15.2-2122 to 15.2-2133.
See SEWAGE DISPOSAL SYSTEMS.
Sewage disposal when sewers not available, §15.2-2157.
Sewerage or water purification company, contracts with, §15.2-2117.
Solid waste disposal by counties, fee, §15.2-2159.
Storm water control program, §15.2-2114.
Street lighting, fee for, §15.2-2158.
Tax on water and sewer charges in certain counties, §15.2-2118.
Water pollution prevention, §15.2-2109.
Water purification company, contracts with, §15.2-2117.
Water supply systems.
Generally, §§15.2-2134 to 15.2-2148.
See WATER SUPPLY SYSTEMS.
Purchasing agents.
County board form of government, §15.2-414.
County executive form of government.
Director of finance to act as, §15.2-524.
County manager form of government.
Director of finance to act as, §15.2-622.
Employment by county, duties, §15.2-1543.
Procurement by county purchasing agent, §§15.2-1233 to 15.2-1240.
Urban county executive form of government.
Director of finance to act as, §15.2-831.
Qualification of local officer for office, §§15.2-1522 to 15.2-1524.
Railroads.
Local taxation of property, §58.1-2607.

LOCALITIES —Cont'd
Real property.
Acquiring for development of business or industry, §15.2-1802.
Acquiring near parks or other public property, §15.2-1801.
Acquisition generally, §15.2-1800.
Authorized acquisitions for public use, §15.2-1814.
Property near parks and other public property, §15.2-1801.
Public hearing, notice, §15.2-1813.
Approval and acceptance of deeds, §15.2-1803.
Business and industry development, acquiring, leasing or selling, §15.2-1802.
Deeds conveying, form, acceptance by governing body, execution, §15.2-1803.
Sale, exchange, lease, etc., or otherwise disposing of, §15.2-1800.
School construction or improvement.
Tenancy in common with school board, §15.2-1800.1.
Real property taxes.
Exempt property generally, §§58.1-3600 to 58.1-3666.
See PROPERTY EXEMPT FROM TAXATION.
Generally, §§58.1-3200 to 58.1-3389.
See REAL PROPERTY TAXES.
Reapportionment.
Governing body elected by district, decennial reapportionment, VA Const Art VII §5.
Receiver to repair derelict and blighted buildings, locality appointed as, §15.2-907.2.
Rechargeable battery disposal and recycling, §10.1-1425.39.
Reciprocal insurance contracts, power to enter into, §38.2-1204.
Recordation tax, §§58.1-3800 to 58.1-3804.
State tax exemption, §58.1-811.
Records.
Reproduction, §15.2-1412.
Recreational facilities authorities, §§15.2-5600 to 15.2-5616.
See RECREATIONAL FACILITIES AUTHORITY.
Recreational facilities, liability in operating.
Agreements with landowners, §29.1-509.
Recycled paper and paper products.
Preference for purchase, §15.2-938.
Recycling.
Grants for recycling, §10.1-1422.04.
Reports by nonresidential solid waste generators and companies, §15.2-939.
Separation for solid waste generally, §15.2-937.
Redevelopment projects.
See REDEVELOPMENT PROJECTS.
Redistricting of election districts.
Decennial reapportionment, VA Const Art VII §5.
Reduction of service by state agency to locality.
Notification, §2.2-612.
Refunding bonds, §§15.2-2643 to 15.2-2649.
Refuse.
Collection and disposal authorities, §§15.2-5100 to 15.2-5159.
See WATER AND WASTE AUTHORITIES.
General powers as to waste and recycling, §§15.2-927 to 15.2-939.
Regional cooperation act, §§15.2-4200 to 15.2-4222.
See PLANNING DISTRICT COMMISSIONS.

LOCALITIES —Cont'd
Regional organizations.
Appropriating funds or supplying goods and services, §15.2-1304.
Regional partnerships.
Regional competitiveness act, §§15.2-1306 to 15.2-1310.
Rehabilitation of buildings.
Preservation and production of low and moderate income housing, other housing experiments.
Local funding, §15.2-958.
Tenant relocation payments.
County manager plan of government, §15.2-737.
Relics, paintings, carvings, etc.
Acquisition and housing, §15.2-945.
Relocation assistance.
County manager plan of government, §15.2-729.
Remote access to local agency information.
Authorizing circuit court clerk to provide, §17.1-226.
Removal of public officers from office, §§24.2-230 to 24.2-238.
See REMOVAL OF PUBLIC OFFICERS FROM OFFICE.
Removal or rehabilitation of derelict structures.
Grants, §36-155.
Removal or repair of building, wall, etc., endangering public health or safety, §§15.2-906, 15.2-907.1.
Rental inspections of units located in rental inspection district.
Residential rental dwelling units.
Building code compliance, §36-105.1:1.
Reproduction of records and documents, §15.2-1412.
Rescue squads.
Establishment of volunteer organization.
Approval of locality, §15.2-955.
Residency of local officers, §§15.2-1505, 15.2-1525.
Removal of residence from jurisdiction officer required to reside, §15.2-1526.
Resources authority.
Issuing and selling local obligations, §62.1-216.
Nonpayment by localities, investigation, withholding state funds, §62.1-216.1.
Restaurants.
Fairs, exemption from provisions by ordinance, §35.1-26.
Retail sales and use tax.
Localities share, §58.1-638.
Municipality entitlement, §58.1-608.3.
Reversion of cities to towns.
City no longer qualifying for city status, §§15.2-4000 to 15.2-4005.
See REVERSION OF CITIES TO TOWNS.
Transition of city to town status generally, §§15.2-4100 to 15.2-4120.
See REVERSION OF CITIES TO TOWNS.
Rewards for arrest and conviction of offender.
Authorization to officer and pay, §15.2-1713.
Crimestoppers information, confidentiality of information, §15.2-1713.1.
Ridesharing.
Municipal licenses and taxes, §46.2-1405.
Shared ride taxi system, §15.2-949.
Riots.
Regulation of assembly or movement of persons in vehicles, §15.2-925.

LOCALITIES —Cont'd
Road construction equipment.
Sale with intent to lease back.
Approval of governing body required, notice, public hearing, §15.2-951.
Road impact fees, §§15.2-2317 to 15.2-2329.
See ROAD IMPACT FEES.
Roads, streets and public rights of way.
Generally, §§15.2-2000 to 15.2-2030.
See ROADS, STREETS AND PUBLIC RIGHTS OF WAY.
Roller skates.
Prohibiting on sidewalks or crosswalks, §46.2-904.
Rolling stock tax distribution, §§58.1-2658, 58.1-2658.1.
Salaries.
City council members, §§15.2-1414.5, 15.2-1414.6.
County boards of supervisors, §§15.2-1414.1 to 15.2-1414.3.
Town council members and mayors, §15.2-1414.7.
Sale of merchandise on highways, public roadways or medians.
Prohibition or regulation, §46.2-931.
Sales taxes, §58.1-605.
School boards.
See LOCAL SCHOOL BOARDS.
School construction or improvement.
Tenancy in common with school board, §15.2-1800.1.
Scooters.
Foot-scooters.
Prohibiting on sidewalks or crosswalks, §46.2-904.
Screening of automobile graveyards and junkyards, §15.2-903.
Seal, §15.2-1402.
Self-insurance.
Liability insurance for officers, employees and volunteers, §15.2-1518.
Local government group self-insurance pools, §§15.2-2700 to 15.2-2709.
See LOCAL GOVERNMENT GROUP SELF-INSURANCE POOLS.
Septic tanks.
Civil penalties.
Uniform schedule, establishment by ordinance.
Specified violations of operation and maintenance of nonconventional sewage disposal systems, §15.2-2157.
Installation permit in Augusta county, §15.2-2157.1.
Loan program for repair of failed septic systems, §15.2-958.6.
Sewage disposal when sewers not available, §15.2-2157.
Service districts, §§15.2-2400 to 15.2-2403.3.
Boundary changes, §15.2-2402.1.
Consolidated cities.
Creation in by court order, §15.2-2401.
Creation, §15.2-2400.
Court order in consolidated cities, §15.2-2401.
Description of proposed district, §15.2-2402.
Powers, §15.2-2403.
Service of process in suit against localities, §15.2-1404.
Setback lines.
Ordinances regulating, §15.2-2279.
Setoff debt collection, income tax, §§58.1-520 to 58.1-535.
See INCOME TAX.

LOCALITIES —Cont'd
Severance tax on coal, gas or oil.
Alternative to specially and separately assessing mineral lands, §58.1-3286.
License tax on persons engaging in business of severing, §§58.1-3712 to 58.1-3713.4.
Local coal severance license taxes, §§58.1-3740 to 58.1-3745.
Sewage disposal authorities, §§15.2-5100 to 15.2-5159.
See WATER AND WASTE AUTHORITIES.
Sewage disposal systems.
Approval of systems by counties, §§15.2-2126 to 15.2-2133.
See SEWAGE DISPOSAL SYSTEMS.
Generally, §§15.2-2122 to 15.2-2125.
See SEWAGE DISPOSAL SYSTEMS.
Sewer authorities, §§15.2-5100 to 15.2-5159.
See WATER AND WASTE AUTHORITIES.
Shared ride taxi system, §15.2-949.
Sheriffs.
Generally, §§15.2-1609 to 15.2-1625.
See SHERIFFS.
Shooting of bows.
Arrow landing upon property of another without permission, §15.2-916.
Sidewalks.
Electric power-assisted bicycles.
Operating on sidewalks, §46.2-904.
Powers, §15.2-2001.
Prohibiting bicycles, roller skates or skateboards, §46.2-904.
Side yards.
Ordinances regulating, §15.2-2279.
Signs.
Loitering on bridges or highway rights-of-way, §46.2-930.
Skateboards.
Prohibiting on sidewalks or crosswalks, §46.2-904.
Smoke detectors in certain buildings, §15.2-922.
Smoking in public places.
Virginia indoor clean air act, §§15.2-2820 to 15.2-2833.
See SMOKING IN PUBLIC PLACES.
Social services.
Adoption.
Generally, §§63.2-1200 to 63.2-1248.
See ADOPTION.
Adult protective services, §§63.2-1603 to 63.2-1610.
Child abuse and neglect, §§63.2-1500 to 63.2-1527.
See CHILD ABUSE AND NEGLECT.
Departments and directors of social services.
Generally, §§63.2-324 to 63.2-336.
See SOCIAL SERVICES.
Foster care generally, §§63.2-900 to 63.2-915.
See SOCIAL SERVICES.
Funding of public assistance and social services, §§63.2-400 to 63.2-412.
See SOCIAL SERVICES.
Local boards of social services.
Generally, §§63.2-300 to 63.2-323.
See SOCIAL SERVICES.
Public assistance.
Generally, §§63.2-500 to 63.2-805.
See PUBLIC AID AND ASSISTANCE.
Temporary assistance for needy families, §§63.2-600 to 63.2-621.
See PUBLIC AID AND ASSISTANCE.
Solicitation of contributions on highways, public roadways, medians.
Prohibition or regulation, §46.2-931.

LOCALITIES —Cont'd
Solid waste management.
General powers as to waste and recycling, §§15.2-901, 15.2-927 to 15.2-939.
Special court.
Annexation, consolidation of localities, transition of localities, etc., §§15.2-3000 to 15.2-3004.
Disputes between jurisdictions involving dams or water impoundment, §§15.2-2135 to 15.2-2141.
Special education.
Power of localities to appropriate and expend funds for handicapped children, §22.1-220.
Special police officers, §§15.2-1737 to 15.2-1746.
See POLICE.
Speed limits.
Highways in cities and towns.
Authority of municipality to increase or decrease speed limits, §46.2-875.
Spills or releases of dangerous or unhealthy substances.
Abatement and removal, §15.2-900.
Sport shooting ranges.
Applicability of noise ordinances, §15.2-917.
Spot blight abatement, §36-49.1:1.
Stadiums.
Providing and operating, §15.2-1808.
State funds collected locally by financial officers.
Disposition, §15.2-1537.1.
Stock subscriptions, VA Const Art X §10.
Storm water control programs, §15.2-2114.
Streets and alleys.
Local authority over highways, §§33.1-224 to 33.1-246.
See LOCAL ROAD AUTHORITIES.
Subdivisions.
Generally, §§15.2-2240 to 15.2-2279.
See SUBDIVISIONS.
Superintendent of public welfare.
See SUPERINTENDENTS OF PUBLIC WELFARE.
Superintendent of schools.
Urban county executive form of government, §15.2-837.
Superintendent of social services.
Urban county executive form of government, §15.2-835.
Supplies and equipment to clerks of courts of record, §15.2-1656.
Swimming pools.
Fencing required, §15.2-921.
Leasing land held or owned by locality for, §15.2-1810.
Operating in sanitary district, §15.2-1811.
System of public recreation and playgrounds.
Election to establish, §15.2-1807.
Tattoo parlors and body-piercing salons, regulation, §15.2-912.
Taxes.
Admission tax, §§58.1-3817, 58.1-3818.
Scott county.
Off-track horse race wagering facilities, §58.1-3818.01.
Stafford county, §58.1-3818.02.
Bawdy places, building and other structure harboring.
Cost of corrective action by locality collected as tax, §15.2-908.1.
Bonds issued by locality.
Levy and collection of tax, §15.2-2624.

LOCALITIES —Cont'd
Taxes —Cont'd
Cigarette tax, §§58.1-3830 to 58.1-3832.
Corporate or partnership officer willful failure to collect and account for, §58.1-3907.
Collection of local taxes generally, §§58.1-3910 to 58.1-3961.
See TAX COLLECTION.
Consumer utility taxes, §§58.1-3814 to 58.1-3816.2.
Correction of erroneous tax assessments, §§58.1-3980 to 58.1-3995.
See CORRECTION OF ERRONEOUS TAX ASSESSMENTS.
Delinquent taxes.
Collection of local taxes generally.
See TAX COLLECTION.
Sale of delinquent tax lands generally, §§58.1-3965 to 58.1-3975.
See SALE OF DELINQUENT TAX LANDS.
Distress.
Collection of local taxes by distress generally, §§58.1-3940 to 58.1-3961.
See TAX COLLECTION.
Drug blight existing on property.
Costs and expenses of locality undertaking corrective action collected as tax, §15.2-907.
Enterprise zone development.
Local enterprise zone development taxation program, §§58.1-3245.6 to 58.1-3245.12.
Excise taxes.
City or town having general taxing powers, §58.1-3840.
Exempt property generally, §§58.1-3600 to 58.1-3666.
See PROPERTY EXEMPT FROM TAXATION.
Food and beverage tax.
City or town excise tax, §58.1-3840.
Counties, §§58.1-3833, 58.1-3834.
Situs for taxation, §58.1-3841.
Generally, §§58.1-3000 to 58.1-3018.
See LOCAL TAXES.
Income tax, §§58.1-540 to 58.1-549.
License taxes, §§58.1-3700 to 58.1-3735.
See LICENSE TAXES.
Local improvements, §§15.2-2404 to 15.2-2413.
See TAXES OR ASSESSMENTS FOR LOCAL IMPROVEMENTS.
Machinery and tools tax, §§58.1-3507, 58.1-3508.
Merchants' capital tax, §§58.1-3509, 58.1-3510.
Natural gas consumption tax.
Imposition when gas service becomes available, §58.1-2905.
Parks, recreational facilities and playgrounds.
System of public recreation and playgrounds.
Annual tax, §15.2-1807.
Tax on property to maintain and operate, §15.2-1806.
Personal property tax relief act of 1998, §§58.1-3523 to 58.1-3535.
See PERSONAL PROPERTY TAX RELIEF ACT OF 1998.
Probate tax, §§58.1-3805 to 58.1-3808.
Public school special tax, §§22.1-102 to 22.1-106.
Real property taxes generally, §§58.1-3200 to 58.1-3389.
See REAL PROPERTY TAXES.
Recordation tax, §§58.1-3800 to 58.1-3804.
Severance tax on coal, gas or oil.
Alternative to specially and separately assessing mineral lands, §58.1-3286.

LOCALITIES —Cont'd
Taxes —Cont'd
Severance tax on coal, gas or oil —Cont'd
License tax on persons engaging in business of severing, §§58.1-3712 to 58.1-3713.4.
Local coal severance license taxes, §§58.1-3740 to 58.1-3745.
Tangible personal property generally, §§58.1-3500 to 58.1-3522.
See PERSONAL PROPERTY TAXES.
Town imposing.
Two-third vote of council members, §15.2-1427.
Transient occupancy tax, §§58.1-3819 to 58.1-3826.
Tax increment financing.
Blighted areas, §§58.1-3245 to 58.1-3245.5.
Tax information.
Tax commissioner authorized to divulge to chief executive officer, §58.1-3.
Telecommunications services, §15.2-2160.
Telegraph or telephone corporation.
Certificate to locality to operate as a telephone utility, §§56-265.4:4, 56-458.
Franchise to occupy parks, streets, etc., §56-462.
Offering of communications services, §56-484.7:1.
Approval, §56-484.7:2.
Revocation, §56-484.7:4.
Wireless service authorities, §§15.2-5431.1 to 15.2-5431.37.
See WIRELESS SERVICE AUTHORITIES.
Telephone or telegraph lines.
Occupation of roads, streets, etc., of counties, cities or towns, §56-458.
Temporary closing public rights of way, §§15.2-2013, 15.2-2014.
Tenant relocation payments.
Rehabilitation of buildings.
County manager plan of government, §15.2-737.
Tennessee Valley Authority, apportionment of payments.
Apportionment among counties and cities in which authority owns property, §58.1-3406.
Terrorism hoax.
Reimbursement of expenses in responding to, §15.2-1716.1.
Tie breakers.
Counties designating, §§15.2-1420, 15.2-1421.
Tour guides and tourist guides, regulation, §15.2-946.
Tourism.
Promoting resources and advantages of localities, §15.2-940.
Tourism zones.
Establishment, tax incentives, regulator flexibility.
Authority, §58.1-3851.
Tax revenues, entitlement, §58.1-3851.1.
Power to designate, §15.2-982.
Towns.
Annulment of charters, §§15.2-3700 to 15.2-3712.
See TOWNS.
Generally.
See TOWNS.
Incorporation by judicial proceedings, §§15.2-3600 to 15.2-3605.
Transition to cities, §§15.2-3800 to 15.2-3834.
See TRANSITION OF TOWNS TO CITIES.
Uniform charter powers and additional powers generally, §§15.2-1100 to 15.2-1133.
See TOWNS.

LOCALITIES —Cont'd
Traffic lights.
Photo-monitoring systems to enforce traffic light signals, §15.2-968.1.
Traffic regulation powers generally, §§15.2-2028, 46.2-1300 to 46.2-1314.
Traffic regulations during state of war, §44-205.
Transient occupancy tax, §§58.1-3819 to 58.1-3826.
Excise tax, city or town having general taxing powers, §58.1-3840.
Transition of city to town status.
City no longer qualifying for city status, §§15.2-4000 to 15.2-4005.
See REVERSION OF CITIES TO TOWNS.
Transition of city to town status generally, §§15.2-4100 to 15.2-4120.
See REVERSION OF CITIES TO TOWNS.
Transition of counties to cities, §§15.2-3900 to 15.2-3919.
See TRANSITION OF COUNTIES TO CITIES.
Transition of towns to cities, §§15.2-3800 to 15.2-3834.
See TRANSITION OF TOWNS TO CITIES.
Transportation board or department disposing of surplus realty.
Notice to local governing body, §33.1-223.2:2.
Transportation districts.
Generally, §§15.2-4500 to 15.2-4534.
See TRANSPORTATION DISTRICTS.
Multicounty transportation improvement districts.
See TRANSPORTATION DISTRICTS.
Transportation improvement district for individual locality.
See TRANSPORTATION DISTRICTS.
Trash.
General powers as to waste and recycling, §§15.2-927 to 15.2-939.
Travel expenses for persons on business of locality, §§15.2-1508.1 to 15.2-1508.4.
Commonwealth bearing portion of expense, §15.2-1508.2.
Generally, §15.2-1508.1.
Rate of reimbursement per mile, §15.2-1508.1.
Supplementation of expenses by certain cities or counties, §§15.2-1508.3, 15.2-1508.4.
Treasurers.
Deputies.
Appointment, powers, removal, §15.2-1603.
Election, powers and duties, §15.2-1608.
Generally, §§58.1-3123 to 58.1-3172.1.
See TREASURERS, LOCAL.
General provisions as to local constitutional officers, §§15.2-1600 to 15.2-1607.
See LOCAL CONSTITUTIONAL OFFICERS.
Insurer's conversion to stock corporation, treatment of money received, §15.2-1608.
Salary of city treasurer, §15.2-1608.1.
Salary of county treasurer, §15.2-1608.2.
Terms, §15.2-1608.
Trees.
Conservation during development process.
Locality located in Planning District 8 classified as nonattainment area for air quality standards, §15.2-961.1.
Planting and replacement during development process, §15.2-961.
Trespass.
Designation of local law-enforcement agency to enforce trespass violations, §15.2-1717.1.

LOCALITIES —Cont'd
Trigon Blue Cross Blue Shield.
Conversion to stock corporation.
Disposition of property received by locality on conversion, §15.2-1512.1.
Unclaimed property in possession of sheriff or police.
Disposition, §15.2-1719.
Bicycles or mopeds, §15.2-1720.
Firearms or other weapons, §15.2-1721.
Urban county executive form of government, §§15.2-800 to 15.2-858.
See URBAN COUNTY EXECUTIVE FORM OF GOVERNMENT.
Urban public-private partnership redevelopment fund, §§15.2-2414 to 15.2-2418.
Use of streets, roads, alleys, etc., §§15.2-2015 to 15.2-2018.
Vacant property.
Cutting grass, weeds and other foreign growth.
Requiring owners, §15.2-901.
Vacation or alteration of public rights of way, §§15.2-2006 to 15.2-2008.
Vandalism.
Willful and malicious damage to or defacement of public or private facilities, §15.2-1812.2.
Vehicle fleet.
Sale with intent to lease back.
Approval of governing body required, notice, public hearing, §15.2-951.
Vehicle license fees and taxes, §46.2-752.
Veterans monuments or memorials, §15.2-1812.
Damage to memorials, actions, §15.2-1812.1.
Veteran's preference for employment, §15.2-1509.
Virginia Beach arena, §§15.2-5921 to 15.2-5927.
See VIRGINIA BEACH ARENA.
Virginia Commonwealth University health system authority.
Authority to lend or donate money or other property, §23-50.16:11.
Virginia infrastructure project loan fund, §§15.2-2430 to 15.2-2440.
See VIRGINIA INFRASTRUCTURE PROJECT LOAN FUND.
Virginia shell building initiative.
Participation, §15.2-941.
Visually handicapped operating stands for sale of newspapers, periodicals, confections, etc., in courthouses, §15.2-1805.
Voluntary cash proffers, use of, §15.2-975.
Voluntary settlement of annexation, transition or immunity issues, §§15.2-3400, 15.2-3401.
Volunteers.
Liability insurance, §15.2-1518.
Property maintenance and zoning inspectors.
Certain cities, §15.2-1132.
Walls.
Endangering public health or safety.
Removal, repair or securing, §15.2-906.
War veterans monuments or memorials, §15.2-1812.
Damage to memorials, actions, §15.2-1812.1.
Waste and recycling, §§15.2-927 to 15.2-939.
Waste management.
Notification of violations, §10.1-1407.1.
Reimbursements to localities for upgrades to treatment works, §10.1-1186.01.
Water authorities, §§15.2-5100 to 15.2-5159.
See WATER AND WASTE AUTHORITIES.

LOCALITIES —Cont'd
Water conservation devices, §15.2-923.
Water shortages or water emergencies, §§15.2-923, 15.2-924.
Water supply systems.
Approval of systems by counties, §§15.2-2149 to 15.2-2156.
See WATER SUPPLY SYSTEMS.
Generally, §§15.2-2134 to 15.2-2148.
See WATER SUPPLY SYSTEMS.
Weapons, unclaimed property disposition, §15.2-1721.
Weeds.
Noxious weed control, §15.2-902.
Vacant property.
Requiring owners to cut, §15.2-901.
Welfare.
Departments and directors of social services.
Generally, §§63.2-324 to 63.2-336.
See SOCIAL SERVICES.
Funding of public assistance and social services, §§63.2-400 to 63.2-412.
See SOCIAL SERVICES.
Generally, §§63.2-500 to 63.2-805.
See PUBLIC AID AND ASSISTANCE.
Local boards of social services.
Generally, §§63.2-300 to 63.2-323.
See SOCIAL SERVICES.
Temporary assistance for needy families, §§63.2-600 to 63.2-621.
See PUBLIC AID AND ASSISTANCE.
Welfare or social services boards.
Adoption.
Agency adoption.
See ADOPTION.
General provisions.
See ADOPTION.
Generally.
See WELFARE BOARDS, LOCAL.
Well covers.
Authority to require and regulate, §18.2-318.
Wetlands.
Condemnation for compensatory mitigation of wetlands, §15.2-1907.1.
Wharves, piers, pilings, etc., constituting obstruction or hazardous use of waters.
Requiring owners to remove, repair, etc., §15.2-909.
Wills and administrations tax, §§58.1-3805 to 58.1-3808.
Wind turbines.
Local property taxation of public service corporations.
Rate of tax on electric suppliers utilizing turbines, §58.1-2606.
Wireless service authorities, §§15.2-5431.1 to 15.2-5431.37.
See WIRELESS SERVICE AUTHORITIES.
Workers' compensation.
Employees defined, §65.2-101.
World War II history relating to Virginians.
Furnishing to state librarian, §42.1-31.
Zoning.
Generally, §§15.2-2280 to 15.2-2316.2.
See ZONING.

LOCAL LAW LIBRARIES.
Circuit court clerks in charge of, §42.1-65.
Circuit courts to enforce rules, §42.1-66.
Computer research services, §42.1-65.
Contributions from bar association, §42.1-70.

LOCAL LAW LIBRARIES —Cont'd
Cost in civil actions, assessment for, §42.1-70.

LOCAL LAWS.
General assembly not to enact, VA Const Art IV §14.

LOCAL OFFICERS AND EMPLOYEES, §§15.2-1500 to 15.2-1543, VA Const Art VII §4.
Absence or disability of officer or employee, §15.2-1503.
Accident and health insurance programs, §15.2-1517.
Administrative leave for elected member of local governing body.
Member also employee of locality, §15.2-1407.
Agricultural agents.
Urban county executive form of government, §15.2-841.
Allowances to injured officials and employees and dependents, §15.2-1511.
Appointment without definite term, §15.2-1503.
Assistants.
Employment, delegation of powers and duties to, §15.2-1502.
Attorney.
Appointment, salary and duties, §15.2-1542.
County executive form of government, §15.2-529.
County manager form of government, §15.2-633.
Creation of office, §15.2-1542.
Locality may appoint or designate, §15.2-1536.
Urban county executive form of government, §15.2-836.
Attorneys for the Commonwealth.
Generally, §§15.2-1626 to 15.2-1633.
See COMMONWEALTH'S ATTORNEYS.
Audit of officers handling public funds.
County board form of government, §15.2-417.
County executive form of government, §15.2-538.
Petition filed in circuit court, §15.2-2512.
Urban county executive form of government, §15.2-844.
Auxiliary police forces, §§15.2-1731 to 15.2-1736.
See POLICE.
Benefit information.
Life-threatening health conditions.
Written benefit information to certain employees, §15.2-1511.1.
Bond, §§15.2-1527 to 15.2-1533.
Blanket surety bond plan.
Risk management division, §2.2-1840.
County board form of government, §15.2-416.
County executive form of government, §15.2-541.
County executives, §15.2-541.
Urban county executives, §15.2-850.
County manager form of government, §15.2-641.
County manager plan form of government, §15.2-707.
Department of general services, division of risk management.
Bonds provided through, §15.2-1527.
Forwarding bond plan to clerk of circuit court and comptroller of Commonwealth, §15.2-1533.
Director of finance.
County executive form of government, §15.2-541.
County manager form of government, §15.2-641.
Urban county executive form of government, §15.2-850.
Discount for advanced payments.
Payment of premiums for more than one year, §15.2-1532.

LOCAL OFFICERS AND EMPLOYEES —Cont'd
Bond —Cont'd
Jointly owned schools for cities and counties.
Treasurer appointed as finance officer, no additional bond, §15.2-1531.
Officers required to give bond, §15.2-1527.
Payment of premium for more than one year in advance, §15.2-1532.
Penalty of bond.
Determination by court or clerk before whom officer qualified, §15.2-1527.
Sheriffs, clerks of circuit court and commissioners of revenue, §15.2-1528.
Treasurer or director of finance of city, §15.2-1530.
Treasurer or director of finance of counties, §15.2-1529.
Plan forwarded to clerk of circuit court and controller of Commonwealth, §15.2-1533.
Requirements, §15.2-1512.
Urban county executive form of government, §15.2-850.
Bonuses for employees, §15.2-1508.
Bribery of public officers generally, §§18.2-438 to 18.2-450.
See PUBLIC OFFICERS AND EMPLOYEES.
Cash match plan for employees of Commonwealth, §§51.1-607 to 51.1-613.
Establishment of local plans, §51.1-610.
Chief administrative officer, §15.2-1540.
Administrative head of government, §15.2-1541.
Authorization to designate officers and employees to perform duties, §15.2-1501.
General duties, §15.2-1541.
Grievance procedure.
Decisions regarding grievability and access to procedure, §15.2-1507.
Locality may appoint or designate, §15.2-1536.
City status granted to town.
Generally, §§15.2-3800 to 15.2-3834.
See TRANSITION OF TOWNS TO CITIES.
Civil service commission.
County manager plan of government, §15.2-721.
Clerk of circuit court.
Bond generally, §§15.2-1527 to 15.2-1533.
Generally.
See CIRCUIT COURT CLERKS.
Clerk of governing body, §15.2-1528.
Compensation where clerk of court serves as governing body, §15.2-1528.
County executive form of government.
Selection, terms and vacancies, §15.2-536.
General duties, §15.2-1529.
Locality to appoint or designate, §15.2-1536.
Urban county executive form of government, §15.2-838.
Collection of state funds locally by financial officers.
Disposition, §15.2-1537.1.
Commissioners of revenue.
Generally, §§58.1-3100 to 58.1-3122.2.
See COMMISSIONERS OF REVENUE.
Commonwealth's attorneys.
Generally, §§15.2-1626 to 15.2-1633.
See COMMONWEALTH'S ATTORNEYS.
Conditioning employment on basis of residency, §15.2-1505.
Conflicts of interest.
Constitutional officers.
Disclosure statements, §2.2-3116.

LOCAL OFFICERS AND EMPLOYEES —Cont'd
Conflicts of interest —Cont'd
Contracts, §2.2-3109.
Members of local governing bodies, §2.2-3107.
Disclosure statements, §2.2-3115.
Constitutional officers, §2.2-3116.
Ethics in public contracting, §§2.2-4367 to 2.2-4377.
Former employees, prohibition from certain activities, §15.2-1408.
Constitutional officers.
Bond generally, §§15.2-1527 to 15.2-1533.
Conflicts of interest.
Disclosure statements, §2.2-3116.
Disclosure statements, §2.2-3116.
Employees.
Grievance procedure, §2.2-3008.
Generally, §§15.2-1600 to 15.2-1637.
See LOCAL CONSTITUTIONAL OFFICERS.
Contacting elected officials.
Right of local employees, §15.2-1512.4.
Contracts.
Conflicts of interest, §2.2-3109.
Members of local governing bodies, §2.2-3107.
County administrators.
County board form of government.
Acting as purchasing agent, §15.2-414.
Appointment, compensation and removal, §15.2-406.
Powers and duties, §15.2-407.
County board form of government.
Generally, §§15.2-400 to 15.2-418.
See COUNTY BOARD FORM OF GOVERNMENT.
County boards of supervisors.
Generally.
See COUNTY BOARDS OF SUPERVISORS.
County clerks.
See COUNTY CLERKS.
County engineer.
County manager form of government, §15.2-625.
County executive form of government.
Generally, §§15.2-500 to 15.2-542.
See COUNTY EXECUTIVE FORM OF GOVERNMENT.
Urban county executive form of government.
Generally, §§15.2-800 to 15.2-858.
See URBAN COUNTY EXECUTIVE FORM OF GOVERNMENT.
County executives.
County executive form of government, §§15.2-509 to 15.2-517.
Urban county executive form of government, §§15.2-804 to 15.2-814.
County manager form of government.
Generally, §§15.2-600 to 15.2-642.
See COUNTY MANAGER FORM OF GOVERNMENT.
County manager plan of government.
Generally, §§15.2-700 to 15.2-750.
See COUNTY MANAGER PLAN OF GOVERNMENT.
County managers.
County manager form of government, §§15.2-609 to 15.2-615.
County manager plan of government, §§15.2-706, 15.2-708, 15.2-710.
County superintendents of public welfare.
County board form of government, §15.2-412.
Criminal background investigations, §§15.2-1503.1, 15.2-1505.1

LOCAL OFFICERS AND EMPLOYEES —Cont'd
Criminal charge arising out of act committed in discharge of duties.
Providing legal fees and expenses, §15.2-1521.
Death of officials and employees.
Allowances to dependents, §15.2-1511.
Defacement of buildings, walls, fences, other structures.
Removal or repair.
Immunity, §15.2-908.
Defense of locality or employee.
Employment of counsel by locality in political subdivision, §15.2-1520.
Deferred compensation plan, §§51.1-600 to 51.1-605.
See PUBLIC OFFICERS AND EMPLOYEES.
Departments and boards of welfare or social services.
Legal services to employees, §15.2-1519.
Liability insurance for employees, §15.2-1519.
Deputies.
Employment, delegation of powers and duties, §15.2-1502.
Designation of officers to perform certain duties, §15.2-1501.
Director of finance.
Bond generally, §§15.2-1527 to 15.2-1533.
Commissioners of revenue.
Commissioner to include director of finance performing duties of commissioner, §58.1-3100.
Generally, §§58.1-3100 to 58.1-3122.2.
See COMMISSIONERS OF REVENUE.
County executive form of government, §§15.2-518 to 15.2-525.
County manager form of government, §§15.2-617 to 15.2-624.
Supplementing salary, §15.2-1605.1.
Treasurers.
Generally, §§58.1-3123 to 58.1-3172.1.
See TREASURERS, LOCAL.
Term to include director when performing duties of treasurer, §58.1-3123.
Urban county executive form of government, §§15.2-826 to 15.2-833.
Disciplinary actions.
Grievance defined, §15.2-1507.
Disclosure statements.
Conflicts of interest, §2.2-3115.
Constitutional officers, §2.2-3116.
Discretionary officers, §15.2-1536.
Discrimination.
Grievance defined, §15.2-1507.
Dismissals, demotions and suspensions.
Grievance defined, §15.2-1507.
Dispute resolution.
Grievance procedure, §§15.2-1506 to 15.2-1507.1.
Dual office holding, §§15.2-1534, 15.2-1535, VA Const Art VII §6.
Elected officers.
Qualification for office, §§15.2-1522 to 15.2-1524.
Election of constitutional and local officers, §§24.2-217 to 24.2-224.
Elective office, qualifications to hold, VA Const Art II §5.
Embezzlement, §18.2-112.
Misuse of public assets, §18.2-112.1.
Employment of council to defend localities and political subdivisions, §15.2-1520.
Employment of officers and other employees as needed, §15.2-1500.

LOCAL OFFICERS AND EMPLOYEES —Cont'd
Ethics in public contracting, §§2.2-4367 to 2.2-4377.
Expenses of public officials.
Generally.
See EXPENSES OF PUBLIC OFFICIALS.
Mileage expenses generally.
See MILEAGE.
Travel expenses generally.
See TRAVEL EXPENSES.
Federal employees prohibited, exception, §2.2-2801.
Fee system abolished.
County executive form of government, §15.2-540.
County manager form of government, §15.2-639.
Urban county executive form of government, §15.2-848.
Financial officer, §15.2-1537.
Financial reports by county officers, §15.2-1230.
Fire marshals generally, §§27-30 to 27-37.1.
Former employees, prohibition from certain activities, §15.2-1408.
Governing bodies of localities generally, §§15.2-1400 to 15.2-1433.
See LOCALITIES.
Grievance procedure, §15.2-1507.
Components and features, §15.2-1507.
County manager plan of government.
Police officers, §15.2-723.
Presence of equal employment opportunity officer, §15.2-738.
Eligibility to file grievances, §15.2-1507.
Establishment, §15.2-1506.
General requirements, §15.2-1507.
Grievance defined, §15.2-1507.
Management steps, §15.2-1507.
Nongrievable complaints, §15.2-1507.
Panel hearings, §15.2-1507.
Responsibilities of local government, §15.2-1507.
Standing panel in counties with county manager form of government, §15.2-1507.1.
Group insurance programs, §§15.2-1517, 51.1-500 to 51.1-514.
See PUBLIC OFFICERS AND EMPLOYEES.
Hazardous materials coordinator, §44-146.38.
Health director.
County executive form of government, §15.2-534.
County manager form of government, §15.2-629.
Health insurance.
Group insurance programs, §§15.2-1517, 51.1-500 to 51.1-514.
Long-term care insurance.
Board of trustees, Virginia Retirement System.
Assumption of responsibility, §51.1-513.3.
Establishment by department of human resource management, §2.2-1207.
Trust fund, §51.1-513.4.
Participation, §2.2-1204.
Health officer.
County board form of government, §15.2-411.
Urban county executive form of government, §15.2-839.
Holding more than one office.
Certain officers prohibited from, §§15.2-1534, 15.2-1535.
Home demonstration agents.
Urban county executive form of government, §15.2-841.
Homesite of county officer becoming part of city tenure and reelection, §15.2-3823.

LOCAL OFFICERS AND EMPLOYEES —Cont'd
Immunity of members of local governmental entities, §15.2-1405.
Defacement of buildings, walls, fences, other structures.
Removal or repair employees or agents, §15.2-908.
Injured officials and employees.
Allowances to, §15.2-1511.
Inquiry into official conduct of office or officer.
County executive form of government, §15.2-506.
County manager form of government, §15.2-606.
County manager plan of government, §15.2-709.
Urban county executive form of government, §15.2-814.
Insurance.
Group life, accident and health insurance programs, §§15.2-1517, 51.1-500 to 51.1-514.
Liability insurance for officers, employees and volunteers, §15.2-1518.
Risk management division.
Risk management plan for claims against, §2.2-1839.
Joint officers and employees, §§15.2-1513 to 15.2-1516.
Agreement between or among employing localities, §15.2-1515.
Employment permitted, §15.2-1513.
Exception as to constitutional officers, §15.2-1516.
Exception to officers elected by voters, §15.2-1515.
Exercise of powers and duties, §15.2-1514.
Salary, retirement, and other benefits, §15.2-1515.
Leaves of absence.
Military duty, §44-93.
State defense force or national defense executive reserve training, §44-204.
Legal fees and expenses for officers and employee.
Criminal charge arising out of act committed in discharge of duties, §15.2-1521.
Local departments and boards of welfare or social services, §15.2-1519.
Liability insurance for officers, employees and volunteers, §15.2-1518.
Departments or boards of welfare and social services, §15.2-1519.
Life insurance programs, §15.2-1517.
Life-threatening health conditions.
Written benefit information to certain employees, §15.2-1511.1.
Lobbying.
Restrictions on former officers and employees.
County executive form of government, §15.2-515.
Urban county executive form of government, §15.2-810.
Local trusts to fund postemployment benefits other than pensions, §§15.2-1544 to 15.2-1549.
Long-term care insurance.
Board of trustees, Virginia Retirement System.
Assumption of responsibility, §51.1-513.3.
Establishment by department of human resource management, §2.2-1207.
Trust fund, §51.1-513.4.
Mayors.
Oaths.
Power to administer, §15.2-1410.
Powers, §15.2-1423.
Presiding officer, §15.2-1422.

LOCAL OFFICERS AND EMPLOYEES —Cont'd
Mayors —Cont'd
Salaries, setting.
City mayors, §15.2-1414.6.
Town mayors, §15.2-1414.7.
Vacancy, §15.2-1424.
Meetings of governmental bodies, §§15.2-1415 to 15.2-1421.
See LOCALITIES.
Mileage expenses generally.
See MILEAGE.
Military duty leaves of absence, §44-93.
Discrimination in hiring prohibited, §44-93.4.
Penalty for employer failure to comply, §44-93.5.
Supplement of military pay and additional life insurance benefits, §44-93.1.
Misuse of public assets, §18.2-112.1.
National defense executive reserve training.
Leaves of absence, §44-204.
Oath before entering upon duties of office, §15.2-1512.
Offices that members of governing body not to be elected or appointed to, §15.2-1535.
Organization of departments of government, §15.2-1500.
Personnel administration system.
Exemptions, §2.2-2905.
Personnel system in certain cities, §15.2-1131.
Police.
Auxiliary police forces, §§15.2-1731 to 15.2-1736.
See POLICE.
Communications system, §§52-16 to 52-19.
County manager form of government, §15.2-632.
County manager plan of government.
Grievances, §15.2-723.
General provisions as to police and public order, §§15.2-1700 to 15.2-1753.
See POLICE.
Special police officers, §§15.2-1737 to 15.2-1746.
See POLICE.
Urban county executive form of government.
Department of law enforcement, §15.2-836.
Department of public safety, §15.2-842.
Preemployment information, §15.2-1505.1.
Preemployment requirements for Arlington County, §15.2-709.1.
Preference for veterans in employment, §15.2-1509.
Public contracting, ethics in, §§2.2-4367 to 2.2-4377.
Purchasing agents.
County board form of government, §15.2-414.
County executive form of government.
Director of finance to act as, §15.2-524.
County manager form of government.
Director of finance to act as, §15.2-622.
Employment by county, duties, §15.2-1543.
Procurement by county purchasing agent, §§15.2-1233 to 15.2-1240.
Urban county executive form of government.
Director of finance to act as, §15.2-831.
Qualification for office.
Failure to qualify vacates office, §15.2-1524.
Record of qualification, §15.2-1523.
Vacancy for failure to qualify, §15.2-1524.
When and how officers qualify, §15.2-1522.
Removal, §§24.2-230 to 24.2-238.
See REMOVAL OF PUBLIC OFFICERS FROM OFFICE.
Removal from locality required to reside in.
Vacancy in office, §15.2-1526

LOCAL OFFICERS AND EMPLOYEES —Cont'd
Required officers, §15.2-1536.
Residency.
Conditioning employment on, §15.2-1505.
County officer, §15.2-1525.
Nonelected officers and nonelected deputies of constitutional officers, §15.2-1525.
Resolution of disputes.
Grievance procedure, §§15.2-1506 to 15.2-1507.1.
Retaliation as result of use or participation in grievance procedure.
Grievance defined, §15.2-1507.
Retirees, group life, accident and health insurance programs, §15.2-1517.
Retirement systems, §§15.2-1510, 51.1-800 to 51.1-823.
See LOCAL RETIREMENT SYSTEMS.
Salaries.
City council members, §§15.2-1414.5, 15.2-1414.6.
County boards of supervisors, §§15.2-1414.1 to 15.2-1414.3.
Severance packages for certain officials.
Public announcement, §15.2-1510.1.
Self-insurance.
Group life, accident and health insurance programs, §15.2-1517.
Liability insurance for officers, employees and volunteers, §15.2-1518.
Sergeants generally.
See SERGEANTS.
Severance packages for certain officials.
Public announcement, §15.2-1510.1.
Sheriffs.
Bond generally, §§15.2-1527 to 15.2-1533.
Generally, §§15.2-1609 to 15.2-1625.
See SHERIFFS.
Smoking or using tobacco products on job, §15.2-1504.
Social security coverage, §§51.1-700 to 51.1-707.
See PUBLIC OFFICERS AND EMPLOYEES.
Special police officers, §§15.2-1737 to 15.2-1746.
See POLICE.
State defense force training.
Leaves of absence, §44-204.
State funds collected by financial officer paid into state treasury, §15.2-1537.1.
Superintendent of social services.
Urban county executive form of government, §15.2-835.
Superintendents of public welfare.
See SUPERINTENDENTS OF PUBLIC WELFARE.
Suspension or removal from office or employment, §15.2-1503.
Grievance defined, §15.2-1507.
Temporary services, tenure, §15.2-1503.
Travel expenses for persons on business of locality, §§15.2-1508.1 to 15.2-1508.4.
Commonwealth bearing portion of expenses, §15.2-1508.2.
Generally, §15.2-1508.1.
Rate of reimbursement per mile, §15.2-1508.1.
Supplementation by certain counties and cities, §§15.2-1508.3, 15.2-1508.4.
Treasurers.
Bond generally, §§15.2-1527 to 15.2-1533.
County manager form of government.
Director of finance to exercise powers, §15.2-620.
County manager plan of government, §§15.2-711 to 15.2-713.

LOCAL OFFICERS AND EMPLOYEES —Cont'd
Treasurers —Cont'd
Election, powers and duties, §15.2-1608.
Generally, §§58.1-3123 to 58.1-3172.1.
See TREASURERS, LOCAL.
General provisions as to local constitutional officers, §§15.2-1600 to 15.2-1607.
See LOCAL CONSTITUTIONAL OFFICERS.
Insurer's conversion to stock corporation.
Treatment of money received, §15.2-1608.1.
Payment of claims.
Governing body requiring, §15.2-1203.
Salary of city treasurer, §15.2-1608.1.
Salary of county treasurer, §15.2-1608.2.
Terms, §15.2-1608.
Urban county executive form of government.
Director of finance to exercise powers, §15.2-829.
Urban county executive form of government.
Generally, §§15.2-800 to 15.2-858.
See URBAN COUNTY EXECUTIVE FORM OF GOVERNMENT.
Vacancy in office.
Failure to qualify, §15.2-1524.
Removal of officer from locality in which required to reside in, §15.2-1526.
Veterans preference in employment, §15.2-1509.
Warrants on state treasury for compensation due and estimated amount allowed.
Comptroller to forward to financial officer, §15.2-1537.1.

LOCAL OFFICES OF CONSUMER AFFAIRS, §15.2-963.

LOCAL OPTION REFERENDA.
ABC law.
Contest of referenda, §4.1-127.
Establishment of government stores, §§4.1-121, 4.1-122.
Sale of mixed beverages, §§4.1-124, 4.1-125.
Pari-mutuel wagering, §59.1-391.

LOCAL PLANNING.
Generally, §§15.2-2200 to 15.2-2239.
See PLANNING AND DEVELOPMENT.
Levies and fees imposed or increased by locality.
Advertisement and enactment of ordinances, §15.2-107.
Pet cemeteries.
Land use restrictions, §§57-39.21, 57-39.24.
Planning commissions, §§15.2-2110 to 15.2-2222.
See PLANNING COMMISSIONS.
Planning district commissions, §§15.2-4200 to 15.2-4222.
See PLANNING DISTRICT COMMISSIONS.
Road impact fees, §§15.2-2317 to 15.2-2329.
See ROAD IMPACT FEES.
Subdivisions and land development, §§15.2-2240 to 15.2-2279.
See SUBDIVISIONS.
Transportation districts, §§15.2-4527, 15.2-4528.
Zoning, §§15.2-2280 to 15.2-2316.2.
See ZONING.

LOCAL PLANNING COMMISSIONS, §§15.2-2210 to 15.2-2222.
See PLANNING COMMISSIONS.

LOCAL RETIREMENT SYSTEMS, §§51.1-800 to 51.1-823.
Assets, §51.1-802.

LOCAL RETIREMENT SYSTEMS —Cont'd
Automatic rollover of mandatory cash-out.
Selection of retirement plan provider and investment product.
Loss resulting, governing body not liable, §51.1-803.
Continuation of laws, §§51.1-804, 51.1-805.
Creditable service.
Portability of service credits, §51.1-801.1.
Disclosure requirements, §§51.1-1000 to 51.1-1004.
Financial reports, §51.1-1003.
Scope, §51.1-1000.
Statement of benefits, §51.1-1002.
Summary plan description, §51.1-1001.
Use of electronic media, §51.1-1004.
Establishment, §§51.1-800, 51.1-801.
Investments, §51.1-803.
Laws continued in effect, §§51.1-804, 51.1-805.
Option to participate in state system, §51.1-800.
Police officers, §§51.1-807 to 51.1-820.
Adoption of system, §§51.1-819, 51.1-820.
Allowance, §51.1-811.
Credited service, §51.1-810.
Disabilities not resulting from discharge of duties, §51.1-812.
Disabilities resulting from discharge of duties, §51.1-813.
Presumption, §51.1-814.
Disability allowance reductions, §51.1-816.
Eligibility, §51.1-811.
Presumption, §51.1-814.
Funds, §51.1-818.
Pension and retirement boards.
Duties, §51.1-808.
Established, §51.1-807.
Powers, §51.1-808.
Treasurer, §51.1-809.
Relief to surviving spouse and children, §51.1-815.
Salary deduction distributions upon death, §51.1-817.
Portability of service credits, §51.1-801.1.
Reimbursements by Commonwealth, §51.1-806.
Setting-up, §§51.1-800, 51.1-801.
State reimbursements, §51.1-806.
Urban county executive governments, §§51.1-821 to 51.1-823.
Amendment of plan and trust, §51.1-822.
Appeals, §51.1-823.
Police retirement system continued, §51.1-821.
Revocation of plan and trust, §51.1-822.
Suspension of plan and trust, §51.1-822.

LOCAL ROAD AUTHORITIES, §§33.1-224 to 33.1-246.
Abandonment of roads, §§33.1-243 to 33.1-245.
Compensation of clerk of board, §33.1-245.
Issuance of process by supervisors, §33.1-244.
Procedure, §33.1-243.
Board of supervisors.
Compensation of supervisors, §33.1-226.
Consent of landowners.
Establishment and alteration of roads, §§33.1-232, 33.1-241.
County road laws.
Continuance of acts in effect for certain counties, §33.1-228.
Discontinuance of gates on public roads, §33.1-246.
Establishment and alteration of roads.
Action of commissioners, §33.1-238.

LOCAL ROAD AUTHORITIES —Cont'd
Establishment and alteration of roads —Cont'd
Alternative procedure, §33.1-229.
Appeal to circuit court, §33.1-239.
Compensation to viewers, commissioners and engineers, §33.1-242.
Condemnation for private road not authorized, §33.1-230.
Consent of landowners, §33.1-232.
Required for roads through cemetery or seminary of learning, §33.1-241.
Continuance of powers of county authorities, §33.1-226.
Duty of viewers, etc., §33.1-231.
Compensation to viewers, §33.1-242.
Employing engineer, §33.1-230.
Pay to engineers, §33.1-242.
Enhancement in value of residue, §33.1-237.
Examination and report, §§33.1-230, 33.1-231, 33.1-233.
How roads and bridges established or altered, §§33.1-229, 33.1-230.
Proceedings on report.
Action of commissioners, §33.1-238.
Appeal to circuit court, §33.1-239.
Appointment of commissioners to assess damages, §33.1-236.
Ascertainment of damages, §33.1-236.
Compensation of commissioners, §33.1-242.
Defense allowed, §33.1-235.
Enhancement in value of residue, §33.1-237.
Notice to owners, §33.1-233.
Payment of costs, compensation and damages, §33.1-240.
Roads established through cemetery or seminary of learning.
Consent of landowners required, §33.1-241.
Width and grade of roads, §33.1-230.
Federal revenue-sharing funds, §§33.1-225.2, 33.1-225.3.
Gates on public roads.
Discontinuance of gates, §33.1-246.
Gifts for construction, etc., of secondary roads, §33.1-225.2.
Levy of road taxes, §33.1-225.
Local legislation.
Compensation of supervisors, §33.1-226.
Railway crossings.
Abandonment, §33.1-243.
Transfer of streets, etc., secondary system to local authorities, §33.1-224.

LOCAL RULES OF COURT.
Authority of district and circuit courts to prescribe, §8.01-4.

LOCAL SALES TAXES, §58.1-605.

LOCAL SCHOOL BOARDS, §§22.1-28 to 22.1-57.5, VA Const Art VIII §7.
Accounting system for county boards.
Centralized system of accounting for counties, §15.2-1541.1.
Actions.
Consent required prior to institution of proceedings, §22.1-82.
Employment of counsel, §22.1-82.
Payment of employee's legal fees, §22.1-83.
Power to sue and be sued, §22.1-71.
Adult education.
Authority of school boards, §22.1-225

LOCAL SCHOOL BOARDS —Cont'd
Adverse agency action.
Judicial review, §22.1-87.
After school programs for at-risk students, §22.1-199.5.
Annual report, §22.1-81.
Appeals.
Court of appeals.
Appellate jurisdiction, §17.1-405.
Appointment.
Public hearing requirement, §22.1-29.1.
Assignment of pupil plans, §22.1-79.
Assistive technology devices, transfer to school division, §22.1-129.1.
Attorney, employment, §22.1-82.
Attorneys' fees.
Employment of attorney, §22.1-82.
Payment of employee's legal fees, §22.1-83.
Auditor of public accounts establishing system of bookkeeping, §30-137.
Automated external defibrillators.
Plan for placement, use and funding for AED in every school, §22.1-274.4.
Bath county.
Staggered terms for elected members, §22.1-57.3:1.1.
Benefits.
Medical benefits.
Fund for payment of hospital, medical, etc., §22.1-85.
Bonds.
Borrowing from Virginia retirement system, §22.1-161.3.
Indebtedness evidenced by bonds, §22.1-161.2.
Legal investments, §22.1-161.8.
Negotiable instruments, §22.1-161.8.
Proceeds from sale of bonds.
Disposition, §22.1-161.4.
Investment pending application to authorized purpose, §22.1-161.5.
Sale of bonds by trustees of retirement system, §22.1-161.8.
Tax to pay principal and interest, §22.1-161.7.
Borrowing from Virginia retirement system, §§22.1-161.1 to 22.1-161.8.
Bonds, §22.1-161.3.
Indebtedness evidenced by bonds, §22.1-161.2.
Legal investments, §22.1-161.8.
Negotiable instruments, §22.1-161.8.
Proceeds from sale of bonds.
Disposition, §22.1-161.4.
Investment pending application to authorized purpose, §22.1-161.5.
Sale of bonds by trustees of retirement system, §22.1-161.8.
Tax to pay principal and interest, §22.1-161.7.
Capital projects for school purposes, §22.1-161.1.
Governing body.
Approval or rejection of resolution, §22.1-161.2.
Resolution by school board, §22.1-161.2.
Budget of school divisions.
Amendment, §15.2-2507.
Contents, §15.2-2504.
Preparation and approval for informative and fiscal planning, §15.2-2503.
Publication and notice, §15.2-2506.
Public hearing, §15.2-2506.
Reserve for contingencies and capital improvements, §15.2-2505.
Time for preparation, §15.2-2503.

LOCAL SCHOOL BOARDS —Cont'd
Career and technical education.
Corporate projects.
Generally, §§22.1-227 to 22.1-237.
See CAREER AND TECHNICAL EDUCATION.
Warranties, §22.1-233.
Sale of projects, §22.1-129.
Centralized competitive purchasing by chief administrative officer, §15.2-1231.
Centralized system for accounting for counties, §15.2-1541.1.
Chairman.
Additional salary, §22.1-32.
Election, §22.1-76.
Charter schools.
General provisions, §§22.1-212.5 to 22.1-212.16.
See CHARTER SCHOOLS.
Child abuse and neglect complaint searches.
Condition of employing personnel, §22.1-296.4.
Claims against counties, §§15.2-1243 to 15.2-1249.
Clerk.
Appointment, §22.1-76.
Duties, §22.1-77.
Commitment of child to institution or agency.
Information to be furnished by and to upon commitment, §16.1-287.
Comprehensive, unified, long-range plan.
Development, §22.1-253.13:6.
Conflicts of interest, §2.2-3119.
Contracts, §2.2-3108.
Dual officeholding.
Membership prohibition, §22.1-30.
Consolidation of schools.
Powers and duties, §22.1-79.
Continuation of special town school districts, §22.1-33.
Corporate powers, §22.1-71.
County board form of government, §15.2-410.
Election of school board members in counties with, §§22.1-47.1 to 22.1-47.4.
Selection in school divisions comprised of counties having, §22.1-47.
County executive form of government.
Elected boards, §15.2-533.
Number, §15.2-531.
Part of department of education, §15.2-531.
Terms, §15.2-532.
Tie breaker, §15.2-531.
County manager form of government.
Election, number of members, terms and vacancies, §§15.2-627, 15.2-628.
Court of appeals.
Appellate jurisdiction, §17.1-405.
Crime prevention.
Development of programs, §22.1-279.9.
Crime stoppers program.
Local school boards authority, §22.1-280.2.
Criminal history record information, dissemination, §19.2-389.
Day programs, establishment outside regular school hours, §22.1-132.1.
Debilitating or life-threatening illness or injury.
Leave without pay for employees with, policies, development, §22.1-296.
Delinquency disposition disclosure, §16.1-305.1.
Department of transportation or commissioner of highways.
Sale of property to by school board in city located in Virginia Beach, §22.1-129.

LOCAL SCHOOL BOARDS —Cont'd
Deputies of local constitutional officers elected as members, §15.2-1534.
Deputy clerk.
Appointment, §22.1-76.
Destruction of property.
Action regarding, §22.1-280.4.
Disabilities, student with.
Assistive technology devices, transfer to school division, §22.1-129.1.
Discipline of students.
Authority of school boards, §22.1-277.2:1.
Division superintendents of schools.
Appointment, §§22.1-60 to 22.1-62.
Designation of representative to attend meetings, §§22.1-69, 22.1-76.
Evaluation, §22.1-60.1.
Terms of contract, §22.1-60.
Vacancies.
Appointment of superintendent after vacancy occurring, §22.1-60.
Dual officeholding.
Membership prohibition, §22.1-30.
Duties of school boards, §§22.1-78, 22.1-79.
Educational technology foundation.
Establishment by board, §22.1-212.2:2.
Educational technology hardware and software.
Donation of obsolete equipment, §22.1-129.
Election of school boards, §§22.1-57.1 to 22.1-57.5.
Applicability of article, §22.1-57.1.
Consolidated cities.
Referendum in certain consolidated cities, §22.1-57.1:1.
Construction of article, §22.1-57.1.
County executive form of government, §15.2-533.
County manager form of government, §15.2-627.
County manager plan of government, §§22.1-47.1 to 22.1-47.4.
Economic interest statement as requirement of candidate, §24.2-502.
Independent candidates' petition of candidacy.
Number of signatures required, §24.2-506.
Nomination petition, §22.1-57.3.
Number of members of initial elected board, §22.1-57.3.
Qualification for office of elected officers, §§15.2-1522 to 15.2-1524.
Referendum on direct election of school board members, §§22.1-57.1 to 22.1-57.5.
Ballot question, §22.1-57.2.
Conduct of election, §§22.1-57.3, 22.1-57.3:3.
Consolidated cities.
Not necessary in certain consolidated cities, §22.1-57.1:1.
Limitation on time of holding subsequent referendum, §22.1-57.5.
Reversion to appointment by school board selection commission, §§22.1-57.4, 22.1-57.5.
Salary of members of elected board.
Increase of salary, §22.1-32.
Students conducting electioneering activities, policies prohibiting, §22.1-79.3.
Term, §§22.1-57.3, 24.2-223.
Tie breaker position, §22.1-57.3.
Transition from appointed to elected board, §22.1-47.3.
Vacancies, §22.1-57.3.
When held, §24.2-223.

LOCAL SCHOOL BOARDS —Cont'd
Eminent domain.
Career and technical education.
Corporate projects, §22.1-234.
Employees of school board.
Fund for payment of medical expenses, §22.1-85.
Payment of legal fees and expenses, §22.1-83.
Exchange, lease or sale of real and personal property, §22.1-129.
Family members or relatives.
Employment, §2.2-3119.
Federal employees prohibited, exception, §2.2-2801.
Fingerprinting applicants for employment, §22.1-296.2.
Firearms safety education programs for students in elementary grades, §22.1-204.1.
Fiscal year.
Uniform fiscal year for localities and school divisions, §15.2-2500.
Freedom of information act, §§2.2-3700 to 2.2-3714.
Excluded records.
Personal information in certain correspondence with public body, §2.2-3705.7.
Funds to provide appropriate accounting and budgetary control.
Establishment of necessity funds, §15.2-2501.
Gifted education.
Advisory committee, §22.1-18.1.
Annual report on, §22.1-18.1.
Grievance procedure for school board employees.
Establishment and administration, §22.1-79.
Group insurance.
Local government group self-insurance pools, §§15.2-2700 to 15.2-2709.
See LOCAL GOVERNMENT GROUP SELF-INSURANCE POOLS.
Highways and roads.
Sale of materials to and use of equipment by school boards, §33.1-195.
Information furnished by departments, offices, divisions, etc., §15.2-2508.
Insurance.
Liability insurance coverage, §22.1-84.
Local government group self-insurance pools, §§15.2-2700 to 15.2-2709.
See LOCAL GOVERNMENT GROUP SELF-INSURANCE POOLS.
Reciprocal insurance contracts, power to enter into, §38.2-1204.
Juvenile commitment to institution or agency.
Information to be furnished to and by boards upon commitment, §16.1-287.
Labor Day opening of school year, §22.1-79.1.
Leases.
Corporate powers, §22.1-71.
Literary fund.
Authority to borrow money from fund, §22.1-153.
General provisions, §§22.1-142 to 22.1-161.
See LITERARY FUND.
Local committees, §22.1-86.
Local government personnel generally, qualification for office, bond, etc., §§15.2-1500 to 15.2-1543.
See LOCAL OFFICERS AND EMPLOYEES.
Loudoun county school board.
Fingerprinting applicants for employment, §22.1-296.2.
Salary of members, §22.1-32.

LOCAL SCHOOL BOARDS —Cont'd
Loudoun county school board —Cont'd
Staggered terms for elected members, §§22.1-57.3:1, 22.1-57.3:1.1.
Meetings, §§22.1-72 to 22.1-75.
Annual organizational meetings, §22.1-72.
Duty to call meetings of people of school division, §22.1-86.
Electronic communication meetings, §2.2-3708.
Minutes, §§22.1-74, 22.1-77.
Procedure in case of tie vote, §22.1-75.
Quorum, §22.1-73.
Special meetings, §22.1-72.
Membership prohibition, §22.1-30.
Mileage expenses, §22.1-32.
Minutes of meetings, §22.1-74.
Duties of clerk, §22.1-77.
Motor vehicle liability insurance.
County providing insurance to protect operators of vehicles owned or leased by county, school board, §15.2-1214.
Nepotism.
Employment of family members or relatives, §2.2-3119.
Number of members.
County board form of government, §15.2-410.
County executive form of government, §15.2-531.
County manager form of government, §15.2-627.
Elected board, §22.1-57.3.
Urban county executive form of government, §15.2-837.
Oath of office, §22.1-31.
Officers.
Election, §22.1-76.
Opening of school year, §22.1-79.1.
Parental consent to release student data, form for, §22.1-79.3.
Park areas.
Development of land adjacent to public schools, §22.1-80.
Personal property.
Corporate powers, §22.1-71.
Power to convey or lease generally, §22.1-129.
Pittsylvania county.
Staggered terms for elected members, §22.1-57.3:1.2.
Policies of school board.
Standards of quality, §22.1-253.13:7.
Powers of school boards, §§22.1-78, 22.1-79.
Power to sue and be sued, §22.1-71.
Principals.
Licensed instructional personnel, employment, §22.1-253.13:2.
Private transportation.
Reimbursement to employees of board, traveling on state business, §22.1-296.
Procurement of goods and services.
Adoption of alternative policies and procedures.
Exemption from general law, §2.2-4343.
Generally, §§2.2-4300 to 2.2-4377.
See PUBLIC PROCUREMENT.
Professional development activities.
Member participation, duty, §22.1-253.13:5.
Public hearing.
Appointment of school board members, §22.1-29.1.
Consolidation of schools, redistricting of school boundaries or adopting pupil assignment plan, §22.1-79.
Public school authority.
General provisions, §§22.1-162 to 22.1-175.
See PUBLIC SCHOOL AUTHORITY.

LOCAL SCHOOL BOARDS —Cont'd
Public school authority —Cont'd
Grants to local school boards, §22.1-166.2.
Loans to local school boards, §22.1-166.1.
Purchase and sale of local school bonds, §22.1-166.
Public school foundation.
Establishment by board, §22.1-212.2:2.
Public school funds, §§22.1-88 to 22.1-124.
See PUBLIC SCHOOL FUNDS.
Public school system.
Administration of schools, §§22.1-2, 22.1-28.
Pulaski county.
Staggered terms for elected members, §22.1-57.3:1.1.
Qualifications of members, §§15.2-1522 to 15.2-1524, 22.1-29.
Qualified voter requirement, §22.1-29.
Quorum, §22.1-73.
Real property.
Corporate powers, §22.1-71.
Power to convey or lease generally, §22.1-129.
Redistricting of school boundaries.
Powers and duties, §22.1-79.
Removal of public officers from office, §§24.2-230 to 24.2-238.
Reporting requirements, §22.1-81.
Failure to appoint superintendents after vacancy occurring, §22.1-60.
Reports.
Gifted education.
Annual report on, §22.1-18.1.
Student ratios reported by superintendents of schools, §22.1-70.1.
Residence requirement, §22.1-29.
Board not to condition employment or feature of employment on basis of, §15.2-1505.
Retirement systems.
Defined contribution plan, §§51.1-617, 51.1-618.
Locality establishing for employees of board, §15.2-1510.
Risk management plan for public liability, §2.2-1837.
Rockbridge county.
Staggered terms for elected members, §22.1-57.3:1.1.
Rulemaking authority.
Bylaws and regulations, §22.1-78.
Salary of members, §22.1-32.
Satellite classrooms, agreements for, §22.1-26.1.
School buses.
Authority of to install signs or devices to indicate bus stops, §33.1-223.2:18.
Decals relating to school bus safety, §22.1-177.
Liability of school board owning or operating vehicle, §22.1-194.
School efficiency review program.
Planning and budget department.
Authority, §2.2-1501.
Generally, §2.2-1502.1.
School trustees.
Federal employees prohibited, exception, §2.2-2801.
Selection in cities and towns constituting school divisions, §§22.1-48 to 22.1-51.
Applicability of article, §22.1-48.
Appointment and terms.
City of Norfolk, §22.1-51.
Generally, §22.1-50.
City school districts, §22.1-49.
Construction of article, §22.1-48.

LOCAL SCHOOL BOARDS —Cont'd
Selection in school divisions composed of less than or more than one county or city, §§22.1-52 to 22.1-57.
Adjudication of ownership of school property, §22.1-56.
Applicability of article, §22.1-52.
Appointment of members, §§22.1-53, 22.1-54.
Compensation of members, §22.1-55.
Composition, §22.1-53.
District appointment of members, §22.1-54.
Effective date for formation of board, §22.1-57.
Formation of board, §22.1-57.
Salary of members, §22.1-55.
Single school board required, §22.1-52.
Terms of members, §22.1-53.
Tie breaker, §22.1-53.
Transfer of title to school property, §22.1-56.
Vacancies, §22.1-53.
Selection in school divisions composed of single county, §§22.1-34 to 22.1-40.
Alternative method, §§22.1-41 to 22.1-46.
Applicability of article, §22.1-34.
Alternative method, §22.1-41.
Appointment of school board, §22.1-36.
Notice of commission meeting, §22.1-37.
Appointment of tie breaker, §22.1-40.
Alternative method, §22.1-44.
Composition of school board, §§22.1-36, 22.1-36.1.
Consolidated divisions, §22.1-38.1.
Construction of article, §22.1-34.
Alternative method, §22.1-41.
Exclusion of town representation, §22.1-36.1.
Expiration of terms of school board members, §22.1-38.
Formation of consolidated county and tier-city, §22.1-38.1.
Limitation on time of holding subsequent referendum.
Referendum on alternative method, §22.1-46.
Referendum on alternative method of selecting school boards, §§22.1-41 to 22.1-46.
Abolition of school board selection commission, §22.1-43.
Applicability of article, §22.1-41.
Circuit court petition, §22.1-42.
Limitations on time of holding subsequent referendum, §22.1-46.
Reversion to appointment by school board selection commission, §22.1-45.
School board selection commission.
Appointment of school board, §22.1-36.
Appointment of tie breaker, §22.1-40.
Composition, §22.1-35.
Filling vacancies in school board, §22.1-39.
Notice of meeting for appointment, §22.1-37.
Referendum on alternative method, §§22.1-43, 22.1-45.
Terms of school board members, §22.1-38.
Vacancies in school board, §22.1-39.
Selection in school divisions comprised of counties having county manager or county board form of government, §22.1-47.
Self insurance.
Local government group self-insurance pools, §§15.2-2700 to 15.2-2709.
See LOCAL GOVERNMENT GROUP SELF-INSURANCE POOLS.
Sexual abuse of student by teacher or school board employee.
Policies of school board to address complaints, §22.1-253.13:7.

LOCAL SCHOOL BOARDS —Cont'd
Single-sex classes.
Authority to establish, §22.1-212.1:1.
Special districts.
Continuation of special town school districts, §22.1-33.
Special education.
General provisions, §§22.1-213 to 22.1-221.
See SPECIAL EDUCATION.
Reimbursement of parents or guardian of children with disabilities in private schools, §22.1-218.
Submission of plan to board, §22.1-215.
Special meetings, §22.1-72.
Standards of learning.
Targeted mathematics remediation and intervention for students showing deficiencies, §22.1-253.13:3.
Standards of quality.
Generally, §§22.1-253.13:1 to 22.1-253.13:9.
See SCHOOLS AND EDUCATION.
State board of education.
Generally, §§22.1-8 to 22.1-20.
See BOARD OF EDUCATION.
Student data, parental consent to release, §22.1-79.3.
Student representatives.
Appointment, §22.1-86.1.
Superintendents.
Juvenile justice department.
Notice to superintendent prior to release of serious offenders, §66-25.2:1.
Licensed instructional personnel, employment, §22.1-253.13:2.
Threat assessment teams, §22.1-79.4.
Supervision of public schools, §§22.1-2, 22.1-28.
Supervision of schools in division vested in, VA Const Art VIII §7.
Surplus real property, §22.1-129.
Surveys requiring student participation.
Boards to adopt policies prohibiting during school day, §22.1-79.3.
Teachers.
Employment of teachers, §22.1-295.
Licensed instructional personnel, §22.1-253.13:2.
Grievance procedures, §§22.1-306 to 22.1-315.
See TEACHERS.
Shortages.
Reporting, §22.1-79.
Strategic compensation grant initiative, §§22.1-318.1, 22.1-318.2.
Temporary loans to school boards, §22.1-111.
Term.
County board form of government, §15.2-410.
County executive form of government, §15.2-532.
County manager form of government, §15.2-628.
Elected board, §§22.1-57.3, 24.2-223.
Urban county executive form of government, §15.2-837.
Establishing different terms, §15.2-824.
Textbooks.
Generally, §§22.1-238 to 22.1-243.
See SCHOOLS AND EDUCATION.
Threat assessment teams, §22.1-79.4.
Tie breaker position, §22.1-57.3.
Tie breakers.
Certain officers prohibited to serve as tie breaker, §22.1-30.
County board form of government, §15.2-410.
County executive form of government, §15.2-531.
County manager form of government, §15.2-627.

LOCAL SCHOOL BOARDS —Cont'd
Tie breakers —Cont'd
Selection, §§22.1-40, 22.1-53.
Alternative method, §22.1-44.
Urban county executive form of government, §15.2-837.
Tie vote.
Procedure in case of tie vote, §22.1-75.
Transition from appointed to elected board, §22.1-47.3.
Transportation department or commissioner of highways.
Sale of property to by school board in city located in Virginia Beach, §22.1-129.
Transportation of nonpublic school pupils.
Agreements to provide, §22.1-176.1.
Travel expenses.
Elected board, §22.1-57.3.
Member ceasing to be resident of district, §22.1-29.
Transition from appointed to elected school board, §22.1-47.3.
Turnaround specialists.
Funding, §22.1-199.1.
Urban county executive form of government.
Appointee from each election district, §15.2-855.
Appointment, number of members, terms, §15.2-837.
Establishing different terms of office, §15.2-824.
Vacancies.
County board form of government, §15.2-410.
County manager form of government, §15.2-627.
Vice-chairman.
Election, §22.1-76.
Violation of education title.
Penalty, §22.1-292.
Violence prevention.
Development of programs, §22.1-279.9.
Virginia index of performance incentive program, §22.1-253.13:9.
Virginia retirement system.
Borrowing from, §§22.1-161.1 to 22.1-161.8. See within this heading, "Borrowing from Virginia retirement system."
Waiver from regulatory requirements regarding accreditation, §22.1-253.13:3.

LOCAL SUPERINTENDENTS OF PUBLIC WELFARE.
See SUPERINTENDENTS OF PUBLIC WELFARE.

LOCAL TAXES, §§58.1-3000 to 58.1-3995.
Admission tax, §§58.1-3817, 58.1-3818.
Excise tax, city or town having general taxing powers, §58.1-3840.
Scott county.
Off-track horse race wagering facilities, §58.1-3818.01.
Stafford county, §58.1-3818.02.
Agreements by third parties to pay, §58.1-3018.
Assessment time limitation waiver, §58.1-3903.1.
Bank franchise tax.
Branch banks, §58.1-1211.
Record of deposits through branches required, §58.1-1212.
City tax, §58.1-1208.
County tax, §58.1-1210.
Credit against state tax, §58.1-1213.
Town tax, §58.1-1209.
Bawdy places, buildings and other structures harboring.
Cost of corrective action by locality collected as tax, §15.2-908.1.

LOCAL TAXES —Cont'd
Boards of equalization, §§58.1-3370 to 58.1-3389.
See REAL PROPERTY TAXES.
Bonds issued by locality.
Levy and collection of annual tax, §15.2-2624.
Businesses, miscellaneous.
Classification of machinery and tools, §§58.1-3508.2, 58.1-3508.3.
Change to fiscal tax year, §58.1-3010.
Changing rate of tax during calendar year, §58.1-3012.
Cigarette tax, §§58.1-3830 to 58.1-3832.
Corporate or partnership officer, willful failure to collect and account for, §58.1-3907.
Excise tax, city or town having general taxing powers, §58.1-3840.
Cities and towns to make city and town levies, §58.1-3005.
Additional tax to pay interest and retire bonds, §58.1-3006.
Funds not available, allocated, etc., until appropriated, §58.1-3005.
City discount for early payment, §15.2-1104.
Classes of property.
Different rates of levy on different classes, §58.1-3008.
Collection generally, §§58.1-3910 to 58.1-3961.
See TAX COLLECTION.
Consumer utility taxes, §§58.1-3814 to 58.1-3816.2.
Corporate or partnership officer liability for failure to pay, §58.1-3906.
Willful failure to collect and account for, §58.1-3907.
Correction of erroneous tax assessments, §§58.1-3980 to 58.1-3995.
See CORRECTION OF ERRONEOUS TAX ASSESSMENTS.
County discount for early payment, §15.2-1201.2.
Delinquent taxes.
Collection of local taxes generally.
See TAX COLLECTION.
Sale of delinquent tax lands generally, §§58.1-3965 to 58.1-3975.
See SALE OF DELINQUENT TAX LANDS.
Different rates of levy on different classes of property, §58.1-3008.
Disasters.
Relief from taxes, §58.1-3014.
Distress.
Collection by distress generally, §§58.1-3940 to 58.1-3961.
See TAX COLLECTION.
Drug blight existing on property.
Costs of locality undertaking corrective action collected as taxes, §15.2-907.
Excise taxes, city and town having general taxing powers, §58.1-3840.
Firefighters.
Volunteer firefighters.
Relief for, §27-47.
Fire zones or districts.
Tax levies, §27-23.1.
Fiscal year.
Levy of taxes on fiscal year basis, §58.1-3010.
Food and beverage tax, §§58.1-3833, 58.1-3834.
City or town, excise tax, §58.1-3840.
Situs for taxation, §58.1-3841.
Guidelines promulgated by department of taxation, §58.1-3701.

LOCAL TAXES —Cont'd
Hearing prior to increase of local levy, §58.1-3007.
Income tax, §§58.1-540 to 58.1-549.
Increase of local tax levy.
Notice and hearing prior to, §58.1-3007.
Injunctions against assessment or collection of taxes, §58.1-3993.
License taxes.
Generally, §§58.1-3700 to 58.1-3735.
See LICENSE TAXES.
Telegraph or telephone companies, §58.1-2690.
Local improvements, §§15.2-2404 to 15.2-2413.
See TAXES OR ASSESSMENTS FOR LOCAL IMPROVEMENTS.
Machinery and tools tax, §§58.1-3507, 58.1-3508.
Miscellaneous businesses, §§58.1-3508.2, 58.1-3508.3.
Meals tax.
County food and beverage tax, §§58.1-3833, 58.1-3834.
Excise tax, city or town having general taxing powers, §58.1-3840.
Situs for taxation, §58.1-3841.
Merchants' capital tax, §§58.1-3509, 58.1-3510.
Mosquito control districts, §32.1-194.
Motor vehicle sales and use tax.
Local taxes prohibited, §58.1-2418.
Notice prior to increase of levy, §58.1-3007.
Occupations, tax on prohibited, §58.1-3009.
Offers of compromise, §58.1-3994.
Omitted local taxes or levies, §58.1-3903.
Forms for assessment, §58.1-3905.
Ordinances.
Affirmative vote of majority of governing body required, VA Const Art VII §7.
Criminal penalties provided for failure to file returns or false statements, §58.1-3916.1.
Providing dates for filing returns, setting penalties, interest, etc., §58.1-3916.
Pari-mutuel wagering on horses.
Admissions tax, §59.1-393.
Parks, recreational facilities and playgrounds.
System of public recreation and playgrounds, annual tax, §15.2-1807.
Tax on property to maintain and operate, §15.2-1806.
Payment agreements, §58.1-3018.
Payrolls, tax on prohibited, §58.1-3009.
Personal property tax relief act of 1998, §§58.1-3523 to 58.1-3535.
See PERSONAL PROPERTY TAX RELIEF ACT OF 1998.
Prepayment, §§58.1-3920, 58.1-3920.1.
Probate tax, §§58.1-3805 to 58.1-3808.
Authorization of city or county probate tax, §58.1-1718.
Public school special tax, §§22.1-102 to 22.1-106.
Public service corporations.
Real and tangible personal property taxation by localities, §58.1-2606.
Railroads, §58.1-2607.
Rates of levy.
Different rates on different classes of property, §58.1-3008.
Real property taxes, §§58.1-3200 to 58.1-3389.
See REAL PROPERTY TAXES.
Recordation tax, §§58.1-3800 to 58.1-3804.
Authority to impose, §58.1-814.
Relief from taxes.
Disasters, §58.1-3014.

LOCAL TAXES —Cont'd
Rescue zones or districts.
Tax levies, §27-23.1.
Sale of delinquent tax lands, §§58.1-3965 to 58.1-3975.
See SALE OF DELINQUENT TAX LANDS.
Sales and use taxes levied by counties and cities, §§58.1-605, 58.1-606.
School purposes.
Special county, district, city or town tax, §§22.1-102 to 22.1-106.
Segregation of property for local taxation, VA Const Art X §4.
Severance tax on coal, gas or oil.
Alternative to specially and separately assessing mineral lands, §58.1-3286.
License tax on persons engaging in business of severing, §§58.1-3712 to 58.1-3713.4.
Local coal severance license taxes, §§58.1-3740 to 58.1-3745.
Social security account numbers.
Disclosure for administrative purposes, §58.1-3017.
Subject of local taxation, §58.1-3000.
Tangible personal property, machinery and tools and merchants capital tax, §§58.1-3500 to 58.1-3522.
See PERSONAL PROPERTY TAXES.
Telegraph or telephone companies, local license tax, §58.1-2690.
Third party payments, §58.1-3018.
Time on assessment limitation waiver, §58.1-3903.1.
Time-shares.
Status of estates, §55-363.
To whom property generally taxed and by whom listed, §58.1-3015.
Retention of property for payment of taxes.
Property listed by and taxed to person other than owner, §58.1-3016.
Town imposing tax.
Two-third votes of council members, §15.2-1427.
Transient occupancy tax, §§58.1-3819 to 58.1-3826.
Excise tax, city or town having general taxing powers, §58.1-3840.
Imposition, §58.1-3843.
Travel campgrounds.
Excise tax, city or town having general taxing powers, §58.1-3840.
Use of July 1 as effective date of assessment, §58.1-3011.
Wills and administrations tax, §§58.1-3805 to 58.1-3808.
Authorization of city or county probate tax, §58.1-1718.
Wind turbines.
Local property taxation of public service corporations.
Rate of tax on electric suppliers utilizing turbines, §58.1-2606.

LOCAL TAX OFFICERS.
Clerks of court, §§58.1-3173 to 58.1-3177.
Commissioners of revenue.
Generally, §§58.1-3100 to 58.1-3122.2.
See COMMISSIONERS OF REVENUE.
Treasurers, §§58.1-3123 to 58.1-3172.1.
See TREASURERS, LOCAL.

LOCAL TECHNOLOGY ZONES, §58.1-3850.

LOCAL TOURISM ZONES.
Establishment, tax incentives, regulatory flexibility.
City, county, town authority, §58.1-3851.
Tax revenues, entitlement, §58.1-3851.1.
Power to designate, §15.2-982.

LOCAL TRANSPORTATION DISTRICTS.
Generally, §§33.1-409 to 33.1-425, 33.1-430 to 33.1-446.
See TRANSPORTATION DISTRICTS.

LOCAL TRUSTS TO FUND POSTEMPLOYMENT BENEFITS OTHER THAN PENSIONS, §§15.2-1544 to 15.2-1549.
Authorized, §15.2-1544.
Exemptions of assets, §15.2-1546.
Finance boards to manage assets.
Creation, §15.2-1547.
Duties, §15.2-1548.
Members, §15.2-1547.
Records, §15.2-1548.
Governing bodies.
Powers, §15.2-1544.
Defining benefits other than pensions, §15.2-1545.
Investment of assets, §§15.2-1548, 15.2-1549.
Powers of governing bodies, §15.2-1544.
Defining benefits other than pensions, §15.2-1545.
Public procurement act.
Exemption from, §15.2-1548.

LOCAL USE TAXES, §58.1-606.

LOCAL VEHICLE TAXES AND LICENSE FEES, §46.2-752.

LOCKOUTS.
Right to work, §40.1-66.

LOCKS.
Burning or destroying, §18.2-80.
Residential landlord obligations, §55-248.13:1.
Landlord's obligations when one co-tenant is excluded from premises, §§55-225.5, 55-248.18:1.

LOCKSMITHS.
Private security services businesses.
Exemptions from provisions, §9.1-140.
General provisions, §§9.1-138 to 9.1-150.
See PRIVATE SECURITY SERVICES BUSINESSES.
Registration.
Waiver of examination, §9.1-140.1.

LOCK-UP ROOM OR WARD.
Detaining juvenile, §16.1-249.

LOCOMOTIVES.
Generally.
See RAILROADS.

LODGES.
Names or insignia, registration, alteration, cancellation, §§2.2-411 to 2.2-417.
See REGISTRATION OF NAMES OR INSIGNIA OF ORGANIZATIONS.

LODGE SYSTEM.
Fraternal benefit societies.
Society operating on, §38.2-4101.

LOGIC WAFER MANUFACTURING PERFORMANCE GRANT PROGRAM, §59.1-284.14.

LOGS.
Drift property generally, §§55-202 to 55-210.
Forest products tax, §§58.1-1600 to 58.1-1622.
See FOREST PRODUCTS TAX.
Vehicles hauling.
Fastening load, §46.2-1155.
Fine for failure to fasten, VA SCt Rule 3B:2.

LOITERING.
Bail bondsmen.
Solicitation of business, §9.1-185.9.
Bridges.
Pedestrians loitering on, §46.2-930.
Fine schedule, VA SCt Rule 3B:2.
Highway rights-of-way.
Pedestrians loitering on, §46.2-930.
Fine schedule, VA SCt Rule 3B:2.
Locality prohibiting, §15.2-926.

LONG-ARM JURISDICTION, §8.01-328.1.

LONG-ARM STATUTE, §8.01-328.1.
Retail sales and use tax.
Tax collectible from dealers.
Jurisdictional standards, §58.1-612.
Trademarks and service marks.
Service on out-of-state registrants, §59.1-92.14.

LONG BOWS.
Locality prohibiting shooting of bows, §15.2-916.

LONG DISTANCE TELEPHONE SERVICE.
Change of carriers, prior authorization, §56-479.1.
Telephonic instruments used to obtain service without payment.
Selling or transferring, §18.2-167.

LONG-TERM CARE FACILITIES.
Actions for personal injuries or wrongful death.
Department paid for services provided injured party or decedent.
Notice to department, §8.01-66.5.
Administrators.
Licensing, §§54.1-3101 to 54.1-3103.1.
Required for operation, death, illness or resignation, continued operation of home, §54.1-3103.
Admissions.
Restriction or prohibition, §32.1-135.
Alterations or additions.
Approval, §32.1-132.
Assisted living facilities, §§63.2-1800 to 63.2-1819.
See ASSISTED LIVING FACILITIES.
Bed supplies.
Applications for increases to be filed in response to requests for applications.
Certificates of public need, §32.1-102.3:2.
Transfer of nursing facility beds, application for, §32.1-102.3:7.
Cafeterias.
County food and beverage tax not levied on nonprofit cafeterias, §58.1-3833.
Certificates of public need for medical care facilities, §§32.1-102.1 to 32.1-102.11.
See MEDICAL CARE FACILITIES.
Certification for purposes of social security, §32.1-137.
Certified nursing facility education initiative, §§32.1-353.1 to 32.1-353.3.

LONG-TERM CARE FACILITIES —Cont'd
Civil penalty.
Failure to conduct background check of compensated employee, §32.1-126.01.
Client residency determinations.
Probating of wills, §64.2-443.
Community-based continuing care providers, §§38.2-4918 to 38.2-4923.
Complainants.
Confidentiality of identity, §32.1-138.5.
Retaliation or discrimination against, §32.1-138.4.
Consideration as precondition for admittance or continued stay, §32.1-317.
Continuing care provider registration and disclosure, §§38.2-4900 to 38.2-4917, 38.2-4924 to 38.2-4932.
Continuing care retirement community nursing home bed projects.
Open admission period, applications for, §32.1-102.3:8.
Requirements for accepting applications, §32.1-102.3:2.
Transfer of nursing facility beds, application for, §32.1-102.3:7.
Utilization of nursing home beds.
Reporting to commissioner of health, §32.1-276.5.
Convictions prohibiting employment of person, §32.1-126.01.
County food and beverage tax.
Tax not levied on food and beverages sold, §58.1-3833.
Criminal conviction clearance.
Obtaining for compensated employees, §32.1-126.01.
Criminal history record information.
Obtaining for compensated employees, §32.1-126.01.
Criminal record history information, dissemination, §19.2-389.
Deficiencies.
Certified nursing facility education initiative, §§32.1-353.1 to 32.1-353.3.
Direct care staffs and other long-term care professional recognition day, §2.2-3311.1.
Disasters, state or local emergencies.
Freedom of information act.
Disaster recovery plans and evacuation plans, exclusions from chapter, §2.2-3705.2.
Disciplinary actions against health professionals.
Reporting required.
Civil penalties for failure to report, §32.1-125.01.
Disease reports.
Infections of dead human bodies, §32.1-37.1.
Disorders of health professional.
Reporting required.
Civil penalties for failure to report, §32.1-125.01.
Education initiative, §§32.1-353.1 to 32.1-353.3.
Authorization to expend penalty funds, §32.1-353.3.
Definitions, §32.1-353.2.
Findings, §32.1-353.1.
Purpose, §32.1-353.1.
Electricity.
Prompt restoration of electrical service during power outages.
Notice to electric utilities of location of licensed nursing homes, §32.1-126.

LONG-TERM CARE FACILITIES —Cont'd
Employment for compensation.
Convictions prohibiting, §32.1-126.01.
Criminal record clearance obtained for compensated employees, §32.1-126.01.
National criminal history record information.
Obtaining for compensated employees, §32.1-126.01.
Sworn statement as to convictions.
Required by applicant, false statement, criminal penalty, §32.1-126.01.
Estate recovery program.
Medicaid recipients, §32.1-326.1.
Fire suppression system.
Licensing requirements, §32.1-126.2.
Fraud as to conditions or operations, §32.1-316.
Freedom of information act.
Disasters, state or local emergencies.
Disaster recovery plans and evacuation plans, exclusions from chapter, §2.2-3705.2.
Gifts or donations by localities to nonprofit organizations, §15.2-953.
Health care data reporting.
Generally, §§32.1-276.2 to 32.1-276.11.
See HEALTH CARE DATA REPORTING.
Hospital or health center commissions, §§15.2-5200 to 15.2-5219.
See HOSPITAL OR HEALTH CENTER COMMISSIONS.
Human research generally, §§32.1-162.16 to 32.1-162.20.
Incompetency.
Conservators.
See CONSERVATORS.
Generally.
See INCOMPETENCY.
Guardian and ward.
See GUARDIAN AND WARD.
Inspections.
Commissioner duties, §32.1-126.
Insurance.
Liability insurance coverage requirements, §32.1-127.
Liability insurance coverage requirements, §32.1-127.
Licensing.
Alterations or additions to nursing homes.
New licenses, §32.1-132.
Applications, §32.1-129.
Commissioner duties, §32.1-126.
Defined, §32.1-123.
Denial of license, §32.1-126.
Display of license, §32.1-133.
Exemption from provisions, §32.1-124.
Expiration, §32.1-131.
Fire suppression systems, §32.1-126.2.
Provision violations.
Penalties, §32.1-136.
Regulations, §32.1-127.
Authorization of sanctions and guidelines, §32.1-127.01.
Renewals, §32.1-131.
Required, §32.1-125.
Revocation, §32.1-135.
Service charges, §32.1-130.
Suspension, §32.1-135.
Transferability of licenses, §32.1-125.
Lien for expenses of treatment.
Person's negligence causing injury, §§8.01-66.2 to 8.01-66.12.
See MEDICAL SERVICES LIEN.

LONG-TERM CARE FACILITIES —Cont'd
Medical malpractice.
Professional services in nursing homes.
Defined, §8.01-581.1.
Medical records.
Storage, §32.1-127.1:01.
Misrepresentations as to conditions or operations, §32.1-316.
National criminal history record information.
Obtaining for compensated employees, §32.1-126.01.
Nonprofit health entities.
Disposition of assets for sale or transfer, §§55-531 to 55-533.
Patient rights and responsibilities, §§32.1-138 to 32.1-138.3.
Patient trust funds.
Knowing failures to deposit, transfer or maintain, §32.1-318.
Personal injury action against home.
Notice to department of medical assistance services, response by department.
Department having paid for services provided injured party or decedent, §8.01-66.5.
Police powers over lands lying beyond localities boundaries, §15.2-1725.
Policy of Commonwealth.
Coordination by secretary of health and human resources, §2.2-212.
Preadmission screening.
Medicaid recipients, §32.1-330.
Prescription drugs.
Re-dispensing of returned drugs, §54.1-3411.1.
Provision violations.
Penalties, §32.1-27.1.
Public information campaign, §2.2-213.1.
Quality of care.
Certified nursing facility education initiative, §§32.1-353.1 to 32.1-353.3.
Receivers.
Appointment, §32.1-135.
Records.
Information required to be kept, §32.1-274.
Religious affiliations.
Application of provisions, §32.1-128.
Residency of patients.
Probating of wills, §64.2-443.
Resignation, restriction or expiration of privileges of health professional.
Reporting required.
Civil penalty for failure, §32.1-125.01.
Retaliation or discrimination against complainants, §32.1-138.4.
Confidentiality of complainant's identity, §32.1-138.5.
Smoke detectors and other fire detection or suppression systems, §36-99.5:1.
Unethical fraudulent or unprofessional conduct by health professional.
Reporting required.
Civil penalty for failure, §32.1-125.01.
Written verification of Medicaid applications, statements or forms, §32.1-319.
Wrongful death action against home.
Notice to department of medical assistance services, response by department.
Department having paid for services provided injured party or decedent, §8.01-66.5.

LONG-TERM CARE INSURANCE, §§38.2-5200 to 38.2-5210.
Hybrid retirement program.
Disability program for participants.
Long-term care benefits provided by board, §51.1-1178.
Income tax credit, §58.1-339.11.
Local employees, officers, teachers.
Establishment by department of human resource management, §2.2-1207.
Assumption of responsibility.
Board of trustees, Virginia Retirement System, §51.1-513.3.
Trust fund, §51.1-513.4.
National Guard.
Rights and benefits on being called to active duty, §44-102.1.
Pre-PACE prepaid health plans.
Applicability of insurance title.
Exceptions, §38.2-226.2.
Public information campaign, §2.2-213.1.
Sickness and disability program for employees of Commonwealth, §51.1-1135.2.
State employees and persons with 5 years creditable coverage under Virginia Retirement System.
Department of human resource management to develop and administer, §2.2-1208.
Assumption of responsibility.
Board of trustees, Virginia Retirement System, §51.1-513.2.
Trust fund, §51.1-513.4.
Virginia retirement system.
Coverage programs established and administered by department of human resource management, §§2.2-1207, 2.2-1208.
Assumption of responsibility by board of trustees, §§51.1-513.2, 51.1-513.3.
Trust fund, §51.1-513.4.
Group insurance program, §51.1-513.1.
Hybrid retirement program.
Disability program for participants.
Long-term care benefits provided by board, §51.1-1178.

LONG TERM CARE OMBUDSMAN.
Freedom of information act.
Excluded records, §2.2-3705.5.

LONG-TERM CARE PREPAID HEALTH PLANS.
PACE plans.
Oversight by medical assistance services department, §32.1-330.3.
Pre-PACE plans.
Oversight by medical assistance services department, §32.1-330.3.

LONG TERM CARE SERVICES FOR THE AGING.
Office of the state long term care ombudsmen.
Freedom of information act.
Excluded records, §2.2-3705.5.

LONG-TERM DISABILITY.
Sickness and disability program for state employees.
Generally, §§51.1-1100 to 51.1-1140.
See SICKNESS AND DISABILITY PROGRAM.

LONGWOOD UNIVERSITY, §§23-182 to 23-191.
Board of visitors, §§23-182 to 23-188.
Campus police departments, §§23-232 to 23-238.
Reporting campus crime, §23-9.1:1.

LONGWOOD UNIVERSITY —Cont'd
Colleges generally, §§23-1.01 to 23-9.2:8.
See COLLEGES AND UNIVERSITIES.
Conferring of degrees, §23-190.
Corporate name, §23-183.
Special license plates, §46.2-749.
Teacher curriculum, §23-191.
Transfer of property to university, §23-184.
Tuition, fees and other charges, §23-189.

LOOSE LEAF TOBACCO.
Tobacco products tax, §§58.1-1021.01 to 58.1-1021.05.
See TOBACCO PRODUCTS TAX.

LOSSES FROM GAMBLING.
Bill in equity for repayment, §11-16.
Recovery, §11-15.
Repayment discharging winner from punishment, §11-16.

LOSS OF CIVIL RIGHTS.
Restoration to persons convicted of felonies, §§53.1-231.1, 53.1-231.2.

LOSS OF ECONOMIC DAMAGES.
Life expectancy tables, §8.01-419.

LOSS OF HEARING.
Workers' compensation.
Medical attention to be furnished, §65.2-603.

LOSS OF INCOME.
Damages not diminished by reimbursement, §8.01-35.
Life expectancy tables, §8.01-419.
Motor vehicle insurance, optional provisions for, §38.2-2201.
Wrongful death, §8.01-52.

LOSS OR CLAIM RESERVES.
Insurance companies, §38.2-1314.

LOST INSTRUMENTS AND RECORDS.
Bills of lading.
Lost or missing bills, §8.7-601.
Court order book or equivalent.
How contents of lost records proved, §8.01-394.
Records filed in clerk's office, §8.01-393.
Reentry of original records, §8.01-392.
Records filed in clerk's office, §8.01-393.
Validation of proved lost records, §8.01-395.
Debts, notes and bonds.
Indemnifying bond required for action, §8.01-32.
Documents of title.
Lost and missing documents, §8.7-601.
Investment securities.
Notice to issuer, §8.8A-406.
Replacement, §8.8A-405.
Original pleadings and papers.
Procedure in civil cases, §8.01-374.
Public finance act.
Mutilated, lost or destroyed bonds, §15.2-2621.
Warehouse receipts.
Lost and missing receipts, §8.7-601.
Wireless service authorities.
Lost or mutilated bond, §15.2-5431.17.

LOST PAST DUE EVIDENCE OF DEBT.
Action on, §8.01-32.

LOTS.
Manufactured home lots.
Leases.
See LEASES.

LOTS —Cont'd
Parking lots or other facilities.
See PARKING LOTS OR OTHER FACILITIES.

LOTTERY PROMOTING PRODUCTS, §18.2-242.

LOTTERY, RAFFLES.
Charitable gaming.
General provisions, §§18.2-340.15 to 18.2-340.37.
See CHARITABLE GAMING.

LOTTERY, STATE, §§58.1-4000 to 58.1-4027.
Altering ticket or share, §58.1-4017.
Assignment of prize as collateral for loan, §58.1-4020.1.
Assignment of right to prize, §58.1-4013.
Audit or post-audit of accounts and transactions of department, §58.1-4023.
Background investigation of director, §58.1-4005.
Background investigation of lottery sales agents, §58.1-4009.
Background investigations of employees, §58.1-4008.
Cash or debit cards.
Only method of payment for tickets or shares, §58.1-4014.1.
Check or draft from sales agents dishonored.
Service charge, §58.1-4021.
Collection of debt owed licensed agent.
Venue of action, §58.1-4021.
Collection of money or proceeds jeopardized, §58.1-4021.
Compulsive gamblers organizations.
Ticket to bear toll-free telephone number, §58.1-4007.1.
Counterfeit tickets or shares, presentation, §58.1-4017.
Deceased prize winners.
Assignment according to terms deceased prize winner beneficiary designation, §58.1-4013.
Definitions, §58.1-4002.
Deposit of money received by agents, §58.1-4021.
Distribution of revenues.
Lottery proceeds fund, VA Const Art X §7-A.
Eligible persons to purchase tickets or shares or receive prizes, §58.1-4019.
Embezzlement of public money or funds associated with lottery, §58.1-4019.
Establishment, §58.1-4001.
Exemption from gambling article, §18.2-334.3.
Exemption from state and local taxation.
Lottery prizes and sales of tickets, §58.1-4025.
Forfeited prizes, unclaimed prizes, §58.1-4020.
Forging ticket or share, §58.1-4017.
Fraudulent notification of prizes, §58.1-4018.1.
Gamblers anonymous.
Tickets to bear toll-free telephone number, §58.1-4007.1.
Income tax on individuals.
Subtraction of prize amount, §58.1-322.
Instant ticket games or contests.
License required for, §58.1-4019.1.
Interest on money not timely paid by sales agents, §58.1-4021.
Internet ticket sales.
Prohibition, §58.1-4007.2.
Investment of prize proceeds to fund payment of annuitized prize, §58.1-4013.
Jeopardized collection of money or proceeds, §58.1-4021.

LOTTERY, STATE —Cont'd
Larceny of ticket, prize or share, §58.1-4018.1.
Licensing of lottery sales agents, §58.1-4009.
Authority, §58.1-4010.
Fictitious or fraudulent statements or representation, §58.1-4009.
Gross receipts, meaning of, §58.1-4011.
Instant ticket games or contests, §58.1-4019.1.
Refusal to issue license, §58.1-4009.
Suspension or revocation, §58.1-4012.
Judicial review, §58.1-4027.
Lottery board.
Bond of members, §58.1-4004.
Closed meetings.
Licensing appeal, §2.2-3711.
Disclosure statement by members.
Filing, time, form, §§2.2-3114, 2.2-3117.
Ineligible to purchase tickets or shares or receive prizes, §58.1-4019.
Membership, §58.1-4004.
Oath of office, §58.1-4004.
Powers, §58.1-4007.
Secretary and executive officer.
Director of lottery department, §58.1-4006.
Terms of members, §58.1-4004.
Vacancies, §58.1-4004.
Lottery department.
Audit or post-audit of accounts, §58.1-4023.
Director.
Appointment, qualifications and salary, §58.1-4005.
Oath of office, §58.1-4005.
Powers, §58.1-4006.
Sheriff powers, §58.1-4006.
Employees, §58.1-4008.
Exempt from personnel act, §58.1-4024.
Ineligible to purchase tickets or shares or receive prizes, §58.1-4019.
Established, §58.1-4003.
Freedom of information act.
Excluded records, §2.2-3705.7.
Independent agency of Commonwealth, §58.1-4003.
Personnel exemption for employees of department, §58.1-4024.
Tax information.
Tax commissioner authorized to divulge, §58.1-3.
Lottery fund, §58.1-4022.
Deposit of money received by agents, §58.1-4021.
Forfeited prizes paid into, §58.1-4020.
Proceeds funds, §58.1-4022.1.
Lottery proceeds fund, VA Const Art X §7-A.
Merchants' capital tax.
Valuing lottery tickets as part of dealers' inventory, §58.1-3510.
Military personnel.
Exemption from 180-day ticket redemption requirement, §58.1-4020.
Officers, public safety medal of valor, §§9.1-800, 9.1-801.
180-day redemption requirement, §58.1-4020.
Prizes.
Assignment of prize as collateral for loan, §58.1-4020.1.
Assignment of right to, §58.1-4013.
Exemption from state and local taxation, §58.1-4025.
Fraudulent notification of prizes, §58.1-4018.1.
Garnishment, §58.1-4013.
Ineligible persons to receive, §58.1-4019.

LOTTERY, STATE —Cont'd
Prizes —Cont'd
Investment of proceeds to fund payment of annuitized prize, §58.1-4013.
Larceny, §58.1-4018.1.
Liens upon, §58.1-4013.
Set-off of debts to Commonwealth, §58.1-4026.
Unclaimed prizes, §58.1-4020.
Prohibited actions, §58.1-4018.
Public school funds.
Lottery proceeds non-recurring costs escrow accounts, §22.1-100.1.
Purposes of revenue generated, §58.1-4001.
Redemption of tickets.
180-day requirements, §58.1-4020.
Regulations governing establishment and operation of lottery.
Powers of lottery board, §58.1-4007.
Sales agents licensing, §58.1-4009.
Authority, §58.1-4010.
Fictitious or fraudulent statements or representation, §58.1-4009.
Gross receipts, meaning of, §58.1-4011.
Instant ticket games or contests, §58.1-4019.1.
Refusal to issue license, §58.1-4009.
Suspension or revocation of license, §58.1-4012.
Judicial review, §58.1-4027.
Set-off of debts to Commonwealth from prizes, §58.1-4026.
Short title, §58.1-4000.
State lottery law, §58.1-4000.
Tampering with equipment or machinery, §58.1-4018.
Tax exemption.
Lottery prizes and sales of tickets, §58.1-4025.
Temporary assistance for needy families (TANF).
Prohibited uses of benefits, §63.2-621.
Tickets or shares.
Cash or debit cards.
Only method of payment for, §58.1-4014.1.
Exemption from sales of tickets from state and local taxation, §58.1-4025.
Forging, altering or fraudulently making, §58.1-4017.
Gifts to minors prohibited, §58.1-4016.
Ineligible persons to purchase, §58.1-4019.
Internet sales prohibited, §58.1-4007.2.
Larceny, §58.1-4018.1.
Presentation of counterfeit or altered ticket or shares, §58.1-4017.
Prices, §58.1-4014.
Redemption, 180-day requirement, §58.1-4020.
Sales to persons under eighteen, §58.1-4015.
Temporary assistance for needy families (TANF).
Prohibited uses of benefits, §63.2-621.
Toll-free telephone number for gamblers anonymous, §58.1-4007.1.
Who may sell, §58.1-4014.
Toll-free telephone number for gamblers anonymous or other compulsive gambler organization.
Tickets to bear, §58.1-4007.1.
Trust fund, proceeds from sale of lottery tickets or shares, §58.1-4021.
Unclaimed prizes, §58.1-4020.
Venue.
Action for collection of debt owed licensed agent, §58.1-4021.

LOUDOUN COUNTY.
Affordable housing dwelling units.
Zoning ordinances, §15.2-2304.

LOUDOUN COUNTY —Cont'd
Agricultural and forestal districts.
County executive form and certain other counties, §§15.2-4400 to 15.2-4407.
Boundary with Jefferson county, West Virginia, §1-313.
Circuit court clerk.
Serving also as clerk of general district court and juvenile and domestic relations district court.
Supplementing salary, §15.2-1635.1.
Confederate cemeteries and graves.
Disbursement of funds appropriated for upkeep, §10.1-2211.
Highways and roads.
Dirt and gravel roads.
Maximum speed limits on nonsurface treated highways, §46.2-873.1.
Inoperable motor vehicles, keeping on residential property, §15.2-905.
Land use proceedings.
Disclosure of business or financial relationships required.
Board of Supervisors, planning commission, board of zoning appeals, §15.2-2287.1.
Local licensing of motor vehicles, trailers and semitrailers.
Payment of fines for ordinance and parking violations.
Evidence required before issuing license, §46.2-752.
Metropolitan Washington airports authority.
Jurisdiction of county police over authority facilities, §5.1-158.
Microcomputer devices.
Use to measure speed of automobile, §46.2-882.
Northern Virginia transportation authority.
Counties included, §15.2-4831.
Parking on secondary highways, §46.2-1222.
Parking violations.
Removal or immobilization of vehicles.
Outstanding parking violations, §46.2-1216.
Pedestrian crosswalks.
Signs requiring vehicles to yield right-of-way.
Ordinance requiring, authority to enact, penalty for violation, §46.2-924.
Public defenders office.
Established, §19.2-163.04.
Real property taxes.
Special assessment for land preservation.
Additional provisions concerning zoning classification, §58.1-3237.1.
Recordation tax, state.
Regional congestion relief fee, §58.1-802.2.
Retail sales and use tax.
Additional sales tax for Northern Virginia and Hampton Roads, §58.1-603.1.
Additional use tax for Northern Virginia and Hampton Roads, §58.1-604.01.
Repair of motor vehicles.
Authority to impose on labor or services, §58.1-605.
Revolutionary war cemeteries and graves.
Disbursement of funds appropriated for upkeep, §10.1-2211.1.
School board.
Fingerprinting applicants for employment, §22.1-296.2.
Salary of members, §22.1-32.
Staggered terms for elected members, §§22.1-57.3:1, 22.1-57.3:1.1.

LOUDOUN COUNTY —Cont'd
Semi-automatic firearms and shotguns.
Carrying loaded firearms in public areas, §18.2-287.4.
Snow and ice removal from public sidewalk, §15.2-2025.
State department of health employees.
Supplementing salaries and travel expenses, §15.2-1508.3.
Subdivision regulations.
Application of county regulations in area subject to municipal jurisdiction, §15.2-2249.
Application of municipal regulations beyond corporate limits, §15.2-2248.
Disagreement between county and municipality, §15.2-2250.
Subdivisions.
Expedited land development review procedures, §15.2-2263.
Taxes or assessments for local improvements.
Construction of electric transmission line, §15.2-2404.
Crooked Bridge Lane, construction, repair and maintenance of bridge, §15.2-2404.
Tax map reference number.
Circuit court clerk indexing by, §17.1-252.
Transient occupancy tax, §58.1-1742.
Disposition of revenues, §58.1-3819.
Well abandonment ordinance.
Duty of owner to cap or close well.
Locality adopting ordinance, §32.1-176.5.
Well construction.
Standards, §32.1-176.4.
Testing requirements, §32.1-176.5.
Zoning ordinances.
Affordable housing dwelling units, §15.2-2304.

LOUDOUN COUNTY ECONOMIC DEVELOPMENT AUTHORITY.
Generally.
See ECONOMIC DEVELOPMENT AUTHORITIES.

LOUDSPEAKERS.
Polling places.
Prohibited on election day, §24.2-605.

LOUISA COUNTY.
Confederate cemeteries and graves.
Disbursement of funds appropriated for upkeep, §10.1-2211.
Dams.
Restrictions, §29.1-532.
Fingerprinting school employees, §22.1-296.2.
Revolutionary war cemeteries and graves.
Disbursement of funds appropriated for upkeep, §10.1-2211.1.
School board.
Fingerprinting applicants for employment, §22.1-296.2.
Salary of members, §22.1-32.

LOW AND MODERATE INCOME HOUSING.
Affordable rental housing.
Assessment for property tax purposes.
Fair market value, determining, §58.1-3295.
Building permits.
Wavier for permit fees, §15.2-958.4.
Comprehensive plan.
Study of need for, §15.2-2224.
County manager plan of government, §15.2-735.
Density of affordable housing units.
Permitting certain densities in comprehensive plan, §15.2-735.1

LOW AND MODERATE INCOME HOUSING —Cont'd
Local funding for repair or production, §15.2-958.
Low-income housing tax credit, §36-55.63.
Corporations, §58.1-435.
Housing and community development department, §36-139.5.
Housing development authority, §36-55.63.
Retail sales and use tax.
Refund authorized for building materials, §58.1-608.1.
Zoning ordinances.
Affordable dwelling unit ordinances, §§15.2-2304 to 15.2-2305.
Creation and preservation of affordable housing.
Purpose of ordinances, §15.2-2283.

LOW-HEAD DAMS.
Recreational premises liability, §29.1-509.

LOW-INCOME HOUSING TAX CREDIT, §36-55.63.
Corporations, §58.1-435.
Housing and community development department, §36-139.5.
Housing development authority, §36-55.63.

LOW-INCOME TAXPAYERS.
Income tax credits, §58.1-339.8.

LOW-LEVEL RADIOACTIVE WASTE MANAGEMENT.
Southeast interstate compact, §§10.1-1500 to 10.1-1504.

LOW-SPEED VEHICLES.
Equipment, §46.2-908.2.
License plates.
Designated license plates, §46.2-711.
Motor vehicle safety inspections.
Exemption from inspection requirement, §46.2-1158.01.
Operation, §46.2-908.3.

LOW TUBAL OVUM TRANSFER.
Status of children of assisted conception.
Generally, §§20-156 to 20-165.

LOYALTY OATHS.
Emergency management organizations, §44-146.25.

LSD.
Drug control act.
Generally, §§54.1-3400 to 54.1-3472.
See DRUG CONTROL.
Drug offenses.
Generally, §§18.2-247 to 18.2-264.
See DRUG OFFENSES.
Schedule I controlled drug, §54.1-3446.

LUBRICATING OILS, §§59.1-149 to 59.1-167.3.
Chemical analysis as evidence, §59.1-165.
Commercial motor vehicles.
Direct fueling of commercial vehicles, §59.1-162.1.
Complaints to commissioner, §59.1-157.
Conflict of laws, §59.1-167.
Cooperation by state agencies, §59.1-162.
Defined terms, §59.1-149.
Delegation of authority, §59.1-167.3.
Enforcement by commissioner, §59.1-166.
Inspections.
Commissioner supervision, §59.1-154.
Methods of making, §59.1-153.

LUBRICATING OILS —Cont'd
Inspections —Cont'd
Samples.
Collection and analysis, §59.1-152.
Provision violations.
Commonwealth's attorneys.
Duties of, §59.1-164.
Penalties, §59.1-163.
Civil penalties, §59.1-167.2.
Rules and regulations, §59.1-156.
Sales offenses.
Assisting in violation, §18.2-230.
False trade name or mixing brand, §18.2-229.
Fraud and misrepresentation, §18.2-226.
Imitating indicia of other brands, §18.2-228.
Label required for lubricating oil, §18.2-231.
Misdemeanor for violation of provision, §18.2-232.
Sale from pump indicating other brand, §18.2-227.
Samples.
Collection and analysis, §59.1-152.
Tank vehicles.
Direct fueling of commercial vehicles, §59.1-162.1.
Testing.
Commissioner supervision, §59.1-154.

LUMBER.
Logtrailers.
Exempt from safety inspection, §46.2-1159.
Vehicles hauling.
Fastening load, §46.2-1155.
Fine for failure to fasten, VA SCt Rule 3B:2.

LUNENBURG COUNTY.
Meherrin river.
Dams.
Restrictions, §29.1-532.
Taking methods, restrictions, §29.1-531.
Nottoway river.
Dams.
Restrictions, §29.1-532.
Public defenders office.
Established, §19.2-163.04.
School board.
Salary of members, §22.1-32.
Southside regional airport authority at Blackstone, 1992 ch 371.

LUNG TRANSPLANTS.
Medical assistance service plans, §32.1-325.

LYE.
Malicious bodily injury by, §18.2-52.
Lesser offenses, conviction under certain indictments, §18.2-54.

LYING IN WAIT, KILLING BY.
Murder of the first degree, §18.2-32.

LYME DISEASE.
Healing arts professionals.
Lyme disease testing, disclosures required, §54.1-2963.2.

LYMPHEDEMA.
Health insurance coverage, §38.2-3418.14.

LYMPHOGRANULOMA VENEREUM.
Venereal diseases generally, §§32.1-55 to 32.1-60.

LYMPHOMA.
High-dose chemotherapy and bone marrow transplants.
Medical assistance service plans, §32.1-325.

LYNCHBURG.
Blue Ridge regional tourism council, §§2.2-2609, 2.2-2610.

LYNCHBURG —Cont'd
Circuit court.
Establishment, §17.1-500.
Confederate cemeteries and graves.
Disbursement of funds appropriated for upkeep, §10.1-2211.
James River.
Dams.
Restrictions, §29.1-532.
Fish passage grant and revolving loan fund.
Requirement for fishways, §29.1-101.9.
Medical care facilities.
Certificates of public need.
Moratorium exceptions, §32.1-102.3:2.
Mentally ill, or persons with intellectual or developmentally disability.
Zoning of group homes of eight or fewer single-family residences, §15.2-2291.
Public defenders office.
Established, §19.2-163.04.
Referendum elections.
Specific charter authorization required, §24.2-684.
Revolutionary war cemeteries and graves.
Disbursement of funds appropriated for upkeep, §10.1-2211.1.
Safety belt systems.
Ordinance requiring use.
Authority to adopt, violation, penalty, §46.2-1094.
School board.
Fingerprinting applicants for employment, §22.1-296.2.

LYNCHBURG PARKING AUTHORITY, 1974 ch 76, 1995 ch 289.

LYNCHING.
Apprehension and prosecution of participants, §18.2-43.
Civil liability, §18.2-44.
Persons suffering death from mob attempting to lynch another, §18.2-45.
Deemed murder, §18.2-40.
Defined, §18.2-39.
Discretionary felony sentencing guidelines, §17.1-805.
Noose, displaying on property of another or in public place.
Criminal offense, §18.2-423.2.

LYNNHAVEN RIVER.
Oysters.
Planting grounds.
Excusing rent payment on condemned oyster grounds, §28.2-623.

M

MACE.
Illegal use of tear gas, phosgene and other gases, §18.2-312.
Malicious bodily injury by means of a caustic substance or agent, §18.2-52.

MACHETES.
Brandishing with intent to intimidate, §18.2-282.1.

MACHINE GUN MANUFACTURERS AND DEALERS.
Inspection of stock, §18.2-294.
Register, §18.2-294.

MACHINE GUNS, §§18.2-288 to 18.2-298.
Aggressive purposes.
Use for, §18.2-290.
What constitutes, §18.2-291.
Applicability of article.
What article does not apply to, §18.2-293.
What article does not prohibit, §18.2-293.1.
Article construction, §18.2-297.
Construction of article, §18.2-297.
Crime of violence.
Use for, §18.2-289.
Definitions, §18.2-288.
Inapplicability of article, §18.2-293.
Inspection of stock of manufacturer or dealer, §18.2-294.
Manufacturer's and dealer's register, §18.2-294.
Plastic firearms, manufacture, import, etc., §18.2-308.5.
Presumption of offensiveness or aggressiveness, §18.2-291.
Prima facie evidence, §18.2-292.
Register of manufacturer and dealer, §18.2-294.
Registration, §18.2-295.
State police department function, §52-4.
Search warrant, §18.2-296.
Serial number or other identification.
Removing, altering, etc., §18.2-311.1.
Short title.
Uniform machine gun act, §18.2-298.
Use for aggressive purposes, §18.2-290.
What constitutes aggressive purpose, §18.2-291.
Use for crime of violence, §18.2-289.
Crime of violence defined, §18.2-288.
What article applies to, §18.2-293.
What article does not prohibit, §18.2-293.1.

MACHINERY AND TOOLS TAX, §§58.1-3507, 58.1-3508.
Situs for taxation, §§58.1-3511 to 58.1-3514.
Tangible personal property taxation generally, §§58.1-3500 to 58.1-3522.
See PERSONAL PROPERTY TAXES.

MAD DOGS.
General provisions.
See DOGS.

MADISON COLLEGE.
James Madison University.
General provisions, §§23-164.1 to 23-164.10.
See JAMES MADISON UNIVERSITY.

MADISON COUNTY.
Combined transient occupancy and food and beverage tax, §58.1-3842.
Confederate cemeteries and graves.
Disbursement of funds appropriated for upkeep, §10.1-2211.
Corn board, §3.2-1410.
District courts.
Establishment of districts, §16.1-69.6.
Historic resources department.
Confederate cemeteries and graves, §10.1-2211.
Societies receiving appropriations, §10.1-2212.
Local school boards.
Salary of members, §22.1-32.
School board.
Salary of members, §22.1-32.
Transient occupancy tax.
Disposition of revenues, §58.1-3819.
Virginia small grains board, §§3.2-2200 to 3.2-2211.

MAGAZINES.
False publications.
Stating, delivering or transmitting to publisher or employee, §18.2-209.
License tax upon privilege or right of printing or publishing.
Localities prohibited from levying, §58.1-3703.
Litter tax imposed on manufacturers, wholesalers, distributors or retailers, §58.1-1708.
Obscene magazines generally, §§18.2-372 to 18.2-388.
See OBSCENITY AND RELATED OFFENSES.
Subscription solicitation.
Child labor, §40.1-112.
Home solicitation sales generally, §§59.1-21.1 to 59.1-21.7:1.
See HOME SOLICITATION SALES.

MAGISTERIAL DISTRICTS.
Boundaries and redistricting of county district, §15.2-1211.
Consolidation of like units of local government, §15.2-3513.

MAGISTRATES, §§19.2-26 to 19.2-48.1.
Abolition of justice of the peace system.
Offices of issuing justice abolished, §19.2-31.
Statutory references to justices of the peace, §19.2-32.
Advisory committee.
Appointment by committee on district courts, §16.1-69.33.
Appointment.
Bond requirement, §19.2-39.
Chief magistrates, §19.2-36.
Eligibility, §19.2-37.
Generally, §19.2-35.
Number in judicial districts, §19.2-34.
Probationary period, §19.2-38.
Qualifications, §19.2-37.
Revocation, §19.2-38.
Training prerequisite to reappointment, §19.2-38.1.
Arrest warrants.
Issuance powers, §19.2-45.
Issued for child.
Limitations on issuance, §16.1-256.
Who may issue process of arrest, §19.2-71.
Assault and battery against, §18.2-57.
Audits, §19.2-48.
Authority vested in office of magistrate, §19.2-33.
Bail and recognizance.
Court-determined terms of bail.
Magistrate to set terms in accordance with, §19.2-130.1.
Power to admit persons to bail, §19.2-45.
Bonds, surety.
Appointment, §19.2-39.
Chief magistrates.
Appointment, §19.2-36.
Children, arrest warrants issued for.
Limitations on issuance by magistrates, §16.1-256.
Civil case fees, §16.1-69.48:2.
Civil warrants.
Issuance powers, §19.2-45.
Compelling attendance of witnesses, §8.01-407.
Compensation, §§19.2-38, 19.2-46.
Committee on district courts to fix salaries, §19.2-46.1.
Mileage allowance, §19.2-46.1.

MAGISTRATES —Cont'd
Competency to testify.
Criminal or civil proceedings, §19.2-271, VA SCt Rule 2:605.
Conservator of the peace, §§19.2-12, 19.2-45.
Construction of statutes, §§19.2-26 to 19.2-29.
Detention orders, §16.1-256.
Disposition of funds paid to or collected by, §19.2-47.1.
District courts, dual officeholding prohibited, §16.1-69.19.
Eligibility for appointment, §19.2-37.
Evidences of debt for collection.
Receipt of claim unlawful, §19.2-47.
Family abuse.
Emergency protective orders, §§16.1-253.4, 19.2-81.3.
Fire investigations.
Issuance of warrants, §27-32.2.
Fire marshals, local.
Entry to investigate releases of hazardous or regulated substances, §27-37.1.
Former Title 39.1.
Effect of repeal on prior acts, offenses, etc., §19.2-27.
Notices, recognizances and processes.
Validation, §19.2-28.
Funds paid to or collected by or on behalf of.
Disposition, §19.2-47.1.
General assembly providing for, VA Const Art VI §8.
Jury service.
Automatic exemption, §8.01-341.
Legal services to employees, §16.1-69.39:1.
License plates.
Special license plates, §46.2-746.9.
Number of magistrates, §19.2-34.
Oaths.
Power to administer, §19.2-45.
Obstructing justice by threats or force, §18.2-460.
Office of issuing justice.
Abolished, §19.2-31.
Office space, §19.2-48.1.
Personal liability by reason of robbery or burglary of office.
Reimbursement by committee on district courts, §16.1-69.33.
Powers enumerated, §19.2-45.
Prisoners' health care.
Involuntary admission and treatment, §53.1-40.1.
Probationary period, §19.2-38.
Protective orders.
Emergency protective orders, §§16.1-253.4, 19.2-81.3.
Quarters, §19.2-48.1.
Reappointment.
Training prerequisites, §19.2-38.1.
References to former sections, articles and chapters in Title 39.1, §19.2-29.
Repeal of former Title 39.1 on prior acts, offenses, etc., §19.2-27.
Repeal of inconsistent statutes, municipal charters, etc., §19.2-26.
Retirement.
Full-time magistrates.
Certification for retirement coverage, §19.2-46.2.
Revocation of appointment, §19.2-38.
Salaries, §§19.2-38, 19.2-46.
Committee on district courts to fix salaries, §19.2-46.1.

MAGISTRATES —Cont'd
Salaries —Cont'd
Mileage allowance, §19.2-46.1.
Search warrants.
Issuance powers, §19.2-45.
Supervision.
Duty of executive secretary of supreme court, §19.2-43.
Generally, §19.2-35.
Territorial jurisdiction, §19.2-44.
Training standards, §19.2-38.1.
Transitional provisions, §§19.2-26 to 19.2-29.
Unlawful entry and detainer.
Issuance of summons, §8.01-126.
Validation of former Tile 39.1 notices, recognizances and processes, §19.2-28.
Vested of authority of prior office, §19.2-33.
Warrantless arrests.
Personal appearance before magistrate, §19.2-82.
Warrant or process issued in complaint of relative prohibited, §19.2-37.

MAGNESIUM.
Agricultural liming materials, §3.2-3706.
Defined terms, §3.2-3700.
Pesticide control, §§3.2-3939, 3.2-3940.

MAIDEN NAME.
Restoration upon decree of divorce, §20-121.4.
Recording and indexing, §55-106.1.
State corporation commission.
Documents filed with commission containing information concerning.
Deletion, removal, refusal to accept documents, §12.1-19.

MAIL.
ABC board.
Notice by mail, §4.1-101.1.
Absentee ballot applications made by, §24.2-701.
Early absentee ballot, §24.2-702.
Multiple election ballot, §24.2-703.
Absentee ballots returned by mail, §24.2-707.
Address confidentiality program.
Victims of domestic violence.
Forwarding mail to address provided by participant, §2.2-515.2.
Adult protective services.
Initial notice by certified mail, subsequent notices by regular mail, §63.2-100.1.
Agriculture and consumer services department.
Initial notice by certified mail, subsequent notices by regular mail, §3.2-101.1.
Air pollution control board.
Initial notice by certified mail, subsequent notices by regular mail, §10.1-1300.1.
Arrest warrants.
Motorist summons, §19.2-76.2.
Behavioral health and developmental services.
Rights of individuals receiving services, §37.2-400.
Campgrounds.
Initial notice by certified mail, subsequent notices by regular mail, §35.1-1.1.
Certified mail.
Equivalent to registered mail, §1-206.
Child custody proceeding.
Uniform child custody jurisdiction and enforcement act.
Giving notice of exercise of jurisdiction to person outside state, §20-146.7.

MAIL —Cont'd
Cigarette delivery sales, §§18.2-246.6 to 18.2-246.15.
See CIGARETTES.
Corporations, notice communicated by, §13.1-610.
Shareholders who share common address, §13.1-610.1.
Corrections department.
Initial notice by certified mail, subsequent notices by regular mail, §53.1-1.01.
Council of higher education.
Initial notice by certified mail, subsequent notices by regular mail, §23-276.1:1.
Criminal justice services department.
Initial notice by certified mail, subsequent notices by regular mail, §9.1-101.1.
Dam safety, flood prevention and protection assistance fund.
Initial notice by certified mail, subsequent notices by regular mail, §10.1-603.16:1.
Derelict buildings.
Notice to property owners.
Plans to remove, demolish or renovate derelict building, §15.2-907.1.
Domestic violence victims.
Address confidentiality program.
Forwarding mail to address provided by participant, §2.2-515.2.
Elections.
State board of elections.
Initial notice by certified mail, subsequent notices by regular mail, §24.2-101.01.
Electronic information delivery.
Condominiums' resale by purchasers, §55-79.97.
Satisfaction of certain information delivery requirements, §59.1-486.
Eminent domain.
Sale of condemned property to former owner.
Offer to sell, method of sending, §25.1-108.
Environmental quality department.
Initial notice by certified mail, subsequent notices by regular mail, §10.1-1182.1.
Financial institutions.
Initial notice by certified mail, subsequent notices by regular mail, §6.2-101.1.
Fire insurance policies, notice of cancellation or refusal to renew, §38.2-2113.
Forensic science department.
Initial notice by certified mail, subsequent notices by regular mail, §9.1-1100.1.
Forestry department.
Initial notice by certified mail, subsequent notices by regular mail, §10.1-1100.1.
Goods sent by mail, §11-2.1.
Groundwater management.
Water control board.
Initial notice by certified mail, subsequent notices by regular mail, §62.1-255.1.
Hotels.
Initial notice by certified mail, subsequent notices by regular mail, §35.1-1.1.
Insurance commissioner.
Initial notice by certified mail, subsequent notices by regular mail, §38.2-100.1.
Inventories and accounts of fiduciaries.
Copies of inventories to be provided, §64.2-1303.
Copies of reports to be provided, §64.2-1211.
Juvenile justice department.
Initial notice by certified mail, subsequent notices by regular mail, §66-10.01.

MAIL —Cont'd
Labor and industry department.
Initial notice by certified mail, subsequent notices by regular mail, §40.1-2.01.
Localities.
Initial notice by certified mail, subsequent notices by regular mail, §15.2-107.2.
Manufactured housing.
Licensing of manufactured housing industry.
Initial notice by certified mail, subsequent notices by regular mail, §36-85.16:1.
Membership camping.
Initial notice by certified mail, subsequent notices by regular mail, §59.1-313.1.
Mines, minerals and energy department.
Initial notice by certified mail, subsequent notices by regular mail, §45.1-161.1:1.
Motor vehicle dealers.
Copy of promulgated regulations, §46.2-1506.
Motor vehicle insurance.
Cancellation or refusal to renew, §38.2-2212.
Notice of cancellation or refusal to renew, §38.2-2208.
Motor vehicles department and commissioner.
Initial notice by certified mail, subsequent notices by regular mail, §46.2-100.1.
Nonprofit corporations.
Notice by mail, when effective, §13.1-810.
Pleadings.
Copies of pleadings.
Furnishing copies to counsel, VA SCt Rule 1:12.
Professional and occupational regulation department.
Regulatory boards.
Initial notice by certified mail, subsequent notices by regular mail, §54.1-101.1.
Public aid and assistance.
Notice of earned income tax credit to recipients.
Mailing annually, §63.2-527.
Real and personal property tax bills, §58.1-3912.
Registered mail.
Certified mail equivalent to, §1-206.
Restaurants.
Initial notice by certified mail, subsequent notices by regular mail, §35.1-1.1.
Rural mail carriers stopping on highways.
Exemption to prohibition, §46.2-892.
Secretary of the Commonwealth.
Initial notice by certified mail, subsequent notices by regular mail, §2.2-401.1.
Service of notice, process and other papers.
Attachment in district court, §16.1-105.
Computation of time, VA SCt Rule 1:7.
Request for waiver of service of process, §8.01-286.1.
State corporation commission, §12.1-19.1.
Unlicensed insurers process.
Alternative method of service, §38.2-803.
Social Security numbers.
Government data collection and dissemination practices act.
Mail not to display or reveal, §2.2-3808.
Social services, local departments.
Initial notice by certified mail, subsequent notices by regular mail, §63.2-100.1.
Soil and water conservation board.
Initial notice by certified mail, subsequent notices by regular mail, §10.1-500.1.
State board of elections.
Initial notice by certified mail, subsequent notices by regular mail, §24.2-101.01.

MAIL —Cont'd
State corporation commission.
Service of process by commission, §12.1-19.1.
Tax assessments, report forms and correspondence mailed by commission deemed delivered, §12.1-43.
State departments and agencies.
Centralized mail handling.
Division of support services, general services department, §2.2-1169.
Subsequent notices sent by regular mail, §1-206.
Summer camps.
Initial notice by certified mail, subsequent notices by regular mail, §35.1-1.1.
Supreme court.
Filing by mail, VA SCt Rule 5:5.
Tax commissioner or department of taxation.
Initial notice by certified mail, subsequent notices by regular mail, §58.1-105.1.
Tax returns or payment of taxes.
Filing by mail, §58.1-9.
Time computation.
Service of notice, process and other papers, VA SCt Rule 1:7.
Toll bridges and roads.
Invoice for failure to pay toll, mailing, §46.2-819.7.
Transportation board.
Initial notice by certified mail, subsequent notices by regular mail, §33.1-13.04.
Transportation department.
Initial notice by certified mail, subsequent notices by regular mail, §33.1-13.04.
Trusts.
First-class mail.
Permissible method of notice or sending documents, §64.2-707.
U. S. mail vehicles.
Flashing amber warning lights, §46.2-1025.
Victims of domestic violence.
Address confidentiality program.
Forwarding mail to address provided by participant, §2.2-515.2.
Voter registration, §§24.2-416.1 to 24.2-416.6.
See VOTER REGISTRATION.
Waste management.
Initial notice by certified mail, subsequent notices by regular mail, §10.1-1400.1.
Water control board.
Initial notice by certified mail, subsequent notices by regular mail, §§62.1-44.3:1, 62.1-255.1.
Workers' compensation commission.
Initial notice by certified mail, subsequent notices by regular mail, §65.2-101.1.

MAIL BOMBS.
Manufacture, possession, use, etc., of fire bombs or explosive devices, §18.2-85.

MAILBOX RULE.
Fire insurance policies, notice of cancellation or refusal to renew, §38.2-2113.

MAIL CARRIERS.
Carrying concealed weapons.
Inapplicability of provisions to rural mail carriers, §18.2-308.
Militia duty exemption, §44-5.
Notaries public.
Federal employees prohibited, exception, §2.2-2801.

MAIL CARRIERS —Cont'd
Rural or star route mail carriers.
Mail vehicles.
Flashing amber warning lights, §46.2-1025.
Stopping on highways, §46.2-892.

MAILING LISTS.
Motor vehicle registration and title, §46.2-210.
Personal information privacy, §§59.1-442 to 59.1-444.

MAIL ORDERS.
Cigarette delivery sales, §§18.2-246.6 to 18.2-246.15.
See CIGARETTES.

MAIMING.
Aggravated malicious wounding, §18.2-51.2.
Animal or fowl, §18.2-144.
Boating under the influence.
Watercraft operation, §18.2-51.5.
Discretionary felony sentencing guidelines, §17.1-805.
Driving while intoxicated, §18.2-51.4.
Emergency medical services personnel.
Malicious wounding, §18.2-51.1.
Law enforcement officers, malicious bodily injury to, §18.2-51.1.
Lesser offenses, conviction under certain indictments, §18.2-54.
Mayhem act, §18.2-51.
Mobs, shooting, stabbing, etc., with intent to maim, kill, etc., §§18.2-41, 18.2-42.1.
Person twice previously convicted of certain violent felonies, §19.2-297.1.
Search and rescue personnel.
Malicious wounding, §18.2-51.1.
Shooting, stabbing, etc., with intent to maim, kill, etc., §18.2-51.

MAINTENANCE CONTRACTS.
Retail sales and use tax service exemptions, §58.1-609.5.

MAIZE.
Corn, §§3.2-1400 to 3.2-1414.
See CORN.

MAJOR BUSINESS FACILITY JOB TAX CREDIT, §58.1-439.

MAJOR EMPLOYMENT AND INVESTMENT PROJECT SITE PLANNING GRANT FUND, §2.2-2240.2.

MAJOR INFORMATION TECHNOLOGY PROJECT.
Secretary of technology.
Agency responsibility, §2.2-225.

MAJOR LEAGUE BASEBALL.
Admissions tax to games and events, §§58.1-3817, 58.1-3818.
Surcharge on admissions, §58.1-3840.
Virginia baseball stadium authority, §§15.2-5800 to 15.2-5819.

MAKEHAMIZED MORTALITY TABLE.
Commutation and valuation of certain estates and interests, §55-274.

MALFEASANCE.
Centralized purchasing violations by officers, §2.2-1115.
Commissioners of revenue.
False entries in books, §58.1-3121.

MALFEASANCE —Cont'd
County or city treasurers.
Omission of taxes from delinquent list, §58.1-3936.
Impeachment of appointed or elected officers, VA Const Art IV §17.
Limitation of prosecutions, §19.2-8.
Prisoner employment and training.
Intentional violations, §53.1-51.
Prison-made goods and services.
Intentional violations of sale requirements, §53.1-51.
Public officers and employees.
Conflicts of interest.
Knowing violations, §2.2-3122.
Public school funds.
Limitation on expenditures, §22.1-91.
Removal from office.
Governor's power to remove, §2.2-108.
Search warrants.
Issuing general search warrant, §19.2-55.
Issuing search warrant without affidavit, §19.2-55.
Search without warrant, §19.2-59.
Statute of limitations.
Criminal prosecutions, §19.2-8.
Transportation districts.
Liability of Commonwealth, counties or cities, §15.2-4526.
Tort liability, §33.1-442.
Virginia Commonwealth University health system authority.
Removal of members of board of directors, §23-50.16:5.
Warrants issued by school board members, clerks or deputy clerks.
Violations of provisions, §22.1-122.

MALICE.
Intoxicated drivers injuring persons.
Exemplary damages, §8.01-44.5.

MALICIOUS MISCHIEF.
Warrantless arrests.
Arrest without warrant authorized, §19.2-81.

MALICIOUS PROSECUTION.
Audiovisual recording of motion picture in commercial theater.
Unlawful, arrest or detention by theater owner.
No civil liability, §18.2-187.2.
Bad checks, drafts or orders.
Evidence and presumptions, §18.2-185.
Limitation of actions.
When action deemed to accrue, §8.01-249.
Shoplifting suspect's arrest or detention.
Exemption from civil liability of merchant, agent or employee, §8.01-226.9.
Statute of limitations.
When cause of action deemed to accrue, §8.01-249.

MALICIOUS WOUNDING.
Aggravated malicious wounding, §18.2-51.2.
Attempts to poison, §18.2-54.1.
Caustic substance or agent or explosive or fire causing malicious bodily injury, §18.2-52.
Discretionary felony sentencing guidelines, §17.1-805.
Driving while intoxicated, §18.2-51.4.
Emergency medical services personnel, §18.2-51.1.
Firefighters, §18.2-51.1.
Juvenile serious or habitual offender comprehensive action program (SHOCAP), §§16.1-330.1, 16.1-330.2

MALICIOUS WOUNDING —Cont'd
Law enforcement officers, malicious bodily injury to, §18.2-51.1.
Lesser offenses, conviction under certain indictments, §18.2-54.
Pregnant women.
Aggravated malicious wounding, §18.2-51.2.
Prisoners, probationers or parolees.
Bodily injuries caused by, §18.2-55.
Reckless endangerment by throwing objects from places higher than one story, §18.2-51.3.
Search and rescue personnel, §18.2-51.1.
Sentencing of person twice previously convicted of certain violent felonies, §19.2-297.1.
Shooting, stabbing, etc., in committing or attempting felony, §18.2-53.
Shooting, stabbing, etc., with intent to maim, kill, etc., §18.2-51.
Use or display of firearm in committing felony, §18.2-53.1.

MALL GUARDS.
Private security services businesses.
Exceptions, §9.1-140.

MALLS.
Energy allocation equipment, §§56-245.2, 56-245.3.
Fire alarms.
Maliciously activating, §18.2-212.
List of tenants.
Filing requirements, §58.1-3901.
Removal of carts from store premises, §18.2-102.1.
Smoke bombs.
Setting off in public buildings, §18.2-87.1.
Submetering, §§56-245.2, 56-245.3.

MALPRACTICE.
Attorneys at law, offense resulting in loss of property.
Retention of license conditioned on maintenance of malpractice insurance, §54.1-3935.
Birth-related neurological injury compensation, §§38.2-5000 to 38.2-5021.
See BIRTH-RELATED NEUROLOGICAL INJURY COMPENSATION.
Definitions.
Term has filed, §8.01-581.12:2.
Medical malpractice.
General provisions, §§8.01-581.1 to 8.01-581.20.
See MEDICAL MALPRACTICE.
Medical malpractice insurance.
Joint underwriting association, §§38.2-2800 to 38.2-2814.
Real estate settlement agents.
Malpractice insurance.
Duty to maintain, amount, §55-525.20.
Sexual sterilization, §54.1-2979.

MALT BEVERAGES.
ABC act.
Generally, §§4.1-100 to 4.1-354.
Administration of licenses.
Generally, §§4.1-200 to 4.1-240.
Alcoholic beverages.
Generally.
See ALCOHOLIC BEVERAGES.
Licenses.
See ALCOHOLIC BEVERAGE LICENSES.

MALT BEVERAGES —Cont'd
Beer bottler licenses.
Authorized conduct, §4.1-208.
Local license taxes, §4.1-233.
State license fees, §§4.1-231, 4.1-232.
Beer franchises, §§4.1-500 to 4.1-517.
See BEER FRANCHISES.
Beer importer licenses.
Authorized conduct, §4.1-208.
Limitation on license, §4.1-218.
Local license taxes, §4.1-233.
State license fees, §§4.1-231, 4.1-232.
Litter tax imposed on manufacturers, wholesalers, distributors or retailers, §58.1-1708.

MALT VINEGAR.
Generally, §§3.2-5500 to 3.2-5507.

MAMMOGRAMS.
Development of film.
Time limits, §32.1-229.
Health insurance.
Public officers and employees.
Required coverage, §2.2-2818.
Health insurance coverage, §38.2-3418.1.
Inspections of mammography centers, §32.1-229.
Medical service plans, §32.1-325.
Notice to be included for patients with dense breast tissue, §32.1-229.
Time limits for development of film, §32.1-229.

MANAGED CARE HEALTH INSURANCE PLANS, §§38.2-5800 to 38.2-5811.
Access to care, §38.2-5807.
Certificates of quality assurance, §§32.1-137.1 to 32.1-137.6.
Application by licensee for, §32.1-137.2.
Civil penalties for violations, §32.1-137.5.
Complaint system, §32.1-137.6.
Definitions, §32.1-137.1.
Denial, §32.1-137.2.
Examination or review of licensees certified under provisions, §32.1-137.4.
Issuance, §32.1-137.2.
Penalties for noncompliance with provisions, §32.1-137.5.
Regulations, §32.1-137.3.
Renewal, §32.1-137.2.
Revocation or nonrenewal, §32.1-137.5.
Suspension, §32.1-137.5.
Claims submission.
Failure of in-network provider to submit claims.
Liability of patient for unbilled health care services, §8.01-27.5.
Complaint system, §38.2-5804.
Conflict of laws, §38.2-5810.
Contracts.
Controversies involving contracts, §38.2-5811.
Provider contracts, §38.2-5805.
Definitions, §§38.2-5800, 38.2-5806.
Certificates of quality assurance, §32.1-137.1.
Disclosures and representations to enrollees, §38.2-5803.
Discrimination.
Prohibited practices, §38.2-5806.
Enrollees.
Disclosures and representations to, §38.2-5803.
Establishment, §38.2-5802.
Examinations, §38.2-5808.
General provisions, §38.2-5801.

MANAGED CARE HEALTH INSURANCE PLANS —Cont'd
Health maintenance organizations.
Compliance by health maintenance organizations, §38.2-5801.
Internal appeal process and external review.
Utilization review, §§38.2-3556 to 38.2-3571.
See HEALTH INSURANCE.
Laboratory tests or other examinations.
Copy of results to insurer, §54.1-2409.4.
Licenses of health carriers.
Suspension or revocation, §38.2-5809.
Prohibited practices, §38.2-5806.
Provider contracts, §38.2-5805.
Utilization review.
See HEALTH INSURANCE.
Virginia Commonwealth University health system authority.
General provisions, §§23-50.16:1 to 23-50.16:35.
See VIRGINIA COMMONWEALTH UNIVERSITY HEALTH SYSTEM AUTHORITY.

MANAGEMENT AND EXCLUSIVE AGENCY CONTRACTS.
Insurance companies, approval by state corporation commission, §38.2-203.

MANAGEMENT, LIMITED LIABILITY COMPANIES, §§13.1-1022 to 13.1-1028.

MANAGEMENT OF INSTITUTIONAL FUNDS, §§64.2-1100 to 64.2-1108.
Applicability of act.
Electronic signatures in global and national commerce act, §64.2-1107.
Existing funds, §64.2-1106.
Uniform application, §64.2-1108.
Appropriate and reasonable costs.
Incurring, §64.2-1101.
Appropriate or accumulate endowment.
Decision, §64.2-1102.
Care of ordinarily prudent person.
Decision to appropriate or accumulate endowment fund, §64.2-1102.
Delegation of management and investment functions, §64.2-1103.
Standard in managing and investing funds, §64.2-1101.
Charitable purposes.
Considered in managing and investing funds, §64.2-1101.
Defined, §64.2-1100.
Committees, officers or employees.
Delegation of functions to, §64.2-1103.
Compliance with article.
Determining, §64.2-1105.
Construction of act, §64.2-1108.
Decisions after receiving property, §64.2-1101.
Definitions, §64.2-1100.
Delegation of management and investment functions, §64.2-1103.
Diversification of investments, §64.2-1101.
Donor-restricted assets.
Assets in endowment fund considered, §64.2-1102.
Duty of loyalty.
Standard in managing and investing funds, §64.2-1101.
Effective date of act, §64.2-1106.
Electronic signatures in global and national commerce act.
Applicability, §64.2-1107.

MANAGEMENT OF INSTITUTIONAL FUNDS —Cont'd
Existing funds.
Applicability of article, §64.2-1106.
External agent to manage and invest fund.
Selecting, review of actions, duty owed, §64.2-1103.
Factors considered, §64.2-1101.
Decision to appropriate or accumulate endowment fund, §64.2-1102.
Good faith.
Decision to appropriate or accumulate endowment fund, §64.2-1102.
Delegation of management and investment functions, §64.2-1103.
Standard in managing and investing funds, §64.2-1101.
Impracticable or wasteful restriction.
Modification, application to court, §64.2-1104.
Individual asset decision.
Making in isolation, §64.2-1101.
Kinds of investments allowed, §64.2-1101.
Modification of restriction in gift instrument, §64.2-1104.
Permanent duration.
Words in gift instrument creating endowment fund of, §64.2-1102.
Pooling funds, §64.2-1101.
Restrictions contained in gift instrument.
Release, modification, §64.2-1104.
Rules applicable to managing and investing, §64.2-1101.
Special skills or expertise.
Duty of persons with, §64.2-1101.
Standard of conduct in managing and investing, §64.2-1101.
Uniformity of application and construction, §64.2-1108.
Unlawful, impracticable, impossible, wasteful restriction.
Modification, application to court, §64.2-1104.
Verification of facts.
Reasonable effort, §64.2-1101.

MANAGING GENERAL INSURANCE AGENTS.
Felony conviction.
Report to commission, §38.2-1357.
Fictitious name.
Report to commission, §38.2-1357.
Licensing, §§38.2-1357 to 38.2-1364.
Continuing education requirements, §38.2-1866.
Contract provisions, §38.2-1360.
Definitions, §38.2-1358.
Duties of insurers utilizing, §38.2-1361.
Examinations, §38.2-1362.
Generally, §38.2-1357.
Penalties, §38.2-1363.
Renewal, §38.2-1363.
Reports to commission, §§38.2-1357, 38.2-1364.
Required, §38.2-1359.
Revocation or suspension of license, §38.2-1363.
Reports to commission, §38.2-1357.

MANASSAS.
Arts and cultural district.
Creation, tax incentives, regulatory flexibility, powers, §15.2-1129.1.
Confederate cemeteries and graves.
Disbursement of funds appropriated for upkeep, §10.1-2211.
Fingerprinting school employees, §22.1-296.2.

MANASSAS —Cont'd
Mental health clinics.
Employees of state mental health clinics.
Supplementation of salaries and reimbursement of travel expenses, §15.2-1508.4.
Microcomputer devices.
Use to measure speed of automobile, §46.2-882.
Northern Virginia transportation authority.
Cities included, §15.2-4831.
Parking violations.
Removal or immobilization of vehicles.
Outstanding parking violations, §46.2-1216.
Personal property tax relief for elderly or handicapped.
Alternative tax rates on motor vehicles.
Ordinance to raise income and financial worth limitations, §58.1-3506.2.
Recordation tax, state.
Regional congestion relief fee, §58.1-802.2.
Retail sales and use tax.
Additional sales tax for Northern Virginia and Hampton Roads, §58.1-603.1.
Additional use tax for Northern Virginia and Hampton Roads, §58.1-604.01.
Repair of motor vehicles.
Authority to impose on labor or services, §58.1-605.
School board.
Fingerprinting applicants for employment, §22.1-296.2.
Salary of members, §22.1-32.
Snow and ice removal from public sidewalk, §15.2-2025.
Speed limit in residence district, §46.2-874.1.
Transient occupancy tax, §58.1-1742.
Well abandonment ordinance.
Duty of owner to cap or close well.
Locality adopting ordinance, §32.1-176.5.
Well construction.
Testing requirements, §32.1-176.5.

MANASSAS AIRPORT AUTHORITY, 1966 ch 288.

MANASSAS BATTLEFIELD CONFEDERATE PARK.
Property exempt from taxation, §58.1-3607.

MANASSAS PARK.
Mental health clinics.
Employees of state mental health clinics.
Supplementation of salaries and reimbursement of travel expenses, §15.2-1508.4.
Microcomputer devices.
Use to measure speed of automobile, §46.2-882.
Northern Virginia transportation authority.
Cities included, §15.2-4831.
Parking violations.
Removal or immobilization of vehicles.
Outstanding parking violations, §46.2-1216.
Personal property tax relief for elderly or handicapped.
Motor vehicles, alternative tax rates.
Ordinance raising income and financial worth limitations, §58.1-3506.2.
Recordation tax, state.
Regional congestion relief fee, §58.1-802.2.
Retail sales and use tax.
Additional sales tax for Northern Virginia and Hampton Roads, §58.1-603.1.
Additional use tax for Northern Virginia and Hampton Roads, §58.1-604.01.

MANASSAS PARK —Cont'd
Retail sales and use tax —Cont'd
Repair of motor vehicles.
Authority to impose on labor or services, §58.1-605.
School board.
Salary of members, §22.1-32.
Snow and ice removal from public sidewalk, §15.2-2025.
Transient occupancy tax, §58.1-1742.
Water and sewage systems.
Lien for charges and taxes imposed, §15.2-2118.
Well abandonment ordinance.
Duty of owner to cap or close well.
Locality adopting ordinance, §32.1-176.5.
Well construction.
Testing requirements, §32.1-176.5.

MANDAMUS.
Annexation.
Compelling city or town to carry out provisions, §15.2-3220.
Application for writ, §8.01-644.
Supreme court forum, §8.01-649.
Verified complaint or petition under oath, §8.01-644.
What petition to state, §8.01-643.
Where presented, §8.01-645.
Award of writ.
Defendant failure to appear or make defense, §8.01-646.
What judgment to be rendered, §8.01-648.
Circuit courts.
Jurisdiction, §17.1-513.
Comptroller of state.
Transportation obligations.
Writ to secure construction of act granting power to incur debt, §8.01-653.1.
Writ to secure construction of act directing payment out of state treasury, §8.01-653.
Construction of acts.
Disbursement of funds in state treasury, §8.01-653.
Incurring obligations for transportation needs, §8.01-653.1.
Courthouse repairs.
Orders of circuit court, §15.2-1643.
Court of appeals.
Jurisdiction, §17.1-404.
Dams for hydroelectric power.
Licenses.
Violation of terms, §62.1-97.
Defendant's responsive pleading, §8.01-647.
District court civil jurisdiction.
Freedom of information act proceedings, §16.1-77.
Election districts.
Reapportionment of local election districts.
Failure to reapportion, §24.2-304.4.
Franchise, privilege, lease or right to use city or town property.
Enforcing obedience, §15.2-2106.
Freedom of information act.
District court civil jurisdiction, §16.1-77.
Enforcement, §2.2-3713.
Open meetings.
Enforcement of rights and privileges, §2.2-3713.
Penalties, §2.2-3714.
Groundwater management.
Provision violations, §62.1-269.
Health.
Provision violations, §32.1-27.

MANDAMUS —Cont'd
Hydroelectric power dams.
Licenses.
Violation of terms, §62.1-97.
Jurisdiction of circuit courts, §17.1-513.
Jurisdiction of court of appeals, §17.1-404.
Jurisdiction of supreme court, §17.1-309.
Limitation of actions.
Petition for mandamus, §8.01-644.1.
Open meetings.
Freedom of information act.
Enforcement of rights and privileges, §2.2-3713.
Port authority.
Remedies of bondholders and trustees, §62.1-144.
Prisoner litigation.
Applicability of provisions, §8.01-690.
Public school funds.
Proceedings to compel settlement of accounts, §22.1-121.
Public school quality standards.
Petition for compliance with standards, §22.1-253.13:8.
Public service companies.
Remedies of persons aggrieved by, §56-6.
Public works.
Transportation obligations.
Writ to secure construction of act granting power to incur debt, §8.01-653.1.
Renewable energy.
Small renewable energy projects.
Enforcement of provisions, §10.1-1197.9.
Sanitation districts law of 1938.
Discharges into tidal waters, §21-220.
Service district commission.
Jurisdiction of circuit courts in matters or proceedings, §17.1-131.
Small renewable energy projects.
Enforcement of provisions, §10.1-1197.9.
State board of elections.
Power to petition for, §24.2-103.
State corporation commission.
Remedies of persons aggrieved by public service companies, §56-6.
Writs lie from supreme court to commission, §12.1-39.
State departments and agencies.
Refusal to adopt uniform system of financial accounting, §2.2-803.
Statute of limitations.
Petition for mandamus, §8.01-644.1.
Supreme court.
Jurisdiction, §17.1-309, VA SCt Rule 5:7, VA Const Art VI §1.
When writ to issue and be tried, §17.1-311.
Taxes on suits or writ taxes generally, §§58.1-1727 to 58.1-1729.
Transportation district bondholders.
Protection and enforcement of rights, §15.2-4519.
Treasurer of state.
Writ to secure construction of act directing payment out of state treasury, §8.01-653.
Urban county executive form of government.
Election districts.
Reapportionment, change of boundaries of election districts, §15.2-857.
Venue.
Preferred forum, §8.01-261.
Virginia Commonwealth University health system authority.
Remedies of obligees of authority, §23-50.16:29.

MANDAMUS —Cont'd
Water pollution control enforcement, §62.1-44.23.

MANDATES.
Assessment of mandates imposed on localities.
State agencies to assess, §2.2-613.
Implementation of federal mandates act, §§2.2-615 to 2.2-619.
Temporary suspension by governor, §2.2-113.

MANDATORY MINIMUM.
Anabolic steroids.
Manufacturing, selling or distributing, §18.2-248.5.
Controlled substances.
Distribution to persons under 18, §18.2-255.
Manufacturing, selling, distributing or possessing, §18.2-248.
Possession of firearm while in possession of controlled substance, §18.2-308.4.
Sale, gift, distribution or possession, §18.2-248.1.
Sale near certain properties, §18.2-255.2.
Transporting into Commonwealth, §18.2-248.01.
Convicted felons possessing firearms or explosives, §18.2-308.2.
Driving while intoxicated, §18.2-270.
Firearm, stun weapon or other weapon.
Possession of firearm while in possession of controlled substance, §18.2-308.4.
Possession on school property, §18.2-308.1.
Forcible sodomy of person less than 13.
Offender more than 3 years older than victim, §18.2-67.1.
Gang activity in school zone.
Enhanced punishment, §18.2-46.3:3.
Rape of child under age of 13.
Offender more than 3 years older than victim, §18.2-61.
Sentencing.
Assault and battery, §18.2-57.
Definition, court required to impose full punishment, §18.2-12.1.
Entering property of another for purposes of damaging.
Property intentionally selected because of race, religion, color or national origin of owner, §18.2-121.
Shooting at law enforcement, fire, rescue or emergency medical vehicles, §18.2-154.
Use or display of firearm in committing felony, §18.2-53.1.

MANDATORY RETIREMENT.
State corporation commission, VA Const Art IX §1.

MAN-MADE DISASTERS.
Architects.
Rescue or relief assistance.
Civil immunity for licensed professional architects, §8.01-226.2.
Emergency management and disaster law generally, §§44-146.13 to 44-146.28.
See EMERGENCY MANAGEMENT.
Engineers.
Rescue or relief assistance.
Civil immunity for licensed professional engineers, §8.01-226.2.

MANSLAUGHTER.
Bar to claiming property rights of decedent, §§64.2-2500 to 64.2-2511.

MANSLAUGHTER —Cont'd
Commercial motor vehicles.
Disqualification to drive.
Death direct result of operating commercial vehicle, §46.2-341.18.
Declared felony, §18.2-30.
Discretionary felony sentencing guidelines, §17.1-805.
Driver license compact.
Statutes and ordinances deemed to cover offense, §46.2-487.
Drivers' licenses.
Disqualification to drive commercial vehicle.
Death direct result of operating commercial vehicle, §46.2-341.18.
One year revocation upon suspension, §46.2-389.
Persons convicted not to be licensed, §46.2-316.
Indictments, presentments or informations.
Statutory short form of indictment, §19.2-221.
Involuntary manslaughter.
Certain conduct punishable as, §18.2-36.1.
Discharging firearm or missile within building or dwelling.
Death resulting, act not malicious, §18.2-279.
Injuring railroad signals.
Death resulting, act not malicious, §18.2-155.
Obstructing or injuring canal, railroad, power line, etc.
Death resulting, §18.2-153.
Operating watercraft or motorboat while under the influence, §18.2-36.2.
Punishment, §18.2-36.
Shooting at or throwing missiles at trains, cars, vessels, etc.
Death resulting, act not malicious, §18.2-154.
Limitation of prosecutions.
No limitation, §19.2-8.1.
Mob crimes, §18.2-42.1.
Murder indictment.
Verdict when accused found guilty of punishable homicide, §19.2-288.
Residential property transfer disclosures.
Actions for failure to disclose, §55-524.
Slayer's act, §§64.2-2500 to 64.2-2511.
Voluntary manslaughter.
Punishment, §18.2-35.
Sentencing of person twice previously convicted of certain violent felonies, §19.2-297.1.

MANUAL FOR COURTS-MARTIAL, UNITED STATES.
Incorporated as part of military laws, §44-40.
Trials and proceedings of national guard courts-martial to be in accordance with, §44-48.

MANUAL WHEELCHAIRS.
Assistive technology device warranties, §§59.1-470 to 59.1-474.

MANUFACTURED HOME LOT RENTAL, §§55-248.41 to 55-248.52.
Abandoned homes, §55-248.44:1.
Applicability of residential landlord and tenant provisions, §55-248.48.
Commission on sale of home located in park.
Landlord demanding or collecting, §55-248.45.
Commission prohibitions, §55-248.45.
Defined terms, §55-248.41.
Reasonable charges in addition to rent, §55-248.44:1.
Security interests, §55-248.44:1.

MANUFACTURED HOME LOT RENTAL —Cont'd
Entrance fee.
Prohibition, §55-248.45.
Evictions, §55-248.50:1.
Limitations, §55-248.46.
Right to sell home upon, §55-248.50:2.
Exit fee.
Prohibition, §55-248.45.
Fee prohibitions, §55-248.45.
Utility service charges, §55-248.45:1.
Free access to tenant's home site, §55-248.45.
Injunctive relief for violations, §55-248.52.
Landlord's obligations, §55-248.43.
Leases of home by owner, §55-248.47.
Local government powers, §55-248.49.
Notice to vacate the premises.
Rental agreement changes shall constitute, §55-248.42.
Rent, §55-248.44:1.
Home sales upon eviction.
Liability for rent, §55-248.50:2.
Retaliatory conduct prohibitions, §55-248.50.
Rental agreements.
Automatic renewal, §55-248.42:1.
Copies to tenants, §55-248.42.
Period of tenancy, §55-248.42:1.
Provisions, §55-248.42.
Retaliatory conduct prohibitions, §§55-248.50, 55-248.50:1.
Terminations, §55-248.46.
Waiver of landlord's right to terminate, §55-248.46:1.
Writing required, §55-248.42.
Retaliatory conduct, §§55-248.50 to 55-248.52.
Sale of home by owner, §55-248.47.
Security deposits, §55-248.42:1.
Security interests.
Abandoned homes, §55-248.44:1.
Home sales upon eviction.
Rent liability, §55-248.50:2.
Notice to landlord of changes, §55-248.42.
Rent liability, §55-248.44:1.
Tenant's obligations, §55-248.44.
TV services providers.
Fee or charge from.
Landlord demanding or collecting, §55-248.45.
Service agreement with, §55-248.45.
Utility service charges, §55-248.45:1.
Vendor restriction prohibitions, §55-248.45.

MANUFACTURED HOUSING, §§36-85.2 to 36-85.36.
Burning or destroying manufactured homes, §18.2-77.
Construction and safety standards, §§36-85.2 to 36-85.15.
Applicability of local ordinances, §36-85.11.
Citation of title, §36-85.2.
Civil and criminal penalties, §36-85.12.
Definitions, §36-85.3.
Enforcement, §§36-85.5, 36-85.11.
Federal standards and regulations, §36-85.6.
Fees, §36 85.14.
Length, §46.2-1115.
Rulemaking authority, §§36-85.7 to 36-85.10.
Authority of board, §36-85.7.
Notice and hearing, §36-85.8.
Printing and distribution, §36-85.9.
Public access to rules, §36-85.10.
Severability of act, §36-85.15.

MANUFACTURED HOUSING —Cont'd
Construction and safety standards —Cont'd
Short title, §36-85.2.
Staff, equipment or supplies, §36-85.13.
Title of act, §36-85.2.
Violations, §36-85.12.
Definitions.
Construction and safety standards, §36-85.3.
Licensing of manufactured housing industry, §36-85.16.
Disabled vehicle in highway, §46.2-111, VA SCt Rule 3B:2.
Ejectment.
Authority of law enforcement personnel to remove or dispose of manufactured home, §8.01-156.
Entering dwelling with intent to commit larceny, assault and battery or other felony, §18.2-91.
Fair housing law, §§36-96.1 to 36-96.23.
Federal standards and regulations.
Construction and safety standards, §36-85.6.
Homeowner's insurance policies.
Set-up requirements, §36-85.22.
Length, §46.2-1115.
Licensing of manufactured housing industry, §§36-85.16 to 36-85.30.
Board.
Creation, §36-85.17.
Defined, §36-85.16.
Membership, §36-85.17.
Powers and duties, §36-85.18.
Common law remedies not excluded, §36-85.30.
Dealer alterations, §36-85.26.
Definitions, §36-85.16.
Disciplinary action against licensees.
Grounds, §36-85.20.
Notice and hearing, §36-85.21.
Disclosure to buyer, §36-85.28.
Failure of buyer to accept delivery.
Actual damages retained by dealer, §36-85.28.
Grounds for disciplinary action against licensees, §36-85.20.
Inspection of service records, §36-85.29.
Insurance policies.
Effect of set-up requirements, §36-85.22.
License required, §36-85.19.
Limitation on damages, §36-85.28.
Notices by mail, §36-85.16:1.
Presentment of claim for warranties and defects, §36-85.24.
Revocation upon payment from fund, §36-85.36.
Set-up requirements, §36-85.22.
Towing assembly (hitch).
Advertisement or communication regarding length, §36-85.27.
Unlicensed operation, §36-85.19.
Warranties.
Dealer alterations, §36-85.26.
Limitation on damages, §36-85.28.
Presentment claims for warranties and defects, §36-85.24.
Service agreements, §36-85.25.
Warranty requirements for manufacturer, dealer and supplier, §36-85.23.
Warranty service, §36-85.25.
Notices by mail.
Licensing of manufactured housing industry, §36-85.16:1.
Permit before moving to place where to be used as place of residence, §58.1-3520.

MANUFACTURED HOUSING —Cont'd
Personal property taxes.
Assessment method, §58.1-3522.
Classification of manufactured homes, §58.1-3503.
Moving manufactured home to place to be used as place of residence.
Payment of property taxes before moving, §58.1-3520.
Proration of tax, §58.1-3521.
Rulemaking authority.
Federal standards and regulations, §36-85.6.
Skirting, §36-99.8.
Subdivisions.
Applicability of subdivision ordinance, §15.2-2247.
Transaction recovery fund, §§36-85.31 to 36-85.36.
Administrative regulations, §36-85.36.
Appeals from decision of board, §36-85.35.
Claim process, §36-85.32.
Disciplinary action by board, §§36-85.33 to 36-85.36.
Appeals from adverse decisions, §36-85.35.
Revocation of license upon payment from fund, §36-85.36.
Violation of provisions, §36-85.34.
Establishment, §36-85.31.
Maximum claim, §36-85.32.
Recovery from fund generally, §36-85.32.
Revocation of license.
Upon payment from fund, §36-85.33.
Rulemaking authority, §36-85.36.
Schedule of assessment fees, §36-85.31.
Zoning.
Mobile home parks.
Replacement of home due to nonconforming use, §15.2-2307.
Regulations to be uniform, §15.2-2290.

MANUFACTURED HOUSING BOARD.
Creation, §36-85.17.
Defined, §36-85.16.
Membership, §36-85.17.
Powers and duties, §36-85.18.

MANUFACTURED HOUSING TRANSACTION RECOVERY FUND, §§36-85.31 to 36-85.36.

MANUFACTURERS OF AIRCRAFT ENGINE.
Grants.
Aerospace engine manufacturer workforce training grant fund, §59.1-284.22.
Aerospace engine manufacturing performance grant program, §59.1-284.20.
Aerospace engine manufacturing supplier bonus performance grant program, §59.1-284.21.

MANUFACTURERS OF CIGARETTES IN STATE.
Certification of compliance with escrow requirement, §3.2-4201.
Civil action for failure to place funds into escrow, §3.2-4201.
Civil penalty for failure to comply, §3.2-4201.
Fire-safe cigarettes, §§59.1-293.1 to 59.1-293.9.
See FIRE-SAFE CIGARETTES.
Master settlement agreement, §§3.2-4200 to 3.2-4219.
Defined, §3.2-4200.
Generally.
See TOBACCO PRODUCTS MANUFACTURERS' RESPONSIBILITIES.
Required to become participating manufacturer, §3.2-4201.

MANUFACTURERS OF CIGARETTES IN STATE —Cont'd
Prohibition from selling cigarettes to consumers.
Second violation, §3.2-4201.
Qualified escrow fund, §3.2-4200.
Assignment and contribution of escrow funds to Commonwealth, §§3.2-4202, 3.2-4203.
Required to placed funds into, §3.2-4201.
Release of funds from escrow, §3.2-4201.
Requirements generally, §3.2-4201.

MANUFACTURERS OF CLEAN ENERGY PRODUCTS.
Clean energy manufacturing incentive grant program, §§59.1-284.25 to 59.1-284.27.

MANUFACTURERS OF MACHINE GUNS.
Inspection of stock, §18.2-294.
Register, §18.2-294.

MANUFACTURERS OF PRESCRIPTION DRUGS.
Distribution of drugs by manufacturer or wholesalers.
Generally, §54.1-3415.
Indigent patient programs offered by pharmaceutical manufacturers.
Practitioner of medicine or osteopathy participating in, §54.1-3301.
Permits, §§54.1-3437 to 54.1-3442.

MANUFACTURERS OF SAWED-OFF FIREARMS.
Inspection of stock upon demand, §18.2-304.
Register, §18.2-304.

MANUFACTURING DEVELOPMENT COMMISSION.
Annual report, §30-276.
Chairman and vice-chairman, §30-275.
Energy plan for Commonwealth.
Development, §30-276.
Established in legislative branch, §30-275.
Executive summary, §30-276.
Meetings, quorum, recommendations, voting on, §30-275.
Membership, §30-275.
Powers and duties, §30-276.
Purpose, §30-275.
Staffing, §30-275.

MANUFACTURING, MACHINERY AND TOOLS TAX, §§58.1-3507, 58.1-3508.

MANUFACTURING MARIJUANA, §18.2-248.1.
Synthetic cannabinoids, §18.2-248.1:1.

MANURE.
Nutrient management plans.
See NUTRIENT MANAGEMENT PLANS.
Renewable electricity production program.
Grants, §§67-900 to 67-903.
Tenant removal or manufacture.
Waste, §55-215.

MANURE APPLICATORS.
Income tax credit for purchase of advanced technology equipment, §58.1-337.

MAPLE SYRUP URINE DISEASE, §§32.1-65 to 32.1-67.1.
Commissioner to notify physician, §32.1-66.
Records.
Confidentiality, §32.1-67.1.

MAPLE SYRUP URINE DISEASE —Cont'd
Reports.
Physicians discovering to report to commissioner, §32.1-66.
Tests.
Subjection of infants to tests, §32.1-65.
Treatment.
Provision by board of health, §32.1-67.
MAPS.
Agricultural and forestal districts.
Application for creation or addition to district, §15.2-4303.
Comprehensive plan, §15.2-2224.
Coordinate system of Virginia.
Use of names, §55-295.
Dam safety.
Dam break inundation zones, §10.1-606.2.
Drainage projects.
Drainage map, §21-330.
Profile of each levee, etc., §21-331.
Geographic information network, §§2.2-2025 to 2.2-2030.
See INFORMATION TECHNOLOGIES AGENCY.
Highways and roads, §33.1-36.
Secondary system of state highways, §33.1-84.
Indexing subdivision plats or maps, §17.1-251.
Mineral mine licenses.
Failure to submit.
Authority of director to have one made at operator's expense, §45.1-161.292:38.
Required, §45.1-161.292:37.
Mineral mine safety.
Denial of entry, §45.1-161.292:59.
Planning and development.
Official maps, §§15.2-2233 to 15.2-2238.
Prescribed burn prescription.
Inclusion of map, §10.1-1150.4.
Recording in plat book, §17.1-236.
Validation of recording, §17.1-237.
Sanitation districts law of 1938.
Plans, maps, etc., to be available to commission, §21-214.
Sanitation districts law of 1946.
Plans, maps, etc., to be available to commission, §21-283.
State highway plat book, §17.1-238.
Subdivision maps, indexing, §17.1-251.
Transportation department.
Preparation at request and expense of local governing bodies or other groups, §33.1-222.
Unified or centralized system for geographic information.
Locality requiring by ordinance, §15.2-962.
Uranium ore exploration.
Maps or plats of proposed exploration activity area, §45.1-275.
Winter sports safety act.
Trail maps, §8.01-227.13.

MARIJUANA.
Carrying concealed weapons.
Disqualification for concealed weapons permit, §18.2-308.09.
Chemical analysis of plant material.
Motion by accused prior to trial.
Full chemical analysis, §19.2-188.1.
Custody of substances, law-enforcement agencies, §19.2-386.25.
Disposal of seized substances, marijuana and paraphernalia, §19.2-386.23.
Destruction prior to trial, §19.2-386.24.

MARIJUANA —Cont'd
Distribution or sale, §18.2-248.1.
Synthetic cannabinoids, §18.2-248.1:1.
Drug houses.
Maintaining fortified drug houses, §18.2-258.02.
Drug offenses generally, §§18.2-247 to 18.2-264.
See DRUG OFFENSES.
Drug paraphernalia.
Offenses generally, §§18.2-265.1 to 18.2-265.5.
Field tests conducted by law enforcement.
Testimony as to results, §19.2-188.1.
Testimony at preliminary hearing, §19.2-188.1.
Firearms.
Possession of firearm while committing offense, §18.2-308.4.
Purchase or transportation by person convicted of certain misdemeanor drug offenses, §18.2-308.1:5.
First time offenders.
Substance abuse screening, assessment or testing, §18.2-254.
Forfeiture of property used in connection with or derived from illegal drug transaction, §19.2-386.22.
Fraud, deceit, misrepresentation, embezzlement or subterfuge.
Obtaining drugs or procuring administration by, §18.2-258.1.
Juvenile detention and other care facilities.
Detainees, delivery to, §18.2-474.1.
Medical purposes, possession or distribution for, §18.2-251.1.
Minors, distributing instruments for use in administering to, §18.2-255.1.
Minors, liability of drug dealers, §§8.01-227.4 to 8.01-227.7.
Minors, selling or distributing to, §18.2-255.
Noxious weed law.
Powers and duties of commissioners, §3.2-801.
Nuisances.
Premises deemed common nuisance, §§18.2-258, 18.2-258.01, 48-16, 48-17.
Obstructing justice by threats or force, §18.2-460.
Presumption as to ownership or occupancy of premises.
Unlawful possession, §18.2-250.1.
Prisoners, crimes by.
Felonies, §53.1-203.
Prisoners, delivery to, §18.2-474.1.
Accommodation distribution, §18.2-248.1.
Probationer or parolee suspected of illegal use.
Probation or parole officer's power to order testing, §53.1-145.
Local community-based probation officers, §9.1-176.1.
Probation for first time offenders, §18.2-251.
Removal of public officer from office.
Manufacture, sale, etc., §24.2-233.
Sale, §18.2-248.1.
Synthetic cannabinoids, §18.2-248.1:1.
School property, colleges campuses, libraries, etc.
Sales on or near properties, §18.2-255.2.
Schools and education.
Expulsion of students for certain drug offenses, §22.1-277.08.
Seizure of property used in connection with or derived from illegal drug transaction, §19.2-386.22.
Custody maintained by law enforcement agency.
Court ordering, §19.2-386.25.

MARIJUANA —Cont'd
Seizure of property used in connection with or derived from illegal drug transaction —Cont'd
Disposal of seized substances, marijuana and paraphernalia, §19.2-386.23.
Destruction prior to trial, §19.2-386.24.
Seizure of substances in connection with violations.
Destruction of part of substances prior to trial, §19.2-386.24.
Disposal, §19.2-386.23.
Substance abuse screening, assessment or testing.
Conviction of person not previously convicted, §18.2-254.
Defeating drug and alcohol screening tests, §18.2-251.4.
Suspension of sentence, §18.2-252.
Suspension of sentence.
Substance abuse screening, assessment or testing, §18.2-252.
Synthetic cannabinoids.
See SYNTHETIC CANNABINOIDS.
Third or subsequent felony conviction.
Distribution or selling, §18.2-248.1.
Transporting into Commonwealth, §18.2-248.01.
Unlawful possession, §18.2-250.1.
Field tests regarding identification of plant material.
Testimony by law enforcement officer as to results, §19.2-188.1.
Full chemical analysis of plant material.
Motion by accused prior to trial, §19.2-188.1.

MARIJUANA PRESCRIBED FOR MEDICAL PURPOSES, §18.2-251.1.

MARINAS.
Defrauding keepers of watercraft, §18.2-189.
Dump stations.
Signs or notices, §32.1-246.1.
Liens of keepers, §43-32.
Appeals, §43-36.
Enforcement, §43-34.
Validity, §43-35.
Lists of owners of boats.
Filing with commissioner of revenue, §58.1-3902.
Lists of tenants.
Owners or operators to file with commissioner of revenue, §58.1-3901.
Sewage facilities, §32.1-246.
State owned bottomlands.
Permits for marinas and boatyards, §28.2-1205.

MARINE ANTIFOULANT PAINTS, §§3.2-3935 to 3.2-3937.

MARINE CORPS LEAGUE.
Special license plates, §46.2-746.4.

MARINE HABITAT AND WATERWAYS IMPROVEMENT FUND, §28.2-1204.2.

MARINE INSURANCE.
Defined, §38.2-126.
Provisions relating to insurance policies and contracts generally.
Inapplicability to marine insurance other than private pleasure vessels, §38.2-300.
Rates.
Generally, §§38.2-1900 to 38.2-1928.
See INSURANCE RATES

MARINE INSURANCE AGENTS.
Licensing of agents generally, §§38.2-1822 to 38.2-1836.1.
Ocean marine agents.
Licensing without examination, §38.2-1814.

MARINE PILOTS.
Militia duty exemption, §44-5.

MARINE POLICE.
Patrol of federal safety zones, §28.2-106.1.
Radio dispatch system, §28.2-107.
Responsibilities generally, §28.2-106.
Water safety zones and restricted areas.
Authority to patrol and enforce, §28.2-106.2.

MARINE PRODUCTS BOARD, §§3.2-2700 to 3.2-2705.

MARINE PRODUCTS FUND, §3.2-2705.
Dedicated revenues, diversion, §3.2-1100.

MARINE RESOURCES COMMISSION, §§28.2-100 to 28.2-105.
Administrative process act.
Emergency regulations, exclusion from provisions, §2.2-4011.
Advisory board, §28.2-246.
Arrest without warrant, §19.2-81.
Award of grants, §28.2-245.
Bathing grounds.
Assignments, §28.2-633.
Beach assignments, §28.2-633.
Beach replenishment projects.
Expedited review of proposal and permit process, §28.2-1205.2.
Blue crab fishery management plan, §28.2-203.1.
Boating safety.
Enforcement of provisions, §29.1-745.
Coastal primary sand dunes and beaches.
Duties, §28.2-1401.
Inspections, §28.2-1417.
Monitoring, §28.2-1417.
Permits.
Exemption, Sandbridge Beach subdivision, §28.2-1408.2.
Issuance, §28.2-1406.
Time for, §28.2-1414.
Procedures, §28.2-1407.
Review, §28.2-1410.
Judicial review, §28.2-1415.
Modifications, §28.2-1413.
Procedure, §28.2-1412.
Remands, §28.2-1413.
Reversal of decisions, §28.2-1413.
When, §28.2-1411.
Standards for use, §28.2-1408.
Powers, §28.2-1401.
Provision violations.
Prosecutions, §28.2-1416.
Restoration, §28.2-1417.
Commercial fishing advisory board, §28.2-208.1.
Commissioner, §28.2-102.
Powers and duties, §28.2-104.
Crabs.
Size restrictions, §28.2-708.
Defined terms, §28.2-100.
Districts.
Creation, §28.2-222.
Officers.
Appointment, §28.2-223.
Collection of license fees, §28.2-224.

MARINE RESOURCES COMMISSION —Cont'd
Emergency regulations, exclusion from provisions, §2.2-4011.
Employees.
Legal representation in criminal prosecutions, §28.2-105.
Enforcement division, §28.2-106.
Patrol of federal safety zones, §28.2-106.1.
Establishment of fund, §28.2-245.
Federal aid in sport fish restoration act.
Assent of Commonwealth to provision, commission powers, §28.2-201.
Fishery management plans, §§28.2-201, 28.2-203.
Fishery resource grant program, §§28.2-245 to 28.2-247.
Fishery statistics.
Collection, §28.2-204.
Fishing, tidal waters generally.
See FISHING, TIDAL WATERS.
Gear licenses.
Limitations on sales, §28.2-204.1.
Handgun purchases by, §59.1-148.3.
Health and sanitation provisions.
Destruction of shellfish or crustacea, §28.2-802.
Importing fish for introduction into waters of the Commonwealth.
Approval, §28.2-825.
Inspections, §28.2-802.
Regulations, §28.2-801.
Seizures, §28.2-802.
Hearings, §28.2-216.
Findings, §28.2-218.
Judicial review, §28.2-219.
Appeals, §28.2-220.
Posting of notices, proof of, §28.2-221.
Procedure, §28.2-217.
Regulations, §28.2-211.
Jurisdiction, §28.2-101.
Law officers' retirement system.
Generally, §§51.1-211 to 51.1-221.
See LAW OFFICERS' RETIREMENT SYSTEM.
Licenses, §28.2-201.
Line of duty act, §§9.1-400 to 9.1-408.
Living shorelines.
General permit, use for stabilizing tidal shorelines, §28.2-104.1.
Meetings, §28.2-102.
Members, §28.2-102.
Office, permanent, §28.2-104.
Oysters and clams.
Area restrictions, §28.2-524.
Chesapeake Bay restrictions, §§28.2-524, 28.2-525.
Dredge contracts, §28.2-550.
Dredging claims for replanting in public clamming areas, §28.2-650.
Dredging or scraping on private ground, §28.2-515.
Failure to pay oyster resource user fees, action for, §28.2-549.
Hydraulic dredges, use, §28.2-520.
Permits to carry oysters out of state, §28.2-546.
Planting grounds, clams, §§28.2-631, 28.2-632.
Planting grounds, oysters.
Assignments, §28.2-601.
General planting grounds.
Assignments.
Recordation of plats, §28.2-617.
Leasing, §28.2-603.
Rent.
Refunds, §28.2-626.
Relief, §28.2-627.

MARINE RESOURCES COMMISSION —Cont'd
Oysters and clams —Cont'd
Public rocks.
Opening and closing, §28.2-507.
Shells.
Conversion into lime, §28.2-529.
Sales, §28.2-505.
Permits.
Limitations on sales, §28.2-204.1.
Scientific collection permits, §28.2-205.
Powers, §§28.2-103, 28.2-202.
Public policy, §28.2-245.
Public safety medal of valor, §§9.1-800, 9.1-801.
Radio system.
Implementation, §28.2-107.
Regulations, §28.2-103.
Amendment petitions, §28.2-214.
Authority, §28.2-208.
Commercial fishermen registration, §28.2-243.
Emergency regulations, §28.2-210.
Promulgation petitions, §28.2-214.
Repeal petitions, §28.2-214.
Surf clams.
Enforcement, §28.2-201.
Reporting requirement, §28.2-247.
Sale of firearms by law-enforcement agencies, §59.1-148.4.
Saltwater recreational fishing.
Cooperative programs, §28.2-302.2.
Secretary of natural resources.
Agency responsibility, §2.2-215.
Submerged lands.
Authority, §28.2-1204.
Development of guidelines as to vegetation, §28.2-1204.1.
Easements, §28.2-1208.
Permits, §28.2-1205.
Encroachments, §28.2-1207.
Renewable energy leases, §28.2-1208.
Ungranted shores of the sea.
Management of lands, §28.2-1503.
Powers and duties, §28.2-1501.
Preparation of management plan, §28.2-1504.
Virginia saltwater sport fishing tournament.
Advisory committee, §28.2-207.
Promotion and development, §28.2-206.
Water safety zones and restricted areas.
Establishment of state zones, enforcement, penalty for violating, §28.2-106.2.
Wetlands.
Duties, §28.2-1301.
Inspections, §28.2-1317.
Monitoring, §28.2-1317.
Permits.
Issuance, §28.2-1306.
Time for, §28.2-1314.
Review, §§28.2-1310 to 28.2-1313.
Judicial review, §28.2-1315.
Powers, §28.2-1301.
Provision violations.
Injunctions, §28.2-1319.
Prosecutions, §28.2-1316.
Restoration, §28.2-1317.

MARINE RESOURCES DEPARTMENT.
Civil actions against employees.
Attorney general or assistant representing, §2.2-507.

MARION.
Smyth-Marion authority.
Generally.
See ECONOMIC DEVELOPMENT AUTHORITIES.

MARITAL AGREEMENTS, §20-155.

MARITAL DISSOLUTION.
Annulment generally.
See ANNULMENT OF MARRIAGE.
Divorce generally.
See DIVORCE.
Legal separation generally.
See LEGAL SEPARATION.

MARITAL FORCIBLE SODOMY, §18.2-67.1.
Discretionary felony sentencing guidelines, §17.1-805.
Jail prisoner escape or release notice, §53.1-116.1.
Prisoner intake notice, §53.1-116.1:01.
Punishment upon conviction of certain subsequent violent felony sexual assault, §18.2-67.5:3.
Person twice previously convicted of violent felony, §19.2-297.1.

MARITAL OBJECT SEXUAL PENETRATION, §18.2-67.2.
Discretionary felony sentencing guidelines, §17.1-805.
Jail prisoner escape or release notice, §53.1-116.1.
Person twice previously convicted of violent felony, §19.2-297.1.
Prisoner intake notice, §53.1-116.1:01.
Punishment upon conviction of certain subsequent violent felony sexual assault, §18.2-67.5:3.

MARITAL PROPERTY.
Agreements.
Nonprobate transfers, §64.2-620.
Dissolution of marriage, §20-107.3.
Homestead allowance waivers, §64.2-314.
Local retirement system assets.
Amenable to division or transfer by court, §51.1-802.
Virginia retirement system.
Assets, §51.1-124.4.

MARITAL RAPE, §18.2-61.
Convict escape or release notice, §53.1-160.1.
Discretionary felony sentencing guidelines, §17.1-805.
Jail prisoner escape or release notice, §53.1-116.1.
Prisoner intake notice, §53.1-116.1:01.
Punishment upon conviction of certain subsequent violent felony sexual assault, §18.2-67.5:3.
Sentencing of person twice previously convicted of certain violent felonies, §19.2-297.1.

MARITAL SEXUAL ASSAULT.
Commonwealth's attorneys.
Multidisciplinary response to sexual assault, §15.2-1627.4.
Death of victim, §18.2-63.1.
Discretionary felony sentencing guidelines, §17.1-805.
Dispositions of complaining witnesses, §18.2-67.
Physical resistance, proof not required, §18.2-67.9.
Preliminary hearings, §§19.2-218.1, 19.2-218.2.
Closing, §18.2-67.8.
Sentencing of person twice previously convicted of certain violent felonies, §19.2-297.1.

MARITAL SEXUAL ASSAULT —Cont'd
Unchaste character or prior sexual conduct of complaining witness, §18.2-67.7.
Venue, person transported through or across Commonwealth, §18.2-359.

MARITAL SHARE.
Dissolution of marriage, §20-107.3.

MARITAL STATUS DISCRIMINATION.
Discrimination generally.
See DISCRIMINATION.
Equal credit opportunities, §§6.2-500 to 6.2-513.
See EQUAL CREDIT OPPORTUNITIES.
Fair housing law, §§36-96.1 to 36-96.23.
See FAIR HOUSING.
Fire insurance policies, §§38.2-2114, 38.2-2115.
Motor vehicle insurance, §38.2-2213.
Refusal to renew, §38.2-2212.

MARKERS OF HISTORIC SITES, §§10.1-2209, 10.1-2210.

MARKET ANALYSES.
Hearsay exceptions.
Market quotations, VA SCt Rule 2:803.
Insurance companies or insurance transactions.
Confidentiality, §38.2-1317.2.

MARKETING ASSOCIATIONS.
Agricultural cooperative associations, §§13.1-313 to 13.1-345.
See AGRICULTURAL COOPERATIVE ASSOCIATIONS.

MARKETING CONTRACTS.
Agricultural cooperative associations, §13.1-329.
Recordation, §13.1-330.

MARKETING SURVEYS.
Insurance information, §38.2-605.

MARKETS, NATIONAL GUARD.
Localities providing and operating, §15.2-971.

MARKET VALUE.
Inventories and accounts of fiduciaries.
Listing property, §64.2-1300.
Sales, UCC, §§8.2-724, 8.2-725.

MARKS, AGRICULTURAL.
Generally, §§3.2-4300 to 3.2-4327.
See AGRICULTURAL GRADES, MARKS AND BRANDS.

MARKS ON CERTAIN CONTAINERS, §§59.1-93 to 59.1-102.
Appeals, §59.1-99.
Trial on appeal, §59.1-100.
Defined terms.
Person, §59.1-93.
Deposits, §59.1-101.
Description filing and publication, §59.1-94.
Certified copy as evidence, §59.1-95.
Refiling and publishing, §59.1-102.
Fees to cover expenses, §59.1-95.1.
Presumptions, §59.1-97.
Provision violations, §59.1-96.
Procedure when violation charged, §59.1-98.
Records, §59.1-102.

MARKS ON TIMBER, §§59.1-103 to 59.1-115.
See TIMBER BRANDS.

MARRIAGE, §§20-13 to 20-49.
Adultery, §18.2-365.
Committed with daughter or granddaughter, son or grandson, etc., §18.2-366.

MARRIAGE —Cont'd
Adultery —Cont'd
Divorce.
Effect of cohabitation after knowledge of adultery, §20-94.
Grounds for divorce from bond of matrimony, §20-91.
HIV or hepatitis B or C.
Testing of persons charged, §18.2-62.
Persons forbidden to marry, §18.2-366.
Prostitution, §18.2-346.
Venereal disease testing, §32.1-58.
Affirmation of marriage.
See AFFIRMATION OF MARRIAGE.
Amendment of marriage records, §20-16.1.
Annulment of marriage.
See ANNULMENT OF MARRIAGE.
Bigamy, §18.2-362.
Dissolution of prior marriage continues prohibition, §20-39.
Exceptions to provisions, §18.2-364.
Leaving Commonwealth to evade law against, §§18.2-363, 20-40.
Prohibition, §20-38.1.
Punishment for violation of prohibition, §20-40.
Void marriage, §§20-38.1, 20-43.
Breach of promise.
Action abolished, §8.01-220.
Celebration. See within this heading, "Solemnization."
Certificates. See within this heading, "License."
Change of name by reason of marriage.
Recording and indexing, §55-106.1.
Restoration by former name upon decree of divorce, §20-121.4.
Civil unions between persons of same sex.
Prohibition, arrangements performed in other states void, §20-45.3.
Common law marriage, §20-13.
Consanguineous marriages, §20-38.1.
Constitution of Virginia.
Marriage restriction, VA Const Art I §15-A.
Counselors.
Marriage and family therapists, §§54.1-3500 to 54.1-3506.
See COUNSELORS.
District court judges prohibited from serving as celebrant, §16.1-69.19.
Divorce.
See DIVORCE.
Emancipation of minor.
Entry of minor into valid marriage, necessary findings, §16.1-333.
Marriage without parental, judicial or other consent, §16.1-334.
Engagement gifts.
Limitation of suits to avoid voluntary conveyances, etc., §8.01-253.
False entry in record or registration, §18.2-207.
False statement in record or registration, §18.2-208.
Family life education in school, §22.1-207.1.
Federal reservations.
Licenses of persons on federal reservations, §20-30.
Fee for celebrating marriage, §20-27.
Gifts in consideration of marriage.
Limitation of suits to avoid voluntary conveyances, etc., §8.01-253.
Health information.
Distribution to license applicants, §32.1-69.1:1.

MARRIAGE —Cont'd
Homosexual marriages.
Marriage restriction, VA Const Art I §15-A.
Prohibition, §20-45.2.
Incestuous marriages.
Dissolution of previous marriage continues prohibition, §20-39.
Leaving Commonwealth to avoid prohibition, §20-40.
Prohibition, §20-38.1.
Punishment for violation of prohibition, §20-40.
Legitimation of children born out of wedlock.
Marriage between parents, §20-31.1.
License.
By whom to be issued, §20-14.
Criteria for issuance, §20-16.
Distribution of health information to applicants, §32.1 69.1:1.
Duration, §20-14.1.
Failure of minister to return license, §§20-21, 20-22.
Fees for issuing, §17.1-275.
Filing requirements, §20-20.
Hearsay exceptions.
Marriage licenses and certificates, VA SCt Rule 2:803.
New license, §20-14.1.
Oath of parties before clerk, §20-16.
Penalty on clerk issuing license contrary to law, §20-33.
Persons on federal reservations, §20-30.
Recording and indexing, §55-106.1.
Recording in marriage register, §17.1-233.
Required, §20-13.
Return of license.
Filing requirements, §20-20.
Sixty-day duration, §20-14.1.
Tax on license, §20-15.
Validation of marriages when license issued by clerk of county court, §20-37.
Ministers.
Attorney for the Commonwealth's ascertainment of name of minister failing to return license and certificate, §20-22.
Authorized to celebrate rites, §20-23.
Celebrating marriage without license, §20-28.
Fee for celebrating marriage, §20-27.
List of licenses not returned by minister.
Clerk to furnish to attorney for the Commonwealth, §20-21.
Penalty for failure to certify record of marriage, §20-24.
Qualifications for appointment to celebrate rite, §20-23.
Religious society having no minister, §20-26.
Name change by reason of marriage.
Recording and indexing, §55-106.1.
Restoration of former name upon decree of divorce, §20-121.4.
Performing marriage without license, §20-28.
Perjury to obtain marriage license, §18.2-434.
Persons other than ministers who may perform rites, §20-25.
Pleadings.
Effect of marriage of party, §§8.01-19, 8.01-20.
Premarital agreements, §§20-147 to 20-155.
See PREMARITAL AGREEMENTS.
Prohibited marriages, §§20-38.1, 20-45.1, 20-45.2.
Marriage restriction, VA Const Art I §15-A.
Record of marriage, §32.1-267.
Certified copies as evidence, §20-20.

MARRIAGE —Cont'd
Record of marriage —Cont'd
Corrections authorized, §20-16.1.
Failure to certify record, §20-24.
Indexing names of parties, §20-20.
Information taken under oath, §20-16.
Register.
Documents recorded in, §17.1-233.
Rites of marriage. See within this heading, "Solemnization."
Same sex marriages, §20-45.2.
Marriage restriction, VA Const Art I §15-A.
Seduction.
Action abolished, §8.01-220.
Social security numbers, blocking access to, §32.1-267.
Solemnization.
Celebrating marriage without license, §20-28.
Failure of minister to certify record of marriage, §20-24.
Federal reservations, §20-30.
Fee for celebrating marriage, §20-27.
License tax on persons authorized to solemnize.
Limitation on localities authority, §58.1-3703.
Ministers qualifying for appointment to perform ceremony, §20-23.
Order authorizing ministers to perform ceremony, §20-23.
Persons other than ministers who may perform rites, §20-25.
Religious societies having no ministers, §20-26.
Required, §20-13.
Validation of certain defects, §20-31.
Validation of certain marriages solemnized outside of Commonwealth, §20-37.1.
Validation of marriages when license issued by clerk of county court, §20-37.
Taking or detaining person with intent to compel, §18.2-355.
Tax on license, §20-15.
Trusts.
Life events affecting administration or distribution of trust.
Trustees' liability, §64.2-798.
Underage marriage with consent of parents, §§20-48, 20-49.
How consent given, §20-49.
Minimum age requirement, §20-48.
When consent required, §20-49.
Validation of marriage.
Affirmation, §20-90.
Carrying certain defects on belief of parties in lawful marriage, §20-31.
Licenses issued by clerk of county court, §20-37.
Remedial remarriage statute, §20-118.
Void marriages, §20-45.1.
Bigamous marriages, §§20-38.1, 20-43.
Consanguineous marriages, §20-38.1.
Effect of premarital agreement, §20-151.
Homosexual marriages, §20-45.2.
Incestuous marriages, §20-38.1.
Legitimation of children, §20-31.1.
Underage marriage without parental consent, §20-48.
Workers' compensation.
Report of remarriage, §65.2-712.

MARRIAGE AND FAMILY THERAPISTS, §54.1-3500.
Donation of services.
Tax credit, §58.1 439.22.

MARRIAGE AND FAMILY THERAPISTS —Cont'd
Health insurance.
Policy coverage for services, §38.2-3408.
Health services plans, coverage of services, §38.2-4221.
Licensure generally, §§54.1-3500 to 54.1-3506.
See COUNSELORS.
Privileged communications, §8.01-400.2, VA SCt Rule 2:506.
Tax credit.
Donation of services, §58.1-439.22.

MARRIAGE CONTRACTS.
Breach of promise.
Action abolished, §8.01-220.
Void contracts as to creditors and purchasers unless in writing, §11-1.
Written evidence required, §11-2.

MARRIAGE REGISTER.
Documents recorded in, §17.1-233.

MARRIED WOMEN.
Separate property of spouse.
Bank or trust company powers, §§6.2-820, 6.2-1002.

MARRIED WOMEN'S PROPERTY RIGHTS, §§55-35 to 55-47.1.
Acquiring property.
Right to, §55-35.
Attorneys-in-fact.
Appointment and powers, §55-43.
Community property.
Generally, §§64.2-315 to 64.2-324.
See COMMUNITY PROPERTY RIGHTS AT DEATH.
Contracts.
Power to contract, §55-36.
Responsibility of one spouse for contracts of the other, §55-37.
Conveyances in writing of property by husband and wife.
Effect on spouse, §55-41.
Death intestate.
Passing of estate, §55-46.
Debts of husband.
Liability of wife, §55-35.
Desertion.
Application of doctrine, §55-37.
Disposing of property.
Right to, §55-35.
Doctrine of necessaries, §55-37.
Entry into land, §55-38.
Equitable separate estates, §55-47.01.
Holding property.
Right to, §55-35.
Inherited lands.
Affect upon by husband's acts only, §55-39.
Defense of, §55-38.
Minor spouses.
Release of interest in spouse's property, §55-42.1.
Presumption of ownership of tangible personal property, §55-47.1.
Profits from real estate.
Rights of husbands, §55-35.
Residents held as tenants by the entirety.
Liens upon, §55-37.
Separate property.
Bank or trust company powers, §§6.2-820, 6.2-1002.

MARRIED WOMEN'S PROPERTY RIGHTS —Cont'd
Suits by and against, §55-36.
Right of entry into land, §55-38.
Torts of husband.
Liability, §55-37.
Using property.
Right to, §55-35.

MARSHALLING ASSETS.
Decedents' estates, §§64.2-528 to 64.2-530.
Executors and administrators.
Order in which debts of decedents to be paid, §§64.2-528 to 64.2-530.
Judgments and decrees.
Judgment liens.
Order of liability between alienees of different parts of estate, §8.01-464.

MARSHALS.
Impersonating, §18.2-174.
Machine gun manufacturer's and dealer's stock inspection, §18.2-294.
State fire marshal.
Fire prevention code.
Enforcement, §27-98.
Injunctions, §27-101.

MARSHES.
Carelessly damaging property by fire, §18.2-88.
Coastal primary sand dunes and beaches, §§28.2-1400, 28.2-1403.
Fire hazards, §10.1-1159.
State forester.
Waste and unappropriated lands, §10.1-1108.
Ungranted shores of the sea, marshes and meadowlands, §§28.2-1500 to 28.2-1514.
See UNGRANTED SHORES OF THE SEA.
United States acquired lands.
Conveyance of certain marshlands to United States, §1-403.
Waterfowl blinds, §29.1-350.
Wetlands, §§28.2-1300 to 28.2-1320.
See WETLANDS.

MARTIAL ARTS.
Defined, §54.1-828.
Regulation of events generally, §§54.1-828 to 54.1-835.
See BOXING, MARTIAL ARTS AND WRESTLING EVENTS.

MARTIAL ARTS WEAPONS.
Carrying concealed weapons, §18.2-308.
Convicted felons, possession or transportation or concealing, §18.2-308.2.
Courthouse, carrying weapon into, §18.2-283.1.
School property, possession on, §18.2-308.1.
Selling or having in possession, §18.2-311.

MARTIN LUTHER KING, JR. DAY.
Legal holidays, §2.2-3300.

MARTIN LUTHER KING MEMORIAL COMMISSION.
Dr. Martin Luther King, Jr. memorial commission.
See DR. MARTIN LUTHER KING, JR. MEMORIAL COMMISSION.

MARTINSVILLE.
Blue Ridge airport authority, 1964 ch 25, 1978 ch 633, 1996 ch 465.
Circuit court, establishment, §17.1-500.

MARTINSVILLE —Cont'd
Circuit court of county to constitute circuit court of city.
Inapplicability of provision to Martinsville, §17.1-505.
Confederate cemeteries and graves.
Disbursement of funds appropriated for upkeep, §10.1-2211.
Jail farms, §19.2-309.1.
New College Institute, §§23-231.30 to 23-231.36.
Public defender offices, §19.2-163.04.
School board.
Salary of members, §22.1-32.
Western Virginia public education consortium, §22.1-354.1.

MARTINSVILLE PARKING AUTHORITY, 1968 ch 365.

MARYLAND.
Boundary line and compact between Virginia and Maryland.
Eluding police or arrests, §28.2-904.
Boundary with, §1-308.
Eastward from Assateague Island, §1-309.
Pocomoke river.
Lower reaches of, §1-310.
Pocomoke sound.
Upper reaches of, §1-310.
Chesapeake Bay commission.
General provisions, §§30-240 to 30-255.
Chesapeake regional Olympic games compact, §§2.2-5900, 2.2-5901.

MARY WASHINGTON COLLEGE.
University of Mary Washington, §§23-91.34 to 23-91.44.
See UNIVERSITY OF MARY WASHINGTON.

MASKS.
Prohibition of wearing masks in certain places, §18.2-422.

MASONS.
Benevolent associations generally.
See BENEVOLENT ASSOCIATIONS OR ORGANIZATIONS.
Exemption from fraternal benefit society chapter provisions, §38.2-4135.
Land conveyances to Free Masons, §57-19.
Land quantity limitations, §57-20.
Special license plates for members, §46.2-746.7.

MASSACHUSETTS TRUSTS.
Business trusts, §§13.1-1200 to 13.1-1285.
See BUSINESS TRUSTS.

MASSAGE PARLORS.
License tax.
Rate limitation, §58.1-3706.

MASSAGE THERAPISTS, §54.1-3000.
ABC day spa licenses, §4.1-206.
Day spa defined, §4.1-100.
Local license tax, §4.1-233.
State license tax, §4.1-231.
Advisory board on massage therapy, §54.1-3029.1.
Certified massage therapist.
Defined, §54.1-3000.
Qualifications, §54.1-3029.
Massage therapy, defined, §54.1-3000.
Medicine and other healing arts professions.
Exceptions and exemptions from licensure, §54.1-2901.

MASSANUTTEN MILITARY ACADEMY.
Officers to be officers of militia, §44-117.

MASS KILLINGS, §18.2-31.
Venue in multiple murder prosecution, §19.2-247.

MASS-MARKET TRANSACTIONS.
Uniform computer information transactions act, §§59.1-501.1 to 59.1-509.2.

MASS TRANSIT.
Actions to increase transit use and reduce highway congestion.
Report by secretary of transportation, §33.1-223.2:24.
Charlottesville-Albemarle regional transit authority, §§15.2-7022 to 15.2-7035.
See CHARLOTTESVILLE-ALBEMARLE REGIONAL TRANSIT AUTHORITY.
Counties, cities or towns.
Designation of source of revenue for, §15.2-948.
Shared ride taxi systems, §15.2-949.
System of transportation for locality not member of transportation district, §15.2-947.
Local income tax.
Revenues distributed to be applied and expended for, §58.1-548.
Mass transit fund.
Retail sales and use tax revenue disposition, §58.1-638.
Motor vehicle fuel sales tax, §§58.1-1718.1 to 58.1-1724.4.
Recordation tax, state.
Distributions to cities and counties for transportation purposes, §58.1-816.
Service districts, §§15.2-2400 to 15.2-2403.3.
Transportation districts.
Multicounty transportation improvement districts.
See TRANSPORTATION DISTRICTS.
Transportation improvement district for individual locality.
See TRANSPORTATION DISTRICTS.
Transportation service districts.
See TRANSPORTATION DISTRICTS.
Transportation infrastructure bank, §§33.1-23.6 to 33.1-23.13.

MASTECTOMY.
Health insurance.
Coverage for reconstructive breast surgery, §38.2-3418.4.
Minimum hospital stay for mastectomy and certain lymph node dissection patients, §38.2-3418.6.
Public officers and employees.
Required coverage, §2.2-2818.

MASTER DEEDS OF TRUST.
Recording, §17.1-259.
Form and requisite, §17.1-259.
Incorporating deed, §17.1-260.

MASTER PLAN.
State parks, §10.1-200.1.

MASTER SETTLEMENT AGREEMENT.
Tobacco manufacturers' responsibilities, §§3.2-4200 to 3.2-4219.
See TOBACCO PRODUCTS MANUFACTURERS' RESPONSIBILITIES.

MASTERS IN CHANCERY, §§8.01-607 to 8.01-619.
See COMMISSIONERS IN CHANCERY.

MASTURBATION.
Obscene sexual display.
Masturbation in public place, §18.2-387.1.

MATCHING CONTRIBUTIONS.
Cash match plan for employees of Commonwealth, §§51.1-607 to 51.1-613.

MATCHMAKERS.
Boxing, martial arts and wrestling events.
Defined, §54.1-828.
Generally, §§54.1-828 to 54.1-835.
See BOXING, MARTIAL ARTS AND WRESTLING EVENTS.

MATERIALITY TO RISK.
Insurance applicants' statements, declarations and descriptions, §38.2-309.

MATERIALMEN'S LIENS.
Generally, §§43-1 to 43-23.2.
See MECHANICS' AND MATERIALMEN'S LIENS.

MATERIAL WITNESSES.
Conditions of release, §19.2-127.

MATERNAL AND CHILD HEALTH SERVICES PLAN, §§32.1-77, 32.1-78.

MATHEWS COUNTY.
Coastal primary sand dunes and beaches.
Zoning ordinance, §28.2-1403.
Middle Peninsula regional airport authority, 1997 ch 871.
Northern Neck-Middle Peninsula public education consortium.
Inclusion in region, §22.1-354.6.
Public oyster rocks, beds and shoals, §§28.2-641 to 28.2-644, 28.2-648.
Riparian rights, oyster planting grounds, §28.2-629.
School board.
Salary of members, §22.1-32.

MATTAPONI INDIAN TRIBE.
Motor vehicle sales and use tax exemption, §58.1-2403.

MATTRESSES.
Bedding and upholstered furniture generally, §§32.1-212 to 32.1-226.
See BEDDING AND UPHOLSTERED FURNITURE.

MAURY SERVICE AUTHORITY, 1972 ch 388.

MAUSOLEUMS.
Cemeteries.
See CEMETERIES.

MAXILLOFACIAL SURGEONS, §§54.1-2700, 54.1-2709.1 to 54.1-2709.5.

MAXIMUM FINE FOR TRAFFIC INFRACTIONS, §46.2-113.
Serious traffic violation.
Vehicles of certain gross weight, §46.2-113.

MAXIMUM SAFE SPEED, §46.2-861.

MAXIMUM SPEED LIMITS.
Generally, §46.2-870.
Highways in cities and towns, §§46.2-874, 46.2-875.
Nonsurface treated highways, §46.2-873.1.
Operation of vehicle at 20 miles per hour or more over applicable speed.
Certain town ordinance prohibiting, §46.2-874.1.

MAXIMUM SPEED LIMITS —Cont'd
Passenger vehicles towing certain trailers, §46.2-876.
Prepayment of fines, §46.2-878.3.
Residence district.
Operation of vehicle at 15 miles per hour or more over applicable speed.
Certain city ordinance prohibiting, §46.2-874.1.
School buses, §46.2-871.
School crossings, §46.2-873.
Vehicles operating under special permit, §46.2-872.

MAYORS.
Acknowledgments, §55-126.
Coordinator of emergency management.
Appointment with consent of council, §44-146.19.
Election, §24.2-222.
Economic interest statement as requirement of candidate, §24.2-502.
Vacancy.
Special election, §24.2-226.
Local personnel, bond, qualification of office, etc., §§15.2-1500 to 15.2-1543.
See LOCAL OFFICERS AND EMPLOYEES.
Militia duty exemption, §44-5.
Oaths.
Powers to administer, §15.2-1410.
Powers, §15.2-1423.
Oaths, §15.2-1410.
Presiding officers, §15.2-1422.
Removal of public officers from office generally, §§24.2-230 to 24.2-238.
Resignation.
Date resignation becomes not revocable, §24.2-226.
Salaries, setting.
City mayors, §15.2-1414.6.
Town mayors, §15.2-1414.7.
Term, §24.2-222.
Towns, transition of towns to cities.
Mayor of town to continue in office, §15.2-3814.
Vacancy, §15.2-1424.
Interim appointment, §24.2-228.
Special election to fill, §24.2-226.
Time to qualify and give bond if required, §24.2-229.

MAY V. JOYNES.
Rule modified, §55-7.

MCHIP.
General provisions, §§38.2-5800 to 38.2-5811.
See MANAGED CARE HEALTH INSURANCE PLANS.

MEADOWLANDS.
Ungranted shores of the sea, marshes and meadowlands, §§28.2-1500 to 28.2-1514.
See UNGRANTED SHORES OF THE SEA.

MEALS ON WHEELS.
Motor vehicle sales and use tax exemption for vehicles, §58.1-2403.

MEALS TAX.
City or town having general taxing powers.
Excise tax, §58.1-3840.
Corporate officer or partnership officer liability for failure to pay, §58.1-3906.
Willful failure to collect and account for, §58.1-3907.
County food and beverage tax, §§58.1-3833, 58.1-3834.

MEALS TAX —Cont'd
Situs for taxation, §58.1-3841.

MEASLES.
Health care provider reports, §32.1-116.3.
Immunizations.
Required immunizations of children, §32.1-46.
Virginia immunization information system (VIIS), §32.1-46.01.
Student immunizations, §23-7.5.

MEASURES AND WEIGHTS, §§3.2-5600 to 3.2-5648.
See WEIGHTS AND MEASURES.

MEAT AND POULTRY PRODUCTS INSPECTION, §§3.2-5400 to 3.2-5418.
Adulterated livestock or poultry product, §3.2-5401.
Agriculture and consumer services board.
Duties, §3.2-5404.
Agriculture and consumer services commissioner.
Powers, §§3.2-5405, 3.2-5416.
Injunctions, §3.2-5417.
Right of access to plants, §3.2-5412.
Rules and regulations, §3.2-5406.
Agriculture and consumer services department.
Cooperation with United States secretary of agriculture, §3.2-5403.
Appeals.
Judicial review of certain orders, §3.2-5405.
Applicability of provisions.
Federal act.
Limitation on applicability to matters regulated under, §3.2-5418.
Bribery.
Prohibited acts, §3.2-5410.
Condemnation, §3.2-5414.
Confidentiality of information.
Improper disclosure of information obtained under provisions, §3.2-5416.
Containers.
When inspection of product placed in container completed, §3.2-5412.
Counterfeiting.
Official marks, devices or certificates.
Prohibited acts, §3.2-5408.
Criminal penalties, §§3.2-5415, 3.2-5416.
Definitions, §3.2-5400.
Equine products.
Prohibition on intrastate distribution, §3.2-5409.
Forgery.
Official marks, devices or certificates.
Prohibited acts, §3.2-5408.
Horses.
Equine products.
Prohibition on intrastate distribution, §3.2-5409.
Human food.
Limitation of inspection to plants preparing products for, §3.2-5411.
Injunctions.
Violations of provisions, §3.2-5417.
Misbranded livestock or poultry product, §3.2-5402.
Prohibited acts, §§3.2-5407 to 3.2-5410.
Rules and regulations, §3.2-5406.
Searches and seizures, §3.2-5414.
Subpoenas.
Agriculture and consumer services commissioner, §3.2-5416.

MEAT AND POULTRY PRODUCTS INSPECTION —Cont'd
Violations of provisions.
Administrative detention of violative animals and products, §3.2-5413.
Criminal penalties, §§3.2-5415, 3.2-5416.
Injunctions, §3.2-5417.
Prohibited acts, §§3.2-5407 to 3.2-5410.
Seizure and condemnation provisions, §3.2-5414.
Warning letter, §3.2-5415.
Witnesses.
Agriculture and consumer services commissioner.
Powers as to, §3.2-5416.

MEAT MARKETS.
Sanitary requirements for food establishments, §§3.2-5105 to 3.2-5119.

MECHANICAL BREAKDOWN OF VEHICLE ON HIGHWAY.
Emergency flashing lights and moving of vehicle, §46.2-888.

MECHANICALLY-RECORDED CONVERSATIONS.
Limitation on use as evidence, §8.01-420.2.

MECHANICS.
Lien for repairs of personal property, §46.2-644.02.
Liens for repairs, §§43-33 to 43-36.
Motor vehicle repair facilities generally, §§59.1-207.1 to 59.1-207.6.
See MOTOR VEHICLE REPAIR FACILITIES.

MECHANICS' AND MATERIALMEN'S LIENS, §§43-1 to 43-71.
Affidavit of general contractor, §43-5.
Affidavit of payment.
Required of owner prior to sale or refinance, §43-13.3.
Affidavit of person performing labor or furnishing services, §43-10.
Affidavit of subcontractor, §43-8.
Affidavits prior to sale, §43-13.2.
Agents.
Defined, §43-1.
Funds.
Handling, §43-4.01.
Notice to, §43-4.01.
Succession upon death or resignation, §43-4.01.
Assignments.
Lien validity and priority unaffected by, §43-19.
Protection of assignees, §43-65.
Boat titling certificates.
Priority of interest shown on certificates, §29.1-727.
Building code.
Designation of mechanic's lien agent on building permit, §36-98.01.
Building permits.
Posting, §43-4.01.
Condominiums.
Assessment liens.
Priority, §55-79.84.
Release of liens at time of first conveyance, §55-79.46.
Creation, §43-3.
Defined terms, §43-1.
A contract for the sale of real estate, §43-20.
Agent, §43-7.
Site development improvements, §43-3.
Enforcement, §43-22.
Limitations on suit, §43-17.

MECHANICS' AND MATERIALMEN'S LIENS —Cont'd
Extent of liens, §43-20.
Forfeiture, §43-23.1.
Forms.
Notice of possible filing of mechanic's lien, §11-2.4.
Fraudulent conveyances.
Void as to creditors and purchasers until recorded.
Priority, §55-96.
Where to be recorded, §55-97.
Fund improprieties, §43-13.
License of contractor.
Building permit to contain information regarding, §43-4.01.
Improperly licensed or unlicensed contractor not entitled to lien, §43-3.
Memorandum and affidavit, contents, §43-5.
Subcontractor memorandum, §43-8.
Sub-subcontractor memorandum, §43-10.
Perfection of lien, requirements as to license or certificate numbers, §43-4.
Material permanently annexed to freehold.
Classification, §43-2.
Motor vehicle titling.
Priority of security interests shown on certificates of title, §46.2-640.
Notice of possible filing of mechanic's lien, §11-2.4.
Owner expenditures to complete undertaking.
Priority, §43-16.
Perfection.
General contractor, §43-4.
Affidavits, sufficiency of, §43-5.
Inuring to benefit of subcontractors, §43-18.
Memorandums.
Inaccuracies, §43-15.
Sufficiency of, §43-5.
Notice.
Service, §43-14.1.
Hearings on validity, §43-17.1.
Persons performing labor or furnishing materials for subcontractor, §43-9.
Affidavits.
Sufficiency, §43-10.
Memorandums.
Inaccuracies, §43-15.
Sufficiency, §43-10.
Notice.
Service, §43-14.1.
Sufficiency, §43-10.
Subcontractors, §43-7.
Affidavits.
Sufficiency, §43-8.
Lien of general contractor to inure to benefit of, §43-18.
Memorandums.
Inaccuracies, §43-15.
Sufficiency, §43-8.
Notice.
Service, §43-14.1.
Sufficiency, §43-8.
Personal liability of owners or general contractors, §43-11.
Fund improprieties, §43-13.
Personal property, repairs, §46.2-644.02.
Priority.
Mechanics' *versus* mechanics' liens, §43-23.
Mechanics' *versus* other liens, §43-21.
Property owners' associations.
Liens for assessments, §55-516.

MECHANICS' AND MATERIALMEN'S LIENS —Cont'd
Protection of assignees, transferees or indorsees of debts secured by, §43-65.
Real estate cooperatives.
Remedies for nonpayment of assessments, §55-472.
Recording in deed book, §17.1-229.
Releases.
Bond filings, §§43-70, 43-71.
Payment, §43-67.
Into court payments, §§43-70, 43-71.
Satisfaction, §43-67.
Remedies cumulative, §43-23.2.
Repairs of personal property, §46.2-644.02.
Residential real property purchases.
Notice of possible filing of mechanic's lien, §11-2.4.
Sale of property subject to lien, §46.2-644.03.
Sale or refinance.
Affidavit of payment required of owner prior to, §43-13.3.
Service of notices, §43-14.1.
Structures permanently annexed to freehold.
Classification, §43-2.
Subdivided land sales.
Property owners' association liens, §55-344.
Unlicensed contractor not entitled to lien, §43-3.
Waivers.
Forged signatures, §43-13.1.
Rights, §43-3.

MECKLENBURG-BRUNSWICK AIRPORT COMMISSION, 1975 ch 211, 1982 ch 42.

MECKLENBURG COUNTY.
Confederate cemeteries and graves.
Disbursement of funds appropriated for upkeep, §10.1-2211.
Fishing, inland waters.
Taking methods, restrictions, §29.1-531.
Meherrin river.
Dams.
Restrictions, §29.1-532.
Port of Virginia economic and infrastructure development zone grant fund, §62.1-132.3:2.
Public defenders office.
Established, §19.2-163.04.
School board.
Salary of members, §22.1-32.
Subdivision regulations.
Application of county regulations in area subject to municipal jurisdiction, §15.2-2249.
Application of municipal regulations beyond corporate limits, §15.2-2248.
Disagreement between county and municipality, §15.2-2250.
Transient occupancy tax.
Disposition of revenues, §58.1-3819.

MEDAL OF HONOR RECIPIENTS.
Special license plates, §46.2-745.

MEDAL OF VALOR FOR PUBLIC SAFETY.
Definition of public safety officer, §9.1-801.
Established, §9.1-800.

MEDALS AND DECORATIONS, MILITARY.
Required to be made in United States, §44-120.1.

MEDIAN STRIPS.
Controlled access highways.
Use of crossover by unauthorized vehicles, §46.2-808.1.

MEDIAN STRIPS —Cont'd
Public mass transportation.
Acquisition and disposition of land in median strips, §33.1-97.
Routing of school buses to avoid pupils crossing divided highway, §46.2-918.
Stopping for school buses.
Roadway separated by barrier or unpaved area, §46.2-859.
Transportation districts.
Acquisition of strips on interstate highways for district, §15.2-4523.

MEDIATION, §§8.01-581.21 to 8.01-581.26.
Alternative dispute resolution, §§8.01-576.4 to 8.01-576.12.
See ALTERNATIVE DISPUTE RESOLUTION.
Arbitration.
General provisions, §§8.01-577 to 8.01-581.016.
See ARBITRATION.
Attorneys at law.
Third party neutral service, VA SCt Rule Pt 6 §II Rule 2.11.
Child custody and visitation arrangements, §20-124.4.
Child support guidelines, §8.01-581.24.
Included in written settlement agreements, §8.01-581.25.
Commission on local government.
Mediator between localities, §15.2-2903.
Confidentiality of information, §§8.01-581.22, 8.01-581.24.
Definitions, §8.01-581.21.
Dispute resolution proceedings.
Administrative dispute resolution, §§2.2-4115 to 2.2-4119.
General provisions, §§8.01-576.4 to 8.01-576.12.
District courts.
Establishment of voluntary civil program for alternative resolution of disputes, §16.1-69.35.
Donation of professional services by mediators.
Tax credit, §58.1-439.22.
Environmental quality department.
Boards, §10.1-1186.3.
Exceptions to confidentiality, §8.01-581.22.
Franchise disputes.
Motor vehicle dealers, §46.2-1572.2.
Immunity.
Mediators and mediation programs, §§8.01-576.9, 8.01-581.23.
Labor disputes, §§40.1-70 to 40.1-75.
Mediation programs.
Civil immunity, §§8.01-576.9, 8.01-581.23.
Mediators.
Civil immunity, §§8.01-576.9, 8.01-581.23.
Confidentiality, §8.01-581.24.
Donation of professional services.
Tax credit, §58.1-439.22.
Standards and duties, §8.01-581.24.
Motor vehicle dealers.
Franchise disputes, §46.2-1572.2.
Procurement by public bodies, §2.2-4366.
Special education.
Dispute resolution for placement of handicapped children, §22.1-214.
Vacating orders and agreements, §8.01-581.26.
Written settlement agreements.
Effect of, §8.01-581.25.

MEDIATOR BETWEEN LOCALITIES.
Commission on local government, §15.2-2903.

MEDICAID.
Abuse or neglect complaints, authority to investigate, §32.1-310.
Admittance preconditions.
Charging, soliciting, accepting or receiving considerations, §32.1-317.
Attorney general.
Duties, §32.1-320.
Audits, §32.1-320.
Benefits.
Concealment of facts, §32.1-321.4.
Determination of rights.
False statements or misrepresentations, §32.1-321.4.
False statements or misrepresentations on applications, §32.1-321.4.
Fraudulently issued benefits.
Liability for, §32.1-321.3.
Fraudulently obtaining, §§32.1-312, 32.1-321.3.
Unintentionally obtaining excess benefits, §32.1-313.
Bribery, §32.1-315.
Change in residence, §63.2-521.
Claims against indigents' estates, §32.1-327.
Commission of social services.
Determination of eligibility for medical assistance and medical care, §63.2-405.
Confidentiality of information, §32.1-325.3.
Consideration of eligibility, §38.2-508.3.
Health insurance coverage, §38.2-508.3.
Continued stays in facilities.
Charging, soliciting, accepting or receiving considerations.
Precondition for, §32.1-317.
Continuing care retirement communities.
Participation in medical assistance program, §32.1-102.3:1.1.
Declaration of purpose, §32.1-310.
Desertion and nonsupport.
Spousal support.
Limitations on orders resulting in eligibility for medical assistance, §20-88.02:1.
Transfer of assets to qualify for assistance, §20-88.02.
Discounts or reduction in prices, §32.1-315.
Duties of attorney general, §32.1-320.
Eligibility.
Commission of social services.
Determination of eligibility for medical assistance and medical care, §63.2-405.
Determination of assets, §32.1-325.02.
Proof of legal presence in the United States, §32.1-325.03.
Estate recovery program, §32.1-326.1.
Facility conditions or operations.
False statements or representations, §32.1-316.
Fraudulently obtaining benefits, §32.1-321.3.
Limitation of action, §32.1-312.
Unintentionally obtaining excess benefits, §32.1-313.
Health insurance.
Commonwealth's right to reimbursement, §38.2-3405.1.
Consideration of Medicaid eligibility, §38.2-508.3.
Exclusion of individuals eligible for Medicaid, §32.1-325.2.
Health maintenance organizations.
Commonwealth's right to reimbursement, §38.2-3405.1.
Consideration of Medicaid eligibility, §38.2-508.3.

MEDICAID —Cont'd
Health services plans.
Commonwealth's right to reimbursement, §38.2-3405.1.
Consideration of Medicaid eligibility, §38.2-508.3.
Implied consent to audit of records, §32.1-310.
Individual and family developmental disabilities and support Medicaid waiver.
Elimination of waiting lists for certain waivers, §32.1-323.2.
Innovation and reform commission, §30-347.
Institutions, conditions or operations.
False statements or representations, §32.1-316.
Intellectual disability Medicaid waiver.
Elimination of waiting lists for certain waivers, §32.1-323.2.
Investigations, §32.1-320.
Licensure of physicians of medicine and osteopathic medicine, chiropractors and podiatrists.
Third-party reimbursement program participation not condition of licensure, §54.1-2910.3.
Limitation of action.
Fraudulently obtaining benefits, §32.1-312.
Unintentionally obtaining excess benefits, §32.1-313.
Long-term care services.
Preadmission screening, §32.1-330.
Managed care programs.
Plain English requirement, §32.1-330.2.
Nursing facilities.
Preadmission screening, §32.1-330.
Overpayments to providers, §32.1-325.1.
Recovery, §32.1-325.1:1.
Paternity proceedings.
Reimbursement of expenses to Commonwealth, §20-49.8.
Patient trust funds.
Failure to deposit, transfer or maintain, §32.1-318.
Payments.
Concealment of facts, §32.1-314.
Determination of rights.
False statements or representations, §32.1-314.
Eligible persons in state-owned medical facilities.
Directed to make payments to or for, §32.1-326.
Excess service charges, §32.1-317.
False statements or representations in applications, §32.1-314.
Fraudulently obtaining or attempting to obtain excess payments, §32.1-312.
Unintentionally obtaining excess payments.
Liability for, §§32.1-313, 32.1-321.2.
Plan for medical assistance services.
State plan, §32.1-325.
Power of attorney.
Authority of agent.
Benefits from governmental programs or civil or military service, §64.2-1635.
Preadmission screening, §32.1-330.
Prior authorization advisory committee, §§32.1-331.12 to 32.1-331.17.
Prosecution of cases by attorney general, §32.1-321.
Records or information provided, exemption from disclosure, §32.1-321.01.
Provision violations.
Penalties, §32.1-325.4.
Rebates, §32.1-315.
Referrals, remuneration for.
Criminal penalties, §32.1-315.

MEDICAID —Cont'd
Reform.
Innovation and reform commission, §30-347.
Remuneration for certain services.
Criminal penalties, §32.1-315.
Right of Commonwealth to reimbursement, §38.2-3405.1.
Savings accounts for educational expenses.
Established by individuals receiving assistance under certain programs, §63.2-505.
Solicitation prohibitions, §32.1-315.
State plan for medical assistance services, §32.1-325.
State programs to implement, §§2.2-617, 2.2-618.
Termination of medical assistance services contracts or agreements.
Powers of director, §32.1-325.
Voter registration agencies designated by state, §24.2-411.2.
Persons authorized to receive applications, §24.2-415.1.
Waiting lists.
Elimination of waiting lists for certain waivers, §32.1-323.2.
Written verification of applications, statements or forms of medical care suppliers, §32.1-319.

MEDICAID INNOVATION AND REFORM COMMISSION, §30-347.

MEDICAID PRIOR AUTHORIZATION ADVISORY COMMITTEE, §§32.1-331.12 to 32.1-331.17.

MEDICAL ADVISORY BOARD.
Motor vehicles department.
Advisory opinions to department, §46.2-204.

MEDICAL ASSISTANCE.
Generally, §§32.1-310 to 32.1-321.4.
See MEDICAID.

MEDICAL ASSISTANCE SERVICES BOARD, §32.1-324.
Confidentiality of information, §32.1-325.3.
Freedom of information act.
Excluded records, §2.2-3705.6.
Plan for medical assistance services, §32.1-325.

MEDICAL ASSISTANCE SERVICES DEPARTMENT, §§32.1-323 to 32.1-330.3.
Assets.
Determination, §32.1-325.02.
Claims against indigents' estates, §32.1-327.
Determination of assets, §32.1-325.02.
Director.
Appointment, §32.1-323.
Benefits.
Fraud or misrepresentation, §32.1-321.4.
Facilitation of communication.
General assembly and governor, reports to, §32.1-324.2.
Payments to or for eligible persons in state-owned medical facilities, §32.1-326.
Plan for medical assistance services.
Administration, §32.1-325.
Powers, §32.1-324.1.
Disclosure of information.
Exemptions from disclosure, §32.1-321.01.
Duties, §32.1-321.1.
Eligibility for services.
Determinations of assets, §32.1-325.02.

MEDICAL ASSISTANCE SERVICES DEPARTMENT —Cont'd
Eligibility for services —Cont'd
Proof of legal presence in the United States, §32.1-325.03.
Establishment, §32.1-323.
Estate recovery program, §32.1-326.1.
Family access to medical insurance security plan, §§32.1-351 to 32.1-353.
Forecast of expenditures.
Submissions, §32.1-323.1.
Health maintenance organizations.
Explanation of benefits for certain enrollees, §38.2-4320.1.
HIV-positive individuals, §32.1-330.1.
Indigent hospitalization program, §§32.1-343 to 32.1-350.
Individual and family developmental disabilities and support Medicaid waiver.
Elimination of waiting lists for certain waivers, §32.1-323.2.
Intellectual disability Medicaid waiver.
Elimination of waiting lists for certain waivers, §32.1-323.2.
Life insurance.
Consideration in making eligibility determinations for institutional or community-based care, §32.1-325.01.
Long-term care prepaid health plans.
Applicability of insurance title.
Exceptions, §38.2-226.2.
Medicaid managed care programs.
Explanation of benefits for certain enrollees, §38.2-4320.1.
Plain English requirement, §32.1-330.2.
Notice of action against nursing home.
Personal injury or wrongful death.
Department having paid for services to injured or decedent, §8.01-66.5.
Nursing homes.
Actions for injuries or wrongful death against.
Notice to department, response.
Department having paid for services to injured or decedent, §8.01-66.5.
Overpayments to providers, §32.1-325.1.
Recovery of overpayments, §32.1-325.1:1.
PACE plans.
Operation and oversight, §32.1-330.3.
Payor of last resort, §32.1-325.2.
Personal injury action against nursing home.
Notice to department.
Department having paid for services to injured or decedent, §8.01-66.5.
Powers, §32.1-321.1.
Preadmission screening, §32.1-330.
Pre-PACE plans.
Operation and oversight, §32.1-330.3.
Records.
Disclosure of information.
Exemptions from disclosure, §32.1-321.01.
Reports.
Facilitation of communication.
General assembly and governor, reports to, §32.1-324.2.
Schools.
Pilot school/community health centers, §32.1-326.2.
Secretary of health and human resources.
Agency responsibility, §2.2-212.
Special education health services.
Interagency agreement, §32.1-326.3.

MEDICAL ASSISTANCE SERVICES DEPARTMENT —Cont'd
Submission of forecast of expenditures, §32.1-325.1.
Termination of medical assistance services contracts or agreements.
Powers of director, §32.1-325.
Uninsured medical catastrophe fund.
Establishment, §32.1-324.3.
Waiting lists.
Elimination of waiting lists for certain waivers, §32.1-323.2.
Wrongful death action against nursing home.
Notice to department.
Department having paid for services to injured or decedent, §8.01-66.5.

MEDICAL BILLS.
Authenticity and reasonableness, §8.01-413.01.

MEDICAL CARE FACILITIES.
Birth defects.
Folic acid's role in prevention.
Distribution of information, §32.1-69.1:1.
Cancer registry.
Information to be provided to, §32.1-70.
Certificate of public need, §§32.1-102.1 to 32.1-102.11.
Administrative procedures, §32.1-102.6.
Designation of judge, §32.1-102.9.
Application of provisions, §32.1-102.11.
Computed tomographic (CT) scanning.
Structured batching process, applications, §32.1-102.2.
Continuing care retirement communities.
Participation in medical assistance program, §32.1-102.3:1.1.
Criteria, §32.1-102.3.
Defined terms, §32.1-102.1.
Completion, §32.1-102.4.
Formal plan of construction, §32.1-102.11.
Good cause, §32.1-102.6.
Initiated construction, §32.1-102.11.
Leased, §32.1-102.11.
Purchased, §32.1-102.11.
Exemptions.
Regulations may provide, §32.1-102.2.
Fees for applications, §32.1-102.2.
Indigents or patients requiring specialized care.
Conditioning approval of certificate on providing care for, §32.1-102.2.
Injunctions, §32.1-102.8.
Designation of judge, §32.1-102.9.
Issuance conditions, §32.1-102.4.
Issuance refusal, §32.1-102.10.
Medical equipment.
Registration of certain equipment, §32.1-102.1:1.
Monitoring, §32.1-102.4.
Moratorium, §32.1-102.3:2.
Nuclear imaging.
Structured batching process, applications, §32.1-102.2.
Position emission tomographic (PET) scanning.
Structured batching process, applications, §32.1-102.2.
Radiation therapy.
Structured batching process, applications, §32.1-102.2.
Regulations, §32.1-102.2.
Required, §32.1-102.3.
Nursing home exemption, §32.1-102.3:1.

MEDICAL CARE FACILITIES —Cont'd
Certificate of public need —Cont'd
Revocation, §32.1-102.4.
Rural areas.
Regulations establishing specific criteria, §32.1-102.2.
State medical facilities plan.
Task force to review, §32.1-102.2:1.
Structured batching process.
Applications, filing, review, §32.1-102.2.
Time limitations for schedules.
Promulgation of regulations, §32.1-102.2.
Transferability, §32.1-102.5.
Communicable disease reports, §32.1-116.3.
Complainants, retaliation or discrimination against, §32.1-125.4.
Confidentiality of complainant's identity, §32.1-125.5.
Confidentiality of complainant's identity, §32.1-125.5.
Conscience clause.
Abortions, §18.2-75.
Consideration as precondition for admittance or continued stay, §32.1-317.
Disciplinary actions against health professionals.
Reporting required.
Civil penalties for failure to report, §32.1-125.01.
Discrimination against complainant or person cooperating with government agency, §32.1-125.4.
Confidentiality of complainant's identity, §32.1-125.5.
Disorders of health professional.
Reporting required.
Civil penalties for failure to report, §32.1-125.01.
Driving while intoxicated.
Person under suspicion for taken to facility.
Issuance of summons on premises, §19.2-73.
False statements as to conditions or operations, §32.1-316.
Health maintenance organizations.
General provisions, §§38.2-4300 to 38.2-4323.
See HEALTH MAINTENANCE ORGANIZATIONS.
Home care organization licensing, §§32.1-162.7 to 32.1-162.15.
Hospice program licensing, §§32.1-162.1 to 32.1-162.6.
Hospitals.
See HOSPITALS.
Human research generally, §§32.1-162.16 to 32.1-162.20.
Long-term care facilities.
See LONG-TERM CARE FACILITIES.
Medical equipment.
Registration of certain equipment, §32.1-102.1:1.
Medical malpractice.
General provisions, §§8.01-581.1 to 8.01-581.20.
See MEDICAL MALPRACTICE.
Medical records.
Evidentiary effect of copies, §8.01-413.
Generally.
See MEDICAL RECORDS.
Medical referrals for profits, §18.2-502.
Medical services lien.
Generally, §§8.01-66.2 to 8.01-66.12.
See MEDICAL SERVICES LIEN.

MEDICAL CARE FACILITIES —Cont'd
Mental health facilities.
General provisions.
See MENTAL HEALTH.
Misrepresentations as to conditions or operations, §32.1-316.
Nursing homes.
See LONG-TERM CARE FACILITIES.
Patient trust funds.
Failures to deposit, transfer or maintain, §32.1-318.
Records.
Information required to be kept, §32.1-274.
Resignation, restriction or expiration of privileges of health professional.
Reporting required.
Civil penalty for failure, §32.1-125.01.
Retaliation against complainant or person cooperating with government agency, §32.1-125.4.
Confidentiality of complainant's identity, §32.1-125.5.
State medical facilities plan.
Task force to review, §32.1-102.2:1.
Summons, issuance on premises.
Person under suspicion of DWI taken to facility, §19.2-73.
Unethical fraudulent or unprofessional conduct by health professional.
Reporting required.
Civil penalty for failure, §32.1-125.01.
Virginia Commonwealth University health system authority.
General provisions, §§23-50.16:1 to 23-50.16:35.
See VIRGINIA COMMONWEALTH UNIVERSITY HEALTH SYSTEM AUTHORITY.
Whistleblower protection.
Discrimination or retaliation against complainant or person cooperating with government agency, §32.1-125.4.
Confidentiality of complainant's identity, §32.1-125.5.
Written verification of Medicaid applications, statements or forms, §32.1-319.

MEDICAL CENTER AT UNIVERSITY OF VIRGINIA.
Management generally, §§23-77.3, 23-77.4.

MEDICAL CLINIC RENDERING FREE SERVICES.
Immunity, §32.1-127.3.

MEDICAL CLINICS FOR INDIGENT OR UNINSURED.
Purchases directly from state agencies or public bodies, §2.2-1120.
Surplus state materials, selling to, §2.2-1124.

MEDICAL COLLEGE OF HAMPTON ROADS.
See EASTERN VIRGINIA MEDICAL SCHOOL.

MEDICAL COLLEGE OF VIRGINIA.
Birth-related neurological injury compensation.
Plan for review of claims, §38.2-5008.
Grants for students, §32.1-122.6.
Nursing scholarships, §23-36.2.
Virginia Commonwealth University.
General provisions, §§23-50.4 to 23-50.16.
See VIRGINIA COMMONWEALTH UNIVERSITY.

MEDICAL COLLEGE OF VIRGINIA —Cont'd
Virginia Commonwealth University —Cont'd
Northern Virginia division, §23-50.16:01.
Transfer of property, rights, duties, etc., §23-50.5.
Virginia Commonwealth University health system authority.
General provisions, §§23-50.16:1 to 23-50.16:35.
See VIRGINIA COMMONWEALTH UNIVERSITY HEALTH SYSTEM AUTHORITY.

MEDICAL COLLEGE OF VIRGINIA HOSPITALS AUTHORITY.
See VIRGINIA COMMONWEALTH UNIVERSITY HEALTH SYSTEM AUTHORITY.

MEDICAL DIRECTIVES.
Anatomical gifts.
Advance health care directive, effect of gift, §32.1-291.21.
Living wills generally, §§54.1-2981 to 54.1-2993.
See LIVING WILLS.

MEDICAL DOCTORS.
Generally.
See PHYSICIANS OR SURGEONS.
Licensing generally, §§54.1-2900 to 54.1-2993.
See MEDICINE AND OTHER HEALING ARTS PROFESSIONS.

MEDICAL EQUIPMENT.
Retail sales and use tax exemption, §58.1-609.10.

MEDICAL EQUIPMENT SUPPLIERS.
Permits, §§54.1-3435.2, 54.1-3435.3.

MEDICAL EXAMINERS, §§32.1-277 to 32.1-288.
Adult fatality review team, §32.1-283.5.
Anatomical gifts.
Cooperation with procurement organization, §32.1-291.22.
Procedures regarding decedent under jurisdiction of medical examiner, §32.1-291.23.
Appointment, §32.1-278.
Assistants, §32.1-280.
Autopsies, §32.1-285.
Causes of death requiring investigation, §32.1-283.
Confidential information.
Information and records maintained by the office, §32.1-283.4.
Cremations.
Prerequisites to allowing, §32.1-284.
Death certificates.
Medical certification completion, §32.1-263.
Duties, §32.1-279.
Evidence.
Records and autopsy reports made by chief medical examiner, §8.01-390.2.
Exhumations, §32.1-286.
Facilities, §32.1-277.
Fee for death investigation, §32.1-283.
Fetal death reports.
Filing time extensions, §32.1-266.
Medical certification completion, §32.1-264.
Investigations of death, §32.1-283.
Confidentiality of information maintained by the office, §32.1-283.4.
Exhumations, §32.1-286.
Local medical examiners.
Appointment, §32.1-282.
Marriage record or registration.
False entry, §18.2-207.

MEDICAL EXAMINERS —Cont'd
Mental health facility patients.
Delivery of death investigation report, §32.1-283.
Offices, §32.1-277.
Organs, glands, eyes.
Removal, obtaining consent, §32.1-283.
Pathologist.
Designation, §32.1-281.
Prerequisites to allowing, §32.1-284.
Preliminary hearings.
Admissibility of reports and records, §19.2-188.
Qualifications, §32.1-278.
Reports.
Investigation as to death.
Persons delivered to, §32.1-283.
Sudden infant death syndrome.
Causes of death requiring investigation, §32.1-283.
Teaching duties, §32.1-279.
Traffic accidents, death resulting from.
Investigation report furnished ti state police, §32.1-283.

MEDICAL EXPENSES.
Bills for medical services.
Authenticity and reasonableness, §8.01-413.01.
District court civil cases.
Evidence of medical reports or records, §16.1-88.2.
Motor vehicle insurance.
Assignment of benefits, §38.2-2201.
Insurer not to receive credit for other medical expense insurance, §38.2-2211.
Medical benefit insurer not to retain right of subrogation to recover from third party, §38.2-2209.
Medical benefit offset against liability or uninsured motorist coverage prohibited, §38.2-2216.
Optional provisions for payment, §38.2-2201.
Presumption of authenticity and reasonableness of medical bills, §8.01-413.01.
Sex offenses, payment of fees in gathering evidence, §19.2-165.1.

MEDICAL LIBRARIES.
Property tax exemptions, §58.1-3606.

MEDICAL MALPRACTICE, §§8.01-581.1 to 8.01-581.20.
Arbitration of malpractice claims, §8.01-581.12.
Attorney-client privilege, §8.01-399.
Birth-related neurological injury compensation, §§38.2-5000 to 38.2-5021.
See BIRTH-RELATED NEUROLOGICAL INJURY COMPENSATION.
Cap on damages, §8.01-581.15.
Certification of expert witness opinion, §8.01-20.1.
Charitable or tax exempt hospitals.
Limit on recovery against, §8.01-38.
Claims reported to state corporation commission.
Duty of insurers of health care providers, §38.2-2228.2.
Competency assessment of licensee.
Three medical malpractice judgments or settlements in ten year period, §54.1-2912.3.
Damages.
Determination of standard in action for damages, §8.01-581.20.
Limitation on recovery, §8.01-581.15.
Charitable or tax exempt hospitals, recovery against, §8.01-38.

MEDICAL MALPRACTICE —Cont'd
Definitions, §8.01-581.1, MedMal Rule 1.
Disclosure of health records, §32.1-127.1:03.
District courts.
Expert witness opinion.
Certification at time of service of process, §16.1-83.1.
Expert testimony, §8.01-581.6, MedMal Rule 6.
Certification of expert witness opinion, §8.01-20.1.
Certification of expert witness opinion at time of service of process, §16.1-83.1.
Number of expert witnesses each party may call, §8.01-581.20.
Standard of care, §8.01-581.20.
Treating health care provider witnesses, number not limited, §8.01-581.20.
Foreign object left in patient's body.
Extension of limitations period, §8.01-243.
Fraud, concealment, intentional misrepresentation.
Extension of limitations period, §8.01-243.
Health care providers.
Defined, §8.01-581.1.
Records.
Copies as evidence, §8.01-413.
Right of patient, attorney or authorized insurer to copies, §8.01-413.
Subpoenas, §8.01-413.
Health professionals.
Defined, §8.01-581.13.
Hospitals.
Charitable or tax exempt institutions, limit on recovery against, §8.01-38.
Immunity.
Health professionals, §8.01-581.13.
Health professionals serving on certain committees, §8.01-581.19.
Health profession students, §8.01-581.13.
Laboratory tests and other examinations not authorized by physician, §§8.01-581.18, 8.01-581.18:1.
Persons providing information to certain committees, §8.01-581.19:1.
Professional consultants to certain boards or committees, §8.01-581.16.
In camera review of expert witness opinion, §8.01-20.1.
Insurance.
Joint underwriting association, §§38.2-2800 to 38.2-2814.
Joint underwriting association, §§38.2-2800 to 38.2-2814.
Laboratory test results.
Immunity for unauthorized tests, §§8.01-581.18, 8.01-581.18:1.
Licensure of physicians.
Reports on judgments or settlements.
Regulations concerning, adoption, §54.1-2910.1.
Limitation of actions, §8.01-243.
Injuries to minors, §8.01-243.1.
Tort claims act, §§8.01-195.6, 8.01-195.7.
Limitation on recovery, §8.01-581.15.
Malignant tumors.
Negligent failure to diagnose.
Extension of limitations period, §8.01-243.
Malpractice.
Defined, §8.01-581.1.
Medical records.
Copies admissible as evidence, §8.01-413.
Disclosure, §32.1-127.1:03.
Right of patient or attorney to copies, §8.01-413.

MEDICAL MALPRACTICE —Cont'd
Medical records —Cont'd
Subpoenas, §8.01-413.
Minors.
Limitation of actions.
Action against health care providers, §8.01-243.1.
Number of expert witnesses each party may call, §8.01-581.20.
Nursing homes.
Professional services in nursing homes.
Defined, §8.01-581.1.
Ore tenus hearing.
Assembly of record, §8.01-581.4:1.
Conduct of, MedMal Rule 6.
Notice to parties, §8.01-581.5, MedMal Rule 6.
Procedure at hearing, MedMal Rule 6.
Request for, MedMal Rule 5.
When hearing to be held, §8.01-581.5, MedMal Rule 5.
Persons with disability.
Tolling limitations period.
Actions by, §8.01-243.
Physician-patient privilege, §8.01-399.
Privileged communications.
Attorney-client privilege, §8.01-399.
Board or committee proceedings, §8.01-581.17.
Physician-patient coverage, §8.01-399.
Professional consultants to certain boards or committees.
Immunity from liability, §8.01-581.16.
Reporting of information to certain committees.
Immunity of persons, §8.01-581.19:1.
Review panels.
Access to material, §8.01-581.4.
Appearance of panel members as witnesses, §8.01-581.8.
Applicability of article, §8.01-581.12:2.
Applicability of rules, MedMal Rule 1.
Arbitration of claims, §8.01-581.12.
Assembly of record, §8.01-581.4:1, MedMal Rule 6.
Attorney-issued summons, §8.01-407.
Attorney list.
Submission of names, §8.01-581.3.
Withdrawal of name, MedMal Rule 3.
Attorney members, §8.01-581.3, MedMal Rule 3.
Certificate of parties, MedMal Rule 3.
Claimant submission of evidence, §8.01-581.4, MedMal Rule 4.
Compensation, MedMal Rule 7.
Completion of discovery, §8.01-581.3:1, MedMal Rule 4.
Composition of panel, §8.01-581.3, MedMal Rule 3.
Conduct of proceedings, §8.01-581.6, MedMal Rule 6.
Construction of article, §8.01-581.12:2.
Convening panel, §8.01-581.3:1, MedMal Rule 4.
Designation of panel, §8.01-581.3, MedMal Rule 3.
Duties of chairman, §8.01-581.4.
Expenses and costs, §8.01-581.10, MedMal Rule 7.
Expert testimony.
Standard of care, §8.01-581.20.
Extension of time for submission of evidence, MedMal Rule 4.
Health care provider list.
Submission of names, §8.01-581.3.
Withdrawal of name, MedMal Rule 3.
Health care provider members, §8.01-581.3, MedMal Rule 3.

MEDICAL MALPRACTICE —Cont'd
Review panels —Cont'd
Health care provider submission of evidence, §8.01-581.4, MedMal Rule 4.
Hearing date, §8.01-581.3:1.
Immunity from civil liability, §8.01-581.8.
Manner of panel selection, §8.01-581.3, MedMal Rule 3.
Oath of panel members, §8.01-581.3:1, MedMal Rule 4.
Objections not waived by participation, §8.01-581.11:1.
Opinion of panel, §8.01-581.7, MedMal Rule 6.
Admissibility as evidence, §8.01-581.8.
Late panel opinions, §8.01-581.7:1.
Conclusions, §8.01-581.7.
Filing requirements, §8.01-581.7.
Limitation on panel opinion, §8.01-581.7:1.
Ore tenus hearing, §§8.01-581.4:1, 8.01-581.5, MedMal Rules 5, 6.
Per diem and expenses of panel, §8.01-581.10, MedMal Rule 7.
Quorum, §8.01-581.6, MedMal Rule 6.
Records.
Assembly of record, §8.01-581.4:1.
Removal of record for inspection and copying, §8.01-581.4:2, MedMal Rule 6.
Request for ore tenus hearing, MedMal Rules 5, 6.
Request for review by panel, §8.01-581.2, MedMal Rule 2.
Additional parties, §8.01-581.2:1.
Amendment of request, §8.01-581.2:1.
Contents of request, MedMal Rule 2.
Copy filed with clerk, sent to counsel of record, §8.01-581.2.
Determination on request, §8.01-581.2.
Joinder of parties or causes of action, §8.01-581.2:1.
Multiple parties, MedMal Rule 2.
Notice of appointment, MedMal Rule 4.
Notice of claim, MedMal Rule 2.
Amendment of notice, MedMal Rule 4.
Objection to notice of claim, MedMal Rule 2.
Action on objection, MedMal Rule 4.
Request for panel, §8.01-581.2, MedMal Rule 2.
Rescission of request, §8.01-581.2.
Rulemaking authority, §8.01-581.11.
Selection of panel, §8.01-581.3, MedMal Rule 3.
Standard of care in proceedings, §8.01-581.20.
Submission of evidence to panel, §8.01-581.4, MedMal Rule 4.
Summons.
Attorney-issued summons, §8.01-407.
Sympathy, admissibility of expressions of, §8.01-581.20:1.
Wrongful death actions against health care providers, §8.01-52.1.
Wrongful death actions against health care providers.
Sympathy, admissibility of expressions of, §8.01-52.1.
Rules of practice.
Applicability of rules, MedMal Rule 1.
Convening of review panel, MedMal Rule 4.
Designation of review panel, MedMal Rule 3.
Expenses and costs, MedMal Rule 7.
Ore tenus hearing, MedMal Rules 5, 6.
References, MedMal Rule 1.
Request for review by medical malpractice review panel, MedMal Rule 2.

MEDICAL MALPRACTICE —Cont'd
Standard of care.
Proceedings before review panel, §8.01-581.20.
Statute of limitations, §8.01-243.
Health care providers, §8.01-243.
Injuries to minors, §8.01-243.1.
Tort claims act, §§8.01-195.6, 8.01-195.7.
Sympathy, admissibility of expressions of, §8.01-581.20:1.
Wrongful death actions against health care providers, §8.01-52.1.
Tolling limitations period.
Actions by persons under disability, §8.01-243.
Tort claims act.
Statute of limitations, §§8.01-195.6, 8.01-195.7.
Treating health care provider witnesses, number not limited, §8.01-581.20.
Verdicts.
Limitation on recovery of damages, §8.01-581.15.
Witnesses.
Expert witnesses.
Certification of expert witness opinion, §8.01-20.1.
Certification of expert witness opinion at time of service of process, §16.1-83.1.
Number each party may call, §8.01-581.20.
Treating health care provider witnesses, number not limited, §8.01-581.20.
Workers' compensation.
Employer liability for medical services ordered by commission, §65.2-605.

MEDICAL MALPRACTICE INSURANCE.
Birth-related neurological injury compensation.
Credits against malpractice insurance premium, §38.2-5020.1.
Joint underwriting association, §§38.2-2800 to 38.2-2814.
Activation, §38.2-2801.
Annual statement, §38.2-2810.
Appeal of actions or decisions of associations, §38.2-2809.
Applicants to be issued policies, §38.2-2806.
Appointment of director, §38.2-2803.
Cancellation, §38.2-2806.
Commissions for placing and servicing risk with association, §38.2-2813.
Definitions, §38.2-2800.
Directors, §38.2-2803.
Administration of stabilization reserve fund, §38.2-2807.
Public officers and employees, §38.2-2812.
Quorum, §38.2-2807.
Review of actions or decisions, §38.2-2809.
Submission of plan of operation, §38.2-2804.
Dissolution, §38.2-2802.
Examination into affairs of association, §38.2-2811.
Examination of business of association, §38.2-2806.
Hospital advisory committee, §38.2-2805.
Immunity for actions made in good faith, §38.2-2814.
Insurer's participation, §38.2-2808.
Manager of stabilization reserve fund, §38.2-2807.
Medical advisory committee, §38.2-2805.
Members, §38.2-2801.
Participation in association, §38.2-2808.
Placing and servicing risk with association, commissions for, §38.2-2813.

MEDICAL MALPRACTICE INSURANCE —Cont'd
Joint underwriting association —Cont'd
Plan of operation, §38.2-2804.
Policies, §38.2-2806.
Powers, §38.2-2801.
Public officers or employees as directors of stabilization reserve fund, §38.2-2812.
Purposes, §38.2-2801.
Rates, §38.2-2806.
Review of actions or decisions, §38.2-2809.
Stabilization reserve fund, §38.2-2807.

MEDICAL NECESSITY.
Abortion when necessary to save life of woman, §18.2-74.1.

MEDICAL OR SURGICAL SERVICE PLANS, §38.2-4203.
Health service plans generally, §§38.2-4200 to 38.2-4235.
See HEALTH SERVICES PLANS.

MEDICAL RECORDS.
Agents.
Disclosure to, §32.1-127.1:03.
Attorney appointed by court to represent patient.
Disclosure to, §32.1-127.1:03.
Behavioral health and developmental services.
Rights of individuals receiving services, §37.2-400.
Bills for medical services.
Authenticity and reasonableness, §8.01-413.01.
Birth-related neurological injury compensation.
Confidential information, §38.2-5002.2.
Delivery of records to injured person, §38.2-5004.
Blood alcohol tests conducted in regular course of emergency medical treatment.
Reports or records of tests admissible under business records exception to hearsay rule, §8.01-413.02.
Breach of medical information, notice to be given, §32.1-127.1:05.
Child abuse or neglect.
Evidence in juvenile and domestic relations district courts, §16.1-245.1.
Child custody and visitation arrangements.
Access to by either parent, §20-124.6.
Child fatality review team access to, §§32.1-283.1, 32.1-283.2.
Closed meetings.
Meetings considering, §2.2-3711.
Commissioner of labor and industry.
Prehospital patient care reports.
EMS agency to release to commissioner, protection, §40.1-8.
Computerized storage, §54.1-2403.2.
Confidential information.
Consent to release of confidential health care information, §32.1-127.1:03.
Patient's right to privacy, §32.1-127.1:03.
Consent to allow release, form, §32.1-127.1:03.
Copies, requests, §32.1-127.1:03.
Court appointed attorney representing patient.
Disclosure to, §32.1-127.1:03.
Death of patient in hospital.
Disclosure for purposes of identifying organ donors, §32.1-127.1:03.
Disclosure of records, §32.1-127.1:03.

MEDICAL RECORDS —Cont'd
Disease prevention and control.
Disclosure of certain information required, §32.1-127.1:04.
District court civil cases.
Evidence of medical reports or records, §16.1-88.2.
Drug diversion investigations.
Copying and removing records, §54.1-3405.
Electronic storage, §54.1-2403.2.
Emergency medical services patient care information system.
Disclosures, §32.1-116.1:1.
Emergency medical services personnel.
Disclosure to law enforcement.
Prehospital patient reports, §§32.1-116.1, 32.1-127.1:03.
Evidence.
Blood alcohol tests conducted in regular course of emergency medical treatment.
Reports or records of tests admissible under business records exception to hearsay rule, §8.01-413.02.
Child abuse or neglect or spousal abuse proceedings.
Admissibility in juvenile and domestic relations district courts, §16.1-245.1.
Copies, §8.01-413.
District court civil cases, §16.1-88.2.
Executors and administrators.
Disclosure to, §32.1-127.1:03.
Falsifying patient records, §18.2-260.1.
Form of consent to release, §32.1-127.1:03.
Form of subpoena.
Records subpoenaed those of pro se parties or nonparty witnesses, §32.1-127.1:03.
Fraud.
Falsifying patient records, §18.2-260.1.
Freedom of information act exclusion.
Health records, §2.2-3705.5.
Guardian ad litem.
Disclosure to, §32.1-127.1:03.
Health care professional licensing.
Reports to licensing authorities.
Use of medical records, §§54.1-2908, 54.1-2909.
Health commissioner.
Authority to examine, §32.1-40.
Immunization, sharing of information, §32.1-46.
Inborn errors of metabolism.
Confidentiality, §32.1-67.1.
Injurious to patient's health or well-being.
Records not furnished patient, state by physician, §32.1-127.1:03.
Insurance information and privacy.
Generally, §§38.2-600 to 38.2-620.
See INSURANCE INFORMATION AND PRIVACY PROTECTION.
Juvenile proceedings.
Juvenile placed in secure facility or shelter care facility, §16.1-248.3.
Law enforcement officers.
Disclosure by emergency medical services personnel.
Prehospital patient reports, §§32.1-116.1, 32.1-127.1:03.
Living wills.
Directive or copy to become part of medical record, §54.1-2983.
Malpractice.
Medical malpractice, §8.01-413.
Medical malpractice proceedings.
Disclosure of patient's records, §32.1-127.1:03.

MEDICAL RECORDS —Cont'd
Minor patients.
Disclosure to, §32.1-127.1:03.
Minor's records.
Parental access, denial, §20-124.6.
Notice to patient.
Breach of medical information, notice to be given, §32.1-127.1:05.
Subpoena of pro se party or nonparty witness records, §32.1-127.1:03.
Notice to provider.
Subpoena duces tecum for patient's medical records, §32.1-127.1:03.
Nursing homes.
Storage, §32.1-127.1:01.
Ophthalmia neonatorum.
Prevention of blindness from.
Recordation of procedure, §32.1-62.
Organ donations.
Death of patient in hospital.
Disclosure for purposes of identifying organ donors, §32.1-127.1:03.
Ownership, §54.1-2403.3.
Phenylketonuria.
Confidentiality, §32.1-67.1.
Prenatal care.
HIV test refusal, §54.1-2403.01.
Prisoners' health care.
Involuntary admission and treatment.
Court ordered release of records, §53.1-40.2.
Privacy, §32.1-127.1:03.
Pro se parties or nonparty witnesses to proceedings.
Subpoena of medical records, §32.1-127.1:03.
Quarantine and isolation of persons with communicable diseases of public health threat.
Disclosure of health records, §32.1-48.015.
Requests for copies, §32.1-127.1:03.
Right of patient, attorney or authorized insurer to copies, §§8.01-413, 54.1-2403.3.
Spousal abuse.
Evidence in juvenile and domestic relations district courts, §16.1-245.1.
Storage, §54.1-2403.2.
Subpoena duces tecum, §§16.1-89, 16.1-265.
Form of notice to provider, §32.1-127.1:03.
Subpoenas.
Compliance, §8.01-413.
Duces tecum, §32.1-127.1:03.
Records of pro se party or nonparty witness, §32.1-127.1:03.
Substance abuse by practitioners.
Disclosure, §54.1-2406.
Teachers.
Cost of furnishing records as condition to continued employment, §22.1-301.
Transfers in conjunction with closure, sale or relocation of practice, §54.1-2405.
Viatical settlements.
Prerequisites to contracting, §38.2-6008.
Waiver of right to privacy, §32.1-127.1:03.
Workers' compensation.
Furnishing copy of medical report, §65.2-604.

MEDICAL REFERRAL FOR PROFIT, §18.2-502.

MEDICAL SAVINGS ACCOUNTS.
Conversion to health savings accounts, §38.2-5602.
Exemption from creditors' claims, §38.2-5604.

MEDICAL SAVINGS ACCOUNTS —Cont'd
Financial institution custodial powers, §6.2-603.

MEDICAL SCHOOLS.
Anatomical gifts.
Recipients of gift, §32.1-291.11.
Clinical training programs.
Participation by students in supervised training programs, §54.1-2959.
Council of higher education.
Health professions and occupations.
Coordinating agency for programs for health professions and occupations, §23-9.10:1.
Grants by state to students, §§32.1-122.5:1, 32.1-122.6.
Dental students.
Dental hygiene, §32.1-122.10.
Physician loan repayment program, §32.1-122.6:1.
Medical College of Virginia.
See MEDICAL COLLEGE OF VIRGINIA.
Pelvic examinations of anesthetized or unconscious females.
Restrictions on and requirements for student performing, §54.1-2959.
Preceptorship programs.
Participation by students, §54.1-2959.
Supervised training programs.
Participation by students, §54.1-2959.
University of Virginia.
Grants for students, §32.1-122.6.

MEDICAL SERVICES LIEN, §§8.01-66.2 to 8.01-66.12.
Attorneys at law.
Lien inferior to claim of attorney, §8.01-66.3.
Charges for services.
Claims of unreasonableness, §8.01-66.7.
Liability for reasonable charges, §8.01-66.6.
Commonwealth, lien in favor of, §8.01-66.9.
Death claims settled by compromise or suit, §8.01-66.10.
Decedents' estates.
Lien inferior to claim of personal representative, §8.01-66.3.
Enforcement of petition, §8.01-66.8.
Injury caused by negligence, §8.01-66.2.
Liability for reasonable charges, §8.01-66.6.
Necessity for settlement or judgment, §8.01-66.11.
Notice.
Written notice required, §8.01-66.5.
Person's negligence causing injury, §8.01-66.2.
Petition to enforce lien, §8.01-66.8.
Physician.
Definition to include chiropractor, §8.01-66.12.
Priority of claims.
Decedents' estates, §8.01-66.3.
Professional services, §8.01-66.3.
State institutions, §8.01-66.9.
Prisons.
Personal recovery in personal injury action, §8.01-66.9:1.
Service of written notice required, §8.01-66.5.
State programs, institutions or departments.
Lien in favor of, §8.01-66.9.
Subrogation.
Death claims settled by compromise or suit, §8.01-66.10.
Municipal or business corporations, §8.01-66.4.
Unreasonableness of charges.
Claim for, hearing and disposal, §8.01-66.7.

MEDICAL SERVICES LIEN —Cont'd
Written notice required, §8.01-66.5.

MEDICAL TESTING KITS.
Warnings required for kits designed for consumer home use, §18.2-502.2.

MEDICAL TREATISES, PERIODICALS OR PAMPHLETS.
Hearsay exception.
Opinion testimony by experts, §8.01-401.1.

MEDICAL TREATMENT.
Hearsay exceptions.
Medical treatment, statement for purposes of, VA SCt Rule 2:803.

MEDICAL USE OF MARIJUANA, §18.2-251.1.

MEDICAL WASTE.
Ships, barges or other vessels transporting upon navigable waters, §10.1-1454.1.

MEDICARE.
Defined, §38.2-100.
Power of attorney.
Benefits from governmental programs or civil or military service, authority of agent, §64.2-1635.

MEDICARE SUPPLEMENT POLICIES, §§38.2-3600 to 38.2-3609.

MEDICATION AIDES.
Administration of drugs to residents in assisted living facilities.
Authority to administer drugs, §54.1-3408.
Competency evaluation.
Application for registration by, §54.1-3042.
Continuing training required, §54.1-3043.
Registration required, §54.1-3041.

MEDICINE AND OTHER HEALING ARTS PROFESSIONS, §§54.1-2900 to 54.1-2993.
Adult abuse, neglect or exploitation.
Photographs, x-rays or medical imaging of incapacitated person.
Taking without consent as part of medical evaluation, §63.2-1606.1.
Report to local department of social services, §63.2-1606.
Aircraft pilots.
Disability reports to licensing authority.
Physician liability, §54.1-2966.
Anatomical gifts.
Advance health care directive, effect of gift, §32.1-291.21.
Death determinations, §32.1-296.
Aqueous solutions.
Sales of to physicians, §54.1-3418.
Assault and battery of health care provider.
Emergency room or other facility providing emergency care, §18.2-57.
Behavior analysts, §§54.1-2957.16, 54.1-2957.17.
Birth-related neurological injury compensation.
Review of claims by board of medicine, §38.2-5004.
Board of medicine, §§54.1-2911 to 54.1-2928.1.
Brain death.
Criteria for determining, §54.1-2972.
Child abuse or neglect reports.
Reason to suspect, required reports, fine for failure, §63.2-1509.

MEDICINE AND OTHER HEALING ARTS PROFESSIONS —Cont'd
Clinical training programs.
Medical students participating in supervised training programs.
Programs at medical schools, §54.1-2959.
Communicable disease reports, §32.1-116.3.
Competency assessment.
Three medical malpractice judgments or settlements in ten year period, §54.1-2912.3.
Congenital anomalies reporting and education system.
Contacts with, §§32.1-69.1, 32.1-69.2.
Continued competency requirements, §54.1-2912.1.
Controlled substances.
Dispensing restrictions, §§54.1-3302 to 54.1-3304.1.
Personnel trained to assist doctors.
Administering, §54.1-3408.
Sale of controlled substances, §54.1-2914.
Crime victims, compensation.
Debt collection activities by health care providers after claim filed.
Prohibited until award made or claim determined noncompensable, §19.2-368.5:2.
Debt collection activities defined, §19.2-368.5:2.
Statute of limitation for debt collection tolled, §19.2-368.5:2.
Death certificates.
Completion of medical certification, §32.1-263.
Death determinations, §54.1-2972.
Anatomical gifts.
Application to, §32.1-296.
Defined terms, §54.1-2900.
Certified respiratory therapy practitioner, §54.1-2954.
Dentist loan repayment program, §32.1-122.9:1.
Dialysis patient care technicians, §§54.1-2729.1 to 54.1-2729.3.
Disabled persons.
Physician reporting, §54.1-2966.
Disasters, state or local emergencies.
Immunity when responding to disasters.
Abandonment of person owed duty of health care to respond, §8.01-225.01.
Unable to provide required care because of lack of resources, §8.01-225.02.
Disciplinary action against practitioner.
Grounds, §54.1-2915.
Posting information concerning on department website, §54.1-2910.2.
Disciplinary proceedings.
Advisory boards, participation, §54.1-2409.3.
Disease reporting.
Immunity from liability, §32.1-38.
Infections of dead human bodies, §32.1-37.1.
Laboratory directors, §32.1-36.
Non-physicians, §32.1-37.
Physicians, §32.1-36.
District court civil cases.
Evidence of medical reports or records.
Testimony of health care provider, §16.1-88.2.
Doctor or Dr..
Use of title, §54.1-3616.
Do not resuscitate orders, §§54.1-2981 to 54.1-2993.
See LIVING WILLS.
Drug analysis.
Exemption from control provisions, §54.1-3407.

MEDICINE AND OTHER HEALING ARTS PROFESSIONS —Cont'd
Drug dispensation requirements, §54.1-3408.
Exceeding recommended dosages, §54.1-2971.01.
Educational programs, approval of, §§54.1-2958 to 54.1-2961.
Endorsement of certain documents by board, §54.1-2912.2.
Exceptions and exemptions generally, §54.1-2901.
Eyeglasses and contact lenses.
Prescriptions.
Filling at establishment of patient's choice.
Right of patient, informing patient, §54.1-2914.
Sales and dispensing by licensed practitioner, §54.1-2914.
Fee division, §54.1-2962.
Fetal death reports, §32.1-264.
Filing time extensions, §32.1-266.
Food supplements.
Sales in conjunction with practice, §54.1-2963.
Free clinics.
Immunity for services provided, §54.1-106.
Notice to licensees of board of medicine, §54.1-106.1.
Free health care to underserved populations.
Providing, §54.1-2901.
Good Samaritan statute.
Generally.
See GOOD SAMARITANS.
Immunity when responding to disasters.
Abandonment of person owed duty of health care to respond, §8.01-225.01.
Unable to provide required care because of lack of resources, §8.01-225.02.
Persons rendering emergency care, obstetrical services, §8.01-225.
Grants to medical students, §§32.1-122.5:1, 32.1-122.6.
Dental students, §32.1-122.9.
Dental hygiene, §32.1-122.10.
Physician loan repayment program, §32.1-122.6:1.
Health care data reporting generally, §§32.1-276.2 to 32.1-276.11.
See HEALTH CARE DATA REPORTING.
Health care decisions act, §§54.1-2981 to 54.1-2993.
See LIVING WILLS.
Health insurance plan not accepted by doctor.
Patient subject to full charge.
Information provided patient, §54.1-2910.01.
Health workforce recruitment, §32.1-122.20.
Hearing aid specialist licenses.
Exemptions for physicians, §54.1-1501.
Hepatitis.
Health care provider exposure.
Deemed consent to release of test results, §32.1-45.1.
HIV, health care provider exposure to.
Consent deemed given to release test results, §32.1-45.1.
Hospital privileges for podiatrists, §32.1-134.2.
Applications, responses to, §32.1-134.3.
Injunctions, §32.1-134.4.
Hospital referrals.
Payments for, §32.1-135.2.
Hospital staff membership or privileges.
Explanations for denial, exclusion or curtailment, §32.1-134.1.
Podiatrists, §§32.1-134.2 to 32.1-134.4.

MEDICINE AND OTHER HEALING ARTS PROFESSIONS —Cont'd

Immunity.
Criminal procedure.
Emergency treatment prior to trial.
Disclosures by health care providers, §19.2-169.6.
Disasters, state or local emergencies.
Abandonment of person owed duty of health care in response to disaster, §8.01-225.01.
Unable to provide required care because of lack of resources, §8.01-225.02.
Persons rendering emergency care, obstetrical services, §8.01-225.

Immunizations.
Certificates, §32.1-46.
Influenza vaccine, administration to minors by pharmacists or nurses, §32.1-46.02.
Virginia immunization information system (VIIS), §32.1-46.01.

Inborn errors of metabolism.
Detection and control reports, §§32.1-65, 32.1-66.
Compliance failures, §32.1-73.

Incapacitated persons.
Consent to medical treatment, §54.1-2970.
Sexual assault victims incapable of making informed decision.
Physical evidence recovery kit for, §54.1-2970.1.

Indigent patient programs offered by pharmaceutical manufacturers.
Practitioner of medicine or osteopathy participating in, §54.1-3301.

Infertility treatments.
Disclosure requirements, §54.1-2971.1.

Information provided patient upon request.
Doctors of medicine, osteopathy and podiatry, §54.1-2910.01.

Interns in hospitals, §54.1-2961.

Laboratory tests or other examinations.
Copy of results, providing patient or legal guardian.
Request by patient, laboratory providing directly, practitioner authorizing, §54.1-2409.4.

Laser surgery.
Health professions department, §54.1-2400.01.

Licensed assistants.
See PHYSICIAN ASSISTANTS.

Licensure and certification of other practitioners of the healing arts, §§54.1-2950.1 to 54.1-2957.01.
Controlled substances and medical devices and appliances.
Sales, §54.1-2914.
Copies of licenses, §54.1-2904.
Disciplinary proceedings.
Advisory boards, participation, §54.1-2409.3.
Examinations, §§54.1-2913.1, 54.1-2931.
Exceptions, §54.1-2901.
Experts in disciplinary proceedings, §54.1-2925.
International medical school graduates, §54.1-2933.
Issuance of license to practice, §54.1-2932.
Out-of-state applicants, §54.1-2927.
Practice, unlawful without license, §54.1-2902.
Lapsed license, practice prohibited, §54.1-2904.
Practice, what constitutes, §54.1-2903.
Qualifications of candidates, §54.1-2930.
Refusal to license, grounds, §§54.1-2915 to 54.1-2918.
Reinstatement of licenses, §54.1-2904.

MEDICINE AND OTHER HEALING ARTS PROFESSIONS —Cont'd

Licensure and certification of other practitioners of the healing arts —Cont'd
Renewal of licenses, §54.1-2904.
Reports on health professionals, §§54.1-2908, 54.1-2909.
Revocation of license, §§54.1-2915 to 54.1-2918.
Notice and opportunity to be heard, §54.1-2920.
Supplemental training or study, §54.1-2935.
Suspension of license, §§54.1-2915 to 54.1-2918.
Notice and opportunity to be heard, §54.1-2920.
Volunteer license, restricted, §54.1-2928.1.

Licensure of physicians of medicine and osteopathic medicine, chiropractors and podiatrists, §§54.1-2929 to 54.1-2941.
Controlled substances and medical devices and appliances.
Sales, §54.1-2914.
Copies of licenses, §54.1-2904.
Data required by board of medicine, §54.1-2910.1.
Disciplinary information.
Posting on department website, §54.1-2910.2.
Disciplinary proceedings.
Advisory boards, participation, §54.1-2409.3.
Examinations, §§54.1-2913.1, 54.1-2931.
Exemptions, §54.1-2901.
Experts in disciplinary proceedings, §54.1-2925.
Foreign licensees.
Temporary licensure to obtain training, §54.1-2933.1.
International medical school graduates, §54.1-2933.
Issuance of license to practice, §54.1-2932.
Medical malpractice judgments or settlements.
Reports, regulations on, adoption, §54.1-2910.1.
Out-of-state applicants, §54.1-2927.
Practice, unlawful without license, §54.1-2902.
Lapsed license, practice prohibited, §54.1-2904.
Practice, what constitutes, §54.1-2903.
Qualifications of candidates, §54.1-2930.
Refusal to license grounds, §§54.1-2915 to 54.1-2918.
Reinstatement of licenses, §54.1-2904.
Renewal of licenses, §54.1-2904.
Reports on health professionals, §§54.1-2908, 54.1-2909.
Revocation of license, §§54.1-2915 to 54.1-2918.
Notice and opportunity to be heard, §54.1-2920.
Supplemental training or study, §54.1-2935.
Suspension of license, §§54.1-2915 to 54.1-2918.
Notice and opportunity to be heard, §54.1-2920.
Temporary licensure of certain foreign graduates to obtain training, §54.1-2933.1.
Third-party reimbursement program participation not condition of licensure, §54.1-2910.3.
Volunteer license, restricted, §54.1-2928.1.

Living wills, §§54.1-2981 to 54.1-2993.
See LIVING WILLS.

Lyme disease testing, disclosures required, §54.1-2963.2.

Manage care health insurance plan.
Doctor not participant.
Patient subject to full charge.
Information provided patient, §54.1-2910.01.

Medical devices and appliances.
Sale, §54.1-2914.

Medical history protocol, §54.1-2403.1.

Medical malpractice.
General provisions, §§8.01-581.1 to 8.01-581.20.
See MEDICAL MALPRACTICE.

MEDICINE AND OTHER HEALING ARTS PROFESSIONS —Cont'd
Medical malpractice judgments or settlements.
Competency assessment, §54.1-2912.3.
Physicians of medicine and osteopathic medicine, chiropractors and podiatrists.
Reports, regulations on, adoption, §54.1-2910.1.
Medical malpractice review panels.
Health care provider members, §8.01-581.3, MedMal Rule 3.
Medical reports or records as evidence in district court civil cases.
Testimony of health care provider, §16.1-88.2.
Medical students in hospitals, §54.1-2960.
Medical students participating in supervised training programs.
Programs at medical schools, §54.1-2959.
Midwives.
Licensure, §§54.1-2957.7 to 54.1-2957.13.
Minors, surgical and medical treatment of.
Authority to consent, §54.1-2969.
Motor vehicle drivers.
Disability reports to licensing authority.
Physician liability, §54.1-2966.1.
Natural death, §§54.1-2981 to 54.1-2993.
See LIVING WILLS.
Occupational therapy.
Advisory board, §§54.1-2956.2 to 54.1-2956.5.
Oleaginous solutions.
Sales to physicians, §54.1-3418.
Ophthalmia neonatorum.
Prevention of blindness from.
Duties of professionals, §32.1-63.
Procedure upon birth, §32.1-62.
Failure to comply, §32.1-73.
Optician licenses.
Exemptions for physicians, §54.1-1501.
Pelvic examinations on anesthetized or unconscious females.
Medical students performing.
Restrictions on and requirements for performing, §54.1-2959.
Pharmacy board.
Drug licensing authority, §§54.1-3304, 54.1-3304.1.
Phenylketonuria.
Detection and control.
Reports, §§32.1-65, 32.1-66.
Compliance failures, §32.1-73.
Phototherapy devices.
Application of tanning facility provisions, §59.1-310.2.
Physician assistants.
See PHYSICIAN ASSISTANTS.
Podiatrists, surgery by, §54.1-2939.
Polysomnographic technologists, §§54.1-2957.14, 54.1-2957.15.
Postmortem examinations.
Persons who may authorize, §54.1-2973.
Prenatal test for venereal disease, §32.1-60.
Failure to comply, §32.1-73.
Prescriptions, §54.1-3408.
Biosimilars.
Adulterated drugs, prohibited acts, §54.1-3457.
Interchangeable biosimilars dispensed, §54.1-3408.04.
Nonresident pharmacies, compliance with provisions, §54.1-3434.1.
By professional counselors, §54.1-3502.
By psychologists, §54.1-3602.
By social workers, §54.1-3702.

MEDICINE AND OTHER HEALING ARTS PROFESSIONS —Cont'd
Prescriptions —Cont'd
Compounding, §54.1-3410.2.
Electronic or fax transmissions, §54.1-3408.02.
Exceeding recommended dosages, §54.1-2971.01.
Relief of intractable pain, medical necessity, §54.1-3408.1.
Generally.
See PRESCRIPTIONS.
Monitoring program, §§54.1-2519 to 54.1-2526.
Radiopharmaceuticals, §54.1-3410.1.
Requirements for, §54.1-3408.01.
Therapeutically equivalent drug products, §54.1-3408.03.
Prisoners' health care.
Involuntary admission and treatment.
Advice, §§53.1-40.1, 53.1-40.2.
Witness fees, §53.1-40.8.
Professional corporations, §§13.1-542.1 to 13.1-556.
See PROFESSIONAL CORPORATIONS.
Professional limited liability companies.
Generally, §§13.1-1100 to 13.1-1123.
See PROFESSIONAL LIMITED LIABILITY COMPANIES.
Professions and occupations regulation.
Generally.
See HEALTH PROFESSIONS DEPARTMENT.
Prohibited acts by licensees generally, §54.1-2409.1.
Radiopharmaceuticals, §54.1-3410.1.
Recruitment and retention of health care providers, §32.1-122.20.
Referral facilities.
Disclosure of interest in, §54.1-2964.
Referrals.
Payments by hospitals for, §32.1-135.2.
Solicitation or receipt of remuneration, §54.1-2962.1.
Reports.
Disabled persons, §54.1-2966.
Disease reporting.
Immunity from liability, §32.1-38.
Infections of dead human bodies, §32.1-37.1.
Laboratory directors, §32.1-36.
Non-physicians, §32.1-37.
Physicians, §32.1-36.
Fetal death reports, §§32.1-264, 32.1-266.
Motor vehicle driver disability reports.
Physician liability, §54.1-2966.1.
Wounds inflicted by weapons, §54.1-2967.
Residents in hospitals, §54.1-2961.
Scrap metal purchasers.
Exemption of material used in provision of health care, §59.1-136.7.
Self-referrals.
Practitioner self-referral act, §§54.1-2410 to 54.1-2414.
Sexual sterilization, §§54.1-2974 to 54.1-2980.
Solicitation of charitable or civic contributions.
Provision exemptions, §57-60.
Student loans.
Dentist loan repayment program, §32.1-122.9:1.
Suspension of license for delinquency, §54.1-2400.5.
Supervision of assistants by licensed physician.
What services may be performed, §54.1-2952.
Surgery by podiatrist, §54.1-2939.

MEDICINE AND OTHER HEALING ARTS PROFESSIONS —Cont'd
Surgery, who may perform generally, §54.1-2400.01:1.
Tanning facility provisions.
Application to phototherapy device use, §59.1-310.2.
Therapeutic pharmaceutical agents, §§54.1-3222 to 54.1-3224.
Title restrictions.
Applicability, §54.1-3513.
Sex offender treatment provider, §54.1-3611.
Unlawful procurement of licensure, §54.1-102.
Unlawful use of licensure, §54.1-111.
Unprofessional conduct.
Grounds for disciplinary action, §54.1-2915.
Venereal diseases.
Information to be provided patients, §32.1-56.
Prenatal test, §32.1-60.
Failure to comply, §32.1-73.
Vitamins.
Sales in conjunction with practice, §54.1-2963.
Witnesses.
Medical reports or records as evidence in district court proceedings.
Testimony of health care providers, §16.1-88.2.
Workers' compensation.
Charges for services, §65.2-714.
False statements or representations, §65.2-312.
Independent medical examinations, §65.2-606.
Medical examinations ordered by employer or commission, §65.2-607.
Peer review of medical costs, §§65.2-1300 to 65.2-1310.
Wounds inflicted by weapons.
Physician reporting, §54.1-2967.
Wrongful death actions against health care providers.
Expert witness opinion, certification of, §8.01-50.1.
Sympathy, admissibility of expressions of, §8.01-52.1.

MEDICINE FOR ANIMALS, §§3.2-4900 to 3.2-4914.
See ANIMALS.

MEDICINES.
Prescriptions.
See PRESCRIPTIONS.
Retail sales and use tax exemptions, §58.1-609.10.

MEDITATION.
Silent meditation in public schools.
Daily observance of one minute of silence, §22.1-203.

MED-PAY BENEFITS.
Medical expense payment provisions.
See MOTOR VEHICLE INSURANCE.

MEETING HOUSES.
Burning or destroying, §18.2-79.

MEETINGS OF GENERAL ASSEMBLY.
Convening extra sessions, §30-3.
Place and time, §30-1.
Appointed by governor, §30-2.

MEETINGS OF LOCAL GOVERNMENTAL BODIES, §§15.2-1415 to 15.2-1421.
Annual of organizational meeting.
Establishing days, times and places of regular meetings, §15.2-1416.

MEETINGS OF LOCAL GOVERNMENTAL BODIES —Cont'd
Authorities, boards and commissions.
Regular meeting times, §15.2-1419.
Call or request for special meeting, §15.2-1417.
Disrupting, preventing orderly conduct, §18.2-415.
Exercise of powers conferred, §15.2-1415.
First amendment right of freedom of speech.
Expressions by members and public prior to convening meeting consistent with, §15.2-1416.1.
Industrial development authority board meetings.
Open meetings, §15.2-4904.
Notice of special meeting, §15.2-1417.
Questions determined, §15.2-1420.
Quorum, §15.2-1415.
Regular meetings, §15.2-1416.
Authorities, boards and commissions, §15.2-1419.
Special meetings, §§15.2-1417, 15.2-1418.
Tie breakers.
Counties designating, §§15.2-1420, 15.2-1421.
Transportation districts.
Open meetings, §15.2-4511.
Virginia freedom of information act.
Applicability, §15.2-1415.

MEETINGS OF MEMBERS OF NONPROFIT CORPORATIONS.
Generally.
See NONPROFIT CORPORATIONS.

MEETINGS OF PUBLIC BODIES.
Disrupting, preventing orderly conduct, §18.2-415.
Family violence fatality review teams.
Death investigations, §32.1-283.3.
Virginia Commonwealth University health system authority.
Board of directors, §23-50.16:32.
Workers' compensation commission, §65.2-204.

MEETINGS OF SHAREHOLDERS OF CORPORATIONS.
Generally.
See CORPORATIONS.

MEGAN'S LAW.
Sex offender and crimes against minors registry.
Generally, §§9.1-900 to 9.1-922.
See SEX OFFENDER REGISTRATION AND NOTIFICATION.
Maintenance, §19.2-390.1.

MEHERRIN RIVER.
Dams.
Restrictions, §29.1-532.
Scenic river, §10.1-418.3.
Taking methods, restrictions, §29.1-531.

MEI PROJECT APPROVAL COMMISSION, §§30-309 to 30-312.
Established, §30-309.
Freedom of information act.
Excluded records, §2.2-3705.6.
Membership, §30-309.
Purpose, §30-309.
Report to General Assembly, §30-312.
Review of individual incentive packages, §30-310.
Staff, §30-311.

MEI PROJECTS.
Public building authority, §2.2-2260.

MELONS.
Farm produce.
Dealers in agricultural produce.
Farm produce sales, §§3.2-4738 to 3.2-4752.

MEMBER OR DIRECTOR AGREEMENTS.
Nonprofit corporations, §13.1-852.1.
Voting agreements, §13.1-852.2.

MEMBERSHIP CAMPING, §§59.1-311 to 59.1-335.
Application of provisions, §59.1-312.
Severability of provisions, §59.1-315.
Cease and desist orders, §59.1-324.
Citation of chapter, §59.1-311.
Conflict of laws, §§59.1-312, 59.1-314.
Promotional prizes and gifts, §59.1-332.
Consumer protection, prohibited practices, §59.1-200.
Contracts, §59.1-328.
Defined, §59.1-313.
Fraud, §59.1-330.2.
Inducements, §59.1-332.
Noncomplying contracts voidable, §59.1-330.1.
Nondisturbance provisions, §59.1-333.
Resales of memberships, §59.1-331.
Rights of purchasers, §59.1-327.
Defined terms, §59.1-313.
Home solicitation sales.
Application of provisions, §59.1-322.
Investigations, §59.1-334.
Mail notice.
Initial notice by certified mail, subsequent notices by regular mail, §59.1-313.1.
Property owners' associations.
Applicability of provisions, §55-508.
Protection of purchasers.
Contracts, §59.1-328.
Fraud, §59.1-330.2.
Noncomplying contracts voidable, §59.1-330.1.
Deposits, §59.1-329.
Disclosure statements, §59.1-326.
Inducements, §59.1-332.
Nondisturbance provisions, §59.1-333.
Resale of memberships, §59.1-331.
Rights of purchasers, §59.1-327.
Surety bonds, §59.1-329.
Provision violations.
Penalties, §59.1-335.
Ratio restrictions, §59.1-317.
Registration, §§59.1-317 to 59.1-325.
Administration, §59.1-317.
Applications, §59.1-318.
Review, §59.1-320.1.
Denial, §59.1-323.
Duration, §59.1-320.1.
Exemptions, §59.1-321.
Fees, §59.1-325.
Home solicitation sales requirements.
Compliance, §59.1-322.
Required, §59.1-317.
Revocation, §59.1-323.
Suspension, §59.1-323.
Severability of provisions, §59.1-315.
Temporary orders, §59.1-324.
Travel clubs.
Application of provisions, §59.1-453.

MEMBERSHIP IN CRIMINAL STREET GANG, §18.2-46.2.

MEMORANDUM ASSESSMENTS.
Individual income tax.
Individual desiring to pay in currency, §58.1-352.

MEMORANDUM OF LIEN.
Collection of state taxes, §58.1-1805.
Collection of taxes assessed by state corporation commission, §58.1-2021.
Income tax.
Jeopardy assessment, §58.1-313.
Retail sales and use tax, delinquent taxes, §58.1-632.

MEMORIAL DAY.
Legal holidays, §2.2-3300.

MEMORIALS BY HIGHWAYS AND ROADS, §33.1-206.1.

MEMORIAL SERVICES.
Disrupting or preventing orderly conduct of funeral.
Disorderly conduct, §18.2-415.

MEMORIALS FOR WAR VETERANS.
Counties, cities or towns, §15.2-1812.
Damage to memorials, actions, §15.2-1812.1.

MENHADEN.
Use of purse nets for taking, §§28.2-400 to 28.2-411.
Area restrictions, §28.2-409.
Biological sampling program and adult survey index, §28.2-400.6.
Closure of Chesapeake Bay purse seine fishery for Atlantic menhaden, §28.2-1000.2.
Food fish restrictions, §28.2-408.
Landings reports, §28.2-400.5.
Licenses.
Appeals, §§28.2-403, 28.2-404.
Applications, §28.2-400.
Commissioner action, §28.2-403.
Dredge.
Carrying while fishing for menhaden, §28.2-405.
Fees, §28.2-402.
Forfeiture of property, §28.2-407.
Patent tongs.
Carrying while fishing for menhaden, §28.2-405.
Qualification for limited entry license, §28.2-400.1.
Scrape.
Carrying while fishing for menhaden, §28.2-405.
Service of notice, process and other papers, §28.2-401.
Transfers, §28.2-403.
Net restrictions, §28.2-410.
Season restrictions, §28.2-410.
Total allowable landings, §28.2-400.2.
Allocation, §28.2-400.3.
Closure when certain percentage of landings taken, §28.2-400.4.
Landings reports, §28.2-400.5.
Monitoring and administration of management program, §28.2-400.4.
Vessel restrictions, §28.2-411.

MENINGITIS.
Colleges and universities.
Vaccination of in-coming student against meningococcal disease, §23-7.5.
Workers' compensation.
Presumption on death or disability, §65.2-402.1.

MENINGOCOCCAL MENINGITIS.
Workers' compensation.
Presumption on death or disability, §65.2-402.1.

MENOKIN FOUNDATION, INCORPORATED.
Historical resources department.
Appropriations, §10.1-2212.

MENTAL ANGUISH.
Amount of damages, §8.01-52.

MENTAL EXAMINATIONS.
Child abuse or neglect.
Psychological, psychiatric and physical examinations of child.
Court may order, §63.2-1524.
Child custody or visitation proceedings.
Custody or visitation at issue, court may order, §20-124.2.
Examination of person standing in loco parentis to child, §16.1-278.15.
Children under supervision of detention homes.
Transportation to psychological and psychiatric evaluations, §16.1-254.
Judicial inquiry and review commission.
Physical or mental examination of judge, §17.1-912.
Juvenile proceedings, §16.1-275.
Children taken into custody, §16.1-248.2.
Statements made, §16.1-261.
Prisoners' health care.
Involuntary admission and treatment, §53.1-40.2.
Psychiatric inpatient treatment of minors.
Involuntary commitment, §16.1-342.
Parental admission of minor younger than fourteen or nonobjecting minor, §16.1-338.
Parental admission of objecting minor, §16.1-339.

MENTAL HEALTH.
Abuse or neglect of incapacitated adult, §18.2-369.
Accounts and accounting.
Access to records, accounts and reports, §37.2-703.
Private funds provided for individuals receiving services, §37.2-705.
Social Security and other federal payments.
Commissioner authorized to receive and expend for individuals receiving services in state facilities, §37.2-704.
System of records, accounts and reports to be prescribed, §37.2-703.
Admissions.
Maliciously or knowingly contriving or conspiring to admit person without reasonable cause, §37.2-431.
Maliciously or knowingly contriving or conspiring to obtain.
Behavioral health and developmental services, §37.2-431.
Prisoners incapable of consenting to treatment, §§53.1-40.1 to 53.1-40.10.
Adult abuse or neglect.
Incapacitated adult, §18.2-369.
Alcoholic beverages, provision or sale to individuals receiving services, §37.2-430.
Aliens.
District court judges.
Power to commit, §16.1-69.28.
Juvenile court disposition of child with mental illness or intellectual disability, §§16.1-278.11, 16.1-280.

MENTAL HEALTH —Cont'd
Aliens —Cont'd
Psychiatric treatment of minors, §§16.1-335 to 16.1-348.
Alternative treatment.
Spiritual means without drugs or material remedy, §37.2-414.
Appeals.
Judicial authorization of treatment.
Appeals from order, §37.2-1105.
Attorneys at law.
Rules of professional conduct.
Client under a disability, VA SCt Rule Pt 6 §II Rule 1.14.
Background check of children's residential facility employees, §37.2-408.1.
Banks.
Effect of incompetence of customer, §8.4-405.
Payment of deposits, §6.2-893.
Powers of banks, §6.2-820.
Behavioral health authorities.
General provisions, §§37.2-600 to 37.2-615.
See BEHAVIORAL HEALTH AUTHORITIES.
Board.
See BEHAVIORAL HEALTH AND DEVELOPMENTAL SERVICES BOARD.
Board of elections.
List of incompetents furnished monthly to state board, §24.2-410.
Burning or destroying mental health facilities, §18.2-77.
Capital punishment.
Defendant's mental condition relevant to capital sentencing.
Expert testimony, §19.2-264.3:1.
Caregivers grant program.
Grants for care providers, §§63.2-2200 to 63.2-2204.
See CAREGIVERS GRANT PROGRAM.
Certificates of need for medical care facilities, §§32.1-102.1 to 32.1-102.11.
See MEDICAL CARE FACILITIES.
Children or minors.
Background check of residential facility employees, §37.2-408.1.
Children taken into custody, §16.1-248.2.
Statements made, §16.1-261.
Children under supervision of detention homes.
Psychological or psychiatric evaluation of children.
Transportation responsibilities of detention home, §16.1-254.
Juvenile proceedings.
Mental examinations and treatment, §16.1-275.
Residence of children born in state facilities, §37.2-714.
School-age children in state facilities, §37.2-713.
Children, psychiatric treatment, §§16.1-335 to 16.1-348.
Admission forms, §16.1-336.1.
Appeal of final orders, §16.1-345.6.
Applicability generally, §16.1-337.
Application and consent of parent.
Admission of minor younger than fourteen, §16.1-338.
Admission of nonobjecting minors fourteen years of age or older, §16.1-338.
Admission of objecting minor fourteen years or older, §16.1-339.
Attorneys for minors on involuntary commitment.
Appointment, §16.1-341.

MENTAL HEALTH —Cont'd
Children, psychiatric treatment —Cont'd
Attorneys for minors on involuntary commitment —Cont'd
Appointment of attorney for unrepresented minor filing appeal, §16.1-345.6.
Duties, §16.1-343.
Availability of judges, §16.1-348.
Clinical evaluation on involuntary commitment petition, §16.1-342.
Confidentiality of files, papers and records, §16.1-337.
Criteria for involuntary commitment, §16.1-345.
Definitions, §16.1-336.
Department of behavioral health and developmental services.
Preparation of prescreening and other clinical forms, §16.1-336.1.
Detention homes, minors in, §16.1-339.1.
Discharge of minor younger than fourteen or nonobjecting minor.
Revocation of parental consent or objections by minor, §16.1-338.
Discharge of objecting minor.
Revocation of parental consent to admission, §16.1-339.
Discharge plan, §16.1-346.1.
Duration of inpatient treatment.
Involuntary commitment, §16.1-345.
Minors younger than fourteen or nonobjecting minors, §16.1-338.
Electronic communications.
Use for petitions and orders, §16.1-345.1.
Emergency custody orders, §16.1-340.
Involuntary temporary detention, §16.1-340.1.
Transportation of minor during, §16.1-340.2.
Evidence at hearing on involuntary commitment, §16.1-344.
Fees and expenses for qualified evaluators, §16.1-347.
Guardian ad litem.
Appointment on judicial approval of admission of objecting minor, §16.1-339.
Hearing on involuntary commitment, §§16.1-341, 16.1-344.
Release of minor to parents prior to hearing, §16.1-340.3.
Immunity.
Health care provider disclosing records to certain persons, §16.1-337.
Involuntary commitment, §16.1-341.
Appeal of final orders, §16.1-345.6.
Attorney for minor, duties, §16.1-343.
Appointment of attorney for unrepresented minor filing appeal, §16.1-345.6.
Clinical evaluation, §16.1-342.
Criteria, §16.1-345.
Electronic communications.
Use for petitions and orders, §16.1-345.1.
Hearings, §16.1-344.
Mandatory outpatient treatment.
Appeal of final orders, §16.1-345.6.
Continuation of order, §16.1-345.5.
Criteria, §16.1-345.2.
Monitoring, §16.1-345.3.
Orders, §16.1-345.2.
Continuation, §16.1-345.5.
Review.
Court review, §16.1-345.4.
Motion for, §16.1-345.3.
Preadmission screening report, §16.1-340.4.

MENTAL HEALTH —Cont'd
Children, psychiatric treatment —Cont'd
Involuntary commitment —Cont'd
Release of minor to parents prior to hearing, §16.1-340.3.
Treatment plans, §16.1-346.
Involuntary temporary detention, §16.1-340.1.
Transportation of minor during, §16.1-340.2.
Judge availability, §16.1-348.
Juvenile court commitment.
Generally, §16.1-280.
Juvenile proceedings, §16.1-275.
Law enforcement officers.
Emergency custody orders, execution, §16.1-340.
Notice of hearing on involuntary commitment, §16.1-341.
Outpatient treatment.
Involuntary commitment.
Mandatory outpatient treatment, §§16.1-345.2 to 16.1-345.6.
Parental admission of minor younger than fourteen and nonobjecting minors, §16.1-338.
Parental admission of objecting minors, §16.1-339.
Parental notification of information regarding minor's health care, §16.1-337.
Petition for involuntary commitment, §16.1-341.
Petition for judicial approval.
Admission of objecting minor, §16.1-339.
Preadmission screening.
Conduct in lieu of examination for admission to state hospital, §16.1-338.
Involuntary commitment, report required, §16.1-340.4.
Mandatory outpatient treatment.
Duties upon receipt of motion for review, §16.1-345.5.
Preparation of forms, §16.1-336.1.
Qualified evaluator.
Clinical evaluation on involuntary commitment petition, §16.1-342.
Examination of objecting minor, §16.1-339.
Fees and expenses, §16.1-347.
Release of minor to parents prior to hearing on involuntary admission, §16.1-340.3.
Release on expiration of involuntary commitment order, §16.1-345.
Service of notice of hearing on involuntary commitment, §16.1-341.
Shelter care facilities, minors in, §16.1-339.1.
Short title, §16.1-335.
Supreme court.
Preparation of admission forms, §16.1-336.1.
Temporary detention, §16.1-340.1.
Transportation of minor during, §16.1-340.2.
Transportation to medical facility.
Emergency custody orders, §16.1-340.
Involuntary commitment, §16.1-345.
Involuntary temporary detention, §16.1-340.2.
Treatment plan.
Discharge plan, §16.1-346.1.
Individualized plan for involuntarily committed minor, §16.1-346.
Individualized plan for minors younger than fourteen or nonobjecting minors, §16.1-338.
Individualized plan for objecting minor fourteen years of age or older, §16.1-339.
Witnesses at hearing on involuntary commitment, §16.1-344.
Circuit court clerks.
List of incompetents furnished monthly to state board of elections, §24.2-410.

MENTAL HEALTH —Cont'd
Civil commitment of mentally ill persons.
General provisions, §§37.2-800 to 37.2-920.
See CIVIL COMMITMENT OF MENTALLY ILL PERSONS.
Colleges and universities.
Community college mental health policies, §23-219.1.
Policies and memorandum of agreement to expand services of students seeking treatment, §23-9.2:8.
School records of student upon attendance at institution of higher education, §23-2.1:3.
Community college mental health policies, §23-219.1.
Community mental health services boards.
General provisions, §§37.2-500 to 37.2-512.
See COMMUNITY MENTAL HEALTH SERVICES BOARDS.
Competency to stand trial.
Generally.
See COMPETENCY TO STAND TRIAL.
Insanity defense, §§19.2-167 to 19.2-182.
See INSANITY DEFENSE.
Confidential information.
Exchange of information about individuals receiving services, §37.2-711.
Religious preferences and affiliations of individuals receiving services, §37.2-712.
Conservators of the peace.
Authority, §37.2-426.
Construction of state facilities.
Razing buildings, §37.2-700.
Controlled substances.
Methamphetamines.
Allowing child, mentally incapacitated or physically helpless person to be present during manufacture, §18.2-248.02.
Criminal background check of children's residential facility employees, §37.2-408.1.
Criminal law and procedure.
Acquittal by reason of insanity, §§19.2-182.2 to 19.2-182.16.
See ACQUITTAL BY REASON OF INSANITY.
Drug sales on or near state hospitals, §18.2-255.2.
Financial exploitation of mentally incapacitated persons, §18.2-178.1.
Insanity defense, §§19.2-167 to 19.2-182.
See INSANITY DEFENSE.
Crisis intervention teams, §§9.1-187 to 9.1-190.
Critical incidents or deaths of individuals receiving services.
Notice to designated protection and advocacy system director, §37.2-709.
Notice to representative of individual, §37.2-709.1.
Death of person in custody.
Payments to persons standing in loco parentis, §64.2-558.
Deferral of elderly or handicapped from real property taxation, §§58.1-3210 to 58.1-3217.
Deferral of sentencing.
Person convicted of offense indicating sexual abnormality, §§19.2-300 to 19.2-302.
Definitions, §37.2-100.
Judicial authorization of treatment, §37.2-1100.
Department of behavioral health and developmental services.
See BEHAVIORAL HEALTH AND DEVELOPMENTAL SERVICES DEPARTMENT.

MENTAL HEALTH —Cont'd
Directors of state facilities.
Duties, §37.2-707.
Employment, §37.2-707.
Qualifications, §37.2-707.
Salaries, §37.2-708.
Discharge, release, etc.
Reports to motor vehicles department, §46.2-401.
Discrimination as to insurance coverage because of mental impairment, §38.2-508.
Disorderly conduct on grounds of facility, §37.2-429.
Disposition of real estate of persons under disability, §§8.01-67 to 8.01-80.
See PERSONS WITH DISABILITY.
District court judges.
Power to commit insane, drug-addicted and inebriated persons, §16.1-69.28.
Drivers' licenses.
Examination of applicants believed incapacitated, §46.2-322.
License not issued to applicant adjudged incapacitated, §46.2-314.
Suspension of license of incapacitated persons, §46.2-400.
One year suspension after hearing, §46.2-402.
Drug offenders.
Commitment for treatment of drug or alcohol abuse, §18.2-254.
Treatment or education programs as condition of probation, §18.2-258.1.
Drug sales on or near state hospital property, §18.2-255.2.
Duty to protect third parties from violent behavior or serious harm.
Mental health service providers, §54.1-2400.1.
Elderly individuals.
Separate state facilities for, §37.2-702.
Employees of state facilities.
Salaries, §37.2-708.
Encumbrance of real estate.
Disposition of real estate of persons under disability generally, §§8.01-67 to 8.01-80.
See PERSONS WITH DISABILITY.
Escape from facility.
Aiding and abetting, §37.2-428.
Resident required to register with sex offender and crimes against minors registry.
Notification by department to state police, §37.2-921.
Evidence.
Hearsay exceptions.
Then existing mental, emotional, or physical condition, VA SCt Rule 2:803.
Examination of condition of facilities, §37.2-701.
Exchange of information about individuals receiving services, §37.2-711.
Exchange of real estate.
Disposition of real estate of persons under disability generally, §§8.01-67 to 8.01-80.
See PERSONS WITH DISABILITY.
Exemption of elderly or handicapped from real property taxation, §§58.1-3210 to 58.1-3217.
Expenses of care, treatment or training, and maintenance.
Amount.
Limitations, §37.2-715.
Assessments and contracts by department, §37.2-717.

MENTAL HEALTH —Cont'd
Expenses of care, treatment or training, and maintenance —Cont'd
Collection by department.
When not required, §37.2-720.
Decedents' estates.
Liability of estate of individual receiving services, §37.2-721.
Investigation by department of financial ability to pay, §37.2-717.
Liability for, §37.2-715.
Estate of individual receiving services, §37.2-721.
Statement forms to be completed by person liable for support of individual receiving services, §37.2-719.
Order to compel payment, §37.2-718.
Revenue fund, §37.2-716.
Statement forms to be completed by person liable for support of individual receiving services, §37.2-719.
Financial exploitation of mentally incapacitated persons, §18.2-178.1.
Firearm.
Disqualification for concealed weapons permit, §18.2-308.09.
Purchase, possession or transportation by mentally incapacitated, §18.2-308.1:2.
Fishing licenses.
Issuance to patients in state institutions, §29.1-313.
Freestanding state facilities.
Authorized, §37.2-702.
Grants for care providers.
Virginia caregivers grant program, §§63.2-2200 to 63.2-2204.
Health care data reporting.
Generally, §§32.1-276.2 to 32.1-276.11.
See HEALTH CARE DATA REPORTING.
Health care professionals.
Reports on to licensing authorities, §§54.1-2908, 54.1-2909.
Health insurance coverage.
Biologically based mental illness, §38.2-3412.1:01.
Public officers and employees, §2.2-2818.
Family access to medical insurance security plan, §§32.1-351 to 32.1-353.
Services, §38.2-3412.1.
Hearsay exceptions.
Then existing mental, emotional, or physical condition, VA SCt Rule 2:803.
Human research.
Board regulations, §37.2-402.
Human rights.
Rights of individuals receiving services, §37.2-400.
Incompetency.
Conservators.
See CONSERVATORS.
Generally.
See INCOMPETENCY.
Guardian and ward.
See GUARDIAN AND WARD.
Insanity defense.
Acquittal by reason of insanity, §§19.2-182.2 to 19.2-182.16.
See ACQUITTAL BY REASON OF INSANITY.
General provisions, §§19.2-167 to 19.2-182.
See INSANITY DEFENSE.
Insurance discrimination because of mental impairment, §38.2-508.

MENTAL HEALTH —Cont'd
Interference with officers and employees, §37.2-429.
Internet posting of licensed providers by corporate, assumed or fictitious names, §37.2-405.1.
Involuntary admission.
Children, psychiatric inpatient treatment, §§16.1-341 to 16.1-346.
Criminal defendants.
Acquittal of defendant by reason of insanity, §19.2-182.3.
Psychiatric hospitalization of defendant prior to trial or sentencing, §19.2-169.6.
Firearms possessed by person involuntarily admitted or ordered.
Disqualification for concealed weapons permit, §18.2-308.09.
Purchase, possession or transportation, §18.2-308.1:3.
Jail inmates, §19.2-169.6.
Prisoners with mental illness, §§53.1-40.1 to 53.1-40.10.
Discharge, §53.1-40.7.
Jail residents, §19.2-169.6.
Release from custody imminent, civil admission proceeding, §53.1-40.9.
Psychiatric inpatient treatment of minors, §§16.1-341 to 16.1-346.
Jails.
Emergency medical, dental and psychiatric care for local prisoners.
Compact, authority of state to enter, §53.1-133.10.
Judicial authorization of treatment, §§37.2-1100 to 37.2-1109.
Actions not authorized by chapter, §37.2-1102.
Antipsychotic medication, electroconvulsive therapy.
Ordering, time restrictions, §37.2-1102.
Appeals from order, §37.2-1105.
Appointment of attorney to represent interests of person for whom treatment sought, §37.2-1101.
Authority of circuit or district courts, §37.2-1101.
Clear and convincing evidence.
Standard of proof, §37.2-1101.
Costs of detention, testing or treatment, payment, §37.2-1107.
Definitions, §37.2-1100.
Electronic filing of petitions and orders, §37.2-1109.
Emergency custody order, §37.2-1103.
Findings required for authorizing treatment, §37.2-1101.
Incapable of making an informed decision.
Standard of proof required, §37.2-1101.
Lack of capacity to consent to treatment, claim based on.
Health professional or hospital not liable on, §37.2-1106.
Lack of consent to treatment, claim based on.
Health professional or hospital not liable on, §37.2-1106.
Law-enforcement officers sent beyond territorial jurisdiction.
Execution of emergency custody order, §37.2-1103.
Order authorizing treatment.
Requirements, §37.2-1101.
Other laws, effect of chapter on, §37.2-1108.

MENTAL HEALTH —Cont'd
Judicial authorization of treatment —Cont'd
Petition.
Request for authorization of treatment, §37.2-1101.
Request for authorization of treatment, §37.2-1101.
Risks and benefits of treatment.
Investigation by appointed attorney, §37.2-1101.
Standard of proof.
Clear and convincing evidence, §37.2-1101.
Temporary detention in hospital, §37.2-1104.
Training center or hospital.
Admission to, ordering, §37.2-1102.
Jury service.
Persons disqualified from service, §8.01-338.
Voluntary exemption for person responsible for continuous care, §8.01-341.1.
Juvenile court commitment.
Disposition of persons adjudged mentally ill or intellectually disabled, §16.1-278.11.
Generally, §16.1-280.
Juvenile proceedings.
Children taken into custody, §16.1-248.2.
Statements made at, §16.1-261.
Court-ordered counseling or treatment.
Payment of costs, §16.1-290.1.
Disposition of persons adjudged mentally ill or intellectually disabled, §16.1-278.11.
Victim impact statements.
Cases involving substance abuse, §16.1-273.
Lease of real estate.
Disposition of real estate of persons under disability generally, §§8.01-67 to 8.01-80.
See PERSONS WITH DISABILITY.
Legal representatives of individuals receiving services.
Persons prohibited from becoming, §37.2-401.
Licensing of mental health facilities, §§37.2-403 to 37.2-422.
See LICENSING OF MENTAL HEALTH FACILITIES.
Life-sharing communities, §63.2-1808.1.
Limitation of actions.
Disabilities which toll statute of limitations, §8.01-229.
Limited partnerships.
Power of incompetent partner to assigned partnership interest, §50-73.48.
Living wills, §§54.1-2981 to 54.1-2993.
See LIVING WILLS.
Medical records.
Treatment of practitioners.
Disclosure, §54.1-2406.
Who may consent, §8.01-413.
Medical treatment for incapacitated persons, §54.1-2970.
Mental or physical disorders.
Judicial authorization of treatment, §§37.2-1100 to 37.2-1109.
Methamphetamines.
Allowing child, mentally incapacitated or physically helpless person to be present during manufacture, §18.2-248.02.
Minors, psychiatric treatment, §§16.1-335 to 16.1-348.
Juvenile court jurisdiction, §16.1-241.
Taking child into immediate custody, §16.1-246.
Mistreatment of individuals receiving services, §37.2-427.

MENTAL HEALTH —Cont'd
Nonresidents.
Property transfers of nonresidents, §§64.2-1426 to 64.2-1432.
Opiate addiction treatment providers.
Conditions for initial licensure, §37.2-406.
Parole.
Contributions by parolee towards cost of program, §53.1-150.1.
Treatment or education programs as condition of parole, §18.2-258.1.
Physician-patient privilege.
Psychologists.
Clinical psychologists as healing art practitioners, §8.01-399, VA SCt Rule 2:505.
Pregnant women.
Medical history protocol, §54.1-2403.1.
Substance abuse, rulemaking authority, §37.2-407.
Prisoners.
Involuntary commitment, §§53.1-40.1 to 53.1-40.10.
Psychiatric hospitalization of defendant prior to trial or sentencing.
Jail residents, §19.2-169.6.
Private funds provided for individuals receiving services, §37.2-705.
Property transfers of nonresidents, §§64.2-1426 to 64.2-1432.
Provider supervision of persons maintaining or operating services, §37.2-413.
Psychologists.
Physician-patient privilege.
Clinical psychologists as healing art practitioners, §8.01-399, VA SCt Rule 2:505.
Public officers.
Vacancy in office.
Determination person incapacitated in judicial proceeding, §24.2-232.
Razing buildings.
Construction of state facilities, §37.2-700.
Real property taxes.
Elderly and handicapped exemption or deferral, §§58.1-3210 to 58.1-3217.
Listing and taxing property to committee, §58.1-3015.
Recognizance taken by insane or mentally incompetent person, §19.2-141.
Records.
Access to, §37.2-703.
Colleges and universities.
School records of students upon attendance at institution of higher education, §23-2.1:3.
Facilities, §32.1-274.
System to be prescribed, §37.2-703.
Redemption of real estate.
Disposition of real estate of persons under disability generally, §§8.01-67 to 8.01-80.
See PERSONS WITH DISABILITY.
Religious practices.
Spiritual means of treatment without drugs or material remedy, §37.2-414.
Religious preferences and affiliations of individuals receiving services.
Collection and dissemination of information concerning, §37.2-712.
Reports.
Access to records, accounts and reports, §37.2-703.
Patient-level data and financial data, §37.2-710.
Psychiatric treatment of children.
Involuntary commitment.
Preadmission screening report, §16.1-340.4.

MENTAL HEALTH —Cont'd
Reports —Cont'd
System of records, accounts and reports to be prescribed, §37.2-703.
Representatives.
Persons representing and binding others, §§64.2-714 to 64.2-718.
Residence.
Children born in state facilities, §37.2-714.
Individuals in state facilities, §37.2-713.
Rights of individuals receiving services, §37.2-400.
Salaries of state mental health clinic employees.
Supplementing by certain counties and cities, §15.2-1508.4.
Sale of real estate.
Disposition of real estate of persons under disability generally, §§8.01-67 to 8.01-80.
See PERSONS WITH DISABILITY.
Secretary of health and human resources.
Responding to needs of substance abusing women and their children, §2.2-213.
Sex offender and crimes against minors registry.
Committed residents required to register with state police on release or discharge.
Duty of department of behavioral health and developmental services, §37.2-921.
Social Security and other federal payments.
Commissioner authorized to receive and expend for individuals receiving services in state facilities, §37.2-704.
Special education.
Dispute resolution for placement of handicapped children, §§22.1-214, 22.1-214.1.
Generally, §§22.1-213 to 22.1-221.
See SPECIAL EDUCATION.
Programs for innovative methods of teaching mentally ill children, §22.1-217.1.
Statute of limitations.
Disabilities which toll statute of limitations, §8.01-229.
Substance abusing women and their children.
Secretary of health and human resources.
Responding to needs, §2.2-213.
Supervision of persons maintaining or operating services, §37.2-413.
Surplus property.
Certain property not to be declared surplus, §37.2-701.
Tax on property owned by mentally ill or incompetent person.
Listed and taxed to committee, §58.1-3015.
Termination of residual parental rights, §16.1-283.
Third party protection.
Mental health service providers.
Protection from violent or serious harm by client, §54.1-2400.1.
Treatment of mental or physical disorders.
Judicial authorization of treatment, §§37.2-1100 to 37.2-1109.
Trust companies.
Powers, §§6.2-820, 6.2-1002.
Trust fund.
Administration, §37.2-319.
Definitions, §37.2-317.
Use of net proceeds, §37.2-319.
Unclaimed personal property of individuals receiving services.
Disposal, §37.2-706.

MENTAL HEALTH —Cont'd
Venereal disease testing upon admittance, §32.1-59.
Veterans, national guard or military reserve members.
Community corrections.
Special treatment procedures, §9.1-173.1.
Department of veterans services.
Establishment of mental health and rehabilitative services program, §2.2-2001.1.
Violations.
Admission of person without reasonable cause.
Maliciously or knowingly contriving or conspiring to obtain, §37.2-431.
Authority of personnel appointed conservators of the peace, §37.2-426.
Disorderly conduct, §37.2-429.
Escape from facility.
Aiding and abetting, §37.2-428.
Interference with officers and employees, §37.2-429.
Mistreatment of individuals receiving services, §37.2-427.
Provision or sale of alcoholic beverages to individuals receiving services, §37.2-430.
Violent behavior or serious bodily harm.
Mental health service providers duty to protect third parties, §54.1-2400.1.
Virginia caregivers grant program.
Grants for care providers, §§63.2-2200 to 63.2-2204.
Voter qualifications.
Adjudicated mentally incompetent not qualified to vote, VA Const Art II §1.
Voter registration.
Cancellation upon incapacity determination, §24.2-427.
Wills.
Persons who may execute, §64.2-401.
Probate.
Bills to impeach or establish.
Tolling, §64.2-448.
Zoning of group homes for mentally ill, or intellectually or developmentally disabled persons, §15.2-2291.

MENTAL HEALTH, INTELLECTUAL DISABILITY AND SUBSTANCE ABUSE SERVICES BOARD.
See BEHAVIORAL HEALTH AND DEVELOPMENTAL SERVICES BOARD.

MENTAL HEALTH, INTELLECTUAL DISABILITY AND SUBSTANCE ABUSE SERVICES DEPARTMENT.
See BEHAVIORAL HEALTH AND DEVELOPMENTAL SERVICES DEPARTMENT.

MENTAL HEALTH PROFESSIONALS.
Adult abuse, neglect or exploitation.
Report to local department of social services, §63.2-1606.
Child abuse or neglect reports.
Reason to suspect, required reports, fine for failure, §63.2-1509.
Disclosure of patient information to third party payors by professionals.
See MENTAL HEALTH.
Duty to protect third parties.
Violent behavior or serious harm by client, §54.1-2400.1.

MENTALLY ILL.
Caregivers grant program.
See CAREGIVERS GRANT PROGRAM.
Civil commitment of mentally ill persons.
General provisions, §§37.2-800 to 37.2-920.
See CIVIL COMMITMENT OF MENTALLY ILL PERSONS.
Generally.
See MENTAL HEALTH.
Sale, lease, exchange, redemption or other disposition of realty.
Disposition of real estate of persons under disability generally, §§8.01-67 to 8.01-80.
See PERSONS WITH DISABILITY.

MENTALLY INCOMPETENT OR INCAPACITATED.
Caregivers grant program.
See CAREGIVERS GRANT PROGRAM.
Civil commitment of mentally ill persons.
General provisions, §§37.2-800 to 37.2-920.
See CIVIL COMMITMENT OF MENTALLY ILL PERSONS.
Generally.
See MENTAL HEALTH.
Sale, lease, exchange, redemption or other disposition of realty.
Disposition of real estate of persons under disability generally, §§8.01-67 to 8.01-80.
See PERSONS WITH DISABILITY.
Treatment and other mental health or substance abuse services.
See MENTAL HEALTH.

MENTAL OR PHYSICAL DISORDERS.
Judicial authorization of treatment.
See MENTAL HEALTH.

MERCHANTABILITY.
Leases, UCC.
Implied warranty, §8.2A-212.
Exclusion or modification, §8.2A-214.
Sales, UCC.
Implied warranty, §8.2-314.
Exclusion or modification, §8.2-316.
Uniform computer information transactions act.
Implied warranties, §59.1-504.3.

MERCHANT MARINE.
Absentee voter registration, §24.2-419.
Absentee voting.
Generally, §§24.2-700 to 24.2-713.
See ABSENTEE AND EARLY VOTING.
Military and overseas voters act, §§24.2-451 to 24.2-470.
See ABSENTEE AND EARLY VOTING.
Persons entitled to vote by absentee ballots, §24.2-700.
Voter registration.
Extended time for members to register, §24.2-420.1.

MERCHANTS AT WHOLESALE.
License taxes, §58.1-3716.

MERCHANTS CAPITAL TAX.
Capital subject to local taxation, §58.1-3509.
License tax in lieu of, §58.1-3704.
Merchants' capital defined, §58.1-3510.
Pharmaceutical wholesalers.
Separate classification of merchant capital, §58.1-3510.01.
Rate limits, §58.1-3509.

MERCHANTS CAPITAL TAX —Cont'd
Situs for taxation, §§58.1-3511 to 58.1-3514.
Tangible personal property taxation generally, §§58.1-3500 to 58.1-3522.
See PERSONAL PROPERTY TAXES.

MERCHANTS, ITINERANT, §§54.1-4300 to 54.1-4306.

MERCURY THERMOSTAT RECYCLING, §10.1-1425.26.

MERCY KILLINGS.
Living wills.
Construction of article, §54.1-2990.

MERGER.
Banks.
Interstate bank mergers, §§6.2-849 to 6.2-859.
See BANKS.
Business trusts, §§13.1-1257 to 13.1-1263.
Foreign business trusts, §13.1-1250.
Property title records.
Organizational changes generally, §13.1-1285.
Corporations, §§13.1-715.1 to 13.1-721.1.
Abandonment of merger, §13.1-721.1.
Action on plan, §13.1-718.
Affiliated transactions, §§13.1-725 to 13.1-727.1.
Appraisal rights, §§13.1-729 to 13.1-741.1.
Articles of merger, §13.1-720.
Fee, §13.1-616.
Definitions, §13.1-715.1.
Effect, §13.1-721.
Foreign corporations authorized to transact business, §13.1-766.1.
Holding company.
Merger between constituent corporation and indirect subsidiary, §13.1-719.
Plan of merger, §13.1-716.
Property title records, §13.1-781.
Shareholders, action on plan, §13.1-718.
Subsidiaries.
Merger between constituent corporation of holding company and indirect subsidiary, §13.1-719.1.
Merger between parent and subsidiary or between subsidiaries, §13.1-719.
Credit unions, §6.2-1318.
Share insurance.
Failure to maintain, §6.2-1332.
Supervisory merger or transfer of assets, §6.2-1317.
Voluntary merger, §6.2-1344.
Foreign corporations.
Foreign corporation authorized to transact business in Commonwealth, §13.1-766.1.
Foreign limited partnerships, §50-73.57:2.
Foreign nonprofit corporations.
Articles of merger.
Fees, §13.1-816.
Foreign trust institutions, §6.2-1068.
Fraternal benefit societies, §38.2-4114.
Health services plans.
Nonprofit corporation operating plan, §38.2-4204.
Liability of participating providers upon, §38.2-4213.
Prepaid hospital, medical and surgical service plans.
Approval of state corporation commission, §38.2-4204.1.
Insurance companies, §§38.2-1017, 38.2-1018.
Acquisition of control of insurers, §§38.2-1323 to 38.2-1328.

MERGER —Cont'd
Insurance companies —Cont'd
Approval of state corporation commission required, §38.2-216.
License tax on telegraph, telephone, water, heat, light, power and pipeline companies.
Gross receipts in cases of merger, §58.1-2631.
Limited liability companies, §§13.1-1070 to 13.1-1073.
Approval, §13.1-1071.
Articles of merger, §13.1-1072.
Articles of organization or operating agreement.
Prohibition, §13.1-1070.
Certificate of merger, §13.1-1072.
Effect of merger, §13.1-1073.
Foreign limited liability companies, §13.1-1060.
Law governing, §13.1-1060.
Foreign stock corporation merging with, §13.1-766.1.
Plan of merger, §§13.1-1070 to 13.1-1073.
Surviving business organization, §13.1-1073.
Limited partnerships, §§50-73.48:1 to 50-73.48:4.
Corporations.
Foreign corporations, §13.1-766.1.
Nonprofit corporations, §§13.1-893.1 to 13.1-897.1.
Abandonment of merger, §13.1-897.1.
Articles of merger, §13.1-896.
Fee, §13.1-816.
Authorization, §13.1-894.
Definitions, §13.1-893.1.
Effect, §13.1-897.
Foreign corporations, §13.1-928.1.
Articles of merger.
Fees, §13.1-816.
Plan of merger, §13.1-894.
Action by directors or members, §13.1-895.
Property title records.
Corporate changes generally, §13.1-945.
Partnerships, §50-73.128.
Effect, §50-73.129.
Statement of merger, §50-73.131.
Planning district commissions, §15.2-4221.
Professional corporations.
Merger with foreign professional corporation or foreign professional limited liability company, §13.1-545.1.
Requirements, §13.1-555.
Professional limited liability companies, §§13.1-1106, 13.1-1121.
Railroad corporations, §56-345.1.
Savings institutions.
Association and bank, §6.2-1146.
Telephone cooperatives, §56-500.
Fees, §56-505.

MERRIMAC PARK COMMISSION, 1958 ch 618.

MESCALINE.
Drug control act.
Generally, §§54.1-3400 to 54.1-3472.
See DRUG CONTROL.
Drug offenses.
Generally, §§18.2-247 to 18.2-264.
See DRUG OFFENSES.
Schedule I controlled drug, §54.1-3446.

MESNE PROFITS.
Ejectment.
Claim for mesne profits.
Assessment, §§8.01-158, 8.01-159.
Postponement of assessment, §8.01-162.

MESNE PROFITS —Cont'd
Ejectment —Cont'd
Claim for mesne profits —Cont'd
Recovery from persons other than defendant, §8.01-164.

MESSAGES BY TELEGRAPH OR TELEPHONE.
Generally.
See TELEGRAPH OR TELEPHONE MESSAGES.

MESSENGER SERVICES.
State departments and agencies.
Division of support services, general services department, duties, §2.2-1169.

METABOLIC DISEASES.
Detection and control of phenylketonuria and other inborn errors of metabolism, §§32.1-65 to 32.1-67.1.
Virginia immunization information system (VIIS).
Linkages to other databases containing certain health records, §32.1-67.1.
Voluntary program for control, §§32.1-68, 32.1-69.

METAL.
Industrial, manufacturing or public utility metal.
Buying with intent to defraud, §18.2-238.
Reduction of heavy metals in packaging, §§10.1-1425.20 to 10.1-1425.25.
Scrap metal purchasers, §§59.1-136.1 to 59.1-136.7.
See SCRAP METAL PURCHASERS.

METAL CONTAINERS.
Litter tax imposed on manufacturers, wholesalers, distributors or retailers, §58.1-1708.

METAL KNUCKS.
Carrying concealed weapons, §18.2-308.
Convicted felons, possession, transportation or concealing, §18.2-308.2.
Courthouses, carrying weapon into, §18.2-283.1.
School property, possession on, §18.2-308.1.
Selling or having in possession, §18.2-311.
Use in commission of crime.
Forfeiture, §19.2-386.29.

METEOROLOGICAL LABORATORIES.
Locality regulating outdoor lighting near, §15.2-920.

METERS, UTILITY.
Defined terms, §56-245.2.
Good working condition requirements, §56-245.1.
Landlord and tenant.
Submetering equipment use, §55-226.2.
Prepaid metering equipment and system.
Electric utilities.
Installation upon customer requests, §56-247.1.
Standards, §56-245.3.

METHADONE.
Opiate addiction treatment providers.
Conditions for initial licensure, §37.2-406.
Schedule II controlled drug, §54.1-3448.

METHAMPHETAMINES.
Allowing child, mentally incapacitated or physically helpless person to be present during manufacture, §18.2-248.02.

METHAMPHETAMINES —Cont'd
Driving while intoxicated.
Blood concentration level, §18.2-266.
Presumption accused under influence, §18.2-269.
Drug control, §§54.1-3400 to 54.1-3472.
See DRUG CONTROL.
Drug offenses.
Generally, §§18.2-247 to 18.2-264.
See DRUG OFFENSES.
Health, state board.
Guidelines for cleanup of residential property used as clandestine methamphetamine laboratories, §32.1-11.7.
Landlord and tenant.
Disclosures by landlord for property previously used to manufacture methamphetamine, §§55-225.17, 55-248.12:3.
Localities, cleanup of methamphetamine labs.
Liability of offender in separate civil action for costs, §15.2-1716.2.
Manufacture, sale, possession or distribution, §18.2-248.03.
Methamphetamine cleanup fund, §18.2-248.04.
Methamphetamine precursor drugs.
Defined, §18.2-248.
Retail sales of products containing, §18.2-248.8.
Sale of ephedrine or related compounds, §§18.2-265.6 to 18.2-265.18.
See EPHEDRINE.
Possession of substances with intent to manufacture, §18.2-248.
Residential property transfer disclosures.
Required disclosures, property previously used to manufacture methamphetamine, §55-519.4.
Schedule II controlled drug, §54.1-3448.

METHANE GAS.
Building or facility to collect and use for electric energy.
Loans to local governments, §§15.2-2430 to 15.2-2440.
See VIRGINIA INFRASTRUCTURE PROJECT LOAN FUND.
Coal mines, surface coal mines, §§45.1-161.256 to 45.1-161.258, 45.1-161.288.
Coal mines, underground coal mines.
Actions for excess methane, §45.1-161.222.
Electric equipment, §45.1-161.193.
Examination for explosive gas and other hazardous conditions, §45.1-161.231.
On-shift examinations, §45.1-161.209.
Pre-shift examinations, §45.1-161.208.
Weekly examinations, §45.1-161.210.
Gas and oil exploration.
Coalbed methane gas, ownership rights not affected, §45.1-361.21:1.

METHANE MONITORING DEVICES OR EQUIPMENT.
Coal mines, underground coal mines.
Allowing persons to work in mine when equipment disconnected, §45.1-161.233.
Checking and testing, §45.1-161.195.
Notice of tampering prohibition, §45.1-161.215.
Tampering with devices, §45.1-161.232.
Flame safety lamps, §45.1-161.297.

METHANOL.
Alternative fuels revolving fund, §§33.1-223.3 to 33.1-223.9.
Labelling of motor fuels, §59.1-167.1.

METHANOL —Cont'd
Motor vehicle emissions inspections.
Clean alternative fuel fleet standards, §46.2-1179.1.
School buses.
Alternative fuel.
Defined terms, §46.2-1089.1.

METHCATHINONE.
Possession of substances with intent to manufacture, §18.2-248.

METHYL BROMIDE.
State forester.
Seedling plant beds, fumigation, §10.1-1114.

METHYL TERTIARY-BUTYL ETHER (MTBE).
Water supply systems.
Inspection of public and private water supply for MTBE, §15.2-2144.

METRIC SYSTEM.
Highways and roads.
Saving provision, §33.1-190.3.
Signs bearing metric units of measure.
Expenditure of funds prohibited in connection with certain signs, §33.1-190.2.
Statutory construction.
Weights and measures deemed to include metric equivalents, §1-256.

METROPOLITAN AREAS.
Transportation districts.
Generally, §§15.2-4500 to 15.2-4534.
See TRANSPORTATION DISTRICTS.

METROPOLITAN PLANNING ORGANIZATIONS.
General assembly members.
Expanding membership to include, §33.1-223.2:23.
Planning duties and responsibilities, §33.1-223.2:25.

METROPOLITAN TRANSPORTATION DISTRICTS, 1970 ch 697.

METROPOLITAN UNIFORM LAWS COMMISSION, 1968 ch 329.

METROPOLITAN WASHINGTON AIRPORTS AUTHORITY, §§5.1-152 to 5.1-177.
Acquisition of airports from United States.
Authorization, §5.1-154.
Acquisition of property, eminent domain, §5.1-160.
Audit of financial transactions, §5.1-170.
Bond issues.
Credit of Commonwealth or political subdivision not pledge, §5.1-166.
Fees and charges, authorization to fix and collect.
Payment of bonds, §5.1-168.
Legal investments, §5.1-165.
Marketability of bonds, powers, §5.1-164.
Members not personally liable, §5.1-155.
Pledge of funds, §5.1-163.
Power to issue revenue bonds, §5.1-156.
Refunding bonds, §5.1-162.
Remedies of holders, §5.1-171.
Revenue bonds, §5.1-161.
Securities for public deposit, §5.1-165.
Tax exemption, §5.1-172.
Trust agreement securing, §5.1-167.
Trust funds, §5.1-169.
Votes required to approve, §5.1-155.
Budget.
Votes required to approve, §5.1-155.

METROPOLITAN WASHINGTON AIRPORTS AUTHORITY —Cont'd
Contract liability, §5.1-173.
Created, §5.1-153.
Criminal penalties.
Violations of rule or regulation, §5.1-157.
Definitions, §5.1-152.
Eminent domain, power, §5.1-160.
Exemption from taxation, §5.1-172.
Fairfax county police.
Jurisdiction of over authority facilities, §5.1-158.
Fees and charges, authorization to fix.
Trust funds, §5.1-169.
Foreign trade zones.
Operation of, §5.1-159.
Immunity of members from liability, §5.1-155.
Inconsistent law inapplicable, §5.1-177.
Independence of authority, §5.1-156.
Jurisdiction of courts of Commonwealth, §5.1-173.
Liberal construction of act, §5.1-175.
Loudoun county police.
Jurisdiction of over authority facilities, §5.1-158.
Membership, terms, officers, quorum, §5.1-155.
Noise limitation on aircraft.
Violation of rule or regulation, §5.1-157.
Notice of intention to adopt rule or regulation.
Publication, §5.1-157.
Powers and duties, §5.1-156.
Publication.
Notice of intention to adopt rule or regulation, §5.1-157.
Public hearings.
Rules or regulations, §5.1-157.
Public procurement act exemption, §5.1-174.
Refunding bonds, §5.1-162.
Revenue bonds, §5.1-161.
Rules and regulations, §5.1-157.
Severability of provision, §5.1-176.
Strikes by employees prohibited, §5.1-156.
Tax exemption, §5.1-172.
Tort liability, §5.1-173.
Traffic and parking.
Rules or regulations, §5.1-157.
Trust funds.
Proceeds from sale of bonds and collection of revenues, §5.1-169.

METROPOLITAN WASHINGTON AIRPORTS AUTHORITY RULES OR REGULATIONS.
Judicial notice.
Rules and regulations, §5.1-157.
Police.
Authorization to establish and maintain force, powers, §5.1-157.
State police department.
Powers upon facilities elsewhere in Commonwealth, §5.1-157.

MEXICO.
Criminal records.
Information exchange program.
Secretary of public safety to establish, §2.2-224.1.

MIAS.
Tuition and fees for state supported colleges or universities.
Waiver for spouses and children, §23-7.4:1.

MICROBES AND PATHOGENS.
Disease prevention and control.
Laboratory reporting on, §32.1-36.

MICROBES AND PATHOGENS —Cont'd
Disease prevention and control —Cont'd
Nonsocomial infections, reporting information on, §32.1-35.1.
Promulgation of list, §32.1-35.
Virginia immunization information system (VIIS), §32.1-46.01.

MICROCOMPUTER DEVICES.
Determining speed of motor vehicles, §46.2-882.
Division of purchases and supply.
Determining proper equipment for monitoring, §2.2-1112.

MICROFILMING OR MICROPHOTOGRAPHING RECORDS AND DOCUMENTS.
Circuit court clerks.
Costs, certification and payment, §17.1-246.
Full faith and credit to reproduction, §17.1-244.
Maintaining indexes by, §17.1-249.
Recording by microphotographic process, §17.1-240.
Removing books from clerk's office, §17.1-245.
Standards for using process, §17.1-239.

MICROWAVE RADIO SYSTEMS.
Cable television.
See CABLE TELEVISION AND SERVICE.
Unlawful use of or injury to signals and equipment, §18.2-165.

MIDDLE ATLANTIC INTERSTATE FOREST FIRE PROTECTION COMPACT.
Forest wardens and fires, §10.1-1150.

MIDDLE PENINSULA CHESAPEAKE BAY PUBLIC ACCESS AUTHORITY, §§15.2-6600 to 15.2-6625.
Actions by or against, §15.2-6606.
Applicability of local ordinances, codes, taxes, etc, §15.2-6623.
Authority to create, §15.2-6601.
Board of directors, §15.2-6604.
Bond issues, §15.2-6612.
Legal investments, §15.2-6618.
Liability limitation, §15.2-6615.
Not debt of Commonwealth, §15.2-6614.
Political subdivisions, §15.2-6619.
Agreement regarding bonds, §15.2-6621.
Security for payment, §15.2-6616.
Tax exemption, §15.2-6617.
Construction of provisions, §15.2-6622.
Definitions, §15.2-6602.
Existing contracts not impaired, §15.2-6624.
Fees, §15.2-6613.
Funds of authority, §15.2-6611.
Jurisdiction of appeals, §15.2-6606.
Liability of political subdivisions, §15.2-6603.
Meetings, §15.2-6605.
Name, §15.2-6607.
Officers, §15.2-6605.
Pecuniary liability of political subdivisions, §15.2-6603.
Political subdivisions.
Agreement regarding bonds, §15.2-6621.
Appropriations and bond issuance, §15.2-6619.
Contracts with, §15.2-6620.
Powers generally, §15.2-6606.
Procurement, §15.2-6610.
Purposes, §15.2-6601.
Quorum, §15.2-6605.
Records, §15.2-6609.

MIDDLE PENINSULA CHESAPEAKE BAY PUBLIC ACCESS AUTHORITY —Cont'd
Rents and charges, authority to collect, §15.2-6613.
Rulemaking, §15.2-6608.
Title of provisions, §15.2-6600.
Traffic regulations, adopting, §15.2-6608.
Withdrawal of membership, §15.2-6625.

MIDDLE PENINSULA REGIONAL AIRPORT AUTHORITY, 1997 ch 871.

MIDDLE SCHOOLS.
Athletic events.
Immunity for team physicians, §8.01-225.1.

MIDDLESEX COUNTY.
Coastal primary sand dunes and beaches.
Zoning ordinances, §28.2-1403.
Middle Peninsula regional airport authority, 1997 ch 871.
Northern Neck-Middle Peninsula public education consortium.
Inclusion in region, §22.1-354.6.
Piankatank river.
Public oyster rocks, beds and shoals, §28.2-646.
School board.
Fingerprinting applicants for employment, §22.1-296.2.
Salary of members, §22.1-32.

MIDWIVES, §§54.1-2957.7 to 54.1-2957.13.
Advisory board on midwifery, §54.1-2957.10.
Business relationship with licensed midwife.
Negligent, grossly negligent or willful and wanton acts or omissions by midwife.
Liability for, §54.1-2957.12.
Certified nurse midwife.
Liability, §54.1-2957.03.
Medically underserved areas.
Pilot programs for obstetrical and pediatric care in underserved areas, §32.1-11.5.
Pilot programs.
Practice without physician supervision, §54.1-2901.
Prescribing schedule III through VI controlled substances, §54.1-2957.01.
Conditional grants, §32.1-122.6:02.
Definitions, §54.1-2957.7.
Delegating activities or functions.
Apprentices or supervised employees, §54.1-2957.13.
Disclosure of health risks, §§54.1-2957.03, 54.1-2957.9.
Disclosure of specific information to client, §54.1-2957.11.
Exceptions to provisions, §54.1-2957.13.
Health insurance.
Policy coverage for services, §38.2-3408.
Health services plans.
Coverage provided, §38.2-4221.
Hospital privileges, §32.1-134.2.
Injunctions, §32.1-134.4.
Response to applications, §32.1-134.3.
Immunity of persons other than licensed midwife.
Negligent, grossly negligent or willful and wanton acts or omissions by midwife, §§54.1-2957.03, 54.1-2957.12.
Inborn errors of metabolism.
Detection and control reports, §32.1-65.
Compliance failures, §32.1-73.

MIDWIVES —Cont'd
Liability of certified nurse midwife, §54.1-2957.03.
License.
Certified professional midwife credential.
Required, §54.1-2957.8.
Exceptions, §54.1-2957.13.
Renewal, §54.1-2957.9.
Required, §54.1-2957.8.
Medically underserved areas.
Certified nurse midwife.
Pilot programs for obstetrical and pediatric care in underserved areas, §32.1-11.5.
Negligent, grossly negligent or willful and wanton acts or omissions.
Liability for, §§54.1-2957.03, 54.1-2957.12.
Ophthalmia neonatorum.
Prevention of blindness from.
Duty of midwife, §32.1-63.
Procedure upon birth, §32.1-62.
Failure to comply, §32.1-73.
Phenylketonuria.
Detection and control reports, §32.1-65.
Compliance failures, §32.1-73.
Postpartum blues or perinatal depression.
Information to maternity patient prior to releasing, §32.1-134.01.
Regulation of practice, §54.1-2957.9.
Unlawful to practice without license, §54.1-2957.8.

MIGRANT LABOR CAMPS, §§32.1-203 to 32.1-211.
Defined terms, §32.1-203.
Notice of intention to construct, remodel or enlarge, §32.1-204.
Operators' responsibilities, §32.1-210.
Permits.
Applications, §32.1-206.
Denial, §32.1-209.
Issuance, §32.1-207.
Provisional permits, §32.1-208.
Required, §32.1-205.
Revocation, §32.1-209.
Suspension, §32.1-209.
Transferability, §32.1-207.
Regulations, §32.1-211.

MILEAGE.
Board for people with disabilities, §51.5-32.
County police.
Transporting violator to jail.
Jail of another county or city adopted as jail of county, §15.2-1609.6.
District court judges and clerks, §16.1-69.47:1.
Election officers, §24.2-116.
Electoral board members, §24.2-108.
Electors for president and vice-president, §24.2-205.
Ethics advisory panels, senate and house of general assembly, §30-112.
General assembly.
Attending legislative committees during recess of assembly, §30-19.15.
Distance ascertained from place other than courthouse of counties or certain cities, §30-19.18.
Jail boards, §53.1-108.
Jurors allowances for attendance and travel expenses, §§17.1-618 to 17.1-623.
Juvenile and domestic relations district court service staff, §§16.1-238, 16.1-239.

MILEAGE —Cont'd
Magistrates.
Allowance, §19.2-46.1.
Sheriffs and deputies, §15.2-1609.3.
Report by sheriff as to mileage incurred, §15.2-1609.4.
Witnesses.
Allowances, §§17.1-611 to 17.1-617.
Juvenile proceedings, §16.1-276.
Tax commissioner, allowance to witnesses summoned before, §58.1-218.

MILITARY.
Abandoned motor vehicles.
Vehicles registered to active duty military personnel, §46.2-1200.2.
Absentee and early voting.
Generally, §§24.2-700 to 24.2-713.
See ABSENTEE AND EARLY VOTING.
Military and overseas voters, §§24.2-451 to 24.2-470.
See ABSENTEE AND EARLY VOTING.
Acknowledgments, §§55-114.1, 55-115.
Who may perform notarial acts, §55-118.1.
Active duty.
Child custody, visitation or support adjudication.
Changed circumstance because of call to active duty.
Petition expedited on docket, §20-108.
Delegation of visitation to family member, §20-124.8.
Military parents equal protection act, §§20-124.7 to 20-124.10.
Continuance or extension of time for filing pleading, etc., where party or attorney on active duty, §44-97.1.
Registration or titling of motor vehicle.
Nonresident active duty member's vehicle registered or titled in another state, §46.2-600.
Rights and benefits, §44-102.1.
State militia.
Regulations generally, §§44-75.1 to 44-84.
Teachers and other school employees.
Compensation of public school employees called to active duty, §22.1-289.2.
Airports.
Military air installations, properties adjacent to.
Landlord obligations, disclosure, §55-248.12:1.
Armories generally, §§44-123 to 44-140.
See ARMORIES.
Assault and battery against family or household member.
Armed forces members found guilty.
Reporting findings to military family advocacy representative, §18.2-57.4.
Assisting armed forces in unlawful detention of United States citizens, §2.2-614.2:1.
Attorneys at law.
Registered military legal assistance attorneys, VA SCt Rule 1A:6.
Attorneys-in-fact.
Deeds and writings executed for personnel under defective powers, §55-56.
Bail and recognizance.
Forfeiture of recognizance while in military or naval service, §19.2-144.
Banking facilities in federal areas, §6.2-835.
Carrying concealed weapons permits.
Expiration during active duty deployment.
Continued validity, time period, §18.2-308.

MILITARY —Cont'd
Child custody, visitation or support adjudication.
Changed circumstance because of call to active duty.
Petition expedited on docket, §20-108.
Delegation of visitation to family member, §20-124.8.
Military parents equal protection act, §§20-124.7 to 20-124.10.
City or town power to aid military units organized in municipality, §15.2-1112.
Civilian contractors.
Motor vehicle registration and license plates.
Grace period for civilian contractors stationed outside the United States, §46.2-221.4.
College and university tuition and required fees.
Dependents of active duty personnel stationed in Virginia.
Domicile for in-state tuition, §23-7.4.
Military duty requiring withdrawal from enrollment.
Tuition relief, refunds and reinstatement.
Guidelines issued, §23-9.6:2.
Virginia military survivors and dependents education program.
Waiver for spouses and children of certain military personnel, §23-7.4:1.
Colleges and universities.
Course credit for active duty and veterans, §23-9.2:3.7.
Restructured financial and administrative operations.
Active military duty.
Employees called to, §23-38.118.
Commission in service not to vacate civil office, §44-102.
Community corrections.
Special treatment procedures, §9.1-173.1.
Compelling attendance as witnesses.
Prior permission required for admiral or general rank, §8.01-407.
Continuance or extension of time for filing pleading where party or attorney on active duty, §44-97.1.
Courts-martial.
National guard, §§44-42 to 44-54.
Naval militia, §§44-67 to 44-74.
Death in line of duty.
Half mast display of state and local flags, §18.2-488.1.
Deeds executed for personnel.
Attorneys-in-fact under defective powers, §55-56.
Default judgments.
Servicemembers civil relief act, §8.01-15.2.
Setting aside default judgments, §8.01-428.
Dentists serving on active duty.
Liability exemption for clinic work, §54.1-106.
Department.
See MILITARY AFFAIRS DEPARTMENT.
Detention of citizens.
Assisting armed forces in unlawful detention of United States citizens, §2.2-614.2:1.
Discrimination as to insurance, §38.2-508.1.
Dishonorable discharge from armed forces of the United States.
Disqualification for concealed weapons permit, §18.2-308.09.
Divorce.
Domicile of military personnel residing abroad, §20-97.

MILITARY —Cont'd
Drivers' licenses.
Commercial drivers' licenses, military experience considered, §46.2-341.9.
Exemption of armed services personnel, §§46.2-305, 46.2-306, 46.2-308.
Extension of licenses for armed services or foreign service personnel, §46.2-221.2.
Motorcycle classification.
Issuance by mail to military members, spouses and dependents, §46.2-328.
Temporary motorcycle classification, completion of safety course, §46.2-328.
Educational opportunity for military children, §§22.1-360, 22.1-361.
Emancipation of minor.
Active duty with armed forces, findings necessary, §16.1-333.
Fire insurance policies.
Discrimination in issuing or refusal to renew, §§38.2-2114, 38.2-2115.
Fishing licenses.
Disabled active duty military personnel, §29.1-302.01.
Military personnel on official leave, exception, §29.1-301.
Flags.
Death in line of duty, half mast display of state and local flags, §18.2-488.1.
Free tuition and fees to state supported colleges and universities.
Virginia military survivors and dependents education program.
Spouses and children of certain military personnel, §23-7.4:1.
Government data collection and dissemination practices act.
Recruiter access to student information and school facilities, §2.2-3804.
Governor.
Military aides, §2.2-102.
Grave markers.
Sale of military grave markers.
Civil penalty, §18.2-511.
Highways and roads.
Speed limits, authority to change, roads within confines of a US military base, §46.2-878.
HOV lanes on interstate 264 and interstate 64.
Utilization by active duty members traveling to military facility in Hampton Roads planning district, §33.1-46.2.
Income tax.
Individual income tax.
Estimated tax, payments, §58.1-491.1.
Extension of time for filing returns.
Desert shield participants, §58.1-344.
Penalty, interest and addition to tax nonapplicable, §58.1-344.1.
Reserve components, §58.1-344.
Insurance discrimination, §38.2-508.1.
Interstate 264 and interstate 64.
HOV lanes.
Utilization by active duty members traveling to military facility in Hampton Roads planning district, §33.1-46.2.
Jails.
Mental health and rehabilitation services support program, establishment, §2.2-2001.1.
Jury service.
Exemption upon request, §8.01-341.1.

MILITARY —Cont'd
Jury service —Cont'd
Federal military personnel not considered residents, §8.01-337.
Landlord and tenant.
Military air installations, properties adjacent to.
Landlord obligations, disclosure, §55-248.12:1.
Leases.
Rental agreements.
Early termination, §55-248.21:1.
Leaves of absence for employees of Commonwealth or political subdivisions, §44-93.
Discrimination in hiring prohibited, §44-93.4.
Penalty for employer failure to comply, §44-93.5.
Reemployment rights, §44-93.3.
Supplement of military pay and additional life insurance benefits, §44-93.1.
Leaves of absence for nongovernmental employees, §44-93.2.
Discrimination in hiring prohibited, §44-93.4.
Penalty for employer failure to comply, §44-93.5.
Reemployment rights, §44-93.3.
Legal separation.
Domicile of military personnel residing abroad, §20-97.
License plates.
Special license plates, §§46.2-746.1 to 46.2-746.4.
Active duty, honorably discharged or retired, §46.2-743.
License taxes.
Armed forces personnel returning from duty outside the United States.
Grace period for business credentialing, §46.2-221.2.
Life insurance discrimination, §38.2-508.1.
Medals and decorations.
Requirement that medals and decorations be made in United States, §44-120.1.
Medical officers serving on active duty.
Liability exemption for clinic work, §54.1-106.
Mental health and rehabilitation services.
Community corrections.
Special treatment procedures, §9.1-173.1.
Support program for Virginia veterans, Virginia national guard members and Virginia residents in reserves.
Establishment by department of veterans services, §2.2-2001.1.
Military assault forces.
Special license plates, §46.2-746.1.
Military family relief fund, §44-102.2.
Tax refunds, voluntary contributions to, §58.1-344.3.
Military parents equal protection act, §§20-124.7 to 20-124.10.
Militia.
Generally, §§44-1 to 44-122.
See MILITIA.
Motorcycles.
Drivers' licenses, motorcycle classification.
Issuance by mail to military members, spouses and dependents, §46.2-328.
Temporary motorcycle classification, completion of safety course, §46.2-328.
Motorcycle classification.
Issuance by mail to military members, spouses and dependents, §46.2-328.
Motor vehicle insurance.
Discrimination in issuance, §38.2-2213.
Discrimination in refusing to renew, §38.2-2212.

MILITARY —Cont'd
Motor vehicle insurance —Cont'd
Refusal to renew based on military service, §38.2-2212.
Motor vehicle registration.
Abandoned motor vehicles.
Vehicles registered to active duty military personnel, §46.2-1200.2.
Grace period for active duty military personnel stationed outside the United States, §46.2-221.4.
Nonresident active duty member's vehicle registered or titled in another state, §46.2-600.
Motor vehicles, abandoned.
Vehicles registered to active duty military personnel, §46.2-1200.2.
Motor vehicle safety inspections.
Extension of validity of stickers for active duty members of the armed services, §46.2-1158.1.
Names and discharges of men serving during war, recording.
Circuit court clerks, §§17.1-261 to 17.1-265.
Names or insignia, registration, alteration, cancellation, §§2.2-411 to 2.2-417.
See REGISTRATION OF NAMES OR INSIGNIA OF ORGANIZATIONS.
National guard.
Generally, §§44-25 to 44-54.3.
See NATIONAL GUARD.
Naval militia.
Generally, §§44-55 to 44-74.
See NAVAL MILITIA.
Notaries.
Armed services member registered and commissioned as notary.
Eligibility, §47.1-4.
Nursing.
Expediting licensure process.
Relocating to state pursuant to spouse's military orders.
Applicant licensed or certified in another state, §54.1-3005.
Oath of office.
Person required to take on active duty in armed forces.
Person who may administer, §49-3.
Payday loans.
Prohibited business methods against military personnel, §6.2-1816.
Powers of attorney and agency agreements.
Laws continued in effect, §44-207.
Professions and occupations.
Expediting issuance of licenses to military spouses, §54.1-119.
Expiration of documents issued to persons in service in armed services, §54.1-117.
Military experience, training and education as substantially equivalent to qualifications for licensure, §54.1-118.
Public officers and employees.
Carry forward of accrued annual leave.
State employee in organized reserve or national guard, §2.2-1201.
Federal employees prohibited, exception.
Active-duty or engaged in war service, §2.2-2802.
Members of Armed Forces and reserve forces, §2.2-2805.
Selective service system, §2.2-2803.

MILITARY —Cont'd
Public officers and employees —Cont'd
Health insurance for state employees.
Supplemental coverage under state program.
Employees eligible for benefits under TRICARE military health system, §2.2-2818.1.
Personnel administration system.
Restoration to position upon termination of service, §2.2-2901.
Selective service compliance required, §2.2-2804.
State employees ordered to active military duty.
Use of accrued annual leave, §2.2-2903.1.
Recordation of names, discharges, etc., of war servicemen, §§17.1-261 to 17.1-265.
Registered military legal assistance attorneys, VA SCt Rule 1A:6.
Registration of name or insignia of organization.
Illegal use of registered insignia, §18.2-177.
Rental agreements.
Early termination, §55-248.21:1.
Reserve military organizations.
Special license plates, §46.2-746.3.
School buildings and grounds.
Government data collection and dissemination practices act.
Recruiter access to student information and school facilities, §2.2-3804.
Schools and education.
Educational opportunity for military children, §§22.1-360, 22.1-361.
Eligibility for interscholastic programs, §§22.1-5, 22.1-5.1.
When tuition charged or not charged, §§22.1-3, 22.1-5.
Selective service.
Public officers and employees.
Compliance required, §2.2-2804.
Federal employees prohibition.
Exception for selective service system, §2.2-2803.
Registration required for issuance of drivers' licenses, §46.2-221.1.
Servicemembers civil relief act.
Default judgments, §8.01-15.2.
Special license plates.
Grace period for active duty military personnel stationed outside the United States, §46.2-221.4.
Military assault forces, §46.2-746.1.
Reserve military organizations, §46.2-746.3.
Veterans' organizations, §46.2-746.4.
Standing armies in time of peace, avoidance, VA Const Art I §13.
State defense force, §§44-54.4 to 44-54.12.
See STATE DEFENSE FORCE.
State employee in organized reserve or national guard.
Carry forward of accrued annual leave, §2.2-1201.
State lottery.
Exemption from 180-day ticket redemption program, §58.1-4020.
Subordinate to civil power, VA Const Art I §13.
Teachers and other school employees.
Active duty service.
Compensation of public school employees called to active duty, §22.1-289.2.
Tuition and required fees for state supported colleges and universities.
Dependents of active duty personnel stationed in Virginia.
Domicile for in-state tuition, §23-7.4.

MILITARY —Cont'd
Tuition and required fees for state supported colleges and universities —Cont'd
Virginia military survivors and dependents education program.
Waiver for spouses and children of certain military personnel, §23-7.4:1.
Unemployment.
Veterans services department, programs to reduce unemployment among veterans, §2.2-2001.2.
Unemployment compensation.
Employer taxation.
Interest.
Abatement for taxes which accrued while employer was in armed forces, §60.2-520.
Uniform of armed forces of United States, protection, §44-120.
Unorganized militia, §§44-85 to 44-90.
Vacancies in office, §24.2-228.1.
Veterans' organizations.
Special license plates, §46.2-746.4.
Virginia military family relief fund, §44-102.2.
Virginia military parents equal protection act, §§20-124.7 to 20-124.10.
Virginia military survivors and dependents education program.
Tuition and required fees for state supported colleges and universities.
Waiver for spouses and children of certain military personnel, §23-7.4:1.
Virginia retirement system.
Service credit for service rendered on active duty on leave from covered position, §51.1-142.2.
Voters during election, privilege from service, VA Const Art II §9.
Wills.
Personalty, disposition of, §64.2-408.
Presumption of formal execution, §64.2-408.

MILITARY ADVISORY COUNCIL, §§2.2-2666.1 to 2.2-2666.3.
Closed meetings, §2.2-3711.
Federal employees prohibited, exception, §2.2-2801.
Freedom of information act.
Records excluded from application of act, §2.2-3705.2.
Oceana/Fentress military advisory council, §2.2-2666.3.
Reports.
Annual executive summary of interim activity, §2.2-2666.1.
Secretary of veterans affairs and homeland security.
Agencies for which responsible, §2.2-230.

MILITARY AFFAIRS DEPARTMENT.
Adjutant general.
Appointment by governor, §44-11.
Assistant adjutant general (army), §44-20.
Auditing accounts, §44-22.
Bond, §44-21.
Charge of department, §44-11.
Charge of military property, §44-19.
Deputy adjutant general (air), §44-20.
Deputy adjutant general (army), §44-20.
Efficiency board for National Guard officers.
Appointment, §44-33.
Expenditures, §44-14.
Military judges.
Designation on case-by-case basis to preside over courts-martial, §44-46.1.

MILITARY AFFAIRS DEPARTMENT —Cont'd
Adjutant general —Cont'd
Personal staff of governor and commander in chief, §2.2-102.
Powers, §44-13.
Preservation of public property, regulations as to reports and care, §44-17.
Qualifications for appointment, §44-11.
Rank, §44-11.
Records, §44-16.
Reports to secretary of defense, §44-15.
Review of judgments of courts-martial, §44-48.
Seal, §44-18.
United States property and fiscal officer.
Ineligibility to serve, §44-24.
Armories generally, §§44-123 to 44-140.
See ARMORIES.
Auditing accounts of adjutant general, §44-22.
Bond of adjutant general and fiscal clerks, §44-21.
Created, §44-11.
Duties, §44-11.1.
Expenditures made by state treasurer, §44-14.
Fort Pickett police, §44-123.3.
Group health and hospitalization insurance for employees.
Adjutant general may provide, §44-24.1.
Military property in charge of adjutant general, §44-19.
National guard.
Generally, §§44-25 to 44-54.3.
See NATIONAL GUARD.
Powers and duties, §44-11.1.
Preservation of public property.
Regulations by adjutant general as to reports and care, §44-17.
Records of adjutant general, §44-16.
Reports by adjutant general to secretary of defense, §44-15.
Seal of adjutant general, §44-18.
Secretary of public safety.
Agency responsibility, §2.2-221.
State defense force, §§44-54.4 to 44-54.12.
See STATE DEFENSE FORCE.

MILITARY AFFAIRS ORGANIZATIONS.
Local or regional.
Freedom of information act.
Records excluded from application of act, §2.2-3705.2.

MILITARY AIDES TO GOVERNOR, §2.2-102.

MILITARY FAMILY RELIEF FUND, §44-102.2.
Tax refunds, voluntary contributions to, §58.1-344.3.

MILITARY GRAVE MARKERS.
Sale, civil penalty, §18.2-511.

MILITARY INSTALLATIONS.
Authorities for development of former federal areas, §§15.2-6300 to 15.2-6322.
Approval of governor for undertakings, §15.2-6308.1.
Board of commissioners, §15.2-6304.
Bond issues, §15.2-6312.
Authorization of bonds, §15.2-6313.
Investment in, §15.2-6318.
Rights and remedies of obligees, §15.2-6316.
Security for payment, §§15.2-6315, 15.2-6317.
Tax exemption, §15.2-6314.
Borrowing money, §15.2-6311.

MILITARY INSTALLATIONS —Cont'd
Authorities for development of former federal areas —Cont'd
Branch offices, §15.2-6306.
Conflict of laws.
Provisions controlling, §15.2-6321.
Cooperative exercise of powers, §15.2-6309.
Definitions, §15.2-6301.
Director, §15.2-6304.
Powers and duties, §15.2-6305.
Dissolution, §15.2-6319.
Establishment, §15.2-6302.
Legal services, §15.2-6307.
Legislative declarations.
Authorities created by governor, §15.2-6300.
Authorities created by localities, §15.2-6300.1.
Payments to Commonwealth or political subdivisions, §15.2-6310.
Personnel act.
Applicability, §15.2-6314.1.
Powers, §§15.2-6308 to 15.2-6312.
Additional and supplemental nature, §15.2-6320.
Principal office, §15.2-6306.
Procurement act.
Applicability, §15.2-6314.1.
Reports.
Annual report, §15.2-6303.
Severability of provisions, §15.2-6320.
Sovereign immunity not waived, §15.2-6322.
Tax exemption, §15.2-6314.
Residential property transfer disclosures.
Military air installations, §55-519.1.
Zoning ordinances.
Encroachment upon, protection against, §15.2-2283.

MILITARY JUDGES, §44-46.1.
Courts-martial, national guard, §§44-42 to 44-54.

MILITARY LAWS OF VIRGINIA.
Active service, regulations as to, §§44-75.1 to 44-84.
Citation of chapter, §44-122.
Classification of militia, §§44-1 to 44-7.
Federal service, orders inducting militia into, §§44-114.1 to 44-114.4.
General administrative officer, §§44-8 to 44-24.1.
Generally, §§44-115 to 44-122.
Military property.
See MILITARY PROPERTY.
National guard, §§44-25 to 44-41.1.
Courts-martial, §§44-42 to 44-54.
National guard mutual assistance compact, §§44-54.1 to 44-54.3.
Naval militia, §§44-55 to 44-66.
Courts-martial, §§44-67 to 44-74.
Privileges of United States reserve, national guard and naval militia, §§44-93 to 44-102.
State defense force, §§44-54.4 to 44-54.12.
Support of militia, §§44-112 to 44-114.
Unorganized militia, §§44-85 to 44-90.

MILITARY PARENTS EQUAL PROTECTION ACT, §§20-124.7 to 20-124.10.
Definitions, §20-124.7.
Temporary custody or visitation order.
Contents, §20-124.10.
Expedited hearing, §20-124.9.
Generally, §20-124.8.
When order in place, §20-124.9.

MILITARY POLICE.
Carrying concealed weapons, inapplicability of provisions, §18.2-308.

MILITARY PROPERTY, §§44-103 to 44-111.
Adjutant general to have charge of, §44-19.
Exemption from levy and sale, §44-96.
Exemption from taxation, §44-131.
State police acquisition, §52-11.3.

MILITARY RECRUITERS.
Schools and education.
Access to high schools and high school students, §22.1-130.1.

MILITARY RESERVATIONS.
Impoundment of motor vehicles.
Motor vehicle insurance, suspension at insured's request, §38.2-2205.1.

MILITARY STAFF OF GOVERNOR.
Divisions, §44-10.

MILITIA, §§44-1 to 44-122, VA Const Art I §13.
Acknowledgments, §§55-114.1, 55-115.
Who may perform notarial acts, §55-118.1.
Actions, power to maintain suit, §44-99.
Active duty, §§44-75.1 to 44-84.
Appointment of rendezvous, §44-77.
Calling forth to state active duty, §44-75.1.
Classes of militia called into service, order, §44-80.
Continuance or time for filing pleading where party or attorney on active duty, §44-97.1.
Employment of members, interference with, §44-98.
Enlisted persons, pay and allowance, §44-83.
Equipment, §44-76.
Exemption from arrest, §44-97.
Governor.
Calling forth to state active duty, §44-75.1.
Length of service when called out, §44-81.
Localities, requests for assistance by, §44-78.1.
Military justice opinions.
In force on actual service, §44-84.
Movement of troops and supplies not to be delayed, §44-82.
National guard mutual assistance counter drug activities compact.
Calling into active duty, §44-75.1.
Enactment into law, §44-75.1:1.
Officers, pay and allowance, §44-83.
Order in which classes of militia called into services, §44-80.
Orders to officers, §44-77.
Payment while in service, §§44-82, 44-83.
Regulations enforced by national service, §44-84.
Retention in service when called out, §44-81.
Support, §44-76.
Training duties, §44-75.2.
Transportation, §44-76.
Transportation companies to furnish transportation, §44-82.
Adjutant general.
See MILITARY AFFAIRS DEPARTMENT.
Age requirement, §44-1.
Armories, §§44-123 to 44-140.
See ARMORIES.
Arrest, exemption from, §44-97.
Artillery, cavalry or infantry existing on passage of act.
Entitlement to retain privileges, §44-7.
Attorneys, employment as special counsel to defend members, §44-100.

MILITIA —Cont'd
Care of military property, §§44-103 to 44-111.
City or town power to aid military units, §15.2-1112.
Commander in chief of armed forces of Commonwealth.
Governor, §44-8.
Regulations, power to prescribe, §44-9.
Commanding officer of militia of Commonwealth.
Adjutant general, §44-13.
Commission not to vacate civil office, §44-102.
Composition, §44-1.
Corps entitled to retain privileges, §44-7.
County, city and town appropriation, §44-113.
Courts-martial.
National guard, §§44-42 to 44-54.
Naval militia, §§44-67 to 44-74.
Defense of members sued civilly or criminally prosecuted, §44-100.
Division, §44-1.
Employment of members, interference with, §44-98.
Execution of process.
Power of governor to summon, §18.2-410.
Exemption from duty, §44-5.
Exemption of uniforms, arms and equipment from levy and sale, §44-96.
Federal employees prohibited, exception, §2.2-2801.
Federal funds, requisition for, §44-112.
Federal service, orders inducting into, §§44-114.1 to 44-114.4.
Fishburne Military Academy officers, §44-117.
Governor.
Commander in chief of armed forces of Commonwealth, §44-8.
Immunity for acts done while in discharge of military duty, §44-100.
Jury duty exemption, §44-94.
Leaves of absence for employees of Commonwealth or political subdivisions, §44-93.
Discrimination in hiring prohibited, §44-93.4.
Penalty for employer failure to comply, §44-93.5.
Reemployment, §44-93.3.
Supplement of military pay and additional life insurance benefits, §44-93.1.
Maintenance of other troops in time of peace, §44-6.
Massanutten Military Academy officers, §44-117.
Military staff of governor.
Divisions, §44-10.
National guard.
Generally, §§44-25 to 44-54.3.
See NATIONAL GUARD.
Naval militia generally, §§44-55 to 44-74.
See NAVAL MILITIA.
Officers.
Prohibition on federal employees, exception, §2.2-2801.
Orders inducing militia into federal service, §§44-114.1 to 44-114.4.
Other troops maintained in time of peace, §44-6.
Pay, active duty, §§44-82, 44-83.
Privileges, corps entitled to retain, §44-7.
Qualifications for enlistment, §44-1.
Recognizances.
Forfeiture of recognizance while in military or naval service, §19.2-144.

MILITIA —Cont'd
Regulations, power of commander in chief to prescribe, §44-9.
Retired list of national guard officers, warrant officers and enlisted persons, §44-119.
Right to own and keep real and personal property, §44-99.
Riot.
Dispersal, duty, §18.2-411.
Immunity of officers quelling, §18.2-412.
Power of governor to summon to preserve peace, §18.2-410.
State appropriations, allowances made to organizations, §44-114.
State defense force, §§44-54.4 to 44-54.12.
See STATE DEFENSE FORCE.
Training duty, §44-75.2.
Unorganized militia, §§44-85 to 44-90.
Composition, §44-4.
Virginia Military Institute officers, §44-117.
Virginia Polytechnic Institute and State University officers, §44-117.
Virginia Women's Institute for Leadership at Mary Baldwin College, §44-117.

MILK AND MILK PRODUCTS, §§3.2-5200 to 3.2-5233.
Accounting system for distributors, §3.2-3210.
Adulteration.
Ice cream and similar products.
Condemnation of adulterated products, §3.2-5216.
Detention of adulterated products, §3.2-5215.
Agriculture and consumer services board.
Rules and regulations, §3.2-5206.
Ice cream and similar products, §3.2-5212.
Machine tests, §§3.2-5223, 3.2-5224.
Agriculture and consumer services commissioner.
Duty to foster dairy industry, §3.2-5200.
Obstruction of commissioner, §3.2-5207.
Machine tests, §3.2-5232.
Powers and duties of commissioner, §3.2-5207.
Warning of persons using or furnishing impure milk, §3.2-5204.
Animal-drug residue in milk.
Excessive residue.
Civil penalties, §3.2-5211.
Appeals.
Milk commission orders, §3.2-3217.
Assessments.
Disposition of receipts, §3.2-3220.
Babcock test.
Machine tests generally, §§3.2-5219 to 3.2-5233.
Cities or towns.
Powers generally, §15.2-1109.
Civil penalties for violation, assessment, §§3.2-5210, 3.2-5211.
Machine test violations, §3.2-5233.
Compact.
Southern dairy compact, §§3.2-3300 to 3.2-3303.
Criminal penalties, §§3.2-3222, 3.2-5209.
Accounting system for distributors.
Violations of provision, §3.2-3210.
Ice cream and similar products, §3.2-5217.
Machine tests.
False manipulation and reading of tests, §3.2-5229.
Violations of provisions, §3.2-5232.
Warning of persons using or furnishing impure milk.
Failure to obey warning, §3.2-5204.

MILK AND MILK PRODUCTS —Cont'd
Dairy milk cases.
Unauthorized use, §18.2-102.2.
Uniform fine schedule, VA SCt Rules 3C:1, 3C:2.
Definitions.
Machine tests.
Person or holder, §3.2-5218.
Milk commission, §3.2-3200.
Drug residue in milk.
Animal-drug residue.
Civil penalties, §§3.2-5210, 3.2-5211.
Excessive residue.
Civil penalties, §3.2-5211.
Fact-finding conferences.
Excessive animal-drug residue in milk, §3.2-5211.
Federal regulations.
Conformity with US Department of Health and Human Services regulations, §3.2-5201.
Generally.
See MILK AND MILK PRODUCTS.
Health commissioner.
Obstruction of commissioner prohibited, §3.2-5208.
Powers and duties, §3.2-5208.
Ice cream and similar products, §§3.2-5212 to 3.2-5217.
Adulteration.
Condemnation of adulterated products, §3.2-5216.
Detention of adulterated products, §3.2-5215.
Criminal penalties, §3.2-5217.
Enforcement of provisions, §3.2-5213.
Misbranded products.
Condemnation, §3.2-5216.
Detention, §3.2-5215.
Permits, §3.2-5214.
Rules and regulations, §3.2-5212.
Importing, §3.2-5203.
Injunctions, §3.2-5205.
Powers of milk commission, §3.2-3221.
Intangible personal property tax.
Extent taxable, §58.1-1104.
Generally, §§58.1-1100 to 58.1-1118.
See PERSONAL PROPERTY TAXES.
Interstate commerce.
Provisions inapplicable, §3.2-3224.
Licenses, §3.2-3212.
Additional nature of licenses, §3.2-3216.
Applications, §3.2-3215.
Reports of licensees, §3.2-3213.
Local regulation, restrictions, §3.2-5202.
Machinery and tools tax, §§58.1-3507, 58.1-3508.
Machine tests, §§3.2-5219 to 3.2-5233.
Approval of test or contrivance other than Babcock or other centrifugal machines, §3.2-5219.
Butterfat.
Sampling to determine butterfat by composite test, §3.2-5227.
Capacity of standard measurers, §3.2-5225.
Certificates.
Manipulators of machines, §§3.2-5221 to 3.2-5223.
Civil penalties for violations, §3.2-5233.
Cream.
Units for testing, §3.2-5226.
Criminal penalties.
False manipulation and reading of tests, §3.2-5229.
Violations of provisions, §3.2-5232.
MILK AND MILK PRODUCTS —Cont'd
Machine tests —Cont'd
Definitions.
Person or holder, §3.2-5218.
Enforcement of provisions, §3.2-5231.
Inspection of machines and scales, §3.2-5228.
Obstruction of commissioner, §3.2-5232.
Rules and regulations, §§3.2-5223, 3.2-5224.
Tender of payment as evidence of test, §3.2-5230.
Manipulators.
Certificates, §§3.2-5221 to 3.2-5223.
Marks on certain containers, §§59.1-93 to 59.1-102.
See MARKS ON CERTAIN CONTAINERS.
Milk commission, §§3.2-3200 to 3.2-3224.
Accounting system for distributors, §3.2-3210.
Appeals from, §3.2-3217.
Bond of officers and employees who handle money, §3.2-3219.
Budgets, §3.2-3219.
Definitions, §3.2-3200.
Hearings.
Exercise or withdrawal of exercise of powers, §3.2-3206.
Injunctions.
Power to seek, §3.2-3221.
Inspections, §3.2-3211.
Books and records of distributors, §3.2-3210.
Market areas.
Defining, §3.2-3207.
Meetings, §3.2-3203.
Members, §§3.2-3201, 3.2-3202.
Powers, §§3.2-3204, 3.2-3205.
Public hearing before withdrawal of exercise of powers, §3.2-3206.
Prices.
Fixing of prices, §3.2-3208.
Minimum retail price, §3.2-3209.
Quorum, §3.2-3203.
Subpoenas.
Noncompliance, §3.2-3218.
Milk commission assessments fund, §3.2-3220.
Dedicated revenues, diversion, §3.2-1100.
Monopolies and restraint of trade.
Marketing agreements not deemed to be, §3.2-3223.
Official beverage of Commonwealth, §1-510.
Ordinances.
Local regulation, restrictions, §3.2-5202.
Prices.
Milk commission.
Fixing of prices, §3.2-3208.
Minimum retail price, §3.2-3209.
Public hearing on violations and civil penalty, §3.2-5210.
Machine test violation, §3.2-5233.
Purchases through division of purchases and supply.
Provisions not mandatory, §2.2-1119.
Rules and regulations.
Agriculture and consumer services board, §3.2-5206.
Ice cream and similar products, §3.2-5212.
Machine tests, §§3.2-5223, 3.2-5224.
Sales.
Unlawful buying and selling, §3.2-3214.
Sanitary requirements for food establishments, §§3.2-5105 to 3.2-5119.
Southern dairy compact, §§3.2-3300 to 3.2-3303.
US Department of Health and Human Services.
Conformity with regulations, §3.2-5201.

MILK BUYING STATIONS.
Licenses.
Creameries, plants and stations generally.
See MILK AND MILK PRODUCTS.

MILK COMMISSION.
Administrative process act.
Exemptions, §2.2-4002.
Generally, §§3.2-3200 to 3.2-3224.
See MILK AND MILK PRODUCTS.

MILK CRATES.
Unauthorized use, §18.2-102.2.
Uniform fine schedule, VA SCt Rules 3C:1, 3C:2.

MILK DISTRIBUTING PLANTS.
Licenses.
Creameries, plants and stations generally.
See MILK AND MILK PRODUCTS.

MILL CANALS.
Drainage rights.
Construction of culverts, etc., under mill canals, §21-432.

MILLER SCHOOL OF ALBEMARLE, §§23-51 to 23-53.

MILLS.
Applications for leave to build or rebuild, §62.1-116.
Commission.
Appointment, §62.1-118.
New commissioners, §62.1-121.
Duties, §62.1-119.
Meetings, §62.1-118.
Oath, §62.1-119.
Reports, §62.1-119.
Granting of leave, §62.1-122.
Damages, unforeseen, §62.1-127.
Forfeiture of works damaged or destroyed, §62.1-126.
Payment of damages, §62.1-123.
Time limitations, §62.1-125.
Vested rights unaffected, §62.1-124.
Notice, §62.1-117.
Further notice, §62.1-120.
Refusal to grant leave, §62.1-122.
Forest fires.
Failure to clean premises, §10.1-1144.
Hydroelectric power generally, §§62.1-80 to 62.1-103.
See HYDROELECTRIC POWER.
Impoundment of surface waters.
Application of provisions, §62.1-114.
Surface water management areas generally, §§62.1-242 to 62.1-253.
See SURFACE WATER MANAGEMENT AREAS.

MINED LAND RECLAMATION.
Abandoned mine reclamation, §§45.1-260 to 45.1-270.
See COAL SURFACE MINING.
Coal surface mining reclamation fund, §§45.1-270.1 to 45.1-270.7.
Minerals reclamation fund, §§45.1-197.8 to 45.1-197.18.
Orphaned lands, §§45.1-197.3 to 45.1-197.7.

MINE FOREMAN.
Certification of coal mine workers.
Generally, §§45.1-161.24 to 45.1-161.41.
First-class mine foreman certification, §45.1-161.38.
Surface foreman certification, §45.1-161.39.

MINE FOREMAN —Cont'd
Operator of coal mines.
Requirement to employ, §45.1-161.38.
Underground coal mines.
Duties generally, §45.1-161.249.
Mine safety requirements applicable to underground mines generally.
See COAL MINE SAFETY.

MINE INSPECTIONS.
Advance notice of inspections, §45.1-161.84.
Certificates of inspection, §45.1-161.89.
Chief of division of mines.
Record of inspections of coal mines, §45.1-161.21.
Denial of entry, §45.1-161.86.
Duties of inspectors, §45.1-161.88.
Duties of operator, §45.1-161.87.
Entry to premises.
Denial of entry, §45.1-161.86.
Evaluation of risks, §45.1-161.82.
Frequency, §45.1-161.81.
Inspector's duties, §45.1-161.88.
Operator's duties, §45.1-161.87.
Records.
Review of inspection reports and records, §45.1-161.83.
Reports.
Review of inspection reports and records, §45.1-161.83.
Risk evaluation, §45.1-161.82.
Scheduling, §45.1-161.85.
Trade secret confidentiality, §45.1-161.84.

MINE INSPECTORS.
Accident, fires or explosions, duties, §45.1-161.80.
Age requirements, §45.1-161.19.
Air flows and gas and oxygen deficiency, tests, §45.1-161.88.
Appointment by director of department of mines, minerals and energy, §45.1-161.18.
Areas and places inspected, §45.1-161.88.
Certification of coal mine workers generally, §§45.1-161.24 to 45.1-161.41.
Closure orders, §45.1-161.91.
Coal mine inspections.
Qualifications, §45.1-161.20.
Corrections notice, §45.1-161.90.
Duties, §§45.1-161.80, 45.1-161.88.
Fires in underground coal mines.
Response to scene, §45.1-161.203.
Inspections at mines last employed, §45.1-161.17.
Mineral mine inspections.
Qualifications, §45.1-161.20.
Mineral mine safety.
Appointment, §45.1-161.292:10.
Conflicts of interest, §45.1-161.292:9.
Duties, §45.1-161.292:53.
Inspections, §45.1-161.292:61.
Qualifications, §45.1-161.292:11.
Conducting inspections of mines, §45.1-161.292:12.
Notice of correction, §45.1-161.90.
Notices of violations, §45.1-161.90.
Qualifications, §45.1-161.19.
Inspectors of coal mines and mineral mines, §45.1-161.20.
Reports of violations, §45.1-161.97.
Rescue stations.
State-designated mine rescue teams, §45.1-161.75.
Violations notice, §45.1-161.90.

MINE LICENSING.
Affidavits.
Annual affidavit as to payment of taxes, §45.1-161.62.
Annual reports, §45.1-161.62.
Applications, §45.1-161.59.
Denial or revocation, §45.1-161.60.
Fees, §45.1-161.58.
Denial, §45.1-161.60.
Disposition of fees, §45.1-161.58.
False statements, §45.1-161.66.
Fees, §45.1-161.58.
Fraud, §45.1-161.66.
Identity of operator, §45.1-161.59.
Maps of mines, §45.1-161.64.
Payment of expense of making, §45.1-161.65.
Required to be made, §45.1-161.65.
Misdemeanors, §45.1-161.61.
Making false statements, §45.1-161.66.
Notice.
Notices to department, §45.1-161.63.
Operating without license, §45.1-161.61.
Operators.
Application for license, §45.1-161.59.
Ownership.
Annual reports following transfer of ownership, §45.1-161.62.
Payment of map expenses, §45.1-161.65.
Penalties, §45.1-161.61.
Posting of maps, §45.1-161.64.
Reports, §45.1-161.62.
Required for operation, §45.1-161.57.
Resumption of mining following discontinuance, §45.1-161.63.
Revocation, §45.1-161.60.
Term, §45.1-161.57.

MINE OPENINGS AND ESCAPEWAYS.
Underground coal mines, §§45.1-161.162 to 45.1-161.170.

MINE OPERATORS.
Foremen.
Employment required, §45.1-161.38.
Liens of employees or suppliers, §§43-24 to 43-26.
Retail sales and use tax direct payment permits, §58.1-624.

MINE PROP SUPPLIERS.
Intangible personal property tax.
Generally, §§58.1-1100 to 58.1-1118.
See PERSONAL PROPERTY TAXES.
Suppliers subject to tax, §58.1-1105.
Liens of suppliers, §§43-24 to 43-26.

MINERAL LANDS.
Real property tax assessment.
Lands and minerals included in general reassessment, §58.1-3287.
Specially and separately assessed, §58.1-3286.
Segregation for local taxation, VA Const Art X §4.

MINERAL LEASES.
Securities generally, §§13.1-501 to 13.1-527.3.
See SECURITIES.

MINERAL MINE LICENSES, §§45.1-161.292:30 to 45.1-161.292:39.
Abandonment.
Notice of intent, §45.1-161.292:36.
Notice to department, §45.1-161.292:36.

MINERAL MINE LICENSES —Cont'd
Applications, §45.1-161.292:32.
Fees, §45.1-161.292:31.
Denial, §45.1-161.292:33.
Discontinuation of work.
Notice to department, §45.1-161.292:36.
False statements.
Penalty, §45.1-161.292:39.
Fees.
Application fee, §45.1-161.292:31.
Disposition, §45.1-161.292:31.
Maps.
Failure to submit.
Authority of director to have one made at operator's expense, §45.1-161.292:38.
Required, §45.1-161.292:37.
Notice.
Intent to abandon or discontinue mine, §45.1-161.292:36.
Operating without a license, §45.1-161.292:34.
Penalties for violation.
Operating without a license, §45.1-161.292:34.
Renewal.
Contents of application, §45.1-161.292:32.
Reports.
Annual report, §45.1-161.292:35.
Transfers of ownership, §45.1-161.292:35.
Required, §45.1-161.292:30.
Revocation, §45.1-161.292:33.
Terms, §45.1-161.292:30.
Transfer of ownership of mine.
Reports to department, §45.1-161.292:35.

MINERAL MINES.
Adjacent property owners.
Consent required before working mine, §45.1-161.311:1.
Mining rights.
Generally, §45.1-161.311.
Right to survey, §45.1-161.311:2.
Discontinuation of work.
Notice of intent, §45.1-161.292:36.
Examinations.
Refuse piles, water and silt retaining dams, §45.1-225.2.
Inspections, §§45.1-161.292:54 to 45.1-161.292:62.
Licensing, §§45.1-161.292:30 to 45.1-161.292:39.
Mine inspections.
See MINE INSPECTIONS.
Mine licensing.
See MINE LICENSING.
Miner training, §§45.1-161.101 to 45.1-161.103.
Refuse piles, water and silt retaining dams, §§45.1-225.1 to 45.1-225.3.
Construction and design requirements, §45.1-225.1.
Definitions, §45.1-225.3.
Examinations, §45.1-225.2.
Rescue crews.
See MINERAL MINE SAFETY.
Safety, §§45.1-161.292:1 to 45.1-161.292:73.
See MINERAL MINE SAFETY.
Surface coal mines.
Mine safety requirements, §§45.1-161.253 to 45.1-161.292.
Surface mineral mining.
Mineral mine safety act, §§45.1-161.292:1 to 45.1-161.292:73.
See MINERAL MINE SAFETY.
Mine safety requirements, §§45.1-161.304 to 45.1-161.309.

MINERAL MINES —Cont'd
Underground mineral mines.
Mineral mine safety act, §§45.1-161.292:1 to 45.1-161.292:73.
See MINERAL MINE SAFETY.
Mine safety requirements, §§45.1-161.293 to 45.1-161.303.
Waste management.
Conditional exemption for mineral mining overburden or solid waste, §10.1-1406.2.

MINERAL MINE SAFETY, §§45.1-161.292:1 to 45.1-161.292:73.
Accidents.
Duty of mine inspector, §45.1-161.292:53.
Investigations, §45.1-161.292:51.
Reports, §45.1-161.292:51.
Maintenance of records, §45.1-161.292:52.
Age restrictions.
Qualifications to work in mines, §45.1-161.292:5.
Appeals.
Tolling of time for abatement, §45.1-161.292:65.
Applicability of act, §45.1-161.292:3.
Certificates of inspection, §45.1-161.292:62.
Certified employees.
Certification required, §45.1-161.292:19.
Examinations for certification, §45.1-161.292:20.
Fees, §45.1-161.292:22.
Reexamination, §45.1-161.292:27.
Foreman certification, §45.1-161.292:29.
General mineral miners certification, §45.1-161.292:28.
Performance of tasks by uncertified persons.
Penalty for violation, §45.1-161.292:21.
Reciprocity, §45.1-161.292:24.
Reexamination, §45.1-161.292:27.
Renewal of certificates, §45.1-161.292:25.
Revocation of certificates, §45.1-161.292:26.
Closure orders, §45.1-161.292:64.
Commonwealths' attorneys.
Prosecution for violations, §45.1-161.292:68.
Compliance with act.
Duty of operators, §45.1-161.292:8.
Required by miners, §45.1-161.292:6.
Confidential information.
Protection of trade secrets during inspections, §45.1-161.292:57.
Conflict of laws.
Other safety and health regulations, §45.1-161.292:3.
Costs.
Enforcement, §45.1-161.292:69.
Definitions, §45.1-161.292:2.
Departmental employees.
Conflicts of interest, §45.1-161.292:9.
Director, §§45.1-161.292:9 to 45.1-161.292:14.
Appointment of technical specialists, §45.1-161.292:14.
Conflicts of interest, §45.1-161.292:9.
Duties, §45.1-161.292:13.
Maps.
Having map made at operator's expense, §45.1-161.292:38.
Enforcement of provisions, §§45.1-161.292:63 to 45.1-161.292:70.
Explosions.
Duties of mine inspectors, §45.1-161.292:53.
Reports, §45.1-161.292:50.
Fees.
Violations of provisions, §45.1-161.292:69.

MINERAL MINE SAFETY —Cont'd
Fires.
Duties of mine inspectors, §45.1-161.292:53.
Reports, §45.1-161.292:50.
First aid stations, §45.1-161.292:40.
Foreman.
Certification, §45.1-161.292:29.
General mineral miner certificate, §45.1-161.292:28.
Immunity.
State-designated mine rescue teams, §45.1-161.292:49.
Independent contractors.
Safety examinations of work area, §45.1-161.292:29.
Injunctions.
Violations, §45.1-161.292:66.
Inspections, §§45.1-161.292:54 to 45.1-161.292:62.
Advance notice of inspections, §45.1-161.292:57.
Certificates of inspection, §45.1-161.292:62.
Confidentiality of trade secrets, §45.1-161.292:57.
Denial of entry, §45.1-161.292:59.
Duplication by mine safety and health administration, §45.1-161.292:54.
Frequency, §45.1-161.292:54.
Mine inspector's duties, §45.1-161.292:61.
Operator's duties, §45.1-161.292:60.
Records, §45.1-161.292:13.
Rescue stations, §45.1-161.292:48.
Review of inspection reports and records, §45.1-161.292:56.
Risk evaluations, §45.1-161.292:55.
Scheduling, §45.1-161.292:58.
Investigations.
Accidents, §45.1-161.292:51.
Labor unions.
Conflicts of interest, §45.1-161.292:9.
Licensing of mineral mines, §§45.1-161.292:30 to 45.1-161.292:39.
See MINERAL MINE LICENSES.
Maps.
Denial of entry, §45.1-161.292:59.
Mine inspectors.
Appointment, §45.1-161.292:10.
Conflicts of interest, §45.1-161.292:9.
Duties, §45.1-161.292:53.
Duties regarding inspections, §45.1-161.292:61.
Qualifications, §45.1-161.292:11.
Conducting inspections of mines, §45.1-161.292:12.
Mineral mining examiners' fund, §45.1-161.292:22.
Miners.
Trading programs.
Mineral mining safety training plan, §45.1-161.292:73.
Training programs, §45.1-161.292:71.
Mineral mining safety training, §45.1-161.292:72.
Mining inspectors, §§45.1-161.292:9 to 45.1-161.292:14.
Notice.
Advance notice of inspections, §45.1-161.292:57.
Notify miners of violations, §45.1-161.292:8.
Violations, §45.1-161.292:63.
Operators.
Duties.
Inspections, §45.1-161.292:60.
Safety materials and supplies.
Duty to keep on hand, §45.1-161.292:7.
Securing compliance with act, §45.1-161.292:8.

MINERAL MINE SAFETY —Cont'd
Operators —Cont'd
Special safety rules, §45.1-161.292:4.
Penalties for violations, §45.1-161.292:67.
Plan for training programs, §45.1-161.292:73.
Prohibited acts generally, §45.1-161.292:6.
Prosecution of violations, §45.1-161.292:68.
Reciprocity.
Certified employees, §45.1-161.292:24.
Records.
Accident reports, §45.1-161.292:52.
Denial of entry, §45.1-161.292:59.
Inspection records.
Review, §45.1-161.292:56.
Inspections, §45.1-161.292:13.
Renewal of certificates, §45.1-161.292:25.
Reports.
Accidents, §45.1-161.292:51.
Maintenance of records, §45.1-161.292:52.
Explosions or fires, §45.1-161.292:50.
Inspection reports.
Review, §45.1-161.292:56.
Violations, §45.1-161.292:70.
Rescues, §§45.1-161.292:40 to 45.1-161.292:49.
Explosions and fires, §45.1-161.292:50.
Inspection of rescue stations, §45.1-161.292:48.
Mine rescue coordinator, §45.1-161.292:48.
Mine rescue crews, §45.1-161.292:41.
Backup crews, §45.1-161.292:45.
Compensation, §45.1-161.292:44.
Deemed to be employees of mine where emergency exists, §45.1-161.292:44.
Duty to train, §45.1-161.292:42.
Good Samaritan statute, §8.01-225.
Jurisdiction, §45.1-161.292:43.
Qualifications, §45.1-161.292:43.
Mine rescue fund, §45.1-161.292:47.
Mine rescue teams, §45.1-161.292:46.
Immunity from liability, §45.1-161.292:49.
Workers' compensation, §45.1-161.292:49.
Requirements of recovery work, §45.1-161.292:45.
Rescue and first aid stations, §45.1-161.292:40.
State-designated mine rescue teams, §45.1-161.292:46.
Immunity from liability, §45.1-161.292:49.
Workers' compensation, §45.1-161.292:49.
Revocation of certificate, §45.1-161.292:26.
Safety materials and supplies, §45.1-161.292:7.
Salaries.
Mine rescue crews, §45.1-161.292:44.
Short title, §45.1-161.292:1.
Special safety rules, §45.1-161.292:4.
Surface mines, §§45.1-161.304 to 45.1-161.309.
Air borne toxic contaminants.
Health regulations, §45.1-161.309.
Applicability of chapter, §45.1-161.304.
Gas and oil wells.
Mining in proximity, §45.1-161.307.
Health regulations, §45.1-161.309.
Respiratory equipment, §45.1-161.308.
Rulemaking authority.
Standards, §§45.1-161.305, 45.1-161.306.
Scope of chapter, §45.1-161.304.
Standards for rules promulgation, §§45.1-161.305, 45.1-161.306.
Technical specialists, §45.1-161.292:14.
Title of act, §45.1-161.292:1.
Trade secrets.
Protection of confidential trade secrets during inspections, §45.1-161.292:57.

MINERAL MINE SAFETY —Cont'd
Training programs for miners, §45.1-161.292:71.
Plan, §45.1-161.292:73.
Safety training, §45.1-161.292:72.
Underground mineral mines, §§45.1-161.293 to 45.1-161.303.
Air quality control.
Respiratory equipment, §45.1-161.302.
Applicability of chapter, §45.1-161.293.
Automatic circuit interrupting devices.
Fire precautions in transporting mining equipment, §45.1-161.303.
Bare wires and cables, §45.1-161.299.
Ear protectors, §45.1-161.302.
Electrical power conductors.
Avoiding accidental contact with power lines, §45.1-161.303.
Disconnecting switches, §45.1-161.301.
Use of rails and track switches, §45.1-161.300.
Explosions.
Procedure, §45.1-161.292:50.
Fire precautions.
Transportation of mining equipment, §45.1-161.303.
Flame safety lamps, §45.1-161.297.
Gas and oil wells.
Mining in proximity, §45.1-161.296.
Installation of bare wires and cables.
Cables not encased in armor, §45.1-161.299.
Man-trip cars.
Transportation of miners, §45.1-161.298.
Methane detection.
Flame safety lamp prohibition, §45.1-161.297.
Noise levels.
Ear protectors for miners, §45.1-161.302.
Off-track mining equipment.
Fire precautions, §45.1-161.303.
Rails and track switches.
Disconnecting switches, §45.1-161.301.
Use as electrical power conductor, §45.1-161.300.
Respiratory equipment and ear protectors, §45.1-161.302.
Rulemaking authority.
Standards, §§45.1-161.294, 45.1-161.295.
Scope of chapter, §45.1-161.293.
Standards for rules promulgation, §§45.1-161.294, 45.1-161.295.
Track switches.
Disconnecting switches, §45.1-161.301.
Use as electrical power conductor, §45.1-161.300.
Transportation of miners, §45.1-161.298.
Transporting mining equipment.
Fire precautions, §45.1-161.303.
Trolley phones.
Fire precautions in transporting mining equipment, §45.1-161.303.
Violations.
Closure orders, §45.1-161.292:64.
Fees and costs, §45.1-161.292:69.
Injunctions, §45.1-161.292:66.
Notice of violations, §45.1-161.292:63.
Tolling during pendency of appeal, §45.1-161.292:65.
Penalties, §45.1-161.292:67.
Performance of certain tasks by uncertified persons, §45.1-161.292:21.
Prosecution, §45.1-161.292:68.
Reports, §45.1-161.292:70.
Tolling of time for abatement, §45.1-161.292:65.

MINERAL MINE SAFETY —Cont'd
Workers' compensation.
Mine rescue crews, §45.1-161.292:44.
Mine rescue teams, §45.1-161.292:49.

MINERAL MINING EXAMINERS' FUND, §45.1-161.292:22.

MINERALS.
Coal mineral estate.
Retention of rights after coal removed, §55-154.2.
Comprehensive plan.
Mineral resources.
Inclusion in plan, §15.2-2224.
Conservation and recreation department.
Disposition of department lands.
Removal of minerals, §10.1-111.
Employee liens, §§43-24 to 43-26.
Heavy equipment dealers generally, §§59.1-353 to 59.1-363.
See HEAVY EQUIPMENT DEALERS.
Management plan.
Exploration activities on state owned uplands, §2.2-1157.
Motor vehicle registration.
Vehicles exempt from registration, §§46.2-671, 46.2-675.
Partition of land.
Validation of certain partitions of mineral rights, §8.01-81.
Presumed to exist in certain lands, §55-154.
Suits to extinguish claim or right, §55-155.
Presumption regarding estate of owner of mineral rights, §55-154.2.
State corrections board contracts to sell or lease, §53.1-31.
Supplier liens, §§43-24 to 43-26.

MINERALS RECLAMATION FUND, §§45.1-197.8 to 45.1-197.18.

MINE REFUSE PILES, WATER AND SILT RETAINING DAMS, §§45.1-221.1 to 45.1-224.1.
Mineral mines, §§45.1-225.1 to 45.1-225.3.

MINE RESCUE CREWS.
Coal mine safety, §§45.1-161.68 to 45.1-161.73.
Good Samaritan statute, §8.01-225.
Mineral mine safety, §§45.1-161.292:41 to 45.1-161.292:45.

MINE RESCUE FUND, §45.1-161.292:47.

MINER TRAINING, §§45.1-161.101 to 45.1-161.103.
Additional training programs, §45.1-161.103.
Certification of workers.
Coal mines, §§45.1-161.24 to 45.1-161.41.
See COAL MINE WORKER CERTIFICATION.
Fees to cover costs of administering program, §45.1-161.102.
First aid training, §45.1-161.101.
Safety awareness for coal miners, §45.1-161.103.
Training programs, §45.1-161.102.
Voluntary on-site safety awareness training program for coal mines, §45.1-161.103.

MINES AND MINING.
Adjacent property owners.
Mineral mines, §§45.1-161.311:1, 45.1-161.311:2.
Mining rights, §§45.1-161.310, 45.1-161.311.
Board of coal mining examiners, §§45.1-161.24 to 45.1-161.41.
See COAL MINE WORKER CERTIFICATION.

MINES AND MINING —Cont'd
Certification of coal mine workers, §§45.1-161.24 to 45.1-161.41.
Coal mine safety board, §§45.1-161.98 to 45.1-161.100.
Coal mine safety generally, §§45.1-161.7 to 45.1-161.322.
See COAL MINE SAFETY.
Coal mine worker certification, §§45.1-161.24 to 45.1-161.41.
Department of mines, minerals and energy.
See MINES, MINERALS AND ENERGY DEPARTMENT.
Emergency seizure of coal properties by Commonwealth, §§45.1-161.312 to 45.1-161.322.
See COAL MINES.
Mine inspections.
See MINE INSPECTIONS.
Mine inspectors.
See MINE INSPECTORS.
Mine licensing.
See MINE LICENSING.
Mineral mine safety, §§45.1-161.292:1 to 45.1-161.292:73.
See MINERAL MINE SAFETY.
Miner training, §§45.1-161.101 to 45.1-161.103.
Principal and income.
Allocations to principal and income, §64.2-1019.
Surface coal mines.
Mine safety requirements, §§45.1-161.253 to 45.1-161.292.
See COAL MINE SAFETY.
Surface mineral mining.
Mine safety requirements, §§45.1-161.304 to 45.1-161.309.
Surveys.
Adjacent property owners.
Right to survey.
Mineral mines, §45.1-161.311:2.
Training of miners, §§45.1-161.101 to 45.1-161.103.
Trust for coal interests.
Known owners, §45.1-161.311:8.
Missing owners, §§45.1-161.311:3 to 45.1-161.311:7.
Underground coal mines.
Safety requirements applicable to, §§45.1-161.105 to 45.1-161.252.
See COAL MINE SAFETY.
Underground mineral mines.
Mine safety requirements, §§45.1-161.293 to 45.1-161.303.
See COAL MINE SAFETY.
Worker certification.
Coal mine workers, §§45.1-161.24 to 45.1-161.41.

MINES DIVISION.
Generally.
See MINES, MINERALS AND ENERGY DEPARTMENT.

MINES, MINERALS AND ENERGY DEPARTMENT.
Administrative rulemaking procedure.
Regulations exempt, §2.2-4006.
Appointment of state geologist, §45.1-383.
Chief.
Mines division. See within this heading, "Mines division."
Coal companies.
Affiliations with by personnel prohibited, §45.1-161.17.

MINES, MINERALS AND ENERGY DEPARTMENT —Cont'd
Coal safety act generally, §§45.1-161.7 to 45.1-161.322.
See COAL MINE SAFETY.
Confidentiality of information gathered, §45.1-385.
Conflicts of interest, state and local government act.
Compliance with provisions, §45.1-161.17.
Continued as agency within secretariat of commerce and trade, §45.1-161.2.
Definitions, §45.1-161.1.
Director, §45.1-383.
Appointment by governor, §45.1-161.2.
Appointment of division heads, §45.1-161.5.
Appointment of mine inspectors, §45.1-161.18.
Closure orders, §45.1-161.91.
Defined, §45.1-161.1.
Duties, §45.1-161.4.
Head of department, §45.1-161.2.
Powers, §45.1-161.4.
State-designated mine rescue teams, §45.1-161.73.
Technical specialists in areas of roof control, electricity, etc.
Appointment by director, §45.1-161.23.
Discontinuance of operations, notice to department, §45.1-161.63.
Disposal of collected data, §45.1-388.
Distribution of reports, §45.1-387.
Division heads.
Appointment by director, §45.1-161.5.
Divisions.
Duties and functions of division, §45.1-386.
Establishment, §45.1-161.5.
Energy division, §§45.1-161.5, 45.1-390.
Establishment, §45.1-390.
Findings and policy, §45.1-390.
Powers and duties, §45.1-390.
Solar energy center, §45.1-391.
Solar photovoltaic manufacturing incentive grant program, §45.1-392.
Virginia energy plan.
Completion date, §67-202.
Definitions, §67-200.
Development, responsibility, requirements, §67-201.
Submission upon completion, §67-203.
Environmental impact assessments.
Drilling for oil or gas in Tidewater, §62.1-195.1.
Fund consisting of mine licensing fees, §45.1-161.58.
Gas and oil division, §45.1-161.5.
Gas drilling in Tidewater.
Environmental impact assessments, §62.1-195.1.
Geology and mineral resources division, §§45.1-161.5, 45.1-383 to 45.1-389.
Dissemination of materials, §45.1-388.
Establishment, §45.1-383.
Intergovernmental cooperation, §45.1-386.
Grants.
Power to accept, §45.1-161.3.
Head of department, §45.1 161.2.
Immunity from trespass prosecution, §45.1-389.
Interest in coal mines prohibited by officers, §45.1-161.17.
Labor unions.
Affiliations of personnel with prohibited, §45.1-161.17.
Lead agency for inspections undertaken pursuant to permits, §45.1-161.6.

MINES, MINERALS AND ENERGY DEPARTMENT —Cont'd
Limitation on authority.
Erosion and sediment control, §62.1-44.15:66.
Mined land reclamation division, §45.1-161.5.
Mine licensing.
See MINE LICENSING.
Mineral mine safety act, §§45.1-161.292:1 to 45.1-161.292:73.
See MINERAL MINE SAFETY.
Mineral mining division, §45.1-161.5.
Miner training, §§45.1-161.101 to 45.1-161.103.
Mines division, §45.1-161.5.
Chief.
Affiliation with operating coal company, operator's association or labor union prohibited, §45.1-161.17.
Age requirements, §45.1-161.16.
Appointment by governor, §45.1-161.15.
Board of coal mining examiners.
Chairman of board, §45.1-161.24.
Member of board, §45.1-161.24.
Closure orders, §45.1-161.91.
Coal mining examiners' fund.
Administration and payments from fund, §45.1-161.31.
Defined, §45.1-161.1.
Experience or education background, §45.1-161.16.
Fires in coal mines, response, §45.1-161.203.
First aid training of coal miners, §45.1-161.101.
Frequency of mine inspections, §45.1-161.81.
Health and safety of persons employed within or at coal mines.
Duties and powers, §45.1-161.21.
Inspections at sites last employed, §45.1-161.17.
Interest in coal mine prohibited, §45.1-161.17.
Map requirements for mine licensing, §45.1-161.65.
Mine license denial or revocation, §45.1-161.60.
Notice of correction, §45.1-161.90.
Notice of violations, §45.1-161.90.
Qualifications, §45.1-161.16.
Record of inspections of coal mines, §45.1-161.21.
Safety awareness training program for coal miners, §45.1-161.103.
Stock ownership in coal mine prohibited, §45.1-161.17.
Maps, §§45.1-161.64, 45.1-161.65.
Safety requirements applicable to underground coal mines, §§45.1-161.105 to 45.1-161.252.
See COAL MINE SAFETY.
New mine opening, notice to department, §45.1-161.63.
Notice.
Initial notice by certified mail, subsequent notices by regular mail, §45.1-161.1:1.
Oil drilling in Tidewater.
Environmental impact assessments, §62.1-195.1.
Operator's associations.
Affiliations with by employees prohibited, §45.1-161.17.
Personnel.
Affiliations with labor unions, coal companies, etc., prohibited, §45.1-161.17.
Power to employ, §45.1-161.3.
Powers, §45.1-161.3.
State geologist, §45.1-384.
Public policy.
Division of energy, §45.1-390.

MINES, MINERALS AND ENERGY DEPARTMENT —Cont'd
Regulations necessary or incidental to performance of duties.
Power to promulgate, §45.1-161.3.
Resumption of operations, notice to department, §45.1-161.63.
Secretary of commerce and trade.
Agency responsibility, §2.2-204.
Solar energy.
Voluntary solar resource development fund, §§67-1300 to 67-1305.
Solar energy center, §45.1-391.
Solar photovoltaic manufacturing incentive grant program, §45.1-392.
State minerals management plan.
Exploration activities on state owned uplands, §2.2-1157.
Stock ownership by officers in coal mines prohibited, §45.1-161.17.
Surface coal mines.
Mine safety requirements, §§45.1-161.253 to 45.1-161.292.
Surface mineral mining.
Mine safety requirements, §§45.1-161.304 to 45.1-161.309.
See COAL MINE SAFETY.
Underground coal mines.
Safety requirements applicable to, §§45.1-161.105 to 45.1-161.252.
See COAL MINE SAFETY.
Underground mineral mines.
Mine safety requirements, §§45.1-161.293 to 45.1-161.303.

MINE TECHNICAL SPECIALISTS.
Appointment by director of department of mines, minerals and energy, §45.1-161.23.

MINE VEHICLES.
Liens of employees or suppliers, §§43-24 to 43-26.

MINI-BIKES.
Exhaust system, §46.2-1051.
Lights, §46.2-1016.
Local government restrictions, §46.2-1051.

MINIMUM CONTACTS.
Long-arm statute, §8.01-328.1.

MINIMUM SPEED LIMITS, §46.2-877.

MINIMUM WAGE ACT, §§40.1-28.8 to 40.1-28.12.
Amount, §40.1-28.10.
Employee.
Defined, §40.1-28.9.
Employee's remedies, §40.1-28.12.
Employer.
Defined, §40.1-28.9.
Fines, §40.1-28.11.
Payment, §40.1-28.10.
Penalties, §40.1-28.11.
Rate of minimum wage, §40.1-28.10.
Ridesharing.
Inapplicability of overtime compensation and minimum wage laws, §46.2-1406.
Rights of persons with disabilities.
Employment discrimination.
Construction of section, §51.5-41.
Violation of provisions.
Employee's remedies, §40.1-28.12.
Wages.
Defined, §40.1-28.9.

MINING COMPACT, §45.1-271.

MINING COMPANY CREDIT FOR TONS OF COAL MINED, §58.1-439.2.

MINING FACILITIES.
Liens of employees or suppliers, §§43-24 to 43-26.

MINING MACHINERY AND TOOLS.
Liens of employees or suppliers, §§43-24 to 43-26.
Machinery and tools tax, §§58.1-3507, 58.1-3508.
Underground mineral mines.
Fire precautions in transporting mining equipment, §45.1-161.303.

MINING TAXES.
Subsurface substances proved to exist.
Imposition of tax, §55-155.

MINISTERIAL DISTRICTS.
District road bonds, §§33.1-321 to 33.1-335.
See DISTRICT ROAD BONDS.

MINISTERS.
Arrest under civil process.
Privileged from civil arrest, §§8.01-327.1, 8.01-327.2.
Cleric-penitent privilege, §8.01-400, VA SCt Rule 2:503.
Contract or tort immunity, §8.01-220.1:3.
License tax.
Limitations on locality's authority, §58.1-3703.
Marriage.
Attorney for the Commonwealth ascertainment of name of minister failing to return license and certificate, §20-22.
Authorized to perform ceremony, §20-23.
Celebrating marriage without license, §20-28.
False entry, §18.2-207.
Fee for celebrating marriage, §20-27.
List of licenses not returned by minister.
Clerk to furnish to Commonwealth's attorney, §20-21.
Penalty for failure to certify record of marriage, §20-24.
Qualifications for appointment to perform ceremony, §20-23.
Records.
Duties as to, §32.1-267.
Religious society having no minister, §20-26.
Privileges, §§8.01-400, 19.2-271.3, VA SCt Rule 2:503.
Property exempt from taxation, VA Const Art X §6.

MINNOWS.
Persons independently selling, bartering or trading.
Exemption from definition of commercial fisherman, §28.2-241.

MINORITY BUSINESS ENTERPRISE DEPARTMENT.
Small business and supplier diversity department, §§2.2-1603 to 2.2-1617.
See SMALL BUSINESS AND SUPPLIER DIVERSITY DEPARTMENT.

MINORITY BUSINESS ENTERPRISE DEPARTMENT (EFF UNTIL 1/1/2014), §§2.2-1400 to 2.2-1405.
Capital access fund for disadvantaged businesses.
Management, §2.2-1402.

MINORITY BUSINESS ENTERPRISE DEPARTMENT (EFF UNTIL 1/1/2014) —Cont'd
Center for development.
Powers of department, §2.2-1402.
Certification programs, §2.2-1403.
Creation, §2.2-1400.
Data collection system.
Development, §2.2-1405.
Defined terms, §2.2-1401.
Director, §2.2-1400.
Powers, §2.2-1403.
FOI act exclusion, §2.2-3705.6.
General provisions regarding state agencies and general operation of government, §§2.2-600 to 2.2-614.3.
See STATE DEPARTMENTS AND AGENCIES.
Interdepartmental board.
Composition, §2.2-1404.
Establishment, §2.2-1403.
Interdepartmental cooperation, §2.2-1404.
Main office, §2.2-1400.
Powers of department, §2.2-1402.
Powers of director, §2.2-1403.
Procurement by public bodies.
Businesses from department's list, §2.2-4310.
Participation of minority businesses, §2.2-4310.
Recommendations, §2.2-1405.
Reports, §2.2-1405.
Secretary of commerce and trade.
Agency responsibility, §2.2-204.

MINORITY BUSINESS ENTERPRISES.
Procurement by public bodies.
Small business and supplier diversity department.
Businesses from department's list, §2.2-4310.

MINORITY BUSINESS ENTERPRISES (EFF UNTIL 1/1/2014).
Colleges and universities.
Procurement of goods and services from, §2.2-1404.1.
Deception in obtaining certificate, §18.2-213.1.
Local ordinances supporting, §15.2-965.1.
Procurement by public bodies.
Minority business enterprise department.
Businesses from department's list, §2.2-4310.

MINORS.
Abortion.
Order authorizing physician to perform abortion.
Minor electing not to seek consent of authorized person, §16.1-241.
Abuse.
Generally, §§63.2-1500 to 63.2-1527.
See CHILD ABUSE AND NEGLECT.
Actions.
How minors may sue, §8.01-8.
Interstate family support.
Action by minor parent, §20-88.45.
Adoption.
Generally.
See ADOPTION.
Adult treatment of children for criminal offenses, §§16.1-269.1 to 16.1-272.
Anti-smoking health awareness.
Virginia foundation for healthy youth, §§32.1-354 to 32.1-367.
See VIRGINIA FOUNDATION FOR HEALTHY YOUTH.
Apprenticeship, §§40.1-117 to 40.1-126.
See APPRENTICESHIP.

MINORS —Cont'd
Arrest of child.
Taking child into custody generally.
See JUVENILE PROCEEDINGS.
Bank accounts of deceased minors.
Personal representatives, access to digital accounts.
Definitions, §64.2-109.
Power granted to personal representative, §64.2-110.
Banks.
Checks, §6.2-896.
Deposits of minors, §§6.2-893, 6.2-896.
Powers, §6.2-820.
Change of name.
Application procedure, §8.01-217.
Charitable gaming.
Instant bingo, pull tabs, seal cards.
Selling to, §18.2-340.28.
Network bingo cards.
Selling to, §18.2-340.28:1.
Wrongful ticket sales, §18.2-340.33.
Child labor.
Apprenticeship, §§40.1-117 to 40.1-126.
See APPRENTICESHIP.
General provisions, §§40.1-78 to 40.1-116.
See CHILD LABOR.
Children or minors.
See CHILDREN OR MINORS.
Child welfare agencies.
Generally.
See CHILD WELFARE AGENCIES.
Compromise of claims, §8.01-424.
Computers.
Monitored usage by parent or guardian.
Excluding from computer trespass crime, §18.2-152.4.
Contributing to delinquency of minors.
See CONTRIBUTING TO DELINQUENCY OF MINORS.
Credit unions.
Transfers to minors.
Acceptance of money under act, §6.2-1364.
Criminal offenses, adult treatment of child, §§16.1-269.1 to 16.1-272.
Cruelty and injuries to children.
Child labor, §40.1-103.
Debts as traders.
Liability of minors.
When plea of infancy not allowed, §8.01-278.
Disposition of real estate of persons under disability, §§8.01-67 to 8.01-80.
See PERSONS WITH DISABILITY.
Emancipation of minors, §§16.1-331 to 16.1-334.1.
Encumbrance of real estate.
Disposition of real estate of persons under disability generally, §§8.01-67 to 8.01-80.
See PERSONS WITH DISABILITY.
Exchange of real estate.
Disposition of real estate of persons under disability generally, §§8.01-67 to 8.01-80.
See PERSONS WITH DISABILITY.
Family and children's trust fund, §§63.2-2100 to 63.2-2103.
Foster care generally, §§63.2-900 to 63.2-915.
See FOSTER CARE.
Generally.
See CHILDREN OR MINORS.
Gifts to minors, §§64.2-1900 to 64.2-1922.
See TRANSFERS TO MINORS.

MINORS —Cont'd
Guardian and ward.
See GUARDIAN AND WARD.
Guardians, §§64.2-1700 to 64.2-1922.
Interstate compact on the placement of children, §63.2-1000.
Implementation, §§63.2-1100 to 63.2-1105.
Interstate family support.
Action by minor parent, §20-88.45.
Nondisclosure of information in exceptional circumstances, §20-88.55.
Juvenile community crime control, §§16.1-309.2 to 16.1-309.10.
See JUVENILE COMMUNITY CRIME CONTROL.
Juvenile detention and other care facilities generally, §§16.1-315 to 16.1-322.7.
See JUVENILE DETENTION AND OTHER CARE FACILITIES.
Juvenile proceedings generally, §§16.1-246 to 16.1-309.1.
See JUVENILE PROCEEDINGS.
Lease of real estate.
Disposition of real estate of persons under disability generally, §§8.01-67 to 8.01-80.
See PERSONS WITH DISABILITY.
Lighters.
Sale of novelty lighters to minors prohibited, §18.2-371.4.
Limitation of actions.
Disabilities which toll statute of limitations, §8.01-229.
Medical treatment.
Consent authority, §54.1-2969.
Motor vehicle accidents.
Defense of lack of consent of owner, §8.01-65.
Liability of owner, §8.01-64.
Neglect.
Generally, §§63.2-1500 to 63.2-1527.
See CHILD ABUSE AND NEGLECT.
Negotiable instruments.
Checks, §6.2-896.
Novelty lighters.
Sale to minors prohibited, §18.2-371.4.
Parental liability.
Damage to private property by minor child, §8.01-44.
Damage to public property by minor child, §8.01-43.
Parents.
Interstate family support.
Action by minor parent, §20-88.45.
Paternity proceedings, §§20-49.1 to 20-49.10.
See PATERNITY PROCEEDINGS.
Plea of infancy.
When not allowed, §8.01-278.
Precious metals dealers.
Prohibited purchases, §54.1-4103.
Prostitution.
Solicitation of prostitution from a minor, §18.2-346.
Psychiatric treatment of minors act, §§16.1-335 to 16.1-348.
See MENTAL HEALTH.
Public assistance.
Temporary assistance for needy families, §§63.2-600 to 63.2-621.
See PUBLIC AID AND ASSISTANCE.
Redemption of real estate.
Disposition of real estate of persons under disability generally, §§8.01-67 to 8.01-80.
See PERSONS WITH DISABILITY.

MINORS —Cont'd
Registry of criminal offenders generally.
See SEX OFFENDER REGISTRATION AND NOTIFICATION.
Sale of real estate.
Disposition of real estate of persons under disability generally, §§8.01-67 to 8.01-80.
See PERSONS WITH DISABILITY.
Savings institutions.
Savings account issued in name of minor, §6.2-1172.
Scrap metal purchasers.
Purchases from minors prohibited, §59.1-136.4.
Settlement of claims, §8.01-424.
Guardian ad litem, §8.01-9.
Small amounts paid through court, §8.01-606.
Sexual sterilization.
Children incapable of informed consent, §54.1-2975.
Shelter care for children.
Juvenile detention and other care facilities generally, §§16.1-315 to 16.1-322.7.
See JUVENILE DETENTION AND OTHER CARE FACILITIES.
Signs warning of children at play, §33.1-210.2.
Smoking.
Virginia foundation for healthy youth, §§32.1-354 to 32.1-367.
See VIRGINIA FOUNDATION FOR HEALTHY YOUTH.
Special education, §§22.1-213 to 22.1-221.
See SPECIAL EDUCATION.
Status of children of assisted conception.
Surrogacy contracts, §§20-156 to 20-165.
See SURROGACY CONTRACTS.
Statute of limitations.
Disabilities which toll statute of limitations, §8.01-229.
Surgical treatment.
Consent authority, §54.1-2969.
Teenage smoking.
Virginia foundation for healthy youth, §§32.1-354 to 32.1-367.
See VIRGINIA FOUNDATION FOR HEALTHY YOUTH.
Temporary assistance for needy families, §§63.2-600 to 63.2-621.
See PUBLIC AID AND ASSISTANCE.
Tobacco products.
Sales to minors, §18.2-371.2.
Novelty lighters, sale prohibited, §18.2-371.4.
Uniform fine schedule, VA SCt Rules 3C:1, 3C:2.
Teenage smoking.
Virginia foundation for healthy youth, §§32.1-354 to 32.1-367.
See VIRGINIA FOUNDATION FOR HEALTHY YOUTH.
Torts.
Joinder of action of tort to infant.
Action for recovery of expenses, §8.01-36.
Recovery of loss wages.
Action for injuries to emancipated infant, §8.01-37.
Transfers to minors, §§64.2-1900 to 64.2-1922.
See TRANSFERS TO MINORS.
Trust companies.
Powers as trustee, §§6.2-820, 6.2-1002.
Welfare.
Temporary assistance for needy families, §§63.2-600 to 63.2-621.
See PUBLIC AID AND ASSISTANCE.

MINORS —Cont'd
Winter sports safety act.
Common law regarding capacity and standard of measuring conduct not abrogated, §8.01-227.21.
Wrongful death.
General provisions, §§8.01-50 to 8.01-56.
See WRONGFUL DEATH.
Youth, commission on, §§30-174 to 30-177.

MINORS' SETTLEMENTS.
Court approval, §8.01-424.
Guardian ad litem, §8.01-9.
Payment of small amounts through court without intervention of fiduciary, §8.01-606.

MIRANDA RIGHTS.
Suppression of evidence.
Written pretrial motion, §19.2-266.2.

MIRROR IMAGE RULE.
Sales, UCC.
Variation of rule, §8.2-207.

MISBRANDED COMMERCIAL FEED.
Assessments, §3.2-4810.
Distribution prohibited, §3.2-4807.

MISBRANDED COSMETICS, §54.1-3465.
Color additives, §54.1-3460.
Condemnations, §54.1-3459.
Deleterious substances, §54.1-3460.
Prohibited acts, §54.1-3457.
Penalties for violations, §54.1-3458.
Tagging, §54.1-3459.

MISBRANDED DRUGS AND DEVICES, §54.1-3462.
Color additives, §54.1-3460.
Condemnation, §54.1-3459.
Deleterious substances, §54.1-3460.
Prescription exemption, §54.1-3463.
Prohibited acts, §54.1-3457.
Penalties for violations, §54.1-3458.
Tagging, §54.1-3459.

MISBRANDED FERTILIZER.
Distribution prohibited, §3.2-3612.

MISBRANDED LUBRICATING OILS.
Prevention by inspection and testing, §59.1-150.

MISBRANDED MEAT AND POULTRY PRODUCTS, §3.2-5402.

MISBRANDED MOTOR FUELS, §59.1-167.1.
Prevention by inspection and testing, §59.1-150.

MISCARRIAGE.
Conscience clause against causing miscarriage, §18.2-75.
Consent of pregnant woman, §18.2-76.
Encouraging or promoting inducing of miscarriage, §18.2-76.1.
First trimester of pregnancy.
When causing miscarriage lawful, §18.2-72.
Necessity to save life of woman.
Causing miscarriage, §18.2-74.1.
Producing miscarriage, §18.2-71.
Second trimester of pregnancy.
When causing miscarriage after lawful, §18.2-74.
When causing miscarriage lawful, §18.2-73.

MISCELLANEOUS CASUALTY INSURANCE.
Defined, §38.2-111.

MISCELLANEOUS PROPERTY INSURANCE.
Defined, §38.2-111.

MISCONDUCT IN OFFICE.
County board form of government.
Inquiry by supervisors into official conduct of office or officer, §15.2-403.
County executive form of government.
Inquiry into official conduct of office or officer, §15.2-506.
County manager form of government.
Inquiry into official conduct of office or officer, §15.2-606.
County manager plan of government.
Inquiry into official conduct of office or officer, §15.2-709.
Removal from office.
Governor's power to remove, §2.2-108.
Retirement, censure or removal of judge, VA Const Art VI §10.
Sheriff, deputy or other officer, §§15.2-1623 to 15.2-1625.
Urban county executive form of government.
Inquiry into official conduct of office or officer, §15.2-814.

MISDEMEANORS.
Abandoned wells or pits.
Person causing not filling, §18.2-316.
ABC offenses.
Advertising, §4.1-320.
Aiding or abetting misdemeanor violators, §4.1-323.
Attempts to commit misdemeanor offenses, §4.1-323.
Delivery of alcoholic beverages to jail inmates, §4.1-321.
Disobeying subpoena of board, §4.1-319.
Drinking alcoholic beverages in public place, §4.1-308.
Uniform fine schedule, VA SCt Rules 3C:1, 3C:2.
Drinking alcoholic beverages while on duty, §4.1-325.2.
Drinking or possessing alcoholic beverages in or on public school grounds, §4.1-309.
Drinking or possessing alcoholic beverages while operating a school bus, §4.1-309.1.
Failure to deliver, keep and preserve records and accounts, §4.1-331.
Failure to pay taxes, §§4.1-331, 4.1-332.
Falsifying license applications, §4.1-325.1.
Hindering conduct of board hearing, §4.1-319.
Importation, shipment and transportation of alcoholic beverages, §4.1-310.
Keeping or drinking alcoholic beverages upon club premises, §4.1-316.
Keeping, possessing or storing still or distilling apparatus without a permit, §4.1-314.
Limitations on carrying alcoholic beverages in motor vehicles transporting passengers for hire, §4.1-312.
Limitations on transporting lawfully purchased alcoholic beverages, §4.1-311.
Maintaining common nuisances, §4.1 317.
Nonpayment of excise tax on beer and wine coolers, §4.1-332.
Offering to another alcoholic beverages in public place, §4.1-308.
Persons by whom alcoholic beverages may not be sold or served for on-premises consumption, §4.1-307.
Persons to whom alcoholic beverages may not be sold, §4.1-304.

MISDEMEANORS —Cont'd
ABC offenses —Cont'd
Possessing, transporting, etc., alcoholic beverages illegally acquired, §4.1-313.
Possession of alcoholic beverages by interdicted persons, §4.1-322.
Possession to sell alcoholic beverages without license upon restaurant premises, §4.1-315.
Prohibited acts by mixed beverage licensees, §4.1-325.
Drinking alcoholic beverages while on duty, §4.1-325.2.
Falsifying license applications, §4.1-325.1.
Prohibiting transfer of wine or beer by licensees, §4.1-327.
Purchase for one to whom sales unlawful, §4.1-306.
Purchase for resale of wine or beer from unlicensed person, §4.1-326.
Purchase of alcoholic beverages from person not authorized to sell, §4.1-303.
Refusal to allow examination and inspection, §4.1-331.
Sale of wine or beer from unlicensed person, §4.1-326.
Sales of alcoholic beverages generally, §4.1-302.
Sales to minors, §§4.1-304, 4.1-307.
Selling or keeping of alcoholic beverages by licensees, §4.1-324.
Solicitation by persons interested in manufacture, etc., of alcoholic beverages, §4.1-330.
Unclassified offenses as misdemeanors, §4.1-349.
Unlawful consumption, purchase or possession of alcoholic beverages, §4.1-305.
Unlawful trade practices, §4.1-328.
Abduction by parent punishable as contempt in any pending proceeding, §18.2-47.
Abduction, disclosure of information and assistance to law enforcement, §18.2-50.
Abortion.
Encouraging or promoting, §18.2-76.1.
Order authorizing when minor elects not to seek consent of authorized person.
Physician performing abortion in violation of provisions, §16.1-241.
Abuse and neglect of incapacitated adult, §18.2-369.
Abusive language to another, §18.2-416.
Accessories to gambling, §18.2-330.
Accommodation drug sales.
Marijuana, §18.2-248.1.
Accord and satisfaction.
Assault or other misdemeanor for which civil action available.
Satisfaction for injury, discharge or recognizance or dismissal of prosecution, §19.2-151.
Adult abuse and neglect.
Incapacitated adult, §18.2-369.
Adulterating drugs, devices and cosmetics, §54.1-3458.
Adultery, §18.2-365.
Persons forbidden to marry, §18.2-366.
Advances of money or other thing of value.
Fraudulent promise to perform agricultural labor, advances secured by, §18.2-201.
Advertising.
Agricultural products misrepresentations, §18.2-225.
Automobiles or trucks, new or used, §18.2-221.
Failure to indicate goods seconds, irregulars, secondhand, etc., §18.2-210.

MISDEMEANORS —Cont'd
Advertising —Cont'd
Intent not to sell at price or terms advertised, §18.2-217.
Misrepresentation as to source of merchandise.
Article made for or acquired from United States government, military force or agency, §18.2-222.
Obscene items, exhibitions or performances, §§18.2-376, 18.2-380.
Unauthorized use of name or picture of person, §18.2-216.1.
Untrue, deceptive or misleading, §18.2-216.
Wholesale or wholesaler use of word, §18.2-220.
Aging and rehabilitative services, department for.
Disclosure of confidential information, §51.5-122.
Agricultural labor.
Advances secured by fraudulent promise to perform, §18.2-201.
Agricultural liming materials, §3.2-3715.
Agricultural products.
Grades, marks and brands, §3.2-4310.
Misrepresentations, §18.2-225.
Misuse or unauthorized use of Virginia quality label, §3.2-4321.
Air cannons, carbide cannons or other loud explosive devices used to repel birds.
Locality prohibiting use, §15.2-918.
Aircraft.
Breaking or preventing operation, §18.2-146.
Entering or setting in motion, §18.2-147.
Interference with aircraft, §5.1-22.
Operation while under the influence, §5.1-13.
Pointing laser at aircraft, §5.1-22.
Procuring with intent to defraud, §18.2-206.
Rented or leased, injury to, §18.2-149.
Tampering, §5.1-16.
Unauthorized use, §18.2-102.
Use for hunting, §5.1-17.
Air pollution violations, §10.1-1320.
Alcohol and substance abuse screening and assessment for designated Class 1 misdemeanor convictions, §19.2-299.2.
Alcohol vaporizing device.
Licensees, keeping or selling.
Prohibition, penalty, §4.1-324.
Use prohibited, penalty, §4.1-302.1.
Ambulances.
Calling or summoning without just cause, §18.2-212.
Anabolic steroids.
Manufacturing, selling, etc., with intent to manufacture, sell, etc., §18.2-248.5.
Animal liens.
Defrauding persons having, §18.2-188.1.
Animals.
Abandonment of animals, §§3.2-6504, 18.2-403.2.
Agricultural animals, care of, §3.2-6503.1.
Baby fowl.
Sale in certain quantities, §§3.2-6510, 18.2-403.2.
Boarding establishments.
Failure to display or provide consumer with written notice of remedies, §3.2-6519.
Violation of veterinary care requirement, §§3.2-6518, 18.2-403.1.
City ordinance violations, §18.2-403.3.
Companion animals, disposal of dead animals, §§3.2-6554, 18.2-403.3.
Willful torture or inhumane injuries, §3.2-6570.

MISDEMEANORS —Cont'd
Animals —Cont'd
Cruelty to animals, §§3.2-6570, 18.2-403.1.
Sale of animals after conviction, §3.2-6570.1.
Disabled or dead animal left in road or unburied, §18.2-323.
Driving animal on railroad track to recover damages, §18.2-158.
False pretense in obtaining registration or giving false pedigree, §18.2-205.
False representation of ownership to animal shelter, §18.2-144.2.
Groomers.
Mistreatment of animals, §3.2-6503.
Veterinary care requirements, §3.2-6518.
Humane investigators.
Interference with, §§3.2-6566, 18.2-403.3.
Mistreatment of animals by owner, §§3.2-6503, 18.2-403.3.
Agricultural animals, §3.2-6503.1.
Pet dealers.
Failure to provide adequate care, etc., §§3.2-6511, 18.2-403.2.
Local ordinances as to permits, §3.2-6537.
Pigeon shooting for amusement, §3.2-6573.
Procuring with intent to defraud, §18.2-206.
Rabid animals, withholding information about, §18.2-313.1.
Remedies, §3.2-4914.
Obstructing or hindering commissioner, §3.2-4909.
Rented or leased, injury to, §18.2-149.
Running at large.
Permitting animals to run at large in county under quarantine, §18.2-121.1.
Sales.
Misrepresentation of animal's condition, §§3.2-6509, 18.2-403.2.
Shelters and boarding establishments.
Mistreatment of animals, §§3.2-6503, 18.2-403.3.
Shooting enclosures, §3.2-6042.
Soring horses, §§3.2-6570, 18.2-403.2.
Transporting animals, §§3.2-6508, 18.2-403.1.
Unauthorized release, §18.2-403.4.
Unauthorized use, §18.2-102.
Unweaned mammalian companion animals, §3.2-6510.
Animals running at large.
Unincorporated communities and villages.
Boundaries within which animals may not run at large, §55-328.
Annoying telephone or pager calls.
Causing telephone or pager to ring with intent to annoy, §18.2-429.
Antitrust act.
Civil investigative demand.
Perjury, false swearing or contempt, §59.1-9.10.
Appearances in court by employees.
Penalizing for, §18.2-465.1.
Apples.
Controlled atmosphere storage of apples and peaches, §3.2-4613.
Excise tax on commercial production of apples.
Producers.
Violations as to records and reports, §3.2-1217.
Unlawful commercial movement, §3.2-4506.
Appointment of counsel for indigent accused.
False swearing to statement of indigence, §19.2-161.

MISDEMEANORS —Cont'd
Archaeological objects and sites, §10.1-2306.
Archaeological permit violations, §10.1-2302.
Armed forces identification card.
Fictitious, facsimile or simulated official identification.
Fraudulent use to obtain alcoholic beverages, §46.2-347.
Arrest.
Resisting lawful arrest, §18.2-479.1.
Arrest report to central criminal records exchange, §19.2-390.
Virginia crime code references, required use, §19.2-390.01.
Arson and related crimes.
Carelessly damaging property by fire, §18.2-88.
Chemical smoke bombs, setting off in certain public buildings, §18.2-87.1.
Other buildings or structures, burning or destroying, §18.2-80.
Personal property, standing grain, etc., burning or destroying, §18.2-81.
Threats to bomb or damage buildings or means of transportation.
Persons under fifteen years of age, §18.2-83.
Woods, brush, leaves, etc.
Setting on fire intentionally whereby another damaged or jeopardized, §18.2-87.
Asbestos contractors and workers.
Licensing provision violations, §54.1-517.
Asbestos NESHAP, §40.1-51.39.
Assault and battery, §18.2-57.
Against family or household member, §18.2-57.2.
By mob, §18.2-42.
Assistance to police officers in execution of office.
Refusal, §18.2-463.
Attempts to commit misdemeanors, §18.2-27.
Attorneys.
Legal aid societies.
Governance violations, §54.1-3916.
Practicing law without authority, §54.1-3904.
Furnishing advice and services for compensation in connection with debt-pooling plans, §54.1-3905.
Unlawful solicitation of professional employment, §54.1-3944.
Aviation contract carrier license violations, §5.1-9.8.
Aviation permit violations, §5.1-9.9.
Bad checks, issuance, §18.2-181.
Wage payments.
Issuance on behalf of business firm or corporation, §18.2-182.
Bail bondsmen, §9.1-185.18.
Bail enforcement agents, §9.1-186.13.
Bait and switch, §18.2-217.
Ballast water discharge.
Failure to comply with filing requirements, §28.2-110.
Bank employee offenses, §6.2-944.
Barratry, §18.2-452.
Bawdy places.
Keeping, residing in or frequenting, §18.2-350.
Beaches and sand dunes, §28.2-1418.
Bedding and upholstered furniture, §32.1-226.
Beekeeping, §3.2-4414.
Behavioral health and developmental services.
Admission of person without reasonable cause.
Maliciously or knowingly contriving or conspiring to obtain, §37.2-431.

MISDEMEANORS —Cont'd
Behavioral health and developmental services —Cont'd
Aiding and abetting escape, §37.2-428.
Alcoholic beverages, provision or sale to individuals receiving services, §37.2-430.
Disorderly conduct or interfering with officer or employee, §37.2-429.
Mistreatment of individuals receiving services, §37.2-427.
Bicycle helmets.
Local ordinances, §46.2-906.1.
Billboards.
Hindering commissioner or agent in the performance of their functions and duties, §33.1-354.
Birds.
Homing pigeons, hunting, pursuing, taking, etc., §18.2-145.
Maiming, killing or poisoning, §18.2-144.
Shooting pigeons, etc., for amusement, §§3.2-6573, 18.2-403.3.
Birth certificates.
Fraudulent use, §18.2-204.1.
Blackjacks, metal knucks, switchblades, etc.
Possession on school property, §18.2-308.1.
Selling or having in possession, §18.2-311.
Blind or visually impaired.
Sale of goods made by, §51.5-105.
Unlawful for person not blind to carry white cane, §18.2-212.1.
Boat dealers, §29.1-807.
Boats.
Breaking or preventing operation, §18.2-146.
Certificate of title.
Failure to surrender when security interest paid, §29.1-730.
Possession of title issued to another, §29.1-732.
Uniform certificate of title for watercraft.
Fraudulent assignment or transfer of title, §29.1-733.14.
Defrauding keepers of watercraft, §18.2-189.
Disregarding signal by law-enforcement officer to stop, §29.1-739.1.
Eluding law-enforcement officer, §29.1-739.1.
Entering or setting in motion, §18.2-147.
Failure to appear for trial, §29.1-210.
Failure to stop and render assistance, §29.1-740.
Impeding conservation police officer, §29.1-207.
Jetskis.
Permitting person under the age of 14 to operate, §29.1-749.
Unlawful operation, §29.1-748.
Motorboating or waterskiing in public swimming areas, §29.1-734.
Operating boat during suspension period, §29.1-738.
Operating boat in improper manner, §29.1-738.01.
Operating boat, waterskiing or spearfishing in reckless manner, §29.1-738.
Operating boat while intoxicated, §29.1-738.
Pass-through zone ordinance violation, §29.1-744.4.
Personal water craft.
Minimum distance from shoreline.
City ordinance regulating, penalty for violation, §29.1-748.1.
Procuring with intent to defraud, §18.2-206.
Reckless or intoxicated operation, §29.1-738.4.
Rented or leased, injury to, §18.2-149.
Unauthorized use, §18.2-102.

MISDEMEANORS —Cont'd
Boats —Cont'd
Violations of chapter, §29.1-746.
Willfully destroying with intent to defraud owner or insurer, §18.2-150.
Body piercing of minors, §18.2-371.3.
Boiler and pressure vessel safety, §40.1-51.39.
Bomb threats.
Persons under fifteen years of age, §18.2-83.
Bootleg recordings, §59.1-41.2.
Boxing and wrestling events, §§54.1-834, 54.1-835.
Branch pilots.
Licensing violations, §§54.1-924, 54.1-927.
Brands and marks.
Cattle brands, §3.2-6109.
False branding of tobacco, §61.1-44.
Tobacco.
False branding, §61.1-44.
Trees and timber.
Defacement of mark, §59.1-107.
Fraudulent use of mark, §59.1-107.
Breed of bull or cattle.
Fraudulent misrepresentation, §18.2-190.
Bribery.
Corruptly influencing or being influenced.
Agents, employees or servants, §18.2-444.
Service of notice, process and other papers.
Bribery to officers to prevent, §18.2-440.
Vote influencing or procuring vote, §24.2-1007.
Voters, §§24.2-1005, 24.2-1007.
Bridges, locks, dams or other structures, burning or destroying, §18.2-80.
Brown v. Board of Education scholarship program and fund.
False or fictitious name or address on application, §30-231.3.
Building code, §36-106.
Smoke detectors for deaf and hearing-impaired.
Violations of provisions, §36-99.5.
Burial grounds.
Injuries to, §18.2-127.
Burial or cremation of dead animal or fowl violation, §18.2-510.
Burning or destroying other buildings or structures, §18.2-80.
Burning or destroying personal property, standing grain, etc., §18.2-81.
Business machines.
Failure to report removal or alteration of identification or serial number, §18.2-214.1.
Business opportunity sales.
False statements, §59.1-269.
Cable television.
Obtaining or attempting to obtain service without payment, §18.2-187.1.
Tampering with or unlawful use, §18.2-165.1.
Cable television lines or signals.
Unlawful use of or injury to, §18.2-165.
Caffeine.
Distributing or selling to minors, §18.2-248.5.
Campgrounds.
Membership camping, §59.1-335.
Capitol grounds.
Injuries to trees, fences or herbage on, §18.2-139.
Carelessly damaging property by fire, §18.2-88.
Carrying concealed weapons, §18.2-308.
Cats, §3.2-6587.
Concealing cat on which license tax not paid, §§3.2-6587, 18.2-403.3.

MISDEMEANORS —Cont'd
Cats —Cont'd
Diseased cats.
Violations of provisions, §3.2-6587.
Improper disposal of diseased animal's body, §3.2-6587.
Leash ordinance violations, §3.2-6587.
License applications, false statements, §§3.2-6587, 18.2-403.3.
License tax.
Failure to pay, §3.2-6587.
Rabies regulations violation, §3.2-6587.
Removal of collar or tag by person other than owner or custodian, §§3.2-6587, 18.2-403.3.
Cattle.
Brands, §3.2-6109.
Cattle stops along railroads.
Injury to, §18.2-157.
Causing or encouraging acts rendering child delinquent, abused, etc., §18.2-371.
Cave protection, §10.1-1003.
Disturbing naturally occurring organisms, §10.1-1006.
Permits for excavation and scientific investigation, §10.1-1003.
Pollution, §10.1-1005.
Speleothem sales, §10.1-1007.
Vandalism, §10.1-1004.
Cemeteries.
Injuries to, §18.2-127.
Pet cemeteries, §§57-39.22, 57-39.25.
Trespass at night, §18.2-125.
Uniform fine schedule, VA SCt Rules 3C:1, 3C:2.
Cemetery operators, perpetual care trust funds and preneed burial contracts, §54.1-2342.
Change of name.
Unlawful change, §18.2-504.1.
Charitable gaming, §§18.2-33, 18.2-340.37.
Check casher registration violation, §6.2-2109.
Child abuse or neglect.
Protective order violations, §16.1-253.2.
Child custody.
Court order violations, §18.2-49.1.
Child injured by act of member of household.
Failing to secure medical attention, §18.2-314.
Chlorofluorocarbons violations, §10.1-1424.1.
Churches.
Injuries to churches and church property, §18.2-127.
Trespass upon church property, §18.2-128.
Uniform fine schedule, VA SCt Rules 3C:1, 3C:2.
Cigarettes.
Counterfeit cigarettes, sale or possession, §18.2-246.14.
Delivery sales report.
False statements in report, penalties, §18.2-246.13.
Taxes. See within this heading, "Taxes."
Circuit court clerks.
Depositing money collected into personal account or intermingling with personal funds, §17.1-271.
Circuit court jurisdiction, §16.1-126.
Clams.
Harvesting or shipping undersized clams, §28.2-537.
Labeling out-of-state clams as Virginia clams, §28.2-532.
Nonresidents taking or planting clams, §28.2-634.
Residents associated, §28.2-635.

MISDEMEANORS —Cont'd
Clams —Cont'd
Taking clams in certain areas, §28.2-536.
Taking on Sunday or at night, §28.2-531.
Use of hydraulic dredges, §28.2-520.
Clandestine organizations.
Failure to file information with state corporation commission, §18.2-421.
Class 1 misdemeanor, §18.2-9.
Punishment for, §18.2-11.
No punishment or maximum punishment prescribed, §18.2-12.
Punishment by reference, §18.2-13.
Class 2 misdemeanor, §18.2-9.
Punishment for, §18.2-11.
Class 3 misdemeanor, §18.2-9.
Punishment for, §18.2-11.
Class 4 misdemeanor, §18.2-9.
Punishment for, §18.2-11.
Closed highways.
Injury to barriers, signs, etc., §33.1-193.
Coal mine worker certification.
Performance of certain tasks by uncertified persons, §45.1-161.30.
Coin and coin silver sales, §18.2-234.
Colleges and universities.
Regulation of private and out-of-state institutions of higher education, §23-276.12.
Combinations to injure others in reputation, trade, business or professions, §18.2-499.
Communications sales and use tax.
Failure, neglect or refusal to collect or remit, §58.1-659.
Services providers.
Doing business without registering or after certificate revoked or suspended, §58.1-653.
Community corrections, §§9.1-173 to 9.1-183.
See COMMUNITY CORRECTIONS.
Community criminal justice boards, §§9.1-178, 9.1-180.
Commuter buses.
Maintenance of records, §46.2-1175.
Compounding offenses, §18.2-462.
Computer crimes.
Encryption abuses, §18.2-152.15.
Harassment by computer, §18.2-152.7:1.
Computer fraud, §18.2-152.3.
Computer invasion of privacy, §18.2-152.5.
Computer services theft, §18.2-152.6.
Computer trespass, §18.2-152.4.
Concealed weapons, carrying, §18.2-308.
Concealing offenses, §18.2-462.
Condominiums, §55-79.28.
False advertising, §55-79.28.
Unlawful sale, §55-79.103.
Confidential information.
Disciplinary proceedings.
Health regulatory boards, §54.1-2400.2.
Juvenile proceeding disclosure violation, §16.1-309.
Confidential tax documents.
Disseminating or publishing, §58.1-3.
Conflicts of interest.
General assembly, §30-123.
Public officers and employees.
Knowing violations, §2.2-3120.
Conservation department violations, §10.1-104.
Conservation officers.
Killing wildlife damaging crops, livestock or personal property.
Impeding person engaged in lawful killing, §29.1-529.

MISDEMEANORS —Cont'd
Conservators of the peace.
Failure to obey, §18.2-464.
Special conservators of the peace.
Unlawful conduct, §9.1-150.4.
Conspiracy to trespass after having been forbidden to do so, §18.2-23.
Consumer affairs.
Investigative orders, §59.1-201.
Consumer finance companies, violations generally, §6.2-1540.
Containers.
Names, marks and devices, §59.1-96.
Contractors.
Failure to obtain certificate of occupancy, §54.1-1101.
Licensing or certification violations, §54.1-1115.
School contracts, background investigation required for.
False statements, §22.1-296.1.
Tradesmen certification violations, §54.1-1135.
Contributing to delinquency of minor, §18.2-371.
Controlled atmosphere storage of apples and peaches, §3.2-4613.
Controlled substances.
Distributing instruments for use in administering to minors, §18.2-255.1.
Fraud, deceit, embezzlement, forgery, etc.
Obtaining drugs or procuring administration by, §18.2-258.1.
Manufacturing, selling, etc., with intent to manufacture, sell, etc., §18.2-248.
Unlawful possession, §18.2-250.
Cooperative in corporate or business name.
Misuse, §13.1-336.
Corporate officer's willful failure to collect and account for local taxes, §58.1-3907.
Corporations.
Signing false documents, §13.1-612.
Unauthorized transaction of business as a corporation, §13.1-613.
Corporation transacting business under assumed name, §59.1-75.
Corruptly influencing or being influenced.
Agents, employees or servants, §18.2-444.
Cosmetics.
Adulterating, §54.1-3458.
Misbranding, §54.1-3458.
Cotton gins, cotton merchants and cotton warehouses, §3.2-4775.
County procurement by county purchasing agent, §15.2-1240.
County treasurer bond violations, §21-388.
Crabs, §28.2-701.
Catch limit violation, §28.2-713.
Crab pots.
Identification number not displayed or maintained, §28.2-712.
Placement in certain channels, §28.2-710.
Use during prohibited period, §28.2-711.
Dredging restrictions, §28.2-707.
Harvesting restrictions, §28.2-705.
Out-of-season catching, §28.2-709.
Scraping restrictions, §28.2-706.
Size limitations, §28.2-708.
Credit cards.
Factoring, §18.2-195.1.
Fraud, §18.2-195.
Criminally receiving goods and services fraudulently obtained, §18.2-197.

MISDEMEANORS —Cont'd
Credit cards —Cont'd
Fraud —Cont'd
Fraudulent applications, §18.2-195.2.
Credit counseling licenses.
Violations of provisions, §§6.2-2001, 6.2-2022.
Crime commission disclosures, §30-162.
Criminal justice information system.
Willful and intentional violations of chapter, §9.1-136.
Criminal street gangs.
Recruiting individual to participate in gang activities, §18.2-46.3.
Crops.
Removal by tenant before rents and advances satisfied, §18.2-100.
Cruelty to animals, §§3.2-6570, 18.2-403.1.
Sale of animals after conviction, §3.2-6570.1.
Soring horses, §§3.2-6570, 18.2-403.2.
Customers of telephone companies.
Disclosing or inducing disclosure of certain information concerning, §18.2-166.
Dairy milk cases or milk crates.
Unauthorized use, §18.2-102.2.
Uniform fine schedule, VA SCt Rules 3C:1, 3C:2.
Damaging antiquities, §10.1-2306.
Dams.
Failure to keep in good order, §33.1-176.
Dam safety, §10.1-613.1.
Dangerous dog owners, §3.2-6540.
Dangerous weapons.
Airports.
Carrying weapon into air carrier airport terminal, §18.2-287.01.
Carrying into courthouses, §18.2-283.1.
Carrying to place of religious worship, §18.2-283.
Children or minors, furnishing to, §18.2-309.
Dead bodies, disposal on private property without permission, §18.2-323.01.
Dead bodies used for scientific study.
Failure to perform duty imposed, §32.1-304.
Trafficking in bodies, §32.1-303.
Defamation of savings institutions, §6.2-1107.
Defined, §18.2-8.
Dentistry.
Practice of in a commercial or mercantile establishment, §54.1-2716.
Derogatory statements affecting banks, §6.2-940.
Derogatory statements affecting credit unions, §6.2-1305.
Derogatory statements affecting trust companies, §6.2-1042.
Desertion of spouse or children, §20-61.
Destruction of private property, §18.2-137.
Destruction of trees, shrubs, etc., §18.2-140.
Dialysis patient care technicians, §54.1-2729.2.
Dietitians and nutritionists, §54.1-2731.
Diplomas from post-secondary educational institutions.
Falsifying or altering and fraudulently using, §18.2-172.1.
Disabilities, schools for students with.
License, operation without, §22.1-331.
License, summary order of suspension.
Failure to comply, §22.1-329.
Disarming a law-enforcement or correctional officer, §18.2-57.02.
Discovery and inspection by accused and Commonwealth.
Applicability of rule, VA SCt Rule 3A:11.

MISDEMEANORS —Cont'd
Disobeying alcoholic beverage subpoena, §4.1-319.
Disorderly conduct in public places, §18.2-415.
Display of obscene materials which can be seen from outside of the vehicle, §46.2-1077.01.
District court jurisdiction, §16.1-123.1.
District courts, fees in certain criminal cases, §16.1-69.48:1.
Divorce advertising violation, §20-122.
DNA data bank violations, §19.2-310.6.
Dogs, §3.2-6587.
Collar, removal, §18.2-97.1.
Commercial dog breeders.
Pet shops, procurement from unlicensed commercial dog breeders, §3.2-6511.1.
Violations, §3.2-6507.5.
Concealing dog on which license tax not paid, §§3.2-6587, 18.2-403.3.
Diseased dogs permitted to stray from premises, §§3.2-6587, 18.2-403.3.
Hybrid canine ordinance violations, §3.2-6582.
Improper disposal of diseased animal, §3.2-6587.
Killing, injuring or chasing poultry or livestock, §18.2-403.1.
Leash ordinance violation, §3.2-6587.
False statements, §3.2-6587.
License applications, false statements, §§3.2-6587, 18.2-403.3.
License tax.
Failure to pay, §3.2-6587.
Pet shops, procurement from unlicensed commercial dog breeders, §3.2-6511.1.
Rabies regulations violations, §3.2-6587.
Removal of collar or tag by person other than owner or custodian, §§3.2-6587, 18.2-403.3.
Removal of transmitting device from dog, falcon, hawk or owl, §18.2-97.1.
Uniform fine schedule, VA SCt Rules 3C:1, 3C:2.
Drainage ditches.
Obstruction, §33.1-345.
Drinking alcoholic beverages, §4.1-308.
Drinking while operating motor vehicle, §18.2-323.1.
Drivers' licenses.
Fraudulent use, §18.2-204.1.
Manufacture, sale, etc., of fictitious, facsimile or simulated license, §18.2-204.2.
Driving after illegally consuming alcohol.
Persons under age twenty-one, §18.2-266.1.
Driving while intoxicated.
Chemical tests of blood.
Reuse of single-use-only needles or syringes, §18.2-268.5.
Driving after forfeiture of license, §18.2-272.
Driving while license suspended or revoked, §46.2-301.1.
Allowing person to operate vehicle knowing license suspended or revoked, §§46.2-301, 46.2-301.1.
Dropping load material, §10.1-1424.
Drug adulteration or misbranding, §54.1-3458.
Drug and alcohol screening tests.
Defeating tests, §18.2-251.4.
Drug offenses.
Advertisement of imitation controlled substances, §18.2-248.4.
Attempts, §18.2-257.
Caffeine and ephedrine sulfate.
Selling or distributing to minor without prescription, §18.2-248.5.

MISDEMEANORS —Cont'd
Drug offenses —Cont'd
Distributing instruments for use in administering to minors, §18.2-255.1.
Ephedrine or related compounds.
Failure to report sales, §18.2-265.18.
Recordkeeping and limitations on amount sold, violations, §18.2-265.7.
Falsifying patient records, §18.2-260.1.
Fraud, deceit, embezzlement, forgery, etc.
Obtaining drugs or procuring administration by, §18.2-258.1.
Inhaling drugs or other noxious chemicals, §18.2-264.
Manufacturing, selling, etc., with intent to manufacture, sell, etc.
Anabolic steroids, §18.2-248.5.
Controlled substances or imitation controlled substances, §18.2-248.
Marijuana, §18.2-248.1.
Synthetic cannabinoids, §18.2-248.1:1.
Owners, lessors, agents, etc., of premises deemed nuisance, §18.2-258.
Pharmacists filling prescription before receiving in writing, §18.2-248.
Synthetic cannabinoids.
Manufacturing, selling, etc., with intent to manufacture, sell, etc, §18.2-248.1:1.
Unlawful possession of controlled substances, §18.2-250.
Unlawful possession of marijuana, §18.2-250.1.
Violations for which no penalty provided, §18.2-260.
Drug paraphernalia.
Advertising, §18.2-265.5.
Dispensing condition violations, §54.1-3468.
Disposal violations, §54.1-3469.
Obtaining by deceit, §54.1-3470.
Possession and distribution of, §54.1-3466.
Selling or distributing, §18.2-265.3.
Storage violations, §54.1-3469.
Usage violations, §54.1-3469.
Dump creating fire hazard to bridge, §33.1-347.
Dwelling places, picketing, §18.2-419.
Election offenses.
Advice of assistance in casting ballot, §24.2-1006.
Willful violations, §24.2-649.
Bribery, intimidation, etc., of person receiving ballot, §24.2-1005.
Campaigning at registration locations, §24.2-1003.
Carrying ballot away from voting booth, §24.2-1011.
Communication of false information to voter, §24.2-1005.1.
Destruction of or failure to mail or deliver voter registration application, §24.2-1002.01.
General penalty, §24.2-1017.
Hindering, intimidating or interfering with qualified voter, §24.2-607.
Interference with voter registration, §24.2-1002.
Intimidation of voters, §24.2-607.
Keys to voting equipment, unauthorized possession, §24.2-1010.
Loudspeakers at polls, §24.2-605.
Neglect of duty by election officers, electoral board members, etc., §24.2-1001.
Penalties not specifically provided elsewhere, §24.2-1017.
Prohibited activities at polls, §24.2-604.
Soliciting or accepting bribe to influence or procure vote, §24.2-1007.

MISDEMEANORS —Cont'd
Election offenses —Cont'd
Unqualified person voting, §24.2-1004.
Voting ballot other than one received, §24.2-1011.
Willful neglect, §24.2-1001.
Electric fences, §18.2-324.1.
Unlawful sale, construction, installation, maintenance or use, §55-298.5.
Electricians.
Certification violations, §54.1-1135.
Electric utility restructuring.
Electric energy emergencies, §56-586.1.
Electronic communication service.
Obtaining service without payment, §18.2-187.1.
Electronic notary's software or hardware.
Possessing, concealing, damaging or destroying, §47.1-29.1.
Electronic tracking devices, unauthorized use, §18.2-60.5.
Eluding police, §46.2-817.
Elvis statute violation, §18.2-216.1.
Embalmers.
Licensing violations, §54.1-2809.
Emblems.
Unauthorized wearing or displaying on motor vehicles.
Emblems of certain associations or societies, §18.2-176.
Emergency telephone calls.
Harassment or annoyance of emergency personnel, §18.2-429.
Emergency two-way radio communications.
Unlawful interference with, §18.2-165.2.
Employee court appearances or jury panel service.
Penalizing for, §18.2-465.1.
Endangered plants and insects, §3.2-1011.
Taking, transportation or sale, §29.1-567.
Entering property of another for purposes of damaging, §18.2-121.
Entrances to state highways from commercial establishments, §33.1-198.
Ephedrine or related compounds.
Failure to report sales, §18.2-265.18.
Recordkeeping and limitations on amount sold, violations, §18.2-265.7.
Ephedrine sulfate.
Selling or distributing to minors, §18.2-248.5.
Escape.
Aiding escape of prisoner or child, §18.2-473.
Officer willfully and deliberately permitting prisoner not convicted of or charged with felony to escape, §18.2-476.
Residential care facilities or juvenile facilities, §18.2-477.1.
Without force or violence or setting fire to jail, §18.2-479.
Ethics in public contracting.
False statement by public employee.
Certificate of compliance, §2.2-4375.
Generally, §2.2-4377.
Examination of bank books, §6.2-1203.
Execution of process.
Officer refusing, delaying, etc., §18.2-469.
Resisting or obstructing, §18.2-409.
Expectorating in public places, §18.2-322.
Explosions and explosives.
Failure to comply with provisions, §59.1-141.
Reports of stolen explosives.
Failure to comply with provisions, §59.1-141

MISDEMEANORS —Cont'd
Expunged records violations, §§19.2-392.3, 19.2-392.4.
Extended service contracts, §59.1-441.
Extortion.
By officers, §18.2-470.
Extradition procedural violations.
Generally, §19.2-96.
Failure to aid forest warden, §10.1-1139.
Uniform fine schedule, VA SCt Rules 3C:1, 3C:2.
Failure to appear, §19.2-128.
Failure to clean certain mills, §10.1-1144.
Falcons, hawks and owls.
Removal of transmitting device from dog, falcon, hawk or owl, §18.2-97.1.
Taking, trapping, holding, transportation, carriage and shipment without permit, §29.1-412.
False advertising, §18.2-216.
Agricultural products misrepresentations, §18.2-225.
Bait and switch, §18.2-217.
Failure to indicate goods seconds, irregulars, secondhand, etc., §18.2-218.
Misrepresentation as to source of merchandise.
Article made for or acquired from United States government, military force or agency, §18.2-222.
Motor vehicles, new or used, §18.2-221.
Wholesale or wholesaler use of word, §18.2-220.
False alarms, §18.2-461.
False bank reports, §6.2-1104.
False certification of checks, §6.2-942.
False identity, establishing, §18.2-204.1.
False impersonation.
Peace officers, §18.2-174.
Public safety personnel, §18.2-174.1.
False publications, §18.2-209.
False reports to police officers, §18.2-461.
False representations to obtain property or credit, §18.2-186.
False swearing to statement of indigence, §19.2-161.
Family abuse.
Protective order violations, §16.1-253.2.
Family or household member.
Assault and battery against, §18.2-57.2.
Family violence fatality review teams.
Death investigations, §32.1-283.3.
Farm machinery and equipment.
Removing, defacing or obliterating serial number, §3.2-5000.
Farm produce sales, §3.2-4708.
Commission merchants.
Violation of provisions, §3.2-4737.
Dealers in agricultural produce.
Violation of article, §3.2-4751.
Dealers in grain products.
Violation of article, §3.2-4763.
Fee bills, fraudulent issue, §18.2-471.
Feed, commercial, §3.2-4817.
Fences.
Pulling down fences or leaving open gates, §18.2-143.
Railroad fences, injury to, §18.2-157.
Fertilizer.
Criminal penalties for violations, §3.2-3625.
Obstructing or hindering commissioner, §3.2-3618.
Filming another unlawfully, §18.2-386.1.
Fines.
Non-traffic prepayable offenses, VA SCt Rules 3C:1, 3C:2.

MISDEMEANORS —Cont'd
Fines —Cont'd
Traffic infractions, VA SCt Rules 3B:1, 3B:2.
Fire alarms.
Maliciously activating in public buildings, §18.2-212.
Firearm dealers.
Licensing violations, §§54.1-4201.1, 54.1-4202.
Firearms.
Acquittal by reason of insanity.
Possession or transportation by persons so acquitted, §18.2-308.1:1.
Airports.
Carrying weapon into air carrier airport terminal, §18.2-287.01.
Carrying concealed weapons, §18.2-308.
Carrying into courthouses, §18.2-283.1.
Carrying loaded firearm in public area, §18.2-287.4.
Carrying to place of religious worship, §18.2-283.
Child access to loaded firearms, §18.2-56.2.
Children, possession or transportation, §18.2-308.7.
Criminal history background check, firearm transfers.
Requesting under false pretenses or disseminating, §18.2-308.2:2.
Discharging in public places, §18.2-280.
Hunting while under influence of intoxicant or narcotic drug, §18.2-285.
Machine gun manufacturer's and dealer's register violation, §18.2-294.
Machine gun registration violations, §18.2-295.
Persons adjudicated legally incompetent or mentally incapacitated.
Purchase, possession or transportation of firearm, §18.2-308.1:2.
Persons involuntarily admitted or ordered to mandatory outpatient treatment.
Purchase, possession or transportation of firearm, §18.2-308.1:3.
Persons subject to protective order.
Purchase or transportation of firearm, §18.2-308.1:4.
Pointing, holding or brandishing, §18.2-282.
Reckless handling, §18.2-56.1.
Sawed-off shotguns or sawed-off rifles.
Manufacturer's and dealer's register violations, §18.2-304.
Serial number or identification on firearm.
Removing, alteration, etc., §18.2-311.1.
Shooting in or along road or in street, §18.2-286.
Toy firearms.
Discharging blank or ball charges.
Selling or giving, §18.2-284.
Firearm shows.
Notice violations, §54.1-4201.1.
Fire chief's orders, disobeying, §§27-15.1, 27-19.
Firefighters.
Assault and battery against, §18.2-57.
Firefighting apparatus.
Calling or summoning without just cause, §18.2-212.
Fire hydrants.
Tampering with, §18.2-162.1.
Fire prevention code violation, §27-100.
Fire protection.
Failure to provide suitable and sufficient exits, §27-53.
Failure to remedy combustible, inflammable or unsafe conditions, §27-61.

MISDEMEANORS —Cont'd
Fire protection —Cont'd
Local officer's violation of law, §27-62.
Fishing, inland waters, §29.1-546.
Collecting specimens without permit, §29.1-412.
Failure to appear for trial, §29.1-210.
Impeding conservation police officer, §29.1-207.
Impeding lawful fishing, §29.1-554.1.
License.
Failure to carry, §29.1-336.
Failure to exhibit upon demand of conservation police officer, §29.1-337.
Failure to obtain, §29.1-335.
False statements, altering, borrowing or lending, §29.1-337.1.
National forests.
Failure to obtain permit, §29.1-408.
Net fishing without permit, §29.1-412.
Taking fish during closed season or exceeding limit, §29.1-550.
Trespass by fishers, §18.2-132.
Posted property, §18.2-134.
Destruction of posted signs or posting land of another, §18.2-135.
Refusal of person on land of another to identify himself, §18.2-133.
Unlawful methods, §29.1-531.
Unlawful sale or purchase of freshwater fish, §29.1-553.
Unlawful storage of fish, §29.1-541.
Use of substances injurious to fish, §29.1-533.
Use of unlawful devices, §29.1-556.
Violation of sanctuaries, refuges, preserves and water used for propagation, §29.1-554.
Fishing, tidal waters, §§28.2-903, 29.1-546.
Carrying patent tongs, etc., while fishing for menhaden, §28.2-405.
Closed season fishing for menhaden, §28.2-410.
Closure of Chesapeake Bay purse seine fishery for Atlantic menhaden.
Taking following closure, §28.2-1000.2.
Concealing name or number of vessel, §28.2-238.
Failure to appear for trial, §28.2-902.
Failure to apply for new license tag in case of loss, §28.2-235.
Failure to attach or display license tag or identification number, §28.2-234.
Failure to display or present fishing license, §28.2-231.
Failure to remove abandoned pole or stake, §28.2-237.
False statements on or altering fishing license, §28.2-230.
Fishing in restricted area.
Chickahominy river, §28.2-311.
Rappahannock river, §28.2-312.
Fishing without a license, §28.2-225.
Nonresident harvester's license, §28.2-227.
Food fish taken, bought or sold above allowable percentage, §28.2-408.
Illegal use of nets, §28.2-305.
Impeding lawful fishing, §28.2-903.1.
Importing fish, shellfish or crustacea for introduction into Virginia waters, §28.2-825.
Improper setting of gill nets in oceanfront, §28.2-308.
Improper use of fixed fishing devices, §28.2-307.
Killing fish by means of explosives, drugs or poisons, §28.2-313.
Net fishing within 300 yards of commercial fishing pier, §28.2-302.

MISDEMEANORS —Cont'd
Fishing, tidal waters —Cont'd
Nets extended improper distance across body of water or channel, §28.2-309.
Officer's failure to perform duty, §28.2-906.
Resistance to officer or authorized person, §28.2-905.
Sale of shellfish from condemned areas, §28.2-821.
Scientific collection without permit, §28.2-205.
Taking and sale of sturgeon, §28.2-303.
Taking, catching, possessing, selling or transporting channel bass (red drum), §28.2-304.
Taking fish during closed season or exceeding limit, §29.1-550.
Trawling boat licensed for other fishing devices, §28.2-316.
Trawling without a license, §28.2-314.
Trotline use on oceanside of Eastern Shore, §28.2-310.
Use of certain hooks, §28.2-306.
Use of forbidden purse net while fishing for menhaden, §28.2-410.
Use of purse nets for vessels less than 70 gross tons, §28.2-411.
Flags, uniform flag act.
Exhibition or display of flag with word, mark, figure, etc., on, §18.2-487.
Mutilating, defacing, etc., §18.2-488.
Punishment generally, §18.2-490.
Flood damage violations, §62.1-44.15:48.
Food and drink.
Adulteration, misbranding and false advertising.
Removal of date labels from meat packaging, §3.2-5127.
Violation of provisions, §3.2-5126.
Failure to comply with requirements of chapter, §3.2-5145.
Hindering commissioner, §3.2-5142.
Obstructing inspection, §3.2-5145.
Operation of facility without inspection by commissioner, §3.2-5130.
Sales at retail.
Acceptance of promissory notes, §18.2-241.
Sanitary requirements, §3.2-5117.
Failure to sterilize bottles and containers, §3.2-5118.
Notice and warning to place premises in sanitary condition.
Failure to obey, §3.2-5133.
Obstructing inspection, §3.2-5119.
Transporting or storage under unsanitary conditions, §3.2-5119.
Forest fire poster destruction, §10.1-1112.
Forest fires, §10.1-1159.
Throwing inflammatory objects from vehicles on highways, §10.1-1143.
Forgery.
Coin or bank notes.
Having in possession, §18.2-173.
Signature of another, maliciously affixing to writing, §18.2-172.2.
Transcripts or diplomas from post-secondary educational institutions.
Falsifying or altering and fraudulently using, §18.2-172.1.
Fornication, §18.2-344.
Persons forbidden to marry, §18.2-366.
Fowl.
Homing pigeons, hunting, pursuing, taking, etc., §18.2-145.

MISDEMEANORS —Cont'd
Fowl —Cont'd
Maiming, killing or poisoning, §18.2-144.
Franchise, privilege, lease or right to use city or town property.
Persons occupying property without consent, §15.2-2107.
Fraud.
Mine licensing, §45.1-161.66.
Fraudulent conveyance.
Watercraft, §29.1-731.
Fuel taxes, §58.1-2203.
Sales tax in certain transportation districts.
Absorption of tax, prohibited, §58.1-2299.4.
Failure of distributor to collect, §58.1-2299.3.
Prohibited acts, §58.1-2299.9.
Willful commission, §58.1-2299.10.
Funeral directors.
Licensing violations, §54.1-2809.
Fur dealers.
Failure to obtain permit, §29.1-406.
Furlough violations, §§53.1-37, 53.1-132.
Fusion intelligence center information.
Unauthorized release or dissemination, §52-48.
Gambling.
Accessories to gambling, §18.2-330.
Illegal possession of gambling device, §18.2-331.
Penalty for illegal gambling generally, §18.2-326.
Premises used as place of gambling.
Owners, lessees, tenants, etc., permitting continuance, §18.2-329.
Uniform fine schedule, illegal gambling, VA SCt Rules 3C:1, 3C:2.
Games, lotteries, etc., for promoting sale of products, §18.2-242.
Garnishment of exempt wages, §34-32.
Gasoline and lubricating oil.
Adulteration of product, §59.1-163.
Sales and inspections, §59.1-163.
Gates across private roads.
Unauthorized leaving open of gates, §§33.1-203, 33.1-204.
General assembly.
Unauthorized use of Senate armorial bearings, §30-15.1:1.
Geothermal energy, §45.1-179.10.
Giving false identity to law enforcement officer, §19.2-82.1.
Glue sniffing, §18.2-264.
Gold sales, §18.2-235.
Grain handlers, §3.2-4327.
Grand larceny, §18.2-95.
Ground water management, §62.1-270.
Gunshot wounds.
Failure to report by health care professionals, §54.1-2967.
Halal food.
Labeling, violation, penalty, §3.2-5124.
Harassment by computer, §18.2-152.7:1.
Hazardous materials.
HAZMAT hauling through tunnels, §46.2-815.
Hazing.
Youth gang members, §18.2-55.1.
Hazing of students, §18.2-56.
Health commissioner and department of health.
Violation of regulation or order, §32.1-27.
High-occupancy vehicle lanes.
Unauthorized use, §33.1-46.2.
Highways.
Closed highways.
Injury to barriers, signs, etc., §33.1-193.

MISDEMEANORS —Cont'd
Highways —Cont'd
Drag racing.
Aiders and abettors, §46.2-866.
Dumping trash, etc.
Highway, right-of-way or private property, §33.1-346.
Entrances to state highways from commercial establishments, §33.1-198.
Livestock and poultry on state highway, §33.1-210.
Reduction of limits, §46.2-1104.
Repair work, §46.2-1303.
Trees and timber.
Cutting or injuring near highways, §33.1-345.
Highway signs.
Displacement, removal or destruction, §33.1-345.
Historical markers.
Displacement, removal or destruction, §33.1-345.
Historic property.
Underwater historic property, §10.1-2214.
Home care organization and hospice employees.
False statements as to convictions, §32.1-162.9:1.
Home/electronic incarceration program, §53.1-131.2.
Homing pigeons.
Hunting, pursuing, taking, etc., §18.2-145.
Horizontal property regimes.
False advertising, §55-79.28.
Horse industry board.
Equine feed assessment.
Manufacturer.
Failure to report or false reporting, §3.2-1722.
Horse racing.
Pari-mutuel wagering.
Accepting wager from minor, §59.1-403.
Wagering by minor, §59.1-403.
Possession of unauthorized drugs within racing enclosure, §59.1-401.
Soring horses, §18.2-403.2.
Touting, §59.1-398.
Horses.
Soring horses, §§3.2-6570, 18.2-403.2.
Hotels, motels, campgrounds, boarding houses, etc.
Defrauding, §18.2-188.
Household electrical appliances.
Removal or alteration of identification numbers and possession of such appliances, §18.2-215.
Housing assistance programs.
False statements or failure to disclose material facts in order to obtain aid, §18.2-186.2.
Humane investigators.
Interference with, §§3.2-6566, 18.2-403.3.
Human immunodeficiency virus testing of convicted prostitutes, §18.2-346.1.
Hunting and fishing seasons in forest lands.
Fire hazards and closing of, §10.1-1158.
Hunting and trapping, §§10.1-1157, 29.1-546.
Bear.
Unlawful killing, §29.1-530.2.
Blaze orange clothing not worn, §29.1-530.1.
Capturing, holding, propagating and disposing of wildlife without permit, §29.1-412.
Carrying axe used for purposes of cutting, felling, etc., trees without permission of landowner, §18.2-141.
Collecting specimens without permit, §29.1-412.
Computer-assisted remote hunting, §29.1-530.3.

MISDEMEANORS —Cont'd
Hunting and trapping —Cont'd
Deer.
Enclosures intended to confine deer, §29.1-525.1.
Exceeding bag limit, §29.1-548.
Hunting from watercraft, §29.1-549.
Out-of-season killing, §29.1-548.
Sights, using after dark, §29.1-523.1.
Spotlighting, §§29.1-523, 29.1-525.
Drugs.
Use on vertebrate wildlife, §29.1-508.1.
Failure to appear for trial, §29.1-210.
Failure to obtain damage stamp, §29.1-354.
Hunting during probation period, §29.1-521.2.
Impeding conservation police officer, §29.1-207.
Impeding lawful hunting or trapping, §29.1-521.1.
License.
Failure to carry, §29.1-336.
Failure to exhibit upon demand of conservation police officer, §29.1-337.
Failure to obtain, §29.1-335.
False statements, alteration, borrowing or lending, §29.1-337.1.
Revoked, reckless handling of firearm.
Hunting while in possession of firearm after privilege revoked, §18.2-56.1.
Migratory game birds, §29.1-547.
National forests.
Failure to obtain permit, §29.1-408.
Shooting preserves.
Removal of shot game without attached seal, §29.1-606.
Taking of game before compliance with requirements, §29.1-603.
Violation of chapter, §29.1-611.
Taking game during closed season or exceeding limit, §29.1-550.
Trespass by hunters, §18.2-132.
Enforcement of provisions, §18.2-136.1.
Posted property, §18.2-134.
Destruction of posted signs or posting land of another, §18.2-135.
Method of posting, §18.2-134.1.
Refusal of person on land of another to identify himself, §18.2-133.
Right to go on land of another to retrieve dogs, §18.2-136.
Unauthorized weapons use, §29.1-519.
Under influence of intoxicant or narcotic drug, §18.2-285.
Unlawful hunting, trapping, possessing, selling or transporting wild birds and animals, §29.1-521.
Unlawful sale or purchase of wild bird or animal, §29.1-553.
Unlawful storage of wild birds and animals, §29.1-541.
Use of dogs without permit, §29.1-412.
Use of falcons, hawks or owls without permit, §29.1-412.
Use of unlawful devices, §29.1-556.
Violation of sanctuaries, refuges, preserves and water used for propagation, §29.1-554.
Waterfowl.
Hunting without license, §29.1-351.1.
Unlicensed blinds, §29.1-351.1.
Wild turkey.
Out-of-season killing, §29.1-552.
Hunting and trapping in state forests, §10.1-1157.

MISDEMEANORS —Cont'd
HVAC contractors.
Certification violations, §54.1-1135.
Hybrid canines.
Violation of ordinances, §3.2-6582.
Iceboxes, refrigerators or other airtight containers.
Discarding or abandoning, §18.2-319.
Identification cards.
DMV identification cards.
False information, §46.2-345.
Manufacture, sale, etc., of fictitious, facsimile or simulated cards, §18.2-204.2.
Identification marks.
Business machines, failure to report removal or alteration, §18.2-214.1.
Changing or removing with intent to defraud, §18.2-214.
Household electrical appliances, removal or alteration and possession of such appliance, §18.2-215.
Personalty permanently marked with social security number preceded by letters VA.
Possession of personalty with removed, altered, etc., mark, §18.2-96.1.
Removal, alteration, etc., §18.2-96.1.
Identifying information.
Use of person's identity with intent to coerce, intimidate or harass, §18.2-186.4.
Identity theft, §18.2-186.3.
Ignition interlock system violations, §18.2-270.1.
Driving or operating a motor vehicle without the required ignition interlock system, §18.2-272.
Illicit sexual intercourse.
Aiding, §18.2-350.
Imitation controlled substances.
Advertising, §18.2-248.4.
Manufacturing, selling, etc., with intent to manufacture, sell, etc., §18.2-248.
Immigrants.
Employment of illegal immigrants, §40.1-11.1.
Impeachment of appointed or elected officers.
High crimes or misdemeanors, VA Const Art IV §17.
Impeding lawful fishing in tidal waters, §28.2-903.1.
Impersonating peace officer, §18.2-174.
Impersonating public safety personnel, §18.2-174.1.
Income tax withholding or payment.
Evading.
False declaration or claim of employment status, §58.1-485.1.
Indecent exposure, §18.2-387.
Minors involved in act, §18.2-370.01.
Indictments, presentments and informations.
Name and address of complaining witness, §19.2-228.
Process on indictment or presentment, §19.2-237.
Security for costs, complaining witness, §19.2-229.
Indigent accused, appointment of counsel.
False swearing to statement of indigence, §19.2-161.
Indigent hospitalization program.
Fraudulently obtaining benefits, §32.1-350.
Industrialized building safety law, §36-83.
Industrial sick benefit company.
False statement for purposes of defrauding, §18.2-204.

MISDEMEANORS —Cont'd
Infected sexual battery.
Sex by person knowingly infected with another, §18.2-67.4:1.
Inquiry into official conduct of office or officer.
County executive form of government.
Witness failing or refusing to obey lawful order, §15.2-506.
County manager form of government.
Witness failing or refusing to obey lawful order, §15.2-606.
County manager plan of government.
Failure or refusal to obey lawful order, §15.2-709.
Urban county executive form of government.
Failure or refusal to obey lawful order, §15.2-814.
Insignia.
Illegal use of registered insignia of certain associations or societies, §18.2-177.
Unauthorized wearing or displaying on motor vehicles.
Insignia of certain associations or societies, §18.2-176.
Unlawful wearing of officer's insignia, §18.2-175.
Insurance.
Fraternal benefit societies.
Application for benefits or membership.
False or fraudulent statements, §38.2-4134.
Solicitation of membership for unlicensed society, §38.2-4134.
Group policies.
Failure to remit funds to insurer, §38.2-3542.
Investigative demand by attorney general.
Perjury, false swearing or contempt, §38.2-1916.1.
Loans to officers and directors, §38.2-213.
Mutual assessment property and casualty insurers.
Risks limitations.
Violations of provisions, §38.2-2505.
Surplus lines insurance.
License taxes, failure of licensee to pay, §38.2-4809.
Violations of provisions, §38.2-4814.
Title insurance.
Kickbacks or rebates.
Prohibition against payment or receipt, §38.2-4614.
Unauthorized reinsurance by domestic insurer, §38.2-216.
Unauthorized removal or transference of property by domestic insurer, §38.2-216.
Insurance agents.
Acting as agent for unlicensed insurer, §38.2-1802.
Interception or monitoring customer telephone calls, §18.2-167.1.
Interference with aircraft, §5.1-22.
Intimidation of voters, §24.2-1005.
Intoxication in public, §18.2-388.
Invasion of privacy.
Computers, §18.2-152.5.
Irish potatoes.
Reports and records.
Falsifying, failure to complete or failure to preserve, §3.2-1814.
Itinerant merchants.
Prohibited sales, §§54.1-4300, 54.1-4305, 54.1-4306.

MISDEMEANORS —Cont'd
Jackrocks.
Manufacturing, distributing or possessing, §18.2-147.2.
Jail prisoners.
Communications by persons outside of jail with, §18.2-473.1.
Work by on property of jailors, §53.1-130.
Work release program, §53.1-131.
Jail superintendent reports.
Falsification, §53.1-115.1.
Jet skis.
Owners of personal watercraft permitting violations, §29.1-749.
Permitting person under the age of 14 to operate, §29.1-749.
Unlawful operation, §29.1-748.
Joyriding, §18.2-102.
Judgment creditors.
Fraud and deceit.
Docketing of judgments and decrees, §8.01-446.1.
Judicial sales.
Special commissioners.
Bond.
Failure to give, §18.2-209.1.
False certificate of clerk, §18.2-209.1.
Failure of clerk to give notice of appointment, §18.2-209.2.
Junkyards, §33.1-348.
Jurisdiction of circuit courts, §16.1-126.
Jurisdiction of district courts, §16.1-123.1.
Jurors.
Corruptly procuring to be summoned, §18.2-466.
Fraudulently drawing jurors, §18.2-467.
Officer summoning to act impartially, §18.2-465.
Service by employees.
Penalizing for, §18.2-465.1.
Juvenile detention and other care facilities.
Communications by persons outside of jail with, §18.2-473.1.
Delivery of articles to without permission of authorities, §18.2-474.
Escape.
Officer allowing detainee charged with nonfelonious offense to escape, §18.2-476.
Monthly reports, falsifying information, §16.1-322.3.
Juvenile justice information system confidentiality violations, §16.1-225.
Juvenile proceedings.
Concealment or removal of child, §16.1-257.
Confidentiality exception.
Commission of delinquent act which would be misdemeanor if committed by adult, §16.1-309.1.
Disclosure violations, §16.1-309.
Interference with or obstruction of officer, §16.1-257.
Keeping a still without permit, §4.1-314.
Kennels.
Mistreatment of animals, §§3.2-6503, 18.2-403.3.
Keys to public buildings.
Possession or duplication, §18.2-503.
Kidnapping and related offenses.
Abduction by parent punishable as contempt in any pending proceeding, §18.2-47.
Disclosure of information and assistance to law enforcement officer violations, §18.2-50.
Kissing.
Penetration of mouth of child with lascivious intent, §18.2-370.6.

MISDEMEANORS —Cont'd
Kosher food.
Labeling, violation, penalty, §3.2-5124.
Labor and employment.
Child labor.
Solicitation, §40.1-112.
Employment of illegal immigrants, §40.1-11.1.
Examinations and inspections by commissioner.
Interference with, §40.1-10.
Labor unions.
Payment of charges by carriers or shippers to benefit labor organization, §40.1-54.
Picketing.
Illegal picketing, §40.1-53.
Minimum wages.
Violations of provisions, §40.1-28.11.
Pay.
Violation of section, §40.1-29.
Polygraph tests for employment.
Prohibited questions, §40.1-51.4:3.
Prevention of employment, §40.1-27.
Registration of certain nonresident employers.
Failure to register, §40.1-30.
Right to work.
Violations of provisions, §40.1-69.
Safety and health.
Inspections, advance notice, §40.1-51.3:1.
Making false statements, §40.1-51.4:2.
Violations of provisions, §40.1-49.4.
Strikes.
Interference by picketers, §40.1-53.
Labor and industry department, §§40.1-10, 40.1-11.1.
Larceny.
False statements to obtain property or credit, §18.2-186.
Grand larceny, §18.2-95.
Petit larceny, §18.2-96.
Shoplifting, §18.2-104.
Laser, laser gun sight or device simulating laser.
Pointing at aircraft, §5.1-22.
Pointing at law enforcement officer, probation or parole officer, etc., §18.2-57.01.
Law enforcement officers.
Assault and battery against, §18.2-57.
Learners' permits, §46.2-335.
Legal aid societies.
Governance violations, §54.1-3916.
Legal services plans.
Subscription contracts.
Violation of provisions, §59.1-441.6.
Lemon law.
Disclosure of returned vehicles, §59.1-207.16:1.
Libel, §18.2-417.
Libraries.
Concealment of book or other property while on premises, §42.1-73.
Failure to return library property, §42.1-74.
Injuring or destroying library property, §42.1-72.
Public records.
Failure of custodians to deliver records at expiration of term, §42.1-8.
Removal of book or other property from library, §42.1-73.
Limitation of prosecution, §19.2-8.
Limited liability companies.
Signing false documents, §13.1-1006.
Unlawful transaction of business, §13.1-1007.
Limited partnerships.
Signing document containing false information, §50-73.15.

MISDEMEANORS —Cont'd
Limited partnerships —Cont'd
Unauthorized partnership transacting business in Commonwealth, §50-73.10:1.
Liquefied petroleum gas containers.
Unlawful use of, filling or refilling or trafficking in, §§18.2-494, 18.2-496.
Liquid fuels, lubricating oils and similar products sales, §18.2-232.
Litter control and recycling, §§18.2-324, 33.1-386.
Motor vehicles.
Escape of load material, §10.1-1424.
Livery stable keeper's lien.
Defrauding person having, §18.2-188.1.
Livestock and poultry.
Beef industry council.
Violations of provisions, §3.2-1102.
Diseases and quarantines, §3.2-6018.
Altering or substituting brands, marks or tags, §3.2-6016.
Bringing into state infected animals or poultry, §3.2-6011.
Failure to comply with rules and regulations, §3.2-6012.
Failure to disinfect vehicles used to transport diseased animals, §3.2-6011.
Egg board.
Reports and records.
Falsifying, failure to complete or failure to preserve, §3.2-1610.
Eggs and hatchery products, §3.2-5312.
False pretense in obtaining registration or giving false pedigree, §18.2-205.
Feeding garbage to swine, §3.2-6034.
Injury or death of livestock.
Failure to notify owner, §56-439.1.
Inspections.
General criminal penalty, §3.2-5415.
Livestock purchase from unknown person, §59.1-195.
On right-of-way of state highways, §33.1-210.
Pork industry board.
Reports and records.
Falsifying or failing to keep, §3.2-2009.
Local officer bids on seized goods, §8.01-498.
Local taxes.
Withholding income.
False or fraudulent information on certificate of residency, §58.1-547.
Local tax officers.
Disclosure of secret information, §58.1-3.
Local wine and beer sales, §4.1-129.
Logging equipment violations, §10.1-1145.
Long distance telephone service.
Telephonic instruments used to obtain without payment.
Selling or transferring, §18.2-167.
Lottery, state.
Gift of ticket to minor, §58.1-4016.
Instant ticket licenses, §58.1-4019.1.
License applications.
False or fraudulent statements, §58.1-4009.
Sale of tickets.
To minors, §58.1-4015.
Unlawful price or location, §58.1-4014.
Unlicensed sellers, §58.1-4014.
Machetes or other bladed weapons.
Brandishing with intent to intimidate, §18.2-282.1.

MISDEMEANORS —Cont'd
Machine gun registration violations, §18.2-295.
Manufacturer's and dealers, §18.2-294.
Magistrate compensation violations, §19.2-47.
Manufactured homes.
Permits required before moving, §58.1-3520.
Manufactured housing construction and safety standards, §36-85.12.
Engaging in business without a license, §36-85.19.
Marijuana.
Distributing instruments for use in administering to minors, §18.2-255.1.
Fraud, deceit, embezzlement, forgery, etc.
Obtaining drugs or procuring administration by, §18.2-258.1.
Selling, giving, etc., with intent to sell, give, etc., §18.2-248.1.
Unlawful possession, §18.2-250.1.
Marriage record or registration.
False entry, §18.2-207.
False statement, §18.2-208.
Masturbation in public place.
Obscene sexual display, §18.2-387.1.
Meat and meat products.
Failure to comply with requirements of chapter, §3.2-5145.
General criminal penalty, §3.2-5415.
Inspections.
False reports or records, §3.2-5416.
Obstructing inspection, §3.2-5145.
Mechanics' and materialmen's liens.
Affidavit of payment required of owner prior to sale or refinance, §43-13.3.
Medical assistance.
Failure to deposit, transfer or maintain patient trust funds in separate account, §32.1-318.
False or misleading information on application, statement or form, §32.1-319.
Applications for eligibility or for use in determining rights to benefits, §32.1-321.4.
Applications for payment or for use in determining rights for payment, §32.1-314.
Medical assistance services department.
Failure to comply with regulation or order, §32.1-325.4.
Failure to comply with subpoena, §32.1-324.1.
Medical referral for profit, §18.2-502.
Medical testing kits designed for consumer home use.
Warning violations, §18.2-502.2.
Membership camping.
Violations of provisions, §59.1-335.
Menhaden.
Closure of Chesapeake Bay purse seine fishery for Atlantic menhaden.
Taking following closure, §28.2-1000.2.
Mental health facilities.
Group homes and residential facilities for children.
Suspension of licenses, failure to comply with, §37.2-418.
Microwave radio system lines or signals.
Unlawful use of or injury to, §18.2-165.
Military.
Air raid precautions.
Violations of provisions, §44-150.
Impersonating a member of the armed forces by wearing the duly prescribed uniform thereof, §44-120.
Military property.
Illegal sale of military property, §44-110.

MISDEMEANORS —Cont'd
Military property —Cont'd
Injuries to military property, §44-109.
Receipt of military property in violation of provisions, §44-109.
Military reserves.
Interference with employment of members, §44-98.
Militia.
Transportation of troops and military supplies.
Failure to furnish transportation when called upon, §44-82.
Milk, milk products and dairies, §3.2-5145.
Accounting system for distributors.
Failure to use or allow inspection, §3.2-3210.
Ice cream and similar products.
Violation of article, §3.2-5217.
License violation, §3.2-3222.
Machine tests.
False manipulation and reading of tests, §3.2-5229.
Hindering commissioner, §3.2-5232.
Milk commission.
Subpoenas.
Failure to comply with subpoenas of milk commission, §3.2-3218.
Violation of article, §3.2-3222.
Obstructing inspection, §3.2-5145.
Standards of quality, grading, sanitary standards, etc.
Violation of article, §3.2-5209.
Warning to persons using or furnishing impure milk.
Failure to obey, §3.2-5204.
Mine licensing, §§45.1-161.61, 45.1-161.66.
Mineral mine licenses.
Making false statements, §45.1-161.292:39.
Operating without a license, §45.1-161.292:34.
Mineral mine safety, §45.1-161.292:67.
Mine safety violations, §§45.1-161.94, 45.1-161.129.
Mines and mining.
Coal surface mining.
False statements generally, §45.1-246.
Permit violations, §45.1-246.
Gas and oil development, §45.1-361.8.
Permits, §45.1-191.
Misbranding drugs, devices and cosmetics, §54.1-3458.
Miscarriages, encouraging or promoting inducing, §18.2-76.1.
Mobile homes.
Permits required before moving, §58.1-3520.
Mobs, assault or battery by, §18.2-42.
Money changing machines, stealing from or tampering with, §18.2-152.
Money laundering, §18.2-246.3.
Money order sales without license, §6.2-1921.
Monopolies and corporate trust.
Civil investigative demand.
Perjury, false swearing or contempt, §59.1-9.10.
Mopeds.
Safety equipment, §46.2-915.2.
Stickers affixed by retail dealer, §46.2-915.
Motion picture equipment.
Display of obscene materials which can be seen from outside of the vehicle, §46.2-1077.01.
Motion picture previews, showing, §18.2-386.
Motor carriers, passengers.
Contract carriers.
Specific operating requirements, §46.2-2099.1.

MISDEMEANORS —Cont'd
Motor carriers, passengers —Cont'd
Disorderly passengers, §46.2-2011.18.
Identification markers.
Prohibited acts, §46.2-2011.21.
Registration.
Prohibited acts, §46.2-2011.21.
Taxicabs.
Violation of provisions, §46.2-2066.
Violations of chapter.
Enforcement of provisions, §46.2-2011.22.
Motor carriers, property.
Convictions of misdemeanors involving dishonesty, §46.2-2133.
Evasion of regulation, §46.2-2131.
Identification markers.
Criminal enforcement, §46.2-2130.
Records, §46.2-2131.
Registration.
Criminal enforcement, §46.2-2130.
Reports, §46.2-2131.
Motorcycle dealers.
Coercing purchaser to provide insurance, §46.2-1993.30.
Inspection of motorcycle prior to sale, §46.2-1993.33.
License plates, §46.2-1993.54.
Temporary license plates issued by dealer, §46.2-1993.63.
License requirement violations, §46.2-1993.6.
Odometer disclosure, §46.2-1993.25.
Motorcycle helmet law.
Prohibited sales, §46.2-910.
Motor vehicle dealers.
Certificate of title for dealers, §46.2-1544.
Coercing purchaser to provide insurance coverage, §46.2-1536.
Coercion of retail franchise dealer, §§46.2-1568, 46.2-1569.
Foreign dealer's license, §46.2-1565.1.
Inspection of vehicles, §46.2-1539.
Licenses, §46.2-1508.
Odometer disclosure, §46.2-1532.
Motor vehicle equipment.
Display of obscene materials which can be seen from outside of the vehicle, §46.2-1077.01.
Motor vehicle keepers.
Defrauding, §18.2-189.
Motor vehicles.
Abandoning motor vehicles, §46.2-1200.1.
Accidents.
Duty of driver to stop, §46.2-900.
Duty of passenger to report, §46.2-900.
Failure to give notice to law-enforcement officer, §46.2-371.
Failure to report.
Suspension of driver's license, §46.2-901.
Proof of insurance or payment of uninsured motor vehicle registration, §46.2-902.1.
Witnesses.
Failure to appear, §46.2-939.
Advertising new or used, §18.2-221.
Aggressive driving, §46.2-868.1.
Air bags.
Installation of noncompliant or previously used air bags or components, §46.2-1088.3.
Alternative fuel fleet standards.
Failure of vehicles to comply, §46.2-649.2.
Blind pedestrians crossing highway, §46.2-933.
Blocking access to premises, §46.2-818.
Breaking or preventing operation, §18.2-146.

MISDEMEANORS —Cont'd
Motor vehicles —Cont'd
Cargo.
Escape of contents, §10.1-1424.
Certificate of title.
Levy of execution.
Fraudulent assignment or transference of title, §46.2-644.
Obtaining when not entitled thereto, §46.2-105.2.
Odometers.
Reading to be reported, §46.2-629.
Possession of certificate issued to another, §46.2-618.
Sale of vehicle without certificate, §46.2-617.
Transfer of title.
Endorsements, §46.2-628.
Sale of vehicle without certificate of title, §46.2-617.
Security interest.
Failure to surrender certificate when security interest paid, §46.2-643.
Taxicabs.
Failure to provide information, §46.2-624.
City and county local license sticker.
Failure to display, §46.2-752.
Commercial drivers' licenses.
Driving commercial motor vehicle with any alcohol in blood, §46.2-341.31.
Driving while disqualified, §46.2-341.21.
Driving while intoxicated.
Blood alcohol content equal to or greater than 0.04, §46.2-341.29.
Blood samples.
Reuse of single-use-only needles, §46.2-341.26:5.
Penalty, §46.2-341.28.
Instruction permits, §46.2-341.10.
Serious traffic violations, §46.2-341.20.
Use of commercial vehicle in controlled substance felony, §46.2-341.19.
Violations, §§46.2-341.7, 46.2-341.17.
Commercial driver training schools.
Unlawful acts, §46.2-1707.
Commercial vehicles.
Damaging or threatening, §46.2-818.
Commuter buses.
Maintenance of records, §46.2-1175.
Cruising ordinances, §46.2-1219.1.
Damaging commercial vehicle, §46.2-818.
Dealer license plates.
Misuse, §46.2-1557.2.
Decals.
Revocation.
Failure to surrender, §46.2-612.
Devices used to supply nitrous oxide to engines, §46.2-1088.4.
Disregarding signal by law-enforcement officer to stop, §46.2-817.
Drinking while operating, §18.2-323.1.
Drivers' licenses, §46.2-350.
Applications.
False certification of Virginia residency, §§46.2-323, 46.2-323.1.
False statements, §§46.2-322, 46.2-348.
Driving while license suspended or revoked, §§46.2-301, 46.2-301.1.
Permitting to drive, §46.2-301.1.
Endorsements, classifications and restrictions authorizing operation of certain vehicles.
Operation without, §46.2-328.

MISDEMEANORS —Cont'd
Motor vehicles —Cont'd
Drivers' licenses —Cont'd
Examination.
Cheating, §46.2-105.1.
Failure to carry, §46.2-104.
Failure to surrender on demand, §46.2-346.
Fake licenses, §46.2-105.1.
Fictitious, canceled, revoked, suspended or altered license.
Displaying, §46.2-346.
Fictitious, facsimile or simulated license.
Fraudulent use to obtain alcoholic beverages, §46.2-347.
Financial responsibility.
Driving while license suspended or revoked, §46.2-302.
Forging evidence of financial responsibility, §46.2-463.
Habitual offenders, §46.2-357.
Learners' permits, §46.2-335.
Lending to another, §46.2-346.
Obtaining when not entitled thereto, §46.2-105.2.
Probation, §46.2-499.
Restrictions on particular licensees.
Violations, §46.2-329.
Special identification card.
Fraudulent use to obtain alcoholic beverages, §46.2-347.
Unlawful procurement of permit, §46.2-105.1.
Unlicensed driving.
Driving without having obtained a driver's license, §46.2-300.
Failure to provide proof of financial responsibility, §46.2-302.
License suspended or revoked, §46.2-301.
Permitting person to drive, §46.2-301.1.
Using the driver's license of another, §46.2-346.
Earphones.
Operation while using, §46.2-1078.
Eluding police, §46.2-817.
Emissions inspections, §46.2-1187.
Employment of lights or spotlights.
Under certain circumstances, §18.2-509.
Entering or setting in motion, §18.2-147.
Farm machinery and equipment.
Removing, defacing or obliterating serial number, §3.2-5000.
Fines collected for violations of traffic ordinances.
Disposition, §46.2-1308.
General penalty for violating title, §46.2-113.
Highways.
Signs.
Unofficial traffic control devices, §46.2-831.
Traffic control devices.
Damaging or removing, §46.2-832.
Highway work zone.
Decreased maximum speed limit, §46.2-878.1.
Hit and run, §46.2-894.
Improper driving, §46.2-869.
Inclement weather.
Operation of vehicles, §46.2-1302.
Law-enforcement officers.
Fees for arrest prohibited, §46.2-218.
License plates.
Alteration or forgery, §46.2-722.
Dealer plates.
Misuse, §46.2-1557.2.
Revocation.
Failure to surrender, §46.2-612.

MISDEMEANORS —Cont'd
Motor vehicles —Cont'd
Loads.
Escape of contents, §10.1-1424.
Mopeds.
Stickers affixed by retail dealer, §46.2-915.
Motor vehicles department, §46.2-113.
Administrative regulations, §46.2-203.
Nonrepairable vehicles, §46.2-1609.
Odometers.
Sale of resetting device, §46.2-112.
Tampering with, §46.2-112.
Overweight vehicles.
Operation in violation of provisions, §46.2-704.
Procuring with intent to defraud, §18.2-206.
Racing on highways, §46.2-865.
Aiders or abettors, §46.2-866.
Seizure of motor vehicle, §46.2 867.
Rebuilt vehicles, §46.2-1609.
Reciprocal agreements.
Operation without payment of reciprocity fees, §46.2-703.
Reckless driving, §46.2-868.
On parking lots, §46.2-864.
Records of convictions or of judgments for damages.
Failure to forward records, §46.2-387.
Registration.
Clean alternative fuel fleet standards.
Failure of certain vehicles to comply, §46.2-649.2.
Decals.
Alteration or forgery, §46.2-722.
Fees.
Farm vehicles.
Failure to pay fees, §46.2-698.
Passenger vehicles.
Failure to pay fees, §46.2-687.
Obtaining when not entitled thereto, §46.2-105.2.
Overweight vehicles.
Operation in violation of provisions, §46.2-704.
Reciprocity.
Operation without payment of reciprocity fees, §46.2-703.
Uninsured motor vehicles, §46.2-707.
Registration card.
Failure to carry, §46.2-104.
Renting vehicles.
Injury to, §18.2-149.
Insurance requirement, §46.2-108.
Reversal of conviction.
Effect, §46.2-413.
Revocation.
Failure to surrender registration card, license plates and decals, §46.2-612.
Safety belts.
Occupants of front seats, §46.2-1094.
School bus drivers.
Failure of drivers to wear, §46.2-1091.
Salvage vehicles, §46.2-1609.
School buses.
Warning devices, §46.2-1090.
Signs.
Damaging or removing, §46.2-832.
Erecting unofficial traffic control devices, §46.2-831.
Unofficial traffic control devices, §46.2-831.
Size.
Excessive size permits, §46.2-1139.

MISDEMEANORS —Cont'd
Motor vehicles —Cont'd
Size —Cont'd
Height.
Damage to overhead obstructions.
Failure to give notice, §46.2-1110.
Driving or attempting to drive oversized vehicle or load through tunnel, §46.2-1110.
Reduction of limits, §46.2-1104.
Snowmobiles, §46.2-1302.
Special identification card.
Obtaining when not entitled thereto, §46.2-105.2.
Stopping vehicle of another, §46.2-818.
Storage batteries, §59.1-191.
Summons.
Failure to appear, §46.2-938.
Taxation.
Local license sticker.
Arlington county ordinance, §46.2-754.
Failure to display, §46.2-752.
Threatening operator of commercial vehicle, §46.2-818.
Tires.
Cleats and other non-rubber protuberances.
Sale of tires having, §46.2-1045.
Puncturing devices, §18.2-147.2.
Regrooved or recut tires.
Prohibited acts, §46.2-1042.
Traffic control devices.
Damaging or removing, §46.2-832.
Traffic infractions.
Misdemeanors for arrest purposes, §46.2-937.
Traffic schools.
Failure to attend, §46.2-1314.
Trespassing vehicles, §46.2-1231.
Consumer protection, prohibited practices, §59.1-200.
Trucks and tractor trucks, civil penalty cases for certain violations.
Failure to comply with instruction to move vehicle and not operate it until judgment satisfied, §46.2-613.4.
Tunnels.
Hauling certain cargoes through tunnels in violation of posted signs, §46.2-815.
Unattended or immobile vehicles, §46.2-1209.
Unauthorized use, §18.2-102.
Uniform demerit point system, §46.2-492.
Uninsured motor vehicle.
Operation without payment of fee, §46.2-707.
Unlawful sublease, §18.2-115.1.
Vehicle registration. See within this subheading, "Registration."
Weight.
Excessive weight permits, §46.2-1139.
Gross vehicle weight ratings.
Tampering with, §46.2-1075.1.
Overweight vehicles.
Seizures.
Violation of special overweight seizure provisions, §46.2-1134.
Weighing vehicles.
Refusal of driver, §46.2-1137.
Uniform fine schedule, VA SCt Rule 3C:2.
Windshields and windows.
Signs, decals and stickers, §46.2-1052.
Sunshading material, §46.2-1052.
Yellow motor vehicles of certain seating capacity.
Operation on state highways, §46.2-917.

MISDEMEANORS —Cont'd
Motor vehicles —Cont'd
Yielding right of way to stationary emergency vehicles, §46.2-921.1.
Motor vehicle sales and use tax.
Evading tax, §58.1-2402.
Motor vehicle title loans.
Violations, §6.2-2223.
Motor vehicle warranties.
Disclosure of returned vehicles, §59.1-207.16:1.
Navigable waters.
Buoys, beacons and daymarks, §62.1-187.
Anchoring on range of range lights, §62.1-189.
Garbage.
Casting garbage, refuse, trash, etc., into waters of the state, §§62.1-194, 62.1-194.2, 62.1-194.3.
Neglect of duty.
Election officers, electoral board members, etc., §24.2-1001.
Newspapers.
Stamping on newspapers word to cause belief done by publisher and circulating newspaper, §18.2-210.
Nonprofit corporations.
Signing of false documents, §13.1-811.
Unauthorized transaction of business as corporation, §13.1-812.
Nonsupport of wife or children, §§20-61, 20-88.
Notaries.
Failure to surrender commission, §47.1-24.
Software or hardware of electronic notary.
Possessing, concealing, damaging or destroying, §47.1-29.1.
Willful misconduct, §47.1-28.
Noxious weeds, §3.2-809.
Nursing.
Licensing violations, §54.1-3008.
Nursing home employees.
False statements as to criminal convictions, §32.1-126.01.
Nutritionists and dietitians, §54.1-2731.
Obscenity and related offenses.
Advertising obscene exhibitions or performances, §§18.2-376, 18.2-380.
Coercing acceptance of obscene articles or publications, §§18.2-378, 18.2-380.
Employing or permitting minor to assist in offense, §§18.2-379, 18.2-380.
Photographs, slides and motion pictures, §18.2-382.
Placards, posters, bills, etc., §§18.2-377, 18.2-380.
Production, publication, sale, etc., of obscene items, §§18.2-374, 18.2-380.
Advertising, §§18.2-376, 18.2-380.
Sales and loans to juveniles, §18.2-391.
Use of computer, enhanced penalties, §18.2-376.1.
Obstructing execution of legal process, §18.2-409.
Obstructing free passage of others, §18.2-404.
Obstructing justice by threats, force or false statements, §18.2-460.
Officers of election.
Employer discriminating against person serving as officer, §24.2-118.1.
Oil discharges into waters of state, §62.1-44.34:20.
Oil, electric, gas, water, service.
Obtaining or attempting to obtain without payment, §18.2-187.1.
Open burning violations, §10.1-1158.

MISDEMEANORS —Cont'd
Operation of aircraft by unlicensed persons, §5.1-15.
Ordinance violations enforced by proceedings as in misdemeanors, §15.2-1429.
Appeals, §15.2-1431.
Oysters.
Buying and selling in unapproved quantities, §28.2-526.
Buying or carrying seed oysters from certain grounds without permit, §28.2-535.
Buying, selling or possessing unculled oysters, §28.2-510.
Carrying oysters out of state without permit, §28.2-549.
Converting shells into lime, §28.2-529.
Failure to keep record of oysters handled, §28.2-538.
Failure to pay oyster resource user fees, §28.2-549.
Failure to scatter or post bond for unculled oysters, §28.2-511.
Interference with surveyor of oyster grounds, §28.2-557.
Interfering with oyster inspections, §28.2-512.
Labeling out-of-state oysters as Virginia oysters, §28.2-532.
Nonresidents taking or planting oysters, §28.2-634.
Residents associated, §28.2-635.
Off season taking from public rocks, §28.2-506.
Possession of oysters on crab dredging boat, §28.2-533.
Possession of oysters while taking clams, §28.2-534.
Possession of patent tongs exceeding approved weight or teeth length, §28.2-509.
Possession of shucked oysters, §28.2-514.
Removal of oyster ground survey markers, §28.2-561.
Shucking or packing without license, §28.2-504.
Staking off public oyster beds, §28.2-624.
Taking or loading on vessel on Sunday or at night, §28.2-530.
Use of patent tongs in prohibited areas, §28.2-508.
Use of rakes or scrapes on ocean side of Eastern Shore, §28.2-519.
Parachute jump training school violations, §5.1-88.6.
Park authority rule or regulation violation, §15.2-5705.
Parking for disabled or handicapped.
License plates or placards.
Alteration, §46.2-1249.
Counterfeiting, §46.2-1247.
Use of counterfeit item, §46.2-1248.
Fraudulently obtaining, §46.2-1251.
Providing, §46.2-1253.
Selling or exchanging, §46.2-1252.
Unauthorized use, §46.2-1250.
Use of counterfeit item, §46.2-1248.
Parking meters.
Slugs manufactured, sold, etc., for unlawful uses, §18.2-180.
Stealing from or tampering with, §18.2-152.
Unlawful operation, §18.2-179.
Parks, refuges or sanctuaries.
Destruction of trees, shrubs, etc., §18.2-140.
Partnership officer willful failure to collect and account for local taxes, §58.1-3907.

MISDEMEANORS —Cont'd
Partnerships.
Signing document containing false information, §50-73.83.
Passports.
Fictitious, facsimile or simulated official identification.
Fraudulent use to obtain alcoholic beverages, §46.2-347.
Manufacture, sale, etc., of fictitious, facsimile or simulated passports, §18.2-204.2.
Pawnbrokers.
Licensing violations, §§54.1-4001, 54.1-4014.
Reporting failures, §54.1-4010.
Payment card scanning devices and re-encoders.
Unlawful use, §18.2-196.1.
Pay telephones.
Slugs manufactured, sold, etc., for unlawful uses, §18.2-180.
Stealing from or tampering with, §18.2-152.
Unlawful operation, §18.2-179.
Peaches.
Controlled atmosphere storage of apples and peaches, §3.2-4613.
Peanuts.
Taxation.
Failure to make returns or keep records, §3.2-1910.
Making false reports or falsifying records, §3.2-1909.
Pedestrian bridges.
Destruction, §33.1-345.
Peeping or spying into restroom, hotel or dressing room, §18.2-130.
Peeping or spying into structure occupied as dwelling, §18.2-130.
Penetration of mouth of child with lascivious intent, §18.2-370.6.
Pen register and trap device violation, §19.2-70.1.
Personal property, standing grain or other crops.
Burning or destroying, §18.2-81.
Personalty permanently marked.
Possession of property with removed, altered, etc., mark, §18.2-96.1.
Removal, alteration, etc., of mark, §18.2-96.1.
Personal watercraft.
Minimum distance from shoreline.
City ordinance regulating, penalty for violation, §29.1-748.1.
Owners of personal watercraft permitting violations, §29.1-749.
Reckless operation, §29.1-738.03.
Pesticide control, §3.2-3947.
Pet cemeteries, §§57-39.22, 57-39.25.
Petit larceny, §18.2-96.
Pet shops.
Dogs, procurement from unlicensed commercial dog breeders, §3.2-6511.1.
Failure to provide adequate care, §§3.2-6511, 18.2-403.2.
Local ordinances governing, §3.2-6537.
Mistreatment of animals, §§3.2-6503, 18.2-403.3.
Pharmacists.
Prescriptions filled before receipt in writing, §18.2-248.
Photographing another unlawfully, §18.2-386.1.
Picketing.
Dwelling place, §18.2-419.

MISDEMEANORS —Cont'd
Picketing —Cont'd
Illegal picketing, §40.1-53.
Piercing.
Body piercing of minors, §18.2-371.3.
Place of punishment, §18.2-15.
Plants.
Inspection.
Obstructing right of entry on premises, §3.2-3810.
Refusal to allow inspection or provide information, §3.2-3810.
Violation of article, §3.2-3810.
Pest control, §3.2-710.
Plastic bag warning violations, §18.2-320.
Plumbers.
Certification violations, §54.1-1135.
Police lines, perimeters or barricades.
Crossing, §18.2-414.2.
Police radio.
Use during commission of crime, §18.2-462.1.
Police vehicles.
Unlawful use of vehicle with word police shown, §18.2-175.
Potatoes, violation of provisions, §3.2-1822.
Precious metals dealers.
Licensing violations, §54.1-4110.
Prescriptions.
Forgery, §18.2-258.1.
Pharmacists filling before receipt in writing, §18.2-248.
Previews of certain motion pictures, showing, §18.2-386.
Prisoners.
Communications by persons outside of jail with prisoners, §18.2-473.1.
Delivery of articles to without permission of authorities, §18.2-474.
Furlough violations, §53.1-37.
Refusing to receive prisoners, §18.2-476.
Work by jail prisoners on property of jailors, §53.1-130.
Work release programs.
Movements outside the program's scope, §53.1-60.
Prison made goods, non-Virginia.
Sale or exchange, §53.1-55.
Privacy invasion.
Computers, §18.2-152.5.
Private property, destruction of, §18.2-137.
Destruction of trees, shrubs, etc., §18.2-140.
Private security services businesses.
Unlawful conduct, §9.1-147.
Unlawful procurement of license, §9.1-148.
Unlicensed activity, §9.1-149.
Probation officers.
Juvenile and domestic relations district courts.
Interference with or obstruction of officer, §16.1-257.
Professions and occupations licensure, §54.1-111.
Unlawful procurement, §54.1-102.
Prohibited acts by mixed beverage licensees, §4.1-325.
Promissory notes.
Acceptance in payment for food sold at retail, §18.2-241.
Prostitution, §18.2-346.
Aiding, §18.2-350.
Injunctions.
Contempt, §48-11.

MISDEMEANORS —Cont'd
Prostitution —Cont'd
Solicitation of prostitution, §18.2-346.
Venereal disease testing, §32.1-58.
Vehicles to promote, §18.2-350.
Venereal disease testing, §32.1-58.
Protective order violations, §16.1-253.2.
Stalking, §18.2-60.4.
Public accommodations.
Health and safety violations, §35.1-7.
Public account inspection violations, §30-135.
Public buildings.
Damaging, §18.2-138.
Public officers and employees.
Conflicts of interest.
Knowing violations, §2.2-3120.
Public property used without consent or franchise, §15.2-2018.
Public records.
False entries or destruction by officers, §18.2-472.
Public school funds.
Ordering the issuance of warrants, §22.1-122.
Purchase of warrants for less than face value, §22.1-124.
Public school transportation.
Misuse of toll exemption cards, §22.1-187.
Public service companies.
Damage or trespass to, §18.2-162.
Free services to members of general assembly and others, §56-8.1.
Relations with affiliated interests.
Unlawful contract or arrangement, loan or assumption, declaration or payment of dividends, §56-85.
Stocks and bonds.
False statements to state corporation commission, §56-73.
State approval represented as opinion of value, §56-74.
Unlawful issuance, execution or negotiation, §56-73.
Tampering with metering devices or diverting service, §18.2-163.
Public squares.
Injuries to trees, fences or herbage on, §18.2-139.
Public utilities.
Acquisition or disposition of utility assets or securities, §56-91.
Damage or trespass to, §18.2-162.
State operation.
Employment of utility employees by state.
Violation of provisions, §56-524.
Tampering with metering devices or diverting service, §18.2-163.
Punishment for, §18.2-11.
No punishment or maximum punishment prescribed, §18.2-12.
Punishment by reference, §18.2-13.
Purchasing alcohol for minors, §4.1-306.
Putative father registry.
Unauthorized release of information, §63.2-1251.
Pyramid promotional schemes, §18.2-239.
Rabid animals.
Withholding information about, §18.2-313.1.
Racing on highways.
Aiders or abettors, §46.2-866.
Railroad crossings.
Erecting signs similar to crossing signs, §56-408.
Failure to maintain crossings of public roads and approaches, §56-405.

MISDEMEANORS —Cont'd
Railroad fences or cattle stops.
Injury to, §18.2-157.
Railroads.
Bells, whistles or horns.
Failure to provide, §56-415.
Failure to sound, §56-415.
Driving animal on track to recover damages, §18.2-158.
Duplicating switch keys, §56-419.
Entering or setting locomotive in motion, §18.2-147.
Trespassing on tracks, §18.2-159.
Trespassing on train, §18.2-160.
Uniform fine schedule, VA SCt Rules 3C:1, 3C:2.
Real estate cooperatives.
Unlawful sale, administration or registration, §55-506.
Real estate settlement services.
Prohibited payments, §55-525.12.
Reckless handling of firearms, §18.2-56.1.
Records, tapes and recorded devices, §59.1-41.6.
Recreational facilities violations, §10.1-1619.
Recreational waysides.
Rules and regulations for use, §33.1-218.
Refusal to aid police officers, §18.2-463.
Renewable energy.
Small renewable energy projects, §10.1-1197.9.
Reptiles.
Keeping in manner that will permit escape, §29.1-569.
Rescue squads, obstructing in performance of mission, §18.2-414.1.
Research farm product.
Damaging or destroying, §18.2-145.1.
Resisting lawful arrest, §18.2-479.1.
Retention of ended case files by circuit court clerk, time, destruction, §17.1-213.
Right to work, §40.1-69.
Riot or unlawful assembly.
Law enforcement agencies, national guard, etc., summoned by governor to preserve peace.
Refusal or neglect to obey command, §18.2-410.
Obstructing free passage of others, §18.2-404.
Riot, §18.2-405.
Unlawful assembly, §18.2-406.
Warning to disperse.
Remaining at place of riot or unlawful assembly after, §18.2-407.
Running at large.
Permitting animals to run at large in county under quarantine, §18.2-121.1.
Safety belts.
School bus drivers.
Failure of drivers to wear, §46.2-1091.
Safety inspection violations, §46.2-1171.
Sales.
Misrepresentations and other offenses connected with generally, §18.2-246.
Unweaned or immature animals, §§3.2-6510, 18.2-403.2.
Salvage vehicles.
General penalty provision, §46.2-1609.
Sand and gravel.
Removal and carrying away prohibited, §62.1-191.
Satisfaction and discharge of assault or other misdemeanors, §19.2-151.
Sawed-off shotguns and sawed-off rifles manufacturers and dealers.
Register violations, §18.2-304.

MISDEMEANORS —Cont'd
School buses.
Pupils crossing divided highways, §46.2-918.
Warning devices, §46.2-1090.
Yellow motor vehicles of certain seating capacity, §46.2-917.
School property.
Refusal to leave after direction to vacate, §18.2-128.
Trespass upon, §18.2-128.
Schools and education, §22.1-292.
Contractors, criminal background checks.
False statements, §22.1-296.1.
Employees failure to disclose conviction for certain crimes, §22.1-296.1.
Failure to attend school, §22.1-263.
False statements as to student's school status, §22.1-3.2.
Inducing children to absent themselves, §22.1-265.
Making false statements as to age of child, §22.1-264.
Residence of child.
False statements, §22.1-264.1.
Unlawful disclosure of scholastic records, §22.1-289.
Scrap metal purchasers, §59.1-136.6.
Seafood landing license, §28.2-228.1.
Secondhand dealers and secondhand goods.
Building fixtures, §59.1-124.
Failure to indicate goods seconds, irregulars, secondhand, etc., §18.2-218.
Railroads and other companies.
Equipment, §59.1-127.
Secondhand grate baskets, keys, bells and bell fixtures, etc.
Buying or receiving with intent to defraud, §18.2-237.
Watches, §59.1-135.
Securities violations, §13.1-520.
Seeds.
Illegal use of word certified, §3.2-4026.
Violation of article, §3.2-4020.
Seed tree violations, §10.1-1167.
Self-propelled machinery.
Operation by habitual offender, §46.2-357.
Septic system inspectors.
Use of title accredited septic system inspector without meeting requirements, §59.1-310.10.
Serial numbers.
Business machines, failure to report removal or alteration, §18.2-214.1.
Changing or removing with intent to defraud, §18.2-214.
Household electrical appliances, removal or alteration and possession of such appliance, §18.2-215.
Sewage disposal, §§21-223, 21-290.
Approval of sewage system by counties.
Noncompliance with provisions, §15.2-2133.
Sex offender and crimes against minors registry.
Failure to register or provision of false information, §18.2-472.1.
Misuse of registry information, §9.1-918.
Notice of penalty on forms and documents, §9.1-919.
Sex offenses prohibiting proximity to children, §18.2-370.2.
Punishment authorized for misdemeanor offense, §18.2-11.

MISDEMEANORS —Cont'd
Sexual abuse of a child 13 to 15 years of age, §18.2-67.4:2.
Sexual battery, §18.2-67.4.
Attempts, §18.2-67.5.
Sharp objects placed in public road, §33.1-345.
Sheep industry board.
Failure to pay assessments, §3.2-2114.
Sheriffs uniforms worn by unauthorized persons, §15.2-1612.
Shipping solid waste or medical waste upon navigable waters of Commonwealth.
Allowing liquids, waste and odors to escape, §10.1-1454.1.
SHOCAP committee.
Records or reports disclosures, §16.1-330.1.
Shooting enclosures, §3.2-6042.
Shooting preserves.
Removal of shot game without attached seal, §29.1-606.
Taking of game before compliance with requirements, §29.1-603.
Trespass upon licensed preserve, §18.2-131.
Violation of chapter, §29.1-611.
Shoplifting, §18.2-104.
Electronic detection devices to shield against.
Manufacture, sale, etc., §§8.01-226.9, 18.2-105.2.
Shopping carts.
Removal from store premises, §18.2-102.1.
Signature of another, maliciously affixing to writing, §18.2-172.2.
Signs.
False and misleading, §33.1-380.
Posting no trespassing signs on property of another, §18.2-119.1.
Simulation of warrants, processes, writs and notices, §18.2-213.
Slander, §18.2-417.
Slugs.
Manufacturing, selling, etc., for unlawful uses, §18.2-180.
Unlawful operation of pay telephones, parking meters, vending machines, etc., §18.2-179.
Small grains.
Reports and records.
Falsifying or failing to preserve, §3.2-2214.
Small renewable energy projects, §10.1-1197.9.
Small, women or minority owned business or disadvantaged business enterprise.
Obtaining certification by deception, §18.2-213.1.
Smithfield hams.
Mislabeling or advertising, §3.2-5421.
Smoke bombs, setting off in certain public buildings, §18.2-87.1.
Smoking in proximity to gas pumps, §46.2-819.4.
Smoking near medical oxygen sources in health care facilities, §18.2-511.1.
Snakehead fish.
Introducing into waters of Commonwealth, §18.2-313.2.
Snakes, handling or using so as to endanger human life or health, §18.2-313.
Snowmobiles.
Violations of local ordinances, §46.2-1302.
Soil scientists and wetland professionals.
Misrepresentation, §54.1-2208.
Solicitation of charitable or civic contributions, §57-59.
Solicitation of prostitution, §18.2-346.
Venereal disease testing, §32.1-58.

MISDEMEANORS —Cont'd
Source of merchandise.
Misrepresentation that article acquired from United States government, military force or agency, §18.2-222.
Southern Cross of Honor.
Wearing when not entitled, §18.2-176.
Soybeans.
Reports and records.
Falsifying or failing to preserve, §3.2-2314.
Special conservators of the peace.
Unlawful conduct, §9.1-150.4.
Speedy trial, §19.2-243.
Speleothems sales, §10.1-1007.
Spitting in public places, §18.2-322.
Spotlight on agricultural land.
Trespass by, §18.2-121.2.
Stalking, §18.2-60.3.
Violation of protective orders, §18.2-60.4.
State agency fraud reporting, §30-138.
State forest damage, §10.1-1111.
State forest violations, §10.1-1110.
State police criminal investigation records and reports.
Disclosure, §52-8.3.
State police officers.
Acceptance of fees and rewards, §52-10.
State police uniforms.
Wearing of same or similar uniforms by non-officers, §52-9.2.
Statute of limitations, §19.2-8.
Sterling and sterling silver sales, §18.2-233.
Steroids.
Manufacturing, selling, etc., anabolic steroids with intent to manufacture, sell, etc., §18.2-248.5.
Storage batteries.
Violations of sales provisions, §59.1-191.
Subdivided land.
Unlawful sale, §55-347.
Submerged lands.
Unlawful use of subaqueous beds, §28.2-1203.
Substance abuse screening and assessment for designated Class 1 misdemeanor convictions, §19.2-299.2.
Summons issued in lieu of warrant, §19.2-74.
Sunshading material.
Motor vehicle windshields and windows, §46.2-1052.
Surrogate brokers prohibited, §20-165.
Swearing in public, §18.2-388.
Synthetic cannabinoids.
Distributing instruments for use in administering to minors, §18.2-255.1.
T&M vehicle dealers.
Licenses required, §46.2-1908.
Tanning facilities.
Operation in violation of provisions, §59.1-310.6.
Tattooing or body piercing of minors, §18.2-371.3.
Tax collection, local.
Corporate or partnership officer willful failure to collect and account for local taxes, §58.1-3907.
Marinas.
Failure to file list of boat owners, §58.1-3902.
Tenants.
Failure to file list of tenants, §58.1-3901.
Treasurers.
Failure to deliver receipts upon collection of taxes, §58.1-3914.
Failure to mail bills to taxpayers, §58.1-3912.

MISDEMEANORS —Cont'd
Tax collection, local —Cont'd
Treasurers —Cont'd
Omission of taxes from delinquent list, §58.1-3936.
Tax collection, state.
Failure to collect and account for tax, §58.1-1815.
Failure to file return, §58.1-1814.
Failure to keep records, §58.1-1814.
Padlocked businesses.
Entering premises without prior approval, §58.1-1805.
Tax documents.
Disseminating or publishing confidential documents, §58.1-3.
Taxes.
Aircraft sales and use tax.
Misrepresenting value of aircraft or amount of tax due, §58.1-1503.
Carnivals, circuses or speedways.
License tax.
Failure to obtain, §58.1-3728.
Cigarettes.
Corporate or partnership officer willful failure to collect and account for, §58.1-3907.
Evading tax, §58.1-1017.
Failure to file monthly report, §58.1-1008.
Failure to preserve records for three years, §58.1-1007.
Interference with enforcement of chapter, §58.1-1006.
Possession with intent to distribute tax-paid cigarettes, §58.1-1017.1.
Refusal to allow audit or inspection of records, §58.1-1007.
Sale of unstamped cigarettes by wholesale dealers.
Violation of provisions, §58.1-1010.
Stamping agents' application for licensure, §58.1-1011.
Use tax.
Failure to preserve records for three years, §58.1-1021.
Refusal to allow audit or inspection of records, §58.1-1021.
Estimated tax.
Failure or refusal to file declaration, §58.1-496.
False or fraudulent statements in declaration, §58.1-496.
False returns, §§58.1-11, 58.1-498.
Forest products.
Failure to make return, keep records or permit examination of records, §58.1-1618.
Failure to make transporter's report, §58.1-1614.
Income.
Failure or refusal to file return, §58.1-348.
Local taxes.
False or fraudulent information on certificate of residency, §58.1-547.
Rental payments to nonresidents.
Supplying false or fraudulent information, §58.1-316.
Sale of real property by nonresident.
Supplying false or fraudulent information, §58.1-317.
Livestock and poultry.
Violations of provisions, §3.2-1102.
Mobile homes.
Permits required before moving.
Violation of provisions, §58.1-3520.

MISDEMEANORS —Cont'd
Taxes —Cont'd
Motor carriers.
Road tax.
False statements, §58.1-2710.
Motor vehicle sales and use tax.
Evading tax, §58.1-2402.
Peanuts.
Failure to make returns or keep records, §3.2-1910.
Making false reports or falsifying records, §3.2-1909.
Public service corporations.
Boundaries of political units.
Failure by commissioner of revenue to furnish, §58.1-2601.
Real estate.
Boards of equalization.
Failure to obey summons, §58.1-3387.
Recordation tax, state.
Misrepresentations to clerk, §58.1-812.
Records and documents.
Failure to make available for inspection, §58.1-103.
Retail sales and use tax.
Absorption of tax, §58.1-626.
Dealers' certificate of registration.
Engaging in business without certificate, §58.1-613.
Failure to pay or collect, §58.1-625.
Misuse of exemption certificate, §58.1-623.1.
Records.
Failure to keep, §58.1-633.
Refusal to permit examination, §58.1-633.
Returns.
Failure to file, §58.1-636.
False or fraudulent, §58.1-636.
Road tax on motor carriers.
False statements, §58.1-2710.
Tobacco.
Bright flue-cured.
Violation of article, §3.2-2411.
Watercraft sales and use tax.
Misrepresenting value of watercraft or amount of tax due, §58.1-1403.
Withholding income.
Employer's failure to make return, withhold tax, pay tax or furnish employee with withholding statement, §58.1-485.
Fraudulent withholding exemption certificate or failure to supply information, §58.1-471.
Taxicabs.
Transfer of title.
Failure to provide required information, §46.2-624.
Taxidermy.
Failure to obtain permit, §29.1-412.
Tax officers.
Commissioners of revenue.
Failure to deliver personal property books, §58.1-3118.
Improper destruction of returns, §58.1-3112.
Refusal to permit access to records or information to commissioner, §58.1-3111.
Disclosure of secret information, §58.1-3.
Treasurers, §58.1-3144.
Failure to account for interest, §58.1-3142.
Refusal to answer treasurer's questions concerning tax liability, §58.1-3128.
Tax preparers.
Disclosure of information, §58.1-4.

MISDEMEANORS —Cont'd
Telegraph and telephone companies.
Endangering life or limb by stringing wires across other works, §56-468.
Obstructing commission in discharge of duties, §56-483.
Obtaining or attempting to obtain service without payment, §18.2-187.1.
Refusal or neglect to make reports, §56-483.
Telephone company customers.
Disclosing or inducing disclosure of certain information concerning, §18.2-166.
Telephone long distance service.
Instruments, obtaining long distance service without payment.
Selling or transferring, §18.2-167.
Telephone or telegraph lines.
Unlawful use of or injury to, §18.2-164.
Telephone or telegraph messages.
Copying or obstructing, §18.2-164.
False information to another, §18.2-428.
Interception or monitoring customer telephone calls, §18.2-167.1.
Telephone records.
Fraudulent sale or receipt, §18.2-152.17.
Television equipment.
Display of obscene materials which can be seen from outside of the vehicle, §46.2-1077.01.
Term papers, thesis, dissertation, etc.
Preparation for profit, §§18.2-505, 18.2-508.
Threats.
Voters, §24.2-1005.
Throwing inflammatory objects near forests, §10.1-1143.
Tires.
Cleats and other non-rubber protuberances.
Sale of tires having, §46.2-1045.
Regrooved or recut tires.
Prohibited acts, §46.2-1042.
Tobacco.
Bright flue-cured, §3.2-2411.
Burley tobacco.
Fees for sale, §61.1-56.
Handling and sale, §61.1-61.
Distributors of tobacco products.
Fraud or misrepresentation in application, §58.1-1021.04:1.
False branding, §61.1-44.
Fraud and deceit, §§61.1-51, 61.1-52.
Manufactured tobacco.
False branding, §61.1-44.
Nesting prohibited, §61.1-45.
Tobacco product manufacturers' responsibilities.
Enforcement of requirements, §3.2-4212.
Tobacco products distributors.
Fraud or misrepresentation in application, §58.1-1021.04:1.
Tobacco sales records.
Inspection by ABC board.
Misuse of information obtained, §4.1-103.01.
Refusal to allow, §4.1-103.01.
Tobacco warehouses.
Itemized statements furnished seller, §61.1-39.
Toll bridges.
Misuse of toll pass, §33.1-252.
Toll facility operators.
Dulles access highway.
Photo-monitoring or automatic vehicle identification systems, misuse of information, §46.2-819.5.

MISDEMEANORS —Cont'd
Toll facility operators —Cont'd
Video-monitoring systems, misuse of information collected, §46.2-819.3:1.
Tollgate keeper.
Refusal to permit toll pass holder to cross bridge, §33.1-252.
Toxic substance inspection refusals, §19.2-397.
Toy firearms.
Discharging blank or ball charges.
Selling or giving, §18.2-284.
Trade and commerce.
Assumed name.
Transacting business, §59.1-75.
Containers.
Names, marks and devices, §59.1-96.
Explosives.
Failure to comply with provisions, §59.1-141.
Extended service contracts.
Violations of provisions, §59.1-441.
Gasoline and lubricating oil.
Sales and inspections violations, §59.1-163.
Livestock purchase from unknown person, §59.1-195.
Secondhand goods.
Building fixtures, §59.1-124.
Watch sales, §59.1-135.
Septic system inspectors.
Use of title accredited septic system inspector without meeting requirements, §59.1-310.10.
Storage battery sales, §59.1-191.
Tanning facilities, §59.1-310.6.
Timber brands.
Fraudulently impressing brand on timber, §59.1-112.
Using recorded brand or trademark without authority, §59.1-110.
Trees and timber.
Detinue.
Unbranded timber, §59.1-115.
Trademarks.
Changing or removing with intent to defraud, §18.2-214.
Tradesmen certification violations, §54.1-1135.
Trailer dealers.
Coercion of dealers by manufacturers or distributors.
Retail installment sales contract, §46.2-1992.68.
Inspection of trailers prior to sale, §§46.2-1992.32, 46.2-1992.34.
License plates, §46.2-1992.54.
Temporary license plates issued by dealers, §46.2-1992.64.
Transcripts from post-secondary educational institutions.
Falsifying or altering and fraudulently using, §18.2-172.1.
Transportation board rules and regulations, violations, §33.1-19.
Transportation companies.
Failure to make necessary repairs, §56-130.
Violation of chapter, orders, rules or regulations, §56-140.
Transportation district trains.
Boarding without lawful payment of fare or with fraudulent or counterfeit ticket, §18.2-160.1.
Transportation of alcoholic beverages, §4.1-310.
Trees and timber.
Carrying axe while hunting without permission of landowner, §10.2-141.

MISDEMEANORS —Cont'd
Trees and timber —Cont'd
Detinue.
Unbranded timber, §59.1-115.
Timber brands.
Conversion, §§59.1-107, 59.1-113.
Fraudulently impressing brand on timber, §59.1-112.
Using recorded brand or trademark without authority, §59.1-110.
Trees near highways.
Cutting or injuring, §33.1-345.
Trespass.
After having been forbidden to do so, §18.2-119.
Instigating trespass, §18.2-120.
Preventing service to persons not forbidden to trespass, §18.2-120.
Cemeteries.
Injuries to, §18.2-127.
Trespass at night, §18.2-125.
Uniform fine schedule, VA SCt Rules 3C:1, 3C:2.
Churches, §18.2-128.
Uniform fine schedule, VA SCt Rules 3C:1, 3C:2.
Computers, §18.2-152.4.
Personal trespass by computer, §18.2-152.7.
Entering property of another for purposes of damaging, §18.2-121.
Hunters, fishers or trappers, §18.2-132.
Posted property, §18.2-134.
Destruction of posted signs or posting land of another, §18.2-135.
Refusal of person on land of another to identify himself, §18.2-133.
Injuries to churches, church property, cemeteries, burial grounds, etc., §18.2-127.
Peeping or spying into structure occupied as dwelling, §18.2-130.
Permitting animals to run at large, §18.2-121.
Posting no trespassing signs on property of another, §18.2-119.1.
Public services or utilities, §18.2-162.
Public transportation, §18.2-160.2.
Railroad tracks, §18.2-159.
Railroad trains, §18.2-160.
School property, §18.2-128.
Shooting preserves, §18.2-131.
Spotlight on agricultural land, §18.2-121.2.
Trial without jury, §19.2-258.
Trust subsidiaries.
Employee offenses, §6.2-1063.
Unauthorized alcoholic beverage sales, §4.1-303.
Unclaimed property.
Unlawful agreements to locate, §55-210.27:1.
Underwater historic property violations, §10.1-2214.
Unemployment compensation, §60.2-121.
Agreements.
Payment of employer's taxes other than by employer, §60.2-107.
Waiver of rights void, §60.2-107.
Benefits.
False statements to obtain or increase, §60.2-632.
Fees by commission prohibited, §60.2-122.
Reports and records.
False statements, §60.2-518.
Subpoenas.
Failure to obey, §60.2-627.
Taxation reports.
False statements, §60.2-518.

MISDEMEANORS —Cont'd
Uniform fine schedules.
Non-traffic prepayable offenses, VA SCt Rules 3C:1, 3C:2.
Traffic infractions, VA SCt Rules 3B:1, 3B:2.
Uniforms.
Unlawful wearing of officer's uniform, §18.2-175.
Unlawful use of credit union designation, §6.2-1306.
Unlicensed aircraft operation, §5.1-14.
Usurped government.
Attempting or instigating others to establish, §18.2-483.
Vandalism.
Destruction of private property, §18.2-137.
Destruction of trees, shrubs, etc., §18.2-140.
Injuries to churches, church property, cemeteries, burial grounds, etc., §18.2-127.
Vehicles, aircraft or boats.
Breaking or preventing operation, §18.2-146.
Vehicles to promote prostitution or unlawful sexual intercourse, §18.2-350.
Vending machines.
Slugs manufactured, sold, etc., for unlawful uses, §18.2-180.
Stealing from or tampering with, §18.2-152.
Unlawful operation, §18.2-179.
Veterinary medicine.
Licensing violations, §54.1-3809.
Vicious dog owners, §3.2-6540.1.
Videotaping another unlawfully, §18.2-386.1.
Vinegar.
Violations of provisions, §3.2-5507.
Virginia corn act.
Tax records and documents.
False statements, §3.2-1414.
Virginia Institute of Marine Science property.
Destruction, §28.2-1102.
Virginia port authority.
Violation of rules and regulations, §62.1-132.11.
Virginia retirement system.
Falsification of records, §51.1-124.10.
Visas.
Manufacture, sale, etc., of fictitious, facsimile or simulated visas, §18.2-204.2.
Volunteer firefighters' and rescue squad workers' service award fund.
Falsification of records, §51.1-1211.
Warehouse receipts.
Delivery.
Delivery of goods without obtaining negotiable receipt, §61.1-5.
Deposit of goods in warehouse.
Fraudulent negotiation of warehouse receipt, §61.1-6.
Fraudulent negotiation of receipt for mortgaged goods, §61.1-6.
Issue of receipts.
Duplicate receipts.
Failure to mark, §61.1-3.
Goods not received, §61.1-1.
Receipts containing false statements, §61.1-2.
Warehouseman's interest in goods not shown, §61.1-4.
Warehouses and warehousemen.
Tobacco.
Burley tobacco.
Fees for sale, §61.1-56.
Itemized statements furnished seller, §61.1-39.
Waste management violations, §10.1-1455.

MISDEMEANORS —Cont'd
Wastewater lines.
Diverting, §18.2-162.1.
Wasting public water supply, §18.2-162.1.
Watercourse obstructions, §21-364.
Water safety zones and restricted areas in tidal waters.
Penalty for violation, §28.2-106.2.
Waters of the state.
Big Sandy river.
Dumping refuse into, §62.1-194.3.
Obstructing tributaries, §62.1-194.3.
Buoys, beacons or daymarks.
Anchoring on range of range lights, §62.1-189.
Casting garbage into waters, §62.1-194.
Discharge of oil in the waters, §62.1-44.34:20.
Ground water management.
Violations of provisions, §62.1-270.
Navigation aids protection, §62.1-187.
Obstructing or contaminating state waters, §62.1-194.1.
Throwing trash into or obstructing river, creek, stream or swamp, §62.1-194.2.
Water supplies.
Approval by county of establishment or extension of existing system.
Noncompliance with provisions, §15.2-2156.
Diverting or wasting, §18.2-162.1.
Weighing stations.
Refusal of driver to weigh vehicle, §46.2-1137.
Uniform fine schedule, VA SCt Rule 3C:2.
Weight loss centers or clinics.
Disclosure violations, §18.2-502.1.
Weights and measures.
Acts declared misdemeanor, §3.2-5645.
Impersonating commissioner or local sealer, §3.2-5644.
Obstructing commissioner or local sealer, §3.2-5643.
Point-of-sale system.
Pricing of retail merchandise, §3.2-5627.
Consumer protection, prohibited practices, §59.1-200.
Public weighmasters, §3.2-5820.
Delegation of authority to unlicensed person, §3.2-5819.
Service agencies and technicians, §3.2-5713.
Stop-sale, stop-use and stop-removal orders, §3.2-5612.
Weight certificate.
Falsification of weight certificate by licensed weighmaster, §3.2-5819.
Issuance by unlicensed person, §3.2-5818.
Presealing of weight certificate by licensed weighmaster, §3.2-5819.
Requesting false weighing or false weight certificate, §3.2-5818.
Well covers, duty of person owning or occupying land, §18.2-317.
Wetlands, §28.2-1318.
White cane law.
Unlawful for person not blind to carry, §18.2-212.1.
Wholesale or wholesaler use of word, §18.2-220.
Wildlife.
Killing wildlife damaging crops, livestock or personal property.
Impeding person engaged in lawful killing, §29.1-529.
Parts not to be used for taxidermy or public display, §29.1-529.

MISDEMEANORS —Cont'd
Will advertisements, §64.2-402.
Wine and beer excise tax violations, §4.1-332.
Wine and beer transfers, §4.1-327.
Wiretap device possession violations, §19.2-63.1.
Wiretapping, §19.2-62.
Unlawful disclosure of existence of order authorizing, §18.2-460.1.
Wolves.
Hybrid canine ordinance violations, §3.2-6582.
Woods, brush, leaves, etc., setting on fire intentionally.
Another damaged or jeopardized, §18.2-87.
Workers' compensation.
Employer violations, §65.2-806.
Payroll reports.
Withholding or providing false or misleading information, §65.2-1006.
Workers' compensation insurance.
Agent violations, §65.2-819.
Payroll reports.
Withholding or providing false or misleading information, §65.2-1006.
Work release program for jail inmates, §53.1-131.
Work release program furloughs, §53.1-132.
Wounds caused by concealable weapons.
Report duties of health care professionals, §54.1-2967.
X-rays, fluoroscopes, etc., in fitting of footwear, §18.2-321.
Zebra mussel.
Introducing into waters of Commonwealth, §18.2-313.2.
Zoning ordinance violations, §15.2-2286.

MISDOINGS OF OTHERS.
Promise to answer for, written evidence required, §11-2.

MISFEASANCE.
Removal from office.
Governor's powers to remove, §2.2-108.
Statute of limitations.
Criminal prosecution, §19.2-8.
Transportation districts.
Liability of Commonwealth, counties or cities, §15.2-4526.
Tort liability, §33.1-442.
Virginia Commonwealth University health system authority.
Removal of members of board of directors, §23-50.16:5.

MISJOINDER.
Parties.
Effect, §8.01-5.

MISLEADING EVIDENCE.
Exclusion of relevant evidence, VA SCt Rule 2:403.

MISNOMER.
Amending pleading to correct, §8.01-6.
Indictments, presentments or informations.
Effect of defects in indictments, §19.2-226.

MISPRISION OF TREASON, §18.2-482.

MISREPRESENTATION.
Aircraft sales and use tax, §58.1-1503.
Animal's condition in sales, §§3.2-6509, 18.2-403.2.
Bedding and upholstered furniture.
Tags, §32.1-221.

MISREPRESENTATION —Cont'd
Boat registration and identification, §29.1-702.1.
Breed of bull or cattle.
Fraudulent misrepresentation, §18.2-190.
Business opportunity sales, §59.1-266.
Condominiums.
Penalties, §55-79.103.
Revocation of registration for misrepresentation, §55-79.101.
Consumer protection.
Prohibited practices, §59.1-200.
Credit card applications, §18.2-195.2.
Credit counseling.
License discipline, grounds, §6.2-2018.
Credit services businesses.
Prohibited acts, §59.1-335.5.
Devices on certain containers, §59.1-96.
Disabilities, schools for students with.
Commitment concerning misrepresentation, §22.1-325.
Discipline of licensees, grounds, §22.1-329.
Drug offenses.
Obtaining drugs or procuring administration by, §18.2-258.1.
Drug paraphernalia.
Obtaining controlled paraphernalia by misrepresentation, §54.1-3470.
False statements to obtain property or credit, §18.2-186.
Fishing, tidal waters.
Licensing, §28.2-230.
Governmental fraud, §18.2-498.3.
Ground water management, §62.1-270.
Health insurance.
Statements as to insurability of person, §38.2-3403.
Health spas.
Contracts, §59.1-296.2:1.
Contracts rendered void, §59.1-302.
Purpose to prevent, §59.1-295.
Home solicitation sales.
Cancellation of sale, §59.1-21.7.
Horizontal property regimes, §55-79.28.
Housing assistance programs.
False statements in order to obtain aid, §18.2-186.2.
Indigent hospitalization program, §§32.1-349, 32.1-350.
Industrial sick benefit companies.
False statements for purposes of defrauding, §18.2-204.
Insurance agency relationships, §38.2-1801.
Insurance agents license refusal, revocation or suspension, §38.2-1831.
Insurance consultants, refusal or revocation of license, §38.2-1843.
Insurance documents or communications, §§38.2-309, 38.2-512.
Insurance policies, §38.2-502.
Insurance unfair trade practices generally, §§38.2-500 to 38.2-518.
See INSURANCE, UNFAIR TRADE PRACTICES.
Life insurance policy procurement, §38.2-3103.
Lubricating oil.
Prevention by inspection and testing, §59.1-150.
Marks on certain containers, §59.1-96.
Marriage record or registration.
False statement, §18.2-208.
Mechanics' and materialmen's liens.
Affidavits prior to sale, §43-13.2.

MISREPRESENTATION —Cont'd
Medicaid.
Benefits, §§32.1-312, 32.1-321.3.
Applications, §32.1-321.4.
Concealment of facts, §32.1-321.4.
Determination of rights, §32.1-321.4.
Facility operations or conditions, §32.1-316.
Payments.
Applications, §32.1-314.
Concealment of events, §32.1-314.
Determination of rights, §32.1-314.
Obtaining or attempting to obtain excess payments, §32.1-312.
Medical care facilities.
Certificates of public need.
Revocation, §32.1-102.4.
Membership camping.
Contracts, §59.1-330.2.
Inducements, §59.1-332.
Motorcycle rider safety.
Disciplinary action against licensee, §46.2-1190.6.
Motor fuels.
Prevention by inspection and testing, §59.1-150.
Names on certain containers, §59.1-96.
Pet cemeteries.
Perpetual care, §§57-39.22, 57-39.25.
Pollution control offenses, §§62.1-44.31, 62.1-44.32.
Procurement in public contracting, §2.2-4376.
Public service companies, §56-73.
Public utilities.
Certificates of public convenience and necessity, §56-265.6.
Radiation control.
Radon screening, testing or mitigation, §32.1-229.01:1.
Radon control.
Proficiency as to screening, testing or mitigation, §32.1-229.01:1.
Real estate brokers and salespersons, §§54.1-2142, 54.1-2142.1.
Real estate cooperatives.
Application, §55-431.
Public offering statements, §55-477.
Special declarant rights, transfers of, §55-461.
Recordation tax, state, §58.1-812.
Residential property transfer disclosures, §55-524.
Sales.
Misrepresentations and other offenses connected with sales, §§18.2-214 to 18.2-246.
See SALES OFFENSES.
Sales, UCC.
Buyer's insolvency, §8.2-702.
Remedies, §8.2-721.
Securities.
Unlawful offers and sales, §13.1-502.
Soil scientists and wetland professionals.
Certification, §54.1-2208.
Solicitation of charitable or civic contributions.
Prohibited acts, §57-57.
Telephone solicitation sales.
Cancellation of sale, §59.1-21.7.
Travel clubs, §59.1-449.
Unemployment compensation.
Benefits, §60.2-632.
Unfair insurance trade practices generally, §§38.2-500 to 38.2-518.
See INSURANCE, UNFAIR TRADE PRACTICES.

MISREPRESENTATION —Cont'd
Virginia retirement system.
Record falsification, §51.1-124.10.
Recovery of payments procured by fraud, false statement, etc., §51.1-124.11.
Vital records, §32.1-276.
Watercraft sales and use tax, §58.1-1403.
Workers' compensation.
Awards, §65.2-312.
Uninsured employer's fund.
Payments procured by, §65.2-1206.
Workers' compensation insurance and self-insurance.
Carrier business or conditions, §65.2-819.

MISSILES.
Carrying weapon into courthouse, §18.2-283.1.
Shooting or throwing missiles, etc., at cars, trains, etc., §18.2-154.
Throwing within or at building or dwelling, §18.2-279.

MISSING CHILDREN.
Amber Alert program.
Activation, §52-34.3.
Definitions, §52-34.1.
Established, §52-34.2.
Duty of police or sheriff to immediately enter identifying and descriptive data, §15.2-1718.
Information clearinghouse, §§52-31 to 52-34.
Schools and education.
Cooperation with local law-enforcement agencies, §22.1-288.1.
Notation in school records, §22.1-288.1.
Transfer of scholastic records, §22.1-289.
Vital records registrar.
Duties as to, §32.1-275.2.
Waiting period before accepting missing child report.
Police or sheriff's department not to establish or maintain policy, §15.2-1718.

MISSING CHILDREN INFORMATION CLEARINGHOUSE, §§52-31 to 52-34.
Defined terms, §52-32.
Duties, §52-33.
Establishment, §52-31.
Network to implement reports, §52-31.1.
Notification when missing child located, §52-34.
Police or sheriff to immediately forward identifying and descriptive data about child, §15.2-1718.
Powers, §52-33.

MISSING IN ACTION.
Tuition and required fees for state supported colleges or universities.
Waiver for spouses and children of military personnel, §23-7.4:1.

MISSING LAW ENFORCEMENT OFFICERS.
Blue Alert program, §§52-34.7 to 52-34.9.
Activation of alert, §§52-34.8, 52-34.9.
Definitions, §52-34.7.
Establishment of program, §52-34.8.

MISSING SENIOR ADULT.
Senior alert program, §§52-34.4 to 52-34.6.

MISSTATEMENT OF AGE ON INSURANCE POLICIES.
Health insurance.
Group insurance policy provisions, §38.2-3532.

MISSTATEMENT OF AGE ON INSURANCE POLICIES —Cont'd
Health insurance —Cont'd
Individual policy provisions, §38.2-3504.
Misstatement on policy with age limit, §38.2-3513.
Life insurance, §38.2-3108.
Group life insurance, §38.2-3329.
Individual life insurance, §38.2-3306.
Industrial life insurance, §38.2-3346.

MISS UTILITY.
Underground utility damage prevention, §§56-265.14 to 56-265.32.
See UNDERGROUND UTILITY LINE DAMAGE PREVENTION.

MISUSE OF OFFICE.
Removal of public officer from office, §24.2-233.

MITIGATING FACTORS.
Capital cases.
Sentencing proceeding, §19.2-264.4.

MITIGATION OF DAMAGES.
All-terrain vehicle violations, §46.2-915.1.
Bicyclist helmet ordinance violations, §46.2-906.1.
Defamation, §8.01-46.
Newspapers or print media, §8.01-48.
Landlord and tenant.
Residential landlords and tenants.
Post-termination remedies of landlord, §55-248.35.
Moped safety equipment violations, §46.2-915.2.
Railroad corporations.
Failure to give statutory signals, §56-416.
Seat belt violations, §§46.2-1092, 46.2-1094.
Watercraft, personal.
Operation restriction violations, §29.1-748.

MITIGATION OF PUNISHMENT.
Slanderous or libelous words provoking, §18.2-417.

MIXED BEVERAGE LICENSES.
Authorized conduct, §4.1-210.
Blue Ridge Parkway establishment, §4.1-126.
Carriers, §4.1-210.
Caterers, §4.1-210.
Falsifying applications, §4.1-325.1.
Grounds for refusal to grant, §4.1-223.
Limitation on license, §4.1-221.
Tasting licenses, §4.1-221.1.
Local license taxes, §4.1-233.
Nude dancing.
Grounds for refusal to grant, §4.1-223.
Prohibited acts by licensee, §4.1-325.
Prohibited acts, §4.1-325.
Agents and employees, §4.1-325.2.
Falsifying applications, §4.1-325.1.
Review of licensee operation, §4.1-114.
Soju.
Delivery of soju, §4.1-305.
Special events, §4.1-210.
Drinking alcoholic beverages while on duty, §4.1-325.2.
Falsifying applications, §4.1-325.1.
State license fees, §§4.1-231, 4.1-232.
Stripteases, §4.1-325.
Grounds for refusal to grant, §4.1-223.
Suspension or revocation.
Nude dancing and stripteases, §4.1-226.

MIXED BEVERAGES.
Generally.
See ALCOHOLIC BEVERAGES.
Licenses.
See ALCOHOLIC BEVERAGE LICENSES.

MOBILE COMPUTERIZED AXIAL TOMOGRAPHY SCANNER.
Motor vehicle sales and use tax exemption, §58.1-2403.

MOBILE HOME PARKS.
Fair housing law, §§36-96.1 to 36-96.23.
See FAIR HOUSING.
Manufactured home lot rental, §§55-248.41 to 55-248.52.
See MANUFACTURED HOME LOT RENTAL.
Zoning.
Replacement of home due to nonconforming use, §15.2-2307.

MOBILE HOMES, §§36-85.2 to 36-85.36.
Construction and safety standards generally, §§36-85.2 to 36-85.15.
See MANUFACTURED HOUSING.
Construction sites.
License plates for transporting mobile homes used as temporary offices, §46.2-723.
Dealer's license plates, §46.2-1549.
Defined, §46.2-100.
Disabled vehicle in highway.
Failure to use proper warning device, §46.2-111, VA SCt Rule 3B:2.
Maximum fine for violating Title 46.2, §46.2-113.
Length of vehicles.
Maximum vehicle lengths, §46.2-1115.
Licensing of industry generally, §§36-85.16 to 36-85.30.
See MANUFACTURED HOUSING.
Motor vehicle sales and use tax exemption.
Mobile home permanently attached to real estate, §58.1-2403.
Permit before moving mobile home to place where to be used as place of residence, §58.1-3520.
Personal property tax special provisions.
Assessment method, §58.1-3522.
Moving mobile home to place to be used as place of residence.
Payment of property taxes before moving, §58.1-3520.
Proration of tax, §58.1-3521.
Retail sales and use tax exemption, §58.1-609.1.

MOBILE INFRARED TRANSMITTERS.
Unlawful possession, §46.2-1077.1.

MOBILE PHONES.
See CELLULAR TELEPHONES.

MOBILE RADIO.
Wiretapping exceptions, §19.2-62.

MOBJACK BAY.
Public oyster rocks, beds and shoals, §§28.2-508, 28.2-640, 28.2-648.

MOBS, CRIMES BY, §§18.2-38 to 18.2-46.
Assault or battery by mob, §18.2-42.
Discretionary felony sentencing guidelines, §17.1-805.
Firearm used or displayed, §18.2-53.1.
Interception of wire, electronic or oral communication.
Order authorizing.
When attorney general may apply, §19.2-66.

MOBS, CRIMES BY —Cont'd
Jurisdiction of actions and prosecutions, §18.2-46.
Lynching, apprehension and prosecution of participants, §18.2-43.
Lynching, civil liability, §18.2-44.
Lynching deemed murder, §18.2-40.
Lynching defined, §18.2-39.
Lynching of another, person suffering death from mob attempting, §18.2-45.
Mob defined, §18.2-38.
Sentencing of persons twice previously convicted of certain violent felonies, §19.2-297.1.
Shooting, stabbing, etc., with intent to maim, kill, etc., §18.2-41.
Violent acts generally, §18.2-42.1.

MOCCASIN GAP SANITATION COMMISSION, 1948 ch 523, 1971 ch 178, 1978 ch 464, 1986 ch 398.

MODEL AIRPLANE GLUE.
Inhaling drugs or other noxious chemical substances, §18.2-264.

MODEL BOILERS.
Boiler and pressure vessel safety, §§40.1-51.8, 40.1-51.19:1 to 40.1-51.19:5.

MODELING AND SIMULATION ADVISORY COUNCIL, §§2.2-2698, 2.2-2699.

MODEL INTERSTATE PAROLE AND PROBATION HEARING ACT, §§53.1-168 to 53.1-176.

MODEL STUDENT CONDUCT POLICIES, §22.1-279.6.

MODIFICATION OF SENTENCE, §19.2-303.
Payment of fine or cost, §19.2-356.
Revocation or suspension, §19.2-306.

MODIFIED GUARANTEED ANNUITIES.
Authority to issue, §38.2-3113.1.
Defined, §38.2-107.1.
Investments of insurers allocated to separate accounts, §38.2-1443.1.
Separate accounts established by insurers, §38.2-3113.1.
Statements required, regulations to be issued, etc., §38.2-3113.1.

MODIFIED GUARANTEED LIFE INSURANCE.
Authority to issue, §38.2-3113.1.
Defined, §38.2-105.1.
Investments of insurers allocated to separate accounts, §38.2-1443.1.
Separate accounts established by insurers, §38.2-3113.1.
Statements, §38.2-3113.1.

MODULAR BUILDING MANUFACTURERS AND RETAILERS.
Definitions, §58.1-602.
Retail sales and use tax, §58.1-610.1.

MOIST SNUFF.
Tobacco products tax, §§58.1-1021.01 to 58.1-1021.05.
See TOBACCO PRODUCTS TAX.

MOLD.
Landlord and managing agent.
Residential landlords and tenants.
Defined, §55-248.4.

MOLD —Cont'd
Landlord and managing agent —Cont'd
Residential landlords and tenants —Cont'd
Visible mold in unit, §55-248.11:2.
Visible evidence of mold within dwelling unit, §8.01-226.12.
Definitions, §55-225.8.
Relocation of tenants, §55-225.9.
Tenant and guest, distinguished, §55-225.8.
Tenant taking or remaining in possession, §55-225.7.
Landlord and tenant.
Definitions, §55-248.4.
Residential dwelling units subject to chapter, §55-225.8.
Disclosure of mold in dwelling unit.
Tenant obligations, §55-248.16.
Duty to prevent, §§55-225.3, 55-225.4.
Move-in inspection report.
Disclosure, §55-248.11:2.
Mold disclosure statement, §55-225.7.
Relocation of tenant, remediation, §55-248.18:2.
Tenant and guest, distinguished, §55-225.8.
Visible mold.
Duty of landlord or managing agent, §8.01-226.12.
Relocation of tenants, remediation, §55-225.9.
Tenant's option, §55-225.7.
Tenant's option to terminate or take possession, §55-248.11:2.

MOLESTING CHILDREN.
See CHILD MOLESTATION.

MOLOTOV COCKTAILS.
Manufacture, possession, use, etc., of fire bombs or explosive devices, §18.2-85.

MONEY.
Circulation of illegal currency.
Contracts and securities for dealing in void, §6.2-203.
Capital stock of void entities vested in Commonwealth, §6.2-204.
Disclosures made by defendants, limitations on use, §6.2-204.
Each member of company personally liable, §6.2-204.
Issuance of currency prohibited, §6.2-202.
Dollar, cent and mill.
Money of account of Commonwealth, §6.2-200.
Extorting money, etc., by threats, §18.2-59.
Foreign currency.
Money of account.
Ascertaining value for money expressed in, §6.2-201.
Forging account coin or bank notes, §18.2-170.
Having in possession, §18.2-173.
Intangible personal property tax, §§58.1-1100 to 58.1-1118.
See PERSONAL PROPERTY TAXES.
Issuance of currency, prohibited, §6.2-202.
Money of account.
Accounts by public officers, §6.2-200.
Dollar, cent and mill, §6.2-200.
Foreign currency.
Ascertaining value for money expressed in, §6.2-201.
Money order sales.
See MONEY ORDERS.
Money order sellers and money transmitters, §§6.2-1900 to 6.2-1921.
See MONEY ORDERS.

MONEY —Cont'd
Obtaining by false pretense, §18.2-178.

MONEY CHANGING MACHINES.
Stealing from or tampering with, §18.2-152.

MONEY DEPOSITED IN COURT.
Payment into court generally.
See PAYMENT INTO COURT.

MONEY LAUNDERING, §§18.2-246.1 to 18.2-246.5.
Definitions, §18.2-246.2.
Forfeitures.
Business license, §18.2-246.5.
Property used in connection with, §19.2-386.19.
Penalties, §18.2-246.3.
Racketeering activities.
Transmission of money derived from, §18.2-516.
Short title, §18.2-246.1.
Unlawful acts, §18.2-246.3.

MONEY MARKET FUNDS.
Insurance companies investments, §38.2-1432.

MONEY ORDERS.
Abandonment presumed, §55-210.3:02.
Bonds, surety.
Money order sellers and money transmitters.
Licenses, §6.2-1904.
Alternative security device, §6.2-1904.
Fees, fines and penalties collected by clerks of courts of record.
Acceptance as payment, §17.1-222.1.
Licenses.
Selling without license, §6.2-1921.
Money order sellers and money transmitters, §§6.2-1900 to 6.2-1921.
Acquisition of control of licensed business, §6.2-1914.
Authorized delegates.
Conducting business through authorized delegates, §6.2-1911.
License not required, §6.2-1901.
Bearer money orders, §6.2-1915.
Books and accounts.
Examination by commission, §6.2-1910.
Cease and desist orders.
Licensing violations, §6.2-1909.
Civil penalties for violation, §6.2-1920.
Conducting business at more than one location, §6.2-1911.
Construction and interpretation, §6.2-1902.
Definitions, §6.2-1900.
Examination of books and records, §6.2-1910.
Liability of licensee for payment, §6.2-1912.
Licenses.
Acquisition of control of licensed business, §6.2-1914.
Alternative security device, §6.2-1904.
Application, §6.2-1903.
Authorized delegates of licensee.
Bearer money order duties, §6.2-1915.
Authorized delegates of licensee, not required, §6.2-1901.
Bonds, surety.
To accompany application, §6.2-1904.
Books, accounts and records of licensee.
Retention, §6.2-1916.
Cease and desist orders, §6.2-1909.
Conditions prerequisite to issuance, §6.2-1906.
Exceptions, §6.2-1902.
Fees.
Annual renewal fee, §6.2-1905.

MONEY ORDERS —Cont'd
Money order sellers and money transmitters —Cont'd
Licenses —Cont'd
Fees —Cont'd
Application fee, §6.2-1903.
Financial statements to accompany application, §6.2-1903.
Investments by licensees.
Permissible investments, maintenance of, §6.2-1918.
Permissible investments, types, §6.2-1919.
Issuance.
Conditions prerequisite, §6.2-1906.
Liability of licensee for payment, §6.2-1912.
Name of licensee.
Money order to bear name, §6.2-1912.
Reinstatement after revocation, §6.2-1907.
Renewal, §6.2-1905.
Reports by licensees, §6.2-1917.
Annual report, §6.2-1905.
Required, §6.2-1901.
Revocation.
Grounds, §6.2-1907.
Hearings, §6.2-1907.
Request for, §6.2-1908.
Inability to meet obligations, §6.2-1907.
Notice of proposed revocation, §6.2-1908.
Reinstatement after revocation, §6.2-1907.
United States government exempt, §6.2-1902.
Name of licensee.
Money order to bear, §6.2-1912.
Negotiable instruments law applicable, §6.2-1912.
Payment.
Liability of licensee, §6.2-1912.
Records.
Books, accounts and records of licensee.
Retention, §6.2-1916.
Examination by commission, §6.2-1910.
Rules and regulations, §6.2-1913.
Scope of chapter, §6.2-1902.
Violations.
Civil penalties for violation, §6.2-1920.
Unclaimed property, disposition of, §55-210.3:02.

MONEY TRANSMISSION.
See MONEY ORDERS.

MONOPOLIES AND RESTRAINT OF TRADE, §§59.1-9.1 to 59.1-9.17.
Actions, §59.1-9.8.
Instituted on behalf of Commonwealth or localities, §59.1-9.15.
Limitation of actions, §59.1-9.14.
Personal suits, §59.1-9.12.
Remedies cumulative, §59.1-9.16.
Venue, §59.1-9.9.
Activities not prohibited, §59.1-9.4.
Acts not prohibited, §59.1-9.4.
Agricultural cooperative associations not deemed illegal monopoly, §13.1-331.
Agricultural cooperative associations not in restraint of trade, §13.1-331.
Combinations to injure others in reputation, trade, business or profession, §§18.2-499 to 18.2-501.
Conflict of laws, §59.1-9.4.
Construction of chapter, §59.1-9.17.
Dairies and dairy products.
Marketing agreements not deemed to be, §3.2-3223.

MONOPOLIES AND RESTRAINT OF TRADE —Cont'd
Defined terms, §59.1-9.3.
Discriminatory practices, §59.1-9.7.
Effect of conviction, §59.1-9.13.
Electric utility restructuring.
Application of antitrust laws, §56-591.
Insurance antitrust provisions, §§38.2-700 to 38.2-705.
Insurance business boycott, coercion or intimidation, §38.2-505.
Insurance rates.
Prohibited conduct by insurers and rate service organizations, §38.2-1916.
Investigations by attorney general, §59.1-9.10.
Monopolies unlawful, §59.1-9.6.
Penalties for violations, §59.1-9.11.
Price-gouging.
Post-disaster anti-price gouging act, §§59.1-525 to 59.1-529.1.
Purpose, §59.1-9.2.
Remedies cumulative, §59.1-9.16.
Restraint of trade, §59.1-9.5.
Agricultural cooperative associations, §13.1-331.
Combinations to injure others in reputation, trade, etc., §§18.2-499 to 18.2-501.
Insurance antitrust provisions, §§38.2-700 to 38.2-705.
Insurance business boycott, coercion or intimidation, §38.2-505.
Insurance rate service organizations, §38.2-1916.
Motion pictures.
Fair competition, §59.1-256.
Short title of chapter, §59.1-9.1.
Unfair and deceptive trade practices.
See UNFAIR AND DECEPTIVE TRADE PRACTICES.

MONTGOMERY COUNTY.
Blue Ridge regional tourism council, §§2.2-2609, 2.2-2610.
Confederate cemeteries and graves.
Disbursement of funds appropriated for upkeep, §10.1-2211.
County attorney.
Prosecution of violations of county ordinances, §15.2-1542.
Dams.
Restrictions, §29.1-532.
Dirt and gravel roads.
Maximum speed limits on nonsurface treated highways, §46.2-873.1.
Medical care facility certificates of need, §32.1-102.3:2.
Parking on secondary highways, §46.2-1222.
Port of Virginia economic and infrastructure development zone grant fund, §62.1-132.3:2.
School board.
Salary of members, §22.1-32.
Terms of members appointed to represent towns, §22.1-57.3:2.
Subdivisions.
Expedited land development review procedures, §15.2-2263.
Tax map reference number.
Circuit court clerk indexing by, §17.1-252.
Transient occupancy tax.
Disposition of revenues, §58.1-3819.
Western Virginia public education consortium.
Inclusion in western Virginia, §22.1-354.1.

MONTH.
Defined, §1-223.

MONTH FOR CHILDREN, §2.2-3320.

MONTPELIER.
National trust for historic preservation.
James Madison home.
Appropriations for maintenance, §10.1-2212.

MONUMENTS.
Counties, cities or towns.
Acquiring real property near monuments, §15.2-1801.
War veterans, §15.2-1812.
Damage to monuments, actions, §15.2-1812.1.
Injury or destruction to, §18.2-137.
Warrantless arrests.
Malicious mischief, §19.2-81.

MOORMANS RIVER.
Scenic river, §10.1-413.1.

MOPEDS.
Attaching to vehicle on highway, §46.2-932.
Carrying articles improperly on moped, §46.2-906.
Controlled access highways.
Prohibited use, §46.2-808.
County, city or town regulating noise, §15.2-919.
Decals required on mopeds, §46.2-915.
Defined, §46.2-100.
Driving while intoxicated.
Generally, §§18.2-266 to 18.2-273.
See DRIVING WHILE INTOXICATED.
Earphones, §46.2-1078.
Exhaust system, §46.2-1051.
Fees.
Motor vehicle registration, §46.2-694.
Fines schedule, VA SCt Rule 3B:2.
Goggles, face shield or safety glasses, §46.2-915.2.
Head lights, §46.2-1015.
Helmet violation, §46.2-915.2.
Identification.
Persons operating to carry, §46.2-914.
Improper left turns, §46.2-847.
Improper passing, §46.2-839.
Interstate highways.
Operation on, prohibition, §46.2-914.
Left turns.
Improper position or method of turning at intersection, §46.2-847.
License plates.
Display required, §46.2-715.
Licensing, §15.2-1720.
Limitations on operation, §46.2-914.
Local government restrictions, §46.2-1051.
Localities regulating noise, §15.2-919.
Maximum fine for violating Title 46.2, §46.2-113.
Motor vehicle registration.
Exemptions from registration.
New resident operating vehicle registered in another state or country, §46.2-662.
Fees, §46.2-694.
Offenses relating to registration, §46.2-613.
Required before operating vehicle on highway, §46.2-600.
Motor vehicle safety inspections.
Exemption from inspection requirement, §46.2-1158.01.
Mufflers.
Straight exhaust or gutted mufflers, §46.2-1047.

MOPEDS —Cont'd
Noise limitation, §§15.2-919, 46.2-1050.
Odometers.
Reporting odometer reading on certificate of title, §46.2-629.
Operating violations, penalty, §46.2-914.
Overtaking and passing vehicles, §46.2-907.
Improper passing, §46.2-839.
Personal property taxes.
Classification, §§58.1-3503, 58.1-3504.
Persons under age 16 years.
Operating on highways, prohibition, §46.2-914.
Prepayment of fine, §16.1-69.40:1.
Red light, proceeding through intersection at, §46.2-833.
Riding on highway.
Improper riding, §46.2-905.
Rights and duties applicable to driver of a motor vehicle, §46.2-800.
Roadways and bicycle paths, riding on, §46.2-905.
Safety equipment for mopeds, §46.2-915.2.
Speed limitations, §46.2-914.
Statewide system of trails, §10.1-204.
Stickers required on mopeds, §46.2-915.
Tailgating vehicles by pedestrians, §46.2-932.
Tail lights, §46.2-1015.
Traffic signals.
Red light, proceeding through intersection at, §46.2-833.
Two vehicles abreast in single lane, §46.2-857.
Unclaimed mopeds in possession of sheriff or police.
Disposal, §§15.2-1719, 15.2-1720.
Vehicle approaching or passing, §46.2-839.

MORPHINE.
Drug control act.
Generally, §§54.1-3400 to 54.1-3472.
See DRUG CONTROL.
Drug offenses.
Generally, §§18.2-247 to 18.2-264.
See DRUG OFFENSES.
Schedule I controlled drug, §54.1-3446.
Schedule II controlled drug, §54.1-3448.
Schedule III controlled drug, §54.1-3450.

MORTALITY TABLES.
Evidence, §8.01-419.
Makehamized mortality table.
Commutation and valuation of certain estates and interests, §55-274.
Standard nonforfeiture provisions for life insurance.
Generally, §§38.2-3200 to 38.2-3229.
See LIFE INSURANCE.

MORTGAGE GUARANTY INSURANCE.
Defined, §38.2-128.
Mortgage guaranty insurance contingency reserve, §38.2-1315.
Rates.
Generally, §§38.2-1900 to 38.2-1928.
See INSURANCE RATES.

MORTGAGE GUARANTY INSURANCE AGENTS.
Licensing of agents generally, §§38.2-1822 to 38.2-1836.1.
Licensing without examination, §38.2-1814.

MORTGAGE GUARANTY INSURANCE CONTINGENCY RESERVE.
Insurance companies, §38.2-1315.

MORTGAGE LENDERS AND BROKERS, §§6.2-1600 to 6.2-1629.
Accounts.
Escrow accounts, §6.2-1618.
Maintenance of required accounts, §6.2-1609.
Acquisition of control.
Application to commissioner, §6.2-1608.
Conditions, §6.2-1608.
Actions.
Private action still maintainable, §6.2-1627.
Advertising.
Prohibited practices, §6.2-1614.
Appraiser's fee for appraisal services.
Failure to pay when due.
Suspension or revocation of license, §6.2-1619.
Assignments.
Licenses.
No assignment, §6.2-1607.
Attorney general.
Enforcement of chapter, §§6.2-1626, 6.2-1628, 6.2-1629.
Attorneys at law.
Exempt from chapter, §6.2-1602.
Attorneys' fees.
Enforcement of chapter, §6.2-1628.
Banks.
Lender authorized to engage in business as.
Exempt from chapter, §6.2-1602.
State bank acting as mortgage broker or lender.
Transacting real estate brokerage business through controlled subsidiary corporation, §6.2-888.
Bonds, surety.
Licenses.
Required, §6.2-1604.
Cease and desist orders, §6.2-1622.
Collateral other than real estate or residential property.
Taking an interest in.
Prohibited practice, §6.2-1614.
Consumer protection.
Application of provisions, §59.1-199.
Credit unions.
Lender authorized to engage in business as.
Exempt from chapter, §6.2-1602.
Criminal background checks.
Acquisition of control, prerequisites, §6.2-1608.
Central criminal records exchange, authority to disseminate information, §19.2-389.
License applicants, §6.2-1605.
Damages.
Attorney general may seek, §§6.2-1626, 6.2-1629.
Definitions, §6.2-1600.
Employees of licensees.
Censure, suspension or barring of person from position of employment, management or control, §6.2-1620.
Negotiating, placing or finding mortgage without license, §6.2-1601.
Escrow.
Accounts, §6.2-1618.
Examinations.
Affairs, business, premises and records of any lender or broker, §6.2-1611.
Exclusive agents of licensees.
Negotiating, placing or finding mortgage without license, §6.2-1601.
Exclusive dealing or agency agreement.
Prohibited practice, §6.2-1614.
Exemptions from chapter, §6.2-1602.

MORTGAGE LENDERS AND BROKERS —Cont'd
Fees.
Annual fees, §6.2-1612.
License, §6.2-1603.
Fiduciaries.
Exempt from chapter, §6.2-1602.
Flipping prohibited, §6.2-1614.
Injunctions, §§6.2-1626, 6.2-1629.
Insurance companies.
Exempt from chapter, §6.2-1602.
Investigations.
Affairs, business, premises and records of lender or broker, §6.2-1611.
Licenses.
Applications, §6.2-1605.
Licenses.
Application, §6.2-1603.
Assignments.
Not assignable, §6.2-1607.
Bonds, surety, §6.2-1604.
Contents.
Requirements, §6.2-1607.
Display, §6.2-1607.
Employees or exclusive agents of licensees.
Censure, suspension or barring of person from position of employment, management or control, §6.2-1620.
License not required, §6.2-1601.
Exemption from requirement, §6.2-1602.
Fees, §6.2-1603.
Investigation of applications, §6.2-1605.
Management or control of licensees.
Censure, suspension or barring of person from position of employment, management or control, §6.2-1620.
Notice.
Suspension or revocation, §6.2-1623.
Qualifications, §6.2-1606.
Requirement, §6.2-1601.
Revocation.
Grounds, §6.2-1619.
Notice, §6.2-1623.
Suspension.
Grounds, §6.2-1619.
Notice, §6.2-1623.
Transferability.
Not transferable, §6.2-1607.
Municipal corporations.
Agencies of exempt from chapter, §6.2-1602.
Notice.
Licenses.
Suspension or revocation, §6.2-1623.
Required notice to borrower, §§6.2-1615, 6.2-1616.
Orders.
Cease and desist orders, §6.2-1622.
Penalties.
Criminal penalties, §6.2-1625.
Fines for violations, §6.2-1624.
Prohibited practices, §§6.2-1614 to 6.2-1617, 6.2-1629.
Attorney general, enforcement, §6.2-1628.
Attorneys' fees, §6.2-1628.
Brokers, §§6.2-1616, 6.2-1617.
Flipping, §6.2-1614.
Lenders, §6.2-1615.
Real estate brokers.
Exempt from chapter, §6.2-1602.
Records.
Maintenance of required records, §6.2-1609.

MORTGAGE LENDERS AND BROKERS —Cont'd
Reports.
Annual report, §6.2-1610.
Events impacting activities of registrants, §6.2-1621.
Rules and regulations.
Promulgation, §6.2-1613.
Savings institutions.
Lender authorized to engage in business as.
Exempt from chapter, §6.2-1602.
Settlement statements.
Failure to provide.
Prohibited practice, §6.2-1615.
Small business investment companies.
Exempt from chapter, §6.2-1602.
State.
Agencies of exempt from chapter, §6.2-1602.
Truth-in-lending.
Failure to comply with.
Prohibited practice, §6.2-1614.
United States.
Agencies of exempt from chapter, §6.2-1602.

MORTGAGE LOAN ORIGINATORS, §§6.2-1700 to 6.2-1721.
Advertising.
Prohibited acts, §6.2-1715.
Bonds, surety, §6.2-1703.
Continuing education, §6.2-1710.
Criminal history record checks.
License applicants, §6.2-1704.
Definitions, §6.2-1700.
Education.
Continuing education, §6.2-1710.
Pre-licensing education, §6.2-1708.
Examinations, §6.2-1713.
Expenses.
Liability of licensee, §6.2-1714.
False advertising.
Prohibited acts, §6.2-1715.
Fees.
Licenses.
Annual renewal fee, §6.2-1714.
Application fee, §6.2-1702.
Fines for violations, §6.2-1719.
Independent contractors, license required, §6.2-1701.
Injunctions.
Cease and desist orders, §6.2-1721.
Investigations, §6.2-1713.
Expenses.
Liability of licensee, §6.2-1714.
Licenses.
Applications, §6.2-1702.
Background check, §6.2-1704.
Bond to accompany, §6.2-1703.
Coordination of licensing, §6.2-1705.
Provisions of written agreement with registry, §6.2-1720.
Denial, §6.2-1706.
Duration, §6.2-1711.
Education.
Continuing education, §6.2-1710.
Pre-licensing education, §6.2-1708.
Exceptions to requirement, §6.2-1701.
Expiration, §6.2-1711.
Fees.
Annual renewal fee, §6.2-1714.
Application fee, §6.2-1702.

MORTGAGE LOAN ORIGINATORS —Cont'd
Licenses —Cont'd
Issuance.
Findings required, §§6.2-1706, 6.2-1707.
Nonprofit organizations.
Determination of bona fide organization, §6.2-1701.1.
Place of business.
License to state, §6.2-1711.
Renewal, §6.2-1711.
Annual renewal fee, §6.2-1714.
Reports.
Events impacting licensee, §6.2-1717.
Required, §6.2-1701.
Revocation.
Grounds, §6.2-1716.
Notice of proposed revocation or suspension, §6.2-1718.
Suspension.
Grounds, §6.2-1716.
Notice of proposed revocation or suspension, §6.2-1718.
Testing of applicants, §6.2-1709.
Transfer or assignment prohibited, §6.2-1711.
Nationwide mortgagee licensing system and registry.
Coordination with, §§6.2-1705, 6.2-1720.
Nonprofit organizations.
Determination of bona fide organization, §6.2-1701.1.
Place of business.
Change, §6.2-1711.
License to state, §6.2-1711.
Reports.
Events impacting licensee, §6.2-1717.
Rules and regulations, §6.2-1720.
Unique identifier, use of, §6.2-1715.

MORTGAGE PASS-THROUGH SECURITIES.
Insurance companies investments, §38.2-1437.1.
Renewal or extension when property value decreases, §38.2-1438.
Insurance companies investments and business entity obligations, §38.2-1421.

MORTGAGE REDEMPTION INSURANCE AGENTS.
Licensing of agents generally, §§38.2-1822 to 38.2-1836.1.

MORTGAGES AND DEEDS OF TRUST, §§6.2-406 to 6.2-423, 55-58 to 55-66.6.
Acceleration.
Sale or conveyance of property.
Notice that debt is subject to call or modification, §6.2-417.
Accounts of sales under, fiduciaries, §64.2-1309.
Acknowledgments.
Validating certain acts, §§55-122 to 55-137.2.
Additional encumbrance.
Certain mortgages not to prohibit, §6.2-416.
Advertisements before sale, §55-59.2.
Construction of compliance requirements, §55-63.
Contents, §55-59.3.
Agricultural cooperative association assets, §13.1-340.
Application for mortgage.
Disclosure of terms, §6.2-406.
Appraisals.
Copy of appraisal, lender to furnish, §6.2-407.
Assets of nonprofit corporations, §13.1-899.

MORTGAGES AND DEEDS OF TRUST —Cont'd
Assignments.
Protection of assignees of debts secured by real estate, §55-66.01.
Protection of assignees or transferees of debt secured by real estate, §55-66.01.
Assumption of loan.
Disclosure of terms of assumption, §6.2-419.
Attorneys at law.
Borrowers not required to employ particular attorney, §6.2-410.
Bail bondsmen.
Proof of collateral.
Licensing requirements, §9.1-185.5.
Banks.
Holding and conveying mortgage property, §6.2-872.
Billing obligee for property taxes, §58.1-3912.
Brokers, §§6.2-1600 to 6.2-1629.
See MORTGAGE LENDERS AND BROKERS.
Mortgage lender and broker act, §§6.2-1600 to 6.2-1629.
See MORTGAGE LENDERS AND BROKERS.
Certificate of satisfaction or partial satisfaction.
Recordation, §55-66.4:2.
Release of deed of trust, §55-66.3.
Certificate of transfer.
Protection of assignees or transferees of debt secured by real estate, §55-66.01.
Child or minor purchasing real property.
Servicemen's readjustment act of 1944, eligibility for guaranty of credit, §11-8.
Church property, §§57-14 to 57-15.1.
Circuit courts.
Electronic filing of land records, §17.1-258.3:1.
Condominiums.
Amendment of condominium instrument.
Mortgagee consent required by provision in instrument, §55-79.73:1.
Release of liens at time of first conveyance, §55-79.46.
Rights of holders, §55-79.72:2.
Rights of mortgagees, §55-79.72:2.
Special declarant rights.
Transfers, §55-79.74:3.
Construction, §55-59.
Phrases in trust deeds, §55-60.
Consumer protection.
Foreclosure rescue services, §59.1-200.1.
Consumer real estate settlement protection act.
See CONSUMER REAL ESTATE SETTLEMENT PROTECTION ACT.
Conveyance of property.
Notice that debut is subject to call or modification upon conveyance, §6.2-417.
Cooperative associations.
Liens on rotating stocks, §13.1-310.
Coordinate systems of Virginia.
Reliance on description depending on systems, §55-296.
Reliance upon description depending on systems, §55-296.
Covenants to pay interest, §55-59.
Credit line deed of trust, §55-58.2.
Fraudulent conveyances.
Void as to creditors and purchasers until recorded.
Priority, §55-96.
Where to be recorded, §55-97.

MORTGAGES AND DEEDS OF TRUST —Cont'd
Credit line deed of trust —Cont'd
Limitation on enforcement when no date fixed for maturity, §8.01-242.
Deed books.
Documents to be recorded in, §§17.1-227, 17.1-229.
Deeds of release.
Execution and deliverance, §55-59.4.
Execution effect, §55-18.
Default, §55-59.
Defined terms.
Credit line deed of trust, §55-58.2.
Release of deeds of trust or other liens, §55-66.3.
Satisfaction.
Document of rescission, §55-66.10.
Satisfaction of mortgages, §55-66.9.
Security trusts, §55-58.1.
Disclosure of terms of mortgage application, §6.2-406.
Drafter's name to appear on first page, §17.1-223.
Duties of parties, §55-59.
Ejectment.
When mortgagee not to recover, §8.01-147.
Electronic billing of property taxes, §58.1-3912.
Electronic filing of land records.
Circuit courts, §17.1-258.3:1.
Emblements.
Applicability, §55-249.
Enforcement.
Limitation of enforcement, §8.01-241.
Permissible form for extension, §8.01-241.1.
Escheat of estates, §55-193.
Escrow account.
Obligation of person maintaining to pay taxes and insurance, §6.2-414.
Evictions.
Mortgagee relief from forfeiture, §55-241.
Evidence.
Recitals, §8.01-389.
Extension of limitation of enforcement, §8.01-241.
Permissible form, §8.01-241.1.
Federal farm loan mortgages.
Recording in federal farm loan mortgage book, §17.1-235.
Fiduciaries.
Accounts of sales under, §64.2-1309.
Foreclosure.
Child support enforcement by department of social services.
Lien asserted by commissioner, §63.2-1934.
Condominiums, §55-79.72:1.
Special declarant rights.
Transfers, §55-79.74:3.
Consumer protection.
Foreclosure rescue services, §59.1-200.1.
Hospital or health center commission property exempt from, §15.2-5212.
Housing development authority.
Powers, §36-55.31.
Membership camping.
Nondisturbance provisions, §59.1-333.
Notice to tenant, §55-225.10.
Real estate cooperatives.
Association transmittal of notice, §55-473.
Nonpayment of assessments, §55-472.
Special declarant rights, transfers of, §55-461.
Receivers.
Special receivers.
Effect of suit against receiver, §8.01-597.

MORTGAGES AND DEEDS OF TRUST —Cont'd
Foreclosure —Cont'd
Sales under deed of trust, §§55-59 to 55-66.
Secured transactions.
Defaults.
Enforcement after default, §8.9A-601.
Southwest Virginia health facilities authority.
Exemption of property of, §15.2-5381.
Time-shares.
Purchaser's rights under developer's foreclosure, §55-388.
Termination of time-share not constituted, §55-373.
Foreclosure rescue services.
Consumer protection, prohibited practices, §59.1-200.1.
Form, §55-58.
Form for extending limitation of enforcement, §8.01-241.1.
Fraudulent conveyances.
Void as to creditors and purchasers until recorded, §55-96.
Where to be recorded, §55-97.
Further encumbrances.
Certain mortgages not to prohibit, §6.2-416.
Grantors and grantees to be listed, §17.1-223.
Horizontal property regimes.
Recordation, §55-79.7.
Housing authorities.
Bonds, trust indentures and mortgages, §§36-29 to 36-35.
See HOUSING AUTHORITIES.
Improvements to land.
Exception as to mortgagees, §8.01-174.
Incorporating deed.
Recording of master deed, §17.1-260.
Indexing, §17.1-249.
Indexing deed books, §17.1-223.
Insurance.
Borrowers not required to employ particular insurer, §6.2-410.
Escrow account.
Obligation of person maintaining to pay, §6.2-414.
Fire insurance, §6.2-412.
Mortgage guaranty insurance.
Lender to reimburse unused premiums, §6.2-413.
Refinancing, restrictions on lender canceling policy, §6.2-415.
Subordinate mortgage loans, §6.2-411.
Temporary contracts, §38.2-205.1.
Temporary contracts permitted, §38.2-205.1.
Insurance company investments, §38.2-1434.
Limitation on mortgages, §38.2-1437.
Limitations, §38.2-1437.
Mortgage pass-through security, §38.2-1437.1.
Participation interest, §38.2-1436.
Renewal or extension on decrease in property value, §38.2-1438.
Second deeds of trust, §38.2-1435.
Second mortgages, §38.2-1435.
Wrap-around mortgages, §38.2-1435.
Interest.
Addition of unpaid interest to principal balance, §6.2-409.
Contract rate more than legal rate, §6.2-325.
Loan fees and charges, §6.2-326.
Subordinate deed of trust or mortgage, §6.2-328.

MORTGAGES AND DEEDS OF TRUST —Cont'd
Interest —Cont'd
Contract rate more than legal rate —Cont'd
Subordinate deed of trust or mortgage, §6.2-327.
Loan fees and charges, §6.2-328.
Rebate of unearned interest.
Applicability, §6.2-405.
Rule of 78, §§6.2-402 to 6.2-404.
Rule of 78, §6.2-403.
Applicability, §6.2-405.
Notice of loan or sale on credit using method, §6.2-402.
Prohibition on use, §6.2-404.
Rebate of unearned interest, §§6.2-402 to 6.2-404.
Subordinate mortgage loans.
Rebates for unearned interest, §6.2-423.
Applicability, §6.2-405.
Rule of 78, §§6.2-402 to 6.2-404.
Keeper liens.
Extent of lien, §43-32.
Landlord and tenant.
Mortgagee relief from forfeiture, §55-241.
Late charges, §6.2-400.
Limitation of actions.
Enforcement of lien, §8.01-241.
Extension of limitation forms, §8.01-241.1.
No maturity date given, §8.01-242.
Unpaid purchase money.
No maturity date given, §8.01-242.
Lost notes, §55-59.1.
Maps or plats attached to deed.
Notation as to recording in plat book, §17.1-236.
Master deed, recording, §17.1-259.
Form and requisite, §17.1-259.
Incorporating deed, §17.1-260.
Minor or unmarried widow purchasing real property.
Servicemen's readjustment act of 1944, eligibility for guaranty of credit, §11-8.
Mortgage lender and broker act, §§6.2-1600 to 6.2-1629.
See MORTGAGE LENDERS AND BROKERS.
Mortgage loan originators, §§6.2-1700 to 6.2-1721.
See MORTGAGE LOAN ORIGINATORS.
No maturity date given.
Limitation of enforcement, §8.01-242.
Nonlisting of secured notes for taxation.
Affect on title, §55-64.1.
Nonprobate transfer on death, §64.2-620.
Nonprofit corporation assets, §13.1-899.
Notice.
Before sales.
Advertisements, §§55-59.1, 55-59.2, 55-63.
Form, §55-62.
Foreclosure, §55-225.10.
Release of deeds of trust or other liens, §55-66.3.
Numbering of pages, §17.1-223.
Partial satisfaction.
Release, §55-66.3.
Payment.
Acceleration.
Notice, §6.2-417.
Prepayment.
Certain contracts to permit, §6.2-421.
Notice of acceleration clause to be contained in deed or mortgage, §6.2-417.
Payoff amount, property owner entitled to, §6.2-418.

MORTGAGES AND DEEDS OF TRUST —Cont'd
Payment —Cont'd
Prepayment —Cont'd
Penalties.
Limits, home occupied by borrower, §6.2-422.
No collection in certain cases, §6.2-420.
Subordinate mortgage loans, §6.2-423.
Rebate of unearned interest.
Applicability, §6.2-405.
Rule of 78, §§6.2-402 to 6.2-404.
Release, §55-66.3.
Payoff amount.
Property owner entitled to, §6.2-418.
Penalties.
Late charges, §6.2-400.
Phrases in deeds construed, §55-60.
Port authority.
Bond issues.
Trust agreement securing, §62.1-141.
Power of attorney.
Authority of agent as to real property, §64.2-1625.
Preparer's name to appear on first page, §17.1-223.
Prepayment.
Certain contracts to permit, §6.2-421.
Payoff amount.
Property owner entitled to, §6.2-418.
Penalties.
Limits, home occupied by borrower, §6.2-422.
No collection in certain cases, §6.2-420.
Subordinate mortgage loans, §6.2-423.
Rebates for unearned interest.
Applicability, §6.2-405.
Rule of 78, §§6.2-402 to 6.2-404.
Priorities of encumbrances.
Credit line deed of trust, §55-58.2.
Priorities of indebtedness.
Disposition of surplus after death of grantor, §55-64.
Evidences of indebtedness placed on equal footing, §55-60.1.
Priority of interest on debts secured by mortgage, §6.2-408.
Property tax bills mailed to obligee, §58.1-3912.
Electronic billing, §58.1-3912.
Property taxes.
Escrow account.
Obligation of person maintaining to pay taxes and insurance, §6.2-414.
Public service companies.
Sale of company under deed of trust, §56-9.
Sale of company under mortgage, §56-9.
Purchase money mortgages, §55-104.
Real estate cooperatives.
Applicability of provisions, §55-425.
Real estate settlements and settlement agents.
Generally, §§55-525.8 to 55-525.32.
See REAL ESTATE SETTLEMENTS.
Real property transfer on death act, §§64.2-621 to 64.2-638.
See REAL PROPERTY TRANSFER ON DEATH ACT.
Recordation.
Acknowledgments, improper.
Recordation in separate book, §55-111.
Certification of counterparts, §55-109.1.
Continued, §55-112.
Copy used where original lost, §§55-109, 55-110.
Drafter's name to appear on first page, §17.1-223.
Electronic recordation of real property documents.
Uniform standards, §55-66.14.

MORTGAGES AND DEEDS OF TRUST —Cont'd
Recordation —Cont'd
Extension of limitation of enforcement, §8.01-241.
Permissible form, §8.01-241.1.
Form and requisites, §17.1-259.
Grantors and grantees names to be listed, §17.1-223.
Incorporating deed, §17.1-260.
Indexing, §17.1-249.
Maps or plats attached to deed of trust.
Notation as to recording in plat book, §17.1-236.
Master deed, §17.1-259.
Numbering of pages, §17.1-223.
Presumption of proper form, §55-106.2.
Refusal by clerk to record, §55-106.5.
Requirements generally, §17.1-223.
Scrivener's act, §17.1-223.
Standards for writings to be recorded, §55-108.
Surname of individual to be underscored or written entirely in capital letters, §17.1-223.
Torrens system, §55-112.
When and where writings admitted to record generally, §55-106.
Recordation tax, local, §§58.1-3800 to 58.1-3804.
Recordation tax, state, §58.1-803.
Construction loan deeds of trust or mortgages, §58.1-804.
Exemptions, §58.1-811.
Notice of assignment of note secured by.
Deed not taxable, §58.1-810.
Not taxable, §58.1-810.
Supplemental writings, when not taxable, §58.1-809.
Recording.
Certification of counterparts, §55-109.1.
Documents recorded in deed books, §17.1-227.
Extension of limitation of enforcement, §8.01-241.
Permissible form, §8.01-241.1.
Federal farm loan mortgage book, §17.1-235.
Refinance mortgages.
Credit line deeds of trust, priority, §55-58.2.
Insurance.
Restrictions on lender canceling policy, §6.2-415.
Subordinate mortgages, priority, §55-58.3.
Release, §55-66.3.
Affidavit by lien creditor, §55-66.3.
Certificates of satisfaction or partial satisfaction.
Delivery by lien creditor, time period, §55-66.3.
Duty of lien creditor to issue, §55-66.3.
Failure of lien creditor to timely deliver.
Forfeiture to lien obligor, §55-66.3.
Form, §55-66.4:1.
Penalty.
Failure of lien creditor to timely deliver, §55-66.3.
Permissibility, §55-66.4.
Recordation, §55-66.6.
Cities and counties using microfilm, marginal notations, §17.1-228.
Placement on grantor index, §55-66.4:2.
Releases by financial institutions, §55-66.3:1.
Settlement agent or title insurance company releasing deed of trust, §55-66.3.
Subsequent holders of lien.
Requirements, §55-66.3.
Time requirement for lien creditor to issue, §55-66.3.
Court releases, §55-66.5.
Definitions, §55-66.3.
Financial institution releases, §55-66.3:1.
Marginal releases, §55-66.4.

MORTGAGES AND DEEDS OF TRUST —Cont'd
Release —Cont'd
Original grantor rather living or dead, §55-66.2.
Recording in deed book, §17.1-227.
Satisfaction of mortgage.
General provisions, §§55-66.8 to 55-66.14.
Settlement agent or title insurance company, §55-66.3.
Affidavit, §55-66.3.
Certificate of satisfaction, §55-66.3.
Filing, §55-66.3.
Wrongful or erroneous certificate executed and filed, §55-66.3.
Damages.
Wrongful or erroneous certificate executed and filed, §55-66.3.
Notice of intent delivered to lien creditor, §55-66.3.
Optional method, §55-66.3.
Religious organizations, §§57-14 to 57-15.1.
Request for payoff amount.
Property owner entitled to, §6.2-418.
Reverse mortgages.
Banks, investment in, §6.2-881.
Rights of parties, §55-59.
Rule of 78, §6.2-403.
Applicability, §6.2-405.
Notice on loan or sale on credit using method, §6.2-402.
Prohibition on use, §6.2-404.
Rebate of unearned interest, §§6.2-402 to 6.2-404.
Rule of 78's.
Notice on loan or sale on credit using method, §6.2-402.
Sales.
Account of sales under deed, §64.2-1309.
Advertisements before, §55-59.2.
Construction of compliance requirements, §55-63.
Advertisements' contents, §55-59.3.
Assumption of loan.
Disclosure of terms of assumption, §6.2-419.
Deeds of release.
Execution and deliverance, §§55-59.4, 55-64.
Evidences of indebtedness placed on equal footing, §55-60.1.
Maturity date absent from deed of trust, §55-61.
Notice before, §55-59.1.
Advertisements, §§55-59.2, 55-63.
Form, §55-62.
Notice of sale under deed of trust, §15.2-979.
Notice that debt is subject to call or modification upon conveyance, §6.2-417.
Postponement of sales.
Notice, §55-59.2.
Prepayment penalties.
No collection in certain cases, §6.2-420.
Provisions authorizing absent, §55-61.
Validation of conveyance, §55-61.1.
Title not affected by nonlisting for taxation, §55-64.1.
Trustee powers and duties, §55-59.4.
Validation of certain sales, §§55-65 to 55-66.
Satisfaction, §§55-66.8 to 55-66.14.
Applicability of procedure, §55-66.8.
Definitions, §55-66.9.
Document of rescission, §55-66.10.
Document of rescission, §55-66.10.
Effect, §55-66.12.
Electronic signatures in global and national commerce act.
Relation of provisions to federal act, §55-66.13.

MORTGAGES AND DEEDS OF TRUST —Cont'd
Satisfaction —Cont'd
Form, §55-66.12.
Release, §55-66.3.
Submission for recording.
Failure to submit, liability, §55-66.11.
Secured creditor to submit, §55-66.11.
Wrongful recording, liability, §55-66.10.
Savings banks.
Real estate loans, §6.2-1187.
Savings institutions.
Power to encumber property, §6.2-1111.
Real estate loans generally, §§6.2-1179 to 6.2-1185.
Trustees on loans secured by deed of trust, §6.2-1185.
Scrivener's act, §17.1-223.
Second or subsequent mortgage or deed of trust.
Certain mortgages not to prohibit, §6.2-416.
Security trusts, §55-58.1.
Settlement agents.
Release of deed of trust, §55-66.3.
Statute of limitations.
Enforcement of lien, §8.01-241.
Extension of limitation forms, §8.01-241.1.
Enforcement of liens, §8.01-241.
Limitation of enforcement.
Extension of limitation form, §8.01-241.1.
No maturity date given, §8.01-242.
Unpaid purchase money.
No maturity date given, §8.01-242.
Subordinate mortgage loans.
Certain mortgages not to prohibit, §6.2-416.
Defined, §55-58.3.
Insurance requirements, §6.2-411.
Interest.
Contract rate more than legal rate, §6.2-327.
Loan fees and charges, §6.2-328.
Prepayment, §6.2-423.
Rebates.
Applicability, §6.2-405.
Rule of 78, §§6.2-402 to 6.2-404.
Rebates for unearned interest.
Applicability, §6.2-405.
Rule of 78, §§6.2-402 to 6.2-404.
Refinance mortgages, priority, §55-58.3.
Surname of individual to be underscored or written in capital letters, §17.1-223.
Surveyors.
Borrowers not required to employ particular surveyor, §6.2-410.
Telephone cooperatives, §56-496.
Title insurance companies.
Release of deed of trust, §55-66.3.
Transfers.
Nonprobate transfers on death, §64.2-620.
Protection, transferees of debt secured by real estate, §55-66.01.
Real property transfer on death act, §§64.2-621 to 64.2-638.
See REAL PROPERTY TRANSFER ON DEATH ACT.
Transfer fee covenants, effect of, §55-70.2.
Trust companies.
Powers as trustees, §§6.2-820, 6.2-1002.
Trustees.
Sale powers and duties, §55-59.4.
Substitute trustees, §55-59.
Unpaid purchase money.
Limitation of actions.
No maturity date given, §8.01-242.

MORTGAGES AND DEEDS OF TRUST —Cont'd
Website access to property tax bills, §58.1-3912.
Widows purchasing real property.
Servicemen's readjustment act of 1944, eligibility for guaranty of credit, §11-8.
Wrap-around mortgages.
Insurance companies investments, §38.2-1435.

MORTICIANS.
Burial society contracts with forbidden, §38.2-4022.
Licensing generally, §§54.1-2800 to 54.1-2825.

MOSQUES.
See CHURCHES AND OTHER PLACES OF WORSHIP.

MOSQUITO CONTROL DISTRICTS, §§32.1-187 to 32.1-197.
Vector control, §32.1-247.

MOST WORSHIPFUL PRINCE HALL GRAND LODGE OF VIRGINIA.
Special license plates, §46.2-746.7.

MOTELS.
Baggage, removal while lien exists, §18.2-188.
Deaf and hearing-impaired.
Smoke detectors, §36-99.5.
Defrauding, §18.2-188.
Digital media purchase or rental fee.
Collection, §58.1-1732.
Disposition of proceeds, §58.1-1733.
Imposition, §58.1-1731.
Liens of keepers, §43-31.
Appeals, §43-36.
Enforcement, §43-34.
Sales of personal property, §43-37.
Proceeds distributions, §43-39.
Subsequent payment of surplus proceeds, §43-40.
Withdrawal from sale upon payment of charges, §43-38.
Validity, §43-35.
Obtaining service without payment, §18.2-188.
Peeping or spying, §18.2-130.
Real property tax exemptions.
Rehabilitated, renovated or replacement structures, §58.1-3220.1.
Rehabilitated, renovated or replacement structures.
Real property tax exemptions, §58.1-3220.1.
Retail sales and use tax.
Service exemptions, §58.1-609.5.
Smoke detectors.
Deaf and hearing-impaired, §36-99.5.
Locality requiring, §15.2-922.
Transient occupancy tax, §§58.1-3819 to 58.1-3826.
See TRANSIENT OCCUPANCY TAX.

MOTHERHOOD AND APPLE PIE DAY, §2.2-3303.

MOTHER'S DAY.
Display of flags, §2.2-3304.

MOTION PICTURES.
Audiovisual recording of motion picture in commercial theater.
Unlawful, penalty, detention of person by owner, §18.2-187.2.
Drive-in theaters.
County regulating motion pictures shown at, §15.2-1222.

MOTION PICTURES —Cont'd
Fair competition, §§59.1-255 to 59.1-260.
Bidding.
Blind bidding, §59.1-258.
Procedures, §59.1-259.
Citation of chapter, §59.1-255.
Defined terms, §59.1-257.
Enforcement of provisions, §59.1-260.
Provision violations.
Remedies, §59.1-260.
Purpose, §59.1-256.
Income tax.
Motion picture production tax credit, §58.1-439.12:03.
Motor vehicles.
Display of obscene materials which can be seen from outside of the vehicle, §46.2-1077.01.
Viewing motion pictures or similar displays while driving, §46.2-1077.
Obscenity and related offenses generally, §§18.2-372 to 18.2-388.
See OBSCENITY AND RELATED OFFENSES.
Previews of certain motion pictures, misdemeanor for showing, §18.2-386.
Retail sales and use tax.
Media-related exemptions, §58.1-609.6.
Theaters.
See THEATERS.

MOTIONS.
Amended pleadings.
Relation back to original pleading, §8.01-6.
Anonymous plaintiff.
Motion for identification, factors considered, §8.01-15.1.
Bail, increase of bond amount, §19.2-132.
Bill of particulars.
Criminal cases before general district courts.
Time for motion, §16.1-69.25:1.
Briefs.
Size of paper, VA SCt Rule 1:16.
Circuit courts.
Civil actions.
Responsive pleadings, VA SCt Rule 3:8.
Computation of time.
Prescribed amount of time to perform act before motion or proceeding, §1-210.
Costs on motion, §17.1-609.
Court of appeals.
Form, VA SCt Rule 5A:4.
Writing and filing requirements, VA SCt Rule 5A:2.
Criminal cases.
Motions for trial, VA SCt Rule 3A:9.
Newly discovered or untested evidence.
Scientific analysis, §19.2-327.1.
Dismissal of indictment, VA SCt Rule 3A:5.
Exclusion of illegally seized evidence.
Written pretrial motion, §19.2-266.2.
Expungement of court records.
Juvenile records, §16.1-306.
Frivolous actions.
Oral motions.
Attorney's representation, §8.01-271.1.
Signing pleading motions.
Attorney's certificate, §8.01-271.1.
Indictment, faulty counts.
Striking, §19.2-291.
Judgment, motions for.
See MOTIONS FOR JUDGMENT.

MOTIONS —Cont'd
Juvenile and domestic relations district courts.
Motion to reduce support arrearages to judgment.
Service of notice, process and other papers, VA SCt Rule 8:4.
Misnomer.
Amending pleading to correct misnomer, §8.01-6.
Motions practice, VA SCt Rule 4:15.
New trial.
District court civil case.
Hearings on, §16.1-97.1.
Nonlawyer not allowed to argue, §16.1-88.03.
Oral motions.
Representations deemed certified, §8.01-271.1.
Pleading in alternative.
Separate trial or motion of party, §8.01-281.
Practice, VA SCt Rule 4:15.
Pretrial motions.
Suppression of evidence.
Writing requirement, §19.2-266.2.
Probating of wills, §64.2-446.
Protective orders.
Preliminary order.
Protection of child's life, health, etc., §16.1-253.
Quash process, §§8.01-277, 8.01-277.1.
Objections to personal jurisdiction, §8.01-277.1.
What constitutes waiver, §8.01-277.1.
Relation back to original pleading, §8.01-6.
Return of seized property, §19.2-60.
Set aside verdict.
Criminal case, VA SCt Rule 3A:15.
Signing of pleadings, §8.01-271.1.
Size of paper, VA SCt Rule 1:16.
Striking pleadings.
See MOTIONS TO STRIKE.
Suppression of evidence.
See MOTIONS TO SUPPRESS EVIDENCE.
Supreme court.
Form, VA SCt Rule 5:6.
Writing and filing requirements, VA SCt Rule 5:4.
Transfer.
General district court, VA SCt Rule 7B:1.
Juvenile and domestic relations district court, VA SCt Rule 8:10.
Wills.
Probate, §64.2-446.

MOTIONS FOR EXPUNGEMENT OF COURT RECORDS.
Juvenile records, §16.1-306.

MOTIONS FOR JUDGMENT.
Abatement of action for want of form.
What defects not to be regarded, §8.01-275.
Amendments, VA SCt Rule 1:8.
Bonds issued by localities.
Judicial determination of validity, §15.2-2651.
Boundary lines.
Motion for judgment to establish boundary lines, §§8.01-179 to 8.01-183.
Corporations preparing without attorney intervention.
District court civil cases, §16.1-88.03.
Defendant's response.
Pleas in abatement.
Judicial discretion, VA SCt Rule 1:9.
District court civil actions brought by, §16.1-81.
Corporations or partnerships preparing without attorney intervention, §16.1-88.03.
Interpleader, §16.1-77.

MOTIONS FOR JUDGMENT —Cont'd
District court civil actions brought by —Cont'd
Service of notice, process and other papers, §16.1-82.
When action deemed brought, §16.1-86.
Ejectment.
Contents, §8.01-135.
Description of premises, §8.01-136.
Several counts and several plaintiffs, §8.01-138.
Endorsement of drafts of orders and decrees.
Electronic filing and service, VA SCt Rule 1:17.
General rules as to pleadings, VA SCt Rule 1:4.
Interpleader in district courts.
Initial pleading, §16.1-77.
Partnerships preparing without attorney intervention.
District court civil cases, §16.1-88.03.
Pleas in abatement.
Judicial discretion, VA SCt Rule 1:9.
Receivers.
Special receivers.
Trial in general district court, §8.01-599.
Service of notice, process and other papers.
District court civil actions, §16.1-82.
Simulation of notice of, §18.2-213.
Size of paper, VA SCt Rule 1:16.
Unlawful entry and detainer.
Motion for judgment in circuit court, §8.01-124.
Venue improperly laid, §8.01-264.

MOTIONS FOR NEW TRIAL.
District court civil cases.
Hearings on, §16.1-97.1.

MOTIONS PRACTICE, VA SCt Rule 4:15.
Briefs.
Filing and service, VA SCt Rule 4:15.
Hearings on motions.
Conduct of hearings, VA SCt Rule 4:15.
Scheduling, VA SCt Rule 4:15.
Notice, VA SCt Rule 4:15.

MOTIONS TO INCREASE AMOUNT OF BAIL BOND, §19.2-132.

MOTIONS TO STRIKE.
Claim fails to state grounds upon which relief may be granted, §8.01-273.
Defensive pleading, §8.01-274.
Unverified pleading, VA SCt Rule 1:10.
Effect of court overruling motion, §8.01-282.
Sufficiency of plaintiff's evidence, §8.01-276, VA SCt Rule 1:10.
Criminal cases, VA SCt Rules 1:10, 3A:15.
Depositions as basis, §8.01-420.
Renewal of motion upon hung jury, VA SCt Rule 1:11.
Unverified pleading, VA SCt Rule 1:10.

MOTIONS TO SUPPRESS EVIDENCE.
Objections raised before trial, §19.2-266.2.
Pretrial motions.
Writing requirement, §19.2-266.2.
Return of seized property and suppression, §19.2-60.
Wiretapping.
Contents of intercepted communication, §19.2-68.
Writing requirement.
Pretrial motions, §19.2-266.2.

MOTIONS TO TRANSFER.
Venue.
General district courts, VA SCt Rule 7B:1.

MOTIONS TO TRANSFER —Cont'd
Venue —Cont'd
Juvenile and domestic relations district courts, VA SCt Rule 8:10.

MOTION TO DISMISS.
Indictments, VA SCt Rule 3A:5.

MOTION TO QUASH PROCESS.
Defective process, §§8.01-277, 8.01-277.1.
Objections to personal jurisdiction, §8.01-277.1.
What constitutes waiver, §8.01-277.1.

MOTION TO REFER TO WORKERS' COMPENSATION COMMISSION.
Birth-related neurological injury compensation act.
Determining whether action satisfies, §8.01-273.1.

MOTION TO SET ASIDE VERDICT.
Criminal cases, VA SCt Rule 3A:15.

MOTION TO STRIKE FAULTY COUNT IN INDICTMENT, §19.2-291.

MOTORBOAT AND WATER SAFETY FUND.
Boat registration and identification fees, §29.1-701.

MOTORBOATS.
Boat dealers generally, §§29.1-800 to 29.1-827.
See BOAT DEALERS.
Boating safety, §§29.1-734 to 29.1-746.
Boating under the influence, §§29.1-738.1 to 29.1-738.3.
Involuntary manslaughter, §18.2-36.2.
Boat registration and identification, §§29.1-700 to 29.1-711.
Boats and other watercraft generally.
See BOATS AND OTHER WATERCRAFT.
Boat titling certificates, §§29.1-712 to 29.1-733.1.
Uniform certificate of title for watercraft, §§29.1-733.2 to 29.1-733.29.
Slacking speed and controlling wakes near structures, §29.1-744.3.
Watercraft sales and use tax, §§58.1-1400 to 58.1-1410.
See WATERCRAFT SALES AND USE TAX.

MOTOR CARRIER ROLLING STOCK TAX, §§58.1-2652 to 58.1-2659.
See PUBLIC SERVICE CORPORATION TAXATION.

MOTOR CARRIERS.
Passengers.
See MOTOR CARRIERS, PASSENGERS.
Property.
See MOTOR CARRIERS, PROPERTY.

MOTOR CARRIERS, PASSENGERS, §§46.2-2000 to 46.2-2099.44.
Abandonment.
License, permit or certificate.
Notice of abandonment, §46.2-2011.14.
Advertising.
Limitations on advertising by licensees, permittees and certificate holders, §46.2-2011.10.
Taxicabs.
Limitations on advertising, §46.2-2060.
Baggage.
Authority to transport baggage of passengers, §46.2-2011.12.
Common carriers.
Duties of carriers, §46.2-2088.

MOTOR CARRIERS, PASSENGERS —Cont'd
Baggage —Cont'd
Stowing, §46.2-2011.13.
Brokers, §§46.2-2099.17 to 46.2-2099.19.
Certificates.
Licensing no substitute for certificates, §46.2-2099.19.
Defined, §46.2-2000.
Licenses.
Certificates not substituted for by licensing, §46.2-2099.19.
Requirement of license, §46.2-2099.18.
Regulation of brokers, §46.2-2099.17.
Car pools.
Exclusions, §46.2-2000.1.
Certificate of fitness.
Contract passenger carriers.
Requirement of certificate, §46.2-2096.
Defined, §46.2-2000.
Nonemergency medical transportation carriers, §46.2-2099.44.
Sight-seeing carriers.
Requirement of certificate, §46.2-2099.4.
Certificate of public convenience and necessity.
Common carriers.
Adequate service existing, §46.2-2078.
Applications, §46.2-2076.
Factors considered, §46.2-2077.
Interstate highway operations, §46.2-2079.
Irregular route certificates, §46.2-2080.
Required certificate, §46.2-2075.
Defined, §46.2-2000.
Services.
Holders to provide service under terms of certificate, §46.2-2011.7.
Transfers, §46.2-2011.8.
Certificates.
Abandonment.
Notice, §46.2-2011.14.
Advertising.
Limitations on advertising by licensees, permittees and certificate holders, §46.2-2011.10.
Altering terms of license, permit or certificate, §46.2-2011.25.
Applications, §46.2-2001.3.
Action without hearing, §46.2-2005.
Hearings, §46.2-2005.
Baggage.
Authority to transport baggage of passengers, §46.2-2011.12.
Bonds, surety or other security, §46.2-2011.9.
Brokers.
Licensing no substitute for certificates, §46.2-2099.19.
Defined, §46.2-2000.
Denial or discipline.
Grounds, §46.2-2011.24.
Procedure, §46.2-2011.26.
Relicensing after discipline, §46.2-2011.28.
Surrender of plates, markers, registration cards, etc., §46.2-2011.29.
Duration, §46.2-2011.3.
Excursion trains.
Application and certification process, §46.2-2099.41.
Expiration, §46.2-2011.3.
Fees, §46.2-2011.5.
Issuance, §46.2-2005.1.
Criteria, §46.2-2011.

MOTOR CARRIERS, PASSENGERS —Cont'd
Certificates —Cont'd
Negligence.
Provisions not to relieve licensees, permittees or certificate holders from liability, §46.2-2011.17.
Place of business of certificate holders.
Requirements, §46.2-2011.11.
Reinstatement, §46.2-2011.27.
Renewal, §46.2-2011.3.
Applications, §46.2-2001.3.
Self-insurers.
Unfair claims settlement practices.
Violations by self-insurers jeopardize certificate or permit, §46.2-2056.
Services.
Holders to provide service under terms of certificate, §46.2-2011.7.
Temporary authority, §46.2-2011.1.
Emergencies, §46.2-2011.2.
Charter buses.
Defined, §46.2-2000.
Citations.
Registration and identification markers.
Prohibited acts, §46.2-2011.21.
Common carriers.
Abandonment or deviation of service, §46.2-2085.
Applicability of provisions, §46.2-2074.
Baggage.
Duties of carriers, §46.2-2088.
Certificate of public convenience and necessity.
Adequate service existing, §46.2-2078.
Applications, §46.2-2076.
Factors considered, §46.2-2077.
Interstate highway operations, §46.2-2079.
Irregular route certificates, §46.2-2080.
Required, §46.2-2075.
Defined, §46.2-2000.
Interruption of service, §46.2-2086.
Preferences.
Undue preferences, §46.2-2089.
Rates, fares, etc.
Duties of carriers, §46.2-2088.
Tariffs showing rates, fares, etc., §46.2-2090.
Changes in tariffs, §46.2-2092.
Charging rate other than in tariff, §46.2-2091.
Filing prerequisite to operation, §46.2-2094.
Joint tariffs, §46.2-2093.
Refusal of service, §46.2-2087.
Routes.
Duties of carriers, §46.2-2088.
Safety.
Duties of carriers, §46.2-2088.
Schedules.
Change of schedules.
Process and communication, §46.2-2082.
Requirements, §46.2-2081.
Title page, §46.2-2083.
Taxicabs.
Provisions to not make cabs into common carriers, §46.2-2061.
Terminals.
Local licensing, §46.2-2095.
Undue preferences, §46.2-2089.
Contract bus carriers.
Conversion of certificates, §46.2-2011.4.
Contract carriers.
Certificate of fitness, requirements, §46.2-2096.
Compliance with provisions, §46.2-2099.
Defined, §46.2-2000.
Department regulation, §46.2-2098.

MOTOR CARRIERS, PASSENGERS —Cont'd
Contract carriers —Cont'd
Generally, §§46.2-2096 to 46.2-2099.1.
Specific operating requirements, §46.2-2099.1.
Contract passenger carriers.
Defined, §46.2-2000.
Conversion of certificates.
Contract bus carriers, §46.2-2011.4.
Definitions, §46.2-2000.
Department of motor vehicles.
Altering terms of license, permit or certificate, §46.2-2011.25.
Applications, §46.2-2001.3.
Denial, §46.2-2011.24.
Fees, §46.2-2011.5.
Hearings, §46.2-2005.
Issuance of license, permit or certificate, §46.2-2005.1.
Issues considered, §46.2-2011.
Brokers.
Regulation of brokers, §46.2-2099.17.
Contract carriers.
Regulation, control, etc., §46.2-2098.
Definition of department, §46.2-2000.
Fees collected under chapter.
Disposition, §46.2-2000.3.
Identification markers.
Issuance, §46.2-2001.2.
Inspections.
Authority as to, §46.2-2011.16.
Insurance or bond.
Filing policy, bond, etc., with department, §46.2-2054.
Ratemaking.
Refunds by carriers.
Enforcement by department, §46.2-2011.15.
Records.
Authority as to, §46.2-2011.16.
Regulation of carriers, §46.2-2001.
Reports.
Authority to require, §46.2-2011.16.
Temporary authority, §46.2-2011.1.
Emergencies, §46.2-2011.2.
Discrimination.
Common carriers.
Undue preferences, §46.2-2089.
Department enforcement, §46.2-2001.
Disorderly passengers, §46.2-2011.18.
Ejecting disorderly passengers, §46.2-2011.18.
Emergency temporary authority, §46.2-2011.2.
Employee haulers.
Defined, §46.2-2000.
Permits.
Application, §46.2-2069.
Required, §46.2-2068.
Restrictions on permit, §46.2-2070.
Evasion.
Criminal enforcement, §46.2-2011.22.
Exclusions, §46.2-2000.1.
Excursion trains, §§46.2-2099.41 to 46.2-2099.44.
Assignment of liability, §46.2-2099.42.
Notice on tickets, §46.2-2099.43.
Certification, §46.2-2099.41.
Defined, §46.2-2000.
Liability of operator, §46.2-2099.42.
Notice on tickets, §46.2-2099.43.
Railroad companies.
Use of company facilities, §46.2-2099.42.
Tickets.
Notice on tickets, §46.2-2099.43.

MOTOR CARRIERS, PASSENGERS —Cont'd
Execution of judgments.
Seizure of vehicles, §46.2-2011.19.
Executive sedans generally.
See LIMOUSINES AND EXECUTIVE SEDAN CARRIERS.
Fees.
Disposition of proceeds, §46.2-2000.3.
Licenses, permits and certificates, §46.2-2011.5.
Nonprofit/tax exempt passenger carriers.
Permit filing fee exemptions, §46.2-2073.
Provisions of chapter provide no relief from fees, taxes, etc., §46.2-2011.31.
Reinstatement of licenses, permits and certificates, §46.2-2011.27.
Violations as to.
Fines, §46.2-2011.23.
Financial responsibility.
Criteria for issuance of license, permit or certificate, §46.2-2011.
Defined, §46.2-2000.
Insurance requirements generally, §§46.2-2051 to 46.2-2058.
Fines.
Taxicabs.
Violation of provisions, §46.2-2066.
Violations of chapter, §46.2-2011.22.
Civil enforcement, §46.2-2011.23.
Fishing boats.
Sight-seeing carriers by boat.
Exemptions from provisions, §46.2-2099.21.
Special or charter party by boat.
Exemptions from provisions, §46.2-2099.21.
Government vehicles.
Exclusions, §46.2-2000.1.
Highways.
Defined, §46.2-2000.
Right to use.
Provisions of chapter convey no special rights as to, §46.2-2011.30.
Hotels.
Shuttles operated by.
Exclusions, §46.2-2000.1.
Identification markers.
Applications, §46.2-2001.3.
Defined, §46.2-2000.
Display, §46.2-2001.2.
Issuance, §46.2-2001.2.
Prohibited acts, §46.2-2011.21.
Property of department, §46.2-2011.32.
Surrender of plates, markers, registration cards, etc., upon discipline, §46.2-2011.29.
Unlawful use, §46.2-2011.20.
Inspections.
Department's authority as to inspections, §46.2-2011.16.
Insurance, §§46.2-2051 to 46.2-2058.
Amounts of coverage, §46.2-2053.
Applicability of requirements, §46.2-2051.
Authorized insurers.
Defined, §46.2-2000.
Conditions of coverage, §46.2-2055.
Filing bond, policy, etc., with department, §46.2-2054.
Keeping insurance, bond, etc., in force, §46.2-2052.
Personal injuries.
Conditions of coverage, §46.2-2055.
Policies.
Filing with department, §46.2-2054.

MOTOR CARRIERS, PASSENGERS —Cont'd
Insurance —Cont'd
Property damage.
Conditions of coverage, §46.2-2055.
Registration.
Coverage prerequisite to issuance, §46.2-2053.
Self-insurers.
Unfair claims settlement practices.
Violations by self-insurers jeopardize certificate or permit, §46.2-2056.
Sight-seeing carriers by boat, §46.2-2099.30.
Single state insurance receipts.
Defined, §46.2-2000.
Special or charter party by boat, §46.2-2099.30.
Substitutes for insurance coverage, §46.2-2053.
Taxicabs, §46.2-2057.
Self-insurers, §46.2-2058.
Interruption of service.
Common carriers, §46.2-2086.
Interstate.
Defined, §46.2-2000.
Intrastate.
Defined, §46.2-2000.
Leases.
Department regulation, §46.2-2001.
License plates.
Surrender of plates, markers, registration cards, etc., upon discipline, §46.2-2011.29.
Licenses.
Abandonment.
Notice, §46.2-2011.14.
Advertising.
Limitations on advertising by licensees, permittees and certificate holders, §46.2-2011.10.
Altering terms of license, permit or certificate, §46.2-2011.25.
Applications, §46.2-2001.3.
Hearings, §46.2-2005.
Bonds, surety or other security, §46.2-2011.9.
Brokers.
Certificates not substituted for by licensing, §46.2-2099.19.
Requirement of license, §46.2-2099.18.
Common carriers.
Terminals.
Local licensing, §46.2-2095.
Defined, §46.2-2000.
Denial or discipline.
Grounds, §46.2-2011.24.
Relicensing after discipline, §46.2-2011.28.
Surrender of plates, markers, registration cards, etc., §46.2-2011.29.
Duration, §46.2-2011.3.
Expiration, §46.2-2011.3.
Fees, §46.2-2011.5.
Issuance, §46.2-2005.1.
Criteria, §46.2-2011.
Negligence.
Provisions not to relieve licensees, permittees or certificate holders from liability, §46.2-2011.17.
Place of business of licensees.
Requirements, §46.2-2011.11.
Provisions of chapter provide no relief from fees, taxes, etc., §46.2-2011.31.
Reinstatement, §46.2-2011.27.
Renewal, §46.2-2011.3.
Applications, §46.2-2001.3.
Required to operate, §46.2-2001.1.

MOTOR CARRIERS, PASSENGERS —Cont'd
Licenses —Cont'd
Taxicabs.
Locally regulated, §46.2-2063.
Restrictions on requiring, §46.2-2064.
Lists of vehicles used for rent or hire.
Furnishing list to commissioner, §46.2-107.
Minibuses.
Defined, §46.2-2000.
Motor carriers.
Defined, §46.2-2000.
Motor launches.
Carriers by motor launch.
Defined, §46.2-2000.
Defined, §46.2-2000.
Negligence.
Provisions not to relieve licensees, permittees or certificate holders from liability, §46.2-2011.17.
Nonemergency medical transportation carriers, §46.2-2099.44.
Nonprofit, subsidized entities.
Exclusions, §46.2-2000.1.
Nonprofit/tax exempt passenger carriers.
Defined, §46.2-2000.
Permits, §46.2-2071.
Fee exemptions, §46.2-2073.
Restrictions on operations, §46.2-2072.
Operation.
Contract carriers.
Compliance with provisions, §46.2-2099.
Defined, §46.2-2000.
Fees.
Vehicle fees, §46.2-2011.6.
License, certificate, etc., required, §46.2-2001.1.
Operators.
Defined, §46.2-2000.
Excursion trains.
Liability of operator, §46.2-2099.42.
Permits.
Abandonment.
Notice, §46.2-2011.14.
Advertising.
Limitations on advertising by licensees, permittees and certificate holders, §46.2-2011.10.
Altering terms of license, permit or certificate, §46.2-2011.25.
Applications, §46.2-2001.3.
Defined, §46.2-2000.
Denial or discipline.
Grounds, §46.2-2011.24.
Procedure, §46.2-2011.26.
Relicensing after discipline, §46.2-2011.28.
Surrender of plates, markers, registration cards, etc., §46.2-2011.29.
Duration, §46.2-2011.3.
Employee haulers.
Application, §46.2-2069.
Required, §46.2-2068.
Restrictions on permit, §46.2-2070.
Expiration, §46.2-2011.3.
Fees, §46.2-2011.5.
Issuance, §46.2-2005.1.
Criteria, §46.2-2011.
Negligence.
Provisions not to relieve licensees, permittees or certificate holders from liability, §46.2-2011.17.
Nonprofit/tax exempt passenger carriers, §46.2-2071.
Fee exemptions, §46.2-2073.

MOTOR CARRIERS, PASSENGERS —Cont'd
Permits —Cont'd
Reinstatement, §46.2-2011.27.
Renewal, §46.2-2011.3.
Applications, §46.2-2001.3.
Required to operate, §46.2-2001.1.
Self-insurers.
Unfair claims settlement practices.
Violations by self-insurers jeopardize certificate or permit, §46.2-2056.
Taxicabs.
Requirement of permit, §46.2-2059.
Persons.
Defined, §46.2-2000.
Place of business.
Requirements, §46.2-2011.11.
Ratemaking.
Common carriers.
Duties of carriers, §46.2-2088.
Tariffs showing rates, fares, etc., §46.2-2090.
Changes in tariffs, §46.2-2092.
Charging rate other than in tariff, §46.2-2091.
Filing prerequisite to operation, §46.2-2094.
Joint tariffs, §46.2-2093.
Refunds by carriers.
Enforcement by department, §46.2-2011.15.
Taxicabs.
Locally regulated, §46.2-2062.
Records.
Criminal enforcement of requirements, §46.2-2011.22.
Department's authority as to, §46.2-2011.16.
Fines.
Civil penalties, §46.2-2011.23.
Refusal of service.
Common carriers, §46.2-2087.
Sight-seeing carriers, §46.2-2099.11.
Registration.
Cards.
Property of department, §46.2-2011.32.
Prohibited acts, §46.2-2011.21.
Surrender of plates, markers, registration cards, etc., upon discipline, §46.2-2011.29.
Unlawful use, §46.2-2011.20.
Reports.
Criminal enforcement of requirements, §46.2-2011.22.
Department's authority to require, §46.2-2011.16.
Fines.
Civil penalties, §46.2-2011.23.
Restricted common carriers.
Defined, §46.2-2000.
Ridesharing.
Inapplicability of motor carrier laws, §46.2-1401.
Right to use highways.
Provisions of chapter convey no special rights as to, §46.2-2011.30.
Routes.
Common carriers.
Duties of carriers, §46.2-2088.
Defined, §46.2-2000.
Irregular routes.
Common carriers.
Certificate of public convenience and necessity, §46.2-2080.
Sight-seeing carriers.
Specific routes authorized, §46.2-2099.5.
Rulemaking, §46.2-2001.
Safety.
Common carriers.
Duties of carriers, §46.2-2088.

MOTOR CARRIERS, PASSENGERS —Cont'd
Schedules.
Common carriers.
Change of schedules.
Process and communication, §46.2-2082.
Requirements, §46.2-2081.
Title page of schedule, §46.2-2083.
School transportation.
Exclusions, §46.2-2000.1.
Self-insurers.
Unfair claims settlement practices.
Violations by self-insurers jeopardize certificate or permit, §46.2-2056.
Services.
Certificate holders to provide service under terms of certificate, §46.2-2011.7.
Defined, §46.2-2000.
Sight-seeing carriers.
Certificate of fitness.
Requirement of certificate, §46.2-2099.4.
Defined, §46.2-2000.
Refusal of service, §46.2-2099.11.
Routes.
Specific routes authorized, §46.2-2099.5.
Tickets, §46.2-2099.5.
Sight-seeing carriers by boat.
Defined, §46.2-2000.
Exemptions from provisions, §46.2-2099.21.
Insurance coverage, §46.2-2099.30.
Special or charter party carriers by boat.
Defined, §46.2-2000.
Exemptions from provisions, §46.2-2099.21.
Insurance coverage, §46.2-2099.30.
Taxes.
Nonprofit/tax exempt passenger carriers.
Defined, §46.2-2000.
Permits, §46.2-2071.
Fee exemptions, §46.2-2073.
Restrictions on operations, §46.2-2072.
Provisions of chapter provide no relief from fees, taxes, etc., §46.2-2011.31.
Taxicabs.
Local license taxes, §46.2-2063.
Restrictions on imposition, §46.2-2064.
Taxicabs.
Advertising.
Limitations, §46.2-2060.
Common carriers.
Provisions to not make cabs into common carriers, §46.2-2061.
Criminal enforcement of provisions, §46.2-2066.
Defined, §46.2-2000.
Definition of taxicab or motor vehicle performing taxicab service, §46.2-2000.
Insurance, §46.2-2057.
Licenses.
Locally regulated, §46.2-2063.
Locally regulated.
Exclusions, §46.2-2000.1.
Licensing and license taxation, §46.2-2063.
Restrictions on imposition, §46.2-2064.
Number of cabs, §46.2-2067.
Operator qualifications, §46.2-2065.
Rates, regulations, etc., §46.2-2062.
Stand regulation, §46.2-2065.
Permits.
Requirement, §46.2-2059.
Self-insurers, §46.2-2058.
Temporary authority, §46.2-2011.1.
Emergencies, §46.2-2011.2.

MOTOR CARRIERS, PASSENGERS —Cont'd
Terminals.
Common carriers.
Local licensing, §46.2-2095.
Tickets.
Sight-seeing carriers, §46.2-2099.5.
Transfers of certificates of public convenience and necessity, §46.2-2011.8.
Transportation.
Defined, §46.2-2000.
Transportation districts.
Exclusions, §46.2-2000.1.
Trip sheets.
Contract carriers.
Specific operating requirements, §46.2-2099.1.
Unruly passengers, §46.2-2011.18.
Violations of chapter.
Criminal enforcement, §46.2-2011.22.

MOTOR CARRIERS, PROPERTY, §§46.2-2100 to 46.2-2176.
Advertising.
Household goods carriers.
Liability of carriers, §46.2-2162.
Misleading advertising, §46.2-2133.
Agricultural products.
Exemptions from provisions, §46.2-2101.
Air carriers.
Exemptions from provisions, §46.2-2101.
Authorized insurers.
Defined, §46.2-2100.
Bills of lading.
Household goods carriers, §46.2-2158.
Combination freight bill/bills of lading, §46.2-2159.
Handling of copy and original of bill, §46.2-2160.
Bonds, surety.
Forms of coverage, §46.2-2143.1.
Brokers, §§46.2-2174 to 46.2-2176.
Certificates.
Holding license not to substitute for appropriate certificate or permit, §46.2-2176.
Defined, §46.2-2100.
Licenses.
Holding license not to substitute for appropriate certificate or permit, §46.2-2176.
Requirement of license, §46.2-2175.
Permits.
Holding license not to substitute for appropriate certificate or permit, §46.2-2176.
Regulation by department, §46.2-2174.
Bulk commodities.
Defined, §46.2-2100.
Bulk property carriers.
Defined, §46.2-2100.
Cargo theft, §18.2-147.1.
Certificate of fitness.
Altering or amending, §46.2-2135.
Applications, §46.2-2108.4.
Bond or letter of credit, §46.2-2122.
Fees, §46.2-2120.
Hearing, §46.2-2109.
Brokers.
Holding license not to substitute for appropriate certificate or permit, §46.2-2176.
Defined, §46.2-2100.
Denial.
Grounds, §46.2-2133.
Discipline.
Due process and procedure, §46.2-2136.

MOTOR CARRIERS, PROPERTY —Cont'd
Certificate of fitness —Cont'd
Discipline —Cont'd
Freight bills.
Persistently underestimating, §46.2-2127.
Grounds for imposing, §46.2-2133.
Imposition in lieu of fine, §46.2-2132.
Relicensing after discipline, §46.2-2138.
Surrender of registration, plates, markers, etc., §46.2-2139.
Duration, §46.2-2118.
Expiration, §46.2-2118.
Factors considered, §46.2-2108.6.
Household goods carriers.
Factors considered for issuance, §46.2-2151.
Requirement of certificate, §46.2-2150.
Soliciting business.
Certificate required, §46.2-2156.
Issuance, §46.2-2115.
License taxes.
Compliance with, §46.2-2108.5.
Misrepresentations to obtain.
Fines, §46.2-2132.
Negligence.
Compliance with chapter.
Effect on liability of licensee, permittee or certificate holder, §46.2-2126.
Prerequisite to doing business, §46.2-2108.2.
Reinstatement, §46.2-2137.
Relicensing after discipline, §46.2-2138.
Renewal, §46.2-2118.
Road tax.
Compliance with requirements, §46.2-2108.5.
Self-insurers.
Unfair claims settlement practices jeopardize certificate, §46.2-2146.
Citations.
Identification markers or registration offenses, §46.2-2130.
Civil penalty for certain violations by trucks and tractor trucks, §46.2-613.1.
Attachment and seizure of vehicle for unpaid fees and penalties, §46.2-613.4.
Service of process.
Operator as agent for, §46.2-613.2.
Procedures for issuance and service, §46.2-613.5.
Special processing of penalties, §46.2-613.3.
Compliance with provisions.
Prerequisite to operation, §46.2-2102.
Contracts.
Indemnification provisions in motor carrier transportation contracts.
Certain provisions void, §11-4.5.
Cooperative associations.
Exemptions from provisions, §46.2-2101.
Deceptive business practices, §46.2-2133.
Department of motor vehicles.
Applications, §46.2-2108.4.
Hearing, §46.2-2109.
Brokers.
Regulation by department, §46.2-2174.
Fees.
Disposition of proceeds, §46.2-2108.1.
Household goods carriers.
Ratemaking.
Department's powers as to, §46.2-2155.
Regulation by department, §46.2-2152.
Powers of department as to, §46.2-2155.
Reports, records, etc.
Setting requirements, §46.2-2125.

MOTOR CARRIERS, PROPERTY —Cont'd
Discontinuance of service.
Household goods carriers, §46.2-2154.
Notice, §46.2-2124.
Documents of title.
General provisions, §§8.7-101 to 8.7-603.
See DOCUMENTS OF TITLE.
Emergencies.
Temporary emergency operation, §46.2-2117.
Estimates of costs.
Household goods carriers, §46.2-2157.
Evasion of regulation.
Criminal enforcement, §46.2-2131.
Execution of judgments.
Holding or seizing vehicles, §46.2-2128.
Exemptions from provisions, §46.2-2101.
Fees.
Application and filing fees, §46.2-2120.
Disposition of proceeds, §46.2-2108.1.
Failure to pay, §§46.2-2133, 46.2-2134.
Fines and civil enforcement, §46.2-2132.
Reinstatement of license, permit or certificate, §46.2-2137.
Vehicle fees, §46.2-2121.
Felony convictions, §46.2-2133.
Fertilizer.
Exemptions from provisions, §46.2-2101.
Financial responsibility.
Applicants for license or certificate.
Bond or letter of credit to accompany, §46.2-2122.
Defined, §46.2-2100.
Failure to maintain, §§46.2-2133, 46.2-2134.
Insurance, §§46.2-2141 to 46.2-2146.
Fish.
Requirements to carry and ship, §29.1-540.
Forest products.
Exemptions from provisions, §46.2-2101.
Fraud, §46.2-2133.
Freight bills.
Household goods carriers, §46.2-2159.
Persistently underestimating, §46.2-2127.
Game.
Requirements to carry and ship, §29.1-540.
Government vehicles.
Exemptions from provisions, §46.2-2101.
Highway.
Defined, §46.2-2100.
Household goods.
Defined, §46.2-2100.
Household goods carriers, §§46.2-2149 to 46.2-2173.
Bills of lading, §46.2-2158.
Combination freight bill/bills of lading, §46.2-2159.
Handling of copy and original of bill, §46.2-2160.
Certificate of fitness.
Factors considered for issuance, §46.2-2151.
Requirement of certificate, §46.2-2150.
Soliciting business.
Certificate required, §46.2-2156.
Claims for loss or damage.
Process for handling claims, §46.2-2168.
Conflict of laws.
Motor carriers chapter prevails, §46.2-2153.
Constructive weight, §46.2-2164.
Damaged property.
Claims for loss or damage.
Process for handling claims, §46.2-2168.
Defined, §46.2-2100.

MOTOR CARRIERS, PROPERTY —Cont'd
Household goods carriers —Cont'd
Discontinuance of service, §46.2-2154.
Discounts, §46.2-2161.
Estimates of costs, §46.2-2157.
Exemptions.
Certain household goods carriers from property carriers article, §46.2-2147.
Short distance carriers, §46.2-2149.
Freight bills, §46.2-2159.
Interchange or interline shipments, §46.2-2156.
Liability of carriers, §46.2-2162.
Lost property.
Claims for loss or damage.
Process for handling claims, §46.2-2168.
Minimum weight shipments, §46.2-2166.
Rates, charges, etc.
Department's powers as to, §46.2-2155.
Discounts, §46.2-2161.
Payment prior to delivery of possession, §46.2-2161.
Reweighing charges, §46.2-2167.
Tariffs showing rates, charges, etc., §46.2-2169.
Change in tariff, §46.2-2171.
Charges to conform to tariff, §46.2-2170.
Contents, §46.2-2173.
Joint tariff, §46.2-2172.
Regulation by department, §46.2-2152.
Powers of department as to, §46.2-2155.
Reweighing, §46.2-2167.
Short distance carriers.
Exemptions, §46.2-2149.
Soliciting business.
Certificate required, §46.2-2156.
Storage-in-transit arrangements, §46.2-2156.
Weight.
Constructive weight, §46.2-2164.
Minimum weight shipments, §46.2-2166.
Process to determine weight, §46.2-2163.
Reweighing, §46.2-2167.
Tickets.
Obtaining weight tickets, §46.2-2165.
Identification markers.
Considered property of department, §46.2-2140.
Criminal enforcement, §46.2-2130.
Defined, §46.2-2100.
Display, §46.2-2108.3.
Insurance, bond, etc., required, §46.2-2143.
Issuance, §46.2-2108.3.
Surrender when disciplined, §46.2-2139.
Unlawful use, §46.2-2129.
Inactivity, §§46.2-2133, 46.2-2134.
Indemnification.
Motor carrier transportation contracts.
Certain indemnification provisions void, §11-4.5.
Insurance, §§46.2-2141 to 46.2-2146.
Amount of coverage, §46.2-2143.1.
Applicability of requirements, §46.2-2141.
Conditions of coverage, §46.2-2145.
Entities covered, §46.2-2145.
Failure to maintain coverage, §§46.2-2133, 46.2-2134.
Filing policies, bonds, etc., with department, §46.2-2144.
Forms of coverage, §46.2-2143.1.
Keeping in force, §46.2-2142.
Policies.
Filing with department, §46.2-2144.
Prerequisite to registration, identification markers, plates, etc., §46.2-2143.

MOTOR CARRIERS, PROPERTY —Cont'd
Insurance —Cont'd
Self-insurers.
Unfair claims settlement practices, §46.2-2146.
Interchange or interline shipments.
Household goods carriers, §46.2-2156.
Interstate.
Defined, §46.2-2100.
Intrastate.
Defined, §46.2-2100.
Judgments.
Execution of judgments.
Holding or seizing vehicles, §46.2-2128.
Licenses.
Altering or amending, §46.2-2135.
Applications, §46.2-2108.4.
Bond or letter of credit, §46.2-2122.
Fees, §46.2-2120.
Hearing, §46.2-2109.
Brokers.
Holding license not to substitute for appropriate certificate or permit, §46.2-2176.
Requirement of license, §46.2-2175.
Defined, §46.2-2100.
Denial.
Grounds, §46.2-2133.
Discipline.
Due process and procedure, §46.2-2136.
Grounds, §46.2-2133.
Imposition in lieu of fine, §46.2-2132.
Relicensing after discipline, §46.2-2138.
Surrender of registration, plates, markers, etc., §46.2-2139.
Expiration, §46.2-2118.
Factors considered, §46.2-2108.6.
Issuance, §46.2-2115.
License taxes.
Compliance with, §46.2-2108.5.
Misrepresentations to obtain.
Fines, §46.2-2132.
Negligence.
Compliance with chapter.
Effect on liability of licensee, permittee or certificate holder, §46.2-2126.
Prerequisite to doing business, §46.2-2108.2.
Reinstatement, §46.2-2137.
Relicensing after discipline, §46.2-2138.
Renewal, §46.2-2118.
Road tax.
Compliance with requirements, §46.2-2108.5.
License taxes.
Licensees, permittees and certificate holders.
Licensing for payment of tax, §46.2-2108.5.
Lists of vehicles used for rent or hire.
Furnishing list to commissioner, §46.2-107.
Livestock.
Exemptions from provisions, §46.2-2101.
Motor carriers.
Defined, §46.2-2100.
Motor vehicles.
Defined, §46.2-2100.
Negligence.
Compliance with chapter.
Effect on liability of licensee, permittee or certificate holder, §46.2-2126.
Motor carrier transportation contracts.
Certain indemnification provisions void, §11-4.5.
Newspaper carriers.
Exemptions from provisions, §46.2-2101.
Operation.
Compliance with provisions required, §46.2-2102.

MOTOR CARRIERS, PROPERTY —Cont'd
Operation —Cont'd
Temporary emergency operation, §46.2-2117.
Permits.
Altering or amending, §46.2-2135.
Applications, §46.2-2108.4.
Brokers.
Holding license not to substitute for appropriate certificate or permit, §46.2-2176.
Defined, §46.2-2100.
Denial.
Grounds, §46.2-2134.
Discipline.
Due process and procedure, §46.2-2136.
Grounds, §46.2-2134.
Imposition in lieu of fine, §46.2-2132.
Relicensing after discipline, §46.2-2138.
Surrender of registration, plates, markers, etc., §46.2-2139.
Duration, §46.2-2118.
Expiration, §46.2-2118.
Factors considered, §46.2-2108.6.
Issuance, §46.2-2115.
License taxes.
Compliance with, §46.2-2108.5.
Misrepresentations to obtain.
Fines, §46.2-2132.
Negligence.
Compliance with chapter.
Effect on liability of licensee, permittee or certificate holder, §46.2-2126.
Prerequisite to doing business, §46.2-2108.2.
Property carriers, §46.2-2148.
Reinstatement, §46.2-2137.
Relicensing after discipline, §46.2-2138.
Renewal, §46.2-2118.
Road tax.
Compliance with requirements, §46.2-2108.5.
Self-insurers.
Unfair claims settlement practices jeopardize certificate, §46.2-2146.
Person.
Defined, §46.2-2100.
Petroleum tank truck carriers.
Employee liens, §§43-24 to 43-26.
Not required to incorporate as public service companies, §13.1-620.
Public service companies generally, §§56-1 to 56-87.
See PUBLIC SERVICE COMPANIES.
Supplier liens, §§43-24 to 43-26.
Property carriers, §§46.2-2147, 46.2-2148.
Defined, §46.2-2100.
Exemptions from article, §46.2-2147.
Household goods carriers.
Exemption of certain household goods carriers from property carriers article, §46.2-2147.
Permits, §46.2-2148.
Property taxes on rolling stock.
Local taxation prohibited, §58.1-2658.
Ratemaking.
Household goods carriers.
Department's powers as to, §46.2-2155.
Discounts, §46.2-2161.
Payment prior to delivery of possession, §46.2-2161.
Reweighing charges, §46.2-2167.
Tariffs showing rates, charges, etc., §46.2-2169.
Change in tariff, §46.2-2171.
Charges to conform to tariff, §46.2-2170.
Contents, §46.2-2173.

MOTOR CARRIERS, PROPERTY —Cont'd
Ratemaking —Cont'd
Household goods carriers —Cont'd
Tariffs showing rates, charges, etc. —Cont'd
Joint tariff, §46.2-2172.
Records.
Authority of department as to, §46.2-2125.
Fines and criminal enforcement, §46.2-2131.
Registration.
Cards considered property of department, §46.2-2140.
Criminal enforcement, §46.2-2130.
Failure to properly register, §46.2-2133.
Insurance, bond, etc., required, §46.2-2143.
Surrender when disciplined, §46.2-2139.
Unlawful use, §46.2-2129.
Reports.
Authority of department as to, §46.2-2125.
Fines and civil enforcement, §46.2-2132.
Fines and criminal enforcement, §46.2-2131.
Restricted common carriers.
Defined, §46.2-2100.
Road tax.
Licensees, permittees and certificate holders.
Registration, §46.2-2108.5.
Seafood.
Bill of lading, §28.2-824.
Removal from condemned areas, §§28.2-810 to 28.2-815.
Self-insurers.
Unfair claims settlement practices, §46.2-2146.
Services.
Defined, §46.2-2100.
Discontinuance of service.
Household goods carriers, §46.2-2154.
Notice, §46.2-2124.
Failure to provide, §46.2-2133.
Shellfish.
Bill of lading requirement, §28.2-824.
Removal from condemned areas.
Sealing of motor vehicles, §28.2-812.
Single state insurance receipt.
Defined, §46.2-2100.
Solid waste management.
Exemptions from provisions, §46.2-2101.
Storage-in-transit arrangements.
Household goods carriers, §46.2-2156.
Taxes.
Failure to pay, §§46.2-2133, 46.2-2134.
Temporary emergency operation, §46.2-2117.
Transportation.
Defined, §46.2-2100.
Vehicle fees, §46.2-2121.
Violations of provisions.
Fines and civil enforcement, §46.2-2132.
Fines and criminal enforcement, §46.2-2131.
Water carriers.
Exemptions from provisions, §46.2-2101.
Weight.
Constructive weight.
Defined, §46.2-2100.
Gross weight.
Defined, §46.2-2100.
Household goods carriers.
Constructive weight, §46.2-2164.
Minimum weight shipments, §46.2-2166.
Process to determine weight, §46.2-2163.
Reweighing, §46.2-2167.
Tickets.
Obtaining weight tickets, §46.2-2165.

MOTOR CARRIERS, PROPERTY —Cont'd
Weight —Cont'd
Net weight.
Defined, §46.2-2100.
Tare weight.
Defined, §46.2-2100.
Workers' compensation.
Noncompliance with provisions, §46.2-2133.

MOTOR CARRIERS ROAD TAX, §§58.1-2700 to 58.1-2712.2.
Amount of tax, §58.1-2701.
Assistance of department of taxation, §58.1-2711.
Cooperative agreements between states, §§46.2-703, 58.1-2712.1.
Credit for payment of diesel fuel tax, §58.1-2706.
Credit for payment of liquefied gases tax, §58.1-2706.
Credit for payment of motor fuel tax, §58.1-2706.
False statements, §58.1-2710.
Definitions, §58.1-2700.
Exemptions and exceptions, §58.1-2702.
False statements, §58.1-2710.
Fuel used in Commonwealth, ascertaining amount, §58.1-2704.
Identification markers, §58.1-2700.1.
Defined, §58.1-2700.
Placement, §58.1-2700.2.
Inspection of books and records, §58.1-2708.
International fuel tax agreement, §58.1-2712.1.
Information exchanges under agreement, §58.1-2712.2.
Licenses, §58.1-2700.1.
Payment, §58.1-2703.
Penalties, §58.1-2709.
Refunds to carriers giving bond, §58.1-2707.
False statements, §58.1-2710.
Reports, §58.1-2705.
Waiver of provisions, §58.1-2700.3.

MOTOR CAR SPORTING EVENT FACILITIES.
ABC license, §4.1-206.
Taxes, §4.1-233.

MOTORCYCLE DEALERS, §§46.2-1993 to 46.2-1993.82.
Advertising.
Civil penalty, §46.2-1993.82.
False advertising, §46.2-1993.75.
Regulated practices, §46.2-1993.81.
Regulations and enforcement, §46.2-1993.82.
VA DLR to be included in advertisement, §46.2-1993.29.
Auctions.
Dealers licensed in another state selling at wholesale auctions in Commonwealth.
Certificate of dealer registration required, §46.2-1993.6.
Inspection not required prior to sale at auctions, §46.2-1993.34.
Audit of records to be maintained, §46.2-1993.21.
Bill of sale.
Completed buyer's order, §46.2-1993.23:1.
Bonding requirements for applicants for license, §46.2-1993.20.
Business hours, §46.2-1993.27.
Buyers order, §46.2-1993.23.

MOTORCYCLE DEALERS —Cont'd
Certificate of qualification.
Dealer-operator, §46.2-1993.19.
Continued operation on loss of certificate, §46.2-1993.11.
Salesperson, §46.2-1993.10.
Certificate of title.
Dealer to obtain on purchase, §46.2-1993.37.
Certificates of ownership.
Temporary certificate delivered to purchaser.
Dealer unable to deliver certificate of origin or certificate of title, §46.2-1993.35.
Certificates of title.
Off-road motorcycles, §§46.2-644.1 to 46.2-644.3.
Cessation of business notice, §46.2-1993.38.
Change in form of ownership, §46.2-1993.15.
Change of location of business, §46.2-1993.13.
Civil penalty for violations, §46.2-1993.5.
Coercing purchaser to provide insurance coverage, §46.2-1993.30.
Commission or compensation paid to person in connection with sale, §46.2-1993.31.
Consignment sales, §46.2-1993.24.
Continued operation on loss of dealer-operator certificate of qualification, §46.2-1993.11.
Definitions, §46.2-1993.
Depositions taken by commissioner of motor vehicles, §46.2-1993.2.
Disclosures by manufacturers and distributors, §46.2-1993.26.
Driver education programs.
Display of dealers license plates, §46.2-1993.52.
Foreign motorcycle dealers plates, display in boarder divisions, §46.2-1993.52.
Immunity of dealer from liability, §46.2-1993.52.
Enjoining violations, §46.2-1993.3.
Family member designated as successor to dealership, §46.2-1993.67.
Fees.
Licenses and registration, §46.2-1993.17.
Manual transaction fee, §46.2-1993.23:2.
On-line systems filing fee, §46.2-1993.23:1.
Financing arranged by dealer.
Notice in buyer's order, §46.2-1993.23.
Foreign dealers license plates, operation under, §46.2-1993.51.
Franchises, §§46.2-1993.64 to 46.2-1993.74.
Additional franchise granted in relevant market areas, §46.2-1993.67.
Civil penalties, §46.2-1993.73.
Coercion of dealers by manufacturers or distributors, §§46.2-1993.66, 46.2-1993.67.
Discontinuation of distributor, §46.2-1993.69.
Distinction between dealer plates, §46.2-1993.42.
Distributors discontinuation, §46.2-1993.69.
Exemption from retail franchising act, §46.2-1993.65.
Family member, designated successor to dealership, §46.2-1993.67.
Filing, §46.2-1993.64.
Hearings and other remedies, §46.2-1993.73.
Late model and factory repurchase franchises, §46.2-1993.74.
Manufacturer operating dealership, §46.2-1993.71.
New, mended, modified, etc., franchises.
Filing, §46.2-1993.64.
Operation of dealerships by manufacturer, §46.2-1993.71.
Retail franchising act.
Exemption, §46.2-1993.65.

MOTORCYCLE DEALERS —Cont'd
Franchises —Cont'd
Sale or transfer of dealership, §46.2-1993.67.
First refusal by manufacturer or distributor, §46.2-1993.68.
Service facilities ownership, §46.2-1993.72.
Termination, cancellation or refusal, §46.2-1993.67.
Fairness, §46.2-1993.67:1.
Involuntary discontinuation, cancellation or nonrenewal, §46.2-1993.67:2.
Repurchase of vehicles, parts and equipment, §46.2-1993.67:2.
When unfair, §46.2-1993.67:1.
Two year waiting period for replacing franchise dealer, §46.2-1993.67.
Warranty obligations of manufacturer, factory branch, distributor or distributor branch, §46.2-1993.70.
Hours of business, §46.2-1993.27.
Immunity of dealers.
License plates of dealers displayed by Virginia schools systems in driver education programs, §46.2-1993.52.
Independent dealers.
Distinction between types of dealer plates, §46.2-1993.42.
Inspection of vehicles prior to sale, §46.2-1993.33.
Not required of certain sellers, §46.2-1993.34.
Insurance.
Coercing purchaser to provide, §46.2-1993.30.
Jurisdiction of courts, §46.2-1993.3.
Late model and factory repurchase franchises, §46.2-1993.74.
License, §§46.2-1993.6 to 46.2-1993.19.
Addition or deletion of franchise, §46.2-1993.15.
Addition or deletion of partner, §46.2-1993.15.
Appeals, §§46.2-1993.78, 46.2-1993.79.
Application, §46.2-1993.7.
Bonding requirements, §46.2-1993.20.
Certificate of qualification for dealer-operator required for issuance, §46.2-1993.9.
Continued operation after loss of certificate, §46.2-1993.11.
Certificate of qualification for salesperson required for issuance, §46.2-1993.10.
Change in form of ownership, §46.2-1993.15.
Change in name of dealer, §46.2-1993.15.
Change of licensed location, §46.2-1993.13.
Collection of fees, §46.2-1993.18.
Corporations officers or directors, responsibility for acts of, §46.2-1993.75.
Denial, suspension and revocation.
Hearing, §§46.2-1993.12, 46.2-1993.17.
Display, §46.2-1993.13.
Salespersons license, §46.2-1993.16.
Equitable remedies.
Not impaired, §46.2-1993.80.
Established place of business required for issuing, §46.2-1993.8.
Expiration, §46.2-1993.19.
Fee, §46.2-1993.17.
Franchiser license required, §46.2-1993.6.
Grounds, §46.2-1993.76.
Information required in application, §46.2-1993.7.
Location of place of business specified, §46.2-1993.13.
Multi-year licenses, §46.2-1993.19.
Nonresident dealer selling at wholesale auctions in Commonwealth.
Certificate of dealer registration required, §46.2-1993.6.

MOTORCYCLE DEALERS —Cont'd
License —Cont'd
Nonresident licensed dealers, fee, §46.2-1993.17.
Partnerships officers or directors, responsibility for acts of, §46.2-1993.75.
Permanent supplemental license, §46.2-1993.14.
Prerequisite to issuance of dealer license plates, §46.2-1993.40.
Renewal, §46.2-1993.19.
Required to engage in business, §46.2-1993.6.
Responsibility of partnership or corporations.
Officers or directors of acts, §46.2-1993.75.
Salesperson to display license, §46.2-1993.16.
Supplemental license, §46.2-1993.14.
Fee, §46.2-1993.17.
Temporary supplemental license, §46.2-1993.14.
Term of license, §46.2-1993.19.
Time for acting on applications, §46.2-1993.12.
License plates, §§46.2-1993.39 to 46.2-1993.63.
Cancellation, §46.2-1993.53.
Criminal penalty, §46.2-1993.54.
Dealer license required before issuance, §46.2-1993.40.
Dealers moving to salesroom, §46.2-1993.50.
Display, §46.2-1993.41.
Distinction between various types of dealers, §46.2-1993.42.
Driver education programs, §46.2-1993.52.
Foreign dealers license, operation under, §46.2-1993.51.
Manufacturer moving to place of shipment or delivery, §46.2-1993.49.
Multi-year license plate, §46.2-1993.41.
Newly purchased motorcycles.
Use of plates on, §46.2-1993.47.
Operation without license plate, dealer permitting, §46.2-1993.48.
Promotional license plates, §46.2-1993.43.
Reissuance after cancellation, §46.2-1993.53.
Removal by department of motor vehicles, §46.2-1993.53.
Required before commencing operation, §46.2-1993.39.
Revocation by commissioner of motor vehicles, §46.2-1993.40.
Temporary license plates issued by dealers, §§46.2-1993.55 to 46.2-1993.63.
Alternative print-on-demand program, §46.2-1993.55:1.
Application, §§46.2-1993.55, 46.2-1993.57.
Bona fide purchasers or owners, issuance to, §46.2-1993.58.
Criminal penalty, §46.2-1993.63.
Destruction of plates on expiration, §46.2-1993.61.
Expiration, §46.2-1993.62.
Forward of application for current title and registration, §46.2-1993.58.
Identification number of vehicle, §46.2-1993.59.
Insertion of dealer's name, date of issuance and expiration, §46.2-1993.59.
Inspection of records by department of motor vehicles, §46.2-1993.56.
Issuance, §46.2-1993.55.
Misstatement and false information, §46.2-1993.58.
Records to be kept by dealers, §46.2-1993.56.
Refunds or credit prohibited, §46.2-1993.62.
Suspension of right of dealer to issue, §46.2-1993.60.
To whom plates issued, §46.2-1993.58.

MOTORCYCLE DEALERS —Cont'd
License plates —Cont'd
Term of plates, §46.2-1993.41.
Transferable dealer plates, §46.2-1993.41.
Transport plates.
Temporary transport plates, §§46.2-1993.45, 46.2-1993.46.
Use generally, §46.2-1993.44.
Location of business to be specified in license, §46.2-1993.13.
Manufacturer operating dealership, §46.2-1993.71.
Manufacturers moving motorcycles to place of shipment of delivery.
Permit obtained from local law-enforcement authority, §46.2-1993.49.
Movement by dealers of motorcycles to salesrooms.
Permit obtained from local law-enforcement authorities, §46.2-1993.50.
Newly purchased motorcycles, use of dealer plates on, §46.2-1993.47.
No liability insurance included.
Stamped on bill of sale, §46.2-1993.23:1.
Nonprofit organizations.
Consigning donated motorcycles to dealers.
Certificate authorizing, §46.2-1993.6:1.
Fees, §46.2-1993.17.
Nonresident dealers licensed in another state.
Certificate of dealer registration required for sales at wholesale auctions, §46.2-1993.6.
Fee for dealer licensed in other states, §46.2-1993.17.
Notice of cessation of business, §46.2-1993.38.
Odometer disclosure, §46.2-1993.25.
Off-road motorcycles.
Certificates of title, §§46.2-644.1 to 46.2-644.3.
On-line systems filing fee, §46.2-1993.23:1.
Operation of motorcycle without license plate, §46.2-1993.48.
Place of assembly or manufacture of new motorcycle.
Disclosure by manufacturers and distributors, §46.2-1993.26.
Powers of commissioner of motor vehicles, §§46.2-1993.1, 46.2-1993.2.
Processing fee.
Disclosure of charge, §46.2-1993.23.
Promotional license plates, §46.2-1993.43.
Records required to be maintained, §46.2-1993.22.
Examination by commissioner or authorized representative, §46.2-1993.21.
Temporary license plates of dealers, §46.2-1993.56.
Registration.
Certificate of dealer registration.
Application, §46.2-1993.17.
Certificate of vehicle registration.
Required before commencing operation, §46.2-1993.39.
Regulations promulgated by commissioner of motor vehicles, §46.2-1993.4.
Retail installment sales contracts.
Coercion by manufacturers or distributors, §46.2-1993.66.
Notice in buyers order, §46.2-1993.23.
Sale or transfer of dealership, §46.2-1993.67.
Manufacturer or distributor permitted first right of refusal, §46.2-1993.68.

MOTORCYCLE DEALERS —Cont'd
Sales by salesperson for other than employer, §46.2-1993.32.
Salesperson.
Certificate of qualification, §46.2-1993.10.
Display of license, §46.2-1993.16.
List maintained by dealer, §46.2-1993.16.
Notice of termination, §46.2-1993.16.
Selling for other than employer, §46.2-1993.32.
Service facility ownership, §46.2-1993.72.
Service of summons for license plate violations, §46.2-1993.54.
Signs, §46.2-1993.28.
Soliciting sales through person with pecuniary interest, §46.2-1993.31.
Special orders placed with manufacturer outside Virginia on behalf of customer.
Nonresident of Virginia.
Inspection of motorcycle prior to sale not required, §46.2-1993.34.
Subpoenas by commissioner of motor vehicles, §46.2-1993.2.
Supplemental licenses, §46.2-1993.14.
Temporary certificates of ownership issued to purchaser.
Dealer unable to deliver certificate of title or certificate of origin, §46.2-1993.35.
Temporary license plates issued by dealers, §§46.2-1993.55 to 46.2-1993.63.
Alternative print-on-demand program, §46.2-1993.55:1.
Application, §§46.2-1993.55, 46.2-1993.57.
Criminal penalty, §46.2-1993.63.
Destruction of plates on expiration, §46.2-1993.61.
Expiration, §46.2-1993.62.
Forwarding of application for current title and registration, §46.2-1993.58.
Identification number of vehicle, §46.2-1993.59.
Insertion of dealers name, date of issuance and expiration, §46.2-1993.59.
Issuance, §46.2-1993.55.
Misstatement or false information, §46.2-1993.58.
Records to be kept by dealers, §46.2-1993.56.
Refunds or credit, §46.2-1993.62.
Suspension of right of dealer, §46.2-1993.60.
To whom plates issued, §46.2-1993.58.
Termination of business, notice to department of motor vehicles, §46.2-1993.38.
Transport plates.
Temporary transport plates, §§46.2-1993.45, 46.2-1993.46.
Warranty obligations of manufacturer, factory branch, distributor or distributor branch, §46.2-1993.70.
Witness fees and mileage for attendance at hearings under chapter, §46.2-1993.2.

MOTORCYCLE RIDER SAFETY, §§46.2-1188 to 46.2-1192.
Administrative and reporting requirements, §46.2-1190.4.
Course completion status of participants, §46.2-1190.4.
Curricula requirements, §46.2-1190.1.
Disciplinary action against licensee, §§46.2-1190.5, 46.2-1190.6.
Experienced rider course, §46.2-1190.1.
Fines, §46.2-1190.7.
Instructor qualifications, §46.2-1190.3.
Licenses, issuance and renewal, §46.2-1192.
Novice rider courses, §46.2-1190.1.

MOTORCYCLE RIDER SAFETY —Cont'd
Penalties, §§46.2-1190.5 to 46.2-1190.7.
Regional training centers.
Administrative and reporting requirements, §46.2-1190.4.
Awarding of contracts, §46.2-1192.
Disciplinary action against licensees, §§46.2-1190.5, 46.2-1190.6.
Establishment, §46.2-1190.
Instructor qualifications, §46.2-1190.3.
Requirements and approval, §46.2-1190.2.
Safety equipment for participants, §46.2-1190.1.
Regulatory violations.
Sanctions, §§46.2-1190.5, 46.2-1190.6.
Rulemaking authority, §46.2-1189.
Sidecar and three-wheeled motorcycle course, §46.2-1190.1.
Training courses, §46.2-1188.
Training program fund, §46.2-1191.
Unsafe equipment, authority to designate, §46.2-1190.2.
Verification of participants eligibility, §46.2-1190.4.

MOTORCYCLES.
Auxiliary head lights, §46.2-1012.
Brake lights, §§46.2-1012, 46.2-1014.
Brakes, §46.2-1069.
Certificates of title.
Off-road motorcycles, §§46.2-644.1 to 46.2-644.3.
County, city or town regulating noise, §15.2-919.
Dealers.
Generally, §§46.2-1993 to 46.2-1993.82.
Defined, §46.2-100.
Drivers' licenses.
Endorsements, classifications and restrictions authorizing operation, §46.2-328.
Fee, §46.2-332.
Examination.
Applicants intending to drive, §46.2-328.
Special examination and road test, §46.2-337.
Learners' permits, §46.2-335.
Applications, §46.2-323.
Military members, spouses and dependents.
Issuance of classification by mail, §46.2-328.
Temporary motorcycle classification, completion of safety course, §46.2-328.
Temporary motorcycle classification, §46.2-328.
Driving two abreast in single lane, §46.2-857.
Fines, VA SCt Rule 3B:2.
Maximum fine for violation of title, §46.2-113.
Headlights, §46.2-1012.
Helmet violation, §46.2-910.
High-occupancy lane designation, inapplicability, §33.1-46.2.
Highways, transportation facilities or projects.
Discriminatory actions, policies or regulations as to use prohibited, §33.1-13.1.
Inspection stickers, §46.2-1163.
Learners' permits, §46.2-335.
License plates.
Dealer's license plates, §46.2-1549.
Generally, §§46.2-1993.39 to 46.2-1993.63.
See MOTORCYCLE DEALERS.
Harley-Davidson owners, §46.2-749.8.
Operation without license plate, manufacturer, distributor or dealer permitting, §46.2-1993.48.
Temporary license plates issued by dealers, §§46.2-1993.55 to 46.2-1993.63.
See MOTORCYCLE DEALERS.

MOTORCYCLES —Cont'd
License plates —Cont'd
Transfer of old license plates and registration number.
Owner selling or transferring registered motorcycle, §46.2-1993.36.
Localities regulating noise, §15.2-919.
Maximum fine for violating Title 46.2, §46.2-113.
Military members, spouses and dependents.
Drivers' licenses.
Issuance of classification by mail, §46.2-328.
Temporary motorcycle classification, completion of safety course, §46.2-328.
Motorcycle rider safety training course.
Drivers' licenses.
Completion required, §46.2-337.
Temporary motorcycle classification, §46.2-328.
Waiver of road test portion of special examination, §46.2-337.
Motor vehicle titling.
Motorcycle purchased by manufacturer for parts, documentation, §46.2-626.2.
Mufflers, §46.2-1050.
Noise limitation, §§15.2-919, 46.2-1050.
Off-road motorcycles.
Certificates of title, §§46.2-644.1 to 46.2-644.3.
Personal property taxes.
Classification, §§58.1-3503, 58.1-3504.
Trail systems established by localities.
Authority, protection of property interest and personal liability.
No liability to locality or property owners, §15.2-1809.1.
Authority, protection of property interests and personal liability, §15.2-1806.
Operating without headlight, horn or rearview mirror, §46.2-912.
Fine schedule, VA SCt Rule 3B:2.
Prepayment of fine, §16.1-69.40:1.
Parking two to a space, §46.2-1220.
Personal property taxes.
Classification, §§58.1-3503, 58.1-3504.
Rebuilt vehicles.
Generally, §§46.2-1600 to 46.2-1610.
See SALVAGE VEHICLES.
Red light, proceeding through intersection at, §46.2-833.
Registration requirements.
Dealers required to register vehicles before commencing operation, §46.2-1993.39.
Fee for motorcycle with sidecar, §46.2-694.
Vendors to furnish statements of registration, §46.2-913.
Riding on generally, §46.2-909.
Sale or transfer of registered motorcycle by owner.
Transfer of old license plates and registration number, §46.2-1993.36.
Stopping vehicles for inspection, motorcycle-only checkpoints not allowed, §46.2-103.
Tailgating vehicles by pedestrians, §46.2-932.
Titling.
Motorcycle purchased by manufacturer for parts, documentation, §46.2-626.2.
Traffic signals.
Red light, proceeding through intersection at, §46.2-833.
Unregistered or unlicensed motorcycles.
Ordinances providing for their disposition, §46.2-910.

MOTORCYCLES —Cont'd
Vendors to furnish statements of licensing, §46.2-913.

MOTOR-DRIVEN CYCLES.
Operation of public highways, §46.2-911.1.

MOTOR FUELS, §§59.1-149 to 59.1-167.3.
Alternative fuels and energy efficient motor vehicles.
Energy policy of Commonwealth, §§67-102, 67-103.
Biodiesel fuel.
Biofuels production incentive grant program, §§45.1-393, 45.1-394.
Energy policy of Commonwealth, §§67-102, 67-103.
Public transportation vehicles.
Use encouraged, §§67-500, 67-501.
CAFE standards.
Federal actions to increase, support, policy of Commonwealth, §§67-800, 67-801.
Chemical analysis as evidence, §59.1-165.
Commercial motor vehicles.
Direct fueling of commercial vehicles, §59.1-162.1.
Complaints to commissioner, §59.1-157.
Conflict of laws, §59.1-167.
Cooperation by state agencies, §59.1-162.
Defective gasoline.
Sale prohibitions, §59.1-155.
Defined terms, §59.1-149.
Delegation of authority, §59.1-167.3.
Energy policy of Commonwealth, §§67-102, 67-103.
Inspections, §59.1-150.
Commissioner supervision, §59.1-154.
Methods of making, §59.1-153.
Rules and regulations, §59.1-156.
Samples.
Collection and analysis, §59.1-152.
Labeling, §59.1-167.1.
License tax imposed on peddlers, itinerant merchants and peddlers at wholesale.
Tax not to be imposed on distributors or vendors of motor fuels, §58.1-3719.
License tax on gasoline retailers.
Limitation on rate, §58.1-3706.
Oxygenated gasoline.
Rules and regulations, §59.1-156.
Petroleum products franchises generally, §§59.1-21.8 to 59.1-21.18:1.
See PETROLEUM PRODUCTS FRANCHISES.
Provision violations.
Commonwealth's attorneys.
Duties of, §59.1-164.
Penalties, §59.1-163.
Civil penalties, §59.1-167.2.
Records.
Statement of desire to do business, §59.1-151.
Retail sales and use tax.
Exemption of motor fuels subject to motor fuel and special fuel tax, §58.1-609.1.
Rules and regulations, §59.1-156.
Sale of liquid fuels, liquidating oils and similar products.
Assisting in violations, §18.2-230.
False trade name or mixing brands, §18.2-229.
Fraud and misrepresentation, §18.2-226.
Imitating indicia of other brand, §18.2-228.
Misdemeanor for violation, §18.2-232.
Sale from pump indicating other brand, §18.2-227.
Samples, §59.1-152.

MOTOR FUELS —Cont'd
Statements.
Filing, §59.1-151.
Storage tanks.
Discharges into waters of the state, §§62.1-44.34:8, 62.1-44.34:9.
Petroleum storage tank fund, §§62.1-44.34:10 to 62.1-44.34:13.
Tank vehicles.
Direct fueling of commercial vehicles, §59.1-162.1.
Testing, §59.1-150.
Commissioner supervision, §59.1-154.
Rules and regulations, §59.1-156.
Samples.
Collection and analysis, §59.1-152.
Virginia energy plan.
Generally, §§67-100 to 67-1003.
See ENERGY.

MOTOR FUEL SALES TAX, §§58.1-1718.1 to 58.1-1724.4.
Definitions, §58.1-1718.1.
Exclusion from professional license tax, §58.1-1722.
Imposition of tax, §58.1-1720.
Rules and regulations promulgation, §58.1-1719.

MOTOR HOMES.
Defined, §46.2-100.
Length of vehicles, §46.2-1112.
Exceptions, §46.2-1113.
Excessive size and weight permits.
Impeding or disrupting vehicles operating under valid highway hauling permit, §46.2-828.2.
Towing motor homes or travel trailers, §46.2-1139.
Motor vehicle registration.
Fees for vehicles designed and used for transporting passengers, §46.2-694.
Motor vehicle safety inspections.
Inapplicability of inspection provisions, §46.2-1162.
Personal property taxes.
Classification, §58.1-3506.
T&M vehicle dealers, §§46.2-1900 to 46.2-1991.
See T&M VEHICLE DEALERS.

MOTORIZED SCOOTERS.
Assistive technology device warranties, §§59.1-470 to 59.1-474.
Crosswalks, operating in, §46.2-908.1.
Highways.
Operating on, restrictions, §46.2-908.1.
Mufflers.
Straight exhaust or gutted mufflers, §46.2-1047.
Overtaking and passing vehicles, §46.2-907.
Persons less than 14 years old.
Operating, supervision required, §46.2-908.1.
Roadways and bicycle paths, riding on, §46.2-905.
Sidewalks or crosswalks, locality may prohibit use, §46.2-904.

MOTORIZED SKATEBOARDS.
Crosswalks, operating in, §46.2-908.1.
Highways.
Operating on, restrictions, §46.2-908.1.
Mufflers.
Straight exhaust or gutted mufflers, §46.2-1047.
Overtaking and passing vehicles, §46.2-907.
Persons less than 14 years old.
Operating, supervision required, §46.2-908.1.

MOTORIZED WHEELCHAIRS.
Assistive technology device warranties, §§59.1-470 to 59.1-474.

MOTOR LAUNCH CARRIERS.
Employee liens, §§43-24 to 43-26.
Public service companies generally, §§56-1 to 56-87.
See PUBLIC SERVICE COMPANIES.
Supplier liens, §§43-24 to 43-26.
Workers' compensation coverage.
Employee defined, §65.2-101.

MOTORMEN.
Issuance of summons for boarding without paying, §15.2-4503.

MOTOR OIL.
Highways construction machinery and equipment.
Specifications in purchasing, §33.1-189.1.

MOTOR OIL PUMPS.
Opening or carrying away, §18.2-151.

MOTOR SPORTS FACILITIES.
Mixed beverage license, §4.1-210.
Fee, §§4.1-231, 4.1-233.

MOTOR VEHICLE ACCIDENTS, §§46.2-894 to 46.2-902.
Abstract or transcript of conviction record.
Drivers arrested for serious traffic offenses, §46.2-384.
Electronic transmission, §46.2-383.
Forms and information contained in abstracts, §46.2-386.
Penalty for failure to forward record, §46.2-387.
Accident reports.
Abstracts or transcripts of driver's conviction records, §46.2-384.
Admissibility as evidence, §46.2-378.
Certification of abstracts of conviction record, §46.2-386.
Certification of financial responsibility, §46.2-372.
Citations, §46.2-388.
Clerk's fee for reports, §46.2-383.
Commercial motor vehicles, §46.2-382.1.
Copies of reports required local ordinance, §46.2-381.
Driver's immediate notice of certain accidents, §46.2-371.
Driver's written reporting of certain accidents, §46.2-372.
Electronic transmission of transcript or abstract of conviction records, §46.2-383.
Forms for and information to be contained in abstracts, §46.2-386.
Garage or repair shop reports, §§46.2-376, 46.2-377.
Inspection by certain persons, §46.2-380.
Judicial recordkeeping requirements, §46.2-382.
Law-enforcement officer investigating accident, §46.2-373.
Medical examiner's report, §46.2-375.
Penalty for failure to forward record of conviction or judgment for damages, §46.2-387.
Prescription and supply of report forms, §46.2-374.
Prosecuting attorneys to appear in certain cases, §46.2-385.
Reports in addition to others required by title, §46.2-898.

MOTOR VEHICLE ACCIDENTS —Cont'd
Accident reports —Cont'd
Reports open to public inspection.
DMV records, §46.2-383.
Reports required by local ordinance, §46.2-381.
Supplemental reports of driver, §46.2-372.
Uniform summons for reportable motor vehicle law violations, §46.2-388.
Unknown owners or operators, §38.2-2206.
Used as evidence, §46.2-378.
Use made by investigating officers, §46.2-379.
Witness reports, §46.2-372.
Action for death sustained as result of accident.
Limits of liability insurance.
Request by personal representative to insurer prior to bringing action, §8.01-417.
Action for personal injuries sustained as result of accident.
Limits of liability insurance.
Request by person injured to insurer prior to bringing action, §8.01-417.
Affidavit as to damages.
Proof of damages, §8.01-416.
Appearance in traffic infraction cases.
No written appearance in waiver of court hearing, §19.2-254.1.
Appraisal of damages.
Sworn appraisal as proof, §8.01-416.
Arbitrary refusal of insurance claim, §8.01-66.1.
Attorneys.
Inspection of accident reports, §46.2-380.
Cargo removal and disposition, §46.2-1212.1.
Certification of financial responsibility, §46.2-372.
Citations.
Uniform summons for reportable motor vehicle law violations, §46.2-388.
Commercial drivers' licenses.
Disqualification for multiple serious traffic violations, §46.2-341.20.
Commercial motor vehicles.
Judicial findings, §46.2-382.1.
Confidentiality.
Garage or repair shop reports, §46.2-377.
Reports open to public inspection.
DMV records, §46.2-383.
Use of accident reports by investigation officers, §46.2-379.
Construction of article.
Applicability to accidents on private or public property, §46.2-899.
Reports in addition to others required by title, §46.2-898.
County or municipal ordinances.
Accident reports required, §46.2-381.
Crash investigation team, department of motor vehicles.
Privileged communications, §8.01-402.
Damage only to unattended property.
Duty of certain persons accompanying driver to report accidents, §46.2-897.
Duty of driver, §46.2-896.
Damages.
Sworn appraisal or estimate as proof, §8.01-416.
Death resulting from accidents.
Limits of liability insurance.
Request by personal representative to insurer prior to bringing action, §8.01-417.
Medical examiners' reports, §46.2-375.
Death to guest in vehicle, §8.01-63.

MOTOR VEHICLE ACCIDENTS —Cont'd
Demerit points, §46.2-492.
Driver information.
Commissioner of DMV.
Supplying attorney representing person involved in accident, §46.2-208.
Driver license compact.
Failure to stop and render aid in an accident resulting in death or bodily injury of another.
Statutes and ordinances deemed to cover offense, §46.2-487.
Drivers' licenses.
Persons convicted of failure to stop and disclose identity at scene, §46.2-316.
Suspension of driver's license for failure to report certain accidents, §46.2-901.
Suspension of licenses for unsatisfied judgments and after certain accidents, §§46.2-417 to 46.2-429.
See DRIVERS' LICENSES.
Driver to stop, etc.
Accident involving injury, death or damage to attended property, §46.2-894.
Driving while intoxicated.
Arresting officer to request abstracts or transcripts of driver's conviction records, §46.2-384.
Reimbursement to locality or volunteer rescue squad for emergency response, §15.2-1716.
Duty of certain persons accompanying driver to report accidents.
Accidents involving damage only to unattended property, §46.2-897.
Accidents involving injury, death or damage to attended property, §46.2-895.
Duty of driver in accident involving damage only to unattended property, §46.2-896.
Emergency care and assistance immunity, §8.01-225.
Emergency flashing lights on vehicle stopped on highway, §46.2-888.
Estimate of damages.
Sworn estimate as proof, §8.01-416.
Evidence.
Damages, sworn appraisal as estimate, §8.01-416.
Use of accident reports, §46.2-378.
Use of by investigation officer, §46.2-379.
Failure to stop and render aid in an accident resulting in death or bodily injury of another, §46.2-894.
Driver license compact.
Statutes and ordinances deemed to cover offense, §46.2-487.
Fine schedule, VA SCt Rule 3B:2.
Maximum fine for violating Title 46.2, §46.2-113.
Forms.
Department to prescribe and supply report forms, §46.2-374.
Uniform summons for reportable motor vehicle law violations, §46.2-388.
Garages and repair shops.
Accident reports, §§46.2-109, 46.2-376, 46.2-377.
Glass or other injurious substances dropped upon highway.
Removing, §18.2-324.
Good Samaritan statute, §8.01-225.
Immobilized or unattended vehicles.
Authority to provide for removal and disposition of cargo, §46.2-1212.1.
Temporary removal and disposition of vehicles, §46.2-1212.

MOTOR VEHICLE ACCIDENTS —Cont'd
Injury or death or damage to attended property.
Duty of certain persons accompanying driver to report accidents, §46.2-895.
Duty of driver to stop, etc., §46.2-894.
Injury to guest in vehicle, §8.01-63.
Insurance carriers.
Inspection of accident report, §46.2-380.
John Doe actions.
Owner or operator of vehicle causing injury or damage unknown, §38.2-2206.
Judgment unsatisfied.
Suspension of driver's license, §46.2-417.
Judicial recordkeeping requirements, §46.2-382.
Law-enforcement officers.
Accident reports, §46.2-373.
Leaving the scene of an accident.
Arresting officer to request abstracts or transcripts of driver's conviction record, §46.2-384.
Duty to stop, §46.2-894.
One year revocation of driver's license, §46.2-389.
Pretrial payment of fine, §16.1-69.40:1.
When directed to do so by law-enforcement officer, §46.2-902.
Limits of liability insurance.
Request for, prior to bringing action for injury or death, §8.01-417.
Loss of use of vehicle, §8.01-66.
Medical examiners' reports, §46.2-375.
Memorials by highways and roads, §33.1-206.1.
Minor operating vehicle.
Defense of lack of consent of owner, §8.01-65.
Liability of owner, §8.01-64.
Motor vehicle insurance.
Refusal to renew based on, §38.2-2212.
Moving vehicle to shoulder of road, §46.2-888.
Nonresident motor vehicle operators.
Failure to report accident, §46.2-432.
Service on commissioner of motor vehicles, §§8.01-307 to 8.01-313.
Appointment binding, §8.01-310.
Continuance of action where service made on commissioner, §8.01-311.
Copy to be sent to defendant and certificate filed with court, §8.01-326.1.
Duties of statutory agent, §8.01-312.
Effective date of service, §8.01-326.1.
Effect of service on statutory agent, §8.01-312.
Fee, §8.01-310.
How service made on commissioner, §8.01-310.
Motor vehicle, defined, §8.01-307.
Nonresident, defined, §8.01-307.
Operator's consent to appointment, §8.01-308.
Specific addresses for mailing by statutory agent, §8.01-313.
Time for nonresident to respond for process from statutory agent, §8.01-312.
Notice.
Driver to give immediate notice of certain accidents, §46.2-371.
Parental liability.
Minor operating vehicle, §8.01-64.
Defense of lack of consent of owner, §8.01-65.
Penalties, §46.2-900.
Personal representatives of persons involved or injured in accident.
Inspection of accident report, §46.2-380.

MOTOR VEHICLE ACCIDENTS —Cont'd
Persons involved or injured in accident.
Inspection of accident report, §46.2-380.
Photographs.
Maintenance, §46.2-380.
Pretrial payment of fine, §16.1-69.40:1.
Prevention courses, insurance rate reductions, §38.2-2217.
Private or public property.
Applicability of article to accidents on property, §46.2-899.
Privileged communications.
Crash investigation team, department of motor vehicles, §8.01-402.
Proof of damages.
Sworn estimate or appraisal, §8.01-416.
Proof of insurance or payment of uninsured motor vehicle registration, §46.2-902.1.
Prosecuting attorneys.
Appearance in certain cases, §46.2-385.
Reckless driving.
Arresting officer to request abstracts or transcripts of driver's conviction record, §46.2-384.
Removal and disposition of vehicles and cargo, §46.2-1212.1.
Removing wrecked or damaged vehicle and glass or other substances from highway, §18.2-324.
Rental car reimbursement.
Recovery of cost of hiring substitute vehicle.
Person entitled to recover for damages or destruction of vehicle, §8.01-66.
Repair shops.
Accident reports, §§46.2-109, 46.2-376, 46.2-377.
Safety service patrol.
Exemption from certain traffic regulations, §46.2-920.1.
Statements by injured persons.
Copies of transcriptions to be delivered to injured person, §8.01-417.
State police arrests.
Warrantless arrests, §52-20.
Procedure after, §52-21.
Stopping in vicinity of fire or emergency, §46.2-890.
Subpoena.
Authority of law-enforcement officers to issue subpoena, §46.2-939.
Subsequent remedial measures.
Inadmissible to prove negligence, §8.01-418.1.
Substitute vehicle provided insured by insurer.
Person entitled to recover cost for hiring substitute vehicle, §8.01-66.
Supplemental reports.
Driver's written reporting requirements, §46.2-372.
Suspension of driver's license and registration.
Uninsured motorist involved in reportable accident, §46.2-708.
Tow trucks or DOT vehicles en route to or from scene.
Exemption from certain traffic regulations, §46.2-920.1.
Unsatisfied judgments, §46.2-417.
Suspension of driver's license, §46.2-417.
Warrantless arrests.
Arrest without warrant authorized, §19.2-81.
Witness reports, §46.2-372.

MOTOR VEHICLE AND TRAFFIC OFFENSES.
Abandoning motor vehicles, §46.2-1200.1.
ABC offenses.
Armed person violations, §4.1-318.
Carrying alcohol in vehicles transporting passengers, §4.1-312.
Confiscation, §§4.1-339 to 4.1-348.
See MOTOR VEHICLE CONFISCATION.
Abstract of driver's conviction record, §46.2-384.
Accidents.
Duty of driver to stop, §46.2-900.
Duty of passenger to report, §46.2-900.
Failure to give notice to law-enforcement officer, §46.2-371.
Failure to report.
Suspension of driver's license, §46.2-901.
Witness' failure to appear, §46.2-939.
Aggressive driving, §46.2-868.1.
Restricted permit to operate, §46.2-392.
Suspension of driver's license, §46.2-392.
Alternative fuel fleet standards.
Failure of vehicles to comply, §46.2-649.2.
Blind pedestrians crossing highway.
Failure to stop, §46.2-933.
Blocking access to premises, §46.2-918.
Breaking and preventing operation, §18.2-146.
Burglary.
Entering with intent to commit murder, rape, robbery or arson, §18.2-90.
Cargo.
Escape of contents, §§10.1-1424, 46.2-1156.
Fines and costs, VA SCt Rule 3B:2.
Fastening loads, §46.2-1155.
Fines and costs, VA SCt Rule 3B:2.
Carjacking, §18.2-58.1.
Cell phones or other wireless telecommunications devices.
Using while operating vehicle.
Emailing or texting while driving, §46.2-1078.1.
Commercial drivers' licenses, disqualifications, §§46.2-341.20, 46.2-341.20:5.
Reckless driving, mandatory fine, §46.2-868.
Holders of provisional drivers' licenses, §46.2-334.01.
Certificate of title.
Forgery and counterfeiting, §46.2-605.
Levy of execution.
Fraudulent assignment or transference of title, §46.2-644.
Obtaining when not entitled to, §46.2-105.2.
Odometers.
Reading to be reported, §46.2-629.
Possession of certificate issued to another, §46.2-618.
Sale of vehicle without certificate, §46.2-617.
Transfer of title.
Endorsements, §46.2-628.
Sale of vehicle without certificate, §46.2-617.
Security interest.
Failure to surrender certificate when interest paid, §46.2-643.
Taxicabs.
Failure to provide information, §46.2-624.
Vehicles damaged by water.
Failure to provide information, §46.2-624.
Child charged with traffic infractions, disposition, §16.1-278.10.
City and county local license sticker.
Failure to display, §46.2-752.

MOTOR VEHICLE AND TRAFFIC OFFENSES —Cont'd
Commercial driver training schools, §46.2-1707.
Commercial vehicles.
Damaging or threatening, §46.2-818.
Commuter buses.
Maintenance of record, §46.2-1175.
Commuter parking lots owned by VDOT.
Parking not in conformance with signs, §46.2-1219.2.
Cruising ordinances, §46.2-1219.1.
Damaging commercial vehicles, §46.2-818.
Dealer franchises.
Coercion, §46.2-1569.
Dealer license plates.
Misuse, §46.2-1557.2.
Dealers, §46.2-1507.
Decals.
Removing without consent of department, §46.2-1074.
Revocation.
Failure to surrender, §46.2-612.
Delinquent children operating vehicle in violation of restrictions, §16.1-278.8.
Disregarding signal by law enforcement officer to stop, §46.2-817.
Distracted driving.
Sending or reading email by handheld communications device, §46.2-1078.1.
Commercial drivers' licenses, disqualifications, §§46.2-341.20, 46.2-341.20:5.
Holders of provisional drivers' licenses, §46.2-334.01.
Reckless driving, mandatory fine, §46.2-868.
District court jurisdiction, §16.1-123.1.
Driving after illegally consuming alcohol.
Persons under age twenty-one, §18.2-266.1.
Driving while license suspended or revoked, §46.2-301.1.
Allowing person to operate vehicle knowing license suspended or revoked, §§46.2-301, 46.2-301.1.
Second conviction, intervention, VASAP compliance, §46.2-355.1.
DWI, §§18.2-266 to 18.2-273.
See DRIVING WHILE INTOXICATED.
Earphones.
Operating while using, §46.2-1078.
Eluding police, §46.2-817.
Email.
Sending or reading email by handheld communications device, §46.2-1078.1.
Commercial drivers' licenses, disqualifications, §§46.2-341.20, 46.2-341.20:5.
Holders of provisional drivers' licenses, §46.2-334.01.
Reckless driving, mandatory fine, §46.2-868.
Emissions inspections, §46.2-1187.
Employment of lights or spotlights, §18.2-509.
Entering automobile, truck, etc.
Intent to commit larceny, assault and battery or other felony, §18.2-91.
Intent to commit murder, rape, robbery or arson, §18.2-90.
Expungement of court records.
Juvenile records, §16.1-306.
Farm machinery and equipment.
Removing, defacing or obliterating serial number, §3.2-5000.
Fines, general penalty for violating title, §46.2-113.

MOTOR VEHICLE AND TRAFFIC OFFENSES —Cont'd
Fines, pretrial waiver of appearance, plea of guilty and payment of fines, §16.1-69.40:1.
Uniform fine schedule, VA SCt Rules 3B:1, 3B:2.
Flamethrowers.
Possession or driving of vehicle equipped with, §46.2-1086.
Forfeiture of motor vehicles used in commission of certain crimes, §19.2-386.16.
Felony DWI, §19.2-386.34.
Forgery and counterfeiting.
Certificate of title and registration card, §46.2-605.
Fraudulent conversion or removal of property subject to lien or title in another, §18.2-115.
Gas projectors.
Possession or driving of vehicle equipped with, §46.2-1086.
General penalty for violating title, §46.2-113.
Habitual offenders, §§46.2-356 to 46.2-363.
Impoundment of motor vehicle, §46.2-301.1.
Handheld communications devices.
Emailing or texting while driving, §46.2-1078.1.
Commercial drivers' licenses, disqualifications, §§46.2-341.20, 46.2-341.20:5.
Reckless driving, mandatory fine, §46.2-868.
Highway signs, §§46.2-831, 46.2-832.
Highway traffic control devices, §46.2-831.
Highway work zone.
Decreased maximum speed limit, §46.2-878.1.
Ignition interlock system, §18.2-270.1.
Impoundment of motor vehicle, §46.2-301.1.
DWI or habitual offender offenses, §46.2-301.1.
Improper driving, §46.2-869.
Inclement weather.
Operation of vehicles in violation of local ordinances, §46.2-1302.
Joyriding, §18.2-102.
Jurisdiction of district courts, §16.1-123.1.
Juvenile violations.
Summons issued by officer.
Juvenile and domestic relations district court may proceed on, §16.1-260.
Law enforcement officers.
Fees for arrest prohibited, §46.2-218.
License plates.
Dealer plates misuse, §46.2-1557.2.
Revocation.
Failure to surrender, §46.2-612.
Lien or title in another.
Fraudulent conversion or removal of property, §18.2-115.
Loads.
Escape of contents, §§10.1-1424, 46.2-1156.
Fines and costs, VA SCt Rule 3B:2.
Fastening loads, §46.2-1155.
Fines and costs, VA SCt Rule 3B:2.
Maximum fine for traffic infraction, §46.2-113.
Mopeds.
Stickers affixed by retail dealers, §46.2-915.
Moving violations generally.
See TRAFFIC INFRACTIONS.
Nonrepairable vehicle, §46.2-1609.
Obtaining documents from department when not entitled to, §46.2-105.2.
Odometers.
Sale of resetting device, §46.2-112.
Tampering with, §46.2-112.
Operation of vehicle by habitual offender, §46.2-357.

MOTOR VEHICLE AND TRAFFIC OFFENSES —Cont'd
Overweight vehicles.
Operation in violation of provision, §46.2-704.
Pickup trucks.
Transportation of persons less than 16 years old in pickup truck beds, §46.2-1156.1.
Port authority property, §62.1-132.11.
Pretrial payment of fines, §16.1-69.40:1.
Uniform fine schedule, VA SCt Rules 3B:1, 3B:2.
Racing on highways, §§46.2-865 to 46.2-867.
Rebuilt vehicles, §46.2-1609.
Receipt or transfer of possession of stolen vehicle, §18.2-109.
Reciprocal agreements.
Operation without payment of reciprocity fees, §46.2-703.
Reckless driving, §46.2-868.
Reckless driving on parking lot, §46.2-864.
Records of convictions or of judgments for damages.
Failure to forward record, §46.2-387.
Registration.
Clean alternative fuel fleet standards.
Failure of certain vehicles to comply, §46.2-649.2.
Decals.
Alteration or forgery, §46.2-722.
Fees.
Farm vehicles.
Failure to pay, §46.2-698.
Passenger vehicles.
Failure to pay, §46.2-687.
License plates.
Alteration or forgery, §46.2-722.
Obtaining when not entitled, §46.2-105.2.
Overweight vehicles, §46.2-704.
Reciprocity.
Operation without payment of reciprocity fees, §46.2-703.
Uninsured motor vehicles, §46.2-707.
Registration card.
Failure to carry, §46.2-104.
Presentation to court or production in court, compliance with provisions, §46.2-104.
Forgery and counterfeiting, §46.2-605.
Removal of property subject to lien or title in another, §18.2-115.
Renting vehicles.
Insurance requirement, §46.2-108.
Reversal of conviction.
Affect, §46.2-413.
Safety belts.
Occupants of front seats, §46.2-1094.
School bus drivers, §46.2-1091.
Safety inspection violations, §§46.2-1158.02, 46.2-1171.
Salvage/nonrepairable certificate.
Altering or forging, §46.2-605.
Salvage vehicles, §46.2-1609.
School buses.
Warning devices, §46.2-1090.
Serial or other identification numbers.
Removal or alteration, §§46.2-1074, 46.2-1075.
Serious traffic violation.
Additional fine for vehicles of certain gross weight, §46.2-113.
Signs, §§46.2-831, 46.2-832.
Size.
Excessive size permits, §46.2-1139.
Impeding or disrupting vehicles operating under valid highway hauling permit, §46.2-828.2.

MOTOR VEHICLE AND TRAFFIC OFFENSES —Cont'd
Size —Cont'd
Height.
Damage to overhead obstructions.
Failure to give notice, §46.2-1110.
Driving or attempting to drive oversized vehicle or load through tunnel, §46.2-1110.
Reduction of limit, §46.2-1104.
Smoke screen equipment.
Possessing or driving of vehicle equipped with, §46.2-1086.
Snowmobiles, §46.2-1302.
Special identification card.
Obtaining when not entitled to, §46.2-105.2.
Stolen vehicles.
Receipt or transfer of possession, §18.2-109.
Stopping vehicle of another, §46.2-818.
Storage batteries, §59.1-191.
Summons.
Failure to appear, §46.2-938.
Texting while driving, §46.2-1078.1.
Commercial drivers' licenses, disqualifications, §§46.2-341.20, 46.2-341.20:5.
Reckless driving, mandatory fine, §46.2-868.
Threatening operator of commercial vehicle, §46.2-818.
Tires.
Cleats and other non-rubber protuberances.
Sales of tires having, §46.2-1045.
Regrooved or recut tires.
Prohibited act, §46.2-1042.
Traffic control devices, §46.2-832.
Traffic infractions defined, §18.2-8.
Traffic infractions generally, §§46.2-800 to 46.2-947.
See TRAFFIC INFRACTIONS.
Traffic infractions, general penalty, §46.2-113.
Traffic schools.
Failure to attend, §46.2-1314.
Trespassing vehicles, §46.2-1231.
Tunnels.
Hauling certain cargoes through, §46.2-815.
Unattended or immobile vehicles, §46.2-1209.
Unauthorized use, §18.2-102.
Uniform demerit point system, §46.2-492.
Uninsured motor vehicle.
Operation without payment of fee, §46.2-707.
Vehicle identification numbers (VIN).
Removal or alteration, §§46.2-1074, 46.2-1075.
Waiver of appearance.
Child charged with traffic infractions, §16.1-302.
Weight.
Excessive weight permits, §46.2-1139.
Impeding or disrupting vehicles operating under valid highway hauling permit, §46.2-828.2.
Gross vehicle weight ratings.
Tampering with, §46.2-1075.1.
Overweight vehicles.
Seizures.
Violation of special overweight seizure provisions, §46.2-1134.
Weighing vehicles.
Refusal of driver, §46.2-1137.
Uniform fine schedule, VA SCt Rule 3C:2.
Windshields and windows.
Signs, decals and stickers, §46.2-1052.
Sunshading materials, §46.2-1052.
Yellow motor vehicles of certain seating capacity.
Operation on state highways, §46.2-917.

MOTOR VEHICLE AND TRAFFIC OFFENSES —Cont'd
Zero tolerance law, §18.2-266.1.

MOTOR VEHICLE CONFISCATION.
ABC offenses, §§4.1-339 to 4.1-348.
Arrests, §4.1-339.
Beverages not licensed under act, §4.1-348.
Contraband beverages, §4.1-346.
Drivers' licenses suspended or revoked for intoxication, §46.2-301.1.
Search and seizure of conveyances or vehicles used in violation of law, §4.1-339.
Drivers' licenses suspended or revoked for intoxication, §46.2-301.1.
Overweight vehicles, forfeiture, §§46.2-1134, 46.2-1135.

MOTOR VEHICLE DEALER BOARD, §§46.2-1503 to 46.2-1507.
Secretary of transportation.
Agency responsibility, §2.2-228.

MOTOR VEHICLE DEALER PROCESSING FEES.
Subject to motor vehicle sales and use tax, §58.1-2402.

MOTOR VEHICLE DEALERS, §§46.2-1500 to 46.2-1582.
Advertising, §§46.2-1580 to 46.2-1582.
Abbreviations VA DLR, §46.2-1535.
Enforcement of agency regulations, §46.2-1582.
New or used automobiles or trucks, §18.2-221.
Regulated advertising practice, §46.2-1581.
Rules promulgation, §46.2-1582.
Agents of commissioner, §46.2-205.
Audits, §46.2-1528.
Bill of sale, §46.2-1530.
Board.
Additional training.
Certification or licensure, §46.2-1506.1.
Application of provisions.
State personnel and public procurement acts, §46.2-1503.2.
Biennial report, §46.2-1503.5.
Composition, §46.2-1503.
Creation, §46.2-1503.
Disbursements from fund, §46.2-1503.3.
Duties, §46.2-1503.4.
Executive director, §46.2-1503.1.
Application of provisions, §46.2-1503.2.
Fund, §46.2-1503.3.
Hearings, §46.2-1504.
Injunctions, §46.2-1505.
Motor vehicle dealer board fund, §46.2-1503.3.
Penalties, §46.2-1507.
Powers, §46.2-1503.4.
Records, §46.2-1503.1.
Regulations, §46.2-1506.
Additional training, §46.2-1506.1.
Reports, §46.2-1503.5.
Suit to enjoin violations, §46.2-1505.
Bonds, surety.
Original dealer's license, §46.2-1527.1.
Business hours, §46.2-1533.
Buyer's order, §46.2-1530.
Cancellation of dealer franchises, §46.2-1569.
Cancellation of purchase contract.
Dealer's right to possession of vehicle, §46.2-1542.
Certificates of dealer registration.
Application, §46.2-1509.
Fund fee, §46.2-1527.1.

MOTOR VEHICLE DEALERS —Cont'd
Certificates of dealer registration —Cont'd
Grounds for disciplinary action, §46.2-1575.
Issuance, expiration and renewal, §46.2-1521.
Refusal to renew, §46.2-1576.
Required, §46.2-1508.
Revocation on payment from transaction recovery fund, §46.2-1527.7.
Certificates of ownership.
Temporary certificate, §46.2-1542.
Certificates of qualification.
Dealer-operators, §§46.2-1511, 46.2-1513.
Revocation on payment from transaction recovery fund, §46.2-1527.7.
Salespersons, §46.2-1512.
Certificates of title.
Off-road motorcycles, §§46.2-644.1 to 46.2-644.3.
Certificates of title for dealers, §46.2-1544.
Certificates of title registration.
Revocation on payment from transaction recovery fund, §46.2-1527.7.
Cessation of business, §46.2-1545.
Changes in form of ownership, make or name.
New application, license and fee, §46.2-1517.
Coercing purchaser to provide insurance coverage, §46.2-1536.
Coercion of retail dealers.
Franchises, §§46.2-1568, 46.2-1569.
Consignment vehicles, §46.2-1531.
Contracts.
Bill of sale, §46.2-1530.
Buyer's order, §46.2-1530.
Cancellation of purchase contract.
Dealer's right to possession of vehicle, §46.2-1542.
Consignment vehicles, §46.2-1531.
Interest, contract rate more than legal rate.
Motor vehicle purchases, §6.2-314.
Dealer-arranged financing, purchase conditioned on.
Notice to customer, §46.2-1530.
Dealer license plates.
Cancellation, §46.2-1557.1.
Dealer license prerequisite to dealer's license plates, §46.2-1547.
Fees, §46.2-1546.
Promotional license plates, §46.2-1549.1.
Insurance requirements, §46.2-1547.
Optional multi-year registration, §46.2-1548.
Promotional plates, §46.2-1549.1.
Registration of dealers, §46.2-1546.
Reissuance, §46.2-1557.1.
Revocation of plates, §46.2-1547.
Transferable plates, §46.2-1548.
Types of plates, §46.2-1549.
Dealer-operators.
Certificate of qualification, §§46.2-1511, 46.2-1513.
Salespersons, §46.2-1512.
Deceptive practices.
Commissioner's enforcement powers, §46.2-1501.
Penalties, §46.2-1507.
Definitions, §46.2-1500.
Regulated advertising practices, §46.2-1581.
Demonstrating trucks.
Use of dealer's license plates or temporary transport plates, §46.2-1552.1.
Demonstrators.
Defined, §46.2-1500.
Sale as new vehicles, notice required, §46.2-1530.
Temporary transfer of license plates from another vehicle, §46.2-720.

MOTOR VEHICLE DEALERS —Cont'd
Disciplinary action against licensee or registrant, §§46.2-1527.7, 46.2-1527.8.
Acts of officers, directors, etc., §46.2-1574.
Agency appeal, §46.2-1577.
Appeals, §§46.2-1577, 46.2-1578.
Enumeration of grounds, §46.2-1575.
Equitable remedies not impaired, §46.2-1579.
Grounds, §46.2-1575.
Judicial review, §46.2-1578.
Notice and hearing, §46.2-1576.
Payments from transaction recovery fund, §§46.2-1527.7, 46.2-1527.8.
Payments under fund not deemed waiver of disciplinary action, §46.2-1527.8.
Refusal to renew license or certificate, §46.2-1576.
Disclosures.
Manufacturers and distributors, §46.2-1532.1.
Odometer disclosure, §46.2-1532.
Discontinuation of franchise distributors, §46.2-1570.
Discrimination by manufacturers or distributors against dealers, §46.2-1568.1.
Display of license, §§46.2-1515, 46.2-1518.
Distributor disclosures, §46.2-1532.1.
Distributor's right of first refusal.
Franchise ownership, §46.2-1569.1.
Electronic filing of documentation.
Manual transaction fee for non-participating dealers, §46.2-1530.2.
On-line systems filing fee, §46.2-1530.1.
Equitable remedies not impaired.
Disciplinary action against dealer licenses, §46.2-1579.
Established place of business.
Business hours, §46.2-1533.
Change of location, §46.2-1515.
Denial of license application for failure to have, §46.2-1514.
Required for license, §46.2-1510.
Signs, §46.2-1534.
Specification of location, §46.2-1515.
Supplemental sales locations, §46.2-1516.
Termination of business, §46.2-1545.
Extended service contracts.
Application of provisions, §59.1-436.
Fees.
License and registration fees, §§46.2-1509, 46.2-1519, 46.2-1520.
Promotional license plates, §46.2-1549.1.
Registration of dealers, §46.2-1546.
Financing.
Coercion concerning financing, §46.2-1568.
Dealer-arranged financing, purchase conditioned on.
Notice to customer, §46.2-1530.
Foreign dealer's license.
Operation under prohibited, §46.2-1556.
Violation of provisions, §46.2-1565.1.
Foreign-registered motor vehicles.
Use in driver education programs, §46.2-1557.
Forms.
Buyer's order, §46.2-1530.
Franchises, §§46.2-1566 to 46.2-1573.1.
Approval of form of franchise or sales agreement, §46.2-1566.
Cancellation of dealer franchises, §46.2-1569.
Cessation to dealer franchises, §46.2-1569.
Civil penalties, §46.2-1573.
Coercion, §§46.2-1568, 46.2-1569.

MOTOR VEHICLE DEALERS —Cont'd
Franchises —Cont'd
Delivery of vehicles, parts and accessories, §46.2-1569.
Discontinuation of distributors, §46.2-1570.
Distributor's right of first refusal, §46.2-1569.1.
Exceptions to manufacturer's operation of dealership, §46.2-1572.
Exemption from retail franchising act, §46.2-1567.
Filing requirements.
Franchise or sale agreement, §46.2-1566.
Grant of dealer franchises, §46.2-1569.
Hearings and other remedies, §46.2-1573.
Attorneys' fees, §46.2-1573.01.
Improvements to facilities or installment of signs.
Coercion as to, prohibited, §46.2-1569.
Manufacturer's operation of dealership, §46.2-1572.
Manufacturer's right of first refusal, §46.2-1569.1.
Mediation of disputes, §46.2-1572.2.
Motorcycle dealers, §§46.2-1993.64 to 46.2-1993.74.
See MOTORCYCLE DEALERS.
Operation of dealership by manufacturer, §46.2-1572.
Ownership of service facilities, §46.2-1572.1.
Site control over premises of dealer.
Agreement between dealer and manufacturer, §46.2-1569.
Termination.
Limited right of dealers to sell new vehicles following, §46.2-1573.02.
Trailer dealers, §§46.2-1992.66 to 46.2-1992.77.
See TRAILER DEALERS.
Warranty obligations, §46.2-1571.
Incentives.
Discrimination by manufacturers or distributors against dealers, §46.2-1568.1.
Injunctions.
Suits to enjoin violations, §46.2-1505.
Inspections.
Compliance with safety inspection requirements, §46.2-1539.
Vehicle inspection prior to sale, §46.2-1540.
Installation of parts or accessories.
Use of dealer's license plates or temporary transport plates, §§46.2-1550.2, 46.2-1551.
Insurance.
Coercing purchaser to provide insurance coverage, §46.2-1536.
Late model and factory repurchase franchises, §46.2-1573.1.
Leads for sales.
Discrimination by manufacturers or distributors against dealers, §46.2-1568.1.
Leasing.
Coercion concerning leasing, §46.2-1568.
License plates, §§46.2-1546 to 46.2-1557.2.
Emergency use of license plates, §§46.2-719 to 46.2-721.
Loaner or demonstration vehicles.
Temporary transfer of plates from another vehicle, §46.2-720.
Temporary plates, §§46.2-1558 to 46.2-1565.
Use of plates, §§46.2-1550 to 46.2-1552.1.
Auction vehicles, §46.2-1550.1.
Demonstrating trucks, §46.2-1552.1.
Generally, §46.2-1550.
General repair service, §46.2-1550.1.
Newly purchased vehicles, §46.2-1552.
Special equipment installation, §46.2-1551.

MOTOR VEHICLE DEALERS —Cont'd
License plates —Cont'd
Use of plates —Cont'd
Unlawful uses, §46.2-1550.
Licenses, §§46.2-1508 to 46.2-1521.
Action on applications, §46.2-1514.
Annual fee for original license, §46.2-1527.1.
Application, §46.2-1509.
Bonding requirements for original license applicants, §46.2-1527.2.
Certificates of dealer registration, §§46.2-1508, 46.2-1509, 46.2-1521.
Certificates of qualification, §§46.2-1511 to 46.2-1513.
Change in form of ownership, make or name, §46.2-1517.
Collection of fees, §46.2-1520.
Contents of application, §46.2-1509.
Dealer's movement to salesrooms, §46.2-1555.
Denial, suspension and revocation generally, §§46.2-1574, 46.2-1575.
Deposit of fees, §46.2-1527.1.
Determining fitness of applicant, §46.2-1509.
Disciplinary action against licensee or registrant.
Payments under fund not deemed waiver of disciplinary action, §46.2-1527.8.
Display of license, §§46.2-1515, 46.2-1518.
Requirements, §46.2-1553.
Salesperson's license, §46.2-1518.
Disposition of fees, §46.2-1520.
Double fee, §46.2-1527.1.
Established place of business.
Change of location, §46.2-1515.
Required, §§46.2-1510, 46.2-1514.
Specification of location, §46.2-1515.
Supplemental sales locations, §46.2-1516.
Exemption from license fee, §46.2-1527.1.
Expiration, §46.2-1521.
Fee to accompany application, §46.2-1509.
Foreign dealer's license, §46.2-1556.
Violation of provisions, §46.2-1565.1.
Foreign-registered vehicles in driver education programs, §46.2-1557.
Hearing on denial, §46.2-1514.
Issuance, §46.2-1521.
License and registration fees, §§46.2-1509, 46.2-1519, 46.2-1520.
Mandatory, §46.2-1508.
Manufacturer movement to place of shipment or delivery, §46.2-1554.
Multi-year licenses, §46.2-1521.
Notice of termination, §46.2-1518.
Operation under foreign dealer's license, §46.2-1556.
Operation without license plates, §46.2-1553.
Prerequisite to receiving dealer's license plates, §46.2-1547.
Removal of plates by DMV, §46.2-1557.1.
Renewal, §46.2-1521.
Renewal fee, §46.2-1527.1.
Required, §46.2-1508.
Revocation on payment from transaction recovery fund, §46.2-1527.7.
Payments from fund not deemed waiver of disciplinary action, §46.2-1527.8.
Salesperson license issued applicant not employed by dealer, §46.2-1521.
Schedule of fees, §46.2-1519.
Service of summons for violations, §46.2-1557.2.
Suspension and revocation generally, §§46.2-1574, 46.2-1575.
Insufficient bonding of applicant for original license, §46.2-1527.2.

MOTOR VEHICLE DEALERS —Cont'd
Licenses —Cont'd
Violations of article, §46.2-1557.2.
License tax, §58.1-3734.
Trade-in sales, §58.1-3734.1.
Line-make defined, §46.2-1500.
Loaner or demonstration vehicles.
Temporary transfer of plates from another vehicle, §46.2-720.
Manual transaction fee, §46.2-1530.2.
Manufacturer disclosures, §46.2-1532.1.
Manufacturer's right of first refusal.
Franchise ownership, §46.2-1569.1.
Mediation.
Franchise disputes, §46.2-1572.2.
Motorcycle dealers, §§46.2-1993 to 46.2-1993.82.
See MOTORCYCLE DEALERS.
Newly purchased vehicles.
Use of dealer's license plates, §46.2-1552.
New motor vehicles.
Demonstrators or returned vehicles.
Sale as new, disclosure required, §46.2-1530.
Sale by dealer following termination of franchise.
Limited right, §46.2-1573.02.
Nonprofit corporations.
Consigning donated motor vehicles to dealers.
Certificate authorizing, §46.2-1508.1.
Fee, §46.2-1519.
Organizations providing vehicles or transportation for indigent persons, §46.2-1508.1.
Notice of termination, §46.2-1518.
Odometer disclosure, §46.2-1532.
Off-road motorcycles.
Certificates of title, §§46.2-644.1 to 46.2-644.3.
Old license plates and registration number.
Use on another vehicle, §46.2-1543.
On-line systems filing fee, §46.2-1530.1.
Partnerships.
Disciplinary action against dealer licenses.
Acts of partners, §46.2-1574.
Performance standards.
Fairness in setting and use by manufacturer, etc., §46.2-1572.4.
Prices.
Coercion of retail dealers, §46.2-1569.
Discrimination by manufacturers or distributors against dealers, §46.2-1568.1.
Private security services businesses.
Exemptions from provisions.
Locksmith services, §9.1-140.
Processing fees charged by dealers.
Subject to motor vehicle sales and use tax, §58.1-2402.
Promotional dealer's license plates, §46.2-1549.1.
Promotional programs.
Discrimination by manufacturers or distributors against dealers, §46.2-1568.1.
Records.
Dealer temporary license plates, §46.2-1559.
Preservation of original dealer records, §46.2-1529.
Refunds or credit.
Expiration of temporary license plates, §46.2-1565.
Repossessed vehicles.
Sale of vehicles repossessed in another state, §46.2-633.1.
Retail franchising act.
Exemption of franchises, §46.2-1567.

MOTOR VEHICLE DEALERS —Cont'd
Retail installment sales contracts.
Coercion of retail franchise dealer, §46.2-1568.
Returned vehicles.
Sale as new, notice required, §46.2-1530.
Rulemaking authority, §46.2-1506.
Sale of vehicles repossessed in another state, §46.2-633.1.
Sales leads.
Discrimination by manufacturers or distributors against dealers, §46.2-1568.1.
Salespersons.
Breach of fiduciary relationship, §46.2-1538.
Certificate of qualification.
Revocation on payment from transaction recovery fund, §46.2-1527.7.
Disciplinary action, §46.2-1574.
Display of license, §46.2-1518.
License issued applicant not employed by dealer, §46.2-1521.
Prohibited solicitation and compensation, §46.2-1537.
Self-dealing, §46.2-1538.
Salesrooms.
Movement of vehicles by dealers.
Displaying license plate, §46.2-1555.
Service contracts, extended.
Application of provisions, §59.1-436.
Service facilities.
Franchises.
Ownership of service facilities, §46.2-1572.1.
Shipment or delivery of vehicles.
Movement by manufacturer.
Display of license plates, §46.2-1554.
Signs.
Improvements to facilities or installment of signs.
Coercion as to, prohibited, §46.2-1569.
Visible permanent sign, §46.2-1534.
Site control over premises of dealer.
Agreement between dealer and manufacturer, §46.2-1569.
Solicitation.
Prohibited solicitation and compensation, §46.2-1537.
Special license plates.
Persons delivering unladen vehicles, §46.2-733.
Standards for performance.
Fairness in setting and use by manufacturer, etc., §46.2-1572.4.
Temporary certificates of ownership, §46.2-1542.
Temporary license plates, §§46.2-1558 to 46.2-1565.
Alternative print-on-demand program, §46.2-1558.1.
Application, §§46.2-1560, 46.2-1561.
Duty of dealer to insert information on plate, §46.2-1562.
Expiration.
Dealer to insert date of expiration, §46.2-1562.
Destruction upon expiration, §46.2-1564.
Time of expiration, §46.2-1565.
Insertion of name, date of issuance, etc., by dealer, §46.2-1562.
Inspection of records, §46.2-1559.
Issuance to dealers and vehicle owners, §46.2-1558.
Suspension of dealer's right, §46.2-1563.
Recordkeeping requirements, §46.2-1559.
Refunds or credit, §46.2-1565.
Suspension of right of dealer to issue, §46.2-1563.

MOTOR VEHICLE DEALERS —Cont'd
Temporary license plates —Cont'd
Vehicle owners.
Issuance, §46.2-1558.
Written application requirement, §§46.2-1560, 46.2-1561.
Temporary transport plates, §§46.2-1550.1 to 46.2-1552.1.
Antique vehicles, §46.2-1550.1.
Demonstrating trucks, §46.2-1552.1.
General repair service, §46.2-1550.1.
Installation of parts or accessories, §§46.2-1550.1, 46.2-1551.
Issuance, §46.2-1550.2.
Print-on-demand, using, §46.2-1550.3.
Newly purchased vehicles, §46.2-1552.
Print-on-demand program, §46.2-1550.3.
Special equipment installation, §46.2-1551.
Use generally, §46.2-1550.2.
Termination of business, §46.2-1545.
Threats.
Waiver of dealer rights.
Threats, etc., by manufacturer, etc., to obtain, §46.2-1572.3.
Titling of vehicles.
Certificate of title for dealers, §46.2-1544.
Trailer dealers, §§46.2-1992 to 46.2-1992.85.
See TRAILER DEALERS.
Transaction recovery fund, §§46.2-1527.1 to 46.2-1527.11.
Assessments, §46.2-1527.1.
Assignment of claimant's rights to department, §46.2-1527.6.
Bond for dealers not participating, §46.2-1527.9.
Recovery on bond, §46.2-1527.10.
Deposit of fees, §46.2-1527.1.
Disciplinary action against licensee or registrant.
No waiver by department, §46.2-1527.8.
Disposition of license and registration fees, §46.2-1520.
Establishment, §46.2-1527.1.
Judgment creditors' claims.
Filing, time, §46.2-1527.3.
Limitations on recovery from fund, §46.2-1527.5.
Maximum claim of one judgment creditor, §46.2-1527.5.
Minimum balance, §46.2-1527.1.
Opportunity to intervene, §46.2-1527.4.
Original license.
Bonding requirements for applicants, §46.2-1527.2.
Payment claims.
Consideration by board, §46.2-1527.3.
Payment from fund.
Revocation of license or certificate of registration, §46.2-1527.7.
Payment of assigned claims, §46.2-1527.6.
Payment of claims, §46.2-1527.6.
Purpose, §46.2-1527.1.
Recovery from fund.
Generally, §46.2-1527.3.
Time period for filing claim, §46.2-1527.5.
Verified claim process, §46.2-1527.5.
Waiver of disciplinary action, §46.2-1527.11.
Transferable dealer's license plates, §46.2-1548.
Transfer of old license plate and registration number.
Use on another vehicle, §46.2-1543.
Unfair competition.
Commissioner's enforcement powers, §46.2-1501.
Penalties, §46.2-1507.

MOTOR VEHICLE DEALERS —Cont'd
Unfair, deceptive or misleading acts or practices.
Advertising, §46.2-1581.
Unladen vehicles.
Special license plates for persons delivering vehicles, §46.2-733.
Used motor vehicles.
Prohibited acts.
Display, parking, selling or advertising sale of certain used vehicles, §46.2-1508.2.
Vehicle inspections, §§46.2-1539, 46.2-1540.
Vehicle shipment or delivery.
Coercion of dealer franchises, §46.2-1569.
Waiver of dealer rights.
Threats, etc., by manufacturer, etc., to obtain, §46.2-1572.3.
Warranty obligation.
Franchises, §46.2-1571.

MOTOR VEHICLE DISABLED IN HIGHWAY.
Failure to use proper warning device, §46.2-111, VA SCt Rule 3B:2.
Maximum fine for violating Title 46.2, §46.2-113.

MOTOR VEHICLE EMISSIONS INSPECTIONS, §§46.2-1176 to 46.2-1187.3.
Administration of emissions inspection program, §§46.2-1177, 46.2-1178.
Inspection program coordinator, §46.2-1177.1.
Biennial inspection program, §46.2-1177.
Frequency of inspection, §46.2-1183.
Inspection program coordinator, §46.2-1177.1.
Board.
Compelling compliance with regulations, §46.2-1187.2.
Defined, §46.2-1176.
Rulemaking authority.
Clean alternative fuel fleet standards, §46.2-1179.1.
Emissions standards, §46.2-1179.
Exemption of certain vehicles, §46.2-1180.
Certificate of inspection.
False certificate, §§46.2-1186, 46.2-1187.
Fleet emissions inspection stations, §46.2-1184.
Clean alternative fuel fleet standards.
Rulemaking authority, §46.2-1179.1.
Compelling compliance with regulations, §46.2-1187.2.
Cost of repairs covered by warranties, §46.2-1181.
Counterfeit certificates of inspection, §46.2-1186.
Definitions, §46.2-1176.
Emissions standards.
Rulemaking authority, §46.2-1179.
Fees.
Emissions inspection fees, §46.2-1182.
Exemption, §§46.2-1182, 46.2-1182.1.
On-road testing of vehicle emissions, §46.2-1182.
Registration fee, §46.2-1182.1.
Vehicle emissions inspection program fund, §46.2-1182.2.
Fleet emissions inspection stations.
Defined, §46.2-1176.
Issuance of permits, §46.2-1184.
Frequency of inspection, §46.2-1183.
Biennial inspections, §46.2-1177.
Imitation certificates of inspection, §46.2-1186.
Inspection program coordinator, §46.2-1177.1.
Inspection stations.
Fleet emissions inspection stations, §46.2-1184.

MOTOR VEHICLE EMISSIONS INSPECTIONS —Cont'd
Inspection stations —Cont'd
Revocation or suspension of permits, §46.2-1185.
Investigations.
Compelling compliance with regulations, §46.2-1187.2.
Fleet emissions inspection stations, §46.2-1184.
Inspection stations, §46.2-1185.
Right of entry, §46.2-1187.1.
Vehicles used for investigations, §46.2-1187.3.
Local emissions inspection programs.
Administration and scope, §46.2-1178.
Recordkeeping requirements, §46.2-1183.
On-road clean screen program, §46.2-1178.1.
On-road testing of vehicle emissions, §46.2-1178.1.
Bilateral agreements with other states, §46.2-1180.
Enforcement actions involving.
Vehicle owner data supplied DEQ, §46.2-208.
Fees, §46.2-1182.
Repairs, subsidy program, §46.2-1178.2.
Separate emissions standards, §46.2-1179.
Registration of vehicles.
Emissions inspection required prior to registration of certain vehicles, §46.2-1183.
Extension for satisfaction of emissions inspection requirements, §46.2-1183.1.
Reinspection of motor vehicle, §46.2-1181.
Repairs, subsidy program.
On-road testing of vehicle emissions, §46.2-1178.2.
Revocation of permit.
Emissions inspection stations, §46.2-1185.
Fleet emissions inspection stations, §46.2-1184.
Rulemaking authority.
Clean alternative fuel fleet standards, §46.2-1179.1.
Emissions standards, §46.2-1179.
Exemption of certain vehicles, §46.2-1180.
Safety inspections generally, §§46.2-1157 to 46.2-1175.1.
See MOTOR VEHICLE SAFETY INSPECTIONS.
Scope of emissions inspection program.
Certain localities, §46.2-1178.
Suspension of permit.
Emissions inspection stations, §46.2-1185.
Fleet emissions inspection stations, §46.2-1184.
Vehicle emissions inspection program fund, §46.2-1182.2.
Waiver of emissions inspection, §46.2-1181.

MOTOR VEHICLE EQUIPMENT, §§46.2-1000 to 46.2-1100.
Absence of or inadequate rearview mirror.
Fine schedule, VA SCt Rule 3B:2.
Pretrial payment of fine, §16.1-69.40:1.
Acetylene lights on antique motor vehicles, §46.2-1036.
Air bags.
Installation of noncompliant or previously used air bags or components, §46.2-1088.3.
Air conditioning units, §46.2-1088.
Improper cooling unit, §46.2-1088.
Fine schedule, VA SCt Rule 3B:2.
Maximum fine for violating Title 46.2, §46.2-113.
Approval certificates, §§46.2-1005 to 46.2-1009.
Auxiliary lights.
Fine schedule, improper use, VA SCt Rule 3B:2.
Maximum fine for violating Title 46.2, §46.2-113.

MOTOR VEHICLE EQUIPMENT —Cont'd
Auxiliary lights —Cont'd
Firefighting, transportation development and other emergency vehicles, §46.2-1028.
Law-enforcement vehicles, §46.2-1029.
Back-up audible warnings.
Ice cream, snack, etc., trucks, §46.2-1088.2.
Brake lights, §46.2-1014.
Fines, VA SCt Rule 3B:2.
Maximum fine for violating Title 46.2, §46.2-113.
Pretrial payment, §16.1-69.40:1.
Brakes, §§46.2-1066 to 46.2-1071.
Approval of brake testing methods and equipment, §46.2-1006.
Braking distances, §46.2-1067.
Emergency or parking brakes, §§46.2-1068, 46.2-1071.
Fine schedule, VA SCt Rule 3B:2.
Maximum fine for violating title, §46.2-113.
Hand brake.
Failure to set hand brake and turn wheels to curb on parked vehicle, §46.2-1071.
Inadequate brakes, §§46.2-1066, 46.2-1068 to 46.2-1070.
Fine schedule, VA SCt Rule 3B:2.
Pretrial payment of fine, §16.1-69.40:1.
Motorcycles, §46.2-1069.
Requirements for parking, §46.2-1071.
Trailers, §46.2-1070.
Braking distances, §46.2-1067.
Chains, §46.2-1044.
Child restraints, §§46.2-1095 to 46.2-1100.
Commercial vehicles.
Additional lights permitted, §46.2-1021.
Dealer's odometer disclosure statement, §46.2-1532.
Defective or unsafe equipment.
Fine schedule, VA SCt Rule 3B:2.
Maximum fine for violating title, §46.2-113.
Pretrial payment of fine, §16.1-69.40:1.
Illegal use, §46.2-1003.
Demonstrator vehicles.
Warning lights, §46.2-1027.
Dimension or marker lights, §§46.2-1017, 46.2-1018.
Fine schedule, VA SCt Rule 3B:2.
Pretrial payment of fine, §16.1-69.40:1.
Dimming headlights, §§46.2-1034, 46.2-1035.
Fine schedule, VA SCt Rule 3B:2.
Maximum fine for violation of Title 46.2, §46.2-113.
Ditch lights, §46.2-1019.
Earphones.
Fine schedule, VA SCt Rule 3B:2.
Pretrial payment of fine, §16.1-69.40:1.
Unlawful use while operating vehicle, §46.2-1078.
Electric vehicles.
Converted electric vehicles, special equipment, §46.2-1001.1.
Exemption from testing procedure, §46.2-1009.
Emergency or parking brakes, §46.2-1068.
Exhaust system, §§46.2-1047 to 46.2-1051.
Chambered pipes, §46.2-1049.
Good working order exhaust system, §46.2-1049.
Improper pollution control device, §46.2-1048.
Inadequate exhaust system, §§46.2-1047 to 46.2-1051.
Fine schedule, VA SCt Rule 3B:2.
Maximum fine for violating Title 46.2, §46.2-113.

MOTOR VEHICLE EQUIPMENT —Cont'd
Exhaust system —Cont'd
Inadequate exhaust system —Cont'd
Fine schedule —Cont'd
Pretrial payment of fine, §16.1-69.40:1.
Local government restrictions on certain mobile equipment, §46.2-1051.
Muffler cutout, etc., §46.2-1047.
Mufflers on motorcycles, §46.2-1050.
Pollution control systems or devices, §46.2-1048.
Straight exhaust on gutted muffler, §46.2-1047.
Faulty brakes.
Reckless driving, §46.2-853.
Flame throwers, §§46.2-1086, 46.2-1087.
Flashing amber, purple or green warning lights, §46.2-1025.
Flashing blue or red and blue warning lights, §46.2-1022.
Emergency vehicle exemption from traffic regulations.
When exemption applicable, §46.2-920.
Flashing high-intensity amber warning lights, §46.2-1026.
Flashing of headlights on designated vehicles, §46.2-1029.1.
Flashing or steady-burning red or red and white warning lights, §46.2-1024.
Flashing red or red and white warning lights, §46.2-1023.
Emergency vehicle exemption from traffic regulations.
When exemption applicable, §46.2-920.
Fog lights, §46.2-1020.
For hire vehicles.
Lettering, §46.2-1076.
Gas projectors, §§46.2-1086, 46.2-1087.
Hazard lights, §46.2-1040.
Fine schedule, VA SCt Rule 3B:2.
Maximum fine for violating Title 46.2, §46.2-113.
Pretrial payment of fine, §16.1-69.40:1.
Headlights, §§46.2-1011, 46.2-1012.
Dimming requirements, §46.2-1034.
Failure to dim, §46.2-1034.
Failure to display at night or during time of poor visibility, §46.2-1030.
Fine schedule, VA SCt Rule 3B:2.
Maximum fine for violating title, §46.2-113.
Pretrial payment of fine, §16.1-69.40:1.
Flashing of headlights on designated vehicles, §46.2-1029.1.
Multiple-beam headlights, §46.2-1032.
Required display, §46.2-1030.
Single-beam headlights, §46.2-1031.
Hood scoops, §46.2-1088.1.
Horns, sirens and whistles, §§46.2-1059 to 46.2-1062.
Approval of warning devices, §46.2-1062.
Emergency vehicles, §46.2-1061.
Fine schedule, VA SCt Rule 3B:2.
Maximum fine for violation of title, §46.2-113.
Pretrial payment, §16.1-69.40:1.
Illegal siren, whistle or horn, §46.2-1060.
Inadequate horn, §46.2-1059.
Rulemaking authority, §46.2-1062.
Unlawful use of warning devices, §46.2-1060.
Ice cream trucks.
Warning devices, §46.2-1088.2.
Identification numbers, §§46.2-1072 to 46.2-1075.
Fees for examination, verification or identification, §46.2-1072.1.

MOTOR VEHICLE EQUIPMENT —Cont'd
Illegible engine or serial numbers, §46.2-1073.
Indicator lights, §46.2-1033.
Law-enforcement vehicles.
Auxiliary lights, §46.2-1029.
Flashing blue or red and blue warning lights, §46.2-1022.
Flashing of headlights, §46.2-1029.1.
Horns, sirens and whistles, §46.2-1061.
Lettering.
For hire vehicles, §46.2-1076.
Vehicles used to transport property, §46.2-1075.
Lift blocks to modify front-end suspension, §46.2-1064.
Lights and turn signals, §§46.2-1010 to 46.2-1040.
Acetylene lights on antique motor vehicles, §46.2-1036.
Approval of headlight testing methods and equipment, §46.2-1006.
Auxiliary headlights, §46.2-1012.
Auxiliary lights on firefighting, transportation development and other emergency vehicles, §46.2-1028.
Auxiliary lights on law-enforcement vehicles, §46.2-1029.
Bicycles and mopeds, §46.2-1015.
Brake lights, §46.2-1014.
Commercial vehicles.
Additional lights permitted, §46.2-1021.
Dimension or marker lights, §§46.2-1017, 46.2-1018.
Dimming headlights, §§46.2-1034, 46.2-1035.
Ditchlights, §46.2-1019.
Driving with excessive headlights, §46.2-1030.
Employment of lights or spotlights.
Under certain circumstances, §18.2-509.
Exceptions to turn signal requirement, §46.2-1038.
Fifteen candlepower interior lights, §46.2-1020.
Fine schedule, VA SCt Rule 3B:2.
Maximum fine for violation of title, §46.2-113.
Flashing amber, purple or green warning lights, §46.2-1025.
Flashing blue or red and blue warning lights, §46.2-1022.
Emergency vehicle exemption from traffic regulations.
When exemption applicable, §46.2-920.
Flashing high-intensity amber warning lights, §46.2-1026.
Flashing lights on other vehicles, §46.2-1029.1.
Flashing or steady-burning red or red and white warning lights, §46.2-1024.
Flashing red or red and white warning lights, §46.2-1023.
Emergency vehicle exemption from traffic regulations.
When exemption applicable, §46.2-920.
Fog lights, §46.2-1020.
Hazard lights, §46.2-1040.
Improper display of warning lights, §46.2-1030.
Indicator lights, §46.2-1033.
Insufficient lighting equipment, §46.2-1010.
Fine schedule, VA SCt Rule 3B:2.
Pretrial payment of fine, §16.1-69.40:1.
Lack of or inadequate signal device, §§46.2-1038, 46.2-1039.
Less than two proper headlights, §46.2-1011.
Motorcycle without proper headlights, §46.2-1012.
Multiple-beam headlights, §46.2-1032.

MOTOR VEHICLE EQUIPMENT —Cont'd
Lights and turn signals —Cont'd
Number of lights to be lighted at any time, §46.2-1030.
Parked vehicles, §46.2-1037.
Permissible lights, §46.2-1020.
Privately owned vehicles.
Additional lights permitted, §46.2-1021.1.
Reflectors, §46.2-1016.
Requirements of turn signals, §§46.2-1038, 46.2-1039.
Secondary warning lights, §46.2-1029.2.
Side lights, §46.2-1020.
Single-beam headlights, §46.2-1031.
Spotlights, §46.2-1019.
Supplemental high mount stop light, §46.2-1014.1.
Tail lights, §46.2-1013.
Use of warning lights, §46.2-1030.
Warning lights on certain demonstrator vehicles, §46.2-1027.
When lights to be lighted, §46.2-1030.
Litter tax imposed on manufacturers, wholesalers, etc., of motor vehicle parts, §58.1-1708.
Maximum fine for violating Title 46.2, §46.2-113.
Mirrors.
Absence of or inadequate rearview mirror, §46.2-1082.
Fine schedule, VA SCt Rule 3B:2.
Maximum fine for violating Title 46.2, §46.2-113.
Mobile infrared transmitters, §46.2-1077.1.
Mudflaps, §46.2-1112.
Mufflers.
Confiscation, §46.2-1000.
Exhaust system generally, §§46.2-1047 to 46.2-1051.
Fine schedule, VA SCt Rule 3B:2.
Maximum fine for violating Title 46.2, §46.2-113.
Motorcycles, §46.2-1050.
Straight exhaust or gutted mufflers, §46.2-1047.
Multiple-beam headlights, §46.2-1032.
Nitrous oxide devices connected to engines, §46.2-1088.4.
Noise-cancellation devices, §46.2-1078.
Obliterated engine or serial numbers, §46.2-1073.
Odometers.
Dealers disclosure statement, §46.2-1532.
Reporting odometer reading on certificate of title, §46.2-629.
Tampering, §46.2-112.
Onboard recording devices, §46.2-1088.6.
Permits.
Electrically powered vehicles, §46.2-1009.
Traction engines and tractors, §46.2-1046.
Pollution control systems or devices.
Exhaust system generally, §§46.2-1047 to 46.2-1051.
Fine schedule, VA SCt Rule 3B:2.
Maximum fine for violating Title 46.2, §46.2-113.
Requirements, §46.2-1048.
Pretrial payment of fine, §16.1-69.40:1.
Uniform fine schedule, VA SCt Rules 3B:1, 3B:2.
Privately owned vehicles.
Additional lights permitted, §46.2-1021.1.
Radar detection devices.
Fine schedule, VA SCt Rule 3B:2.
Pretrial payment of fine, §16.1-69.40:1.

MOTOR VEHICLE EQUIPMENT —Cont'd
Radar detection devices —Cont'd
Unlawful use, §46.2-1079.
Rear fenders, flaps or guards, §46.2-1083.
Fine schedule, VA SCt Rule 3B:2.
Maximum fine for violating Title 46.2, §46.2-113.
Pretrial payment of fine, §16.1-69.40:1.
Recording devices, §46.2-1088.6.
Reflectors, §§46.2-1016, 46.2-1017.
Regrooved or recut tires.
Sale, etc., prohibited, §46.2-1042.
Removal of engine or serial numbers, §46.2-1073.
Replacement glass.
Fine schedule, VA SCt Rule 3B:2.
Pretrial payment of fine, §16.1-69.40:1.
Improper repair, §46.2-1058.
Safety belts, §§46.2-1091 to 46.2-1094.
Child restraints, §§46.2-1095 to 46.2-1100.
Uniform fine schedule for violations, VA SCt Rules 3C:1, 3C:2.
Safety glass.
Absence of required safety glass, §46.2-1056.
Fine schedule, VA SCt Rule 3B:2.
Maximum fine for violating Title 46.2, §46.2-113.
Pretrial payment of fine, §16.1-69.40:1.
Seats.
Operator's seat improperly affixed, §46.2-1084.
Fine schedule, VA SCt Rule 3B:2.
Maximum fine for violating Title 46.2, §46.2-113.
Pretrial payment of fine, §16.1-69.40:1.
Serial or identification numbers.
Fees for examination, verification or identification, §46.2-1072.1.
Illegible, removed or obliterated engine or serial numbers, §46.2-1073.
Possession of vehicle with removed or altered serial numbers, §46.2-1075.
Removal or alteration without consent of department, §46.2-1074.
Requirements for stamping, cutting or embossing numbers, §46.2-1072.
Single-beam headlights, §46.2-1031.
Sirens, §§46.2-1059 to 46.2-1062.
Size and weight limitations, §46.2-1112.
Slow-moving vehicle emblems, §46.2-1081.
Smoke screen emission devices, §§46.2-1086, 46.2-1087.
Snack trucks, ice cream trucks, etc.
Warning devices, §46.2-1088.2.
Solid rubber tire restrictions, §46.2-1041.
Fine schedule, VA SCt Rule 3B:2.
Maximum fine for violating Title 46.2, §46.2-113.
Pretrial payment of fine, §16.1-69.40:1.
Speedometers.
Good working order requirement, §46.2-1080.
Spotlights, §46.2-1019.
Fine schedule, VA SCt Rule 3B:2.
Pretrial payment of fine, §16.1-69.40:1.
Standards.
Electrically powered vehicles, §46.2-1009.
Steering and suspension systems, §§46.2-1063 to 46.2-1065.
Bumper height limits, §46.2-1063.
Fine schedule, VA SCt Rule 3B:2.
Maximum fine for violating Title 46.2, §46.2-113.

MOTOR VEHICLE EQUIPMENT —Cont'd
Steering and suspension systems —Cont'd
Front-end suspension.
Modification by use of lift blocks, §46.2-1064.
Improper alteration, §§46.2-1063, 46.2-1064.
Fine schedule, VA SCt Rule 3B:2.
Pretrial payment of fine, §16.1-69.40:1.
Modification of front-end suspension by use of lift blocks, §46.2-1063.
Preventive maintenance kit for use on part of steering gear, §46.2-1065.
Repair kit for use on part of steering gear, §46.2-1063.
Steering gear repair kits, §46.2-1065.
Stop lights.
Supplemental high mount stop light, §46.2-1014.1.
Fine schedule, VA SCt Rule 3B:2.
Maximum fine for violation of Title 46.2, §46.2-113.
Studded tires.
Fine schedule, VA SCt Rule 3B:2.
Pretrial payment of fine, §16.1-69.40:1.
Sun-shading or tinting films or applications, §§46.2-1052, 46.2-1053.
Supplemental high mount stop light, §46.2-1014.1.
Fine schedule, VA SCt Rule 3B:2.
Maximum fine for violating Title 46.2, §46.2-113.
Suspension systems, §§46.2-1063 to 46.2-1065.
Tail lights, §46.2-1013.
Fine schedule, VA SCt Rule 3B:2.
Maximum fine for violating Title 46.2, §46.2-113.
Pretrial payment of fine, §16.1-69.40:1.
Tampering with gross vehicle weight ratings, §46.2-1075.1.
Television-equipped vehicles, §46.2-1077.
Display of obscene materials which can be seen from outside of the vehicle, §46.2-1077.01.
Viewing motion pictures or similar displays while driving, §46.2-1077.
Testing, evaluation and approval of equipment, §§46.2-1005 to 46.2-1009.
Brake and headlight testing methods and equipment, §46.2-1006.
Electrically powered vehicles, §46.2-1009.
Exemptions for certain electrically powered vehicles, §46.2-1009.
Fees for certificates of approval, §46.2-1008.
Issuance of certificates of approval, §46.2-1005.
Procedure, §46.2-1005.
Retesting of devices, §46.2-1007.
Revocation of certificates of approval, §46.2-1007.
Rulemaking authority, §46.2-1005.
Tires, §§46.2-1041 to 46.2-1046.
Chains, §46.2-1044.
Cleats, etc., on tires, §§46.2-1044, 46.2-1045.
Devices for puncturing.
Manufacturing, distributing or possessing, §18.2-147.2.
Police use authorized, §33.1-345.
Improper or inadequate tires, §§46.2-1041, 46.2-1043, 46.2-1044.
Fine schedule, VA SCt Rule 3B:2.
Maximum fine for violating Title 46.2, §46.2-113.
Pretrial payment of fine, §16.1-69.40:1.
Loading of tires, §46.2-1043.1.
Regrooved or recut tires, §46.2-1042.
Solid rubber tire restrictions, §46.2-1041.

MOTOR VEHICLE EQUIPMENT —Cont'd
Tires —Cont'd
Studded tires, §§46.2-1044, 46.2-1045.
Tire tax, §§58.1-640 to 58.1-644.
Tire tread depth, §46.2-1043.
Tractor engines and tractors, §46.2-1046.
Tire tread depth.
Fine schedule, VA SCt Rule 3B:2.
Pretrial payment of fine, §16.1-69.40:1.
Tow trucks.
Lettering, §46.2-1076.
Traction engines and tractors.
Issuance of special permits for operation on highway, §46.2-1046.
Trademark or trade name.
Required for sale of certain unapproved equipment, §46.2-1004.
Trailers.
Reflectors and reflectorized material required, §46.2-1088.5.
Unapproved equipment.
Fine schedule, VA SCt Rule 3B:2.
Maximum fine for violating Title 46.2, §46.2-113.
Pretrial payment of fine, §16.1-69.40:1.
Illegal possession or sale, §46.2-1002.
Trademark or name and instructions required, §46.2-1004.
Uniformed law-enforcement officers.
Stopping vehicles for inspection, §46.2-103.
Unsafe equipment.
Illegal use, §46.2-1003.
Fine schedule, VA SCt Rule 3B:2.
Maximum fine for violating Title 46.2, §46.2-113.
Unsafe vehicles.
Confiscation of registration card, license plates and decals, §46.2-1000.
Removal from streets, §46.2-1001.
Suspension of registration, §46.2-1000.
Warning devices.
Ice cream, snack, etc., trucks, §46.2-1088.2.
School buses, §46.2-1090.
Warning lights.
School buses, §46.2-1090.1.
Whistles, §§46.2-1059 to 46.2-1062.
Windshields and windows, §§46.2-1052 to 46.2-1058.
Absence of required safety glass, §46.2-1056.
Absence of windshield, §46.2-1057.
Driver's view obstructed because of suspended object or altered vehicle, §46.2-1054.
Fine schedule, VA SCt Rule 3B:2.
Improper replacement of glass in vehicle, §46.2-1058.
Improper signs on windshields, etc., §46.2-1052.
Inadequate windshield wipers, §46.2-1055.
Missing windshield, §46.2-1057.
Replacement of glass in vehicle, §46.2-1058.
Signs, decals and stickers on windshields, etc., §46.2-1052.
Sun-shading or tinting films or applications, §§46.2-1052, 46.2-1053.
Suspension of objects or alteration of vehicle so as to obstruct driver's view, §46.2-1054.
Windshield defroster or defogger, §46.2-1055.1.
Windshield missing, §46.2-1057.

MOTOR VEHICLE FINANCIAL RESPONSIBILITY, §§46.2-435 to 46.2-463.
Acceptance by owner in lieu of driver, §46.2-437.

MOTOR VEHICLE FINANCIAL RESPONSIBILITY —Cont'd
Affidavit of nonexistence affects, §46.2-461.
Bond duly executed.
Action on bond, §46.2-451.
Bond to constitute lien on real estate of surety, §46.2-447.
Cancellation not to affect recovery rights, §46.2-446.
Cancellation of bond with individual sureties, §46.2-449.
Certificates of cancellation, §46.2-449.
Conditions of bond, §46.2-445.
Consent of commissioner to cancellation of bond, §46.2-460.
Discharging lien of bond, §46.2-450.
How bond to be conditioned, §46.2-445.
Individual sureties, §§46.2-449, 46.2-452.
Method of proving, §46.2-436.
Notice of cancellation, §46.2-448.
Notice prerequisite to cancellation, §46.2-446.
Order discharging lien of bond, §46.2-450.
Parties to suit on bond with individual sureties, §46.2-452.
Suit on bond, §46.2-451.
Surety requirements of bond, §46.2-444.
Cancellation or return of old proof, §46.2-457.
Certificate of insurance carrier, §46.2-439.
Default of foreign insurance carrier, §46.2-442.
Nonresidents, §§46.2-440, 46.2-441.
Construction of article, §46.2-443.
Conviction of certain offenses.
Proof required for issuance or reinstatement of driver's license, §46.2-316.
Default of foreign insurance carrier, §46.2-442.
Deposit of money or securities.
Additional security if funds impaired, §46.2-456.
Assessment for expenses of holding deposits, §46.2-455.
Certification of value upon delivery, §46.2-454.
Consent of commissioner to return of money or securities, §46.2-460.
Defraying expenses of safe keeping and handling, §46.2-455.
Delivering to commissioner, §46.2-453.
Impairment of security, §46.2-456.
Interpleader to determine rights in deposits, §46.2-458.
Method of proving, §46.2-436.
Subject to execution, §46.2-454.
Sum equal to liability coverage, §46.2-453.
Drivers' licenses.
Driving while restoration of license or permit contingent on furnishing proof, §46.2-302.
Requirement of proof for persons convicted of certain offenses, §46.2-316.
Suspension.
Nonresidents.
Compliance with requirements, §46.2-431.
Pending furnishing of proof required, §46.2-459.
Reinstatement, §46.2-411.
Relief from furnishing proof of financial responsibility, §46.2-427.
Unsatisfied judgments.
Order for installment payments of judgment, §46.2-421.
Foreign insurance carrier.
Defaults on undertakings or agreements, §46.2-442.
Forging evidence of proof, §46.2-463.
Furnishing for each vehicle, §46.2-435.

MOTOR VEHICLE FINANCIAL RESPONSIBILITY —Cont'd
Habitual offender status.
Restoration of driving privileges, §46.2-361.
Interpleader to determine rights in deposits, §46.2-458.
Interpretation of article, §46.2-443.
Liability insurance policies.
Certificate of insurance carrier, §46.2-439.
Consent of commissioner to cancellation of policy, §46.2-460.
Inapplicability of chapter provisions, §46.2-443.
Method of proving, §46.2-436.
Lien of bond, §46.2-447.
Discharging, §46.2-450.
Methods of proving, §46.2-436.
Motor vehicle registration.
Suspension.
Reinstatement, §46.2-411.
New driver's license or registration card.
Person to whom proof surrendered, §46.2-462.
Nonresident.
Certificate of insurance carrier, §§46.2-440, 46.2-441.
Permit or certificate of convenience and necessity.
Issuance by state corporation commission, §46.2-438.
Persons convicted of certain offenses.
Proof required for issuance or reinstatement of driver's license, §46.2-316.
Release of proof when commissioner not to release proof, §46.2-461.
Requirement for each vehicle, §46.2-435.
When other proof required, §46.2-459.
Risk retention groups and purchasing groups.
Groups not exempt, §38.2-5113.
Self-insurance certificate.
Method of proving, §46.2-436.
Substitution of new proof, §46.2-457.
Surrender of proof.
New license or registration to person, §46.2-462.
Uninsured motor vehicles.
When other proof required, §46.2-709.
Vehicles operated under permit or certificate of state corporation commission, §46.2-438.

MOTOR VEHICLE FUELS SALES TAX ACT.
Sales tax in certain transportation districts, §§58.1-2291 to 58.1-2299.20.
See FUEL TAXES.

MOTOR VEHICLE GRAVEYARDS OR JUNKYARDS, §33.1-348.

MOTOR VEHICLE INSURANCE.
Accidents.
Refusal to renew based on, §38.2-2212.
Affiliated insurer willing to provide coverage at a lower premium than expiring policy.
Policy issued deemed renewal, §38.2-231.
After market parts.
Estimating costs of automobile repairs, §38.2-510.
Agents' moratorium in soliciting, negotiating, etc.
Disclosure required, §38.2-613.1.
Agents selling medical, hospital, surgical, etc., benefits as part of policy.
Life and health insurance agents license not required, §38.2-1828.
Age of motor vehicle.
Failure to issue or renew insurance on basis of, §38.2-2215.

MOTOR VEHICLE INSURANCE —Cont'd
Age, sex, race, color, creed, national origin.
Refusal to renew based on.
Prohibition, §38.2-2212.
Antisubrogation statute.
Medical benefit insurer not to retain right of subrogation to recover from third party, §38.2-2209.
Appeal of premium increase or points charged by main insured, §38.2-1905.
Appeal to state corporation commission on cancellation or refusal to renew, §38.2-2212.
Applicability of other valid and collectible insurance, §38.2-2205.
Arbitrary refusal of accident claim, §8.01-66.1.
Arbitration.
Physical damage.
Arbitration between insurers, §38.2-2231.
Arbitration under underinsured or uninsured motorist endorsement, §38.2-2206.
Assessment to fund program to reduce losses from motor vehicle thefts, §38.2-414.
Assignment of benefits, §38.2-2201.
Assignment of insurance risks, §§46.2-464 to 46.2-471.
Applicability of article, §§46.2-470, 46.2-471.
Application, §46.2-464.
Authority of commission, §46.2-467.
Confidentiality of information, §46.2-468.
Action within power of commission, §46.2-469.
Construction of article, §46.2-471.
Family optional coverage, §46.2-465.
Filing requirements by insurance carriers, §46.2-468.
Liability of commission for acts or omissions, §46.2-469.
Nondisclosure of action within power of commission, §46.2-467.
Nonresidents, §46.2-470.
Optional coverage, §46.2-465.
Power of commission, §46.2-467.
Rate classification, §46.2-466.
Rates generally.
Workers' compensation, automobiles, home protection, etc., §§38.2-2000 to 38.2-2027.
See INSURANCE RATES.
Rating schedules, §46.2-466.
Right of application, §46.2-464.
Rulemaking authority, §46.2-466.
Breach of terms or conditions, insurer to rely on defense.
Notice to claimant, §38.2-2226.
Cancellation.
Grounds and procedure, §38.2-2212.
Notice, mailing or electronic delivery requirements of insurer, §38.2-2208.
Notice requirements generally, §§38.2-231, 38.2-2212.
Reason required on application, §38.2-2210.
Warning concerning to appear on application, §38.2-2210.
Capping.
Defined, engaging in practice prohibited, §38.2-517.
Certificates of insurance, requirements, §38.2-518.
Change in occupation materially increasing risk.
Refusal to renew, §38.2-2212.
Change of address of insurer.
Grounds for cancellation, §38.2-2212.

MOTOR VEHICLE INSURANCE —Cont'd
Chiropractors.
Policy providing for reimbursement for services, §38.2-2203.
Claims submitted.
Refusal to renew based on.
Prohibition, §38.2-2212.
Collision damage waiver on rentals, §§59.1-207.28 to 59.1-207.33.
Conviction of certain offenses.
Proof of financial responsibility in form of liability policy.
Required to issue or reinstate driver's license, §46.2-316.
Copies of orders to companies affected, §38.2-2225.
County providing insurance to protect operators of vehicles owned or leased by county, school board, etc., §15.2-1214.
Coverage reduction, notice of, §38.2-231.
Credit for other medical expense insurance, insurer not to receive, §38.2-2211.
Credit reports.
Grounds for termination of policy, §38.2-2212.
Use of credit information, §38.2-2234.
Death occurring as result of motor vehicle accident.
Limits of liability insurance.
Request of insurer to provide prior to bringing action, §8.01-417.
Defense of breach of terms or conditions, reliance by insurer.
Notice to claimant, §38.2-2226.
Defined, §38.2-124.
Designated replacement or repair facilities or products.
Insured not obligated to use.
Failure to disclose, §38.2-517.
Disclosure required, §38.2-514.1.
Motor vehicle rental contract insurance agents and enrollers, §38.2-514.2.
Discrimination, §§38.2-508, 38.2-2215.
Issuance, §38.2-2213.
Refusal to renew, §38.2-2212.
Driver's license.
Conviction of certain offenses.
Proof of financial responsibility in form of liability policy.
Required to issue or reinstate driver's license, §46.2-316.
Suspension, revocation.
Cancellation of policy, §38.2-2212.
Drivers' policy coverage, §46.2-473.
Driving experience.
Refusal to renew based on.
Prohibition, §38.2-2212.
Elderly, reduction in rates, §38.2-2217.
Employees, policies not to exclude coverage to, §38.2-2207.
Estimates of repair costs when using after market parts, §38.2-510.
Failure to pay premium.
Cancellation of policy, §38.2-2212.
False or fraudulent claim.
Refusal to renew, §38.2-2212.
Fleet vehicles.
Self-insurance, §46.2-368.
Form of notice of cancellation or refusal to renew, §38.2-2212.
Form of notice of optional coverage available, §38.2-2202.

MOTOR VEHICLE INSURANCE —Cont'd
Form of warning concerning cancellation on application, §38.2-2210.
Forms, standard forms, §§38.2-2218 to 38.2-2224.
Adoption, §38.2-2218.
Amendment of standard form, §38.2-2221.
Objections, hearing on, §38.2-2219.
Use of form after adoption, §38.2-2220.
Variations of or additions to, §38.2-2223.
Withdrawal of form, §38.2-2222.
Future financial responsibility of licensed property and casualty insurers.
Proof required at request of insured, §38.2-228.
Glass claims.
Third party representative acting on behalf of insurer.
Failure to disclose, §38.2-517.
Guidelines for filing readable forms.
State corporation commission to establish, §38.2-2224.
HEAT fund, §38.2-414.
Help eliminate automobile theft fund, §38.2-414.
Immunity of persons furnishing insurer information as to reasons for cancellation or refusal to renew, §38.2-2212.
Impoundment of vehicle, suspension of coverage at insured's request, §38.2-2205.1.
Income loss benefits, provisions for, §38.2-2201.
Increase in premium.
Insurer not to increase unless accident caused by insured, §38.2-1905.
Notice of, §38.2-231.
Insurers, licensed property and casualty insurers.
Proof of future financial responsibility at request of insured, §38.2-228.
John Doe actions.
Owner or operator of vehicle causing injury or damage unknown, §38.2-2206.
Law enforcement officers.
Premium increases, §38.2-1905.
Lawful occupation.
Refusal to renew based on.
Prohibition, §38.2-2212.
Liability insurance generally, §§38.2-2200 to 38.2-2234.
See LIABILITY INSURANCE.
Limits of liability insurance.
Request in action resulting from automobile accident of insurer to provide, §8.01-417.
Local government group self-insurance pools, §§15.2-2700 to 15.2-2709.
Loss of income benefits, provisions for, §38.2-2201.
Low-speed vehicles.
Required, §46.2-908.3.
Manifestation of willingness to renew policy, §38.2-2212.
Marital status.
Refusal to renew based on.
Prohibition, §38.2-2212.
Medical expense payment provisions, §38.2-2201.
Assignment of benefits, §38.2-2201.
Insurer not to receive credit for other medical expense insurance, §38.2-2211.
Medical benefit insurer not to retain right of subrogation to recover from third party, §38.2-2209.

MOTOR VEHICLE INSURANCE —Cont'd
Medical expense payment provisions —Cont'd
Offset of benefit against liability or uninsured motorist coverage prohibited, §38.2-2216.
Presumption of authenticity and reasonableness of medical bills, §8.01-413.01.
Military service.
Refusal to renew based on.
Prohibition, §38.2-2212.
Moratorium on agents soliciting, negotiating, etc.
Disclosure required, §38.2-613.1.
Nonresidents.
Assignment of risks, §46.2-470.
Nonwaiver of rights agreements.
Notice to claimant, §38.2-2226.
Notice.
Cancellation or refusal to renew, §§38.2-231, 38.2-2212.
Mailing or electronic delivery, insurer's requirements, §38.2-2208.
Increase in rates, §38.2-1905.
Intention to rely on defenses and execution of nonwaiver of rights agreement, §38.2-2226.
Optional coverage available, required notice, §38.2-2202.
Settlement of claim, §38.2-2226.1.
Occupational or membership requirements of insurer.
Failure to conform.
Refusal to renew, §38.2-2212.
Offset of medical benefit against liability or uninsured coverage prohibited, §38.2-2216.
Omnibus clause, standard liability insurance, §38.2-2204.
Operation of vehicle by other than named insured with expressed or implied consent of named insured.
Omnibus clause, §38.2-2204.
Optional provisions.
Assignment of benefits, §38.2-2201.
Medical expense payment and loss of income benefits, §38.2-2201.
Required notice of optional coverage available, §38.2-2202.
Other valid and collectible insurance, applicability, §38.2-2205.
Owners' policy coverage, §46.2-472.
Particular profession, trade, occupation or business.
Policies limited to class or group engaged in, §38.2-2212.
Paying greater than prevailing competitive charges for repair services or products.
Not required of insurer, §38.2-517.
Personal injury action by person injured in automobile accident.
Limits of liability insurance.
Request by person injured in automobile accident of insurer to provide prior to bringing action, §8.01-417.
Points under safe driver insurance plan.
Insurer not to charge unless accident caused by insured, §38.2-1905.
Policies and contracts generally, §§38.2-300 to 38.2-326.
See INSURANCE POLICIES AND CONTRACTS.
Policy coverage, §§46.2-472 to 46.2-482.
Additional coverage, §46.2-474.
Binder in lieu of policy, §46.2-481.
Cancellation of certified policy, §46.2-482.

MOTOR VEHICLE INSURANCE —Cont'd
Policy coverage —Cont'd
Compliance with law, §46.2-475.
Driver's policy, §46.2-473.
Endorsement in lieu of policy, §46.2-481.
Liability covered by workers' compensation, §46.2-476.
Multiple policies.
Meeting requirements of chapter, §46.2-478.
Noncompliance with law, §46.2-475.
Optional provisions to which policy subject but need not contain, §46.2-479.
Owner's policy, §46.2-472.
Proration of insurance, §46.2-480.
Provisions to which policy subject but need not contain, §46.2-479.
Reimbursement of carrier, §46.2-480.
Several policies.
Meeting requirements of chapter, §46.2-478.
Statutory agreement, §46.2-474.
Termination of certified policy, §46.2-482.
When chapter applicable to policy, §46.2-477.
Presumption motor vehicle uninsured, §38.2-2206.
Proof of financial responsibility, §§46.2-435 to 46.2-463.
See MOTOR VEHICLE FINANCIAL RESPONSIBILITY.
Proration of insurance, §46.2-480.
Rates.
Classifications, statement defining provided insured, §38.2-2214.
Generally, §§38.2-1900 to 38.2-1928.
See INSURANCE RATES.
Increase in premium, accidents caused by insured, §38.2-1905.
Increase, notice of, §38.2-231.
Reduction for persons fifty-five years of age and older, §38.2-2217.
Refusal of owner to allow access to data from recording device.
Increase in premiums prohibited, §38.2-2213.1.
Workers' compensation, automobiles, home protection, etc., §§38.2-2000 to 38.2-2027.
See INSURANCE RATES.
Readable policy forms.
Guidelines to be established by state corporation commission, §38.2-2224.
Recording device.
Refusal of owner to allow access to data from.
Prohibited actions by insurer, §38.2-2213.1.
Refusal to renew based on, prohibition, §38.2-2212.
Records, retention.
Cancellation, refusal to renew, reduction in coverage, §§38.2-231, 38.2-2212.
Reduction in coverage, notice of, §38.2-231.
Reduction in rates for persons fifty-five years of age and older, §38.2-2217.
Refusal to renew.
Age of motor vehicle as basis, §38.2-2215.
Grounds and procedure, §38.2-2212.
Notice, mailing or electronic delivery requirements of insurer, §38.2-2208.
Notice requirements generally, §§38.2-231, 38.2-2212.
Reason required on application, §38.2-2210.
Release of insurance data.
Department of motor vehicles, §46.2-208.
Renewal.
Refusal to renew, §38.2-2212.

MOTOR VEHICLE INSURANCE —Cont'd
Rental reimbursement coverage.
Mandatory offer, §38.2-2230.
Rentals.
Collision damage waiver, §§59.1-207.28 to 59.1-207.33.
Replacement or repair facilities or services.
Unfair settlement practices, §38.2-517.
Replacement policies, §38.2-2212.1.
Review by state corporation commission on cancellation or refusal to renew, §38.2-2212.
Review of insurer action.
Cancellation, refusal to renew, reduction in coverage, §38.2-231.
Risk retention groups and purchasing groups.
Motor vehicle financial responsibility insurance law of Commonwealth.
Groups not exempt, §38.2-5113.
Self-insurance.
Fleet vehicles, §46.2-368.
Sending copies of orders to companies affected, §38.2-2225.
Settlement of claim, notice required, §38.2-2226.1.
Standard forms.
Adoption, §38.2-2218.
Amendment, §38.2-2221.
Objections, hearing on, §38.2-2219.
Use of form after adoption, §38.2-2220.
Variations of or additions to, §38.2-2223.
Withdrawal, §38.2-2222.
Standard provisions.
Applicability of other valid and collectible insurance, §38.2-2205.
Liability insurance generally, §38.2-2204.
Subrogation.
John Doe actions, §38.2-2206.
Medical benefit insurer.
Right of subrogation not retained against third party, §38.2-2209.
Payment of claims under uninsured or underinsured motorist endorsement, §38.2-2206.
Workers' compensation liability carriers, §65.2-309.1.
Substitute vehicle provided insured by insurer.
Person entitled to recover cost for hiring substitute vehicle, §8.01-66.
Suspension of coverage at insured's request, §38.2-2205.1.
Underinsured motorist coverage, §38.2-2206.
Arbitration under endorsement, §38.2-2206.
Required notice of optional coverage available, §38.2-2202.
Unfair insurance trade practices generally, §§38.2-500 to 38.2-518.
See INSURANCE, UNFAIR TRADE PRACTICES.
Uninsured motorist coverage, §38.2-2206.
Arbitration under endorsement, §38.2-2206.
Medical benefit offset against prohibited, §38.2-2216.
Notice of optional coverage available, §38.2-2202.
Rates.
Workers' compensation, automobiles, home protection, etc., §§38.2-2000 to 38.2-2027.
See INSURANCE RATES.
Uninsured motorist fund, §§38.2-3000, 38.2-3001.
Use of license plates from another vehicle.
Application of liability insurance policy, §46.2-721.

MOTOR VEHICLE INSURANCE —Cont'd
Vanpools, renewal of liability coverage, §38.2-2217.1.
Virginia property and casualty insurance guaranty association, §§38.2-1600 to 38.2-1623.
Warning concerning cancellation to appear on application, §38.2-2210.
Workers' compensation.
Liability covered by workers' compensation law, §46.2-476.
Uninsured or underinsured motorist benefits.
Lien of employer, §65.2-309.1.

MOTOR VEHICLE LEASES.
Driver information.
Commissioner of department of motor vehicles.
Supplying leasing company on request, §46.2-208.
Injury to vehicles leased, §18.2-149.
Personal property taxes.
Payment of tax by lessee, §58.1-3516.2.
Unlawful sublease.
A vehicle subject to lease, security interest or lien, §18.2-115.1.

MOTOR VEHICLE LICENSE PLATES, §§46.2-711 to 46.2-749.130.
Address correction.
Updating addresses by persons completing forms, §46.2-203.1.
AFL-CIO supporters.
Special license plates, §46.2-746.10.
Agricultural or horticultural.
Exemption of vehicles used for, §46.2-664.
Air Force Cross recipients.
Special license plates, §46.2-742.2.
Air force retirees.
Special license plates, §46.2-743.
Altered or forged plates, §46.2-722.
Altering appearance of plates, §46.2-716.
Amateur radio operators.
Special license plates, §46.2-738.
Antique motor vehicles.
Special license plates, §46.2-730.
Antique trailers, §46.2-730.
Appointed officials.
Special license plates, §46.2-736.2.
Attachment to vehicle, §§46.2-715, 46.2-716.
Attorney general.
Special license plate, §46.2-736.1.
Autism.
Unlocking autism, §46.2-749.60.
Aviation.
Special license plates, §46.2-746.11.
Battle of Chosin Reservoir.
Special license plates for survivors, §46.2-740.
Bicentennial special license plates and decals, §46.2-727.
Bicycle enthusiasts, §46.2-749.111.
BoatU.S. members, §46.2-749.54.
Bronze Star recipients.
Special license plates, §46.2-742.1.
Business entity logo on plate.
Fleet vehicles, business entities with, §46.2-725.2.
Carpooling.
Special license plates, §46.2-749.10.
Children or minors.
Special license plates.
Supporters of certain children's programs, §46.2-749.2:1.

MOTOR VEHICLE LICENSE PLATES —Cont'd
Child's handprint.
Special license plates.
Supporters of certain children's programs, §46.2-749.2:1.
Circuit court clerks.
Special license plates, §46.2-737.
City special license plates, §46.2-749.4.
Commemorative license plates for counties, cities and towns, §46.2-749.4:4.
City treasurers.
Special license plates, §46.2-737.
Civic organizations.
Special license plates, §46.2-746.1.
Class-J No. 611 steam locomotive.
Special plates commemorating, §46.2-749.40.
Clean special fuel vehicles.
Special license plates, §46.2-749.3.
Clerk of the House of Delegates.
Special license plate, §46.2-736.1.
Clerk of the Virginia Senate.
Special license plate, §46.2-736.1.
College fraternities and sororities.
Special license plates, §46.2-746.7.
Combat infantryman badge, §46.2-742.4.
Commercial vehicles.
Revocation of plates or decals, §46.2-609.
Commissioners of the revenue.
Special license plates, §46.2-737.
Commonwealth's attorneys.
Special license plates, §46.2-737.
Communiplates, §§46.2-711 to 46.2-749.130.
Confiscation for equipment safety violations, §46.2-1000.
Constitutional officers.
Special license plates, §§46.2-736.1, 46.2-737.
County attorneys.
Special license plates, §46.2-737.
County special license plates, §46.2-749.4.
Commemorative license plates for counties, cities and towns, §46.2-749.4:4.
County treasurers.
Special license plates, §46.2-737.
Credit unions.
Special license plates, §46.2-746.12.
Dealer license plates.
Generally, §§46.2-1546 to 46.2-1557.2.
See MOTOR VEHICLE DEALERS.
Temporary plates, §§46.2-1558 to 46.2-1565.
See MOTOR VEHICLE DEALERS.
Decals.
Altered or forged decals, §46.2-722.
Appeal of revocation, §46.2-611.
Bicentennial decals, §46.2-727.
Confiscation for equipment safety violations, §46.2-1000.
Display requirements, §46.2-712.
Failure to surrender revoked decals, §46.2-612.
Fee for replacement of lost, mutilated or illegible decal, §46.2-692.
Grace period for replacement of decals.
Renewal of registration of vehicles, §46.2-647.
Lost or mutilated decal, §46.2-607.
Offenses related to decals, §46.2-613.
Permanent decals, §46.2-714.
Physically handicapped persons, §46.2-731.
Property of department, §46.2-713.
Revocation, §46.2-609.
Use of old decals after application for new decal, §46.2-718.
Defined, §46.2-100.

MOTOR VEHICLE LICENSE PLATES —Cont'd
Demonstration vehicles.
Temporary transfer of plates from another vehicle, §46.2-720.
Department to furnish number and design of plates, §46.2-711.
Disabled parking license plates, §46.2-731.
Disabled veterans.
Special license plates, §46.2-739.
Displaying on vehicles required, §§46.2-711, 46.2-715.
Distinguished Flying Cross recipients.
Special license plates, §46.2-742.2.
Distinguished Service Cross recipients.
Special license plates, §46.2-742.2.
Drive smart.
Special license plates, §46.2-749.2:10.
Ducks Unlimited.
Special license plates, §46.2-749.7.
Duplicates for lost or mutilated plates, §46.2-607.
Education begins at home.
Special license plates, §46.2-749.80.
Emergency use of license plates, §§46.2-719 to 46.2-721.
Application of liability insurance policy, §46.2-721.
Issuance of special permit, §46.2-719.
Evidence.
Certificate of license plate number as prima facie evidence of ownership, §46.2-213.
Exchange of plates.
Fee, §46.2-692.2.
Executive officers.
Special license plates, §46.2-736.1.
Exemption from requirement.
Agricultural or horticultural.
Vehicles used for, §46.2-664.
Failure to display, §46.2-711.
Fine schedule, VA SCt Rule 3B:2.
Maximum fine for violating Title 46.2, §46.2-113.
Pretrial payment of fine, §16.1-69.40:1.
Farm use.
Exempt vehicles, §46.2-665.
Fastening to vehicle, §46.2-716.
Improper fastening.
Fine schedule, VA SCt Rule 3B:2.
Fees.
Amateur radio operators, §46.2-738.
Antique motor vehicles, §46.2-730.
Bicentennial license plates and decals, §46.2-727.
Business entity logo on plate.
Fleet vehicles, business entities with, §46.2-725.2.
Clean special fuel vehicles, §46.2-749.3.
Colleges and universities, §46.2-749.
Counties, cities or towns.
Commemorative license plates for counties, cities and towns, §46.2-749.4:4.
County or city logotype, §46.2-749.4.
Deaf and hearing impaired, §46.2-732.
Disabled veterans, §46.2-739.
Exchange of plates, §46.2-692.2.
Friend of the Chesapeake, §46.2-749.2.
Handicapped persons, §46.2-731.
National air and space museum, §46.2-746.11.
Persons delivering unladen vehicles, §46.2-733.
Professional or volunteer firefighters and members of volunteer fire department auxiliaries, §46.2-736.
Purple Heart recipients, §46.2-742.

MOTOR VEHICLE LICENSE PLATES —Cont'd
Fees —Cont'd
Replacement of lost, mutilated or illegible plates or decals, §46.2-692.
Sample license plates, §46.2-692.1.
Special license plates, §46.2-725.
Amateur radio operators, §46.2-738.
Bronze Star or Silver Star recipients, §46.2-742.1.
Dog and cat sterilization program supporters, §46.2-749.2:7.
Family and children's trust fund supporters, §46.2-749.48.
National air and space museum, §46.2-746.11.
Professional or volunteer fire fighters and members of volunteer fire department auxiliaries, §46.2-736.
Purple Heart recipients, §46.2-742.
Virginia breast cancer foundation, §46.2-749.45.
Virginians for the Arts, §46.2-749.2:2.
Volunteer rescue squad and volunteer rescue squad auxiliary members, §46.2-735.
Special plates displaying official insect, §46.2-728.3.
Special plates displaying scenic design, §46.2-728.2.
State bird and floral emblem incorporated, §46.2-728.1.
State-owned motor vehicles, §46.2-750.
Supporters of certain children's programs, §46.2-749.2:1.
Trailers sold or transferred.
Transfer of license plates by owners selling or transferring registered trailer, §46.2-1992.36.
Virginia National Guard, §46.2-744.
Virginia's tobacco heritage, §46.2-749.5.
Volunteer rescue squad and volunteer rescue squad auxiliary members, §46.2-735.
Wildlife conservationists, §46.2-749.1.
Fight terrorism, §46.2-749.62.
Fire department vehicles.
Volunteer fire departments, §46.2-649.1:1.
Firefighters.
Special license plates, §46.2-736.
Five-point star.
Special license plates.
Supporters of certain children's programs, §46.2-749.2:1.
Fleet vehicles, business entities with.
Business entity logo on plate, §46.2-725.2.
For-hire license plates.
Displaying not-for-hire plates, §46.2-724.
Exemption for pickup or panel trucks, §46.2-711.
Forms for applications, §46.2-203.
Fox hunting, §46.2-749.58.
Friend of the Chesapeake.
Special license plates, §46.2-749.2.
Friends of Tibet, §46.2-749.89.
Governor.
Special license plates, §46.2-736.1.
Grace period for replacement of license plates.
Renewal of registration of vehicles, §46.2-647.
Great Seal of Virginia.
Special license plates, §46.2-728.
Greyhound adoption program supporters.
Special plates, §46.2-749.14.
Handicapped persons.
Special license plates, §46.2-731.
Harley-Davidson motorcycle owners.
Special license plates, §46.2-749.8.

MOTOR VEHICLE LICENSE PLATES —Cont'd
Heart emblem.
Special license plates.
Supporters of certain children's programs, §46.2-749.2:1.
Honorably discharged veterans.
Special license plates, §46.2-743.
Honorary consuls.
Special license plates, §46.2-736.2.
Horse enthusiasts.
Special plates, §46.2-749.18.
House of Delegates.
Special license plates, §46.2-736.1.
Improper display, §46.2-715.
Fine schedule, VA SCt Rule 3B:2.
Maximum fine for violating Title 46.2, §46.2-113.
Pretrial payment of fine, §16.1-69.40:1.
Insect of state.
Special license plates, §46.2-728.3.
Institutions of higher education.
Special license plates, §46.2-749.
Internet commerce industry.
Special plates, §46.2-749.13.
Jamestown settlement.
Special plates commemorating 400th anniversary of establishment, §46.2-749.2:13.
Juvenile diabetes research foundation, §46.2-749.115.
Legibility requirements, §46.2-712.
Letter and numeral requirements, §46.2-712.
License agents, §46.2-205.
Lieutenant governor.
Special license plate, §46.2-736.1.
Loaner vehicles.
Temporary transfer of license plates from another vehicle, §46.2-720.
Lost or mutilated plates, §46.2-607.
Replacement fee, §46.2-692.
Low-speed vehicles.
Designated license plates, §46.2-711.
Required, §46.2-908.3.
Manufacturers' license plates.
Distinguishing between various types of dealers, §46.2-1549.
Transferable license plates, §46.2-1548.
Use of, §46.2-1550.
Medal of Honor recipients.
Special license plates, §46.2-745.
Medical transportation carriers, nonemergency.
Exemption from displaying for-hire license plates, §46.2-711.
Military affairs.
Grace period for active duty military personnel stationed outside the United States, §46.2-221.4.
Military assault forces.
Special license plates, §46.2-746.1.
Military veterans' organizations.
Special license plates, §46.2-746.4.
Mobile homes used as temporary offices at construction sites.
Plates for transporting, §46.2-723.
Motorcycle dealers, §§46.2-1993.39 to 46.2-1993.63.
See MOTORCYCLE DEALERS.
NASA Langley research center.
Special license plates, §46.2-749.81.
NASCAR.
Virginia motor sports initiative, §46.2-749.69:1.

MOTOR VEHICLE LICENSE PLATES —Cont'd
National air and space museum.
Special license plates for supporters, §46.2-746.11.
National Rifle Association Supporters.
Special license plates, §46.2-749.6.
Natural Bridge of Virginia.
Special plates, §46.2-749.26.
Naval aviators.
Special plates, §46.2-749.46.
Navy Cross recipients.
Special license plates, §46.2-742.2.
Not-for-hire plates.
Vehicles operated for-hire displaying not-for-hire plates, §46.2-724.
Obscured plate.
Fine schedule, VA SCt Rule 3B:2.
Occupational associations.
Special license plates, §46.2-746.8.
Occupations.
Special license plates, §46.2-746.9.
Oceana Naval Air Station.
Special plates, §46.2-749.28.
Offenses relating to licensing, §46.2-613.
Old license plates or decals.
Use after application for new, §46.2-718.
Operation Desert Shield veterans.
Special license plates, §46.2-743.
Operation Desert Storm veterans.
Special license plates, §46.2-743.
Operation Iraqi Freedom veterans.
Special license plates, §46.2-743.
Operation Wildflower supporters.
Special plates, §46.2-749.29.
Organ donations, encouraging participation in the organ donor program, §46.2-749.105.
Panel trucks.
Exemption from displaying for-hire license plates, §46.2-711.
Parrothead club, §46.2-749.68.
Passenger-carrying vehicles for rent or hire.
Issuance of designated plates, §46.2-711.
Passenger-carrying vehicles operated by common carriers.
Issuance of designated plates, §46.2-711.
Pearl Harbor survivors.
Special license plates, §46.2-741.
Permanent license plates, §46.2-714.
Issuance for trailers and semitrailers, §46.2-712.
Personalized plates, §§46.2-711 to 46.2-749.130.
Pickup trucks.
Exemption from displaying for-hire license plates, §46.2-711.
Presidential inauguration license plates.
Display on vehicles registered in state, §46.2-729.1.
Prisoners of war.
Special license plates, §46.2-746.
Professional firefighters.
Special license plates, §46.2-736.
Promotional license plates.
Motorcycle dealers, §46.2-1993.43.
Property-carrying vehicles operated by private carriers.
Issuance of designated plates, §46.2-711.
Property of department.
Subject to repossession, §46.2-713.
Purple Heart recipients.
Special license plates, §46.2-742.
REACT Teams.
Special license plates, §46.2-748.

MOTOR VEHICLE LICENSE PLATES —Cont'd
Reconstructed and specially constructed vehicles.
Special license plates, §46.2-734.
Rental vehicles.
Designated license plates for rental vehicles, §46.2-711.
Requirements of license plates and decals, §46.2-712.
Rescue squad vehicles.
Volunteer rescue squads, §46.2-649.1:1.
Reservation of plates with certain registration numbers or letters, §46.2-726.
Reserve military organizations.
Special license plates, §46.2-746.3.
Revocation of plates.
Commencement of period, §46.2-414.
Failure to surrender revoked plates, §46.2-612.
Judicial review, §46.2-611.
Return to commissioner, §46.2-370.
Unlawful uses, §46.2-609.
Ride-sharing vehicles.
Special license plates, §46.2-749.10.
Ruritan National.
Special license plates for members, §46.2-746.7.
Sample license plates, §46.2-692.1.
Scenic design.
Special license plates, §46.2-728.2.
Silver Star recipients.
Special license plates, §46.2-742.1.
Size requirements, §46.2-712.
Society of the 173rd airborne brigade.
Special plates, §46.2-746.2:2.
Sons of Confederate veterans.
Special plates, §46.2-746.22.
Speaker of the House of Delegates.
Special license plates, §46.2-736.1.
Special forces association, §46.2-746.2:4.
Special license plates, §§46.2-725 to 46.2-749.130.
Administrative fee, §46.2-725.
AFL-CIO supporters, §46.2-746.10.
Air Force cross recipients, §46.2-742.2.
Air force retirees, §46.2-743.
Amateur radio operators, §46.2-738.
Ambulances.
Operated by private ambulance services, §46.2-726.
Antique motor vehicles, §46.2-730.
Antique trailers, §46.2-730.
Applicability of article to passenger cars, motor homes and pick-up or panel trucks, §46.2-725.
Appointed officials, §46.2-736.2.
Attorney general, §46.2-736.1.
Aviation.
National air and space museum supporters, §46.2-746.11.
Aviation education facilities supporters, §46.2-746.11.
Aviation enthusiasts, §46.2-746.14.
Battle of Chosin Reservoir survivors, §46.2-740.
Bicentennial plates and decals, §46.2-727.
Bicycle enthusiasts, §46.2-749.111.
BoatU.S. members, §46.2-749.54.
Bronze Star recipients, §46.2-742.1.
Business entity logo on plate.
Fleet vehicles, business entities with, §46.2-725.2.
Carpooling, §46.2-749.10.
Circuit court clerks, §46.2-737.
City treasurers, §46.2-737.
Civic organizations, §46.2-746.7.

MOTOR VEHICLE LICENSE PLATES —Cont'd
Special license plates —Cont'd
Class-J No. 611 steam locomotive, §46.2-749.40.
Clean special fuel vehicles, §46.2-749.3.
Clerk of the House of Delegates, §46.2-736.1.
Clerk of the Virginia Senate, §46.2-736.1.
College fraternities and sororities, §46.2-746.7.
Combat infantryman badge, §46.2-742.4.
Combination of series, §46.2-725.
Commemorative license plates for counties, cities and towns, §46.2-749.4:4.
Commissioners of the revenue, §46.2-737.
Commonwealth's attorneys, §46.2-737.
Constitutional officers, §§46.2-736.1, 46.2-737.
County attorneys, §46.2-737.
County treasurers, §46.2-737.
Credit unions, §46.2-746.12.
Criteria for issuance or reissuance of series, §46.2-725.
Deaf and hearing impaired persons, §46.2-732.
Disabled parking license plates, §46.2-731.
Disabled veterans, §46.2-739.
Distinguished Flying Cross recipients, §46.2-742.2.
Distinguished Service Cross recipients, §46.2-742.2.
Dog and cat sterilization program supporters, §46.2-749.2:7.
Drive smart, §46.2-749.2:10.
Ducks Unlimited, §46.2-749.7.
Eastern shore tourism, §46.2-749.7:3.
Education begins at home, §46.2-749.80.
Executive officers, §46.2-736.1.
Family and children's trust fund supporters, §46.2-749.48.
Fees, §46.2-725.
Amateur radio operators, §46.2-738.
Bronze Star or Silver Star recipients, §46.2-742.1.
Dog and cat sterilization program supporters, §46.2-749.2:7.
Family and children's trust fund supporters, §46.2-749.48.
National air and space museum, §46.2-746.11.
Professional or volunteer fire fighters and members of volunteer fire department auxiliaries, §46.2-736.
Purple Heart recipients, §46.2-742.
Virginia breast cancer foundation, §46.2-749.45.
Virginians for the Arts, §46.2-749.2:2.
Volunteer rescue squad and volunteer rescue squad auxiliary members, §46.2-735.
Fight terrorism, §46.2-749.62.
Flag design incorporated into, §46.2-749.62.
Fleet vehicles, business entities with, §46.2-725.2.
Floral emblem, §46.2-728.1.
Fox hunting, §46.2-749.58.
Friend of the Chesapeake, §46.2-749.2.
Friends of Tibet, §46.2-749.89.
Generally, §46.2-725.
Governor, §46.2-736.1.
Great Seal of Virginia, §46.2-728.
Greyhound adoption program supporters, §46.2-749.14.
Handicapped persons, §46.2-731.
Harley-Davidson motorcycle owners, §46.2-749.8.
Honorably discharged veterans, §46.2-743.
Honorary consuls, §46.2-736.2.
Horse enthusiasts, §46.2-749.18.
House of Delegates, §46.2-736.1.
Institutions of higher education, §46.2-749.

MOTOR VEHICLE LICENSE PLATES —Cont'd
Special license plates —Cont'd
Internet commerce industry, §46.2-749.13.
Jamestown settlement.
Commemoration of 400th anniversary of establishment, §46.2-749.2:13.
Juvenile diabetes research foundation, §46.2-749.115.
Lieutenant governor, §46.2-736.1.
Localities, §46.2-749.4.
Commemorative license plates for counties, cities and towns, §46.2-749.4:4.
Medal of Honor recipients, §46.2-745.
Military, active duty, honorably discharged or retired, §46.2-743.
Military assault force members, §46.2-746.1.
Military veterans' organizations, §46.2-746.4.
NASA Langley research center, §46.2-749.81.
NASCAR.
Virginia motor sports initiative, §46.2-749.69:1.
National air and space museum, §46.2-746.11.
National Rifle Association Supporters, §46.2-749.6.
Natural Bridge of Virginia, §46.2-749.26.
Naval aviators, §46.2-749.46.
Navy Cross recipients, §46.2-742.2.
Occupational associations, §46.2-746.8.
Occupations, §46.2-746.9.
Oceana Naval Air Station, §46.2-749.28.
Operation Desert Shield veterans, §46.2-743.
Operation Desert Storm veterans, §46.2-743.
Operation Iraqi Freedom veterans, §46.2-743.
Operation Wildflower supporters, §46.2-749.29.
Organ donations, encouraging participation in the organ donor program, §46.2-749.105.
Parrothead club, §46.2-749.68.
Peace corps volunteers, §46.2-746.12.
Pearl Harbor survivors, §46.2-741.
Persons delivering unladen vehicles, §46.2-733.
Presidential inauguration license plates, §46.2-729.1.
Prisoners of war, §46.2-746.
Professional firefighters, §46.2-736.
Purple Heart recipients, §46.2-742.
REACT Teams, §46.2-748.
Reconstructed vehicles, §46.2-734.
Reserved numbers or letters, §46.2-726.
Reserve military organizations, §46.2-746.3.
Ride-sharing vehicles, §46.2-749.10.
Scenic design, §46.2-728.2.
Schedule of fees.
Reserved numbers or letters, §46.2-726.
Silver Star recipients, §46.2-742.1.
Society of the 173rd airborne brigade, §46.2-746.2:2.
Sons of Confederate veterans, §46.2-746.22.
Speaker of the House of Delegates, §46.2-736.1.
Special forces association, §46.2-746.2:4.
Specially constructed vehicles, §46.2-734.
State bird emblem, §46.2-728.1.
State commissions and boards, §46.2-736.2.
State insect, §46.2-728.3.
Street rods, §46.2-747.
Supporters of Virginia agriculture, §46.2-749.102.
Surfrider foundation, §46.2-749.130.
Surviving spouses of honorably discharged veterans, §46.2-743.
3rd infantry regiment (old guard), §46.2-746.2:3.
United States Congressmen, §46.2-736.1.
United States Senators, §46.2-736.1.
United We Stand, §46.2-749.78.
University presidents, §46.2-746.1.

MOTOR VEHICLE LICENSE PLATES —Cont'd
Special license plates —Cont'd
Unlocking autism, §46.2-749.60.
Urban league of Hampton Roads, §46.2-749.86.
USS Cole attack victims, §46.2-749.66.
Vanpooling, §46.2-749.10.
Vehicles specially equipped to transport handicapped persons, §46.2-731.
Veterans of foreign wars of the United States, §46.2-746.2:6.
Virginia association for community conflict resolution, §46.2-749.119.
Virginia Bowler, §46.2-749.9.
Virginia breast cancer foundation, §46.2-749.45.
Virginia defense force, §46.2-743.
Virginia lighthouses, §46.2-749.31.
Virginia motor sports initiative, §46.2-749.69:1.
Virginia National Guard, §46.2-744.
Retired members, §46.2-746.5.
Virginians for the Arts, §46.2-749.2:2.
Virginia sheriffs' institute, §46.2-749.110.
Virginia's tobacco heritage, §46.2-749.5.
Volunteer fire department auxiliaries, §46.2-736.
Volunteer firefighters, §46.2-736.
Volunteer rescue squads and volunteer rescue squad auxiliary members, §46.2-735.
Volunteer search and rescue organizations, §46.2-746.6.
Washington redskins supporters, §46.2-749.73.
Wildlife conservationists, §46.2-749.1.
Special permits.
Emergency use of license plates, §§46.2-719 to 46.2-721.
State bird.
Special license plates incorporating the official bird, §46.2-728.1.
State commissions and boards.
Special license plates, §46.2-736.2.
State floral emblem.
Special license plates, §46.2-728.1.
State-owned motor vehicles.
Display requirements, §46.2-750.
Passenger vehicles, §46.2-751.
Vehicles used for police work, §46.2-750.1.
Vehicles used for security or transportation purposes involving governor or members of general assembly, §46.2-750.
Storage of unlicensed vehicles.
Reconstructed and specially constructed vehicles, §46.2-734.
Street rods.
Special license plates, §46.2-747.
Supporters of Virginia agriculture, §46.2-749.102.
Surfrider foundation.
Special license plates, §46.2-749.130.
Surviving spouses of honorably discharged veterans.
Special license plates, §46.2-743.
Suspension of plates.
Commencement of period, §46.2-414.
Judicial review, §46.2-611.
Nonresidents.
Conviction of or judgment against resident in another jurisdiction, §46.2-434.
Suspension or revocation of driver's license, §46.2-391.1.
Uninsured motor vehicles, §§46.2-706, 46.2-708, 46.2-709.
Taxicabs.
Issuance of designated plates, §46.2-711.

MOTOR VEHICLE LICENSE PLATES —Cont'd
Temporary license plates.
Motorcycle dealers issuing, §§46.2-1993.55 to 46.2-1993.63.
See MOTORCYCLE DEALERS.
Trailer dealers issuing, §§46.2-1992.56 to 46.2-1992.65.
Temporary transfer to another vehicle.
When permitted, §46.2-720.
3rd infantry regiment (old guard).
Special license plates, §46.2-746.2:3.
Trailer dealers, §§46.2-1992.39 to 46.2-1992.65.
See TRAILER DEALERS.
Trailers.
Transfer of license plates by owner selling or transferring registered trailer, §46.2-1992.36.
Transfer to another vehicle, §46.2-1543.
Uniformed law-enforcement officers.
Patrolling landowner's property to enforce, §46.2-102.
United States Congressmen.
Special license plates, §46.2-736.1.
United States Senators.
Special license plates, §46.2-736.1.
United We Stand.
Special license plates, §46.2-749.78.
Unladen vehicles.
Special license plates for person delivering vehicles, §46.2-733.
Unlocking autism, §46.2-749.60.
Urban league of Hampton Roads, §46.2-749.86.
Use of old plates and registration number on another vehicle.
Registration and transfer fees, §46.2-693.
Use of plates from another vehicle, §§46.2-719 to 46.2-721.
Application of liability insurance policy, §46.2-721.
USS Cole attack victims, §46.2-749.66.
Vanity plates, §§46.2-711 to 46.2-749.130.
Vanpooling.
Special license plates, §46.2-749.10.
Veterans of foreign wars of the United States, §46.2-746.2:6.
Veterans of the battle of Iwo Jima.
Special license plates, §46.2-746.4.
Virginia association for community conflict resolution.
Special license plates, §46.2-749.119.
Virginia Bowler.
Special license plates, §46.2-749.9.
Virginia breast cancer foundation.
Special license plates for supporters, §46.2-749.45.
Virginia lighthouses.
Special plates, §46.2-749.31.
Virginia motor sports initiative, §46.2-749.69:1.
Virginia National Guard.
Special license plates, §46.2-744.
Retired members, §46.2-746.5.
Virginia sheriffs' institute, §46.2-749.110.
Virginia's tobacco heritage.
Special license plates, §46.2-749.5.
Volunteer fire department vehicles, §46.2-649.1:1.
Volunteer firefighters.
Special license plates, §46.2-736.
Volunteer rescue squad members.
Special license plates, §46.2-735.
Volunteer rescue squad vehicles, §46.2-649.1:1.
Volunteer search and rescue organizations.
Special license plates, §46.2-746.6.

MOTOR VEHICLE LICENSE PLATES —Cont'd
Voter registration.
Electronic transfer of information in department records for purposes of, §46.2-208.1.
Washington redskins supporters, §46.2-749.73.
Wildlife conservationists.
Special license plates, §46.2-749.1.

MOTOR VEHICLE LOADS AND CARGO.
Escape of contents, §10.1-1424.
Clean up of escaped objects constituting obstruction or endangering travel, §§10.1-1424, 46.2-1156.
Fine for failure to prevent, VA SCt Rule 3B:2.
Load covers, §46.2-1156.
Fine for failure to prevent escape of contents, VA SCt Rule 3B:2.
Logs, poles, lumber, etc., hauling.
Fastening loads, §46.2-1155.
Fine for failure to fasten, VA SCt Rule 3B:2.
Size and weight of vehicles generally, §§46.2-1101 to 46.2-1156.
See MOTOR VEHICLE SIZE AND WEIGHT.

MOTOR VEHICLE RECORDING DEVICES, §46.2-1088.6.

MOTOR VEHICLE RECORDS.
Abstracts of conviction records, §§46.2-383 to 46.2-387.
Motor vehicles department.
See MOTOR VEHICLES DEPARTMENT.

MOTOR VEHICLE REGISTRATION, §§46.2-645 to 46.2-710, 46.2-750 to 46.2-756.
Address of owner or lessee of vehicle.
Applicants to supply DMV, §46.2-600.
Agricultural vehicle exemption from registration.
Farm machinery and tractors, §46.2-667.
Harvesting operation vehicles, §46.2-668.
Insurance coverage for exempted vehicles, §46.2-684.1.
Land owned or leased by vehicle's owner, §46.2-665.
Nocturnal use of highways by exempted vehicles, §46.2-684.
Return trips of exempted farm vehicles, §46.2-673.
Seasonal transportation of farm products and livestock, §46.2-666.
Spraying fruit trees and other plants, §46.2-664.
Transporting fertilizer, cotton or peanuts, §46.2-672.
Wood products transported by vehicles owned by farmers, §46.2-670.
All-terrain vehicles.
Exemption from registration, §46.2-679.1.
Antique motor vehicles.
Suspension, unsafe to operate, not properly equipped, §46.2-730.
Application for registration.
Department filing requirement, §46.2-645.
Appointment of agent for process, §46.2-601.
Backhoes.
Exemption from registration, §46.2-663.
Buses.
Fees for vehicles designed and used for passenger transportation, §46.2-694.
Change of address, §46.2-606.
Church buses.
Fees for vehicles designed and used for passenger transportation, §46.2-694.

MOTOR VEHICLE REGISTRATION —Cont'd
City or county decals, §§46.2-752 to 46.2-756.
Additional license fees in certain localities, §46.2-753.
Free of charge, issuance, §46.2-752.
Limitations on imposition of local license taxes and fees, §§46.2-752, 46.2-755.
Local license fees in Arlington county, §46.2-754.
One-time, one-month extension to satisfy local requirements, §46.2-752.1.
Prohibiting display after expiration, §46.2-752.
Requiring evidence of payment of personal property taxes, §46.2-752.
State defense force, vehicles owned or leased by members, §46.2-752.
Collection by department of certain license fees, §46.2-756.
Combination tractor trucks and semitrailers.
Registration fees, §46.2-701.
Commercial fishing vehicles.
Exemption from registration, §46.2-674.
Commercial vehicles.
Civil penalty for violations by trucks and tractor trucks, §46.2-613.1.
Attachment and seizure of vehicle for unpaid fees and penalties, §46.2-613.4.
Service of process.
Operator as agent for, §46.2-613.2.
Procedures for issuance and service, §46.2-613.5.
Special processing of penalties, §46.2-613.3.
Rejection of application, §46.2-608.
Revocation of registration, §46.2-609.
Vehicles not designed or used for passenger transportation.
Registration fees, §46.2-697.
Common carriers of passengers.
Fees for vehicles designed and used for passenger transportation, §46.2-694.
Company vehicles of automotive manufacturers, §46.2-602.2.
Confidential information.
Records in office of department of motor vehicles.
Privileged records, release, conditions, §46.2-208.
Deactivation, §46.2-646.1.
Dealer temporary license plates.
Duty of dealer to forward application for current titling and registration, §46.2-1561.
Death of owner.
Time period effective after death, §46.2-615.
Definitions.
Uninsured motor vehicles, §46.2-704.
Electric vehicles.
Converted electric vehicles, §§46.2-602.3, 46.2-625.
Exemptions from registration.
Locomotives or electric cars operating on rails, §46.2-683.
Embezzlement of vehicle.
Suspension of registration, §46.2-610.
Emissions inspections.
Extension for the satisfaction of emissions inspection requirements, §46.2-1183.1.
Engine number.
Stopping vehicles for inspection, §46.2-103.
Exemptions from registration, §§46.2-662 to 46.2-684.
Agricultural or horticultural vehicles.
Farm machinery and tractors, §46.2-667.
Harvesting operations, §46.2-668.

MOTOR VEHICLE REGISTRATION —Cont'd
Exemptions from registration —Cont'd
Agricultural or horticultural vehicles —Cont'd
Land owned or leased by vehicle's owner, §46.2-665.
Return trips for exempted farm vehicles, §46.2-673.
Seasonal transportation of farm produce and livestock, §46.2-666.
Spraying fruit trees and other plants, §46.2-664.
Transporting fertilizer, cotton or peanuts, §46.2-672.
Transport of wood products of farmers, §46.2-670.
Backhoes, §46.2-663.
Certain vehicles required to show evidence of exemption, §46.2-649.
Commercial fishing vehicles, §46.2-674.
Forklift trucks, §46.2-678.
Golf carts, §46.2-676.
Heavy machinery used for highway purposes, §46.2-682.
Insurance coverage for exempted vehicles, §46.2-684.1.
Locomotives or electric cars operating on rails, §46.2-683.
Mining vehicles, §§46.2-671, 46.2-675.
New resident operating vehicle registered in another state or country, §46.2-662.
Nocturnal use of highways by exempted vehicles, §46.2-684.
Oyster shells hauling vehicles, §46.2-680.
Self-propelled wheel chairs, §46.2-677.
Snowmobiles, §46.2-679.
Temporary exemption, §46.2-662.
Traction engines, §46.2-683.
Tractors or similar vehicles by sawmill operators, §46.2-669.
Utility vehicles, §46.2-676.
Exhibiting registration card, §46.2-104.
Presentation to court or production in court, compliance with provision, §46.2-104.
Expiration of registration, §§46.2-613, 46.2-646.
Extension.
One-time, one-month extension to satisfy local requirements, §46.2-752.1.
Satisfaction of emissions inspection requirements, §46.2-1183.1.
Failure to carry registration card, §46.2-104.
Presentation to court or production in court, compliance with provision, §46.2-104.
Failure to obtain registration, §46.2-600.
Farm tractors.
Defined, §46.2-100.
Registration not required, §46.2-600.
Farm use.
Exempt vehicles, §46.2-665.
Farm vehicles.
Exemption of agricultural vehicles generally, §§46.2-664 to 46.2-673.
Registration fees, §46.2-698.
Return trips of exempted farm vehicles, §46.2-673.
Fees, §§46.2-685 to 46.2-704.
Additional revenue generated by fee increases.
Disposition, §46.2-702.1.
Assessment and collection of fees.
Pursuant to reciprocal agreement, §46.2-703.
Change of address.
Failure to comply with notice requirement, §46.2-606.

MOTOR VEHICLE REGISTRATION —Cont'd
Fees —Cont'd
Combination tractor trucks and semitrailers, §46.2-701.
Commercial vehicles not designed or used for passenger transportation, §46.2-697.
Customer service centers of department.
Registration renewal in.
Service charge, §46.2-214.3.
Deactivation, §46.2-646.1.
Disposition of fees, §§46.2-685, 46.2-686.
Failure to pay certain fees, §46.2-687.
Farm vehicles, §46.2-698.
Five-year registration for trailer fleets, §46.2-701.
Fleet vehicles registered pursuant to reciprocal agreement, §46.2-703.1.
For-hire carriers, §46.2-697.
Highway maintenance and operating fund.
Disposition of additional revenue generated by fee increases, §46.2-702.1.
Jointly operated small rented vehicles, §46.2-695.
One-trip permit, §46.2-651.
Payment of fees into special fund, §§46.2-685, 46.2-686.
Penalty for failure to pay certain fees, §46.2-687.
Private carriers, §46.2-697.
Prohibited operations for failure to pay fees, §46.2-704.
Reactivation, §46.2-646.1.
Reciprocal agreement with other states, §§46.2-703, 46.2-703.1.
Refund, §§46.2-688 to 46.2-690.
For-hire vehicles, §46.2-690.
Passenger vehicles, §46.2-689.
Pro rata refund of fees paid, §46.2-688.
Registration of tow vehicles, §46.2-649.1.
Replacement of lost, mutilated or illegible indicia of titling and registration, §46.2-692.
Single-trip temporary registration or permit, §46.2-652.
Fee, §46.2-652.1.
Small rented vehicles jointly operated, §46.2-695.
Specialized mobile equipment, §46.2-700.
Temporary registration.
Oversize or overweight vehicles, §46.2-652.1.
Transportation of oversized manufactured homes, §46.2-653.
Trailers and semitrailers not designed and used for passenger transportation, §46.2-694.1.
Truck owners inducted into armed forces, §46.2-691.
Use of old plates and registration number on another vehicle, §46.2-693.
Vehicles and access of gross weight, §46.2-704.
Vehicles designed and used for transporting passengers, §46.2-694.
Vehicles specially equipped to accommodate persons with disabilities.
Determination of fee, §46.2-702.2.
Well-drilling machinery, §46.2-700.
Wrecking vehicles, §46.2-702.
Fire department vehicles.
Volunteer fire departments, §46.2-649.1:1.
Fleet trailers.
Registration fees, §46.2-701.
Fleet vehicles.
Additional registration fees, §46.2-703.1.
Compliance with clean alternative fuel standards prior to registration, §46.2-649.2.
Foreign market vehicles, §46.2-602.

MOTOR VEHICLE REGISTRATION —Cont'd
Foreign-registered vehicles.
Nonresident owners, §§46.2-655 to 46.2-661.
Use in driver education programs, §46.2-1557.
Foreign vehicles, §46.2-625.
For-hire vehicles.
Refund of fees, §46.2-690.
Forms for certificates, §46.2-203.
Fraud and deceit.
Obtaining card from department when not legally entitled, §46.2-105.2.
Unlawful procurement of certification, §46.2-105.1.
Use of false name or address in application for registration card, §46.2-613.
Vehicle compliance with clean alternative fuel fleet standards, §46.2-649.2.
Golf carts.
Exemption from registration, §46.2-676.
Highway machinery.
Vehicles exempt from registration, §46.2-682.
Identification of holder of registration card.
Presentation of card at officer's request, signing name in presence of officer, §46.2-104.
Interstate passenger transportation.
Fees for vehicles used and designed for passenger transportation, §46.2-694.
Jointly operated small rented vehicles.
Registration fees, §46.2-695.
Law-enforcement officers.
Patrolling landowner's property to enforce, §46.2-102.
Stopping vehicles for inspection and to secure information, §46.2-103.
License agents, §46.2-205.
License plates.
Generally, §§46.2-711 to 46.2-749.130.
See MOTOR VEHICLE LICENSE PLATES.
List of registrations.
Furnishing to local commissioners of the revenue, §46.2-210.
Local license fees.
City or county decals, §§46.2-752 to 46.2-756.
Logging vehicles, §46.2-648.
Lost, mutilated or illegible registration card.
Fee for replacement, §46.2-692.
Mailing list of registrations.
List of registrations offered for sale to public, §46.2-210.
Mail-in renewals.
Reduction in registration fees, §46.2-697.
Manufactured homes.
Temporary registration or permit for transportation of oversize homes, §46.2-653.
Manufacturer's serial number.
Stopping vehicles for inspection, §46.2-103.
Military affairs.
Abandoned motor vehicles.
Vehicles registered to active duty military personnel, §46.2-1200.2.
Grace period for active duty military personnel stationed outside the United States, §46.2-221.4.
Nonresident active duty military personnel.
Registration of vehicle registered in another state not required, §46.2-600.
Mining vehicles.
Exemption from registration, §§46.2-671, 46.2-675.
Mopeds.
Fees, §46.2-694.

MOTOR VEHICLE REGISTRATION —Cont'd
Motor carriers, passengers.
See MOTOR CARRIERS, PASSENGERS.
Motor carriers, property.
See MOTOR CARRIERS, PROPERTY.
Motorcycle dealers.
Registration of vehicle required before commencing operation, §46.2-1993.39.
Motorcycles.
Fee for motorcycle with sidecar, §46.2-694.
Off-road motor vehicles.
Exemption from registration, §46.2-679.2.
Motor homes.
Fees for vehicles designed and used for transporting passengers, §46.2-694.
National change of address system.
Contract with postal service to use, §46.2-606.
New resident operating vehicle registered in another state or country.
Temporary exemption from registration, §46.2-662.
Nocturnal use of highways by exempted vehicles, §46.2-684.
Nonresident owners of foreign vehicles.
Active duty military personnel.
Registration of vehicle registered in another state not required, §46.2-600.
Business operation of vehicles in state, §46.2-660.
Commercial vehicles doing business in state, §46.2-660.
Extension of reciprocal privileges, §46.2-661.
Multiple vehicle operation other than for pleasure, §46.2-655.
Privileges extended, §46.2-655.
Reciprocal privileges, §§46.2-655, 46.2-661.
Reciprocity required, §46.2-655.
Six month operation without registration, §46.2-656.
State not requiring registration of like vehicles, §46.2-657.
Temporary operation without registration, §46.2-656.
When registration not required, §46.2-657.
Off-road motor vehicles.
Exemption from registration, §46.2-679.2.
Old registration number.
Used on another vehicle, §46.2-1543.
One-trip permit, §46.2-651.
Out-of-business dealers.
Temporary registration, title for person other than the dealer, §46.2-654.1.
Oversize or overweight vehicles.
Temporary registration, §46.2-652.
Fee, §46.2-652.1.
Oyster shells.
Hauling vehicles.
Exemption from registration, §46.2-680.
Panel trucks.
Additional fee, §46.2-694.
Passenger vehicles.
Registration fees, §46.2-694.
Personal property taxes.
Imposition by localities, §46.2-752.
Local license fees generally, §§46.2-752 to 46.2-756.
Pickup trucks.
Additional fee, §46.2-694.
Possession of registration cards, §46.2-104.
Privileged records.
Records in office of department of motor vehicles, release, conditions, §46.2-208.

MOTOR VEHICLE REGISTRATION —Cont'd
Proof of financial responsibility.
New registration to person to whom proof surrendered, §46.2-462.
Quarry operators.
Vehicles exempt from registration, §§46.2-671, 46.2-675.
Reactivation, §46.2-646.1.
Reciprocity for nonresidents, §§46.2-655 to 46.2-661.
Reconstructed and specially constructed vehicles, §§46.2-625, 46.2-734.
Refund of fees, §§46.2-688 to 46.2-690.
For-hire vehicles, §46.2-690.
Passenger vehicles, §46.2-689.
Pro rata refund of fees paid, §46.2-688.
Registration card.
Altering or forging, §46.2-605.
Appeal of suspension, revocation, etc., §46.2-611.
Change of address, §46.2-606.
Confiscation for equipment safety violations, §46.2-1000.
Contents, §46.2-604.
Duplicates for lost or mutilated card, §46.2-607.
Effective after death of owner, §46.2-615.
Electronic titling program, §46.2-603.1.
Failure to surrender revoked card, §46.2-612.
Issuance, §46.2-603.
Lost or mutilated cards, §46.2-607.
Fee for replacement, §46.2-692.
Offenses relating to registration, §46.2-613.
Owner to secure, §46.2-600.
Rejection of application, §46.2-608.
Revocation, §46.2-609.
Suspension on theft or embezzlement of vehicle, §46.2-610.
Reinstatement of suspended or revoked registration, §46.2-411.
Renewal of registration, §46.2-646.
Grace period for replacement of license plates or decals, §46.2-647.
Replica vehicle, §§46.2-602.1, 46.2-625.
Required before operating vehicle on highway, §46.2-600.
Rescue squad vehicles.
Volunteer rescue squads, §46.2-649.1:1.
Residence address of owner of vehicle.
Individual applicants to supply DMV, §46.2-600.
Revocation of cards.
Commencement of period, §46.2-414.
Return to commissioner, §46.2-370.
Revocation of registration.
Judicial review, §46.2-410.
Ridesharing, small vehicles rented for, §46.2-695.
Right to recover damages not affected by chapter, §46.2-614.
Salvage vehicles.
Registration of nonrepairable vehicle, §46.2-1603.2.
Sawmill operators.
Exemption from registration of tractors and similar vehicles, §46.2-669.
School buses.
Fees for vehicles designed for transportation of passengers, §46.2-694.
Seafood.
Transporting harvested seafood.
Exemption of vehicle from registration, §46.2-674.

MOTOR VEHICLE REGISTRATION —Cont'd
Service of notice, process and other papers.
Appointment of agent, §46.2-601.
Single-trip temporary registration or permit, §46.2-652.
Fee, §46.2-652.1.
Transportation of manufactured home exceeding size permitted, §46.2-653.
Snowmobiles.
Exemption from registration, §46.2-679.
Special construction and forestry equipment.
Defined, §46.2-100.
Registration not required, §46.2-600.
Specialized mobile equipment.
Registration fees, §46.2-700.
Specially constructed vehicles, §§46.2-625, 46.2-734.
State-owned motor vehicles, §§46.2-750 to 46.2-751.
Street address of owner or lessee of vehicle.
Business applicants to supply DMV, §46.2-600.
Suspension of cards.
Commencement of period, §46.2-414.
Suspension of certificate.
Effect of reversal of conviction, §46.2-413.
Equipment safety violations, §46.2-1000.
Judicial review, §46.2-410.
Nonresidents.
Conviction of or judgment against resident in another jurisdiction, §46.2-434.
Suspension or revocation of driver's license, §46.2-391.1.
Theft or embezzlement of vehicle, §46.2-610.
Uninsured motor vehicles, §§46.2-706, 46.2-708, 46.2-709.
Suspension of license for unpaid judgments.
Creditor's consent to registration despite default in installment payments, §46.2-423.
Suspension of licenses for nonresidents.
Power over nonresidents, §46.2-430.
Taxes.
Evidence of payment of taxes or exemption from taxes, §46.2-649.
Taxicabs.
Fees for vehicles used and designed for passenger transportation, §46.2-694.
Temporary registration, §§46.2-650 to 46.2-654.1.
Auction sales of motor vehicles, §46.2-654.
Duplicate applications of certificate of title and registration, §46.2-650.
Manufactured home exceeding size permitted by law.
Transportation of, §46.2-653.
One-trip permit, §46.2-651.
Out-of-business dealers, title for person other than the dealer, §46.2-654.1.
Oversize or overweight vehicles, §46.2-652.
Fee, §46.2-652.1.
Rulemaking authority, §46.2-650.
Theft.
Unlawful procurement of certificate, §46.2-105.1.
Theft of vehicle.
Suspension of registration, §46.2-610.
Tow dolly or converter gear, optional registration, §46.2-648.1.
Tow trucks, §46.2-649.1.
Trailers.
Dealer to obtain certificate of vehicle registration and license plates, §46.2-1992.39.
Evidence of tax payments required, §46.2-649.

MOTOR VEHICLE REGISTRATION —Cont'd
Truck owner inducted into armed forces.
Refund of fees, §46.2-691.
Trucks and tractor trucks.
Civil penalty for violations, §46.2-613.1.
Attachment and seizure of vehicle for unpaid fees and penalties, §46.2-613.4.
Service of process.
Operator as agent for, §46.2-613.2.
Procedures for issuance and service, §46.2-613.5.
Special processing of penalties, §46.2-613.3.
Uninsured motor vehicles, §§46.2-705 to 46.2-710.
Additional fee, §46.2-706.
Certificates required of applicants for registration, §46.2-706.
Confidentiality of insurance information, §46.2-706.1.
Definitions, §46.2-705.
Disposition of collected funds, §46.2-710.
False evidence of insurance, §46.2-707.
Furnishing certificate of insurance, §46.2-707.
Furnishing insurance information, §46.2-706.1.
Hearing prior to suspension, §46.2-708.
Operating vehicle without payment of fee, §46.2-707.
Proof of financial responsibility, §46.2-709.
Return of suspended driver's license and indicia of titling and registration, §46.2-709.
Suspension of driver's license and indicia of titling and registration for certain violations, §46.2-706.
Suspension of driver's license and registration for reportable accident, §46.2-708.
Verification of certificates, §46.2-706.
Utility vehicles.
Exemption from registration, §46.2-676.
Vehicles designed and used for transportation of passengers, §46.2-694.
Vehicles not designed or used for transportation of passengers.
Fees, §46.2-694.1.
Volunteer rescue squad or volunteer fire department vehicles, §46.2-649.1:1.
Voter registration.
Electronic transfer of information in department records for purposes of, §46.2-208.1.
Well-drilling machinery.
Registration fees, §46.2-700.
Wrecking vehicles.
Registration fees, §46.2-702.

MOTOR VEHICLE RENTALS.
Collision damage waiver, §§59.1-207.28 to 59.1-207.33.
Citation of chapter, §59.1-207.28.
Defined terms, §59.1-207.30.
Enforcement of provisions, §59.1-207.33.
Notice, §59.1-207.31.
Prohibited exclusions, §59.1-207.32.
Provision violations.
Penalties, §59.1-207.33.
Scope, §59.1-207.29.
Cost of hiring substitute vehicle.
Recovery by person entitled to recover for damages or destruction to vehicle, §8.01-66.
Driver information.
Commissioner of department of motor vehicles.
Supplying company on request, §46.2-208.
Injury to rented vehicles, §18.2-149.

MOTOR VEHICLE RENTALS —Cont'd
License plates.
Designated license plates for rental vehicles, §46.2-711.
Lists of vehicles used for rent or hire.
Furnishing list to commissioner, §46.2-107.
Merchants' capital tax, §§58.1-3509, 58.1-3510.
Personal information privacy, §§59.1-442 to 59.1-444.
Registration fees.
Small ridesharing vehicles, §46.2-695.
Tax upon rental of vehicle, §§58.1-1734 to 58.1-1741.
Administration of tax, §58.1-1738.
Amount, §58.1-1736.
Applicability, §58.1-1738.
Collected by rentor, §58.1-1738.
Credits, §58.1-1740.
Definitions, §58.1-1735.
Disposition of revenue, §58.1-1741.
Exemptions, §58.1-1737.
Forwarding tax information to law enforcement, §58.1-1739.
Government agencies.
Exemption, §58.1-1737.
Levy, §58.1-1736.
Mobile diagnostic units.
Exemption, §58.1-1737.
Payment by person renting, §58.1-1738.
Rates against gross proceeds.
Amount determined, §58.1-1736.
Rentors' responsibilities, §58.1-1738.
Time for remitting, §58.1-1738.
Truck, tractor truck, trailer, semitrailer.
Exemption, §58.1-1737.
Use of revenue, purposes, §58.1-1741.
Virginia motor vehicle rental tax act.
Title, §58.1-1734.
Titling of motor vehicles.
Priority of security interests, §46.2-640.1.
Vehicles without drivers.
Recordkeeping requirements, §46.2-108.

MOTOR VEHICLE RENTAL TAX, §§58.1-1734 to 58.1-1741, MOTOR VEHICLE RENTALS.

MOTOR VEHICLE REPAIR FACILITIES, §§59.1-207.1 to 59.1-207.6.
Accident reports.
Garage owners and repair shops, §§46.2-109, 46.2-376, 46.2-377.
Appraisal or estimate as to damage to vehicle.
Sworn appraisal or estimate as proof, §8.01-416.
Bills, written, §59.1-207.5.
Bullet-proof glass.
Reporting vehicles equipped with glass, §46.2-109.
Citation of chapter, §59.1-207.1.
Consumer protection, prohibited practices, §59.1-200.
Defined terms, §59.1-207.2.
Enforcement of provisions, §59.1-207.6.
Estimate or appraisal of damages.
Sworn, proof of damages, §8.01-416.
Glass.
Bullet-proof glass.
Reporting vehicles equipped with glass, §46.2-109.
Sale or installation of motor vehicle glass, §59.1-207.5:1.
Inspection of parts.
Customer right, §59.1-207.4.

MOTOR VEHICLE REPAIR FACILITIES —Cont'd
Inspections.
Department's right to inspect vehicles in garages, §46.2-110.
License plates.
Emergency use, §§46.2-719 to 46.2-721.
Loaner vehicles.
Temporary transfer of plates from another vehicle, §46.2-720.
Liens.
Enforcement, §46.2-644.03.
Keeper of garage or person keeping vehicle.
Storage, towing and recovery, care, §46.2-644.01.
Mechanics for repairs, §46.2-644.02.
Liens of keepers and mechanics.
Appeals, §43-36.
Validity, §43-35.
Loaner vehicles.
Temporary transfer of license plates from another vehicle, §46.2-720.
Local regulation of sanitary conditions.
Application of public gathering place provisions, §32.1-202.
Replaced parts.
Returning of, §59.1-207.4.
Reports.
Vehicles equipped with bullet-proof glass or smoke screening devices, §46.2-109.
Vehicles struck by bullets, §46.2-109.
Sale of vehicle subject to lien, §46.2-644.03.
Sign requirements, §59.1-207.3.
Smoke screen devices.
Reporting vehicles equipped with device, §46.2-109.
Titling of motor vehicles.
Priority of security interests shown on certificates of title, §46.2-640.
Unclaimed vehicles.
Reporting requirements, §46.2-1218.
Violations of provisions.
Penalties, §59.1-207.6.
Written estimates, §59.1-207.3.
Written invoices, §59.1-207.5.

MOTOR VEHICLE REPAIRS.
After market parts.
Estimates by insurer for costs of repair when using, §38.2-510.
Appraisal or estimate as to damage to vehicle.
Sworn appraisal or estimate as proof, §8.01-416.
County manager plan of government.
Zoning ordinances regulating, §15.2-730.
Insurance unfair settlement practices, §38.2-517.

MOTOR VEHICLE REPOSSESSION.
Criminal provisions pertaining to unauthorized use, preventing operation and setting in motion.
Inapplicability to bona fide repossession, §18.2-148.
Motor vehicle sales and use tax exemption, §58.1-2403.

MOTOR VEHICLES.
Abandoned motor vehicles, §§46.2-1200 to 46.2-1207.
ABC offenses.
Confiscation, §§4.1-339 to 4.1-348.
See MOTOR VEHICLE CONFISCATION.

MOTOR VEHICLES —Cont'd
ABC offenses —Cont'd
Driving after illegally consuming alcohol.
Persons under age twenty-one, §18.2-266.1.
Limitation on carrying alcoholic beverages in vehicle transporting passengers for hire, §4.1-312.
Violations by armed persons, §4.1-318.
Accessories.
Standards.
State police department function, §52-4.
Accidents generally, §§46.2-894 to 46.2-902.
See MOTOR VEHICLE ACCIDENTS.
Advertising new or used vehicles, §18.2-221.
Affidavit as to damages.
Proof of damages, §8.01-416.
After market parts.
Estimates by insurer for repair costs when using, §38.2-510.
Aggressive driving, §46.2-868.1.
Restricted permit to operate, issuance, §46.2-392.
Suspension of driver's license, §46.2-392.
Alternative fuels and energy efficient vehicles.
Energy policy of Commonwealth, §§67-102, 67-103.
State owned motor vehicles.
Alternative fuel vehicle conversion fund, §2.2-1176.1.
Centralized fleet, conversion to alternative fuel vehicles, §2.2-1176.
Alternative fuels revolving fund.
General provisions, §§33.1-223.3 to 33.1-223.9.
Antique motor vehicles.
Limited uses, §46.2-730.
Revocation of privilege to register vehicle.
Violations, §46.2-730.
Special license plates, §46.2-730.
Unsafe vehicles, not properly equipped.
Suspension of registration, §46.2-730.
Violations, misdemeanors, §46.2-730.
Appliances, standards.
State police department function, §52-4.
Appraisal of damages.
Sworn appraisal as proof, §8.01-416.
Armored vehicles.
Used by bank to deliver or pick up deposits, §6.2-814.
Arrest of motorists.
Impoundment of vehicle, §19.2-80.1.
Assignment of insurance risks, §§46.2-464 to 46.2-471.
See MOTOR VEHICLE INSURANCE.
Attorney general.
Special license plates, §46.2-736.1.
Auction sales of motor vehicles.
Issuance of temporary registration certificates, §46.2-654.
Automatic vehicle identification system.
Toll roads or toll bridges, §§46.2-819.1, 46.2-819.3.
Dulles access highway, §46.2-819.1.
Video-monitoring system installed in conjunction with, §46.2-819.3:1.
Automobile clubs, §§13.1-400.1 to 13.1-400.9.
Automobile graveyards.
Ordinances taxing and regulating, §15.2-903.
Bailees failure to return vehicle, §18.2-117.
Bears.
Keeping bear if struck by motor vehicle, §29.1-539.
Biodiesel fuels.
Biofuels production incentive grant program, §§45.1-393, 45.1-394.

MOTOR VEHICLES —Cont'd
Biodiesel fuels —Cont'd
Energy policy of Commonwealth, §§67-102, 67-103.
Public transportation vehicles.
Use encouraged, §§67-500, 67-501.
Blind pedestrians.
Effect of failure to use cane or guide dog, §46.2-934.
Liability for injuries to, §46.2-932.1.
Pedestrians generally, §§46.2-923 to 46.2-935.
See PEDESTRIANS.
Vehicles to stop for pedestrians guided by dog or carrying recognized cane, §46.2-933.
Bona fide purchasers of motor vehicles.
Distress for local taxes levied and assessed.
Liability to levy or distress, §58.1-3942.
Brakes, §§46.2-1066 to 46.2-1071.
See MOTOR VEHICLE EQUIPMENT.
Breaking, injuring, etc., or preventing operation of vehicle, §18.2-146.
Bona fide repossession, inapplicability of provisions to, §18.2-148.
CAFE standards.
Federal actions to increase, support, policy of Commonwealth, §§67-800, 67-801.
Cargo.
Cleanup of escaped objects constituting obstruction or endangering travel, §10.1-1424.
Escape of contents, §46.2-1156.
Fine for failure to prevent, VA SCt Rule 3B:2.
Hauling logs, poles, lumber, etc.
Fastening loads.
Fine for failure to fasten, VA SCt Rule 3B:2.
Load covers, §46.2-1156.
Fine for failure to prevent escape of contents, VA SCt Rule 3B:2.
Size and weight of vehicles generally, §§46.2-1101 to 46.2-1156.
See MOTOR VEHICLE SIZE AND WEIGHT.
Vehicle loading to prevent escape of contents, §10.1-1424.
Car seats.
Child restraints, §§46.2-1095 to 46.2-1100.
Cell phones or other wireless telecommunications devices.
Using while operating vehicle.
Emailing or texting while driving, §46.2-1078.1.
Commercial drivers' licenses, disqualifications, §§46.2-341.20, 46.2-341.20:5.
Reckless driving, mandatory fine, §46.2-868.
Holders of provisional drivers' licenses, §46.2-334.01.
Child labor.
Restrictions on employment as driver or helper, §40.1-100.
Children or minors.
Failure to ensure child is properly secured.
Uniform fine schedule, VA SCt Rule 3C:2.
Classification plates.
Uniform fine schedule, failure to obtain, VA SCt Rules 3C:1, 3C:2.
Clean fuel vehicle and advanced cellulosic biofuels job creation tax credit, §58.1-439.1.
Color of vehicles.
Data included on registration and certificate of title, §46.2-604.
Commercial drivers' licenses, §§46.2-341.1 to 46.2-341.34.
See COMMERCIAL DRIVERS' LICENSES.

MOTOR VEHICLES —Cont'd
Commercial driver training schools, §§46.2-1700 to 46.2-1707.
Concealed weapons, carrying in, §18.2-308.
Confidential information.
Records in office of department of motor vehicles.
Privileged records, release, conditions, §46.2-208.
Cost of hiring substitute vehicle.
Recovery by person entitled to recover for damages or destruction of vehicle, §8.01-66.
County manager plan of government.
Removal or immobilization of trespassing vehicle, §15.2-719.
Zoning ordinances regulating storage of junked and repair of motor vehicles.
Civil penalties for violations, §15.2-730.
County ordinances.
Uniformity with general laws of Commonwealth, §15.2-1201.
Criminal forfeiture.
Felony DWI, vehicle used in, §19.2-386.34.
Vehicles used in commission of certain specified crimes, §19.2-386.16.
Damages.
Sworn appraisal or estimate as proof, §8.01-416.
Dealers.
Generally, §§46.2-1500 to 46.2-1582.
See MOTOR VEHICLE DEALERS.
Motorcycle dealers, §§46.2-1993 to 46.2-1993.82.
See MOTORCYCLE DEALERS.
Trailer dealers.
Generally, §§46.2-1992 to 46.2-1992.85.
See TRAILER DEALERS.
Deer.
Hazards, creating, §29.1-529.
Keeping deer if struck by motor vehicle, §29.1-539.
Definitions, §46.2-100.
Defrauding keeper of motor vehicles, §18.2-189.
Delinquent children.
Loss of driving privileges, §16.1-278.8.
Alcohol, drug and handgun offenses, §16.1-278.9.
Department of motor vehicles.
Generally.
See MOTOR VEHICLES DEPARTMENT.
Devices for puncturing tires.
Manufacturing, distributing or possessing, §18.2-147.2.
Police use authorized, §33.1-345.
Disability or handicap.
Parking for disabled or handicapped, §§46.2-1240 to 46.2-1259.
See PARKING FOR DISABLED OR HANDICAPPED.
Personal property on vehicles, alternative tax rates, §§58.1-3506.1 to 58.1-3506.8.
Disabled vehicles.
Flares or other signals, §46.2-111.
Distracted driving.
Cell phones or other wireless telecommunications devices, using while operating vehicle, §46.2-1078.1.
Commercial drivers' licenses, disqualifications, §§46.2-341.20, 46.2-341.20:5.
Holders of provisional licenses, §46.2-334.01.
Reckless driving, mandatory fine, §46.2-868.
Distress for local taxes levied or assessed.
Bona fide purchaser for value liability, §58.1-3942.

MOTOR VEHICLES —Cont'd
Drinking while operating motor vehicle, §18.2-323.1.
Open container, passenger area, defined, §18.2-323.1.
Rebuttable presumption, §18.2-323.1.
Drive-by shootings.
Shooting from vehicle so as to endanger persons, §18.2-286.1.
Disqualification for concealed weapons permit, §18.2-308.09.
Shooting in or along road or street, §18.2-286.
Hunting, §29.1-521.2.
Driver improvement programs, §§46.2-489 to 46.2-506.
See DRIVER IMPROVEMENT PROGRAMS.
Drivers' licenses.
Commercial drivers' licenses, §§46.2-341.1 to 46.2-341.34.
See COMMERCIAL DRIVERS' LICENSES.
Generally.
See DRIVERS' LICENSES.
Driver training schools, §§46.2-1700 to 46.2-1707.
Driving after illegally consuming alcohol.
Persons under age twenty-one, §18.2-266.1.
Driving records.
Certification and admissibility in evidence, §46.2-215.
Charges for information supplied by department of motor vehicles, §§46.2-214, 46.2-214.1.
Additional charge, §46.2-214.1.
Release of information for research purposes, §46.2-209.
Release of privileged information, §46.2-208.
Accident reports, §§46.2-379, 46.2-380.
Driving while intoxicated.
Generally, §§18.2-266 to 18.2-273.
See DRIVING WHILE INTOXICATED.
Driving while license suspended or revoked.
See DRIVING WHILE LICENSE SUSPENDED OR REVOKED.
Dropping substances on highways.
Allowing escape of load material, §10.1-1424.
Drug transactions.
Closure of nuisance premises, §§48-16, 48-17.
Common nuisance, §§18.2-258, 18.2-258.01.
DWI, §§18.2-266 to 18.2-273.
See DRIVING WHILE INTOXICATED.
Elderly.
Personal property taxes on motor vehicles, alternative tax rates, §§58.1-3506.1 to 58.1-3506.8.
Electric vehicles.
See ELECTRIC VEHICLES.
Electronic filings or submissions to department, §46.2-216.1.
Emailing while driving.
Using handheld communications devices, §46.2-1078.1.
Commercial drivers' licenses, disqualifications, §§46.2-341.20, 46.2-341.20:5.
Holders of provisional licenses, §46.2-334.01.
Reckless driving, mandatory fine, §46.2-868.
Emergency medical services, §32.1-111.4.
Inspections, §32.1-111.7.
Permits, §32.1-111.6.
Revocation and suspension, §32.1-111.8.
Emergency vehicles.
Generally, §§46.2-920 to 46.2-922.
Emissions inspections, §§46.2-1176 to 46.2-1187.3.
See MOTOR VEHICLE EMISSIONS INSPECTIONS.

MOTOR VEHICLES —Cont'd
Energy policy of Commonwealth, §§67-102, 67-103.
Enforcement of motor vehicles title, §46.2-102.
Entering vehicle to commit crime, malicious mischief or injury, §18.2-147.
Equipment generally, §§46.2-1000 to 46.2-1100.
See MOTOR VEHICLE EQUIPMENT.
Estimate of damages.
Sworn estimate as proof, §8.01-416.
Evidence.
Damages, sworn appraisal as estimate, §8.01-416.
Driving records, §46.2-215.
Exhaust system, §§46.2-1047 to 46.2-1051.
See MOTOR VEHICLE EQUIPMENT.
Financial responsibility, §§46.2-435 to 46.2-463.
See MOTOR VEHICLE FINANCIAL RESPONSIBILITY.
Fines, general penalty, §46.2-113.
Fines, pretrial waiver of appearance, plea of guilty and payment of fines, §16.1-69.40:1.
Traffic infractions and uniform fine schedule, VA SCt Rules 3B:1, 3B:2.
Fines, uniform fine schedule, VA SCt Rules 3B:1, 3B:2.
Firearms and ammunition possessed by employee.
Storing at workplace in locked private motor vehicle, §15.2-915.
Forest fires.
Throwing inflammatory objects from vehicles, §10.1-1143.
Fort Monroe authority.
Responsibility for vehicles within area of operation, §2.2-2341.1.
Fraud in procuring, §18.2-206.
Fraudulent conversion or removal of property subject to lien or title in another, §18.2-115.
Fuel efficiency standards.
CAFE standards.
Federal actions to increase, support, policy of Commonwealth, §§67-800, 67-801.
Fuels, §§59.1-149 to 59.1-167.3.
See MOTOR FUELS.
Garage keeper's lien, §46.2-644.01.
Enforcement, §46.2-644.03.
General penalty for violating title, §46.2-113.
Global positioning systems.
Search warrant to permit use of tracking device, §19.2-56.2.
Governor, reciprocal agreements by, §46.2-106.
Habitual offenders, §§46.2-356 to 46.2-363.
Handicapped persons.
Parking for disabled or handicapped, §§46.2-1240 to 46.2-1259.
See PARKING FOR DISABLED OR HANDICAPPED.
Personal property on vehicles, alternative tax rates, §§58.1-3506.1 to 58.1-3506.8.
Hazardous materials transportation, §§10.1-1450 to 10.1-1454.
Headlights.
See MOTOR VEHICLE EQUIPMENT.
Heavy equipment dealers generally, §§59.1-353 to 59.1-363.
See HEAVY EQUIPMENT DEALERS.
Horns, sirens and whistles, §§46.2-1059 to 46.2-1062.
See MOTOR VEHICLE EQUIPMENT.
Hunting.
Deer.
Forfeiture, §29.1-524.

MOTOR VEHICLES —Cont'd
Hunting —Cont'd
Deer —Cont'd
Lights, use of, §§29.1-523, 29.1-525.
Disability or handicap.
Shooting from stationary vehicles, §29.1-521.3.
Shooting or attempting to take wild birds or animals from, §29.1-521.
Ignition interlock system, §18.2-270.1.
Illegal drug transactions.
Closure of nuisance premises, §§48-16, 48-17.
Immobilized or unattended vehicles.
Generally, §§46.2-1209 to 46.2-1217.
See ABANDONED MOTOR VEHICLES.
Impoundment of vehicle.
Arrest of motorists, §19.2-80.1.
Driving while license suspended or revoked, §46.2-301.1.
DWI or habitual offender offenses, §46.2-301.1.
Indigency.
Nonprofit organizations providing vehicles or transportation for indigent persons, §46.2-1508.1.
Inoperable motor vehicles on residential or commercial property.
Authority of locality to restrict keeping, removal, §§15.2-904, 15.2-905.
Inspections.
Emissions inspections, §§46.2-1176 to 46.2-1187.3.
See MOTOR VEHICLE EMISSIONS INSPECTIONS.
Safety inspections, §§46.2-1157 to 46.2-1175.1.
See MOTOR VEHICLE SAFETY INSPECTIONS.
State police department.
Functions, §52-4.
Stopping vehicles for inspection or to secure information, §46.2-103.
Insurance.
Generally.
See MOTOR VEHICLE INSURANCE.
Liability insurance policies generally, §§38.2-2200 to 38.2-2234.
See LIABILITY INSURANCE.
Interest.
Contract rate more than legal rate.
Motor vehicle purchases, §6.2-314.
Internet self-service options, §46.2-216.4.
Access through state library, §46.2-216.5.
Jackrocks.
Manufacturing, distributing or possessing, §18.2-147.2.
John Doe actions.
Owner or operator of vehicle causing injury or damage unknown, §38.2-2206.
Joyriding.
Bona fide repossession, inapplicability of provisions to, §18.2-148.
Judgment unsatisfied.
Suspension of driver's license, §46.2-417.
Judicial conference for district courts.
Special sessions concerning, §16.1-220.
Junked vehicles.
County manager plan of government.
Zoning ordinances regulating storage, §15.2-730.
Junkyards, §33.1-348.
Ordinances taxing and regulating, §15.2-903.
Leased vehicles.
Certificate of title.
New indicia of title.
Procedure as to leased vehicles, §46.2-619.

MOTOR VEHICLES —Cont'd
Leased vehicles —Cont'd
Driver information.
Commissioner of department of motor vehicles.
Supplying leasing company on request, §46.2-208.
Injury to, §18.2-149.
Personal property taxes.
Classification, §58.1-3506.
Payment of tax by lessee, §58.1-3516.2.
Rental car reimbursement.
Recovery of cost of hiring substitute vehicle.
Recovery for damaged or destroyed vehicle, §8.01-66.
Sublease, §18.2-115.1.
Lease-purchase agreements.
Application of provisions, §59.1-207.19.
Lemon law, §§59.1-207.9 to 59.1-207.16:1.
License agents, §46.2-205.
License plates.
Generally, §§46.2-711 to 46.2-749.130.
See MOTOR VEHICLE LICENSE PLATES.
License taxes upon owner of motor vehicle.
Alternative fuel vehicles, §58.1-2249.
Liability for tax, due date, §58.1-2251.
Localities imposing, §15.2-973.
Licensure of drivers.
Commercial drivers' licenses, §§46.2-341.1 to 46.2-341.34.
See COMMERCIAL DRIVERS' LICENSES.
Generally.
See DRIVERS' LICENSES.
Lien or title in another.
Fraudulent conversion or removal of property, §18.2-115.
Liens.
Impounded vehicles.
Repossession or removal by lienholder, §46.2-301.1.
Keeper of garage or other person keeping vehicle.
Towing and recovery, storage, care, §46.2-644.01.
Enforcement, §46.2-644.03.
Mechanics for repairs, §46.2-644.02.
Enforcement, §46.2-644.03.
Sale of vehicle by person acquiring lien, §46.2-644.03.
Liens of keepers.
Appeals, §43-36.
Validity, §43-35.
Lieutenant governor.
Special license plates, §46.2-736.1.
Lights and turn signals, §§46.2-1010 to 46.2-1040.
See MOTOR VEHICLE EQUIPMENT.
Lights or spotlights employed under certain circumstances, §18.2-509.
Load material.
Allowing escape, §10.1-1424.
Loads.
Covers, §46.2-1156.
Fine for failure to prevent escape of contents, VA SCt Rule 3B:2.
Escape of contents, §46.2-1156.
Fine for failure to prevent, VA SCt Rule 3B:2.
Hauling logs, poles, lumber, etc.
Fastening loads.
Fine for failure to fasten, VA SCt Rule 3B:2.
Size and weight of vehicles generally, §§46.2-1101 to 46.2-1156.
See MOTOR VEHICLE SIZE AND WEIGHT.

MOTOR VEHICLES —Cont'd
Localities regulating and controlling operation, §15.2-2028.
Powers generally, §§46.2-1300 to 46.2-1314.
See LOCALITIES.
Locality selling vehicle fleet with intent to lease back.
Approval, notice, public hearing, §15.2-951.
Low-speed vehicles, §§46.2-908.2, 46.2-908.3.
Motor vehicle safety inspections.
Exemption from inspection requirement, §46.2-1158.01.
Mailing list of registrations and titles.
List of registrations and titles offered for sale to public, §46.2-210.
Maximum fine for traffic infraction, §46.2-113.
Mechanic's lien for repairs, §46.2-644.02.
Enforcement, §46.2-644.03.
Motorcycle dealers, §§46.2-1993 to 46.2-1993.82.
See MOTORCYCLE DEALERS.
Motorcycle rider safety, §§46.2-1188 to 46.2-1192.
Motorcycles.
Generally.
See MOTORCYCLES.
Rider safety, §§46.2-1188 to 46.2-1192.
See MOTORCYCLE RIDER SAFETY.
Motor vehicle rental tax, §§58.1-1734 to 58.1-1741.
See MOTOR VEHICLE RENTALS.
Motor vehicle tire puncturing devices.
Manufacturing, distributing or possessing, §18.2-147.2.
Police use authorized, §33.1-345.
NADA yellow or black books.
Motor vehicle value, §8.01-419.1.
Odometer.
Acquisition of vehicle from vendor.
Reporting odometer reading, §46.2-629.
Motorcycle dealer odometer disclosure, §46.2-1993.25.
Reporting odometer reading on certificate of title, §46.2-629.
Tampering, §46.2-112.
T&M vehicle dealers.
Disclosure, §46.2-1932.
Open container law, §18.2-323.1.
Open container, passenger area, defined, §18.2-323.1.
Rebuttable presumption, §18.2-323.1.
Uniform fine schedule, VA SCt Rules 3C:1, 3C:2.
Parking.
Disabled or handicapped persons, §§46.2-1240 to 46.2-1259.
See PARKING FOR DISABLED OR HANDICAPPED.
Generally, §§46.2-1216 to 46.2-1239.
See PARKING.
Pedestrians.
General provisions, §§46.2-923 to 46.2-935.
See PEDESTRIANS.
Personal property taxes.
Classification, §58.1-3506.
Tangible personal property, §58.1-3503.
Elderly and handicapped, alternative tax rates, §§58.1-3506.1 to 58.1-3506.8.
Generally, §§58.1-3500 to 58.1-3522.
See PERSONAL PROPERTY TAXES.
Lessee of leased vehicle paying tax, §58.1-3516.2.
Proration of tax, §58.1-3516.
Returns.
Alternative method for filing, §58.1-3518.1.

MOTOR VEHICLES —Cont'd
Personal property taxes —Cont'd
Situs for assessment, §58.1-3511.
Tax relief act of 1998, §§58.1-3523 to 58.1-3535.
See PERSONAL PROPERTY TAX RELIEF ACT OF 1998.
Physician reports on disabilities of drivers, §54.1-2966.1.
Port authority property.
Regulations, §62.1-132.11.
Pretrial payment of fines, §16.1-69.40:1.
Traffic infractions and uniform fine schedule, VA SCt Rules 3B:1, 3B:2.
Private highways.
Application, §56-550.
Privileged records.
Records in office of department of motor vehicles, release, conditions, §46.2-208.
Proof of financial responsibility, §§46.2-435 to 46.2-463.
See MOTOR VEHICLE FINANCIAL RESPONSIBILITY.
Public utility vehicles.
Extension of loads beyond front of vehicles.
Self-propelled pole carriers, §46.2-1120.
Racing.
ABC license.
Motor car sporting event licenses, §4.1-206.
Taxes, §4.1-233.
Radar and similar speed determining devices, §46.2-882.
Certificate of accuracy, §46.2-882.
Division of purchases and supply.
Determining proper equipment for monitoring, §2.2-1112.
Evidence in criminal prosecutions, §46.2-942.
Railroad corporations.
Safety requirements for vehicles transporting railroad employees, §56-419.2.
Reckless driving, §§46.2-852 to 46.2-868.
See RECKLESS DRIVING.
Registration, §§46.2-645 to 46.2-710, 46.2-750 to 46.2-756.
See MOTOR VEHICLE REGISTRATION.
Reimbursement for hiring substitute vehicle.
Person entitled to recover for damages or destruction of vehicle, §8.01-66.
Removal of property subject to lien or title in another, §18.2-115.
Rental car reimbursement.
Recovery of cost of hiring substitute vehicle.
Recovery for damaged or destroyed vehicle, §8.01-66.
Rented or leased, injury to, §18.2-149.
Repairs.
After market parts.
Estimates by insurer for costs when using, §38.2-510.
County manager plan of government.
Zoning ordinances regulating, §15.2-730.
Garage keeper's lien, §46.2-644.01.
Enforcement, §46.2-644.03.
Insurance unfair settlement practices, §38.2-517.
Lien.
Enforcement of liens, §46.2-644.03.
Garage keepers, §46.2-644.01.
Mechanics, §46.2-644.02.
Mechanic's lien, §46.2-644.02.
Enforcement, §46.2-644.03.
Replica vehicle.
Antique vehicle license plates.
Not automatically eligible for, §46.2-602.1.

MOTOR VEHICLES —Cont'd
Replica vehicle —Cont'd
Defined, §46.2-100.
Miles driven per year, restriction, §46.2-602.1.
Model year, requirements, §46.2-602.1.
New vehicle ID number, line-make and model year.
Assignment by DMV, §46.2-602.1.
Safety and emission inspections.
Vehicle subject to, §46.2-602.1.
Titling and registration, §§46.2-602.1, 46.2-625.
Repossession.
Criminal provisions pertaining to unauthorized use, preventing operation or setting in motion.
Inapplicability to bona fide repossession, §18.2-148.
Sale of vehicle repossessed in another state by dealer, §46.2-633.1.
Retail sales and use tax.
Exemption of motor vehicles, §58.1-609.1.
Motor vehicles brought into Virginia for use in performing construction contracts, §§58.1-604.1 to 58.1-604.3.
Revocation of drivers' licenses.
See DRIVERS' LICENSES.
Ridesharing, §§46.2-1400 to 46.2-1407.
Rules of the road.
Traffic regulation generally, §§46.2-800 to 46.2-947.
See TRAFFIC INFRACTIONS.
Safety belts, §§46.2-1091 to 46.2-1094.
Child restraints, §§46.2-1095 to 46.2-1100.
Safety devices.
Standards.
State police department function, §52-4.
Safety inspections, §§46.2-1157 to 46.2-1175.1.
See MOTOR VEHICLE SAFETY INSPECTIONS.
Sale of vehicle by person acquiring lien.
Keepers of garage or mechanics for repairs, §46.2-644.03.
Salvage vehicles.
Generally, §§46.2-1600 to 46.2-1610.
See SALVAGE VEHICLES.
Seat belts, §§46.2-1091 to 46.2-1094.
Child restraints, §§46.2-1095 to 46.2-1100.
Self-service options via Internet, §46.2-216.4.
Access through state library, §46.2-216.5.
Self-service storage liens, §§55-418, 55-419.
Serious traffic violation.
Additional fine for vehicles of certain gross weight, §46.2-113.
Setting in motion with intent to commit crime, malicious mischief or injury, §18.2-147.
Bona fide repossession, inapplicability of provisions to, §18.2-148.
Shellfish, removal from condemned area.
Sealing of motor vehicles, §28.2-812.
Sheriffs.
Auxiliary, reserve, or special deputies.
Vehicles used by.
Personal property tax classification, §58.1-3506.
Equipment on vehicles.
Auxiliary lights, §46.2-1029.
Flashing blue or red and blue warning lights, §46.2-1022.
Flashing of headlights, §46.2-1029.1.
Warnings, sirens and whistles, §46.2-1061.
Markings, §15.2-1610.

MOTOR VEHICLES —Cont'd
Shooting at or throwing missiles at motor vehicles, §18.2-154.
Shooting from vehicle so as to endanger persons, §18.2-286.1.
Disqualification for concealed weapons permit, §18.2-308.09.
Sidewalks.
Driving on sidewalks, §46.2-903.
Size and weight.
Generally, §§46.2-1101 to 46.2-1156.
See MOTOR VEHICLE SIZE AND WEIGHT.
Slow moving traffic vehicles.
Designation of lanes for.
Commonwealth transportation board or local authorities, §46.2-804.
Solid waste management.
Local regulation of vehicle construction, parking, etc., §46.2-1304.1.
Speeding.
Eluding police, §46.2-817.
General provisions.
See SPEEDING.
State owned motor vehicles.
See STATE OWNED MOTOR VEHICLES.
Steering and suspension systems, §§46.2-1063 to 46.2-1065.
Stolen vehicles.
See MOTOR VEHICLE THEFT.
Stopping distance tables, §46.2-880.
Stopping or standing.
Municipal regulations, §46.2-1220.
Storage.
Lien, §46.2-644.01.
Enforcement, §46.2-644.03.
Sublease of motor vehicle.
Vehicle to lease, security interest or lien, §18.2-115.1.
Substitute vehicle provided insured by insurer.
Recovery of cost of hiring substitute vehicle, §8.01-66.
Suspension of drivers' licenses.
See DRIVERS' LICENSES.
Tables of speed and stopping distances, §46.2-880.
T&M vehicle dealers, §§46.2-1900 to 46.2-1991.
See T&M VEHICLE DEALERS.
Tangier, town of.
Inapplicability of motor vehicles Title 46.2, §46.2-115.
Temporary assistance for needy families (TANF) recipients.
Surplus state motor vehicle resale to recipients.
Vehicles sold to social services departments, §2.2-1124.
Testing, evaluation and approval of equipment, §§46.2-1005 to 46.2-1009.
Texting while driving.
Using handheld communications devices, §46.2-1078.1.
Commercial drivers' licenses, disqualifications, §§46.2-341.20, 46.2-341.20:5.
Holders of provisional licenses, §46.2-334.01.
Reckless driving, mandatory fine, §46.2-868.
Tires.
Generally.
See MOTOR VEHICLE EQUIPMENT.
Waste tires.
See WASTE TIRES.

MOTOR VEHICLES —Cont'd
Titling, §§46.2-616 to 46.2-644.
See MOTOR VEHICLE TITLING.
Towing.
Complaints against tow truck drivers, §46.2-119.
Lien, §46.2-644.01.
Enforcement, §46.2-644.03.
Prohibited acts, §46.2-118.
Registration of tow truck drivers, §46.2-116.
Revocation or suspension of registration, §46.2-117.
Toy vehicles.
Defined, §46.2-100.
Electrically powered vehicles.
Battery requirements to operate, §46.2-908.1.
Interstate highways, operating on, §46.2-908.1.
Use on highways, restrictions, §46.2-932.
Tracking devices.
Search warrant to permit use of tracking device, §19.2-56.2.
Traffic regulation generally, §§46.2-800 to 46.2-947.
See TRAFFIC INFRACTIONS.
Trailer dealers, §§46.2-1992 to 46.2-1992.85.
See TRAILER DEALERS.
Trespassing motor vehicles, §46.2-1231.
Unattended vehicles, §§46.2-1209 to 46.2-1217.
See ABANDONED MOTOR VEHICLES.
Unauthorized use, §18.2-102.
Bona fide repossession, inapplicability of provisions to, §18.2-148.
Underinsured motor vehicle owner or operator.
Institution of action against, §38.2-2206.
Uniformed officer enforcement of title, §46.2-102.
Uniform fine schedule, traffic infractions, VA SCt Rules 3B:1, 3B:2.
Uninsured motor vehicle owner or operator.
Institution of action against, §38.2-2206.
Unsafe vehicles.
Removal from highway, §46.2-1001.
Unsatisfied judgment.
Suspension of driver's license, §46.2-417.
Usury.
Interest, contract rate more than legal rate.
Motor vehicle purchases, §6.2-314.
Value in issue.
NADA yellow or black books, §8.01-419.1.
Vandalism.
Breaking or preventing operation of vehicle, §18.2-146.
War, traffic regulations during, §44-205.
Weighmasters, public.
Determining weight of vehicle or combination of vehicles, §3.2-5812.
Wildlife Center of Virginia.
Vehicles owned or controlled by.
Exemption from certain traffic regulations, §46.2-920.2.
Windshields and windows, §§46.2-1052 to 46.2-1058.
See MOTOR VEHICLE EQUIPMENT.
Zero tolerance law, §18.2-266.1.
Zoning, §15.2-730.

MOTOR VEHICLE SAFETY INSPECTIONS, §§46.2-1157 to 46.2-1175.1.
Antique motor vehicles.
Exception from requirement, §46.2-1158.01.

MOTOR VEHICLE SAFETY INSPECTIONS —Cont'd
Armed forces personnel.
Extension of validity of stickers for active duty members of the armed services, §46.2-1158.1.
Commercial motor vehicles.
Exception from requirement, §46.2-1158.01.
Commuter buses.
Recordkeeping requirements by operators, §46.2-1175.
Correcting defects found by inspection, §46.2-1157.
Fine schedule, VA SCt Rule 3B:2.
Maximum fine for violating Title 46.2, §46.2-113.
Pretrial payment of fine, §16.1-69.40:1.
Counterfeit inspection stickers, §46.2-1173.
Dealer inspection of vehicles, §§46.2-1539, 46.2-1540.
Emissions inspections, §§46.2-1176 to 46.2-1187.3.
See MOTOR VEHICLE EMISSIONS INSPECTIONS.
Exemption from inspection requirement.
Generally, §46.2-1158.01.
Logtrailer, §46.2-1159.
Towed vehicle, §46.2-1160.
Extension of validity of stickers for active duty members of the armed services, §46.2-1158.1.
Failure to comply, §46.2-1158.02.
Fees and charges, §§46.2-1167, 46.2-1168.
Fine schedule, VA SCt Rule 3B:2.
Maximum fine for violation of title, §46.2-113.
Fire departments or fire companies.
Donation of vehicles, §27-15.2.
Frequency of inspection, §46.2-1158.
Extension of validity of stickers for active duty members of the armed services, §46.2-1158.1.
Highway maintenance vehicles, §46.2-1175.1.
Imitation inspection stickers, §46.2-1173.
Infraction, failure to comply, §46.2-1158.02.
Inspection, defined, §46.2-1169.
Inspection stations.
Administrative process act.
Actions of superintendent subject to, §46.2-1163.
Advertising, etc., when not authorized, §46.2-1170.
Designation, §46.2-1163.
Minimum standards required, §46.2-1163.
Posting of regulations, §46.2-1165.
Revocation of designation.
Surrender of inspection stickers and other forms and papers, §46.2-1172.
Rulemaking authority, §46.2-1163.
Suspension of designation, §46.2-1171.
Inspection stickers.
Display requirements, §46.2-1163.
Imitation or counterfeit, §46.2-1173.
Lost or damaged stickers, §46.2-1164.
Removal, §46.2-1173.
Replacement of lost or damaged stickers, §46.2-1164.
Transfer to new windshield, §46.2-1164.
Unauthorized taking, possession or use, §46.2-1172.
Law enforcement officers certified to perform.
Removal of unsafe vehicles from highway, §46.2-1001.
Logtrailers.
Exempt from inspection, §46.2-1159.
Maximum fine for violating Title 46.2, §46.2-113.
Misdemeanor, §46.2-1171.

MOTOR VEHICLE SAFETY INSPECTIONS —Cont'd
Motorcycles inspected prior to sale by dealers, §46.2-1993.33.
Not required by certain sellers, §46.2-1993.34.
Motor homes.
Inapplicability of inspection provisions, §46.2-1162.
Posting of regulations.
Official inspection stations, §46.2-1165.
Reciprocal agreements, §46.2-1174.
Recreational vehicles.
Inapplicability of inspection provisions, §46.2-1162.
Refuse collection vehicles, §46.2-1175.1.
Registration fee, §46.2-1168.
Reinspection.
Charges, §46.2-1167.
Making of repairs or adjustments, §46.2-1169.
Rulemaking authority.
Official inspection stations, §§46.2-1163, 46.2-1165, 46.2-1166.
Scope of inspection, §46.2-1158.
Semitrailers equipped with heating or cooking appliances, §46.2-1161.1.
Standards.
Minimum standards for inspection stations, §46.2-1166.
State police department.
Commuter bus operators.
Inspection of records and buses, §46.2-1175.
Functions, §52-4.
Submitting vehicle to inspection, §46.2-1157.
Fine schedule, VA SCt Rule 3B:2.
Maximum fine for violating Title 46.2, §46.2-113.
Pretrial payment of fine, §16.1-69.40:1.
T&M vehicle dealers.
Inspection of vehicles required, §46.2-1940.
Exceptions, §46.2-1941.
Towed vehicles.
Exempt from inspection, §46.2-1160.
Trailers and semitrailers equipped with heating or cooking appliances, §46.2-1161.1.
Trailers sold by trailer dealers prior to sale, §§46.2-1992.32, 46.2-1992.34.
Itemization of deficiencies made available to purchaser, §46.2-1992.34.
Not required of certain sellers, §46.2-1992.33.
Uniform vehicle inspection reciprocity agreement.
Authority of superintendent, §46.2-1174.
Violations, §§46.2-1158.02, 46.2-1171.
Windshield replacement.
Reinspection not required, §46.2-1164.
Transfer of inspection sticker to new windshield, §46.2-1164.

MOTOR VEHICLE SALES AND USE TAX, §§58.1-2400 to 58.1-2426.
Action for recovery, §58.1-2406.
Aliens.
Refund to foreign nationals, §58.1-2423.
Amount of tax, §58.1-2402.
Appeals from order or decision of commissioner of department of motor vehicles, §58.1-2426.
Basis of tax, §58.1-2405.
Collection, §58.1-2406.
Correction of assessment.
Application to commissioner.
Filing, time, §58.1-2426.

MOTOR VEHICLE SALES AND USE TAX —Cont'd
Credits against tax, §58.1-2424.
Dealer processing fee subject to tax, §58.1-2402.
Definitions, §58.1-2401.
Disposition of revenues, §58.1-2425.
Estimated tax.
Insufficient payment, §58.1-2406.
Examination of dealer's records, books, papers or documents, §58.1-2420.
Exemptions, §58.1-2403.
Falsely stating selling price with intent to evade, §58.1-2402.
Forwarding of tax information to officials charged with enforcing tax laws of other states, §58.1-2422.
Information forwarded to officials of other states, §58.1-2422.
Levy, §58.1-2402.
Local sales and use taxes prohibited, §58.1-2418.
Overcollection of tax administered by DMV, §58.1-16.
Payment.
Time for, §58.1-2404.
Processing fees by dealers subject to tax, §58.1-2402.
Records.
Examination of dealer's records, §58.1-2420.
Refunds, §58.1-2423.
Rentals.
Basis of tax, §58.1-2405.
Payment, time for, §58.1-2404.
Rules and regulations, §58.1-2421.
Separately stated rental price, §58.1-2419.
Tax levied upon, §58.1-2402.
Tax upon rental of vehicles, §§58.1-1734 to 58.1-1741.
See MOTOR VEHICLE RENTALS.
Rules and regulations, §58.1-2421.
Sale price, basis of tax, §58.1-2405.
Separate statement of tax on sale or rental price, §58.1-2419.
Tax on sale or rental price to be separately stated, §58.1-2419.
Time for payment, §58.1-2404.
Title of chapter, §58.1-2400.
Used vehicles, basis of tax, §58.1-2405.
Venue of appeals from commissioner of department of motor vehicles, §58.1-2426.
Virginia motor vehicle sales and use tax act, §58.1-2400.
Virginia retail sales and use tax.
Generally, §§58.1-600 to 58.1-639.
See RETAIL SALES AND USE TAX.
Motor vehicles, machinery, etc., brought into Virginia for use in performing contracts, §§58.1-604.1 to 58.1-604.3.

MOTOR VEHICLES DEPARTMENT.
Absentee voting.
Casting ballots in-person, §24.2-707.
Accident reports.
General provisions, §§46.2-371 to 46.2-388.
See MOTOR VEHICLE ACCIDENTS.
Reporting duties, §52-4.2.
Address corrections.
Notification by applicants and license holders, §46.2-324.
Administrators.
Surety bond, §46.2-219.

MOTOR VEHICLES DEPARTMENT —Cont'd
Agreements with other agencies.
Collection of fees, §46.2-205.2.
Anatomical gifts.
Drivers' licenses or identification cards.
Designation by applicant, duties, §46.2-342.
Assessments, fees, penalties, etc.
Delinquent accounts, posting of names on website, §46.2-208.2.
Assistant commissioners.
Authority of officers, §46.2-217.
Surety bond, §46.2-219.
Automatic payments, §46.2-212.2.
Bad check fees.
Uncollected checks tendered for license fees or taxes, §46.2-207.
Blind and visually impaired persons.
Department to report names of persons refused licenses for defective vision, §46.2-221.
Bonds, surety.
Branch office personnel, §46.2-205.
Branch offices, §46.2-205.
License agents, §46.2-205.
Personnel hiring, §46.2-205.
Carriers of passengers or property in vehicles.
Responsibilities, §46.2-200.
Certificates of public convenience and necessity.
Household goods carriers.
See MOTOR CARRIERS, PROPERTY.
Limousines and executive sedan carriers.
See LIMOUSINES AND EXECUTIVE SEDAN CARRIERS.
Motor launch carriers.
See MOTOR LAUNCH CARRIERS.
Sight-seeing carriers.
See SIGHT-SEEING CARRIERS.
Special or charter party carriers.
See SPECIAL OR CHARTER PARTY CARRIERS.
Certificates of title.
General provisions, §§46.2-616 to 46.2-644.
See MOTOR VEHICLE TITLING.
Change of address notification, §46.2-324.
Fee for failure to notify department, §46.2-324.
Civil actions against employees.
Attorney general or assistant representing, §2.2-507.
Collection of fees.
Agreements with other agencies, §46.2-205.2.
Commercial driver license system.
Authority to enter into agreements, §46.2-341.32.
Commercial driver training schools.
General provisions, §§46.2-1700 to 46.2-1707.
Commissioner.
Advising local commissioners of revenue of situs of certain vehicles, §46.2-211.
Advisory opinions from medical advisory board, §46.2-204.
Appointment, §46.2-201.
Authority of officers, §46.2-217.
Compelling attendance of witnesses, §46.2-369.
Employment of special counsel for defense of officers, §46.2-220.
Enforcement of laws, §46.2-217.
License agents, §46.2-205.
Location of office, §46.2-205.
Mail notice.
Initial notice by certified mail, subsequent notices by regular mail, §46.2-100.1.

MOTOR VEHICLES DEPARTMENT —Cont'd
Commissioner —Cont'd
Motor vehicle accidents.
Service of notice, process and other papers, §§8.01-307 to 8.01-313.
See MOTOR VEHICLE ACCIDENTS.
Oath and bond, §46.2-202.
Rulemaking authority, §46.2-203.
Licensure of drivers, §46.2-369.
Salary, §46.2-202.
Subpoena powers, §46.2-369.
Summoning witnesses and taking testimony, §46.2-369.
Transportation safety, §§46.2-222, 46.2-223.
Crash investigation team.
Privileged communications, §8.01-402.
Credit cards.
Payments by payment device, §46.2-212.1.
Crime solvers' rewards.
Department law-enforcement officers.
Acceptance or receipt prohibition, §46.2-218.
Criminal forfeitures.
Duties of commissioner, §19.2-386.2:1.
Dealers.
General provisions, §§46.2-1500 to 46.2-1582.
See MOTOR VEHICLE DEALERS.
Licensing.
Responsibilities, §46.2-200.
Transaction recovery fund, §§46.2-1527.1 to 46.2-1527.11.
See MOTOR VEHICLE DEALERS.
Delinquent accounts, posting of names on website, §46.2-208.2.
Department offices and agencies.
Compensation of personnel, §46.2-205.
Deputy commissioners.
Authority of officers, §46.2-217.
Surety bond, §46.2-219.
Disposition of fees and money collected, §§46.2-205, 46.2-206.
Driver improvement programs.
General provisions, §§46.2-489 to 46.2-506.
See DRIVER IMPROVEMENT PROGRAMS.
Driver license compact.
Department as licensing authority, §46.2-484.
Voter registration cancellation, §24.2-427.
Drivers' licenses.
General provisions, §§46.2-300 to 46.2-340.
See DRIVERS' LICENSES.
Responsibilities, §46.2-200.
Driving records.
Admissibility of records, §46.2-215.
Charges for information supplied by department, §§46.2-214, 46.2-214.1.
Additional charge, §46.2-214.1.
Release of information for research purposes, §46.2-209.
Release of privileged information, §46.2-208.
Driving while intoxicated.
Report of conviction to, §18.2-273.
Duties generally, §46.2-200.
Electronic filings or submissions to department, §46.2-216.1.
Electronic documents provided by department, §46.2-216.1.
Electronic payments.
Fees for insufficient funds transactions, §46.2-207.
Electronic transfer of information.
Sex offender and crimes against minors registry.
Change of address notification, §46.2-324.
DMV identification cards, §46.2-345.

MOTOR VEHICLES DEPARTMENT —Cont'd
Electronic transfer of information —Cont'd
Sex offender and crimes against minors registry —Cont'd
Driver education program, §46.2-323.
Expiration of drivers' license, §46.2-330.
Voter registration purposes, §46.2-208.1.
Established as executive department, §46.2-200.
Evidence.
Admissibility of department records, §46.2-215.
Effect of certified records in court proceedings, §46.2-215.
Fieri facias.
Notice.
Sale of property subject to prior security interest, §8.01-480.
Forfeiture of vehicle for criminal offense.
Duties of commissioner, §19.2-386.2:1.
Fuel tax laws.
Responsibilities, §46.2-200.
ID cards.
Fraud or false statement in application, §46.2-348.
Fraudulent use to obtain alcoholic beverages, §46.2-347.
Issuance, §46.2-345.
Obtaining card when not legally entitled, §46.2-105.2.
Revocation.
Return to commissioner, §46.2-370.
Veterans identification cards, §46.2-345.1.
Identification card issued to emancipated minor, §16.1-334.1.
Immunity.
Anatomical gifts.
Drivers' licenses or identification cards.
Failure to note designation, §46.2-342.
Insurance.
Liability insurance policies, §46.2-219.
Internet self-service options, §46.2-216.4.
Access through state library, §46.2-216.5.
Issuance of licenses, §46.2-328.
Law-enforcement officers.
Disallowance of certain fees, §46.2-218.
Line of duty act, §§9.1-400 to 9.1-408.
Powers of appointed officers, §46.2-217.
Right to inspect vehicles in garages, §46.2-110.
Size and weight compliance officers, §46.2-217.
Civil penalty for certain violations by trucks and tractor trucks.
Special processing of penalties, §46.2-613.3.
Reciprocal agreements.
Operation without payment of reciprocity fees.
Authority to hold vehicle, §46.2-703.
Special counsel for defense, §46.2-220.
Surety bond, §46.2-219.
License agents, §46.2-205.
License plates.
General provisions, §§46.2-711 to 46.2-749.130.
See MOTOR VEHICLE LICENSE PLATES.
License, registration and title laws.
Responsibilities, §46.2-200.
List of registrations and titles.
Furnishing list to local commissioners of the revenue, §46.2-210.
Medical advisory board.
Creation, §46.2-204.
Motor carriers.
Service centers.
Responsibilities of department, §46.2-200.

MOTOR VEHICLES DEPARTMENT —Cont'd
Motor carriers, passengers.
See MOTOR CARRIERS, PASSENGERS.
Motor carriers, property.
See MOTOR CARRIERS, PROPERTY.
Motorcycle dealers.
Generally, §§46.2-1993 to 46.2-1993.82.
See MOTORCYCLE DEALERS.
Motorcycle rider safety.
Rulemaking authority, §46.2-1189.
Motor vehicle accidents.
Generally.
See MOTOR VEHICLE ACCIDENTS.
Reporting duties of department, §52-4.2.
Service of notice, process and other papers.
Commissioner generally, §§8.01-307 to 8.01-313.
See MOTOR VEHICLE ACCIDENTS.
Motor vehicle dealers.
General provisions, §§46.2-1500 to 46.2-1582.
See MOTOR VEHICLE DEALERS.
Motor vehicles records.
Charges for information supplied by department, §§46.2-214, 46.2-214.1.
Additional charge, §46.2-214.1.
Motor vehicle use and sales tax generally, §§58.1-2400 to 58.1-2426.
See MOTOR VEHICLE SALES AND USE TAX.
National change of address system.
Contract with postal service to use, §§46.2-324, 46.2-342, 46.2-416, 46.2-606.
Notice.
Fieri facias.
Sale of property subject to prior security interest, §8.01-480.
Initial notice by certified mail, subsequent notices by regular mail, §46.2-100.1.
Records supplied to third persons, §46.2-212.
Officers vesting with police powers, §46.2-217.
Line of duty act, §§9.1-400 to 9.1-408.
Ownership of the vehicle.
Certificate of license plate number as prima facie evidence of ownership, §46.2-213.
Payment device.
Defined, §46.2-100.
Payments by, §46.2-212.1.
Payment of assessments, fees, penalties, etc.
Automatic payments, §46.2-212.2.
Delinquent accounts, posting of names on website, §46.2-208.2.
Personnel.
Compensation, §46.2-205.
License agents, §46.2-205.
Plain view violations of criminal laws.
Authority of DMV officers, §46.2-217.
Powers generally, §46.2-200.
Privileged communications.
Accident reports, §§46.2-379, 46.2-380.
Crash investigation team, §8.01-402.
Releases, §46.2-208.
Privileged records, release, conditions, §46.2-208.
Property and casualty insurers, future financial responsibility.
Proof required at request of named insured, §38.2-228.
Records.
Destruction of records, §46.2-216.
Driving records. See within this heading, "Driving records."
Electronic filings or submissions to department, §46.2-216.1.
Electronic documents provided by department, §46.2-216.1.

MOTOR VEHICLES DEPARTMENT —Cont'd
Records —Cont'd
Inspection, §46.2-208.
Accident reports, §§46.2-379, 46.2-380.
Maintenance of records of licenses and learners' permits, §46.2-327.
Notice of records supplied to third persons, §46.2-212.
Privileged records, release, conditions, §46.2-208.
Release of information in department records for research purposes, §46.2-209.
Release of vehicle information to prospective vehicle purchasers, §46.2-209.1.
Use of names of persons refused licenses for defective vision, §46.2-221.
Registration of motor vehicles.
General provisions, §§46.2-645 to 46.2-710, 46.2-750 to 46.2-756.
See MOTOR VEHICLE REGISTRATION.
Release of information for research purposes, §46.2-209.
Release of privileged information, §46.2-208.
Accident reports, §§46.2-379, 46.2-380.
Release of vehicle information to prospective vehicle purchasers, §46.2-209.1.
Reports.
Discharge of patients from state institutions, §46.2-401.
Driving while intoxicated.
Conviction reported to department, §18.2-273.
Research, release of information in records, §46.2-209.
Rewards for apprehension of criminals.
Department law-enforcement officers.
Acceptance or receipt prohibition, §46.2-218.
Rulemaking authority.
Examination of school bus drivers, §46.2-339.
Safety responsibility laws.
Responsibilities, §46.2-200.
Secretary of transportation.
Agency responsibility, §2.2-228.
Self-service options via Internet, §46.2-216.4.
Access through state library, §46.2-216.5.
Service of notice, process and other papers.
Motor vehicle accidents.
Generally, §§8.01-307 to 8.01-313.
See MOTOR VEHICLE ACCIDENTS.
Situs of certain vehicles.
Commissioner to advise local commissioners of revenue of situs, §46.2-211.
Taxes administered by.
Overcollection, §58.1-16.
Taxes on fuel.
Fuel taxes, §§58.1-2200 to 58.1-2299.20.
See FUEL TAXES.
Titling motor vehicles.
General provisions, §§46.2-616 to 46.2-644.
See MOTOR VEHICLE TITLING.
Trailer dealers.
Generally, §§46.2-1992 to 46.2-1992.85.
See TRAILER DEALERS.
Transaction recovery fund, §§46.2-1527.1 to 46.2-1527.11.
See MOTOR VEHICLE DEALERS.
Transportation safety, §46.2-222.
Powers and duties of commissioner, §46.2-223.
Vital records, issuing certified copies.
Authorization, §32.1-272.
Fees, §32.1-273.
Procedures and requirements generally, §32.1-272.

MOTOR VEHICLES DEPARTMENT —Cont'd
Vital records, issuing certified copies —Cont'd
Security paper required, considered as original record, §32.1-252.
Subject to rules and audit requirements of state registrar, §32.1-252.
Violations, §32.1-276.
Voter registration, §24.2-411.1.
Citizenship status.
Department of motor vehicles to furnish lists of noncitizens, §24.2-410.1.
Driver license compact.
Cancellation of registration, §24.2-427.
Electronic transfer of information in department records for purposes of, §46.2-208.1.
Location accessibility, §24.2-413.
Persons authorized to receive applications, §24.2-415.1.

MOTOR VEHICLE SEIZURES.
ABC offenses, confiscation, §§4.1-339 to 4.1-348.
Drivers' licenses suspended or revoked for intoxication, §46.2-301.1.
Overweight vehicles, §§46.2-1134, 46.2-1135.

MOTOR VEHICLE SIZE AND WEIGHT, §§46.2-1101 to 46.2-1156.
Agricultural multi-purpose drying units.
Applicability of size limitations, §46.2-1102.
Alteration by local authorities, §46.2-1101.
Arlington county.
Overweight permits for certain trucks operated by county, §46.2-1145.
Automobile transporters.
Maximum vehicle lengths, §46.2-1114.
Auxiliary power unit or other idle reduction technology utilized by vehicles.
Extension of weight limits, §46.2-1129.1.
Auxiliary power unit and idle reduction technology defined, §46.2-1129.1.
Buses.
Length exceptions for certain passenger buses, §46.2-1113.
Length generally, §46.2-1113.
Maximum widths, §§46.2-1107, 46.2-1108.
Permits for excessive size and weight for articulated buses, §46.2-1147.
Certified escort vehicle drivers, §§46.2-2900 to 46.2-2910.
Citation for certain motor vehicle law violations, §46.2-388.
City ordinances fixing weight limits, §46.2-1138.1.
Coal haulers.
Overweight permits, §46.2-1143.
Commercial vehicles.
Widths, §46.2-1109.
Compliance officers, §46.2-217.
Civil penalty for certain violations by trucks and tractor trucks.
Special processing of penalties, §46.2-613.3.
Line of duty act, §§9.1-400 to 9.1-408.
Reciprocal agreements.
Operation without payment of reciprocity fees.
Authority to hold vehicle, §46.2-703.
Concrete haulers.
Excessive size and weight permits, §§46.2-1142, 46.2-1142.1.
Connection between vehicles.
Maximum length between vehicles connected, §46.2-1118.
Other requirements, §46.2-1118.

MOTOR VEHICLE SIZE AND WEIGHT —Cont'd
Cotton modules haulers.
Excess tandem axle weight permits, §46.2-1149.1.
Crossing bridge or culvert.
Emergency response vehicles responding to emergency calls.
Overweight permits granted, §46.2-1130.1.
Vehicle exceeding weight limit, §46.2-1130.
Definitions.
Maximum vehicle weights, §46.2-1122.
Enforcement of provisions.
Motor vehicles department.
Line of duty act, §§9.1-400 to 9.1-408.
Size and weight compliance officers, §46.2-217.
Civil penalty for certain violations by trucks and tractor trucks.
Special processing of penalties, §46.2-613.3.
Reciprocal agreements, operation without payment of reciprocity fees.
Authority to hold vehicle, §46.2-703.
Erection of weight signs.
Crossing bridge or culvert, §46.2-1130.
Escort vehicles.
Certified escort vehicle drivers, §§46.2-2900 to 46.2-2910.
Excessive size and weight permits, §§46.2-1139 to 46.2-1149.5.
Applications, §46.2-1139.
Articulated buses, §46.2-1147.
Authority to use certain streets and highways, §46.2-1140.
Certified escort vehicle drivers, §§46.2-2900 to 46.2-2910.
Coal haulers, §46.2-1143.
Concrete haulers, §§46.2-1142, 46.2-1142.1.
Containerized freight, §46.2-1141.
Cotton modules haulers, §46.2-1149.2.
Delegation of authority by commissioner, §46.2-1139.1.
Distance limitations of permits, §46.2-1149.
Emergency response vehicles.
Overweight permits to cross bridges and culverts granted, §46.2-1130.1.
Escort vehicles.
Certified escort vehicle drivers, §§46.2-2900 to 46.2-2910.
Excavated materials haulers, §46.2-1143.1.
Farm animal feed haulers.
Overweight permits, §46.2-1144.2.
Generally, §46.2-1139.
Haulers of imported goods, §46.2-1146.
Route designations, §46.2-1139.
Rubber-tired, self-propelled hauler or loader, §46.2-1149.
Scope, §46.2-1139.
Solid waste haulers, §46.2-1144.
Special fund for fees collected, §46.2-1149.3.
Specialized mobile equipment, §46.2-1149.4.
Tank wagons.
Overweight permits, §46.2-1144.1.
Towing motor homes or travel trailers, §46.2-1139.
Tree-length log transportation, §46.2-1149.2.
Trucks operated by Arlington County, §46.2-1145.
Underground pipe cleaning, hydroexcavating and water blasting equipment.
Overweight permits, §46.2-1149.5.
Violations, §46.2-1139.
Virginia-grown farm produce, §46.2-1148.
Extension of weight limits, §46.2-1128.
Auxiliary power unit or other idle reduction technology utilized by vehicles, §46.2-1129.1.

MOTOR VEHICLE SIZE AND WEIGHT —Cont'd
Extension of weight limits —Cont'd
Vehicles hauling Virginia-grown farm or forest products, §46.2-1129.
Farm animal feed haulers.
Overweight permits, §46.2-1144.2.
Farm machinery.
Applicability of size limitations, §46.2-1102.
Federal regulation of interstate commerce, §46.2-1103.
Fees.
Annual overweight permit fee, §46.2-1140.1.
Cotton modules haulers.
Excess tandem axle weight permits, §46.2-1149.1.
Excessive size and weight permits.
Special fund for fees collected, §46.2-1149.3.
Overweight permits for containerized freight, §46.2-1141.
Firefighting equipment.
Size limitations inapplicable, §46.2-1102.
Freight.
Overweight permits for containerized freight, §46.2-1141.
Gravel, sand or crushed stone, trucks hauling.
Excessive size and weight permits, applicability, §46.2-1143.
Gross weight, §46.2-1126.
Highways, commissioner of.
Reduction of size limits, §46.2-1104.
House trailers.
Maximum vehicle lengths, §46.2-1115.
Imports.
Excess height and length permits for haulers of imported goods, §46.2-1146.
Interstate commerce.
Federal regulation of interstate commerce, §46.2-1103.
Interstate highways.
Weight limits for vehicles using highway, §46.2-1127.
Lengths, §§46.2-1112 to 46.2-1121.
Automobile transporters, §46.2-1114.
Connection between vehicles, §46.2-1118.
Converter gear, §46.2-1119.
Exceeding length requirement, §46.2-1117.
Fine schedule, VA SCt Rule 3B:2.
Maximum fine for violating Title 46.2, §46.2-113.
Pretrial payment of fine, §16.1-69.40:1.
Exceptions for certain passenger buses, §46.2-1113.
Extension of load beyond front of vehicles, §46.2-1120.
Flag or light at end of load, §46.2-1121.
Generally, §46.2-1112.
Mobile homes or house trailers, §46.2-1115.
More than one trailer attached to vehicle, §46.2-1116.
Passenger bus exception, §46.2-1113.
Special permits, §46.2-1112.
Tow dolly, §46.2-1119.
Tractor truck semitrailer combinations, etc., §§46.2-1112, 46.2-1117.
Vehicles having more than one trailer, etc., attached, §46.2-1116.
Watercraft transporters, §46.2-1114.
Limitations applicable throughout Commonwealth, §46.2-1101.
Federal regulation of interstate commerce, §46.2-1103.

MOTOR VEHICLE SIZE AND WEIGHT —Cont'd
Loads.
Extension of load beyond line of fender or body, §46.2-1111.
Extension of loads beyond front of vehicles, §46.2-1120.
Fastening load of logs, barrels, etc., §46.2-1155.
Fine schedule, VA SCt Rule 3B:2.
Maximum fine for violation of title, §46.2-113.
Pretrial payment of fine, §16.1-69.40:1.
Flag or light at end of load, §46.2-1121.
Load covers, §46.2-1156.
Maximum fine for violating Title 46.2, §46.2-113.
Prevention of escape of contents, §46.2-1156.
Fine schedule, VA SCt Rule 3B:2.
Maximum fine, §46.2-113.
Pretrial payment of fine, §16.1-69.40:1.
Unloading excess load, §46.2-1137.
Weight of vehicles and loads, §46.2-1123.
Wide-load escort.
Law enforcement vehicles.
Exemption from certain traffic regulations, §46.2-920.
Local authorities.
Alteration of size and weight limits, §46.2-1101.
Reduction of size limits, §46.2-1104.
Local ordinances fixing weight limits, §§46.2-1138.1, 46.2-1138.2.
Mobile homes.
Maximum vehicle lengths, §46.2-1115.
Motor vehicles department.
Size and weight compliance officers, §46.2-217.
Civil penalty for certain violations by trucks and tractor trucks.
Special processing of penalties, §46.2-613.3.
Line of duty act, §§9.1-400 to 9.1-408.
Reciprocal agreements.
Operation without payment of reciprocity fees.
Authority to hold vehicle, §46.2-703.
Multiple-trailers attached to vehicle.
Maximum vehicle lengths, §46.2-1116.
Oversize or overweight vehicles, temporary registration, §46.2-652.
Fee, §46.2-652.1.
Overweight vehicle cases.
Certificate as to accuracy of scales, §46.2-1137.
Forfeiture of vehicle and cargo, §46.2-1135.
Liquidated damages, §46.2-1135.
Powers of enforcement officers, §46.2-1135.
Service of notice, process and other papers, §§46.2-1132, 46.2-1136.
Special processing provisions, §46.2-1133.
Special seizure provisions, §46.2-1134.
Unloading excess load, §46.2-1137.
Weighing vehicles, §46.2-1137.
Refusing officer's order to drive to weighing station, uniform fine schedule, VA SCt Rules 3C:1, 3C:2.
Passenger buses.
Maximum length exceptions, §46.2-1113.
Passenger vehicles.
Maximum widths and heights, §46.2-1105.
Permits for excessive size and weight, §§46.2-1139 to 46.2-1149.5.
Rear fenders, flaps or guards.
When required, §46.2-1083.
Record of conviction, etc.
Vehicle weight violations.
Forwarding requirements, §46.2-1131.
Reduction of size limits, §46.2-1104.

MOTOR VEHICLE SIZE AND WEIGHT —Cont'd
Registration of overweight or oversize vehicles.
Temporary registration, §46.2-652.
Fee, §46.2-652.1.
Schedule of fees.
Extension of weight limits, §46.2-1128.
Serious traffic violation.
Additional fine for vehicles of certain gross weight, §46.2-113.
Service of notice, process and other papers.
Overweight vehicle cases, §§46.2-1132, 46.2-1136.
Single axle weight, §46.2-1124.
Single-trip temporary registration or permit.
Oversize or overweight vehicles, §46.2-652.
Fee, §46.2-652.1.
Size and weight compliance officers, §46.2-217.
Civil penalty for certain violations by trucks and tractor trucks.
Special processing of penalties, §46.2-613.3.
Line of duty act, §§9.1-400 to 9.1-408.
Reciprocal agreements.
Operation without payment of reciprocity fees.
Authority to hold vehicle, §46.2-703.
Solid waste.
Overweight permits for solid waste haulers, §46.2-1144.
Special overweight processing provisions, §46.2-1133.
Special overweight seizure provisions, §46.2-1134.
Tampering with gross vehicle weight ratings, §46.2-1075.1.
Tandem axle weight, §46.2-1125.
Tank wagons.
Overweight permits, §46.2-1144.1.
Tire loading, limits, §46.2-1043.1.
Tow dolly and converter gear.
Maximum vehicle lengths, §46.2-1119.
Towing and towed vehicles, §§46.2-1150 to 46.2-1154.
Town ordinances fixing weight limits, §46.2-1138.2.
Tractor truck semitrailer combinations, etc.
Maximum vehicle lengths, §§46.2-1112, 46.2-1117.
Tree-length log transportation permits, §46.2-1149.2.
Underground pipe cleaning, hydroexcavating and water blasting equipment.
Overweight permits, §46.2-1149.5.
Validity of permits, §46.2-1140.1.
Violation of weight limits, §46.2-1131.
Citation for certain motor vehicle law violations, §46.2-388.
Size and weight compliance officers, §46.2-217.
Line of duty act, §§9.1-400 to 9.1-408.
Special processing of penalties, §46.2-613.3.
Virginia-grown farm or forest products.
Extension of weight limits, §46.2-1129.
Virginia-grown farm produce.
Overweight permit for hauling, §46.2-1148.
Watercraft transporters.
Maximum vehicle lengths, §46.2-1114.
Weighing fee, §46.2-1137.
Weigh stations.
Civil penalty for certain violations by trucks and tractor trucks, §46.2-613.1.
Attachment and seizure of vehicle for unpaid fees and penalties, §46.2-613.4.
Service of process.
Operator as agent for, §46.2-613.2.

MOTOR VEHICLE SIZE AND WEIGHT —Cont'd
Weigh stations —Cont'd
Civil penalty for certain violations by trucks and tractor trucks —Cont'd
Service of process —Cont'd
Procedures for issuance and service, §46.2-613.5.
Special processing of penalties, §46.2-613.3.
Weight per inch of tire width, §46.2-1124.
Weights, §§46.2-1122 to 46.2-1138.1.
Weight violation cases, §§46.2-1132 to 46.2-1137.
Widths and heights, §§46.2-1105 to 46.2-1111.
Bus widths, §§46.2-1107, 46.2-1108.
Commercial vehicles, §46.2-1109.
Damage to overhead obstruction, §46.2-1110.
Exceeding limitations, §§46.2-1105, 46.2-1110.
Fine schedule, VA SCt Rule 3B:2.
Maximum fine for violating Title 46.2, §46.2-113.
Pretrial payment of fine, §16.1-69.40:1.
Exceptions to limitations, §46.2-1105.
Extension of loads beyond line of fender or body, §46.2-1111.
Height of vehicles, §46.2-1110.

MOTOR VEHICLES OWNED BY STATE.
Centralized fleet management, §§2.2-1173 to 2.2-1181.
Drivers' licenses.
Partial application of chapter to vehicles, §46.2-366.
Persons included within scope of chapter, §46.2-367.
Insurance for state motor vehicles.
Risk management division, §2.2-1838.
License plates, §§46.2-750 to 46.2-751.
Registration, §§46.2-750 to 46.2-751.

MOTOR VEHICLE TAXES.
Alternative fuel vehicles, annual license tax, §58.1-2249.
Liability for tax, due date, §58.1-2251.
Emissions inspection fees, §§46.2-1182, 46.2-1182.1.
License plate fees.
See MOTOR VEHICLE LICENSE PLATES.
License tax, alternative fuel vehicles, §58.1-2249.
Liability for tax, due date, §58.1-2251.
License taxes imposed by localities, §15.2-973.
Motor titling certificates, §46.2-627.
Personal property taxes.
Classification, §58.1-3506.
Tangible personal property, §58.1-3503.
Elderly and handicapped, alternative tax rates, §§58.1-3506.1 to 58.1-3506.8.
Generally, §§58.1-3500 to 58.1-3522.
See PERSONAL PROPERTY TAXES.
Proration of tax, §58.1-3516.
Returns.
Alternative method for filing, §58.1-3518.1.
Situs for assessment, §58.1-3511.
Tax relief act of 1998, §§58.1-3523 to 58.1-3535.
See PERSONAL PROPERTY TAX RELIEF ACT OF 1998.
Registration.
City or county decals, §§46.2-752 to 46.2-756.
Fees, §§46.2-685 to 46.2-704.
See MOTOR VEHICLE REGISTRATION.
Retail sales and use tax.
Exemption of motor vehicles, §58.1-609.1.

MOTOR VEHICLE TAXES —Cont'd
Retail sales and use tax —Cont'd
Generally, §§58.1-600 to 58.1-639.
See RETAIL SALES AND USE TAX.
Motor vehicles brought into Virginia for use in performing construction contracts, §§58.1-604.1 to 58.1-604.3.
Safety inspection fees and charges, §§46.2-1167, 46.2-1168.
Sales and use tax generally, §§58.1-2400 to 58.1-2426.
See MOTOR VEHICLE SALES AND USE TAX.

MOTOR VEHICLE THEFT.
Driver's license.
Suspension of driver's license for conviction, §46.2-390.
Help eliminate automobile theft fund, §38.2-414.
Receipt or transfer of possession of stolen vehicle, §18.2-109.
Salvage.
Unrecovered stolen vehicles, §46.2-1603.
State police arrests.
Warrantless arrests, §52-20.
Suspension of registration card, §46.2-610.

MOTOR VEHICLE TITLE LOANS, §§6.2-2200 to 6.2-2227.
Acquisition of corporation, §6.2-2208.
Advertising, §6.2-2218.
Applicability of chapter, §6.2-2202.
Internet loans, §6.2-2225.
Attorney General.
Enforcement authority, §6.2-2226.
Bonds, surety.
Licenses, §6.2-2204.
Cease and desist orders, §6.2-2220.
Change of location or additional location.
Notice to commissioner, §6.2-2207.
Consumer protection.
Violation of Virginia consumer protection act, §6.2-2227.
Criminal convictions of members, partners, directors, officers or principals.
Reports, §6.2-2211.
Suspension or revocation of licenses, §6.2-2219.
Criminal penalty for violations, §6.2-2223.
Definitions, §6.2-2200.
Disclosures, required, §6.2-2215.
Enforcement.
Attorney General, §6.2-2226.
Noncompliant loan agreement, validity, §6.2-2224.
Fees.
Annual fees, §6.2-2213.
Interest and other charges, §6.2-2216.
Licenses.
Applications, §6.2-2203.
Fines for violations, §6.2-2222.
Interest, §6.2-2216.
Internet loans.
Applicability of chapter, §6.2-2225.
Investigations.
License applications, §6.2-2205.
Reimbursement of expenses of investigation, §6.2-2213.
State corporation commission, §6.2-2212.
Licenses.
Applications, §6.2-2203.
Investigation of applications, §6.2-2205.
Bonds, surety, §6.2-2204.
Changes in places of business, §6.2-2207.

MOTOR VEHICLE TITLE LOANS —Cont'd
Licenses —Cont'd
Fees.
Applications, §6.2-2203.
Issuance, §6.2-2206.
Places of business, §6.2-2207.
Posting, §6.2-2207.
Qualifications, §6.2-2206.
Required, §6.2-2201.
Suspension or revocation, §6.2-2219.
Notice of proposed suspension or revocation, §6.2-2221.
Notice.
Change of location or additional location, §6.2-2207.
Repossession and sale of vehicle, §6.2-2217.
Suspension or revocation of licenses.
Notice of proposed suspension or revocation, §6.2-2221.
Prohibited business practices, §6.2-2215.
Records.
Retention of books, accounts and records, §6.2-2209.
Regulations, §6.2-2214.
Reports.
Annual report, §6.2-2210.
Criminal convictions of members, partners, directors, officers or principals, §6.2-2211.
Other reporting requirements, §6.2-2211.
Repossession of vehicle.
Limited recourse, §6.2-2217.
Sale of vehicle.
Limited recourse, §6.2-2217.
Scope of chapter, §6.2-2202.
State corporation commission.
Acquisition of corporation, §6.2-2208.
Cease and desist orders, §6.2-2220.
Investigations, §6.2-2212.
Notice.
Change of location or additional location, §6.2-2207.
Regulations, §6.2-2214.
Suspension or revocation of licenses, §6.2-2219.
Notice of proposed suspension or revocation, §6.2-2221.
Suspension or revocation of licenses, §6.2-2219.
Notice of proposed suspension or revocation, §6.2-2221.
Title loan agreements.
Noncompliant loan agreement, validity, §6.2-2224.
Requirements, §6.2-2215.

MOTOR VEHICLE TITLING, §§46.2-616 to 46.2-644.
Abandoned motor vehicles.
Person in possession obtaining title, §46.2-1202.1.
Purchaser of vehicle from person in possession.
Application for title, §46.2-1202.1.
Acquiring vehicle from vendor.
Questionable certificate of title, §46.2-616.
Address correction.
Updating addresses by persons completing forms, §46.2-203.1.
Altering or forging, §46.2-605.
Application for certificate of title, §46.2-621.
Statements in application, §46.2-623.
Certificate of ownership.
Owner to secure, §46.2-600.
Certificate of title.
Abandoned motor vehicles.
Purchaser of vehicle from person in possession, §46.2-1202.1.

MOTOR VEHICLE TITLING —Cont'd
Certificate of title —Cont'd
Acquiring vehicle from vendor without certificate, §46.2-616.
Appeal of suspension, revocation, etc., §46.2-611.
Application, §46.2-621.
Change of address, §46.2-606.
Contents, §46.2-604.
Correction of errors in title, §46.2-621.1.
Disposition of fees, §46.2-627.
Duplicates for lost or mutilated certificate, §46.2-607.
Electronic record in lieu of paper certificate, §46.2-603.
Electronic titling program, §46.2-603.1.
Errors in title.
Correction, §46.2-621.1.
Failure to surrender revoked certificate, §46.2-612.
Fee, §46.2-627.
Foreign vehicles, §46.2-625.
Forwarding transferred certificate to department, §§46.2-630, 46.2-631.
How transferred, §46.2-628.
Insurance companies.
Application for certificate to vehicle not a salvage vehicle.
Company unable to present certificate of title, §46.2-632.
Issuance, §46.2-603.
Joint owners, §46.2-622.
National motor vehicle title information system, notification, §46.2-208.
Lost or mutilated certificates, §46.2-607.
Fee for replacement, §46.2-692.
Transfer when certificate lost, §46.2-632.
New indicia of title, §46.2-619.
No qualification on estate, §46.2-634.
Offenses relating to titling, §46.2-613.
Owner to secure, §46.2-600.
Period of validity, §46.2-620.
Purchaser, petitioning court to obtain title, procedure, §46.2-618.
Rejection of application, §46.2-608.
Reporting odometer reading, §46.2-629.
Acquisition of vehicle from vendor.
Reporting odometer reading, §46.2-629.
Sale of vehicle without certificate, §46.2-617.
Security interests generally, §§46.2-636 to 46.2-644.
Specially constructed vehicles, §46.2-625.
Statements in application, §46.2-623.
Surrender of certificates for demolished vehicles, §46.2-635.
Transfer of title by operation of law, §46.2-633.
Transfer of title on death, §46.2-633.2.
Transfer of title when qualification on estate, §46.2-634.
Transfer when certificate lost, §46.2-632.
Unlawful possession of certificate issued to another, §46.2-618.
Change of address, §46.2-606.
Commercial vehicles.
Rejection of application, §46.2-608.
Company vehicles of automotive manufacturers, §46.2-602.2.
Correction of errors in certificate of title, §46.2-621.1.
Dealer's certificate of title, §46.2-1544.
Decedents' estates.
Transfer of title when no qualification on estate, §46.2-634

MOTOR VEHICLE TITLING —Cont'd
Demolished vehicles.
New certificate of title, §46.2-635.
Duplicate indicia of title, §46.2-607.
Electric vehicles.
Converted electric vehicles, §§46.2-602.3, 46.2-625.
Errors in title.
Correction of errors in certificate of title, §46.2-621.1.
Farm tractors.
Defined, §46.2-100.
Titling or registration in state.
Not required, §46.2-600.
Fees.
Change of address.
Failure to comply with notice requirement, §46.2-606.
Replacement of lost, mutilated or illegible certificates, §46.2-692.
Foreign market vehicles, §46.2-602.
Foreign vehicles, §46.2-625.
Forms for certificates, §46.2-203.
Fraud and deceit.
Making false affidavit or swearing falsely, §46.2-105.
Obtaining certificate from department when not legally entitled, §§46.2-105.1, 46.2-105.2, 46.2-750 to 46.2-751.
Use of false name or address in application for certificate of title, §46.2-613.
Insurance companies.
Application for certificate to vehicle not a salvage vehicle.
Company unable to present certificate of title, §46.2-632.
Joint owners.
Issuance of certificate of title in names of joint owners, §46.2-622.
Leased vehicles.
New indicia of title, §46.2-619.
License agents, §46.2-205.
List of titles.
Furnishing to local commissioners of the revenue, §46.2-210.
Lost certificate of title.
Transfer when certificate lost, §46.2-632.
Mailing list.
List of titles offered for sale to public, §46.2-210.
Manufactured homes.
Cancellation of title, §46.2-653.
Military personnel.
Nonresident active duty members.
Registration of vehicle registered in another state not required, §46.2-600.
Motorcycles.
Motorcycle purchased by manufacturer for parts, documentation, §46.2-626.2.
National change of address system.
Contract with postal service to use.
DMV, §46.2-606.
New certificate of title.
Demolished vehicles, §46.2-635.
New indicia of title, §46.2-619.
Odometer reading.
Reporting on certificate of title, §46.2-629.
Period of validity of certificate of title, §46.2-620.
Reconstructed and specially constructed vehicles, §46.2-734.
Reconstructed vehicles, §46.2-625.
Replica vehicle, §§46.2-602.1, 46.2-625.

MOTOR VEHICLE TITLING —Cont'd
Repossessed vehicles.
Sale of vehicle repossessed in another state by dealer, §46.2-633.1.
Revocation of certificates.
Return to commissioner, §46.2-370.
Right to recover damages not affected by chapter, §46.2-614.
Sale of vehicle repossessed in another state by dealer, §46.2-633.1.
Sale of vehicle without certificate of title, §46.2-617.
Salvage vehicles.
Branding of titles, §46.2-1605.
Cancellation of title upon DMV receipt, §46.2-1603.2.
Certificates of title issued by other states, §46.2-1606.
Insurance company unable to present certificate of title, §46.2-1603.
Rebuilders required to possess certificate of title, §46.2-1604.
Title requirements upon transfer, §46.2-1603.1.
Titling of nonrepairable vehicle, §46.2-1603.2.
Unrecovered stolen vehicle, §46.2-1603.
Security interests in certificates of title, §§46.2-636 to 46.2-644.
Adequate notice of certificate, §46.2-638.
Certificate as notice of security interest, §46.2-638.
Designated in order of priority, §46.2-636.
Disclosure on application, §46.2-636.
Filing requirements, §46.2-639.
Levy of execution, §46.2-644.
Possession of certificate subject to security interest, §46.2-641.
Priority of security interests shown on certificates, §46.2-640.
Recording subsequent security interests, §46.2-637.
Release of security interest shown on certificate, §§46.2-642, 46.2-643.
Retention of certificate subject to security interest, §46.2-641.
Subsequently created security interests, §46.2-637.
Surrender of certificate required when security interest paid, §46.2-643.
Thirty-day filing period, §46.2-639.
Vehicle leases that are not sales or security interests, §46.2-640.1.
Service of notice, process and other papers.
Appointment of agent for process, §46.2-601.
Specially constructed vehicles, §46.2-625.
Survivorship.
Issuance of certificate of title in names of joint owners, §46.2-622.
Taxicabs.
Information required on transfer of title, §46.2-624.
Transfer of title.
Appeal of denial of application, §46.2-611.
By operation of law, §46.2-633.
Death, §46.2-633.2.
Death of certificate holder.
No qualification of estate, §46.2-634.
Forwarding transferred certificate to department, §§46.2-630, 46.2-631.
How certificate of title transferred, §46.2-628.
Information required of taxicabs or vehicles damaged by water, §46.2-624.

MOTOR VEHICLE TITLING —Cont'd
Transfer of title —Cont'd
Lost certificate of title, §46.2-632.
Repossessed vehicle from another state.
Sale by dealer, §46.2-633.1.
Transfer of vehicle ownership.
Odometer reading reported on certificate of title, §46.2-629.
Water-damaged vehicles.
Information required on transfer of title, §46.2-624.

MOTOR VEHICLE TRANSACTION RECOVERY FUND, §§46.2-1527.1 to 46.2-1527.11.
See MOTOR VEHICLE DEALERS.

MOTOR VEHICLE VALUE.
NADA yellow or black books, §8.01-419.1.

MOTOR VEHICLE WARRANTIES.
Disclosure of returned vehicles, §59.1-207.16:1.
Enforcement, §§59.1-207.9 to 59.1-207.16:1.
Actions, §59.1-207.14.
Limitations, §59.1-207.16.
Citation of chapter, §59.1-207.9.
Conformity to all warranties, §59.1-207.12.
Nonconforming motor vehicles, §59.1-207.13.
Defined terms, §59.1-207.11.
Intent of general assembly, §59.1-207.10.
Purpose, §59.1-207.10.
Extended warranties of manufacturers, §§59.1-207.34 to 59.1-207.39.
Defined terms, §59.1-207.34.
Disclosures, §59.1-207.36.
Enforcement of provisions, §59.1-207.38.
Provision violations.
Penalties, §59.1-207.38.
Regulations, §59.1-207.39.
Reimbursements, §59.1-207.37.
Requirements, §59.1-207.35.
Manufacturers' warranty adjustment, §§59.1-207.34 to 59.1-207.39.
Consumer protection, prohibited practices, §59.1-200.
Defined terms, §59.1-207.34.
Disclosures, §59.1-207.36.
Enforcement of provisions, §59.1-207.38.
Provision violations.
Penalties, §59.1-207.38.
Regulations, §59.1-207.39.
Reimbursements, §59.1-207.37.
Requirements, §59.1-207.35.
Nonconformity of motor vehicle, §59.1-207.13.
Presumption reasonable number of attempts undertaken to conform to warranty, §59.1-207.13.
Replacement, return of motor vehicles, refund.
Nonconformity of motor vehicle within lemon law rights period, §59.1-207.13.

MOTOR VOTER REGISTRATION, §24.2-411.1.

MOUNTAIN RIDGES.
Zoning.
Regulation of construction, §15.2-2295.1.

MOUNT VERNON.
Name reserved, locality not granted right to use, §15.2-103.

MOVE-IN INSPECTION.
Landlord and tenant.
Report itemizing damage to unit, §55-225.6.
Mold disclosure statement, §55-225.7.

MOVE OVER LAW.
Drivers approaching stationary emergency vehicles, §46.2-921.1.
Failure to yield right of way.
Fine schedule, VA SCt Rule 3B:2.

MOVERS.
Household goods carriers.
See HOUSEHOLD GOODS CARRIERS.
Motor carriers of property generally, §§46.2-2100 to 46.2-2176.
See MOTOR CARRIERS, PROPERTY.

MOVIES.
Audiovisual recording of motion picture in commercial theater.
Unlawful, penalty, detention of person by owner, §18.2-187.2.
Drive-in theaters.
County regulating motion pictures shown at, §15.2-1222.
Fair competition, §§59.1-255 to 59.1-260.
See MOTION PICTURES.
Fee for purchase or rental in hotels, motels, etc..
Collection, §58.1-1732.
Disposition of proceeds, §58.1-1733.
Imposition, §58.1-1731.
Income tax.
Motion picture production tax credit, §58.1-439.12:03.
Obscene movies generally, §§18.2-372 to 18.2-388.
See OBSCENITY AND RELATED OFFENSES.
Previews of certain motion pictures, misdemeanor for showing, §18.2-386.
Retail sales and use tax.
Media-related exemption, §58.1-609.6.

MOVIE THEATERS.
See THEATERS.

MOVING TRAFFIC VIOLATIONS.
Accidents.
Generally, §§46.2-894 to 46.2-902.
See MOTOR VEHICLE ACCIDENTS.
Aggravated involuntary manslaughter, §18.2-36.1.
Aggressive driving, §46.2-868.1.
Restricted permit to operate, issuance, §46.2-392.
Suspension of driver's license, §46.2-392.
Circular intersections.
Path of travel, §46.2-807.
Yielding right-of-way, §46.2-822.
Coasting in neutral, §46.2-811.
Controlled access highways.
Prohibited vehicle uses, §46.2-808.
Criminal procedure.
Arrest warrants, §§19.2-75 to 19.2-76.3.
Generally, §§46.2-936 to 46.2-947.
Crossing double solid line, §46.2-804.
Cruising ordinance violations, §46.2-1219.1.
Demerit points, §46.2-492.
Disabled vehicle in highway.
Failure to use proper warning device, §46.2-111, VA SCt Rule 3B:2.
Distracted driving.
Sending or reading email by handheld communications device, §46.2-1078.1.
Commercial drivers' licenses, disqualifications, §§46.2-341.20, 46.2-341.20:5.
Holders of provisional drivers' licenses, §46.2-334.01.

MOVING TRAFFIC VIOLATIONS —Cont'd
Distracted driving —Cont'd
Sending or reading email by handheld communications device —Cont'd
Reckless driving, mandatory fine, §46.2-868.
Drag racing, §§46.2-865 to 46.2-867.
Driving in center lane, §46.2-804.
Driving in center of three-lane highway, §46.2-804.
Driving more than thirteen hours in a twenty-four hour period, §46.2-812.
Driving on right side of road, §46.2-802.
Driving through safety zone, §46.2-814.
Driving too fast for highway and traffic conditions, §46.2-861.
Driving while intoxicated.
Generally, §§18.2-266 to 18.2-273.
See DRIVING WHILE INTOXICATED.
Evasion of traffic control devices, §46.2-833.1.
Fine schedule, VA SCt Rule 3B:2.
Maximum fine for violation of title, §46.2-113.
Fleeing or eluding police, §46.2-817.
Following too closely, §46.2-816.
Hauling hazardous cargo through tunnels in violation of posted signs, §46.2-815.
Highway sign violations, §§46.2-830, 46.2-830.1.
Highway work zone violations, §46.2-878.1.
Horse-driven vehicles on controlled access highways, §46.2-808.
HOV lane restrictions, §33.1-46.2.
Improperly stopped or parked on highway, §46.2-888.
Improper passing, §§46.2-837 to 46.2-844.
Involuntary manslaughter, §18.2-36.1.
Keeping to right in crossing intersection or railroads, §46.2-803.
Lane changing without first ascertaining safety of move, §46.2-804.
Maximum fine for violating Title 46.2, §46.2-113.
Maximum safe speed violations, §46.2-861.
Minimum safe speed violations, §46.2-877.
Minors.
Public passenger-carrying vehicles operated by minors, §46.2-810.
Mopeds.
Generally.
See MOPEDS.
Motorcycles.
Generally.
See MOTORCYCLES.
Rider safety, §§46.2-1188 to 46.2-1192.
See MOTORCYCLE RIDER SAFETY.
No-cruising ordinances, §46.2-1219.1.
Occupying trailer being towed on highway, §46.2-813.
One-way streets and roads, §§46.2-836, 46.2-892.
Overtaking violations, §§46.2-837 to 46.2-844.
Passing violations, §§46.2-837 to 46.2-844.
Pretrial payment of fine, §16.1-69.40:1.
Private roads.
Yielding right-of-way before entering public highway or sidewalk, §46.2-826.
Railroad crossings, §§46.2-884 to 46.2-887.
Reckless driving.
Generally, §§46.2-852 to 46.2-868.
See RECKLESS DRIVING.
Riding animals on highway after sunset, §46.2-801.
Rights-of-way violations, §§46.2-820 to 46.2-829.
Right turn on red light, §46.2-835.
Running a red light, §46.2-805.

MOVING TRAFFIC VIOLATIONS —Cont'd
School buses.
Passing a stopped school bus, §§46.2-844, 46.2-859.
Signal violations, §§46.2-848 to 46.2-851.
Signs, lights and markings, §§46.2-830 to 46.2-836.
Size, weight and length violations.
Height limitations, §46.2-1110.
Length limitations, §46.2-1112.
Vehicles exceeding weight limitations, §§46.2-1123 to 46.2-1127.
Width limitations, §46.2-1105.
Slow-moving traffic to keep right, §46.2-804.
Speeding violations.
See TRAFFIC INFRACTIONS.
Stopping in vicinity of fire or emergency, §46.2-890.
Stopping violations.
See TRAFFIC INFRACTIONS.
Towing vehicles generally, §§46.2-1150 to 46.2-1154.
Traffic circles.
Path of travel, §46.2-807.
Yielding right-of-way, §46.2-822.
Traffic control devices on highways, violations, §46.2-830.
Traffic infractions generally.
See TRAFFIC INFRACTIONS.
Traffic lights, §46.2-833.
Turning violations, §§46.2-845 to 46.2-847.
Uncontrolled T intersections.
Yielding right-of-way, §46.2-824.
U-turns improperly executed, §46.2-845.
Vehicular homicide, §18.2-36.1.

MRS. MURPHY LAW.
Fair housing exception, §36-96.2.

MUDFLAPS.
Motor vehicle size and weight, §46.2-1112.

MUFFLERS.
Fine schedule, VA SCt Rule 3B:2.
Maximum fine for violation of title, §46.2-113.
Firearm mufflers, carrying into courthouses, §18.2-283.1.
Firearms offenses.
Courthouses, carrying weapon into, §18.2-283.1.
Maximum fine for violating Title 46.2, §46.2-113.
Mopeds.
Locality regulating noise of mopeds not equipped with muffler, §15.2-919.
Motorboats, §29.1-737.
Motorcycles, §46.2-1050.
Locality regulating noise of motorcycle not equipped with muffler, §15.2-919.
Motor vehicle equipment.
Confiscation, §46.2-1000.
Exhaust system, §§46.2-1047 to 46.2-1051.
Generally, §§46.2-1047 to 46.2-1051.
Straight exhaust or gutted mufflers, §46.2-1047.
Straight exhaust or gutted mufflers, §46.2-1047.

MULCH.
Equipment used to grind trees, underbrush and other vegetative cover for reuse as.
Property exempt from taxation, §58.1-3660.

MULES.
Larceny, §18.2-97.
Maiming, killing or poisoning, §18.2-144.

MULLAHS.
Clergy.
Generally.
See CLERGY.

MULLET.
Taking methods, restrictions, §29.1-531.

MULTIFLORA ROSE.
Noxious weed control.
Counties, cities or towns, §15.2-902.

MULTI-JURISDICTION GRAND JURIES, §§19.2-215.1 to 19.2-215.11.
See GRAND JURIES.

MULTILINE TELEPHONE SYSTEMS (MLTS).
Emergency calls, §§56-484.19 to 56-484.25.
See EMERGENCY TELEPHONE CALLS.

MULTIMEDIA AND TELECOMPUTING PACKAGES.
Programs designed to promote educational opportunities, §22.1-199.1.

MULTIPLE CLAIMANT LITIGATION, §§8.01-267.1 to 8.01-267.9.
See PARTIES.

MULTIPLE DEFENDANTS, SPLIT VERDICTS, §19.2-287.

MULTIPLE KILLINGS.
Capital murder, §18.2-31.
Venue of capital murder prosecution, §19.2-247.

MULTIPLE PARTIES.
General provisions, §§8.01-267.1 to 8.01-267.9.
See PARTIES.
Venue, §8.01-263.

MULTIPLE-PARTY ACCOUNTS, §§6.2-604 to 6.2-620.
Agency relationship of parties, §6.2-619.
Applicability of provisions, §6.2-605.
Attachment, §6.2-606.
Change of form of account upon written order to financial institution, §6.2-609.
Decedents' estates.
Liability of surviving party for debts, §6.2-611.
Definitions, §6.2-604.
Disclaimer of property interests.
Disclaimer of rights of survivorship in jointly held property, §64.2-2605.
Divorce.
Effect, §6.2-607.
Effective date of provisions, §6.2-620.
Financial institution protection, §6.2-612.
Discharge, §6.2-616.
Payment of joint accounts, §6.2-613.
Payment of P.O.D. account, §6.2-614.
Payment of trust account, §6.2-615.
Setoff, §6.2-617.
Garnishment, §6.2-606.
Identification of joint accounts, §6.2-618.
Joint accounts.
Attachment and garnishment, §6.2-606.
Nontestamentary transfers, §6.2-610.
Ownership during lifetime, §6.2-606.
Principal/agency relationship of parties, §6.2-619.
Right of survivorship, §6.2-608.
Scope of provisions, §6.2-605.
Survivorship.
Disclaimer of rights of survivorship in jointly held property, §64.2-2605.

MULTIPLE-PARTY ACCOUNTS —Cont'd
Survivorship —Cont'd
Right of survivorship, §6.2-608.
Transfers nontestamentary, §6.2-610.

MULTISTATE TRUST INSTITUTIONS, §§6.2-803, 6.2-1065 to 6.2-1073.
See TRUSTS.

MUMPS.
Health care provider reports, §32.1-116.3.
Immunizations.
Required immunizations of children, §32.1-46.
Virginia immunization information system (VIIS), §32.1-46.01.

MUNICIPAL AIRPORTS.
Generally, §§5.1-31 to 5.1-47.
See AIRPORTS.

MUNICIPAL BONDS.
Classes not included in determining debt limitation, VA Const Art VII §10.
Debt limitation, VA Const Art VII §10.
Insurance.
Limitation of risks of insurers, §38.2-208.
Limitation on debt, VA Const Art VII §10.

MUNICIPAL COURTS.
Continued as general district courts, §16.1-69.8.
General district courts generally.
See DISTRICT COURTS.

MUNICIPALITIES.
Administrative process act.
Exemptions, §2.2-4002.
Admission tax.
City or town having general taxing powers, §58.1-3840.
Advanced shipbuilding training facility grants, §59.1-284.23.
Agricultural and forestal districts, §§15.2-4300 to 15.2-4314.
Aircraft.
Locality acquiring through forfeiture.
List published by secretary of public safety, §2.2-224.
Air raid precautions, §§44-147 to 44-151.
Alcoholic beverage sales at licensed establishment.
Temporary injunction.
Meeting place for persons committing serious criminal violations, §48-17.1.
Alley use by public service companies without consent or compensation, §56-14.
Animals.
City pounds, §3.2-6546.
Sales of animals from, §3.2-6545.
Cruelty to animals, §3.2-6544.
Ordinances, §§3.2-6543 to 3.2-6545.
Dangerous dogs, control, §3.2-6540.
Dog and cat licensing, §§3.2-6521 to 3.2-6536.
Dogs running at large.
Prohibiting, §3.2-6538.
Permits for pet shops and dealers in companion animals, §3.2-6537.
Rabid animals, §3.2-6522.
Rabies control, §3.2-6525.
Vicious dogs, control, §3.2-6540.1.
Animals running at large and keeping of animals and fowl, powers, §3.2-6544.
Annexation.
Generally, §§15.2-3200 to 15.2-3235.
See ANNEXATION.

MUNICIPALITIES —Cont'd
Armories.
Conveyance of public grounds for armory building purposes, §44-130.
Financial assistance by cities, §44-137.
Joint use of public buildings for, §44-129.
Associations of political subdivisions, §§15.2-1303 to 15.2-1305.
Attorneys for the Commonwealth.
Generally, §§15.2-1626 to 15.2-1633.
See COMMONWEALTH'S ATTORNEYS.
Auditor of public accounts establishing system of bookkeeping, §30-137.
Bad check passed to locality.
Fee, ordinances providing for, §15.2-106.
Bank franchise tax.
Branch banks, §§58.1-1211, 58.1-1212.
City tax, §58.1-1208.
Credit against state tax, §58.1-1213.
Town tax, §58.1-1209.
Banks.
Deposits.
Pledging assets to secure, §6.2-890.
Fiscal or transfer agents, §6.2-820.
Blighted areas.
Tax increment financing, §§58.1-3245 to 58.1-3245.5.
Boards of equalization, §§58.1-3370 to 58.1-3389.
See REAL PROPERTY TAXES.
Boards of social services.
Local boards generally, §§63.2-300 to 63.2-323.
See SOCIAL SERVICES.
Boat traffic congesting waterway.
Pass-through zones.
Authority to adopt ordinance, §29.1-744.4.
Bonds.
Debt limitation, VA Const Art VII §10.
Bonds of local officers, §§15.2-1527 to 15.2-1533.
Boundaries.
Annexation.
Generally, §§15.2-3200 to 15.2-3235.
See ANNEXATION.
Establishment of boundary lines by commissioners, §§15.2-3100 to 15.2-3105.
See BOUNDARIES.
Relocation or change by agreement, §§15.2-3106 to 15.2-3109.
See BOUNDARIES.
Budgets, audits and reports, §§15.2-2500 to 15.2-2513.
Building code.
Statewide code generally, §§36-97 to 36-119.1.
See BUILDING CODE.
Buildings.
Persons with physical disabilities.
Access to public buildings, §§2.2-1159 to 2.2-1161.
Cable television systems.
Localities providing services, §§15.2-2108.2 to 15.2-2108.17.
See CABLE TELEVISION AND SERVICE.
Capital improvement programs, §15.2-2239.
Cash match plan for employees of Commonwealth, §§51.1-607 to 51.1-613.
Cat licensing, §§3.2-6521 to 3.2-6536.
Child welfare agencies.
Appropriations to, contracts with, §63.2-1816.
Cigarette tax, §§58.1-3830 to 58.1-3832.
Corporate officer willful failure to collect and account for, §58.1-3907.

MUNICIPALITIES —Cont'd
Cigarette tax —Cont'd
Excise tax, city or town having general taxing powers, §58.1-3840.
Cities.
Generally.
See CITIES.
City and town defined, VA Const Art VII §1.
City status granted county, §§15.2-3900 to 15.2-3919.
See TRANSITION OF COUNTIES TO CITIES.
City status granted to towns, §§15.2-3800 to 15.2-3834.
See TRANSITION OF TOWNS TO CITIES.
Clean energy improvements.
Financing, §15.2-958.3.
Commissioners of revenue.
Generally, §§58.1-3100 to 58.1-3122.2.
See COMMISSIONERS OF REVENUE.
Commission on local government, §§15.2-2900 to 15.2-2908.
See COMMISSION ON LOCAL GOVERNMENT.
Commonwealth's attorneys.
Generally, §§15.2-1626 to 15.2-1633.
See COMMONWEALTH'S ATTORNEYS.
Comprehensive plan, §§15.2-2222.1 to 15.2-2232.
Conditional zoning, §§15.2-2296 to 15.2-2303.
See CONFLICTS OF INTEREST.
Condominiums.
Conversion condominiums.
Ordinances, enactment, authority, §55-79.94.
Consent of city or town to use public property, VA Const Art VII §8.
Consolidation.
Counties, cities or towns consolidating into single county or city, §§15.2-3520 to 15.2-3550.
See CONSOLIDATION OF LOCALITIES.
Like units of local government, §§15.2-3500 to 15.2-3519.
See CONSOLIDATION OF LOCALITIES.
Consumer utility taxes, §§58.1-3814 to 58.1-3816.2.
Corporation or company, terms not to include municipal corporations, VA Const Art IX §7.
Courthouses, §§15.2-1638 to 15.2-1655.
See COURTHOUSES.
Criminal justice training academies, §§15.2-1747 to 15.2-1753.
See CRIMINAL JUSTICE TRAINING ACADEMIES.
Dams.
Construction for purposes of providing public water supply, §§15.2-2134, 15.2-2142.
Disputes between jurisdictions.
Special court proceedings, §§15.2-2135 to 15.2-2141.
Dance halls.
Ordinances regulating, §15.2-912.3.
Debt limitation, VA Const Art VII §10.
Departments and directors of social services.
Generally, §§63.2-324 to 63.2-336.
See SOCIAL SERVICES.
Directional signs.
Integrated directional sign program.
Participation fees, §33.1-12.01.
Directors of emergency management, §44-146.19.
Disabled or handicapped persons.
Access to public buildings, §§2.2-1159 to 2.2-1161.
Disabled vehicle in roadway.
Flares or torches placed in roadway.
Inapplicability to cities artificially lighted at night, §46.2-111.

MUNICIPALITIES —Cont'd
Disorderly conduct in public places.
Authority to adopt ordinance prohibiting, §18.2-415.
Dispute resolution proceedings.
Administrative dispute resolution, §§2.2-4115 to 2.2-4119.
Election of constitutional and local officers, §§24.2-217 to 24.2-224.
Election of governing bodies, VA Const Art VII §5.
Electrical energy requirements.
Aggregating for purposes of negotiating purchase of electricity, §56-589.
Electric authorities, §§15.2-5400 to 15.2-5431.
See ELECTRIC AUTHORITIES.
Electric power and energy.
Purchase of, §15.2-1133.
Embezzlement by officers, agents or employees, §18.2-112.
Misuse of public assets, §18.2-112.1.
Emergency management and disasters.
Declaration of local emergency, §44-146.21.
Director, §44-146.19.
Generally, §§44-146.13 to 44-146.28.
See EMERGENCY MANAGEMENT.
Immunity from liability, §44-146.23.
Joint action by political subdivisions, §44-146.20.
Powers and duties of political subdivisions generally, §44-146.19.
Emergency medical services.
Fire/EMS departments.
Ordinances relating to powers and duties of fire/EMS departments, §27-14.
Eminent domain.
Generally, §§15.2-1901 to 15.2-1906.
See LOCALITIES.
Energy conservation and costs savings.
Facilities owned by state and local governments.
Energy and operational efficiency performance-based contracting act, §§11-34.1 to 11-34.4.
Financing clean energy improvements, §15.2-958.3.
Excise taxes.
City or town having general taxing powers, §58.1-3840.
Explosives or inflammables.
Local regulation, §59.1-140.
Fire programs fund, allocation to, §38.2-401.
Fishways.
Grants and loans to local governments for construction, §29.1-101.5.
Food tax.
City or town having general taxing powers, §58.1-3840.
Situs for taxation, §58.1-3840.
Forest products tax.
Allocation to cities, §58.1-1611.
Former federal areas, authorities for development, §§15.2-6300 to 15.2-6322.
Franchise, privilege, lease or right to use city or town property, §§15.2-2100 to 15.2-2108.1:1.
Freedom of information act.
Exclusions from chapter, §§2.2-3705.1 to 2.2-3705.8.
Gambling devices, illegal possession.
Failure to enforce, enforcement by governor and attorney general, §18.2-338.

MUNICIPALITIES —Cont'd
Garbage removal and disposal.
General powers of locality as to waste and recycling, §§15.2-901, 15.2-927 to 15.2-939.
General assembly power to provide for organization and government, VA Const Art VII §2.
General powers of local government, §§15.2-900 to 15.2-982.
See LOCALITIES.
General provisions as to localities, §§15.2-100 to 15.2-107.2.
See LOCALITIES.
Going out of business special sale permits.
Issuance, inspections, etc., §18.2-224.
Golf carts and utility vehicles.
Designation of highways for operation on, §46.2-916.2.
Governing bodies of localities.
Generally, §§15.2-1400 to 15.2-1433.
See LOCALITIES.
Governmental fraud, §§18.2-498.1 to 18.2-498.5.
Grievance procedure.
Local government officers generally, §§15.2-1506 to 15.2-1507.1.
Group insurance.
Local government group self-insurance pools, §§15.2-2700 to 15.2-2709.
See LOCAL GOVERNMENT GROUP SELF-INSURANCE POOLS.
Hampton Roads sports facility authority, §§15.2-5900 to 15.2-5916.
Handbills, leaflets, bulletins, literature, advertisements.
Distribution on highways, public roadways and medians, prohibition or regulation, §46.2-931.
Hazardous materials emergency response.
Coordinator of emergency management to enter into agreements with, §44-146.36.
Hazardous materials coordinator, appointment, §44-146.38.
High-occupancy lanes, authority to designate, §33.1-46.2.
Highway design, right-of-way acquisition and construction.
Assumption of responsibility.
Agreement with Commonwealth transportation board, §33.1-12.1.
Hospital authorities.
Generally, §§15.2-5300 to 15.2-5367.
See HOSPITAL AUTHORITIES.
Hospital or health center commissions, §§15.2-5200 to 15.2-5219.
See HOSPITAL OR HEALTH CENTER COMMISSIONS.
Housing revitalization zones, §§36-157 to 36-170.
See HOUSING REVITALIZATION ZONES.
HOV lanes, authority to designate, §33.1-46.2.
Hunting.
Prohibiting hunting in heavily populated areas, §15.2-1113.1.
Immunity of counties from city-initiated annexation and city incorporation, §§15.2-3300 to 15.2-3308.
See IMMUNITY OF COUNTIES FROM CITY-INITIATED ANNEXATION AND CITY INCORPORATION.
Impoundment of water.
Disputes between jurisdictions.
Special court proceedings, §§15.2-2135 to 15.2-2141.

MUNICIPALITIES —Cont'd
Income tax, §§58.1-540 to 58.1-549.
Indoor clean air act, §§15.2-2820 to 15.2-2833.
See SMOKING IN PUBLIC PLACES.
Industrial development authorities.
Generally, §§15.2-4900 to 15.2-4920.
See INDUSTRIAL DEVELOPMENT AUTHORITIES.
Virginia regional industrial facilities authorities, §§15.2-6400 to 15.2-6416.
See VIRGINIA REGIONAL INDUSTRIAL FACILITIES AUTHORITIES.
Insurance.
Local government group self-insurance pools, §§15.2-2700 to 15.2-2709.
See LOCAL GOVERNMENT GROUP SELF-INSURANCE POOLS.
Internet use by library employees and patrons.
Acceptable Internet use policies, establishment.
Local governments without library boards, §42.1-36.1.
Joint activities.
Regional competitiveness act, §§15.2-1306 to 15.2-1310.
Joint exercise of powers, §§15.2-1300 to 15.2-1302, VA Const Art VII §3.
Joint officers and employees, §§15.2-1513 to 15.2-1516.
Juvenile detention and other care facilities.
Operating and maintaining generally, §§16.1-315 to 16.1-322.7.
See JUVENILE DETENTION AND OTHER CARE FACILITIES.
Keys to buildings of political subdivision.
Possession or duplication, §18.2-503.
Land preservation special assessment.
Real property taxes, §§58.1-3229 to 58.1-3244.
See REAL PROPERTY TAXES.
Law libraries.
Assessment as part of cost in civil action, §42.1-70.
Local law libraries, §§42.1-65 to 42.1-71.
Regional law libraries, established by city or county, §42.1-71.
Lending of credit, VA Const Art X §10.
Libraries, grants to municipal library, §42.1-49.
Libraries, local and regional, §§42.1-33 to 42.1-45.
Library property, transfer to city in which library situated, §42.1-45.
License taxes.
Generally, §§58.1-3700 to 58.1-3735.
See LICENSE TAXES.
Telephone or telegraph companies, §58.1-2690.
Limitation on debt, VA Const Art VII §10.
Litter prevention and recycling grants, §10.1-1422.04.
Loans for repair of failed septic systems, §15.2-958.6.
Local income tax, §§58.1-540 to 58.1-549.
Localities generally.
See LOCALITIES.
Machinery and tools tax, §§58.1-3507, 58.1-3508.
Mandates prescribed by state government.
Application for temporary suspension, §2.2-113.
Maps.
Official map, §§15.2-2233 to 15.2-2238.
Meals tax.
City or town having general taxing powers, §58.1-3840.
Situs for taxation, §58.1-3840.

MUNICIPALITIES —Cont'd
Merchants' capital tax, §§58.1-3509, 58.1-3510.
Methane or other combustible gas.
Building or facility to collect and use for electric power.
Loans to local governments, §§15.2-2430 to 15.2-2440.
See VIRGINIA INFRASTRUCTURE PROJECT LOAN FUND.
Militia, appropriations, §44-113.
Militia, requests for assistance by locality, §44-78.1.
Misuse of public assets, §18.2-112.1.
Mortgage lender and broker act.
Agencies of exempt from chapter, §6.2-1602.
Motor carriers, passengers.
Common carriers.
Terminals.
Local licensing, §46.2-2095.
Government vehicles.
Exclusions, §46.2-2000.1.
Taxicabs.
Licensing and license taxation, §46.2-2063.
Restrictions on imposition, §46.2-2064.
Number of cabs, §46.2-2067.
Operator qualifications, §46.2-2065.
Regulation by localities, §46.2-2062.
Stand regulation, §46.2-2065.
Motor carriers, property.
Government vehicles.
Exemptions from provisions, §46.2-2101.
Motorcycles, use of transportation facilities or projects.
Discrimination as to use of facilities or projects prohibited.
State or federal funds used by locality, §33.1-13.1.
Motor vehicle and traffic regulation powers.
Generally, §§46.2-1300 to 46.2-1314.
See LOCALITIES.
Motor vehicle sales and use tax.
Local tax prohibited, §58.1-2418.
Revenue disposition, §58.1-2425.
Natural gas consumption tax.
Imposition when gas service becomes available, §58.1-2905.
Noise ordinances.
Civil penalties for noise ordinance violations.
Adoption of uniform schedule, §15.2-980.
Obscenity.
Adoption of ordinances prohibiting, §15.2-926.2.
Officers and employees.
Bonds of local officers generally, §§15.2-1527 to 15.2-1533.
Circuit court clerks generally.
See CIRCUIT COURT CLERKS.
Commissioners of revenue of cities generally.
See COMMISSIONERS OF REVENUE.
Commonwealth's attorneys generally.
See COMMONWEALTH'S ATTORNEYS.
Grievance procedure.
Local government personnel generally, §§15.2-1506 to 15.2-1507.1.
Joint officers and employees, §§15.2-1513 to 15.2-1516.
Local government personnel generally, qualifications for office, etc., §§15.2-1500 to 15.2-1543.
See LOCAL OFFICERS AND EMPLOYEES.
Local trusts to fund postemployment benefits other than pensions, §§15.2-1544 to 15.2-1549.

MUNICIPALITIES —Cont'd
Officers and employees —Cont'd
Mayors.
See MAYORS.
Military duty leave, §§44-93.1 to 44-93.5.
Qualification of local officer for office, §§15.2-1522 to 15.2-1524.
Removal of public officers generally, §§24.2-230 to 24.2-238.
See REMOVAL OF PUBLIC OFFICERS FROM OFFICE.
Sheriffs generally.
See SHERIFFS.
Telecommuting, §15.2-1512.3.
Travel expenses, §§15.2-1508.1 to 15.2-1508.4.
Treasurers of cities generally.
See TREASURERS, LOCAL.
Official map, §§15.2-2233 to 15.2-2238.
Ordinances generally.
See ORDINANCES.
Park authorities, §§15.2-5700 to 15.2-5714.
See PARK AUTHORITIES.
Parks, recreational facilities and playgrounds, §§15.2-1806 to 15.2-1811.
See LOCALITIES.
Pass-through zones.
Boat traffic congesting waterway.
Authority to adopt ordinance, §29.1-744.4.
Personal property taxes.
Exempt property generally, §§58.1-3600 to 58.1-3666.
See PROPERTY EXEMPT FROM TAXATION.
Generally, §§58.1-3500 to 58.1-3522.
See PERSONAL PROPERTY TAXES.
Machinery and tools tax, §§58.1-3507, 58.1-3508.
Merchants' capital tax, §§58.1-3509, 58.1-3510.
Tax relief act of 1998, §§58.1-3523 to 58.1-3535.
See PERSONAL PROPERTY TAX RELIEF ACT OF 1998.
Personal watercraft.
Minimum distance from shoreline.
City ordinance regulating, penalty for violation, §29.1-748.1.
Personnel generally, qualifications for office, bond, etc., §§15.2-1500 to 15.2-1543.
See LOCAL OFFICERS AND EMPLOYEES.
Persons with physical disabilities.
Access to public buildings, §§2.2-1159 to 2.2-1161.
Planning and development.
Generally, §§15.2-2200 to 15.2-2239.
See PLANNING AND DEVELOPMENT.
Subdivisions generally, §§15.2-2240 to 15.2-2279.
See SUBDIVISIONS.
Zoning generally, §§15.2-2280 to 15.2-2316.2.
See ZONING.
Planning commissions, §§15.2-2210 to 15.2-2222.
Planning district commissions, §§15.2-4200 to 15.2-4222.
See PLANNING DISTRICT COMMISSIONS.
Police.
Auxiliary police forces, §§15.2-1731 to 15.2-1736.
See POLICE.
Generally, §§15.2-1700 to 15.2-1753.
See POLICE.
Interjurisdictional law-enforcement authority and agreements, §§15.2-1724 to 15.2-1730.
See POLICE.
Special police officers in localities, §§15.2-1737 to 15.2-1746.
See POLICE.

MUNICIPALITIES —Cont'd
Powers.
General powers of local government, §§15.2-900 to 15.2-982.
See LOCALITIES.
Joint exercise, §§15.2-1300 to 15.2-1302.
Pretrial services program, §§19.2-152.2 to 19.2-152.7:1.
Probate tax, city, §§58.1-3805 to 58.1-3808.
Prompt payment of bills, §§2.2-4352, 2.2-4354.
Property records.
When writings to be recorded in corporation, §55-102.
Property taxes.
Exempt property generally, §§58.1-3600 to 58.1-3666.
See PROPERTY EXEMPT FROM TAXATION.
Machinery and tools tax, §§58.1-3507, 58.1-3508.
Merchants' capital tax, §§58.1-3509, 58.1-3510.
Personal property taxes generally, §§58.1-3500 to 58.1-3522.
See PERSONAL PROPERTY TAXES.
Personal property tax relief act of 1998, §§58.1-3523 to 58.1-3535.
See PERSONAL PROPERTY TAX RELIEF ACT OF 1998.
Real property taxes generally, §§58.1-3200 to 58.1-3389.
See REAL PROPERTY TAXES.
Public assistance.
Departments and directors of social services.
Generally.
See SOCIAL SERVICES.
Funding of public assistance and social services, §§63.2-400 to 63.2-412.
See SOCIAL SERVICES.
Local boards generally, §§63.2-300 to 63.2-323.
See SOCIAL SERVICES.
Temporary assistance for needy families, §§63.2-600 to 63.2-621.
See PUBLIC AID AND ASSISTANCE.
Publications.
State publications depository program.
Generally, §§42.1-92 to 42.1-97.
See STATE PUBLICATIONS DEPOSITORY PROGRAM.
Public property use, consent of city or town required, VA Const Art VII §8.
Public service company using without consent or compensation, §56-14.
Public records generally, §§42.1-76 to 42.1-90.1.
See STATE RECORDS MANAGEMENT.
Public school special tax, §§22.1-102 to 22.1-106.
Public service corporation assessments against property.
Review by governing bodies, §58.1-2602.
Public service corporations, local taxation of property, §58.1-2606.
Railroads, §58.1-2607.
Public utilities.
Generally, §§15.2-2109 to 15.2-2121.
See LOCALITIES.
Sewage disposal systems, §§15.2-2122 to 15.2-2133.
See SEWAGE DISPOSAL SYSTEMS.
Water supply systems, §§15.2-2134 to 15.2-2156.
See WATER SUPPLY SYSTEMS.
Qualification of local officer for office, §§15.2-1522 to 15.2-1524.
Railroads.
Local taxation of property, §58.1-2607.

MUNICIPALITIES —Cont'd
Real property taxes.
Exempt property generally, §§58.1-3600 to 58.1-3666.
See PROPERTY EXEMPT FROM TAXATION.
Generally, §§58.1-3200 to 58.1-3389.
See REAL PROPERTY TAXES.
Reapportionment of districts or wards, VA Const Art VII §5.
Rechargeable battery disposal and recycling, §10.1-1425.39.
Reciprocal insurance contracts, power to enter into, §38.2-1204.
Recordation tax, §§58.1-3800 to 58.1-3804.
Recordation tax, state.
Exemption, §58.1-811.
Records.
When writings to be recorded in, §55-102.
Recreational facilities.
Liability in operating.
Agreements with landowners, §29.1-509.
Recycling.
Grants, §10.1-1422.04.
Refuse collection and disposal authorities, §§15.2-5100 to 15.2-5159.
See WATER AND WASTE AUTHORITIES.
Refuse removal and disposal.
General powers of locality as to waste and recycling, §§15.2-901, 15.2-927 to 15.2-939.
Regional cooperation act, §§15.2-4200 to 15.2-4222.
See PLANNING DISTRICT COMMISSIONS.
Regional partnerships.
Regional competitiveness act, §§15.2-1306 to 15.2-1310.
Removal of public officers from office, §§24.2-230 to 24.2-238.
See REMOVAL OF PUBLIC OFFICERS FROM OFFICE.
Rental inspections of unit located in rental inspection district.
Residential rental dwelling units.
Building code compliance, §36-105.1:1.
Restaurants.
Fairs, exemption from provisions by ordinance, §35.1-26.
Retail sales and use tax.
Localities share, §58.1-638.
Roads, streets and public rights of way.
Generally, §§15.2-2000 to 15.2-2030.
See ROADS, STREETS AND PUBLIC RIGHTS OF WAY.
Local authority over highways, §§33.1-224 to 33.1-246.
See LOCAL ROAD AUTHORITIES.
Rolling stock tax distribution, §§58.1-2658, 58.1-2658.1.
Salaries of city council members, §§15.2-1414.5, 15.2-1414.6.
Salaries of town council members and mayors, §15.2-1414.7.
Sale of merchandise on highways, public roadways or medians.
Prohibition or regulation, §46.2-931.
Sale of property, VA Const Art VII §9.
Self insurance.
Local government group self-insurance pools, §§15.2-2700 to 15.2-2709.
See LOCAL GOVERNMENT GROUP SELF-INSURANCE POOLS.
Septic system repair loan program, §15.2-958.6.

MUNICIPALITIES —Cont'd
Service districts, §§15.2-2400 to 15.2-2403.3.
Service of notice, process and other papers.
How process served, §8.01-300.
Setoff debt collection, income tax, §§58.1-520 to 58.1-535.
See INCOME TAX.
Severance tax on coal, gas or oil.
Alternative to specially and separately assessing mineral lands, §58.1-3286.
License tax on persons engaging in business of severing, §§58.1-3712 to 58.1-3713.4.
Local coal severance license taxes, §§58.1-3740 to 58.1-3745.
Sewage disposal authorities, §§15.2-5100 to 15.2-5159.
See WATER AND WASTE AUTHORITIES.
Sewage disposal systems.
Generally, §§15.2-2122 to 15.2-2133.
See SEWAGE DISPOSAL SYSTEMS.
Sewer authorities, §§15.2-5100 to 15.2-5159.
See WATER AND WASTE AUTHORITIES.
Signs.
Loitering on bridges or highway rights-of-way, §46.2-930.
Smoking in public places.
Virginia indoor clean air act, §§15.2-2820 to 15.2-2833.
See SMOKING IN PUBLIC PLACES.
Social services.
Adoption.
Generally, §§63.2-1200 to 63.2-1248.
See ADOPTION.
Adult protective services, §§63.2-1603 to 63.2-1610.
Child abuse and neglect, §§63.2-1500 to 63.2-1527.
See CHILD ABUSE AND NEGLECT.
Departments and directors of social services.
Generally.
See SOCIAL SERVICES.
Foster care generally, §§63.2-900 to 63.2-915.
See SOCIAL SERVICES.
Funding of public assistance and social services, §§63.2-400 to 63.2-412.
See SOCIAL SERVICES.
Local boards generally, §§63.2-300 to 63.2-323.
See SOCIAL SERVICES.
Temporary assistance for needy families, §§63.2-600 to 63.2-621.
See PUBLIC AID AND ASSISTANCE.
Solicitation of contributions on highways, public roadways, medians.
Prohibition or regulation, §46.2-931.
Solid waste management.
General powers of locality as to waste and recycling, §§15.2-901, 15.2-927 to 15.2-939.
Special police officers, §§15.2-1737 to 15.2-1746.
See POLICE.
Speed limits.
Highways in cities and towns.
Authority of municipality to increase or decrease speed limits, §46.2-875.
Stock subscriptions, VA Const Art X §10.
Subdivisions generally, §§15.2-2240 to 15.2-2279.
See SUBDIVISIONS.
Superintendents of public welfare.
See SUPERINTENDENTS OF PUBLIC WELFARE.
Taxes.
Cigarette tax, §§58.1-3830 to 58.1-3832.
Corporate or partnership officer willful failure to collect and account for, §58.1-3907.

MUNICIPALITIES —Cont'd
Taxes —Cont'd
Collection of local taxes generally, §§58.1-3910 to 58.1-3961.
See TAX COLLECTION.
Consumer utility taxes, §§58.1-3814 to 58.1-3816.2.
Correction of erroneous tax assessments, §§58.1-3980 to 58.1-3995.
See CORRECTION OF ERRONEOUS TAX ASSESSMENTS.
Delinquent taxes.
Collection of local taxes, §§58.1-3921 to 58.1-3938.
See TAX COLLECTION.
Sale of delinquent tax lands, §§58.1-3965 to 58.1-3975.
See SALE OF DELINQUENT TAX LANDS.
Distress.
Collection of local taxes by distress generally, §§58.1-3940 to 58.1-3961.
See TAX COLLECTION.
Excise taxes.
City or town having general taxing powers, §58.1-3840.
Exempt property generally, §§58.1-3600 to 58.1-3666.
See PROPERTY EXEMPT FROM TAXATION.
Income tax, §§58.1-540 to 58.1-549.
License taxes, §§58.1-3700 to 58.1-3735.
See LICENSE TAXES.
Local taxes generally, §§58.1-3000 to 58.1-3018.
See LOCAL TAXES.
Machinery and tools tax, §§58.1-3507, 58.1-3508.
Merchants' capital tax, §§58.1-3509, 58.1-3510.
Natural gas consumption tax.
Imposition when gas service becomes available, §58.1-2905.
Personal property taxes generally, §§58.1-3500 to 58.1-3522.
See PERSONAL PROPERTY TAXES.
Personal property tax relief act of 1998, §§58.1-3523 to 58.1-3535.
See PERSONAL PROPERTY TAX RELIEF ACT OF 1998.
Probate tax, city, §§58.1-3805 to 58.1-3808.
Public school special tax, §§22.1-102 to 22.1-106.
Real property taxes generally, §§58.1-3200 to 58.1-3389.
See REAL PROPERTY TAXES.
Recordation tax, §§58.1-3800 to 58.1-3804.
Severance tax on coal, gas or oil.
License tax on persons engaging in business of severing, §§58.1-3712 to 58.1-3713.4.
Local coal severance license taxes, §§58.1-3740 to 58.1-3745.
Taxes or assessments for local improvements, §§15.2-2404 to 15.2-2413.
See TAXES OR ASSESSMENTS FOR LOCAL IMPROVEMENTS.
Tax increment financing.
Blighted areas, §§58.1-3245 to 58.1-3245.5.
Telecommunications services.
Providing, §15.2-2160.
Telephone or telegraph companies, local license tax, §58.1-2690.
Tennessee Valley Authority, apportionment of payments.
Apportionment among cities in which authority owns property, §58.1-3406.

MUNICIPALITIES —Cont'd
Tourism zones.
Establishment, tax incentives, regulator flexibility.
Authority, §58.1-3851.
Tax revenues, entitlement, §58.1-3851.1.
Power to designate, §15.2-982.
Towns.
Generally.
See TOWNS.
Traffic regulation.
During state of war, §44-205.
Motor vehicle and traffic regulation powers generally, §§46.2-1300 to 46.2-1314.
See LOCAL GOVERNMENT.
Transient occupancy tax.
Excise tax, city or town having general taxing powers, §58.1-3840.
Imposed on rooms suitable or intended for occupancy purposes, §58.1-3843.
Transition of city to town.
City no longer qualifying for city status, §§15.2-4000 to 15.2-4005.
See REVERSION OF CITIES TO TOWNS.
Generally, §§15.2-4100 to 15.2-4120.
See REVERSION OF CITIES TO TOWNS.
Transition of counties to cities, §§15.2-3900 to 15.2-3919.
See TRANSITION OF COUNTIES TO CITIES.
Transition of towns to cities, §§15.2-3800 to 15.2-3834.
See TRANSITION OF TOWNS TO CITIES.
Transportation board or department disposing of surplus realty.
Notice to local governing body, §33.1-223.2:2.
Transportation districts, §§15.2-4500 to 15.2-4534, 33.1-409 to 33.1-425.
See TRANSPORTATION DISTRICTS.
Trash removal and disposal.
General powers of locality as to waste and recycling, §§15.2-901, 15.2-927 to 15.2-939.
Travel expenses to persons traveling on business of locality, §§15.2-1508.1 to 15.2-1508.4.
Treasurers, §§58.1-3123 to 58.1-3172.1.
See TREASURERS, LOCAL.
Trust companies.
Fiscal or transfer agents, §§6.2-820, 6.2-1002.
Unclaimed property, disposition.
Intangible property held for owner, §55-210.9.
Uniform charter powers, §§15.2-1100 to 15.2-1126.
Virginia Beach arena, §§15.2-5921 to 15.2-5927.
See VIRGINIA BEACH ARENA.
Virginia Commonwealth University health system authority.
Authority to lend or donate money or other property, §23-50.16:11.
Virginia infrastructure project loan fund, §§15.2-2430 to 15.2-2440.
See VIRGINIA INFRASTRUCTURE PROJECT LOAN FUND.
Waste and recycling.
General powers, §§15.2-901, 15.2-927 to 15.2-939.
Water authorities, §§15.2-5100 to 15.2-5159.
See WATER AND WASTE AUTHORITIES.
Water supply systems.
Generally, §§15.2-2134 to 15.2-2156.
See WATER SUPPLY SYSTEMS.
Welfare.
Departments and directors of social services.
Generally.
See SOCIAL SERVICES.

MUNICIPALITIES —Cont'd
Welfare —Cont'd
Funding of public assistance and social services, §§63.2-400 to 63.2-412.
See SOCIAL SERVICES.
Local boards generally, §§63.2-300 to 63.2-323.
See SOCIAL SERVICES.
Temporary assistance for needy families, §§63.2-600 to 63.2-621.
See PUBLIC AID AND ASSISTANCE.
Welfare or social services boards.
Generally.
See WELFARE BOARDS, LOCAL.
Well covers.
Authority to require and regulate, §18.2-318.
World War II history relating to Virginians.
Furnishing to state librarian, §42.1-31.
Zoning generally, §§15.2-2280 to 15.2-2316.2.
See ZONING.

MURDER.
Accessory before the fact or principal in second degree, how punished.
Capital murder, §18.2-18.
Bar to claiming property rights of decedent, §§64.2-2500 to 64.2-2511.
See SLAYER'S ACT.
Canals, railroads, power lines, etc.
Obstructing or injuring, death resulting, §18.2-153.
Capital murder, §18.2-31.
Accessory before the fact or principal in second degree, how punished, §18.2-18.
Appointment of counsel in capital cases, §§19.2-163.7, 19.2-163.8.
Arrest warrants.
Law enforcement officers not to seek without prior approval of attorney for the Commonwealth, §19.2-71.
Attempt to commit capital offense, §18.2-25.
Declared felony, §18.2-30.
Indictments, central file, §19.2-217.1.
Lynching deemed murder, §18.2-40.
Multiple murder, venue, §19.2-247.
Conviction of lesser offense, §19.2-288.
Criminal solicitation to commit murder, §18.2-29.
Declared felony, §18.2-30.
Discretionary felony sentencing guidelines, §17.1-805.
Entering dwelling with intent to commit, §18.2-90.
Firearm or missile discharged within or at building or dwelling.
Death resulting, §18.2-279.
Firearm used or displayed, §18.2-53.1.
Indictments, presentments or informations.
Statutory short form of indictment, §19.2-221.
Injuring railroad signals.
Death resulting, §18.2-155.
Juvenile serious offenders, commitment, §16.1-285.1.
Release and review hearings, §16.1-285.2.
Juvenile serious or habitual offender comprehensive action program (SHOCAP), §§16.1-330.1, 16.1-330.2.
Killing a fetus, §18.2-32.2.
Killing for hire, §18.2-31.
Killing of pregnant women, §18.2-32.1.
Capital murder, §18.2-31.

MURDER —Cont'd
Limitation of prosecutions.
No limitation, §19.2-8.1.
Lynching, §18.2-40.
Mob crimes, §18.2-42.1.
Multiple murder prosecution, venue, §19.2-247.
Murder of the first degree, §18.2-32.
Murder of the second degree, §18.2-32.
Pregnant women, §18.2-32.1.
Capital murder, §18.2-31.
Residential property transfer disclosures.
Actions for failure to disclose, §55-524.
Sentence of person twice previously convicted of certain violent felonies, §19.2-297.1.
Shooting at or throwing missiles at trains, cars, vessels, etc.
Death resulting, §18.2-154.
Slayer's act, §§64.2-2500 to 64.2-2511.
See SLAYER'S ACT.
Solicitation to commit murder, §18.2-29.
Third-time conviction, §19.2-297.1.
Three strikes, §19.2-297.1.
Venue of certain homicide cases, §19.2-247.
Wiretapping.
Court-ordered interception of communications.
When authorized by state police, §19.2-66.

MURDER OF PREGNANT WOMEN, §18.2-32.1.
Capital murder, §18.2-31.

MURDER OF THE FIRST DEGREE, §18.2-32.
Declared felony, §18.2-30.
Discretionary felony sentencing guidelines, §17.1-805.
Lynching deemed murder, §18.2-40.
Mob crimes, §18.2-42.1.
Third-time conviction, §19.2-297.1.

MURDER OF THE SECOND DEGREE, §18.2-32.
Declared felony, §18.2-30.
Discretionary felony sentencing guidelines, §17.1-805.
Lynching deemed murder, §18.2-40.
Mob crimes, §18.2-42.1.
Third-time conviction, §19.2-297.1.

MUSEUM AUTHORITIES.
Virginia Naval museum authority, 1975 ch 488, 1980 ch 334.

MUSEUM OF FINE ARTS, §§23-253.1 to 23-253.7.
Closed meetings.
Board of trustees, §2.2-3711.
Retail sales and use tax exemption, §58.1-609.1.
Secretary of education.
Agency responsibility, §2.2-208.

MUSEUM OF NATURAL HISTORY, §§10.1-2000 to 10.1-2012.
Agents, §10.1-2010.
Board, §10.1-2002.
Acceptance of gifts, §10.1-2011.
Bonds, surety, §10.1-2006.
Closed meetings, §2.2-3711.
Meetings, §10.1-2007.
Oaths, §10.1-2005.
Officers, §10.1-2004.
Powers and duties, §10.1-2009.
Quorum, §10.1-2008.
Vacancies, §10.1-2003.
Bonds, surety.
Board, §10.1-2006.
Created, §10.1-2000.

MUSEUM OF NATURAL HISTORY —Cont'd
Director.
Agents and employees, §10.1-2010.
Gifts.
Acceptance by board, §10.1-2011.
Purposes, §10.1-2001.
Reports, §10.1-2012.
Secretary of natural resources.
Agency responsibility, §2.2-215.
Terms of members.
Board, §10.1-2003.

MUSEUMS.
ABC licenses.
Authorized conduct, §4.1-206.
Admission tax, §§58.1-3817, 58.1-3818.
Damaging property located in, §18.2-138.
Emergency medical services museum.
Official emergency medical services museum of Commonwealth, §1-510.
Frontier culture museum of Virginia, §§23-296 to 23-298.
Hampton Roads museum consortium, §§22.1-356, 22.1-357.
Living historical farm museums.
Locality operating and maintaining, §15.2-943.
Locality acquiring and housing relics, paintings, carvings, etc., §15.2-945.
Motor sports museum.
Official motor sports museum of Commonwealth, §1-510.
Natural history, §§10.1-2000 to 10.1-2012.
Property loaned to museums, §§55-210.31 to 55-210.38.
Definitions, §55-210.31.
Notice, §55-210.33.
Statute of limitations on recovery, §55-210.32.
Termination of loans, §§55-210.35, 55-210.36.
Title to property, §55-210.37.
Owners' responsibilities, §55-210.36.
Property loaned prior to July 1, 2002, §55-210.38.
Publication requirements, §§55-210.36, 55-210.37.
Statute of limitations on recovery, §55-210.32.
Termination of loans, §§55-210.35, 55-210.36.
Title to property, §§55-210.34, 55-210.37.
Property tax exemptions to nonprofit museums, §58.1-3606.
Science museum of Virginia, §§23-239 to 23-253.
State aid.
Estimates by nonstate agencies for annual budget, §2.2-1505.
Virginia Museum of Fine Arts, §§23-253.1 to 23-253.7.
War memorial museum.
Official war memorial museum of Commonwealth, §1-510.

MUSHROOM FESTIVAL, §2.2-3321.

MUSIC.
Recorded device piracy, §§59.1-41.1 to 59.1-41.6.
Authority of attorney general, §59.1-68.2.
Truth in music advertising act, §§59.1-466.1 to 59.1-466.4.

MUSICAL INSTRUMENTS.
Personal property taxes.
Classification, §58.1-3504.

MUSIC LICENSING FEES.
Actions.
Violations of chapter, §59.1-464.
Applicability of chapter, §59.1-466.

MUSIC LICENSING FEES —Cont'd
Attorneys' fees.
Violations of chapter, §59.1-464.
Contracts.
Requirements, §59.1-462.
Damages.
Violations of chapter, §59.1-464.
Defined terms, §59.1-460.
Exceptions to chapter, §59.1-466.
Injunctions.
Violations of chapter, §59.1-464.
Notice, §59.1-461.
Performing rights society.
Prohibited conduct, §59.1-463.
Schedule of fees, §59.1-461.
Prohibited conduct, §59.1-463.
Schedules.
Providing by performing rights society, §59.1-461.

MUSIC PLAYERS.
Portable electronics insurance, §§38.2-1875 to 38.2-1880.

MUSKRAT.
Hunting.
Times, §29.1-520.
Sale of game, §29.1-536.

MUSK THISTLE.
Counties, cities, towns.
Authority to control, §15.2-902.
Defined, §15.2-902.
Ordinances, §15.2-902.

MUSSELS.
Nuisance species.
Nonindigenous aquatic nuisance species act, §§29.1-571 to 29.1-577.
See NONINDIGENOUS AQUATIC NUISANCE SPECIES ACT.
Oysters and clams generally.
See OYSTERS AND CLAMS.
Zebra mussels.
Introducing into waters of Commonwealth, §18.2-313.2.

MUTUAL AID ASSOCIATIONS.
Insurance title provisions not to apply to certain associations, §38.2-226.

MUTUAL AID IN EMERGENCIES, COMPACT, §44-146.28:1.

MUTUAL AID IN FIRE OR MEDICAL SERVICE EMERGENCIES, §§27-2 to 27-4.
Compact, §44-146.28:1.

MUTUAL ASSESSMENT FIRE INSURANCE COMPANIES.
License tax on insurance companies.
Exemptions and exclusions, §58.1-2502.

MUTUAL ASSESSMENT LIFE, ACCIDENT AND SICKNESS INSURER, §§38.2-3900 to 38.2-3923.
Accident and sickness insurance, class of insurance written by, §38.2-3902.
Accident and sickness policy reserves, §38.2-3923.
Agents license required, §38.2-3919.
Amount of payment and when to be paid, policy to specify, §38.2-3914.
Annuities, class of insurance written by, §38.2-3902.
Applicability of chapter, §38.2-3900.
Applicable laws, §38.2-3903.

MUTUAL ASSESSMENT LIFE, ACCIDENT AND SICKNESS INSURER —Cont'd
Assessment contract, §38.2-3915.
Assessment liability, right to limit, §38.2-3917.
Assessment notice, §38.2-3918.
Classes of insurance written by, §38.2-3902.
Classification of risks, §38.2-3916.
Contingent assessment liability, when waived, §38.2-3917.
Continuance of businesses transacting business on July 1, 1985.
Additional companies, licensing prohibited, §38.2-3906.
Contract, §38.2-3915.
Conversion of insurers, §38.2-3904.
Approval of state corporation commission required, §38.2-1005.
Domestic insurers, §38.2-1005.1.
Defenses, time limit on, §38.2-3911.
Definitions, §38.2-3901.
Directors, §38.2-3907.
Executive committee, §38.2-3907.
Filing of forms, §38.2-3910.
Forms to be filed, §38.2-3910.
Fraudulent misstatements, time limit on defenses, §38.2-3911.
General insurance laws, applicability, §38.2-3903.
Grace period, §38.2-3913.
Incontestability of policy, §38.2-3912.
Incorporation, §38.2-3905.
Inspection of books and papers, §38.2-3909.
Licensing of additional companies prohibited, §38.2-3906.
Life insurance, class of insurance written by, §38.2-3902.
Life policy reserves, §38.2-3923.
Limitation on single risk to be assumed, §38.2-3921.
Members right to inspect books and papers, §38.2-3909.
Minimum surplus, §38.2-3920.
Notice of assessment, §38.2-3918.
Officers, §38.2-3908.
Rates, §38.2-3916.
Reinsurance, §38.2-3922.
Reserves required, §38.2-3923.
Right to limit assessment liabilities, §38.2-3917.
Scope of chapter, §38.2-3900.
Secretary and treasurer, §38.2-3908.
Single risk assumed, limitation on, §38.2-3921.
Specification of amount of payment and when to pay, §38.2-3914.
Surplus to policyholder, §38.2-3920.
Time limit on certain defenses, §38.2-3911.

MUTUAL ASSESSMENT LIFE AND HEALTH INSURANCE AGENTS.
License required, §38.2-3919.
Licensing of insurance agents generally, §§38.2-1822 to 38.2-1836.1.

MUTUAL ASSESSMENT PROPERTY AND CASUALTY INSURANCE AGENTS.
License required, §38.2-2525.
Licensing of insurance agents generally, §§38.2-1822 to 38.2-1836.1.
Licensing without examination, §38.2-1814.

MUTUAL ASSESSMENT PROPERTY AND CASUALTY INSURERS, §§38.2-2500 to 38.2-2529.
Action to recover assessments, §38.2-2522.

MUTUAL ASSESSMENT PROPERTY AND CASUALTY INSURERS —Cont'd
Agents, license required, §38.2-2525.
Annual meeting, §38.2-2509.
Applicability of chapter, §38.2-2500.
Applicable laws, §38.2-2506.
Assessment contract, §38.2-2518.
Assessment liability, right to limit, §38.2-2520.
Assessment notice, §38.2-2521.
Assessments, action to recover, §38.2-2522.
Assumption of limitation on single risk, §38.2-2527.
Authorization of mutual assessment insurance, §38.2-2502.
Authorized territory, property beyond, §38.2-2504.
Borrowing money to pay loss or damage, §38.2-2524.
Bylaws as part of contract, §38.2-2516.
Classes of insurance that may be written, §38.2-2503.
Classification of risks, §38.2-2519.
Contract, §38.2-2518.
Conversion, §38.2-2507.
Definitions, §38.2-2501.
Directors, §38.2-2509.
Executive committee, §38.2-2509.
Filing of forms, §38.2-2517.
Forms, filing, §38.2-2517.
General insurance law, applicability, §38.2-2506.
General powers imposed and conferred upon corporations by law, §38.2-2508.
Income earned on surplus.
Used to pay losses, §38.2-2526.
Incorporation, §38.2-2508.
Issuance of policies, §38.2-2516.
License, how obtained, §38.2-2511.
License suspension or revocation.
Failure to maintain required memberships, §38.2-2515.
Limitation on risk to those specified in chapter, §38.2-2505.
Limitation on single risk to be assumed, §38.2-2527.
Loss and adjustment, notice of, §38.2-2523.
Loss or damage exceeding cash on hand, proceeding, §38.2-2524.
Members.
Exclusion, §38.2-2513.
Procedure upon, §38.2-2514.
Notice of exclusion, §38.2-2514.
Number of memberships to be maintained by insurers, §38.2-2515.
Who may become, §38.2-2512.
Withdrawal, §38.2-2513.
Minimum surplus to policyholders required, §38.2-2503.
Mutual assessment insurance authorized, §38.2-2502.
Notice of assessment, §38.2-2521.
Notice of loss and adjustment, §38.2-2523.
Officers, §38.2-2510.
Personal liability for loss, §38.2-2505.
President, §38.2-2510.
Property beyond authorized territory, §38.2-2504.
Proxies, §38.2-2509.
Rates, §38.2-2519.
Rehabilitation or liquidation.
Failure to maintain required membership, revocation or suspension of license, §38.2-2515.

MUTUAL ASSESSMENT PROPERTY AND CASUALTY INSURERS —Cont'd
Reinsurance, §38.2-2528.
Requirement of unearned premium reserves, §38.2-2529.
Right to limit assessment liability, §38.2-2520.
Risks limited to those specified in chapter, §38.2-2505.
Scope of chapter, §38.2-2500.
Secretary, §38.2-2510.
Surplus to policyholders, §38.2-2526.
Minimum surplus required, §38.2-2503.
Treasurer, §38.2-2510.
Unearned premium reserves required, §38.2-2529.
Who may become members, §38.2-2512.

MUTUAL ASSISTANCE COMPACT, NATIONAL GUARD, §§44-54.1 to 44-54.3.

MUTUAL CONSENT ADOPTION REGISTRY.
See ADOPTION.

MUTUAL EXCHANGE OF INSURANCE CONTRACTS.
Reciprocal insurance, §§38.2-1200 to 38.2-1231.

MUTUAL FUNDS.
Insurance companies investments, §38.2-1432.
Investment of public funds.
Restrictions, §2.2-4508.

MUTUAL INSURERS.
Articles of incorporation.
Additional requirement, §38.2-1002.
Bylaws to be filed with state corporation commission, §38.2-1003.
Conversion of mutual holding companies to stock holding companies, §§38.2-1005.1:1 to 38.2-1005.1:13.
Conversion of stock insurer to mutual insurer, §§38.2-1006 to 38.2-1018.
Conversion to stock companies.
Approval of state corporation commission required, §38.2-1005.
Domestic insurers, §38.2-1005.1.
Formation of mutual insurance holding companies, §§38.2-1005.1:1 to 38.2-1005.1:13.
Incorporation of domestic insurers, §38.2-1001.
Legal existence upon recording charter with state corporation commission, §38.2-1003.
Licensing of insurers.
Generally, §§38.2-1024 to 38.2-1039.1.
Refusal, suspension or revocation, §§38.2-1040 to 38.2-1044.
Surplus requirement, §38.2-1029.
Acquisition of initial surplus, §38.2-1034.
Mergers, §§38.2-1017, 38.2-1018.
Public or private corporations as members, §38.2-206.
Voting by members, §38.2-1004.

MUTUAL SAVINGS BANKS.
Enterprise zones.
Eligibility, §59.1-279.

MUZZLE LOADERS.
Hunting.
Blaze orange clothing required.
Exception for Muzzleloading rifles, §29.1-530.1.
Licenses, §29.1-307.
Sportsman's hunting and fishing license, §29.1-310.1.
Restrictions, §§29.1-519, 29.1-528.

MYELOMA.
High-dose chemotherapy and bone marrow transplants.
Medical assistance service plans, §32.1-325.

N

NADA YELLOW OR BLACK BOOKS.
Motor vehicle value, §8.01-419.1.

NAIC.
Annual statement by insurers to national association of insurance commissioners, §38.2-1300.
Valuation of investments and other assets of insurance companies, §38.2-1306.2.

NAIL CARE.
Barbers, §§54.1-700 to 54.1-706.

NAME CHANGE, §8.01-217.
Adoptive child's name.
Interlocutory order of adoption, §63.2-1209.
Petition for adoption and change of name.
Filing, venue, proceedings, §63.2-1201.
Amendments to vital records, §32.1-269.
Application to circuit court, §8.01-217.
BVU authority, §15.2-7203.
Corporations.
Issuing certificate, §13.1-616.
Property title records, §13.1-781.
Divorce.
Restoration of former name upon decree of divorce, §20-121.4.
Recording and indexing, §55-106.1.
Fee of circuit court clerk for services, §17.1-275.
Filing case with clerk, §16.1-260.
Identifying information.
Order of court containing, §8.01-217.
Incarcerated persons.
Procedure, §8.01-217.
Insurance agents.
Report to state corporation commission, §38.2-1826.
Insurance consultants, §38.2-1842.
Marriage, change of name by reason of.
Restoration of former name upon decree of divorce, §20-121.4.
Minors.
Procedure, §8.01-217.
Nonprofit corporations.
Issuing certificate, §13.1-816.
Notaries.
Name change during term of office, §47.1-17.
Notice.
Prisoners name change.
Victims of crime, §53.1-133.02.
Registered voters, §24.2-423.
Order of court, §8.01-217.
Pleadings.
Effect, §§8.01-19, 8.01-20.
Prisoners.
Notice to victims of crime, §53.1-133.02.
Probationers.
Procedure, §8.01-217.
Procedure, §8.01-217.
Registered voter, §24.2-423.
Registrar of vital records and central criminal records exchange.
Transmittal of order to, §8.01-217.

NAME CHANGE —Cont'd
Retention of ended case files by circuit court clerk, time, destruction, §17.1-213.
Sealing records.
Threat to health and safety of applicant, §8.01-217.
Sex changes.
Amendments to vital records, §32.1-269.
Threat to health and safety of applicant, §8.01-217.
Trademarks and service marks.
Applicant for registration, §59.1-92.8.
Unlawful change, §18.2-504.1.
Utility consumer services cooperatives.
Amendments to articles of incorporation, §56-231.22.
Venue of proceeding, §8.01-217.
Voter registration.
Notice of change of name of registered voter, §24.2-423.

NAMES.
Advertising.
Unauthorized use of name of person, §18.2-216.1.
Agricultural cooperative associations.
Limitation of use of word cooperative, §13.1-336.
Anonymous litigant.
Pseudonym, use, §8.01-15.1.
Assumed or fictitious names.
Business transactions under assumed name, §§59.1-69 to 59.1-76.
See TRANSACTING BUSINESS UNDER ASSUMED NAME.
Proceeding anonymously.
Pseudonym, use, §8.01-15.1.
Banks.
Branch offices.
Operation under different name, §6.2-834.
Unlawful use of terms bank, savings bank, etc., §6.2-939.
Use in marketing materials or solicitation, §6.2-941.
Use of name in prohibited manner, §59.1-92.22.
Business transactions under assumed name, §§59.1-69 to 59.1-76.
See TRANSACTING BUSINESS UNDER ASSUMED NAME.
Business trusts, §13.1-1214.
Change of name.
Property title records.
Organizational changes generally, §13.1-1285.
Foreign business trusts, §13.1-1244.
Reserved name, §13.1-1215.
BVU authority, §15.2-7203.
Captive insurers, §38.2-1103.
Change of name.
See NAME CHANGE.
Computers.
Using computer to gather identifying information, §18.2-152.5:1.
Consumer finance companies.
Restrictions on name, §6.2-1504.
Cooperative associations.
Cooperative to be included in name, §13.1-301.
Limitation of use of cooperative in corporate name, §13.1-308.
Coordinate system of Virginia.
Use, §55-295.
Corporations, §§13.1-630 to 13.1-632.
Assumed or fictitious names, §13.1-630.

NAMES —Cont'd
Corporations —Cont'd
Change of name.
Fee for issuing certificate, §13.1-616.
Property title records, §13.1-781.
Distinguishable upon records of state corporation commission, §13.1-630.
Foreign corporations, §13.1-762.
Registered names, §13.1-632.
Indistinguishable name, application for use, §13.1-630.
Fee, §13.1-616.
Requirements for corporate name, §13.1-630.
Reserved name, §13.1-631.
Application fee, §13.1-616.
Special kinds of businesses, language stating or implying, §13.1-630.
Credit unions.
Bylaws to state name, §6.2-1322.
Inclusion of words credit union required, §6.2-1320.
Unlawful use of words credit union, §6.2-1306.
Use in marketing materials or solicitation, §6.2-1307.
Use of name in prohibited manner, §59.1-92.22.
Dentistry practices, §54.1-2718.
Display of name of practitioner, §54.1-2720.
Divorce.
Restoration of former name, §20-121.4.
Recording and indexing, §55-106.1.
Doctor.
Use of title, §54.1-3616.
Dr.
Use of title, §54.1-3616.
Fees.
Corporations.
Change of name, issuing certificate, §13.1-616.
Foreign corporation, registered name.
Filing with commission, §13.1-632.
Indistinguishable name, application for use, §13.1-616.
Reserved name, application, §13.1-616.
Reserved name, notice of transfer, §13.1-616.
Limited liability companies.
Certificate reciting change, §13.1-1005.
Reserved name, application, §13.1-1005.
Reserved name, notice of transfer, §13.1-1005.
Nonprofit corporations.
Change of name, issuing certificate, §13.1-816.
Indistinguishable name.
Application for use, §13.1-816.
Registered name of foreign corporation, §13.1-831.
Reserved name, §13.1-816.
Foreign corporations, §13.1-762.
Registered names, §13.1-632.
Foreign limited partnerships.
Certificate of registration, §50-73.56.
Foreign nonprofit corporations, §13.1-924.
Registered name, §13.1-831.
Horse races.
Pari-mutuel wagering on horses.
Racing under false name, §59.1-402.
Identification of holder of driver's license or permit or vehicle registration card.
Signing name in presence of officer, §46.2-104.
Identity theft, §§18.2-186.3, 18.2-186.3:1, 18.2-186.5.
Industrial development corporation, §13.1-984.
Industrial loan associations.
Requirements as to, §6.2-1402.

NAMES —Cont'd
Industrial loan associations —Cont'd
Use of words bank, banking, savings bank, trust company, etc., §6.2-1402.
Insurance agents, change of name, §38.2-1826.
Insurance companies.
Captive insurers, §38.2-1103.
Reciprocal insurers, §38.2-1205.
Insurance consultants.
Change of name, §38.2-1842.
Joint names, securities registered in, §§13.1-434 to 13.1-436.
Letters of credit.
Change of beneficiary's name, §8.5A-113.
Limited liability companies, §13.1-1012.
Limited partnerships.
Assumed or fictitious names in certificate, §50-73.21.
Distinguishable upon records of commission, §50-73.2.
Requirements, §50-73.2.
Reservation of name, §50-73.3.
Words or abbreviations in certificate, §50-73.2.
Liquid fuels, lubricating oils and similar products sales.
Trade names, §§18.2-226 to 18.2-232.
Middle Peninsula Chesapeake Bay public access authority, §15.2-6607.
Motor vehicle dealers.
Changes in form of ownership, make or name, §46.2-1517.
Mount Vernon.
Name reserved, locality not granted right to use, §15.2-103.
Nonprofit corporations, §§13.1-829 to 13.1-831.
Assumed or fictitious names, §13.1-829.
Change of name.
Fee for issuing certificate, §13.1-816.
Property title records, §13.1-945.
Corporate names, §13.1-829.
Distinguishable upon records of state corporation commission, §13.1-829.
Foreign corporations, §13.1-924.
Indistinguishable name.
Application for use, §13.1-829.
Fees, §13.1-816.
Registered names.
Foreign corporations, §13.1-831.
Reserved name, §13.1-830.
Application fee, §13.1-816.
Notice of transfer.
Fees, §13.1-816.
Northern Neck Chesapeake Bay public access authority, §15.2-6633.
Organizations, registration, alteration, cancellation, §§2.2-411 to 2.2-417.
See REGISTRATION OF NAMES OR INSIGNIA OF ORGANIZATIONS.
Personal information privacy, §§59.1-442 to 59.1-444.
Political action committees.
Use of candidate's name in name of committee, §24.2-949.3.
Professional corporations.
Use of initials P.C. or PC following corporate name, §13.1-544.1.
Professional limited liability companies.
Use of certain initials, §13.1-1104.
Pseudonym, use.
Proceeding anonymously, §8.01-15.1.
Reciprocal insurers, §38.2-1205.

NAMES —Cont'd
Recordation of document requirement, §§17.1-223, 55-106.5.
Recordation of men serving in war.
Circuit court clerks, §§17.1-261 to 17.1-265.
Registered limited liability partnerships, §50-73.133.
Restoration of former name upon divorce, §20-121.4.
Recording and indexing, §55-106.1.
Savings institutions.
Corporate names, §6.2-1116.
Use in marketing materials or solicitation, §6.2-1105.
Use of certain terms prohibited, §6.2-1106.
Securities registered in joint names, §§13.1-434 to 13.1-436.
Sex changes.
Change of name.
Amendments to vital records, §32.1-269.
Solicitation of charitable or civic contributions.
Prohibited acts, §57-57.
Streets, roads and alleys.
Localities may name, §15.2-2019.
Telephone cooperatives.
Limitation on use of words, §56-489.
Trade names.
Liquid fuels, lubricating oils and similar products sales, §§18.2-226 to 18.2-232.
Transacting business under assumed name, §§59.1-69 to 59.1-76.
See TRANSACTING BUSINESS UNDER ASSUMED NAME.
Trust companies.
Unlawful use of name, §6.2-1040.
Use in marketing materials or solicitation, §6.2-1043.
Unauthorized use of name of person, §18.2-216.1.
Utility aggregation cooperatives, §56-231.40.
Articles of incorporation to contain, §56-231.41.
Utility consumer services cooperatives.
Articles of incorporation to contain, §56-231.17.
Change of name.
Amendment to articles of incorporation, §56-231.22.
Other corporations' names not to include certain terms, §56-231.18.
Voter registration.
Notice of change of name of registered voter, §24.2-423.
War servicemen.
Recordation of names of men serving in war.
Circuit court clerks, §§17.1-261 to 17.1-265.

NAMES ON CERTAIN CONTAINERS, §§59.1-93 to 59.1-102.
Appeals, §59.1-99.
Trial on appeal, §59.1-100.
Defined terms.
Person, §59.1-93.
Deposits, §59.1-101.
Description filing and publication, §59.1-94.
Certified copy as evidence, §59.1-95.
Refiling in publication, §59.1-102.
Fees to cover expenses, §59.1-95.1.
Presumptions, §59.1-97.
Prohibited acts, §59.1-96.
Procedure when violation charged, §59.1-98.
Records, §59.1-102.

NASA LANGLEY RESEARCH CENTER.
Motor vehicle license plates.
Special license plates, §46.2-749.81.

NASCAR.
Special license plates.
License plates bearing name, numbers and color schemes used by professional drivers, §46.2-749.69:1.

NATIONAL AFFORDABLE HOUSING ACT OF 1990.
Counties, cities or towns.
Participation in federal development programs, §15.2-956.

NATIONAL AIR AND SPACE MUSEUM.
Special license plates for supporters, §46.2-746.11.

NATIONAL ASSOCIATION OF INSURANCE COMMISSIONERS.
Annual statement to, §38.2-1300.
Information sharing with commission, §38.2-234.
Valuation of investments and other assets, §38.2-1306.2.

NATIONAL AUTOMOBILE DEALERS ASSOCIATION YELLOW OR BLACK BOOKS.
Motor vehicle value, §8.01-419.1.

NATIONAL BASKETBALL ASSOCIATION FRANCHISE.
Hampton Roads sports facility authority, §§15.2-5900 to 15.2-5916.
Virginia Beach arena, §§15.2-5921 to 15.2-5927.
See VIRGINIA BEACH ARENA.

NATIONAL CHANGE OF ADDRESS SYSTEM.
DMV.
Contract with postal service to use, §§46.2-324, 46.2-342, 46.2-416, 46.2-606.

NATIONAL CRIME INFORMATION CENTER.
Criminal justice information system.
Generally, §§9.1-126 to 9.1-137.

NATIONAL CRIME INFORMATION CENTER COMPUTER.
Missing children reports.
Duty of police or sheriff to immediately enter identifying and descriptive data, §15.2-1718.

NATIONAL DEFENSE EXECUTIVE RESERVE.
Leaves of absence for employees of Commonwealth or political subdivisions, §44-204.

NATIONAL DRIVER REGISTER SERVICE.
Drivers' licenses.
Suspension or revocation of driving privileges.
Notification of register by DMV, §46.2-208.

NATIONAL EMISSION STANDARDS FOR HAZARDOUS AIR POLLUTANTS.
Asbestos NESHAP, §§40.1-51.23 to 40.1-51.41.

NATIONAL FOREST PERMITS, §29.1-100.
Hunting, fishing and trapping, §§29.1-408 to 29.1-411.
Multiple-year licenses, §29.1-328.
Terms, §29.1-328.

NATIONAL FORESTS.
ABC mixed beverage license.
Establishments located on Jefferson and George Washington national forests, §4.1-126.

NATIONAL GUARD, §§44-25 to 44-41.1.
Absence without leave.
Annual active duty training, §44-41.1.
Vacation of commissions of officers, §44-33.
Acknowledgments, §§55-113 to 55-115.
Who may perform notarial acts, §55-118.1.
Actions or suits, power to maintain, §44-99.
Active duty.
Annual active duty training, §44-41.
Failure to attend, §44-41.1.
Registration or titling of vehicle.
Nonresident guard members' vehicles registered or titled in another state, §46.2-600.
Regulations generally, §§44-75.1 to 44-84.
Rights and benefits, §44-102.1.
Age requirement, §44-2.
Appointment of officers by governor, §44-27.
Armories generally, §§44-123 to 44-140.
See ARMORIES.
Armory drills, §44-41.
Arms, §44-39.
Exemption from levy and sale, §44-96.
Arrest, exemption from, §44-97.
Privileged from civil arrest, §§8.01-327.1, 8.01-327.2.
Attorneys, employment of special counsel for members sued civilly or criminally prosecuted, §44-100.
Bail and recognizance.
Absence without leave, §44-41.1.
Care of military property, §§44-103 to 44-111.
Carry forward of accrued annual leave.
State employee in organized reserve or national guard, §2.2-1201.
City or town power to aid military units, §15.2-1112.
Colleges and universities.
Dependents of active duty personnel stationed in Virginia.
Domicile for in-state tuition, §23-7.4.
Tuition grants for members, §23-7.4:2.
Commanding officers.
Qualifications, §44-28.
Commissioned officers.
Administration of oath of office and enlistment, §44-32.1.
Administration of oaths in connection with investigations, §44-40.2.
Oath, §44-32.
Commission not to vacate civil office, §44-102.
Commission of officers by governor, §44-27.
Composition, §§44-2, 44-25.
Continuation of membership after discharge or separation from military service of United States, §44-38.
Courts-martial, §§44-42 to 44-54.
Absence without leave, §44-41.1.
Adjutant general, review of judgments, §44-48.
Arrest warrants, powers to issue, §44-47.
Attachment attendance of witnesses.
Enforcement, §44-47.
Certificate on imposition of sentence to fine or imprisonment, §44-51.
Collection of fines, §44-53.
Commitments in carrying out sentences of confinement.
Powers to issue, §44-47.
Confinement imposed by military court.
Where sentence to be executed, §44-49.
Contempt, power to punish for, §44-47.
Disposition of fines, §44-54.

NATIONAL GUARD —Cont'd
Courts-martial —Cont'd
Fines.
Collection, §44-53.
Disposition, §44-54.
Governor, review of judgments.
Dismissal from service or dishonorable discharge, §44-48.
How constituted and powers, §44-42.
Kinds of courts-martial, §44-42.
Manual for courts-martial United States.
Proceedings by, §44-48.
Military judges, §44-46.1.
Process, how executed, §44-50.
Production of books and papers.
Powers, §44-47.
Refusal to be sworn or to answer, sentencing for, §44-47.
Review of judgments, §44-48.
Sentences, how executed, §44-50.
Sentences, where executed, §44-49.
Sheriffs, deputy sheriffs, sergeants or police officers.
Delivery of certificate on sentencing to fine or imprisonment, §44-51.
Execution of processes and sentences, §44-50.
Special courts-martial.
Commissioned officers may not be tried, §44-44.
Convening, §44-44.
Punishment, powers, §44-44.
Subpoenas and subpoenas duces tecum.
Powers to issue, §44-47.
Summary courts-martial.
Convening, §44-45.
Sentencing, powers, §44-45.
Criminal prosecutions under laws of Virginia.
Bar to prosecution under military laws of Virginia, §44-40.
Customs and usage in United States Army, Air Force or Navy, §44-115.
Defense of members sued civilly or criminally prosecuted, §44-100.
Discharge of enlisted persons, §44-37.
Discharge of officers.
Moral character, capacity and general fitness, §44-33.
Discipline, §44-40.
Absence without leave, §44-41.1.
Efficiency board, determination of moral character, capacity and general fitness for service, §44-33.
Elimination of officers, §44-33.
Emergency management assistance compact, §44-146.28:1.
Employment of members, interference with, §44-98.
Enlistment contract and oath, §44-36.
Enlistments, §44-35.
Equipment, §44-39.
Exemption from levy and sale, §44-96.
Examining board to test officers for physical, moral and professional fitness, §44-30.
Execution of process.
Power of governor to summon for, §18.2-410.
Exemption of military property from levy and sale, §44-96.
Federal service, orders inducting into, §§44-114.1 to 44-114.4.
Headquarters, §44-26.
Health insurance.
Rights and benefits on being called to active duty, §44-102.1.

NATIONAL GUARD —Cont'd
Highways.
Failure to yield right-of-way, §46.2-847.
Fine schedule, VA SCt Rule 3B:2.
Prepayment of fine, §16.1-69.40:1.
Immunity for acts done while in discharge of military duty, §44-100.
Impoundment of motor vehicles.
Motor vehicle insurance, suspension at insured's request, §38.2-2205.1.
Inactive duty training, §44-41.
Failure to report, §44-41.1.
Income tax on individuals.
Active or inactive wages and salaries deducted from taxable income, §58.1-322.
Investigations, administration of oaths by commissioned officers, §44-40.2.
Jury duty exemption for active officers and members, §44-94.
Leases of personnel.
Early termination, §55-248.21:1.
Leaves of absence for employees of Commonwealth or political subdivisions, §44-93.
Discrimination in hiring prohibited, §44-93.4.
Penalty for employer failure to comply, §44-93.5.
Reemployment, §44-93.3.
Supplement of military pay and additional life insurance benefits, §44-93.1.
Life and long-term care insurance.
Rights and benefits on being called to active duty, §44-102.1.
Line of duty act, §§9.1-400 to 9.1-408.
Location of units, §44-26.
Mental health and rehabilitation services support program.
Community corrections.
Special treatment procedures, §9.1-173.1.
Establishment by department of veterans services, §2.2-2001.1.
Military laws, persons subject to, §44-40.1.
Militia generally.
See MILITIA.
Motor vehicle registration or title.
Nonresident activated or mobilized guard members.
Vehicles registered or titled in another state, §46.2-600.
Mutual assistance compact, §§44-54.1 to 44-54.3.
Oath of enlistment, §44-36.
Oath of office and enlistment, administration, §44-32.1.
Oath of officers, §44-32.
Oaths, administration by commissioned officers in connection with investigations, §44-40.2.
Organization, §44-25.
Personnel administration system.
Preferences, §2.2-2903.
Persons subject to military laws, §44-40.1.
Powers of officers and soldiers in performance of duty, §44-40.
Presumption of membership upon discharge or separation from military service of United States, §44-38.
Promotion of officers by governor, §44-27.
Public safety medal of valor, §§9.1-800, 9.1-801.
Qualification, §44-2.
Prescribed in National Guard regulations, §44-29.
Rank of officers.
Relative rank, §44-31.

NATIONAL GUARD —Cont'd
Recognizances.
Forfeiture of recognizance while in military service, §19.2-144.
Regulations to prescribe qualifications of officers, §44-29.
Relative rank of officers, §44-31.
Retired list of officers, warrant officers and enlisted persons, §44-119.
Right to own and keep real and personal property, §44-99.
Riot.
Dispersal, duty, §18.2-411.
Immunity of officers quelling, §18.2-412.
Power of governor to summon to preserve peace, §18.2-410.
Second lieutenants.
Appointments, §44-27.
Special license plates, §46.2-744.
Retired members, §46.2-746.5.
Staff officers.
Qualifications, §44-28.
Surplus officers, disbandment of organization.
Disposition, §44-33.
Tests as to physical, moral and professional fitness for officers, §44-30.
Training, §44-40.
Training duty, §44-75.2.
Tuition grants for members, §23-7.4:2.
Uniforms, §44-39.
Exemption from levy and sale, §44-96.
United States property and fiscal officer.
Appointment, designation or detailing by governor, §44-24.
Vacation of commissions of officers upon resignation, §44-33.
Virginia Military Institute.
National guard service required for military scholarship cadets, §23-107.2.
Warrant officers.
Administration of oath of office and enlistment, §44-32.1.
Workers' compensation.
Average weekly wage of member, §65.2-101.
Coverage, §65.2-103.
Employee defined, §65.2-101.

NATIONAL GUARD MUTUAL ASSISTANCE COUNTER DRUG ACTIVITIES COMPACT.
Enactment of compact into law, terms, §44-75.1:1.
Governor's power to provide for national guard to support drug interdiction, §44-75.1.

NATIONAL HOCKEY LEAGUE FRANCHISE.
Hampton Roads sports facility authority, §§15.2-5900 to 15.2-5916.

NATIONAL MEDICAL SUPPORT NOTICE.
Support orders providing health care coverage for dependent children.
Enforcement of coverage by, §63.2-1924.1.

NATIONAL MOTOR VEHICLE TITLE INFORMATION SYSTEM.
Certificate of title, issuance, notification, §46.2-208.

NATIONAL ORIGIN.
Discrimination.
Equal credit opportunities, §§6.2-500 to 6.2-513.
See EQUAL CREDIT OPPORTUNITIES.

NATIONAL ORIGIN —Cont'd
Discrimination —Cont'd
Fair employment contracting act, §§2.2-4200, 2.2-4201.
Human rights act, §§2.2-3900 to 2.2-3903.
Procurement by public bodies, §2.2-4310.
Employment discrimination by contractors, §2.2-4311.

NATIONAL PARKS.
ABC mixed beverage license.
Establishments located on Blue Ridge Parkway property, §4.1-126.
Park police.
Agreements to enforce state and county laws on federal property, §15.2-1729.

NATIONAL RIFLE ASSOCIATION.
Special license plates for supporters, §46.2-749.6.

NATIONAL RIFLE ASSOCIATION FIREARM SAFETY OR TRAINING COURSE.
Carrying concealed weapons permit application.
Demonstration of competence with handgun, §18.2-308.02.
Nonresidents, §18.2-308.06.

NATIONAL SKI PATROL SYSTEMS, INC.
Volunteers.
Immunity of certified volunteers rendering emergency care, §8.01-225.

NATIONAL TEACHER CERTIFICATION INCENTIVE PROGRAM AND FUND, §22.1-299.2.

NATIONAL TOBACCO TRUST.
Directors and officers.
Attorney general, service on board, §2.2-515.
Commissioner of agriculture and consumer services.
Authorized to serve on board of directors, §3.2-104.
Immunity from civil liability for acts taken, §8.01-220.1:4.
Governor, service on board, §2.2-116.

NATIONAL VOTER REGISTRATION ACT.
Commissioner of elections, state coordinator, §24.2-404.1.
Notice of felony convictions.
State board to notify general registrar, §24.2-409.1.
Secretary of state board of elections, state coordinator, §24.2-404.1.
State programs to implement, §§2.2-617, 2.2-618.

NATIVE AMERICANS.
Birth certificates.
Correction of racial classification, §32.1-272.
Fishing license exemption, §29.1-301.
Fur-bearing animals, possession of parts from, §29.1-521.
Fur dealer permit exemptions, §29.1-401.
Hunting license exemption, §29.1-301.
Motor vehicle sales and use tax exemption for tribes living on reservation, §58.1-2403.
Taxation, US Const Art I §2, Amd 14.
Trapping license exemption, §29.1-301.

NATURAL AREA PRESERVES, §§10.1-209 to 10.1-217.
Dedication, §10.1-213.
Defined, §10.1-209.

NATURAL AREA PRESERVES —Cont'd
Definitions, §10.1-209.
Department of conservation and recreation.
Additional powers, §§10.1-210, 10.1-211.
Establishment, §10.1-214.
Fund.
Defined, §10.1-209.
Establishment of fund, §10.1-215.
Gifts, devises and bequests, §10.1-217.
Instrument of dedication.
Defined, §10.1-209.
Islands.
Unappropriated islands which rise from common lands, §28.2-1201.
Natural area.
Defined, §10.1-209.
Natural area registry, §10.1-216.
Natural heritage program, §10.1-212.
Natural heritage resources.
Defined, §10.1-209.
Owner.
Defined, §10.1-209.
Program.
Defined, §10.1-209.
Registry.
Defined, §10.1-209.
System.
Defined, §10.1-209.

NATURAL BRIDGE.
Special license plates, §46.2-749.26.

NATURAL DEATH, §§54.1-2981 to 54.1-2993.
See LIVING WILLS.

NATURAL DISASTERS.
Architects.
Rescue or relief assistance.
Civil immunity for licensed professional architects, §8.01-226.2.
Emergency management and disaster law generally, §§44-146.13 to 44-146.28.
See EMERGENCY MANAGEMENT.
Engineers.
Rescue or relief assistance.
Civil immunity for licensed professional engineers, §8.01-226.2.
Farmer major drought, flood and hurricane disaster assistance, §§3.2-500 to 3.2-506.

NATURAL GAS.
Conservation and ratemaking efficiency, §§56-600 to 56-602.
Alternative rate designs and other mechanisms, §56-601.
Authority given gas utilities, §56-601.
Construction of chapter, §56-601.
Definitions, §56-600.
Generally, §56-601.
Option to file plan, §56-602.
Plans, §56-602.
Revenue-neutral plans, §56-602.
Consumption tax, §§58.1-2904 to 58.1-2907.
Counties.
Natural gas distribution service within any underserved area or county, §15.2-2109.3.
Energy policy of Commonwealth, §§67-102, 67-103.
Mining in proximity to gas and oil wells, §45.1-161.121.
Offshore energy resources, §67-300.
Coastal energy research consortium, §§67-600 to 67-604.

NATURAL GAS —Cont'd
Offshore energy resources —Cont'd
Royalties from offshore natural gas and oil resources, §67-301.
Performance-based regulation of gas utilities, §56-235.6.
Qualified projects of natural gas utilities, §§56-605 to 56-608.
Deferral of costs, §56-607.
Defined terms, §56-605.
Infrastructure development, §56-606.
Investment limit, §56-607.
Transportation and storage contracts, prudent and reasonable, §56-608.
Ratemaking based on performance, §56-235.6.
Retail sales and use tax exemptions.
Machinery or tools used for drilling, extracting, etc., §58.1-609.3.
Retail supply choice for natural gas customers, §56-235.8.
Safety.
Recovery of eligible safety activity costs, §56-235.10.
State corrections board contracts to sell or lease, §53.1-31.
Steps to advance Virginia's energy plan.
Natural gas utilities.
SAVE plans, §§56-603, 56-604.
Strategic facility placed into service.
Recovery of costs through rates charged, §56-235.9.
Virginia energy plan.
Generally, §§67-100 to 67-1003.
See ENERGY.

NATURAL GAS COMPANIES.
Generally.
See GAS COMPANIES.

NATURAL GAS CONSERVATION AND RATEMAKING EFFICIENCY ACT, §§56-600 to 56-602.

NATURAL GAS CONSUMPTION TAX, §§58.1-2904 to 58.1-2907.
Collection and remittance, §58.1-2905.
Imposition of tax, §58.1-2904.
Special regulatory tax, §§58.1-2906, 58.1-2907.

NATURAL GAS EXPLORATION, §§45.1-361.1 to 45.1-361.44.
See GAS AND OIL EXPLORATION.

NATURAL GAS SEVERANCE TAX.
Local license tax on persons engaging in business of severing gases, §§58.1-3712 to 58.1-3713.4.

NATURAL GUARDIAN ACT, §64.2-1700.

NATURAL HISTORY MUSEUM, §§10.1-2000 to 10.1-2012.
See MUSEUM OF NATURAL HISTORY.

NATURALIZATION.
Constitutional provisions, US Const Art I §§8, 9.

NATURAL RESOURCES.
Abandoned mine reclamation, §§45.1-260 to 45.1-270.
See COAL SURFACE MINING.
Beach conservation and development, §§10.1-705 to 10.1-711.
Chesapeake Bay preservation, §§62.1-44.15:67 to 62.1-44.15:79.

NATURAL RESOURCES —Cont'd
Coal surface mining, §§45.1-226 to 45.1-270.7.
See COAL SURFACE MINING.
Conservation as policy of state, VA Const Art XI §1.
Development or utilization, VA Const Art XI §2.
Erosion and sediment control, §§62.1-44.15:51 to 62.1-44.15:66.
Forest fires generally, §§10.1-1135 to 10.1-1150.
See FOREST WARDENS AND FIRES.
Forest management of state-owned lands fund, §§10.1-1120 to 10.1-1123.
Forest protection for cities and counties, §§10.1-1124 to 10.1-1130.
See FOREST PROTECTION FOR CITIES AND COUNTIES.
Forestry services for landowners, §§10.1-1131 to 10.1-1134.
See FORESTRY SERVICES FOR LANDOWNERS.
Gas and oil exploration, §§45.1-361.1 to 45.1-361.44.
See GAS AND OIL EXPLORATION.
Natural area preserves, §§10.1-209 to 10.1-217.
Open space land act, §§10.1-1700 to 10.1-1705.
See OPEN-SPACE LAND.
Parks and recreation generally.
See PARKS AND RECREATION.
Principal and income.
Allocations to principal and income, §64.2-1019.
Reforestation of timberlands, §§10.1-1170 to 10.1-1176.
Scenic rivers, §§10.1-400 to 10.1-418.8.
See SCENIC RIVERS.
Shore erosion control, §§10.1-700 to 10.1-704.
Soil and water conservation districts, §§10.1-506 to 10.1-559.
See SOIL AND WATER CONSERVATION DISTRICTS.
Waters of the state.
See WATERS OF THE STATE.
Wetlands generally, §§28.2-1300 to 28.2-1320.
See WETLANDS.

NATURAL RESOURCES, SECRETARY OF, §§2.2-200 to 2.2-202, 2.2-215 to 2.2-220.3.
Chesapeake Bay preservation, §§62.1-44.15:67 to 62.1-44.15:79.
Oil and gas drilling in Tidewater Virginia.
Report assessing environmental risk, §62.1-195.1.
Spill response council.
Reports, §62.1-44.34:28.
Selection of members, §62.1-44.34:25.
Water quality information provided citizens of Commonwealth.
Lead secretary to ensure, §2.2-216.

NATUROPATHY.
Healing arts.
Exemption of persons licensed to practice, §54.1-2901.

NAUTICAL SCHOOL.
Virginia Polytechnic Institute and State University, §§23-142 to 23-146.

NAVAL CRIMINAL INVESTIGATION SERVICE.
Carrying concealed weapons by law-enforcement agents, §18.2-308.

NAVAL MILITIA, §§44-55 to 44-66.
Acknowledgments, §§55-113 to 55-115.
Who may perform notarial acts, §55-118.1.

NAVAL MILITIA —Cont'd
Actions or suits, power to maintain, §44-99.
Active duties.
Regulations generally, §§44-75.1 to 44-84.
Time of war or national emergency.
Relief from service or duty in naval militia, §44-63.
Age requirement, §44-3.
Armories generally, §§44-123 to 44-140.
See ARMORIES.
Arms, §44-57.
Exemption from levy and sale, §44-96.
Arrest, exemption from, §44-97.
Privileged from civil arrest, §§8.01-327.1, 8.01-327.2.
Attorneys, employment of special counsel to defend member sued civilly or criminally prosecuted, §44-100.
Care of military property, §§44-103 to 44-111.
Commander in chief, governor, §44-60.
Command of senior officer when in field or afloat upon actual service, §44-60.
Composition, §§44-2, 44-55.
Courts-martial, §§44-67 to 44-74.
Arrest warrants, powers to issue, §44-70.
Confinement in lieu of fine, §44-72.
Deck courts.
Punishment, powers of, §44-69.
Dishonorable discharge, §44-73.
Dismissal from service, §44-73.
Disposition of fine, §44-74.
General courts-martial.
Punishment, powers of, §44-69.
Jurisdiction, §44-68.
Procedure, §44-68.
Processes, execution, §44-71.
Punishment, §44-69.
Subpoenas, powers to issue, §44-70.
Summary courts-martial.
Punishment, powers of, §44-69.
Summons, execution, §44-71.
Types of, §44-67.
Courts of, §44-66.
Defense of member sued civilly or criminally prosecuted, §44-100.
Disbandment, §44-62.
Discipline, §44-61.
Subject to military discipline of United States Army, Air Force or Navy, §44-115.
Efficiency in naval militia, §44-63.
Employment of members, interference with, §44-98.
Equipment, §44-57.
Exemption from levy and sale, §44-96.
Exemption of uniforms, arms and equipment from levy and sale, §44-96.
Federal service, orders inducting into, §§44-114.1 to 44-114.4.
Immunity for acts done while in discharge of military duty, §44-100.
Interpretation of state laws governing naval militia.
United States laws concerning United States Navy to be followed, §44-65.
Jury duty exemption for active officers and members, §44-94.
Leaves of absence for employees of Commonwealth or political subdivisions, §44-93.
Discrimination in hiring prohibited, §44-93.4.
Penalty for employer failure to comply, §44-93.5.

NAVAL MILITIA —Cont'd
Leaves of absence for employees of Commonwealth or political subdivisions —Cont'd
Reemployment, §44-93.3.
Supplement of military pay and additional life insurance benefits, §44-93.1.
Membership in other military or naval organizations, §44-59.
Naval reserve, §44-62.
Oath of officers and enlisted persons, §44-64.
Organization, §44-56.
Other naval or military organizations, membership in, §44-59.
Precedence of officers, §44-58.
Qualifications, §§44-3, 44-55.
Recognizances.
Forfeiture of recognizance while in naval service, §19.2-144.
Regulations governing precedence of officers, §44-58.
Regulations of United States naval reserve to govern matters, §44-56.
Relief from service or duty in naval militia, §44-63.
Right to own and keep real and personal property, §44-99.
Senior officer to command.
When in field or afloat upon actual service, §44-60.
Uniforms.
Exemption from levy and sale, §44-96.
United States laws concerning United States Navy to be followed, §44-65.
United States Navy and Marine Corps, discipline prescribed for, §44-61.
Workers' compensation.
Average weekly wage of member, §65.2-101.
Employee defined, §65.2-101.

NAVIGABLE WATERS.
Dam construction across navigable streams.
Certain localities permitted, §15.2-2142.
General assembly power to declare stream navigable, VA Const Art IV §14.
Improvement of stream navigability, §§62.1-155 to 62.1-158.
Solid waste or medical waste transported by ship, barge or other vessel, §10.1-1454.1.

NAVIGATION AIDS.
Protection of, §§62.1-187 to 62.1-189.

NAVIGATORS.
Health insurance.
Definitions, §38.2-3455.
Prohibited activities, §38.2-3456.

NAVY CROSS RECIPIENTS.
Special license plates, §46.2-742.2.

NECESSARIES, DOCTRINE OF, §55-37.

NEEDLES.
Disposal, §54.1-3469.
Driving while intoxicated.
Chemical tests of blood.
Reuse of single-use-only needles or syringes, §18.2-268.5.
Drug paraphernalia, §§18.2-265.1 to 18.2-265.5.
Possession and distribution of controlled paraphernalia, §§54.1-3466 to 54.1-3468.
Storage, §54.1-3469.

NEGLECT OF AGED OR INCAPACITATED ADULTS.
Adult protective services, §§63.2-1603 to 63.2-1610.

NEGLECT OF CHILDREN.
Generally, §§63.2-1500 to 63.2-1527.
See CHILD ABUSE AND NEGLECT.

NEGLECT OF DUTY.
Election officers, electoral board members, etc., §24.2-1001.
Impeachment of appointed or elected officers, VA Const Art IV §17.
Removal of public officer from office, §24.2-233.
Governor's power to remove, §2.2-108.
Statute of limitations.
Criminal prosecutions, §19.2-8.

NEGLIGENCE.
Air carriers.
Certificate or permit holder not relieved of liability for negligence, §5.1-144.
Assumption of risk.
Bicycle helmet ordinance violations not considered, §46.2-906.1.
Hunting gear.
Blaze orange clothing requirement, §29.1-530.1.
Railroad employees, injuries to, §8.01-59.
Workers' compensation.
Compliance filing violations, §65.2-805.
Rejection of coverage.
Employer defenses, §65.2-300.
Attorney liability to client, §54.1-3906.
Loss of debts or money, §64.2-1415.
Bank deposits and collections.
Unauthorized signature or alteration, §8.4-406.
Bicycle helmet ordinance violations not considered, §46.2-906.1.
Child labor.
Cruelty and injuries to children, §40.1-103.
Circuit courts.
Allegations of negligence, VA SCt Rule 3:18.
Claims against the United States.
Medical services provided by federal government, §8.01-37.1.
Comparative negligence.
Bank deposits and collections.
Unauthorized signature or alteration, §8.4-406.
Negotiable instruments.
Forged or altered instrument, §§8.3A-405, 8.3A-406.
Compromise of claims.
Persons with disability, §8.01-424.
Construction contract indemnification provisions, void, §§11-4.1, 11-4.4.
Contributory negligence.
See CONTRIBUTORY NEGLIGENCE.
Credit services businesses.
Liability to consumers, §59.1-335.10.
Damages generally.
See DAMAGES.
Death by wrongful act, §§8.01-50 to 8.01-56.
Dram shop liability not in Virginia, §4.1-304.
Driving while intoxicated.
Chemical tests of blood.
Withdrawing of blood samples, §18.2-268.5.
Dry cleaners.
Loss or injury to clothing, §8.01-42.
Dyeing clothing.
Loss or injury to clothing, §8.01-42.

NEGLIGENCE —Cont'd
Employers of persons with disabilities.
Hiring liability, §51.5-41.
Family purpose doctrine.
Parental liability for damage by minor child, §§8.01-43, 8.01-44.
Fiduciaries.
Loss of debts or money, §64.2-1415.
Fire damaging property, carelessly damaging, §18.2-88.
Fishing, landowner's duty of care, §29.1-509.
Gross negligence.
Athletic team physicians, §8.01-225.1.
County, city or town liability in operating recreational facilities.
Agreements with landowners, §29.1-509.
Disease reporting, §32.1-38.
Health care professional rendering services to clinic patients, §54.1-106.
HIV test confidentiality, §32.1-36.1.
Nonprofit crime information-gathering organizations, §8.01-226.3.
Rescue or relief assistance.
Licensed professional engineers and architects, §8.01-226.2.
Sports team physicians, §8.01-225.1.
Teachers.
Withdrawal of civil immunity, §8.01-220.1:2.
Vaccine-related injury or death, §8.01-44.2.
Health care professionals rendering service to clinic patients.
Liability exemption, §54.1-106.
Hold harmless clauses in construction contracts, void, §§11-4.1, 11-4.4.
Hospitals.
Charitable or tax exempt institutions, liability, §8.01-38.
Hotels.
Liability of guests for hotel damage, §8.01-42.2.
Loss or injury to clothing.
Delivered for dyeing, dry cleaning or laundering, §8.01-42.
Hunting and fishing, §29.1-509.
Blaze orange clothing requirement, §29.1-530.1.
Landowners' duty of care, §29.1-509.
Law enforcement officers, §8.01-226.
Indemnification provisions in construction contracts, void, §§11-4.1, 11-4.4.
Indemnification provisions in motor carrier transportation contracts, void, §11-4.5.
John Doe actions.
Owner or operator of vehicle causing injury or damage unknown, §38.2-2206.
Laundries.
Loss or injury to clothing, §8.01-42.
Lien for expenses of treatment.
Person's negligence causing injury, §8.01-66.2.
Limitation of actions, §8.01-243.
Accrual of right of action, §8.01-230.
Medical malpractice.
General provisions, §§8.01-581.1 to 8.01-581.20.
See MEDICAL MALPRACTICE.
Medical malpractice review panels.
Standard of care in proceedings, §8.01-581.20.
Medical services lien.
Lien against person whose negligence caused injury, §8.01-66.2.
Moped safety equipment violations not considered, §46.2-915.2.
Motor carriers, passengers.
Excursion trains.
Assignment of liability, §46.2-2099.42.

NEGLIGENCE —Cont'd
Motor carriers, passengers —Cont'd
Provisions not to relieve licensees, permittees or certificate holders from liability, §46.2-2011.17.
Motor carriers, property.
Compliance with chapter.
Effect on liability of licensee, permittee or certificate holder, §46.2-2126.
Indemnification provisions in motor carrier transportation contracts.
Certain provisions void, §11-4.5.
Motor carrier transportation contract indemnification provisions, void, §11-4.5.
Motor vehicle accidents.
Generally, §§8.01-63 to 8.01-66.1.
Negotiable instruments.
Forged signature or alteration of instrument.
Liability for negligence contributing to, §8.3A-406.
Oil discharges.
Good Samaritan liability for assistance in containment and cleanup, §62.1-44.34:18.
Penalties, §62.1-44.34:20.
Overhead high voltage line safety.
Application of provisions, §59.1-414.
Parental liability for minor child, §§8.01-43, 8.01-44.
Minor operating vehicle, §§8.01-64, 8.01-65.
Partnerships.
Liability of partnership for partner's actionable conduct, §50-73.95.
Persons with disability.
Compromise of claims, §8.01-424.
Pharmacists.
Dispensing drugs without safety closure containers, §54.1-3427.
Premises liability.
Firefighters, §8.01-226.
Prescribed burning.
Liability of owner or agent for negligent or improper conduct, §10.1-1150.5.
Preservation of right of action.
Violation of statutory duty, §8.01-221.
Public utilities.
Underground utility line damage prevention.
Liability of operators and excavators, §56-265.25.
Railroad corporations.
Employee injuries.
Liability for, §56-441.
Enclosed tracks.
Liability for injury on, §56-431.
Fires set by engines or trains, §56-428.
Injuries to employees, §§8.01-57 to 8.01-62.
See RAILROADS.
Non-enclosed tracks.
Liability for injuries, §56-432.
Recreational activities.
Landowners' duty of care, §29.1-509.
Rescission of release of liability in personal injury action or claim.
Release executed as condition of settlement, §8.01-425.1.
Right of action.
Violation of statutory duty, §8.01-221.
Security freezes.
Consumer credit reports.
Noncompliance with law, §59.1-444.2.
Settlement of claims.
Persons with disability, §8.01-424.

NEGLIGENCE —Cont'd
Sexual sterilization, §54.1-2979.
Space flight activities liability and immunity.
Limitation of immunity of space flight entity, §8.01-227.9.
Statute of limitations, §8.01-243.
Accrual of right of action, §8.01-230.
Subsequent remedial measures.
Inadmissible to prove negligence, §8.01-418.1.
Teachers.
Gross negligence.
Withdrawal of civil immunity, §8.01-220.1:2.
Trapping.
Landowners' duty of care, §29.1-509.
Underground utility line damage prevention.
Liability of operators and excavators, §56-265.25.
Vaccine-related injury or death.
Action for gross negligence, §8.01-44.2.
Verbal statements by injured persons.
Furnishing copies of transcription to declarant, §8.01-417.
Veterinarians.
Rendering services without charge, §54.1-3811.
Vicarious liability.
Parental liability for minor child, §§8.01-43, 8.01-44.
Minor operating vehicle, §§8.01-64, 8.01-65.
Wanton negligence.
County, city or town liability in operating recreational facilities.
Agreements with landowners, §29.1-509.
Watercraft, personal.
Operation restriction violations, §29.1-748.
Winter sports safety act.
Liability of operator, §8.01-227.20.
Failure to fulfill duty not negligence per se, §8.01-227.22.
Workers' compensation.
Compliance filing violations, §65.2-805.
Generally, §§65.2-100 to 65.2-1310.
See WORKERS' COMPENSATION.
Rejection of provisions.
Employer defenses, §65.2-300.
Written statements by injured person to declarant, §8.01-417.
Wrongful death.
General provisions, §§8.01-50 to 8.01-56.
See WRONGFUL DEATH.

NEGLIGENCE PER SE.
Motor vehicle safety belts.
Failure to use child restraint devices, §46.2-1098.
Riding animals on highways after sunset, §46.2-800.1.
Towing trailer on highway.
Occupancy prohibited, §46.2-813.
Violation of statutory duty.
Right to recover damages, §8.01-221.

NEGLIGENT HOMICIDE.
Driver license compact.
Statutes and ordinances deemed to cover offense, §46.2-487.

NEGOTIABLE INSTRUMENTS, §§8.3A-101 to 8.3A-605.
Acceptor.
Defined, §8.3A-103.
Obligation.
Liability, §8.3A-413.
Accommodation party.
Discharge of accommodation parties, §8.3A-605.

NEGOTIABLE INSTRUMENTS —Cont'd
Accommodation party —Cont'd
Instrument signed for accommodation.
Liability, §8.3A-419.
Accord and satisfaction.
By use of instrument, §8.3A-311.
Agency.
Deposit of checks to personal account, §6.2-897.
Alteration.
Defined, §8.3A-407.
Liability for negligence contributing to, §8.3A-406.
Applicability of article, §8.3A-102.
As originally drawn, defined, §8.3A-413.
Assignments.
False assignment, §6.2-943.
Bills of lading, §8.7-104.
Breach of fiduciary duty.
Notice, §8.3A-307.
Cancellation.
Discharge by cancellation, §8.3A-604.
Cashier's check.
Defined, §8.3A-104.
Effect on obligation for which taken, §8.3A-310.
Lost, destroyed or stolen, §8.3A-312.
Obligation of issuer.
Liability, §8.3A-412.
Refusal to pay.
Liability, §8.3A-411.
Certificate of deposit.
Defined, §8.3A-104.
Certified checks.
Acceptance.
Liability, §8.3A-409.
Defined, §8.3A-409.
Effect on obligation for which taken, §8.3A-310.
False certification, §6.2-942.
Lost, destroyed or stolen, §8.3A-312.
Refusal to pay.
Liability, §8.3A-411.
Checks.
Bad checks.
See BAD CHECKS.
Defined, §§8.3A-104, 8.3A-312.
Deposit by fiduciary or agent to personal account, §6.2-897.
Dishonor.
Rules governing, §8.3A-502.
Effect on obligation for which taken, §8.3A-310.
False certification of check, §6.2-942.
Minors, §6.2-896.
Citation of title, §8.3A-101.
Claimant.
Defined, §8.3A-312.
Claims.
Claimant, defined, §8.3A-312.
Person taking instrument, §8.3A-306.
Recoupment, §8.3A-305.
Comparative negligence.
Forged signature or alteration of instrument, §8.3A-406.
Conflict of laws, §8.3A-102.
Consideration.
Defined, §8.3A-303.
Contradictory terms of instrument, §8.3A-114.
Contribution.
Joint and several liability, §8.3A-116.
Contributory negligence.
Forged signature or alteration of instrument, §8.3A-406.
Conversion of instrument.
Liability, §8.3A-420.

NEGOTIABLE INSTRUMENTS —Cont'd
Criminal procedure.
Disposition of money, securities or documents seized upon arrest, etc., §19.2-270.2.
Date of instrument, §8.3A-113.
Deceased persons, validity of writing payable to, §11-9.
Declaration of loss.
Defined, §8.3A-312.
Defenses.
Recoupment, §8.3A-305.
Definitions, §8.3A-103.
Acceptance, §8.3A-409.
Alteration, §8.3A-407.
As originally drawn, §8.3A-413.
Certified check, §8.3A-409.
Check, §§8.3A-104, 8.3A-312.
Claimant, §8.3A-312.
Consideration, §8.3A-303.
Declaration of loss, §8.3A-312.
Employee, §8.3A-405.
Fiduciary, §8.3A-307.
Fraudulent indorsement, §8.3A-405.
Holder in due course, §8.3A-302.
Index of definitions, §8.3A-103.
Negotiation, §8.3A-201.
Obligated bank, §§8.3A-312, 8.3A-411.
Payable at a definite time, §8.3A-108.
Payable on demand, §8.3A-108.
Person entitled to enforce, §8.3A-301.
Presentment, §8.3A-501.
Represented person, §8.3A-307.
Responsibility, §8.3A-405.
Without recourse, §8.3A-415.
Destroyed instrument, §8.3A-309.
Discharge of obligation.
Accommodation parties, §8.3A-605.
Cancellation, §8.3A-604.
Effect, §8.3A-601.
Indorsers, §8.3A-605.
Renunciation, §8.3A-604.
Dishonor.
Evidence of dishonor, §8.3A-505.
Notice of dishonor.
Evidence of, §8.3A-505.
Excused presentment, §8.3A-504.
How given, §8.3A-503.
Protest.
Defined, §8.3A-505.
Rules governing, §8.3A-502.
Presumption of, §8.3A-505.
Protest.
Defined, §8.3A-505.
Rules governing, §8.3A-502.
Special provisions, §8.3A-502.
Documents of title, §8.7-104.
Drafts.
Acceptance.
Acceptance varying draft.
Liability, §8.3A-410.
Liability, §8.3A-409.
Defined, §8.3A-104.
Dishonor.
Rules governing, §8.3A-502.
False assignment, §6.2-943.
Power of banks to negotiate, §6.2-814.
Unaccepted draft.
Drawee liability on, §8.3A-408.
Drawee.
Defined, §8.3A-103.
Liability on unaccepted draft, §8.3A-408.

NEGOTIABLE INSTRUMENTS —Cont'd
Drawer.
Defined, §8.3A-103.
Obligation.
Liability, §8.3A-414.
Educational facilities authority.
Issuance of negotiable notes, §23-30.46.
Electronic transactions.
Instruments for which electronically filed document not acceptable, §17.1-258.6.
Transferable records, §59.1-494.
Embezzlement, §6.2-943.
Employee.
Defined, §8.3A-405.
Fraudulent indorsement.
Employer's responsibility for, §8.3A-405.
Erroneous acceptance, §8.3A-418.
Evidence.
Disposition of money, securities or documents seized upon arrest, etc., §19.2-270.2.
Notice of dishonor, §8.3A-505.
Parol evidence.
Other agreements affecting instrument, §8.3A-117.
Excused presentment.
Notice of dishonor, §8.3A-504.
False pretenses and cheats.
False assignment, §6.2-943.
False certification of check, §6.2-942.
Fictitious payees.
Liability, §8.3A-404.
Fiduciaries.
Breach of fiduciary duty.
Notice of, §8.3A-307.
Defined, §8.3A-307.
Foreign money.
Instrument payable in, §8.3A-107.
Fraud and deceit.
Employee's fraudulent indorsement.
Employer's responsibility for, §8.3A-405.
False assignment, §6.2-943.
False certification of check, §6.2-942.
Fictitious payees, §8.3A-404.
Forged signature or alteration of instrument.
Liability for negligence contributing to, §8.3A-406.
Impostors, §8.3A-404.
Unauthorized signature.
Liability, §8.3A-403.
Funds transfers.
General provisions, §§8.4A-101 to 8.4A-507.
See FUNDS TRANSFERS.
General provisions of commercial code, §§8.1A-101 to 8.1A-310.
See COMMERCIAL CODE.
Good faith.
Defined, §8.3A-103.
Holder in due course.
Defined, §8.3A-302.
Proof of signatures and status as, §8.3A-308.
Signatures and status.
Proof of, §8.3A-308.
Special provisions, §8.3A-302.
Identification of person to whom instrument payable, §8.3A-110.
Impostors.
Liability, §8.3A-404.
Incomplete instrument.
Defined, §8.3A-115.
Indorsement.
Anomalous indorsement, §8.3A-205.

NEGOTIABLE INSTRUMENTS —Cont'd
Indorsement —Cont'd
Blank indorsement, §8.3A-205.
Defined, §8.3A-204.
Employee.
Fraudulent indorsement.
Employer's responsibility for, §8.3A-405.
Restrictive indorsement, §8.3A-206.
Special indorsement, §8.3A-205.
Without recourse.
Obligation of indorser, §8.3A-415.
Indorser.
Discharge of indorsers, §8.3A-605.
Joint and several liability, §8.3A-116.
Obligation of indorser, §8.3A-415.
Instrument.
Accord and satisfaction.
By use of instrument, §8.3A-311.
Alteration of instrument.
Liability for negligence contributing to, §8.3A-406.
Claims to an instrument, §8.3A-306.
Contradictory terms of instrument, §8.3A-114.
Date of, §8.3A-113.
Effect on obligation for which taken, §8.3A-310.
Identification of person to whom payable, §8.3A-110.
Incomplete instrument.
Defined, §8.3A-115.
Issue of, §8.3A-105.
Lost, destroyed or stolen, §8.3A-309.
Other agreements affecting instrument, §8.3A-117.
Overdue instrument, §8.3A-304.
Payable in foreign money, §8.3A-107.
Person entitled to enforce.
Defined, §8.3A-301.
Place of payment, §8.3A-111.
Reacquisition, §8.3A-207.
Stolen instrument.
Payment, §8.3A-602.
Transfer of instrument.
Value and consideration, §8.3A-303.
Interest.
Instrument not payable with interest, §8.3A-112.
Interest-bearing instrument.
Date on which payable, §8.3A-112.
Judgment entered for sum due, §8.01-382.
Issue.
Defined, §8.3A-105.
Issuer.
Defined, §8.3A-105.
Joint and several liability, §8.3A-116.
Lease-purchase agreements.
Prohibited practices, §59.1-207.22.
Liability.
Contribution, §8.3A-116.
Joint and several liability, §8.3A-116.
Limitation of actions, §8.3A-118.
Deposit accounts and certificates of deposit, §8.3A-118.1.
Lost instrument, §8.3A-309.
Maker.
Defined, §8.3A-103.
Minors.
Checks, §6.2-896.
Mistake.
Payment or acceptance by mistake, §8.3A-418.
Money orders.
Money order sellers and money transmitters, §§6.2-1900 to 6.2-1921.
See MONEY ORDERS.

NEGOTIABLE INSTRUMENTS —Cont'd
Money orders —Cont'd
Sales.
See MONEY ORDERS.
Negligence.
Forged signature or alteration of instrument.
Liability for negligence contributing to, §8.3A-406.
Negotiation.
Defined, §8.3A-201.
Power of banks, §6.2-814.
Rescission, §8.3A-202.
Transfer of instrument, §8.3A-201.
Rights acquired by transfer, §8.3A-203.
Notes.
Defined, §8.3A-104.
Dishonor.
Rules governing, §8.3A-502.
Effect on obligation for which taken, §8.3A-310.
Obligation of issuer.
Liability, §8.3A-412.
Notice.
Third party.
Written notice.
Right to defend action, §8.3A-119.
Obligated bank.
Defined, §§8.3A-312, 8.3A-411.
Wrongful refusal to pay negotiable instrument.
Liability, §8.3A-411.
Order.
Defined, §8.3A-103.
Payable at definite time.
Defined, §8.3A-108.
Payable on demand.
Defined, §8.3A-108.
Payable to bearer or to order.
Defined, §8.3A-109.
Unconditional order.
Defined, §8.3A-106.
Ordinary care.
Defined, §8.3A-103.
Overdue instrument, §8.3A-304.
Parties.
Defined, §8.3A-103.
Payment by mistake, §8.3A-418.
Payment of obligation, §8.3A-602.
Tender of payment, §8.3A-603.
Place of payment of instrument, §8.3A-111.
Port authority.
Bond issues.
Characteristics, §62.1-140.
Presentment.
Defined, §8.3A-501.
Excused presentment, §8.3A-504.
Notice of dishonor, §8.3A-504.
Rules governing dishonor, §8.3A-501.
Warranties, §8.3A-417.
Presumptions.
Incomplete instrument, §8.3A-115.
Notice of dishonor, §8.3A-505.
Power of banks to negotiate, §6.2-814.
Promise.
Defined, §8.3A-103.
Payable at definite time.
Defined, §8.3A-108.
Payable on demand.
Defined, §8.3A-108.
Payable to bearer or to order.
Defined, §8.3A-109.
Unconditional promise.
Defined, §8.3A-106.

NEGOTIABLE INSTRUMENTS —Cont'd
Protest.
Defined, §8.3A-505.
Prove.
Defined, §8.3A-103.
Public finance act.
All bonds, §15.2-2615.
Reacquisition of instrument, §8.3A-207.
Recoupment.
Defenses and claims in recoupment, §8.3A-305.
Remitter.
Defined, §8.3A-103.
Renunciation.
Discharge by renunciation, §8.3A-604.
Represented person.
Defined, §8.3A-307.
Return of instrument following payment, §8.3A-602.
Scope of article, §8.3A-102.
Short title, §8.3A-101.
Signatures.
Forged signature.
Liability for negligence contributing to, §8.3A-406.
Person liable on instrument, §8.3A-401.
Representative signature.
Liability, §8.3A-402.
Unauthorized signature.
Liability, §8.3A-403.
Small estates.
Payment or delivery of small asset by affidavit, power of successor to indorse or negotiate, §64.2-601.
Statute of limitations, §8.3A-118.
Deposit accounts and certificates of deposit, §8.3A-118.1.
Stolen instrument, §8.3A-309.
Teller's check.
Defined, §8.3A-104.
Effect on obligation for which taken, §8.3A-310.
Lost, destroyed or stolen, §8.3A-312.
Refusal to pay.
Liability, §8.3A-411.
Tender of payment, §8.3A-603.
Third parties.
Notice of right to defend action, §8.3A-119.
Threats and threatening letters, §18.2-59.
Title of article, §8.3A-101.
Transfer of instrument.
Negotiation, §8.3A-201.
Reacquisition, §8.3A-207.
Rights acquired, §8.3A-203.
Value and consideration, §8.3A-303.
Warranties, §8.3A-416.
Traveler's check.
Defined, §8.3A-104.
Unauthorized signature.
Liability, §8.3A-403.
Warranties.
Presentment warranties, §8.3A-417.
Transfer warranties, §8.3A-416.

NEIGHBORHOOD ASSISTANCE ACT.
Tax credit, §§58.1-439.18 to 58.1-439.24.
Amount of credits, §§58.1-439.20, 58.1-439.21.
Individuals, §58.1-439.24.
Carry over, §58.1-439.21.
Individuals, §58.1-439.24.
Contracting services.
Donation of, §58.1-439.23.

NEIGHBORHOOD ASSISTANCE ACT —Cont'd
Tax credit —Cont'd
Definitions, §58.1-439.18.
Individual, §58.1-439.24.
Individuals.
Donations by, §58.1-439.24.
Professional services.
Donation of, §58.1-439.22.
Proposals, §58.1-439.20.
Public policy, §58.1-439.19.

NEIGHBORHOOD WATCH GROUPS.
Freedom of information act.
Criminal records not disclosed, §2.2-3706.
Patrol vehicles.
Flashing amber warning lights, §46.2-1025.

NELSON COUNTY.
Blue Ridge regional tourism council, §§2.2-2609, 2.2-2610.
Confederate cemeteries and graves.
Disbursement of funds appropriated for upkeep, §10.1-2211.
Dirt and gravel roads.
Maximum speed limits on nonsurface treated highways, §46.2-873.1.
Minerals.
Presumed to exist in certain lands, §55-154.
Suits to extinguish claim or right, §55-155.
Revolutionary war cemeteries and graves.
Disbursement of funds appropriated for upkeep, §10.1-2211.1.
School board.
Fingerprinting applicants for employment, §22.1-296.2.
Salary of members, §22.1-32.
Transient occupancy tax.
Condominiums, apartments townhouses or like rental buildings.
Authority to levy, rate, designation of revenues, §58.1-3821.
Disposition of revenues, §58.1-3819.

NEONATAL INJURY.
Birth-related neurological injury compensation, §§38.2-5000 to 38.2-5021.
See BIRTH-RELATED NEUROLOGICAL INJURY COMPENSATION; INSURANCE.

NEPOTISM.
General registrar's appointment, §24.2-110.
Appointment of assistants, §24.2-112.
Local school boards.
Employment of family members or relatives, §2.2-3119.
Procurement transactions by public employees.
Prohibited participation, §2.2-4369.

NETS TO TAKE MENHADEN, §§28.2-400 to 28.2-411.
Closure of Chesapeake Bay purse seine fishery for Atlantic menhaden, §28.2-1000.2.

NETWORKING OF PUBLIC LIBRARIES, §§42.1-32.1 to 42.1-32.6.

NETWORKS.
Computer crimes, §§18.2-152.1 to 18.2-152.15.
See COMPUTER CRIMES.
Individual health insurance coverage.
Failure of in-network provider to submit claims.
Liability of patient for unbilled health care services, §8.01-27.5.

NETWORKS —Cont'd
Individual health insurance coverage —Cont'd
Network plans, §38.2-3430.4.
Property capable of embezzlement, §18.2-152.8.

NEUROLOGICAL INJURY.
Birth-related neurological injury compensation, §§38.2-5000 to 38.2-5021.
See BIRTH-RELATED NEUROLOGICAL INJURY COMPENSATION; INSURANCE.

NEUTERING DOGS AND CATS, §§3.2-6574 to 3.2-6580.

NEWBORNS.
Birth-related neurological injury compensation, §§38.2-5000 to 38.2-5021.
See BIRTH-RELATED NEUROLOGICAL INJURY COMPENSATION.
Blood samples.
Hospitals to offer to obtain blood sample from newborn infants and provide to mother, §32.1-134.02.
Death shortly after birth.
Family compensation, §38.2-5009.1.
Health insurance coverage, §38.2-3411.
Hearing screenings.
Medical assistance services plans, §32.1-325.
Postpartum services insurance coverage, §38.2-3414.1.
Medical assistance services plans, §32.1-325.
Virginia immunization information system (VIIS).
Linkages to other databases containing certain health records.
Newborn screenings, §32.1-46.01.

NEW COLLEGE INSTITUTE, §§23-231.30 to 23-231.36.
Board of directors.
Creation and membership, §23-231.31.
Curriculum development, §23-231.33.
Powers and duties, §23-231.32.
Real property, powers as to, §23-231.34.
Cooperation with other agencies, §23-231.36.
Creation, §23-231.30.
Curriculum, §23-231.33.
Duties, §23-231.30.
Employees.
Personnel administration system, exemptions, §2.2-2905.
Executive director, §23-231.35.
Gifts, grants and donations, §23-231.36.
Purpose, §23-231.30.

NEW HOME BUYERS.
Planned development units.
County requiring information to prospective buyers, §15.2-1216.

NEW HOME WARRANTIES, §55-70.1.

NEW KENT COUNTY.
Coastal primary sand dunes and beaches.
Zoning ordinances, §28.2-1403.
Development agreements, §15.2-2303.1.
Middle Peninsula regional airport authority, 1997 ch 871.
Port of Virginia economic and infrastructure development zone grant fund, §62.1-132.3:2.
School board.
Fingerprinting applicants for employment, §22.1-296.2.
Salary of members, §22.1-32.

NEW KENT COUNTY —Cont'd
Water and sewage systems.
Lien for charges and taxes imposed, §15.2-2118.

NEW LONDON ACADEMY.
Public school funds.
Handling funds of joint school, §22.1-118.

NEWLY DISCOVERED EVIDENCE.
Criminal procedure.
Motion for scientific analysis, §19.2-327.1.
Writ of actual innocence, §§19.2-327.2 to 19.2-327.6, VA SCt Rule 5:7B.
Form, VA SCt Rules Part 5A Appx Form 12.
Nonbiological evidence, writ based on, §§19.2-327.10 to 19.2-327.14.

NEW MONMOUTH PRESBYTERIAN CHURCH.
Confederate cemeteries and graves.
Disbursement of funds for upkeep, §10.1-2211.

NEW MOTOR VEHICLES.
Advertising, §18.2-221.
Motor vehicle dealers, §46.2-1581.
T&M vehicle dealers, §46.2-1990.
Motor vehicle dealers, §§46.2-1500 to 46.2-1582.
See MOTOR VEHICLE DEALERS.
Motor vehicle warranties, §§59.1-207.9 to 59.1-207.16:1, 59.1-207.34 to 59.1-207.39.
See MOTOR VEHICLE WARRANTIES.

NEW PARTIES.
When court may add, §8.01-7.

NEWPORT NEWS.
Aerospace engine manufacturer's grants.
Advanced shipbuilding training facility grant program, §59.1-284.23.
Circuit court.
Establishment, §17.1-500.
Clerks of circuit courts, compensation and expenses, §17.1-288.
Coastal primary sand dunes and beaches.
Zoning ordinances, §28.2-1403.
Confederate cemeteries and graves.
Disbursement of funds appropriated for upkeep, §10.1-2211.
Drug treatment court.
Established, §18.2-254.1.
Fishing, tidal waters.
Generally.
See FISHING, TIDAL WATERS.
Regulations.
Publication, §28.2-209.
Grass, weeds, other foreign growth on occupied or vacant property.
Cutting by property owners, ordinance prescribing, §15.2-901.
Improvements.
Taxes or assessments for local improvements.
Authority to impose, §15.2-2404.
Jail farms, §19.2-309.1.
Oyster point development corporation.
See OYSTER POINT DEVELOPMENT CORPORATION.
Port authority.
Board of commissioners, §62.1-129.
Port of Virginia economic and infrastructure development zone grant fund, §62.1-132.3:2.
Public service corporations, taxation of property.
Restriction of imposition of additional tax, §58.1-2606.

NEWPORT NEWS —Cont'd
Referendum elections.
Specific charter authorization required, §24.2-684.
Retail sales and use tax.
Additional sales tax for Northern Virginia and Hampton Roads, §58.1-603.1.
Additional use tax for Northern Virginia and Hampton Roads, §58.1-604.01.
Revolutionary war cemeteries and graves.
Disbursement of funds appropriated for upkeep, §10.1-2211.1.
Sale of delinquent tax lands.
Special masters.
Appointment, special provisions applicable, §58.1-3970.1.
School board.
Fingerprinting applicants for employment, §22.1-296.2.
Salary of members, §22.1-32.
Semi-automatic firearms and shotguns.
Carrying loaded firearms in public areas, §18.2-287.4.
Sports authority of Hampton Roads, Virginia, 1986 ch 426.
Vacant and abandoned property.
Screening ordinance authorized, §15.2-903.
Voluntary property maintenance and zoning inspectors, §15.2-1132.
Water and sewage systems.
Lien for charges and taxes imposed, §15.2-2118.

NEWPORT NEWS-HAMPTON PARKING AUTHORITY, 1968 ch 200, 1983 ch 57, 1983 ch 69, 1984 ch 596.

NEWPORT NEWS PARK AND INDUSTRIAL AUTHORITY.
Name changed to peninsula ports authority of Virginia, 1964 ch 39.

NEWPORT NEWS SHIPBUILDING AND DRY DOCK COMPANY.
Motor vehicles of security personnel.
Flashing red or red and white warning lights, §46.2-1023.

NEW PROVIDENCE PRESBYTERIAN CHURCH.
Confederate cemeteries and graves.
Disbursement of funds for upkeep, §10.1-2211.

NEW RIVER BASIN.
Preparation of plans and programs for management, §62.1-44.38.

NEWSLETTERS.
License tax upon privilege or right of printing.
Localities prohibited from levying, §58.1-3703.

NEWS MEDIA.
Campaign disclosures.
Advertisements.
See CAMPAIGN FINANCE DISCLOSURE.
Criminal trials.
Judicial discretion to permit radio or television coverage, §19.2-266.
Defamation.
Newspapers or print media, §8.01-48.
Radio and television broadcasts, §8.01-49.
Election polling places.
Visiting, photographing or filming inside, §24.2-604.
False publications.
Stated, delivered or transmitted to, §18.2-209.

NEWS MEDIA —Cont'd
Newspapers.
Generally.
See NEWSPAPERS.
Police lines or barricades.
Exemption from provisions, §15.2-1714.
Radio.
Generally.
See RADIO.
Retail sales and use tax exemption, §58.1-609.6.
Television.
Generally.
See TELEVISION.

NEWSPAPER CARRIERS.
Child labor, §40.1-109.
Motor carriers, property.
Exemptions from provisions, §46.2-2101.

NEWSPAPER REPORTERS.
Police lines or barricades.
Exemption from provisions, §15.2-1714.

NEWSPAPERS.
Banks.
Publication of statements, §6.2-907.
Campaign disclosures.
Advertisements.
See CAMPAIGN FINANCE DISCLOSURE.
Consumer protection.
Application of provisions, §59.1-199.
Defamation.
Mitigation of damages against newspapers or print media, §8.01-48.
Election polling places.
News media visiting, photographing or filming inside, interviews, §24.2-604.
False publications.
Stating, delivering or transmitting to publisher or employee, §18.2-209.
Highway route boxes.
Erection and maintenance, §33.1-206.
License tax upon privilege or right of printing or publishing.
Localities prohibited from levying, §58.1-3703.
Litter tax imposed on manufacturers, wholesalers, distributors or retailers, §58.1-1708.
Service by publication.
City or county newspapers deemed published for purpose of legal advertisements, §8.01-323.
Newspapers which may be used for legal notices and publications, §8.01-324.
What order publication to state, §8.01-317.
When publication in newspaper dispensed with, §8.01-317.
Stamping on newspaper word to cause belief done by publisher and circulating newspaper, §18.2-210.

NEWSPAPER STANDS.
Locality authorizing visually handicapped to operate in courthouse, §15.2-1805.

NEW TIRES.
Tire tax, §§58.1-640 to 58.1-644.

NEW TOWN IMPROVEMENT AND CIVIC CLUB, INC.
Little England Chapel.
Appropriations for maintenance, §10.1-2212.

NEW TRIAL.
Additur.
New trial for inadequate damages, §8.01-383.1.

NEW TRIAL —Cont'd
After-discovered evidence.
Right not impaired, §8.01-430.
Attachments.
Restitution to defendant, §8.01-576.
Award of new trial.
How often awarded, §8.01-383.
Costs, payment when granted, §17.1-610.
Court of appeals.
Reversing and remanding case for new trial.
Petition for appeal to supreme court upon award, §17.1-412.
Criminal cases.
Grant of motion to set aside verdict, VA SCt Rule 3A:15.
Criminal procedure.
Accused not tried for higher offense, §19.2-285.
Evidence admitted erroneously, §19.2-324.1.
Damages inadequate, §8.01-383.1.
District court civil cases.
When granted, §16.1-97.1.
Eminent domain.
Just compensation.
Appointment of new body to determine just compensation, §25.1-242.
Hearings on motion.
District court civil cases, §16.1-97.1.
Inadequate damages, §8.01-383.1.
Judicial discretion.
Power to grant new trial, §8.01-383.
Motion for new trial.
District court civil cases, §16.1-97.1.
When unnecessary in certain cases, §8.01-384.

NEW YEAR'S DAY.
ABC stores.
Closed, §4.1-120.
Legal holidays, §2.2-3300.

NEW YORK STOCK EXCHANGE.
Securities listed or approved for listing, security registration exemption, §13.1-514.

NEXT FRIEND.
Birth certificates.
Delayed birth certificate registration, §32.1-260.
Change of name, §8.01-217.
Fiduciaries generally.
See FIDUCIARIES.
Inventories and accounts.
Who may insist or object, §64.2-1209.
Pleadings, §8.01-8.
Sterilization of adults incapable of informed consent, §54.1-2976.
Sterilization of children incapable of informed consent, §54.1-2975.
Suits by minors, §8.01-8.

NEXT OF KIN.
Coal mines.
Underground coal mines.
List of next of kin, §45.1-161.202.

NICKELSVILLE.
Confederate cemeteries and graves, §10.1-2211.

NIGHT SCHOOLS.
Public school programs, §22.1-210.

NIGHT SKY PROTECTION.
Outdoor lighting, locality regulating near certain facilities, §15.2-920.

900 NUMBERS.
Pay-per-call services, §§59.1-429 to 59.1-434.

911 EMERGENCY TELEPHONE SYSTEMS.
Audit.
Wireless E-911 fund.
Grant funding received by recipients, §56-484.17.
Date localities required to be served by 9-1-1 system, §56-484.16.
Definitions.
Prepaid wireless E-911 charge.
Collection, §56-484.17:1.
E-911 tax, §58.1-1730.
Enhanced public safety telephone services act, §§56-484.12 to 56-484.17:1.
Definitions, §56-484.12.
E-911 tax, §58.1-1730.
Voice-over-Internet protocol service providers.
Notice to subscribers of lack of access to E-911, §56-484.12:1.
Plan for access to E-911, §56-484.12:2.
E-911 services board.
Division of public safety communication.
Staff support for board, providing, §2.2-2031.
Local emergency telecommunications requirements, §56-484.16.
Multiline telephone systems (MLTS).
Emergency calls, §§56-484.19 to 56-484.25.
See EMERGENCY TELEPHONE CALLS.
Prepaid wireless E-911 charge.
Collection at point of sale, §56-484.17:1.
Defined, §56-484.17:1.
Rate established, §56-484.17:1.
Use of digits 9-1-1.
Advertising or promoting use.
Required use of digits 9-1-1, §56-484.16.
Wireless E-911 cost recovery subcommittee, §56-484.15.
Wireless E-911 fund, §56-484.17.
Wireless E-911 surcharge.
Collection by CMRS providers, §56-484.17.

NITROGEN.
Fertilizer generally.
See FERTILIZER.
Sale of deicing agents containing urea, nitrogen or phosphorus prohibited, §3.2-3607.2.

NITROUS OXIDE.
Dental hygienists, administration, §§54.1-2722, 54.1-3408.
Motor vehicles.
Devices used to supply nitrous oxide to engines, §46.2-1088.4.

NOBILITY.
Titles of prohibited, US Const Art I §§9, 10.

NO-CRUISING ORDINANCES, §46.2-1219.1.

NO-FAULT DIVORCE, §20-91.
Divorce from bond of matrimony.
See DIVORCE.

NO-FAULT PLANS FOR BIRTH INJURIES.
Birth-related neurological injury compensation, §§38.2-5000 to 38.2-5021.
See BIRTH-RELATED NEUROLOGICAL INJURY COMPENSATION.

NO FENCE LAW, §§55-310 to 55-316.

NOISE CONTROL.
Building code.
Acoustical treatment measures, standards.
Installation in certain buildings and structures, §36-99.10:1.

NOISE CONTROL —Cont'd
Criminal procedure.
Determining decibel levels for evidentiary purposes, §19.2-270.7.
Mine safety.
Underground coal mines.
Noise levels, §45.1-161.176.
Motorcycle, moped, and motorized skateboard or foot-scooter noise, §15.2-919.
Proper equipment to determine decibel level of sound.
Standards established by division of purchases and supply, §2.2-1112.
Sports shooting ranges.
Applicability of local noise ordinance, §15.2-917.

NO KNOCK ENTRY.
Search warrants, §19.2-56.

NOLLE PROSEQUI.
Clerk's report to central criminal records exchange, §19.2-390.
Virginia crime code references, required use, §19.2-390.01.
Criminal cases, §19.2-265.3.
Expungement of police and criminal records, §19.2-392.2.
Parole revocation hearings.
Preliminary hearing requirements, §53.1-165.
Plea bargaining, VA SCt Rule 3A:8.
Retention of ended case files by circuit court clerk, time, destruction, §17.1-213.
Teacher reinstatement of suspension, §22.1-315.

NOLO CONTENDERE.
Arraignment.
Court acceptance of plea, §19.2-254.
Contents of judgment order, §19.2-307, VA SCt Rules Part 3A Appx Form 10.
Substantial compliance with form required, VA SCt Rule 3A:22.
Corporation's plea in district court, VA SCt Rule 7C:6.
Determining voluntariness, VA SCt Rule 3A:8.
Nontraffic offenses for which prepayment authorized, §19.2-254.2.
Plea admissible in civil actions, §8.01-418.
Plea bargaining agreement procedure, VA SCt Rule 3A:8.
Traffic infraction cases, §19.2-254.1.
Voluntariness of plea.
Judicial determination, VA SCt Rule 3A:8.
Withdrawal of plea.
Before imposition of sentence, §19.2-296.

NOMINATION OF CANDIDATES.
Political party nominations, §§24.2-508 to 24.2-511.
Primaries generally, §§24.2-512 to 24.2-538.
See PRIMARY ELECTIONS.

NOMINEES.
Shares of corporations held by nominees, §13.1-664.
Appraisal rights.
Assertion of rights by nominees, §13.1-731.
Voting entitlement.
Trustee or fiduciary holding share registered in name of nominee, §13.1-662.

NONCLAIM ACT, §64.2-556.

NONCLAIM STATUTE, §8.01-250.
Limitation of actions, §8.01-244.
Improvements to real property.
Damages arising out of defective or unsafe condition of improvement, §8.01-250.

NONCOMPETE CLAUSES.
Attorneys.
Employment contracts or settlement agreements, VA SCt Rule Pt 6 §II Rule 5.6.

NON COMPOS MENTIS.
See MENTAL HEALTH.

NONCONFORMING USES.
Zoning, §15.2-2307.

NONCORPORATIONS.
Nonprofit corporations.
Generally.
See NONPROFIT CORPORATIONS.

NONCRIMINAL INCIDENT RECORDS.
Records to be kept by chiefs of police and sheriffs, §15.2-1722.

NON-ENGLISH SPEAKING PERSONS.
Civil commitment of mentally ill persons.
Interpreters.
Admission or certification proceedings, §37.2-802.
Interpreter privilege, VA SCt Rule 2:507.
Interpreters in civil cases, §8.01-384.1:1.
Interpreters in criminal cases, §19.2-164.

NONFEASANCE.
Highways and roads, §33.1-23.03:7.
Housing development authority.
Bond issues, §36-55.44.
Property taxes.
Tax commissioner and department of taxation, §58.1-210.
Resources authority, §62.1-221.
Solicitation of charitable or civic contributions.
Professional fundraisers, §57-61.
Transportation districts.
Liability of Commonwealth, counties or cities, §15.2-4526.
Tort liability, §§33.1-421, 33.1-442.

NONFIREFIGHTER REGIONAL FIRE HAZARDOUS MATERIALS EMERGENCY RESPONSE TEAM.
Premises liability.
Duty of care owed to law enforcement officers, §8.01-226.

NONFORFEITURE PROVISIONS.
Life insurance policies, §§38.2-3200 to 38.2-3229.
See LIFE INSURANCE.
Long-term care insurance, §38.2-5210.

NONINDIGENOUS AQUATIC NUISANCE SPECIES ACT, §§29.1-571 to 29.1-577.
Civil penalty for violation, §29.1-577.
Cooperation with other governmental agencies, §29.1-573.
Costs of eradicating.
Liability of persons violating provisions, §29.1-577.
Definition of nonindigenous aquatic nuisance species, §29.1-571.
Designation of other nuisance species.
Authority of board, §29.1-572.

NONINDIGENOUS AQUATIC NUISANCE SPECIES ACT —Cont'd
Importing, transporting, sale, purchase, etc.
Permit authorizing, §29.1-575.
Prohibitions, §29.1-574.
Inspections.
Authority of director, §29.1-576.
Regulations, authority of board to adopt, §29.1-572.
Seizure or eradication of species.
Authority of director after entering property, §29.1-576.
Suppression, control, eradication, prevention or retardation.
Power of department to conduct operation, §29.1-573.
Zebra mussel, quagga mussel and snakehead fishes, §29.1-571.

NONJOINDER OF PARTIES, §8.01-5.

NONPOINT-SOURCE-POLLUTION MANAGEMENT.
Agricultural best management practices tax credit, §58.1-339.3.
Stormwater management, §§62.1-44.15:24 to 62.1-44.15:50.
See STORMWATER MANAGEMENT.

NONPRESCRIPTION DRUGS.
Retail sales and use tax exemption, §58.1-609.10.

NONPROFIT CIVIC ORGANIZATIONS.
Prisoners performing work for, §53.1-59.

NONPROFIT CORPORATIONS, §§13.1-801 to 13.1-945.
Abandonment of property presumption.
Intangible interest in business associations, §55-210.6:1.
Property of dissolved associations, §55-210.7.
Refunds, §55-210.6:2.
Acceptance of votes by corporation, §13.1-848.
Accounting records, §13.1-932.
Actions.
Amending pleading to reflect correct name.
Confusing and similar names, §8.01-6.2.
Actions of members without meeting, §13.1-841.
Advance for expenses incurred as party to proceeding, §13.1-878.
Agent indemnification, §13.1-881.
Agent insurance, §13.1-882.
Agricultural cooperative associations, §§13.1-313 to 13.1-345.
See AGRICULTURAL COOPERATIVE ASSOCIATIONS.
Aliens.
Pattern or practice of employing unauthorized aliens.
Foreign corporations.
Revocation of certificate of authority, §13.1-931.
Involuntary termination of corporate existence, §13.1-915.
Amending pleading to reflect correct name.
Confusing and similar names, §8.01-6.2.
Amendment of articles of incorporation.
Articles of amendment, §13.1-888.
Fee, §13.1-816.
Authority, §13.1-884.
By directors and members, §§13.1-885, 13.1-886.
Effect, §13.1-891.

NONPROFIT CORPORATIONS —Cont'd
Amendment of articles of incorporation —Cont'd
Prior to organization, §13.1-887.1.
Voting groups, voting on, §13.1-887.
Annual meeting of members, §13.1-838.
Annual registration fees, §13.1-936.1.
Automatic termination of corporate existence, §13.1-914.
Collection of unpaid bills, §13.1-936.2.
Failure to pay.
Automatic revocation of foreign corporation's certificate of authority, §13.1-930.
Penalty for late payment, §13.1-914.
Foreign corporation, §13.1-930.
Annual report of domestic and foreign corporation, §13.1-936.
Failure to file.
Revocation of foreign corporation certificate of authority, §13.1-930.
Termination of corporate existence, §13.1-914.
Antitrust laws.
Applicability, §59.1-9.4.
Applicability of provisions to existing corporations, §13.1-937.
Applicability to social, patriotic and benevolent societies incorporated before 1900, §13.1-938.
Articles of amendment, §13.1-888.
Converting to stock corporation, §13.1-942.
Fee, §13.1-816.
Articles of consolidation.
Foreign corporations.
Fees, §13.1-816.
Articles of correction.
Correcting filed articles, §13.1-807.
Fee, §13.1-816.
Articles of dissolution, §13.1-904.
Fee, §13.1-816.
Articles of incorporation, §13.1-819.
Amendment.
Articles of amendment, §13.1-888.
Fee, §13.1-816.
Authority, §13.1-884.
By directors, §13.1-885.
By directors and members, §13.1-886.
Converting to stock corporation.
Filing articles of amendment, §13.1-942.
Effect, §13.1-891.
Prior to organization, §13.1-887.1.
Restated articles, §13.1-889.
Voting groups, §13.1-887.
Content requirements, §13.1-819.
Fee, §13.1-816.
Incorporators to sign and file with state corporation commission, §13.1-818.
Restatement, §13.1-889.
Articles of restatement, §13.1-889.
Fee, §13.1-816.
Articles of merger, §13.1-896.
Foreign corporations.
Fees, §13.1-816.
Articles of restatement, §13.1-889.
Fee, §13.1-816.
Articles of revocation of dissolution, §13.1-905.
Articles of termination of corporate existence, §13.1-912.
Asset sales, §§13.1-899 to 13.1-901.
Other than in regular course of business, §13.1-900.
Regular course of business, §13.1-899.

NONPROFIT CORPORATIONS —Cont'd
Assumed or fictitious names, §13.1-829.
Authorization to transact or offer to transact business.
Required, §13.1-812.
Automatic termination of corporate existence, §13.1-914.
Automobile clubs, §§13.1-400.1 to 13.1-400.9.
Bylaws, §13.1-823.
Amendment, §13.1-892.
Emergency bylaws, §13.1-824.
Quorum or voting requirements for directors, increasing, §13.1-893.
Certificate of correction.
Correcting filed articles, §13.1-807.
Certificate of good standing, §13.1-809.
Certificates issued by state corporation commission, §13.1-805.
Effective time and date of document, §13.1-806.
Certificates of authority.
Foreign corporations.
Amendment, §13.1-922.
Application fee, §13.1-816.
Application, §13.1-921.
Fee, §13.1-816.
Automatic revocation, §13.1-930.
Commission revocation, §13.1-931.
Effect, §13.1-923.
Fees, §§13.1-815.1, 13.1-816.
Reentry after certificate of authority surrendered or revoked, §13.1-931.1.
Required to transact business, §13.1-919.
Transacting business without, §13.1-920.
Certificates of incorporation.
Issuance, §13.1-820.
Challenging validity of corporate action.
Ultra vires, §13.1-828.
Change of name.
Property title records, §13.1-945.
Charitable gaming generally, §§18.2-340.15 to 18.2-340.37.
See CHARITABLE GAMING.
Charter fees, §13.1-815.1.
Claims against dissolved corporations, §§13.1-908, 13.1-908.1.
Court proceedings, §13.1-908.2.
Director duties, §13.1-908.3.
Collection of fees by state corporation commission, §13.1-815.
Commencement of existence, §13.1-820.
Community action statewide organizations, §2.2-5406.
Community associations.
Special provisions, §13.1-814.1.
Consents of members, action without meeting, §13.1-841.
Consent to electronic transmission of notice or other communication, §13.1-810.
Consolidation.
Foreign corporations.
Articles of consolidation.
Fees, §13.1-816.
Conversion to stock corporation, §§13.1-942 to 13.1-944.
Articles of amendment, §13.1-942.
Controlling law and continuity, §13.1-944.
Domestic stock corporation, §13.1-941.01.
Fees, §13.1-943.
Cooperative associations, §§13.1-301 to 13.1-311.1.
See COOPERATIVE ASSOCIATIONS.

NONPROFIT CORPORATIONS —Cont'd
Copies of file documents, evidentiary effect, §13.1-808.
Corporate name, requirements, §13.1-829.
Correcting filed articles, §13.1-807.
Fee or articles of correction, §13.1-816.
Counties, cities or towns.
Gifts and donations to, §15.2-953.
Court-ordered meetings of members, §13.1-840.
Court orders for advances, reimbursement or indemnification, §13.1-879.1.
Cumulative voting.
Voting for directors, §13.1-852.
Date documents become effective, §13.1-806.
Definitions, §13.1-803.
Domestic nonstock corporations, §13.1-603.
Foreign nonstock corporations, §13.1-603.
Merger, §13.1-893.1.
Dental or optometric services plans, §§38.2-4500 to 38.2-4523.
Directors, §§13.1-853 to 13.1-874.
Action without meeting, §13.1-865.
Agreements among directors, §13.1-852.1.
Amendment of articles of incorporation, §13.1-885.
By directors and members, §13.1-886.
Amendment of bylaws, §13.1-892.
Bylaws.
Adoption, §13.1-823.
Emergency bylaws, §13.1-824.
Committees, §13.1-869.
Community associations.
Limitation on directors' liability, §13.1-870.2.
Compensation, §13.1-863.
Conduct, standards of, §13.1-870.
Conflicts of interest, §13.1-871.
Business opportunities, §13.1-871.1.
Consent to be named or elected director required, §13.1-855.
Correcting filed articles, §13.1-807.
Direct or indirect personal interest, conflict of interest, §13.1-871.
Business opportunities, §13.1-871.1.
Dissolution, §§13.1-902, 13.1-903.
Duties, §13.1-833.
Election, §13.1-855.
Classes of members, §13.1-856.
Inspectors of elections, §13.1-847.1.
Judicial review, §13.1-861.
Emergency bylaws, §13.1-824.
Emergency powers, §13.1-827.
Fixing compensation, §13.1-863.
Good faith judgment.
Standard of conduct, §13.1-870.
Increasing or decreasing number, §13.1-855.
Indemnification.
Advance for expenses, §13.1-878.
Authority to indemnify, §13.1-876.
Court orders, §13.1-879.1.
Determination and authorization, §13.1-880.
Generally, §§13.1-875 to 13.1-883.
Mandatory indemnification, §13.1-877.
Initial directors.
Terms, §13.1-857.
Inspection of records by, §13.1-935.1.
Insurance, §13.1-882.
Judicial review of elections, §13.1-861.
Limitation on liability, §13.1-870.1.
Community association director, §13.1-870.2.
Meetings, §13.1-864.
Actions without meeting, §13.1-865.

NONPROFIT CORPORATIONS —Cont'd
Directors —Cont'd
Meetings —Cont'd
Notice, §13.1-866.
Waiver, §13.1-867.
Organizational meeting, §13.1-822.
Quorum, §13.1-868.
Notice of resignation, §13.1-859.
Number, §13.1-855.
Personal interest direct or indirect, conflict of interest, §13.1-871.
Business opportunities, §13.1-871.1.
Plan of merger.
Action on plan by directors, §13.1-895.
Adoption, §13.1-894.
Qualifications, §13.1-854.
Quorum, §13.1-868.
Removal, §13.1-860.
Requirement for, §13.1-833.
Residency of Commonwealth not required, §13.1-854.
Resignation, §13.1-859.
Sale of assets in regular course of business, §13.1-899.
Sale of assets other than in regular course of business, §13.1-900.
Staggered terms, §13.1-858.
Standards of conduct, §13.1-870.
Termination of corporate existence by initial directors, §13.1-913.
Terms, §13.1-857.
Uniformity, §13.1-858.
Vacancy, §13.1-862.
Variable range for size of directors.
Fixing minimum and maximum number, §13.1-855.
Voting by directors, §13.1-868.
Voting for, §13.1-852.
Disability or handicap.
Protection and advocacy system.
Establishment of nonprofit entity to provide protection, advocacy, etc, services, §51.5-39.13.
Disposition of assets by nonprofit health care entities, §55-531.
Obligations of entities, §55-532.
Dissolution, §§13.1-902 to 13.1-917.
Articles of dissolution, §13.1-904.
Fee, §13.1-816.
Articles of revocation, §13.1-905.
Fee, §13.1-816.
By directors, §13.1-903.
By directors and members, §13.1-902.
Claims against corporation, §§13.1-908, 13.1-908.1.
Court proceedings, §13.1-908.2.
Director duties, §13.1-908.3.
Decree for dissolution, §13.1-911.
Distribution of assets, §13.1-907.
Effect, §13.1-906.
Involuntary dissolution, §§13.1-909 to 13.1-911.
Judicial dissolution, §13.1-909.
Decree, §13.1-911.
Receivers or custodians, appointment, §13.1-910.
Plan of distribution, §13.1-907.
Receivers or custodians, appointment, §13.1-910.
Reinstatement of corporation after ceasing to exist, §13.1-916.
Revocation, §13.1-905.

NONPROFIT CORPORATIONS —Cont'd
Dissolution —Cont'd
Telephone cooperatives, §56-503.
Fees, §56-505.
Termination of corporate existence.
Articles of termination, §13.1-912.
Automatic termination, §13.1-914.
Incorporators or initial directors, §13.1-913.
Involuntary termination, §13.1-915.
Reinstatement, §13.1-916.
Survival of remedy, §13.1-917.
Voluntary dissolution, §§13.1-902, 13.1-903.
Distribution of assets, dissolution, §13.1-907.
Dividends.
Prohibited, §13.1-814.
Documents required or permitted to be filed.
Dependent on fact objectively ascertainable outside plan or filed document, §13.1-804.
Effective time and date of document, §13.1-806.
Electronic filing, §13.1-804.
Evidentiary effect of copies, §13.1-808.
Filing fee.
Documents accompanied by required fee, §13.1-804.
Filing requirements generally, §13.1-804.
Reorganization of corporations, §13.1-804.1.
Domestication.
Foreign nonprofit corporations, §§13.1-898.2 to 13.1-898.7.
Economic development partnership authority.
Assistance with economic development, §2.2-2240.
Educational institutions, sale of certain real property, §13.1-901.
Electronic notice, §13.1-810.
Electronic signatures in global and national commerce act.
Chapter to control conflicting provisions, §13.1-939.
Emergency bylaws, §13.1-824.
Emergency powers, §13.1-827.
Employee indemnification, §13.1-881.
Employee insurance, §13.1-882.
Entrance fees, §13.1-815.1.
Evidentiary effect of certificates of incorporation, §13.1-820.
Evidentiary effect of copy of filed documents, §13.1-808.
Existence begins when certificate of corporation becomes effective, §13.1-820.
Existing corporations.
Applicability of provisions to, §13.1-937.
Saving provision, §13.1-939.
Facts to be certified by clerk of state corporation commission upon request, §12.1-20.
False documents, penalty for signing, §13.1-811.
Fees, §§13.1-815 to 13.1-816.
Annual registration fees, §13.1-936.1.
Penalty for late payment, §13.1-914.
Article of incorporation, §13.1-816.
Articles of amendment or restatement, §13.1-816.
Articles of consolidation.
Foreign corporations, §13.1-816.
Articles of correction, §13.1-816.
Articles of dissolution, §13.1-816.
Articles of merger, §13.1-816.
Foreign corporations, §13.1-816.
Articles of revocation of dissolution, §13.1-816.
Articles of termination of corporate existence, §13.1-816.

NONPROFIT CORPORATIONS —Cont'd
Fees —Cont'd
Certificates of authority.
Foreign corporations, §13.1-815.1.
Amended certificate application, §13.1-816.
Application, §13.1-816.
Change of name.
Issuing certificate, §13.1-816.
Charter and entrance fees, §13.1-815.1.
Collection by state corporation commission, §13.1-815.
Converting to stock corporation, §13.1-943.
Filing documents or issuing certificates, §13.1-816.
Foreign corporations.
Certificates of authority, §13.1-815.1.
Amended certificate application, §13.1-816.
Application, §13.1-816.
Registered name, §13.1-831.
Withdrawal.
Statement, §13.1-816.
Indistinguishable name.
Application for use, §13.1-816.
Payment as prerequisite to action by state corporation commission, §13.1-815.
Registered name of foreign corporation, §13.1-831.
Reserved name, §13.1-816.
Withdrawal of foreign corporations.
Statement, §13.1-816.
Filing of documents required or permitted to be filed.
Dependent on fact objectively ascertainable outside plan or filed document, §13.1-804.
Effective time and date of document, §13.1-806.
Electronic filing, §13.1-804.1.
Evidentiary effect of copies, §13.1-808.
Fees, §13.1-816.
Filing fee.
Documents accompanied by required fee, §13.1-804.1.
Reorganization of corporations, §13.1-804.1.
Requirements generally, §13.1-804.
Finality of state corporation commission actions, §13.1-813.
Food.
Adulteration, misbranding and false advertising.
Exemptions to regulations, §3.2-5101.
Foreign corporations, §§13.1-919 to 13.1-931.1.
Aliens.
Pattern or practice of employing unauthorized aliens.
Revocation of certificate of authority, §13.1-931.
Certificates of authority.
Amendment, §13.1-922.
Application fee, §13.1-816.
Applications, §13.1-921.
Fees, §13.1-816.
Automatic revocation, §13.1-930.
Commission revocation, §13.1-931.
Effect, §13.1-923.
Fees, §§13.1-815.1, 13.1-816.
Reentry after certificate of authority surrendered or revoked, §13.1-931.1.
Required to transact business, §13.1-919.
Transacting business without, §13.1-920.
Conversion.
Entity conversion of foreign corporation authorized to transact business in Commonwealth, §13.1-928.2.
Definition.
Foreign nonstock corporation, §13.1-603.

NONPROFIT CORPORATIONS —Cont'd
Foreign corporations —Cont'd
Domestication, §§13.1-898.2 to 13.1-898.7.
Entity conversion of foreign corporation authorized to transact business in Commonwealth, §13.1-928.2.
Fees, §13.1-816.
Certificate of authority, §13.1-815.1.
Registration fees.
Collection of unpaid bills, §13.1-936.2.
Failure to pay.
Automatic revocation of certificate of authority, §13.1-930.
Penalty for late payment, §13.1-930.
Time for payment, §13.1-930.
Merger, §13.1-928.1.
Name.
Corporate name generally, §13.1-924.
Registered name, §13.1-831.
Reentry after certificate of authority surrendered or revoked, §13.1-931.1.
Registered name, §13.1-831.
Registered office and registered agent.
Change of office or agent, §13.1-926.
Merger of agent into qualified entity, notice, §13.1-926.
Name change, §13.1-926.
Required to maintain in Commonwealth, §13.1-925.
Resignation of agent, §13.1-927.
Service on agent, §13.1-928.
Agent required to forward notice to corporation, §13.1-925.
Statement of change, §13.1-926.
Termination of certificate of authority.
Failure to file statement of change after agent's resignation, §13.1-930.
Registration fees.
Collection of unpaid bills, §13.1-936.2.
Failure to pay.
Automatic revocation of certificate of authority, §13.1-930.
Penalty for late payment, §13.1-930.
Time for payment, §13.1-930.
Service of notice, process and other papers on, §13.1-928.
Transacting business, activities not constituting, §13.1-919.
Transacting business, authority required, §13.1-919.
Consequences of transacting without authority, §13.1-920.
Withdrawal, §13.1-929.
Fee, §13.1-816.
General assembly, reservation of power, §13.1-802.
General powers, §13.1-826.
Geographic information system.
Establishment to assist in development, §2.2-2030.
GIS.
Establishment to assist in development, §2.2-2030.
Good standing, certificate of, §13.1-809.
Health services plans, §§38.2-4200 to 38.2-4235.
See HEALTH SERVICES PLANS.
Income tax on corporations.
Exemptions, §58.1-401.
Incorporators, §13.1-818.
Bylaws.
Adoption, §13.1-823.

NONPROFIT CORPORATIONS —Cont'd
Incorporators —Cont'd
Organizational meeting, §13.1-822.
Termination of corporate existence, §13.1-913.
Indemnification, §§13.1-875 to 13.1-883.
Advance for expenses, §13.1-878.
Applicability of article, §13.1-883.
Authority to indemnify, §13.1-876.
Continuation as to persons ceasing to have capacity as director or officer, §13.1-883.
Court orders, §13.1-879.1.
Definitions, §13.1-875.
Determination and authorization, §13.1-880.
Further indemnity, power of corporation to make, §13.1-883.
Heirs, executors, administration.
Right to receive inuring to, §13.1-883.
Insurance, §13.1-882.
Limitation to reasonable expenses, §13.1-876.
Mandatory indemnification, §13.1-877.
Obligation in advance of act or omission, §13.1-883.
Officers, employees and agents.
Generally, §13.1-881.
Provision obligating corporation to fullest extent of law, §13.1-883.
Indictment, service of summons to answer, §19.2-238.
Injunctions, §13.1-813.
Innovation and entrepreneurship investment authority.
Auxiliaries, §2.2-2232.
Inspection of members' list for notice, §13.1-845.
Court-ordered inspection, §13.1-845.
Inspection of records by directors, §13.1-935.1.
Inspection of records by members, §13.1-933.
Court-ordered inspections, §13.1-935.
Scope of rights, §13.1-934.
Inspectors of elections, §13.1-847.1.
Insurance on behalf of directors, officers, etc., §13.1-882.
Involuntary dissolution, §§13.1-909 to 13.1-911.
Involuntary termination of corporate existence, §13.1-915.
Issuance of certificates by state corporation commission, §13.1-805.
Effective time and date of document, §13.1-806.
Jail industry program goods and services.
Purchases, §53.1-133.8.
Joint and several liability.
Preincorporation transactions, §13.1-821.
Joint ventures.
Powers to enter into, §13.1-826.
Judicial dissolution, §§13.1-909 to 13.1-911.
Lawful purposes, engaging in, §13.1-825.
Lease of assets.
Other than regular course of business, §13.1-900.
Regular course of business, §13.1-899.
Legal services plans, §§38.2-4400 to 38.2-4418.
Liability for preincorporation transaction, §13.1-821.
List of members for meetings, §13.1-845.
Mail notice.
When effective, §13.1-810.
Mandatory indemnification, §13.1-877.
Meetings of directors, §13.1-864.
Actions without meeting, §13.1-865.
Minutes, §13.1-932.
Notice, §13.1-866.
Oral notice, §13.1-810.

NONPROFIT CORPORATIONS —Cont'd
Meetings of directors —Cont'd
Notice —Cont'd
Waiver, §13.1-867.
Organizational meeting, §13.1-822.
Meetings of members.
Actions without meeting, §13.1-841.
Annual meeting, §13.1-838.
Chairman, §13.1-844.1.
Conduct of meeting, §13.1-844.1.
Court-ordered meetings, §13.1-840.
List of members, §13.1-845.
Minutes, §13.1-932.
Notice, §13.1-842.
List of members for notice, §13.1-845.
Waiver, §13.1-843.
Quorum, §13.1-849.
Change in, §13.1-851.
Record date for voting groups, §13.1-844.
Remote participation, §13.1-844.2.
Special meetings, §13.1-839.
Remote participation, §13.1-844.2.
Members, §§13.1-837 to 13.1-852.2.
Acceptance of votes by corporation, §13.1-848.
Actions without meeting, §13.1-841.
Agreements among members, §13.1-852.1.
Voting agreements, §13.1-852.2.
Amendment of articles of incorporation, §13.1-886.
Amendment of bylaws, §13.1-892.
Annual meetings, §13.1-838.
Certificates evidencing membership, issuance, §13.1-837.
Classes of members, §13.1-837.
Court-ordered meetings, §13.1-840.
Cumulative voting, voting for directors, §13.1-852.
Dissolution, §13.1-902.
Election of directors, §13.1-855.
Classes of members, §13.1-856.
Voting for, §13.1-852.
Generally, §13.1-837.
Inspection of members' list for notice, §13.1-845.
Court-ordered inspection, §13.1-845.
Inspection of records, §13.1-933.
Court-ordered inspections, §13.1-935.
Scope of right, §13.1-934.
List of members for meeting, §13.1-845.
Meetings. See within this heading, "Meetings of members."
Notice of meetings, §13.1-842.
Waiver, §13.1-843.
Number of members, §13.1-810.1.
Plan of merger.
Action on plan, §13.1-895.
Approval, §13.1-894.
Proxies, §13.1-847.
Determination of validity of proxies, §13.1-847.1.
Quorum, §13.1-849.
Change, §13.1-851.
Record date for voting groups, §13.1-844.
Records of, §13.1-932.
Removal of director, §13.1-860.
Residency of Commonwealth not required, §13.1-854.
Sale of assets other than in regular course of business.
Approval required, §13.1-900.
Special meetings, §13.1-839.
Vacancies on board of directors, filling, §13.1-862.
Voting entitlements, §13.1-846.

NONPROFIT CORPORATIONS —Cont'd
Members —Cont'd
Voting groups.
Action by single and multiple groups, §13.1-850.
Amendments, voting on, §13.1-887.
Voting requirements, §13.1-849.
Change in requirements, §13.1-851.
Merger, §§13.1-893.1 to 13.1-897.1.
Abandonment of merger, §13.1-897.1.
Articles of merger, §13.1-896.
Fee, §13.1-816.
Authorization, §13.1-894.
Definitions, §13.1-893.1.
Effect, §13.1-897.
Foreign corporations, §13.1-928.1.
Plan of merger, §13.1-894.
Action by directors or members, §13.1-895.
Property title records.
Corporate changes generally, §13.1-945.
Mortgage loan originators.
Determination of bona fide nonprofit organizations, §6.2-1701.1.
Mortgage of assets, §13.1-899.
Motorcycle dealers.
Consigning donated motorcycles to dealers.
Certificate authorizing, §46.2-1993.6:1.
Fees, §46.2-1993.17.
Motor vehicle dealers.
Consigning donated motor vehicles to dealers.
Certificate authorizing, §46.2-1508.1.
Fee, §46.2-1519.
Organizations providing vehicles or transportation for indigent persons, §46.2-1508.1.
Names, §§13.1-829 to 13.1-831.
Amending pleading to reflect correct name.
Confusing and similar names, §8.01-6.2.
Assumed or fictitious names, §13.1-829.
Change of name.
Fee for issuing certificate, §13.1-816.
Property title records, §13.1-945.
Corporate names, §13.1-829.
Distinguishable upon records of state corporation commission, §13.1-829.
Foreign corporations, §§13.1-831, 13.1-924.
Indistinguishable name.
Application for use, §13.1-829.
Fees, §13.1-816.
Reserved name, §13.1-830.
Application fee, §13.1-816.
Notice of transfer.
Fees, §13.1-816.
Notice, §13.1-810.
Impending termination of corporate existence, §13.1-914.
Meetings, §13.1-842.
Waiver, §13.1-843.
Number of members, §13.1-810.1.
Officers, §§13.1-853 to 13.1-874.
Authority, §13.1-873.
Duties, §13.1-873.
Holding other office, §13.1-872.
Indemnification, §13.1-881.
Generally, §§13.1-875 to 13.1-883.
Insurance, §13.1-882.
Removal, §13.1-874.
Required officers, §13.1-872.
Resignation, §13.1-874.
Oral notice.
Meeting of board of directors, §13.1-810.
Organization, §13.1-822.
Organizational meeting, §13.1-822.

NONPROFIT CORPORATIONS —Cont'd
Partnership agreements.
Powers to enter into, §13.1-826.
Payment of fees as prerequisite to action by state corporation commission, §13.1-815.
Pleadings.
Amending pleading to reflect correct name.
Confusing and similar names, §8.01-6.2.
Powers, §13.1-826.
Preincorporation transactions, liability for, §13.1-821.
Prison made goods and services, purchases of, §§53.1-47 to 53.1-55.
Professional corporations generally, §§13.1-542.1 to 13.1-556.
See PROFESSIONAL CORPORATIONS.
Prohibition of shares of stock and dividends, §13.1-814.
Property owners' associations.
Applicability of provisions, §55-508.
Proxies, §13.1-847.
Determination of validity of proxies, §13.1-847.1.
Publication of notice, §13.1-810.
Purposes, §13.1-825.
Real estate cooperatives.
Association organizations, §55-458.
Recordation of documents.
Duties of state corporation commission, §13.1-805.
Record date for voting groups, §13.1-844.
Records, §13.1-932.
Court-ordered inspections, §13.1-935.
Directors.
Inspection of records by, §13.1-935.1.
Inspection by members, §13.1-933.
Scope of right, §13.1-934.
Property title records.
Corporate changes, §13.1-945.
Registered name of foreign corporation, §13.1-831.
Registered office and registered agent, §§13.1-833 to 13.1-836.
Change of registered office or change of agent, §13.1-834.
Statement of change, §13.1-833.
Termination of corporate existence.
Failure to file after resignation of agent, §13.1-914.
Discontinuance of registered office, §13.1-835.
Foreign corporations.
Change of office or agent, §13.1-926.
Discontinuance of registered office, §13.1-927.
Merger of agent into qualified entity, notice, §13.1-926.
Name change, §13.1-926.
Required to maintain in Commonwealth, §13.1-925.
Resignation of agent, §13.1-927.
Service on agent, §13.1-928.
Agent required to forward notice to corporation, §13.1-925.
Statement of change, §13.1-926.
Merger of agent into qualified entity.
Notice, §13.1-834.
Name change, §13.1-834.
Required to maintain in Commonwealth, §13.1-833.
Resignation of registered agent, §13.1-835.
Statement of change.
Termination of corporate existence.
Failure to file after resignation of agent, §13.1-914.

NONPROFIT CORPORATIONS —Cont'd
Registered office and registered agent —Cont'd
Service of process on agent, §13.1-836.
Designation by agent of person to receive service, §13.1-836.
Duty to forward notice to corporation, §13.1-833.
Foreign corporations, §13.1-928.
Statement of change of registered office or agent, §13.1-834.
Statement of resignation of agent, §13.1-835.
Written notice directed to agent, §13.1-810.
Registration fees.
Annual payment, §13.1-936.1.
Applied against unpaid fees, §13.1-815.
Collection of unpaid bills, §13.1-936.2.
Failure to pay.
Automatic revocation of foreign corporation's certificate of authority, §13.1-930.
Automatic termination of corporate existence, §13.1-914.
Penalty for late payment, §13.1-914.
Foreign corporations, §13.1-930.
Rehearings by state corporation commission, §13.1-813.
Reinstatement of corporation after ceasing to exist, §13.1-916.
Rejection of votes by corporation, §13.1-848.
Removal of director, §13.1-860.
Removal of officer, §13.1-874.
Reorganization.
Filings with commission pursuant to, §13.1-804.1.
Reports.
Annual report, §13.1-936.
Failure to file.
Automatic revocation of foreign corporation's certificate of authority, §13.1-930.
Automatic termination of corporate existence, §13.1-914.
Reserved name, §13.1-830.
Residency of director or member not required, §13.1-854.
Resignation of director, §13.1-859.
Resignation of officer, §13.1-874.
Restated articles of incorporation, §13.1-889.
Articles of restatement, §13.1-889.
Fee, §13.1-816.
Sale of assets, §§13.1-899 to 13.1-901.
Other than regular course of business, §13.1-900.
Regular course of business, §13.1-899.
Saving provision, §13.1-939.
Service of notice, process and other papers, §13.1-836.
Designation by agent of person to receive, §13.1-836.
Foreign corporations, §13.1-928.
Foreign corporations, §13.1-928.
Withdrawal, §13.1-929.
Registered agent as agent for service, §13.1-836.
Foreign corporations, §13.1-928.
Summons to answer indictment, §19.2-238.
Shares of stock prohibited, §13.1-814.
Short title, §13.1-801.
Signing false documents, penalty, §13.1-811.
Small business assistance.
Establishment of corporation to assist.
Department of business assistance authorized to establish (eff until 1/1/2014), §2.2-903.
Social, patriotic and benevolent societies incorporated before 1900.
Applicability of provisions, §13.1-938.

NONPROFIT CORPORATIONS —Cont'd
Special meetings of members, §13.1-839.
State corporation commission generally, §§12.1-1 to 12.1-43.
See STATE CORPORATION COMMISSION.
Summons to answer indictment, §19.2-238.
T&M vehicle dealers.
Consigning donated T&M vehicles to dealers.
Certificate authorizing, §46.2-1908.1.
Telephone cooperatives.
Application of provisions to, §56-490.
Termination of corporate existence, §§13.1-912 to 13.1-917.
Articles of termination, §13.1-912.
Fee, §13.1-816.
Automatic termination, §13.1-914.
By incorporators or initial directors, §13.1-913.
Involuntary termination, §13.1-915.
Reinstatement, §13.1-916.
Survival of remedy after termination, §13.1-917.
Time documents become effective, §13.1-806.
Time-shares.
Association formation provisions, §55-368.
Title.
Property title records.
Corporate changes, §13.1-945.
Trailer dealers.
Consigning donated trailers to dealers.
Certificate authorizing, §46.2-1992.6:1.
Fees, §46.2-1992.17.
Ultra vires, §13.1-828.
Unclaimed property, disposition of, §55-210.6:1.
Property of dissolved associations, §55-210.7.
Records, §§55-210.24 to 55-210.24:2.
Refunds, §55-210.6:2.
Unemployment compensation.
Employer taxation.
Financing of benefits to employees, §60.2-501.
Authority to terminate elections, §60.2-503.
Unlawfully transacting or offering to transact business, §13.1-812.
Virginia nonprofit corporation act, §13.1-801.
Voting by members.
Action by single and multiple voting groups, §13.1-850.
Corporation's acceptance of votes, §13.1-848.
Cumulative voting, voting for directors, §13.1-852.
Directors, §13.1-852.
Entitlement, §13.1-846.
Inspectors of elections, §13.1-847.1.
Proxies, §13.1-847.
Determination of validity of proxies, §13.1-847.1.
Voting agreements, §13.1-852.2.
Voting requirements, §13.1-849.
Change in, §13.1-851.
Voting groups.
Action by single and multiple groups, §13.1-850.
Amendments, voting on, §13.1-887.
Record date, §13.1-844.
Voting requirements, §13.1-849.
Change in, §13.1-851.
Winding up and liquidating business.
Effect of dissolution, §13.1-906.
Withdrawal of foreign corporation, §13.1-929.
Written notice, §13.1-810.

NONPROFIT CRIME INFORMATION GATHERING ORGANIZATIONS.
Civil immunity, §8.01-220.3.

NONPROFIT DEBT COUNSELING AGENCIES.
Credit counseling generally, §§6.2-2000 to 6.2-2025.
See CREDIT COUNSELING.

NONPROFIT ENTITIES, RETAIL SALES AND USE TAX EXEMPTIONS, §58.1-609.11.
Reports to general assembly on tax exemptions, §58.1-609.12.

NONPROFIT FRATERNAL ORGANIZATIONS.
Alcoholic beverages.
Mixed beverage banquet licenses, §4.1-210.

NONPROFIT HEALTH CARE ENTITIES.
Disposition of assets, §§55-531 to 55-533.
Applicability of chapter, §55-533.
Definitions, §55-531.
Notice to attorney general, §55-532.
Obligations, §55-532.
Publication of public notice, §55-532.
Public meeting, §55-532.

NONPROFIT ORGANIZATIONS PROMOTING VOTER PARTICIPATION.
Persons who may obtain lists of registered voters, §24.2-405.

NONREPAIRABLE VEHICLES, §§46.2-1600 to 46.2-1610.
See SALVAGE VEHICLES.

NONRESIDENTS.
Aircraft.
Operation of aircraft, §5.1-25.
Aircraft accidents.
Service of notice, process and other papers, §§8.01-307 to 8.01-313.
Attachment.
Attachment against remainders, §8.01-547.
Pretrial levy or seizure of attachment, §§8.01-533, 8.01-534.
Service in district court proceedings, §16.1-105.
Auctions and auctioneers.
Licensing applicants, §54.1-603.
Bail bondsmen.
Licensing, §9.1-185.7.
Bail enforcement agents.
Licenses, §9.1-186.7.
Bond for costs upon suit by nonresident, §17.1-607.
Indemnity of obligor in bond, §17.1-608.
Broker-dealers, investment advisors, investment advisor representatives or agents.
Service of process on, appointment of clerk of state corporation commission, §13.1-517.
Child custody proceeding.
Uniform child custody jurisdiction and enforcement act.
Generally, §§20-146.1 to 20-146.38.
See CHILD CUSTODY.
Ordering to appear with or without child, §20-146.21.
Civil commitment of mentally ill persons.
Disposition of nonresidents, §37.2-826.
Clam licenses, §28.2-500.
Coal mine worker certification.
Reciprocal acceptance of other certificates, §45.1-161.33.
Commercial drivers' licenses, §46.2-341.8.
Compulsory school attendance.
Nonresident children, §§22.1-255, 22.1-263.
Concealed weapons permits, §18.2-308.06.

NONRESIDENTS —Cont'd
Conservators.
Property transfers to nonresident fiduciary, §§64.2-1426 to 64.2-1432.
Consumer finance companies.
Collection of loans made outside state, §6.2-1529.
Court costs and fees.
Security for costs upon suit by, §17.1-607.
Indemnity obtained by obligor on bonds, §17.1-608.
Decedents' estates.
Money transfers, §64.2-609.
Personal property transfers, §64.2-609.
Security transfers, §64.2-608.
Descent and distribution.
Money transfers, §64.2-609.
Personal property transfers, §64.2-609.
Security transfers, §64.2-608.
Driver improvement programs.
Scope of article, §46.2-491.
Drivers' licenses.
Issuance of driver's license prohibited, §46.2-323.1.
Restricted driver's privilege.
Issuance to out-of-state licensees, §46.2-398.1.
When license not required.
Military privately-owned vehicle driver's license, §46.2-308.
Nonresidents licensed in home state, §46.2-307.
Temporary exemption for new resident licensed under laws of another state, §46.2-308.
Eminent domain.
Service of notice.
Nonresident owner, §25.1-212.
Estate tax.
Defined, §58.1-903.
Duty of resident representative of nonresident decedent, §58.1-910.
Imposition on transfer of taxable estate, §58.1-903.
Payment to other states, §§58.1-913 to 58.1-919.
Evidence.
Affidavit prima facie evidence of nonresidence, §8.01-414.
Fiduciaries, §§64.2-1426 to 64.2-1432.
Property transfers to nonresident fiduciary, §§64.2-1426 to 64.2-1432.
Service of notice, process and other papers.
Designation of clerk of court as agent for service, §64.2-1419.
Firearms.
Concealed weapons permits, §18.2-308.06.
Fishing.
Inland waters.
Interjurisdictional inland waters, §§29.1-534, 29.1-535.
Licensing.
Exemptions, §29.1-301.
Required, §29.1-321.
Trip fishing licenses, §29.1-311.
Saltwater recreational licenses.
Lifetime permit, §28.2-302.10:1.
Tidal waters.
Fees for licenses, §28.2-201.
Harvesters' licenses, §28.2-227.
Menhaden taking with purse nets.
Applications, §28.2-400.
Service of notice, process and other papers, §28.2-401.
Hunting.
Licensing.
Bear hunting, §29.1-305.

NONRESIDENTS —Cont'd
Hunting —Cont'd
Licensing —Cont'd
Deer hunting, §29.1-305.
Exemptions, §29.1-301.
Fees, §29.1-303.
Foxhound training preserves, §29.1-304.
Nonresident trip hunting license, §29.1-303.1.
Required, §29.1-321.
Shooting preserves, §29.1-304.
Turkey hunting, §29.1-305.
Husband and wife.
Appointments of attorneys-in-fact by married women, §55-43.
Income tax.
Estates or trust.
Share of income from Virginia sources, §58.1-363.
Estimated tax upon sale of real property, filing, §58.1-317.
Individual income tax, §58.1-325.
Commuters into state daily, filing not required, §58.1-342.
Credit for taxes paid state of residence, §58.1-332.
One spouse nonresident, §58.1-326.
Information reporting on rental payments to nonresident payees, §58.1-316.
Partnerships.
Nonresident owners, §58.1-395.
Income tax withholding.
Reciprocity with other states, §58.1-482.
Virginia source income of nonresident owners, §58.1-486.2.
Insurance adjusters.
Nonresident licenses, reciprocal agreements, §38.2-1845.5.
Person moving into Commonwealth from another jurisdiction, §38.2-1845.6.
Unlicensed public adjusters process, §§38.2-812 to 38.2-815.
Insurance agents.
Continuing education, exemptions from requirements, §38.2-1871.
Insurance brokers and agents process, §§38.2-808 to 38.2-811.
Licensing, §38.2-1836.
Portable electronics insurance, §38.2-1878.
Service of process, clerk of state corporation commission as agent, §38.2-1836.
Insurance companies.
Unlicensed insurers, §§38.2-800 to 38.2-807.
Insurance consultant licensing, §38.2-1845.
Intangible personal property tax.
Situs of business domicile, §58.1-1106.
Jurisdiction.
Suits against state, US Const Amd 11.
Landlord and tenant.
Service of process agent appointment, §55-218.1.
Married women's property rights.
Appointments of attorneys-in-fact, §55-43.
Mental health or substance abuse.
Property transfers of nonresidents, §§64.2-1426 to 64.2-1432.
Mortgages and deeds of trust.
Trustees for security trusts, §55-58.1.
Motorcycle dealers.
Licensed in other states.
Fee for license of motorcycle dealer, §46.2-1993.17.

NONRESIDENTS —Cont'd
Motorcycle dealers —Cont'd
Licensed in other states —Cont'd
Sale at wholesale auction.
Certificate of dealer registration required, §46.2-1993.6.
License plates.
Operation under foreign dealers license, §46.2-1993.51.
Motor vehicle insurance.
Assignment of risks, §46.2-470.
Motor vehicle operators.
Service of notice, process and other papers, §§8.01-307 to 8.01-313.
Motor vehicle proof of financial responsibility.
Certificate of insurance carrier, §§46.2-440, 46.2-441.
Motor vehicle registration.
Active duty military personnel.
Vehicles registered or titled in another state, §46.2-600.
Nonresident owners of foreign vehicles, §§46.2-655 to 46.2-661.
Notaries.
Notice of change of address, §47.1-18.
Registered and commissioned as notary.
Qualifications, §47.1-4.
Removal of notary's residence from Commonwealth.
Maintaining commission, §47.1-22.
Oysters.
Licenses, §28.2-500.
Planting grounds.
General oyster planting grounds.
Assignments.
Eligibility, §28.2-604.
Residents not to be associated with nonresidents, §28.2-635.
Prohibitions on planting or taking, §28.2-634.
Partnerships.
Income tax.
Nonresident owners, §58.1-395.
Party served by publication and not appearing.
Time period for rehearing of case to correct injustice, §8.01-322.
Personal injury actions against estates of deceased nonresidents.
Appointment of administrator, §64.2-454.
Personal property taxes.
Intangible personal property tax.
Situs of business domicile, §58.1-1106.
Situs for assessment, §58.1-3511.
Personal representatives, §§64.2-1426 to 64.2-1432.
Personal service on nonresident outside Virginia equivalent to order of publication, §8.01-320.
Pharmacies shipping, mailing or delivering drugs or devices into Commonwealth.
Registration, disclosures, toll-free telephone service, prescription monitoring program compliance, §54.1-3434.1.
Application for registration, renewal, §54.1-3434.2.
Denial, revocation or suspension of registration, §54.1-3434.3.
Prohibited acts, unregistered pharmacies, §54.1-3434.4.
Powers of attorney to insurer or contractor.
Fee charged by secretary of Commonwealth, §2.2-409.

NONRESIDENTS —Cont'd
Private investigators.
Private security services businesses.
Exceptions, §9.1-140.
Property rights of married women.
Appointments of attorneys-in-fact, §55-43.
Public accountants.
Licenses.
Substantial equivalency, §54.1-4411.
Publication, service by, when available, §8.01-316.
Public procurement.
Nonresident contractors with absolute preference, §2.2-4324.
Real property.
Rental payments to nonresident payees.
Tax information reporting on, §58.1-316.
Sale of real property.
Estimated tax, filing, §58.1-317.
Retail franchisors, service of process on, §13.1-566.
Securities.
Transfers upon death, §64.2-608.
Security for costs upon suit by nonresident, §17.1-607.
Indemnity obtained by obligor in bond, §17.1-608.
Service of notice, process and other papers.
Aircraft accidents, §§8.01-307 to 8.01-313.
Attachment in district court, §16.1-105.
Broker-dealers, investment advisors, investment advisor representatives or agents.
Clerk of state corporation commission as agent for receipt, §13.1-517.
Fiduciaries.
Designation of clerk of court as agent for service, §64.2-1419.
Insurance adjusters.
Unlicensed public adjusters process, §§38.2-812 to 38.2-815.
Insurance agents.
Clerk of state corporation commission as agent for service, §38.2-1836.
Insurance brokers and agents process, §§38.2-808 to 38.2-811.
Insurance companies, unlicensed insurers, §§38.2-800 to 38.2-807.
Issuers of securities.
Appointment of clerk of state corporation commission as agent, §13.1-517.
Landlord and tenant, §55-218.1.
Motor vehicle accidents, §§8.01-307 to 8.01-313.
Party served by publication and not appearing.
Time period for rehearing, §8.01-322.
Personal service on nonresident outside state equivalent to order of publication, §8.01-320.
Publication, service by, when available, §8.01-316.
Retail franchisors, §13.1-566.
Sex offender and crimes against minors registry.
Registration, when required, §9.1-905.
Surplus lines insurance.
Licensing of brokers, §38.2-1857.9.
Taxes or assessments for local improvements.
Notice to nonresidents, §15.2-2409.
Traffic infractions.
Arrest of nonresidents.
Definitions, §46.2-944.
Issuance of citation to motorist, §46.2-945.
Noncompliance with citation, §§46.2-945, 46.2-946.

NONRESIDENTS —Cont'd
Trailer dealers.
Fee for registration of dealers licensed in other state, §46.2-1992.17.
Trapping.
Licensing.
Exemptions, §29.1-301.
Issuance, §29.1-321.
Trustees, §§64.2-1426 to 64.2-1432.
Viatical settlements.
Broker licensing, §38.2-1865.4.
Providers, §38.2-6002.
Weapons.
Concealed weapons permits, §18.2-308.06.
Wills.
Money transfers, §64.2-609.
Personal property transfers, §64.2-609.
Personalty, disposition of, §64.2-407.
Probate.
Bills to impeach or establish.
Tolling of period, §64.2-448.
Foreign proved wills, §64.2-450.
Security transfers upon death, §64.2-608.
Trust devises or bequests, §64.2-426.
Wrongful death action against estates of deceased nonresidents.
Appointment of administrator, §64.2-454.

NONRESIDENT VIOLATOR COMPACT, §§46.2-483 to 46.2-488.

NONSTOCK CORPORATIONS, §§13.1-801 to 13.1-945.
See NONPROFIT CORPORATIONS.

NONSUIT.
Actions generally.
See ACTIONS.
Additional nonsuit, court allowing, stipulation, §8.01-380.
Consent of adverse party required.
Adverse party filing counterclaim, cross-claim or third-party claim, §8.01-380.
Dismissal of action by nonsuit generally, §8.01-380.
Improper venue chosen after nonsuit, transfer, §8.01-380.
Landlord and tenant.
Recoveries for rent and for use and occupation, §55-227.
New proceeding after nonsuit, with court, §8.01-380.
One nonsuit taken as matter of right, §8.01-380.
Reimbursement of expert witness fees and travel costs.
Determination of reasonableness of expenses, §8.01-380.
Retention of ended case files by circuit court clerk, time, destruction, §17.1-213.
Statute of limitations.
Suspension or tolling of statute, §8.01-229.
Subsequent nonsuits, §8.01-380.
Suspension or tolling of statute of limitations, §8.01-229.
Time for allowing party to suffer, §8.01-380.

NONSUPPORT.
Desertion and nonsupport generally, §§20-61 to 20-88.02:1.
See DESERTION AND NONSUPPORT.

NONTIDAL WATERS.
Sanitation districts law of 1946, §§21-224 to 21-290.

NONVIOLENT FELONIES.
Community based probation agency.
Sentencing to, conditions, imposition, revocation, §19.2-303.3.
Sentencing to detention center incarceration program, §19.2-316.2.
Sentencing to diversion center incarceration program, §19.2-316.3.

NOOSE.
Displaying on property of another or in public place.
Criminal offense, §18.2-423.2.

NO-PAR STOCK, §6.2-808.

NORFOLK.
Branch pilot licensing.
Provision violations.
Court jurisdiction, §54.1-924.
Circuit court, §17.1-500.
Jurisdiction over river, watercourse or bay lying between county or city.
Inapplicability of provisions, §17.1-516.
Coastal primary sand dunes and beaches.
Zoning ordinances, §28.2-1403.
Confederate cemeteries and graves.
Disbursement of funds appropriated for upkeep, §10.1-2211.
Delinquent real estate card system record and index, §58.1-3932.
Fishing, tidal waters.
Regulations.
Publication, §28.2-209.
Housing authorities.
Eminent domain.
Limitation on city of Norfolk, §36-27.2.
Improvements.
Taxes or assessments for local improvements.
Authority to impose, §15.2-2404.
Judgment records in office of circuit court clerk, validation, §17.1-254.
Local school boards.
Appointment and terms, §22.1-51.
Magistrates, appointment from adjoining judicial districts, §19.2-37.
Medical care facilities.
Certificates of public need.
Moratorium exceptions, §32.1-102.3:2.
Metropolitan transportation district, 1970 ch 697.
Metropolitan uniform laws commission, 1968 ch 329.
Motor carriers, passengers.
Irregular route passenger certificates.
Presumption of need, §46.2-2080.
Port authority.
Board of commissioners, §62.1-129.
Port of Virginia economic and infrastructure development zone grant fund, §62.1-132.3:2.
Public defenders office.
Established, §19.2-163.04.
Public service corporations, taxation of property.
Restriction of imposition of additional tax, §58.1-2606.
Railroads.
Light rail system, extension to Virginia Beach, §33.1-221.1:8 (note).
Referendum elections.
Specific charter authorization required, §24.2-684.

NORFOLK —Cont'd
Retail sales and use tax.
Additional sales tax for Northern Virginia and Hampton Roads, §58.1-603.1.
Additional use tax for Northern Virginia and Hampton Roads, §58.1-604.01.
Revolutionary war cemeteries and graves.
Disbursement of funds appropriated for upkeep, §10.1-2211.1.
Sale of delinquent tax lands.
Special masters.
Appointment, special provisions applicable, §58.1-3970.1.
School board.
Fingerprinting applicants for employment, §22.1-296.2.
Salary of members, §22.1-32.
Semi-automatic firearms and shotguns.
Carrying loaded firearms in public areas, §18.2-287.4.
Sports authority of Hampton Roads, Virginia, 1986 ch 426.
Summons and process.
Who may serve process, §8.01-293.
Zoning.
Retail alcoholic beverage control licensees.
Special exception, expiration, change of ownership, §15.2-2286.
Zoning ordinance.
Coastal primary sand dunes and beaches, §28.2-1403.

NORFOLK AREA MEDICAL CENTER AUTHORITY.
See EASTERN VIRGINIA MEDICAL SCHOOL.

NORFOLK COUNTY.
Cemeteries.
Location restrictions, §57-26.

NORFOLK PARKING AUTHORITY, 1964 ch 208.

NORFOLK PORT AND INDUSTRIAL AUTHORITY.
Created, 1948 ch 463.
Amended in 1954, 1954 ch 564.
Amended in 1956, 1956 ch 391.
Amended in 1958, 1958 ch 131.
Amended in 1960, 1960 ch 408.
Amended in 1964, 1964 ch 287.
Amended in 1968, 1968 ch 196.
Amended in 1970, 1970 ch 484.
Amended in 1972, 1972 ch 760.
Amended in 1978, 1978 ch 186.
Amended in 1980, 1980 ch 36, 1980 ch 42.

NORFOLK STATE UNIVERSITY, §§23-174.1 to 23-174.7.
Board of visitors, §§23-174.4 to 23-174.6.
Campus police departments, §§23-232 to 23-238.
Reporting campus crime, §23-9.1:1.
Coastal energy research consortium, §§67-600 to 67-604.
Conferring of degrees, §23-174.7.
Control of general assembly, §23-174.1.
Corporate name, §23-174.2.
Special license plates, §46.2-749.
Transfer of property, §23-174.3.
Tuition, fees and other charges, §23-174.7.
Universities generally, §§23-1.01 to 23-9.2:8.
See COLLEGES AND UNIVERSITIES.

NORTHAMPTON COUNTY.
Circuit court judges exercising appointment power to local post, board or commission.
Exercise of appointment powers, §17.1-501.

NORTHAMPTON COUNTY —Cont'd
Coastal primary sand dunes and beaches.
Zoning ordinance, §28.2-1403.
Crabs.
Dredging restrictions, §28.2-707.
Fishing nets.
Restrictions, §28.2-309.
Fish trotlines, §28.2-310.
Oysters.
Planting grounds.
General oyster planting grounds.
Rights of assignees, §28.2-618.
Riparian oyster planting grounds.
Assignments, §28.2-602.
Seed oysters.
Permits to buy or carry, §28.2-535.
Use of dredges, scrapes or rakes on ocean side of Eastern Shore, §28.2-519.
School board.
Salary of members, §22.1-32.
Waterfowl blinds.
Application of provisions, §29.1-350.
Zoning ordinance.
Coastal primary sand dunes and beaches, §28.2-1403.

NORTH CAROLINA.
Boundary with, §1-304.
Eastward from low-water mark of Atlantic ocean, §1-305.
Roanoke river basin bi-state commission, §§62.1-69.36 to 62.1-69.44.

NORTHERN NECK CHESAPEAKE BAY PUBLIC ACCESS AUTHORITY, §§15.2-6626 to 15.2-6651.
Agreement with Commonwealth and participating political subdivisions, §15.2-6647.
Alternative method for doing things authorized.
Act provides, §15.2-6648.
Appropriation by political subdivisions, §15.2-6645.
Audit, §15.2-6635.
Board of directors.
Appointment, removal, §15.2-6630.
Bylaws, adoption, §15.2-6631.
No personal liability on bonds issued by authority, §15.2-6641.
Officers, election, §15.2-6631.
Quorum, §15.2-6631.
Bonds, §§15.2-6638 to 15.2-6644.
Bylaws, adoption, §15.2-6631.
Contracts with political subdivisions, §15.2-6646.
Creation, §15.2-6627.
Credit of Commonwealth and participating political subdivision not pledged, §15.2-6640.
Definitions, §15.2-6628.
Deposit of money of authority, §15.2-6637.
Dissolution, §15.2-6632.
Donations by political subdivisions, §15.2-6645.
Exemption from taxation, §15.2-6643.
Existing contracts, leases or franchises not impaired, §15.2-6650.
Fees, rents and other charges, §15.2-6639.
Fire protection codes and building regulations.
Authority subject to, §15.2-6649.
Investment of funds of authority, §15.2-6637.

NORTHERN NECK CHESAPEAKE BAY PUBLIC ACCESS AUTHORITY —Cont'd
Legal investments.
Bonds of authority, §15.2-6644.
Liberal construction of provisions, §15.2-6648.
Meetings of authority, §15.2-6631.
Minutes of proceedings.
Keeping, requirement, open to public inspection, §15.2-6635.
Motor vehicles and traffic.
Rules and regulations, §15.2-6634.
Name, §15.2-6633.
Notice.
Rules, regulations, minimum standards.
Adoption, §15.2-6634.
Pecuniary liability not imposed on participating political subdivision, §15.2-6629.
Powers, §15.2-6632.
Procurement of professional service, nonprofessional services and materials.
Subjection public procurement act, §15.2-6636.
Public purpose, declaration, §15.2-6627.
Purposes, §15.2-6627.
Records of financial transactions, §15.2-6635.
Regional entity of government, §15.2-6627.
Region for which authority to exist, §15.2-6627.
Rules, regulations, minimum standards.
Adoption, force and effect of law, §15.2-6634.
Severability of provisions, §15.2-6648.
Title of act, §15.2-6626.
Withdrawal of membership, §15.2-6651.
Zoning, subdivision, erosion and sediment control ordinances.
Authority subject to, §15.2-6649.

NORTHERN NECK-MIDDLE PENINSULA PUBLIC EDUCATION CONSORTIUM, §§22.1-354.6 to 22.1-354.10.
Cooperation of other agencies, §22.1-354.10.
Creation, §22.1-354.6.
Definition of region, §22.1-354.6.
Duties, §22.1-354.7.
Cooperation of other agencies in performance of, §22.1-354.10.
Executive director, §22.1-354.8.
Functions, §22.1-354.7.
Gifts and grants.
Application for and acceptance of, §22.1-354.9.
Governing board, §22.1-354.6.
Staff support, §22.1-354.8.

NORTHERN REGIONAL PARK AUTHORITY, 1977 ch 64.

NORTHERN VIRGINIA BICENTENNIAL CENTER.
Construction, maintenance, etc., of access roads, §33.1-221.

NORTHERN VIRGINIA PARK AND PLANNING DISTRICT, 1930 ch 420, 1932 ch 338, 1938 ch 181.

NORTHERN VIRGINIA PLANNING DISTRICT.
Recordation tax, state.
Regional congestion relief fee, §58.1-802.2.
Retail sales and use tax.
Additional sales tax for Northern Virginia and Hampton Roads, §58.1-603.1.
Additional use tax for Northern Virginia and Hampton Roads, §58.1-604.01.
Repair of motor vehicles.
Authority to impose on labor or services, §58.1-605.

NORTHERN VIRGINIA PLANNING DISTRICT —Cont'd
Snow and ice removal from public sidewalk, §15.2-2025.
Transient occupancy tax, §58.1-1742.

NORTHERN VIRGINIA TRANSPORTATION AUTHORITY, §§15.2-4829 to 15.2-4840.
Advisory committees, §15.2-4837.
Allocation of expenses, §15.2-4835.
Bond issues, §15.2-4839.
Use of certain revenues, §15.2-4838.1.
Chairpersons, §15.2-4832.
Compensation of members, §15.2-4836.
Counties included, §15.2-4831.
Creation of authority, §15.2-4830.
Fund, §15.2-4838.01.
General duties and responsibilities, §15.2-4840.
Long-range planning responsibilities, §15.2-4838.
Members, §15.2-4832.
Planning coordination advisory committee, §15.2-4837.
Policies and priorities, §15.2-4838.
Powers and functions, §15.2-4830.
Quorum, §15.2-4834.
Real estate taxes.
Commercial and industrial real property, classification of, §58.1-3221.3.
Retail sales and use tax.
Repair of motor vehicles.
Authority to impose on labor or services, §58.1-605.
Short title, §15.2-4829.
Staff, §15.2-4833.
Technical advisory committee, §15.2-4837.
Transportation department.
Analysis of transportation projects in Northern Virginia transportation district, §33.1-13.03:1.
Voting requirements, §15.2-4834.

NORTHERN VIRGINIA TRANSPORTATION COMMISSION.
Administrative expenses, allocation, §15.2-4515.
Tax information.
Tax commissioner authorized to divulge, §58.1-3.

NORTHERN VIRGINIA TRANSPORTATION DISTRICT, 1964 ch 630, 1968 ch 449, 1974 ch 251, 1980 ch 144, 1981 ch 227.
Established pursuant to state code, §15.2-4503.1.

NORTHERN VIRGINIA TRANSPORTATION DISTRICT FUND, §58.1-815.1.

NORTHERN VIRGINIA TRANSPORTATION DISTRICT PROGRAM, §33.1-221.1:3.

NORTH LANDING RIVER.
Board of game and inland fisheries.
Control of land, §29.1-103.
Scenic river, §10.1-413.2.

NORTH MAYO RIVER.
Scenic river, §10.1-418.4.

NORTH MEHERRIN RIVER.
Scenic river, §10.1-418.1.

NORTHUMBERLAND COUNTY.
Circuit court.
Port of Reedville.
Appointment of agent, §62.1-163.
Coastal primary sand dunes and beaches.
Zoning ordinance, §28.2-1403.

NORTHUMBERLAND COUNTY —Cont'd
Franchise, privilege, lease or right-to-use public property.
Ferry service for automobiles, §15.2-2105.1.
Northern Neck Chesapeake Bay public access authority, §§15.2-6626 to 15.2-6651.
See NORTHERN NECK CHESAPEAKE BAY PUBLIC ACCESS AUTHORITY.
Northern Neck-Middle Peninsula public education consortium.
Inclusion in region, §22.1-354.6.
School board.
Salary of members, §22.1-32.

NORTHWEST TERRITORY.
Cession of territory northwest of Ohio river, §1-303.

NORTON.
Cumberlands airport commission, 1958 ch 439.
School board.
Salary of members, §22.1-32.
Tax map reference number.
Circuit court clerk indexing by, §17.1-252.
Virginia coalfield economic development authority, §§15.2-6000 to 15.2-6015.

NORTON INDUSTRIAL DEVELOPMENT AUTHORITY, 1962 ch 632.

NOTARIES, §§47.1-1 to 47.1-30.
Acknowledgments.
Corporate acknowledgments, §55-121.
Defined, §47.1-2.
Electronic signatures, §59.1-489.
Military personnel, §§55-114.1, 55-115.
Outside the United States, §§55-114, 55-130.
Seal affixing failures, §55-129.
Proof of authority of person performing notarial acts, §55-118.2.
Validating certain acts, §§55-122 to 55-137.2.
Who may perform notarial acts, §55-118.1.
Within United States, §55-113.
Administrative removal process, §47.1-24.
Appointment.
Power of governor to appoint, §47.1-3.
Armed forces or department of defense personnel.
Administering oath of office to, §49-3.
Armed services members.
Registered and commissioned as notary.
Eligibility, §47.1-4.
Assisting another in drafting, completing, selecting or understanding document, §47.1-15.
Carrying concealed weapons.
Permit required, §18.2-308.
Ceasing to be legal resident.
Revocation of commission, §47.1-23.
Certificate.
Act evidenced by, §47.1-16.
Change of address, §47.1-18.
Change of name, §47.1-17.
Civil liability, §§47.1-26, 47.1-27.
Clerk of circuit court.
Appearance before to qualify.
Generally, time period, return of unclaimed commission, cancellation, §47.1-9.
Commission.
Appearance before clerk of circuit court to qualify.
Generally, time limit, return of unclaimed commission, cancellation, §47.1-9.

NOTARIES —Cont'd
Commission —Cont'd
Application, §47.1-5.
Electronic notary public, §47.1-7.
Misrepresentation as to felony conviction, §47.1-28.
Misstatement of fact.
Revocation of commission, §47.1-23.
Recommission, §47.1-5.1.
Records kept by secretary, retention period, §47.1-10.
Cancellation.
Failure to appear before clerk in timely manner, §47.1-9.
Disqualification to hold.
Removal from office, time period, §47.1-25.
Electronic notary public, §47.1-7.
Issuance of commission, §47.1-8.
Expiration date, §47.1-21.
Statement by notary upon notarial act, §47.1-16.
Issuance, §47.1-8.
Notification that commission granted and where it may be secured, §47.1-8.
Oath of notary, §47.1-9.
Qualifications, §47.1-4.
Recommission, §47.1-5.1.
Removal from Commonwealth.
Consent of secretary to maintain, §47.1-22.
Resignation of commission, §47.1-22.
Revocation.
Grounds, §47.1-23.
Secretary of the Commonwealth to commission, §47.1-3.
Surrender, §47.1-24.
Term, §47.1-21.
Time limit.
Appearance before clerk to qualify, §47.1-9.
Unclaimed commission.
Return, §47.1-9.
Commonwealth at large.
Fee for issuing commission, §2.2-409.
Compelling attendance of witnesses, §8.01-407.
Conflicts of interest, §47.1-30.
County or city and state act performed.
Notarization to include, §47.1-16.
Date act performed.
Notarization to include, §47.1-16.
Date of expiration of commission.
Writings subject of notarial act to state, §47.1-16.
Declining to notarize document.
Authority, §47.1-15.
Defined, §§1-226, 47.1-2.
Disqualification from office, §47.1-25.
Duties of clerks, §47.1-9.
Duty of care, §47.1-14.
Electoral board members or registrars.
Collecting notary fees during time of appointment.
Prohibition, §47.1-19.
Electronic notary public.
Appearance before clerk to qualify, §47.1-9.
Application for commission, §47.1-5.
Authenticity of electronic notarial act.
Evidence of, §47.1-11.1.
Certificate.
Act evidenced by, §47.1-16.
Certificate of authority for an electronic notarial act, §47.1-11.1.
Change of name.
New commission, application, time limit, §47.1-17.

NOTARIES —Cont'd
Electronic notary public —Cont'd
Defined, §47.1-2.
Device used to create electronic signature.
Duties concerning, §47.1-14.
Duties of notaries performing electronic notarial acts, §47.1-14.
Equipment and technical aspects of electronic notarization.
Assistance to secretary in developing standards, §47.1-6.1.
Fees, §47.1-19.
Lost or stolen record, signature or seal.
Duty upon discovering, §47.1-14.
Notarization requirements, §47.1-16.
Oath, §47.1-9.
Possessing, concealing, damaging or destroying notary's software or hardware.
Criminal penalty, §47.1-29.1.
Prohibited acts, §47.1-15.
Records of notarial acts.
Duty to keep, requirements, §47.1-14.
Registration with and commission by secretary.
Authority upon being commissioned, §47.1-8.
Issuance of commission, §47.1-8.
Requirements, §47.1-7.
Resignation or ceasing to be notary.
Destruction of coding, disk, certification, card, software or seal, §47.1-22.
Retention of electronic records.
Time period, §47.1-14.
Standards for electronic notarization, §47.1-6.1.
Use of record, signature or seal by person other than notary.
Duty upon discovering, §47.1-14.
Employer fee agreements, §47.1-20.
Employer inducing notary to commit official misconduct, §47.1-28.
English language.
Becoming incapable of reading or writing.
Revocation of commission, §47.1-23.
Extraterritorial powers.
Powers outside Commonwealth, §47.1-13.
For use in Commonwealth, §47.1-13.1.
Federal employees.
Notarial acts.
Authority to perform within Commonwealth, §47.1-13.
Federal employees prohibited, exception, §2.2-2801.
Fees, §§47.1-19, 47.1-20.
Charging more than established fee.
Unlawful, §47.1-19.
Commission to notary for Commonwealth at large, §2.2-409.
Safe deposit boxes.
Opening after nonpayment of rent, §6.2-2309.
Felony conviction.
Misrepresentation on application for commission, §47.1-28.
Revocation of commission, §47.1-23.
Fraud or deceit.
Performance of official act with intent to deceive or defraud, §47.1-15.
Identity of subject.
Means of identification, §47.1-14.
Satisfactory evidence of identity, §§47.1-2, 47.1-14.
Impersonation of a notary, §47.1-29.
Issuance of notary commission, §47.1-8.
Jurisdiction.
Territorial jurisdiction, §47.1-13.

NOTARIES —Cont'd
Mail carriers.
Federal employees prohibited, exception, §2.2-2801.
Mentally incompetent.
Adjudication.
Revocation of commission, §47.1-23.
Names of notaries and date of registration and qualification.
Records kept by secretary of the Commonwealth, §47.1-10.
Nonattorney notaries.
Prohibitions, §47.1-15.
Nonresidents.
Notice of change of address, §47.1-18.
Registered and commissioned as notary.
Qualifications, §47.1-4.
Removal of notary's residence from Commonwealth.
Maintaining commission, §47.1-22.
Notarial acts.
Civil liability, §47.1-26.
Conflict of interest, §47.1-30.
Defined, §47.1-12.
Duty of care, §47.1-14.
Electronic notarial act.
Authenticity, evidence of, §47.1-11.1.
Certificate of authority, §47.1-11.1.
Defined, §47.1-2.
Duties of notaries performing, §47.1-14.
Records of notarial acts.
Duty to keep, requirements, §47.1-14.
Evidence of, §47.1-16.
Expiration date of commission.
Statement by notary, §47.1-16.
Federal government employees.
Authority to perform within Commonwealth, §47.1-13.
Fees, §47.1-19.
Agreements with employers, §47.1-20.
Persons authorized to perform outside the Commonwealth.
For use in Commonwealth, §47.1-13.1.
Powers, §47.1-12.
Powers outside the Commonwealth, §47.1-13.
For use in Commonwealth, §47.1-13.1.
Prohibitions, §47.1-15.
Revocation of commission, §47.1-23.
Requirements of notarization, §47.1-16.
Validation of prior acts, §47.1-20.1.
Notarial certificate wording on same page as signature, §47.1-15.
Notarization requirements, §47.1-16.
Oath, §47.1-9.
Military or department of defense personnel.
Administering oath of office to, §49-3.
Official misconduct.
Conflict of interest, §47.1-30.
Defined, §47.1-2.
Removal from office by administrative process, §47.1-24.
Revocation of commission, §47.1-23.
Powers, §47.1-12.
Outside Commonwealth, §47.1-13.
For use in Commonwealth, §47.1-13.1.
Territorial jurisdiction, §47.1-13.
Presence of signer at time of notarization.
Requirement, exception, §47.1-15.
Prohibitions, §47.1-15.
Revocation of commission, §47.1-23.

NOTARIES —Cont'd
Qualification for appointment.
Fee for qualifying notaries, §17.1-275.
Qualifications to be commissioned as notary, §47.1-4.
Reasonable care in performance of duties.
Duty to exercise, §47.1-14.
Records kept by secretary, retention period, §47.1-10.
Reference materials for notaries.
Secretary to prepare, copies, availability, §47.1-11.
Registered with secretary of the Commonwealth, §47.1-3.
Electronic notary public, §47.1-7.
Removal by administrative process, §47.1-24.
Disqualification to hold office.
Time period, §47.1-25.
Removal of residence from Commonwealth, §47.1-22.
Resignation, §47.1-22.
Retention of records.
Secretary of the Commonwealth, §47.1-10.
Revocation of commission, §§47.1-23 to 47.1-25.
Administrative process, §47.1-24.
Disqualification from office, §47.1-25.
Grounds, §47.1-23.
Surrender of commission, §47.1-24.
Safe deposit boxes.
Opening after notice for nonpayment of rent, §§6.2-2306 to 6.2-2309.
Seal affixed to notarial certificate.
Requirement, §47.1-16.
Short title, §47.1-1.
Signature of notary.
Specimen of each notary commissioned.
Secretary of the Commonwealth to keep, §47.1-10.
Software or hardware of electronic notary.
Possessing, concealing, damaging or destroying.
Criminal penalty, §47.1-29.1.
Statement of fee at bottom of document, §17.1-270.
Surrender of commission, §47.1-24.
Territorial jurisdiction, §47.1-13.
Title of act, §47.1-1.
Travel expenses.
Agreement to recover, §47.1-19.
Unauthorized practice of law.
Revocation of commission, §47.1-23.
Validation of certain acts, §47.1-20.1.
Willful misconduct, §47.1-28.

NOTATION CREDIT.
Letters of credit, §8.5A-108.

NOTES.
Colleges and universities.
Restructured financial and administrative operations.
Bonds, notes or other obligations.
Authority of covered institution, §§23-38.107, 23-38.108.
Deceased persons, validity of writing payable to, §11-9.
Defined as negotiable instrument, §8.3A-104.
Dishonor, §8.3A-502.
Electronic transactions.
Transferable records, §59.1-494.
Embezzlement, §18.2-111.
Forging coin or bank notes, §18.2-170.
Having in possession, §18.2-173.

NOTES —Cont'd
Insurance companies investments generally, §§38.2-1400 to 38.2-1447.
Intangible personal property tax, §§58.1-1100 to 58.1-1118.
See PERSONAL PROPERTY TAXES.
Investment of public funds.
Corporate notes, §2.2-4510.
Joint names, securities registered in, §§13.1-434 to 13.1-436.
Larceny of bank notes, §18.2-98.
Lost evidence of debt.
Action on, §8.01-32.
Negotiable instruments generally, §§8.3A-101 to 8.3A-605.
See NEGOTIABLE INSTRUMENTS.
Obligation for which taken, §8.3A-310.
Obligation of issuer, §8.3A-412.
Promissory notes.
See PROMISSORY NOTES.
Securities generally, §§13.1-501 to 13.1-527.3.
See SECURITIES.
Signatures on notes issued by corporation, §13.1-647.

NOTES IN ANTICIPATION OF BOND ISSUE.
Bonds issued by locality, §§15.2-2628 to 15.2-2631.

NOT FIRST CLASS GOODS.
Advertising or offering for sale, prohibited practices, §59.1-200.

NOT GUILTY BY REASON OF INSANITY, §§19.2-182.2 to 19.2-182.16.
See ACQUITTAL BY REASON OF INSANITY.

NOT GUILTY PLEAS.
Arraignment.
Court refusal to accept plea of guilty.
Lesser offense included in charge, §19.2-254.
Judicial examination of accused.
Suggested questions to be put by court to accused, VA SCt Rules Part 3A Appx Form 7.
Nontraffic offenses for which prepayment authorized, §19.2-254.2.
Pretrial diversion, §19.2-303.2.
Traffic infraction cases, §19.2-254.1.
Writ of actual innocence, §§19.2-327.2 to 19.2-327.6, VA SCt Rule 5:7B.
Form, VA SCt Rules Part 5A Appx Form 12.
Nonbiological evidence, writ based on, §§19.2-327.10 to 19.2-327.14.

NOTICE.
Abandoned motor vehicles.
Removal and disposition of unattended or immobilized vehicles, §§46.2-1213, 46.2-1215.
Vehicle taken into custody, §46.2-1202.
Abandonment of manufactured home, §55-248.44:1.
ABC board.
Applications for licenses and permits.
Notice to localities, §4.1-230.
Initial notice by certified mail, subsequent notices by regular mail, §4.1-101.1.
Interdiction of intoxicated driver or habitual drunkard, §4.1-333.
Refusal to grant licenses, §4.1-224.
Suspension or revocation of licenses, §4.1-227.
Suspension or revocation of permits, §4.1-229.
Absconding persons.
Publication of interim notice.
Party who changes residence without filing forwarding address with clerk, §8.01-319.

NOTICE —Cont'd
Absentee voting.
Rejected ballots, §24.2-711.1.
Abutting landowners taxed or assessed for improvement, §15.2-2405.
Amount of assessment, §§15.2-2408, 15.2-2409.
Acceptance of service by another.
Notice to be mailed to defendant, §8.01-315.
Accounts in financial institutions, adverse claim, §6.2-602.
Actions without meeting of directors, §13.1-865.
Administrative process.
Formal hearings, §2.2-4020.
Hearings.
Decision is due, §2.2-4021.
Regulations.
Evidentiary hearings, §2.2-4009.
Fast-track rulemaking process.
Noncontroversial regulation, §2.2-4012.1.
Notice of intended regulatory action, §2.2-4007.01.
Petitions, §2.2-4007.
Revisions, §§2.2-4007.03, 2.2-4007.06.
Adoption of 1950 code.
Effect on notice given, taken or issued before code in force, §1-8.
Adoption of children.
Consent of birth parent withheld.
Notice of right to be represented by counsel, §63.2-1203.
Adult day care centers.
Summary order of suspension and other proceedings, §63.2-1709.
Adult protective services.
Hearing as to emergency protective services, §63.2-1608.
Initial notice by certified mail.
Subsequent notices by regular mail, §63.2-100.1.
Adverse claim to account in financial institution, §6.2-602.
Adverse insurance underwriting decisions, §38.2-610.
Advertising notice generally.
See PUBLICATION.
Agricultural and forestal districts, §15.2-4303.
Application for creation or addition, §15.2-4307.
Proposals as to land acquisition or construction within district, §15.2-4313.
Public hearing, §15.2-4309.
Agricultural cooperative associations.
Amendments to articles of incorporation, §13.1-318.
Bylaw adoption, amendment or revision, §13.1-319.
Meetings, §13.1-323.
Agriculture and consumer services department.
Initial notice by certified mail, subsequent notices by regular mail, §3.2-101.1.
Agritourism activity liability.
Limited liability, warning required, §3.2-6402.
Air pollution control board.
Initial notice by certified mail, subsequent notices by regular mail, §10.1-1300.1.
Permits.
Public hearings on, §10.1-1322.01.
Qualified fumigation facilities.
Notice and operational requirements, §10.1-1308.1.

NOTICE —Cont'd
Alcoholic beverage sales at licensed establishment.
Temporary injunction sought by locality.
Establishment meeting place for committing serious criminal violations.
Hearing, §48-17.1.
Aliens, commitment to correctional facilities, §53.1-218.
Animal boarding establishments.
Confinement and disposition of abandoned or stray animals, §§3.2-6546, 3.2-6548.
Written notice of consumer remedies, §3.2-6519.
Annexation, §15.2-3204.
Agreements between towns and counties defining town's annexation rights.
Public hearing before commission on local government, §15.2-3232.
Immunity of county from city-initiated annexation and city incorporation.
Determination of county eligibility, §15.2-3303.
Order fixing additional parties, §15.2-3205.
Annulment of marriage.
Revocation of death benefits by annulment, §20-111.1.
Annulment of town charter, §15.2-3703.
Arbitration.
Change of award by arbitrators, §8.01-581.08.
Asbestos notification, §§40.1-51.20 to 40.1-51.22.
Assignments for the benefit of creditors.
Income assignments, §55-162.
Fees, §55-167.
Termination of assignments, §55-166.
Property assignments, §55-156.
Assisted living facilities.
Summary order of suspension and other proceedings, §63.2-1709.
Attachment.
Hearing on claim of exemption, §8.01-546.2.
Attorney discipline, VA SCt Rule Pt 6 §IV Par 13-12.
Appeal of board determination, VA SCt Rule Pt 6 §IV Par 13-19.
Appeals from board proceedings, VA SCt Rule Pt 6 §IV Par 13-26.
Criminal adjudication or guilty plea, VA SCt Rule Pt 6 §IV Par 13-22.
District committees proceedings, VA SCt Rule Pt 6 §IV Par 13-16.
Notice of impairment evidence, VA SCt Rule Pt 6 §IV Par 13-12.
Reinstatement, VA SCt Rule Pt 6 §IV Par 13-25.
Subcommittee actions, VA SCt Rule Pt 6 §IV Par 13-15.
Attorney licensing.
Forfeiture of license for failure to pay fees, §54.1-3914.
Proceedings pending disciplinary actions, §54.1-3936.
Bad checks.
Check returned unpaid, §8.01-27.2.
Bail and recognizance.
Denial of bail.
Notice of right to appeal, §19.2-120.
Bail bondsmen.
Recovery of bailee.
Notice to law enforcement, §9.1-185.15.
Banks.
Acquisition of interests in financial institutions.
Notice of intent to acquire out-of-state bank, §6.2-715.

NOTICE —Cont'd
Banks —Cont'd
FDIC receivership.
Notice and proof of claim, §6.2-931.
Posting of notice, effect, §6.2-928.
Impairment of capital stock, §6.2-906.
Interstate bank mergers.
Notice of subsequent merger, §6.2-859.
Interstate branch banks.
Notice of subsequent merger, §6.2-847.
State bank becoming national bank.
Notice to state corporation commission, §6.2-825.
Baseball stadium authority.
Selection of site of stadium, public hearing, §15.2-5806.
Bawdy place.
Building and other structure harboring.
Locality requiring removal, repair, etc., §15.2-908.1.
Beekeeping.
Diseased bees, §3.2-4404.
Beer franchises.
Cancellation of agreement, §4.1-506.
Behavioral health and developmental services department.
Notice by mail, §37.2-101.
Biotechnology research act.
Regulated introduction.
Public notice of proposed introductions, §2.2-5504.
Birth-related neurological injury compensation.
Awards, §38.2-5009.
Notification of possible beneficiaries, §38.2-5004.1.
Blue Alert program.
Missing law enforcement officers, §§52-34.7 to 52-34.9.
Boards of equalization.
Increase and assessment, §58.1-3381.
Notice when increase requested after taxpayer filed appeal, §58.1-3379.
Sittings by boards, §58.1-3378.
Boat titling certificates.
Security interests, §§29.1-725, 29.1-726.
Bonds issued by localities, §15.2-2606.
Judicial determination of validity of bonds.
Publication of motion for judgment, §15.2-2652.
Boundaries of localities relocated or changed by agreement.
Publication of agreed boundary line, §15.2-3107.
Branch pilots.
Notice of need for pilots, §54.1-911.
Breach of personal information, §18.2-186.6.
Budgets of localities and school divisions, §15.2-2506.
Amendment, §15.2-2507.
Building code.
Lessor or sublessor receiving summons or ticket for violation.
Notice also to be served on owner, §36-106.
Burial societies.
Assessment, §38.2-4017.
Bus or vehicle fleet, road construction equipment.
Sale by locality with intent to lease back.
Approval of governing body required, public hearing, §15.2-951.
Cable television.
Localities providing services.
Actions by private providers, §15.2-2108.11.

NOTICE —Cont'd
Cable television —Cont'd
Localities providing services —Cont'd
Public hearing on feasibility study, §15.2-2108.7.
Campgrounds.
Notice by mail, §35.1-1.1.
Cancellation of insurance policy, §38.2-231.
Fire insurance, §§38.2-2113, 38.2-2114.
Motor vehicle insurance, §§38.2-2208, 38.2-2212, 46.2-482.
Cancer registry.
Notice to patients included in registry, §32.1-71.02.
Car rentals.
Collision damage waiver, §59.1-207.31.
Casualty insurance.
Revocation of agent's license, notice to criminal justice services department if surety bail bondsman, §38.2-2412.1.
Violations by agent, notice to criminal justice services department if surety bail bondsman, §38.2-2412.1.
Cemeteries.
Access to private cemeteries, §57-27.1.
Cemetery operators, perpetual care trust funds and preneed burial contracts.
Resale of interment rights, notice of contingency, §54.1-2312.1.
Change of address.
Failure to inform clerk of change of address.
Publication of interim notice, §8.01-319.
Change of city to town.
Citizen petition, §15.2-4102.
Copy of notice and ordinance, §15.2-4101.
Change of name.
Children.
Parental notice, §8.01-217.
Registered voters, §24.2-423.
Charge-off of state taxes, §58.1-1802.
Charitable gaming.
Denial, suspension or revocation of permit, §18.2-340.20.
Suspension of permit by officer charged with enforcement power, §18.2-340.36.
Check cashers.
Notice of proposed registration revocation, §6.2-2111.
Child abuse or neglect.
Notice to school board if teacher is subject of founded complaint, §63.2-1503.
Notice to superintendent of public instruction.
Board of education licensee as subject of founded complaint of child abuse or neglect, §63.2-1503.
Child changing name.
Parental notice, §8.01-217.
Child custody proceedings.
Relocation or change of address, §20-124.5.
Uniform child custody jurisdiction and enforcement act.
Enforcement proceeding, §20-146.29.
Service of petition and order of court, §20-146.30.
Giving notice of exercise of jurisdiction to person outside state, §20-146.7.
Requirement of notice and opportunity to be heard, §20-146.16.
Child may be conceived and man entitled to legal rights and obligations.
Legal notice to man engaging in sexual intercourse with woman, §63.2-1250.

NOTICE —Cont'd
Child pornography image registry.
Penalty for unlawful use of images, §19.2-390.3.
Children, psychiatric treatment.
Appeal of final orders, §16.1-345.6.
Child support.
Reopening of proceedings, §20-112.
Subsequent enforcement proceedings.
Delivery of notice to party at last known address, §20-60.6.
Child support enforcement by department of social services.
Administrative hearing on debt, §63.2-1943.
Administrative support order, §63.2-1916.
Delivery of notice to last known address, sufficiency, §63.2-1917.
Appeal from decision of hearing officer, §63.2-1943.
Income withholding.
Administrative order, §§63.2-1923, 63.2-1924.
Lien asserted by commissioner.
Distraint, seizure and sale of property, §63.2-1933.
Review of support order, §63.2-1921.
Service of lien asserted by department, §63.2-1928.
Service of order to withhold and deliver property, §63.2-1929.
Child visitation proceedings.
Relocation or change of address, §20-124.5.
Child welfare agencies.
Summary order of suspension and other proceedings, §63.2-1709.
Churches and religious organizations.
Resale of interment rights, notice of contingency, §54.1-2312.2.
Circuit courts.
Motion raising defenses and objections, VA SCt Rule 3A:9.
City status granted county.
Service of notice of petition alleging eligibility, §15.2-3903.
Civil aircraft of the United States.
Instruments affecting title to or interest in, §55-100.
Claims against counties.
Disallowance, §15.2-1246.
To claimant, §15.2-1245.
Claims against the state.
Tort claims act, §8.01-195.6.
Coal mine worker certification.
Revocation of certificate, §45.1-161.35.
Coal surface mining.
Abandoned mine reclamation.
State lien for reclamation work, §§45.1-266, 45.1-268.
Violations of act.
Administrative review of notice or order, §45.1-249.
Collection of state taxes.
Intent to file lien, §58.1-1805.
Colleges and universities.
Acquisitions, conveyances and transfers of property.
Notice of sale of certain property, §2.2-1153.
Regulation of private and out-of-state postsecondary schools.
Notice of school closures, §23-276.16.
Commercial code.
When notice given, §8.1A-202.

NOTICE —Cont'd
Commercial drivers' licenses.
Change of address, §46.2-341.11.
Third party testers.
Notice to department, when required, §46.2-341.14:7.
Commercial real estate brokers' liens.
Perfection or attachment of lien, §55-527.
Commissioners in chancery.
Adjournment of proceedings, §8.01-614.
Commission on local government.
Notice to commission deemed to institute action or proceeding, §15.2-2908.
Required notice before proceedings instituted, §15.2-2907.
Committees.
Property transfers to foreign committees, §64.2-1429.
Commonwealth's attorneys.
Criminal fines and penalties.
Petition for relief, §19.2-364.
Community-based corrections system for state-responsible offenders.
Construction of new facility, notice requirements, §53.1-67.4.
Community corrections.
Withdrawal from program, §9.1-179.
Community mental health services boards.
Withdrawal of county or city from joint services board, §37.2-510.
Compensation board appeals, §15.2-1636.9.
Comprehensive plan, §15.2-2225.
Computer information transactions.
Breach of personal information, notice required, §18.2-186.6.
Termination of obligations, §59.1-506.17.
Condominiums.
Cancellation of contract of sale by purchaser.
Resale of unit by unit owner other than declarant, §55-79.97.
Cease and desist orders, §55-79.100.
Common elements.
Pesticide application, §55-79.80:01.
Conversion condominiums, §55-79.94.
Tenants' notice, §55-79.94.
Lien for assessments, §55-79.84.
Meetings of unit owners' association, §55-79.75.
Registration filing, §55-79.92.
Confession of judgment.
Appointment of substitute for attorney-in-fact, §8.01-435.
Form of notice, §8.01-433.1.
Confidential information.
Sale of purchaser information by merchant, §59.1-442.
Conservation easements.
Recording of instrument, §10.1-1012.
Conservatorship of estate of incapacitated persons.
Appointment of conservator.
Hearing on petition, §64.2-2004.
Consolidation of county, city or town into single county or city, §15.2-3521.
Consumer finance companies.
Commencing business at new location, closing location, §6.2-1508.
Contractors, complaints against.
Findings of board, §54.1-1114.
Contractor transaction recovery act.
Notice to regulants of assessments, §54.1-1119.

NOTICE —Cont'd
Contractor transaction recovery proceedings.
Determinations of payment, §54.1-1122.
Cooperative associations.
Amendments of articles of incorporation, §13.1-301.1.
Bylaw adoption, amendment or revision, §13.1-301.2.
Corporations, §13.1-610.
Appraisal rights, §13.1-732.
Appraisal notice, §13.1-734.
Intent to demand payment, §13.1-733.
Directors' meetings, §§13.1-686, 13.1-687.
Directors' resignation, §13.1-679.
Dissolution.
Claims against corporation, §13.1-746.1.
Known claims, §13.1-746.
Officers' resignation and removal, §13.1-695.
Shareholder meetings, §13.1-658.
Waiver, §13.1-659.
Shareholders who share common address, §13.1-610.1.
Correction of erroneous state tax assessments.
Intent to file application for correction with tax commissioner, §58.1-1821.
Corrections department.
Initial notice by certified mail, subsequent notices by regular mail, §53.1-1.01.
Council of higher education.
Initial notice by certified mail, subsequent notices by regular mail, §23-276.1:1.
County food and beverage tax referendum, §58.1-3833.
County manager plan of government.
Litter control ordinance violations, §15.2-733.
County police force, election on establishing, §15.2-1702.
Court-appointed special advocate.
Required, §9.1-155.
Courthouses.
Posting, §1-211.1.
Court of appeals.
Decisions, VA SCt Rule 5A:29.
Court officers.
Motion on bond, §8.01-227.
Credit services businesses.
Contracts, §59.1-335.8.
Information statements, §59.1-335.7.
Credit unions.
Closing offices, time for giving, §6.2-1326.
Crime victim and witness assistance.
Release of defendant.
Notice to victim, §19.2-11.01.
Crime victims and witnesses.
Rights generally, §19.2-11.01.
Criminal fines and penalties.
Commonwealth's attorneys.
Petition for relief, §19.2-364.
Criminal forfeiture.
Commissioner of department of motor vehicles, §19.2-386.2:1.
Criminal justice services department.
Initial notice by certified mail, subsequent notices by regular mail, §9.1-101.1.
Custodial trust.
Resignation of trustee, §64.2-912.
Dams.
Applications for leave to build or rebuild, §§62.1-117, 62.1-120.
Dam break inundation zones.
High or significant hazard potential structure proposed, notice to public, §10.1-606.4.

NOTICE —Cont'd
Dams —Cont'd
Hydroelectric power.
Notice to owners of existing developments, §62.1-92.
Dam safety, flood prevention and protection assistance fund.
Initial notice by certified mail, subsequent notices by regular mail, §10.1-603.16:1.
Death penalty.
Defendant's mental condition relevant to capital sentencing.
Expert testimony on issue, §19.2-264.3:1.
Evidence of unadjudicated criminal conduct, §19.2-264.3:2.
Expert testimony, notice of intention to introduce, §19.2-264.3:4.
Death presumption.
Petition seeking judicial determination of death.
Order that presumption made out, publication, §64.2-2304.
Decertification of law enforcement officer, §15.2-1708.
Delinquent local treasurers, §58.1-3171.
Dental plan organizations.
Enrollee's membership, termination of, §38.2-6106.
License renewal, §38.2-6104.
Department of agriculture and consumer services.
Suspension of permit, §18.2-340.36.
Depositions.
Audio-visual depositions, §8.01-412.3.
Upon oral examination.
Special notice, VA SCt Rule 4:5.
Derelict buildings.
Locality appointment as receiver to repair derelict and blighted buildings.
Enforcement of receiver's lien by sale at public auction, §15.2-907.2.
Written notice to property owners.
Plans to remove, demolish or renovate, §15.2-907.1.
Descent and distribution.
Notice to interested parties, §64.2-508.
Desertion and nonsupport.
Income deduction of support orders, §20-79.1.
Disability or handicap.
Protection and advocacy system.
Critical incidents and deaths in state facilities, §51.5-39.12.
Discipline of law enforcement officers.
Law enforcement officers procedural guarantee act.
Notice of charges, §9.1-502.
Discrimination.
Antidiscrimination policy, posting, §2.2-4201.
Dispute resolution proceedings.
Objections, §8.01-576.6.
Resolution of dispute prior to return date, §8.01-576.5.
Distress for local taxes and levies.
Secured parties prior to sale, §58.1-3942.
Divorce.
Revocation of death benefits by divorce, §20-111.1.
Dog and cat sales by dealers.
Written notice of consumer remedies, §3.2-6515.
Drainage projects.
Appointment of board of viewers, §21-299.
Notice of issuance of bonds, §21-393.
Redemption of land sold for taxes, §21-391.

NOTICE —Cont'd
Drainage projects —Cont'd
Sale of tax delinquent lands, §21-377.
Drainage rights.
Application to acquire drainage rights, §21-428.
Ascertainment of damages by commissioners, §21-429.
Drift property, §55-204.
Driver improvement programs.
Attendance notice, §46.2-501.
Clinic or instructor licenses.
Disciplinary action against licensee, §46.2-490.6.
Drivers' licenses.
Change of address, §46.2-324.
Suspension or revocation of license, §46.2-416.
Mental incompetence, §46.2-322.
Nonresidents, §46.2-433.
Unsatisfied judgments.
Order for installment payments of judgment, §46.2-420.
Driving while intoxicated.
Administrative suspension of driver's license, §§46.2-391.2, 46.2-391.3, 46.2-391.5.
Content of notice, §46.2-391.3.
Forms, §46.2-391.5.
Requirements, §46.2-391.2.
Revocation of probation, education and rehabilitation of person convicted, §18.2-271.1.
Drug blight existing on property.
Corrective action by owner, §15.2-907.
Drug control.
Delivery of prescription drug order, §54.1-3420.2.
Destruction of part of seized substances prior to trial, §19.2-386.24.
Pharmacy closings, §54.1-3434.01.
Suspension or revocation of registration or forfeiture of controlled substances.
Notification to DEA, §54.1-3424.
Ejectment.
Defendant's claim for improvements, §8.01-160.
Recovery of possession by owner, §8.01-156.
Election contest to general assembly election.
Intent to contest, §24.2-803.
Election contest to governor, lieutenant governor or attorney general elections.
Intent to contest, §24.2-804.
Election districts.
Precinct or polling place change, §24.2-306.
Elections.
Adopting or changing county form of government, §15.2-301.
County executive form of government.
Election of county chairman from county at large, §15.2-503.
County police force, establishing, §15.2-1702.
Disqualification of party nominees, §24.2-612.1.
Presidential electors.
Notice of disqualification, §24.2-543.
State board of elections.
Initial notice by certified mail, subsequent notices by regular mail, §24.2-101.01.
Tie vote.
Determination by lot in case of tie, §24.2-674.
Electoral board changes in membership or officers.
Secretary of board to send notice to state board of elections, §24.2-106.
Electoral board meetings, §24.2-107.
Eminent domain.
County entering upon and taking possession of property prior to conclusion of proceedings, §15.2-1905.

NOTICE —Cont'd
Eminent domain —Cont'd
Filing of petition, §25.1-209.
Form of notice by publication, §25.1-211.
Inspection of property to be condemned, §25.1-203.
Owner under a disability, §25.1-215.
Right of entry after filing of petition, §25.1-223.
Service of notice, §25.1-210.
Service on nonresident owner, §25.1-212.
Title transfer by certificate.
Certificate of deposit, §25.1-306.
Petition for distribution of funds, §25.1-310.
Environmental covenants, §10.1-1243.
Environmental quality department.
Initial notice by certified mail, subsequent notices by regular mail, §10.1-1182.1.
Equal credit opportunities.
Notice of action on application, §6.2-502.
Escape of convict, notice to state police, §53.1-116.1.
Escheats.
Certification of lands escheated, §55-183.
Inquests, §55-172.
Residuum of decedent's estate.
Publication of suits, §55-198.
Estate tax.
Deficiency assessed, §58.1-906.
Payments by nonresident decedents to other states.
Proof of payment not filed, notice to domiciliary state, §58.1-919.
Recapture tax on certain use valuations.
Disposition or change in use of property, §58.1-933.
Estrays, §55-204.
Evictions, §55-239.
Exchange facilitators.
Change in control of facilitator, §55-525.2.
Executions.
Receipt of money by officer under execution, §8.01-500.
Safe deposit boxes.
Access denied except by court order, §6.2-2304.
Expert testimony, notice of intention to introduce in capital cases, §19.2-264.3:4.
Explosives.
Theft, §59.1-139.
Expungement of court records.
Juvenile records, §16.1-306.
Fair employment contracting act.
Antidiscrimination policy, posting, §2.2-4201.
Family day homes.
Liability insurance coverage, §63.2-1809.1.
Farm machinery dealerships.
Termination.
By suppliers, §59.1-352.3.
Fences.
Division fences.
How given, §55-322.
Notice to build, §55-318.
Repair, §55-319.
Lawful fence.
Constituted by water or canal, §55-300.
Fertilizer.
Notice of violation, §3.2-3625.
Warning in lieu of instituting proceedings, §3.2-3624.
Fidelity and surety insurer's license revocation.
Supreme court clerk and circuit court clerks to be given notice, §38.2-2412.

NOTICE —Cont'd
Fiduciaries.
Property transfers to foreign fiduciaries, §64.2-1429.
Fieri facias.
Sale of property subject to prior security interest, §8.01-480.
Service of notice where no judgment exists.
Penalty, §8.01-504.
Financial institutions.
Acquisition of interests in financial institutions.
Notice of intent to acquire out-of-state bank, §6.2-715.
Adverse claims to accounts.
Criteria for recognition, §6.2-602.
Initial notice by certified mail, subsequent notices by regular mail, §6.2-101.1.
Firearm shows.
State and local police to receive notice by sponsor, §54.1-4201.1.
Firearms sales.
Disposition of firearms surrendered to locality, §15.2-915.5.
Fire insurance.
Change in deductible, §38.2-2127.
Earthquake exclusion, §38.2-2129.
Fire insurance policy cancellation or refusal to renew, §§38.2-2113, 38.2-2114.
Fire insurance, use of credit information, §38.2-2126.
Fishing, tidal waters.
Health and sanitation provisions.
Polluted ground, §28.2-804.
Cessation of activities, §28.2-805.
Hearings, §28.2-216.
Importing fish for introduction into waters of the Commonwealth, §28.2-825.
Foreclosures, §55-225.10.
Forensic science department.
Hazardous materials, disposal, §9.1-1106.
Initial notice by certified mail, subsequent notices by regular mail, §9.1-1100.1.
Forestry department.
Initial notice by certified mail, subsequent notices by regular mail, §10.1-1100.1.
Foster care placement.
Notice to school in which student to be enrolled, of status of parental rights, §63.2-900.
Franchise, privilege, lease or right to use city or town property.
Amendment or extension of franchise, §15.2-2105.
Ordinance proposing grant of franchise, §15.2-2101.
Fraudulent conveyances.
United States civil aircraft.
Recordation of instruments affecting, §55-100.
Void as to creditors and purchasers until recorded, §55-96.
Freedom of information.
Electronic communication meetings, §2.2-3708.
Freedom of information act.
Notice of chapter, §2.2-3702.
Open meetings required, §2.2-3707.
Fuel taxes.
Sales tax in certain transportation districts.
Jeopardy assessment, §58.1-2299.12.
Relief from assessment or adverse decision, §58.1-2299.15.
Funds transfers.
Payment orders.
Obligation of beneficiary's bank to give notice to beneficiary, §8.4A-404.

NOTICE —Cont'd
Funds transfers —Cont'd
Rejection of payment order, §8.4A-210.
Garnishment.
Notice of exemption form, §8.01-512.4.
Gas and oil exploration.
Appeal of agency's decisions, §45.1-361.23.
Coalbed methane gas wells.
Arbitration of conflicting claims of ownership, §45.1-361.22:1.
Meetings of the board, §45.1-361.14.
Notice of hearing before board, §45.1-361.19.
Notice of permit applications, §45.1-361.30.
Gas companies.
Entry onto property.
Natural gas companies, §56-49.01.
Genetically engineered organisms.
Regulated introduction.
Public notice of proposed introductions, §2.2-5504.
Groundwater management.
Water control board.
Initial notice by certified mail, subsequent notices by regular mail, §62.1-255.1.
Guardians.
Property transfers to foreign guardians, §64.2-1429.
Standby guardianship, §§16.1-354, 16.1-355.
Guardianship of incapacitated persons.
Appointment of guardian.
Hearing on petition, §64.2-2004.
Hampton Roads sports facility authority.
Public hearing on selecting site, §15.2-5906.
Hazardous materials.
Forensic science department.
Disposal, §9.1-1106.
Health.
Initial notice by certified mail, subsequent notices by regular mail, §32.1-3.1.
Health care professional referrals.
Disclosure of interest in referral facilities, §54.1-2964.
Health care sharing ministries.
Publication not insurance, §38.2-6300.
Health commissioner and department of health.
Initial notice by certified mail, subsequent notices by regular mail, §32.1-3.1.
Health insurance.
Claims notice.
Group insurance policy provisions, §38.2-3534.
Individual policies, §38.2-3503.
Federal market reforms.
Notice of rescission, §38.2-3441.
Group insurance policy provisions.
Claim notice, §38.2-3534.
Termination of coverage, §38.2-3542.
Individual policies.
Acknowledgment of notice by insurer not waiver of right, §38.2-3512.
Claim notice, §38.2-3503.
Printing on policy, §38.2-3502.
Lapse, §38.2-232.
Premium increases, §38.2-3407.14.
Reconstructive breast surgery coverage, §38.2-3418.4.
Retroactive denial of claims, §38.2-3407.15.
Utilization review.
Internal appeal process and external review.
Notice of eligibility for standard external review, §38.2-3561.

NOTICE —Cont'd
Health insurance —Cont'd
Utilization review —Cont'd
Internal appeal process and external review —Cont'd
Notice of right to external review, §38.2-3559.
Health maintenance organization.
Exercise of certain powers, §38.2-4303.
Health spas.
Buyers' rights, §59.1-304.
Closing or relocation, §59.1-296.2:1.
Contracts, §59.1-298.
Cancellation, §59.1-296.3.
Tanning facilities, §§59.1-310.3, 59.1-310.4.
Heavy equipment dealers.
Agreements.
Cancellation, §59.1-354.
Termination, §59.1-355.
Forms of notice, §59.1-357.
Transfers of business, §59.1-356.
Higher education council.
Initial notice by certified mail, subsequent notices by regular mail, §23-276.1:1.
Highway construction contracts.
Adjustment of claims, §33.1-386.
Highways and roads.
Eminent domain and damages.
Right to enter land to ascertain suitability for highway purposes, §33.1-94.
Home service contract providers.
Reimbursement insurance policies.
Cancellation, §38.2-2625.
Home solicitation sales.
Cancellations, §§59.1-21.3, 59.1-21.4.
Hospital discharge procedures.
Information to be provided to patient and family, §32.1-137.02.
Hotels.
Initial notice by certified mail, subsequent notices by regular mail, §35.1-1.1.
Hunting and fishing seasons in forestlands.
Fire hazards and closing, §10.1-1161.
Hunting incident reports.
Duty of law-enforcement agency or emergency medical service provider to report, §29.1-530.4.
Hydroelectric power dams.
Notice to owners of existing developments, §62.1-92.
Implied warranties on new homes, §55-70.1.
Impoundment of surface waters.
Riparian owner rights.
Application for leave to store floodwaters, §62.1-107.
Income tax.
Employment.
Earned income tax credit.
Notice by employer to employee, §40.1-28.7:3.
Jeopardy assessment, §58.1-313.
Liens, §58.1-314.
Local income tax referendums, §58.1-540.
Income tax setoff debt collection.
Claimant agency to notify department of taxation, §58.1-524.
Final setoff, §58.1-529.
Intention to setoff, §58.1-525.
Industrial development authorities.
Public hearings, §15.2-4906.
Industrial loan associations.
Requirements as to notice to borrower, §6.2-1416.

NOTICE —Cont'd
Industrial waste discharges to state waters.
Application for discharge, §62.1-44.16.
Initial notice by certified mail.
Subsequent notices sent by regular mail, §1-206.
Injunctions.
Dissolution of injunctions, §8.01-625.
Required, §8.01-629.
Insurance adjusters.
Refusal of license, §38.2-1845.7.
Unlicensed public adjusters process, §§38.2-812 to 38.2-815.
Insurance agents, appointment, §38.2-1833.
Insurance antitrust provisions, cease and desist orders, §38.2-702.
Insurance brokers and agents.
Property and casualty insurance.
Revocation of agent's license, notice to criminal justice services department if surety bail bondsman, §38.2-2412.1.
Violations by agent, notice to criminal justice services department if surety bail bondsman, §38.2-2412.2.
Termination of license.
Failure to comply with continuing education requirements, §38.2-1869.
Unlicensed nonresident brokers and agents process, §§38.2-808 to 38.2-811.
Insurance commissioner.
Initial notice by certified mail, subsequent notices by regular mail, §38.2-100.1.
Insurance companies.
Conversion of mutual holding companies to stock holding companies, §38.2-1005.1:12.
Conversion of stock insurer to mutual insurer.
Meeting to approve conversion, policyholders to receive notice, §38.2-1007.
Electronic notifications, §38.2-325.
Fire insurance.
Notice of cancellation or refusal to renew, §38.2-2113.
Motor vehicle insurance.
Notice of cancellation or refusal to renew, §38.2-2208.
Financial condition hazardous.
Order to take appropriate action to remedy, §38.2-1038.
License suspension or revocation, §38.2-1041.
Rehabilitation and liquidation.
Disbursement of assets by receiver, §38.2-1506.
Retroactive denial of claims, §38.2-3407.15.
Risk-based capital, §38.2-5513.
Unlicensed insurers process, §§38.2-800 to 38.2-807.
Insurance information collection and disclosure practices, §38.2-604.
Financial information, §38.2-604.1.
Insurance policies.
Cancellation, refusal to renew, reduction in coverage or increase in rate, §38.2-231.
Electronic notifications, §38.2-325.
Fire insurance.
Notice of cancellation or refusal to renew, §38.2-2113.
Motor vehicle insurance.
Notice of cancellation or refusal to renew, §38.2-2208.
Fire insurance, §§38.2-2113, 38.2-2114.
Forms approved or disapproved by state corporation commission, §38.2-316.

NOTICE —Cont'd
Insurance policies —Cont'd
Motor vehicle insurance, §§38.2-2208, 38.2-2212, 46.2-482.
Settlements, notice of settlement payments, §38.2-236.
Insurance rates.
Workers' compensation, automobiles, home protection, etc.
Publication of filing, §38.2-2007.
Interdiction, §4.1-333.
Interment rights in cemetery.
Abandonment, §57-39.1:1.
Interstate family support.
Orders.
Contest of validity or enforcement, §20-88.70.
Modification.
Notice to issuing tribunal, §20-88.77:2.
Invention development services, §59.1-210.
Investment advisor representative.
Beginning or terminating connection with investment advisor, §13.1-504.
Investment securities.
Adverse claims, §8.8A-105.
Defects or defenses, §§8.8A-202, 8.8A-203.
Lost, destroyed or wrongfully taken certificate.
Obligation to notify issuer, §8.8A-406.
Jail.
Escape of convict, notice to state police, §53.1-116.1.
Prisoner intake, §53.1-116.1:01.
Prisoner releases, §53.1-116.1.
Jeopardy assessment.
Income tax, §58.1-313.
Liens, §58.1-314.
Judicial emergency declaration, §17.1-331.
Judicial retirement system.
Disability retirement, §§51.1-307, 51.1-507.
Judicial sales.
Persons appointed to receive purchase money, etc., §§8.01-101, 8.01-103.
Failure of clerk to give notice, §18.2-209.2.
Juvenile and domestic relations district courts.
Trial rights of parties.
Notification and waiver, VA SCt Rule 8:17.
Juvenile case removed to circuit court, §16.1-269.1.
Juvenile delinquency.
Interstate compact relating to juveniles.
Commission meetings, §16.1-323.
Juvenile justice department.
Initial notice by certified mail, subsequent notices by regular mail, §66-10.01.
Release of serious offenders, §66-25.2.
School superintendent, §66-25.2:1.
Juvenile petition alleging offense that would be felony if committed by adult.
Disclosure of notice of filing of petition and certain reports, §16.1-305.2.
Intake officer responsibilities, §16.1-260.
Juvenile residential care facilities in localities without zoning ordinance.
Persons planning to establish to give notice, §15.2-2207.
Labor and industry department.
Initial notice by certified mail, subsequent notices by regular mail, §40.1-2.01.
Labor dispute mediation and conciliation.
Collective bargaining contracts.
Proposed termination or modification, §40.1-71.

NOTICE —Cont'd
Labor dispute mediation and conciliation —Cont'd
Notice to governor, §40.1-72.
Landlord and tenant.
Defective drywall, §55-225.11.
Desertion by tenant.
Entry prerequisite by landlord, §55-224.
Ejectment.
Writs of possession, §8.01-470.
Evictions, §55-239.
Failure to pay rent after 5 days' notice.
Forfeiture of possession, §55-225.
Foreclosure, §55-225.10.
Manufactured home lot rental.
Owner sale or lease of home, §55-248.47.
Rental agreement changes, §55-248.42.
Termination of tenancy, §55-248.46.
Material noncompliance or danger.
Written notice requirement, §§55-225.12, 55-225.13.
Methamphetamine.
Disclosures by landlord for property previously used to manufacture methamphetamine, §§55-225.17, 55-248.12:3.
Pesticide control.
Notice to tenant for insecticide or pesticide use, §55-248.13:3.
Rent defaults.
Forfeiture of right of possession, §55-225.
Residential landlords and tenants, §55-248.6.
Abandonment of personal property by tenants.
Disposal of, §55-248.38:1.
Absence of tenant, §55-248.33.
Acceptance of rent with reservation, §55-248.34:1.
Casualty damage to unit, §55-248.24.
Deceased tenants.
Disposal of property of, §55-248.38:3.
Defined, §55-248.4.
Early termination of lease by military personnel, §55-248.21:1.
Ejectment.
Writs of possession, §8.01-470.
Electronic delivery of notice, §55-248.6.
Entries by landlord, §55-248.18.
Essential services.
Wrongful failure to supply, §55-248.23.
Fire damage to unit, §55-248.24.
Intent of landlord to enter premises, §55-248.18.
Landlord remedies for noncompliance with lease or rent agreements, §55-248.31.
Material noncompliance or danger, §55-248.27.
Methamphetamine.
Disclosures by landlord for property previously used to manufacture methamphetamine, §§55-225.17, 55-248.12:3.
Noncompliance by landlord.
Tenant remedies, §55-248.21.
Periodic tenancy termination notice, §55-248.37.
Service by sheriffs, §55-248.31:1.
Temporary vacation of property.
Nonemergency property condition, §55-248.18.
Tenancy at will.
Notice of change of provisions, effect, §55-248.15.
Unlawful entry and detainer.
Writs of possession, §8.01-470.
Service by sheriffs, §55-248.31:1.

NOTICE —Cont'd
Landlord and tenant —Cont'd
Termination of rental agreement.
Tenant's breach not remedial by landlord, §55-248.31.
Termination of tenancies, §55-222.
Early termination by victims of family abuse, sexual abuse or criminal sexual assault, §§55-225.16, 55-248.21.
Unlawful entry and detainer.
Writs of possession, §8.01-470.
Lapse of insurance policies.
Life and health insurance, §38.2-232.
Law enforcement expenditures.
Minimum training standards, compliance, §9.1-168.
Law enforcement officers.
Decertification, §15.2-1708.
Law enforcement officers procedural guarantee act.
Notice of charges, §9.1-502.
Lease of gas, oil or minerals on state corrections board property, §53.1-31.
Legal notices.
Localities.
Website publication as well as newspaper, §15.2-107.1.
Newspapers which may be used for legal notices, §8.01-324.
Lemon law.
Disclosure of returned vehicles, §59.1-207.16:1.
Nonconformity of motor vehicles, §59.1-207.13.
Letters of credit.
Terms of notice to transferee beneficiary, §8.5A-107.
Lie detector tests.
Criminal procedure.
Written notice prior to examination, §19.2-9.1.
Liens.
Release of deeds of trust or other liens, §55-66.3.
Service generally, §43-64.
Life insurance.
Standard nonforfeiture provisions.
Election to apply provisions on a contract-form-by-contract-form, §38.2-3229.
Life insurance policy lapse, §38.2-232.
Limited liability companies.
Dissolution of claims, notice and request for presentation of claims, §13.1-1049.2.
Court proceedings following notice, §13.1-1049.3.
Failure to pay registration fee, §13.1-1064.
Impending cancellation of existence, §13.1-1050.2.
Resignation of member, §13.1-1032.
Limited partnerships.
Certificate of limited partnership.
Scope of notice, §50-73.19.
Dissolution and winding up.
Disposal of known claims, §50-73.52:1.
Disposal of other claims, §50-73.52:2.
Litter control ordinance violations.
County manager plan of government, §15.2-733.
Livestock.
Injury or death of stock.
Notice to owner, §56-439.1.
Living wills.
Notification to attending physician, §54.1-2983.
Local constitutional officers.
Employment positions, §15.2-1604.
Local income tax.
Referendum, §58.1-540.

NOTICE —Cont'd
Local tax collection.
Distress.
Secured parties prior to sale, §58.1-3942.
Lease of real estate for collection, §58.1-3948.
Local taxes due, §58.1-3911.
Local tax levy increase, §58.1-3007.
Local treasurers, delinquent treasurers, §58.1-3171.
Local treasurer securing final discharge from liability, §58.1-3146.
Mammograms.
Notice to be included for patients with dense breast tissue, §32.1-229.
Manufactured home lot rental.
Abandonment, §55-248.44:1.
Owner sale or lease of home, §55-248.47.
Termination of tenancy, §55-248.46.
Manufactured housing.
Licensing of manufactured housing industry.
Initial notice by certified mail, subsequent notices by regular mail, §36-85.16:1.
Mechanics' and materialmen's liens.
Perfection.
General contractors.
Service, §43-14.1.
Persons performing labor or furnishing materials for subcontractor, §43-9.
Service, §43-14.1.
Sufficiency, §43-10.
Service generally, §43-14.1.
Subcontractors, §43-7.
Service, §43-14.1.
Sufficiency, §43-8.
Personal liability of owners or general contractors, §43-11.
Possible filing of mechanics' lien, §11-2.4.
Medical malpractice review panels.
Amendment of notice of claim, MedMal Rule 4.
Notice of appointment, §8.01-581.3:1, MedMal Rule 4.
Notice of claim, MedMal Rule 2.
Ore tenus hearing, §8.01-581.5.
Removal of record for inspection and copying, §8.01-581.4:2, MedMal Rule 6.
Medical records.
Evidence in district court.
Intention to present evidence by, §16.1-88.2.
Production of documents and things, §8.01-413.
Subpoena duces tecum, §32.1-127.1:03.
Subpoena of pro se party or nonparty witness records, §32.1-127.1:03.
Transfers of in conjunction with closure, sale or relocation of practice, §54.1-2405.
Medical referrals for profit.
Injunctions, §18.2-502.
Medical services lien.
Hearing on claim of unreasonableness, §8.01-66.7.
Written notice required, §8.01-66.5.
Medicare supplement policies.
Free look notice provision required, §38.2-3604.
Meetings of local governing bodies.
Special meeting, §15.2-1417.
Membership camping.
Initial notice by certified mail, subsequent notices by regular mail, §59.1-313.1.
Mental health.
Children, psychiatric treatment.
Appeal of final orders, §16.1-345.6.
Critical incidents or deaths of individuals receiving services at state facilities, §§37.2-709, 37.2-709.1.

NOTICE —Cont'd
Metropolitan Washington airports authority.
Intention to adopt rule or regulation.
Publication, §5.1-157.
Migrant labor camps.
Intention to construct, remodel or enlarge, §32.1-204.
Mills.
Applications for leave to build or rebuild, §§62.1-117, 62.1-120.
Mine inspections.
Advance notice of inspections, §45.1-161.84.
Mineral mine licenses.
Intent to abandon or discontinue mine, §45.1-161.292:36.
Mineral mine safety.
Advance notice of inspections, §45.1-161.292:57.
Notify miners of violations, §45.1-161.292:8.
Violations, §45.1-161.292:63.
Mine safety.
Smoking in underground coal mines, §45.1-161.179.
Smoking warning sign, §45.1-161.179.
Substance abuse testing, notice to chief of positive results, §45.1-161.87.
Underground coal mines.
Dangerous conditions, §45.1-161.214.
Monitor tampering prohibition, §45.1-161.215.
Smoking, §45.1-161.179.
Violations, §45.1-161.90.
Notice of correction, §45.1-161.90.
Mines, minerals and energy department.
Initial notice by certified mail, subsequent notices by regular mail, §45.1-161.1:1.
Missing law enforcement officers.
Blue Alert program, §§52-34.7 to 52-34.9.
Mortgage lender and broker act.
Licenses, suspension or revocation, §6.2-1623.
Required notice to borrower, §§6.2-1615, 6.2-1616.
Mortgages and deeds of trust.
Foreclosure, §55-225.10.
Release of deeds of trust or other liens, §55-66.3.
Sales, §§55-59.1, 55-62.
Advertising, §§55-59.2, 55-59.3, 55-63.
Motion on bond.
Court officers, §8.01-227.
Motor carriers.
Rates.
New rates, §46.2-1937.
Motorcycle dealers.
Cessation of business, §46.2-1993.38.
Motorcycle franchises.
Hearings and other remedies, §46.2-1993.73.
Motor vehicle accidents.
Driver to give immediate notice of certain accidents, §46.2-371.
Motor vehicle dealers.
Disciplinary action against dealer licenses, §46.2-1576.
Termination of business, §46.2-1545.
Termination of license of salesperson's or representative's employment, §46.2-1518.
Transaction recovery fund.
Claims against dealer's bond, §46.2-1527.2.
Motor vehicle insurance.
Cancellation or refusal to renew, §38.2-2212.
Certified policy, §46.2-482.
Mailing or electronic delivery requirements of insurer, §38.2-2208.
Collision damage waiver on rentals, §59.1-207.31.
Notice of settlement of claim, §38.2-2226.1.

NOTICE —Cont'd
Motor vehicle insurance —Cont'd
Optional coverage available, §38.2-2202.
Premium increase, §38.2-1905.
Motor vehicle proof of financial responsibility.
Notice as prerequisite to cancellation of bond, §46.2-448.
Notice of cancellation, §46.2-448.
Motor vehicle registration.
Change of address, §46.2-606.
Suspension of registration on theft or embezzlement of vehicle, §46.2-610.
Motor vehicle rentals.
Collision damage waiver, §59.1-207.31.
Motor vehicles department.
Initial notice by certified mail, subsequent notices by regular mail, §46.2-100.1.
Records supplied to third persons, §46.2-212.
Motor vehicle title loans.
Change of location or additional location, §6.2-2207.
Repossession and sale of vehicle, §6.2-2217.
Suspension or revocation of licenses.
Notice of proposed suspension or revocation, §6.2-2221.
Motor vehicle titling.
Change of address, §46.2-606.
Motor vehicle warranties.
Disclosure of returned vehicles, §59.1-207.16:1.
Enforcement.
Nonconformity of motor vehicles, §59.1-207.13.
Manufacturers' warranty adjustment, §§59.1-207.35, 59.1-207.36.
Reimbursements, §59.1-207.37.
Museums.
Property loaned to museums, §55-210.33.
Statute of limitations on recovery, §55-210.32.
Termination of loans, §§55-210.35, 55-210.36.
Title to property, §55-210.37.
Mutual assessment life, accident and sickness insurers.
Assessments, §38.2-3918.
Mutual assessment property and casualty insurers.
Assessment, §38.2-2521.
Loss and adjustment, §38.2-2523.
Natural gas companies.
Entry onto property, §56-49.01.
Newspapers.
Legal notices, newspapers which may be used for, §8.01-324.
Nonprofit corporations, §13.1-810.
Claims against dissolved corporations, §§13.1-908, 13.1-908.1.
Directors committees, §13.1-869.
Directors' conduct standards, §13.1-870.
Directors meetings, §§13.1-866, 13.1-867.
Directors' resignation, §13.1-859.
Impending termination of corporate existence, §13.1-914.
Foreign corporations, §13.1-930.
Members meetings, §§13.1-842, 13.1-843.
Officers' resignation, §13.1-874.
Nonprofit health care entities.
Disposition of assets, §55-532.
Northern Neck Chesapeake Bay public access authority.
Rules, regulations, minimum standards.
Adoption, §15.2-6634.
Notaries.
Change of address, §47.1-18.

NOTICE —Cont'd
Notice of breach of personal information.
Security freezes on consumer credit reports, §59.1-444.2.
Nurse licensure compact.
Notice of actions taken, §54.1-3032.
Nursing schools.
Discontinuation of education programs, due process requirements, §54.1-3014.
Obscene books, proceeding against.
Temporary restraining orders, §18.2-384.
Occupational safety and health.
Penalty for giving advance notice of inspections, §40.1-51.3:1.
Oil discharges, §62.1-44.34:19.
Open meetings.
Electronic communication meetings, §2.2-3708.
Freedom of information act, §2.2-3707.
Ordinances.
Counties, descriptive notice of intention to propose, §15.2-1427.
Outdoor advertising.
Beautification projects likely to obstruct signs.
Notice by locality, §33.1-371.1.
Overhead electrical transmission line construction, §56-46.1.
Overhead high voltage line safety, §§59.1-410, 59.1-411.
Oyster planting grounds.
Temporary enclosures on leased ground.
Notice of authorization for, §28.2-603.2.
Parental notice.
Change of name of child, §8.01-217.
Parking for disabled or handicapped.
Confiscation of placards, §46.2-1255.
Revocation of placards and license plates, §46.2-1256.
Parking ordinance violation.
Law-enforcement notice, §46.2-941.
Parks and recreation.
State parks.
Planning, solicitation of public comment on, §10.1-200.1.
Parole.
Crime victims to receive, §§53.1-116.1, 53.1-155, 53.1-160, 53.1-160.1.
Partnerships.
When person has notice of fact, §50-73.80.
Payday loans.
Cease and desist orders, §6.2-1822.
Closing business location, §6.2-1807.
Commencement of business at new office, §6.2-1807.
Proposed suspension or revocation of license, §6.2-1823.
Personal information privacy, §59.1-442.
Notice of breach of personal information, §18.2-186.6.
Personal property tax relief programs for elderly or handicapped, §58.1-3506.6.
Personal representative, appointment.
Public assistance recipient unable to manage funds.
Hearing on petition, §63.2-507.
Persons with disability.
Disposition of real estate.
Alternate procedure for sale of real estate, §8.01-79.
Pesticide application.
Condominiums.
Common elements, §55-79.80:01.

NOTICE —Cont'd
Pesticide control.
Landlord and tenant.
Notice to tenant for insecticide or pesticide use, §55-248.13:3.
Pet cemeteries.
Removal of restriction on land, §57-39.24.
Petroleum products franchises.
Agreement termination, cancellation or failure to renew, §59.1-21.14.
Transfer of franchise by dealer, §59.1-21.11.
Pharmacists' licensing.
Revocation, §54.1-3318.
Pharmacy closings, §54.1-3434.01.
Pharmacy engaging in compounding drugs.
Notice of intent to dispense or deliver sterile compounded drug, §54.1-3410.2.
Planning and development.
Additional notice of planning matters, §15.2-2205.
Adoption of plan, ordinance or amendment.
Required notice before adopting or recommending, §15.2-2204.
Comprehensive plan, §15.2-2225.
Juvenile residential care facilities.
Persons planning to establish in locality without zoning ordinance, §15.2-2207.
Locality requiring applicants to make, §15.2-2206.
Polling places.
Prohibited areas, §24.2-604.
Unusable or inaccessible, §24.2-310.
Polygraph tests.
Criminal procedure.
Written notice prior to examination, §19.2-9.1.
Port authority.
Option date, §62.1-129.1.
Potato board.
Seed potatoes, violation of provisions, §3.2-1821.
Power of attorney.
Resignation of agent, §64.2-1616.
Powers of appointment to property.
Releases, §64.2-2703.
Prescribed burn.
Department of forestry to be notified prior to burn, §10.1-1150.4.
Presumption of death.
Petition seeking judicial determination of death.
Order that presumption made out, publication, §64.2-2304.
Primary elections.
Adoption of direct primary by political party, §24.2-516.
Order of election by state board, §24.2-517.
Principal and income.
Total return unitrust, conversion to, §64.2-1003.
Prisoner construction and maintenance of highways.
Local law enforcement to receive, §53.1-56.
Prisoner escapes, §53.1-160.1.
Prisoner estates.
Actions against, §53.1-222.
Prisoner releases, §§53.1-116.1, 53.1-160.1.
Prisoner work for localities, state agencies or nonprofit organizations.
Local law enforcement to receive, §53.1-59.
Procurement by public bodies.
Contractor's intention to file dispute claim, §2.2-4363.
Ineligibility of bidder, offeror or contractor, §2.2-4357.
Nonresponsibility of low bidder, §2.2-4359.

NOTICE —Cont'd
Professional and occupational regulation department.
Regulatory boards.
Initial notice by certified mail, subsequent notices by regular mail, §54.1-101.1.
Notice to regulant of right to request informal fact-finding conference, §54.1-201.
Professions and occupations.
License suspension, §54.1-104.
Property insurance.
Revocation of agent's license, notice to criminal justice services department if surety bail bondsman, §38.2-2412.1.
Violations by agent, notice to criminal justice services department if surety bail bondsman, §38.2-2412.1.
Property owners' associations.
Liens for assessments, §55-516.
Pesticide application in common areas, §55-510.3.
Property taxes due, §58.1-3911.
Psychiatric treatment of children.
Appeal of final orders, §16.1-345.6.
Public aid and assistance.
Notice of change in contact information, §63.2-501.1.
Notice of earned income tax credit to recipients, §63.2-527.
Publication generally.
See PUBLICATION.
Public procurement.
Competitive negotiation.
Request for proposal, §2.2-4302.2.
Competitive sealed bidding.
Invitation to bid, §2.2-4302.1.
Public rights-of-way, vacating or alteration, §15.2-2006.
Public school absence, §22.1-258.
Public school funds.
Petition for referendum for special tax levy, §22.1-104.
Public service companies.
Dissolution, §56-13.
First stockholder meeting after sale, §56-10.
Public utilities.
Nuclear emergency evacuation plans.
Customers to be notified, §56-245.1:1.
Rates.
Changes, §56-237.1.
Sewage disposal.
Sewerage systems not regulated as public utilities.
Notice that such system includes a sewage treatment plant, §56-265.11:1.
Sewerage companies.
Notice that such system includes a sewage treatment plant, §56-261.
Suspension of service to sewerage companies, §56-236.2.
Small water or sewer utilities.
Rates.
Changes, §56-265.13:5.
Underground utility line damage prevention.
Designers, §56-265.17:1.
Operators' responses, §56-265.17:3.
Duty of operator upon, §56-265.19.
Elements, §56-265.18.
Recordation if made by telephone, §56-265.22.
Required, §56-265.17.
Special project notice, §56-265.17.

NOTICE —Cont'd
Quarantine.
Livestock and poultry.
Contagious and infectious diseases, §3.2-6005.
Railroad company mergers, §56-345.1.
Railroad corporations.
Maintenance of grade crossings, §56-405.
Real estate board.
Cease and desist orders.
Condominium provision violations, §55-79.100.
Real estate cooperatives.
Cancellation right of purchasers, §55-483.
Conversion buildings, §55-487.
Meetings, §55-465.
Sale of interest for nonpayment of assessments, §55-472.
Voting, §55-467.
Real estate tax exemption or deferral for elderly or handicapped program, §58.1-3213.1.
Real estate transaction recovery fund.
Board findings, §54.1-2114.
Real property tax apportionment, §58.1-3226.
Real property tax assessment.
Appeals of board of equalization decisions to circuit court.
Notice provided taxpayer by assessing official, §58.1-3331.
Change in assessment, §58.1-3330.
Easement acquired by public service corporation.
Deduction from value of real estate to state corporation commission and department of taxation, §58.1-3355.
Increase by boards of equalization, §58.1-3381.
Notice when increase requested after taxpayer filed appeal, §58.1-3379.
Real property taxes, collection of taxes.
Lease of real estate, §58.1-3948.
Real property tax service charge in lieu of payments.
Notice to governor or educational institutions, §58.1-3404.
Receivers.
Special receivers.
Appointment, §8.01-591.
Emergency appointment, §8.01-592.
List of creditors, §8.01-595.
Parties served with process, §8.01-594.
Sale of assets, §8.01-596.
Recognizances.
Commitment for trial.
Notice to attorney for Commonwealth, §19.2-135.
Denial of bail.
Notice of right to appeal, §19.2-120.
Recreational facilities authorities.
Public hearing on creating, §15.2-5602.
Redevelopment projects.
Spot blight abatement, §36-49.1:1.
Regulations.
Notice of intended regulatory action, §2.2-4007.01.
Petitions for new or amended regulations, §2.2-4007.
Revisions, §§2.2-4007.03, 2.2-4007.06.
Release of deeds of trust or other liens, §55-66.3.
Removal of juvenile case to circuit court, §16.1-269.1.
Renewable energy.
Small renewable energy projects.
Permits by rule, notice of intent, §10.1-1197.6.

NOTICE —Cont'd
Rental inspection ordinance and rental inspection districts.
Locality adopting and establishing, §36-105.1:1.
Rentals, motor vehicles.
Collision damage waiver, §59.1-207.31.
Representation.
Persons representing and binding other, §§64.2-714 to 64.2-718.
Rescission of release of liability, right to.
Release executed by person not represented by counsel, §8.01-425.1.
Restaurants.
Initial notice by certified mail, subsequent notices by regular mail, §35.1-1.1.
Retail sales and use tax.
Dealers collecting.
Revocation or suspension of certificate of registration, §58.1-613.
Exemption certificates.
Suspension of exemption for misuse, §58.1-623.1.
Jeopardy assessment, §58.1-631.
Reversion of city to town.
Citizen petition, §15.2-4102.
Petition by governing body, §15.2-4101.
Risk retention groups and purchasing groups.
Policy notice, §38.2-5103.
Purchasing group requirements, §38.2-5108.
Road impact fees.
Road improvements plan.
Public hearing, §15.2-2321.
Safe deposit boxes and storage.
Notice of lien of fieri facias denying access to box, §6.2-2304.
Notice to lessee that safe or box will be opened for nonpayment of rent, §6.2-2305.
Sale of delinquent tax lands, §58.1-3965.
Sale of gas, oil or minerals on state corrections board property, §53.1-31.
Sales of self-service storage property, §§55-418, 55-419.
Sales, UCC.
Breach of obligations, §8.2-607.
Termination of contracts, §8.2-309.
Sales under deed of trust, §§55-59.1, 55-62.
Advertising, §§55-59.2, 55-59.3, 55-63.
Notice of sale under deed of trust, §15.2-979.
Sanitation districts law of 1938.
Withdrawals from district, §21-203.
Scholarships.
Soil scientist scholarships.
Notice to attorney general upon breach of contract, §23-38.10.
Schools and education.
Change in school divisions, §22.1-25.
Expulsion of students, §22.1-277.06.
Nonrenewal of teacher contract, §22.1-305.
Parental responsibility and involvement requirements, §22.1-279.3.
Public notice regarding certain resource guides, §22.1-17.5.
Teacher grievances.
Hearing before school board or hearing officer.
Decision generally, §22.1-313.
Secretary of the Commonwealth.
Initial notice by certified mail, subsequent notices by regular mail, §2.2-401.1.
Security sales agent.
Beginning or terminating connection with broker-dealer or issuer, §13.1-504.

NOTICE —Cont'd
Sentence of person twice previously convicted for certain violent felonies.
Intention to seek punishment pursuant to sections, §19.2-297.1.
Service by publication.
Publication of interim notice, §8.01-319.
Service districts.
Creation, §15.2-2400.
Court order in consolidated cities, §15.2-2401.
Service of notice, process and other papers generally.
See SERVICE OF NOTICE, PROCESS AND OTHER PAPERS.
Setoff debt collection, income tax.
Claimant agency to notify department of taxation, §58.1-524.
Final setoff, §58.1-529.
Intention to setoff, §58.1-525.
Settlements.
Insurance claims, notice of settlement payments, §38.2-236.
Sewage disposal.
Land application, marketing and distribution of sewage sludge, §62.1-44.19:3.
Sewerage systems not regulated as public utilities.
Notice that such system includes a sewage treatment plant, §56-265.11:1.
Sewage system to be established in county or extension of existing system in county.
Governing body of county to be notified, §§15.2-2126, 15.2-2129.
Sewerage companies.
Public utilities.
Notice that such system includes a sewage treatment plant, §56-261.
Suspension of service to sewerage companies, §56-236.2.
Sewer use standards violations.
Hearing.
Civil penalty, imposition by locality, §15.2-2122.
Sex offender and crimes against minors registry.
Automatic notification of registration to certain entities, §9.1-914.
Electronic notification to requesting persons, §9.1-914.
Misuse of registry information.
Notice of penalty on forms and documents, §9.1-919.
Sheriffs' jail duties.
Jail duty failure complaint, §53.1-125.
Simulation of notice, §18.2-213.
Small business financing authority.
Public hearings.
Tax exemptions on bond issues, §2.2-2292.
Small claims courts, §16.1-122.3.
Small renewable energy projects.
Permits by rule, notice of intent, §10.1-1197.6.
Smoking in underground coal mines, §45.1-161.179.
Social services, local departments.
Initial notice by certified mail, subsequent notices by regular mail, §63.2-100.1.
Soil and water conservation board.
Initial notice by certified mail, subsequent notices by regular mail, §10.1-500.1.
Soil and water conservation districts.
Directors, notice of election, §10.1-523.

NOTICE —Cont'd
Solicitation of charitable or civic contributions.
Publication of warnings, §§57-52, 57-52.1.
Special exception, zoning, §15.2-2310.
Spousal support.
Remarriage, §20-110.
Reopening of proceedings, §20-112.
Stalking victim to receive notice of release of person incarcerated upon conviction, §18.2-60.3.
State agencies.
Discontinuance or reduction of service to locality, §2.2-612.
State board of elections.
Initial notice by certified mail, subsequent notices by regular mail, §24.2-101.01.
State corporation commission.
Orders, rules and regulations promulgated by commission, §12.1-28.
Returnable to location of commission, §12.1-5.
State departments and agencies.
Initial notice by certified mail, subsequent notices by regular mail, §2.2-601.1.
State parks.
Planning, solicitation of public comment on, §10.1-200.1.
Statutory agent for service of process or notice.
Address for mailing of process, §8.01-312.
Specific addresses, §8.01-313.
Certificate filed with court, §8.01-326.1.
Copy of process sent to defendant, §8.01-326.1.
Defined, §8.01-285.
Duties of agent, §8.01-312.
Effective date of service, §8.01-326.1.
Effect of service on, §8.01-312.
Legal force and validity, §8.01-312.
Motor vehicle weight violation.
Operator of vehicle statutory agent, §46.2-1132.
Nonresident aircraft operator or owner.
Secretary of Commonwealth, §8.01-309.
Nonresident motor vehicle operator.
Address for mailing process, §8.01-313.
Commissioner of DMV, §8.01-308.
Secretary of Commonwealth.
Service on generally, §8.01-329.
State corporation commission.
Service on clerk generally, §12.1-19.1.
Time for nonresident to respond for process from statutory agent, §8.01-312.
Unincorporated associations or orders or unincorporated common carriers.
Principal office outside state and transacting business in state, §8.01-306.
Stormwater control program.
Public hearing, §15.2-2114.
Subdivisions and land development.
Advertisement of plans, ordinances and amendments generally, §15.2-2204.
Interest granted to locality as condition of site plan approval.
Vacation by locality, §15.2-2270.
Subdivision ordinances.
Public hearings on, §15.2-2251.
Subdivision plat vacated after sale of lot, §15.2-2272.
Subdivision plat vacated before sale of lot, §15.2-2271.
Subdivisions ordinances changed, amended, etc., by codification, §15.2-1433.

NOTICE —Cont'd
Subsequent notices sent by regular mail, §1-206.
Summary jury trial, §8.01-576.2.
Summer camps.
Initial notice by certified mail, subsequent notices by regular mail, §35.1-1.1.
Superintendents of schools.
Renegotiation of contract.
Notice to board members, §22.1-60.
Surface mining.
National pollutant discharge elimination system permits.
Violations, §45.1-254.
Notice of noncompliance served on operator, §45.1-186.1.
Surplus lines insurance.
Policy procured or placed with insurer approved to issue surplus lines insurance but not licensed or regulated by commission, §38.2-4806.
Suspension of professions and occupations license, §54.1-104.
Tanning facilities, §§59.1-310.3, 59.1-310.4.
Tax collection, local taxes.
Prior to referral to attorney, local collector or sheriff, §58.1-3934.
Prior to referral to private collection agent, §58.1-3919.1.
Tax collection, state taxes.
Charge-off of state taxes, §58.1-1802.
Intent to file lien, §58.1-1805.
Tax commissioner.
Service of notices, §§58.1-216, 58.1-217.
Taxes or assessments for local improvements.
Amount of assessment, §§15.2-2408, 15.2-2409.
Tax regulations issued by tax commissioner, §58.1-203.
Teachers.
Grievance procedures.
Hearing before school board or hearing officer.
Decision generally, §22.1-313.
Nonrenewal of contract, §22.1-305.
Telegraph or telephone companies.
Carrier identification, §59.1-426.
Telephone solicitation sales.
Cancellations, §§59.1-21.3, 59.1-21.4.
Theft.
Explosives, §59.1-139.
Timber cutting encroachment.
Damage recovery, §55-332.
Time-shares.
Conversion time-share projects, §55-374.
Protection of lienholders, §55-389.
Purchaser cancellation, §55-376.
Termination of time-shares, §55-373.
Title insurance of owner, availability to buyer in real property transaction, §38.2-4616.
Tobacco warehouses.
Discontinuance, §61.1-38.
Tort claims for damages.
Notice to be given counties, cities and towns, §15.2-209.
Town charters annulled, §15.2-3703.
Trademarks and service marks.
Applicant not to be entitled to registration, §59.1-92.5.
Trailer dealer franchises.
Hearings and other remedies by commissioner of motor vehicles, §46.2-1992.75.
Trailer dealers.
Denial, suspension or revocation of license, §46.2-1992.80.

NOTICE —Cont'd
Transcripts filed with appellate court.
Court of appeals, VA SCt Rule 5A:8.
Supreme court, VA SCt Rule 5:11.
Transition of city to town.
Citizen petition, §15.2-4102.
Petition by governing body, §15.2-4101.
Transportation board.
Initial notice by certified mail, subsequent notices by regular mail, §33.1-13.04.
Location of routes, §33.1-18.
Transportation companies.
Freight arrival, §56-117.
Transportation department.
Initial notice by certified mail, subsequent notices by regular mail, §33.1-13.04.
Transportation districts.
Transportation plan, §15.2-4528.
Transportation improvement districts.
District within city of Charlottesville and county of Albemarle.
Public hearing on creating district, §33.1-448.
Public hearing on creating.
Counties with population of more than 500,000, §33.1-431.
Trespass.
Timber cutting encroachment, §55-332.
Trustees.
Substituted trustees.
Appointment, §64.2-1406.
Trusts.
Establishment of trust.
Duty of trustee, §64.2-775.
Judicial proceedings involving trusts, §64.2-713.
Knowledge of fact, §64.2-702.
Methods and waiver, §64.2-707.
Resignation of trustee, §64.2-758.
Transfer of principal place of business, §64.2-706.
Unclaimed property.
Sales, §55-210.18.
Unemployment compensation.
Claims adjudication, §60.2-619.
Ungranted shores of the sea.
Filing notice of lis pendens, §28.2-1513.
Uniform computer information transactions act.
Termination of obligations, §59.1-506.17.
United States civil aircraft.
Instruments affecting title to or interest in, §55-100.
Unlicensed insurers process, §§38.2-800 to 38.2-807.
Unlicensed nonresident insurance brokers and agents process, §§38.2-808 to 38.2-811.
Unlicensed public adjusters process, §§38.2-812 to 38.2-815.
Vacation and alteration of public rights-of-way, §15.2-2006.
Variances, zoning, §15.2-2310.
Viatical settlements.
Prerequisites to contracting, §38.2-6008.
Virginia retirement system.
Group insurance program.
Opting out, §51.1-507.
Loss of benefits for convicted felons.
Review of determination made by employer, §51.1-124.13.
Visitation proceedings.
Relocation or change of address, §20-124.5.
Voter registration.
Advance notice.
Other times and locations, §24.2-415.

NOTICE —Cont'd
Voter registration —Cont'd
Change of address within Commonwealth, §24.2-424.
Change of name of registered voter, §24.2-423.
Denial of registration, §24.2-114.
Electronic notice.
Change of address within Commonwealth, §24.2-424.
Change of voter's name, pilot program, §24.2-423.
Improper registration, cancellation for, §24.2-429.
Internet postings required, §24.2-415.
Objections, §24.2-432.
Other times and locations.
Advance notice, §24.2-415.
Record reconstruction, §24.2-446.
When notice not required, §24.2-415.
Voting or counting equipment for elections.
Preparation, §24.2-633.
Wages.
Failure of employer to make payment, §40.1-29.
Waste management.
Initial notice by certified mail, subsequent notices by regular mail, §10.1-1400.1.
Violation of provisions.
Notice to local governments, §10.1-1407.1.
Water and waste authorities.
Ordinance, agreement or resolution and notice of hearing, §15.2-5104.
Water control board.
Initial notice by certified mail, subsequent notices by regular mail, §§62.1-44.3:1, 62.1-255.1.
Meetings, §62.1-44.11.
Watercraft sales and use tax, dealers certificate of registration.
Suspension or revocation, §58.1-1406.
Watershed improvements districts.
Hearing on petition for establishment, §10.1-616.
Waters of the state.
Oil discharges, §62.1-44.34:19.
Provision violations.
Notification of local governments and property owners, §62.1-44.15:4.
Toxic impaired waters, §62.1-44.19:6.
Waste discharges, §62.1-44.5.
Water supply systems.
Approval by counties of establishment or extension of existing systems, §§15.2-2149 to 15.2-2152.
Weapons sales.
Disposition of firearms surrendered to locality, §15.2-915.5.
Whistleblowing.
Fraud and abuse whistleblower protection act.
Notice of protection to employees, §2.2-3013.
Wills.
Bona fide purchasers.
Devises of real estate without notice, §64.2-456.
Intestacy, §64.2-458.
Later wills, §64.2-457.
Notice to interested parties, §64.2-508.
Recordation.
Effect, §64.2-455.
Wine franchises.
Cancellation of agreement, §4.1-407.
Winter sports safety act.
Warnings required on tickets, passes and contracts, §8.01-227.12.
Wireless service authorities.
Rates and charges, hearing on, §15.2-5431.25.

NOTICE —Cont'd
Wireless service authorities —Cont'd
Resolution creating, §15.2-5431.5.
Wiretapping.
Court-ordered interception of communications.
Application for and issuance of order, §19.2-68.
Workers' compensation.
Accidents, §65.2-600.
Occupational diseases, §65.2-405.
Policy clause requirements, §65.2-809.
Rejection of coverage, §65.2-300.
Tolling of statute of limitations, §65.2-602.
Workers' compensation commission.
Initial notice by certified mail, subsequent notices by regular mail, §65.2-101.1.
Workers' compensation insurance and self-insurance.
Cancellations, §65.2-804.
Provision violations, §§65.2-805, 65.2-806.
Service requirements, §65.2-810.
Work release programs.
Law enforcement to receive, §53.1-160.
Works on watercourses.
Applications for leave to build or rebuild, §§62.1-117, 62.1-120.
Zoning.
Additional notice of zoning matters, §15.2-2205.
Advertisement of plans, ordinances and amendments generally, §15.2-2204.
Amendments and variations of conditions, notice to landowners subject to, §15.2-2302.
Ordinances changed, amended, etc., by codification, §15.2-1433.
Public hearing on proposed ordinance and map and adoption of ordinance, §15.2-2285.
Special exceptions or variances, §15.2-2310.

NOTICE BY PUBLICATION.
See PUBLICATION.

NOTICE OF APPEAL.
Administrative agency appeals, VA SCt Rule 2A:2.
Appeal by Commonwealth in criminal case, §19.2-400.
Cross appeals, §19.2-401.
Appeals from general district courts in civil cases, §16.1-112.
Birth-related neurological injury compensation claims, §38.2-5011.
Child support enforcement by department of social services.
Appeal from decision of hearing officer, §63.2-1943.
Compensation board appeal.
Board decisions, §15.2-1636.9.
Court of appeals, §17.1-407.
Appeals from trial court, VA SCt Rule 5A:6.
Extension of time, VA SCt Rule 5A:3.
Time for filing, §17.1-408.
Workers' compensation commission.
Special rule applicable to appeals, VA SCt Rule 5A:11.
District courts, §16.1-112.
Corporation or partnership preparing without attorney intervention, §16.1-88.03.
What constitutes noting an appeal, VA SCt Rule 7A:13.
Juvenile case transferred to circuit court, §16.1-269.1.
Supreme court, VA SCt Rule 5:9.
Appeal from court of appeals, VA SCt Rule 5:11.

NOTICE OF APPEAL —Cont'd
Supreme court —Cont'd
Appeals from the state corporation commission, VA SCt Rule 5:21.
Extension of time, VA SCt Rule 5:5.
Transfer of juvenile case to circuit court, §16.1-269.1.
Withdrawal of appeal.
General district courts, juvenile and domestic relations district courts, §16.1-133.

NOTICE OF HEARING.
Agricultural and forestal districts, §15.2-4309.
Annexation.
Agreements between towns and counties as town's annexation rights.
Public hearing before commission on local government, §15.2-3232.
Arbitration, §8.01-581.04.
Baseball stadium authority.
Selection of site of stadium, §15.2-5806.
Bonds issued by localities, §15.2-2606.
Judicial determination of validity.
Publication of motion for judgment, §15.2-2652.
Broker-dealers, investment advisors, investment advisor representatives and agents.
Revocation of registration, §13.1-506.
Budgets of localities and school divisions.
Public hearing, §15.2-2506.
Amendment, §15.2-2507.
Bus or vehicle fleet, road construction equipment.
Sale by locality with intent to lease back.
Approval of governing body required, public hearing, §15.2-951.
Cable television.
Localities providing services.
Public hearing on feasibility study, §15.2-2108.7.
Charters of local government.
Public hearings, §15.2-202.
Child abuse or neglect.
Preliminary protective orders, §16.1-253.
Removal orders, child taken into custody, §16.1-252.
Commissioners in chancery.
Notice of time and place of taking account, §8.01-611.
Comprehensive plan.
Public hearing, §15.2-2225.
Correction of taxes assessed by state corporation commission, §58.1-2031.
Detention hearing for child taken into custody, §16.1-250.
District courts.
Minimum time limit, §16.1-83.
Drivers' licenses.
Suspension or revocation of license, §§46.2-402, 46.2-403, 46.2-408.
Ethics advisory panels, senate and house of general assembly, §30-114.
Fishing, tidal waters, §28.2-216.
Foster care placement review, §16.1-282.
Garbage and refuse pickup and disposal services.
Ordinance displacing private company, §§15.2-930, 15.2-934.
Gas and oil exploration, §45.1-361.19.
Hampton Roads sports facility authority.
Selecting facility site, §15.2-5906.

NOTICE OF HEARING —Cont'd
Industrial development authorities.
Public hearings, §15.2-4906.
Insurance agents, refusal to issue and revocation of license, §38.2-1832.
Insurance consultants, refusal or revocation of license, §38.2-1844.
Juvenile proceedings.
Detention hearings, §16.1-250.
Foster care placement review, §16.1-282.
Preliminary protective orders, §16.1-253.
Removal orders, abuse or neglect of child, §16.1-252.
Termination of residual parental rights, §16.1-283.
Transfer to circuit court, §16.1-269.1.
Medical malpractice review panels.
Written notification of parties and panel members, §8.01-581.3:1, MedMal Rule 4.
Medicine and other healing arts professions.
Licensing hearings, §54.1-2920.
Membership camping.
Registration, §59.1-323.
Mental health facility admissions.
Involuntary commitment.
Psychiatric inpatient treatment of minors, §16.1-341.
Psychiatric inpatient treatment of minors.
Involuntary commitment, §16.1-341.
Mental health or substance abuse.
Legally incompetent or incapacitated persons.
Notice and hearing.
See MENTAL HEALTH.
Official map to be amended or modified, §15.2-2235.
Parental rights termination, §16.1-283.
Park authorities.
Creating, §15.2-5702.
Parks, recreational facilities or playgrounds.
Established, operated or maintained by locality.
Public hearing, §15.2-1813.
Planning and development.
Comprehensive plan, §15.2-2225.
Protective orders.
Preliminary order to protect child's life, health or normal development, §16.1-253.
Public rights-of-way, vacation and alterations, §15.2-2006.
Public service corporation tax assessment review, §58.1-2671.
Notice to Commonwealth, §58.1-2674.
Real property acquired by locality.
Public hearings, §15.2-1813.
Real property tax increase proposal, §58.1-3321.
Recreational facilities authorities.
Creating, §15.2-5602.
Redevelopment projects.
Spot blight abatement, §36-49.1:1.
Rental inspection ordinance and rental inspection districts.
Locality adopting and establishing, §36-105.1:1.
Retail franchise registration revocation, §13.1-562.
Road impact fees.
Road improvements plan, §15.2-2321.
Sanitation districts law of 1938.
Creation of districts, §21-146.
Sanitation districts law of 1946.
Creation of districts, §21-229.
Service districts.
Creation, §15.2-2400.
Court order in consolidated cities, §15.2-2401.

NOTICE OF HEARING —Cont'd
Small claims courts, §16.1-122.3.
Special exception, zoning, §15.2-2310.
Stormwater control program.
Adopting, §15.2-2114.
Public hearing, §15.2-2114.
Subdivision ordinances.
Public hearing, §15.2-2251.
Taxes or assessments for local improvements.
Appeal of assessment, §15.2-2411.
Termination of residual parental rights, §16.1-283.
Transfer of juvenile case to circuit court, §16.1-269.1.
Transportation districts.
Transportation plan, §15.2-4528.
Transportation improvement districts.
District within city of Charlottesville and county of Albemarle.
Public hearing on creating district, §33.1-448.
Public hearing on creating.
Counties with population of more than 500,000, §33.1-431.
Vacation and alteration of public right-of-way, §15.2-2006.
Wireless service authorities.
Resolution creating, §15.2-5431.5.
Zoning.
Proposed ordinance and map and adoption of ordinance, §15.2-2285.
Special exceptions or variances, §15.2-2310.

NO-TILL PLANTERS OR DRILLS.
Income tax credit for purchase of conservation tillage equipment.
Corporations, §58.1-432.
Individuals, §58.1-334.

NOT-TO-EXCEED-PRICE CONTRACTS.
Procurement by public bodies.
Juvenile correctional facilities, §2.2-4307.

NOTTOWAY COUNTY.
Confederate cemeteries and graves.
Disbursement of funds appropriated for upkeep, §10.1-2211.
Nottoway river.
Dam restrictions, §29.1-532.
School board.
Salary of members, §22.1-32.
Southside regional airport authority at Blackstone, 1992 ch 371.

NOTTOWAY RIVER.
Dam restrictions, §29.1-532.
Scenic river, §10.1-414.

NOXIOUS CHEMICAL SUBSTANCES.
Inhaling, §18.2-264.

NOXIOUS OR NAUSEATING GASES.
Illegal use, §18.2-312.

NOXIOUS WEEDS, §§3.2-800 to 3.2-809.
Counties, cities or towns, §15.2-902.

NSU, §§23-174.1 to 23-174.7.

NUCLEAR ACCIDENTS.
Emergency management and disaster law generally, §§44-146.13 to 44-146.28.
See EMERGENCY MANAGEMENT.
Evacuation plans.
Public utilities to notify customers, §56-245.1:1.

NUCLEAR ENERGY.
Emergency plans prepared by local government, §44-146.19.

NUCLEAR ENERGY —Cont'd
Evacuation plans, utilities to notify customers, §56-245.1:1.
Inspections of nuclear vessels, §40.1-51.10.
Radiation control.
Fire insurance policies, excluding loss or damage caused by, §38.2-2102.
Generally, §§32.1-227 to 32.1-238.
See RADIATION CONTROL.
Radiological emergency preparedness fund.
One-time and annual fees to, §44-146.32.
Virginia nuclear energy consortium, §§67-1400 to 67-1406.
Articles of incorporation, §67-1404.
Audit of accounts, §67-1406.
Board of directors, §67-1403.
Definitions, §67-1400.
Deposit of funds, §67-1405.
Established, §67-1401.
Executive director, §67-1404.
Formation by board, §67-1404.
Funds, §67-1405.
Governance, §67-1403.
Members, §67-1404.
Performance of essential government function for purposes of expending public funds, §67-1401.
Periodic external review, §67-1406.
Powers, §67-1402.
Purpose, §§67-1402, 67-1404.
Reporting on nonproprietary activities, §67-1404.
Strategic plan and summary of activities.
Submission, §67-1403.

NUDE DANCING.
ABC law.
Licenses.
Suspension or revocation, §4.1-226.
Mixed beverage licenses.
Grounds for refusal to grant, §4.1-223.
Prohibited acts by licensee, §4.1-325.

NUDIST CAMPS FOR JUVENILES.
Hotel, campground or summer camp conducting.
License not to be issued to owner or lessee, §35.1-18.

NUDITY.
Obscenity and related offenses generally, §§18.2-372 to 18.2-388.
See OBSCENITY AND RELATED OFFENSES.

NUISANCE BIRD LAW, §§3.2-900, 3.2-901.

NUISANCES, §§48-1 to 48-17.1.
Abating public nuisance, §§48-1 to 48-6.
Counties, cities or towns, §§15.2-900, 15.2-1115.
Defense by interested person, §48-4.
Derelict buildings, §§15.2-906, 15.2-907.1.
Locality appointed as receiver to repair derelict and blighted buildings, §15.2-907.2.
Enforcement of judgment in rem, §§48-6, 48-16.
Fines and costs, §48-5.
Investigation of complaint by special grand jury, §48-1.
Judgment of abatement, §48-5.
Outdoor advertising, §33.1-375.
Permitting continuation of nuisance, §48-3.
Presentment against person causing nuisance, §48-2.
Presentment against premises, §48-3.
Reimbursement to locality for costs of abatement, §48-5.

NUISANCES —Cont'd
Abating public nuisance —Cont'd
Service of copy of presentment, §48-4.
ABC offenses.
Enjoining nuisances, §4.1-335.
Interdiction of illegal alcoholic beverages, §4.1-334.
Maintaining common nuisances, §4.1-317.
Alcoholic beverage sales at licensed establishment.
Temporary injunction.
Establishment meeting place for committing serious criminal violations, §48-17.1.
Aquatic species.
Nonindigenous aquatic nuisance species act, §§29.1-571 to 29.1-577.
See NONINDIGENOUS AQUATIC NUISANCE SPECIES ACT.
Birds, §§3.2-900, 3.2-901.
Buildings used for purpose of lewdness, assignation, prostitution or criminal street gang activities, §§48-7 to 48-15.
Abatement of houses and contents, §48-7.
Sale of furniture, etc., §48-12.
Cancellation of order of abatement, §48-14.
Closing of building, §48-12.
Contempt proceedings, §48-10.
Dismissal of case, §48-9.
Disposition of proceeds of sale, §48-13.
Immunity to witnesses, §48-15.
Injunctive relief, §48-8.
Order of abatement, §48-12.
Punishment for contempt, §48-11.
Redemption of sold property, §48-14.
Sale of furniture, etc., §48-12.
Disposition of proceeds of sale, §48-13.
Substitution of complainant, §48-9.
Trial of case, §48-9.
Counties, cities or towns.
Abatement or removal, recovery of cost, §§15.2-900, 15.2-907.1, 15.2-1115.
Dams, §29.1-532.
Derelict buildings.
Authority to remove, demolish or renovate, §§15.2-906, 15.2-907.1.
Locality appointed as receiver to repair derelict and blighted buildings, §15.2-907.2.
Drug offenses.
Premises deemed common nuisance, §18.2-258.
Enjoining, §§18.2-258.01, 48-17.
Easements.
Interference with use and enjoyment, §55-50.1.
Farms, §3.2-302.
Illegal drug transactions.
Closure of nuisance premises, §§48-16, 48-17.
Lien for charge of costs, §15.2-1115.
Outdoor advertising.
Abatement, §33.1-375.
Public property used without consent or franchise, §15.2-2018.
Removal.
Counties, cities or towns, §§15.2-900, 15.2-1115.
Derelict buildings, §§15.2-906, 15.2-907.1.
Statute of limitations, §8.01-243.
Waters of the state.
Court powers limited to grant leave to erect obstructions, §§62.1-8, 62.1-9.

NUMBER.
Signatures on referenda petitions.
Adopting or changing county form of government, §15.2-301.

NUMBER —Cont'd
Statutory construction, §1-227.

NUNCHAHKA, NUNCHAKU OR NUNCHUCK.
See MARTIAL ARTS WEAPONS.

NUNCUPATIVE WILLS.
Military personnel, §64.2-408.

NUNNERY.
Property tax exemptions, §§58.1-3402, 58.1-3606.

NURSE LICENSURE COMPACT, §§54.1-3030 to 54.1-3040.
Administration of compact, §54.1-3037.
Adverse actions, §54.1-3034.
Amendment of compact, §54.1-3039.
Application for license in party state, §54.1-3033.
Arbitration authority, §54.1-3040.
Authority of party state licensing boards, §54.1-3035.
Change of primary state of residence, §54.1-3033.
Construction, §54.1-3040.
Coordinated licensure information system, §54.1-3036.
Definitions, §54.1-3030.
Enactment to make effective, §54.1-3039.
Exchange of information, §54.1-3037.
Findings, §54.1-3031.
Immunity, §54.1-3038.
Notice of actions taken, §54.1-3032.
Party state licensing boards.
Authority, §54.1-3035.
Purpose, §54.1-3031.
Recognition of license to practice, §54.1-3032.
Report of adverse actions, §54.1-3034.
Severability, §54.1-3040.
Withdrawal from compact, §54.1-3039.

NURSERIES.
Intangible personal property tax.
Exemptions, §58.1-1103.
License tax on sale of nursery products.
Localities prohibited from imposing, §58.1-3703.

NURSERY SCHOOLS.
Accredited private school program.
Child welfare agency licensure and regulation.
Exemption from provision, conditions for exemption, §63.2-1717.
Board of education.
Accreditation regulations, §22.1-19.
Certification of private school program, §63.2-1717.
Child welfare agency licensure and regulation.
Exemption from provision, conditions for exemption, §63.2-1717.
Immunizations required for attendance at, §32.1-46.

NURSING, §§54.1-3000 to 54.1-3028.1.
Adult abuse, neglect or exploitation.
Photographs, x-rays or medical imaging of incapacitated person.
Taking without consent as part of medical evaluation, §63.2-1606.1.
Report to local department of social services, §63.2-1606.
Advisory council on the future of nursing in Virginia.
Secretary of health and human resources.
Responsibilities, §2.2-212.

NURSING —Cont'd
Assault and battery of health care provider.
Emergency room or other facility providing emergency care, §18.2-57.
Bills for medical services.
Presumption of authenticity and reasonableness, §8.01-413.01.
Board of nursing, §§54.1-3000 to 54.1-3015.
Powers and duties, §54.1-3005.
Workforce information, §54.1-3012.1.
Child abuse or neglect reports.
Education programs on child abuse recognition and intervention, §54.1-3013.1.
Reason to suspect, required reports, fine for failure, §63.2-1509.
Compact on nurse licensure, §§54.1-3030 to 54.1-3040.
Controlled substances.
Dispensing restrictions, §54.1-3303.
Correctional health assistants, §54.1-3016.1.
Death, authority to pronounce, §54.1-2972.
Disasters, state or local emergency.
Immunity.
Abandonment of person owed duty of health care in response to disaster, §8.01-225.01.
Unable to provide required care because of lack of resources, §8.01-225.02.
Disclosure of patient information to third party payors by professionals.
See MENTAL HEALTH.
Donation of services.
Tax credit, §58.1-439.22.
Driving while intoxicated.
Chemical test for alcohol or drug content of blood.
Persons qualified to take blood samples, §18.2-268.5.
Drugs.
Dispensation requirements, §54.1-3408.
Nurse practitioners.
Prescription of controlled substances and devices, §54.1-2957.01.
Prohibited acts by licensees generally, §54.1-2409.1.
Sexual assault nurse examiners.
Administration of preventive medication, §54.1-3408.
Duty to protect third parties.
Violent behavior or serious harm by client, §54.1-2400.1.
Escrow fund protection, §54.1-2506.2.
Exemption from provisions, §54.1-3001.
Expediting licensure process.
Relocating to state pursuant to spouse's military orders.
Applicant licensed or certified in another state, §54.1-3005.
Fluoride varnish.
Administering topical varnish to teeth of child aged 6 months to 3 years, §54.1-3408.
Foreign nursing school graduates.
Practice of nursing, §54.1-3001.
Free health care to underserved population.
Practice nursing by nurses rendering, §54.1-3001.
Graduate nursing scholarships, §§23-35.9 to 23-36.2.
Fund, §54.1-3011.2.
Health service plans, coverage, §38.2-4221.
Holders of current unrestricted licenses from other states or countries.
Practice of nursing, §54.1-3001.

NURSING —Cont'd
Identification badges.
Use of first name and first letter only of last name, §54.1-3005.
Immunity.
Disasters, state or local emergency.
Abandonment of person owed duty of health care in response to disaster, §8.01-225.01.
Unable to provided required care because of lack of resources, §8.01-225.02.
Immunization of children.
Influenza vaccine, administration to minors by pharmacists or nurses, §§32.1-46.02, 54.1-3408.
Inborn errors of metabolism.
Detection and control reports, §§32.1-65, 32.1-66.
Compliance failures, §32.1-73.
Income tax credit.
Donation of services, §58.1-439.22.
Interstate compact on nurse licensure, §§54.1-3030 to 54.1-3040.
Licensure compact, §§54.1-3030 to 54.1-3040.
Liens.
Medical services lien, §§8.01-66.2 to 8.01-66.12.
See MEDICAL SERVICES LIEN.
Loan repayment fund, §54.1-3011.2.
Medical bills.
Presumption of authenticity and reasonableness, §8.01-413.01.
Medical malpractice.
General provisions, §§8.01-581.1 to 8.01-581.20.
See MEDICAL MALPRACTICE.
Nurse aides, certification, §§54.1-3022 to 54.1-3025.1.
Advanced certification, §54.1-3025.1.
Competency evaluation, certification by, §54.1-3023.
Denial of certification, §54.1-3007.
Lapsed certifications, §54.1-3011.
Nurse aide education programs, §§54.1-3006.2, 54.1-3028.1.
Renewals, §54.1-3011.
Revocations, §54.1-3007.
Suspensions, §54.1-3007.
Nurse practitioners.
Defined, §54.1-3000.
Donation of services.
Tax credit, §58.1-439.22.
Licensure, §54.1-2957.
Medically underserved areas.
Pilot programs for obstetrical and pediatric care in underserved areas, §§32.1-11.5, 54.1-2901.
Patient care team members, §54.1-2957.
Prescription endorsement, signature or stamp, §54.1-2957.02.
Prescription of controlled substances and devices, §54.1-2957.01.
Ophthalmia neonatorum.
Prevention of blindness from.
Duty of nurses, §32.1-63.
Procedure upon birth, §32.1-62.
Failure to comply, §32.1-73.
Phenylketonuria.
Detection and control reports, §§32.1-65, 32.1-66.
Compliance failures, §32.1-73.
Practical nurses, duty to protect third parties.
Violent behavior or serious harm by client, §54.1-2400.1.
Practical nurses, licensure, §§54.1-3019 to 54.1-3021.
Denial of license, §54.1-3007.

NURSING —Cont'd
Practical nurses, licensure —Cont'd
Fee, additional, §54.1-3011.1.
Lapsed licenses, §54.1-3011.
Qualifications, §54.1-3020.
Renewal of license, §54.1-3011.
Revocations, §54.1-3007.
Suspensions, §54.1-3007.
Prescriptions, §54.1-3408.
Nurse practitioners.
Acceptance of signature, §54.1-2957.02.
Controlled substances and devices, §54.1-2957.01.
Professional limited liability companies.
Generally, §§13.1-1100 to 13.1-1123.
See PROFESSIONAL LIMITED LIABILITY COMPANIES.
Professions and occupations regulation generally.
See HEALTH PROFESSIONS DEPARTMENT.
Prohibited acts by licensees generally, §54.1-2409.1.
Records of patients.
Admissibility of copies, §8.01-413.
Right of patient, attorney or authorized insurer to copies, §8.01-413.
Subpoenas, §8.01-413.
Registered nurses, duty to protect third parties.
Violent behavior or serious harm by client, §54.1-2400.1.
Registered nurses, licensure, §54.1-3018.
Denial of license, §54.1-3007.
Fee, additional, §54.1-3011.1.
Lapsed licenses, §54.1-3011.
Provisional license, §54.1-3017.1.
Qualifications, §54.1-3017.
Renewal of license, §54.1-3011.
Revocations, §54.1-3007.
Suspensions, §54.1-3007.
Scholarships, §§23-35.9 to 23-36.2, 32.1-122.6:01, 32.1-122.6:02.
Fund, §54.1-3011.2.
Schools and education.
Employment of nurses by school board, §22.1-274.
Schools of nursing.
Education programs, §54.1-3006.1.
Approval, §54.1-3013.
Child abuse recognition and intervention, §54.1-3013.1.
Discontinuation of education programs, due process requirements, §54.1-3014.
Nurse aide education program, §54.1-3006.2.
Survey, §54.1-3014.
Self-referrals.
Practitioner self-referral act, §§54.1-2410 to 54.1-2414.
Sexual assault nurse examiners.
Administration of preventive medication, §54.1-3408.
Standardized HCFA-1500 health insurance claims forms for services.
Acceptance by insurers required, §38.2-322.
Student loans.
Tuition loan repayment program, §32.1-122.6:04.
Tax credit.
Donation of services, §58.1-439.22.
Title restrictions.
Applicability, §54.1-3513.
Sex offender treatment provider, §54.1-3611.

NURSING —Cont'd
Topical fluoride varnish.
Administering to teeth of child aged 6 months to 3 years, §54.1-3408.
Tuberculin purified protein derivative.
Nurses possessing and administering.
Polices and guidelines, adoption, §32.1-50.2.
Tuberculosis.
Treating person with active tuberculosis.
Report required, §32.1-50.
Tuberculosis diagnosis, obtaining specimens for.
Exemption from licensing requirement, §54.1-2901.
Tuberculosis nurses.
License continuance, §54.1-3015.
Undergraduate nursing scholarships, §§23-35.9 to 23-36.2.
Fund, §54.1-3011.2.
Unlawful procurement of licensure, §54.1-102.
Unlawful use of licensure, §54.1-111.
Venereal disease.
Pregnant women.
Prenatal test required by, §32.1-60.
Virginia health workforce development authority, §§32.1-122.7 to 32.1-122.7:2.
Workforce information, §54.1-3012.1.

NURSING HOME AND ASSISTED LIVING FACILITY ADMINISTRATORS, §§54.1-3100 to 54.1-3103.1.
Board of long-term care administrators, §54.1-3101.
Experiential or practicum requirements.
Waiver, §54.1-3102.1.
Licensing, §§54.1-3100 to 54.1-3103.1.
Professions and occupations regulation generally.
See HEALTH PROFESSIONS DEPARTMENT.
Prohibited acts by licensees generally, §54.1-2409.1.
Unlawful procurement of licensure, §54.1-102.
Unlawful use of licensure, §54.1-111.

NURSING HOME PATIENTS' RIGHTS AND RESPONSIBILITIES, §§32.1-138 to 32.1-138.3.
Incompetency.
Conservators.
See CONSERVATORS.
Generally.
See INCOMPETENCY.
Guardian and ward.
See GUARDIAN AND WARD.
Living wills generally, §§54.1-2981 to 54.1-2993.
See LIVING WILLS.

NURSING HOMES.
See LONG-TERM CARE FACILITIES.

NURSING LOANS.
Student loans.
State board repayment program, §32.1-122.6:01.

NUTRIENT MANAGEMENT PLANS.
Conservation and recreation department.
Golf courses, §10.1-104.5.
Training and certification, §10.1-104.2.
Voluntary program, §10.1-104.2.
Database of critical data attributes.
Nutrients and sediments entering state waters.
Onsite best management practices implemented by state to limit, §2.2-220.3.

NUTRIENT MANAGEMENT PLANS —Cont'd
Golf courses, §10.1-104.5.
Income tax credit.
Purchase of advanced technology pesticide and fertilizer application equipment.
Corporations, §§58.1-337, 58.1-436.
Nitrogen application rates, §10.1-104.2:1.
Resource management plans, §§10.1-104.7 to 10.1-104.9.
Soil and water conservation board.
Nitrogen application rates, §10.1-104.2:1.
Voluntary program, §10.1-104.2.
State lands, required for, §10.1-104.4.

NUTRIENT MANAGEMENT TRAINING AND CERTIFICATION.
Conservation and recreation department, §10.1-104.2.

NUTRIENT REMOVAL TECHNOLOGY.
Design and installation at treatment works.
Reimbursements to localities for upgrades, §10.1-1186.01.

NUTRITIONAL INFORMATION.
Misbranded food items.
Failure to comply with federal requirements for nutritional information, etc., §3.2-5123.

NUTRITIONISTS AND DIETITIANS, §§54.1-2730, 54.1-2731.

NUTRITION THERAPY.
Medical nutrition therapy.
Public officers and employees.
Required health insurance coverage, §2.2-2818.

O

OATH OF OFFICE.
Armed forces or state department personnel.
Administering oath to deployed personnel, §49-3.
Board of education, §22.1-12.
Congress.
Oath of office, US Const Art VI.
Electoral board members, registrars and officers of election, §24.2-120.
Failure to take oath, §49-11.
Local governing body or school board member, vacancy in office not created, §24.2-228.
Form of general oath required, §49-1.
General assembly members or officers.
Who may administer, §49-3.
Governor, US Const Art VI.
Grand juries, §19.2-197.
Judges, US Const Art VI.
Juvenile and domestic relations district court clerks, §16.1-69.17.
Juvenile and domestic relations district court judges, §16.1-69.17.
Juvenile and domestic relations district court probation officers, §16.1-69.17.
Lieutenant governor, US Const Art VI, Amd 14.
Local governing body, elected member.
Failure to take oath, effect, §24.2-228.
Local school boards, §22.1-31.
Failure to take oath, effect, §24.2-228.
Lottery board members, §58.1-4004.
Lottery director, §58.1-4005.
Medical malpractice review panels.
Oath of office, MedMal Rule 4.
Notary public, §47.1-9.

OATH OF OFFICE —Cont'd
Officers elected or appointed under or pursuant to constitutions, VA Const Art II §7, US Const Art VI.
Out-of-state commissioners, §49-2.
Probation officers.
Local probation officers, §9.1-177.
State corporation commission, §12.1-11.
Superintendent of public instruction.
Oath of office, §22.1-22.
Tax commissioner, §58.1-201.
Vice-president of the United States, US Const Art VI, Amd 14.

OATHS AND AFFIRMATIONS, §§49-1 to 49-11.
Administration of oaths, §§49-3, 49-4.
Administrators, §§64.2-501, 64.2-503.
Affidavits.
Taking affidavits, §§49-4 to 49-7.
Affirmation in lieu of oath, §49-9.
Affirmations.
Defined as including, §1-228.
Alcohol safety action program.
Oath of office of case managers and employees, §18.2-271.4.
Attachment.
Examination on oath of codefendant, §8.01-562.
Attorney licensing.
Board power, §54.1-3925.3.
Attorneys.
Board of bar examiners.
Power to administer, §54.1-3925.3.
Qualification for practice, §54.1-3903.
Bail and recognizance.
Pretrial services officers, §19.2-152.4:1.
Banks.
Directors, §§6.2-863, 6.2-901.
Examiners.
Directors' oaths administered by examiners, §6.2-901.
Building code technical review board, §36-111.
Change of name.
Applications under oath, §8.01-217.
Circuit court clerks.
Power to administer, §17.1-217.
Condominiums.
Real estate board.
Investigations of complaints, §55-79.99.
Consumer finance companies.
Investigation by state corporation commission, §6.2-1530.
Court of appeals judges, §17.1-400.
Defined as including affirmations, §1-228.
Deputy treasurer, sheriff, commissioner of revenue or clerk of circuit court, §15.2-1603.
District court clerks, §16.1-69.17.
Power to administer, §16.1-69.40.
District court judges, §16.1-69.17.
Power to administer, §16.1-69.27.
Election officers, §24.2-611.
Electors.
Presidential elections.
Political party selection of electors, §24.2-542.
Selected by groups other than political parties, §24.2-543.
Emergency management organizations.
Loyalty oath required, §44-146.25.
Eminent domain.
Just compensation.
Oath of impartiality, §25.1-230.

OATHS AND AFFIRMATIONS —Cont'd
Executors, §64.2-501.
Failure to take oath, §49-11.
Fire insurance appraisers and umpires, §38.2-2122.
Fire marshals and assistants, §27-37.
General assembly.
Who may administer oath, §49-3.
Witnesses.
Administration, §30-11.
Grand juries.
Multi-jurisdiction.
Administration of witness oath by foreman, §19.2-215.5.
Regular grand juries.
Statutory oath of office, §19.2-197.
Special grand juries.
Administration of witness oath by foreman, §19.2-208.
Health professions department investigations.
Personnel powers, §54.1-2506.
Holy Bible.
Use in administration of oaths, §49-10.
Industrial development authority directors, §15.2-4904.
Industrial loan association.
Directors, §6.2-1403.
Insurance companies examinations.
Powers of state corporation commission, §38.2-1318.
Interpreters, VA SCt Rule 2:604.
Jail farm superintendents and guards, §53.1-100.
Jail superintendents and officers, §§53.1-95.8, 53.1-110.
Judicial officers.
Who may administer oath to officer, §49-3.
Local government officers and employees.
Failure to take oath, effect, §24.2-228.
Oath of office required before entering duty, §15.2-1512.
Power to administer oaths, §15.2-1410.
Qualification of elected officer for office, §15.2-1522.
Loyalty oath.
Emergency management organizations, §44-146.25.
Magistrates and other officers.
Who may administer oaths to officers, §§49-3, 49-4.
Medical malpractice review panels.
Administration of oaths by panelists, §8.01-581.6.
Motor vehicle dealers.
Powers of board, §46.2-1504.
Motor vehicles department.
Commissioner, §46.2-203.
Museum of natural history, §10.1-2005.
National guard.
Administered by commissioned officers or warrant officers, §44-32.1.
Administration by commissioned officers during investigations, §44-40.2.
Enlistment, §44-36.
Officers, §44-32.
Naval militia officers and enlisted persons, §44-64.
Nonprofit corporations.
Inspectors of elections, §13.1-847.1.
Notary public, §47.1-9.
Officers elected or appointed under or pursuant to constitution, VA Const Art II §7

OATHS AND AFFIRMATIONS —Cont'd
Officers of election, §24.2-611.
Optometry board, §54.1-3209.
Perjury, §§18.2-434 to 18.2-437.
Personal representatives, §§64.2-501, 64.2-503.
Pleadings sworn before clerk or court officer, §8.01-280.
Presidential elections.
Oaths of electors.
Electors selected by political parties, §24.2-542.
Selected by groups other than political parties, §24.2-543.
Quo warranto.
Petition verified under oath, §8.01-637.
Real estate board.
Condominiums.
Investigations of complaints, §55-79.99.
Real estate cooperatives.
Investigations, §55-503.
Real estate cooperatives.
Investigative powers of agency, §55-503.
Recordation where fact of oaths recorded, §49-8.
Religious objection to oaths, §49-9.
Sanitation districts law of 1938.
Commission members, §21-163.
Sanitation districts law of 1946.
Commission members, §21-243.
Science museum of Virginia.
Oath of board members, §23-246.
Search warrants.
Supported by oath or affirmation, US Const Amd 4.
Sewage handling and disposal appeal review board, §32.1-166.3.
Solicitation of charitable or civic contributions.
Investigations, §57-59.
State board of corrections.
Administration powers, §53.1-6.
Investigations.
Corrections department director power, §53.1-15.
State corporation commission.
Consumer finance companies.
Investigation by commission, §6.2-1530.
Power to administer, §12.1-13, VA Const Art IX §3.
State defense force.
Administration of oaths by commissioned officers and others, §44-54.8.
State police officers.
Power to administer, §52-9.
State police superintendents, §52-3.
Taking affidavits, §§49-4 to 49-7.
Corporations and other entities, §49-7.
Officer of another state or country, §49-5.
Partnerships and other entities, §49-7.
Purchaser of fuel, etc., §49-6.
Who may take affidavits, §49-4.
Tax commissioner, §58.1-201.
Tax returns.
Unnecessary, §58.1-11.
Transportation board.
Oath of members, §33.1-9.
Trust companies.
Who may take oath for corporate fiduciary, §6.2-1004.
Voter challenged, §24.2-651.
Voter who is shown as having already voted, §24.2-651.1.

OATHS AND AFFIRMATIONS —Cont'd
Voter registration.
Information on application provided under oath, VA Const Art II §2.
Weighmasters, public, §3.2-5808.
Witnesses, VA SCt Rule 2:603.
Who may administer, §8.01-405.
Zoning.
Oath regarding property interests of local officers, §15.2-2287.

OATLANDS, INCORPORATED.
Appropriations for maintenance of Oatlands, §10.1-2212.

OATS.
Generally, §§3.2-2200 to 3.2-2214.
See SMALL GRAINS.

OBESITY.
Health commissioner and department of health.
Combating childhood obesity, §32.1-19.
Morbid obesity.
Public officers and employees.
Required coverage, §2.2-2818.
Prader-Willi syndrome.
Defined, §51.5-116.
Virginia youth obesity prevention.
Division of Virginia foundation for healthy youth, §32.1-355.

OBJECTIONS.
Acquittal by reason of insanity.
Modification or removal of conditional release, §19.2-182.11.
Arbitration.
Award, §8.01-581.07.
Change of award, §8.01-581.08.
Bench trial.
Motion raising objections, VA SCt Rule 3A:9.
Certificates of analysis.
Objection to admission of certificate of analysis in lieu of testimony, §19.2-187.1.
Circuit courts.
Criminal cases, VA SCt Rule 3A:9.
Contemporaneous objection rule.
Court of appeals, VA SCt Rule 5A:18.
Supreme court, VA SCt Rule 5:25.
Court of appeals.
Contemporaneous objection rule, VA SCt Rule 5A:18.
Record on appeal.
Transcript or written statement, VA SCt Rule 5A:8.
Depositions.
Audio-visual depositions, §8.01-412.4.
Dispute resolution proceedings.
Notice and opportunity to object, §8.01-576.6.
Double jeopardy.
Written pretrial motion, §19.2-266.2.
Evidence.
Certificates of analysis.
Objection to admission of certificate of analysis in lieu of testimony, §19.2-187.1.
Fieri facias.
Interrogatories to judgment debtor, §8.01-506.
Former jeopardy.
Written pretrial motion, §19.2-266.2.
Illegal search and seizure.
Written pretrial motion, §19.2-266.2.
Indictments, presentments and informations.
Defective indictment.
Written pretrial motion, §19.2-266.2.

OBJECTIONS —Cont'd
Jury instructions.
Counsel's opportunity to object, VA SCt Rule 3A:16.
How made, VA SCt Rule 3A:16.
Jury selection.
Irregularities in jury lists or for legal disability, §8.01-352.
Jury trial.
Motion raising objections, VA SCt Rule 3A:9.
Medical malpractice review panels.
Notice of claim, MedMal Rules 2, 4.
Objections not waived by participation, §8.01-581.11:1.
Miranda rights.
Written pretrial motion, §19.2-266.2.
Polygraph examination, §8.01-418.2.
Pretrial motions.
Suppression of evidence, §19.2-266.2.
Rulings of court.
When formal exceptions unnecessary, §8.01-384.
Self-incrimination, privilege against.
Written pretrial motion, §19.2-266.2.
Sex offender registration and notification.
Failure to register or reregister.
Objection to affidavit of state police in lieu of testimony, §18.2-472.1.
Speedy trial.
Written pretrial motion, §19.2-266.2.
Suppression of evidence.
Written requirement, §19.2-266.2.
Supreme court.
Contemporaneous objection rule, VA SCt Rule 5:25.
Record on appeal.
Transcript or written statement, VA SCt Rule 5:11.
Unconstitutionality of statute.
Defense objections raised before trial, §19.2-266.2.
Unreasonable search and seizure.
Written pretrial motion, §19.2-266.2.
Venue.
Frivolous motion to transfer.
Award of court costs, §8.01-266.
Improperly laid venue, §8.01-264.

OBJECT SEXUAL PENETRATION, §18.2-67.2.
Attempts, §18.2-67.5.
Jail prisoner escape or release notice, §53.1-116.1.
Prisoner intake notice, §53.1-116.1:01.
Capital murder.
Killing person in commission of or attempt to commit, §18.2-31.
Carnal knowledge of child.
Between thirteen and fifteen years of age, §18.2-63.
Convict escape or release notice, §53.1-160.1.
Jail prisoner escape or release notice, §53.1-116.1.
Prisoner intake notice, §53.1-116.1:01.
Suspension of sentence, placing on probation, §19.2-303.
Juvenile detained in jail, detention facility or committed to juvenile justice department, §18.2-64.1.
Jail prisoner escape or release notice, §53.1-116.1.
Prisoner intake notice, §53.1-116.1:01.
Punishment upon conviction of certain subsequent felony sexual assault, §18.2-67.5:2.

OBJECT SEXUAL PENETRATION —Cont'd
Child victims' testimony.
Using two-way closed-circuit television, §18.2-67.9.
Correctional employee carnal knowledge of defendant or convicted person, §18.2-64.2.
Death of victim, §18.2-63.1.
Murder in first degree, §18.2-32.
Deferral of proceedings, defendant placed on probation.
Counseling or therapy, completion.
Violation against spouse, §18.2-67.2.
Deposition of complaining witness, §18.2-67.
Discretionary felony sentencing guidelines, §17.1-805.
Firearm used or displayed, §18.2-53.1.
HIV or hepatitis B or C.
Testing of persons charged, §18.2-62.
Jail prisoner escape or release notice, §53.1-116.1.
Murder of the first degree, killing in commission of, §18.2-32.
Physical resistance, proof not required, §18.2-67.6.
Preliminary hearings, closing, §18.2-67.8.
Prisoner intake notice, §53.1-116.1:01.
Probation, conditions, §19.2-303.
Punishment upon conviction of certain subsequent violent felony sexual assault, §18.2-67.5:3.
Sentence of person twice previously convicted of certain violent felonies, §19.2-297.1.
Suspension of sentence, §19.2-303.
Counseling or therapy, completion.
Violation against spouse, §18.2-67.2.
Unchaste character or prior sexual conduct of complaining witness, §18.2-67.7.
Venue, person transported through or across Commonwealth, §18.2-359.

OBSCENITY AND RELATED OFFENSES, §§18.2-372 to 18.2-388.
Advertising.
Obscene items, exhibitions or performances, §18.2-376.
Use of computer, enhanced penalties, §18.2-376.1.
Application of article.
Exceptions to, §18.2-383.
Books alleged to be obscene.
Inapplicability of provisions to motion pictures, §18.2-385.
Proceeding against, §18.2-384.
Child pornography.
Abduction of child for purposes of manufacturing child pornography, §18.2-48.
Child pornography image registry, §19.2-390.3.
Computer or electronic data seized as evidence.
Reasonable opportunity for defense review, §19.2-270.1:1.
Display of pornography or grooming video to child under 13, §18.2-374.4.
Distribution, §18.2-374.1:1.
Facilitation of payment for access, §18.2-374.1:1.
Forfeiture.
Property used in connection with exploitation and solicitation of children, §19.2-386.31.
Persuading or commanding another to provide in child pornography in order to gain entry into a group trading or sharing child pornography, §18.2-374.1:1.

OBSCENITY AND RELATED OFFENSES —Cont'd
Child pornography —Cont'd
Possession, §18.2-374.1:1.
Production, publication, etc., with intent to distribute, financing, etc., §18.2-374.1.
Electronic means used to facilitate, §18.2-374.3.
Receiving money for procuring person for manufacture of child pornography, §18.2-356.
Sentencing.
Mandatory restitution to victims as condition, §19.2-305.1.
Taking indecent liberties with children, §18.2-370.
Jail prisoner escape or release notice, §53.1-116.1.
Person in custodial or supervisory relation, §18.2-370.1.
Prisoner intake notice, §53.1-116.1:01.
Coercing acceptance of obscene articles or publications, §18.2-378.
Computer, harassment by.
Transmittal of obscene communication, §18.2-152.7:1.
Computer or electronic data seized as evidence.
Reasonable opportunity for defense review, §19.2-270.1:1.
Discretionary felony sentencing guidelines, §17.1-805.
Enumeration of obscene items, §18.2-373.
Exceptions to application of article, §18.2-383.
Exhibitions and performances, §18.2-375.
Advertising, §18.2-376.
Use of computer, enhanced penalties, §18.2-376.1.
First offense, punishment, §18.2-380.
Harassment by computer.
Transmittal of obscene communication, §18.2-152.7:1.
Indecent exposure, §18.2-387.
Minors involved in act, §18.2-370.01.
Intoxication in public, §18.2-388.
Uniform fine schedule, VA SCt Rules 3C:1, 3C:2.
Masturbation in public place.
Obscene sexual display, §18.2-387.1.
Minors, employing or permitting to assist in offense, §18.2-379.
Minors, prohibited sales and loans to.
Definitions, §18.2-390.
Exceptions to application of article, §18.2-391.1.
Unlawful acts, §18.2-391.
Motion pictures, §18.2-382.
Proceeding against alleged obscene book inapplicable to, §18.2-385.
Showing previews of certain motion pictures, §18.2-386.
Obscene defined, §18.2-372.
Obscene items enumerated, §18.2-373.
Ordinances prohibiting obscenity, adoption, §15.2-926.2.
Photographs, §18.2-382.
Placards, posters, bills, etc., §18.2-377.
Previews of certain motion pictures.
Showing, §18.2-386.
Proceeding against obscene book, §18.2-384.
Inapplicability to motion pictures, §18.2-385.
Production, publication, sale, etc., of obscene items, §18.2-374.
Use of computer, enhanced penalties, §18.2-376.1.
Profane swearing in public, §18.2-388.
Uniform fine schedule, VA SCt Rules 3C:1, 3C:2.
Punishment for first offense, §18.2-380.

OBSCENITY AND RELATED OFFENSES —Cont'd
Punishment for subsequent offenses, §18.2-381.
Sales and loans to juveniles, §§18.2-390 to 18.2-391.1.
Definitions, §18.2-390.
Exceptions to application of article, §18.2-391.1.
Unlawful acts, §18.2-391.
Sentencing guidelines for violent felony offenses.
Discretionary felony sentencing guidelines, §17.1-805.
Sexually explicit items involving children.
Child pornography image registry, §19.2-390.3.
Display of pornography or grooming video to child under 13, §18.2-374.4.
Possession, §18.2-374.1:1.
Production, publication, etc., with intent to distribute, financing, etc., §18.2-374.1.
Electronic means used to facilitate, §18.2-374.3.
Sentencing.
Mandatory restitution to victims as condition, §19.2-305.1.
Slides, §18.2-382.
Subsequent offenses, punishment, §18.2-381.
Taking indecent liberties with children, §§18.2-370, 18.2-370.1.
Jail prisoner escape or release notice, §53.1-116.1.
Prisoner intake notice, §53.1-116.1:01.
Punishment upon conviction of certain subsequent felony sexual assault, §18.2-67.5:2.
Suspension of sentence, placing on probation, §19.2-303.
Telephones or citizens band radio.
Use of obscene, vulgar, etc., language, §18.2-427.
Temporary assistance for needy families (TANF).
Prohibited uses of benefits, §63.2-621.

OBSERVANCES.
Special days and observances.
See HOLIDAYS.

OBSERVATORIES.
Locality regulating near astronomical observatories, §15.2-920.

OBSESSIVE-COMPULSIVE DISORDER.
Health insurance.
Coverage for biologically based mental illness, §38.2-3412.1:01.
Public officers and employees.
Required coverage, §2.2-2818.

OBSTETRIC AND GYNECOLOGIC SERVICES.
Health insurance.
Access to services, §38.2-3407.11.
Federal market reforms.
Choice of health care professional.
Prior authorization or referral not required, §38.2-3443.
Optional coverage, §38.2-3414.
Postpartum services, §38.2-3414.1.
Public officers and employees.
Required coverage, §2.2-2818.
Requirements for obstetrical care, §38.2-3407.16.
Postpartum services insurance coverage, §38.2-3414.1.
Medical assistance services plans, §32.1-325.

OBSTETRICIANS.
Birth-related neurological injury compensation, §§38.2-5000 to 38.2-5021.
See BIRTH-RELATED NEUROLOGICAL INJURY COMPENSATION.

OBSTRUCTING FREE PASSAGE OF OTHERS, §18.2-404.

OBSTRUCTING JUSTICE BY THREATS, FORCE OR FALSE STATEMENTS, §18.2-460.
Bail, presumption against admitting to bail for certain offense, §19.2-120.

OBSTRUCTION OF ADMINISTRATION OF JUSTICE, §§18.2-460 to 18.2-472.1.
Aiding officer in execution of office, refusal, §18.2-463.
Concealing or compounding offenses, §18.2-462.
Corruptly procuring juror, §18.2-466.
Employee court appearance or service on jury panel, penalizing, §18.2-465.1.
Execution of criminal process, officer refusing, delaying, etc., §18.2-469.
Extortion by officer, §18.2-470.
False alarms, §18.2-461.
False entries or destruction of records, §18.2-472.
False reports to police officers, §18.2-461.
False statements to law enforcement officers conducting investigation, §18.2-460.
Fee bills, fraudulent issue, §18.2-471.
Fraud in drawing juror, §18.2-467.
Officers summoning juror to act impartially, §18.2-465.
Orders of conservators of the peace, failure to obey, §18.2-464.
Police radio, use during commission of crime, §18.2-462.1.
Sex offender registry.
Failure to register or provision of false information, §18.2-472.1.
Sound recordings of jury deliberations, §18.2-468.
Threats, force or false statements to obstruct justice, §18.2-460.
Bail, presumption against admitting to bail for certain offense, §19.2-120.
Wire or oral interception of communications.
Disclosure of existence of order authorizing, §18.2-460.1.

OBSTRUCTION OF PROBATION OFFICERS.
Juvenile and domestic relations district court probation officers, §16.1-257.

OBSTRUCTION OF ROAD, STREET OR PUBLIC RIGHTS-OF-WAY, §§15.2-2009 to 15.2-2012.

OBTAINING INFORMATION UNDER FALSE PRETENSES.
Insurance information, §38.2-619.

OBTAINING PROPERTY BY FALSE PRETENSES.
Computer fraud, §18.2-152.3.

OCCASIONAL SALES OF PERSONAL PROPERTY.
Retail sales and use tax exemption, §58.1-609.10.

OCCUPATIONAL DISEASES, §§65.2-400 to 65.2-407.
See WORKERS' COMPENSATION.

OCCUPATIONAL SAFETY AND HEALTH, §§40.1-44.1 to 40.1-51.4:5.
Administrative search warrants.
Duration, §40.1-49.10.

OCCUPATIONAL SAFETY AND HEALTH —Cont'd
Appeals, §40.1-49.5.
Attorney general.
Assistants to attorneys for the Commonwealth, §40.1-49.6.
Attorneys for the Commonwealth.
Attorney general's office.
Assistants in enforcement proceedings, §40.1-49.6.
Enforcement of provisions, §40.1-49.6.
Circuit court.
Defined, §40.1-49.3.
Commission.
Defined, §40.1-49.3.
Commissioner.
Defined, §40.1-49.3.
Technical aid from state health commissioner, §40.1-51.
Confidentiality of information, §40.1-51.4:1.
Court of appeals, §40.1-49.5.
Discrimination.
Employees' exercising of rights, §§40.1-51.2:1, 40.1-51.2:2.
Duties of employees, §40.1-51.2.
Duties of employers, §40.1-51.1.
Employee.
Defined, §40.1-49.3.
Duties, §40.1-51.2.
Employees' rights and duties, §40.1-51.2.
Discrimination, §§40.1-51.2:1, 40.1-51.2:2.
Employer.
Defined, §40.1-49.3.
Duties, §40.1-51.1.
Enforcement of provisions, §40.1-49.4.
Evidence.
Civil penalties against employers, §40.1-51.3:2.
Fraud, §40.1-51.2:2.
Health and safety inspectors.
Duties, §40.1-51.3.
Penalty for giving advance notice of inspection, §40.1-51.3:1.
Immunity of employee.
Reporting threatening conduct, §40.1-51.4:5.
Industrial hygiene and safety profession.
Protection of job title, §§40.1-139 to 40.1-142.
Inspections, §40.1-49.8.
Conduct, §40.1-49.11.
Inspectors.
Duties of health and safety inspectors, §40.1-51.3.
Penalty for giving advance notice of inspection, §40.1-51.3:1.
Lifting devices.
Rules and regulations, §40.1-44.1.
Occupational safety and health standard.
Defined, §40.1-49.3.
Orders.
Publication, §40.1-49.7.
Penalties.
Fraud, §40.1-51.4:2.
Person.
Defined, §40.1-49.3.
Polygraph tests, §40.1-51.4:3.
Publication of orders, §40.1-49.7.
Reporting threatening conduct.
Immunity of employee, §40.1-51.4:5.
Rights of employees, §40.1-51.2.
Discrimination for exercising, §§40.1-51.2:1, 40.1-51.2:2.
Rules and regulations.
Safety and health generally, §40.1-49.4.

OCCUPATIONAL SAFETY AND HEALTH —Cont'd
Rules and regulations —Cont'd
Tramways, hauling and lifting devices, §40.1-44.1.
Sample analysis, collection or testing, §40.1-49.11.
Serious violation.
Defined, §40.1-49.3.
State health commissioner.
Technical aid, §40.1-51.
Trade secrets, §40.1-51.4:1.
Tramways.
Rules and regulations, §40.1-44.1.
Trials.
Evidence of civil penalty against employers, §40.1-51.3:2.
Warrants.
Administrative search warrants, §40.1-49.10.
Review by courts, §40.1-49.12.
Workplace inspections, §40.1-49.8.

OCCUPATIONAL THERAPY.
Advisory board, §§54.1-2956.2 to 54.1-2956.5.
Health insurance.
Family access to medical insurance security plan, §§32.1-351 to 32.1-353.
Public officers and employees.
Required coverage, §2.2-2818.
License required, §54.1-2956.5.
Licensing generally, §§54.1-2950.1 to 54.1-2957.01.
Respiratory therapy advisory board.
Powers as to occupational therapy, §54.1-2956.1.
Schools and education.
Employment by school board, §22.1-274.
Unlicensed practice, §54.1-2956.5.

OCCUPATIONAL THERAPY ADVISORY BOARD, §§54.1-2956.2 to 54.1-2956.5.

OCCUPATIONAL THERAPY ASSISTANTS.
Defined, §54.1-2900.
License required, §54.1-2956.5.
Unlicensed practice, §54.1-2956.5.

OCCUPATIONS.
See PROFESSIONS AND OCCUPATIONS.

OCCUPYING TRAILER BEING TOWED ON HIGHWAY, §46.2-813.
Fine schedule for violation, VA SCt Rule 3B:2.
Maximum fine for violating Title 46.2, §46.2-113.
Prepayment of fine, §16.1-69.40:1.

OCEANA/FENTRESS MILITARY ADVISORY COUNCIL, §2.2-2666.3.

OCEANA NAVAL AIR STATION.
Special license plates, §46.2-749.28.

OCTANE.
Motor fuels labeling, §§17.1-413, 59.1-167.1.

OCULAR PROSTHESES.
Medical assistance services plans, §32.1-325.

ODD FELLOWS.
Exemption from fraternal benefit society chapter provisions, §38.2-4135.
Land conveyances to, §57-19.
Land quantity limitations, §57-20.

ODOMETERS.
Acquisition of vehicle from vendor.
Reporting odometer reading, §46.2-629.
Motorcycle dealer odometer disclosure, §46.2-1993.25.

ODOMETERS —Cont'd
Reporting odometer reading on certificate of title, §46.2-629.
Tampering, §46.2-112.
T&M vehicle dealers.
Disclosure, §46.2-1932.

ODU, §§23-49.11 to 23-49.22:4.
See OLD DOMINION UNIVERSITY.

OFFAL.
Adulterated food, §3.2-5122.

OFF-DUTY POLICE OFFICERS.
Employment, §15.2-1712.

OFFER AND ACCEPTANCE.
Leases, UCC, §8.2A-206.
Firm offers, §8.2A-205.
Sales, UCC, §8.2-206.
Auctions, §8.2-328.
Firm offers, §8.2-205.
Uniform computer information transactions act.
Acceptance that varies terms, §59.1-502.4.
Conditional offer or acceptance, §59.1-502.5.
Contracts, §59.1-502.3.
Electronic agents, §59.1-502.6.

OFFERS TO COMPROMISE.
Evidence, relevancy, VA SCt Rule 2:408.

OFFICE BUILDINGS.
Energy allocation equipment, §§56-245.2, 56-245.3.
Fire alarms.
Maliciously activating, §18.2-212.
Fortified drug houses.
Penalty, §18.2-258.02.
Lists of tenants.
Owners or operators to file with commissioner of revenue, §58.1-3901.
Smoke bombs.
Setting off in certain public buildings, §18.2-87.1.
Submetering, §§56-245.2, 56-245.3.

OFFICE FOR PROTECTION AND ADVOCACY SERVICES.
Conversion of Virginia office for protection and advocacy to a private, nonprofit entity, §51.5-39.13.
Protection and advocacy system generally, §§51.5-39.1 to 51.5-39.13.
See DISABILITY OR HANDICAP.

OFFICE FURNITURE AND EQUIPMENT.
Commonwealth's attorneys, treasurers or commissioners of revenue purchasing.
Manner of payment, §15.2-1636.15.
Executive agencies.
Acquisition and maintenance.
Division of support services, general services department, §2.2-1170.
Sheriffs purchasing.
Payment for items, §15.2-1615.1.
State departments and agencies.
Acquisition and maintenance.
Division of support services, general services department, §2.2-1170.

OFFICEHOLDING PROHIBITION.
District court judges, §16.1-69.19.
Electoral board members, §24.2-106, VA Const Art II §8.
Fee bills, fraudulent issue, §18.2-471.
General assembly members, VA Const Art IV §4.

OFFICEHOLDING PROHIBITION —Cont'd
Justices or judges of courts of record, §17.1-102, VA Const Art VI §11.
Local government officers or governing body members.
Holding more than one office, VA Const Art VII §6.
Members of congress, US Const Art I §6.
Officers of election, VA Const Art II §8.
Perjury, persons convicted of, §18.2-434.
Registrars of election, §§24.2-110, 24.2-119, VA Const Art II §8.
United States officers.
Holding more than one office, US Const Art I §6.

OFFICE OF COMPREHENSIVE SERVICES FOR AT-RISK YOUTH AND FAMILIES.
Director.
Hiring and supervision, §2.2-2648.
Powers and duties, §2.2-2649.

OFFICE OF EXECUTIVE SECRETARY TO SUPREME COURT.
Administrator of circuit court system, §17.1-502.

OFFICE OF SEXUALLY VIOLENT PREDATOR SERVICES.
Establishment, §37.2-900.1.

OFFICE OF TELEWORK PROMOTION AND BROADBAND ASSISTANCE, §2.2-225.1.

OFFICE OF THE GOVERNOR.
Assistant to the Governor for intergovernmental affairs, office of, §§2.2-300 to 2.2-303.
Executive reorganization, §§2.2-127 to 2.2-133.
Extradition of criminals, §§19.2-84 to 19.2-118.
See EXTRADITION.
Governor generally, §§2.2-100 to 2.2-135.
See GOVERNOR.
Governor's secretaries, §§2.2-200 to 2.2-229.
Workforce development coordination, §§2.2-435.6, 2.2-435.7.

OFFICE OF THE STATE LONG TERM CARE OMBUDSMAN.
Freedom of information act.
Excluded records, §2.2-3705.5.

OFFICERS OF ELECTION.
Generally, §§24.2-115 to 24.2-118.
See ELECTIONS.

OFFICERS OF NATIONAL GUARD.
Generally, §§44-25 to 44-54.3.
See NATIONAL GUARD.

OFFICES OF CONSUMER AFFAIRS.
County or city establishing local office, §15.2-963.

OFFICE SPACE IN STATE BUILDINGS.
Assignment to agencies, §2.2-1140.

OFFICIAL CONDUCT OF OFFICE OR OFFICER.
County board form of government.
Inquiries by board of county supervisors, §15.2-403.
County executive form of government.
Inquiry into, §15.2-506.
County manager plan of government.
Inquiry into, §15.2-709.
Urban county executive form of government.
Inquiry into, §15.2-814.

OFFICIAL MAP.
Counties, cities or towns, §§15.2-2233 to 15.2-2238.
Additions and modifications, §15.2-2235.
Adoption, §15.2-2234.
Building permit application for area shown as future or proposed right-of-way.
Granting or denying by locality, §15.2-2233.
Certification by commission to governing body, §15.2-2234.
Consultation with Commonwealth transportation board, §15.2-2237.
Copies sent to Commonwealth transportation board, §15.2-2237.
Counties withdrawing roads from secondary system of state highways.
Provisions not to affect exercise of authority, §15.2-2238.
Defined, §15.2-2201.
Filing in office of clerk of court, §15.2-2234.
Preparations, §15.2-2233.
Readoption, §15.2-2236.
Review, §15.2-2236.
What map to show, §15.2-2233.

OFFICIAL OPINIONS OF ATTORNEY GENERAL, §2.2-505.

OFF-ROAD MOTORCYCLES.
All-terrain vehicle traffic regulation, §46.2-915.1.
Certificates of title, §§46.2-644.1 to 46.2-644.3.
Dealer acquisition of motorcycles, §46.2-644.3.
Department of motor vehicles.
Recordkeeping requirements, §46.2-644.2.
Department recordkeeping requirements, §46.2-644.2.
Titling of motorcycles, §46.2-644.1.
Exhaust system, §46.2-1051.
Helmet law, all-terrain vehicles, §46.2-915.1.
Light, §46.2-1016.
Local government restrictions, §46.2-1051.
Trail systems established by localities.
Authority, protection of property interest and personal liability.
No liability to locality or property owners, §15.2-1809.1.
Authority, protection of property interests and personal liability, §15.2-1806.

OFF-ROAD VEHICLES.
Certificates of title.
Off-road motorcycles, §§46.2-644.1 to 46.2-644.3.
Limitations on operation, §46.2-915.1.
Motor vehicle dealer, §46.2-1500.
Motor vehicle registration.
Exemption from registration, §46.2-679.2.
Southwest regional recreation authority.
Operation of off-road recreation vehicles in localities embraced by authority, §46.2-800.2.

OFFSET.
Collection of accounts receivable by the Commonwealth.
Treasury offset programs of United States.
Participation, §§2.2-4806, 2.2-4809.
Eminent domain.
Highways and roads.
Enhancement to be offset against damages, §33.1-130.
Insurance companies, rehabilitation and liquidation.
Mutual debts or credits, §38.2-1515.

OFFSET —Cont'd
Partnerships.
Buyout price to dissociated partner.
Damages for wrongful dissociation, §50-73.112.

OFFSHORE ENERGY RESOURCES, §67-300.
Coastal energy research consortium, §§67-600 to 67-604.
Royalties from offshore natural gas and oil resources, §67-301.

OFFSHORE WIND DEVELOPMENT AUTHORITY, §§67-1200 to 67-1211.
Confidentiality of information, §67-1210.
Creation, §67-1201.
Data collection, §67-1203.
Definitions, §67-1200.
Director, §67-1208.
Employees, §67-1207.
Federal loan guarantees, §67-1205.
Members, §67-1202.
Port facilities upgrades, §67-1204.
Powers and duties, §§67-1203 to 67-1207.
Purpose, §67-1201.
Declaration of public purpose, §67-1211.
Reports.
Annual report, §67-1209.
Staff, §67-1208.
Tax exemption, §67-1211.
Transmission of power from offshore wind energy projects, §67-1206.
Vacancies, §67-1202.

OFFSHORE WIND ENERGY.
Virginia offshore wind development authority, §§67-1200 to 67-1211.
See OFFSHORE WIND DEVELOPMENT AUTHORITY.

OFF-STREET PARKING FACILITIES.
Locality providing, §15.2-967.

OFF TRACK BETTING.
Satellite facility.
Defined, §59.1-365.
Local referendum on operating, §59.1-391.
Owners or operators license, §§59.1-375 to 59.1-386.
Percentage retained, §59.1-392.
Powers and duties of commission, §59.1-369.
Simulcast horse racing.
Commission to promulgate regulations and conditions, §59.1-369.
Defined, §59.1-365.
Percentage retained, §59.1-392.
Satellite facility.
Number of facilities authorized, §59.1-369.

OHIO RIVER.
Cession of territory northwest of, §1-303.

OHIO RIVER BASIN COMMISSION.
Members, §62.1-79.2.
Participation by Commonwealth, §62.1-79.1.
Purpose, §62.1-79.1.

OHIO RIVER VALLEY WATER SANITATION COMMISSION, §§62.1-70 to 62.1-79.
Appropriations, §62.1-79.
Assistants, §62.1-77.
Chairman, §62.1-77.
Compact.
Effect of signing, §62.1-72.
Execution, §62.1-70.
Form, §62.1-71.

OHIO RIVER VALLEY WATER SANITATION COMMISSION —Cont'd
Compact —Cont'd
Terms, §62.1-71.
Conflict of laws.
Supplemental to other laws and powers, §62.1-75.
Effective date, §62.1-78.
Meetings, §62.1-77.
Members.
Appointment, §62.1-73.
Expenses, §62.1-76.
Removal, §62.1-73.
Powers, §62.1-74.
Supplemental to other laws and powers, §62.1-75.
Secretary, §62.1-77.

OIL.
Coal mines.
Underground coal mines.
Flammable or combustible materials at surface areas, §45.1-161.238.
Storage and use, §45.1-161.205.
Emergency petroleum products supplies, §§59.1-21.18:2 to 59.1-21.18:4.
Fines.
Used motor oil management and recycling program, violations, §10.1-1422.6.
Mining in proximity to gas and oil wells, §45.1-161.121.
Petroleum products franchises generally, §§59.1-21.8 to 59.1-21.18:1.
See PETROLEUM PRODUCTS FRANCHISES.
Presumed to exist in certain lands, §55-154.
Suits to extinguish claim or right, §55-155.
Retail sales and use tax exemptions.
Machinery, tools, etc., used in drilling, extraction, etc., §58.1-609.3.
State corrections board contracts to sell or lease, §53.1-31.
Used motor oil.
Management and recycling program, §10.1-1422.6.
Surplus state materials, disposition.
Recycling encouraged, §2.2-1124.
Virginia energy plan.
Generally, §§67-100 to 67-1003.
See ENERGY.

OIL AND GAS CONSERVATION COMPACT, §§45.1-381, 45.1-382.

OIL COMPANIES.
Obtaining or attempting to obtain service without payment, §18.2-187.1.
Retail sales and use tax exemptions.
Machinery or tools used in drilling, extracting, etc., §58.1-609.3.
Workers' compensation coverage.
Employee defined, §65.2-101.

OIL DISCHARGES INTO WATERS OF STATE.
Aboveground storage tanks.
Registration, §62.1-44.34:19.1.
Regulations for, §62.1-44.34:15.1.
Exemptions from, §62.1-44.34:17.
Access to records and facilities, §62.1-44.34:19.2.
Applicability of administrative process act, §62.1-44.34:22.
Contingency plans, §62.1-44.34:15.
Contribution claims by persons or operators incurring cost or paying cost or damages, §62.1-44.34:18.
Defined terms, §62.1-44.34:14.

OIL DISCHARGES INTO WATERS OF STATE —Cont'd
Discharge prohibition and liability, §62.1-44.34:18.
Discharge reporting, §62.1-44.34:19.
Enforcement of provisions, §62.1-44.34:20.
Exemption from provisions, §62.1-44.34:23.
Fees, §62.1-44.34:21.
Financial responsibility for vessels and facilities, §62.1-44.34:16.
Exemptions, §62.1-44.34:17.
Ohio river valley water sanitation commission.
Jurisdiction, §62.1-74.
Provision violations.
Penalties, §62.1-44.34:20.
Records, §62.1-44.34:19.2.
Spill response council, §§62.1-44.34:24 to 62.1-44.34:28.
Storage tanks, §§62.1-44.34:8, 62.1-44.34:9.
Petroleum storage tank fund, §§62.1-44.34:10 to 62.1-44.34:13.

OIL EXPLORATION.
Chesapeake Bay drilling, §62.1-195.1.
Generally, §§45.1-361.1 to 45.1-361.44.
See GAS AND OIL EXPLORATION.
Tidewater drilling, §62.1-195.1.

OIL FILTERS.
Management and recycling program, §10.1-1422.6.

OILING OF HIGHWAYS, §33.1-196.

OIL LEASES.
Securities generally, §§13.1-501 to 13.1-527.3.
See SECURITIES.

OIL SEVERANCE TAX.
Local license tax on persons engaging in business of severing oil, §§58.1-3712.1, 58.1-3713.4.

OILS, LUBRICATING, §§59.1-149 to 59.1-167.3.
See LUBRICATING OILS.

OIL SPILLS.
Discharges into waters of the state, §§62.1-44.34:14 to 62.1-44.34:23.
See OIL DISCHARGES INTO WATERS OF STATE.
Spill response council, §§62.1-44.34:24 to 62.1-44.34:28.
See SPILL RESPONSE COUNCIL.

OIL SUPPLIES.
Emergency petroleum products supplies, §§59.1-21.18:2 to 59.1-21.18:4.
See EMERGENCY PETROLEUM PRODUCTS SUPPLIES.

OIL TANK TRUCK CARRIERS.
Petroleum tank truck carriers.
Employee liens, §§43-24 to 43-26.
Not required to incorporate as public service companies, §13.1-620.
Public service companies generally, §§56-1 to 56-87.
See PUBLIC SERVICE COMPANIES.
Supplier liens, §§43-24 to 43-26.
Public service companies generally, §§56-1 to 56-87.
See PUBLIC SERVICE COMPANIES.

OLD DOMINION UNIVERSITY, §§23-49.11 to 23-49.22:4.
Board of visitors, §§23-49.12 to 23-49.17.

OLD DOMINION UNIVERSITY —Cont'd
Campus police departments, §§23-232 to 23-238.
Reporting campus crime, §23-9.1:1.
Center for graduate and undergraduate studies, §§23-49.22:1 to 23-49.22:4.
Coastal energy research consortium, §§67-600 to 67-604.
Commercial space flight authority.
Advice and assistance, §2.2-2204.
Conferring of degrees, §23-49.19.
Corporate name, §23-49.11.
Lease or sale of real estate, §23-49.21.
Payroll and other transactions.
Processing, §2.2-803.1.
Special license plates, §46.2-749.
Teacher curriculum, §23-49.20.
Tuition, fees and other charges, §23-49.11.
Universities generally, §§23-1.01 to 23-9.2:8.
See COLLEGES AND UNIVERSITIES.

OLEAGINOUS SOLUTIONS.
Sales, §54.1-3418.

OLYMPICS.
Athletic leaves of absence for state employees, §2.2-124.
Chesapeake regional Olympic games compact, §§2.2-5900, 2.2-5901.

OLYMPIC SYMBOLS.
Prohibitions on use to induce sale of goods or services or to promote performance or competition, §59.1-92.21.

OMBUDSMAN.
Clean air act, §§10.1-1324, 10.1-1326.
Disability or handicap.
Protection and advocacy services, §51.5-39.7.
Health care facilities, §32.1-138.

OMER L. HIRST-ADELARD L. BRAULT EXPRESSWAY.
HOV-3 vehicles may use without paying toll, §33.1-46.2.

OMITTED CHILDREN, §§64.2-419, 64.2-420.

OMNIBUS CLAUSE.
Liability insurance on motor vehicles, aircraft and watercraft.
Standard provisions, §38.2-2204.

ONANCOCK.
Water and sewage systems.
Lien for charges and taxes imposed, §15.2-2118.

ONE CALL.
Underground utility line damage prevention, §§56-265.14 to 56-265.32.
See UNDERGROUND UTILITY LINE DAMAGE PREVENTION.

ONE HUNDRED DOLLARS OR LESS, PLAINTIFF ENTITLED TO JUDGMENT FOR DEFENDANT.
Circuit courts, §17.1-514.

ONE-WAY STREETS AND ROADS, §46.2-806.
Fine schedule for violating, VA SCt Rule 3B:2.
Maximum fine for violating Title 46.2, §46.2-113.
Left on steady red light after stopping, §46.2-836.
Demerit points, §46.2-492.
Prepayment of fines for violations, §16.1-69.40:1.

ONLINE CONFERENCES.
Open meetings.
Freedom of information act.
Electronic communication meetings, §2.2-3708.
Exceptions to prohibition, §2.2-3708.1.
General assembly, electronic mode prohibited, §2.2-3707.01.
Minutes, §2.2-3707.

ONLINE SERVICES.
Access contracts, §59.1-506.11.

ONLINE SHOPPING.
Uniform computer information transactions act, §§59.1-501.1 to 59.1-509.2.
Uniform electronic transactions act, §§59.1-479 to 59.1-497.

ONSITE SEWAGE SYSTEM PROFESSIONALS.
Generally, §§54.1-2300 to 54.1-2302.
See WATERWORKS OPERATORS.

OPEN ACCOUNT AGREEMENT.
Lost evidence of debt, action on, §8.01-32.

OPEN AIR PERFORMANCES.
License tax on traveling performances, §58.1-3728.

OPEN BURNING.
Fire prevention code enforcement, §27-98.

OPEN CONTAINER LAW, §18.2-323.1.
Open container defined, §18.2-323.1.
Passenger area defined, §18.2-323.1.
Rebuttable presumption, §18.2-323.1.
Uniform fine schedule, VA SCt Rules 3C:1, 3C:2.

OPEN-END CREDIT BALANCE.
Failure to provide written notice to consumer, §59.1-200.

OPEN-END CREDIT PLANS, §§6.2-433 to 6.2-435.
Amendments to contract or plan, §6.2-433.
Law governing, plans by bank or savings institution, §6.2-434.
Law governing, plans by sellers or lenders, §6.2-435.

OPENING OF SCHOOL YEAR, §22.1-79.1.

OPENING STATEMENTS.
Attorneys at law.
Informing jury of amount of damages sought by plaintiff, §8.01-379.1.
Preservation of right to argument before jury, §8.01-379.
Criminal cases, §19.2-265.

OPEN MEETINGS.
Freedom of information act.
Closed meetings.
Limited purposes, §2.2-3711.
Procedures, §2.2-3712.
Denial of rights or privileges conferred by chapter.
Enforcement, procedure, §2.2-3712.
Electronic communication meetings, §2.2-3708.
Exceptions to prohibition, §2.2-3708.1.
General assembly, electronic mode prohibited, §2.2-3707.01.
Minutes, §2.2-3707.
Required, §2.2-3707.
Transaction of business other than by votes at meetings, §2.2-3710.

OPEN MEETINGS —Cont'd
State board of elections, local electoral boards.
Security of ballots or voting and counting equipment.
Protocols for maintaining.
Closed meetings, §24.2-625.1.

OPEN PRICE TERM.
Sales, UCC, §8.2-305.

OPEN SOURCE INITIATIVE.
Public officers and employees.
Ownership of copyrights developed by state employees, §2.2-2822.

OPEN-SPACE LAND, §§10.1-1700 to 10.1-1705.
Acquisition or designation of property, §10.1-1701.
Water facilities revolving fund.
Loans for land conservation, §62.1-229.3.
Assessments of fee interest in land subject to perpetual conservation easement, §10.1-1011.
Community development authorities.
Power to purchase development rights, §15.2-5158.
Defined, §10.1-1700.
Diversion from open-space use, §10.1-1704.
Easements, §10.1-1703.
Farming.
Acquisition of title subject to, §10.1-1703.
Interpretation of provisions.
Chapter controlling over other laws, §10.1-1705.
Land preservation tax credits, §58.1-512.
Preservation easement fund, §10.1-2202.2.
Public body.
Acquisition or designation of property, §10.1-1701.
Defined, §10.1-1700.
Further powers, §10.1-1702.
Real property taxes.
Assessment in planned development subdivisions, §58.1-3284.1.
Assessment of property where interest less than fee held by public body, §58.1-3205.
Land preservation tax credits, §58.1-512.
Special assessment for land preservation, §§58.1-3229 to 58.1-3244.
See REAL PROPERTY TAXES.
Taxation of interest in land subject to perpetual conservation easement, §10.1-1011.
Timber.
Acquisition of title subject to, §10.1-1703.
Title.
Acquisition subject to farming or timber rights, §10.1-1703.
Urban area.
Defined, §10.1-1700.

OPEN-SPACE LANDS PRESERVATION TRUST FUND, §10.1-1801.1.

OPERA HOUSES.
Fire protection, §27-51.

OPERATION DESERT SHIELD.
Veterans.
Special license plates for veterans, §46.2-743.

OPERATION DESERT STORM.
Veterans.
Special license plates for veterans, §46.2-743.

OPERATION IRAQI FREEDOM.
Veterans.
Special license plates for veterans, §46.2-743.

OPERATION WILDFLOWER.
Special license plates for supporters, §46.2-749.29.

OPERATOR ASSISTANCE AT PAY STATIONS, §56-480.2.

OPERATORS' LICENSES.
Generally.
See DRIVERS' LICENSES.

OPHTHALMIA NEONATORUM, §§32.1-61 to 32.1-64.

OPHTHALMOLOGISTS.
Hearing aid specialists and opticians.
Optical prescriptions, refractions or other practices, §54.1-1508.

OPIATE ADDICTION TREATMENT PROVIDERS.
Conditions for initial licensure, §37.2-406.

OPINIONS OF ATTORNEY GENERAL, §2.2-505.

OPIUM.
Drug control act.
Generally, §§54.1-3400 to 54.1-3472.
See DRUG CONTROL.
Drug offenses.
Generally, §§18.2-247 to 18.2-264.
See DRUG OFFENSES.
Schedule II controlled drug, §54.1-3448.
Schedule III controlled drug, §54.1-3450.
Schedule V controlled drug, §54.1-3454.

OPOSSUM.
Sale of game, §29.1-536.

OPPORTUNITY EDUCATIONAL INSTITUTION, §§22.1-27.1 to 22.1-27.6.
See SCHOOLS AND EDUCATION.

OPTICAL SCANNERS.
Assistive technology device warranties, §§59.1-470 to 59.1-474.

OPTICIANS.
Free clinics.
Immunity for services provided, §54.1-106.
Health benefit programs.
Provider willing to meet terms and conditions not to be excluded, §38.2-3407.
Health services plans, coverage of services, §38.2-4221.
License, §54.1-1507.
Permissible practices, §54.1-1509.
Practices requiring prescription of optometrist or ophthalmologist, §54.1-1508.
Professional limited liability companies, §§13.1-1100 to 13.1-1123.
See PROFESSIONAL LIMITED LIABILITY COMPANIES.
Standardized HCFA-1500 health insurance claims forms for services.
Acceptance by insurers required, §38.2-322.
Unlawful procurement of licensure, §54.1-102.
Unlawful use of licensure, §54.1-111.

OPTIONAL FORMS OF COUNTY GOVERNMENT.
County board form of government, §§15.2-400 to 15.2-418.
See COUNTY BOARD FORM OF GOVERNMENT.
County executive form of government, §§15.2-500 to 15.2-542.
See COUNTY EXECUTIVE FORM OF GOVERNMENT.

OPTIONAL FORMS OF COUNTY GOVERNMENT —Cont'd
County manager form of government, §§15.2-600 to 15.2-642.
See COUNTY MANAGER FORM OF GOVERNMENT.
County manager plan of government, §§15.2-700 to 15.2-750.
See COUNTY MANAGER PLAN OF GOVERNMENT.
General provisions, §§15.2-300 to 15.2-307.
See COUNTIES.
Urban county executive form of government, §§15.2-800 to 15.2-858.
See URBAN COUNTY EXECUTIVE FORM OF GOVERNMENT.

OPTIONS.
Corporations.
Share options, §13.1-646.
Options to purchase real estate, §§55-57.1, 55-57.2.
Power of attorney.
Authority of agent, §64.2-1628.

OPTOMETRIC SERVICES AGENTS.
Licensing of insurance agents generally, §§38.2-1822 to 38.2-1836.1.

OPTOMETRIC SERVICES PLANS, §§38.2-4205, 38.2-4500 to 38.2-4523.
Agents, licensing, §38.2-4519.
Applicability of chapter, §38.2-4500.
Applicability of general insurance laws, §38.2-4509.
Benefits and limitations, subscriber to be advised, §38.2-4514.
Board of directors, §38.2-4508.
Change of participants, §38.2-4507.
Compensation to officers or directors for purchase or sale of property or obtaining loan, §§38.2-211, 38.2-213.
Contracts between participating optometrists, §38.2-4512.
Contracts with participating optometrists, §38.2-4511.
Controversies involving subscription contracts, §38.2-4523.
Corporate restrictions, §38.2-4520.
Definitions, §38.2-4501.
Filing of policy forms with state corporation commission required, §38.2-316.
Free choice of practitioners available, §38.2-4513.
Geographical area, §38.2-4515.
Health care provider panels, §38.2-3407.10.
Health services plans generally, §§38.2-4200 to 38.2-4235.
See HEALTH SERVICES PLANS.
Information and privacy protection generally, §§38.2-600 to 38.2-620.
See INSURANCE INFORMATION AND PRIVACY PROTECTION.
Interplan arrangements, §38.2-4516.
Liability of participants, §38.2-4505.
Licensing, §38.2-4517.
Renewal, §38.2-4518.
Loans to officers or directors, §38.2-210.
Violations, §38.2-213.
Misleading applications or contracts, §38.2-4522.
Nonprofit corporation required, §38.2-4504.

OPTOMETRIC SERVICES PLANS —Cont'd
Plan generally, §38.2-4503.
Provider panels, §38.2-3407.10.
Rehabilitation, liquidation, conservation, etc., §38.2-4509.1.
Reports, §38.2-4510.
Standardized HCFA-1500 health insurance claims forms.
Acceptance by plans required, §38.2-322.
Taxes, §38.2-4521.
Terms of participants, §38.2-4506.
Unlicensed insurers process, §§38.2-800 to 38.2-807.

OPTOMETRISTS, §§54.1-3200 to 54.1-3221.
Bills for medical services.
Presumption of authenticity and reasonableness, §8.01-413.01.
Board of optometry, §§54.1-3207 to 54.1-3211.
Court reports, §54.1-3206.
Commercial or mercantile establishments.
Practicing, §54.1-3205.
Conduct, prohibited, §54.1-3204.
Supervision by unlicensed persons, §54.1-3205.1.
Defined terms, §54.1-3200.
Commercial or mercantile establishment, §54.1-3205.
Diagnostic pharmaceutical agents, §54.1-3221.
Diagnostic pharmaceutical agents.
Certification for administration, §§54.1-3220, 54.1-3221.
Disasters, state or local emergencies.
Immunity.
Abandonment of person owed duty of health care in response to disaster, §8.01-225.01.
Unable to provide required care because of lack of resources, §8.01-225.02.
Display of license, §54.1-3203.
Exemption from licensure, §54.1-3202.
Free clinics.
Immunity for services provided, §54.1-106.
Free health care to underserved population, §54.1-3202.
Health benefit programs.
Provider willing to meet terms and conditions not to be excluded, §38.2-3407.
Health services plans, coverage of services, §38.2-4221.
Hearing aid specialists and opticians.
Optical prescriptions, refractions or other practices, §54.1-1508.
Immunity.
Disasters, state or local emergencies.
Abandonment of person owed duty of health care in response to disaster, §8.01-225.01.
Unable to provide required care because of lack of resources, §8.01-225.02.
Licensure of optometrists, §§54.1-3212 to 54.1-3219.
Display of license, §54.1-3203.
Exemptions, §54.1-3202.
Medical bills.
Presumption of authenticity and reasonableness, §8.01-413.01.
Medical malpractice.
General provisions, §§8.01-581.1 to 8.01-581.20.
See MEDICAL MALPRACTICE.
Practice of optometry, what constitutes, §54.1-3201.
Practicing in a commercial or mercantile establishment, §54.1-3205.

OPTOMETRISTS —Cont'd
Professional corporations, §§13.1-542.1 to 13.1-556.
See PROFESSIONAL CORPORATIONS.
Professional limited liability companies.
Generally, §§13.1-1100 to 13.1-1123.
See PROFESSIONAL LIMITED LIABILITY COMPANIES.
Professions and occupations regulation generally.
See HEALTH PROFESSIONS DEPARTMENT.
Prohibited acts, §54.1-3204.
Supervision by unlicensed persons, §54.1-3205.1.
Prohibited acts by licensees generally, §54.1-2409.1.
Records or papers of patients.
Admissibility of copies, §8.01-413.
Right of patient or attorney to copies, §8.01-413.
Subpoenas, §8.01-413.
Self-referrals.
Practitioner self-referral act, §§54.1-2410 to 54.1-2414.
Standardized HCFA-1500 health insurance claims forms for services.
Acceptance by insurers required, §38.2-322.
Therapeutic pharmaceutical agents, §§54.1-3222 to 54.1-3224.
Title restrictions.
Applicability, §54.1-3513.
Unlawful procurement of licensure, §54.1-102.
Unlawful use of licensure, §54.1-111.

OPTOMETRY BOARD, §§54.1-3207 to 54.1-3211.
Court reports, §54.1-3206.

ORAL AND MAXILLOFACIAL SURGEONS, §§54.1-2700, 54.1-2709.1 to 54.1-2709.5.
Defined, §32.1-276.3.
Health care data reporting.
Generally, §§32.1-276.2 to 32.1-276.11.
See HEALTH CARE DATA REPORTING.
Health insurance.
Mandated reimbursements applicable only to covered services, §38.2-3407.17.
Patient level data.
Submission to board, §32.1-276.6.

ORAL ARGUMENT.
Attorney discipline.
District committees proceedings, VA SCt Rule Pt 6 §IV Par 13-16.
Court of appeals.
Argument made on brief not waived by oral argument, §8.01-679.1.
Criminal cases and traffic infractions, VA SCt Rule 5A:12.
Length, VA SCt Rule 5A:28.
Notice, VA SCt Rule 5A:28.
Supreme court.
Length, VA SCt Rule 5:33.
Notice, VA SCt Rule 5:33.
Waiver, VA SCt Rule 5:33.
Waiver, VA SCt Rule 5A:28.

ORAL COMMUNICATIONS INTERCEPTION, §§19.2-61 to 19.2-70.3.
See ELECTRONIC SURVEILLANCE.

ORAL MOTIONS, §8.01-271.1.

ORAL TRUSTS.
Clear and convincing evidence to establish, §64.2-725.

ORANGE COUNTY.
Confederate cemeteries and graves.
Disbursement of funds appropriated for upkeep, §10.1-2211.
Fingerprinting school employees, §22.1-296.2.
Grass, weeds, other foreign growth on occupied or vacant property.
Cutting by property owners, ordinance prescribing, §15.2-901.
School board.
Fingerprinting applicants for employment, §22.1-296.2.
Salary of members, §22.1-32.
Water and sewage systems.
Lien for charges and taxes imposed, §15.2-2118.
Well abandonment ordinance.
Duty of owner to cap or close well.
Locality adopting ordinance, §32.1-176.5.
Well construction.
Testing requirements, §32.1-176.5.

ORDER BOOKS, CIRCUIT COURTS, §17.1-124.
Chancery order book, §17.1-124.
Common law order book, §17.1-124.
Recording and signing orders making up days proceedings, §17.1-123.
Trust fund order book, §17.1-125.

ORDER OF GOVERNOR.
Return, §2.2-112.

ORDER OF REFERENCE.
Sale of delinquent tax lands, §58.1-3969.

ORDER OF THE EASTERN STAR.
Special license plates for members, §46.2-746.7.

ORDERS OF COURT.
Address confidentiality program.
Victims of domestic violence.
Disclosure of actual address, §2.2-515.2.
Adoption records and information.
Identity of biological family of adopted person.
Access by adopter person, §63.2-105.
Agricultural liming materials.
Stop sale, use, removal or seizure orders, §3.2-3708.
Animals running at large.
Unincorporated communities and villages.
Boundaries within which animals may not run at large, §§55-325, 55-327.
Appointment of counsel in juvenile proceedings, §16.1-268.
Authentication of circuit courts orders, §17.1-123.
Bail and recognizance, §19.2-137.
Bankruptcy orders.
Recordation, §§55-140 to 55-142.01.
Behavioral health and developmental services.
Expenses of care, treatment or training, and maintenance.
Order to compel payment, §37.2-718.
Birth certificates.
Delayed birth certificates.
Registration by court order, §32.1-260.
Bonds, surety.
Who may execute bond for writ or order, §8.01-4.2.
Cease and desist orders.
See CEASE AND DESIST ORDERS.
Changing place of holding circuit court.
Posting of order, §17.1-115.
Child abuse or neglect.
Protective orders.
See PROTECTIVE ORDERS.

ORDERS OF COURT —Cont'd
Child abuse or neglect —Cont'd
Removal orders, child taken into custody.
Dispositional hearing, §16.1-278.2.
Emergency removal order, §16.1-251.
Preliminary removal order, §16.1-252.
Child-placing agency records and information.
Identity of biological family of adopted person.
Access by adopter person, §63.2-105.
Computation of time.
Performance required by specified date or prescribed period of time, §1-210.
Conservatorship of estate of incapacitated persons.
Appointment of conservator, §64.2-2009.
Consolidation of actions generally.
See CONSOLIDATION OF ACTIONS.
Coordination of actions.
Multiple claimant litigation, §8.01-267.3.
Court of appeals.
Form, VA SCt Rule 5A:4.
Furnishing to counsel, VA SCt Rule 5A:2.
Decedents' estates.
Creditors to show cause against distributions, §64.2-556.
Form, §64.2-557.
Desertion and nonsupport.
Support orders.
See DESERTION AND NONSUPPORT.
Detention orders issued for child.
Limitation on issuance, §§16.1-255, 16.1-256.
Dispute resolution proceedings.
Incorporation of mediation agreement, §8.01-576.11.
Vacating orders and agreements, §8.01-576.12.
Distress warrants.
Title to property levied on, district court proceedings, §16.1-121.
District court civil cases.
Entry of formal orders, §16.1-94.
Title to property levied on under distress or execution, §16.1-121.
Domestic violence victims.
Address confidentiality program.
Disclosure of actual address, §2.2-515.2.
Drafts of orders.
Endorsement by counsel of record.
Electronic filing and service, VA SCt Rule 1:17.
Emancipation of minors, §16.1-332.
Endorsement.
Drafts endorsed by counsel.
Electronic filing and service, VA SCt Rule 1:17.
Entry.
District court civil cases, §16.1-94.
Execution.
Title to property levied on, district court proceedings, §16.1-121.
Family abuse.
Protective orders.
See PROTECTIVE ORDERS.
Fences.
Lawful fences constituted by water or canal.
Revocation of orders, §55-301.
Fiduciaries.
Investments.
Court orders, §64.2-1500.
Finality of orders, VA SCt Rule 1:1.
Foreign support orders.
Interstate family support act generally, §§20-88.32 to 20-88.82.
See INTERSTATE FAMILY SUPPORT ACT.

ORDERS OF COURT —Cont'd
Guardianship of incapacitated persons.
Appointment of guardian, §64.2-2009.
Joinder.
See JOINDER.
Judicial emergency declaration, §17.1-331.
Juvenile and domestic relations district courts.
Endorsements of orders, VA SCt Rule 8:19.
Juvenile proceedings.
Any person, §16.1-292.
Detention orders, limitation on issuance, §16.1-255.
Removal orders, abuse or neglect of child.
Dispositional hearing, §16.1-278.2.
Emergency removal order, §16.1-251.
Preliminary removal order, §16.1-252.
Review of orders, §16.1-289.
Violations by child.
Revocation or modification, §16.1-291.
Warrants, limitation on issuance, §16.1-256.
Military parents equal protection act.
Temporary custody or visitation order, §§20-124.8 to 20-124.10.
Motor vehicle proof of financial responsibility.
Order discharging lien of bond, §46.2-450.
Multiple claimant litigation, §8.01-267.1.
Pet cemeteries.
Removal of restriction on land, §57-39.24.
Prostitution.
Houses of prostitution.
Order of abatement of nuisance, §48-12.
Protective orders.
Elder abuse, neglect or exploitation.
See PROTECTIVE ORDERS.
Recording evidences and incidents of trial in civil cases.
Circuit court judge ordering, §17.1-128.
Recording orders making up each days proceedings of circuit court, §§17.1-123 to 17.1-125.
Sentencing orders, VA SCt Rules Part 3A Appx Form 10.
Substantial compliance with form required, VA SCt Rule 3A:22.
Stalking.
Protective orders, §19.2-152.10.
Emergency orders authorized, §19.2-152.8.
Law enforcement officers, prohibition on orders against, §19.2-152.8.
Preliminary orders, §19.2-152.9.
Venue, §19.2-152.11.
Violation of orders, §18.2-60.4.
Standby guardian for incompetent children, §16.1-350.
Supreme court.
Furnishing to counsel, VA SCt Rule 5:4.
Title to land.
Recordation of decrees affecting, §55-138.
Transfer of actions.
Multiple claimant litigation, §§8.01-267.4, 8.01-267.8.
Trusts.
Judicial proceedings involving trusts, §64.2-713.
United States courts.
Recordation, §§55-140 to 55-142.01.
Victims of domestic violence.
Address confidentiality program.
Disclosure of actual address, §2.2-515.2.
Water supplies.
Emergency orders, §32.1-175.

ORDERS OF COURT —Cont'd
Wetlands.
Provision violations, §28.2-1317.

ORDERS OF PUBLICATION, §§8.01-316, 8.01-317.
Service by publication generally.
See SERVICE BY PUBLICATION.

ORDERS OF TAX COMMISSIONER.
Service, §§58.1-216, 58.1-217.
Taxpayer problem resolution program.
Taxpayer assistance order, §58.1-1818.

ORDINANCES, §§15.2-1425 to 15.2-1433.
Abandoned motor vehicles.
Authority of governing bodies to enact, §46.2-1201.
Removal and disposition of unattended vehicles, §§46.2-1213, 46.2-1215.
Towing vehicles, §46.2-1217.
ABC law.
Local regulation or prohibitions, §4.1-128.
Time of sale of wine and beer, §4.1-129.
Accounts due pursuant to ordinance.
Penalty and interest for failure to pay, §15.2-105.
Adoption in performance of duties, obligations and functions, §§15.2-1425, 15.2-1427.
Advertisement.
Certain fees and levies, §15.2-107.
Affordable dwelling units, §§15.2-2304, 15.2-2305.
Agricultural stewardship, §3.2-409.
Air cannons, carbide cannons or other loud explosives used to repel birds, §15.2-918.
Alarm company operators, regulating, §15.2-911.
All-terrain vehicles.
Limitations on operation, §46.2-915.1.
Protective head gear, §46.2-915.1.
Amateur radio antennas.
Height restrictions, §15.2-2293.1.
Amendments.
Identification of section to be amended, §15.2-1426.
Procedure generally, §15.2-1427.
Animal ordinances, §3.2-6543.
County regulation of keeping animals and fowl, §3.2-6544.
Dangerous dogs, §3.2-6540.
Dogs running at large, §3.2-6538.
Licensing of dogs and cats, §§3.2-6521 to 3.2-6536.
Permits for pet shops and dealers in companion animals, §3.2-6537.
Pounds.
Sales of animals from, §3.2-6545.
Rabid animal, §3.2-6522.
Rabies control, §3.2-6525.
Running at large, §3.2-6544.
Vicious dogs, §3.2-6540.1.
Annexation, §15.2-3202.
Immunity of county from city-initiated annexation and city incorporation, §15.2-3301.
Annulment of town charter, §15.2-3702.
Appeal from fine or imprisonment as in misdemeanor cases, §15.2-1431.
Appropriations, affirmative vote of majority of governing body required, VA Const Art VII §7.
Appropriations, ordinances or resolutions.
Procedure generally, §15.2-1428.
Arrests by state police for violations, §52-22.

ORDINANCES —Cont'd
Attack dogs.
County with urban county executive form of government.
Authority to prohibit training on residential property, §3.2-6541.
Automobile graveyards.
Taxing and regulating, §15.2-903.
Bad checks.
Fee for passing bad checks to localities, §15.2-106.
Bail bonds, §15.2-1430.
Bicycle helmets, §46.2-906.1.
Bicycles.
Licensing, disposition of unclaimed bicycles, §15.2-1720.
Biotechnology research act.
Limitations on local regulation, §2.2-5509.
Blighted areas.
Tax increment financing, §§58.1-3245 to 58.1-3245.5.
Body-piercing salons and tattoo parlors, §15.2-912.
Boiler and pressure vessel operator certification, §15.2-910.
Bond issues.
County issuing bonds, §§15.2-2640, 15.2-2641.
Municipalities issuing bonds, §15.2-2636.
Provisions contained in ordinance or resolution, adoption, filing with court, §15.2-2607.
Borrowing money.
Affirmative vote of majority of council members required, VA Const Art VII §7.
Resolution or ordinance authorizing, §15.2-1428.
Building of houses, §15.2-2279.
Campgrounds.
Local ordinances superseded, §35.1-9.
Cat licensing, §§3.2-6521 to 3.2-6536.
Checks.
Bad checks.
Fee for passing bad checks to localities, §15.2-106.
Chesapeake Bay preservation areas.
Designation by counties, cities or towns in Tidewater Virginia, §62.1-44.15:74.
Enforcement of provisions, authority of local governments, §62.1-44.15:73.
Outside Tidewater area, adoption of provisions, §62.1-44.15:75.
State agency consistency, §62.1-44.15:78.
Child-care services and facilities.
Certain counties and cities, §15.2-914.
Cigarette tax.
Administration and enforcement of taxes on sale or use of cigarettes, §58.1-3833.
City council members' salaries, setting, §15.2-1414.6.
City councils.
Alternative election of mayor, §24.2-222.1.
City status granted to counties.
Petitioning court to declare eligibility, §15.2-3901.
City status granted to town.
Petitioning court for city status, §15.2-3800.
Clear expression of object in title, §15.2-1426.
Codification, §15.2-1433.
Community revitalization, local funding.
Richmond, §15.2-958.5.
Computation of time.
Act requiring performance by specified date or prescribed period of time, §1-210.
Condominiums.
Conversion condominiums, §55-79.94.

ORDINANCES —Cont'd
Conservation of trees during development process.
Locality located in Planning District 8 classified as nonattainment area for air quality standards, §15.2-961.1.
Consolidation of like units of local government.
Ordinances in force in localities at time of consolidation, §15.2-3517.
Constitutionality or validity.
Appeals from general district courts in civil cases, §16.1-106.
Consumer affairs.
Offices established by locality, §15.2-963.
Contraction of corporate limits of city or town limits, §15.2-3236.
Counties to publish notice of intention to propose ordinance for passage, §15.2-1427.
County boards of supervisors salaries.
Establishing annually by ordinance and payment in monthly installments, §15.2-1414.3.
Criminal justice training academies.
Creating, §15.2-1747.
Crosswalks.
Authority to regulate crosswalks, §46.2-916.2.
Curled thistle, §15.2-902.
Cutting grass or lawn in certain counties, §15.2-1215.
Dairies and dairy products.
Local regulation, restrictions, §3.2-5202.
Dance halls.
Regulation by localities, §15.2-912.3.
Defacement of buildings, walls, fences and other structures on private property.
Removal or repair, §15.2-908.
Derelict buildings.
Authority to remove, demolish or renovate, §15.2-907.1.
Locality appointed as receiver to repair derelict and blighted buildings, §15.2-907.2.
Discrimination.
County manager plan of government, §15.2-725.
Urban county executive form of government.
Human rights ordinance, §15.2-853.
Disorderly conduct in public places.
Authority of locality to adopt ordinance, §18.2-415.
District court jurisdiction of offenses against, §16.1-123.1.
Dog ordinances.
Dangerous dogs, §3.2-6540.
Hybrid canines, §3.2-6582.
Leash ordinance, referendum, §3.2-6539.
Licensing, §§3.2-6521 to 3.2-6536.
Rabid animals, §3.2-6522.
Running at large, §3.2-6538.
Vicious dogs, §3.2-6540.1.
Door-to-door vendors, §15.2-913.
Driving under the influence.
Chemical testing to determine alcohol or drug content of blood.
Authorization of ordinances paralleling provisions, §18.2-268.12.
Municipal regulation by ordinances, §46.2-1313.
Reimbursement for emergency response, §15.2-1716.
Electric authorities.
Creation, §15.2-5403.
Emergency ordinances.
Counties generally, §15.2-1427.

ORDINANCES —Cont'd
Emergency ordinances —Cont'd
Imposition or increase of certain levies or fees, §15.2-107.
Regulating assemblies or movement of persons or vehicles during riot, §15.2-925.
Eminent domain.
County entering upon and taking possession prior to conclusion of proceedings.
Powers of county after ordinance or resolution declaring intent, §15.2-1905.
Resolution or ordinance prior to initiating, §15.2-1903.
Enterprise zone development.
Local enterprise zone development taxation program, §58.1-3245.8.
Copies of ordinance to local assessing officers, §58.1-3245.9.
Fairfax county.
Publication of notice of intention to proposed passage, §15.2-1201.
Rabies.
Distribution of oral vaccine to prevent spread, §3.2-6525.
Fair housing.
Civil action by attorney general.
Legality of land use ordinance, §36-96.17.
Local enforcement and regulation, §36-96.21.
Federal law.
Supremacy of, §1-248.
Fencing of swimming pools, §15.2-921.
Final vote, recording, §15.2-1427.
Fine for violations, §15.2-1429.
Nonpayment, §15.2-1431.
Firearm regulation, §15.2-915.
Ordinances governing transportation of loaded rifle or shotgun, §15.2-915.2.
Fire/EMS department, §27-14.
Fires.
Regulating or prohibiting making of fires, §15.2-922.1.
Fire suppression systems connected to local water utilities, §15.2-2113.
Form generally, §15.2-1426.
Franchise, privilege, lease or right to use city or town property.
Adoption as advertised, §15.2-2102.
Generally, §§15.2-2100 to 15.2-2108.1:1.
Publication of notice, §15.2-2102.
Gambling, county ordinances, §18.2-340.
Garbage and refuse collection and disposal.
General powers of locality for waste and recycling, §§15.2-927 to 15.2-939.
Urban county executive form of government, §15.2-815.
General powers of local government, §§15.2-900 to 15.2-982.
See LOCALITIES.
Green roof incentive programs, §15.2-977.
Height restrictions on amateur radio antennas, §15.2-2293.1.
Helicopter landings.
Zoning ordinances, §15.2-2293.2.
Helmet law.
All-terrain vehicles, §46.2-915.1.
Historic structures, demolition, razing or moving.
Urban county executive form of government, §15.2-819.
Hotels.
Local ordinances superseded, §35.1-9.

ORDINANCES —Cont'd
Human rights ordinance.
Power of locality to enact, §15.2-965.
Urban county executive form of government, §15.2-853.
Hunting.
Bow and arrow, hunting with, §29.1-528.1.
Firearms, hunting with, §29.1-528.
Prohibiting hunting in heavily populated areas, §15.2-1113.1.
Hybrid canines, §3.2-6582.
Illegal gambling, county ordinances, §18.2-340.
Incorporating state law by reference, §1-220.
Industrial development authorities.
Creation, §15.2-4903.
Industrialized building safety.
Application of local ordinances, §36-81.
Injunctive relief against continuing violation, §15.2-1432.
Inoperable motor vehicles.
Residential or commercial property, removal, §§15.2-904, 15.2-905.
Interference with students at schools, §15.2-1717.
Itinerant merchants.
Enactment of ordinances by localities not prohibited, §54.1-4303.
Joint aid agreements by localities, §15.2-1300.1.
Junkyards.
Taxing and regulating, §15.2-903.
Jurisdiction over ordinance violations.
District courts, §16.1-123.1.
Law library assessment as part of cost in civil action, §42.1-70.
Levies and fees imposed or increased by locality.
Advertisement and enactment of ordinances for certain fees and levies, §15.2-107.
License taxes.
Uniform ordinance provisions, §58.1-3703.1.
Lighting of exterior of buildings and property.
County executive form of government, §15.2-504.1.
County manager plan of government, §15.2-742.
Limited access streets, §15.2-2026.
Litter control.
County manager plan of government, §15.2-733.
Local sales or use taxes by cities or counties, §§58.1-605, 58.1-606.
Local taxes.
Assessments, use of July 1 as effective date, §58.1-3011.
Criminal penalties for failure to file returns or false statements, §58.1-3916.1.
Dates for filing returns, setting penalties, interest, etc., §58.1-3916.
Levies based on fiscal year, §58.1-3010.
License taxes.
Uniform ordinance provisions, §58.1-3703.1.
Majority vote, §15.2-1427.
Manufactured housing.
Construction and safety standards.
Application of local ordinances, §36-85.11.
Misdemeanors.
Appeals as in misdemeanor cases, §15.2-1431.
County manager form of government.
Ordinances to parallel criminal laws of Commonwealth, §15.2-605.
County manager plan of government.
Ordinance to parallel criminal laws of Commonwealth, §15.2-747.
Enforcement of violations as, §15.2-1429.

ORDINANCES —Cont'd
Mopeds.
Licensing, disposition of unclaimed mopeds, §15.2-1720.
Motorcycles.
Disposition of unregistered or unlicensed motorcycles, §46.2-916.
Noise ordinance, §15.2-919.
Motor vehicle and traffic regulation.
Local powers generally, §§46.2-1300 to 46.2-1314.
See LOCAL GOVERNMENT.
Size and weight.
City ordinances fixing weight limits, §46.2-1138.1.
Musk thistle, §15.2-902.
Noise control.
Civil penalties for noise ordinance violations.
Adoption of uniform schedule, §15.2-980.
Motorcycle, moped, and motorized skateboard or foot-scooter noise, §15.2-919.
Sports shooting ranges, §15.2-917.
Nonpayment of fines, §15.2-1431.
Notice of intention to propose ordinance for passage.
Publication by county, §15.2-1427.
Noxious weed control, §15.2-902.
Object clearly expressed in title, §15.2-1426.
Obscenity.
Adoption of ordinances prohibiting, §15.2-926.2.
Official map of locality.
Adopting, additions and modifications, §§15.2-2234, 15.2-2235.
Outdoor lighting near planetariums, astronomical observatories and meteorological laboratories, §15.2-920.
Parking.
Authority of localities to issue parking permits, §46.2-1230.
Buses.
Restrictions on idling of engines, §46.2-1224.1.
Conditions precedent to issuance of summons for violation, §46.2-941.
Counties of Arlington, Fairfax, Stafford and Prince William.
Regulation or prohibition of parking of certain vehicles, §46.2-1222.1.
County ordinances prohibiting parking on certain streets and highways, §46.2-1224.
Issuance of summons, §46.2-941.
Limiting length of time of parking adjacent to commercial business areas.
Vehicles of certain weight and length, §46.2-1222.2.
Mailing summons, §19.2-76.2.
Municipal enforcement provisions, §46.2-1225.
Municipal parking regulations, §§46.2-1220, 46.2-1221.
Regulation of vehicular traffic on certain privately-owned public parking areas, §46.2-1219.1.
Towing vehicles, §46.2-1217.
Towns of Clifton, Herndon and Vienna.
Regulation or prohibition of parking of certain vehicles, §46.2-1222.1.
Unsettled parking violations.
Removal or immobilization of vehicles, §46.2-1216.
Vehicular and pedestrian traffic on certain parking lots, §46.2-1217.
Within boundaries of state-supported institutions, §15.2-968.

ORDINANCES —Cont'd
Pass-through zones.
Locality authorized to adopt ordinance, congested boat traffic, §29.1-744.4.
Peddlers and itinerant merchants.
County manager plan of government, §15.2-732.
Pedestrians.
Authority to regulate crosswalks, §46.2-916.2.
Authority to regulate pedestrian traffic, §46.2-935.
Prohibiting distribution of handbills, etc., §46.2-931.
Penalties for violations, §15.2-1429.
Personal property tax proration, §58.1-3516.
Personal property tax relief for elderly or handicapped.
Alternative tax rates on motor vehicles, §§58.1-3506.1 to 58.1-3506.8.
Personal property tax returns, penalties, interest, etc.
Counties, cities and towns providing for, §58.1-3916.
Personal watercraft.
Minimum distance from shoreline.
City ordinance regulating, penalty for violation, §29.1-748.1.
Photo-monitoring systems to enforce traffic light signals, §15.2-968.1.
Planting and replacement of trees during development process, §15.2-961.
Police forces, organization, §15.2-1701.
Powers of local government generally, §§15.2-900 to 15.2-982.
See LOCALITIES.
Prescribing criminal penalties for failure to file returns or false statements, §58.1-3916.1.
Property tax exemptions.
Triennial application for exemption, §58.1-3605.
Property tax returns.
Criminal penalties for failure to file or false statements, §58.1-3916.1.
Publication of notice of intention to propose ordinance for passage.
Counties generally, §15.2-1427.
Public procurement.
Implementation, §2.2-4302.
Rabies.
Emergency ordinances.
Rabid animals, §3.2-6522.
Regulations to prevent spread, §3.2-6525.
Real property improvements.
Financing clean energy programs, §15.2-958.3.
Green roof incentive programs, §15.2-977.
Real property tax assessments or reassessments.
Annual and biennial assessment, §58.1-3253.
Annual assessment and reassessment in cities having not more than 30,000 population, §58.1-3251.
General reassessment in towns, §58.1-3256.
Real property taxes.
Credits.
Rehabilitated, renovated or replacement structures.
Residential structures, §58.1-3220.01.
Deferral programs, §58.1-3219.
Elderly or handicapped, §§58.1-3210 to 58.1-3217.
Energy-efficient buildings.
Levy of tax at different rate, §58.1-3221.2.

ORDINANCES —Cont'd
Real property taxes —Cont'd
Exemptions.
Elderly or handicapped, §§58.1-3210 to 58.1-3217.
Rehabilitated, renovated or replacement structures.
Commercial or industrial structures, §58.1-3221.
Hotel or motel structures, §58.1-3220.1.
Residential structures, §58.1-3220.
Liens.
Release on portion of real estate upon payment of taxes, §58.1-3226.1.
Prince William county senior citizens and disabled persons.
Ordinance prescribing alternative due dates, §58.1-3916.02.
Special assessment for land preservation, §§58.1-3229 to 58.1-3244.
Rechargeable battery disposal and recycling, §10.1-1425.39.
Recodification, §15.2-1433.
Recording final vote, §15.2-1427.
Recreational facilities authorities.
Creating, §15.2-5602.
Recycled paper and paper products purchases.
Preference for, §15.2-938.
Recycling, §§15.2-937 to 15.2-939.
Separation of solid waste generally, §15.2-937.
Refund of local taxes erroneously paid, §58.1-3990.
Rental inspection ordinance and rental inspection districts.
Locality adopting and establishing, §36-105.1:1.
Repeals.
Identification of section to be repealed, §15.2-1426.
Procedure generally, §15.2-1427.
Resale of tickets, §15.2-969.
Restaurants.
Fairs, exemption from provisions by local ordinance, §35.1-26.
Local ordinances superseded, §35.1-9.
Reversion of city to town status.
Petitioning court for town status, §15.2-4101.
Richmond.
Community revitalization, local funding, §15.2-958.5.
Riot.
Regulating assemblies or movement of persons or vehicles, §15.2-925.
Road impact fees.
Generally, §§15.2-2317 to 15.2-2329.
See ROAD IMPACT FEES.
Salaries of city council members, §15.2-1414.6.
Salaries of county boards of supervisors.
Annual salary established and payment in monthly installments, §15.2-1414.3.
Sale of city or town property, §15.2-200, VA Const Art VII §9.
Sales and use taxes by cities or counties, §§58.1-605, 58.1-606.
Sanitation districts law of 1938.
Bond issues, §§21-191, 21-194.
Creation of districts, §21-153.
Sanitation districts law of 1946.
Bond issues, §§21-271, 21-274.
Creation of districts, §21-236.
Service districts, §§15.2-2400 to 15.2-2403.3.
Setback lines established, §15.2-2279.

ORDINANCES —Cont'd
Severance tax on coal, gas or oil, §§58.1-3712 to 58.1-3713.4.
Alternative to specially and separately assessing mineral lands, §58.1-3286.
Local coal severance license taxes, §§58.1-3740 to 58.1-3745.
Sewage disposal.
Land application, marketing and distribution of sludge, §62.1-44.19:3.
Small businesses.
Minority and women owned businesses.
Local ordinances supporting, §15.2-965.1.
Smoke detectors in certain buildings, §15.2-922.
Smoking in public places.
Clean air act, §§15.2-2828 to 15.2-2833.
See SMOKING IN PUBLIC PLACES.
Snow and ice removal from public sidewalks.
Counties in northern Virginia Planning District 8, §15.2-2025.
Solid waste management facility siting, §15.2-929.
Sports shooting ranges.
Applicability of noise ordinances, §15.2-917.
State law.
Incorporating state law by reference, §1-220.
Supremacy of, §1-248.
State police arrests for violations, §52-22.
Stopping or standing, §46.2-1220.
Stormwater control programs, §15.2-2114.
Stormwater management.
Localities, reporting need for more stringent ordinances, §62.1-44.15:33.
Subdivisions.
Generally, §§15.2-2240 to 15.2-2279.
Summer camps.
Local ordinances superseded, §35.1-9.
Summons in lieu of warrant.
Ordinance violations, §19.2-74.
Supplements for codification or recodification, §15.2-1433.
Swimming pools.
Fencing required, §15.2-921.
Swine.
Garbage feeding.
Prohibited feeding of certain putrescible wastes, §3.2-6033.
Tangier, town of.
Motor vehicle regulation.
Authority to adopt local ordinances, §46.2-115.
Tattoo parlors and body-piercing salons, §15.2-912.
Tax imposed by city.
Affirmative vote of majority of council members required, VA Const Art VII §7.
Tax imposed by town.
Two-third votes required, §15.2-1427.
Tax imposed generally, §15.2-1428.
Tax increment financing.
Blighted areas, §§58.1-3245 to 58.1-3245.5.
Ticket scalping, §15.2-969.
Towing vehicles.
Authority of localities to regulate certain towing, §46.2-1217.
Town councils.
Alternative election of mayor, §24.2-222.1.
Town imposing tax.
Two-third votes required, §15.2-1427.
Tracking of mud and debris upon highways.
Counties adopting, §15.2-2022.

ORDINANCES —Cont'd
Traffic light signals.
Photo-monitoring systems to enforce, §15.2-968.1.
Transient occupancy tax, §§58.1-3819 to 58.1-3826.
Transition of city to town status.
Petitioning court for town status, §15.2-4101.
Transition of counties to cities.
Petitioning court to declare eligibility, §15.2-3901.
Transition of towns to cities.
Petitioning court for city status, §15.2-3800.
Transportation districts.
Creation, §15.2-4504.
Triennial application for exemption, §58.1-3605.
Unclaimed property in possession of sheriff or police.
Disposal, §15.2-1719.
Validity of adoptions, §15.2-1427.
Veto of ordinances or resolutions.
Appropriations, tax imposition or authorization to borrow money, §15.2-1428.
Violations.
Appeals as in misdemeanor cases, §15.2-1431.
Bonds of persons convicted, §15.2-1430.
Injunctive relief against continuing violation, §15.2-1432.
Penalties, §15.2-1429.
State police arrests, §52-22.
Visually handicapped operating stand for sale of newspapers, periodicals, etc., in courthouse, §15.2-1805.
Voluntary settlement of annexation, transition or immunity issues, §15.2-3400.
Water conservation devices, §15.2-923.
Waterfront, wharves, public landings, etc.
Sale by city or town, §15.2-2100.
Water shortages or water emergencies, §§15.2-923, 15.2-924.
Well abandonment ordinance.
Certain localities adopting, §32.1-176.5.
Well covers.
Authority of counties, cities and towns, §18.2-318.
Zoning.
Civil penalties, §15.2-2209.
Codification or recodification, §15.2-1433.
Generally, §§15.2-2280 to 15.2-2316.2.

ORES.
Conservation and recreation department, §10.1-108.
Presumed to exist in certain lands, §55-154.
Suits to extinguish claim or right, §55-155.
Surface mining.
Permits, §45.1-181.
Uranium ore exploration, §§45.1-272, 45.1-278.

ORGAN AND TISSUE DONOR REGISTRY.
Virginia donor registry, §§32.1-291.20, 32.1-292.2.

ORGAN DONATIONS.
Anatomical gifts generally, §§32.1-291.1 to 32.1-291.25.
See ANATOMICAL GIFTS.
Criminal proceedings.
Removal of organs or other body parts for transplant.
Certificate of surgeon as evidence, §19.2-188.2.
Death certificates.
Disclosure of information to nonprofit organ, eye or tissue procurement organization, §32.1-271.

ORGAN DONATIONS —Cont'd
Funeral services.
Immunity from liability for failure to restore features to acceptable manner for viewing.
Preparation of body following organ, tissue or eye donation, §54.1-2818.4.
Hospitals.
Donation protocol, §32.1-127.
Immunity from liability, §32.1-127.1.
Implied warranty in connection with transfer, §32.1-297.
Medical records.
Death of patient in hospital.
Disclosure for purposes of identifying organ donors, §32.1-127.1:03.
Registry.
Virginia donor registry, §§32.1-291.20, 32.1-292.2.
Request duties of custodial parties, §32.1-283.
Special license plates to encourage participation in the organ donor program, §46.2-749.105.
State employees.
Bone marrow or organ donation.
Leave for, §2.2-2821.1.
Virginia donor registry, §§32.1-291.20, 32.1-292.2.
Virginia transplant council.
Established, membership, duties, §32.1-297.1.

ORGAN DONORS.
Bone marrow donors recognition day, §2.2-3312.

ORGANIC ACETATES.
Inhaling drugs or other noxious chemical substances, §18.2-264.

ORGANIC BY-PRODUCTS.
Renewable electricity production program.
Grants, §§67-900 to 67-903.

ORGANIZATION OF STATE GOVERNMENT.
Acquisitions, conveyances and transfers of property.
State departments and agencies generally, §§2.2-1147 to 2.2-1156.
See STATE DEPARTMENTS AND AGENCIES.
Assistant to the Governor for intergovernmental affairs, office of, §§2.2-300 to 2.2-303.
Authorities.
See AUTHORITIES.
Boards.
See BOARDS.
Collection and dissemination of information by state agencies.
Personal information, privacy protection.
Government data collection and dissemination practices act, §§2.2-3800 to 2.2-3809.
See GOVERNMENT DATA COLLECTION AND DISSEMINATION PRACTICES ACT.
Social security numbers, protection, §§2.2-3815, 2.2-3816.
Commissions.
See COMMISSIONS.
Committees.
See COMMITTEES, STATE GOVERNMENT.
Councils.
See COUNCILS.
Department for the aging and rehabilitative services.
Generally, §§51.5-116 to 51.5-181.
See AGING AND REHABILITATIVE SERVICES, DEPARTMENT FOR.

ORGANIZATION OF STATE GOVERNMENT —Cont'd
Department of accounts.
Claims against the state, §§2.2-814 to 2.2-816.
Generally, §§2.2-800 to 2.2-813.2.
See COMPTROLLER.
Department of business assistance (eff until 1/1/2014), §§2.2-900 to 2.2-904.1.
Department of criminal justice services.
Center for school safety, §9.1-184.
Comprehensive community-corrections act for local responsible offenders, §§9.1-173 to 9.1-183.
See COMMUNITY CORRECTIONS.
Court-appointed special advocate program, §§9.1-151 to 9.1-157.
Criminal justice information system, §§9.1-126 to 9.1-137.
See CRIMINAL JUSTICE INFORMATION SYSTEM.
Department of forensic science, §§9.1-1100 to 9.1-1113.
See FORENSIC SCIENCE DEPARTMENT.
Generally, §§9.1-100 to 9.1-116.
See CRIMINAL JUSTICE SERVICES DEPARTMENT.
Law enforcement expenditures, §§9.1-165 to 9.1-172.
Private security services businesses.
Licensing, certifying, registering and regulation, §§9.1-138 to 9.1-150.
See PRIVATE SECURITY SERVICES BUSINESSES.
Department of fire programs, §§9.1-200 to 9.1-208.
Department of general services.
Abatement of risk of asbestos.
State-owned and public school buildings.
See ASBESTOS ABATEMENT.
Asbestos abatement.
State-owned and public school buildings, §§2.2-1162 to 2.2-1167.
Division of consolidated laboratory services, §§2.2-1103 to 2.2-1108.
See GENERAL SERVICES DEPARTMENT.
Division of engineering and buildings, §§2.2-1129 to 2.2-1161.1.
See ENGINEERING AND BUILDINGS DIVISION.
Division of purchases and supply, §§2.2-1109 to 2.2-1128.
See PURCHASES AND SUPPLY DIVISION.
Division of support services, §§2.2-1168 to 2.2-1172.
Generally, §§2.2-1100 to 2.2-1102.
Department of human resources management, §§2.2-1200 to 2.2-1208.
See HUMAN RESOURCES MANAGEMENT DEPARTMENT.
Department of law.
Division of consumer council, §2.2-517.
Division of debt collection, §2.2-518.
Generally, §§2.2-500 to 2.2-516.
See ATTORNEY GENERAL.
Department of minority business enterprise (eff until 1/1/2014), §§2.2-1400 to 2.2-1405.
See MINORITY BUSINESS ENTERPRISE DEPARTMENT (EFF UNTIL 1/1/2014).
Department of planning and budget, §§2.2-1500 to 2.2-1514.
See PLANNING AND BUDGET DEPARTMENT.

ORGANIZATION OF STATE GOVERNMENT —Cont'd
Department of small business and supplier diversity, §§2.2-1603 to 2.2-1617.
See SMALL BUSINESS AND SUPPLIER DIVERSITY DEPARTMENT.
Department of treasury.
Disbursement from state treasury, §§2.2-1819 to 2.2-1827.
Division of risk management, §§2.2-1832 to 2.2-1843.
Generally, §§2.2-1800 to 2.2-1812.
See STATE TREASURER.
Revenue stabilization fund, §§2.2-1828 to 2.2-1831.
State depositories.
Deposit of money paid into state treasury, §§2.2-1813 to 2.2-1818.
Discrimination.
Human rights act, §§2.2-3900 to 2.2-3903.
Employment and training department.
See GOVERNOR'S EMPLOYMENT AND TRAINING DEPARTMENT.
Executive reorganization, §§2.2-127 to 2.2-133.
Foundations.
See FOUNDATIONS.
Freedom of information act, §§2.2-3700 to 2.2-3714.
See FREEDOM OF INFORMATION.
General provisions regarding state agencies and general operation of government, §§2.2-600 to 2.2-614.3.
See STATE DEPARTMENTS AND AGENCIES.
Government performance and results act, §§2.2-5510, 2.2-5511.
Governor.
Generally, §§2.2-100 to 2.2-135.
See GOVERNOR.
Governor's secretaries, §§2.2-200 to 2.2-229.
Human rights act, §§2.2-3900 to 2.2-3903.
Implementation of federal mandates act, §§2.2-615 to 2.2-619.
Information technologies agency, §§2.2-2005 to 2.2-2031.
See INFORMATION TECHNOLOGIES AGENCY.
Secretary of the Commonwealth.
Generally, §§2.2-400 to 2.2-410.
See SECRETARY OF THE COMMONWEALTH.
Social security numbers, protection, §§2.2-3815, 2.2-3816.
State officers and employees.
Conflict of interests.
State and local government generally, §§2.2-3100 to 2.2-3127.
See PUBLIC OFFICERS AND EMPLOYEES.
Fraud and abuse whistleblower protection act, §§2.2-3009 to 2.2-3014.
See WHISTLEBLOWING.
Generally, §§2.2-2800 to 2.2-2831.
See PUBLIC OFFICERS AND EMPLOYEES.
Grievance procedure, §§2.2-3000 to 2.2-3008.
See PUBLIC OFFICERS AND EMPLOYEES.
Termination or layoffs from employment with Commonwealth.
Workforce transition act of 1995, §§2.2-3200 to 2.2-3206.
See PUBLIC OFFICERS AND EMPLOYEES.
Virginia personnel act.
Personnel administration system generally, §§2.2-2900 to 2.2-2905.
See PUBLIC OFFICERS AND EMPLOYEES.

ORGANIZATION OF STATE GOVERNMENT —Cont'd
Strategic plans.
Development and maintenance, §2.2-5510.
Review, §2.2-5511.
Veterans services department, §§2.2-2000 to 2.2-2004.
See VETERANS SERVICES DEPARTMENT.
Volunteers in state service.
State government volunteers act, §§2.2-3600 to 2.2-3605.

ORIENTAL DARTS.
See MARTIAL ARTS WEAPONS.

ORIGINALS.
Best evidence rule exceptions.
See BEST EVIDENCE RULE EXCEPTIONS.
Docketing or recording of writings, §55-108.
Use of copies admitted elsewhere, §55-109.
West Virginia court records, §55-110.

ORPHANED LANDS, §§45.1-197.3 to 45.1-197.7.
See SURFACE MINING.

ORPHANED WELL FUND, §45.1-361.40.

ORTHOPEDIC APPLIANCES.
Retail sales and use tax exemption, §58.1-609.10.

ORTHOTIC APPLIANCES.
Workers' compensation.
Medical attention to be furnished, §65.2-603.

OSTEOPATHIC MEDICINE.
Indigent patient programs offered by pharmaceutical manufacturers.
Practitioner of medicine or osteopathy participating in, §54.1-3301.
Licensing generally, §§54.1-2900 to 54.1-2993.
See MEDICINE AND OTHER HEALING ARTS PROFESSIONS.

OTTER.
Defined, §29.1-100.

OUSTER.
Ejectment generally, §§8.01-131 to 8.01-165.
See EJECTMENT.
Landlord and tenant, §§55-225.2, 55-248.26.

OUSTER PROCEEDINGS AGAINST LOCAL TREASURERS.
Institution of proceedings by governor, §58.1-3164.
Substitute, appointment of, §58.1-3165.
Continuance in office upon removal of predecessor, §58.1-3166.
Suspension of officer proceeded against, §58.1-3165.

OUTDOOR ADVERTISING, §§33.1-351 to 33.1-381.
Abatement of nuisance, §33.1-375.
Administration by commissioner, §33.1-352.
Advertiser's license.
Bond required for out-of-state licensee, §33.1-359.
Disposition of fees, §33.1-376.
Expiration, §33.1-356.
Judicial review of revocation, §33.1-358.
Out-of-state licensee, §33.1-359.
Renewal fee, §33.1-356.
Required, §33.1-356.
Revocation, §§33.1-357, 33.1-358.
Transferability, §33.1-367.

OUTDOOR ADVERTISING —Cont'd
Advertising structures.
Defined, §33.1-351.
Identification, §33.1-368.
Prohibitions, §33.1-369.
Rocks, stones, trees, etc., §33.1-373.
Agreements for enforcement and collection of penalties, §33.1-375.1.
Alcoholic beverages.
Compliance with transportation department integrated directional sign program and outdoor advertising provisions, §4.1-113.1.
Limitations on placement locations, §4.1-112.2.
Notice of violation, penalty for failure to take corrective action, §4.1-320.
Regulation of outdoor advertising by ABC board, §4.1-111.
Area of advertising structure, §33.1-363.
Exempted advertising structures, §33.1-355.
Construction of article, §33.1-378.
Definitions, §33.1-351.
Display, use, etc., permits.
Appeal from refusal or renewal, §33.1-366.
Application, §33.1-361.
Disposition of fees, §33.1-376.
Duration, §33.1-362.
Fees, §§33.1-361, 33.1-362.
Off-premises sign, etc., §33.1-360.
Renewal, §33.1-362.
Required, §33.1-360.
Revocation, §§33.1-364, 33.1-366.
Temporary permit, §33.1-365.
Transferability, §33.1-367.
Disposition of fees, §33.1-376.
Enforcement by commissioner, §33.1-352.
Exempt signs and advertising structures, §33.1-355.
False and misleading signs, §§33.1-379 to 33.1-381.
Penalty, §33.1-380.
Prohibition, §33.1-379.
Removal, §33.1-381.
Federal-aid primary highways.
Special provisions, §§33.1-370, 33.1-371.
Fees.
License fees, §33.1-356.
Permit fees, §33.1-361.
Selective pruning permits, §33.1-371.1.
Highway billboard signs.
Adjustment or relocation, §33.1-95.2.
Interstate highways.
Special provisions, §§33.1-370, 33.1-371.
Liberal construction of article, §33.1-378.
National highway system.
Special provisions, §§33.1-370, 33.1-371.
Nonconforming billboard signs.
Maintenance and repair, §33.1-370.2.
Personal property taxes.
Classification of tangible personal property, §58.1-3503.
Posting advertisements, §33.1-372.
Prohibited advertisements and structures, §33.1-369.
Pruning of vegetation that obstructs motorist view of signs.
Selective pruning permits, §33.1-371.1.
Public policy, §33.1-351.
Recordation tax, state.
Limit on amount for outdoor advertising sign, §58.1-807.

OUTDOOR ADVERTISING —Cont'd
Removal of signs.
Violations, §33.1-377.1.
Right of entry upon land.
Hindering commissioner or agent, §33.1-354.
Rocks, poles, etc., advertising on, §33.1-373.
Agreement for enforcement and collection of penalties and cost, §33.1-375.1.
Rulemaking authority, §§33.1-371, 33.1-374.
Selective pruning permits, §33.1-371.1.
Special provisions.
Interstate highway system, §§33.1-370, 33.1-371.
State preemption, §33.1-374.
Temporary permits, §33.1-365.
Territorial jurisdiction, §33.1-353.
Tree trimming.
Policies to be developed, §33.1-84.1.
Violations of article.
Abatement of nuisance, §33.1-375.
False or misleading signs, §§33.1-379 to 33.1-381.
Penalty, §33.1-377.1.

OUTDOOR DRAMAS.
Official outdoor dramas of Commonwealth, §1-510.

OUTDOOR LIGHTING.
Locality regulating near certain facilities, §15.2-920.
State public bodies.
Purchase of shielded outdoor light fixtures, §2.2-1111.

OUTDOOR MOTOR SPORTS ROAD RACING CLUB.
Mixed beverage license, §4.1-410.
Fee, §§4.1-231, 4.1-233.

OUTDOOR PERFORMING ARTS AMPHITHEATERS.
Food concessions.
Beer and wine licenses, §4.1-208.
On-premises licenses, §4.1-209.
Mixed beverage license, §4.1-210.
Fee, §§4.1-231, 4.1-233.

OUTDOOR RECREATION.
Acquisition of property, §10.1-208.
Certain counties regulating persons and traffic, §15.2-1220.
Cooperation of departments, §10.1-207.
Department of conservation and recreation to establish long-range plan, §10.1-200.
Recreational use of land, §10.1-208.
Timber and agricultural use of land, §10.1-208.

OUTDOORS FOUNDATION, §§10.1-1800 to 10.1-1804.
Administration, §10.1-1800.
Cooperation of state agencies, §10.1-1804.
Employee retirement, §51.1-126.7.
Establishment, §10.1-1800.
Farmland preservation office.
Cooperative development with, §3.2-201.
Gifts, §10.1-1803.
Open-space easements.
Fee for recording, §58.1-817.
Open-space lands preservation trust fund, §10.1-1801.1.
Powers, §10.1-1801.
Reports, §10.1-1802.
Taxation, §10.1-1803.
Virginia retirement system, §51.1-126.7.

OUTLAWRY.
Abolished, §19.2-10.

OUTPUT CONTRACTS.
Sales, UCC, §8.2-306.

OVA DONORS, HIV TESTS, §32.1-45.3.

OVARIAN CANCER.
Clinical trials.
Public officers and employees.
Required health insurance coverage, §2.2-2818.
Workers' compensation.
Presumption as to death or disability, §65.2-402.

OVERCROWDED PRISONS.
Incarceration in jails.
Compensation, §53.1-20.1.

OVERDRAFTS.
Bank deposits and collections.
Charging account of customer, §8.4-401.
Banks.
By directors, §6.2-877.
Electronic funds transfer rejected for insufficient funds.
Rights and remedies from bad check law applicable, §§8.01-27.1, 8.01-27.2.
Savings institutions.
Overdrafts by directors, §6.2-1129.

OVERHEAD ELECTRICAL LINE CONSTRUCTION.
Notice and determination by state corporation commission, §56-46.1.

OVERHEAD HIGH VOLTAGE LINE SAFETY, §§59.1-406 to 59.1-414.
Application of provisions, §59.1-414.
Defined terms, §59.1-407.
Enforcement of provisions, §59.1-412.
Exemption from provisions, §59.1-413.
Prohibited conduct, §59.1-408.
Scope of provisions, §59.1-406.
Temporary safety arrangements, §59.1-410.
Notice requirements, §59.1-411.
Warning signs, §59.1-409.

OVER INVOICE.
Motorcycle dealers advertising, §46.2-1993.81.

OVERRIDING VETO OF GOVERNOR.
Vote required, VA Const Art V §6.

OVERTAKING AND PASSING.
Motor vehicles generally, §§46.2-837 to 46.2-844.
See TRAFFIC INFRACTIONS.

OVER-THE-COUNTER MEDICINES.
Adulteration, §18.2-54.2.
Attempts to poison, §18.2-54.1.

OVERTHROW OF GOVERNMENT.
Advocating change by force, violence or other unlawful means, §18.2-484.
Emergency management organization employment.
Persons advocating not to be employed or associated in, §44-146.25.

OVERTIME COMPENSATION.
Law-enforcement employees, firefighters and emergency medical technicians, §§9.1-700 to 9.1-706.

OVERWEIGHT PERMITS.
Motor vehicle size and weight.
Excessive size and weight permits, §§46.2-1139 to 46.2-1149.5.
See MOTOR VEHICLE SIZE AND WEIGHT.

OWLS.
Permits to take, hold and transport, §29.1-419.
Issuance, §29.1-413.
By whom, §29.1-420.
Required, §29.1-412.
Removal of transmitting device from dog, falcon, hawk or owl, §18.2-97.1.
Right to go on land of another to retrieve falcon, hawk or owl, §18.2-136.

OWN RECOGNIZANCE.
Release on unsecured bond or promise to appear, §19.2-123.

OX ACTIVITY LIABILITY, §§3.2-6300 to 3.2-6302.
Actions prohibited, §3.2-6301.
Definitions, §3.2-6300.
Limited liability, §3.2-6301.
Ox activity sponsors, §3.2-6302.
Ox professionals, §3.2-6302.

OXYGENATED GASOLINE.
Rules and regulations regarding, §59.1-156.

OXYGEN SOURCES, HEALTH CARE FACILITIES.
Smoking, §18.2-511.1.

OYSTER PLANTING GROUNDS, §§28.2-600 to 28.2-650.
Aquaculture opportunity zones, §28.2-603.1.
Assignments, §28.2-625.
General oyster-planting grounds, §§28.2-603 to 28.2-622. See within this heading, "General oyster-planting grounds."
Riparian oyster-planting grounds, §§28.2-600 to 28.2-602.
Boundary oyster stakes.
Removal, §28.2-561.
Buoys.
Removal, §28.2-561.
Channel dredging.
Gubernatorial authority to authorize, §28.2-638.
Chesapeake Bay.
Public oyster rocks, beds, and shoals declared, §28.2-643.
Condemnation, §28.2-628.
Condemnation of oyster bottoms and grounds by locality, §15.2-1902.
Conflict of laws, §28.2-649.
Crassostrea ariakesis.
Placement in state-owned bottomlands, §28.2-826.
Dredging.
Equipment on boats, §28.2-516.
Marked ground, §28.2-517.
Ocean side of Eastern Shore, §28.2-519.
Private grounds, §28.2-515.
Eminent domain.
Condemnation of oyster bottoms and grounds by locality, §15.2-1902.
General oyster-planting grounds, §§28.2-603 to 28.2-622.
Aquaculture opportunity zones, §28.2-603.1.
Assignments.
Applications, §28.2-605.
Eligibility, §28.2-604.
Lapses, §28.2-609.
Posting of notice of application, §28.2-606.
Chesapeake Bay acreage, §28.2-611.
Consolidations, §28.2-622.
Duration, §28.2-613.
Fees, §28.2-608.
Ground becoming vacant, §28.2-619.

OYSTER PLANTING GROUNDS —Cont'd
General oyster-planting grounds —Cont'd
Assignments —Cont'd
Marking of ground, §28.2-607.
Navigation projects.
Effect of proposal, §28.2-621.
Preferences, §28.2-616.
Renewal, §28.2-613.
Rent, §28.2-612.
Delinquent ground, §28.2-620.
Restrictions, §§28.2-609, 28.2-610.
Rights of assignees, §28.2-618.
Rights of riparian owners to build bulkheads or wharves, §28.2-630.
Surveys, §28.2-607.
Resurveys, §§28.2-614, 28.2-615.
Transfers, §28.2-613.
Temporary enclosures on leased ground, §28.2-603.1.
Notice requirement, §28.2-603.2.
Use, §28.2-603.
Hill's Bay.
Public oyster rocks, beds, and shoals declared, §§28.2-641, 28.2-642.
Hole in the Wall.
Public oyster rocks, beds, and shoals declared, §28.2-644.
Lynnhaven river.
Excusing rent payment on condemned oyster grounds, §28.2-623.
Maps, §28.2-562.
Mobjack Bay.
Public oyster rocks, beds, and shoals declared, §§28.2-640, 28.2-648.
Natural beds held in trust for benefit of people, VA Const Art XI §3.
Nonresident planting or taking, §28.2-634.
Permits.
Private, noncommercial piers traversing, §28.2-1205.
Joint application and review process.
Coordinated review water resources projects, §28.2-1205.1.
Piankatank river.
Public oyster rocks, beds and shoals declared, §28.2-646.
Pocomoke Sound.
Public oyster rocks, beds and shoals declared, §28.2-644.
Poquoson river.
Public oyster rocks, beds and shoals declared, §28.2-647.
Posts.
Removal, §28.2-561.
Public rocks.
Use or staking off, §28.2-624.
Raking.
Ocean side of Eastern Shore, §28.2-519.
Range monuments.
Removal, §28.2-561.
Rappahannock river.
Declaration of public oyster rocks, beds and shoals, §28.2-639.
Leasing prohibitions, §28.2-636.
Removal of oysters planted by mistake, §28.2-559.
Rent paid under mistake.
Refund, §28.2-626.
Rent relief, §28.2-627.
Residents not to be associated with nonresidents, §28.2-635.

OYSTER PLANTING GROUNDS —Cont'd
Riparian oyster-planting grounds, §§28.2-600 to 28.2-602.
Assignments.
Eligibility, §28.2-600.
Entitlements, §28.2-601.
Fees, §28.2-600.
Obligations, §28.2-601.
Recordation, §28.2-600.
Special terms and conditions, §28.2-602.
Surveys, §28.2-600.
Rights of owners to build bulkheads or wharves, §28.2-630.
Riparian rights, §§28.2-629, 28.2-630.
Scraping.
Marked ground, §28.2-517.
Ocean side of Eastern Shore, §28.2-519.
Private grounds, §28.2-515.
Signal beacons.
Removal, §28.2-561.
Surveys.
Removal of oysters planted by mistake, §28.2-559.
Resurveys, §28.2-552.
Transfers, §28.2-625.
General oyster planting grounds, §28.2-613.
Riparian oyster planting grounds, §28.2-601.

OYSTER POINT DEVELOPMENT CORPORATION.
Created, 1972 ch 726.
Amended in 1976, 1976 ch 524.
Amended in 1979, 1979 ch 285.
Amended in 1980, 1980 ch 46.
Amended in 1987, 1987 ch 58.
Amended in 1988, 1988 ch 717.
Amended in 1992, 1992 ch 233.
Amended in 1993, 1993 ch 682.

OYSTERS AND CLAMS, §§28.2-500 to 28.2-562.
Area restrictions, §28.2-524.
Boundary oyster stakes.
Removal, §28.2-561.
Buoys.
Removal, §28.2-561.
Chesapeake Bay restrictions, §§28.2-524, 28.2-525.
Clam planting grounds, §§28.2-631, 28.2-632.
Crab dredging boats.
Oyster possession limitations, §28.2-533.
Crassostrea ariakesis.
Planting in state-owned bottomlands, §28.2-826.
Culled oysters.
Penalty, §28.2-511.
Prima facie evidence of culling violations, §28.2-513.
Damages to oyster and clamming grounds.
Improvement of navigability of streams.
Claims for damages, §62.1-158.
Dredge contracts, §28.2-550.
Dredge license or permit revocation, §28.2-521.
Dredges, hydraulic.
Use, §28.2-520.
Dredging by boat, §28.2-516.
Dredging equipment on boat, §28.2-516.
Dredging in the James river, §28.2-518.
Dredging or scraping marked ground, §28.2-517.
Dredging or scraping on private ground, §28.2-515.
Dredging, scraping or raking on ocean side of Eastern Shore, §28.2-519.

OYSTERS AND CLAMS —Cont'd
Fees.
Oyster resource user fees, §28.2-541.
Fines, uniform schedule, VA SCt Rules 3C:1, 3C:2.
Fishing, tidal waters generally.
See FISHING, TIDAL WATERS.
Grants.
Oyster growers transferring oysters to sanctuary, §28.2-201.1.
Growers transferring oysters to sanctuary.
Grant eligibility, §28.2-201.1.
Health and sanitation provisions generally, §§28.2-800 to 28.2-826.
See FISHING, TIDAL WATERS.
Inspection duties of officers, §28.2-548.
Inspection interferences, §28.2-512.
Inspections when loaded on conveyance or sold, §28.2-547.
Labels, §28.2-532.
Larceny, §28.2-560.
Licenses, §§28.2-500 to 28.2-505.
Applications, §28.2-501.
Dredging equipment on boat, §28.2-516.
Fees, §28.2-502.
Packing or shucking, §28.2-504.
Residency requirements, §28.2-500.
Revocation, §28.2-521.
Theft, §28.2-528.
Taking with tongs, §28.2-503.
Maps, §28.2-562.
Maturity requirement, §28.2-532.
Natural oyster beds held in trust for benefit of people, VA Const Art XI §3.
Issuance of grants, §28.2-1200.
Night taking or loading restrictions, §§28.2-530, 28.2-531.
Oyster growing activities fund, §28.2-201.1.
Oyster planting grounds, §§28.2-600 to 28.2-650.
See OYSTER PLANTING GROUNDS.
Oyster resource user fees, §28.2-541.
Failure to pay, §28.2-549.
Patent tongs.
Area restrictions, §28.2-508.
Penalty for violations, §28.2-523.
Possession.
Out of season.
Prima facie evidence of violation, §28.2-506.
Teeth length, §28.2-509.
Weight restrictions, §28.2-508.
Permit to carry oysters out of state, §28.2-546.
Polluted grounds.
Health and sanitation provisions generally, §§28.2-800 to 28.2-826.
See FISHING, TIDAL WATERS.
Possession of oysters out of season while taking clams, §28.2-534.
Posts.
Removal, §28.2-561.
Potomac river compact.
Authority to regulate dredging, §§28.2-1003, 28.2-1005.
Experimental oyster hatchery program, §28.2-1004.
Possession, marketing and disposal of shellfish out of commission's jurisdiction, §28.2-1006.
Provision violations, §28.2-549.
Penalty, §28.2-523.
Prima facie evidence, §28.2-522.
Public rocks.
Closing, §28.2-507.

OYSTERS AND CLAMS —Cont'd
Public rocks —Cont'd
Opening, §28.2-507.
Patent tongs.
Restrictions, §28.2-508.
Seasons for taking, §28.2-506.
Purchasing oysters from catcher.
License fee, §28.2-228.
Range monuments.
Removal, §28.2-561.
Records, §28.2-538.
Replenishment fund, §28.2-542.
Reports.
Conclusive evidence, §28.2-551.
Seasons for taking from public rocks, §28.2-506.
Seed oysters.
Permit to buy or carry, §28.2-535.
Shells.
Conversion into lime, §28.2-529.
Sales, §28.2-505.
Shucked oyster possession limitations, §28.2-514.
Signal beacons.
Removal, §28.2-561.
Size restrictions, §28.2-537.
Standards of measure, §28.2-526.
Sunday taking or loading restrictions, §§28.2-530, 28.2-531.
Surf clams.
Enforcement of regulations, §28.2-201.
Surveyors, §28.2-557.
Surveys.
Baylor survey.
Crossings, §28.2-555.
Erosion control devices, §28.2-556.
Reestablishment of lines, §§28.2-552, 28.2-553.
Removal of oysters planted by mistake, §28.2-559.
Sale of charts and plats, §28.2-554.
Conclusive evidence, §28.2-551.
Maps, §28.2-562.
Marker removal, §28.2-561.
Permanent markers, §28.2-558.
Resurveys, §28.2-552.
Removal of oysters planted by mistake, §28.2-559.
Taking restrictions, §28.2-536.
Theft, §28.2-527.
Transfer of grown oysters to sanctuary.
Grant eligibility, §28.2-201.1.
Unculled oysters.
Buying, selling or possessing, §28.2-510.
Interfering with inspections, §28.2-512.
Uniform fine schedule, VA SCt Rules 3C:1, 3C:2.
Vehicles transporting oyster shells.
Exemption from motor vehicle registration, §46.2-680.

OYSTER SHELL.
Official shell of Commonwealth, §1-511.

P

PACKAGING OF DRUGS, §54.1-3427.

PACKING APPLES FOR SALE, §§3.2-4502 to 3.2-4504.

PACKINGHOUSES.
Sanitary requirements for food establishments, §§3.2-5105 to 3.2-5119.
See FOOD.

PAC'S.
Campaign finance disclosure generally.
See CAMPAIGN FINANCE DISCLOSURE.

PADLOCKING BUSINESS ENTERPRISES.
Collection of delinquent state taxes, §58.1-1805.

PAGE COUNTY.
Cabin capital of Virginia.
Official designation, §1-510.
Dirt and gravel roads.
Maximum speed limits on nonsurface treated highways, §46.2-873.1.
Industrial development authority.
Board of supervisors.
Appointment of members to board of authority, §15.2-4904.
Minerals.
Presumed to exist in certain lands, §55-154.
Suits to extinguish claim or right, §55-155.
Port of Virginia economic and infrastructure development zone grant fund, §62.1-132.3:2.
Public defenders office.
Established, §19.2-163.04.
Revolutionary war cemeteries and graves.
Disbursement of funds appropriated for upkeep, §10.1-2211.1.
School board.
Salary of members, §22.1-32.
Transient occupancy tax.
Disposition of revenues, §58.1-3819.

PAGERS.
Annoying calls.
Causing pager to ring with intent to annoy, §18.2-429.
Insurance.
Portable electronics insurance, §§38.2-1875 to 38.2-1880.

PAGING COMPANIES.
Unlawful electronic communication devices, §§18.2-190.1 to 18.2-190.8.

PAID-UP NONFORFEITURE BENEFITS.
Standard nonforfeiture provisions for life insurance generally, §§38.2-3200 to 38.2-3229.
See LIFE INSURANCE.

PAIN RELIEF.
Physical therapists.
Administration of certain topical drugs, §54.1-3408.
Prescribing drug dosage in excess of recommended dosage.
Medical necessity, §54.1-3408.1.

PAINT.
Lead-based paint, §36-107.1.
Marine antifoulant paints, §§3.2-3935 to 3.2-3937.

PAINTBALL GUNS.
Local regulation, §15.2-915.4.

PAINTINGS.
Locality acquiring and housing, §15.2-945.

PALEONTOLOGY.
Cave protection, §§10.1-1000 to 10.1-1008.
See CAVE PROTECTION.

PALMISTRY PRACTITIONERS.
License tax, §58.1-3726.

PAMPHLETS.
Hearsay exception.
Opinion testimony by experts, §8.01-401.1.

PAMUNKEY INDIAN TRIBE.
Motor vehicle sales and use tax exemption, §58.1-2403.

PAN AMERICAN GAMES.
Athletic leaves of absence for state employees, §2.2-124.

PANCREATIC CANCER.
Presumption as to death or disability.
Firefighters, §65.2-402.

PANDERING, §18.2-355.
Pimping.
See PIMPING.

PANEL TRUCKS.
Defined, §46.2-100.
Motor vehicle license plates.
Exemption from displaying for-hire license plates, §46.2-711.
Motor vehicle registration.
Additional fee, §46.2-694.

PANHANDLING.
Solicitation of contributions on highways, public roadways, medians.
Localities and VDOT may prohibit or regulate, §46.2-931.

PANIC DISORDER.
Health insurance.
Coverage for biologically based mental illness, §38.2-3412.1:01.
Public officers and employees.
Required coverage, §2.2-2818.

PAPER AND PAPER PRODUCTS.
Recycled paper and paper products.
Preference for purchase by locality, §15.2-938.
Surplus state materials, disposition.
Recycling encouraged, §2.2-1124.

PAPER ROUTES.
Child labor, §40.1-109.

PAP SMEARS.
Health insurance, §38.2-3418.1:2.
Public officers and employees.
Required coverage, §2.2-2818.

PARACHUTE JUMP TRAINING SCHOOLS.
Disclosure of liability insurance coverage, §5.1-88.6.

PARADES.
Equine activity liability generally, §§3.2-6200 to 3.2-6203.

PARAMEDICS.
AIDS exposure.
Deemed consent to release of test results, §32.1-45.1.
Anatomical gifts.
Search of individual for document of gift, §32.1-291.12.
Child abuse or neglect.
Persons required to report, §63.2-1509.
Communicable disease reporting, §32.1-116.3.
Hepatitis.
Exposure to body fluids.
Deemed consent to release of test results, §32.1-45.1.
Hepatitis, meningitis, tuberculosis and HIV.
Workers' compensation.
Presumption on death or disability from, §65.2-402.1.

PARAMEDICS —Cont'd
Influenza vaccine, administration to minors, §32.1-46.02.

PARAMILITARY ACTIVITY UNLAWFUL, §§18.2-433.1 to 18.2-433.3.
Applicability of article.
Exceptions, §18.2-433.3.
Definition, §18.2-433.1.
Exceptions to article, §18.2-433.3.
Prohibited activities generally, §18.2-433.2.

PARAPHERNALIA, DRUGS.
See DRUG PARAPHERNALIA.

PARASAIL OPERATORS.
Regulation, promulgation, §29.1-735.3.

PARCEL CHECKING MACHINES.
License tax on coin machine operators.
Exemption of operators, §58.1-3721.

PARCEL IDENTIFICATION NUMBER.
Circuit court clerk indexing by, §17.1-252.

PARCEL SERVICES.
State departments and agencies.
Division of support services, general services department, §2.2-1169.

PARCENERS.
Waste, §55-212.

PARDON.
Absolute pardon.
Expungement of criminal records, §19.2-392.2.
Commutation of capital punishment, §53.1-230.
Execution of death sentences, §53.1-232.
Executive clemency.
Commutation of capital punishment, §53.1-230.
Investigation of cases for executive clemency by parole board, §53.1-231.
Powers vested in governor, §53.1-229.
Expungement of criminal records.
Absolute pardon, §19.2-392.2.
Governor's power, VA Const Art V §12.
President, US Const Art II §2.

PARENS PATRIAE.
Governor instituting action or suit in name of Commonwealth, §2.2-111.

PARENTAGE PROCEEDINGS.
Generally, §§20-49.1 to 20-49.10.
See PATERNITY PROCEEDINGS.

PARENTAL ABDUCTION, §18.2-49.1.
Abduction punishable as contempt in pending proceedings, §18.2-47.
Seizure and forfeiture of property used in connection with abduction, §19.2-386.32.

PARENTAL CARE, CHILDREN WITHOUT.
Disposition to protect welfare of child, §16.1-278.2.
Juvenile proceedings generally, §§16.1-246 to 16.1-309.1.
See JUVENILE PROCEEDINGS.

PARENTAL CONSENT.
Blood donation by minors, §54.1-2969.
Hepatitis B or C exposure incident.
School employee exposed to or exposing others.
Testing of minors, §32.1-45.1.
HIV exposure incident.
School employee exposed to or exposing others.
Testing minor, §32.1-45.1.

PARENTAL CONSENT —Cont'd
Judicial consent in lieu of, when authorized, §16.1-278.12.
Juvenile and domestic relations district court jurisdiction, §16.1-241.
Marriage, minimum age, §20-48.
Medical or surgical procedures on minors, §54.1-2969.
Psychiatric inpatient treatment of minors, §§16.1-338, 16.1-339.
Underage marriage, §§20-48, 20-49.

PARENTAL LIABILITY FOR DAMAGE BY MINOR.
Minor operating vehicle, §8.01-64.
Defense of lack of consent of owner, §8.01-65.
Private property, §8.01-44.
Public property, §8.01-43.

PARENTAL NOTIFICATION.
Abortion.
Judicial authorization without notifying parents.
Jurisdiction of juvenile and domestic relations court, §16.1-241.
Psychiatric treatment of minors.
Parental notification of information regarding minor's health care, §16.1-337.

PARENTAL PLACEMENT ADOPTION.
Birth parent or legal guardian placing directly with adoptive parents.
See ADOPTION.

PARENTAL RELIEF OF CARE AND CUSTODY OF CHILD.
Juvenile proceedings generally, §§16.1-246 to 16.1-309.1.
See JUVENILE PROCEEDINGS.
Trespass after having been forbidden to do so, §§18.2-119, 18.2-120.

PARENTAL RESPONSIBILITY AND INVOLVEMENT.
Enforcing standards of student conduct and attendance, §22.1-279.3.

PARENTAL RIGHTS TERMINATION.
See TERMINATION OF PARENTAL RIGHTS.

PARENT AND CHILD.
Actions.
Suit by either or both parents on behalf of minor as his next friend, §8.01-8.
Amusement device rider safety.
Duties of parent or guardian, §59.1-521.
Anatomical gifts.
Actions permitted by parent of minor after minor's death, §32.1-291.8.
Reasonable search for parents of unemancipated minor, §32.1-291.14.
Who may make gift of body or body part of decedent, §32.1-291.9.
Who may make gift prior to donor's death, §32.1-291.4.
Birth-related neurological injury compensation.
Notification of possible beneficiaries, §38.2-5004.1.
Construction of statutes.
Rights of parents to make decisions concerning upbringing, education and care of child, §1-240.1.
Disclaimer of property interests.
Parent's power to disclaim for minor child, §64.2-2009.

PARENT AND CHILD —Cont'd
Establishment of relationship to determine succession or taking by, through or from person, §64.2-102.
Immunization of child.
Required immunizations, duty of child, §32.1-46.
Internet access by child.
Denial by parent or legal guardian.
Not considered computer trespass, §18.2-152.4.
Partial birth infanticide.
Mother not to be prosecuted, §18.2-71.1.
Representation.
Persons representing and binding others, §§64.2-714 to 64.2-718.
Suicide.
Student at imminent risk of suicide.
Parental contact by public school, §22.1-272.1.

PARENT AS NATURAL GUARDIAN OF CHILDREN, §64.2-1700.

PARENTING EDUCATION CLASSES.
Requirement in child custody disputes, §16.1-278.15.

PARENT'S DERIVATIVE ACTION FOR TORT TO INFANT, §8.01-36.

PARENTS OF UNDISCIPLINED CHILDREN.
Proceedings against, §16.1-241.2.

PARENTS SUPPORT BY CHILDREN, §20-88.

PARENT-TEACHER ASSOCIATIONS.
Advisory board on teacher education and licensure.
One member to be member of a parent-teacher association, §22.1-305.2.

PARI-MUTUEL WAGERING, §§59.1-364 to 59.1-405.
Administration of drugs or devices.
Prohibited conduct, §59.1-400.
Advance deposit account wagering.
Defined, §59.1-365.
Alcohol and drug testing of personnel, §59.1-369.
Attempts to commit violations of provisions.
Prohibited conduct, §59.1-405.
Audits, §59.1-394.
Award of prize money not deemed to be part of gaming contract, §59.1-364.
Background investigations, §59.1-371.
Bribery.
Prohibited conduct, §59.1-399.
Campaign contributions.
Licensees, §59.1-375.
Limited licensees, §59.1-376.
Conspiracies.
Prohibited conduct, §59.1-405.
Contracts for purses and prizes, §59.1-369.
Defined terms, §59.1-365.
Drug possession.
Prohibited conduct, §59.1-401.
Ejection or exclusion from enclosure.
Persons reflecting on honesty and integrity of racing, §59.1-369.
Exemption from gambling article, §18.2-334.4.
Fees.
Permits, §59.1-388.
Fingerprinting, §59.1-371.
Gamblers anonymous or other organization.
Hosting toll-free telephone number for, §59.1-369.
Gaming contracts.
Award of prize money not deemed to be part of, §59.1-364.

PARI-MUTUEL WAGERING —Cont'd
Injunctions, §59.1-374.
Inspection of personnel and personal property by racing commission, §59.1-369.
Licenses, §§59.1-375 to 59.1-386.
ABC equine event licenses.
Authorized conduct, §4.1-206.
Local license taxes, §4.1-233.
State license fees, §4.1-231.
Acquisition of interest in licensee, §59.1-386.
Applications, §59.1-377.
Approval, §59.1-378.
Denial, §59.1-378.
Corporations, §59.1-379.
Hearings and appeals, §§59.1-373, 59.1-384.
Operator's licenses, §59.1-381.
Conducted pari-mutuel wagering without license, §59.1-395.
Corporations.
Refusal, §59.1-379.
Duration, §59.1-380.
Operator's license, §59.1-383.
Fraudulent use of credential, §59.1-396.
Issuance, §59.1-378.
Operator's license, §59.1-382.
Limited licenses, §59.1-376.
Operator's license.
Acquisition of interest in licensee, §59.1-386.
Application, §59.1-381.
Denial.
Appeals, §§59.1-373, 59.1-384.
Duration, §59.1-383.
Form, §59.1-383.
Issuance, §59.1-382.
Surety bonds, §59.1-383.
Renewal.
Denial.
Corporations, §59.1-379.
Required, §59.1-375.
Revocation, §59.1-385.
Fraudulent use of credential, §59.1-396.
Hearings and appeals, §59.1-373.
Steeplechase facilities, §59.1-378.1.
Surety bonds, §59.1-380.
Operator's license, §59.1-383.
Suspension, §59.1-385.
Hearings and appeals, §59.1-373.
License tax, limitation on gross receipts, §58.1-3732.1.
Live horse racing compact, §§59.1-394.1 to 59.1-394.4.
Compact committee.
Established, §59.1-394.1.
Members, §59.1-394.2.
Powers and duties, §59.1-394.1.
Cooperation of departments, agencies and officers, §59.1-394.3.
Racing commission.
Effect on powers, §59.1-394.4.
Terms of compact, §59.1-394.1.
Local referendum, §59.1-391.
Minors, wagering by.
Prohibited conduct, §59.1-403.
Permits, §§59.1-387 to 59.1-390.
Applications, §59.1-388.
Consideration of, §59.1-389.
Denial.
Hearings and appeals, §59.1-373.
Duration, §59.1-389.
Expiration automatically on holders leaving employment of licensee, §59.1-389.

PARI-MUTUEL WAGERING —Cont'd
Permits —Cont'd
Fees, §59.1-388.
Required, §59.1-387.
Revocation, §59.1-390.
Hearings and appeals, §59.1-373.
Summary suspension, §59.1-390.
Suspension, §59.1-390.
Hearings and appeals, §59.1-373.
Summary suspension, §59.1-390.
Transferability, §59.1-387.
Prohibited conduct.
Administration of drugs or devices, §59.1-400.
Attempts to commit violations of provisions, §59.1-405.
Bribery, §59.1-399.
Conspiracies, §59.1-405.
Drug possession, §59.1-401.
Fraudulent use of credential, §59.1-396.
Minors, wagering by, §59.1-403.
Racing under false name, §59.1-402.
Touting, §59.1-398.
Unlawful conduct of wagering, §59.1-395.
Unlawful transmission of information, §59.1-397.
Public assistance.
Temporary assistance for needy families (TANF).
Prohibited uses of benefits, §63.2-621.
Racing commission, §§59.1-364 to 59.1-374.
Background investigations, §59.1-371.
Campaign contributions, §§59.1-368, 59.1-370.
Conflicts of interest, §59.1-368.
Control, §59.1-364.
Creation, §59.1-366.
Duties, §59.1-369.
Executive secretary, §59.1-370.
Fingerprinting, §59.1-371.
Hearings, §59.1-373.
Injunctions, §59.1-374.
Legal representation, §59.1-367.
Licenses, §§59.1-375 to 59.1-386.
Steeplechase facilities, §59.1-378.1.
Local referendum, §59.1-391.
Members, §59.1-366.
Permits, §§59.1-387 to 59.1-390.
Powers, §59.1-369.
Staff, §59.1-370.
Steeplechase facilities.
Licensing, §59.1-378.1.
Transfers of meets, §59.1-376.
Virginia breeders fund, §59.1-372.
Racing under false name.
Prohibited conduct, §59.1-402.
Retainage by licensees, §59.1-392.
Simulcast horse racing.
Commission to promulgate regulations and conditions, §59.1-369.
Defined, §59.1-365.
State racing operations fund, §59.1-370.1.
Steeplechase facilities.
Licenses, §59.1-378.1.
Stewards.
Appointment by racing commission, §59.1-370.
Summary suspension of permits, §59.1-390.
Summary suspension of permits, §59.1-390.
Taxes.
Admissions tax, §59.1-393.
Percentage retained, §59.1-392.
Temporary assistance for needy families (TANF).
Prohibited uses of benefits, §63.2-621.

PARI-MUTUEL WAGERING —Cont'd
Touting.
Prohibited conduct, §59.1-398.
Transfers of meets, §59.1-376.
Virginia breeders fund, §59.1-372.
Wiretapping.
Court-ordered interception, §19.2-66.

PARK AND PLANNING DISTRICTS.
Northern Virginia park and planning district, 1930 ch 420, 1932 ch 338, 1938 ch 181.

PARK AUTHORITIES, §§15.2-5700 to 15.2-5714.
Applicability to all localities of Commonwealth, §15.2-5700.
Board, §15.2-5703.
Bonds, §§15.2-5712 to 15.2-5714.
Authority to issue, terms, conditions, etc., §15.2-5712.
Mutilated, lost or destroyed bonds, §15.2-5714.
Water and sewer systems, §15.2-5713.
Conservators of the peace.
Appointment of special conservator, §15.2-5706.
Contracts for park services, §15.2-5711.
Conveyance or lease of park to authority, §15.2-5711.
Creation, §15.2-5702.
Definitions, §15.2-5701.
Exemption from taxation, §15.2-5708.
Funds, §15.2-5710.
Joining authority, §15.2-5702.
Member of local governing body named to position, §15.2-1535.
Members, §15.2-5703.
Northern regional park authority, 1977 ch 64.
Ordinance or resolution creating, §15.2-5702.
Park authorities act.
Chapter known and cited as, §15.2-5700.
Powers, §15.2-5704.
Rates and charges, §15.2-5709.
Recordation of conveyances to authority, §15.2-5707.
Urban county executive form of government.
Establishing different terms for members, §15.2-824.
Violation of rules and regulations, §15.2-5705.
Water and sewer systems.
Bonds for, §15.2-5713.
Withdrawal from authority, §15.2-5702.

PARK COMMISSIONS.
Merrimac park commission, 1958 ch 618.

PARKING.
Advisory board.
Municipal regulation of towing fees, §46.2-1233.2.
Ambulances.
Parking near, §46.2-921.
Booting vehicles.
Immobilization of trespassing vehicles.
Regulation by localities, §46.2-1232.
Unsettled parking violations, removal or immobilization of vehicles, §46.2-1216.
Brakes, emergency or parking brakes, §§46.2-1068, 46.2-1071.
Buses.
Local ordinances regulating idling of engines, §46.2-1224.1.
Capitol Square, §46.2-1226.
Division of support services, duties, §2.2-1172.
Colleges and universities.
Enforcement of parking regulations of board of visitors, §46.2-1228.

PARKING —Cont'd
Colleges and universities —Cont'd
Rulemaking authority, §23-9.2:3.
Commuter parking lots owned by VDOT.
Parking not in conformance with signs and pavement markings.
Traffic infraction, §46.2-1219.2.
Contested or delinquent citations, §§46.2-1225 to 46.2-1229.
County, city or town powers.
Motor vehicle and traffic regulation generally, §§46.2-1300 to 46.2-1314.
See LOCAL GOVERNMENT.
Ordinances, §46.2-1225.
Parking within boundaries of state-supported institutions, §15.2-968.
Providing and operating places for parking or storage of vehicles, §15.2-1122.
Curb ramps, §46.2-1306.1.
Decal holders, §46.2-731.
Department of game and inland fisheries owned facilities or department-leased land.
Collection of parking fees, §§29.1-103, 29.1-113.
Restrictions, §29.1-113.
Disabled or handicapped persons, §§46.2-1240 to 46.2-1259.
See PARKING FOR DISABLED OR HANDICAPPED.
Disabled persons. See within this heading, "Handicapped parking spaces."
Driver's license.
Examination of applicants, §46.2-325.
Enforcement of regulations.
Board of visitors of educational institutions, §46.2-1228.
Capitol Square, §46.2-1226.
City or county parking ordinances, §46.2-1225.
State behavioral health and developmental services board, §46.2-1229.
State primary and secondary highways, §46.2-1227.
Fine schedule, VA SCt Rule 3B:2.
Maximum fine for violation of article, §46.2-113.
Fire apparatus, parking near, §46.2-921.
Fire hydrants, distance restrictions, §46.2-1306.
Free parking accommodations.
Liability for personal property left in vehicle, §46.2-1234.
Handicapped license plates, §§46.2-731, 46.2-739.
Handicapped parking spaces.
Holders of special plates or decals, §46.2-731.
Identification by above grade signage, §36-99.11.
Improper use, §46.2-731.
Headlights, dimming, §46.2-1035.
Hydrants.
Fire hydrant distance restrictions, §46.2-1306.
Immobilization of trespassing vehicles.
Parking lot owners or operators, §46.2-1231.
Regulation by localities, §46.2-1232.
Impeding access to fire hydrant, private driveway, etc., §46.2-1239.
Fine schedule, VA SCt Rule 3B:2.
Pretrial payment of fine, §16.1-69.40:1.
License plates.
Handicapped persons, §§46.2-731, 46.2-739.
Lights on parked vehicles, §46.2-1037.
Limiting length of time of parking adjacent to commercial business areas.
Vehicles of certain weight and length.
Authority of local government, §46.2-1222.2.
Local parking permits, §46.2-1230.

PARKING —Cont'd
Location of parked vehicles, §46.2-889.
Maximum fine for violating Title 46.2, §46.2-113.
Motor vehicle traffic.
Regulation on certain parking lots, §46.2-1219.
Regulation on certain privately-owned public parking areas, §46.2-1219.1.
Municipal parking permits, §46.2-1230.
Municipal regulation of vehicular and pedestrian traffic, §§46.2-1219, 46.2-1305.
No-parking signs.
County authority to erect, §46.2-1225.
County ordinance regulations, §46.2-1224.
Ordinances.
Authority of localities to issue parking permits, §46.2-1230.
Buses.
Restrictions on idling of engines, §46.2-1224.1.
Counties of Arlington, Fairfax, Stafford and Prince William.
Regulation or prohibition of parking of certain vehicles, §46.2-1222.1.
County ordinances prohibiting parking on certain streets and highways, §46.2-1224.
Issuance of summons, §46.2-941.
Limiting length of time of parking adjacent to commercial business areas.
Vehicles of certain weight and length, §46.2-1222.2.
Local enforcement provisions, §46.2-1225.
Local parking regulations, §§46.2-1220, 46.2-1221.
Mailing summons, §19.2-76.2.
Regulation of vehicular traffic on certain privately-owned public parking areas, §46.2-1219.1.
Stopping or standing, §46.2-1220.
Towing vehicles, §46.2-1217.
Towns of Clifton, Herndon and Vienna.
Regulation or prohibition of parking of certain vehicles, §46.2-1222.1.
Unsettled parking violations.
Removal or immobilization of vehicles, §46.2-1216.
Vehicular and pedestrian traffic on certain parking lots, §46.2-1219.
Pedestrian traffic.
Regulation on certain parking lots, §46.2-1219.
Personal property left in vehicles.
Liability of persons furnishing free parking accommodations, §46.2-1234.
Private driveways, §46.2-1239.
Removal of trespassing vehicles.
Parking lot owners or operators, §46.2-1231.
Regulation by localities, §46.2-1232.
Requirements, §46.2-1071.
Rescue squad vehicles, parking near, §46.2-921.
Service districts, §§15.2-2400 to 15.2-2403.3.
Setting hand brake and turning wheel to curb, §46.2-1071.
Solid waste hauling vehicles.
Local regulation of construction, parking, etc., §46.2-1304.1.
Special license plate holders, §46.2-731.
State behavioral health and developmental services board.
Enforcement of parking regulations, §46.2-1229.
State highway system, §46.2-1223.
State parks, §10.1-200.3.
State primary and secondary highways.
Enforcement of state regulations, §46.2-1227.
Stopping or standing, §46.2-1220.

PARKING —Cont'd
Storage charges.
Municipal regulation of towing and storage fees, §46.2-1233.1.
Summons for violations.
Condition precedent for issuance, §46.2-941.
Mailing summons, §19.2-76.2.
Ticketing trespassing vehicles.
Parking lot owners or operators, §46.2-1231.
Regulation by localities, §46.2-1232.
Too close to intersection, §46.2-1239.
Towing fees.
Municipal regulation, §§46.2-1233 to 46.2-1233.2.
Towing trespassing vehicles.
Immunity from liability, §46.2-1231.1.
Towing vehicles.
Municipal regulation of towing fees, §§46.2-1233 to 46.2-1233.2.
Unsettled parking violations.
Removal or immobilization of vehicles, §46.2-1216.
Vehicles of certain weight and length.
Limiting length of time of parking adjacent to commercial business areas.
Authority of local government, §46.2-1222.2.

PARKING AUTHORITIES.
Alexandria parking authority, 1956 ch 406, 1958 ch 348.
Arlington county parking authority, 1958 ch 383, 1972 ch 337.
Bristol parking authority, 1968 ch 555.
Culpeper parking authority, 1976 ch 584.
Fairfax county parking authority, 1972 ch 337.
Fairfax parking authority, city of, 1958 ch 526, 1991 ch 21.
Fredericksburg parking authority, 1978 ch 691.
Front Royal parking authority, 1970 ch 413.
Repeal of chapter 413, 1970 acts, 1987 ch 31.
Harrisonburg parking authority, 1958 ch 517, 1968 ch 544.
Herndon parking authority, town of, 1991 ch 142.
Lynchburg parking authority, 1974 ch 76, 1995 ch 289.
Martinsville parking authority, 1968 ch 365.
Newport News-Hampton parking authority, 1968 ch 200, 1983 ch 57, 1983 ch 69, 1984 ch 596.
Norfolk parking authority, 1964 ch 208.
Portsmouth parking authority, 1964 ch 351, 1970 ch 229, 1975 ch 258.
Pulaski and Wytheville parking authority, 1968 ch 682.
Vienna parking authority, town of, 1991 ch 446.
Winchester parking authority, 1964 ch 221, 1966 ch 515.

PARKING BRAKES.
Motor vehicles, §§46.2-1068, 46.2-1071.

PARKING FOR DISABLED OR HANDICAPPED, §§46.2-1240 to 46.2-1259.
Definitions, §46.2-1240.
Drivers' licenses.
Enforcement of provisions, §46.2-1254.
Enforcement of provisions, §46.2-1243.
Confiscation of placards, §46.2-1255.
Drivers' licenses, §46.2-1254.
Volunteer parking enforcement units, §46.2-1244.
Identification cards.
Enforcement of provisions, §46.2-1254.

PARKING FOR DISABLED OR HANDICAPPED —Cont'd
Issuance of disabled parking placards, §46.2-1241.
License plates.
Alteration, §46.2-1249.
Counterfeit plates, §46.2-1247.
Use of, §46.2-1248.
Fraudulently obtaining, §46.2-1251.
Providing to unauthorized persons, §46.2-1253.
Reciprocity, §46.2-1258.
Revocation, §46.2-1256.
Selling or exchanging, §46.2-1252.
Unauthorized use, §46.2-1250.
Metered spaces.
Four hours free parking, §46.2-1245.
Notice.
Confiscation of placards, §46.2-1255.
Revocation of placards and license plates, §46.2-1256.
Placards.
Alteration, §46.2-1249.
Confiscation, §46.2-1255.
Construction, §46.2-1259.
Counterfeit placards, §46.2-1247.
Use of, §46.2-1248.
Definitions, §46.2-1240.
Fraudulently obtaining, §46.2-1251.
Issuance, §§46.2-1241, 46.2-1259.
Providing to unauthorized persons, §46.2-1253.
Reciprocity, §46.2-1258.
Revocation, §46.2-1256.
Selling or exchanging, §46.2-1252.
Unauthorized use, §46.2-1250.
Private security guards.
Enforcement of provisions, §46.2-1243.
Reciprocity, §46.2-1258.
Placards and license plates, §46.2-1258.
Time-restricted or metered spaces.
Four hours free parking, §46.2-1245.
Towing of unauthorized vehicles, §46.2-1246.
Unauthorized vehicles, §46.2-1242.
Prepayment of fine, §16.1-69.40:1.
Towing, §46.2-1246.
Volunteer parking enforcement units, §46.2-1244.

PARKING LOTS OR OTHER FACILITIES.
Applicability of motor vehicles title, §46.2-101.
City or town providing and operating, §15.2-1122.
Commuter parking lots owned by VDOT.
Parking not in conformance with signs and pavement markings.
Traffic infraction, §46.2-1219.2.
Handicapped parking spaces.
Identification by above grade signage, §36-99.11.
Locality providing off-street parking facilities, §15.2-967.
Reckless driving, §46.2-864.
Regulating traffic in parking lots, §§46.2-1219, 46.2-1219.1.
Shopping carts, removal, §18.2-102.1.
Ticketing trespassing vehicles, §§46.2-1231, 46.2-1232.
Towing fees, municipal regulations, §§46.2-1233 to 46.2-1233.2.
Towing trespassing vehicles.
Immunity from liability, §46.2-1231.1.
Trespassing vehicles.
Ticketing, removal or immobilization, §§46.2-1231, 46.2-1232.

PARKING LOTS OR OTHER FACILITIES —Cont'd
Unclaimed vehicles.
Reporting requirements, §46.2-1218.

PARKING METERS.
Disabled or handicapped persons.
Four hours free parking, §46.2-1245.
Municipal parking regulations, §§46.2-1220, 46.2-1221.
County-owned or leased property, §46.2-1221.
Slugs manufactured, sold, etc., for unlawful uses, §18.2-180.
Stealing from or tampering with, §18.2-152.
Unlawful operation, §18.2-179.

PARKS AND RECREATION.
ABC mixed beverage license.
Establishments located on Blue Ridge Parkway and Jefferson and George Washington national forests, §4.1-126.
Access roads and bikeways to public recreation areas, §33.1-223.
Counties, cities or towns.
Acquiring real property near parks, §15.2-1801.
City or town immunity for operating, §15.2-1809.
Collecting fees, §15.2-1806.
Establishing, §15.2-1806.
Elections, §15.2-1807.
Franchise, privilege, lease or right to use city or town property, §§15.2-2100 to 15.2-2108.1:1.
Liability in operating.
Agreements with landowners, §29.1-509.
Police powers over lands lying beyond localities boundaries, §15.2-1725.
Sale by city or town, restrictions, §15.2-2100.
Sales, VA Const Art VII §9.
Sanitary districts, operating in, §15.2-1811.
Sport facilities, §15.2-1808.
Swimming pools.
Leasing lands owned or held by locality for, §15.2-1810.
Taxing property for maintenance and operation, §15.2-1806.
Destruction of trees, shrubs, etc., in public parks, refuges or sanctuaries, §18.2-140.
Drug sales on or near property, §18.2-255.2.
Firearms.
Semi-automatic firearms and shotguns.
Carrying loaded firearms in public areas, §18.2-287.4.
Highways and roads.
Eminent domain damages.
Authority to acquire land to replace parkland, §33.1-91.1.
Hunting and fishing seasons in forestlands, §§10.1-1158 to 10.1-1161.
Hunting and trapping in state forests, §§10.1-1151 to 10.1-1157.
Liability of county, city or town in operating.
Agreements with landowners, §29.1-509.
Natural area preserve, §§10.1-209 to 10.1-217.
Offenses prohibiting residing in proximity to children.
Boundary line of public parks, §18.2-370.3.
Outdoor recreation.
Acquisition of property, §10.1-208.
Cooperation of other departments, §10.1-207.
Property exempt from taxation, VA Const Art X §6.
Parks or playgrounds held by trustees for perpetual use, §58.1-3606.

PARKS AND RECREATION —Cont'd
Real property taxes.
Land preservation special assessments.
Generally, §§58.1-3229 to 58.1-3244.
See REAL PROPERTY TAXES.
Scenic rivers, §§10.1-400 to 10.1-418.8.
See SCENIC RIVERS.
Shenandoah national park.
Jurisdiction.
Commonwealth and United States, §1-402.
Southwest regional recreation authority, §§15.2-6016 to 15.2-6024.
State parks, §§10.1-200 to 10.1-205.
Development revenue bonds, §§10.1-300 to 10.1-312.
Tax exempt property, VA Const Art X §6.
Parks held by trustees for perpetual use, §58.1-3606.
Water quality tests, §32.1-248.1.

PARKS AND RECREATION LAND PRESERVATION SPECIAL ASSESSMENT.
Real property taxes, §§58.1-3229 to 58.1-3244.
See REAL PROPERTY TAXES.

PAROCHIAL SCHOOLS.
Alcoholic beverages, outdoor advertising.
Limitations on placement locations, §4.1-112.2.
Notice of violation, penalty for failure to take corrective action, §4.1-320.
Criminal background checks and fingerprinting of employees, §22.1-296.3.
Criminal history record information, dissemination, §19.2-389.
Private schools generally.
See PRIVATE SCHOOLS.
School bus operators.
Requirements, §§22.1-178, 22.1-180.

PAROL CONTRACTS.
Contracts void as to creditors and purchasers unless in writing, §11-1.
Written evidence required to maintain action, §11-2.

PAROLE AND POSTRELEASE SUPERVISION.
Aged prisoners.
Conditional release, §53.1-40.01.
Violent offenders, §19.2-297.1.
Arrests, §53.1-161.
Considered as escapee, §53.1-163.
Warrantless arrests, §53.1-162.
Board, §§53.1-134 to 53.1-140.
Bodily injuries caused by parolees, §18.2-55.
Central criminal records exchange.
Report of parole violators, §19.2-390.
Community-based corrections system for state-responsible offenders.
Generally.
See COMMUNITY-BASED CORRECTIONS SYSTEM FOR STATE-RESPONSIBLE OFFENDERS.
Community corrections, §§9.1-173 to 9.1-183.
See COMMUNITY CORRECTIONS.
Community programs, §53.1-155.1.
Conditional release of geriatric prisoners, §53.1-40.01.
Persons convicted under three strikes you're out law, §19.2-297.1.
Director authority to recommend review, §53.1-154.1.
Districts, §53.1-141.
Officer assignments, §53.1-142.

PAROLE AND POSTRELEASE SUPERVISION —Cont'd
Districts —Cont'd
Post-release supervision of felons.
Contribution by persons on parole, §53.1-150.1.
Program operated through parole and probation districts, §§19.2-295.2, 53.1-150.
DNA analysis.
Requiring persons to submit sample.
Parole officers, §53.1-145.
Felons sentenced for offenses committed on and after January 1, 1995, or July 1, 2000, §19.2-295.2.
Felons sentenced for offenses committed on and after July 1, 2006.
Sex offender registration violations, §19.2-295.2:1.
Felony convictions, §§53.1-151, 53.1-152.
Geriatric prisoners, §§19.2-297.1, 53.1-40.01.
Good conduct credits for persons convicted after October 1, 1942.
Effect of credit upon eligibility for parole, §53.1-196.
Good conduct credits for persons convicted prior to October 1, 1942.
Effect of credit upon eligibility for parole, §§53.1-193, 53.1-194.
Halfway houses.
Juvenile, placing in, §16.1-293.
Hearings, §§53.1-168 to 53.1-176.
Foreign parolees, §53.1-172.
Preliminary hearings, §53.1-173.
Reincarceration procedure, §53.1-168.
Hearing officers, §53.1-169.
Record, §53.1-171.
Revocation of parole by foreign states, §53.1-176.
Revocation of parole by Virginia, §53.1-175.
Rights of parolees, §53.1-170.
Ineligibility.
Felony offenses committed on or after January 1, 1995, §53.1-165.1.
Intensive parole supervision.
Community-based corrections system for state-responsible offenders.
Programs included in system, §53.1-67.6.
Interstate compact for the supervision of adult offenders, §§53.1-176.1 to 53.1-176.3.
Investigations prior to release, §53.1-155.
Jail inmate sentenced to more than twelve months, §53.1-153.
Juveniles.
Halfway houses, placing in, §16.1-293.
Independent living services on release from commitment, §16.1-293.
Mental health services transition plan, §16.1-293.1.
Placing in foster home or with institution, §16.1-293.
Revocation or modification, §16.1-291.
Supervision, §16.1-293.
Transfer of supervision from one county or city to another or to another state, §16.1-295.
Limitation on application of statutes, §53.1-165.1.
Local-responsible offenders.
Community corrections, §§9.1-173 to 9.1-183.
See COMMUNITY CORRECTIONS.
Misdemeanor and felony offenses, §53.1-152.
Modification.
Juveniles, §16.1-291.
Notice prior to release of parolees, §§53.1-116.1, 53.1-160, 53.1-160.1.

PAROLE AND POSTRELEASE SUPERVISION —Cont'd
Officers.
See PAROLE OFFICERS.
Out-of-state parolee supervision.
Form of compact, §53.1-167.
Governor to execute compact, §53.1-166.
Revocation hearings, §§53.1-168 to 53.1-176.
Parole board review periods, §53.1-154.
Period of parole, §53.1-156.
Public assistance.
Temporary assistance for needy families.
Parolee recipient failing drug test, §63.2-605.
Public procurement.
Exemptions from chapter, §2.2-4343.
Release, §§53.1-116.1, 53.1-158 to 53.1-160.1.
Mandatory releases, §53.1-159.
Notice prior to, §§53.1-116.1, 53.1-160, 53.1-160.1.
Representation of parolee at hearings.
Attorney appointment, §53.1-165.
Residential community programs, §53.1-155.1.
Return to facility, §53.1-164.
Review authority of director, §53.1-154.1.
Revocation, §53.1-165.
Hearings, §§53.1-137, 53.1-168 to 53.1-176.
Juveniles, §16.1-291.
Sex offender registration violations.
Felons sentenced for offenses committed on and after July 1, 2006, §19.2-295.2:1.
Substance abuse treatment.
Contribution by parolee towards cost of program, §53.1-150.1.
Temporary assistance for needy families.
Parolee recipient failing drug test, §63.2-605.
Terms and conditions.
Compliance, copy furnished, §53.1-157.
Three time losers, §53.1-151.
Violent felonies, §19.2-297.1.

PAROLE BOARD, §§53.1-134 to 53.1-140.
Access to prisoners, §53.1-138.
Arrests of parolees, §53.1-161.
Case review periods, §53.1-154.
Chairman, §53.1-135.
Powers and duties, §53.1-139.
Civil actions against members or employees.
Attorney general or assistant representing, §2.2-507.
Creation, §53.1-134.
Department of corrections.
Director.
Parole administration, §53.1-140.
Duties, §53.1-136.
Freedom of information act.
Exclusions from chapter, §2.2-3703.
Hearings, revocation, §53.1-137.
Investigations prior to parole, §53.1-155.
Mandatory parole, §53.1-159.
Members.
Appointment, §53.1-134.
Chairman, §53.1-135.
Powers and duties, §53.1-139.
Vice chairman, §53.1-135.
Powers, §53.1-136.
Prisons.
Access to prisoners by parole board, §53.1-138.
Reports of prison officials to parole board, §53.1-138.
Reports by prison officials, §53.1-138.
Revocation of parole.
Hearings, §53.1-137.

PAROLE BOARD —Cont'd
Revocation of parole —Cont'd
Powers, §53.1-175.
Requests to other states, §53.1-176.
Secretary of public safety.
Agency responsibility, §2.2-221.
Vice chairman, §53.1-135.

PAROLE OFFICERS.
Appointment.
Term, §53.1-144.
Arrest of parolees without warrant, §53.1-162.
Arrest powers, §§53.1-145, 53.1-146.
Assignment to districts, §53.1-142.
Authorization, §53.1-143.
Carnal knowledge of defendant or convicted person, §18.2-64.2.
Carrying concealed weapons, §53.1-145.
Compensation, §53.1-147.
DNA analysis.
Requiring persons to submit sample, §53.1-145.
Drug and alcohol screening tests.
Authority to order, §53.1-145.
Duties, §53.1-145.
As to persons convicted of local violations, §53.1-146.
Expenses, §53.1-147.
Laser, laser gun sights or device simulating laser.
Pointing at law enforcement officer, probation or parole officer, etc., §18.2-57.01.
Powers, §53.1-145.
As to persons convicted of local violations, §53.1-146.
Sexual battery of defendant or convicted person, §18.2-67.4.
Weapons.
Carrying concealed weapons, §53.1-145.

PAROL EVIDENCE.
Computer information transactions, §59.1-503.1.
Landlord and tenant.
Remedies for rent and for use and occupation, §55-227.
Leases, UCC, §8.2A-202.
Negotiable instruments, §8.3A-117.
Sales, UCC, §8.2-202.

PARROTHEAD CLUB.
Motor vehicle license plates, §46.2-749.68.

PARTIAL BIRTH INFANTICIDE, §18.2-71.1.

PARTIAL DISABILITY.
Sickness and disability program for state employees.
Generally, §§51.1-1100 to 51.1-1140.
See SICKNESS AND DISABILITY PROGRAM.

PARTIALLY PROVED DEEDS AND OTHER DOCUMENTS.
Recording in writings partially proved book, §17.1-234.

PARTICIPATION IN CRIMINAL STREET GANG, §18.2-46.2.

PARTIES.
Address change.
Notice to court clerk, §8.01-319.
Annexation.
Additional parties, §15.2-3205.
Anonymous plaintiff.
Motion for identification, factors considered, §8.01-15.1.

PARTIES —Cont'd
Appraisal rights, corporations.
Fair value determinations by courts, §13.1-740.
Assignments.
Allowance of certain discounts against intermediate assignor or transferor, §8.01-13.
Assignee may sue in own name, §8.01-13.
Suit against assignor, §8.01-14.
Attachments.
Defendant not served and fails to appear, §8.01-571.
Examination on oath of codefendant, §8.01-562.
Procedure when codefendant fails to appear, §8.01-564.
Suggestion that codefendant has not made full disclosure, §8.01-565.
Who made defendants, §8.01-539.
Beneficial owners.
Action against assignor, §8.01-14.
Action in own name, §8.01-13.
Suit when legal title in another, §8.01-12.
Big Sandy river.
Obstructing or dumping refuse into, §62.1-194.3.
Birth-related neurological injury compensation hearing, §38.2-5006.
Bonds issued by localities.
Judicial determination of validity.
Parties defendant, §§15.2-2651, 15.2-2652.
Bonds, surety.
Who may execute bond for writ or order, §8.01-4.2.
Cemeteries.
Improvement of abandoned and neglected cemeteries, §57-39.1.
Proceedings for removal of remains and sale of land vacated, §57-39.
Removal of remains from abandoned family graveyard, §§57-38.1, 57-38.2.
Change of address.
Notice to clerk of court.
When required, §8.01-319.
Change of parties, §§8.01-19, 8.01-20.
Continuance by new parties, §8.01-16.
Church property.
Suits by members against trustees, §57-13.
Circuit courts.
Intervention, VA SCt Rule 3:14.
Joinder of parties, VA SCt Rule 3:12.
New parties, VA SCt Rule 3:16.
Statutory interpleader, VA SCt Rule 3:15.
Substitution of parties, VA SCt Rule 3:17.
Third party claims, VA SCt Rule 3:13.
Coal.
Suits to extinguish claim or right, §55-155.
Consolidation of counties, cities or towns into single county or city, §15.2-3523.
Constitutional rights.
Use of claim against party, §8.01-223.1.
Contraction of corporate limits of cities or towns.
Town located in two or more counties, §15.2-3242.
Corporations, appraisal rights.
Fair value determinations by courts, §13.1-740.
Criminal cases.
Severance of parties, VA SCt Rule 3A:10.
Dam or water impoundment disputes.
Disputes between jurisdictions.
Adding additional parties, §15.2-2138.
Death of parties, §§8.01-16 to 8.01-23.
After verdict but before judgment, §8.01-21.
Cessation of defendant powers, §8.01-17.

PARTIES —Cont'd
Death of parties —Cont'd
Continuance for new parties, §8.01-16.
Marriage.
Effect of marriage of party, §8.01-20.
Multiple parties, §8.01-22.
Suit involving a decedent's estate or trust in which number of parties exceeds thirty and one dies, §8.01-23.
Pendency of appeal, §8.01-20.
Plaintiff cessation of suit, §8.01-18.
Proceedings in writing binding deceased person, §8.01-11.
Survival of causes of action, §§8.01-25, 8.01-56.
Death presumption.
Defendants to real or personal property proceedings, §64.2-2300.
Deceased persons.
Proceedings on writing binding deceased person, §8.01-11.
Deeds.
After-acquired property, §55-52.
Effectual deeds binding between parties, §55-51.
Delinquent tax lands sales proceedings, §58.1-3967.
Eminent domain.
Dropping of parties improperly joined, §25.1-251.
Substitution of parties.
Owner incapable of defending, §25.1-217.
Impoundment of surface waters.
Riparian owner rights.
Application for leave to store floodwaters, §62.1-108.
Indispensable parties.
When court may add new parties to suit, §8.01-7.
Insurance companies.
Limitation on joinder of, §8.01-5.
Interpleader, §8.01-364.
Intervention.
Child custody proceeding.
Uniform child custody jurisdiction and enforcement act.
Laws of Commonwealth applicable, §20-146.16.
Jail facilities, substandard.
Prisoner confinement limitations and transfers.
Joining of state, §53.1-70.
Joinder.
Child custody proceeding.
Uniform child custody jurisdiction and enforcement act.
Laws of Commonwealth applicable, §20-146.16.
Death or change of parties, §8.01-16.
Limitation on joinder of insurance company, §8.01-5.
Multiple claimants, §8.01-267.5.
Suit against joint assignors, §8.01-14.
Tenants in common, §8.01-10.
Limited liability companies.
Derivative actions.
Proper plaintiff, §13.1-1043.
Limited partnerships.
Derivative actions.
Proper plaintiff, §50-73.63.
Lost shareholders, proceeding for determination, §13.1-777.
Mechanics' and materialmen's liens, §43-33.
Enforcement, §43-22.
Releases, §43-71.

PARTIES —Cont'd
Military affairs.
Servicemembers civil relief act.
Default judgments, §8.01-15.2.
Military service.
Continuance or extension of time for filing pleading, §44-97.1.
Minerals.
Suits to extinguish claim or right, §55-155.
Minors.
How minors may sue, §8.01-8.
Misjoinder.
Effect, §8.01-5.
Misnomer.
Amending pleading to correct misnomer, §8.01-6.
Multiple claimant litigation, §§8.01-267.1 to 8.01-267.9.
Actions pending in same court, §8.01-267.2.
Application for transfer, §8.01-267.4.
Conflict of laws, §8.01-267.9.
Consolidation proceedings, §8.01-267.3.
Standards, §8.01-267.1.
Effect on other laws, §8.01-267.9.
Interrogatory appeals, §8.01-267.8.
Joinder, §8.01-267.5.
Later-filed actions, §8.01-267.7.
Ongoing litigation.
Joinder of later-filed actions, §8.01-267.7.
Pending in same court, §8.01-267.2.
Separate trials, §8.01-267.6.
Severance, §8.01-267.5.
Special interrogatories, §8.01-267.6.
Transfer, §8.01-267.4.
Standards, §8.01-267.1.
Multiple parties.
Venue, §8.01-263.
New parties.
When court may add, §8.01-7.
Nonjoinder.
Effect, §8.01-5.
Oil.
Suits to extinguish claim or right, §55-155.
Oral motions.
Representations deemed certified, §8.01-271.1.
Ores.
Suits to extinguish claim or right, §55-155.
Partition of land.
When name or share of parties unknown, §8.01-90.
Paternity proceedings.
Commencement of action, §20-49.2.
Personal property proceedings where death presumed, §64.2-2300.
Persons with disability.
Definition, §8.01-2.
Disposition of real estate, §8.01-69.
Presumption of death.
Defendants in real or personal property proceedings, §64.2-2300.
Presumption of death determination revoked.
Substitution of supposed decedent in pending actions, §64.2-2308.
Proceeding anonymously, §8.01-15.1.
Pseudonym.
Proceeding anonymously, use, §8.01-15.1.
Real party in interest.
Suit by beneficial owner when legal title in another, §8.01-12.
When defendant powers cease, §8.01-17.
Real property proceedings where death presumed, §64.2-2300.

PARTIES —Cont'd
Relation back to original pleading, §8.01-6.
Religious organizations.
Suits by members against trustees, §57-13.
Reversion of cities to towns, §15.2-4103.
Sale of delinquent tax land proceedings, §58.1-3967.
Service by publication and not appearing.
Time period for petition for rehearing to correct injustice, §8.01-322.
Servicemembers civil relief act.
Default judgments, §8.01-15.2.
Service of notice, process and other papers.
General provisions, §§8.01-285 to 8.01-327.2.
See SERVICE OF NOTICE, PROCESS AND OTHER PAPERS.
Severance of parties.
Criminal cases, VA SCt Rule 3A:10.
Multiple claimant litigation, §8.01-267.5.
Shareholder determination proceedings, §13.1-777.
Signing of pleadings, §8.01-271.1.
Standing.
See STANDING.
State corporation commission.
Commonwealth to be complainant and party against whom complaint preferred defendant, §12.1-27.
Meetings and communications between commissioners and parties, §12.1-30.1.
Stock insurers conversion to mutual insurer.
Compelling completion of mutualization, §38.2-1014.
Substitution of parties.
Cessation of defendant powers, §8.01-17.
Death or change of parties, §8.01-16.
Presumption of death determination revoked.
Substitution of supposed decedent in pending actions, §64.2-2308.
When suit discontinued unless revived, §8.01-18.
Town seeking city status, §15.2-3804.
Towns incorporated by judicial proceedings, §§15.2-3600, 15.2-3601.
Transition of counties to cities, §15.2-3904.
Trusts.
Judicial proceedings involving trusts, §64.2-713.
Unemployment compensation.
Claims adjudication.
Appeals.
Commission review of tribunal decisions, §60.2-622.
Judicial review of board of review, §60.2-631.
Judicial review of commission decision, §60.2-625.
Unincorporated associations or orders.
Suits by and against entities, §8.01-15.
United States.
Actions to which United States a party, US Const Art III §2.
Waters of the state.
Big Sandy river.
Obstructing or dumping refuse into, §62.1-194.3.
Contaminating state waters, §62.1-194.1.
Obstructing state waters, §62.1-194.1.
Surface water withdrawal actions, §62.1-44.23:1.
Wills.
Probate.
Appearance, §64.2-446.
Process against, §64.2-449.

PARTIES —Cont'd
Workers' compensation.
Principal joining subcontractor, §65.2-304.

PARTIES UNKNOWN.
Service by publication, §8.01-316.

PARTITION OF LAND, §§8.01-81 to 8.01-93.
Act of 1922.
Validation of certain petitions prior to act, §8.01-87.
Allotment to one or more parties, §8.01-83.
Death presumption.
Parties to proceedings, §64.2-2300.
Deeds.
Recordation tax, state, §58.1-806.
Disposition of share in proceeds.
Application to payment of lien, §8.01-84.
Persons with disability, §8.01-85.
When proceeds of sale deemed personal estate, §8.01-89.
Election of shares.
Shares laid off together, §8.01-82.
Horizontal property regimes, §55-79.34.
In kind distribution impractical.
Partition of goods, etc., by sale, §8.01-93.
Lessee's rights.
Effect of partition or sale on rights, §8.01-91.
Lists of judgments for partition or recovery of lands.
Delivery by clerks to commissioners of revenue, §58.1-3304.
Failure to deliver, §58.1-3305.
Mineral rights, §8.01-81.
Persons with disability.
Disposition of real estate, §§8.01-67 to 8.01-80.
See PERSONS WITH DISABILITY.
Disposition of share in proceeds, §8.01-85.
Presumption of death.
Parties to proceedings, §64.2-2300.
Real property taxes, apportionment, §58.1-3225.
Recordation tax, state.
Deeds of partition, §58.1-806.
Recording decree, §55-138.
In deed book, §17.1-227.
Sale in lieu of petition, §8.01-83.
Shares laid off together, §8.01-82.
Tax liens of Commonwealth.
Jurisdiction over Commonwealth for purposes of determining validity, amount and priority, §58.1-1809.
Time-shares, §55-372.
Unknown parties.
When name or share of parties unknown, §8.01-90.
Unrepresented shares.
Allowance of attorneys' fees out of shares, §8.01-92.
Utility transfers.
Sale of assets, §56-90.1.
Validation of partitions prior to act of 1922, §8.01-87.
Venue.
Preferred forum, §8.01-261.
Vesting of legal title, §8.01-88.
Who may institute action, §8.01-81.

PARTITION OF PERSONAL PROPERTY.
Appeal, §16.1-77.2.
Jurisdiction of general district court, §16.1-77.2.
Petition to compel, §16.1-77.2.

PARTITION OF PERSONAL PROPERTY —Cont'd
Venue.
Permissible forum, §8.01-262.

PARTNERSHIP INCOME TAX, §§58.1-390.1 to 58.1-395.
Credits.
Historic rehabilitation tax credit, §58.1-339.2.
Defined terms, §58.1-390.1.
Investment partnership carried interest income.
Subtraction from taxable income, §§58.1-322, 58.1-402.
Nonresident owners, §58.1-395.
Pass-through entities.
Defined, §58.1-390.1.
Extension of time for filing returns, §58.1-393.1.
Taxation, §58.1-390.2.
Reports, §58.1-392.
Returns.
Extension of time for filing, §58.1-393.1.
Failure to make, §58.1-394.1.
Fraudulent returns, §58.1-394.2.
Pass-through entity items, §58.1-394.3.
Taxable income, §58.1-391.

PARTNERSHIP OFFICER LIABILITY.
Conversion of trust taxes, §58.1-1816.
Failure to pay, collect or account for taxes, §§58.1-1813 to 58.1-1815.
Local taxes, failure to pay, §58.1-3906.
Willful failure to collect and account for, §58.1-3907.

PARTNERSHIPS.
Abandonment of property presumption.
Intangible interest in business associations, §55-210.6:1.
Property of dissolved associations, §55-210.7.
Refunds, §55-210.6:2.
Accounts and accounting.
Partners deemed to have accounts, §50-73.99.
Winding up partnership business.
Settlement of accounts and contributions among partners, §50-73.123.
Actions.
By and against partnership and partners, §§50-73.97, 50-73.103.
Dissociation by partner when business not woundup.
Buyout of partners interest.
Action by dissociated partner to determine buyout price, §50-73.112.
District court civil cases.
Preparing, executing and serving pleadings and papers without attorney intervention, §16.1-88.03.
Savings clause, §50-73.149.
Agents.
Partner as agent of partnership, §50-73.91.
Alley use without consent or compensation, §56-14.
Amendment of provisions.
Partnerships subject to, §50-73.86.
Applicability of provisions, §50-73.147.
Uniformity of application, §50-73.144.
Arrest warrants.
Execution of warrant or summons.
Arrest outside county or city where charged to be tried, §19.2-76.

PARTNERSHIPS —Cont'd
Banking corporations.
Limitation on power to enter agreement, §13.1-627.
Nonprofit corporations, §13.1-826.
Business trusts, §§13.1-1200 to 13.1-1285.
See BUSINESS TRUSTS.
Buyout of dissociated partners interest, §50-73.112.
Cancellation of statement partnership authority, §50-73.93.
Care, partner's duty of, §50-73.102.
Certificate reciting change, correction, merger, conversion or domestication.
Request, admitted to record in deed books, continuity of title records, §50-73.150.
Change, correction, merger, conversion or domestication.
Certificate reciting.
Admitted to record in deed books, continuity of title records, §50-73.150.
Citation of act.
Short title, §50-73.145.
Competing with partnership, partner prohibited, §50-73.102.
Conflict of laws.
Internal relations, §50-73.84.
Construction of provisions.
Uniformity of construction, §50-73.144.
Continuation of partnership after dissolution, §50-73.118.
Continuation of partnership beyond definite term or particular undertaking, §50-73.104.
Contributions.
Nature of partner's liability, §50-73.96.
Winding up partnership business.
Settlement of accounts and contributions among partners, §50-73.123.
Contributions of partners upon winding up, §50-73.123.
Conversion.
Business trusts to new entity, §§13.1-1272 to 13.1-1277.
Effect, §50-73.127.
General partnership to limited partnership, §§50-73.11:3, 50-73.11:4.
Limited partnership to partnership, §50-73.126.
Partnership to limited liability company, §13.1-1010.1.
Effect, §13.1-1010.2.
Conveyance of partnership property, §50-73.92.
Limitation on partners authority to transfer.
Statement of partnership authority, §50-73.93.
Corporations.
Power to enter into partnership agreement, §13.1-627.
Single shareholder, §13.1-611.
Credit unions.
Limitations on power to enter into partnership agreement, §13.1-627.
Nonprofit corporations, §13.1-826.
Dealing with partnership, partner prohibited, §50-73.102.
Definitions, §50-73.79.
Conversions and mergers, §50-73.124.
Determining whether partnership formed, rules, §50-73.88.
Dissociation by partner, §§50-73.109 to 50-73.111.
Action by dissociated partner to determine buyout price, §50-73.112.

PARTNERSHIPS —Cont'd
Dissociation by partner —Cont'd
Business not wound up, §§50-73.112 to 50-73.116.
Buyout of dissociated partners interest, §50-73.112.
Continued use of partnership name, §50-73.116.
Liability of dissociated partner to other persons, §50-73.114.
Power of dissociated partner to bind partnership, §50-73.113.
Purchase of dissociated partners interest, §50-73.112.
Statement of dissociation, §50-73.115.
Buyout of partner's interest, §50-73.112.
Deferred payment of buyout price, §50-73.112.
Effect, §50-73.111.
Events causing, §50-73.109.
Indemnification of dissociated partner, §50-73.112.
Offset against buyout price for dissociated partner's interest.
Damages for wrongful dissociation, §50-73.112.
Power of partner to dissociate, §50-73.110.
Price for buying out dissociated partner's interest, §50-73.112.
Wrongful dissociation, §50-73.110.
Buyout of interest of partner who dissociates when business not wound up.
Damages for wrongful dissociation offset against buyout price, §50-73.112.
Dissolution.
Winding up partnership business, §§50-73.117 to 50-73.123. See within this heading, "Winding up partnership business."
Distributions.
Defined, §50-73.79.
In-kind distributions, §50-73.100.
District court civil cases.
Preparing, executing and serving pleadings and papers without attorney intervention, §16.1-88.03.
Effective date of provisions, §50-73.147.
Electronic filing of required information, §50-73.83.
English.
Statement filed to be in English language, §50-73.83.
Limited partnerships, §50-73.17.
Enterprise zones.
Eligibility, §59.1-279.
Entity distinct from partners.
Partnership as, §50-73.87.
Execution against assets of partner to satisfy judgment against partnership, §50-73.97.
False information, signing document containing, §50-73.83.
Fees.
Statements.
Filing and recordation, §50-73.83.
Fiduciary duty of loyalty and care, §50-73.102.
Formation, §50-73.88.
Factors in determining whether partnership formed, §50-73.88.
Fuel taxes.
Sales tax in certain transportation districts.
Corporate or partnership officers, liability, §58.1-2299.19.
Giving notification, §50-73.80.
Good faith and fair dealing.
Discharge of duties by partner, §50-73.102.
Income tax, §§58.1-390.1 to 58.1-395.
Credit for agricultural best management practices, §58.1-339.3.

PARTNERSHIPS —Cont'd
Income tax —Cont'd
Credit for purchase of advanced technology pesticide and fertilizer application equipment, §58.1-337.
Credit for purchase of conservation tillage equipment, §58.1-334.
Defined terms, §58.1-390.1.
Investment partnership carried interest income.
Subtraction from taxable income, §§58.1-322, 58.1-402.
Nonresident owners, §58.1-395.
Pass-through entities.
Defined, §58.1-390.1.
Extension of time for filing returns, §58.1-393.1.
Taxation, §58.1-390.2.
Reports, §58.1-392.
Returns.
Extension of time for filing, §58.1-393.1.
Failure to make, §58.1-394.1.
Fraudulent returns, §58.1-394.2.
Pass-through entity items, §58.1-394.3.
Taxable income, §58.1-391.
Indemnification.
Dissociated partner, §50-73.112.
Nature of partner's liability, §50-73.96.
In-kind distributions, §50-73.100.
Insurance agents.
License.
Business entities acting as, §38.2-1822.
Insurance consultants.
Business entities acting as.
License required, §38.2-1838.
Insurance corporations.
Limitation on power to enter into partnership agreement, §13.1-627.
Nonprofit corporations, §13.1-826.
Interest.
Applicable rate of interest, §50-73.82.
Usury.
Prohibited from pleading, §6.2-308.
Internal relations, law governing, §50-73.84.
Judgments and decrees.
Effect of judgments against partnership, §50-73.97.
Partners transferable interest subject to charging order, §50-73.108.
Knowledge.
When person has knowledge of facts, §50-73.80.
Liability of officers.
Local taxes, failure to pay, §58.1-3906.
Willful failure to collect and account for, §58.1-3907.
Taxes, conversion of trust taxes, §58.1-1816.
Taxes, failure to pay, collect or account, §§58.1-1813 to 58.1-1815.
Liability of partners, §50-73.96.
Dissociation by partner when business not wound up.
Liability of dissociated partner to other persons, §50-73.114.
Winding up partnership business.
Partners liability to other partners after dissolution, §50-73.122.
Liability of partnership.
Partner's actionable conduct, §50-73.95.
Liability of purported partner, §50-73.98.
Liens.
Charging order on partners transferable interest, §50-73.108.

PARTNERSHIPS —Cont'd
Limitation of actions.
Settlement of accounts, §8.01-246.
Limitation on partners authority to transfer property.
Statement of partnership authority, §50-73.93.
Limited liability companies.
Conversion of partnership to limited liability company, §13.1-1010.1.
Effect, §13.1-1010.2.
General provisions, §§13.1-1000 to 13.1-1080.
See LIMITED LIABILITY COMPANIES.
Professional limited liability companies, §§13.1-1100 to 13.1-1123.
See PROFESSIONAL LIMITED LIABILITY COMPANIES.
Limited partnerships.
Conversion of limited partnership to partnership, §50-73.126.
Effect, §50-73.127.
Conversion of partnership to limited partnership.
Effect, §50-73.127.
Defined, §50-73.124.
Transition provisions, §50-73.148.
Limited partnerships generally, §§50-73.1 to 50-73.78.
See LIMITED PARTNERSHIPS.
Loans.
Transactions between partner and partnership, §50-73.85.
Loss or injury, liability of partnership, §50-73.95.
Loyalty, partner's duty of, §50-73.102.
Merger, §50-73.128.
Effect, §50-73.129.
Statement of merger, §50-73.131.
Misapplication of money or property.
Liability of partnership, §50-73.95.
Motorcycle dealers license denied, suspended or revoked.
Acts of officers or directors, §46.2-1993.75.
Motor vehicle dealers.
Disciplinary action against dealer licenses.
Acts of partners, §46.2-1574.
Negligence.
Liability of partnership for partner's actionable conduct, §50-73.95.
Nonprofit corporations.
Power to enter into agreements, §13.1-826.
Notice.
Giving and receiving, §50-73.80.
When person has notice of fact, §50-73.80.
Oaths.
Self-authentication of affidavits, §49-7.
Offset against buyout price for dissociated partner's interest.
Damages for wrongful dissociation, §50-73.112.
Partnership agreement.
Defined, §50-73.79.
Effect, §50-73.81.
Waiver of provisions.
Nonwaivable provisions, §50-73.81.
Partnership at will.
Defined, §50-73.79.
Winding up partnership business.
Events causing dissolution and winding up, §50-73.117.
Partnership authority.
Statement of, §50-73.93.
Statement of denial by person named as partner in, §50-73.94.

PARTNERSHIPS —Cont'd
Partnership interest.
Defined, §50-73.79.
Transferable interest of partner in partnership, §50-73.106.
Dissociation by partner when all or substantially all interest transferred, §50-73.109.
Subject to charging order, §50-73.108.
Transfer of, §50-73.107.
Person.
Defined as including partnerships, §§1-230, 1-231.
Pleadings.
District court civil cases.
Preparing, executing and serving without attorney intervention, §16.1-88.03.
Ownership, §8.01-279.
Presumptions.
Partnership property.
When property presumed to be, §50-73.90.
Receiving share of profits, §50-73.88.
Price for buying out dissociated partner's interest, §50-73.112.
Property.
Partnership property, §50-73.89.
Partner not co-owner of, §50-73.105.
Transfer, §50-73.92.
Defined, §50-73.79.
What constitutes, §50-73.90.
Property title records.
Change, correction, merger, conversion or domestication.
Certificate reciting.
Admitted to record in deed books, continuity of title records, §50-73.150.
Public ground use without consent or compensation, §56-14.
Public-private partnership advisory commission, §§30-278 to 30-281.
Public service companies.
Limitations on power to enter into partnership agreement, §13.1-627.
Purported partners.
Liability, §50-73.98.
Real estate cooperatives.
Organization of associations, §55-458.
Real property.
Limitation on partners authority to transfer.
Statement of partnership authority, §50-73.93.
Real property taxes.
Land conservation incentives, §58.1-513.
Receiving notification, §50-73.80.
Receiving share of profits.
Presumption person partner, §50-73.88.
Recordation of documents.
Statements, §50-73.83.
Recordation tax, state.
Exemption, §58.1-811.
Records.
Access of partners to books and records, §50-73.101.
Keeping of books and records, §50-73.101.
Recovery of transferred partnership property from transferee, §50-73.92.
Registered limited liability partnerships, §§50-73.132 to 50-73.143.
See REGISTERED LIMITED LIABILITY PARTNERSHIPS.
Relation among and between partners and partnership.
Law governing, §50-73.84.

PARTNERSHIPS —Cont'd
Repeal of provisions.
Partnerships subject to, §50-73.86.
Reports.
Income tax, §58.1-392.
Rights and duties of partners, §50-73.99.
Information, §50-73.101.
Standards of conduct, §50-73.102.
Rules for determining whether partnership formed, §50-73.88.
Savings and loan associations.
Limitations on power to enter into partnership agreement, §13.1-627.
Nonprofit corporations, §13.1-826.
Savings clause, §50-73.149.
Sealed writing, §11-3.
Secured transactions.
Applicability of certain provisions, §50-73.84.
Self-dealing by partner, §50-73.102.
Service of notice, process and other papers.
Arrest warrants, §19.2-76.
How process served, §8.01-304.
Settlement of accounts and contributions on winding up, §50-73.123.
Severability of provisions, §50-73.146.
Shareholders in corporations.
Single shareholder, §13.1-611.
Shares of corporations, voting entitlement, §13.1-662.
Small claims courts.
Representation, §16.1-122.4.
Standards of partner's conduct, §50-73.102.
Statements.
Amendment, §50-73.83.
Cancellation, §50-73.83.
Statement of partnership authority, §50-73.93.
Defined, §50-73.79.
Delayed effective date, §50-73.83.
Denial, §50-73.94.
Effective date, §50-73.83.
Execution, §50-73.83.
Fees, §50-73.83.
Filing, §50-73.83.
Merger, §50-73.131.
Partnership authority, §50-73.93.
Denial, statement, §50-73.94.
Recordation, §50-73.83.
Renewal, §50-73.83.
Winding up partnership business.
Statement of dissolution, §50-73.121.
Status.
Entity distinct from partners, §50-73.87.
Statute of limitations.
Settlement of accounts, §8.01-246.
Street use without consent or compensation, §56-14.
Supplemental principles of law, §50-73.82.
Supplement to partners authority.
Statement of partnership authority, §50-73.93.
Surplus lines insurance brokers.
License.
Business entities acting as, §38.2-1857.2.
Tax liability of officers.
Fuel taxes, §58.1-2288.
Term of partnership.
Continuation beyond definite term, §50-73.104.
Time-shares, §§55-360 to 55-400.
See TIME-SHARES.
Title of act.
Short title, §50-73.145.

PARTNERSHIPS —Cont'd
Title records.
Change, correction, merger, conversion or domestication.
Certificate reciting.
Admitted to record in deed books, continuity of title records, §50-73.150.
Torts.
Liability of partnership for partner's actionable conduct, §50-73.95.
Trade secrets, §§59.1-336 to 59.1-343.
Trailer dealer license denied, suspended or revoked.
Acts of officers or directors, §46.2-1992.78.
Transacting business under assumed name.
Certificate, §59.1-69.
Failure to file.
Effect on right of action, §59.1-76.
Transactions between partner and partnership, §50-73.85.
Transferable interest of partner in partnership, §50-73.106.
Dissociation by partner when all or substantially all interest transferred, §50-73.109.
Subject to charging order, §50-73.108.
Transfer of, §50-73.107.
Transfer of partnership property, §50-73.92.
Limitation of partners authority.
Statement of partnership authority, §50-73.93.
Transition provisions, §50-73.148.
Trusts.
Liability of trustees and rights of persons dealing with trustees.
Interest as a general partner, §64.2-802.
Unclaimed property, disposition of, §55-210.6:2.
Property of dissolved associations, §55-210.7.
Records, §§55-210.24 to 55-210.24:2.
Refunds, §55-210.6:2.
Usury.
Prohibited from pleading, §6.2-308.
Viatical settlement broker license.
Business entity acting as broker, §38.2-1865.1.
Winding up partnership business, §§50-73.117 to 50-73.123.
Binding effect of partner's acts, §50-73.120.
Continuation of partnership after dissolution, §50-73.118.
Contributions of partners, §50-73.123.
Events causing dissolution and winding up, §50-73.117.
Judicial supervision, order of court for, §50-73.119.
Liability of partner to other partners after dissolution, §50-73.122.
Partnership at will.
Events causing dissolution and winding up, §50-73.117.
Partnership for definite term.
Events causing, §50-73.117.
Power of partner to bind partnership after dissolution, §50-73.120.
Preservation of business or property for reasonable time while winding up, §50-73.119.
Right to windup business after dissolution, §50-73.119.
Settlement of accounts and contributions among partners, §50-73.123.
Statement of dissolution, §50-73.121.
Withdrawal.
Events of withdrawal on general partners, §50-73.28.

PARTNERSHIPS —Cont'd
Wrongful act or omission, liability of partnership, §50-73.95.
Wrongful dissociation, §50-73.110.
Offset against buyout price for dissociated partner's interest, §50-73.112.

PART PERFORMANCE.
Extinguishing obligation, §11-12.

PASSBOOKS.
Time savings passbook.
Account defined as including, §8.4-104.

PASSENGER COMMON CARRIERS.
Air carriers, §§5.1-89 to 5.1-151.
See AIR CARRIERS.
Buses generally.
See BUSES.
License tax limitation on county, city or town, §58.1-3703.
Limousines and executive sedan carriers.
See LIMOUSINES AND EXECUTIVE SEDAN CARRIERS.
Motor carriers, §§46.2-2000 to 46.2-2099.44.
See MOTOR CARRIERS, PASSENGERS.
Motor launch carriers.
See MOTOR LAUNCH CARRIERS.
Motor vehicle sales and use tax exemption, §58.1-2403.
Railroads.
Generally, §§56-345.1 to 56-451.1.
See RAILROADS.
Special or charter party carriers.
See SPECIAL OR CHARTER PARTY CARRIERS.
Special regulatory revenue tax, §§58.1-2660 to 58.1-2665.
Transportation companies.
Generally, §§56-99.2 to 56-140.
See TRANSPORTATION COMPANIES.

PASSING, MOTOR VEHICLE.
Generally, §§46.2-837 to 46.2-844.
See TRAFFIC INFRACTIONS.

PASSPORTS.
Criminal history record information, dissemination, §19.2-389.
Extortion by threats.
Threatening to withhold, §18.2-59.
Fictitious, facsimile or simulated passports.
Manufacture, sale, possession, etc., §18.2-204.2.

PASS-THROUGH ZONES.
Locality authorized to adopt ordinance, congested boat traffic, §29.1-744.4.

PASSWORDS.
Computers.
Using computer to gather identifying information, §18.2-152.5:1.
Identity theft, §§18.2-186.3, 18.2-186.3:1, 18.2-186.5.

PAST DUE LOST EVIDENCE OF DEBT.
Action on, §8.01-32.

PASTURE MANAGEMENT.
Resource management plans, §10.1-104.8.

PATENT AND TRADEMARK ATTORNEYS.
Admittance to practice.
Foreign attorneys admitted without examination, VA SCt Rule 1A:2.

PATENTS.
Colleges and universities.
Adoption of intellectual property policies, §23-4.3.

PATENTS —Cont'd
Colleges and universities —Cont'd
Authorization of transfer interest, §23-4.4.
Congress, US Const Art I §8.
Innovation and entrepreneurship investment authority.
Administration of materials developed by or for state agencies, public institutions or political subdivisions, §2.2-2221.
Inventions, US Const Art I §8.
Invention development services generally, §§59.1-208 to 59.1-215.
See INVENTION DEVELOPMENT SERVICES.
Practice of patent law, §54.1-3901.
Foreign attorneys, VA SCt Rule 1A:2.
Public officers and employees.
Ownership of patents developed by state employees, §2.2-2822.
Sales, UCC.
Buyer's obligation against infringement, §8.2-312.
Notice of claim or litigation to person answerable over, §8.2-607.
Warranty against infringement, §8.2-312.
Water and waste authorities.
Powers, §15.2-5114.

PATENTS FOR LAND, §§41.1-1 to 41.1-20.
See LAND OFFICE.

PATERNITY PROCEEDINGS.
Acknowledgment by putative father under oath.
Evidence relating to parentage, §20-49.5.
Admission by putative father.
Evidence relating to parentage, §20-49.4.
Assisted conception, status of child, §§20-156 to 20-165.
Parentage of child, §20-158.
Relation of parent and child, §20-164.
Birth certificates.
Amendments to show paternity, §32.1-269.
Determination of paternity.
New birth certificates established on determination of paternity, §32.1-261.
Transmittal to state registrar, §20-49.8.
Burden of proof.
Evidence relating to parentage, §20-49.4.
Child support.
Proceedings to establish paternity or enforce support obligations.
Males between the ages of fourteen and eighteen, §20-49.6.
Support of children of unwed parents by father, §20-49.5.
Child support enforcement by department of social services.
Acknowledgment by father or mother.
Establishment by, §63.2-1913.
Establishment by department.
Request filed, §63.2-1913.
Genetic tests.
Establishment by, §63.2-1913.
Hospital paternity establishment plans, §63.2-1914.
Names and addresses of persons alleged to be putative fathers.
Department requesting, §63.2-1902.
Summons by department to appear, §63.2-1913.
Child with father's surname.
Evidence relating to parentage, §20-49.4.
Commencement of actions, §20-49.2.
Competency of parents to testify, §20-49.7.

PATERNITY PROCEEDINGS —Cont'd
Deductions on income tax.
Evidence relating to parentage, §20-49.4.
Descent and distribution.
Delineation of parent-child relationship, §64.2-102.
Evidence of paternity, §64.2-103.
DNA testing, §§20-49.3, 20-49.4.
Drivers' licenses.
Suspension or refusal to renew, failure to comply with a paternity test order, §46.2-320.1.
Evidence.
Admissibility of evidence related to parentage, §§20-49.3, 20-49.4.
Competency of parties to testify, §20-49.7.
Full faith and credit.
Out-of-state paternity determinations, §20-49.8.
Genetic testing.
Child support enforcement by department of social services.
Establishment by, §63.2-1913.
Genetic tests, §§20-49.3, 20-49.4.
Establishing exclusion of individual as father.
Relief from determination, §20-49.10.
Hospital paternity establishment plans.
Child support enforcement by department of social services, §63.2-1914.
Income tax personal exemption.
Evidence relating to parentage, §20-49.4.
Interstate family support, §20-88.78.
Judgments and decrees.
Determination of parentage, §20-49.8.
Jurisdiction.
Commencement of action, §20-49.2.
Juvenile and domestic relations district court, §16.1-241.
Labor and delivery expenses.
Payment or apportionment of unpaid expenses between parties, §20-49.8.
Males between the ages of fourteen and eighteen.
Admission of paternity, §20-49.4.
Proceedings to establish paternity or enforce support obligations, §20-49.6.
Maternal relationship.
How established, §20-49.1.
Medical or anthropological evidence.
Admissibility, §20-49.4.
Open cohabitation.
Evidence relating to parentage, §20-49.4.
Orders.
Determination of parentage, §20-49.8.
Parent and child relationship.
How established, §20-49.1.
Parties.
Commencement of action, §20-49.2.
Paternal relationship.
How established, §20-49.1.
Personal exemptions on income tax.
Evidence relating to parentage, §20-49.4.
Petition for relief from determination, §20-49.10.
Physician-patient privilege.
Waiver of privilege, §20-49.7.
Relief from legal determination of paternity, §20-49.10.
Setting aside legal determination.
Genetic test establishing individual not father, §20-49.10.
Sexual intercourse between mother and putative father.
Evidence relating to parentage, §20-49.4.

PATERNITY PROCEEDINGS —Cont'd
Surrogacy contracts, §§20-156 to 20-165.
Determination of parentage generally, §20-158.
Relation of parent and child, §20-164.

PATHOLOGICAL SPECIMENS.
State laboratory for testing specimens submitted by medical profession.
Division of consolidated laboratory services, §2.2-1104.

PATHOLOGISTS.
Postmortem examinations.
Employment to make autopsies, §32.1-281.

PATIENT HEALTH RECORDS PRIVACY.
Breach of medical information, notice to be given, §32.1-127.1:05.
Disease prevention and control.
Disclosure of certain information required, §32.1-127.1:04.
Records generally.
See MEDICAL RECORDS.

PATIENT LEVEL DATA SYSTEM, §32.1-276.6.

PATIENTS AT MENTAL HEALTH.
Admissions and dispositions generally.
See MENTAL HEALTH.

PATIENTS' RECORDS.
Generally.
See MEDICAL RECORDS.

PATRICK COUNTY.
Blue Ridge airport authority, 1964 ch 25, 1978 ch 633, 1996 ch 465.
Confederate cemeteries and graves.
Disbursement of funds appropriated for upkeep, §10.1-2211.
Official covered bridge festival of Commonwealth, §1-510.
Public defenders office.
Established, §19.2-163.04.
School board.
Salary of members, §22.1-32.
Transient occupancy tax.
Disposition of revenues, §58.1-3819.
Western Virginia public education consortium, §22.1-354.1.

PATRICK HENRY MEMORIAL FOUNDATION.
Brookneal home.
Appropriations for maintenance, §10.1-2212.
Property exempt from taxation, §58.1-3607.

PATRICK HOSPITAL AUTHORITY.
Procurement.
Exceptions to competitive procurement, §2.2-4345.

PATRIOTIC MEMBERSHIP ORGANIZATIONS.
Alcoholic beverages.
Mixed beverage banquet licenses, §4.1-210.

PAUPERS.
Indigency generally.
See INDIGENCY.

PAVING SECONDARY ROADS, §33.1-70.1.

PAWNBROKERS, §§54.1-4000 to 54.1-4014.
Actions on bond, §54.1-4003.
Auctions.
Sale of goods pawned, §54.1-4005.
Watch resales.
Application of provisions, §59.1-136.
Bonds, surety, §54.1-4003.
Care of tangible personal property, §54.1-4013.

PAWNBROKERS —Cont'd
City or town power to regulate conduct of and prescribe number, §15.2-1114.
Consumer finance companies.
Exemption from act, §6.2-1503.
County power to regulate, §15.2-1232.1.
Criminal offenses.
Licensing violations, §54.1-4014.
Daily reporting requirements, §54.1-4010.
Defined, §54.1-4000.
Destroying identity of pawned property, §54.1-4012.
Digital image of identification of customers, retaining, §54.1-4009.
Disfiguring pawned property, §54.1-4012.
Examination of records by law enforcement, §54.1-4011.
Interest rates, §54.1-4008.
Law enforcement officers, admission to place of business, §54.1-4011.
License authorization by court, §54.1-4001.
License required, §54.1-4001.
Local limitation of number of shops, §54.1-4002.
Lost ticket charge, §54.1-4004.
Memorandum to pledgor, §54.1-4004.
Misdemeanors.
Licensing violations, §54.1-4014.
Penalties for violations, §54.1-4014.
Records, §54.1-4009.
Examinations, §54.1-4011.
Seizure authorized, §54.1-4011.
Reports, §54.1-4010.
Sale of pawned goods, §54.1-4005.
Search for stolen or missing articles, §54.1-4011.
Service fee.
Record service fee, §54.1-4009.
Storage fee, §54.1-4013.
Unlawful procurement of licensure, §54.1-102.
Unlawful use of licensure, §54.1-111.
Watch resales, §§59.1-131 to 59.1-136.
Advertising, §59.1-134.
Auction sales exempted, §59.1-136.
Displaying, §59.1-134.
Invoice to purchaser, §59.1-133.
Provision violations.
Penalties, §59.1-135.
Tagging, §59.1-132.
When watch deemed secondhand, §59.1-131.

PAYABLE ON DEATH ACCOUNTS.
Multiple-party accounts.
Generally, §§6.2-604 to 6.2-620.
See MULTIPLE-PARTY ACCOUNTS.

PAY ANY BANK.
Items endorsed, §8.4-201.

PAYDAY LOANS, §§6.2-1800 to 6.2-1829.
Acquisition of controlling share of business, §6.2-1808.
Action against borrower outside Commonwealth.
Agreement with borrower allowing.
Prohibition, §6.2-1816.
Action by person suffering loss, §6.2-1826.
Additional office, opening, approval, §6.2-1807.
Administrative or regulatory proceeding against licensee.
Reporting to commissioner, §6.2-1812.
Advertising.
Disclosure statements to be included, §6.2-1816.

PAYDAY LOANS —Cont'd
Advertising —Cont'd
  Restrictions, §6.2-1819.
Amount of obligation to licensee.
  Limitation, §6.2-1816.
Annual report to commissioner, §6.2-1811.
Application for license, §6.2-1803.
Application for loan.
  Query to database by licensee, §6.2-1810.
Arranging or brokering loans.
  Engaging in business of, prohibition, §6.2-1801.
Attorney general.
  Referral of violations to, investigation, duties, §6.2-1828.
Bankruptcy, reorganization, receivership.
  Reporting to commissioner, §6.2-1812.
Bond required by applicant for license, §6.2-1804.
Books, accounts and records.
  Maintenance, retention, §6.2-1809.
Business methods, required and prohibited, §6.2-1816.
Cap on amount of obligation owed licensee, §6.2-1816.
Cease and desist orders, §6.2-1822.
Check as security, §6.2-1816.
Closing business location.
  Notice, §6.2-1807.
Collection.
  Fair debt collection practices act compliance, §6.2-1816.
Commencement of business at new office.
  Notice, §6.2-1807.
Conducting in same place as other business conducted, §6.2-1820.
Consumer protection act.
  Violations constitute violation of act, §6.2-1829.
Contents of license, §6.2-1807.
Costs of examination, supervision and regulation.
  Fee to defray costs, §6.2-1814.
Court costs and attorneys' fees.
  Action by person suffering loss, §6.2-1826.
  Judgment obtained against borrower, §6.2-1818.
Database inquiry.
  Eligibility of applicant for new loan, §6.2-1810.
Database inquiry fee, §6.2-1810.
Dating check accepted as security, §6.2-1816.
Default.
  Legal proceeding initiated by licensee.
    Time period after default, §6.2-1816.
Definitions, §6.2-1800.
Deposit item return fee, §6.2-1818.
Disbursement of loan proceeds, §6.2-1816.
Doing business without license, §§6.2-1801, 6.2-1825.
Electronically debiting borrower's deposit account, §6.2-1816.
Eligibility of applicant for new loan.
  Query to database by licensee, §6.2-1810.
Endorsing check upon receipt as security, §6.2-1816.
Entry into loan.
  Reporting event to database, §6.2-1810.
Examination of licensees, §6.2-1813.
Extended payment plan.
  Payment of loan by, §6.2-1816.
Fair debt collection practices act compliance, §6.2-1816.
Fees, §6.2-1817.
  Additional charges, §6.2-1818.

PAYDAY LOANS —Cont'd
Fees —Cont'd
  Application fee, §6.2-1803.
  Cashing loan proceeds check.
    Prohibition, §6.2-1816.
  Opening additional office or relocating office, approval, §6.2-1807.
  Paid to defray costs of examination, supervision and regulation, §6.2-1814.
Felony indictment or conviction.
  Reporting to commissioner, §6.2-1812.
Fifth loan made to borrower within 180 days, §6.2-1816.
Financial institutions.
  Electing not to become licensed under provisions.
    Inapplicability of provision, §6.2-1802.
  Electing to become licensed under provisions.
    Effect, §6.2-1802.
Fine or penalty for violations, §6.2-1824.
Hearings.
  Cease and desist orders, §6.2-1822.
  Proposed suspension or revocation, request, §6.2-1823.
Information to borrower, providing, §6.2-1816.
Interest in property, limitations on taking, §6.2-1816.
Interest rate, §6.2-1817.
Internet-accessible database, §6.2-1810.
Internet loans made to residents.
  Applicability of provisions, §6.2-1827.
Investigation and examination of business affairs, §6.2-1813.
Investigation of applicant for license, §6.2-1805.
License required to engage in business of making, §6.2-1801.
  Suspension or revocation of license, §6.2-1821.
Loan fee, §6.2-1817.
Making new loan following payment or satisfaction of loan, §6.2-1816.
Maximum amount of obligation, §6.2-1816.
Media advertisements.
  Conspicuous disclosures, §6.2-1816.
Military personnel.
  Prohibited business methods against, §6.2-1816.
Negotiating check to third party, prohibition, §6.2-1816.
Noncompliant loan agreement.
  Unenforceable, §6.2-1826.
Notice.
  Cease and desist orders, §6.2-1822.
  Closing business location, §6.2-1807.
  Commencement of business at new office, §6.2-1807.
  Proposed suspension or revocation of license, §6.2-1823.
Obligated upon more than one loan, §6.2-1816.
Pamphlet explaining rights and liabilities.
  Giving borrower, §6.2-1816.
Partial payments to be allowed, §6.2-1816.
Payment other product or service of licensee.
  Loan for, prohibition, §6.2-1816.
Post-dated check as security, prohibition, §6.2-1816.
Posting or display of license, §6.2-1807.
Power of attorney or authority to confess judgment.
  Licensee not to obtain from borrower, §6.2-1816.
Private right of action, §6.2-1826.
Product or service sold at licensee's business location.
  Loan to enable borrower to pay for, §6.2-1816.

PAYDAY LOANS —Cont'd
Prohibited business methods, §6.2-1816.
Qualifications for issuance of license, §6.2-1806.
Query to database by licensee.
Eligibility of applicant for new loan, §6.2-1810.
Rate of interest, §6.2-1817.
Receipts, §6.2-1816.
Refinancing, renewal or extension, prohibition, §6.2-1816.
Relocation of office, approval, §6.2-1807.
Repayment in full, §6.2-1816.
Reports.
Annual report to commissioner, §6.2-1811.
Other events where report required, §6.2-1812.
Required business methods, §6.2-1816.
Rules and regulations, §6.2-1815.
Satisfaction of loan.
Reporting event to database, §6.2-1810.
Schedule of fee and interest charges, posting, §6.2-1816.
Surrender of license.
License in force until, preexisting legal right or obligation not affected, §6.2-1807.
Suspension or revocation of license, §6.2-1821.
License in force until, preexisting legal right or obligation not affected, §6.2-1807.
Notice of proposed suspension or revocation, §6.2-1823.
Threatening criminal proceedings against borrower, prohibition, §6.2-1816.
Toll-free number of commissions.
Giving borrower, §6.2-1816.
Transfer or assignment of license.
Prohibition, §6.2-1807.
Unfair, misleading, deceptive or fraudulent acts or practices, §6.2-1816.
Verification fee, §6.2-1817.
Waiver of borrower's rights.
Agreement calling for, prohibition, §6.2-1816.
Web page promoting licensee.
Conspicuous disclosures, §6.2-1816.
Written loan agreement, §6.2-1816.

PAYMENT BONDS.
Public construction contracts, §2.2-4337.
Actions on, §2.2-4341.
Alternative forms of security, §2.2-4338.
Public contracts for goods and services, §2.2-4339.

PAYMENT IN FULL.
Banks.
Finance charges.
Credit union loans, §6.2-1302.
Checks.
Restrictive indorsements generally, §8.3A-206.
Savings institutions.
Shares and shareholders, §6.2-1117.

PAYMENT INTO COURT, §8.01-421.
Eminent domain.
Highways.
Awards in greater or lesser amounts, §33.1-128.
Release of mechanics' lien, §§43-70, 43-71.
Small amounts to certain persons through court without intervention of fiduciary, §8.01-606.

PAYMENT ORDERS.
Bad check law generally, §§18.2-181 to 18.2-185.
Funds transfers.
See FUNDS TRANSFERS.

PAYMENTS IN LIEU OF PROPERTY TAXES.
Electric authorities, §15.2-5423.

PAYOR BANKS.
Bank deposits and collections generally.
See BANK DEPOSITS AND COLLECTIONS.

PAY-PER-CALL SERVICES, §§59.1-429 to 59.1-434.
Consumer protection, prohibited practices, §59.1-200.
Defined terms, §59.1-429.
Delayed timing periods, §59.1-430.
Disclosures, §59.1-430.
Duties of telephone company and long distance carriers, §59.1-431.
Enforcement of provisions, §59.1-434.
Investigations, §59.1-433.
Promotional prizes and gifts, §59.1-417.
Provision violations.
Penalties, §59.1-434.
Rates, §59.1-430.
Duties of telephone companies and long distance carriers, §59.1-431.
Regulations, §59.1-432.

PAY-PER-VIEW.
Boxing and wrestling events.
Tax on gross receipts or proceeds, §54.1-833.

PAY PHONES.
Communications sales and use tax, §§58.1-645 to 58.1-662.
See COMMUNICATIONS SALES AND USE TAX.

PAYROLL DEDUCTIONS.
Desertion and nonsupport.
Enforcement of support orders, §§20-79.1 to 20-79.3.
Income tax withholding, §§58.1-460 to 58.1-486.3.
See INCOME TAX WITHHOLDING.
Medicaid.
Unintentionally obtaining excess payments, §32.1-321.2.
Support of child or spouse.
Employer embezzling deduction, §18.2-111.2.
Failure to comply with support obligation, §16.1-278.16.
Unemployment compensation, §60.2-114.1.
Wage purchases, §6.2-1525.
Withholding by pass-through entities, §§58.1-486.1 to 58.1-486.3.

PAYROLL FACTOR.
Allocation and apportionment of corporate taxable income, §§58.1-412, 58.1-413.

PAY TELEPHONES.
Communications sales and use tax, §§58.1-645 to 58.1-662.
See COMMUNICATIONS SALES AND USE TAX.
Registration, §§56-508.15, 56-508.16.
Slugs, manufacturing, selling, etc., for unlawful uses, §18.2-180.
Stealing from or tampering with, §18.2-152.
Unlawful operation, §18.2-179.

P.C.
Professional corporations.
Generally, §§13.1-542.1 to 13.1-556.
See PROFESSIONAL CORPORATIONS.
Use of initials following corporate name, §13.1-544.1.

PEACE BONDS, §§19.2-19 to 19.2-25.
See RECOGNIZANCE TO KEEP THE PEACE.

PEACE CORPS.
Special license plates for returned volunteers, §46.2-746.12.

PEACE OFFICERS.
Conservation police officers.
Generally, §§29.1-200 to 29.1-218.
See CONSERVATION POLICE OFFICERS.
Conservators of the peace.
Generally, §§19.2-12 to 19.2-18.
See CONSERVATORS OF THE PEACE.
Special conservators of the peace, §§9.1-150.1 to 9.1-150.4.
Interjurisdictional law-enforcement authority and agreements, §§15.2-1724 to 15.2-1730.
Law enforcement officers generally.
See LAW ENFORCEMENT OFFICERS.
Police generally, §§15.2-1700 to 15.2-1753.
See POLICE.
Rewards.
Apprehension of escaped inmates, §19.2-7.
Sheriffs.
See SHERIFFS.
Special conservators of the peace, §§9.1-150.1 to 9.1-150.4.

PEACHES.
Controlled atmosphere storage, §§3.2-4600 to 3.2-4613.

PEANUTS, §§3.2-1900 to 3.2-1910.
Bonds, surety.
Virginia peanut board.
Secretary and other employees, §3.2-1904.
Definitions, §3.2-1900.
Excise tax.
Criminal penalties, §§3.2-1909, 3.2-1910.
Delinquent taxes.
Penalty and interest, §3.2-1102.
Action to recover, §3.2-1102.
Expenditure of moneys collected, §3.2-1906.
Levy, §3.2-1905.
Peanut fund, §3.2-1910.
Processors.
Liability for collection and payment, §3.2-1907.
Records, §3.2-1908.
Falsifying records as misdemeanor, §3.2-1909.
Virginia peanut board.
Administration of funds levied and collected, §3.2-1904.
Peanut fund.
Dedicated revenues, diversion, §3.2-1100.
Excise tax, Expenditure of moneys collected, §3.2-1906.
Virginia peanut board.
Bond of secretary and other employees, §3.2-1904.
Chairman, §3.2-1903.
Commission continued as board, §3.2-1901.
Compensation, §3.2-1903.
Members, §3.2-1901.
Expenses, §3.2-1903.
Terms, §3.2-1902.
Powers and duties, §3.2-1904.
Vacancies, §3.2-1902.

PEARL HARBOR REMEMBRANCE DAY, §2.2-3309.

PEARL HARBOR SURVIVORS.
Special license plates, §46.2-741.

PEDDLERS.
City or town power to regulate or prohibit peddling, §15.2-1114.

PEDDLERS —Cont'd
County manager plan of government, §15.2-732.
County power to regulate, §15.2-1232.1.
License taxes, §58.1-3717.
Limitations on license taxes imposed, §58.1-3719.
Peddlers at wholesale, §58.1-3718.
Ordinances regulating door-to-door vendors, §15.2-913.

PEDESTRIANS, §§46.2-923 to 46.2-935.
Blind pedestrians.
Effect of failure to use cane or guide dog, §46.2-934.
Intentional interference with guide dog, §3.2-6588.
Liability for injuries to, §46.2-932.1.
Vehicles to stop for pedestrians guided by dog or carrying recognized cane, §46.2-933.
Boarding or alighting from bus, §46.2-927.
Careless interference with vehicle passage, §46.2-923.
Controlled access highways.
Prohibited use, §46.2-808.
Control signals.
Failure to observe pedestrian control signals, §46.2-925.
Failure to yield right of way, §46.2-924.
Pedestrian boarding or alighting from a bus, §46.2-927.
Fine schedule, VA SCt Rule 3B:2.
Maximum fine for violating Title 46.2, §46.2-113.
Handbills, leaflets, literature, advertisements.
Distribution along highways, public roadways, medians.
Localities and VDOT may prohibit or regulate, §46.2-931.
Highways and roads.
Funding to undertake pedestrian projects, §33.1-223.2:6.
Hitchhiking, §46.2-929.
Jaywalking, §46.2-923.
Juvenile offenses.
Summons issued by officer.
Juvenile and domestic relations district court may proceed on, §16.1-260.
Local regulation of pedestrian traffic, §§46.2-1219, 46.2-1305.
Loitering on bridges or highway rights-of-way, §46.2-930.
Fine schedule, VA SCt Rule 3B:2.
Malicious interference with vehicle passage, §46.2-923.
Manner of crossing highway, §46.2-923.
No sidewalk.
Keeping to left side of roadway, §46.2-928.
Ordinances.
Authority to regulate pedestrian traffic, §46.2-935.
Parking lots.
Regulation of pedestrian traffic, §46.2-1219.
Playing on streets or highways, §46.2-932.
Policy statewide, §33.1-23.03:001.
Prepayment of fine, §16.1-69.40:1.
Roller skates on highways, §46.2-932.
Sale of merchandise on highways, public roadways, medians.
Localities and VDOT may prohibit or regulate, §46.2-931.
Sidewalks for pedestrian traffic, §33.1-205.
Signs at marked crosswalks, §46.2-924.
Skateboards on highways, §46.2-932.
Solicitation of contributions on highways, public roadways, medians.
Localities and VDOT may prohibit or regulate, §46.2-931.

PEDESTRIANS —Cont'd
Soliciting rides, §46.2-929.
Statewide policy, §33.1-23.03:001.
Stepping into street where driver's vision obscured, §46.2-926.
Tailgating.
Persons riding bicycles, mopeds, etc., not to attach to vehicles, §46.2-932.
Toys or other devices on wheels.
Playing on highways, §46.2-932.
Walking on left edge of roadway where no sidewalk, §46.2-928.
Walk or Don't walk signal, §46.2-925.
Walkways for pedestrian traffic, §33.1-205.

PEDIGREE.
False livestock pedigree, §18.2-205.

PEDIGREE SYSTEM.
Controlled substances.
Establishment and implementation by board of pharmacy, pedigree defined, §54.1-3307.

PEEPHOLES IN APARTMENT DOORS.
Residential landlord obligations, §55-248.13:1.

PEEPING TOMS, §18.2-130.
Third misdemeanor conviction, punishment, §18.2-67.5:1.

PEER REVIEW OF MEDICAL COSTS.
Workers' compensation generally, §§65.2-1300 to 65.2-1310.
See WORKERS' COMPENSATION.

PELHAM CHAPEL.
Leasing, §57-5.

PELLET GUNS.
Local regulation, §15.2-915.4.
Pointing, holding or brandishing air or gas operated weapon, §18.2-282.

PELVIC EXAMINATIONS.
Medical students performing.
Examinations of anesthetized or unconscious females, §54.1-2959.

PENDENTE LITE SUPPORT, §16.1-278.17.
Divorce proceedings.
Contents of decree, §20-79.
Hearings, §20-103.
Formula for determination, §16.1-278.17:1.

PENDING ACTIONS.
Adoption of 1950 code.
Effect generally, §§1-4, 1-9.

PENINSULA AIRPORT COMMISSION.
Created, 1946 ch 22.
Amended in 1946-47, 1946-47 ch 46.
Amended in 1948, 1948 ch 1.
Amended in 1954, 1954 ch 568.
Amended in 1956, 1956 ch 489.
Amended in 1958, 1958 ch 68.
Amended in 1964, 1964 ch 270.
Amended in 1968, 1968 ch 777.
Amended in 1971, 1971 ch 134.
Amended in 1975, 1975 ch 385.
Amended in 1979, 1979 ch 167.
Amended in 1980, 1980 ch 370.
Amended in 1984, 1984 ch 114.
Amended in 1987, 1987 ch 60.
Amended in 1989, 1989 ch 270.

PENINSULA CIVIC RECREATION CENTER AUTHORITY, 1960 ch 579.

PENINSULA PORTS AUTHORITY OF VIRGINIA.
Created, 1952 ch 46.
Amended in 1956, 1956 ch 42.
Amended in 1964, 1964 ch 39.
Amended in 1973, 1973 ch 185.
Amended in 1974, 1974 ch 495.
Amended in 1977, 1977 ch 68, 1977 ch 599.
Amended in 1978, 1978 ch 86.
Amended in 1984, 1984 ch 249.
Amended in 1998, 1998 ch 211.
Amended in 2000, 2000 ch 670, 2000 ch 698.

PENINSULA TRANSPORTATION DISTRICT.
Commission members, §15.2-4507.
Transportation districts generally, §§15.2-4500 to 15.2-4534.

PENITENTIARY.
Prisons generally.
See PRISONS.

PENNSYLVANIA.
Chesapeake Bay commission.
General provisions, §§30-240 to 30-255.

PEN REGISTERS.
Application for and issuance of order, §19.2-70.2.
General prohibition of use, §19.2-70.1.

PENSIONS, BENEFITS AND RETIREMENT.
Abandonment of funds presumption, §55-210.8.
Attorneys.
Mass retirement program of state bar, §54.1-3917.
Colleges and universities.
Voluntary early retirement.
Authority to establish incentives, §23-9.2:3.1.
Credit unions.
Power to act as trustee or custodian, §6.2-1363.
Disclaimer of property interests.
Disclaimer of beneficiary designation, §64.2-2610.
Employee trusts.
Restraints on delineation of property construed, §55-13.1.
Firefighters.
Relief for firefighters and dependents, §§27-39 to 27-50.
See FIREFIGHTERS.
General assembly power to grant, VA Const Art IV §14.
Income tax.
Amended returns.
Federal, state or local employees, §58.1-1823.
Interest.
Loans by pension plans to participants, §6.2-319.
Judicial retirement system, §§51.1-300 to 51.1-309.
See JUDICIAL RETIREMENT SYSTEM.
Law officers' retirement system, §§51.1-211 to 51.1-221.
See LAW OFFICERS' RETIREMENT SYSTEM.
Loans.
Pension plans to participants.
Interest, contract rate more than legal rate, §6.2-319.
Retirement system of Virginia, §§51.1-124.1 to 51.1-169.
See VIRGINIA RETIREMENT SYSTEM.
Security registration exemption, §13.1-514.
State bar of Virginia.
Master retirement program, §54.1-3917.
State corporation commission, VA Const Art IX §1.

PENSIONS, BENEFITS AND RETIREMENT —Cont'd
State police retirement system, §§51.1-200 to 51.1-210.
See STATE POLICE RETIREMENT SYSTEM.
Transferability of pension plan.
Nonprobate transfer on death, §64.2-620.
Unclaimed funds, disposition of, §§55-210.8, 55-210.28:1.
Unemployment compensation.
Benefits reduction, §60.2-604.
Virginia retirement system, §§51.1-124.1 to 51.1-169.
See VIRGINIA RETIREMENT SYSTEM.
Volunteer firefighters' and rescue squad workers' service award fund, §§51.1-1200 to 51.1-1211.
See VOLUNTEER FIREFIGHTERS' AND RESCUE SQUAD WORKERS' SERVICE AWARD FUND.

PEOPLE AS SOURCE OF POWER, VA Const Art I §2.

PEOPLE WITH DISABILITIES.
See DISABILITY OR HANDICAP.

PEPPER SPRAY.
Illegal use of tear gas, phosgene and other gases, §18.2-312.
Malicious bodily injury by means of a caustic substance or agent, §18.2-52.

PER CAPITA.
Descent and distribution.
When parties take, §64.2-202.
Wills.
Descendants of devisees or legatees.
When parties take, §64.2-418.

PERCENTAGE RETAINED BY PARI-MUTUEL LICENSEES, §59.1-392.

PER DIEM EXPENSES.
See EXPENSES OF PUBLIC OFFICIALS.

PERFECTION OF LIENS.
Hangar keeper liens.
Aircraft subject to chattel mortgage, §43-34.1.
Mechanic's and materialmen's liens.
General contractors.
Affidavits, §43-5.
Inuring to benefit of subcontractor, §43-18.
Memorandums, §§43-5, 43-15.
Hearings on validity, §43-17.1.
Persons performing labor or furnishing materials for subcontractors, §43-9.
Affidavits, §43-10.
Memorandums, §§43-10, 43-15.
Notice, §§43-10, 43-14.1.
Subcontractors, §43-7.
Affidavit, §43-8.
Lien of general contractor to inure to benefit of subcontractor, §43-18.
Memorandum, §§43-8, 43-15.
Notice, §§43-8, 43-14.1.

PERFECTION OF SECURITY INTERESTS.
Canal employee or supplier liens, §§43-24, 43-25.
Manufacturing employee or supplier liens, §§43-24, 43-25.
Mechanics' and materialmen's liens.
General contractors, §43-4.

PERFECTION OF SECURITY INTERESTS —Cont'd
Mechanics' and materialmen's liens —Cont'd
Persons performing labor or furnishing materials for subcontractor, §43-9.
Subcontractors, §43-7.
Mining employee or supplier liens, §§43-24, 43-25.
Railway employee or supplier liens, §§43-24, 43-25.
Secured transactions.
See SECURED TRANSACTIONS.
Transportation company employee or supplier liens, §§43-24, 43-25.

PERFORMANCE BONDS.
Public construction contracts, §2.2-4337.
Action on, §2.2-4340.
Alternative forms of security, §2.2-4338.
Public contracts for goods and services, §2.2-4339.

PERFORMANCE EVALUATION INFORMATION.
Employment-related information disclosure.
Prospective or current employer disclosing.
Immunity, presumption of good faith, §8.01-46.1.

PERFORMANCE OF CONTRACTS.
Leases, UCC.
Adequate assurance, §8.2A-401.
Excused performance, §§8.2A-405, 8.2A-406.
Substituted performance, §8.2A-404.
Part performance extinguishing obligation, §11-12.
Sales, UCC.
Assurance, §8.2-609.
Cooperation, §8.2-311.
Delegation, §8.2-210.
Generally, §§8.2-501 to 8.2-515.
Options, §8.2-311.
Substituted performance, §8.2-614.
Suspension until adequate assurance of performance, §8.2-609.

PERFORMING ARTS.
Arts commission.
Duties, §2.2-2509.

PERFORMING ARTS CENTERS.
Drinking or possessing alcoholic beverages in or on school grounds, §4.1-309.
Mixed beverages licenses, §4.1-210.
Local license taxes, §4.1-233.
State license fees, §4.1-231.

PERINATAL CARE.
Health insurance.
Public officers and employees.
Required coverage, §2.2-2818.
Postpartum services insurance coverage, obstetrical services, §38.2-3414.1.
Medical assistance services plans, §32.1-325.

PERINATAL DEPRESSION.
Information to maternity patient prior to releasing.
Hospital or nurse midwife, §32.1-134.01.

PERIODICALS.
Hearsay exception.
Opinion testimony by experts, §8.01-401.1.
Tourism authority.
Authority to issue and carry and charge for advertising, §2.2-2318.

PERIODIC TESTING FOR DRUG OR ALCOHOL ABUSE.
Condition of suspended sentence or probation.
Drug conviction, §§18.2-252, 18.2-254.
Felony conviction generally, §18.2-251.01.
Defeating drug and alcohol screening tests, §18.2-251.4.

PERISHABLE PROPERTY.
Purchases through division of purchases and supply.
Provisions not mandatory, §2.2-1119.
Sales, UCC, §§8.2-603, 8.2-604.

PERITONEAL DIALYSIS EQUIPMENT AND SUPPLIES.
Retail sales and use tax exemption, §58.1-609.10.

PERJURY, §§18.2-434 to 18.2-437.
Absentee and early voting.
Military and overseas voters.
Declaration regarding what constitutes perjury, §24.2-463.
Agricultural cooperative associations.
Persons signing instrument containing misstatement, §13.1-345.
Antitrust laws.
Investigations by attorney general, §59.1-9.10.
Appointment of attorney for accused.
False swearing regarding statement of indigency, §19.2-161.
Auditor of public accounts examinations.
Willfully swearing falsely in, §30-136.
Boat registration.
False affidavit or swearing, §29.1-702.1.
Crime victim and witness assistance programs.
Filing false claim under oath, §19.2-368.16.
Drivers' licenses.
Persons convicted of unlawful procurement of license or permit, §46.2-316.
Giving conflicting testimony on separate occasions as to same matter, §18.2-435.
Grand juries.
Grand juror testifying as to witnesses testimony, §19.2-192.
Special grand jury testimony.
Limitation of prosecution for perjury, §19.2-212.
Immunity of witnesses, §18.2-437.
Impeachment of witnesses.
Unadjudicated perjury, VA SCt Rule 2:608.
Inducing another to give false testimony, §18.2-436.
Industrial sick benefit companies.
False statements for purposes of defrauding, §18.2-204.
Insurance rate investigations, §38.2-1916.1.
Motor vehicle certificate, license or permit.
Making false affidavit or swearing falsely, §46.2-105.
Motor vehicles department.
False affidavit to department.
One year revocation of driver's license, §46.2-389.
Officeholding prohibited of person convicted, §18.2-434.
Public assistance.
False application or false swearing, §63.2-502.
Punishment and penalty generally, §18.2-434.
What deemed perjury, §18.2-434.
Witnesses.
Impeachment of witnesses, unadjudicated perjury, VA SCt Rule 2:608.

PERMANENT INJUNCTIONS.
Injunctions generally, §§8.01-620 to 8.01-634.
See INJUNCTIONS.

PERMITS.
ABC law.
Applications for permits, §4.1-230.
Continuing operation.
Person becoming lawfully entitled to operate a licensed establishment, §4.1-212.
Delivery of wine and beer permits, §4.1-212.1.
State license fees, §4.1-231.
Fees, §4.1-230.
Issuance by board, §4.1-212.
Publication, §4.1-230.
Suspension or revocation, §4.1-229.
Agricultural liming materials.
Contractors, §3.2-3704.
Distributors, §3.2-3702.
Aircraft.
Contract carriers, §5.1-9.2.
Application and fee, §5.1-9.3.
Duration, §5.1-9.9.
Suspension or revocation, §5.1-9.9.
Willful misrepresentation of facts, §5.1-9.9.
Air pollution control board.
See AIR POLLUTION CONTROL BOARD.
Airports.
Dangerous structures, §§5.1-25.1 to 5.1-25.4.
Animals.
Pet shops and dealers in companion animals.
Local ordinances, §3.2-6537.
Archaeological objects and sites.
Excavation of human remains, §10.1-2305.
Beach replenishment projects.
Expedited review of proposal and permit process, §28.2-1205.2.
Bedding and upholstered furniture.
Fees, §32.1-218.
Process to sanitize or sterilize, §32.1-216.
Refusal to issue, suspension or revocation, §32.1-224.
Biomass.
Small-scale conversion of biomass to alternative fuel.
Special exception or special use permit not required, §15.2-2288.01.
Building fixtures.
Secondhand article sales.
Issuance and revocation, §59.1-118.
Required, §59.1-117.
Building permits.
Erosion and sediment control, §62.1-44.15:57.
Residential property.
Wavier of building permit fees for affordable housing, §15.2-958.4.
Sewage disposal considerations in issuance, §32.1-165.
Carrying concealed weapons, §18.2-308.
Appeal of denial of permit, §18.2-308.08.
Application for permit, §18.2-308.02.
Processing, §18.2-308.04.
Supreme Court website, inclusion on application, §18.2-308.015.
Carrying concealed handgun with permit, §18.2-308.01.
Central criminal records exchange.
Entering information into system, §18.2-308.07.
Denial of permit, §18.2-308.08.
Fees, §18.2-308.03.
Issuance of de facto permit, §18.2-308.05.

PERMITS —Cont'd
Carrying concealed weapons —Cont'd
Issuance of permit, §18.2-308.04.
Nonresident concealed handgun permits, §18.2-308.06.
Petition for appeal to court of appeals from final decision of circuit court, §17.1-406.
Reciprocity, §18.2-308.014.
Renewal of permit, §18.2-308.010.
Replacement permits, §18.2-308.011.
Retention of applications by circuit court clerk, time, destruction, §17.1-213.
Suspension or revocation of permit, §18.2-308.013.
Cave protection.
Excavation and scientific investigation, §10.1-1003.
Charitable gaming.
See CHARITABLE GAMING.
Chesapeake Bay watershed nutrient credit exchange program.
General permit, §62.1-44.19:14.
New or expanded facilities, §62.1-44.19:15.
Child labor.
Theatrical permits, §40.1-102.
Cigarette excise tax.
Stamping agent's permit, §58.1-1011.
City or town powers.
Requiring issuance in connection with enforcement of ordinance or regulation, §15.2-1125.
Clams.
Revocation, §28.2-521.
Coal surface mining, §§45.1-234 to 45.1-241.
See COAL SURFACE MINING.
Coastal primary sand dunes and beaches.
Exemption, Sandbridge Beach subdivision, §28.2-1408.2.
Issuance, §28.2-1406.
Time for, §28.2-1414.
Procedures, administrative, §28.2-1407.
Required, §28.2-1406.
Review, §28.2-1410.
Judicial review, §28.2-1415.
Modifications, §28.2-1413.
Procedure, §28.2-1412.
Remands, §28.2-1413.
Reversal of decisions, §28.2-1413.
When, §28.2-1411.
Standards for use, §28.2-1408.
Communications sales and use tax.
Direct payment permit, §58.1-658.
Dead bodies or fetuses.
Permits to transport, disinter or reinter, §§32.1-265, 32.1-266.
Deer.
Bonus deer permits, §29.1-305.1.
Dental hygienists, §54.1-2726.
Dentistry.
Clinician permits, §54.1-2715.
Oral and maxillofacial surgeons.
Sedation or anesthesia, §54.1-2709.5.
Door-to-door vendors.
Permit fees, §15.2-913.
Drug control.
Distributors, §§54.1-3429, 54.1-3430.
Limited permit for repackaging drugs, §54.1-3437.1.
Manufacturers, §§54.1-3429, 54.1-3430, 54.1-3437 to 54.1-3442.
Medical equipment suppliers, §§54.1-3435.2, 54.1-3435.3.

PERMITS —Cont'd
Drug control —Cont'd
Pharmacies, §§54.1-3432 to 54.1-3434.
Registration of nonresident pharmacies, §54.1-3434.2.
Warehousers, §54.1-3435.4.
Wholesalers, §§54.1-3429, 54.1-3430.
Drug paraphernalia.
Issuance of to non-pharmacists, §54.1-3471.
Eel pots, use in Back Bay and its tributaries, §29.1-416.1.
Electricity.
Electrical utility facility construction, §56-46.1.
Electric utility restructuring, §56-580.
Emergency medical services.
Agency, §32.1-111.6.
Revocation and suspension of permits, §32.1-111.8.
Emergency medical services vehicles, §32.1-111.6.
Revocation and suspension of permits, §32.1-111.8.
Endangered species.
Taking, possessing or transporting, §29.1-568.
Violations, §29.1-567.
Erosion and sediment control, §62.1-44.15:57.
Explosives.
Manufacturing, storage, handling, use or sales, §27-97.2.
Falcons.
Taking, holding and transporting, §29.1-419.
Issuance, §29.1-413.
By whom, §29.1-420.
Required, §29.1-412.
Fertilizer.
Contractor-applicator, §§3.2-3605 to 3.2-3608.
Field trial, §29.1-422.
Firearms.
Carrying concealed handgun with permit, §18.2-308.01.
Carrying concealed weapon.
Appeal of denial of permit, §18.2-308.08.
Application for permit, §18.2-308.02.
Processing, §18.2-308.04.
Supreme Court website, inclusion on application, §18.2-308.015.
Central criminal records exchange.
Entering information into system, §18.2-308.07.
Denial of permit, §18.2-308.08.
Issuance of de facto permit, §18.2-308.05.
Issuance of permit, §18.2-308.04.
Nonresident concealed handgun permits, §18.2-308.06.
Reciprocity, §18.2-308.014.
Renewal of permit, §18.2-308.010.
Replacement permits, §18.2-308.011.
Suspension or revocation of permit, §18.2-308.013.
Fees, §18.2-308.03.
Firearm sales or purchases.
Certain counties requiring for sale or purchase of pistols or revolvers, §15.2-1208.
Destruction of records of permits to sell, §15.2-1208.
Fishing, inland waters.
Eel pots, use in Back Bay and its tributaries, §29.1-416.1.
Fish and wildlife educational events.
Youth special permits, §29.1-315.1.
Multiple-year licenses or permits, §29.1-328.
National forest permits, §§29.1-408 to 29.1-411.

PERMITS —Cont'd
Fishing, inland waters —Cont'd
Netting of fish permits, §29.1-416.
Issuance, §29.1-413.
Required, §29.1-412.
Special permits for handicapped persons, §29.1-314.
Special permits for residents of juvenile learning centers, §29.1-317.
Special permits for school classes, §29.1-315.
Special permits for youth camps, §29.1-316.
Terms, §29.1-328.
Veterans.
Special permits, §29.1-312.
Youth special permits.
Fish and wildlife educational events, §29.1-315.1.
Fishing, tidal waters.
Health and sanitation provisions.
Removal of shellfish from condemned areas, §28.2-811.
Special permits, §28.2-815.
Limitation on sales, §28.2-204.1.
Scientific collection permits, §28.2-205.
Fur dealer permits, §§29.1-400 to 29.1-407.
Game and inland fisheries department.
Credit cards.
Payment of license and permit fees, §29.1-112.
Gas and oil exploration.
Regulation of development and production, §§45.1-361.27 to 45.1-361.38.
See GAS AND OIL EXPLORATION.
Geothermal energy.
Cancellation or suspension of permit, §45.1-179.8.
Going out of business special sales permits.
Failure to acquire, §18.2-223.
Issuance by counties, cities or towns, §18.2-224.
Groundwater management.
Withdrawal permits, §§62.1-262, 62.1-266.
Existing ground water withdrawals in existing ground water management areas, §62.1-260.
Existing ground water withdrawals in newly established ground water management areas, §62.1-261.
Issuance criteria, §62.1-263.
Issuance of special exceptions, §62.1-267.
Issuance of special orders, §62.1-268.
Not required, §62.1-259.
Provision violations.
Penalties, §§62.1-269, 62.1-270.
Public water supplies, §62.1-264.
Drought relief wells, §62.1-265.
Guns.
Carrying concealed weapon, §18.2-308.
Hawks.
Taking, holding and transporting, §29.1-419.
Issuance, §29.1-413.
By whom, §29.1-420.
Required, §29.1-412.
Hazardous waste management, §§10.1-1426, 10.1-1427.
Highways.
Construction or repair work within right-of-way lines, §46.2-1303.
Intermittent closing of roads subject to flooding.
Application and issuance of permit, §33.1-223.2.
Hunting.
Disability or handicap.
Shooting from stationary vehicles, §29.1-521.3.

PERMITS —Cont'd
Hunting —Cont'd
Fish and wildlife educational events.
Youth special permits, §29.1-315.1.
Multiple-year licenses or permits, §29.1-328.
National forest permits, §§29.1-408 to 29.1-411.
State forest permits, §§10.1-1151 to 10.1-1153.
Fees, §17.1-275.
Terms, §29.1-328.
Veterans.
Special permits for veterans, §29.1-312.
Youth special permits.
Fish and wildlife educational events, §29.1-315.1.
Ice cream, etc., manufacturing, §3.2-5214.
Manufactured homes.
Moving to place where to be used as place of residence, §58.1-3520.
Migrant labor camps.
Applications, §32.1-206.
Denial, §32.1-209.
Issuance, §32.1-207.
Provisional permits, §32.1-208.
Required, §32.1-204.
Revocation, §32.1-209.
Suspension, §32.1-209.
Transferability, §32.1-207.
Mobile homes.
Moving to place where to be used as place of residence, §58.1-3520.
Motor carriers, passengers.
See MOTOR CARRIERS, PASSENGERS.
Motor vehicle equipment.
Electrically powered vehicles, §46.2-1009.
Traction engines and tractors, §46.2-1046.
Motor vehicle size and weight.
Excessive size and weight permits, §§46.2-1139 to 46.2-1149.5.
See MOTOR VEHICLE SIZE AND WEIGHT.
Impeding or disrupting vehicles operating under valid highway hauling permit, §46.2-828.2.
National forest permits, §§29.1-408 to 29.1-411.
Netting of fish permits, §29.1-416.
Issuance, §29.1-413.
By whom, §29.1-420.
Required, §29.1-412.
Nonindigenous aquatic nuisance species act.
Authorizing, importing, transporting, sale, purchase, etc., §29.1-575.
Owls.
Taking, holding and transporting, §29.1-419.
Issuance, §29.1-413.
By whom, §29.1-420.
Required, §29.1-412.
Oysters.
Carrying oysters out of state, §28.2-546.
Dredging equipment on boats, §28.2-516.
Dredging in James river, §28.2-518.
Dredging or scraping on private ground, §28.2-515.
Revocation, §28.2-521.
Seed oysters.
Permits to buy or carry, §28.2-535.
Pari-mutuel wagering on horses, §§59.1-387 to 59.1-390.
See PARI-MUTUEL WAGERING.
Pest control, plants.
Sale or transporting of plant pests, §3.2-712.
Pet shops.
Local ordinances, §3.2-6537.

PERMITS —Cont'd
Pharmacies.
Drug control, §§54.1-3432 to 54.1-3434.
Pheasants.
Raising or purchasing, §29.1-514.
Pistol sales or purchases.
Certain counties requiring, §15.2-1208.
Plants and plant products inspection.
Sale or transporting of plant pests, §3.2-3802.
Precious metals dealers, §§54.1-4106, 54.1-4108.
Prerequisite to obtaining by contractor, §54.1-1111.
Public service companies, §56-15.
Renewable energy.
Small renewable energy projects.
Permits by rule, §10.1-1197.6.
Retail sales and use tax.
Direct payment permits, §58.1-624.
Revolver sales or purchases.
Certain counties requiring, §15.2-1208.
Roads, streets or public rights-of-way.
Use permits for transportation and utilities, §15.2-2015.
Salvage vehicles.
Crushing or flattening of vehicle into unrecognizable state.
Permit requirements, §46.2-1603.1.
Secondhand article sales.
Building fixtures.
Issuance and revocation, §59.1-118.
Required, §59.1-117.
Septage disposal.
Application backlogs, §32.1-163.4.
Letters in lieu of permits, §32.1-164.
Septic tanks.
Appeals from denials, §32.1-164.1.
Validity, §32.1-164.1:1.
Voluntary system upgrades for systems that are not failing, §32.1-164.1:3.
Small businesses.
One-stop small business permitting program, §2.2-1617.
One-stop small business permitting program (eff until 1/1/2014), §2.2-904.1.
Small renewable energy projects.
Permits by rule, §10.1-1197.6.
Solid waste management.
Closure of landfill.
Postclosure monitoring, maintenance and plans, §10.1-1410.2.
Landfill siting review, §10.1-1408.4.
Requirement, §10.1-1408.1.
Revocation or amendment, §10.1-1409.
Wetlands.
Special provisions regarding, §10.1-1408.5.
Specimen collection permits, §29.1-418.
Issuance, §29.1-413.
Required, §29.1-412.
Stormwater management.
Application, §62.1-44.15:34.
Regulated activities, §62.1-44.15:34.
Review and evaluation schedule, §62.1-44.15:38.
Revocation of approval, §62.1-44.15:38.
Security for permit, §62.1-44.15:34.
Terms, §62.1-44.15:26.
Submerged lands.
Cessation of activities, §28.2-1212.
Compliance, §28.2-1212.
Encroachments, §28.2-1207.
Fees, §28.2-1206.
Inspections, §28.2-1212.

PERMITS —Cont'd
Submerged lands —Cont'd
Joint application and review process.
Coordinated review of water resources projects, §28.2-1205.1.
Monitoring, §28.2-1212.
Use of state-owned bottom lands, §28.2-1205.
Surface mining.
Regulation of mining activity, §§45.1-181 to 45.1-185.
Surface water management areas.
Withdrawal permits, §62.1-248.
Application requirements, §62.1-248.1.
Cancellation, §62.1-251.
Not required, §62.1-243.
Riparian rights, §62.1-253.
State agency review, §62.1-250.
Suspension, §62.1-251.
Taxidermy permits, §29.1-415.
Issuance, §29.1-413.
By whom, §29.1-420.
Required, §29.1-412.
Sale of unclaimed or mounted specimens, §29.1-415.
Threatened species.
Permits to take, transport or possess, §29.1-568.
Transportation department.
Land use permits.
Issuance to company other than public service company, §2.2-1151.1.
Trapping.
Falcons, §29.1-419.
Hawks, §29.1-419.
Multiple-year licenses or permits, §29.1-328.
National forest permits, §§29.1-408 to 29.1-411.
Owls, §29.1-419.
Terms, §29.1-328.
Utility lines, §56-15.
Waste management, §§10.1-1402.1, 10.1-1402.2.
Water control board.
Stormwater management.
Terms, §62.1-44.15:26.
Waters of the state.
Confined animal feeding operations, §62.1-44.17:1.
Chesapeake Bay watershed nutrient credit exchange program, §62.1-44.19:21.
Discharge of sewage, industrial waste or other wastes.
Applications.
When application considered complete, §62.1-44.15:3.
Public hearings and permit procedures before the board, §62.1-44.15:02.
Fees.
Conformance with federal requirements, §62.1-44.15:8.
Permit program fund, §62.1-44.15:7.
Industrial waste discharges, §62.1-44.18:2.
Sewage discharges, §62.1-44.18:2.
Violations, §§62.1-44.31, 62.1-44.32.
Virginia water protection permits, §62.1-44.15:20.
Coordinated review of water resources projects, §62.1-44.15:5.01.
General permit for water quality improvement activities, §62.1-44.15:5.1.
Instream flow, preservation of, §62.1-44.15:22.
Potomac river.
Low-flow protections, §62.1-44.15:5.02.
Public hearings and permit procedures before the board, §62.1-44.15:5.02.
Water withdrawals, §62.1-44.15:22.

PERMITS —Cont'd
Waters of the state —Cont'd
Virginia water protection permits —Cont'd
Wetland and stream mitigation banks, §62.1-44.15:23.
Wetlands, impacts to, §62.1-44.15:21.
Wastes, non-industrial non-sewage.
Discharges, §62.1-44.18:2.
Water supplies, §32.1-172.
Additional or amended permits, §32.1-173.
Revocation, §32.1-174.
Weapons.
Carrying concealed weapons, §18.2-308.
Appeal of denial of permit, §18.2-308.08.
Application for permit, §18.2-308.02.
Processing, §18.2-308.04.
Supreme Court website, inclusion on application, §18.2-308.015.
Carrying concealed handgun with permit, §18.2-308.01.
Central criminal records exchange.
Entering information into system, §18.2-308.07.
Denial of permit, §18.2-308.08.
Fees, §18.2-308.03.
Issuance of de facto permit, §18.2-308.05.
Issuance of permit, §18.2-308.04.
Nonresident concealed handgun permits, §18.2-308.06.
Petition for appeal to court of appeals from final decision of circuit court, §17.1-406.
Reciprocity, §18.2-308.014.
Renewal of permit, §18.2-308.010.
Replacement permits, §18.2-308.011.
Suspension or revocation of permit, §18.2-308.013.
Well construction, §32.1-176.5.
Express geothermal permits, §32.1-176.4.
Fees, §32.1-176.4.
Wetlands.
Expedited permits, §28.2-1307.
Issuance, §28.2-1306.
Time for, §28.2-1314.
Modification of board decision, §28.2-1313.
Procedures, administrative, §28.2-1307.
Remand of board decision, §28.2-1313.
Required, §28.2-1306.
Reversal of board decision, §28.2-1313.
Review, §§28.2-1310, 28.2-1311.
Judicial review, §28.2-1315.
Procedure, §28.2-1312.
Standards for use and development of wetlands, §28.2-1308.
Utilization of guidelines, §28.2-1308.
Wildlife capturing, holding, propagating and disposing of, §29.1-417.
Issuance, §29.1-413.
Required, §29.1-412.
Withdrawal permits.
Groundwater management. See within this heading, "Groundwater management."

PERPETUAL CARE TRUST FUNDS.
Generally, §§54.1-2310 to 54.1-2342.

PERPETUAL EASEMENTS PERMITTING INUNDATION BY WATER.
Property exempt from taxation, VA Const Art X §6.

PERPETUATION OF TESTIMONY.
Abolition of common-law proceeding, §8.01-420.1.

PERPETUITIES, RULE AGAINST, §§55-13.2, 55-13.3.
Uniform statutory rule against perpetuities, §§55-12.1 to 55-12.6.

PERSONAL EFFECTS.
Property exempt from taxation, VA Const Art X §6.

PERSONAL FLOTATION DEVICES.
Personal watercraft, required to operate, §29.1-748.

PERSONAL IDENTIFIABLE INFORMATION.
Foster care children aged 16 or older, credit checks of.
Identification of cases of identity theft or misuse of personal identifying information, §63.2-905.2.
Identification generally.
See IDENTIFICATION.
Identity theft generally.
See IDENTITY THEFT.
Personal information privacy, §§59.1-442 to 59.1-444.
See PERSONAL INFORMATION PRIVACY.
State corporation commission.
Information contained in documents filed with commission.
Deletion, removal, refusal to accept documents, §12.1-19.

PERSONAL IDENTIFICATION NUMBERS.
Computers.
Using computer to gather identifying information, §18.2-152.5:1.
Identity theft, §§18.2-186.3, 18.2-186.3:1, 18.2-186.5.
Use of person's identity with intent to coerce, intimidate or harass, §18.2-186.4.

PERSONAL INFORMATION PRIVACY, §§59.1-442 to 59.1-444.
Collection and dissemination of information by state agencies.
Privacy protection.
Government data collection and dissemination practices act, §§2.2-3800 to 2.2-3809.
See GOVERNMENT DATA COLLECTION AND DISSEMINATION PRACTICES ACT.
Social security numbers, protection, §§2.2-3815, 2.2-3816.
Department of motor vehicle records.
Release of personal information, §46.2-208.
Accident reports, §§46.2-379, 46.2-380.
Domestic and sexual violence services.
Confidentiality of records of persons receiving, §63.2-104.1.
Employee personal identifying information, employer prohibition from releasing, §40.1-28.7:4.
Identification cards issued by DMV.
Confidentiality, §46.2-345.
Insurance information and privacy protection generally, §§38.2-600 to 38.2-620.
See INSURANCE INFORMATION AND PRIVACY PROTECTION.
Internet publication of personal information of public officials, §18.2-186.4:1.
Medical records.
Breach of medical information, notice to be given, §32.1-127.1:05.

PERSONAL INFORMATION PRIVACY —Cont'd
Medical records —Cont'd
Generally.
See MEDICAL RECORDS.
Notice of breach of personal information, §18.2-186.6.
Social security numbers, protection, §§2.2-3815, 2.2-3816.
Student records.
Public school pupils.
Disclosure of personal identifying information, §22.1-287.

PERSONAL INJURY LIABILITY INSURANCE.
Carbon monoxide exclusions, §38.2-235.
Certified escort vehicle drivers.
Insurance required, §46.2-2902.
Defined, §38.2-117.
Liability insurance generally, §§38.2-2200 to 38.2-2234.
See LIABILITY INSURANCE.
Motor vehicle insurance generally.
See MOTOR VEHICLE INSURANCE.
Notice of cancellation, refusal to renew, reduction in coverage or increase in rate, §38.2-231.
Rates.
Generally, §§38.2-1900 to 38.2-1928.
See INSURANCE RATES.

PERSONALIZED LICENSE PLATES, §§46.2-711 to 46.2-749.130.

PERSONAL JURISDICTION.
Jurisdiction generally.
See JURISDICTION.

PERSONAL LEAVE.
Sickness and disability program for state employees.
Generally, §§51.1-1100 to 51.1-1140.
See SICKNESS AND DISABILITY PROGRAM.

PERSONAL PROPERTY.
Abandoned motor vehicles.
Sale of personal property found in vehicles, §46.2-1214.
Abandoned property.
Disposition of unclaimed property.
Generally, §§55-210.1 to 55-210.30.
See UNCLAIMED PROPERTY.
Action for wrongful detention.
General provisions, §§8.01-114 to 8.01-123.
See DETINUE.
Aircraft keeper liens, §43-32.
Animal keeper liens, §43-32.
Appointment powers.
Release of, §§64.2-2700 to 64.2-2704.
Assignments for benefit of creditors, §§55-156 to 55-160.
Attachments.
General provisions, §§8.01-533 to 8.01-576.
See ATTACHMENT.
Banks.
Ownership and lease of personal property, §6.2-884.
Bequests.
Wills generally, §§64.2-400 to 64.2-458.
See WILLS.
Boat keeper liens, §43-32.
Burning or destroying, §18.2-81.
Cats.
Deemed personal property, §3.2-6585.

PERSONAL PROPERTY —Cont'd
Charitable gifts generally.
See CHARITABLE GIFTS.
Child or minor purchasing.
Servicemen's readjustment act of 1944, eligibility for guaranty of credit, §11-8.
Church property, §§57-7.1 to 57-17.
Commercial space flight authority.
Conveyance, lease or transfer by city or county to authority, §2.2-2217.
Community property rights at death, §§64.2-315 to 64.2-324.
See COMMUNITY PROPERTY RIGHTS AT DEATH.
Commutation and valuation of certain estates and interests, §§55-269.1 to 55-277.
Counties, cities or towns.
General power as to acquisition, disposition and use, §15.2-951.
Crimes relating to property.
Proof of ownership, §19.2-284.
Death presumption.
Parties to proceedings, §64.2-2300.
Decedents' estates.
Nonresidents.
Transfers, §64.2-609.
Small estates.
Defined terms, §64.2-600.
Descent and distribution.
Generally, §§64.2-200 to 64.2-206.
See DESCENT AND DISTRIBUTION.
Nonresident decedents.
Transfers, §64.2-609.
Destruction of private property, §18.2-137.
Detinue generally, §§8.01-114 to 8.01-123.
See DETINUE.
Disclaimer of property interests, §§64.2-2600 to 64.2-2614.
See DISCLAIMER OF PROPERTY INTERESTS.
Dogs.
Deemed personal property, §3.2-6585.
Drift property, §§55-202 to 55-210.
Economic development partnership authority.
Sale, lease or transfer of property to authority, §2.2-2246.
Educational gifts generally.
See CHARITABLE GIFTS.
Embezzlement, §18.2-111.
Payroll deductions intended for child support, §18.2-111.2.
Emblements, §§55-249 to 55-252.
Federal lien registrations, §§55-142.1 to 55-142.9.
Fieri facias.
Writs on judgments for personal property, §8.01-472.
Fire departments and companies.
Destruction of property to prevent spread of fire, §§27-20 to 27-22.
Fraudulent conversion of leased personal property, §18.2-118.
Fraudulent conversion or removal of property subject to lien or title in another, §18.2-115.
Fraudulent conveyances generally, §§55-80 to 55-105.
See FRAUDULENT CONVEYANCES.
Gifts for educational, literary or charitable purposes.
Generally.
See CHARITABLE GIFTS.
Hangar keeper liens, §43-32.

PERSONAL PROPERTY —Cont'd
Homestead exemption of householder.
Form of homestead deed, §34-14.
Setting apart exemption in personal estate, §§34-13, 34-14.
When exemption may be set apart, §34-17.
Identified with social security number preceded by letters VA, §18.2-96.1.
Possession with removed, altered, etc., mark, §18.2-96.1.
Removal, alteration, etc., §18.2-96.1.
Innkeeper liens, §43-31.
Insurance companies investments, §38.2-1440.
Intestate succession, §§64.2-200 to 64.2-206.
See DESCENT AND DISTRIBUTION.
Jails.
Inmate payments for damaged property, §53.1-228.1.
Joint ownership, §55-20.1.
Lease-purchase agreements, §§59.1-207.17 to 59.1-207.27.
See LEASE-PURCHASE AGREEMENTS.
Leases, UCC, §§8.2A-101 to 8.2A-532.
See LEASES, UCC.
Legacies.
Wills, §§64.2-400 to 64.2-458.
See WILLS.
Lien or title in another.
Fraudulent conversion or removal, §18.2-115.
Lien registration by federal government, §§55-142.1 to 55-142.9.
Limitation of actions.
Criminal prosecutions, §19.2-8.
Damage actions, §8.01-243.
Limited liability companies.
Membership interest.
Nature of, §13.1-1038.
Limited partnerships.
Nature of partnership interest, §50-73.44.
Literary gifts generally.
See CHARITABLE GIFTS.
Livery stable keeper liens, §43-32.
Local school boards.
Corporate powers, §22.1-71.
Exchange, lease or sale of real and personal property, §22.1-129.
Marina keeper liens, §43-32.
Married women's property rights.
Generally, §§55-35 to 55-47.1.
See MARRIED WOMEN'S PROPERTY RIGHTS.
Mechanics' liens, §§43-33 to 43-36.
Military personnel.
Wills, disposition by, §64.2-408.
Military property, care of, §§44-103 to 44-111.
Militia, right to own and keep, §44-99.
Murderers.
Bar to acquiring property rights of decedent, §§64.2-2500 to 64.2-2511.
See SLAYER'S ACT.
Museums.
Property loaned to museums, §§55-210.31 to 55-210.38.
See MUSEUMS.
Nonresidents.
Wills, disposition by, §64.2-407.
Ownership proof.
Criminal offenses, §19.2-284.
Presumption of ownership, §55-47.1.
Partition.
Jurisdiction of district court and proceedings, §16.1-77.2.

PERSONAL PROPERTY —Cont'd
Partition —Cont'd
Venue.
Permissible forum, §8.01-262.
Personal actions for damages.
Statute of limitations, §8.01-243.
Port authority.
Acquisition, §§62.1-132.18, 62.1-132.19.
Power of attorney.
Authority of agent.
Tangible personal property, §64.2-1626.
Presumption of death.
Parties to proceedings, §64.2-2300.
Presumption of ownership of tangible personal property, §55-47.1.
Principle and income.
Uniform principle and income act, §§64.2-1000 to 64.2-1032.
See PRINCIPAL AND INCOME.
Prisoner estates.
Disposal of unclaimed personal property, §53.1-228.
Prisons.
Inmate payments for damaged property, §53.1-228.1.
Prostitution.
Houses of prostitution.
Sale of furniture, etc., §48-12.
Real estate trusts.
Recorded deeds of conveyance to trustees.
Classification of interest of beneficiary, §55-17.1.
Registration of federal liens, §§55-142.1 to 55-142.9.
Religious organizations, §§57-7.1 to 57-17.
Transfers to, §57-7.1.
Removal of property subject to lien or title in another, §18.2-115.
Rent-to-own agreements, §§59.1-207.17 to 59.1-207.27.
See LEASE-PURCHASE AGREEMENTS.
Rights of married women generally, §§55-35 to 55-47.1.
See MARRIED WOMEN'S PROPERTY RIGHTS.
Sales, UCC, §§8.2-101 to 8.2-725.
See SALES, UCC.
Savings banks.
Investments.
Generally, §6.2-1187.
Segregation of property for local taxation, VA Const Art X §4.
Self-service storage, §§55-416 to 55-423.
Servicemen's readjustment act of 1944.
Minors or unmarried widows eligibility for guaranty of credit, §11-8.
Slayers, bar to property rights, §§64.2-2500 to 64.2-2511.
See SLAYER'S ACT.
Statute of limitations.
Damages actions, §8.01-243.
Tangible personal property.
Criminal prosecutions, §19.2-8.
Tangible personal property.
Presumption of ownership, §55-47.1.
Tenancy by the entireties, §§55-20.1, 55-20.2.
Trade secrets, §§59.1-336 to 59.1-343.
Trusts of real property.
Recorded deeds of conveyance to trustee, §55-17.1.
Unclaimed property, disposition of.
Generally, §§55-210.1 to 55-210.30.
See UNCLAIMED PROPERTY.

PERSONAL PROPERTY —Cont'd
Venue.
Partition.
Permissible forum, §8.01-262.
Widow purchasing.
Servicemen's readjustment act of 1944, eligibility for guaranty of credit, §11-8.
Wills.
Nonresident decedents.
Transfers, §64.2-609.
Writs on judgments for personal property, §§8.01-470, 8.01-472.
Sale of property subject to prior security interest, §8.01-480.
Territorial extent of lien, §8.01-481.
Wrongful detention.
Civil action, §§8.01-114 to 8.01-123.
See DETINUE.

PERSONAL PROPERTY TAXES, §§58.1-3500 to 58.1-3522.
Alternative tax rates for elderly and handicapped, §§58.1-3506.1 to 58.1-3506.8.
Applications under article, §58.1-3506.5.
Change in circumstances, §58.1-3506.7.
Classification of motor vehicles, §58.1-3506.1.
Effective date, §58.1-3506.7.
Model ordinance, §58.1-3506.4.
Notice of relief program, §58.1-3506.6.
Permanently and totally disabled defined, §58.1-3506.3.
Restrictions and conditions, §§58.1-3506.2, 58.1-3506.4.
Assessment, VA Const Art X §2.
Manufactured homes, §58.1-3522.
Situs for assessment, §§58.1-3511 to 58.1-3514.
Bills to taxpayers.
Electronic billing, §58.1-3912.
Mailing, §58.1-3912.
Website access, §58.1-3912.
Boats, filing returns.
Alternative methods, §58.1-3518.1.
Classification of property.
Elderly or handicapped, alternative tax rates, §§58.1-3506.1 to 58.1-3506.8.
Farm animals, grains, agricultural products, etc., §58.1-3505.
General classification, §58.1-3503.
Household goods and personal effects, §58.1-3504.
Machinery and tools used in cleaning of motor vehicles, §58.1-3508.5.
Machinery and tools used in manufacturing or processing materials for national defense, §58.1-3508.4.
Machinery and tools used in other businesses, §§58.1-3508.2, 58.1-3508.3.
Machinery and tools used in semiconductor manufacturing, §58.1-3508.1.
Other classifications, §58.1-3506.
Precision investment castings.
Machinery and tools used in manufacture of, §58.1-3508.3.
Collection of local taxes generally, §§58.1-3910 to 58.1-3961.
See TAX COLLECTION.
Correction of erroneous tax assessments, §§58.1-3980 to 58.1-3995.
See CORRECTION OF ERRONEOUS TAX ASSESSMENTS.
County executive form of government.
Public service corporations, special provisions for assessments, §§58.1-2680 to 58.1-2683.

PERSONAL PROPERTY TAXES —Cont'd
County manager form of government.
Public service corporations, special provisions for assessments, §§58.1-2680 to 58.1-2683.
Credit in prorating jurisdiction.
Moving from nonprorating locality to prorating locality, §58.1-3516.
Daily rental property tax.
Corporate officer or partnership officer liability for failure to pay, §58.1-3906.
Willful failure to collect and account for, §58.1-3907.
Delinquent taxes.
Collection of local taxes generally, §§58.1-3921 to 58.1-3938.
See TAX COLLECTION.
When taxes delinquent, §58.1-3922.
Distress.
Collection of local taxes by distress generally, §§58.1-3940 to 58.1-3961.
See TAX COLLECTION.
Elderly and handicapped, alternative tax rates, §§58.1-3506.1 to 58.1-3506.8.
Applications under article, §58.1-3506.5.
Change in circumstances, §58.1-3506.7.
Classification of motor vehicles generally, §58.1-3506.1.
Effective date, §58.1-3506.7.
Notice of relief program, §58.1-3506.6.
Permanently and totally disabled defined, §58.1-3506.3.
Restrictions and conditions, §§58.1-3506.2, 58.1-3506.4.
Electronic billing of property taxes, §58.1-3912.
Enterprise zone development.
Local enterprise zone development taxation program, §§58.1-3245.6 to 58.1-3245.12.
Exemptions, VA Const Art X §6.
Farm animals, grains, etc.
Governing body may exempt, §58.1-3505.
Generally, §§58.1-3600 to 58.1-3666.
See PROPERTY EXEMPT FROM TAXATION.
Failure to file returns.
Ordinances prescribing criminal penalties, §58.1-3916.1.
Failure to pay by December 5th, §58.1-3915.
False statements in returns.
Ordinances prescribing criminal penalties, §58.1-3916.1.
Federal government, property leased, loaned or otherwise made available to private party from, §58.1-3502.
Federal government, property leased to agency of, §58.1-3501.
Filing returns, §58.1-3900.
Boats, alternative methods, §58.1-3518.1.
Motor vehicles, alternative methods, §58.1-3518.1.
Taxpayers, §58.1-3518.
Assessment if taxpayer fails to file return, §58.1-3519.
Trailers, alternative methods, §58.1-3518.1.
General classification of tangible personal property, §58.1-3503.
Household goods.
Classification, §§58.1-3503, 58.1-3504.
Insurance companies.
Taxes applicable to companies, §58.1-2508.
Intangible personal property tax.
Assessment and payment of deficiencies, §58.1-1114.
Assessment sheets or forms, §58.1-1118.

PERSONAL PROPERTY TAXES —Cont'd
Intangible personal property tax —Cont'd
Audit of returns, §58.1-1110.
Department of taxation, §58.1-1112.
Branches outside of Commonwealth, §58.1-1106.
Classification of subjects of taxation, §58.1-1101.
Collection, §58.1-1117.
Dairies.
To what extent taxable on intangible personal property, §58.1-1104.
Date property returned for taxation, §58.1-1107.
Deficiencies, assessment and payment, §58.1-1114.
Delinquent taxpayers, §58.1-1113.
Estimate of tax.
Delinquent taxpayers, §58.1-1113.
Exempt professions and businesses, §58.1-1103.
Extension of time for filing returns, §58.1-1109.
Failure to file return, §58.1-1113.
Failure to pay, §58.1-1116.
Fiduciaries, application to generally, §58.1-1111.
Filing returns, §58.1-1108.
Extension, §58.1-1109.
Interest on deficiencies, §58.1-1114.
Limitation on imposing tax, §58.1-1114.
List of delinquent taxes.
Local treasurers to make, §58.1-1800.
Local treasurers to transmit to department of taxation, §58.1-1801.
Livestock producers, §58.1-1102.
Memorandum of lien, §58.1-1117.
Mine prop suppliers, §58.1-1105.
Nonresidents doing business in Commonwealth, §58.1-1106.
Payment, §58.1-1108.
Deficiencies, §58.1-1114.
Failure to pay, §58.1-1116.
Penalty.
Deficiency, §58.1-1114.
Failure to file returns, §58.1-1113.
Failure to pay, §58.1-1116.
Personal property segregated for state taxation, §58.1-1100.
Poultry producers, §58.1-1102.
Property subject to state taxation, §58.1-100.
Pulpwood suppliers, §58.1-1105.
Railroad crosstie suppliers, §58.1-1105.
Railroads, §58.1-2608.
Rate of tax, §58.1-1101.
Receipt of state taxes by local treasurer, §58.1-1800.
Refund of overpayment, §58.1-1115.
Returns.
Audits of returns, §58.1-1110.
Date property returned for taxation, §58.1-1107.
Extension of time for filing, §58.1-1109.
Failure to file, §58.1-1113.
Forwarded to department of taxation by commissioners of revenue, §58.1-3113.
Forwarding to and audit by department, §58.1-1112.
Time for filing, §58.1-1108.
Where filed, §58.1-1110.
Segregation of personal property for state taxation, §58.1-1100.
Situs of business domicile, nonresidents, §58.1-1106.
Telecommunications companies, §58.1-2608.
Time limit for imposing tax, §58.1-1114.
Transmittal of assessment sheets or forms, §58.1-1118.
Veneer log suppliers, §58.1-1105.

PERSONAL PROPERTY TAXES —Cont'd
January 1, tax day, §58.1-3515.
Joint bill for real and personal property taxes, §58.1-3912.
Jurisdiction.
Personal jurisdiction for tax liabilities, §8.01-328.1.
Leased, loaned or property otherwise made available to private party from agency of federal, state or local government, §58.1-3502.
Leased tangible personal property to agency of federal, state or local government, §58.1-3501.
Lessee of motor vehicle paying tax, §58.1-3516.2.
Local government, property leased, loaned or otherwise made available to private party from, §58.1-3502.
Local government, property leased to agency of, §58.1-3501.
Local taxes generally, §§58.1-3000 to 58.1-3018.
See LOCAL TAXES.
Machinery and tools tax, §§58.1-3507, 58.1-3508.
Miscellaneous businesses, §§58.1-3508.2, 58.1-3508.3.
Semiconductor manufacturing, §58.1-3508.1.
Mailing tax bills to taxpayers, §58.1-3912.
Manufactured homes, §§58.1-3520, 58.1-3521.
Assessment method, §58.1-3522.
Payment before moving home, §58.1-3520.
Proration, §58.1-3521.
Merchants capital tax, §§58.1-3509, 58.1-3510.
Capital subject to taxation, §58.1-3509.
Merchants' capital defined, §58.1-3510.
Pharmaceutical wholesalers, separate classification, §58.1-3510.01.
Rate limits, §58.1-3509.
Mobile homes.
Assessment method, §58.1-3522.
Payment before moving home, §58.1-3520.
Proration of tax, §58.1-3521.
Mosquito control, §32.1-194.
Motor vehicle carrier rolling stock.
Local taxation prohibited, §58.1-2658.
Motor vehicle cleaning.
Machinery and tools used directly in cleaning of motor vehicles, §58.1-3508.5.
Motor vehicle leases.
Lessee paying tax, §58.1-3516.2.
Motor vehicles, §§58.1-3523 to 58.1-3535.
See PERSONAL PROPERTY TAX RELIEF ACT OF 1998.
Motor vehicles department.
Commissioner to advise local commissioners of revenue of situs of certain vehicles, §46.2-211.
Motor vehicles, filing returns.
Alternative method, §58.1-3518.1.
National defense.
Machinery and tools used in manufacturing or processing materials for, classification, §58.1-3508.4.
Notice of taxes due, §58.1-3911.
Ordinances.
Providing dates for filing returns, setting penalties, interest, etc., §58.1-3916.
Payment.
Lessees of motor vehicles, §58.1-3516.2.
Prorated taxes, §58.1-3516.1.
Personal effects.
Classification, §§58.1-3503, 58.1-3504.

PERSONAL PROPERTY TAXES —Cont'd
Personal property book.
Alteration by commissioner of revenue after delivery to local treasurer, §58.1-3119.
Arrangement by commissioner of revenue in contents, §58.1-3115.
Books for preceding year not made out.
How supplied, §58.1-3120.
Delivery of copies to local treasurers and department of taxation, §58.1-3118.
False entries, §58.1-3121.
Furnished to commissioner of revenue by department of taxation, §58.1-3114.
Reproductions of books, §58.1-3118.
Retention of original in commissioner of revenue's office, §58.1-3118.
Separate books for state and local levies, department of taxation may prescribe, §58.1-3116.
Pharmaceutical wholesalers.
Separate classification of merchants' capital, §58.1-3510.01.
Prepayment of taxes, §58.1-3920.
Interest on funds received, §58.1-3920.1.
Property subject to local taxation, §58.1-3000.
Proration, §58.1-3516.
Mobile homes, §58.1-3521.
Payment of prorated taxes, §58.1-3516.1.
Public school special tax, §§22.1-102 to 22.1-106.
Public service corporations.
County executive or county manager governments, special provisions for assessments, §§58.1-2680 to 58.1-2683.
Intangible personal property.
No state or local tax, §58.1-2690.
Local taxation, §58.1-2606.
Railroads, §58.1-2607.
Assessment by tax commissioner, §§58.1-2655 to 58.1-2657.
Railroads.
Assessment of property by tax commissioner, §§58.1-2655 to 58.1-2657.
Local taxation of tangible personal property, §58.1-2607.
Receipts to taxpayers when taxes collected, §58.1-3914.
Refund of tax already paid, §58.1-3516.
Returns.
Boats, alternative method of filing, §58.1-3518.1.
Filing with commissioner of revenue, §58.1-3900.
Forms, §58.1-3517.
Motor vehicles, alternative method of filing, §58.1-3518.1.
Taxpayers to file, §58.1-3518.
Assessment if taxpayer fails to file, §58.1-3519.
Trailers, alternative method of filing, §58.1-3518.1.
Segregation of property for local taxation, §58.1-3500, VA Const Art X §4.
Semiconductor manufacturing.
Classification of machinery and tools, §58.1-3508.1.
Short-term rental property, §§58.1-3510.4 to 58.1-3510.7.
Certificate of registration, §58.1-3510.5.
Exemptions, §58.1-3510.7.
Imposition and collection of tax, §58.1-3510.6.
Penalties, §58.1-3510.7.
Qualifications for engagement in short-term rental business, §58.1-3510.4.

PERSONAL PROPERTY TAXES —Cont'd
Situs for taxation.
Apportioned assessment, §58.1-3511.
Cargo in transit, §58.1-3514.
Generally, §58.1-3511.
Imports, §58.1-3513.
Nonresident exception, §58.1-3511.
Refund of tax paid to city or county by nonresident, §58.1-3511.
Vessels and containers used in interstate and foreign commerce, §58.1-3512.
State government, property leased, loaned or otherwise made available to private party from, §58.1-3502.
State government, property leased to agency of, §58.1-3501.
Tangible personal property defined, §58.1-3500.
Tax day, §58.1-3515.
Tax relief act of 1998, §§58.1-3523 to 58.1-3535.
See PERSONAL PROPERTY TAX RELIEF ACT OF 1998.
Trailers, filing returns.
Alternative methods, §58.1-3518.1.
Website access to property tax bills, §58.1-3912.

PERSONAL PROPERTY TAX RELIEF ACT OF 1998, §§58.1-3523 to 58.1-3535.
Definitions, §58.1-3523.
Furnishing of information.
Commissioners of revenue to treasurer, §58.1-3535.
Department to commissioners of revenue, §58.1-3534.
Qualifying vehicles.
Defined, §58.1-3523.
Identification, §58.1-3524.
Reimbursement to localities for administrative costs, §15.2-1636.20.
Reports and records.
Furnishing of information between agencies, §§58.1-3534, 58.1-3535.
State payment to treasurers.
Treasurers, defined, §58.1-3523.
State reimbursement to taxpayers, §58.1-3524.

PERSONAL PROTECTION SPECIALISTS.
Private security services businesses, §§9.1-138 to 9.1-150.

PERSONAL RECOGNIZANCE.
Motor vehicles, §46.2-944.
Wildlife violators compact, §29.1-530.5.

PERSONAL REPRESENTATIVES.
Decedents' estates.
Generally.
See DECEDENTS' ESTATES.
Estate tax generally, §§58.1-900 to 58.1-938.
See ESTATE TAX.
Fiduciaries generally.
See FIDUCIARIES.
Generally, §§64.2-500 to 64.2-620.
See EXECUTORS AND ADMINISTRATORS.
Partition of land.
Generally, §§8.01-81 to 8.01-93.
See PARTITION OF LAND.
Public assistance recipients.
Appointment for, unable to manage funds, §63.2-507.
Representation.
Persons representing and binding others, §§64.2-714 to 64.2-718.

PERSONAL REPRESENTATIVES —Cont'd
Suits upon judgment and contracts of decedent, §64.2-519.
Tax responsibilities of fiduciaries generally, §§58.1-21 to 58.1-24.
Wills.
Generally, §§64.2-400 to 64.2-458.
See WILLS.

PERSONAL TRESPASS BY COMPUTER, §18.2-152.7.

PERSONAL WATERCRAFT, §§29.1-748 to 29.1-750.
Boating safety education program.
Completion required, rules, promulgation, §29.1-735.2.
Conservation police officers.
Arrests, §§29.1-205, 29.1-210.
Impeding in discharge of duty, §29.1-207.
Defined terms, §§29.1-100, 29.1-700.
Instruction by rental agents, §29.1-749.2.
Insurance on rentals, §29.1-749.3.
Minimum distance from shoreline.
City ordinance regulating, penalty for violation, §29.1-748.1.
Owners permitting violations, §29.1-749.
Reckless operation, §29.1-738.03.
Restrictions on operating, §29.1-748.
Safety education course required prior to renting, §29.1-736.

PERSONNEL ACT.
Personnel administration system generally, §§2.2-2900 to 2.2-2905.
See PUBLIC OFFICERS AND EMPLOYEES.

PERSONNEL AND TRAINING DEPARTMENT.
See HUMAN RESOURCES MANAGEMENT DEPARTMENT.

PERSONNEL OF LOCAL GOVERNMENT.
Generally, qualifications for office, bond, etc., §§15.2-1500 to 15.2-1543.
See LOCAL OFFICERS AND EMPLOYEES.

PERSONNEL RECORDS.
Employment-related information disclosure.
Prospective or current employer disclosing.
Immunity, presumption of good faith, §8.01-46.1.
Records to be kept by sheriffs and chiefs of police, §15.2-1722.

PERSONNEL SYSTEMS.
Certain cities, §15.2-1131.

PERSON NOT FOUND.
Fee of sheriff for effort to serve order, notice, etc., §17.1-268.

PERSONS WITH DISABILITY.
Actions.
When guardian ad litem need not be appointed, §8.01-9.
Appeal bond.
Exemption from requirement, §8.01-676.1.
Compromise of claims, §8.01-424.
Defined, §8.01-2.
Delinquent tax lands sales.
Appointment of guardian ad litem, §58.1-3967.
Dental plan organizations.
Children with mental or physical incapacity, §38.2-6106.
Disposal of real estate, §§8.01-67 to 8.01-80.
Abatement of suit by death of person, §8.01-72.

PERSONS WITH DISABILITY —Cont'd
Disposal of real estate —Cont'd
Alternate procedure for sale of real estate, §8.01-78.
Application of proceeds of transaction, §8.01-78.
Court action on report, §8.01-80.
Reference of petition to commissioner, §8.01-79.
Application of proceeds, §8.01-76.
Appointment of guardian ad litem, §8.01-73.
Circuit court jurisdiction, §8.01-68.
Commencement of action, §8.01-69.
Disposition of proceeds, §8.01-76.
What proceeds to pass as real estate, §8.01-77.
Disqualification of certain purchasers, §8.01-75.
Fiduciary, defined, §8.01-67.
Leases, §8.01-74.
New leases, §8.01-74.
Partition of land, §8.01-85.
Payment of excess proceeds, §8.01-76.
Person under a disability, defined, §8.01-67.
Proceeds of sale to pass as real estate, §8.01-77.
Venue.
Preferred forum, §8.01-261.
Drainage projects.
Guardian ad litem for infants and incapacitated adults, §21-310.
Improvements to land.
When value deemed real estate, §8.01-177.
Jury selection.
Objections to jury list on account of legal disability, §8.01-352.
Jury service.
Disqualification from service, §8.01-338.
Limitation of actions.
Effect of disabilities upon right of entry, §8.01-237.
Sexual abuse.
When cause of action deemed to accrue, §8.01-249.
Local road authorities.
Establishment and alteration of roads.
Appointment of guardian ad litem, §33.1-234.
Partition of land.
Disposition of share in proceeds, §8.01-85.
Public utilities.
Discounted fees and charges for low-income and disabled customers, §15.2-2119.
Receivers.
Moneys deposited in court.
Deposit of certain funds with general receiver under supervision of fiduciary, §8.01-601.
Recognizances.
How recognizance taken, §19.2-141.
Removal of political disabilities consequent upon conviction for offense.
Governor's powers, VA Const Art V §12.
Sale of delinquent tax lands.
Appointment of guardian ad litem, §58.1-3967.
Settlement of claims, §8.01-424.
Sexual battery of mentally incapacitated person, §18.2-67.4.
Statute of limitations, §8.01-249.
Statute of limitations.
Effect of disabilities upon right of entry, §8.01-237.
Sexual abuse.
When cause of action deemed to accrue, §8.01-249.
Ungranted shores of the sea.
Effect of disability, §28.2-1512.

PERSONS WITH DISABILITY —Cont'd
Venue.
Disposition of real estate.
Preferred forum, §8.01-261.

PER STIRPES.
Descent and distribution.
When parties take, §64.2-202.
Wills.
Descendants of devisees or legatees.
When take, §64.2-418.

PERTUSSIS VACCINE.
Immunizations.
Required immunizations of children, §32.1-46.

PEST CONTROL COMPACT, §§3.2-714 to 3.2-731.

PEST CONTROL, PLANTS, §§3.2-700 to 3.2-713.
Abundance surveys, §3.2-702.
Administration, §3.2-701.
Appeals.
Judicial review, §3.2-713.
Authority to compensate growers in infested areas, §3.2-709.
Compensation to growers in infested areas, §3.2-709.
Cooperation with agencies and private organizations, §3.2-707.
Cooperative suppression program fund, §3.2-708.
Costs, §3.2-711.
Definitions, §3.2-700.
Emergencies.
Authority for abatement and other emergency measures, §3.2-705.
Inspections, §3.2-706.
Intergovernmental cooperation, §3.2-707.
New pests, actions, §3.2-702.
Penalties for violations, §3.2-710.
Permits.
Sale or transporting of plant pests, §3.2-712.
Quarantine, §§3.2-703, 3.2-704.
Rules and regulations, §3.2-701.

PESTICIDE APPLICATION EQUIPMENT.
Income tax credit for purchase of advanced technology equipment, §58.1-337.
Corporate tax credit, §58.1-436.

PESTICIDES, §§3.2-3900 to 3.2-3947.
Application of pesticides.
Enforcement of provisions, §3.2-3942.
Exemptions from provisions, §3.2-3931.
Commercial applicators.
Certification, §3.2-3930.
Delinquent renewals, §3.2-3933.
Reciprocity, §3.2-3934.
Defined, §3.2-3900.
Commissioner of agriculture and consumer services.
Complaints to commissioner, §3.2-3910.
Interference with commissioner or agents, §3.2-3939.
Commonwealth's attorneys.
Prosecution of violations, §3.2-3946.
Complaints to commissioner or board, §3.2-3910.
Condominiums.
Common elements.
Notice of pesticide application, §55-79.80:01.
Fees.
Certification of applicators.
Late fee for delinquent renewals, §3.2-3933.

PESTICIDES —Cont'd
Fees —Cont'd
Disposition, §3.2-3912.
Licenses, §3.2-3925.
Registration, §3.2-3919.
Injunctions.
Violations of provisions, §3.2-3947.
Labels.
Defined, §3.2-3900.
Prohibited acts, §§3.2-3939, 3.2-3940.
Landlord and tenant.
Notice to tenant for insecticide or pesticide use, §55-248.13:3.
Licenses, §§3.2-3924 to 3.2-3928.
Revocation or suspension, §§3.2-3939, 3.2-3940.
Summary suspension by commissioner, §3.2-3940.
Marine antifoulant paints, §§3.2-3935 to 3.2-3937.
Medicinal and toilet preparations.
Exemption of drugs or chemicals intended for, §3.2-3913.
Penalties.
Disposition, §3.2-3912.
Exemptions, §3.2-3941.
Violations of provisions, §3.2-3947.
Private applicators.
Certification, §3.2-3932.
Delinquent renewals, §3.2-3933.
Reciprocity, §3.2-3934.
Defined, §3.2-3900.
Prohibited acts, §3.2-3939.
Administrative violations, §3.2-3940.
Property owners' associations.
Application of pesticides in common areas, posting of notice, §55-510.3.
Real estate cooperatives.
Pesticide application notice.
Posting in or upon common elements, §55-464.1.
Reciprocity.
Certification of applicators, §3.2-3934.
Registration, §§3.2-3914 to 3.2-3928.
Reports.
Accidents, incidents or loss, §3.2-3909.
Restricted use pesticides.
Defined, §3.2-3900.
Prohibited, §3.2-3929.
Rules and regulations.
Board, §3.2-3906.
Schools and education.
Integrated pest management, §22.1-132.2.
Searches and seizures.
Noncomplying lots, §3.2-3945.
Stop-sale or removal or stop-use orders, §3.2-3944.
Trade secrets.
Protection of trade secrets, §3.2-3908.
Violations of provisions.
Administrative violations, §3.2-3940.
Commonwealth's attorneys.
Prosecution of violations, §3.2-3946.
Injunctions, §3.2-3947.
Penalties, §3.2-3947.
Proceedings upon, §3.2-3946.
Prohibited acts, §3.2-3939.
Seizure, condemnation and sale, §3.2-3945.
Stop-sale or removal or stop-use orders, §3.2-3944.
Warning instead of report of violation, §3.2 3946.

PET CEMETERIES, §§57-39.20 to 57-39.25.
Change of address of owner of burial right, §57-39.23.

PET CEMETERIES —Cont'd
Declaration of land use restriction.
Duty to file, §57-39.21.
Removal of restriction, §57-39.24.
Definitions, §57-39.20.
Owner of burial right.
Change of address, §57-39.23.
Perpetual care.
Trust fund requirement, §57-39.22.
Unlawful representations, §57-39.22.
Violation of provisions, §57-39.25.
Restriction of land use.
Duty to file declaration, §57-39.21.
Removal of restriction, §57-39.24.
Violations of provisions, §57-39.25.

PET DEALERS.
Sale of dogs and cats, §§3.2-6512 to 3.2-6517.

PETERSBURG.
Arts and cultural district.
Creation, tax incentives, regulatory flexibility, powers, §15.2-1129.1.
Bridge authority of the city of, 1952 ch 529, 1962 ch 259.
Circuit court, establishment, §17.1-500.
Coastal primary sand dunes and beaches.
Zoning ordinances, §28.2-1403.
Confederate cemeteries and graves.
Disbursement of funds appropriated for upkeep, §10.1-2211.
Day care programs during school hours, §22.1-132.1.
Port of Virginia economic and infrastructure development zone grant fund, §62.1-132.3:2.
Public defenders office.
Established, §19.2-163.04.
Sale of delinquent tax lands.
Special masters.
Appointment, special provisions applicable, §58.1-3970.1.
School board.
Fingerprinting applicants for employment, §22.1-296.2.
Salary of members, §22.1-32.
Water and sewage systems.
Lien for charges and taxes imposed, §15.2-2118.

PETERSBURG, BRIDGE AUTHORITY OF THE CITY OF, 1952 ch 529, 1962 ch 259.

PETITION FOR REDRESS OF GRIEVANCES, VA Const Art I §12.

PETITIONS.
Access to abandoned waste site, §10.1-1406.1.
Acquittal by reason of insanity.
Temporary custody and evaluation, release, §19.2-182.6.
Actual innocence.
Petition for writ of actual innocence, VA SCt Rule 5:7B, VA SCt Rule Pt 5A Appx Form 12, VA SCt Rule Pt 5 Appx Form 12.
Adopting or changing county form of government.
Referenda, §15.2-301.
Adoption.
Petition for restoration of parental rights.
Pre-adoptive parents not identified, §16.1-283.2.
Adult protective services.
Emergency protective services, §63.2-1608.
Agricultural cooperative associations.
Referendum of members, §13.1-328.

PETITIONS —Cont'd
Agricultural cooperative associations —Cont'd
Removal of director, §13.1-325.
Removal of officers, §13.1-327.
Voluntary dissolution, matters adjudged in circuit court, §13.1-332.
Alcoholic beverage sales at licensed establishment.
Temporarily enjoining, locality seeking.
Establishment meeting place for committing serious criminal violations, §48-17.1.
Animals running at large.
Unincorporated communities and villages.
Boundaries within which animals may not run at large, §55-324.
Contest of petition, §55-326.
Costs of petition, §55-329.
Annexation.
Agreements between towns and counties defining town's annexation rights.
Inability to reach voluntary agreement.
Town's petition to commission on local government for order establishing rights of town, §15.2-3234.
Review by circuit court of order of commission on local government, §15.2-3235.
Conflicting petitions for same territory, §15.2-3206.
Petition seeking territory lying in two or more counties, §15.2-3206.
Voters of adjacent territory or governing body of adjacent county or town, §15.2-3203.
Appeals.
By Commonwealth in criminal cases, §19.2-402.
Court of appeals, §17.1-406.
Time for filing, §17.1-408.
Appraisal rights, corporations.
Fair value determinations by courts, §13.1-740.
Attorney discipline.
Reinstatement, VA SCt Rule Pt 6 §IV Par 13-25.
Audit of accounts of county officers, boards and commissions, §15.2-2512.
Autopsies, §32.1-285.
Beer franchises.
Contemplated actions by brewery or wholesaler.
Petition to board to determine lawfulness of specified action, §4.1-509.1.
Birth certificates.
Delayed birth certificate registration.
Required allegations, §32.1-260.
Bonds issued by localities.
Contesting validity, §15.2-2653.
Boundaries of localities relocated or changed by agreement.
Petition to circuit court for approval, §15.2-3108.
Boundary lines established by commissioner.
Procedure when commissioners fail to agree, §15.2-3104.
Change of city to town.
Citizen petition for town status, §15.2-4102.
Petition by governing body, §15.2-4101.
Child custody, §16.1-278.15.
Child or minor purchasing real or personal property.
Servicemen's readjustment act of 1944, eligibility for guaranty of credit.
Approval of circuit court of execution of contract, note, etc., to obtain benefits, §11-8.
Child visitation, §16.1-278.15.
City no longer qualifying for city status.
Determination of city status, §15.2-4002.

PETITIONS —Cont'd
City status granted county, §15.2-3901.
Coal interests, trusts for.
Known owners, §45.1-161.311:8.
Unknown owners, §45.1-161.311:3.
Conditional release of geriatric felons, §§19.2-297.1, 53.1-40.01.
Conditional zoning.
Review of decision, §15.2-2301.
Conservatorship of estate of incapacitated persons.
See CONSERVATORSHIP OF ESTATE OF INCAPACITATED PERSONS.
Consolidation of counties, cities or towns into single county or city, §15.2-3522.
Voters' petitions requesting consolidation agreement and referendum, §15.2-3531.
Consolidation of like units of local government.
Voters requesting agreement, §15.2-3503.
Consumer finance companies.
Petition of aggrieved licensee for review, §6.2-1539.
Contraction of corporate limits of cities or towns, §15.2-3237.
Towns located in two more counties, §15.2-3241.
Corporations, appraisal rights.
Fair value determinations by courts, §13.1-740.
Corporations, rehearings by state corporation commission, §13.1-614.
Correction of taxes assessed by state corporation commission, §58.1-2030.
County food and beverage tax, §58.1-3833.
County manager plan of government.
Establishment of department of real estate assessments.
Referendum for, §15.2-716.
Referenda on certain questions, §15.2-749.
County supervisor election and term referenda.
Alternative for biennial elections and staggered terms, §24.2-219.
Reversion to quadrennial elections, §24.2-220.
Courthouses, removal of county courthouse, §15.2-1644.
Court of appeals.
Petition for appeal.
See COURT OF APPEALS.
Petition for rehearing, VA SCt Rules 5A:32 to 5A:35.
Criminal fines and penalties.
Petition of defendant for installment payment, §19.2-355.
Relief from fines and penalties, §§19.2-362 to 19.2-368.
Death row prisoners.
Habeas corpus writs.
Limitation on consideration, §8.01-654.1.
Petition for writ in cases where death sentence imposed, VA SCt Rule 5:7A.
Delinquent real estate taxes, ascertain, §58.1-3959.
Detinue.
Commencement of action, §8.01-114.
Driving while intoxicated.
Persons convicted in another state.
Admission to probation and assignment to alcohol safety action program, §18.2-271.1.
Election contests of governor, lieutenant governor or attorney general elections, §24.2-804.

PETITIONS —Cont'd
Election contests to general assembly election, §24.2-803.
Election recounts, §24.2-801.
Presidential electors, §24.2-801.1.
Elections.
Address change to another county or city.
Inactive status assignment, §24.2-428.1.
Candidates name to be printed on official primary ballot, §§24.2-521, 24.2-522.
Independent candidates' petition of candidacy, §§24.2-506, 24.2-507.
Presidential electors.
Groups other than political parties submitting name, §24.2-543.
Primary candidates' petition of candidacy, §§24.2-521 to 24.2-524.
Special election to fill vacancy in elected constitutional and local offices, §24.2-226.
Electric utility restructuring.
Coal-fired generation facilities.
Construction by default service provider, §56-585.
Emancipation of minors, §16.1-331.
Eminent domain.
Amendments, §25.1-216.
Commencement of proceedings, §25.1-205.
Consolidation for trial, §25.1-221.
Contents, §25.1-206.
County, city or town initiating, §15.2-1903.
Joinder of separate parcels, §25.1-208.
Notice of filing, §25.1-209.
Request for right of entry, §25.1-207.
Title transfer by certificate.
Agreement on amount of compensation, §25.1-317.
Distribution of funds, §25.1-310.
Petition for determination of just compensation, §25.1-318.
Estate tax payment by nonresident decedents to other states.
Accountings to domiciliary state, §58.1-915.
Expungement of criminal records, §19.2-392.2.
Foster care.
Annual review, §16.1-282.2.
Permanency planning hearing, §16.1-282.1.
Placement review, §16.1-282.
Freedom of information act.
Open meetings.
Denial of rights or privileges, §2.2-3712.
Geriatric felons.
Conditional release, §§19.2-297.1, 53.1-40.01.
Guardian and ward.
See GUARDIAN AND WARD.
Habeas corpus writs.
Death row prisoners.
Limitation on consideration, §8.01-654.1.
Petition for writ in cases where death sentence imposed, VA SCt Rule 5:7A.
Hospital authorities.
Assertion that need for authority exists, §15.2-5304.
Hospital or health center commission no longer necessary, §15.2-5216.
Immunity of county from city-initiated annexation and city incorporation, §15.2-3301.
Urban-type services.
Immunity of part or parts of county, §15.2-3304.
Income tax.
Local income tax referendums, §58.1-540.

PETITIONS —Cont'd
Incompetency.
Conservators.
See CONSERVATORS.
Generally.
See INCOMPETENCY.
Guardian and ward.
See GUARDIAN AND WARD.
Independent candidates, §24.2-506.
Deadline for filing, §24.2-507.
Insurance companies, rehabilitation and liquidation.
Disbursement of assets by receiver, §38.2-1506.
Interstate family support act, §20-88.54.
Juvenile and domestic relations district courts.
Matters alleged to be within jurisdiction.
Commenced by filing, §16.1-260.
Juvenile proceedings.
Commencement of matters within jurisdiction of court, §16.1-260.
Form and content, §16.1-262.
Filed by party with legitimate interest, §16.1-241.
Obtaining treatment, rehabilitation or other services, §16.1-278.13.
Preliminary protective order, §16.1-253.
Review of foster care placement, §16.1-282.
Revocation or modification of probation, protective supervision or parole, §16.1-291.
Termination of parental rights, §16.1-283.
Less toxic goods and products.
Purchases by public bodies, §2.2-4314.
Local income tax.
Referendum, §58.1-540.
Medical services lien.
Petition to enforce lien, §8.01-66.8.
Meetings of members of nonprofit corporations.
Court-ordered meetings, §13.1-840.
Mental health facility admissions.
Psychiatric inpatient treatment of minors.
Involuntary commitment, §16.1-341.
Nonprofit corporation members meetings.
Court-ordered meetings, §13.1-840.
Obscene books, proceeding against, §18.2-384.
Open meetings.
Freedom of information act.
Denial of rights or privileges, §2.2-3712.
Parental rights termination, §16.1-283.
Pari-mutuel wagering on horses.
Local referendum, §59.1-391.
Parole.
Revocation or modification.
Juveniles, §16.1-291.
Partition of personal property, §16.1-77.2.
Personal representatives, appointment.
Public assistance recipients.
Recipient unable to manage funds, §63.2-507.
Power of attorney.
Petition for construction of power, §64.2-1614.
Presidential electors.
Groups other political parties submitting names of electors, §24.2-543.
Primary elections.
Candidates name to be printed on official primary ballot, §24.2-521.
Filing, §§24.2-521, 24.2-522.
Filing fees, §§24.2-523, 24.2-524.
Principal and income.
Income trust conversion to total return unitrust, §64.2-1003.

PETITIONS —Cont'd
Prisoners' health care.
Involuntary admission and treatment, §53.1-40.2.
Private waterworks, appointment of receivers for, §32.1-174.3.
Probation.
Revocation or modification.
Juveniles, §16.1-291.
Prohibition.
Verified petition under oath, §8.01-644.
What petition to state, §8.01-645.
Where presented, §8.01-645.
Protective orders.
Ex parte preliminary protective orders.
Protection of child's life, health or normal development, §16.1-253.
Preliminary protective orders in cases of family abuse, §16.1-253.1.
Public assistance recipients.
Appointment of personal representative for, §63.2-507.
Public records not in authorized possession, return of, §42.1-89.
Public service corporation tax assessment review, §58.1-2670.1.
Railroad crossings.
Consolidation or closure, §33.1-145.1.
Real estate taxes.
Ascertaining delinquent taxes, §58.1-3959.
Proration of delinquent taxes after purchase of part of tract, §58.1-3227.
Recounts in elections, §24.2-801.
Recycled goods and products.
Purchases by public bodies, §2.2-4313.
Referendum.
Address change to another county or city.
Inactive status assignment, §24.2-428.1.
Request for abolition of constitutional offices, §24.2-685.
Change in form of government having effect of abolishing office, §24.2-686.
Sheep industry board, §3.2-2104.
Voter petitions calling for, §24.2-684.1.
Removal of county courthouse, §15.2-1644.
Removal of public officer from office, §24.2-233.
Appointed officer for term certain, §24.2-234.
Requirements, §24.2-235.
Reversion of city to town.
Citizen petition, §15.2-4102.
City no longer qualifying for city status.
Determination of city status, §15.2-4002.
Petition by governing body, §15.2-4101.
Right to petition for redress of grievances.
Constitution of the United States, US Const Amd 1.
Sanitation districts law of 1938.
Creation of districts, §§21-146 to 21-149.
Sanitation districts law of 1946.
Creation of districts, §§21-229 to 21-232.
Sentence of persons twice previously convicted of certain violent felonies.
Conditional release of certain elder felons, §§19.2-297.1, 53.1-40.01.
Service districts.
Creation by court order in consolidated cities, §15.2-2401.
Servicemen's readjustment act of 1944, eligibility of minor to obtain benefits.
Circuit approval of execution of contract, note, etc., §11-8.

PETITIONS —Cont'd
Sexually violent predators, civil commitment.
Conditional or unconditional release, §37.2-911.
Shareholder meetings, court-ordered, §13.1-656.
Sharing of local constitutional officers.
Referendum, §15.2-1602.
Sheep industry board.
Referendum, §3.2-2104.
Soil and water conservation districts.
See SOIL AND WATER CONSERVATION DISTRICTS.
Special elections.
Vacancies in elected constitutional and local offices, §24.2-226.
Standby guardianship for incompetent children, §16.1-350.
State corporation commission.
Appeals, §12.1-39.
Writs of supersedeas, §12.1-41.
Subdivision covenants.
Modification in certain counties, §15.2-2257.
Subdivisions.
Restricting access to certain public streets, §15.2-2267.
Supreme court.
Petition for appeal.
See SUPREME COURT.
Petition for rehearing, VA SCt Rules 5:20, 5:31, 5:37.
Surrogacy contracts.
Court-approved contracts, §20-160.
Taxes or assessments for local improvements, §15.2-2405.
Telegraph or telephone companies.
Offering of communications services, §56-484.7:1.
Approval, §56-484.7:2.
Revocation, §56-484.7:4.
Termination of residual parental rights, §16.1-283.
Town seeking city status.
Filing with circuit court, §15.2-3800.
Towns incorporated by judicial proceedings, §15.2-3600.
Transition of city to town status.
Citizen petition for town status, §15.2-4102.
Petition by governing body, §15.2-4101.
Transition of counties to cities, §15.2-3901.
Transportation improvement districts.
Creation in counties with population of more than 500,000, §33.1-431.
District within city of Charlottesville and county of Albemarle, §33.1-448.
Abolition of district, §33.1-462.
Enlargement of district, §33.1-461.
Visitation of child, §16.1-278.15.
Voluntary settlement of annexation, transition or immunity issues by localities.
Affirmance of order by circuit court, §15.2-3400.
Voter registration.
Appeal of denial, §24.2-422.
Objections, §24.2-431.
Waste sites.
Access to abandoned waste sites, §10.1-1406.1.
Waterworks.
Private waterworks, appointment of receivers for, §32.1-174.3.
Zoning.
Conditional zoning.
Review of decision, §15.2-2301.

PETIT LARCENY.
Conviction.
Property worth more than two hundred dollars, §19.2-290.
Prosecution for grand larceny, §19.2-289.
Elements of offense, §18.2-96.
Statute of limitations, §19.2-8.

PETROLEUM GAS.
Liquefied petroleum gas fitters, §§54.1-1128 to 54.1-1135.
See LIQUEFIED PETROLEUM GAS FITTERS.

PETROLEUM LEASES FROM UNDERGROUND STORAGE TANKS.
Virginia petroleum storage tank fund, §62.1-44.34:11.

PETROLEUM PRODUCTS FRANCHISES, §§59.1-21.8 to 59.1-21.18:1.
Actions.
Authority of attorney general, §59.1-68.2.
Agreements.
Assignments.
Continued rights of dealers upon assignment, §59.1-21.15:1.
Disclosure before conclusion, §59.1-21.15.
Exemption from provisions, §59.1-21.18:1.
Notice to terminate, cancel or fail to renew, §59.1-21.14.
Provisions, §59.1-21.11.
Waiver of constitutional rights, §59.1-21.11:1.
Applicability.
Effective date of provisions, §59.1-21.17.
Authority of attorney general, §59.1-68.2.
Defined terms, §59.1-21.10.
Effective date of provisions, §59.1-21.17.
Findings of general assembly, §59.1-21.9.
Operation by refiner, §59.1-21.16:2.
Powers of attorney general, §59.1-21.16.
Provision violations.
Civil actions, §59.1-21.12.
Purpose of provisions, §59.1-21.9.
Repurchases upon termination, §59.1-21.13.
Short title of chapter, §59.1-21.8.
Waiver of constitutional rights, §59.1-21.11:1.

PETROLEUM PRODUCTS SUPPLIES, EMERGENCY, §§59.1-21.18:2 to 59.1-21.18:4.
Authority of attorney general, §59.1-68.2.
Defined terms, §59.1-21.18:2.
Prohibited acts, §59.1-21.18:3.
Exemptions, §59.1-21.18:4.

PETROLEUM STORAGE TANK FUND.
Defined terms, §62.1-44.34:10.
Established, §62.1-44.34:11.
Financial responsibility, §62.1-44.34:12.
Levy of fee for maintenance, §62.1-44.34:13.

PETROLEUM TANK TRUCK CARRIERS.
Employee liens, §§43-24 to 43-26.
Not required to incorporate as public service companies, §13.1-620.
Public service companies generally, §§56-1 to 56-87.
See PUBLIC SERVICE COMPANIES.
Supplier liens, §§43-24 to 43-26.
Transportation companies generally, §§56-99.2 to 56-140.
See TRANSPORTATION COMPANIES.

PETS.
Campground regulations, §35.1-17.

PETS —Cont'd
Cats generally.
See CATS.
Cemeteries, §§57-39.20 to 57-39.25.
See PET CEMETERIES.
Comprehensive animal laws generally, §§3.2-6500 to 3.2-6590.
See ANIMALS.
Dogs generally.
See DOGS.
Hybrid canines, §§3.2-6581 to 3.2-6584.
Importation into Commonwealth.
Veterinary inspection certificate or examination without certificate, §3.2-5902.
Poor debtor's exemption, §34-26.
Rabies control generally.
See RABIES.
Sterilization, §§3.2-6574 to 3.2-6580.
Trust created for care of animal or animals, §64.2-726.

PET SHOPS.
Commercial dog breeders.
Defined, §3.2-6500.
Procurement from unlicensed commercial dog breeders, penalty, §3.2-6511.1.
Mistreatment of animals, §§3.2-6503, 18.2-403.3.
Failure to provide adequate care, §§3.2-6511, 18.2-403.2.
Permits.
Local ordinances, §3.2-6537.
Sale of dogs and cats by dealers, §§3.2-6512 to 3.2-6517.

PETTY CASH FUNDS.
Counties, §15.2-1229.

PEYOTE.
Drug control act.
Generally, §§54.1-3400 to 54.1-3472.
See DRUG CONTROL.
Drug offenses.
Generally, §§18.2-247 to 18.2-264.
See DRUG OFFENSES.
Schedule I controlled drug, §54.1-3446.

PHARMACEUTICAL WHOLESALERS.
Merchants' capital tax.
Separate classification of merchants' capital, §58.1-3510.01.

PHARMACISTS AND PHARMACIES, §§54.1-3300 to 54.1-3321.
Advertising.
Allowed words, §54.1-3433.
Nonresident pharmacies.
Prohibited acts, §54.1-3434.1.
Analysis of controlled substances.
Exemption from control provisions, §54.1-3407.
Aqueous solutions.
Sales, §54.1-3418.
Authenticity and reasonableness of medical bills, §8.01-413.01.
Automated drug dispensing systems, §54.1-3434.02.
Defined, §54.1-3401.
Bills for medical services.
Presumption of authenticity and reasonableness, §8.01-413.01.
Board of medicine powers, §54.1-2926.
Board of pharmacy, §§54.1-3304 to 54.1-3309.
Administration of standards and schedules, §54.1-3443.

PHARMACISTS AND PHARMACIES —Cont'd
Board of pharmacy —Cont'd
Controlled substances registration certificates, §§54.1-3422 to 54.1-3424.
Dissemination of information, §54.1-3428.
Executive director, §54.1-3305.
Medicine and other healing arts practitioners.
Authority to regulate, §54.1-3304.1.
Drug dispensing licenses, §54.1-3304.
Powers and duties, §54.1-3307.
Collaborative agreements.
Defined, §54.1-3300.
Participation in, §54.1-3300.1.
Compounding drugs, §54.1-3410.2.
Continuous quality improvement program, §54.1-3434.03.
Contraband.
Controlled substances.
Nonresident pharmacies ordering or shipping in violation of chapter, §54.1-3434.4.
Counseling customers, §54.1-3319.
Criminal record checks.
Hospital pharmacy employees, §32.1-126.02.
Defined terms, §54.1-3300.
Discipline.
Refusal, revocation, suspension and denial.
License, permit, certificate or registration, §54.1-3316.
Disposing of stocks, §54.1-3417.
Donated drugs.
Indigent patient programs offered by pharmaceutical manufacturers, §54.1-3301.
Drug control permits, §54.1-3434.2.
Drug violations but not criminally prosecuted.
Monetary penalty, §18.2-261.
Ephedrine and pseudoephedrine.
Retail sale of products containing, §18.2-248.8.
Sale of ephedrine or related compounds, §§18.2-265.6 to 18.2-265.18.
See EPHEDRINE.
Exceptions to licensing, §54.1-3301.
Free clinics.
Immunity for services provided, §54.1-106.
Tax credit.
Donation of services to patients of free clinic, §58.1-439.22.
Freedom of choice.
Health insurance, §38.2-3407.7.
Health services plans, §38.2-4209.1.
Free health care to underserved populations.
Providing, §54.1-3301.
Gelatin capsules.
Disposal, §54.1-3469.
Disposition, §54.1-3469.
Distribution, §§54.1-3467, 54.1-3468.
Storage, §54.1-3469.
Generic drugs.
Workers' compensation.
Use of therapeutically equivalent drug product instead of brand name, §65.2-603.1.
Health insurance.
Freedom of choice, §38.2-3407.7.
Health services plans.
Freedom of choice, §38.2-4209.1.
Historic buildings that formerly housed drugstore or pharmacy.
Exception to restrictions on advertising signs, §54.1-3433.
Hospital pharmacy employees.
Criminal record checks, §32.1-126.02.

PHARMACISTS AND PHARMACIES —Cont'd
Hypodermic needles or syringes.
Disposal, §54.1-3469.
Distribution, §§54.1-3467, 54.1-3468.
Storage, §54.1-3469.
Income tax credit.
Donation of services to patients of free clinic, §58.1-439.22.
Indigent patient programs offered by pharmaceutical manufacturers, §54.1-3301.
Influenza vaccine.
Administration to minors by pharmacists or nurses, §§32.1-46.02, 54.1-3408.
Insulin preparations.
Dispensation, §54.1-3419.
Internet pharmacies.
Registration with board, §54.1-3434.1.
Interns.
Definition of pharmacy intern, §54.1-3300.
Supervision.
Acts restricted to pharmacists, §54.1-3320.
Defined, §54.1-3300.
Licensure, §§54.1-3310 to 54.1-3321.
Exceptions, §54.1-3301.
Revocations, §54.1-3318.
Lien for expenses of medicine.
Person's negligence causing injury, §§8.01-66.2 to 8.01-66.12.
See MEDICAL SERVICES LIEN.
Mail order pharmacies.
Designation of single exclusive provider permitted.
Health insurance, §38.2-3407.7.
Health maintenance organizations, §38.2-4312.1.
Health services plans, §38.2-4209.1.
Manufacturing supervision, §54.1-3438.
Marijuana.
Dispensing or distributing to person holding valid prescription, §18.2-251.1.
Medical bills.
Presumption of authenticity and reasonableness, §8.01-413.01.
Medical malpractice.
General provisions, §§8.01-581.1 to 8.01-581.20.
See MEDICAL MALPRACTICE.
Medicine and other healing arts practitioners.
Authority to license and regulate, §54.1-3304.1.
Licensing to dispense drugs, §54.1-3304.
Medical or therapeutic purpose requirement, §54.1-3303.
Restrictions, §54.1-3302.
Monetary penalty for drug violations where not criminally prosecuted, §18.2-261.
Nonresident pharmacies shipping, mailing or delivering drugs or devices into Commonwealth.
Registration, disclosures, toll-free telephone service, prescription monitoring program compliance, §54.1-3434.1.
Application for registration, renewal, §54.1-3434.2.
Denial, revocation or suspension of registration, §54.1-3434.3.
Prohibited acts, unregistered pharmacies, §54.1-3434.4.
Oleaginous solutions.
Sales, §54.1-3418.
Oral prescriptions.
Acts restricted to pharmacists, §54.1-3320.

PHARMACISTS AND PHARMACIES —Cont'd
Patient safety organization participation.
Continuous quality improvement program compliance, §54.1-3434.03.
Permitting to control drugs, §§54.1-3432 to 54.1-3434.
Powers of board of medicine, §54.1-2926.
Practice of pharmacy.
Acts restricted to pharmacists, §54.1-3320.
Defined, §54.1-3300.
Prescription monitoring program, §§54.1-2519 to 54.1-2526.
Prescriptions.
Acts restricted to pharmacists, §54.1-3320.
Delivery of prescription drug order, §54.1-3420.2.
Filling, §54.1-3410.
Before receipt in writing, §18.2-248.
Filling before receipt in writing, §18.2-248.
Identification requirements, §54.1-3420.1.
Marijuana.
Dispensing or distributing marijuana to, §18.2-251.1.
Monitoring program, §§54.1-2519 to 54.1-2526.
Out-of-state prescriptions.
Pre-issuance requirements, §54.1-3303.
Recording, §54.1-3412.
Refilling, §54.1-3411.
Returns, exchanges or re-dispensing of drugs.
Prohibition, §54.1-3411.1.
Schedule V drugs, §54.1-3416.
Technicians.
Acts performed by technicians, §54.1-3321.
Workers' compensation.
Use of therapeutically equivalent drug product instead of brand name, §65.2-603.1.
Professional corporations, §§13.1-542.1 to 13.1-556.
See PROFESSIONAL CORPORATIONS.
Professional limited liability companies.
Generally, §§13.1-1100 to 13.1-1123.
See PROFESSIONAL LIMITED LIABILITY COMPANIES.
Professions and occupations regulation generally.
See HEALTH PROFESSIONS DEPARTMENT.
Prohibited acts by licensees generally, §54.1-2409.1.
Quality improvement program, continuous, §54.1-3434.03.
Quinine.
Disposal, §54.1-3469.
Distribution, §§54.1-3467, 54.1-3468.
Storage, §54.1-3469.
Records.
Controlled paraphernalia distribution, §54.1-3468.
Re-dispensing of returned drugs.
Suitability determination, §54.1-3411.1.
Refusal, revocation, suspension and denial.
License, permit, certificate or registration, §54.1-3316.
Registration of nonresident pharmacies to control drugs, §§54.1-3434.01 to 54.1-3434.4.
Returns, exchanges or re-dispensing of drugs.
Prohibition, §54.1-3411.1.
Safety closure containers for drugs, §54.1-3427.
Self-referrals.
Practitioner self-referral act, §§54.1-2410 to 54.1-2414.
Special license plates, §46.2-746.9.
Supervision of manufacturing, §54.1-3438.

PHARMACISTS AND PHARMACIES —Cont'd
Tax credit.
Donation of services to patients of free clinic, §58.1-439.22.
Technicians.
Definition of pharmacy technician, §54.1-3300.
Registration, §54.1-3321.
Supervision.
Acts restricted to pharmacists, §54.1-3320.
Defined, §54.1-3300.
TPA-certified optometrist.
Controlled substances.
Dispensing restrictions, §54.1-3303.
Unlawful procurement of licensure, §54.1-102.
Unlawful use of licensure, §54.1-111.
Unprofessional conduct.
Refusal, revocation, suspension and denial.
License, permit, certificate or registration, §54.1-3316.
Vaccinations.
Influenza vaccine.
Administration to minors by pharmacists or nurses, §§32.1-46.02, 54.1-3408.
Workers' compensation.
Use of therapeutically equivalent drug product instead of brand name, §65.2-603.1.

PHARMACY BOARD, §§54.1-3304 to 54.1-3309.

PHEASANTS.
Hunting, §29.1-514.
Permits to raise or purchase, §29.1-514.

PHENCYCLIDINE.
Driving while intoxicated.
Blood concentration level, §18.2-266.
Presumption accused under influence, §18.2-269.

PHENYLKETONURIA, §§32.1-65 to 32.1-67.1.
Virginia immunization information system (VIIS).
Linkages to other databases containing certain health records, §32.1-67.1.

PHONOGRAPHS.
Personal property taxes.
Classification, §58.1-3504.
Recorded device piracy, §§59.1-41.1 to 59.1-41.6.
Authority of attorney general, §59.1-68.2.
Records, tapes and recorded devices, §§59.1-41.1 to 59.1-41.6.
See CRIMINAL LAW AND PROCEDURE.

PHOSGENE.
Illegal use, §18.2-312.

PHOSPHORUS.
Fertilizer generally.
See FERTILIZER.
Sale of deicing agents containing urea, nitrogen or phosphorus prohibited, §3.2-3607.2.

PHOSPHORUS USE IN CLEANING AGENTS, §§62.1-193.1 to 62.1-193.3.

PHOTOGRAPHERS.
License tax, no regularly established place of business, §58.1-3727.

PHOTOGRAPHIC COPIES AS EVIDENCE, §8.01-391.

PHOTOGRAPHS.
Adult abuse, neglect or exploitation.
Photographs, x-rays or medical imaging of incapacitated person.
Taking without consent as part of medical evaluation, §63.2-1606.1.

PHOTOGRAPHS —Cont'd
Agricultural and forestal districts.
Aerial photographs, application for creation or addition to district, §15.2-4303.
Arrest, photographs of arrestees.
Freedom of information act.
Criminal records, disclosure, §2.2-3706.
Bad checks.
Use to identify party presenting bad check, §19.2-270.3.
Bail, release of accused on secured or unsecured bond.
Conditions of release on bond, §19.2-123.
Burglary.
Use of photographs as evidence, §19.2-270.1.
Child abuse or neglect.
Photographs and X-rays of child, evidence, §63.2-1520.
Child charged with delinquent act or certain serious crimes, §16.1-299.
Commercial drivers' licenses.
Application to include photo of applicant, §46.2-341.12.
Licensee, §46.2-341.15.
Criminal trials.
Judicial discretion to permit taking of photographs, §19.2-266.
Destruction, donation or return of exhibits received in evidence, §19.2-270.4.
DMV issued special identification cards, §46.2-345.
Drivers' licenses.
Application to include photo of applicant, §46.2-323.
Commercial drivers' licenses, §46.2-341.12.
Licensee, §46.2-341.15.
Commercial drivers' licenses, §46.2-341.15.
Elections.
Presentation of voter identification, requirements for voting, §24.2-643.
Voter registration.
Department of motor vehicles to provide assistance in providing voter registration cards with, §24.2-411.1.
Photograph of voter, duties of registrars, §24.2-404.
Fish and game violations.
Photographic evidence, §29.1-553.
Identification cards issued by DMV, §46.2-345.
Larceny.
Use of photographs as evidence, §19.2-270.1.
Motor vehicle accidents.
Maintenance, §46.2-380.
Obscene photographs generally, §§18.2-372 to 18.2-388.
See OBSCENITY AND RELATED OFFENSES.
Police authorities of counties, cities and towns.
When authorized to take, §§19.2-392, 19.2-392.01.
Prisoners in state correctional facilities.
Identification procedure, §53.1-23.
Shoplifting.
Use of photographs as evidence, §19.2-270.1.
Toll roads or toll bridges.
Use of photo-monitoring system, §§46.2-819.1, 46.2-819.3.
Unauthorized use of picture or portrait of person, §18.2-216.1.
Unlawfully photographing another, §18.2-386.1.

PHOTO LINEUPS.
Written policies and procedures for conducting.
Establishment by law enforcement, required, §19.2-390.02.
Training standards and model policy, §9.1-102.

PHOTO-MONITORING SYSTEMS.
Enforcement of traffic light signals.
Local powers, §15.2-968.1.
High-occupancy toll lanes.
Enforcement by photo-enforcement system, procedure, §33.1-56.3.
Toll facilities.
Dulles access highway, §46.2-819.5.
Installation by locality within, §46.2-819.1.
Vehicle owner data.
Commissioner of DMV.
Supplying traffic light photo-monitoring system operator, §46.2-208.

PHOTOVOLTAIC, SOLAR AND WIND ENERGY UTILIZATION GRANT PROGRAM, §§67-1000 to 67-1003.
Definitions, §67-1000.
Grants for installation.
Application, requirements for grants, §67-1003.
Eligibility, §67-1001.
Photovoltaic, solar and wind energy utilization grant fund, §67-1002.

PHRENOLOGY PRACTITIONERS.
License tax, §58.1-3726.

PHYSICAL AND HEALTH EDUCATION.
Course of public school instruction, §22.1-207.
Required to be taught in public schools, activities included, §22.1-200.

PHYSICAL CONDITION.
Evidence.
Hearsay exceptions.
Then existing mental, emotional, or physical condition, VA SCt Rule 2:803.

PHYSICAL EXAMINATIONS.
Child abuse or neglect.
Psychological, psychiatric and physical examinations of child.
Court may order, §63.2-1524.
Drivers' licenses.
Applicants for license, §46.2-322.
Commercial drivers' licenses, §46.2-341.12.
Employee protection and safety.
Requiring payment for as condition of employment, §40.1-28.
Firefighters.
Relief for firefighters and dependents, §27-40.1:1.
Health insurance.
Group insurance policy provisions, §38.2-3539.
Individual policy provisions, §38.2-3503.
Judicial inquiry and review commission.
Physical or mental examination of judge, §17.1-912.
Juvenile proceedings, §16.1-275.
Prisoners, §53.1-33.
Teachers.
Cost of medical examinations as condition to continued employment, §22.1-301.

PHYSICAL FITNESS CLUBS, §§59.1-294 to 59.1-310.
See HEALTH CLUBS.

PHYSICAL THERAPIST ASSISTANTS.
Direction and control of licensed physical therapist.
Performance of duties under, requirements, §54.1-3482.
Licensing.
Generally, §§54.1-2950.1 to 54.1-2957.01.
See MEDICINE AND OTHER HEALING ARTS PROFESSIONS.
Unlawful designation as, §54.1-3481.
Unprofessional conduct, §54.1-3483.

PHYSICAL THERAPISTS, §§54.1-3473 to 54.1-3483.
Assistants.
Direction and control of licensed physical therapist.
Performance of duties under, requirements, §54.1-3482.
Unlawful designation as assistant, §54.1-3481.
Unprofessional conduct, §54.1-3483.
Bills for medical services.
Presumption of authenticity and reasonableness, §8.01-413.01.
Board.
Generally, §54.1-3475.
Certification to provide services without referral, §54.1-3482.1.
Continuing competency requirements, §§54.1-3474, 54.1-3480.1.
Definitions, §54.1-3473.
Direction and referral by physician, §54.1-3482.
Disasters, state or local emergencies.
Immunity.
Abandonment of person owed duty of health care in response to disaster, §8.01-225.01.
Unable to provide required care because of lack of resources, §8.01-225.02.
Donation of services.
Tax credit, §58.1-439.22.
Exemptions from provisions, §54.1-3476.
Failure to refer patient.
Medical condition beyond scope of practice, §54.1-3482.
Health benefit programs.
Provider willing to meet terms and conditions not to be excluded, §38.2-3407.
Health insurance.
Family access to medical insurance security plan, §§32.1-351 to 32.1-353.
Public officers and employees.
Required coverage, §2.2-2818.
Health services plans, coverage of services, §38.2-4221.
Immunity.
Disasters, state or local emergencies.
Abandonment of person owed duty of health care in response to disaster, §8.01-225.01.
Unable to provide required care because of lack of resources, §8.01-225.02.
Invasive procedures within scope of practice.
Performing, requirements, §54.1-3482.
Licensing.
Examination or endorsement, §54.1-3479.
Generally, §§54.1-2900 to 54.1-2993.
See MEDICINE AND OTHER HEALING ARTS PROFESSIONS.
Refusal, revocation or suspension, §54.1-3480.
Required, §54.1-3474.
Requirements for licensure, §54.1-3477.
Physical therapist assistant, §54.1-3478.

PHYSICAL THERAPISTS —Cont'd
Lien for expenses of treatment.
Person's negligence causing injury, §§8.01-66.2 to 8.01-66.12.
See MEDICAL SERVICES LIEN.
Medical bills.
Presumption of authenticity and reasonableness, §8.01-413.01.
Medical malpractice.
General provisions, §§8.01-581.1 to 8.01-581.20.
See MEDICAL MALPRACTICE.
One-time evaluation of patient, §54.1-3482.
Practice of physical therapy.
Scope of practice, §54.1-3482.
Prevention of impairments, functional limitations and disabilities.
Services rendered without referral, §54.1-3482.
Records or papers of patients.
Admissibility of copies, §8.01-413.
Right of patient, attorney or authorized insurer to copies, §8.01-413.
Subpoenas, §8.01-413.
Referral and direction by physician, §54.1-3482.
Refusal, revocation or suspension of licensure, §54.1-3480.
Regulation by board, §54.1-3475.
Requirements for licensure, §54.1-3477.
Physical therapist assistant, §54.1-3478.
Schools and education.
Employment by school board, §22.1-274.
Services authorized without referral, §54.1-3482.
Certification to provide services without referral, §54.1-3482.1.
Special education students.
Services rendered without referral, §54.1-3482.
Standardized HCFA-1500 health insurance claims forms for services.
Acceptance by insurers required, §38.2-322.
Student athletes.
Services rendered without referral, §54.1-3482.
Tax credit.
Donation of services, §58.1-439.22.
Topical drugs, administration, §54.1-3408.
Traineeships, §54.1-3479.
Treatment without referral order, §54.1-3482.
Certification to provide services without referral, §54.1-3482.1.
Unlawful designation as, §54.1-3481.
Unprofessional conduct, §54.1-3483.
Unlawful to practice without license, §54.1-3474.
Wellness, fitness and health screenings.
Services rendered without referral, §54.1-3482.
Workplace ergonomics.
Services rendered without referral, §54.1-3482.

PHYSICIAN ASSISTANTS.
Activities delegated.
Practice supervision agreement, §54.1-2952.
Advisory board on physician assistants, §54.1-2950.1.
Conditional grants for students, §32.1-122.6:03.
Controlled substances and devices.
Prescribing, §54.1-2952.1.
Death, authority to pronounce, §54.1-2972.
Donation of services.
Tax credit, §58.1-439.22.
Education and training required, §54.1-2950.
Emergency department of hospital.
Practicing in, §54.1-2952.

PHYSICIAN ASSISTANTS —Cont'd
Issuance of license, §54.1-2951.2.
Licensing generally, §§54.1-2950.1 to 54.1-2957.01.
Number physician allowed to supervise, §54.1-2952.
Practice supervision agreement, §54.1-2952.
Prescribing controlled substances and devices, §54.1-2952.1.
Professional corporation, partnerships of licensees, hospitals.
Employment, §54.1-2952.
Radiologic technology procedures.
Practices permitted, §54.1-2952.
Requirements for licensure as physician assistant, §54.1-2951.1.
Restricted volunteer license for certain physician assistants, §54.1-2951.3.
Revocation, suspension or refusal to renew license.
Grounds, §54.1-2953.
Services performed by, §54.1-2952.
Signature, when accepted, §54.1-2952.2.
Supervision by licensed physician, §54.1-2952.
Tax credit.
Donation of services, §58.1-439.22.
Tuberculosis.
Treating person with active tuberculosis.
Report required, §32.1-50.
Unlicensed practice, §54.1-2949.
Venereal disease.
Pregnant women.
Prenatal test required by, §32.1-60.

PHYSICIAN-PATIENT PRIVILEGE, §8.01-399, VA SCt Rule 2:505.
Child abuse or neglect.
Inapplicability in legal proceedings, §63.2-1519.
Disabled drivers.
Physician reports on, §54.1-2966.1.
Emergency medical treatment.
Termination of privilege upon patient discharge, §54.1-2962.2.
Paternity proceedings.
Waiver of privilege, §20-49.7.
Workers' compensation.
Medical examinations ordered by employers or commission.
Applicability of privilege, §65.2-607.

PHYSICIANS' CURRENT PROCEDURAL TERMINOLOGY.
Use by health insurance providers, §38.2-322.

PHYSICIANS OR SURGEONS.
Abortions.
Generally, §§18.2-71 to 18.2-76.1.
See ABORTION.
Informed written consent.
Required to obtain, civil penalty for failure, §18.2-76.
Partial birth infanticide.
Medical necessity to prevent death of mother, §18.2-71.1.
Performing on unemancipated minor, §16.1-241.
Adult abuse, neglect or exploitation.
Photographs, x-rays or medical imaging of incapacitated person.
Taking without consent as part of medical evaluation, §63.2-1606.1.
Report to local department of social services, §63.2-1606.

PHYSICIANS OR SURGEONS —Cont'd
Aircraft pilot disabilities.
Reporting to licensing authorities, §54.1-2966.
Alternative or experimental therapeutic options.
Disclosure requirements, §54.1-2963.1.
Anatomical gifts.
Participation in removal or transplant of part, §32.1-291.14.
Assault and battery of health care provider.
Emergency room or other facility providing emergency care, §18.2-57.
Assessments.
Birth-related neurological injury compensation, §38.2-5020.
Automatic external defibrillators.
Immunity of physician supervising, §8.01-225.
Behavioral health and developmental services.
Supervision of persons maintaining or operating services, §37.2-413.
Behavioral health and developmental services department.
Employment of unlicensed physician, limitations, §37.2-313.
State training centers with certified skilled nursing beds.
Licensed physician on duty at all times, §37.2-313.1.
Bills for medical services.
Presumption of authenticity and reasonableness, §8.01-413.01.
Birth defects.
Folic acid's role in prevention.
Distribution of information, §32.1-69.1:1.
Birth-related neurological injury compensation, §§38.2-5000 to 38.2-5021.
See BIRTH-RELATED NEUROLOGICAL INJURY COMPENSATION.
Cancer registry.
Information to be provided to, §32.1-70.
Child abuse or neglect.
Reason to suspect, required reports, fine for failure, §63.2-1509.
Taking child into temporary custody, §63.2-1517.
Communicable disease reporting, §32.1-116.3.
Competency assessment.
Three medical malpractice judgments or settlements in ten year period, §54.1-2912.3.
Conscience clause.
Abortions, §18.2-75.
Controlled substances.
Personnel properly trained to assist doctors.
Administering, §54.1-3408.
Sale, §54.1-2914.
Crime victims, compensation.
Debt collection activities by health care providers after claim filed, §19.2-368.5:2.
Dentistry.
Oral or maxillofacial surgeons, §§54.1-2700, 54.1-2709.1 to 54.1-2709.5.
Dialysis patient care technicians, §§54.1-2729.1 to 54.1-2729.3.
Disasters, state or local emergencies.
Immunity.
Abandonment of person owed duty of health care in response to disaster, §8.01-225.01.
Unable to provide required care because of lack of resources, §8.01-225.02.
Disciplinary information concerning licensees.
Posting on department website, §54.1-2910.2.

PHYSICIANS OR SURGEONS —Cont'd
Disciplinary proceedings.
Confidentiality of information, §54.1-2400.2.
Disclosure of medical treatment options, §54.1-2963.1.
Disclosure of mental health patient information to third party payors.
See MENTAL HEALTH.
Disease reporting, §§32.1-36 to 32.1-38.
Communicable disease reporting, §32.1-116.3.
Immunity from liability, §32.1-38.
Doctor..
Use of title, §54.1-3616.
Donation of professional services.
Tax credit, §58.1-439.22.
Driving while intoxicated.
Chemical test for alcohol or drug content of blood.
Persons qualified to draw blood, §18.2-268.5.
Duty to protect third parties.
Violent behavior or serious harm by client, §54.1-2400.1.
Emergency medical care.
Generally.
See MEDICINE AND OTHER HEALING ARTS PROFESSIONS.
Spousal liability, §8.01-220.2.
Team physician, §8.01-225.1.
Emergency medical services.
Good Samaritan statute, §8.01-225.
Physician-patient privilege.
Termination upon discharge of patient, §54.1-2962.2.
Escrow fund protection, §54.1-2506.2.
Evidence.
Hearsay exceptions.
Medical treatment, statement for purposes of, VA SCt Rule 2:803.
Eyeglasses or sunglasses.
Sale of nonprescription eyeglasses and sunglasses, §54.1-3202.
Fetal death reports, §32.1-264.
Extension of time for filing, §32.1-266.
Free health clinic services.
Immunity from liability, §54.1-106.
Notice to licensees of board of medicine, §54.1-106.1.
Good Samaritan statute, §8.01-225.
Gunshot wound reports, §54.1-2967.
Health benefit programs.
Provider willing to meet terms and conditions not to be excluded, §38.2-3407.
Health care data reporting.
Generally, §§32.1-276.2 to 32.1-276.11.
See HEALTH CARE DATA REPORTING.
Health insurance claim submission.
Failure of in-network provider to submit claims.
Liability of patient for unbilled health care services, §8.01-27.5.
Health insurance plan not accepted by doctor.
Patient subject to full charge.
Information provided patient, §54.1-2910.01.
Health insurance reform.
Choice of health care professional.
Federal market reforms, §38.2-3443.
Health insurance reimbursement for services.
Licensed practitioner rendering services that might be reimbursed if performed by other health care provider, §38.2-3408.
Health practitioners' monitoring program, §§54.1-2515 to 54.1-2518.

PHYSICIANS OR SURGEONS —Cont'd
Hearsay exceptions.
Medical treatment, statement for purposes of, VA SCt Rule 2:803.
Human immunodeficiency virus reporting.
Persons testing positive for exposure, §32.1-36.
Husband and wife.
Spousal liability for emergency medical care, §8.01-220.2.
Immunity.
Aircraft pilots, §54.1-2966.
Disasters, state or local emergencies.
Abandonment of person owed duty of health care in response to disaster, §8.01-225.01.
Unable to provide required care because of lack of resources, §8.01-225.02.
Disciplinary actions, reports of, §54.1-2908.
Free health clinic services, §54.1-106.
Notice to licensees of board of medicine, §54.1-106.1.
Good Samaritan statute, §8.01-225.
Medical malpractice, §§8.01-581.13, 8.01-581.19.
Team physicians, §8.01-225.1.
Withdrawal of life-sustaining procedures pursuant to living wills, §54.1-2988.
Wounds caused by concealable weapons, §54.1-2967.
Income tax credit.
Donation of professional services, §58.1-439.22.
Indigent patient programs offered by pharmaceutical manufacturers.
Practitioner of medicine or osteopathy participating in, §54.1-3301.
Information provided patient upon request, §54.1-2910.01.
Juvenile detention homes having custody or responsibility for supervision of children.
Transportation of children to medical appointments, §16.1-254.
Lab test results.
Copy provided patient.
Request by patient, lab providing directly, practitioner authorizing, §54.1-2409.4.
Licensing generally, §§54.1-2900 to 54.1-2993.
See MEDICINE AND OTHER HEALING ARTS PROFESSIONS.
Lien for expenses of treatment.
Person's negligence causing injury, §§8.01-66.2 to 8.01-66.12.
See MEDICAL SERVICES LIEN.
Loan repayment program, §32.1-122.6:1.
Lyme disease testing, disclosures required, §54.1-2963.2.
Managed care health insurance plan.
Doctor not participant.
Patient subject to full charge.
Information provided patient, §54.1-2910.01.
Marijuana.
Prescribing for medical purposes, §18.2-251.1.
Marriage record or registration.
False entry, §18.2-207.
Medical bills.
Presumption of authenticity and reasonableness, §8.01-413.01.
Medical devices and appliances.
Sale, §54.1-2914.
Medically underserved areas.
Pilot programs for obstetrical and pediatric care in underserved areas, §32.1-11.5.
Medical malpractice.
General provisions, §§8.01-581.1 to 8.01-581.20.
See MEDICAL MALPRACTICE.

PHYSICIANS OR SURGEONS —Cont'd
Medical malpractice judgments or settlements.
Competency assessment, §54.1-2912.3.
Reporting, regulations concerning, adoption, §54.1-2910.1.
Medical records.
Generally.
See MEDICAL RECORDS.
Medical referrals for profit, §18.2-502.
Metabolic disease screening, §§32.1-65, 32.1-66.
Motor vehicle driver disabilities.
Reporting to licensing authorities, §54.1-2966.1.
Negligence.
Vaccine-related injury or death.
Action for gross negligence, §8.01-44.2.
Oral or maxillofacial surgeons, §§54.1-2700, 54.1-2709.1 to 54.1-2709.5.
Partial birth infanticide.
Medical necessity to prevent death of mother, §18.2-71.1.
Patient level data.
Submission to board, §32.1-276.6.
Physical therapists generally, §§54.1-3473 to 54.1-3483.
See PHYSICAL THERAPISTS.
Physician assistants.
See PHYSICIAN ASSISTANTS.
Prescription monitoring program, §§54.1-2519 to 54.1-2526.
Prescriptions.
See PRESCRIPTIONS.
Professional corporations, §§13.1-542.1 to 13.1-556.
See PROFESSIONAL CORPORATIONS.
Professional limited liability companies, §§13.1-1100 to 13.1-1123.
See PROFESSIONAL LIMITED LIABILITY COMPANIES.
Referrals for profit, §18.2-502.
Schools and education.
Employment by school board, §22.1-274.
Immunization of students, §22.1-271.2.
Self-referrals.
Practitioner self-referral act, §§54.1-2410 to 54.1-2414.
Standardized HCFA-1500 health insurance claims forms for services.
Acceptance by insurers required, §38.2-322.
Surgery, who may perform generally, §54.1-2400.01:1.
Tax credit.
Donation of professional services, §58.1-439.22.
Team physicians.
Immunity from liability, §8.01-225.1.
Third-party reimbursement program participation not condition of licensure, §54.1-2910.3.
Treatment options, restrictions on disclosure by insurer prohibited, §38.2-3405.
Tuberculosis.
Reports of active tuberculosis, §32.1-50.
Treating person with active tuberculosis.
Report required, §32.1-50.
Treatment planning, §32.1-50.1.
Vaccine-related injury or death.
Negligence.
Action for gross negligence, §8.01-44.2.
Venereal disease diagnosed in child twelve years of age or younger.
Reporting requirements, §32.1-36.

PHYSICIANS OR SURGEONS —Cont'd
Venereal disease tests for pregnant women.
Prenatal test required by, §32.1-60.
Virginia health workforce development authority, §§32.1-122.7 to 32.1-122.7:2.
Weight loss centers or clinics.
Duties of physicians affiliated with, §18.2-502.1.
Wound reports, §54.1-2967.

PIANKATANK RIVER.
Oysters and clams.
Patent tongs.
Area prohibitions, §28.2-508.
Planting grounds.
Public oyster rocks, beds and shoals declared, §28.2-646.
Taking restrictions, §28.2-524.

PIANOS.
Personal property taxes.
Classification, §58.1-3504.

PICKEREL.
Game fish defined as including, §29.1-100.

PICKETING.
Dwelling places, §§18.2-418, 18.2-419.
Illegal picketing.
Labor unions, §40.1-53.
Obstructing free passage of others.
Lawful picketing not prohibited, §18.2-404.

PICKUP TRUCKS.
Defined, §46.2-100.
Motor vehicle license plates.
Exemption from displaying for-hire license plates, §46.2-711.
Motor vehicle registration.
Additional fee, §46.2-694.
Transportation of persons less than 16 years old in pickup truck beds, §46.2-1156.1.

PICTURES.
See PHOTOGRAPHS.

PIERCING BODY.
Minors, §18.2-371.3.

PIERS, §§62.1-164, 62.1-165.
Boundaries of localities to embrace.
Localities bordering Chesapeake Bay or Atlantic Ocean, §15.2-3105.
Motorboats to slacken speed and control wakes near structures, §29.1-744.3.
Obstruction or hazard to lawful use of waters.
Removal, repair, etc., §15.2-909.
Personal watercraft to slacken speed and control wakes when near structures, §29.1-748.
Placement of private piers for noncommercial purposes by owners by riparian lands, §28.2-1203.
Boat lift and open-sided roof designed to shelter boat, §28.2-1203.
Removal of obstructions or hazards from state waters, §28.2-1210.
Saltwater recreational fishing license, §28.2-302.9.

PIGEONS.
Nuisance bird law, §§3.2-900, 3.2-901.
Protection of homing pigeons, §18.2-145.

PIG IRON.
Buying with intent to defraud, §18.2-238.

PIGS.
Destruction of swine affected with hog cholera.
Shooting enclosures, §§3.2-6035 to 3.2-6042.
Estrays, §§55-202 to 55-206.
False pedigree, §18.2-205.
False pretense in obtaining registration, §18.2-205.
Garbage feeding, §§3.2-6031 to 3.2-6034.
Hog cholera.
Unlawful acts as to, §3.2-6017.
Larceny, §18.2-97.
Livestock.
Diseases.
See LIVESTOCK AND ANIMAL DISEASES.
Generally.
See LIVESTOCK.
Maiming, killing or poisoning, §18.2-144.
Pork industry board, §§3.2-2000 to 3.2-2009.
See PORK INDUSTRY BOARD.
Smithfield hams, §§3.2-5419 to 3.2-5421.

PIKE.
Game fish defined as including, §29.1-100.

PILINGS.
Obstruction or hazard to lawful use of waters.
Removal, repair, etc., §15.2-909.
Removal of obstructions or hazards from state waters, §28.2-1210.

PILLOWS.
Bedding and upholstered furniture generally, §§32.1-212 to 32.1-226.
See BEDDING AND UPHOLSTERED FURNITURE.

PILOT PROGRAMS.
Administrative process act.
Regulations imposing local government mandates, §2.2-4010.

PILOTS.
Aircraft.
See AIRCRAFT.
Branch pilots, §§54.1-900 to 54.1-927.
See BRANCH PILOTS.

PIMPING.
Competency of persons to testify, §18.2-360.
Receiving money for procuring person, §18.2-356.
Receiving money from earnings of male or female prostitute, §18.2-357.

PIN.
Circuit court clerk indexing by parcel identification number, §17.1-252.
Computers.
Using computer to gather identifying information, §18.2-152.5:1.
Identity theft, §§18.2-186.3, 18.2-186.3:1, 18.2-186.5.
Use of person's identity with intent to coerce, intimidate or harass, §18.2-186.4.

PINBALL MACHINES.
License tax on amusement machines and amusement machine operators, §§58.1-3720 to 58.1-3723.

PIPE BOMBS.
Manufacture, possession, use, etc., of fire bombs or explosive devices, §18.2-85.

PIPELINE COMPANY LICENSE TAX.
Estimated tax, §§58.1-2640 to 58.1-2651.
See PUBLIC SERVICE CORPORATION TAXATION.
Generally, §§58.1-2620 to 58.1-2635.
See PUBLIC SERVICE CORPORATION TAXATION.

PIPELINES.
Authority to permit, §56-258.
Compensation for damages, §56-260.
Distribution companies.
Taxes, §58.1-400.2.
Estimated tax, §§58.1-2640 to 58.1-2651.
See PUBLIC SERVICE CORPORATION TAXATION.
Gas pipeline construction, §56-265.2:1.
Hazardous liquid pipeline safety, §§56-553 to 56-555.
Citation of chapter, §56-553.
Definitions, §56-554.
Implementation of federal act, §56-555.
State corporation commission.
Implementation of federal act, §56-555.
Title of act, §56-553.
Landfill gas pipelines.
Placement within highway-right-of-way.
Department of transportation permission.
Notice to counties through which pipeline passes, §33.1-223.2:11.
Liability exemption provisions, §56-260.1.
License tax generally, §§58.1-2620 to 58.1-2635.
See PUBLIC SERVICE CORPORATION TAXATION.
Manner of laying, §56-257.
Means of locating, §56-257.1.
Natural gas pipeline safety, §56-257.2.
Oil discharges into waters of the state, §§62.1-44.34:14 to 62.1-44.34:23.
Public service companies.
Generally, §§56-1 to 56-46.3.
See PUBLIC SERVICE COMPANIES.
Retail sales and use tax.
Exemption of gas, electricity or water delivered to customers through mains, lines or pipes, §58.1-609.1.
Rights-of-way, §56-259.
Submerged lands.
Structures, maintenance or removal, §28.2-1209.
Underground utility line damage prevention, §§56-265.14 to 56-265.32.
See UNDERGROUND UTILITY LINE DAMAGE PREVENTION.

PIPELINE TRANSMISSION COMPANIES, §§56-257 to 56-260.1.
Public service corporations or companies.
Defined to include pipeline companies, §56-1.

PIPES.
Drug paraphernalia, §§18.2-265.1 to 18.2-265.5.

PIPE TOBACCO.
Tobacco generally.
See TOBACCO.
Tobacco products tax, §§58.1-1021.01 to 58.1-1021.05.
See TOBACCO PRODUCTS TAX.

PIRACY.
Authority of attorney general, §59.1-68.2.
Powers of congress, US Const Art I §8.

PIRACY OF RECORDINGS, §§59.1-41.1 to 59.1-41.6.
Audiovisual recording of motion picture in commercial theater.
Unlawful, penalty, detention of person by owner, §18.2-187.2.

PISTOLS.
Carrying concealed weapons, §18.2-308.
Firearms dealers, §§54.1-4200 to 54.1-4202.
See FIREARMS DEALERS.
Firearms generally.
See FIREARMS.
Firearms offenses, §§18.2-279 to 18.2-287.4, 18.2-308 to 18.2-311.1.
See FIREARMS OFFENSES.
Permits to sell or purchase.
Counties requiring, §15.2-1208.
Use in commission of crime.
Forfeiture, §19.2-386.29.

PITS.
Abandoned pits, duty of person causing to fill, §18.2-316.

PITTSYLVANIA COUNTY.
Confederate cemeteries and graves.
Disbursement of funds appropriated for upkeep, §10.1-2211.
Disabled veterans, exemption from solid waste disposal fee, §15.2-2159.
Fishing, inland waters.
Taking methods, restrictions, §29.1-531.
Former officers and employees.
Restrictions on activities, §15.2-1408.
Outdoor performing arts amphitheater, area or similar facility.
Retail on-premises wine and beer license, §4.1-209.
Revolutionary war cemeteries and graves.
Disbursement of funds appropriated for upkeep, §10.1-2211.1.
School board.
Fingerprinting applicants for employment, §22.1-296.2.
Salary of members, §22.1-32.
Staggered terms for elected members, §22.1-57.3:1.2.
Solid waste disposal fee, §15.2-2159.
Uranium mining and development study, §§45.1-285.1 to 45.1-285.10.

PLACARDS, MOTOR VEHICLE PARKING.
See PARKING FOR DISABLED OR HANDICAPPED.

PLACEBOS.
Professional use of imitation controlled substances, §18.2-248.3.

PLACE OF ASSEMBLY, DISCLOSURE.
Motorcycle manufacturers and distributors, §46.2-1993.26.
Trailer manufacturers and distributors, §46.2-1992.25.

PLAIN ENGLISH REQUIREMENT.
Medicaid managed care programs.
Information documents, §32.1-330.2.
Referenda, §§24.2-684, 24.2-687.
Proposed constitutional amendments, §30-19.9.
Questions submitted to voters, §30-19.10.

PLAINTIFF ENTITLED TO LESS THAN $100, JUDGMENT FOR DEFENDANT.
Circuit courts, §17.1-514.

PLANETARIUMS.
Locality regulating outdoor lighting near, §15.2-920.

PLANNED DEVELOPMENTS.
County requiring information to be provided prospective buyers, §15.2-1216.
Real property tax assessment of lots and open spaces, §58.1-3284.1.
Subdivided land sales.
Generally, §§55-336 to 55-347.
See SUBDIVIDED LAND SALES.
Subdivisions and land development generally, §§15.2-2240 to 15.2-2279.
See SUBDIVISIONS.

PLANNED FIRE TREATMENT.
Prescribed burning and certified prescribed burn managers, §§10.1-1150.1 to 10.1-1150.6.

PLANNING AND BUDGET DEPARTMENT, §§2.2-1500 to 2.2-1514.
Administrative process act.
Proposed regulations.
Economic impact analysis, §2.2-4007.04.
Anticipated revenues.
Estimates by state agencies, §2.2-1504.
Appropriations.
Monitoring and adjustment, §2.2-1501.
Assistant to the Governor for intergovernmental affairs, office of.
Cooperation with department, §2.2-303.
Boundaries.
District systems boundaries, approval, §2.2-1501.
Budget bill.
Land preservation.
Bill to include, §2.2-1509.4.
Major information technology projects.
Bill to include, §2.2-1509.3.
Submission, §2.2-1509.
Budget highlights.
Publication, §2.2-1510.
Capital outlay projects.
Regulations, establishment, §2.2-1502.
Chief planning and budget officer.
Governor, §2.2-103.
Commercial activities list, §2.2-1501.1.
Comptroller.
Financial statements, §2.2-1512.
Council on Virginia's future, §§2.2-2683 to 2.2-2689.
Courts.
Estimates of financial needs, §2.2-1506.
Creation, §2.2-1500.
Debt capacity advisory committee, §§2.2-2712 to 2.2-2714.
Director.
Appointment, §2.2-1500.
District systems boundaries, approval.
Duties of department, §2.2-1501.
Duties of department, §2.2-1501.
Electronic funds transfers.
Payment of amounts due and owing Commonwealth, §2.2-211.
Estimates by nonstate agencies, §2.2-1505.
Estimates by state agencies, §2.2-1504.
Executive agencies.
Budget development, participation, §2.2-1507.
District systems boundaries, approval.
Duties of department, §2.2-1501.
Executive budget.
Budget bill.
Submission, §2.2-1509.

PLANNING AND BUDGET DEPARTMENT —Cont'd
Executive budget —Cont'd
Formulation, §2.2-1501.
Submission to General assembly, §2.2-1508.
Federal budget.
Assessment and review, §2.2-1501.
General assembly.
Consideration of budget by committees, §2.2-1511.
Estimates of financial needs, §2.2-1506.
Executive budget.
Submission to General assembly, §2.2-1508.
Submission of additional information to legislative committees, §2.2-1513.
General provisions regarding state agencies and general operation of government, §§2.2-600 to 2.2-614.3.
See STATE DEPARTMENTS AND AGENCIES.
Imprisonment term increases.
Evaluation of effect on operating costs, §30-19.1:4.
Integrated policy analysis, planning and budgeting process.
Duties of department, §2.2-1501.
Performance management.
Roadmap for Virginia's future.
Council on Virginia's future, §§2.2-2683 to 2.2-2689.
Performance management system for financial services, §2.2-1501.
Policy analysis, §2.2-1501.
Preplanning justification.
Capital outlay projects, §2.2-1502.
Privatization analyses, §2.2-1501.1.
Program evaluation, §2.2-1501.
Roadmap for Virginia's future.
Council on Virginia's future, §§2.2-2683 to 2.2-2689.
Publication of budget highlights, §2.2-1510.
Public hearings on budget bill, §2.2-1510.
Regulations.
Capital outlay projects, §2.2-1502.
Reports.
Comptroller.
Financial statements, §2.2-1512.
Standardized system of financial reports, §2.2-1501.
Roadmap for Virginia's future.
Council on Virginia's future, §§2.2-2683 to 2.2-2689.
School efficiency review program.
Authority of department, §2.2-1501.
Generally, §2.2-1502.1.
Secretary of finance.
Agency responsibility, §2.2-211.
Six-year financial outline.
Filing by governor, §2.2-1503.1.
Six-year revenue plan.
Filing by Governor, §2.2-1503.
State aid.
Estimates by nonstate agencies for annual budget, §2.2-1505.
Statistical data.
Coordination and review, §2.2-1501.
Virginia's future, council on, §§2.2-2683 to 2.2-2689.

PLANNING AND BUDGET SYSTEM OF STATE.
Balance budget.
Duty of governor, VA Const Art X §7.
Juvenile community crime control.
Appropriations for operating costs of programs
How determined, §16.1-309.6.

PLANNING AND DEVELOPMENT, §§15.2-2200 to 15.2-2329.
Advertisement of plans, ordinances or amendments, §15.2-2204.
Advisory plans examiner board.
Urban county executive form of government.
Expedited land development review, §15.2-851.
Capital construction project by state agency.
Furnishing locality preliminary plans, §15.2-2202.
Capital improvement programs, §15.2-2239.
Commercial real estate.
Approval of plats, site plans and development plans, §15.2-2259.
Comprehensive plan, §§15.2-2222.1 to 15.2-2232.
Adjacent unincorporated territory included in municipal plan, §15.2-2231.
Adoption of parts of plan, §15.2-2228.
Affordable housing.
Study of need for, §15.2-2224.
Amendment, §15.2-2229.
Approval or disapproval of plans, §15.2-2226.
Coastal resource management guidance, §15.2-2223.2.
Consistent with statewide transportation plan and improvement program, §15.2-2223.
Control of general or approximate location, character and extent of feature shown on plan, §15.2-2232.
Coordination of state and local transportation planning, §15.2-2222.1.
Future economic and population growth.
Inclusion, §15.2-2224.
General in nature, §15.2-2223.
Historic areas included in plan, §15.2-2224.
Implementation of plan, §15.2-2224.
Incorporated towns included in county plan, §15.2-2231.
Legal status of plan, §15.2-2232.
Long-range recommendations for general development, §15.2-2223.
Maps included in plan, §15.2-2224.
Matters studied in preparation of plan, §15.2-2224.
Methods of implementation, §15.2-2224.
Mineral resources.
Inclusion, §15.2-2224.
Notice and hearing on plan, §15.2-2225.
Overruling action of commission, §15.2-2232.
Preparation and recommendation by planning commission, §15.2-2223.
Public facilities study, §15.2-2230.1.
Resubmission of plan by planning commission, §15.2-2227.
Return of plan to planning commission, §15.2-2227.
Review of plan, §15.2-2230.
Status of plan, §15.2-2232.
Surveys and studies in preparation, §§15.2-2223, 15.2-2224.
Time for reviewing plan, §15.2-2230.
Urban development areas, §15.2-2223.1.
Dam break inundation zone.
Development within.
Contract-ready costs for conducting upgrades to impounding structure.
Study, estimate provided, payment by developer, §15.2-2243.1.
Land of proposed subdivision within.
Fact set forth in plat, §15.2-2258.
Declaration of intent, §15.2-2200.
Definitions, §15.2-2201.

PLANNING AND DEVELOPMENT —Cont'd
Department of environmental quality.
Distribution of environmental impact reports for major state projects, §15.2-2202.
Duties of state agencies, §15.2-2202.
Expedited land development review.
Urban county executive form of government, §15.2-851.
Hospital authorities.
Compliance with planning laws, §15.2-5317.
Intention of general assembly, §15.2-2200.
Juvenile residential care facilities.
Notice by person planning to establish in locality without zoning ordinance, §15.2-2207.
Levies and fees imposed or increased by locality.
Advertisement and enactment of ordinances, §15.2-107.
Master plan of state agency affecting comprehensive plan, §15.2-2202.
Notice by applicants, when locality may require, §15.2-2206.
Notice by direct mail or any other means of planning or zoning matter, §15.2-2205.
Notice of intention to adopt plan, ordinance or amendment.
Publication required prior to recommendation or adopting, §15.2-2204.
Official maps, §§15.2-2233 to 15.2-2238.
Additions and modifications, §15.2-2235.
Adoption by governing body, §15.2-2234.
Building permit application made for area shown as future or proposed right-of-way.
Granting or denying by locality, §15.2-2233.
Certification by planning commission to governing body, §15.2-2234.
Consultation with Commonwealth transportation board, §15.2-2237.
Copy of map and ordinance sent to Commonwealth transportation board, §15.2-2237.
Counties that have withdrawn roads from secondary system of state highways.
Provisions not to affect exercise of authority, §15.2-2238.
Filing in office of clerk of circuit court, §15.2-2234.
Preparation by local planning commission, §15.2-2233.
Readoption, §15.2-2236.
Report by commission as to additions or modifications, §15.2-2235.
Review, §15.2-2236.
What map to show, §15.2-2233.
Planning commissions.
Generally, §§15.2-2210 to 15.2-2222.
See PLANNING COMMISSIONS.
Planning district commissions, §§15.2-4200 to 15.2-4222.
See PLANNING DISTRICT COMMISSIONS.
Plans examiner board.
Urban county executive form of government.
Expedited land development review, §15.2 851.
Public hearing on plans, ordinances or amendments, §15.2-2204.
Restraining violation, §15.2-2208.
Scenic rivers.
Evaluation of planning, use and development proposals, §10.1-402.
Subdivisions and land development generally, §§15.2-2240 to 15.2-2279.
See SUBDIVISIONS.

PLANNING AND DEVELOPMENT —Cont'd
Transportation districts, §§15.2-4527, 15.2-4528.
Trees.
Planting and conserving during development process, §§15.2-961, 15.2-961.1.
Urban county executive form of government.
Business or financial relationship disclosures in land use proceedings.
Board of supervisors, planning commission and board of zoning appeals, §15.2-852.
Expedited land development review, §15.2-851.
Zoning, §§15.2-2280 to 15.2-2316.2.
See ZONING.

PLANNING COMMISSIONS.
Advisory members, §15.2-2213.
Agricultural and forestal districts.
Review of application, §15.2-4307.
Capital improvement programs.
Preparation and submission to governing bodies, §15.2-2239.
Comprehensive plans, §§15.2-2222.1 to 15.2-2232.
See PLANNING AND DEVELOPMENT.
Cooperation, §15.2-2211.
County commission surveying as town commission, §15.2-2218.
Creation, §15.2-2210.
Defined, §15.2-2201.
Duplicate commission in Chesapeake and Hampton, §15.2-2220.
Duties, §15.2-2221.
Existing commissions.
Continuation to operate, §15.2-2203.
Expenditures, §15.2-2222.
Facilities for holding of meetings and preservation of documents.
Governing body providing, §15.2-2216.
Gifts and donations, §15.2-2222.
Joint local planning commission, §15.2-2219.
Majority vote required for actions, §15.2-2215.
Meetings, §15.2-2214.
Notice of intention to adopt plan, ordinance or amendment required prior to recommending, §15.2-2204.
Officers, §15.2-2217.
Official maps, §§15.2-2233 to 15.2-2238.
Public hearings on plans, ordinances or amendments, §15.2-2204.
Qualifications, appointment, removal, terms and compensation, §15.2-2212.
Quorum, §15.2-2215.
Rules for transaction of business, adoption, §15.2-2217.
Special meetings, §15.2-2214.
Special surveys, §15.2-2217.
Subdivisions and development of land.
Generally, §§15.2-2240 to 15.2-2279.
See SUBDIVISIONS.
Town designating county commission as local commission, §15.2-2218.
Urban county executive form of government.
Appointee from each election district, §15.2-855.
Establishing different terms of office, §15.2-824.
Zoning.
Generally, §§15.2-2280 to 15.2-2316.2.
See ZONING.

PLANNING DISTRICT COMMISSIONS, §§15.2-4200 to 15.2-4222.
Appropriating or lending funds, §15.2-4218.
Charter agreement, §15.2-4203.
Compensation, §15.2-4203.

PLANNING DISTRICT COMMISSIONS —Cont'd
Cooperation and consultation with other agencies, §15.2-4214.
Definitions, §15.2-4202.
Disposition of assets and earnings, §15.2-4204.
Dual membership, §15.2-4220.
Duties, §15.2-4208.
Housing and community development director.
Oversight responsibilities, §36-139.6.
Inconsistent laws inapplicable, §15.2-4222.
Member of local governing body named to position, §15.2-1535.
Merger of two commissions, §15.2-4221.
Organization of commission, §15.2-4203.
Powers, §15.2-4205.
Additional powers, §15.2-4206.
Purposes of commission, §15.2-4207.
Purposes of provisions, §15.2-4201.
Regional cooperation act.
Short title, §15.2-4200.
Regional cooperation incentive fund, §15.2-4217.
Regional strategic plan.
Actions to be in conformity with plan, §15.2-4210.
Amendment, §15.2-4211.
Preparation and adoption, §15.2-4209.
Review, §15.2-4212.
Report, §15.2-4215.
Specialized transportation incentive fund, §15.2-4217.1.
State aid, receipt by commission, §15.2-4216.
State or federal aid applications by localities.
Commission to be informed, §15.2-4213.
Tax exemption, §15.2-4219.
Tourism development authority.
LENOWISCO and Cumberland plateau planning district commissions, §§15.2-5500 to 15.2-5508.

PLANNING DISTRICTS.
Boundaries, §36-139.7.
Planning District 1 or Planning District 2.
Water and waste authorities.
Enforcement charges, §15.2-5138.1.
Planning District 8.
Grass, weeds, other foreign growth on occupied or vacant property.
Cutting by property owners.
Ordinance prescribing, §15.2-901.
Planning district 15.
Disclosures by builders or owners of residential property.
Mining operations, §55-518.

PLANTING OF TREES.
Counties, cities or towns.
Planting and replacement during development process, §15.2-961.
Trees destroyed during construction process, §15.2-960.

PLANT PEST CONTROL, §§3.2-700 to 3.2-713.
See PEST CONTROL, PLANTS.

PLANT POLLINATION ADVISORY BOARD, §§3.2-2800 to 3.2-2806.
Definitions, §3.2-2800.
Plant pollination fund, §3.2-2806.
Dedicated revenues, diversion, §3.2-1100.
Powers and duties of commissioner, §3.2-2805.
Reports to board, §3.2-2805.

PLANTS.
Biotechnology research act, §§2.2-5500 to 2.2-5509.

PLANTS —Cont'd
Deer causing damage to residential plants.
Authorization to kill deer, §29.1-529.
Destruction of plants on private property, public parks, refuges or sanctuaries, §18.2-140.
Endangered plant and insect species, §§3.2-1000 to 3.2-1011.
Genetically engineered organisms.
Biotechnology research act, §§2.2-5500 to 2.2-5509.
Sale on highways.
Counties prohibiting, §15.2-1219.

PLANTS AND PLANT PRODUCTS INSPECTION, §§3.2-3800 to 3.2-3811.
Allowing of inspection.
Required upon request of commissioner, §3.2-3806.
Penalty for violation, §3.2-3810.
Appeals.
Judicial review, §3.2-3811.
Certificates.
Nursery stock brought into Commonwealth, §3.2-3804.
Commissioner of agriculture and consumer services.
Duties, §§3.2-3801, 3.2-3807.
Orders as to eradication or control of infestation, §3.2-3807.
Right of entry, §3.2-3806.
Stop delivery or stop sale orders, §3.2-3808.
Definitions, §3.2-3800.
Fees, §3.2-3803.
Disposition of money collected, §3.2-3801.
Information to be furnished upon request of commissioner, §3.2-3806.
Licenses.
Nurserymen, dealers or agents to sell nursery stock, §3.2-3803.
Penalties for violations, §3.2-3810.
Permits.
Sale or transporting of plant pests, §3.2-3802.
Reciprocal agreements with other states, §3.2-3801.
Reciprocity, §3.2-3801.
Requests for inspection.
Inspection by commissioner upon, §3.2-3805.
Right of entry, §3.2-3806.
Refusal of entry, penalty, §3.2-3810.
Searches and seizures, §3.2-3809.
Stop delivery or stop sale orders, §3.2-3808.

PLASMA.
Implied warranty in connection with transfer, §32.1-297.

PLASTIC BAGS.
Sales.
Warning required, §18.2-320.

PLASTIC COATED BULLETS.
Use or attempted use in commission or attempted commission of crime, §18.2-308.3.

PLASTIC CONTAINERS.
Litter tax imposed on manufacturers, wholesalers, etc., §58.1-1708.

PLASTIC FIREARMS.
Manufacture, sale, etc., §18.2-308.5.

PLAT BOOK.
State highway plat book, §17.1-238.

PLAT BOOK —Cont'd
Validation of recordings, §17.1-237.

PLATINUM.
Precious metals dealers.
General provisions, §§54.1-4100 to 54.1-4111.
See PRECIOUS METALS DEALERS.

PLATS.
Boundary lines established by commissioners, §15.2-3101.
Condominiums.
Boundaries between units, relocation of, §55-79.69.
Contents of plats, §55-79.58.
Subdivision of units, §55-79.70.
Indexing subdivision plats, §17.1-251.
Recording in plat book, §17.1-236.
Validation of recording, §17.1-237.
State highway plat book, §17.1-238.
Subdivision plats, indexing, §17.1-251.
Subdivisions generally, §§15.2-2240 to 15.2-2279.
See SUBDIVISIONS.
Towns incorporated by judicial proceedings.
Plat to accompany petitions, §15.2-3600.
Transportation department.
Preparation at request and expense of local governing bodies or other groups, §33.1-222.

PLAYGROUNDS.
Alcoholic beverages, outdoor advertising.
Limitations on placement locations, §4.1-112.2.
Notice of violation, penalty for failure to take corrective action, §4.1-320.
Counties, cities or towns, §§15.2-1806 to 15.2-1811.
City or town immunity for operating, §15.2-1809.
Collecting fees, §15.2-1806.
Establishing, §15.2-1806.
Liability of county, city or town in operating.
Agreements with landowners, §29.1-509.
Sanitary districts, operating playgrounds in, §15.2-1811.
Sports facilities, providing and operating, §15.2-1808.
Swimming pools.
Leasing land owned or held by locality for, §15.2-1810.
System of playgrounds, election to establish, §15.2-1807.
Taxing property for operation and maintenance, §15.2-1806.
Offense prohibiting proximity to children.
Contact with children near playground or athletic facility, §18.2-370.2.
Offense prohibiting residing in proximity to children.
Boundary line of public parks, §18.2-370.3.
Property tax exemptions, VA Const Art X §6.
Held by trustees for perpetual use, §58.1-3606.

PLAYS, DRAMAS AND CONCERTS.
Child labor, §§40.1-101, 40.1-102.

PLEA AGREEMENTS.
Disqualification of judge.
Rejecting plea bargain submitted by parties, §19.2-153.
Evidence.
Withdrawn pleas and offers to plead, VA SCt Rule 2:410.
Procedure, VA SCt Rule 3A:8.
Victim of felony.
Consulting, §19.2-11.01.

PLEADINGS.
Abatement of action for want of form.
When action or suit not to abate, §8.01-274.
Adding claim or defense.
Relation back of amended pleadings, §8.01-6.1.
Affidavit.
Verification.
Electronic filing and service, VA SCt Rule 1:17.
Affirmative defenses.
Statute of limitations.
Manner of pleading statute of limitations, §8.01-235.
Alternative pleading, §8.01-281, VA SCt Rule 1:4.
Amended pleadings, VA SCt Rule 1:8.
Confusion in similar trade or corporate name, §8.01-6.2.
Defective process, §§8.01-277, 8.01-277.1.
Objections to personal jurisdiction, §8.01-277.1.
Demurrer, §8.01-273.
District courts, VA SCt Rule 7A:9.
Fiduciaries, actions against, §8.01-6.3.
Misnomer, §8.01-6.
Variance between evidence and allegations.
Remedy, §8.01-377.
What constitutes waiver, §8.01-277.1.
Answers.
Amendment, VA SCt Rule 1:8.
Election contest of general assembly election, §24.2-803.
Election contests of governor, lieutenant governor or attorney general elections, §24.2-804.
Election contests of primaries and elections generally, §24.2-809.
General rules as to pleadings, VA SCt Rule 1:4.
Obscene books, proceeding against, §18.2-384.
Residential landlords and tenants.
Landlord noncompliance as defense to action for possession or rent, §55-248.25.
Material noncompliance or dangerous charges, §55-248.27.
Size of paper, VA SCt Rule 1:16.
Small claims courts.
Pleadings allowed, §16.1-122.3.
Attachment, §8.01-536.
Answer under oath, §8.01-562.
Attorney certificate of service, VA SCt Rule 1:12.
Bonds issued by localities.
Judicial determination of validity.
Motion for judgment, §15.2-2651.
Contesting issuance, §15.2-2653.
Reply by party defendant, §15.2-2654.
Boundaries.
Motion for judgment to establish boundaries, §8.01-180.
Changing claim or defense.
Relation back of amended pleadings, §8.01-6.1.
Child custody proceeding.
Information required to be submitted, §20-146.20.
Circuit courts.
Ad damnum clause required, VA SCt Rule 3:2.
Answers, VA SCt Rule 3:8.
Bill of particulars, VA SCt Rule 3:7.
Captions, VA SCt Rule 3:2.
Commencement of proceedings, VA SCt Rule 3:2.
Counterclaims, VA SCt Rule 3:9.
Criminal cases, VA SCt Rules 3A:9, 3A:15.
Cross-claims, VA SCt Rule 3:10.
Demurrers, VA SCt Rule 3:8.
Filing of pleadings, VA SCt Rule 3:3.
General provisions, VA SCt Rule 3:18.
Negligence, allegations, VA SCt Rule 3:18.

PLEADINGS —Cont'd
Circuit courts —Cont'd
Reply.
Civil actions, VA SCt Rule 3:11.
Responsive pleadings, VA SCt Rule 3:8.
Complaints.
Censure, retirement or removal of judge.
Judicial inquiry and review commission to file with Supreme Court, VA Const Art VI §10.
Election contests of primaries or elections.
Contents, §24.2-807.
Enlargement or amendment, §24.2-808.
Time of filing and service, §24.2-808.
Election law offenses, §24.2-1019.
Motions for judgment.
See MOTIONS FOR JUDGMENT.
Compliance with rules of supreme court, §8.01-271.
Confusion in similar trade or corporate name.
Amending pleading to reflect correct name, §8.01-6.2.
Continuances generally.
See CONTINUANCES.
Corporations.
Amending pleading to reflect correct name.
Confusion in similar names, §8.01-6.2.
District court civil cases.
Preparing, executing and serving without attorney intervention, §16.1-88.03.
Ownership, §8.01-279.
Correction of defects.
District court civil cases, §16.1-93.
Counterclaims.
See COUNTERCLAIMS.
Criminal cases generally, VA SCt Rule 3A:9.
General district courts.
Filing format and procedure, VA SCt Rule 7C:7.
Crossclaims.
See CROSS-CLAIMS.
Date and time filed noted on papers, §17.1-129.
Defects.
Correction in district court civil cases, §16.1-93.
District courts in civil cases.
Appeals from district courts, §16.1-114.1.
Notice of defects, VA SCt Rule 1:17.
Defenses.
Adding or changing.
Relation back of amended pleadings, §8.01-6.1.
Defensive pleadings.
Motion to strike, §8.01-274.
Demurrer to evidence abolished, §8.01-276.
District courts.
Amendments, VA SCt Rule 7A:9.
Civil cases generally, §§16.1-76 to 16.1-122.7.
See DISTRICT COURTS.
Copies of pleadings.
Furnishing to counsel, VA SCt Rule 7A:10.
Criminal cases generally, §§16.1-123.1 to 16.1-137.
See DISTRICT COURTS.
Filing format and procedure, VA SCt Rule 7A:7.
General rules as to pleadings, VA SCt Rule 7A:8.
Specific rule for pleading in general district courts, VA SCt Rule 7B:2.
Verification, VA SCt Rule 7B:6.
Division of legislative services.
Extensions for members, §30-5.
Divorce.
No-fault divorce.
Decree of divorce without amended bill or amended cross-bill, §20-121.02.

PLEADINGS —Cont'd
Election contest of primaries or elections.
Answers, §24.2-809.
Complaints, §§24.2-807, 24.2-808.
Election contests of general assembly election, §24.2-803.
Election contests of governor, lieutenant governor or attorney general elections, §24.2-804.
Electronic filing and service, §8.01-271.01, VA SCt Rule 1:17.
Circuit courts.
Civil procedure, VA SCt Rule 3:3.
General district courts, VA SCt Rule 7A:7.
Equity.
Answers in equity proceedings, §8.01-283.
Motion to strike evidence, §8.01-282.
Escheats.
Condemnation proceedings during pendency of escheat proceedings, §55-201.1.
Proceedings to claim lands escheated, §55-176.
Exceptions abolished, §8.01-274.
Executors and administrators.
Suits against, §64.2-548.
Extension of time.
Judicial discretion, VA SCt Rule 1:9.
Military active duty of party or attorney, §44-97.1.
Fiduciaries, actions against.
Amended pleadings, §8.01-6.3.
Filing.
Filing date and time noted on papers, §17.1-129.
Frivolous actions.
Signing pleadings.
Attorney's certificate, §8.01-271.1.
General assembly.
Extensions for members, §30-5.
General rules as to pleadings, VA SCt Rule 1:4.
Handwriting.
When proof necessary, §8.01-279.
Imperfection in pleadings.
When action or suit not to abate, §8.01-274.
Impoundment of surface waters.
Riparian owner rights.
Application for leave to store floodwaters, §62.1-107.
Interpleader in district courts.
Initial pleading, §16.1-77.
Interstate family support, §20-88.54.
Judicial discretion.
Size of paper, VA SCt Rule 1:16.
Jury deliberations.
What jury may not carry from courtroom, §8.01-381.
Juvenile and domestic relations district courts.
Electronic filing and service, VA SCt Rule 8:8.
Format, VA SCt Rule 8:7.
General rules as to pleadings, VA SCt Rule 8:8.
Judicial discretion, VA SCt Rule 8:9.
Motion or petition in certain proceedings.
Contents of pleadings, VA SCt Rule 8:3.
Legal separation.
No-fault divorce.
Decree of divorce without amended bill or amended cross-bill, §20-121.02.
Limited liability companies.
Derivative actions, §13.1-1044.
Third-party liability of members.
Proper parties to actions, §13.1-1020.
Limited partnerships.
Derivative actions, §50-73.64.

PLEADINGS —Cont'd
Lost original papers.
Procedure in civil cases, §8.01-374.
Marriage.
Effect of marriage of party, §§8.01-19, 8.01-20.
Mechanics' and materialmen's liens.
Enforcement, §43-22.
Military active duty of party or attorney.
Extension of time for filing pleading, §44-97.1.
Misnomer.
Amending pleading to correct misnomer, §8.01-6.
Mortgages and deeds of trust.
Sale authorization, §55-61.
Motions.
See MOTIONS.
Motions for judgment.
See MOTIONS FOR JUDGMENT.
Multiple matters, §8.01-272.
Name.
Mistake in name.
Amending pleading to correct misnomer, §8.01-6.
New parties to suit.
When court may add, §8.01-7.
Next friend suits, §8.01-8.
Nonlawyers filing, issuing, etc., §16.1-88.03.
Obscene books, proceeding against, §18.2-384.
Ownership.
Business associations, §8.01-279.
Paper.
Size of paper.
Electronic filing and service.
Applicability of provisions, VA SCt Rule 1:17.
Partnerships.
District court civil cases.
Preparing, executing and serving without attorney intervention, §16.1-88.03.
Ownership, §8.01-279.
Payment of a debt, §8.01-421.
Persons with disability.
Disposition of real estate.
Commencement of suit, §8.01-69.
Plea in abatement abolished, §8.01-276.
Plea of infancy.
When not allowed, §8.01-278.
Pretrial scheduling order, VA SCt Rule 1:18.
Uniform pretrial scheduling order, VA SCt Rule Pt 1 Appx Form 3.
Promises not to plead statute of limitations, §8.01-232.
Quo warranto.
Defendant's pleading.
Pleading when defendant appears, §8.01-642.
Relation back to original pleading, §8.01-6.
Replies.
Election contests to general assembly election, §24.2-803.
Responsive pleadings.
Manner of pleading statute of limitations, §8.01-235.
Service of notice, process and other papers.
General provisions, §§8.01-285 to 8.01-327.2.
See SERVICE OF NOTICE, PROCESS AND OTHER PAPERS.
Mail service.
Furnishing copies to counsel, VA SCt Rule 1:12.
Signing of pleadings, §8.01-271.1.
Similar trade or corporate name, confusion.
Amending pleading to reflect correct name, §8.01-6.2.

PLEADINGS —Cont'd
Size of paper, VA SCt Rule 1:16.
Circuit courts, VA SCt Rule 1:16.
Court of appeals, VA SCt Rule 5A:4.
General district courts, VA SCt Rule 7A:7.
Juvenile and domestic relations district courts, VA SCt Rule 8:7.
Supreme court, VA SCt Rule 5:6.
Small claims courts, §16.1-122.3.
Standards for writings to be docketed, §55-108.
Use of copies admitted to record elsewhere, §55-109.
Striking pleadings.
Refusal of adverse party to testify, §8.01-401.
Subject to rules of supreme court, §8.01-271.
Supreme court.
Authority to prepare system of pleading, §8.01-3.
Trade names.
Amending pleading to reflect correct name.
Confusion in similar names, §8.01-6.2.
Trial evidence.
Variance between evidence and allegations.
Amendment of pleadings.
Remedy, §8.01-377.
Trusts.
Judicial proceedings involving trusts, §64.2-713.
Unemployment compensation.
Claims adjudication.
Appeals.
Judicial review of board of review, §60.2-631.
Judicial review of commission decisions, §60.2-625.
Unincorporated associations.
Ownership, §8.01-279.
Variance between evidence and allegations, §8.01-377.
Verification, VA SCt Rule 1:10.
Warrants.
District court civil cases brought on, §16.1-79.
When action deemed brought, §16.1-86.
Small claims courts.
Civil warrant to commence actions, §16.1-122.3.
Wrong person.
Amending pleading to correct misnomer, §8.01-6.

PLEA IN ABATEMENT.
Abolished, §8.01-276.
Motions for judgment.
Judicial discretion, VA SCt Rule 1:9.

PLEA IN INFANCY.
When not allowed, §8.01-278.

PLEAS, VA SCt Rule 3A:8.
Alternative pleas.
Allowance of defendant to plea several matters of law or fact, §19.2-255.
Arraignment, §19.2-254.
Corporation.
Acting by counsel or through agent, VA SCt Rule 3A:8.
Court-entered plea for accused.
Felony arraignment, §19.2-259.
District courts.
Criminal and traffic cases, VA SCt Rule 7C:6.
Evidence.
Withdrawn pleas and offers to plead, VA SCt Rule 2:410.
Guilty pleas.
Admissible in civil actions, §8.01-418.
Arraignment.
Court refusal to accept, §19.2-254.

PLEAS —Cont'd
Guilty pleas —Cont'd
Bench trial.
Trial without jury in felony case, §19.2-257.
Conditional pleas of guilty.
Felony case, §19.2-254.
Contents of judgment order, §19.2-307, VA SCt Rules Part 3A Appx Form 10.
Substantial compliance with form required, VA SCt Rule 3A:22.
Corporations, district court criminal and traffic cases, VA SCt Rule 7C:6.
Determining voluntariness, VA SCt Rule 3A:8.
Felony convictions.
How accused convicted of felony, §19.2-283.
Judicial examination of accused.
Suggested questions, VA SCt Rules Part 3A Appx Form 6.
Juvenile and domestic relations district courts.
Permissible pleas by child, VA SCt Rule 8:18.
Plea bargaining agreement procedure, VA SCt Rule 3A:8.
Prepayment of fines, §§16.1-69.40:1, 16.1-69.40:2.
Non-traffic prepayable offenses and uniform fine schedule, VA SCt Rules 3C:1, 3C:2.
Traffic infractions and uniform fine schedule, VA SCt Rules 3B:1, 3B:2.
Pretrial diversion, §19.2-303.2.
Right of accused to plead guilty, VA Const Art I §8.
Traffic infraction cases, §19.2-254.1.
Withdrawal of plea.
Before imposition of sentence, §19.2-296.
Conditional plea, §19.2-254.
Juvenile and domestic relations district courts, VA SCt Rule 8:18.
Nolo contendere.
Admissible in civil action, §8.01-418.
Arraignment.
Court acceptance of plea, §19.2-254.
Contents of judgment order, §19.2-307, VA SCt Rules Part 3A Appx Form 10.
Substantial compliance with form required, VA SCt Rule 3A:22.
Corporation's plea in district court, VA SCt Rule 7C:6.
Determining voluntariness, VA SCt Rule 3A:8.
Plea bargaining agreement procedure, VA SCt Rule 3A:8.
Traffic infraction cases, §19.2-254.1.
Withdrawal before imposition of sentence, §19.2-296.
Nontraffic offenses for which prepayment authorized, §19.2-254.2.
Traffic infraction cases, §19.2-254.1.
Voluntariness.
Determining voluntariness, VA SCt Rule 3A:8.
Juvenile and domestic relations district courts, VA SCt Rule 8:18.

PLEDGEES.
Holders of stock corporation shares as collateral security.
Pledgee not liable as shareholder, §13.1-644.

PLEDGE OF ALLEGIANCE.
Guidelines on constitutional rights and restrictions relating to recitation in public schools, §22.1-202.
Administrative rulemaking exemptions, §2.2-4006.

PLEDGE OF SECURITY AS COLLATERAL FOR PUBLIC FUNDS.
Virginia security for public deposits act, §§2.2-4400 to 2.2-4411.
See SECURITY FOR PUBLIC DEPOSITS.

PLUMBERS.
Building code, §§36-97 to 36-119.1.
See BUILDING CODE.
License, §§54.1-1128 to 54.1-1135.
Applications, §54.1-1130.
Continuing education, §54.1-1133.
Defined terms, §54.1-1128.
Denial grounds, §54.1-1134.
Examinations, §54.1-1130.
Exemptions, §54.1-1131.
Expiration, §54.1-1132.
Prohibited acts, §54.1-1135.
Renewal, §54.1-1132.
Requirement, §54.1-1129.
Revocation grounds, §54.1-1134.

PLUMBING FIXTURES.
Secondhand fixtures, §§59.1-116.1 to 59.1-124.
Buying or receiving with intent to defraud, §18.2-237.
Company equipment, §§59.1-125 to 59.1-130.

PNEUMATIC GUNS.
Local regulation, §15.2-915.4.

PNEUMOCOCCAL VACCINE.
Hospitals.
Administration under standing order or protocol, §32.1-126.4.
Required immunizations of children, §32.1-46.

PNEUMOCONIOSIS.
Workers' compensation.
Compensation for disability from, §65.2-504.
Death benefits, §65.2-513.
Special provisions, §65.2-514.
Limitations upon total compensation, §§65.2-518, 65.2-519.
Notice to employee, §65.2-405.
Permanent, partial or total disability.
Compensation for, §65.2-503.

POCOMOKE SOUND.
Oysters.
Planting grounds.
Public oyster rocks, beds, and shoals declared, §28.2-645.

P.O.D. ACCOUNTS.
Generally, §§6.2-604 to 6.2-620.
See MULTIPLE-PARTY ACCOUNTS.

PODIATRIST ASSISTANT.
Generally.
See PHYSICIAN ASSISTANTS.
Licensing generally, §§54.1-2950.1 to 54.1-2957.01.

PODIATRISTS.
Assistants.
See PHYSICIAN ASSISTANTS.
Bills for medical services.
Presumption of authenticity and reasonableness, §8.01-413.01.
Controlled substances.
Sale, §54.1-2914.
Disasters, state or local emergency.
Immunity.
Abandonment of person owed duty of health care in response to disaster, §8.01-225.01.

PODIATRISTS —Cont'd
Disasters, state or local emergency —Cont'd
Immunity —Cont'd
Unable to provide required care because of lack of resources, §8.01-225.02.
Disciplinary information concerning licensees.
Posting on department website, §54.1-2910.2.
Expert witnesses.
Qualified to testify as expert, §8.01-401.2:1.
Health benefit programs.
Provider willing to meet terms and conditions not to be excluded, §38.2-3407.
Health insurance plan not accepted by doctor.
Patient subject to full charge.
Information provided patient, §54.1-2910.01.
Health maintenance organizations.
Exclusions, §38.2-3407.6.
Health services plans, coverage of services, §38.2-4221.
Hospital privileges, §32.1-134.2.
Applications, responses to, §32.1-134.3.
Injunctions, §32.1-134.4.
Immunity.
Disasters, state or local emergency.
Abandonment of person owed duty of health care in response to disaster, §8.01-225.01.
Unable to provide required care because of lack of resources, §8.01-225.02.
Information provided patient upon request, §54.1-2910.01.
Licensing generally, §§54.1-2900 to 54.1-2993.
See MEDICINE AND OTHER HEALING ARTS PROFESSIONS.
Managed care health insurance plan.
Doctor not participant.
Patient subject to full charge.
Information provided patient, §54.1-2910.01.
Medical bills.
Presumption of authenticity and reasonableness, §8.01-413.01.
Medical devices and appliances.
Sale, §54.1-2914.
Medical malpractice.
General provisions, §§8.01-581.1 to 8.01-581.20.
See MEDICAL MALPRACTICE.
Medical malpractice judgments and settlements.
Reporting, regulations concerning, adoption, §54.1-2910.1.
Preferred provider plans.
Exclusions, §38.2-3407.6.
Records or papers of patients.
Medical records generally.
See MEDICAL RECORDS.
Standardized HCFA-1500 health insurance claims forms for services.
Acceptance by insurers required, §38.2-322.
Surgery on patients under general anesthesia, limitations, §54.1-2939.
Third-party reimbursement program participation not condition of licensure, §54.1-2910.3.
Witnesses.
Podiatrists as expert witness, §8.01-401.2:1.

POE FOUNDATION, INCORPORATED.
Poe Shrine at Richmond.
Appropriations for maintenance, §10.1-2212.

POET LAUREATE OF VIRGINIA, §1-512.

POINTS OF CONTACT TEST.
Venue in criminal cases.
Conspiracy, §18.2-22.

POINTS OF CONTACT TEST —Cont'd
Venue in criminal cases —Cont'd
Credit card fraud, §18.2-198.1.
Forgery, §19.2-245.1.
Larceny and embezzlement, §19.2-245.

POINT SYSTEM, SAFE-DRIVER INSURANCE POLICY.
Motor vehicle insurer not to charge unless accident caused by insured, §38.2-1905.

POINT SYSTEM, TRAFFIC INFRACTIONS.
See DEMERIT POINT SYSTEM.

POISON.
Animals or fowl, poisoning, §18.2-144.
Attempts to poison, §18.2-54.1.
Caustic substances or agents.
Malicious bodily injury by, §18.2-52.
Lesser offenses, conviction under certain indictments, §18.2-54.
Cosmetics.
Use of poisons in cosmetics, §54.1-3460.
Devices.
Use of poisons in devices, §54.1-3460.
Drugs.
Use of poisons in drugs, §54.1-3460.
Economic poisons.
Applicability of drug control provisions, §54.1-3403.
Fish, killing or capturing by, §28.2-313.
Murder of the first degree, §18.2-32.
State laboratory for testing economic poisons.
Division of consolidated laboratory services, §2.2-1104.
Statewide poison control system, §32.1-111.15.

POISONOUS ANIMALS RUNNING AT LARGE.
Fee by owner to cover locality's cost in locating and capturing, §3.2-6544.

POLES.
Vehicles hauling.
Fastening loads, §46.2-1155.
Fine for failure to fasten, VA SCt Rule 3B:2.

POLICE, §§15.2-1700 to 15.2-1753.
Abduction, disclosure of information and assistance to, §18.2-50.
Abolition of county police force.
Referenda, §15.2-1703.
Absence without leave from National Guard.
Power to take person into custody, §44-41.1.
Adjoining counties, cities or towns.
Calling upon law enforcement officers for assistance, §15.2-1730.
Age requirement, §15.2-1705.
Airports.
Local police jurisdiction, §5.1-23.
Allowances to injured officials and employees.
Authorization of governing body of locality to make, §15.2-1511.
Amber Alert program.
Activation, §52-34.3.
Definitions, §52-34.1.
Established, §52-34.2.
Animals, enforcement authority, §3.2-6567.
Animals owned, used or trained by law enforcement agencies.
Killing or injuring, §18.2-144.1.
Arrest records.
Records kept by chiefs of police, §15.2-1722.
Arrests without warrant, §19.2-81.
Domestic violence situations, §19.2-81.3.

POLICE —Cont'd
Arrests without warrant —Cont'd
Stalking, §19.2-81.3.
Assault and battery against, §18.2-57.
Assistance to officer in execution of office, refusal, §18.2-463.
Assistance to officers of other counties, cities or towns.
Calling upon law enforcement officers for assistance, §15.2-1730.
Auxiliary police forces in localities, §§15.2-1731 to 15.2-1736.
Acting beyond limits of jurisdiction, §15.2-1735.
Aiding and assisting regular officers in performance of duties, §15.2-1734.
Air raid precautions, §44-149.
Appointing or providing for appointments, §15.2-1733.
Appropriations for equipment and maintenance, §15.2-1732.
Calling into service or providing for calling into service, §15.2-1734.
Carrying concealed weapon, §18.2-308.
Clothing appropriate for duties to be performed.
Wearing of regular uniform would adversely limit effectiveness, §15.2-1734.
Contiguous localities, mutual aid agreements, §15.2-1736.
Defending or going beyond limits of jurisdiction, §15.2-1735.
Establishment, equipping and maintaining, §15.2-1731.
Immunities of full-time law-enforcement officers, §15.2-1731.
Local vehicle licenses.
Issuance free of charge, §46.2-752.
Minimum standards, §9.1-102.
Mutual aid agreements among governing bodies of contiguous locality, §15.2-1736.
Number to be fixed by ordinance, §15.2-1733.
Powers and authority when called into service, §15.2-1731.
Training requirements, §15.2-1731.
Undercover work.
Wearing clothing appropriate for duties to be performed, §15.2-1734.
Uniform, organization and rules prescribed by governing body, §15.2-1733.
Uniforms generally, §15.2-1734.
Barricades, lines and perimeters established.
Crossing, §18.2-414.2.
Bicycles.
Disposition of unclaimed bicycles in possession of police, §15.2-1720.
Boating safety.
Disregarding signals to stop, §29.1-739.1.
Enforcement of provisions, §29.1-745.
Bribery of public officers generally, §§18.2-438 to 18.2-450.
See PUBLIC OFFICERS AND EMPLOYEES.
Calling upon law enforcement officers of counties, cities or towns for assistance, §15.2-1730.
Campus police departments.
Generally, §§23-232 to 23-238.
See CAMPUS POLICE.
Capital murder, killing law enforcement officer, §18.2-31.
Capitol police.
Authority for offenses committed on Capitol Square, §18.2-124.

POLICE —Cont'd
Capitol police —Cont'd
Duties, §30-34.2:1.
Firearms or weapons in possession of division.
Destruction of unclaimed weapons, §30-34.2:2.
Handgun purchases by, §59.1-148.3.
Powers, §30-34.2:1.
Carnal knowledge of defendant or convicted person, §18.2-64.2.
Carrying concealed weapons, §18.2-308.
Central criminal records exchange, reports to, §19.2-390.
Virginia crime code references, required use, §19.2-390.01.
Certification through training required, §15.2-1706.
Chief of police.
Chief law enforcement officer of locality, §15.2-1701.
Disclosure of information about former officers.
Immunity from liability, §15.2-1709.
Parole of prisoners.
Notice to prior to release, §53.1-160.
Records kept by police, §15.2-1722.
Strip search policy, development, §19.2-59.1.
Child abuse or neglect.
Reason to suspect, required reports, fine for failure, §63.2-1509.
Child taken into custody.
Duties, §16.1-247.
When and how child taken into immediate custody, §16.1-246.
Civil commitment of mentally ill persons.
Emergency custody orders.
Authority to execute and serve, §15.2-1704.
Involuntary temporary detention orders.
Authority to execute and serve, §15.2-1704.
Civilian protection, police misconduct, §9.1-600.
Civil matters, authority, §15.2-1704.
College and university tuition and required fees.
Waiver for child or spouse of officer killed in line of duty, §23-7.4:1.
College or university criminal justice courses.
Payments to institutions, §23-9.2:4.
College or university grounds.
Campus police generally, §§23-232 to 23-238.
See CAMPUS POLICE.
Communicable disease reports, §32.1-116.3.
Communications system, joint state and local system, §§52-16 to 52-19.
Contracts with counties, cities and towns, §52-17.
Districts, §52-18.
Establishment of radio and teletype systems, §52-16.
Rules and regulations, §52-19.
Community corrections, §§9.1-173 to 9.1-183.
See COMMUNITY CORRECTIONS.
Confidentiality of records concerning child, §16.1-301.
Conservation police officers.
Ex officio wardens, §29.1-202.
Generally, §§29.1-200 to 29.1-218.
See CONSERVATION POLICE OFFICERS.
Conservators of the peace.
Generally, §§19.2-12 to 19.2-18.
See CONSERVATORS OF THE PEACE.
Special conservators of the peace, §§9.1-150.1 to 9.1-150.4.
Use of title police, §19.2-13.

POLICE —Cont'd
Cooperation in furnishing of police services.
Reciprocal agreements, §15.2-1726.
County police.
County executive form of government, §15.2-528.
County manager form of government, §15.2-632.
County manager plan of government.
Grievances, §15.2-723.
Mileage for transporting violator to jail.
Jail of another county or city adopted as jail of county, §15.2-1609.6.
Referenda to abolish force, §15.2-1703.
Referendum prior to establishing force, §15.2-1702.
Urban county executive form of government.
Department of law enforcement, §15.2-836.
Department of public safety, §15.2-842.
Courts-martial processes and sentences, execution, §44-50.
Criminal justice training academies, §§15.2-1747 to 15.2-1753.
See CRIMINAL JUSTICE TRAINING ACADEMIES.
Critical incident stress management team-EMS or public safety personnel privilege, §19.2-271.4.
Death in line of duty.
Allowances by governing body of locality, §15.2-1511.
Half mast display of state and local flags, §18.2-488.1.
Decertification, §15.2-1707.
Notice, §15.2-1708.
Decibel level of sound.
Proper equipment to determine.
Standards established by division of purchases and supply, §2.2-1112.
Detoxification centers.
Transporting public inebriates to, §18.2-388.
Direction of traffic.
Authority to deputize persons, §46.2-1310.
Hand signals, §46.2-1309.
Disclosure of information about former officers.
Immunity from liability, §15.2-1709.
Dogs.
Killing or injuring animals used by police, §18.2-144.1.
Sale by locality, §15.2-981.
Surplus dogs sold to handlers, §2.2-1124.
Driving while intoxicated.
Preliminary analysis of breath.
Duties and responsibilities, §18.2-267.
Procedure generally, §§18.2-266 to 18.2-273.
See DRIVING WHILE INTOXICATED.
Drug enforcement.
Intensified drug enforcement jurisdictions, §15.2-1715.
Drug screening.
Refusal to submit or production of positive result.
Decertification, §15.2-1707.
Educational requirement, §15.2-1705.
Eluding police, §46.2-817.
Employment of off-duty officers, §15.2-1712.
Establishment of county police.
Referendum prior to, §15.2-1702.
Explosives.
Notice of theft to, §59.1-139.
False alarms, §18.2-461.
False impersonation, §18.2-174.
False reports to officers, §18.2-461.

POLICE —Cont'd
Family abuse.
Arrest without warrant, §19.2-81.3.
Emergency protective orders, §16.1-253.4.
Protective orders.
Authority to execute and serve, §15.2-1704.
Transportation to hospital, shelter, etc., §19.2-81.3.
Federal authorities, mutual aid agreements with, §15.2-1728.
Federal officers enforcing state and county laws on federal property, §15.2-1729.
Fees and other compensation not to be received, §15.2-1710.
Felony conviction.
Decertification, §15.2-1707.
Firearms.
Carrying concealed, §18.2-308.
Disposal of unclaimed firearms in possession, §15.2-1721.
Firearm or object similar in appearance pointed, held or brandished.
Immunity from liability in making arrest under provision, §18.2-282.
Purchases, §59.1-148.3.
Firearm shows.
Notice, §54.1-4201.1.
Fleeing or eluding police, §46.2-817.
Forces in existence on July 1, 1980, validation, §15.2-1723.
Free tuition and required fees to state supported colleges or universities.
Child or spouse of officer killed in line of duty, §23-7.4:1.
Funeral processions under police escort.
Fine schedule, VA SCt Rule 3B:2.
Impeding or disrupting, §46.2-828.1.
Prepayment of fine, §16.1-69.40:1.
Yielding right-of-way, §46.2-828.
Furloughed prisoners.
Notice to, §53.1-37.
Grievance procedures.
County manager plan of government, §15.2-723.
Gunshot wounds.
Reports on by health care professionals, §54.1-2967.
Handgun purchases by, §59.1-148.3.
Hand signals for direction of traffic, §46.2-1309.
Heart disease.
Presumption as to death or disability, §§15.2-1511, 65.2-402.
Workers' compensation presumption, §65.2-402.
Hepatitis C test, positive results.
Convicted prostitutes or injection drug users tested.
Limited disclosure to, §18.2-346.1.
Hepatitis, meningitis, tuberculosis and HIV.
Workers' compensation.
Presumption on death or disability from, §65.2-402.1.
Hepatitis testing, §32.1-45.2.
Highway construction and maintenance by prisoners.
Notice to chief of police, §53.1-56.
Highway corporations.
Powers of corporations, §56-550.
HIV testing, §32.1-45.2.
Hostage or barricaded person situation.
Emergency control of telephone service, §18.2-50.2.

POLICE —Cont'd
Hunting incident reports.
Duty of law-enforcement agency or emergency medical service provider to report, §29.1-530.4.
Hunting while under influence of intoxicant or narcotic drug.
Enforcement of provision, §18.2-285.
Hypertension.
Presumption to be suffered in line of duty, §15.2-1511.
Workers' compensation presumption, §65.2-402.
Impersonating, §18.2-174.
Incident records.
Records kept by chiefs of police, §15.2-1722.
In person and photo lineups.
Written policies and procedures for conducting.
Establishment, required, §19.2-390.02.
Training standards and model policy, §9.1-102.
Intensified drug enforcement jurisdictions, §15.2-1715.
Interjurisdictional law-enforcement authority and agreements, §§15.2-1724 to 15.2-1730.
Calling upon law enforcement officers of counties, cities or towns for assistance, §15.2-1730.
Cooperation in furnishing police services.
Reciprocal agreements, §15.2-1726.
Extending police power over lands lying beyond boundaries, §15.2-1725.
Federal authorities enforcing state and county laws on federal property, §15.2-1729.
Going and being sent beyond territorial limits of locality, §15.2-1724.
Immunity from liability and exemptions from laws, ordinances and regulations.
Police and other polices sent beyond territorial limits of locality, §15.2-1724.
Lands lying beyond boundaries.
Extending police power, §15.2-1725.
Localities outside Commonwealth.
Reciprocal agreements, §15.2-1727.
Mutual aid agreements between police departments and federal authorities, §15.2-1728.
Public property beyond limits of locality.
Extending police power, §15.2-1725.
Reciprocal agreements.
Localities outside Commonwealth, §15.2-1727.
Other law enforcement agencies, §15.2-1726.
Tripartite contract with governing body of town.
Sheriff furnishing law enforcement services to town, §15.2-1726.
Investigative records.
Records kept by chiefs of police, §15.2-1722.
Isolation and quarantine.
Authority to execute and serve orders, §15.2-1704.
Job performance information disclosed to prospective employer of former officer.
Immunity of chief for disclosure, §15.2-1709.
Jurisdiction beyond boundaries of cities and towns, §§19.2-249, 19.2-250.
Jurisdiction over lands, buildings and structures, §15.2-1124.
Jury service exemption, §8.01-341.
Juvenile proceedings.
Service of summons, §16.1-264.
Juvenile records confidentiality, §16.1-301.
Killed in line of duty.
Allowances to dependents by governing body of locality, §15.2-1511.

POLICE —Cont'd
Killed in line of duty —Cont'd
Free tuition and required fees to state supported colleges and universities.
Child or spouse, §23-7.4:1.
Lands lying beyond boundaries of locality.
Extending police power over, §15.2-1725.
Law enforcement expenditures.
State assistance to local government, §§9.1-165 to 9.1-172.
Law enforcement officers generally.
See LAW ENFORCEMENT OFFICERS.
Law officers' retirement system, §§51.1-211 to 51.1-221.
See LAW OFFICERS' RETIREMENT SYSTEM.
Legal fees and expenses for officers.
Prosecution for act admitted in discharge of duties, §15.2-1711.
Lines, perimeters or barricades, establishing.
Crossing, §18.2-414.2.
Lineups.
In person and photo lineups.
Written policies and procedures for conducting.
Establishment, required, §19.2-390.02.
Training standards and model policy, §9.1-102.
Localities outside Commonwealth.
Reciprocal agreements with, §15.2-1727.
Machine gun manufacturer's and dealer's stock.
Inspection upon demand, §18.2-294.
Malicious bodily injury to, §18.2-51.1.
Firearm used or displayed, §18.2-53.1.
Metropolitan Washington airports authority rules or regulations.
Authorization to establish and maintain force, powers, §5.1-157.
Minimum qualifications for office, §15.2-1705.
Misconduct.
Civilian protection, §9.1-600.
Missing child reports.
Duty to immediately enter identifying and descriptive data, §15.2-1718.
Missing law enforcement officers.
Blue Alert program, §§52-34.7 to 52-34.9.
Missing senior adults.
Duties on receipt of report, §15.2-1718.1.
Senior alert program, §§52-34.4 to 52-34.6.
Mopeds.
Disposition of unclaimed mopeds in possession of police, §15.2-1720.
Motor vehicles.
Auxiliary lights, §46.2-1029.
Flashing blue or red and blue warning lights, §46.2-1022.
Flashing of headlights, §46.2-1029.1.
Generally.
See EMERGENCY VEHICLES.
Local vehicle licenses.
Issuance free of charge for vehicles owned by officers, §46.2-752.
Move over or reduce speed.
Drivers approaching stationary emergency vehicles, §46.2-921.1.
Secondary warning lights, §46.2-1029.2.
Unlawful use of vehicle with police shown, §18.2-175.
Warnings, sirens and whistles, §46.2-1061.
Yielding right of way to stationary emergency vehicles, §46.2-921.1.

POLICE —Cont'd
Motor vehicle titling.
Enforcement by uniformed officers, §46.2-102.
Mutual aid agreements between police and campus police, §23-234.
Mutual aid agreements between police and federal authorities, §15.2-1728.
Noise levels.
Proper equipment to determine decibel level of sound.
Standards established by division of purchases and supply, §2.2-1112.
Notice of decertification, §15.2-1708.
Obstructing justice by threats, force or false statements, §18.2-460.
Off-duty officers.
Employment, §15.2-1712.
Ordinance providing for organization, §15.2-1701.
Organization of police forces, §15.2-1701.
Pawnbrokers.
Records, §54.1-4011.
Reports, §54.1-4010.
Peace and good order, preservation, §15.2-1700.
Personnel records.
Records kept by chiefs of police, §15.2-1722.
Police lines or barricades, §15.2-1714.
Polling places.
Preservation of order inside and outside, §24.2-606.
Port authority, §62.1-132.12.
Powers and duties, §15.2-1704.
Precious metals dealers.
Exemptions from provisions, §54.1-4109.
Permits, §54.1-4108.
Record requirements, §§54.1-4101, 54.1-4101.1.
Premises liability.
Duty of care owed to law enforcement officers, §8.01-226.
Preservation of peace and good order, §15.2-1700.
Prisoner construction and maintenance of highways.
Notice to chief of police, §53.1-56.
Prisoner furloughs.
Notice of to chief of police, §53.1-37.
Prisoner work for localities, state agencies or nonprofit organizations.
Notice to chief of police, §53.1-59.
Private highways.
Police powers of highway corporations, §56-550.
Privileged communications.
Critical incident stress management team-EMS or public safety personnel privilege, §19.2-271.4.
Prosecution for act committed in discharge of duties.
Legal fees and expenses, §15.2-1711.
Protective orders.
Emergency orders, family violence, §19.2-81.3.
Emergency protective orders, §16.1-253.4.
Family abuse.
Authority to execute and serve, §15.2-1704.
Public inebriates.
Transporting to detoxification centers, §18.2-388.
Public-private education facilities and infrastructure act.
Violations of law, §56-575.14.
Qualifications for office, §15.2-1705.
Radio signal, message or transmission.
Use during commission of crime, §18.2-462.1.

POLICE —Cont'd
Railroad corporations.
Conductors as conservators of the peace, §56-354.
Depot agents as conservators of the peace, §56-354.
Motormen as conservators of the peace, §56-354.
Power to appoint, §56-353.
Station agents as conservators of the peace, §56-354.
Reciprocal agreements.
Cooperation in furnishing of police services, §15.2-1726.
Localities outside Commonwealth, §15.2-1727.
Records confidentiality concerning children, §16.1-301.
Records to be kept by chief of police, §15.2-1722.
Referenda to abolish county police force, §15.2-1703.
Referendum prior to establishing county police force, §15.2-1702.
Refusal to aid officer, §18.2-463.
Report of family abuse, §19.2-81.3.
Reports to central criminal records exchange, §19.2-390.
Retention of unclaimed property in possession of police, §15.2-1719.
Retired officers.
Carrying concealed weapon, §18.2-308.
Retirement systems, §§51.1-807 to 51.1-820.
Adoption of system, §§51.1-819, 51.1-820.
Allowance, §51.1-811.
Credited service, §51.1-810.
Disabilities not resulting from discharge of duties, §51.1-812.
Disabilities resulting from discharge of duties, §51.1-813.
Presumption, §51.1-814.
Disability allowance reductions, §51.1-816.
Eligibility, §51.1-811.
Presumption, §51.1-814.
Funds, §51.1-818.
Locality establishing for local police, §15.2-1510.
Pension and retirement boards.
Duties, §51.1-808.
Established, §51.1-807.
Powers, §51.1-808.
Treasurer, §51.1-809.
Reduction of disability retirement allowance, §51.1-816.
Relief to surviving spouse and children, §51.1-815.
Salary deduction payments upon death, §51.1-817.
Retirement system, state.
Generally, §§51.1-124.1 to 51.1-169.
See VIRGINIA RETIREMENT SYSTEM.
Reward offers.
Apprehension of escaped inmates, §19.2-7.
Claiming and receiving, §15.2-1710.
Riot or unlawful assembly.
Dispersal, duty, §18.2-411.
Immunity of officers quelling, §18.2-412.
Sale of firearms by law-enforcement agencies, §59.1-148.4.
Sale of unclaimed property in possession of police, §15.2-1719.
Search warrants, execution, §19.2-56.
Secondhand article sales.
Building fixtures.
Inspections by police, §59.1-122.
Permits.
Issuance and revocation, §59.1-118.

POLICE —Cont'd
Secondhand article sales —Cont'd
Building fixtures —Cont'd
Reports, §59.1-121.
Sending or going beyond territorial limits of locality, §15.2-1724.
Senior alert program.
Missing senior adult, §§52-34.4 to 52-34.6.
Sexual battery of defendant or convicted person, §18.2-67.4.
Sexually violent predators, civil commitment.
Database of prisoners incarcerated for sexually violent offenses.
Access to records, §37.2-905.2.
Special conservators of the peace, §§9.1-150.1 to 9.1-150.4.
Use of title police, §19.2-13.
Special police, §§15.2-1737 to 15.2-1746.
Application for appointment, §15.2-1738.
Appointment of officers, §15.2-1737.
Arrest powers, §§15.2-1745, 18.2-81.
Background investigations, §15.2-1737.
Bond, §15.2-1743.
Certain officers not employees of Commonwealth or locality, §15.2-1740.
Circuit courts.
Appointment upon application and showing a necessity, §15.2-1737.
Compensation, §15.2-1739.
Conservators of the peace, §15.2-1737.
District judges before whom person arrested is brought shall examine case and dispose in accordance to law, §15.2-1746.
Duties and powers, §15.2-1745.
Extension of authority when in actual pursuit of persons accused of crime, §15.2-1744.
Jurisdiction and authority, §15.2-1744.
Limiting jurisdiction and authority to specific place or places in locality, §15.2-1744.
Otherwise regularly employed officers not employees of Commonwealth or locality, §15.2-1740.
Pursuit of persons accused of crime.
Extension of authority, §15.2-1744.
Qualifications, §15.2-1738.
Removal, §15.2-1741.
Office vacated, §15.2-1742.
Search warrants, executing, §15.2-1745.
Specific place or places in locality, limiting jurisdiction and authority, §15.2-1744.
Summons in lieu of arrest warrant, issuance, §19.2-74.
Supervision of person or agency making application for appointment, §15.2-1737.
Toll bridges, §§33.1-258 to 33.1-260.
Vacancies, §15.2-1741.
Removal from locality, §15.2-1742.
State police arrests, §§52-20 to 52-22.
State police communications system, §§52-12 to 52-15.
State police department, §§52-1 to 52-11.5.
See STATE POLICE DEPARTMENT.
State police retirement system, §§51.1-200 to 51.1-210.
See STATE POLICE RETIREMENT SYSTEM.
Strip search procedures development, §19.2-59.1.
Summons.
Authority to issue, §19.2-267.1.
Tire puncturing device use authorized, §33.1-345.

POLICE —Cont'd
Toll bridges.
Special police, §§33.1-258 to 33.1-260.
Traffic infractions.
Arrest of nonresidents, §§46.2-944 to 46.2-947.
Training.
Criminal justice training academies, §§15.2-1747 to 15.2-1753.
See CRIMINAL JUSTICE TRAINING ACADEMIES.
Transportation of prisoners, §53.1-31.1.
Trespass.
Hunters, fishers or trappers.
Enforcement of provisions, §18.2-136.1.
Local law-enforcement agency.
Designation to enforce trespass violations, §15.2-1717.1.
Tuition and required fees to state supported colleges or universities.
Waiver to child or spouse of officer killed in line of duty, §23-7.4:1.
Unclaimed property in possession of police.
Bicycles or mopeds, §15.2-1720.
Firearms or other weapons, §15.2-1721.
Uniforms.
Unlawful wearing of officer's uniform, §18.2-175.
Validation of certain police forces, §15.2-1723.
Virginia Amber Alert program.
Activation, §52-34.3.
Definitions, §52-34.1.
Established, §52-34.2.
Virginia Commonwealth University health system authority.
Authority to employ police officers and auxiliary forces, §23-232.
Volunteer citizen support units.
Local vehicle licenses.
Issuance free of charge, §46.2-752.
Waiver of minimum qualification requirements, §15.2-1705.
Warrants and summons.
Authority to execute and serve, §15.2-1704.
Weapons.
Disposal of unclaimed firearms or other weapons in possession of police, §15.2-1721.
Witnesses' fees received by officer, §15.2-1710.
Workers' compensation.
Employee defined, §65.2-101.
Heart disease.
Presumptions as to death or disability from, §65.2-402.
Hepatitis, meningitis, tuberculosis and HIV.
Presumption on death or disability from, §65.2-402.1.
Hypertension.
Presumptions as to death or disability from, §65.2-402.
Injury where weather constitutes particular risk of employment of public safety officer, §65.2-301.1.
Off-duty coverage, §65.2-102.
Wounds caused by concealable weapons.
Reports by health care providers, §54.1-2967.

POLICE DOGS.
Killing or injuring, §18.2-144.1.
Sale by locality, §15.2-981.
Surplus dogs sold to handlers, §2.2-1124.

POLICE LINES OR BARRICADES, §15.2-1714.
Crossing, §18.2-414.2.

POLICE OFFICER RETIREMENT, LOCAL, §§51.1-807 to 51.1-820.
See LOCAL RETIREMENT SYSTEMS.

POLICE RADIO.
Joint state and local police communications system, §§52-16 to 52-19.
Use during commission of crime, §18.2-462.1.

POLICE SCHOOL.
Department of state police.
Functions, §52-4.

POLICE VEHICLES.
Generally.
See EMERGENCY VEHICLES.
Shooting at marked vehicles, §18.2-154.
State owned motor vehicles.
Centralized fleet management.
Exceptions, §2.2-1174.
Unlawful use of vehicle with word police shown, §18.2-175.

POLICY RESEARCH.
Nonpartisan research on United States policy.
Retail sales and use tax exemption.
Miscellaneous exemptions, §58.1-609.10.

POLIOMYELITIS.
Immunizations.
Required immunizations of children, §32.1-46.
Virginia immunization information system (VIIS), §32.1-46.01.

POLITICAL ACTION COMMITTEES.
Campaign finance disclosure generally.
See CAMPAIGN FINANCE DISCLOSURE.
List of registered voters.
Obtaining, §24.2-405.

POLITICAL CONTRIBUTIONS TO CANDIDATES.
Campaign finance disclosure generally.
See CAMPAIGN FINANCE DISCLOSURE.

POLITICAL PARTIES.
Ascertaining vote after polls closed.
Presence of representatives on request, §24.2-655.
Bribery of party officials.
Certain matters not to constitute defense, §18.2-448.
Definition, §18.2-446.
Immunity of witness, §18.2-450.
Punishment, §18.2-449.
When person deemed guilty of bribery, §18.2-447.
Campaign finance disclosure.
See CAMPAIGN FINANCE DISCLOSURE.
Certification of candidates to state board and electoral boards, §24.2-511.
Chairman.
Lobbyist, employment as, prohibition, §2.2-435.
Defined, §24.2-101.
Election officers.
Representation, §24.2-115.
Electoral boards.
Members prohibited from serving as committee chairman, §24.2-106.
Representation, §24.2-106.
General assembly candidates.
Method of nominating, §24.2-509.
Lists of registered voters or persons voting at primary or elections.
Persons who may obtain lists, §§24.2-405, 24.2-406.

POLITICAL PARTIES —Cont'd
Lobbyists, employment of chairman, prohibition, §2.2-435.
Nomination of candidates.
Certification of candidates to state board and secretary of electoral board, §24.2-511.
Deadlines for parties to nominate by methods other than primary, §24.2-510.
General assembly candidates.
Method of nominating, §24.2-509.
Method determined by party, §24.2-509.
Methods other than primary.
Deadlines for nominating, §24.2-510.
Powers, §24.2-508.
Primaries generally, §§24.2-512 to 24.2-538.
See PRIMARY ELECTIONS.
Party committees.
Campaign finance disclosure generally.
See CAMPAIGN FINANCE DISCLOSURE.
Election at same time as primary candidate, §24.2-518.
Powers, §24.2-508.
Registrars.
Prohibited from serving as committee chairman, §24.2-110.
State board of elections.
Representation, §24.2-102.

POLITICAL REFUGEES.
Colleges and universities.
In-state tuition, establishing eligibility for, §23-7.4.

POLITICAL SUBDIVISIONS.
Admission tax, §§58.1-3817, 58.1-3818.
Scott county.
Off-track horse race wagering facilities, §58.1-3818.01.
Stafford county, §58.1-3818.02.
Air raid precautions, §§44-147 to 44-151.
Alleghany Highlands economic development authority, §§15.2-6200 to 15.2-6214.
Animal ordinances generally.
See LOCALITIES.
Annexation.
Generally, §§15.2-3200 to 15.2-3235.
See ANNEXATION.
Annulment of town charters, §§15.2-3700 to 15.2-3712.
See TOWNS.
Assisting armed forces in unlawful detention of United States citizens, §2.2-614.2:1.
Associations of political subdivisions, §§15.2-1303 to 15.2-1305.
Baseball stadium authority, §§15.2-5800 to 15.2-5819.
Blighted areas.
Tax increment financing, §§58.1-3245 to 58.1-3245.5.
Boards of equalization, §§58.1-3270 to 58.1-3389.
See REAL PROPERTY TAXES.
Bond issues.
Counties, cities or towns generally, §§15.2-2600 to 15.2-2663.
See PUBLIC FINANCE ACT.
Bonds of local officers, §§15.2-1527 to 15.2-1533.
Boundaries.
Annexation.
Generally, §§15.2-3200 to 15.2-3235.
See ANNEXATION.
Contraction of corporate limits of cities or towns, §§15.2-3236 to 15.2-3245.
See BOUNDARIES.

POLITICAL SUBDIVISIONS —Cont'd
Boundaries —Cont'd
Establishment of boundary lines by commissioners, §§15.2-3100 to 15.2-3105.
See BOUNDARIES.
Relocation or change by agreement, §§15.2-3106 to 15.2-3109.
See BOUNDARIES.
Budgets, audits and reports.
Localities generally, §§15.2-2500 to 15.2-2513.
Cash match plan for employees of Commonwealth, §§51.1-607 to 51.1-613.
Establishment by political subdivision.
Contract with VRS, §51.1-611.
Cigarette tax, §§58.1-3830 to 58.1-3832.
Corporate or partnership officer.
Willful failure to collect and account for, §58.1-3907.
Cities generally.
See CITIES.
City status granted to towns, §§15.2-3800 to 15.2-3834.
See TRANSITION OF TOWNS TO CITIES.
Coalfield economic development authority, §§15.2-6000 to 15.2-6015.
Collection of local taxes generally, §§58.1-3910 to 58.1-3961.
See TAX COLLECTION.
Commissioners of revenue generally, §§58.1-3100 to 58.1-3122.2.
See COMMISSIONERS OF REVENUE.
Commission on local government, §§15.2-2900 to 15.2-2908.
See COMMISSION ON LOCAL GOVERNMENT.
Consolidation of localities.
Counties, cities or towns consolidating into single county or city, §§15.2-3520 to 15.2-3550.
See CONSOLIDATION OF LOCALITIES.
Like units of local government, §§15.2-3500 to 15.2-3519.
See CONSOLIDATION OF LOCALITIES.
Consumer utility taxes, §§58.1-3814 to 58.1-3816.2.
Contraction of corporate limits of cities or towns, §§15.2-3236 to 15.2-3245.
See BOUNDARIES.
Contracts.
Performance agreements.
Extension of performance period, §11-7.1.
Corporation or company not to include political subdivisions, VA Const Art IX §7.
Correction of assessments generally, §§58.1-3980 to 58.1-3995.
See CORRECTION OF ERRONEOUS TAX ASSESSMENTS.
Counties generally.
See COUNTIES.
County attorneys generally.
See COUNTY ATTORNEYS.
Criminal justice training academies, §§15.2-1747 to 15.2-1753.
See CRIMINAL JUSTICE TRAINING ACADEMIES.
Electrical energy requirements.
Aggregating for purposes of negotiating purchase of electricity, §56-589.
Electric authorities, §§15.2-5400 to 15.2-5431.
See ELECTRIC AUTHORITIES.
Emergency management and disaster law generally, §§44-146.13 to 44-146.28.
See EMERGENCY MANAGEMENT.

POLITICAL SUBDIVISIONS —Cont'd
Eminent domain.
Counties, cities or towns generally, §§15.2-1901 to 15.2-1906.
See LOCALITIES.
Employment of counsel to defend, §15.2-1520.
Former federal areas, authorities for development, §§15.2-6300 to 15.2-6322.
Franchise, privilege, lease or right to use city or town property, §§15.2-2100 to 15.2-2108.1:1.
Freedom of information act.
Exclusions from chapter, §§2.2-3705.1 to 2.2-3705.8.
Governing bodies of localities.
Generally, §§15.2-1400 to 15.2-1433.
See LOCALITIES.
Governmental fraud, §§18.2-498.1 to 18.2-498.5.
Grievance procedure.
Local government personnel generally, §§15.2-1506 to 15.2-1507.1.
Hampton Roads area refuse collection and disposal system authority, §15.2-5102.1.
Hampton Roads sports facility authority, §§15.2-5900 to 15.2-5916.
Hospital authorities.
Cities generally, §§15.2-5300 to 15.2-5367.
See HOSPITAL AUTHORITIES.
Hospital or health center commissions, §§15.2-5200 to 15.2-5219.
See HOSPITAL OR HEALTH CENTER COMMISSIONS.
Immunity of counties from city-initiated annexation and city incorporation, §§15.2-3300 to 15.2-3308.
See IMMUNITY OF COUNTIES FROM CITY-INITIATED ANNEXATION AND CITY INCORPORATION.
Incorporation of towns by judicial proceedings, §§15.2-3600 to 15.2-3605.
Indoor clean air act, §§15.2-2820 to 15.2-2833.
See SMOKING IN PUBLIC PLACES.
Inhabitants.
Defined, §1-235.
Insurance.
Local government group self-insurance pools, §§15.2-2700 to 15.2-2709.
See LOCAL GOVERNMENT GROUP SELF-INSURANCE POOLS.
Joint exercise of powers, §§15.2-1300 to 15.2-1302.
Joint local officers and employees, §§15.2-1513 to 15.2-1516.
Juvenile detention and other care facilities.
Operating and maintaining.
Generally, §§16.1-315 to 16.1-322.7.
See JUVENILE DETENTION AND OTHER CARE FACILITIES.
Land preservation special assessment.
Real property taxes, §§58.1-3229 to 58.1-3244.
See REAL PROPERTY TAXES.
Libraries, local and regional, §§42.1-33 to 42.1-45.
License taxes generally, §§58.1-3700 to 58.1-3735.
See LICENSE TAXES.
Localities generally.
See LOCALITIES.
Local personnel generally, qualifications for office, bond, etc., §§15.2-1500 to 15.2-1543.
See LOCAL OFFICERS AND EMPLOYEES.

POLITICAL SUBDIVISIONS —Cont'd
Local taxes generally, §§58.1-3000 to 58.1-3018.
See LOCAL TAXES.
Meals tax.
County food and beverage tax, §§58.1-3833, 58.1-3834.
Excise tax, city or town having general taxing powers, §58.1-3840.
Situs for taxation, §§58.1-3840, 58.1-3841.
Merchants capital tax, §§58.1-3509, 58.1-3510.
Motor vehicle and traffic regulation powers, §§46.2-1300 to 46.2-1314.
See LOCALITIES.
Ordinances and other actions by local governing body, §§15.2-1425 to 15.2-1433.
See ORDINANCES.
Park authorities, §§15.2-5700 to 15.2-5714.
See PARK AUTHORITIES.
Parks, recreational facilities and playgrounds.
Locality establishing, operating, etc., §§15.2-1806 to 15.2-1811.
See LOCALITIES.
Personal property taxes.
Exempt property generally, §§58.1-3600 to 58.1-3666.
See PROPERTY EXEMPT FROM TAXATION.
Generally, §§58.1-3500 to 58.1-3522.
See PERSONAL PROPERTY TAXES.
Machinery and tools tax, §§58.1-3507, 58.1-3508.
Merchants capital tax, §§58.1-3509, 58.1-3510.
Tax relief act of 1998, §§58.1-3523 to 58.1-3535.
See PERSONAL PROPERTY TAX RELIEF ACT OF 1998.
Planning commissions, §§15.2-2210 to 15.2-2222.
See PLANNING COMMISSIONS.
Planning district commissions, §§15.2-4200 to 15.2-4222.
See PLANNING DISTRICT COMMISSIONS.
Planning, subdivision of land and zoning.
Generally, §§15.2-2200 to 15.2-2239.
See PLANNING AND DEVELOPMENT.
Road impact fees, §§15.2-2317 to 15.2-2329.
See ROAD IMPACT FEES.
Subdivisions generally, §§15.2-2240 to 15.2-2279.
See SUBDIVISIONS.
Zoning generally, §§15.2-2280 to 15.2-2316.2.
See ZONING.
Police.
Auxiliary police forces, §§15.2-1731 to 15.2-1736.
See POLICE.
Generally, §§15.2-1700 to 15.2-1753.
See POLICE.
Interjurisdictional law-enforcement authority and agreements, §§15.2-1724 to 15.2-1730.
See POLICE.
Special police officers in localities, §§15.2-1737 to 15.2-1746.
See POLICE.
Population.
Classifications, §1-236.
Defined, §1-235.
Pretrial services programs.
Assistance to judicial officers in carrying out bail and pretrial release duties, §§19.2-152.2 to 19.2-152.7:1.
See BAIL AND RECOGNIZANCE.
Probate tax, §§58.1-3805 to 58.1-3808.
Prompt payment of bills, §§2.2-4352, 2.2-4354.
Property exempt from taxation generally, §§58.1-3600 to 58.1-3666, VA Const Art X §6.
See PROPERTY EXEMPT FROM TAXATION.

POLITICAL SUBDIVISIONS —Cont'd
Publications.
State publications depository program.
Duties of local agencies generally, §42.1-94.
Generally, §§42.1-92 to 42.1-97.
See STATE PUBLICATIONS DEPOSITORY PROGRAM.
Public records generally, §§42.1-76 to 42.1-90.1.
See STATE RECORDS MANAGEMENT.
Public utilities.
Locality establishing, maintaining, operating, etc., §§15.2-2109 to 15.2-2121.
See LOCALITIES.
Qualification of local officer for office, §§15.2-1522 to 15.2-1524.
Real property tax credit.
When land acquired by political subdivision, §§58.1-3360 to 58.1-3363.
Real property taxes.
Exempt property generally, §§58.1-3600 to 58.1-3666.
See PROPERTY EXEMPT FROM TAXATION.
Generally, §§58.1-3200 to 58.1-3389.
See REAL PROPERTY TAXES.
Recordation tax, §§58.1-3800 to 58.1-3804.
Exemption, §58.1-811.
Recreational facilities authorities, §§15.2-5600 to 15.2-5616.
See RECREATIONAL FACILITIES AUTHORITY.
Regional partnerships.
Regional competitiveness act, §§15.2-1306 to 15.2-1310.
Resources authority, §§62.1-197 to 62.1-223.
See RESOURCES AUTHORITY.
Road impact fees, §§15.2-2317 to 15.2-2329.
See ROAD IMPACT FEES.
Roads, streets and public rights of way.
Counties, cities or towns generally, §§15.2-2000 to 15.2-2030.
See ROADS, STREETS AND PUBLIC RIGHTS OF WAY.
Local authority over highways, §§33.1-224 to 33.1-246.
See LOCAL ROAD AUTHORITIES.
Sale of delinquent tax lands generally, §§58.1-3965 to 58.1-3975.
See SALE OF DELINQUENT TAX LANDS.
Service districts, §§15.2-2400 to 15.2-2403.3.
Sewage disposal systems.
Localities generally, §§15.2-2122 to 15.2-2133.
See SEWAGE DISPOSAL SYSTEMS.
Special police officers in localities, §§15.2-1737 to 15.2-1746.
See POLICE.
Statutory construction.
Delegation of duties assigned to political subdivisions, §1-213.
Subdivisions, §§15.2-2240 to 15.2-2279.
See SUBDIVISIONS.
Superintendents of public welfare.
See SUPERINTENDENTS OF PUBLIC WELFARE.
Tangible personal property tax generally, §§58.1-3500 to 58.1-3522.
See PERSONAL PROPERTY TAXES.
Taxes or assessments for local improvements, §§15.2-2404 to 15.2-2413.
See TAXES OR ASSESSMENTS FOR LOCAL IMPROVEMENTS.
Tax increment financing, §§58.1-3245 to 58.1-3245.5.

POLITICAL SUBDIVISIONS —Cont'd
Towns generally.
See TOWNS.
Transient occupancy tax, §§58.1-3819 to 58.1-3826.
Transition of city to town status.
City no longer qualifying for city status, §§15.2-4000 to 15.2-4005.
See REVERSION OF CITIES TO TOWNS.
Generally, §§15.2-4100 to 15.2-4120.
See REVERSION OF CITIES TO TOWNS.
Transition of counties to cities, §§15.2-3900 to 15.2-3919.
See TRANSITION OF COUNTIES TO CITIES.
Transition of towns to cities, §§15.2-3800 to 15.2-3834.
See TRANSITION OF TOWNS TO CITIES.
Transportation districts, §§33.1-409 to 33.1-425, 33.1-430 to 33.1-446.
Travel expenses.
Persons on business of locality, §§15.2-1508.1 to 15.2-1508.4.
Persons traveling on business of locality, §§15.2-1508.1 to 15.2-1508.4.
Treasurers of counties or cities, §§58.1-3123 to 58.1-3172.1.
See TREASURERS, LOCAL.
United States acquired lands.
Concurrent jurisdiction over certain lands leased to, §1-407.
Conveyance of lands ceded to and no longer used by United States, §1-406.
United States property.
Acquisition of property from United States, §15.2-952.
Virginia Beach arena, §§15.2-5921 to 15.2-5927.
See VIRGINIA BEACH ARENA.
Virginia retirement system, participation in, §§51.1-130 to 51.1-139.
See VIRGINIA RETIREMENT SYSTEM.
Water supply systems.
Localities generally, §§15.2-2134 to 15.2-2156.
See WATER SUPPLY SYSTEMS.
Welfare or social services boards generally.
See WELFARE BOARDS, LOCAL.
Workers' compensation.
Employee defined, §65.2-101.
Zoning, §§15.2-2280 to 15.2-2316.2.
See ZONING.

POLLBOOKS.
Accuracy, verification, registrar, §24.2-114.
Entry of voter's name on, §24.2-643.
Form and signing of, §24.2-611.
Paper ballots exceeding names on, §24.2-662.
Preservation, §24.2-114.
Primaries, §24.2-531.
Registrars.
Duties, §24.2-114.
Sealing and delivering to clerk after ascertaining results, §24.2-668.
Transfer or return to state board, §24.2-114.

POLLING PLACES.
Accessibility to elderly, disabled or handicapped, §24.2-310.
Alternative upon polling place being unusable or inaccessible, §24.2-310.
Signs for special entrances, §24.2-604.1.
Building and facilities requirements, §24.2-310.
Campaigning near polling place, §24.2-604.
Candidates entering to vote or visit, §24.2-604.

POLLING PLACES —Cont'd
Changes not to be enacted within sixty days of general election, §24.2-306.
Children or minors.
Election pages.
Children serving as, §24.2-604.
Closing polls, §24.2-603.
Defined, §24.2-101.
Election pages.
Children serving as, §24.2-604.
Emergency making unstable or inaccessible.
Alternative provided, notice, §24.2-310.
Entrances for disabled or elderly.
Signs for special entrances, §24.2-604.1.
Grants to non-governmental entity furnishing facilities for use as polling place, §24.2-310.
Hindering or delaying qualified voter from entering or leaving, §24.2-604.
Hours polls to be open, §24.2-603.
Lines of voters waiting to vote.
Extension outside polling place, §24.2-643.
Locating in building of private organization, §24.2-310.1.
Loitering or congregating near entrance, §24.2-604.
Loudspeakers prohibited, §24.2-605.
Materials at polling places, §24.2-610.
Minors entering polling place to vote in simulated election, §24.2-604.
Noisy or riotous manner at or about polls, §24.2-607.
Notice of change, §24.2-306.
Polling place unusable or inaccessible, §24.2-310.
Number for each precinct, §§24.2-307, 24.2-308.
Officers of election.
Generally, §§24.2-115 to 24.2-118.
See ELECTIONS.
Pages.
Children serving as, §24.2-604.
Presence of representatives of parties or candidates, §24.2-604.
Preservation of order at elections, §24.2-606.
Prohibited activities, §24.2-604.
Prohibited area notices, §24.2-604.
Requirements, §24.2-310.
Additional requirement, §24.2-310.1.
Sample ballots.
Restrictions on giving, tendering or exhibiting while in polling place, §24.2-622.
Taking into voting booth or enclosure, §24.2-622.
Simulated elections.
Minors entering to vote in, §24.2-604.
Voting booth requirements, §24.2-609.
Voting equipment, electronic voting or counting systems.
Demonstration of voting equipment on election day, §24.2-647.
Furniture and equipment to be at, §24.2-637.
Wireless communication between voting machines or with outside equipment while polls open, §24.2-625.2.

POLL TAX.
Failure to pay poll or other tax.
Denial or abridgment of right to vote, US Const Amd 24.

POLLUTION.
Agricultural stewardship, §§3.2-400 to 3.2-410.
See AGRICULTURAL STEWARDSHIP.
Air pollution.
Generally.
See AIR POLLUTION.

POLLUTION —Cont'd
Air pollution control board, §§10.1-1300 to 10.1-1322.4.
See AIR POLLUTION CONTROL BOARD.
Brownfields restoration and land renewal, §§10.1-1230 to 10.1-1237.
Casting solid waste into waters, §§62.1-194 to 62.1-194.3.
Clams.
Dredging clams in polluted areas for replanting, §28.2-650.
Clean coal projects, §§67-400, 67-401.
Cleaning agents, §§62.1-193.1 to 62.1-193.3.
Confined animal feeding operations, §62.1-44.17:1.
Chesapeake Bay watershed nutrient credit exchange program, §62.1-44.19:21.
Environmental laboratory certification program.
Division of consolidated laboratory services to establish, §2.2-1105.
Equipment.
Property exempt from taxation.
Certified equipment and facilities, §58.1-3660.
Retail sales and use tax.
Commercial and industrial exemptions, §58.1-609.3.
Ground water management, §§62.1-254 to 62.1-270.
Immunity.
Voluntarily disclosed violations, §10.1-1199.
Industrial discharges into waters of the state, §§62.1-44.16, 62.1-44.17.
Instream toxics removal or remediation technologies.
Evaluation and review, §62.1-44.17:4.
Motor vehicles.
Exhaust systems generally, §§46.2-1047 to 46.2-1051.
Fine schedule, VA SCt Rule 3B:2.
Maximum fine for violating Title 46.2, §46.2-113.
Requirements generally, §46.2-1048.
Oil discharges into waters of the state, §§62.1-44.34:14 to 62.1-44.34:23.
See OIL DISCHARGES INTO WATERS OF STATE.
Permit fees, water, §§62.1-44.15:7, 62.1-44.15:8.
Policy of state, VA Const Art XI §1.
Prevention program, §§10.1-1425.10 to 10.1-1425.19.
Sanitation districts law of 1938.
Discharges into tidal waters causing pollution, §21-218.
Relief from pollution as purpose of commission, §21-169.
Sanitation districts law of 1946.
Relief from pollution as purpose of commission, §21-249.
Sewage discharges into waters of the state, §§62.1-44.18 to 62.1-44.19:3.4.
Spill response council, §§62.1-44.34:24 to 62.1-44.34:28.
State policy as to waters, §§62.1-10 to 62.1-13.
Storage tank discharges into waters of the state, §§62.1-44.34:8, 62.1-44.34:9.
Petroleum storage tank fund, §§62.1-44.34:10 to 62.1-44.34:13.
Toxics discharge reduction, §§62.1-44.17:2, 62.1-44.17:3.
Water pollution.
See WATER POLLUTION.

POLLUTION —Cont'd
Waters of the state.
State water control generally, §§62.1-44.2 to 62.1-44.34:28.
See WATERS OF THE STATE.

POLLUTION PREVENTION PROGRAM, §§10.1-1425.10 to 10.1-1425.19.
Advisory panel, §10.1-1425.13.
Confidential information.
Trade secret protection, §10.1-1425.16.
Defined, §10.1-1425.10.
Enforcement actions, §10.1-1425.19.
Establishment of prevention policy, §10.1-1425.11.
Evaluation reports, §10.1-1425.17.
Grants.
Pollution prevention grants, §10.1-1425.19.
Inspections, §10.1-1425.19.
Panels.
Advisory panel, §10.1-1425.13.
Pilot projects, §10.1-1425.14.
Policies.
Establishment of prevention policy, §10.1-1425.11.
Prevention assistance program, §10.1-1425.12.
Reports.
Evaluation report, §10.1-1425.17.
Toxic or hazardous substance.
Defined, §10.1-1425.10.
Trade secrets, §10.1-1425.16.
Waste exchange, §10.1-1425.15.

POLYGRAPH EXAMINERS, §§54.1-1800 to 54.1-1806.
Approval of schools, §54.1-1803.
Defined terms, §54.1-1800.
Evidence of polygraph examination.
Admissible in disciplinary action against polygrapher, §8.01-418.2.
Fingerprints, §54.1-1804.
Instruments, §54.1-1805.
License requirements, §54.1-1801.
Powers and duties of department, §54.1-1802.1.
Question prohibitions, §54.1-1806.
Schools.
Approval, §54.1-1803.
Tools of the trade, §54.1-1805.
Unlawful procurement of licensure, §54.1-102.
Unlawful use of licensure, §54.1-111.

POLYGRAPH TESTS.
Criminal procedure.
Written notice prior to examination, §19.2-9.1.
Evidence.
Admissibility, VA SCt Rule 2:402.
Occupational safety and health.
Prohibition of questions on tests for employment, §§40.1-51.4:3, 40.1-51.4:4, 54.1-1806.
Teachers refusal to submit to.
Teacher not to be dismissed or placed on probation, §22.1-307.

POLYSOMNOGRAPHIC TECHNOLOGISTS, §§54.1-2957.14, 54.1-2957.15.

POLYTETRAFLUOROETHYLENE.
Bullets coated with or containing.
Use or attempted use in commission or attempted commission of crime, §18.2-308.3.

PONDS.
Deer.
Killing a deer in, §29.1-516.

PONDS —Cont'd
Dredging sand and gravel, §§62.1-190 to 62.1-193.
Impoundment of surface waters generally, §§62.1-104 to 62.1-115.
See IMPOUNDMENT OF SURFACE WATERS.
Surface water management areas, §§62.1-242 to 62.1-253.
See SURFACE WATER MANAGEMENT AREAS.
Waters of the state generally.
See WATERS OF THE STATE.

PONIES.
Larceny, §18.2-97.
Maiming, killing or poisoning, §18.2-144.

PONZI SCHEMES.
Pyramid promotional schemes, §§18.2-239, 18.2-240.

POOLROOMS.
Child labor.
Age of workers, §40.1-100.
Drug houses.
Maintaining fortified drug houses, §18.2-258.02.
Drug transactions on premises.
Closure of nuisance premises, §§48-16, 48-17.
Common nuisance, §§18.2-258, 18.2-258.01.

POOR.
Indigency generally.
See INDIGENCY.

POOR DEBTORS ACT, §§34-26 to 34-28.

POPLAR FOREST.
Thomas Jefferson home.
Appropriations to corporation for maintenance, §10.1-2212.

POPPY STRAW.
Drug control act.
Generally, §§54.1-3400 to 54.1-3472.
See DRUG CONTROL.
Drug offenses.
Generally, §§18.2-247 to 18.2-264.
See DRUG OFFENSES.
Schedule II controlled drug, §54.1-3448.

POPULAR NAMES AND SHORT TITLES.
Administrative procedure act, §2.2-4000.
Agricultural and forestal districts act, §15.2-4300.
Agricultural cooperative association act, §13.1-313.
Aircraft sales and use tax act, §58.1-1500.
Antitrust act, §59.1-9.1.
Appalachian region interstate compact, §15.2-5700.
Arson reporting immunity act, §27-85.3.
Asbestos neshap act, §40.1-51.23.
Auditor of public accounts, duties, §30-133.
Automatic dialing-announcing devices, §§59.1-518.1 to 59.1-518.4.
Automobile repair facilities act, §59.1-207.1.
Bank franchise tax act, §58.1-1200.
Birth-related neurological injury compensation act, §38.2-5000.
Boiler and pressure vessel safety act, §40.1-51.5.
Broadband infrastructure loan fund, §§15.2-2419 to 15.2-2429.
Business opportunity sales act, §59.1-262.
Business trust act, §13.1-1200.

POPULAR NAMES AND SHORT TITLES —Cont'd
Charlottesville-Albemarle regional transit authority act, §15.2-7022.
Chesapeake Bay preservation, §§62.1-44.15:67 to 62.1-44.15:79.
Chesapeake Bay watershed nutrient credit exchange program, §§62.1-44.19:12 to 62.1-44.19:23.
Child protection accountability system, §63.2-1530.
Coal mine safety act, §45.1-161.7.
College building authority act, §23-30.23.
Collision damage waiver law, §59.1-207.28.
Commercial driver license act, §46.2-341.1.
Commercial space flight authority act, §2.2-2201.
Communications sales and use tax act, §58.1-645.
Community action act, §2.2-5400.
Comprehensive money laundering act, §18.2-246.1.
Computer crimes act, §18.2-152.1.
Concealed carry permits, §§18.2-307.1 to 18.2-308.015.
Condominium act, §55-79.39.
Consumer protection act, §59.1-196.
Credit services businesses act, §59.1-335.1.
Drug control act, §54.1-3400.
Drug treatment court, §18.2-254.1.
Economic development partnership act, §2.2-2234.
Educational facilities authority act, §23-30.40.
Electric authorities act, §15.2-5400.
Emergency services and disaster law, §44-146.13.
Employment security act, §60.2-100.
Energy and operational efficiency performance-based contracting act, §§11-34.1 to 11-34.4.
Enterprise zone grant act, §59.1-538.
Estate tax act, §58.1-900.
Foreign country money judgments recognition act, §8.01-465.6.
Forest products tax act, §58.1-1600.
Foundation for healthy youth, §§32.1-354 to 32.1-367.
Fraud against taxpayers act, §8.01-216.1.
Fraud and abuse whistleblower protection act, §§2.2-3009 to 2.2-3014.
Freedom of information act, §2.2-3700.
Fuels tax act, §§58.1-2200 to 58.1-2299.20.
Geothermal resources conservation act, §45.1-179.1.
Governmental frauds act, §18.2-498.1.
Government data collection and dissemination practices act, §2.2-3800.
Government non-arbitrage investment, §2.2-4700.
Green roofing, §58.1-3852.
Hazardous liquid pipeline safety act, §56-553.
Health care decisions act, §54.1-2981.
Health practitioners' monitoring program, §§54.1-2515 to 54.1-2518.
Health spa act, §59.1-294.
Heavy equipment dealer act, §59.1-353.
Highway corporation act, §56-535.
Home solicitation sales act, §59.1-21.1.
Housing authorities law, §36-1.
Housing development authority act, §36-55.24.
Housing revitalization zone act, §36-157.

POPULAR NAMES AND SHORT TITLES —Cont'd
Human rights act, §§2.2-3900 to 2.2-3903.
Implementation of federal mandates act, §2.2-615.
Industrial development and revenue bond act, §15.2-4900.
Industrial development corporation act, §13.1-981.
Industrialized building safety law, §36-70.
Innovative and entrepreneurship investment authority, §2.2-2218.
Innovative technology authority act, §2.2-2218.
Insurance unfair trade practices, §§38.2-500 to 38.2-518.
Interstate compact for the supervision of adult offenders, §53.1-176.2.
Interstate compact on educational opportunity for military children, §22.1-360.
Interstate wildlife violator compact, §§29.1-103, 29.1-530.5.
Investment partnership act, §2.2-5100.
Judicial determination of death, §§64.2-2304 to 64.2-2309.
Juvenile and domestic relations district court law, §16.1-226.
Lease-purchase agreement act, §59.1-207.17.
Limited liability company act, §13.1-1000.
Line of duty act, §§9.1-400 to 9.1-408.
Litter tax act, §58.1-1706.
Local agricultural and forestal districts act, §15.2-4400.
Local government investment pool act, §2.2-4600.
Luggage for children in foster care, §63.2-914.
Manufactured housing construction and safety standards law, §36-85.2.
Marine tourism activity liability act, §§28.2-1105 to 28.2-1107.
Membership campground act, §59.1-311.
Middle peninsula Chesapeake bay public access authority, §15.2-6600.
Military and overseas voters act, §§24.2-451 to 24.2-470.
Military code, §44-122.
Mineral mine safety act, §45.1-161.292:1.
Model policies for codes of student conduct, §22.1-279.6.
Money laundering act, §18.2-246.1.
Motion picture fair competition act, §59.1-255.
Motor vehicle sales and use tax act, §58.1-2400.
Motor vehicle warranty enforcement act, §59.1-207.9.
Northern Neck Chesapeake bay public access authority, §15.2-6626.
Northern Virginia transportation authority act, §15.2-4829.
Notary public act, §47.1-1.
Park authorities act, §15.2-5700.
Personnel act, §2.2-2900.
Petroleum products franchise act, §59.1-21.8.
Post-disaster anti-price gouging act, §59.1-525.
Potomac river compact, §62.1-44.113.
Prescription monitoring program act, §§54.1-2519 to 54.1-2526.
Prisoner litigation reform act, §8.01-689.
Private well construction act, §32.1-176.1.
Prizes and gifts act, §59.1-415.
Psychiatric inpatient treatment of minors act, §16.1-335.
Publications depository program, §42.1-92.

POPULAR NAMES AND SHORT TITLES —Cont'd
Public building authorities act, §2.2-2260.
Public finance act, §15.2-2600.
Public-private transportation act, §56-556.
Public procurement act, §2.2-4300.
Public records act, §42.1-76.
Public recreational facilities authorities act, §15.2-5600.
Public school security equipment grant act of 2013, §22.1-280.2:2.
Public telephone information act, §59.1-424.
Racketeer-influenced and corrupt organizations act, §18.2-512.
Real estate cooperative act, §55-424.
Real estate time-share act, §55-360.
Recordation tax act, §58.1-800.
Regional cooperation act, §15.2-4200.
Register act, §2.2-4100.
Residential landlord and tenant act, §55-248.2.
Resources authority act, §62.1-197.
Retail sales and use tax act, §58.1-600.
Retirement system oversight act, §30-78.
Revised uniform limited partnership act, §50-73.73.
Right to farm act, §§3.2-300 to 3.2-302.
Risk-based capital act, §38.2-5500.
Sanitation district act, §§21-141, 21-224.
Sawed-off shotgun and sawed-off rifle act, §18.2-307.
Securities act, §13.1-527.
Security for public deposits act, §2.2-4400.
Self-service storage facility act, §55-416.
Self storage insurance, §§38.2-1881 to 38.2-1886.
Senior citizens higher education act, §23-38.54.
Simultaneous death act, §§64.2-2200 to 64.2-2208.
Slayer's act, §§64.2-2500 to 64.2-2511.
Small business financing, §2.2-2279.
Small estate act, §§64.2-600 to 64.2-605.
Small investor-owned telephone utility act, §56-531.
Small water or sewer public utility act, §56-265.13:1.
Soft drink excise tax act, §58.1-1700.
Solar easement act, §55-352.
State government volunteers act, §2.2-3600.
State lottery act, §58.1-4000.
State publications depository program, §42.1-92.
State revenue bond act, §33.1-267.
State water control law, §62.1-44.2.
Statewide fire prevention code act, §27-94.
Stormwater management program, §§62.1-44.15:24 to 62.1-44.15:50.
Subdivided land sales act, §55-336.
TANF, §§63.2-600 to 63.2-621.
Tax on wills and administrations act, §58.1-1711.
Telephone cooperative act, §56-485.
Temporary assistance for needy families (TANF), §§63.2-600 to 63.2-621.
Text messaging while driving, §46.2-1078.1.
Time share act, §55-360.
Tort claims act, §8.01-195.1.
Tourism authority act, §2.2-2315.
Tourism financing development authority act, §15.2-5516.
Transportation district act, §15.2-4500.
Tuition assistance grant act, §23-38.11.

POPULAR NAMES AND SHORT TITLES —Cont'd
Underground utility damage prevention act, §56-265.14.
Unemployment compensation act, §60.2-100.
Unfair insurance trade practices, §§38.2-500 to 38.2-518.
Uniform act on interstate arbitration and compromise of death taxes, §58.1-920.
Uniform act to secure the attendance of witnesses from without a state in criminal proceedings, §19.2-282.
Uniform adult guardianship and protective proceedings jurisdiction act, §§64.2-2100 to 64.2-2120.
Uniform anatomical gift act, §32.1-291.1.
Uniform audio-visual deposition act, §8.01-412.7.
Uniform certificate of title for watercraft act, §§29.1-733.2 to 29.1-733.29.
Uniform commercial code-bank deposits and collections, §8.4-101.
Uniform commercial code-documents of title, §8.7-101.
Uniform commercial code-funds transfers, §8.4A-101.
Uniform commercial code-general provisions, §8.1A-101.
Uniform commercial code-investment securities, §8.8A-101.
Uniform commercial code-leases, §8.2A-101.
Uniform commercial code-letters of credit, §8.5A-101.
Uniform commercial code-negotiable instruments, §8.3A-101.
Uniform commercial code-sale of goods, §8.2-101.
Uniform commercial code-secured transactions, §8.9A-101.
Uniform computer information transactions act, §59.1-501.1.
Uniform criminal extradition act, §19.2-118.
Uniform custodial trusts act, §§64.2-900 to 64.2-918.
Uniform disclaimer of property interests act, §§64.2-2600 to 64.2-2614.
Uniform disposition of unclaimed property act, §55-210.1.
Uniform electronic transactions act, §59.1-479.
Uniform federal lien registration act, §55-142.7.
Uniform flag act, §18.2-492.
Uniform international wills act, §§64.2-433 to 64.2-442.
Uniform interstate depositions and discovery act, §§8.01-412.8 to 8.01-412.15.
Uniform interstate family support act, §20-88.82.
Uniform machine gun act, §18.2-298.
Uniform partnership act, §50-73.145.
Uniform power of attorney act, §§64.2-1600 to 64.2-1642.
Uniform principal and income act, §§64.2-1000 to 64.2-1032.
Uniform prudent investor act, §§64.2-780 to 64.2-791.
Uniform prudent management of institutional funds act, §§64.2-1100 to 64.2-1108.
Uniform real property transfer on death act, §§64.2-621 to 64.2-638.
Uniform recognition of acknowledgments act, §55-118.9.

POPULAR NAMES AND SHORT TITLES —Cont'd
Uniform trade secrets act, §59.1-336.
Uniform traffic control devices on highways, §46.2-830.
Uniform transfers on death (TOD) securities registration act, §§64.2-612 to 64.2-619.
Uniform transfers to minors act, §§64.2-1900 to 64.2-1922.
Utility aggregation cooperatives act, §56-231.52.
Utility consumer services cooperatives act, §56-231.37.
Utility facilities act, §56-265.9.
Utility transfers act, §56-92.
Vietnam human rights day, §2.2-3310.3.
Virginia Beach arena, §§15.2-5921 to 15.2-5927.
Virginia broadband infrastructure loan fund, §§15.2-2419 to 15.2-2429.
Virginia Commonwealth University health system authority act, §23-50.16:1.
Virginia jobs investment program, §2.2-1611.
Virginia new jobs program, §2.2-1612.
Virginians with disabilities act, §51.5-1.
Virginia nuclear energy consortium, §§67-1400 to 67-1406.
Virginia stormwater management program, §§62.1-44.15:24 to 62.1-44.15:50.
Virginia unemployment compensation act, §60.2-100.
Virginia waste management act, §§10.1-1400 to 10.1-1458.
Virginia water resources and wetlands protection program, §§62.1-44.15:20 to 62.1-44.15:23.1.
Water and waste authorities act, §15.2-5100.
Water control law, §62.1-44.2.
Watercraft dealer licensing act, §29.1-800.
Watercraft sales and use tax act, §58.1-1400.
Water resources and wetlands protection program, §§62.1-44.15:20 to 62.1-44.15:23.1.
Wildlife violator compact, §29.1-530.5.
Williamsburg area transit authority, §15.2-6800.
Winter sports safety act, §§8.01-227.11 to 8.01-227.23.
Wireless service authorities act, §15.2-5431.1.
Workers' compensation act, §65.2-100.

POPULATION OF LOCALITY.
Constitutional officers' salaries based upon.
Determined by preceding census, §15.2-1636.11.
Legal enumeration, §15.2-1414.

POQUOSON.
Buses.
Restricting nonscheduled buses over designated streets, §46.2-1304.
Coastal primary sand dunes and beaches.
Zoning ordinances, §28.2-1403.
Joint court system with York county.
Removal, approval of electorate required.
Inapplicability of provisions, §15.2-1646.
Port of Virginia economic and infrastructure development zone grant fund, §62.1-132.3:2.
Real property taxes.
Improvements to real property separate class of property, §58.1-3221.1.
Retail sales and use tax.
Additional sales tax for Northern Virginia and Hampton Roads, §58.1-603.1.
Additional use tax for Northern Virginia and Hampton Roads, §58.1-604.01.

POQUOSON —Cont'd
School board.
Salary of members, §22.1-32.
Social services.
District board of social services.
Local director serving as board, §63.2-307.
Underground relocation of electric, telephone and cable TV distribution lines.
Taxes and assessments on abutting property owners, §15.2-2404.

POQUOSON RIVER.
Oyster-planting grounds.
Public oyster rocks, beds and shoals declared, §28.2-647.

PORK INDUSTRY BOARD, §§3.2-2000 to 3.2-2009.
Bonds, surety.
Employees handling money, §3.2-2001.
Commission continued as board, §3.2-2001.
Definitions, §3.2-2000.
Educational and research programs, §3.2-2004.
Excise tax, §§3.2-2006 to 3.2-2009.
Members, §3.2-2001.

PORK INDUSTRY FUND, §3.2-2005.
Dedicated revenues, diversion, §3.2-1100.

PORNOGRAPHY.
Discretionary felony sentencing guidelines, §17.1-805.
Obscenity and related offenses generally, §§18.2-372 to 18.2-388.
See OBSCENITY AND RELATED OFFENSES.
Public officers and employees.
Computers.
Restricted access to sexually explicit material, §2.2-2827.
Sales and loans to juveniles, §§18.2-390 to 18.2-391.1.
Taking indecent liberties with children, §18.2-370.
Jail prisoner escape or release notice, §53.1-116.1.
Person in custodial or supervisory relationship, §18.2-370.1.
Prisoner intake notice, §53.1-116.1:01.
Punishment upon conviction of certain subsequent felony sexual assault, §18.2-67.5:2.
Suspension of sentence, placing on probation, §19.2-303.
Temporary assistance for needy families (TANF).
Prohibited uses of benefits, §63.2-621.

PORTABLE ELECTRONICS INSURANCE, §§38.2-1875 to 38.2-1880.
Applicability of other laws, §38.2-1880.
Charges to customer, §38.2-1878.
Definitions, §38.2-1875.
Disclosures to customers, §38.2-1877.
Employees and representatives of vendors, §38.2-1878.
Licensure of vendors, §38.2-1876.
Revocation or suspension of license, §38.2-1879.
Month-to-month or periodic basis, §38.2-1877.
Nonresident licensees, §38.2-1878.
Rulemaking, §38.2-1880.
Vendors.
Employees and representatives of vendors, §38.2-1878.
Licensure, §38.2-1876.
Revocation or suspension of license, §38.2-1879.

PORTABLE ELECTRONICS INSURANCE —Cont'd
Vendors —Cont'd
Requirements for sale of insurance, §38.2-1877.

PORT AUTHORITIES, UNCODIFIED.
Chesapeake port authority, 1987 ch 397, 1992 ch 700.
Norfolk port and industrial authority.
See NORFOLK PORT AND INDUSTRIAL AUTHORITY.
Peninsula ports authority of Virginia.
See PENINSULA PORTS AUTHORITY OF VIRGINIA.

PORT AUTHORITY, §§62.1-128 to 62.1-147.2.
Accounts, §62.1-139.
Annual operating plan and budget, §62.1-139.
Board of commissioners, §62.1-129.
Employment terms and conditions, §§62.1-129.1, 62.1-129.2.
Executive director, §62.1-129.
Powers, §62.1-130.
Maritime advisory council.
Authority to form, §62.1-129.
Trust for postemployment benefits authorized, §62.1-129.2.
Bond issues, §62.1-140.
Credit of Commonwealth or political subdivisions not pledged, §62.1-147.
Legal investments, §62.1-146.
Prior actions legalized, §62.1-147.1.
Proceeds held in trust, §62.1-143.
Remedies of holders and trustees, §62.1-144.
Trust agreement securing, §62.1-141.
Budget, §62.1-139.
Bylaws, §62.1-132.2.
Charges, §62.1-132.16.
Proceeds held in trust, §62.1-143.
Use of port facilities, §62.1-142.
Coal.
Expediting shipments, §62.1-134.1.
Construction of provisions, §62.1-147.2.
Cooperation with federal agencies, §62.1-132.13.
Corps of engineers, §62.1-132.14.
Corporation commission powers unaffected, §62.1-138.
Corps of engineers cooperation, §62.1-132.14.
Craney Island disposal area, §62.1-132.20.
Creation, §62.1-128.
Defined terms.
Bonds, §62.1-140.
Cost, §62.1-140.
Craney Island disposal area, §62.1-132.20.
Port facility, §62.1-140.
Revenue bonds, §62.1-140.
Dispute resolution, §62.1-163.
Duties, §62.1-132.1.
Planning, §62.1-132.5.
Stimulation of commerce, §62.1-132.3.
Terminal operations, consolidation of, §62.1-132.8.
Eminent domain, §62.1-136.
Employment of personnel, §62.1-132.7.
Personnel administration system.
Exemptions, §2.2-2905.
Police officers, §62.1-132.12.
Employment terms and conditions, §§62.1-129.1, 62.1-129.2.
Executive director.
Duties, §62.1-130.
Exemption from Virginia personnel act, §62.1-132.6.

PORT AUTHORITY —Cont'd
Fees, §62.1-132.16.
Finances.
Oversight, §62.1-139.
Fire prevention and suppression, §62.1-132.11:1.
Foreign trade zones, §62.1-132.9.
Freedom of information act exclusion.
Proprietary information gathered by, §2.2-3705.6.
Grants from federal agencies, §62.1-132.15.
Grants of funds and property, §62.1-132.17.
Information technologies agency.
Exemption from certain procedures, §62.1-147.1:1.
Loans from federal agencies, §62.1-132.15.
Local authority subordinate to, §62.1-132.
Maritime advisory council.
Authority to form, §62.1-129.
Ocean disposal areas.
Location and establishment, §62.1-132.20.
Offices, §62.1-131.
Operating plan.
Annual operating plan and budget, §62.1-139.
Organization, §62.1-132.2.
Planning, §62.1-132.5.
Police officers, §62.1-132.12.
Workers' compensation.
Presumption on death or disability from blood borne diseases, §§65.2-402, 65.2-402.1.
Port of Virginia economic and infrastructure development zone grant fund, §62.1-132.3:2.
Port opportunity fund, §62.1-132.3:1.
Powers, §62.1-132.1.
Exercise constitutes governmental functions, §62.1-145.
Foreign trade zones, §62.1-132.9.
Non-restrictive, §62.1-132.6.
Police powers, §62.1-132.11.
Special police officers, §62.1-132.12.
Private terminal operators.
Agreements with, §62.1-132.12:1.
Property.
Acquisition, §§62.1-132.18, 62.1-132.19.
Leases, §62.1-132.19.
Publications, §62.1-132.10.
Rates, §62.1-132.4.
Records.
Form, §62.1-139.
Location, §62.1-131.
Reports.
Annual report, §62.1-139.
Retail sales and use tax.
Exemptions, §58.1-609.1.
Secretary of transportation.
Agency responsibility, §2.2-228.
Stimulation of commerce, §62.1-132.3.
Taxes, §62.1-145.
Terminal operations, consolidation of, §62.1-132.8.
Terminal operators.
Agreements with private terminal operators, §62.1-132.12:1.
Title to property, §62.1-131.

PORT COMMISSIONS.
Alexandria port commission, 1962 ch 392, 1964 ch 480.

PORT FUND.
Motor vehicle sales and use tax revenue disposition, §58.1-2425.
Retail sales and use tax revenue disposition, §58.1-638.

PORTS.
Barge and rail usage tax credit.
International trade facilities using, §58.1-439.12:09.
Foreign trade zones, §§62.1-159 to 62.1-162.
Authority powers, §62.1-132.9.
Private corporations.
Applications, §62.1-161.
Authority to establish and operate zone, §62.1-162.
Public corporations.
Applications, §62.1-160.
Authority to establish and operate zone, §62.1-162.
Defined, §62.1-159.
Management, §62.1-163.
Offshore wind development authority.
Port facilities upgrades, §67-1204.
Recordation tax, state.
Distributions to cities and counties for, §58.1-816.
Reedville.
Appointment of agent, §62.1-163.
Virginia ports volume increase tax credit, §58.1-439.12:10.
Waters of the state generally.
See WATERS OF THE STATE.

PORTSMOUTH.
Circuit court, establishment, §17.1-500.
Coastal primary sand dunes and beaches.
Zoning ordinances, §28.2-1403.
Confederate cemeteries and graves.
Disbursement of funds appropriated for upkeep, §10.1-2211.
Historic areas, landmarks, buildings or structures.
Ramps to serve handicapped.
Approval of agency or board not required for construction, §15.2-2306.
Metropolitan transportation district, 1970 ch 697.
Metropolitan uniform laws commission, 1968 ch 329.
Outdoor performing arts amphitheater, area or similar facility.
Mixed beverages license, §4.1-210.
Personal property tax relief for elderly or handicapped.
Motor vehicles, alternate tax rates.
Ordinance to raise income and financial worth limitations, §58.1-3506.2.
Port authority.
Board of commissioners, §62.1-129.
Port of Virginia economic and infrastructure development zone grant fund, §62.1-132.3:2.
Public defenders office.
Established, §19.2-163.04.
Public service corporations, taxation of property.
Restriction of imposition of additional tax, §58.1-2606.
Retail sales and use tax.
Additional sales tax for Northern Virginia and Hampton Roads, §58.1-603.1.
Additional use tax for Northern Virginia and Hampton Roads, §58.1-604.01.
Revolutionary war cemeteries and graves.
Disbursement of funds appropriated for upkeep, §10.1-2211.1.
School board.
Salary of members, §22.1-32.

PORTSMOUTH —Cont'd
Sports authority of Hampton Roads, Virginia, 1986 ch 426.
Tidewater airport commission, 1962 ch 606, 1964 ch 45.
Unsafe vehicle removal, §46.2-1001.
Voluntary property maintenance and zoning inspectors, §15.2-1132.

PORTSMOUTH PARKING AUTHORITY, 1964 ch 351, 1970 ch 229, 1975 ch 258.

PORTSMOUTH PORT AND INDUSTRIAL COMMISSION.
Created, 1954 ch 157.
Amended in 1964, 1964 ch 29.
Amended in 1966, 1966 ch 468.
Amended in 1968, 1968 ch 688.
Amended in 1970, 1970 ch 138.
Amended in 1977, 1977 ch 420.
Amended in 1978, 1978 ch 287.

POSSESSION OF BURGLARIOUS TOOLS, §18.2-94.

POSSESSION OF DRUGS.
Controlled substances, §18.2-250.
With intent to manufacture, sell, etc., §18.2-248.
Drug blight existing on property.
Locality requiring owner to take corrective action to abate, §15.2-907.
Marijuana, §18.2-250.1.
With intent to manufacture, sell, etc., §18.2-248.1.
Synthetic cannabinoids, §18.2-248.1:1.

POSSESSION OF INFECTIOUS BIOLOGICAL SUBSTANCES, §18.2-52.1.

POSSESSION, WRIT OF.
See WRIT OF POSSESSION.

POSTAGE.
Commonwealth's attorneys, treasurers or commissioners of revenue purchasing.
Manner of payment, §15.2-1636.15.
Sheriffs, payment, §15.2-1615.1.

POSTAL SERVICE, US Const Art I §8.
Highways.
Rural post roads.
Federal aid, §33.1-215.
Mail.
Generally.
See MAIL.
National change of address systems.
DMV.
Contract with postal service to use, §§46.2-324, 46.2-342, 46.2-416, 46.2-606.

POSTED PROPERTY.
Hunting, fishing or trapping prohibited.
Destruction of posted signs or posting land of another, §18.2-135.
Method of posting lands, §18.2-134.1.
Right of hunters to go on land of another to retrieve dogs, §18.2-136.
Trespass on, §18.2-134.

POSTHUMOUS CHILDREN.
Descent and distribution, §64.2-419.
Future interests.
Sale, lease or exchange of land subject to.
Effect of decree, §8.01-94.

POSTING ORDERS.
Changing place of holding circuit court, §17.1-115.

POSTMARITAL AGREEMENTS, §20-155.

POSTMORTEM EXAMINATIONS, §§32.1-277 to 32.1-288.
Autopsies, §32.1-285.
Infant death suspected of being attributable to sudden infant death syndrome, §32.1-285.1.
Chief medical examiner.
Appointment, §32.1-278.
Assistants, §32.1-280.
Duties, §32.1-279.
Evidence.
Records and reports made by, §8.01-390.2.
Qualifications, §32.1-278.
Teaching duties, §32.1-279.
Disposition of remains, §32.1-288.
Evidence.
Autopsy reports made by chief medical examiner, §8.01-390.2.
Exhumations, §32.1-286.
Facilities, §32.1-277.
Investigations of death, §32.1-283.
Exhumations, §32.1-286.
Local medical examiners.
Appointment, §32.1-282.
Offices, §32.1-277.
Pathologist, employment, §32.1-281.
Persons who may authorize, §54.1-2973.
Removal of organs or body parts for transplant.
Certificate of surgeon as evidence, §19.2-188.2.
Workers' compensation.
Powers of employers or commission to order, §65.2-607.

POSTNUPTIAL AGREEMENTS, §20-155.

POST OFFICES, US Const Art I §8.
Highways.
Rural post roads.
Federal aid, §33.1-215.
Mail.
Generally.
See MAIL.

POSTPAID CALLING SERVICE.
Communications sales and use tax, §§58.1-645 to 58.1-662.
See COMMUNICATIONS SALES AND USE TAX.

POSTPARTUM BLUES OR PERINATAL DEPRESSION.
Information to maternity patient prior to releasing.
Hospital or nurse midwife, §32.1-134.01.

POSTPARTUM SERVICES, INSURANCE COVERAGES, §38.2-3414.1.
Medical assistance services plans, §32.1-325.
Public officers and employees.
Required coverage, §2.2-2818.

POSTRELEASE SUPERVISION.
General provisions.
See PAROLE AND POSTRELEASE SUPERVISION.

POSTSECONDARY SCHOOLS.
Regulation of private and out-of-state postsecondary schools, §§23-276.1 to 23-276.16.
See COLLEGES AND UNIVERSITIES.

POTATOES, §§3.2-1800 to 3.2-1815.
Board.
Compensation, §3.2-1803.

POTATOES —Cont'd
Board —Cont'd
Composition, §3.2-1801.
Definitions, §3.2-1800.
Elections.
Referendum on question of levying tax, §§3.2-1805 to 3.2-1809.
Legislative declarations, §3.2-1801.
Meetings, §3.2-1803.
Members, §3.2-1801.
Officers, §3.2-1803.
Powers and duties, §3.2-1804.
Referendum.
Question of levying tax, §§3.2-1805 to 3.2-1809.
Terms of members, §3.2-1802.
Vacancies, §3.2-1802.
Criminal penalty for violation of provisions, §3.2-1822.
Seed potatoes.
Experimental varieties, permission to sell, §3.2-1820.
Inspection, §3.2-1818.
Regulations to establish standards, §3.2-1804.
Sales exempted, §3.2-1817.
Seizure of shipments in violation of provisions, §3.2-1819.
Standards required, §3.2-1816.
Stop sale orders, §3.2-1819.
Substandard potatoes, permission to sell, §3.2-1820.
Tax.
Delinquent taxes.
Collection, §3.2-1812.
Expenditure of moneys collected, §3.2-1811.
Handlers.
Criminal penalties for certain acts, §3.2-1814.
Deduction of tax from payment to farmer, §3.2-1811.
Records, §3.2-1813.
Report and payment, §3.2-1811.
Revocation of license for failure, §3.2-1815.
Who deemed handler, §3.2-1800.
Interest, §3.2-1812.
Referendum on question of levying, §§3.2-1805 to 3.2-1809.
Virginia Potato fund, §3.2-1810.
Violation of provisions, §§3.2-1821, 3.2-1822.
Virginia Potato fund, §3.2-1810.
Dedicated revenues, diversion, §3.2-1100.

POTOMAC AND RAPPAHANNOCK TRANSPORTATION COMMISSION.
Members, §15.2-4507.

POTOMAC RIVER.
Basin commission, §§62.1-64 to 62.1-69.
Riparian rights, §§62.1-44.113 to 62.1-44.116.
Water protection permits.
Low-flow protections, §62.1-44.15:5.02.

POTOMAC RIVER BASIN COMMISSION, §§62.1-64 to 62.1-69, 1970 ch 464, 1979 ch 114.
Compact.
Authority to execute, §62.1-64.
Form, §62.1-65.
Terms, §62.1-65.
Creation, §62.1-66.
Duties, §62.1-69.
Members, §62.1-66.
Alternate members, §62.1-67.
Appointment, §62.1-67.
Expenses, §62.1-68.

POTOMAC RIVER BASIN COMMISSION —Cont'd
Members —Cont'd
Qualifications, §62.1-67.
Term, §62.1-67.
Voting restrictions, §62.1-69.
Powers, §62.1-69.
Structures upon the river or its tributaries.
Voting restrictions, §62.1-69.

POTOMAC RIVER COMPACT, §§28.2-1001 to 28.2-1007.
Agency cooperation, §28.2-1002.
Dredging of oysters.
Authority to regulate, §28.2-1005.
Dredging of soft shell clams.
Authority to regulate, §28.2-1003.
Experimental oyster hatchery program.
Authority to regulate, §28.2-1004.
Possession, marketing and disposal of shellfish out of commission's jurisdiction, §28.2-1006.

POTOMAC RIVER FISHERIES COMMISSION.
Regulation of leasing of river bottom, §28.2-1007.

POTOMAC RIVER RIPARIAN RIGHTS, §§62.1-44.113 to 62.1-44.116.
Citation of chapter, §62.1-44.113.
Riparian rights.
Use of river, §62.1-44.114.
Use of river, §62.1-44.114.
Dispute assistance by board, §62.1-44.116.
Review of uses, §62.1-44.115.

POTOMAC-SHENANDOAH RIVER BASIN.
Preparation of plans and programs for management, §62.1-44.38.

POULTRY.
Agricultural and forestal districts, §§15.2-4300 to 15.2-4407.
Agricultural cooperative associations, §§13.1-313 to 13.1-345.
See AGRICULTURAL COOPERATIVE ASSOCIATIONS.
Agriculture and consumer services board.
Diseases.
Laboratory for diagnosis, §3.2-5903.
Powers and duties as to, §§3.2-6001, 3.2-6002.
Law enforcement officers.
Duty to execute orders of board, §3.2-6013.
Animals generally.
See ANIMALS.
Avian influenza prevention and control measures, §3.2-6023.
Bioterrorism.
Penalties, §18.2-46.7.
Burial or cremation of dead fowl, §18.2-510.
Contagious and infectious diseases, §§3.2-6000 to 3.2-6023.
Altering disease control identification, §3.2-6016.
Anthrax, possession.
Unlawful activities, §3.2-6017.
Biological residues.
Abatement, §3.2-6002.
Bringing infected animals into Commonwealth, §3.2-6011.
Circuit court judges.
Enforcement of orders, §3.2-6014.
Compensation for euthanized or slaughtered animals, §3.2-6021.
Damages, §3.2-6019.

POULTRY —Cont'd
Contagious and infectious diseases —Cont'd
Enforcement of orders.
Circuit court judges, §3.2-6014.
Law enforcement officers, §3.2-6013.
Euthanasia or slaughter.
By owner, §3.2-6009.
Compensation, §3.2-6021.
Indemnity to owner, §3.2-6022.
Importation, proclamation prohibiting, §3.2-6010.
Violation, §3.2-6011.
Law enforcement officers.
Authority to execute orders, §3.2-6013.
Prevention and eradication, §3.2-6002.
Regulations, penalty for violations, §3.2-6023.
Protection of livestock and poultry, §3.2-6001.
Quarantine.
Disposition of quarantined animals with potential to impact livestock or poultry, §3.2-6008.
Domestic animals not permitted to enter or leave quarantine, §3.2-6007.
Individuals exposed, §3.2-6006.
Notice of quarantine, §3.2-6005.
Regulations.
Prevention and eradication, §3.2-6002.
Separation and caring for diseased animals, §3.2-6004.
Right of entry, §3.2-6000.
Separation and caring for diseased animals.
Regulations, §3.2-6004.
Slaughter facility operators, duties, §3.2-6012.
State veterinarian.
Duty when animals suspected of having disease, §3.2-6003.
Unlawful activities.
Altering disease control identification, §3.2-6016.
Anthrax, possession, §3.2-6017.
USDA, cooperation with, §3.2-6015.
Vaccine, authority to test, §3.2-6017.
Violations.
Liability for damages, §3.2-6019.
Penalty, §3.2-6018.
Prevention and control measures, §3.2-6023.
Damages.
Violations of certain provisions, §3.2-6019.
Definitions, §3.2-5900.
Disposal of dead poultry, §3.2-6024.
Diseases.
Importation.
Certificate of veterinary inspection required for importation of certain poultry, §3.2-5902.
Prohibited acts, §3.2-6011.
Laboratory for diagnosis of diseases, §3.2-5903.
Poultry slaughter yards.
Duties of operators, §3.2-6012.
Powers and duties of agriculture and consumer services board, §§3.2-6001, 3.2-6002.
Quarantine, §§3.2-6003 to 3.2-6008.
Disposal of dead poultry, §§3.2-6024 to 3.2-6030.
Damages for violations of provisions, §3.2-6019.
Dogs killing, injuring or chasing poultry, §§3.2-6552, 3.2-6553.
Hybrid canines, §3.2-6583.
Compensation for livestock and poultry killed, §3.2-6584.
Misdemeanor, §18.2-403.1.
Domestic animals generally, §§3.2-5900 to 3.2-5905.

POULTRY —Cont'd
Egg board, §§3.2-1600 to 3.2-1610.
See EGG BOARD.
Eggs and hatchery products.
See EGGS.
Estrays, §§55-202 to 55-206.
Feed generally, §§3.2-4800 to 3.2-4817.
See FEED.
Intangible personal property tax.
Certain livestock producers, §58.1-1102.
Generally, §§58.1-1100 to 58.1-1118.
See PERSONAL PROPERTY TAXES.
Larceny, §18.2-97.
Live-bird marketing system.
Avian influenza prevention and control measures, §3.2-6023.
Livestock.
Diseases.
See LIVESTOCK AND ANIMAL DISEASES.
Generally.
See LIVESTOCK.
Maiming, killing or poisoning fowl, §18.2-144.
Motor vehicle lights or spotlights employed causing animals to panic, §18.2-509.
Personal property taxes.
Classification of tangible personal property, §§58.1-3503, 58.1-3505.
Products inspection generally, §§3.2-5400 to 3.2-5418.
See MEAT AND POULTRY PRODUCTS INSPECTION.
Quarantine.
Contagious and infectious diseases, §§3.2-6003 to 3.2-6008.
Retail sales and use tax.
Agricultural exemptions, §58.1-609.2.
Rules and regulations.
Disposal of dead poultry, §3.2-6029.
Sale of unborn young, §8.2-105.
Unborn young, sale of, §8.2-105.
Weights and measures, §3.2-5634.

POULTRY WASTE MANAGEMENT PROGRAM, §62.1-44.17:1.1.

POULTRY WASTE RESOURCES.
Renewable electricity production program.
Grants, §§67-900 to 67-903.

POUNDS.
Abandoned, animal past holding period deemed, §3.2-6546.
Companion animal rescue agencies.
Contact information, §§3.2-6546, 3.2-6548.
Mistreatment of animals, §3.2-6503.
Confinement and disposition of animals, §3.2-6546.
Contact information, §§3.2-6546, 3.2-6548.
Destruction of animals, §3.2-6546.
Fees.
Owners, fees for confinement or repeated confinement of companion animal, §3.2-6546.
Feral dog or cat, destruction, §3.2-6546.
Foster care providers.
Affiliation with, §3.2-6546.
Foster homes.
Defined, §3.2-6500.
Mistreatment of animals, §3.2-6503.
Gift, sale or delivery of animals.
Animals past holding period, §3.2-6546.
Holding period, §3.2-6546.

POUNDS —Cont'd
Identification, duty of operator to ascertain, §3.2-6546.
Limit on delivery of animals to one person, §3.2-6546.
Maintenance by county or city, §3.2-6546.
Owners readily identifiable, notification, §3.2-6546.
Releasing agencies other than pounds or animal shelters, §3.2-6549.
Sale or gift to federal or state agency or federal dealer.
Animals past holding period, §3.2-6546.
Time period for keeping animals, §3.2-6546.

POUR-OVER ACT, §64.2-426.

POVERTY.
Indigency generally.
See INDIGENCY.

POWER COMPANIES.
Articles of incorporation.
Conducting business as public service company, statement required, §13.1-620.
Consumer utility tax, §58.1-3814.
Estimated tax, §§58.1-2640 to 58.1-2651.
See PUBLIC SERVICE CORPORATION TAXATION.
Generally, §§58.1-3814 to 58.1-3816.2.
License tax.
Generally, §§58.1-2620 to 58.1-2635.
See PUBLIC SERVICE CORPORATION TAXATION.
Municipal license taxes, §58.1-3731.
Meters.
Good working condition requirements, §56-245.1.
Pipelines, §§56-257 to 56-260.1.
Public service companies.
Generally, §§56-1 to 56-46.3.
See PUBLIC SERVICE COMPANIES.
Public utilities.
Generally, §§56-232 to 56-265.
See PUBLIC UTILITIES.
Special regulatory revenue tax, §§58.1-2660 to 58.1-2665.
Use of city or town property, consent required, VA Const Art VII §8.

POWER COMPANY LICENSE TAX.
Estimated tax, §§58.1-2640 to 58.1-2651.
See PUBLIC SERVICE CORPORATION TAXATION.
Generally, §§58.1-2620 to 58.1-2635.
See PUBLIC SERVICE CORPORATION TAXATION.

POWER LINES.
Application of provisions, §59.1-414.
Certificates of public convenience and necessity.
Issuance, §56-265.2.
Crossing of railroads, §56-16.1.
Municipalities, §56-16.2.
Defined terms, §59.1-407.
Duty where wires cross other works, §56-33.
Enforcement of provisions, §59.1-412.
Environmental, economic and service reliability considerations and construction, §56-46.1.
Exemption from provisions, §59.1-413.
Notice requirements, §59.1-411.
Obstructing or injuring, §18.2-153.

POWER LINES —Cont'd
Overhead high voltage line safety, §§59.1-406 to 59.1-414.
Permits to place, §56-15.
Pole use rates, §56-41.1.
Private highways, crossing, §56-547.
Prohibited conduct, §59.1-408.
Scope of provisions, §59.1-406.
Secondhand article sales.
Company equipment, §§59.1-125 to 59.1-130.
Submerged lands.
Structures, maintenance or removal, §28.2-1209.
Temporary safety arrangements, §59.1-410.
Underground utility line damage prevention, §§56-265.14 to 56-265.32.
See UNDERGROUND UTILITY LINE DAMAGE PREVENTION.
Warning signs, §59.1-409.

POWER OF APPOINTMENT.
Release, §§64.2-2700 to 64.2-2704.
Representation.
Persons representing and binding other.
Generally, §§64.2-714 to 64.2-718.
Holder of general testamentary power of appointment.
Authority to represent and bind another, §64.2-715.
Trusts.
Exercise in favor of trustee.
Method of creating trust, §64.2-719.
Revocable trusts.
Holder of power of withdrawal.
Rights of settlor, §64.2-752.
Power of withdrawal defined, §64.2-701.
Wills.
Construed to refer to federal gift tax exclusion, §64.2-431.
Exceptions, §§64.2-407, 64.2-408.
Murderers barred from claiming property rights of decedent, §64.2-2507.
Residuary clauses construed, §64.2-423.
Validity when executed by, §64.2-406.

POWER OF APPOINTMENT OF CIRCUIT JUDGES, §17.1-501.

POWER OF ATTORNEY.
Acceptance of acknowledged power of attorney, §64.2-1617.
Liability for refusal to accept, §64.2-1618.
Acceptance of appointment as agent, §64.2-1611.
Acknowledgments issued for principal, §55-118.6.
Additional nature of remedies, §64.2-1621.
Agents.
Acceptance of appointment as, §64.2-1611.
Authority, §§64.2-1622 to 64.2-1638.
Certification.
Form, §64.2-1639.
Co-agent, §64.2-1609.
Compensation, §64.2-1610.
Court-appointed fiduciary.
Relation to, §64.2-1606.
Defined, §64.2-1600.
Delegation of duties, §64.2-1612.
Disclosures, §64.2-1612.
Duties, §64.2-1612.
Exoneration, §64.2-1613.
Immunity from liability, §64.2-1612.
Judicial review of conduct, §64.2-1614.

POWER OF ATTORNEY —Cont'd
Agents —Cont'd
Liability, §64.2-1615.
Reimbursement, §64.2-1610.
Resignation, §64.2-1616.
Successor agents, §64.2-1609.
Termination of agent's authority, §64.2-1608.
Anatomical gifts.
Advance health care directive, effect of gift, §32.1-291.21.
Annuities.
Authority of agent as to insurance and annuities, §64.2-1631.
Applicability of act, §64.2-1601.
Existing powers of attorney, §64.2-1642.
Uniformity of application and construction, §64.2-1640.
Armed forces members.
Deeds and writings executed for personnel while under defective powers, §55-56.
Authority of agent, §§64.2-1622 to 64.2-1638.
Banks and financial institutions, §64.2-1629.
Benefits from governmental programs or civil or military service, §64.2-1635.
Claims and litigation, §64.2-1633.
Commodities, §64.2-1628.
Construction of authority, §64.2-1624.
Estates, trusts and other beneficial interests, §64.2-1632.
Family and household management, §64.2-1634.
General authority.
Grant of, §64.2-1622.
Gifts, §64.2-1638.
Taxes, §64.2-1637.
Incorporation by reference, §64.2-1623.
Insurance and annuities, §64.2-1631.
Operation of entity or business, §64.2-1630.
Options, §64.2-1628.
Personal and family maintenance, §64.2-1634.
Personal property.
Tangible personal property, §64.2-1626.
Real property, §64.2-1625.
Retirement plans, §64.2-1636.
Scope of authority, §64.2-1624.
Specific grant.
Authority that requires, §64.2-1622.
Stocks and bonds, §64.2-1627.
Operation of entity or business, §64.2-1630.
Taxes, §64.2-1637.
Banks and financial institutions.
Applicability of other laws, §64.2-1620.
Authority of agent with respect to, §64.2-1629.
Co-agent, §64.2-1609.
Condominiums.
Owners' associations.
Control of common elements, §55-79.80.
Variations of chapter by agreement, §55-79.41:1.
Confession of judgment.
Attorney-in-fact, §§8.01-432 to 8.01-441.
See CONFESSION OF JUDGMENT.
Conflict of laws.
Financial institutions and entities.
Applicability of other laws, §64.2-1620.
Governing law, §64.2-1605.
Conservator.
Nomination, §64.2-1606.
Construction and interpretation.
Reference to former section or provision of code, §64.2-108.2.
Consumer finance companies.
Power not to be taken by licensee for certain purposes, §6.2-1524.

POWER OF ATTORNEY —Cont'd
Conveyances.
Authority of agent as to real property, §64.2-1625.
Credit counseling.
Business practices and methods, §6.2-2014.
Death of principal.
Termination of power, §64.2-1608.
Deeds.
Execution for military personnel while under defective powers, §55-56.
Informalities in deeds by attorney-in-fact, §55-23.
Definitions, §64.2-1600.
Acknowledged, §64.2-1617.
Benefits from governmental programs or civil or military service, §64.2-1635.
Estates, trusts and other beneficial interests, §64.2-1632.
Retirement plan, §64.2-1636.
Disability of principal, when power not terminated by.
Safe deposit boxes.
Limited access to safe deposit boxes, §6.2-2303.
Domestic reciprocals.
Subscribers agreement and power of attorney, §38.2-1223.
Modification, §38.2-1224.
Durable power of attorney.
Definition of durable, §64.2-1600.
Health care durable powers.
Anatomical gifts.
Advance health care directive, effect of gift, §32.1-291.21.
Living wills, §§54.1-2981 to 54.1-2993.
See HEALTH CARE DURABLE POWER OF ATTORNEY.
Power of attorney durable unless expressly provided otherwise, §64.2-1602.
Electronic signatures in global and national commerce act.
Relation of uniform act to, §64.2-1641.
Electronic transmission.
Effect same as original, §64.2-1604.
Execution of power, §64.2-1603.
Effect, §§64.2-1604, 64.2-1607.
Existing powers of attorney.
Effect of act on, §64.2-1642.
Exoneration of agent, §64.2-1613.
Fidelity and surety insurers, power of agent to execute bonds.
Attachment to bond or obligation, §38.2-2416.
Bonds executed under power binding on insurer, §38.2-2420.
Continuance of power, §38.2-2417.
Recording, §38.2-2416.
Revocation, §38.2-2417.
Marginal notation, §38.2-2419.
Recording, §38.2-2418.
Fiduciaries generally.
See FIDUCIARIES.
Financial institutions and entities.
Applicability of other laws, §64.2-1620.
Authority of agent with respect to, §64.2-1629.
Forms.
Agent's certification, §64.2-1639.
Future contingencies.
Effect, §64.2-1604.
General provisions, §§64.2-1600 to 64.2-1642.
Governing law to determine meaning and effect, §64.2-1605.
Grandfather clause.
Existing powers of attorney, effect of act on, §64.2-1642.

POWER OF ATTORNEY —Cont'd
Guardian.
Nomination, §64.2-1606.
Health care durable power of attorney.
Anatomical gifts.
Advance health care directive, effect of gift, §32.1-291.21.
Living wills, §§54.1-2981 to 54.1-2993.
See HEALTH CARE DURABLE POWER OF ATTORNEY.
Incapacity of principal.
When power terminated, §64.2-1608.
Incorporation by reference.
Letters and memoranda, §64.2-104.
Insurance.
Authority of agent as to insurance and annuities, §64.2-1631.
Judicial relief, §64.2-1614.
Liability.
Agent, §64.2-1615.
Immunity from liability, §64.2-1612.
Refusal to accept acknowledged power of attorney, §64.2-1618.
Married women.
Appointment of attorney-in-fact and powers, §55-43.
Membership camping.
Registration.
Application accompaniments, §59.1-318.
Military and emergency laws.
Laws continued in effect, §44-207.
Mortgages.
Authority of agent as to real property, §64.2-1625.
Motor carriers, passengers.
Ratemaking.
Common carriers.
Tariffs showing rates, fares, etc.
Joint tariffs, §46.2-2093.
Motor carriers, property.
Household goods carriers.
Rates, charges, etc.
Tariffs showing rates, charges, etc.
Joint tariff, §46.2-2172.
Nonresident insurer or contractor.
Fee charged by secretary of Commonwealth, §2.2-409.
Notice.
Resignation of agent, §64.2-1616.
Personal property.
Authority of agent.
Tangible personal property, §64.2-1626.
Petition for construction of power, §64.2-1614.
Photocopy same effect as original, §64.2-1604.
Principal, execution for, §55-118.6.
Principles of law and equity to supplement, §64.2-1619.
Real property.
Authority of agent, §64.2-1625.
Reciprocal insurers generally, §§38.2-1200 to 38.2-1231.
Reciprocal insurers, service of process on.
Appointment of clerk of state corporation commission as agent, §38.2-1216.
Recordation, §55-107.
Recording in deed book, §17.1-227.
Reference to former section or provision of code.
Construction and interpretation, §64.2-108.2.
Reliance on acknowledged power of attorney, §64.2-1617

POWER OF ATTORNEY —Cont'd
Remedies and judicial relief available, §64.2-1614.
Under other laws, §64.2-1621.
Revocation of power, §64.2-1608.
Safe deposit boxes.
Incapacity of sole lessee.
Limited access to safe deposit boxes, §6.2-2303.
Savings institutions.
Savings account, §6.2-1173.
Signatures.
Execution of power, §64.2-1603.
Special skills of agent, §64.2-1612.
Successor agents, §64.2-1609.
Surety bail bondsmen.
Licensing application, §9.1-185.5.
Taxation.
Authority of agent as to taxes, §64.2-1637.
Taxpayer meetings.
Representation of taxpayer, §58.1-1834.
Termination of power, §64.2-1608.
Trusts and trustees.
Agent authorized to create trust on settlor's behalf.
Method of creating trust, §64.2-719.
Authority of agent.
Estates, trusts and other beneficial interests, §64.2-1632.
Revocable trusts.
Agent under power exercising settlor's powers, §64.2-751.
Uniformity of application and construction, §64.2-1640.
Uniform power of attorney act, §§64.2-1600 to 64.2-1642.
Validity of power, §64.2-1604.
Voter registration.
Prohibition on use of power of attorney, §24.2-123.
When power effective, §64.2-1607.

POWERS OF LOCAL GOVERNMENT.
Cities.
Uniform charter powers and other powers generally, §§15.2-1100 to 15.2-1133.
See CITIES.
Counties.
Miscellaneous powers, §§15.2-1200 to 15.2-1232.
See COUNTIES.
General powers, §§15.2-900 to 15.2-982.
See LOCALITIES.
Towns.
Uniform charter powers and other powers generally, §§15.2-1100 to 15.2-1133.
See TOWNS.

POWHATAN COUNTY.
Confederate cemeteries and graves.
Disbursement of funds appropriated for upkeep, §10.1-2211.
School board.
Salary of members, §22.1-32.
Well abandonment ordinance.
Duty of owner to cap or close well.
Locality adopting ordinance, §32.1-176.5.
Well construction.
Permits, §32.1-176.4.
Testing requirements, §32.1-176.5.

POW/MIA FLAG.
Display, §2.2-3310.1.

PRACTICAL NURSES.
Correctional health assistants, §54.1-3016.1.

PRACTICAL NURSES —Cont'd
Duty to protect third parties.
Violent behavior or serious harm by client, §54.1-2400.1.
Influenza vaccine.
Administration to minors by pharmacists or nurses, §§32.1-46.02, 54.1-3408.
Licensing, §§54.1-3019 to 54.1-3021.
Records of patients.
Admissibility of copies, §8.01-413.
Medical records generally.
See MEDICAL RECORDS.
Right of patient, attorney or authorized insurer to copies, §8.01-413.
Subpoenas, §8.01-413.

PRACTICE OF COUNSELING.
Professional counseling and marriage and family therapy, §54.1-3500.

PRACTICE OF LAW.
Attorneys generally.
See ATTORNEYS AT LAW.
Commonwealth's attorneys.
Full-time attorneys in certain counties.
Private practice prohibited, §15.2-1628.
Full-time devotion to duties in certain cities.
Private practice of law prohibited, §15.2-1630.
Part-time attorneys electing full-time status.
Private practice prohibited, §§15.2-1629, 15.2-1631.
Professional corporations, §54.1-3902.
Proceedings pending disciplinary action, §54.1-3936.
Revocation of certificate of registration, §54.1-3937.
Professional limited liability companies, §54.1-3902.
Proceedings pending disciplinary action, §54.1-3936.
Revocation of certificate of registration, §54.1-3937.
Registered limited liability partnerships, §54.1-3902.
Unauthorized practice of law, VA SCt Rule Pt 6 §I UPR 4.
See ATTORNEYS AT LAW.

PRACTICE OF LAW LIMITATION.
Court of appeals judges, §17.1-400.
District court judges, §16.1-69.12.
Judges generally, VA SCt Rule Pt 6 §III Canon 4.
Justices or judges of courts of record, §17.1-102, VA Const Art VI §11.
Juvenile and domestic relations district court judges, §16.1-69.12.
Supreme court clerk, deputy clerk or court employee, §17.1-102.

PRACTICE OF MARRIAGE AND FAMILY THERAPY, §54.1-3500.

PRACTICE OF MEDICINE.
Clinical psychologist.
Defined as psychological assessment and psychotherapy not amounting to practice of medicine, §54.1-3600.
Conditional grants for certain medical students, §32.1-122.6.
Defined, §54.1-2900.
Health maintenance organization not engaged in unlawful practice, §38.2-4319.
Physician and podiatrist assistants.
See PHYSICIAN ASSISTANTS.

PRACTICE OF MEDICINE —Cont'd
Professional counselors.
Provisions not construed as infringing on practice of medicine, §54.1-3502.
Psychologists.
Provisions not construed as infringing on practice of medicine, §54.1-3602.
Social workers.
Provisions not construed as infringing on practice of medicine, §54.1-3702.

PRACTITIONER SELF-REFERRALS, §§54.1-2410 to 54.1-2414.
Disclosures of interest in referral facilities, §54.1-2964.
Receipt of remuneration, §54.1-2962.1.
Solicitation of remuneration, §54.1-2962.1.

PRADER-WILLI SYNDROME.
Defined, §51.5-116.

PRAECIPE.
Local rules of court.
Forms, VA SCt Rules Part 1 Appx Form 1.
Use of praecipe to manage civil docket, VA SCt Rule 1:15.
Use of prescribed form required, VA SCt Rule 1:15.

PRAYER IN SCHOOLS.
Daily observance of one minute of silence, §22.1-203.
Guidelines for constitutional compliance, §22.1-203.2.
Student-initiated prayer, §22.1-203.1.

PRECINCTS.
Absentee voting.
Central absentee voter precinct, §24.2-712.
Defined, §24.2-101.
Changes not to be enacted within sixty days of general election, §24.2-306.
City precinct requirements, §24.2-307.
Composition, §24.2-305.
County precinct requirements, §24.2-307.
Defined, §24.2-101.
Notice of changes, §24.2-306.
Population requirements, §24.2-307.
Less than minimum number of voters where voters do not have same choice of candidates, §24.2-309.
Revision to comply with population requirements, §24.2-307.
Town precinct requirements, §24.2-308.
Voters not having same choice of candidates.
Establishment with less than minimum number of voters, §24.2-309.

PRECIOUS METALS.
Personal property taxes.
Classification, §58.1-3504.

PRECIOUS METALS DEALERS, §§54.1-4100 to 54.1-4111.
Defined terms, §54.1-4100.
Digital image of identification of customer, retaining, §54.1-4101.
Examination of records by law enforcement, §54.1-4101.1.
Exemptions from provisions, §54.1-4109.
Law enforcement officers, admission to place of business, §54.1-4101.1.
Letters of credit, §54.1-4106.
Private action on letter, §54.1-4107.

PRECIOUS METALS DEALERS —Cont'd
Local ordinances, §54.1-4111.
Permits, §§54.1-4106, 54.1-4108.
Prohibited purchases, §54.1-4103.
Provision violations.
Penalties, §54.1-4110.
Records, §§54.1-4101, 54.1-4101.1.
Disposition records, §54.1-4105.
Retention of purchases, §54.1-4104.
Search for missing or stolen articles, §54.1-4101.1.
Statements of ownership.
Dealer purchasing prerequisite, §54.1-4102.
Surety bonds, §54.1-4106.
Private action on bonds, §54.1-4107.
Unlawful procurement of licensure, §54.1-102.
Unlawful use of licensure, §54.1-111.

PRECIOUS STONES.
Personal property taxes.
Classification, §58.1-3504.

PRECISION INVESTMENT CASTINGS.
Personal property taxes.
Separate classification of machinery and tools used in manufacturing, §58.1-3508.3.

PREEMPTION OF FEDERAL SECURITIES LAW, §13.1-514.2.

PREEMPTIVE RIGHTS OF SHAREHOLDERS, §13.1-651.

PREEXISTING CONDITIONS.
Credit life insurance rates, §38.2-3726.
Health insurance.
Adoption.
Coverage of adopted children required, §38.2-3411.2.
Credit for previous coverage, §38.2-3514.1.
Federal market reforms.
Exclusions prohibited, §38.2-3444.
Individual policy provision, §38.2-3503.
Continuing coverage, §38.2-3430.3.
Minimum standards for coverage, §38.2-3520.
When liability not denied because of preexisting disease, physical impairment or defect, §38.2-3514.
Small employer market, §38.2-3432.3.
Health maintenance organizations.
Affiliation period, §38.2-4322.
Long-term care insurance, §38.2-5204.
Medicare supplement policy coverage, §38.2-3605.

PREFABRICATED HOUSING.
See MANUFACTURED HOUSING.

PREFERENCES.
Coal.
Virginia coal used in state facilities, §2.2-4325.
Community reinvestment.
Contracts for investment of funds, §2.2-4327.
Public procurement.
Contracts for investment of funds.
Affordable housing considerations, §2.2-4327.
Recycled paper and paper products.
Purchasing programs for state agencies, §2.2-4323.
Use by state agencies, §2.2-4326.
Veterans.
Local government employment, §15.2-1509.
Virginia products and Virginia firms.
Products with recycled content, §2.2-4324

PREFERRED PROVIDER PLANS.
Health benefit programs, §38.2-3407.
Individual or group exclusive provider policies and contract, §38.2-3407.
Health services plans, §38.2-4209.
Podiatrists.
Exclusions, §38.2-3407.6.

PREFERRED STOCK.
Insurance companies investments, §38.2-1423.

PREGNANCY.
AIDS.
HIV testing, §54.1-2403.01.
Blood samples.
Hospitals to offer to obtain blood sample from newborn infants and provide to mother, §32.1-134.02.
Contraceptives.
Health insurance coverage, §38.2-3407.5:1.
Cord blood bank initiative.
Established, §32.1-69.3.
Providing information to pregnant women, §54.1-2403.02.
Publication of information, §32.1-69.4.
Criminal offenses.
Aggravated malicious wounding, §18.2-51.2.
Killing a fetus, §18.2-32.2.
Murder of pregnant women, §18.2-32.1.
Capital murder, §18.2-31.
Descent and distribution.
Pretermitted children, §§64.2-419, 64.2-420.
Discrimination.
Human rights act, §§2.2-3900 to 2.2-3903.
Down syndrome or other prenatally diagnosed conditions.
Counseling for women with positive test results, §54.1-2403.01.
Health insurance.
Public officers and employees.
Required coverage, §2.2-2818.
Human cloning, §§32.1-162.21, 32.1-162.22.
Maternal and child health services plan, §§32.1-77, 32.1-78.
Midwives generally.
See MIDWIVES.
Minor deemed adult for purposes of consent.
Medical or health services required, §54.1-2969.
Postpartum services insurance coverages, §38.2-3414.1.
Medical assistance services plans, §32.1-325.
Substance abuse.
Rulemaking authority, §37.2-407.
Surrogacy contracts, §§20-156 to 20-165.
See SURROGACY CONTRACTS.
Termination of pregnancy.
Abortion generally, §§18.2-71 to 18.2-76.1.
See ABORTION.
Aggravated malicious wounding, §18.2-51.2.
Venereal test, §32.1-60.
Virginia pregnant women support fund, §32.1-11.6.
Wills.
Pretermitted children, §§64.2-419, 64.2-420.

PREJUDGMENT INTEREST, §8.01-382.

PREJUDICE.
Discrimination generally.
See DISCRIMINATION.
Evidence.
Exclusion of relevant evidence, VA SCt Rule 2:403.
Witnesses, VA SCt Rule 2:610.

PRELIMINARY HEARINGS, §§19.2-183 to 19.2-190.
Adjournment.
Power to adjourn case, §19.2-183.
Attorneys.
Appointment of counsel, §19.2-183.
Autopsy records and reports.
Admissibility of evidence, §19.2-188.
Bail.
When accused to be bailed by judge, §19.2-186.
Certificates of analysis.
Admissibility of evidence, §19.2-187.
Chain of custody evidence, §19.2-187.01.
Right to examine person involved in chain of custody, §19.2-187.1.
Procedure for subpoena duces tecum of analysis evidence, §19.2-187.2.
Closed hearing.
Victims or witnesses of sex offenses.
Informing of right to, §19.2-11.01.
Commitment of accused.
Order for commitment for further examination, §19.2-189.
Subsequent examination, §19.2-189.
When accused to be committed by judge, §19.2-186.
Contemporaneous and related acts or occurrences.
Joint preliminary hearings, §19.2-183.1.
Controlled substances.
Law-enforcement field test results, §19.2-188.1.
Criteria for judicial action, §19.2-186.
Discharge of accused.
Criteria, §19.2-186.
District courts.
Powers to conduct preliminary examinations, §16.1-127.
Speedy trial on felony charge, §19.2-243.
Election recounts, §24.2-802.
Evidence.
Blood alcohol tests conducted in regular course of providing emergency medical treatment.
Admissibility of records or reports, §19.2-187.02.
Certificate of surgeon.
Removal of organs or other body parts for transplant, §19.2-188.2.
Certificates of analysis.
Admissibility, §19.2-187.
Without testimony of preparer, §19.2-183.
Chain of custody evidence, §19.2-187.01.
Procedure for subpoena duces tecum of analysis evidence, §19.2-187.2.
Right to examine person performing analysis, §19.2-187.1.
Controlled substances.
Law-enforcement field test results, §19.2-188.1.
Evidentiary matters and remedies, §19.2-183.
Government records search, affidavit of government official, §19.2-188.3.
Reports of medical examiner, §19.2-188.
Admissibility without testimony of preparer, §19.2-183.
Subscription and reduction of writing of testimony, §19.2-185.
Government records search.
Admissibility of affidavit of government official, §19.2-188.3.
Inanimate object sexual penetration, §§19.2-218.1, 19.2-218.2.
Indictments, presentments and informations.
General provisions, §§19.2-216 to 19.2-238.
See INDICTMENTS, PRESENTMENTS AND INFORMATIONS.

PRELIMINARY HEARINGS —Cont'd
Joint preliminary hearings, §19.2-183.1.
Juvenile transferred for proper criminal proceedings, §16.1-269.1.
Marital sexual assault, §§19.2-218.1, 19.2-218.2.
Production of documents and things.
Certificates of analysis.
Procedure for subpoena duces tecum of analysis evidence, §19.2-187.2.
Rape.
Spousal rape, §§19.2-218.1, 19.2-218.2.
Recognizances.
Certification of examination and recognizance, §19.2-190.
Required unless waived, §19.2-218.
Right to counsel.
Informing accused, §19.2-183.
Sexual assault cases, exclusion of public, §18.2-67.8.
Sodomy.
Forcible sodomy, §§19.2-218.1, 19.2-218.2.
Spousal sexual crimes, §§19.2-218.1, 19.2-218.2.
Two-way video testimony.
Certificates of analysis, presenting, §19.2-187.01.
Victims or witnesses of sex offenses.
Closed hearing.
Informing of right to, §19.2-11.01.
Witnesses.
Examination of witnesses, §19.2-183.
Sequestration of witnesses, §19.2-184.

PREMARITAL AGREEMENTS, §§20-147 to 20-155.
Amendment, §20-153.
Applicability of act, §20-147.
Construction of act, §20-147.
Contents, §20-150.
Defenses to enforcement.
Laches and estoppel, §20-152.
Void marriage, §20-151.
Definitions, §20-148.
Electronic filing of documents.
Instruments for which electronic medium not acceptable, §17.1-258.6.
Enforcement, §20-151.
Formalities, §20-149.
Homestead allowance waivers, §64.2-314.
Limitation of actions, §20-152.
Marital agreements, §20-155.
Postnuptial agreements, §20-155.
Prior agreements, §20-154.
Revocation, §20-153.
Signatures requirement, §20-149.
Unconscionability issue, §20-151.
Validity of prior agreements, §20-154.
Writing requirement, §20-149.

PREMISES LIABILITY.
Firefighters and law enforcement officers.
Duty of care owed, §8.01-226.
Hunting and fishing, §29.1-509.
Landlord and tenant.
Limitation of landlord's liability, §55-248.14.

PREMIUM FINANCE COMPANIES, INSURANCE, §§38.2-4700 to 38.2-4712.
See INSURANCE PREMIUM FINANCE COMPANIES.

PRENATAL CARE.
Down syndrome or other prenatally diagnosed conditions.
Counseling women with positive test results, §54.1-2403.01.

PRENATAL CARE —Cont'd
HIV testing, §54.1-2403.01.

PRENEED BURIAL CONTRACTS.
Generally, §§54.1-2310 to 54.1-2342.

PRENEED FUNERAL CONTRACTS, §§54.1-2820 to 54.1-2825.
Annuity contracts used to fund.
Requirements, §38.2-3100.3.
Declarations of trust, §54.1-2824.
Deposits of money received, §54.1-2822.
Exemption from levy, garnishment and distress, §54.1-2823.
Designation of person to make arrangements, §54.1-2825.
Exemptions, §54.1-2821.
Irrevocable trust, §54.1-2820.
Life insurance contracts used to fund.
Requirements, §38.2-3100.3.
Records, §54.1-2822.1.
Requirements, §54.1-2820.
Trust accounts.
Deposits of money received, trustees, restrictions on persons serving as, §54.1-2822.

PRENUPTIAL AGREEMENTS.
See PREMARITAL AGREEMENTS.

PREORGANIZATION CERTIFICATE OF SUBSCRIPTION.
Securities generally, §§13.1-501 to 13.1-527.3.
See SECURITIES.

PRE-PACE LONG-TERM CARE PREPAID HEALTH PLANS.
Applicability of insurance title.
Exceptions, §38.2-226.2.
Operation and oversight, §32.1-330.3.

PREPAID CALLING SERVICE.
Communications sales and use tax, §§58.1-645 to 58.1-662.
See COMMUNICATIONS SALES AND USE TAX.

PREPAID COLLEGE TUITION AND SAVINGS, §§23-38.72 to 23-38.87:1.
See COLLEGE SAVINGS PLAN.

PREPAID METERING EQUIPMENT AND SYSTEM.
Electric utilities.
Installation upon customer requests, §56-247.1.

PREPARER'S NAME ON RECORDED DOCUMENTS, §17.1-223.

PREPARING FOR THE TOP JOBS OF THE 21ST CENTURY.
Virginia higher education opportunity act of 2011, §§23-38.87:10 to 23-38.87:21.
See COLLEGES AND UNIVERSITIES.

PREPAYMENT OF FINES.
Non-traffic offenses, §16.1-69.40:2.
Non-traffic prepayable offenses and uniform fine schedule, VA SCt Rules 3C:1, 3C:2.
Traffic infractions, §16.1-69.40:1.
Traffic infractions and uniform fine schedule, VA SCt Rules 3B:1, 3B:2.

PREPAYMENT OF LOANS.
Industrial loan association borrowers, §6.2-1409.
Penalties.
Industrial loan association borrowers, §6.2-1409.
Subordinate mortgage loans, §6.2-103.

PRE-RELEASE FACILITIES.
Community-based corrections system for state-responsible offenders.
Generally, §§53.1-67.2 to 53.1-67.6.
See COMMUNITY-BASED CORRECTIONS SYSTEM FOR STATE-RESPONSIBLE OFFENDERS.
Program included, §53.1-67.6.
Community corrections.
Generally, §§9.1-173 to 9.1-183.
See COMMUNITY CORRECTIONS.
Optional programs, §9.1-176.
Public procurement.
Exemptions from chapter, §2.2-4343.

PRESCHOOLS.
Accredited private school program.
Child welfare agency licensure and regulation.
Exemption from provision, conditions for exemption, §63.2-1717.
Board of education.
Accreditation regulations, §22.1-19.
Certification and conditions for operating, §63.2-1717.
Child welfare agency licensure and regulation.
Exemption from provision, conditions for exemption, §63.2-1717.
Physical examinations, §22.1-270.
Program for at-risk four-year-olds, §22.1-199.1.
Special education.
Reimbursement to school board operating preschool special education program, §22.1-218.

PRESCRIBED BURNING, §§10.1-1150.1 to 10.1-1150.6.
Certified prescribed burn manager.
Defined, §10.1-1150.1.
Requirements for voluntary certification, §10.1-1150.3.
Revocation of certification, §10.1-1150.6.
Defined, §10.1-1150.1.
Elements of prescribed burn, §10.1-1150.4.
Landowner or agent not liable, §10.1-1150.5.
Manner in which prescribed burn to be performed, §10.1-1150.4.
Map of area to be burned.
Prescription to include, §10.1-1150.4.
Negligent or improper conduct of prescribed burn, §10.1-1150.5.
Notice to department of forestry prior to burn, §10.1-1150.4.
Nuisance.
Burning in public interest and not nuisance, §10.1-1150.5.
Prescription.
Defined, §10.1-1150.1.
Preparation by prescribed burn manager and requirements, §10.1-1150.4.
Smoke management plan, prescription to include, §10.1-1150.4.
State forester to develop and administer certification process and training course, §10.1-1150.2.
Training program, §10.1-1150.2.

PRESCRIBED BURN MANAGERS.
Certified managers, §§10.1-1150.1 to 10.1-1150.6.

PRESCRIPTION DRUG DONATION PROGRAM.
Accepting unused previously dispensed prescription drugs, §54.1-3411.1.

PRESCRIPTION MONITORING PROGRAM, §§54.1-2519 to 54.1-2526.
Access to database.
Delegation of authority, §54.1-2523.2.
Advisory committee.
Establishment by director, §54.1-2520.
Applicability, §54.1-2520.
Confidential information, §54.1-2523.
Immunity from liability, accidental disclosure, §54.1-2524.
Unlawful disclosure of information, §54.1-2525.
Defined terms, §54.1-2519.
Director.
Immunity from liability, §54.1-2524.
Powers and duties, §54.1-2520.
Establishment of program, §54.1-2520.
Freedom of information.
Exemption, §54.1-2523.
Immunity from liability, §54.1-2524.
Information technologies agency requirements.
Exemptions, §54.1-2526.
Misuse by recipients of covered substances.
Criteria, development, disclosure of information, §54.1-2523.1.
Reports, §54.1-2521.
Confidential information, §54.1-2523.
Exemptions, §54.1-2522.

PRESCRIPTIONS.
Assisting person in unlawfully procuring prescription drugs, §18.2-258.2.
Biosimilars.
Adulterated drugs, prohibited acts, §54.1-3457.
Interchangeable biosimilars dispensed, §54.1-3408.04.
Nonresident pharmacies, compliance with provisions, §54.1-3434.1.
Cards, §32.1-325.
Civil commitment of mentally ill persons.
Drugs and medicines.
Providing person discharged from state facilities, §37.2-843.
Compounding, §54.1-3410.2.
Contraband.
Controlled substances.
Nonresident pharmacies ordering or shipping in violation of chapter, §54.1-3434.4.
Delivery of prescription drug order, §54.1-3420.2.
Distribution by manufacturers and wholesalers.
Generally, §54.1-3415.
Donations.
Indigent patient programs offered by pharmaceutical manufacturers, §54.1-3301.
Prescription drug donation program.
Accepting unused previously dispensed prescription drugs, §54.1-3411.1.
Drug control act.
Generally, §§54.1-3400 to 54.1-3472.
See DRUG CONTROL.
Drug offenses.
Generally, §§18.2-247 to 18.2-264.
See DRUG OFFENSES.
Electronic or fax transmission, §54.1-3408.02.
Electronic prescribing clearinghouse.
Secretary of health and human resources.
Duties regarding, §2.2-213.3.
Exceeding recommended dosages, §54.1-2971.01.

PRESCRIPTIONS —Cont'd
Eyeglasses.
Filling at establishment of patient's choice.
Right of patient, informing patient, §54.1-2914.
Facsimile machines, §54.1-3408.
Filling and refilling, §§54.1-3410, 54.1-3411.
Recordation by pharmacists, §54.1-3412.
Forgery or alteration, §18.2-258.1.
Free or discount drug programs offered by drug companies.
Toll-free number maintained by commissioner of health, §32.1-23.
Generic substitutes.
Workers' compensation.
Use of therapeutically equivalent drug product instead of brand name, §65.2-603.1.
Health insurance.
Public officers and employees.
Required coverage for prescription drugs, §2.2-2818.
Healthy lives prescription fund, §2.2-214.1.
Identification requirements, §54.1-3420.1.
Indigent patient programs offered by pharmaceutical manufacturers.
Practitioner of medicine or osteopathy participating in, §54.1-3301.
Interchangeable biosimilars dispensed, §54.1-3408.04.
Nonresident pharmacies, compliance with provisions, §54.1-3434.1.
Marijuana, possession or distribution for medical purposes, §18.2-251.1.
Medical insurance benefits.
Contraceptives, §38.2-3407.5:1.
Denial for certain drugs, §38.2-3407.5.
Prescription benefit cards, requirements, §38.2-3407.4:2.
Midwives.
Certified nurse midwife.
Pilot programs.
Prescribing schedule III through VI controlled substances, §54.1-2957.01.
Misbranded drug or device exemption, §54.1-3463.
Monitoring program, §§54.1-2519 to 54.1-2526.
Nurse practitioners.
Acceptance of signature, §54.1-2957.02.
Controlled substances and devices, §54.1-2957.01.
Pain relief, medical necessity.
Exceeding recommended dosage, §54.1-3408.
Pharmacists.
Professional regulation generally, §§54.1-3300 to 54.1-3321.
See PHARMACISTS AND PHARMACIES.
Pharmacists filling before receipt in writing, §18.2-248.
Pharmacy identification cards, §32.1-325.
Physician assistants.
Prescription by, §54.1-2952.1.
Prescription drug donation program.
Accepting unused previously dispensed prescription drugs, §54.1-3411.1.
Prescription monitoring program, §§54.1-2519 to 54.1-2526.
Professional counselors.
Drug prescriptions, §54.1-3502.
Psychologists.
Administration of drugs by psychologists, §54.1-3602.
Radiopharmaceuticals, §54.1-3410.1.

PRESCRIPTIONS —Cont'd
Relief of intractable pain, medical necessity, §54.1-3408.1.
Requirements for elements, §§54.1-3408, 54.1-3408.01.
Electronic or fax transmissions, §54.1-3408.02.
Retail sales and use tax exemptions, §58.1-609.10.
Returns, exchanges or re-dispensing of drugs.
Prohibition, §54.1-3411.1.
Schedule V drugs, §54.1-3416.
Schedule VI controlled drugs, §54.1-3455.
Social workers.
Administration or prescription of drugs by social workers, §54.1-3702.
Therapeutically equivalent drug products, §54.1-3408.03.
Virginia Medicaid prior authorization advisory committee.
Administrative process act.
Exemptions, §2.2-4002.
Workers' compensation.
Use of therapeutically equivalent drug product instead of brand name, §65.2-603.1.

PRESCRIPTIVE EASEMENTS.
Political subdivision establishing easement involving provision of water and sewer services.
Period of continued to be demonstrated, §15.2-2109.1.

PRESENCE AT TRIAL, §19.2-259, VA Const Art I §8, US Const Amd 6.

PRESENTENCING PROCEDURE.
Investigations and reports by probation officers, §19.2-299.
Presentence reports, §19.2-299.
Victim impact statement included, §19.2-299.1.
Sexual abnormality of offender indicted, §§19.2-300 to 19.2-302.
Victim impact statements, §§19.2-299, 19.2-299.1.
Investigations and reports by probation officers, §19.2-299.
When required, §19.2-299.1.

PRESENTMENT.
Bank deposits and collections.
Documentary drafts.
Duty to send for presentment, §8.4-501.
On arrival drafts, §8.4-502.
Electronic presentment, §8.4-110.
Responsibility of presenting banks, §8.4-503.
Criminal procedure, §§19.2-216 to 19.2-238.
See INDICTMENTS, PRESENTMENTS AND INFORMATIONS.
Negotiable instruments.
Defined, §8.3A-501.
Excused presentment, §8.3A-504.
Rules governing, §8.3A-501.
Warranties, §8.3A-417.

PRESENT SENSE IMPRESSION.
Hearsay exceptions, VA SCt Rule 2:803.

PRESERVATION EASEMENT FUND, §10.1-2202.2.

PRESERVATION OF COURT RECORDS.
Circuit court records.
Case files of ended cases, §17.1-213.
Receipt books, canceled checks and statements, §17.1-211.

PRESERVATION OF LAND.
Farmland preservation, office of, §§3.2-200 to 3.2-203.
Land preservation.
Budget bill, contents, §2.2-1509.4.
Special assessments for.
Real property taxes, §§58.1-3229 to 58.1-3244.
See REAL PROPERTY TAXES.

PRESERVES.
Shooting preserves generally, §§29.1-600 to 29.1-612.
See SHOOTING PRESERVES.
Wildlife habitat, refuge or sanctuary.
Destruction of trees, shrubs, etc., §18.2-140.

PRESIDENTIAL ELECTIONS.
Abstract of votes, §24.2-675.
Ballots.
Preparation and form, §24.2-614.
Separate ballot, §24.2-615.
Certification of persons expected to be nomination.
National conventions.
Furnishing state board, §24.2-542.1.
Choosing electors, §24.2-202.
Convening electors, §24.2-203.
Different day prescribed by congress for choosing electors or for meeting, §24.2-204.
Election contests.
Election of electors, §24.2-805.
Procedure generally, §§24.2-803 to 24.2-814.
Electors generally, §§24.2-202 to 24.2-205.
Groups other than political parties submitting names of electors, §24.2-543.
Nominations.
Certification of persons expected to be nomination.
National conventions.
Furnishing state board, §24.2-542.1.
Electors selected by other groups.
How names of electors submitted, §24.2-543.
Electors selected by political parties.
State board to be furnished names, §24.2-542.
National conventions, §24.2-542.1.
Number of electors, §24.2-202.
Oaths of electors.
Political party selection of electors, §24.2-542.
Selected by groups other than political parties, §24.2-543.
Pay of electors, §24.2-205.
Persons moving from precincts, §24.2-401.
Petition selected electors.
How required to vote, §24.2-203.
Petitions to submit names of electors.
Groups other than political parties, §24.2-543.
Political party selection of electors.
Oaths of electors, §24.2-542.
State board to be furnished names, §24.2-542.
Primary elections.
Presidential election year primaries, §§24.2-515, 24.2-544, 24.2-545.
Recount of election of electors, petition, §24.2-801.1.
Separate ballots, §24.2-615.
Statewide convention selected electors.
How required to vote, §24.2-203.
Vacancies, §24.2-203.
Voting for presidential electors, §24.2-644.
Voting of electors.
How required to vote, §24.2-203.
Write-in votes, §24.2-644.

PRESIDENTIAL INAUGURATION LICENSE PLATES.
Display on vehicles registered in state, §46.2-729.1.

PRESIDENT OF THE UNITED STATES.
Age, US Const Art II §1.
Aliens.
Ineligible for presidency, US Const Art II §1.
Ambassadors and consuls, US Const Art II §§2, 3.
Appointment of officers, etc., US Const Art II §2.
Approval of laws, US Const Art I §7.
Approval of order, resolution or vote of congress, US Const Art I §7.
Arrest under civil process.
Privileged from civil arrest, §§8.01-327.1, 8.01 327.2.
Bribery, US Const Art II §4.
Commander in chief, US Const Art II §2.
Compelling attendance as witness.
Prior court permission required, §8.01-407.
Compensation, US Const Art II §1.
Congress.
Adjourning congress, US Const Art II §3.
Convening congress, US Const Art II §3.
Declaration of president's disability.
Determination of issue, US Const Amd 25 §4.
By two-thirds vote of both houses, US Const Amd 25 §4.
Messages to congress, US Const Art II §3.
Special sessions of congress, US Const Art II §3.
Death.
Duty of congress, US Const Art II §1.
President-elect.
Provision in case of, US Const Amd 20.
Succession upon death, US Const Amd 25 §1.
Disability, US Const Art II §1.
Declaration by president.
Inability to perform duties, US Const Amd 25 §3.
Declaration by vice-president and other officers, US Const Amd 25 §4.
Determination of issue by congress, US Const Amd 25 §4.
Duties, US Const Art II §3.
Declaration by president of inability to perform duties, US Const Amd 25 §3.
Transmittal to senate and house of representatives, US Const Amd 25 §4.
Elections.
See PRESIDENTIAL ELECTIONS.
Eligibility, US Const Art II §1.
Execution of laws, US Const Art II §3.
Executive power, US Const Art II §1.
Failure to qualify, US Const Amd 20.
Impeachment, US Const Art II §4.
Inability, US Const Art II §1.
Jury service.
Automatic exemption, §8.01-341.
Limitation on terms, US Const Amd 22.
Message to congress, US Const Art II §3.
Ministers.
Receiving, US Const Art II §3.
Pardons, US Const Art II §2.
Powers of president, US Const Art II §§2, 3.
Public officers.
Commissions, US Const Art II §3.
Qualifications, US Const Art II §1.
Removal, US Const Art II §§1, 4.
Succession upon removal, US Const Amd 25 §1.

PRESIDENT OF THE UNITED STATES —Cont'd
Resignation, US Const Art II §1.
Succession upon resignation, US Const Amd 25 §1.
Signing bills, US Const Art I §7.
State of the union.
Message to congress, US Const Art II §3.
Statutes.
Approval of laws by president, US Const Art I §7.
Veto, US Const Art I §7.
Succession to office, US Const Art II §1, Amd 20.
Upon death, resignation or removal of president, US Const Amd 25 §1.
Supreme court.
Appointment of justices, US Const Art II §2.
Terms of office, US Const Art II §1, Amds 20, 21.
Limitation on terms, US Const Amd 22.
Time of taking office, US Const Amd 20.
Treason, US Const Art II §4.
Treaties, US Const Art II §2.
Vacancies during senate recess, US Const Art II §2.
Veto, US Const Art I §7.

PRESS, FREEDOM OF, VA Const Art I §12, US Const Amd 1.

PRESUMPTION OF DEATH, §§64.2-2300 to 64.2-2309.
Absences generally, §64.2-2300.
Aircraft disappearances, §64.2-2300.
Clerk probate or administration restrictions, §64.2-2303.
Court proceedings.
Refunding bond failures, §64.2-2306.
Curator for estate of resident.
Appointment, presumption not applicable, §64.2-2302.
Clerk of court not to grant, §64.2-2303.
Disappearances generally, §64.2-2300.
Fund distributions.
Presumption not applicable, §64.2-2301.
Judicial determination of death.
Costs, §64.2-2309.
Distribution of property on determination.
Refunding bond by person entitled to property, §64.2-2306.
Evidence at hearing, §64.2-2304.
Notice of hearing, publication, §64.2-2304.
Order determining person dead.
Entry, requirements, §64.2-2305.
Notice, publication, §64.2-2304.
Revocation of determination, §64.2-2307.
Refunding bond by person entitled to property, §64.2-2306.
Revocation of determination, §64.2-2307.
Substitution of supposed decedent in pending actions, §64.2-2308.
Less than seven year absence.
Exposure to sufficient peril, §64.2-2300.
Party defendants to real or personal property proceedings, §64.2-2300.
Refunding bonds, §64.2-2306.
Revocation of death determination, §64.2-2307.
Substitution of supposed decedent in pending actions, §64.2-2308.
Ship disappearances, §64.2-2300.
Substitution of supposed decedent in pending actions.
Revocation of death determination, §64.2-2308.

PRESUMPTION OF DEATH —Cont'd
Terrorist attacks on September 11, 2001, §64.2-2300 (note).

PRESUMPTIONS.
Abandoned motor vehicles.
Immobilized or unattended vehicles, §46.2-1209.
Rebuttable presumption, §46.2-1200.1.
Abandonment of property generally, §§55-210.2:1 to 55-210.10:2.
See UNCLAIMED PROPERTY.
Acknowledgments.
Officer who took as spouse of grantee.
Validity, §55-131.
Adoption.
Expiration of revocation periods.
No presumption in favor of parent, §63.2-1206.
Man father of child, §63.2-1202.
Agricultural equipment warranties, §59.1-207.8.
Anatomical gifts.
Presumption of validity, §32.1-291.19.
Animals.
Agricultural animals, care of, §3.2-6503.1.
Authorities for development of former federal areas.
Establishment and authority to transact business, §15.2-6302.
Bad checks, drafts or orders.
Intent to defraud, §18.2-183.
Malicious prosecution actions, §18.2-185.
Notation attached to check, §18.2-184.
Bail for illegal aliens.
Presumption of no bail for illegal aliens charged with certain crimes, §19.2-120.1.
Bail in offenses giving rise to rebuttable presumption against bail.
Commonwealth's attorney concurrence required, §19.2-120.
Bail involving schedule I or II controlled substance offense.
Previous conviction as drug kingpin or act of violence, §19.2-120.
Bank deposits and collections.
Stop payment orders.
Losses resulting from violation of orders, §8.4-403.
Bills for medical services.
Authenticity and reasonableness, §8.01-413.01.
Birth-related neurological injury compensation, §38.2-5008.
Boards of equalization.
Valuation, §58.1-3379.
Boards of equalization's assessment determinations.
Correctness, §58.1-3381.
Boating under the influence.
Alcoholic content of blood, §29.1-738.3.
Boat titling certificates.
Ownership, §29.1-733.
Bonds issued by locality.
Validity, §15.2-2627.
Casting solid waste into waters, §62.1-194.
Child pornography.
Production, publication, etc., with intent to distribute, financing, etc.
Age of person depicted, §18.2-374.1.
Child support.
Rebuttable presumption of child support, §§20-108.1, 20-108.2.
Child support enforcement by department of social services.
Amount of support, §63.2-1918.

PRESUMPTIONS —Cont'd
Civil commitment of mentally ill persons.
Admission raises no presumption of legal incapacity, §37.2-825.
Coal.
Existence in certain lands, §55-154.
Suits to extinguish claim or right, §55-155.
Commercial code.
General provisions.
Presumptions, when created, §8.1A-206.
Rule of law continues unchanged, §8.11-104.
Commercial drivers' licenses.
Driving while intoxicated.
Alcohol content of blood, §46.2-341.27.
Communications sales and use tax.
All sales subject to tax, §58.1-657.
Community property rights at death, §64.2-316.
Competency to stand trial.
Juvenile transfer to circuit court, §16.1-269.1.
Condominiums.
Contents of plats and plans, §55-79.58.
Contractors.
Knowledge of licensing or certification requirements.
Failure to renew license or certificate, §54.1-1115.
Controlled substances, unlawful possession.
Ownership or occupancy of premises or vehicles, §18.2-250.
Conveyances without words of limitation, §55-11.
Crab pots.
Tidal tributary placement, §28.2-711.
Credit card fraud used to obtain tickets from transportation company.
Person obtaining tickets at discount price from other than agent of company.
Presumption ticket acquired in violation of provisions, §18.2-198.
Credit cards.
Federal fair credit billing act.
Place where transaction occurred, §6.2-430.
Dam safety.
Record drawings of impounding structure.
Presumption of compliance, §10.1-605.
Death, §§64.2-2300 to 64.2-2309.
See PRESUMPTION OF DEATH.
Decedents' estates.
Community property rights at death, §64.2-316.
Deer hunting.
Lights, use of, §29.1-523.
Descent and distribution.
Presumption of death, §§64.2-2300 to 64.2-2309.
See PRESUMPTION OF DEATH.
Desertion and nonsupport.
Desertion and abandonment, §20-81.
Devices on certain containers.
Evidence of unlawful use and trafficking in, §59.1-97.
Dogs.
Force used against dog to protect pet from attack, §3.2-6570.
Domicile of dependent students.
Establishing eligibility for in-state tuition, §23-7.4.
Drinking while driving, §18.2-323.1.
Driving while intoxicated.
Alcoholic content of blood, §18.2-269.
Actions for exemplary damages for persons injured by intoxicated driver, §8.01-44.5.

PRESUMPTIONS —Cont'd
Drug offense involving schedule I or II controlled substance.
Bail, previous conviction as drug kingpin or act of violence, §19.2-120.
Employment-related information disclosure.
Good faith, §8.01-46.1.
Fee simple presumed in conveyances without words of limitation, §55-11.
Firearms offenses.
Bail, presumption against admitting to bail, §19.2-120.
Firefighters.
Relief for firefighters and dependents, §§27-40.1, 27-40.2.
Fishing, tidal waters.
Crab pots.
Tidal tributary placement, §28.2-711.
Proof of posting of notices, §28.2-221.
Fraudulent conveyances, §55-80.
Guardians.
Custody, care and education of wards, §64.2-1800.
Health care decisions.
Capable of making informed decision, §54.1-2983.2.
Presumption not created by directive, §54.1-2983.3.
Health care services coverage providers, jurisdiction over, §38.2-3420.
Hepatitis, meningitis, tuberculosis and HIV.
Workers' compensation.
Death or disability from, §65.2-402.1.
Highway tables of speed and stopping distances, §46.2-880.
HOV lane violations.
Registered owner of vehicle, §33.1-46.2.
Hunting.
Deer.
Lights, use of, §29.1-523.
Hypertension or heart disease suffered in line of duty.
Police, sheriff or sheriff deputy suffering, §15.2-1511.
Invention development services.
Remedies, §59.1-214.
Juvenile case transferred to circuit court.
Competency of child to stand trial, §16.1-269.1.
Landlord and tenant.
Manufactured home lot rental.
Owner sale or lease of home restrictions, §55-248.47.
Material noncompliance or danger, §55-225.12.
No mold existed at time of move-in inspection, §8.01-226.12.
Residential landlords and tenants.
Abandoned premises by tenant, §55-248.33.
Defenses to landlord actions for possession or rent, §55-248.25.
Material noncompliance or danger, §55-248.27.
Personal property abandonment, §55-248.38:1.
Tenancy periods, §55-248.7.
Lemon law.
Nonconforming motor vehicles, §59.1-207.13.
Reasonable number of attempts undertaken to conform motor vehicle to warranty, §59.1-207.13.
Liens, release of, §43-68.
Liquefied petroleum gas containers.
Unlawful use of, filling, refilling or trafficking in, §18.2-495.
Living wills, §54.1-2988.

PRESUMPTIONS —Cont'd
Machine guns.
Offensive or aggressive purposes, §18.2-291.
Manufactured home lot rental.
Owner sale or lease of home restrictions, §55-248.47.
Marijuana, unlawful possession.
Ownership or occupancy of premises or vehicle, §18.2-250.1.
Marks on certain containers.
Evidence of unlawful use and trafficking in, §59.1-97.
Medical bills.
Authenticity and reasonableness, §8.01-413.01.
Medical evidence.
Authenticity and reasonableness of medical bills, §8.01-413.01.
Medical referrals for profit, §18.2-502.
Military personnel.
Wills.
Formal execution, §64.2-408.
Minerals.
Existence in certain lands, §55-154.
Extent of owners estate to mineral rights, §55-154.2.
Suits to extinguish claim or right, §55-155.
Mortgages and deeds of trust.
Court releases, §55-66.5.
Recordation of security trusts, §55-58.1.
Motor vehicle license plates.
Altered or forged plates or decals, §46.2-722.
Motor vehicle uninsured, §38.2-2206.
Motor vehicle warranties.
Enforcement.
Nonconforming motor vehicles, §59.1-207.13.
Motor vehicle warranty enforcement.
Reasonable number of attempts undertaken to conform vehicle to warranty, §59.1-207.13.
Name on certain containers.
Evidence of unlawful use and trafficking in, §59.1-97.
Negotiable instruments.
Incomplete instrument, §8.3A-115.
Notice of dishonor, §8.3A-505.
Nonprofit corporations.
Inspectors of elections.
Report deemed correct, §13.1-847.1.
Obscene books, proceeding against.
Knowledge book obscene, §18.2-384.
Oil.
Existence in certain lands, §55-154.
Suits to extinguish claim or right, §55-155.
Open container while operating vehicle, §18.2-323.1.
Ores.
Existence in certain lands, §55-154.
Suits to extinguish claim or right, §55-155.
Ownership of tangible personal property, §55-47.1.
Parking.
Municipal parking ordinances.
Violations of ordinances, §§46.2-1220, 46.2-1221.
Partnerships.
Partnership property.
When property presumed to be, §50-73.90.
Receiving share of profits, §50-73.88.
Personal property ownership, §55-47.1.
Photo-monitoring systems to enforce traffic light signals.
Traffic light violation, vehicle operated by owner, lessee, renter, §15.2-968.1.

PRESUMPTIONS —Cont'd
Power of attorney.
Signature presumed to be genuine, §64.2-1603.
Power to direct.
Holder of power fiduciary.
Person other than beneficiary holding power, §64.2-770.
Prima facie evidence.
See PRIMA FACIE EVIDENCE.
Property abandonment, §55-210.2:1.
Generally, §§55-210.2:1 to 55-210.10:2.
See UNCLAIMED PROPERTY.
Radar devices.
Signs indicated legal rate of speed and measurement by radar, §46.2-883.
Rape.
Capacity of child over the age of 10 but less than 12 to commit violation, §18.2-61.
Real property taxation of apartments.
Sale of apartment not presumed for conversion to condominium, §58.1-3202.
Recordation of documents.
Presumption of proper form, §55-106.2.
Release of liens, §43-68.
Resource management plans.
Presumption of full compliance, §10.1-104.7.
Respiratory disease, hypertension, heart disease or cancer.
Presumption as to death or disability from, §65.2-402.
Retail sales and use tax.
Dealers, tax collectible from.
Presumption of activity within Commonwealth to require registration, §58.1-612.
Sales or leases subject to tax, §58.1-623.
Sales, UCC.
Breaches with accepted goods, §8.2-607.
Sexually explicit items involving children.
Production, publication, etc., with intent to distribute, finance, etc.
Age of person depicted, §18.2-374.1.
Sexually violent predators, civil commitment.
Assessment of prisoner for possible commitment, §37.2-905.1.
Simultaneous death.
Survival by 120 hours, §64.2-2201.
Donative dispositions in governing instruments, §64.2-2202.
Slayers barred from claiming property rights of decedent.
Convictions, §64.2-2510.
Solid waste.
Casting into waters, §62.1-194.
Spearfishing under the influence.
Alcoholic content of blood, §29.1-738.3.
State corporation commission.
Tax assessments, report forms and correspondence mailed by commission deemed delivered, §12.1-43.
Stopping or standing motor vehicle.
Municipal ordinances, §46.2-1220.
Surfboarding under the influence.
Alcoholic content of blood, §29.1-738.3.
Tangible personal property ownership, §55-47.1.
Tax assessment pursuant to ruling.
Correctness, §58.1-205.
Telegraph or telephone companies.
Questions as to reasonableness, justice or validity of rates, rules and regulations, §56-480.

PRESUMPTIONS —Cont'd
Tobacco products manufacturers' responsibilities.
Enforcement of requirements, §3.2-4217.1.
Traffic light signal violation monitoring system.
Traffic light violation, vehicle operated by owner, lessee, renter, §15.2-968.1.
Transfer of juvenile to circuit court.
Competency of child to stand trial, §16.1-269.1.
Trusts.
Conflict between trustee's fiduciary and personal interest.
Transaction affected by, §64.2-764.
Holder of power to direct fiduciary.
Person other than beneficiary holding power, §64.2-770.
Unclaimed property.
Presumption of abandonment generally, §§55-210.2:1 to 55-210.10:2.
See UNCLAIMED PROPERTY.
Unemployment compensation.
Benefit eligibility, §60.2-612.
Claims adjudication.
Appeals.
Commission review of tribunal decisions, §60.2-622.
Board of review, §60.2-631.
Judicial review of commission decisions, §60.2-625.
Viatical settlement brokers.
Agents of settlement providers, §38.2-1865.1.
Voter registration.
Petition objecting to registration not brought within six months of registration, §24.2-434.
Water and waste authority bonds.
Validity, §15.2-5126.
Waterskiing under the influence.
Alcoholic content of blood, §29.1-738.3.
Waters of the state.
Casting solid waste into waters, §62.1-194.
Weights and measures.
Use of weight, measure or weighing or measuring device.
Presumptive proof, §3.2-5648.
Wills.
Formal execution by military personnel, §64.2-408.
Generic terms.
Construction, §64.2-101.
Presumption of death, §§64.2-2300 to 64.2-2309.
See PRESUMPTION OF DEATH.
Probate.
Foreign proved wills, §64.2-450.
Winter sports safety act.
Applicability of article, §8.01-227.23.
Assumption of risks, §8.01-227.19.
Wireless service authorities.
Bond issues.
Contest of validity, §15.2-5431.15.
Witnesses.
Competency of witness to testify, §8.01-396.
Workers' compensation.
Acceptance of provisions, §65.2-300.
Cancer.
Death or disability from, §65.2-402.
Dependency.
Wholly dependent, §65.2-515.
Heart disease.
Death or disability from, §65.2-402.

PRESUMPTIONS —Cont'd
Workers' compensation —Cont'd
Hepatitis, meningococcal meningitis, tuberculosis or HIV.
Death or disability, §65.2-402.1.
Hypertension.
Death or disability from, §65.2-402.
Infectious disease, death or disability from, §65.2-402.1.
Injuries arose out of and were in course of employment.
Employee physically or mentally unable to testify, §65.2-105.
Pneumoconiosis presumed over silicosis, §65.2-504.
Respiratory disease.
Death or disability from, §65.2-402.
Writings admitted to record.
Proper form, §55-106.2.
Zoning appeals.
Decisions of board, §15.2-2314.

PRETERMITTED CHILDREN, §§64.2-419, 64.2-420.

PRETEXT INSURANCE INTERVIEWS.
Defined, §38.2-602.
Use to obtain insurance information, §38.2-603.

PRETRIAL CONFERENCES, VA SCt Rule 4:13.
Annexation.
Matters considered, §15.2-3207.
Consolidation of counties, cities or towns into single county or city, §15.2-3525.
Eminent domain proceedings, §25.1-219.
Reversion of cities to towns, §15.2-4105.
Town seeking city status, §15.2-3806.
Transition of counties to cities.
Matters considered, §15.2-3906.

PRETRIAL DISCOVERY.
Generally.
See DISCOVERY.

PRETRIAL DIVERSION, §§19.2-303.2, 19.2-303.4.

PRETRIAL PAYMENT OF FINES.
Nontraffic offenses.
Uniform fine schedule, VA SCt Rules 3C:1, 3C:2.
Written appearance and waiver of court hearing, §19.2-254.2.
Traffic infraction cases.
Uniform fine schedule, VA SCt Rules 3B:1, 3B:2.
Written appearance and waiver of court hearing, §19.2-254.1.

PRETRIAL RELEASE ON UNSECURED BOND OR PROMISE TO APPEAR, §19.2-123.

PRETRIAL SCHEDULING ORDER, VA SCt Rule 1:18.
Uniform pretrial scheduling order, VA SCt Rule Pt 1 Appx Form 3.

PRETRIAL SERVICES ACT.
Assistance to judicial officers in discharging bail and pretrial release duties, §§19.2-152.2 to 19.2-152.7:1.
See BAIL AND RECOGNIZANCE.

PRETRIAL SERVICES PROGRAMS TO ASSIST JUDICIAL OFFICERS, §§19.2-152.2 to 19.2-152.7:1.
Act of violence, force or threat defined, §19.2-152.7:1.

PRETRIAL SERVICES PROGRAMS TO ASSIST JUDICIAL OFFICERS —Cont'd
Biennial plan submitted by county or city to department of criminal justice services, §19.2-152.3.
Community criminal justice boards, §19.2-152.5.
Definitions, §19.2-152.7:1.
Establishment of services and services agencies, §19.2-152.2.
Failure to comply, §19.2-152.7.
Funding, §19.2-152.7.
Local pretrial services officers.
Duties, §19.2-152.4:3.
Mandated services, §19.2-152.4.
Notification to department of criminal justice services on withdrawal, §19.2-152.6.
Oath of office.
Local pretrial services officer, §19.2-152.4:1.
Pretrial services officers.
Capias.
Authorization to seek, §19.2-152.4:1.
Local officers, duties, §19.2-152.4:3.
Oath of office, §19.2-152.4:1.
Purposes, §19.2-152.2.
Records and reports.
Confidentiality, §19.2-152.4:2.
Standards prescribed by department of criminal justice services, §19.2-152.3.
Withdrawal by city or county from services, §19.2-152.6.

PRETRIAL WAIVER OF APPEARANCE.
Payment of fines.
Nontraffic offenses.
Nontraffic prepayable offenses and uniform fine schedule, VA SCt Rules 3C:1, 3C:2.
Non-traffic offenses, §16.1-69.40:2.
Traffic infractions, §16.1-69.40:1.
Traffic infractions and uniform fine schedule, VA SCt Rules 3B:1, 3B:2.

PREVIEWS OF MOTION PICTURES.
Misdemeanor for showing certain previews, §18.2-386.

PRICE ADVERTISING.
Comparison price advertising act, §§59.1-207.40 to 59.1-207.44.

PRICE FIXING.
Agricultural cooperative associations not deemed to be formed for purposes of, §13.1-331.
Antitrust laws, §§59.1-9.1 to 59.1-9.17.
See ANTITRUST.

PRICE-GOUGING.
Post-disaster anti-price gouging act, §§59.1-525 to 59.1-529.1.
Definitions, §59.1-526.
Determination of price unconscionability, §59.1-527.
Emergency orders, §59.1-529.1.
Enforcement, §59.1-529.
Investigation of complaints, §59.1-528.
Orders.
Emergency orders, §59.1-529.1.
Prohibited acts, §59.1-527.
Title of act, §59.1-525.

PRICE OF GOODS.
Hearsay exceptions, VA SCt Rule 2:803.

PRIEST-PENITENT PRIVILEGE, §§8.01-400, 19.2-271.3, VA SCt Rule 2:503.

PRIESTS.
Clergy generally.
See CLERGY.

PRIMA FACIE CORRECT STATEMENT OF TRIAL.
Transcript certified by reporter or other designated individual, §17.1-128.

PRIMA FACIE EVIDENCE.
Acknowledgments.
Recordation certificates not signed by clerk, §§55-137.1, 55-137.2.
Advertising merchandise for sale with intent not to sell at price or terms advertised, §18.2-217.
Animal, aircraft, vehicle, etc., procured with intent to defraud, §18.2-206.
Antitrust laws.
Convictions in other proceedings, §59.1-9.13.
Discriminatory practices, §59.1-9.7.
Automatic vehicle identification system.
Toll roads or toll bridges, §§46.2-819.1, 46.2-819.3.
Bad checks, drafts or orders.
Intent and knowledge, §18.2-183.
Notation attached to, §18.2-184.
Bailee's failure to return animal, aircraft, vehicle or boat, §18.2-117.
Bait and switch, §18.2-217.
Blackjacks, metal knucks, switchblades, etc.
Selling or having in possession, §18.2-311.
Boat titling certificates, §29.1-717.
Ownership, §29.1-733.
Burglary tool possession.
Intent to commit burglary, robbery or larceny, §18.2-94.
Cable television service, tampering with or unlawful use, §18.2-165.1.
Child abuse or neglect.
Removal of custody of suspected abused or neglected child.
Prima facie evidence, §63.2-1525.
Child support.
Social services department.
Admissibility and identification of support payment records, §20-60.2.
Cigarette excise tax.
Failing to affix stamps, §58.1-1013.
Commercial drivers' licenses.
Driving while intoxicated.
Refusal of chemical test to determine alcohol or drug content of blood, §46.2-341.26:3.
Compulsory school attendance.
Daily attendance records maintained by teachers, §22.1-259.
Consumer protection.
Willful violations, §59.1-206.
Cooperative nonprofit life benefit companies.
Constitution, laws or bylaws, §38.2-3808.
Court records, §8.01-389.
Crabs.
Taking limitations, §28.2-713.
Credit card forgery.
Unauthorized possession of two or more signed credit cards or card numbers, §18.2-194.
Criminal fines and penalties.
Embezzlement.
Misuse, misappropriation or willful failure to account for fines, §19.2-361.
Cross burning, §18.2-423.
Decedents' estates.
Beneficiary liability, §64.2-536.

PRIMA FACIE EVIDENCE —Cont'd
Decedents' estates —Cont'd
List of heirs, §64.2-509.
Deed or deeds of trust, §8.01-389.
Devices on certain containers.
Certified copy, §59.1-95.
Drivers' licenses.
Abstract data of conviction, §46.2-409.
Driving while intoxicated.
Commercial drivers' licenses.
Refusal of chemical test, §46.2-341.26:3.
Embezzlement.
Criminal fines and penalties.
Misuse, misappropriation or willful failure to account for fines, §19.2-361.
Public officers, agents or employees.
Default in paying over funds, §18.2-112.
Enterprise zones.
Eligibility form, §59.1-279.
Facts certified by state corporation commission clerk, §12.1-20.
Fishing, tidal waters.
Crabs.
Taking limitations, §28.2-713.
Licensing.
Failure to present, §28.2-231.
Oysters and clams.
Culling violations, §28.2-513.
Patent tongs.
Possession out of season, §28.2-506.
Teeth length violations, §28.2-509.
Weight violations, §28.2-509.
Possession of oysters out of season while taking clams, §28.2-534.
Provision violations, §28.2-522.
Restrictions on taking or loading on Sunday or at night, §28.2-530.
Trawling restrictions.
Violations, §28.2-317.
Fraudulent conversion of farm products.
Subject to lien or title in another.
Failure to pay proceeds of sale, §18.2-115.
Fraudulent conversion of leased personal property, §18.2-118.
Highways and roads.
Existence of a public road, §33.1-184.
Hunting.
Deer.
Lights, use of, §29.1-525.
Income tax.
Individual taxpayer failing or refusing to file return or making false statements, §58.1-349.
Judicial records, §8.01-389.
Larceny.
Intent to sell or distribute, §18.2-108.01.
Machine guns.
Use of machine gun by person occupying premises, §18.2-292.
Marks on certain containers.
Certified copy, §59.1-95.
Mechanics' and materialmen's liens.
Fund improprieties, §43-13.
Notice to agents, §43-4.01.
Personal liability of owners or general contractors.
Receipt of notice, §43-11.
Service of notice, §43-14.1.
Metering devices of public services or utilities.
Tampering with or diverting service, §18.2-163.
Mining.
Presumption rebutted, §55-154.

PRIMA FACIE EVIDENCE —Cont'd
Motor vehicle license plates.
Certificate of license plate number as prima facie evidence of ownership, §46.2-213.
Names on certain containers.
Certified copy, §59.1-95.
Obscene items, production, publication, sale, etc., §18.2-374.
Pig iron or industrial, manufacturing or public utility iron, brass, etc.
Buying or receiving with intent to defraud, §18.2-238.
Public road existence, §33.1-184.
Recordation certificates not signed by clerk, §§55-137.1, 55-137.2.
Records of the court, §8.01-389.
Retail sales and use tax.
Fraudulent return, §58.1-635.
Secondhand grate baskets, keys, bells and bell fixtures.
Buying or receiving with intent to defraud, §18.2-237.
Sex offender registration and notification.
Failure to register or reregister.
Affidavit of state police prima facie evidence of failure to register, §18.2-472.1.
Shoplifting.
Willful concealment of goods or merchandise while still on premises, §§18.2-23, 18.2-103.
Slugs manufactured, sold, etc., for unlawful purposes, §18.2-180.
Spousal support.
Social services department.
Admissibility and identification of support payment records, §20-60.2.
Swastikas, placing on certain property, §18.2-423.1.
Tax commissioner's affidavit, §58.1-110.
Telegraph or telephone companies.
Questions as to reasonableness, justice or validity of rates, rules or regulations, §56-480.
Telephone cooperatives.
Certificates of incorporation, §56-490.
Termination of residual parental rights, §16.1-283.
Timber brands.
Certificates.
Evidence of right to use marks, §59.1-105.
Toll roads or toll bridges.
Use of photo-monitoring systems, §§46.2-819.1, 46.2-819.3.
Trademarks and service mark registration.
Certificate of registration, §59.1-92.6.
Trademarks and service marks.
Distinctive nature, §59.1-92.3.
Vital records.
Certified copies, §32.1-272.

PRIMARY ELECTIONS, §§24.2-512 to 24.2-538.
Absentee and early voting.
Military and overseas voters.
Elections to which provisions applicable, §24.2-454.
Abstract of votes, §24.2-532.
Acknowledgment of declaration of candidacy, §24.2-520.
Adoption of direct primary.
Notice to state board, §24.2-516.
Alternative method of nominating candidate.
No declaration of candidacy filed, §24.2-526.
Applicability of article, §24.2-514.

PRIMARY ELECTIONS —Cont'd
Applicability of general elections law, §24.2-513.
Ballot containers, §24.2-531.
Ballots, §24.2-529.
Candidates' qualifications, §24.2-519.
Chairman of parties entitled to copy pollbooks, §24.2-532.
Chairman of parties to furnish names of candidates, §§24.2-516, 24.2-527.
Closing registration records before election, §24.2-416.
Conducted in accordance with provisions of article, §24.2-512.
Constitutional and local officers.
Schedule for primaries in year 2001 and each tenth year thereafter, §24.2-515.1.
Convention nominations.
Primary candidates not to be nominated by, §24.2-528.
Costs.
Payment by county and city treasurer, §24.2-518.
Death of opposed candidate prior to primary, §24.2-538.
Death or withdrawal of nominee by default, §24.2-537.
Death, resignation or removal of incumbent.
Vacancy in office occurring less than sixty days before primary date, §24.2-536.
Declaration of candidacy.
Filing, §24.2-522.
Filing fees paid by candidates, §§24.2-523, 24.2-524.
Required, §24.2-520.
Declaration of nominee.
One declaration of candidacy filed, §24.2-526.
When nominee declared, §24.2-534.
Defined, §24.2-101.
Election contests.
Generally, §24.2-806.
Procedure generally, §§24.2-803 to 24.2-814.
United States senate or statewide office, §24.2-805.
Procedure generally, §§24.2-803 to 24.2-814.
Election machinery costs.
Payment by political party committee, §24.2-518.
Entitlement to have name printed on ballot, §24.2-525.
Fraud of candidate.
Setting aside nomination, §24.2-537.
General elections law.
Applicability of provisions, §24.2-513.
Law enforcement officers to obtain returns not forwarded, §24.2-532.
Name printed on ballot.
Persons entitled to have, §24.2-525.
Names of candidates to be furnished state board and local electoral boards, §24.2-527.
Nomination by convention.
Primary candidate not to be nominated by, §24.2-528.
Nominations article applicable to, §24.2-514.
Notice of vacancy in office occurring less than sixty days before primary date, §24.2-536.
Notice ordering primary, §24.2-517.
Notice to state board of adoption of direct primary, §24.2-516.
Number of candidates for primary to be held, §24.2-526.
One declaration of candidacy filed.
Nominee declared, §24.2-526.

PRIMARY ELECTIONS —Cont'd
Opposing candidate for nomination dying prior to primary, §24.2-538.
Order of holding of election.
State board to order, §24.2-517.
Party committee members.
Election at same time as party's candidate, §24.2-518.
Persons eighteen years of age at next general election.
Advanced registration and voting in intervening primaries, §24.2-403.
Petition by candidate for name to be printed on official primary ballot, §24.2-521.
Filing fees paid by candidates, §§24.2-523, 24.2-524.
Filings to be made, §24.2-522.
Plurality of votes cast required to nominate, §24.2-535.
Pollbooks, §24.2-531.
Presidential election year primaries, §§24.2-515, 24.2-544, 24.2-545.
Qualification of primary candidates, §24.2-519.
Qualifications to vote, §24.2-530.
References in chapter to primaries, §24.2-512.
Returns.
Law enforcement officer to obtain returns not forwarded, §24.2-532.
Tabulation by state board, §24.2-534.
Setting aside nomination prior to primary, §24.2-537.
State board to order election, §24.2-517.
Tabulation of returns by state board, §24.2-534.
Time primaries to be held.
Presidential election year primaries, §§24.2-515, 24.2-544.
Treasurers of cities or counties.
Payment of primary expenses, §24.2-518.
Vacancy in office occurring less than sixty days before primary date, §24.2-536.
Vote required to nominate, §24.2-535.
Voter qualifications, §24.2-530.
Voter registration records closed before election, §24.2-416.
Voting in primary, §24.2-530.
When nominee declared, §24.2-534.
One declaration of candidacy filed, §24.2-526.

PRIMARY HEALTH CARE SYSTEM, §§32.1-122.5 to 32.1-122.8.

PRIME QUALITY COMMERCIAL PAPER.
Investment of public funds, §2.2-4502.

PRINCE EDWARD COUNTY.
Confederate cemeteries and graves.
Disbursement of funds appropriated for upkeep, §10.1-2211.
Fishing, inland waters.
Taking methods, restrictions, §29.1-531.
School board.
Salary of members, §22.1-32.
Southside regional airport authority at Blackstone, 1992 ch 371.
Transient occupancy tax.
Disposition of revenues, §58.1-3819.

PRINCE GEORGE COUNTY.
Admission tax, §§58.1-3817, 58.1-3818.
Aerospace engine manufacturer's grants.
Aerospace engine manufacturer workforce training grant fund, §59.1-284.22.

PRINCE GEORGE COUNTY —Cont'd
Aerospace engine manufacturer's grants —Cont'd
Aerospace engine manufacturing performance grant program, §59.1-284.20.
Aerospace engine manufacturing supplier bonus performance grant program, §59.1-284.21.
Coastal primary sand dunes and beaches.
Zoning ordinances, §28.2-1403.
Confederate cemeteries and graves.
Disbursement of funds appropriated for upkeep, §10.1-2211.
Parking on secondary highways, §46.2-1222.
Port of Virginia economic and infrastructure development zone grant fund, §62.1-132.3:2.
School board.
Salary of members, §22.1-32.
Transient occupancy tax.
Disposition of revenues, §58.1-3819.

PRINCE WILLIAM COUNTY.
Agricultural and forestal districts.
County executive form and certain other counties, §§15.2-4400 to 15.2-4407.
Circuit court clerk fees.
Secure remote access to land records, convenience fee program, §17.1-276.
Coastal primary sand dunes and beaches.
Zoning ordinances, §28.2-1403.
County attorney.
Prosecuting violations of county ordinances, §15.2-1542.
Cutting grass or lawn area of residential real property.
Requiring owner of occupied property, §15.2-1215.
Fingerprinting school employees, §22.1-296.2.
Inoperable motor vehicles, keeping on residential property, §15.2-905.
Local licensing of motor vehicles, trailers and semitrailers.
Payment of fines for ordinance and parking violations.
Evidence required before issuing license, §46.2-752.
Microcomputer devices.
Use to measure speed of automobile, §46.2-882.
Northern Virginia transportation authority.
Counties included, §15.2-4831.
Outdoor performing arts amphitheater, area or similar facility.
Mixed beverages license, §4.1-210.
Retail on-premises wine and beer license, §4.1-209.
Parking of vehicles.
Secondary highways, §46.2-1222.
Parking ordinances.
Regulation or prohibition of parking of certain vehicles, §46.2-1222.1.
Parking violations.
Removal or immobilization of vehicles.
Outstanding parking violations, §46.2-1216.
Poles or subsurface structures.
Placing under or along road or street not in state highway system.
Permit from county engineer.
Ordinance requiring, authority to adopt, §56-15.
Public service corporations.
Special provisions for assessment of real or personal property, §§58.1-2680 to 58.1-2683.

PRINCE WILLIAM COUNTY —Cont'd
Real estate taxes.
Senior citizens and disabled persons.
Ordinance prescribing alternative due dates, §58.1-3916.02.
Recordation tax, state.
Regional congestion relief fee, §58.1-802.2.
Retail sales and use tax.
Additional sales tax for Northern Virginia and Hampton Roads, §58.1-603.1.
Additional use tax for Northern Virginia and Hampton Roads, §58.1-604.01.
Repair of motor vehicles.
Authority to impose on labor or services, §58.1-605.
School board.
Fingerprinting applicants for employment, §22.1-296.2.
Salary of members, §22.1-32.
Semi-automatic firearms and shotguns.
Carrying loaded firearms in public areas, §18.2-287.4.
Snow and ice removal from public sidewalk, §15.2-2025.
State department of health employees.
Supplementing salaries and travel expenses, §15.2-1508.3.
Subdivisions.
Expedited land development review procedures, §15.2-2263.
Tax map reference number.
Circuit court clerk indexing by, §17.1-252.
Transient occupancy tax, §58.1-1742.
Disposition of revenues, §58.1-3819.
Well abandonment ordinance.
Duty of owner to cap or close well.
Locality adopting ordinance, §32.1-176.5.
Well construction.
Standards, §32.1-176.4.
Testing requirements, §32.1-176.5.

PRINCIPAL AND INCOME.
Allocation of receipts and disbursements.
Character of receipts, §64.2-1009.
Disbursements from income, §64.2-1024.
Disbursements from principal, §64.2-1025.
Distribution from trust or estate, §64.2-1010.
Fiduciary duties, §64.2-1001.
Obligation to pay money, allocation to income, §64.2-1014.
Rental property, allocation to income, §64.2-1013.
Total return unitrust, §64.2-1003.
Trust administration, §64.2-1011.
Annuities.
Allocations to principal and income, §64.2-1017.
Applicability of act.
Existing trusts, decedent's estates, and nontrust estates, §64.2-1032.
Nontrust estates, §64.2-1030.
Existing nontrust estates, §64.2-1032.
Uniformity of application and construction, §64.2-1031.
Apportionment of receipts and disbursements.
Death of decedent or beginning of income interest, §64.2-1007.
End of income interests, §64.2-1008.
Receipts normally apportioned, §§64.2-1016 to 64.2-1023.
Receipts not normally apportioned, §§64.2-1012 to 64.2-1015.

PRINCIPAL AND INCOME —Cont'd
Business and other activities conducted by trustees, §64.2-1011.
Construction of act.
Uniformity of application and construction, §64.2-1031.
Deferred compensation.
Allocations to principal and income, §64.2-1017.
Definitions, §64.2-1000.
Depreciation.
Defined, §64.2-1026.
Transfers from income to principal for, §64.2-1026.
Derivatives and options.
Allocations to principal and income, §64.2-1022.
Disbursements during administration of trust.
Allocation.
Disbursements from income, §64.2-1024.
Disbursements from principal, §64.2-1025.
Total return unitrust, §64.2-1003.
Distribution from trust or estate, §64.2-1010.
Fiduciaries.
Adjustments between principal and income, §64.2-1002.
Defined, §64.2-1000.
Distribution to residuary and remainder beneficiaries, §64.2-1005.
Duties, §64.2-1001.
Determination and distribution of net income, §64.2-1004.
Income beneficiary.
Defined, §64.2-1006.
When right to income begins and ends, §64.2-1006.
Income tax.
Payment of income taxes, §64.2-1028.
Income trust conversion to total return unitrust, §64.2-1003.
Insubstantial allocations not required, §64.2-1016.
Insurance.
Allocation of dividends and other proceeds, §64.2-1015.
Liquidating asset.
Allocation, §64.2-1018.
Defined, §64.2-1018.
Mines and mining.
Allocations to principal and income, §64.2-1019.
Natural resources.
Allocations to principal and income, §64.2-1019.
Net income.
Defined, §64.2-1000.
Determination and distribution, §64.2-1004.
Nontrust estates, §64.2-1030.
Existing nontrust estates, §64.2-1032.
Obligation to pay money.
Allocation to income, §64.2-1014.
Principal receipts, §64.2-1012.
Property not productive of income, §64.2-1021.
Prudent person rule.
Adjustments between principal and income.
Guidelines for fiduciary, §64.2-1002.
Reimbursement of principal.
Transfers from income to, §64.2-1027.
Remainder beneficiaries.
Defined, §64.2-1000.
Distribution to, §64.2-1005.
Rental property.
Allocations to income, §64.2-1013.
Securities.
Asset-backed securities.
Allocations to principal and income, §64.2-1023.

PRINCIPAL AND INCOME —Cont'd
Securities —Cont'd
Asset-backed securities —Cont'd
Defined, §64.2-1023.
Taxes.
Adjustments between principal and income because of taxes, §64.2-1029.
Income taxes.
Payment, §64.2-1028.
Special taxes or assessments for improvement representing addition of value to principal, §64.2-1030.
Timber.
Allocations to principal and income, §64.2-1020.
Total return unitrust, §64.2-1003.
Transfers from income to principal, §§64.2-1026, 64.2-1027.
Water.
Allocations of interest in, §64.2-1019.

PRINCIPALS IN THE FIRST DEGREE.
Deer hunting with lights, §§29.1-523, 29.1-525.

PRINCIPALS IN THE SECOND DEGREE.
Deer hunting with lights, §§29.1-523, 29.1-525.
How punished, §18.2-18.

PRINCIPALS, PUBLIC SCHOOLS.
Alcohol or drug use, incidents involving.
Immunity for personnel reporting, §8.01-47.
Assault and battery, actions not constituting, §18.2-57.
Assault and battery against, §18.2-57.
Assignment by division superintendent, §22.1-297.
Assistant principals.
Assignment by division superintendent, §22.1-297.
Employment by school boards, §22.1-293.
Fingerprinting required, §22.1-296.2.
Interstate agreement on qualification of educational personnel, §§22.1-316 to 22.1-318.
License required, §22.1-293.
Payment of salary, §22.1-296.
Performance evaluation process, §22.1-294.
Probationary terms of service, §22.1-294.
Reassigning to teaching position, §22.1-294.
Tuberculosis certificate, §22.1-300.
Asthma medications, self-administration by student.
Immunity of principal supervising, §8.01-226.5:1.
Policies, §22.1-274.2.
Auto-injectable epinephrine, self-administration by student.
Immunity of principal supervising, §8.01-226.5:1.
Bomb threats, firebombs or explosives, incidents involving.
Immunity for personnel reporting, §8.01-47.
Child abuse and neglect complaint searches.
Condition of employment, §22.1-296.4.
Compacts.
Interstate agreement on qualification of educational personnel, §§22.1-316 to 22.1-318.
Convictions for certain crimes, disclosure, §22.1-296.1.
Criminal records checks, §§22.1-296.1, 22.1-296.2.
Employee personnel files, §22.1-295.1.
Employment by school boards, §22.1-293.
Epinephrine, self-administration by student.
Immunity of principal supervising, §8.01-226.5:1.
Evaluation, §22.1-294.

PRINCIPALS, PUBLIC SCHOOLS —Cont'd
Evaluation of administrators.
Performance objectives, §22.1-253.13:5.
Fingerprinting applicants for employment, §22.1-296.2.
Fingerprinting required, §22.1-296.2.
Immunity for investigating or reporting.
Student conduct involving explosive or drugs and alcohol, §8.01-47.
Inhaled asthma medications, student's self-administration.
Immunity of principal supervising, §8.01-226.5:1.
Policies, §22.1-274.2.
Interstate agreement on qualification of educational personnel, §§22.1-316 to 22.1-318.
License required, §22.1-293.
Standards of quality, §22.1-253.13:2.
Payment of salary, §22.1-296.
Performance evaluation process, §22.1-294.
Powers and duties, §22.1-293.
Probationary terms of service, §22.1-294.
Professional development programs, §22.1-253.13:5.
Reassigning to teaching position, §22.1-294.
Supervisors.
Criminal records checks, §§22.1-296.1, 22.1-296.2.
Defined, §22.1-294.
Evaluation, §22.1-294.
Interstate agreement on qualification of educational personnel, §§22.1-316 to 22.1-318.
Reassigning to teaching position, §22.1-294.
Tuberculosis certificate, §22.1-300.
Tuberculosis certificate, §22.1-300.

PRINTING SERVICES, PURCHASES BY STATE AGENCIES.
Purchases through division of purchases and supply, §§2.2-1109 to 2.2-1128.
See PURCHASES AND SUPPLY DIVISION.

PRIOR INCONSISTENT STATEMENTS.
Criminal cases, §19.2-268.1, VA SCt Rule 2:613.
Impeachment of witness, §§8.01-403, 8.01-404, VA SCt Rule 2:613.

PRIORITY OF JUDGMENTS, §8.01-459.

PRIORITY OF LIENS.
Assignments of income for the benefit of creditors, §§55-156, 55-164, 55-165.
Attachments.
Holders in due course, §8.01-557.
Boat titling certificates.
Levies made by proper court order, §29.1-731.
Priority of interest shown on certificates, §29.1-729.
Canal employee or supplier liens, §43-24.
Commercial real estate brokers' liens, §55-527.
Commercial brokers, §55-527.
Condominiums.
Assessment liens, §55-79.84.
Credit line deeds of trust, §55-58.2.
Void as to creditors and purchasers until recorded, §55-96.
Where to be recorded, §55-97.
Creditor's suits.
Fraudulent conveyances, §§55-82, 55-82.1.
Decedents' estates.
Debt payment order, §§64.2-528 to 64.2-530.
Distress.
Landlord and tenant, §55-231.

PRIORITY OF LIENS —Cont'd
Escheated lands.
Payment of creditors, §55-195.
Fraudulent conveyances.
Creditor's suits, §§55-82, 55-82.1.
First in time, §55-101.
Liens of subsequent purchasers, §55-104.
Void as to creditors and purchasers until recorded.
Credit line deeds of trust, §§55-96, 55-97.
Keeper liens, §43-32.
Landlord and tenant.
Distress, §55-231.
Manufactured home lot rental.
Abandoned homes, §55-248.44:1.
Manufacturing employee or supplier liens, §43-24.
Mechanics' and materialmen's liens.
Mechanics'*versus* mechanics' liens, §43-23.
Mechanics'*versus* other liens, §43-21.
Owner expenditures to complete undertaking, §43-16.
Mining employee or supplier liens, §43-24.
Mortgages and deeds of trust.
Credit line deed of trust, §§55-58.2, 55-96, 55-97.
Debts secured by mortgage or deed of trust, §6.2-408.
Disposition of surplus after death of grantor, §55-64.
Indebtedness placed on equal footing, §55-60.1.
Property owners' associations.
Liens for assessments, §55-516.
Railway employee or supplier liens, §43-24.
Real estate cooperatives.
Nonpayment of assessments, §55-472.
Termination sale proceeds, §55-454.
Resources authority.
Pledges, §62.1-210.
Security interests.
See PRIORITY OF SECURITY INTERESTS.
Self-service storage, §55-418.
Subdivided land sales.
Property owners' associations.
Unpaid assessments, §55-344.
Transportation company employee or supplier liens, §43-24.
Unemployment compensation.
Employer taxation.
Collection, §60.2-523.
Writings admitted to record same day, §55-101.

PRIORITY OF SECURITY INTERESTS.
Distress for local taxes.
Security interest perfected prior to distraint, §58.1-3942.
Secured transactions.
Accessions, §8.9A-335.
Agricultural liens.
Agricultural liens on same collateral, §8.9A-322.
Filed financing statement providing certain incorrect information.
Agricultural lien perfected by, §8.9A-338.
Interests that take priority over or take free of, §8.9A-317.
Law governing, §8.9A-302.
Buyer of goods, §8.9A-320.
Certificate of title.
Security interest in goods covered by, §8.9A-337.
Chattel paper or instrument.
Priority of purchaser, §8.9A-330.
Commingled goods, §8.9A-336.
Conflicting security interests, §8.9A-322.

PRIORITY OF SECURITY INTERESTS —Cont'd
Secured transactions —Cont'd
Consignee.
Rights and title with respect to creditors and purchasers, §8.9A-319.
Crops.
Security interest in, §8.9A-334.
Deposit account, §8.9A-327.
Transfer of funds from, §8.9A-332.
Filed financing statement providing certain incorrect information.
Security interest perfected by, §8.9A-338.
Financial asset.
Priority of certain interests in, §8.9A-331.
Fixtures.
Security interest in, §8.9A-334.
Future advances, §8.9A-323.
Investment property, §8.9A-328.
Law governing, §8.9A-301.
Agricultural liens, §8.9A-302.
Deposit accounts, §8.9A-304.
Goods covered by certificate of title, §8.9A-303.
Investment property, §8.9A-305.
Letter-of-credit rights, §8.9A-306.
Lessee of goods in ordinary course of business, §8.9A-321.
Letter-of-credit right, §8.9A-329.
Law governing, §8.9A-306.
Licensee of general intangible, §8.9A-321.
Liens arising by operation of law, §8.9A-333.
New debtor.
Security interests created by, §8.9A-326.
Purchase-money security interests, §8.9A-324.
Purchasers of instruments, documents, and securities under other provisions.
Priority of rights of, §8.9A-331.
Sale of right to payment, §8.9A-318.
Subordination.
Priority subject to, §8.9A-339.
Transfer of money.
Transferee takes money free of security interest, §8.9A-332.
Transferred collateral, §8.9A-325.
Transition provisions, §8.9A-709.
Unperfected security interest.
Interests that take priority over or take free of, §8.9A-317.

PRIORITY TRANSPORTATION FUND.
Allocation of trust fund, §33.1-23.03:8.

PRIOR SEXUAL CONDUCT.
Rape shield law, §18.2-67.7.

PRISONER LITIGATION REFORM, §§8.01-689 to 8.01-697.
Applicability of provisions, §8.01-690.
Declaratory relief.
Applicability of provisions, §8.01-690.
Discovery requests, §8.01-695.
In forma pauperis.
When status denied, §8.01-692.
When status granted, §8.01-691.
Injunctive relief.
Applicability of provisions, §8.01-690.
Mandamus relief.
Applicability of provisions, §8.01-690.
Oral arguments.
Heard at request of court, §8.01-695.
Payment of filing fees and costs, §8.01-691.
Pro se representation.
Applicability of provisions, §8.01-690.

PRISONER LITIGATION REFORM —Cont'd
Records of the department of corrections, access, §8.01-697.
Responsive pleadings, §8.01-694.
Service of notice, process and other papers, §8.01-694.
Short title, §8.01-689.
Subpoena requests, §8.01-695.
Summary judgment, §8.01-696.
Venue, §8.01-693.

PRISONERS OF WAR.
Special license plates, §46.2-746.
Tuition and required fees for state supported colleges and universities.
Waiver for spouses and children of military personnel, §23-7.4:1.

PRISONS.
Abduction by prisoner, §18.2-48.1.
Seizure and forfeiture of property used in connection with abduction, §19.2-386.32.
Absentee voting by prisoners.
Certain persons in confinement entitled to vote absentee, §24.2-700.
Generally, §§24.2-700 to 24.2-713.
See ABSENTEE AND EARLY VOTING.
Actions by prisoners.
Litigation reform for prisoners, §§8.01-689 to 8.01-697.
Actual innocence.
Prisoner petition for writ of actual innocence, VA SCt Rule 5:7B, VA SCt Rule Pt 5A Appx Form 12, VA SCt Rule Pt 5 Appx Form 12.
Adults, juveniles sentenced as, §53.1-63.1.
Aliens, commitment, §§53.1-218 to 53.1-220.1.
Inquiries as to citizenship, §53.1-218.
Records pertaining to case, §53.1-219.
Transfers, §§53.1-220, 53.1-220.1.
Appointment of council for indigent prisoners, §53.1-40.
Arrest without warrant.
Corrections officers, §19.2-81.1.
Artistic products made by prisoners.
Exemption from retail sales and use tax, §58.1-609.1.
Sale, §53.1-46.
Assignment of prisoners to programs, §53.1-32.1.
Attorney appointment for indigent prisoners, §53.1-40.
Attorney visits to prisoners, §53.1-30.
Bank deposits.
Felony convicts serving one year or more in state correctional institution, §6.2-894.
Bank's power to act as comity, §6.2-820.
Board of corrections generally, §§53.1-2 to 53.1-6.
See CORRECTIONS BOARD.
Board of corrections visits, §53.1-30.
Bodily injuries caused by prisoners, §18.2-55.
Payment by inmate, §53.1-32.01.
Boot camp incarceration program, §53.1-67.1.
Burning or destroying occupied prison, §18.2-77.
Capital murder, killing of person by prisoner, §18.2-31.
Carrying concealed weapons.
Inapplicability to officers or guards of correctional institutions, §18.2-308.
Cellular telephones.
Illegal conveyance to or possession by, §18.2-431.1.

PRISONS —Cont'd
Certificate of execution, §53.1-235.
Change of name.
Applications of incarcerated persons, §8.01-217.
Chaplains.
Risk management plan for public liability, §2.2-1837.
Child support owed by prisoners.
Notification by department of corrections, §53.1-31.2.
Civil commitment of mentally ill persons.
Federal prisoners.
Receiving and maintaining in state facilities, §37.2-828.
Civil commitment of sexually violent predators, §§37.2-900 to 37.2-920.
See SEXUALLY VIOLENT PREDATORS, CIVIL COMMITMENT.
Claims against the state.
Tort claims act.
When claim exempt from act, §8.01-195.3.
Wrongful incarceration for a felony conviction, compensation, §§8.01-195.10 to 8.01-195.12.
Classification of prisoners, §53.1-32.1.
Clemency, §§53.1-229 to 53.1-231.
Death sentence procedures, §53.1-232.
Commencement of term, §53.1-186.
Commitment of convicted persons to custody of director, §53.1-20.
Commitment of sexually violent predators.
Civil commitment generally, §§37.2-900 to 37.2-920.
See SEXUALLY VIOLENT PREDATORS, CIVIL COMMITMENT.
Committees, estates of prisoners.
Appointment, §53.1-221.
Liability, §53.1-222.
Powers, §53.1-222.
Surety bond, §53.1-221.
Communicable disease reports to transportation agencies, §32.1-116.3.
Community-based programs for adults committed to correctional institutions, §53.1-10.
Community corrections, §§9.1-173 to 9.1-183.
See COMMUNITY CORRECTIONS.
Comprehensive reentry plan, §53.1-32.2.
Conduct of execution by director, §§53.1-233, 53.1-234.
Conduct records, §53.1-188.
Confiscation of articles, §53.1-26.
Contraband.
Delivery of articles to prisoners without authority, §18.2-474.
Delivery of drugs, firearms, etc., §18.2-474.1.
Contracts.
Procurement, §53.1-262.
Convictions register, §53.1-24.
Convicts as witnesses.
Competency to testify, §19.2-269.
Court order for release, §19.2-269.1.
Correctional officers.
Jury service exemption, guards, §8.01-341.
Warrantless arrests, §19.2-81.1.
Weapons authority, §53.1-29.
Corrections compact, interstate.
Director authority, §53.1-217.
Form, §53.1-216.
Governor to execute, §53.1-216.
Corrections department generally, §§53.1-8 to 53.1-17.
See CORRECTIONS DEPARTMENT.

PRISONS —Cont'd
Courts-martial sentences, where, §44-49.
Credits.
Earned sentence credits, §§53.1-202.2 to 53.1-202.4.
Commencement of eligibility, §53.1-202.2.
Condition for earning, §53.1-202.3.
Defined, §53.1-202.2.
Eligibility, §53.1-202.2.
Forfeiture and restoration, §53.1-189.
Juveniles convicted as adults and sentenced as serious juvenile offenders, §53.1-202.2.
Condition for earning, report by department of juvenile justice, §53.1-202.3.
Prerequisites, §53.1-202.3.
Rate earned, §53.1-202.3.
Refusal to participate in mandatory programs, §53.1-32.1.
Rules, criteria, etc., established by board of corrections, §53.1-202.4.
Time spent in confinement while awaiting trial in addition to, §53.1-187.
Good conduct allowances, §§53.1-186 to 53.1-202.
Injuries or extraordinary services, §53.1-191.
Time confined awaiting trial, §53.1-187.
Youthful offender facilities, §53.1-67.
Crimes by persons other than prisoners.
Cellular telephones.
Illegal conveyance to, §18.2-431.1.
Communications by persons outside of jail with prisoners, §18.2-473.1.
Delivery of certain articles to prisoners, §18.2-474.
Delivery of drugs, firearms, explosives, etc., to, §18.2-474.1.
Accommodation distribution of marijuana, §18.2-248.1.
Officers carnal knowledge of convicted person, §18.2-64.2.
Officers sexual battery of convicted person, §18.2-67.4.
Officers voluntarily allowing prisoner convicted of or charged with felony to escape, §18.2-475.
Officers willfully and deliberately permitting prisoner not convicted of or charged with felony to escape, §18.2-476.
Refusing to receive prisoner, §18.2-476.
Crimes by prisoners, §§53.1-203 to 53.1-205.
Abduction by prisoner, §18.2-48.1.
Seizure and forfeiture of property used in connection with abduction, §19.2-386.32.
Bodily injuries caused by, §18.2-55.
Burning or destroying occupied prisons, §18.2-77.
Capital murder, killing of person by prisoner, §18.2-31.
Cellular telephones.
Possession by, §18.2-431.1.
Felonies, §§53.1-203, 53.1-204.
Trials, §53.1-205.
Criminal justice information system.
Correctional information.
Information not subject to review or correction, §9.1-133.
Custody of property in name of board, §53.1-18.
Database of prisoners incarcerated for sexually violent offenses.
Access to records, §37.2-905.2.
Director to keep, requirements, review identification of prisoners scheduled for release, §§37.2-903, 37.2-905.1.
Death chamber, §53.1-233.

PRISONS —Cont'd
Death of inmates.
Dispositions of bodies, §32.1-288.
Investigations of death.
Copy of autopsy report to department of corrections, §32.1-283.
Death sentence procedures, §§53.1-232 to 53.1-236.
Fixing date, §53.1-232.
When execution date required, §53.1-232.1.
Defendants, prisoners as.
Foreign crimes, §53.1-208.
Foreign prisoners, §53.1-209.
Transportation costs, §53.1-207.
Defined terms, §53.1-1.
Appropriate court.
Agreement on detainers, §53.1-211.
Correctional services.
Private management of prisons, §53.1-261.
Intractable behavior.
Youthful offender facilities and programs.
Transfer of prisoners, §53.1-66.
Prison contractor.
Private management of prisons, §53.1-261.
Prison facility.
Private management, §53.1-261.
Delegation of private management powers and duties, §53.1-265.
Delivery of articles to prisoners without authority, §18.2-474.
Delivery of drugs, firearms, explosives, etc., to, §18.2-474.1.
Department of corrections, §§53.1-8 to 53.1-17.
See CORRECTIONS DEPARTMENT.
Description of prisoners, §53.1-23.
Detainer agreement, §§53.1-210 to 53.1-215.
Appropriate court.
Defined, §53.1-211.
Central administrator.
Designation, §53.1-215.
Cooperation in enforcement, §53.1-212.
Enactment, §53.1-210.
Escape of detained persons, §53.1-213.
Facility officers.
Powers and duties, §53.1-214.
Information agent.
Designation, §53.1-215.
Detention center incarceration program.
Establishment, §53.1-67.8.
Discharges.
Allowances, transportation and clothing, §53.1-190.
Crime victim notification, §53.1-133.02.
HIV testing of inmates prior to discharge, §53.1-33.1.
Mental health treatment of prisoners incapable of consenting.
Discharge of prisoner involuntarily admitted, §53.1-40.7.
Prisoners without government-issued identification.
Issuance of special identification card upon release, §53.1-116.1:02.
Release registration notice, §53.1-160.1.
Disease reports.
Infections of dead human bodies, §32.1-37.1.
Disposition of real estate of persons under disability, §§8.01-67 to 8.01-80.
See PERSONS WITH DISABILITY.
Disposition of remains, §53.1-236.

PRISONS —Cont'd
Disrobing, prisoner required by circumstances.
Correctional officer to be of same gender, §53.1-25.1.
Diversion center incarceration program.
Establishment, §53.1-67.7.
DNA analysis of convicted felons.
Blood, saliva or tissue samples, §§19.2-310.2, 19.2-310.3.
DNA data bank exchange.
Expungement of DNA profile, §19.2-310.7.
Forensic samples, §19.2-310.6.
Operation, §19.2-310.5.
Rulemaking authority, §19.2-310.5.
Unauthorized uses, §19.2-310.6.
Procedures for conducting DNA analysis of blood, saliva or tissue sample, §19.2-310.4.
Procedures for withdrawal of blood, saliva or tissue sample, §19.2-310.3.
Drivers' licenses.
Suspension or nonrenewal of license for nonpayment of fees to local correctional facilities or jails, §46.2-320.2.
Drugs, delivery to prisoners, §18.2-474.1.
Earned sentence credits, §§53.1-202.2 to 53.1-202.4.
Condition for earning, §53.1-202.3.
Eligibility, §53.1-202.2.
Forfeiture and restoration, §53.1-189.
Juveniles convicted as adults and sentenced as serious juvenile offenders, §53.1-202.2.
Condition for earning, report by department of juvenile justice, §53.1-202.3.
Prerequisites, §53.1-202.3.
Rate earned, §53.1-202.3.
Refusal to participate in mandatory programs, §53.1-32.1.
Rules, criteria, etc., established by board of corrections, §53.1-202.4.
Time spent in confinement while awaiting trial in addition to, §53.1-187.
Electronic incarceration.
See HOME/ELECTRONIC INCARCERATION.
Employees.
Personnel administration system.
Exemptions, §2.2-2905.
Employment and training of prisoners, §§53.1-41 to 53.1-62.
By-products, §53.1-53.
Career education.
Classification and assignment of prisoners, §53.1-32.1.
Good time credits, §53.1-197.
Opportunities for, §53.1-41.
Catalogue of prison goods and services, §53.1-54.
Charges of prison goods and services, §53.1-54.
Court-imposed debt.
Duties of director in collecting, §53.1-60.1.
Funds, investments, §53.1-44.
Grass cutting and other work in highway maintenance, §53.1-56.
Highway construction and maintenance, §53.1-56.
Highway employees as guards, §53.1-58.
Payments by transportation department, §53.1-57.
Pay incentives, §53.1-43.
Preferences for prisoners paying certain amount of child support obligations, §53.1-41.
Public works projects, §§53.1-56 to 53.1-59.

PRISONS —Cont'd
Employment and training of prisoners —Cont'd
Purchase by division of purchases and supply.
Correctional facilities products or services, §2.2-1116.
Restitution and other costs and fees to be paid while participating in work program, §53.1-41.
Road construction and maintenance, §53.1-59.
Sale of non-Virginia prison goods and services, §53.1-55.
Sale of prison goods and services, §53.1-45.
Artistic products, §53.1-46.
By-products, §53.1-53.
Purchases by Commonwealth and nonprofit organizations, §53.1-47.
Evasion by variance from specifications, §53.1-49.
Exceptions, §53.1-48.
Intentional violations, §53.1-51.
Procedure, §53.1-52.
Questioning of vouchers, certificates and warrants, §53.1-50.
Work program agreements, §53.1-45.1.
Street construction and maintenance, §53.1-59.
Technical education.
Classification and assignment of prisoners, §53.1-32.1.
Good time credits, §53.1-197.
Opportunities for, §53.1-41.
Trust accounts for inmates, §53.1-43.1.
Work allowances, §53.1-42.
Work opportunities, §53.1-41.
Work program agreements, §53.1-45.1.
Work release programs, §53.1-60.
Ineligibility, §53.1-62.
Use of earnings, §53.1-61.
Encumbrance of real estate.
Disposition of real estate of persons under disability generally, §§8.01-67 to 8.01-80.
See PERSONS WITH DISABILITY.
Escape.
Crime victim notification, §53.1-133.02.
Furlough violations, §53.1-37.
Generally, §§18.2-473 to 18.2-480.1.
See ESCAPE.
Reward for apprehension, §19.2-7.
Work release restrictions, §53.1-60.
Escape of prisoner subject to registration.
Notice to state police, §53.1-160.1.
Establishment, §53.1-19.
Establishment of youthful offender facilities and programs, §§53.1-63, 53.1-64.
Estates of prisoners.
Accounting upon discharge, §53.1-225.
Commitment of estate to sheriff, §53.1-226.
Committee.
Appointment, §53.1-221.
Liabilities, §53.1-222.
Powers, §53.1-222.
Surety bonds, §53.1-221.
Maintenance of prisoner's family, §53.1-224.
Personal property, §53.1-228.
Prisoner's capacity, rights, powers and authority over, §53.1-221.
Real estate.
Selling or encumbering, §53.1-227.
Suits against prisoners, §53.1-223.
Will, capacity to make, §53.1-221.
Exchange of real estate.
Disposition of real estate of persons under disability generally, §§8.01-67 to 8.01-80.
See PERSONS WITH DISABILITY.

PRISONS —Cont'd
Executive clemency, §§53.1-229 to 53.1-231.
Death sentence procedures, §53.1-232.
Explosives, delivery to prisoners, §18.2-474.1.
Extradition of criminals.
Application for requisition for return of escaped convict, etc., §§19.2-111, 19.2-112.
Confinement in jail for prisoners being taken through Commonwealth, §19.2-98.
Extraordinary services rendered by prisoners.
Credits, §53.1-191.
Felonies, place of punishment, §18.2-15.
Fingerprints of prisoners, §53.1-23.
Firearms, delivery to prisoners, §18.2-474.1.
Food services, medical services or cosmetological services.
Work assignments for prisoners.
Physical examination, exclusion, §53.1-33.
Freedom of information act.
Exclusions from chapter.
Inmate medical records, §2.2-3705.5.
Furloughs, §§53.1-37, 53.1-58.
Gang members committing offenses in correctional facilities.
Notice of gang membership to prosecuting attorney, §53.1-10.
GED certificates.
Testing for general education development, §22.1-254.2.
General assemblymen visits, §53.1-30.
Geriatric prisoners.
Conditional release, §53.1-40.01.
Persons convicted under three strikes you're out law, §19.2-297.1.
Good conduct allowances.
Computation of confinement period, §53.1-186.
Credit for time confined awaiting trial.
Cumulative nature of credit, §53.1-187.
Felonies committed on or after January 1, 1995.
Inapplicability to sentence imposed upon conviction, §§53.1-197.1, 53.1-202.1.
Forfeiture, §53.1-189.
Persons committed on or after July 1, 1981, §§53.1-198 to 53.1-202.
Application, §53.1-199.
Choice of system, §53.1-198.
Classification system, §53.1-201.
Conditions, §53.1-200.
Confinement awaiting transfer.
Credit, §53.1-202.
Eligibility, §53.1-199.
Persons committed prior to July 1, 1981, §§53.1-192 to 53.1-197.
Article applicability, §53.1-192.
Career education, §53.1-197.
Credits earned prior to 1944, §53.1-195.
Educational training credits, §53.1-197.
Persons convicted after October 31, 1942, §53.1-196.
Persons convicted prior to October 1, 1942, §§53.1-193, 53.1-194.
Technical education, §53.1-197.
Refusal to participate in mandatory programs, §53.1-32.1.
Restoration, §53.1-189.
Youthful offender facilities, §53.1-67.
Goods made by prisoners, sale of, §§53.1-45 to 53.1-55.
Guard authority under private management, §53.1-263.

PRISONS —Cont'd
Guardian ad litem.
Expenses in civil action against incarcerated felon.
Damages arising from criminal act, §8.01-9.
Process on convict defendant, §8.01-297.
Gubernatorial visits, §53.1-30.
Habeas corpus.
Generally, §§8.01-654 to 8.01-668.
See HABEAS CORPUS.
Supreme court, §53.1-232.1.
Suspension of execution of judgment.
Admittance of prisoner to bail, §8.01-665.
Health care.
Medical treatment of prisoners incapable of consenting, §53.1-40.1.
Exchange of medical information and records, §53.1-40.10.
Periodic review of prisoner retention, §53.1-40.6.
Procedure, §53.1-40.3.
Expenses, §53.1-40.8.
Mental health treatment of prisoners incapable of consenting.
Exchange of mental health information and records, §53.1-40.10.
Involuntary admission, §53.1-40.2.
Appeal of order authorizing, §53.1-40.4.
Commitment proceedings.
Prior to release, §53.1-40.9.
Discharge of prisoner involuntarily admitted, §53.1-40.7.
Pre-release commitment proceedings, §53.1-40.9.
Procedure, §53.1-40.3.
Expenses, §53.1-40.8.
Transfer of prisoners, §53.1-40.5.
Periodic review of prisoner retention, §53.1-40.6.
Hepatitis C test, positive results.
Convicted prostitutes or injection drug users tested.
Limited disclosure, §18.2-346.1.
Hepatitis testing of employees, §32.1-45.2.
Highway construction and maintenance by prisoners, §§53.1-56, 53.1-59.
Highway employees as guards, §53.1-58.
Payments by transportation department, §53.1-57.
HIV testing of employees, §32.1-45.2.
HIV testing of inmates prior to discharge, §53.1-33.1.
Home/electronic incarceration.
See HOME/ELECTRONIC INCARCERATION.
Identification cards.
Prisoners without government-issued identification.
Issuance of special identification card upon release, §53.1-116.1:02.
Immigration alien inquiry, §53.1-218.
Indigent prisoners.
Appointment of counsel, §53.1-40.
Injuries to or extraordinary services performed by prisoners.
Credits allowed, §53.1-191.
Inmate payment for damaged property, §53.1-228.1.
Jails, §§53.1-68 to 53.1-133.9.
See JAILS.
Jury service exemption.
Guards and superintendents, §8.01-341.
Juvenile detention and other care facilities generally, §§16.1-315 to 16.1-322.7.
See JUVENILE DETENTION AND OTHER CARE FACILITIES.

PRISONS —Cont'd
Juveniles sentenced as adults.
Facilities for, §53.1-63.1.
Lease of real estate.
Disposition of real estate of persons under disability generally, §§8.01-67 to 8.01-80.
See PERSONS WITH DISABILITY.
Letter writing privileges of prisoners, §53.1-35.
Limitation of actions.
Actions by confined persons.
Exhaustion of administrative remedies, §8.01-243.2.
Disabilities which toll statute of limitations, §8.01-229.
Litigation reform for prisoners, §§8.01-689 to 8.01-697.
Local correctional facilities, §§53.1-68 to 53.1-133.9.
See JAILS.
Mandatory participation by prisoners in programs, §53.1-32.1.
Marijuana, delivery to prisoners, §18.2-474.1.
Marijuana distributed as accommodation to inmates, §18.2-248.1.
Master program listing of available permanent and temporary positions, §53.1-32.1.
Medical expenses.
Payment for bodily injury.
Intentional infliction on any person by inmate, §53.1-133.01:1.
Medical research on prisoners, §53.1-36.
Medical services lien.
Recovery in personal injury action, §8.01-66.9:1.
Medical treatment of prisoners incapable of consenting, §53.1-40.1.
Exchange of medical information and records, §53.1-40.10.
Periodic review of prison retention, §53.1-40.6.
Petition for appeal to court of appeals, §17.1-406.
Procedure, §§53.1-40.3, 53.1-40.8.
Mental health treatment of prisoners incapable of consenting.
Exchange of information and records, §53.1-40.10.
Involuntary admission, §53.1-40.2.
Appeal, §53.1-40.4.
Commitment proceedings prior to release, §53.1-40.9.
Discharge, §53.1-40.7.
Procedure, §§53.1-40.3, 53.1-40.8.
Transfer of prisoner, §53.1-40.5.
Periodic review of retention, §53.1-40.6.
Petition for appeal to court of appeals from final judgment of circuit court.
Finality of decisions, §17.1-410.
Psychiatric hospitalization of defendant prior to trial or sentencing.
Jail inmates, §19.2-169.6.
Name change of prisoner.
Notification to crime victim, §53.1-133.02.
Notice to prisoners of registration upon release, §53.1-160.1.
Overcrowded prisons.
Incarceration in jails, compensation for, §53.1-20.1.
Parole, §§53.1-134 to 53.1-176.
See PAROLE AND POSTRELEASE SUPERVISION.
Parties to be present, §53.1-234.
Pay incentives for prisoners, §53.1-43.
Assignment to certain programs, §53.1-32.1.

PRISONS —Cont'd
Payment for bodily injury.
Intentional infliction on any person by inmate, §53.1-32.01.
Personnel administration system.
Exemptions, §2.2-2905.
Photographs of prisoners, §53.1-23.
Physical contact between inmate and officer.
Officer to be of same gender, §53.1-25.1.
Physical examination of prisoners, §53.1-33.
Prisoner descriptions.
Recordation for identification, §53.1-23.
Prisoner estates, §§53.1-221 to 53.1-228.
Prisoner litigation reform, §§8.01-689 to 8.01-697.
Prisoner programs and treatment in jails, §§53.1-128 to 53.1-133.
Prisoner release registration notice, §53.1-160.1.
Prisoner transfers into and between correctional facilities, §53.1-21.
Prison guards.
Jury service.
Automatic exemption, §8.01-341.
Private management, §§53.1-261 to 53.1-266.
Contractor powers and duties.
Delegation, §53.1-265.
Contracts, §53.1-262.
Criminal law.
Application to contractor-operated facilities, §53.1-264.
Defined terms, §53.1-261.
Juvenile corrections, §§66-25.3 to 66-25.7.
Regulations, §53.1-266.
Security employee authority, §53.1-263.
Probation.
See PROBATION.
Process on convict defendant, §8.01-297.
Procurement.
Contracts, §53.1-262.
Exceptions to competitive procurement, §2.2-4345.
Program assignments, §53.1-32.1.
Property damage.
Inmate payment for intentional damaged property, §53.1-228.1.
Public assistance benefits.
Ineligibility of prisoner for benefits due to incarceration.
Notice by department to social services department, §53.1-31.3.
Public works projects, prisoners working on, §§53.1-56 to 53.1-59.
Rape and sexual assault.
Treatment program for prisoners convicted of, §37.2-903.
Records.
Exchange of medical and mental health information, §53.1-133.03.
Recreation programs.
Treatment and privileges of prisoners, §53.1-32.
Redemption of real estate.
Disposition of real estate of persons under disability generally, §§8.01-67 to 8.01-80.
See PERSONS WITH DISABILITY.
Reentry planning, §53.1-32.2.
Refusing to receive prisoners, §18.2-476.
Release of prisoners, §53.1-28.
Geriatric prisoners, §53.1-40.01.
Notification to crime victims, §53.1-133.02.
Prisoners without government-issued identification.
Issuance of special identification card upon release, §53.1-116.1:02.

PRISONS —Cont'd
Religious services.
Treatment and privileges of prisoners, §53.1-32.
Retail sales and use tax.
Exemption of sales by prisoners of artistic products personally made, §58.1-609.1.
Rules, §53.1-25.
Sale of prison goods and services, §§53.1-45 to 53.1-55.
Sale of real estate.
Disposition of real estate of persons under disability generally, §§8.01-67 to 8.01-80.
See PERSONS WITH DISABILITY.
Schools of correctional centers, §53.1-10.
Searches of visitors, §53.1-30.
Secretary of health and human resources.
System for providing services to children with incarcerated parents, §2.2-213.2.
Secretary of public safety.
Offender transition and reentry services, system for, §2.2-221.1.
Sentencing generally, §§19.2-295 to 19.2-310.01.
See SENTENCING.
Services provided by prisoners, sale of, §§53.1-45 to 53.1-55.
Sex offenders, receipt into department of corrections.
Duties, §53.1-23.2.
Sex offenders, treatment program, §53.1-32.
Sexually violent predators.
Civil commitment generally.
See SEXUALLY VIOLENT PREDATORS, CIVIL COMMITMENT.
Smoking in public places, indoor clean air act.
Inapplicability to department of corrections areas not entered by general public, §15.2-2823.
State board of corrections generally, §§53.1-2 to 53.1-6.
See CORRECTIONS BOARD.
Statute of limitations.
Disabilities which toll statute of limitations, §8.01-229.
Stores, §53.1-27.
Superintendents.
Crime victims notification, §53.1-133.02.
Jury service.
Automatic exemption, §8.01-341.
Telephone systems within correctional facilities, §53.1-1.1.
Time served.
Credit for time spent in confinement while awaiting trial, §53.1-187.
Earned sentence credits, §§53.1-202.2 to 53.1-202.4.
Transfer of prisoners, §53.1-234.
Crime victim notification, §53.1-133.02.
Into and between correctional facilities, §53.1-21.
Mental health treatment of prisoners incapable of consenting, §53.1-40.5.
Transition and reentry services, system for, §2.2-221.1.
Transportation of prisoners, §53.1-31.1.
Collection of court costs by towns, §19.2-338.
Treatment and privileges of prisoners, §§53.1-32 to 53.1-40.
Ability to work, §53.1-33.
Appointment of counsel, §53.1-40.
Classification system, §53.1-32.1.
Contagious disease control, §53.1-34.
Correspondence privileges, §53.1-35.

PRISONS —Cont'd
Treatment and privileges of prisoners —Cont'd
Denial of medically necessary services prohibited, §53.1-32.
Fees for nonemergency medical services, §53.1-32.
Furloughs, §53.1-37.
Ineligibility, §53.1-38.
Mandatory participation in programs, §53.1-32.1.
Medical research programs.
Assistance in by prisoners, §53.1-36.
Physical examinations, §53.1-33.
Program assignments, §53.1-32.1.
Purpose of prison, §53.1-32.
Recreation programs, §53.1-32.
Religious services, §53.1-32.
Trust accounts for inmates, §53.1-43.1.
Trust companies.
Power to act as comity, §§6.2-820, 6.2-1002.
Unemployment compensation.
Benefits.
Eligibility, §60.2-612.
Venereal disease testing.
Admittees, §32.1-59.
Victim seeking visit with offender.
Department policy to assist victims, §53.1-30.
Warrantless arrests.
Arrest without warrant by correctional officers, §19.2-81.1.
Power of correctional officers to detain, §19.2-81.2.
Weapons authority for correction officers and employees, §53.1-29.
Welfare benefits.
Ineligibility of prisoner for benefits due to incarceration.
Notice by department to social services department, §53.1-31.3.
Will, capacity to make, §53.1-221.
Witnesses, inmates as.
Civil actions, §8.01-410.
Foreign prisoners, §53.1-209.
Surrender certificate, §53.1-206.
Transportation costs, §53.1-207.
Work allowances of prisoners, §53.1-42.
Work assignments.
Exclusion of prisoners, §53.1-33.
Physical examination prior to, §53.1-33.
Workers' compensation.
Employee imprisonment.
Suspension of benefits, §65.2-510.1.
Reporting of imprisonment, §65.2-712.
Work release programs, §53.1-60.
Ineligibility, §53.1-62.
Notification to crime victims, §53.1-133.02.
Use of earnings, §53.1-61.
Youthful offender facilities and programs, §§53.1-63 to 53.1-67.
Admissions, §53.1-67.
Consideration of report, §53.1-65.
Elements of program, §53.1-63.
Establishment, §§53.1-63, 53.1-64.
Good conduct allowances, §53.1-67.
Juveniles sentenced as adults, §53.1-63.1.
Prisoner transfers, §53.1-66.

PRIVACY, INVASION OF.
Computers, §18.2-152.5.
Peeping or spying into dwelling or enclosure.
Violation of occupant's reasonable expectation of privacy, §18.2-130.
Unauthorized use of name or picture, §8.01-40.

PRIVACY, INVASION OF —Cont'd
Unsolicited facsimile transmissions, §8.01-40.2.
Consumer protection violations, §59.1-200.
Virginia telephone privacy protection act, §§59.1-510 to 59.1-518.

PRIVACY OF INFORMATION.
Collection and dissemination of information by state agencies.
Personal information, privacy protection.
Government data collection and dissemination practices act, §§2.2-3800 to 2.2-3809.
See GOVERNMENT DATA COLLECTION AND DISSEMINATION PRACTICES ACT.
Social security numbers, protection, §§2.2-3815, 2.2-3816.
Identification generally.
See IDENTIFICATION.
Identity theft generally.
See IDENTITY THEFT.
Insurance information and privacy protection generally, §§38.2-600 to 38.2-620.
See INSURANCE INFORMATION AND PRIVACY PROTECTION.
Medical records.
Breach of medical information, notice to be given, §32.1-127.1:05.
Disease prevention and control.
Disclosure of certain information required, §32.1-127.1:04.
Right to privacy, §32.1-127.1:03.
Personal information privacy, §§59.1-442 to 59.1-444.
See PERSONAL INFORMATION PRIVACY.
Social security numbers, protection, §§2.2-3815, 2.2-3816.
Tax information secrecy.
See TAX INFORMATION SECRECY.

PRIVATE ACTIVITY BONDS, §§15.2-5000 to 15.2-5005.

PRIVATE CEMETERIES.
Access to private cemeteries, §57-27.1.
Official local register of places of burial, §15.2-978.
Property exempt belonging to memorial or monumental association, §15.2-978.

PRIVATE COLLEGE ADVISORY BOARD.
Creation, §23-9.10:2.

PRIVATE FOUNDATIONS.
State aid.
Estimates by nonstate agencies for annual budget, §2.2-1505.

PRIVATE HIGHWAYS, §§56-535 to 56-552.
See HIGHWAY CORPORATIONS.

PRIVATE INVESTIGATORS.
Private security services businesses, §§9.1-138 to 9.1-150.
Nonresidents, exceptions, §9.1-140.

PRIVATE JUVENILE DETENTION OR OTHER CARE FACILITY.
Establishment in locality without zoning ordinance.
Public notice and hearing, §15.2-2207.

PRIVATE LAWS.
General assembly not to enact local, special or private law, VA Const Art IV §14.

PRIVATELY OWNED SEWERAGE SYSTEMS.
Street or public ground use without consent or compensation, §56-14.
Systems not regulated as public utilities, §§56-265.10 to 56-265.13.

PRIVATELY OWNED WATER SYSTEMS.
Public ground use without consent or compensation, §56-14.
Street use without consent or compensation, §56-14.
Systems not regulated as public utilities, §§56-265.10 to 56-265.13.

PRIVATE MANAGEMENT OF JUVENILE CORRECTIONS, §§66-25.3 to 66-25.7.

PRIVATE MANAGEMENT OF PRISONS, §§53.1-261 to 53.1-266.

PRIVATE OPERATION OF JUVENILE DETENTION FACILITIES, §§16.1-322.5 to 16.1-322.7.

PRIVATE PIERS.
Placement for noncommercial purposes by owners of riparian lands, §28.2-1203.
Inclusion of attached boat lift, §28.2-1203.

PRIVATE PROPERTY, DESTRUCTION, §18.2-137.
Destruction of trees, shrubs, etc., §18.2-140.
Vandalism generally.
See VANDALISM.

PRIVATE PROPERTY, TAKING, VA Const Art I §11, US Const Amd V.
Eminent domain generally.
See EMINENT DOMAIN.

PRIVATE REGIONAL JAILS.
Construction requirements and limitations, §53.1-71.1.
Criminal laws.
Applicability, §53.1-71.3.
Non-delegable powers and duties, §53.1-71.4.
Operation requirements and limitations, §53.1-71.1.
Rules.
Board promulgation, §53.1-71.5.
Security employees.
Authority, §53.1-71.2.
State reimbursement to localities, §53.1-71.6.

PRIVATE ROADS.
Connections over shoulders of highways for intersecting private roads, §33.1-197.
Damages to personal property by reason of work projects, etc., §33.1-200.
Dumping trash, etc., §33.1-346.
Erection and maintenance of gates by landowners, §§33.1-202 to 33.1-204.
Highway corporations, §§56-535 to 56-552.
See HIGHWAY CORPORATIONS.
Leaving gates open, §§33.1-203, 33.1-204.
Multi-family residential developments.
Regulation by localities, §15.2-2027.
Repairing entrances destroyed by work projects, etc., §33.1-199.
Residential developments.
Designation as highways for law enforcement purposes.
Authority of local government, §46.2-1307.
State improvements to certain public roads, §33.1-201.

PRIVATE SCHOOLS.
Aid to nonpublic higher education, VA Const Art VIII §11.
Alcoholic beverages, outdoor advertising.
Limitations on placement locations, §4.1-112.2.
Notice of violation, penalty for failure to take corrective action, §4.1-320.
Appropriations to schools or institutions of learning not owned or exclusively controlled by state or subdivision, VA Const Art VIII §10.
Athletic events.
Immunity for team physician, §8.01-225.1.
Child abuse or neglect reports.
Complaints against school personnel, §63.2-1511.
Interagency agreement, child abuse and neglect investigations, §63.2-1511.
Investigation procedures and release of information, §63.2-1516.1.
Standard for determining if report unfounded, §63.2-1511.
Reason to suspect, required reports, fine for failure, §63.2-1509.
Posting notice of employee obligations, §22.1-291.3.
Child welfare agencies.
Regulation and licensure provisions.
Inapplicability of provisions to private schools, §63.2-1815.
Council of higher education.
Advisory services to private nonprofit institutions, §23-9.10:2.
Criminal record checks of employees, §22.1-296.3.
Dissemination of information, §19.2-389.
Day care programs established by school boards outside regular school hours.
Eligibility of private school students to attend, §22.1-132.1.
Disabilities, schools for students with, §§22.1-319 to 22.1-332.
See DISABILITIES, SCHOOLS FOR STUDENTS WITH.
Disorderly conduct in public places.
Disrupting school, §18.2-415.
Drivers' licenses for minors at least 16 years 3 months old.
Certification of compliance with attendance laws, §46.2-334.
Drug sales on or near property, §18.2-255.2.
Fingerprinting employees, §22.1-296.3.
Firearms.
Discharging, §18.2-280.
Disqualification for concealed weapons permit, §18.2-308.09.
Pointing, holding or brandishing in school or on school grounds, §18.2-282.
Possession on school property, §18.2-308.1.
Gang activity in school zone.
Enhanced punishment, §18.2-46.3:3.
Handicap or disability.
Schools for students with disabilities, §§22.1-319 to 22.1-332.
See DISABILITIES, SCHOOLS FOR STUDENTS WITH.
Immunizations required for attendance at schools, §32.1-46.
Internet.
Acceptable Internet use policies for public and private schools, §22.1-70.2.

PRIVATE SCHOOLS —Cont'd
Preschool or nursery school program.
Certifications and condition for operating, §63.2-1717.
Property exempt from taxation, nonprofit, VA Const Art X §6.
Remediation program for at-risk public school students, §22.1-253.13:1.
School bus operators.
Requirements, §§22.1-178, 22.1-180.
Special education.
Reimbursement of parents or guardian of children with disabilities in private schools, §22.1-218.
Transportation of handicapped pupils, §22.1-221.
Use of private facilities and personnel under contract, §22.1-216.
Student records.
Furnishing information to private school, §22.1-288.
Suspension or expulsion of pupils, §§22.1-277 to 22.1-277.2.
Swastika, placing on property, §18.2-423.1.
Transportation of pupils.
Local school boards, agreements to provide, §22.1-176.1.

PRIVATE SECURITY SERVICES BUSINESSES, §§9.1-138 to 9.1-150.
Advisory board, §9.1-143.
Armed security officers.
Limitation of powers, §9.1-146.
Armored car personnel training standards, §9.1-139.
Background checks, §9.1-139.
Powers of department, §9.1-142.
Bonds, surety.
Licensing, certification registration, §9.1-144.
Certification, §9.1-139.
Bonds, surety, §9.1-144.
Fingerprints, §9.1-145.
Insurance, §9.1-144.
Misrepresentations.
Unlawful conduct, §9.1-147.
Unlicensed activity, §9.1-149.
Compliance agents.
Designation, §9.1-139.
Fingerprints, §9.1-145.
Qualifications, §9.1-139.
Unlicensed activity, §9.1-149.
Concealed weapons.
Armed security officers, §9.1-146.
Employee of electronic security business, authority to carry, §9.1-141.
Criminal justice services board.
Powers and duties, §9.1-141.
Criminal offenses.
Unlawful conduct, §9.1-147.
Unlawful procurement of license, §9.1-148.
Unlicensed activity, §9.1-149.
Defined terms, §9.1-138.
Department.
Powers, §9.1-142.
Exceptions, §9.1-140.
Fees.
Powers of department, §9.1-142.
Fines, §9.1-150.
Fingerprints.
Employees, §9.1-139.
Required, §9.1-145.
Injunctions.
Powers of department, §9.1-142.

PRIVATE SECURITY SERVICES BUSINESSES —Cont'd
Insurance.
Licensing, certification registration, §9.1-144.
Investigations.
Powers of department, §9.1-142.
Licensing, §9.1-139.
Bonds, surety, §9.1-144.
Fingerprints, §9.1-145.
Insurance, §9.1-144.
Misrepresentations.
Unlawful conduct, §9.1-147.
Unlawful procurement, §9.1-148.
Unlicensed activity, §9.1-149.
Locksmith services.
Exemptions from provisions, §9.1-140.
Registration.
Waiver of examination, §9.1-140.1.
Motor vehicle owner information.
Commissioner of DMV.
Supplying licensee upon request, §46.2-208.
Qualifications.
Licensing, certification or registration, §9.1-139.
Reciprocity.
Powers of board, §9.1-141.
Records.
Compliance, §9.1-139.
Registration, §9.1-139.
Bonds, surety, §9.1-144.
Fingerprints, §9.1-145.
Insurance, §9.1-144.
Locksmith services.
Waiver of examination, §9.1-140.1.
Misrepresentations.
Unlawful conduct, §9.1-147.
Unlicensed activity, §9.1-149.
Temporary licenses, §9.1-139.
Unarmed security officers.
Fingerprint requirements, §9.1-145.
Unauthorized practice.
Enforcement.
Powers of department, §9.1-142.
Unlawful conduct, §9.1-147.
Unlawful conduct, §9.1-147.
Fines, §9.1-150.
Unlicensed activity, §9.1-149.
Fines, §9.1-150.

PRIVATE SECURITY SERVICES TRAINING SCHOOLS.
Certification, §9.1-139.
School director.
Designation, §9.1-139.
Qualifications, §9.1-139.

PRIVATE TRUST COMPANY ACT, §§6.2-1074 to 6.2-1080.
See TRUST COMPANIES.

PRIVATE WELL CONSTRUCTION, §§32.1-176.1 to 32.1-176.7.

PRIVATIZATION OF STATE PROGRAMS OR ACTIVITIES.
Loss of jobs due to.
Report to governor, §2.2-203.2:1.

PRIVILEGE.
Arrest under civil process.
Persons exempt from arrest, §8.01-327.2.
Attorney-client privilege.
Confidentiality of information, VA SCt Rule Pt 6 §II Rule 1.6.

PRIVILEGE —Cont'd
Attorney-client privilege —Cont'd
Evidence, VA SCt Rule 2:502.
Insanity defense.
Evaluator's report, §19.2-169.5.
Limitations on waiver of attorney-client privilege and work product protection, §8.01-420.7.
Receiver appointed to protect client's interest, §54.1-3900.01.
Attorney licensing.
Information and testimony furnished to board, §54.1-3925.3.
Attorney-work product privilege, VA SCt Rule 4:1.
Dispute resolution proceedings, §8.01-576.10.
Banks.
Voluntary regulatory self-assessment reports, §6.2-948.
Effect on other privileges, §6.2-950.
Exceptions, §6.2-949.
Civil arrest.
Privilege from civil arrest, §§8.01-327.1, 8.01-327.2.
Cleric-penitent privilege, §8.01-400, VA SCt Rule 2:503.
Criminal procedure, §19.2-271.3.
Crash investigation team, department of motor vehicles, §8.01-402.
Critical incident stress management team-EMS or public safety personnel privilege, §19.2-271.4.
Deaf and hearing impaired persons.
Interpreters for the deaf, §§8.01-400.1, 19.2-164.
Deeds.
Inclusion in deeds, §55-50.
Department of motor vehicle records, release, conditions, §46.2-208.
Disease reporting, §32.1-38.
Electronic communications.
Interception of, §19.2-67.
Evidence, rules of, VA SCt Rules 2:501 to 2:507.
Attorney-client privilege, VA SCt Rule 2:502.
Cleric-penitent privilege, VA SCt Rule 2:503.
Common law interpretation, VA SCt Rule 2:501.
General rule, VA SCt Rule 2:501.
Interpreters for deaf or non-English speaking persons, VA SCt Rule 2:507.
Marriage and family therapist-client privilege, VA SCt Rule 2:506.
Physician-patient privilege, VA SCt Rule 2:505.
Preliminary determinations, VA SCt Rule 2:104.
Professional counselor-client privilege, VA SCt Rule 2:506.
Psychologist-client privilege, VA SCt Rule 2:506.
Social worker-client privilege, VA SCt Rule 2:506.
Spousal privilege, VA SCt Rule 2:504.
General assembly, VA Const Art IV §9.
Arrest, §30-6.
Qualifications of privilege, §30-7.
Words spoken or written, §30-9.
Civil proceedings for or against members and clerks, §30-4.
Witness duty, §30-6.
Healing arts privilege.
Communications between physicians and patients, §8.01-399, VA SCt Rule 2:505.
Husband and wife, VA SCt Rule 2:504.
Child abuse or neglect.
Inapplicability of privilege in legal proceeding, §63.2-1519.
Competency of spouse to testify, §8.01-398.

PRIVILEGE —Cont'd
Husband and wife —Cont'd
Confidential communications between spouses during marriage.
Privilege to refuse to disclose and to prevent disclosure, §19.2-271.2.
Evidence, VA SCt Rule 2:504.
Spousal communications, §8.01-398.
Insurance adjusters.
Confidential and privileged documents, §38.2-1845.20.
Insurance information and privacy protection generally, §§38.2-600 to 38.2-620.
See INSURANCE INFORMATION AND PRIVACY PROTECTION.
Insurers reports of acts of larceny by agents or surplus lines brokers, §38.2-1810.
Interpreters.
Deaf and hearing impaired persons, §§8.01-400.1, 19.2-164.
Deaf or non-English speaking persons, VA SCt Rule 2:507.
Non-English speaking persons, §8.01-384.1:1.
Judge of court of record holding case under advisement for unreasonable length.
Designation of judge to assist regular judge, §17.1-107.
Judicial inquiry and review commission.
Filing of papers with commission, §17.1-914.
Juvenile court reports of court officials and employees, §16.1-303.
Lieutenant governor.
Arrest, §30-6.
Qualifications of privilege, §30-7.
Proceedings while general assembly is in session, §30-4.
Witness duty, §30-6.
Marriage and family therapist-client privilege, §8.01-400.2, VA SCt Rule 2:506.
Medical malpractice.
Board or committee proceedings, §8.01-581.17.
National guard, state defense force or naval militia member.
Arrest, §44-97.
No exclusive emoluments or privileges, VA Const Art I §4.
Nursing homes.
Appointment of receivers, §32.1-27.1.
Oral communications.
Interception of, §19.2-67.
Physician-patient privilege, §8.01-399, VA SCt Rule 2:505.
Child abuse or neglect.
Inapplicability in legal proceedings, §63.2-1519.
Disabilities of drivers.
Physician reports on, §54.1-2966.1.
Emergency medical treatment.
Termination of privilege upon patient discharge, §54.1-2962.2.
Priest-penitent privilege, §§8.01-400, 19.2-271.3, VA SCt Rule 2:503.
Professional corporations.
Confidential relationship between person rendering service and person receiving not affected, §13.1-547.
Professional counselor-client privilege, §8.01-400.2, VA SCt Rule 2:506.
Psychologist-client privilege, §8.01-400.2, VA SCt Rule 2:506.
Clinical psychologists, §8.01-399, VA SCt Rule 2:505.

PRIVILEGE —Cont'd
Public utilities, §56-256.
Rabbi-penitent privilege, §§8.01-400, 19.2-271.3, VA SCt Rule 2:503.
Religious sects or denominations, general assembly not to confer upon, VA Const Art I §16.
Self-incrimination.
See SELF-INCRIMINATION, PRIVILEGE AGAINST.
Social worker-client privilege, §8.01-400.2, VA SCt Rule 2:506.
Spousal privilege, §8.01-398, VA SCt Rule 2:504.
Child abuse or neglect.
Inapplicability of privilege in legal proceeding, §63.2-1519.
Tax information.
Assessment cards and sheets, public disclosure, §58.1-3331.
Attorney general's authority to request and share information, §58.1-3.2.
Availability of information to audit local tax returns, §58.1-3.1.
Motor carrier road tax.
International fuel tax agreement.
Information exchanges under agreement, §58.1-2712.2.
Motor vehicle fuel sales tax, §58.1-1724.1.
Real property tax.
Income-producing realty, reports by owners, §58.1-3294.
Retail sales and use tax.
Report of gross misuse of exemption certificates, §58.1-623.1.
Road tax on motor carriers.
International fuel tax agreement.
Information exchanges under agreement, §58.1-2712.2.
Secrecy generally, §58.1-3.
Setoff debt collection act.
Exemption, use of information, §58.1-533.
Tax commissioner's authority to request and share information, §58.1-3.2.
Taxpayer bill of rights, §58.1-1845.
Tax preparers not to disclose information without consent, §58.1-4.
Town officers provided information by commissioners of revenue, §58.1-3109.
Transfer of credit or other tax attribute.
Deemed consent to disclosure, §58.1-3.3.
Treasurers books and papers pertaining to office, §58.1-3127.
Wills and administration, tax on.
Return filed, §58.1-1714.
Trauma registry.
Information transmitted to, §32.1-116.1.
Unemployment compensation.
Claims adjudication.
Self-incrimination, §60.2-628.
Reservation of right to amend or appeal, §60.2-104.
Voluntary environmental assessment.
Hazardous waste cleanup, §10.1-1198.
Voters during election, VA Const Art II §9.
Wire, electronic or oral communication.
Interception of privileged communication, §19.2-67.
Workers' compensation.
Peer review of medical costs.
Statewide coordinating committee, §65.2-1308.

PRIVILEGE AGAINST SELF-INCRIMINATION.
See SELF-INCRIMINATION, PRIVILEGE AGAINST.

PRIVILEGE FROM ARREST.
Arrest under civil process, §§8.01-327.1, 8.01-327.2.
Congressional members, US Const Art I §6.
General assembly members, §§30-6, 30-7, 30-9, VA Const Art IV §9.
Lieutenant governor, §§30-6, 30-7.
National guard, state defense force or naval militia member, §44-97.
Voters during election, VA Const Art II §9.

PRIVILEGE TAXES.
Insurance companies, license tax generally, §§58.1-2500 to 58.1-2533.
See INSURANCE COMPANIES LICENSE TAX.
License taxes generally, §§58.1-3700 to 58.1-3735.
See LICENSE TAXES.
Local license tax on telegraph or telephone companies, §58.1-2690.
Telegraph, telephone, water, heat, light, power and pipeline companies, §§58.1-2620 to 58.1-2635.
See PUBLIC SERVICE CORPORATION TAXATION.

PRIVITY OF CONTRACT.
Condominiums.
Special declarant rights.
Transfers, §55-79.74:3.
Health spas.
Defenses to actions, §59.1-305.
Lack of privity no defense to certain actions, §8.01-223.
Real estate cooperatives.
Special declarant rights, transfers of, §55-461.
Res judicata, preclusion of claims, effect, VA SCt Rule 1:6.
Sales, UCC, §8.2-318.

PRIZES.
Promotional prizes, §§59.1-415 to 59.1-423.
See PROMOTIONAL PRIZES AND GIFTS.
State lottery.
Assignment of right to prize, §58.1-4013.
Garnishment, §58.1-4013.
Ineligible persons to receive, §58.1-4019.
Liens upon, §58.1-4013.
Set-off of debts to Commonwealth, §58.1-4026.
Tax exemption, §58.1-4025.
Unclaimed prizes, §58.1-4020.
Time-shares.
Advertising practices regulated, §55-374.1.

PROBABLE CAUSE.
Arrest warrant, issuance, §19.2-72.
Arrest warrants for children issued by magistrates, §16.1-256.
Boating under the influence.
Consent to blood or breath test, §29.1-738.2.
Child taken into custody.
When and how child taken into immediate custody, §16.1-246.
Detention orders for children issued by magistrate, §16.1-256.
Juvenile and domestic relations district court felony jurisdiction.
Limited to probable cause determination, §16.1-241.
Obscene books, proceeding against, §18.2-384.

PROBABLE CAUSE —Cont'd
Prisoners' health care.
Involuntary admission and treatment, §53.1-40.2.
Search warrant based upon complaint and affidavit, §19.2-52.
Search warrant to permit use of tracking device, §19.2-56.2.
Transfer of juvenile case to circuit court, §16.1-269.1.
Wiretapping.
Issuance of order authorizing interception, §19.2-68.

PROBATE OF WILLS, §§64.2-443 to 64.2-454.
See WILLS.

PROBATE TAX, LOCAL, §§58.1-3805 to 58.1-3808.
Authority of city or county, §§58.1-1718, 58.1-3805.
Charter provisions of cities.
Article construed not to affect or repeal, §58.1-3808.
Circuit court clerk.
Collection and compensation, §58.1-3806.
City charter provisions, article not construed as effecting or repealing, §58.1-3808.
Collection of tax, §58.1-3806.
City having no court for probate of wills or issuance of grants of administration, §58.1-3807.
Compensation of clerk collecting, §58.1-3806.
Imposition, §58.1-3805.
In addition to state tax, §58.1-3805.
Interpretation of article, §58.1-3808.
Levy in addition to state tax, §58.1-3805.

PROBATE TAX, STATE, §§58.1-1711 to 58.1-1718.
City or county probate tax.
Authorize, §58.1-1718.
Collection of additional tax.
Undervaluation of estate, §58.1-1717.
Fee on recording of list of heirs or affidavit.
Tax in lieu of probate tax, §58.1-1717.1.
Filing of return, §58.1-1714.
Levy, §58.1-1712.
Payment requisite to qualification, §58.1-1715.
Payment when estate committed to court-appointed administrator, §58.1-1716.
Rate, §58.1-1712.
Refund on overvaluation of estate, §58.1-1717.
Time of valuation of estate, §58.1-1713.
Title of article, §58.1-1711.
Undervaluation of estate, §58.1-1717.
Value of estate, tax based on, §58.1-1713.
Overvaluation of estate, §58.1-1717.
Undervaluation of estate, §58.1-1717.
Virginia tax on wills and administrations act, §58.1-1711.

PROBATION.
Arrests of probationers, §53.1-149.
Assault and battery against family or household member, §18.2-57.3.
Blood, saliva or tissue samples.
Taking of as condition of probation, §19.2-303.
Bodily injuries caused by probationers, §18.2-55.
Boot camp incarceration program, §§19.2-316.1, 53.1-67.1.
Change of name.
Applications of probationers, §8.01-217.
Child in need of supervision, §16.1-278.5.

PROBATION —Cont'd
Community-based probation agency.
Conditions, imposition, revocation, §19.2-303.3.
Community corrections.
Generally, §§9.1-173 to 9.1-183.
See COMMUNITY CORRECTIONS.
Probation supervision as mandated service, §9.1-176.
Community service.
Property damage or loss, §19.2-305.1.
Requiring for damages or support, §19.2-305.
Roadway litter pick-up program for probationers.
Civil immunity, §8.01-226.8.
Conditions of probation.
Blood, saliva or tissue samples, §19.2-303.
Fingerprinting, §19.2-303.
Modification, §19.2-304.
Reckless driving offense which is alcohol-related or drug-related, §46.2-392.
Release from detention center incarceration program, §19.2-316.2.
Release from diversion center incarceration program, §19.2-316.3.
Contributions by parolee towards cost of a program, §53.1-150.
Conviction of aliens.
Duties of probation officer, §19.2-294.2.
Criminal fines and penalties.
Installment payment as condition of probation, §19.2-356.
Criminal street gang.
Conviction as participant or member.
Suspension of sentence and placing on probation.
Restrictions placed on accused, §19.2-303.
Delinquent children, §16.1-278.8.
Detention center incarceration program.
Establishment, §53.1-67.8.
Release from, §19.2-316.2.
Sentence of nonviolent felons to, §19.2-316.2.
Districts, §53.1-141.
Officer assignments, §53.1-142.
Post-release supervision of felons.
Operated through probation and parole districts, §19.2-295.2.
Diversion center incarceration program.
Establishment of program, §53.1-67.7.
Release from, §19.2-316.3.
Sentencing of nonviolent felons to, §19.2-316.3.
DNA analysis.
Requiring persons to submit sample.
Probation officers, §53.1-145.
Drivers' licenses probation, §46.2-499.
Driving while intoxicated.
Education and rehabilitation of persons charged or convicted, §18.2-271.1.
Drug offenses.
First time offenders, §18.2-251.
Possession of firearm, §18.2-308.4.
Fingerprints.
Taking of fingerprints as condition of probation, §19.2-303.
First offenders, §19.2-303.2.
Property crimes, misdemeanors, §19.2-303.2.
Forcible sodomy.
Deferral of proceedings, defendant placed on probation.
Counseling or therapy, completion.
Violation against spouse, §18.2-67.1.
Global positioning system.
Wearing device as condition of probation, §19.2-303.

PROBATION —Cont'd
Hearings, §§53.1-168 to 53.1-176.
Foreign probationers.
Reincarceration procedure, §53.1-168.
Hearing officers, §53.1-169.
Probationers in foreign states, §53.1-172.
Record, §53.1-171.
Rights of probationers, §53.1-170.
Immediate sanction probation programs, §19.2-303.5.
Intensive probation supervision.
Community-based corrections system for state-responsible offenders.
Programs included in system, §53.1-67.6.
Release from detention center incarceration program, §19.2-316.2.
Release from diversion center incarceration program, §19.2-316.3.
Interstate compact for the supervision of adult offenders, §§53.1-176.1 to 53.1-176.3.
Juveniles.
Bodily injuries caused by juvenile probationers, §18.2-55.
Revocation or modification, §16.1-291.
Transfer of supervision from one county or city to another or to another state, §16.1-295.
Marijuana convictions.
First time offenders, §18.2-251.
Modification, §19.2-304.
Juveniles, §16.1-291.
Sentence suspension or modification, §19.2-303.
Object sexual penetration, §19.2-303.
Deferral of proceedings, defendant placed on probation.
Counseling or therapy, completion.
Violation against spouse, §18.2-67.2.
Officers.
See PROBATION OFFICERS.
Postrelease supervision of felons.
Felons sentenced for offenses committed on and after January 1, 1995, or July 1, 2000, §19.2-295.2.
Felons sentenced for offenses committed on and after July 1, 2006.
Sex offender registration violations, §19.2-295.2:1.
General provisions.
See PAROLE AND POSTRELEASE SUPERVISION.
Sex offender registration violations.
Felons sentenced for offenses committed on and after July 1, 2006, §19.2-295.2:1.
Presentence reports.
Preparation by probation officers in certain cases, §19.2-299.
Property crime, first offenders, §19.2-303.2.
Public assistance.
Temporary assistance for needy families.
Probationer recipient failing drug test, §63.2-605.
Rape.
Counseling or therapy, completion.
Deferral of proceedings, defendant placed on probation.
Violation against spouse, §18.2-61.
Reckless driving offense which is alcohol-related or drug-related.
Conditions, §46.2-392.
Reimbursement for cost of program.
Contributions by parolee, §53.1-150.

PROBATION —Cont'd
Restitution.
Amount of restitution, §19.2-305.2.
Enforcement of restitution order, §19.2-305.2.
Interest to be paid on award, §19.2-305.4.
Partial restitution as condition, §19.2-303.
Property damage or loss, §19.2-305.1.
Requiring for damages or support, §19.2-305.
Revocation or suspension of sentence, §§19.2-303, 19.2-306.
Boot camp incarceration program, §§19.2-316.1, 53.1-67.1.
Detention center incarceration program.
Withdrawal, removal or failure to comply with terms and conditions of probation, §19.2-316.2.
Diversion center incarceration program.
Voluntary withdrawal, removal or failure to comply with terms and conditions, §19.2-316.3.
Juveniles, §16.1-291.
Roadway litter pick-up program for probationers.
Civil immunity, §8.01-226.8.
Substance abuse screening and assessment on felony conviction, §18.2-251.01.
Supervision transfers of probationers, §53.1-148.
Temporary assistance for needy families.
Probationer recipient failing drug test, §63.2-605.

PROBATION OFFICERS.
Appointment.
Terms, §53.1-144.
Arrest of probationers, §53.1-149.
Arrest powers, §53.1-145.
Arrests of parolees without warrant, §53.1-162.
Assignment to districts, §53.1-142.
Authorization, §53.1-143.
Carnal knowledge of defendant or convicted person, §18.2-64.2.
Carrying concealed weapons, §53.1-145.
Child abuse or neglect reports.
Reason to suspect, required reports, fine for failure, §63.2-1509.
Community corrections.
Confidentiality of investigation reports, §9.1-177.1.
Local probation officers.
Duties, §9.1-176.1.
Oath of office, §9.1-177.
Compensation, §53.1-147.
Confidentiality of investigation reports, §9.1-177.1.
Conviction of aliens.
Duties of probation officers, §19.2-294.2.
Discretionary sentencing guideline worksheets.
Preparation, §19.2-298.01.
DNA analysis.
Requiring persons to submit sample, §53.1-145.
Drug and alcohol screening tests.
Authority to order, §53.1-145.
Duties, §53.1-145.
As to persons convicted of local violations, §53.1-146.
Expenses, §53.1-147.
Investigations and reports in certain cases, §19.2-299.
Juvenile and domestic relations district courts.
Compensation and expenses, §§16.1-238, 16.1-239.

PROBATION OFFICERS —Cont'd
Juvenile and domestic relations district courts —Cont'd
Detention orders, authorization to issue, §16.1-255.
Filing of reports, §16.1-274.
How services provided, §16.1-235.
Intake duties and responsibilities, §16.1-260.
Interference with or obstruction of officer, §16.1-257.
Local court service units, §16.1-235.
Oath of office, §16.1-69.17.
Powers, duties and functions, §16.1-237.
Replacement intake officers, §16.1-235.1.
State court service units, §16.1-235.
Studying report prior to transfer hearing, §16.1-269.2.
Supervisory officers, §16.1-236.
Laser, laser gun sights or device simulating laser.
Pointing at law enforcement officer, probation or parole officer, etc., §18.2-57.01.
Local community-based probation officers.
Duties, §9.1-176.1.
Oath of office, §9.1-177.
Powers, §53.1-145.
As to persons convicted of local violations, §53.1-146.
Presentence reports.
Preparation in certain cases, §19.2-299.
Sexual battery of defendant or convicted person, §18.2-67.4.
Supervision transfers, §53.1-148.
Weapons.
Carrying concealed, §53.1-145.

PRO BONO NEUTRALS.
Dispute resolution proceedings, §8.01-576.7.

PRO BONO PUBLIC SERVICE, VA SCt Rule Pt 6 §II Rule 6.1.

PROCEEDING ANONYMOUSLY, §8.01-15.1.

PROCESS.
Defined, §1-237.
Execution of process for criminal.
Officer refusing, delaying, etc., §18.2-469.
Fees generally, §17.1-272.
Resisting or obstructing execution of legal process, §18.2-409.
Service of notice, process and other papers generally.
See SERVICE OF NOTICE, PROCESS AND OTHER PAPERS.
Simulation of process, §18.2-213.
Tax commissioner, §§58.1-216, 58.1-217.

PROCESS BOOK, §17.1-215.

PROCESSING FEE.
Consumer finance companies, §6.2-1520.
Motorcycle dealers.
Disclosure of charge, §46.2-1993.23.
Motor vehicle dealers.
Subject to motor vehicle sales and use tax, §58.1-2402.

PROCUREMENT BY COUNTIES.
Centralized competitive purchasing by chief administrative officer, §15.2-1231.
Purchasing agents, §§15.2-1233 to 15.2-1240.
Certification of sufficient funds, §15.2-1238.
Competition, purchases and sales based on, §15.2-1236.

PROCUREMENT BY COUNTIES —Cont'd
Purchasing agents —Cont'd
Definitions, §15.2-1234.
Provisions not applicable until agent employed, §15.2-1233.
Review and filing of contract, §15.2-1237.
Rules and regulations governing, §15.2-1235.
Violations, §§15.2-1239, 15.2-1240.

PROCUREMENT BY PUBLIC BODIES.
Ballots and election materials exemption, §24.2-602.
Bid rigging, §§59.1-68.6 to 59.1-68.8.
Central electronic procurement system.
Purchases and supply division, maintenance, §2.2-1110.
Colleges and universities.
Restructured financial and administrative operations.
Procurement policies, §23-38.110.
Vendors, use.
Small business and supplier diversity department, determination of criteria, §2.2-1609.
Competition exemptions.
Ballots and other election materials, §24.2-602.
Competitive government act, §§2.2-5512, 2.2-5513.
Computers.
Information technologies agency, §2.2-2012.
Conspiracies to rig bids.
Combinations to rig bids, §59.1-68.7.
Defined terms, §59.1-68.6.
Enforcement of provisions, §59.1-68.8.
Contractor bidding prerequisites, §54.1-1112.
Division of purchases and supply.
Purchases equipment, supplies, etc., through division generally, §§2.2-1109 to 2.2-1128.
See PURCHASES AND SUPPLY DIVISION.
Election materials and services.
Exemptions, §24.2-602.
Electric authorities.
Applicability of act to certain authorities, §15.2-5405.1.
Energy performance-based contracts, §§11-34.1 to 11-34.4.
Governmental fraud, §§18.2-498.1 to 18.2-498.5.
Information technology.
Information technologies agency, §2.2-2012.
Public procurement act, §§2.2-4300 to 2.2-4377.
See PUBLIC PROCUREMENT.
Purchases and supply division.
Central electronic procurement system, maintenance, §2.2-1110.
Telecommunications goods and services.
Information technologies agency, §2.2-2012.
University of Virginia medical center.
Exemption from provisions, §23-77.4.
Urban county executive form government.
Purchases generally, §15.2-831.
Virginia Commonwealth University health system authority.
Exemption from procurement act, §23-50.16:34.
Virginia retirement system.
Exemption, §51.1-124.32.

PRODUCER-CONTROLLED PROPERTY AND CASUALTY INSURERS, §§38.2-1341 to 38.2-1346.

PRODUCTION OF DOCUMENTS AND THINGS.
Arbitration, §8.01-581.06.

PRODUCTION OF DOCUMENTS AND THINGS —Cont'd
Circuit courts.
Criminal cases, VA SCt Rule 3A:12.
Criminal cases, VA SCt Rule 3A:12.
Subpoena duces tecum.
Form, VA SCt Rules Part 3A Appx Form 9.
Department of agriculture and consumer services.
Authority to compel production, §18.2-340.18.
Depositions upon oral examination, VA SCt Rule 4:5.
Drug offenses.
Witnesses not excused from producing because of self-incrimination, §18.2-262.
Electronic storage of documents or information.
Criminal cases, VA SCt Rule 3A:12.
Ethics advisory panels, senate and house of general assembly.
Power to compel, §30-115.
Failure or refusal to comply, VA SCt Rule 4:9.
Fiduciaries.
Subpoena powers of fiduciaries, §64.2-1203.
Fieri facias.
Interrogatories to judgment debtor, §8.01-506.1.
Governor's power to require, §2.2-109.
Inspections by auditor of public accounts of state officers, §30-135.
Insurance companies examinations, power of state corporation commission, §38.2-1318.
Insurance rate investigations by attorney general, §38.2-1916.1.
Investigation by local governmental bodies into governmental affairs, §15.2-1409.
County board form of government.
Inquiry into official conduct of office or officer, §15.2-403.
County executive form of government.
Inquiry into official conduct of office or officer, §15.2-506.
County manager form of government.
Inquiry into official conduct of office or officer, §15.2-606.
County manager plan of government.
Inquiry into official conduct of office or officer, §15.2-709.
Urban county executive form of government.
Inquiry into official conduct of office or officer, §15.2-814.
Juvenile and domestic relations district courts.
Requests for subpoenas for witnesses and records, VA SCt Rule 8:13.
Medical malpractice review panels, §8.01-581.6, MedMal Rule 6.
Medical records.
Evidentiary effect of copies, §8.01-413.
Non-parties.
Production by a person not party, VA SCt Rule 4:9A.
Procedure, VA SCt Rule 4:9.
Sanctions.
Failure to respond to request for inspection, VA SCt Rule 4:12.
Scope, VA SCt Rule 4:9.
Size of paper, VA SCt Rule 1:16.
State corporation commission.
Power to compel, §12.1-13, VA Const Art IX §3.
Subpoenas duces tecum.
See SUBPOENAS DUCES TECUM.

PRODUCTION OF DOCUMENTS AND THINGS —Cont'd
Tax commissioner and department of taxation.
Writs, notices, etc., compelling production of books and papers, §58.1-216.
Time limitations.
Waiver by parties, §8.01-384.2.
Uniform interstate depositions and discovery act.
Electronically stored information.
Production of, subject to act, VA SCt Rule 4:9.
Wills.
Probate, §64.2-446.
Compelling production of wills, §64.2-449.

PRODUCTS LIABILITY.
Consolidation of issues or claims, §8.01-374.1.
Risk retention groups and purchasing groups, §§38.2-5100 to 38.2-5115.
See RISK RETENTION GROUPS AND PURCHASING GROUPS.
Statute of limitations, §8.01-243.
Accrual of right of action, §8.01-230.
Personal actions based on contract, §8.01-246.
When cause of action deemed to accrue, §8.01-249.
Trial.
Bifurcated trial, §8.01-374.1.
Consolidation of issues or claims, §8.01-374.1.

PROFANITY, ABUSIVE LANGUAGE TO ANOTHER, §18.2-416.
Action for insulting words, §8.01-45.
Harassment by computer.
Profane communication, §18.2-152.7:1.
Uniform fine schedule, VA SCt Rules 3C:1, 3C:2.

PROFANITY, SWEARING IN PUBLIC, §18.2-388.
Uniform fine schedule, VA SCt Rules 3C:1, 3C:2.

PROFANITY, TELEPHONE OR CITIZENS BAND RADIO, §18.2-427.

PROFESSIONAL AND OCCUPATIONAL REGULATION DEPARTMENT.
Architects.
Professions and occupations regulation, §§54.1-400 to 54.1-411.
See ARCHITECTS.
Asbestos contractors and workers, §§54.1-500 to 54.1-517.
See ASBESTOS CONTRACTORS AND WORKERS.
Auctioneers, §§54.1-600 to 54.1-607.
Barbers, §§54.1-700 to 54.1-706.
Board for professional and occupational regulation, §54.1-309.
Degrees of regulation, §54.1-311.
Duties, §54.1-310.
Generally, §§54.1-200 to 54.1-204.
Powers, §54.1-310.
Boxing, martial arts and wrestling events generally, §§54.1-828 to 54.1-835.
See BOXING, MARTIAL ARTS AND WRESTLING EVENTS.
Branch pilots, §§54.1-900 to 54.1-927.
See BRANCH PILOTS.
Cash bonds interest, §54.1-308.1.
Cemetery operators, perpetual care trust funds and preneed burial contracts, §§54.1-2310 to 54.1-2342.
Complaints.
Filing, §54.1-307.1.
Continuation of department, §54.1-301.

PROFESSIONAL AND OCCUPATIONAL REGULATION DEPARTMENT —Cont'd
Contractors, §§54.1-1100 to 54.1-1127.
See CONTRACTORS.
Criminal background investigations.
Record information, dissemination, §19.2-389.
Defined terms, §54.1-300.
Dialysis patient care technicians, §§54.1-2729.1 to 54.1-2729.3.
Director.
Agent for service of process.
Nonresident contractors, §54.1-1113.
Appointment, §54.1-301.
Compensation, §54.1-308.
Contractors, complaints against.
Investigations, §54.1-1114.
Contractors, nonresident.
Agent for service of process, §54.1-1113.
Defined, §54.1-300.
Duties, §54.1-304.
Supervision of department, §54.1-302.
Powers, §§54.1-303, 54.1-304.
Supervision of department, §54.1-302.
Real estate transaction recovery fund, §§54.1-2112 to 54.1-2120.
Register of applicants for contractors' licenses, §54.1-1104.
Service of process agent.
Appointment by nonresident real estate appraisers, §54.1-2019.
Nonresident real estate brokers, salespersons and rental agents, §54.1-2111.
Surety bond, §54.1-305.
Transaction recovery act, §§54.1-1118 to 54.1-1127.
Engineers, §§54.1-400 to 54.1-411.
See ENGINEERS.
Expenses, §54.1-308.
Fingerprints of polygraph examiners.
Submission, §54.1-1804.
Interest on cash bonds held by regulatory boards, §54.1-308.1.
Interior designers, §§54.1-412 to 54.1-414.
Investigations, §54.1-306.
Landscape architects, §§54.1-400 to 54.1-411.
See LANDSCAPE ARCHITECTS.
Opticians.
See OPTICIANS.
Polygraph examiners, §§54.1-1800 to 54.1-1806.
See POLYGRAPH EXAMINERS.
Real estate appraisal management companies, §§54.1-2020 to 54.1-2023.
Real estate appraisers, §§54.1-2009 to 54.1-2019.
See REAL ESTATE APPRAISERS.
Real estate brokers, salespersons and rental agents, §§54.1-2100 to 54.1-2145.
See REAL ESTATE BROKERS, SALESPERSONS AND RENTAL AGENTS.
Regulatory boards.
Composition, §54.1-200.
Consent agreements.
Delegating to director authority to enter into, §54.1-202.
Costs, recovery of, §54.1-203.
Duties, §54.1-201.
General provisions, §§54.1-100 to 54.1-114.
Initial notice by certified mail, subsequent notices by regular mail, §54.1-101.1.
Interest on cash bonds held by boards, §54.1-308.1.
Monetary penalties, §54.1-202.

PROFESSIONAL AND OCCUPATIONAL REGULATION DEPARTMENT —Cont'd
Regulatory boards —Cont'd
Notice to regulant of right to request informal fact-finding conference, §54.1-201.
Powers, §54.1-201.
Prior convictions.
Abridgement of rights, §54.1-204.
Temporary licenses and certifications.
Issuance to persons licensed in another state, §54.1-201.1.
Rental location agents, §§54.1-2100 to 54.1-2145.
See REAL ESTATE BROKERS, SALESPERSONS AND RENTAL AGENTS.
Secretary of commerce and trade.
Agency responsibility, §2.2-204.
Soil scientists, wetland professionals and geologists, §§54.1-2200 to 54.1-2208.4.
Subpoenas, §54.1-307.
Supervision of department, §54.1-302.
Surveyors, §§54.1-400 to 54.1-411.
See SURVEYORS.
Tax information.
Tax commissioner authorized to divulge, §58.1-3.
Temporary licenses and certifications.
Issuance to persons licensed in another state, §54.1-201.1.
Waterworks operators, §§54.1-2300 to 54.1-2302.

PROFESSIONAL ATHLETES.
Beer and wine advertising.
Display incorporating use of, §4.1-209.
Bribery of participants, §§18.2-442, 18.2-443.

PROFESSIONAL ATHLETIC TEAMS.
Beer and wine advertising.
Display incorporating use of, §4.1-209.

PROFESSIONAL BONDSMEN.
Acceptance of collateral, §9.1-185.10.
Applicability of provisions.
Exception, §9.1-185.1.
Bail enforcement agents, §§9.1-186 to 9.1-186.13.
See BAIL ENFORCEMENT AGENTS.
Criminal justice services department.
Investigations, §9.1-185.3.
Licensing, powers, §9.1-185.3.
List of licensed bondsmen.
To correctional facilities, §9.1-185.17.
To state corporation commission, §9.1-185.16.
Regulatory authority, §§9.1-102, 9.1-185.2.
Criminal violations, §9.1-185.18.
Definitions, §9.1-185.
Fees charged, §9.1-185.8.
Firearms training and usage, §9.1-185.11.
Information required on bonds, §9.1-185.8.
License granted by county or city, §58.1-3724.
Licensing.
Application, §9.1-185.5.
Criminal justice services department powers, §9.1-185.3.
Examination requirement, §9.1-185.5.
Grounds for license discipline, §9.1-185.8.
Ineligible persons, §9.1-185.4.
Nonresidents, §9.1-185.7.
Qualifications, §9.1-185.4.
Renewal, §9.1-185.6.
Term, §9.1-185.6.
List of licensed bondsmen.
To correctional facilities, §9.1-185.17.
To state corporation commission, §9.1-185.16.
Premiums, amount to be charged, §9.1-185.8.

PROFESSIONAL BONDSMEN —Cont'd
Prohibited acts, §9.1-185.8.
Criminal violations, §9.1-185.18.
Proof of collateral for licensing, §9.1-185.5.
Recordkeeping requirements, §9.1-185.13.
Recovery of bailee, §9.1-185.15.
Reports, §9.1-185.14.
Solicitation of business, §9.1-185.9.
Uniform, §9.1-185.12.

PROFESSIONAL BOXING AND WRESTLING.
Generally, §§54.1-828 to 54.1-835.
See BOXING, MARTIAL ARTS AND WRESTLING EVENTS.

PROFESSIONAL BOXING, WRESTLING AND MARTIAL ARTS ADVISORY BOARD, §54.1-831.01.

PROFESSIONAL CORPORATIONS, §§13.1-542.1 to 13.1-556.
Accounting, special provisions for corporations engaged in, §13.1-549.1.
Applicability of general corporations laws, §13.1-556.
Architects, board of directors, §13.1-553.
Architects, special provisions for corporations rendering services, §13.1-549.
Authority to render professional services, §13.1-542.1.
Authorized entities, §13.1-542.1.
Board of directors, §13.1-553.
Confidential relationship between person rendering services and person receiving not affected, §13.1-547.
Conflict of laws, §13.1-556.
Conversion into nonprofessional corporation, §§13.1-552, 13.1-553.
Deceased shareholders, disposition of shares, §13.1-552.
Definitions, §13.1-543.
Disposition of shares of deceased or disqualified shareholders, §13.1-552.
Disqualification of shareholder, §13.1-551.
Disposition of shares, §13.1-552.
Engaging in other business prohibited, §13.1-548.
Engineers, board of directors, §13.1-553.
Engineers, special provisions for corporations rendering services, §13.1-549.
Fiduciaries, professional law corporation qualifying as, §13.1-546.1.
Foreign professional corporation.
Certificate of authority, §13.1-544.2.
Merger with, §13.1-545.1.
General corporations laws, applicability, §13.1-556.
Income taxes, §13.1-554.1.
Interior designers, board of directors, §13.1-553.
Interior designers, special provisions for corporations using title of, §13.1-549.
Investing funds in real estate, mortgages, stocks, etc., §13.1-548.
Landscape architects, board of directors, §13.1-553.
Landscape architects, special provisions for corporations rendering services, §13.1-549.
Law corporations qualifying as executor, administrator or other fiduciary, §13.1-546.1.

PROFESSIONAL CORPORATIONS —Cont'd
Law corporations, registration certificate required, §13.1-549.2.
Liability for debts of corporation, directors, officers and employees, §13.1-547.
Merger.
Foreign professional corporation or foreign professional limited liability company, §13.1-545.1.
Requirements, §13.1-555.
Nonprofessional employees and officers, §13.1-546.
Organizers need not be employees, §13.1-546.
P.C., use of initials following corporate name, §13.1-544.1.
Practice of law, §54.1-3902.
Proceedings pending disciplinary actions, §54.1-3936.
Revocation of certificate of registration, §54.1-3937.
Professional limited liability companies, §§13.1-1100 to 13.1-1123.
See PROFESSIONAL LIMITED LIABILITY COMPANIES.
Professional relationships between persons furnishing services and persons receiving not affected, §13.1-547.
Property taxes, §13.1-554.1.
Qualified charitable remainder trust.
Shareholder transferring shares to, §13.1-550.
Rendering professional services, §13.1-546.
Shareholders.
Disposition of shares of deceased or disqualified shareholders, §13.1-552.
Disqualification, §13.1-551.
Need not be employees, §13.1-546.
Qualifications, §13.1-549.
Transfer of shares, §13.1-550.
Who may become, §13.1-544.
Surveyors, board of directors, §13.1-553.
Surveyors, special provisions for corporations rendering services, §13.1-549.
Transfer of shares, §13.1-550.
Who may organize, §13.1-544.

PROFESSIONAL COUNSELOR-CLIENT PRIVILEGE, §8.01-400.2, VA SCt Rule 2:506.

PROFESSIONAL COUNSELORS.
Bills for medical services.
Presumption of authenticity and reasonableness, §8.01-413.01.
Board certification of rehabilitation providers, §54.1-3514.
Renewal of certification, §54.1-3515.
Counselors generally.
See COUNSELORS.
Disasters, state or local emergency.
Immunity.
Abandonment of person owed duty of health care in response to disaster, §8.01-225.01.
Unable to provide required care because of lack of resources, §8.01-225.02.
Donation of services.
Tax credit, §58.1-439.22.
Duty to protect third parties.
Violent behavior or serious harm by client, §54.1-2403.2.
Immunity.
Disasters, state or local emergency.
Abandonment of person owed duty of health care in response to disaster, §8.01-225.01.

PROFESSIONAL COUNSELORS —Cont'd
Immunity —Cont'd
Disasters, state or local emergency —Cont'd
Unable to provide required care because of lack of resources, §8.01-225.02.
Licensing, §§54.1-3500 to 54.1-3506.
Medical bills.
Presumption of authenticity and reasonableness, §8.01-413.01.
Medical malpractice.
Health professional civil immunity, §8.01-581.13.
Privileged communications, §8.01-400.2, VA SCt Rule 2:506.
Prohibited acts by licensees generally, §54.1-2409.1.
Tax credit.
Donation of services, §58.1-439.22.
Title restrictions.
Applicability, §54.1-3513.
Sex offender treatment provider, §54.1-3611.

PROFESSIONAL EMPLOYER ORGANIZATIONS.
Defined, §65.2-101.
Insurance rates, §38.2-1921.1.
Registration, requirements before offering services, service agreements, §65.2-803.1.
Civil penalty for noncompliance, §65.2-805.

PROFESSIONAL LIMITED LIABILITY COMPANIES, §§13.1-1100 to 13.1-1123.
Agents.
Disqualification, §13.1-1116.
Liability for debts, etc., §13.1-1109.
Nonprofessional agents, §13.1-1107.
Architects, engineers, surveyors and landscape architects.
Special provisions, §13.1-1111.
Attorneys.
Registration certificate required, §13.1-1113.
Authority to render professional services, §13.1-1101.1.
Authorized entities, §13.1-1101.1.
Certificate of authority.
Foreign professional companies, §13.1-1105.
Conduct of business.
Not authorized to engage in other business, §13.1-1110.
Conversion to nonprofessional company, §13.1-1117.
Decedents' estates.
Disposition of membership interests, §13.1-1117.
Defined, §§13.1-1102, 13.1-1123.
Dentistry, practice of, §54.1-2717.
Employees.
Disqualification, §13.1-1116.
Liability for debts, etc., §13.1-1109.
Nonprofessional employees, §13.1-1107.
Executors and administrators.
Authorized to act in fiduciary capacity, §13.1-1108.
Fiduciaries.
Company authorized to act in fiduciary capacity, §13.1-1108.
Foreign professional companies.
Certificate of authority, §13.1-1105.
General assembly.
Reservation of power to amend or repeal, §13.1-1100.
Income taxes, §13.1-1120.
Independent contractors.
Professional practice, §13.1-1107.

PROFESSIONAL LIMITED LIABILITY COMPANIES —Cont'd
Interior designers.
Special provisions for companies using title of, §13.1-1111.
Investment of funds, §13.1-1110.
Legislative purpose, §13.1-1101.
Limited liability companies generally, §§13.1-1000 to 13.1-1080.
See LIMITED LIABILITY COMPANIES.
Limited liability company act.
Applicability to professional companies, §13.1-1122.
Management.
Vested in members, §13.1-1118.
Managers.
Disqualification, §13.1-1116.
Employee status not required, §13.1-1107.
Liability for debts, etc., §13.1-1109.
Management authority, §13.1-1118.
Membership.
Deceased members.
Disposition of membership interests, §13.1-1117.
Disqualification of member, §13.1-1116.
Disposition of membership interests, §13.1-1117.
Employee status not required, §13.1-1107.
Liability of members for debts, etc., §13.1-1109.
Qualifications, §§13.1-1103, 13.1-1111.
Who may become a member, §13.1-1103.
Transfer of interests, §13.1-1115.
Who may become a member, §13.1-1103.
Merger, §13.1-1106.
Statutory requirements, §13.1-1121.
Surviving entity requirement, §13.1-1121.
Name.
Use of certain initials, §13.1-1104.
Practice of law, §54.1-3902.
Proceedings pending disciplinary actions, §54.1-3936.
Revocation of certificate of registration, §54.1-3937.
Professional business entity.
Defined, §13.1-1102.
Professional services.
Defined, §13.1-1102.
Property taxes, §13.1-1120.
Public accountancy.
Special provisions, §13.1-1112.
Public policy, §13.1-1101.
Purposes, §13.1-1101.
Qualified charitable remainder trust.
Transfer membership interest, §13.1-1115.
Reservation of power.
General assembly.
Power to amend or repeal act, §13.1-1100.
Taxation.
Income and property taxes, §13.1-1120.
Transfer of membership interests, §13.1-1115.

PROFESSIONAL RESPONSIBILITY, CODE OF.
See ATTORNEYS AT LAW.

PROFESSIONS AND OCCUPATIONS.
Accessibility mechanics.
Certification, §§54.1-1140 to 54.1-1143.
Architects, §§54.1-400 to 54.1-411.
See ARCHITECTS.
Asbestos contractors and workers, §§54.1-500 to 54.1-517.
See ASBESTOS CONTRACTORS AND WORKERS.
Athletic trainers, §§54.1-2957.4 to 54.1-2957.6.

PROFESSIONS AND OCCUPATIONS —Cont'd
Attorneys.
Licensing, §§54.1-3900 to 54.1-3944.
See ATTORNEYS AT LAW.
Auctioneers, §§54.1-600 to 54.1-607.
Audiologists, §§54.1-2600 to 54.1-2604.
Barbers, §§54.1-700 to 54.1-706.
Boxing, martial arts and wrestling events, §§54.1-828 to 54.1-835.
See BOXING, MARTIAL ARTS AND WRESTLING EVENTS.
Branch pilots, §§54.1-900 to 54.1-927.
See BRANCH PILOTS.
Cemetery operators, perpetual care trust funds and preneed burial contracts, §§54.1-2310 to 54.1-2342.
Certificates generally.
Social security numbers, §54.1-116.
Child support enforcement by department of social services.
License, certificate or registration.
Suspension, delinquency in payments, §63.2-1937.
Chiropractors.
Generally.
See CHIROPRACTORS.
Licensing generally, §§54.1-2929 to 54.1-2941.
See MEDICINE AND OTHER HEALING ARTS PROFESSIONS.
Clinical psychologists.
Licensing generally, §§54.1-2929 to 54.1-2941.
See MEDICINE AND OTHER HEALING ARTS PROFESSIONS.
Coal mine worker certification, §§45.1-161.24 to 45.1-161.41.
Common interest community managers, §§54.1-2345 to 54.1-2354.
Contractors, §§54.1-1100 to 54.1-1127.
See CONTRACTORS.
Cosmetology.
Barbers, §§54.1-700 to 54.1-706.
Counselors, §§54.1-3500 to 54.1-3506.
Dentistry, §§54.1-2700 to 54.1-2729.
See DENTISTRY.
Dialysis patient care technicians, §§54.1-2729.1 to 54.1-2729.3.
Diplomats.
Expiration of documents issued to persons in diplomatic service, §54.1-117.
Doctors of medicine.
Generally.
See PHYSICIANS OR SURGEONS.
Licensing generally, §§54.1-2929 to 54.1-2941.
See MEDICINE AND OTHER HEALING ARTS PROFESSIONS.
Drug control, §§54.1-3400 to 54.1-3472.
See DRUG CONTROL.
Elevator mechanics.
Certification, §§54.1-1140 to 54.1-1143.
Engineers, §§54.1-400 to 54.1-411.
See ENGINEERS.
False occupation, establishing, §18.2-204.1.
Firearm dealers, §§54.1-4200 to 54.1-4202.
Funeral services, §§54.1-2800 to 54.1-2825.
See FUNERAL SERVICES.
Home inspectors.
Board for asbestos, lead and home inspectors, §§54.1-500.1, 54.1-501.
Certification of inspectors, §54.1-517.2.
Defined, §54.1-500.

PROFESSIONS AND OCCUPATIONS —Cont'd
Home inspectors —Cont'd
Certificate to practice.
Requirements, §54.1-517.2.
Certified home inspections.
Defined, §54.1-500.
Requirements for certified inspection, §54.1-517.1.
Licenses.
Disciplinary actions against licensees, §§54.1-516, 54.1-516.1.
Unlawful use of licensure, §§54.1-111, 54.1-517.1.
Industrial hygiene and safety profession.
Protection of job title, §§40.1-139 to 40.1-142.
Intangible personal property tax.
Exemption of professions regulated by Commonwealth, §58.1-1103.
Interior designers, §§54.1-412 to 54.1-414.
Itinerant merchants, §§54.1-4300 to 54.1-4306.
Landscape architects, §§54.1-400 to 54.1-411.
See LANDSCAPE ARCHITECTS.
License applications generally.
Social security numbers, §54.1-116.
Licensed substance abuse treatment practitioners, §§54.1-3507, 54.1-3508.
License taxes generally, §§58.1-3700 to 58.1-3735.
See LICENSE TAXES.
Lie detector test examiners, §§54.1-1800 to 54.1-1806.
See POLYGRAPH EXAMINERS.
Limited liability companies.
General provisions, §§13.1-1000 to 13.1-1080.
See LIMITED LIABILITY COMPANIES.
Professional limited liability companies, §§13.1-1100 to 13.1-1123.
See PROFESSIONAL LIMITED LIABILITY COMPANIES.
Localities.
Violations of professional license requirements, statute of limitations, §19.2-8.
Marriage and family therapists, §§54.1-3500 to 54.1-3506.
See COUNSELORS.
Medical equipment suppliers.
Permits, §§54.1-3435.2, 54.1-3435.3.
Medicine and other healing arts professions, §§54.1-2900 to 54.1-2993.
See MEDICINE AND OTHER HEALING ARTS PROFESSIONS.
Military affairs.
Expediting issuance of licenses to military spouses, §54.1-119.
Expiration of documents issued to persons in service in armed services, §54.1-117.
Military experience, training and education as substantially equivalent to qualifications for licensure, §54.1-118.
Mortgage loan originators, §§6.2-1700 to 6.2-1721.
See MORTGAGE LOAN ORIGINATORS.
Motorcycle dealers, §§46.2-1993 to 46.2-1993.82.
See MOTORCYCLE DEALERS.
Nail care.
Barbers, §§54.1-700 to 54.1-706.
Nursing, §§54.1-3000 to 54.1-3028.1.
See NURSING.
Nursing home and assisted living facility administrators, §§54.1-3100 to 54.1-3103.1.
Optometrists, §§54.1-3200 to 54.1-3221.
See OPTOMETRISTS.

PROFESSIONS AND OCCUPATIONS —Cont'd
Osteopathic medicine.
Licensing generally, §§54.1-2929 to 54.1-2941.
See MEDICINE AND OTHER HEALING ARTS PROFESSIONS.
Pawnbrokers, §§54.1-4000 to 54.1-4014.
See PAWNBROKERS.
Payday loans.
Licensing and regulation of person making, §§6.2-1800 to 6.2-1829.
See PAYDAY LOANS.
Pharmacists, §§54.1-3300 to 54.1-3321.
See PHARMACISTS AND PHARMACIES.
Physical therapists.
General provisions, §§54.1-3473 to 54.1-3483.
See PHYSICAL THERAPISTS.
Licensing generally, §§54.1-2950.1 to 54.1-2957.01.
See MEDICINE AND OTHER HEALING ARTS PROFESSIONS.
Physical therapists' assistants.
Licensing generally, §§54.1-2950.1 to 54.1-2957.01.
See MEDICINE AND OTHER HEALING ARTS PROFESSIONS.
Physician assistants.
Licensing generally, §§54.1-2950.1 to 54.1-2957.01.
See MEDICINE AND OTHER HEALING ARTS PROFESSIONS.
Physicians or surgeons.
Generally.
See PHYSICIANS OR SURGEONS.
Licensing generally, §§54.1-2929 to 54.1-2941.
See MEDICINE AND OTHER HEALING ARTS PROFESSIONS.
Pilots.
Branch pilots, §§54.1-900 to 54.1-927.
See BRANCH PILOTS.
Podiatrists.
Generally.
See PODIATRISTS.
Licensing generally, §§54.1-2929 to 54.1-2941.
See MEDICINE AND OTHER HEALING ARTS PROFESSIONS.
Podiatrists' assistants.
Licensing generally, §§54.1-2950.1 to 54.1-2957.01.
See MEDICINE AND OTHER HEALING ARTS PROFESSIONS.
Polygraph examiners, §§54.1-1800 to 54.1-1806.
See POLYGRAPH EXAMINERS.
Precious metals dealers, §§54.1-4100 to 54.1-4111.
See PRECIOUS METALS DEALERS.
Professional corporations generally, §§13.1-542.1 to 13.1-556.
See PROFESSIONAL CORPORATIONS.
Professional limited liability companies.
General provisions, §§13.1-1100 to 13.1-1123.
See PROFESSIONAL LIMITED LIABILITY COMPANIES.
Psychologists, §§54.1-3600 to 54.1-3606.1.
See PSYCHOLOGISTS.
Public weighmasters, §§3.2-5800 to 3.2-5820.
See WEIGHMASTERS, PUBLIC.
Real estate appraisal management companies, §§54.1-2020 to 54.1-2023.
Real estate appraisers, §§54.1-2009 to 54.1-2019.
See REAL ESTATE APPRAISERS.

PROFESSIONS AND OCCUPATIONS —Cont'd
Real estate brokers, salespersons and rental agents, §§54.1-2100 to 54.1-2145.
See REAL ESTATE BROKERS, SALESPERSONS AND RENTAL AGENTS.
Rental location agents, §§54.1-2100 to 54.1-2145.
See REAL ESTATE BROKERS, SALESPERSONS AND RENTAL AGENTS.
Residential building energy analysts, §§54.1-1144 to 54.1-1146.
Social security numbers.
Applicants for licensure, certification, registration or authorization to provide, §63.2-1937.
Social workers, §§54.1-3700 to 54.1-3709.
Soil scientists, wetland professionals and geologists, §§54.1-2200 to 54.1-2208.4.
Speech pathologists, §§54.1-2600 to 54.1-2604.
Substance abuse treatment practitioners, §§54.1-3507, 54.1-3508.
Surveyors, §§54.1-400 to 54.1-411.
See SURVEYORS.
Trailer dealers, §§46.2-1992 to 46.2-1992.85.
See TRAILER DEALERS.
Unlawful acts generally, §54.1-111.
Time limitation on prosecution, §19.2-8.
Veterinarians.
See VETERINARIANS.
Veterinary medicine, §§54.1-3800 to 54.1-3813.
Warehousers of prescription drugs.
Permits, §54.1-3435.4.
Waste management facility operators, §§54.1-2209 to 54.1-2212.
Water well systems providers.
Certification, §§54.1-1128 to 54.1-1130.
Waterworks operators, §§54.1-2300 to 54.1-2302.
Weighmasters, public, §§3.2-5800 to 3.2-5820.
See WEIGHMASTERS, PUBLIC.
Wholesale distributors of prescription drugs.
Licensing, §§54.1-3435, 54.1-3435.1.
Exemptions, §54.1-3435.02.
Registration, §54.1-3435.01.

PROFFERED CASH PAYMENTS AND EXPENDITURES.
Conditional zoning, §15.2-2303.
Locality accepting as part of rezoning application.
Alternative improvements.
Utilization of proffered cash payments for, §15.2-2303.2.
Amount of proffered cash payments received during fiscal year.
Inclusion in capital improvement program, §15.2-2303.2.
Cash payments not accepted during fiscal year.
Notification to commission on local government, §15.2-2303.2.
Collecting or accepting after final inspection, §15.2-2303.1:1.
Commission on local government, report by, §15.2-2303.2.
Forfeiture by locality of cash payments.
Failure to timely begin work on improvements for which cash payments proffered, §15.2-2303.2.
Reports to commission on local government, §15.2-2303.2.
Voluntary agreement to earlier payment date, §15.2-2303.3.
Waiver of future rights as part of proffer, severable and void, §15.2-2303.3.

PROFFERED CASH PAYMENTS AND EXPENDITURES —Cont'd
Locality accepting as part of rezoning application —Cont'd
When locality may require payment, §15.2-2303.3.

PROFITS FROM CRIME.
Criminal forfeiture, §§19.2-368.19 to 19.2-368.22.

PROFIT-SHARING PLANS.
Security registration exemption, §13.1-514.

PRO HAC VICE, §54.1-3900.
Out-of-state attorneys, VA SCt Rule 1A:4.
Application to appear pro hoc vice before a Virginia tribunal, VA SCt Rules Part 1A Appx Form 1.

PROHIBITING PROXIMITY TO CHILDREN, SEX OFFENSES, §18.2-370.2.
Punishment authorized for felony, §18.2-10.
Punishment authorized for misdemeanor offense, §18.2-11.

PROHIBITION, VA Const Art VI §1, US Const Amds 18, 21.
Annexation.
Compelling city or town to carry out provisions, §15.2-3220.
Application for writ, §8.01-644.
Suspension of proceedings, §8.01-650.
Verified petition under oath, §8.01-644.
What petition to state, §8.01-645.
Where presented, §8.01-645.
Award of writ.
Defendant failure to appear or make defense, §8.01-646.
What judgment to be rendered, §8.01-648.
Circuit courts.
Jurisdiction, §17.1-513.
Contempt.
Enforcement of writ, §8.01-652.
Court of appeals.
Jurisdiction, §17.1-404.
Stay of proceedings by judge of court of appeals, §8.01-651.
Defendant's responsive pleading, §8.01-647.
Enforcement of writ, §8.01-652.
Jurisdiction of circuit courts, §17.1-513.
Jurisdiction of court of appeals, §17.1-404.
Jurisdiction of supreme court, §17.1-309.
Service of writ, §8.01-652.
State board of elections.
Power to petition for, §24.2-103.
State corporation commission.
Writ lies from supreme court to commission, §12.1-39.
Supreme court.
Jurisdiction, §17.1-309, VA SCt Rule 5:7, VA Const Art VI §1.
Stay of proceedings by justice of supreme court, §8.01-651.
When writ to issue and be tried, §17.1-311.
Suspension of proceedings.
Application for writ, §8.01-650.
Trial court failure to stay proceedings.
Appellate court suspension of proceedings, §8.01-651.
Venue.
Preferred forum, §8.01-261.

PROHIBITION OF LIQUOR, US Const Amds 18, 21.

PROJECT DISCOVERY.
Block grants, §22.1-199.1.

PROJECT YES.
Block grants, §22.1-199.1.

PROMISE.
Actions.
By one not a party thereto, §55-22.
Contracts.
See CONTRACTS.
Covenants.
See COVENANTS.
Frauds, statute of, §11-2.
Limitation of actions.
New promise.
Effect, §8.01-229.
New promise.
Effect, §8.01-229.
Seduction.
See SEDUCTION.
Statute of frauds, §11-2.
Third-party beneficiary may sue, §55-22.
Written evidence required to maintain action, §11-2.

PROMISE TO APPEAR.
Summons issued in lieu of warrant, §19.2-74.

PROMISSORY NOTES.
Electronic transactions.
Transferable records, §59.1-494.
False statements to obtain property or credit, §18.2-186.
Food sold at retail.
Acceptance of promissory notes in payment for, §18.2-241.
Lost notes, other evidences of debt.
Indemnifying bond required for action, §8.01-32.
Shares in stock corporation.
Note as consideration, §13.1-643.
Transferability.
Nonprobate transfer on death, §64.2-620.

PROMOTERS.
Boxing, martial arts and wrestling events.
Defined, §54.1-828.
Generally, §§54.1-828 to 54.1-835.
See BOXING, MARTIAL ARTS AND WRESTLING EVENTS.
License and bond requirements, §54.1-829.
Firearms shows.
Notice prior to show, vendor or exhibitor list, duty to maintain, copy to law enforcement, §54.1-4201.1.

PROMOTIONAL LICENSE PLATES.
Motorcycle dealers, §46.2-1993.43.
Trailer dealers, §46.2-1992.43.

PROMOTIONAL PRIZES AND GIFTS, §§59.1-415 to 59.1-423.
Actions, §59.1-421.
Checks, simulated, §59.1-419.
Consumer protection, prohibited practices, §59.1-200.
Defined terms, §59.1-415.
Enforcement of provisions, §59.1-422.
Exemption from provisions, §59.1-423.
Handling charges.
Conditions for, §59.1-420.
Invoices, simulated, §59.1-419.
Membership camping, §59.1-332.
Pay-per-call service telephone numbers, §59.1-417.

PROMOTIONAL PRIZES AND GIFTS —Cont'd
Provision violations.
Penalties, §59.1-422.
Representation of being specially selected, §59.1-418.
Representations of eligibility to win, §59.1-417.
Representations of having won, §59.1-416.
Shipping charges.
Conditions for, §59.1-420.
Travel clubs.
Prohibited practices, §59.1-449.

PROMOTION OF UNIFORMITY OF LEGISLATION.
Commissioners, §§30-196, 30-197.

PROMPT COLLECTION OF ACCOUNT RECEIVABLE.
Division of debt collection, §2.2-519.

PROMPT PAYMENT.
Insurance claims.
Life, accident and sickness insurance guaranty association, §§38.2-1700 to 38.2-1721.
See LIFE, ACCIDENT AND SICKNESS INSURANCE GUARANTY ASSOCIATION.
Virginia property and casualty insurance guaranty association, §§38.2-1600 to 38.2-1623.
Localities, §§2.2-4352, 2.2-4354.
State agencies, §§2.2-4347 to 2.2-4356.
Defect or impropriety in invoice, §2.2-4351.
Definitions, §2.2-4347.
Exemptions, §2.2-4348.
Generally, §2.2-4350.
Interest penalty, §2.2-4355.
Localities generally, §2.2-4352.
Payment clauses to be included in contract, §2.2-4354.
Payment clauses to be included in contracts, §2.2-4354.
Postmark date deemed payment date, §2.2-4353.
Reports by comptroller, §2.2-4356.
Retainage to remain valid, §2.2-4349.
Separate payment dates, §2.2-4350.
Virginia Commonwealth University health system authority, §23-50.16:6.

PROOF OF FINANCIAL RESPONSIBILITY, MOTOR VEHICLES, §§46.2-435 to 46.2-463.
See MOTOR VEHICLE FINANCIAL RESPONSIBILITY.

PROOF OF INSURANCE.
Cotton warehouses, §3.2-4765.

PROOF OF LOSS.
Forms furnished by insurer, §38.2-320.
Health insurance.
Group insurance policy provision, §38.2-3536.
Individual policies, §38.2-3503.
Insurance policy requiring to be filed within specified time.
Time consumed in adjusting claim not considered, §38.2-314.

PROPANE.
Liquefied petroleum gas containers, §§18.2-493 to 18.2-498.
Retail sales and use tax exemption.
Domestic consumption, §§58.1-609.10, 58.1-609.13.
Exception, local sales or use tax, §58.1-609.13.

PROPERTY.
Abandoned property.
Disposition of unclaimed property.
Escheat, §§55-168 to 55-201.1.
See ESCHEAT.
Generally, §§55-210.1 to 55-210.30.
See UNCLAIMED PROPERTY.
After-acquired property.
Deed validity, §55-52.
Appointment powers.
Release of, §§64.2-2700 to 64.2-2704.
Assignments for benefit of creditors, §§55-156 to 55-160.
Carriers.
Motor carriers of property generally, §§46.2-2100 to 46.2-2176.
See MOTOR CARRIERS, PROPERTY.
Cattle guards, §§55-304, 55-305.
Church property, §§57-7.1 to 57-17.
Community property rights at death, §§64.2-315 to 64.2-324.
See COMMUNITY PROPERTY RIGHTS AT DEATH.
Commutation and valuation of certain estates and interests, §§55-269.1 to 55-277.
Condominiums, §§55-79.39 to 55-79.103.
See CONDOMINIUMS.
Cooperatives, §§55-424 to 55-506.
See REAL ESTATE COOPERATIVES.
Custodial trusts, §§64.2-900 to 64.2-918.
See CUSTODIAL TRUSTS.
Deeds generally, §§55-48 to 55-79.
See DEEDS.
Descent and distribution generally, §§64.2-200 to 64.2-206.
See DESCENT AND DISTRIBUTION.
Disclaimer of property interests, §§64.2-2600 to 64.2-2614.
See DISCLAIMER OF PROPERTY INTERESTS.
Drift property, §§55-202 to 55-210.
Emblements, §§55-249 to 55-252.
Escheat, §§55-168 to 55-201.1.
See ESCHEAT.
Estates in land, §§55-1 to 55-25.1.
See ESTATES IN LAND.
Estrays, §§55-202 to 55-206.
Federal lien registrations, §§55-142.1 to 55-142.9.
Fences.
Cattle guards, §§55-304, 55-305.
Division fences, §§55-317 to 55-322.
Electric fences, §§55-298.1 to 55-298.5.
Gates across rights-of-way, §§55-304, 55-305.
Lawful fences, §§55-299 to 55-303.
Trespass in crossing, §§55-306 to 55-309.
No-fence law, §§55-310 to 55-316.
Fraudulent conveyances, §§55-80 to 55-105.
See FRAUDULENT CONVEYANCES.
Gifts for educational, literary or charitable purposes.
Generally.
See CHARITABLE GIFTS.
Ground rent, §§55-79.01 to 55-79.06.
Intervening, §38.2-315.
Intestate succession generally, §§64.2-200 to 64.2-206.
See DESCENT AND DISTRIBUTION.
Landlord and tenant, §§55-217 to 55-248.
See LANDLORD AND TENANT.
Lien registrations by federal government, §§55-142.1 to 55-142.9.

PROPERTY —Cont'd
Manufactured home lot rental, §§55-248.41 to 55-248.52.
See MANUFACTURED HOME LOT RENTAL.
Married women's property rights, §§55-35 to 55-47.1.
See MARRIED WOMEN'S PROPERTY RIGHTS.
Membership camping, §§59.1-311 to 59.1-335.
See MEMBERSHIP CAMPING.
Mortgages and deeds of trust, §§6.2-406 to 6.2-423, 55-58 to 55-66.6.
See MORTGAGES AND DEEDS OF TRUST.
Murderers.
Bar to claiming property rights of decedent, §§64.2-2500 to 64.2-2511.
See SLAYER'S ACT.
Museums.
Property loaned to museums, §§55-210.31 to 55-210.38.
See MUSEUMS.
Owners' associations, §§55-508 to 55-516.2.
See PROPERTY OWNERS' ASSOCIATIONS.
Partnerships.
Partnership property, §50-73.89.
Partner not co-owner of, §50-73.105.
Transfer, §50-73.92.
Defined, §50-73.79.
What constitutes, §50-73.90.
Principal and income.
Uniform principal and income act, §§64.2-1000 to 64.2-1032.
See PRINCIPAL AND INCOME.
Real estate cooperatives, §§55-424 to 55-506.
See REAL ESTATE COOPERATIVES.
Recordation of documents generally, §§55-106 to 55-142.9.
See RECORDATION OF DOCUMENTS.
Registration of federal liens, §§55-142.1 to 55-142.9.
Residential ground rent, §§55-79.01 to 55-79.06.
Residential property transfer disclosures, §§55-517 to 55-525.
See RESIDENTIAL PROPERTY TRANSFER DISCLOSURES.
Rights of married women, §§55-35 to 55-47.1.
See MARRIED WOMEN'S PROPERTY RIGHTS.
Self-service storage, §§55-416 to 55-423.
Slayers, bar to property rights, §§64.2-2500 to 64.2-2511.
See SLAYER'S ACT.
Solar easements, §§55-352 to 55-354.
Submerged lands, §§28.2-1200 to 28.2-1213.
See SUBMERGED LANDS.
Time-shares, §§55-360 to 55-400.
See TIME-SHARES.
Trade secrets, §§59.1-336 to 59.1-343.
Unclaimed property, disposition of.
Escheat, §§55-168 to 55-201.1.
See ESCHEAT.
Generally, §§55-210.1 to 55-210.30.
See UNCLAIMED PROPERTY.
Utility aggregation cooperatives.
Powers as to property, §56-231.43.
Utility consumer services cooperatives.
Powers as to property, §§56-231.23, 56-231.24.
Waste, §§55-211 to 55-216.

PROPERTY AND CASUALTY INSURANCE GUARANTY ASSOCIATION, §§38.2-1600 to 38.2-1623.
Access to records, §38.2-1616.

PROPERTY AND CASUALTY INSURANCE GUARANTY ASSOCIATION —Cont'd
Account for all other insurance, §38.2-1604.
Applicability of chapter, §38.2-1601.
Automobile insurance account, §38.2-1604.
Board of directors, §38.2-1605.
Certificates of contribution, tax write-offs, §38.2-1611.1.
Claims recoverable from more than one association, §38.2-1610.
Construction of chapter, §38.2-1602.
Created, §38.2-1604.
Definitions, §38.2-1603.
Detection and prevention of insurer insolvencies, §38.2-1611.
Directors, §38.2-1605.
Duties, §38.2-1606.
Duties of state corporation commission, §38.2-1608.
Examination and regulation by state corporation commission, §38.2-1612.
Exceptions from chapter, §38.2-1601.
Exemption from payment of fees and taxes, §38.2-1613.
Exhaustion of remedies under policy, §38.2-1610.
Expiration of chapter, §38.2-1617.
Financial report annually, §38.2-1612.
Fines and penalties for violations of insurance title.
Credit to, §38.2-225.
Good faith actions, no liability, §38.2-1615.
Immunity for action taken in good faith, §38.2-1615.
Insolvencies, aids in detection and prevention, §38.2-1611.
Insured's rights and liabilities, §38.2-1609.
Investment and obligations by insurers, §38.2-1442.
Liberal construction of chapter, §38.2-1602.
Members, §38.2-1604.
Operation plan, §38.2-1607.
Plan of operation, §38.2-1607.
Powers, §38.2-1606.
Powers of state corporation commission, §38.2-1608.
Priority of claims, §38.2-1609.
Prompt payment of covered claims.
Purposes of chapter, §38.2-1600.
Purposes of chapter, §38.2-1600.
Rights and liabilities of insureds, §38.2-1609.
Safety fund, §§38.2-1618 to 38.2-1623.
Setting aside judgments, §38.2-1616.
Settlements binding on receiver or liquidator, §38.2-1609.
State corporation commission duties and powers, §38.2-1608.
Statements filed with receiver or liquidator, §38.2-1609.
Stay of proceedings against insolvent insurer, §38.2-1616.
Tax and fee exemptions, §38.2-1613.
Tax write-offs of certificates of contribution, §38.2-1611.1.
Termination of operation, §38.2-1617.
Workers' compensation insurance account, §38.2-1604.

PROPERTY CARRIERS.
Motor carriers of property generally, §§46.2-2100 to 46.2-2176.
See MOTOR CARRIERS, PROPERTY.

PROPERTY DAMAGE LIABILITY INSURANCE.
Carbon monoxide exclusions, §38.2-235.
Certified escort vehicle drivers.
Insurance required, §46.2-2902.
Defined, §38.2-118.
Liability insurance generally, §§38.2-2200 to 38.2-2234.
See LIABILITY INSURANCE.
Motor vehicle insurance generally.
See MOTOR VEHICLE INSURANCE.
Notice of cancellation, refusal to renew, reduction in coverage or increase in rate, §38.2-231.

PROPERTY EXEMPT FROM TAXATION, §§58.1-3600 to 58.1-3666, VA Const Art X §6.
Application for exemption, §58.1-3605.
Benevolent or charitable organizations, §58.1-3606.
Building source of revenue.
Exemption not applicable, §58.1-3603.
Cemeteries or burial grounds, §58.1-3606.
Certified stormwater management developments and property, §58.1-3660.1.
Churches or religious bodies, §58.1-3606.
Classification on and after July 1, 1971, §§58.1-3609 to 58.1-3622.
American National Red Cross, §58.1-3616.
Boys and girls clubs, §58.1-3611.
Boy scouts and girl scouts, §58.1-3614.
Churches, religious associations or denominations, §58.1-3617.
Classification exemption, §58.1-3609.
College alumni associations and foundations, §58.1-3618.
Exemption by classification, §58.1-3609.
Farm club associations, §58.1-3621.
Habitat for Humanity and local affiliates, §58.1-3622.
Home demonstration clubs, 4-H clubs and Future Farmers of America, §58.1-3615.
Property inundating by waters, §58.1-3620.
Societies for the prevention of cruelty to animals, §58.1-3613.
State Future Farmers of America, Future Homemakers of America and Future Business Leaders of America, §58.1-3619.
Veterans of World War I auxiliaries, §58.1-3612.
Volunteer fire departments and rescue squads, §58.1-3610.
Water inundating property, §58.1-3620.
Classification or designation before July 1, 1971, §§58.1-3606 to 58.1-3608.
American Legion, §58.1-3607.
Association for Preservation of Virginia Antiquities, §58.1-3607.
Association for the Preservation of Petersburg Antiquities, §58.1-3607.
Clarke County Historical Association, §58.1-3607.
Colonial Williamsburg, Incorporated, §58.1-3607.
Commonwealth or political subdivision, §58.1-3606.
Confederate Memorial Literary Society, §58.1-3607.
Disabled American Veterans, §58.1-3607.
Exempt by classification, §58.1-3606.
Exempt by designation, §58.1-3607.
Exempt organizations use of property owned by another, §58.1-3608.
Fleet Reserve Association, §58.1-3607.

PROPERTY EXEMPT FROM TAXATION —Cont'd
Classification or designation before July 1, 1971 —Cont'd
4-H Clubs, §58.1-3607.
Future Farmers of America, §58.1-3607.
General Organization of the United Daughters of Confederacy, §58.1-3607.
George Washington's Boyhood Home Restoration, §58.1-3607.
Historic Alexandria Foundation, §58.1-3607.
Historic Fredericksburg, Incorporated, §58.1-3607.
Historic Richmond Foundation, §58.1-3607.
Home Demonstration Clubs, §58.1-3607.
Lynchburg Fine Arts Centers, §58.1-3607.
Lynchburg Historical Foundation, §58.1-3607.
Manassas Battlefield Confederate Park, §58.1-3607.
Memorial Foundation of the Germanna Colonies in Virginia, §58.1-3607.
Mount Vernon Ladies' Association of the Union, §58.1-3607.
National Trust for Historic Preservation in the United States, §58.1-3607.
Norfolk Historic Foundation, §58.1-3607.
Patrick Henry Memorial Foundation, §58.1-3607.
Robert E. Lee Memorial Foundation, §58.1-3607.
Society of the Cincinnati in the State of Virginia, §58.1-3607.
Stonewall Jackson Memorial, §58.1-3607.
Thomas Jefferson Memorial Foundation, §58.1-3607.
United Daughters of the Confederacy, §58.1-3607.
United Spanish War Veterans, §58.1-3607.
Use of property owned by another by exempt organizations, §58.1-3608.
Veterans of Foreign Wars, §58.1-3607.
Veterans of World War I, §58.1-3607.
Virginia Historical Society, §58.1-3607.
Virginia Home, §58.1-3607.
Waterford Foundation, §58.1-3607.
Westmoreland Davis Foundation, §58.1-3607.
Women's Home Incorporated, §58.1-3607.
Commercial or industrial structures.
Rehabilitated, renovated or replaced, §58.1-3221.
Consumer utility taxes.
Exemption from consumer utility taxes, §58.1-3816.2.
Damaged, razed or destroyed buildings by fortuitous happenings.
Abatement of levies, §58.1-3222.
Death, sickness or accident benefits paid.
Exemption not applicable to associations, corporations, etc., paying, §58.1-3602.
Definitions, §58.1-3600.
Designation on or after January 1, 2003, §58.1-3651.
Designation on or after July 1, 1971, §§58.1-3650 to 58.1-3650.960.
Academy of Music Theater, Inc., §58.1-3650.17.
Accessible Apartments of Newport News, Inc., City of Newport News, §58.1-3650.355.
Accomack County Nursing Home Commission, Inc., Accomack County, §58.1-3650.847.
Action in the Community Through Service, Prince William county, §58.1-3650.108.
Adult Day Care Center of Martinsville and Henry county, City of Martinsville, §58.1-3650.382.
Adult Development Center, Inc., City of Richmond, §58.1-3650.314.

PROPERTY EXEMPT FROM TAXATION —Cont'd
Designation on or after July 1, 1971 —Cont'd
Al-Anon Family Group Headquarters, Inc., City of Virginia Beach, §58.1-3650.620.
Alcoholic Counseling Service of Martinsville, Inc., Franklin county, §58.1-3650.22.
Alexandria Community Y, Inc., §58.1-3650.22.
Alliance for the Physically Disabled, Inc., Fairfax County, §58.1-3650.805.
Altavista Sheltered Workshop, Inc., Town of Altavista, §58.1-3650.480.
Alternative Community Properties, Inc., Chesterfield County, §58.1-3650.637.
Alternative House, Inc., Fairfax county, §58.1-3650.365.
Alternatives for Abused Adults, Inc., City of Staunton, §58.1-3650.389.
Amalgamated Clothing and Textile Workers' Retirees Club, Warren county, §58.1-3650.405.
American Horse Protection Association, Loudoun county, §58.1-3650.229.
American Horticultural Society, §58.1-3650.19.
American Lung Association, City of Richmond, §58.1-3650.442.
American Roentgen Ray Society, Loudoun County, §58.1-3650.808.
American Type Culture Collection, Prince William County, §58.1-3650.835.
AMVETS-Post No. 40, City of Roanoke, §58.1-3650.720.
A. P. Carter Birthplace Foundation, Inc., Scott county, §58.1-3650.227.
A. P. Carter Museum Foundation, Inc., Scott county, §58.1-3650.236.
Appalachian Educational Communications Corporation, City of Bristol, §58.1-3650.653.
Appalachian Family Ministries, Inc., Wise county, §58.1-3650.422.
Appalachian Traditions, Inc., Wise county, §58.1-3650.539.
Appalachian Trail Conference, Augusta and Nelson counties, §58.1-3650.317.
Appalachian Trail Conference, Clarke county, §58.1-3650.190.
Arlington Assembly of God Housing Corporation, Fairfax county, §58.1-3650.124.
Arlington-Fairfax Chapter, Inc., of the Izaak Walton League of America, Fairfax County, §58.1-3650.608.
Arlington-Fairfax Jewish Congregation, Arlington county, §58.1-3650.195.
Arlington Hospital Properties, Inc., §58.1-3650.166.
Arlington Lodge No. 58, Free and Accepted Masons, Prince Hall Affiliation, Arlington County, §58.1-3650.631.
Arts Enter Cape Charles, Inc., Northampton County, §58.1-3650.874.
Asbury Centers, Inc., Town of Wytheville, §58.1-3650.511.
Asbury Centers, Inc., Wythe county, §58.1-3650.543.
Ashland War Memorial Association, §58.1-3650.2.
Assisted Housing Development Corporation, City of Newport News, §58.1-3650.283.
Assist, Inc., City of Falls Church, §58.1-3650.107.
Association for Retarded Citizens of the Peninsula, Inc., City of Newport News, §58.1-3650.541.

PROPERTY EXEMPT FROM TAXATION —Cont'd
Designation on or after July 1, 1971 —Cont'd
Association for Retarded Citizens, Petersburg area, §58.1-3650.112.
Association for the Preservation of Civil War Sites, Dinwiddie county, §58.1-3650.395.
Association for the Preservation of Civil War Sites, Inc., City of Fredericksburg, §58.1-3650.534.
Association for the Preservation of Civil War Sites, Inc., Rockingham County, §58.1-3650.609.
Association for the Preservation of Civil War Sites, Inc., Spotsylvania County, §58.1-3650.438.
Association of Retarded Citizens of the Peninsula, Inc., City of Newport News, §58.1-3650.648.
Athletes for Jesus, City of Richmond, §58.1-3650.639.
Atlantic Rural Exposition, Inc., Henrico county, §58.1-3650.153.
Audubon Naturalist Society of the Central Atlantic States, Inc., §58.1-3650.920.
Audubon Naturalist Society of the Central Atlantic States, Inc., Fairfax county, §58.1-3650.759.
Augusta Agriculture Rural-Industrial Exposition, Inc., §58.1-3650.28.
Augusta Hospital Corporation, Augusta County, §58.1-3650.601.
Avenel Foundation, City of Bedford, §58.1-3650.760.
Bainbridge Blackwell Family Counseling Services, Inc., City of Richmond, §58.1-3650.469.
Ballston Baptist Church, Arlington county, §58.1-3650.194.
Baptist General Convention of Virginia, City of Richmond, §58.1-3650.333.
Barter Foundation, Inc., Washington county, §58.1-3650.188.
Baycliff Civic League, Inc., City of Virginia Beach, §58.1-3650.855.
Bay Island Yacht Club, §58.1-3650.552.
Beach Community Grange and Woodpecker Grange, Chesterfield county, §58.1-3650.66.
Beach Health Clinic, Inc., City of Virginia Beach, §58.1-3650.823.
Bedford Breakfast Lions Club, §58.1-3650.915.
Bedford Christian Ministries, Bedford County, §58.1-3650.887.
Belle Grove, Inc., Shenandoah County, §58.1-3650.797.
Belleville Senior Housing, Inc., City of Suffolk, §58.1-3650.280.
Bellevue, Inc., City of Danville, §58.1-3650.359.
Benevolent and Protective Order of Elks Lodge No. 875, Spotsylvania county, §58.1-3650.768.
Berkley Aerie No. 795, Fraternal Order of the Eagles, City of Chesapeake, §58.1-3650.319.
Bethany House of Northern Virginia, Inc., Fairfax County, §58.1-3650.613.
Bethel Way Adult Center, Pittsylvania county, §58.1-3650.504.
Bethlehem Center, City of Richmond, §58.1-3650.89.
Beth Sholom Assisted Living, Henrico County, §58.1-3650.862.
Beth Sholom Home of Eastern Virginia, city of Virginia Beach, §58.1-3650.763.
Beth Sholom Home of Virginia, §58.1-3650.24.

PROPERTY EXEMPT FROM TAXATION —Cont'd

Designation on or after July 1, 1971 —Cont'd

Beth Sholom Housing Corporation, City of Virginia Beach, §58.1-3650.222.
Beth Sholom Housing Corporation, Henrico county, §58.1-3650.81.
Beth Sholom Sands, City of Virginia Beach, §§58.1-3650.897, 58.1-3650.904.
Bible Broadcasting Network, Inc., City of Chesapeake, §§58.1-3650.177, 58.1-3650.214.
Big Caney Water Corporation, Dickenson County, §58.1-3650.598.
Big Stone Gap Housing Corporation, §58.1-3650.83.
Birdneck Point Community League, Inc., City of Virginia Beach, §58.1-3650.551.
Birdsong Trust Fund, City of Suffolk, §58.1-3650.685.
BizNet, Inc., City of Virginia Beach, §58.1-3650.901.
Black History Museum and Cultural Center of Virginia, Inc., City of Richmond, §58.1-3650.349.
Blackwater Creeds Foundation, City of Virginia Beach, §58.1-3650.730.
Bland County Historical Society, Bland County, §58.1-3650.593.
Blanks Memorial Foundation, Ltd., Halifax County, §58.1-3650.829.
Blue Mountain School, Floyd county, §58.1-3650.495.
Blue Ridge Alliance of the Performing Arts., Inc., Loudoun county, §58.1-3650.130.
Blue Ridge Area Foodbank, Inc., City of Staunton, §58.1-3650.240.
Blue Ridge Area Foodbank, Inc., county of Augusta, §58.1-3650.246.
Blue Ridge Chapel, Inc., Franklin county, §§58.1-3650.173, 58.1-3650.210.
Blue Ridge Christian Home, Inc., Fauquier County, §58.1-3650.580.
Blue Ridge Federation of the Blind, City of Charlottesville, §58.1-3650.146.
Blue Ridge Housing Development Corp., City of Roanoke, §58.1-3650.832.
Blue Ridge Legal Services, Harrisonburg, City of, §58.1-3650.270.
Boissevain Coal Miners Memorial Museum, Inc., (a.k.a. Boissevain Coal Miners Museum and Park, Inc.), §58.1-3650.491.
Bolling Haxall House Foundation, City of Richmond, §58.1-3650.468.
Bose Audubon Center of the Fairfax Audubon Society, Fairfax county, §58.1-3650.162.
Boykins Baptist Church, Southampton County, §58.1-3650.798.
Breakthrough, Inc., Loudoun county, §58.1-3650.782.
Bren Mar Recreation Association, Inc., Fairfax County, §58.1-3650.894.
Brethren Housing Corporation, City of Manassas, §58.1-3650.362.
Briarcliff Foundation, Inc., City of Clifton Forge, §58.1-3650.161.
Bridgewater Home, Inc., Rockingham county, §58.1-3650.500.
Bridgewater Home, Inc., Town of Bridgewater, §58.1-3650.434.
Bristol-Goodson Historical Preservationists, Inc., City of Bristol, §58.1-3650.493.

PROPERTY EXEMPT FROM TAXATION —Cont'd

Designation on or after July 1, 1971 —Cont'd

Broyhill Crest Recreation, Inc., Fairfax County, §58.1-3650.857.
Bruton Park Home, Inc., City of Newport News, §58.1-3650.674.
Buckingham County Public Library, Buckingham county, §58.1-3650.461.
Burwell-Van Lennep Foundation, Clarke county, §58.1-3650.372.
Camelot Community Club, Inc., Fairfax County, §58.1-3650.856.
CAMG /- A, Inc., §58.1-3650.943.
CAMG /- B, Inc., §58.1-3650.944.
CAMG /- C, Inc., §58.1-3650.945.
CAMG /- D, Inc., §58.1-3650.946.
CAMG /- E, Inc., §58.1-3650.947.
CAMG /- F, Inc., §58.1-3650.948.
CAMG /- G, Inc., §58.1-3650.949.
CAMG /- H, Inc., §58.1-3650.950.
CANDII, City of Hampton, §58.1-3650.804.
Cape Charles Historical Society, Inc., Northhampton County, §58.1-3650.691.
Cape Charles Rescue Services, Inc., Northampton County, §58.1-3650.852.
Capital Area Agency on the Aging, City of Richmond, §58.1-3650.202.
Capital Area Community Food Bank, Inc., Fairfax County, §58.1-3650.816.
Capital Area Specialized Transportation for the Elderly and Handicapped, Inc., City of Richmond, §58.1-3650.251.
Carolanne Farm Swim Club, Inc., §58.1-3650.957.
Carriage Museum of America, Inc., Loudoun County, §58.1-3650.607.
Carroll County Historical Society, Inc., Carroll county, §58.1-3650.483.
Carroll Wellness Center, Carroll County, §58.1-3650.895.
Cedar Creek Battlefield Foundation, Inc., Frederick county, §58.1-3650.381.
Cedarwoods Residential, Inc., Powhatan County, §58.1-3650.668.
Center for Pastoral Counseling for Virginia, Loudoun County, §58.1-3650.812.
Central Valley Habitat for Humanity, Inc., Rockingham County, §58.1-3650.842.
Central Virginia Education Telecommunication Corporation, Stafford County, §58.1-3650.830.
Central Virginia ETV Corporation, Fairfax county and Chesterfield county, §58.1-3650.149.
Central Virginia Foodbank, Inc., City of Richmond, §58.1-3650.242.
Central Virginia Foodbank, Inc., Henrico county, §58.1-3650.290.
Central Virginia Housing Coalition, Inc., City of Fredericksburg, §58.1-3650.886.
Charles City County Civil League, Inc., §58.1-3650.57.
Charles H. Taylor Arts Center Foundation, Inc., §58.1-3650.960.
Charlottesville-Albemarle Legal Aid Society, City of Charlottesville, §58.1-3650.164.
Chase City Community Services, Inc., §58.1-3650.679.
Chase City Medical Clinic, Inc., Mecklenburg county, §58.1-3650.266.
Chesapeake Bay Foundation, Inc., §58.1-3650.11.
Chesapeake Care, Inc., City of Chesapeake, §58.1-3650.867.

PROPERTY EXEMPT FROM TAXATION —Cont'd

Designation on or after July 1, 1971 —Cont'd

Chesapeake Community Trust, City of Chesapeake, §58.1-3650.320.
Chesapeake Health Investment Program, City of Chesapeake, §58.1-3650.868.
Chesapeake RHF Housing, Inc., City of Chesapeake, §§58.1-3650.458, 58.1-3650.494.
Chesapeake Soccer Foundation, §58.1-3650.929.
Chesterfield Alternative Properties, Chesterfield county, §58.1-3650.532.
Chesterfield Alternatives, Inc., Chesterfield county, §§58.1-3650.425, 58.1-3650.736, 58.1-3650.779, 58.1-3650.815.
Chickahominy Indian Tribe, Inc., Charles City county, §58.1-3650.516.
Child and Family Service of Southwest Hampton Roads, Inc., City of Portsmouth, §58.1-3650.336.
Childhood Language Center, City of Richmond, §58.1-3650.638.
Children, Incorporated, City of Richmond, §58.1-3650.642.
Children's Center, City of Suffolk, §58.1-3650.872.
Children's Oncology Services of Virginia, Inc., City of Richmond, §58.1-3650.98.
Children's Theater of Richmond, Inc., §58.1-3650.5.
Chisholm Foundation, Inc., City of Portsmouth, §58.1-3650.334.
Christel Broadcasting, Inc., Henrico county, §58.1-3650.344.
Christian Charities, Inc., City of Richmond, §58.1-3650.556.
Christian Children's Fund, Inc., Henrico county, §58.1-3650.407.
Christian Relief Services of Virginia, Inc., Fairfax county, §58.1-3650.509.
Citizens Against Family Violence, City of Martinsville, §58.1-3650.432.
City of Light Development Corporation, City of Winchester, §58.1-3650.384.
Civitan Recreation Club of Alexandria, Virginia, §58.1-3650.15.
Client Centered Legal Services of Southwest Virginia, Inc., Town of Cartlewood, §58.1-3650.481.
Clinch River Health Services, Inc., Scott county, §58.1-3650.342.
Closet of the Greater Herndon Area, Inc., §58.1-3650.916.
Club Brittany, Inc., City of Virginia Beach, §58.1-3650.549.
Coastal Conservation Association, §58.1-3650.941.
Cockade City Lodge No. 16, Fraternal Order of Police, Inc., City of Petersburg, §58.1-3650.475.
Colbin Run Citizens Association, Inc., County of Fairfax, §58.1-3650.206.
Colonel John Banister Chapter of the National Society Daughters of the American Revolution, City of Petersburg, §58.1-3650.271.
Colonial Beach Moose Lodge, §58.1-3650.844.
Colonial Community Services, Inc., York county, §58.1-3650.564.
Colony Pines Residents' Association, Inc., City of Newport News, §58.1-3650.675.
Commonwealth Health Services Co., City of Roanoke, §58.1-3650.186.

PROPERTY EXEMPT FROM TAXATION —Cont'd

Designation on or after July 1, 1971 —Cont'd

Community Alternatives, Inc., City of Virginia Beach, §58.1-3650.603.
Community Alternatives Management Group, Inc., §58.1-3650.919.
Community Alternatives Management Group, Inc., City of Virginia Beach, §58.1-3650.604.
Community Arts Center Foundation, Inc., Halifax County, §58.1-3650.866.
Community Fire Company, Inc., Northampton County, §58.1-3650.851.
Community Memorial Hospital, Mecklenburg county, §58.1-3650.368.
Community Resource Network of Chesapeake, City of Chesapeake, §58.1-3650.386.
Community Theatre of the Virginia Peninsula, city of Newport News, §58.1-3650.792.
Compass and Anchor Club, Loudoun County, §58.1-3650.610.
Concerned Black Men of Richmond, Inc., City of Richmond, §58.1-3650.410.
Conservation, Inc., City of Hampton, §58.1-3650.875.
Cooper's Cove Community Club, Franklin county, §58.1-3650.93.
Corporation for Jefferson's Poplar Forest, Bedford County, §58.1-3650.170.
Council for America's First Freedom, City of Richmond, §58.1-3650.585.
Council of United Filipino Organizations of Tidewater, Inc., City of Virginia Beach, §58.1-3650.597.
Council on Alcoholism, Lord Fairfax Community, Inc., City of Winchester, §58.1-3650.562.
Country Club Hills Recreation Corporation, City of Fairfax, §58.1-3650.701.
Court House Players, Inc., Mathews county, §58.1-3650.778.
Crisis Pregnancy Center of Roanoke Valley, Inc., City of Roanoke, §58.1-3650.659.
Cross-Over Ministry, Inc., City of Richmond, §58.1-3650.472.
Crossroads Shelter, Inc., Town of Wytheville, §58.1-3650.788.
Culpeper Calvary Museum, Inc., County of Culpeper, §58.1-3650.684.
Culpeper Community Development Corporation, Inc., Culpeper county, §58.1-3650.454.
Daily Planet, Inc., City of Richmond, §58.1-3650.261.
Dale City Masonic Association, Inc., Prince William county, §58.1-3650.537.
Danville Regional Health System, City of Danville, §58.1-3650.791.
Darvills Community Center, Dinwiddie county, §58.1-3650.790.
Daughters of America, King George county, §58.1-3650.30.
David R. Pinn Community Center, Fairfax county, §58.1-3650.218.
David R. Pinn Community Center, Sideburn Civic Association, Fairfax county, §58.1-3650.181.
Dawn Progressive Association, Inc., Caroline county, §58.1-3650.109.
Deep Creek Lodge No. 46, Knights of Pythias, City of Chesapeake, §§58.1-3650.174, 58.1-3650.211.
DeHart Botanical Gardens, Inc., Patrick County, §58.1-3650.834.

PROPERTY EXEMPT FROM TAXATION —Cont'd
Designation on or after July 1, 1971 —Cont'd
Delta Beta Lambda Building Foundation, Alpha Phi Alpha Fraternity, Inc., city of Hampton, §58.1-3650.789.
Delta Community Service Foundation, §58.1-3650.940.
DePaul Family Services, Inc., §58.1-3650.917.
Diamond Springs/Gardenwood Park Civic League, Inc., City of Virginia Beach, §58.1-3650.602.
Didlake Foundation, county of Prince William, §58.1-3650.116.
Dinwiddie Library Foundation, Dinwiddie county, §58.1-3650.396.
Diocesan Missionary Society of Virginia, City of Harrisonburg, §58.1-3650.488.
Disabled American Veterans Chapter 37, City of Galax, §58.1-3650.294.
Disabled American Veterans Galax Chapter No. 37, Inc., Carroll County, §58.1-3650.594.
Door of Hope, Loudoun County, §58.1-3650.809.
Downtown Greens, Inc., §58.1-3650.907.
Drewryville Woman's Club, Southampton county, §58.1-3650.306.
Drug Action Center, Inc., James City county, §58.1-3650.376.
Dublin Recreation Corporation, Pulaski county, §58.1-3650.305.
Early Works, Inc., City of Chesapeake, §58.1-3650.499.
East End Community Center, City of Richmond, §58.1-3650.61.
Eastern Prince William Sports Club, Prince William county, §58.1-3650.784.
Eastern Shore Community Development Group, Accomack county, §58.1-3650.167.
Eastern Shore Foodbank, Accomack County, §58.1-3650.645.
Eastern Shore of Virginia Barrier Islands, Inc., §58.1-3650.952.
Eastern Shore of Virginia Habitat for Humanity, Inc., Northampton County, §58.1-3650.840.
Eastern Shore Rural Health System, Inc., Accomack County, §58.1-3650.646.
Easter Seal Society of Virginia, Inc., county of Caroline, §58.1-3650.156.
Easter Seal Society of Virginia, King and Queen county, §58.1-3650.159.
ECHO, Loudoun county, §58.1-3650.431.
Ecumenical Community for Helping Others, Inc., Fairfax county, §§58.1-3650.182, 58.1-3650.219.
Edinburgh Square Foundation, Inc., Roanoke county, §58.1-3650.255.
Edsall Park Swim Club, Inc., Fairfax County, §58.1-3650.731.
ElderHomes Corporation, City of Richmond, §58.1-3650.558.
Elks National Home, City of Bedford, §58.1-3650.621.
Emergency Shelter, Inc., City of Richmond, §58.1-3650.260.
Eno Transportation Foundation, Inc., Loudoun county, §58.1-3650.490.
Equine Rescue League Foundation, Loudoun county, §58.1-3650.781.
E-TRON Systems, Inc., County of Fairfax, §58.1-3650.696.
E-TRON Systems, Inc., doing business as Wildflour Breadmill, City of Fairfax, §58.1-3650.694.

PROPERTY EXEMPT FROM TAXATION —Cont'd
Designation on or after July 1, 1971 —Cont'd
Fairfax Cable Access Corporation, §58.1-3650.152.
Fairfax County Housing and Community Development Corporation, Fairfax county, §58.1-3650.522.
Fairfax County Policy Association, Inc., Fairfax County, §58.1-3650.713.
Fairfax County Symphony Orchestra, Inc., Fairfax County, §58.1-3650.612.
Fairfax County Vocational Education Foundation, Inc., §58.1-3650.134.
Fairfax Education Association Retirement Housing Corporation, §58.1-3650.21.
Fairfax Opportunities Unlimited, Inc., Fairfax county, §58.1-3650.97.
Fairfax Swimming Pool, Inc., City of Fairfax, §58.1-3650.702.
Falls Church Housing Corporation, City of Falls Church, §§58.1-3650.265, 58.1-3650.727, 58.1-3650.879.
Falls Church Public Cable TV Access Corporation, Fairfax county and City of Falls Church, §58.1-3650.185.
Family and Children's Service of Richmond, Henrico county, §58.1-3650.103.
Family and Child Services of Washington, D.C., Inc., Fauquier County, §58.1-3650.673.
Family Life Services of Southern Virginia, Inc., City of Danville, §58.1-3650.652.
Family Resource Center, Inc., Town of Wytheville, §58.1-3650.479.
Father McDonald Columbian Center, Inc., §58.1-3650.51.
Fauquier and Loudoun Garden Club, Loudoun County, §58.1-3650.881.
Fauquier Habitat for Humanity, Inc., Fauquier County, §58.1-3650.614.
Fauquier Health Services Corporation, Fauquier county, §58.1-3650.310.
Fauquier Hospital, Inc., Fauquier county, §58.1-3650.191.
Fauquier Temporary Family Shelter, Inc., Fauquier county, §58.1-3650.529.
Fellowship Foundation, Inc., §58.1-3650.10.
FFA-FHA Camp Association, Inc., Isle of Wight county, §58.1-3650.780.
FFA-FHA/HERO Educational and Recreational Center, Isle of Wight county, §58.1-3650.780.
Fine Arts Center for New River Valley, Inc., Town of Pulaski, §58.1-3650.158.
Fine Arts Museum of Southern Virginia, Town of Chase City, §58.1-3650.444.
Flowerdew Hundred Foundation, Prince George County, §58.1-3650.256.
Floyd-Montgomery-Radford Shelter Home, Inc., §58.1-3650.80.
Fluvanna County Historical Society, Fluvanna county, §58.1-3650.478.
Foodbank of Southeastern Virginia, Inc., City of Chesapeake, §58.1-3650.241.
Foodbank of Southeastern Virginia, Inc., City of Norfolk, §§58.1-3650.339, 58.1-3650.795.
Foodbank of the Virginia Peninsula, City of Newport News, §58.1-3650.632.
Food for Others, Inc., Fairfax County, §58.1-3650.747.
F.O.R.E., Inc., Fauquier county, §58.1-3650.169.
Forest Recreation Center, Inc., Forest Community, Bedford county, §58.1-3650.27.

PROPERTY EXEMPT FROM TAXATION —Cont'd

Designation on or after July 1, 1971 —Cont'd

Forest Youth Athletic Association, Bedford County, §58.1-3650.821.
Fort Early Corporation, City of Lynchburg, §58.1-3650.160.
Fort Harrison, Inc., Rockingham county, §58.1-3650.132.
Foundation for Senior Independence, Chesterfield County, §58.1-3650.707.
Foundation of the ARC of Northern Virginia, Prince William county, §58.1-3650.430.
Francis Makemie Society, Accomack County, §58.1-3650.839.
Franklin County Association of Retarded Citizens, Inc., §58.1-3650.49.
Franklin County Sheltered Workshop, Inc., §58.1-3650.48.
Fraternal Order of Eagles, Fredericksburg Aerie 4123, §58.1-3650.905.
Frederick county, §58.1-3650.567.
Fredericksburg Christian Radio, Inc., Spotsylvania county, §58.1-3650.316.
Fredericksburg Food Relief Clearinghouse, Inc., City of Fredericksburg, §58.1-3650.622.
Fredericksburg-Rappahannock Chapter of the Izaak Walton League of America, Spotsylvania county, §58.1-3650.510.
Frederick United Methodist Housing Development Corporation, Frederick county, §58.1-3650.380.
Freedom House, City of Richmond, §58.1-3650.345.
Friendship Industries, Inc., §58.1-3650.906.
Friendship Industries, Inc., City of Harrisonburg, §58.1-3650.225.
Friendship Manor Apartment Village Corporation, City of Roanoke, §58.1-3650.151.
Friendship Manor Apartment Village Corporation, Roanoke county, §58.1-3650.252.
Friends of Anne Spencer Memorial Foundation, Inc., City of Lynchburg, §58.1-3650.133.
Friends of the Homeless, Inc., City of Newport News, §58.1-3650.743.
Friends of the Rappahannock, Inc., Stafford county, §58.1-3650.476.
Friends of Women Prisoners, Inc., City of Alexandria, §58.1-3650.125.
Friends School; Things Unlimited, §58.1-3650.913.
Gabriel Homes, Inc., Fairfax county, §58.1-3650.390.
Gainesville Ruritan Club, Prince William county, §58.1-3650.766.
Galax Community Apartments Corporation, City of Galax, §58.1-3650.436.
Garden Club of Virginia, §58.1-3650.1.
Garfield Childs Memorial Fund, City of Richmond, §58.1-3650.640.
Gateway Farms, Inc., of Greater Richmond, Inc., Chesterfield county, §58.1-3650.464.
Gateway Homes of Greater Richmond, Inc., Chesterfield county, §58.1-3650.463.
George C. Marshall Home Preservation Fund, Inc., Loudoun County, §58.1-3650.665.
George C. Marshall Home Preservation Fund, Inc., Town of Leesburg, §58.1-3650.664.
George Mason University Educational Foundation, Inc., City and county of Fairfax, §58.1-3650.512.

PROPERTY EXEMPT FROM TAXATION —Cont'd

Designation on or after July 1, 1971 —Cont'd

George Mason University Foundation, §58.1-3650.7.
George Washington Boyhood Home Foundation, Stafford county, §58.1-3650.586.
Giles County Historical Society, §58.1-3650.119.
Girls Club of Richmond, City of Richmond, §58.1-3650.346.
Girls Incorporated, Center for Youth of Southwest Hampton Roads, City of Portsmouth, §58.1-3650.618.
Glass-Glen Burnie Foundation, City of Winchester, §58.1-3650.449.
Glenwood Racecourse at Middleburg, Virginia, §58.1-3650.9.
Gloucester-Mathews Humane Society, Inc., Gloucester county, §58.1-3650.228.
Gloucester Women's Club, county of Gloucester, §58.1-3650.535.
God's Storehouse, Inc., City of Danville, §58.1-3650.301.
Goochland County Historical Society, Goochland County, §58.1-3650.698.
Goochland Family Service Society, §58.1-3650.122.
Goochland Recreation Center, Inc., Goochland county, §58.1-3650.220.
Good Neighbor Village, Inc., Henrico county, §58.1-3650.421.
Good News Mission, Arlington county, §58.1-3650.197.
Good Shepherd Alliance, Inc., Loudoun county, §§58.1-3650.775, 58.1-3650.883.
Good Shepherd Housing and Family Services, Inc., Fairfax county, §58.1-3650.750.
Good Shepherd Housing Foundation, Prince William county, §58.1-3650.783.
Goodwill Industries of Tenneva, §58.1-3650.60.
Goodwin House, Inc., City of Alexandria, §58.1-3650.818.
Goodwin House, Inc., Fairfax county, §58.1-3650.234.
Great Bridge Baseball, Inc., City of Chesapeake, §58.1-3650.573.
Greater Annandale Recreation Center, Inc., Fairfax county, §58.1-3650.455.
Greater Orange Community Development Corporation, §58.1-3650.942.
Greater Southeast Development Corporation, §58.1-3650.91.
Greater Washington Educational Telecommunications Association, Inc., county of Arlington, §58.1-3650.165.
Greater Washington Jewish Community Foundation of Virginia, Inc., Fairfax county, §58.1-3650.440.
Greenbriar Civic Association, Inc., §58.1-3650.68.
Greenspring Village, Inc., Fairfax County, §58.1-3650.896.
Greenstone Residence, Inc., Augusta county, §58.1-3650.303.
Greensville County Historical Society, City of Emporia, §58.1-3650.579.
Greensville Memorial Hospital, Inc., City of Emporia, §58.1-3650.199.
Greenwood Homes, Inc., Fairfax county, §58.1-3650.163.
Groome Road Home, Inc., §58.1-3650.954.
Guest House III, Inc., City of Richmond, §58.1-3650.583.

PROPERTY EXEMPT FROM TAXATION —Cont'd

Designation on or after July 1, 1971 —Cont'd

Guest House IV, Inc., City of Richmond, §58.1-3650.584.
Guildfield Housing Development Corporation, Pittsylvania County, §58.1-3650.617.
Guinea Heritage Association, Ltd., Gloucester County, §58.1-3650.889.
Habitat for Humanity in the Roanoke Valley, Inc., City of Roanoke, §58.1-3650.658.
Halifax Educational Foundation, Inc., §58.1-3650.922.
Hampton Ecumenical Lodgings and Provisions, Inc., City of Hampton, §58.1-3650.746.
Hampton Roads Power Squadron, Inc., City of Hampton, §58.1-3650.86.
Hands Across Mathews of Mathews, Virginia, §58.1-3650.937.
Hanging Rock Battlefield and Railway Preservation Foundation, City of Salem, §58.1-3650.740.
Hanging Rock Battlefield and Railway Preservation Foundation, County of Roanoke, §58.1-3650.740.
Happy Acres Foundation, Inc., §58.1-3650.47.
Harrisonburg-Rockingham Association for Retarded Children, Inc., City of Harrisonburg, §58.1-3650.486.
Harrison Museum of African American Culture, City of Roanoke, §58.1-3650.893.
Hartwood Foundation, Inc., Fairfax County, §58.1-3650.624.
Hartwood Group Homes, Inc., Fairfax county, §58.1-3650.136.
Hartwood Place, Inc., Fairfax county, §58.1-3650.366.
Hartwood Terrace, Inc., Fairfax County, §58.1-3650.717.
Hayfield Farm Swim Club, Inc., Fairfax County, §58.1-3650.581.
Head Injury Services Partnership, Inc., Fairfax county, §58.1-3650.540.
Health Care Development Corporation, Fauquier county, §58.1-3650.311.
Health Dynamics, Inc., Fauquier county, §58.1-3650.309.
Hearthstone Children's House, Inc., City of Charlottesville, §58.1-3650.120.
Henrico county.
  Nonprofit organizations located within county, §58.1-3650.44.
Henrico County Education Foundation, Inc., Henrico county, §58.1-3650.525.
Henricus Foundation, County of Chesterfield, §58.1-3650.735.
Heritage Association, Inc., Page county, §58.1-3650.46.
Heritage Haven, Inc., Rockingham county, §58.1-3650.110.
Highland Center, Inc., Highland County, §58.1-3650.826.
Highland county Medical Center, Inc., Highland county, §58.1-3650.772.
Hillsville Masonic Lodge Number 193 A.F. & A.M., Town of Hillsville in Carroll county, §58.1-3650.426.
Hispanic Committee of Virginia, Inc., Fairfax county, §58.1-3650.419.
Historical Society of Mecklenburg County, Mecklenburg county, §58.1-3650.295.

PROPERTY EXEMPT FROM TAXATION —Cont'd

Designation on or after July 1, 1971 —Cont'd

Historical Society of the Pound, Inc., Wise County, §58.1-3650.870.
Historic Buckingham, Inc., Buckingham county, §58.1-3650.117.
Historic Falmouth Town and Stafford County, Inc., Stafford county, §58.1-3650.209.
Historic Farmville, Inc., Town of Farmville or in Prince Edward county, §58.1-3650.356.
Historic Hopewell Foundation, Inc., §58.1-3650.6.
Historic Port Royal, Inc., Caroline County, §58.1-3650.888.
Historic Richmond Theatre Foundation, City of Richmond, §58.1-3650.467.
Historic Staunton Foundation, Inc., City of Staunton, §58.1-3650.237.
Holland Meadows Swim & Racquet Club, Ltd., City of Virginia Beach, §58.1-3650.548.
Holmes Run Acres Recreation Association, Inc., §58.1-3650.955.
Homeless Haven, Inc., t/a The Haven Family Assistance Center, City of Norfolk, §58.1-3650.505.
Homestretch, Inc., §58.1-3650.910.
HOPE in Northern Virginia, Inc., City of Falls Church, §58.1-3650.137.
Hopewell Optimist Club, §58.1-3650.958.
Hopewell Preservation, Inc., City of Hopewell, §58.1-3650.575.
Hopkins House Association of Alexandria, Virginia, §58.1-3650.14.
Hospice of Northern Virginia, Arlington county, §58.1-3650.351.
Hospice Support Care, Inc., City of Fredericksburg, §58.1-3650.758.
House of Care of Southwest Virginia, Inc., City of Roanoke, §58.1-3650.627.
Housing Opportunities Made Equal, Inc., City of Richmond, §58.1-3650.413.
Hughes Memorial Home Trust, Pittsylvania County, §58.1-3650.623.
I. C. Corporation, City of Hampton, §58.1-3650.299.
Imaging Center of Southwest Virginia, Inc., City of Roanoke, §58.1-3650.269.
Immaculate Heart Mission, Arlington county, §58.1-3650.193.
Improved Benevolent Protection Order of Elks of the Word, City of Chesapeake, §§58.1-3650.175, 58.1-3650.212.
Inova Services, Inc., Fairfax county, §58.1-3650.324.
Institute Corporation, Loudoun county, §58.1-3650.298.
Institute for Personal and Professional Development, Warren county, §58.1-3650.189.
International Seamen's Friend House of the Lower Virginia Peninsula, City of Newport News, §58.1-3650.738.
International Society of Air Safety Investigators, §58.1-3650.923.
International Society of Air Safety Investigators, Loudoun County, §58.1-3650.884.
Isle of Wight-Smithfield-Windsor Chamber of Commerce, Isle of Wight County, §58.1-3650.833.
Iverson Properties, Inc., Chesterfield County, §58.1-3650.688.

PROPERTY EXEMPT FROM TAXATION —Cont'd

Designation on or after July 1, 1971 —Cont'd

Izaak Walton League, Montgomery County, §58.1-3650.697.
Izaak Walton League of America, Inc., Park-Alexandria Chapter, Stafford county, §58.1-3650.544.
J.E.B. Stuart Birthplace Preservation Trust, Inc., Patrick County, §58.1-3650.716.
Jefferson Area Board for the Aging, Inc., County of Albemarle, §58.1-3650.657.
Jefferson Area United Transportation, City of Charlottesville, §58.1-3650.99.
Jeremiah House, Inc., Loudoun county, §58.1-3650.776.
Jewish Community Center, Goochland county, §58.1-3650.307.
Jewish Family Services, Inc., Henrico county, §58.1-3650.370.
Jewish Foundation for Group Homes, Inc., Fairfax county, §58.1-3650.765.
John Lynch Lodge 34, Fraternal Order of Police, City of Lynchburg, §58.1-3650.278.
John Paul I Knights of Columbus, Prince William County, §58.1-3650.693.
Judeo-Christian Outreach Center, Inc., City of Virginia Beach, §58.1-3650.820.
Junior Achievement of Richmond, §58.1-3650.139.
Junior League of Hampton Roads, Inc., City of Newport News, §58.1-3650.705.
Junior League of Richmond, City of Richmond, §58.1-3650.559.
Junior Order of United American Mechanics, City of Poquoson, §58.1-3650.322.
Kenmore Association, Inc., City of Fredericksburg, §58.1-3650.507.
Kenmore Association, Inc., Stafford County, §58.1-3650.737.
Kent Gardens Residential Club, Inc., Fairfax County, §58.1-3650.687.
Kernstown Battlefield Association, Inc., §58.1-3650.911.
Khedive Temple A.A.O.N.M.S., City of Chesapeake, §§58.1-3650.176, 58.1-3650.213.
Kilmarnock Museum, Inc., Lancaster County, §58.1-3650.801.
Kingdom Missions, Franklin county, §58.1-3650.332.
King's Grant Community League, Inc., §58.1-3650.921.
King's Grant Retirement Community, Henry county, §58.1-3650.397.
Kings Ridge Swim Club, Inc., Fairfax county, §58.1-3650.787.
King William county, §58.1-3650.291.
Kinsale Foundation, Westmoreland county, §58.1-3650.79.
Kiwanis Club of Chester, Inc., Foundation, §58.1-3650.931.
Kiwanis Foundation, Inc., Chesterfield County, §58.1-3650.859.
Knights of Pythias, City of Poquoson, §58.1-3650.323.
Laburnum Properties, Inc., City of Richmond, §58.1-3650.140.
Lakeview Swim Club, Inc., Fairfax County, §58.1-3650.836.
Lakewood Manor Baptist Retirement Community, Inc., Henrico county, §58.1-3650.184.

PROPERTY EXEMPT FROM TAXATION —Cont'd

Designation on or after July 1, 1971 —Cont'd

Lancaster/Northumberland Habitat for Humanity, Inc., Lancaster County, §58.1-3650.802.
Langley Nonprofit Housing Development Corporation, Fairfax county, §58.1-3650.353.
Larkspur Civic League, Ltd., City of Virginia Beach, §58.1-3650.554.
Larkspur Swim & Racquet Club, Ltd., City of Virginia Beach, §58.1-3650.555.
Larrymore Lawns Community Park Association, City of Norfolk, §58.1-3650.827.
Last Great Waters, Inc., City of Virginia Beach, §58.1-3650.890.
Laurel Shelter, Inc., §58.1-3650.935.
LCCA Company, Brunswick county, §58.1-3650.445.
League of Older Americans, Inc., City of Roanoke, §58.1-3650.860.
Lee Graham Corporation, Fairfax county, §58.1-3650.785.
Leeland Road Group Home, Inc., Stafford county, §58.1-3650.587.
Lend-A-Paw Relief Organization, Fairfax county, §58.1-3650.764.
Leviticus Project Association, Inc., Chesterfield county, §58.1-3650.531.
Lewinsville Retirement Residence, Inc., §58.1-3650.41.
Lewis Ginter Botanical Garden, Inc., Henrico county, §58.1-3650.600.
Light House Ministries, Inc., Accomack county, §58.1-3650.418.
Lincolnia Park Recreational Club, Inc., Fairfax county, §58.1-3650.545.
Lions Mobile Sight and Hearing Unit of District 24-D, Inc., §58.1-3650.928.
Literacy Council of Metropolitan Richmond, Inc., City of Richmond, §58.1-3650.428.
Little Neck Swim & Racquet Club, Inc., City of Virginia Beach, §58.1-3650.592.
Little River Glen Limited Partnership, Fairfax County, §58.1-3650.741.
Little Theatre of Norfolk, §58.1-3650.171.
London House, Inc., City of Portsmouth, §58.1-3650.335.
Long Branch Swim and Racquet Club, Inc., Fairfax county, §58.1-3650.786.
Loudoun Citizens for Social Justice, Inc., Loudoun county, §58.1-3650.328.
Loudoun County Transportation Association, Loudoun County, §58.1-3650.841.
Loudoun Hospital Center, Loudoun County, §58.1-3650.680.
Loudoun Interfaith Relief, Inc., Loudoun County, §58.1-3650.880.
Loudoun Restoration and Preservation Society, Inc., City of Leesburg, §58.1-3650.65.
Loudoun Vocational Education Foundation, Inc., Loudoun county, §58.1-3650.400.
Louisa County Library Foundation, Louisa County, §58.1-3650.663.
Lovettsville Game Protective Association, §58.1-3650.3.
Luther Crest, Inc., Shenandoah county, §58.1-3650.286.
Lynchburg Sheltered Industries, Inc., City of Lynchburg, §58.1-3650.347.
Macedonia Baptist Church of NAUCK, Arlington county, §58.1-3650.106.

PROPERTY EXEMPT FROM TAXATION —Cont'd

Designation on or after July 1, 1971 —Cont'd

Madison House, Inc., City of Charlottesville, §58.1-3650.55.
Manassas Elks Lodge No. 2512, Prince William County, §58.1-3650.626.
Mantua Hills Swimming Association, Inc., §58.1-3650.925.
MARC of Virginia, Inc., Mecklenburg county, §58.1-3650.369.
M.A.R.C. Workshop, Inc., §58.1-3650.39.
Marian Manor, Inc., City of Virginia Beach, §58.1-3650.304.
Marine Corps League, §58.1-3650.38.
Marine Spill Response Corporation, City of Virginia Beach, §58.1-3650.513.
Marine Spill Response Corporation, Fairfax county, §58.1-3650.773.
Martha Jefferson House and Infirmary, City of Charlottesville, §58.1-3650.281.
Mary Ball Washington Museum and Library, Inc., Lancaster county, §58.1-3650.302.
Mary Immaculate Nursing Center, Inc., §58.1-3650.912.
Mary Washington Hospital, Inc., Foundation, Inc., etc., §58.1-3650.501.
Marywood, Inc., Henrico county, §58.1-3650.143.
Mathews county Land Conservancy, §58.1-3650.938.
Mathews County Woman's Club and Mathews County Junior Woman's Club, Mathews County, §58.1-3650.710.
Mathews Youth Center, Inc., Mathews County, §58.1-3650.709.
Maupin-Sizemore Foundation, City of Bedford, §58.1-3650.822.
Meadow Outdoors Foundation, Inc., Fauquier county, §58.1-3650.172.
Meadows Housing Corporation, Albemarle county, §58.1-3650.406.
Meals of Virginia Beach, Inc., City of Virginia Beach, §58.1-3650.892.
Meals on Wheels of Greater Richmond, Inc., County of Henrico, §58.1-3650.838.
M. E. Cox Center for Elder Day Care, Inc., §58.1-3650.914.
Medical Foundation of Roanoke Valley, City of Salem, §58.1-3650.183.
Melrose/Rugby Neighborhood Forum, Inc., City of Roanoke, §58.1-3650.849.
Memorial Child Guidance Clinic, City of Richmond, §58.1-3650.411.
Memorial Child Guidance Clinic, Henrico county, §58.1-3650.533.
Memorial Foundation of the Germanna Colonies in Virginia, Inc., §58.1-3650.926.
Memorial Properties, Inc., City of Danville, §58.1-3650.360.
Mennowood Communities, Inc., City of Newport News, §58.1-3650.521.
Menokin Foundation, Inc., Richmond County, §58.1-3650.676.
Mercy House, Inc., City of Harrisonburg, §58.1-3650.487.
Mid-Atlantic Teen Challenge, Inc., City of Newport News, §58.1-3650.654.
Middlesex County Museum, Inc., County of Middlesex, §58.1-3650.819.
Military Order of the Purple Heart, County of Fairfax, §58.1-3650.115.

PROPERTY EXEMPT FROM TAXATION —Cont'd

Designation on or after July 1, 1971 —Cont'd

Military Retirees Club of Richmond, Virginia, Inc., City of Richmond, §58.1-3650.378.
Minority Youth Appreciation Society, Inc., Learning Center, City of Richmond, §58.1-3650.557.
Montgomery county Christmas Store, §58.1-3650.932.
Montgomery County Community Shelter, Town of Christiansburg, §58.1-3650.722.
Montgomery Museum and Lewis Miller Regional Arts Center, Montgomery county, §58.1-3650.233.
Monticello Area Community Action Agency, City of Charlottesville, §58.1-3650.569.
Montross Moose Lodge, Number 2333, Loyal Order of the Moose, Inc., Westmoreland County, §58.1-3650.728.
Morris Fine and Mammie Fine Foundation, City of Chesapeake, §58.1-3650.247.
Mosby Woods Recreation Association, Inc., City of Fairfax, §58.1-3650.700.
Mothers, Inc., City of Virginia Beach, §58.1-3650.745.
Mountain Empire Older Citizens, Inc., Wise county, §58.1-3650.364.
Mountain Empire Regional Business Incubator, Inc., Scott County, §58.1-3650.850.
Mountain Empire Services of the Southwest, Inc., Pulaski county, §58.1-3650.296.
Mountain Manor Homes, City of Roanoke, §58.1-3650.517.
Mountain Shelter, Inc., County of Wythe, §58.1-3650.729.
Mountain Shelter, Inc., Town of Wytheville, §58.1-3650.729.
Mountain View Bible Camp, Carroll county, §58.1-3650.293.
Mount Carmel Bus Company, City of Newport News, §58.1-3650.485.
Mount Vernon Inn, Inc., §58.1-3650.131.
National Association of Ministers' Wives and Widows, Inc., City of Richmond, §58.1-3650.138.
National Audubon Society and certain local chapters, §58.1-3650.36.
National Center for State Courts, City of Williamsburg, §58.1-3650.75.
National D-Day Memorial Foundation, City of Bedford, §58.1-3650.761.
National Hospital for Orthopaedics and Rehabilitation, Arlington county, §58.1-3650.352.
National Sporting Library, Incorporated, §58.1-3650.909.
National Wildlife Federation, §58.1-3650.933.
National Wildlife Federation, Frederick County, §58.1-3650.711.
Nat the Cat, Inc., City of Richmond, §58.1-3650.414.
Nature Conservancy, §58.1 3650.13.
Naval Submarine League, Fairfax County, §58.1-3650.719.
Needle's Eye Ministries, Inc., City of Richmond, §58.1-3650.858.
New Life Center, Inc., City of Winchester, §58.1-3650.577.
New London Community House, Inc., Bedford county, §58.1-3650.72.

PROPERTY EXEMPT FROM TAXATION —Cont'd
Designation on or after July 1, 1971 —Cont'd
Newport News Green Foundation, Inc., City of Newport News, §58.1-3650.807.
Newport News Link, Inc., City of Newport News, §58.1-3650.799 (1998 ch 646).
New River Community Action, Inc., §58.1-3650.918.
New River Community Sentencing, Inc., Montgomery county, §58.1-3650.572.
New River Historical Society, Pulaski county, §58.1-3650.118.
New River Valley Habitat for Humanity, Inc., Pulaski county, §58.1-3650.599.
Newsome House, Inc., City of Newport News, §58.1-3650.230.
Nickelsville Community Improvement and Development Company, Inc., Scott county, §58.1-3650.341.
1908 Courthouse Foundation, Grayson County and Town of Independence, §58.1-3650.595.
North Alanton Civic League, Inc., City of Virginia Beach, §58.1-3650.553.
Northampton Fire and Rescue, Inc., Northampton County, §58.1-3650.853.
Northern Neck Alliance, Inc., Westmoreland County, §58.1-3650.803.
Northern Neck Elks Lodge No. 2666, §58.1-3650.770.
Northern Neck-Middle Peninsula Area Agency on Aging, Gloucester county, §58.1-3650.226.
Northern Neck-Middle Peninsula Area Agency on Aging, Inc., Middlesex county, §58.1-3650.239.
Northern Shenandoah Valley Association for Retarded Citizens, Frederick county, §58.1-3650.451.
Northern Virginia Association for Retarded Citizens, Inc., City of Falls Church, §58.1-3650.403.
Northern Virginia Dental Clinic, Inc., Fairfax County, §58.1-3650.891.
Northern Virginia Family Service, Inc., City of Falls Church, §58.1-3650.402.
Northern Virginia Family Service, Inc., Fairfax county, §58.1-3650.391.
Northern Virginia Family Service, Prince William county, §58.1-3650.767.
Northern Virginia Youth Symphony Association, Fairfax county, §58.1-3650.497.
North Franklin County Park, §58.1-3650.94.
North King Street Improvement Council, Inc., City of Hampton, §58.1-3650.876.
Northwestern Workshop, Inc., Frederick county, §58.1-3650.568.
Northwest Recreation Club, Inc., City of Roanoke, §58.1-3650.721.
NRV Nursing Center, Inc., Montgomery County, §58.1-3650.863.
O.A.R. of Fairfax county, Inc., §58.1-3650.924.
OASIS Commission on Social Ministry of Portsmouth and Chesapeake, City of Portsmouth, §58.1-3650.576.
Ocean View Democratic and Social Club, Inc., §58.1-3650.959.
Odiero, Ltd., Montgomery County, §58.1-3650.825.
Office of Human Affairs, Inc., City of Newport News, §58.1-3650.744.
Old Church Gallery, Floyd county, §58.1-3650.462.
Old Dominion Chapter, National Railway Historical Society, Chesterfield county, §58.1-3650.263.

PROPERTY EXEMPT FROM TAXATION —Cont'd
Designation on or after July 1, 1971 —Cont'd
Old Dominion Eye Bank and Research, Inc., §58.1-3650.74.
Olde Newberne Foundation, Inc., §58.1-3650.77.
Old Time Gospel Hour, Inc., City of Lynchburg, §58.1-3650.287.
Omega Corporation of Chesterfield, §58.1-3650.113.
121 Verona Corporation, Augusta County, §58.1-3650.845.
Orange County Granges.
Generally, §58.1-3650.123.
Orthopaedic Research of Virginia, Henrico county, §58.1-3650.524.
Our Lady of Hope Health Center, Inc., Henrico County, §58.1-3650.651.
Our Lady of Peace, Albemarle county, §58.1-3650.527.
Our Lady of Perpetual Help Health Center, Inc., city of Virginia Beach, §58.1-3650.769.
Our Lady of the Valley, Inc., City of Roanoke, §58.1-3650.289.
Outreach for Christ, Inc., City of Virginia Beach, §58.1-3650.882.
Oxbow Human Services Consortium, Inc., Wise County, §58.1-3650.692.
Pamplin Foundation, County of Dinwiddie, §58.1-3650.682.
Paramount Theatre and Cultural Center, Inc., City of Charlottesville, §58.1-3650.528.
Parent-Child Development Center, Inc., King William county, §58.1-3650.379.
Parent Educational Advocacy Training Center, Inc., Fairfax County, §58.1-3650.899.
Parklawn Recreation Association, Inc., Fairfax county, §58.1-3650.570.
Park West Lions Club, Prince William County, §58.1-3650.615.
Pathway Homes, Inc., Fairfax county, §58.1-3650.257.
Pathway Living, Inc., Fairfax county, §58.1-3650.258.
Pathway Options, Inc., Fairfax county, §58.1-3650.514.
Pathway Visions, Inc., City of Fairfax, §58.1-3650.662.
Patrick Henry Boys' Plantation, Inc., Bedford county, §58.1-3650.383.
Patrick Henry Boys' Plantation, Inc., Campbell county, §58.1-3650.243.
Patrick Henry Boys' Plantation, Inc., Charlotte county, §58.1-3650.277.
Patrick Henry Boys' Plantation, Inc., Halifax county, §58.1-3650.276.
Peaceful Harbor, Inc., City of Hampton, §58.1-3650.423.
Pembroke Manor Recreation, Inc., City of Virginia Beach, §58.1-3650.546.
Pembroke Meadows Civic League, Inc., City of Virginia Beach, §58.1-3650.550.
Peninsula Arts Association, Inc., §58.1-3650.32.
Peninsula Habitat for Humanity, Inc., City of Newport News, §58.1-3650.619.
Peninsula Institute for Community Health, Inc., City of Newport News, §58.1-3650.903.
Peninsula Legal Aid Center, Inc., City of Hampton, §58.1-3650.128.
Peninsula Nature and Science Center, Inc., §58.1-3650.10.

PROPERTY EXEMPT FROM TAXATION —Cont'd

Designation on or after July 1, 1971 —Cont'd

People Assisting the Homeless, Inc., City of Richmond, §58.1-3650.582.
People-to-People Health Foundation, Inc., §58.1-3650.78.
Petersburg Area Art League, City of Petersburg, §58.1-3650.542.
Petersburg Community Development Corporation, City of Petersburg, §58.1-3650.439.
Petersburg Economic Action Corporation, City of Petersburg, §58.1-3650.591.
Petersburg Foundation, City of Petersburg, §58.1-3650.340.
Phoenix Village Associates, Inc., City of Newport News, §58.1-3650.284.
Pine Ridge Civic League, Inc., City of Virginia Beach, §58.1-3650.547.
Pleasant View Home for the Handicapped, Inc., Rockingham county and City of Harrisonburg, §§58.1-3650.180, 58.1-3650.217.
Pocahontas, Gordonsville and Petersburg Historic Foundations, §58.1-3650.17.
Point of Honor, Inc., City of Lynchburg, §58.1-3650.828.
Police Association of Prince William County, Prince William county, §58.1-3650.417.
Poquoson Woman's Club, City of Poquoson, §58.1-3650.321.
Portsmouth Area Resources Coalition, Inc., City of Portsmouth, §58.1-3650.535.
Portsmouth Lodge No. 898, Loyal Order of the Moose, Inc., City of Chesapeake, §§58.1-3650.178, 58.1-3650.215.
Portsmouth Veterans Home, Inc., City of Portsmouth, §58.1-3650.574.
Potomac Appalachian Trail Club, §58.1-3650.12.
Potomac Conservancy, Fairfax County, §58.1-3650.699.
Powhatan Masonic Temple, Powhatan county, §58.1-3650.588.
Preservation of Historic Suffolk, Inc., City of Suffolk, §58.1-3650.871.
Preservation of Historic Winchester, Inc., City of Winchester, §58.1-3650.450.
Preston Community Center, Henry County, §58.1-3650.715.
Prestonwood Properties, Inc., Chesterfield County, §58.1-3650.635.
Price's Fork Chapter of the Virginia State Grange, §58.1-3650.69.
Prince William Chapter of the Izaak Walton League of America, §58.1-3650.703.
Prince William county.
  Health and hospital associations generally, §§58.1-3650.179, 58.1-3650.217.
  P.W.H. Corporation, Prince William Hospital, Inc., PWH Foundation, Inc. and Long Term Care Corporation, City of Manassas, §58.1-3650.208.
  P.W.H. Personal Care Corporation and P.W.H. Home Health Services, Inc., City of Manassas, §58.1-3650.231.
Prison Fellowship Ministries, Fairfax county, §58.1-3650.606.
Psychiatric Rehabilitation Services, Inc., §58.1-3650.951.
Public Broadcasting Service, Fairfax County, §58.1-3650.725.
Purcellville Preservation Association, Loudoun County, §58.1-3650.670.
Rainbow Center 4-H Therapeutic Equestrian Program, Inc., Prince William County, §§58.1-3650.837, 58.1-3650.846.
Rapidan Habitat for Humanity, Inc., Orange County, §58.1-3650.650.
Rappahannock Area Agency on Aging, Inc., §58.1-3650.59.
Rappahannock Council on Domestic Violence, Stafford county, §58.1-3650.315.
Rappahannock County Citizen's League, County of Rappahannock, §58.1-3650.626.
Rappahannock Refuge, Inc., City of Fredericksburg, §58.1-3650.502.
Rappahannock United Way, Inc., Spotsylvania county, §58.1-3650.605.
Red Cloud Tribe No. 58 I.O.R.M., City of Poquoson, §58.1-3650.374.
Red Fez Club, Inc., City of Galax, §58.1-3650.393.
Regional Properties, Inc., Loudoun County, §58.1-3650.810.
Remington Home, Inc., Fauquier County, §58.1-3650.748.
Residential Youth Service, Inc., Fairfax county, §58.1-3650.259.
Resources for Independence of Virginia, Inc., Fairfax County, §58.1-3650.714.
Resources for Independence of Virginia, Inc., Loudoun County, §58.1-3650.811.
Reston Interfaith Housing Corporation, Inc., Fairfax County, Town of Herndon, §58.1-3650.873.
Reston Interfaith, Inc., Fairfax county, §58.1-3650.427.
Retirees Club ACTWU, Local 371T and Fraternal Order of Police, Warren county, §58.1-3650.578.
Retirement Housing Foundation, City of Chesapeake, §58.1-3650.330.
Richfield Nursing Center, Roanoke county, §58.1-3650.254.
Richfield Retirement Community, Roanoke county, §58.1-3650.253.
Richlands Athletic League, Inc., Tazewell county, §58.1-3650.519.
Richmond Animal League, Chesterfield County, §58.1-3650.813.
Richmond Area Association for Retarded Children, Inc., §58.1-3650.71.
Richmond Area High Blood Pressure Center, City of Richmond, §§58.1-3650.337, 58.1-3650.560.
Richmond Cerebral Palsy Center, City of Richmond, §58.1-3650.279.
Richmond Children's Museum, City of Richmond, §58.1-3650.312.
Richmond Community Action Program, Inc., City of Richmond, §58.1-3650.641.
Richmond Community Senior Center, Inc., City of Richmond, §58.1-3650.88.
Richmond Community Senior Center, Inc., Henrico county, §58.1-3650.433.
Richmond Council of Garden Clubs, Inc., §58.1-3650.23.
Richmond County Community Services Association, Inc., Richmond county, §58.1-3650.274.

PROPERTY EXEMPT FROM TAXATION —Cont'd

Designation on or after July 1, 1971 —Cont'd

Richmond Discoveries, Inc., Henrico county, §58.1-3650.367.
Richmond Goodwill Industries, Inc., City of Richmond, §58.1-3650.350.
Richmond Hill, Inc., City of Richmond, §58.1-3650.348.
Richmond Lakeside Lodge No. 1714, Loyal Order of Moose, Inc., Henrico county, §58.1-3650.446.
Richmond Lodge No. 45 of the Benevolent and Protective Order of Elks of the United States of America, Inc., Henrico county, §58.1-3650.375.
Richmond Metropolitan Blood Service, §58.1-3650.114.
Richmond Metropolitan Habitat for Humanity, Inc., Chesterfield County, §58.1-3650.681.
Richmond Metropolitan Habitat for Humanity, Inc., City of Richmond, §58.1-3650.343.
Richmond Metropolitan Habitat for Humanity, Inc., Henrico County, §58.1-3650.660.
Richmond Residential Services, Inc., City of Richmond, §58.1-3650.377.
Richmond Section, National Council of Jewish Women, Inc., §58.1-3650.40.
Richmond Virginia Seminary, City of Richmond, §58.1-3650.385.
Ridge Run Terrace Properties, Inc., Chesterfield County, §58.1-3650.636.
Rivanna Conservation Society, Fluvanna County, §58.1-3650.878.
Riverfront Management Corp., City of Richmond, §58.1-3650.756.
River's Edge Civic Association, §58.1-3650.64.
Roanoke, City of.
  Fine arts organizations in City of Roanoke, §58.1-3650.141.
Roanoke Foundation for Downtown, Inc., City of Roanoke, §58.1-3650.794.
Roanoke Rebos, Inc., County of Roanoke, §58.1-3650.415.
Roanoke Valley Council of Community Services, Inc., City of Roanoke, §58.1-3650.460.
Roberta Webb Child Care Center, Inc., City of Harrisonburg, §58.1-3650.796.
Robert E. Rose Memorial Foundation, Inc., Frederick county, §58.1-3650.753.
Robert Pierre Johnson Housing Development Corporation, Fairfax county, §58.1-3650.477.
Robert R. Moton Memorial Institute, Gloucester county, §58.1-3650.267.
Rob Lee Family Park, Henry county, §58.1-3650.471.
Rockingham County Fair Association, Inc., §58.1-3650.145.
Rockingham-Harrisonburg Halfway House, Inc., §58.1-3650.52.
Rolling Hills Swim Club, Inc., Fairfax County, §58.1-3650.854.
Roman Eagle Memorial Home, Inc., City of Danville, §58.1-3650.739.
Roman Eagle Properties, Inc., City of Danville, §58.1-3650.361.
Ronald McDonald House Charities of Greater Washington, Inc., Fairfax County, §58.1-3650.742.
Ronald McDonald House, City of Norfolk, §58.1-3650.127.

PROPERTY EXEMPT FROM TAXATION —Cont'd

Designation on or after July 1, 1971 —Cont'd

Rosehill Neighborhood, Inc., Western county, §58.1-3650.456.
Rosewell Foundation, Inc., Gloucester county, §58.1-3650.793.
Rosie Grier Youth Shelter, City of Richmond, §58.1-3650.412.
Rosser Family Foundation, City of Hampton, §58.1-3650.706.
Route One Corridor Housing, Inc., Fairfax county, §58.1-3650.530.
Royal Pool Association, Inc., Fairfax County, §58.1-3650.900.
Rudolph Steiner School in Falls Church, §58.1-3650.18.
Ruritan National, Inc., §58.1-3650.16.
Russell Housing, Inc., City of Virginia Beach, §58.1-3650.224.
Saddler Home, Inc., City of Newport News, §58.1-3650.678.
Safehaven, Inc., City of Newport News, §58.1-3650.571.
St. Alban's Housing Corporation, Fairfax county, §58.1-3650.148.
St. Benedict's Corporation, Tazewell county, §58.1-3650.101.
St. Chivas Corporation, County of Tazewell, §58.1-3650.661.
St. Joseph's Villa Housing Corporation, Henrico county, §58.1-3650.155.
St. Joseph's Villa Housing Corp. II, Henrico county, §58.1-3650.398.
St. Mark's Evangelical Brethren Church, Arlington county, §58.1-3650.192.
St. Mary's Housing Corporation, Fairfax county, §58.1-3650.262.
St. Mary's Woods, Inc., Henrico county, §58.1-3650.300.
St. Peter's Episcopal Church of Arlington, Arlington county, §58.1-3650.198.
Saints Cosma and Damianos House, City of Richmond, §58.1-3650.297.
Salem Historical Society, City of Salem, §58.1-3650.232.
Salem Woods Civic Association, Inc., §58.1-3650.930.
Salvation Army, Inc., City of Staunton, §58.1-3650.325.
Samaritan Helping Hands Home, City of Emporia, §58.1-3650.473.
Samaritan House, Inc., Virginia Beach, Virginia, §58.1-3650.749.
Sanders Common, Ltd., Gloucester county, §58.1-3650.205.
Save Our School Foundation, Inc., Hanover county, §§58.1-3650.429, 58.1-3650.459, 58.1-3650.492.
Save the Railroad Station, Inc., Fauquier County, §58.1-3650.671.
Second Phoenix Village Associates, Inc., City of Newport News, §58.1-3650.285.
Second St. Alban's Housing Corporation, Fairfax county, §58.1-3650.508.
Second St. Mary's Housing Corporation, Prince William county, §58.1-3650.250.
Securing Emergency Resources through Voluntary Efforts, Inc., City of Manassas, §58.1-3650.628.

PROPERTY EXEMPT FROM TAXATION —Cont'd

Designation on or after July 1, 1971 —Cont'd

Sedalia Center, Inc., Bedford County, §§58.1-3650.704, 58.1-3650.734.
Senior Center, Inc., Albemarle county, §58.1-3650.313.
Senior Center, Inc., City of Charlottesville, §58.1-3650.282.
Senior Citizen Center of Prince Edward County, Town of Farmville, §58.1-3650.96.
Serenity House Substance Abuse Recovery Program, Inc., City of Newport News, §58.1-3650.885.
Serenity House Substance Abuse Recovery Program, Inc., Newport News, §58.1-3650.677.
Sergeant Santa of Richmond, Inc., City of Richmond, §58.1-3650.644.
Serve, Inc., Stafford County, §58.1-3650.672.
Service to Abused Families, Inc., Culpeper county, §58.1-3650.453.
Shalom Et Benedictus, Inc., Frederick county, §58.1-3650.754.
Share-A-Homes of the Virginia Peninsula, Inc., City of Hampton, §58.1-3650.647.
Share-A-Homes of the Virginia Peninsula, Inc., City of Newport News, §58.1-3650.633.
Sheltered Home of Alexandria, §58.1-3650.35.
Sheltered Occupational Center of Northern Virginia, Inc., Fairfax county, §58.1-3650.235.
Shelter for Abused Women, City of Winchester, §58.1-3650.448.
ShenanArts, Augusta county, §58.1-3650.561.
Shenandoah county, §58.1-3650.566.
Shenandoah Fellowship Foundation, §58.1-3650.58.
Shenandoah Shared Hospital Services, Inc., City of Harrisonburg, §58.1-3650.135.
Shenandoah Valley Community Residences, Inc., City of Winchester, §58.1-3650.712.
Shenandoah Valley Community Residences, Inc., Frederick County, §58.1-3650.666.
Shenandoah Valley Independent Living Center, City of Winchester, §58.1-3650.424.
Shen-Paco Industries, Inc., Page county, §58.1-3650.752.
Shining Light Masonic Lodge 272 and Order of Eastern Star Chapter 182, §58.1-3650.953.
Showalter Memorial Health Center, Trolinger House and New River House, Montgomery county, §58.1-3650.150.
Showtimers of Roanoke Valley, Inc., City of Roanoke, §58.1-3650.399.
Sleepy Hollow Bath and Racquet Club, Inc., §58.1-3650.956.
Smithfield Little Theater, Inc., Isle of Wight county, §58.1-3650.408.
Somerset-Olde Creek Recreation Club, Inc., Fairfax County, §58.1-3650.831.
Sophia House, Inc., Louisa county, §58.1-3650.757.
Southampton County Historical Society, §58.1-3650.25.
South County Housing Coalition, Inc., Fairfax county, §58.1-3650.326.
South-Eastern Organ Procurement Foundation, City of Richmond, §58.1-3650.90.
Southside Virginia Railroad Society, §58.1-3650.34.
Southwest Development Corporation, §58.1-3650.84.

PROPERTY EXEMPT FROM TAXATION —Cont'd

Designation on or after July 1, 1971 —Cont'd

Special Love, Inc., Frederick County, §58.1-3650.667.
Springboard Recreation Club, Inc., Fairfax County, §58.1-3650.898.
Springfield Swimming and Racquet Club, Fairfax County, §58.1-3650.864.
Springfield, Virginia Youth Club, Inc., Fairfax County, §58.1-3650.865.
Stafford County Vocational Education Foundation, Inc., Stafford County, §58.1-3650.726.
Stafford United Methodist Housing Development Corporation, Stafford county, §58.1-3650.371.
Staunton Fine Arts Association, Inc., City of Staunton, §58.1-3650.388.
Steamer Co. No. 5, The Fire History Museum, City of Richmond, §58.1-3650.392.
Stepping Stones, Inc., City of Martinsville, §58.1-3650.733.
Sterling Park United Methodist Housing Development Corporation, Loudoun county, §58.1-3650.308.
Stone House Foundation, Frederick county, §58.1-3650.452.
Stonewall Estates Group Home, Inc., Spotsylvania county, §58.1-3650.590.
Straight Street-Buckingham, Inc., Buckingham county, §58.1-3650.777.
Strict construction of exemptions, §58.1-3650.
Suffolk Shelter for the Homeless, Inc., City of Suffolk, §58.1-3650.409.
Sugar Plum, Inc., City of Virginia Beach, §58.1-3650.515.
Sunlight Lodge No. 1558, City of Hopewell, §58.1-3650.848.
Sunny Fountain Lodge No. 1897, Grand United Order of Odd Fellows, Culpeper County, §58.1-3650.526.
Sunnyside Presbyterian Home, City of Waynesboro, §58.1-3650.724.
Sunnyside Presbyterian Retirement Community, Rockingham county, §58.1-3650.489.
Sun Ray Farmers Association, §58.1-3650.54.
Sun Ray Parent-Teachers Association, §58.1-3650.53.
Susan Jan Kaneski Corporation, City of Chesapeake, §58.1-3650.248.
Tazewell Little League Baseball, Inc., Tazewell county, §58.1-3650.520.
Tazewell Youth Football, Inc., Tazewell county, §58.1-3650.518.
Temple Foundation, Inc., §58.1-3650.8.
Terjo Properties, Inc., Chesterfield County, §58.1-3650.689.
The Association for the Preservation of Civil War Sites, Inc., Shenandoah county, §58.1-3650.563.
Theater IV, City of Richmond, §58.1-3650.275.
Three Chopt Soccer Association, Inc., Henrico county, §58.1-3650.154.
Thunderbird Research Corporation, Warren county, §58.1-3650.457.
Tidewater Child Care Association, Inc., City of Portsmouth, §58.1-3650.482.
Tidewater Intergroup Services Center, Inc., §58.1-3650.94.
Tidewater Soaring Foundation, §58.1-3650.936.
Tocoma School Community Center, Inc., Wise County, §58.1-3650.718.

PROPERTY EXEMPT FROM TAXATION —Cont'd

Designation on or after July 1, 1971 —Cont'd

Total Action Against Poverty in Roanoke Valley, City of Covington, §58.1-3650.771.
Total Action Against Poverty in the Roanoke Valley, Inc., county of Roanoke, §58.1-3650.416.
Town Hall-Levy Opera House Foundation, Inc., §58.1-3650.45.
Train Station Foundation, §58.1-3650.908.
Transportation and Public Service, Inc., Fairfax county, §58.1-3650.203.
Triad Foundation, Inc., City of Newport News, §58.1-3650.656.
Tri-Area Health Clinic, Inc., Carroll county, §58.1-3650.484.
Tri-County Homes, Inc., Carroll county, §58.1-3650.470.
Tri-County Medical Corporation, King William county, §58.1-3650.331.
Triple-R Holding Corporation, City of Chesapeake, §58.1-3650.498.
Trustees of Fairfax Old Town Hall, §58.1-3650.76.
Tuckahoe Little League, Inc., §58.1-3650.43.
Tuckahoe Lodge No. 1163, Loyal Order of Moose, Henrico county, §58.1-3650.523.
TWBTS, Inc., §58.1-3650.939.
Twig, Junior Auxiliary of the Alexandria Hospital, §58.1-3650.62.
Twin County-Galax Association for Retarded Citizens, City of Galax, §58.1-3650.102.
United Community Center, Inc., King and Queen county, §58.1-3650.157.
United Community Ministries, Inc., Fairfax county, §58.1-3650.329.
United Network for Organ Sharing, Chesterfield county, §58.1-3650.404.
United Rappahannock Tribe, Inc., King and Queen County, §58.1-3650.708.
United States Slow-Pitch Softball Hall of Fame Foundation, Inc., City of Petersburg, §58.1-3650.111.
United Way of Richmond, City of Richmond, §58.1-3650.466.
United Way of South Hampton Roads, City of Norfolk, §58.1-3650.814.
United Way-Thomas Jefferson Area, City of Charlottesville, §58.1-3650.144.
Upper King William Senior Citizens Association, Inc., King & Queen County, §58.1-3650.630.
Upper Mattaponi Indian Tribe, King William county, §58.1-3650.536.
Upper Pohick Community League, §58.1-3650.67.
Valley Program for Aging Services, Inc., City of Harrisonburg, Augusta County, Highland County, Rockingham County, §58.1-3650.861.
Valley Workshops, Inc., §58.1-3650.56.
Varina Masonic Lodge No. 272, A.F. & A.M., Henrico county, §58.1-3650.538.
Vetshouse, Inc., City of Virginia Beach, §58.1-3650.817.
Village View Foundation, City of Emporia, §58.1-3650.272.
Vinson Hall Corporation, §58.1-3650.4.
Vinson Pavilion, Fairfax county, §58.1-3650.327.
Virginia Aeronautical Historical Society, Henrico county, §58.1-3650.221.
Virginia Association of the Blind, Inc., City of Chesapeake, §58.1-3650.843.

PROPERTY EXEMPT FROM TAXATION —Cont'd

Designation on or after July 1, 1971 —Cont'd

Virginia Association of Volunteer Rescue Squads, Inc., Goochland county, §58.1-3650.774.
Virginia Baptist Homes, Inc., §58.1-3650.33.
Virginia Beach Christian Outreach Group, Inc., City of Virginia Beach, §58.1-3650.441.
Virginia Beach Community Development Corporation, City of Virginia Beach, §58.1-3650.401.
Virginia Beach Community Trust Exempt Fund, City of Virginia Beach, §58.1-3650.902.
Virginia Beach Ecumenical Housing, Inc., City of Virginia Beach, §58.1-3650.358.
Virginia Beach Foundation, City of Virginia Beach, §58.1-3650.443.
Virginia Beach, HOME Inc., City of Virginia Beach, §58.1-3650.824.
Virginia Center for the Performing Arts, City of Richmond, §58.1-3650.121.
Virginia Congress of Parents & Teachers, City of Richmond, §58.1-3650.643.
Virginia Congress of Parents & Teachers, Henrico county, §58.1-3650.751.
Virginia Council of Social Welfare, City of Richmond, §58.1-3650.87.
Virginia Division, Sons of Confederate Veterans, §58.1-3650.31.
Virginia Home for Boys, City of Richmond, §58.1-3650.596.
Virginia Home for Boys in Richmond, Inc., county of Henrico, §58.1-3650.200.
Virginia Jaycee, Inc., Bedford county, §58.1-3650.238.
Virginia Mennonite Home, Inc., City of Harrisonburg, §58.1-3650.168.
Virginia Mountain Housing, Inc., Giles and Montgomery counties, Town of Christiansburg or Pembroke, §58.1-3650.394.
Virginia Museum of Transportation, Inc., City of Roanoke, §58.1-3650.732.
Virginia Opera Association, City of Richmond, §58.1-3650.202.
Virginia Peninsula Council Domestic Violence, City of Hampton, §58.1-3650.420.
Virginia Peninsula Shelter for Abused Children, Inc., t/a Safehaven, City of Newport News, §58.1-3650.655.
Virginia Quilt Museum, §58.1-3650.934.
Virginia Synod Lutheran Homes, Inc., City of Roanoke, §58.1-3650.187.
Virginia Tissue Bank, City of Chesapeake, §58.1-3650.318.
Virginia Trust for Historic Preservation, Lee Fendall House in City of Alexandria, §58.1-3650.20.
Virginia United Methodist Homes, Inc., Henrico County, §58.1-3650.695.
Vocational Industrial Clubs of America, Inc., Loudoun county, §58.1-3650.92.
Wakefield Foundation, Inc., town of Wakefield, §58.1-3650.292.
Walden Glen Swim and Racquet Club, Inc., §58.1-3650.927.
Walter Reed Memorial Hospital, county of Gloucester, §58.1-3650.204.
Warren Co. Habitat for Humanity, Inc., Warren County, §58.1-3650.625.
Warren County Workshop, Inc., Warren County, §58.1-3650.631.

PROPERTY EXEMPT FROM TAXATION —Cont'd
Designation on or after July 1, 1971 —Cont'd
Washington Regional Transplant Consortium, Fairfax county, §58.1-3650.503.
Watermen's Museum, York county, §58.1-3650.387.
Watermen's Museum, Yorktown, §58.1-3650.373.
Waynesboro Association for Retarded Citizens, Inc., §58.1-3650.37.
Waynesboro Players, Inc., Waynesboro, §58.1-3650.264.
Wayside Foundation for the Arts, Inc., Frederick County, §58.1-3650.611.
Wayside Museum of American History and Arts, Frederick County, §58.1-3650.683.
Wellspring Ministries, Fairfax county, §58.1-3650.208.
Wesley Agape House, Inc., Fairfax County, §58.1-3650.686.
Wesley Housing Development Corporation of Northern Virginia, Fairfax county, §58.1-3650.354.
West End Community Center, Inc., §58.1-3650.42.
West End Manor and Three Fountains North Civic Associations, Henrico county, §58.1-3650.142.
Westlake Hills Civic Association, City of Richmond, §58.1-3650.268.
West Mathews Community League, Mathews county, §58.1-3650.589.
Westminster-Canterbury Corporation, §58.1-3650.29.
Westminster-Canterbury of Lynchburg, Inc., §58.1-3650.73.
Westminster-Canterbury of Winchester, Inc., City of Winchester and county of Frederick, §58.1-3650.246.
Westover Hills Community Center, Inc., City of Danville, §58.1-3650.363.
Wildlife Center of Virginia and the Wildlife Center of Virginia Foundation, City of Waynesboro, §58.1-3650.723.
William Byrd Community House, Inc., §58.1-3650.70.
Williamsburg Area Child Development Resources, Inc., James City county, §58.1-3650.100.
Williamsburg Land Conservancy, James City county, §58.1-3650.762.
Williamsburg Players, Inc., York county, §58.1-3650.85.
Winchester Chapter of the Izaak Walton League of America, Frederick county, §58.1-3650.506.
Winchester Little Theater, Inc., §58.1-3650.63.
Windmore Foundation of the Arts, Culpeper County, §58.1-3650.669.
Windsordale Civic Association, Henrico county, §58.1-3650.105.
Windy Hill Foundation, Loudoun county, §58.1-3650.565.
Wintergreen Nature Foundation, Nelson County, §58.1-3650.806.
Winters Hill Properties, Inc., Chesterfield County, §58.1-3650.690.
Wise County Historical Society, Inc., Wise County, §58.1-3650.869.
Wise County Humane Society, §58.1-3650.106.
Wise School of Dance, Inc., Town of Wise, §58.1-3650.338.
Wise School of Dance, Inc., Wise county, §58.1-3650.357.

PROPERTY EXEMPT FROM TAXATION —Cont'd
Designation on or after July 1, 1971 —Cont'd
Wolftrap Foundation of the Performing Arts, Fairfax county, §58.1-3650.126.
Woman's Club of King & Queen County, King & Queen County, §58.1-3650.629.
Women's Center, Fairfax County and Town of Vienna, §58.1-3650.877.
Woodley Recreation Association, Inc., Fairfax County, §58.1-3650.649.
Woodrow Wilson Birthplace Foundation, City of Staunton, §58.1-3650.104.
Workshop V, Inc., City of Charlottesville, §58.1-3650.147.
Wytheville Community Apartments Corporation, Town of Wytheville, §58.1-3650.437.
Yoder Preservation Trust, Inc., City of Newport News, §58.1-3650.800.
York County Volunteer Association, Inc., §58.1-3650.26.
Yorktown Arts Foundation, Inc., York county, §58.1-3650.129.
Youth Development Center, Inc., City of Winchester, §58.1-3650.447.
Youth for Tomorrow-New Life Center, Inc., City of Bristol, §58.1-3650.288.
Youth With a Mission, City of Richmond, §58.1-3650.465.
Y's Men's Club of Galax, Virginia, Inc., City of Galax, §58.1-3650.474.
Zion Place, Inc., City of Virginia Beach, §58.1-3650.223.
Zulekia Court Number 35, L.O.S.N.A., City of Chesapeake, §58.1-3650.755.
Disabled veterans.
Real property tax exemption, §§58.1-3219.5 to 58.1-3219.8.
Elderly or handicapped.
Real property tax exemptions, §§58.1-3210 to 58.1-3217.
Environmental restoration sites, §58.1-3664.
Erosion control improvements.
Partial exemption, §58.1-3665.
Farm animals, grains, agricultural products, etc.
Governing body may exempt from personal property tax, §58.1-3505.
Federal transportation grant anticipation revenue notes, §33.1-23.25.
General assembly powers, VA Const Art IV §14.
Generating and cogenerating equipment used for energy, §58.1-3662.
Hotel and motel real estate.
Rehabilitated or renovated or replacement structures, §58.1-3220.1.
Information to be kept by county, city or town, §58.1-3604.
Land source of revenue.
Exemption not applicable, §58.1-3603.
Lease of exempt building or land.
Exemption not applicable when source of revenue, §58.1-3603.
Libraries, §58.1-3606.
Metropolitan Washington airports authority, §5.1-172.
Military property and armory property, §44-131.
Museums, §58.1-3606.
Northern Neck Chesapeake Bay public access authority, §15.2-6643.

PROPERTY EXEMPT FROM TAXATION —Cont'd
Open space land interest held by public body, §58.1-3205.
Parks or playgrounds for perpetual use, §58.1-3606.
Partial taxation by one political subdivision or utility property owned by another, §58.1-3663.
Payment of death, sickness or accident benefits.
Exemptions not applicable to associations, corporations, etc., paying, §58.1-3602.
Pollution control equipment and facilities, §58.1-3660.
Publication.
Total assessed valuations and computation of percentage of exempt and immune property, §58.1-3604.
Public-private transportation act.
Property indirectly owned by government, §58.1-3606.1.
Recycling equipment, facilities or devices, §58.1-3661.
Rehabilitated commercial or industrial structures, §58.1-3221.
Rehabilitated hotel or motel structures, §58.1-3220.1.
Rehabilitated residential real estate, §58.1-3220.
Renovated commercial or industrial structures, §58.1-3221.
Renovated hotel or motel structures, §58.1-3220.1.
Renovated residential real estate, §58.1-3220.
Replacement commercial or industrial structures, §58.1-3221.
Replacement hotel or motel structures, §58.1-3220.1.
Replacement residential real estate, §58.1-3220.
Reports by owners of tax exempt real estate, §58.1-3605.1.
Riparian buffers, §58.1-3666.
Sale by tax exempt owner.
Taxable immediately, §58.1-3601.
Service charge on certain real property, §§58.1-3400 to 58.1-3407.
Service charges in lieu of payments of real property taxes, §§58.1-3400 to 58.1-3407.
Solar energy equipment, facilities or devices, §58.1-3661.
Stormwater management developments and property, §58.1-3660.1.
Taxable immediately upon sale by tax exempt owner, §58.1-3601.
Transportation board.
Federal transportation grant anticipation revenue notes, §33.1-23.25.
Transportation infrastructure bank, §33.1-23.12.
Utility property owned by political subdivision.
Partial taxation by other political subdivision, §58.1-3663.
Veterans.
Disabled veterans.
Real property tax exemption, §§58.1-3219.5 to 58.1-3219.8.
Wetlands, §58.1-3666.
Young Men's Christian Associations, §58.1-3606.

PROPERTY FACTOR.
Allocation and apportionment of corporate taxable income, §§58.1-409 to 58.1-411.

PROPERTY INSURANCE.
Affiliated insurer willing to provide coverage at a lower premium than expiring policy.
Policy issued deemed renewal policy, §38.2-231.
Aircraft insurance.
Defined, §38.2-125.
Animal insurance.
Defined, §38.2-116.
Boiler and machinery insurance.
Defined, §38.2-115.
Burglary and theft insurance.
Defined, §38.2-113.
Certificates of insurance, requirements, §38.2-518.
Commercial multi-peril insurance.
Defined, §38.2-132.
Department of Criminal Justice Services.
Revocation of agent's license, notice to department if surety bail bondsman, §38.2-2412.1.
Violations by agent, notice to department if surety bail bondsman, §38.2-2412.2.
Discrimination, §38.2-508.
Farmowners insurance.
Defined, §38.2-131.
Fire insurance, §§38.2-2100 to 38.2-2130.
Defined, §38.2-110.
Future financial responsibility of licensed property and casualty insurers.
Proof required at request of named insured, §38.2-228.
Glass insurance.
Defined, §38.2-114.
Homeowners insurance.
Defined, §38.2-130.
Home protection insurance.
Defined, §38.2-129.
Information and privacy protection.
Applicability of chapter, §38.2-601.
Generally, §§38.2-600 to 38.2-620.
See INSURANCE INFORMATION AND PRIVACY PROTECTION.
Insurable interest required, §38.2-303.
Insurance consultants.
License examination requirement.
Property and casualty insurance consultants, §38.2-1838.
Internet posting of property and casualty forms and endorsements, §38.2-325.
Joint underwriting association.
Appeals from decisions of association, §38.2-2712.
Ceding basic property insurance to association, §38.2-2709.
Creation, §38.2-2708.
Definitions, §38.2-2701.
Governing bodies, §38.2-2709.
Immunity from liability for action taken in good faith, §38.2-2711.
Implementation of provisions by state corporation commission, §38.2-2707.
Obligations not impaired in event of repealed chapter, §38.2-2713.
Participation of members, §38.2-2709.
Plan of operation, §38.2-2708.
Purposes of chapter, §38.2-2700.
Supervision and regulation by state corporation commission, §38.2-2710.
When commission may implement, §38.2-2707.

PROPERTY INSURANCE —Cont'd
Local government group self-insurance pools, §§15.2-2700 to 15.2-2709.
Pools authorized, §15.2-2703.
Marine insurance.
Defined, §38.2-126.
Miscellaneous property insurance.
Defined, §38.2-111.
Motor vehicle insurance.
Defined, §38.2-124.
Generally.
See MOTOR VEHICLE INSURANCE.
Mutual assessment insurers.
Generally, §§38.2-2500 to 38.2-2529.
See MUTUAL ASSESSMENT PROPERTY AND CASUALTY INSURERS.
Policies and contracts generally, §§38.2-300 to 38.2-326.
See INSURANCE POLICIES AND CONTRACTS.
Producer-controlled property and casualty insurers.
Business transacted with, §§38.2-1341 to 38.2-1346.
Property damage liability insurance.
Certified escort vehicle drivers.
Insurance required, §46.2-2902.
Defined, §38.2-118.
Notice of cancellation, refusal to renew, reduction in coverage or increase in rate, §38.2-231.
Property damage resulting from natural disaster.
Disclosure of information to certain officials, §38.2-324.
Rates.
Generally, §§38.2-1900 to 38.2-1928.
See INSURANCE RATES.
Workers' compensation, automobiles, home protection, etc., §§38.2-2000 to 38.2-2027.
See INSURANCE RATES.
Records, retention.
Cancellation, refusal to renew, reduction in coverage, §38.2-231.
Replacement and repairs.
Unfair settlement practices, §38.2-517.
Residual market facility.
Appeal from decision of inspection service or facility, §38.2-2712.
Approval of state corporation commission.
Rules, rates, etc., §38.2-2703.
Definitions, §38.2-2701.
Director, §38.2-2702.
Establishment, §38.2-2702.
Immunity from liability for action taken in good faith, §38.2-2711.
Inspection of property or facility, §38.2-2704.
Inspection service, operation of, §38.2-2705.
Obligations not impaired in event of repealed chapter, §38.2-2713.
Purposes of chapter, §38.2-2700.
Rules, rates, etc.
Approval of state corporation commission, §38.2-2703.
Service of notice, process and other papers, §38.2-2706.
Supervision and regulation by state corporation commission, §38.2-2710.
Review of insurer action.
Cancellation, refusal to renew, reduction in coverage, §38.2-231.
Revocation of agent's license, notice to criminal justice services department if surety bail bondsman, §38.2-2412.1.

PROPERTY INSURANCE —Cont'd
Self storage insurance, §§38.2-1881 to 38.2-1886.
Surplus lines insurance law, §§38.2-4805.1 to 38.2-4816.
Title insurance.
Defined, §38.2-123.
Travel insurance, §§38.2-1887 to 38.2-1890.
Unfair insurance trade practices generally, §§38.2-500 to 38.2-518.
See INSURANCE, UNFAIR TRADE PRACTICES.
Violations by agent, notice to criminal justice services department if surety bail bondsman, §38.2-2412.2.
Water damage insurance.
Defined, §38.2-112.
Where contracts deemed made.
Contracts with respect to ownership, maintenance and use in Commonwealth, §38.2-313.

PROPERTY INSURANCE AGENTS.
Chartered property and casualty underwriters.
Exempt from education and examination requirements, §38.2-1817.
Continuing education, §§38.2-1866 to 38.2-1874.
Criminal justice services department.
Revocation of agent's license, notice to department if surety bail bondsman, §38.2-2412.1.
Violations by agent, notice to department if surety bail bondsman, §38.2-2412.2.
Licensing of agents generally, §§38.2-1822 to 38.2-1836.1.
Examination required, §38.2-1814.
Mutual assessment agents.
Licensing without examination, §38.2-1814.
Revocation of agent's license, notice to criminal justice services department if surety bail bondsman, §38.2-2412.1.
Surety bail bondsman.
Revocation of agent's license, notice to criminal justice services department, §38.2-2412.1.
Violations by agent, notice to criminal justice services department, §38.2-2412.2.
Temporary licenses and appointments, §38.2-1830.
Violations by agent, notice to criminal justice services department if surety bail bondsman, §38.2-2412.2.

PROPERTY INSURANCE CONSULTANTS.
Licensing of consultants generally, §§38.2-1837 to 38.2-1845.

PROPERTY OWNERS' ASSOCIATIONS, §§55-508 to 55-516.2.
Amendment or repeal of rule or regulation, §55-513.
Amendment to declaration and bylaws.
Consent of mortgagee, §55-515.1.
Corrective amendments, §55-515.2.
Applicability of provisions, §55-508.
Assessments, §55-514.
Blanket fidelity bond or employee dishonesty insurance, §55-514.2.
Late fees, §55-513.3.
Lien for assessments, §55-516.
Requirements, §55-509.3.
Violations.
Assessment of charges against member for, §55-513.
Blanket fidelity bond or employee dishonesty insurance.
Required, association collecting assessments for common expenses, §55-514.2.

PROPERTY OWNERS' ASSOCIATIONS —Cont'd
Board of directors.
Closed sessions, §55-510.1.
Communication by lot owners among selves and with board.
Establishment of method, §55-510.2.
Meetings, §§55-510, 55-510.1.
Notice, §55-510.1.
Rules and regulations, §55-513.
Cancellation of sale contract.
Disclosure lot located in development subject to act, §55-509.4.
Capital components.
Defined, §55-509.
Reserves, §55-514.1.
Charges against lots or lot owners.
Requirements, §55-509.3.
Common interest community board.
Generally, §§54.1-2345 to 54.1-2354.
See COMMON INTEREST COMMUNITY BOARD.
Common interest community manager.
Defined, §54.1-2345.
Fiduciary duty, §54.1-2353.
Generally.
See COMMON INTEREST COMMUNITY MANAGERS.
License required, §54.1-2346.
Communication by lot owners among selves and with board of directors.
Establishment of method, §55-510.2.
Compliance requirements of lot owners, §55-515.
Condemnation of common area, §55-516.2.
Consent of mortgagee to amend declaration and bylaw, §55-515.1.
Contract disclosure statement.
Sale of lot, §55-509.4.
Contracts, declarant control.
Limitations, §55-509.1:1.
Defined terms, §55-509.
Disclosure packets.
Sale of lot.
Contents, §55-509.5.
Contract disclosure statement, §55-509.4.
Delivery by association upon seller's request, §55-509.5.
Exceptions, §55-509.10.
Fees, §§55-509.6, 55-509.7.
Property subject to more than one declaration, §55-509.8.
Discrimination.
Restraints on alienation not to be used to discriminate, §55-515.2.
Documents provided by declarant upon transfer of control, §55-509.2.
Electronic transmission and other equivalent methods.
Use by association, lot owners, others entitled to occupy lot.
Exercise of rights and obligations, §55-515.3.
Eminent domain.
Condemnation of common areas, §55-516.2.
Fees.
Assessments, late fees, §55-513.3.
Services in common areas.
Charges against lots or lot owners, requirements, §55-509.3.
Fiduciary duty.
Common interest community manager, §54.1-2353.

PROPERTY OWNERS' ASSOCIATIONS —Cont'd
Fiduciary trust account.
Funds deposited with managing agent, §55-514.2.
Flag of the United States.
Display by lot owners, §55-513.1.
Action for violation of restrictions, §55-513.1.
Restrictions by association, §55-513.1.
Funds deposited with managing agent.
Handled in fiduciary capacity, §55-514.2.
Home-based businesses.
Allowed, reasonable restrictions, §55-513.2.
Leases, declarant control.
Limitations, §55-509.1:1.
Liens, §§55-514, 55-516.
Lot located in development subject to act.
Contract disclosure.
Sale of lot, §55-509.4.
Pesticide application in common areas.
Posting of notice, §55-510.3.
Real estate taxes.
Developer payments, §55-509.1.
Records, §55-510.
Reports, §55-516.1.
Development, dissemination.
Common interest community board, §54.1-2350.
Reserves for capital components, §55-514.1.
Rule restricting unreasonable restraints on alienation.
Not to be applied to defeat declaration, §55-515.2.
Rules and regulations, §55-513.
Sale of lot.
Contract disclosure statement, §55-509.4.
Exceptions, §55-509.10.
Disclosure packets.
Contents, §55-509.5.
Delivery by association upon seller's request, §55-509.5.
Exceptions, §55-509.10.
Fees, §§55-509.6, 55-509.7.
Property subject to more than one declaration, §55-509.8.
Escrow instructions.
Providing settlement agent, §55-509.9.
Financial update by preparer of disclosure packet.
Providing settlement agent upon request, §55-509.9.
Information provided by settlement agent.
Transmission of funds to association or community, §55-509.9.
Sale of unit for lien for assessment, §55-516.
Stormwater management.
Common interest community ceding responsibility to governmental entity.
Immunity for civil liability, §62.1-44.15:41.
Suspension of member's right to use facilities or services, §55-513.
Transfer of control.
Items provided by declarant, §55-509.2.
United States flag.
Display by lot owners, §55-513.1.
Action for violation of restrictions, §55-513.1.
Restrictions by association, §55-513.1.
Validity of declaration, §55-515.2.

PROPERTY RIGHTS BARRED.
Slayer's act.
Generally, §§64.2-2500 to 64.2-2511.
See SLAYER'S ACT.

PROPERTY RIGHTS OF MARRIED WOMEN, §§55-35 to 55-47.1.
See MARRIED WOMEN'S PROPERTY RIGHTS

PROPERTY SETTLEMENT AGREEMENTS.
Dissolution of marriage, §20-107.3.
Equitable distribution.
Expert witnesses in hearings, §8.01-375.
Incorporation by reference, §20-109.1.
Local retirement system assets, §51.1-802.
Virginia retirement system assets, §51.1-124.4.

PROPERTY TAXES.
Abutting property owners, taxes or assessments upon, VA Const Art X §3.
Affordable rental housing.
Fair market value, determining, §58.1-3295.
Annexation.
Reduced taxation on real estate in territory added, §15.2-3219.
Assessment, VA Const Art X §2.
Acts authorizing.
Provisions for annual general reassessment and equalization of assessments.
Certain cities and counties, §58.1-3260.
Advisory aid and assistance on equalizing assessments.
Duty of tax commissioner render upon request, §58.1-202.
Annual assessment, §58.1-3253.
Biennial assessment, §58.1-3253.
Board of equalization of real estate assessment.
County manager plan of government, §§15.2-716, 15.2-716.1.
County manager plan of government, §15.2-716.
Time for contesting, §15.2-717.
Department of real estate assessment.
County manager plan of government, §15.2-716.
General reassessment by direction of governing body, §58.1-3254.
July 1 as effective date, §58.1-3011.
Time for contesting.
County manager plan of government, §15.2-717.
Urban county executive form of government, §15.2-828.
County providing for department of assessments, §15.2-840.
Bill of rights for taxpayers, §58.1-1845.
Blighted areas.
Tax increment financing, §§58.1-3245 to 58.1-3245.5.
Board of equalization of real estate assessments.
County manager plan of government, §§15.2-716, 15.2-716.1.
Urban county executive form of government, §15.2-840.
Board of real estate review and equalization.
County manager form of government, §15.2-619.
Bonds issued by locality.
Levy and collection of tax, §15.2-2624.
Change to fiscal tax year, §58.1-3010.
Changing rate of tax during calendar year, §58.1-3012.
Children or minors.
Property owned by listed and taxed to guardian or trustee, §58.1-3015.
City status granted town.
Taxes accruing before transition, §15.2-3828.
Classification and segregation, VA Const Art X §1.
Environmental restoration sites, §58.1-3664.
Real property by tax commissioner, §58.1-208.
Collection and publication of data by tax commissioner, §58.1-207.

PROPERTY TAXES —Cont'd
Collection of local taxes generally, §§58.1-3910 to 58.1-3961.
See TAX COLLECTION.
Commissioners of revenue.
Generally, §§58.1-3100 to 58.1-3122.2.
See COMMISSIONERS OF REVENUE.
Conservation easements.
Assessments of fee interest in land subject to perpetual conservation easement, §10.1-1011.
Contesting real estate assessments.
Time for contesting.
County manager plan of government, §15.2-717.
Corporately owned property.
Listed by and taxed to corporation, §58.1-3015.
Correction of erroneous tax assessments, §§58.1-3980 to 58.1-3995.
See CORRECTION OF ERRONEOUS TAX ASSESSMENTS.
County executive form of government.
Department of assessments, §§15.2-518, 15.2-535.
Public service corporations, special provisions for assessments, §§58.1-2680 to 58.1-2683.
Real estate reassessments by director of finance, §15.2-521.
County manager form of government.
Board of real estate review and equalization, §15.2-619.
Public service corporations, special provisions for assessments, §§58.1-2680 to 58.1-2683.
Reassessment of real estate by director of finance, §15.2-619.
Responsibilities of county manager, §15.2-615.
County manager plan of government.
Assessment of real estate, §15.2-716.
Time for contesting, §15.2-717.
Board of equalization of real estate assessments, §§15.2-716, 15.2-716.1.
Department of real estate assessments, §15.2-716.
Installment collection of taxes, §15.2-745.
Reassessment of real estate, §15.2-716.
Deceased persons' property.
Listed to personal representative and taxed to estate, §58.1-3015.
Deferral of real estate tax, §§58.1-3219 to 58.1-3219.3.
Elderly or handicapped exemption or deferral program, §§58.1-3210 to 58.1-3217.
Delinquent taxes.
Collection of local taxes generally, §§58.1-3921 to 58.1-3938.
See TAX COLLECTION.
Sale of delinquent tax lands generally, §§58.1-3965 to 58.1-3975.
See SALE OF DELINQUENT TAX LANDS.
When property taxes delinquent, §58.1-3922.
Department of assessments.
County executive form of government, §§15.2-518, 15.2-535.
Department of real estate assessments.
County manager plan of government, §15.2-716.
Director of finance.
County executive form of government.
Reassessment of real estate, §15.2-521.
County manager form of government.
Reassessment of real estate, §15.2-619.
Disabled veterans.
Real property tax exemption, §§58.1-3219.5 to 58.1-3219.8.
Tax credits, §§58.1-3360 to 58.1-3363.

PROPERTY TAXES —Cont'd
Disasters.
Relief from taxes, §58.1-3014.
Distress.
Collection of local taxes by distress generally, §§58.1-3940 to 58.1-3961.
See TAX COLLECTION.
Elderly and handicapped exemption or deferral, §§58.1-3210 to 58.1-3217.
Electric authorities.
Payments in lieu of property taxes, §15.2-5423.
Enterprise zone development.
Local enterprise zone development taxation program, §§58.1-3245.6 to 58.1-3245.12.
Environmental restoration sites.
Separate classification and exemption, §58.1-3664.
Erosion control improvements.
Partial exemption, §58.1-3665.
Exemptions.
Fraternal benefit societies, §38.2-4124.
Generally, §§58.1-3600 to 58.1-3666, VA Const Art X §6.
See PROPERTY EXEMPT FROM TAXATION.
Military property, §44-131.
Real property taxes.
See REAL PROPERTY TAXES.
Veterans, VA Const Art X §6-A.
Fiscal year.
Levy of taxes on fiscal year basis, §58.1-3010.
Fixing rate for budget year, time, §15.2-2503.
Forwarding copies of certain receipts and reports by circuit court clerks, §58.1-3303.
Guardianship and conservatorship.
Listed by and taxes to guardians or conservators, §58.1-3015.
Incapacitated persons.
Listed by and taxed to guardians or conservators, §58.1-3015.
Installment collection of taxes.
County manager plan of government, §15.2-745.
Insurance companies.
Taxes applicable to companies, §58.1-2508.
Intangible personal property tax, §§58.1-1100 to 58.1-1118.
See PERSONAL PROPERTY TAXES.
Land preservation, special assessment for, §§58.1-3229 to 58.1-3244.
See REAL PROPERTY TAXES.
Leasehold interest, §58.1-3203.
Local taxes generally, §§58.1-3000 to 58.1-3018.
See LOCAL TAXES.
Machinery and tools tax, §§58.1-3507, 58.1-3508.
Mentally ill or incapacitated person owning property.
Listed by and taxed to committee, §58.1-3015.
Merchants' capital tax, §§58.1-3509, 58.1-3510.
Mortgages and deeds of trust.
Escrow account.
Obligation of person maintaining to pay taxes and insurance, §6.2-414.
Mosquito control districts, §32.1-194.
Motor carriers rolling stock.
Local taxation prohibited, §58.1-2658.
Open space land.
Assessment of fee interest in land subject to perpetual conservation easement, §10.1-1011.
Parks, recreational facilities or playgrounds established by locality.
Taxing property for operation and maintenance, §15.2-1806.

PROPERTY TAXES —Cont'd
Payments in lieu of property taxes.
Electric authorities, §15.2-5423.
Personal property taxes.
General provisions, §§58.1-3500 to 58.1-3522.
See PERSONAL PROPERTY TAXES.
Tax relief act of 1998, §§58.1-3523 to 58.1-3535.
See PERSONAL PROPERTY TAX RELIEF ACT OF 1998.
Power of attorney.
Authority of agent as to taxes, §64.2-1637.
Professional corporations, §13.1-554.1.
Professional limited liability companies, §13.1-1120.
Property subject to taxation, VA Const Art X §1.
Local taxes, §58.1-3000.
State taxes, §58.1-100.
Publication showing rates of local levies, §58.1-210.
Public school special taxes, §§22.1-102 to 22.1-106.
Certification of referendum results, §§22.1-105, 22.1-106.
Conduct of referendum, §22.1-105.
Levy in accordance with referendum, §22.1-106.
Levy of tax authorized, §22.1-102.
Order for referendum, §22.1-104.
Petition for referendum, §22.1-103.
Request by school board, §22.1-103.
Uniform county levy in lieu of district taxes, §22.1-103.
Public service companies.
Assessment of real estate and tangible personal property by central state agency, VA Const Art X §2.
Public service corporations.
Assessments in counties having county executive or county manager governments, §§58.1-2680 to 58.1-2683.
Local taxation of real and tangible personal property, §58.1-2606.
Railroads, §58.1-2607.
Taxation generally, §§58.1-2600 to 58.1-2690.
See PUBLIC SERVICE CORPORATION TAXATION.
Railroads.
Local taxation, §58.1-2607.
Assessment of property by tax commissioner, §§58.1-2655 to 58.1-2657.
Rate changes during calendar year, §58.1-3012.
Rate for budget year.
Fixing, time, §15.2-2503.
Rates of local levies, publication by department of taxation, §58.1-210.
Real property taxes, §§58.1-3200 to 58.1-3389.
See REAL PROPERTY TAXES.
Reassessment.
Biennial general reassessments, §58.1-3253.
County manager form of government, §15.2-619.
Board of real estate review and equalization, §15.2-619.
Director of finance, §15.2-619.
County manager plan of government, §15.2-716.
General reassessment by direction of governing body, §58.1-3254.
Manual and guidelines.
Tax commission to make available annually, §58.1-202.
Urban county executive form of government, §15.2-828.

PROPERTY TAXES —Cont'd
Relief.
Disasters, §58.1-3014.
Retention of property for payment of taxes.
Listed by and taxed to person other than owner, §58.1-3016.
Riparian buffers, §58.1-3666.
Sale of delinquent tax lands, §§58.1-3965 to 58.1-3975.
See SALE OF DELINQUENT TAX LANDS.
School purposes.
Special county, district, city or town tax, §§22.1-102 to 22.1-106.
Segregation of property for local taxation, VA Const Art X §4.
Service districts.
Power to levy and collect, §15.2-2403.
Special assessment for land preservation, §§58.1-3229 to 58.1-3244.
See REAL PROPERTY TAXES.
Special levies to pay interest and retire bonds, §58.1-3006.
Tangible personal property, machinery and tools and merchants' capital tax.
General provisions, §§58.1-3500 to 58.1-3522.
See PERSONAL PROPERTY TAXES.
Taxable property, VA Const Art X §1.
Tax increment financing, §§58.1-3245 to 58.1-3245.5.
Tax relief act of 1998, §§58.1-3523 to 58.1-3535.
See PERSONAL PROPERTY TAX RELIEF ACT OF 1998.
Time for contesting real property assessments.
County manager plan of government, §15.2-717.
To whom property generally taxed and by whom listed, §58.1-3015.
Retention of property for payment of taxes.
Listed by and taxed to person other than owner, §58.1-3016.
Town granted city status.
Taxes accruing before transition, §15.2-3828.
Trust property.
Listed by and taxed to trustee, §58.1-3015.
Uniformity, VA Const Art X §1.
Urban county executive form of government.
Assessment of real estate, §15.2-828.
County providing for department of assessments, §15.2-840.
Veterans.
Disabled veterans.
Real property tax exemption, §§58.1-3219.5 to 58.1-3219.8.
Tax credits, §§58.1-3360 to 58.1-3363.
Wetlands, §58.1-3666.
Wind turbines.
Local property taxation of public service corporations.
Rate of tax on electric suppliers utilizing turbines, §58.1-2606.

PROPS.
Larceny of things fixed to freehold, §18.2-99.

PROPYLENE.
Liquefied petroleum gas containers, §§18.2-493 to 18.2-498.

PROSECUTING ATTORNEYS.
Commonwealth's attorneys generally.
See COMMONWEALTH'S ATTORNEYS.
Professional responsibility, VA SCt Rule Pt 6 §II Rule 3.8.

PRO SE REPRESENTATION.
Corporations.
District court civil cases, §16.1-81.1.
District courts.
Corporations, §16.1-81.1.
Warrants in debt, VA SCt Rule 7B:3.
Facsimile signatures, VA SCt Rule 1:4.
Prisoner litigation.
Applicability of provisions, §8.01-690.
Residence of pro se litigant.
Statement of residence and notice of change, §8.01-319.
Small claims courts, §16.1-122.4.
Supreme court.
Prisoners, VA SCt Rule 5:7.

PROSTATE SPECIFIC ANTIGEN.
Health insurance.
Coverage for PSA testing, §38.2-3418.7.
Medical assistance services plans.
PSA testing for high-risk men, §32.1-325.
Presumption as to death or disability.
Firefighters, §65.2-402.

PROSTHETIC DEVICES.
Health insurance coverage, §38.2-3418.15.
Retail sales and use tax exemption, §58.1-609.10.
Workers' compensation.
Medical attention to be furnished, §65.2-603.

PROSTITUTION, §18.2-346.
Abating public nuisances, §§48-7 to 48-15.
Abduction of child for purposes of, §18.2-48.
Seizure and forfeiture of property used in connection with abduction, §19.2-386.32.
Threatening, attempting or assisting, §18.2-49.
Aiding, §§18.2-348, 18.2-350.
Bawdy places.
Abatement of public nuisances, §§48-7 to 48-15.
Defined, §18.2-347.
Keeping, residing in or frequenting, §18.2-347.
Being a prostitute, §18.2-346.
Buildings or other structures harboring bawdy place.
Authority of locality to require removal, repair, etc., §15.2-908.1.
Competency of persons to testify in prosecutions.
Procuring prosecutions, §18.2-360.
Criminal forfeiture.
Motor vehicles used in commission of crimes where prostitute is a minor, §19.2-386.16.
Discretionary felony sentencing guidelines, §17.1-805.
HIV and hepatitis C.
Testing convicted prostitutes, limited disclosure of results, §18.2-346.1.
Houses of prostitution.
Abating public nuisances, §§48-7 to 48-15.
Pandering, §§18.2-355, 18.2-368.
Person transported through or across Commonwealth.
Venue, §18.2 359.
Placing or leaving wife for, §18.2-368.
Receiving money for procuring person, §18.2-356.
Receiving money for procuring person for, §18.2-356.
Receiving money from earnings of male or female prostitute, §18.2-357.
Solicitation of prostitution, §18.2-346.

PROSTITUTION —Cont'd
Taking, detaining, etc., person for or consenting to, §18.2-355.
Vehicles used to promote, §§18.2-349, 18.2-350.
Venereal disease testing, §32.1-58.
Venue, person transported through or across Commonwealth, §18.2-359.

PROTECTION AND DEVELOPMENT OF FOREST RESOURCES STATE FUND.
Forest products tax revenue disposition, §58.1-1609.
Alternative disposition, §58.1-1610.

PROTECTION OF THIRD PARTIES.
Mental health service provider's duty.
Violent behavior or serious harm by client, §54.1-2400.1.

PROTECTIVE ORDERS.
Appeals.
Effect during pendency of appeal, §16.1-106.
Assault and battery upon party protected, §§16.1-253.2, 18.2-60.4.
Breaking and entering home of protected person, §16.1-253.2.
Central criminal records exchange.
Protective order registry, §19.2-387.1.
State police department, duties, §52-45.
Child or spousal support.
Contents of orders, §20-60.3.
Circuit courts, jurisdiction to hear motions, §17.1-513.
Criminal cases.
Discovery, VA SCt Rule 3A:11.
Discovery, VA SCt Rule 4:1.
Criminal cases, VA SCt Rule 3A:11.
Limiting further disclosure of discoverable materials and information, §8.01-420.01.
Uniform interstate depositions and discovery act.
Application to court, §8.01-412.13.
Divorce proceedings.
Pendente lite protective orders, §20-103.
Emergency protective orders.
Authorized, §16.1-253.4.
Domestic violence.
Assault and battery, §18.2-57.2.
Warrantless arrests, §19.2-81.3.
Family abuse, §16.1-279.1.
Assault and battery, §18.2-57.2.
Police officers.
Authority to execute and serve, §15.2-1704.
Preliminary orders, §16.1-253.1.
Virginia criminal information network, §16.1-253.1.
Felony violations, §§16.1-253.2, 18.2-60.4.
Firearms possession by person subject to.
Disqualification for concealed weapons permit, §18.2-308.09.
Purchase or transportation, §18.2-308.1:4.
Guardian and ward.
Uniform adult guardianship and protective proceedings jurisdiction act.
Registration and recognition of orders from another state, §64.2-2117.
Home health and personal care services.
Convictions prohibiting employment, §32.1-162.9:1.
Juvenile and domestic relations district court jurisdiction, §16.1-241.

PROTECTIVE ORDERS —Cont'd
Legal separation.
Cruelty and reasonable apprehension of bodily hurt, §20-103.
Purchase or transportation of firearm by persons subject to protective orders, §18.2-308.1:4.
Misdemeanor for violating, §16.1-253.2.
Preliminary protective orders.
Family abuse, §16.1-253.1.
Offenses resulting in serious bodily injury, §19.2-152.9.
Protection of child's life, health, etc., §16.1-253.
Stalking, §19.2-152.9.
Registry, §19.2-387.1.
State police department, duties, §52-45.
Stalking, §19.2-152.10.
Assault and battery of person protected by protective order, §18.2-60.4.
Emergency orders authorized, §19.2-152.8.
Entry of order in addition to sentence imposed for violation, §18.2-60.4.
In violation, §18.2-60.3.
Law enforcement officers, prohibition on orders against, §19.2-152.8.
Preliminary orders, §19.2-152.9.
Venue, §19.2-152.11.
Violation of orders, §18.2-60.4.
Trespass after having been forbidden to do so, §§18.2-119, 18.2-120.
Uniform adult guardianship and protective proceedings jurisdiction act.
Registration and recognition of orders from another state, §64.2-2117.
Violent offenses.
Offenses resulting in serious bodily injury, §19.2-152.10.
Emergency orders authorized, §19.2-152.8.
Law enforcement officers, prohibition on orders against, §19.2-152.8.
Preliminary protective orders, §19.2-152.9.
Venue, §19.2-152.11.
Virginia criminal information network.
Emergency protective orders, §16.1-253.4.
Family abuse preliminary orders, §16.1-253.1.
Foreign protective orders, §16.1-279.1.
Voter registration lists.
Post office box address, §§24.2-405, 24.2-406.

PROTEST OF AWARD OF PUBLIC CONTRACTS, §2.2-4360.
Effect upon contract, §2.2-4361.
Stay of award during protest, §2.2-4362.

PROTISTS.
Genetically engineered organisms.
Biotechnology research act, §§2.2-5500 to 2.2-5509.

PROTOZOA.
Infectious biological substance crimes, §18.2-52.1.

PROXIES, §13.1-663.
Appointment of proxy, §13.1-663.
Insurance companies.
Regulation of solicitation by state corporation commission, §38.2-202.
Members of nonprofit corporations, §13.1-847.
Determination of validity of proxies, §13.1-847.1.
Mutual assessment property and casualty insurers, §38.2-2509.
Real estate cooperatives, §55-467.

PROXIMITY TO CHILDREN, SEX OFFENSES PROHIBITING, §18.2-370.2.
Punishment authorized for felony, §18.2-10.
Punishment authorized for misdemeanor offense, §18.2-11.

PRUDENT INVESTOR RULE, §§64.2-780 to 64.2-791.
Acceptance of trusteeship.
Duties at inception, §64.2-784.
Agent's duties, §64.2-788.
Alteration by trust provisions, §64.2-781.
Applicability of act.
Existing trust, §64.2-790.
Compliance with act.
Determining compliance, §64.2-787.
Duty of trustees, §64.2-781.
Reviewing compliance, §64.2-787.
Statutory duty, §64.2-781.
Construction of act.
Applicability of act, §64.2-790.
Uniformity of application, §64.2-791.
Custodial trustees.
Standard of care.
Duty to observe, §64.2-906.
Definitions, §64.2-780.
Delegation of duties, §64.2-788.
Criteria for selecting agent, §64.2-788.
Diversification strategy, §64.2-783.
Existing trusts.
Applicability of act, §64.2-790.
Impartiality.
Duty of, §64.2-785.
Investment costs.
Standard of appropriate and reasonable, §64.2-786.
Loyalty.
Duty of, §64.2-785.
Management functions.
Delegation of, §64.2-788.
Portfolio strategy, §64.2-782.
Diversification by trustee, §64.2-783.
Duties at inception of trusteeship, §64.2-784.
Risks and return objective, §64.2-782.
Standard of care, §64.2-782.
Investment cost, §64.2-786.
Trust agreements.
Language invoking standard of care, §64.2-789.
Trust agreements.
Language invoking standard of care, §64.2-789.
Virginia Commonwealth University.
Board of visitors, §23-50.10:01.
Virginia polytechnic institute and state university.
Board of visitors, §23-122.1.
Waiver of rule, §64.2-781.
William and Mary college.
Board of visitors, §23-44.1.

PRUDENT MANAGEMENT OF INSTITUTIONAL FUNDS.
Uniform act, §§64.2-1100 to 64.2-1108.
See MANAGEMENT OF INSTITUTIONAL FUNDS.

PRUDENT PERSON RULE.
College savings plan.
Standard of care in administering and investing, §23-38.80.
Management of institutional funds.
Uniform prudent management of institutional funds act, §§64.2-1100 to 64.2-1108.
See MANAGEMENT OF INSTITUTIONAL FUNDS.

PRUDENT PERSON RULE —Cont'd
Principal and income.
Adjustments between principal and income.
Guidelines for fiduciary, §64.2-1002.
Trusts.
Trustee's duty of prudent administration, §64.2-766.

PRURIENT INTEREST.
Obscenity and related offenses generally, §§18.2-372 to 18.2-388.
See OBSCENITY AND RELATED OFFENSES.

PSA TESTING.
Health insurance.
Coverage, §38.2-3418.7.
Medical assistance services plans.
Coverage, §32.1-325.

PSEUDOEPHEDRINE.
Retail sale of products containing, §18.2-248.8.
Sale of ephedrine or related compounds, §§18.2-265.6 to 18.2-265.18.
See EPHEDRINE.

PSEUDONYM.
Proceeding anonymously, use, §8.01-15.1.

PSYCHIATRIC TREATMENT OF MINORS ACT, §§16.1-335 to 16.1-348.
See MENTAL HEALTH.

PSYCHIATRISTS.
Disclosure of patient information to third party payors by professionals.
See MENTAL HEALTH.
Duty to protect third parties.
Violent behavior or serious harm by client, mental health service provider's duty, §54.1-2400.1.
Insanity defense experts.
Compensation, §19.2-175.
Licensing generally, §§54.1-2929 to 54.1-2941.
See MEDICINE AND OTHER HEALING ARTS PROFESSIONS.
Minors, psychiatric treatment, §§16.1-335 to 16.1-348.
See MENTAL HEALTH.
Prisoners' health care.
Involuntary admission and treatment.
Advice, §§53.1-40.1, 53.1-40.2.
Professional corporations generally, §§13.1-542.1 to 13.1-556.
See PROFESSIONAL CORPORATIONS.

PSYCHOLOGICALLY AFFECTED PROPERTY.
Residential property transfer disclosures.
Actions for failure to disclose, §55-524.

PSYCHOLOGIST-CLIENT PRIVILEGE, §8.01-400.2, VA SCt Rule 2:506.
Clinical psychologist, §8.01-399, VA SCt Rule 2:505.

PSYCHOLOGISTS, §§54.1-3600 to 54.1-3606.1.
Activities that are nondiscretionary.
Delegation to unlicensed persons, §54.1-3614.
Behavioral analysts.
Licensing, §54.1-2957.16.
Exceptions to licensing requirements, §54.1-2957.17.
Medical licensing generally, §§54.1-2900 to 54.1-2993.
Bills for medical services.
Presumption of authenticity and reasonableness, §8.01-413.01.
Board of psychology, §§54.1-3603 to 54.1-3605.

PSYCHOLOGISTS —Cont'd
Clinical psychologists.
Donation of services.
Tax credit, §58.1-439.22.
Immunity.
Disasters, state or local emergencies.
Abandonment of person owed duty in response to disaster, §8.01-225.01.
Unable to provide required care because of lack of resources, §8.01-225.02.
Licensing generally, §§54.1-2900 to 54.1-2993.
See MEDICINE AND OTHER HEALING ARTS PROFESSIONS.
Physician-patient privilege, §8.01-399, VA SCt Rule 2:505.
Plan for medical assistance services.
Contracts with director, §32.1-325.
Prisoners health care.
Involuntary admission and treatment.
Advice, §§53.1-40.1, 53.1-40.2.
Witness fees, §53.1-40.8.
Tax credit.
Donation of services, §58.1-439.22.
Continuing education, §54.1-3606.1.
Defined terms, §54.1-3600.
Delegation to unlicensed persons, §54.1-3614.
Disclosure of patient information to third party payors by professionals.
See MENTAL HEALTH.
Drug administration or prescription, §54.1-3602.
Duty to protect third parties.
Violent behavior or serious harm by client, §54.1-2400.1.
Exemptions from licensing, §54.1-3601.
Free clinics.
Immunity for services provided, §54.1-106.
Functions that are nondiscretionary.
Delegation to unlicensed persons, §54.1-3614.
Health benefit programs.
Providers willing to meet terms and conditions not to be excluded, §38.2-3407.
Health services plans, coverage of services, §38.2-4221.
Insanity defense experts.
Compensation, §19.2-175.
License requirements, §54.1-3606.
Exemptions, §54.1-3601.
Medical bills.
Presumption of authenticity and reasonableness, §8.01-413.01.
Medical malpractice.
General provisions, §§8.01-581.1 to 8.01-581.20.
See MEDICAL MALPRACTICE.
Minors, psychiatric treatment.
Qualified evaluator generally, §§16.1-335 to 16.1-348.
See MENTAL HEALTH.
Privileged communications, §8.01-400.2, VA SCt Rule 2:506.
Clinical psychologists, §8.01-399, VA SCt Rule 2:505.
Professional corporations generally, §§13.1-542.1 to 13.1-556.
See PROFESSIONAL CORPORATIONS.
Professional limited liability companies, §§13.1-1100 to 13.1-1123.
See PROFESSIONAL LIMITED LIABILITY COMPANIES.
Professions and occupations regulation generally.
See HEALTH PROFESSIONS DEPARTMENT.

PSYCHOLOGISTS —Cont'd
Psychiatric treatment of minors.
Qualified evaluator generally, §§16.1-335 to 16.1-348.
See MENTAL HEALTH.
Records or papers of patients.
Admissibility of copies, §8.01-413.
Medical records generally.
See MEDICAL RECORDS.
Right of patient, attorney or authorized insurer to copies, §8.01-413.
Subpoenas, §8.01-413.
Self-referrals.
Practitioner self-referral act, §§54.1-2410 to 54.1-2414.
Standardized HCFA-1500 health insurance claims forms for services.
Acceptance by insurers required, §38.2-322.
Title restrictions.
Applicability, §54.1-3513.
Sex offender treatment provider, §54.1-3611.
Unlawful procurement of licensure, §54.1-102.
Unlawful use of licensure, §54.1-111.

PSYCHOTROPIC DRUGS.
Schools prohibited from recommending for use by students, §22.1-274.3.

PUBIC AREA.
Sexual conduct, defined, §18.2-390.

PUBLIC ACCOMMODATIONS.
Hotels generally.
See HOTELS.
Inns generally.
See INNS.
Motels generally.
See MOTELS.
Restaurants generally.
See RESTAURANTS.

PUBLIC ACCOUNTANTS, §§54.1-4400 to 54.1-4425.
See ACCOUNTANTS.

PUBLIC ADJUSTERS.
General provisions, §§38.2-1845.1 to 38.2-1845.23.
See INSURANCE ADJUSTERS.
Unlicensed public adjusters process, §§38.2-812 to 38.2-815.
See INSURANCE ADJUSTERS.

PUBLIC AID AND ASSISTANCE, §§63.2-500 to 63.2-805.
Adjustments in amount pending board decision, §63.2-514.
Administrative process act.
Court review.
Exemptions, §2.2-4025.
Exemptions from case decisions, §2.2-4018.
Adoption.
Special needs children.
Adoption assistance payments, §§63.2-1300 to 63.2-1304.
Assistance, subsidy payments.
Medical assistance, uniform act, §§63.2-1400 to 63.2-1405.
Advocacy projects.
Legal services in claims for supplemental security income, §63.2-803.
Agent orange settlement agreement or judgment.
Amount received pursuant to disregarded in determining amount of assistance, §63.2-505.

PUBLIC AID AND ASSISTANCE —Cont'd
Amendment or repeal of laws, subject to, §63.2-509.
Amount.
Change or withdrawal of grant, §§63.2-514 to 63.2-519.
Determination by local board, §§63.2-504, 63.2-505.
Regulations to be adopted by local board, §63.2-505.
Appeal to commissioner, board's decision, §§63.2-517 to 63.2-519.
Action by commissioner, §63.2-518.
Appeals review panels, §63.2-517.
Failure of board to make decision within reasonable time, §63.2-517.
Final agency action for purposes of judicial review, §63.2-519.
Food stamp appeals, §63.2-517.
Hearing, notice, investigation, testimony, evidence, §63.2-518.
Hearing officers, delegation of authority to, §63.2-517.
Time for taking appeal after notice of decision, §63.2-517.
Application, §63.2-501.
Completeness and correctness.
Investigation on receipt, §63.2-503.
Contact information for applicants, §63.2-501.1.
False application or false swearing, §63.2-502.
Fee or charge for representing applicant, §63.2-508.
Procedure upon receipt, §63.2-503.
Appropriations by counties and cities, §63.2-400.
Assignment prohibited, §63.2-506.
Assisted living facility residents.
Auxiliary grants, receiving, §63.2-800.
Auditor of public accounts.
Expenses incurred in rendering services.
Administrative expenses of state department, §63.2-404.
Auxiliary grants program, §63.2-800.
Board for the blind and vision impaired.
See BLIND AND VISION IMPAIRED, BOARD FOR.
Board of social services.
See SOCIAL SERVICES BOARD.
Change in amount of grant, §63.2-514.
Decision granting, denying, changing or discontinuing grant, §§63.2-515 to 63.2-519.
Change in circumstances.
Change in amount or withdrawal of grant, §§63.2-514 to 63.2-519.
Notice to local board, §63.2-513.
Change in residence.
TANF or medical assistance recipients, §63.2-521.
Child care services, §63.2-620.
Child support.
Enforcement, §§63.2-1900 to 63.2-1960.
See CHILD SUPPORT ENFORCEMENT BY DEPARTMENT OF SOCIAL SERVICES.
Obligation to support and maintain children living in same home, §63.2-510.
Child support collection.
Generally.
See CHILD SUPPORT.
Collection of accounts receivable by Commonwealth.
Withholding state services for delinquent debtors, §2.2-4808.

PUBLIC AID AND ASSISTANCE —Cont'd
Commissioner of social services.
See COMMISSIONER OF SOCIAL SERVICES.
Comptroller.
Expenses incurred in rendering services.
Administrative expenses of state department, §63.2-404.
Confidentiality of applicant's contact information, §63.2-501.1.
Confidentiality of department or local board records, §§63.2-102 to 63.2-105.
Criminal penalties.
Change in circumstances, failure to give notice, §63.2-513.
Failure to support child, §63.2-510.
False statements, representations, impersonations or fraudulent devices, §63.2-522.
Unauthorized use of food stamps, electronic transfer cards and energy assistance, §63.2-523.
Decision of local board.
Eligibility and amount, §§63.2-504, 63.2-505, 63.2-515 to 63.2-519.
Procedure for granting, denying, changing or discontinuing grant, §§63.2-515 to 63.2-519.
Appeal to commission, §§63.2-517 to 63.2-519.
Notice of decision, §63.2-515.
Record of decision, §63.2-516.
Reconsideration of grants, changing or withdrawing, §63.2-514.
Definitions, §§63.2-100, 63.2-500.
Dental care provided by department of health.
Recipients eligible to receive convict made dentures, §63.2-804.
Department and commissioner of social services.
Generally, §§63.2-200 to 63.2-214.3.
See SOCIAL SERVICES.
Department for the blind and vision impaired.
See BLIND AND VISION IMPAIRED, DEPARTMENT FOR.
Department of social services.
See SOCIAL SERVICES DEPARTMENT.
Deprivation or hazard to recipient.
Inability to manage funds.
Appointment of personal representative, §63.2-507.
Earned income tax credit.
Notice to recipients of public aid, §63.2-527.
Educational expense saving account.
Established by individuals receiving assistance under certain programs, §63.2-505.
Electronic transfer cards.
Unauthorized uses, §63.2-523.
Eligibility.
Citizenship or legal presence required, §63.2-503.1.
Decisions granting, denying, changing or discontinuing grant, §§63.2-515 to 63.2-519.
Determination by local board, §63.2-504.
General relief, §63.2-802.
Erroneous payment of assistance.
Recovery, §63.2-512.
Execution, levy, attachment, garnishment or other legal process.
Not subject to, §63.2-506.
Failure of county or city to provide.
Deductions, withholding payments, §63.2-408.
Failure to manage funds.
Personal representatives for recipients, §63.2-507.
False application or false swearing, §63.2-502.

PUBLIC AID AND ASSISTANCE —Cont'd
False statements, representations, impersonations or fraudulent devices, §63.2-522.
Fee or charge for representing applicant or recipient, §63.2-508.
Food stamps.
Appeal to commissioner, §63.2-517.
Drug-related felony convictions.
Effect on eligibility, §63.2-505.2.
Full employment program (FEP).
Replacement of TANF and food stamp benefits, §63.2-608.
Implementation of program, §63.2-801.
Savings accounts for educational expenses.
Established by individuals receiving assistance under certain programs, §63.2-505.
Transitional benefits, §63.2-505.1.
Unauthorized uses, traffic in, §63.2-523.
Foster care.
Debt owed to department of social services.
Expenditures for dependent children, §63.2-1909.
Fraud, §63.2-522.
Assistant attorney for Commonwealth prosecution fraud cases.
Payment for legal services by department, §63.2-525.
Denial of benefits, §63.2-524.
Fraud prevention and investigation units, §63.2-526.
Fraud recovery special fund, §63.2-526.
Statewide fraud control program, §63.2-526.
Unauthorized use of food stamps, electronic transfer cards and energy assistance, §63.2-523.
Full employment program (FEP).
Temporary assistance for needy families.
Replacement of TANF and food stamp benefits, §63.2-608.
Funding of public assistance and social services, §§63.2-400 to 63.2-412.
Appropriations by counties and cities, §63.2-400.
Children's residential facilities.
Construction and operation by local boards, §63.2-411.
Expenditures by state department.
Purposes, §63.2-403.
Expenses of auditor of public accounts, comptroller and state treasurer, §63.2-404.
Failure of county or city to provide.
Deductions, withholding payments, §63.2-408.
Foster care.
Appropriations by counties and cities, §63.2-400.
Reimbursement of counties and cities, §63.2-401.
Lien on property of applicant or recipient.
No lien to attach, §63.2-409.
Medical assistance, medical care and social services eligibility.
Determination by commissioner, §63.2-405.
Needy persons engage in work or training programs.
Assistance to, costs of administration, §63.2-412.
Other necessary or incidental public assistance or socials services.
County or city providing, §63.2-407.
Payment for by counties and cities.
Appropriations, §63.2-400.
Reimbursement, §63.2-401.

PUBLIC AID AND ASSISTANCE —Cont'd
Funding of public assistance and social services —Cont'd
Pool of funds under comprehensive services act, §63.2-410.
Reimbursement of counties and cities, §63.2-401.
Reimbursement to Commonwealth.
Local boards, §63.2-402.
Social security act or regulations of department of health and human services amendments.
Authority of state board to adopt standards, requirements or procedures, §63.2-406.
Work or training programs.
Assistance to needy persons engage in, cost of administration, §63.2-412.
General relief, eligibility for, §63.2-802.
Granting, denying, changing or discontinuing grants.
Decision of board, procedure, §§63.2-514 to 63.2-519.
Guardian or conservator.
Application made on behalf of applicant.
Condition precluding applicant from signing application, §63.2-501.
Home energy assistance program, §63.2-805.
Savings accounts for educational expenses.
Established by individuals receiving assistance under certain programs, §63.2-505.
Unauthorized benefit from, §63.2-523.
Human services information and referral program, §§63.2-222 to 63.2-227.
See HUMAN SERVICES INFORMATION AND REFERRAL PROGRAM.
Increased assistance.
Fee or charge for representing recipient, §63.2-508.
Investigation by local board.
Completeness and correctness of application, §63.2-503.
Reconsideration of grants, §63.2-514.
Decisions granting, denying, changing or discontinuing grant, §§63.2-515 to 63.2-519.
Jail inmate work release earnings.
Use by dependents, §53.1-131.
Larceny.
Unauthorized use of food stamps, electronic transfer cards and energy assistance, §63.2-523.
Lien on property of applicant or recipient.
No lien to attach, §63.2-409.
Local boards of social services.
Generally, §§63.2-300 to 63.2-323.
See SOCIAL SERVICES.
Local departments and directors of social services.
Generally, §§63.2-324 to 63.2-336.
See SOCIAL SERVICES.
Local superintendents of public welfare.
See SUPERINTENDENTS OF PUBLIC WELFARE.
Local welfare boards.
See WELFARE BOARDS, LOCAL.
Medical care and assistance.
Medicaid generally.
See MEDICAID.
Nonsupport.
Criminal penalty for failure to support child living in same home, §63.2-510.
Proceedings against person liable for support of applicant or recipient, §63.2-511.

PUBLIC AID AND ASSISTANCE —Cont'd
Notice of change in contact information, §63.2-501.1.
Notice of earned income tax credit.
Recipients of public aid, §63.2-527.
Other necessary or incidental public assistance or socials services.
County or city providing, §63.2-407.
Payment by counties and cities.
Appropriations, §63.2-400.
How paid, §63.2-520.
Reimbursement of counties and cities, §63.2-401.
Pending determination of eligibility.
Local board providing necessary assistance, §63.2-504.
Perjury.
False application or false swearing, §63.2-502.
Personal representatives for recipients, §63.2-507.
Prisons.
Ineligibility of prisoner for benefits due to incarceration.
Notice by department to social services department, §53.1-31.3.
Proof of legal presence.
Eligibility for assistance, §63.2-503.1.
Reconsideration of grants, §63.2-514.
Decisions granting, denying, changing or discontinuing grant, §§63.2-515 to 63.2-519.
Reimbursement of counties and cities, §63.2-401.
Reimbursement to Commonwealth.
Local boards, §63.2-402.
Savings accounts for educational expenses.
Established by individuals receiving assistance under certain programs, §63.2-505.
Social security act or regulations of department of health and human services amendments.
Authority of state board to adopt standards, requirements or procedures, §63.2-406.
State treasurer.
Expenses incurred in rendering services.
Administrative expenses of state department, §63.2-404.
Supplemental security income claims.
Legal services, §63.2-803.
Support of applicant or recipient.
Proceedings against persons liable for, §63.2-511.
Support of dependent children and custodians.
Collection of support generally.
See CHILD SUPPORT.
Suspension of assistance pending board decision, §63.2-514.
TANF, §§63.2-600 to 63.2-621.
Temporary assistance for needy families (TANF), §§63.2-600 to 63.2-621.
Administered by state department, §63.2-600.
Appeal of boards decisions, §63.2-618.
Application, §63.2-602.
Assignment to Commonwealth any rights of support, §63.2-602.
Benefits not being used for children.
Personal representatives for recipients, §63.2-507.
Cash assistance, §63.2-617.
Change in residence, §63.2-521.
Child care services, §63.2-620.
Children born to TANF recipients.
Financial benefits paid to family, §63.2-604.

PUBLIC AID AND ASSISTANCE —Cont'd
Temporary assistance for needy families (TANF) —Cont'd
Compulsory school attendance laws, compliance, §63.2-606.
Cooperation in locating parent, §63.2-602.
Creation of program, §63.2-600.
Diversionary cash assistance, §63.2-617.
Drug tests.
Parolees or probationers failing, §63.2-605.
Eligibility, §63.2-602.
Childhood immunizations, §63.2-603.
Children born to TANF recipients, §63.2-604.
Compulsory school attendance laws, compliance, §63.2-606.
Financial eligibility, §63.2-614.
Parolees or probationers failing drug tests, §63.2-605.
Residence of unemancipated minor custodial parent, §63.2-607.
Virginia initiative for employment not welfare (VIEW), §§63.2-608 to 63.2-610.
Evaluation to measure achievements, §63.2-619.
Financial eligibility, §63.2-614.
Full employment program (FEP).
Replacement of TANF and food stamp benefits, §63.2-608.
Fund, §63.2-601.1.
Goals, §63.2-601.
Identification of parents, §63.2-602.
Immunization of eligible child, required, §63.2-603.
Income disregards, §63.2-614.
Income tax.
Corporations.
Credit for certain employers hiring recipients, §58.1-439.9.
Limitations on TANF assistance.
Providing assistance and social services for recipients subject to limitations, §63.2-616.
Misidentification of another as parent.
Criminal penalty, §63.2-602.
Parentage determination, §63.2-602.
Parolees or probationers failing drug tests, §63.2-605.
Personal representatives for recipients.
Benefits not being used for children, §63.2-507.
Prohibited uses of benefits, §63.2-621.
Report by commissioner.
Annual report, §63.2-619.
Residence of unemancipated minor custodial parent, §63.2-607.
Savings accounts for educational expenses.
Established by individuals receiving assistance under certain programs, §63.2-505.
School attendance.
Compulsory school attendance laws, compliance, §63.2-606.
Skill development training.
Tuition and other expenses of recipients, §63.2-615.
Statewide TANF program funding pool program, §63.2-601.2.
Time limit for receipt of financial assistance.
VIEW participants, §63.2-613.
Transitional food stamps benefits following termination of TANF assistance, §63.2-505.1.
Tuition and other expenses.
Recipient enrolled in skill development training, §63.2-615.

PUBLIC AID AND ASSISTANCE —Cont'd
Temporary assistance for needy families (TANF) —Cont'd
Two-parent families and single-parent families treated same, §63.2-602.
Unemancipated minor custodial parent, residence, §63.2-607.
Virginia initiative for employment not welfare (VIEW), §63.2-608.
Case management, §63.2-611.
Child care, transportation, counseling and medical assistance.
Services provided to families, §63.2-611.
Coordinated services, §63.2-610.
Exemptions, §63.2-609.
Hardship exceptions to time limit for receipt of assistance, §63.2-613.
Income disregards, §63.2-614.
Motor vehicle sales to participants, §63.2-611.
Services to families, §63.2-611.
Statewide intensive case management ratio, §63.2-611.
Termination of financial assistance.
Services provided, §63.2-611.
Time limit on receipt of financial assistance, §63.2-612.
Hardship exceptions, §63.2-613.
Workers' compensation.
Ineligibility for certain benefits, §§65.2-500, 65.2-502, 65.2-512.
Transferal prohibited, §63.2-506.
Trusts.
Debtors and creditors.
Public assistance, claims for reimbursement, §64.2-745.
Unable to manage funds.
Personal representatives for recipients, §63.2-507.
VIEW.
Virginia initiative for employment not welfare, §§63.2-608 to 63.2-613.
Virginia initiative for employment not welfare, §§63.2-608 to 63.2-613.
Withdrawal of grant, §63.2-514.
Decisions, granting denying, changing or discontinuing grant, §§63.2-515 to 63.2-519.
Work or training programs.
Assistance to needy persons engage in, cost of administration, §63.2-412.
Work release earnings of jail inmates.
Use by dependents, §53.1-131.

PUBLIC AREAS.
Carrying loaded firearms.
Certain semi-automatic rifles and pistols and shotguns, §18.2-287.4.
Defined terms, §32.1-198.
Firearms, discharging in public places, §18.2-280.
Disqualification for concealed weapons permit, §18.2-308.09.
Powers of localities, §32.1-202.
Regulations, §32.1-200.
Tear gas, phosgene and other gases, illegal use, §18.2-312.
Toilet facilities, §§32.1-198 to 32.1-202.

PUBLICATION.
Abandoned vessels.
Acquiring title, §29.1-733.1.
ABC license applicant.
Notice of application, §4.1-230.

PUBLICATION —Cont'd
Administrative process act.
Emergency regulations, §2.2-4011.
Adopting or changing county form of government.
Notice of referenda, §15.2-301.
Agricultural and forestal districts.
Application for creation or addition, §15.2-4307.
Agricultural cooperative association meetings, notice, §13.1-323.
Annexation.
Agreements between towns and counties on town's annexation rights.
Notice of public hearing before commission on local government, §15.2-3232.
Notice and copy of ordinance, §15.2-3204.
Order fixing additional parties, §15.2-3205.
Annulment of town and charters.
Copy of notice and ordinance, §15.2-3703.
Attachment.
District court proceedings, §16.1-105.
Automobile graveyard or junkyard ordinances, §15.2-903.
Banks.
Bankruptcy and insolvency.
Notice of amount of dividend ordered paid and unclaimed, §6.2-920.
Periodic statements, §6.2-907.
Bicycle in possession of police or sheriff.
Location and description, §15.2-1720.
Boards of equalization.
Notice of sittings of board, §58.1-3378.
Bonds issued by localities.
Judicial determination of validity.
Service by publication of motion for judgment, §15.2-2652.
Notice of public hearing, §15.2-2606.
Boundaries of localities relocated or changed by agreement.
Agreed boundary line, §15.2-3107.
Budgets of localities and school divisions, §15.2-2506.
Amendment, §15.2-2507.
Change of city to town.
Citizen petition, §15.2-4102.
Copy of notice and ordinance, §15.2-4101.
Order limiting time for intervenors, §15.2-4104.
Charters of local governments.
Election on new or amendment to existing charter, §15.2-201.
Public hearing on new or amendment to existing charter, §15.2-202.
Child custody proceeding.
Uniform child custody jurisdiction and enforcement act.
Giving notice of exercise of jurisdiction to person outside state, §20-146.7.
City status granted county.
Copy of notice and ordinance, §15.2-3903.
Order limiting time for intervention, §15.2-3905.
Commissioners of revenue office.
Advertising location prior to date for filing returns with, §58.1-3108.
Committees.
Property transfers to foreign committees, §64.2-1429.
Condominiums.
Lien for assessments, §55-79.84.
Condominium unit to be sold to enforce lien for assessment, §55-79.84.

PUBLICATION —Cont'd
Consolidation of counties, cities or towns into single county or city.
Charter, §15.2-3535.
Consolidation agreements, §15.2-3537.
Notice and consolidation agreements, §15.2-3521.
Consolidation of like units of local government.
Consolidation agreement, §15.2-3504.
Constitution of Virginia, amendment.
Distribution of information on proposed amendments to voters, §30-19.9.
Contraction of corporate limits of cities or towns.
Ordinance, §15.2-3236.
Petition for contraction or town located in two or more counties, §15.2-3242.
County executive form of government.
Notice of referenda on election of county chairman from county at large, §15.2-503.
County police force, establishing.
Notice of election, §15.2-1702.
Death presumption.
Petition seeking judicial determination of death.
Order that presumption made out, publication, §64.2-2304.
Decedents' estates.
Nonresident decedents.
Transfers of money and personal property belonging to, §64.2-609.
Orders to creditors to show cause against distributions, §64.2-556.
Form, §64.2-557.
Settling of accounts of personal representatives.
Proceedings for receiving proof of debts, §64.2-550.
Delinquent tax land sales.
Notice, §58.1-3965.
Service on parties not otherwise served, §58.1-3967.
Devices on certain containers.
Description, §59.1-94.
Drilling for oil or gas in Tidewater.
Environmental impact assessment, §62.1-195.1.
Election notice.
Adopting or changing county form of government, §15.2-301.
Establishment of county police force, §15.2-1702.
Electric authorities.
Ordinance or agreement creating, §15.2-5403.
Evidence.
Affidavit evidence of publication, §8.01-415.
Fairfax county.
Adoption of ordinances.
Notice of intention to proposed passage, §15.2-1201.
False publications, §18.2-209.
Family violence fatality review teams.
Death investigations.
Statistical information, §32.1-283.3.
Fishing, inland waters.
Seasons.
Closing or shortening, §29.1-507.
Fishing, tidal waters.
Regulations, §§29.1-501, 29.1-505.
Franchise, privilege, lease or right to use city or town property.
Amendment or extension of franchise, §15.2-2105.
Ordinance proposing grant of franchise, §15.2-2101.

PUBLICATION —Cont'd
Guardians.
Property transfers to foreign guardians, §64.2-1429.
Hunting.
Regulations, §§29.1-501, 29.1-505.
Seasons.
Closing or shortening, §29.1-507.
Impoundment of surface waters.
Riparian owner rights.
Application for leave to store floodwaters, §62.1-107.
Industrial development authorities.
Public hearings, §15.2-4906.
Industrial waste discharges into state waters.
Application for discharge, §62.1-44.16.
Insurance companies.
Examination reports, §38.2-1320.4.
License suspension or revocation, §38.2-1043.
Insurance rates.
Workers' compensation, automobiles, home protection, etc.
Notice of filing, §38.2-2007.
Juvenile proceedings.
Service of summons, §16.1-264.
Local constitutional officers.
Advertising employment positions, §15.2-1604.
Local delinquent tax list, §58.1-3924.
Locality selling vehicle fleet and road construction equipment with intent to lease back.
Notice of public hearing, §15.2-951.
Local treasurer securing final discharge from liability, notice, §58.1-3146.
Marks on certain containers.
Description, §59.1-94.
Medical care facilities.
Certificates of public need.
Hearings, §32.1-102.6.
Metropolitan Washington airports authority.
Notice of intention to adopt rule or regulation, §5.1-157.
Moped in possession of police or sheriff.
Location and description, §15.2-1720.
Museums.
Property loaned to museums.
Termination of loans, §55-210.36.
Title to property, §55-210.37.
Names on certain containers.
Description, §59.1-94.
Nonprofit corporations.
Notice, §13.1-810.
Nonprofit corporations members meetings, notice, §13.1-842.
Nonprofit health care entities.
Notice of disposition of assets, §55-532.
Obscene books, proceeding against.
Show cause orders, §18.2-384.
Official map of locality, §15.2-2234.
Notice of hearing on adding to or modifying, §15.2-2235.
Oil and gas exploration.
Notice of permit applications, §45.1-361.30.
Ordinances.
Advertisement and enactment of certain fees and levies, §15.2-107.
Notice by county of intention to propose ordinance passage, §15.2-1427.
Overhead transmission line construction, notice, §56-46.1.

PUBLICATION —Cont'd
Oyster planting grounds.
General oyster planting grounds.
Assignments.
Posting notice of application, §28.2-606.
Temporary enclosures on leased ground.
Notice of authorization to place, §28.2-603.2.
Park authorities.
Ordinance or resolution creating, §15.2-5702.
Personal property taxes.
Machinery and tools, change in classification of, §58.1-3507.
Planning and development.
Advertisement of plans, ordinances or amendments, §15.2-2204.
Presumption of death.
Petition seeking judicial determination of death.
Order that presumption made out, publication, §64.2-2304.
Property exempt from taxation.
Total assessed valuations and computation of percentage of exempt and immune property, §58.1-3604.
Property owners' associations.
Sale of unit for lien for assessment, §55-516.
Public-private education facilities and infrastructure act.
Procurement, §56-575.16.
Public rights-of-way, vacating or altering, §15.2-2006.
Questions submitted to voters.
Explanation, §30-19.10.
Register of regulations, §2.2-4031.
Reversion of city to town.
Citizen petition, §15.2-4102.
Copy of notice and ordinance, §15.2-4101.
Order limiting time for intervenors, §15.2-4104.
Sale of delinquent tax lands.
Notice, §58.1-3965.
Service on parties not otherwise served, §58.1-3967.
Savings institutions.
State corporation commission to publish regulations, §6.2-1192.
Service by publication.
See SERVICE BY PUBLICATION.
Service districts.
Creation of district by court order in consolidated cities, §15.2-2401.
Notice of public hearing, §15.2-2400.
Solicitation of charitable or civic contributions.
Warnings, §§57-52, 57-52.1.
Special exception, zoning, §15.2-2310.
State corporation commission.
Orders, rules and regulations promulgated by commission, §12.1-28.
Storm water control program.
Notice of public hearing, §15.2-2114.
Public hearing on adopting, §15.2-2114.
Tax commissioner and department of taxation.
Property tax data, §58.1-207.
Rates of local levies, §58.1-210.
Rulings, decisions, orders and regulations, §58.1-204.
Taxes or assessments for local improvements.
Notice to abutting property owners, §15.2-2409.
Tobacco products distributors, list of licensed, §58.1-1021.04:1.
Tobacco warehouses.
Discontinuance, §61.1-38.

PUBLICATION —Cont'd
Tobacco warehouses —Cont'd
Records, §61.1-42.
Town seeking city status.
Copy of notice and ordinance, §15.2-3803.
Time limit for intervenors, §15.2-3805.
Transition of city to town.
Citizen petition, §15.2-4102.
Copy of notice and ordinance, §15.2-4101.
Order limiting time for intervenors, §15.2-4104.
Transition of counties to cities.
Copy of notice and ordinance, §15.2-3903.
Order limiting time for intervention, §15.2-3905.
Transportation improvement districts.
District within city of Charlottesville and county of Albemarle.
Notice of public hearing on creating district, §33.1-448.
Notice of public hearing on creating.
Counties with population of more than 500,000, §33.1-431.
Transportation plan, §15.2-4528.
Trapping.
Regulations, §§29.1-501, 29.1-505.
Seasons.
Closing or shortening, §29.1-507.
Unclaimed bicycles or mopeds in possession of police or sheriff.
Location and description of bicycle or moped, §15.2-1720.
Vacation or alteration of public right-of-way, §15.2-2006.
Variances, zoning, §15.2-2310.
Vessels, abandoned.
Acquiring title, §29.1-733.1.
Voluntary settlement of annexation, transition or immunity issues.
Ordinance, §15.2-3400.
Voter registration.
Advance notice.
Other times and locations for registration, §24.2-415.
Water and waste authorities.
Ordinance, agreement or resolution and notice of hearing, §15.2-5104.
Waters of the state.
Removal of obstructions or hazards, §28.2-1210.
Wills.
Designation of when made, §64.2-414.
Execution procedure, §§64.2-403, 64.2-404.
Probate.
Interested parties.
Process against, §64.2-449.
Zoning.
Hearing on proposed ordinance and map and adoption of ordinance, §15.2-2285.
Special exceptions or variances, §15.2-2310.

PUBLICATION ORDERS, §§8.01-316, 8.01-317.
Service by publication generally.
See SERVICE BY PUBLICATION.

PUBLICATIONS BY STATE LOCAL OR REGIONAL AGENCIES.
State publications depository program, §§42.1-92 to 42.1-97.
See STATE PUBLICATIONS DEPOSITORY PROGRAM.

PUBLICATION SUBSCRIPTION SALES.
License tax upon privilege or right of printing or publishing.
Localities prohibited from levying, §58.1-3703

PUBLIC BEACH MAINTENANCE AND DEVELOPMENT FUND, §10.1-709.

PUBLIC BROADCASTING BOARD.
Secretary of administration.
Agency responsibility, §2.2-203.

PUBLIC BROADCASTING STATIONS.
Board of education, powers and duties related to, §22.1-20.1.
Purchasing through division of purchases and supply, §2.2-1122.
Surplus state materials.
Sale to public television stations, §2.2-1124.

PUBLIC BUILDING AUTHORITY, §§2.2-2260 to 2.2-2278.
Actions against authority.
Jurisdiction, §2.2-2277.
Service of notice, process and other papers, §2.2-2277.
Audits.
Funds of authority, §2.2-2272.
Board of directors, §2.2-2262.
Bond issues, §2.2-2264.
Funds received deemed trust funds, §2.2-2267.
Investment of public funds.
Securities for investment and deposit, §2.2-2269.
Proceedings to enforce rights, §2.2-2268.
Rates, fees and charges.
Authority to fix, revise, charge and collect, §2.2-2266.
Refunding bonds, §2.2-2270.
Tax exemption, §2.2-2278.
Trust agreement securing, §2.2-2265.
Bonds, surety.
Contractors, §2.2-2275.
Contracts.
Authority to enter into, §§2.2-2263, 2.2-2273.
Competition and award, §2.2-2275.
Terms, §2.2-2275.
Creation, §2.2-2261.
Defined terms, §2.2-2260.
Eminent domain, §2.2-2276.
Expenses, §2.2-2261.
Federal funds.
Authority to receive or disburse, §2.2-2271.
Fees.
Authority to fix, revise, charge and collect, §2.2-2266.
Financing of projects, §2.2-2263.
Funds of authority.
Audits, §2.2-2272.
Funds received deemed trust funds, §2.2-2267.
General services department.
Preapproval of plans and specifications, §2.2-2263.
Grants.
Authority to receive or disburse, §§2.2-2263, 2.2-2271.
Improvements of facilities.
Contracts or leases.
Authority to enter into, §2.2-2273.
Investment of public funds.
Bond issues.
Securities for investment and deposit, §2.2-2269.
Jail projects, powers and duties, §2.2-2263.
Leases.
Authority to enter into, §2.2-2273.
Loans.
Authority to receive or disburse, §§2.2-2263, 2.2-2271.

PUBLIC BUILDING AUTHORITY —Cont'd
MEI project approval commission, §§30-309 to 30-312.
Established, §30-309.
Membership, §30-309.
Purpose, §30-309.
Report to General Assembly, §30-312.
Review of individual incentive packages, §30-310.
Staff, §30-311.
Members, §2.2-2261.
Officers, §2.2-2262.
Powers and duties.
Authority, §2.2-2263.
Board of directors, §2.2-2262.
Eminent domain, §2.2-2276.
Right of entry, §2.2-2276.
Purpose, §2.2-2261.
Rates, fees and charges.
Authority to fix, revise, charge and collect, §2.2-2266.
Receipts.
Funds received deemed trust funds, §2.2-2267.
Refinancing of projects, §2.2-2263.
Refunding bonds, §2.2-2270.
Reports.
Annual financial statement, §2.2-2263.
MEI project approval commission.
Report to General Assembly, §30-312.
Resolutions.
Authority to adopt, §2.2-2274.
Right of entry, §2.2-2276.
Rules and regulations.
Authority to adopt, §2.2-2274.
Seals and seal instruments.
Powers and duties of authority, §2.2-2263.
Service of notice, process and other papers.
Actions against authority, §2.2-2277.
Short title, §2.2-2260.
Tax exemption, §2.2-2278.
Trusts.
Bond issues.
Trust agreement securing, §2.2-2265.
Funds received deemed trust funds, §2.2-2267.

PUBLIC BUILDINGS.
Accommodation.
Human rights act, §§2.2-3900 to 2.2-3903.
Burning or destroying buildings used by public, §18.2-79.
Business enterprises for the blind.
Generally.
See BLIND AND VISUALLY IMPAIRED.
Carrying loaded firearms.
Certain semi-automatic rifles and pistols and shotguns, §18.2-287.4.
Child abduction prevention in state buildings.
Code Adam alert programs, §2.2-1161.1.
Code Adam alert programs.
State building open to public, §2.2-1161.1.
Discrimination.
Human rights act, §§2.2-3900 to 2.2-3903.
Disorderly conduct in public places, §18.2-415.
Division of engineering and buildings, §§2.2-1129 to 2.2-1167.
See ENGINEERING AND BUILDINGS DIVISION.
Energy conservation and costs savings.
Energy and operational efficiency performance-based contracting act, §§11-34.1 to 11-34.4.

PUBLIC BUILDINGS —Cont'd
Excess building space.
Sale or lease by department of general services, §2.2-1156.
Fire alarms.
Maliciously activating, §18.2-212.
Fire protection review of plans and inspections of state buildings, §27-5.5.
Governor's powers over.
Rooms and space in building at seat of government, §2.2-123.
High performance buildings, §§2.2-1182, 2.2-1183.
Indoor clean air act, §§15.2-2820 to 15.2-2833.
See SMOKING IN PUBLIC PLACES.
Inspections.
Asbestos abatement in state-owned and public school buildings, §2.2-1163.
Standards for inspections, §2.2-1164.
Keys, possession or duplication, §18.2-503.
Leases of public lands and buildings, §2.2-1146.
Persons with physical disabilities.
Access to, §§2.2-1159 to 2.2-1161.
Police powers over lands lying beyond localities boundaries, §15.2-1725.
Public-private education facilities and infrastructure act, §§56-575.1 to 56-575.18.
Affected local jurisdictions, §§56-575.1, 56-575.6.
Appropriating body.
Review of proposed comprehensive agreement.
Responsible entity, state agency or institution, §56-575.4.
Approval of qualifying projects, §56-575.4.
Affected local jurisdictions, §56-575.6.
Private entity proposals, §56 575.3.
Procurement, §56-575.16.
Auditor of public accounts.
Electronic filings with, §56-575.18.
Periodic review of agreements entered into, §56-575.18.
Comprehensive agreements, §§56-575.1, 56-575.9.
Default by operator, §56-575.11.
Conceptual proposals.
Posting, public comment, procurement records, access, §56-575.17.
Condemnation, §§56-575.11, 56-575.12.
Utility crossings, §56-575.13.
Contributions and gifts to governor, governor's PAC, governor's secretaries.
Prohibited during approval process, violation, civil penalty, §56-575.17:1.
Dedication of public property, §56-575.7.
Default by private entity.
Material default, remedies, §56-575.11.
Definitions, §56-575.1.
Disapproval of qualifying projects, §56-575.3.
Financing, §56-575.8.
Comprehensive agreements, §§56-575.9, 56-575.11.
Government assistance, §56-575.10.
Freedom of information act.
Excluded records, §2.2-3705.6.
Gifts or contributions from person making bid or offer.
Governor, governor's PAC, governor's secretaries.
Prohibition on accepting, violation, civil penalty, §2.2-3104.01.
Government assistance, §56-575.10.
Guidelines for responsible public entities.
Development prior to requesting or considering proposal, requirements, §§56-575.3:1, 56-575.16.

PUBLIC BUILDINGS —Cont'd
Public-private education facilities and infrastructure act —Cont'd
Legislative intent, §56-575.2.
Operators, §56-575.1.
Police powers and jurisdiction, §56-575.14.
Powers and duties of private entities, §§56-575.8, 56-575.9.
Private entity, §56-575.1.
Comprehensive agreements, §§56-575.9, 56-575.11.
Powers and duties, §§56-575.8, 56-575.9.
Requests for approvals, §§56-575.3, 56-575.4.
Utility crossings, §56-575.13.
Procurement act not applicable, §56-575.16.
Proposals for qualifying projects, §§56-575.3, 56-575.4.
Affected local jurisdictions, §56-575.6.
Conceptual proposals.
Posting, public comment, procurement records, access, §56-575.17.
Procurement, §56-575.16.
Rejection, §56-575.3.
Public entity, §56-575.1.
Approval of qualifying projects, §§56-575.3, 56-575.4.
Comprehensive agreements, §56-575.9.
Remedies, §56-575.11.
Condemnation, §§56-575.11, 56-575.12.
Dedication of public property, §56-575.7.
Government assistance, §56-575.10.
Procurement, §56-575.16.
Service contracts, §56-575.5.
Sovereign immunity, §56-575.15.
Public-private partnership advisory commission.
Submission of copies of proposals to.
Responsible entity, state agency or institution, §56-575.4.
Public property dedication, §56-575.7.
Purpose, §56-575.2.
Remedies of public entity, §56-575.11.
Service contracts, §§56-575.1, 56-575.5.
Sovereign immunity, §56-575.15.
Utility crossings, §56-575.13.
Violations of law.
Police powers and jurisdiction, §56-575.14.
Sanitation districts law of 1938.
Use of public places, §21-173.
Smoke bombs.
Setting off in certain public buildings, §18.2-87.1.
Spitting in public places, §18.2-322.
Vending stands, business enterprises for the blind.
Generally.
See BLIND AND VISUALLY IMPAIRED.

PUBLIC CHARTER SCHOOLS, §§22.1-212.5 to 22.1-212.16.
See CHARTER SCHOOLS.

PUBLIC DEBT.
Bonds, notes or other obligations issued by Commonwealth, §§2.2-4900 to 2.2-4906.
Applicable law, §2.2-4902.1.
Cooperation of Commonwealth instrumentalities, §2.2-4904.
Governor.
Authority to contract debts, §2.2-4900.
Tax-supported debt, considerations, §2.2-4903.
Information necessary to carry out chapter.
Duties of Commonwealth instrumentalities, §2.2-4904.

PUBLIC DEBT —Cont'd
Bonds, notes or other obligations issued by Commonwealth —Cont'd
Interest on obligations, §§2.2-5000 to 2.2-5003.
Conflict of laws, §2.2-5003.
Excess interest rates permitted, §2.2-5000.
Exercise of authority, manner, §2.2-5001.
Federal income tax restrictions, effect, §2.2-5002.
Treatment of net original issue premium as principal, §2.2-5002.1.
Limitation of chapter, §2.2-4905.
Lost bonds or certificates.
Renewal, §2.2-4906.
Ratings of bonds, §2.2-4902.
Rights of instrumentalities.
Limitations of chapter, §2.2-4905.
Security interests in bonds, §2.2-4902.1.
Specific bond issues and certificates of debt.
Continued effectiveness, §2.2-4901.
Tax-supported debt, considerations, §2.2-4903.

PUBLIC DEFENDERS, §§19.2-163.04 to 19.2-163.5.
Appeals.
Accused's right to counsel, §19.2-163.3.
Appointment of counsel, §§19.2-157 to 19.2-163.03.
See ATTORNEYS AT LAW.
Appointment of public defenders.
Circuit court clerk fees, §17.1-275.
Assistant public defenders.
Attorney general assistance, §19.2-163.5.
Attorney general.
Legal services to public defender offices, §19.2-163.5.
Capital cases, counsel in, §§19.2-163.7, 19.2-163.8.
Compensation.
Fees charged by circuit court clerks, §17.1-275.
Supplementing compensation, §19.2-163.01:1.
Conflicts of interest.
Defense services not providable, §19.2-163.4.
Duties of public defenders, §19.2-163.3.
Offices established, §19.2-163.04.
Repayment of representation costs by accused, §19.2-163.4:1.
Supplementing compensation of, §19.2-163.01:1.

PUBLIC DEPOSITS IN PUBLIC DEPOSITORIES.
Security for public deposits, §§2.2-4400 to 2.2-4411.
See SECURITY FOR PUBLIC DEPOSITS.

PUBLIC DRUNKENNESS, §18.2-388.
Community corrections.
Detoxification center programs and public inebriate diversion, §9.1-176.
Delinquent child, loss of driving privilege, §16.1-278.9.
Uniform fine schedule, VA SCt Rules 3C:1, 3C:2.

PUBLIC EDUCATION STANDARDS OF QUALITY/LOCAL REAL ESTATE PROPERTY TAX RELIEF FUND, §58.1-638.1.
Retail sales and use tax.
Revenue disposition, §58.1-638.

PUBLIC FACILITIES DISTRICTS, §§21-427, 21-427.1.

PUBLIC FINANCE ACT, §§15.2-2600 to 15.2-2663.
All bonds, §§15.2-2604 to 15.2-2637.
Adoption of ordinance or resolution for issuance, §15.2-2607.
Anticipation notes, §§15.2-2620, 15.2-2629.
Anticipation of federal and state funds, §15.2-2630.
Terms of temporary loans, §15.2-2631.
Bearer form, §15.2-2614.
Collection of rates, rents, fees or charges, §15.2-2605.
Contesting validity of issue.
Time for contesting, §15.2-2627.
Contracts concerning interest rate, cash flow or other basis desired by locality, §15.2-2626.
Covenants relating to issuance of revenue bonds, §15.2-2609.
Dating bonds, §15.2-2612.
Defeasance of bonds outstanding, §15.2-2623.
Deposit of funds collected for payment of bonds, §15.2-2625.
Destruction of bonds and coupons after payment in full, §15.2-2622.
Discharge of liens on real estate, §15.2-2605.
Election on bond issue.
Holding of election, §15.2-2611.
Request for referendums, §15.2-2610.
Enforcement of liens on real estate, §15.2-2605.
Escrow fund or payment of bonds defeased, §15.2-2623.
Execution.
Form and matter determined by governing body, §15.2-2613.
Facsimile signatures, §15.2-2613.
Filing ordinance or resolution in circuit court, §15.2-2607.
Futures contracts, §15.2-2626.
Interest rates swap agreements, §15.2-2626.
Interim receipts, §15.2-2616.
Investment of money collected for payment of bonds, §15.2-2625.
Investment of proceeds pending application to purposes for which bonds authorized, §15.2-2619.
Investments in bonds by public officers and bodies of Commonwealth, counties, cities and towns, §15.2-2620.
Levy and collection of tax to pay principal and interest, §15.2-2624.
Liens on real estate.
Unpaid rates, rents, fees or charges, §15.2-2605.
Maturity, §15.2-2612.
Mutilated, lost or destroyed bonds, §15.2-2621.
Negotiable instruments, §15.2-2615.
Notes in anticipation of bond issues, §15.2-2628.
Notes in anticipation of issue, §§15.2-2620, 15.2-2629.
Anticipation of federal and state fund, §15.2-2630.
Temporary loans, §15.2-2631.
Notice of public hearing on issuance, §15.2-2606.
Ordinance or resolution for issuance, §15.2-2607.
Place of payment, §15.2-2612.
Powers of localities.
Generally, §15.2-2604.
Presumption of validity, §15.2-2627.
Provisions in ordinance or resolution for issuance, §15.2-2607.
Publication of notice of public hearing on issuance, §15.2-2606.

PUBLIC FINANCE ACT —Cont'd
All bonds —Cont'd
Public hearing before issuance of bond, §15.2-2606.
Rate of interest.
Determining by governing body, §15.2-2612.
Redemption or repurchase, §15.2-2612.
Referendum requested on question of issuance.
Filing with circuit court, §15.2-2610.
Registered or book entry form, §15.2-2614.
Revenue-producing undertakings, issuance of bonds, §15.2-2608.
Rights of owners of outstanding bonds defeased, §15.2-2623.
Sale, §15.2-2617.
Disposition of proceeds, §15.2-2618.
Separate fund for proceeds of sale, §15.2-2618.
Signature of person ceasing to be officer, §15.2-2613.
Tax to pay principal and interest, §15.2-2624.
Temporary bonds, §15.2-2616.
Time for contesting validity of proposed bond issue, §15.2-2627.
Bonds issued by counties, §§15.2-2638 to 15.2-2642.
Elections, §15.2-2638.
Ordinance or resolution requesting, §15.2-2640.
Treatment as city for issuance, §15.2-2639.
Election to be treated as city for issuance, §15.2-2639.
Ordinance or resolution, §15.2-2640.
Subsequent ordinance or resolution authorizing issuance, §15.2-2641.
Powers generally, §15.2-2638.
School district bonds, §15.2-2642.
School purposes.
Request for bond, §15.2-2640.
Voter approval, §15.2-2638.
Ordinance or resolution requesting election, §15.2-2640.
Treatment as city for issuance, §15.2-2639.
Bonds issued by municipalities, §§15.2-2632 to 15.2-2637.
Amount of outstanding bonds, limitation, §§15.2-2634, 15.2-2635.
Contracting debts on transition from town to city, §15.2-2632.
Contracting debts to pay expenses, §15.2-2633.
Danville to incur indebtedness only in accordance with provisions, §15.2-2637.
Expense payments, §15.2-2633.
Limitations on amount of outstanding bonds, §§15.2-2634, 15.2-2635.
Ordinance or resolution providing for issuance, §15.2-2636.
Transition from town to city.
Contracting certain debts on, §15.2-2632.
Charters under which bonds issued or validated.
Provisions not to affect, §15.2-2601.
Contesting issuance of bonds or validity, §15.2-2653.
Default by locality.
Investigation by governor, §15.2-2659.
Definitions, §15.2-2602.
General acts under which bonds issued or validated.
Provisions not to affect, §15.2-2601.
July 1, 1991 validation of bonds, §15.2-2662.
July 1, 1992 validation of bonds, §15.2-2662.

PUBLIC FINANCE ACT —Cont'd
Matured principal, premium or interest.
Disposition of funds due on bonds outstanding, §15.2-2603.
Notice of default and availability of funds, §15.2-2659.
Powers conferred in addition to other powers, §15.2-2661.
Principal, premium or interest matured.
Disposition of unclaimed funds due, §15.2-2603.
Project undertaken.
Bonds not affected by, §15.2-2660.
Provisions controlling, §15.2-2661.
Public finance act of 1991.
Provisions known and cited as, §15.2-2600.
Refunding bonds, §§15.2-2643 to 15.2-2649.
Amount of bonds, §15.2-2645.
Authority to issue, §15.2-2643.
Divestment of rights of owners of outstanding indebtedness to be refunded, §15.2-2644.
Full authority for issuance, sale or exchange, §15.2-2643.
Issuance or exchange for indebtedness to be retired, §15.2-2644.
Limitation on amount of bonds, §15.2-2645.
Participation in funds donated by Commonwealth, §15.2-2646.
Payment of expenses incurred in connection with authorization and issuance, §15.2-2647.
Proceeds of refunding bonds, application, §15.2-2644.
Purchase in open market, §15.2-2648.
Road districts, magisterial districts, sanitary districts or school districts.
County providing for issuance for, §15.2-2649.
Sale, §15.2-2644.
Special and local acts under which bonds issued or validated.
Provisions not to affect, §15.2-2601.
Stormwater control program adopted by locality.
Issuance of bonds to support, §15.2-2114.
Transition provisions, §15.2-2663.
Unclaimed funds due on matured bonds or coupons.
Disposition, §15.2-2603.
Validity of bonds, judicial determination, §§15.2-2650 to 15.2-2658.
Appeals, §15.2-2656.
Consolidation of actions or proceedings, §15.2-2655.
Contesting issuance or validity, §15.2-2653.
Petition, §15.2-2653.
Decree validating bonds binding and conclusive, §15.2-2657.
Determination of question, §15.2-2654.
Intervention by interested party, §15.2-2654.
Joint hearing, §15.2-2655.
Matter of form disregarded, §15.2-2658.
Motion for judgment.
Contesting issuance, §15.2-2653.
Filing, §15.2-2651.
Parties defendant, §§15.2-2651, 15.2-2652.
Petition contesting validity, §15.2-2653.
Priority of proceeding over all business court, §15.2-2654.
Proceeding by political subdivision to establish validity, §15.2-2651.
Provisions controlling as to proceedings, §15.2-2650.
Publication of motion for judgment, §15.2-2652.

PUBLIC FINANCE ACT —Cont'd
Validity of bonds, judicial determination —Cont'd
Reply by party defendant, §15.2-2654.
Service by publication of motion for judgment, §15.2-2652.
Substantial defects, material errors and omissions, §15.2-2658.
Withholding state funds from defaulting locality, §15.2-2659.

PUBLIC FUNDS.
Advanced communications assistance fund, §2.2-2233.
Aerospace engine manufacturer workforce training grant fund, §59.1-284.22.
Aging and rehabilitative services department.
Alzheimer's and related diseases research award fund, §51.5-153.
Commonwealth neurotrauma initiative trust fund, §51.5-179.
Respite care grant fund, §51.5-157.
Special fund for the rehabilitation of persons with disabilities, §51.5-125.
Agricultural dealers fund, §3.2-4743.
Agriculture and consumer services board.
Dedicated funds, §3.2-1100.
Agriculture and forestry industries development fund, §§3.2-303 to 3.2-309.
Airport fund.
Allocation of highway funds, §33.1-23.03:2.
Motor vehicle sales and use tax revenue disposition, §58.1-2425.
Retail sales and use tax revenue disposition, §58.1-638.
Airports revolving fund, §§5.1-30.1 to 5.1-30.10.
See VIRGINIA AIRPORTS REVOLVING FUND.
Alternative fuel vehicle conversion fund, §2.2-1176.1.
Alzheimer's and related diseases research award fund, §51.5-153.
"A Place of My Own" program Fund, §63.2-914.
Arts commission.
Endowment fund.
Development and administration, §2.2-2509.
Arts foundation.
Virginia arts foundation fund, §2.2-2702.
Assisted living facility education, training and technical assistance fund, §63.2-1803.1.
Assistive technology loan fund authority, §51.5-57.
At-risk student academic achievement program and fund, §22.1-199.4.
At-risk youth and families.
Community policy and management team.
State pool of funds, §2.2-5211.
Eligibility, §2.2-5212.
State trust fund, §2.2-5213.
Beach conservation and development.
Public beach maintenance and development fund, §10.1-709.
Beef industry fund, §3.2-1305.
Beehive grant fund, §3.2-4415.
Behavioral health and developmental services revenue fund, §37.2-716.
Behavioral health and developmental services trust fund, §§37.2-317 to 37.2-319.
Biofuels production fund, §45.1-393.
Birth-related neurological injury compensation fund, §38.2-5015.

PUBLIC FUNDS —Cont'd
Breast and cervical cancer prevention and treatment fund, §§32.1-368, 32.1-369.
Bright flue-cured tobacco promotion fund, §3.2-2407.
Brown v. Board of Education scholarship program and fund, §§30-231.01 to 30-231.10.
Capital access fund for disadvantaged businesses, §2.2-2311.
Management.
Minority business enterprise department (eff until 1/1/2014), §2.2-1402.
Capital improvement fund, §29.1-101.01.
Capital school projects fund, §22.1-175.5.
Caregivers grant fund, §63.2-2202.
Charter schools.
Public charter school fund, §22.1-212.5:1.
Christopher Reeve stem cell research fund, §§23-286.1, 23-286.2.
Civics education commission fund, §30-315.
Civil War site preservation fund, §10.1-2202.4.
Clean energy manufacturing incentive grant fund, §59.1-284.26.
Clients' protection fund, §54.1-3913.1.
Coal and gas road improvement fund, §58.1-3713.
Coal mining examiners' fund, §45.1-161.31.
Collections of local income taxes fund, §58.1-548.
Collections of local sales taxes, §58.1-605.
College partnership laboratory school fund, §23-299.1.
Combined sewer overflow matching fund, §§62.1-241.11, 62.1-241.12.
Commission on civics education fund, §30-315.
Common interest community management information fund, §§55-528 to 55-530.
Common interest community management recovery fund, §55-530.1.
Commonwealth health research fund, §§23-277 to 23-286.
Commonwealth neurotrauma initiative trust fund, §51.5-179.
Commonwealth research commercialization fund, §2.2-2233.1.
Commonwealth space flight fund, §33.1-23.03:2.
Retail sales and use tax revenue disposition, §58.1-638.
Communications sales and use tax trust fund, §58.1-662.
Community college incentive scholarship fund, §23-220.3.
Contract collector fund.
State tax collection, §58.1-1803.
Contractor transaction recovery fund, §§54.1-1118 to 54.1-1127.
Cooperative marketing fund.
Administration and management, §2.2-2319.
Cooperative tourism advertising fund.
Administration and management, §2.2-2318.
Corn fund, §3.2-1411.
Counties/cities school construction, renovation, maintenance, capital outlay and debt service fund.
Localities treatment of money received as result of insurer's conversion to stock corporation, §15.2-1608.1.
Counties/cities schools health insurance premium fund.
Treatment of money received by locality as result of insurer's conversion to stock corporation, §15.2-1608.1.

PUBLIC FUNDS —Cont'd
Courts technology fund, §17.1-132.
Criminal justice services department.
Intensified drug enforcement jurisdictions fund, §9.1-105.
Regional criminal justice academy training fund, §9.1-106.
School resource officer incentive grants fund, §9.1-110.
Dam safety.
Soil and water conservation district dam maintenance and small repair fund, §10.1-611.1.
Dam safety administrative fund, §10.1-613.5.
Dark-fired tobacco promotion fund, §3.2-2407.1.
Debt collection recovery fund, §2.2-518.
Defective drywall correction and restoration assistance fund, §§36-156.1, 36-156.2.
Disability insurance trust fund, §51.1-1140.
Disaster response funds.
Disbursements, §44-146.18:1.
Hazardous materials emergency response program disbursement, §44-146.37.
Dr. Martin Luther King, Jr. memorial commission fund, §30-192.7.
Drug investigation special trust account, §52-4.3.
Drug offender assessment and treatment fund, §18.2-251.02.
Egg fund, §3.2-1605.
Employee health insurance fund, §2.2-2818.
Enterprise fund.
Creation by ABC board, §4.1-116.
Environmental covenants fund, §10.1-1248.
Environmental health education and training fund, §32.1-248.3.
Family access to medical insurance security plan trust fund, §32.1-352.
Family and children's trust fund, §§63.2-2100 to 63.2-2103.
Farmland preservation fund, §3.2-201.
Financial institutions special fund.
Check casher registration fee deposit, §6.2-2103.
Fire programs fund, §38.2-401.
Fire services grant fund program, §38.2-401.
Fish passage grant and revolving loan fund, §§29.1-101.2 to 29.1-101.9.
Fleet management internal service fund, §2.2-1181.
Fraud and abuse whistleblower reward fund, §2.2-3014.
Game protection fund, §29.1-101.
Boat registration and identification fees, §29.1-701.
Authority to set and adjust, §29.1-701.1.
Retail sales and use tax revenue disposition, §58.1-638.
Watercraft sales and use tax.
Transfer of collections to, §58.1-1410.
GIS fund, §2.2-2028.
Government non-arbitrage investment, §§2.2-4700 to 2.2-4705.
Governor's agriculture and forestry industries development fund, §§3.2-303 to 3.2-309.
Governor's development opportunity fund, §2.2-115.
Governor's motion picture opportunity fund.
Administration and management, §2.2-2318.
Creation and purposes, §2.2-2320.
Hampton Roads sports facility authority financing fund, §15.2-5911.

PUBLIC FUNDS —Cont'd
Hampton Roads transportation fund, §33.1-23.5:4.
Health insurance fund, §2.2-2818.
Health research fund, §§23-277 to 23-286.
Healthy lives prescription fund, §2.2-214.1.
HEAT fund, §38.2-414.
Help eliminate automobile theft fund (HEAT), §38.2-414.
Highway maintenance and operating fund.
Budget bill.
Amounts diverted from fund included in bill, §2.2-1509.2.
Vehicle registration fee increases.
Disposition of additional revenue generated by, §46.2-702.1.
Historic resources fund, §10.1-2202.1.
Horse industry promotion and development fund, §3.2-1704.
Housing revitalization fund, §36-167.
Hybrid retirement program disability insurance trust fund, §51.1-1183.
Incentive fund.
Regional competitiveness act, §15.2-1308.
Information technology and management internal service fund, §2.2-2013.
Innovation and entrepreneurship investment authority.
Advanced communications assistance fund, §2.2-2233.
Insurance and guarantee fund, §2.2-2290.
Insurance collateral assessment fund, §38.2-1057.
Intensified drug enforcement jurisdictions fund, §§9.1-105, 15.2-1715.
Fees collected by circuit court clerks designated for, §17.1-275.
Intercity passenger rail operating and capital fund.
Establishment, §33.1-221.1:1.3.
Interest on fund belongs to fund, §58.1-3142.
Internet crimes against children fund, §17.1-275.12.
Investment.
Generally, §§2.2-4500 to 2.2-4519.
See INVESTMENT OF PUBLIC FUNDS.
Government non-arbitrage investment, §§2.2-4700 to 2.2-4705.
Local government investment pool, §§2.2-4600 to 2.2-4606.
Investment partnership act.
Virginia investment partnership grant fund, §2.2-5104.
Land conservation fund, §10.1-1020.
Legal aid services fund.
Additional fees collected by circuit court clerks, §17.1-278.
Lifetime hunting and fishing endowment fund, §29.1-101.1.
Litter control and recycling fund, §10.1-1422.01.
Local government investment pool, §§2.2-4600 to 2.2-4606.
See INVESTMENT OF PUBLIC FUNDS.
Lottery fund, §58.1-4022.
Forfeited prizes paid into, §58.1-4020.
Proceeds funds, §58.1-4022.1.
Sales agents to deposit to credit of, §58.1-4021.
Machinery and equipment donation grant fund, §23-231.1:1.
Major employment and investment project site planning grant fund, §2.2-2240.2.

PUBLIC FUNDS —Cont'd
Marine fishing improvement fund, §28.2-208.
Marine habitat and waterways improvement fund, §28.2-1204.2.
Marine patrols fund, §28.2-108.
Marine products fund, §3.2-2705.
Mass transit fund.
Retail sales and use tax revenue disposition, §58.1-638.
Methamphetamine cleanup fund, §18.2-248.04.
Military family relief fund, §44-102.2.
Tax refunds, voluntary contributions to, §58.1-344.3.
Mineral mining examiners' fund, §45.1-161.292:22.
Mine rescue fund, §§45.1-161.74, 45.1-161.292:47.
Minority business enterprise department (eff until 1/1/2014).
Capital access fund for disadvantaged businesses. Management, §2.2-1402.
Motorboat and water safety fund.
Boat registration and identification fees, §29.1-701.
Authority to set and adjust, §29.1-701.1.
Motorcycle rider safety training fund, §46.2-1191.
Motor vehicle transaction recovery fund, §§46.2-1527.1 to 46.2-1527.11.
See MOTOR VEHICLE DEALERS.
National teacher certification incentive program and fund, §22.1-299.2.
Natural area preservation, §10.1-215.
Natural resources commitment fund, §10.1-2128.1.
Northern Virginia transportation authority fund, §15.2-4838.01.
Northern Virginia transportation district fund, §58.1-815.1.
Nursing scholarship fund, §54.1-3011.2.
Nutrient offset fund, §10.1-2128.2.
One-stop small business permitting program.
Comprehensive permitting fund, §2.2-1617.
One-stop small business permitting program (eff until 1/1/2014).
Comprehensive permitting fund, §2.2-904.1.
Open-space lands preservation trust fund, §10.1-1801.1.
Oyster growing activities fund, §28.2-201.1.
Oyster replenishment fund, §28.2-542.
Payments into state treasury, §2.2-1802.
Peanut fund, §3.2-1906.
Pest control insurance fund, §§3.2-717 to 3.2-719.
Petroleum storage tank fund, §§62.1-44.34:10 to 62.1-44.34:13.
Photovoltaic, solar and wind energy utilization grant fund, §67-1002.
Plant pollination fund, §3.2-2806.
Pork industry fund, §3.2-2005.
Port fund.
Motor vehicle sales and use tax revenue disposition, §58.1-2425.
Retail sales and use tax revenue disposition, §58.1-638.
Port opportunity fund, §62.1-132.3:1.
Potato fund, §3.2-1810.
Pregnant women support fund, §32.1-11.6.
Preservation easement fund, §10.1-2202.2.
Pro hac vice fund, §17.1-205.

PUBLIC FUNDS —Cont'd
Protection and development of forest resources of state fund.
Forest products tax revenue disposition, §58.1-1609.
Alternative disposition, §58.1-1610.
Public accountants.
Board of accountancy fund.
Established, §54.1-4405.
Board of accountancy trust account.
Established, §54.1-4405.1.
Public assistance fraud.
Fraud recovery special fund, §63.2-526.
Public beach maintenance and development fund, §10.1-709.
Public charter school fund, §22.1-212.5:1.
Public officers and employees.
Employee health insurance fund, §2.2-2818.
Public school construction grants fund, §22.1-175.2.
Public school educational technology trust fund, §22.1-175.7.
Public school funds, §§22.1-88 to 22.1-124.
See PUBLIC SCHOOL FUNDS.
Putative father registry fund, §63.2-1249.
Radiation control.
Radioactive material perpetual care trust fund, §32.1-232.
Radiological emergency preparedness fund, §§44-146.31 to 44-146.33.
Special trust fund for radioactive materials facility licensure and inspection, §32.1-232.1.
Railway enhancement fund, §33.1-221.1:1.1.
Real estate transaction recovery fund, §§54.1-2112 to 54.1-2120.
Reforestation of timber lands state fund.
Forest products tax revenue disposition, §58.1-1609.
Regional cooperation incentive fund, §15.2-4217.
Regional criminal justice academy training fund, §9.1-106.
Forwarding of fees charged by circuit court clerks to, §17.1-275.
Renewable electricity production grant fund, §67-902.
Rescue squads assistance fund, §32.1-111.12.
Financial assistance and review committee, §32.1-111.12:01.
Resources authority.
Capital reserve funds, §62.1-215.
Respite care grant fund, §51.5-157.
Revenue stabilization fund, VA Const Art X §8.
Saltwater recreational fishing development fund, §28.2-302.3.
School funds, §§22.1-88 to 22.1-124.
See PUBLIC SCHOOL FUNDS.
School resource officer incentive grants fund, §9.1-110.
Seed fund, §3.2-4004.
Semiconductor manufacturing performance grant programs, §§59.1-284.13 to 59.1-284.15:1.
Sewage disposal.
Onsite operation and maintenance fund, §32.1-164.8.
Onsite sewage indemnification fund, §32.1-164.1:01.
Sexual and domestic violence victim fund, §9.1-116.1.

PUBLIC FUNDS —Cont'd
Sheep industry promotion and development fund, §3.2-2111.
Shortline railway preservation and development fund.
Establishment, §33.1-221.1:1.2.
Small business environmental compliance assistance fund, §§10.1-1197.1 to 10.1-1197.4.
Small business financing authority.
Capital access fund for disadvantaged businesses, §2.2-2311.
Insurance and guarantee fund, §2.2-2290.
Virginia export fund.
Creation and management, §2.2-2309.
Virginia small business growth fund, §2.2-2310.
Small business investment grant fund, §§2.2-904.03, 2.2-1616.
Small business jobs grant fund program, §§2.2-904.02, 2.2-1615.
Small grains fund, §3.2-2211.
Small renewable energy project fee fund, §10.1-1197.6.
Solid waste or recycling revolving fund, §§62.1-241.1 to 62.1-241.10.
Soybean fund, §3.2-2311.
Space flight fund, §33.1-23.03:2.
Retail sales and use tax revenue disposition, §58.1-638.
Special fund for the rehabilitation of persons with disabilities, §51.5-125.
Specialized transportation incentive fund, §15.2-4217.1.
Stadium authority financing fund, §15.2-5811.
State bar fund, §54.1-3913.
State forests system fund, §10.1-1119.1.
State insurance reserve trust fund.
Risk management division, §2.2-1835.
State owned motor vehicles.
Fleet management internal service fund, §2.2-1181.
State park acquisition and development fund, §10.1-202.
State park conservation resources fund, §10.1-202.
Proceeds from disposition of state surplus materials.
Deposit into fund, §2.2-1125.
State park projects fund, §10.1-202.
State racing operations fund, §59.1-370.1.
State treasury.
Payments into state treasury, §2.2-1802.
State water control board permit program fund, §62.1-44.15:7.
Stormwater management fund, §62.1-44.15:29.
Strategic compensation grant fund, §22.1-318.1.
Submerged lands.
Marine habitat and waterways improvement fund, §28.2-1204.2.
Tax increment financing fund, §§58.1-3245 to 58.1-3245.5.
Technology infrastructure fund, §§2.2-2022 to 2.2-2024.
Technology initiative in tobacco-dependent localities fund, §58.1-439.15.
Technology partnership fund.
Department of taxation, §58.1-202.2.
Temporary assistance for needy families fund, §63.2-601.1.
Tobacco indemnification and community revitalization fund, §3.2-3106.
Distributions from fund, §3.2-3108.

PUBLIC FUNDS —Cont'd
Tobacco indemnification and community revitalization fund —Cont'd
Endowment fund, §§3.2-3104, 3.2-3106.
Limitations on claims, §3.2-3107.
Payments from fund, §3.2-3107.
Tourism authority.
Cooperative marketing fund.
Administration and management, §2.2-2319.
Cooperative tourism advertising fund.
Administration and management, §2.2-2318.
Governor's motion picture opportunity fund.
Administration and management, §2.2-2318.
Creation and purposes, §2.2-2320.
Transportation improvement program set-aside fund, §58.1-816.1.
Transportation partnership opportunity fund, §33.1-221.1:8.
Transportation trust fund.
Motor vehicle sales and use tax revenue disposition, §58.1-2425.
Northern Virginia transportation district fund, §58.1-815.1.
Retail sales and use tax revenue disposition, §58.1-638.
Transportation improvement program set-aside fund, §58.1-816.1.
U.S. route 58 corridor development fund, §58.1-815.
Trauma center fund.
Created, purpose, §18.2-270.01.
Driving while intoxicated offenders
Payment to fund by multiple offenders, §18.2-270.01.
Treasury board.
Duties, §2.2-2416.
Underground utility damage prevention special fund, §56-265.32.
Unemployment compensation fund, §§60.2-300 to 60.2-317.
Uninsured medical catastrophe fund, §32.1-324.3.
Uninsured motorists fund, §§38.2-3000, 38.2-3001.
Urban public-private partnership redevelopment fund, §§15.2-2414 to 15.2-2418.
U.S. route 58 corridor development fund, §58.1-815.
Vehicle emissions inspection program fund.
Establishment and use of funds, §46.2-1182.2.
Veterans services fund, §2.2-2718.
Virginia agricultural foundation fund, §3.2-2905.
Dedicated revenues, diversion, §3.2-1100.
Virginia airports revolving fund, §§5.1-30.1 to 5.1-30.10.
See VIRGINIA AIRPORTS REVOLVING FUND.
Virginia arts foundation fund, §2.2-2702.
Virginia Beach arena financing fund, §15.2-5925.
Virginia beef industry fund, §3.2-1305.
Virginia bicentennial of the American War of 1812 fund, §30-297.
Virginia breeders fund, §59.1-372.
Virginia caregivers grant fund, §63.2-2202.
Virginia College savings plan, §§23-38.75 to 23-38.87:1.
See COLLEGE SAVINGS PLAN.
Virginia commission on the centennial of the Woodrow Wilson presidency fund, §30-321.

PUBLIC FUNDS —Cont'd
Virginia defective drywall correction and restoration assistance fund, §§36-156.1, 36-156.2.
Virginia export fund.
Creation and management, §2.2-2309.
Virginia farmland preservation fund, §3.2-201.
Virginia health care fund, §§32.1-366, 32.1-367.
Virginia horse industry promotion and development fund, §3.2-1704.
Virginia infrastructure project loan fund, §§15.2-2430 to 15.2-2440.
See VIRGINIA INFRASTRUCTURE PROJECT LOAN FUND.
Virginia investment partnership grant fund, §2.2-5104.
Virginia jobs investment program fund, §2.2-1611.
Virginia jobs investment program fund (eff until 1/1/2014), §2.2-903.1.
Virginia military family relief fund, §44-102.2.
Tax refunds, voluntary contributions to, §58.1-344.3.
Virginia pregnant women support fund, §32.1-11.6.
Virginia public school construction grants fund, §22.1-175.2.
Virginia real estate transaction recovery fund, §§54.1-2112 to 54.1-2120.
Virginia removal or rehabilitation of derelict structures fund, §§36-152 to 36-156.
Virginia Rescue Squads Assistance Fund, §32.1-111.12.
Financial assistance and review committee, §32.1-111.12:01.
Virginia retirement system generally.
See VIRGINIA RETIREMENT SYSTEM.
Virginia sesquicentennial of the American civil war fund, §30-270.
Virginia sexual and domestic violence victim fund, §9.1-116.1.
Virginia small business growth fund, §2.2-2310.
Virginia stormwater management fund, §62.1-44.15:29.
Virginia technology infrastructure fund, §§2.2-2022 to 2.2-2024.
Virginia wine promotion fund, §3.2-3005.
Vital statistics automation fund, §32.1-273.1.
Volunteer firefighters' and rescue squad workers' service award fund, §§51.1-1200 to 51.1-1211.
See VOLUNTEER FIREFIGHTERS' AND RESCUE SQUAD WORKERS' SERVICE AWARD FUND.
Waste kitchen grease fund, §3.2-5514.
Water facilities revolving fund, §§62.1-224 to 62.1-232.
Water quality improvement fund, §§10.1-2128 to 10.1-2130.
Water supply assistance grant fund, §32.1-171.2.
Water supply revolving fund, §§62.1-233 to 62.1-241.
Waterworks technical assistance fund, §32.1-171.1.
Weights and measures fund, §3.2-5628.
Wetland and stream replacement fund, §62.1-44.15:23.1.
Whistleblowing.
Fraud and abuse whistleblower reward fund, §2.2-3014.
Wild Spanish mustangs fund, §10.1-1027.

PUBLIC FUNDS —Cont'd
Wine promotion fund, §3.2-3005.
Workers' compensation.
Commission administrative fund, §§65.2-1000 to 65.2-1008.
Second injury fund, §§65.2-1100 to 65.2-1106.
Uninsured employer's fund, §§65.2-1200 to 65.2-1206.
Workers' compensation uninsured employer's fund, §§65.2-1200 to 65.2-1206.
Workforce development training fund.
Workforce council, duties regarding, §2.2-2670.
Workforce training access fund, §2.2-2674.
Youth Internet safety fund, §2.2-507.2.

PUBLIC GATHERING PLACES.
Carrying loaded firearms.
Certain semi-automatic rifles and pistols and shotguns, §18.2-287.4.
Defined terms, §32.1-198.
Firearms, discharging in public places, §18.2-280.
Disqualification for concealed weapons permit, §18.2-308.09.
Powers of localities, §32.1-202.
Regulations, §32.1-200.
Tear gas, phosgene and other gases, illegal use, §18.2-312.
Toilet facilities, §§32.1-198 to 32.1-202.

PUBLIC GUARDIAN AND CONSERVATOR ADVISORY BOARD, §§2.2-2411, 2.2-2412.
Composition, §2.2-2411.
Creation, §2.2-2411.
Duties, §2.2-2412.
Powers, §2.2-2412.
Purpose, §2.2-2411.
Report, §2.2-2412.

PUBLIC GUARDIAN AND CONSERVATOR PROGRAM.
Aging and rehabilitative services, department for, §§51.5-149 to 51.5-151.

PUBLIC HEARINGS.
Agricultural and forestal districts, §§15.2-4307, 15.2-4309.
Meeting with owners to review district, §15.2-4311.
Annexation.
Agreements between towns and counties defining town's annexation rights.
Hearing before commission on local government, §15.2-3232.
Joint hearing on inability of localities to agree on voluntary agreements, §15.2-3234.
Baseball stadium authority.
Selection of site, §15.2-5806.
Bonds issued by locality, §15.2-2606.
Budgets of localities and school divisions, §15.2-2506.
Amendment, §15.2-2507.
County executive form of government, §15.2-539.
County manager form of government, §15.2-638.
Bus or vehicle fleet, road construction equipment.
Sale by locality with intent to lease back.
Approval of governing body required, notice, public hearing, §15.2-951.
Charters of local government, §15.2-202.
City no longer qualifying for city status.
Report of commission on local government, §15.2-4003.

PUBLIC HEARINGS —Cont'd
Comprehensive plans, §§15.2-2204, 15.2-2225.
Adoption or disapproval, §15.2-2226.
Amendments, §§15.2-2227, 15.2-2229.
Location, character or extent of facility to be constructed, §15.2-2232.
Conditional zoning.
Amendments and variations of conditions, §15.2-2302.
County board of supervisors salaries.
Establishment by ordinance, §15.2-1414.3.
County executive form of government.
Budgets, §15.2-539.
County executives removal.
Urban county executive form of government, §15.2-805.
County manager form of government.
Budgets, §15.2-638.
County manager plan of government.
Removal of county manager, §15.2-708.
County manager's removal.
County manager form of government, §15.2-610.
County manager plan of government, §15.2-708.
Eminent domain.
County entering upon and taking possession prior to conclusion of proceedings.
Ordinance or resolution following public hearing as to intent, §15.2-1905.
Garbage and refuse pickup and disposal services.
Contracting for services displacing private company, §15.2-930.
Ordinance displacing private company, §15.2-934.
Ordinance requiring delivery to certain facilities, §15.2-931.
Hampton Roads sports facility authority.
Selecting facility site, §15.2-5906.
Immunity for statements made at, §8.01-223.2.
Industrial development authorities, §15.2-4906.
Metropolitan Washington airports authority.
Rules or regulations, §5.1-157.
Official map of locality.
Additions and modifications, §15.2-2235.
Adoption, §15.2-2234.
Park authorities.
Creating, §15.2-5702.
Parks, recreational facilities or playground.
Establishment, maintenance and operation by locality.
Notice, §15.2-1813.
Planning and development.
Comprehensive plan, §§15.2-2204, 15.2-2225.
Adoption or disapproval, §15.2-2226.
Amendments, §15.2-2227.
Location, character or extent of facility to be constructed, §15.2-2232.
Recommending and adopting, plans, ordinances or amendments, §15.2-2204.
Planning district commission.
Regional strategic plans, §15.2-4209.
Amendment, §15.2-4211.
Private juvenile detention or other care facility to be established in locality.
Locality without zoning ordinance, §15.2-2207.
Public rights-of-way, vacation and alteration.
Notice of hearing, §15.2-2006.
Real property.
Acquisition, §15.2-1813.
Recreational facilities authorities.
Creation or modification of articles of incorporation, §15.2-5602.

PUBLIC HEARINGS —Cont'd
Reversion of city to town.
City no longer qualifying for city status.
Report by commission on local government, §15.2-4003.
Road impact fees.
Road improvements plan, §15.2-2321.
Salaries of county boards of supervisors.
Establishment by ordinance, §15.2-1414.3.
Service districts.
Creation, §15.2-2400.
Solid waste management facility siting approval, §15.2-929.
Special exception, zoning, §15.2-2310.
Storm water control program, §15.2-2114.
Subdivision ordinances, §15.2-2251.
Amendments, §15.2-2253.
Subdivision ordinances changed, amended, etc., by codification, §15.2-1433.
Towns incorporated by judicial proceedings.
Hearings before commission on local government, §15.2-3601.
Transportation districts.
Transportation plan, §15.2-4528.
Urban county executive form of government.
Budgets, §15.2-847.
Establishment of salaries and expenses of board of supervisors, §15.2-846.
Removal of county executive, §15.2-805.
Vacation and alteration of public right-of-way.
Notice of hearing, §15.2-2006.
Variances, zoning, §15.2-2310.
Virginia shell building initiative.
Participation by locality or other political subdivision, §15.2-941.
Voluntary settlement of annexation, transition or immunity issues, §15.2-3400.
Water and waste authorities, §15.2-5105.
Notice, §15.2-5104.
Wireless service authorities.
Creation of authority, §15.2-5431.3.
Zoning.
Conditional zoning.
Amendments and variations, §15.2-2302.
Proposed ordinance, approval and adoption of ordinance, §15.2-2285.
Special exceptions or variances, §15.2-2310.
Zoning ordinances changed, amended, etc., by codification, §15.2-1433.

PUBLIC HOUSING.
Acceptance of rent with reservation, §55-248.34:1.
Building code.
General provisions, §§36-97 to 36-119.1.
See BUILDING CODE.
Center for housing research, §§23-135.7:14 to 23-135.7:20.
Consolidated housing authorities, §§36-47 to 36-47.2.
Department of housing and community development.
Generally, §§36-131 to 36-139.7.
See HOUSING AND COMMUNITY DEVELOPMENT DEPARTMENT.
Fair housing.
General provisions, §§36-96.1 to 36-96.23.
See FAIR HOUSING.
Housing and community development board, §§36-131 to 36-137.

PUBLIC HOUSING —Cont'd
Housing authorities.
General provisions, §§36-1 to 36-55.
See HOUSING AUTHORITIES.
Housing development authority.
General provisions, §§36-55.24 to 36-55.52.
See HOUSING DEVELOPMENT AUTHORITY.
Housing generally.
See HOUSING.
Housing projects generally.
See HOUSING PROJECTS.
Low and moderate income housing generally.
See LOW AND MODERATE INCOME HOUSING.
Money judgment, attorneys' fees, court costs.
Acceptance of payment with reservation, right to evict not waived, §55-248.34:1.
Redevelopment projects.
Generally, §§36-48 to 36-55.
See REDEVELOPMENT PROJECTS.

PUBLIC INEBRIATE DIVERSION.
Community corrections.
Generally, §§9.1-173 to 9.1-183.
See COMMUNITY CORRECTIONS.

PUBLIC INTOXICATION, §18.2-388.
Delinquent children, loss of driving privileges, §16.1-278.9.
Transporting public inebriates to detoxification center, §18.2-388.
Uniform fine schedule, VA SCt Rules 3C:1, 3C:2.

PUBLICITY.
Crime victim and witness assistance programs.
Public information campaign, §19.2-368.17.
Trial publicity.
Attorneys at law.
Professional responsibility, VA SCt Rule Pt 6 §II Rule 3.5.
Unauthorized use of name or picture, §8.01-40.

PUBLIC LANDS.
Conservation, policy of state, VA Const Art XI §1.
Escheat generally, §§55-168 to 55-201.1.
See ESCHEAT.
Housing revitalization zones.
Sale of public lands.
Designated area, §36-163.
Hunting and fishing seasons in forestlands, §§10.1-1158 to 10.1-1161.
Hunting and trapping in state forest, §§10.1-1151 to 10.1-1157.
Land office, §§41.1-1 to 41.1-20.
See LAND OFFICE.
Leases of public lands and buildings, §2.2-1146.
Nutrient management plans, §10.1-104.4.
Parks and recreation generally.
See PARKS AND RECREATION.
Police powers over lands lying beyond localities boundaries, §15.2-1725.
State parks, §§10.1-200 to 10.1-205.
Development revenue bonds, §§10.1-300 to 10.1-312.
Ungranted shores of the sea, marshes and meadowlands, §§28.2-1500 to 28.2-1514.
See UNGRANTED SHORES OF THE SEA.

PUBLIC LIBRARIES.
Generally.
See LIBRARIES.
Local and regional libraries, §§42.1-33 to 42.1-45.

PUBLIC LIBRARIES —Cont'd
Networking, §§42.1-32.1 to 42.1-32.6.

PUBLIC NUISANCES.
Generally, §§48-1 to 48-17.1.
See NUISANCES.

PUBLIC OFFICERS AND EMPLOYEES.
Acceptance of bribe, §18.2-439.
Activities permitted, §40.1-57.3.
Administrative process act, §§2.2-4000 to 2.2-4031.
Agency administrators.
Employment of personnel, §2.2-2812.
Agency heads.
Appointment, confirmation process, §2.2-106.
Severance benefits provided departing agency head.
Publicly announced, §2.2-106.
Alternative work schedules.
Duties of heads of state agencies, §2.2-2817.1.
Secretary of administration.
Establishment of policy, §2.2-203.1.
Anatomical gifts.
Bone marrow or organ donation.
Leave for, §2.2-2821.1.
Annual review.
Required, §2.2-1202.
Antitrust laws.
Investigations by attorney general.
Duties of officials and employees, §59.1-9.10.
Appeals.
Grievance procedure.
Review of hearing decisions, §2.2-3006.
Health insurance.
Denial of claims, §2.2-2818.
Appearance of state officers before governor.
Governor's power to require, §2.2-109.
Appointments.
Merit and fitness, §2.2-2901.
Signed statements required from appointees.
Severance benefits under workforce transition act, §2.2-109.01.
Architect licensing exemptions, §54.1-402.1.
Asbestos abatement in state-owned and public school buildings.
Immunity from civil liability, §2.2-1167.
Athletic leaves of absence for state employees, §2.2-124.
Attorney general.
Conflicts of interest.
Advisory opinions, §2.2-3121.
Enforcement, §2.2-3126.
Generally.
See ATTORNEY GENERAL.
Legal services provided in civil matters, §2.2-507.
Attorneys at law.
Conflicts of interest.
Successive government and private employment, VA SCt Rule Pt 6 §II Rule 1.11.
Attorneys for the Commonwealth.
Generally, §§15.2-1626 to 15.2-1633.
See COMMONWEALTH'S ATTORNEYS.
Audit of officers handling public funds.
County board form of government, §15.2-417.
County executive form of government, §15.2-538.
Petition filed in circuit court, §15.2-2512.
Urban county executive form of government, §15.2-844.
Auditor of public accounts, §§30-130 to 30-142.
See AUDITOR OF PUBLIC ACCOUNTS.

PUBLIC OFFICERS AND EMPLOYEES —Cont'd
Auditors.
Personnel administration system.
Pay scales, §2.2-2901.
Blind or visually impaired.
Information technology access for blind or visually impaired.
State agencies, institutions of higher education and political subdivision to provide, §§2.2-3500 to 2.2-3504.
Blood-borne pathogens.
Testing for, §32.1-45.2.
Boards.
Officers of state institutions.
Members of institution's board, §2.2-2806.
Bonds of officers.
Blanket surety bond plan.
Risk management division, §2.2-1840.
County, city or town officers.
See BONDS, SURETY.
Filing, §2.2-2811.
Local officers generally, §§15.2-1527 to 15.2-1533.
See LOCAL OFFICERS AND EMPLOYEES.
Premiums paid out of state treasury, §2.2-2810.
Requirements, §2.2-2809.
State and court officers generally.
See BONDS, SURETY.
Bone marrow or organ donation.
Leave for, §2.2-2821.1.
Bribery, §18.2-438.
Acceptance of bribe, §18.2-439.
Commissioners, auditors, arbitrators or jurors.
Giving bribes to or receiving bribes, §18.2-441.
Immunity of witnesses, §§18.2-445, 18.2-450.
Prevention of service of process, §18.2-440.
Public servants.
Defined, §18.2-446.
When person guilty of bribery, §18.2-447.
Certain matters not to constitute defense, §18.2-448.
Immunity of witnesses, §18.2-450.
Punishment, §18.2-449.
Bridges, etc.
Free use, §33.1-252.
Cash match plan, §§51.1-607 to 51.1-613.
Administration, §51.1-608.
Annual report, §51.1-613.
Board of trustees of Virginia retirement system.
Administration, §51.1-608.
Contributions, §51.1-609.
Definitions, §51.1-607.
Generally, §51.1-608.
Immunity from losses suffered.
Board of trustees, retirement system employees and retirement system advisory committee, §51.1-124.22.
Local plans, §51.1-610.
Other systems not affected, §51.1-613.
Political subdivision participation.
Contract with VRS, §51.1-611.
Standards, §51.1-612.
Census.
Prohibition on federal employees, exception, §2.2-2801.
Certified professional secretary examinations.
Classification of persons passing, §2.2-2904.
Circuit court clerks.
See CIRCUIT COURT CLERKS.
Circuit court judges.
See CIRCUIT COURT JUDGES.

PUBLIC OFFICERS AND EMPLOYEES —Cont'd
City officers and employees generally.
See CITY OFFICERS AND EMPLOYEES.
City status granted to town.
Generally, §§15.2-3800 to 15.2-3834.
See TRANSITION OF TOWNS TO CITIES.
Civil service commission.
County manager plan of government, §15.2-721.
Claims against the state.
Tort claims act.
Preservation of immunity, §8.01-195.3.
Classification system for public officers and employees.
Human resources management department, duties, §2.2-1201.
Clerks of circuit courts.
See CIRCUIT COURT CLERKS.
Collection and dissemination of information by state agencies.
Personal information, privacy protection.
Government data collection and dissemination practices act, §§2.2-3800 to 2.2-3809.
See GOVERNMENT DATA COLLECTION AND DISSEMINATION PRACTICES ACT.
Social security numbers, protection, §§2.2-3815, 2.2-3816.
Collective bargaining for governmental employees.
Prohibition, §40.1-57.2.
Color of office.
Acts under color of office, validity, §2.2-2808.
Commercial liability insurance joint underwriting association.
Officers or employees as directors, §38.2-2911.
Commercial space flight authority.
Virginia personnel act, exemption, §2.2-2215.
Commissioner of agriculture and consumer services.
See AGRICULTURE AND CONSUMER SERVICES COMMISSIONER.
Commissioners of revenue.
Generally, §§58.1-3100 to 58.1-3122.2.
See COMMISSIONERS OF REVENUE.
Commonwealth's attorneys.
Generally, §§15.2-1626 to 15.2-1633.
See COMMONWEALTH'S ATTORNEYS.
Compensation of public officials.
Generally.
See COMPENSATION OF PUBLIC OFFICERS AND EMPLOYEES.
Salaries generally.
See SALARIES.
Compensation or payment to which employee not entitled.
Liability of employee receiving and employee authorizing payment, §2.2-804.
Competitive government act, §§2.2-5512, 2.2-5513.
Computers.
Restricted access to sexually explicit material, §2.2-2827.
Confidential information.
Personal information, §2.2-1203.
Conflicts of interest, §§2.2-3100 to 2.2-3127.
Advisory opinions, §2.2-3121.
Applicability, §2.2-3101.
Contracts, §2.2-3105.
Exceptions, §2.2-3110.
Transactions, §2.2-3111.

PUBLIC OFFICERS AND EMPLOYEES —Cont'd
Conflicts of interest —Cont'd
Award or payment in honor of meritorious or exceptional service.
Exclusion from scope of provisions, §2.2-3104.1.
Contracts.
Applicability, §2.2-3105.
Exceptions, §2.2-3110.
Exceptions, §2.2-3110.
Invalidation, §2.2-3123.
Local officers and employees, §2.2-3109.
Members of local governing bodies, §2.2-3107.
Prohibited contracts, §2.2-3106.
Rescission of sales, §2.2-3123.
School boards, §2.2-3108.
Violations, void, §2.2-2808.
Copy of chapter, furnishing, §2.2-3100.1.
Defined terms, §2.2-3101.
Disability to hold state office, §2.2-2800.
Exceptions, §2.2-2801.
Disclosure statements.
Applicability, §2.2-3113.
Constitutional officers, §2.2-3116.
Copy of chapter, furnishing, §2.2-3100.1.
Forms, §§2.2-3117, 2.2-3118.
General assembly members' statements of economic interest, §2.2-3114.1.
Local officers and employees, §2.2-3115.
Persons serving in or seeking multiple positions, or reappointees, §2.2-3118.1.
State officers and employees, §2.2-3114.
District court judges, §16.1-69.19.
Elected offices.
Holding two elected offices simultaneously, prohibited, §2.2-2807.
Electoral board members, §24.2-106, VA Const Art II §8.
Enforcement, §2.2-3126.
Ethics in public contracting, §§2.2-4367 to 2.2-4377.
Exceptions.
Transactions, §2.2-3112.
Federal employees.
Disability to hold state office, §2.2-2800.
Exceptions, §2.2-2801.
Military affairs.
Exception for members of Armed Forces and reserve forces, §2.2-2805.
Exception for selective service system, §2.2-2803.
Exception when called to active-duty or engaged in war service, §2.2-2802.
Fee bills, fraudulent issue, §18.2-471.
Forfeitures, §§2.2-3124, 19.2-386.33.
Former employees, prohibition from certain activities, §15.2-1408.
Furnishing copy of policy of state to officers and employees, §2.2-3100.1.
General assembly members, VA Const Art IV §4.
Generally prohibited conduct, §2.2-3103.
Gifts.
Local ordinances regulating receipt of gifts, §2.2-3104.2.
Public procurement act, public-private transportation act, public-private education facilities and infrastructure act.
Accepting from person making bid or offeror under acts.
Prohibition, governor and governor's secretaries, §§2.2-3104.01, 2.2-4376.1.

PUBLIC OFFICERS AND EMPLOYEES —Cont'd
Conflicts of interest —Cont'd
Justices or judges of courts of record, VA Const Art VI §11.
Limitation of actions, §2.2-3125.
Lobbying restrictions.
Representing person or group before prior agency, §2.2-3104.02.
Local government officers or members of governing bodies, VA Const Art VII §6.
Local ordinances regulating receipt of gifts, §2.2-3104.2.
Officers of election, VA Const Art II §8.
Officers of state institutions.
Members of institution's board, §2.2-2806.
Perjury, persons convicted of, §18.2-434.
Policy of state, §§2.2-3100, 2.2-3100.1.
Prohibited and unlawful conduct enumerated, §2.2-3102.
Prohibited contracts, §2.2-3106.
Public procurement act, public-private transportation act, public-private education facilities and infrastructure act.
Gifts or contributions from person making bid or offeror under acts.
Prohibition on accepting, governor and governor's secretaries, §§2.2-3104.01, 2.2-4376.1.
Registrars of election, §§24.2-110, 24.2-119, VA Const Art II §8.
Review of provisions, §2.2-3100.1.
Revolving door policy, §2.2-3104.
School boards, §2.2-3119.
Teacher awards.
Exclusion from scope of provisions, §2.2-3104.1.
Terminated employees.
Representing clients before agency where previously employed, §2.2-3104.
Transactions.
Applicability, §2.2-3111.
Exceptions, §2.2-3112.
Prohibited conduct generally, §2.2-3112.
Venue, §2.2-3127.
Violations.
Knowing violations, §2.2-3120.
Malfeasance in office or employment, §2.2-3122.
Virginia Commonwealth University health system authority.
Applicability of provisions to board of directors, §23-50.16:5.
Virginia retirement system.
Board of trustees and employees.
Application, §51.1-124.21.
Conservation police officers generally.
See CONSERVATION POLICE OFFICERS.
Constitutional local officers.
Generally, §§15.2-1600 to 15.2-1637.
See LOCAL CONSTITUTIONAL OFFICERS.
Constitutional officers.
Conflicts of interest.
Disclosure statements, §2.2-3116.
Disclosure statements, §2.2-3116.
Employees.
Grievance procedure, §2.2-3008.
Contracts.
Conflicts of interest.
Applicability, §2.2-3105.
Invalidation, §2.2-3123.
Local officers and employees, §2.2-3109.
Members of local governing bodies, §2.2-3107.

PUBLIC OFFICERS AND EMPLOYEES —Cont'd
Contracts —Cont'd
Conflicts of interest —Cont'd
Prohibited contracts, §2.2-3106.
Rescission of sales, §2.2-3123.
School boards, §2.2-3108.
Void contracts, §2.2-2808.
Controlled substances.
Removal for manufacture, sale, etc., §24.2-233.
Copyrights.
Ownership of copyrights developed by state employees, §2.2-2822.
Corrections department.
Grievance procedure, §2.2-3007.
Costs.
Termination or layoff of employees, §2.2-3205.
County board form of government.
Generally, §§15.2-400 to 15.2-418.
See COUNTY BOARD FORM OF GOVERNMENT.
County boards of supervisors.
See COUNTY BOARDS OF SUPERVISORS.
County executive form of government.
Generally, §§15.2-500 to 15.2-542.
See COUNTY EXECUTIVE FORM OF GOVERNMENT.
Urban county executive form of government.
Generally, §§15.2-800 to 15.2-858.
See URBAN COUNTY EXECUTIVE FORM OF GOVERNMENT.
County manager form of government.
Generally, §§15.2-600 to 15.2-642.
See COUNTY MANAGER FORM OF GOVERNMENT.
County manager plan of government.
Generally, §§15.2-700 to 15.2-750.
See COUNTY MANAGER PLAN OF GOVERNMENT.
County officers and employees generally.
See COUNTY OFFICERS AND EMPLOYEES.
Creative commons.
Ownership of copyrights developed by state employees, §2.2-2822.
Criminal background checks.
Sensitive positions in state agencies, §2.2-1201.1.
Criminal offenses.
Conflicts of interest.
Knowing violations, §2.2-3120.
Criminal procedure.
Defense of employees, §2.2-2817.
Debt collection act.
Collection of accounts receivable by Commonwealth, §§2.2-4800 to 2.2-4809.
See COLLECTION OF ACCOUNTS RECEIVABLE BY COMMONWEALTH.
Debts.
Income withholding.
Liability for debt owed to Commonwealth, §2.2-2816.
Deferred compensation plan, §§51.1-600 to 51.1-605.
Additional nature of plan, §51.1-605.
Contract, §51.1-601.
Criteria, §51.1-604.
Defined terms, §51.1-600.
Employees of political subdivisions, §51.1-603.1.
Immunity from losses suffered.
Board of trustees, retirement system employees and retirement system advisory committee, §51.1-124.22.
Local employee plans, §51.1-603.

PUBLIC OFFICERS AND EMPLOYEES —Cont'd
Deferred compensation plan —Cont'd
Participation by employees of political subdivisions, §51.1-603.1.
Plans for local employees, §51.1-603.
Plans for state employees, §51.1-602.
Reemployed employees, participation, §51.1-601.1.
Standards, §51.1-604.
State employee plans, §51.1-602.
Department and commissioner of social services.
Generally, §§63.2-200 to 63.2-214.3.
See SOCIAL SERVICES.
Disability benefits.
Sickness and disability program generally, §§51.1-1100 to 51.1-1140.
See SICKNESS AND DISABILITY PROGRAM.
Disability to hold state office, §2.2-2800.
Exceptions, §2.2-2801.
Disappearance of public officer.
Presumption of vacancy, §2.2-2829.
Disciplinary actions.
Personnel administration system, §§2.2-2900 to 2.2-2905.
Disclosure statements.
Applicability, §2.2-3113.
Constitutional officers, §2.2-3116.
Forms, §§2.2-3117, 2.2-3118.
General assembly members' statements of economic interest, §2.2-3114.1.
Local officers and employees, §2.2-3115.
Orientation for state filers, §§2.2-3128 to 2.2-3131.
Attendance requirements, §2.2-3130.
Equivalent ethics orientation course, §2.2-3131.
Exempt persons, §2.2-3131.
Joint agency orientation sessions, §2.2-3131.
Record of attendance, §2.2-3129.
Semiannual orientation course, §2.2-3128.
State filer, defined, §2.2-3101.
Persons serving in or seeking multiple positions, or reappointees, §2.2-3118.1.
State officers and employees, §2.2-3114.
Discrimination.
Human rights act, §§2.2-3900 to 2.2-3903.
District court clerks.
See DISTRICT COURT CLERKS.
District court judges.
See DISTRICT COURT JUDGES.
District offices.
Prohibition on federal employees, exception, §2.2-2801.
Drug paraphernalia.
Removal for sale, possession, etc., §24.2-233.
Dual officeholding.
Generally.
See DUAL OFFICEHOLDING.
Local officers and members of governing bodies, §§15.2-1534, 15.2-1535.
Elected offices.
Holding two elected offices simultaneously, prohibited, §2.2-2807.
Election of federal, state and local officers generally, §§24.2-100 to 24.2-1019.
See ELECTIONS.
Elective office, qualifications to hold, VA Const Art II §5.
Eligibility for employment.
Strikes, §40.1-55.
Embezzlement, §18.2-112.
Misuse of public assets, §18.2-112.1.

PUBLIC OFFICERS AND EMPLOYEES —Cont'd
Embezzlement —Cont'd
Prima facie evidence.
Default in paying over funds, §18.2-112.
Emergency medical technicians generally.
See EMERGENCY MEDICAL TECHNICIANS.
Employee health insurance fund, §2.2-2818.
Employee management relations.
Human resources management department, duties, §2.2-1201.
Employment of personnel necessary to functioning of agency, §2.2-2812.
Engineer licensing exemptions, §54.1-402.1.
Ethics in public contracting, §§2.2-4367 to 2.2-4377.
Executive agencies.
Personnel necessary to functioning of agency.
Employment, §2.2-2812.
Expenses.
Method of payment, §2.2-2814.
Time of payment, §2.2-2814.
Travel expenses, §2.2-2823.
Expense accounts, §2.2-2826.
Monitoring, §2.2-2824.
Reimbursement for certain expenditures, §2.2-2825.
Expenses of public officials.
Generally.
See EXPENSES OF PUBLIC OFFICIALS.
Mileage expenses generally.
See MILEAGE.
Travel expenses generally.
See TRAVEL EXPENSES.
Extortion by officer, §18.2-470.
Fair employment contracting act, §§2.2-4200, 2.2-4201.
Federal employees.
Disability to hold state office, §2.2-2800.
Exceptions, §2.2-2801.
Military affairs.
Exception for members of Armed Forces and reserve forces, §2.2-2805.
Exception for selective service system, §2.2-2803.
Exception when called to active-duty or engaged in war service, §2.2-2802.
Fee system abolished.
County executive form of government, §15.2-540.
County manager form of government, §15.2-639.
Urban county executive form of government, §15.2-848.
Firefighters generally.
See FIREFIGHTERS.
Fire marshals, §§27-30 to 27-37.1.
See FIRE MARSHALS.
Flex time.
Duties of heads of state agencies, §2.2-2817.1.
Secretary of administration.
Establishment of policy on telecommuting and alternative work schedules, §2.2-203.1.
Foreign office or title, US Const Art I §9.
Forfeiture of office.
Acceptance of bribe by officer or candidate for office, §18.2-439.
Forfeitures.
Conflicts of interest, §§2.2-3124, 19.2-386.33.
Forging public records of, §18.2-168.
Fraud and abuse whistleblower protection act, §§2.2-3009 to 2.2-3014.
See WHISTLEBLOWING.

PUBLIC OFFICERS AND EMPLOYEES —Cont'd
Freedom of information act.
Exceptions for employee information, §2.2-1203.
Generally, §§2.2-3700 to 2.2-3714.
See FREEDOM OF INFORMATION.
Functions and policies of agency discussing, §2.2-603.
Garnishment.
Municipal officials, clerks and employees, §§8.01-524, 8.01-525.
State employees, §8.01-525.
Wages and salaries of state and municipal employees, §§8.01-522, 8.01-524, 8.01-525.
General assembly.
See GENERAL ASSEMBLY.
Gifts.
Conflicts of interest.
Generally prohibited conduct, §2.2-3103.
Local ordinances regulating receipt of gifts, §2.2-3104.2.
Public procurement act, public-private transportation act, public-private education facilities and infrastructure act.
Accepting from person making bid or offeror under acts.
Prohibition, governor and governor's secretaries, §§2.2-3104.01, 2.2-4376.1.
Procurement transactions.
Prohibitions on gifts, §2.2-4371.
Governing bodies of localities.
Generally, §§15.2-1400 to 15.2-1433.
See LOCALITIES.
Governor, §§2.2-100 to 2.2-135.
See GOVERNOR.
Grievance procedure, §§2.2-3000 to 2.2-3008.
Agency's cooperation, §2.2-3005.1.
Alternative programs, §2.2-3001.
Constitutional officers' employees, §2.2-3008.
Corrections department employees, §2.2-3007.
Cost of hearing, §2.2-3005.1.
Costs, §2.2-3006.
County manager plan of government.
Police officers, §15.2-723.
Presence of equal employment opportunity officer, §15.2-738.
Coverage, §2.2-3001.
Executive agencies.
Responsibilities, §2.2-3000.
Exemptions, §2.2-3002.
Exempt issues, §2.2-3004.
Grievance hearings, §2.2-3004.
Hearing officers, §2.2-3005.
Scope of hearing officer's decision, §2.2-3005.1.
Hearing officers, §§2.2-3005, 2.2-3005.1.
Hearings, §2.2-3004.
Human resources management department.
Duties, §2.2-3003.
Juvenile justice department employees, §2.2-3007.
Local government personnel generally, §§15.2-1506 to 15.2-1507.1.
Management's right to exclude, §2.2-3004.
Policy of the Commonwealth, §2.2-3000.
Procedure generally, §2.2-3003.
Review of hearing decisions, §2.2-3006.
Time limits, §2.2-3003.
Whistleblowing.
Fraud and abuse whistleblower protection act, applicability, §2.2-3012.
Group insurance program, §§51.1-500 to 51.1-514.
Accounting to board, §51.1-514.

PUBLIC OFFICERS AND EMPLOYEES —Cont'd
Group insurance program —Cont'd
Additional accidental death and dismemberment benefits, §51.1-505.01.
Additional insurance options, §51.1-512.
Spouse and minor dependents, §51.1-512.1.
Amount of coverage, §51.1-505.
Beneficiaries of payment on death, §51.1-511.
Board authorized to purchase, §51.1-501.
Cessation, §51.1-505.
Contributions by employees, §51.1-506.
Contributions by employers, §51.1-508.
Coverage limitation, §51.1-503.
Death and dismemberment benefits.
Additional benefits, §51.1-505.01.
Defined terms, §51.1-500.
Eligible employees and officers, §51.1-502.
Teaching hospital employees, §51.1-502.1.
Employee contributions, §51.1-506.
Employee eligibility, §§51.1-502, 51.1-502.1.
Employer contributions, §51.1-508.
Employer records and information, §51.1-509.
Limitations in coverage, §51.1-503.
Long-term care insurance, §51.1-513.1.
Officer eligibility, §§51.1-502, 51.1-502.1.
Opting out, §51.1-507.
Optional insurance, §51.1-512.
Spouse and minor dependents, §51.1-512.1.
Payment on death beneficiaries, §51.1-511.
Payments.
Accidental death and dismemberment insurance, §51.1-505.
Payroll deductions, §51.1-506.
Political subdivision participation, §51.1-504.
Process exemption, §51.1-510.
Purchase power of board, §51.1-501.
Reduction of coverage, §51.1-505.
Retired employees.
Amount of life insurance, §51.1-505.
Contributions for life insurance not required, §51.1-506.
Separation from service.
Acceptance of premiums paid.
Employees of institution of higher education or local school board, §51.1-506.
Spouse and minor dependents, §51.1-512.1.
Termination of coverage, §51.1-505.
Virginia retirement system generally, §§51.1-124.1 to 51.1-169.
See VIRGINIA RETIREMENT SYSTEM.
Health insurance.
Appeals.
Denial of claims, §2.2-2818.
Continuing coverage upon termination of provider, §2.2-2818.
Coverage, §2.2-2818.
Employee health insurance fund, §2.2-2818.
Employer contribution rates, §2.2-2818.01.
High deductible health plan option availability, §2.2-2818.
Long-term care insurance.
Board of trustees, Virginia Retirement System.
Assumption of responsibility, §§51.1-513.2, 51.1-513.3.
Program for employees of local governments, local officers and teachers, §2.2-1207.
Program for persons within Virginia retirement system, §2.2-1208.
Trust fund, §51.1-513.4.
Mandated benefits.
Application of insurance mandates to state plan, §2.2-2818.2.

PUBLIC OFFICERS AND EMPLOYEES —Cont'd
Health insurance —Cont'd
Participation, §2.2-1204.
Part-time employees, §2.2-2818.
Purchase options, §2.2-2820.
Pre-existing conditions, §2.2-2818.
Preferred providers, §2.2-2818.
Required, §2.2-2818.
Risk management division.
Risk management plan for claims against, §2.2-1839.
Self-insured group health insurance plans, §2.2-2818.
Sickness and disability program generally, §§51.1-1100 to 51.1-1140.
See SICKNESS AND DISABILITY PROGRAM.
Specialists.
Guaranteed access, §2.2-2818.
Supplemental coverage under state program.
State employees eligible for benefits under TRICARE military health system, §2.2-2818.1.
Surviving spouses and dependents.
Continued coverage purchases through department, §2.2-1205.
Procedure, §2.2-2819.
Qualifications, §2.2-2819.
Termination, §2.2-2819.
Continued coverage purchases through plan sponsor, §2.2-1206.
Terms, §2.2-2818.
Tobacco indemnification and community revitalization commission, §3.2-3106.
TRICARE military health system.
State employees eligible for benefits under.
Supplemental coverage under state program, §2.2-2818.1.
Hearings.
Grievance hearings, §2.2-3004.
Hearing officers, §§2.2-3005, 2.2-3005.1.
HIV exposure.
Consent deemed given to release of test results, §32.1-45.1.
Testing, §32.1-45.2.
Honoraria.
Conflicts of interest.
Generally prohibited conduct, §2.2-3103.
Hourly employees.
Personnel administration system.
Exemptions, §2.2-2905.
Human rights act, §§2.2-3900 to 2.2-3903.
Immunity.
Bribery prosecutions, §18.2-445.
Investigation of elected official, §52-8.2.
Members of local governmental entities, §15.2-1405.
Roadway litter pick-up program for probationers.
Civil immunity, §8.01-226.8.
Income withholding.
Liability for debt owed to Commonwealth, §2.2-2816.
Incompetence in performance of duties.
Removal, §24.2-233.
Information technology access for blind or visually impaired.
State agencies, institutions of higher education and political subdivision to provide, §§2.2-3500 to 2.2-3504.
Innovation and entrepreneurship investment authority.
Virginia personnel act, exemption, §2.2-2231.

PUBLIC OFFICERS AND EMPLOYEES —Cont'd
Inquiry into official conduct of office or officer.
County executive form of government, §15.2-506.
County manager form of government, §15.2-606.
County manager plan of government, §15.2-709.
Urban county executive form of government, §15.2-814.
Inspector general, state.
Cooperation of state agencies and officers, §2.2-310.
Internet.
Internet publication of personal information of public officials, §18.2-186.4:1.
Restricted access to sexually explicit material, §2.2-2827.
Interpreters for deaf in state agency proceeding, §§2.2-3400 to 2.2-3402.
Investigation of elected official.
Immunity of witnesses, §52-8.2.
Investment of public funds, §§2.2-4500 to 2.2-4519.
See INVESTMENT OF PUBLIC FUNDS.
Involuntary separations, §2.2-3201.
Joint local officers and employees, §§15.2-1513 to 15.2-1516.
Judicial inquiry and review commission.
Assistance and information for, §17.1-917.
Juvenile and domestic relations district court judges.
See JUVENILE AND DOMESTIC RELATIONS DISTRICT COURTS.
Juvenile justice department.
Grievance procedure, §2.2-3007.
Land surveyor licensing exemptions, §54.1-402.1.
Law enforcement officers generally.
See LAW ENFORCEMENT OFFICERS.
Law officers' retirement system, §§51.1-211 to 51.1-221.
See LAW OFFICERS' RETIREMENT SYSTEM.
Layoffs, §§2.2-3200 to 2.2-3206.
Costs, §2.2-3205.
Involuntary separations, §2.2-3201.
Personnel administration system, §§2.2-2900 to 2.2-2905.
Preferential treatment, §2.2-3201.
Prerequisites to termination or layoff, §2.2-3201.
Reemployment, §2.2-3201.
Retirement, §2.2-3204.
Review of program, §2.2-3206.
Transitional severance benefits.
Computation and payment, §2.2-3203.
Eligibility, §2.2-3202.
Leaves of absence.
Athletic leaves for state employees, §2.2-124.
Bone marrow or organ donation, §2.2-2821.1.
Military service duty, §44-93.
Discrimination in hiring prohibited, §44-93.4.
Penalty for employer failure to comply, §44-93.5.
Reemployment, §44-93.3.
State employees ordered to active military duty.
Use of accrued annual leave, §2.2-2903.1.
Supplement of military pay and additional life insurance benefits, §44-93.1.
State defense force or national defense executive reserve training, §44-204.
Volunteer fire and rescue services, §2.2-2821.2.
Librarian of Virginia, §§42.1-13 to 42.1-18.
See LIBRARIAN OF VIRGINIA.

PUBLIC OFFICERS AND EMPLOYEES —Cont'd
Lieutenant governor.
See LIEUTENANT GOVERNOR.
Life insurance.
Military duty leaves of absence.
Additional life insurance benefits, §44-93.1.
Limitation of actions.
Conflicts of interest, §2.2-3125.
Lobbying.
Former officers and employees in certain counties, restrictions on activities.
County executive form of government, §15.2-515.
Urban county executive form of government, §15.2-810.
Representing person or group before prior agency, restrictions, §2.2-3104.02.
Local constitutional officers.
Generally, §§15.2-1600 to 15.2-1637.
See LOCAL CONSTITUTIONAL OFFICERS.
Local fire marshals, §§27-30 to 27-37.1.
See FIRE MARSHALS.
Local governing bodies generally, §§15.2-1400 to 15.2-1433.
See LOCALITIES.
Local government personnel generally, qualifications for office, etc., §§15.2-1500 to 15.2-1543.
See LOCAL OFFICERS AND EMPLOYEES.
Local health departments and directors.
Designation, §32.1-31.
Local officers and employees generally.
See LOCAL OFFICERS AND EMPLOYEES.
Local trusts to fund postemployment benefits other than pensions, §§15.2-1544 to 15.2-1549.
Long-term care insurance.
Board of trustees, Virginia Retirement System.
Assumption of responsibility, §§51.1-513.2, 51.1-513.3.
Program for local government employees, officers, teachers, §2.2-1207.
Program for persons within Virginia retirement system, §2.2-1208.
Trust fund, §51.1-513.4.
Malfeasance.
Conflicts of interest.
Knowing violations, §2.2-3122.
Marijuana.
Removal for manufacture, sale, etc., §24.2-233.
Mayors generally.
See MAYORS.
Medal of valor.
Public safety, §§9.1-800, 9.1-801.
Medical malpractice joint underwriting association.
Member of board of directors, §38.2-2812.
Meetings of local governmental bodies, §§15.2-1415 to 15.2-1421.
See LOCALITIES.
Mileage allowances, §2.2-2823.
Mileage expenses generally.
See MILEAGE.
Military and military service, §44-93.
Carry forward of accrued annual leave, §2.2-1201.
Discrimination in hiring prohibited, §44-93.4.
Federal employee prohibition.
Exception for members of Armed Forces and reserve forces, §2.2-2805.
Exception for selective service system, §2.2-2803.

PUBLIC OFFICERS AND EMPLOYEES —Cont'd
Military and military service —Cont'd
Federal employee prohibition —Cont'd
Exception when called to active-duty or engaged in war service, §2.2-2802.
Health insurance for state employees.
Supplemental coverage under state program.
Employees eligible for benefits under TRICARE military health system, §2.2-2818.1.
Leaves of absence for military duty, §44-93.
Discrimination in hiring prohibited, §44-93.4.
Penalty for employer failure to comply, §44-93.5.
Reemployment, §44-93.3.
State employees ordered to active military duty.
Use of accrued annual leave, §2.2-2903.1.
Supplement of military pay and additional life insurance benefits, §44-93.1.
Penalty for employer failure to comply, §44-93.5.
Personnel administration system.
Restoration to position upon termination of service, §2.2-2901.
Reemployment, §44-93.3.
Selective service compliance required, §2.2-2804.
Supplement of military pay and additional life insurance benefits, §44-93.1.
Misdemeanors.
Conflicts of interest.
Knowing violations, §2.2-3120.
Misuse of office.
Removal, §24.2-233.
Misuse of public assets, §18.2-112.1.
Multiple office-holding.
Congress, US Const Art I §6.
Holding two elected offices simultaneously, prohibited, §2.2-2807.
National defense executive reserve training.
Leaves of absence, §44-204.
National guard members.
Personnel administration system.
Preferences, §2.2-2903.
Neglect of duty.
Removal, §24.2-233.
Office hours, §2.2-3322.
Open source initiative.
Ownership of copyrights developed by state employees, §2.2-2822.
Orientation for state filers.
Disclosure statements, §§2.2-3128 to 2.2-3131.
Part-time employees.
Health insurance, §2.2-2818.
Purchase options, §2.2-2820.
Personnel administration system.
Exemptions, §2.2-2905.
Patents.
Ownership of patents developed by state employees, §2.2-2822.
Permitted activities, §40.1-57.3.
Personal identifying information.
Internet publication of personal information of public officials, §18.2-186.4:1.
Personnel administration system, §§2.2-2900 to 2.2-2905.
Appointments.
Merit and fitness, §2.2-2901.
Auditors.
Pay scales, §2.2-2901.
Authorities to develop former federal areas.
Exemption of authorities from personnel act, §15.2-6314.1.

PUBLIC OFFICERS AND EMPLOYEES —Cont'd
Personnel administration system —Cont'd
Certified professional secretary examinations.
Classification of persons passing, §2.2-2904.
Changes in rate of pay.
Prerequisites, §2.2-2901.
Chief personnel officer.
Governor, §2.2-103.
Classification plan.
Governor to establish and maintain, amendments, §2.2-103.
Compensation plan.
Governor to establish and maintain, amendments, §2.2-103.
Contact with elected officials, rights of employees, §2.2-2902.1.
Economic development partnership authority.
Exemption from act, §2.2-2244.
Electric authorities.
Applicability of act to certain authorities, §15.2-5405.1.
Establishment of positions or pay rates.
Prerequisites, §2.2-2901.
Exemptions, §2.2-2905.
Higher education institutions, faculty and administrative positions.
Policies for designation of positions, §2.2-2901.
Innovation and entrepreneurship investment authority.
Exemption, §2.2-2231.
Military affairs.
Preferences for national guard, veterans and surviving spouses or children of veterans, §2.2-2903.
Restoration to position upon termination of service, §2.2-2901.
National guard members.
Preferences, §2.2-2903.
Port authority.
Exemptions from personnel act, §62.1-132.6.
Powers and duties of governor, §2.2-103.
Promotions.
Merit and fitness, §2.2-2901.
Purpose, §2.2-2900.
Rights of employees to contact elected officials, §2.2-2902.1.
Short title, §2.2-2900.
Tenure.
Merit and fitness, §2.2-2901.
Tobacco products.
Use by state employees, §2.2-2902.
Tourism authority.
Exemption from act, §2.2-2325.
Veterans and surviving spouses and children.
Preferences, §2.2-2903.
Virginia Commonwealth University health system authority.
Exemption from personnel act, §23-50.16:34.
Personnel information system.
Establishment and administration, §2.2-1201.
Personnel necessary to functioning of agency.
Employment, §2.2-2812.
Personnel systems in certain cities, §15.2-1131.
Police.
Auxiliary police forces, §§15.2-1731 to 15.2-1736.
See POLICE.
Generally, §§15.2-1700 to 15.2-1753.
See POLICE.
Special police officers, §§15.2-1737 to 15.2-1746.
See POLICE.

PUBLIC OFFICERS AND EMPLOYEES —Cont'd
Pornography.
Computers.
Restricted access to sexually explicit material, §2.2-2827.
Preemployment requirements for Arlington County, §15.2-709.1.
Presents from foreign states, US Const Art I §9.
Private security services businesses.
Exceptions, §9.1-140.
Privatization of commercial activities, loss of jobs due to.
Report to governor, §2.2-203.2:1.
Production of books, accounts, vouchers and other papers.
Power of governor to require, §2.2-109.
Promotions.
Personnel administration system, §§2.2-2900 to 2.2-2905.
Public contracting, ethics in, §§2.2-4367 to 2.2-4377.
Public procurement act, §§2.2-4300 to 2.2-4377.
See PUBLIC PROCUREMENT.
Public records generally, §§42.1-76 to 42.1-90.1.
See STATE RECORDS MANAGEMENT.
Public safety medal of valor, §§9.1-800, 9.1-801.
Public service companies.
Free services to, §56-8.1.
Public utilities, state operation.
Disclosures, §56-234.5.
Employment of utility employees, §56-512.
Established procedure to be maintained, §56-519.
Replacement of utility employees, §56-513.
Status unaffected by acceptance or refusal of state employment, §56-514.
Purchases of equipment, supplies, printing and nonprofessional services.
Division of purchases and supply generally, §§2.2-1109 to 2.2-1128.
See PURCHASES AND SUPPLY DIVISION.
Purchasing agents.
County executive form of government.
Director of finance to act as, §15.2-524.
County manager form of government.
Director of finance to act as, §15.2-622.
Employment by county and duties, §15.2-1543.
Procurement by county purchasing agents, §§15.2-1233 to 15.2-1240.
Urban county executive form of government.
Direction of finance to act as, §15.2-831.
Qualifications to hold elective office, VA Const Art II §5.
Receipt of public funds.
Report to comptroller, §2.2-807.
Records.
False entries or destruction, §18.2-472.
Recruitment.
Human resources department, duties, §2.2-1201.
Religious beliefs.
No religious test for office.
Prohibited, US Const Art VI.
Removal of public officers from office, §§24.2-230 to 24.2-238.
Applicability of article, §24.2-230.
Appointed officers for term certain, §24.2-234.
Appointment of attorney to represent Commonwealth at trial, §24.2-237.
Attorney for the Commonwealth to represent Commonwealth at trial, §24.2-237.
Circuit court removal, §24.2-233.
Appointed officers for term certain, §24.2-234.

PUBLIC OFFICERS AND EMPLOYEES —Cont'd
Removal of public officers from office —Cont'd
Circuit court removal —Cont'd
Procedure, §24.2-235.
Suspension pending hearing and appeal, §24.2-236.
Costs and reasonable attorney fees, §24.2-238.
Determination that person incapacitated in judicial proceeding.
Vacancy occurring, §24.2-232.
Exceptions as to applicability, §24.2-230.
Forfeiture of office.
Sentence for commission of certain crimes, §24.2-231.
Grounds for removal by circuit court, §24.2-233.
Jury trial.
Right to demand, §24.2-237.
Petition to circuit court for removal, §24.2-233.
Appointed officers for term certain, §24.2-234.
Requirements, §24.2-235.
Procedure for removal, §24.2-235.
Right of appeal to supreme court, §24.2-237.
Service of show cause rule upon officer, §24.2-235.
Show cause rule, §24.2-235.
Supreme court review.
Right of appeal, §24.2-237.
Suspension pending hearing and appeal, §24.2-236.
Trial by jury.
Right to demand, §24.2-237.
Reports to governor, §2.2-110.
Resignation of local elected officer.
Date resignation becomes not revocable, §24.2-226.
Resources authority.
Board of directors.
Forfeiture of officer employment, §62.1-201.
Restitution.
Employee receiving payment for not entitled.
Liability of employee receiving and employee authorizing payment, §2.2-804.
Retirement.
General assembly to maintain and administer system, VA Const Art X §11.
Involuntary separation, §2.2-3204.
Retirement system for state police officers, §§51.1-200 to 51.1-210.
See STATE POLICE RETIREMENT SYSTEM.
Retirement system of Virginia, §§51.1-124.1 to 51.1-169.
See VIRGINIA RETIREMENT SYSTEM.
Revolving door policy.
Conflicts of interest, §2.2-3104.
Risk management plan for public liability, §2.2-1837.
Salaries.
Generally.
See SALARIES.
School boards.
Conflicts of interest, §2.2-3119.
Secretaries.
Certified professional secretary examinations.
Classification of persons passing, §2.2-2904.
Secretary of administration, §§2.2-200 to 2.2-202, 2.2-203.
Secretary of commerce and trade, §§2.2-200 to 2.2-202, 2.2-204 to 2.2-207.
Secretary of education, §§2.2-200 to 2.2-202.
Secretary of finance, §§2.2-200 to 2.2-202, 2.2-211.
Secretary of health and human resources, §§2.2-200 to 2.2-202, 2.2-212, 2.2-214.

PUBLIC OFFICERS AND EMPLOYEES —Cont'd
Secretary of natural resources, §§2.2-200 to 2.2-202, 2.2-215 to 2.2-220.3.
Secretary of public safety, §§2.2-200 to 2.2-202, 2.2-221 to 2.2-224.1.
Secretary of technology, §§2.2-200 to 2.2-202, 2.2-225.
Secretary of the Commonwealth.
Generally, §§2.2-400 to 2.2-410.
See SECRETARY OF THE COMMONWEALTH.
Secretary of transportation, §§2.2-200 to 2.2-202, 2.2-228, 2.2-229.
Secretary of veterans affairs and homeland security, §§2.2-200 to 2.2-202, 2.2-230 to 2.2-233.
Security for public deposits, §§2.2-4400 to 2.2-4411.
See SECURITY FOR PUBLIC DEPOSITS.
Selective service.
Compliance required, §2.2-2804.
Federal employee prohibition.
Exception for service in selective service system, §2.2-2803.
Self-insured group health insurance plans, §2.2-2818.
Sensitive positions in state agencies.
Criminal background checks for positions designated as sensitive, §2.2-1201.1.
Sergeants generally.
See SERGEANTS.
Severance benefits.
Departing agency head.
Public announcement, §2.2-106.
Payment to state officers or employees, §2.2-2831.
Transitional severance benefits.
Eligibility for, §2.2-3202.
Sexually explicit material.
Restricted computer access, §2.2-2827.
Sheriffs.
Generally, §§15.2-1609 to 15.2-1625.
See SHERIFFS.
Sickness and disability program, §§51.1-1100 to 51.1-1140.
See SICKNESS AND DISABILITY PROGRAM.
Social security, §§51.1-700 to 51.1-707.
Agreements between states, §51.1-703.
Contributions by state employees, §51.1-704.
Coverage of local employees, §51.1-705.
Defined terms, §51.1-700.
Federal-state agreement, §51.1-702.
Interstate agreements, §51.1-703.
Plan of agreement for extending benefits.
Political subdivisions desiring coverage, §51.1-705.
Rules and regulations, §51.1-701.
Source of contributions, §51.1-706.
State employee contributions, §51.1-704.
State social security administrator.
Authority, §51.1-707.
Director of VRS, §51.1-700.
Social security numbers, protection, §§2.2-3815, 2.2-3816.
Special counsel, employment, §§2.2-510, 2.2-510.1.
Special police officers, §§15.2-1737 to 15.2-1746.
See POLICE.
State defense force training.
Leaves of absence, §44-204

PUBLIC OFFICERS AND EMPLOYEES —Cont'd
State departments and agencies.
General provisions.
State agencies related to operation of government, §§2.2-600 to 2.2-614.3.
See STATE DEPARTMENTS AND AGENCIES.
State forester, §§10.1-1104 to 10.1-1119.
See STATE FORESTER.
State inspector general.
Cooperation of state agencies and officers, §2.2-310.
State police generally.
See STATE POLICE DEPARTMENT.
State police retirement system, §§51.1-200 to 51.1-210.
See STATE POLICE RETIREMENT SYSTEM.
Strikes by government employees, §§40.1-55 to 40.1-57.1.
Appeals.
Reemployment.
Appeal by employer, §40.1-57.1.
Eligibility for employment, §40.1-55.
Appeal from declaration of ineligibility, §40.1-57.
Notice.
Termination, §40.1-56.
Termination, §40.1-55.
Appeal by employer for reemployment, §40.1-57.1.
Notification by department head, §40.1-56.
Superintendent of public instruction.
See SUPERINTENDENT OF PUBLIC INSTRUCTION.
Superintendents of public welfare.
Generally.
See SUPERINTENDENTS OF PUBLIC WELFARE.
Supreme court justices.
See SUPREME COURT JUSTICES.
Surviving spouses and dependents.
Health insurance.
Continued coverage purchases through department, §2.2-1205.
Procedure, §2.2-2819.
Qualifications, §2.2-2819.
Termination, §2.2-2819.
Continued coverage purchases through plan sponsor, §2.2-1206.
Suspension from office.
Pending hearing and appeal on removal petition, §24.2-236.
Telecommuting.
Duties of heads of state agencies, §2.2-2817.1.
Secretary of administration.
Establishment of policy, §2.2-203.1.
Temporary employees.
Personnel administration system.
Exemptions, §2.2-2905.
Terminated employees, §§2.2-3200 to 2.2-3206.
Annual report by human resources department, §2.2-1201.
Conflicts of interest.
Representing clients before agency where previously employed, §2.2-3104.
Costs, §2.2-3205.
Human resource management department.
Duties, §2.2-3201.
Involuntary separations, §2.2-3201.
Personnel administration system, §§2.2-2900 to 2.2-2905.

PUBLIC OFFICERS AND EMPLOYEES —Cont'd
Terminated employees —Cont'd
Preferential treatment, §2.2-3201.
Prerequisites to termination or layoff, §2.2-3201.
Purpose, §2.2-3200.
Reemployment, §2.2-3201.
Retirement, §2.2-3204.
Review of program, §2.2-3206.
Severance benefits announced prior to departure.
Agency heads, §2.2-106.
Governor's secretaries, §2.2-200.
Signed statement from appointees, §2.2-109.01.
Short title, §2.2-3200.
Signed statements required from appointees.
Severance benefits under workforce transition act, §2.2-109.01.
Transitional severance benefits.
Computation and payment, §2.2-3203.
Eligibility, §2.2-3202.
Terms of elected officers.
Attorney general, §24.2-210, VA Const Art V §15.
Circuit court clerks, §24.2-217.
City councils, §24.2-222.
Commissioners of revenue, §24.2-217.
Commonwealth's attorneys, §24.2-217.
County board of supervisors, §24.2-218.
Governor, §24.2-210, VA Const Art V §1.
House of delegates, general assembly, §24.2-215.
House of representatives, United States, §24.2-208.
Lieutenant governor, §24.2-210, VA Const Art V §13.
Mayors, §24.2-222.
School boards, §24.2-223.
Senators, general assembly, §24.2-214.
Senators, United States, §24.2-206.
Sheriffs, §24.2-217.
Treasurers, §24.2-217.
When terms begin.
May general election, §24.2-200.
November general election, §24.2-200.
Special elections to fill vacancies, §24.2-201.
Terrorist acts.
Removal, §24.2-233.
Tobacco indemnification and community revitalization commission, §3.2-3106.
Tobacco products.
Use by state employees, §2.2-2902.
Town councils generally.
See TOWN COUNCILS.
Town mayors generally.
See MAYORS.
Town officers and employees generally.
See TOWN OFFICERS AND EMPLOYEES.
Transfers.
Personnel administration system, §§2.2-2900 to 2.2-2905.
Transitional severance benefits.
Computation and payment, §2.2-3203.
Eligibility, §2.2-3202.
Travel expenses, §2.2-2823.
Expense accounts, §2.2-2826.
Expenses generally.
See TRAVEL EXPENSES.
Monitoring, §2.2-2824.
Persons traveling on business of locality, §§15.2-1508.1 to 15.2-1508.4.
Reimbursement for certain expenditures, §2.2-2825.
Treasurer of state.
See TREASURER OF STATE.

PUBLIC OFFICERS AND EMPLOYEES —Cont'd
Treasurers, local, §§58.1-3123 to 58.1-3172.1.
See TREASURERS, LOCAL.
Unauthorized receipt of compensation or payment.
Liability of employee receiving and employee authorizing payment, §2.2-804.
Unemployment compensation.
Benefits.
Eligibility, §60.2-615.
Employer taxation.
Financing of benefits to employees, §§60.2-506, 60.2-507.
United States.
Appointment, US Const Art II §2.
Bribery, US Const Art II §4.
Commissions, US Const Art II §3.
Emoluments, US Const Art I §9.
Holding more than one office, US Const Art I §6.
Impeachment, US Const Art II §4.
Ineligibility of members of congress, US Const Art I §6.
Presents from foreign states, US Const Art I §9.
Presidential electors.
Eligibility, US Const Art II §1.
Religious tests, US Const Art VI.
Removal, US Const Art II §4.
Treason, US Const Art II §4.
Vacancies, US Const Art II §2.
Urban county executive form of government.
Generally, §§15.2-800 to 15.2-858.
See URBAN COUNTY EXECUTIVE FORM OF GOVERNMENT.
Vacancies in elected office.
Attorney general, §24.2-213.
Congress, §§24.2-207, 24.2-208.
Constitutional (local) and local offices, §§24.2-225 to 24.2-229.1.
Applicability of provisions, §24.2-225.
Election generally, §24.2-226.
Interim appointment.
Court appointment of constitutional or local elected offices other than local governing body, §24.2-227.
Local governing body, §24.2-228.
Legitimacy of votes by appointees, §24.2-229.1.
Mayors.
Interim appointments, §24.2-228.
Time to qualify and give bond, §24.2-229.
General assembly, §24.2-216.
Writs of election issued, VA Const Art IV §7.
Governor.
Discharge of duties when office vacate, §24.2-211.
House of representatives, United States, §24.2-209.
Lieutenant governor.
Discharge of duties, §24.2-212.
Senators, United States, §24.2-207.
Term of officer elected to fill.
Commencement and expiration, §24.2-201.
Vacancies in office.
Constitutional (local) and local officers.
Filling vacancy in constitutional office, §24.2-228.1.
Disappearance of public officer.
Presumption of vacancy, §2.2-2829.
Filling by Governor, §2.2-2830.
Vacancies in state offices.
Boards, commission, etc., appointed by governor.
List prepared by secretary of Commonwealth, §2.2-405.

PUBLIC OFFICERS AND EMPLOYEES —Cont'd
Vacancies in state offices —Cont'd
Incapacitation.
Vacancy occurring when officer determined incapacitated, §24.2-232.
Secretary of the Commonwealth's office, filling, §2.2-400.
Venue.
Conflicts of interest, §2.2-3127.
Veterans and surviving spouses and children.
Personnel administration system.
Preferences, §2.2-2903.
Virginia Commonwealth University health system authority.
Exemption from work transition act, §23-50.16:34.
Virginia retirement system.
General provisions, §§51.1-124.1 to 51.1-169.
See VIRGINIA RETIREMENT SYSTEM.
Group insurance program, §§51.1-500 to 51.1-514.
Volunteer fire and rescue services.
Leave for, §2.2-2821.2.
Wage assignments.
Liability for debt owed to Commonwealth, §2.2-2816.
Whistleblowing.
Fraud and abuse whistleblower protection act, §§2.2-3009 to 2.2-3014.
See WHISTLEBLOWING.
Workers' compensation, §2.2-2821.
Workers' compensation coverage.
Employee defined, §65.2-101.
Workforce transition act of 1995.
Short title, §§2.2-3200 to 2.2-3206.
Signed statements required from appointees regarding severance benefits, §2.2-109.01.

PUBLIC-PRIVATE CONTRACTS.
Tax commissioner.
Financing agency technology needs, §58.1-202.2.

PUBLIC-PRIVATE EDUCATION FACILITIES AND INFRASTRUCTURE ACT, §§56-575.1 to 56-575.18.
See PUBLIC BUILDINGS.

PUBLIC-PRIVATE PARTNERSHIP ADVISORY COMMISSION, §§30-278 to 30-281.
Confidentiality of records, §30-281.
Definitions, §30-278.
Members, §30-279.
Proposals for qualifying projects, §30-280.
Purpose, §30-279.

PUBLIC-PRIVATE PARTNERSHIP CONTRACTS.
Public private partnership oversight advisory committee.
Review and approval of contract terms, §58.1-202.2.

PUBLIC-PRIVATE TRANSPORTATION ACT, §§56-556 to 56-574.
See TRANSPORTATION.

PUBLIC PROCUREMENT, §§2.2-4300 to 2.2-4377.
ABC board.
Exempt purchases, §4.1-104.
Actions by bidders or offerors generally, §2.2-4364.
Actions through designated or authorized officers or employees, §2.2-4302.
Administrative appeals procedure, §2.2-4365.

PUBLIC PROCUREMENT —Cont'd
Agreements for cooperative procurement, §2.2-4304.
Aliens.
Employment of unauthorized aliens.
Prohibition, contract provisions, §2.2-4311.1.
Alternative dispute resolution, §2.2-4366.
Appeals.
Administrative appeals procedure, §2.2-4365.
Denial of bid withdrawal, §2.2-4358.
Effect upon contracts, §2.2-4361.
Authorities to develop former federal areas.
Authority subject to terms of act, §15.2-6314.1.
Award of contract.
Discrimination prohibited, §2.2-4200.
Web publication, §2.2-4303.
Bid bonds, §2.2-4336.
Alternative forms of security, §2.2-4338.
Other than construction projects, §2.2-4339.
Bids and bidding.
Competitive sealed bidding.
Defined, §2.2-4301.
Process, §2.2-4302.1.
Birth-related neurological injury compensation.
Compliance with procurement policies, §38.2-5002.1.
Blind and visually impaired.
Information technology access.
Requirements, §2.2-3503.
Bonds, surety.
Bid bonds, §2.2-4336.
Alternative forms of security, §2.2-4338.
Other than construction projects, §2.2-4339.
Payment bonds, §2.2-4337.
Actions on, §2.2-4341.
Other than construction projects, §2.2-4339.
Performance bonds, §2.2-4337.
Action on, §2.2-4340.
Other than construction projects, §2.2-4339.
Brand names.
Use of, §2.2-4315.
Business authorized to transact business in Commonwealth.
Required, information included in solicitation, §2.2-4311.2.
Cancellation of bids or proposals, §2.2-4319.
Cash escrow in lieu of bond, §2.2-4338.
Cashier's check in lieu of bond, §2.2-4338.
Certified check in lieu of bond, §2.2-4338.
Claims on contracts, §2.2-4363.
Coal.
Virginia coal used in state facilities.
Preference for, §2.2-4325.
Colleges and universities.
Restructured financial and administrative operations.
Exemptions, deviation from provisions, §23-38.110.
Vendors, use.
Small business and supplier diversity department, determination of criteria, §2.2-1609.
Commercial space flight authority.
Exemption, §2.2-2215.
Community reinvestment.
Contracts for investment of funds.
Affordable housing preferences, §2.2-4327.
Competitive exemptions.
Elections materials and services.
Exemptions, §2.2-4346.

PUBLIC PROCUREMENT —Cont'd
Competitive exemptions —Cont'd
Requirements for competitive procurement, §2.2-4344.
Competitive government act, §§2.2-5512, 2.2-5513.
Competitive negotiation.
Defined, §2.2-4301.
Methods of procurement, §2.2-4303.
Process, §2.2-4302.2.
Public school contracts providing for caps and gowns, photographs, etc., §2.2-4346.
Request for proposal, §2.2-4302.2.
Competitive sealed bidding.
Actions by bidders or offerors generally, §2.2-4364.
Award to lowest responsive and responsible bidder, §2.2-4302.1.
Bonds, §2.2-4336.
Alternative forms of security, §2.2-4338.
Other than construction projects, §2.2-4339.
Cancellation or rejection, §2.2-4319.
Defined, §2.2-4301.
Errors in bids.
Action on denial of withdrawal of bid, §2.2-4364.
Appeal of denial of withdrawal of bid, §2.2-4358.
Withdrawal due to error, §2.2-4330.
Evaluation of bids, §2.2-4302.1.
Exemptions from chapter, §2.2-4345.
Invitation to bid, §2.2-4302.1.
Lowest responsible bidder.
Award to lowest responsive and responsible bidder, §2.2-4302.1.
Negotiation with, §2.2-4318.
Methods of procurement, §2.2-4303.
Negotiation with lowest responsible bidder, §2.2-4318.
Nonresponsibility determination, §2.2-4359.
Actions by bidders, §2.2-4364.
Process, §2.2-4302.1.
Public opening and announcement of all bids received, §2.2-4302.1.
Public-private education facilities and infrastructure act, §56-575.16.
Specification comments, §2.2-4316.
State aid projects, §2.2-4305.
Tie bids.
Preference for local products and firms, §2.2-4328.
Transportation department.
Acceptance of bids, §2.2-4322.
Public-private transportation act, §56-573.1.
Computers.
Information technologies agency, §2.2-2012.
Construction contracts.
Methods of procurement, §§2.2-4302.3, 2.2-4303.
Progress payments.
Estimated percentage of completion, §2.2-4333.
Retainage, §2.2-4333.
Unreasonable delays in performance of public contracts.
Provisions barring damages void, §2.2-4335.
Construction management basis.
Method for procuring construction, §§2.2-4302.3, 2.2-4303.
Construction management contracts, §2.2-4306.
Juvenile correctional facilities, §2.2-4307.
Contract formation and administration, §§2.2-4303 to 2.2-4342.
Competitive sealed bidding.
State aid projects, §2.2-4305.

PUBLIC PROCUREMENT —Cont'd
Contract formation and administration —Cont'd
Construction management contracts, §2.2-4306.
Juvenile correctional facilities, §2.2-4307.
Cooperative procurement, §2.2-4304.
Design-build contracts, §2.2-4306.
Juvenile correctional facilities, §2.2-4307.
Public bodies other than Commonwealth, §2.2-4308.
Discrimination in awarding contracts.
Prohibition, §2.2-4200.
Employment discrimination by contractor.
Prohibition, required contract provisions, §2.2-4201.
E-Verify program.
Use required, §2.2-4308.2.
Fixed-price contracts.
Public bodies other than Commonwealth, §2.2-4308.
Insurance.
Owner-controlled insurance program.
Purchase by public body, §2.2-4308.1.
Juvenile correctional facilities.
Fixed-price or not-to-exceed price design-build and construction management contract, §2.2-4307.
Modification of contract, §2.2-4309.
Not-to-exceed-price contracts.
Juvenile correctional facilities, §2.2-4307.
Owner-controlled insurance program.
Purchase by public body, §2.2-4308.1.
Prohibited contracts.
Retail sales and use tax.
Dealers not in compliance with, §2.2-4321.1.
Public works contracts, §2.2-4321.2.
Retail sales and use tax.
Dealers not in compliance with, §2.2-4321.1.
Contractors.
Debarment, §2.2-4321.
Employment discrimination.
Prohibition, required contract provisions, §2.2-4201.
Prequalification, §2.2-4317.
Workers' compensation.
Requirements for contractors and subcontractors, §2.2-4332.
Contract pricing arrangements, §2.2-4331.
Contractual claims or disputes, §2.2-4363.
Cooperative procurement, §2.2-4304.
Correctional facilities products and services, §2.2-1116.
Cost plus percentage of costs contracts, §2.2-4331.
Cost reimbursement basis contracts, §2.2-4331.
Damages for unreasonable delays in performance.
Public construction contracts.
Provisions barring damages void, §2.2-4335.
Debarment of contractors, §2.2-4321.
Definitions, §2.2-4301.
Ethics in public contracting, §2.2-4368.
Prompt payment by state agency, §2.2-4347.
Department for the blind and vision impaired.
Purchases from, §2.2-1117.
Design-build contracts, §2.2-4306.
Juvenile correctional facilities, §2.2-4307.
Public bodies other than Commonwealth, §2.2-4308.
Direct purchases by using agency, §2.2-1120.

PUBLIC PROCUREMENT —Cont'd
Discrimination prohibited, §2.2-4310.
Awarding contracts, §2.2-4200.
Employment discrimination by contractors, §2.2-4311.
Prohibited, required contract provision, §2.2-4201.
Religion.
Contracting with faith-based organizations, §2.2-4343.1.
Division of engineering and buildings.
Generally, §§2.2-1129 to 2.2-1167.
See ENGINEERING AND BUILDINGS DIVISION.
Division of purchases and supply.
Purchases through division generally, §§2.2-1109 to 2.2-1128.
See PURCHASES AND SUPPLY DIVISION.
Drug free workplace.
Contractor provision to maintain, §2.2-4312.
Economic development partnership authority.
Exemption from act, §2.2-2244.
Elections materials and services.
Exemptions, §2.2-4346.
Emergencies.
Awarding of contract without competitive bidding or competitive negotiation, §2.2-4303.
Employment discrimination by contractors, §2.2-4311.
Prohibited, required contract provisions, §2.2-4201.
Energy forward pricing mechanisms, §2.2-4329.1.
Errors in bids.
Action on denial of withdrawal of bid, §2.2-4364.
Appeal of denial of withdrawal of bid, §2.2-4358.
Withdrawal due to error, §2.2-4330.
Escrow account procedure.
Retainage funds of political subdivisions, §2.2-4334.
Ethics in public contracting, §§2.2-4367 to 2.2-4377.
See ETHICS IN PUBLIC CONTRACTING.
E-Verify program.
Prequalification of prospective contractors, §2.2-4317.
Use required, §2.2-4308.2.
Exemptions from chapter, §§2.2-4343 to 2.2-4346.
ABC board.
Purchases by, §4.1-104.
Competitive exceptions.
Requirements for competitive procurement, §2.2-4344.
Competitive sealed bidding, §2.2-4345.
Elections materials and services, §2.2-4346.
Prisons.
Exceptions to competitive procurement, §2.2-4346.
Public school contracts providing for caps and gowns, photographs, etc.
Competitive negotiation, §2.2-4346.
Specific exemptions, §2.2-4346.
Transactions, §2.2-4343.
Fair employment contracting act, §§2.2-4200, 2.2-4201.
Faith-based organizations.
Contracting with faith-based organizations, §2.2-4343.1.
Federal E-Verify program.
Prequalification of prospective contractors, §2.2-4317.

PUBLIC PROCUREMENT —Cont'd
Federal E-Verify program —Cont'd
Use required, §2.2-4308.2.
Financial services.
Treasury board, §2.2-2417.
Fixed-price contracts, §2.2-4331.
Modification, §2.2-4309.
Procurement by public bodies.
Public contracts, §2.2-4331.
Public bodies other than Commonwealth, §2.2-4308.
Fixed price design-build method.
Method for procuring construction, §2.2-4303.
Foreign or domestic business authorized to transact business in Commonwealth.
Required, information included in solicitation, §2.2-4311.2.
Forward pricing mechanisms.
Energy, §2.2-4329.1.
Fraud or corruption in decision to award.
Injunctions, §2.2-4360.
Freedom of information act.
Excluded records, §2.2-3705.6.
Gifts, contributions, other items of value from person making bid or offeror.
Governor, governor's PAC, governor's secretaries.
Prohibition on accepting, §§2.2-3104.01, 2.2-4376.1.
Immigration law.
Compliance, contract provisions, §2.2-4311.1.
E-Verify program.
Prequalification of prospective contractors, §2.2-4317.
Use required, §2.2-4308.2.
Ineligibility notice, §2.2-4357.
Information technology.
Information technologies agency, §2.2-2012.
Injunctions.
Fraud or corruption in decision to award, §2.2-4360.
Security to protect public body, §2.2-4364.
Innovation and entrepreneurship investment authority.
Exempted from provisions, §2.2-2231.
Inspection of records, §2.2-4342.
Insurance.
Exclusion of insurance bids prohibited, §2.2-4320.
Methods of procurement, §2.2-4303.
Owner-controlled insurance program.
Purchase by public body in connection with construction contract, §2.2-4308.1.
Juvenile correctional facilities.
Fixed-price or not-to-exceed price design-build and construction management contract, §2.2-4307.
Limitations of chapter, §2.2-4343.
Local preferences.
Tie bids.
Preference for local products and firms, §2.2-4328.
Lowest responsible bidder.
Negotiation with, §2.2-4318.
Methods of procurement, §§2.2-4302.3, 2.2-4303.
Metropolitan Washington airports authority.
Exemption from act, §5.1-174.
Minority business enterprises.
Participation by businesses owned by women and minorities, §2.2-4310.
Modification of contract, §2.2-4309.
Negotiation of contract.
Without competitive bidding or competitive negotiation, §2.2-4303.

PUBLIC PROCUREMENT —Cont'd
Nonresident contractors with absolute preference, §2.2-4324.
Nonresponsibility determination, §2.2-4359.
Actions by bidders, §2.2-4364.
Notice.
Competitive negotiation.
Request for proposal, §2.2-4302.2.
Competitive sealed bidding.
Invitation to bid, §2.2-4302.1.
Ineligibility, §2.2-4357.
Notice of nonresponsibility, §2.2-4359.
Not-to-exceed-price contracts.
Juvenile correctional facilities, §2.2-4307.
Owner-controlled insurance program.
Purchase by public body in connection with construction contract, §2.2-4308.1.
Paper and paper products.
Preference for recycled products, §2.2-4326.
Payment bonds, §2.2-4337.
Alternative forms of security, §2.2-4338.
Other than construction projects, §2.2-4339.
Performance bonds, §2.2-4337.
Action on, §2.2-4340.
Alternative forms of security, §2.2-4338.
Other than construction projects, §2.2-4339.
Petition for less toxic goods and products, §2.2-4314.
Petition for recycled goods and products, §2.2-4313.
Preferences and priorities.
Community reinvestment.
Contracts for investment of funds.
Affordable housing preferences, §2.2-4327.
Nonresident contractors with absolute preference, §2.2-4324.
Recycled goods and products.
Preference for recycled paper and paper products, §2.2-4326.
Virginia products with recycled content and Virginia firms, §2.2-4324.
Tie bids.
Preference for local products and firms, §2.2-4328.
Virginia coal used in state facilities, §2.2-4325.
Virginia products with recycled content and Virginia firms, §2.2-4324.
Prequalification of prospective contractors, §2.2-4317.
Pricing mechanisms.
Energy forward pricing mechanisms, §2.2-4329.1.
Prisons.
Exceptions to competitive procurement, §2.2-4346.
Professional services.
Competitive negotiation, procurement by, §§2.2-4302.2, 2.2-4302.3, 2.2-4303.
Prompt payment.
Defect or impropriety in invoice, §2.2-4351.
Definitions, §2.2-4347.
Exemptions, §2.2-4348.
Generally, §2.2-4350.
Interest penalty, §2.2-4355.
Localities, §§2.2-4352, 2.2-4354.
Payment clauses to be included in contracts, §2.2-4354.
Postmark date deemed payment date, §2.2-4353.
Reports by comptroller, §2.2-4356.
Retainage to remain valid, §2.2-4349.
Separate payment dates, §2.2-4350.
State agency, §§2.2-4347 to 2.2-4356.
See PROMPT PAYMENT.

PUBLIC PROCUREMENT —Cont'd
Proprietary information.
Disclosure prohibited, §2.2-4342.
Protest of award or decision to award, §2.2-4360.
Effect of appeal upon contract, §2.2-4361.
Stay of award during protest, §2.2-4362.
Public school contracts providing for caps and gowns, photographs, etc.
Competitive negotiation, §2.2-4346.
Public works contracts.
Requirements, §2.2-4321.2.
Purpose of chapter, §2.2-4300.
Records.
Public inspection, §2.2-4342.
Recycled goods and products.
Petition for, §2.2-4313.
Preference for recycled paper and paper products, §2.2-4326.
Preference for Virginia products with recycled content, §2.2-4324.
Purchasing programs for state agencies, §2.2-4323.
Rejection of bids or proposals, §2.2-4319.
Religion.
Contracting with faith-based organizations, §2.2-4343.1.
Remedies, §§2.2-4357 to 2.2-4366.
Restoration of eligibility, §2.2-4357.
Retail sales and use tax.
Dealers not in compliance with.
Prohibited contracts, §2.2-4321.1.
Retainage on construction contracts, §2.2-4333.
Deposit of retained funds with local governments, §2.2-4334.
Prompt payment law.
Retainage to remain valid, §2.2-4349.
Review of procurement standards, §§2.2-4313, 2.2-4314.
Set asides.
Participation by small businesses and businesses owned by women and minorities, §2.2-4310.
Sheltered workshops.
Exceptions to requirement for competitive procurement, §2.2-4344.
Short title, §2.2-4300.
Single or term contracts.
Purchasing procedures not requiring competitive bidding or competitive negotiation, §2.2-4303.
Small business and supplier diversity department.
Vendors, use by public institutions of higher education, §2.2-1609.
Small businesses.
Participation by, §2.2-4310.
Specification comments, §2.2-4316.
State aid projects.
Competitive sealed bidding, §2.2-4305.
Stay of award during protest, §2.2-4362.
Subcontractors.
Workers' compensation.
Requirements for contractors and subcontractors, §2.2-4332.
Telecommunications goods and services.
Information technologies agency, §2.2-2012.
Tie bids.
Preference for local products and firms, §2.2-4328.
Tourism authority.
Exemption from act, §2.2-2325.
Toxic substances.
Petition for less toxic goods and products, §2.2-4314.

PUBLIC PROCUREMENT —Cont'd
Trade secrets.
Public inspection, §2.2-4342.
Transportation department.
Acceptance of bids, §2.2-4322.
Competitive sealed bidding.
Public-private transportation act, §56-573.1.
Treasury board.
Financial services, §2.2-2417.
Unreasonable delays in performance.
Public construction contracts.
Provisions barring damages void, §2.2-4335.
Virginia coal used in state facilities.
Preference for, §2.2-4325.
Virginia firms.
Preferences, §2.2-4324.
Virginia products with recycled content.
Preferences, §2.2-4324.
Waiver of informalities in bids, §2.2-4319.
Web publication.
Award of contract, §2.2-4303.
Withdrawal of bid due to error, §2.2-4330.
Action on denial, §2.2-4364.
Appeal of denial, §2.2-4358.
Women owned businesses.
Participation by, §2.2-4310.
Workers' compensation.
Requirements for contractors and subcontractors, §2.2-4332.
Workshops serving individuals with disabilities.
Purchases from nonprofit workshops, §2.2-1118.

PUBLIC PROPERTY.
Commercial space flight authority.
Conveyance, lease or transfer by city or county to authority, §2.2-2217.

PUBLIC RECORDS.
Generally.
See RECORDS.
Protection of private information, §§42.1-76 to 42.1-90.1.
Generally.
See STATE RECORDS MANAGEMENT.
Vital records, §§32.1-249 to 32.1-276.
See VITAL RECORDS.

PUBLIC RECREATIONAL FACILITIES AUTHORITIES ACT, §§15.2-5600 to 15.2-5616.
See RECREATIONAL FACILITIES AUTHORITY.

PUBLIC RESTROOMS, §§32.1-198 to 32.1-202.

PUBLIC RIGHTS OF WAY.
Localities generally, §§15.2-2000 to 15.2-2030.
See ROADS, STREETS AND PUBLIC RIGHTS OF WAY.

PUBLIC ROAD AUTHORITIES.
Local road authorities, §§33.1-224 to 33.1-246.
See LOCAL ROAD AUTHORITIES.
Transportation board.
Generally, §§33.1-1 to 33.1-23.
See TRANSPORTATION BOARD.

PUBLIC SAFETY.
Communications systems.
Freedom of information act requests.
Excluded records, §2.2-3705.2.
Department of criminal justice services.
Center for school safety, §9.1-184.

PUBLIC SAFETY —Cont'd
Department of criminal justice services —Cont'd
Comprehensive community-corrections act for local responsible offenders, §§9.1-173 to 9.1-183.
See COMMUNITY CORRECTIONS.
Court-appointed special advocate program, §§9.1-151 to 9.1-157.
Criminal justice information system, §§9.1-126 to 9.1-137.
See CRIMINAL JUSTICE INFORMATION SYSTEM.
Generally, §§9.1-100 to 9.1-116.
See CRIMINAL JUSTICE SERVICES DEPARTMENT.
Law enforcement expenditures, §§9.1-165 to 9.1-172.
Private security services businesses.
Licensing, certifying, registering and regulation, §§9.1-138 to 9.1-150.
See PRIVATE SECURITY SERVICES BUSINESSES.
Department of fire programs, §§9.1-200 to 9.1-208.
Department of forensic science, §§9.1-1100 to 9.1-1113.
See FORENSIC SCIENCE DEPARTMENT.
Discrimination.
Human rights act, §§2.2-3900 to 2.2-3903.
Firefighters and emergency medical technicians procedural guarantee act, §§9.1-300 to 9.1-304.
Human rights act, §§2.2-3900 to 2.2-3903.
Law enforcement officers procedural guarantee act, §§9.1-500 to 9.1-507.
Line of duty act, §§9.1-400 to 9.1-408.
Medal of valor.
Definition of public safety officer, §9.1-801.
Established, §9.1-800.
Secretary of public safety, §§2.2-200 to 2.2-202, 2.2-221 to 2.2-224.1.
Sex offender and crimes against minors registry, §§9.1-900 to 9.1-922.
See SEX OFFENDER REGISTRATION AND NOTIFICATION.
Special conservators of the peace, §§9.1-150.1 to 9.1-150.4.

PUBLIC SAFETY COMMUNICATIONS SYSTEMS.
Freedom of information act requests.
Excluded records, §2.2-3705.2.

PUBLIC SAFETY, DEPARTMENTS OF.
County manager form of government, §15.2-632.
Urban county executive form of government, §15.2-842.

PUBLIC SAFETY, SECRETARY OF, §§2.2-200 to 2.2-202, 2.2-221 to 2.2-224.1.

PUBLIC SCHOOL AUTHORITY, §§22.1-162 to 22.1-175.
Administration of funds.
Transferred from literary fund, §22.1-165.
Agency and instrumentality of state, §22.1-163.
Board of commissioners.
Compensation, §22.1-164.
Defined, §22.1-162.
Membership, §22.1-164.

PUBLIC SCHOOL AUTHORITY —Cont'd
Bond issues.
Bonds of the authority, defined, §22.1-162.
Exemption from taxation, §22.1-172.
Issuance of bonds of authority, §22.1-167.
Legal investments, §22.1-173.
Purchase and sale of local school bonds, §22.1-166.
Local school bonds, defined, §22.1-162.
Refunding issues, §22.1-167.1.
Pass-through of savings realized, §22.1-167.1.
Reserve fund, §22.1-168.1.
School security equipment grants, §22.1-280.2:2.
Security for payment, §§22.1-167.2, 22.1-168.
Bonds or notes issued for purpose of making grants, §22.1-167.3.
Chairman.
Designation, §22.1-164.
Creation, §22.1-163.
Definitions, §22.1-162.
Duties of authority.
Enumeration, §22.1-171.
Employee hiring, §22.1-164.
Grants.
Local school boards, §22.1-166.2.
Investment of funds, §22.1-169.
Loans.
Local school boards, §22.1-166.1.
Management of funds transferred from literary fund, §22.1-165.
Powers of authority.
Enumeration, §22.1-171.
Public body corporate, §22.1-163.
Repayments to literary fund, §22.1-170.
School security equipment grants, §22.1-280.2:2.
Service of notice, process and other papers.
Statutory agents, §22.1-174.
Transfers from literary fund to authority, §§22.1-165, 22.1-175.
Trust indenture.
Security for payment and bonds, §22.1-168.
Vice-chairman.
Election, §22.1-164.

PUBLIC SCHOOL CONSTRUCTION GRANTS PROGRAM, §§22.1-175.1 to 22.1-175.5.

PUBLIC SCHOOL EDUCATIONAL TECHNOLOGY GRANTS PROGRAM, §§22.1-175.6 to 22.1-175.9.

PUBLIC SCHOOL EMPLOYEES.
See SCHOOL PERSONNEL.

PUBLIC SCHOOL FOUNDATIONS, §22.1-212.2:2.

PUBLIC SCHOOL FUNDS, §§22.1-88 to 22.1-124.
Accounts and accounting.
Accounts to purchase certain materials and supplies, §22.1-122.1.
Compelling settlement of accounts, §22.1-121.
Credit card payments, §22.1-116.1.
Disbursement of school division funds, §22.1-116.
Fiscal agents of certain school districts, §§22.1-117, 22.1-118.
Petty cash funds, §22.1-123.
Settlement by treasurer, §22.1-120.
System of accounting, §22.1-115.
Warrants for less than face value, §22.1-124.
Annual report of expenditures, §22.1-90.
Apportionment of school funds.
Approval and certification, §22.1-99.
Federal funds apportioned containing lands leased for flood control purposes, §22.1-109.

PUBLIC SCHOOL FUNDS —Cont'd
Appropriations, §§22.1-94, 22.1-97.
Glebe lands and church property, §22.1-107.
Local appropriations for public schools, §22.1-94.
Procedure upon inadequate local funds, §22.1-97.
At-risk student academic achievement program and fund, §22.1-199.4.
Budgets.
Annual report of expenditures, §22.1-90.
Apportionment of school funds, §22.1-99.
Approval of annual budget for school purposes, §22.1-93.
Capital outlay expenditures.
Proration of operating cost, §22.1-96.
Classification of expenditures, §22.1-115.
Estimate of funds needed for public schools, §22.1-92.
Instructional costs, funds allocated for to be included in school performance report card, §22.1-90.1.
Limitation on expenditures, §22.1-91.
Local appropriations for public schools, §§22.1-94, 22.1-97.
Reduction in state aid.
Length of school term below 180 days or 990 hours, §22.1-98.
Statements of funds available, §22.1-115.
Unexpended school and educational funds, §22.1-100.
Building construction.
Proration of operating cost, expenditures, etc., §22.1-96.
Cafeteria funds.
Management of decentralized cafeteria funds, §22.1-89.1.
Capital outlay expenditures.
Proration of operating cost, §22.1-96.
City appropriations, §22.1-94.
Procedure upon insufficient educational funds, §22.1-97.
Classification of expenditures, §22.1-115.
Constituent funds, §22.1-88.
County appropriations.
Procedure upon insufficient educational funds, §22.1-97.
Credit cards.
Funds from credit cards, §22.1-89.3.
Receipt of payment by, §22.1-116.1.
Decentralized cafeteria funds.
Management system, §22.1-89.1.
Disbursement of funds, §22.1-116.
Handling of funds for joint school, §22.1-118.
Donations.
Deposit and disbursement of donations, §22.1-112.
Emergencies.
Reduction of funds for short school term.
Exception for severe weather conditions or other emergencies, §22.1-98.
Extended school year incentive program, §22.1-98.1.
Fiscal agents of certain school districts, §22.1-117.
County or city treasurer as fiscal agent, §22.1-118.
No commission for treasurer, §22.1-119.
Settlement by treasurer, §§22.1-120, 22.1-121.
Forest reserves.
Money derived from forest reserve, §22.1-108.
Glebe lands and church property, §22.1-107.
Instructional costs, funds allocated for to be included in school performance report card, §22.1-90.1.

PUBLIC SCHOOL FUNDS —Cont'd
Leases.
Lands leased for flood control purposes.
Federal funds apportioned to school divisions, §22.1-109.
Limitation on expenditures, §22.1-91.
Literary fund, §§22.1-142 to 22.1-161.
See LITERARY FUND.
Loans.
Temporary loans to school boards, §22.1-110.
Lottery proceeds non-recurring costs escrow accounts, §22.1-100.1.
Management of funds.
Appropriated funds, §22.1-89.
Cafeteria funds, §22.1-89.1.
Constituent funds, §22.1-88.
Control generally, §22.1-89.
Disposition schedule for financial records, §22.1-89.2.
Retention of financial records, §22.1-89.2.
Nonresident students.
Increase of funds, §22.1-101.1.
180 days or 990 hours school term.
Reduction in length of school term.
State aid reduced, §22.1-98.
Out-of-state placing agencies or persons.
Billing for nonresident students, §22.1-101.1.
Payment of claims.
Accounts to purchase certain materials and supplies, §22.1-121.
Approval, §22.1-122.
Petty cash funds, §22.1-123.
Prohibited acts, §22.1-122.
Warrants, §§22.1-122, 22.1-124.
Petty cash funds.
Payment of claims, §22.1-123.
Purchase of school materials and supplies.
Payment of claims, §22.1-122.1.
Records.
Financial records.
Funds from telephone service or credit cards, §22.1-89.3.
Retention and disposition schedule, §22.1-89.2.
Reports.
Annual report of expenditures, §22.1-90.
School term.
Extended school year incentive program, §22.1-98.1.
Length of school term below 180 days or 990 hours.
Reduction of state aid, §22.1-98.
Small schools.
Cost saving agreements with contiguous schools.
Calculation of funding to small school at level owed to contiguous school, §22.1-98.2.
Special taxes, §§22.1-102 to 22.1-106.
Certification of results, §§22.1-105, 22.1-106.
Conduct of referendum, §22.1-105.
Levy in accordance with referendum results, §22.1-106.
Levy of tax authorized, §22.1-102.
Order for referendum, §22.1-104.
Petition for referendum, §22.1-103.
Request by school board, §22.1-103.
Uniform county levy in lieu of district levies, §22.1-103.
State aid reduction.
Length of school term below 180 days or 990 hours, §22.1-98.
System of accounting, §22.1-115.

PUBLIC SCHOOL FUNDS —Cont'd
Taxes.
Duty to levy school tax.
County appropriations for public schools, §22.1-94.
Special taxes, §§22.1-102 to 22.1-106.
Telephones.
Funds from telephone services, §22.1-89.3.
Temporary loans to school boards, §22.1-110.
Town appropriations, §22.1-94.
Procedure upon insufficient educational funds, §22.1-97.
Town school division funds, §§22.1-113, 22.1-114.
Trust funds, §22.1-111.
Unexpended school and educational funds, §22.1-100.
Weather closings.
Reduction of funds for short school term.
Exception for severe weather conditions or other emergencies, §22.1-98.

PUBLIC SCHOOL TAXES.
Special county, district, city or town tax, §§22.1-102 to 22.1-106.

PUBLIC SCHOOL TRANSPORTATION.
School buses.
Generally, §§22.1-176 to 22.1-198.
See SCHOOL BUSES.

PUBLIC SERVICE COMPANIES, §§56-1 to 56-46.3.
Administration and judicial review of assessment in tax, §§58.1-2670 to 58.1-2676.
Affiliated interests, §§56-76 to 56-87.
Appeals from commission decisions, §56-86.
Contract approval, §56-77.
Defined terms, §56-76.
Dividend payments to.
Orders prohibiting, §56-83.
Obligation assumption approval, §56-82.
Payment accounts.
Exclusions from, §56-78.
Payments as operating expenses or capital expenditures.
Orders prohibiting treatment of, §56-81.
Payments to.
Proof of costs, §56-79.
Procedure before commission, §56-84.
Provision violations, §56-85.
Rules of commission to carry out chapter, §56-87.
Supervision by commission, §56-80.
Alley use without consent or compensation, §56-14.
Articles of incorporation.
Statement of kind of business and brief description, §13.1-620.
Assessments against property.
Increase in assessed value, §58.1-2604.
Books, inspections of, §56-36.
Boundaries of political unit furnished to by commissioners of revenue, §58.1-2601.
Boundaries of political units to be furnished company, state corporation commission and department of taxation, §58.1-2601.
Certificates of public convenience and necessity.
Limousines and executive sedan carriers.
See LIMOUSINES AND EXECUTIVE SEDAN CARRIERS.
Public utilities.
Generally, §§56-265.1 to 56-265.9.
See PUBLIC UTILITIES.

PUBLIC SERVICE COMPANIES —Cont'd
Charters.
Repeals, §56-8.
City regulation powers, §56-37.
Claim settlements by commission, §56-38.
Common law remedies not altered or abridged, §56-7.
Companies in which Commonwealth interested, §§56-46.1, 56-46.2.
Environmental, economic and service reliability factors in approving construction, §56-46.1.
Complaint.
Examination by commission, §56-43.
Connections between corporations.
General assembly may require, §56-34.
Consumer protection.
Application of provisions, §59.1-199.
Consumer utility taxes, §§58.1-3814 to 58.1-3816.2.
Cooperatives.
Foreign cooperatives, §13.1-309.1.
Corporations generally, §§13.1-601 to 13.1-779.
See CORPORATIONS.
County executive or county manager governments.
Special provisions for assessments, §§58.1-2680 to 58.1-2683.
County regulation powers, §56-37.
Crossings and connections, §§56-16 to 56-34.
Course changes to avoid crossings, §§56-22, 56-29.
Highways, §56-23.
Applications, §56-27.
Change of highway course to avoid crossings, §56-29.
Construction, §56-25.
Contests by county or Commonwealth, §56-28.
Cost, §56-26.
Damage payments, §56-30.
Effect of, §56-24.
Limitation on rights if altering, closing or obstructing highway or stream involved, §56-32.
Work to proceed, §56-31.
Right of one to cross the works of another, §56-17.
Contests by companies whose works are crossed, §56-19.
Cost, §56-17.
Course changes to avoid crossings, §56-22.
Payment of damages, §56-20.
Submission of plans, §56-18.
Work to proceed, §56-21.
Utility lines crossing railroads, §56-16.1.
Municipalities, §56-16.2.
Wagonway construction, §56-16.
Damage or trespass to, §18.2-162.
Triple damages, §56-5.
Defined terms, §56-1.
Affiliated interest, §56-76.
Environment, §56-46.1.
Historic, §56-46.1.
Interested parties, §56-46.1.
Loan, §56-55.
Public service company, §§56-55, 56-76.
Public utility, §56-46.1.
Qualifying facilities, §56-46.1.
Reasonably accommodate requests to wheel or transmit power, §56-46.1.
Securities, §56-55.
Total capitalization, §56-55.
Designation as, §§56-1.1, 56-1.2.
Diverting service, §§8.01-44.7, 18.2-163.

PUBLIC SERVICE COMPANIES —Cont'd
Duty of corporation whose wires cross other works, §56-33.
Electric vehicle charging services.
Definitions, §56-1.
Regulation by commission, §56-232.2:1.
Retail sale of electricity, §56-1.2:1.
Eminent domain.
Highways and roads.
Acquisition of interest for exchange, §33.1-96.
Hydroelectric power.
Right of eminent domain, §62.1-98.
Enterprise zones.
Eligibility, §59.1-279.
Erosion and sediment control.
General erosion and sediment control specifications, annual filing, §62.1-44.15:55.
Estimated tax.
Water, heat, light, power and pipeline companies, §§58.1-2640 to 58.1-2651.
See PUBLIC SERVICE CORPORATION TAXATION.
Executive sedans generally.
See LIMOUSINES AND EXECUTIVE SEDAN CARRIERS.
Expenses prior to organization, §56-3.
Foreign cooperatives, §13.1-309.1.
Foreign utility companies.
Protection of public interests from adverse effects, §56-46.3.
Free services to public officers and employees, §56-8.1.
General assembly members.
Free services to, §56-8.1.
Governance by provisions of title, §56-2.
Highway corporations, §§56-535 to 56-552.
See HIGHWAY CORPORATIONS.
Household goods carriers.
See HOUSEHOLD GOODS CARRIERS.
Improvement, local taxation, §58.1-2609.
Income tax on corporations.
Clean-fuel vehicle credit, §58.1-438.1.
Exemptions, §58.1-401.
Major business facility job tax credit, §58.1-439.
Intangible personal property.
No state or local tax on, §58.1-2690.
Issuance of stocks, bonds, etc., §§56-55 to 56-75.
Application, §56-60.
Action of commission, §56-61.
Appeal, §56-63.
Fees, §56-75.
Void if order not obtained, §56-67.
Application of chapter, §56-57.
Exceptions, §56-65.
Short-term indebtedness, §56-65.1.
Capitalization of permits, franchises or contracts for consolidation.
Commission power, §56-66.
Commonwealth liability, §56-74.
Defined terms, §56-55.
Joint actions with commission of another state, §56-62.
Licensed salesmen requirements, §56-68.
Officer's acts bind company, §56-72.
Privilege, §56-56.
Proceeds.
Accounting for disposition of, §56-70.
Purposes to which proceeds may be applied, §56-69.
Provision violations, §56-71.
Employee violations, §56-73.

PUBLIC SERVICE COMPANIES —Cont'd
Issuance of stocks, bonds, etc. —Cont'd
Provision violations —Cont'd
Officer violations, §56-73.
Purposes, §56-58.
Short-term indebtedness, §56-65.1.
Sureties.
Order required before acting as, §56-59.
Validity of authorized securities, §56-67.1.
Joint ventures, §13.1-627.
License taxes, §58.1-3731.
Localities generally prohibited from imposing, §58.1-3703.
Telegraph, telephone, water, heat, etc., companies, §§58.1-2620 to 58.1-2635.
See PUBLIC SERVICE CORPORATION TAXATION.
Lien of taxes, §58.1-2612.
Limousines and executive sedan carriers.
See LIMOUSINES AND EXECUTIVE SEDAN CARRIERS.
Metering devices, tampering with, §§8.01-44.7, 18.2-163.
Motor launch carriers.
See MOTOR LAUNCH CARRIERS.
Moving companies.
See HOUSEHOLD GOODS CARRIERS.
Obtaining services without payment, §18.2-187.1.
Organization.
Expenses prior to, §56-3.
Partnership agreements, §13.1-627.
Pay telephone registration, §§56-508.15, 56-508.16.
Personal property taxes, §58.1-2606.
Assessment by central state agency, VA Const Art X §2.
Assessment of property by tax commissioner, §§58.1-2655 to 58.1-2657.
Motor carrier rolling stock, prohibited taxes, §58.1-2658.
Railroads, §58.1-2607.
Petroleum tank truck carriers.
Employee liens, §§43-24 to 43-26.
Not required to incorporate as public service companies, §13.1-620.
Supplier liens, §§43-24 to 43-26.
Transportation companies generally, §§56-99.2 to 56-140.
See TRANSPORTATION COMPANIES.
Powers, §56-49.
Property.
Treble damages for injury to, §56-5.
Provision applicability, §56-2.
Public ground use without consent or compensation, §56-14.
Public-private transportation act.
Crossing utility's facilities, §56-570.
Public utilities.
Generally, §§56-232 to 56-265.
See PUBLIC UTILITIES.
Railroads.
Generally.
See RAILROADS.
Rates.
Appeals, §56-8.2.
Notice when rate is reduced, §56-40.
Passing capital project costs to customers.
Burden of proof, §56-234.3.
Utility pole use, §56-41.1.

PUBLIC SERVICE COMPANIES —Cont'd
Real property taxes, §58.1-2606.
Assessment by central state agency, VA Const Art X §2.
Assessment in localities requiring payment in installments, §58.1-3917.
Assessment of separately owned land and improvements, §58.1-3282.
Easement acquired, deduction from value of real estate, §58.1-3354.
Notice to state corporation commission and department of taxation, §58.1-3355.
Local taxation.
Land and nonutility and noncarrier improvements, §58.1-2609.
Railroads, §58.1-2607.
Assessment of property by tax commissioner, §§58.1-2655 to 58.1-2657.
Taxable real estate, §58.1-3201.
Records, inspections of, §56-36.
Regulation of, §56-35.
Remedies not altered or abridged, §56-7.
Remedies of persons aggrieved by, §56-6.
Reports.
Special reports to commission, §56-36.
Retail sales and use tax direct payment permits, §58.1-624.
Right-of-way easements.
Conveyance to companies by state departments and agencies, §2.2-1150.
Rolling stock tax, §§58.1-2652 to 58.1-2659.
Sale of company, §56-9.
Claims against company, §56-11.
Debts of company, §56-11.
Effect, §§56-10, 56-13.
Holding of property sold under decree of court, §56-12.
Security registration exemptions, §13.1-514.
Sewerage companies, §§56-261 to 56-265.
Small sewer utilities, §§56-265.13:1 to 56-265.13:7.
Sewerage systems not regulated as public utilities, §§56-265.10 to 56-265.13.
Sight-seeing carriers.
Boat carriers.
See SIGHT-SEEING CARRIERS.
Generally.
See SIGHT-SEEING CARRIERS.
Small investor-owned telephone utilities, §§56-531 to 56-534.
Small water or sewer public utilities, §§56-265.13:1 to 56-265.13:7.
Special or charter party carriers.
See SPECIAL OR CHARTER PARTY CARRIERS.
Special regulatory revenue taxes, §§58.1-2660 to 58.1-2665.
State corporation commission generally, §§12.1-1 to 12.1-43.
See STATE CORPORATION COMMISSION.
State operation of public utilities, §§56-509 to 56-528.
See PUBLIC UTILITIES, STATE OPERATION.
Stock corporations generally.
See CORPORATIONS.
Streets and roads.
Occupation of, §§56-14, 56-15.
Regulation of use, §56-14.
Submerged lands.
Structures, maintenance or removal, §28.2-1209.
Taxation generally, §§58.1-2600 to 58.1-2690.
See PUBLIC SERVICE CORPORATION TAXATION.

PUBLIC SERVICE COMPANIES —Cont'd
Telegraph or telephone companies, §§56-458 to 56-484.3.
See TELEGRAPH OR TELEPHONE COMPANIES.
Telephone cooperatives, §§56-485 to 56-508.
See TELEPHONE COOPERATIVES.
Transportation companies.
Generally, §§56-99.2 to 56-140.
See TRANSPORTATION COMPANIES.
Trespass, §18.2-162.
Utility lines.
Construction, §56-46.2.
Environmental, economic and service reliability factors, §56-46.1.
Duty where wires cross other works, §56-33.
Permits, §56-15.
Public-private education facilities and infrastructure act.
Utility crossings, §56-575.13.
Underground utility line damage prevention, §§56-265.14 to 56-265.32.
See UNDERGROUND UTILITY LINE DAMAGE PREVENTION.
Utility plant sales or leases to cities or towns, §56-254.
Voice-over-Internet protocol service.
Defined, §56-1.
E-911 access.
Notice to subscribers of lack of, §56-484.12:1.
Plan for, §56-484.12:2.
Regulation of, §56-1.3.
Water supply companies, §§56-261 to 56-265.
Small water utilities, §§56-265.13:1 to 56-265.13:7.
Water systems not regulated as public utilities, §§56-265.10 to 56-265.13.

PUBLIC SERVICE CORPORATION TAXATION, §§58.1-2600 to 58.1-2690.
Administrative and judicial review of assessment and tax, §§58.1-2670 to 58.1-2676.
Appeals to supreme court, §§58.1-2675, 58.1-2676.
Application for correction of certification of gross receipts, §58.1-2674.1.
Application to court to correct erroneous local assessment ratio, §58.1-2670.1.
Application to state corporation commission or department of taxation, §58.1-2670.
Correction after hearing or investigation, §58.1-2673.
Applications, §58.1-2674.1.
Enforcement of proceedings, §58.1-2673.
Hearings.
Setting for hearings, §58.1-2671.
Mandamus, enforcement of commission orders, §58.1-2673.
Motion of state corporation commission to review, §58.1-2672.
Notice of hearing to adverse parties, §58.1-2671.
Notice of hearing to Commonwealth, §58.1-2674.
Review on motion of state corporation commission, §58.1-2672.
Service of notice to Commonwealth, §58.1-2674.
Supreme court appeals, §§58.1-2675, 58.1-2676.
Time for application to commission or department for review, §58.1-2670.
Assessments against property.
Review by local authorities, §58.1-2602.
Consumer utility taxes, §§58.1-3814 to 58.1-3816.2.

PUBLIC SERVICE CORPORATION TAXATION —Cont'd
County executive or county manager governments, special provisions for assessments, §§58.1-2680 to 58.1-2683.
Definitions, §58.1-2600.
Estimated tax.
Water, heat, light, power and pipeline companies, §§58.1-2640 to 58.1-2651.
Amendments to declaration, §58.1-2642.
Declarations.
Amendments, §58.1-2642.
Late filing, §58.1-2645.
Requirement and contents, §58.1-2640.
Time for filing, §58.1-2641.
Where filed, §58.1-2647.
Extensions of time for payments, §58.1-2646.
Failure to pay, §58.1-2648.
Exceptions, §58.1-2649.
Inconsistency with provisions affecting taxpayers beginning or going out of business, §58.1-2650.
Installment payments, §58.1-2643.
Late filing of declarations, §58.1-2645.
On account of tax for tax year, payments, §58.1-2644.
Other provisions of chapter not affected by article, §58.1-2650.
Overpayment, §58.1-2647.
Payment, §58.1-2643.
Extension of time, §58.1-2646.
Failure to pay, §58.1-2648.
Exceptions, §58.1-2649.
How made, §58.1-2647.
On account of tax for tax year, §58.1-2644.
Provisions not applicable to special revenue taxes, §58.1-2651.
Refunds, §58.1-2647.
Requirement of declaration, §58.1-2640.
Special revenue taxes, provisions not applicable to, §58.1-2651.
Time for filing declaration, §58.1-2641.
Underpayments, §58.1-2648.
Where declarations filed and how payments made, §58.1-2647.
Extension of local levies by commissioners of revenue, §58.1-2603.
Failure to file timely reports, §58.1-2610.
Failure to pay tax, §58.1-2611.
Improvements, local taxation, §58.1-2609.
Income tax on corporations.
Clean-fuel vehicle credit, §58.1-438.1.
Exemptions, §58.1-401.
Major business facility job tax credit, §58.1-439.
Increase in assessed valuation, §58.1-2604.
License taxes imposed by county, city or town, §58.1-3731.
Prohibition generally, §58.1-3703.
License tax on telegraph, telephone, water, heat, light, power and pipeline companies, §§58.1-2620 to 58.1-2635.
Acquisition of business of another corporation.
Applicability of other provisions to, §58.1-2632.
Gross receipts, §58.1-2630.
Annual state license tax.
Companies furnishing water, heat, light or power, §58.1-2620.
Pipeline companies, §58.1-2627.1.
Annual tax on companies, §58.1-2626.
Assessment by state corporation commission, §58.1-2633.
Copies forwarded to interested parties, §58.1-2634.

PUBLIC SERVICE CORPORATION TAXATION —Cont'd
License tax on telegraph, telephone, water, heat, light, power and pipeline companies —Cont'd
Basis of tax, §58.1-2620.
Consolidation or merger.
Applicability of other provisions to, §58.1-2632.
Gross receipts in cases of, §58.1-2631.
Corporations commencing business, §58.1-2629.
Applicability of other provisions to, §58.1-2632.
Credit against tax.
Virginia coal employment and production incentive tax credit, §58.1-2626.1.
Date of payment of taxes, §58.1-2635.
Estimated tax on water, heat, light, power and pipeline companies, §§58.1-2640 to 58.1-2651.
Estimate of gross receipts.
Corporations commencing business, §58.1-2629.
Exemptions, §58.1-2627.
Gross receipts, basis of tax, §58.1-2620.
Gross receipts in cases of acquisition of business of another corporation, §58.1-2630.
Gross receipts in cases of consolidation or merger, §58.1-2631.
Heat companies.
Annual state license tax, §58.1-2620.
Light companies.
Annual state license tax, §58.1-2620.
Local taxation, assessment of value of property subject to, §58.1-2633.
Copies forwarded to interested parties, §58.1-2634.
Local tax on telegraph or telephone companies, §58.1-2690.
Payment of taxes.
Date, §58.1-2635.
Pipeline companies.
Annual state license tax, §58.1-2627.1.
Power companies.
Annual state license tax, §58.1-2620.
Rate of tax on companies furnishing water, heat, light or power, §58.1-2620.
Rate of tax on pipeline companies, §58.1-2627.1.
Reports annually, §58.1-2628.
Virginia coal employment and production incentive tax credit, §58.1-2626.1.
Water companies.
Annual state license tax, §58.1-2620.
Lien of taxes, §58.1-2612.
Local authorities to examine assessments against property, §58.1-2602.
Local levies extended by commissioners of revenue, §58.1-2603.
Major business facility job tax credit, §58.1-439.
Payment of tax.
Failure to pay, §58.1-2611.
Personal property taxes, §58.1-2606.
Assessment of tangible personalty by central state agency, VA Const Art X §1.
Motor carrier rolling stock, property taxes prohibited, §58.1-2658.
Railroads, §58.1-2607.
Assessment of property by tax commissioner, §§58.1-2655 to 58.1-2657.
Railroads.
Personal property taxes, §58.1-2607.
Assessment of property by tax commissioner, §§58.1-2655 to 58.1-2657.
Real property taxes, §58.1-2607.
Assessment of property by tax commissioner, §§58.1-2655 to 58.1-2657.

PUBLIC SERVICE CORPORATION TAXATION —Cont'd
Railroads —Cont'd
State taxation, §58.1-2608.
Real property taxes, §58.1-2606.
Assessment in localities requiring payment in installments, §58.1-3917.
Assessment of separately owned land and improvements, §58.1-3282.
Easement acquired, deduction from value of real estate, §§58.1-3354, 58.1-3355.
Railroads, §58.1-2607.
Assessment of property by tax commissioner, §§58.1-2655 to 58.1-2657.
Taxable real estate, §58.1-3201.
Reports.
Failure to file timely reports, §58.1-2610.
Retail sales and use tax direct payment permits, §58.1-624.
Revenue taxes of public service corporations, §§58.1-2660 to 58.1-2665.
Rolling stock tax, §§58.1-2652 to 58.1-2659.
Assessment of property by department of taxation and state corporation commission, §58.1-2655.
Copies of assessments furnished taxpayers and local officials, §58.1-2657.
Valuation of sidetracks, double tracks, etc., §58.1-2656.
Date of payment, §58.1-2652.
Distribution of taxes, §§58.1-2658, 58.1-2658.1.
Exemptions under federal law.
Article not applicable to, §58.1-2659.
Failure of motor carriers to properly file reports, §58.1-2654.1.
Federal law exemptions.
Article not applicable to, §58.1-2659.
Rate, §58.1-2652.
Report of motor vehicle carriers, §58.1-2654.
Failure to properly file reports, §58.1-2654.1.
Report of railroads and freight car companies, §58.1-2653.
Sidetracks, double tracks, etc., valuation, §58.1-2656.
State tax, §58.1-2652.
Special regulatory revenue taxes, §§58.1-2660 to 58.1-2665.
Assessment, §58.1-2663.
When not assessed or assessed only in part, §58.1-2664.
Collection, §58.1-2663.
Computation of tax on railroads, §58.1-2662.
Exceptions, §58.1-2661.
Gross receipts of telephone and telegraph company, §58.1-2662.1.
Gross receipts of water, heat, light or power companies, §58.1-2662.2.
Levy, §58.1-2660.
Payment, §58.1-2663.
Purposes of taxes collected, §58.1-2665.
Railroads.
Based upon gross transportation receipts, §58.1-2662.
Exceptions, §58.1-2661.
Rates, §58.1-2660.
Telephone and telegraph companies.
Gross receipts, §58.1-2662.1.
Uses of taxes collected, §58.1-2665.
Water, heat, light or power companies.
Gross receipts, §58.1-2662.2.
When assessed or assessed only in part, §58.1-2664.

PUBLIC SERVICE CORPORATION TAXATION —Cont'd
State taxation of railroads, telecommunications companies, §58.1-2608.
Telecommunications companies.
State taxation, §58.1-2608.

PUBLIC SQUARES.
Injuries to trees, fences or herbage on, §18.2-139.

PUBLIC SWEARING, §18.2-388, VA SCt Rules 3C:1, 3C:2.

PUBLIC SWIMMING OR BATHING AREA.
Placement of markers designating.
Petition requesting, costs, motorboating or water skiing prohibited, §29.1-734.

PUBLIC TELEPHONE INFORMATION ACT, §§59.1-424 to 59.1-427.

PUBLIC TRANSPORTATION.
Biodiesel and other alternative fuels.
Use encourage in public transportation vehicles, §§67-500, 67-501.
Charlottesville-Albemarle regional transit authority, §§15.2-7022 to 15.2-7035.
See CHARLOTTESVILLE-ALBEMARLE REGIONAL TRANSIT AUTHORITY.
Counties, cities or towns.
Designation of source of revenue from mass transit, §15.2-948.
Shared ride taxi systems, §15.2-949.
System of transportation for locality not member of transportation district, §15.2-947.
Discrimination against persons with disabilities, §51.5-44.
Local income tax.
Revenues distributed to be applied and expended for, §58.1-548.
Mass transit fund.
Retail sales and use tax revenue disposition, §58.1-638.
Motor vehicle fuel sales tax, §§58.1-1718.1 to 58.1-1724.4.
Recordation tax, state distributions to cities and counties for transportation purposes, §58.1-816.
Richmond metropolitan authority, §§15.2-7000 to 15.2-7021.
See RICHMOND METROPOLITAN AUTHORITY.
Rights of persons with disabilities, §51.5-44.
Service districts, §§15.2-2400 to 15.2-2403.3.
Trespass, §18.2-160.2.

PUBLIC USES.
Taking of private property for, VA Const Art I §11.

PUBLIC UTILITIES, §§56-232 to 56-265.
Abandonment of property.
Presumption.
Deposits held by utilities, §55-210.5.
Acquisition, disposition or sale of assets or securities, §§56-88 to 56-92.
Acts substitution by commission, §56-247.
Affiliated interests.
Regulation of relations with, §§56-76 to 56-87.
See PUBLIC SERVICE COMPANIES.
Air pollution control.
Exemption from enforcement, §10.1-1307.3.
Alley use without consent or compensation, §56-14.

PUBLIC UTILITIES —Cont'd
Articles of incorporation.
Statement of kinds of business and brief description, §13.1-620.
BVU authority, §§15.2-7200 to 15.2-7226.
See BVU AUTHORITY.
Capital resource conservation, §56-235.1.
Certificates of public convenience and necessity, §§56-265.1 to 56-265.9.
Appeals from orders, §56-265.7.
Application of provisions, §56-265.8.
Chapter title, §56-265.9.
Defined terms, §56-265.1.
Effective dates, §56-265.5.
Electric utility facilities of local or state governments, §56-265.4:1.
Engineer inspections of electrical generation facilities, §56-265.8:1.
Gas service, §56-265.4:5.
Non-utility gas service, §56-265.4:6.
Issuance, §56-265.3.
Operation as telephone utility, §56-265.4:4.
Operation in territory of another certificate holder, §56-265.4.
Provision violations.
Penalties, §56-265.6.
Required, §§56-265.2, 56-265.3.
Water and sewer service, §56-265.3:1.
Charges.
Churches, §56-236.1.
Performance-based ratemaking.
Gas and electric utilities, §56-235.6.
Schedules, §56-236.
Complaints.
Procedures, §56-247.1.
Conflict of interest.
Ownership in contractor or subcontractor.
Disclosure by directors or officers, §56-234.5.
Consent of city or town to use public property, §15.2-2017, VA Const Art VII §8.
Use of public property without consent or franchise, §15.2-2018.
Conservation of energy, §56-235.1.
Construction projects.
Certificates of public convenience and necessity required, §56-265.2.
Review by commission, §56-234.3.
Consumer utility taxes, §§58.1-3814 to 58.1-3816.2.
Conveyances.
Easements.
Instruments conveying easements to public service corporations, §56-259.1.
Cooperatives.
Utility aggregation cooperatives, §§56-231.38 to 56-231.52.
See UTILITY AGGREGATION COOPERATIVES.
Utility consumer services cooperatives, §§56-231.15 to 56-231.37.
See UTILITY CONSUMER SERVICES COOPERATIVES.
Corporations generally, §§13.1-601 to 13.1-779.
See CORPORATIONS.
Counties, cities or towns generally, §§15.2-2109 to 15.2-2121.
See LOCALITIES.
Curtailment of service in times of emergency or shortage, §56-250.
Customer deposits.
Interest and return of deposits, §56-247.1.

PUBLIC UTILITIES —Cont'd
Damage or trespass to, §18.2-162.
Triple damages, §56-5.
Deferral portion of increase in fuel tariffs.
Defined, recovery, electric utilities, §56-249.6.
Defined terms, §§56-232, 56-245.2.
Distribution system facilities, §56-265.4:2.
Service, §56-233.
Deposits.
Unclaimed, disposition, §55-210.5.
Director disclosures, §56-234.5.
Shareholder information, §56-249.7.
Disclosure by directors or officers.
Ownership in contractor or subcontractor, §56-234.5.
Diverting service, §§8.01-44.7, 18.2-163.
Easements, §55-50.2.
Electric authorities, §§15.2-5400 to 15.2-5431.
See ELECTRIC AUTHORITIES.
Electric metering and submetering, §§56-245.2, 56-245.3.
Electric utility consumption tax, §§58.1-2900 to 58.1-2903.
Electric utility integrated resource planning, §§56-597 to 56-599.
Electric utility restructuring.
Commission on, §§30-201 to 30-209.
See ELECTRIC UTILITY RESTRUCTURING.
Generally, §§56-576 to 56-596.
See ELECTRIC UTILITY RESTRUCTURING.
Eminent domain.
Commencement of proceedings, §25.1-205.
Highways and roads.
Acquisition of interest for exchange, §33.1 96.
Hydroelectric power, §62.1-98.
Erosion and sediment control.
General erosion and sediment control specifications, annual filing, §62.1-44.15:55.
Estimated tax.
Water, heat, light, power and pipeline companies, §§58.1-2640 to 58.1-2651.
See PUBLIC SERVICE CORPORATION TAXATION.
Existing remedies retained, §56-253.
Extension of service, §56-255.
Facility requirements, §56-234.
Electrical utility facility construction, §56-46.1.
Jurisdiction of commission when federal facility ceases to be customer of electric utility, §56-235.7.
Foreign utility companies.
Protection of public interests, §56-46.3.
Franchise, privilege, lease or right to use city or town property, §§15.2-2100 to 15.2-2108.1:1.
Fuel cost recovery, §56-249.6.
Fuel price and purchase monitoring by commission, §56-248.1.
Gas pipeline construction, §56-265.2:1.
Highway corporations.
Crossings by utilities, §56-547.
Highways and roads.
Eminent domain.
Acquisition of interest for exchange, §33.1-96.
Hydroelectric power.
Application of provisions, §62.1-80.1.
Eminent domain right, §62.1-98.
Immunities, §56-256.
Investigation of operations, §56-234.4.
Issuance of stocks, bonds, etc., §§56-55 to 56-75.
See PUBLIC SERVICE COMPANIES.

PUBLIC UTILITIES —Cont'd
Lease of plants to cities or towns, §56-254.
License tax by counties, cities or towns, §58.1-3731.
License tax on telegraph, telephone, water, heat, light, power and pipeline companies, §§58.1-2620 to 58.1-2635.
See PUBLIC SERVICE CORPORATION TAXATION.
Locality establishing, maintaining, etc.
Generally, §§15.2-2109 to 15.2-2121.
See LOCALITIES.
Meters.
Defined terms, §56-245.2.
Good working condition requirements, §56-245.1.
Landlord and tenant.
Submetering equipment use, §55-226.2.
Standards, §56-245.3.
Tampering with devices, §§8.01-44.7, 18.2-163.
Motor vehicles.
Extension of loads beyond front of vehicles.
Self-propelled pole carriers, §46.2-1120.
Natural gas conservation and ratemaking efficiency act, §§56-600 to 56-602.
Natural gas customers retail supply choice, §56-235.8.
Natural gas distribution service within any underserved area or county, §15.2-2109.3.
Natural gas pipeline safety, §56-257.2.
Natural gas utility placing strategic facility into service.
Recovery of costs through rates charged, §56-235.9.
Natural gas utility safety.
Recovery of eligible safety activity costs, §56-235.10.
New generation facilities.
Review and approval, §56-234.3.
Nonpayment actions.
Procedures, §56-247.1.
Nuclear emergency evacuation plans.
Notification of customers, §56-245.1:1.
Obtaining services without payment, §18.2-187.1.
Officer disclosures, §56-234.5.
Shareholder information, §56-249.7.
Overhead high voltage line safety, §§59.1-406 to 59.1-414.
See OVERHEAD HIGH VOLTAGE LINE SAFETY.
Pay telephone registration, §§56-508.15, 56-508.16.
Performance-based regulation.
Gas and electric utilities, §56-235.6.
Permits for using streets, highways, roads, etc.
City or town providing for issuance, §15.2-2015.
Pipelines, §§56-257 to 56-260.1.
Authority to permit, §56-258.
Compensation for damages, §56-260.
Liability exemption provisions, §56-260.1.
Manner of laying, §56-257.
Means of locating, §56-257.1.
Rights-of-way, §56-259.
Planning and development.
Comprehensive plan, public facilities study, §15.2-2230.1.
Police powers over lands lying beyond localities boundaries, §15.2-1725.
Powers, §56-256.
Prepaid metering equipment and system.
Electric utilities.
Installation upon customer requests, §56-247.1.

PUBLIC UTILITIES —Cont'd
Private highways.
Utility crossings, §56-547.
Privileges, §56-256.
Procedure requirements of commission, §56-247.1.
Projected operation programs of electric utilities, §56-234.3.
Public ground use without consent or compensation, §56-14.
Public-private education facilities and infrastructure act, §§56-575.1 to 56-575.18.
See PUBLIC BUILDINGS.
Public-private transportation act.
Crossing utility's facilities, §56-570.
Public service companies.
Generally, §§56-1 to 56-46.3.
See PUBLIC SERVICE COMPANIES.
Purchased power cost recovery, §56-249.6.
Purchasing practices, §56-233.1.
Rates.
Alternative price regulation, §56-235.2.
Applications for changes.
Investigation procedures, §56-235.3.
Changes, §56-237.
Effective if not suspended, §56-240.
Hearings, §56-237.2.
Notice, §56-237.1.
Suspension of proposed rates, §56-238.
Appeals, §56-239.
Church charges, §56-236.1.
Electric utility restructuring.
Generally, §§56-576 to 56-596.
See ELECTRIC UTILITY RESTRUCTURING.
Fixing by commission, §56-235.
Income tax costs for investor-owned utilities.
Determining.
Utility part of publicly-traded, consolidated group, §56-235.2.
Increases, losses due to excessive temporary reduction, §56-244.
Increases, temporary, §56-245.
Just and reasonable determinations, §56-235.2.
Lowest rate applicable, §56-234.
Liability to customer for violation, §56-234.1.
Multiple rate increases within any twelve-month period, §56-235.4.
Natural gas conservation and ratemaking efficiency act, §§56-600 to 56-602.
Natural gas utility placing strategic facility into service.
Recovery of costs through rates charged, §56-235.9.
Performance-based ratemaking.
Gas and electric utilities, §56-235.6.
Reductions, temporary, §56-242.
Duration, §56-243.
Increases to make up for losses, §56-244.
Review, §56-234.2.
Schedules, §56-236.
Changes, §56-237.
Effective if not suspended, §56-240.
Hearings, §56-237.2.
Notification, §56-237.1.
Suspension of proposed rates, §56-238.
Appeals, §56-239.
Special charges or incentives, §56-235.2.
Stand-by electric service at renewable cogeneration facilities, §56-235.1:1.

PUBLIC UTILITIES —Cont'd
Rates —Cont'd
Suspension of enforcement of proposed rates.
Pending investigation by commission, §56-238.
Uniformity, §56-234.
Ratio utility billing system.
Landlord and tenant, §55-226.2.
Records, §56-249.2.
Remedies retained, §56-253.
Renewable energy resources.
Customers' options to purchase.
Notification by investor owned electric utilities, §56-245.1:2.
Reports, §56-249.
Fuel transactions of electric utilities, §56-249.3.
Filing, §56-249.4.
Retail supply choice for natural gas customers, §56-235.8.
Right-of-way easements.
Conveyance to companies by state departments and agencies, §2.2-1150.
Safety.
Recovery of eligible safety activity costs, §56-235.10.
Sale of plants to cities or towns, §56-254.
Secondhand article sales.
Building fixtures.
Exemption from provisions, §59.1-123.
Provision applicability, §59.1-123.
Company equipment, §§59.1-125 to 59.1-130.
Service districts in localities, §§15.2-2400 to 15.2-2403.3.
Service requirements, §56-234.
Sewage disposal systems, §§15.2-2122 to 15.2-2133.
See SEWAGE DISPOSAL SYSTEMS.
Sewerage companies, §§56-261 to 56-265.
Cooperative associations, §13.1-301.
Notice that such system includes a sewage treatment plant, §56-261.
Small sewer utilities, §§56-265.13:1 to 56-265.13:7.
Suspension of service to sewerage companies.
Required notice, §56-236.2.
Systems not regulated as public utilities, §§56-265.10 to 56-265.13.
Sewerage systems not regulated as public utilities.
Notice that such system includes a sewage treatment plant, §56-265.11:1.
Small investor-owned telephone utilities, §§56-531 to 56-534.
Small water or sewer public utilities, §§56-265.13:1 to 56-265.13:7.
Special regulatory revenue tax, §§58.1-2660 to 58.1-2665.
Standard commercial units.
Prescription, §56-248.
State corporation commission generally, §§12.1-1 to 12.1-43.
See STATE CORPORATION COMMISSION.
State operation of, §§56-509 to 56-528.
See PUBLIC UTILITIES, STATE OPERATION.
Steps to advance Virginia's energy plan.
Natural gas utilities.
SAVE plans, §§56-603, 56-604.
Stock corporations generally.
See CORPORATIONS.
Stormwater control programs adopted by localities, §15.2-2114.

PUBLIC UTILITIES —Cont'd
Streets, alleys or public grounds not to be used without consent of city or town, §15.2-2017, VA Const Art VII §8.
Use of public property without consent or franchise, §15.2-2018.
Submetering, §§56-245.2, 56-245.3.
Surface coal mining.
Applicability of act, §45.1-259.
Tariffs.
Prompt payment law not applicable.
Tariffs prescribed by State Corporation Commission, §2.2-4348.
Taxation of public service corporations generally, §§58.1-2600 to 58.1-2690.
See PUBLIC SERVICE CORPORATION TAXATION.
Telegraph or telephone companies, §§56-458 to 56-484.3.
See TELEGRAPH OR TELEPHONE COMPANIES.
Telephone cooperatives, §§56-485 to 56-508.
See TELEPHONE COOPERATIVES.
Termination of customer service.
Procedures, §56-247.1.
Sewage service, §56-264.1.
Water service, §56-264.1.
Tests by commission, §56-246.
Toll bridges.
Bridges deemed public utilities, §33.1-262.
Transfer of operations, §56-249.1.
Transfers of assets or securities, §§56-88 to 56-92.
Trespass, §18.2-162.
Unclaimed property, disposition, §55-210.5.
Underground utility line damage prevention, §§56-265.14 to 56-265.32.
See UNDERGROUND UTILITY LINE DAMAGE PREVENTION.
Use of public property of city or town, consent required, §56-14, VA Const Art VII §8.
Utility lines generally.
See UTILITY LINES.
Virginia electric utility restructuring act, §§56-576 to 56-596.
See ELECTRIC UTILITY RESTRUCTURING.
Water supply companies, §§56-261 to 56-265.
Small water utilities, §§56-265.13:1 to 56-265.13:7.
Systems not regulated as public utilities, §§56-265.10 to 56-265.13.
Water supply systems, §§15.2-2134 to 15.2-2156.
See WATER SUPPLY SYSTEMS.

PUBLIC UTILITIES, DEPARTMENTS OF.
County manager form of government, §15.2-634.
Urban county executive form of government, §15.2-843.

PUBLIC UTILITIES, STATE OPERATION, §§56-509 to 56-528.
Application of provisions, §56-527.
Attorney general.
Duties of, §56-526.
Collection of revenue, §56-520.
Commonwealth's attorneys.
Duty of, §56-526.
Compensation to utilities, §56-522.
Cooperation, §56-515.
Defined terms, §56-523.
Disposition of revenue, §56-520

PUBLIC UTILITIES, STATE OPERATION —Cont'd
Duties of governor when threat of curtailment or interruption of operation, §56-510.
Entry upon property, §56-515.
Established procedure to be maintained, §56-519.
Expenses of operation, §56-518.
Information to be furnished governor, §56-512.
Injunctions, §56-525.
Obstructing governor or agents, §56-517.
Penalties for provision violations, §56-524.
Possession of utility, §56-516.
Power of governor as commander in chief, §56-528.
Power of governor to possess and operate, §56-511.
Restoration of possession, §56-521.
Utility employees.
Employment by state, §56-512.
Replacement of, §56-513.
Status unaffected by acceptance or refusal, §56-514.

PUBLIC UTILITY TRANSFERS, §§56-88 to 56-92.

PUBLIC WATER SUPPLIES.
Generally, §§32.1-167 to 32.1-176.
See WATER SUPPLY.

PUBLIC WEIGHMASTERS, §§3.2-5800 to 3.2-5820.
See WEIGHMASTERS, PUBLIC.

PUBLIC WELFARE.
Board for the blind and vision impaired.
Generally.
See BLIND AND VISION IMPAIRED, BOARD FOR.
Board of social services.
Generally.
See SOCIAL SERVICES BOARD.
Child welfare agencies.
Generally.
See CHILD WELFARE AGENCIES.
Commissioner of social services.
See COMMISSIONER OF SOCIAL SERVICES.
Department for the blind and vision impaired.
Generally.
See BLIND AND VISION IMPAIRED, DEPARTMENT FOR.
Department of social services.
Generally.
See SOCIAL SERVICES DEPARTMENT.
Local boards of public welfare.
Generally.
See WELFARE BOARDS, LOCAL.
Local superintendents of public welfare.
Generally.
See SUPERINTENDENTS OF PUBLIC WELFARE.
Public aid and assistance generally.
See PUBLIC AID AND ASSISTANCE.
Support of dependent children and caretakers.
Collection of support generally.
See CHILD SUPPORT.

PUBLIC WELFARE, BOARDS OF.
County board form of government, §15.2-412.

PUBLIC WELFARE, SUPERINTENDENTS OF.
County board form of government, §15.2-412.

PUBLIC WORKS, VA Const Art X §10.
Contract requirements, §2.2-4321.2.
Division of engineering and buildings.
Generally, §§2.2-1129 to 2.2-1167.
See ENGINEERING AND BUILDINGS DIVISION.
Energy performance-based contracts, §§11-34.1 to 11-34.4.
Mandamus.
Transportation obligations.
Writ to secure construction of act granting power to incur debt, §8.01-653.1.
Prisoners.
Employment and training of prisoners, §§53.1-56 to 53.1-59.
Procurement by public bodies, §§2.2-4300 to 2.2-4377.
See PUBLIC PROCUREMENT.

PUBLIC WORKS, DEPARTMENTS OF.
County executive form of government, §§15.2-518, 15.2-526.
County manager form of government, §15.2-625.
Urban county executive form of government, §15.2-834.

PUBLISHER'S AFFIDAVIT.
Charters of local governments.
Notice of public hearing in lieu of election, §15.2-202.
Text prior to election, §15.2-201.

PULASKI AND WYTHEVILLE PARKING AUTHORITY, 1968 ch 682.

PULASKI COUNTY.
Blue Ridge regional tourism council, §§2.2-2609, 2.2-2610.
Confederate cemeteries and graves.
Disbursement of funds appropriated for upkeep, §10.1-2211.
Dams.
Restrictions, §29.1-532.
Public defenders office.
Established, §19.2-163.04.
School board.
Salary of members, §22.1-32.
Staggered terms for elected members, §22.1-57.3:1.
Table of town or city lots.
Entries by commissioner of revenue in counties, §58.1-3302.
Transient occupancy tax.
Disposition of revenues, §58.1-3819.
Unsafe vehicle removal, §46.2-1001.
Western Virginia public education consortium.
Inclusion in western Virginia, §22.1-354.1.

PULASKI DEVELOPMENT AUTHORITY.
Generally.
See ECONOMIC DEVELOPMENT AUTHORITIES.

PULPWOOD.
Agricultural and forestal districts, §§15.2-4300 to 15.2-4407.
Forest products tax, §§58.1-1600 to 58.1-1622.
See FOREST PRODUCTS TAX.

PULPWOOD SUPPLIERS.
Intangible personal property tax.
Generally, §§58.1-1100 to 58.1-1118.
See PERSONAL PROPERTY TAXES.

PUMPS.
Dispensing kerosene, gasoline or motor oils.
Opening or carrying away, §18.2-151.

PUNITIVE DAMAGES.
Asbestos-related injuries.
Bifurcated proceedings, §8.01-374.1.
Cap, §8.01-38.1.
Credit services businesses, §59.1-335.10.
Liability of sureties or banks, §59.1-335.4.
Damages generally.
See DAMAGES.
Death of party liable for injury.
Survival of action, §§8.01-25, 8.01-56.
Defamation.
Mitigation of damages against newspapers or print media, §8.01-48.
Discrimination against persons with disabilities, §51.5-46.
Driving intoxicated.
Exemplary damages for persons injured by drivers, §8.01-44.5.
Employee theft.
Civil action for recovery, §8.01-44.4.
Employment-related information disclosure.
Prospective or current employer disclosing.
Bad faith disclosure, punitive damages, §8.01-46.1.
Equal credit opportunities.
Election of remedies, §6.2-512.
Provision violations, §6.2-505.
Ethnic intimidation, §8.01-42.1.
Fair housing law, §§36-96.17, 36-96.18.
Fences.
Livestock crossing lawful fences, §55-306.
Hate crimes, §8.01-42.1.
Insurance providing coverage for punitive damages.
Policy of Commonwealth, §38.2-227.
Intoxicated drivers.
Exemplary damages for persons injured by, §8.01-44.5.
Liability insurance.
Policy of Commonwealth, §38.2-227.
Limitation on recovery, §8.01-38.1.
Livestock.
Crossing lawful fences, §55-306.
Motor vehicle accidents.
Arbitrary refusal of insurance claim, §8.01-66.1.
Picketing dwelling places, §18.2-419.
Products liability.
Bifurcated proceedings, §8.01-374.1.
Racial intimidation, §8.01-42.1.
Real estate cooperatives, §55-436.
Purchaser protection violations, §55-492.
Religious intimidation, §8.01-42.1.
Search without warrant.
Liability of officer or person violating provisions, §19.2-59.
Shoplifting.
Civil action for recovery, §8.01-44.4.
Stalking.
Civil actions against an individual, §8.01-42.3.
Summary judgment motion.
Sustaining as to punitive damages claim only, §8.01-420.
Survival of causes of action, §§8.01-25, 8.01-56.
Death of party liable for injury, §§8.01-25, 8.01-56.
Theft.
Employee theft, §8.01-44.4.

PUNITIVE DAMAGES —Cont'd
Theft —Cont'd
Shoplifting, §8.01-44.4.
Trade secrets, §59.1-338.
Unauthorized use of name or picture, §8.01-40.
Wiretapping.
Civil action for unlawful interception, disclosure or use, §19.2-69.
Wrongful death.
Amount of damages, §8.01-52.

PUNITIVE DAMAGES CAP, §8.01-38.1.

PUPILS' RECORDS, §§22.1-287 to 22.1-289.
Missing children, §§22.1-288.1, 22.1-289.

PUPIL TRANSPORTATION, §§22.1-176 to 22.1-198.
See SCHOOL BUSES.

PURCELLVILLE.
Taxes and assessments on electricity customer.
Construction of electric transmission line, §15.2-2404.

PURCHASE MONEY MORTGAGES, §55-104.

PURCHASE MONEY SECURITY INTERESTS.
Fraudulent conveyances.
Void as to creditors and purchasers until recorded.
Priority, §55-96.
Where to be recorded, §55-97.
Priority of lien.
Attachment or levy, §8.2A-307.
Credit line deed, §§55-58.2, 55-96.
Secured transactions, §8.9A-103.
Priority, §8.9A-324.

PURCHASERS FOR VALUABLE CONSIDERATION.
See BONA FIDE PURCHASERS.

PURCHASES AND SUPPLY DIVISION, §§2.2-1109 to 2.2-1128.
Accounting system.
Prescribed by comptroller, §2.2-1115.
Vendor accounting information, standard, §2.2-1115.1.
Charities.
Direct purchases by certain charitable corporations, §2.2-1120.
Competitive government act, §§2.2-5512, 2.2-5513.
Contracts entered into by division.
Executed in name of Commonwealth, §2.2-1115.
Vendor accounting information, standard, §2.2-1115.1.
Correctional facilities products or services, purchase, §2.2-1116.
Created within department of general services, §2.2-1109.
Department of the blind and vision impaired.
Purchases from, §2.2-1117.
General services department.
Central electronic procurement system, maintenance, §2.2-1110.
Public broadcasting stations and public bodies.
Purchasing through division, §2.2-1122.
Purchases through division.
Cases in which purchases through division not mandatory, §2.2-1119.
Correctional facilities products or services, §2.2-1116.

PURCHASES AND SUPPLY DIVISION —Cont'd
Purchases through division —Cont'd
Decibel level of sound.
Proper equipment used to determine, §2.2-1112.
Department of the blind and vision impaired.
Purchases from, §2.2-1117.
Direct purchases by agency, charitable corporation or institutions of higher education, §2.2-1120.
Estimates, regulations, when submitted, §2.2-1114.
Exceptions, §2.2-1119.
Health care clinics for indigent and uninsured, §2.2-1120.
Motor vehicle speed monitoring devices.
Determination of proper equipment and electrical devices, §2.2-1112.
Nonprofit workshops serving individuals with disabilities.
Purchases from, §2.2-1118.
Payment, manner, funds, §2.2-1115.
Public broadcasting stations and public bodies, §2.2-1122.
Purchase made in violation of provisions.
Malfeasance in office, intentional violations, §2.2-1115.
Warrant upon voucher not to issue, §2.2-1115.
Purchases made in accordance with Virginia public procurement act, §2.2-1111.
Regulations, adoption, requirements, §2.2-1111.
Requisitions, regulations, §2.2-1114.
Standardization of equipment and supplies, §2.2-1112.
State forms, procurement and inventory.
Setting uniform standards, §2.2-1113.
State printing facilities.
Economical operation, powers in obtaining, §2.2-1113.
State treasury.
Prompt payment of money collected to, §2.2-1115.
Transportation services, certain organizations providing.
Purchase directly from contracts established by division, §2.2-1120.
Using agency to purchase all equipment, supplies, etc., through division, §2.2-1110.
Vendor accounting information, standard, §2.2-1115.1.
Virginia public procurement act.
Generally, §§2.2-4300 to 2.2-4346.
See PUBLIC PROCUREMENT.
Purchases made in accordance with, §2.2-1111.
Virginia retirement system.
Inapplicability of article, §2.2-1110.
State flag, sale, §2.2-1128.
Surplus materials.
Acquisition from federal government, §2.2-1123.
Disposition by state agency or institution.
Establishment of procedures, §2.2-1124.
Proceeds from sale or recycling, disposition, §2.2-1125.
Vendor accounting information, standard, §2.2-1115.1.

PURCHASES BY COUNTIES.
Centralized competitive purchasing by chief administrative officer, §15.2-1231.
Purchasing agent, §§15.2-1233 to 15.2-1240.
Certification of sufficient funds, §15.2-1238.
Competition, purchases and sales based on, §15.2-1236.

QUALIFIED CHARITABLE REMAINDER TRUSTS —Cont'd
Shareholder in professional corporation transferring shares to, §13.1-550.

QUALIFIED DOMESTIC RELATIONS ORDER.
Dissolution of marriage or divorce from bonds of matrimony.
Decree as to property of parties, §20-107.3.

QUALIFIED ESCROW FUND.
Tobacco manufacturers' responsibilities, §§3.2-4200, 3.2-4201.
Assignment and contribution of escrow funds to Commonwealth, §§3.2-4202, 3.2-4203.

QUALITY LABELS AND MARKS.
Agricultural grades, marks and brands, §§3.2-4312 to 3.2-4321.
See AGRICULTURAL GRADES, MARKS AND BRANDS.

QUARANTINE.
Animals.
No-fence law, §55-315.
Branch pilots.
Fees for detention, §54.1-921.
Choice of method of treatment, §32.1-44.
Commissioner authority to require, §32.1-43.
Communicable diseases of public health threat, §§32.1-48.05 to 32.1-48.017.
Conditions for invoking provisions, §32.1-48.07.
Declaration of quarantine, §32.1-48.08.
Definitions, §32.1-48.06.
Determination of exceptional circumstances, §32.1-48.05.
Electronic filings to expedite proceedings, §32.1-48.013:1.
Health records.
Disclosure, §32.1-48.015.
Immunity from liability, §32.1-48.016.
Isolation, exceptional circumstances, §32.1-48.011.
Order of isolation, §32.1-48.012.
Appeal, §32.1-48.013.
Appeal of circuit court order, VA SCt Rule 5:41.
Circuit court proceedings, VA SCt Rule 3:24.
Electronic filings to expedite proceedings, §32.1-48.013:1.
Enforcement, §32.1-48.014.
Isolation proceedings, VA SCt Rule 7A:16.
Rules of practice and procedure, §17.1-503.
Order of quarantine, §32.1-48.09.
Appeal, §32.1-48.010.
Appeal of circuit court order, VA SCt Rule 5:41.
Circuit court proceedings, VA SCt Rule 3:24.
Enforcement, §32.1-48.014.
Isolation proceedings, VA SCt Rule 7A:16.
Rules of practice and procedure, §17.1-503.
Property or facilities.
Use of public or private property or facilities, §32.1-48.017.
Contagious and infectious diseases, livestock and poultry.
Disposition of quarantined animals with potential to impact livestock or poultry, §3.2-6008.
Domestic animals not permitted to enter or leave quarantine, §3.2-6007.
Individuals exposed, §3.2-6006.
Notice of quarantine, §3.2-6005.
Counties general powers, §15.2-1200.
Isolation of certain persons with communicable diseases of public health significance, §§32.1-48.01 to 32.1-48.04.
Appeal of circuit court order, VA SCt Rule 5:41.

QUARANTINE —Cont'd
Isolation of certain persons with communicable diseases of public health significance —Cont'd
Circuit court proceedings, VA SCt Rule 3:24.
Isolation proceedings, VA SCt Rule 7A:16.
Orders, rules of practice and procedure, §17.1-503.
Livestock.
Contagious and infectious diseases, §§3.2-6003 to 3.2-6008.
No-fence law, §55-315.
Notice.
Livestock and poultry.
Contagious and infectious diseases, §3.2-6005.
Noxious weeds, §3.2-802.
Permitting animals to run at large in county under quarantine, §18.2-121.1.
Plant pests, §§3.2-703, 3.2-704.
Police offices.
Orders of isolation and quarantine.
Authority to execute and serve orders, §15.2-1704.
Poultry.
Contagious and infectious diseases, §§3.2-6003 to 3.2-6008.
Weeds, noxious, §3.2-802.

QUARRY OPERATORS.
Motor vehicle registration.
Vehicles exempt from registration, §§46.2-671, 46.2-675.

QUARTERING OF SOLDIERS, US Const Amd 3.

QUIETING TITLE, §§55-153 to 55-155.

QUININE.
Disposal, §54.1-3469.
Distribution, §§54.1-3467, 54.1-3468.
Storage, §54.1-3469.

QUITCLAIM DEEDS.
Escheated lands.
Refunds, §55-200.
Recordation in deed books, §17.1-227.
Words of release in deeds.
Effect, §55-75.

QUO WARRANTO.
Application.
By whom filed, §8.01-637.
Verified petition under oath, §8.01-637.
Attorneys' fees, §8.01-643.
Bench trial, §8.01-643.
Case criteria.
Issuance of writ, §8.01-636.
Circuit courts.
Jurisdiction, §17.1-513.
Common-law writ abolished, §8.01-635.
Default judgments.
Failure of defendant to appear, §8.01-640.
Defendant's responsive pleading, §8.01-643.
Issuance of writ.
Case criteria, §8.01-636.
Leave of court, §8.01-637.
Judgments and decrees.
Defendant failure to appear, §8.01-640.
Defendant found guilty on merits, §8.01-643.
Jury trial, §8.01-643.
Pleading of defendant, §8.01-642.
Rendition of judgment.
Service by publication, §8.01-641.
Service by publication.
Motion to set aside judgment, §8.01-641.

PURCHASES BY COUNTIES —Cont'd
Purchasing agent —Cont'd
Definitions, §15.2-1234.
Provisions not applicable until agent employed, §15.2-1233.
Review and filing of contract, §15.2-1237.
Rules and regulations governing, §15.2-1235.
Violations, §§15.2-1239, 15.2-1240.
Urban county executive form of government, §15.2-831.

PURCHASES BY GOVERNMENT FROM NONGOVERNMENT SOURCES.
Fair employment contracting act, §§2.2-4200, 2.2-4201.
Public procurement act, §§2.2-4300 to 2.2-4377.
See PUBLIC PROCUREMENT.

PURCHASES BY GOVERNMENT THROUGH DIVISION OF PURCHASES AND SUPPLY.
Division of purchases and supply generally, §§2.2-1109 to 2.2-1128.
See PURCHASES AND SUPPLY DIVISION.

PURCHASING AGENTS.
County board form of government, §15.2-414.
County executive form of government.
Director of finance to act as, §15.2-524.
County manager form of government.
Director of finance to act as, §15.2-622.
Employment by county and duties, §15.2-1543.
Procurement by purchasing agents, §§15.2-1233 to 15.2-1240.
Urban county executive form of government.
Director of finance to act as, §15.2 831.

PURE ENDOWMENT CONTRACTS.
Annuities generally.
See ANNUITIES.
Life insurance generally, §§38.2-3100 to 38.2-3354.
See LIFE INSURANCE.
Standard nonforfeiture provisions for life insurance.
Generally, §§38.2-3200 to 38.2-3229.
See LIFE INSURANCE.

PURE FOOD ACT, §§3.2-5100 to 3.2-5145.
See FOOD.

PURGING RECORDS.
Criminal records, §§19.2-392.1 to 19.2-392.4.
Destruction of records after transferring to electronic format, §16.1-69.55.
District courts.
Retention, §16.1-69.55.
DNA data bank exchange, §19.2-310.7.
Fingerprints and photographs of children, §16.1-299.
Juvenile and domestic relations district court, §16.1-306.

PURPLE FLASHING WARNING LIGHTS, §46.2-1025.

PURPLE HEART RECIPIENTS.
Special license plates, §46.2-742.

PURSE NETS TO TAKE MENHADEN, §§28.2-400 to 28.2-411.
Closure of Chesapeake Bay purse seine fishery for Atlantic menhaden, §28.2-1000.2.

PUSHCARTS.
Removal of shopping carts from store premises, §18.2-102.1.

PUTATIVE FATHER REGISTRY, §§63.2-1249 to 63.2-1253.
Certificate of search, §63.2-1252.
Confidentiality of information, §63.2-1251.
Copy of notice of registration.
Sent to mother of child subject to registration, §63.2-1251.
Establishment, §63.2-1249.
Evidence in adoption or termination of parental rights proceedings.
Certificate of search, §63.2-1252.
Failure to register, §63.2-1250.
Form for registering.
Department to prepare, §63.2-1250.
Freedom of information act disclosure exemption, §63.2-1251.
Funding.
Adoption petition, filing fee, §63.2-1201.
Informing public of registry.
Duty of department, §63.2-1253.
Legal notice to man engaging in sexual intercourse with woman.
Child may be conceived and man entitled to legal rights and obligations, §63.2-1250.
Notification of adoption or termination of parental right proceeding.
Registration by putative father required to receive, §63.2-1250.
Pamphlet or publication informing public.
Duty of department, §63.2-1253.
Person who may register, §63.2-1250.
Putative father registry fund.
Established, money deposited into, §63.2-1249.
Release of information, §63.2-1251.
Rights not prejudiced by failure to register, §63.2-1250.
Search of registry, §63.2-1252.
Signature of registrant required on form, §63.2-1250.
Time for registering, §63.2-1250.
Unauthorized release of information.
Criminal penalty, §63.2-1251.
Waiver of rights, failure to register, §63.2-1250.

PYRAMID PROMOTIONAL SCHEMES, §§18.2-239, 18.2-240.

Q

QATAR.
University of Virginia.
Branch campus in Qatar, §23-91.23:1.
Virginia Commonwealth university branch campus, §23-50.16:36.

QUAGGA MUSSEL.
Nonindigenous aquatic nuisance species act, §§29.1-571 to 29.1-577.
See NONINDIGENOUS AQUATIC NUISANCE SPECIES ACT.

QUAIL.
Bobwhite quail, §§29.1-514, 29.1-544.

QUALIFICATION OF LOCAL OFFICER FOR OFFICE.
Failure to qualify vacates office, §15.2-1524.
Record of qualification, §15.2-1523.
When and how officers qualify, §15.2-1522.

QUALIFIED CHARITABLE REMAINDER TRUSTS.
Membership interest in professional limited liability company.
Transfer by member, §13.1-1115.

QUO WARRANTO —Cont'd
Service of notice, process and other papers.
How summons served, §8.01-639.
Service by publication, §8.01-641.
Sewerage companies.
Duty failures, §56-264.
Statutory writ established, §8.01-635.
Summons and process.
How summons directed and served, §8.01-639.
Venue.
Preferred forum, §8.01-261.
Water supply companies.
Duty failures, §56-264.

R

RABBI-PENITENT PRIVILEGE, §8.01-400, VA SCt Rule 2:503.

RABBIS.
Clergy generally.
See CLERGY.

RABBITS.
Hunting, §29.1-516.
Pet cemeteries, §§57-39.20 to 57-39.25.
See PET CEMETERIES.
Sale of game, §29.1-536.

RABIES, §§3.2-6521 to 3.2-6525, 32.1-48.1 to 32.1-48.4.
Cats.
Inoculation prerequisite to licensing, §3.2-6521.
Certificate of inoculation.
Availability, §3.2-6521.
Copy to owner, §3.2-6529.
Presentation upon request, §3.2-6521.
Requirements, §3.2-6529.
Treasurers of localities.
Veterinarians to forward copy of information to, §3.2-6529.
Clinics, §3.2-6521.
Confinement of suspected animals, §3.2-6522.
Control, §§3.2-6521 to 3.2-6525.
Licensing of dogs and cats, §§3.2-6526 to 3.2-6536.
Cooperation with local governing bodies and agencies, §32.1-48.4.
Display or publication of regulations declaring existence of rabies, §32.1-48.1.
Dogs.
Inoculation prerequisite to licensing, §3.2-6521.
Licensing required, §3.2-6524.
Emergency ordinances.
Rabid animals, §3.2-6522.
Exposed animals, §3.2-6522.
Local authority and responsibility plan, §3.2-6562.1.
Exposed people, §3.2-6522.
Local authority and responsibility plan, §3.2-6562.1.
Fairfax county.
Ordinances.
Distribution of oral vaccine to prevent spread, §3.2-6525.
Inoculation, §3.2-6521.
Animal shelters, §3.2-6523.
Dogs.
Regulation of state health commissioner, §32.1-48.2.
Prerequisite to dog or cat licensing, §3.2-6521.
Local governing bodies and agencies, cooperation with, §32.1-48.4.

RABIES —Cont'd
Local ordinances and requirements.
Regulations of state health commissioner covering, §32.1-48.3.
Ordinances.
Emergency ordinances.
Rabid animals, §3.2-6522.
Regulations to prevent spread, §3.2-6525.
Outbreak of rabies occurring in county or city.
State health commissioner declaring existence of rabies, §32.1-48.1.
Proceedings as to rabid animals, §3.2-6522.
Rabid animals, §3.2-6522.
Regulations to prevent spread, §3.2-6525.
Reports of rabid animals, §3.2-6522.
Unlicensed dogs prohibited, §3.2-6524.
Vaccination or inoculation of dogs.
Regulation of state health commissioner requiring, §32.1-48.2.
Veterinary records, release, §54.1-3812.
Withholding information about rabid animals, §18.2-313.1.

RACCOONS.
Hunting.
Sundays, §29.1-521.
Weapon restrictions, §29.1-519.
Sale of game, §29.1-536.

RACECOURSES.
Public gathering place requirements, §32.1-198.

RACE INSURRECTION AGAINST ANOTHER RACE.
Conspiracy to incite, §18.2-485.

RACE TRACKS.
ABC license.
Motor car sporting event facility license, §4.1-206.
Taxes, §4.1-233.

RACIAL DISCRIMINATION.
Constitutional prohibition, VA Const Art I §11.
Discrimination generally.
See DISCRIMINATION.
Equal credit opportunities, §§6.2-500 to 6.2-513.
See EQUAL CREDIT OPPORTUNITIES.
Fair employment contracting act, §§2.2-4200, 2.2-4201.
Fair housing law, §§36-96.1 to 36-96.23.
See FAIR HOUSING.
Fire insurance policies, §§38.2-2114, 38.2-2115.
Health maintenance organizations, §38.2-4312.
Human rights act, §§2.2-3900 to 2.2-3903.
Law enforcement officers.
Diversity and biased policing policy to be established, §9.1-102.
Life insurance, §38.2-508.2.
Motor vehicle insurance.
Issuance, §38.2-2213.
Refusal to renew, §38.2-2212.
Procurement by public bodies, §2.2-4310.
Employment discrimination by contractors, §2.2-4311.

RACIAL INTIMIDATION.
Tort liability, §8.01-42.1.

RACIAL PROFILING.
Law enforcement officers.
Diversity and biased policing policy to be established, §9.1-102.

RACING.
Equine activity liability.
Horse racing excluded, §3.2-6201.

RACING —Cont'd
Greyhound racing and simulcasting, §59.1-405.1.
Motor sports facilities.
Mixed beverage license, §4.1-210.
Fee, §§4.1-231, 4.1-233.
Motor vehicles.
ABC license.
Motor car sporting event licenses, §4.1-206.
Taxes, §4.1-233.
Pari-mutuel wagering on horses, §§59.1-364 to 59.1-405.
See PARI-MUTUEL WAGERING.

RACING COMMISSION.
Administrative process act.
Exemptions, §2.2-4002.
Campaign contributions, §§59.1-368, 59.1-370.
Creation, §59.1-366.
Legal representation, §59.1-367.
Members, §59.1-366.
Pari-mutuel wagering on horses, §§59.1-364 to 59.1-374.
Background investigations, §59.1-371.
Conflicts of interest, §59.1-368.
Control, §59.1-364.
Duties, §59.1-369.
Executive secretary, §59.1-370.
Fingerprinting, §59.1-371.
Hearings, §59.1-373.
Injunctions, §59.1-374.
Licenses, §§59.1-375 to 59.1-386.
Steeplechase facilities, §59.1-378.1.
Local referendum, §59.1-391.
Permits, §§59.1-387 to 59.1-390.
Powers, §59.1-369.
Staff, §59.1-370.
State racing operations fund, §59.1-370.1.
Steeplechase facilities licenses, §59.1-378.1.
Transfers of meets, §59.1-376.
Virginia breeders fund, §59.1-372.
Procurement.
Exceptions to competitive procurement, §2.2-4346.
Secretary of commerce and trade.
Agency responsibility, §2.2-204.
Stewards.
Appointment by commission, §59.1-370.

RACKETEERING, §§18.2-512 to 18.2-517.
Conspiracy to commit, §18.2-514.
Criminal penalties, §18.2-515.
Transmission of money derived or traceable from racketeering activity, §18.2-516.
Criminal street gang.
Defined, §18.2-513.
Definitions, §18.2-513.
Dissolution or reorganization of enterprise, §18.2-515.
Divestiture of interest in enterprise or property, §18.2-515.
Drug kingpins, §18.2-248.
Forfeiture of property, §18.2-515.
Transmission of money derived form racketeering activity, §18.2-516.
Maintaining interest or control through racketeering activity, §§18.2-514, 18.2-515.
Racketeering activity defined, §18.2-513.
Racketeering offenses, §§18.2-514, 18.2-515.
Receipt of proceeds derived from racketeering activity, §§18.2-514, 18.2-515.
Suspension or revocation of any license, permit or prior approval, §18.2-515

RACKETEERING —Cont'd
Transmission of money derived or traceable from racketeering activity, §18.2-516.
Use or investment of proceeds derived from racketeering activity.
Acquisition of real property or establishment of enterprise, §§18.2-514, 18.2-515.
Venue for prosecution, §18.2-517.
Virginia racketeer influenced and corrupt organization (RICO) act.
Short title, §18.2-512.

RADAR CALIBRATION, §46.2-882.
Admissibility of results in criminal prosecution, §46.2-942.
Certificate as to accuracy of device, §46.2-882.

RADAR DETECTION DEVICES.
Demerit points, §46.2-1079.
Law enforcement officers.
Compulsory minimum training standards, §9.1-102.
Speed of motor vehicles, §§46.2-882, 46.2-883.
Division of purchases and supply.
Determining proper equipment for monitoring, §2.2-1112.

RADFORD.
Blue Ridge regional tourism council, §§2.2-2609, 2.2-2610.
Circuit court, establishment, §17.1-500.
Confederate cemeteries and graves.
Disbursement of funds appropriated for upkeep, §10.1-2211.
Fingerprinting school employees, §22.1-296.2.
School board.
Fingerprinting applicants for employment, §22.1-296.2.
Salary of members, §22.1-32.
Western Virginia public education consortium.
Inclusion in western Virginia, §22.1-354.1.

RADFORD UNIVERSITY, §§23-155.1 to 23-155.10.
Board of visitors, §§23-155.1 to 23-155.7.
Campus police departments.
General provisions, §§23-232 to 23-238.
See COLLEGES AND UNIVERSITIES.
Reporting campus crime, §23-9.1:1.
Conferring of degrees, §23-155.9.
Corporate name, §23-155.2.
Special license plates, §46.2-749.
Teacher curriculum, §23-155.10.
Transfer of property, §23-155.3.
Tuition, fees and other charges, §23-155.8.
Universities generally, §§23-1.01 to 23-9.2:8.
See COLLEGES AND UNIVERSITIES.

RADIATION CONTROL, §§32.1-227 to 32.1-238.
Advisory board, §32.1-233.
Agreement authority of boards, §32.1-236.
Agreement authority of governor, §32.1-235.
Bonds of licensees, §32.1-231.
Defined terms, §32.1-227.
Department of health.
Designation as state radiation control agency, §32.1-228.1.
Enforcement of provisions, §32.1-234.1.
Exemptions, §32.1-228.
Impoundment of sources of ionizing radiation, §32.1-238.
Injunction of violations, §32.1-234.1.
Licensing of radioactive material, §32.1-229.3.

RADIATION CONTROL —Cont'd
Local ordinances, §32.1-237.
Powers of board, §§32.1-229, 32.1-230.
Radioactive material perpetual care trust fund, §32.1-232.
Radon screening, testing or mitigation.
Prerequisites to conducting or offering, §§32.1-229.01, 32.1-229.01:1.
Rulemaking authority, §32.1-229.
State agency.
Designation of department of health as, §32.1-228.1.
Violations of provisions.
Enforcement by department, §32.1-234.1.
Workers' compensation.
Limitation of actions, §65.2-406.
X-ray machines.
Inspections, §§32.1-229.1, 32.1-229.2.

RADIO.
Advertising.
Consumer protection.
Application of provisions, §59.1-199.
Campaign disclosures.
Advertisements.
See CAMPAIGN FINANCE DISCLOSURE.
Citizens band radios.
Use of profane, threatening or indecent language, §18.2-427.
Criminal trials.
Judicial discretion to permit broadcasting, §19.2-266.
Defamation.
Defamatory statements in broadcasts, §8.01-49.
Election polling places.
News media visiting, photographing or filming inside, interviews, §24.2-604.
Emergency two-way radio communications.
Unlawful interference with, §18.2-165.2.
False publications.
Stated, delivered or transmitted to radio station, §18.2-209.
Intangible personal property tax, §§58.1-1100 to 58.1-1118.
See PERSONAL PROPERTY TAXES.
Joint state and local police communications system.
Generally, §§52-16 to 52-19.
Machinery and tools tax, §§58.1-3507, 58.1-3508.
Microwave radio systems.
Unlawful use of or injury to signals and equipment, §18.2-165.
Personal property taxes.
Classification of radio instruments and equipment, §58.1-3504.
Intangible personal property taxes, §§58.1-1100 to 58.1-1118.
See PERSONAL PROPERTY TAXES.
Police radio.
Use during commission of crime, §18.2-462.1.
Recorded device piracy.
Application of provisions, §59.1-41.2.
Remote broadcasts by radio station.
Amber warning lights on vehicles used in broadcast, §46.2-1025.
Retail sales and use tax.
Media-related exemptions, §58.1-609.6.
State police communications system generally, §§52-12 to 52-19.
See STATE POLICE COMMUNICATIONS SYSTEM.

RADIO —Cont'd
Trial publicity.
Attorneys at law.
Professional responsibility, VA SCt Rule Pt 6 §II Rule 3.5.
Wiretapping exceptions, §19.2-62.

RADIOACTIVE CONTAMINATION.
Fire insurance policies, excluding loss or damage caused by, §38.2-2102.

RADIOACTIVE MATERIAL PERPETUAL CARE TRUST FUND, §32.1-232.

RADIOACTIVE WASTE, §§10.1-1430 to 10.1-1432.
Board.
Agreements with federal government, §10.1-1434.
Further powers, §10.1-1432.
Damage or trespass to facility threatening release, §18.2-162.
Defined, §10.1-1400.
Eminent domain.
Board powers, §10.1-1432.
Federal government agreements, §10.1-1430.
Authority of board, §10.1-1434.
Further powers of board, §10.1-1432.
Hazardous materials emergency response, §§44-146.34 to 44-146.40.
Southeast interstate low-level radioactive waste management compact, §§10.1-1500 to 10.1-1504.
State or interstate agency agreements, §10.1-1431.
Transportation of hazardous materials, §44-146.30.

RADIO COMMON CARRIERS.
Income tax on telecommunications companies, §58.1-400.1.
Credit, §58.1-434.
Modifications to taxable income, §58.1-403.
Public service companies generally, §§56-1 to 56-87.
See PUBLIC SERVICE COMPANIES.
Public utilities generally, §§56-232 to 56-265.
See PUBLIC UTILITIES.
Telegraph or telephone companies generally, §§56-458 to 56-484.3.
See TELEGRAPH OR TELEPHONE COMPANIES.
Telephone cooperatives generally, §§56-485 to 56-508.
See TELEPHONE COOPERATIVES.

RADIO DISTRIBUTION DEVICES.
Sale or lease of state property for communications purposes, §2.2-1151.

RADIOLOGICAL AGENT CRIMES, §18.2-52.1.

RADIOLOGICAL EMERGENCY PREPAREDNESS FUND, §§44-146.31 to 44-146.33.

RADIOLOGICAL TECHNOLOGY ADVISORY BOARD, §54.1-2956.8.
Testing program establishment, §54.1-2956.8:2.

RADIOLOGICAL TECHNOLOGY PRACTITIONERS.
Licensing generally, §§54.1-2950.1 to 54.1-2957.01.
See MEDICINE AND OTHER HEALING ARTS PROFESSIONS.

RADIOLOGIC TECHNOLOGISTS.
Licensing generally, §§54.1-2900 to 54.1-2993.
See MEDICINE AND OTHER HEALING ARTS PROFESSIONS.
Professional corporations generally, §§13.1-542.1 to 13.1-556.
See PROFESSIONAL CORPORATIONS.
Professional limited liability company generally, §§13.1-1100 to 13.1-1123.
See PROFESSIONAL LIMITED LIABILITY COMPANIES.
Professions and occupations regulation generally.
See HEALTH PROFESSIONS DEPARTMENT.

RADIO OR TELEVISION REMOTE BROADCASTS.
Flashing, blinking or alternating amber warning lights on vehicles, §46.2-1025.

RADIO REPORTERS.
Police lines or barricades.
Exemption from provisions, §15.2-1714.

RADON TESTING.
Radiation control companies.
Proficiency licensure, §§32.1-229.01, 32.1-229.01:1.
Schools and education.
Minimum standards, §22.1-138.

RAFFLES.
Charitable gaming.
General provisions, §§18.2-340.15 to 18.2-340.37.
See CHARITABLE GAMING.

RAIL AND PUBLIC TRANSPORTATION DEPARTMENT, §§33.1-391.2 to 33.1-391.5.
Civil actions against employees.
Attorney general or assistant representing, §2.2-507.
Commissioner of highways.
Liaison duties with other organizations, §33.1-190.4.
Contracts for passenger and freight rail and public transportation improvements.
Authority or director to let, §33.1-12.
Creation, §33.1-391.2.
Defense of employees, §33.1-11.
Director.
Appointment, §33.1-391.2.
Powers and duties, §33.1-391.3.
Freedom of information act.
Excluded records, §2.2-3705.6.
General powers of department, §33.1-391.4.
Intercity passenger rail operating and capital fund.
Establishment, §33.1-221.1:1.3.
Investments.
Liability exemption of officers and employees, §33.1-23.03:7.
Main office location, §33.1-7.
Monitoring and approving actions.
Transportation board, §33.1-12.
Responsibilities of department, §33.1-391.5.
Secretary of transportation.
Agency responsibility, §2.2-228.
Shortline railway preservation and development fund.
Administration of fund, §33.1-221.1:1.2.

RAILROAD CROSSINGS, §§56-405 to 56-412.2.
Bells.
Failure to signal, §§56-415, 56-416.
Sounding, §56-414.

RAILROAD CROSSINGS —Cont'd
Bridges.
Proceedings to remodel or replace existing bridges, §56-366.3.
Brush removal, §56-411.
Canals, §56-362.
Cattle guards, §§56-429, 56-430.
Appeals of decisions, §56-435.
Discontinuance, §56-434.
Enclosed lands, §56-433.
Clearance requirements, §56-417.1.
Closing, §56-365.1.
Commercial drivers' licenses.
Disqualification for railroad grade crossing violations, §46.2-341.20:1.
Employer penalty, §46.2-341.20:2.
Consolidation, §56-365.1.
County roads, §56-363.
Adjustments to trackage and roads, §56-405.02.
Closure, §33.1-145.1.
Maintenance by railroad, §56-405.
Maintenance of crossings, §56-405.1.
Proceedings to eliminate or abolish existing grade crossings, §33.1-145.1.
Crossbucks, §56-405.2.
Similar signs prohibited, §56-408.
Crossing tracks without shifting gears, §46.2-886.
Disobeying warning signals, §46.2-884.
Drivers to stop, look and listen, §46.2-886.
Failure to stop vehicle, §46.2-885.
Fine schedule for motor vehicle violations, VA SCt Rule 3B:2.
Gates, §§56-429, 56-430.
Highways, streets and roads, §56-363.
Adjustments to trackage and streets, §56-405.02.
Closing or consolidation of grade crossings, §56-365.1.
Closure of road, §33.1-145.1.
Definitions, §56-355.2.
Elimination of grade crossings by change of alignment of highways, §56-369.
Elimination of grade crossings by construction of replacement public highways, §56-369.
Limitation on establishment of new crossing, §33.1-145.1.
Maintenance of crossing, §§56-405, 56-405.1.
Maintenance of underpasses or overhead structures, §56-368.1.
Proceedings to eliminate or abolish existing grade crossings, §33.1-145.1.
Proceedings to eliminate or remodel existing crossings, §56-366.1.
Traffic infraction. See within this heading, "Traffic infractions."
Horns.
Failure to signal, §§56-415, 56-416.
Sounding, §56-414.
Injuring, destroying, etc., railroad signals, §18.2-155.
Livestock appraisals.
Application of provisions, §56-439.
Board duties, §56-436.
Costs, §§56-437, 56-438.
Effect, §56-437.
Maintenance, §56-405.
Agreements, §56-405.1.
Maximum fine for violating Title 46.2, §46.2-113.
Moving crawler-type tractors, steam shovels, etc., over grade crossings, §46.2-887.
Obstructing road or track, §§56-412.1, 56-412.2.

RAILROAD CROSSINGS —Cont'd
Overhead structures.
Definition of overpass, §56-355.2.
Maintenance of, §56-368.1.
Passing, §46.2-858.
Prepayment of fines for motor vehicle violations, §16.1-69.40:1.
Private highways, §§56-547, 56-548.
Proceedings to eliminate or remodel existing crossings, §56-366.1.
Closing or consolidation of grade crossings, §56-365.1.
Protective devices.
Installation of automatically operated devices, §56-406.1.
Maintenance, §56-406.2.
Train stopping before reaching crossings, §56-412.
Public-private transportation act.
Cost of crossing, §56-570.
Railroads intersecting other railroads, §56-363.
Reckless driving.
Passing at a railroad grade crossing, §46.2-858.
Renewable energy co-location of distribution facilities.
Obligations regarding railroad crossings, §67-1102.
School buses.
Stop, look and listen, §46.2-886.
Signal boards, §56-405.2.
Injuring, etc., railroad signals, §18.2-155.
Similar signs prohibited, §56-408.
State roads.
Elimination of grade crossings by change of alignment of roads, §56-369.
Elimination of grade crossings by construction of replacement public highways, §56-369.
Stopping, §56-412.
Streams, §56-362.
Subsequent maintenance of underpasses or overhead structures, §56-368.1.
Traffic control, §56-363.
Traffic infractions.
Crossing tracks without shifting gears, §46.2-886.
Disobeying warning signals, §46.2-884.
Drivers to stop, look and listen, §46.2-886.
Failure to stop vehicle, §46.2-885.
Fine schedule, VA SCt Rule 3B:2.
Moving crawler-type tractors, steam shovels, etc., §46.2-887.
Passing at a railroad grade crossing, §46.2-858.
Prepayment of fine, §16.1-69.40:1.
Traffic regulations generally, §§46.2-884 to 46.2-887.
Tree removal, §56-411.
Underpasses.
Defined, §56-355.2.
Maintenance of, §56-368.1.
Watercourses, §56-362.
Whistles.
Failures to signal, §§56-415, 56-416.
Sounding, §56-414.

RAILROAD CROSSTIES.
Forest products tax, §§58.1-1600 to 58.1-1622.
See FOREST PRODUCTS TAX.
Intangible personal property tax.
Generally, §§58.1-1100 to 58.1-1118.
See PERSONAL PROPERTY TAXES.
Liens of suppliers, §§43-24 to 43-26.

RAILROAD ROLLING STOCK TAX, §§58.1-2652 to 58.1-2659.
See PUBLIC SERVICE CORPORATION TAXATION.

RAILROADS.
ABC licenses.
Mixed beverages licenses, §4.1-210.
Accident investigations, §56-131.
Aircraft, owning and operating, §56-111.
Articles of incorporation.
Statement and brief description in articles, §13.1-620.
Bells, §§56-414 to 56-416.
Brush removal from right-of-way, §56-411.
Buchanan county.
Roadways within railroad right-of-way, maintenance, §56-412.3.
Cars.
Boarding or riding without paying fare.
Uniform fine schedule, VA SCt Rule 3C:2.
Breaking and entering, cargo theft, §18.2-147.1.
Burglary, §18.2-90.
Burning or destroying occupied cars in which persons dwell or lodge, §18.2-77.
Driving while intoxicated.
Generally, §§18.2-266 to 18.2-273.
See DRIVING WHILE INTOXICATED.
Unlawful, §18.2-266.
Employee liens, §§43-24 to 43-26.
Entering car used as dwelling or place of human habitation.
Intent to commit larceny, assault and battery or other felony, §18.2-91.
Intent to commit murder, rape, robbery or arson, §18.2-90.
Entering with intent to commit crime, malicious mischief or injury, §18.2-147.
Journal boxes.
Taking or removing waste or packing from, §18.2-156.
Obstructing or injuring, §18.2-153.
Obstructing streets or roads, §§56-412.1, 56-412.2.
Setting in motion with intent to commit crime, malicious mischief or injury, §18.2-147.
Shooting at or throwing missiles at, §18.2-154.
Supplier liens, §§43-24 to 43-26.
Trespassing on railroad trains, §18.2-160.
Uniform fine schedule, VA SCt Rules 3C:1, 3C:2.
Cattle guards, §§56-429, 56-430.
Appeals of decisions, §56-435.
Discontinuance, §56-434.
Enclosed lands, §56-433.
Clearance requirements for structures, §56-417.1.
Conductors.
Powers as conservators of the peace, §56-354.
Conflict of laws.
Liability for injuries to employees, §56-441.
Consolidations, §56-345.1.
Corporations generally, §§13.1-601 to 13.1-779.
See CORPORATIONS.
Credit card fraud used to obtain tickets.
Discounted ticket obtained from other than agent of company.
Presumption ticket acquired under violation of statute, §18.2-198.
Crossings and connections.
Connections between corporations.
General assembly may require, §56-34.
Generally, §§56-405 to 56-412.2.
See RAILROAD CROSSINGS.
Highway crossings, §§56-23 to 56-32.
See PUBLIC SERVICE COMPANIES.
Public service companies, §§56-17 to 56-34.

RAILROADS —Cont'd
Crossings and connections —Cont'd
Right of one to cross the works of another, §§56-17 to 56-22.
See PUBLIC SERVICE COMPANIES.
Dead bodies used for scientific study.
Receipts, §32.1-299.
Defined terms.
Limitations on passenger rail transportation liability, §56-446.1.
Railroad crossings, §56-355.2.
State highway system, §56-355.1.
Depot agents.
Powers of conservators of the peace, §56-354.
Discrimination against persons with disabilities, §51.5-44.
Drainage projects.
Assessment of benefits to railroads, §21-361.
Damage, §21-360.
Manner of crossing right-of-way, §21-363.
Notice to railroad, §21-362.
Rights-of-way, §§21-360 to 21-363.
Electric cars operating on rails.
Exemption from motor vehicle registration, §46.2-683.
Eminent domain.
Hydroelectric power dams, §62.1-98.
Right of power, §56-347.
Employee injuries.
Liability for, §56-441.
Employee liens, §§43-24 to 43-26.
Enclosed tracks.
Liability for injuries, §56-431.
Engine bells, whistles and horns, §56-414.
Engineers.
Powers as conservators of the peace, §56-354.
Engine fires.
Liability for, §56-428.
Erosion and sediment control.
General erosion and sediment control specifications, annual filing, §62.1-44.15:55.
Examinations of works and equipment, §56-128.
Excursion trains, §§46.2-2099.41 to 46.2-2099.44.
Failure to remove cause of complaint in cities or towns, §56-440.
Federal railroad administration track safety and inspection program.
Failure to make necessary repairs, §56-130.
Participation by commission, §56-129.1.
Fences.
Injury to, §18.2-157.
No-fence law.
Applicability, §55-312.
Fences along roadbeds, §§56-429, 56-430.
Fires set by engines or trains.
Liability, §56-428.
Flashing amber warning lights.
High-rail vehicles, §46.2-1025.
Forest fires.
Failure to properly maintain locomotives, §10.1-1145.
Inflammable material on lands adjoining right-of-way, §10.1-1147.
Freight arrival, notice requirements, §56-117.
Freight bills, §56-118.
Heavy rail transportation facilities.
Resources authority generally, §§62.1-197 to 62.1-223.
See RESOURCES AUTHORITY.

RAILROADS —Cont'd
High-rail vehicles.
Flashing amber warning lights, §46.2-1025.
Highway crossing.
Generally, §§56-405 to 56-412.2.
See RAILROAD CROSSINGS.
Horns, §§56-414 to 56-416.
Hydroelectric power dams.
Eminent domain right, §62.1-98.
Income tax.
Apportionment of taxable income, §58.1-420.
Modifications to taxable income, §58.1-403.
State taxation, §58.1-2608.
Information to be furnished to commission, §56-446.
Injuries to employees.
Assumption of risk, §8.01-59.
Contributory negligence.
No bar to recovery, §8.01-58.
Exculpatory contracts void, §8.01-60.
Liability of common carriers, §8.01-57.
Common carrier, defined, §8.01-61.
Election of remedies not required, §8.01-62.
Set-off of insurance, §8.01-60.
Violation of safety appliance acts.
Assumption of risk, §8.01-59.
Contributory negligence, §8.01-58.
Injuring, destroying, etc., signals, §18.2-155.
Injury to fences or cattle stops, §18.2-157.
Insurable interest in property along route, §56-352.
Insurance.
Injuries to railroad employees.
Set-off of insurance, §8.01-60.
Insurance companies investments, §38.2-1419.
Intercity passenger rail operating and capital fund.
Establishment, §33.1-221.1:1.3.
Joint ventures.
Entering into, §13.1-627.
Journal boxes.
Taking or removing waste or packing from, §18.2-156.
Liability.
Passenger rail transportation.
Limitations on liability, §56-446.1.
Livestock appraisals.
Application of provisions, §56-439.
Board duties, §56-436.
Costs, §56-437.
Fees of appraisers and clerks, §56-438.
Effect, §56-437.
Notice of injury or death of stock, §56-439.1.
Locomotives.
Exemption from motor vehicle registration, §46.2-683.
Maintenance, §56-413.01.
Mechanics' and materialmen's liens.
Creation for construction, §43-3.
Mergers, §56-345.1.
Motor carriers, passengers, §§46.2-2000 to 46.2-2099.44.
Motor carriers, property, §§46.2-2100 to 46.2-2176.
Motormen.
Powers as conservator of the peace, §56-354.
Motor vehicles.
Owning and operating, §56-111.
No-fence law.
Applicability, §55-312.

RAILROADS —Cont'd
Non-enclosed tracks.
Liability for injuries, §56-432.
Nonresident corporations.
Liability as common carrier, §56-122.
Norfolk.
Light rail system, extension to Virginia Beach, §33.1-221.1:8 (note).
Overhead high voltage line safety.
Application of provisions, §59.1-413.
Partnership agreements, entering into, §13.1-627.
Permits for using streets, highways, roads, etc.
City or town providing for issuance, §15.2-2015.
Police.
Conductors as conservators of the peace, §56-354.
Depot agents as conservators of the peace, §56-354.
Engineers as conservators of the peace, §56-354.
Motormen as conservators of the peace, §56-354.
Power to appoint, §56-353.
Station agents as conservators of the peace, §56-354.
Powers, §56-346.
Condemnation, §56-347.
Insurable interest in property along route, §56-352.
Police agent appointment, §56-353.
Private highways.
Crossings, §§56-547, 56-548.
Property taxes.
Local taxation, §58.1-2607.
Assessment of property by tax commissioner, §§58.1-2655 to 58.1-2657.
Public ground use without consent or compensation, §56-14.
Public-private transportation act, §§56-556 to 56-574.
See TRANSPORTATION.
Rail car maintenance, §56-413.01.
Railway enhancement fund, §33.1-221.1:1.1.
Rates.
Charging other than published tariff, §56-102.
Commission authority over, §56-99.2.
Real property taxes.
Nonoperating (noncarrier) property, §58.1-3201.
Repairs.
Penalties for failure to make, §56-130.
Reports of accident investigations, §56-131.
Retail sales and use tax.
Machinery, tools and equipment brought into state for use in constructing, §§58.1-604.1 to 58.1-604.3.
Railroad rolling stock.
Commercial and industrial exemptions, §58.1-609.3.
Rights-of-way.
Duty of care for recreational activities, §29.1-509.
Rolling stock tax, §§58.1-2652 to 58.1-2659.
See PUBLIC SERVICE CORPORATION TAXATION.
Safety requirements for vehicles transporting railroad employees, §56-419.2.
Sale of corporation.
Effect, §56-10.
Secondhand articles sales generally, §§59.1-125 to 59.1-130.
See SECONDHAND ARTICLE SALES.
Security registration exemptions, §13.1-514.
Shortline railway preservation and development fund.
Establishment, §33.1-221.1:1.2.

RAILROADS —Cont'd
Spark arrestors.
Cleaning and maintaining locomotives designed with, §56-413.01.
Special regulatory revenue tax, §§58.1-2660 to 58.1-2665.
Standards for locomotives and rail cars, §56-413.01.
State operation of public utilities.
Application of provisions to, §56-527.
State recordation tax.
Sales contracts for rolling stock or equipment, §§58.1-808, 58.1-809.
Station agents.
Powers as conservator of the peace, §56-354.
Stations.
Public gathering place requirements, §§32.1-198 to 32.1-202.
Stopping before reaching crossings, §56-412.
Supplier liens, §§43-24 to 43-26.
Switch keys, duplicates, §56-419.
Taxes.
Gross transportation receipts from operations as common carrier by motor vehicle, §56-111.
Property taxes, §§58.1-2655 to 58.1-2657.
Real and tangible personal property, §58.1-2607.
Rolling stock tax, §§58.1-2652 to 58.1-2659.
See PUBLIC SERVICE CORPORATION TAXATION.
Special regulatory revenue tax, §§58.1-2660 to 58.1-2665.
State taxation, §58.1-2608.
Telegraph or telephone lines, §56-383.
Erection parallel to railroads, §56-458.
Tickets acquired in violation of credit card fraud provisions.
Discounted ticket obtained from other than agent of company.
Presumption ticket acquired in violation of provisions, §18.2-198.
Tracks.
Adjustments to trackage and streets, §56-405.02.
Cars obstructing streets or roads, §§56-412.1, 56-412.2.
Driving animal on to recover damages, §18.2-158.
Employee liens, §§43-24 to 43-26.
Enclosed tracks.
Liability for injuries, §56-431.
Non-enclosed tracks.
Liability for injuries, §56-432.
Obstructing or injuring, §18.2-153.
Supplier liens, §§43-24 to 43-26.
Switch keys, duplicates, §56-419.
Trespassing on, §18.2-159.
Unused tracks kept in place, §56-451.1.
Vehicles obstructing, §§56-412.1, 56-412.2.
Traction engines.
Exemption from motor vehicle registration, §46.2-683.
Transportation companies generally, §§56-99.2 to 56-140.
See TRANSPORTATION COMPANIES.
Transportation districts.
Generally, §§15.2-4500 to 15.2-4534.
See TRANSPORTATION DISTRICTS.
Transportation infrastructure bank, §§33.1-23.6 to 33.1-23.13.
Tree removal from right-of-way, §56-411.
Underground utility line damage prevention.
Excavation on railroad owned land, exemption, §56-265.15:1.

RAILROADS —Cont'd
Unused tracks kept in place, §56-451.1.
Utility lines.
Crossing of railroads, §56-16.1.
Municipalities, §56-16.2.
Public-private education facilities and infrastructure act.
Utility crossings, §56-575.13.
Vehicles obstructing tracks, §§56-412.1, 56-412.2.
Vehicles operating on rails.
Exemption from motor vehicle registration, §46.2-683.
Virginia Beach.
Norfolk light rail system, extension to Virginia Beach, §33.1-221.1:8 (note).
Wagonway construction, §56-16.
Whistles, §§56-414 to 56-416.
Workers' compensation.
Employees defined, §65.2-101.

RAILWAY ENHANCEMENT FUND, §33.1-221.1:1.1.

RAINWATER.
Guidelines concerning use of, §32.1-248.2.

RAINY DAY FUND.
Revenue stabilization fund, VA Const Art X §8.

RAMPS ON CURBS.
Specifications for constructing at intersections for use by mobility impaired, §15.2-2021.

RANGE LIGHTS.
Anchoring on range of, §62.1-189.

RAPE, §18.2-61.
Abduction with intent to defile, §§18.2-48, 18.2-49.
Punishment upon conviction of certain subsequent violent felony sexual assault, §18.2-67.5:3.
Seizure and forfeiture of property used in connection with abduction, §19.2-386.32.
Suspension of sentence, placing on probation, §19.2-303.
Threatening, attempting or assisting, §18.2-49.
Abortions.
Funding by state, §32.1-92.1.
Attempted rape, §18.2-67.5.
Jail prisoner escape or release notice, §53.1-116.1.
Payment of medical fees in gathering evidence, §19.2-165.1.
Prisoner intake notice, §53.1-116.1:01.
Burglary.
Entering dwelling with intent to commit, §18.2-90.
Capital murder, §18.2-31.
Childhood sexual abuse, §8.01-249.
Child rape.
Grounds for teacher suspension, §22.1-315.
Jail prisoner escape or release notice, §53.1-116.1.
Minor under age of thirteen, §18.2-61.
Prisoner intake notice, §53.1-116.1:01.
Public school employees.
Criminal records checks, §§22.1-296.1, 22.1-296.2.
Report of convictions, §19.2-291.1.
Child victims' testimony.
Using two-way closed-circuit television, §18.2-67.9.
Civil commitment of sexually violent predators, §§37.2-900 to 37.2-920.
See SEXUALLY VIOLENT PREDATORS, CIVIL COMMITMENT.

RAPE —Cont'd
Commonwealth's attorneys.
Multidisciplinary response to sexual assault, §15.2-1627.4.
Confidentiality of information.
Records of persons receiving domestic or sexual violence services, §63.2-104.1.
Convict escape or release notice, §53.1-160.1.
Database of prisoners incarcerated for sexually violent offenses.
Access to records, §37.2-905.1.
Director to keep, requirements, review identification of prisoners scheduled for release, §§37.2-903, 37.2-905.1.
Death of victim, §18.2-63.1.
Deferral of proceedings, defendant placed on probation.
Counseling or therapy, completion.
Violation against spouse, §18.2-61.
Depositions of complaining witnesses, §18.2-67.
Discretionary felony sentencing guidelines, §17.1-805.
Firearm used or displayed, §18.2-53.1.
Freedom of information act.
Exclusions from chapter.
Rape crisis center records, §2.2-3705.2.
Health insurance coverage for victims, §38.2-3418.
Hearsay exception, recent complaint, §19.2-268.2.
HIV or hepatitis B or C.
Testing of person charged, §18.2-62.
Incest.
See INCEST.
Jail prisoner escape or release notice, §53.1-116.1.
Juvenile proceeding confidentiality exception.
Commission of delinquent act which would be felony if committed by adult, §16.1-309.1.
Juvenile serious offenders, §16.1-285.1.
Release and review hearings, §16.1-285.2.
Mandatory minimum term of confinement.
Rape of child under age of 13.
Offender more than 3 years older than victim, §18.2-61.
Medical fees in gathering evidence.
Payment, §19.2-165.1.
Medical personnel performing physical evidence recovery kit.
Sexual assault victims incapable of making informed decision, §54.1-2970.1.
Minor under age of thirteen.
Convict escape or release notice, §53.1-160.1.
Murder of the first degree, §18.2-32.
Object rape.
See OBJECT SEXUAL PENETRATION.
Personal identifying information.
Confidentiality.
Records of persons receiving domestic or sexual violence services, §63.2-104.1.
Person transported through or across Commonwealth.
Venue, §18.2-359.
Physical resistance, proof not required, §18.2-67.6.
Preliminary hearings.
Closed hearing, §18.2-67.8.
Spousal rape, §§19.2-218.1, 19.2-218.2.
Prisoner intake notice, §53.1-116.1:01.
Probation, conditions, §19.2-303.

RAPE —Cont'd
Punishment upon conviction of certain subsequent violent felony sexual assault, §18.2-67.5:3.
Rape shield law, §18.2-67.7.
Rebuttable presumption.
Capacity of juvenile over age of 10 but less than 12 to commit violation, §18.2-61.
Sentence of person twice previously convicted of certain violent felonies, §19.2-297.1.
Sexual assault, §§18.2-61 to 18.2-67.10.
See SEXUAL ASSAULT.
Sexual battery.
See SEXUAL BATTERY.
Sexually violent predators.
Civil commitment, §§37.2-900 to 37.2-920.
See SEXUALLY VIOLENT PREDATORS, CIVIL COMMITMENT.
Office of sexually violent predator services.
Establishment, §37.2-900.1.
Spousal rape, §18.2-61.
Convict escape or release notice, §53.1-160.1.
Jail prisoner escape or release notice, §53.1-116.1.
Preliminary hearings, §§19.2-218.1, 19.2-218.2.
Prisoner intake notice, §53.1-116.1:01.
Subsequent conviction.
Punishment, §18.2-67.5:3.
Suspension of sentence, §19.2-303.
Counseling or therapy, completion.
Violation against spouse, §18.2-61.
Rape of child under age of 13.
Offender more than 3 years older than victim, §18.2-61.
Treatment program for prisoners convicted of, §37.2-903.
Unchaste character or prior sexual conduct of complaining witness, §18.2-67.7.
Venue.
Person transported through or across Commonwealth, §18.2-359.

RAPE KIT.
Medical personnel performing physical evidence recovery kit.
Sexual assault victims incapable of making informed decision, §54.1-2970.1.

RAPE SHIELD LAW, §18.2-67.7.

RAPID HEAVY RAIL COMMUTER MASS TRANSPORTATION SYSTEM.
Motor vehicle fuel sales tax, §§58.1-1718.1 to 58.1-1724.4.

RAPPAHANNOCK COMMUNITY COLLEGE.
Community colleges generally.
See COMMUNITY COLLEGES.

RAPPAHANNOCK COUNTY.
Circuit court clerks serving also as clerk of general district court and juvenile and domestic relations district court.
Supplementing salary, §15.2-1635.1.
Combined transient occupancy and food and beverage tax, §58.1-3842.
Dirt and gravel roads.
Maximum speed limits on nonsurface treated highways, §46.2-873.1.
Public defenders office.
Established, §19.2-163.04.
School board.
Salary of members, §22.1-32.
Well abandonment ordinance.
Duty of owner to cap or close well.
Locality adopting ordinance, §32.1-176.5.

RAPPAHANNOCK COUNTY —Cont'd
Well construction.
Testing requirements, §32.1-176.5.

RAPPAHANNOCK RIVER.
Gang hooks.
Use in taking or catching fish, §28.2-306.
Grab hooks.
Use in taking or catching fish, §28.2-306.
Haul seine restrictions, §28.2-312.
Oysters and clams.
Patent tongs.
Area prohibitions, §28.2-508.
Planting grounds.
Declaration of public oyster rocks, beds and shoals, §28.2-639.
Leasing prohibitions, §28.2-636.
Rappahannock river basin commission, §§62.1-69.25 to 62.1-69.33:2.
Rivers generally.
See RIVERS.
Scenic river, §10.1-415.
Snatch hooks.
Use in taking or catching fish, §28.2-306.
Waters of the state generally.
See WATERS OF THE STATE.

RAPPAHANNOCK RIVER BASIN.
Preparation of plans and programs for management, §62.1-44.38.

RAPPAHANNOCK RIVER BASIN COMMISSION, §§62.1-69.25 to 62.1-69.33:2.
Accounts and records audited by auditor of public accounts, §62.1-69.33.
Advisory committees, establishing, §62.1-69.28.
Budget, §62.1-69.33.
Chairpersons, §62.1-69.30.
Compensation of members, §62.1-69.33:1.
Cooperation of agencies of Commonwealth, §62.1-69.31.
Created, 1998 ch 553. (expires July 1, 2000), 2000 ch 386 (Sunset provision repealed), 2000 ch 456 (Sunset provision repealed).
Dissolution, §62.1-69.32.
Distribution of cost among local government members, §62.1-69.33.
Established upon passage by two-thirds of basins localities of resolution, §62.1-69.26.
Estimated expenses to be included in budget, §62.1-69.33.
Executive summary of activities, §62.1-69.33:2.
Expense reimbursement, §62.1-69.33:1.
Fiscal agent, designation, §62.1-69.33.
Funding, §62.1-69.33.
Guidance for stewardship and enhancement of water quality and natural resources.
Purposes and mission of commission, §62.1-69.27.
Meetings, §62.1-69.30.
Membership, §62.1-69.29.
Nonprofit corporation.
Establishing as instrumentality to assist in details administering affairs, §62.1-69.28.
Powers, §62.1-69.28.
Purposes and mission, §62.1-69.27.
Rappahannock river basin defined, §62.1-69.25.
Resolution establishing commission, language, §62.1-69.26.
Soil and water conservation district member, §62.1-69.29.
Staffing provided by local governing bodies and planning district commission, §62.1-69.31.

RAPPAHANNOCK RIVER BASIN COMMISSION —Cont'd
Terms and vacancies, §62.1-69.29.
Withdrawal from commission, §62.1-69.32.

RATE OF INTEREST.
Generally.
See INTEREST.

RATE SERVICE ORGANIZATIONS.
Cooperation among organization, §38.2-1924.
Examination of, §38.2-1925.
Insurance rates generally, §§38.2-1900 to 38.2-1928.
See INSURANCE RATES.
Licensing, §38.2-1914.
Operation and control, §38.2-1913.
Prohibited conduct, §38.2-1916.
Workers' compensation, automobiles, home protection, etc., rates.
Cooperation among organizations, §38.2-2019.
Examination of policies or other evidence of insurance, §38.2-2021.
Filings by, §38.2-2004.
Procurement of actuarial, technical or other services, §38.2-2020.

RATES OF AIR CARRIERS.
See AIR CARRIERS.

RATES OF INSURANCE.
Generally, §§38.2-1900 to 38.2-1928.
See INSURANCE RATES.
Workers' compensation, automobiles, home protection, etc., §§38.2-2000 to 38.2-2027.
See INSURANCE RATES.

RATES OF TELEGRAPH OR TELEPHONE COMPANIES.
See TELEGRAPH OR TELEPHONE COMPANIES.

RATES OF TELEPHONE COOPERATIVES.
See TELEPHONE COOPERATIVES.

RATES OF TRANSPORTATION COMPANIES.
See TRANSPORTATION COMPANIES.

RATIO OF STUDENTS TO INSTRUCTIONAL PERSONNEL.
Schools and education, §22.1-253.13:1.

RATITES, §3.2-6500.

RAZING HISTORIC STRUCTURES.
Civil penalty imposed.
Urban county form of government, ordinances, §15.2-819.

RAZORS.
Carrying concealed weapons, §§18.2-308, 18.2-308.2.
Convicted felons, possession or transportation or concealing, §18.2-308.2.
Courthouses, carrying weapon into, §18.2-283.1.
School property, possession on, §18.2-308.1.
Use in commission of crime.
Forfeiture, §19.2-386.29.
Weapons offenses generally.
See WEAPONS OFFENSES.

REACT TEAMS.
Special license plates, §46.2-748.

READING RECOVERY PROGRAM.
Block grants, §22.1-199.1.

READING SPECIALISTS FOR ELEMENTARY SCHOOLS.
Employment by school boards, §22.1-253.13:1.

READING THE LAW PROGRAM, §54.1-3926.

READY-MIXED CONCRETE PLANTS.
Water discharge permits.
General permits for discharges of stormwater and process wastewater, §62.1-44.15:5.2.
Public hearings and permit procedures before the board, §62.1-44.15:02.

REAL ESTATE.
Real property.
Generally.
See REAL PROPERTY.

REAL ESTATE APPRAISAL MANAGEMENT COMPANIES, §§54.1-2020 to 54.1-2023.
Bond or letter of credit, §54.1-2021.1.
Civil penalties for violations, §54.1-2023.
Definitions, §54.1-2020.
Exemptions from chapter, §54.1-2021.
Fees charged, disclosure, §54.1-2022.
License requirement, §§54.1-2021.1, 54.1-2022.
Moral character requirement, §54.1-2021.1.
Persons not subject to chapter, §54.1-2021.
Prohibited acts, §54.1-2022.
Penalties, §54.1-2023.

REAL ESTATE APPRAISER BOARD, §§54.1-2012, 54.1-2013.
Subpoena power, §54.1-2015.

REAL ESTATE APPRAISERS, §§54.1-2009 to 54.1-2019.
Appointment of service of process agent for nonresidents, §54.1-2019.
Appraisal management companies.
Appraiser engaged by, disclosure of fee, §54.1-2011.
Authentication of reports, §54.1-2017.
Board of real estate appraisers, §§54.1-2012, 54.1-2013.
Subpoena power, §54.1-2015.
Categories of licensure, §54.1-2016.
Consent to suits by nonresidents, §54.1-2019.
Defined terms, §54.1-2009.
Examinations, §54.1-2013.
Exemptions from licensing, §54.1-2010.
Licensure categories, §54.1-2016.
Licensure requirements, §54.1-2011.
Continuing education, §54.1-2014.
Exemptions, §54.1-2010.
List, §54.1-2018.
Management companies, §§54.1-2020 to 54.1-2023.
Real estate appraisal management companies, §§54.1-2020 to 54.1-2023.
Residential property transfer disclosure duties, §55-523.
Roster, §54.1-2018.
Terms, use of, §54.1-2017.
Transaction recovery fund, §§54.1-2112 to 54.1-2120.
Unlawful procurement of licensure, §54.1-102.
Unlawful use of licensure, §54.1-111.
Use of terms, §54.1-2017.

REAL ESTATE BOARD, §§54.1-2104, 54.1-2105.
Continuing education, §54.1-2105.
Educational curriculum guidelines, §54.1-2105.
Fair housing.
Disciplinary action against real estate licensees, §§36-96.8, 36-96.20.
General powers, §54.1-2105.

REAL ESTATE BOARD —Cont'd
Horizontal property regimes.
Changes in project by developer, §55-79.26.
Enjoining violations, §55-79.30.
Hearings, §55-79.27.
Inspections, §55-79.18.
Fee, §55-79.19.
Public reports, §55-79.21.
Waiver of initial inspection, §55-79.20.
Investigations of developer violations, §55-79.29.
Notice by developer prior to offering projects, §55-79.16.
Notice by developer prior to offering projects, §55-79.16.
Accompaniments, §55-79.17.
Changes in project by developer, §55-79.26.
Real estate brokers, salespersons and rental agents, §§54.1-2104 to 54.1-2105.1, 54.1-2143.
Residential property transfer disclosures.
Forms, §55-525.
Duty to develop, §54.1-2105.1.
Subdivided land sales, §§55-336 to 55-347.

REAL ESTATE BROKERS, SALESPERSONS AND RENTAL AGENTS, §§54.1-2100 to 54.1-2145.
Adverse facts pertaining to physical condition of property.
Disclosures to prospective buyers.
Duties of licensees engaged by landlord, §54.1-2133.
Duties of licensees engaged by seller, §54.1-2131.
Physical condition of property defined, §§54.1-2131, 54.1-2133.
Alternative properties.
Showing prospective buyers.
Licensee engaged by seller, §54.1-2131.
Showing prospective tenants.
Licensee engaged by landlord providing, §54.1-2133.
Antitrust laws not superseded or impaired, §54.1-2145.
Assistance to buyer or prospective buyer.
Licensee engaged by seller providing, §54.1-2131.
Assistance to tenant or potential tenant.
Licensee engaged by landlord providing, §54.1-2133.
Association of realtors.
License plates.
Issuance of special plates to members, §46.2-746.8.
Audit of brokers.
Renewal of firm license, certification of audit, §54.1-2106.2.
Voluntary compliance program, §54.1-2111.1.
Banks.
Subsidiaries.
Real estate brokerage business of controlled subsidiaries, §6.2-888.
Board, real estate, §§54.1-2104 to 54.1-2105.1.
General powers, regulations, §54.1-2105.
Regulations to be consistent, §54.1-2143.
Brokerage agreements.
Disclosure by licensee, §§54.1-2131, 54.1-2133.
Disclosure of dual representation, §54.1-2139.
Broker compliance program, §54.1-2111.1.
Buyers engaging licensee.
Duties of licensee, §54.1-2132.
Cease and desist orders.
Broker or salesperson not licensed by board, §54.1-2105.2.

REAL ESTATE BROKERS, SALESPERSONS AND RENTAL AGENTS —Cont'd
Commencement of brokerage agreements, §54.1-2137.
Common source information companies.
Use does not create relationship, §54.1-2141.
Compensation shall not imply brokerage agreement, §54.1-2140.
Commercial real estate brokers' liens, §§55-526, 55-527.
Common law abrogated, §54.1-2144.
Common source information companies.
Brokerage relationship not created by using, §54.1-2141.
Compensation shall not imply brokerage agreement, §54.1-2140.
Compliance program for brokers not in compliance, §54.1-2111.1.
Condominiums.
Escrow of deposits, §55-79.95.
Consent to suits, §54.1-2111.
Construction of provisions in relation to antitrust laws, §54.1-2145.
Consumer protection.
Application of provisions, §59.1-199.
Continuing education.
Relicensure of brokers and salespersons, §54.1-2105.03.
Contracts or agreements for services to be performed in sale by party.
Written evidence required to maintain action, §11-2.
Defective drywall.
Disclosures to owner by property manager, §54.1-2135.
Disclosures to prospective buyers, §54.1-2131.
Disclosures to prospective tenants, §§54.1-2133, 54.1-2134.
Definitions.
Duties of brokers and salespersons, §54.1-2130.
Real estate broker, §54.1-2100.
Real estate salesperson, §54.1-2101.
Designated standard agency or designated representation disclosure, §54.1-2139.1.
Disclosures.
Adverse facts pertaining to physical condition of property, §§54.1-2131, 54.1-2133.
Brokerage relationship, §54.1-2138.
Defective drywall.
Disclosures to owner by property manager, §54.1-2135.
Disclosures to prospective buyers, §54.1-2131.
Disclosures to prospective tenants, §§54.1-2133, 54.1-2134.
Designated agency or designated representation, §54.1-2139.1.
Dual agency or dual relationship, §54.1-2139.
Commercial real estate transactions, §54.1-2139.01.
Limited service representatives, §54.1-2138.1.
Discriminatory housing practices.
Fair housing violations.
Actions by real estate board on real estate licenses, §36-96.20.
Liability not limited, §54.1-2142.
Dual agency or dual relationship disclosure, §54.1-2139.
Commercial real estate transactions, §54.1-2139.01.
Duties of real estate brokers and salespersons, §§54.1-2130 to 54.1-2145.
Supervising broker, §54.1-2110.1.

REAL ESTATE BROKERS, SALESPERSONS AND RENTAL AGENTS —Cont'd
Educational requirements as condition of licensure.
Continuing education.
Relicensure of brokers and salespersons, §54.1-2105.03.
Reactivation of inactive license.
Remedial education for brokers and salespersons, §54.1-2105.04.
Regulations, adoption by board, power, requirements, §54.1-2105.
Relicensure of brokers and salespersons, §54.1-2105.03.
Remedial education for brokers and salespersons.
Reactivation of inactive license, §54.1-2105.04.
Salespersons within one year of licensure.
Guidelines, establishment, requirements, §54.1-2105.01.
Schools established to offer courses.
Regulation by board, §54.1-2105.02.
Standards of quality, establishment.
Prelicensure and broker licensure courses, §54.1-2105.
Waiver of requirements by boards, §54.1-2105.
Electronic recordkeeping, §54.1-2146.
Escrow accounts.
Condominiums.
Deposits made in disposition of units, §55-79.95.
Foreclosure, protection of funds in event of, §54.1-2108.1.
Exemptions from licensing, §54.1-2103.
Fair housing violations.
Actions by real estate board on real estate licenses, §36-96.20.
False information, liability for, §54.1-2142.1.
Foreclosure, protection of funds in event of, §54.1-2108.1.
Forms.
Disclosure of brokerage relationship, §54.1-2138.
Disclosure of designated agency or designated representation, §54.1-2139.1.
Disclosure of dual agency or dual relationship, §54.1-2139.
Commercial real estate transactions, §54.1-2139.01.
Fund protection, §54.1-2108.
Foreclosure, protection of funds in event of, §54.1-2108.1.
Gross receipts of brokers for license tax purposes.
Limitations, §58.1-3732.2.
Immunity.
Lead-based paint.
Sale or lease of residential dwelling.
Agent immunity and disclosure requirements, §8.01-226.7.
Inactive license.
Reactivation.
Remedial education for brokers and salespersons, §54.1-2105.04.
Knowledge not to be imputed, §54.1-2142.
Landlord engaging licensee to lease property.
Duties of licensee, §54.1-2133.
Lead-based paint.
Sale or lease of residential dwelling.
Agent immunity and disclosure requirements, §8.01-226.7.
Liability for false information by licensees, §54.1-2142.1.

REAL ESTATE BROKERS, SALESPERSONS AND RENTAL AGENTS —Cont'd
Liability for misrepresentations by licensees, §54.1-2142.
License plates.
Association of realtors.
Issuance of special plates to members, §46.2-746.8.
License taxes, gross receipts limitations, §58.1-3732.2.
Licensure requirements, §54.1-2106.1.
Exemptions, §54.1-2103.
Renewal of firm license, certification of audit, §54.1-2106.2.
Limited service representatives.
Disclosures, §54.1-2138.1.
Managing real estate.
Duties of licensee, §54.1-2135.
Misrepresentations by licensees, §54.1-2142.
Mortgage lender and broker act.
Exempt from chapter, §6.2-1602.
Physical condition of property.
Adverse facts.
Disclosure to prospective buyers, §§54.1-2131, 54.1-2133.
Defined, §§54.1-2131, 54.1-2133.
Place of business for real estate brokers, §54.1-2110.
Preconditions to brokerage agreement, §54.1-2136.
Preparation of real estate contracts, §54.1-2101.1.
Prospective buyers.
Duties of licensees engaged by landlord, §54.1-2133.
Duties of licensees engaged by seller, §54.1-2131.
Prospective tenants.
Duties of landlord engaging licensee, §54.1-2133.
Duties of tenants engaging licensee, §54.1-2134.
Protection of funds, §54.1-2108.
Foreclosure, protection of funds in event of, §54.1-2108.1.
Reactivation of inactive license.
Remedial education for brokers and salespersons, §54.1-2105.04.
Real estate settlements.
Generally, §§55-525.8 to 55-525.32.
See REAL ESTATE SETTLEMENTS.
Settlement agents.
Generally, §§55-525.16 to 55-525.32.
See REAL ESTATE SETTLEMENTS.
Persons who may act as, §55-525.19.
Reciprocal licensing, §54.1-2105.
Records retained in electronic form, §54.1-2146.
Renewal of firm license, certification of audit, §54.1-2106.2.
Residential property transfer disclosure duties, §55-523.
Rules and regulations.
Consistency with article required, §54.1-2143.
Educational requirements for licensure, §§54.1-2105 to 54.1-2105.04.
Seller engaging licensee.
Duties of licensee, §54.1-2131.
Service of process agent.
Designation, §54.1-2111.
Supervising broker, duties, §54.1-2110.1.
Tenants engaging licensee.
Duties of licensee, §54.1-2134.
Termination of brokerage agreements, §54.1-2137.

REAL ESTATE BROKERS, SALESPERSONS AND RENTAL AGENTS —Cont'd
Transaction recovery act, §§54.1-2112 to 54.1-2120.
Travel insurance, §§38.2-1887 to 38.2-1890.
Unlawful procurement of licensure, §54.1-102.
Unlawful use of licensure, §54.1-111.
Unlicensed conduct of business, §54.1-2106.1.
Voluntary compliance program for brokers not in compliance, §54.1-2111.1.

REAL ESTATE COOPERATIVES, §§55-424 to 55-506.
Administration by board, §55-496.
Powers, §§55-502, 55-503.
Advertising signs on common elements, §55-451.
Agreements to varied provisions, §55-427.
Alterations of units, §55-447.
Applicability of chapter, §§55-425, 55-433, 55-476.
Associations.
Approval of budgets, §55-460.
Assumption of debt.
Contents of public offering statement, §55-479.
Limitations, §55-473.1.
Bylaws, §55-463.
Common expense assessments, §55-471.
Common interest community board.
Generally, §§54.1-2345 to 54.1-2354.
See COMMON INTEREST COMMUNITY BOARD.
Contract liability, §55-468.
Conveyance of cooperative, §55-469.
Creation, §55-458.
Encumbrance of cooperative, §55-469.
Executive board, §§55-460, 55-462.
Termination of contracts and leases of declarant, §55-462.
Insurance, §55-470.
Meetings, §55-465.
Membership, §§55-458, 55-460.
Executive board, §55-460.
Nonpayment of assessments.
Remedies, §55-472.
Organizations, §55-458.
Powers, §55-459.
Public offering statements.
Copies to, §55-478.
Quorums, §55-466.
Records, §55-474.
Reports, §55-504.1.
Development, dissemination.
Common interest community board, §54.1-2350.
Tort liability, §55-468.
Transmittal of foreclosure notices, §55-473.
Trustee powers to be exercised without inquiry, §55-475.
Upkeep of cooperatives, §55-464.
Voting, §§55-466, 55-467.
Boundaries of units, §§55-439, 55-448.
Relocation, §55-448.
Building code applicability, §§55-425, 55-429.
Bylaws, §55-463.
Construction and validity, §55-440.
Capital components.
Reserves for capital components, §55-471.1.
Cease and desist orders, §§55-500, 55-501.
Common expense assessments, §55-471.
Reserves for capital components, §55-471.1.

REAL ESTATE COOPERATIVES —Cont'd
Common expense liabilities, §55-444.
Common interest community board.
Generally, §§54.1-2345 to 54.1-2354.
See COMMON INTEREST COMMUNITY BOARD.
Common interest community manager.
Fiduciary duty, §54.1-2353.
Generally.
See COMMON INTEREST COMMUNITY MANAGERS.
Conflict of laws, §§55-431, 55-432.
Consequential damages, §55-436.
Consolidations, §55-457.
Construction of provisions.
Effectuation of purpose, §55-433.
Implicit repeals, §55-432.
Contents of declarations, §55-442.
Contract liability, §55-468.
Conveyance, §55-469.
Creation, §55-438.
Damage awards, §55-436.
Declarations.
Amendments, §55-453.
Association power limitations, §55-459.
Boundary relocations, §55-448.
Construction and validity, §55-440.
Contents, §55-442.
Declarant contracts and leases.
Termination, §55-462.
Declarant control periods, §55-460.
Declarant reports, §55-504.
Declarants' obligations to complete and restore, §55-494.
Development rights, exercise of, §55-446.
Executive board powers to amend, §55-460.
Leasehold cooperatives, §55-443.
Limited common elements allocation, §55-445.
Ownership.
Interest allocations, §55-444.
Secured lender rights, §55-455.
Subdivision of units, §55-449.
Transfers of special rights, §55-461.
Vote allocations, §55-444.
Definition, §55-426.
Disabled, §55-487.
Elderly, §55-487.
Description of units, §55-441.
Development rights.
Exercise of, §55-446.
Public offering statements.
Required information, §§55-478, 55-479.
Upkeep responsibilities, §55-464.
Easement for encroachments, §55-450.
Easements through common elements, §55-452.
Eminent domain, §55-430.
Fiduciary duty to association.
Common interest community manager, §54.1-2353.
General principles of law applicable, §55-431.
Homestead exemptions, §55-428.
Horizontal property regimes generally, §§55-79.1 to 55-79.38.
See HORIZONTAL PROPERTY REGIMES.
Individuals age 55 and over.
Permanent residency restricted to.
Common expense assessments, §55-471.
Insurance, §55-470.
Investigative powers of board, §55-503.
Leasehold cooperatives, §55-443.

REAL ESTATE COOPERATIVES —Cont'd
Liens, §§55-469, 55-473.
Nonpayment of assessments, §55-472.
Release of liens, §55-486.
Limited common elements allocation, §55-445.
Exercise of development rights, §55-446.
Local ordinances.
Applicability, §§55-425, 55-429.
Master associations, §55-456.
Mergers, §55-457.
Obligation of good faith, §55-435.
Ownership interest allocations, §55-444.
Exercise of development rights, §55-446.
Mergers or consolidations of cooperatives, §55-457.
Pesticide application notice.
Posting in or upon common elements, §55-464.1.
Promotional material.
Cease and desist orders, §55-500.
Property owners' associations generally.
Applicability of provisions, §55-508.
Protection of cooperative purchasers, §§55-476 to 55-495.
Applicability of article, §55-476.
Cancellation rights, §55-483.
Conversion buildings, §55-487.
Declarants' obligations, §55-494.
Effect of violations, §55-492.
Escrow of deposits, §55-485.
Express warranties, §55-488.
Statute of limitations, §55-491.
Implied warranties, §55-489.
Exclusion, §55-490.
Modification, §55-490.
Statute of limitations, §55-491.
Promotional material labeling, §55-493.
Public offering statements.
Amendments, §55-478.
Cooperatives containing conversion buildings, §55-481.
Cooperative securities, §55-482.
Cooperative subject to development rights.
Required information, §55-479.
Copies to association, §55-478.
Delivering not required, §55-476.
Liability for, §55-477.
Preparation not required, §55-476.
Provisions, §55-478.
Required information, §55-481.
Requirements, §55-477.
Terms, §55-478.
Time-shares, §55-480.
Release of liens, §55-486.
Resales, §55-484.
Substantial completion of units, §55-495.
Provision violations.
Cease and desist orders, §§55-500, 55-501.
Penalties, §55-506.
Public offering statements.
Agency regulation of, §55-505.
Amendments by association, §55-473.1.
Amendments by declarant, §55-504.
Punitive damages, §55-436.
Registration.
Application, §55-498.
Receipt of, §55-499.
Exemptions, §55-497.
Order of registration, §55-499.
Penalties for violations, §55-506.
Required, §55-497.
Revocation, §55-501.
Uncompleted unit approval, §55-498.

REAL ESTATE COOPERATIVES —Cont'd
Remedies, §55-436.
Resales of cooperative interests, §55-484.
Reserves for capital components, §55-471.1.
Rule against perpetuities, §55-440.
Sales, use for, §55-451.
Secured lender rights, §55-455.
Senior housing communities.
Common expense assessments, §55-471.
Special damages, §55-436.
Statements on resale of cooperative interests, §55-484.
Stormwater management.
Common interest community ceding responsibility to governmental entity.
Immunity for civil liability, §62.1-44.15:41.
Subdivision of units, §55-449.
Taxes, §55-428.
Termination, §55-454.
Executive board powers, §55-460.
Title, §55-440.
Title of chapter, §55-424.
Tort liability, §55-468.
Unconscionable contracts, §55-434.
Unconscionable management contracts, §55-462.
Unit alterations, §55-447.
Unit descriptions, §55-441.
Upkeep duty of associations, §55-464.
Variation of provisions by agreement, §55-427.
Vote allocations, §55-444.
Waiver of rights or remedies, §55-248.9.
Zoning.
Applicability, §§55-425, 55-429.

REAL ESTATE INVESTMENT TRUSTS.
Deeds.
Recordation, §55-106.4.
Interest.
Usury, prohibited from pleading, §6.2-308.
Taxable income, §58.1-402.
Usury.
Prohibited from pleading, §6.2-308.

REAL ESTATE LOAN TRANSACTIONS.
Mortgages and deeds of trust.
See MORTGAGES AND DEEDS OF TRUST.
Savings institutions, §§6.2-1179 to 6.2-1185.

REAL ESTATE SETTLEMENT AGENTS.
Generally, §§55-525.16 to 55-525.32.
See REAL ESTATE SETTLEMENTS.

REAL ESTATE SETTLEMENT PROCEDURES ACT OF 1974.
Violations.
Attorney general, action to enjoin, §6.2-1626.

REAL ESTATE SETTLEMENTS, §§55-525.8 to 55-525.32.
Affiliated business.
Referrals to, disclosure by settlement service provider, §55-525.13.
Applicability of chapter, §55-525.9.
Appraisal or valuation using automated or other valuation mechanism by person not licensed as appraiser.
Fee charged by lender, disclosure, §55-525.14.
Attorney fees.
Failure to cause disbursement, §55-525.15.
Consumer real estate settlement protection act.
See CONSUMER REAL ESTATE SETTLEMENT PROTECTION ACT.

REAL ESTATE SETTLEMENTS —Cont'd
Damages.
Failure to cause disbursement, §55-525.15.
Definitions, §55-525.8.
Settlement agents, §55-525.16.
Disbursement of loan funds.
Defined, §55-525.8.
Duty of lender at or before loan closing, §55-525.10.
Failure to cause, §55-525.15.
Disbursement of settlement proceeds.
Defined, §55-525.8.
Duty of settlement agent, §55-525.11.
Failure to cause, §55-525.15.
Disclosures.
Appraisal or valuation using automated or other valuation mechanism by person not licensed as appraiser.
Fee charged by lender, §55-525.14.
Referrals to affiliated settlement service provider, §55-525.13.
Settlement agents, §55-525.23.
Failure to comply with chapter.
Validity or enforceability of loan documents not effected, §55-525.9.
Kickbacks, rebates, commissions, thing of value, other payment.
Receipt prohibited, exceptions, §55-525.12.
Lenders.
Appraisal or valuation using automated or other valuation mechanism by person not licensed as appraiser.
Fee charged by lender, disclosure, §55-525.14.
Defined, §55-525.8.
Duty, §55-525.10.
Failure to carry out, liability, §55-525.15.
Loan documents.
Defined, §55-525.8.
Validity and enforceability not affected by noncompliance with chapter, §55-525.9.
Noncompliance with chapter.
Validity or enforceability of loan documents not affected, §55-525.9.
Overpayments.
Return to provider of funds, §55-525.11.
Party to real estate transaction.
Authority to provide escrow, closing, settlement services, §55-525.19.
Transaction containing more than 4 residential dwelling units, §55-525.18.
Defined, §55-525.16.
Escrow, closing, settlement services guidelines.
Copy furnished, §55-525.23.
Real estate settlement procedures act of 1974.
Violations.
Attorney General, action to enjoin, §6.2-1626.
Recordation of documents.
Duty of settlement agent, §55-525.11.
Refinancing or other loans where rescission applies.
Disbursement of loan funds by lender, time, §55-525.10.
Settlement agents, §§55-525.16 to 55-525.32.
Accounting by title insurers acting as agents, §55-525.29.
Analysis of escrow accounts.
Title insurance agents acting as settlement agents, §55-525.20.
Applicability of chapter, §55-525.18.
Limitation on, §55-525.17.

REAL ESTATE SETTLEMENTS —Cont'd
Settlement agents —Cont'd
Audit of escrow accounts.
Requirement, frequency, §55-525.20.
Care owed.
Duty to exercise reasonable care, §55-525.20.
Charges for complying with settlement statement requirements, §55-525.26.
Choice of agents, §55-525.22.
Disclosure, §55-525.23.
Compliance with chapter and other requirements.
Duty, §55-525.20.
Conditions for providing services, §55-525.24.
Condominiums' resale by purchasers, §§55-79.97, 55-79.97:3.
Confidentiality of information, §55-525.32.
Definitions, §§55-525.8, 55-525.16.
Disbursement of funds held in escrow, §55-525.24.
Disbursement of settlement proceeds.
Duty of settlement agent, §55-525.11.
Failure to cause, §55-525.15.
Disclosures, §55-525.23.
Duties, §§55-525.11, 55-525.20.
Failure to carry out, liability, §55-525.15.
Educational requirements.
Licensing authority may issue, §55-525.28.
Errors and omissions or malpractice insurance.
Duty to maintain, amount, §55-525.20.
Escrow accounts.
Provisions for maintaining, §55-525.24.
Escrow, closing, settlement services guidelines.
Disclosure, copy furnished party to transaction, §55-525.23.
Escrows held by agent pursuant to instructions or agreement, §55-525.24.
Estimation of charges made in good faith, §55-525.25.
Felony conviction.
Person prohibited from assisting or being employed by, §55-525.21.
Persons prohibited from acting as agent, §55-525.19.
Fidelity bond or employee dishonesty insurance.
Duty to maintain, amount, waiver of bond requirement, §55-525.20.
Fiduciary capacity.
Funds deposited with agent handled in, §55-525.24.
Fiduciary trusts accounts.
Funds deposited in, §55-525.24.
Fraud, deceit, misrepresentation.
Felony conviction involving.
Person prohibited from assisting or being employed by, §55-525.21.
Funds deposited with agent, §55-525.24.
Injunctions, restraining orders.
Violations, §55-525.31.
Interest received on deposited funds.
Agent not to retain, §55-525.24.
Law real estate settlement agents.
Defined, §55-525.16.
Requirements for providing services and receiving compensation, §55-525.18.
Legal advice, authority to provide.
Disclosure, §55-525.23.
Order, rules, regulations, subpoenas, summonses.
Licensing authority may issue, §55-525.28.
Particular agent.
Seller may not require use, §55-525.22.
Disclosure, §55-525.23.
Penalties and liabilities, §55-525.31.

REAL ESTATE SETTLEMENTS —Cont'd
Settlement agents —Cont'd
Person prohibited from assisting or being employed by, §55-525.21.
Persons who may act as, §55-525.19.
Real estate brokers.
Limitation of applicability of chapter to licensees performing settlement services, §55-525.17.
Records of affairs.
Duty to maintain, §55-525.27.
Records pertaining to settlements handled.
Retention, time period, §55-525.27.
Registration with appropriate licensing authority, §55-525.30.
Fee, §55-525.30.
Requirement, §55-525.30.
Termination, grounds, §55-525.31.
Release of deed of trust, §55-66.3.
Certificate of satisfaction or partial satisfaction, delivery to agent, §55-66.3.
Restitution.
Violations, ordering, §55-525.31.
Right to select agent, §55-525.22.
Disclosure, §55-525.23.
Role in closing transaction.
Disclosure, §55-525.23.
Settlement statements.
Charges for complying with requirements.
Prohibition, §55-525.26.
Defined, §55-525.16.
Falsifying, prohibition, §55-525.25.
Requirements, §55-525.24.
Surety bond.
Duty to maintain, amount, waiver of bond requirement, §55-525.20.
Title insurance availability notification to buyer, §38.2-4616.
Title insurance premiums payable to insurers and agents.
Held in agent's settlement account, §55-525.24.
Unauthorized practice of law.
Guidelines to avoid or prevent.
Complaints concerning noncompliance, §55-525.30.
Regulations establishing, §55-525.30.
Injunctions, §55-525.31.
Unlicensed practice, penalties, §55-525.31.
Variation of chapter's provisions by agreement.
Prohibition, disclosure, §55-525.23.
Violations of chapter or rules and regulations, §55-525.31.
Waiver of rights conferred by chapter.
Prohibition, disclosure, §55-525.23.
Settlement defined, §55-525.8.
Settlement service provider.
Defined, §55-525.8.
Referrals to affiliated providers.
Disclosure required, §55-525.13.
Title insurance.
Availability of owner's insurance.
Notification to purchaser by settlement agent, §55-525.11.
Variation of chapter's provisions by agreement.
Disclosure by settlement agent prohibited, §55-525.23.
Waiver of rights conferred by chapter.
Disclosure by settlement agent prohibited, §55-525.23.

REAL ESTATE SETTLEMENTS —Cont'd
Wet settlement act.
See MORTGAGES AND DEEDS OF TRUST.

REAL ESTATE TIME-SHARES, §§55-360 to 55-400.
See TIME-SHARES.

REAL ESTATE TRANSACTION RECOVERY ACT.
Real estate brokers, salespersons and rental agents, §§54.1-2112 to 54.1-2120.

REAL ID ACT.
Computer chips or radio-frequency devices in drivers' licenses or special ID cards.
Refusal of DMV to comply, §46.2-323.01.
State departments and agencies.
Participation limited, §2.2-614.2.

REAL PARTY IN INTEREST.
Beneficial owners.
Suit when legal title in another, §8.01-12.
Cessation of defendant powers, §8.01-17.

REAL PROPERTY.
Abandoned property.
Disposition of unclaimed property.
Escheat, §§55-168 to 55-201.1.
See ESCHEAT.
Generally, §§55-210.1 to 55-210.30.
See UNCLAIMED PROPERTY.
Absolute auction of real property, §54.1-607.
Annulment of marriage.
Consumer finance companies, §6.2-1524.
Appointment powers.
Release of, §§64.2-2700 to 64.2-2704.
Assignments for benefit of creditors, §§55-156 to 55-160.
Attachment.
Removal of district court proceedings to court of record, §16.1-105.
Banks.
Mortgages and deeds of trust.
Holding and conveying mortgage property, §6.2-872.
Purpose for which banks may purchase, hold and convey, §§6.2-872, 6.2-873.
Bequests and legacies.
Limitation on enforcement, §8.01-254.
Boundaries.
Establishing boundary lines, §§8.01-179 to 8.01-188.
Cattle guards, §§55-304, 55-305.
Cave protection.
General provisions, §§10.1-1000 to 10.1-1008.
See CAVE PROTECTION.
Charitable gifts.
Generally.
See CHARITABLE GIFTS.
Child purchasing.
Servicemen's readjustment act of 1944.
Eligibility for guaranty of credit, §11-8.
Church property, §§57-7.1 to 57-17.
Colleges and universities.
Approval for transfer of certain property, §23-4.01.
Borrowing to purchase real estate, §23-30.02.
Register of state property, §23-4.
Sale or lease of interest in real property, §23-4.1.
Commercial space flight authority.
Conveyance, lease or transfer by city or county to authority, §2.2-2217.
Community land trusts.
Defined, §55-221.1.

REAL PROPERTY —Cont'd
Community land trusts —Cont'd
Not considered landlords, §55-221.1.
Community property rights at death.
Generally, §§64.2-315 to 64.2-324.
See COMMUNITY PROPERTY RIGHTS AT DEATH.
Commutation and valuation of certain estates and interests, §§55-269.1 to 55-277.
Condominiums generally, §§55-79.39 to 55-79.103.
See CONDOMINIUMS.
Conservation and recreation department.
Disposition of department lands, §§10.1-108 to 10.1-114.
See CONSERVATION AND RECREATION DEPARTMENT.
Consumer financc companies.
Liens on real estate, §6.2-1524.
Consumer real estate settlement protection act.
See CONSUMER REAL ESTATE SETTLEMENT PROTECTION ACT.
Contracts.
Preparation by real estate licensees, §54.1-2101.1.
Statute of frauds, §11-2.
Void as to creditors and purchasers unless in writing, §11-1.
Conveyances.
Recordation tax as to deeds conveying.
State recordation tax, §§58.1-800 to 58.1-817.
See RECORDATION TAX, STATE.
Transfer fee covenants, §55-70.2.
Cooperatives, §§55-424 to 55-506.
See REAL ESTATE COOPERATIVES.
Counties, cities or towns.
Acquiring property near parks or other public properties, §15.2-1801.
Business and industry, acquiring, leasing or selling for, §15.2-1802.
County manager plan of government.
Purchase, sale, exchange or lease, §15.2-734.
Deed conveying, form, acceptance by governing body, execution, §15.2-1803.
Derelict buildings.
Authority to remove, demolish or renovate, §§15.2-906, 15.2-907.1.
Locality appointed as receiver to repair derelict and blighted buildings, §15.2-907.2.
Drug blight.
Locality requiring owner to take corrective action to abate, §15.2-907.
Financing clean energy improvements, §15.2-958.3.
Liens against real estate, §15.2-104.
Powers to acquire or dispose of generally, §15.2-1800.
School construction or improvement.
Tenancy in common with school board, §15.2-1800.1.
Credit line deed of trust, §55-58.2.
Limitation on enforcement when no date fixed for maturity, §8.01-242.
Credit unions.
Authorized investments, §6.2-1376.
Criminal offenses relating to property.
Proof of ownership, §19.2-284.
Custodial trusts, §§64.2-900 to 64.2-918.
See CUSTODIAL TRUSTS.
Damage actions.
Statute of limitations, §8.01-243.

REAL PROPERTY —Cont'd
Death presumption.
Parties to proceedings, §64.2-2300.
Decedents' estates.
Real estate generally.
See DECEDENTS' ESTATES.
Deeds.
Generally, §§55-48 to 55-79.
See DEEDS.
Recordation tax as to deeds conveying real estate.
State recordation tax generally, §§58.1-800 to 58.1-817.
See RECORDATION TAX, STATE.
Definitions.
Land or real estate, §1-219.
Delinquent tax land sales, §§58.1-3965 to 58.1-3975.
See SALE OF DELINQUENT TAX LANDS.
Descent and distribution generally, §§64.2-200 to 64.2-206.
See DESCENT AND DISTRIBUTION.
Destruction of private property, §18.2-137.
Detinue.
Generally, §§8.01-114 to 8.01-123.
See DETINUE.
Disclaimer of property interests.
Generally, §§64.2-2600 to 64.2-2614.
See DISCLAIMER OF PROPERTY INTERESTS.
Disclosures.
Residential property transfer disclosures, §§55-517 to 55-525.
See RESIDENTIAL PROPERTY TRANSFER DISCLOSURES.
Discrimination.
Human rights act, §§2.2-3900 to 2.2-3903.
Doctrine of worthier title.
Abolished, §55-14.1.
Economic development partnership authority.
Sale, lease or transfer of property to authority, §2.2-2246.
Educational gifts generally.
See CHARITABLE GIFTS.
Educational institutions, sale of real property.
Incorporated nonstock institutions, §13.1-901.
Ejectment actions.
Generally, §§8.01-131 to 8.01-165.
See EJECTMENT.
Electronic recording of documents, §§55-142.10 to 55-142.15.
Emancipation of minor.
Effects of order on minor's ability to buy and sell, §16.1-334.
Emblements, §§55-249 to 55-252.
Eminent domain generally, §§25.1-100 to 25.1-421.
See EMINENT DOMAIN.
Escheat, §§55-168 to 55-201.1.
See ESCHEAT.
Estates in land, §§55-1 to 55-25.1.
See ESTATES IN LAND.
Evidence.
Hearsay exceptions.
Interest in property, records or documents affecting, VA SCt Rule 2:803.
Exchange facilitators act, §§55-525.1 to 55-525.7.
Executions.
Right of daytime entry of dwelling house, §8.01-491.
Federal lien registration, §§55-142.1 to 55-142.9.
Electronic recordation of real property documents.
Uniform standards, §55-142.13.

REAL PROPERTY —Cont'd
Fee simple estates.
Action for termination of determinable fee simple estate, §8.01-255.1.
Fiduciary sales for persons under disability, §§8.01-67 to 8.01-80.
See PERSONS WITH DISABILITY.
Fire departments or companies.
Destruction of property to prevent spread of fire, §§27-20 to 27-22.
Flood control.
Conservation, small watersheds flood control and area development fund.
Lands, easements and rights of way, §§10.1-648, 10.1-649.
Fraudulent conveyances.
Generally, §§55-80 to 55-105.
See FRAUDULENT CONVEYANCES.
General assembly.
Disclosure statements, §30-111.
Ground rent, §§55-79.01 to 55-79.06.
Hearsay exceptions.
Interest in property, records or documents affecting, VA SCt Rule 2:803.
Homestead exemption of householder.
Alienation.
How real estate set apart as exempt may be aliened, §34-9.
Encumbrances.
How real estate set apart as exempt may be encumbered, §34-9.
Setting apart real estate subject to, §34-7.
Form of homestead deed, §34-6.
How exemption secured, §34-6.
Joint tenant.
Partition or sale of real estate held as exempt by, §34-8.
When exemption may be set apart, §34-17.
Illegal drug transactions.
Closure of nuisance premises, §§48-16, 48-17.
Improvements to land.
Generally, §§8.01-166 to 8.01-178.
See IMPROVEMENTS TO LAND.
Interest.
Real estate loan transactions.
See INTEREST.
Investment trusts.
Real estate investment trusts.
See REAL ESTATE INVESTMENT TRUSTS.
Joint ownership, §55-20.1.
Judicial sales.
Generally, §§8.01-96 to 8.01-113.
See JUDICIAL SALES.
Sales of judicial tax lands, §§58.1-3965 to 58.1-3975.
See SALE OF DELINQUENT TAX LANDS.
Labor unions.
Authority to own, encumber and sell, §40.1-52.
Landlord and tenant, §§55-217 to 55-248.
See LANDLORD AND TENANT.
Land subject to a debt.
Preferred forum, §8.01-261.
Land trusts.
Domestic insurer investing in real property.
Ownership through land trusts, §38.2-1441.
Trust not to fail because of lack of specifics, §55-17.1.
Deemed personal property of beneficiary, §55-17.1.
Judgment of lien, §55-17.1.
Power of trust to sell, lease, etc., §55-17.1.

REAL PROPERTY —Cont'd
Larceny of things fixed to freehold, §18.2-99.
Lien registration by federal government, §§55-142.1 to 55-142.9.
Electronic recordation of real property documents.
Uniform standards, §55-142.13.
Liens against real estate.
Alien land apportioned between alienees, §8.01-464.
Child support decree as lien on real estate, §8.01-460.
Decreed sale of real estate, §8.01-462.
Lien on real estate upon recordation, §8.01-458.
Spousal support decree as lien on real estate, §8.01-460.
Support of child or spouse.
Judgment created by operation of law, §16.1-278.15.
Limitation of actions.
Bill in equity to repeal grant of land by state, §8.01-238.
Enforcement of bequests and legacies, §8.01-254.
Entry on or action for land, §8.01-236.
Fee simple estates.
Action for termination of determinable fee simple estate, §8.01-255.1.
Ground rents.
Suit for recovery, §8.01-239.
Improvements to real property.
Damages arising out of defective or unsafe condition of improvement, §8.01-250.
Indemnifying bonds.
Motion for new execution after loss of property sold under indemnity bond, §§8.01-255.2, 8.01-476.
Personal action for damages, §8.01-243.
Persons with disability.
Effect of disabilities upon right of entry, §8.01-237.
Limited liability companies.
Third-party liability of members.
Estate or interest in property, §13.1-1021.
Literary gifts generally.
See CHARITABLE GIFTS.
Local school boards.
Exchange, lease or sale of real and personal property, §22.1-129.
Manufactured home lot rental, §§55-248.41 to 55-248.52.
See MANUFACTURED HOME LOT RENTAL.
Married women's property rights.
Generally, §§55-35 to 55-47.1.
See MARRIED WOMEN'S PROPERTY RIGHTS.
Membership camping, §§59.1-311 to 59.1-335.
See MEMBERSHIP CAMPING.
Mortgages and deeds of trust, §§6.2-406 to 6.2-423, 55-58 to 55-66.6.
See MORTGAGES AND DEEDS OF TRUST.
New College Institute.
Board of directors, powers, §23-231.34.
Nonresidents.
Rental payments to nonresident payees.
Tax information reporting on, §58.1-316.
Sale of real property.
Estimated tax, filing, §58.1-317.
Nonstock incorporated educational institutions.
Sale of real property, §13.1-901.
Open-space land.
General provisions, §§10.1-1700 to 10.1-1705.
See OPEN-SPACE LAND.

REAL PROPERTY —Cont'd
Options to purchase real estate, §§55-57.1, 55-57.2.
Owners' associations, §§55-508 to 55-516.2.
See PROPERTY OWNERS' ASSOCIATIONS.
Ownership.
Chain of title, §§41.1-9 to 41.1-12.
See LAND OFFICE.
Partition of land.
General provisions, §§8.01-81 to 8.01-93.
See PARTITION OF LAND.
Partnership property.
Limitation on partners authority to transfer.
Statement of partnership authority, §50-73.93.
Personal actions for damages.
Statute of limitations, §8.01-243.
Persons with disability.
Disposition of real estate, §§8.01-67 to 8.01-80.
See PERSONS WITH DISABILITY.
Power of attorney.
Authority of agent, §64.2-1625.
Principal and income.
Uniform principal and income act, §§64.2-1000 to 64.2-1032.
See PRINCIPAL AND INCOME.
Prisoner estates.
Selling or encumbering, §53.1-227.
Public road no longer publicly maintained.
Primary access to more than one property owner's property.
Maintenance, repair, improvement by a property owner, §55-50.3.
Real estate board.
See REAL ESTATE BOARD.
Real estate investment trusts.
See REAL ESTATE INVESTMENT TRUSTS.
Real estate loan transactions.
Loan interest.
See INTEREST.
Real estate settlements and settlement agents.
Generally, §§55-525.8 to 55-525.32.
See REAL ESTATE SETTLEMENTS.
Recordation of documents.
Deed of gift.
Recordation tax exemption, §58.1-811.
Electronic recordation of real property documents.
Mortgage satisfaction.
General provisions, §§55-66.8 to 55-66.14.
Uniform standards, §55-66.14.
Federal lien registration, §55-142.13.
General provisions, §§55-106 to 55-142.9.
See RECORDATION OF DOCUMENTS.
Recordation tax as to deeds conveying.
State recordation tax, §§58.1-800 to 58.1-817.
See RECORDATION TAX, STATE.
Registration of federal liens, §§55-142.1 to 55-142.9.
Electronic recordation of real property documents.
Uniform standards, §55-142.13.
Residential ground rent, §§55-79.01 to 55-79.06.
Residential property transfer disclosures, §§55-517 to 55-525.
See RESIDENTIAL PROPERTY TRANSFER DISCLOSURES.
Richmond metropolitan authority.
Acquisition of property, §15.2-7015.
Power of authority to exercise, §15.2-7002.
Rights of married women generally, §§55-35 to 55-47.1.
See MARRIED WOMEN'S PROPERTY RIGHTS.

REAL PROPERTY —Cont'd
Road no longer publicly maintained.
Primary access to more than one property owner's property.
Maintenance, repair, improvement by a property owner, §55-50.3.
Rule against perpetuities, §§55-12.1 to 55-12.6, 55-13.1 to 55-13.3.
Sale of delinquent tax lands, §§58.1-3965 to 58.1-3975.
See SALE OF DELINQUENT TAX LANDS.
Sales, UCC.
Goods to be severed from realty, §8.2-107.
Price payable in realty, §8.2-304.
Savings banks.
Investments, §6.2-1187.
Loans secured by real estate, §6.2-1187.
Power to hold, convey and encumber, §6.2-1111.
Segregation for local taxation, VA Const Art X §4.
Self-service storage, §§55-416 to 55-423.
Servicemen's readjustment act of 1944.
Minors or unmarried widows eligibility for guaranty of credit, §11-8.
Settlement.
Consumer real estate settlement protection act.
See CONSUMER REAL ESTATE SETTLEMENT PROTECTION ACT.
Wet settlement act.
See MORTGAGES AND DEEDS OF TRUST.
Slayers, bar to property rights, §§64.2-2500 to 64.2-2511.
See SLAYER'S ACT.
Solar easements, §§55-352 to 55-354.
State departments and agencies.
Acquisitions, conveyances and transfers of property, §§2.2-1147 to 2.2-1156.
See STATE DEPARTMENTS AND AGENCIES.
Statute of frauds, §11-2.
Contracts void as to creditors or purchases unless in writing, §11-1.
Submerged lands, §§28.2-1200 to 28.2-1213.
See SUBMERGED LANDS.
Taxes.
Generally.
See REAL PROPERTY TAXES.
Sale of delinquent tax lands, §§58.1-3965 to 58.1-3975.
See SALE OF DELINQUENT TAX LANDS.
Tenancy by the entireties, §§55-20.1, 55-20.2.
Time-shares, §§55-360 to 55-400.
See TIME-SHARES.
Title.
Chain of title.
Lord Fairfax, §41.1-2.
Open-space land, §10.1-1703.
Recordation of decrees affecting, §55-138.
Title insurance, §§38.2-4600 to 38.2-4616.
See TITLE INSURANCE.
Trespass to realty, §§18.2-119 to 18.2-136.1.
See TRESPASS.
Trusts.
Domestic insurer investing in real property.
Ownership through land trusts, §38.2-1441.
Failure for lack of specifics.
Deemed personal property of beneficiary, §55-17.1.
Judgment lien, §55-17.1.
Power of trustee to sell, lease, etc., §55-17.1.
Power of trustee, §64.2-778.

REAL PROPERTY —Cont'd
Trusts —Cont'd
Real estate investment trusts.
See REAL ESTATE INVESTMENT TRUSTS.
Uniform trust code, §§64.2-700 to 64.2-808.
See TRUSTS.
Unclaimed property, disposition of.
Escheat, §§55-168 to 55-201.1.
See ESCHEAT.
Generally, §§55-210.1 to 55-210.30.
See UNCLAIMED PROPERTY.
Ungranted shores of the sea, marshes and meadowlands, §§28.2-1500 to 28.2-1514.
See UNGRANTED SHORES OF THE SEA.
Uniform trust code, §§64.2-700 to 64.2-808.
See TRUSTS.
United States acquired lands.
Jurisdiction over lands acquired by United States, §§1-400 to 1-408.
Unlawful entry and detainer.
Generally, §§8.01-124 to 8.01-130.
Waste, §§55-211 to 55-216.
Wasteland.
Sale of unappropriated land, §§41.1-16 to 41.1-20.
See LAND OFFICE.
Wet settlement act.
See MORTGAGES AND DEEDS OF TRUST.
Worthier title.
Doctrine abolished, §55-14.1.
Writs on judgments for real property, §8.01-470.

REAL PROPERTY TAXES, §§58.1-3200 to 58.1-3389.
Abatement of levies.
Razed, destroyed or damaged buildings by fortuitous happenings, §58.1-3222.
Abstracts of grants of land.
Entry by commissioners of abstracts and assessment of value, §58.1-3308.
Librarian of Virginia to furnish commissioners of revenue, §58.1-3306.
Acquired land from United States when beneficial ownership held prior to January 1, §58.1-3204.
Administrative and judicial review, §§58.1-3350 to 58.1-3355.
Assessment not invalid unless rights prejudiced by error, §58.1-3353.
Assessments, §58.1-3350.
Change when easement acquired, §58.1-3354.
Lands in one place assessed in another, error corrected, §58.1-3352.
Value of real estate, change of assessed value, §58.1-3351.
Affordable rental housing.
Fair market value, determining, §58.1-3295.
Agricultural, horticultural, forest and open space uses.
General assembly may define and classify, VA Const Art X §2.
Agricultural use.
Special assessment on real estate devoted to, §§58.1-3229 to 58.1-3244.
Airspace.
Assessment, §58.1-3283.
Annexation.
Reduced taxation on real estate in territory added, §15.2-3219.
Apportionment of taxes.
Partition, §58.1-3225.
Procedure, §58.1-3226.

REAL PROPERTY TAXES —Cont'd
Apportionment of taxes —Cont'd
Release of lien on portion of real estate upon payment of taxes, §58.1-3226.1.
Separately-owned real estate, §58.1-3224.
Appraisal cards or sheets, §58.1-3332.
Appraisers.
Appointment in counties or cities, §58.1-3271.
Certification of appraisers contracted by locality to perform assessments, §58.1-3258.1.
Denial, suspension or revocation of certification, grounds, §58.1-3258.2.
Qualifications, §§58.1-3258, 58.1-3276.
Removal and appointment of substitute, §58.1-3276.
Assessments, VA Const Art X §2.
Additions, §58.1-3291.
Affordable rental housing.
Fair market value, determining, §58.1-3295.
Airspace owned separately from subjacent land surface, §58.1-3283.
Amount, §58.1-3201.
Annual assessment.
Acts authorizing, §§58.1-3260, 58.1-3261.
Cities having not more than 30,000 population, §58.1-3251.
Provisions not repealed, §58.1-3258.
Urban county executive form of government, §15.2-828.
Appeals to circuit court, §58.1-3379.
Written notice provided by assessing official to taxpayer, §58.1-3331.
Appointment of board of assessors and appraiser in counties and cities, §58.1-3271.
Appraisal cards or sheets, §58.1-3332.
Assistance by department of taxation, §58.1-3278.
Biennial assessment.
Provisions not repealed, §58.1-3258.
Boards of equalization, §§58.1-3370 to 58.1-3389.
By whom reassessment made in counties and cities, §58.1-3275.
Certification of supervisors, assessors and appraisers contracted by locality to perform assessments, §58.1-3258.1.
Denial, suspension or revocation of certification, grounds, §58.1-3258.2.
Change of value of real estate assessed, §58.1-3351.
Notice, §58.1-3330.
Commissioner of revenue.
Annual or biennial assessment performed by, §58.1-3270.
Completion of making reassessment, §58.1-3257.
Conservation easements and conservation easements held pursuant to open-space land act.
Assessment of fee interest subject to perpetual easement, §10.1-1011.
Correction of error.
Lands lying in one place assessed in another, §58.1-3352.
County manager plan of government, §15.2-716.
Time for contesting, §15.2-717.
Damage or destruction, value reduced, §58.1-3293.
Death of owner, §58.1-3342.
Defective drywall, residential property containing, §58.1-3284.2.
Department of assessments.
Urban county executive form of government, §15.2-840.

REAL PROPERTY TAXES —Cont'd
Assessments —Cont'd
Derelict building.
Prior to plan to remove, demolish or renovate, §15.2-907.1.
Disclosure of certain records, §58.1-3331.
Duplicate assessment, §58.1-3383.
Easement acquired by public service, highway or street facility.
Change in assessment, §58.1-3354.
Effect on rate when assessment results in increase, §58.1-3321.
Establishment of department of real estate assessment, §58.1-3274.
Exempt building or land source of revenue, §58.1-3603.
Extension of time for making reassessment, §58.1-3257.
Failure to comply with law on general reassessment, §58.1-3259.
Fair market value, §58.1-3280.
One hundred percent, §58.1-3201.
Forms for general reassessment furnished by department of taxation, §58.1-3277.
General reassessment.
Cities, §58.1-3250.
Counties, §58.1-3252.
Not required in certain counties, §58.1-3255.
Towns, §58.1-3256.
How made by board of assessors, §58.1-3272.
Income producing realty.
Report of income data by owner, §58.1-3294.
Land in one place assessed in another, §58.1-3352.
Land preservation special assessment, §§58.1-3229 to 58.1-3244.
Lands appearing on abstracts of grants, §58.1-3308.
Leasehold interest, §58.1-3203.
Lease of exempt building or land, source of revenue, §58.1-3603.
Methodology used to calculate, availability upon request, §58.1-3331.
Mineral lands and minerals included in general reassessment, §58.1-3287.
Mineral lands specially and separately assessed, §58.1-3286.
New buildings, §58.1-3291.
New buildings substantially completed, §58.1-3292.
Urban county executive form of government, city or counties adjacent, §58.1-3292.1.
Notice of change, §58.1-3330.
Notice of increase by boards of equalization, §58.1-3381.
Increase requested after taxpayer filed appeal, §58.1-3379.
Omitted real estate, §§58.1-3383, 58.1-3904.
Open or common space in planned development subdivisions, §58.1-3284.1.
Open space lands held by public body.
Interest less than fee, §58.1-3205.
Ownership, ascertaining by commissioner of revenue, §58.1-3281.
Planned development divisions, lots and open spaces, §58.1-3284.1.
Prejudicial effect of error, omission or irregularity.
Assessment not invalid unless, §58.1-3353.
Presumption valuation correct, §58.1-3379.
Public disclosure of assessment records, §58.1-3331.

REAL PROPERTY TAXES —Cont'd
Assessments —Cont'd
Public service corporations.
Localities requiring taxes paid in installments, §58.1-3917.
Qualifications of assessors and appraisers, §§58.1-3258, 58.1-3276.
Reassessment made by professional assessor, §58.1-3275.
Reduction in value of building, §58.1-3293.
Removal of assessors and appraisers, §58.1-3276.
Repair, §58.1-3291.
Residential rental apartments, §58.1-3295.1.
Review of assessment by person aggrieved, §58.1-3350.
Separate ownership of land and improvements.
Public service corporations or political subdivisions of Commonwealth, §58.1-3282.
Several owners, how land divided among, §58.1-3290.
Special assessment, land preservation, §§58.1-3229 to 58.1-3244.
Standing timber, §58.1-3284.
Apportionment of value between owner of soil and owner of timber, §58.1-3309.
Subdivided or rezoned lots, §58.1-3285.
Taxes extended on basis of, §58.1-3320.
Tax increment financing, §§58.1-3245 to 58.1-3245.5.
Taxpayer problem resolution program, §58.1-1818.
Timberland reduced in value, §58.1-3293.
Trees, standing timber, §58.1-3284.
Unknown owner, §58.1-3288.
Urban county executive form of government, §15.2-828.
County providing for department of assessments, §15.2-840.
Value of building reduced, §58.1-3293.
Wetlands located on property, §58.1-3284.3.
Working papers used by assessing officials.
Request by taxpayer to examine, §58.1-3331.
Assessment tax year, §58.1-3281.
Bills to taxpayers.
Electronic billing, §58.1-3912.
Mailing, §58.1-3912.
Website access, §58.1-3912.
Blighted areas.
Tax increment financing, §§58.1-3245 to 58.1-3245.5.
Board of assessors.
Appointment in counties or cities, §58.1-3271.
General reassessments in towns, §58.1-3256.
How assessments made by, §58.1-3272.
Qualifications, §58.1-3276.
Reassessments made in cities and counties, §58.1-3275.
Removal and appointment of substitute, §58.1-3276.
Review of assessment upon application of aggrieved person, §58.1-3350.
Boards of equalization, §§58.1-3370 to 58.1-3389.
Absence of regular member.
Alternate member, selection to serve, §58.1-3374.
Action of board, §58.1-3381.
Alternate members.
Appointment by circuit court, §58.1-3373.
Service in absence of regular members, §58.1-3374.
Appeals, §§58.1-3379, 58.1-3382.
Notice provided taxpayer by assessing official.
Appeals of board decisions to circuit court, §58.1-3331.

REAL PROPERTY TAXES —Cont'd
Boards of equalization —Cont'd
Applicability of article, §58.1-3389.
Application for equalization, §58.1-3380.
Applications for relief, §58.1-3378.
Appointment by circuit courts, §58.1-3370.
Appointment in counties with county executive or county manager form of government, §58.1-3371.
Assistance, §58.1-3376.
Changes ordered, commissioner of revenue to make, §58.1-3385.
Circuit court appointment, §58.1-3370.
Compensation, §58.1-3375.
Continuing education, §58.1-3374.
Copies of orders, §58.1-3384.
Counties not having general reassessment or annual or biennial assessment.
Taxes extended on basis of last equalization, §58.1-3388.
County executive form of government, §58.1-3371.
County manager form of government, §§15.2-619, 58.1-3371.
County manager plan of government, §§15.2-716, 15.2-716.1.
Course of instruction, §58.1-3374.
Duplicate assessments, §58.1-3383.
Exoneration of taxpayer, §58.1-3385.
Extended taxes on basis of last assessment made.
Counties not having general reassessment or annual or biennial assessments, §58.1-3388.
Failure to obey summons of taxpayer, §58.1-3387.
Hearing complaints and equalizing assessments, §58.1-3379.
Income and expense statements by owners of income producing property.
Consideration of statements in complaints before board, §58.1-3294.
Increasing or decreasing assessments, §58.1-3379.
Land book use, §58.1-3377.
Legal assistance for boards in certain cities, §58.1-3376.
Limit on compensation, §58.1-3375.
Local authority application for equalization, §58.1-3380.
Minutes, §58.1-3384.
Notice before increase made, §58.1-3381.
Notice of sittings, §58.1-3378.
Notice provided taxpayer by assessing official.
Appeals of board decisions to circuit court, §58.1-3331.
Notice when increase requested after taxpayer filed appeal, §58.1-3379.
Number of members, §58.1-3374.
Omitted real estate, §58.1-3383.
Organization, §58.1-3376.
Permanent boards, §58.1-3373.
Presumptive correctness of determinations, §58.1-3381.
Qualifications, §58.1-3374.
Real estate assessable by state corporation commission or department of taxation.
Article not applicable to, §58.1-3389.
Reassessment in towns.
Grievances as to correction of assessments, §58.1-3256.
Reassessment record copy delivered to, §58.1-3300.
Refund on exoneration of taxpayer, §58.1-3385.
Review of assessment upon application by person aggrieved, §58.1-3350.

REAL PROPERTY TAXES —Cont'd
Boards of equalization —Cont'd
Sittings, §58.1-3378.
Summoning taxpayers, §58.1-3386.
Failure to obey, §58.1-3387.
Taxpayer application for equalization, §58.1-3380.
Terms.
Alternate members appointed by circuit court, §58.1-3373.
Members appointed by circuit court, §§58.1-3370, 58.1-3371.
Members of permanent boards, §58.1-3373.
Urban county executive form of government, §15.2-840.
Use of land book, §58.1-3377.
Vacancies, §58.1-3374.
Capital improvement projects.
Local government facilities private capital lending, §15.2-1817.
Change in assessment.
Notice, §58.1-3330.
Change of value of real estate assessed, §58.1-3351.
City reassessments, §58.1-3250.
Annual reassessment in cities having not more than 30,000 population, §58.1-3251.
Biennial general reassessment, §58.1-3253.
Reassessment by direction of governing body, §58.1-3254.
Claims, §58.1-513.
Classification of real property by tax commissioner, §58.1-208.
Collection of local taxes generally, §§58.1-3910 to 58.1-3961.
See TAX COLLECTION.
Commercial and industrial real property, classification of, §58.1-3221.3.
Commercial structures.
Exemption for rehabilitation, renovation or replacement, §58.1-3221.
Condominiums.
Conversion of convertible lands, §55-79.61.
Confidentiality.
Income producing realty.
Reports of income data by owners, §58.1-3294.
Conservation areas.
Partial exemption for new structures or improvements, fee, processing applications, §58.1-3219.4.
Conservation easements.
Assessment of fee interest subject to perpetual conservation easement, §10.1-1011.
Corporations, tax credits for, §58.1-512.
Correction of erroneous tax assessments, §§58.1-3980 to 58.1-3995.
See CORRECTION OF ERRONEOUS TAX ASSESSMENTS.
County executive form of government.
Director of finance.
Reassessment of real estate, §15.2-521.
Public service corporations, special provisions for assessments, §§58.1-2680 to 58.1-2683.
County manager form of government.
Board of real estate review and equalization, §15.2-619.
Public service corporations, special provisions for assessments, §§58.1-2680 to 58.1-2683.
Reassessment of real estate by director of finance, §15.2-619.
County manager plan of government.
Assessment of real estate, §15.2-716.
Time for contesting, §15.2-717.

REAL PROPERTY TAXES —Cont'd
County manager plan of government —Cont'd
Board of equalization of real estate assessments, §§15.2-716, 15.2-716.1.
Contesting real property assessments.
Time for, §15.2-717.
Department of real estate assessments.
Referendum for establish and establishment, §15.2-716.
Installment collection, §15.2-745.
Reassessment of real estate, §15.2-716.
County reassessments, §58.1-3252.
Biennial general reassessment, §58.1-3255.
Not required every four years in certain counties, §58.1-3255.
Reassessment by direction of governing body, §58.1-3254.
Credit.
Enterprise zones.
Real property investment tax credits, §59.1-280.1.
Land conservation incentives, §§58.1-510 to 58.1-513.
Land preservation tax credits, §58.1-512.
Rehabilitated, renovated or replacement residential structures, §58.1-3220.01.
Transfer of unused credit, §58.1-513.
Damaged, destroyed or razed buildings by fortuitous happenings.
Abatement of levies, §58.1-3222.
Death of owner, assessment upon, §58.1-3342.
Deeds and property transfer receipts and reports.
Forwarding by circuit court clerks to local commissioners and department of taxation, §58.1-3303.
Defective drywall.
Assessment of residential property containing, §58.1-3284.2.
Deferral, §§58.1-3219 to 58.1-3219.3.
Conditions, §58.1-3219.1.
Elderly or handicapped property, §§58.1-3210 to 58.1-3217.
General assembly may provide, VA Const Art X §2.
Lien for taxes delinquent twenty years or more.
Deferred taxes not considered delinquent, §58.1-3341.
Lien upon real estate, §58.1-3219.1.
Limitation on collection of local taxes.
Tolling with respect to taxes deferred during pendency of deferral, §58.1-3940.
Waiver of time limitation on assessment, §58.1-3903.1.
Limitations, §58.1-3219.3.
Ordinance adopting deferral program, §58.1-3219.
Payment of deferred amount, §58.1-3219.1.
Portion of increase, §58.1-3219.
Definitions.
Permanently and totally disabled, §58.1-3217.
Taxable real estate, §58.1-3200.
Delinquent taxes.
Ascertaining delinquent taxes, §58.1-3959.
Collection of local taxes generally, §§58.1-3921 to 58.1-3938.
See TAX COLLECTION.
Proration after purchase of part of tract, §58.1-3227.
Release of delinquent lien to facilitate conveyance, §58.1-3228.

REAL PROPERTY TAXES —Cont'd
Delinquent taxes —Cont'd
Sale of delinquent tax lands generally, §§58.1-3965 to 58.1-3975.
See SALE OF DELINQUENT TAX LANDS.
When taxes delinquent, §58.1-3922.
Department of assessments.
County manager plan of government, §15.2-716.
Establishment, §58.1-3274.
Joint department, §58.1-3274.
Urban county executive form of government, §15.2-840.
Director of finance.
County executive form of government.
Reassessment of real estate, §15.2-521.
County manager form of government.
Reassessment of real estate, §15.2-619.
Disabled veterans.
Exemption, §§58.1-3219.5 to 58.1-3219.8.
Absence from residence, effect, §58.1-3219.8.
Administration by department of veterans services, §58.1-3219.7.
Application, §58.1-3219.6.
Generally, §58.1-3219.5.
Tax credits, §§58.1-3360 to 58.1-3363.
Disclosure or access to records, §§58.1-3330 to 58.1-3332.
Distress.
Collection of local taxes by distress generally, §§58.1-3940 to 58.1-3961.
See TAX COLLECTION.
Donation to public or private conservation agency.
Land preservation tax credits, §58.1-512.
Easement acquired by public service, highway or street facility.
Change in assessment, §58.1-3354.
Elderly and handicapped exemptions, §§58.1-3210 to 58.1-3217.
Absence from residence, §58.1-3214.
Affidavit or written statement.
Filed annually by person claiming exemption, §58.1-3213.
Application for exemption, §58.1-3213.
Authorization, §58.1-3210.
Change in circumstances, §58.1-3215.
Deferral program, §58.1-3216.
Deferral programs inapplicable to participants, §58.1-3219.3.
Effective date, §58.1-3215.
Lien, §58.1-3216.
Net financial worth or annual income limitations.
Local restrictions and exemption allowed, §58.1-3212.
Notice of program, §58.1-3213.1.
Permanently and totally disabled defined, §58.1-3217.
Prorated tax exemption or deferral of tax, §58.1-3211.1.
Requirements, §58.1-3210.
Residence in jurisdiction for designated period of time.
No local ordinance to require, §58.1-3212.
Restrictions and exemptions.
Local, §58.1-3212.
Electronic billing, §58.1-3912.
Eminent domain.
Credit on current year's taxes.
Land acquired by United States, Commonwealth, political subdivision or church, §§58.1-3360 to 58.1-3363.

REAL PROPERTY TAXES —Cont'd
Energy-efficient buildings for tax purposes.
Classification of real property, §58.1-3221.2.
Enterprise zone development.
Local enterprise zone development taxation program, §§58.1-3245.6 to 58.1-3245.12.
Enterprise zones.
Real property investment tax credits, §59.1-280.1.
Environmental restoration sites.
Separate classification and exemption, §58.1-3664.
Exemptions.
Assessment of exempt building or land source of revenue, §58.1-3603.
Commercial or industrial structures.
Rehabilitation, renovation or replacement, §58.1-3221.
Disabled veterans, §58.1-3219.5.
Absence from residence, effect, §58.1-3219.8.
Administration by department of veterans services, §58.1-3219.7.
Application, §58.1-3219.6.
Elderly and handicapped, §§58.1-3210 to 58.1-3217.
Absence from residence, §58.1-3214.
Affidavit or written statement.
Filed annually by person claiming exemption, §58.1-3213.
Application for exemption, §58.1-3213.
Authorization, §58.1-3210.
Change in circumstances, §58.1-3215.
Deferral program, §58.1-3216.
Deferral programs inapplicable to participants, §58.1-3219.3.
Disabled veterans, §§58.1-3219.5 to 58.1-3219.8.
Effective date, §58.1-3215.
Lien, §58.1-3216.
Net financial worth or annual income limitations.
Local restrictions and exemption allowed, §58.1-3212.
Notice of program, §58.1-3213.1.
Permanently and totally disabled defined, §58.1-3217.
Prorated tax exemption or deferral of tax, §58.1-3211.1.
Requirements, §58.1-3210.
Residence in jurisdiction for designated period of time.
No local ordinance to require, §58.1-3212.
Restrictions and exemptions, §58.1-3212.
Fraternal benefit societies, §38.2-4124.
Generally, §§58.1-3600 to 58.1-3666.
See PROPERTY EXEMPT FROM TAXATION.
Joint owners who are disabled or individuals at least 65 years of age, exceptions, §58.1-3211.1.
Military property, §44-131.
Property exempt generally, VA Const Art X §6.
Razed, destroyed or damaged buildings by fortuitous happenings.
Abatement of levies, §58.1-3222.
Redevelopment or conservation areas or rehabilitation districts.
Partial exemption for new structures or other improvements to real estate in, §58.1-3219.4.
Covenant running with land, §58.1-3219.4.
Demolition of registered Virginia landmark.
Inapplicability of exemption, §58.1-3219.4.
Fee for processing applications, §58.1-3219.4.
Listing upon land book reduced value due to exemption, prohibition, §58.1-3219.4.

REAL PROPERTY TAXES —Cont'd
Exemptions —Cont'd
Redevelopment or conservation areas or rehabilitation districts —Cont'd
Partial exemption for new structures or other improvements to real estate in —Cont'd
Notification of exempt assessment amount, §58.1-3219.4.
Rehabilitated commercial or industrial structure, §58.1-3221.
Rehabilitated hotel or motel structures, §58.1-3220.1.
Rehabilitated residential real estate, §58.1-3220.
Renovated commercial or industrial structure, §58.1-3221.
Renovated hotel or motel structures, §58.1-3220.1.
Renovated residential structures, §58.1-3220.
Replacement commercial or industrial structure, §58.1-3221.
Replacement hotel or motel structures, §58.1-3220.1.
Replacement residential structures, §58.1-3220.
Service charge in lieu of payment, §§58.1-3400 to 58.1-3407.
Veterans, VA Const Art X §6-A.
Disabled veterans, §§58.1-3219.5 to 58.1-3219.8.
Extended on basis of assessment, §58.1-3320.
Counties not having general reassessment, annual or biennial assessment, §58.1-3388.
Failure to file returns.
Ordinances prescribing criminal penalties, §58.1-3916.1.
Failure to pay taxes by December 5, §58.1-3915.
Fairfax, city of.
Energy-efficient buildings for tax purposes, classification of, §58.1-3221.2.
Improvements to real property as separate class, §58.1-3221.1.
Fair market value, assessment of lands, §58.1-3280.
False statements in returns.
Ordinances prescribing criminal penalties, §58.1-3916.1.
Forest use.
Special assessment on real estate devoted to, §§58.1-3229 to 58.1-3244.
Forms.
Notice of proposed real property tax increase, §58.1-3321.
Fortuitous happenings.
Abatement of levies on buildings razed, destroyed or damaged by, §58.1-3222.
Historical buildings.
Separate class of property for local taxation.
Buildings listed on Virginia landmarks register, §58.1-3221.5.
Horizontal property regimes, §55-79.14.
Horticultural use.
Special assessment on real estate devoted to, §§58.1-3229 to 58.1-3244.
Hotel or motel structure exemption.
Rehabilitated, renovated or replacement structures, §58.1-3220.1.
Improvements to real property as separate class.
Cities of Fairfax, Poquoson, Roanoke, §58.1-3221.1.
Income producing realty.
Reports of income data by owners, §58.1-3294.
Increase in tax.
Effect on rate when assessment results in, §58.1-3321.

REAL PROPERTY TAXES —Cont'd
Individuals, tax credits for, §58.1-512.
Industrial structures.
Exemption for rehabilitation, renovation or replacement, §58.1-3221.
Installment collection.
County manager plan of government, §15.2-745.
Insurance companies.
Taxes applicable to companies, §58.1-2508.
Joint bill for real and personal property taxes, §58.1-3912.
Land book.
Alteration after delivery to local treasurer prohibited, §58.1-3311.
Changes noted in by commissioners of revenue, §58.1-3312.
Copies, disposition, §58.1-3310.
Correction of mistakes by commissioners, §58.1-3313.
Entry of lands on lists to be transferred and charged, §58.1-3309.
Entry of tracts in counties, §58.1-3301.
Fees for entering and transferring lands on, §58.1-3314.
Collection of fees, §58.1-3315.
Form prescribed by department of taxation, §58.1-3301.
Omitted lands, entry on, §58.1-3904.
Original retained by commissioners of revenue, §58.1-3310.
Use by boards of equalization, §58.1-3377.
Land conservation incentives, §§58.1-510 to 58.1-513.
Definitions, §58.1-511.
Effective date, §58.1-510.
Purpose, §58.1-510.
Land preservation special assessment, §§58.1-3229 to 58.1-3244.
Additional provisions concerning zoning classifications, §58.1-3237.1.
Albemarle, Arlington, Augusta, James City, Loudon and Rockingham counties.
Additional provisions concerning zoning classifications, §58.1-3237.1.
Annexed area.
Assessment and taxation in newly annexed area, §58.1-3232.
Application by property owners, §58.1-3234.
Misstatements, §58.1-3238.
Application of other provisions of tax title, §58.1-3243.
Authority to adopt ordinances, §58.1-3231.
Change in use or zoning, §58.1-3227.
Failure to report change in use, §58.1-3238.
Classifications of real estate established and defined, §58.1-3230.
Contiguous real estate located in more than one taxing locality, §58.1-3241.
Continuation of assessment, §58.1-3234.
Deferral programs inapplicable to participants, §58.1-3219.3.
Delinquent taxes, removal of parcels, §58.1-3235.
Determinations by local officers before assessment, §58.1-3233.
Determining whether real estate devoted to agricultural use, horticultural use, etc.
Standards applied uniformly throughout Commonwealth, §58.1-3240.
Eminent domain.
Taking of real estate assessed by right of, §58.1-3242.

REAL PROPERTY TAXES —Cont'd
Land preservation special assessment —Cont'd
General reassessment following adoption of ordinance, §58.1-3231.
Local officers' determinations before assessment, §58.1-3233.
Misstatements in application, §58.1-3238.
Newly annexed areas.
Assessment and taxation in, §58.1-3232.
Removal of parcels.
Delinquent taxes, §58.1-3235.
Requirements for preparation and use of true values, article not in conflict with, §58.1-3244.
Roll-back taxes, §58.1-3237.
Separation of part of real estate assessed, §58.1-3241.
Split-off of lots, §58.1-3241.
Standards applied uniformly throughout Commonwealth, §58.1-3240.
State land evaluation advisory council, §58.1-3239.
Valuation of real estate, §58.1-3236.
Zoning classifications, additional provisions concerning, §58.1-3237.1.
Land preservation tax credits, §58.1-512.
Lands in one place assessed in another.
Correction of error, §58.1-3352.
Leasehold interest, §58.1-3203.
Lease of exempt building or land, source of revenue.
Assessment, §58.1-3603.
Lease of real estate for collection of taxes, §§58.1-3947, 58.1-3948.
Lien, §§58.1-3340 to 58.1-3345.
Accumulated amount of tax deferred and interest, §58.1-3219.1.
Death of owner, assessment upon, §58.1-3342.
Deferral programs for elderly or handicapped, §58.1-3216.
Deferred taxes not considered delinquent, §58.1-3341.
Delinquent taxes.
Real property tax liens for taxes delinquent 20 years or more, §58.1-3341.
Enforcement by suit in equity, §58.1-3340.
Fee simple estate, taxes lien on, §58.1-3344.
Interest of owner, lien not limited to, §58.1-3344.
Jointly owned real estate, effect of lien, §58.1-3343.
Lands purchased by Commonwealth, §58.1-3341.
Limitation of actions.
Real property tax liens for taxes delinquent 20 years or more, §58.1-3341.
Proration of sellers liability for taxes at sales, §58.1-3340.
Purchasers at sales to pay taxes, §58.1-3340.
Real estate for payment of taxes and levies assessed, §58.1-3340.
Release of delinquent taxes 20 years or more, §58.1-3341.
Release on portion of real estate upon payment of taxes, §58.1-3226.1.
Rents of real estate, §58.1-3340.
Sale of delinquent tax land.
Lien on real estate for real property taxes.
Enforcement of lien by suit in equity under provisions, §58.1-3340.
Statute of limitations.
Real property tax liens for taxes delinquent 20 years or more, §58.1-3341.

REAL PROPERTY TAXES —Cont'd
Lien —Cont'd
Tax delinquencies.
Real property tax liens for taxes delinquent 20 years or more, §58.1-3341.
Timber in certain counties, §58.1-3345.
Lien of delinquent real estate taxes.
Recording, §58.1-3930.
Life tenant's interest when remainder held by United States, §58.1-3223.
Limitations, §58.1-513.
Lists of judgments for partition or recovery of lands.
Delivery of lists by circuit court clerks to commissioners of revenue, §58.1-3304.
Failure of clerk to deliver, §58.1-3305.
Local taxes generally, §§58.1-3000 to 58.1-3018.
See LOCAL TAXES.
Mailing tax bills to taxpayers, §58.1-3912.
Mineral lands and minerals included in general reassessment, §58.1-3287.
Mineral lands specially and separately assessed, §58.1-3286.
Mosquito control, §32.1-194.
Multi-unit real estate, §58.1-3202.
New buildings.
Assessment of substantially complete building, §58.1-3292.
Urban county executive form of government, city or county adjacent, §58.1-3292.1.
Valuation for assessment, §58.1-3291.
Notice of change in assessment or reassessment, §58.1-3330.
Notice of proposed real property tax increase, §58.1-3321.
Notice of taxes due, §58.1-3911.
Notice provided taxpayer by assessing official.
Appeals of board of equalization decisions to circuit court, §58.1-3331.
Omitted lands, §58.1-3904.
Open or common space in planned development subdivisions.
Assessment, §58.1-3284.1.
Open space land.
Assessment of fee interest subject to perpetual conservation easement, §10.1-1011.
Assessment of property where interest less than fee held by public body, §58.1-3205.
Special assessment on real estate devoted to, §§58.1-3229 to 58.1-3244.
Ownership, ascertainment by commissioner of revenue, §58.1-3281.
Partition, apportionment of taxes, §58.1-3225.
Petition to ascertain delinquent taxes, §58.1-3959.
Poquoson, city of.
Improvements to real property as separate class, §58.1-3221.1.
Prejudicial effect of error, omission or irregularity of assessment.
Assessment not invalid unless, §58.1-3353.
Prepayment of taxes, §58.1-3920.
Interest on funds received, §58.1-3920.1.
Prince William county senior citizens and disabled persons.
Ordinance prescribing alternative due dates, §58.1-3916.02.
Property owners' associations.
Developer to pay upon transfer of common areas to association, §55-509.1.
Property subject to local taxation, §58.1-3000.

REAL PROPERTY TAXES —Cont'd
Proration of delinquent taxes.
Public taking of private real estate, credit on current year's taxes, §58.1-3360.2.
Purchase of part of tract, §58.1-3227.
Public hearings on proposed real property tax increase, §58.1-3321.
Public school funds.
Duty to levy school tax, §22.1-95.
Public school special tax, §§22.1-102 to 22.1-106.
Public service corporations.
Assessment in localities requiring payment in installments, §58.1-3917.
County executive or county manager governments, special provisions for assessments, §§58.1-2680 to 58.1-2683.
Local taxation, §58.1-2606.
Railroads, §58.1-2607.
Taxable real estate, §58.1-3201.
Public taking of private real estate, §§58.1-3360 to 58.1-3363.
Railroads.
Local taxation, §58.1-2607.
Assessment of property by tax commissioner, §§58.1-2655 to 58.1-2657.
Nonoperating (noncarrier) property.
Property subject to taxation, §58.1-3201.
Rate of levy.
Effect when assessment results in tax increase, §58.1-3321.
Reassessment or assessment, §§58.1-3250 to 58.1-3295.1.
Acts authorizing.
Provisions for annual general reassessments.
Certain cities and counties, §58.1-3260.
Annual assessment and equalization in certain cities and counties.
Acts authorizing, §58.1-3261.
Annual general reassessment in certain cities and counties.
Acts authorizing, §58.1-3260.
Annual or biennial reassessment.
Provisions not repealed, §58.1-3258.
Annual reassessment in cities having not more than 30,000 population, §58.1-3251.
Assistance by department of taxation, §58.1-3278.
Boards of equalization, §§58.1-3370 to 58.1-3389.
County manager form of government, §15.2-619.
By whom made in cities and counties, §58.1-3275.
Completion of work, §58.1-3257.
County manager form of government.
Director of finance, §15.2-619.
County manager plan of government, §15.2-716.
Director of finance.
County manager form of government, §15.2-619.
Extension of time for making, §58.1-3257.
Failure to comply with law on general reassessment, §58.1-3259.
Forms for general reassessment furnished by department of taxation, §58.1-3277.
General reassessment in cities, §58.1-3250.
General reassessment in counties, §58.1-3252.
Not required in certain counties, §58.1-3255.
General reassessment in towns, §58.1-3256.
Mineral lands and minerals included in general reassessment, §58.1-3287.
Notice, §58.1-3330.
Subdivided or rezoned lots, §58.1-3285.
Taxes extended on basis of, §58.1-3320.
Urban county executive form of government, §15.2-828.

REAL PROPERTY TAXES —Cont'd
Reassessment record, §58.1-3300.
Recapitulation sheets.
Forwarding to department of taxation, §58.1-3300.
Receipts to taxpayers when taxes collected, §58.1-3914.
Recording lien of delinquent real estate taxes, §58.1-3930.
Redevelopment areas.
Partial exemption for new structures or improvements, fee, processing applications, §58.1-3219.4.
Refund.
Public taking of private real estate, §58.1-3362.
Rehabilitated commercial or industrial structure exemption, §58.1-3221.
Rehabilitated hotel or motel structures, §58.1-3220.1.
Rehabilitated residential real estate.
Credits, §58.1-3220.1.
Exemptions, §58.1-3220.
Rehabilitation districts.
Partial exemption for new structures or improvements, fee, processing applications, §58.1-3219.4.
Release of lien on portion of real estate upon payment of taxes, §58.1-3226.1.
Release or redemption of property becoming separately owned from lien of taxes, §58.1-3224.
Renewable energy products, property used for design and manufacture of.
Classification of improvements for tax purposes, §58.1-3221.4.
Renovated commercial or industrial structure exemption, §58.1-3221.
Renovated hotel or motel structures, §58.1-3220.1.
Renovated residential structures.
Credits, §58.1-3220.01.
Exemptions, §58.1-3220.
Repairs or additions to buildings.
Valuation for assessment, §58.1-3291.
Replacement commercial or industrial structure exemption, §58.1-3221.
Replacement hotel or motel structures, §58.1-3220.1.
Replacement residential structures.
Credits, §58.1-3220.01.
Exemptions, §58.1-3220.
Residential rental apartments.
Assessments, §58.1-3295.1.
Roanoke.
Energy-efficient buildings for tax purposes, classification of, §58.1-3221.2.
Improvements to real property, classification, §58.1-3221.1.
Sale of delinquent tax lands, §§58.1-3965 to 58.1-3975.
See SALE OF DELINQUENT TAX LANDS.
Segregation of property for local taxation, VA Const Art X §4.
Separately owned real estate.
Apportionment, §58.1-3224.
Assessment of public service corporation or political subdivision, §58.1-3282.
Service charge in lieu of payment, §§58.1-3400 to 58.1-3407.
Appeal from erroneous assessments, §58.1-3407.
Apportionment of payments received from Tennessee Valley Authority, §58.1-3406.

REAL PROPERTY TAXES —Cont'd
Service charge in lieu of payment —Cont'd
Buildings exempted, §58.1-3402.
Calculation of service charge, §58.1-3401.
Commonwealth owned property, §58.1-3403.
Erroneous assessments, §58.1-3407.
Exempted property, §58.1-3400.
Exemptions, §58.1-3402.
Imposition by commissioner of revenue, §58.1-3400.
International or treaty exempted property.
Service charge on, §58.1-3405.
Notice to educational institutions.
Ordinance levying service charge on, §58.1-3404.
Notice to governor of ordinance levying charge on state owned property, §58.1-3404.
Property owned by Commonwealth, §58.1-3403.
Tennessee Valley Authority in lieu of taxes.
Apportionment of payments, §58.1-3406.
Valuation of property, §58.1-3401.
Service of notice of change in assessment, §58.1-3330.
Several owners.
How land divided among to be assessed, §58.1-3290.
Severance tax on coal and gases.
Alternative to procedure for specially and separately assessing mineral lands, §58.1-3286.
Special assessment for land preservation, §§58.1-3229 to 58.1-3244.
Additional provisions concerning zoning classification, §58.1-3237.1.
Albemarle, Arlington, Augusta, James City, Loudon and Rockingham counties.
Additional provisions concerning zoning classifications, §58.1-3237.1.
Annexed areas.
Authority to provide for assessment and taxation in newly annexed areas, §58.1-3232.
Application of other provisions of tax title, §58.1-3243.
Applications by property owners, §58.1-3243.
Misstatements, §58.1-3238.
Authority to adopt ordinance, §58.1-3231.
Change in use or zoning, §58.1-3237.
Failure to report change in use, §58.1-3238.
Classification of real estate established and defined, §58.1-3230.
Contiguous real estate located in more than one taxing locality, §58.1-3241.
Continuation of assessment, §58.1-3234.
Deferral programs inapplicable to participants, §58.1-3219.3.
Delinquent taxes, removal of parcels, §58.1-3235.
Determinations made by local officers before assessment, §58.1-3233.
Determining whether real estate devoted to agricultural use, horticultural use, etc.
Uniform standards applied throughout Commonwealth, §58.1-3240.
Eminent domain.
Taking of real estate assessed by right of, §58.1-3242.
General assessment following adoption of ordinance, §58.1-3231.
Local officers determination before assessment, §58.1-3233.
Misstatements in applications, §58.1-3238.

REAL PROPERTY TAXES —Cont'd
Special assessment for land preservation —Cont'd
Newly annexed areas.
Authority to provide for assessment and taxation, §58.1-3232.
Removal of parcels.
Delinquent taxes, §58.1-3235.
Requirements for preparation and use of true values, article not in conflict with, §58.1-3244.
Roll-back taxes, §58.1-3237.
Separation of part of real estate assessed, §58.1-3241.
Split-off of lots, §58.1-3241.
Standards applied uniformly throughout Commonwealth.
Determining whether real estate devoted to agricultural use, horticultural use, etc., §58.1-3240.
State land evaluation advisory council, §58.1-3239.
Valuation of real estate, §58.1-3236.
Zoning classification provisions, additional provisions, §58.1-3237.1.
Standing timber.
Apportionment of value between owner of soil and owner of timber, §58.1-3309.
Assessment, §58.1-3284.
State land evaluation advisory council, §58.1-3239.
Statute of limitations.
Criminal prosecutions, §19.2-8.
Subdivided or rezoned lots.
Assessment and reassessment, §58.1-3285.
Subjected real estate to taxation, §§58.1-3200 to 58.1-3205.
Surplus revenues.
Return by counties, §15.2-2511.1.
Table of town or city lots, §58.1-3302.
Taxable real estate, §§58.1-3200 to 58.1-3205.
Acquired land from United States when beneficial ownership held prior to January 1, §58.1-3204.
Defined, §58.1-3200.
Leasehold interest, §58.1-3203.
Multi-unit real estate, §58.1-3202.
Open-space land act, interest less than fee held by public body, §58.1-3205.
Public service corporation property, §58.1-3201.
Railroads, nonoperating (noncarrier) property, §58.1-3201.
Subjects of local taxation, §58.1-3200.
What real estate to be taxed, §58.1-3201.
Tax credits.
Credit on current year's taxes.
Land acquired by United States, Commonwealth, etc., §§58.1-3360 to 58.1-3363.
Life tenant's interest when remainder held by United States, §58.1-3223.
Tax increment financing, §§58.1-3245 to 58.1-3245.5.
Tax year for assessment, §58.1-3281.
Time-shares.
Status of estates, §55-363.
Town reassessments, §58.1-3256.
Transfer of unused credit, §58.1-513.
Trees, assessment of standing timber, §58.1-3284.
United States holding remainder interest.
Life tenant's interest, §58.1-3223.

REAL PROPERTY TAXES —Cont'd
Unknown owners, assessment in name of, §58.1-3288.
Urban county executive form of government.
Assessment of real estate, §15.2-828.
County providing for department of assessments, §15.2-840.
Veterans.
Disabled veterans.
Exemption, §§58.1-3219.5 to 58.1-3219.8.
Tax credits, §§58.1-3360 to 58.1-3363.
Virginia landmarks register.
Separate class of property for local taxation.
Buildings listed on, §58.1-3221.5.
Website access to property tax bills, §58.1-3912.
Wetlands.
Assessment of residential property containing, §58.1-3284.3.

REAL PROPERTY TRANSFER ON DEATH ACT, §§64.2-621 to 64.2-638.
Applicability of article, §64.2-622.
Effect on other methods of transfer, §64.2-623.
Relation to federal electronic signatures in global and national commerce act, §64.2-638.
Uniform application and construction of provisions, §64.2-637.
Authorization for transfer on death deed, §64.2-624.
Beneficiaries.
Disclaimer, §64.2-633.
Priority of interests, §64.2-632.
Capacity of transferor, §64.2-627.
Conflicting provision in other instrument.
Transfer on death deed revocable, §64.2-625.
Covenant or warranty of title not transferred, §64.2-632.
Creditor claims, property subject to, §64.2-634.
Debts and obligations, property subject to, §64.2-634.
Definitions, §64.2-621.
Disclaimer by beneficiary, §64.2-633.
Effect of provisions on other methods of transfer, §64.2-623.
Limitation of action to enforce liability for debts and obligations, §64.2-634.
Nonexclusivity of provisions, §64.2-623.
Nontestamentary status of deed, §64.2-626.
Priority of interests of beneficiaries, §64.2-632.
Recordation of transfer on death deeds, §64.2-628.
Recordation tax, state.
Exemptions as to deeds conveyed in real estate, §58.1-811.
Relation to federal electronic signatures in global and national commerce act, §64.2-638.
Rules applicable upon death of transferor, §64.2-632.
Statutory allowances, property subject to, §64.2-634.
Transfer on death deeds.
Authorized, §64.2-624.
Contents, §64.2-628.
Effect at transferor's death, §64.2-632.
Effect during transferor's life, §64.2-631.
Effective without notice, delivery, acceptance or consideration, §64.2-629.
Exemption from recordation tax, §64.2-628.
Form, §64.2-635.
Revocation, optional form, §64.2-636.

REAL PROPERTY TRANSFER ON DEATH ACT —Cont'd
Transfer on death deeds —Cont'd
Instrument revoking, §64.2-630.
Joint owners, revocation, §64.2-630.
Nontestamentary status, §64.2-626.
Optional form, §64.2-635.
Revocation, §64.2-636.
Requirements generally, §64.2-628.
Revocation.
Instrument revoking, §64.2-630.
Optional form, §64.2-636.
Permitted, §64.2-625.
Transfers before, on or after July 1, 2013.
Applicability of article, §64.2-622.
Uniform application and construction of provisions, §64.2-637.

REAPPORTIONMENT.
Action challenging boundaries of election district.
Attorney general, legal services, §2.2-508.
Annexation.
Redistricting, §15.2-3226.
Congressional districts, US Const Art I, Amds 14, 17.
County, city or town district or ward.
Decennial reapportionment, VA Const Art VII §5.
Decennial redistricting measures, §24.2-311.
Other measures, §24.2-312.
Rescheduling of elections following, §24.2-313.
Election districts, VA Const Art II §6.
House of delegates districts, general assembly, §24.2-304.03.
Joint reapportionment committee, §§30-263 to 30-265.
Local election districts.
General provisions, §§24.2-304.1 to 24.2-304.6.
See ELECTION DISTRICTS.
Redistricting of county election district, §15.2-1211.
Senatorial districts, general assembly, §24.2-303.3.
Urban county executive form of government, §15.2-856.

REAR FENDERS, FLAPS OR GUARDS, §46.2-1083.
Fine schedule, VA SCt Rule 3B:2.
Maximum fine for violating Title 46.2, §46.2-113.

REARVIEW MIRRORS.
Absence of or inadequate rearview mirror, §46.2-1082.
Fine schedule, VA SCt Rule 3B:2.
Maximum fine for violating Title 46.2, §46.2-113.
Motorcycles, §46.2-912.
Pretrial payment of fine, §16.1-69.40:1.

REASSESSMENT OF REAL PROPERTY.
Real property tax purposes, §§58.1-3250 to 58.1-3295.1.
See REAL PROPERTY TAXES.

REBATES.
Insurance agents, §38.2-1831.
Insurance consultants, §38.2-1843.
Insurance or annuity contract, §38.2-509.
Small employer health insurance, §38.2-3436.
Medicaid, §32.1-315.
Motorcycle dealer advertising, §46.2-1993.81.
Motor vehicle dealer advertising, §46.2-1581.
Petroleum products franchises.
Agreement provisions concerning, §59.1-21.11.

REBATES —Cont'd
Real estate settlement services, §55-525.12.
Referral transactions in connection with consumer sales or leases, §18.2-242.1.
T&M vehicle dealer advertising, §46.2-1990.
Title insurance, §38.2-4614.
Trailer dealer advertising, §46.2-1992.84.

REBUILT VEHICLES, §§46.2-1600 to 46.2-1610.
See SALVAGE VEHICLES.

REBUTTABLE PRESUMPTIONS.
See PRESUMPTIONS.

RECALL OF RETIRED JUDGES TO SERVICE.
Court of appeals judge absent or unable through sickness, disability or other reason to perform or discharge duties, §17.1-400.
Payment for services, §17.1-327.

RECAPTURE TAX.
Estate tax, certain use valuations, §§58.1-931 to 58.1-934.
State tax, certain use valuations.
Imposition, §58.1-931.
Liability of qualified heir, §58.1-932.
Notice of disposition or change in use of property, §58.1-933.
Purposes of article, §58.1-934.

RECEIPT BOOKS.
Circuit courts.
Receipt books, canceled checks and statements.
Maintenance, §17.1-211.
Clerk of circuit court to maintain in office, §17.1-211.
Sheriffs, §15.2-1614.

RECEIPT OF STOLEN GOODS, §18.2-108.
Firearms, §18.2-108.1.
Proof of ownership to property, §19.2-284.
Vehicles, aircraft or boats, §18.2-109.

RECEIPTS.
Bail bondsmen.
Acceptance of collateral, §9.1-185.10.
Consumer finance companies.
Required for all cash payments, §6.2-1524.
Distress for local taxes levied or assessed.
Motor vehicles purchased by, §58.1-3942.
Embezzlement, §18.2-111.
Home solicitation sales, §59.1-21.4.
Lease-purchase agreements, §59.1-207.24.
Payment device numbers.
Display on receipt, §6.2-429.
Secondhand article sales.
Company equipment, §§59.1-126, 59.1-127.
State corporation commission.
Issuance for receipt of currency for payments, §12.1-17.
Telephone solicitation sales, §59.1-21.4.
Warehouse receipts, §§61.1-1 to 61.1-6.
Workers' compensation.
Persons who may receive payment and written receipts, §65.2-525.

RECEIVERS, §§8.01-582 to 8.01-606.
Advertising.
False advertising.
Receiver's stock, §18.2-216.
Attachments.
Appointment to secure forthcoming property, §8.01-549.

RECEIVERS —Cont'd
Attorney's practice, appointment for.
Protection of client interests.
Attorney unable to properly discharge responsibilities, §54.1-3900.01.
Pending disciplinary action, §54.1-3936.
Banks.
Appointment.
Closing bank upon insolvency, §6.2-913.
Court order of sale and execution of deeds, §6.2-917.
Failure to comply with order of commission, §6.2-906.
Protection of creditors, §6.2-916.
FDIC receivership, §§6.2-925 to 6.2-937.
Appointment of FDIC as receiver, §6.2-926.
Assets held by closed bank as fiduciary, §6.2-934.
Definitions, §6.2-925.
Depositors, subrogation of rights, §6.2-936.
Distribution of assets, §6.2-933.
Emergency sale of assets, §6.2-930.
Executory contracts and leases, termination, §6.2-935.
Notice and proof of claim, §6.2-931.
Posting, effect, §6.2-928.
Payment of claims after prescribed period, §6.2-932.
Powers of receiver, §6.2-929.
Records, destruction, §6.2-937.
Transfer of title to bank assets, §6.2-927.
Interest.
Court to prescribe rate on appointment of receivers, §6.2-919.
Investments, §6.2-924.
Judicial sales and rentals.
Sale and execution of deeds, §6.2-917.
Loans.
Power of receivers to contract for loans, §6.2-924.
Powers of bank, §6.2-820.
Proceedings to bar claims against banks in liquidation, §§6.2-920 to 6.2-923.
Rights and powers, §6.2-918.
Sales, §6.2-917.
Bonds, surety.
General receivers.
Apportionment of bonds to funds, §8.01-588.1.
Generally, §8.01-588.
Recording in bond book, §17.1-230.
Cemetery operators, perpetual care trust funds and preneed burial contracts.
Receiver for cemetery company, §54.1-2313.1.
Collection of money and failing to account, §18.2-114.1.
Common interest community managers.
Unable to discharge fiduciary duties, §54.1-2353.
Condominiums.
Special declarant rights.
Transfers, §55-79.74:3.
Conservation of assets of foreign or alien insurers, §38.2-1521.
Consumer finance companies.
Procedure, §6.2-1537.
Corporations.
Bankruptcy and insolvency.
Shares standing in need of receiver, §13.1-662.
Service of notice, process and other papers.
On whom process served, §8.01-303.
Corporations, dissolution.
Appointment in judicial proceeding, §13.1-748.

RECEIVERS —Cont'd
Credit counseling.
Reports.
Receivership as grounds for licensee reporting, §6.2-2010.
Credit unions.
Insolvency.
Powers of commission, §6.2-1313.
Derelict buildings.
Receiver to repair derelict and blighted buildings, locality appointed as, §15.2-907.2.
Dissolution of nonprofit corporations.
Appointment in judicial dissolution, §13.1-910.
Dissolution of stock corporation.
Appointment in judicial proceeding, §13.1-748.
Emergency appointment.
Special receivers, §§8.01-592, 8.01-593.
Escrow fund protection.
Health care professionals, §54.1-2506.2.
Fiduciaries generally.
See FIDUCIARIES.
General receivers, §§8.01-582 to 8.01-590.
Affidavit.
Holding money for benefit of specifically identified beneficiary, §8.01-582.
Appointment, §8.01-582.
Audit of funds, §8.01-582.
Bonds, surety.
Apportionment of bonds to funds, §8.01-588.1.
Generally, §8.01-588.
Compensation and fees, §8.01-589.
Holding money for benefit of specifically identified beneficiary, §8.01-582.
Inquiries as to unknown owners of funds, §8.01-586.
Interest.
Liability for loss of income, §8.01-587.
Investments.
How dividends and interest collected and invested, §8.01-584.
Liability.
For loss of income, §8.01-587.
Moneys deposited in court.
Funds under supervision of fiduciary and belonging to person under disability, §8.01-601.
Neglect of duty, §8.01-590.
Recordkeeping requirements, §8.01-585.
Reporting requirements.
Apportionment of bonds to funds, §8.01-588.1.
Securities.
How dividends and interest collected and invested, §8.01-584.
How securities taken and kept, §8.01-583.
Power of receivers over securities, §8.01-583.
Unknown owners of funds, §8.01-586.
Health care professionals.
Protection of escrow funds held by, §54.1-2506.2.
Hospital or health center commissions, §15.2-5213.
Insurance companies, rehabilitation and liquidation.
Application for.
By state corporation commission, §38.2-1505.
Qualified financial contracts and netting agreements, §38.2-1522.
Requirements when receiver appointed, §38.2-1506.
Interest.
Banks.
Court to have authority to prescribe limit on appointment, §6.2-919.

RECEIVERS —Cont'd
Interest —Cont'd
General receivers.
Liability for loss of income, §8.01-587.
Investments.
Asset placement in financial institutions, §64.2-1413.
Banks, §6.2-924.
General receivers.
How dividends and interest collected and invested, §8.01-584.
Localities.
Appointment as receiver to repair derelict and blighted buildings, §15.2-907.2.
Moneys deposited in court, §§8.01-600 to 8.01-606.
Accounting requirements, §8.01-604.
Authority of receivers of accounts, §8.01-606.
Duties of clerk of court, §8.01-600.
General receivers.
Funds under supervision of fiduciary and belonging to person under disability, §8.01-601.
How money deposited, §8.01-600.
Liability of clerk of court, §8.01-600.
Payment of small amounts without intervention of fiduciary, §8.01-606.
Procedure for deposit, §8.01-600.
Proceedings where owner of money unknown, §8.01-602.
Recovery of money paid into state treasury, §8.01-605.
Unknown owner of money, §8.01-602.
Neglect of duty.
General receivers, §8.01-590.
Nonprofit corporations, dissolution.
Appointment in judicial dissolution, §13.1-910.
Nursing homes.
Appointment, §§32.1-27.1, 32.1-135.
Public corporations.
Shareholder action to appoint custodian or receiver, §13.1-672.6.
Pyramid promotional scheme.
Distribution of assets, §18.2-240.
Savings institutions.
Bank sales.
Court order, §6.2-917.
Corporations.
Appointment in judicial dissolution proceedings, §13.1-748.
Federal deposit insurance corporation.
Appointment as receiver, §6.2-1199.
Schedule of fees.
General receivers, §8.01-589.
Securities.
General receivers.
How dividends and interest collected and invested, §8.01-584.
How securities taken and kept, §8.01-583.
Power of receivers over securities, §8.01-583.
Service of notice, process and other papers.
Corporations.
On whom process served, §8.01-303.
Execution of bond that designates clerk as attorney for service, §64.2-1419.
Adjudication of due diligence, §64.2-1421.
Duties of clerk, §64.2-1420.
Shares of corporation.
Shares standing in name of receiver in proceedings under bankruptcy, §13.1-662.

RECEIVERS —Cont'd
Small water or sewer utilities.
Failure to provide service, §56-265.13:6.1.
Southwest Virginia health facilities authority, §15.2-5382.
Special receivers, §§8.01-591 to 8.01-599.
Appointment, §8.01-591.
Effect of judgment against receiver, §8.01-598.
Emergency appointments.
Notice not required, §8.01-592.
Subsequent proceedings, §8.01-593.
List of creditors, §8.01-595.
Notice requirements.
Appointment, §§8.01-591, 8.01-592, 8.01-594.
List of creditors, §8.01-595.
Sale of assets, §8.01-596.
Parties served with process.
Notice not required, §8.01-594.
Preparation of list of creditors, §8.01-595.
Settlement of accounts, §§8.01-617 to 8.01-619.
Subsequent proceedings after emergency appointment, §8.01-593.
Suits against receivers in certain cases, §8.01-597.
Trial of warrant or motion for judgment against receiver in district court, §8.01-599.
Tax responsibility of fiduciaries, §§58.1-21 to 58.1-24.
Trust companies.
Appointment.
Protection of creditors, §6.2-1038.
Conservation of assets.
Powers of state corporation commission, §6.2-1036.
Powers, §§6.2-820, 6.2-1002.
Unknown owners of funds.
General receivers, §8.01-586.
Moneys deposited in court, §8.01-602.
Water and sewer utilities.
Certain private waterworks, §32.1-174.3.
Failure to provide service, §56-265.13:6.1.
Water supplies.
Appointment for, §32.1-174.1.

RECENT COMPLAINT HEARSAY EXCEPTION.
Sexual assault, §19.2-268.2.

RECHARGEABLE BATTERY DISPOSAL AND RECYCLING, §10.1-1425.39.

RECIPROCAL INSURANCE, §§38.2-1200 to 38.2-1231.
Domestic reciprocals, §§38.2-1219 to 38.2-1231.
Income tax on corporations.
Exemption of reciprocal insurers paying premium tax to Commonwealth, §58.1-401.
Service of notice, process and other papers on reciprocal insurer.
Fee charged by secretary of Commonwealth, §2.2-409.

RECIPROCITY.
Abandonment of property presumption, §§55-210.11, 55-210.11:01.
Attorneys.
Applications for admission to the Virginia bar without examination, VA SCt Rule 1A:1.
Cable television.
Franchises, §15.2-2108.26.
Charitable organizations that solicit funds.
Registration, §57-50.
Coal mine workers certification, §45.1-161.33.
Concealed weapons, carrying, §18.2-308.014.

RECIPROCITY —Cont'd
Death taxes.
Interstate compromise and arbitration.
Reciprocal application of arbitration provision, §58.1-930.
Discovery.
Uniform interstate depositions and discovery act, §8.01-412.14.
Escort vehicles.
Certified escort vehicle drivers, §46.2-2907.
Firearms.
Carrying concealed weapons, §18.2-308.014.
Fishing, inland waters.
Interjurisdictional inland waters, §29.1-535.
Income tax withholding, §58.1-482.
Insurance adjusters.
Examination waiver, §38.2-1845.4.
Nonresident licenses, §38.2-1845.5.
Person moving into Commonwealth from another jurisdiction, §38.2-1845.6.
Insurance agents.
Licensing nonresident agents, §38.2-1836.
Insurance consultants.
Licensing, §38.2-1845.
Living wills, §54.1-2993.
Medicine and other healing arts professions.
Licensing, §54.1-2927.
Mineral mine safety.
Certified employees, §45.1-161.292:24.
Motor vehicle registration.
Nonresident owners of foreign vehicles, §§46.2-655 to 46.2-661.
See MOTOR VEHICLE REGISTRATION.
Parking for disabled or handicapped.
Placards and license plates, §46.2-1258.
Pesticide control.
Certification of applicators, §3.2-3934.
Pharmacist licensure, §54.1-3313.
Plants and plant products inspection, §3.2-3801.
Police cooperation agreements, §15.2-1726.
Agreements outside Commonwealth, §15.2-1727.
Private security services businesses.
Powers of board, §9.1-141.
Property presumed abandoned or escheated, §§55-210.11, 55-210.11:01.
Public accountants.
Licenses.
Substantial equivalency, §54.1-4411.
Real estate brokers, salespersons and rental agents.
Requirements for license by reciprocity, §54.1-2105.
Real estate cooperatives.
Agency regulation of public offering statements, §55-505.
Schools and education.
Fingerprinting employees and applicants for employment, §22.1-296.2.
Solicitation of charitable or civic contributions.
Out-of-state enforcement proceedings, §57-64.
Registration of charitable organizations, §57-50.
Surplus lines insurance.
Licensing of brokers, §38.2-1857.2.
Nonresidents, §38.2-1857.9.
Teachers.
Licensure by reciprocity, §22.1-298.1.
Unemployment compensation, §§60.2-116, 60.2-609.

RECIPROCITY —Cont'd
Viatical settlements.
Broker licensing, §38.2-1865.4.
Weapons.
Carrying concealed weapons, §18.2-308.014.
Wildlife violators compact, §29.1-530.5.

RECKLESS DRIVING, §§46.2-852 to 46.2-868.
Business driveway or premises, §46.2-864.
Church driveway or premises, §46.2-864.
Class 1 misdemeanor, §46.2-868.
Commercial drivers' licenses.
Disqualification for multiple serious traffic violations, §46.2-341.20.
Commercial parking lots, §46.2-864.
Conduct constituting, §46.2-852.
Death resulting.
Arresting officer to request drivers' conviction records, §46.2-384.
Disqualification for commercial driver's license, §46.2-341.19.
Suspension of license, §46.2-396.
Demerit points, §46.2-492.
Double jeopardy.
Dual charge of driving while intoxicated.
Dismissal of one of dual charges upon conviction of other charge, §19.2-294.1.
Drag racing, §§46.2-865 to 46.2-867.
Aiding or abetting, §46.2-866.
Injuring persons while engaging in a race, §46.2-865.1.
Seizure of motor vehicle, §46.2-867.
Suspension of driver's license, §46.2-865.
Drivers' licenses.
Suspension of license for conviction of serious driving offense, §46.2-396.1.
Suspension of license or issuance of restricted license, §46.2-392.
Death resulting from reckless driving, §46.2-396.
Speeding in excess of twenty or more miles over speed limit, §46.2-393.
Driving in excess of eighty miles per hour, §46.2-862.
Driving too fast for highway and traffic conditions, §46.2-861.
Driving two vehicles abreast in single lane, §46.2-857.
Driving vehicle which is not under control, §46.2-853.
Driving while driver's view obstructed or control impaired, §46.2-855.
Dual charge of driving while intoxicated.
Dismissal of one of dual charges upon conviction of other charge, §19.2-294.1.
Employee parking lots, §46.2-864.
Exceeding speed limit.
Drag racing, §46.2-865.
Driving too fast for highway and traffic conditions, §46.2-861.
Driving twenty or more miles over posted speed limit, §46.2-862.
Speeding in excess of eighty miles per hour, §46.2-862.
Failure to give proper signals, §46.2-860.
Failure to yield right-of-way, §46.2-863.
Faulty brakes, §46.2-853.
Fine schedule, VA SCt Rule 3B:2.
Maximum fine for violating Title 46.2, §46.2-113.
Reckless driving as exception, §§18.2-11, 46.2-868.

RECKLESS DRIVING —Cont'd
Fine schedule —Cont'd
Pretrial payment of fine, §16.1-69.40:1.
General rule, §46.2-852.
Highways under construction, not yet open to the public, §46.2-864.
Improper driving as lesser offense, §46.2-869.
Improper signals, §46.2-860.
Industrial parking lots, §46.2-864.
Maximum fine for criminal offense, §§18.2-11, 46.2-868.
Motor vehicle accidents.
Arresting officer to request drivers' conviction record, §46.2-384.
Overtaking on or at the crest of grade or on a curve, §46.2-854.
Overtaking two vehicles abreast, §46.2-856.
Parking lots, etc., §46.2-864.
Passing a stopped school bus, §46.2-859.
Passing at railroad grade crossing, §46.2-858.
Passing on or at the crest of grade or on a curve, §46.2-854.
Passing two vehicles abreast, §46.2-856.
Probation.
Conditions, §46.2-392.
Railroad grade crossing.
Passing at crossing, §46.2-858.
Recreational facility driveway or premises, §46.2-864.
Reimbursement to localities or volunteer rescue squads, §15.2-1716.
Retail parking lots, §46.2-864.
Right-of-way.
Failure to yield, §46.2-863.
School buses.
Passing a stopped school bus, §§46.2-844, 46.2-859.
School driveway or premises, §46.2-864.
Uniform point system, §46.2-492.

RECKLESS ENDANGERMENT.
Throwing objects from places higher than one story, §18.2-51.3.

RECKLESS FIREARM HANDLING, §18.2-56.1.
Recklessly leaving loaded firearm so as to endanger child's life, §18.2-56.2.

RECKLESS OPERATION OF PERSONAL WATERCRAFT, §29.1-738.03.

RECLAMATION OF MINED LAND.
Abandoned mine reclamation, §§45.1-260 to 45.1-270.
See COAL SURFACE MINING.
Coal surface mining reclamation fund, §§45.1-270.1 to 45.1-270.7.
Generally.
See MINED LAND RECLAMATION.
Minerals reclamation fund, §§45.1-197.8 to 45.1-197.18.

RECODIFICATION OF ORDINANCES, §15.2-1433.

RECOGNITION OF ACKNOWLEDGMENTS ACT, §§55-118.1 to 55-118.9.

RECOGNITION OF FOREIGN COUNTY MONEY-JUDGMENTS, §§8.01-465.6 to 8.01-465.13.
See FOREIGN JUDGMENTS.

RECOGNITION OF FOREIGN CUSTODY DETERMINATION.
Uniform child custody jurisdiction and enforcement act.
Duty of courts of Commonwealth, §20-146.24.
Full faith and credit accorded order issued by another state, §20-146.34.
Generally, §§20-146.1 to 20-146.38.
See CHILD CUSTODY.

RECOGNIZANCES.
See BAIL AND RECOGNIZANCE.

RECOGNIZANCE TO KEEP THE PEACE, §§19.2-19 to 19.2-25.
Accused appears, procedure, §19.2-21.
Appeals, §§19.2-24, 19.2-25.
Arrest without warrant, §19.2-22.
Complaint and warrant, §19.2-20.
When required, §19.2-19.

RECONDITIONED GOODS.
Advertising or offering for sale, prohibited practices, §59.1-200.

RECONSIDERATION OF SENTENCE, §19.2-303.
Payment of fine or costs, §19.2-356.
Revocation or suspension, §19.2-306.

RECONSTRUCTED AND SPECIALLY CONSTRUCTED VEHICLES.
Registration and licensing, §46.2-734.

RECONVENED SESSIONS OF GENERAL ASSEMBLY.
Consideration of bills returned by governor, VA Const Art IV §6.

RECORDATION OF DOCUMENTS, §§55-106 to 55-142.9.
Abstract of judgments.
Judgment docket, §17.1-232.
Acknowledgments, §§55-113 to 55-118.9.
See ACKNOWLEDGMENTS.
Agricultural cooperative association.
Articles of incorporation, §13.1-317.
Amendments to, §13.1-318.
Marketing contracts, §13.1-330.
Annexation.
Order of court, §15.2-3223.
Appeal bonds.
Recording in bond book, §17.1-230.
Attachment bonds.
Recording in bond book, §17.1-230.
Attorneys.
Costs assessed by clerk of disciplinary system.
Orders enforcing may be recorded, §54.1-3910.1.
Bankruptcy.
Order and decrees, §§55-140 to 55-142.01.
Bills of sale.
Recording in deed book, §17.1-229.
Bond book.
Documents recorded in, §17.1-230.
Bonds, surety.
Bonds taken by courts and officers, §49-12.
Boundaries.
Motion for judgment to establish boundary lines.
Recordation and effect of judgment, §8.01-183.
Businesses operating under assumed name.
Certificate, §59.1-69.
Business trusts.
Documents, §13.1-1203.
Certificate of satisfaction or partial satisfaction, §55-66.4:2.
Documents recorded in deed book, §17.1-227.

RECORDATION OF DOCUMENTS —Cont'd
Circuit court clerks.
Recordation and indexing generally, §§17.1-223 to 17.1-254.
Collection of state taxes.
Memorandum of lien, §58.1-1805.
Commercial real estate brokers' liens, §55-527.
Commissioners' bond.
Recording in bond book, §17.1-230.
Commissioners in chancery.
Reports of settlement of accounts.
Special receivers and special commissioners, §8.01-619.
Condominiums.
Assessment liens, §55-79.84.
Assignments of limited elements, §55-79.57.
Boundaries between units, relocation of, §55-79.69.
Contents of plats and plans, §55-79.58.
Contraction of condominiums, §55-79.64.
Conversion of convertible lands, §55-79.61.
Description of units, §55-79.47.
Expansion of, §55-79.63.
Instruments.
Amendment of, §55-79.71.
Plans.
Contents of, §55-79.58.
Plats.
Contents of, §55-79.58.
Preliminary recordation of plats and plans, §55-79.59.
Recordation of condominium instruments, §55-79.49.
Special declarant rights.
Transfers, §55-79.74:3.
Subdivision of units, §55-79.70.
Termination of condominium, §55-79.72:1.
Contracts.
Recording in deed book, §17.1-229.
Contracts in reference to real estate.
Documents recorded in deed book, §17.1-227.
Copy of illegible instrument used for making permanent photostat record, §17.1-224.
Corporations.
Deeds of corporations, §55-119.
State corporation commission duties, §13.1-605.
When writings to be recorded, §55-102.
Cost bonds.
Recording in bond book, §17.1-230.
Costs of recording documents generally.
See FEES.
County recordation, §55-102.
Cover sheets on deeds or other instruments.
Use by certain circuit court clerks, §17.1-227.1.
Custodial trusts.
Instrument vesting title to trust property.
Trustee's duty, §64.2-906.
Daily indexes, §17.1-249.
Deed books.
Documents to be recorded in, §17.1-227.
Additional documents, §17.1-229.
Microfilm process used by city or county rendering marginal notations impractical or impossible, §17.1-228.
Deeds.
Corporation deeds, §55-119.
Cover sheets on deeds or other instruments.
Use by certain circuit court clerks, §17.1-227.1.
Documents recorded in deed books, §17.1-227.
Additional documents recorded, §17.1 229

RECORDATION OF DOCUMENTS —Cont'd
Deeds —Cont'd
Easements.
Notation of relocation of easements, §55-50.
Maps or plats attached to deed.
Notation as to recording in plat book, §17.1-236.
Open-space easements.
Virginia outdoors foundation, fee for recording easement, §58.1-817.
Options to purchase real estate, §§55-57.1, 55-57.2.
Real estate investment trusts, §55-106.4.
Requirements generally, §17.1-223.
Writings partially proved book, §17.1-234.
Deeds of assignment for the benefit of creditors, §55-156.
Substitution of trustee, §55-157.
Deeds of release.
Documents recorded in deed book, §17.1-227.
Delinquent local treasurers, notice, §58.1-3171.
Devices on certain containers.
Description filing and publication, §59.1-94.
Disclaimer of property interests, §64.2-2613.
Divorce decrees.
Recordation and indexing, §55-106.1.
Drafter's name to appear on first page, §17.1-223.
Drift property.
Valuation and description to be recorded, §55-203.
Electronic recordation of real property documents.
Uniform standards, §55-66.14.
Federal lien registration, §55-142.13.
Eminent domain, §25.1-247.
Highways and roads.
Certificates in lieu of payments, §33.1-122.
Order confirming award, §33.1-127.
Title transfer by certificate, §25.1-307.
Order confirming award, §25.1-314.
Property in two or more localities, §25.1-309.
Environmental covenants, §10.1-1244.
Escheats.
Original lost or destroyed, certified copy, §55-186.3.
Removal of parcels from escheat certificate, §55-182.1.
Sale of escheated lands, §55-186.2.
Verdicts of inquest, §55-175.
Estrays.
Valuation and description to be recorded, §55-203.
Evictions, §55-245.
Executions.
Judgment docket, §17.1-232.
Executors' or administrators' bond.
Recording in bond book, §17.1-230.
Expenses for recording documents generally.
See FEES.
Federal farm loan mortgage book, §17.1-235.
Fees for recording generally.
See FEES.
Fences.
Division fences.
Requirements for agreement to bind successors in title, §55-321.
Fiduciaries.
Inventories and accounts, §§64.2-1210 to 64.2-1214, 64.2-1310.
Disposition of papers relating to estates, §64.2-1317.
Recording bond in bond book, §17.1-230.
First in time, §55-101.

RECORDATION OF DOCUMENTS —Cont'd
Fraudulent conveyances.
Civil aircraft of the United States.
Recordation of instruments affecting, §55-100.
First in time, §55-101.
Purchasers unaffected by record of deed or contract, §55-100.
Recorded contracts as valid as deeds, §55-95.
Time stamp machine to note time of recordation, §55-96.
Void as to creditors and purchasers until recorded, §55-96.
Where to be recorded, §55-97.
Gas and oil exploration.
Pooling of interests in drilling units, §45.1-361.26.
General indexes, §17.1-249.
Grantors and grantees to be listed, §17.1-223.
Grants.
Documents recorded in deed books, §17.1-227.
Highways and roads.
Abandonment of county roads, §33.1-163.1.
Eminent domain.
Certificates in lieu of payments, §33.1-122.
Order confirming award, §33.1-127.
Homestead deeds.
Documents recorded in deed books, §§17.1-227, 17.1-229.
Improperly notarized documents.
Not in proper form for recordation, §55-106.2.
Income tax.
Declarations of estimated tax, individuals, §58.1-494.
Incorporating deed.
Master deed of trust, §17.1-260.
Indexing, §17.1-249.
Injunction bonds.
Recording in bond book, §17.1-230.
Judgment docket.
Documents recorded in, §17.1-232.
Landlord and tenant.
Evictions, §55-245.
Service of process agent designation, §55-218.1.
Leases.
Leases of personal property recorded in deed book, §§17.1-227, 17.1-229.
Memoranda of leases, §55-57.1.
Liens.
Commercial real estate brokers, §55-527.
Condominiums.
Lien for assessments, §55-79.84.
Deed book, §§17.1-227, 17.1-229.
Delinquent real estate taxes, §58.1-3930.
Release, §55-66.3.
Limitation of enforcement of deeds of trust, mortgages and unpaid purchase money liens.
Extension of limitation, §8.01-241.
Lis pendens notice.
Documents recorded in deed books, §17.1-227.
List of heirs, §64.2-509.
Fee on recording of list of heirs or affidavit.
Tax in lieu of probate tax, §§58.1-1717.1, 58.1-1718, 58.1-3805.
Literary fund.
Evidence of loan indebtedness, §22.1-151.
Local recordation tax, §§58.1-3800 to 58.1-3804.
See RECORDATION TAX, LOCAL.
Local treasurers.
Notice to delinquent treasurers, §58.1-3171.
Marginal notations rendered impractical or impossible by microfilm process used to record documents.
Documents entered in deed book, §17.1-228.

RECORDATION OF DOCUMENTS —Cont'd
Marketing contracts.
Agricultural cooperative association members, §13.1-330.
Marks on certain containers.
Description filing and publication, §59.1-94.
Marriage licenses.
Recording in marriage register, §17.1-233.
Marriage records, §§32.1-267, 55-106.1.
Certified copies as evidence, §20-20.
Corrections authorized, §20-16.1.
Failure to certify, §20-26.
Indexing names of parties, §20-20.
Information taken under oath, §20-16.
Marriage register.
Documents recorded in, §17.1-233.
Master deed of trust, §17.1 259.
Incorporating deed, §17.1-260.
Mechanics' liens.
Deed book, §17.1-229.
Membership camping.
Nondisturbance provisions, §59.1-333.
Memorandum of lien.
Collection of state taxes, §58.1-1805.
Microfilm process used by cities and counties rendering marginal notations impractical.
Documents recorded in deed book, §17.1-228.
Mortgages and deeds of trust.
Certification of counterparts, §55-109.1.
Documents recorded in deed book, §17.1-227.
Documents recorded in deed books, §17.1-227.
Extension of limitation of enforcement, §8.01-241.
Permissible form, §8.01-241.1.
Federal farm loan mortgage book, §17.1-235.
Maps or plats attached to deed.
Notation as to recording in plat book, §17.1-236.
Master deed.
Form and requisites, §17.1-259.
Incorporating deed, §17.1-260.
Releases, §§55-66.3, 55-66.6.
Requirements generally, §17.1-223.
Security trusts, §55-58.1.
Mortgage satisfaction.
General provisions, §§55-66.8 to 55-66.14.
Municipal corporations, when writings to be recorded in, §55-102.
Names on certain containers.
Description filing and publication, §59.1-94.
Nonprofit corporations.
Duties of state corporation commission, §13.1-805.
Notarization improper.
Not in proper form for recordation, §55-106.2.
Numbering of pages, §17.1-223.
Oaths.
Where fact of oath recorded, §49-8.
Option to purchase real estate, §§55-57.1, 55-57.2.
Orders of circuit courts, order books, §§17.1-123 to 17.1-125.
Original requirement, §55-108.
Records of the courts of West Virginia, §55-110.
Use of copies admitted elsewhere, §55-109.
Overhead high voltage line safety.
Notice compliance, §59.1-411.
Oysters.
General oyster planting grounds, §28.2-617.
Assignments, §§28.2-607, 28.2-608.
Parcel identification number (PIN).
Circuit court clerk indexing by, §17.1-252.
Pari-mutuel wagering on horses.
Local referendum petition, §59.1-391.

RECORDATION OF DOCUMENTS —Cont'd
Park authorities.
Conveyances to authority, §15.2-5707.
Partially proved deeds and other instruments.
Writings partially proved book, §17.1-234.
Partition, final judgments or decrees, §55-138.
Documents recorded in deed book, §17.1-227.
Partnerships.
Statements, §50-73.83.
Pet cemeteries.
Land use restrictions, §57-39.21.
Order removing restriction on land, §57-39.24.
Plat book.
Plats and maps recorded in, §17.1-236.
Validation of recording, §17.1-237.
Port authority.
Charges for use of port facilities, §62.1-142.
Powers of appointment to property.
Releases, §64.2-2703.
Powers of attorney, §55-107.
Fidelity and surety insurer to agent to execute bonds, §38.2-2416.
Revocation, §§38.2-2418, 38.2-2419.
Marginal notation, §38.2-2419.
Powers of attorney to convey real estate.
Documents recorded in deed book, §17.1-227.
Preparer's name to appear on first page, §17.1-223.
Presumption of proper form, §55-106.2.
Priority of writings.
When admitted to record same day, §55-101.
Proper form.
Improperly notarized.
Not in proper form, §55-106.2.
Presumption, §55-106.2.
Property owners' associations.
Liens for assessments.
Perfection, §55-516.
Purchasers unaffected by record of deed or contract, §55-100.
Quitclaim deeds.
Documents recorded in deed book, §17.1-227.
Real estate brokers' liens.
Commercial brokers, §55-527.
Real estate cooperatives.
Consolidations, §55-457.
Conveyance of cooperative, §55-469.
Creation, §55-438.
Declaration amendments, §55-453.
Encumbrance of the cooperative, §55-469.
Mergers, §55-457.
Sale prerequisites, §55-495.
Special declarant rights, transfers of, §55-461.
Termination, §55-454.
Real estate settlements.
Duty of settlement agent, §55-525.11.
Real estate taxes.
Delinquent tax liens, §58.1-3930.
Real property.
Electronic documents, §§55-142.10 to 55-142.15.
Mortgage satisfaction.
General provisions, §§55-66.8 to 55-66.14.
Real property transfer on death act.
Transfer on death deeds, §64.2-628.
Receivers' bond.
Recording in bond book, §17.1-230.
Recordation tax, local, §§58.1-3800 to 58.1-3804.
See RECORDATION TAX, LOCAL.
Recordation tax, state, §§58.1-800 to 58.1-817.
See RECORDATION TAX, STATE.
Refusal by clerk to record, §§17.1-223, 55-106.5.

RECORDATION OF DOCUMENTS —Cont'd
Release of deed of trust or other liens.
Affidavit filed by creditor with certificate, §55-66.3.
Certificate of satisfaction or partial satisfaction, §§55-66.3, 55-66.6.
Releases of mortgages.
Documents recorded in deed book, §17.1-227.
Requirements for filing or recording, §17.1-223.
Resources authority.
Pledges, §62.1-210.
Scrivener's act, §17.1-223.
Septic tanks.
Permits, §32.1-164.1.
Social security numbers.
Deed books.
Documents recorded in, §17.1-227.
Standards for writings, §55-108.
Records of the courts of West Virginia, §55-110.
Use of copies admitted elsewhere, §55-109.
State highway plat book, §17.1-238.
State recordation tax, §§58.1-800 to 58.1-817.
See RECORDATION TAX, STATE.
Subdivided land sales.
Liens, §55-344.
Subdivision interest granted to locality as condition of site plan approval.
Vacation by locality, §15.2-2270.
Subdivision ordinances.
Filing and recording with clerk of circuit court, §15.2-2252.
Time for recording plat after final approval, §15.2-2241.
Subdivision plats, §15.2-2264.
Requisites of preparing plats, §15.2-2262.
Statutory requirements, §15.2-2254.
Time for filing after final approval, §15.2-2241.
Vacation of plat after sale of lot, §15.2-2272.
Vacation of plat before sale of lot, §15.2-2271.
Surname of individuals to be in capital letters, §17.1-223.
Taxation.
General provisions.
Local recordation tax, §§58.1-3800 to 58.1-3804.
See RECORDATION TAX, LOCAL.
State recordation tax, §§58.1-800 to 58.1-817.
See RECORDATION TAX, STATE.
Tax collection, state taxes.
Memorandum of lien, §58.1-1805.
Taxes or assessments for local improvements.
Resolutions or ordinances, §15.2-2412.
Tax map reference number.
Indexing by, §17.1-252.
Telephone cooperatives.
Certificates of incorporation, §56-490.
Timber brands.
Adoption by persons engaged in lumbering or rafting on certain waters, §59.1-103.
Adoption by timber dealers, §59.1-109.
Time-shares.
Possibility of reverter.
Effect of recordation, §55-376.1.
Rejection of recordations, §55-363.
Title.
Decrees affecting title to land, §55-138.
Torrens system.
Acts establishing continued in force, §55-112.
Transfer fee covenants, §55-70.2.
Transfer on death deeds.
Real property transfer on death act, §64.2-628.

RECORDATION OF DOCUMENTS —Cont'd
Trustees.
Custodial trusts.
Instrument vesting title to trust property.
Trustee's duty, §64.2-906.
Recording bond in bond book, §17.1-230.
Substituted trustees.
Notice filing, §64.2-1406.
Underground utility line damage prevention.
Notification centers, §56-265.16:1.
United States civil aircraft.
Recordation of instruments affecting, §55-100.
United States court judgments, §§55-140 to 55-142.01.
Unpaid purchase money liens.
Extension of limitation of enforcement, §8.01-241.
West Virginia records.
Use of copies when original lost, §55-110.
When clerk may refuse document to be recorded, §55-106.5.
When writings admitted to record, §55-106.
Where writings to be admitted to record, §55-106.
Will book.
Documents recorded in, §17.1-231.
Wills, §64.2-455.
World War servicemen, names, discharges, etc., §§17.1-261 to 17.1-265.
Writings not duly acknowledged.
Copying to separate book, §55-111.
Writings partially proved book.
Documents recorded in, §17.1-234.

RECORDATION TAX, LOCAL, §§58.1-3800 to 58.1-3804.
Authority of city or county to levy, §58.1-3800.
Authority to impose, §58.1-814.
Charter provisions, article not construed as affecting or repealing, §58.1-3802.
Circuit court clerk, collection and compensation, §58.1-3803.
City having no court for recordation of deeds and other instruments.
Collection of tax for city, §58.1-3804.
Collection, §58.1-3803.
City having no court for recordation of deeds and other instruments, §58.1-3804.
Instruments relating to property located in more than one jurisdiction, §58.1-3801.
Interpretation of article, §58.1-3802.
Levy in addition to state recordation tax, §58.1-3800.
Property located in more than one jurisdiction.
Tax of instruments relating to, §58.1-3801.
Statute of limitations.
Criminal prosecutions, §19.2-8.

RECORDATION TAX, STATE, §§58.1-800 to 58.1-817.
Additional tax paid by grantor, §58.1-802.
Amendments to charters of corporations, §58.1-801.
Charter of corporations amendments, §58.1-801.
City recordation tax.
Authority to impose, §58.1-814.
Collection, §58.1-812.
Additional tax paid by grantor, §58.1-802.
Department of taxation, §58.1-813.
Construction loan deeds of trust or mortgage, §58.1-804.

RECORDATION TAX, STATE —Cont'd
Contracts, §58.1-807.
Sales contracts for sale of rolling stock or equipment, §58.1-808.
Supplemental writings, when not taxable, §58.1-809.
County recordation tax.
Authority to impose, §58.1-814.
Deeds generally, §58.1-801.
Deeds of confirmation.
Taxability, §58.1-810.
Deeds of correction.
Taxability, §58.1-810.
Deeds of gift.
Exemptions, §58.1-811.
Deeds of partition, §58.1-806.
Deeds of release, §58.1-805.
Distribution of recordation tax.
Northern Virginia transportation district fund, §58.1-815.1.
Transportation-related purposes, §58.1-815.4.
Divorce.
Transfers pursuant to decree, §58.1-806.
Exemption, §58.1-811.
Grantors, additional tax paid by, §58.1-802.
Husband and wife.
Deed to which spouses only parties.
Taxability, §58.1-810.
Leases, §58.1-807.
Supplemental writings, when not taxable, §58.1-809.
Misrepresentation, §58.1-812.
Mortgages and deeds of trust, §58.1-803.
Construction loan deeds of trust or mortgages, §58.1-804.
Exemptions, §58.1-811.
Notice of assignment of note secured by.
Deed not taxable, §58.1-810.
Not taxable, §58.1-810.
Supplemental writings, when not taxable, §58.1-809.
Northern Virginia planning district.
Regional congestion relief fee, §58.1-802.2.
Northern Virginia transportation district fund, §58.1-815.1.
Other deeds not taxable, §58.1-810.
Outdoor advertising.
Limit on amount for outdoor advertising sign, §58.1-807.
Partition of land.
Deeds of partition, §58.1-806.
Payment prerequisite to recordation, §58.1-812.
Regional congestion relief fee, §58.1-802.2.
Releases.
Deeds of release, §58.1-805.
Rolling stock.
Sales contracts, §58.1-808.
Supplemental writings, when not taxable, §58.1-809.
Sales contracts for sale of rolling stock or equipment, §58.1-808.
Separate maintenance.
Transfers pursuant to, §58.1-806.
Spouses.
Deeds to which husband and wife only parties.
Taxability, §58.1-810.
Statute of limitations.
Criminal prosecutions, §19.2-8.
Supplemental writings.
When not taxable, §58.1-809.
Title of chapter, §58.1-800.

RECORDATION TAX, STATE —Cont'd
U.S. route 58 corridor development fund, §58.1-815.
Virginia recordation tax act.
Title of chapter, §58.1-800.

RECORDED CONVERSATIONS.
Limitation on use as evidence, §8.01-420.2.

RECORDED DEVICES, §§59.1-41.1 to 59.1-41.6.
Authority of attorney general, §59.1-68.2.
Confiscation, §59.1-41.5.
Defined terms.
Manufacturer, §59.1-41.4.
Owner, §59.1-41.1.
Prohibited acts, §§59.1-41.2, 59.1-41.3, 59.1-41.6.
True name of manufacturer to be shown, §59.1-41.4.

RECORDING FEES.
Costs.
Generally.
See COSTS.
Generally.
See FEES.
Litigation fees.
Generally.
See COURT COSTS AND FEES.
Local recordation tax, §§58.1-3800 to 58.1-3804.
State recordation tax, §§58.1-800 to 58.1-817.

RECORD ON APPEAL.
Administrative agency appeals, VA SCt Rule 2A:3.
Appeals by Commonwealth in criminal cases, §19.2-405.
Court of appeals.
Authorization of judged act, VA SCt Rule 5A:9.
Contents, VA SCt Rule 5A:7.
Inspection and return, §8.01-675.4.
Omission, §8.01-675.4.
Preparation and transmission, VA SCt Rule 5A:10.
Retention, §8.01-675.4.
Transcript or written statement, VA SCt Rule 5A:8.
Criminal appeals by Commonwealth, §19.2-405.
Failure of trial court to deliver record to appellate court, §8.01-679.
State corporation commission.
Fee charged by clerk.
Making up, certifying, transmitting record, §12.1-21.2.
Supreme court, VA SCt Rule 5:15.
Certification for review.
Appeal from court of appeals, VA SCt Rule 5:15.
Direct appeal from trial court, VA SCt Rules 5:10 to 5:13.
Dispositions, VA SCt Rule 5:16.
Finding of records, §8.01-673.
Inspection of records, §8.01-673.
Omission part of record, §8.01-673.
Retention, §8.01-673.
Return of records, §8.01-673.

RECORD PLAYERS.
Personal property taxes.
Classification, §58.1-3504.

RECORDS.
ABC board.
Auditing, §4.1-115.
ABC licensees.
Business records.
Alternative storage, rules and regulations, §4.1-111.

RECORDS —Cont'd
ABC licensees —Cont'd
Business records —Cont'd
Duty to keep, inspection, §4.1-204.
ABC offenses.
Failure to deliver, keep and preserve records and accounts, §4.1-331.
Licensees, §4.1-204.
Accident and sickness insurance.
Medical records.
Right of patient, attorney or authorized insurer to copies, §§8.01-413, 54.1-2403.3.
Acquittal by reason of insanity.
Copies of orders and notices transmitted to commissioner, §19.2-182.16.
Adjutant general, §44-16.
Administrative process act.
Court review.
Agency records, §2.2-4027.
Adoption, §§63.2-1245 to 63.2-1248.
Adoption records.
See ADOPTION RECORDS.
Air carriers.
Commission may require filing, §5.1-142.
Aircraft sales and use tax.
Retention and examination by commissioner, §58.1-1508.
Animal control officers, §3.2-6557.
Annulment of marriage, §§32.1-268, 32.1-268.1.
Attorney discipline.
Clerk of the disciplinary system, VA SCt Rule Pt 6 §IV Par 13-9.
Confidentiality, VA SCt Rule Pt 6 §IV Par 13-30.
Attorney licensing.
Access to criminal history records, §54.1-3925.2.
Attorneys at law.
Rules of professional conduct.
Safekeeping property, VA SCt Rule Pt 6 §II Rule 1.15.
Banks.
Federal deposit insurance corporation.
Inspection of records of banks insured under, §6.2-812.
Birth certificates, §§32.1-257 to 32.1-261.
Amendments, §32.1-269.
Delayed birth certificates, §32.1-259.
Registration by court order, §32.1-260.
Matching birth and death certificates, §32.1-275.1.
Notation of missing children, §32.1-275.2.
Board of coal mining examiners, §45.1-161.26.
Board of education.
Retention of pupil personnel records, §22.1-20.
Boat registration and identification, §29.1-707.
Boat titling certificates, §29.1-718.
Dealers' records, §29.1-721.
Business trusts.
Contents, §13.1-1278.
Inspection by beneficial owners, §13.1-1279.
Court-ordered inspection, §13.1-1281.
Scope of right, §13.1-1280.
BVU authority, §15.2-7211.
Cable television.
Confidential proprietary information or trade secrets pertaining to municipality's provision of service.
Exemption from disclosure under FOIA, §15.2-2108.18.
Localities providing services, §15.2-2108.11.
Campaign finance disclosure.
See CAMPAIGN FINANCE DISCLOSURE.

RECORDS —Cont'd
Cemetery operators, perpetual care trust funds and preneed burial contracts.
Financial records of cemetery company, §54.1-2323.
Seller, §54.1-2332.
Central criminal records exchange, §§19.2-387 to 19.2-392.
Sex offender and crimes against minors registry, §§9.1-900 to 9.1-922.
See SEX OFFENDER REGISTRATION AND NOTIFICATION.
Charge-off of state taxes, §58.1-1802.
Charitable gaming.
Instant bingo, §18.2-340.28.
Network bingo, §18.2-340.28.1.
Sale of supplies, §18.2-340.34:2.
Recordkeeping requirements.
Suppliers of charitable gaming supplies, §18.2-340.34.
Child abuse or neglect, §§63.2-1514, 63.2-1515.
Child custody and visitation arrangements.
Access to by either parent, §20-124.6.
Child custody proceeding.
Uniform child custody jurisdiction and enforcement act.
Preservation of court records.
Until child attains eighteen years of age, §20-146.11.
Child labor.
Required records, §40.1-81.1.
Cigarette excise tax.
Dealers, §58.1-1003.
Documents touching purchase, sale, etc., of cigarettes, §58.1-1021.
Retention, §58.1-1007.
Cigarettes.
Enforcement of illegal sale or distribution, §58.1-1034.
Fire-safe cigarettes.
Testing and certification of cigarettes, §59.1-293.2.
Circuit courts.
Confidentiality.
Juvenile proceedings, §16.1-307.
Copying or duplicating records becoming illegible, §17.1-212.
Copying records of court, §17.1-208.
Disposition of papers and ended case files, §17.1-213.
Electronic filing of documents, §§8.01-271.01, 17.1-258.2 to 17.1-258.6.
Inspection of records of court, §17.1-208.
Land records.
Secure access, §§17.1-279, 17.1-292 to 17.1-295.
Fee allowed for providing, §17.1-276.
Receipt books, §17.1-211.
Recordation and indexing generally, §§17.1-223 to 17.1-254.
Removal of records or papers, §17.1-210.
Secure remote access to records, §§17.1-292 to 17.1-295.
Fee allowed to clerk for providing, §17.1-276.
Vital records.
Amendment petitions, §32.1-269.
Disclosure petitions, §32.1-271.
Wills, §64.2-455.
Commercial space flight authority, §2.2-2213.
Commissioners of accounts.
Records of fiduciaries, §64.2-1221.

RECORDS —Cont'd
Consumer finance companies, §6.2-1533.
Access of state corporation commission to records, §6.2-1530.
Conversion of records to electronic format, §59.1-495.
Corporations.
Generally, §13.1-770.
Records and reports, §§13.1-770 to 13.1-775.2.
Nonprofit corporations, §§13.1-932 to 13.1-936.2.
Corrections department.
Access for prisoner litigation, §8.01-697.
Escape cases, evidence, §18.2-480.1.
Cotton gins, cotton merchants or cotton warehouses, requirements, §3.2-4770.
Court-appointed special advocate.
Client records, inspection and copying, §9.1-156.
Courts.
Circuit courts generally. See within this heading, "Circuit courts."
Destruction of records after transferring to electronic format, §16.1-69.55.
District courts. See within this heading, "District courts."
Expungement of police and court records, §19.2-392.2.
Juvenile and domestic relations district courts, §16.1-69.55.
Preservation of records, VA SCt Rule 1:14.
Secure remote access to records, §§17.1-292 to 17.1-295.
Transcription of proceedings, VA SCt Rule 1:3.
Credit cards.
Subpoenas duces tecum.
Criminal procedure, §19.2-10.1.
Credit counseling.
Books, accounts and records, §6.2-2008.
Cremations.
Funeral director duties, §54.1-2808.1.
Crime victim and witness assistance programs.
Confidentiality of records, §§19.2-368.6, 19.2-368.14.
Criminal records, §§19.2-387 to 19.2-392.
Expungement, §§19.2-392.1 to 19.2-392.4.
Sex offender and crimes against minors registry, §§9.1-900 to 9.1-922.
See SEX OFFENDER REGISTRATION AND NOTIFICATION.
Custodial trusts.
Trustee duties, §64.2-906.
Dead bodies used for scientific study.
Distributions, §32.1-300.
Death certificates, §32.1-263.
Matching birth and death certificates, §32.1-275.1.
Time extensions, §32.1-266.
Devices on certain containers, §59.1-102.
District courts, §§16.1-69.53 to 16.1-69.58.
Case records retention, §16.1-69.55.
Civil proceeding case record retention, §16.1-69.55.
Committee on district courts to determine form and character, §16.1-69.51.
Construction of records as to period of years, §16.1-69.53.
Criminal and traffic infraction proceedings.
Retention of case records, §16.1-69.55.
Definitions, §16.1-69.53.
Destruction of records, §§16.1-69.57, 16.1-117 to 16.1-118.1.
Destruction of records after transferring to electronic format, §16.1-69.55.

RECORDS —Cont'd
District courts —Cont'd
Disposal of original upon reproduction, §16.1-69.54.
Final disposition entered before January 1, 1985.
Applicability of provisions for retention and destruction, §16.1-69.58.
Financial and administrative records retention, §16.1-69.56.
Methods for processing, retention and reproduction, §16.1-69.58.
Retention and storage, §16.1-69.54.
Secure remote access to records, §§17.1-292 to 17.1-295.
Division of records.
Secretary of the Commonwealth in charge of, §2.2-401.
Divorce, §§32.1-268, 32.1-268.1.
Domestic violence.
Address confidentiality program, §2.2-515.2.
Drainage projects.
Bond issues, §21-399.
Drainage record, §21-346.
Drivers' licenses.
Department's recordkeeping requirements, §46.2-327.
Privileged records.
Records in office of department of motor vehicles, release, conditions, §46.2-208.
Drug control, §§54.1-3404 to 54.1-3406.
New drugs, §54.1-3421.
Economic development partnership authority.
Funds of authority, §2.2-2242.
Elections.
Accuracy and security.
State board to ensure, §24.2-611.
Electronic records.
Acceptance, §59.1-496.
Conversion of records to electronic format, §59.1-495.
Electronic display as satisfying requirements, §59.1-486.
Filing, §59.1-496.
Interoperability with other systems, §59.1-497.
Legal effect and enforceability, §§59.1-485, 59.1-501.7.
Retention, §59.1-490.
Sending and receiving, §59.1-493.
Standardization of formats, §59.1-497.
Transferable records, §59.1-494.
Employment commission, §60.2-114.
Employment records.
Evidentiary effect of copies, §8.01-413.1.
Escheators.
Commissions, §55-192.
Escheats.
Examination of records, §55-190.1.
Evidence.
Hearsay exceptions.
Business records, VA SCt Rule 2:803.
Entry by adverse or interested party as corroboration of testimony, §8.01-397.
Family records, VA SCt Rule 2:803.
Public records or reports, VA SCt Rule 2:803.
Recorded recollection, VA SCt Rule 2:803.
Self-authentication, VA SCt Rule 2:902.
Explosives.
Sales, §59.1-138.
Expungement of records.
See EXPUNGEMENT OF RECORDS.

RECORDS —Cont'd
False entries or destruction of records by officers, §18.2-472.
Farm produce sales.
See FARM PRODUCE SALES.
Fetal death reports, §32.1-264.
Fiduciaries.
Commissioners of accounts.
Records of fiduciaries, §64.2-1221.
Inventories, §§64.2-1214, 64.2-1310.
Reports, §64.2-1214.
Sale of accounts, §64.2-1310.
Financial institutions.
Subpoenas duces tecum.
Criminal procedure, §19.2-10.1.
Firearm dealers, §54.1-4201.
Fire protection.
State police duties, §27-55.
Fishing, tidal waters.
Health and sanitation provisions.
Shellfish removed from condemned areas, §28.2-813.
Forest products tax, §58.1-1617.
Failure to keep or permit examination, §58.1-1618.
Forging public records, §18.2-168.
Freedom of information, §§2.2-3700 to 2.2-3714.
See FREEDOM OF INFORMATION.
Fuel taxes, §58.1-2216.
Failure to keep or retain, §58.1-2270.
Inspection of records, §58.1-2276.
Record-keeping requirements, §58.1-2275.
Sales tax in certain transportation districts.
Records of distributors, §58.1-2299.14.
Full faith and credit clause, US Const Art IV §1.
Funeral services.
Preneed funeral contracts, §54.1-2822.1.
Guardian ad litem.
Authority to inspect and copy, §16.1-266.
Handlers of cotton, §3.2-1513.
Health insurance, utilization review.
Internal appeal process and external review.
Assigned independent review organization, §38.2-3568.
Health maintenance organizations.
Medical records.
Right of patient, attorney or authorized insurer to copies, §§8.01-413, 54.1-2403.3.
Health professions department.
Copies as evidence, §54.1-112.
Health services plans.
Medical records.
Right of patient, attorney or authorized insurer to copies, §§8.01-413, 54.1-2403.3.
Health spas, §59.1-308.1.
Hearsay exceptions.
Business records, VA SCt Rule 2:803.
Entry by adverse or interested party as corroboration of testimony, §8.01-397.
Family records, VA SCt Rule 2:803.
Public records or reports, VA SCt Rule 2:803.
Recorded recollection, VA SCt Rule 2:803.
Hospital or health center commissions, §15.2-5215.
Hospital records.
Child abuse or neglect or spousal abuse, §16.1-245.1.
Hybrid retirement program.
Disability program for participants.
Employer and employee recordkeeping required, §51.1-1180.

RECORDS —Cont'd
Industrial development corporations, §13.1-997.
Industrial loan associations.
Retention of books and records, §6.2-1411.
Inspection of records.
Nonprofit corporations, §§13.1-933 to 13.1-935.1.
Shareholders, §§13.1-771 to 13.1-773.
Insurance adjusters.
Investigation and examination of licensees, §38.2-1845.22.
Maintenance of records, §38.2-1845.15.
Insurance companies.
Examination, §38.2-1321.
Insurance information and privacy protection generally, §§38.2-600 to 38.2-620.
See INSURANCE INFORMATION AND PRIVACY PROTECTION.
Loss records, §38.2-1313.
Medical records.
Right of patient, attorney or authorized insurer to copies, §§8.01-413, 54.1-2403.3.
Interstate insurance product regulation compact.
Compacting states' records, §38.2-6200.
Itinerant merchants, §54.1-4301.
Examination by law-enforcement officers, §54.1-4302.
Jail prisoner tally.
Daily record of sheriff, §53.1-122.
Jails.
Conduct records, §53.1-188.
Exchange of medical and mental health information, §53.1-133.03.
Juvenile and domestic relations district courts.
Case records retention, §16.1-69.55.
Destruction of records after transferring to electronic format, §16.1-69.55.
Expungement, §16.1-306.
Secure remote access to records, §§17.1-292 to 17.1-295.
Juvenile detention or group home or residential care facility commissions, §16.1-322.
Juvenile justice department.
Confidentiality of records of children committed to department, §16.1-300.
Evidence of escape cases, §18.2-480.1.
Juvenile justice information system, §§16.1-222 to 16.1-225.
Juvenile records.
Confidentiality of court records, §16.1-305.
Circuit courts, §16.1-307.
Juvenile justice department records, §16.1-300.
Law enforcement records, §16.1-301.
Delinquency cases, disclosures of dispositions, §16.1-305.1.
Dockets, indices and other books, §16.1-302.
Exceptions as to confidentiality, §16.1-309.1.
Expungement of court records, §16.1-306.
Fingerprinting and photographing children, §16.1-299.
Penalty for confidentiality violations, §16.1-309.
Privacy of records, §16.1-302.
Privilege of reports of court officials and employees, §16.1-303.
School principal, disclosures to, §16.1-301.
Land conservation foundation, §10.1-1025.
Libraries.
State records management, §§42.1-76 to 42.1-90.1.
See STATE RECORDS MANAGEMENT.

RECORDS —Cont'd
Library board.
Minutes and records, §42.1-6.
Limited liability companies.
Property title records, §13.1-1067.
Recordkeeping requirements, §13.1-1028.
Limited partnerships.
Recordkeeping requirements, §50-73.8.
Livestock.
Purchases from unknown persons, §§59.1-193, 59.1-194.
Lobbyists, preservation and retention, time period, §2.2-429.
Local treasurers.
Destruction, §58.1-3129.
Lost instruments or records.
Establishing generally, §§8.01-392 to 8.01-395.
Marks on certain containers, §59.1-102.
Marriage records, §32.1-267.
Certified copies as evidence, §20-20.
Clerk authorized to amend, §20-16.1.
Failure to certify, §20-24.
Indexing names of parties, §20-20.
Information taken under oath, §20-16.
Medical malpractice.
Assembly of record, §8.01-581.4:1.
Medical records.
Authenticity and reasonableness of medical bills, §8.01-413.01.
Child abuse or neglect or spousal abuse, §16.1-245.1.
Child fatality review team access to, §§32.1-283.1, 32.1-283.2.
District court civil cases.
Evidence of medical reports or records, §16.1-88.2.
Evidentiary effect of copies, §8.01-413.
Health records privacy, §32.1-127.1:03.
Immunizations, sharing of information, §32.1-46.
Virginia immunization information system (VIIS), §32.1-46.01.
Malpractice, §8.01-581.4:1.
Prenatal care.
HIV test refusal, §54.1-2403.01.
Quarantine and isolation of persons with communicable diseases of public health threat.
Disclosure of health records, §32.1-48.015.
Right of patient, attorney or authorized insurer to copies, §§8.01-413, 54.1-2403.3.
Mental health facilities.
Access to records, accounts and reports, §37.2-703.
System of records, accounts and reports to be prescribed, §37.2-703.
Middle Peninsula Chesapeake Bay public access authority, §15.2-6609.
Mine inspections.
Chief of division of mines, §45.1-161.21.
Review of inspection reports and records, §45.1-161.83.
Mineral mine safety.
Accident reports, §45.1-161.292:52.
Denial of entry, §45.1-161.292:59.
Inspections, §45.1-161.292:13.
Review, §45.1-161.292:56.
Mine safety.
Underground coal mines.
Examinations for hazardous conditions, §45.1-161.212.
Mortgage lender and broker act.
Maintenance of required records, §6.2-1609.

RECORDS —Cont'd
Motor carrier regulations by state police.
Inspection of required records, §52-8.4.
Motor carriers, passengers.
Criminal enforcement of requirements, §46.2-2011.22.
Department's authority as to records, §46.2-2011.16.
Fines.
Civil penalties, §46.2-2011.23.
Motor carriers, property.
Authority of department as to, §46.2-2125.
Fines and criminal enforcement, §46.2-2131.
Motorcycle dealers, §46.2-1993.22.
Examination of records required to be maintained, §46.2-1993.21.
Temporary license plates issued by dealers, §46.2-1993.56.
Motor fuels.
Statement of desire to do business, §59.1-151.
Motor vehicle dealers.
Board, §46.2-1503.1.
Dealer temporary license plates, §46.2-1559.
Preservation of original dealer records, §46.2-1529.
Motor vehicle sales and use tax.
Examination of dealer's records, §58.1-2420.
Motor vehicles department.
Destruction of records, §46.2-216.
Electronic filings and submissions to department, §46.2-216.1.
Electronic documents provided by department, §46.2-216.1.
Maintenance of records of licenses and learner's permits, §46.2-327.
Notice of records supplied to third persons, §46.2-212.
Privileged records, release, conditions, §46.2-208.
Release of information in department records for research purposes, §46.2-209.
Release of vehicle information to prospective vehicle purchasers, §46.2-209.1.
Use of names of persons refused licenses for defective vision, §46.2-221.
When open for inspection, §46.2-208.
Accident reports, §§46.2-379, 46.2-380.
Motor vehicle title loans.
Retention of books, accounts and records, §6.2-2209.
Names on certain containers, §59.1-102.
Nonprofit corporations, §13.1-932.
Court-ordered inspections, §13.1-935.
Inspection by members, §13.1-933.
Scope of right, §13.1-934.
Oil discharges, §62.1-44.34:19.2.
Oysters.
Record of oysters handled, §28.2-538.
Parole revocation hearings, §53.1-171.
Partnerships.
Access of partners to books and records, §50-73.101.
Keeping of books and records, §50-73.101.
Pawnbrokers, §§54.1-4009, 54.1-4011.
Pharmacies.
Controlled paraphernalia distribution, §54.1-3468.
Pharmacy board inspections, §54.1-3309.
Police.
Confidentiality of records concerning children, §16.1-301.
Port authority.
Form, §62.1-139.

RECORDS —Cont'd
Port authority —Cont'd
Location, §62.1-131.
Precious metals dealers, §§54.1-4101, 54.1-4101.1, 54.1-4105.
Preliminary hearings.
Government records search.
Admissibility of affidavit of government official, §19.2-188.3.
Preneed funeral contracts, §54.1-2822.1.
Prisoners.
Conduct records, §53.1-188.
Conviction records, §53.1-24.
Health care admission and treatment.
Periodic review of prisoner retention, §53.1-40.6.
Prisons.
Exchange of medical and mental health information, §53.1-133.03.
Private security services businesses.
Compliance, §9.1-139.
Probation.
Revocation hearings, §53.1-171.
Procurement by public bodies.
Public inspection of records, §2.2-4342.
Professional and occupational regulation department.
Copies as evidence, §54.1-112.
Promotional prizes and gifts.
Application of provisions, §59.1-423.
Proof, US Const Art IV §1.
Property owners' associations, §55-510.
Public accountants.
Duties of director, §54.1-4406.
Public records as evidence, §§8.01-389 to 8.01-391.
Public safety communications systems.
Freedom of information act requests.
Excluded records, §2.2-3705.2.
Public school funds.
Financial records.
Funds from telephone service or credit cards, §22.1-89.3.
Retention and disposition schedule, §22.1-89.2.
Public school students' records, §§22.1-287 to 22.1-289.
Public utilities, §56-249.2.
Underground utility line damage prevention.
Abandoned lines, §56-265.19.
Record of notification, §56-265.22.
Real estate brokers, salespersons and rental agents.
Electronic records, §54.1-2146.
Real estate cooperatives.
Associations, §55-474.
Real estate settlement agents.
Duty to keep records, retention, time period, §55-525.27.
Real property taxes.
Disclosure of certain assessment records, §58.1-3331.
Reassessment record, §58.1-3300.
Retail sales and use tax, dealers required to make return, §58.1-633.
Road tax on motor carriers.
Inspection, §58.1-2708.
Salvage vehicles.
Inspection of records, §46.2-1607.
Maintenance and contents, §46.2-1608.
Sanitation districts law of 1938.
Commission's recordkeeping requirements, §21-179.

RECORDS —Cont'd
Sanitation districts law of 1946.
Commission's recordkeeping requirements, §21-259.
Register of fees, rents and charges, §21-265.
Savings institutions.
Access to books and records, §§6.2-1125, 6.2-1196.
Examination of books, etc., of persons believed to be doing business without authority, §6.2-1203.
Trust accounts.
Maintenance of books and accounts, §6.2-1087.
Secondhand article sales.
Building fixtures, §59.1-120.
Secretary of the Commonwealth.
Chesapeake regional Olympic games compact.
Records to be filed, §2.2-5901.
Compacts, appointments under, §2.2-403.
Duties generally as to executive branch records, §2.2-402.
Seeds, §3.2-4006.
Service contracts, extended.
Production, §59.1-440.
Sewage handling and disposal appeal review board.
Decisions, §32.1-166.8.
Recommendations for modifications of regulations, §32.1-166.9.
Sex offender and crimes against minors registry, §§9.1-900 to 9.1-922.
See SEX OFFENDER REGISTRATION AND NOTIFICATION.
Sheriffs, §53.1-123.
Confidentiality of records concerning children, §16.1-301.
Expenses incurred, §15.2-1609.4.
Jail prisoner tally, §53.1-122.
Services performed by part-time deputy, §15.2-1609.9.
Sickness and disability program.
Employers, §51.1-1137.
Small business financing authority.
Executive director.
Powers and duties, §2.2-2284.
Solicitation of charitable or civic contributions.
Information filed, §57-56.
Professional fund-raisers, §57-61.
Southwest Virginia health facilities authority, §15.2-5384.
State corporation commission.
Clerk's duties, §12.1-19.
State police criminal investigations.
Confidentiality, §52-8.3.
State records management.
General provisions, §§42.1-76 to 42.1-90.1.
See STATE RECORDS MANAGEMENT.
State treasurer.
Payments into state treasury.
Record of payments, §2.2-1805.
Statewide agencies radio system (STARS).
Freedom of information act requests.
Excluded records, §2.2-3705.2.
Students' records.
Public schools, §§22.1-287 to 22.1-289.
Superintendents of schools.
Recordkeeping requirements, §22.1-68.
Surplus lines insurance, §38.2-4807.
T&M vehicle dealers.
Maintenance, §46.2-1929.
Temporary license plates, §46.2-1965.

RECORDS —Cont'd
Taxation.
State tax collection.
Charge-off of state taxes, §58.1-1802.
Taxpayer records.
Examination by tax commissioner, §58.1-219.
Inspection by department of taxation, §58.1-103.
Retention of records, §58.1-102.
Theft or destruction of public records, §18.2-107.
Threat assessment teams.
Public institutions of higher education.
Freedom of information act requests.
Excluded records, §2.2-3705.4.
Time-shares.
Books and records of association, §55-370.01.
Keeping of financial records, §55-385.
Tobacco indemnification and community revitalization commission.
Freedom of information act requests.
Excluded records, §2.2-3705.6.
Tobacco products distributors.
Recordkeeping requirements, §58.1-1021.04:2.
Tobacco warehouses, §61.1-42.
Leaf tobacco.
Record of purchase or delivery, §§61.1-47, 61.1-48.
Tourism authority.
Executive director.
Powers and duties, §2.2-2317.
Tourism financing development authority.
Board of directors, §15.2-5518.
Trademarks and service marks.
Registered or renewed, §59.1-92.9.
Trailer dealers, §46.2-1992.22.
Transportation districts.
Commission, accounts and records, §15.2-4514.
Travel clubs.
Production of, §59.1-452.
Trusts.
Trustee's recordkeeping duty, §64.2-772.
Unclaimed property, §§55-210.24 to 55-210.24:2.
Disposition of funds received, §55-210.19.
Unemployment compensation, §60.2-114.
Veterans services foundation, §2.2-2717.
Veterinary medicine.
Release of records, §54.1-3812.
Viatical settlements.
Records retention, §38.2-6006.
Virginia regional industrial facilities authorities, §15.2-6413.
Virginia retirement system group insurance program.
Employer duties, §51.1-509.
Hybrid retirement program.
Disability program for participants.
Employer and employee recordkeeping required, §51.1-1180.
Vital records, §§32.1-249 to 32.1-276.
See VITAL RECORDS.
Voter registration generally, §§24.2-400 to 24.2-447.
See VOTER REGISTRATION.
Waste kitchen grease.
Transportation.
Registrants, §3.2-5511.
Watercraft sales and use tax.
Retention of documents, §58.1-1407.
Waters of the state.
Oil discharges, §62.1-44.34:19.2.
Wills, §64.2-455.

RECORDS —Cont'd
Workers' compensation accidents, §65.2-900.
Confidentiality, §65.2-903.

RECORDS, DEPARTMENTS OF.
Urban county executive form of government, §15.2-838.

RECORDS, DIVISION OF.
Secretary of the Commonwealth in charge of, §2.2-401.

RECOUNTS IN ELECTIONS.
Appeals.
Proceeding not subject to appeal, §24.2-802.
Applicability of provisions, §24.2-800.
Bonds, surety.
Petitioner assessed with costs, §24.2-802.
Chief justice of supreme court.
Designation of judges to sit with chief judge of circuit, §24.2-801.
Circuit court judges.
Designation of judges to sit with chief judge, §24.2-801.
Circuit courts.
Recount court, §24.2-801.
Coordinators of recount, §24.2-802.
Costs, §24.2-802.
Election contests.
Contests following, §24.2-814.
Evidence.
Printed return sheets, §24.2-659.
Grounds, §24.2-800.
Hand count when optical scan tabulator counts differ, §24.2-802.
Officials of recount, §24.2-802.
Optical scan tabulators, §24.2-802.
Overvotes, §24.2-802.
Petition, §24.2-801.
Preliminary hearing, §24.2-802.
Printed return sheets.
Evidence, §24.2-659.
Procedure, §24.2-802.
Promulgation of standards, §24.2-802.
Service of notice, process and other papers.
Petitions, §24.2-801.
Standards.
Promulgation of standards, §24.2-802.
Supervision of recount, §24.2-802.
Undervotes, §24.2-802.
Venue.
Filing of petition, §24.2-801.

RECOUPMENT.
Negotiable instruments, §8.3A-305.
Secured transactions.
Banks.
Security interests in deposit accounts, §8.9A-340.
Uniform computer information transactions act.
Remedies, §59.1-508.10.

RECREATIONAL AREAS.
Police powers over lands lying beyond localities boundaries, §15.2-1725.
Southwest regional recreation authority, §§15.2-6016 to 15.2-6024.

RECREATIONAL ASSOCIATION OR ORGANIZATION.
Donations by localities, §15.2-953.

RECREATIONAL AUTHORITIES.
Southwest regional recreation authority, §§15.2-6016 to 15.2-6024.

RECREATIONAL FACILITIES.
Access roads to public recreation areas, §33.1-223.
Acquisition of property for outdoor recreation, §10.1-208.
Authorities, §§15.2-5600 to 15.2-5616.
Bikeways to public recreation areas, §33.1-223.
Cooperation of departments, outdoor recreation, §10.1-207.
Counties, cities or towns, §§15.2-1806 to 15.2-1811.
Agreements with landowners, §29.1-509.
Appropriations to legal entities owning.
Urban county executive form of government, §15.2-820.
City or town immunity for operating, §15.2-1809.
Collecting fees, §15.2-1806.
Establishing, §15.2-1806.
Hiking, biking and horse back riding trial, §15.2-1806.
Sale by city or town, VA Const Art VII §9.
Sanitary districts.
Operating facilities in, §15.2-1811.
Sports facilities, providing and operating, §15.2-1808.
Swimming pools.
Leasing land held or owned by locality for, §15.2-1810.
System of public recreation and playgrounds.
Election to establish, §15.2-1807.
Taxing property for maintenance and operation, §15.2-1806.
Urban county executive form of government.
Appropriations to legal entities owning, §15.2-820.
Destruction of trees, shrubs, etc., §18.2-140.
Drug sales on or near property, §18.2-255.2.
Firearms and shotguns carried loaded in park areas, §18.2-287.4.
Gang activities.
Community or recreation centers, enhanced punishment, §18.2-46.3:3.
Hunting and fishing and trapping in state forests, §§10.1-1151 to 10.1-1161.
Liability of county, city or town in operating.
Agreements with landowners, §29.1-509.
Nature area preserves, §§10.1-209 to 10.1-217.
Outdoor recreational facilities.
Long-range plan developed by department of conservation and recreation, §10.1-200.
Property taxes.
Land preservation special assessments, §§58.1-3229 to 58.1-3244.
See REAL PROPERTY TAXES.
Property tax exemption, VA Const Art X §6.
Parks held by trustees for perpetual use, §58.1-3606.
Public-private education facilities and infrastructure act, §§56-575.1 to 56-575.18.
See PUBLIC BUILDINGS.
Southwest regional recreation authority, §§15.2-6016 to 15.2-6024.
Water quality tests, §32.1-248.1.

RECREATIONAL FACILITIES AUTHORITY, §§10.1-1600 to 10.1-1622, 15.2-5600 to 15.2-5616.
Acquisition, maintenance and operation of projects, §15.2-5606.
Appropriations to authority, §15.2-5605.
Articles of incorporation, §15.2-5602.

RECREATIONAL FACILITIES AUTHORITY —Cont'd
Assessments.
Exemptions, §10.1-1616.
Authority.
Defined, §10.1-1600.
Becoming member of existing authority, §15.2-5602.
Board, §10.1-1602.
Defined, §10.1-1600.
Exercise of powers of authority, §15.2-5603.
Bond issues.
Bonds defined, §10.1-1600.
Form, terms and execution, §10.1-1604.
Interim receipts or temporary bonds, §10.1-1607.
Interpretation of provisions.
Securities for investment and deposit, §10.1-1613.
Revenue refunding bonds, §10.1-1614.
Sale and issuance, §10.1-1605.
Trust agreements securing bonds, §10.1-1610.
Use of proceeds, §10.1-1606.
Bonds, §§15.2-5607 to 15.2-5614.
Authority to issue, §15.2-5607.
Exemption from taxation, §15.2-5613.
Legal investments, §15.2-5614.
Payments, §15.2-5607.
Remedies of bondholders and trustees, §15.2-5612.
Resolution authorizing, §15.2-5608.
Securing payment, §15.2-5609.
Terms, conditions, etc., §15.2-5608.
Complete authority for acts authorized, provisions to constitute, §15.2-5615.
Conveyance, lease or other transfer of property to authority, §15.2-5605.
Conveyances, §§10.1-1621, 10.1-1622.
Creation, §§10.1-1601, 15.2-5602.
Definitions, §15.2-5601.
Dissolution, §15.2-5616.
Exercise of powers constitutes performance of governmental function, §15.2-5613.
Expenses, §10.1-1609.
Federal agency.
Defined, §10.1-1600.
Fees, rents and other charges, §15.2-5610.
Grants.
Public or private funds, §10.1-1615.
Interim receipts.
Bond issues, §10.1-1607.
Interpretation of provisions.
Debts of Commonwealth, §10.1-1608.
Leases, §10.1-1621.
Loans.
Public or private funds, §10.1-1615.
Money of authorities, §10.1-1617.
Deemed trust funds, §10.1-1611.
Money received deemed trust funds, §15.2-5611.
Ordinance or resolution creating, §15.2-5602.
Powers, §§10.1-1603, 15.2-5604.
Project.
Defined, §10.1-1600.
Public recreational facilities authorities act.
Chapter known and cited as, §15.2-5600.
Real property.
Conveyances, §§10.1-1621, 10.1-1622.
Leases, §10.1-1621.
Title, §10.1-1618.
Records.
Real estate conveyances, §10.1-1622.
Referendum on question of creation, §15.2-5602.

RECREATIONAL FACILITIES AUTHORITY —Cont'd
Reserves, §15.2-5610.
Revenue refunding bonds, §10.1-1614.
Rights of bondholders or trustees, §10.1-1612.
Securities.
Bonds for investment and deposit, §10.1-1613.
Severability and liberal construction of provisions, §15.2-5615.
Special conservators of the peace, §10.1-1620.
Taxation.
Exemption from taxes or assessments, §10.1-1616.
Title to property, §10.1-1618.
Trust agreements securing bonds, §10.1-1610.
Trust funds.
Money received, §10.1-1611.
Violation of regulations, §10.1-1619.
Withdrawal from authority, §15.2-5602.

RECREATIONAL VEHICLES.
Lights and reflectors, §46.2-1016.
Motor carrier road tax exemptions, §58.1-2702.
Personal property taxes.
Classification, §58.1-3503.

RECREATIONAL WAYSIDES.
Deemed part of interstate, primary or secondary system, §33.1-219.
Establishment along or across public highways, §33.1-217.
Scenic highways and Virginia byways, §§33.1-62 to 33.1-66.
Use regulations, §33.1-218.

RECREATION LANDOWNER'S LIABILITY.
Airport landing areas.
Limitation of liability of private landing area owner, §5.1-7.3.
Duty of care and liability for hunters, fishermen, sightseers, etc., §29.1-509.
Southwest regional recreation authority.
Contracts to hold landowners harmless, §15.2-6020.
Limiting liability, §15.2-6024.
Trail system for ATVs and off-road motorcycles.
Locality providing.
No liability to locality or property owners, §15.2-1809.1.
Protection of persons property and interest and personal liability, §15.2-1806.

RECREATION SPECIALISTS.
Professions and occupations regulation generally.
See HEALTH PROFESSIONS DEPARTMENT.
Prohibited acts by licensees generally, §54.1-2409.1.
Unlawful procurement of licensure, §54.1-102.
Unlawful use of licensure, §54.1-111.

RECRIMINATION.
Divorce, §20-91.

RECRUITMENT FOR CRIMINAL STREET GANG, §18.2-46.3.

RECTAL CANCER.
Presumption as to death or disability.
Firefighters, §65.2-402.

RECUSAL OF CIRCUIT COURT JUDGES.
Criminal cases, §§19.2-153, 19.2-154.

RECYCLED PAPER AND PAPER PRODUCTS.
Preference for purchase by locality, §15.2-938.

RECYCLING.
Beverage containers.
Plastic holding devices, §10.1-1415.2.
Cathode ray tubes, §10.1-1425.26.
Collection and survey of litter, §10.1-1416.
Community service.
Recycling duties for probationers.
Civil immunity, §8.01-226.8.
Computer recovery and recycling act, §§10.1-1425.27 to 10.1-1425.38.
See COMPUTER RECOVERY AND RECYCLING ACT.
Container.
Defined, §10.1-1414.
Definitions, §10.1-1414.
Recycling residue, §10.1-1400.
Disposable package.
Defined, §10.1-1414.
Duties of department.
Further duties, §10.1-1422.
Duties of state agencies and state universities.
Agency programs, §10.1-1425.6.
Agency purchasing programs, §2.2-4323.
Business assistance department (eff until 1/1/2014), §10.1-1425.7.
Education department duties, §§10.1-1425.6 to 10.1-1425.9.
Small business and supplier diversity department, §10.1-1425.7.
Transportation department, §10.1-1425.8.
Enforcement of provisions, §10.1-1417.
Facilities.
Resources authority generally, §§62.1-197 to 62.1-223.
See RESOURCES AUTHORITY.
Fully halogenated chlorofluorocarbons, §10.1-1424.1.
General powers of localities as to waste and recycling, §§15.2-927 to 15.2-939.
Grants, §10.1-1422.04.
Hardwood floors.
Products containing trichloroethylene prohibited, §10.1-1424.2.
Highways and roads.
Lubricating motor oil for machinery and equipment, §33.1-189.1.
Improper disposal of solid waste, §10.1-1418.1.
Improper disposal of tires, §10.1-1418.2.
Liability for large waste tire pile fires, §10.1-1418.3.
Lien for removal, §10.1-1418.5.
Removal of waste tire piles, §10.1-1418.4.
Income tax credit.
Purchase of machinery and equipment for processing recyclable materials.
Corporations, §58.1-439.7.
Labeling plastic containers, §10.1-1415.1.
Lead acid batteries.
General provisions, §§10.1-1425.1 to 10.1-1425.5.
See LEAD ACID BATTERIES.
Litter.
Defined, §10.1-1414.
Litter bags, §10.1-1420.
Litter control and recycling fund, §10.1-1422.01.
Advisory board, §10.1-1422.02.
Membership, §10.1-1422.03.
Litter control program, §10.1-1415.
Litter receptacle.
Defined, §10.1-1414.
Local governments.
Grants for recycling, §10.1-1422.04.

RECYCLING —Cont'd
Mercury thermostat recycling, §10.1-1425.26.
Motor vehicles.
Allowing escape of load material, §10.1-1424.
Highway and road machinery and equipment.
Lubricating motor oil, §33.1-189.1.
Waste tires, §§10.1-1422.3, 10.1-1424.
Notice.
Public notice of provisions, §10.1-1423.
Oil.
Used motor oil.
Management and recycling program, §10.1-1422.6.
Person.
Defined, §10.1-1414.
Placement of litter receptacles, §10.1-1419.
Preemption of local ordinances, §10.1-1425.
Procurement by public bodies.
Petition for recycled goods and products, §2.2-4313.
Preferences.
Paper and paper products used by state agencies, §2.2-4326.
Virginia firms, §2.2-4324.
Virginia products with recycled content, §2.2-4324.
Public place.
Defined, §10.1-1414.
Public procurement.
Recycled goods and products.
Purchasing programs for state agencies, §2.2-4323.
Rechargeable battery disposal and recycling, §10.1-1425.39.
Recycled paper and paper products.
Preference for purchase by locality, §15.2-938.
Recycling residues, §10.1-1422.2.
Reports by nonresidential solid waste generators and companies, §15.2-939.
Responsibility for removal of litter from receptacles, §10.1-1421.
Sale of the business within the Commonwealth.
Defined, §10.1-1414.
Separation of waste generally.
Ordinances, §15.2-937.
Sold within the Commonwealth.
Defined, §10.1-1414.
Solid waste management.
Recycling survey reports, §10.1-1411.
Solid waste or recycling revolving fund, §§62.1-241.1 to 62.1-241.10.
See SOLID WASTE OR RECYCLING REVOLVING FUND.
State agencies.
Agency purchasing programs, §2.2-4323.
Surplus state materials, disposition.
Recycling paper products, beverage containers, electronics and used motor oil, §2.2-1124.
Televisions.
Cathode ray tubes, §10.1-1425.26.
Tires.
Improper disposal of tires, §10.1-1418.2.
Liability for large waste tire pile fires, §10.1-1418.3.
Lien for removal, §10.1-1418.5.
Removal of waste tire piles, §10.1-1418.4.
Partial reimbursement for waste tires, §10.1-1422.4.
Waste tire trust fund, §10.1-1422.3.

RECYCLING —Cont'd
Trichloroethylene.
Products containing trichloroethylene prohibited, §10.1-1424.2.
Vehicle.
Defined, §10.1-1414.
Violation of article, §10.1-1418.
Watercraft.
Defined, §10.1-1414.

RECYCLING FACILITIES.
Resources authority generally, §§62.1-197 to 62.1-223.
See RESOURCES AUTHORITY.

RECYCLING REPORTS.
Nonresidential solid waste generators and companies, §15.2-939.

RED CROSS.
Driver information.
Commissioner of DMV.
Supplying applicant to be volunteer vehicle operator, §46.2-208.
Property exempt from taxation, §58.1-3616.
Solicitation of contributions.
Exemption from provisions, §57-60.

RED DRUM.
Taking, possessing or sale, §28.2-304.

REDEMPTION.
Control share acquisitions, §13.1-728.7.
Delinquent tax lands.
Prior to date for judicial sale, §58.1-3974.
Drainage projects.
Lands sold for taxes.
Board of viewers to pay treasurer, §21-384.
Deed on failure to redeem, §21-392.
Notice of redemption, §21-391.
Repayment of purchasers, §21-392.
Right of redemption, §21-380.
Who may redeem, §21-383.
Lottery tickets.
180-day redemption requirement, §58.1-4020.
Persons with disability.
Disposition of real estate, §§8.01-67 to 8.01-80.
See PERSONS WITH DISABILITY.
Real estate subject to tax becoming separately owned.
Release or redemption of lien of taxes, §58.1-3224.
Residential ground rent, §55-79.05.
Ground rent, §55-79.05.
Sale of delinquent tax lands.
Nonjudicial sale of properties of minimal size and value, §58.1-3975.
Owners rights, §§58.1-3965, 58.1-3974.
Secured transactions.
Defaults.
Collateral.
Right to redeem, §8.9A-623.

REDEMPTION TENDER.
Defined, §§55-243, 55-248.34:1.
Unlawful detainer cases for nonpayment of rent.
Forfeiture prevention, §§55-243, 55-248.34:1.

REDEVELOPMENT AND HOUSING AUTHORITIES.
Chesapeake redevelopment and housing authority, 1972 ch 455, 1987 ch 229.
Hampton redevelopment and housing authority, 1956 ch 323, 1958 ch 260, 1972 ch 269, 1976 ch 632.

REDEVELOPMENT AREAS.
Real property taxation by localities.
Partial exemption for new structures or improvements, application fee, §58.1-3219.4.

REDEVELOPMENT PROJECTS, §§36-48 to 36-55.
Bonds as legal instruments and securities, §36-55.
Conservation plan.
Acquisition of property prior to adoption, §36-52.2.
Authority similar to redevelopment plans, §36-52.1.
Authority to implement, §36-50.1.
Preparation and adoption by localities, §36-49.1.
Public hearing prior to approval, §36-49.1.
Requirements generally, §36-51.1.
Conservation project.
Authority to implement, §36-49.1.
Defined, §36-49.
Eminent domain.
Acquisition of property prior to adoption of development of conservation plan, §36-52.2.
Downzoned lands, §25.1-107.
Making property available for conservation or redevelopment, §36-53.
Fair housing law, §§36-96.1 to 36-96.23.
See FAIR HOUSING.
Federal government aid, §36-54.
Housing development authority.
General provisions, §§36-55.24 to 36-55.52.
See HOUSING DEVELOPMENT AUTHORITY.
Housing revitalization zones, §§36-157 to 36-170.
See HOUSING REVITALIZATION ZONES.
Intergovernmental cooperation, §36-52.
Land in urban areas.
Urban public-private partnership redevelopment fund, §§15.2-2414 to 15.2-2418.
Legislative findings, §§36-48, 36-48.1.
Local housing rehabilitation zones.
Creation, §36-55.64.
Powers of housing authorities, §§36-49.2, 36-50.
Public policy, §§36-48, 36-48.1.
Redevelopment plans.
Approval, §36-51.
Contents, §36-51.
Reaffirmance, §36-51.
Rehabilitation district.
Adoption and designation, §36-52.3.
Spot blight abatement, §36-49.1:1.
Tax increment financing.
Blighted areas, §§58.1-3245 to 58.1-3245.5.
Undertakings constituting redevelopment projects, §36-49.
Urban public-private partnership redevelopment fund, §§15.2-2414 to 15.2-2418.

RED FLAG OR LIGHT AT END OF LOAD, §46.2-1121.
Disabled vehicle, §46.2-111.
Fine schedule, VA SCt Rule 3B:2.
Maximum fine for violating Title 46.2, §46.2-113.

RED FLARES OR TORCHES.
Disabled vehicle on highway, §46.2-111.

REDISTRICTING.
Action challenging boundaries of election district.
Attorney general, legal services, §2.2-508.
Annexation, §15.2-3226.

REDISTRICTING —Cont'd
Apportionment of election districts, VA Const Art II §6.
County, city, town district reapportionment.
Decennial reapportionment of districts, VA Const Art VII §5.
Effective date of measures, §24.2-311.
County election districts, §15.2-1211.
Effective date of measures.
Decennial redistricting, §24.2-311.
Other measures, §24.2-312.
House of delegates districts, §24.2-304.03.
Rescheduling of elections following, §24.2-313.
School boundaries.
Local school boards.
Powers, §22.1-79.
Senatorial districts, §24.2-303.3.

REDOMESTICATION OF INSURERS, §§38.2-1019 to 38.2-1023.

RED OR RED AND WHITE FLASHING WARNING LIGHTS, §§46.2-1023, 46.2-1024.
Emergency vehicle exemption from traffic regulations.
When exemption applicable, §46.2-920.

REDUCED CIGARETTE IGNITION PROPENSITY, §§59.1-293.1 to 59.1-293.9.
See FIRE-SAFE CIGARETTES.

REDUCTION IN INSURANCE COVERAGE.
Automobile insurance.
Notice requirements, §38.2-231.

REDUCTION OF CORPORATE LIMITS OF CITIES OR TOWNS.
Contraction of corporate limits generally, §§15.2-3236 to 15.2-3245.
See BOUNDARIES.

REDUCTION OF FLOOD DAMAGE ACT, §§10.1-600 to 10.1-603.

REDUCTION OF HEAVY METALS IN PACKAGING, §§10.1-1425.20 to 10.1-1425.25.

RED-WINGED BLACKBIRDS.
Nuisance bird law, §§3.2-900, 3.2-901.

REEDVILLE.
Port.
Agent appointment, §62.1-163.

RE-ENCODERS.
Payment card scanning devices and re-encoders, unlawful use, §18.2-196.1.

REFEREE AT SPORTING EVENTS.
Workers' compensation.
Employee not to include sports official, §65.2-101.

REFERENDUM.
ABC law.
Contests of local option referenda, §4.1-127.
Establishment of government stores, §§4.1-121, 4.1-122.
Sale of mixed beverages, §§4.1-124, 4.1-125.
Sunday wine and beer sales, §4.1-123.
Abolition of constitutional offices, §24.2-685.
Change in form of government having effect of abolishing office, §24.2-686.
Explanation of referendum questions submitted to voters, §24.2-687.
Adopting or changing county form of government, §15.2-301.
Limitations as to frequency, §15.2-306.

REFERENDUM —Cont'd
Apples.
Excise tax on commercial production of apples.
Question of levying, §§3.2-1208 to 3.2-1214.
Ascertaining results, §24.2-684.
Ballots, §24.2-684.
Watershed improvements districts, §10.1-618.
Barratry, inapplicability of article, §18.2-451.
Bonds issued by locality.
Explanation of referendum questions, §24.2-687.
Holding of election, §15.2-2611.
Requests for, §15.2-2610.
Calling, §24.2-684.
Certifying, §24.2-684.
Circulating voter petitions, §24.2-684.1.
City status granted to town.
Question of seeking city status, §15.2-3801.
Constitutional office abolition, §24.2-685.
Change in form of government having effect of, §24.2-686.
Explanation of referendum questions submitted to voters, §24.2-687.
Corn.
Assessment for market development, education and promotion, §§3.2-1405 to 3.2-1409.
Cotton board.
See COTTON BOARD.
County executive form of government.
Chairman board of supervisors.
Electing from county at large, §15.2-503.
County food and beverage tax, §58.1-3833.
County manager plan of government.
Board of supervisors.
Electing by district or at large, §15.2-603.
Establishment of department of real estate assessments, §15.2-716.
Questions upon which referenda provided for by statute, §15.2-749.
County police force, abolishing, §15.2-1703.
County police force, establishing, §15.2-1702.
County supervisor elections and terms.
Alternative for biennial elections and staggered terms, §24.2-219.
Reversion to quadrennial election, §24.2-220.
Time and frequency, §24.2-221.
Court order calling, §24.2-684.
Department of real estate assessments.
County manager plan of government.
Establishing, §15.2-716.
Distribution of information on proposed questions.
Submission to voters, §30-19.10.
Electric authorities.
Governing units participation as member, §15.2-5403.
Explanation of referendum questions, §24.2-687.
Gas or electric facilities acquired by locality, §15.2-2109.
Horse industry board, §§3.2-1705, 3.2-1706.
Equine feed assessment, §§3.2-1713 to 3.2-1718.
Equine infectious anemia test fee.
Subsequent referenda on continuation of, §§3.2-1708 to 3.2-1711.
Income tax.
Local income tax, §58.1-540.
Leash laws.
City ordinances, §3.2-6539.
Local income tax, §58.1-540.
Local school boards.
Election of school boards.
Counties with county manager plan of government, §§22.1-47.1 to 22.1-47.4.

REFERENDUM —Cont'd
Local school boards —Cont'd
Popular election of school boards, §§22.1-57.1 to 22.1-57.5.
Selection in school divisions composed of a single county.
Alternative method, §§22.1-41 to 22.1-46.
Number of signatures required on petition.
Adopting or changing form of county government, §15.2-301.
Park authorities.
Contracts entered into with authority, §15.2-5711.
Question of establishing, §15.2-5702.
Petitions.
Address change to another county or city.
Inactive status assignment, §24.2-428.1.
Request for abolition of constitutional offices, §24.2-685.
Change in form of government having effect of abolishing office, §24.2-686.
Requirements for voter petitions calling for referendum, §24.2-684.1.
Sheep industry board, §3.2-2104.
Potato board.
Question of levying tax, §§3.2-1805 to 3.2-1809.
Recreational facilities authorities.
Creating, §15.2-5602.
Sharing local constitutional officers, §15.2-1602.
Signatures on voter petitions, §24.2-684.1.
Small grains.
Assessment for market development, education and promotion, §§3.2-2205 to 3.2-2209.
Soil and water conservation districts, §10.1-555.
Soybeans.
Question of assessment for research, promotion, etc., §§3.2-2305 to 3.2-2309.
Statewide referendum on matter other than constitutional amendment.
Distribution of information, §30-19.10.
Television transmission and relay facilities.
County authority to equip and maintain, §15.2-1224.
Time for holding, §24.2-682.
Transition of cities to towns.
Question of seeking city status, §15.2-3801.
Venue for filing petitions on request for abolition of constitutional offices, §24.2-685.
Voluntary settlement of annexation, transition or immunity issues.
Contracting of debt by counties in voluntary settlement agreements, §15.2-3401.
Water and waste authorities.
Adoption of ordinance, resolution or agreement, §15.2-5105.
Voters petition requesting agreement and referendum, §15.2-5106.
Watershed improvements districts, §§10.1-617, 10.1-634, 10.1-634.1.

REFERRAL ACTIVITIES.
Professional counseling and marriage and family therapy, §54.1-3500.

REFERRAL SALES.
Consumer sales or leases, §18.2-242.1.

REFERRALS BY HEALTH CARE PROFESSIONALS, §§54.1-2410 to 54.1-2414.
Disclosure of interest in referral facilities, §54.1-2964.
Hospital payments to professionals, §32.1-135.2.

REFERRALS BY HEALTH CARE PROFESSIONALS —Cont'd
Medical referral for profit, §18.2-502.
Division of fees between physicians, §54.1-2962.
Remuneration in exchange for referral, §32.1-135.2.
Receipt of remuneration, §54.1-2962.1.
Solicitation of remunerations, §54.1-2962.1.

REFINERIES.
Taxes on fuel.
Fuel taxes, §§58.1-2200 to 58.1-2299.20.
See FUEL TAXES.

REFLECTORS, MOTOR VEHICLES, §§46.2-1016, 46.2-1017.

REFORESTATION OF TIMBERLANDS, §§10.1-1170 to 10.1-1176.
Administration, §10.1-1170.
Exceptions, §10.1-1171.
Failure of general assembly to appropriate from general fund.
Time when article not effective, §10.1-1176.
Forest products tax levied for, §58.1-1602.
Fund, §10.1-1174.
Disposition of forest products tax revenue, §58.1-1609.
Landowners' rights, §10.1-1175.
Options for reforestation, §10.1-1173.
State forester.
Authority, §10.1-1173.
Time when article is effective, §10.1-1176.

REFORMATION OF TRUST.
Mistake of fact or law, §64.2-733.

REFRIGERATORS.
Discarding or abandoning, §18.2-319.

REFUGEES.
Colleges and universities.
Political refugee establishing eligibility for in-state tuition, §23-7.4.

REFUND ANTICIPATION LOANS, §§6.2-2500 to 6.2-2505.
Advertising, §6.2-2501.
Civil penalty for violation, §6.2-2505.
Definitions, §6.2-2500.
Disclosure required, §6.2-2501.
Failure to process application promptly, §6.2-2502.
Fee schedule.
Facilitator to display, §6.2-2501.
Fines.
Civil penalty for violation, §6.2-2505.
Fraudulent transactions, practices or course of business.
Prohibition, §6.2-2502.
Loan arrangement required to complete tax return.
Prohibition, §6.2-2502.
Local acts, statutes, ordinances or regulations.
Preemption by chapter, §6.2-2504.
Misrepresenting material factor or condition.
Prohibition, §6.2-2502.
Preemption.
Local acts, statutes, ordinances or regulations, §6.2-2504.
Prohibited activities, §6.2-2502.
Right of rescission, time period, §6.2-2503.
Schedule showing current fees.
Facilitator to display, §6.2-2501.

REFUNDING BONDS.
Counties, cities or towns.
Public finance act, §§15.2-2643 to 15.2-2649.
Electric authorities, §15.2-5419.
Water and waste authorities, §15.2-5142.
Purchase on open market or otherwise, §15.2-5143.

REFUNDS.
Cigarette excise or use tax.
Correction of erroneous assessments, §58.1-1022.
Community-based continuing care providers.
Refund on rescission of contract, §38.2-4923.
Credit life insurance and credit health insurance.
Termination of insurance prior to scheduled maturity date, §38.2-3729.
Disclosures required.
Returned goods, §59.1-200.
Fuel taxes.
Uses eligible for refund, §58.1-2259.
Motor vehicle registration fees, §§46.2-688 to 46.2-690.
Tax refunds.
See TAX REFUNDS.
Unemployment compensation.
Employer contribution, §60.2-524.

REFUSAL TO RENEW INSURANCE.
Fire insurance, §38.2-2114.
Mailing or electronic delivery of notice, §38.2-2113.
Motor vehicle insurance.
Grounds and procedure, §38.2-2212.
Notice, insurer's requirements, §§38.2-231, 38.2-2208.
Reason for nonrenewal required on application, §38.2-2210.
Unfair discrimination, §38.2-508.
Armed forces members, §38.2-508.1.
Prohibited, §38.2-508.2.

REFUSE.
Collection vehicles.
Flashing amber warning lights, §46.2-1025.
Parking, ordinances prohibiting or limiting, §46.2-1224.
Safety inspections, §46.2-1175.1.
Counties, cities or towns, §§15.2-901, 15.2-927 to 15.2-939.
Charging and collecting compensation, §15.2-928.
Collection and disposal generally, §15.2-927.
Contracting with other localities or Commonwealth to provide or supply services, §15.2-928.
Fee exemption, §15.2-936.
Fee for solid waste disposal by certain counties, §15.2-2159.
Leaves or grass clippings in landfill, §15.2-935.
Penalties for unauthorized disposal or failure to use facilities, §15.2-928.
Pickup and disposal services.
Contracting for services, §15.2-930.
Authorization to enter into contract, §15.2-932.
Requiring delivery to certain facilities, §15.2-931.
Regulation, §15.2-930.
Requiring delivery to certain facilities, §15.2-931.
Private waste companies, displacement, §15.2-934.

REFUSE —Cont'd
Counties, cities or towns —Cont'd
Prohibiting disposal in unauthorized areas, §15.2-928.
Recycling and waste disposal powers generally, §15.2-928.
Requiring delivery to certain facilities, §15.2-933.
Requiring property owners to remove from property, §15.2-901.
Separation of solid waste generally, §15.2-937.
Service districts, §§15.2-2400 to 15.2-2403.3.
Solid waste management facilities.
Providing and operating, §15.2-928.
Siting approval, §15.2-929.
Urban county executive form of government.
Regulation of pickup and disposal services, contracting for services, §15.2-815.
Mines and mining.
Refuse piles, §§45.1-221.1 to 45.1-224.1.
Mineral mines, §§45.1-225.1 to 45.1-225.3.
Recycling generally.
See RECYCLING.
Solid waste management generally, §§10.1-1408.1 to 10.1-1414.
See SOLID WASTE MANAGEMENT.

REFUSE COLLECTION AND DISPOSAL AUTHORITIES.
Generally, §§15.2-5100 to 15.2-5159.
See WATER AND WASTE AUTHORITIES.

REGIONAL ALTERNATIVE EDUCATION PROGRAMS, §22.1-209.1:2.

REGIONAL CHILD FATALITY REVIEW TEAMS, §32.1-283.2.

REGIONAL COMPETITIVENESS ACT, §§15.2-1306 to 15.2-1310.
Assignment weights for functional activities, §15.2-1310.
Criteria for incentive payments, §15.2-1309.
Definitions, §15.2-1307.
Eligibility for incentive payments, §15.2-1309.
Incentive fund, §15.2-1308.
Incentives for joint activities, §15.2-1308.
Policy of general assembly, §15.2-1306.
Weights assigned for functional activities, §15.2-1310.

REGIONAL COOPERATION ACT, §§15.2-4200 to 15.2-4222.
See PLANNING DISTRICT COMMISSIONS.

REGIONAL COOPERATION INCENTIVE FUND, §15.2-4217.

REGIONAL CRIMINAL JUSTICE ACADEMY TRAINING FUND, §9.1-106.
Forwarding of fees by Circuit court clerks to, §17.1-275.

REGIONAL CRIMINAL JUSTICE TRAINING ACADEMIES, §§15.2-1747 to 15.2-1753.
See CRIMINAL JUSTICE TRAINING ACADEMIES.

REGIONAL EMERGENCY MEDICAL SERVICES COUNCILS, §32.1-111.11.
Charitable solicitations, exemption from provisions, §57-60.

REGIONAL HOUSING AUTHORITIES.
Fair housing law, §§36-96.1 to 36-96.23.
See FAIR HOUSING.

REGIONAL HOUSING AUTHORITIES —Cont'd
General provisions, §§36-40 to 36-46.
See HOUSING AUTHORITIES.
Housing development authority, §§36-55.24 to 36-55.52.
See HOUSING DEVELOPMENT AUTHORITY.

REGIONAL INDUSTRIAL DEVELOPMENT.
Virginia regional industrial facilities authorities, §§15.2-6400 to 15.2-6416.
See VIRGINIA REGIONAL INDUSTRIAL FACILITIES AUTHORITIES.

REGIONAL JAIL AUTHORITIES.
Riverside regional jail authority, 1990 ch 726, 1993 ch 228, 1999 ch 642, 1999 ch 675.

REGIONAL JAILS, §§53.1-105 to 53.1-115.2.
See JAILS.

REGIONAL LAW LIBRARIES.
Establishment by governing body, §42.1-71.

REGIONAL LIBRARIES, §§42.1-33 to 42.1-45.

REGIONAL ORGANIZATIONS.
Appropriations to by localities, §15.2-1304.

REGIONAL PARK AUTHORITIES.
Northern regional park authority, 1977 ch 64.

REGIONAL PARTNERSHIPS.
Regional competitiveness act, §§15.2-1306 to 15.2-1310.

REGIONAL STRATEGIC PLAN.
Planning district commissions, §§15.2-4209 to 15.2-4212.

REGIONAL TRANSPORTATION DISTRICT PROGRAM, §33.1-221.1:7.

REGIONAL WORKFORCE TRAINING CENTERS.
Workforce council, §2.2-2671.
Powers and duties, §2.2-2670.

REGISTERED AGENT AND OFFICE.
Corporations, §§13.1-634 to 13.1-637.
Fee for change of address, §13.1-616.
Foreign corporations, §§13.1-763 to 13.1-766.
Limited liability companies, §§13.1-1015 to 13.1-1018.1.
Limited partnerships, §§50-73.4 to 50-73.7.
Nonprofit corporations, §§13.1-833 to 13.1-836, 13.1-925 to 13.1-928.
Registered limited liability partnerships, §50-73.135.
Automatic cancellation of registration.
Effect on registered agent, §50-73.134.

REGISTERED LIMITED LIABILITY PARTNERSHIPS, §§50-73.132 to 50-73.143.
Agents.
Registered agent, §50-73.135.
Attorneys.
Practice of law.
Registration certificate required for registered limited liability partnership engaged in, §50-73.143.
Automatic cancellation of registration.
Effect, §50-73.134.
Cancellation of registration, §50-73.137.
Disposal of known claims, §50-73.137:2.
Disposal of unknown claims, §50-73.137:3.
Court determination of security, §50-73.137:4.
Effect, §§50-73.134, 50-73.137:1.

REGISTERED LIMITED LIABILITY PARTNERSHIPS —Cont'd
Cancellation of registration —Cont'd
Registered agent resignation, failure to file certificate of change, §50-73.135.
Defined, §50-73.79.
Foreign commerce.
Applicability of provisions to, §50-73.141.
Foreign registered limited liability partnerships.
Defined, §50-73.79.
Registration, §50-73.138.
Failure to register.
Effect, §50-73.140.
Withdrawal, §50-73.139.
Interstate commerce.
Applicability of provisions to foreign and interstate commerce, §50-73.141.
Liability of partners, §50-73.96.
Limited liability companies.
General provisions, §§13.1-1000 to 13.1-1080.
See LIMITED LIABILITY COMPANIES.
Limited partnerships.
Becoming registered limited liability partnerships, §50-73.142.
General provisions, §§50-73.1 to 50-73.78.
See LIMITED PARTNERSHIPS.
Names, §50-73.133.
Practice of law, §54.1-3902.
Professional limited liability companies.
General provisions, §§13.1-1100 to 13.1-1123.
See PROFESSIONAL LIMITED LIABILITY COMPANIES.
Real property taxes.
Land conservation incentives, §58.1-513.
Registered agent, §50-73.135.
Automatic cancellation of registration.
Effect on registered agent, §50-73.134.
Registered office, §50-73.135.
Registration certificate required for registered limited liability partnership engaged in practice of law, §50-73.143.
Registration of foreign registered limited liability partnerships, §50-73.138.
Failure to register.
Effect, §50-73.140.
Registration of partnership as, §50-73.132.
Cancellation of registration, §50-73.137.
Disposal of known claims, §50-73.137:2.
Disposal of unknown claims, §50-73.137:3.
Court determination of security, §50-73.137:4.
Effect, §50-73.137:1.
Registered agent resignation, failure to file certificate of change, §50-73.135.
Reports.
Annual continuation reports, §50-73.134.
Restoration of status, §50-73.134.
Revocation of registration.
Annual continuation report.
Failure to file or pay filing fee, §50-73.134.
Service of process.
Automatic cancellation of registration.
Clerk of commission appointed as agent for process, §50-73.134.
Statement of cancellation of registration, §50-73.137.
Statement of registration, §50-73.132.
Amendment, §50-73.136.
Effect, §50-73.136.
Time-shares.
General provisions, §§55-360 to 55-400.
See TIME-SHARES.

REGISTERED LIMITED LIABILITY PARTNERSHIPS —Cont'd
Withdrawal of foreign registered limited liability partnership, §50-73.139.

REGISTERED MAIL.
Child custody proceeding.
Uniform child custody jurisdiction and enforcement act.
Giving notice of exercise of jurisdiction to person outside state, §20-146.7.

REGISTERED NAME.
Foreign nonprofit corporation, §13.1-831.
Foreign stock corporation, §13.1-632.

REGISTERED NURSES.
Correctional health assistants, §54.1-3016.1.
Duty to protect third parties.
Violent behavior or serious harm by client, §54.1-2400.1.
Influenza vaccine.
Administration to minors by pharmacists or nurses, §32.1-46.02.
Licensing, §54.1-3018.
Records of patients.
Admissibility of copies, §8.01-413.
Medical records generally.
See MEDICAL RECORDS.
Right of patient, attorney or authorized insurer to copies, §8.01-413.
Subpoenas, §8.01-413.

REGISTERED OR BOOK ENTRY FORMS.
Bonds issued by locality, §15.2-2614.

REGISTER OF HISTORIC PLACES.
Historic resources department, §10.1-2206.1.

REGISTER OF MACHINE GUNS.
Manufacturer's and dealer's register, §18.2-294.

REGISTER OF REGULATIONS.
Virginia register act.
Generally, §§2.2-4100 to 2.2-4104.
See ADMINISTRATIVE CODE AND REGISTER OF REGULATIONS.
Water control board, §62.1-44.12.

REGISTER OF THE BLIND, §51.5-68.
Confidentiality, §51.5-69.

REGISTERS.
Hazardous radioactive material shippers, §44-146.30.
Historic places, §10.1-2206.1.
Machine guns.
Manufacturer's and dealer's register, §18.2-294.
Sawed-off firearm manufacturers and dealers, §18.2-304.

REGISTRAR.
Administrative code and register of regulations.
Compilation of code, §2.2-4104.
Administrative process act.
Guidance documents, §2.2-4008.
Proposed regulations.
Notice of intended regulatory action, §2.2-4007.01.
Petitions, §2.2-4007.
Appointment, §2.2-4102.
Powers and duties, §2.2-4102.
Proposed regulations.
Submission, §2.2-4007.05.
Register of regulations, §2.2-4031.

REGISTRARS OF ELECTIONS.
Generally, §§24.2-110 to 24.2-114.
See VOTER REGISTRATION.

REGISTRATION.
Aboveground oil storage tanks, §62.1-44.34:19.1.
Accounting corporations, §13.1-549.1.
Agricultural grades, marks and brands.
Grain handlers, §§3.2-4323, 3.2-4325, 3.2-4326.
Bicycle serial numbers, §46.2-908.
Bingo managers and callers.
Required to receive remuneration, qualification, suspension or revocation, §§18.2-340.33, 18.2-340.34:1.
Boats and other watercraft generally, §§29.1-700 to 29.1-711.
Brokers-dealers, securities, §§13.1-504 to 13.1-506.
Cattle brands, §§3.2-6100 to 3.2-6109.
Charitable gaming suppliers, §18.2-340.34.
Charitable organizations that solicit contributions, §§57-49, 57-51.
Child custody determination issued by court of another state, §20-146.26.
Enforcement, §20-146.27.
Child support enforcement by department of social services.
Suspension, delinquency in payments, §63.2-1937.
Cigarette delivery sales.
Person making, §18.2-246.11.
Commercial fishermen, §§28.2-241 to 28.2-244.
Purchases from those known to be unregistered, §28.2-244.
Regulations, §28.2-243.
Required, §28.2-241.
Transfer of registrations, §28.2-241.
Communications sales and use tax.
Services providers, §58.1-653.
Conservators of the peace.
Special conservators, §19.2-13.
Continuing care providers, §38.2-4901.
Convicted criminals.
Sex offender and crimes against minors registry, §§9.1-900 to 9.1-922.
See SEX OFFENDER REGISTRATION AND NOTIFICATION.
Corporations.
Annual registration fees, §13.1-775.1.
Collection of unpaid bills, §13.1-775.2.
Failure to pay.
Automatic revocation of certificate of authority of corporation, §13.1-768.
Automatic termination of corporate existence, §13.1-752.
Late payment, penalty, §13.1-752.
Penalty for late payment.
Foreign corporations, §13.1-768.
Reinstatement fee after ceasing to exist, §13.1-754.
Corporations unpaid registration fees.
Collection by local treasurers, §58.1-2814.
Credit services businesses, §59.1-335.3.
Dangerous dogs, §3.2-6540.
Dealers collecting retail sales and use tax, §58.1-613.
Elections.
Voter registration, §§24.2-400 to 24.2-447.
See VOTER REGISTRATION.
Electric power-assisted bicycles.
Serial numbers, §46.2-908.
Equine dental technicians, §54.1-3813.

REGISTRATION —Cont'd
Exchange companies offering exchange programs.
Time-shares, §55-374.2.
Extended service contracts, §59.1-436.
Feed, commercial, §3.2-4804.
Firearms.
Machine guns, §§18.2-295, 52-4.
Foreign corporations.
Annual registration fees, §13.1-775.1.
Collection of unpaid bills, §13.1-775.2.
Failure to file.
Automatic revocation of certificate of authority, §13.1-768.
Late payment, penalty, §13.1-768.
Foreign limited liability companies, §§13.1-1052 to 13.1-1056.3.
Foreign limited partnerships.
Generally, §§50-73.53 to 50-73.61.
See LIMITED PARTNERSHIPS.
Foreign nonprofit corporations.
Annual registration fees, §13.1-936.1.
Collection of unpaid bills, §13.1-936.2.
Failure to pay automatic revocation of certificate of authority, §13.1-930.
Penalty for late payment, §13.1-930.
Foreign support orders.
Generally, §§20-88.66 to 20-88.77.
See INTERSTATE FAMILY SUPPORT ACT.
Full faith and credit clause, US Const Art IV §1.
Gas and oil exploration.
Persons required to register, §45.1-361.37.
Health service plan holding companies.
Nonprofit corporation members of system, §38.2-4231.
Health spas, §59.1-296.1.
Insurers members of holding company system, §38.2-1329.
Investment securities.
Assurance that endorsements are effective, §8.8A-402.
Authenticating trustee's duty, §8.8A-407.
Issuers.
Rights with respect to registered owners, §8.8A-207.
Registrar's duty, §8.8A-407.
Replacement of lost, destroyed or wrongfully taken security certificates, §8.8A-405.
Requisites for registration of transfer.
Purchaser's right to, §8.8A-307.
Signature of registrar.
Effect, §8.8A-208.
Transfer.
Duty of issuer to register transfer, §8.8A-401.
Duty of transfer agent, §8.8A-407.
Jointly registered securities, §§13.1-434 to 13.1-436.
Law corporations, §13.1-549.2.
Limited liability companies.
Foreign companies, §§13.1-1052 to 13.1-1056.3.
Registration fees, §§13.1-1061 to 13.1-1066.
Application of payment, §13.1-1061.
Assessments, §13.1-1061.
Collection, §13.1-1061.
Unpaid bills, §13.1-1066.
Filing requirements.
Prerequisite to commission action, §13.1-1065.
Payment, §§13.1-1061, 13.1-1062, 13.1-1064.
Penalty for failure to timely pay, §13.1-1064.
Livestock.
False pretense in obtaining, §18.2-205.

REGISTRATION —Cont'd
Lobbyists.
Registration and reporting requirements, §§2.2-418 to 2.2-435.
See LOBBYISTS.
Machine guns, §§18.2-295, 52-4.
Medical equipment.
Registration of certain medical equipment, §32.1-102.1:1.
Medication aides.
Administration of drugs to residents of assisted living facilities, §§54.1-3041 to 54.1-3043.
Medicine for animals.
See ANIMALS.
Membership camping, §§59.1-317 to 59.1-325.
See MEMBERSHIP CAMPING.
Motor carriers, passengers.
See MOTOR CARRIERS, PASSENGERS.
Motor carriers, property.
See MOTOR CARRIERS, PROPERTY.
Motorcycle dealers.
Certificate of dealer registration.
Application, §46.2-1993.17.
Certificate of vehicle registration.
Required before commencing operation, §46.2-1993.39.
Motor vehicles, §§46.2-645 to 46.2-710, 46.2-750 to 46.2-756.
See MOTOR VEHICLE REGISTRATION.
Nonprofit corporations.
Annual registration fees, §13.1-936.1.
Collection of unpaid bills, §13.1-936.2.
Failure to pay.
Automatic revocation of foreign corporation's certificate of authority, §13.1-930.
Automatic termination of corporate existence, §13.1-914.
Penalty for late payment, §13.1-914.
Foreign corporations, §13.1-930.
Oil storage tanks, aboveground, §62.1-44.34:19.1.
Pay telephones, §§56-508.15, 56-508.16.
Pesticide control, §§3.2-3914 to 3.2-3928.
Prescription drug distributors, wholesale, §54.1-3435.01.
Professional law corporations, §13.1-549.2.
Putative father registry, §§63.2-1249 to 63.2-1253.
See PUTATIVE FATHER REGISTRY.
Real estate settlement agents, §55-525.29.
Termination, grounds, §55-525.31.
Retail franchises.
Bond, §13.1-561.
Fee, §13.1-561.
Procedure, §13.1-561.
Required, §13.1-560.
Revocation or refusal to renew, §13.1-562.
Retail sales and use tax.
Dealers collecting tax, §58.1-613.
Risk retention groups and purchasing groups.
Purchasing group requirements, §38.2-5108.
Securities, §§13.1-507 to 13.1-513.
Coordination, §13.1-509.
Effectiveness of registration statement, §13.1-511.
Exemptions, §§13.1-514, 13.1-514.1.
Investment securities. See within this heading, "Investment securities."
Joint names, §§13.1-434 to 13.1-436.
Notification, §13.1-508.
Qualifications, §13.1-510.

REGISTRATION —Cont'd
Securities —Cont'd
Reports to keep registration statements current, §13.1-511.
Required, §13.1-507.
Stop orders, §13.1-513.
TOD security registration, §§64.2-612 to 64.2-619.
See TOD SECURITY REGISTRATION.
Securities brokers-dealers, §§13.1-504 to 13.1-506.
Seeds.
Lawn and turf seed mixture, §3.2-4009.
Service contracts, extended, §59.1-436.
Service marks.
Generally, §§59.1-92.1 to 59.1-92.22.
See TRADEMARKS AND SERVICE MARKS.
Sex offender and crimes against minors registry, §§9.1-900 to 9.1-922.
See SEX OFFENDER REGISTRATION AND NOTIFICATION.
Social security numbers.
Applicants for renewal to provide, §63.2-1937.
Solicitation of charitable or civic contributions.
Charitable organizations.
Suspension, §57-61.1.
Commercial co-ventures, §57-61.2.
Federated fund-raising organizations.
Withholding from donations designated for member agencies, disclosure, §57-58.
Nonresidents.
Effective date, §57-61.1.
Suspension, §57-61.1.
Professional fund-raisers, §57-61.
Effective date, §57-61.1.
Filing to become public record, §57-56.
Ratio of fund-raising expenses to contributions to be included, §57-58.
Suspension, §57-61.1.
Registration of charitable organizations.
Effective date, §57-61.1.
Special conservators of the peace, §19.2-13.
Time-shares, §§55-390 to 55-394.4.
Exchange companies offering exchange programs, §55-374.2.
Trademarks and service marks.
Generally, §§59.1-92.1 to 59.1-92.22.
See TRADEMARKS AND SERVICE MARKS.
Trailers.
Trailer dealer to obtain certificate of vehicle registration and license plates, §46.2-1992.39.
Travel clubs, §59.1-446.
Vacant buildings.
City or town power, §15.2-1127.
Vicious dogs, §3.2-6540.1.
Voters, §§24.2-400 to 24.2-447.
See VOTER REGISTRATION.
Watercraft sales and use tax.
Dealers certificate of registration, §58.1-1406.
Wholesale distributors of prescription drugs, §54.1-3435.01.
Exemptions, §54.1-3435.02.
X-ray machines, §32.1-229.1.

REGISTRATION AND PROTECTION OF TRADEMARKS AND SERVICE MARKS.
Generally, §§59.1-92.1 to 59.1-92.22.
See TRADEMARKS AND SERVICE MARKS.

REGISTRATION CARDS.
Motor vehicles.
See MOTOR VEHICLE REGISTRATION.

REGISTRATION OF CHILD CUSTODY DETERMINATION.
Made by court of another state, §20-146.26.
Enforcement, §20-146.27.

REGISTRATION OF CONVICTED CRIMINALS.
Sex offender and crimes against minors registry, §§9.1-900 to 9.1-922.
See SEX OFFENDER REGISTRATION AND NOTIFICATION.

REGISTRATION OF FOREIGN SUPPORT ORDERS.
Generally, §§20-88.66 to 20-88.77.
See INTERSTATE FAMILY SUPPORT ACT.

REGISTRATION OF NAMES OR INSIGNIA OF ORGANIZATIONS, §§2.2-411 to 2.2-417.
Application for registration, alteration or cancellation, §2.2-412.
Certificate issued to petitioners, §2.2-414.
Fee charged by secretary of the Commonwealth, §2.2-409.
Illegal use of registered insignia, §18.2-177.
Imitative name or insignia prohibited, §2.2-415.
Labor unions.
Illegal use of names or insignia, §18.2-177.
Mottos or slogans of state agencies, §2.2-416.
Use of registered motto or slogan, §2.2-417.
Organizations or associations which may register, alter or cancel name, §2.2-411.
Record kept by secretary of Commonwealth, §2.2-414.
Registration for use, benefit and on behalf of organization throughout Commonwealth, §2.2-413.

REGISTRATION OF VOTERS, §§24.2-400 to 24.2-447.
See VOTER REGISTRATION.

REGROOVED OR RECUT TIRES.
Sale, etc., prohibited, §46.2-1042.

REGULATIONS OF STATE AGENCIES.
Administrative process act.
Generally, §§2.2-4000 to 2.2-4031.
Virginia register act.
Generally, §§2.2-4100 to 2.2-4104.
See ADMINISTRATIVE CODE AND REGISTER OF REGULATIONS.

REGULATORY REVENUE TAXES.
Public service companies, §§58.1-2660 to 58.1-2665.

REHABILITATED COMMERCIAL OR INDUSTRIAL STRUCTURE PROPERTY TAX EXEMPTION, §58.1-3221.

REHABILITATED HOTEL OR MOTEL STRUCTURE PROPERTY TAX EXEMPTION, §58.1-3220.1.

REHABILITATED RESIDENTIAL REAL ESTATE TAX CREDIT, §58.1-3220.01.

REHABILITATED RESIDENTIAL REAL ESTATE TAX EXEMPTION, §58.1-3220.

REHABILITATION AND LIQUIDATION OF INSURERS, §§38.2-1500 to 38.2-1522.
Dental or optometric services plans, §38.2-4509.1.
Health maintenance organizations, §38.2-4317.
Health services plans, §38.2-4214.1.
Legal services plans, §38.2-4408.1.

REHABILITATION CENTER FOR THE BLIND AND VISUALLY IMPAIRED, §51.5-73.

REHABILITATION COUNCIL FOR THE BLIND AND VISUALLY IMPAIRED, §51.5-71.

REHABILITATION DISTRICTS.
Real property taxation by localities.
Partial exemption for new structures or improvements, application fee, §58.1-3219.4.
Rehabilitation, purchase of owner occupied residences.
Local loans and grants to individuals, §15.2-958.

REHABILITATION OF BUILDINGS.
County manager plan of government.
Tenant relocation payments, §15.2-737.
Local funding.
Preservation of low and moderate income housing, other housing experiments, §15.2-958.

REHABILITATION OF DERELICT STRUCTURES.
Virginia removal or rehabilitation of derelict structures fund, §§36-152 to 36-156.

REHABILITATION OF DISABLED PERSONS, VOCATIONAL.
See DISABILITY OR HANDICAP.

REHABILITATION PROVIDERS ADVISORY BOARD.
Defined terms, §54.1-3510.

REHABILITATION PROVIDERS CERTIFICATION, §54.1-3514.
Renewal, §54.1-3515.

REHABILITATIVE SERVICES, §§51.5-116 to 51.5-181.
See AGING AND REHABILITATIVE SERVICES, DEPARTMENT FOR.

REHEARINGS.
Arbitration.
Vacating award, §§8.01-581.01, 8.01-581.010.
Appeal of order vacating without rehearing, §8.01-581.016.
Attachment judgment rendered on publication, §§8.01-575, 8.01-576.
Birth-related neurological injury compensation claims, §38.2-5010.
Corporations, issuance of certificates, articles, etc., §13.1-614.
Costs when new trial granted, payment, §17.1-610.
Court of appeals.
Petition for rehearing.
Criminal cases and traffic infractions, VA SCt Rules 5A:15, 5A:15A.
En banc, VA SCt Rules 5A:34, 5A:35.
Extension of time, VA SCt Rule 5A:3.
On motion of party, VA SCt Rule 5A:33.
Procedure, VA SCt Rule 5A:35.
Scope of rules, VA SCt Rule 5A:32.
Court of appeals reversing and remanding case for new trial.
Petition for appeal to supreme court upon award, §17.1-412.
Criminal appeals by Commonwealth.
No petition for rehearing may be filed, §§19.2-403, 19.2-404.
District courts.
New trial, §16.1-97.1.
Insurance rate regulations.
Special restrictions on individual insurers, §38.2-1911.

REHEARINGS —Cont'd
Nonprofit corporations, certificates issued by state corporation commission, §13.1-813.
Supreme court, §17.1-308.
Petition for rehearing, §8.01-675.2, VA SCt Rule 5:37.
Color of cover, VA SCt Rule 5:31.
Denial, VA SCt Rule 5:20.
Extension of time, VA SCt Rule 5:5.
Workers' compensation awards, §65.2-705.

REIMBURSEMENT FOR RENTAL VEHICLE.
Recovery of cost of hiring substitute vehicle.
Person entitled to recover for damages or destruction of vehicle, §8.01-66.

REINSURANCE.
Ceding or accepting from other insurer, §38.2-136.
Certification and rate filing of reinsurance with affiliated company, §38.2-1912.
Contracting to reinsure risk for purposes of distributing assets among stockholders, §38.2-217.
Contract provisions required.
Inapplicability to contracts of reinsurance, §38.2-300.
Credits allowed ceding insurers, §§38.2-1316.1 to 38.2-1316.8.
Any ceding insurer, §38.2-1316.4.
Applicability of provisions, §38.2-1316.8.
Definitions, §38.2-1316.1.
Domestic ceding insurers, §38.2-1316.2.
Prerequisites to eligibility.
Any ceding insurer, §38.2-1316.4.
Domestic ceding insurers, §38.2-1316.2.
Reinsurance agreements affected, §38.2-1316.8.
Fraternal benefit societies, §38.2-4113.
Health services plans, §38.2-4229.
Joint reinsurance organizations, §38.2-1915.
Examination of, §38.2-1925.
Workers' compensation, automobiles, home protection, etc., rates, §38.2-2002.
Licensing, §§38.2-1347 to 38.2-1357.
Books and records, §38.2-1350.
Brokers, §38.2-1350.
Defined, §38.2-1347.
Utilizing services, §38.2-1351.
Contract provisions, §§38.2-1349, 38.2-1352.
Definitions, §38.2-1347.
Duties.
Brokers, §38.2-1351.
Managers, §38.2-1354.
Examinations, §38.2-1355.
Managers, §38.2-1352.
Defined, §38.2-1347.
Prohibited acts, §38.2-1353.
Utilization of, §38.2-1354.
Penalties, §38.2-1356.
Prohibited acts, §38.2-1353.
Renewal, §38.2-1356.
Requirements, §38.2-1348.
Revocation or suspension license, §38.2-1356.
Mutual assessment life, accident and sickness insurer, §38.2-3922.
Mutual assessment property and casualty insurers, §38.2-2528.
Restrictions, §38.2-216.

REIT.
See REAL ESTATE INVESTMENT TRUSTS.

REJECTION OF GOODS.
Leases, UCC.
Rejection of goods by lessee, §§8.2A-508 to 8.2A-510.
Sales, UCC.
Rightful rejection, §§8.2-602 to 8.2-604.
Buyer's remedies, §8.2-711.
Wrongful rejection.
Seller's remedies, §8.2-703.

RELATION BACK OF AMENDED PLEADINGS, §8.01-6.1.
Confusion in similar trade or corporate name.
Amending pleading to reflect correct name, §8.01-6.2.

RELATIVES.
Adoption.
Close relative adoption, §§63.2-1242.1 to 63.2-1242.3.
Caregivers grant program.
See CAREGIVERS GRANT PROGRAM.
Custody or visitation of child awarded to person with legitimate interest, §§20-124.1, 20-124.2.
Foster care.
Kinship foster care, §63.2-900.1.
Criminal history and central registry checks.
Approved kinship foster care parents, §63.2-901.1.
Placement and visitation for siblings, §63.2-900.2.

RELEASE.
ABC law.
Storage in warehouses, §§4.1-130, 4.1-132.
Claims against the state.
Tort claims act, §8.01-195.8.
Contribution between joint contractors and co-obligors not affected, §11-13.
Covenant of quiet enjoyment, §55-78.
Deeds of release.
Effect, §55-18.
Execution and deliverance, §55-59.4.
Effect of execution, §55-18.
Recordation tax, state, §58.1-805.
Words of release, §55-75.
Disclaimer of property interests.
Distinguished, §64.2-2603.
Documents recorded in deed books, §17.1-227.
Effect on liability and contribution, §8.01-35.1.
Emancipation of minor.
Minor may execute, §16.1-334.
Estate tax lien for unpaid taxes.
Certificate of release, §58.1-908.
Fidelity and surety insurers, §38.2-2413.
Joint contractors or co-obligors, §§11-10, 11-11.
Leases.
For lessee's enjoyment construed, §55-78.
Liens, §§43-67 to 43-71.
Bond filings, §§43-70, 43-71.
Court releases, §43-68.
Mechanic's liens.
Payment, §43-67.
Into court payments, §§43-70, 43-71.
Satisfaction, §43-67.
Mortgages and deeds of trust.
Certificate of satisfaction or partial satisfaction.
Form, §55-66.4:1.
Recordation, §§55-66.4, 55-66.4:2, 55-66.5.
City and county using microfilm, marginal notations, §17.1-228.
Court releases, §55-66.5.

RELEASE —Cont'd
Mortgages and deeds of trust —Cont'd
Marginal releases, §§55-66.4, 55-66.6.
Original grantor rather living or dead, §55-66.2.
Recording in deed book, §17.1-227.
Part performance extinguishing obligation, §11-12.
Powers of appointment, §§64.2-2700 to 64.2-2704.
Real property tax liens.
Payment of taxes on real estate becoming separately owned, §§58.1-3224, 58.1-3226.1.
Recordation tax, state.
Deeds of release, §58.1-805.
Recording.
Documents to be recorded in deed books.
Counties and cities using microfilm, marginal notations, §17.1-228.
Settlement of personal injury action or claim.
Rescission of release of liability executed as condition of settlement, §8.01-425.1.
Trusts.
Release of beneficiaries.
Trustees' liability, §64.2-800.

RELEASE OF DANGEROUS OR UNHEALTHY SUBSTANCES.
Counties, cities or towns.
General power to abate or remove, §15.2-900.

RELEASE OF LIABILITY AS CONDITION OF SETTLEMENT.
Rescission of release in personal injury action or claim, §8.01-425.1.

RELEASE OF PETROLEUM.
Underground storage tanks releasing petroleum into environment.
Virginia petroleum storage tank fund, §62.1-44.34:11.

R. E. LEE CAMP.
Appropriation of funds, §57-5.

RELICS.
Locality acquiring and housing, §15.2-945.

RELIGION.
Appropriations to, VA Const Art IV §16.
Behavioral health and developmental services.
Spiritual means of treatment without drugs or material remedy, §37.2-414.
Child day center operated by religious institution.
Exemption from licensure, requirements for operating, §63.2-1716.
Child placement.
Agency's religious or moral objections to placement.
Conscience clause, §63.2-1709.3.
Protection of religious affiliation, §16.1-288.
Church electric rates, §56-236.1.
Churches and other places of worship generally.
See CHURCHES AND OTHER PLACES OF WORSHIP.
Clergy generally.
See CLERGY.
Colleges and universities.
Religious preferences and affiliations.
Collection and dissemination of information, §23-2.1.
Religious student organizations.
Right to determine internal affairs, governance and members, §23-9.2:12.

RELIGION —Cont'd
Contract or tort immunity.
Members of churches, synagogues or religious bodies, §8.01-220.1:3.
Evidence.
Hearsay exceptions.
Baptismal certificates, VA SCt Rule 2:803.
Religious organizations, records, VA SCt Rule 2:803.
Free exercise and enjoyment, VA Const Art I §16, US Const Amd 1.
Governmental entity substantially burdening.
Prohibition, definitions, applicability, remedies, §57-2.02.
Health care sharing ministries, §§38.2-6300, 38.2-6301.
Hearsay exceptions.
Baptismal certificates, VA SCt Rule 2:803.
Religious organizations, records, VA SCt Rule 2:803.
Hospices.
Exemption from licensure, §32.1-162.2.
Hospitals.
Application of provisions for practice of religious tenets, §32.1-128.
Behavioral health and developmental services.
Spiritual means of treatment without drugs or material remedy, §37.2-414.
Family planning information, §32.1-134.
Immunizations.
Exemptions from provisions, §§22.1-271.2, 32.1-46.
Inborn errors of metabolism.
Tests to detect and control.
Objections, §32.1-65.
Income tax exemption for religious corporations, §58.1-401.
Juvenile justice department.
Care of children committed to department.
Collection of information concerning preferences, §66-25.
Mental health facilities.
Religious preferences and affiliations of individuals receiving services, §37.2-712.
Militia duty exemption.
Religious beliefs, §44-5.
No establishment of religion, VA Const Art I §16, US Const Amd 1.
Nursing homes.
Application of provisions for practice of religious tenets, §32.1-128.
Phenylketonuria.
Tests to detect and control, §32.1-65.
Privileged communications.
Penitent privilege, §8.01-400, VA SCt Rule 2:503.
Property exempt from taxation, §58.1-3617, VA Const Art X §6.
Public procurement.
Contracting with faith-based organizations, §2.2-4343.1.
Public school instruction.
Comparative religion as elective course, §22.1-202.1.
Emphasis on moral education, §22.1-208.
Public school students.
Expression of religious viewpoint by students, §22.1-203.3.
Religious tests.
Constitution of the United States, US Const Art VI.
Toxic substances.
Diagnosis of employee injuries and illnesses.
Objections to medical treatment or examinations, §32.1-244.

RELIGIOUS DENOMINATIONS.
Corporate charter not granted by general assembly, VA Const Art IV §14.
Health care sharing ministries, §§38.2-6300, 38.2-6301.

RELIGIOUS DISCRIMINATION.
Advertising discrimination, §57-2.1.
Constitutional prohibition, VA Const Art I §11.
Discrimination generally.
See DISCRIMINATION.
Equal credit opportunities, §§6.2-500 to 6.2-513.
See EQUAL CREDIT OPPORTUNITIES.
Fair employment contracting act, §§2.2-4200, 2.2-4201.
Health maintenance organizations, §38.2-4312.
Human rights act, §§2.2-3900 to 2.2-3903.
Life insurance, §38.2-508.2.
Procurement by public bodies, §2.2-4310.
Employment discrimination by contractors, §2.2-4311.

RELIGIOUS FREEDOM, §§57-1 to 57-2.1, VA Const Art I §16, US Const Amd 1.
Act recited, §57-1.
Reaffirmation of rights, §57-2.
Governmental entity substantially burdening free exercise of religion.
Prohibition, definitions, applicability, remedies, §57-2.02.
Religious freedom week and day, §57-2.01.

RELIGIOUS FREEDOM WEEK AND DAY, §57-2.01.

RELIGIOUS INTIMIDATION.
Tort liability, §8.01-42.1.

RELIGIOUS ORGANIZATIONS.
Antitrust laws.
Applicability, §59.1-9.4.
Appropriation of property, §57-3.
Charitable gaming.
General provisions, §§18.2-340.15 to 18.2-340.37.
See CHARITABLE GAMING.
Child day center operated by religious institution.
Exemption from licensure, requirements for operating, §63.2-1716.
Church electric rates, §56-236.1.
Dangerous weapons, carrying to place of religious worship, §18.2-283.
Determination of property rights on division of church or society, §57-9.
Disorderly conduct in public places.
Disrupting place of religious worship, §18.2-415.
Donations to churches or sectarian societies.
Localities, prohibition, §15.2-953.
Donations to vestries for charitable purposes, §57-4.
Ecclesiastical officers.
Property powers and duties, §57-16.
Glebe lands.
Appropriation of, §57-3.
Health care sharing ministries.
Defined, §38.2-6300.
Health care cost sharing arrangement among individuals of same religion, §38.2-6300.
Inapplicability of insurance laws, §38.2-6301.
Not business engaging in the business of insurance, §38.2-6301.
Notice publication not insurance, §38.2-6300.
Income tax exemption for religious corporations, §58.1-401.

RELIGIOUS ORGANIZATIONS —Cont'd
Intimidation.
Tort liability, §8.01-42.1.
Land held in adverse possession, §57-17.
Pelham Chapel.
Leasing, §57-5.
Property of unincorporated church held by corporation, §57-16.1.
Property transfers.
What transfers valid, §57-7.1.
Real property tax credit when land acquired by.
Credit on current year's taxes, §§58.1-3360 to 58.1-3363.
Resale of interment rights, §54.1-2312.2.
Solicitation of charitable or civic contributions.
Generally, §§57-48 to 57-69.
See SOLICITATION OF CHARITABLE OR CIVIC CONTRIBUTIONS.
Suits by members to have land sold or mortgaged, §57-14.
Circuit court clerk's fees, §57-15.
Fiscal officer liability, §57-15.1.
Proceedings by trustees or members for similar purposes, §57-15.
Tort liability for intimidations, §8.01-42.1.
Transfer of property by trustees to church or religious body, §57-15.
Trustees.
Appointment of to effectuate purposes of conveyances, §57-8.
Holding personal property, §57-10.
Suits by and against, §57-11.
Suits by members against trustees, §57-13.
Suits by trustees to have land sold or mortgaged, §57-15.

RELOCATION ASSISTANCE.
Eminent domain, §§25.1-406 to 25.1-421.
See EMINENT DOMAIN.
Housing authorities.
Alternative housing of persons displaced by condemnation, conversion, etc., §36-27.01.

REMAINDERS.
Attachment against remainders, §8.01-547.
Attornment.
Unnecessary, §55-220.
When void, §55-221.
Contingent remainders, §55-15.
Disposition of estates in property, §§8.01-94, 8.01-95.
Fraudulent conveyances.
Pretend reservations to be recorded, §55-87.
Heir limitations construed.
Heirs of his body or words of like import, §55-14.
Life tenancies.
Default or surrender of tenant not to prejudice remainderman, §55-8.
Power of disposal in life tenant not to defeat remainder, §55-7.
Recovery at death of life tenant of taxes paid, §55-25.
Murderers barred from claiming property rights of decedent, §64.2-2506.
Not defeated, §55-16.
Principal and income.
Uniform principal and income act, §§64.2-1000 to 64.2-1032.
See PRINCIPAL AND INCOME.

REMAINDERS —Cont'd
Real property taxes.
When remainder held by United States.
Life tenant's interest, §58.1-3223.
Rule in Shelley's case abolished, §55-14.
Valuation of decedent's property, §64.2-305.
Waste, §§55-211 to 55-216.
When remainders not defeated, §55-16.
Works on watercourses.
Rights upon forfeiture by tenant of works damaged or destroyed, §62.1-126.

REMARRIAGE.
Cessation of spousal support, §§20-109, 20-110.
Legal separation.
Remarriage as bigamy, §20-116.
Prohibition pending appeal from divorce decree, §20-118.
Remedial remarriage statute, §20-118.
Workers' compensation.
Disclosure by employee or dependent receiving payments, §65.2-712.

REMEDIAL MEASURES.
Evidence.
Subsequent remedial measures, relevancy, VA SCt Rule 2:407.

REMEDIAL PROGRAMS IN PUBLIC SCHOOLS.
State funding, §22.1-253.13:1.

REMEDIATION PROGRAM FOR AT-RISK STUDENTS, §22.1-253.13:1.

REMEDIES.
Alternative dispute resolution proceedings.
Generally.
See ALTERNATIVE DISPUTE RESOLUTION.
Arbitration.
Generally, §§8.01-577 to 8.01-581.016.
See ARBITRATION.
Attachment.
Generally, §§8.01-533 to 8.01-576.
See ATTACHMENT.
Computer information transactions, §§59.1-508.1 to 59.1-508.16.
Declaratory judgments.
Generally, §§8.01-184 to 8.01-191.
See DECLARATORY JUDGMENTS.
Detinue.
Generally, §§8.01-114 to 8.01-123.
See DETINUE.
Dispute resolution proceedings.
Generally, §§8.01-576.4 to 8.01 576.12.
Ejectment.
Generally, §§8.01-131 to 8.01-165.
See EJECTMENT.
Equal credit opportunities.
Election of remedies, §6.2-512.
Garnishment.
Generally, §§8.01-511 to 8.01-525.
See GARNISHMENT.
Habeas corpus.
Generally, §§8.01-654 to 8.01-668.
See HABEAS CORPUS.
Improvements to land.
Generally, §§8.01-166 to 8.01-178.
See IMPROVEMENTS TO LAND.
Injunctions.
Generally, §§8.01-620 to 8.01-634.
See INJUNCTIONS.
Interpleader, §8.01-364.

REMEDIES —Cont'd
Interstate family support, §§20-88.32 to 20-88.82.
See INTERSTATE FAMILY SUPPORT ACT.
Judicial sales.
Generally, §§8.01-96 to 8.01-113.
See JUDICIAL SALES.
Landlord and tenant.
Landlord's unlawful ouster, §55-225.2.
Material noncompliance or danger, §§55-225.12, 55-225.13.
Mandamus.
Generally, §§8.01-644 to 8.01-653.1.
See MANDAMUS.
Partition of land.
Generally, §§8.01-81 to 8.01-93.
See PARTITION OF LAND.
Prohibition, writ of.
Generally, §§8.01-644 to 8.01-653.1.
See PROHIBITION.
Quo warranto.
Generally, §§8.01-635 to 8.01-643.
See QUO WARRANTO.
Receivership.
Generally, §§8.01-582 to 8.01-606.
See RECEIVERS.
Tort claims act.
General provisions, §§8.01-195.1 to 8.01-195.9.
See TORT CLAIMS ACT.
Uniform computer information transactions act, §§59.1-508.1 to 59.1-508.16.
Unlawful entry and detainer.
Generally, §§8.01-124 to 8.01-130.
See UNLAWFUL ENTRY AND DETAINER.

REMITTITUR.
Appeal in verdict reduced and accepted under protest, §8.01-383.1.
Final judgment entered after verdict set aside, §8.01-430.

REMOVAL OF CASES.
Attachment levied on real estate, district court proceedings, §16.1-105.
Criminal cases removed from state to federal court, §19.2-9.
District court civil cases.
Attachment levied on real estate, §16.1-105.
Judgment on forthcoming bond, §16.1-77.1.
Juvenile case removed to circuit court, §16.1-269.1.
Appeals by juvenile, §16.1-269.4.
Determinations by circuit court, §16.1-269.6.
Placement of juvenile, §16.1-269.5.
Retention by juvenile court, §16.1-269.3.
Reversion of city to town.
Removal of cases to circuit court of county, §15.2-4119.
Small claims courts.
Removal to general district court, §16.1-122.4.

REMOVAL OF COURT RECORDS.
Circuit court records, §17.1-210.

REMOVAL OF DERELICT STRUCTURES.
Virginia removal or rehabilitation of derelict structures fund, §§36-152 to 36-156.

REMOVAL OF JUDGES OF COURTS OF RECORD.
Supreme court jurisdiction in matters, VA Const Art VI §1.

REMOVAL OF NUISANCES.
Counties, cities or towns, §§15.2-900, 15.2-1115.
Derelict buildings, §§15.2-906, 15.2-907.1.
Locality appointed as receiver to repair derelict and blighted buildings, §15.2-907.2.

REMOVAL OF PROPERTY SUBJECT TO LIEN, §18.2-115.

REMOVAL OF PUBLIC OFFICERS FROM OFFICE, §§24.2-230 to 24.2-238.
Applicability of provisions, §24.2-230.
Appointed officer for term certain, §24.2-234.
Appointment of attorney to represent Commonwealth at trial, §24.2-237.
Attorney for the Commonwealth to represent Commonwealth at trial, §24.2-237.
Circuit court removal from office, §24.2-233.
Appointed officer for term certain, §24.2-234.
Procedure, §24.2-235.
Suspension pending hearing and appeal, §24.2-236.
Costs and attorney fees, §24.2-238.
Determination person incapacitated in judicial proceeding.
Vacancy occurring, §24.2-232.
Exceptions to applicability, §24.2-230.
Forfeiture of office.
Sentence for commission of felony, §24.2-231.
Governor's powers.
Removal of board, commission, etc., members, §2.2-108.
Grounds for removal by circuit court, §24.2-233.
Judges of courts of record.
Supreme court jurisdiction, VA Const Art VI §1.
Jury trial, §24.2-237.
Petition to circuit court for removal from office, §24.2-233.
Appointed officer for term certain, §24.2-234.
Requirements, §24.2-235.
Procedure for removal, §24.2-235.
Right of appeal to supreme court, §24.2-237.
Service of show cause rule, §24.2-235.
Show cause rule, §24.2-235.
State corporation commission.
Conflict of interest violations, §12.1-10.
Supreme court review.
Right of appeal, §24.2-237.
Suspension pending hearing and appeal, §24.2-236.
Trial by jury, §24.2-237.

REMOVAL OF SNOW AND ICE.
City or town powers, §15.2-1115.
Northern Virginia Planning District 8.
Public sidewalks, §15.2-2025.
Service districts, §§15.2-2400 to 15.2-2403.3.

REMOVAL OF STUDENTS FROM CLASSES.
Disruptive behavior, §22.1-276.2.

RENEWABLE ENERGY.
Clean energy manufacturing incentive grant program, §§59.1-284.25 to 59.1-284.27.
Customers' options to purchase.
Notification by investor owned electric utilities, §56-245.1:2.
Energy policy of Commonwealth, §§67-102, 67-103.
Green job creation tax credit, §58.1-439.12:05.
Personal property taxes.
Classification of property, §58.1-3506.

RENEWABLE ENERGY —Cont'd
Real property taxes.
Classification of improvements to property used for design and manufacture of renewable energy products, §58.1-3221.4.
Renewable electricity production program, §§67-900 to 67-903.
Definitions, §67-900.
Grants for electricity produced by qualified energy resources.
Application, requirements for grants, §67-903.
Eligibility, §67-901.
Renewable electricity production grant fund, §67-902.
Renewable energy co-location of distribution facilities, §§67-1100 to 67-1110.
Consent procedures, §67-1106.
Contracting for private right-of-way, §67-1108.
Damage to property, recovery of costs for, §67-1110.
Definitions, §67-1100.
Fees.
Public rights-of-way use fee, §67-1103.
Inspection or coordination costs, payment by generator, §67-1107.
Location and placement of facilities, §67-1109.
Public property, use of, §67-1102.
Railroad crossings, rights and obligations, §67-1102.
Relocation.
Reimbursement for costs, §67-1104.
Restoration of property disturbed upon installation, §67-1110.
Rights-of-way.
Consent to use, §67-1106.
Contracting for private right-of-way, §67-1108.
Imposition of restrictions, §67-1101.
Occupation and use by renewable generators, §67-1101.
Public rights-of-way use fee, §67-1103.
State highway system, §67-1105.
Safety and clearance standards, §67-1109.
Renewable energy portfolio standard program.
Investor-owned incumbent electric utility.
Sale of electricity from renewable sources through, §56-585.2.
Rights-of-way.
Renewable generators, §56-259.
Small renewable energy projects, §§10.1-1197.5 to 10.1-1197.11.
Administrative enforcement, §10.1-1197.9.
Contest of decisions of department, §10.1-1197.7.
Criminal violations, §10.1-1197.9.
Definitions, §10.1-1197.5.
Enforcement of provisions, §10.1-1197.9.
Fees, §10.1-1197.6.
Information to be provided to department, §10.1-1197.11.
Penalties for violations, §10.1-1197.9.
Permits by rule, §10.1-1197.6.
Review of applications, §10.1-1197.7.
Right of entry to inspect, §10.1-1197.10.
State corporation commission, limitation of jurisdiction, §10.1-1197.8.
Stand-by electric service at renewable cogeneration facilities.
Rates for, §56-235.1:1.
Submerged lands.
Renewable energy leases, §28.2-1208.

RENEWABLE ENERGY —Cont'd
Thermal energy.
Renewable energy portfolio standard program.
Investor-owned incumbent electric utility, sale of electricity from renewable sources through, §56-585.2.
Tidal waters.
Submerged lands.
Renewable energy leases, §28.2-1208.
Virginia universities clean energy development and economic stimulus foundation, §§23-300 to 23-303.

RENOVATED COMMERCIAL OR INDUSTRIAL STRUCTURE PROPERTY TAX EXEMPTION, §58.1-3221.

RENOVATED HOTEL OR MOTEL STRUCTURE PROPERTY TAX EXEMPTION, §58.1-3220.1.

RENOVATED RESIDENTIAL REAL ESTATE PROPERTY TAX CREDIT, §58.1-3220.01.

RENOVATED RESIDENTIAL REAL ESTATE PROPERTY TAX EXEMPTION, §58.1-3220.

RENOVATION CONTRACTORS.
Board for asbestos, lead and home inspectors, §§54.1-500.1, 54.1-501.
Disciplinary actions against licensees, §54.1-516.
License required, §54.1-503.
Penalties for license violations, §54.1-517.
Scope of statutory provisions, §54.1-512.

RENT.
Armories.
Temporary renting, §44-135.1.
Attachments.
Pretrial levy or seizure of attachment, §8.01-534.
Bad check.
Notice check for rent returned unpaid, §8.01-27.2.
Beach assignments, §28.2-633.
Boundaries.
Motion for judgment to establish boundaries.
Claims to rents, etc., not considered, §8.01-182.
Condominiums.
Conversion condominiums.
Special provisions for elderly or disabled, §55-79.94.
Damage insurance required by landlord.
Payments for premium costs deemed rent, §55-248.7:2.
Decedents' estates.
Powers of executors and administrators, §64.2-521.
Proceeds, §64.2-522.
Distress for local taxes against landlord.
Credit out of rent, tenant paying taxes or levies, §58.1-3944.
Educational facilities authority, §23-30.50.
Escheats.
Liability of escheator, §55-180.
Provision for enjoyment, §55-194.
Income tax credit for reductions, §58.1-339.9.
Judgment as lien on real estate.
Decreed sale of real estate, §8.01-462.
Landlord and tenant generally.
See LANDLORD AND TENANT.
Manufactured home lot rental, §55-248.44:1.
Home sales upon eviction.
Liability for rent, §55-248.50:2.
Retaliatory conduct, §55-248.50.
Merchants' capital tax, §§58.1-3509, 58.1-3510.

RENT —Cont'd
Oysters.
Planting grounds.
General oyster planting grounds, §§28.2-611, 28.2-612.
Delinquent ground, §28.2-620.
Lynnhaven river.
Excusing payment on condemned grounds, §28.2-623.
Refund of rent paid under mistake, §28.2-626.
Relief from rent, §28.2-627.
Recorded device piracy, §§59.1-41.2, 59.1-41.3.
Redemption tender.
Defined, §§55-243, 55-248.34:1.
Unlawful detainer cases for nonpayment of rent.
Forfeiture prevention, §§55-243, 55-248.34:1.
Renter's insurance required by landlord.
Payment for premium costs.
Deemed rent, §55-248.7:2.
Residential ground rent, §§55-79.01 to 55-79.06.
Sanitation districts law of 1938.
Fees, rents and charges, §§21-180 to 21-188.
Sanitation districts law of 1946.
Fees, rents and charges, §§21-260 to 21-268.
Tenants entitled to emblements.
What rent to be paid, §55-250.

RENTAL AGREEMENTS.
Landlord and tenant generally, §§55-217 to 55-248.
See LANDLORD AND TENANT.
Leases generally.
See LEASES.
Manufactured home lot rental.
Automatic renewal, §55-248.42:1.
Provisions, §55-248.42.
Retaliatory conduct, §§55-248.50, 55-248.50:1.
Termination, §55-248.46.
Waiver of landlord's right to terminate, §55-248.46:1.
Writing required, §55-248.42.
Residential landlord and tenant generally, §§55-248.2 to 55-248.40.
See LANDLORD AND TENANT.

RENTAL CAR REIMBURSEMENT.
Cost of hiring substitute vehicle.
Recovery by person entitled to recover for damages or destruction to vehicle, §8.01-66.
Motor vehicle insurance coverage.
Mandatory offer, §38.2-2230.

RENTAL INSPECTION DISTRICTS.
Residential rental dwelling units.
Rental inspections by localities.
Building code compliance, §36-105.1:1.

RENTAL LOCATION AGENTS.
Generally, §§54.1-2100 to 54.1-2145.
See REAL ESTATE BROKERS, SALESPERSONS AND RENTAL AGENTS.

RENTAL OF BOATS.
Injury to vessel, §18.2-149.
Personal watercraft.
Identification of watercraft rentals, §29.1-749.1.
Instruction by rental agents, §29.1-749.2.
Insurance on rental, §29.1-749.3.
Safety requirements, §29.1-736.

RENTAL OF MOTOR VEHICLES.
Generally.
See MOTOR VEHICLE RENTALS.

RENTAL OF MOTOR VEHICLES —Cont'd
Motor vehicle rental tax, §§58.1-1734 to 58.1-1741.
See MOTOR VEHICLE RENTALS.

RENTERS' INSURANCE.
Residential leases.
Insurance as requisite of lease, §55-248.7:2.

RENT-TO-OWN.
Lease-purchase agreements generally, §§59.1-207.17 to 59.1-207.27.
See LEASE-PURCHASE AGREEMENTS.

RENUNCIATION OF INTEREST.
Wrongful death beneficiaries, §8.01-53.

REORGANIZATION ACT.
Effective date, §1-2.1.

REPAIRS.
County manager plan of government.
Zoning ordinances regulating motor vehicle repairs, §15.2-730.
Insurance unfair settlement practices, §38.2-517.
Motor vehicle repair facilities, §§59.1-207.1 to 59.1-207.6.
See MOTOR VEHICLE REPAIR FACILITIES.

REPEAL OF STATUTES.
Generally, §§1-3 to 1-9.
See STATUTES.

REPEAT OFFENDERS.
Child custody order violations, §18.2-49.1.
Drivers' licenses, §§46.2-356 to 46.2-363.
Driving motor vehicle prohibited, §46.2-357.
Impoundment of motor vehicle.
Driving while license suspended or revoked, §46.2-301.1.
Restoration of driving privileges, §§46.2-358 to 46.2-361.
Revocation of license for fourth conviction, §46.2-394.
Self-propelled machinery or equipment.
Operation prohibited, §46.2-357.
Ten-year denial of license, §46.2-356.
Driving while intoxicated.
Mandatory minimum sentences, §18.2-270.
Family or household member, assault and battery on, §18.2-57.2.
Juvenile offenders.
Commitment, §16.1-285.1.
Release and review hearings, §16.1-285.2.
Comprehensive action program, §§16.1-330.1, 16.1-330.2.
Serving adult sentence, §16.1-285.2.
Juvenile proceedings.
Serious or habitual offenders.
Commitment, §16.1-285.1.
Release and review hearings, §16.1-285.2.
Comprehensive action program, §§16.1-330.1, 16.1-330.2.
Serving adult sentence, §16.1-285.2.
Motor vehicle habitual offenders, §§46.2-356 to 46.2-363.
Driving while intoxicated, §18.2-270.
For-hire passenger vehicle, unlicensed operation, §46.2-316.
Odometer tampering, §46.2-112.
Railroad tracks, trespassing, §18.2-159.
Sentencing violent felons, §19.2-297.1.
Stalking, §18.2-60.3.

REPLACEMENT COMMERCIAL OR INDUSTRIAL STRUCTURE PROPERTY TAX EXEMPTION, §58.1-3221.

REPLACEMENT GLASS.
Improper repair, §46.2-1058.

REPLACEMENT HOTEL OR MOTEL STRUCTURE PROPERTY TAX EXEMPTION, §58.1-3220.1.

REPLACEMENT INSURANCE POLICIES.
Fire insurance, §38.2-2114.1.
Motor vehicle insurance, §38.2-2212.1.

REPLACEMENT RESIDENTIAL REAL ESTATE PROPERTY TAX CREDIT, §58.1-3220.01.

REPLACEMENT RESIDENTIAL REAL ESTATE PROPERTY TAX EXEMPTION, §58.1-3220.

REPLEVIN.
Action abolished, §8.01-218.
Detinue.
General provisions, §§8.01-114 to 8.01-123.
See DETINUE.

REPLICA VEHICLES.
Antique vehicle license plates.
Not automatically eligible for, §46.2-602.1.
Defined, §46.2-100.
Miles driven per year, restriction, §46.2-602.1.
Model year, requirements, §46.2-602.1.
New vehicle ID number, line-make and model year.
Assignment by DMV, §46.2-602.1.
Safety and emission inspections.
Vehicle subject to, §46.2-602.1.
Titling and registration, §§46.2-602.1, 46.2-625.

REPLY.
Election contests to general assembly election, §24.2-803.

REPORTER OF SUPREME COURT, §§17.1-321 to 17.1-323.
Salaries, §17.1-326.

REPORTS.
ABC board.
Auditing, §4.1-115.
Abduction or threat of abduction, §18.2-50.
Accidents.
Railroads, §56-131.
Tabulation and use by departments, §52-4.2.
Acquittal by reason of insanity.
Conditional release, §19.2-182.7.
Review of continuation of confinement hearing, §19.2-182.5.
Temporary custody and evaluation.
Assessment of acquittee mental health, §19.2-182.2.
Adjutant general.
Reports to secretary of defense, §44-15.
Adoption.
Adult adoption, §63.2-1244.
Disclosure of information from file, §§63.2-1246, 63.2-1247.
Disposition upon entry of final order, §63.2-1246.
Fees for home studies, investigations, visitations and reports, §63.2-1248.
Foreign adoptions.
Child admitted to U.S. with IR-3 or IH-3 visa, §63.2-1200.1.
Parental placement adoption.
Return of copies furnished counsel, §63.2-1239.

REPORTS —Cont'd
Adoption —Cont'd
Parental placement adoption —Cont'd
When investigation and report not required, §63.2-1238.
Required, adoption decreed by court, §32.1-262.
Stepparent adoption, §63.2-1242.
Suspected property exchange violation, §63.2-1219.
To circuit court after investigation by agency, §63.2-1208.
Visitation by agency during probationary period, §63.2-1212.
Adult abuse, neglect or exploitation, §63.2-1606.
Adult fatality review team, §32.1-283.5.
Agricultural cooperative associations, §13.1-333.1.
Agricultural liming materials.
Tonnage, §3.2-3705.
Agriculture and consumer services commissioner.
Farmland preservation, office of, §3.2-203.
Wineries and farm wineries.
Nonstock corporation established and operated to assist distribution of wines, §3.2-102.
Agriculture and forestry industries development fund.
Report to legislature, §3.2-309.
Air carriers.
See AIR CARRIERS.
Air pollution control board.
Qualified fumigation facilities.
Notice and operational requirements, §10.1-1308.1.
Airport revolving fund.
Loan report to general assembly and governor, §5.1-30.9.
Amusement device rider safety.
Rider to report injuries to owner or operator, §59.1-520.
Arrest of school employees, §19.2-83.1.
Arrest report to central criminal records exchange, §19.2-390.
Virginia crime code references, required use, §19.2-390.01.
Arrest warrants.
Unexecuted felony and misdemeanor warrants, §19.2-76.1.
Arson reporting immunity, §§27-85.3 to 27-85.6.
Art and architecture review board.
Biennial report, §2.2-2400.
Assignments of income for the benefit of creditors.
Trustee duties, §55-162.
Assistive technology loan fund authority, §51.5-59.
At-risk youth and families.
State executive council for comprehensive services for, §2.2-2648.
Attorney general.
Annual report to governor, §2.2-516.
Attorneys at law.
Rules of professional conduct.
Professional misconduct, VA SCt Rule Pt 6 §II Rule 8.3.
Safekeeping property, VA SCt Rule Pt 6 §II Rule 1.15.
Auditor of public accounts.
Annual report to governor, §30-141.
Retail sales and use tax.
Annual review of collection and distribution, §30-133.2.

REPORTS —Cont'd
Auditor of public accounts —Cont'd
Revenue stabilization fund, §2.2-1829.
Summary of results of audits and oversight responsibilities, §30-133.
Authorities for development of former federal areas, §15.2-6303.
Autism advisory council.
Annual progress report, §30-327.
Bail bondsmen, §9.1-185.14.
Bail enforcement agents, §9.1-186.11.
Ballast water discharge, §28.2-110.
Banks.
Acquisition of interests in financial institutions, §6.2-707.
Federal forms, conformity with, §6.2-709.
Out-of-state bank holding companies and subsidiaries, §6.2-714.
Interstate bank mergers.
Periodic reports, §6.2-855.
Interstate branch banking.
Periodic reports, §6.2-843.
Interstate branching.
Periodic reports, §6.2-843.
Publication of financial statements, §6.2-907.
Report of examination open for inspection, §6.2-904.
Statements to corporation commission, §6.2-907.
Barbers.
Infections discovered through inspection, §54.1-705.
Bar examiners board.
Biennial report, §54.1-114.
Baseball stadium authority.
Site of stadium, §15.2-5806.
Beef industry council.
Annual report, §3.2-1304.
Handlers, reports of cattle handled, §3.2-1306.
Behavioral health and developmental services department.
Background checks, §37.2-314.
Commissioner, duties generally, §37.2-304.
Data on children and adolescents, §37.2-308.
Duties of department relating to substance abuse, §37.2-310.
Benefit corporations.
Annual benefit report, §13.1-791.
Blind and visually impaired.
Manufacturing and service industrial training.
Financial reporting of schools, §51.5-75.
Vending stands, §51.5-92.
Board of education.
Human research projects, §22.1-16.1.
Quality of education standards for school divisions, §22.1-18.
Boundary lines established by commissioners, §15.2-3102.
Failure of commissioners to agree, §15.2-3104.
BVU authority, §15.2-7211.
Cable television.
Localities providing services.
Annual report, §15.2-2108.16.
Campaign finance disclosure.
Contributions and expenditures.
Generally.
See CAMPAIGN FINANCE DISCLOSURE.
Violations, §24.2-946.3.
Capitol projects.
Value engineering reports, §2.2-1133.
Capitol square preservation council, §30-194.

REPORTS —Cont'd
Cemetery operators, perpetual care trust funds and preneed burial contracts.
Financial report required for perpetual care trust funds, §54.1-2324.
Preneed trust accounts.
Financial report required, §54.1-2333.
Center for innovative technology.
Annual report of initiatives, projects and work plan, §2.2-2221.1.
Center for rural Virginia.
Annual status report, §2.2-2723.
Central criminal records exchange.
Local law-enforcement reporting requirements, §19.2-390.
Virginia crime code references, required use, §19.2-390.01.
Charitable gaming.
Qualified organizations.
Joint bingo game operations, §18.2-340.29.
Receipts and disbursements, §18.2-340.30.
Charter schools, §22.1-212.15.
Chesapeake Bay and Virginia waters clean-up and oversight act.
Status reports on progress, §62.1-44.118.
Chesapeake Bay 2000 agreement, §2.2-220.1.
Chesapeake Bay water quality and quality of living resources.
Secretary of natural resources.
Tributary plan report, §2.2-220.
Chesapeake Bay watershed nutrient credit exchange program.
Permittees, §62.1-44.19:18.
Chief medical examiner.
Death investigations.
Family violence fatality review teams, §32.1-283.3.
Child abuse or neglect.
Complaints and reports generally, §§63.2-1508 to 63.2-1513.
Cigarette delivery sales.
Failure to make report or false statements in report, penalties, §18.2-246.13.
Person making, §18.2-246.11.
Cigarette excise tax.
Tobacco product manufacturers, §58.1-1008.1.
Materially false statements in reports, §58.1-1008.2.
Wholesaler's monthly report, §58.1-1008.
Cigarettes.
Fire-safe cigarettes.
Testing and certification of cigarettes, §59.1-293.2.
Circuit courts.
Business of court for month, clerk's duties, §§17.1-221, 17.1-222.
Sexual sterilization, §54.1-2978.
Civics education commission, §30-316.
Civil commitment of mentally ill persons.
Preadmission screening reports.
Involuntary admissions, §37.2-816.
Involuntary temporary detention, §37.2-809.
Rulemaking authority, §37.2-823.
Clams.
Conclusive evidence of boundaries of beds, §28.2-551.
Coal and energy commission, §30-189.
Coal surface mining.
Refuse piles, water and silt retaining dams.
Submission of designs and other data, §§45.1-222, 45.1-224.

REPORTS —Cont'd
Collection of accounts receivable by Commonwealth.
Annual reports, §2.2-4804.
College building authority.
Annual report, §23-30.36.
Colleges and universities.
Annual reports required of boards of visitors, §§23-1.01, 23-2.
Athletic receipts and disbursements, §23-1.1.
Boards of visitors.
Annual executive summary report, §23-2.05.
Hazing of students causing bodily injury.
Officials to report to attorney for Commonwealth, §18.2-53.
Student fees, use, §23-2.3.
Visa applicant's failure to enroll or visa violations, §23-2.2.
College savings plan.
Annual report, §23-38.84.
Joint legislative audit and review commission oversight, §30-332.
Collegial bodies.
Annual reports to governor and general assembly.
Consolidated reports, §2.2-608.
Governor may require any agency to submit, §2.2-608.
Posting on agency or department website, §2.2-608.
Commercial liability insurance joint underwriting association.
Annual statements, §38.2-2909.
Commercial space flight authority.
Annual report, §2.2-2213.
Commissioners in chancery.
Settlement of accounts of special receivers and special commissioners, §§8.01-618, 8.01-619.
Commissioners of accounts.
Fiduciaries' bonds, §64.2-1221.
Commission on electric utility restructuring.
Annual report to general assembly and governor, §30-205.
Commission on local government, §15.2-2908.
Common interest community board.
Horizontal property regimes.
Copies of public reports, §55-79.25.
Preliminary reports, §55-79.22.
Public reports of examinations, §§55-79.21, 55-79.24.
Commonwealth health research board, §23-286.
Communicable diseases, §32.1-116.3.
Community colleges.
Annual report by chancellor, §23-227.
Comptroller.
Report to governor, §2.2-813.
Compulsory school attendance.
Opening of school year, §§22.1-260, 22.1-261.
Computer recovery and recycling act.
Manufacturers, §10.1-1425.30.
Condominiums.
Declarant reports, §55-79.93.
Unit owners' association reports, §55-79.93:1.
Congenital anomalies reporting and education system, §§32.1-69.1, 32.1-69.2.
Conservatorship of estate of incapacitated persons.
Evaluation report, §64.2-2005.
Consumer finance act, §6.2-1534.
Consumer reports.
Investigative consumer reports.
Insurance institutions, agents or insurance-supported organizations, §38.2-607.

REPORTS —Cont'd
Corporations.
Annual report.
Foreign corporation.
Automatic revocation of certificate of authority, §13.1-768.
Domestic and foreign corporations, §13.1-775.
Failure to file report, §13.1-752.
Council of higher education.
Community colleges, transfer and graduation of students, §23-9.2:3.02.
Duties to report generally, §23-9.6:1.
Reports of expenditures of state funds, §23-9.9:01.
County officers.
Financial reports, §15.2-1230.
Credit counseling.
Licensee's annual report to commissioner, §6.2-2009.
Special reports.
Grounds for reporting, §6.2-2010.
Credit unions.
Annual report to corporation commission, §6.2-1311.
Out-of-state credit unions.
Periodic reports, §6.2-1380.
Crime commission, §30-158.
Crime reporting program generally, §§52-25 to 52-30.
See CRIME REPORTING PROGRAM.
Criminal fines and penalties.
Unsatisfied fines, etc., §19.2-349.
Criminal street gang membership.
Entering on criminal gang file of Virginia criminal information network, §52-8.6.
Crisis intervention teams.
Assessment of programs, §9.1-190.
Status reports, §9.1-187.
Custodial trustees, §64.2-914.
Damage stamp program, §29.1-356.
Localities to report claims and reimbursements, §29.1-358.
Death penalty.
Defendant's mental condition relevant to capital sentencing.
Disclosure of contents of mental health expert's report, §19.2-264.3:1.
Intellectual disability, defendants with.
Determination of disability, §19.2-264.3:1.2.
Post-sentence reports, §19.2-264.5.
Debt capacity advisory committee.
Estimated amount of prudent tax-supported debt, §2.2-2714.
Dental services plans, §38.2-4510.
Department of agriculture and consumer services.
Annual reporting requirements, §18.2-340.18.
Criminal violations to prosecuting attorney, §18.2-340.18.
Financial reporting and audit requirements, §18.2-340.23.
Diseases, §§32.1-35 to 32.1-38.
Domestic reciprocal insurers.
Attorney's financial statement, §38.2-1231.
Drainage projects.
Preliminary report, §§21-312 to 21-315.
Driving while intoxicated.
Conviction reported to department of motor vehicles, §18.2-273.
Drug control.
Fraud or deceit in obtaining substance or prescription, §54.1-3408.2.

REPORTS —Cont'd
Economic development partnership authority.
Audited annual financial statements, §2.2-2242.
Nonprofit corporations, §2.2-2240.
Elections.
Results, changes, §24.2-671.
Electric authorities, §15.2-5426.
Electric utility restructuring.
State corporation commission.
Advancement of competition, §56-596.
Emergency management.
Annual statewide drill, §44-146.17:2.
Emergency medical services patient care information system, §§32.1-116.1 to 32.1-116.3.
Eminent domain.
Condemnation commissioners' report.
See EMINENT DOMAIN.
Just compensation, §25.1-232.
Confirmation or setting aside, §25.1-233.
Contracts regarding property to be made part of, §25.1-236.
Employment commission, §60.2-114.
Engineering and buildings division.
Performance standards for use of property, §2.2-1131.1.
Environmental excellence program, §10.1-1187.5.
Environmental impact reports of state agencies, §§10.1-1188 to 10.1-1192.
See ENVIRONMENTAL IMPACT REPORTS.
Environmental quality department.
Watershed planning and permitting activities, §10.1-1193.
Erosion and sediment control, §§62.1-44.15:58, 62.1-44.15:59.
Escheats.
State treasurer to receive and report to governor, §§55-189, 55-190.
Treasurer reports to escheators, §55-171.
Evidence.
Hearsay exceptions.
Public records or reports, VA SCt Rule 2:803.
Explosives.
Reports of stolen explosives, §27-97.1.
Family abuse, law enforcement officers, §19.2-81.3.
Farm and forest land protection.
Plans by certain agencies to implement policies.
Secretary of agriculture and forestry, §3.2-206.
Farmland preservation, office of, §3.2-203.
Feed, commercial, §3.2-4804.
Fertilizer contractor-applicators.
Application of regulated products to nonagricultural land, §3.2-3602.1.
Fiduciaries.
Commissioners of accounts.
Fiduciaries' bonds, §64.2-1221.
Inventories and accounts, §64.2-1210.
Confirmation, effect of, §64.2-1213.
Copies to be provided, §64.2-1211.
Examination, §64.2-1212.
Filing, §64.2-1211.
Recordation, §64.2-1214.
Return to court, §64.2-1214.
Financial institutions.
Acquisition of interests in financial institutions, §6.2-707.
Federal forms, conformity with, §6.2-709.
Fire marshals, local.
Investigations, §27-33.

REPORTS —Cont'd
Fires.
Coal mines.
Underground coal mines, §45.1-161.203.
Fishermen, commercial.
Harvest, §28.2-242.
Fishing, inland waters.
Licensing.
Sale of licenses, §29.1-333.
Fishing, tidal waters.
Licensed buyers.
Harvest reports, §28.2-242.
Menhaden, use of purse nets for taking.
Landings reports, §28.2-400.5.
Saltwater recreational fishing.
Recreational boat catch reports, §28.2-302.7.
Self marketers.
Harvest reports, §28.2-242.
Shellfish removed from condemned areas, §28.2-814.
Foreign nonprofit corporations.
Annual report, §13.1-936.
Failure to file automatic revocation of certificate of authority, §13.1-930.
Foreign stock corporation.
Annual report, §13.1-775.
Failure to file automatic revocation of certificate of authority, §13.1-768.
Forest products tax.
Shippers of forest products, §58.1-1614.
Fraternal benefit societies.
Annual statement, §38.2-4126.
False or fraudulent statement, §38.2-4134.
Valuation report, §38.2-4125.
Freedom of information.
Electronic communication meetings, §2.2-3708.
Freedom of information advisory council, §30-179.
Funds transfers.
Execution of payment order.
Erroneous execution, §8.4A-304.
Unauthorized payment order.
Duty of customer to report, §8.4A-204.
Fur dealer permittees, §29.1-405.
Gas and oil exploration.
Production activities, §45.1-361.38.
General assembly.
Reports required or requested by law or resolution.
Submission to division of legislative automated services, §30-34.15.
Virginia state crime commission, §30-158.
Gifted education.
Annual report by local school board, §22.1-18.1.
Government data collection and dissemination practices act.
Dissemination, §2.2-3805.
Systems operating or in development, §2.2-3807.
Governor.
Revenue collections, economic outlook.
Submission to legislative committees, §2.2-1513.
State officers to make reports to governor, §2.2-110.
Virginia state crime commission, §30-158.
Workforce improvements, §2.2-435.7.
Grand juries.
Special grand jury report, §19.2-213.
Guardianship of incapacitated persons.
Annual report by guardian, §64.2-2020.
Evaluation report, §64.2-2005.

REPORTS —Cont'd
Gubernatorial commissions.
Governor's report, §2.2-135.
Gunshot wounds.
Health care professionals, §54.1-2967.
Hampton Roads sports facility authority, §15.2-5906.
Handlers of cotton, §3.2-1514.
Hate crimes, §52-8.5.
Hazing of students causing bodily injury.
School officials to report to attorney for Commonwealth, §18.2-53.
Health board, state, §32.1-14.
Health care data reporting, §§32.1-276.2 to 32.1-276.11.
See HEALTH CARE DATA REPORTING.
Health care professionals.
Disability or handicap reports to Commonwealth by physicians, §54.1-2968.
Disciplinary action against health care professionals, §54.1-2908.
Gunshot wounds, §54.1-2967.
To licensing authorities, §§54.1-2908, 54.1-2909.
Health insurance.
Mandated benefits.
Costs and utilization, §38.2-3419.1.
Utilization review.
Internal appeal process and external review.
Assigned independent review organization, §38.2-3568.
Health insurance reform commission.
Executive summary of activity, §30-345.
Health maintenance organizations.
Additional report, §38.2-4307.1.
Annual statements, §38.2-4307.
Health professions department.
Biennial report, §54.1-114.
Prescription monitoring program, §54.1-2521.
Confidential information, §54.1-2523.
Exemptions, §54.1-2522.
Health services plans, §38.2-4217.
Hearsay exceptions.
Public records or reports, VA SCt Rule 2:803.
Highway corporations.
Annual report, §56-542.
Historic resources department.
Stewardship of state-owned historic properties, §10.1-2202.3.
Horizontal property regimes.
Common interest community board.
Copies of public reports, §55-79.25.
Preliminary reports, §55-79.22.
Public reports of examinations, §§55-79.21, 55-79.24.
Real estate board.
Copies of public reports, §55-79.25.
Preliminary reports, §55-79.22.
Public reports of examinations, §§55-79.21, 55-79.24.
Hospital authorities.
Audit report, §15.2-5318.
Hospital or health center commissions, §15.2-5215.
Hospitals.
Health care data reporting generally, §§32.1-276.2 to 32.1-276.11.
See HEALTH CARE DATA REPORTING.
Hunting.
Sale of licenses, §29.1-333.
Income tax.
Change in federal taxable income, taxpayer report, §58.1-311.

REPORTS —Cont'd
Income tax —Cont'd
Change in taxes paid other states, §58.1-311.1.
Corporations, §58.1-441.
Failure to make, §58.1-450.
Forms furnished, §58.1-448.
Supplemental reports, §58.1-449.
Education improvement scholarships tax credits.
Duties of foundation receiving donation, §58.1-439.28.
Partnerships, §58.1-392.
Industrial loan associations.
Annual report, §6.2-1412.
Information technologies agency.
CIO's annual report, §2.2-2007.
Insanity defense.
Competency report, §19.2-169.1.
Sanity report, §19.2-169.5.
Unrestorably incompetent defendant, §19.2-169.3.
Inspector general, state, §2.2-313.
Fraudulent transactions discovered by state agencies, courts, §30-138.
Insurance adjusters.
Reporting to commission, §38.2-1845.17.
Insurance agents.
Administrative actions against.
Reporting requirements, §38.2-1826.
Insurance companies.
Actuarial opinion and summary, annual submission to commissioner, §38.2-1315.1.
Alien insurers.
Regulatory cost comparison report, §38.2-1026.
Annual statements and other reports, §§38.2-1300 to 38.2-1306.1.
Examination reports, §§38.2-1320 to 38.2-1320.4.
Gross premium income, §38.2-406.
Insurance information and privacy protection generally, §§38.2-600 to 38.2-620.
See INSURANCE INFORMATION AND PRIVACY PROTECTION.
Larcenous acts by agents or surplus lines brokers, §38.2-1810.
License tax, §§58.1-2506, 58.1-2507.
Medical malpractice claims.
Report to state corporation commission, §38.2-2228.2.
Receivers.
Report filing with state corporation commission, §38.2-1516.
Risk-based capital, §38.2-5502.
Foreign insurers, §38.2-5510.
Invention development services, §59.1-212.
Investigative consumer reports.
Insurance institutions, agents or insurance-supported organizations, §38.2-607.
Jail boards, §53.1-107.
Jail farm superintendents, §53.1-104.1.
Jail superintendents, §53.1-115.1.
Joint commission on health care, §30-168.3.
Executive summary of activity and work, §30-168.5.
Joint legislative audit and review commission, §30-58.2.
State spending, §30-58.3.
Judicial council, §17.1-705.
Judicial inquiry and review commission.
Annual report, §17.1-905.
Judicial retirement system.
Annual financial report, §51.1-1003.
Juvenile and domestic relations district courts.
Court-ordered reports, VA SCt Rule 8:5.

REPORTS —Cont'd
Juvenile case transferred to circuit court.
Studying report prior to transfer hearing, §16.1-269.2.
Juvenile community crime control.
Quarterly report, §16.1-309.3.
Superintendent, §16.1-309.10.
Juvenile detention and other care facilities.
Localities or commissions eligible to receive state funds, §16.1-322.3.
Juvenile detention home, group home or residential care facility commissions, §16.1-322.
Juvenile justice department.
Confidentiality of reports of children committed to department, §16.1-300.
Juvenile offender demographics.
Secretary of public safety to provide, §2.2-222.
Juvenile proceedings.
Filing, §16.1-274.
Labor and industry department.
Annual report, §40.1-4.1.
Land conservation foundation.
Executive summary, §10.1-1018.1.
Law enforcement officers.
Writing reports.
Compulsory minimum training standards, §9.1-102.
Legal services plans.
Quarterly reports, §38.2-4410.
Legislative program review and evaluation, §30-70.
Liquefied petroleum gas fitters.
Building officials and others, §54.1-1134.
Lobbyists.
Registration and reporting requirements, §§2.2-418 to 2.2-435.
See LOBBYISTS.
Localities audited financial report.
Filing with auditor of public accounts, §15.2-2510.
Local retirement systems.
Annual financial report, §51.1-1003.
Local school boards.
Annual report, §22.1-81.
Gifted education.
Annual report on, §22.1-18.1.
Local treasurer's report to finance board, §58.1-3160.
Managing general agents insurance licensing, §38.2-1364.
Manufacturing development commission, §30-276.
Marine resources commission.
Fishery resource grant program, §28.2-247.
Medical examiners.
Investigation as to death.
Persons delivered to, §32.1-283.
Medical malpractice claims.
Report to state corporation commission, §38.2-2228.2.
Medical malpractice joint underwriting association annual statement, §38.2 2810.
Medicine and other healing arts professions.
Disabled persons, §54.1-2966.
Disease reporting.
Immunity from liability, §32.1-38.
Infections of dead human bodies, §32.1-37.1.
Laboratory directors, §32.1-36.
Non-physicians, §32.1-37.
Physicians, §32.1-36.
Fetal death reports, §§32.1-264, 32.1-266.

REPORTS —Cont'd
Medicine and other healing arts professions —Cont'd
Motor vehicle driver disability reports.
Physician liability, §54.1-2966.1.
Wounds inflicted by weapons, §54.1-2967.
MEI project approval commission.
Report to General Assembly, §30-312.
Mental health facilities.
Access to records, accounts and reports, §37.2-703.
Critical incidents or deaths of individuals receiving services, §§37.2-709, 37.2-709.1.
Patient-level data and financial data, §37.2-710.
Psychiatric treatment of children.
Involuntary commitment.
Preadmission screening report, §16.1-340.4.
System of records, accounts and reports to be prescribed, §37.2-703.
Military advisory council.
Annual executive summary of interim activity, §2.2-2666.1.
Mine inspections.
Review of inspection reports and records, §45.1-161.83.
Mine licensing.
Annual reports, §45.1-161.62.
Mineral mine licenses.
Annual report, §45.1-161.292:35.
Transfers of ownership, §45.1-161.292:35.
Mineral mine safety.
Accidents, §45.1-161.292:51.
Maintenance of records, §45.1-161.292:52.
Explosions or fires, §45.1-161.292:50.
Inspection reports.
Review, §45.1-161.292:56.
Violations, §45.1-161.292:70.
Mine safety.
Accidents and injuries, §45.1-161.79.
Explosions, §45.1-161.77.
Operators' reports of accidents, §45.1-161.78.
Underground coal mines.
Fire reports, §45.1-161.203.
Roof falls, §45.1-161.117.
Violations, §45.1-161.97.
Minority business enterprise department (eff until 1/1/2014), §2.2-1405.
Money order sellers and money transmitters.
Licensees, §6.2-1917.
Annual report, §6.2-1905.
Mortgage lender and broker act.
Annual report, §6.2-1610.
Events impacting activities of registrants, §6.2-1621.
Mortgage loan originators.
Events impacting licensee, §6.2-1717.
Motor carriers, passengers.
Criminal enforcement of requirements, §46.2-2011.22.
Department's authority to require reports, §46.2-2011.16.
Fines.
Civil penalties, §46.2-2011.23.
Motor carriers, property.
Authority of department as to, §46.2-2125.
Fines and civil enforcement, §46.2-2132.
Fines and criminal enforcement, §46.2-2131.
Motor vehicle dealers.
Biennial report of board, §46.2-1503.5.
Motor vehicle repair facilities.
Vehicles equipped with bullet-proof glass or smoke screening devices, §46.2-109.

REPORTS —Cont'd
Motor vehicle repair facilities —Cont'd
Vehicles struck by bullets, §46.2-109.
Motor vehicles department.
Discharge of patients from state institutions, §46.2-401.
Driving while intoxicated.
Conviction reported to department, §18.2-273.
Motor vehicle title loans.
Annual report, §6.2-2210.
Criminal convictions of members, partners, directors, officers or principals, §6.2-2211.
Other reporting requirements, §6.2-2211.
Museum of natural history, §10.1-2012.
Nonprofit corporations.
Annual report, §13.1-936.
Failure to file automatic termination of corporate existence, §§13.1-914, 13.1-930.
Nuclear energy consortium.
Reporting on nonproprietary activities, §67-1404.
Strategic plan and summary of activities.
Submission, §67-1403.
Nurse licensure compact.
Report of adverse actions, §54.1-3034.
Office of telework promotion and broadband assistance.
Annual report on telework participation levels and trends, §2.2-225.1.
Offshore wind development authority.
Annual report, §67-1209.
Oil discharges, §62.1-44.34:19.
Open meetings.
Electronic communication meetings, §2.2-3708.
Optometric services plans, §38.2-4510.
Outdoors foundation, §10.1-1802.
Oysters, §28.2-551.
Partnerships.
Income tax, §58.1-392.
Pawnbrokers, §54.1-4010.
Payday loans.
Annual report by licensee, §6.2-1811.
Other events requiring licensee to report, §6.2-1812.
Pesticide control.
Accidents, incidents or loss, §3.2-3909.
Pharmacy board inspections, §54.1-3308.
Planning and budget department.
Standardized system of financial reports, §2.2-1501.
Planning district commissions, §15.2-4215.
Plant pollination advisory board.
Reports to board, §3.2-2805.
Pollution prevention program.
Evaluation report, §10.1-1425.17.
Port authority.
Annual report, §62.1-139.
Prescription monitoring program, §54.1-2521.
Confidential information, §54.1-2523.
Exemptions, §54.1-2522.
Presentence reports.
Investigations and reports by probation officers, §19.2-299.
Victim impact statements, when required, §19.2-299.1.
Prisons.
Youthful offender facilities and programs.
Consideration of reports, §53.1-65.
Professional and occupational regulation department.
Biennial report, §54.1-114.

REPORTS —Cont'd
Professional and occupational regulation report.
Biennial report.
Disciplinary actions, §54.1-2400.3.
Prompt payment of bills by state agencies.
Comptroller's reports, §2.2-4356.
Property owners' associations, §55-516.1.
Property tax exemptions.
Owners of tax exempt real estate, §58.1-3605.1.
Public accountants.
Board's biennial report, §54.1-4421.
Public building authority.
Annual financial statement, §2.2-2263.
MEI project approval commission.
Report to General Assembly, §30-312.
Public charter schools, §22.1-212.15.
Public guardian and conservator advisory board, §2.2-2412.
Public school funds.
Annual report of expenditures, §22.1-90.
Instructional costs, funds allocated for to be included in school performance report card, §22.1-90.1.
Public service companies.
License tax, §58.1-2628.
Special reports to commission, §56-36.
Public service corporation taxation.
Failure to file timely reports, §58.1-2610.
Public utilities, §56-249.
Fuel transactions of electric utilities, §§56-249.3, 56-249.4.
Rabies.
Reports of rabid animals, §3.2-6522.
Railroad accident investigations, §56-131.
Real estate board.
Horizontal property regimes.
Copies of public reports, §55-79.25.
Preliminary reports, §55-79.22.
Public reports of examinations, §§55-79.21, 55-79.24.
Real estate cooperatives.
Association reports, §55-504.1.
Declarant annual reports, §55-504.
Real property tax assessments.
Income producing realty reports, §58.1-3294.
Receivers.
General receivers.
Apportionment of bonds to funds, §8.01-588.1.
Recycling reports.
Nonresidential solid waste generators and companies, §15.2-939.
Registered limited liability partnerships.
Annual continuation reports, §50-73.134.
Remediation programs.
Schools and education, §22.1-199.2.
Resources authority, §62.1-222.
Retail sales and use tax.
Auditor of public accounts.
Annual review of collection and distribution, §30-133.2.
Road tax on motor carriers, §58.1-2705.
Roanoke river basin advisory committee.
Annual executive summary of interim activity, §62.1-69.35:2.
Roanoke river basin bi-state commission.
Annual report, §62.1-69.44.
Independent reports to commission, §62.1-69.38.
Rolling stock tax.
Motor vehicle carriers, §§58.1-2654, 58.1-2654.1
Railroads and freight car companies, §58.1-2653.

REPORTS —Cont'd
Salvage vehicles.
Demolishing or dismantling of vehicles.
Updating records of department, §46.2-1608.2.
Reports to law enforcement, §46.2-1608.1.
Savings institutions.
Associations to furnish financial statements and reports, §6.2-1194.
Audits, §6.2-1126.
Schools and education.
Arrest of teachers and other employees, §19.2-83.1.
Discipline of students.
Reports of certain acts to school authorities, §22.1-279.3:1.
Hazing of students causing bodily injury.
Officials to report to attorney for Commonwealth, §18.2-53.
Opportunity educational institution.
Reports of schools within institution, §22.1-27.2.
Threat assessment teams, §22.1-79.4.
Science museum of Virginia.
Annual report, §23-253.
Scrap metal purchasers.
Purchases by, §59.1-136.5.
Secondhand article sales.
Building fixtures, §59.1-121.
Secretary of commerce and trade.
Legislative report, §2.2-207.
Urban issues, §2.2-206.
Secretary of natural resources.
Chesapeake Bay 2000 agreement, §2.2-220.1.
Chesapeake Bay water quality and quality of living resources.
Tributary plan report, §2.2-220.
Secretary of public safety.
Juvenile offender demographics, §2.2-222.
Secretary of the Commonwealth.
Compacts, appointments under, §2.2-403.
Identifying for governor boards, commissions, etc., appointed by governor, §2.2-402.
Persons appointed to boards, commissions, etc., §2.2-406.
Secretary of transportation.
Actions to increase transit use and reduce highway congestion, §33.1-223.2:24.
Securities brokers-dealers, §13.1-518.1.
Security for public deposits, §2.2-4411.
Sentencing.
Mental health examination.
Psychiatrist's report, §19.2-301.
Presentence reports, §19.2-299.
Victim impact statements, when required, §19.2-299.1.
Sexual sterilization, §54.1-2978.
Sheriffs.
Court requested report, §53.1-124.
Expenses incurred, §15.2-1609.4.
Jail prisoner tally, §53.1-121.
Services performed by part-time deputies, §15.2-1609.9.
Travel expenses statement, §15.2-1609.5.
Small business and supplier diversity department, §2.2-1610.
Small business commission.
Annual report to governor and general assembly, §30-183.
Small business financing authority.
Annual report, §2.2-2312.
Southwest Virginia health facilities authority, §15.2-5384.

REPORTS —Cont'd
Spill response council, §62.1-44.34:28.
State corporation commission.
Annual report to governor, §12.1-4.
Hearing examiners, findings, §12.1-31.
State departments and agencies.
Annual reports.
Consolidated reports, §2.2-608.
Governor may require any agency to submit, §2.2-608.
Posting on agency or department website, §2.2-608.
Required reports to governor or general assembly.
Governor may require any agency to submit, §2.2-607.
Time for submitting, §2.2-607.
Transfer of employees, §2.2-607.
State forester.
General assembly, §10.1-1119.
State inspector general, §2.2-313.
Fraudulent transactions discovered by state agencies, courts, §30-138.
State police criminal investigations.
Confidentiality, §52-8.3.
State police retirement system.
Annual financial report, §51.1-1003.
State publications depository program.
Annual report by Librarian of Virginia.
Agencies not furnishing or providing information, §42.1-97.
Stormwater management, §62.1-44.15:37.
Stream restoration assistance.
Damage inspections and reports, §10.1-654.
Superintendents of schools.
Student ratios reported to local school boards, §22.1-70.1.
Surplus lines insurance.
Quarterly business transactions report, §38.2-4806.
Tax commissioner's annual report, §58.1-202.
Tax exemptions.
Retail sales and use tax, §58.1-609.12.
Telegraph or telephone companies.
Interexchange telephone companies, §56-482.1.
Penalties for violations, §56-482.2.
Time-shares.
Owners' association annual report, §55-370.1.
Registration reports, §55-394.1.
Tobacco products tax.
Manufacturers' reports, §58.1-1021.02:1.
Tobacco warehouses, §61.1-41.
Tourism authority.
Annual report, §2.2-2323.
Toxic substances information.
Health board duties, §32.1-245.
Operator duties, §32.1-244.
Traffic infractions.
Arrest of nonresidents, §§46.2-944 to 46.2-947.
Transfer of child to circuit court.
Studying report prior to transfer hearing, §16.1-269.2.
Transportation board.
Statistics and information gathering and reporting, §33.1-13.05.
Transportation department.
Annual report, §33.1-13.03.
Transportation infrastructure bank, §33.1-23.13.
Trapping.
Sale of licenses, §29.1-333.
Trust companies, §6.2-1031.

REPORTS —Cont'd
Trusts.
Duty of trustee, §64.2-775.
Tuberculosis.
Reports of active tuberculosis, §32.1-50.
Unclaimed property.
Holder of property reports, §§55-210.10:2, 55-210.12.
Verified reports, §55-210.24.
Unemployment compensation, §60.2-114.
Commission on unemployment compensation.
Annual report to general assembly and governor, §30-222.
Executive summary of activities and work, §30-224.
Failure to file, §60.2-513.
Payroll and tax reports, §60.2-512.
Urban public-private partnership redevelopment fund, §15.2-2418.
Value engineering reports.
Capitol projects, §2.2-1133.
Veterans service organizations, joint leadership council.
Annual executive summary of interim activity, §2.2-2682.
Veterans services foundation.
Quarterly report on funding levels and services, §2.2-2715.
Veterinary medicine.
Practicing violations, §54.1-3810.
Viatical settlements.
Broker licensing, §38.2-1865.5.
Reports of licensees, §38.2-6004.
Virginia Beach arena.
Acquisition, lease or contract involving facility site.
Report and plan regarding funding, §15.2-5923.
Virginia foundation for healthy youth, §32.1-364.
Virginia-Israel advisory board.
Annual executive summary, §2.2-2424.
Virginia retirement system.
Annual financial report, §51.1-1003.
Benefit restoration plan, §51.1-1304.
Virginia Roanoke river basin advisory committee.
Annual executive summary of interim activity, §62.1-69.35:2.
Virginia sesquicentennial of the American civil war commission, §30-272.
Virginia's future, council on.
Annual executive summary of interim activity, §2.2-2689.
Balanced accountability scorecard.
Publication, §2.2-2686.
Voluntary settlements by localities of annexation, transition or immunity issues.
Commission on local government, §15.2-3400.
Volunteer Rescue Squads, Virginia Association of.
Financial report, §32.1-111.13.
Water control board.
Water resources policy and status, §62.1-44.40.
Water quality improvement act.
Directors of departments of environmental quality and conservation and recreation, §10.1-2134.
State comptroller, §10.1-2133.
Waters of the state.
Oil discharges, §62.1-44.34:19.
Quality monitoring, information and restoration, §62.1-44.19:5.

REPORTS —Cont'd
Waters of the state —Cont'd
Toxics discharge reduction, §§62.1-44.17:2, 62.1-44.17:3.
Weapons.
Wounds caused by concealable weapons.
Health care professionals, §54.1-2967.
Weights and measures.
Service agencies and technicians.
Service report, §3.2-5711.
Wineries and farm wineries.
Agriculture and consumer services commissioner.
Nonstock corporation established and operated to assist distribution of wines, §3.2-102.
Wireless service authorities.
Financial statement, §15.2-5431.33.
Wiretapping.
Filing requirements, §19.2-70.
Woodrow Wilson presidency centennial commission, §30-323.
Workers' compensation, §65.2-712.
Accidents, §65.2-900.
Days of operation of business, §65.2-901.
Employee numbers and hours of labor, §65.2-901.
Failure to make, §65.2-902.
Workforce development improvements.
Governor, §2.2-435.7.
Youthful offender facilities and programs.
Consideration of reports, §53.1-65.

REPORTS OF SUPREME COURT, §§17.1-316 to 17.1-320.
Advance sheets, printing and distribution, §17.1-317.
Custody and distribution, §17.1-319.
Law school libraries destroyed by fire.
Furnishing reports to, §17.1-320.
Printing and binding volumes, §17.1-316.
Reporter of court, §§17.1-321 to 17.1-323.

REPOSE, STATUTE OF, §8.01-250.
Banking.
Objections to debiting of accounts, §8.4A-505.
Mines and minerals, §55-154.

REPOSSESSED GOODS.
Advertising or offering for sale, prohibited practices, §59.1-200.

REPOSSESSION.
Boat titling certificates.
Transfers by operation of law, §29.1-717.2.
Consumer goods.
When not allowed, §11-4.3.
Lease-purchase agreements.
Prohibited practices, §59.1-207.22.
Reinstatement, §59.1-207.23.
Motor vehicle dealer advertising, §46.2-1581.
Motor vehicles.
Criminal unauthorized use, §18.2-148.
Motor vehicle sales and use tax exemption, §58.1-2403.
Sale of vehicle repossessed in another state by dealer, §46.2-633.1.
Private property.
Private security services businesses.
Exceptions, §9.1-140.
Retail sales and use tax.
Credit for tax paid on repossession by dealers, §58.1-620.
Secured transactions.
Defaults.
Collateral.
Disposition after default, §8.9A-610.
Application of proceeds, §8.9A-615.

REPOSSESSION —Cont'd
Secured transactions —Cont'd
Defaults —Cont'd
Collateral —Cont'd
Disposition after default —Cont'd
Notice before disposition, contents and form, §§8.9A-611, 8.9A-613, 8.9A-614.
Notice before disposition, timeliness, §8.9A-612.
Surplus or deficiency calculations, §8.9A-616.
Right to possession after default, §8.9A-609.
T&M vehicle dealer advertising, §46.2-1990.

REPRESENTING AND BINDING OTHERS, §§64.2-714 to 64.2-718.
Agents, §64.2-716.
Appointment of representative, §64.2-718.
Consent of person who may represent and bind another.
Effect, §64.2-714.
Conservators, §64.2-716.
Fiduciaries and parents, §64.2-716.
Guardians, §64.2-716.
Holder of general testamentary power of appointment.
Representation by, §64.2-715.
Identity or location of person unknown.
Substantially identical interest.
Representation by person having, §64.2-717.
Matters representative may act on, §64.2-718.
Minor, incapacitated or unborn individual.
Substantially identical interest.
Representation by person having, §64.2-717.
Notice to person who may represent and bind another.
Effect, §64.2-714.
Parents, §64.2-716.
Personal representatives, §64.2-716.
Persons designated by settlor or beneficiaries, §64.2-716.
Several persons or interests.
Appointment of representative for, §64.2-718.
Substantially identical interest.
Representation by person having, §64.2-717.
Trustees, §64.2-716.

REPRIEVES BY GOVERNOR, VA Const Art V §12.

REPRODUCTION OF RECORDS AND DOCUMENTS.
Counties, cities or towns, §15.2-1412.

REPTILES.
Keeping of reptiles, §29.1-569.
Snakes.
Handling or using so as to endanger human life or health, §18.2-313.

REPUBLICAN FORM OF GOVERNMENT, US Const Art IV §4.

REPUDIATION.
Leases, UCC.
Anticipatory repudiation, §§8.2A-402, 8.2A-403.
Retraction, §8.2A-403.
Sales, UCC.
Anticipatory repudiation, §§8.2-610, 8.2-611.
Proof of market price, §8.2-723.
Buyer's damages, §8.2-713.
Buyer's repudiation of contract.
Seller's damages, §8.2-708.
Seller's remedies, §8.2-703.

REPUDIATION —Cont'd
Sales, UCC —Cont'd
Seller's repudiation of contract.
Buyer's remedies, §8.2-711.
Uniform computer information transactions act.
Anticipatory repudiation.
Breach of contract, §59.1-507.9.
Retraction, §59.1-507.10.

REPURCHASE AGREEMENTS.
Investment of public funds.
Overnight, term and open repurchase agreements, §2.2-4507.

REPUTATION EVIDENCE.
Hearsay exceptions.
Reputation as to character trait, VA SCt Rule 2:803.
Impeachment of witnesses.
Reputation for truthtelling, VA SCt Rule 2:608.

REQUESTS FOR ADMISSION, VA SCt Rule 4:11.
Administrative process act.
Hearings, §2.2-4022.
Responses submitted in support of motion for summary judgment.
Depositions as basis for request for admission, §8.01-420.
Size of paper, VA SCt Rule 1:16.
Waiver of time limitations by parties, §8.01-384.2.

RESCISSION.
Accrual of cause of action, §8.01-249.
Civil commitment of mentally ill persons.
Involuntary admissions.
Rescission of mandatory outpatient treatment order, §37.2-817.3.
Community-based continuing care providers.
Right to rescind contract, §38.2-4923.
Health insurance.
Federal market reforms.
Rescission of coverage, prohibition, §38.2-3441.
Home solicitation sales, §§59.1-21.3, 59.1-21.7.
Leases, UCC, §8.2A-208.
Rights and remedies for default, §8.2A-505.
Public contracts.
Conflicts of interest of government officers and employees, §30-125.
Refund anticipation loans, §6.2-2503.
Release of liability as condition of settlement of personal injury action or claim, §8.01-425.1.
Sales, UCC, §8.2-209.
Time-share contract, §55-383.
Viatical settlement contracts, §38.2-6007.
Right to rescind, §38.2-6008.

RESCUES.
Licensed professional engineers and architects.
Civil immunity, §8.01-226.2.
Mineral mine safety, §§45.1-161.292:40 to 45.1-161.292:49.
Explosions and fires, §45.1-161.292:50.
Inspection of rescue stations, §45.1-161.292:48.
Mine rescue coordinator, §45.1-161.292:48.
Mine rescue crews, §45.1-161.292:41.
Backup crews, §45.1-161.292:45.
Compensation, §45.1-161.292:44.
Deemed to be employees of mine where emergency exists, §45.1-161.292:44.

RESCUES —Cont'd
Mineral mine safety —Cont'd
Mine rescue crews —Cont'd
Duty to train, §45.1-161.292:42.
Jurisdiction, §45.1-161.292:43.
Qualifications, §45.1-161.292:43.
Mine rescue fund, §45.1-161.292:47.
Mine rescue teams, §45.1-161.292:46.
Immunity from liability, §45.1-161.292:49.
Workers' compensation, §45.1-161.292:49.
Requirements of recovery work, §45.1-161.292:45.
Rescue and first aid stations, §45.1-161.292:40.
State-designated mine rescue teams, §45.1-161.292:46.
Immunity from liability, §45.1-161.292:49.
Workers' compensation, §45.1-161.292:49.
Refusal to aid officer in execution of office, §18.2-463.

RESCUE SQUADS.
Abused, neglected or endangered infants.
Immunity for accepting, §8.01-226.5:2.
Assistance fund, §32.1-111.12.
Auxiliary lights.
Rescue and lifesaving vehicles, §46.2-1028.
Boat registration, exemption.
Volunteer squads, §29.1-702.
Boat title certificates.
Fee exemption for volunteer squads, §29.1-718.
Charitable gaming.
General provisions, §§18.2-340.15 to 18.2-340.37.
See CHARITABLE GAMING.
Child abuse or neglect.
Persons required to report, §63.2-1509.
Communicable disease reports to, §32.1-116.3.
Counties, cities or towns.
Approval by local governing body for establishing, §15.2-955.
Gifts or donations to volunteer and nonprofit organizations, §15.2-953.
Loans to volunteer rescue organizations, §15.2-954.
Tuition reimbursement for personnel, §15.2-954.1.
Criminal history record information free of charge to volunteer applicant, §19.2-389.
Critical incident stress management team-EMS or public safety personnel privilege, §19.2-271.4.
Death in line of duty.
Half mast display of state and local flags, §18.2-488.1.
Driver information.
Commissioner of DMV.
Supplying member or applicant for membership in volunteer squad, §46.2-208.
Driving under the influence reimbursement, §15.2-1716.
Emergency medical services patient care information system, §§32.1-116.1 to 32.1-116.3.
Fine schedule, VA SCt Rule 3B:2.
Flashing amber warning lights.
Rescue and lifesaving vehicles, §§46.2-1025, 46.2-1029.1.
Flashing red or red and white warning lights.
Rescue and lifesaving vehicles, §§46.2-1023, 46.2-1029.1.
Following or parking near rescue squad vehicle, §46.2-921.
Highways and roads.
Snow removal from driveways, §33.1-200.1.

RESCUE SQUADS —Cont'd
Immunity.
Accepting abused, neglected or endangered infants, §8.01-226.5:2.
Killed in line of duty.
Tuition and required fees to state supported colleges or universities.
Waiver for child or spouse of member, §23-7.4:1.
Line of duty act, §§9.1-400 to 9.1-408.
Local vehicle licenses.
Issuance free of charge.
Volunteer squads, §46.2-752.
Motor vehicle license plate.
Special license plates for volunteer rescue organizations, §46.2-746.6.
Volunteer rescue squads, §46.2-649.1:1.
Motor vehicle registration.
Volunteer rescue squads, §46.2-649.1:1.
Motor vehicle sales and use tax exemption, §58.1-2403.
Move over or reduce speed.
Drivers approaching stationary emergency vehicles, §46.2-921.1.
Obstructing members in performance of mission, §18.2-414.1.
Parking in front of rescue squad building, §46.2-1239.
Personal property taxes.
Classification of vehicles, §58.1-3506.
Prepayment of fine, §16.1-69.40:1.
Prison made goods and services, §§53.1-47 to 53.1-55.
Privileged communications.
Critical incident stress management team-EMS or public safety personnel privilege, §19.2-271.4.
Property tax exemptions, §58.1-3610.
Public safety medal of valor, §§9.1-800, 9.1-801.
Secondary warning lights, §46.2-1029.2.
Special license plates for members, §46.2-735.
Statewide emergency medical services and systems generally, §§32.1-111.1 to 32.1-111.16.
See EMERGENCY MEDICAL SERVICES.
Surplus state materials.
Sale to volunteer squads, §2.2-1124.
Terrorism hoax.
Reimbursement of expenses in responding to, §15.2-1716.1.
Tuition and required fees to state supported colleges or universities.
Waiver for child or spouse of member killed in line of duty, §23-7.4:1.
Virginia Association of Volunteer Rescue Squads.
Financial report, §32.1-111.13.
Virginia Rescue Squads Assistance Fund, §32.1-111.12.
Financial assistance and review committee, §32.1-111.12:01.
Volunteer firefighters' and rescue squad workers' service award fund, §§51.1-1200 to 51.1-1211.
See VOLUNTEER FIREFIGHTERS' AND RESCUE SQUAD WORKERS' SERVICE AWARD FUND.
Warning lights on certain demonstrator vehicles.
Rescue and lifesaving vehicles, §46.2-1027.
Workers' compensation.
Average weekly wage of volunteer rescue squad member, §65.2-101.

RESCUE SQUADS —Cont'd
Workers' compensation —Cont'd
Employee defined as including volunteer member, §65.2-101.
Yielding right-of-way to approaching rescue vehicles, §46.2-829.
Yielding right of way to stationary emergency vehicles, §46.2-921.1.

RESEARCH.
Aging and rehabilitative services commissioner.
Human research, regulations regarding, §51.5-132.
Anatomical gifts, §§32.1-291.1 to 32.1-291.25.
See ANATOMICAL GIFTS.
Animals.
Unauthorized release of research animals, §18.2-403.4.
Use of animal bearing tag, license or tattooed identification.
Consent of owner required, §3.2-6547.
Behavioral health and developmental services.
Rights of individuals receiving services.
Not to be subjects of research without consent, §37.2-400.
Behavioral health and developmental services department.
Duties of commissioner, §37.2-306.
Biotechnology research act, §§2.2-5500 to 2.2-5509.
Commonwealth health research board, §§23-277 to 23-286.
Dead human bodies used for scientific study, §§32.1-298 to 32.1-304.
Economic development partnership authority.
Grants to promote research, development, and commercialization of products, §2.2-2240.1.
Powers and duties, §2.2-2239.
Forensic science academy, §9.1-1103.
Human research, §§32.1-162.16 to 32.1-162.20.
Application of federal policies, §32.1-162.20.
Board of education, §22.1-16.1.
Defined terms, §32.1-162.16.
Exemption from provisions, §32.1-162.17.
Informed consent, §32.1-162.18.
Defined, §32.1-162.16.
Juvenile justice board.
Promulgation of regulations, §66-10.1.
Review committees, §32.1-162.19.
State board of social services.
Adoption of regulation, §63.2-218.
Innovative and entrepreneurship investment authority.
Research and technology investment advisory committee, §2.2-2220.1.
Research and technology strategic roadmap, §2.2-2221.2.
Development, §2.2-2221.
Insurance information surveys, §38.2-605.
Nuclear energy consortium, §§67-1400 to 67-1406.
Articles of incorporation, §67-1404.
Audit of accounts, §67-1406.
Board of directors, §67-1403.
Definitions, §67-1400.
Deposit of funds, §67-1405.
Established, §67-1401.
Executive director, §67-1404.
Formation by board, §67-1404.
Funds, §67-1405.

RESEARCH —Cont'd
Nuclear energy consortium —Cont'd
Governance, §67-1403.
Members, §67-1404.
Performance of essential government function for purposes of expending public funds, §67-1401.
Periodic external review, §67-1406.
Powers, §67-1402.
Purpose, §§67-1402, 67-1404.
Reporting on nonproprietary activities, §67-1404.
Strategic plan and summary of activities.
Submission, §67-1403.
Research and development tax credit, §58.1-439.12:08.
Retail sales and use tax.
Commercial and industrial exemptions, §58.1-609.3.
Sexually explicit material.
Public officers and employees.
Restricted computer access, exceptions, §2.2-2827.
Stem cell research.
Christopher Reeve stem cell research fund, §§23-286.1, 23-286.2.
Tobacco indemnification and community revitalization commission, §3.2-3103.
Women, council on.
Powers and duties, §2.2-2631.

RESEARCH AND DEVELOPMENT TAX CREDIT, §58.1-439.12:08.

RESEARCH FARM PRODUCT.
Damaging or destroying, §18.2-145.1.

RESERVED NAMES.
Corporations, §§13.1-616, 13.1-631.
Nonprofit corporation, §13.1-830.

RESERVES OF INSURANCE COMPANIES, §§38.2-1311 to 38.2-1315.
Life insurance, §§38.2-3126 to 38.2-3144.

RESERVOIRS.
Attempts to poison, §18.2-54.1.
Retail sales and use tax.
Machinery, tools and equipment brought into state for use in constructing or repairing, §§58.1-604.1 to 58.1-604.3.

RESIDENCY REQUIREMENTS.
Assignments of property for the benefit of creditors.
Substitute trustees, §55-157.
Candidates for elected office, §24.2-500.
Circuit court judges, §17.1-507.
Corporations, §13.1-674.
Court of appeals judges, §17.1-400.
District court judges, §§16.1-69.6:1, 16.1-69.16.
Eldercare facility patients.
Probating of wills, §64.2-443.
Elective office, qualifications to hold, VA Const Art II §5.
Firearms transfers, §18.2-308.2:2.
Fire insurance appraisers and umpires, §38.2-2122.
General assembly members, VA Const Art IV §4.
Governor, VA Const Art V §3.
Grants by Commonwealth, requiring employer reports of certification of employees as condition, §2.2-621.
Industrial development authority directors, §15.2-4904.
Insurance agents, §38.2-1800.1.

RESIDENCY REQUIREMENTS —Cont'd
Judges of circuit courts, §17.1-103.
Lieutenant governor, VA Const Art V §13.
Local constitutional officers, §15.2-1601.
Local government personnel, §§15.2-1505, 15.2-1525.
Removal of residence from jurisdiction officer required to reside, §15.2-1526.
Local income tax, §§58.1-541, 58.1-547.
Lottery board members, §58.1-4004.
Magistrates, §19.2-37.
Mortgages and deeds of trust.
Security trust, §55-58.1.
Nonprofit corporations, §13.1-854.
Qualifications of voters, VA Const Art II §1.
Resources authority.
Board of directors, §62.1-201.
State board of corrections, §53.1-2.
Voter qualifications, VA Const Art II §1.
Water control board.
Members.
Qualifications, §62.1-44.9.

RESIDENTIAL BUILDING ENERGY ANALYSTS, §§54.1-1144 to 54.1-1146.
Board regulations, §54.1-1146.
Definitions, §54.1-1144.
License required, §54.1-1145.
Rules and regulations, §54.1-1146.
Training and other qualifications, §54.1-1145.

RESIDENTIAL CARE FACILITIES FOR CHILDREN, §§16.1-315 to 16.1-322.7.
See JUVENILE DETENTION AND OTHER CARE FACILITIES.

RESIDENTIAL COMMUNITY BASED PROBATION PROGRAMS.
Participation in, §53.1-155.1.

RESIDENTIAL CUT-THROUGH TRAFFIC.
Restrictive regulation, §46.2-809.1.

RESIDENTIAL DEVELOPMENTS.
Maximum speed limits in certain residence districts, §46.2-878.2.

RESIDENTIAL GROUND RENT, §§55-79.01 to 55-79.06.

RESIDENTIAL LANDLORDS AND TENANTS, §§55-248.2 to 55-248.40.
See LANDLORD AND TENANT.

RESIDENTIAL PROPERTY TRANSFER DISCLOSURES, §§55-517 to 55-525.
Actions, §55-524.
Adjacent parcels.
No representations with respect to, §55-519.
Applicability of provisions, §55-517.
Building code enforcement actions.
No pending actions, §55-519.
Building code violations.
Builders of new dwellings, §55-518.
Changed circumstances, §55-522.
Condition of property and improvements on.
Defective drywall, §55-519.2.
No representations or warranties, §55-519.
Contract cancellation, §55-520.
Damages suffered as result of violation.
Action to recover actual damages, §55-524.
Dam break inundation zone.
Property located within, §55-519.
Defective drywall.
Disclosures by owner of property.
Sale of residential real property, §55-519.2.

RESIDENTIAL PROPERTY TRANSFER DISCLOSURES —Cont'd
Defined terms.
Acceptance, §55-520.
Real estate purchase contract, §55-520.
Disclaimer statement.
Delivery to purchaser, time, late delivery, remedy, §55-520.
Disclosures by owner of property.
Permissive disclosure, tourism activity zone, §55-519.3.
Sale of residential real property, §55-519.2.
Disclosure statement, §55-519.
Error, inaccuracy or omission of delivered information.
Owner not liable, §55-521.
Exemptions, §55-518.
Forms to be developed by board, §§54.1-2105.1, 55-525.
Historic district ordinance.
Effect, §55-519.
Material change in condition of property, §55-522.
Methamphetamine.
Required disclosures, property previously used to manufacture methamphetamine, §55-519.4.
Military air installations, §55-519.1.
Mining operations.
Property in planning district 15, §55-518.
Owner liability, §55-521.
Real estate contract defined, §55-517.
Real estate licensee duties, §55-523.
Remedies of purchaser.
Failure of owner to comply, §55-524.
Defective drywall, §55-519.2.
Report or opinion by engineer, surveyor, geologist, insect control expert contractor or home inspector.
Satisfaction of chapter's requirements, §55-521.
Required disclosures, §55-519.
Defective drywall, §55-519.2.
Military air installations, §55-519.1.
Resource protection areas.
Established by ordinance implementing Chesapeake Bay Preservation Act, §55-519.
Sexual offenders required to register, §55-519.
Solar energy.
Right to install solar energy collection devices, §55-519.
Termination of purchase.
Failure of owner to comply, §55-524.
Untimely delivery of disclosure statement, §55-520.
Time for disclosure, §55-520.
Tourism.
Permissive disclosure, tourism activity zone, §55-519.3.
Wastewater system located on property.
No representations by owner with respect to, §55-519.

RESIDENTIAL REAL PROPERTY TRANSACTIONS.
Consumer real estate settlement protection act.
See CONSUMER REAL ESTATE SETTLEMENT PROTECTION ACT.
Disclosures, §§55-517 to 55-525.
Discrimination generally.
See DISCRIMINATION.

RESIDENTIAL REAL PROPERTY TRANSACTIONS —Cont'd
Discriminatory housing practices, §§36-96.3 to 36-96.6.
Lead-based paint.
Sale of residential structure with levels exceeding building code standards, §36-107.1.
Sale or lease of residential dwelling.
Agent immunity and disclosure requirements, §8.01-226.7.
Mechanics' liens, notice of possible filing, §11-2.4.
New home sales.
Implied warranties, waiver of warranties, as is sale, §55-70.1.
Notice of possible filing of mechanics' lien required, §11-2.4.
Notification to buyers of availability of owner's title insurance.
Settlement agents duty, §38.2-4616.
Property owners' associations.
Sale of lot subject act, §§55-509.4 to 55-509.10.
Real estate settlement procedures act of 1974.
Violations.
Attorney general, action to enjoin, §6.2-1626.
Real estate settlements and settlement agents.
Generally, §§55-525.8 to 55-525.32.
See REAL ESTATE SETTLEMENTS.
Settlement services.
Agents.
Title insurance availability notification to buyer, §38.2-4616.
Title insurance.
Notification to buyers of availability of owner's title insurance, §38.2-4616.
Transfer fee covenants, §55-70.2.
Wet settlement act.
See MORTGAGES AND DEEDS OF TRUST.

RESIDUAL MARKET FACILITY.
Basic property insurance, §§38.2-2700 to 38.2-2713.

RESIDUAL PARENTAL RIGHTS.
Termination, §16.1-283.

RESISTING LAWFUL ARREST, §18.2-479.1.

RES JUDICATA.
Civil actions, preclusion of claims, VA SCt Rule 1:6.
Criminal procedure.
Acquittal on merits of case, §19.2-292.

RESOLUTIONS BY LOCALITIES.
Ordinances and other actions by local governing body generally, §§15.2-1425 to 15.2-1433.
See ORDINANCES.

RESORT COMPLEX.
Wine and beer sales in hotel classified as.
Retail on-premises wine and beer licenses, §4.1-209.

RESOURCE CONSERVATION AND RECOVERY ACT.
State programs to implement, §§2.2-617, 2.2-618.

RESOURCE MANAGEMENT PLANS, §§10.1-104.7 to 10.1-104.9.
Criteria for plans, §10.1-104.8.
Effect of compliance, §10.1-104.7.
Eligibility for matching grants, §10.1-104.7.

RESOURCE MANAGEMENT PLANS —Cont'd
Freedom of information act exemptions, §10.1-104.7.
Haylands, §10.1-104.8.
On-farm assessment of best management practices, §10.1-104.8.
Pasture management, §10.1-104.8.
Presumption of full compliance, §10.1-104.7.
Soil and water conservation board regulations, §§10.1-104.8, 10.1-104.9.

RESOURCES AUTHORITY, §§62.1-197 to 62.1-223.
Administrative powers, §62.1-203.
Airports revolving fund, §§5.1-30.1 to 5.1-30.10.
Collection of money due, §5.1-30.4.
Construction of chapter, §5.1-30.10.
Creation of fund, §5.1-30.2.
Definitions, §5.1-30.1.
Deposit of money, §5.1-30.3.
Expenditures, §5.1-30.3.
Investments, §5.1-30.3.
Loans to local government, §5.1-30.5.
Annual report on loans, §5.1-30.9.
Pledging loans to secure bonds, §5.1-30.6.
Sale of loans, §5.1-30.7.
Management of fund, §§5.1-30.2, 5.1-30.8.
Audits, §62.1-222.
Authorization to perform acts, §62.1-240.2.
Board of directors, §62.1-201.
Authorization of bonds and credit enhancements by resolution, §62.1-208.
Executive director, §62.1-202.
Liability for bonds or credit enhancements, §62.1-207.
Bond issues and credit enhancements.
Authorization by resolution of board, §62.1-208.
Bondholder protection, §62.1-214.
Capital reserve fund limitation, §62.1-215.
Character of negotiable instruments, §62.1-212.
Contract powers, §62.1-221.
Defined, §62.1-199.
Legal investments, securities.
Character as, §62.1-220.
Liability of Commonwealth, political subdivision and members of board of directors, §62.1-207.
Limitations on amount of bonds issued and local obligations guaranteed, §62.1-204.
Nonpayment by localities.
Investigation by governor, withholding state funds, §62.1-216.1.
Pledges generally, §62.1-210.
Pledging revenue or funds, §62.1-206.
Powers to issue, §62.1-204.
Provisions of resolution or trust indenture authorizing issuance, §62.1-209.
Purchase and credit enhancements of local obligations, §62.1-216.
Purchases of bonds by authority, §62.1-211.
Refunding bonds, §62.1-205.
Resolution or trust indenture, provisions, §62.1-209.
Solid waste or recycling revolving fund.
Pledge of loans to secure bonds of authority, §62.1-241.9.
Sources of payment and security, §62.1-206.
Tax exemption, §62.1-219.
Terms and conditions, §62.1-208.
Validity of proposed issuance, actions to determine, §62.1-208.

RESOURCES AUTHORITY —Cont'd
Bond issues and credit enhancements —Cont'd
Validity of signatures of prior members or officers, §62.1-213.
Water facilities revolving fund.
Pledge of loans to secure bonds of authority, §62.1-231.
Water supply revolving fund.
Pledge of loans to secure bonds of authority, §62.1-240.
Capital reserve funds.
Establishment, §62.1-215.
Citation of provisions, §62.1-197.
Construction of provisions, §62.1-223.
Creation, §62.1-200.
Defective drywall correction and restoration assistance fund, §§36-156.1, 36-156.2.
Defined terms, §62.1-199.
Deposit of money, §62.1-221.
Airport revolving fund, §5.1-30.3.
Established, §62.1-200.
Executive director, §62.1-202.
Exemption from taxation, §62.1-219.
Fees.
Authority to establish and collect, §62.1-203.
Freedom of information act.
Excluded records, §2.2-3705.6.
Grants from Commonwealth, §62.1-217.
Grants to local governments, §62.1-218.
Investment of public funds.
Legal and prudent investments, §2.2-4519.
Legislative findings, §62.1-198.
Loans.
Airport revolving fund.
Annual report on loans, §5.1-30.9.
Local government loans, §5.1-30.5.
Pledging loans to secure bonds, §5.1-30.6.
Sale of loans, §5.1-30.7.
Sale of loans, §62.1-240.1.
Airport revolving fund, §5.1-30.7.
Nonpayment by localities.
Investigation by governor, withholding state funds, §62.1-216.1.
Pledges generally, §62.1-210.
Powers, §§62.1-203, 62.1-240.2.
Bonds and credit enhancements, issuance, §62.1-204.
Borrowing money, §62.1-204.
Purchase and credit enhancements of local obligations, §62.1-216.
Purposes, §62.1-198.
Reports, §62.1-222.
Rules and regulations.
Authority to adopt, §62.1-203.
Secretary of commerce and trade.
Agency responsibility, §2.2-204.
Solid waste or recycling revolving fund.
Collection of money, §62.1-241.5.
Loans to local governments, §62.1-241.6.
Management, §62.1-241.2.
Pledge of loans to secure bonds of authority, §62.1-241.9.
Powers of authority, §62.1-241.9:2.
Tax exemption, §62.1-219.
Virginia infrastructure project loan fund, §§15.2-2430 to 15.2-2440.
See VIRGINIA INFRASTRUCTURE PROJECT LOAN FUND.
Water facilities revolving fund.
Bond issues, §62.1-231.
Collection of money, §62.1-228.

RESOURCES AUTHORITY —Cont'd
Water supply revolving fund.
Bond issues, §62.1-240.
Collection of money, §62.1-237.
Loans, §62.1-238.
Management, §62.1-234.
Pledge of loans to secure bonds of authority, §62.1-240.

RESPIRATORY CARE.
Licensing generally, §§54.1-2950.1 to 54.1-2957.01.
See MEDICINE AND OTHER HEALING ARTS PROFESSIONS.

RESPIRATORY DISEASES.
Presumption as to death or disability.
Volunteer or salaried firefighters, §65.2-402.
Statewide asthma management, §§32.1-73.5, 32.1-73.6.

RESPIRATORY EQUIPMENT.
Underground coal mines.
Miners exposed to inhalation of gas, dust, etc., to wear, §45.1-161.175.

RESPIRATORY THERAPY ADVISORY BOARD, §§54.1-2956, 54.1-2956.1.

RESPITE CARE GRANT PROGRAM.
Aging and rehabilitative services, department for.
Definitions, §51.5-155.
Established, §51.5-156.

RESTAURANTS, §§35.1-1 to 35.1-28.
ABC law.
Beer licenses, §4.1-208.
Mixed beverage restaurant licenses, §4.1-210.
Outdoor dining areas.
Mixed beverage restaurant licenses, §4.1-210.
Possession without license to sell alcoholic beverages upon premises, §4.1-315.
Tasting conducted by manufacturers, §4.1-201.1.
Wine and beer licenses, §4.1-209.
Administrative process.
Applicability of administrative process act, §35.1-4.
Notice, by mail, §35.1-1.1.
Alcoholic beverages.
Beer licenses, §4.1-208.
Carrying concealed weapons.
Club or restaurant serving alcohol, limitations, §18.2-308.12.
Mixed beverages licenses.
See MIXED BEVERAGE LICENSES.
Possession without license to sell, §4.1-315.
Wine and beer licenses, §4.1-209.
Carrying concealed weapons.
Club or restaurant serving alcohol, limitations, §18.2-308.12.
Charitable donations of food, §35.1-14.2.
Definitions, §35.1-1.
Discrimination against persons with disabilities, §51.5-44.
Disease reporting, §32.1-37.
Diseases.
Prevention of transmission of disease, §§35.1-10, 35.1-15.
Drug houses.
Maintaining fortified drug houses, §18.2-258.02.
Drug transactions on premises.
Closure of nuisance premises, §§48-16, 48-17.
Common nuisance, §§18.2-258, 18.2-258.01.

RESTAURANTS —Cont'd
Enforcement of provisions, §35.1-2.
Exemptions from provisions, §35.1-25.
Fairs, §35.1-26.
Food and beverage tax.
Excise tax on meals.
City or town having general taxing powers, §58.1-3840.
Counties, §§58.1-3833, 58.1-3834.
Situs for taxation, §58.1-3841.
Food and drug administration's food code.
Authority of board to adopt, §35.1-14.
Food products with alcoholic content of more than one-half of one percent by volume.
Selling on premises, §4.1-324.
Health board, state.
Commissioner vested with board's authority, §35.1-3.
Enforcement of provisions, §35.1-2.
Orders, §35.1-6.
Rules and regulations, §§35.1-11, 35.1-12, 35.1-14.
Health commissioner and department of health.
Board's authority vested in commissioner, §35.1-3.
Disease transmission.
Authority of commissioner to prevent, §§35.1-10, 35.1-15.
Enforcement of provisions, §35.1-2.
Right of entry, §35.1-5.
Indoor clean air act, §§15.2-2820 to 15.2-2833.
See SMOKING IN PUBLIC PLACES.
Injunctions.
Violations, §35.1-7.
Inspections, §35.1-22.
Right of entry, §35.1-5.
State institutions with dining accommodations to request inspections, §35.1-23.
Licensing, §§35.1-18, 35.1-20.
Advice and assistance to applicants, §35.1-24.
Display of license, §35.1-21.
Mixed beverage licenses.
See MIXED BEVERAGE LICENSES.
Notice, by mail, §35.1-1.1.
Obtaining food without payment, §18.2-188.
Ordinances.
Fairs, exemption from provisions by local ordinance, §35.1-26.
Local ordinances superseded, §35.1-9.
Outdoor dining areas.
Mixed beverage restaurant licenses, §4.1-210.
Penalties for violations, §35.1-7.
Retail sales and use tax.
Exemption to meals furnished to employees as part of wages, §58.1-609.3.
Rights of persons with disabilities, §51.5-44.
Rules and regulations, §§35.1-11, 35.1-12, 35.1-14.
Administrative process act.
Applicability, §35.1-4.
Penalties for violations, §35.1-7.
Sanitary requirements for food establishments, §§3.2-5105 to 3.2-5119.
Smoking regulated.
Indoor clean air act, §§15.2-2820 to 15.2-2833.
See SMOKING IN PUBLIC PLACES.
Sulfiting agents.
Certain uses prohibited, §35.1-14.1.

RESTITUTION.
Animals.
Removal of transmitting device from dog, falcon, hawk or owl.
Loss or death of animal resulting, §18.2-97.1.

RESTITUTION —Cont'd
Assault and battery.
Dismissal of prosecution, §19.2-151.
Attachments.
Order of court on rehearing or new trial, §8.01-576.
Cable television service.
Obtaining without payment, §18.2-187.1.
Child pornography.
Mandatory restitution to victims as condition of sentence, §19.2-305.1.
Church or cemetery property.
Willfully and maliciously damaging, §18.2-127.
Consumer protection.
Assurances of voluntary compliance, §59.1-202.
Unintentional violations, §59.1-207.
Crime victims and witnesses.
Compensating victims of crime, §§19.2-368.1 to 19.2-368.18.
See CRIME VICTIM AND WITNESS ASSISTANCE.
Delinquent children, §16.1-278.8.
Dog transmitting device removal.
Loss or death of dog resulting, §18.2-97.1.
Electronic communication devices.
Unlawful use, §18.2-190.6.
Electronic communication services.
Obtaining without payment, §18.2-187.1.
Falcons, hawks or owls.
Removal of transmitting device from dog, falcon, hawk or owl.
Loss or death of animal resulting, §18.2-97.1.
Fire investigations.
Seized property, §27-34.1.
Gambling winner repaying loser.
Discharge of winner from punishment, §11-16.
Identity theft, §18.2-186.3.
Indigent hospitalization program.
Liability for excess payments, §32.1-349.
Installment payment of criminal fines and penalties, §§19.2-354 to 19.2-358.
Insurance title violations, §§38.2-218, 38.2-1916.2.
Interest to be paid on award of restitution, §19.2-305.4.
Jail inmate work release earnings.
Use, §53.1-131.
Judicial sales.
Disturbance of purchaser's title, §8.01-113.
Medicaid.
Fraudulently obtained benefits, §32.1-321.3.
Obtaining excess payments, §32.1-312.
Unintentionally obtaining excess payments, §§32.1-313, 32.1-321.2.
Medical students.
Conditional grant breaches, §32.1-122.6.
Metering devices of public services or utilities.
Tampering with or diverting service, §18.2-163.
Oil, electric, gas or water service.
Obtaining without payment, §18.2-187.1.
Prisoner employment program earnings, §53.1-41.
Prisoner work release earnings, §§53.1-60, 53.1-61.
Probation.
Amount of restitution, §19.2-305.2.
Enforcement of restitution order, §19.2-305.2.
Property damage or loss, §19.2-305.1.
Requiring for damages or support, §19.2-305.
Public officers and employees.
Employee receiving payment not entitled to, §2.2-804.

RESTITUTION —Cont'd
Real estate settlement agents.
Violations, ordering, §55-525.31.
Research farm product.
Damaging or destroying, §18.2-145.1.
Sales, UCC.
Buyer's remedies, §8.2-718.
Suspension of sentence and placing on probation.
Partial restitution as condition, §19.2-303.
Telegraph or telephone services.
Obtaining without payment, §18.2-187.1.
Timber, larceny of, §55-334.1.
Trade secrets.
Conflict of laws, §59.1-341.
Work release earnings of jail inmates, §53.1-131.

RESTORATION OF CIVIL RIGHTS.
Persons convicted of felonies.
Notification, processing applications, §53.1-231.1.
Voter registration, right to register, §53.1-231.2.
Removal of political disabilities felony conviction.
Governor's powers, VA Const Art V §12.

RESTORATION OF FORMER NAME UPON DIVORCE, §20-121.4.
Recording and indexing, §55-106.1.

RESTORATION TAX CREDIT, §58.1-339.2.

RESTRAINING ORDERS.
Cease and desist orders generally.
See CEASE AND DESIST ORDERS.
Injunctions generally.
See INJUNCTIONS.
Protective orders.
See PROTECTIVE ORDERS.

RESTRAINT OF TRADE.
Agricultural cooperative associations, §13.1-331.
Antitrust laws.
General provisions, §§59.1-9.1 to 59.1-9.17.
See ANTITRUST.
Insurance companies, §§38.2-700 to 38.2-705.
Combinations to injure others in reputation, trade, etc., §§18.2-499 to 18.2-501.
Insurance antitrust provisions, §§38.2-700 to 38.2-705.
Insurance business boycott, coercion or intimidation, §38.2-505.
Insurance rate service organizations, §38.2-1916.
Motion pictures.
Fair competition.
Purpose of provisions, §59.1-256.

RESTRICTED DRIVERS' PERMITS.
Aggressive driving, §46.2-392.
Child support delinquency, §46.2-320.1.
Driver's license probation, §46.2-499.
Driving while intoxicated, §18.2-271.1.
Administrative suspension of license, §46.2-391.2.
Revocation of license for conviction, §46.2-391.
Driving while license, permit, privilege to drive suspended or revoked.
Restricted license, issuance, duration, violations, penalty, §46.2-301.
Drug offense conviction, §18.2-259.1.
Habitual offenders, restoration of driving privilege, §§46.2-358, 46.2-360

RESTRICTED DRIVERS' PERMITS —Cont'd
Local correctional facilities or jails, nonpayment of fees, §46.2-320.2.
Out-of-state licensees.
Issuance of restricted driving privilege, §46.2-398.1.
Reckless driving conviction, §46.2-392.
Refusal of application, §46.2-320.
Special restrictions on licenses, §46.2-329.
Ten or more consecutive unexcused absences from school.
Suspension of license.
Issuance of restricted license, conditions, violations, penalty, §46.2-334.001.

RESTRICTED FIREARM AMMUNITION.
Use or attempted use in commission or attempted commission of crime, §18.2-308.3.

RESTRICTED PARCEL CARRIERS.
Employee liens, §§43-24 to 43-26.
Not required to incorporate as public service companies, §13.1-620.
Public service companies generally, §§56-1 to 56-87.
See PUBLIC SERVICE COMPANIES.
Supplier liens, §§43-24 to 43-26.
Transportation companies generally, §§56-99.2 to 56-140.
See TRANSPORTATION COMPANIES.

RESTRICTIVE COVENANTS.
Fair housing.
Discriminatory housing practices, §36-96.3.
Restrictive covenant, defined, §36-96.1:1.
Void as against public policy, §36-96.6.
Subdivided land sales, §55-343.

RESTRICTIVE INDORSEMENTS.
Negotiable instruments, §8.3A-206.

RESTROOMS.
Highways and roads.
Rest stops, §§33.1-217 to 33.1-219.
Family restrooms, required, §33.1-223.2:7.
Peeping or spying, §18.2-130.
Public gathering places, §§32.1-198 to 32.1-202.

RESTRUCTURED HIGHER EDUCATION FINANCIAL AND ADMINISTRATIVE OPERATIONS ACT, §§23-38.88 to 23-38.121.
See COLLEGES AND UNIVERSITIES.

REST STOPS, §§33.1-217 to 33.1-219.
Family restrooms, required, §33.1-223.2:7.

RESUMPTION OF FORMER NAME UPON DIVORCE, §20-121.4.
Recording and indexing, §55-106.1.

RETAIL FRANCHISING, §§13.1-557 to 13.1-574.
Applicability of chapter.
Effective date, §13.1-574.
Civil remedies, §13.1-571.
Complaint or record of violation transmitted to locality, §13.1-569.1.
Confidentiality of information, §13.1-567.
Copies of records of commission, evidence, §13.1-569.
Declaration by franchisee that franchise void, §13.1-565.
Definitions, §13.1-559.
Effective date of chapter, §13.1-574.
Expense of regulation.
Fees to cover, §13.1-561.1.

RETAIL FRANCHISING —Cont'd
Fair dealing with franchisees, policy of Commonwealth, §13.1-558.
Forms provided by state corporation commission, §13.1-572.
Heavy equipment dealers.
Application of provisions, §59.1-363.
Injunctions, §13.1-568.
Investigations by state corporation commission, §13.1-567.
Misrepresentation of material facts, §13.1-570.
Motorcycle dealers.
Exemption from act, §46.2-1993.65.
Nonresident franchisors, service of process, §13.1-566.
Offenses punishable by commission, §13.1-570.
Offers to sell franchises, unlawful offers, §13.1-563.
Penalties imposed by commission, §13.1-570.
Petroleum products franchises.
Application of provisions, §59.1-21.18:1.
Policy of Commonwealth, §13.1-558.
Records of commission, availability to public, §13.1-573.
Registration.
Bond, §13.1-561.
Fee, §§13.1-561, 13.1-561.1.
Hearing on revocation or refusal to renew, §13.1-562.
Procedure, §13.1-561.
Renewal.
Fee, §13.1-561.
Refusal, §13.1-562.
Required, §13.1-560.
Revocation, §13.1-562.
Summary suspension, §13.1-562.
Retail franchising act, §13.1-557.
Rulemaking power of state corporation commission, §13.1-572.
Service of process on nonresident franchisors, §13.1-566.
Short title, §13.1-557.
Surrender of right, undue influence to induce, §13.1-564.
T&M vehicle dealers.
Exemption of franchises from act, §46.2-1974.
Transmittal of record or complaint to locality where violation occurred, §13.1-569.1.
Undue influence to induce surrender of right, §13.1-564.
Unlawful cancellation, §13.1-564.
Unlawful offers to sell franchises, §13.1-563.
Voidable franchises, §13.1-565.

RETAIL FRANCHISING ACT, §§13.1-557 to 13.1-574.
See RETAIL FRANCHISING.

RETAIL OFF-PREMISES BEER LICENSES.
Authorized conduct, §4.1-208.
Local license taxes, §4.1-233.
State license fees, §§4.1-231, 4.1-232.

RETAIL OFF-PREMISES WINE AND BEER LICENSES.
Authorized conduct, §4.1-209.
Local license taxes, §4.1-233.
State license fees, §§4.1-231, 4.1-232.

RETAIL OFF-PREMISES WINERY LICENSES.
Authorized conduct, §4.1-207.
Local license taxes, §4.1-233.
State license fees, §§4.1-231, 4.1-232.

RETAIL ON-AND-OFF PREMISES BEER LICENSES.
Authorized conduct, §4.1-208.
Local license taxes, §4.1-233.
State license fees, §§4.1-231, 4.1-232.

RETAIL ON-AND-OFF PREMISES WINE AND BEER LICENSES.
Authorized conduct, §4.1-209.
Local license taxes, §4.1-233.
State license fees, §§4.1-231, 4.1-232.

RETAIL ON-PREMISES BEER LICENSES.
Authorized conduct, §4.1-208.
Local license taxes, §4.1-233.
State license fees, §§4.1-231, 4.1-232.

RETAIL ON-PREMISES WINE AND BEER LICENSES.
Authorized conduct, §4.1-209.
Local license taxes, §4.1-233.
State license fees, §§4.1-231, 4.1-232.

RETAIL SALES AND USE TAX, §§58.1-600 to 58.1-639.
Absorption of tax prohibited, §58.1-626.
Adjustment of rate based on percentage of sales of eleven cents or more, §58.1-628.2.
Administration of chapter, §58.1-601.
Advertising or holding out to public absorption of tax, §58.1-626.
Agricultural exemptions, §58.1-609.2.
Amnesty.
School supplies, limited exemption, §58.1-611.2.
Absorption of tax, advertising, prohibition, inapplicability, §58.1-626.
Collection of tax by dealer during limited period, §58.1-625.
Auditor of public accounts.
Annual review of collection and distribution, §30-133.2.
Bad checks, §§18.2-182.1, 58.1-637.
Bad debt credit, §58.1-621.
Bond of person subject to tax, §58.1-630.
Bracket of prices used for collection.
Adjustment based on sales of eleven cents or more, §58.1-628.2.
Building materials.
Refund authorized for certain materials, §58.1-608.1.
Burden of proving sales or leases not subject to tax, §58.1-623.
Certificates of exemption, §58.1-623.
Misuse of certificates, §58.1-623.1.
Suspension for misuse, §58.1-623.1.
Collection.
Dealers, §§58.1-612 to 58.1-622.
Public procurement, prohibited contracts.
Dealers not in compliance with, §2.2-4321.1.
Generally, §58.1-625.
Commercial exemptions, §58.1-609.3.
Communications sales and use tax, §§58.1-645 to 58.1-662.
See COMMUNICATIONS SALES AND USE TAX.
Enforcement procedures, applicability, §58.1-661.
Contractors, §58.1-610.
Credits.
Bad debts, §58.1-621.
Repossessions of property by dealers, §58.1-620.
Taxes paid to another state, §58.1-611.
Dealers, tax collectible from, §58.1-612.
Bad check, §58.1-637.
Bad debts, §58.1-621.

RETAIL SALES AND USE TAX —Cont'd
Dealers, tax collectible from —Cont'd
Bond of person subject to tax, §58.1-630.
Certificate of registration for place of business, §58.1-613.
Cessation of business at place specified in certificate, §58.1-613.
Collection generally, §58.1-625.
Commissioners of revenue electing to provide services.
Guidelines, rules, procedures to follow, §58.1-613.
Credit for bad debts, §58.1-621.
Credit for tax paid upon repossessions, §58.1-620.
Dealer.
Defined, §58.1-612.
Deduction in submitting return, §58.1-622.
Discounts, §58.1-622.
Electronic submission of consolidated returns, §58.1-615.
Engaging in business after certificate of registration suspended or revoked, §58.1-613.
Estimate for taxable period.
Failure to make return or fraudulent return, §58.1-618.
Failure, neglect or refusal to collect, §58.1-625.
Failure to make or fraudulent return, §58.1-618.
Jurisdiction over dealers, §58.1-612.
Payment to accompany return, §58.1-616.
Presumption of activity within Commonwealth to require registration, §58.1-612.
Public procurement, prohibited contracts.
Dealers not in compliance with, §2.2-4321.1.
Records, §58.1-633.
Reimbursement for returned goods, §58.1-619.
Repossessions, credit for tax paid, §58.1-620.
Returned goods, §58.1-619.
Returns, §58.1-615.
Electronic submission of consolidated returns, §58.1-615.
Extensions, §58.1-617.
Failure to file, false or fraudulent returns, §§58.1-635, 58.1-636.
Estimate for taxable period, §58.1-618.
Revocation or suspension of certificate of registration, §58.1-613.
Sale of business by dealers liable for tax, §58.1-629.
Vending machine sales, §58.1-614.
Definitions, §58.1-602.
Dealer, §58.1-612.
Delinquent taxes.
Memorandum of lien, §58.1-632.
Direct payment permits, §58.1-624.
Discount allowed dealer, §58.1-622.
Disposition of revenues, §58.1-638.
Municipality entitlement, §58.1-608.3.
Election.
Local sales or use taxes, §§58.1-605, 58.1-606.
Energy star qualified products.
Exemption, §58.1-609.1.
Enforcement of chapter, §58.1-601.
Estimated tax.
Failure to file or fraudulent return by dealers, §58.1-618.
Exceptions to exemptions, §58.1-609.13.
Exemption certificates, §58.1-623.
Misuse, §58.1-623.1.
Suspension for misuse, §58.1-623.1.
Exemptions.
Agricultural exemptions, §58.1-609.2.

RETAIL SALES AND USE TAX —Cont'd
Exemptions —Cont'd
Commercial exemptions, §58.1-609.3.
Energy star qualified products, §58.1-609.1.
Exceptions, local sales and use taxes, §58.1-609.13.
Gift transactions, §58.1-604.6.
Governmental and commodities, §58.1-609.1.
Hurricane preparedness equipment, limited exemption, §58.1-611.3.
Industrial exemptions, §58.1-609.3.
Information required from persons relating to, §58.1-601.
Media-related exemptions, §58.1-609.6.
Miscellaneous exemptions, §58.1-609.10.
Reports to general assembly on tax exemptions studies, §58.1-609.12.
Motor vehicles, machinery, etc., brought into Virginia for use in performing contracts, §58.1-604.3.
Nonprofit entities, §58.1-609.11.
Reports to general assembly on tax exemptions, §58.1-609.12.
Port authority agents or lessees, §62.1-145.
Railroad rolling stock.
Commercial and industrial exemptions, §58.1-609.3.
School supplies, limited exemption, §58.1-611.2.
Absorption of tax, advertising, prohibition, inapplicability, §58.1-626.
Collected by dealer during limited period, §58.1-625.
Service exemptions, §58.1-609.5.
Suspension of exemption, §58.1-608.4.
Failure, neglect or refusal to collect tax, §58.1-625.
Failure to file return.
Civil penalty, §58.1-635.
Criminal penalty, §58.1-636.
False returns.
Civil penalty, §58.1-635.
Criminal penalty, §58.1-636.
Food purchased for human consumption, §58.1-611.1.
Fraudulent returns.
Civil penalty, §58.1-635.
Criminal penalty, §58.1-636.
Gift transactions, §58.1-604.6.
Governmental and commodities exemptions, §58.1-609.1.
Hampton roads transportation authority.
Repair of motor vehicles.
Authority to impose on labor or services, §58.1-605.
Hurricane preparedness equipment.
Limited exemption, §58.1-611.3.
Imposition of sales tax, §58.1-603.
Imposition of use tax, §58.1-604.
Increase in sales and use tax rate, transitional provision, §58.1-639.
Industrial exemptions, §58.1-609.3.
Jeopardy assessments, §58.1-631.
Jurisdiction.
Collection of tax from dealers, §58.1-612.
Limitation on assessment, §58.1-634.
Localities' share of revenues, §58.1-638.
Local sales tax, §58.1-605.
Suspension of exemption, §58.1-608.4.
Local treasurers, authority to require production of information, §58.1-3128.1.

RETAIL SALES AND USE TAX —Cont'd
Local use tax, §58.1-606.
Exception to exemption of propane gas, firewood, etc., used for heating homes, §58.1-609.13.
Suspension of exemption, §58.1-608.4.
Long arm statute.
Tax collectible from dealers.
Jurisdictional standards, §58.1-612.
Low-income housing.
Refund authorized for building materials, §58.1-608.1.
Media-related exemptions, §58.1-609.6.
Memorandum of lien, §58.1-632.
Miscellaneous exemptions, §58.1-609.10.
Reports to general assembly on tax exemptions studies, §58.1-609.12.
Modular building manufacturers and retailers, §58.1-610.1.
Motor vehicles, machinery, etc., brought into Virginia for use in performing contracts.
Use tax on, §58.1-604.1.
Exemptions, §58.1-604.3.
Filing return, §58.1-604.2.
Payment of tax, §58.1-604.2.
Registration by owners or lessees of property, §58.1-604.2.
Moving residence or business into Commonwealth, §58.1-607.
Municipality entitlement to revenues, §58.1-608.3.
Nonprofit entities, exemptions, §58.1-609.11.
Reports to general assembly on tax exemptions, §58.1-609.12.
Northern Virginia transportation authority.
Repair of motor vehicles.
Authority to impose on labor or services, §58.1-605.
Payment of tax.
Accompanying dealer's return, §58.1-616.
Bad checks, §58.1-637.
Direct payment permits, §58.1-624.
Motor vehicles, machinery, etc., brought into Virginia for use in performing contracts, use tax on, §58.1-604.2.
Period of limitations on assessment, §58.1-634.
Port authority agents or lessees.
Exemptions, §62.1-145.
Presumed sales or leases subject to tax, §58.1-623.
Prima facie evidence.
Failure to file return or fraudulent return, §58.1-635.
Public education standards of quality/local real estate property tax relief fund.
Revenue disposition, §58.1-638.
Public procurement.
Dealers not in compliance with.
Prohibited contracts, §2.2-4321.1.
Railroad rolling stock.
Commercial and industrial exemptions, §58.1-609.3.
Records of dealers, §58.1-633.
Refunds.
Building materials, §58.1-608.1.
Registration of dealers.
Certificates, §58.1-613.
Reports.
Auditor of public accounts.
Annual review of collection and distribution, §30-133.2.

RETAIL SALES AND USE TAX —Cont'd
Repossessions of property by dealer.
Credit for tax paid, §58.1-620.
Returned goods.
Reimbursement to dealer, §58.1-619.
Returns by dealers, §58.1-615.
Electronic submission of consolidated returns, §58.1-615.
Extensions, §58.1-615.
Failure to file, false returns or fraudulent returns, §§58.1-635, 58.1-636.
Estimate for taxable period, §58.1-618.
Sale of business, §58.1-629.
Sale of business by dealers, §58.1-629.
Sales tax.
Disposition of revenues, §58.1-638.
Imposition, §58.1-603.
Local sales tax, §58.1-605.
Exception to exemption of propane gas, firewood, etc., used for heating homes, §58.1-609.13.
School supplies.
Limited exemption, §58.1-611.2.
Absorption of tax, advertising, prohibition, inapplicability, §58.1-626.
Collection by dealer during limited period, §58.1-625.
Service exemptions, §58.1-609.5.
Short title, §58.1-600.
Statute of limitations.
Criminal prosecutions, §19.2-8.
Taxes paid to another state.
Credit for, §58.1-611.
Tire tax.
Generally, §§58.1-640 to 58.1-644.
Provisions of chapter to apply to tire tax, §58.1-644.
Transitional provision, §58.1-639.
Transportation companies.
Examination of books, records and other documents, §58.1-633.
Use tax.
Disposition of revenues, §58.1-638.
Imposition, §58.1-604.
Local use tax, §58.1-606.
Motor vehicles, machinery, tools and equipment brought into Virginia for performing contract, §58.1-604.1.
Exemptions, §58.1-604.3.
Filing return, §58.1-604.2.
Payment of tax, §58.1-604.2.
Registration by owners or lessees of property, §58.1-604.2.
Moving residence or business into Commonwealth, §58.1-607.
Vending machine sales.
Tax collectible from dealers, §58.1-614.
Virginia communications sales and use tax act, §§58.1-645 to 58.1-662.
See COMMUNICATIONS SALES AND USE TAX.

RETAIL STORES.
Electronic security equipment sales.
Private security services businesses, exceptions, §9.1-140.
Payment device numbers.
Display on receipt, §6.2-429.
Peeping or spying, §18.2-130.
Sale of food.
Acceptance of promissory notes in payment, §18.2-241.

RETAINAGE BY PARI-MUTUEL LICENSEES, §59.1-392.

RETAINAGE ON PUBLIC CONSTRUCTION CONTRACTS.
Prompt payment law.
Retainage to remain valid, §2.2-4349.
Public contracts for construction, §2.2-4333.
Deposit of retained funds with local governments, §2.2-4334.

RETAINED ASSET ACCOUNTS.
Life insurance, §§38.2-3117.1 to 38.2-3117.4.
Definitions, §38.2-3117.1.
Disclosures to beneficiary prior to selection of option, §38.2-3117.4.
Information to beneficiary describing settlement options, §38.2-3117.2.
Supplemental contract required, §38.2-3117.3.

RETALIATION.
Beer franchises.
Retaliatory action against wholesaler, §4.1-512.
Complaints against adult or child care agencies.
Against complainant, §63.2-1730.
Continuing care facilities.
Self organization by residents, §38.2-4910.
Foreign or alien insurers.
Domestic insurers subject to retaliatory costs in other states, §38.2-1026.
Grievance procedure for local government personnel.
Definition of grievance, §15.2-1507.
Manufactured home lot rentals, §§55-248.50 to 55-248.52.
Whistleblowing.
Fraud and abuse whistleblower protection act.
Retaliation against whistleblowers prohibited, §2.2-3011.
Wine franchises.
Retaliatory action against wholesaler, §4.1-413.

RETALIATORY DISCHARGE.
Asbestos workers and contractors.
Employer discrimination for compliance with provisions, §54.1-515.
Workers' compensation.
Employee exercise of rights, §65.2-308.

RETALIATORY EVICTIONS, §§55-248.39, 55-248.40.
Manufactured home lot rentals, §§55-248.50 to 55-248.52.

RETENTION OF COURT RECORDS.
Case files of ended cases in circuit court, §17.1-213.

RETIRED JUDGES, COURTS OF RECORD.
Designation of judges to hold courts and assist other judges, §§17.1-105 to 17.1-107.

RETIRED JUDGES RECALLED TO SERVICE.
Court of appeals judge absent or unable through sickness, disability or other reason to perform duties, §17.1-400.

RETIRED OFFICERS ASSOCIATION.
Special license plates, §46.2-746.4.

RETIREMENT.
Abandonment of funds presumption, §55-210.8.
Attorneys.
Master retirement program of state bar, §54.1-3917.

RETIREMENT —Cont'd
Colleges and universities.
Voluntary early retirement.
Authority to establish incentives, §23-9.2:3.1.
Commercial space flight authority.
Retirement contributions for personnel, §2.2-2203.3.
Credit unions.
Power to act as trustee or custodian, §6.2-1363.
Employee trusts.
Restraints on the alienation of property construed, §55-13.1.
Firefighters.
Relief for firefighters and dependents, §§27-39 to 27-50.
See FIREFIGHTERS.
General assembly power to grant pensions, VA Const Art IV §14.
Governmental employee retirement.
General assembly to maintain and administer system, VA Const Art X §11.
Income tax.
Amended returns.
Federal, state or local employees, §58.1-1823.
Credit for taxes paid to foreign country on retirement income, §58.1-332.1.
Definition of income tax, §58.1-332.2.
Judicial retirement system, §§51.1-300 to 51.1-309.
See JUDICIAL RETIREMENT SYSTEM.
Law officers' retirement system, §§51.1-211 to 51.1-221.
See LAW OFFICERS' RETIREMENT SYSTEM.
Local government personnel.
Retirement systems generally, §15.2-1510.
Magistrates.
Full-time magistrates.
Certification for retirement coverage, §19.2-46.2.
Outdoors foundation, §51.1-126.7.
Power of attorney.
Authority of agent as to retirement plans, §64.2-1636.
Retirement system of Virginia, §§51.1-124.1 to 51.1-169.
See VIRGINIA RETIREMENT SYSTEM.
Security registration exemption, §13.1-514.
State bar of Virginia.
Master retirement program, §54.1-3917.
State corporation commission, VA Const Art IX §1.
State police retirement system, §§51.1-200 to 51.1-210.
See STATE POLICE RETIREMENT SYSTEM.
Unclaimed funds, disposition of, §§55-210.8, 55-210.28:1.
Unemployment compensation.
Benefit reduction, §60.2-604.
Virginia port authority.
Establishment of plan for employees, §51.1-126.4.
Group insurance, §51.1-502.3.
Virginia retirement system, §§51.1-124.1 to 51.1-169.
See VIRGINIA RETIREMENT SYSTEM.
Virginia state bar.
Master retirement program, §54.1-3917.
Volunteer firefighters' and rescue squad workers' service award fund, §§51.1-1200 to 51.1-1211.
See VOLUNTEER FIREFIGHTERS' AND RESCUE SQUAD WORKERS' SERVICE AWARD FUND.

RETIREMENT COMMUNITIES.
Continuing care retirement community nursing home bed projects.
Open admission period, applications for, §32.1-102.3:8.
Requirements for accepting applications, §32.1-102.3:2.
Transfer of nursing facility beds, application for, §32.1-102.3:7.
Utilization of nursing home beds.
Reporting to commissioner of health, §32.1-276.5.

RETIREMENT SYSTEM FOR STATE POLICE OFFICERS, §§51.1-200 to 51.1-210.
See STATE POLICE RETIREMENT SYSTEM.

RETIREMENT SYSTEM OF THE JUDICIARY, §§51.1-300 to 51.1-309.
See JUDICIAL RETIREMENT SYSTEM.

RETIREMENT SYSTEM OF VIRGINIA, §§51.1-124.1 to 51.1-169.
See VIRGINIA RETIREMENT SYSTEM.

RETRAINING OF WORKERS.
Income tax on corporations.
Worker retraining tax credit, §58.1-439.6.

RETROACTIVE DETERMINATION OF CHILD SUPPORT LIABILITY, §20-108.1.

RETROACTIVE LAWS.
Ex post facto laws, US Const Art I §§9, 10.

RETURN OF GOODS FOR REFUND, EXCHANGE OR CREDIT.
Disclosures required, §59.1-200.

RETURN OF ORDER OR WARRANT OF GOVERNOR, §2.2-112.

REVENUE SHARING.
Alleghany Highlands economic development authority.
County of Alleghany and city of Clifton Forge, §15.2-6214.
Regional cooperation act, §15.2-4207.
State highway systems in certain localities.
Revenue-sharing funds.
Annual allocation of funds to localities, §33.1-23.05.
Limitation of yearly amount, §33.1-23.05.
Virginia regional industrial facilities authorities, §15.2-6407.
Voluntary settlement of annexation, transition or immunity issues, §§15.2-3400, 15.2-3401.

REVENUE STABILIZATION FUND, VA Const Art X §8.

REVENUE STAMPS.
Cigarette excise tax generally, §§58.1-1000 to 58.1-1022.
See CIGARETTE TAX.

REVERSE MORTGAGES.
Banks, investment in, §6.2-881.

REVERSION OF CITIES TO TOWNS, §§15.2-4100 to 15.2-4120.
Actions pending, effect, §15.2-4118.
Annexation.
Temporary restrictions, §15.2-4117.
Appeals, §15.2-4108.
Appointment of special court to hear case, §15.2-4101.

REVERSION OF CITIES TO TOWNS —Cont'd
Assistance of state agencies in gathering and presenting evidence, §15.2-4107.
Authorization to change to town status, §15.2-4100.
Charter for resulting town, §15.2-4112.
Citizen petition for town status, §15.2-4102.
City no longer qualifying for city status, judicial determination, §§15.2-4000 to 15.2-4005.
Appointment of special court to hear case, §15.2-4002.
Certification of findings of commission to governing body, §15.2-4001.
Continuance in office of officers, agents and employees, §15.2-4005.
Determination of status by special court, §15.2-4004.
Effect when city becomes town, §15.2-4005.
Election of town council and other elected officers of town after change to town status, §15.2-4005.
Enjoyment of city status until requirements of provisions fulfilled, §15.2-4000.
Imposition of terms and conditions to ensure orderly transition, §15.2-4004.
Investigation by commission on local government, §15.2-4001.
Investigation by special court, §15.2-4003.
Notice to adjoining counties of petition for determination, §15.2-4002.
Order changing city to town, §15.2-4004.
Petitioning circuit court for determination of city status, §15.2-4002.
Public hearing on report of commission on local government, §15.2-4003.
Report by commission to be certified to circuit court, §15.2-4002.
Terms of officers, §15.2-4005.
Continuance of service of officers, agents and employees, §15.2-4115.
Continued jurisdiction of court granting transition, §15.2-4120.
Court granting transition to exist for ten years, §15.2-4120.
Courts jurisdiction, §15.2-4119.
Declining grant of town status, §15.2-4109.
Effective date of transition, §15.2-4111.
Effect on pending suits, §15.2-4118.
Effect when city becomes town, §15.2-4115.
Election of town council and other elected officers after change in status, §15.2-4115.
Five year finality limitation, §15.2-4110.
Hearing and decision by court, §15.2-4106.
Intervention.
Time limit, §15.2-4104.
Jurisdiction of courts, §15.2-4119.
Liabilities and assets of city, §15.2-4114.
Library aid continued, §15.2-4116.
Order granting town status, §15.2-4106.
Ordinance declining to accept eligibility for town status, §15.2-4109.
Ordinance petitioning court for town status, §15.2-4101.
Parties, §15.2-4103.
Petition to circuit court granting town status.
Citizen petition, §15.2-4102.
Governing body, §15.2-4101.
Pretrial conferences, §15.2-4105.
Proceedings final for five years, §15.2-4110.

REVERSION OF CITIES TO TOWNS —Cont'd
Prohibition on return to previous independent city status, §15.2-4113.
Publication of citizen petition for town status, §15.2-4102.
Publication of copy of notice and ordinance, §15.2-4101.
Publication of order limiting time for intervenors, §15.2-4104.
Removal of causes and proceedings to court or courts of concurrent or like jurisdiction of county, §15.2-4119.
Restriction on annexation, §15.2-4117.
Restrictions on subsequent change in status, §15.2-4113.
Service of citizen petition for town status, §15.2-4102.
Service of notice of petition to circuit court, §15.2-4101.
Subsequent change in status, restrictions, §15.2-4113.
Terms and conditions for granting town status, §15.2-4106.
Terms of officers after change in status, §15.2-4115.
Two year limitation on annexation, §15.2-4117.

REVERSIONS.
Attornment.
Unnecessary, §55-220.
When void, §55-221.
Fraudulent conveyances.
Pretend reservations to be recorded, §55-87.
Landlord and tenant.
Grantee rights, §55-217.
Lessee rights, §55-218.
Murderers barred from claiming property rights of decedent, §64.2-2504.
Principal and income.
Uniform principal and income act, §§64.2-1000 to 64.2-1032.
See PRINCIPAL AND INCOME.
Tenants entitled to emblements.
What rent to be paid, §55-250.
Waste, §§55-211 to 55-216.
Works on watercourses.
Rights upon forfeiture by tenant of works damaged or destroyed, §62.1-126.

REVISION OF CONSTITUTION OF VIRGINIA, VA Const Sched §§1 to 5.
Constitutional convention, VA Const Art XII §2.
Effect generally, §1-4.

REVIVAL OF ACTIONS.
Personal suits, §§59.1-68.3, 59.1-68.5.
Sale offenses.
Authority of attorney general, §59.1-68.2.
Suits by Commonwealth's attorneys, §59.1-68.4.
Suspension or tolling of statute of limitations, §8.01-229.

REVIVAL OF WILLS, §§64.2-411, 64.2-412, 64.2-414.

REVOCATION OF DRIVERS' LICENSES.
See DRIVERS' LICENSES.

REVOLVERS.
Carrying concealed weapons, §18.2-308.
Dealers.
County requiring reports of sales.
Power repealed, destruction of records, §15.2-1207

REVOLVERS —Cont'd
Firearms dealers, §§54.1-4200 to 54.1-4202.
See FIREARMS DEALERS.
Firearms generally.
See FIREARMS.
Firearms offenses, §§18.2-279 to 18.2-287.4, 18.2-308 to 18.2-311.1.
See FIREARMS OFFENSES.
Permits to sell or purchase.
Certain counties requiring, §15.2-1208.

REVOLVING CREDIT.
Interest.
Credit union charges, §6.2-1302.
Open-end credit plans, §§6.2-433 to 6.2-435.
Amendments to contract or plan, §6.2-433.
Law governing, plans by bank or savings institution, §6.2-434.
Law governing, plans by sellers or lenders, §6.2-435.

REWARDS.
Crime solvers' rewards.
See CRIME SOLVERS' REWARDS.
Localities authorized to offer and pay rewards, §15.2-1713.
Police officer claiming and receiving, §15.2-1710.

RICHARD BLAND COLLEGE.
College of William and Mary generally, §§23-39 to 23-49.1:1.
See COLLEGE OF WILLIAM AND MARY.

RICHLANDS COAL MINERS' MEMORIAL.
Tazewell county.
Official designation, §1-510.

RICHMOND.
Bar examinations, §54.1-3927.
Behavioral health authorities.
Authorized to establish, §37.2-601.
Generally, §§37.2-600 to 37.2-615.
See BEHAVIORAL HEALTH AUTHORITIES.
Blighted structures.
Sale of certain property, §15.2-958.1.
Capitol district.
Establishment as seat of government of Commonwealth, §2.2-620.
Cemeteries, §57-27.
Chancery court.
Recordation of documents.
When and where writings generally admitted to record, §55-106.
Circuit court.
Antitrust actions.
Investigations by attorney general, §59.1-9.10.
Condominiums.
Investigations by board of complaints.
Orders to compel, §55-79.99.
Dams for hydroelectric power, §62.1-97.
Escheats.
Duty failures by escheators, §§55-189, 55-190.
Establishment, §17.1-500.
Fidelity and surety insurers.
Institution of civil proceedings against, §38.2-2415.
Health spas.
Investigations, §59.1-308.2.
Hydroelectric power dams.
Provision violations, §62.1-97.
Insurance companies, rehabilitation and liquidation.
Application for receiver by state corporation commission, §38.2-1505.

RICHMOND —Cont'd
Circuit court —Cont'd
Insurance companies, rehabilitation and liquidation —Cont'd
Filing in Richmond circuit court, §38.2-1502.
Insurers' deposits with state treasurer.
Bill to enforce policyholder or general creditors lien, §38.2-1046.
Jurisdiction over offenses committed in Capitol Square, §18.2-124.
Jurisdiction over river, watercourse or bay lying between county or city.
Inapplicability of provisions, §17.1-516.
Medical assistance services director.
Subpoena applications, §32.1-324.1.
Membership camping
Investigations, §59.1-334.
Motor carrier road tax penalty appeals, §58.1-2709.
Motor vehicle sales and use tax appeals, §58.1-2426.
Pari-mutuel wagering on horses.
Racing commission.
Appeals of decisions, §59.1-373.
Pay-per-call services.
Orders to compel, §59.1-433.
Public service corporation tax assessment review, §58.1-2670.1.
Public utilities, state operation.
Injunctions against violation of provisions, §56-525.
Racing commission.
Pari-mutuel wagering on horses.
Appeals of decisions, §59.1-373.
Real estate board.
Investigations of complaints.
Orders to compel, §55-79.99.
Release of liens, §43-68.
Road tax on motor carriers, appeals of penalties, §58.1-2709.
Service contracts, extended.
Orders to compel, §59.1-439.
Solicitation of charitable or civic contributions.
Obstruction of investigations, §57-59.
Subpoenas of ethics advisory panels of senate and house.
Application to Richmond circuit court, §30-115.
Travel clubs.
Orders to compel, §59.1-451.
Unemployment compensation.
Employer taxation.
Collection of taxes.
Injunctions, §60.2-522.
Evaluation of employing unit as employer, §60.2-500.
Venue.
See VENUE.
Vital records.
Amendment petitions, §32.1-269.
Disclosure petitions, §32.1-271.
Wills.
Probate.
Jurisdiction, §64.2-443.
Circuit court clerks.
Compensation and expenses, §17.1-288.
Employee liens.
Perfection, §43-25.
Mutual assurance society's liens, §43-66.
Supplier liens.
Perfection, §43-25.

RICHMOND —Cont'd
Coastal primary sand dunes and beaches.
Zoning ordinances, §28.2-1403.
Community revitalization, local funding, §15.2-958.5.
Confederate cemeteries and graves.
Disbursement of funds appropriated for upkeep, §10.1-2211.
Corporation court.
Recordation of documents.
When and where writings generally admitted to record, §55-106.
Credit union voluntary merger.
Further recordation not required in county, §6.2-1344.
District court.
Jurisdiction over offenses committed in Capitol Square, §18.2-124.
Economic development.
Community revitalization, local funding, §15.2-958.5.
Fingerprinting school employees, §22.1-296.2.
Fishing, tidal waters.
Regulations.
Publication, §28.2-209.
General district court.
Separate division maintained south of James river, §16.1-69.35.
Health spas.
Situs of investigation, §59.1-308.2.
Health, state board.
Meeting location, §32.1-6.
Improvements.
Taxes or assessments for local improvements.
Authority to impose, §15.2-2404.
Jail facilities, substandard.
Prisoner confinement limitations and transfers.
Court jurisdiction, §53.1-70.
James river.
Dams.
Restrictions, §29.1-532.
Library system.
Cooperative system for Henrico and Chesterfield counties and city of Richmond, §42.1-44.
Membership camping.
Situs of investigations, §59.1-334.
Pay-per-call services.
Situs of investigations, §59.1-433.
Port of Virginia economic and infrastructure development zone grant fund, §62.1-132.3:2.
Public defenders office.
Established, §19.2-163.04.
Public utilities, state operation.
Compensation to utilities.
Action venue, §56-522.
Injunctions against violation of provisions.
Action venue, §56-525.
Restoration of possession to utility.
Action venue, §56-521.
Revolutionary war cemeteries and graves.
Disbursement of funds appropriated for upkeep, §10.1-2211.1.
Sale of delinquent tax lands.
Special masters.
Appointment, special provisions applicable, §58.1-3970.1.
School board.
Fingerprinting applicants for employment, §22.1-296.2.
Salary of members, §22.1-32.

RICHMOND —Cont'd
Semi-automatic firearms and shotguns.
Carrying loaded firearms in public areas, §18.2-287.4.
Service contracts, extended.
Situs of investigations, §59.1-439.
Solicitation of charitable or civic contributions.
Investigation proceedings, §57-59.
State board of corrections.
Main office, §53.1-4.
Time-shares.
Board proceedings, §55-399.1.
Travel clubs.
Situs of investigations, §59.1-451.
Virginia war memorial carillon.
Agreement for use of, proceeds from use, §2.2-1130.
Voluntary property maintenance and zoning inspectors, §15.2-1132.
Water and sewage systems.
Lien for charges and taxes imposed, §15.2-2118.
Zoning.
Retail alcoholic beverage control licensees.
Special exception, review, change of ownership, §15.2-2286.

RICHMOND AMBULANCE AUTHORITY, 1991 ch 431.

RICHMOND COUNTY.
Coastal primary sand dunes and beaches.
Zoning ordinances, §28.2-1403.
Northern Neck Chesapeake Bay public access authority, §§15.2-6626 to 15.2-6651.
See NORTHERN NECK CHESAPEAKE BAY PUBLIC ACCESS AUTHORITY.
Northern Neck-Middle Peninsula public education consortium.
Inclusion in region, §22.1-354.6.
School board.
Salary of members, §22.1-32.

RICHMOND EYE AND EAR HOSPITAL AUTHORITY, 1970 ch 742, 1974 ch 64, 1977 ch 229.

RICHMOND METROPOLITAN AUTHORITY, §§15.2-7000 to 15.2-7021.
Board of directors.
Governance of authority, §15.2-7001.
Bond issues.
City of Richmond and counties of Henrico and Chesterfield, §15.2-7013.
Covenants to secure bonds, §15.2-7008.
Enforcement of bonds, §15.2-7010.
Facsimile signatures, §15.2-7003.
Issuance by resolution, §15.2-7003.
Negotiable instruments, §15.2-7010.
Payment of principal and interest, §§15.2-7003, 15.2-7005.
Rates and charges, §15.2-7004.
Refunding bonds.
Investment instruments, §15.2-7006.
Issuance and redemption, §15.2-7006.
Revenue bonds eligible for investment, §15.2-7009.
Tax-exempt status, §15.2-7011.
Trust agreements, §§15.2-7007, 15.2-7008.
Unclaimed money for payment principal and interest.
Reversion to state treasury, §15.2-7017.
Use and disposition of bond revenues, §15.2-7008.

RICHMOND METROPOLITAN AUTHORITY —Cont'd
City of Richmond and counties of Henrico and Chesterfield.
Acquisition of property, §15.2-7015.
Bond issues, §15.2-7013.
General powers, §15.2-7012.
Commonwealth transportation board.
Appointment of board of directors, §15.2-7001.
General powers, §15.2-7014.
Limited access toll highway.
Approval required by board, §15.2-7018.
Members on board of directors, §15.2-7001.
State highway maintenance and constructions funds.
Use for authority facilities, §15.2-7005.
Comptroller of the Commonwealth.
Custodian of accounts, §15.2-7017.
Conflict of laws.
Inconsistent laws, §§15.2-7019, 15.2-7020.
Construction of act.
Liberal construction, §15.2-7019.
Severability, §15.2-7020.
Contracts.
Covenants to secure bonds, §15.2-7008.
Police services, §15.2-7017.
Creation, §15.2-7001.
Definitions, §15.2-7000.
Limited access highway or highways.
Commonwealth transportation board.
Approval required by board, §15.2-7018.
Transfer to City of Richmond, §15.2-7016.
Powers of the authority, §15.2-7002.
Public body corporate and political subdivision, §15.2-7001.
Real property.
Acquisition of property, §15.2-7015.
Power of authority to exercise, §15.2-7002.

RICHMOND PROFESSIONAL INSTITUTE.
Virginia Commonwealth University.
General provisions, §§23-50.4 to 23-50.16.
See VIRGINIA COMMONWEALTH UNIVERSITY.
Transfer of property, rights, duties, etc., §23-50.5.

RICKETTSIAE.
Infectious biological substance crimes, §18.2-52.1.

RICO.
Virginia racketeer influenced and corrupt organization (RICO) act, §§18.2-512 to 18.2-517.
See RACKETEERING.

RIDERS.
Insurance policies and contracts.
Generally, §§38.2-300 to 38.2-326.
See INSURANCE POLICIES AND CONTRACTS.

RIDESHARING, §§46.2-1400 to 46.2-1407.
Inapplicability of laws.
Motor carriers, §46.2-1401.
Overtime compensation and minimum wage, §46.2-1406.
Workers' compensation, §46.2-1402.
Liability of employer, §§46.2-1402, 46.2-1403.
Motor vehicle liability coverage, renewal, §38.2-2217.1.
Motor vehicle registration.
Small vehicles rented for ridesharing, §46.2-695.

RIDESHARING —Cont'd
Municipal licenses and taxes, §46.2-1405.
Reduced transit fares, §46.2-1404.
Ridesharing arrangement, defined, §46.2-1400.
Ridesharing payments, §46.2-1404.
Shared ride taxi system, §15.2-949.
Special license plates for vehicles, §46.2-749.10.
Vehicles deemed not commercial vehicles or buses, §46.2-1407.

RIDING ANIMALS ON HIGHWAY.
After sunset, §46.2-800.1.
Controlled access highways, §46.2-808.
Fine schedule for violation, VA SCt Rule 3B:2.
Maximum fine for violating Title 46.2, §46.2-113.
Prepayment of fines for violations, §16.1-69.40:1.

RIFLES.
Concealed weapons and concealed handgun permits, §§18.2-307.1 to 18.2-308.015.
Criminal history background check, firearms transfers, §18.2-308.2:2.
Hunting restrictions, §§29.1-519, 29.1-528.
Sawed-off rifles generally, §§18.2-299 to 18.2-307.
Semiautomatic rifles.
Aliens, possession or transportation, §18.2-308.2:01.
Carrying loaded firearms in public areas, §18.2-287.4.
Children or minors, possession or transportation, §18.2-308.7.
Serial number or other identification.
Removing, altering, etc., §18.2-311.1.
Transportation of loaded rifle or shotgun.
Ordinances regulating, §15.2-915.2.
Use in commission of crime.
Forfeiture, §19.2-386.29.
Use or display in committing felony, §18.2-53.1.
Weapons generally.
See WEAPONS.
Weapons offenses generally.
See WEAPONS OFFENSES.

RIGHT OF ACCUSED TO TESTIFY, §19.2-268.

RIGHT OF ASSEMBLY, US Const Amd 1.

RIGHT OF ENTRY.
Agricultural stewardship.
Enforcement, §3.2-404.
Beekeeping.
Enforcement of provisions, §3.2-4409.
Boiler safety, §40.1-51.10.
Brownfields restoration and land renewal.
Abandoned sites, access to, §10.1-1236.
Voluntary remediation program, §10.1-1232.
Cemeteries.
Access to private cemeteries, §57-27.1.
Coal surface mining.
Abandoned mine reclamation, §§45.1-251, 45.1-263.
Condominiums.
Conversion condominiums, §55-79.94.
Cotton gin, cotton merchant or cotton warehouse.
Inspection by commissioner, §3.2-4769.
Descent and distribution.
Descent cast, §64.2-205.
Family residence rights, §64.2-307.
Distress.
Landlord and tenant.
Officer entry by force to levy or attach, §55-235.

RIGHT OF ENTRY —Cont'd
Dogs.
Commercial dog breeders.
Right of entry for inspections, §3.2-6507.3.
Eggs and hatchery products.
Agriculture and consumer services commissioner, §3.2-5310.
Eminent domain.
Abandonment of condemnation after entry, §25.1-225.
After filing of petition, §25.1-223.
Conditions for approval, §25.1-224.
Interest on award, §25.1-244.
Highways and roads, §§33.1-94, 33.1-120.
Inspection of property to be condemned, §25.1-203.
Request contained in petition, §25.1-207.
Sheriff's removal of forcible resistance, §25.1-246.
Title vested in petitioner, §25.1-237.
Erosion and sediment control.
VESCP authority, §62.1-44.15:60.
Evictions.
Limitation of suits against landlord, §55-248.
Farm produce sales.
Commission merchants.
Agriculture and consumer services commissioner, §3.2-4723.
Fire departments or companies, §27-17.
Fire investigations.
Remedying inflammable or unsafe conditions, §27-61.
State police, §27-58.
Fire marshals, local, §§27-32.1, 27-37.1.
Fire prevention code.
Conduct of inspections, examinations, testing or collection of samples, §27-98.4.
Enforcement, §27-98.1.
Fishing, tidal waters.
Health and sanitation provisions.
Enforcement, §28.2-802.
Gas companies.
Natural gas companies, §56-49.01.
Health commissioner, §32.1-25.
Highways and roads.
Eminent domain, §§33.1-94, 33.1-120.
Housing development authority.
Right to enter and inspect housing development, §36-55.34:1.
Husband and wife.
Rights of wife not affected by husband's acts only, §55-39.
Wife's right of entry into land inherited, §55-38.
Industrialized building safety.
Enforcement mechanism, §36-82.
Inspection warrants, toxic substances, §§19.2-393 to 19.2-397.
Landlord and tenant.
Abuse of access, §55-248.10:1.
Desertion by tenant, §55-224.
Distress.
Officer entry by force to levy or attach, §55-235.
Evictions, §§55-239 to 55-248.
Fees, §55-246.
Limitation of suits against landlord, §55-248.
Recordation, §55-245.
Reentry time limitations, §55-244.
Grantee rights, §55-217.
Lessee rights, §55-218.
Passing of power to grantees or devisees, §55-220.
Recovery of possession limited, §55-225.1.
Rent defaults, §55-225.

RIGHT OF ENTRY —Cont'd
Landlord and tenant —Cont'd
Residential landlords and tenants.
Absent tenants, §55-248.33.
Limitations to landlord recovery of possession, §55-248.36.
Maintenance failures by tenant, §55-248.32.
Residential tenant obligations to landlord, §55-248.18.
Lease-purchase agreements.
Prohibited practices, §59.1-207.22.
Married women's property rights.
Right of entry into land inherited, §55-38.
Rights not affected by husband's acts only, §55-39.
Mines and mining.
Adjacent property owners.
Survey rights, §45.1-161.311.
Motor vehicle emissions inspections.
Public or private property, §46.2-1187.1.
Natural gas companies, §56-49.01.
Oysters.
Surveyors, §28.2-557.
Plants and plant products inspection, §3.2-3806.
Refusal of entry, penalty, §3.2-3810.
Pressure vessel safety, §40.1-51.10.
Property rights of married women.
Right of entry into land inherited, §55-38.
Rights not affected by husband's acts only, §55-39.
Public building authority, §2.2-2276.
Radiation control.
Enforcement actions, §32.1-234.1.
Real estate cooperatives.
Conversion buildings, §55-487.
Schools and education.
Condemnation of land for school purposes, §22.1-127.
Small renewable energy projects.
Right of entry to inspect, §10.1-1197.10.
State police.
Fire investigations, §27-58.
State veterinarian, §3.2-6000.
Commercial dog breeders.
Right of entry for inspections, §3.2-6507.3.
Livestock and poultry contagious and infectious diseases, §3.2-6000.
Stormwater management.
Department, §62.1-44.15:39.
Surveyors.
Oysters, §28.2-557.
Tires.
Removal of waste tire piles, §10.1-1418.4.
Tobacco distributor's premises.
Inspection of records, §58.1-1021.04:2.
Water control board, §62.1-44.20.

RIGHT OF FIRST REFUSAL.
Real estate cooperatives.
Conversion buildings, §55-487.
Time-shares.
Conversion time-share projects, §55-374.

RIGHT OF TRIAL BY JURY, US Const Art III §2.
Jury trials generally.
See JURY TRIAL.

RIGHT SIDE OF HIGHWAY.
Driving on, §46.2-802.
Fine schedule for violations, VA SCt Rule 3B:2.
Maximum fine for violating Title 46.2, §46.2-113.
Prepayment of fines for violations, §16.1-69.40:1.

RIGHTS OF ACCUSED, VA Const Art I §8.
Certificates of analysis.
Right of accused to require testimony in lieu of certificate of analysis, §19.2-187.1.

RIGHTS OF ASSISTED LIVING FACILITIES RESIDENTS, §63.2-1808.

RIGHTS OF NURSING HOME PATIENTS, §§32.1-138 to 32.1-138.3.

RIGHTS OF PERSONS WITH DISABILITIES, §§51.5-40 to 51.5-46.
See DISABILITY OR HANDICAP.

RIGHTS-OF-WAY.
Cable TV companies, utility companies, public service corporations and political subdivisions.
Conveyance of right-of-way easements by state departments, agencies and institutions, §2.2-1151.
Conservation, small watersheds flood control and area development fund, §§10.1-648, 10.1-649.
Drainage projects, §21-331.
Railroads, §§21-360 to 21-363.
Eminent domain and damages.
Identification and acquisition of rights-of-way, §33.1-89.3.
Firearms.
Semi-automatic rifles, pistols and shotguns.
Carrying loaded firearms in public areas, §18.2-287.4.
Highway right-of-way fund.
Acquisition of properties for future use, §§33.1-137 to 33.1-143.
Motor vehicles. See within this heading, "Traffic regulations."
Pipelines, §56-259.
Liability exemption provisions, §56-260.1.
Public service companies.
Powers, §56-49.
Railroad drainage projects, §§21-360 to 21-363.
Renewable energy co-location of distribution facilities.
Occupation and use of rights-of-way by renewable generators, §67-1101.
Renewable generators, §56-259.
Telegraph or telephone companies, §56-463.
Public rights-of-way use fee, §56-468.1.
Reimbursement for relocation costs, §56-468.2.
Traffic regulations, §§46.2-820 to 46.2-829.
Demerit points, §46.2-492.
Designation of stop and yield right-of-way intersections, §46.2-1301.
Driver approaching or entering circular intersection, §46.2-822.
Driver on left to yield to driver on right entering intersection, §46.2-820.
Driver turning left to yield to oncoming vehicle, §46.2-825.
Fine schedule for violations, VA SCt Rule 3B:2.
Firehose, driving over, §46.2-922.
Following or parking near fire apparatus, §46.2-921.
Maximum fine for violating Title 46.2, §46.2-113.
Obeying yield right-of-way sign at intersection, §46.2-821.
Pedestrian, §46.2-924.
Prepayment of fine, §16.1-69.40:1.
Reckless driving, §46.2-863.

RIGHTS-OF-WAY —Cont'd
Traffic regulations —Cont'd
Stopping and yielding when approaching intersection of highway controlled by stop sign, §46.2-821.
Stopping and yielding when entering public highway or sidewalk from private road, §46.2-826.
Uncontrolled T intersections, §46.2-824.
Yielding or stopping when approaching intersection controlled by yield right-of-way sign, §46.2-821.
Yielding right-of-way to emergency vehicles, §46.2-829.
Yielding right of way to stationary emergency vehicles, §46.2-921.1.
Yielding to funeral procession under police escort, §46.2-828.
Yielding to left turning vehicle giving right-of-way automatic signal device, §46.2-825.
Yielding to pedestrian boarding or alighting from bus, §46.2-927.
Yielding to U.S. armed services, national guard, etc.
Members, §46.2-827.
Transportation board.
Furnishing information regarding right-of-way transactions, §33.1-16.

RIGHT TO ASSEMBLE PEACEFULLY, VA Const Art I §12.

RIGHT TO BAIL, §19.2-120.

RIGHT TO BEAR ARMS, VA Const Art I §13, US Const Amd 2.

RIGHT TO CARRY LAW.
Carrying concealed weapons, §18.2-308.

RIGHT TO COUNSEL, US Const Amd 6.
Administrative process act.
Hearings, §2.2-4020.
Adoption of children.
Withholding consent by birth parent.
Notice of right to be represented by counsel, §63.2-1203.
Appointment of counsel for accused, §§19.2-157 to 19.2-163.03.
Preliminary hearings.
Informing accused, §19.2-183.
Writ of actual innocence.
Hearings regarding, §19.2-327.3, VA SCt Rule 5:7B.

RIGHT TO DIE.
Anatomical gifts.
Advance health care directive, effect of gift, §32.1-291.21.
Living wills, §§54.1-2981 to 54.1-2993.
See LIVING WILLS.

RIGHT TO FARM ACT, §§3.2-300 to 3.2-302.
Defined terms, §3.2-300.
Nuisances, §3.2-302.
Purpose, §3.2-302.
Restrictive ordinances, prohibited, §3.2-301.

RIGHT TO HUNT, VA Const Art XI §4.

RIGHT TO PETITION FOR REDRESS OF GRIEVANCES, VA Const Art I §12, US Const Amd 1.

RIGHT TO PRIVACY ACT, §8.01-40.

RIGHT TO WORK, §§40.1-58 to 40.1-69.
Abstention from membership or officeholding in unions, §40.1-61.
Actions.
Recovery of unlawfully denied employment, §40.1-63.
Agreements designed to violate article, §40.1-65.
Application of provisions, §40.1-58.1.
Contracts, §40.1-64.
Contracts.
Application of article, §40.1-64.
Damages.
Recovery, §40.1-67.
Fees.
Employer not to require payment.
Labor organizations, §40.1-62.
Injunctions, §40.1-67.
Interpretation of provisions.
Agreements designed to violate article, §40.1-65.
Payment of union dues, §40.1-62.
Policy of article, §40.1-58.
Service of notice, process and other papers.
State corporation commissions as attorney for union, §40.1-68.
State corporation commission.
Service of notice, process and other papers, §40.1-68.
Unions.
Abstention from membership, §40.1-61.
Dues, §40.1-62.
Peaceful solicitation to join, §40.1-66.
Requirements, §40.1-60.
Unlawful agreements or combinations, §40.1-59.
Unlawfully denied employment, §40.1-63.
Violations of provisions.
Agreements to violate law, §40.1-65.
Conduct causing designated as illegal, §40.1-66.
Injunctions, §40.1-67.
Penalty, §40.1-69.
Yellow dog contracts, §40.1-61.

RIGHT-TURN ON RED, §46.2-835.

RIGHT, WRIT OF.
Abolished, §8.01-165.
Ejectment.
General provisions, §§8.01-131 to 8.01-165.
See EJECTMENT.

RIOT OR UNLAWFUL ASSEMBLY, §§18.2-404 to 18.2-414.2.
Banks.
Suspension of business during riots, §6.2-815.
Conduct constituting.
Riot, §18.2-405.
Unlawful assembly, §18.2-406.
Conspiracy to riot, §18.2-408.
Crimes by mobs, §§18.2-38 to 18.2-46.
Crossing police lines, etc., §18.2-414.2.
Discretionary felony sentencing guidelines, §17.1-805.
Dispersal of unlawful or riotous assemblies, §§18.2-411, 18.2-412.
Governor summoning law enforcement agencies, §18.2-410.
Immunity of officers and others in quelling riot or unlawful assembly, §18.2-412.
Incitement to riot, §18.2-408.
Injury to property or persons by persons unlawfully or riotously assembled, §18.2-414.

RIOT OR UNLAWFUL ASSEMBLY —Cont'd
Legal process.
Resisting or obstructing execution, §§18.2-409, 18.2-410.
Locality declared in state of riot or insurrection.
Commission of certain offenses, §18.2-413.
Locality regulating assemblies or movement of persons or vehicles, §15.2-925.
Mob crimes, §§18.2-38 to 18.2-46.
Obstructing free passage of others, §18.2-404.
Paramilitary activity unlawful, §§18.2-433.1 to 18.2-433.3.
Police lines or barricades, §§15.2-1714, 15.2-1744.
Preservation of peace.
Power of governor to summon law enforcement agencies, §18.2-410.
Rescue squads, obstructing members in performance of mission, §18.2-414.1.
Trust companies.
Suspension of business during riots, §6.2-1002.
Warning to disperse.
Remaining at place of riot or unlawful assembly after, §18.2-407.

RIPARIAN OYSTER-PLANTING GROUNDS.
Oyster planting grounds generally, §§28.2-600 to 28.2-650.
See OYSTER PLANTING GROUNDS.

RIPARIAN RIGHTS.
Buffers.
Riparian forest buffer protection for waterways tax credit, §58.1-339.10.
Clam planting grounds.
Owner rights to build bulkheads or wharves, §28.2-630.
Construction of provisions, §62.1-44.44.
Floodwater impoundment, §§62.1-107 to 62.1-115.
Application for leave to store, §62.1-107.
Board to examine, §62.1-109.
Court to hear and determine, §62.1-110.
Denial, §62.1-111.
Expiration of leave, §62.1-112.
Hearings, §62.1-108.
Application of provisions, §62.1-114.
Use of bed of watercourse, §62.1-113.
Use of water stored, §62.1-115.
Forest buffers.
Riparian forest buffer protection for waterways tax credit, §58.1-339.10.
Impoundment of surface waters, §§62.1-104 to 62.1-115.
See IMPOUNDMENT OF SURFACE WATERS.
Irrigation or watering of animals on riparian lands.
Conditions, §28.2-1203.
Oysters.
Building bulkheads or wharves, §28.2-630.
Sewing or planting, §28.2-629.
Potomac river, §§62.1-44.113 to 62.1-44.116.
Public service companies.
Powers, §56-49.
Shellfish.
Sewing or planting, §28.2-629.
Submerged lands.
Boundaries to extend to mean low-water mark, §28.2-1202.
Surface water management areas, §§62.1-242 to 62.1-253.
See SURFACE WATER MANAGEMENT AREAS.

RIPARIAN RIGHTS —Cont'd
Waterfowl blinds, §29.1-344.
Application of provisions, §29.1-350.
Forfeiture of rights, §29.1-345.
Stationary blinds, §29.1-344.1.
Time for obtaining, §29.1-344.2.

RISK-BASED CAPITAL FOR INSURERS, §§38.2-5500 to 38.2-5514.
See INSURANCE COMPANIES.

RISK MANAGEMENT INSURANCE.
Risk retention groups and purchasing groups, §§38.2-5100 to 38.2-5115.
See RISK RETENTION GROUPS AND PURCHASING GROUPS.

RISK MANAGEMENT PLAN FOR PUBLIC LIABILITY, §2.2-1837.

RISK OF LOSS.
Landlord and tenant.
Residential landlords and tenants.
Abandoned property by tenant, §55-248.38:1.
Leases, UCC, §8.2A-219.
Casualty to identified goods, §8.2A-221.
Default, §8.2A-220.
Preneed funeral contracts.
Stored supplies, §54.1-2820.
Sales, UCC.
Absence of breach, §8.2-509.
Casualty to identified goods, §8.2-612.
Effect of breach, §8.2-510.

RISK RETENTION GROUPS AND PURCHASING GROUPS, §§38.2-5100 to 38.2-5115.
Agents or brokers, duties, §38.2-5112.
Applicability of state laws, §38.2-5114.
Authority of state corporation commission, §38.2-5110.
Binding effect of orders issued in United States district courts, §38.2-5115.
Charter and license as liability insurance company.
Risk retention groups chartered in Commonwealth, §38.2-5102.
Definitions, §38.2-5101.
Equitable apportionment of liability insurance losses and expenses, participation in mechanism established, §38.2-5104.
Exemption of purchasing groups from laws relating to group purchase of insurance, §§38.2-5106, 38.2-5107.
Foreign risk retention groups, §38.2-5103.
Group purchase of insurance.
Exemption of insurers, §38.2-5107.
Purchasing groups exemptions, §38.2-5106.
Restrictions, §38.2-5109.
Licensing of risk retention groups, §38.2-1039.1.
Motor vehicle financial responsibility insurance law.
Groups not exempt from, §38.2-5113.
Notice requirements of purchasing groups, §§38.2-5103, 38.2-5108.
Penalties for violating chapter, §38.2-5111.
Plan of operation, approval by state corporation commission, §38.2-5102.
Powers of state corporation commission, §38.2-5110.
Property and casualty insurance guaranty association provisions.
Inapplicability of provisions of chapter to risk retention groups, §38.2-5104.

RISK RETENTION GROUPS AND PURCHASING GROUPS —Cont'd
Purposes of chapter, §38.2-5100.
Registration requirements of purchasing groups, §38.2-5108.
Restrictions on insurance purchased by purchasing groups, §38.2-5109.
Risk retention groups chartered in Commonwealth, §38.2-5102.
Risk retention groups not chartered in Commonwealth, §38.2-5103.
State laws, applicability to persons or corporations, §38.2-5114.
United States district courts, binding effect of orders issued, §38.2-5115.
Violations of chapter, §38.2-5111.

RIVANNA RIVER.
Rivanna river basin commission, §§62.1-69.45 to 62.1-69.52.
Budget, §62.1-69.49.
Chairpersons, §62.1-69.47.
Compensation, §62.1-69.48.
Definitions, §62.1-69.45.
Dissolution, §62.1-69.52.
Establishment, §62.1-69.46.
Expense reimbursement, §62.1-69.48.
Fiscal management, §62.1-69.49.
Meetings, §62.1-69.47.
Members, §62.1-69.47.
Powers and duties, §62.1-69.50.
Purpose, §62.1-69.46.
Staff support, §62.1-69.51.
Withdrawal of locality, §62.1-69.52.
Scenic river, §10.1-416.

RIVERS.
Annexation.
Boundary line where territory fronts river, §15.2-3210.
Big Sandy river.
Obstructing or dumping solid waste into, §62.1-194.3.
Boundaries.
Lawful fences constituted by, §§55-299 to 55-303.
Bulkheads, §§62.1-164, 62.1-165.
Casting solid waste into, §62.1-194.2.
Closing upon finding of toxic substances, §32.1-248.
Crab dredging restrictions, §28.2-707.
Dam construction across navigable streams.
Certain localities, §15.2-2142.
District court judges.
Jurisdiction over, §16.1-69.29.
Docks, §§62.1-164, 62.1-165.
Dredging sand and gravel, §§62.1-190 to 62.1-193.
Fences constituted by, §§55-299 to 55-303.
Fish consumption advisories, §32.1-248.01.
Hydroelectric power, §§62.1-80 to 62.1-103.
See HYDROELECTRIC POWER.
Impoundment of surface waters generally, §§62.1-104 to 62.1-115.
See IMPOUNDMENT OF SURFACE WATERS.
Landings, §§62.1-164, 62.1-165.
Menhaden taken with purse nets.
Area restrictions, §28.2-409.
Nets.
Distance extension restrictions, §28.2-309.
Piers, §§62.1-164, 62.1-165.
Potomac river basin commission, §§62.1-64 to 62.1-69.
See POTOMAC RIVER BASIN COMMISSION.

RIVERS —Cont'd
Rappahannock river basin commission, §§62.1-69.25 to 62.1-69.33:2.
Rivanna river basin commission, §§62.1-69.45 to 62.1-69.52.
Roanoke river basin bi-state commission, §§62.1-69.36 to 62.1-69.44.
Scenic rivers.
Generally, §§10.1-400 to 10.1-418.8.
See SCENIC RIVERS.
Submerged lands generally, §§28.2-1200 to 28.2-1213.
Surface water management areas, §§62.1-242 to 62.1-253.
Virginia Roanoke river basin advisory committee, §§62.1-69.34 to 62.1-69.35:2.
Waters of the state generally.
See WATERS OF THE STATE.
Wharves, §§62.1-164, 62.1-165.

RIVERSIDE REGIONAL JAIL AUTHORITY, 1990 ch 726, 1993 ch 228.

ROACH CLIPS.
Drug paraphernalia, §§18.2-265.1 to 18.2-265.5.

ROAD DISTRICTS.
District road bonds, §§33.1-321 to 33.1-335.
See DISTRICT ROAD BONDS.
Refunding bonds.
County providing for issuance for districts, §15.2-2649.

ROAD IMPACT FEES, §§15.2-2317 to 15.2-2329.
Adoption of impact fee and schedule, §15.2-2322.
Advisory committee.
Establishment prior to adoption of ordinance, §15.2-2319.
Amending impact fee, §15.2-2325.
Amount of impact fees imposed on specific development or subdivision, determining, §15.2-2323.
Applicability of provisions, §15.2-2317.
Urban transportation service districts, §15.2-2328.
Assessment of road improvement fees prior to adopting system of impact fees, §15.2-2321.
Authority to assess and impose, §15.2-2319.
Credits, §15.2-2324.
Definitions, §15.2-2318.
Maximum impact fee imposed, determining, §15.2-2323.
Public hearing road improvement plan, §15.2-2321.
Refund of impact fees, §15.2-2327.
Road improvement plan, §15.2-2321.
Updating, §15.2-2325.
Service areas to be established, §15.2-2320.
Updating plan and amending impact fee, §15.2-2325.
Urban transportation service districts.
Applicability of provisions, §15.2-2328.
Imposition of impact fees, §15.2-2329.
Use of proceeds, §15.2-2326.
When impact fees assessed and imposed, §15.2-2323.

ROADMAP FOR VIRGINIA'S FUTURE.
Council on Virginia's future, §§2.2-2683 to 2.2-2689.

ROAD RAGE.
Aggressive driving, §46.2-868.1.
Restricted permit to operate, issuance, §46.2-392.

ROAD RAGE —Cont'd
Aggressive driving —Cont'd
Suspension of driver's license, §46.2-392.

ROADSIDE STANDS.
Retail sales and use tax exemption.
Farm produce and egg sales, §58.1-609.2.

ROADS, STREETS AND PUBLIC RIGHTS OF WAY, §§15.2-2000 to 15.2-2030.
Abutting property owners to purchase fractional portion of public right of way and easements.
Condition to vacation or abandonment, §15.2-2008.
Acquisition in connection with changes, §15.2-2002.
Acquisition of land outside corporate limits, §15.2-2003.
Acquisitions, conveyances and transfers of property.
Transportation board.
Request to board for transfer to authority, §33.1-223.2:17.
Air space over public streets, public rights-of-way, etc.
Sale or lease, §15.2-2030.
Alteration and vacation, §15.2-2006.
Fee for processing application, §15.2-2007.
Fractional portion of public right-of-way and easements purchased by a abutting property owner, §15.2-2008.
Viewers, §15.2-2006.
Virginia Beach, §15.2-2007.1.
Appeal of alteration or vacation, §15.2-2006.
Bicycle paths.
Converting sidewalks to, §15.2-2001.
Closing rights-of-way temporarily to public use, §15.2-2013.
Public safety requiring, §15.2-2014.
Compensation for damages, §56-260.
Conditional vacation.
Recording after condition met, §15.2-2006.
Consent or franchise to used streets.
Occupying or using without consent, §15.2-2018.
Utilities not to use streets without consent, §15.2-2017.
Constructing, improving and maintaining streets, highways, etc., outside city or town, §15.2-2004.
Construction of public roads not in state highway or secondary system.
Expenditures by county, §15.2-2023.
Curb ramps.
Construction at intersections, §15.2-2021.
Dedication for public use.
Subdivision ordinance provision, §15.2-2241.
Bonding requirements for acceptance of dedication, §15.2-2241.1.
Dirt and gravel roads.
Maximum speed limit on nonsurface treated highways for certain counties, §46.2-873.1.
Disorderly conduct in public places, §18.2-415.
Display of numbers on buildings fronting public right-of-way, §15.2-2024.
District road bonds, §§33.1-321 to 33.1-335.
See DISTRICT ROAD BONDS.
Encroachments, §15.2-2009.
Awnings, fire escapes, shutters, etc., §15.2-2010.
Existing encroachments, §15.2-2011.
Fee for processing application to permit, §15.2-2012.
County manager plan of government, §15.2-743.

ROADS, STREETS AND PUBLIC RIGHTS OF WAY —Cont'd
Expansion or development of business.
Vacation to accommodate, §15.2-2006.
Expenditure of county revenues.
Road not in state highway system or secondary system, §15.2-2023.
Fee for processing application for alteration and vacation, §15.2-2007.
Firearms.
Discharging, §18.2-280.
Disqualification for concealed weapons permit, §18.2-308.09.
Semi-automatic rifles, pistols or shotguns.
Carrying loaded firearms in public areas, §18.2-287.4.
Shooting in or along street, §§18.2-286, 29.1-521.2.
Hunting, §29.1-521.2.
Franchise, privilege, lease or right to use city or town property, §§15.2-2100 to 15.2-2108.1:1.
Handbills, leaflets, literature, advertisements.
Distribution on highways, public roadways, medians.
Localities and VDOT may prohibit and regulate, §46.2-931.
Hay, coal, gasoline, explosives or other articles through streets.
Regulation of transportation, §15.2-2029.
Highway corporations, §§56-535 to 56-552.
See HIGHWAY CORPORATIONS.
Highways and roads generally.
See HIGHWAYS AND ROADS.
Hydroelectric power dams.
Eminent domain right, §62.1-98.
Improvement of navigability of streams.
City assurances to United States, §62.1-156.
Lights on public rights-of-way.
Installation by counties, §15.2-2020.
Limited access street, §15.2-2026.
Littering, §18.2-324.
Local road authorities, §§33.1-224 to 33.1-246.
See LOCAL ROAD AUTHORITIES.
Mobility impaired persons.
Curb ramps to be constructed at intersection, §15.2-2021.
Mud and debris upon highways and secondary highways within county boundary.
County ordinance regulating tracking, §15.2-2022.
Naming streets, roads and alleys, §15.2-2019.
Numbering of buildings fronting public right-of-way.
Display of numbers, §15.2-2024.
Obstruction or encroachment, §15.2-2009.
Awnings, fire escapes, shutters, etc., §15.2-2010.
Existing encroachment, §15.2-2011.
Fee for processing application, §15.2-2012.
Occupying or using streets without consent, §15.2-2018.
Official map, §§15.2-2233 to 15.2-2238.
Opening or maintaining through, on or over land belonging to Commonwealth, §15.2-2005.
Ordinance of vacation.
Recording as deeds recorded, §15.2-2006.
Outdoor advertising, §§33.1-351 to 33.1-381.
See OUTDOOR ADVERTISING.
Permits for use of streets of transportation and utilities, §15.2-2015.
Picketing.
Illegal picketing, §40.1-53.

ROADS, STREETS AND PUBLIC RIGHTS OF WAY —Cont'd
Pipelines, §§56-257 to 56-260.1.
Authority to permit, §56-258.
Liability exemption provisions, §56-260.1.
Manner of laying, §56-257.
Means of locating, §56-257.1.
Rights-of-way, §56-259.
Underground utility line damage prevention, §§56-265.14 to 56-265.32.
See UNDERGROUND UTILITY LINE DAMAGE PREVENTION.
Police, fire and rescue vehicle access to developments.
Regulating and controlling private roadways within residential development, §15.2-2027.
Powers and authority of locality generally, §15.2-2001.
Private roadways within multi-family residential developments.
Regulating and controlling, §15.2-2027.
Publication of notice to alter and vacate, §15.2-2006.
Public hearing on altering or vacating, §15.2-2006.
Public right-of-way defined, §15.2-2000.
Public transportation, use permits, §15.2-2015.
Railroad crossings.
Adjustments to trackage, §56-405.02.
Bells, §56-414.
Failure to signal, §§56-415, 56-416.
Cattle guards, §§56-429, 56-430.
Appeals of decisions, §56-435.
Discontinuance, §56-434.
Clearance requirements, §56-417.1.
Crossbucks, §56-405.2.
Similar signs prohibited, §56-408.
Gates, §§56-429, 56-430.
Generally, §§56-405 to 56-412.2.
See RAILROAD CROSSINGS.
Horns, §56-414.
Failure to signal, §§56-415, 56-416.
Maintenance, §56-405.
Agreements, §56-405.1.
Protective devices.
Installation of automatically operated devices, §56-406.1.
Maintenance cost of automatically operated devices, §56-406.2.
Signal boards, §56-405.2.
Similar signs prohibited, §56-408.
Whistles, §56-414.
Failure to signal, §§56-415, 56-416.
Ramps on curbs.
Construction and intersection, §15.2-2021.
Rates charged by person using streets.
Regulation by city or town, §15.2-2016.
Recording ordinance of vacation, §15.2-2006.
Regulation of traffic, §15.2-2028.
Repair of public roads not in state highway system or secondary system.
Expenditure by county, §15.2-2023.
Retail sales and use tax.
Machinery, tools and equipment brought into state for use in performing contracts, §§58.1-604.1 to 58.1-604.3.
Road impact fees, §§15.2-2317 to 15.2-2329.
See ROAD IMPACT FEES.
Sale of city or town property, VA Const Art VII §9.

ROADS, STREETS AND PUBLIC RIGHTS OF WAY —Cont'd
Sale of merchandise on highways, public roadways, medians.
Localities and VDOT may prohibit or regulate, §46.2-931.
Service districts, §§15.2-2400 to 15.2-2403.3.
Services render to public by persons using street.
Regulation by city or town, §15.2-2016.
Shooting in or along street, §§18.2-286, 29.1-521.2.
Hunting, §29.1-521.2.
Sidewalks.
Powers of locality generally, §15.2-2001.
Snow and ice removal.
Northern Virginia planning district date, §15.2-2025.
Solicitations of contributions on highways, public roadways, medians.
Localities and VDOT may prohibit and regulate, §46.2-931.
Spitting in public places, §18.2-322.
State highway system.
Inapplicability of provisions to highway, road, street or public right-of-way constituting part of, §15.2-2000.
State land.
Opening or maintaining through, on or over, §15.2-2005.
Stop and yield right-of-way intersections.
Designation by municipal governments, §46.2-1301.
Subdivisions and developments generally, §§15.2-2240 to 15.2-2279.
See SUBDIVISIONS.
Taxes or assessments for local improvements, §§15.2-2404 to 15.2-2413.
Telegraph or telephone companies.
Lines.
Endangering life or limb by stringing wires across other works, §56-468.
Erection, §56-458.
Consent of appropriate authorities, §56-460.
Franchises to occupy public ground, §56-462.
Height of, §56-466.
Location of, §56-466.
Relocation of, §§56-458.1, 56-459.
Restoring condition of ground, §56-467.
Temporarily closing rights-of-way to public use, §15.2-2013.
Public safety requiring, §15.2-2014.
Through traffic.
Limited access street, §15.2-2026.
Town jurisdiction over public rights of way lying within boundaries, §15.2-2000.
Tracking of mud and debris upon highways and secondary highways within county boundary.
County ordinance regulating, §15.2-2022.
Traffic regulations, §15.2-2028.
Transportation board.
Generally, §§33.1-1 to 33.1-23.
See TRANSPORTATION BOARD.
Transportation revenue bonds, §§33.1-267 to 33.1-295.
See TRANSPORTATION REVENUE BONDS.
Use permits, transportation and utilities, §15.2-2015.
Using or occupying streets without consent, §15.2-2018.

ROADS, STREETS AND PUBLIC RIGHTS OF WAY —Cont'd
Utilities, consent to use, §15.2-2017.
Utilities, use permits, §15.2-2015.
Vehicles for hire, use permits, §15.2-2015.
Viewers.
Alteration and vacation, §15.2-2006.
Virginia Beach, §15.2-2007.1.
Whole of lot or other subdivision acquired.
Remnant unsuitable of erection of building, §15.2-2002.

ROAD TAX ON MOTOR CARRIERS, §§58.1-2700 to 58.1-2712.2.
Amount of fuel used in Commonwealth, §58.1-2704.
Amount of tax, §58.1-2701.
Appeals.
Penalties, §58.1-2709.
Assistance of department of taxation, §58.1-2711.
Bond of motor carriers.
Refund to motor carriers giving bond, §58.1-2707.
False statements, §58.1-2710.
Cooperative agreements between states, §46.2-703.
Credit for payment of diesel fuel tax, §58.1-2706.
Credit for payment of liquefied gases tax, §58.1-2706.
Credit for payment of motor fuel tax, §58.1-2706.
False statements, §58.1-2710.
Definition, §58.1-2700.
Exemptions and exceptions, §58.1-2702.
False statements, §58.1-2710.
Identification markers, §58.1-2700.1.
Defined, §58.1-2700.
Placement, §58.1-2700.2.
Inspection of books and records, §58.1-2708.
International fuel tax agreement, §58.1-2712.1.
Information exchanges under agreement, §58.1-2712.2.
Licenses, §58.1-2700.1.
Motor carriers, property.
Licensees, permittees and certificate holders.
Registration, §46.2-2108.5.
Payment, §58.1-2703.
Penalties, §58.1-2709.
Records.
Inspection, §58.1-2708.
Refunds to motor carriers giving bond, §58.1-2707.
False statements, §58.1-2710.
Reports, §58.1-2705.
Supreme court.
Appeals by motor carriers, §58.1-2709.
Waiver of provisions, §58.1-2700.3.

ROADWAY LITTER PICK-UP PROGRAM FOR PROBATIONERS.
Civil immunity, §8.01-226.8.

ROANOKE.
Bar examinations, §54.1-3927.
Blue Ridge regional tourism council, §§2.2-2609, 2.2-2610.
Circuit court, establishment, §17.1-500.
Confederate cemeteries and graves.
Disbursement of funds appropriated for upkeep, §10.1-2211.

ROANOKE —Cont'd
Mental health clinics.
Employees of state mental health clinics.
Supplementation of salaries and reimbursement of travel expenses, §15.2-1508.4.
Outdoor performing arts amphitheater, area or similar facility.
Retail on-premises wine and beer license, §4.1-209.
Public defenders office.
Established, §19.2-163.04.
Real property taxes.
Energy-efficient buildings for tax purposes, classification of, §58.1-3221.2.
Improvements to real property, classification, §58.1-3221.1.
School board.
Fingerprinting applicants for employment, §22.1-296.2.
Salary of members, §22.1-32.
Water and sewage systems.
Lien for charges and taxes imposed, §15.2-2118.
Western Virginia public education consortium.
Inclusion in western Virginia, §22.1-354.1.

ROANOKE CITY DEVELOPMENT AUTHORITY.
Generally.
See ECONOMIC DEVELOPMENT AUTHORITIES.

ROANOKE COUNTY.
Agricultural and forestal districts.
County executive form and certain other counties, §§15.2-4400 to 15.2-4407.
Blue Ridge regional tourism council, §§2.2-2609, 2.2-2610.
Confederate cemeteries and graves.
Disbursement of funds appropriated for upkeep, §10.1-2211.
Cutting grass or lawn area of residential real property.
Requiring owner of occupied property, §15.2-1215.
Mines and minerals.
Presumed to exist in certain lands, §55-154.
Suits to extinguish claim or right, §55-155.
Revolutionary war cemeteries and graves.
Disbursement of funds appropriated for upkeep, §10.1-2211.1.
School board.
Fingerprinting applicants for employment, §22.1-296.2.
Salary of members, §22.1-32.
Subdivisions.
Expedited land development review procedures, §15.2-2263.
Tax map reference number.
Circuit court clerk indexing by, §17.1-252.
Transient occupancy tax.
Disposition of revenues, §58.1-3819.1.
Unsafe vehicles.
Law enforcement officers certified to perform vehicle safety inspections, §46.2-1001.
Western Virginia public education consortium.
Inclusion in western Virginia, §22.1-354.1.

ROANOKE COUNTY DEVELOPMENT AUTHORITY.
Generally.
See ECONOMIC DEVELOPMENT AUTHORITIES.

ROANOKE HIGHER EDUCATION AUTHORITY, §§23-231.13 to 23-231.18, 1997 ch 813.

ROANOKE HIGHER EDUCATION CENTER.
Executive director, staff, §23-231.17.

ROANOKE REGIONAL AIRPORT COMMISSION, 1986 ch 140, 1996 ch 385.

ROANOKE RIVER.
Scenic river, §10.1-418.

ROANOKE RIVER BASIN.
Preparation of plans and programs for management, §62.1-44.38.
Roanoke river basin bi-state commission, §§62.1-69.36 to 62.1-69.44.
Virginia Roanoke river basin advisory committee, §§62.1-69.34 to 62.1-69.35:2.

ROANOKE RIVER BASIN BI-STATE COMMISSION, §§62.1-69.36 to 62.1-69.44.
Ad hoc committees, §62.1-69.40.
Authority to establish, §62.1-69.39.
Appropriations.
Annual budget, §62.1-69.42.
Audits.
Annual audit, §62.1-69.42.
Budget.
Annual budget, §62.1-69.42.
Compensation of members, §62.1-69.43.
Composition, §62.1-69.38.
Cooperation by state agencies, §62.1-69.41.
Definitions, §62.1-69.36.
Duties, §62.1-69.39.
Established, §62.1-69.37.
Fiscal agent.
Designation, §62.1-69.42.
Funding, §62.1-69.42.
Members, §62.1-69.38.
Compensation and expenses, §62.1-69.43.
Powers, §62.1-69.39.
Purpose, §62.1-69.37.
Reports.
Annual report, §62.1-69.44.
Independent reports to commission, §62.1-69.38.
Staffing, §62.1-69.41.
Standing committees, §62.1-69.40.
Authority to establish, §62.1-69.39.

ROANOKE TECHNICAL INSTITUTE, §§23-135.8 to 23-135.11.

ROBBERY, §18.2-58.
Bank robbery, §18.2-93.
Capital murder, killing in commission of, §18.2-31.
Carjacking, §18.2-58.1.
Convicted ineligible for furloughs, §53.1-38.
Discretionary felony sentencing guidelines, §17.1-805.
District court offices, personal liability of judge.
Reimbursement by committee on district courts, §16.1-69.33.
Entering dwelling with intent to commit, §18.2-90.
First degree murder, killing in commission of, §18.2-32.
Interception of wire, electronic or oral communication.
Order authorizing.
When attorney general may apply, §19.2-66.

ROBBERY —Cont'd
Juvenile proceeding confidentiality exception.
Commission of delinquent act which would be felony if committed by adult, §16.1-309.1.
Juvenile serious offenders, §16.1-285.1.
Release and review hearings, §16.1-285.2.
Serious or habitual offender comprehensive action program (SHOCAP), §§16.1-330.1, 16.1-330.2.
Magistrate's office, personal liability of magistrate.
Reimbursement by committee on district courts, §16.1-69.33.
Mob crimes, §18.2-42.1.
Possession of burglarious tools, prima facie evidence of intent to commit, §18.2-94.
Prisoner work release programs.
Eligibility, §53.1-62.
Sentence of person twice previously convicted of certain violent felonies, §19.2-297.1.

ROBERT E. LEE MEMORIAL ASSOCIATION, INCORPORATED.
Continuation of association, §57-6.
Stratford, Westmoreland County.
Appropriations for development, §10.1-2212.

ROBERT E. LEE MEMORIAL FOUNDATION.
Property tax exemption, §58.1-3607.

ROCKBRIDGE, CITY OF.
Revolutionary war cemeteries and graves.
Disbursement of funds appropriated for upkeep, §10.1-2211.1.

ROCKBRIDGE COUNTY.
Automobile graveyards, screening ordinance, §15.2-903.
Blue Ridge regional tourism council, §§2.2-2609, 2.2-2610.
Confederate cemeteries and graves.
Disbursement of funds for upkeep, §10.1-2211.
Fingerprinting school employees, §22.1-296.2.
Public defenders office.
Established, §19.2-163.04.
School board.
Fingerprinting applicants for employment, §22.1-296.2.
Salary of members, §22.1-32.
Staggered terms for elected board, §22.1-57.3:1.
Transient occupancy tax.
Additional transient occupant tax, §58.1-3825.
Disposition of revenues, §58.1-3819.

ROCK CLIMBING.
Duty of care and liability for damages of landowners to participants, §29.1-509.

ROCK DUST.
Workers' compensation.
Death benefits, §65.2-513.
Special provisions, §65.2-514.
Notice to employee, §65.2-405.

ROCKFISH RIVER.
Scenic river, §10.1-415.1.

ROCKINGHAM COUNTY.
Agricultural and forestal districts.
County executive form and certain other counties, §§15.2-4400 to 15.2-4407.
Cutting grass or lawn area of residential real property.
Requiring owner of occupied property, §15.2-1215.
Mines and minerals.
Presumed to exist in certain lands, §55-154.
Suits to extinguish claim or right, §55-155.

ROCKINGHAM COUNTY —Cont'd
Outdoor performing arts amphitheater, area or similar facility.
Retail on-premises wine and beer license, §4.1-209.
Real property taxes.
Special assessment for land preservation.
Additional provisions concerning zoning classification, §58.1-3237.1.
Revolutionary war cemeteries and graves.
Disbursement of funds appropriated for upkeep, §10.1-2211.1.
School board.
Salary of members, §22.1-32.
Shenandoah valley regional airport commission, 1956 ch 628, 1958 ch 396, 1978 ch 18, 1988 ch 209, 1994 ch 773.
Small claims court authorized, §16.1-122.1.
Unsafe vehicles.
Law enforcement officers certified to perform vehicle safety inspections, §46.2-1001.
Water and sewage systems.
Lien for charges and taxes imposed, §15.2-2118.
Mandatory connection, §15.2-2110.

RODENT DISEASES, VECTOR CONTROLS, §32.1-247.

RODEOS.
Equine activity liability act, §§3.2-6200 to 3.2-6203.
See HORSES.

ROHYPNOL.
Date rape drug.
Possession and distribution, enhanced penalty, §18.2-251.2.
Possession and distribution.
Enhanced penalty, §18.2-251.2.

ROLLBACK TAXES.
Correction of erroneous local taxes.
Correction by commissioner, §58.1-3981.
Real estate tax special assessment for land preservation.
Change in use or zoning of real estate, §58.1-3237.

ROLLER SKATING.
Attaching to vehicle on highway, §46.2-932.
Locality prohibiting roller skating on sidewalks or crosswalks, §46.2-904.
Tailgating vehicles by pedestrians, §46.2-932.

ROLLING STOCK.
Railroad cars.
See RAILROADS.
Recordation tax, state.
Sales contracts, §§58.1-808, 58.1-809.

ROLLING STOCK TAX, §§58.1-2652 to 58.1-2659.
See PUBLIC SERVICE CORPORATION TAXATION.

ROLL-YOUR-OWN CIGARETTE MACHINES.
Excise tax on cigarettes, §58.1-1003.3.

ROLL-YOUR-OWN TOBACCO.
Excise tax on cigarettes.
Amount constituting one cigarette, §58.1-1000.
Generally, §§58.1-1000 to 58.1-1022.
See CIGARETTE TAX.
Invoice, manufacturers, stamping agents, §58.1-1003.2.
Payment, §58.1-1003.2.
Rate of tax, §58.1-1001.
Return, §58.1-1003.2.

ROLL-YOUR-OWN TOBACCO —Cont'd
Excise tax on cigarettes —Cont'd
Stamping process, §58.1-1003.2.

RONALD REAGAN WASHINGTON NATIONAL AIRPORT.
Arlington county.
Jurisdiction of police force, §5.1-158.
Metropolitan Washington airports authority.
Acquisition from United States, authorization, §5.1-154.
Generally, §§5.1-152 to 5.1-177.
See METROPOLITAN WASHINGTON AIRPORTS AUTHORITY.

ROOFIES.
Possession and distribution.
Enhanced penalty, §18.2-251.2.

ROOFING CONTRACTORS.
Building code, §§36-97 to 36-119.1.
See BUILDING CODE.

ROOFING SHEATHING.
New home construction.
Fire-retardant treated plywood used in lieu of fire-retardant plywood.
Vendee's action for breach of manufacturer's warranty, §55-70.1.

ROOF, RIBS AND FACES, UNDERGROUND COAL MINES.
Safety requirements, §§45.1-161.108 to 45.1-161.119.

ROOFTOPS.
Green roofing.
Incentives and regulatory flexibility, §58.1-3852.
Throwing objects from places higher than one story.
Reckless endangerment, §18.2-51.3.

ROOMING HOUSES.
Smoke detectors.
Locality requiring, §15.2-922.

ROTARY INTERNATIONAL.
Special license plates, §46.2-746.7.

ROTARY TRAFFIC ISLANDS, §46.2-807.
Circular intersections, path of travel, §46.2-807.
Fine schedule, VA SCt Rule 3B:2.
Maximum fine for violating Title 46.2, §46.2-113.

ROUND THE MOUNTAIN.
Southwest Virginia cultural heritage foundation, §§2.2-2734 to 2.2-2737.

ROUTINE PRACTICE, §8.01-397.1.

ROYALTIES.
Music licensing fees, §§59.1-460 to 59.1-466.
See MUSIC LICENSING FEES.
Securities generally, §§13.1-501 to 13.1-527.3.
See SECURITIES.

RUBELLA.
Immunization.
Required immunization of children, §32.1-46.
Virginia immunization information system (VIIS), §32.1-46.01.

RUDEE INLET AUTHORITY, 1960 ch 227.

RULE AGAINST GOVERNING BODIES.
Judicial sales.
Awarding rule against special commissioner, purchaser, etc., for judgment for amounts due, §§8.01-105 to 8.01-108.
Execution, §8.01-105.

RULE AGAINST GOVERNING BODIES —Cont'd
Judicial sales —Cont'd
Awarding rule against special commissioner, purchaser, etc., for judgment for amounts due —Cont'd
Hearing, §8.01-106.
Issuance, §8.01-105.
Rendering of judgment, §8.01-106.
Trial by jury of issues, §8.01-107.
When sureties proceeded against by rule, §8.01-108.

RULE AGAINST JUDGMENT FOR AMOUNT DUE, §§8.01-105 to 8.01-108.

RULE AGAINST PERPETUITIES, §55-13.3.
Cemeteries.
Disposition of property for maintenance and care.
In perpetuity allowed, §57-31.
Condominiums.
Validity of condominium instruments, §55-79.52.
Determination of lives in being, §55-13.2.
Employee trusts, §55-13.1.
Horizontal property regimes, §55-79.36.
Real estate cooperatives, §55-440.
Trusts of real estate, §55-17.1.
Uniform statutory rule against perpetuities, §§55-12.1 to 55-12.6.
Applicability, §§55-12.5, 55-12.6.
Construction and interpretation, §55-12.6.
Effective date, §55-12.5.
Exclusions, §55-12.4.
General rule, §55-12.1.
Nonvested property interest or power of appointment.
Time of creation, §55-12.2.
Reformation, §55-12.3.
Remedies.
Reformation, §55-12.3.
Time of creation of nonvested property interest or power of appointment, §55-12.2.

RULE 11 SANCTION.
Signing of pleadings, §8.01-271.1.

RULE IN SHELLEY'S CASE.
Abolishment of rule, §55-14.

RULE OF 78, §6.2-403.
Applicability, §6.2-405.
Notice on loan or sale of credit using method, §6.2-402.

RULE ON WITNESSES, VA SCt Rule 2:615.
Civil trials, §8.01-375.
Criminal trials, §§19.2-265.01, 19.2-265.1, 19.2-265.5.
Preliminary hearing, §19.2-187.1.

RULES AND REGULATIONS.
Administrative process generally, §§2.2-4000 to 2.2-4031.
Families, stability and autonomy.
Consideration in developing state agency regulations, §2.2-606.
Jamestown-Yorktown foundation.
Adoption of regulations, §23-289.
Juvenile delinquency.
Interstate compact relating to juveniles, §16.1-323.
Metropolitan Washington airports authority, §5.1-157.
Mortgage loan originators, §6.2-1720.
One-stop small business permitting program, §2.2-1617.

RULES AND REGULATIONS —Cont'd
One-stop small business permitting program (eff until 1/1/2014), §2.2-904.1.
Schools and education.
Nutritional guidelines for competitive foods sold to students.
Promulgation of regulations, §22.1-207.4.

RULES OF COURT, ADOPTION BY SUPREME COURT.
Authority, §8.01-3.
Availability, §8.01-3.
Effective date, §8.01-3.
Evidence rules.
Authority, submission to code commission, §8.01-3.
Modification or annulment.
Enactment by general assembly, §8.01-3.
Publication, §8.01-3.
Variance with enactment of general assembly.
Enactment given effect, §8.01-3.

RULES OF STATUTORY CONSTRUCTION.
See STATUTORY CONSTRUCTION.

RULES OF THE ROAD.
Traffic regulation generally, §§46.2-800 to 46.2-947.
See TRAFFIC INFRACTIONS.

RULE TO SHOW CAUSE.
Local treasurer securing final discharge from liability, §58.1-3146.
Nonlawyer not allowed to issue, §16.1-88.03.

RUNAWAYS.
Arrest of child, §16.1-246.
Interstate compact relating to juveniles, §§16.1-323, 16.1-323.1.

RUNNERS.
Attorneys.
Unlawful solicitation of professional employment, §§54.1-3941, 54.1-3943.

RUNNING AT LARGE, §§55-202 to 55-206.
Counties preventing animals running at large on highways, §15.2-1218.
Estrays and drift property generally, §§55-202 to 55-210.
General assembly power to regulate stock, VA Const Art IV §14.
No-fence law.
Animal restrictions, §55-316.
Permitting animals to run at large in county under quarantine, §18.2-121.1.
Unincorporated communities and villages, §§55-323 to 55-330.
See ANIMALS RUNNING AT LARGE.

RUNNING RED LIGHT, §46.2-805.
Fine schedule, VA SCt Rule 3B:2.
Maximum fine for violating Title 46.2, §46.2-113.
Prepayment of fines, §16.1-69.40:1.

RURAL COMMUNITIES.
Center for rural Virginia, §§2.2-2720 to 2.2-2724.
See CENTER FOR RURAL VIRGINIA.
Economic development partnership authority.
Powers and duties.
Special services, §2.2-2238.1.
Strategic plan for rural communities, §2.2-2238.1.

RURAL ENTERPRISE ZONES.
Generally, §§59.1-279 to 59.1-284.01.
See ENTERPRISE ZONES.

RURAL HEALTH PLAN, §32.1-122.07.

RURAL HOSPITALS.
Designation as, §§32.1-122.07, 32.1-125.3.

RURAL HOUSING PROJECTS.
Fair housing law, §§36-96.1 to 36-96.23.
See FAIR HOUSING.
Farmers of low income, §§36-36 to 36-38.
Homestead exemption, §36-37.
Housing applications by farmers, §36-38.
Powers of county and regional authorities, §§36-36, 36-37.
Tenant selection limitations, §36-37.
Housing development authority.
General provisions, §§36-55.24 to 36-55.52.
See HOUSING DEVELOPMENT AUTHORITY.
Housing revitalization zones, §§36-157 to 36-170.
See HOUSING REVITALIZATION ZONES.

RURAL MAIL CARRIERS.
Stopping on highways.
Exemption to prohibition, §46.2-892.

RURAL REHABILITATION CORPORATION.
Asset return and administration, §§3.2-600 to 3.2-604.

RURAL RUSTIC ROADS.
Designation, §33.1-70.1.
Maximum speed limit on, §46.2-873.2.

RURITAN NATIONAL.
Motor vehicle license plates.
Special license plates for members, §46.2-746.7.

RUSSELL COUNTY.
Cumberlands airport commission, 1958 ch 439.
Dams.
Restrictions, §29.1-532.
Electric utility restructuring.
Transmission and distribution of electric energy.
Applicability of provisions suspended, §56-580.
Industrial development authority.
Board of supervisors.
Appointment of members to board of authority, §15.2-4904.
Revolutionary war cemeteries and graves.
Disbursement of funds appropriated for upkeep, §10.1-2211.1.
School board.
Salary of members, §22.1-32.
Virginia coalfield economic development authority, §§15.2-6000 to 15.2-6015.

RUSSELL FORK STATE SCENIC RIVER, §10.1-411.2.

RYE.
Generally, §§3.2-2200 to 3.2-2214.
See SMALL GRAINS.

S

SABBATICAL LEAVE.
Public officers and employees.
Benefits based on employment, §60.2-615.

SACRAMENTAL WINE.
Schools and education.
Drinking or possessing alcoholic beverages in or on public school grounds, §4.1-309.
Winery licenses.
Authorized conduct, §4.1-207.

SADOMASOCHISM.
Obscenity and related offenses generally, §§18.2-372 to 18.2-388.
See OBSCENITY AND RELATED OFFENSES.

SAFE BOATING, §§29.1-734 to 29.1-746.

SAFE-DEPOSIT BOXES, §§6.2-2300 to 6.2-2314.
See SAFE-DEPOSIT OR STORAGE BUSINESSES.

SAFE-DEPOSIT OR STORAGE BUSINESSES, §§6.2-2300 to 6.2-2314.
Abandonment of property presumption, §55-210.3:3.
Intangible interest in business associations, §55-210.6:1.
Property of dissolved associations, §55-210.7.
Refunds, §55-210.6:2.
Co-lessee.
Removal of attached property.
Effect, §6.2-2304.
Cumulative remedy, §6.2-2314.
Death of sole lessee.
Limited access to safe deposit box, §6.2-2302.
Documents.
Pretium affectionis, §6.2-2313.
Garnishment.
Denying access to box, §§6.2-2301, 6.2-2304.
Incapacity of sole lessee.
Limited access to safe deposit boxes, §6.2-2303.
Joint use, §6.2-2301.
Lease-purchase agreements.
Application of provisions, §59.1-207.19.
Lessee's right to contents after opening, §6.2-2309.
Limited access to safe deposit box.
Death of lessee, §6.2-2302.
Incapacity of lessee, §6.2-2302.
Marking contents when box opened, §6.2-2306.
Notary public.
Certificate, §6.2-2308.
Duties when box opened after notice, §§6.2-2306, 6.2-2307.
Notice.
Lessee notified that safe or box will be opened for nonpayment of rent, §6.2-2305.
Lien of fieri facias.
Denying access to box, §6.2-2304.
Opening after notice, §§6.2-2306, 6.2-2308.
Opening box after notice.
Certificate of notary public as evidence, §6.2-2308.
In presence of notary public, §6.2-2306.
Packages or boxes stored in vault.
Sale after rental unpaid for three years, §6.2-2312.
Recovery of debt beyond proceeds of sale of contents of box, §§6.2-2300 to 6.2-2314.
Rental for packages stored in vault unpaid for three years, §6.2-2312.
Sale of contents for nonpayment of rent, §§6.2-2310, 6.2-2311.
Disposition of proceeds of sale, §6.2-2311.
Storage by bank after box opened, §6.2-2307.
Unclaimed property, disposition of, §55-210.3:3.
Intangible interest in business associations, §55-210.6:1.
Property of dissolved associations, §55-210.7.
Records, §§55-210.24 to 55-210.24:2.
Refunds, §55-210.6:2.

SAFE DRINKING WATER ACT.
Laboratories mandated by federal act.
Inspection and certification program.
Division of consolidated laboratory services to establish, §2.2-1104.
State programs to implement, §§2.2-617, 2.2-618.

SAFE HAVEN LAW.
Causing or encouraging acts rendering children, delinquent, abused, etc.
Leaving infant with hospital or rescue squad.
Defense to prosecution, §18.2-371.
Child abuse and neglect.
Leaving infant with hospital or rescue squad.
Defense to prosecution, §18.2-371.1.

SAFEKEEPING OF WILLS, §64.2-409.

SAFETY.
Amusement devices.
Rider safety, §§59.1-519 to 59.1-524.
Natural gas utilities.
Recovery of eligible safety activity costs, §56-235.10.
School safety center, §9.1-184.

SAFETY BELTS.
Bus drivers.
Requirement to wear, §46.2-1091.
Child restraint devices, §§46.2-1095 to 46.2-1100.
Immunity of volunteer installers or inspectors, §8.01-226.5.
Combination lap belt and shoulder harness, §§46.2-1092, 46.2-1093.
Front seat occupants.
Required use, §46.2-1094.
Installation, §§46.2-1092, 46.2-1093.
Lap belts, §§46.2-1092, 46.2-1093.
Maximum fine for violating Title 46.2, §46.2-113.
Shoulder harnesses, §§46.2-1092 to 46.2-1094.
Uniform fine schedule for violations, VA SCt Rules 3B:2, 3C:1, 3C:2.
Use in lieu of child restraint devices.
Permitted use of standard seat belt, §46.2-1100.

SAFETY GLASS.
Absence of required safety glass on motor vehicle, §46.2-1056.
Fine schedule, VA SCt Rule 3B:2.
Maximum fine for violating Title 46.2, §46.2-113.
Moped safety equipment, §46.2-915.2.

SAFETY INSPECTIONS, MOTOR VEHICLES, §§46.2-1157 to 46.2-1175.1.
See MOTOR VEHICLE SAFETY INSPECTIONS.

SAFETY ZONES, DRIVING THROUGH, §46.2-814.
Fine schedule, VA SCt Rule 3B:2.
Maximum fine for violating Title 46.2, §46.2-113.
Prepayment of fine, §16.1-69.40:1.

SAILBOATS.
Watercraft sales and use tax, §§58.1-1400 to 58.1-1410.
See WATERCRAFT SALES AND USE TAX.

SAILORS.
Acknowledgments, §§55-113 to 55-115.
Who may perform notarial acts, §55-118.1.
Naval militia generally, §§44-55 to 44-74.
See NAVAL MILITIA.
Wills.
Personalty, disposition of, §64.2-408.
Presumption of formal execution, §64.2-408.

ST. MARY'S RIVER.
Scenic river, §10.1-418.2.

SAINT PAUL.
Industrial development authority.
Board of supervisors.
Appointment of members to board of authority, §15.2-4904.

SALARIES.
Budget of state.
Budget bill, contents, §2.2-1509.
Circuit court clerks, §17.1-287.
Circuit court judges, §17.1-523.
Comparability to private sector, §2.2-1202.
Emergency medical technicians.
Overtime compensation, §§9.1-700 to 9.1-706.
Firefighters.
Overtime compensation, §§9.1-700 to 9.1-706.
Garnishment.
General provisions, §§8.01-511 to 8.01-525.
See GARNISHMENT.
General assembly.
Powers as to salaries of public officers, VA Const Art IV §14.
Goals.
Comparability to private sector, §2.2-1202.
Human resources management department.
Duties, §2.2-1201.
Income tax withholding, §§58.1-460 to 58.1-486.3.
See INCOME TAX WITHHOLDING.
Law enforcement officers.
Enforcement of motor vehicles title.
Officers to be paid fixed salaries, §46.2-102.
Overtime compensation, §§9.1-700 to 9.1-706.
Local constitutional officers.
Generally, §§15.2-1636.1 to 15.2-1636.20.
See LOCAL CONSTITUTIONAL OFFICERS.
Local school boards.
Annual salary of members, §22.1-32.
Mine rescue crews, §45.1-161.292:44.
Public officers and employees.
Administration, §2.2-1201.
Changes in rate of pay.
Prerequisites, §2.2-2901.
Goals, §2.2-1202.
Income withholding.
Liability for debt owed to Commonwealth, §2.2-2816.
Increases in salaries.
Procedure, §2.2-2815.
Members of boards, commissions, committees, councils and other collegial bodies, §2.2-2813.
Method of payment, §2.2-2814.
Time of payment, §2.2-2814.
Wage assignments.
Liability for debt owed to Commonwealth, §2.2-2816.
Supreme court clerk and deputy clerk, §17.1-325.
Withholding income tax, §§58.1-460 to 58.1-486.3.
See INCOME TAX WITHHOLDING.

SALEM.
Blue Ridge regional tourism council, §§2.2-2609, 2.2-2610.
Circuit court, establishment, §17.1-500.
Circuit court of county to constitute circuit court of city.
Inapplicability of provision to Salem, §17.1-505.
Confederate cemeteries and graves.
Disbursement of funds appropriated for upkeep, §10.1-2211.
School board.
Salary of members, §22.1-32.

SALEM, CITY OF.
Western Virginia public education consortium.
Inclusion in western Virginia, §22.1-354.1.

SALE OF DELINQUENT TAX LANDS,
§§58.1-3965 to 58.1-3975.
Additional authority to sell, §58.1-3965.1.
Certain special delinquent taxes or special assessments, §58.1-3965.2.
Alternative dispute resolution, circuit court option to refer, §58.1-3965.
Attorney employed to sale, §58.1-3969.
Attorney, employment to institute proceedings, §58.1-3966.
Attorneys' fees, §58.1-3969.
Bill in equity, institution of proceedings, §58.1-3967.
Bond of attorney to institute proceedings, §58.1-3966.
Commissioner in chancery.
Referral of case to, §58.1-3969.
Community development authorities.
Additional authority to sell land in, §58.1-3965.2.
County, city, etc., may purchase, §58.1-3970.
Drainage projects.
Acquisition of land by board of viewers, §21-385.
Consequences of change of ownership, §21-389.
Deed to purchaser, §21-387.
Delinquent tax assessments, §§21-375, 21-376.
Laws governing sales, §§21-386, 21-390.
Notice of sale, §21-377.
Payments of interest in principals of bond, §21-388.
Place of sale.
When land lies in more than one county, §21-378.
Redemption.
Board of viewers to pay treasurer, §21-384.
Deed on failure to redeem, §21-392.
Notice, §21-391.
Repayment to purchaser, §21-392.
Right, §21-380.
Who may redeem, §21-383.
Sale and collection in accordance with general law, §21-386.
Sufficiency of bid, §21-381.
Time of sale, §21-379.
Evidence of value of property for purposes of approval of sale, §58.1-3969.
Former owners, heirs or assigns.
Relief for by ordinance, §58.1-3967.
Form of notice of sale, §58.1-3965.
Guardian ad litem appointed for persons under disability, §58.1-3967.
Improper placement of property on delinquent land books, §58.1-3971.
Institution of proceedings, §58.1-3967.
Lien for taxes paid by owners, §58.1-3974.
Limitation on enforcement by sale, §58.1-3940.
Waiver of time limitation on assessment, §58.1-3903.1.
More than one parcel covered by one bill, §58.1-3968.
Nonjudicial sales properties of minimal size and value, §58.1-3975.
Notice of sale, §58.1-3965.
Additional authority to sell, §58.1-3965.1.
Order of reference to commission in chancery or special master, §58.1-3969.
Parties, §58.1-3967.
Procedure, §58.1-3967.
Purchase by county, city or town, §58.1-3970.
Purchases of certain land in name of Commonwealth.
Reversion to owner subject to lien of delinquent taxes, §58.1-3973.

SALE OF DELINQUENT TAX LANDS —Cont'd
Redemption, owners rights, §§58.1-3965, 58.1-3974.
Relief for former owner, heir or assigns, §58.1-3967.
Report of property in improperly placement in delinquent land books, §58.1-3971.
Reversion to owners of purchases under repealed statutes in name of Commonwealth, §58.1-3973.
Service by publication.
Parties not otherwise served, §58.1-3967.
Service of notice of sale, §58.1-3965.
Special commissioner, appointment to sell property, §58.1-3969.
Special masters.
Appointment, §58.1-3970.1.
Referral of case, §58.1-3969.
Surplus received from sale, disposition, §58.1-3967.
Title acquired by purchaser, §58.1-3967.
Two or more parcels covered by one bill, §58.1-3968.
Venue of proceeding, §58.1-3967.
When lands may be sold, §58.1-3965.

SALE ON APPROVAL TRANSACTIONS,
§§8.2-326, 8.2-327.
Goods sent by mail, §11-2.1.
Unsolicited goods, §11-2.2.

SALES.
Abandoned property, §§55-210.18 to 55-210.22.
ABC act.
Generally, §§4.1-100 to 4.1-354.
See ALCOHOLIC BEVERAGES.
Advertising.
See ADVERTISING.
Agricultural cooperative association assets, §13.1-340.
Aircraft keepers' liens, §43-34.
Animal keepers' liens.
Enforcement, §43-34.
Animals.
Immature or unweaned animals, §§3.2-6510, 18.2-403.2.
Antitrust laws, §§59.1-9.1 to 59.1-9.17.
See ANTITRUST.
Approval sales.
Goods sent by mail, §11-2.1.
Armories, §44-136.
Assets of nonprofit corporations, §§13.1-899, 13.1-900.
Automatic dialing-announcing devices, §§59.1-518.1 to 59.1-518.4.
Banks.
Receivers, §6.2-917.
Beekeeping.
Bill of sale.
Certificate of health to accompany, §3.2-4407.
Beer franchises.
Generally, §§4.1-500 to 4.1-517.
See BEER FRANCHISES.
Birds, §29.1-547.
Blind and vision impaired, sale of goods made by, §§51.5-101 to 51.5-105.
Boat dealers.
Installment sales, §29.1-826.
Boat keepers' liens.
Enforcement, §43-34.
Boats and other watercraft.
License required, §29.1-808.

SALES —Cont'd
Boats and other watercraft —Cont'd
Selling, assigning or transfer of title, §29.1-717.
Certificate lost or unavailable, §29.1-717.1.
Death of holder, no qualification on estate, §29.1-717.3.
Transfer by operation of law, §29.1-717.2.
Bobwhite quail, §29.1-544.
Body fluids.
HIV infected fluids, §32.1-289.2.
Business opportunity sales, §§59.1-262 to 59.1-269.
See BUSINESS OPPORTUNITY SALES.
Cancellation of door-to-door sales contracts, §§59.1-21.3, 59.1-21.7.
Career and technical education.
Corporate projects.
Sale of completed projects and other school board property, §22.1-234.
Cats.
Sale by dealers, §§3.2-6512 to 3.2-6517.
Cigarettes.
Counterfeit cigarettes.
Unlawful to sell or possess, civil penalty, §18.2-246.14.
Delivery sales, §§18.2-246.6 to 18.2-246.15.
See CIGARETTES.
Fire-safe cigarettes, §§59.1-293.1 to 59.1-293.9.
See FIRE-SAFE CIGARETTES.
Illegal sales or distribution.
Consumer protection violations, §59.1-200.
Enforcement, §§58.1-1031 to 58.1-1037.
Tobacco products to minors, §18.2-371.2.
Uniform fine schedule, VA SCt Rules 3C:1, 3C:2.
Cleaning agents.
Enforcement of provisions, §62.1-193.3.
Prohibitions, §§62.1-193.1 to 62.1-193.3.
Coal interests, trusts for.
Trustee sale of lease, §45.1-161.311:5.
Colleges and universities.
Sale of interest in real property, §23-4.1.
Commercial code generally, §§8.2-101 to 8.2-725.
See SALES, UCC.
Contracts, sizes of type in printed contracts, §11-4.
Counterfeit cigarettes.
Unlawful to sell or possess, civil penalty, §18.2-246.14.
Credit cards, §§6.2-424 to 6.2-432.
Open-end credit plans, §§6.2-433 to 6.2-435.
Truth-in-lending.
Compliance with federal law, §6.2-436.
Criminal offenses generally, §§18.2-214 to 18.2-246.
See SALES OFFENSES.
Customer information lists, §§59.1-442 to 59.1-444.
Dairies and dairy products.
Unlawful buying and selling, §3.2-3214.
Dead bodies, §§32.1-302, 32.1-303.
Decedents' estates.
Real estate.
Goods, §64.2-526.
Powers of executors and administrators, §§64.2-521, 64.2-522.
Restrictions, §64.2-526.
Distress, §§55-230 to 55-232.2.
Dogs.
Sale by dealers, §§3.2-6512 to 3.2-6517.
Door-to-door.
Home solicitation sales generally, §§59.1-21.1 to 59.1-21.7:1.
See HOME SOLICITATION SALES.

SALES —Cont'd
Door-to-door —Cont'd
Ordinances regulating vendors in counties, cities or towns, §15.2-913.
Drug offenses generally, §§18.2-247 to 18.2-264.
See DRUG OFFENSES.
E-commerce.
Uniform electronic transactions act, §§59.1-479 to 59.1-497.
Electronic communication devices.
Unlawful devices, §18.2-190.3.
Material or equipment used to manufacture, §18.2-190.3.
Electronic transactions.
Uniform electronic transactions act, §§59.1-479 to 59.1-497.
Endangered species, §§29.1-564, 29.1-567.
Escheated lands, §§55-184.1 to 55-191.
Explosives, §59.1-138.
Farm produce, §§3.2-4700 to 3.2-4775.
See FARM PRODUCE SALES.
Fertilizer, §§3.2-3600 to 3.2-3625.
Fiduciary sale of real property for persons under disability, §§8.01-67 to 8.01-80.
See PERSONS WITH DISABILITY.
Fish, §§29.1-531, 29.1-536, 29.1-553.
Fraudulent conveyances.
Generally, §§55-80 to 55-105.
See FRAUDULENT CONVEYANCES.
Recorded contracts as valid as deeds, §55-95.
Game, §29.1-536.
Penalties for provision violations, §29.1-553.
Going out of business sale, §§18.2-223, 18.2-224.
Goods, §§8.2-101 to 8.2-725.
See SALES, UCC.
Goods distrained or levied on, §18.2-101.
Goods sent by mail, §11-2.1.
Hangar keepers' liens.
Enforcement, §43-34.
Home solicitation sales.
General provisions, §§59.1-21.1 to 59.1-21.7:1.
See HOME SOLICITATION SALES.
Housing.
New homes.
Implied warranties, waiver of warranties, as is sale, §55-70.1.
Transfer fee covenant, effect, §55-70.2.
Ignition interlock systems, §18.2-270.2.
Innkeepers' liens.
Enforcement, §43-34.
Personal property sales, §§43-37 to 43-40.
Jail industry program goods and services, §§53.1-133.6, 53.1-133.7.
Landlord and tenant.
Distress, §§55-230 to 55-238.
Liquid fuels, lubricating oils and similar products, §§18.2-226 to 18.2-232.
Livery stable keepers' liens.
Enforcement, §43-34.
Manufactured homes.
Owner sales, §55-248.47.
Marina keepers' liens.
Enforcement, §43-34.
Mechanics' liens.
Enforcement, §43-34.
Migratory game birds.
Prohibited sales, §29.1-547.
Misrepresentations and other offenses in connection with, §§18.2-214 to 18.2-246.
See SALES OFFENSES.

SALES —Cont'd
Money orders.
See MONEY ORDERS.
Money order sellers and money transmitters, §§6.2-1900 to 6.2-1921.
See MONEY ORDERS.
New homes.
Implied warranties, waiver of warranties, as is sale, §55-70.1.
Transfer fee covenant, effect of, §55-70.2.
Nonprofit corporation assets, §§13.1-899, 13.1-900.
Nutria.
Restrictions upon, §29.1-545.
Obscene materials to juveniles, §§18.2-390 to 18.2-391.1.
Offenses generally, §§18.2-214 to 18.2-246.
See SALES OFFENSES.
Online shopping.
Uniform electronic transactions act, §§59.1-479 to 59.1-497.
Open-end credit plans, §§6.2-433 to 6.2-435.
Partition of land.
Application of proceeds of sale to payment of lien, §8.01-84.
Effect of partition or sale on lessee's rights, §8.01-91.
General provisions, §§8.01-81 to 8.01-93.
See PARTITION OF LAND.
In kind distribution impractical, §8.01-93.
Sale in lieu of partition, §8.01-83.
When proceeds of sale deemed personal estate, §8.01-89.
Persons with disability.
Disposition of real estate.
Alternate procedure for sale of real estate, §§8.01-78 to 8.01-80.
General provisions, §§8.01-67 to 8.01-80.
See PERSONS WITH DISABILITY.
Petroleum products franchises.
Agreement provisions concerning, §59.1-21.11.
Prison made goods and services, §§53.1-45 to 53.1-55.
Property owners' associations.
Sale of lot subject act, §§55-509.4 to 55-509.10.
Public utilities.
Plant sales to cities or towns, §56-254.
Real estate cooperatives.
Declarant rights, §55-451.
Nonpayment of assessments, §55-472.
Resales, §55-484.
Substantial completion requirement, §55-495.
Recorded device piracy, §§59.1-41.2, 59.1-41.3.
Rescission of door-to-door sales contracts, §§59.1-21.3, 59.1-21.7.
Residential property transfer disclosures, §§55-517 to 55-525.
See RESIDENTIAL PROPERTY TRANSFER DISCLOSURES.
Safe deposit boxes.
Contents after two years, §6.2-2310.
Secondhand articles, §§59.1-116.1 to 59.1-136.
See SECONDHAND ARTICLE SALES.
Securities generally, §§13.1-501 to 13.1-527.3.
See SECURITIES.
Sizes of type in printed contracts, §11-4.
Stock corporation assets.
In regular course of business, §13.1-723.
Other than in regular course of business, §13.1-724.

SALES —Cont'd
Stock corporation assets —Cont'd
Shareholder approval, §13.1-724.
Disposition not requiring, §13.1-723.
Stolen property, §18.2-108.01.
Telephone solicitation sales, §§59.1-21.1 to 59.1-21.7:1.
See TELEPHONE SOLICITATION SALES.
Timber.
Sale of unclaimed timber, §59.1-106.
Tobacco.
Cigarette delivery sales, §§18.2-246.6 to 18.2-246.15.
See CIGARETTES.
Counterfeit cigarettes.
Unlawful to sell or possess, civil penalty, §18.2-246.14.
Illegal sales or distribution.
Consumer protection violations, §59.1-200.
Enforcement, §§58.1-1031 to 58.1-1037.
Tobacco products to minors, §18.2-371.2.
Uniform fine schedule, VA SCt Rules 3C:1, 3C:2.
Type size in printed contracts, §11-4.
Uniform commercial code generally, §§8.2-101 to 8.2-725.
See SALES, UCC.
Unsolicited goods.
Deemed gift to recipient, §11-2.2.
Used goods, §§59.1-116.1 to 59.1-136.
See SECONDHAND ARTICLE SALES.
Vinegar.
Prohibited sales, §§3.2-5503, 3.2-5504, 3.2-5506.
Watercraft.
License required, §29.1-808.
Weights and measures.
Bulk sale and delivery of commodities, §3.2-5635.
How certain commodities to be sold, §3.2-5622.
Information to be shown on packages, §§3.2-5623, 3.2-5624.
Livestock.
Day and hour of livestock sale.
Announcement, §3.2-5639.
Determination of weight of livestock on date of sale, §3.2-5638.
Misleading containers prohibited, §3.2-5625.
Wine franchises.
Generally, §§4.1-400 to 4.1-418.
See WINE FRANCHISES.
Wiretapping.
Electronic, mechanical or other devices, §19.2-63.

SALES FACTOR.
Allocation and apportionment of corporate taxable income, §§58.1-414 to 58.1-416.

SALES OFFENSES, §§18.2-214 to 18.2-246.
Actions, §§59.1-68.2, 59.1-68.3.
Personal suits, §59.1-68.5.
Suits by attorneys for the Commonwealth and city and county attorneys, §59.1-68.4.
Advertising.
Intent not to sell at price or terms advertised, §18.2-217.
New or used automobiles or trucks, §18.2-221.
Untrue, deceptive or misleading, §18.2-216.
Agricultural products misrepresentations, §18.2-225.
Authority of attorney general, §59.1-68.2.
Automobiles or trucks, advertising new or used, §18.2-221.
Bait and switch, §18.2-217.

SALES OFFENSES —Cont'd
Business machines.
Failure to report removal or alteration of identification or serial number, §18.2-214.1.
Clientele right to select, §18.2-244.
Coin and coin silver sales, §18.2-234.
Customers right to select, §18.2-244.
Drug offenses generally, §§18.2-247 to 18.2-264.
See DRUG OFFENSES.
Electronic communication devices.
Unlawful devices, §18.2-190.3.
Material or equipment used to manufacture, §18.2-190.3.
Elvis statute violation, §18.2-216.1.
False advertising, §18.2-216.
Food sold at retail.
Acceptance of promissory notes in payment for, §18.2-241.
Games, lotteries, etc., for promoting sale of products, §18.2-242.
Going out of business sales.
Failure to acquire permit, §18.2-223.
Gold sales, §18.2-235.
Household electrical appliances.
Removal or alteration of identification number, §18.2-215.
Inadvertent error in advertising, §18.2-243.
Injunctions, §18.2-245.
Liquid fuels, lubricating oils and similar products, §§18.2-226 to 18.2-232.
Assisting in violations of provision, §18.2-230.
False trade name or mixing brand, §18.2-229.
Fraud and misrepresentation, §18.2-226.
Imitating indicia of other brands, §18.2-228.
Label requirement, §18.2-231.
Punishment for violations of provision, §18.2-232.
Sale from pump indicating other brand, §18.2-227.
Misdemeanor generally, §18.2-246.
Obscene materials to juveniles, §§18.2-390 to 18.2-391.1.
Pig iron or industrial iron, brass, copper, metal, etc.
Buying with intent to defraud, §18.2-238.
Pyramid promotional schemes, §18.2-239.
Referral transactions in connection with consumer sales or leases, §18.2-242.1.
Reliance upon information supplied by advertiser, §18.2-243.
Residential real estate transactions.
Discrimination, §36-96.4.
Secondhand grate baskets, keys, bells and bell fixtures, etc.
Buying or receiving with intent to defraud, §18.2-237.
Seconds, irregulars, secondhand, etc.
Failure to indicate, §18.2-218.
Source of merchandise, misrepresentation, §18.2-222.
Sterling and sterling silver, §18.2-233.
Stolen property, sale, §18.2-108.01.
Suits by attorneys for the Commonwealth and city and county, §59.1-68.4.
Trademarks, identification marks, etc.
Changing or removing with intent to defraud, §18.2-214.
Unauthorized use of name or picture of person, §18.2-216.1.
Wholesale or wholesaler use of word, §18.2-220.

SALES REPRESENTATIVES, INDEPENDENT, §§59.1-455 to 59.1-459.
Contracts, §59.1-456.
Absence no defense, §59.1-459.

SALES REPRESENTATIVES, INDEPENDENT —Cont'd
Contracts —Cont'd
Waiver of rights, §59.1-458.
Defined terms, §59.1-455.
Payment of commissions, §§59.1-457, 59.1-458.
Waiver of rights, §59.1-458.

SALES TAXES.
Aircraft, §§58.1-1500 to 58.1-1510.
See AIRCRAFT SALES AND USE TAX.
Baseball stadium authority.
Entitlement to sales tax revenues, §15.2-5814.
Cigarette excise tax, §§58.1-1000 to 58.1-1022.
See CIGARETTE TAX.
Cigarette tax, localities, §§58.1-3830 to 58.1-3832.
Corporate or partnership officer willful failure to collect and account for, §58.1-3907.
Communications sales and use tax, §§58.1-645 to 58.1-662.
See COMMUNICATIONS SALES AND USE TAX.
Forest products tax, §§58.1-1600 to 58.1-1622.
See FOREST PRODUCTS TAX.
Fuel taxes, §§58.1-2200 to 58.1-2299.20.
See FUEL TAXES.
Hampton Roads sports facility authority.
Entitlement to sales tax revenues derived from stadium, §15.2-5914.
Local sales tax, §58.1-605.
Motor vehicle fuel sales tax, §§58.1-1718.1 to 58.1-1724.4.
Motor vehicles, §§58.1-2400 to 58.1-2426.
See MOTOR VEHICLE SALES AND USE TAX.
Retail sales and use tax generally, §§58.1-600 to 58.1-639.
See RETAIL SALES AND USE TAX.
Tire tax, §§58.1-640 to 58.1-644.
Tobacco products tax, §§58.1-1021.01 to 58.1-1021.05.
Towns granted city status.
County sales and use tax to become city sales and use tax, §15.2-3828.
Watercraft, §§58.1-1400 to 58.1-1410.
See WATERCRAFT SALES AND USE TAX.

SALES, UCC, §§8.2-101 to 8.2-725.
Acceptance of goods.
Breach in regard to accepted goods.
Buyer's damages, §8.2-714.
Effect of acceptance, §8.2-607.
Nonacceptance.
Seller's damages, §8.2-708.
Obligation of buyer, §8.2-301.
Revocation in whole or in part, §§8.2-607, 8.2-608.
Buyer's remedies.
Enumerated, §8.2-711.
Seller's remedies.
Enumerated, §8.2-703.
What constitutes, §8.2-606.
Action for price.
Seller's remedies, §8.2-709.
Affirmations.
Express warranties, §8.2-313.
Antecedent breach.
Effect of cancellation or rescission on claims, §8.2-720.
Anticipatory repudiation, §8.2-610.
Proof of market price, §8.2-723.
Retraction, §8.2-611.
Seller's repudiation.
Buyer's right to goods, §8.2-502.

SALES, UCC —Cont'd
Approval.
Sale on approval, §§8.2-326, 8.2-327.
Assignment of rights, §8.2-210.
Assortment of goods.
Buyer's option, §8.2-311.
Assurance of performance.
Right to adequate assurance, §8.2-609.
Auction sales, §8.2-328.
Breach of obligations.
Antecedent breach.
Effect of cancellation or rescission on claims, §8.2-720.
Installment contracts, §8.2-612.
Limitation of actions, §8.2-725.
Notice requirements, §8.2-607.
Burden of proof.
Breaches with respect to accepted goods, §8.2-607.
Buyer's remedies.
Acceptance of goods.
Breach in regard to accepted goods, §8.2-714.
Collateral contracts.
Remedies for breach unimpaired, §8.2-701.
Consequential damages, §8.2-715.
Cover, §8.2-712.
Detinue, §8.2-716.
Fraud, §8.2-721.
Incidental damages, §8.2-715.
Modification or limitation by contract, §8.2-719.
Nondelivery of goods, §8.2-713.
Options and cooperation respecting performance.
Additional remedies, §8.2-311.
Repudiation of contract by seller, §8.2-713.
Buyer's right to goods, §8.2-502.
Restitution, §8.2-718.
Specific performance, §8.2-716.
Cancellation of contract.
Buyer's remedies.
Enumerated, §8.2-711.
Seller's remedies, §8.2-703.
C. & F. terms, §§8.2-320, 8.2-321.
Casualty to identified goods, §8.2-613.
C.I.F. terms, §§8.2-320, 8.2-321.
Citation of article, §8.2-101.
Collateral contracts.
Remedies for breach not impaired, §8.2-701.
Contracts allowing possession to remain with seller.
Void as to creditors and purchasers unless in writing, §11-1.
Cooperation respecting performance, §8.2-311.
Course of dealing.
Implied warranties, §8.2-314.
Cover.
Buyer's procurement of substitute goods, §8.2-712.
Credit.
Confirmed credit, §8.2-325.
Letters of credit, §8.2-325.
Creditors' rights and remedies.
Sale on approval and sale or return transactions, §8.2-326.
Sold goods.
Rights of seller's creditors, §8.2-402.
Cure.
Improper tender or delivery of goods.
Seller's right to cure, §8.2-508.
Damages.
Acceptance of goods.
Buyer's damages for breach in regard to accepted goods, §8.2-714.

SALES, UCC —Cont'd
Damages —Cont'd
Antecedent breach.
Effect of cancellation or rescission on claims, §8.2-720.
Consequential damages.
Buyer's consequential damages, §8.2-715.
Contractual limitations, §8.2-719.
Cover by buyer.
Right to cover, §8.2-712.
Deduction from price, §8.2-717.
Delivery of goods.
Buyer's damages for nondelivery, §8.2-713.
Incidental damages.
Buyer's incidental damages, §8.2-715.
Recovery by person in position of seller, §8.2-707.
Seller's incidental damages, §8.2-710.
Limitation, §8.2-718.
Liquidation, §8.2-718.
Nonacceptance of goods.
Seller's damages, §8.2-708.
Repudiation by buyer.
Seller's damages, §8.2-708.
Repudiation by seller.
Buyer's damages, §8.2-713.
Resale of goods by seller, §§8.2-703, 8.2-706.
Warranty breaches, §8.2-714.
Decedents' estates, §64.2-526.
Definitions.
Agreement, §8.2-106.
Banker's credit, §8.2-325.
Between merchants, §8.2-104.
Buyer, §8.2-103.
Cancellation, §8.2-106.
Commercial unit, §8.2-105.
Confirmed credit, §8.2-325.
Conforming to contract, §8.2-106.
Contract, §8.2-106.
Contract for sale, §8.2-106.
Cover, §8.2-712.
Entrusting, §8.2-403.
Financing agency, §8.2-104.
Future goods, §8.2-105.
Good faith, §8.2-103.
Goods, §8.2-105.
Identification, §8.2-501.
Index of definitions, §8.2-103.
Installment contract, §8.2-612.
Letter of credit, §8.2-325.
Lot, §8.2-105.
Merchant, §8.2-104.
Overseas, §8.2-323.
Person in position of seller, §8.2-707.
Present sale, §8.2-106.
Receipt, §8.2-103.
Sale, §8.2-106.
Sale on approval, §8.2-326.
Sale or return, §§8.2-326, 8.2-327.
Seller, §8.2-103.
Termination, §8.2-106.
Delegation of performance, §8.2-210.
Description of goods.
Express warranties by description, §8.2-313.
Detinue of goods.
Right of buyer, §8.2-716.
Disputed goods.
Preservation of evidence, §8.2-515.
Documents against which draft is drawn.
When deliverable, §8.2-514.
Entrusters and entrustees, §8.2-403.

SALES, UCC —Cont'd
Evidence.
Breaches with respect to accepted goods, §8.2-607.
Disputed goods.
Preserving evidence, §8.2-515.
Excludable security and other transactions, §8.2-102.
Exclusive dealings, §8.2-306.
Executory portion of contract.
Waiver, §8.2-209.
Extrinsic evidence, §8.2-202.
Finality of written expression, §8.2-202.
Financing agencies.
Shipment of goods.
Drafts paid or purchased by agency, §8.2-506.
Firm offers, §8.2-205.
Fitness for particular purpose.
Implied warranties, §8.2-315.
Exclusion or modification, §8.2-316.
Formal requirements, §8.2-201.
Formation of contract.
Generally, §8.2-204.
Offer and acceptance.
Additional terms in acceptance or confirmation, §8.2-207.
Auctions, §8.2-328.
Firm offers, §8.2-205.
Fraudulent conveyances.
Recorded contracts as valid as deeds, §55-95.
Void as to creditors and purchasers until recorded, §§55-96, 55-97.
General provisions of commercial code, §§8.1A-101 to 8.1A-310.
See COMMERCIAL CODE.
Good faith purchasers, §8.2-403.
Goods severed from realty, §8.2-107.
Identification of goods, §8.2-501.
Casualty to identified goods, §8.2-613.
Seller's right notwithstanding breach of contract, §8.2-704.
Improper tender or delivery.
Buyer's rights on improper delivery, §8.2-601.
Infringement of enjoyment of goods.
Warranty against infringement, §8.2-312.
Insolvency of buyer.
Remedies of seller on discovery, §8.2-702.
Insolvency of seller.
Buyer's right to goods, §8.2-502.
Inspection of goods.
Buyer's right, §8.2-513.
Buyer's right to inspect goods after arrival of goods but before payment is due, §8.2-310.
Payment by buyer before inspection, §8.2-512.
Installment contracts, §8.2-612.
Insurable interest in goods, §8.2-501.
Interpretation and construction.
Cancellation.
Effect of term on claims for antecedent breach, §8.2-720.
Delivery of goods.
Absence of specified place for delivery, §8.2-308.
Time for delivery.
Absence of specified time, §8.2-309.
Open price terms, §8.2-305.
Rescission.
Effect of term on claims for antecedent breach, §8.2-720.
Risks.
Allocation or division, §8.2-303.
Shipment of goods.
Time for shipment.
Absence of specified time, §8.2-309.

SALES, UCC —Cont'd
Letters of credit, §8.2-325.
Merchantability of goods.
Implied warranties, §8.2-314.
Exclusion or modification, §8.2-316.
Minerals.
Applicability of chapter, §8.2-107.
Modification, §8.2-209.
Notice.
Breach of obligations, §8.2-607.
Termination of contract, §8.2-309.
Obligations of parties.
Generally, §8.2-301.
Offer and acceptance, §8.2-206.
Additional terms in acceptance or confirmation, §8.2-207.
Auctions, §8.2-328.
Firm offers, §8.2-205.
Oil and gas.
Applicability of chapter, §8.2-107.
Open price terms, §8.2-305.
Options respecting performance, §8.2-311.
Output contracts, §8.2-306.
Parol evidence, §8.2-202.
Payment.
Accepted goods, §8.2-607.
Before inspection, §8.2-512.
By check, §8.2-511.
Confirmed credit, §8.2-325.
Credit.
Running of credit, §8.2-310.
Failure of buyer to pay.
Person in position of seller.
Recovery of incidental damages, §8.2-707.
Seller's remedies.
Action for price, §8.2-709.
Enumerated, §8.2-703.
Incidental damages, §8.2-710.
Letters of credit, §8.2-325.
Obligation of buyer, §8.2-301.
On arrival of goods, §8.2-321.
Open time for payment, §8.2-310.
Price payable in money, goods, realty, etc., §8.2-304.
Tender by buyer, §8.2-511.
When due, §8.2-310.
Performance.
Assurance.
Right to adequate assurance, §8.2-609.
Cooperation, §8.2-311.
Delegation, §8.2-210.
Generally, §§8.2-501 to 8.2-515.
Options, §8.2-311.
Specific performance.
Right of buyer, §8.2-716.
Substituted performance, §8.2-614.
Suspension until adequate assurance of performance, §8.2-609.
Person in position of seller, §8.2-707.
Price.
Action for price.
Seller's remedies, §§8.2-703, 8.2-709.
Admissibility of market quotations, §8.2-724.
Proof of market price, §8.2-723.
Deduction of damages, §8.2-717.
Failure of buyer to pay.
Person in position of seller.
Recovery of incidental damages, §8.2-707.
Seller's remedies.
Action for price, §§8.2-703, 8.2-709.
Incidental damages, §8.2-710.

SALES, UCC —Cont'd
Price —Cont'd
Net landed weights, §8.2-321.
Open price terms, §8.2-305.
Payable in money, goods, realty, etc., §8.2-304.
Proof of market price, §8.2-723.
Admissibility of market quotations, §8.2-724.
Promises.
Express warranties, §8.2-313.
Reclamation of goods.
Seller's remedies on discovery of buyer's insolvency, §8.2-702.
Rejection of goods.
Rightful rejection.
Buyer's options as to salvage of rightfully rejected goods, §8.2-604.
Buyer's remedies.
Enumerated, §8.2-711.
Effect, §8.2-602.
Manner, §8.2-602.
Merchant buyer's duties as to rightfully rejected goods, §8.2-603.
Waiver of buyer's objections by failure to particularize, §8.2-605.
Wrongful rejection.
Seller's remedies.
Enumerated, §8.2-703.
Repudiation.
Anticipatory repudiation, §§8.2-610, 8.2-611.
Proof of market price, §8.2-723.
Buyer's damages, §8.2-713.
Buyer's repudiation of contract.
Enumeration of seller's remedies, §8.2-703.
Seller's damages, §8.2-708.
Buyer's right to goods, §8.2-502.
Seller's repudiation of contract.
Buyer's remedies.
Enumerated, §8.2-711.
Buyer's right to goods, §8.2-502.
Requirements contracts, §8.2-306.
Resale of goods.
Remedy of person in position of seller, §8.2-707.
Seller's remedies, §8.2-706.
Rescission, §8.2-209.
Restitution.
Buyer's remedies, §8.2-718.
Return of goods.
Sale or return transactions, §§8.2-326, 8.2-327.
Risk of loss.
Absence of breach, §8.2-509.
Casualty to identified goods, §8.2-613.
Effect of breach, §8.2-510.
Sale on approval transactions, §§8.2-326, 8.2-327.
Sale or return transactions, §§8.2-326, 8.2-327.
Salvaging unfinished goods.
Right of seller, §8.2-704.
Samples of goods.
Express warranties by sample, §8.2-313.
Scope of chapter, §8.2-102.
Seals.
Inoperability, §8.2-203.
Seller's remedies.
Action for price, §8.2-709.
Buyer's insolvency, §8.2-702.
Delivery of goods.
Stoppage in transit or otherwise, §8.2-705.
Fraud, §8.2-721.
Generally, §8.2-703.
Identification of goods.
Notwithstanding breach of contract, §8.2-704.

SALES, UCC —Cont'd
Seller's remedies —Cont'd
Incidental damages, §8.2-710.
Modification or limitation by contract, §8.2-719.
Nonacceptance of goods by buyer, §8.2-708.
Options and cooperation respecting performance.
Additional remedies, §8.2-311.
Repudiation of contract by buyer, §8.2-708.
Resale of goods, §8.2-706.
Salvaging unfinished goods, §8.2-704.
Shipment and delivery.
C. & F. terms, §§8.2-320, 8.2-321.
Bill of lading required in overseas shipments, §8.2-323.
Casualty to identified goods, §8.2-613.
C.I.F. terms, §§8.2-320, 8.2-321.
Bill of lading required in overseas shipments, §8.2-323.
Condition.
Delivery on, §8.2-507.
Cure by seller of improper tender or delivery, §8.2-508.
Delay in delivery.
Excuse by failure of presupposed conditions, §§8.2-615, 8.2-616.
Ex-ship delivery, §8.2-322.
F.A.S. terms, §8.2-319.
Financing agency's rights.
Drafts paid or purchased by agency, §8.2-506.
F.O.B. terms, §8.2-319.
Bill of lading required in overseas shipments, §8.2-323.
Improper tender or delivery.
Cover by buyer, §8.2-712.
Cure by seller, §8.2-508.
Damages of buyer for nondelivery, §8.2-713.
Excuse by failure of presupposed conditions, §§8.2-615, 8.2-616.
Inspection of goods, §§8.2-512, 8.2-513.
Net landed weights, §8.2-321.
No arrival, no sale terms, §8.2-324.
Casualty to identified goods, §8.2-613.
Obligation of seller to transfer and deliver goods, §8.2-301.
Overseas shipments, §8.2-323.
Payment on arrival, §8.2-321.
Place for delivery.
Absence of specified place, §8.2-308.
Refusal of delivery.
Buyer's remedies.
Enumerated, §8.2-711.
Seller's remedies on discovery of buyer's insolvency, §8.2-702.
Reservation.
Authority to ship under reservation, §8.2-310.
Risk of loss.
Absence of breach, §8.2-509.
Effect of breach, §8.2-510.
Sale on approval transactions, §§8.2-326, 8.2-327.
Sale or return transactions, §§8.2-326, 8.2-327.
Seller's options.
Specifications or arrangements relating to shipment, §8.2-311.
Shipment by seller, §8.2-504.
Under reservation, §8.2-505.
Single lot or several lots, §8.2-307.
Stoppage of goods in transit or otherwise.
Remedy of person in position of seller, §8.2-707.
Remedy of seller, §§8.2-703, 8.2-705.
Substituted performance, §8.2-614.

SALES, UCC —Cont'd
Shipment and delivery —Cont'd
Tender of delivery.
Buyer's rights on improper delivery, §8.2-601.
Cover by buyer where tender improper, §8.2-712.
Cure by seller of improper tender, §8.2-508.
Effect of seller's tender, §8.2-507.
Excuse by failure of presupposed conditions, §§8.2-615, 8.2-616.
Manner of seller's tender, §8.2-503.
Time for shipment or delivery.
Absence of specified time, §8.2-309.
Warranty of condition on arrival, §8.2-321.
Withholding delivery.
Seller's remedies, §8.2-703.
Specific performance.
Right of buyer, §8.2-716.
Statute of frauds, §8.2-201.
Statute of limitations, §8.2-725.
Substituted performance, §8.2-614.
Termination of contract.
Contracts of indefinite duration, §8.2-309.
Definition of termination, §8.2-106.
Notice of termination, §8.2-309.
Third party actions.
Who can sue third parties for injury to goods, §8.2-722.
Timber.
Applicability of chapter, §8.2-107.
Title of article.
Short title, §8.2-101.
Title to goods.
Passing of title, §8.2-401.
Power to transfer title, §8.2-403.
Reservation for security, §8.2-401.
Warranty of title, §8.2-312.
Transfer of goods.
Requisites, §8.2-105.
Unconscionability, §8.2-302.
Unfinished goods.
Seller's right to salvage, §8.2-704.
Usage of trade.
Implied warranties, §8.2-314.
Waiver of executory portion of contract, §8.2-209.
Warranties.
Damages for breach, §8.2-714.
Express warranties.
Cumulation and conflict, §8.2-317.
Exclusions.
Generally, §8.2-316.
Generally, §8.2-313.
Modification.
Generally, §8.2-316.
Implied warranties.
Course of dealing or usage of trade, §8.2-314.
Cumulation and conflict, §8.2-317.
Exclusions.
Generally, §8.2-316.
Fitness for particular purpose, §8.2-315.
Exclusion or modification, §8.2-316.
Merchantability.
Exclusion or modification, §8.2-316.
Modification generally, §8.2-316.
Infringement of enjoyment of goods.
Warranty of title and against infringement, §8.2-312.
Merchantability, §8.2-314.
Registration card, conditioning warranty upon return by purchaser, §8.2-317.1.

SALES, UCC —Cont'd
Warranties —Cont'd
Title.
Warranty of title and against infringement, §8.2-312.

SALES UNDER DEED OF TRUST.
Advertising.
Contents, §55-59.3.
Newspaper advertising, §55-63.
Required, §55-59.2.
Construction of phrases, §55-60.
Deed of release.
Execution and deliverance, §55-59.4.
Disposition of surplus, §55-64.
Evidences of indebtedness placed on equal footing, §55-60.1.
Maturity date absent, §55-61.
Notice, §55-59.1.
Advertising, §§55-59.2, 55-59.3, 55-63.
Form, §55-62.
Notice of sale under deed of trust, §15.2-979.
Postponement of sale.
Notice, §55-59.2.
Provisions authorizing absent, §55-61.
Validation of conveyances, §55-61.1.
Title not affected by nonlisting for taxation, §55-64.1.
Trustee powers and duties, §55-59.4.
Validation of certain sales, §§55-65 to 55-66.

SALTWATER RECREATIONAL FISHING LICENSES, §§28.2-302.1 to 28.2-302.10:1.

SALTWATER SPORT FISHING TOURNAMENT, §28.2-206.

SALVAGE.
Sales, UCC.
Buyer's options, §8.2-604.
Seller's rights, §8.2-704.
Secondhand article sales.
Building fixtures, exemption from provisions, §59.1-123.

SALVAGE VEHICLES, §§46.2-1600 to 46.2-1610.
Alteration of vehicle identification number.
Duties of licensees, §46.2-1603.1.
Certificates of title.
Cancellation upon receipt by DMV, §46.2-1603.2.
Insurance company unable to present certificate of title, §46.2-1603.
Out-of-state certificates, §46.2-1606.
Rebuilders required to possess, §46.2-1605.
Titling of nonrepairable vehicle prohibited, §46.2-1603.2.
Unrecovered stolen vehicle, §46.2-1603.
Civil penalties, §46.2-1609.
Crushing or flattening of vehicle into unrecognizable state.
Holding period, §46.2-1608.1.
Permit requirements, §46.2-1603.1.
Definitions, §46.2-1600.
Demolishing or dismantling of vehicles.
Updating records of department, §46.2-1608.2.
Exemption from chapter.
Repairable vehicles, §46.2-1602.2.
Good faith exceptions.
Sales prohibitions, §46.2-1602.
Holding period prior to crushing or flattening vehicle, §46.2-1608.1.
Insurance companies.
Duties upon acquiring certain vehicles, §46.2-1602.1.

SALVAGE VEHICLES —Cont'd
Insurance companies —Cont'd
Nonrepairable certificates.
Duty to obtain, §46.2-1603.2.
Unable to present certificate of title, §46.2-1603.
Inventory.
Examination of inventory, §46.2-1607.
Licensing of dealers, §46.2-1601.
Duties of licensees, §46.2-1603.1.
Revocation or suspension of license, §46.2-1609.
Missing vehicle identification number.
Duties of licensees, §46.2-1603.1.
Nonrepairable vehicles.
Defined, §46.2-1600.
Owner's declaration, §46.2-1603.2.
Sales prohibitions, §46.2-1602.
Titling and registration prohibited, §46.2-1603.2.
Penalties, §46.2-1609.
Rebuilders.
Defined, §46.2-1600.
Required to possess certificate of title, §46.2-1604.
Rebuilt vehicles.
Branding of titles, §46.2-1605.
Defined, §46.2-1600.
Examination of vehicles for highway use, §46.2-1605.
Sales prohibitions, §46.2-1602.
Vehicles repaired or rebuilt for highway use, §46.2-1605.
Records.
Demolishing or dismantling of vehicles.
Updating records of department, §46.2-1608.2.
Inspection of records, §46.2-1607.
Maintenance and contents, §46.2-1608.
Repairable vehicles.
Exemption from chapter, §46.2-1602.2.
Reports to law enforcement, §46.2-1608.1.
Revocation or suspension of license, §46.2-1609.
Sales prohibitions, §46.2-1602.
Salvage certificates.
Application, §46.2-1603.
Duty of insurance companies to obtain, §§46.2-1602.1, 46.2-1603.
Duty of licensees to obtain, §46.2-1603.1.
Schedule of fees.
Licensing of dealers, §46.2-1601.
Tampering with vehicle identification number.
Duties of licensees, §46.2-1603.1.
Transfer of vehicle.
Titling requirements, §46.2-1603.1.
Unlicensed dealers, §46.2-1601.
Vehicle identification numbers.
Duties of licensees, §46.2-1603.1.

SAME ACT STATUTE, §19.2-294.

SAME SEX MARRIAGES, §20-45.2.
Civil unions between persons of same sex.
Prohibition, arrangements performed in other states void, §20-45.3.

SANCTIONS.
Attorneys at law.
Frivolous actions, §8.01-271.1.
Oral motions, §8.01-271.1.
Signing of pleadings, §8.01-271.1.
Discovery.
Criminal cases.
Noncompliance with continuing duty to disclose, VA SCt Rule 3A:11.
District courts.
Criminal and traffic cases, VA SCt Rule 7C:6.

SANCTIONS —Cont'd
Discovery —Cont'd
Failure to make discovery, VA SCt Rule 4:12.
District courts.
Discovery.
Criminal and traffic cases, VA SCt Rule 7C:6.
Frivolous actions, §8.01-271.1.
Parties.
Refusal of adverse party to testify, §8.01-401.

SANCTUARIES.
See WILDLIFE HABITAT, REFUGE OR SANCTUARY.

SANDBRIDGE BEACH SUBDIVISION.
Coastal primary sand dunes and beaches.
Permits and standards of use, exemption, §28.2-1408.2.

SAND, DREDGING, §§62.1-190 to 62.1-193.
Beach replenishment projects.
Expedited review of proposal and permit process, §28.2-1205.2.

SAND DUNES.
Coastal primary sand dunes and beaches generally, §§28.2-1400 to 28.2-1420.
See COASTAL PRIMARY SAND DUNES AND BEACHES.

SAND, VEHICLES CARRYING.
Load covers, §46.2-1156.
Fine for failure to prevent escape of contents, VA SCt Rule 3B:2.
Overweight permits, §46.2-1143.

SANGRIA.
Defined, §4.1-100.
Pre-mixing containers to be served and sold on licensed premises, §4.1-325.

SANITARIUMS.
Certificates of public need for medical care facilities, §§32.1-102.1 to 32.1-102.11.
See MEDICAL CARE FACILITIES.
Hospitals generally.
See HOSPITALS.

SANITARY DISTRICTS, §§21-112.22 to 21-140.3.
Abolishing sanitary districts, §21-117.1.
Assumption of districts bonded indebtedness.
County or city purchasing water supply or sewage disposal system from district, §15.2-2116.
Authority of governing body.
Acquisition of federal and state property, §21-118.1.
Additional powers, §21-118.4.
Levy and expenditure of taxes, §21-118.3.
Powers and duties generally, §21-118.
Special taxing districts, §21-119.
Unified water supply and sewerage systems, §21-118.5.
Use of sanitary district funds, §21-118.2.
Validation of proceedings, §21-121.4.
Boards of supervisors.
Validation of proceedings, §21-121.4.
Bond issues.
Generally, §§21-122 to 21-140.3.
See SANITARY DISTRICTS BONDS.
Validation of proceedings, §21-121.2:1.
Boundaries.
Alteration of boundaries in certain counties, §21-116.1.
Conflicts of law.
Powers of districts created under other laws, §21-121.3.

SANITARY DISTRICTS —Cont'd
County manager plan of government.
Exercise of powers in name of district or in name of county or both, §15.2-724.
Creation, §21-113.
Definitions, §21-112.22.
Eminent domain.
Authority of governing body, §21-118.
Enlargement of sanitary districts, §21-116.
Inclusion of town in new or enlarged district, §21-113.
Validation of certain actions, §21-121.5.
Filing of petition, §21-114.
Abolishing sanitary districts, §21-117.1.
Answer and defense, §21-115.
Merger of sanitary districts, §21-117.
Governing body.
Additional powers, §21-118.4.
Authority to acquire federal and state property, §21-118.1.
Authority to use sanitary district funds, §21-118.2.
Powers and duties generally, §21-118.
Taxing authority, §21-118.3.
Hearing of petition, §21-114.
Abolishing sanitary districts, §21-117.1.
Merger of sanitary districts, §21-117.
Improvements.
Nature of improvements of special taxing districts, §21-119.
Joint agreements for sewage or water service, §15.2-2112.
Merger of sanitary districts, §21-117.
Validation of certain actions, §21-121.5.
Motor vehicle liability insurance.
County providing to protect operators of vehicles owned or leased by sanitary district, §15.2-1214.
New or enlarged district.
Inclusion of town in district, §21-113.
Notice of petition, §21-114.
Abolishing sanitary districts, §21-117.1.
Merger of sanitary districts, §21-117.
Parks, recreational facilities and swimming pools.
Operations by counties and cities in, §15.2-1811.
Powers and duties of governing body.
Special taxing districts, §21-119.
Unified water supply and sewerage systems, §21-118.5.
Validation of proceedings, §21-121.4.
Reduction of area of sanitary districts, §21-116.1.
Reduction of sanitary districts, §21-120.
Refunding bonds.
County providing for issuance for districts, §15.2-2649.
Sanitation districts law of 1938.
General provisions, §§21-141 to 21-223.
See SANITATION DISTRICTS LAW OF 1938.
Sanitation districts law of 1946.
General provisions, §§21-224 to 21-290.
See SANITATION DISTRICTS LAW OF 1946.
Sewerage systems.
Unified water supply and sewerage systems, §§21-118.5 to 21-118.8.
Special taxing districts, §21-119.
Transfer of certain districts to towns, §21-119.1.
Unified water supply and sewerage systems, §§21-118.5 to 21-118.8.
Applicability of public finance act, §21-118.5.
Application of revenues, §§21-118.6, 21-118.7.

SANITARY DISTRICTS —Cont'd
Unified water supply and sewerage systems —Cont'd
Payment to county of revenues held by district, §21-118.7.
Power of county governing body to fix rates, §21-118.5.
Ratification of prior agreements, §21-118.8.
Tax levy where revenues insufficient, §21-118.6.
Validation of prior agreements, §21-118.8.
United States property.
Acquiring property from United States, §15.2-952.
Urban county executive form of government, §15.2-858.
Administered by department of public utilities, §15.2-843.
Validation of expenditures, §21-118.3.
Validation of proceedings, §§21-121 to 21-121.6.
Additional districts, §21-121.2.
Bond issues, §21-121.2:1.
Districts created prior to January 1, 1970, §21-121.
Districts created prior to June 30, 1954, §21-121.1.
Enlargement of sanitary districts, §21-121.5.
Merger of sanitary districts, §21-121.5.
Powers of boards of supervisors and other governing bodies, §21-121.4.
Powers of districts created under other laws, §21-121.3.
Water and sewer authority, §21-121.6.
Water and sewer authority.
Validation of proceedings, §21-121.6.
Water supply system or sewage system acquired by locality from, §15.2-2116.

SANITARY DISTRICTS BONDS.
Advances to sanitary districts, §21-134.1.
Agents for sale of bonds, §21-129.
Allocation of county funds to sanitary districts, §21-134.01.
Amount of bonds, §21-127.
Authority to issue bonds, §21-122.
Agents for sale of bonds, §21-129.
Borrowing in anticipation of bond issue, §21-127.1.
Failure or refusal to issue bonds, §21-128.
Bond of depository, §21-136.
Bonds for special purpose, §21-122.1.
Borrowing in anticipation of bond issue, §21-127.1.
Canvass of returns, etc., §21-124.
Inquiry into returns, §21-126.
Circuit court order requiring election, §21-123.
Conduct of election, §21-124.
Conflict of laws.
Laws continued in effect, §21-139.
Cost of giving surety on additional bonds required, §21-133.
County fund allocations, §21-134.01.
Coupon bonds, §21-130.
Delivery to purchasers, §21-131.
Delivery to treasurer, §21-131.
Deposit of proceeds, §21-134.
Liability, §21-132.
Deposit of proceeds, §21-134.
Bond of depository, §21-136.
Insolvency of depository, §21-135.
Destroyed bonds, §21-130.1.
Drainage projects, §§21-396 to 21-422.
See DRAINAGE PROJECTS.

SANITARY DISTRICTS BONDS —Cont'd
Elections.
Bonds for special purpose, §21-122.1.
Canvass of returns, etc., §21-124.
Conduct of election, §21-124.
Inquiry into election and returns, §21-126.
Order requiring election, §21-123.
Procedure after election, §§21-125, 21-126.
Failure or refusal to issue bonds, §21-128.
Form of bonds, §21-130.
Insolvency of depository, §21-135.
Levy of tax.
Serial bonds, §21-138.
Liability of treasurer, §21-132.
Limitation of amount, §21-122.
Lost bonds, §21-130.1.
Maximum amount of bonds, §21-127.
Mutilated bonds, §21-130.1.
Order requiring election, §21-123.
No election required for special purpose bonds, §21-122.1.
Procedure after election, §21-125.
Inquiry into election and returns, §21-126.
Registered bonds, §21-130.
Reimbursement of county for advances to sanitary district, §21-134.1.
Validation of advances, §21-134.2.
Sale of bonds.
Agents for sale of bonds, §21-129.
Sanitation districts law of 1938, §§21-189 to 21-202.
See SANITATION DISTRICTS LAW OF 1938.
Sanitation districts law of 1946, §§21-269 to 21-282.
See SANITATION DISTRICTS LAW OF 1946.
Serial bonds.
No sinking fund required, §21-137.2.
Payment of interest, §§21-137.2, 21-138.
What constitutes, §21-137.1.
Sinking fund for term bonds, §21-137.1.
No sinking fund required for serial bonds, §21-137.2.
Special purpose bonds, §21-122.1.
Surety cost on additional bonds, §21-133.
Taxes.
Payment of interest on serial bonds, §§21-137.2, 21-138.
Sinking fund for term bonds.
Payment of interest on term bonds, §21-137.1.
Term bonds.
What constitutes, §21-137.1.
Use of excess revenues.
Serial bonds, §21-137.2.
Validation of advances to sanitary districts, §21-134.2.
Validation of certain bonds, §21-140.3.
Validation of proceedings, §§21-140 to 21-140.3.
Additional sanitary districts, §21-140.2.
Districts prior to January 1, 1947, §21-140.
Districts prior to June 30, 1954, §21-140.1.

SANITARY DISTRICTS, NONCODIFIED.
Created, 1926 ch 161.
Amended in 1933, 1933 ch 42.
Amended in 1936, 1936 ch 426.
Amended in 1940, 1940 ch 117.
Amended in 1942, 1942 ch 15, 1942 ch 139.
Amended in 1944, 1944 ch 232, 1944 ch 300, 1944 ch 304, 1944 ch 305.
Amended in 1946, 1946 ch 84, 1946 ch 372.

SANITARY DISTRICTS, NONCODIFIED —Cont'd
Amended in 1948, 1948 ch 70, 1948 ch 71, 1948 ch 94, 1948 ch 465.
Amended in 1950, 1950 ch 198, 1950 ch 442.
Amended in 1952, 1952 ch 300.
Amended in 1954, 1954 ch 324.
Amended in 1956, 1956 ch 139, 1956 ch 691.
Amended in 1958, 1958 ch 454, 1958 ch 521.
Amended in 1960, 1960 ch 561.
Amended in 1962, 1962 ch 554.
Amended in 1964, 1964 ch 344.
Amended in 1968, 1968 ch 678.
Amended in 1970, 1970 ch 253, 1970 ch 597.
Amended in 1972, 1972 ch 219, 1972 ch 222.
Amended in 1977, 1977 ch 303.
Amended in 1981, 1981 ch 294.
Amended in 1984, 1984 ch 732.
Amended in 1989, 1989 ch 51, 1989 ch 357, 1989 ch 394.

SANITARY REQUIREMENTS FOR FOOD, §§3.2-5105 to 3.2-5119.
See FOOD.

SANITATION.
Eggs and hatchery products, §3.2-5308.
Fishing, tidal waters.
Health and sanitation provisions generally, §§28.2-800 to 28.2-826.
See FISHING, TIDAL WATERS.
Food establishments, §§3.2-5105 to 3.2-5119.

SANITATION COMMISSIONS.
Moccasin Gap sanitation commission, 1948 ch 523, 1971 ch 178, 1978 ch 464, 1986 ch 398.

SANITATION DISTRICTS LAW OF 1938, §§21-141 to 21-223.
Bond issues, §§21-189 to 21-202.
Bondholders' special remedies, §21-200.
Bonds constitute legal investments, §21-199.
Destroyed bonds, §21-200.1.
Election prior to issuance, §21-190.
Interim bonds, §21-201.
Exemption of bonds from taxation, §21-156.
Form and contents, §21-192.
Negotiability, §21-195.
How sold, §21-193.
Interim certificates, §21-201.
Inviolability of rights and remedies, §21-202.
Issuance.
Election prior to issuance, §21-190.
Form and contents, §21-192.
Interim certificates, §21-201.
Liability of state and localities, §§21-196, 21-197.
Lost bonds, §21-200.1.
Matters determined by resolution, §21-191.
Mutilated bonds, §21-200.1.
Negotiability, §21-195.
Form and contents, §21-192.
Outstanding bonds limitation, §21-189.
Personal liability, §21-197.
Liability of state and localities, §21-196.
Purchase by commission, §21-198.
Resolutions, §§21-191, 21-194.
Determination of bond matters, §21-191.
Part of bondholders' contract, §21-194.
Sale of bonds, §21-193.
Purchase by commission, §21-198.
Special remedies of bondholders, §21-200.
Ten million dollars outstanding bond limitation, §21-189.

SANITATION DISTRICTS LAW OF 1938
—Cont'd
Territorial jurisdiction.
Creation of districts, §21-145.
Title of act, §21-141.
Uniformity of fees, rents and charges, §21-181.
Withdrawals from district, §§21-203 to 21-213.
Additional rights conferred on localities withdrawing, §21-208.
Commission members, §§21-212, 21-213.
Compliance with steps for withdrawal, §21-205.
Election on issuance of bonds, §21-209.
Erection of disposal system by separate district, §21-210.
Nonappointment of commission members on withdrawal, §21-212.
Nonresident commission members, §21-213.
Notice of intention, §21-203.
One year limitation, §21-207.
Power of localities electing to set up separate district, §21-206.
Proof of compliance with steps, §21-205.
Rights conferred on localities withdrawing, §§21-206, 21-208.
Right to withdraw and set up separate district, §21-204.
Setting up separate district, §§21-204, 21-206.
Sewage disposal system, §§21-210, 21-211.
Six month limitation on issuance of bonds, §21-209.
Withdrawal within one year, §21-207.
Withdrawing city to provide disposal system, §21-211.

SANITATION DISTRICTS LAW OF 1946,
§§21-224 to 21-290.
Bids and bidding.
Manner of letting contracts, §21-245.
Bond issues, §§21-269 to 21-282.
Bondholders' special remedies, §21-280.
Bond matters determined by resolution, §21-270.
Bonds constitute legal investments, §21-279.
Destroyed bonds, §21-280.1.
Election prior to issuance, §21-270.
Form and contents, §21-272.
How sold, §21-273.
Interim certificates, §21-282.
Inviolability of rights and remedies, §21-281.
Issuance.
Election prior to issuance, §21-270.
Form and contents, §21-272.
Interim certificates, §21-282.
Negotiability, §21-275.
Liability of state and localities on bonds, §§21-276, 21-277.
Lost bonds, §21-280.1.
Mutilated bonds, §21-280.1.
Negotiability, §21-275.
Outstanding bonds limitation, §21-269.
Personal liability on bonds, §21-277.
Purchase by commission, §21-278.
Resolutions, §§21-271, 21-274.
Resolutions as part of bondholders' contract, §21-274.
Sale of bonds, §21-273.
Purchase by commission, §21-278.
Special remedies of bondholders, §21-280.
Ten million dollar outstanding bond limitation, §21-269.
Unabridgement of rights and remedies, §21-281.

SANITATION DISTRICTS LAW OF 1946
—Cont'd
Boundaries.
Territory which may be embraced in district, §21-228.
Citation of title, §21-224.
Commission, §§21-237 to 21-259.
Accounts and records, §21-259.
Agents and employees, §21-257.
Authority to collect fees, rents or charges, §21-260.
Bond of members, §21-243.
Compensation of members, §21-239.
Creation, §21-237.
Election of officers, §21-238.
Eminent domain powers, §21-246.
Enumeration of powers, §21-248.
Establishment, §21-237.
Expenses of members, §21-239.
Funds of commission, §21-258.
Immunity of localities from acts of commission, §21-247.
Manner of letting contracts, §21-245.
Meetings, §§21-240, 21-241.
Quorum, §21-241.
Oath of members, §21-243.
Personnel hiring, §21-257.
Public sewerage systems generally, §§21-151 to 21-256.
Purpose of commission, §21-249.
Quorum, §21-241.
Removal of members, §21-242.
Suspension of members, §21-242.
Contracts.
Collection of fees, rents and charges, §21-268.
Manner of letting contracts, §21-245.
Special contracts for disposal of sewage and other waste, §21-254.
Court proceedings, §21-227.
Creation of districts.
Approval of state health commissioner, §21-235.
Contents of petition, §21-230.
Exclusion from district of localities voting against establishment, §21-234.
Governing bodies adoption of resolutions, §21-236.
Hearing and determination, §21-232.
Notice of hearing on petition, §21-229.
Ordering election, §21-232.
Order when election favors establishment, §21-233.
Signatures on petition, §21-231.
Territory which may be embraced in district, §21-228.
Definitions, §21-225.
Discharges into nontidal waters, §§21-287 to 21-290.
Deleterious to system, §21-288.
Injurious or deleterious to system, §21-288.
Jurisdiction to enforce remedies against violations, §21-289.
Pollution causing agents, §21-287.
Punishment for violations, §21-290.
Elections.
Creation of districts, §§21-232 to 21-234.
Ordering and conduct of elections, §21-226.
Fees, rents and charges, §§21-260 to 21-268.
Actions for collection, §21-267.
Appeal from action fixing fees, etc., §21-266.
Authority to collect, §21-260.
Contracts for collection, §21-268.
Effect of failure to pay, §21-264.

SANITATION DISTRICTS LAW OF 1938
—Cont'd
Bond issues —Cont'd
Unabridgement of rights and remedies, §21-202.
Boundaries.
Territory which may be embraced in district, §21-145.
Citation of title, §21-141.
Commission.
Accounts and records, §21-179.
Agents and employees of commission, §21-177.
Authority, §21-155.
Bond of members, §21-163.
Compensation of members, §21-159.
Creation of board or commission to control corporation, §21-157.
Deposit of commission funds, §21-178.
Eminent domain powers, §21-166.
Enumeration of commission powers, §21-168.
Eminent domain, §21-166.
Exemption of bonds from taxation, §21-156.
Expenses of members, §21-159.
Fees, rents and charges.
Generally, §§21-180 to 21-188.
Funds of commission, §21-178.
Immunity of local governments for acts of commission, §21-167.
Manner of letting contracts, §21-165.
Meetings, §§21-160, 21-161.
Quorum, §21-161.
Oath of members, §21-163.
Officers of board or commission, §21-158.
Personnel hiring, §21-177.
Powers, §21-155.
Public sewer and disposal facilities, §§21-170 to 21-176.
Purpose of commission, §21-169.
Quorum, §21-161.
Relief from pollution as purpose of commission, §21-169.
Removal of members, §21-162.
Suspension of members, §21-162.
Corporate body and politic.
Name and style, §21-154.
Court proceedings, §21-144.
Creation of districts, §§21-145 to 21-153.
Adoption of resolutions by governing bodies, §21-153.
Approval of state health commissioner, §21-152.
Contents of petition, §21-147.
Exclusion from district of localities voting against establishment, §21-151.
Hearing on determination, §21-149.
Notice of hearing on petition, §21-146.
Ordering election, §21-149.
Election favors establishment, §21-150.
Signatures on petition, §21-148.
Territory which may be embraced in district, §21-145.
Definitions, §21-142.
Discharges into tidal waters, §§21-218 to 21-223.
Causing pollution, §21-218.
Deleterious to system, §21-219.
Injurious or deleterious to system, §21-219.
Jurisdiction to enforce remedies, §21-221.
Marine sewerage from vessels, §21-222.
Punishment for violations, §21-223.
Remedies to prevent discharge violations, §21-220.
Elections.
Ordering and conduct of elections, §21-143.

SANITATION DISTRICTS LAW OF 1938
—Cont'd
Eminent domain.
How power of eminent domain exercised, §21-166.
Exclusion from district.
Local municipalities voting against establishment, §21-151.
Fees, rents and charges, §§21-180 to 21-188.
Actions for collection, §§21-187, 21-188.
Appeal from action fixing fees, etc., §21-186.
Authorization, §21-180.
Contracts for collection, §21-188.
Effect of failure to pay, §21-184.
Payments by localities, §21-215.
Register open to public inspection, §21-185.
Schedule, §21-182.
Time and place of payment, §21-183.
Effect of failure to pay, §21-184.
Uniformity and basis, §21-181.
Hearing on petition.
Creation of districts, §§21-149 to 21-151.
Jurisdiction.
Court proceedings, §21-144.
Nontidal waters.
General provisions, §§21-224 to 21-290.
See SANITATION DISTRICTS LAW OF 1946.
Notice of hearing on petition.
Creation of districts, §21-146.
Ordinances.
Creation of districts, §21-153.
Powers and duties of localities, §§21-214 to 21-217.
Additional powers conferred on localities, §21-217.
Contracts with localities outside of district, §21-216.
Payments by localities, §21-215.
Plans, maps, etc., to be available to commission, §21-214.
Powers conferred on localities, §21-217.
Prohibitions and penalties, §§21-218 to 21-223.
Public buildings.
Use of public places, §21-173.
Public sewer and disposal facilities, §§21-170 to 21-176.
Acquisition and use of pipes, sewers, etc., §21-170.
Approval of disposal methods, §21-175.
Collection from public sewage systems, §21-171.
Prohibition of sale or encumbrance of system, §21-176.
Sale or encumbrance of system, §21-176.
Special contracts for disposal of sewage and other wastes, §21-174.
Use of public places, §21-173.
Use of public sewer and disposal facilities, §21-172.
Register of fees, rents and charges, §21-185.
Rents.
Generally, §§21-180 to 21-188.
Resolutions.
Bond issues, §§21-191, 21-194.
Creation of districts.
Governing bodies, §21-153.
Sanitary districts.
General provisions, §§21-112.22 to 21-140.3.
See SANITARY DISTRICTS.
Schedule of fees and charges, §21-182.
Short title, §21-141.
State health commissioner.
Approval of creation of districts, §21-152.
Taxes.
Exemption of bonds from taxation, §21-156.

SANITATION DISTRICTS LAW OF 1946 —Cont'd
Fees, rents and charges —Cont'd
Register open to public inspection, §21-265.
Schedule, §21-262.
Time and place of payment, §21-263.
Effect of failure to pay, §21-264.
Uniformity and basis, §21-261.
Ordinances.
Creation of districts, §21-236.
Powers and duties of localities, §§21-283 to 21-286.
Additional powers conferred on localities, §21-286.
Contracts with localities outside of district, §21-284.
Payments by localities, §21-284.
Plans, maps, etc., to be available to commission, §21-282.
Powers conferred on localities, §21-286.
Public sewer and disposal facilities, §§21-250 to 21-256.
Acquisition of pipes, sewers, etc., §21-250.
Approval of disposal methods, §21-255.
Collection from public sewage systems, §21-251.
Prohibition of sale or encumbrance of system, §21-256.
Sale or encumbrance of system, §21-256.
Special contracts for disposal of sewage and other wastes, §21-254.
Use of pipes, sewers, plants, etc., §21-250.
Use of public places, §21-253.
Use of public sewage systems, §21-252.
Rents.
Generally, §§21-260 to 21-268.
Resolutions.
Creation of districts, §21-236.
Sanitary districts.
General provisions, §§21-112.22 to 21-140.3.
See SANITARY DISTRICTS.
Schedule of fees, rents and charges, §21-262.
Short title, §21-224.
Tidal waters.
General provisions, §§21-141 to 21-223.
See SANITATION DISTRICTS LAW OF 1938.
Title of act, §21-224.
Uniformity of fees, rents and charges, §21-261.
Use of public places, §21-253.

SATELLITE CLASSROOMS, §22.1-26.1.

SATELLITE TELEVISION.
Cable TV generally.
See CABLE TELEVISION AND SERVICE.
Manufactured home lot rental.
Fee prohibitions, §55-248.45.
Residential landlord obligations, §55-248.13:2.

SATISFACTION FOR INJURY.
Assault or other misdemeanor for which civil actions available.
Discharge of recognizance or dismissal of prosecution, §19.2-151.

SATISFACTION OF JUDGMENTS, §§8.01-453 to 8.01-457.
Child support enforcement by department of social services.
Lien asserted by commissioner, §63.2-1934.
After foreclosure, §63.2-1935.
Docketing.
Entry of payment or discharge on judgment docket, §§8.01-453, 8.01-455.

SATISFACTION OF JUDGMENTS —Cont'd
Docketing —Cont'd
Marking satisfied judgments in favor of state, §8.01-457.
Judgment creditor not located, §8.01-456.
Notation of payment by judgment creditor, §8.01-454.
Payment by third parties for releasing recognizance, §8.01-457.
Priority, §8.01-459.
Recognizances and bonds having force of judgment, §8.01-465.

SATURDAYS.
Banks.
Closing, §6.2-806.
Computation of time.
Last day to perform act falling on, §1-210.
Employee protection and safety.
Employees entitled to choose as day of rest.
See EMPLOYEE PROTECTION AND SAFETY.
Holidays falling on, §2.2-3300.
Service of notice, process and other papers.
Return of process, §8.01-294.
Tax returns and payment of taxes.
Filing or payment date falling on, §58.1-8.

SAVE.
Steps to advance Virginia's energy plan.
Natural gas utilities.
SAVE plans, §§56-603, 56-604.

SAVINGS AND LOAN ASSOCIATIONS.
Articles of incorporation.
Statement of kind of business in article, §13.1-620.
Brokerage services, making available to customers.
When registration not required, §13.1-504.1.
Consumer protection.
Application of provisions, §59.1-199.
Depositories for money received by local treasurers.
See TREASURERS, LOCAL.
Enterprise zones.
Eligibility, §59.1-279.
Freedom of information act requests.
Records containing account numbers or routing information.
Excluded records, §2.2-3705.1.
Income tax on corporation.
Modifications to taxable income, §58.1-403.
Insurance premium finance companies.
Not subject to restrictions and obligations imposed by chapter, §38.2-4700.
Joint ventures.
Limitations on entering into, §13.1-627.
Nonprofit corporations.
Limitations on powers to enter into, §13.1-826.
License tax, §58.1-3730.
Loans.
Lending practices generally, §§6.2-400 to 6.2-437.
Partnership agreements.
Limitations on entering into, §13.1-627.
Nonprofit corporations.
Limitations on power to enter into, §13.1-826.
Security brokerage services made available to customers.
When registration not required, §13.1-504.1.
Security for public deposits.
Authority to secure, §2.2-4409.

SAVINGS AND LOAN ASSOCIATIONS —Cont'd
Security for public deposits —Cont'd
Qualified public depositories.
Mandatory, §2.2-4407.
Security registration exemption, §13.1-514.
Trust powers, §§6.2-1081 to 6.2-1099.
Trusts.
Exception to trustee's bond requirement, §64.2-755.
Unclaimed property.
Disposition, §55-210.3:01.

SAVINGS BANKS.
Abandonment of property presumption.
Intangible interest in business associations, §55-210.6:1.
Property of dissolved associations, §55-210.7.
Refunds, §55-210.6:2.
Commercial banks.
State savings banks.
Conversion from state savings bank to state association or commercial bank, §6.2-829.
Fiduciaries.
Trust powers, §6.2-1099.
Investments, §6.2-1187.
Loans, §6.2-1187.
Real estate loans, §6.2-1187.
Repeal or amendment of statute or regulation.
Effect on existing loan or investment, §6.2-1188.
Local government bonds.
Repeal or amendment of statute or regulation.
Effect on existing loan or investment, §6.2-1188.
Mortgages and deeds of trust and deeds of trust.
Real estate loans, §6.2-1187.
Personal property.
Investments.
Generally, §6.2-1187.
Real property.
Investments.
Generally, §6.2-1187.
Loans secured by real estate, §6.2-1187.
Rules and regulations.
State corporation commission, §6.2-1192.
Security for public deposits.
Qualified public depositories.
Mandatory, §2.2-4407.
State corporation commission.
Rules and regulations, §6.2-1192.
State savings banks.
Formation.
Authorized, §6.2-1115.
State association or commercial bank.
Conversion from state savings bank to, §6.2-829.
Conversion to state savings bank, §6.2-829.
Trusts and trustees.
Trust powers, §6.2-1099.
Unclaimed property, §55-210.3:01.
Disposition of records, §§55-210.24 to 55-210.24:2.
Intangible interest in business associations, §55-210.6:1.
Property of dissolved associations, §55-210.7.
Refunds, §55-210.6:2.

SAVINGS INSTITUTIONS, §§6.2-1100 to 6.2-1205.
Accounts, §§6.2-1166 to 6.2-1178.
Defined, §6.2-1100.
Depositories for federal taxes, §6.2-1170.
Establishment by board, §6.2-1166.
Federal employee retirement security act of 1974, §6.2-1171.

SAVINGS INSTITUTIONS —Cont'd
Accounts —Cont'd
Federal self-employed individuals tax retirement act, §6.2-1171.
Fiduciary accounts, §§6.2-1176, 6.2-1177.
Payment of accounts of deceased or incompetent, §6.2-1174.
Freedom of information act requests.
Records containing account numbers or routing information.
Excluded records, §2.2-3705.1.
Health savings accounts.
Trustee or custodian of, §6.2-603.
Interest.
Amount paid, §6.2-1166.
Legal investments, §6.2-1169.
Medical savings accounts.
Trustee or custodial services, §6.2-603.
Minors.
Accounts issued in name of minor, §6.2-1172.
Payment of account through fiduciary, etc., §6.2-1174.
Powers of attorney, §6.2-1173.
Redemption, §6.2-1168.
Security.
Accounts as security, §6.2-1169.
Trust accounts.
Same beneficiary, separate accounts, §6.2-1178.
Types, §6.2-1166.
Withdrawals.
Rules governing withdrawal, §6.2-1167.
Acquisition by out-of-state institutions or holding companies, §§6.2-1148 to 6.2-1165.
Acquisition of control of state savings bank.
Approval of commission, §6.2-1147.
Acquisition of interests in financial institutions.
Savings institution holding company seeking to acquire bank or bank holding company deemed a bank holding company, §6.2-712.
Advertising.
Misleading advertising, §6.2-1109.
Affiliates.
Examination, §6.2-1195.
Applicability to commercial paper and depository activities, §6.2-1112.
Assets.
Insolvent or financially unstable associations.
Merger, consolidation or transfer of assets, §6.2-1205.
Association.
Defined, §6.2-1100.
Audit, §§6.2-1126, 6.2-1198.
Bankruptcy and insolvency.
Merger, consolidation or transfer of assets.
Insolvent or financially unstable associations, §6.2-1205.
Banks or banking holding companies.
Association acquired by bank or bank holding company, §6.2-1146.
Consolidation.
Association and bank, §6.2-1146.
Conversion from bank to stock association, §§6.2-830, 6.2-1144.
General provisions.
See BANKS.
Merger.
Association and bank, §6.2-1146.
Stock association.
Conversion from stock association to bank, §§6.2-830, 6.2-1144.

SAVINGS INSTITUTIONS —Cont'd
Banks or banking holding companies —Cont'd
Trust powers.
Financial institution stock.
Voting, §6.2-1091.
Bonds, surety.
Officers and employees, §6.2-1127.
Trust powers.
When security not required, §6.2-1085.
Books.
Access to books, §§6.2-1125, 6.2-1196.
Examination of books, etc., of persons believed to be doing business without authority, §6.2-1203.
Branch offices.
Approval, §6.2-1133.
Change of location, §6.2-1135.
Closing.
During actual or threatened emergency, §6.2-1138.
Defined, §6.2-1100.
Drive-in or pedestrian office, §6.2-1134.
Remote service units, §6.2-1136.
Certificates of authority to do business, §6.2-1118.
Foreign savings institutions, §§6.2-1149, 6.2-1154.
Child support enforcement by department of social services.
Data exchange agreements authorized, §63.2-1932.
Lien or orders to withhold and deliver.
Joint accounts, support debtor's interest in, §63.2-1931.
Commercial banks.
Conversion from state savings bank to state association or commercial bank, §6.2-1143.
Commercial paper.
Applicability to commercial paper, §6.2-1112.
Commissioner.
Supervisory powers generally, §6.2-1191.
Committee.
Payment of savings accounts to, §6.2-1174.
Compliance review committees.
Definitions, §6.2-1113.
Records, reports or other documents, §6.2-1113.
Discovery or admissibility, §§6.2-807, 6.2-1113.
Consolidation.
Association and bank, §6.2-1146.
Fees.
Investigation of application, §6.2-1202.
Generally, §6.2-1145.
Insolvent or financially unstable associations, §6.2-1205.
Trust powers.
Continuation in the event of consolidation, §6.2-1084.
Construction of chapter, §6.2-1101.
Consumer finance act.
See CONSUMER FINANCE.
Consumer finance companies, §§6.2-1500 to 6.2-1543.
See CONSUMER FINANCE COMPANIES.
Contracts.
Foreign savings institutions.
Law applicable to contracts, §6.2-1152.
Conversion from bank to stock association, §§6.2-830, 6.2-1144.
Conversion from mutual to stock association, §6.2-1139.

SAVINGS INSTITUTIONS —Cont'd
Conversion from state into federal association and vice versa.
Effect of conversion.
Federal savings institution into state association.
Property rights, obligations, etc., §6.2-1142.
State association into federal savings institutions, §§6.2-828, 6.2-1141.
Former federal savings institution may do business as state institution, §6.2-1142.
How federal savings institutions may convert into state association, §6.2-1142.
How state association may convert into federal savings institution, §§6.2-828, 6.2-1141.
Conversion from state savings bank to state association or commercial bank, §6.2-1143.
Conversion from stock association to bank, §§6.2-830, 6.2-1144.
Conversion to state savings from bank state association or commercial bank, §6.2-1143.
Corporate names, §6.2-1116.
Corporation acts.
Applicability of Virginia stock corporation act and Virginia nonprofit corporation act, §6.2-1114.
Foreign savings institutions, §6.2-1151.
Credit.
Revolving credit.
Open-end credit plans, §§6.2-433 to 6.2-435.
Credit cards and devices.
Open-end credit plans, §§6.2-433 to 6.2-435.
Credit unions, §§6.2-1300 to 6.2-1380.
See CREDIT UNIONS.
Curator.
Payment of savings accounts to, §6.2-1174.
Defamation of institutions and certain federal agencies, §6.2-1107.
Definitions, §6.2-1100.
Affiliate of any savings institution, §6.2-1195.
Compliance review committees, §6.2-1113.
Foreign savings institutions, §6.2-1148.
Trust powers, §6.2-1081.
Deposits.
Association as depository for federal taxes, §6.2-1170.
Commercial code.
Applicability to depository activities, §6.2-1112.
Federal insurance of deposits.
Required for all banks or savings and loan associations, §6.2-601.
Directors.
Examination of directors, §6.2-1196.
Generally, §6.2-1121.
Loans.
Limitation on loans to director, §6.2-1128.
Meetings, §6.2-1122.
Quorum, §6.2-1122.
Number, §6.2-1121.
Oaths, §6.2-1121.
Overdrafts.
Limitation on overdraft by director, §6.2-1129.
Ownership of shares required, §6.2-1121.
Qualifications, §6.2-1121.
Quorum, §6.2-1122.
Removal, §6.2-1200.
Dissolution.
Trust powers.
Effect on trust accounts, §6.2-1097.
Drive-in office, §6.2-1134.
Electronic funds transfer.
Home financial services, §6.2-1137.

SAVINGS INSTITUTIONS —Cont'd
Electronic funds transfer —Cont'd
Remote service units, §6.2-1136.
Emergencies.
Suspension of business during actual or threatened emergency, §6.2-1138.
Equal savings and loan associations.
Closing of membership, §6.2-1123.
Examinations.
Affiliates, §6.2-1195.
Books, etc., of persons believed to be doing business without authority, §6.2-1203.
Commission's examinations, §6.2-1195.
Fees, §6.2-1202.
Foreign savings institutions, §6.2-1153.
Institution to give examiners access to books, etc., §6.2-1196.
Special examinations, §6.2-1201.
Executors and administrators.
Accounts of fiduciaries, §6.2-1176.
Payment of savings account to, §6.2-1174.
Facilitating organizations or instrumentalities, membership in, §6.2-1110.
False pretenses and cheats.
False statement or willful overvaluation of property for purposes of influencing lending institution, §6.2-1104.
Officers and employees, §6.2-1197.
Federal deposit insurance corporation.
Appointment as receiver, §6.2-1199.
Membership in, §6.2-1108.
Federal employee retirement security act.
Trustees or custodians.
Association may act, §6.2-1171.
Federal financial institutions.
Applicability of provisions.
Federal savings banks, §6.2-1101.
Federal home loan bank.
Membership in, §6.2-1108.
Federal institutions.
Applicability of chapter, §6.2-1101.
Federal saving institution.
Defined, §6.2-1100.
Federal self-employed individuals tax retirement act.
Trusts and trustees.
Investments in savings accounts, §6.2-1171.
Fees.
Examinations and investigations, §6.2-1202.
Supervision and regulation, §6.2-1202.
Fiduciaries.
Accounts of fiduciaries, §6.2-1176.
Inquiry as to funds deposited in fiduciary's personal account.
Institution need not inquire, §6.2-1177.
Payment of accounts of deceased or incompetent persons, §6.2-1174.
Financial institution holding company.
Defined, §6.2-1100.
Financial statements, §6.2-1194.
Foreign savings banks.
Applicability of provisions, §6.2-1101.
Foreign savings institutions, §§6.2-1148 to 6.2-1165.
Acquisitions of state savings bank or holding companies, §6.2-1164.
Activities not considered doing business, §6.2-1156.
Applicability of chapter, §6.2-1101.
Certificate of authority, §6.2-1149.
Revocation, §6.2-1154.

SAVINGS INSTITUTIONS —Cont'd
Foreign savings institutions —Cont'd
Commissioner.
General supervisory powers, §6.2-1191.
Contracts.
Law applicable to contracts, §6.2-1152.
Corporation acts.
Applicability of Virginia stock corporation act and Virginia nonprofit corporation act, §6.2-1151.
Defined, §6.2-1100.
Definitions, §6.2-1148.
Nonseverability of article, §6.2-1165.
Offices, §6.2-1133.
Branch offices, change of location, §6.2-1135.
Supervision, §6.2-1153.
Unapproved institutions.
Injunction to prevent doing business, §6.2-1155.
When operation in state prohibited, §6.2-1150.
Formation.
Capital requirements.
Minimum capital requirement, §6.2-1120.
Certificate of authority to do business, §6.2-1118.
Mutual savings and loan associations, §6.2-1115.
Stock savings and loan association, §6.2-1115.
Fraudulent entries by officers or clerks, §18.2-113.
Freedom of information act requests.
Records containing account numbers or routing information.
Excluded records, §2.2-3705.1.
General provisions, §§13.1-501 to 13.1-527.3.
See SECURITIES.
Guardian and ward.
Accounts of fiduciaries, §6.2-1176.
Payment of savings accounts to guardian, §6.2-1174.
Holding companies.
Acquisition of interests in financial institutions.
Savings institution holding company seeking to acquire bank or bank holding company deemed a bank holding company, §6.2-712.
Acquisitions.
Out-of-state financial institutions.
Acquisitions of state savings bank or holding companies, §6.2-1164.
Bank or bank holding company.
Acquisition of savings institution or savings institution holding company, §6.2-1163.
Mutual savings and loan associations.
Reorganization into mutual holding companies, §6.2-1140.
Regulation, §§6.2-1147, 6.2-1192, 6.2-1204.
Home financial services, §6.2-1137.
Home loan.
Defined, §6.2-1100.
Injunctions.
Foreign savings institutions.
Enjoining unapproved institutions from doing business, §6.2-1155.
Insurance.
Deposits.
Federal insurance of deposits.
Required for all banks or savings and loan associations, §6.2-601.
Federal deposit insurance.
Required for all banks or savings and loan associations, §6.2-601.
Statement by institutions that its shares are insured or guaranteed, §6.2-1109.

SAVINGS INSTITUTIONS —Cont'd
Insured savings institutions.
Defined, §6.2-1100.
Interest.
Contract rate more than legal rate.
Educational loans by banks or savings institutions, §6.2-323.
Installment loans, §6.2-309.
Loans of $5000 or more made by financial institution, §6.2-316.
Open-end credit plans, §6.2-313.
State savings institutions, §6.2-310.
Stock or commodity purchases.
Loans having term up to one year, §6.2-315.
Permissible rate, §6.2-1166.
Revolving credit.
Open-end credit plans, §§6.2-433 to 6.2-435.
Interpretation and construction.
Construction of chapter, §6.2-1101.
Investments.
Federal self-employed individuals tax retirement act, §6.2-1171.
General investment authority, §6.2-1186.
Legal investments.
Accounts as legal investment, §6.2-1169.
Real estate loans.
Required investments, §6.2-1179.
Trust powers.
Collective investment funds, §6.2-1094.
Custody, §6.2-1093.
Funds and assets held as fiduciary, §6.2-1088.
Funds awaiting investment or distribution, §6.2-1089.
Liability.
Members of mutual savings institutions, §6.2-1131.
Libel and slander.
Defamation of institutions and certain federal agencies prohibited, §6.2-1107.
Liquid assets.
Defined, §6.2-1100.
Loans.
Consumer finance act.
See CONSUMER FINANCE.
Consumer finance companies, §§6.2-1500 to 6.2-1543.
See CONSUMER FINANCE COMPANIES.
Directors.
Limitation on loans to directors, §6.2-1128.
Employees.
Limitation on loans to employees, §6.2-1128.
General investment authority, §6.2-1186.
Lending practices generally, §§6.2-400 to 6.2-437.
Liability of institutions.
Limitation on liability of institutions making loans for certain purposes, §6.2-1189.
Officers and employees.
Limitation on loans to officers, directors and employees, §6.2-1128.
Real estate loans, §§6.2-1179 to 6.2-1185.
Security interests.
Perfection of certain security interests, §6.2-1190.
Statutes or regulations.
Effect of repeal or amendment on existing loan on investment, §6.2-1188.
Logo or symbol.
Use in marketing materials or solicitation, §6.2-1105.
Losses.
Liability of members of mutual savings institutions, §6.2-1131.

SAVINGS INSTITUTIONS —Cont'd
Main office.
Defined, §6.2-1100.
Manufactured buildings.
Defined, §6.2-1100.
Marketing materials or solicitation.
Use of institution's name, logo or symbol, §6.2-1105.
Members.
Closing of membership, §6.2-1123.
Communication with members, §6.2-1125.
Defined, §6.2-1100.
Notice of meetings of members, §6.2-1123.
Record date.
Determination of membership, §6.2-1123.
Merger.
Association and bank, §6.2-1146.
Fees.
Investigation of application for merger, §6.2-1202.
Generally, §6.2-1145.
Insolvent or financially unstable associations.
Merger, consolidation or transfer of assets, §6.2-1205.
Trust powers.
Continuation in the event of merger, §6.2-1084.
Minors.
Savings account issued in name of minor, §6.2-1172.
Mortgages and deeds of trust.
Generally, §§6.2-406 to 6.2-423.
See MORTGAGES AND DEEDS OF TRUST.
Power to encumber property, §6.2-1111.
Trustees on loans secured by deed of trust, §6.2-1185.
Mortgages and deeds of trust and deeds of trust.
Lender authorized to engage in business as.
Exempt from chapter, §6.2-1602.
Power to encumber property, §6.2-1111.
Trustees on loans secured by deed of trust, §§6.2-1185, 6.2-1186.
Mutual capital certificates, §6.2-1132.
Mutual savings and loan associations.
Conversion from mutual to stock association, §6.2-1139.
Definition of mutual association, §6.2-1100.
Formation, §6.2-1115.
Liability of members, §6.2-1131.
Meetings.
Notice of meetings of members, §6.2-1123.
Mutual capital certificates, §6.2-1132.
Proxies, §6.2-1124.
Record date.
Determination of membership, §6.2-1123.
Reorganization into mutual holding companies, §6.2-1140.
Shares and shareholders.
Reorganization of mutual association into mutual holding company, §6.2-1140.
Voting rights.
Generally, §6.2-1124.
Mutual savings institution.
Defined, §6.2-1100.
Name.
Corporate name, §6.2-1116.
Use in marketing materials or solicitation, §6.2-1105.
Use of certain names prohibited, §6.2-1106.
Officers and employees.
Bonds, surety, §6.2-1127.

SAVINGS INSTITUTIONS —Cont'd
Officers and employees —Cont'd
Examination under oath, §6.2-1196.
False statements by, §6.2-1197.
Loans.
Limitation on loans to officers, directors or employees, §6.2-1128.
Overdrafts.
Limitation on overdrafts by officers and employees, §6.2-1129.
Removal, §6.2-1200.
Offices.
Branch offices.
Approval, §6.2-1133.
Change of location, §6.2-1135.
Drive-in or pedestrian offices, §6.2-1134.
Closing.
During actual or threatened emergency, §6.2-1138.
Drive-in offices, §6.2-1134.
Establishment, §6.2-1133.
Pedestrian offices, §6.2-1134.
Remote service units, §6.2-1136.
Open-end credit plans, §§6.2-433 to 6.2-435.
Amendments to contract or plan, §6.2-433.
Law governing, plans by bank or savings institution, §6.2-434.
Law governing, plans by sellers or lenders, §6.2-435.
Out-of-state institutions or holding companies.
Acquisitions by.
Applicable laws, rules and regulations, §6.2-1161.
Definitions, §6.2-1148.
Enforcement of article, §6.2-1161.
Hearing, §6.2-1159.
Interstate agreements, §6.2-1162.
Investigations of application, §6.2-1159.
Notice of intent to acquire out-of-state savings institution, §6.2-1160.
Out-of-state savings institution holding company, §6.2-1157.
Out-of-state savings institutions, §6.2-1158.
Reports, §6.2-1162.
Nonseverability of article, §6.2-1165.
Notice of intent to acquire out-of-state savings institution, §6.2-1160.
Overdrafts.
Directors.
Limitation on overdraft by directors, §6.2-1129.
Officers and employees.
Limitation on overdrafts by officers, directors or employees, §6.2-1129.
Payday loans.
Election not to become licensed under provisions.
Inapplicability of provisions, §6.2-1802.
Election to become licensed under provisions.
Effect, §6.2-1802.
Generally, §§6.2-1800 to 6.2-1829.
See PAYDAY LOANS.
Payment in full.
Shares and shareholders, §6.2-1117.
Pedestrian offices, §6.2-1134.
Powers of attorney.
Savings account, §6.2-1173.
Preexisting institutions.
Effect of chapter on, §6.2-1102.
Profits.
Undivided profit, §6.2-1130.
Publication.
State corporation commission to publish regulations, §6.2-1192.

SAVINGS INSTITUTIONS —Cont'd
Real estate loans, §§6.2-1179 to 6.2-1185.
Adjustable loans, §6.2-1182.
Appraisals, §6.2-1180.
Authority of associations, §6.2-1179.
Deed of trust.
Power to encumber, §6.2-1111.
Trustees on loans secured by, §6.2-1185.
Defined, §6.2-1100.
Home loans.
Special provisions, §6.2-1183.
Initial repayments, §6.2-1181.
Loan-to-value ratios, §6.2-1180.
Repayments.
Initial repayments, §6.2-1181.
Required investments, §6.2-1179.
Successors in interest.
Dealings with, §6.2-1184.
Real property.
Power to hold, convey and encumber, §6.2-1111.
Receivers.
Federal deposit insurance corporation.
Appointment as receiver, §6.2-1199.
Trust powers.
Effect on trust accounts of appointment of receiver, §6.2-1097.
Records.
Access to records, §§6.2-1125, 6.2-1196.
Examination of books, etc., of persons believed to be doing business without authority, §6.2-1203.
Freedom of information act requests.
Records containing account numbers or routing information.
Excluded records, §2.2-3705.1.
Trust accounts.
Maintenance of books and accounts, §6.2-1087.
Redemption, §6.2-1168.
Regulations.
Holding companies, §6.2-1192.
Remote service units, §6.2-1136.
Reorganization of mutual association into mutual holding company, §6.2-1140.
Reports.
Associations to furnish financial statements and reports, §6.2-1194.
Audits, §6.2-1126.
Reserves, §6.2-1130.
Revolving credit.
Open-end credit plans, §§6.2-433 to 6.2-435.
Rules and regulations.
State corporation commission.
Adoption, §6.2-1192.
Duration, §6.2-1192.
Permitting associations to have powers comparable to federal savings institutions, §6.2-1192.
Publication, §6.2-1192.
Savings accounts.
Defined, §6.2-1100.
Fiduciary accounts, §6.2-1176.
Deposit into personal account.
Duties of institution, §6.2-1177.
Payment of accounts of deceased or incompetent persons, §6.2-1174.
Investments.
Legal investments, §6.2-1169.
Legal investments, §6.2-1169.
Minors.
Accounts issued in name of minor, §6.2-1172.

SAVINGS INSTITUTIONS —Cont'd
Savings accounts —Cont'd
Payment of savings accounts through personal representatives, guardian, curator or committee, §6.2-1174.
Powers of attorney, §6.2-1173.
Redemption, §6.2-1168.
Security.
Accounts as security, §6.2-1169.
Trustees.
Shares held by various trustees for same beneficiary, §6.2-1178.
Types of accounts authorized, §6.2-1166.
Withdrawal.
Rules governing, §6.2-1167.
Savings banks.
Defined, §6.2-1100.
General provisions.
See SAVINGS BANKS.
Savings institution holding company.
Defined, §6.2-1100.
Securities.
Accounts as security, §6.2-1169.
Perfection of certain security interests, §6.2-1190.
Service corporations.
Defined, §6.2-1100.
Severability of provisions, §6.2-1101.
Shares and shareholders.
Acceptance of shares of security, §6.2-1117.
Commissions, fees, etc., for sale of stock not permitted, §6.2-1118.
Directors to own shares, §6.2-1121.
Disposition of money received before institution opens, §6.2-1117.
Mutual capital certificates, §6.2-1132.
Mutual savings and loan associations.
Reorganization of mutual association into mutual holding company.
Issuance of stock, §6.2-1140.
Paid in full, §6.2-1117.
Par value of shares, §6.2-1117.
Reorganization of mutual association into mutual holding company.
Issuance of stock, §6.2-1140.
Requisition with own shares by association, §6.2-1117.
Sale of stock.
Commissions, fees, etc., for sale of stock not permitted, §6.2-1118.
Stock option plans, §6.2-1117.
Subscriptions to stock.
Payment, §6.2-1117.
Trust powers.
Financial institution stock.
Voting of stock held by association as fiduciary, §6.2-1091.
State association.
Defined, §6.2-1100.
State bank.
Defined, §6.2-1100.
State corporation commission.
Acquisition of control of state savings bank.
Approval of commission, §6.2-1147.
Examinations, §6.2-1195.
Powers in case of violations of law, irregularities, etc., §6.2-1199.
Regulations.
Adoption, §6.2-1192.
Duration, §6.2-1192.
Permitting associations to have powers comparable to federal savings institutions, §6.2-1192.

SAVINGS INSTITUTIONS —Cont'd
State corporation commission —Cont'd
Regulations —Cont'd
Publication, §6.2-1192.
Statements to be furnished by commission to directors of institutions, §6.2-1193.
Statements.
Associations to furnish financial statements and reports, §6.2-1194.
Statements to be furnished by state corporation commission to directors of institutions, §6.2-1193.
State savings banks.
Acquisition by out-of-state financial institutions, §6.2-1164.
Defined, §6.2-1100.
State savings institution.
Defined, §6.2-1100.
Stock and stockholders.
Interest, contract rate more than legal rate.
Loans having term up to one year, §6.2-315.
Minimum capital requirement, §6.2-1120.
Stock association.
Defined, §6.2-1100.
Stock institution.
Defined, §6.2-1100.
Surplus, §6.2-1130.
Taxation.
Depositories for federal taxes and United States treasury tax and loan account, §6.2-1170.
Trust powers.
Acceptance of fiduciary account, §6.2-1086.
Affiliates.
Dealings with self or affiliates, §6.2-1090.
Applications.
Permission to offer trust services, §6.2-1082.
Appointment of receiver.
Effect on trust accounts, §6.2-1097.
Assets.
Custody, §6.2-1093.
Bonds, surety.
When security not required, §6.2-1085.
Books and accounts.
Separate from other records, §6.2-1087.
Certificate authorizing exercise.
Issuance, §6.2-1083.
Collective investment funds, §6.2-1094.
Establishment, §6.2-1094.
Common trust funds.
Establishment, §6.2-1094.
Compensation of association acting as fiduciary, §6.2-1095.
Consolidation or merger of associations.
Continuation of trust powers, §6.2-1084.
Custody of assets and investments, §6.2-1093.
Dealings with self or affiliates, §6.2-1090.
Definitions, §6.2-1081.
Dissolution.
Voluntary dissolution of association.
Effect on trust accounts, §6.2-1097.
Distributions.
Funds awaiting investment or distribution, §6.2-1089.
Investments, §6.2-1088.
Collective investment funds, §6.2-1094.
Custody, §6.2-1093.
Funds awaiting investment or distribution, §6.2-1089.
Operation of trust department, §6.2-1086.
Permission to offer trust services.
Applications, §6.2-1082.

SAVINGS INSTITUTIONS —Cont'd
Trust powers —Cont'd
Powers and privileges, §6.2-1083.
Records.
Contents, §6.2-1087.
Separate from other records, §6.2-1087.
Review of accounts, §6.2-1086.
Revocation, §6.2-1098.
Rights of associations, §6.2-1083.
Shares and shareholders.
Voting of financial institution stock held by association as fiduciary, §6.2-1091.
Supervision of trust department, §6.2-1086.
Surrender of powers, §6.2-1096.
Transactions between trust accounts, §6.2-1092.
Trusts and trustees.
Accounts of fiduciaries, §6.2-1176.
Beneficiaries.
Savings accounts held by various trustees for same beneficiary, §6.2-1178.
Federal employee retirement security act.
Association may act as trustee, §6.2-1171.
Federal self-employed individual tax retirement act.
Association may act as trustee, §6.2-1171.
Real estate loans.
Trustees on loans secured by deed of trust, §6.2-1185.
Unauthorized conduct of business.
Doing business without authority, §6.2-1203.
Examination of books, etc., of persons believed to be doing business without authority, §6.2-1203.
Prohibitions and restrictions on conduct, §6.2-1103.
Terms.
Use of certain terms prohibited, §6.2-1106.
Unclaimed property, §55-210.3:01.
Disposition, §55-210.3:01.
Withdrawals.
Rules governing, §6.2-1167.
Withdrawal value.
Defined, §6.2-1100.

SAWDUST.
Fish.
Prohibition against use of substances injurious to fish, §29.1-533.
Motor vehicle registration.
Vehicles owned by farmers and used to transport certain wood products, §46.2-670.
Saw mills, stave mills, etc.
Cleaning of premises, §10.1-1144.

SAWED-OFF SHOTGUNS AND SAWED-OFF RIFLES, §§18.2-299 to 18.2-307.
Applicability of article.
What article does not apply to, §18.2-303.
Concealed weapons and concealed handgun permits, §§18.2-307.1 to 18.2-308.015.
Curiosity, ornament or keepsake, possession for, §18.2-303.1.
Definitions, §18.2-299.
Inapplicability of article, §18.2-303.
Inspection of manufacturer's and dealer's stock, §18.2-304.
Manufacturer's and dealer's register, §18.2-304.
Plastic firearms, manufacture, import, etc., §18.2-308.5.
Possession, §18.2-300.
Sawed-off shotgun and sawed-off rifle act, §18.2-307.

SAWED-OFF SHOTGUNS AND SAWED-OFF RIFLES —Cont'd
Scientific purposes, possession for, §18.2-303.1.
Search warrants, §18.2-306.
Short title, §18.2-307.
Use, §18.2-300.
What article does not apply to, §18.2-303.
What article does not prohibit, §18.2-303.1.

SAXIS, TOWN OF.
Golf carts or utility vehicles.
Designating public highways for operation, authority, §46.2-916.2.

SCAFFOLDING.
Homing pigeons.
Use of scaffolding to injure pigeons prohibited, §18.2-145.
Underground coal mines, §45.1-161.241.

SCALLOPS.
Defined as shellfish, §28.2-800.

SCALPING OF TICKETS.
Ordinances prohibiting, §15.2-969.

SCAM BOXING CONTESTS, §54.1-834.

SCANDALOUS MATTER.
Trademark and service mark registrability.
Ineligibility for registration of marks containing, §59.1-92.3.

SCANNERS.
Use of police radio signal, message or transmission during commission of crime, §18.2-462.1.

SCANNING DEVICES.
Payment card scanning devices and re-encoders, unlawful use, §18.2-196.1.

SCENIC HIGHWAYS AND VIRGINIA BYWAYS, §§33.1-62 to 33.1-66.

SCENIC RIVERS, §§10.1-400 to 10.1-418.8.
Acquisition of property.
Powers and duties of director, §10.1-401.
Advisory committees.
Local governments.
Powers, §10.1-406.1.
Powers and duties of director, §10.1-401.
Appomattox state scenic river, §10.1-409.
Banister state scenic river, §10.1-411.3.
Blackwater state scenic river, §10.1-418.6.
Board.
Defined, §10.1-400.
Catoctin creek state scenic river, §10.1-410.
Chickahominy state scenic river, §10.1-410.1.
Clinch-Guest state scenic river, §10.1-411.1.
Clinch state scenic river, §10.1-410.2.
Conservation and recreation board.
Duties, §10.1-107.
Conservation police officers.
Daylight hours patrol of lakes from Memorial Day through Labor Day, §29.1-739.2.
Construction, §10.1-407.
Dan state scenic river, §10.1-413.3.
Defined, §10.1-400.
Department.
Defined, §10.1-400.
Duties, §10.1-405.
Powers and duties, §10.1-405.
Designation.
Powers and duties of director, §10.1-401.
Recommendation for, §10.1-404.

SCENIC RIVERS —Cont'd
Development and evaluation as scenic resource, §10.1-402.
Director.
Defined, §10.1-400.
Powers and duties, §10.1-401.
Eminent domain, §10.1-405.
Evaluation of planning, use and development proposals, §10.1-402.
Goose creek scenic river, §10.1-411.
Hearings, §10.1-403.
Historic falls of the James scenic river, §10.1-412.
Hughes state scenic river, §10.1-418.8.
James river, §10.1-413.
Historic falls, §10.1-412.
Jordan state scenic river, §10.1-418.7.
Local governments.
Powers, §10.1-406.1.
Meherrin river, §10.1-418.3.
Moormans river, §10.1-413.1.
North Landing and tributaries scenic river, §10.1-413.2.
North Mayo river, §10.1-418.4.
North Meherrin river, §10.1-418.1.
Nottoway river, §10.1-414.
Planning and development.
Department's powers and duties, §10.1-405.
Evaluation of planning, use and development proposals, §10.1-402.
Rappahannock river, §10.1-415.
Recommendations.
Powers and duties of director, §10.1-401.
Riparian uses, §10.1-408.
Rivanna river, §10.1-416.
River.
Defined, §10.1-400.
Roanoke river, §10.1-418.
Rockfish river, §10.1-415.1.
Russell Fork state scenic river, §10.1-411.2.
St. Mary's river, §10.1-418.2.
Shenandoah river, §10.1-417.
South Mayo river, §10.1-418.5.
Staunton river, §10.1-418.
Studies.
Powers and duties of director, §10.1-401.
Virginia scenic rivers system.
Defined, §10.1-400.

SCHEDULE OF FEES.
Circuit court clerks.
Fees generally, §17.1-275.
Court of appeals clerk, §17.1-418.
Supreme court clerk, §17.1-328.

SCHEDULE OF REVISED CONSTITUTION, VA Const Sched §§1 to 5.

SCHEDULE I DRUGS, §54.1-3446.
Administering, §54.1-3413.
Controlled substances registration certificates, §§54.1-3422 to 54.1-3424.
Designer drugs, §54.1-3456.
Manufacturing, §54.1-3413.
Placement of substance in, §54.1-3445.

SCHEDULE II DRUGS, §54.1-3448.
Confirmation of receipt for distribution, §54.1-3420.
Controlled substances registration certificates, §§54.1-3422 to 54.1-3424.
Designer drugs, §54.1-3456.
Disposing of stocks, §54.1-3417.

SCHEDULE II DRUGS —Cont'd
Distribution by manufacturers and wholesalers, §54.1-3415.
Identification requirement for prescriptions, §54.1-3420.1.
Official orders for, §54.1-3414.
Placement of substance in, §54.1-3447.
Prescription requirements, §§54.1-3410, 54.1-3411.
Written requests for distribution, §54.1-3420.

SCHEDULE III DRUGS, §54.1-3450.
Confirmation of receipt for distribution, §54.1-3420.
Controlled substances registration certificates, §§54.1-3422 to 54.1-3424.
Designer drugs, §54.1-3456.
Disposing of stocks, §54.1-3417.
Distribution by manufacturers and wholesalers, §54.1-3415.
Identification requirement for prescriptions, §54.1-3420.1.
Placement of substance in, §54.1-3449.
Prescription requirements, §§54.1-3410, 54.1-3411.
Prisoner crimes, §53.1-203.
Juvenile corrections facilities, §18.2-477.2.
Written requests for distribution, §54.1-3420.

SCHEDULE IV DRUGS, §54.1-3452.
Confirmation of receipt for distribution, §54.1-3420.
Controlled substances registration certificates, §§54.1-3422 to 54.1-3424.
Designer drugs, §54.1-3456.
Disposing of stocks, §54.1-3417.
Distribution by manufacturers and wholesalers, §54.1-3415.
Identification requirement for prescriptions, §54.1-3420.1.
Placement of substance in, §54.1-3451.
Prescription requirements, §§54.1-3410, 54.1-3411.
Written requests for distribution, §54.1-3420.

SCHEDULE V DRUGS, §54.1-3454.
Controlled substances registration certificates, §§54.1-3422 to 54.1-3424.
Designer drugs, §54.1-3456.
Disposing of stocks, §54.1-3417.
Distribution by manufacturers and wholesalers, §54.1-3415.
Identification requirement for prescriptions, §54.1-3420.1.
Placement of substance in, §54.1-3453.
Prescription requirements, §§54.1-3410, 54.1-3411.
Prescriptions, §54.1-3416.
Written requests for distribution, §54.1-3420.
Confirmation of receipt for distribution, §54.1-3420.

SCHEDULE VI DRUGS, §54.1-3455.
Designer drugs, §54.1-3456.
Distribution by manufacturers and wholesalers, §54.1-3415.
Prescription requirements, §§54.1-3410, 54.1-3411.

SCHIZOAFFECTIVE DISORDER.
Health insurance.
Coverage for biologically based mental illness, §38.2-3412.1:01.

SCHIZOAFFECTIVE DISORDER —Cont'd
Health insurance —Cont'd
Public officers and employees.
Required coverage, §2.2-2818.

SCHIZOPHRENIA.
Health insurance.
Coverage for biologically based mental illness, §38.2-3412.1:01.
Public officers and employees.
Required coverage, §2.2-2818.

SCHOLARSHIPS, §§23-31 to 23-38.10:1.
Alumni scholarships, §23-35.
Arts commission.
Duties, §2.2-2509.
Brown v. Board of Education scholarship program and fund, §§30-231.01 to 30-231.10.
Awards committee.
Award of scholarships, §§30-231.2, 30-231.8.
Compensation and expenses, §30-231.7.
Establishment, §30-231.5.
FOI act exclusion.
Records relating to personally identifiable information, §2.2-3705.4.
Legal, research and policy analysis services, §30-231.9.
Meetings, §30-231.6.
Membership, §30-231.5.
Powers and duties, §30-231.8.
Quorum, §30-231.6.
Reporting requirements, §30-231.10.
Support staff, §30-231.9.
Voting on recommendations, §30-231.6.
College level examination program (CLEP) examinations and costs.
Use of awards for, §30-231.2.
Definitions, §30-231.01.
Establishment, §§30-231.1, 30-231.4.
Professional degree programs.
Use of awards for, §30-231.2.
Purpose, §30-231.1.
Scholarship awards.
Amount, §30-231.3.
Applicant required to sign, §30-231.3.
Balance surrendered to Commonwealth.
Withdrawal from education agency, failure to complete program, §30-231.3.
Criteria for award, §30-231.2.
Disbursement of funds to student accounts, §30-231.3.
Eligible students, §30-231.2.
False or fictitious name or address in application, criminal penalty, §30-231.3.
Notice by agency acting on behalf of recipient or assistance received, §30-231.3.
Renewal of scholarships, §30-231.2.
Right or entitlement not created, §30-231.3.
Terms and conditions, §30-231.3.
Use of scholarships, §30-231.3.
Theological education or religious training.
Ineligibility of students enrolled in, §30-231.2.
Community college incentive scholarship program, §§23-220.2 to 23-220.4.
Dental hygienists, §§23-37.1 to 23-37.5, 32.1-122.10.
Contracts signed before awards, §23-37.3.
Duration, §23-37.4.
Effect of military service, §23-38.
Establishment, §23-37.1.
How awarded, §23-37.2.
How payments made, §23-37.5.

SCHOLARSHIPS —Cont'd
Dental hygienists —Cont'd
Number, §23-37.1.
Payments to student or account, §23-37.5.
Qualifications of applicants, §23-37.2.
Signed contracts before award, §23-37.3.
Yearly renewal, §23-37.4.
Dental students, §32.1-122.9.
Dental hygiene, §§23-37.1 to 23-37.5, 32.1-122.10.
Donations.
Investment of funds donated for scholarships, §23-32.
Irrevocable donations, §23-33.
Right of nomination by donor, §23-33.
Selection when donor fails to nominate, §23-34.
Health workforce recruitment, §32.1-122.20.
Income tax credits.
Education improvement scholarships tax credits, §§58.1-439.25 to 58.1-439.28.
Investment of funds.
Donated for scholarships, §23-32.
Medical College of Virginia.
Nursing scholarships, §23-36.2.
Medical students, §§32.1-122.5:1, 32.1-122.6.
Military service.
Effect of armed forces service on obligation to state, §23-38.
Nursing scholarships, §§23-35.9 to 23-36.2.
Advisory committee, §23-35.9.
Award by board, §§32.1-122.6:01, 32.1-122.6:02.
Basis of awards, §23-35.10.
Contract signed before award, §23-35.11.
Effect of military service, §23-38.
Establishment, §23-35.9.
Fund, §54.1-3011.2.
How payments made, §23-35.13.
Medical college of Virginia, §23-36.2.
Number, §23-35.9.
Payments to student or account, §23-35.13.
Recipients to be bona fide residents, §23-35.10.
Renewals, §23-35.12.
Signed contract before award, §23-35.11.
University of Virginia, §23-36.2.
Yearly renewals, §23-35.12.
Physician assistants.
Conditional grants, §32.1-122.6:03.
Scholarship assistance program, §§23-38.45 to 23-38.52.
Acceptance of gifts, §23-38.52.
Administration, §§23-38.45, 23-38.46.
Amount of grants, §23-38.48.
Bona fide residence, §23-38.46.
Creation, §23-38.45.
Criteria for making grants, §23-38.47.
Determining amount of grants, §§23-38.47, 23-38.48.
Eligibility, §23-38.46.
Employment of staff, §23-38.52.
Financial assistance programs established by restricted endowment and gifts.
Administration by council of higher education, §23-38.52.
Promulgation of rules, §23-38.51.
Rulemaking authority, §23-38.51.
Terms and conditions of grants, §23-38.49.
Tuition and room and board, §23-38.50.
Use of grants, §23-38.50.
Soil scientist scholarships, §§23-38.3 to 23-38.10.
Basis of awards, §23-38.4.
Contract signed before award, §23-38.5.
Disposition of funds repaid, §23-38.10.

SCHOLARSHIPS —Cont'd
Soil scientist scholarships —Cont'd
Effect of military service, §§23-38, 23-38.8.
Establishment, §23-38.3.
Failure to abide by contract, §23-38.10.
How payments made, §23-38.7.
Number, §23-38.3.
Payments to student or account, §23-38.7.
Recipients to be bona fide residents, §23-38.4.
Relief from obligation of contract, §23-38.9.
Renewals, §23-38.6.
Signed contract before award, §23-38.5.
Termination of contract, §23-38.9.
Yearly renewals, §23-38.6.
Special education traineeships, §23-38.10:1.
Stephen J. Wright scholars program, §23-38.53:11.
Teachers.
Teaching scholarship loans, §22.1-290.
Traineeships for education of special education personnel, §23-38.10:1.
Tuition remission.
Unfunded scholarships, §23-31.
Unfunded scholarships, §23-31.
University of Virginia.
Nursing scholarships, §23-36.2.
Virginia behavioral health and developmental services scholarship fund, §23-38.2.
Virginia Military Institute.
Military scholarship cadets, §§23-107.1, 23-107.2.
Virginia Polytechnic Institute and State University.
Soil scientist scholarships, §§23-38.3 to 23-38.10.
Virginia teaching scholarship loan program, §22.1-290.01.
Collaboration between council of higher education and state board of education, §23-38.10:1.
Women, council on.
Establishment, §2.2-2631.

SCHOLASTIC RECORDS.
Freedom of information act exclusions.
Military recruiters, §22.1-288.
Schools and education.
Student records generally, §§22.1-287 to 22.1-289.

SCHOOL BOARDS, LOCAL, §§22.1-28 to 22.1-57.5.
See LOCAL SCHOOL BOARDS.

SCHOOL BUILDINGS AND FACILITIES, §§22.1-125 to 22.1-140.
Acquisition of property.
Authority to acquire property from federal government, §22.1-130.
Condemnation of land for school purposes, §22.1-127.
Counties, cities and towns, §22.1-126.1.
Exchange of real and personal property, §22.1-129.
Property given, devised or bequested to school board, §22.1-126.
Title to property, §§22.1-125, 22.1-128.
Approval of plans for buildings by division superintendent, §22.1-140.
Arrest of child.
Carrying weapon on school property, §16.1-246.
Asbestos abatement.
Inspections, §§2.2-1163, 2.2-1165.
Labels or marks where asbestos found, §2.2-1166.
Standards for inspections, §2.2-1164.

SCHOOL BUILDINGS AND FACILITIES —Cont'd
Authority to acquire property from federal government, §22.1-130.
Buildings unfit for occupancy.
Duty to close buildings, §22.1-136.
Burning or destroying schoolhouses, §18.2-79.
Career and technical education projects and associated land.
Power of school board to sell, §22.1-129.
Carrying weapons on school property.
Arrest of child, §16.1-246.
Condemnation of land for school purposes, §22.1-127.
Counties, cities and towns, §22.1-126.1.
Construction grants, §§22.1-175.1 to 22.1-175.5.
Application, §22.1-175.4.
Capital school projects fund, §22.1-175.5.
Fund, §22.1-175.2.
Guidelines, §22.1-175.3.
Program established, §22.1-175.1.
County department of public works.
Maintenance, etc., of school buildings and buses, §22.1-134.
Damaging property located in, §18.2-138.
Damaging public buildings, §18.2-138.
Daycare programs in certain localities, §22.1-132.1.
Development of park areas adjacent to public schools, §22.1-80.
Discharging firearm in or near school property, §18.2-280.
Disqualification for concealed weapons permit, §18.2-308.09.
Donation of obsolete educational technology hardware and software, §22.1-129.
Drug sales on or near property, §18.2-255.2.
Exception to title vesture, §22.1-125.
Extent of school board's authority, §22.1-125.
Firearms.
Arrest of child carrying weapon on school property, §16.1-246.
Discharging in or near school property, §18.2-280.
Disqualification for concealed weapons permit, §18.2-308.09.
Pointing, holding or brandishing, §18.2-282.
Possession on school property, §18.2-308.1.
Fire drills, §22.1-137.
Flags, §22.1-133.
Grants.
Construction grants, §§22.1-175.1 to 22.1-175.5.
Application, §22.1-175.4.
Capital school projects fund, §22.1-175.5.
Health standards, §22.1-135.
Inspections.
Asbestos abatement.
Labels or marks where asbestos found, §2.2-1166.
State-owned and public school buildings, §§2.2-1163, 2.2-1165.
Standards for inspections, §2.2-1164.
Integrated pest management, §22.1-132.2.
Literary fund.
Power of board to make loans for erection of school buildings, §22.1-146.
Local governments.
Property acquisition for educational purposes by counties, cities and towns, §22.1-126.1.
Location of school outside boundaries of school division, §22.1-127.
Lock-down drills, §22.1-137.2.

SCHOOL BUILDINGS AND FACILITIES —Cont'd
Maintenance, etc., by county department of public works, §22.1-134.
Military affairs.
Government data collection and dissemination practices act.
Recruiter access to student information and school facilities, §2.2-3804.
Minimum standards.
Health and environmental standards, §§22.1-135, 22.1-136, 22.1-138.
Opportunity educational institution, §22.1-27.6.
Pest management, §22.1-132.2.
Property given, devised or bequested to school board, §22.1-126.
Public-private education facilities and infrastructure act, §§56-575.1 to 56-575.18.
See PUBLIC BUILDINGS.
Radon testing, §22.1-138.
Refusal to leave after direction to vacate, §18.2-128.
Right of entry, §22.1-127.
Sale, exchange or lease of real and personal property, §22.1-129.
Sanitary standards, §22.1-135.
Sex offenses prohibiting entry onto school property, §18.2-370.5.
Sex offenses prohibiting working on school property, §18.2-370.4.
Smoke bombs.
Setting off in schools, §18.2-87.1.
Surplus real property, §22.1-129.
Swastika, placing on certain property, §18.2-423.1.
Title to property vested in school board, §22.1-125.
Title to school board real estate, §22.1-128.
Trespass upon school property, §18.2-128.
Unfit for occupancy.
Duty to close buildings, §22.1-136.
Use of school property, §§22.1-131, 22.1-132.
Weapons.
Arrest of child for carrying on property, §16.1-246.
Discharging firearm in or near school property, §18.2-280.
Disqualification for concealed weapons permit, §18.2-308.09.
Pointing, holding or brandishing firearms, air or gas operated weapons or similar object, §18.2-282.
Possession of firearms or other weapons on school property, §18.2-308.1.

SCHOOL BUSES, §§22.1-176 to 22.1-198.
Age limit for drivers, §§22.1-178, 46.2-919.
Alcohol or drug use.
Drinking or possessing alcoholic beverages while operating a school bus, §4.1-309.1.
Alternative fuels.
Authority of local school divisions to use, §22.1-177.
Signs and markings on buses using fuels, §46.2-1089.1.
Applicability of insurance article, §22.1-198.
Career and technical education.
Corporate projects.
Transportation of students, §22.1-235.
Child restraint exemption, §§46.2-1096, 46.2-1099.
Compliance with insurance article, §22.1-189.

SCHOOL BUSES —Cont'd
Contributions, §22.1-176.
County department of public works.
Maintenance, etc., §22.1-134.
Decals relating to school bus safety, §22.1-177.
Definitions, §46.2-100.
Insurance, §22.1-188.
Divided highways.
Pupils' crossing divided highways.
Avoidance of routes, §46.2-918.
Drivers.
Age requirement, §§22.1-178, 46.2-919.
Automated external defibrillators.
Proof of training or certification, §22.1-178.
Cardiopulmonary resuscitation.
Proof of training or certification, §22.1-178.
Character statement, §22.1-178.
Drivers' licenses.
Current driver's license, §22.1-178.
Endorsements, classifications and restrictions authorizing operation, §46.2-328.
Examination of school bus drivers, §46.2-339.
Suspension or revocation, DMV to notify school district, §46.2-340.
First-aid training or certification, §22.1-178.
Hiring school buses to transport children, §46.2-917.1.
Ignition interlock system.
Operating school bus without installation, prohibition, §18.2-270.1.
Information concerning drivers submitted by school division to DMV, §46.2-340.
Physical examination requirement, §22.1-178.
Requirements generally, §§22.1-178 to 22.1-181.
Sex offender and crimes against minors registry.
Commercial driver's licenses.
Cancellation of endorsement for conviction of offense requiring registration, §46.2-341.18:3.
Instruction permit to drive school bus.
Non-eligibility while registration required, §46.2-341.10.
Prohibition from driving school bus while registration required, §46.2-339.
Statement or copy of driving record, §22.1-178.
Training program, §22.1-181.
Twelve-month employees generally.
See SCHOOLS AND EDUCATION.
Wireless telecommunications devices.
Use by persons driving school buses, §46.2-919.1.
Drug sales on school buses or at bus stops, §18.2-255.2.
Emergency drills, §22.1-184.
Extracurricular activities.
Acceptance of contributions for transportation, §22.1-176.
Fees and charges.
Payment for transportation of pupils, §22.1-186.
When fee may be charged, §22.1-176.
Fine schedule, VA SCt Rule 3B:2.
Maximum fine for violating Title 46.2, §46.2-113.
Firearms or other weapons, possession on, §18.2-308.1.
Guest doctrine, §8.01-63.
Inapplicability of doctrine, §22.1-193.
Handicapped children.
Transportation of handicapped pupils attending public or private programs, §22.1-221
Identification.
When letter identification to be covered, §22.1-183.

SCHOOL BUSES —Cont'd
Improper painting and lettering, §46.2-1089.
Insurance, §§22.1-188 to 22.1-198.
Amount required, §22.1-190.
Applicability of insurance article, §22.1-198.
Compliance with article prerequisite to receiving state school funds, §22.1-189.
Applicability of insurance article, §22.1-198.
Coverage required, §22.1-190.
Injury and damage coverage, §22.1-190.
Definitions, §22.1-188.
Distribution of funds when superintendent effects insurance, §22.1-197.
Guest doctrine not applicable, §22.1-193.
Injury and damage policy coverage, §22.1-192.
Lapsed insurance, §22.1-196.
Liability of locality or school board owning or operating vehicle, §22.1-194.
Recovery when vehicle operated under contract, §22.1-195.
Sufficiency of proof in action on policy, §22.1-193.
Taxicabs providing transportation of students, coverages, §22.1-190.
When required, §22.1-190.
When superintendent to obtain insurance, §22.1-191.
Lapsed insurance, §22.1-196.
Literary fund.
Alternative fuel conversion.
Power of board to make loans, §22.1-146.
Locality selling bus fleet with intent to lease back.
Approval, notice, public hearing, §15.2-951.
Maximum speed limit, §46.2-871.
Motor vehicle registration.
Fees for vehicles designed for transportation of passengers, §46.2-694.
New buses placed in service on or after July 1, 2007.
Warning devices required, §46.2-1090.
Nonpublic school pupils.
Agreements to provide transportation, §22.1-176.1.
Operation of yellow passenger vehicles.
Hiring school buses to transport children, §46.2-917.1.
Transportation of students required, §46.2-917.
Painting and lettering, §46.2-1089.
Parochial or private schools.
Requirements for school bus drivers, §22.1-180.
Passing a stopped school bus, §§46.2-844, 46.2-859.
Prepayment of fine, §16.1-69.40:1.
Public school system.
Transportation of pupils authorized, §22.1-176.
Pupils crossing divided highways.
Avoidance of routes, §46.2-918.
Reckless driving.
Passing a stopped school bus, §46.2-859.
Rulemaking authority, §22.1-177.
Safety belts.
Drivers required to wear, §46.2-1091.
School pupils and personnel.
Defined, §22.1-188.
Shelters on bus routes, §22.1-185.
Signs and markings on buses using alternative fuels, §46.2-1089.1.
Signs or devices to indicate bus stops.
Authority of local school board to install, §33.1-223.2:18.

SCHOOL BUSES —Cont'd
Special education children.
Transportation of children with disabilities to and from program, §22.1-221.
Special or charter party certificate, §46.2-917.2.
Stopped buses.
Exemption to prohibition on stopping on highway, §46.2-893.
Passing, §§46.2-844, 46.2-859.
Toll roads.
Exemption from payment of tolls, §22.1-187.
Traffic infractions.
Passing a stopped school bus, §§46.2-844, 46.2-859.
Training program for drivers, §22.1-181.
Trespass upon school property.
School property defined to include school bus, §18.2-128.
Use of school buses for public purposes, §§22.1-176, 22.1-182.
Video-monitoring systems.
Passing a stopped school bus, §46.2-844.
Warning devices, §§46.2-1090, 46.2-1090.1.
Warning lights, §46.2-1090.1.
When to be covered, §22.1-183.
Weapons.
Possession of firearms or other weapons, §18.2-308.1.
Width of vehicles, §46.2-1105.
Wireless telecommunications devices.
Use by persons driving school buses, §46.2-919.1.

SCHOOL CAFETERIAS.
Cafeteria workers.
Tuberculosis certificate, §22.1-300.
County food and beverage tax not levied, §58.1-3833.
Recycling programs of state agencies.
Duties of department of education, §10.1-1425.9.

SCHOOL CRISIS AND EMERGENCY MANAGEMENT PLANS, §22.1-279.8.

SCHOOL CROSSINGS.
Fine schedule, VA SCt Rule 3B:2.
Maximum fine for violating Title 46.2, §46.2-113.
Maximum speed limits, §46.2-873.
Prepayment of fine, §16.1-69.40:1.

SCHOOL DISTRICTS.
Bond issues.
County acting for on behalf of school district, §15.2-2642.
Consolidation of like units of local government, §15.2-3513.
Refunding bonds.
County providing for issuance for districts, §15.2-2649.

SCHOOL DIVISIONS.
Local school boards.
Generally, §§22.1-28 to 22.1-57.5.
See LOCAL SCHOOL BOARDS.

SCHOOL DIVISION SUPERINTENDENTS.
Generally, §§22.1-58 to 22.1-70.3.
See SUPERINTENDENTS OF SCHOOLS.

SCHOOL FOR THE DEAF AND BLIND.
Admissions procedures, §22.1-348.
Board of visitors.
Establishment, §22.1-346.2.
Secretary of education, powers and duties, §2.2-208.

SCHOOL FOR THE DEAF AND BLIND —Cont'd
Educational programs, §22.1-348.
Employment of teachers.
Terms of employment, §22.1-349.
Exclusion of children not immunized, §32.1-47.
General provisions, §§22.1-346 to 22.1-349.
Persons eligible, §22.1-348.
Teachers.
Terms of employment of teachers, §22.1-349.

SCHOOL LUNCH PROGRAM AND SCHOOL BREAKFAST PROGRAM.
Family access to medical insurance security plan.
Agreements with department of education, §32.1-351.2.
Retail sales and use tax exemptions, §58.1-609.10.
State programs to implement, §§2.2-617, 2.2-618.
Superintendent of public instruction.
Administration of National School Lunch Act, §22.1-24.

SCHOOL NURSES.
Employment by school board, §22.1-274.

SCHOOL PERSONNEL.
Alcohol or drug use, incidents involving.
Immunity for personnel reporting, §8.01-47.
Assault and battery, actions not constituting, §18.2-57.
Assault and battery against teachers, principal or guidance counselor, §18.2-57.
Assistant principals.
See PRINCIPALS, PUBLIC SCHOOLS.
Asthma medications, self-administration by student.
Immunity of school board employees supervising, §8.01-226.5:1.
Policies, §22.1-274.2.
Athletic coaches.
Child abuse or neglect.
Persons required to report, §63.2-1509.
Separate contract, §22.1-302.
Auto-injectable epinephrine, self-administration by student.
Immunity of principal supervising, §8.01-226.5:1.
Automated external defibrillators.
Teacher licensure requirements, §22.1-298.1.
Bomb threats, firebombs or explosives, incidents involving.
Immunity for personnel reporting, §8.01-47.
Cardiopulmonary resuscitation.
Teacher licensure requirements, §22.1-298.1.
Child abuse and neglect complaint searches.
Condition of employment, §22.1-296.4.
Child abuse or neglect reports.
Complaints against school personnel, §63.2-1511.
Investigation procedures and release of information, §63.2-1516.1.
Standard for determining if report unfounded, §63.2-1511.
Reason to suspect, required reports, fine for failure, §63.2-1509.
Posting notice of employee obligations, §22.1-291.3.
College partnership laboratory schools.
Immunity from liability, §23-299.10.
Requirements, §23-299.8.
Convictions for certain crimes, disclosure on application for employment, §22.1-296.1.

SCHOOL PERSONNEL —Cont'd
Corporal punishment against student.
Restriction on using, §63.2-1511.
Criminal records checks, §§22.1-296.1, 22.1-296.2.
Debilitating or life-threatening illness or injury.
Leave without pay for employees with, policies, development, §22.1-296.
Disclosure of convictions for certain crimes on application for employment, §22.1-296.1.
Emergency first aid.
Teacher licensure requirements, §22.1-298.1.
Epinephrine.
Administration by school nurse, §54.1-3408.
Self-administration by student.
Immunity of principal supervising, §8.01-226.5:1.
Fingerprinting applicants for employment, §22.1-296.2.
First aid.
Teacher licensure requirements, §22.1-298.1.
Grievance procedure for school board employees.
Local school board to establish, §22.1-79.
Hepatitis B or C exposure incident.
School board employee exposed to or exposing another.
Consent to testing and release of information, §32.1-45.1.
HIV exposure incident.
School board employee exposed to or exposing another.
Consent to testing and release of information, §32.1-45.1.
HIV exposure-prone incident.
Employee involved, §22.1-271.3.
HIV prevention training, §22.1-271.3.
Human trafficking, awareness and training materials, §22.1-16.5.
Immunity for investigating or reporting.
Student conduct involving explosive or drugs and alcohol, §8.01-47.
Inhaled asthma medications, student's self-administration.
Immunity of school board employees supervising, §8.01-226.5:1.
Policies, §22.1-274.2.
Institutes for training teachers, administrators and librarians.
Guidelines to be developed by state council of higher education, §23-9.13:1.
Insulin or glucagon administered to student by employee.
Immunity, §8.01-225.
Interstate agreement on qualification of educational personnel, §§22.1-316 to 22.1-318.
Military service.
Active duty.
Compensation of public school employees called to active duty, §22.1-289.2.
Payment of wages, §22.1-296.
Personnel files, §22.1-295.1.
Principals.
See PRINCIPALS, PUBLIC SCHOOLS.
Private transportation.
Reimbursement, traveling on state business, §22.1-296.
Supervisors.
See PRINCIPALS, PUBLIC SCHOOLS.

SCHOOL PERSONNEL —Cont'd
Teachers.
Generally.
See TEACHERS.
Tuberculosis certificate, §22.1-300.

SCHOOL PROCUREMENT.
Procurement by public bodies generally, §§2.2-4300 to 2.2-4377.
See PUBLIC PROCUREMENT.

SCHOOL PROPERTY AND BUILDINGS, §§22.1-125 to 22.1-140.
See SCHOOL BUILDINGS AND FACILITIES.

SCHOOL PSYCHOLOGISTS.
Duty to protect third parties.
Violent behavior or serious harm by client, §54.1-2400.1.
Licensing, §§54.1-3600 to 54.1-3606.1.

SCHOOL RESOURCE OFFICER INCENTIVE GRANTS FUND, §9.1-110.

SCHOOL SAFETY AUDITS, §22.1-279.8.

SCHOOL SAFETY CENTER, §9.1-184.

SCHOOLS AND EDUCATION.
Absence from school.
Court action for parents' failure to comply with law, §22.1-262.
Duty of law enforcement officer, §22.1-266.
Inducing children to absent themselves, §22.1-265.
Notification requirement, §22.1-258.
Proceedings against habitually absent child, §22.1-267.
Ten or more consecutive unexcused absences.
Suspension of student's driver's license, §46.2-334.001.
Access to student records, §22.1-287.
Accident prevention instruction, §22.1-204.
Accounting for schools' performance, §22.1-253.13:3.
Accreditation and evaluation.
Opportunity educational institution for schools denied accreditation or given accreditation with warning, §§22.1-27.1 to 22.1-27.6. See within this heading, "Opportunity educational institution."
Quality standards, §22.1-253.13:3.
Address information on admission document, §22.1-4.1.
Admission.
Birth certificates required, §22.1-3.1.
Foster care, children placed in, §22.1-3.4.
Scholastic records, transfer, §22.1-289.
Levy of fees and charges, §22.1-6.
Notice of student's school status, §22.1-3.2.
Race or ethnicity.
Designation by public elementary school students, §22.1-4.2.
Residence of child.
False statements, criminal penalty, §22.1-264.1.
Street address or route number on admission document, §22.1-4.1.
Tuition charges, §22.1-5.
Adult education, §§22.1-223 to 22.1-225.
Adult education programs for individuals functioning below high school completion level.
Local school boards to implement, §22.1-253.13:1.
Adult students.
Arrest.
Report of arrest of student age 18 or older for specified crimes, §19.2-83.1.

SCHOOLS AND EDUCATION —Cont'd
Advanced studies high school diplomas.
Requirements, §22.1-253.13:4.
Advancement via individual determination.
Block grants, §22.1-199.1.
After-school session.
Students required to attend, §22.1-254.01.
Alcoholic beverages, outdoor advertising.
Limitations on placement locations, §4.1-112.2.
Notice of violation, penalty for failure to take corrective action, §4.1-320.
Alcohol or drug use.
Drinking or possessing alcoholic beverages in or on public school grounds, §4.1-309.
Delinquent children, loss of driving privileges, §16.1-278.9.
Drinking or possessing alcoholic beverages while operating a school bus, §4.1-309.1.
Alcohol or drug use, incidents involving.
Immunity for personnel reporting, §8.01-47.
Algebra readiness intervention services.
Standard of learning, §22.1-253.13:1.
Teachers to provide, §22.1-253.13:2.
Alternative education, §22.1-209.1:2.
Authority of school boards, §22.1-277.2:1.
AVID programs, §22.1-209.1:3.
Compulsory attendance exemptions, §22.1-254.
Alternative school year schedules, §22.1-79.1.
American Sign Language instruction, §22.1-207.5.
College foreign language course credit to entering students who have completed, §23-9.2:3.9.
Anabolic steroids.
Use by student during athletic training period.
Ineligibility to compete in athletic competitions, §22.1-276.3.
Anatomical gifts.
Recipients of gift, §32.1-291.11.
Animal dissection.
Alternatives to animal dissection, §22.1-200.01.
Appropriations to private schools, VA Const Art VIII §10.
Arrest.
Carrying weapon on school property, §16.1-246.
Report of arrest of student age 18 or older for specified crimes, §19.2-83.1.
Report of arrest of teachers or other employees, §19.2-83.1.
Assault and battery against teachers, principal or guidance counselor, §18.2-57.
Assault and battery by certain employees.
Actions not constituting, §18.2-57.
Assault and battery by employees.
Actions not constituting, §18.2-57.
Assignment of pupil plans.
Local school boards powers and duties, §22.1-79.
Asthma.
Possession and self-administration of inhaled asthma medications by asthmatic students, §22.1-274.2.
Immunity of school board employees supervising, §8.01-226.5:1.
Asthma medications, self-administration by student.
Immunity of school board employees supervising, §8.01-226.5:1.
Possession and self-administration of inhaled asthma medications by asthmatic students, §22.1-274.2.

SCHOOLS AND EDUCATION —Cont'd
Athletic competition.
Anabolic steroids used by student during athletic training period.
Ineligibility to compete in athletic competitions, §22.1-276.3.
Concussions in student-athletes, §22.1-271.5.
Athletic events.
Team doctor immunity, §8.01-225.1.
At-risk students.
After school programs for, §22.1-199.5.
At-risk student academic achievement program and fund, §22.1-199.4.
Reading intervention services, §22.1-253.13:1.
Reduction of pupil-teacher ratios and class sizes for grades K through 3, §22.1-199.1.
Remediation, §22.1-253.13:1.
School boards to implement programs of prevention, intervention or remediation for, §22.1-253.13:1.
Standards of quality, §22.1-253.13:1.
Autistic.
Special education, §§22.1-213 to 22.1-221.
See SPECIAL EDUCATION.
Auto-injectable epinephrine.
Self-administration by student, §22.1-274.2.
Immunity of principal supervising, §8.01-226.5:1.
Automated external defibrillators.
Advanced studies diploma, requirements, §22.1-253.13:4.
Number of personnel with certification and training required per school building, §22.1-274.
Plan for placement, use and funding for AED in every school, §22.1-274.4.
Standards of learning for health instruction, §22.1-253.13:1.
Teacher licensure requirements, §22.1-298.1.
Average daily membership.
Students enrolled in school on less than full-time basis, §22.1-253.13:1.
AVID.
Block grants, §22.1-199.1.
Banks.
School thrift or savings plans.
Participation, §6.2-813.
Basic skills, selected programs and instructional personnel.
Quality standards, §22.1-253.13:1.
Birth certificates.
Required upon admission, §22.1-3.1.
Blood-borne pathogens.
Prevention training for personnel, §22.1-271.3.
Board of education.
Generally, §§22.1-8 to 22.1-20.
See BOARD OF EDUCATION.
Opening of the school year.
Waiver of the Labor Day restriction, §22.1-79.1.
Uniforms in public schools.
Guidelines, §22.1-79.2.
Bomb threats, firebombs or explosives, incidents involving.
Expulsion, §22.1-277.07.
Immunity for personnel reporting, §8.01-47.
Boy scouts, discrimination against, §22.1-79.3.
Breakfast programs, §22.1-207.3.
Public school funds.
See PUBLIC SCHOOL FUNDS.
Buildings, §§22.1-134 to 22.1-140.
See SCHOOL BUILDINGS AND FACILITIES.

SCHOOLS AND EDUCATION —Cont'd
Bullying.
Center for school safety, duties, §9.1-184.
Discipline of students generally, §§22.1-276.01 to 22.1-280.4. See within this heading, "Discipline of students."
Model policies for codes of student conduct, §22.1-279.6.
Prevention and prohibition of bullying, policies and procedures for, §22.1-291.4.
Burning or destroying schoolhouses, §18.2-79.
Buses generally, §§22.1-176 to 22.1-198.
See SCHOOL BUSES.
Cafeteria workers.
Tuberculosis certificate, §22.1-300.
Cardiopulmonary resuscitation.
Advanced studies diploma, requirements, §22.1-253.13:4.
Number of personnel with certification and training required per school building, §22.1-274.
Standards of learning for health instruction, §22.1-253.13:1.
Teacher licensure requirements, §22.1-298.1.
Career and technical education.
Generally, §§22.1-227 to 22.1-237.
See CAREER AND TECHNICAL EDUCATION.
Standards of learning for, §§22.1-253.13:1, 22.1-253.13:4.
Career and technical education projects.
Generally, §§22.1-227 to 22.1-237.
See CAREER AND TECHNICAL EDUCATION.
Character education, §22.1-208.01.
Charter schools, §§22.1-212.5 to 22.1-212.16.
See CHARTER SCHOOLS.
Charter schools generally, §§22.1-212.5 to 22.1-212.16.
See CHARTER SCHOOLS.
Child abuse or molestation.
Condition of employment.
Conviction data required, §22.1-296.1.
Search of registry for complaints of child abuse and neglect.
Condition of employment, §22.1-296.4.
Student at imminent risk of suicide.
Notice to social services if parental abuse or neglect, §22.1-272.1.
Child abuse or neglect reports.
Complaints against school personnel, §63.2-1511.
Interagency agreement, child abuse and neglect investigations, §63.2-1511.
Investigation procedures and release of information, §63.2-1516.1.
Standard for determining if report unfounded, §63.2-1511.
Reason to suspect, required reports, fine for failure, §63.2-1509.
Posting notice of employee obligations, §22.1-291.3.
Children in custody of state institutions.
Responsibility for providing education, §22.1-7.
Class rankings, §22.1-253.13:4.
Class size reduction.
Programs designed to promote educational opportunities, §22.1-199.1.
College partnership laboratory schools, §§23-299 to 23-299.10.
Application for formation, §23-299.4.
Final decision of board of education, §23-299.6.
Review, §23-299.5.

SCHOOLS AND EDUCATION —Cont'd
College partnership laboratory schools —Cont'd
Collaborative partnerships with public school divisions, §23-299.2.
Contents of application for formation, §23-299.4.
Contracts for establishment, §23-299.3.
Decision of board of education final, §23-299.6.
Definitions, §23-299.
Discrimination laws, applicability, §23-299.2.
Employment of professional, licensed personnel, §23-299.8.
Enrollment eligibility, §23-299.2.
Fund, established, §23-299.1.
Funding of schools, §23-299.9.
Governing board.
Administration and management by, §23-299.2.
Defined, §23-299.
Gifts, donations, grants, etc., authorization to receive, §23-299.9.
Immunity from liability, §23-299.10.
Innovation technical advisory group, §22.1-212.8:1.
Legislative intent, §23-299.
Local education agency, designation as, §23-299.2.
Operations, responsibility for, §23-299.2.
Renewals, §23-299.7.
Review of application, §23-299.5.
Revocations, §23-299.7.
Teachers.
Immunity from liability, §23-299.10.
Requirements, §23-299.8.
Tuition, §23-299.2.
Commercial, promotional and corporate partnerships and sponsorships.
Policies regarding, §22.1-89.4.
Community colleges.
Associate's degree or certificate of general studies, dual enrollment for.
Articulation agreements with public high schools, §23-9.2:3.02.
Compacts.
Interstate agreement on qualification of educational personnel, §§22.1-316 to 22.1-318.
Southern regional education compact, §§22.1-358, 22.1-359.
Comparative religion as elective course, §22.1-202.1.
Competency-based career and technical education programs, §22.1-253.13:1.
Compulsory school attendance, §§22.1-254 to 22.1-269.1, VA Const Art VIII §3.
Age requirements.
False statements, §22.1-264.
Alternative attendance programs, §22.1-269.1.
Alternative education program attendance, §22.1-254.
Attendance officers.
Appointment, §22.1-258.
Complaints filed or noncompliance with law, §22.1-262.
Duties, §22.1-261.
Child in need of services or supervision.
Excusal from compliance with legal requirement, §§16.1-278.4, 16.1-278.5.
Court complaints.
Parents' failure to comply with law, §22.1-262.
Criminal offenses.
Inducing children to absent themselves from school, §22.1-265.
Criminal prosecutions.
Duties of Commonwealth's attorney, §22.1-268.

SCHOOLS AND EDUCATION —Cont'd
Compulsory school attendance —Cont'd
Criminal prosecutions —Cont'd
Exclusive original jurisdiction, §22.1-268.
Daily attendance records.
Teachers to keep, §22.1-259.
Emancipation of minor.
Relief of obligation, §16.1-334.
Excuses, §22.1-254.
Exempt from compulsory attendance, §22.1-254.
Alternative attendance program, §22.1-269.1.
Children in need of services or supervision, §§16.1-278.4, 16.1-278.5.
Emancipated minor, §16.1-334.
Habitually absent child.
Complaint to court for parents' failure to comply with law, §22.1-262.
Misdemeanor offense, §22.1-263.
Proceedings against, §22.1-267.
High school equivalency certificate.
Testing for general educational development, §22.1-254.2.
HIV infected children.
Guidelines for attending, §22.1-271.3.
Home schooling.
Public policy, §22.1-254.1.
Requirements, §22.1-254.1.
Testing for general educational development, §22.1-254.2.
Inducing children to absent themselves from school, §22.1-265.
Investigation of nonenrollment cases by attendance officer, §22.1-261.
Knowing and willful violations of provisions, §22.1-263.
Law enforcement officers.
Delivery of truant child to school, §22.1-266.
List of children not enrolled.
Maintenance by division superintendent, §22.1-261.
Report after opening of school, §22.1-260.
Misdemeanors.
Inducing children to absent themselves from school, §22.1-265.
Misdemeanor violation, §§22.1-263 to 22.1-265.
Nonresident children, §§22.1-255, 22.1-263.
Notification when pupil fails to report to school, §22.1-258.
Opening of school year.
List of children not enrolled, §22.1-261.
Report of children enrolled and not enrolled, §22.1-260.
Opportunity educational institution.
Attendance of students in school under supervision, §22.1-27.3.
Parental responsibility and involvement, §22.1-279.3.
Previous violations of provisions, §22.1-263.
Public assistance.
Temporary assistance for needy families.
Compliance with laws required, §63.2-606.
Pupils absence or failure to report to school.
Court action for parents' failure to comply with law, §22.1-262.
Duty of law enforcement officer, §22.1-266.
Inducing children to absent themselves, §22.1-265.
Notification requirement, §22.1-258.
Proceedings against habitually absent child, §22.1-267.

SCHOOLS AND EDUCATION —Cont'd
Compulsory school attendance —Cont'd
Report of children enrolled and not enrolled.
List of children not enrolled.
Opening of school year, §22.1-261.
Opening of school year, §22.1-260.
Required, §22.1-254.
Residence of child.
False statements, §22.1-264.1.
School aged children.
Nonresidents, §22.1-255.
Social security numbers.
Students to present, §22.1-260.
Statewide enforcement, §22.1-269.
Summer school.
Students required to attend, §22.1-254.01.
Temporary assistance for needy families.
Compliance with laws required, §63.2-606.
Truancy centers.
Defined, §22.1-266.
Delivery of child to, §22.1-266.
Truant officers.
Appointment, §22.1-258.
Delivery of child to school, §22.1-266.
Duties, §22.1-261.
Filing of complaint or noncompliance, §22.1-262.
Waivers, §22.1-254.
Computers.
Donation of obsolete educational technology hardware and software, §22.1-129.
Donation of surplus state computers to, §2.2-1124.
Programs designed to promote educational opportunities, §22.1-199.1.
Concussions in student-athletes, §22.1-271.5.
Constitution of Virginia.
Teaching bill of rights in school, §§22.1-208.01, 22.1-253.13:1.
Construction grants, §§22.1-175.1 to 22.1-175.5.
Contractors having direct contact with students.
Criminal background information required, §22.1-296.1.
Contracts between school divisions.
Joint public school facilities and services, §22.1-27.
Contracts with publishers of textbooks, §22.1-241.
Controlled substances.
Expulsion of students for certain drug offenses, §22.1-277.08.
Reports of certain acts to school authorities, §22.1-279.3:1.
Corporal punishment.
Prohibition, §22.1-279.1.
Corporal punishment against student.
Restriction on using, §63.2-1511.
Correctional facilities.
Schools for persons committed to correctional institutions, §53.1-10.
Costs of maintaining educational program.
State and local support of public schools, VA Const Art VIII §2.
County food and beverage tax.
Tax not levied on food and beverages sold, §58.1-3833.
Courses of instruction, §§22.1-199 to 22.1-212.2.
Accident prevention, §22.1-204.
Alternative education programs, §22.1-209.1:2.
American Sign Language, §22.1 207.5.
College foreign language course credit to entering students who have completed, §23-9.2:3.9.

SCHOOLS AND EDUCATION —Cont'd
Courses of instruction —Cont'd
Animal dissection.
Alternatives to animal dissection, §22.1-200.01.
At-risk student academic achievement program and fund, §22.1-199.4.
Basic skills, selected programs and instructional personnel, §22.1-253.13:1.
Character education, §22.1-208.01.
Comparative religion as elective course, §22.1-202.1.
Daily observance of one minute of silence, §22.1-203.
Dissection.
Alternatives to animal dissection, §22.1-200.01.
Driver education programs, §22.1-205.
Drugs, alcohol and substance abuse education, §22.1-206.
Economic education and financial literacy, §22.1-200.03.
Elementary school subjects, §22.1-200.
Employment counseling and placement services, §22.1-209.
English language instruction.
No obligation on school boards to instruct in other than English language, §22.1-212.1.
Environmental instruction.
Green schools program of education in waste reduction and resource efficiency, §22.1-212.1:2.
Family life education, §§22.1-207.1, 22.1-207.2.
Standards of learning regarding dating violence and characteristics of abusive relationships, §22.1-207.1:1.
Green schools program of education in waste reduction and resource efficiency, §22.1-212.1:2.
History and principles of flags of United States and Virginia, §22.1-202.
Kindergarten programs, §22.1-199.
Moral education emphasis, §22.1-208.
Night schools, §22.1-210.
Optional education programs for kindergarten through grade five, §22.1-200.1.
Physical and health education, §22.1-207.
Physical education.
Required, activities included, §22.1-200.
Programs and teachers in state agencies and institutions, §22.1-209.2.
Reading intervention services, §22.1-253.13:1.
Religion.
Comparative religion as elective course, §22.1-202.1.
Resource efficiency.
Green schools program of education in waste reduction and resource efficiency, §22.1-212.1:2.
School breakfast programs, §22.1-207.3.
Sexual assault avoidance, treatment, and counseling.
Family life education, §§22.1-207.1, 22.1-207.1:1.
Single-sex classes, §22.1-212.1:1.
Statewide Electronic Classroom Program, §22.1-212.2.
Vacation schools and summer camps, §§22.1-211, 22.1-212.
Virginia history and United States Constitution, §22.1-201.
Waste reduction.
Green schools program of education in waste reduction and resource efficiency, §22.1-212.1:2.

SCHOOLS AND EDUCATION —Cont'd
Courses of instruction in public schools.
Generally, §§22.1-199 to 22.1-212.2.
Crime prevention.
Development of programs, §22.1-279.9.
Crime stoppers program, §22.1-280.2.
Crime victims.
Transfer of students to other school within division, §22.1-3.3.
Criminal prosecution of juveniles as adults for commission of certain crimes.
School boards to provide information to students, §22.1-279.4.
Criminal records checks.
School officers and employees, §§22.1-296.1, 22.1-296.2.
Critical incident response.
Center for school safety to develop training program, §9.1-184.
Cyberbullying.
Model policies for codes of student conduct, §22.1-279.6.
Prevention and prohibition of bullying, policies and procedures for, §22.1-291.4.
Damaging school houses, §18.2-138.
Data coordinator/instructional resource teachers.
Standards of quality, §22.1-253.13:2.
Dating violence.
Family life education, §22.1-207.1.
Standards of learning, §22.1-207.1:1.
Daycare programs in certain localities, §22.1-132.1.
Definitions, §22.1-1.
Corporal punishment, §22.1-279.1.
Health of students, §22.1-271.1.
Industrial quality eye protective devices, §22.1-275.
School crime line, §22.1-280.2.
Transfer of scholastic records, §22.1-289.
Department of juvenile justice.
Reenrollment of children who have been in custody of department.
Promulgation of regulations, §22.1-17.1.
Destruction of property.
School board action regarding, §22.1-280.4.
Destructive devices.
Expulsion, §22.1-277.07.
Diabetes.
School employee administering insulin or glucagon to student.
Immunity, §8.01-225.
Diploma.
Quality standards, §22.1-253.13:4.
Secondary school students earning prescribed units of credit, §22.1-253.13:4.
Withholding because of nonpayment of fees and charges, §22.1-6.
Disabilities, schools for students with, §§22.1-319 to 22.1-332.
See DISABILITIES, SCHOOLS FOR STUDENTS WITH.
Disabled children.
Early identification, §22.1-253.13:1.
Special education, §§22.1-213 to 22.1-221.
See SPECIAL EDUCATION.
Discharging firearms, §18.2-280.
Disqualification for concealed weapons permit, §18.2-308.09.
Discipline of students, §§22.1-276.01 to 22.1-280.4.
Attendance of alternative education program.
Authority of school boards, §22.1-277.2:1.

SCHOOLS AND EDUCATION —Cont'd
Discipline of students —Cont'd
Attendance of alternative education program —Cont'd
Exclusion from admission, §22.1-277.2.
Authority of school boards, §22.1-277.2:1.
Civil penalties.
Parents' failure in parental responsibility and involvement requirements, §22.1-279.3.
Corporal punishment.
Restrictions on using, §63.2-1511.
Definitions, §22.1-276.01.
Destruction of property.
School board action regarding, §22.1-280.4.
Expulsion of pupils, §§22.1-277, 22.1-277.06 to 22.1-277.08.
Alternative education program.
Exclusion from admission, §22.1-277.2.
Exclusion from admission, §22.1-277.2.
Guidelines for school board policies, §22.1-279.6.
Hazing, §18.2-56.
Readmission, §22.1-277.06.
Guidelines for school board policies, §22.1-279.6.
Guidelines for student searches, §22.1-279.7.
Interagency agreement, child abuse and neglect investigations, §63.2-1511.
Model student conduct policies, §22.1-279.6.
Notification of parent of violation of school board policy, §22.1-279.3.
Parental responsibility and involvement requirements, §22.1-279.3.
Prevention of crime and violence.
Development of programs, §22.1-279.9.
Proceedings against parents for failure to comply with provisions, §16.1-241.2.
Prosecution of juveniles as adults for certain crimes.
Information provided to students, §22.1-279.4.
Removal of students from classes, §22.1-276.2.
Reports of certain acts to school authorities, §22.1-279.3:1.
School board regulations, §22.1-279.6.
School crime line, §22.1-280.2.
School crisis and emergency management plans, §22.1-279.8.
School safety audits, §22.1-279.8.
Searches.
Guidelines for student searches, §22.1-279.7.
Suspension of pupils, §22.1-277.
Exclusion from admission, §22.1-277.2.
Guidelines for school board policies, §22.1-279.6.
Long-term suspension, §22.1-277.05.
Readmission, §§22.1-277.04, 22.1-277.05.
Short-term suspension, §22.1-277.04.
Uniforms in public schools.
Guidelines, §22.1-79.2.
Discrimination.
Persons with disabilities, §51.5-42.
Disorderly conduct in public places.
Disrupting school, §18.2-415.
Removal of students from classes, §22.1-276.2.
Dissection.
Alternatives to animal dissection, §22.1-200.01.
Driver education programs.
Courses of instruction, §22.1-205.
Motorcycle dealers, display of license plates, §46.2-1993.52.
Use of foreign-registered motor vehicles, §46.2-1557.
Dropout prevention.
Block grants, §22.1-199.1.

SCHOOLS AND EDUCATION —Cont'd
Drug offenses.
Employees.
Report of convictions, §19.2-291.1.
Expulsion of students for certain drug offenses, §22.1-277.08.
Reports of certain acts to school authorities, §22.1-279.3:1.
Drug or alcohol abuse.
Courses of instruction, §22.1-206.
Drug sales on or near property, §18.2-255.2.
Drug sales on or near school property, §18.2-255.2.
Drug testing, policy standards, §22.1-279.6.
Eating disorders, information to be provided to parents, §22.1-273.2.
Economic education and financial literacy, §22.1-253.13:1.
Instruction requirements, §22.1-200.03.
Educational technology foundation.
Establishment by school board, §22.1-212.2:2.
Elections.
Policies regarding certain activities, §22.1-79.3.
Students conducting electioneering activities, policies prohibiting, §22.1-79.3.
Electronic records and electronic signatures from parents.
Boards to adopt policies regarding, §22.1-79.3.
Elementary school subjects, §22.1-200.
Emergency first aid.
Advanced studies diploma, requirements, §22.1-253.13:4.
Number of personnel with certification and training required per school building, §22.1-274.
Standards of learning for health instruction, §22.1-253.13:1.
Teacher licensure requirements, §22.1-298.1.
Emergency management operations plan.
Coordinator of emergency management, §44-146.18.
Eminent domain.
Condemnation of land for school purposes, §22.1-127.
Counties, cities and towns, §22.1-126.1.
Emotionally disturbed.
Special education, §§22.1-213 to 22.1-221.
See SPECIAL EDUCATION.
Employees.
Generally.
See SCHOOL PERSONNEL.
Teachers generally.
See TEACHERS.
Employment counseling and placement services, §22.1-209.
Endangered species.
Wildlife, possession and display by teachers for educational purposes, §29.1-417.
End-of-course assessments for grades 3, 5 and 8, §22.1-253.13:1.
English as second language.
Block grants for program, §22.1-199.1.
School boards to provide instruction in English language designed to promote, §22.1-212.1.
English language instruction.
No obligation of school boards to teach in other than English language, §22.1-212.1.
Enrollment, open policy, §22.1-7.1.
Entrepreneurship education program.
Established, administered by board of education, §22.1-208.2:4.

SCHOOLS AND EDUCATION —Cont'd
Environmental instruction.
Green schools program of education in waste reduction and resource efficiency, §22.1-212.1:2.
Epinephrine.
Administration by school nurse, §54.1-3408.
Self-administration by student, §22.1-274.2.
Immunity of principal supervising, §8.01-226.5:1.
Exclusion of children not immunized, §32.1-47.
Explosives.
Expulsion, §22.1-277.07.
Expulsion of students. See within this heading, "Suspension and expulsion of pupils."
Family life education, §§22.1-207.1, 22.1-207.2.
Standards of learning regarding dating violence and characteristics of abusive relationships, §22.1-207.1:1.
Family literacy.
Programs designed to promote educational opportunities, §22.1-199.1.
Fees and charges.
Effect of nonpayment on report card or diploma, §22.1-6.
Textbooks, damage to, §22.1-243.
Tuition charges, §22.1-5.
Financial literacy, §22.1-253.13:1.
Fingerprinting applicants for employment, §22.1-296.2.
Fingerprinting employees, §22.1-296.2.
Fire alarms.
Maliciously activating, §18.2-212.
Firearms.
Arrest for carrying on school property, §16.1-246.
Discharging, §18.2-280.
Disqualification for concealed weapons permit, §18.2-308.09.
Expulsion of students, §22.1-277.07.
Pointing, holding or brandishing, §18.2-282.
Policies prohibiting possession of firearms, §22.1-277.07:1.
Reports of certain acts to school authorities, §22.1-279.3:1.
Safety education programs for students in elementary grades, §22.1-204.1.
Firearms and other weapons.
Discharging in school, §18.2-280.
Machete or other bladed weapon.
Brandishing with intent to intimidate upon school property, §18.2-282.1.
Possession on school property, §18.2-308.1.
Fire drills, §22.1-137.
First aid.
Advanced studies diploma, requirements, §22.1-253.13:4.
Number of personnel with certification and training required per school building, §22.1-274.
Standards of learning for health instruction, §22.1-253.13:1.
Teacher licensure requirements, §22.1-298.1.
Fishing, inland waters.
Fish and wildlife educational events.
Youth special permits, §29.1-315.1.
Special fishing permits, §29.1-315.
Flags.
Commonwealth and United States flags to be flown at every public school, §22.1-133.
Public school instruction, §22.1-202.
Forensic science academy, §9.1-1103.

SCHOOLS AND EDUCATION —Cont'd
Foster care children.
Enrollment in receiving school divisions, §22.1-3.4.
Scholastic records, transfer, §22.1-289.
Notice to school in which student to be enrolled, of status of parental rights, §63.2-900.
School placement, §63.2-900.3.
Freedom of information act.
Excluded records.
Personal information in certain correspondence with public body, §2.2-3705.7.
Free public education.
General assembly to provide for, VA Const Art VIII §1.
Persons residing within school division, §22.1-3.
Public policy, §22.1-2.
Free textbooks, etc., VA Const Art VIII §3.
Full-time equivalent instructional positions, §22.1-253.13:1.
Gang activity in school zone.
Enhanced punishment, §18.2-46.3:3.
General achievement diploma requirements, §22.1-253.13:4.
General assembly to provide, VA Const Art VIII §1.
Gifted students.
Early identification and enrollment in appropriate program, §22.1-253.13:1.
Gifts to for educational purposes.
Generally.
See CHARITABLE GIFTS.
Girl scouts, discrimination against, §22.1-79.3.
Glucagon.
School employee administering insulin or glucagon to student.
Immunity, §8.01-225.
Governor's award for outstanding achievement.
Virginia index of performance incentive program, §22.1-253.13:9.
Graduation requirements, §22.1-253.13:4.
Grants.
Block grants.
Programs designed to promote educational opportunities, §22.1-199.1.
Construction grants, §§22.1-175.1 to 22.1-175.5.
Security equipment grants, §22.1-280.2:2.
Teachers, strategic compensation grant initiative, §§22.1-318.1, 22.1-318.2.
Green schools program of education in waste reduction and resource efficiency, §22.1-212.1:2.
Grievance procedure for school board employees.
School board to establish, §22.1-79.
Handicap or disability of students.
Schools for students with disabilities, §§22.1-319 to 22.1-332.
See DISABILITIES, SCHOOLS FOR STUDENTS WITH.
Hazing of students, §18.2-56.
Crime and violence prevention programs, §22.1-279.9.
Discipline of student, report to attorney for Commonwealth, §18.2-56.
Model policies for codes of student conduct, §22.1-279.6.
Headstart.
Promotion of educational opportunities, §22.1-199.1.

SCHOOLS AND EDUCATION —Cont'd
Health care facilities.
Pilot school/community health centers.
Medical assistance services department, §32.1-326.2.
Health of students, §§22.1-270 to 22.1-275.1.
Asthma.
Immunity of school board employees supervising, §8.01-226.5:1.
Possession and self-administration of inhaled asthma medications by asthmatic students, §22.1-274.2.
Auto-injectable epinephrine.
Self-administration by student, §22.1-274.2.
Immunity of principal supervising, §8.01-226.5:1.
Concussions in student-athletes, §22.1-271.5.
Contagious and infectious diseases, §22.1-272.
Definitions, §22.1-271.1.
Eating disorders, information to be provided to parents, §22.1-273.2.
HIV infected children, §22.1-271.3.
Home-instructed, exempted and excused children, §22.1-271.4.
Home schooling, §22.1-271.4.
Immunization requirements, §22.1-271.2.
Inhalers.
Immunity of school board employees supervising, §8.01-226.5:1.
Possession and self-administration of inhaled asthma medications by asthmatic students, §22.1-274.2.
Memorandum of agreement relating to special education health services, §22.1-274.02.
Pilot school/community health centers.
Medical assistance services department, §32.1-326.2.
Preschool physical examinations, §22.1-270.
Protective eye devices, §22.1-275.
Psychotropic drugs, schools prohibited from recommending, §22.1-274.3.
School health advisory board, §22.1-275.1.
School health services, §22.1-274.
Scoliosis screening, §22.1-273.1.
Sight and hearing testing of pupils, §22.1-273.
Survey of student health risk behaviors.
Boards to adopt policies regarding notification to parents, §22.1-79.3.
Toxic art materials, §22.1-274.1.
Health provisions applicable to students, §§22.1-270 to 22.1-275.1.
Hearing impaired.
Special education, §§22.1-213 to 22.1-221.
See SPECIAL EDUCATION.
Hepatitis B.
Prevention training for school personnel, §22.1-271.3.
Hepatitis B or C exposure incident.
School board employee exposed to or exposing another.
Consent to testing and release of information, §32.1-45.1.
High school diplomas.
Advanced studies diploma, requirements, §22.1-253.13:4.
Associate's degree or certificate of general studies, dual enrollment for.
Articulation agreements with public high schools, §23-9.2:3.02.
Korean war veteran honorary diploma, §22.1-17.4.

SCHOOLS AND EDUCATION —Cont'd
High school diplomas —Cont'd
Vietnam war veteran honorary diploma, §§2.2-3310, 22.1-17.4.
World War II veteran honorary high school diploma, §22.1-17.4.
High school equivalency certificate.
Testing for general educational development, §22.1-254.2.
High school to work partnerships.
Career and technical education, §22.1-227.1.
History.
United States Constitution.
Public school instruction, §22.1-201.
Virginia history.
Public school instruction, §22.1-201.
HIV exposure-prone incident.
School board employee exposed to or exposing another.
Consent to testing and release of information, §32.1-45.1.
School employees possibly involved, §22.1-271.3.
HIV infected children.
Guidelines for school attendance, §22.1-271.3.
HIV prevention training for personnel, §22.1-271.3.
Homeless students.
Enrollment notwithstanding lack of records, §22.1-3.1.
Immunization requirements, §22.1-271.2.
Preschool physical examinations, §22.1-270.
Waiver of address requirement for certain documents, §22.1-4.1.
Home schooling, §22.1-254.1.
Health of students, §22.1-271.4.
Testing for general educational development, §22.1-254.2.
Homework assistance program.
Block grants, §22.1-199.1.
Human trafficking, awareness and training materials for school division staff, §22.1-16.5.
Immunization requirements, §22.1-271.2.
Public health emergency involving vaccine-preventable disease, §32.1-47.1.
Immunizations required for attendance at schools, §32.1-46.
Individual school accreditation plans, §22.1-253.13:3.
Inhaled asthma medications, student self-administration.
Immunity of school board employees supervising, §8.01-226.5:1.
Possession and self-administration of inhaled asthma medications by asthmatic students, §22.1-274.2.
Inhaled asthma medications, student's self-administration.
Immunity of school board employees supervising, §8.01-226.5:1.
Possession and self-administration of inhaled asthma medications by asthmatic students, §22.1-274.2.
Inspection walk-through of school as part of school safety audit, §22.1-279.8.
Insulin.
School employee administering insulin or glucagon to student.
Immunity, §8.01-225.
Intellectual disability.
Special education, §§22.1-213 to 22.1-221.
See SPECIAL EDUCATION.

SCHOOLS AND EDUCATION —Cont'd
Interference with pupils at school.
Localities preventing by ordinance, §15.2-1717.
Ordinances preventing, §15.2-1717.
Internet.
Acceptable Internet use policies for public and private schools, §22.1-70.2.
Cyberbullying.
Model policies for codes of student conduct, §22.1-279.6.
Prevention and prohibition of bullying, policies and procedures for, §22.1-291.4.
Internship programs for students.
Identification of programs exempt from federal and state laws, §22.1-17.3.
Interscholastic programs.
Organizations governing, school membership in.
Eligibility of certain children of military personnel required, §22.1-5.1.
Interstate agreement on qualification of educational personnel, §§22.1-316 to 22.1-318.
Interstate compact on educational opportunity for military children, §§22.1-360, 22.1-361.
Janitors.
Tuberculosis certificate, §22.1-300.
Joint facilities and services, §22.1-27.
Joint schools.
Establishment with consent of state board, §22.1-26.
Juvenile justice department.
Education division, §66-13.1.
Notice to school superintendent prior to release of serious offenders, §66-25.2:1.
Reenrollment of children who have been in custody of department.
Promulgation of regulations, §22.1-17.1.
Kindergarten programs, §22.1-199.
Optional education programs for kindergarten through grade five, §22.1-200.1.
Labor day law.
Opening of the school year, §22.1-79.1.
Law-enforcement agency.
Failure to produce birth certificate upon admission.
Required notification to local law-enforcement agency, §22.1-3.1.
Library media centers.
Automation and providing network capabilities, §22.1-199.1.
Library networking, §§42.1-32.1 to 42.1-32.6.
Literary fund, §§22.1-142 to 22.1-161.
See LITERARY FUND.
Local detention homes.
Programs and courses of instruction, §22.1-209.2.
Local school boards.
Generally, §§22.1-28 to 22.1-57.5.
See LOCAL SCHOOL BOARDS.
Lock-down drills, §22.1-137.2.
Lockers.
Searches.
Guidelines for student searches, §22.1-279.7.
Machete or other bladed weapon.
Brandishing with intent to intimidate upon school property, §18.2-282.1.
Medical assistance services department.
Pilot school/community health centers, §32.1-326.2.
Middle school teacher corps, §22.1-199.1.
Military personnel, children of.
Eligibility for interscholastic programs, §§22.1-5, 22.1-5.1.

SCHOOLS AND EDUCATION —Cont'd
Military personnel, children of —Cont'd
When tuition to be charged or not charged, §§22.1-3, 22.1-5.
Military recruiters.
Access to high schools and high school students, §22.1-130.1.
Access to student information, school buildings, etc., §22.1-288.
Miller School of Albemarle, §§23-51 to 23-53.
Missing children information clearinghouse.
Network, notification to school of missing child, §52-31.1.
Model student conduct policies, §22.1-279.6.
Moment of silence.
Daily observance of one minute of silence, §22.1-203.
Moral education.
Emphasis on instruction, §22.1-208.
Night schools.
Public school programs, §22.1-210.
Noncustodial parents.
Participation in certain school activities, emergency contact, listing as, §22.1-4.3.
Northern Neck-Middle Peninsula public education consortium, §§22.1-354.6 to 22.1-354.10.
Notice.
Expulsion of students, §22.1-277.06.
Parental responsibility and involvement requirements, §22.1-279.3.
Public notice regarding certain resource guides, §22.1-17.5.
Nurses.
Employment by school board, §22.1-274.
Nutritional guidelines for competitive foods sold to students, §22.1-207.4.
Occupational therapists.
Employment by school board, §22.1-274.
Online course, §§22.1-212.23 to 22.1-212.27.
See VIRTUAL SCHOOLS.
Open enrollment policy, §22.1-7.1.
Opening of the school year, §22.1-79.1.
Opportunity educational institution, §§22.1-27.1 to 22.1-27.6.
Accreditation with warning.
Disclosure of information and documentation from schools receiving, §22.1-27.2.
Supervision of school receiving for certain number of consecutive years, §22.1-27.2.
Administration and supervision, §22.1-27.1.
Attendance of students in school under supervision, §22.1-27.3.
Average daily membership calculations, §22.1-27.5.
Board, §22.1-27.1.
Buildings and facilities, §22.1-27.6.
Certification of enrollment for funding purposes, §22.1-27.5.
Considered as statewide school division, §22.1-25.
Created, §22.1-27.1.
Decision to transfer school back to local school division, time frame for, §22.1-27.2.
Denial of accreditation, supervision of school, §22.1-27.2.
Department of education, members to assist board, §22.1-27.1.
Executive director, §22.1-27.1.
Operation of schools under board supervision, §22.1-27.2.

SCHOOLS AND EDUCATION —Cont'd
Opportunity educational institution —Cont'd
Per pupil funding transferred to institution, §22.1-27.5.
Reports of schools within institution, §22.1-27.2.
Staff members, §22.1-27.4.
Teachers of schools under supervision, §22.1-27.4.
Parental responsibility and involvement.
Enforcement of standards of student conduct and attendance, §22.1-279.3.
Parents.
Defined, §22.1-1.
Discipline of students.
Notification of violation of school board policy, §22.1-279.3.
Parental responsibility and involvement requirements, §22.1-279.3.
Rights of parents to make decisions concerning upbringing, education and care of child, §1-240.1.
Performance of schools.
Accounting for schools' performance, §22.1-253.13:3.
College partnership laboratory schools, §§23-299 to 23-299.10. See within this heading, "College partnership laboratory schools."
Virginia index of performance incentive program, §22.1-253.13:9.
Personnel files of employees, §22.1-295.1.
Personnel generally.
See SCHOOL PERSONNEL.
Persons deemed residing within school division, §22.1-3.
Physical and health education, §22.1-207.
Required to be taught, activities included, §22.1-200.
Physical therapists.
Employment by school board, §22.1-274.
Physicians.
Employment by school board, §22.1-274.
Planning and public involvement.
Quality standards, §22.1-253.13:6.
Pledge of allegiance.
Guidelines on constitutional rights and restrictions relating to recitation, §22.1-202.
Administrative rulemaking exemptions, §2.2-4006.
Police powers over lands lying beyond localities boundaries, §15.2-1725.
Policies of school board.
Bullying prevention and prohibition, policies and procedures for, §22.1-291.4.
Sexual abuse of student by teacher or school board employee.
Policies of school board to address complaints, §22.1-253.13:7.
Standards of quality, §22.1-253.13:7.
Student conduct, §22.1-279.6.
Prayer in public schools.
Daily observance of one minute of silence, §22.1-203.
Guidelines for constitutional compliance, §22.1-203.2.
Student-initiated prayer, §22.1-203.1.
Preschool physical examinations, §22.1-270.
Preschool programs for at-risk four-year-olds, §22.1-199.1.
Preschools.
See PRESCHOOLS.
Private business or professional schools.
Furnishing student records, §22.1-288.

SCHOOLS AND EDUCATION —Cont'd
Private school remediation program for at-risk students, §22.1-253.13:1.
Private schools, appropriations for, VA Const Art VIII §10.
Problem children.
Alternative education programs, §22.1-209.1:2.
Project discovery.
Block grants, §22.1-199.1.
Project YES.
Block grants, §22.1-199.1.
Promotion of educational opportunities.
Programs for, §22.1-199.1.
Property generally, §§22.1-125 to 22.1-134.
See SCHOOL BUILDINGS AND FACILITIES.
Prosecution of juveniles as adults for commission of certain crimes.
School boards to provide information to students, §22.1-279.4.
Protective eye devices, §22.1-275.
Psychotropic drugs, schools prohibited from recommending, §22.1-274.3.
Public charter schools, §§22.1-212.5 to 22.1-212.16.
See CHARTER SCHOOLS.
Public-private education facilities and infrastructure act, §§56-575.1 to 56-575.18.
See PUBLIC BUILDINGS.
Public school authority.
Generally, §§22.1-162 to 22.1-175.
See PUBLIC SCHOOL AUTHORITY.
Public school foundations, §22.1-212.2:2.
Public school funds.
Generally, §§22.1-88 to 22.1-124.
See PUBLIC SCHOOL FUNDS.
Public school security equipment grant act of 2013, §22.1-280.2:2.
Pupil-teacher ratio reduction.
Programs designed to promote educational opportunities, §22.1-199.1.
Quality standards, §§22.1-253.13:1 to 22.1-253.13:9.
Reports, §22.1-18.
Review, §22.1-18.01.
Questionnaires requiring student participation.
Boards to adopt policies prohibiting during school day, §22.1-79.3.
Student health risk behaviors.
Boards to adopt policies regarding notification to parents, §22.1-79.3.
Race or ethnicity.
Designation by public elementary school students, §22.1-4.2.
Ratios of students to instructional personnel, §22.1-253.13:1.
Reading intervention services, §22.1-253.13:1.
Reading recovery.
Block grants, §22.1-199.1.
Reading specialists for elementary school.
Employment by school boards, §22.1-253.13:1.
Recordation tax, state.
Distributions to cities and counties for public education purposes, §58.1-816.
Records of students, §§22.1-287 to 22.1-289.
Redistricting of school boundaries.
Local school boards powers and duties, §22.1-79.
Refusal to leave property after direction to vacate, §18.2-128.
Regional alternative education programs, §22.1-209.1:2.

SCHOOLS AND EDUCATION —Cont'd
Regional detention homes.
Programs and courses of instruction, §22.1-209.2.
Regional schools, §22.1-26.
Release of school from state regulation regarding accreditation, §22.1-253.13:3.
Religion.
Expression of religious viewpoint by students, §22.1-203.3.
Public school instruction.
Comparative religion as elective course, §22.1-202.1.
Emphasis on moral education, §22.1-208.
Remedial programs.
Reading intervention services, §22.1-253.13:1.
State funding, §22.1-253.13:1.
Remediation for at-risk students, §22.1-253.13:1.
Regulations for establishing standards for, §22.1-199.2.
Removal of student for disruptive behavior from class, §22.1-276.2.
Report cards.
Withholding because of nonpayment of fees and charges, §22.1-6.
Residence of child.
False statements, criminal penalty, §22.1-264.1.
Resource efficiency.
Green schools program of education in waste reduction and resource efficiency, §22.1-212.1:2.
Resource guides.
Public notice and comment regarding, §22.1-17.5.
Safety.
Employment of security officers, §22.1-280.2:1.
Employment, job entry and training requirements, establishing, §9.1-102.
Lock-down drills, §22.1-137.2.
School safety audits, §22.1-279.8.
School safety center, §9.1-184.
Security equipment grants, §22.1-280.2:2.
Threat assessment teams, §22.1-79.4.
Sale of real and personal property, §22.1-129.
Satellite classrooms, §22.1-26.1.
School boards.
Generally, §§22.1-28 to 22.1-57.5.
See LOCAL SCHOOL BOARDS.
School breakfast programs, §22.1-207.3.
School buses, §§22.1-176 to 22.1-198.
See SCHOOL BUSES.
School crime line, §22.1-280.2.
School crisis and emergency management plans, §22.1-279.8.
School divisions.
How school divisions made, §22.1-25.
Opportunity educational institution, statewide school division, §22.1-25.
Persons deemed residing within, §22.1-3.
Transfer of students from division.
Documentation, §22.1-254.02.
School health advisory board, §22.1-275.1.
School health services, §22.1-274.
School prayer.
Daily observance of one minute of silence, §22.1-203.
Guidelines for constitutional compliance, §22.1-203.2.
Student-initiated prayer, §22.1-203.1.
School psychologists.
Duty to protect third parties.
Violent behavior or serious harm by client, §54.1-2400.1.

SCHOOLS AND EDUCATION —Cont'd
School psychologists —Cont'd
Licensing, §§54.1-3600 to 54.1-3606.1.
School records.
Copies received as evidence, §8.01-390.1.
Student criminal records.
Dissemination and maintenance, §22.1-288.2.
School safety audits, §22.1-279.8.
School safety center, §9.1-184.
School year.
Opening after Labor Day, §22.1-79.1.
Scoliosis screening, §22.1-273.1.
Searches and seizures.
Guidelines for student searches, §22.1-279.7.
Model policies for codes of student conduct, §22.1-279.6.
Security officers, §22.1-280.2:1.
Employment, job entry and training requirements, establishing, §9.1-102.
Special conservators of the peace.
All appointments void, §19.2-13.
Service of notice, process and other papers.
Service of teachers or school employees, §8.01-294.
Sex education.
Family life education, §§22.1-207.1, 22.1-207.2.
Sex offender and crimes against minors registry.
Automatic notification of registration to certain entities, §9.1-914.
Boards to adopt policies regarding notification to parents, §22.1-79.3.
Sex offenders within school division.
Registration of school to receive notice of offender registration, §22.1-79.
Sex offenses prohibiting entry onto school property, §18.2-370.5.
Sex offenses prohibiting residing in proximity to, §18.2-370.3.
Sex offenses prohibiting working on school property, §18.2-370.4.
Sexual abuse of student by teacher or school board employee.
Policies of school board to address complaints, §22.1-253.13:7.
Sexual assault avoidance, treatment, and counseling.
Family life education, §§22.1-207.1, 22.1-207.1:1.
Sexually violent predators, civil commitment.
Database of prisoners incarcerated for sexually violent offenses.
Access to records, §37.2-905.2.
Sign language.
American Sign Language instruction, §22.1-207.5.
Single-sex education, §22.1-212.1:1.
Six-year educational technology plan for Virginia, §22.1-199.1.
Smoke bombs.
Setting off in certain public buildings, §18.2-87.1.
Setting off in schools, §18.2-87.1.
Smoking in public places.
Public elementary, intermediate and high schools.
Prohibition on smoking, §15.2-2824.
Social history reports prepared by intake officers.
Superintendent of division to provide information, §22.1-288.2.
Southern regional education compact, §§22.1-358, 22.1-359.
Special education, §§22.1-213 to 22.1-221.
See SPECIAL EDUCATION.
Special tax, §§22.1-102 to 22.1-106.

SCHOOLS AND EDUCATION —Cont'd
Speech impaired.
Special education, §§22.1-213 to 22.1-221.
See SPECIAL EDUCATION.
Speech therapists.
Employment by school board, §22.1-274.
Standards of learning, §22.1-253.13:1.
Test security, §22.1-253.13:3.
FOI exclusion.
Records furnished board of education investigating security breach, §2.2-3705.3.
Standards of quality, §§22.1-253.13:1 to 22.1-253.13:9.
Accounting for schools' performance, §22.1-253.13:3.
Accreditation and evaluation, §22.1-253.13:3.
Opportunity educational institution for schools denied accreditation or given accreditation with warning, §§22.1-27.1 to 22.1-27.6. See within this heading, "Opportunity educational institution."
Additional standards, §22.1-253.13:8.
Basic skills, selected programs and instructional personnel, §22.1-253.13:1.
Board of public education to determine and prescribe, VA Const Art VIII §2.
Choice within school divisions, reporting on, §22.1-18.
Diplomas and certificates, §22.1-253.13:4.
Elementary resources teachers, §22.1-253.13:2.
Fund.
Public education standards of quality/local real estate property tax relief fund.
Retail sales and use tax, revenue disposition, §58.1-638.
Guidance counselors, §22.1-253.13:2.
High quality educational program to be ensured by general assembly, VA Const Art VIII §1.
Librarians, §22.1-253.13:2.
Opportunity educational institution for schools denied accreditation or given accreditation with warning, §§22.1-27.1 to 22.1-27.6. See within this heading, "Opportunity educational institution."
Planning and public involvement, §22.1-253.13:6.
Policies of school board, §22.1-253.13:7.
Principals.
Licensing requirements, §22.1-253.13:2.
Quality of classroom instruction and educational leadership, §22.1-253.13:5.
Report by board of education, §22.1-18.
Review by board of education, §22.1-18.01.
Statewide compliance with standards, §22.1-253.13:8.
Superintendents.
Licensing requirements, §22.1-253.13:2.
Support services positions, §22.1-253.13:2.
Teachers.
Licensing requirements, §22.1-253.13:2.
Ratio of students to teachers, §22.1-253.13:2.
State boards, agencies and institutions.
Child in residence or custody.
Responsibility for providing education, §22.1-7.
Programs and courses of instruction, §22.1-209.2.
Statewide voluntary pupil-teacher ratio and class size reduction program, §22.1-199.1.
Street address or route number on admission document, §22.1-4.1.
Strip searches.
Guidelines for student searches, §22.1-279.7.
Student immunization record, §22.1-271.2.

SCHOOLS AND EDUCATION —Cont'd
Student internship programs.
Identification of programs exempt from federal and state laws, §22.1-17.3.
Student records.
Access to records, §22.1-287.
Cooperation with local law-enforcement agencies, §22.1-288.1.
Copies received as evidence, §8.01-390.1.
Directory information, §22.1-287.1.
Furnishing information to public or private schools, colleges, etc., §22.1-288.
Immunization, §22.1-271.2.
Limitations on access to records, §22.1-287.
Missing children notation, §22.1-288.1.
Personal identifying information, disclosure, §22.1-287.
Transfer of scholastic records, §22.1-289.
Student's status.
Notice of status required as condition of admission, §22.1-3.2.
Student teachers.
Compensation of cooperating teachers, §23-8.2:1.
Suicide.
Student at imminent risk of suicide.
Duties of administrative or instructional personnel, §22.1-272.1.
Summer camps, §§22.1-211, 22.1-212.
Summer school.
Failure of literacy tests, §22.1-253.13:1.
Programs for at-risk students, §22.1-253.13:1.
Reading intervention services, §22.1-253.13:1.
Remediation program for at-risk students, §22.1-253.13:1.
Students required to attend, §22.1-254.01.
Superintendent of public instruction, §§22.1-21 to 22.1-24.
Superintendents of schools, §§22.1-58 to 22.1-70.3.
See SUPERINTENDENTS OF SCHOOLS.
Support by state or local government, VA Const Art VIII §2.
Surplus real estate, §22.1-129.
Surveys requiring student participation.
Boards to adopt policies prohibiting during school day, §22.1-79.3.
Student health risk behaviors.
Boards to adopt policies regarding notification to parents, §22.1-79.3.
Suspension and expulsion of pupils.
Alternative education program.
Authority of school boards, §22.1-277.2:1.
Exclusion from admission, §22.1-277.2.
Children not immunized, §32.1-47.
Drug offenses, §22.1-277.08.
Exclusion of expelled student from admission, §22.1-277.2.
Firearms, §22.1-277.07.
Generally, §22.1-277.
Hazing, §18.2-56.
Long-term suspension, §22.1-277.05.
Readmission, §§22.1-277.04 to 22.1-277.06.
Short-term suspension, §22.1-277.04.
Swastika, placing on property, §18.2-423.1.
Swastikas, placing on property, §18.2-423.1.
Teachers.
Generally.
See TEACHERS.
Technical diplomas.
Requirements, §22.1-253.13:4.
Technological studies program, §22.1-253.13:1.

SCHOOLS AND EDUCATION —Cont'd
Technology plans for individuals, §22.1-199.1.
Testing sight and hearing of pupils, §22.1-273.
Test security procedures.
Action for violating test security procedures.
FOI exclusion.
Records furnished board of education investigating security breach, §2.2-3705.3.
Mandatory tests required by board, §22.1-19.1.
Pursuit of remedies, §22.1-253.13:3.
Actions for violations, §22.1-19.1.
Revocation of administrative or teaching license for violations, §22.1-292.1.
Textbooks, §§22.1-238 to 22.1-243.
Approval of textbooks, §22.1-238.
Basal textbooks, §22.1-239.
Contracts with publishers, §22.1-241.
Damage, fees, §22.1-243.
Distribution of textbooks and consumable materials, §22.1-243.
Free textbooks, etc., VA Const Art VIII §3.
Generally, §§22.1-238 to 22.1-243.
Regulations, §22.1-242.
Threat assessment teams, §22.1-79.4.
Center for school safety to develop procedures, §9.1-184.
Juvenile records, disclosure, §16.1-301.
Threats to commit serious bodily harm to persons on school property, §18.2-60.
Tornado drills, §22.1-137.1.
Toxic art materials.
Identification and labeling, §22.1-274.1.
Transfer of scholastic records on transfer of student to school, §22.1-289.
Transfer of students from division.
Documentation, §22.1-254.02.
Transfer of students to schools within division.
Student victim of crime, §22.1-3.3.
Transportation of pupils, §§22.1-176 to 22.1-198.
See SCHOOL BUSES.
Generally, §§22.1-176 to 22.1-198.
See SCHOOL BUSES.
Trespass upon school property, §18.2-128.
Model policies for codes of student conduct, §22.1-279.6.
Truancy.
Complaint to court for parent's failure to comply with compulsory attendance law, §22.1-262.
Misdemeanor offense, §22.1-263.
Proceedings against child, §22.1-267.
Truant officers.
Appointment, §22.1-258.
Delivery of child to school, §22.1-260.
Duties, §22.1-261.
Tuberculosis certificate, employees, §22.1-300.
Tuition charges, §22.1-5.
Turnaround specialists.
Funding, §22.1-199.1.
Twins or multiples, placement, §22.1-79.3.
Unexcused absences from school.
Ten or more consecutive unexcused absences.
Suspension of student's driver's license, §46.2-334.001.
Uniforms.
Board of education guidelines, §22.1-79.2.
United States Constitution.
Study of documents, §22.1-201.
United States Flag.
Instruction in history and principles, §22.1-202.

SCHOOLS AND EDUCATION —Cont'd
United States Flag —Cont'd
Pledge of allegiance to.
Guidelines on constitutional rights and restrictions relating to recitation, §22.1-202.
Administrative rulemaking exemptions, §2.2-4006.
Universities and colleges.
Furnishing student records to public or private institutions, §22.1-288.
Use of school property, §§22.1-131, 22.1-132.
Vacation schools, §§22.1-211, 22.1-212.
Valentine Museum at Richmond.
Appropriations for providing exhibits to the public schools, §10.1-2212.
Vandalism.
Model policies for codes of student conduct, §22.1-279.6.
Victim of crime.
Transfer of students to other school within division, §22.1-3.3.
Vietnam war veteran honorary high school diploma, §§2.2-3310, 22.1-17.4.
Violence prevention.
Development of programs, §22.1-279.9.
Virginia flag.
Instruction and history and principles, §22.1-202.
Virginia history.
Study of documents, §22.1-201.
Subjects taught in elementary grades, §22.1-200.
Virginia retirement system.
Borrowing by school boards from Virginia retirement system, §§22.1-161.1 to 22.1-161.8.
See LOCAL SCHOOL BOARDS.
Certain employees of public school divisions, §51.1-126.6.
School division superintendents.
Prior service or membership credits, §51.1-142.3.
Virginia teaching scholarship loan program, §22.1-290.01.
Collaboration between council of higher education and state Board of Education, §23-38.10:1.
Virtual schools, §§22.1-212.23 to 22.1-212.27.
Accreditation standards, §22.1-253.13:3.
Innovation technical advisory group, §22.1-212.8:1.
Virtual Virginia program, §22.1-212.2.
Visually impaired.
Special education, §§22.1-213 to 22.1-221.
See SPECIAL EDUCATION.
Waivers of regulatory requirements for accreditation, §22.1-253.13:3.
Warrantless arrests.
Carrying weapon on school property, §19.2-81.
Waste reduction.
Green schools program of education in waste reduction and resource efficiency, §22.1-212.1:2.
Weapons violation.
Arrest for carrying on school property, §16.1-246.
Discharging firearm, §18.2-280.
Disqualification for concealed weapons permit, §18.2-308.09.
Pointing, holding or brandishing firearm, air or gas operated weapons or object similar in appearance, §18.2-282.
Possession of firearm or weapon on school property, §18.2-308.1.
Western Virginia public education consortium, §§22.1-354.1 to 22.1-354.5.

SCHOOLS AND EDUCATION —Cont'd
Wildlife, possession and display by teachers for educational purposes, §29.1-417.
World War II veteran honorary high school diploma, §22.1-17.4.

SCHOOLS PERSONNEL.
Arrest.
Report of arrest of teachers or other employees, §19.2-83.1.
Conviction of certain offenses.
Reports, §19.2-291.1.
Criminal records checks, §§22.1-296.1, 22.1-296.2.
Drugs.
Conviction of offenses involving.
Reports, §19.2-291.1.
Fingerprinting required, §22.1-296.2.
Medical examinations and medical records.
Costs as condition to continued employment, §22.1-301.
Payment of wages, §22.1-296.
Personnel files, §22.1-295.1.
Tuberculosis certificate, §22.1-300.

SCHOOL SUPPLIES.
Retail sales and use tax exemption.
Limited exemption, §58.1-611.2.
Absorption of tax, advertising, inapplicability, §58.1-626.
Collection by dealer during limited period, §58.1-625.

SCIENCE MUSEUM OF VIRGINIA, §§23-239 to 23-253.
Acceptance of gifts, §23-252.
Annual report, §23-253.
Board of trustees.
Acceptance of gifts, §23-252.
Appointment, §23-243.
Bonds of members, §23-247.
Chairman, §23-245.
Composition, §23-243.
Duties, §23-250.
Meetings, §23-248.
Closed meetings, §2.2-3711.
Oath of members, §23-246.
Officers, §23-245.
Powers, §23-250.
Quorum, §23-249.
Reporting requirements, §23-253.
Terms of members, §23-244.
Vacancies, §23-244.
Vice-chairman, §23-245.
Creation, §23-239.
Director.
Appointment, §23-250.
Personnel hiring, §23-251.
Divisions, §23-242.
Employees.
Personnel administration system.
Exemptions, §2.2-2905.
Expenditures, §23-252.
Financial statement.
Annual report by board, §23-253.
Organization, §23-242.
Public policy, §§23-239, 23-240.
Purpose, §23-240.
Secretary of education.
Agency responsibility, §2.2-208.

SCIENTIFIC ADVISORY COMMITTEE, §§9.1-1111 to 9.1-1113.

SCIENTIFIC STUDIES.
See RESEARCH.

SCIENTIFIC TREATISES, PERIODICALS OR PAMPHLETS.
Hearsay exception.
Opinion testimony by experts, §8.01-401.1.

SCIRE FACIAS, WRIT OF.
Abolished, §8.01-24.
Administrators de bonis non, §64.2-547.

SCOFFLAWS.
Habitual offenders generally.
See HABITUAL OFFENDERS.

SCOLIOSIS.
Schools and education.
Screening of students, §22.1-273.1.

SCOOTERS.
Assistive technology device warranties, §§59.1-470 to 59.1-474.
Crosswalks, operating in, §46.2-908.1.
Foot-scooters.
Defined, §46.2-100.
Highways.
Operating on, restrictions, §46.2-908.1.
Mufflers.
Straight exhaust or gutted mufflers, §46.2-1047.
Overtaking and passing vehicles, §46.2-907.
Persons less than 14 years old.
Operating, supervision required, §46.2-908.1.
Roadways and bicycle paths, riding on, §46.2-905.
Sidewalks or crosswalks, locality may prohibit use, §46.2-904.

SCOREKEEPERS AT SPORTING CONTESTS.
Worker' compensation.
Employee not to include sports official, §65.2-101.

S CORPORATIONS.
Income tax on corporations.
Credit for purchase of advanced technology pesticide and fertilizer application equipment, §58.1-436.
Credit for purchase of conservation tillage equipment, §58.1-432.
Exemptions, §58.1-401.
Individual income tax.
Credit for purchase of advanced technology pesticide and fertilizer application equipment, §58.1-337.
Credit for purchase of conservation tillage equipment, §58.1-334.
Credit for taxes paid other states, §58.1-332.
Low-income housing credit, §58.1-435.
Major business facility job tax credit, §58.1-439.
Worker retraining tax credit, §58.1-439.6.
Individual income tax.
Credit for agricultural best management practices, §58.1-339.3.
Nonresident individual shareholders, §58.1-325.

SCOTCHTOWN.
Patrick Henry home.
Historical societies receiving appropriations, §10.1-2212.

SCOTT COUNTY.
Admissions tax.
Off-track horse race wagering facilities, §58.1-3818.01.
Confederate cemeteries and graves.
Disbursement of funds appropriated for upkeep, §10.1-2211.

SCOTT COUNTY —Cont'd
Electric utility restructuring.
Transmission and distribution of electric energy.
Applicability of provisions suspended, §56-580.
School board.
Salary of members, §22.1-32.
Staggered membership and term of office, §15.2-410.
Virginia coalfield economic development authority, §§15.2-6000 to 15.2-6015.

SCRAP METAL PURCHASERS, §§59.1-136.1 to 59.1-136.7.
Abandoned motor vehicles.
Recordkeeping requirements, §46.2-1206.
Definitions, §59.1-136.1.
Exemptions from provisions, §59.1-136.7.
Ferrous scrap.
Purchasing directly, §59.1-136.2.
Health care.
Exemption of material used in, §59.1-136.7.
Minors.
Purchases from prohibited, §59.1-136.4.
Nonferrous scrap.
Purchases of, §59.1-136.3.
Penalties for violations, §59.1-136.6.
Purchases by.
Ferrous scrap, §59.1-136.2.
Metal articles, §59.1-136.3.
Minors.
Purchases from prohibited, §59.1-136.4.
Nonferrous scrap, §59.1-136.3.
Proprietary articles, §59.1-136.3.
Reports of purchases, §59.1-136.5.
Secondhand article sales.
Building fixtures.
Exemption from provisions, §59.1-123.
Company equipment.
Exemption from provisions, §59.1-129.

SCRAP SELLERS.
Secondhand article sales.
Building fixtures, exemption from provisions, §59.1-123.

SCREENING OF DRIVE-IN THEATERS.
Movies shown for adult audiences, counties requiring, §15.2-1222.

SCRIP.
Corporations.
Issuance in registered or bearer form, §13.1-641.
Land scrip.
Counties' subscriptions and individual donations, §23-141.
Institutions receiving interest accruing on proceeds, §23-136.

SCRIVENER'S ACT, §17.1-223.

SCUBA DIVING.
Boating safety, §29.1-734.1.
Spearfishing.
Engaging in while intoxicated, §§29.1-738 to 29.1-738.6.

SCULPTURE.
Child pornography image registry, §19.2-390.3.
Locality acquiring and housing, §15.2-945.
Sexually explicit items involving children.
Production, sale, possession with intent to distribute, etc., §18.2-374.1.

SEAFOOD.
Crabs generally, §§28.2-700 to 28.2-713.
See CRABS.

SEAFOOD —Cont'd
Fishing, tidal waters.
See FISHING, TIDAL WATERS.
License taxes.
Tax not imposed on distributor or vendor catching seafood and selling, §58.1-3719.
Motor vehicle registration.
Transporting harvested seafood.
Exemption of vehicle from registration, §46.2-674.
Oyster planting grounds.
Generally, §§28.2-600 to 28.2-650.
See OYSTER PLANTING GROUNDS.
Oysters and clams.
Generally, §§28.2-500 to 28.2-562.
See OYSTERS AND CLAMS.
Retail sales and use tax.
Agricultural exemptions, §58.1-609.2.
Zoning ordinances.
Commercial fishermen and seafood buyers operating from waterfront residences.
Protection of businesses from zoning ordinances, §15.2-2307.1.

SEAFOOD LANDING LICENSE, §28.2-228.1.

SEALED WRITING, §11-3.

SEALING OF RECORDS.
Attorneys at law.
Proceedings pending disciplinary action, §54.1-3936.
Birth certificates.
New birth certificates upon proof of adoption, legitimation or determination of paternity, §32.1-261.
Change of name.
When records may be sealed, §8.01-217.
Child custody proceeding.
Health, safety or liberty of child jeopardized.
Disclosure of information required to be submitted to court, §20-146.20.
Criminal justice information system.
Criminal history records, §9.1-134.
District court records.
Maintaining records sealed in expungement proceedings, §16.1-69.55.
Divorce, §20-124.
Eavesdropping and wiretapping.
Information obtained to be sealed, §19.2-68.
Grand juries.
Multi-jurisdiction grand juries.
Perjury prosecution, §19.2-212.
Legal separation, §20-124.
Public records.
Provisions not to require opening of sealed record, §42.1-78.
Sentencing.
Presentencing investigation and report, §19.2-299.
Victim impact statements, §19.2-299.1.

SEALING WORKED-OUT AREAS.
Underground coal mines, §45.1-161.228.

SEALS AND SEALED INSTRUMENTS.
Acknowledgments.
Foreign countries.
Seal affixing failures, §55-129.
Adjutant general, §44-18.
Ballots, §24.2-619.
Bonds taken by courts and officers.
Agent or attorney of surety company signing without seal, §49-18.

SEALS AND SEALED INSTRUMENTS —Cont'd
Bonds taken by courts and officers —Cont'd
Seal not required, §49-18.1.
Circuit courts.
Electronic filing of documents.
Digital signatures and seals, §17.1-258.4.
Commercial space flight authority, §2.2-2204.
Commonwealth of Virginia.
Seals of the Commonwealth, §§1-500 to 1-505.
Counties, cities or towns, §15.2-1402.
Credit unions.
Powers as to corporate seal, §6.2-1302.
Definition of seal, §1-241.
Economic development partnership authority, §2.2-2237.
Electoral boards.
Custody of secretary, §24.2-107.
Forging or keeping instrument for forging, §18.2-169.
Leases, UCC.
Inoperative, §8.2A-203.
Pleadings.
Instruments under seal, VA SCt Rule 1:4.
Public building authority.
Powers and duties of authority, §2.2-2263.
Sales, UCC.
Inoperative, §8.2A-203.
Sealed writing, §11-3.
Shooting preserves.
Attachment to shot game, §29.1-606.
Small business financing authority.
Powers and duties of authority, §2.2-2285.
State board of elections, §24.2-103.
State corporation commission, §12.1-3.
Facts certified by clerk to be under seal, §12.1-20.
Tourism authority.
Powers and duties, §2.2-2318.
Voting or counting equipment for elections, §24.2-633.
Writings not purporting to be sealed, §11-3.

SEALS OF THE COMMONWEALTH, §§1-500 to 1-505.
Coins, commemorative.
Commercial purposes, authorizing use for, §2.2-122.
Commercial purposes, authorizing use for.
Governor's power, §2.2-122.
Custody, §1-502.
Fee for affixing, §2.2-409.
Great seal, §1-500.
Tax on, §1-503.
Use, §1-503.
Lesser seal, §1-501.
Tax on, §1-504.
Uses, §1-504.
Library of Virginia.
Impressions displayed in, §1-502.
Property of Commonwealth, §1-505.
Special license plates, §46.2-728.
Use.
Great seal, §1-503.
Lesser seal, §1-504.
Unauthorized use, §1-505.

SEALS TAX, §§58.1-1725, 58.1-1726.

SEAPLANES.
Airplanes generally.
See AIRPLANES.
Conservation police officers.
Daylight hours patrol of lakes from Memorial Day through Labor Day, §29.1-739.2.

SEAPLANES —Cont'd
Conservation police officers —Cont'd
Disregarding signals by officer to stop, §29.1-739.1.
Fleeing or eluding police, §29.1-739.1.
Game and inland fisheries.
Regulations, §29.1-735.1.

SEARCH AND RESCUE PERSONNEL.
Malicious bodily injury to, §18.2-51.1.

SEARCHES AND SEIZURES, US Const Amd 4.
ABC offenses.
Confiscation proceedings, §§4.1-336 to 4.1-338.
Motor vehicles, §§4.1-339 to 4.1-348.
See MOTOR VEHICLE CONFISCATION.
Search warrants, §4.1-337.
Agricultural liming materials.
Appeal from assessment, seizure and sale, §3.2-3712.
Assessments not paid, §3.2-3711.
Anatomical gifts.
Search of donor registry.
Rights and duties of procurement organizations, §32.1-291.14.
Search of individual for document of gift, §32.1-291.12.
Attorney's office, §19.2-56.1.
Body cavity searches, §19.2-59.1.
Cigarette excise tax.
Counterfeit stamps, §58.1-1015.
Cigarettes.
Fire-safe cigarettes.
Nonconforming cigarettes seized as contraband, §59.1-293.6.
Conservation police officers, §29.1-208.
Cruelty to animals, §3.2-6568.
Disposition of property seized, §19.2-58.
Driving while intoxicated.
Vehicle subject to seizure and forfeiture, §18.2-270.
Felony DWI, vehicle used in, §19.2-386.34.
Eggs and hatchery products.
Violations of provisions, §3.2-5309.
Endangered species, §29.1-567.
Exclusionary rule, §19.2-60.
Feed, commercial.
Detained commercial feeds, §3.2-4813.
Fertilizer, §§3.2-3619, 3.2-3620.
Firearm dealers.
Records, §54.1-4201.
Food, §3.2-5135.
Forfeiture proceedings, §§3.2-5137, 3.2-5138.
Sale of seized goods, §3.2-5138.
Disposition of proceeds, §3.2-5139.
Health professions department investigations.
Personnel power to serve and execute warrants, §54.1-2506.
Illegal searches and seizures.
Written pretrial motion, §19.2-266.2.
Inventory of property seized, §19.2-57.
Jails.
Persons entering, §53.1-127.
Law enforcement officers.
Compulsory minimum training standards, §9.1-102.
Local correctional facilities.
Persons entering, §53.1-127.
Meat and poultry products inspection, §3.2-5414.
Motion for return of seized property, §19.2-60.

SEARCHES AND SEIZURES —Cont'd
Motor vehicles.
ABC confiscation proceedings, §§4.1-339 to 4.1-348.
Driving while intoxicated.
Vehicle subject to seizure and forfeiture, §18.2-270.
Felony DWI, vehicle used in, §19.2-386.34.
Trucks and tractor trucks, civil penalty for certain violations.
Attachment and seizure of vehicle for unpaid fees and penalties, §46.2-613.4.
No knock entry, §19.2-56.
Noncomplying lots, §3.2-4013.
Pawnbroker records and shops, §54.1-4011.
Pesticide control.
Noncomplying lots, §3.2-3945.
Plants and plant products inspection, §3.2-3809.
Potato board.
Seed potatoes.
Seizure of shipments in violation of provisions, §3.2-1819.
Precious metals dealers.
Records and articles, §54.1-4101.1.
Prison visitors, §53.1-30.
Schools and education.
Guidelines for student searches, §22.1-279.7.
Model policies for codes of student conduct, §22.1-279.6.
Search warrants generally, §§19.2-52 to 19.2-60.
See SEARCH WARRANTS.
Strip searches, §19.2-59.1.
Schools and education.
Guidelines for student searches, §22.1-279.7.
Suppression of unlawfully seized evidence, §19.2-60.
Underground coal mines.
Entry as consent to search for smoking materials, §45.1-161.177.
Uniform of officer making, §19.2-78.
Unreasonable search and seizure.
Suppression of evidence.
Written pretrial motion requirement, §19.2-266.2.
Warrantless searches.
Department of motor vehicles.
Authority of law enforcement officers, §46.2-217.
Fireworks dealers' records, §54.1-4201.
Game law enforcement, §19.2-56.
Conservation police officers, §29.1-208.
Pawnbrokers' records and shops, §54.1-4011.
Precious metals dealers' records, etc., §54.1-4101.1.
Toxic substances, inspection warrants, §§19.2-393 to 19.2-397.
Unlawful searches, §19.2-59.
Suppression of evidence, pretrial motion, §19.2-266.2.
Warrants.
Search warrants generally, §§19.2-52 to 19.2-60.
See SEARCH WARRANTS.
Weights and measures.
Agriculture and consumer services commissioner, §3.2-5612.
Written pretrial motion.
Suppression of evidence.
Unreasonable search and seizure, §19.2-266.2.

SEARCHES WITHOUT WARRANT.
Department of motor vehicles.
Authority of law enforcement officers, §46.2-217.

SEARCHES WITHOUT WARRANT —Cont'd
Fireworks dealers' records, §54.1-4201.
Game law enforcement, §19.2-56.
Conservation police officers, §29.1-208.
Pawnbrokers' records and shops, §54.1-4011.
Precious metals dealers' records, etc., §54.1-4101.1.
Toxic substances, inspection warrants, §§19.2-393 to 19.2-397.
Unlawful searches, §19.2-59.
Suppression of evidence, pretrial motion, §19.2-266.2.

SEARCH WARRANTS, §§19.2-52 to 19.2-60.
Attorney's office, issuance for search of, §19.2-56.1.
Certified affidavit requirement.
Prerequisite to issuance of search warrant, §19.2-54.
Complaint and affidavit.
Effect of failure to file affidavit, §19.2-54.
Issuing search warrant without affidavit deemed malfeasance, §19.2-55.
Probable cause requirement for issuance, §19.2-52.
Copy of affidavit part of warrant, §19.2-56.
Directed to, §19.2-56.
Electronically transmitted facsimile process.
Filing affidavit by authorized, §19.2-54.
Exception to strip search prohibition, §19.2-59.1.
Exception to warrantless search prohibition, §19.2-59.
Exclusionary rule, §19.2-60.
Execution, §§19.2-56, 19.2-57.
Effect of warrants not executed within fifteen days, §19.2-56.
Fifteen days, warrant not executed within, §19.2-56.
Fire prevention code.
Appeals, §27-98.5.
Conduct of search, §27-98.4.
Issuance, §27-98.2.
Game laws.
Enforcement as exception to warrantless search prohibition, §19.2-59.
General search warrants.
Issuance deemed malfeasance, §19.2-55.
Issuance prohibition, §19.2-54, VA Const Art I §10.
GPS.
Tracking devices, warrant to permit use of, §19.2-56.2.
Inventory of property seized, §19.2-57.
Issuance.
Affidavit preliminary to issuance, §19.2-54.
Probable cause requirement, §19.2-52.
What may be searched and seized, §19.2-53.
Machine guns, §18.2-296.
Magistrates.
Power to issue, §19.2-45.
Malfeasance in office.
Issuing general search warrant, §19.2-55.
Issuing search warrant without affidavit, §19.2-55.
Motion for return of seized property, §19.2-60.
No-knock entry, §19.2-56.
Oath or affirmation, US Const Amd 4.
Persons subject to search and seizure, §§19.2-53, 19.2-56.
Disposition of property seized, §§19.2-58, 19.2-60.
Motion for return of seized property, §19.2-60.
Exception to strip search prohibition, §19.2-59.1.

SEARCH WARRANTS —Cont'd
Persons subject to search and seizure —Cont'd
Exception to warrantless search prohibition, §19.2-59.
Execution and return of warrant, §§19.2-56, 19.2-57.
List of property seized, §19.2-57.
To whom search warrant directed, §19.2-56.
Warrant to show date and time of issuance, §19.2-56.
General search warrant prohibition, §19.2-54.
Issuing general search warrant deemed malfeasance, §19.2-55.
Strip searches prohibited, §19.2-59.1.
Suppression of evidence, §19.2-60.
Warrantless searches prohibited, §19.2-59.
Warrants not executed within fifteen days, §19.2-56.
Places subject to search and seizure, §§19.2-53, 19.2-56.
Attorney's office, §19.2-56.1.
Disposition of property seized, §§19.2-58, 19.2-60.
Motion for return of seized property, §19.2-60.
Exception to warrantless search prohibition, §19.2-59.
Execution and return of warrant, §§19.2-56, 19.2-57.
List of property seized, §19.2-57.
To whom search warrant directed, §19.2-56.
Warrant to show date and time of issuance, §19.2-56.
General search warrant prohibition, §19.2-54.
Issuing general search warrant deemed malfeasance, §19.2-55.
Suppression of evidence, §19.2-60.
Warrantless searches prohibited, §19.2-59.
Warrants not executed within fifteen days, §19.2-56.
Property subject to search and seizure, §19.2-53.
Attorney's office, §19.2-56.1.
Disposition of property seized, §19.2-58.
Motion for return of seized property, §19.2-60.
Exception to warrantless search prohibition, §19.2-59.
Execution and return of warrant, §§19.2-56, 19.2-57.
List of property seized, §19.2-57.
To whom search warrant directed, §19.2-56.
Warrant to show date and time of issuance, §19.2-56.
General search warrant prohibition, §19.2-54.
Issuing general search warrant deemed malfeasance, §19.2-55.
No knock entry, §19.2-56.
Suppression of evidence, §19.2-60.
Warrantless searches prohibited, §19.2-59.
Warrants not executed within fifteen days, §19.2-56.
Requirements for affidavit, §19.2-54.
Sawed-off shotguns and sawed-off rifles, §18.2-306.
Sealing affidavit, §19.2-54.
Search without warrant.
Generally.
See SEARCHES WITHOUT WARRANT.
Unlawful, §19.2-59.
Special police officer executing, §15.2-1745.
State veterinarian.
Inspection of premises where animals are kept, §3.2-6502.

SEARCH WARRANTS —Cont'd
Strip searches prohibition, §19.2-59.1.
Suppression of evidence.
Unlawfully seized evidence, §19.2-60.
Unreasonable search and seizure.
Written pretrial motion requirement, §19.2-266.2.
Things subject to search and seizure, §§19.2-53, 19.2-56.
Disposition of property seized.
Motion for return of seized property, §19.2-60.
Exception to warrantless search prohibition, §19.2-59.
Execution and return of warrant, §§19.2-56, 19.2-57.
List of property seized, §19.2-57.
To whom search warrant directed, §19.2-56.
Warrant to show date and time of issuance, §19.2-56.
General search warrant prohibition, §19.2-54.
Issuing general search warrant deemed malfeasance, §19.2-55.
Warrantless searches prohibited, §19.2-59.
Warrants not executed within fifteen days, §19.2-56.
To whom directed, §19.2-56.
Tracking devices, warrant to permit use of, §19.2-56.2.
Unlawful search without warrant, §19.2-59.
Unreasonable search and seizure.
Suppression of evidence.
Written pretrial motion requirement, §19.2-266.2.
Wiretapping.
Obtaining records concerning electronic communication service or remote computing service, §19.2-70.3.
Execution of warrants, §19.2-56.
Written pretrial motion.
Suppression of evidence.
Unreasonable search and seizure, §19.2-266.2.

SEASONAL WORKERS.
Migrant labor camps, §§32.1-203 to 32.1-211.
See MIGRANT LABOR CAMPS.

SEATBELTS, §§46.2-1091 to 46.2-1100.
Bus drivers.
Requirement to wear, §46.2-1091.
Child safety restraint system, §§46.2-1095 to 46.2-1100.
Appropriate safety belt system.
Children secured in, §46.2-1095.
Children less than age eighteen.
Properly secured by safety belt system, §46.2-1095.
Children up to age eight.
Securing in child restraint device, §46.2-1095.
Evidence, comment by counsel.
Violation not admissible or subject to, §46.2-1095.
Exemptions for certain children, §§46.2-1096, 46.2-1099.
Failure to ensure child is properly secured.
Uniform fine schedule, VA SCt Rule 3C:2.
Immunity of installers or inspectors.
Installing or inspecting without compensation, §8.01-226.5.
Impractical use exemption, §46.2-1099.
Indigent persons, §46.2-1097.
Mandatory, §46.2-1095.
Negligence per se, §46.2-1098.

SEATBELTS —Cont'd
Child safety restraint system —Cont'd
Negligence to be considered in mitigation of damages.
Violation not to constitute, §46.2-1095.
Rear facing child restraint devices.
Placed in back seat, exception, §46.2-1095.
Required, §46.2-1095.
Special fund for indigents, §46.2-1097.
Standard seatbelts.
Use permitted, §46.2-1100.
Taxicabs, school buses, executive sedans or limousines.
Inapplicability to, §46.2-1095.
Uniform traffic summons.
Violation charged by, §46.2-1095.
Violations not negligence per se, §46.2-1098.
Combination lap belt and shoulder harness.
Installation in certain vehicles, §46.2-1092.
Requirements, §46.2-1093.
Failure to ensure child is properly secured.
Uniform fine schedule, VA SCt Rule 3C:2.
Front seat occupants.
Required use of safety lap belt and shoulder harness, §46.2-1094.
Installation, §§46.2-1092, 46.2-1093.
Maximum fine for violating Title 46.2, §46.2-113.
Safety lap belts.
Installation in certain vehicles, §46.2-1092.
Required for occupants of front seats, §46.2-1094.
Requirements, §46.2-1093.
Shoulder harnesses.
Combination of lap belt and shoulder harnesses, §46.2-1092.
Required for occupants of front seats, §46.2-1094.
Requirements, §46.2-1093.
Uniform fine schedule for violations, VA SCt Rules 3B:2, 3C:1, 3C:2.
Use in lieu of child restraint devices.
Permitted use of standard seatbelt, §46.2-1100.

SEAT OF MOTOR VEHICLE.
Improperly affixed, §46.2-1084.
Fine schedule, VA SCt Rule 3B:2.
Maximum fine for violating Title 46.2, §46.2-113.

SEAWALLS.
Beach conservation and development, §§10.1-705 to 10.1-711.
See BEACH CONSERVATION AND DEVELOPMENT.
Coastal primary sand dunes and beaches, §§28.2-1400 to 28.2-1420.
See COASTAL PRIMARY SAND DUNES AND BEACHES.
Construction by locality, §15.2-970.
Erosion and sediment control, §§62.1-44.15:51 to 62.1-44.15:66.
Shore erosion control, §§10.1-700 to 10.1-704.
See SHORE EROSION CONTROL.

SECOBARBITAL.
Schedule III controlled substance, §54.1-3450.

SECONDARY SCHOOLS.
Schools and education generally.
See SCHOOLS AND EDUCATION.

SECONDARY SYSTEM OF STATE HIGHWAYS, §§33.1-67 to 33.1-88.
See HIGHWAYS AND ROADS.

SECONDHAND ARTICLE SALES, §§59.1-116.1 to 59.1-136.
Advertising or offering for sale, prohibited practices, §59.1-200.

SECONDHAND ARTICLE SALES —Cont'd
Building fixtures, §§59.1-116.1 to 59.1-124.
Dealers.
Business to open to inspection, §59.1-122.
Defined, §59.1-119.
Records, §59.1-120.
Open to inspection, §59.1-122.
Reports, §59.1-121.
Showing of permits and identification, §59.1-119.1.
Definitions, §59.1-116.1.
Permits.
Dealers required to show, §59.1-119.1.
Issuance and revocation, §59.1-118.
Required, §59.1-117.
Provision exemptions, §59.1-123.
Provision violations, §59.1-124.
Sellers, proof of ownership prior to sale, §59.1-120.
City or town power to regulate dealers, §15.2-1114.
Company equipment, §§59.1-125 to 59.1-130.
Bills of sale, §59.1-126.
Violations, §59.1-127.
Buying, when lawful, §§59.1-125, 59.1-127.
Check as form of payment.
Required for purchases over $1,000, §59.1-126.
Items which may be bought or accepted, §59.1-125.
Secondhand copper or aluminum wire, §§59.1-128 to 59.1-130.
Requirement, §59.1-129.
Violations, §59.1-130.
Violations, §59.1-127.
Receipts, §§59.1-126, 59.1-127.
Violations, §59.1-127.
Secondhand copper or aluminum wire, §§59.1-128 to 59.1-130.
Requirement, §59.1-129.
Violations, §59.1-130.
County power to regulate, §15.2-1232.1.
Grate baskets, keys, bells and bell fixtures, gas fixtures, etc.
Buying or receiving with intent to defraud, §18.2-237.
Names, marks and devices on certain containers and articles.
Generally, §§59.1-93 to 59.1-102.
See MARKS ON CERTAIN CONTAINERS.
Terms seconds, irregulars, secondhand, etc.
Failure to indicate on goods, §18.2-218.
Watches, §§59.1-131 to 59.1-136.
Advertising, §59.1-134.
Auction sales exempted, §59.1-136.
Displaying, §59.1-134.
Invoice to purchaser, §59.1-133.
Provision violations.
Penalties, §59.1-135.
Tagging, §59.1-132.
When watched deemed secondhand, §59.1-131.

SECOND INJURY FUND, §§65.2-1100 to 65.2-1106.

SECOND LIEUTENANTS.
National Guard, appointment, §44-27.

SECONDS.
Advertising or offering for sale goods which are seconds, prohibited practices, §59.1-200.

SECOND TRIMESTER OF PREGNANCY.
Lawful abortions, §§18.2-73, 18.2-74.

SECRECY OF TAX INFORMATION, §58.1-3.
Attorney general's authority to request and share information, §58.1-3.2.
Availability to audit local tax returns, §58.1-3.1.
Motor vehicle fuel sales tax, §58.1-1724.1.
Real property tax.
Assessment cards and sheets, public disclosure, §58.1-3331.
Income-producing realty, reports by owners, §58.1-3294.
Retail sales and use tax.
Report of gross misuse of exemption certificates, §58.1-623.1.
Road tax on motor carriers.
International fuel tax agreement.
Information exchanges under agreement, §58.1-2712.2.
Setoff debt collection act.
Exemption, use of information, §58.1-533.
Tax commissioner's authority to request and share information, §58.1-3.2.
Taxpayer bill of rights, §58.1-1845.
Taxpayers not to disclose without consent, §58.1-4.
Town officers provided information by commissioners of revenue, §58.1-3109.
Transfer of credit or other tax attribute.
Deemed consent to disclosure, §58.1-3.3.
Treasurers' books and papers pertaining to office, §58.1-3127.
Wills and administration, tax on.
Return filed, §58.1-1714.

SECRETARIES.
Public officers and employees.
Certified professional secretary examinations.
Classification of persons passing, §2.2-2904.

SECRETARIES OF GOVERNOR, §§2.2-200 to 2.2-229.

SECRETARY OF ADMINISTRATION.
Agencies for which responsible, §2.2-203.
Alternative dispute resolution.
Ad hoc working groups to promote, §2.2-203.2:2.
Alternative work schedules.
Secretary to establish policy, §2.2-203.1.
Appointment by governor, §2.2-200.
Compensation, §2.2-201.
Economic development policy for Commonwealth.
Cabinet level committee to assist.
Committee membership, §2.2-205.
Flex time.
Establishment of policy on telecommuting and alternative work schedules, §2.2-203.1.
General powers of governor's secretaries, §2.2-200.
Office expenses, payment, §2.2-201.
Position established, §2.2-203.
Privatization of commercial activities, loss of jobs due to.
Report to governor, §2.2-203.2:1.
Telecommuting.
Secretary to establish policy, §2.2-203.1.

SECRETARY OF AGRICULTURE AND FORESTRY, §§2.2-200 to 2.2-202.
Agency responsibilities, §2.2-203.3.
Duties, §2.2-203.3.
Established, §2.2-203.3.
Farm and forest land protection.
Plans by certain agencies to implement policies.
Review, report, time for filing, §3.2-206.

SECRETARY OF AGRICULTURE AND FORESTRY —Cont'd
Invasive species.
Development of strategies to eradicate and prevent, §2.2-220.2.
Nutrients and sediments entering state waters.
Onsite best management practices implement by state to limit.
Database of critical data attributes, §2.2-220.3.

SECRETARY OF COMMERCE AND TRADE.
Agencies responsible for, §2.2-204.
Appointment by governor, §2.2-200.
Biotechnology research act.
Implementation of provisions, §2.2-204.
Compensation, §2.2-201.
Comprehensive economic development policy for Commonwealth.
Development, §2.2-205.
Economic crisis strike force, §2.2-205.1.
General powers of secretaries, §2.2-200.
Legislative report, §2.2-207.
Office expenses, payment, §2.2-202.
Position established, §2.2-204.
Urban areas report, §2.2-206.
Virginia liaison office.
Support, §2.2-206.

SECRETARY OF EDUCATION.
Agency responsibilities, §2.2-208.
Alternative policies, plans and budgets for education.
Authorized to direct preparation, §2.2-208.
Appointment by governor, §2.2-200.
Compensation, §2.2-201.
Conflicts between agencies and officers.
Power to resolve, §2.2-208.
Cultural affairs.
Formulation of comprehensive program budget, §2.2-208.
Economic development policy for Commonwealth.
Cabinet level committee to assist.
Committee membership, §2.2-205.
General powers of secretaries, §2.2-200.
Office expenses, payment, §2.2-202.
Position established, §2.2-208.

SECRETARY OF FINANCE.
Agency responsibilities, §2.2-211.
Appointment by governor, §2.2-200.
Compensation, §2.2-201.
Electronic transfers of funds.
Agencies assigned to secretary to pay Commonwealth by, §2.2-211.
General powers of secretaries, §2.2-200.
Office expense, payment, §2.2-202.
Position created, §2.2-211.

SECRETARY OF HEALTH AND HUMAN RESOURCES.
Agency responsibility, §2.2-212.
Agency rules discriminating against individuals infected with HIV.
Review of rules to eliminate, §2.2-214.
Appointment by governor, §2.2-200.
Children with incarcerated parents.
System for providing services to, §2.2-213.2.
Compensation, §2.2-201.
Comprehensive services act for at-risk youth and families.
Service as lead secretary, §2.2-212.

SECRETARY OF HEALTH AND HUMAN RESOURCES —Cont'd
Economic development policy for Commonwealth.
Cabinet level committee to assist.
Committee membership, §2.2-205.
Electronic prescribing clearinghouse.
Duties regarding, §2.2-213.3.
General powers of secretaries, §2.2-200.
Long-term care public information campaign.
Cooperation with commissioner of insurance, §2.2-213.1.
Office expenses, payment, §2.2-202.
Position established, §2.2-212.
Prescriptions.
Electronic prescribing clearinghouse.
Duties regarding, §2.2-213.3.
Substance abusing women and their children.
Development of criteria, other duties, §2.2-213.

SECRETARY OF NATURAL RESOURCES.
Agency responsibility, §2.2-215.
Appointment by governor, §2.2-200.
Chesapeake Bay 2000 agreement, §2.2-220.1.
Chesapeake Bay and tributaries.
Comprehensive program to monitor quality of waters, habitat and living resources.
Duties, §2.2-216.
Development of tributary plans to, §§2.2-218 to 2.2-220.
Duty to monitor water, habitat, and living resources, §2.2-216.
Friend of the bay award, establishment, §2.2-217.
Compensation, §2.2-201.
Economic development policy for Commonwealth.
Cabinet level committee to assist.
Committee membership, §2.2-205.
General powers of secretaries, §2.2-200.
Invasive species.
Development of strategies to eradicate and prevent, §2.2-220.2.
Nutrients and sediments entering state waters.
Onsite best management practices implement by state to limit.
Database of critical data attributes, §2.2-220.3.
Office expenses, payment, §2.2-202.
Position established, §2.2-215.
Reports.
Chesapeake Bay 2000 agreement, §2.2-220.1.

SECRETARY OF PUBLIC SAFETY.
Agency responsibility, §2.2-221.
Aircraft acquired by localities through forfeiture.
Publication of list, §2.2-224.
Appointment by governor, §2.2-200.
Compensation, §2.2-201.
General powers of secretaries, §2.2-200.
Information exchange program, secretary to establish, §2.2-224.1.
Juvenile demographics report, §2.2-222.
Offender transition and reentry services, system for, §2.2-221.1.
Office expenses, payment, §2.2-202.
Position established, §2.2-221.

SECRETARY OF TECHNOLOGY.
Agency responsibility, §2.2-225.
Alternative work schedules.
Establishment of policy, §2.2-203.1.
Appointment by governor, §2.2-200.

SECRETARY OF TECHNOLOGY —Cont'd
Compensation, §2.2-201.
Economic development policy for Commonwealth.
Cabinet level committee to assist.
Committee membership, §2.2-205.
Flex time.
Establishment of policy on telecommuting and alternative work schedules, §2.2-203.1.
General powers of secretaries, §2.2-200.
Information technology advisory council.
Chairman, §2.2-2699.5.
Major information technology projects.
Develop criteria and requirements defining, §2.2-225.
Procurement.
Review and approve or terminate, §2.2-225.
Office expenses, payment, §2.2-202.
Position established, §2.2-225.
Strategy development, planning and budgeting.
Powers, §2.2-225.
Telecommuting.
Establishment of policy, §2.2-203.1.

SECRETARY OF THE COMMONWEALTH, §§2.2-400 to 2.2-410.
Appointment by governor, §2.2-400.
Authentication and certification of records.
Records to be used in other states, §2.2-404.
Boundary changes.
Collection of data from political subdivisions, §2.2-408.
Central criminal records exchange.
Reports to, §19.2-390.
Chesapeake regional Olympic games compact.
Records to be filed, §2.2-5901.
Compacts to which Commonwealth party.
Compilation, records and report on appointments, §2.2-403.
Division of records, charge of, §2.2-401.
Duties generally, §2.2-402.
Electronic database of collegial bodies.
Secretary to maintain, transfer to governor-elect upon request, §2.2-406.1.
Ex officio secretary to governor, §2.2-401.
Fees charged for services rendered in office, §2.2-409.
Collection, §2.2-402.
Landlord and tenant.
Service of notice, process and other papers.
Nonresident property owners, §55-218.1.
Lobbyists.
Registration and reporting requirements, §§2.2-418 to 2.2-435.
See LOBBYISTS.
Mail notice.
Initial notice by certified mail, subsequent notices by regular mail, §2.2-401.1.
Notaries.
Generally.
See NOTARIES.
Registered with and commissioned by, §47.1-3.
Notice.
Initial notice by certified mail, subsequent notices by regular mail, §2.2-401.1.
Oath to keep secret matters required by governor to conceal, §2.2-400.
Order or warrant of governor.
Return to secretary, §2.2-112.

SECRETARY OF THE COMMONWEALTH —Cont'd
Organizational chart of state government, §2.2-402.
Records.
Chesapeake regional Olympic games compact.
Records to be filed, §2.2-5901.
Records of executive branch, duties, §2.2-402.
Registration, alteration or cancellation of names or insignia of organizations, §§2.2-411 to 2.2-417.
See REGISTRATION OF NAMES OR INSIGNIA OF ORGANIZATIONS.
Registration of names and insignia.
Illegal use of registered insignia, §18.2-177.
Report to general assembly on persons accepted to boards, commission, etc., §2.2-406.
Report to governor identifying boards, commissions, etc., §2.2-402.
Seals of the Commonwealth.
Keeper, §2.2-402.
Secrecy of matters required by governor.
Oath, §2.2-400.
Secretary of administration.
Agency responsibility, §2.2-203.
Service of notice, process and other papers.
Appointed agent for service.
Lobbyists and principals, §2.2-423.
Exercise of personal jurisdiction, §8.01-329.
Initial notice by certified mail, subsequent notices by regular mail, §2.2-401.1.
Landlord and tenant.
Nonresident property owners, §55-218.1.
Term, §2.2-400.
Town seeking city status.
Copy of special court order certified to, §15.2-3807.
Vacancies arising on boards, commission, etc.
List prepared, §2.2-405.
Vacancy in office, filling, §2.2-400.

SECRETARY OF TRANSPORTATION.
Agency responsibility, §2.2-228.
Appointment by governor, §2.2-200.
Compensation, §2.2-201.
Economic development policy for Commonwealth.
Cabinet level committee to assist.
Committee membership, §2.2-205.
General powers of secretaries, §2.2-200.
Office expenses, payment, §2.2-202.
Position established, §2.2-228.
Report on actions to increase transit use and reduce highway congestion, §33.1-223.2:24.

SECRETARY OF VETERANS AFFAIRS AND HOMELAND SECURITY, §§2.2-200 to 2.2-202, 2.2-230 to 2.2-233.
Agencies for which responsible, §2.2-230.
Appointment by governor, §2.2-200.
Duties, §2.2-231.
Secure Commonwealth panel, §2.2-233.
Statewide interoperability strategic plan, §2.2-232.
Establishment of position, §2.2-230.
General powers of secretaries, §2.2-200.
Powers, §2.2-231.
Secure Commonwealth panel.
Duties, §2.2-233.
Statewide interoperability strategic plan.
Duties, §2.2-232.

SECRET SOCIETIES.
Clandestine organizations.
Defined, §18.2-420.
Information to be filed with state corporation commission, §18.2-421.

SECTARIAN SOCIETIES.
Appropriations to, VA Const Art IV §16.
Donations by locality.
Prohibition, §15.2-908.

SECURE COMMONWEALTH PANEL.
Secretary of veterans affairs and homeland security.
Agencies for which responsible, §2.2-230.
Duties, §2.2-233.

SECURED TRANSACTIONS, §§8.9A-101 to 8.9A-809.
Acceleration of payment.
When not allowed, §11-4.3.
Accessions.
Perfection and priority of security interest in, §8.9A-335.
Accounting.
Defined, §8.9A-102.
Request for, §8.9A-210.
After-acquired property.
Security interest in, §8.9A-204.
Agricultural liens.
Default.
Time of default, §8.9A-606.
Defined, §8.9A-102.
Perfection and priority.
Filed financing statement providing certain incorrect information.
Priority of agricultural lien perfected by, §8.9A-338.
Filing.
When required to perfect lien, §8.9A-310.
Interests that take priority over or take free of agricultural lien, §8.9A-317.
Law governing, §8.9A-302.
Priorities among agricultural liens on same collateral, §8.9A-322.
When perfected, §8.9A-308.
Applicability of provisions, §§8.9A-109, 8.9A-110.
Attachment of security interest, §8.9A-203.
Effect on delegation of performance and assignment of rights, §8.9A-210.
Financial asset.
Security interest arising in purchase or delivery of, §8.9A-206.
Perfection.
Security interests perfected upon attachment, §8.9A-309.
Bank deposits and collections.
Depositary and collecting banks.
Collection of items, §8.4-208.
Documentary drafts.
Dishonor.
Privilege of presenting bank to deal with goods, §8.4-504.
Banks.
Defined, §8.9A-102.
Rights of banks.
Control agreement.
Refusal to enter into or disclose existence of, §8.9A-342.
Deposit accounts, §§8.9A-340, 8.9A-341.
Security interests in deposit accounts.
Control agreements.
Rights of banks with respect to agreements, §8.9A-342.

SECURED TRANSACTIONS —Cont'd
Banks —Cont'd
Security interests in deposit accounts —Cont'd
Perfection and priority, §8.9A-304.
Rules of priority, §8.9A-327.
Rights and duties of banks, §8.9A-341.
Set-off or recoupment, §8.9A-340.
Transfer of funds from deposit account, §8.9A-332.
Boats and other watercraft.
Security interests, §§29.1-723 to 29.1-732.
See BOATS AND OTHER WATERCRAFT.
Boat titling certificates.
Certificate as notice, §29.1-725.
Holding of certificate, §29.1-728.
Issuance effect, §29.1-713.
Listing upon certificate, §29.1-723.
Security interests subsequently created, §29.1-724.
Possession.
Application of provisions, §29.1-723.
Priority, §29.1-727.
Release of interest shown on certificate, §29.1-729.
Surrender of certificate when security interest paid, §29.1-730.
Chattel paper.
Perfection of security interests in, §8.9A-312.
Purchaser of chattel paper or instrument.
Priority, §8.9A-330.
Citation of provisions, §8.9A-101.
Collateral.
Control of collateral.
Rights and duties of secured party having, §§8.9A-207, 8.9A-208.
Default.
Acceptance in full or partial satisfaction of obligation, §§8.9A-620 to 8.9A-622.
Disposition after default, §§8.9A-610 to 8.9A-617.
Redemption.
Right to redeem collateral, §8.9A-623.
Transfer of record or legal title, §8.9A-619.
Description.
Sufficiency, §8.9A-108.
Disposition.
Permissible, §8.9A-205.
Rights of secured party on, §8.9A-315.
List of collateral.
Request regarding, §8.9A-210.
Possession of collateral.
Rights and duties of secured party having, §8.9A-207.
Title immaterial, §8.9A-202.
Transferred collateral.
Priority of security interests in, §8.9A-325.
Use permissible, §8.9A-205.
Commercial code general provisions.
See COMMERCIAL CODE.
Commingled goods, §8.9A-336.
Consolidation of debts.
Consumer goods purchased in separate transactions.
Security interest in consumer goods, §8.9A-204.1.
Consumer goods.
Security interest in consumer goods, §8.9A-204.1.
Contracts creating, law governing validity, §11-1.
Crops.
Priority of security interests in, §8.9A-334.

SECURED TRANSACTIONS —Cont'd
Debtor.
Defined, §8.9A-102.
Location, §8.9A-307.
Default.
Acceptance of collateral in full or partial satisfaction of obligation, §8.9A-620.
Effect, §8.9A-622.
Notification, §8.9A-621.
Agricultural lien.
Time of default, §8.9A-606.
Collateral.
Acceptance in full or partial satisfaction of obligation, §§8.9A-620 to 8.9A-622.
Disposition after default, §§8.9A-610 to 8.9A-617.
Redemption.
Right to redeem collateral, §8.9A-623.
Transfer of record or legal title, §8.9A-619.
Collection and enforcement by secured party, §8.9A-607.
Application of proceeds, §8.9A-608.
Commercially reasonable conduct.
Determination whether conduct commercially reasonable, §8.9A-627.
Disposition of collateral after, §8.9A-610.
Compulsory disposition, §8.9A-620.
Deficiency.
Action in which deficiency is in issue, §8.9A-626.
Explanation of calculation of, §8.9A-616.
Liability for, §8.9A-615.
Notification before, §8.9A-611.
Contents and form, §§8.9A-613, 8.9A-614.
Timeliness, §8.9A-612.
Proceeds.
Application, §8.9A-615.
Surplus.
Action in which surplus is an issue, §8.9A-626.
Explanation of calculation of, §8.9A-616.
Right to, §8.9A-615.
Transferee of collateral.
Rights, §8.9A-617.
Fixtures.
Procedure if security agreement covers, §8.9A-604.
Judicial enforcement, §8.9A-601.
Noncompliance with provisions by secured party.
Remedies, §8.9A-625.
Possession.
Rights of secured party to take possession after default, §8.9A-609.
Real property.
Procedure if security agreement covers, §8.9A-604.
Rights after default, §8.9A-601.
Agreement on standards concerning, §8.9A-603.
Waiver and variance, §8.9A-602.
Secondary obligors.
Liability, §8.9A-628.
Limitation on liability of secured party, §8.9A-628.
Rights and duties, §8.9A 618.
Unknown debtor or secondary obligor, §8.9A-605.
Waiver of certain rights, §8.9A-624.
Definitions, §§8.9A-102, 8.9A-103.
Deposit account.
Bank's rights and duties with respect to, §8.9A-341.
Right of recoupment or set-off against deposit account.
Effectiveness, §8.9A-340.

SECURED TRANSACTIONS —Cont'd
Deposit account —Cont'd
Control, §8.9A-104.
Defined, §8.9A-102.
Perfection and priority of security interest in, §8.9A-312.
Law governing, §8.9A-304.
Perfection by control, §8.9A-314.
Priority of security interests, §8.9A-327.
Transfer of funds from deposit account.
Transferee takes funds free of security interest, §8.9A-332.
Description of property.
Sufficiency, §8.9A-108.
Distress for local taxes levied or assessed.
Security interest not bar to, §58.1-3942.
Signatures of both parties not discriminatory, §6.2-504.
Duties of secured party.
Account debtor notified of assignment, §8.9A-209.
Control or possession of collateral.
Secured party having, §§8.9A-207, 8.9A-208.
Effective date of provisions, §8.9A-701.
Action taken before.
Effectiveness, §8.9A-705.
Financing statement.
Pre-effective-date financing statement, §8.9A-707.
Security interest perfected before effective date, §8.9A-703.
Security interest unperfected before effective date, §8.9A-704.
Electronic chattel paper.
Control, §8.9A-105.
Perfection by control, §8.9A-314.
Defined, §8.9A-102.
Enforceability of security interest, §8.9A-203.
Farm tractors.
Defined, §46.2-100.
Perfecting security interests, §46.2-636.1.
Fees charged by circuit court clerk, §17.1-275.
Fieri facias.
Sale of property subject to prior security interest, §8.01-480.
Filing office, §8.9A-501.
Delay by, §8.9A-524.
Destruction of records, §8.9A-522.
Duties, §§8.9A-519, 8.9A-520, 8.9A-522, 8.9A-523.
Fees, §8.9A-525.
Format of statements and records, §8.9A-521.1.
Information from, §8.9A-523.
Refusal to accept record, §§8.9A-520, 8.9A-521.
Reports on operation, §8.9A-527.
Uniform form of written financing statement and amendment, §8.9A-521.
Filing-office rules, §8.9A-526.
Financial asset.
Priority of certain interests in, §8.9A-331.
Purchase or delivery of.
Security interest arising in, §8.9A-206.
Financing statement.
Amendments, §§8.9A-501, 8.9A-512.
Change of place of filing.
Transition provision, §8.11-105.
Change of requirement of filing.
Transition provision, §8.11-104.
Pre-effective-date financing statement, §8.9A-707.
Required refilings.
Transitional provision, §8.11-106.
Assignment, §8.9A-501.

SECURED TRANSACTIONS —Cont'd
Financing statement —Cont'd
Collateral.
Indication of collateral, §8.9A-504.
Contents, §8.9A-502.
Duration of effectiveness, §§8.9A-501, 8.9A-515.
Effective date of provisions.
Pre-effective-date financing statement, §8.9A-707.
Errors and omissions.
Claims concerning inaccurate or wrongfully filed record, §8.9A-518.
Effect, §8.9A-506.
Indexing errors, §8.9A-517.
Events with impact on effectiveness, §8.9A-507.
Farm tractors.
Filing to perfect security interest, §46.2-636.1.
Filing, §§8.9A-501, 8.9A-502, 8.9A-505.
Continuation statement.
Persons entitled to file, §8.9A-708.
Effectiveness, §8.9A-516.
Effectiveness of filed record, §8.9A-510.
Initial financing statement.
Persons entitled to file, §8.9A-708.
When filing suffices to continue effectiveness of financing statement, §8.9A-706.
Persons entitled to file, §8.9A-509.
What constitutes, §8.9A-516.
Wrongfully filed record.
Claims concerning, §8.9A-518.
Lapsed financing statement.
Effect, §8.9A-515.
Mortgages and deeds of trust.
Record of mortgage as financing statement, §8.9A-502.
Name of debtor and secured party, §8.9A-503.
Errors and omissions.
Effect, §8.9A-506.
New debtor becoming bound by security agreement.
Effectiveness of financing statement, §8.9A-508.
Rejection of wrongfully filed record, §8.9A-516.
Replacement financing statement, §8.9A-501.
Secured party of record, §8.9A-511.
Assignment of powers of, §8.9A-514.
Special construction and forestry equipment.
Filing to perfect security interest, §46.2-636.1.
Termination statement, §8.9A-513.
Time of filing, §8.9A-502.
Fixtures.
Defaults.
Procedure when fixtures involved, §8.9A-604.
Priority of security interests in, §8.9A-334.
Fraudulent conveyances.
Recorded contracts as valid as deeds, §55-95.
Void as to creditors and purchasers until recorded, §55-96.
Where to be recorded, §55-97.
Future advances.
Priority of security interests, §8.9A-323.
Security interest in, §8.9A-204.
General provisions of commercial code, §§8.1A-101 to 8.1A-310.
See COMMERCIAL CODE.
Health-care-insurance receivables.
Defined, §8.9A-102.
Third parties.
Assignments.
Modification of assigned contract, §8.9A-405.
Restrictions on assignments, §§8.9A-406, 8.9A-408.

SECURED TRANSACTIONS —Cont'd
Identification and proof of assignment, §8.9A-406.
Leases.
Restrictions on security interest in leasehold interest or in lessor's residual interest, §8.9A-407.
Investment property.
Control, §8.9A-106.
Perfection by control, §8.9A-314.
Defined, §8.9A-102.
Perfection and priority of security interests in, §8.9A-312.
Law governing, §8.9A-305.
Perfection by control, §8.9A-314.
Priority of security interests, §8.9A-328.
Investment securities.
Security entitlements.
Priority among security interest and entitlement holders, §8.8A-511.
Judgment creditors.
Sale of property subject to prior security interest, §8.01-480.
Law governing validity of contracts creating, §11-1.
Lease-purchase agreements.
Application of provisions, §59.1-207.19.
Prohibited practices, §59.1-207.22.
Leases, UCC.
Creation, §8.2A-303.
Creation of security interest in party's interest under lease contract, §8.2A-303.
General provisions, §§8.2A-101 to 8.2A-532.
See LEASES, UCC.
Priority of goods, §8.2A-307.
Priority of security interest in goods, §8.2A-307.
Security interests distinguished from leases, §8.1A-203.
Letter-of-credit right.
Assignment.
Restrictions on assignment ineffective, §8.9A-409.
Control, §8.9A-107.
Defined, §8.9A-102.
Perfection and priority of security interests in, §8.9A-312.
Law governing, §8.9A-306.
Perfection by control, §8.9A-314.
Priority of security interests, §8.9A-329.
Letters of credit.
Security interest of issuers or nominated persons, §8.5A-117.1.
Motor vehicle sublease.
Unlawful sublease of vehicle subject to security interest, §18.2-115.1.
Motor vehicle titling.
Certificates of title, §§46.2-636 to 46.2-644.
See MOTOR VEHICLE TITLING.
Partnerships.
Applicability of certain provisions, §50-73.84.
Perfection of security interests.
Attachment.
Security interests perfected upon attachment, §8.9A-309.
Chattel paper.
Security interests in, §8.9A-312.
Continuity of perfection, §8.9A-308.
Change in governing law, §8.9A-316.
Control.
Perfection by, §8.9A-314.

SECURED TRANSACTIONS —Cont'd
Perfection of security interests —Cont'd
Delivery to secured party.
Perfection of security interest without filing, §8.9A-313.
Deposit accounts.
Perfection by control, §8.9A-314.
Security interests in, §8.9A-312.
Documents.
Security interests in, §8.9A-312.
Effective date of provisions.
Security interest perfected before, §8.9A-703.
Security interest unperfected before, §8.9A-704.
Effect on delegation of performance and assignment of rights, §8.9A-210.
Electronic chattel paper.
Perfection by control, §8.9A-314.
Filing.
Not required to perfect security interest in property subject to certain statutes, regulations, and treaties, §8.9A-311.
Permissive filing, §8.9A-312.
When required, §8.9A-310.
Instruments.
Security interests in, §8.9A-312.
Investment property.
Perfection by control, §8.9A-314.
Security interests in, §8.9A-312.
Law governing, §8.9A-301.
Agricultural liens, §8.9A-302.
Deposit accounts, §8.9A-304.
Goods covered by certificate of title, §8.9A-303.
Investment property, §8.9A-305.
Letter-of-credit rights, §8.9A-306.
Letter-of-credit rights.
Law governing, §8.9A-306.
Perfection by control, §8.9A-314.
Security interests in, §8.9A-312.
Money.
Security interests in, §8.9A-312.
Possession by secured party.
Perfection of security interest without filing, §8.9A-313.
Treaties.
Security interest in property subject to certain treaties, §8.9A-311.
When perfected, §8.9A-308.
Power of attorney.
Authority of agent as to security interests.
Tangible personal property, §64.2-1626.
Priority of security interests.
Accessions, §8.9A-335.
Agricultural liens.
Agricultural liens on same collateral, §8.9A-322.
Filed financing statement providing certain incorrect information.
Agricultural lien perfected by, §8.9A-338.
Interests that take priority over or take free of, §8.9A-317.
Law governing, §8.9A-302.
Buyer of goods, §8.9A-320.
Certificate of title.
Security interest in goods covered by, §8.9A-337.
Chattel paper or instrument.
Priority of purchaser, §8.9A-330.
Commingled goods, §8.9A-336.
Conflicting security interests, §8.9A-322.
Consignee.
Rights and title with respect to creditors and purchasers, §8.9A-319.

SECURED TRANSACTIONS —Cont'd
Priority of security interests —Cont'd
Crops.
Security interest in, §8.9A-334.
Deposit account, §8.9A-327.
Transfer of funds from, §8.9A-332.
Filed financing statement providing certain incorrect information.
Security interest perfected by, §8.9A-338.
Financial asset.
Priority of certain interests in, §8.9A-331.
Fixtures.
Security interest in, §8.9A-334.
Future advances, §8.9A-323.
Investment property, §8.9A-328.
Law governing, §8.9A-301.
Agricultural liens, §8.9A-302.
Deposit accounts, §8.9A-304.
Goods covered by certificate of title, §8.9A-303.
Investment property, §8.9A-305.
Letter-of-credit rights, §8.9A-306.
Lessee of goods in ordinary course of business, §8.9A-321.
Letter-of-credit right, §8.9A-329.
Law governing, §8.9A-306.
Licensee of general intangible, §8.9A-321.
Liens arising by operation of law, §8.9A-333.
New debtor.
Security interests created by, §8.9A-326.
Purchase-money security interests, §8.9A-324.
Purchasers of instruments, documents, and securities under other provisions.
Priority of rights of, §8.9A-331.
Sale of right to payment, §8.9A-318.
Subordination.
Priority subject to, §8.9A-339.
Transfer of money.
Transferee takes money free of security interest, §8.9A-332.
Transferred collateral, §8.9A-325.
Transition provisions, §8.9A-709.
Unperfected security interest.
Interests that take priority over or take free of, §8.9A-317.
Proceeds.
Rights of secured party in, §8.9A-315.
Purchase-money security interests, §8.9A-103.
Priority, §8.9A-324.
Resources authority.
Pledges.
Perfection, §62.1-210.
Savings clause, §8.9A-702.
Scope of provisions, §§8.9A-109, 8.9A-110.
Security agreement.
Effectiveness, §8.9A-201.
Special construction and forestry equipment.
Defined, §46.2-100.
Perfecting security interests, §46.2-636.1.
Statement of account.
Request regarding, §8.9A-210.
Third parties.
Alienability of debtor's rights, §8.9A-401.
Assignments.
Agreement not to assert defenses against assignee, §8.9A-403.
Claims and defenses against assignee, §8.9A-404.
Discharge of account debtor, §8.9A-406.
Modification of assigned contract, §8.9A-405.
Restrictions on certain assignments, §8.9A-406.
Certain restrictions ineffective, §§8.9A-408, 8.9A-409.

SECURED TRANSACTIONS —Cont'd
Third parties —Cont'd
Assignments —Cont'd
Rights acquired by assignee, §8.9A-404.
Contract of debtor.
Secured party not obligated on, §8.9A-402.
Torts of debtor.
Secured party not obligated on, §8.9A-402.
Transitional provisions.
Amendments effective July 1, 2013, §§8.9A-801 to 8.9A-809.
Effectiveness of action before July 1, 2013, §8.9A-805.
Initial financing statement continuing effectiveness, §8.9A-806.
Pre-effective-date financing statement, amending, §8.9A-807.
Priority of conflicting claims, §8.9A-809.
Savings clause, §8.9A-802.
Security interest perfected before July 1, 2013, §8.9A-803.
Security interest unperfected before July 1, 2013, §8.9A-804.
Who may file initial financing statement or continuation statement, §8.9A-808.
Change of place of filing, §8.11-105.
Change of requirement of filing, §8.11-104.

SECURITIES, §§13.1-501 to 13.1-527.3.
Advertising, §13.1-515.
Advice unlawful, §13.1-503.
Agent.
Defined, §13.1-501.
Air carriers.
Contract carriers by aircraft.
Duration and custody of securities, §5.1-9.6.
Issuance of license.
Securities deposited in lieu of insurance or bonds, §5.1-9.5.
Asset-backed securities facilitation.
No interest retained by transferor, §6.2-2401.
Securitization transaction defined, §6.2-2400.
Treatment of securitization transactions, §6.2-2402.
Banks.
See BANKS.
Bond issues.
Security interests in bonds, §2.2-4902.1.
Brokers-dealers.
Civil liabilities, §13.1-522.
Consumer protection.
Application of provisions, §59.1-199.
Defined, §13.1-501.
Extensions of credit under securities and exchange act of 1934.
Contract rate of interest.
Exceptions to, §6.2-322.
Interest.
Extensions of credit under securities and exchange act of 1934.
Exceptions to contract rate of interest, §6.2-322.
Investigations of state corporation commission, §13.1-518.
Nonresidents, service of process on, §13.1-517.
Registration.
Credit unions providing broker-dealer services, §13.1-504.2.
Exempt transactions from registration requirement, §13.1-514.
Procedure for registration, §13.1-505.

SECURITIES —Cont'd
Brokers-dealers —Cont'd
Registration —Cont'd
Required, §13.1-507.
Revocation of registration, §13.1-506.
Savings and loan associations and savings banks providing brokerage services, §13.1-504.1.
Reports filed with state corporation commission, §13.1-518.1.
Business opportunity sales, §§59.1-262 to 59.1-269.
See BUSINESS OPPORTUNITY SALES.
Civil liabilities for violations, §13.1-522.
College building authority.
Investment of funds, §23-30.30.
Commercial code.
Investment securities, §§8.8A-101 to 8.8A-601.
See INVESTMENT SECURITIES.
Commonwealth's attorneys.
Record or complaint concerning violation.
Transmitted to by state corporation commission, §13.1-520.1.
Condominiums, §55-79.90.
Confidentiality of information and documents obtained in commission investigation, §13.1-518.
Contribution as in cases of contract among persons jointly and severally liable, §13.1-522.
Cooperative housing corporation.
Defined, §13.1-501.
Copies of commission records as evidence in lieu of original, §13.1-524.
Costs of supervising and administering provisions.
Fees and funds collected to be deposited into special fund for, §13.1-525.1.
Crimes, §13.1-520.
Offenses punishable by commission, §13.1-521.
Prosecution instituted by indictment, §13.1-520.
Debt capacity advisory committee, §§2.2-2712 to 2.2-2714.
Decedents' estates.
Filings by executors or administrators.
Continuation of powers, §64.2-607.
Transfers upon death.
Nonresident decedents, §64.2-608.
Definitions, §13.1-501.
Descent and distribution.
Filings by administrators.
Continuation of powers, §64.2-607.
Transfers upon death.
Nonresident decedents, §64.2-608.
Disclaimer of property interests.
Disclaimer of beneficiary designation, §64.2-2610.
Division of securities counsel.
Created in office of attorney general, §13.1-527.1.
Duties, §13.1-527.1.
Employment of attorneys, employees and consultants, §13.1-527.2.
Technical assistance provided by state corporation commission, §13.1-527.3.
Domestic stock insurers.
Equity securities.
Restrictions upon purchase and sale, §38.2-214.
Effective date.
Transition provisions, §13.1-526.
Electronic transactions.
Transferable records, §59.1-494.

SECURITIES —Cont'd
False or misleading statements to commission, §13.1-516.
Federal securities and obligations.
Accounts of banks, trust companies or trust subsidiaries.
Separate holdings, §6.2-1006.
Fee for commission interpretations, §13.1-525.
Fees to cover expenses of regulation, §13.1-525.1.
Fiduciaries.
Inventories and accounts, §64.2-1312.
Investments.
Permissible securities, §64.2-1502.
Retention upon cessation of eligibility, §64.2-1505.
Trustees.
Substituted trustees.
Securities transferred to successor, §64.2-1425.
Forms, commission's power to make, amend and rescind, §13.1-523.
General assembly.
Disclosure statements, §30-111.
Injunctions.
Securities violations, §13.1-519.
Injunctions for violations, §13.1-518.
Insurance companies investments generally, §§38.2-1400 to 38.2-1447.
Insurers' deposits with state treasurer, §§38.2-1045 to 38.2-1058.
Interest.
Broker-dealers.
Extensions of credit under securities and exchange act of 1934.
Exceptions to contract rate of interest, §6.2-322.
Damages recovered in civil action, §13.1-522.
Interpretations by commission, §13.1-525.
Invalidity of provision not to affect other provisions, §13.1-527.01.
Investigations by commission, §13.1-518.
Investment advisor.
Defined, §13.1-501.
Unlawful advice, §13.1-503.
Investment advisor representative.
Defined, §13.1-501.
Investment advisory contracts.
Requirements, §13.1-503.
Investment of public funds.
Asset-backed securities, §2.2-4511.
Legal investments.
Funds other than sinking funds, §2.2-4501.
Public sinking funds.
Legal investments, §2.2-4500.
Investment securities.
Commercial code, §§8.8A-101 to 8.8A-601.
See INVESTMENT SECURITIES.
Issuance of stocks, bonds, etc.
Defined terms, §56-55.
Issuer.
Defined, §13.1-501.
Joint and several liability in civil actions, §13.1-522.
Joint names, registration in, §§13.1-434 to 13.1-436.
License taxes.
Security brokers and dealers.
Limitation on gross receipts, §58.1-3732.5.
Limitation on civil actions, §13.1-522.
Limitation on criminal prosecutions, §13.1-520.

SECURITIES —Cont'd
Literary fund.
Investment of fund, §22.1-145.
Membership camping.
Application of provisions, §59.1-321.
Minerals reclamation fund.
Release of bonds and other securities, §45.1-197.10.
Misleading filing, §13.1-516.
Mortgages and deeds of trust, §§6.2-406 to 6.2-423, 55-58 to 55-66.6.
See MORTGAGES AND DEEDS OF TRUST.
Motor vehicle proof of financial responsibility.
Deposit of money or securities generally.
See MOTOR VEHICLE FINANCIAL RESPONSIBILITY.
Nonresident broker-dealer, investment advisor, investment advisor representative or agent.
Consent to service of process, §13.1-517.
Offenses punishable by commission, §13.1-521.
Offers unlawful, §13.1-502.
Penalties imposed by commission for violations, §13.1-521.
Port authority bonds, §62.1-146.
Power of attorney.
Authority of agent as to stocks and bonds, §64.2-1627.
Operation of entity or business, §64.2-1630.
Primacy of Virginia law, §13.1-514.2.
Principal and income.
Asset-backed securities.
Allocations to principal and income, §64.2-1023.
Defined, §64.2-1023.
Public school authority.
Investment of funds, §22.1-169.
Public service companies.
Issuance of stocks, bonds, etc., §§56-55 to 56-75.
Application, §56-60.
Action of commission, §56-61.
Appeal, §56-63.
Fees, §56-75.
Void if order not obtained, §56-67.
Application of chapter, §56-57.
Exceptions, §56-65.
Short-term indebtedness, §56-65.1.
Capitalization of permits, franchises or contracts for consolidation.
Commission power, §56-66.
Commonwealth liability, §56-74.
Joint actions with commission of another state, §56-62.
Licensed salesmen requirements, §56-68.
Officer acts bind company, §56-72.
Privilege, §56-56.
Proceeds.
Accounting for disposition of, §56-70.
Purposes to which proceeds may be applied, §56-69.
Provision violations, §56-71.
Employee violations, §56-73.
Officer violations, §56-73.
Purposes, §56-58.
Short-term indebtedness, §56-65.1.
Sureties.
Order required before acting as, §56-59.
Validity of authorized securities, §56-67.1.
Real estate cooperatives.
Public offering statements, §55-482.
Receivers.
General receivers.
How dividends and interest collected and invested, §8.01-584.

SECURITIES —Cont'd
Receivers —Cont'd
General receivers —Cont'd
Powers of receivers over securities, §8.01-583.
Records available to public, §13.1-524.
Registration of brokers-dealers, investment advisors, investment advisor representatives and agents, §§13.1-504 to 13.1-506.
Brokerage services of savings and loan associations or savings banks.
When registration not required, §13.1-504.1.
Credit unions, broker-dealer services provided by.
When registration not required, §13.1-504.2.
Exempt transactions from registration requirements, §13.1-514.
Post-registration provisions, §13.1-505.1.
Procedure for registration, §13.1-505.
Required, §13.1-504.
Revocation of registration, §13.1-506.
Registration of securities, §§13.1-507 to 13.1-513.
Coordination, §13.1-509.
Effectiveness of registration statements, §13.1-511.
Exemptions, §13.1-514.
Order of commission exempting, §13.1-514.1.
Joint names, §§13.1-434 to 13.1-436.
Notification, §13.1-508.
Qualification, §13.1-510.
Reports to keep current.
Information in registration statements, §13.1-511.
Requirements, §13.1-507.
Stop orders.
Denying effectiveness or revoking effectiveness of registration statement, §13.1-513.
Unlawful to offer or sell unless registered, §13.1-507.
Regulatory authority of commission, §13.1-523.1.
Reports by broker-dealers filed with commission, §13.1-518.1.
Resources authority.
Bonds, §62.1-220.
Rulemaking power of commission, §13.1-523.
Sales unlawful, §13.1-502.
Savings institutions.
Accounts as security, §6.2-1169.
Perfection of certain security interests, §6.2-1190.
Securities counsel, division of, §§13.1-527.1 to 13.1-527.3.
Service of process on nonresident registered broker-dealer, investment advisor, investment advisor representative or agent.
Consent to service, §13.1-517.
Severability clause, §13.1-527.01.
Shares of corporations generally, §§13.1-638 to 13.1-653.
See CORPORATIONS.
Short title, §13.1-527.
Solicitation of advisory clients, unlawful advice, §13.1-503.
State treasurer.
Authority to transfer or sell, §2.2-1808.
Title of act, §13.1-527.
Transfer on death security registration, §§64.2-612 to 64.2-619.
See TOD SECURITY REGISTRATION.
Transfers.
Nonprobate transfer after death, §64.2-620.

SECURITIES —Cont'd
Transition provisions, §13.1-526.
Transmission of record or complaint of violation to locality where occurring, §13.1-520.1.
Trust companies.
Nominee for fiduciary holding, §6.2-1010.
Trustees.
Substituted trustees.
Transfers, §64.2-1425.
Trust subsidiaries.
Nominee for fiduciary holding, §6.2-1010.
Unclaimed property, disposition of.
Sales, §55-210.18.
Transfer of record of ownership, §55-210.18:1.
Unlawful practices, §§13.1-502, 13.1-503.
Viatical settlements.
Applicability of securities act, §38.2-6016.
Wills.
Construction of bequests, §64.2-415.
Filings by executors.
Continuation of powers, §64.2-607.
Transfers.
Nonresident decedents, §64.2-608.

SECURITIES BROKERS-DEALERS.
Civil liabilities, §13.1-522.
Investigations of by state corporation commission, §13.1-518.
Nonresidents, service of process on, §13.1-517.
Registration.
Changing connection from one broker-dealer or issuer to another, §13.1-504.
Exempt transactions from registration requirements, §13.1-514.
Notice of beginning or terminating connection with broker-dealer, §13.1-504.
Procedure, §13.1-505.
Required, §13.1-504.
Revocation, §13.1-506.
Securities generally, §§13.1-501 to 13.1-527.3.
See SECURITIES.

SECURITIES COUNSEL, DIVISION OF, §§13.1-527.1 to 13.1-527.3.

SECURITIES LENDING.
Investment of public funds, §2.2-4506.

SECURITIES REGISTERED IN JOINT NAMES, §§13.1-434 to 13.1-436.

SECURITIZATION TRANSACTIONS.
Asset-backed securities facilitation.
Treatment of securitization transactions, §6.2-2402.
Defined, §6.2-2400.
No interest retained by transferor, §6.2-2401.

SECURITY AUDIT OF GOVERNMENT DATABASE.
Chief information officer, §2.2-2008.

SECURITY AUDIT OF STATE PUBLIC BODIES.
Information technologies agency, §2.2-2009.

SECURITY DEPOSITS.
Public utilities.
Interest and return of deposit, §56-247.1.
Real estate brokers, salespersons and rental agents.
Protection of funds in event of foreclosure, §54.1-2108.1.
Residential landlords and tenants, §55-248.15:1.

SECURITY DEPOSITS —Cont'd
Transfers upon purchase, §55-507.

SECURITY FOR APPEAL, §8.01-676.1, VA SCt Rules 5:24, 5A:17.

SECURITY FOR PUBLIC DEPOSITS, §§2.2-4400 to 2.2-4411.
Administration.
Treasury board, duties, §2.2-2416.
Administration of chapter, §2.2-4405.
Applicability of chapter, §2.2-4400.
Authority to deposit public funds, §2.2-4408.
Authority to secure, §2.2-4409.
Bonds, surety.
Not required, §2.2-4402.
Citation of chapter, §2.2-4400.
Collateral, §2.2-4402.
Additional collateral, requiring, §2.2-4405.
Dedicated method.
Defined, §2.2-4401.
Deposits secured by, §2.2-4402.
Payment of losses, procedure, §2.2-4404.
Defaulting depository.
Defined, §2.2-4401.
Payment of losses, §2.2-4405.
Dedicated method, §2.2-4404.
Pooled method, §2.2-4403.
Defined terms, §2.2-4401.
Eligible collateral.
Defined, §2.2-4401.
Deposits secured by, §2.2-4402.
Securities and instruments acceptable, determining, §2.2-4405.
Intent, §2.2-4400.
Liabilities and duties.
Acceptance by public depositor, §2.2-4409.
Liability of public depositors, §2.2-4410.
Losses.
Dedicated method.
Payment of losses, §2.2-4404.
Liability of public depositors, §2.2-4410.
Pooled method.
Payment of losses, §2.2-4403.
Pooled method.
Defined, §2.2-4401.
Deposits secured by, §2.2-4402.
Payment of losses, procedure, §2.2-4403.
Qualified public depositories.
Authority of public depositors to make deposits in, §2.2-4408.
Defined, §2.2-4401.
Mandatory, §2.2-4407.
Reports by public depositors, §2.2-4411.
Rules and regulations.
Adoption, enforcement by board, §2.2-4405.
Short title, §2.2-4400.
Subrogation.
Treasury board.
Subrogation to depositor's rights, §2.2-4406.
Treasury board.
Duties, §2.2-2416.
Powers, §2.2-4405.
Subrogation to depositor's rights, §2.2-4406.

SECURITY FREEZES.
Consumer credit reports, §§59.1-444.1, 59.1-444.2.
Definitions, §59.1-444.1.
Practice and operation, §59.1-444.2.

SECURITY GUARDS.
Armed security officers.
Limitation of powers, §9.1-146.

SECURITY GUARDS —Cont'd
Private security services businesses, §§9.1-138 to 9.1-150.

SECURITY INTERESTS.
Boats and other watercraft, §§29.1-723 to 29.1-732.
See BOATS AND OTHER WATERCRAFT.
Generally.
See SECURED TRANSACTIONS.

SECURITY SERVICES VEHICLES.
Flashing amber warning lights, §46.2-1025.

SECURITY SYSTEMS.
Commercial rental property.
Tenant installation, §55-226.1.

SECURITY TO KEEP PEACE, §§19.2-19 to 19.2-25.
See RECOGNIZANCE TO KEEP THE PEACE.

SEDUCTION.
Action abolished, §8.01-220.

SEED BOARD, §§3.2-4021 to 3.2-4027.
Certification, §3.2-4024.
Department, commissioner or board.
Certification by not affected, §3.2-4027.
Illegal use of word certified, §3.2-4026.
Duties, §3.2-4024.
Fees.
Use of brands, labels and tags, §3.2-4024.
Members, §3.2-4022.
Compensation and expenses, §3.2-4023.
Meetings, §3.2-4022.
Office, §3.2-4022.
Powers, §3.2-4024.
Quorum, §3.2-4022.
Rules and regulations, §3.2-4025.

SEED POTATOES.
See POTATOES.

SEEDS, §§3.2-4000 to 3.2-4027.
Advertising.
Disclaimers, nonwarranties and limited warranties, §3.2-4017.
Requirements, §§3.2-4008, 3.2-4016.
Assessments.
Variance from guarantee, §3.2-4014.
Board of agriculture and consumer services.
Authority, §3.2-4001.
Second generation hybrids.
Naming in regulations, §3.2-4001.
Commissioner of agriculture and consumer services.
Duties, §3.2-4003.
Rules for testing seeds, §3.2-4002.
Commonwealth's attorneys.
Prosecution of violations, §3.2-4019.
Cool-season lawn and turf seeds.
Defined, §3.2-4000.
Requirements as to labeling, §3.2-4008.
Definitions, §3.2-4000.
Disposition of fees and assessments, §3.2-4004.
Funds.
Seed fund.
Disposition of fees and assessments, §3.2-4004.
Guaranty of farm or garden seed.
Effect, §3.2-4007.
Inspection fees, §3.2-4010.
Labels.
Lawn and turf seed mixture.
Change in labeling or specifications, §3.2-4009.

SEEDS —Cont'd
Labels —Cont'd
Requirements as to labeling, §§3.2-4008, 3.2-4016.
Transgenetic seeds, §3.2-4008.
Licensing.
Sales or distribution, §3.2-4005.
Prohibited acts, §§3.2-4015, 3.2-4016.
Records, §3.2-4006.
Registration.
Lawn and turf seed mixture, §3.2-4009.
Retail sales and use tax.
Agricultural exemptions, §58.1-609.2.
Searches and seizures.
Noncomplying lots, §3.2-4013.
Second generation hybrids.
Naming in regulations, §3.2-4001.
Testing rules, §3.2-4002.
Tolerances.
Establishment and use in enforcement, §3.2-4001.
Transgenetic seeds.
Labeling requirements, §3.2-4008.
Variance from guarantee.
Assessments, §3.2-4014.
Violations of provisions.
Assessments, §3.2-4020.
Notice, §3.2-4018.
Penalties, §3.2-4020.
Proceedings on, §3.2-4018.
Prosecution, §3.2-4018.
Warranties.
Disclaimers, nonwarranties and limited warranties, §3.2-4017.

SEED TREES, §§10.1-1162 to 10.1-1169.
Diameter defined, §10.1-1162.
Exemptions, §10.1-1163.
Management plan.
Failure to carry out, §10.1-1169.
Notice, §10.1-1166.
Penalties, §10.1-1167.
Person defined, §10.1-1162.
Pine trees.
Uncut for reseeding purposes, §10.1-1164.
Posting or publication of notices, §10.1-1166.
Reseeding purposes.
Pine trees to be left uncut, §10.1-1164.
When trees may be cut, §10.1-1165.
State forester.
Failure to carry out planting, cutting or management plan, §10.1-1169.
Inspection or planting.
Failing to leave seed trees uncut, §10.1-1168.
Trees left for reseeding purposes, §§10.1-1164, 10.1-1165.
Failure to leave uncut, §10.1-1168.
Tree defined, §10.1-1162.
Violation of article, §10.1-1167.

SEEING EYE DOGS.
See GUIDE DOGS.

SEIZURE AND IMPOUNDMENT OF ANIMALS, §3.2-6569.

SEIZURE OF COAL PROPERTIES BY COMMONWEALTH, §§45.1-161.312 to 45.1-161.322.
Acquisition expenses, §45.1-161.321.
Applicability of provisions, §45.1-161.318.
Condemnation proceedings, §45.1-161.320.
Declaration of policy, §45.1-161.313.
Gubernatorial powers of operation, §45.1-161.315.

SEIZURE OF COAL PROPERTIES BY COMMONWEALTH —Cont'd
Leases of properties, §45.1-161.319.
Operating expenses, §45.1-161.321.
Proclamation of seizure, §45.1-161.314.
Public uses.
Defined, §45.1-161.313.
Interruption, §45.1-161.314.
Purchases of properties, §45.1-161.319.
Restoration of property to owner or operator, §45.1-161.322.
Subjects of seizure, §45.1-161.312.
Virginia fuel commission.
Duties, §45.1-161.316.
Members, §45.1-161.317.
Powers, §45.1-161.316.

SELECTIVE SERVICE.
Two-year college transfer grant program.
Selective service requirements, effect of failure to meet, §23-38.10:10.

SELF-HELP.
Manufactured home lot rental.
Termination of tenancy limitations, §55-248.46.

SELF-INCRIMINATION, PRIVILEGE AGAINST, US Const Amd 5.
ABC offenses.
Witness not excused from testimony, §4.1-350.
Antitrust laws, §59.1-9.10.
Combinations to injure others in reputation, trade, business or profession.
Protection of persons testifying or producing evidence, §18.2-501.
Boats and other watercraft.
Provision violations, §29.1-561.
Bribery prosecutions.
Immunity of witnesses, §§18.2-445, 18.2-450.
Drug offenses.
Witnesses not excused from testifying, §18.2-262.
Fishing, inland waters.
Provision violations, §29.1-561.
Former trial testimony of accused not received as evidence, §19.2-270.
Gambling prosecutions.
Immunity of witness, §18.2-337.
Game and inland fisheries.
Provision violations, §29.1-561.
Grand juries.
Multi-jurisdiction grand juries.
Use of testimony compelled after witness invokes privilege, §19.2-215.7.
Special grand juries.
Compelling witness to testify or produce evidence, §19.2-208.
Hunting.
Provision violations, §29.1-561.
Interstate family support act.
Refusal to answer, adverse inference, §20-88.59.
Investigations of elected officials.
Witnesses called by court or attorney for the Commonwealth, §52-8.2.
Perjury prosecutions.
Immunity of witnesses, §18.2-437.
Suppression of evidence.
Written pretrial motion, §19.2-266.2.
Trapping.
Provision violations, §29.1-561.
Unemployment compensation.
Claims adjudication, §60.2-628.

SELF-INCRIMINATION, PRIVILEGE AGAINST —Cont'd
Use of claim against party in civil action, §8.01-223.1.
Waiver of privilege, §19.2-268.

SELF-INSURANCE.
Local government employees and retirees.
Group life, accident and health insurance.
Locality providing through program of self-insurance, §15.2-1517.
Liability insurance for officers, employees and volunteers.
Locality providing, §15.2-1518.
Local government group self-insurance pools, §§15.2-2700 to 15.2-2709.
Scc LOCAL GOVERNMENT GROUP SELF-INSURANCE POOLS.

SELF-PROPELLED MACHINERY OR EQUIPMENT.
Controlled access highways.
Prohibited use, §46.2-808.

SELF-PROVING WILLS, §§64.2-452, 64.2-453.

SELF REFERRALS.
Practitioner self-referral act, §§54.1-2410 to 54.1-2414.

SELF REPRESENTATION.
District courts.
Warrants in debt, VA SCt Rule 7B:3.
Facsimile signatures, VA SCt Rule 1:4.
Residence of pro se litigant.
Statement of residence and notice of change, §8.01-319.
Small claims courts, §16.1-122.4.
Supreme court.
Prisoners, VA SCt Rule 5:7.

SELF-SERVICE STORAGE, §§55-416 to 55-423.
Application of chapter, §55-423.
Care of property, §55-420.
Control of property, §55-420.
Custody of property, §55-420.
Defined terms, §55-417.
Effective date of chapter, §55-423.
Liens, §55-418.
Enforcement, §55-419.
Other remedies not preempted, §55-419.1.
Rental agreements to remain valid, §55-421.
Savings clause, §55-421.
Self storage insurance, §§38.2-1881 to 38.2-1886.
Short title of chapter, §55-416.

SELF STORAGE INSURANCE, §§38.2-1881 to 38.2-1886.
Applicability of law, §38.2-1886.
Charges outside of rental agreement, §38.2-1884.
Definitions, §38.2-1881.
Home state, §38.2-1884.
Employees and authorized representatives, §38.2-1884.
Information provided to customers, §38.2-1883.
Licenses.
Required, §38.2-1882.
Suspension or revocation, §38.2-1885.
List of locations where lessor offers coverage, §38.2-1882.
Producer removed, effect, §38.2-1884.
Rulemaking authority, §38.2-1886.
Sale, requirements, §38.2-1883.

SELF STORAGE INSURANCE —Cont'd
Suspension or revocation of license, §38.2-1885.
Training, employees and authorized representatives, §38.2-1884.
Violations.
Suspension or revocation of license, §38.2-1885.

SEMI-AUTOMATIC RIFLE OR PISTOL.
Aliens, possession or transportation, §18.2-308.2:01.
Carrying loaded firearms in public areas, §18.2-287.4.
Children or minors, possession or transportation, §18.2-308.7.
Criminal history background check, firearms transfers, §18.2-308.2:2.

SEMI-AUTOMATIC SHOTGUNS.
Importation, sale, etc., §18.2-308.8.

SEMICONDUCTOR MANUFACTURING.
Machinery and tools tax, §58.1-3508.1.
Performance grant programs, §§59.1-284.13 to 59.1-284.15:1.
Definitions, §§59.1-284.13 to 59.1-284.15:1.
Goochland county, §59.1-284.13.
Grants for capital investments made and jobs created, §59.1-284.14:1.
Additional employment and new capital investment, §59.1-284.15:1.
Memory or logic wafers, §59.1-284.15.
Manassas, city of, §59.1-284.14.
Retail sales and use tax exemption, §58.1-609.3.

SEMINARIES.
Local road authorities.
Establishment and alteration of roads.
Consent required for establishment through seminary, §33.1-241.

SEMITRAILERS.
Defined, §46.2-100.
Garage keeper's lien.
Towing, recovering and storage costs, §46.2-644.01.
Parking, ordinances prohibiting or limiting, §46.2-1224.
Registration card.
Operator required to carry, exhibition to law enforcement, failure to carry, penalty, §46.2-104.
Retail sales and use tax exemption, §58.1-609.1.
T&M vehicle dealers, §§46.2-1900 to 46.2-1991.
See T&M VEHICLE DEALERS.
Vehicle leases that are not sales or security interests, §46.2-640.1.

SENATE OF THE GENERAL ASSEMBLY.
See GENERAL ASSEMBLY.

SENATE OF THE UNITED STATES.
See CONGRESS.

SENIOR ALERT PROGRAM, §§52-34.4 to 52-34.6.
Activation upon incident of missing senior adult, §52-34.6.
Cancellation of alert, §52-34.6.
Conference with state police.
Prior to making local alert, §52-34.6.
Decision to make alert.
Law enforcement agency decision, §52-34.6.
Definitions, §52-34.4.
Establishment, §52-34.5.
Information contained in alert, §52-34.6.

SENIOR ALERT PROGRAM —Cont'd
Local, regional or statewide alerts, §52-34.6.
Location of missing senior.
Notification to state police.
Duty of law enforcement agency, §52-34.6.
Missing senior adult defined, §52-34.4.
Uniform standards for creation.
Development by state police, §52-34.5.
Voluntary establishment, §52-34.4.

SENIOR CITIZENS.
Adult abuse, neglect and exploitation.
Abuse of aged or incapacitated adults, §18.2-369.
Adult protective services, §§63.2-1603 to 63.2-1610.
Financial exploitation of mentally incapacitated persons, §18.2-178.1.
Adult day care centers, §§63.2-1700 to 63.2-1819.
See ADULT DAY CARE CENTERS.
Adult protective services.
Protection of aged and incapacitated adults, §§63.2-1603 to 63.2-1610.
Deferral of real property taxes, §§58.1-3210 to 58.1-3217.
Department for the aging and rehabilitative services.
Generally, §§51.5-116 to 51.5-181.
See AGING AND REHABILITATIVE SERVICES, DEPARTMENT FOR.
DMV identification cards.
Persons 70 years or older.
Exchange of driver's license for card, §46.2-345.
Equal credit opportunities generally, §§6.2-500 to 6.2-513.
See EQUAL CREDIT OPPORTUNITIES.
Exemption from real property taxes, §§58.1-3210 to 58.1-3217.
Fishing licenses.
Lifetime license, fee, §29.1-302.1.
Higher education for senior citizens, §§23-38.54 to 23-38.60.
Hunting licenses.
Lifetime license, fee, §29.1-302.1.
Local transportation services serving.
Nonprofit operating.
Exemption from local license tax on taxicabs, §15.2-967.1.
Missing senior adult.
Senior Alert program, §§52-34.4 to 52-34.6.
Motor vehicle personal property tax alternative rates, §§58.1-3506.1 to 58.1-3506.8.
Personal property taxes.
Alternative rates, motor vehicles, §§58.1-3506.1 to 58.1-3506.8.
Prisons.
Release of geriatric prisoners, §53.1-40.01.
Real property taxes.
Exemptions, §§58.1-3210 to 58.1-3217.
Prince William county senior citizens and disabled persons.
Ordinance prescribing alternative due dates, §58.1-3916.02.
Sale, lease, exchange, redemption or other disposition of realty.
Disposition of real estate of persons under disability generally, §§8.01-67 to 8.01-80.
See PERSONS WITH DISABILITY.
Senior Alert program, §§52-34.4 to 52-34.6.
Solid waste disposal fee.
Locality may charge discounted rate, §15.2-2159.

SENIOR CITIZENS —Cont'd
State departments and agencies.
Designation of officials to review effect of decisions on senior citizens, §2.2-604.1.
Transportation board.
Goals for addressing transportation needs of populations.
Establishment of specific mobility goals, §33.1-23.03:002.

SENIOR CITIZENS' HIGHER EDUCATION ACT OF 1974, §§23-38.54 to 23-38.60.

SENIOR JUDGE.
Court of appeals, §17.1-401.

SENIOR JUSTICE OF SUPREME COURT, §17.1-302.

SENTENCING, §§19.2-295 to 19.2-310.01, US Const Amd 7.
Abduction with intent to extort money or defile.
Suspended sentence.
Imposition in addition to active sentence, §18.2-48.
Acquittal of higher offense.
Accused guilty of part of offense charged, §19.2-285.
Additional term upon conviction for felony offenses.
Post-release supervision.
Felons sentenced for offenses committed on and after January 1, 1995, or July 1, 2000, §19.2-295.2.
Felons sentenced for offenses committed on and after July 1, 2006.
Sex offender registration violations, §19.2-295.2:1.
Adult sentencing of child, §16.1-284.
Circuit court power over juvenile offender, §16.1-272.
Alcohol and substance abuse screening and assessment for designated Class 1 misdemeanor convictions, §19.2-299.2.
Allocution.
Defendant's right of allocution, §19.2-298.
Alternative sentencing.
Community-based corrections system for state-responsible offenders, §§53.1-67.2 to 53.1-67.6.
Community corrections, §§9.1-173 to 9.1-183.
See COMMUNITY CORRECTIONS.
Ascertainment of punishment, §19.2-295.
Jury trial.
Separate proceeding, §19.2-295.1.
Bench trial.
Court ascertainment of punishment, §19.2-295.
Boot camp incarceration program, §§19.2-316.1, 53.1-67.1.
Habitual motor vehicle offenders, §46.2-357.
Capital cases, US Const Amd 5.
Fixing execution dates, §53.1-232.
When execution dates required, §53.1-232.1.
Stay of execution, §53.1-232.1.
When capital punishment inflicted, §18.2-17.
Capital punishment.
See DEATH PENALTY.
Child sentenced as adult, §16.1-284.
Child support.
Recognizance for compliance with order or decree.
Confinement for noncompliance, §20-115.

SENTENCING —Cont'd
Come-back time.
Revocation or suspension of sentence, §19.2-306.
Commission, §§17.1-800 to 17.1-806.
See SENTENCING COMMISSION.
Commitment of convicted persons to custody of director of department of corrections, §53.1-20.
Common-law offenses, how punished, §18.2-16.
Community-based corrections system for state-responsible offenders, §§53.1-67.2 to 53.1-67.6.
Community-based probation agency.
Conditions, imposition, revocation, §19.2-303.3.
Community corrections, §§9.1-173 to 9.1-183.
See COMMUNITY CORRECTIONS.
Community criminal justice boards, §§9.1-178, 9.1-180.
Community service.
Criminal fines and penalties.
Community work in lieu of payment, §19.2-354.
Probation, §§19.2-305, 19.2-305.1.
Commutation of capital punishment.
Governor's powers, VA Const Art V §12.
Computation of imprisonment period, §53.1-186.
Concurrent sentences.
Expressly ordered requirement, §19.2-308.
Running, generally, §19.2-308.
Sentence imposed in another state, §19.2-308.1.
Conditional release.
Geriatric prisoners, §53.1-40.01.
Person twice previously convicted of violent felony, §19.2-297.1.
Contempt.
Summarily punishment for contempt.
Imprisonment limited unless jury impaneled, §18.2-457.
Corrections department.
Receipt of sentencing documents, §19.2-310.01.
Transfer of prisoners to custody of department, §19.2-310.
Courts-martial.
How process and sentence executed, §44-50.
Naval militia.
Confinement in lieu of fine, §44-72.
Powers of punishment, §44-69.
Special courts-martial, national guard, §44-44.
Summary courts-martial, national guard, §44-45.
Where sentences executed, §44-49.
Credit for time confined awaiting trial, §53.1-187.
Criminal fines and penalties.
Community service in lieu of payment, §19.2-354.
Installment payment as condition of suspension of sentence, §19.2-358.
Recovery generally, §§19.2-339 to 19.2-368.
See CRIMINAL FINES AND PENALTIES.
Requiring peace and good behavior of defendant, §19.2-357.
Criminal street gang.
Conviction as participant or member.
Suspension of sentence and placing on probation.
Restrictions placed on accused, §19.2-303.
Cruel and unusual punishment, VA Const Art I §9.
Custodial transfer of prisoners.
Director of department of corrections, §19.2-310.
Death penalty.
See DEATH PENALTY.

SENTENCING —Cont'd
Deck courts, naval militia.
Powers of punishment, §44-69.
Deferred sentencing.
First drug conviction, §18.2-251.
First offense of assault and battery against family or household member, §18.2-57.3.
Forcible sodomy.
Deferral of proceedings, defendant placed on probation.
Counseling or therapy, completion.
Violation against spouse, §18.2-67.1.
Mental health examination.
Construction of provisions, §19.2-302.
Expenses of psychiatrist, §19.2-301.
Offense indicating sexual abnormality, §19.2-300.
Report of findings and conclusions, §19.2-301.
Object sexual penetration.
Deferral of proceedings, defendant placed on probation.
Counseling or therapy, completion.
Violation against spouse, §18.2-67.2.
Payment of costs, §19.2-303.4.
Person convicted of offense indicating sexual abnormality, §§19.2-300 to 19.2-302.
Pretrial diversion, §19.2-303.2.
Payment of costs, §19.2-303.4.
Rape.
Counseling or therapy, completion.
Deferral of proceedings, defendant placed on probation.
Violation against spouse, §18.2-61.
Desertion and nonsupport.
Commitment to workhouse, city farm or work squad, §20-62.
Continuance of failure to support after completion of sentence, §20-78.
Deduction of certain time from sentence, §20-77.
Probation on support order to pay and entry of recognizance, §20-72.
Condition of recognizance, §20-73.
Violation of support orders, §20-80.
When authority to suspend sentence may be exercised, §20-77.
Detention center incarceration program, §19.2-316.2.
Establishment of program, §53.1-67.8.
Discretionary sentencing guideline midpoints, §17.1-805.
Use, §19.2-298.01.
Diversion center incarceration program, §19.2-316.3.
Establishment of program, §53.1-67.7.
Program included in community-based corrections system for state-responsible offenders, §53.1-67.6.
Driving while intoxicated.
Mandatory minimum sentences, §18.2-270.
Subsequent offense, §18.2-270.
Dual felony and misdemeanor offenses.
Confinement priority, §19.2-309.
Earned sentence credits, §§53.1-202.2 to 53.1-202.4.
Commencement of eligibility, §53.1-202.2.
Condition for earning, §53.1-202.3.
Credit for time confined awaiting trial in addition to, §53.1-187.
Defined, §53.1-202.2.
Eligibility, §53.1-202.2.
Forfeiture and restoration, §53.1-189.

SENTENCING —Cont'd
Earned sentence credits —Cont'd
Juveniles convicted as adults and sentenced as serious juvenile offenders.
Condition for earning, report by department of juvenile justice, §53.1-202.3.
Eligibility, §53.1-202.2.
Prerequisites, §53.1-202.3.
Rate earned, §53.1-202.3.
Rules, criteria, etc., established by board of corrections, §53.1-202.4.
Evidence.
Prior criminal convictions, §19.2-295.1.
Executive clemency, VA Const Art V §12.
Explanation of departure from sentencing guidelines.
Court to file with record of case, §19.2-298.01.
Fees towards cost of participation in parole, probation and work release programs, §53.1-150.
Felonies, punishment for, §18.2-10.
Felons sentenced for offenses committed on and after January 1, 1995, or July 1, 2000.
Post-release supervision, §19.2-295.2.
Felons sentenced for offenses committed on and after July 1, 2006.
Post-release supervision.
Sex offender registration violations, §19.2-295.2:1.
Fines, uniform schedule.
Nontraffic prepayable offenses, VA SCt Rules 3C:1, 3C:2.
Traffic infractions, VA SCt Rules 3B:1, 3B:2.
Firearm possession while in possession of controlled substance or committing drug offense.
Mandatory minimum, §18.2-308.2.
Fiscal impact statements.
Increases in terms of imprisonment, §30-19.1:4.
Forms for use of sentencing courts.
Contents of sentencing orders, VA SCt Rules Part 3A Appx Form 10.
Substantial compliance with form required, VA SCt Rule 3A:22.
Gambling, illegal, §18.2-326.
Gambling winner repaying loser.
Discharge from punishment, §11-16.
Gang activity in school zone.
Enhanced punishment, §18.2-46.3:3.
General assembly power to provide for punishment of crime, VA Const Art IV §14.
General courts-martial, naval militia.
Powers of punishment, §44-69.
Geriatric prisoners.
Conditional release, §53.1-40.01.
Person twice previously convicted for violent felonies, §19.2-297.1.
Good conduct allowances.
Felonies committed on or after January 1, 1995.
Inapplicability to sentence imposed upon conviction, §§53.1-197.1, 53.1-202.1.
Persons committed on or after July 1, 1981.
Application, §53.1-199.
Choice of system, §53.1-198.
Classification system, §53.1-201.
Conditions, §53.1-200.
Confinement prior to transfer.
Credits, §53.1-202.
Eligibility, §53.1-199.
Persons committed prior to July 1, 1981.
Article applicability, §53.1-192.

SENTENCING —Cont'd
Good conduct allowances —Cont'd
Persons committed prior to July 1, 1981 —Cont'd
Career education, §53.1-197.
Credits earned prior to 1944, §53.1-195.
Educational training credits, §53.1-197.
Persons convicted after October 1, 1942, §53.1-196.
Persons convicted prior to October 1, 1942, §§53.1-193, 53.1-194.
Technical education, §53.1-197.
Guidelines in felony cases.
Discretionary sentencing guideline midpoints, §17.1-805.
Use, §19.2-298.01.
Guilty pleas.
Withdrawal of guilty plea, §19.2-296.
Habitual offenders.
Motor vehicles.
Tampering with odometer, §46.2-112.
Serious or habitual juvenile offenders.
Commitment, §16.1-285.1.
Release and review hearings, §16.1-285.2.
Comprehensive action program, §§16.1-330.1, 16.1-330.2.
Serving adult sentence, §16.1-285.2.
Home/electronic incarceration program for jail inmates, §53.1-131.2.
Criminal fines and penalties.
Installment payments as condition to program, §19.2-354.
Immediate sanction probation programs, §19.2-303.5.
Imposition of punishment, §19.2-295.
Increases in terms of imprisonment, §30-19.1:4.
Indeterminate commitment, §§19.2-311 to 19.2-316.
Compliance with terms and conditions of parole, §19.2-315.
Concurrence by corrections department, §19.2-311.
Diagnostic evaluation, §19.2-316.
Duration and character of commitment, §19.2-311.
Eligibility criteria, §19.2-311.
Eligibility for release, §§19.2-313, 19.2-314.
Evaluation for rehabilitation, §19.2-316.
Mental health evaluation, §19.2-316.
Supervision of persons released, §19.2-314.
Time on parole not counted as part of commitment period, §19.2-315.
Youthful offender facilities and programs, §§53.1-63 to 53.1-67.
Initial discretionary sentencing guideline midpoints, §17.1-805.
Insanity defense.
Restoration of sanity of prisoner, §19.2-180.
Involuntary manslaughter.
Victim impact statements.
When required, §19.2-299.
Jail, nonconsecutive days in, §53.1-131.1.
Jury trial.
Ascertainment of punishment by jury, §19.2-295.
Modification of sentence by court.
Written explanation, §19.2-295.
Separate proceeding, §19.2-295.1.
Mandatory minimum.
Anabolic steroids.
Manufacturing, selling or distributing, §18.2-248.5.
Assault and battery, §18.2-57.
Controlled substances.
Distribution to persons under 18, §18.2-255.

SENTENCING —Cont'd
Mandatory minimum —Cont'd
Controlled substances —Cont'd
Manufacturing, selling, distributing or possessing, §18.2-248.
Possession of firearm while in possession of controlled substance, §18.2-308.4.
Sale, gift, distribution or possession, §§18.2-248.1, 18.2-248.1:1.
Sale near certain properties, §18.2-255.2.
Transporting into Commonwealth, §18.2-248.01.
Convicted felons possessing firearms or explosives, §18.2-308.2.
Definition, court required to impose full punishment, §18.2-12.1.
Driving while intoxicated, §18.2-270.
Entering property of another for purposes of damaging.
Property intentionally selected because of race, religion, color or national origin of owner, §18.2-121.
Firearm, stun weapon or other weapon.
Possession of firearm while in possession of controlled substance, §18.2-308.4.
Possession on school property, §18.2-308.1.
Forcible sodomy of person less than 13.
Offender more than 3 years older than victim, §18.2-67.1.
Gang activity in school zone.
Enhanced punishment, §18.2-46.3:3.
Rape of child under age of 13.
Offender more than 3 years older than victim, §18.2-61.
Shooting at law enforcement, fire, rescue or emergency medical vehicles, §18.2-154.
Use or display of firearm in committing felony, §18.2-53.1.
Mental health examination.
Deferral of sentencing.
Construction of provisions, §19.2-302.
Expenses of psychiatrist, §19.2-301.
Offense indicating sexual abnormality, §19.2-300.
Report of findings and conclusions, §19.2-301.
Midpoint of initial recommended sentencing range.
Discretionary sentencing guideline midpoints, §17.1-805.
Misdemeanors, punishment for, §18.2-11.
Alcohol and substance abuse screening and assessment for designated Class 1 misdemeanor convictions, §19.2-299.2.
No punishment or maximum punishment prescribed, §18.2-12.
Punishment by reference, §18.2-13.
Modification of sentence, §19.2-303.
Nolo contendere.
Withdrawal of plea, §19.2-296.
Nonconsecutive days in jail, §53.1-131.1.
Nonviolent felonies.
Detention center incarceration program, §19.2-316.2.
Diversion center incarceration program, §19.2-316.3.
Operating costs.
Increases in terms of imprisonment, §30-19.1:4.
Orders of circuit court, VA SCt Rules Part 3A Appx Form 10.
Substantial compliance with form required, VA SCt Rule 3A:22.

SENTENCING —Cont'd
Other states.
Sentence imposed in another state.
Concurrent sentences, §19.2-308.1.
Parole.
Generally.
See PAROLE AND POSTRELEASE SUPERVISION.
Peace and good behavior of defendant.
Installment payment of criminal fines and penalties, §19.2-357.
Plea bargaining.
Sentence recommendations, VA SCt Rule 3A:8.
Postrelease supervision.
Felons sentenced for offenses committed on and after January 1, 1995, or July 1, 2000, §19.2-295.2.
Felons sentenced for offenses committed on and after July 1, 2006.
Sex offender registration violations, §19.2-295.2:1.
General provisions.
See PAROLE AND POSTRELEASE SUPERVISION.
Sex offender registration violations.
Felons sentenced for offenses committed on and after July 1, 2006, §19.2-295.2:1.
Presentence reports, §19.2-299.
Victim impact statements, when required, §19.2-299.1.
Pretrial diversion, §19.2-303.2.
Payment of costs, §19.2-303.4.
Previous criminal convictions.
Introduction as evidence, §19.2-295.1.
Violent felonies, §19.2-297.1.
Priority of sentence of confinement.
Conviction for combination of felony and misdemeanor offenses, §19.2-309.
Prison crimes, §53.1-204.
Probation.
Generally.
See PROBATION.
Pronouncement of sentence, §19.2-298.
Protective order violations, §16.1-253.2.
Punishment for felonies, §18.2-10.
Punishment for misdemeanors, §18.2-11.
By reference, §18.2-13.
No punishment or maximum punishment prescribed, §18.2-12.
Registration of convicted criminals.
Sex offender and crimes against minors registry, §§9.1-900 to 9.1-922.
See SEX OFFENDER REGISTRATION AND NOTIFICATION.
Release from sentence.
Indeterminate commitment.
Eligibility for release, §§19.2-313, 19.2-314.
Reprieves by governor, VA Const Art V §12.
Sex offender and crimes against minors registry, §§9.1-900 to 9.1-922.
See SEX OFFENDER REGISTRATION AND NOTIFICATION.
Sex offender registration violations.
Post-release supervision.
Felons sentenced for offenses committed on and after July 1, 2006, §19.2-295.2:1.
Sexual assault.
Punishment upon conviction of certain subsequent felony sexual assault, §18.2-67.5:2.
Punishment upon conviction of certain subsequent violent felony sexual assault, §18.2-67.5:3.

SENTENCING —Cont'd
Special courts-martial, national guard.
Authority, §44-44.
Spousal support.
Recognizance for compliance with order or decree.
Confinement for noncompliance, §20-115.
Substance abuse screening and assessment for designated Class 1 misdemeanor convictions, §19.2-299.2.
Substance abuse screening and assessment, suspension of sentence.
Drug conviction, §18.2-252.
Felony conviction generally, §18.2-251.01.
Summary courts-martial, national guard.
Authority, §44-45.
Summary courts-martial, naval militia.
Powers of punishment, §44-69.
Support of child or spouse.
Failure to comply with support obligation, §16.1-278.16.
Suspension of execution of sentence, §19.2-303.
Come-back time, §19.2-306.
Defendant sentenced to detention center incarceration program, §19.2-316.2.
Defendant sentenced to diversion center incarceration program, §19.2-316.3.
Fixing period of suspension, §19.2-303.1.
Forcible sodomy.
Complaining witness less than 13.
Offender more than 3 years older than victim, §18.2-67.1.
Counseling or therapy, completion.
Violation against spouse, §18.2-67.1.
Global positioning system.
Wearing device as condition of suspended sentence, §19.2-303.
Installment payment of criminal fines and penalties, §19.2-356.
Mandatory minimum.
Definition, suspension prohibited, §18.2-12.1.
Object sexual penetration.
Counseling or therapy, completion.
Violation against spouse, §18.2-67.2.
Rape by spouse.
Counseling or therapy, completion, §18.2-61.
Rape of child under age of 13.
Offender more than 3 years older than victim, §18.2-61.
Restitution.
Partial restitution as condition, §19.2-303.
Revocation or suspension, §19.2-303.
Detention center incarceration program.
Voluntary withdrawal, removal or failure to comply with terms and conditions, §19.2-316.2.
Diversion center incarceration program.
Voluntary withdrawal, removal or failure to comply with terms and conditions, §19.2-316.3.
Substance abuse screening and assessment.
Drug conviction, §18.2-252.
Felony conviction generally, §18.2-251.01.
Three time loser law.
Violent felonies, §19.2-297.1.
Traffic infractions.
Consideration of defendant's prior traffic record, §46.2-943.
Transfer of prisoners.
Custodial transfer to director of department of corrections, §19.2-310.

SENTENCING —Cont'd
Transmission of sentencing documents, §19.2-310.01.
Truth in sentencing, §19.2-295.1.
Unclassified offenses, how punished, §18.2-14.
Uniform fine schedule.
Nontraffic prepayable offenses, VA SCt Rules 3C:1, 3C:2.
Traffic infractions, VA SCt Rules 3B:1, 3B:2.
Victim impact statement prior to, §19.2-11.01.
Victim impact statements.
Admission, §19.2-295.3.
When required, §19.2-299.1.
Victim testimony prior to, §19.2-11.01.
Violent felonies.
Persons previously convicted of violent felonies, §19.2-297.1.
Sentence of person twice previously convicted of certain felonies, §19.2-297.1.
Virginia criminal sentencing commission, §§17.1-800 to 17.1-806.
See SENTENCING COMMISSION.
Work release program.
Criminal fines and penalties.
Installment payments as condition to program, §19.2-354.
Worksheets.
Discretionary sentencing guideline worksheets, §19.2-298.01.
Writ of actual innocence, §§19.2-327.2 to 19.2-327.6, VA SCt Rule 5:7B.
Nonbiological evidence, writ based on, §§19.2-327.10 to 19.2-327.14.

SENTENCING COMMISSION, §§17.1-800 to 17.1-806.
Compensation, §17.1-802.
Created, §17.1-800.
Discretionary sentencing guideline midpoints.
Adoption of initial midpoints, §17.1-805.
Modifications, report, effective date, §17.1-806.
Duties, §17.1-803.
Expenses, §17.1-802.
Goals, §17.1-801.
Increases in terms of imprisonment.
Duties, §30-19.1:4.
Meetings, §17.1-804.
Membership, §17.1-802.
Powers, §17.1-803.
Purposes, §17.1-801.
Sex offender and crimes against minors registry.
Requests for registry data, §9.1-916.
Staff, §17.1-804.

SENTENCING GUIDELINES IN FELONY CASES.
Discretionary midpoints, §17.1-805.
Use, §19.2-298.01.

SEPARATE MAINTENANCE.
Custody, visitation and support.
Authority of court to make decree, §20-107.2.
Filing case with clerk, §16.1-260.
Jurisdiction of claims for, §20-96.
Petition not necessary, §16.1-260.
Recordation tax, state.
Transfers pursuant to, §58.1-806.
Transfer of venue, §16.1-243.

SEPARATE TRIALS.
Civil cases, §§8.01-272, 8.01-281.
Criminal cases, VA SCt Rules 3A:10, 7C:4.

SEPARATION OF POWERS, VA Const Art I §5, Art III §1.

SEPTEMBER 11, 2001.
Presumption of death.
Terrorist attacks on September 11, 2001, §64.2-2300 (note).
Workers' compensation.
Occupational disease coverage, §65.2-406.

SEPTIC SYSTEM INSPECTORS, §§59.1-310.7 to 59.1-310.10.
Applicability of provisions.
Exceptions, §59.1-310.8.
Definitions, §59.1-310.7.
Exceptions to provisions, §59.1-310.8.
Title accredited septic system inspector..
Requirements for use, §59.1-310.9.
Penalty for use without meeting requirements, §59.1-310.10.

SEPTIC TANKS.
Application fees, §32.1-164.
Civil penalties.
Uniform schedule, establishment by local ordinance.
Specified violations of operation and maintenance of nonconventional sewage disposal systems, §15.2-2157.
Failing systems.
Betterment loans to repair or replace failing systems, §32.1-164.1:2.
Inspection upon installation, §32.1-164.1.
Installation permit in Augusta county, §15.2-2157.1.
Loans.
Betterment loans to repair or replace failing systems, §32.1-164.1:2.
Locality financing for repair of failed septic systems, §15.2-958.6.
Mechanics' and materialmen's liens.
Structures permanently annexed to freehold.
Classification, §43-2.
Onsite sewage indemnification fund, §32.1-164.1:1.
Onsite sewage system professionals.
Designs by professional engineers, §32.1-163.6.
Regulation and licensing generally, §§54.1-2300 to 54.1-2302.
See WATERWORKS OPERATORS.
Onsite soil evaluators, §§32.1-163.1, 32.1-164.
Permits.
Denials.
Appeals from, §32.1-164.1.
Validity, §32.1-164.1:1.
Voluntary system upgrades for systems that are not failing, §32.1-164.1:3.
Private site sewage evaluations, §32.1-163.5.
Repair.
Betterment loans to repair or replace failing systems, §32.1-164.1:2.
Sewage disposal when sewers not available.
Localities requiring installation, maintenance and operation, §15.2-2157.

SEPULTURE.
Violation of, §18.2-127.
Civil action to recover damages, §8.01-44.6.

SEQUESTRATION OF JURORS.
Criminal cases, §19.2-264.

SEQUESTRATION OF WITNESSES, VA SCt Rule 2:615.
Civil trials, §8.01-375.

SEQUESTRATION OF WITNESSES —Cont'd
Criminal trials, §§19.2-265.01, 19.2-265.1, 19.2-265.5.
Preliminary hearings, §19.2-184.

SERGEANTS.
Absence without leave from National Guard.
Taking person into custody, §44-41.1.
Courts-martial.
Processes and sentences, execution, §44-50.
Naval militia, §44-71.
Escheats.
Inquests.
Jury of inquests, §55-173.
Heart disease.
Presumption as to death or disability, §65.2-402.
Hepatitis, meningitis, tuberculosis and HIV.
Workers' compensation.
Presumption on death or disability from, §65.2-402.1.
Powers and duties of sheriffs.
Sheriffs generally.
See SHERIFFS.
Service of notice, process and other papers.
Courts-martial processes and sentences, §§44-50, 44-71.
Workers' compensation commission subpoenas, §65.2-202.
Sheriffs generally.
See SHERIFFS.
Workers' compensation.
Hepatitis, meningitis, tuberculosis and HIV.
Presumption on death or disability from, §65.2-402.1.
Presumptions as to death or disability from hypertension or heart disease, §65.2-402.
Workers' compensation commission subpoenas.
Service, §65.2-202.

SERIAL KILLINGS, §18.2-31.
Venue in multiple murder prosecution cases, §19.2-247.

SERIAL NUMBERS.
Changing or removing with intent to defraud, §18.2-214.
Secondhand watches, §59.1-133.
Firearms.
Removing, altering, etc., §18.2-311.1.
Household electrical appliances.
Removal or alteration and possession of such appliance, §18.2-215.
Identification marks.
See IDENTIFICATION MARKS.
Motor vehicles.
Fees for examination, verification or identification, §46.2-1072.1.
Illegible, removed or obliterated engine or serial numbers, §46.2-1073.
Possession of vehicle with removed or altered serial number, §46.2-1075.
Removal or alteration without consent of department, §46.2-1074.
Requirements for stamping, cutting or embossing numbers, §46.2-1072.
Personalty permanently marked, §18.2-96.1.
Possession with removed, altered, etc., mark, §18.2-96.1.
Removal, alteration, etc., §18.2-96.1.
Secondhand watches, §59.1-133.

SERIOUS OR HABITUAL JUVENILE OFFENDERS.
Commitment, §16.1-285.1.
Release and review hearings, §16.1-285.2.

SERIOUS OR HABITUAL JUVENILE OFFENDERS —Cont'd
Comprehensive action program, §§16.1-330.1, 16.1-330.2.
Earned sentence credit.
Condition for earning, report by department of juvenile justice, §53.1-202.3.
Eligibility, §53.1-202.2.
Serving adult sentence, §16.1-285.2.

SERVICE ANIMALS.
Failure to use not contributory negligence, §46.2-934.
Intentional interference with, §3.2-6588.
Pedestrian guided by dog, §46.2-933.
Liability for injuries to, §46.2-932.1.
Rights of persons with disabilities in public places and places of public accommodation, §51.5-44.
Rights of persons with disabilities to housing accommodations, §51.5-45.

SERVICE AUTHORITIES.
Augusta county service authority, 1969 Ex Sess ch 12.
Maury service authority, 1972 ch 388.
Southeastern public service authority of Virginia, 1977 ch 544, 2000 ch 580, 2000 ch 596.

SERVICE BY PUBLICATION.
Affirmation of marriage, §§20-104 to 20-105.1.
Alternative procedures, §20-105.1.
Order of publication against nonresident defendant, §20-104.
Permissible form for orders of publication, §20-105.
Aircraft accidents.
Nonresident operator or owner of aircraft, §§8.01-307 to 8.01-313.
Annulment of marriage, §§20-104 to 20-105.1.
Alternative procedures, §20-105.1.
Combining orders of publication, §20-104.1.
Order of publication against nonresident defendant, §20-104.
Permissible form for orders of publication, §20-105.
Attachment, §8.01-544.
Courts not of record, §16.1-105.
District courts, §16.1-105.
Attorney disbarment, §54.1-3938.
Child support.
Reopening proceeding, §20-112.
Church trustees, §57-11.
Constructive service, §8.01-296.
Costs, §8.01-316.
Criminal forfeiture, §§19.2-386.3, 19.2-386.9.
Death presumption, §64.2-2300.
Delinquent tax land sales.
Parties not otherwise served, §58.1-3967.
Divorce, §§20-104 to 20-105.1.
Alternative procedures, §20-105.1.
Combining orders of publication, §20-104.1.
Order of publication against nonresident defendant, §20-104.
Permissible form for orders of publication, §20-105.
Drainage projects.
Proceedings on petitions, §§21-296, 21-297.
Publication against unknown owners, §21-307.
Family graveyards, removal of remains, §57-38.2.

SERVICE BY PUBLICATION —Cont'd
Fieri facias service on judgment better, §8.01-487.1.
Foreign corporations, §8.01-301.
Garnishment, §8.01-511.
Interim notice, §8.01-319.
Impoundment of surface water, §§62.1-108, 62.1-110.
John Doe actions, §38.2-2206.
Judgments, payment entered, §8.01-455.
Juvenile proceedings.
Summons, §16.1-264.
Land office.
Chain of title, lost links, §41.1-9.
Legal separation, §§20-104 to 20-105.1.
Alternative procedures, §20-105.1.
Order of publication against nonresident defendant, §20-104.
Permissible form for orders of publication, §20-105.
Lost instruments, §8.01-394.
Lost shareholders, §13.1-777.
Motor vehicle accidents.
Newspapers deemed published for purpose of legal advertisements, §8.01-323.
Newspapers used for legal notices and publications, §8.01-324.
Nonresident motor vehicle operator, §§8.01-307 to 8.01-313.
Nonresidents, service on equivalent to order of publication, §8.01-320.
Nuisances.
Presentment against premises causing nuisance, §48-4.
Parental rights termination, §16.1-283.
Proceedings to enforce tax liens, §8.01-321.
Personal service outside of Virginia equivalent to order of publication, §8.01-320.
Property settlement agreements, §20-109.1.
Quo warranto.
Motion to set aside judgment, §8.01-641.
Return of service, §8.01-327.
Sale of delinquent tax lands.
Parties not otherwise served, §58.1-3967.
Service of process or notice on statutory agent, §8.01-326.1.
Unknown defendants or parties.
Limitation on rehearing to correct injustice, §8.01-322.
Notice of subsequent proceedings, §8.01-318.
What order of publication to state, §8.01-317.
When available, §8.01-316.
When publication in newspaper dispensed with, §8.01-317.
Tax commissioner, §58.1-216.
Unincorporated associations, §8.01-306.
Will probate, §§64.2-446, 64.2-449.
Minors, §64.2-448.

SERVICE CHARGE IN LIEU OF PAYMENT OF TAX.
Real property taxes, §§58.1-3400 to 58.1-3407.

SERVICE CHARGES AND USER FEES.
Insurance premium finance companies.
Maximum charge, §38.2-4705.
Retail sales and use tax, §58.1-609.5.

SERVICE CONTRACTS, EXTENDED, §§59.1-435 to 59.1-441.
Consumer protection, prohibited practices, §59.1-200.

SERVICE CONTRACTS, EXTENDED —Cont'd
Defined terms, §59.1-435.
Investigations, §59.1-439.
Letters of credit, §59.1-437.
Motor vehicles, §§59.1-207.34 to 59.1-207.39.
Penalties, §59.1-441.
Records, production of, §59.1-440.
Registration, §59.1-436.
Regulations, §59.1-438.
Surety bonds, §59.1-437.

SERVICE DISTRICTS, §§15.2-2400 to 15.2-2403.3.
Boundary changes, §15.2-2402.1.
Consolidated cities.
Creation by court order, §15.2-2401.
Creation by locality, §15.2-2400.
Court order in consolidated cities, §15.2-2401.
Description of proposed district, §15.2-2402.
Mandamus in matters pertaining to actions of commissions.
Jurisdiction of circuit courts to issue writs, §17.1-131.
Powers, §15.2-2403.

SERVICE DOGS.
Rights of persons with disabilities in public places and places of public accommodations, §51.5-44.

SERVICE MARKS.
Business opportunity sales.
Prohibited acts, §59.1-266.
Virginia trademark and service mark act (1998), §§59.1-92.1 to 59.1-92.22.
See TRADEMARKS AND SERVICE MARKS.

SERVICEMEMBERS CIVIL RELIEF ACT.
Default judgments, §8.01-15.2.

SERVICEMEN'S READJUSTMENT ACT OF 1944.
Minors or unmarried widows, eligibility for guaranty of credit.
Qualification to contract for and purchase real or personal property, §11-8.

SERVICE OF NOTICE, PROCESS AND OTHER PAPERS, §§8.01-285 to 8.01-327.2.
Acceptance of service by another.
Notice to be mailed defendant, §8.01-315.
Acceptance of service of process, §8.01-327.
Actual innocence.
Petition for writ of actual innocence, VA SCt Rule 5:7B.
Address of defendants, §8.01-290.
Administrative process act.
Final orders, §2.2-4023.
Adoption of 1950 code.
Effect on process given, taken or issued before code in force, §1-8.
Affirmation of marriage.
How process may be served, §20-99.2.
Agencies of state, how process served, §8.01-300.
Alcoholic beverage sales at licensed establishment.
Notice of hearing on temporary injunction sought by locality.
Establishment meeting place for committing serious criminal violations, §48-17.1.
Annexation.
Notice and copy of ordinance, §15.2-3204.
Annulment of marriage.
How defendant may accept service, §20-99.1:1.

SERVICE OF NOTICE, PROCESS AND OTHER PAPERS —Cont'd
Annulment of marriage —Cont'd
How process may be served, §20-99.2.
Personal service of process outside Commonwealth.
Validation of service prior to October 1, 1977, §8.01-320.
Timely receipt of process though not served or accepted, §8.01-288.
Annulment of town charters.
Copy of notice and ordinance, §15.2-3703.
Arrest under civil process, §§8.01-327.1, 8.01-327.2.
Defined, §8.01-327.1.
Attachment.
District court proceedings, §16.1-105.
Fee for service on person of attachment under which body taken, §17.1-272.
Order of publication, §8.01-544.
Return by officer, §8.01-559.
Attorney discipline, VA SCt Rule Pt 6 §IV Par 13-12.
Attorney licensing.
Revocation proceedings, §54.1-3938.
Attorneys at law.
Foreign attorneys, VA SCt Rules 1:5, 1A:4.
Law firms, VA SCt Rule 1:5.
Service after entry of general appearance, §8.01-314.
Bad check.
Notice check returned unpaid, §8.01-27.2.
Banks.
Acquisition of interests in financial institutions.
Consent to service of process, §6.2-704.
Boards of state, how process served, §8.01-300.
Bonds issued by localities.
Judicial determination of validity.
Service by publication of motion for judgment, §15.2-2652.
Bribery to officers to prevent, §18.2-440.
Business trusts.
Registered office and agent, §§13.1-1220 to 13.1-1223.
Change of city to town.
Citizen petition, §15.2-4102.
Petition by governing body, §15.2-4101.
Charitable organizations that solicit contributions, §57-51.
Child custody proceeding.
Uniform child custody jurisdiction and enforcement act.
Enforcement.
Service of petition and order of court, §20-146.30.
Giving notice of exercise of jurisdiction to person outside state, §20-146.7.
Limited immunity from service when participating in proceeding, §20-146.8.
Requirement of notice and opportunity to be heard, §20-146.16.
Child support enforcement by department of social services.
Lien asserted by department, §63.2-1928.
Notice of administrative support order, §63.2-1916.
Delivery of notice to last known address, sufficiency, §63.2-1917.
Income withholding, §§63.2-1923, 63.2-1924.
Notice of review of order, §63.2-1921.

SERVICE OF NOTICE, PROCESS AND OTHER PAPERS —Cont'd
Child support enforcement by department of social services —Cont'd
Order to withhold and deliver property, §63.2-1929.
Circuit court clerks.
Delivering or sending process to sheriff, §17.1-214.
Process book, §17.1-215.
Transmittal of fee for service to sheriff, §17.1-216.
Circuit courts.
Civil actions.
Proof of service, VA SCt Rule 3:6.
Summons, VA SCt Rule 3:5.
Delivery or sending process to sheriff.
Clerk's duties, §17.1-214.
Process book, §17.1-215.
Transmittal of fee with paper served to sheriff, §17.1-216.
City status granted county.
Notice of petition alleging eligibility, §15.2-3903.
Civil actions.
Circuit courts.
Proof of service, VA SCt Rule 3:6.
Summons, VA SCt Rule 3:5.
Civil arrest.
Defined, §8.01-327.1.
Claims against counties.
How process served, §8.01-300.
Claims against the state.
Fraudulent claims.
Civil investigative demands, §8.01-216.13.
Tort claims act.
Service on Commonwealth or locality, §8.01-195.4.
College building authority.
On whom process served, §23-30.38.
Commissioner of motor vehicles.
Nonresident motor vehicle operators, §§8.01-307 to 8.01-313.
Appointment binding, §8.01-310.
Continuance of action where service made on commissioner, §8.01-311.
Copy to be sent to defendant and certificate filed with court, §8.01-326.1.
Due diligence affidavit, §8.01-313.
Duties of statutory agent, §8.01-312.
Effective date of service, §8.01-326.1.
Effect of service on statutory agent, §8.01-312.
Fee, §8.01-310.
Former resident defined as nonresident, §8.01-307.
How process served, §8.01-310.
Motor vehicle, defined, §8.01-307.
Nonresident defendant licensed by Commonwealth, §8.01-313.
Nonresident defendant not licensed by Commonwealth, §8.01-313.
Nonresident, defined, §8.01-307.
Operator's consent to appointment, §8.01-308.
Specific addresses for mailing by statutory agent, §8.01-313.
Party seeking service to provide addresses, §8.01-312.
Time for nonresident to respond for process from statutory agent, §8.01-312.
Commissions of state, how process served, §8.01-300.
Committees.
Execution of bond that designates clerk as attorney for service, §64.2-1419.
Adjudication of due diligence, §64.2-1421.

SERVICE OF NOTICE, PROCESS AND OTHER PAPERS —Cont'd
Committees —Cont'd
Execution of bond that designates clerk as attorney for service —Cont'd
Duties of clerk, §64.2-1420.
Common carriers.
Unincorporated common carriers.
How process served, §§8.01-305, 8.01-306.
Compelling attendance of witnesses.
Execution of process in another locality, §8.01-409.
Computation of time.
Electronic filing and service, VA SCt Rule 1:17.
Condominiums.
Registration application, §55-79.89.
Confession of judgment.
Judgment confessed by attorney-in-fact.
Service of copy on judgment debtor, §8.01-438.
Conservation police officers.
Powers, §29.1-203.
Conservators.
Execution of bond designates clerk as attorney for service, §64.2-1419.
Nonresidents, §64.2-1426.
Consolidation of counties, cities or towns into single county or city.
Notice of consolidation, §15.2-3521.
Constructive service, §8.01-296.
Garnishment, §8.01-511.
Contractors, nonresident.
Appointment of agent, §54.1-1113.
Contractor transaction recovery fund.
Actions against, §54.1-1120.
Convict defendant, §8.01-297.
Copies of pleadings.
Furnishing copy to counsel, VA SCt Rule 3A:21.
Number of copies, §8.01-291.
Corporations.
Arrest warrants, §19.2-76.
Clerk of state corporation commission as agent for service.
Failure to maintain registered agent or agent not found at registered office, §13.1-637.
Designation by agent of person to receive service, §13.1-637.
Foreign corporations, §13.1-766.
Facsimile serviced by sheriff, §13.1-637.
Foreign corporations, §§8.01-301, 13.1-766.
Designation by registered agent of person to receive service, §13.1-766.
Publication, when available, §8.01-316.
Withdrawn corporations, §13.1-767.
Generally, §8.01-299.
Registered agent is corporate agent for service of process, §13.1-637.
Duty to forward notice to corporation, §13.1-634.
Foreign corporations, §13.1-766.
Summons to answer indictment, §19.2-238.
Trustee or receiver, §8.01-303.
Correction of taxes assessed by state corporation commission.
Notice of hearing, §58.1-2031.
Costs.
Failure to comply with request to waive service of process, §8.01-286.1.
Counties, actions by or against.
How process served, §8.01-300.
Counties, cities or towns, suits against, §15.2-1404.
Court of appeals, VA SCt Rule 5A:1.

SERVICE OF NOTICE, PROCESS AND OTHER PAPERS —Cont'd
Court officers.
Motion on bond, §8.01-227.
Courts-martial, naval militia.
Execution, §44-71.
Courts-martial processes, execution, §44-50.
Criminal forfeiture, §19.2-386.3.
Curators.
Execution of bond that designates clerk as attorney for service, §64.2-1419.
Adjudication of due diligence, §64.2-1421.
Duties of clerk, §64.2-1420.
Decedents' estates.
Executors, administrators or officers unable to receive service or defend suit.
Authority excludes defending actions or expiration of duties.
Filing tolls statute of limitations if suit names proper estate of deceased, §8.01-6.2.
Decertification of law enforcement officer, notice, §15.2-1708.
Default judgments.
Substitute service mailing requirements, §8.01-296.
Validation of posted service, §8.01-296.
Defective process.
Motion to quash process, §§8.01-277, 8.01-277.1.
Objections to personal jurisdiction, §8.01-277.1.
What constitutes waiver, §8.01-277.1.
Delinquent tax lands sales.
Notice, §58.1-3965.
Depositions and discovery.
Uniform interstate depositions and discovery act.
Subpoenas, §8.01-412.11.
Distress warrants.
Summons in proceedings to try title to property levied on.
District court proceedings, §16.1-120.
District court civil cases.
Summons in proceedings to try title to property levied on under distress or execution, §16.1-120.
District court criminal cases.
Filing format and procedure, VA SCt Rule 7A:7.
Service and filing of papers, VA SCt Rule 7C:7.
District courts.
Where process returnable, §16.1-69.36.
Divorce.
How defendant may accept service, §20-99.1:1.
How process may be served, §20-99.2.
Personal service outside Commonwealth.
Validation of service prior to October 1, 1977, §8.01-320.
Timely receipt of process though not served or accepted, §8.01-288.
Drainage projects.
Proceedings on petitions, §21-297.
Driver improvement program.
Order of probation, suspension or revocation, §46.2-504.
Due diligence.
Change of address.
Failure to inform clerk of change, §8.01-319.
Corporations, §8.01-319.
Fiduciaries.
Execution of bond that designates clerk as attorney for service.
Adjudication of due diligence, §64.2-1421.
Nonresident vehicle operators.
Affidavit as to due diligence, §8.01-313.
Aircraft operators, §8.01-329.

SERVICE OF NOTICE, PROCESS AND OTHER PAPERS —Cont'd
Due diligence —Cont'd
Parentage proceedings, §20-49.8.
Election contest of governor, lieutenant governor or attorney general elections.
Notice of intent to contest, §24.2-804.
Election contests of primaries and elections.
Time of filing and service of complaint, §24.2-808.
Election contest to general assembly election.
Notice of intent to contest, §24.2-803.
Election recounts.
Petitions, §24.2-801.
Electronic filing and service, §8.01-271.01, VA SCt Rule 1:17.
Eminent domain.
Funds paid into court.
Petition for pro rata share, §25.1-243.
Notice of petition filed, §25.1-210.
Nonresident owner, §25.1-212.
Owner under a disability, §25.1-215.
Title transfer by certificate.
Petition for determination of just compensation, §25.1-318.
Petition for distribution of funds, §25.1-310.
Exceptions to Sunday prohibition, §8.01-289.
Execution.
Officer refusing, delaying, etc., §18.2-469.
Process appearing to be duly served by sheriff, §8.01-295.
Resisting or obstructing legal process, §18.2-409.
Summons in proceedings to try title to property levied on.
District court proceedings, §16.1-120.
Territorial limits, §8.01-295.
To whom process directed and where executed, §8.01-292.
Executors and administrators.
Executors, administrators or officers unable to receive service or defend suit.
Authority excludes defending actions or expiration of duties.
Filing tolls statute of limitations if suit names proper estate of deceased, §8.01-6.2.
Nonresidents, §64.2-1426.
Extradition of criminals.
Immunity from process in civil actions, §19.2-113.
Extradition of witnesses.
Securing attendance from another state in criminal proceedings.
Exemption of witnesses from service of process, §19.2-280.
Facsimile process in criminal proceedings, §19.2-3.1.
Fees, §17.1-272.
High constables in Norfolk, §17.1-273.
Secretary of the Commonwealth serving, §2.2-409.
Fiduciaries.
Execution of bond that designates clerk as attorney for service, §64.2-1419.
Adjudication of due diligence, §64.2-1421.
Duties of clerk, §64.2-1420.
Nonresidents, §64.2-1426.
Designation of clerk of court as agent for service, §64.2-1419.
Fieri facias.
Garnishment of estate of debtor, §8.01-503.
Filing of papers, VA SCt Rule 3A:21.
Electronic filing and service, criminal actions, VA SCt Rule 3A:23.

SERVICE OF NOTICE, PROCESS AND OTHER PAPERS —Cont'd
Financial institutions.
Acquisition of interests in financial institutions.
Consent to service of process, §6.2-704.
Fishing, tidal waters.
Menhaden taking with purse nets.
Nonresidents, §28.2-401.
Foreign corporations, §13.1-766.
Designation by agent of person to receive, §13.1-766.
Generally, §8.01-301.
Publication, when available, §8.01-316.
Service on registered agent, §13.1-766.
Trustee or receiver, §8.01-303.
Withdrawn corporations, §13.1-767.
Foreign limited partnerships.
Service on partnership whose registration has been canceled, §50-73.58.
Clerk of commission as agent upon automatic cancellation of certificate, §50-73.58:1.
Transaction of business without registration.
Initiating actions against foreign limited partnerships transacting without registration, §50-73.59.
Foreign nonprofit corporations, §13.1-928.
Service on registered agent, §13.1-928.
Designation by agent of person to receive, §13.1-928.
Withdrawal, §13.1-929.
Forms of writs.
Prescription by supreme court, §8.01-286.
Funds transfers.
Creditor process on receiving bank, §8.4A-502.
Fusion intelligence center.
Immunity, §52-48.
Garnishment.
Constructive service, §8.01-511.
Corporations, §8.01-513.
Fieri facias lien on estate of debtor, §8.01-503.
Institution of proceedings, §8.01-511.
Limited liability companies, §8.01-513.
Service upon federal government, §8.01-523.
Substitute service, §8.01-511.
Guardians.
Execution of bond that designates clerk as attorney for service, §64.2-1419.
Adjudication of due diligence, §64.2-1421.
Duties of clerk, §64.2-1420.
Nonresidents, §64.2-1426.
Habeas corpus.
Service of writ, §§8.01-657, 8.01-658.
Health professional department investigations.
Personnel powers, §54.1-2506.
High constable, Norfolk.
Fees adopted by local ordinance, §17.1-273.
Hospital authority commissioners.
Removal proceedings.
Service by mail, §15.2-5313.
How process to be served, §§8.01-287 to 8.01-289.
Exceptions to Sunday prohibition, §8.01-289.
Manner set forth by rules of supreme court, §8.01-287.
Sunday prohibition, §8.01-289.
Timely service, §8.01-288.
Valid service, §8.01-288.
Identification of defendants, §8.01-290.
Income tax.
Jeopardy assessment, §58.1-313.
Income tax setoff debt collection.
Notice of intention to setoff, §58.1-525.

SERVICE OF NOTICE, PROCESS AND OTHER PAPERS —Cont'd
Insurance adjusters.
Unlicensed public adjusters process, §§38.2-812 to 38.2-815.
Appointment of agent for service, §38.2-813.
Method of service or notice, §38.2-814.
Other legal service not affected, §38.2-815.
Insurance agents and brokers.
Nonresidents, clerk of state corporation commission as agent, §38.2-1836.
Unlicensed nonresident brokers and agents, §§38.2-808 to 38.2-811.
Appointment as agent for service, §38.2-809.
Definitions, §38.2-808.
Method of service, §38.2-810.
Other legal service not limited, §38.2-811.
Insurance companies.
Conversion of stock insurer to mutual insurer.
Compelling completion of mutualization, §38.2-1014.
Reciprocal insurers.
Clerk of state corporation commission appointed as agent, §38.2-1216.
Unlicensed insurers, §§38.2-800 to 38.2-807.
Appointment as agent for service, §38.2-801.
Attorneys' fees against unlicensed insurers, §38.2-807.
Defense of action by unlicensed insurer, §38.2-806.
Definitions, §38.2-800.
Judgment entered on default of appearance, time of entry, §38.2-805.
Method of service, §§38.2-802, 38.2-803.
Alternative, §38.2-803.
Other legal service not limited, §38.2-804.
Insurance consultants.
Clerk of commission.
Agent for service, appointment, §38.2-1838.
Insurance consultants, refusal or revocation of license.
Notice of hearing, §38.2-1844.
Insurance rate investigations by attorney general.
Investigation demand, §38.2-1916.1.
Insurance-supported organizations, §38.2-616.
Investigative demands.
Insurance rate investigations by attorney general, §38.2-1916.1.
Investment advisor representatives, nonresidents, §13.1-517.
Investment advisors, nonresidents, §13.1-517.
Issuance of process, §§8.01-290 to 8.01-293.
Jeopardy assessment.
Income tax, §58.1-313.
Retail sales and use tax, §58.1-631.
John Doe actions.
Owner or operator of vehicle causing injury or damage unknown, §38.2-2206.
Judicial inquiry and review commission, §17.1-919.
Order compelling attendance and testimony of witness, §17.1-909.
Scope of process, §17.1-908.
Jurors.
How summons served, §8.01-298.
Juvenile proceedings.
Motion to reduce support arrearages to judgment, VA SCt Rule 8:4.
Protective orders for family abuse, §16.1-279.1.
Summons, §§16.1-263, 16.1-264.

SERVICE OF NOTICE, PROCESS AND OTHER PAPERS —Cont'd
Juvenile proceedings —Cont'd
Termination of residual parental rights, §16.1-283.
Waiver, §16.1-263.
Landlord and tenant.
Appointment of resident agent by nonresident property owners, §55-218.1.
Notice, §55-248.6.
Rental agreements.
Notices required by, §8.01-296.
Late return of process or service.
Effect of, §8.01-294.
Law firms.
Service on one member or associate of firm, VA SCt Rule 1:5.
Legal separation.
How defendant may accept service, §20-99.1:1.
Limitation of actions.
Service of process prevented by defendant, §8.01-229.
Limited liability companies.
Foreign limited liability companies.
Agent for service.
Automatic cancellation of certificate of registration, clerk of commission appointed, §13.1-1056.1.
Registered agent for service of process and papers, §13.1-1018.
Registered agent is agent for service, §13.1-1018.
Limited partnerships.
Clerk of commission agent to receive.
Failure to appoint registered agent, agent not found, §50-73.7.
Designation by agent of person to receive, §50-73.7.
Foreign limited partnerships.
Service on partnership whose registration has been canceled, §50-73.58.
Clerk of commission as agent upon automatic cancellation of certificate, §50-73.58:1.
Transaction of business without registration.
Initiating actions against foreign limited partnerships transacting without registration, §50-73.59.
How process served, §8.01-304.
Office of registered agent, §50-73.7.
Lobbyists and principal.
Secretary of Commonwealth agent for service, §2.2-423.
Local road authorities.
Establishment and alteration of roads.
Issuance of process by supervisors, §33.1-244.
Long-arm statute, §8.01-328.1.
Mail service.
Attachment in district court, §16.1-105.
Computation of time, VA SCt Rule 1:7.
State corporation commission, §12.1-19.1.
Unlicensed insurers process.
Alternative method of service, §38.2-803.
Mandamus.
Service of writ, §8.01-652.
Mental health facility admissions.
Psychiatric inpatient treatment of minors.
Petition for involuntary commitment, §16.1-341.
Motion on bond.
Court officers, §8.01-227.
Motions for judgment.
District court civil actions, §16.1-82.
Motions practice.
Briefs.
Filing and service of briefs, VA SCt Rule 4:15.

SERVICE OF NOTICE, PROCESS AND OTHER PAPERS —Cont'd
Motions practice —Cont'd
Definition of served for purposes of rule, VA SCt Rule 4:15.
Motion to quash process.
Defective process, §§8.01-277, 8.01-277.1.
Objections to personal jurisdiction, §8.01-277.1.
What constitutes waiver, §8.01-277.1.
Motorcycle dealers.
Summons for license plate violations, §46.2-1993.54.
Motor vehicle dealers.
Transaction recovery fund.
Claims against the fund, §46.2-1527.4.
Motor vehicle registration.
Civil penalty for certain violations by trucks and tractor trucks.
Service of process.
Operator as agent for, §46.2-613.2.
Procedures for issuance and service, §46.2-613.5.
Motor vehicle size and weight.
Overweight vehicle cases, §§46.2-1132, 46.2-1136.
Motor vehicle titling.
Appointment of agent for process, §46.2-601.
Municipal governments.
How process served, §8.01-300.
Name and address of defendants, §8.01-290.
Natural persons, §8.01-296.
Nonprofit corporations, §13.1-836.
Designation by agent of person to receive, §13.1-836.
Foreign corporations, §13.1-928.
Foreign corporations, §13.1-928.
Withdrawal, §13.1-929.
Registered agent as agent for service, §13.1-836.
Foreign corporations, §13.1-928.
Summons to answer indictment, §19.2-238.
Nonresident motor vehicle operators.
Continuance of action where service made on commissioner, §8.01-311.
Duties of statutory agent, §8.01-312.
Effect of service on statutory agent, §8.01-312.
Fee, §8.01-310.
How service made on commissioner, §8.01-310.
Motor vehicle, defined, §8.01-307.
Nonresident, defined, §8.01-307.
Service on commissioner of motor vehicles, §8.01-308.
Specific addresses for mailing by statutory agent, §8.01-313.
Time for nonresident to respond for process from statutory agent, §8.01-312.
Nonresident operator or owner of aircraft.
Continuance of action where service made on secretary, §8.01-311.
Duties of statutory agent, §8.01-312.
Effect of service on statutory agent, §8.01-312.
Fee, §8.01-310.
How service made on secretary, §8.01-310.
Service on secretary of state, §8.01-309.
Specific addresses for mailing by statutory agent, §8.01-313.
Time for nonresident to respond for process from statutory agent, §8.01-312.
Nonresidents.
Attachment in district court, §16.1-105.
Broker-dealers, investment advisors, investment advisor representatives or agents.
Appointment of clerk of state corporation commission as agent for receipt, §13.1-517.

SERVICE OF NOTICE, PROCESS AND OTHER PAPERS —Cont'd
Nonresidents —Cont'd
Contractors.
Appointment of agent for service of process, §54.1-1113.
Fiduciaries, §64.2-1426.
Designation of clerk of court as agent for service, §64.2-1419.
Insurance adjusters.
Unlicensed public adjusters process, §§38.2-812 to 38.2-815.
Insurance agents.
Clerk of state corporation commission as agent for service, §38.2-1836.
Insurance brokers and agents process, §§38.2-808 to 38.2-811.
Insurance companies, unlicensed insurers, §§38.2-800 to 38.2-807.
Issuers of securities.
Appointment of clerk of state corporation commission as agent, §13.1-517.
Personal service on nonresident outside state equivalent to order of publication, §8.01-320.
Publication, when available, §8.01-316.
Retail franchisors, §13.1-566.
Notice of appeal.
Appeals from general district courts in civil cases, §16.1-112.
Nuisances.
Presentment against person or premises causing nuisance, §48-4.
Number of copies, §8.01-291.
Obscene books, proceeding against, §18.2-384.
Obstructing legal process, §18.2-409.
Orders of publication, §§8.01-316, 8.01-317.
Papers returnable out of state.
Process and service fee, §17.1-272.
Parental rights termination, §16.1-283.
Parties unknown.
Service by publication, §8.01-316.
Partition of personal property, petitions, §16.1-77.2.
Partnerships.
Arrest warrants, §19.2-76.
How process served, §8.01-304.
Personal representatives.
Execution of bond that designates clerk as attorney for service, §64.2-1419.
Adjudication of due diligence, §64.2-1421.
Duties of clerk, §64.2-1420.
Personal service outside of Commonwealth, §8.01-320.
Person not found.
Fee for sheriff's effort to serve, §17.1-268.
Plaintiff suing on sworn claim in district court, §16.1-88.
Pleadings.
Service by mail.
Certificate of counsel, VA SCt Rule 1:12.
Power of attorney.
Authority of agent as to claims and litigation, §64.2-1633.
Prisons and prisoners.
Process on convict defendant, §8.01-297.
Process book, §17.1-215.
Process, defined, §8.01-285.
Prohibition, writ of.
Service of writ, §8.01-652.

SERVICE OF NOTICE, PROCESS AND OTHER PAPERS —Cont'd
Proof of service.
Child custody proceeding.
Uniform child custody jurisdiction and enforcement act.
Giving notice of exercise of jurisdiction to person outside state, §20-146.7.
Circuit courts.
Civil actions, VA SCt Rule 3:6.
Juvenile proceedings, §16.1-264.
Protective orders.
Emergency protective orders, §16.1-253.4.
Ex parte preliminary protective order, family abuse, §16.1-253.1.
Offenses resulting in serious bodily injury, §19.2-152.10.
Publication orders, §§8.01-316, 8.01-317.
Public building authority.
Actions against authority, §2.2-2277.
Public officers, removal.
Show cause rules, §24.2-235.
Public school authority.
Statutory agents, §22.1-174.
Public service corporation tax assessment review.
Hearing notice, §58.1-2671.
Notice to Commonwealth, §58.1-2674.
Quasi-governmental entities.
How process served, §8.01-300.
Quo warranto.
How summons served, §8.01-639.
Real estate appraisers.
Appointment of agents, §54.1-2019.
Real estate brokers, salespersons and rental agents.
Appointment of agent, §54.1-2111.
Real property tax assessment.
Notice of change in assessment, §58.1-3330.
Receivers.
Execution of bond that designates clerk as attorney for service, §64.2-1419.
Adjudication of due diligence, §64.2-1421.
Duties of clerk, §64.2-1420.
Reciprocal insurers.
Clerk of state corporation commission appointed as agent, §38.2-1216.
Recounts in elections.
Petitions, §24.2-801.
Registered agents.
Corporations, §13.1-637.
Duty to forward notice, §13.1-634.
Foreign corporations, §13.1-766.
Withdrawn corporations, §13.1-767.
Designation of person other than agent to receive.
Corporations, §13.1-637.
Foreign corporations, §13.1-766.
Limited liability company, §13.1-1018.
Limited partnerships, §50-73.7.
Nonprofit corporations, §13.1-836.
Foreign nonprofit corporations, §13.1-928.
Limited liability company, §13.1-1018.
Limited partnerships, §50-73.7.
Nonprofit corporations, §13.1-836.
Foreign nonprofit corporations, §13.1-928.
Withdrawn corporation, §13.1-929.
Registered limited liability partnerships.
Automatic cancellation of registration.
Clerk of commission appointed as agent for process, §50-73.134.

SERVICE OF NOTICE, PROCESS AND OTHER PAPERS —Cont'd
Removal of public officer from office.
Show cause rules, §24.2-235.
Request for waiver of service of process, §8.01-286.1.
Residual market facility, basic property insurance, §38.2-2706.
Resisting or obstructing execution of legal process, §18.2-409.
Retail franchisors, nonresidents, §13.1-566.
Retail sales and use tax jeopardy assessment, §58.1-631.
Return of process, §8.01-294.
Late return, effect of, §8.01-294.
Return, defined, §8.01-285.
Saturday, Sunday or legal holiday, §8.01-294.
Return of service, §§8.01-325, 8.01-326.
Late return, effect of, §8.01-294.
Proof of service, §§8.01-294, 8.01-325.
Evidentiary effect, §8.01-326.
Reversion of city to town.
Citizen petition, §15.2-4102.
Petition by governing body, §15.2-4101.
Right to work.
Clerk of state corporation commission, §40.1-68.
Safe deposit box.
Access denied except by court order, §6.2-2304.
Sale of delinquent tax lands, notice, §58.1-3965.
Schools.
Service of teachers or school employees, §8.01-294.
Search warrants.
Tracking device, use of, §19.2-56.2.
Secretary of the Commonwealth.
Appointed agent for service.
Lobbyists and principals, §2.2-423.
Fee for service on parties, §2.2-409.
Initial notice by certified mail, subsequent notices by regular mail, §2.2-401.1.
Nonresident operator or owner of aircraft, §§8.01-307 to 8.01-313.
Continuance of action where service made on secretary, §8.01-311.
Copy to be sent to defendant and certificate filed with court, §8.01-326.1.
Due diligence affidavit, §8.01-313.
Duties of statutory agent, §8.01-312.
Effective date of service, §8.01-326.1.
Effect of service on statutory agent, §8.01-312.
Exercise of personal jurisdiction, §8.01-329.
Fee, §8.01-310.
Former resident defined as nonresident, §8.01-307.
How process served, §8.01-310.
Nonresident defendant licensed by Commonwealth, §8.01-313.
Nonresident defendant not licensed by Commonwealth, §8.01-313.
Nonresident, defined, §8.01-307.
Operator's consent to appointment, §8.01-309.
Specific addresses for mailing by statutory agent, §8.01-313.
Party seeking service to provide addresses, §8.01-312.
Time for nonresident to respond for process from statutory agent, §8.01-312.
Security brokers-dealers, nonresidents, §13.1-517.
Security issuers, nonresidents, §13.1-517.
Security sales agents, nonresidents, §13.1-517.

SERVICE OF NOTICE, PROCESS AND OTHER PAPERS —Cont'd
Sergeants.
Courts-martial processes and sentences, §§44-50, 44-71.
Workers' compensation commission subpoenas, §65.2-202.
Service by posting, §8.01-296.
Service by publication.
See SERVICE BY PUBLICATION.
Setoff debt collection, income tax.
Notice of intention to setoff, §58.1-525.
Sexual sterilization.
Adults incapable of informed consent, §54.1-2976.
Children incapable of informed consent, §54.1-2975.
Sheriffs.
Clerk of circuit court to deliver or send process to sheriff, §17.1-214.
Deputy acting in place of sheriff, §15.2-1616.
Drivers' license suspension or revocation notice, §46.2-416.
Fee for service, §46.2-370.
Fee for effort to serve order, notice, etc., when person not found, §17.1-268.
Fee transmitted by circuit court clerk to sheriff, §17.1-216.
Process sent by mail, §15.2-1620.
Returns, §8.01-294.
State corporation commission writs, processes and orders, §12.1-29.
Tax commissioner, writs, processes and orders from, §58.1-217.
Show cause rules.
Removal of public officers from office, §24.2-235.
Simulation of warrants, processes, writs and notices, §18.2-213.
Small claims courts, §16.1-122.3.
Solicitation of charitable or civic contributions.
Nonresidents, §57-51.
State corporation commission.
Clerk appointed as agent for service.
Corporations.
Failure to maintain registered agent or agent not found at registered office, §13.1-637.
Foreign corporations, failure to maintain registered office in Commonwealth, §13.1-766.
Foreign stock corporation, withdrawn corporation, §13.1-767.
Nonprofit corporations.
Failure to maintain registered agent in Commonwealth, §13.1-836.
Foreign corporations, §§13.1-928, 13.1-929.
Nonresident broker-dealers, investment advisors, investment advisor representatives or agents, §13.1-517.
Nonresident insurance agents, §38.2-1836.
Nonresident issuers of securities, §13.1-517.
Reciprocal insurers, §38.2-1216.
Trademark and service mark registration.
Service on out-of-state registrants, §59.1-92.14.
Unlicensed insurers, §38.2-801.
Clerk as statutory agent, §12.1-19.1.
Execution of writs, processes and orders, §12.1-29.
Method of service by commission, §12.1-19.1.
Nonresident retail franchisors.
Appointment of clerk as agent, §13.1-566.
Returnable to location of commission, §12.1-5.

SERVICE OF NOTICE, PROCESS AND OTHER PAPERS —Cont'd
State corporation commission —Cont'd
Territorial limits, §8.01-295.
State departments and agencies.
How process served, §8.01-300.
Initial notice by certified mail, subsequent notices by regular mail, §2.2-601.1.
Statewide execution, §8.01-292.
Statute of limitations.
Service of process prevented by defendant, §8.01-229.
Statutory agent.
Address for mailing of process, §8.01-312.
Specific addresses, §8.01-313.
Certificate filed with court, §8.01-326.1.
Copy of process sent to defendant, §8.01-326.1.
Defined, §8.01-285.
Duties of agent, §8.01-312.
Effective date of service, §8.01-326.1.
Effect of service on, §8.01-312.
Legal force and validity, §8.01-312.
Motor vehicle weight violation.
Operator of vehicle statutory agent, §46.2-1132.
Nonresident aircraft operator or owner.
Secretary of Commonwealth, §8.01-309.
Nonresident motor vehicle operator.
Address for mailing process, §8.01-313.
Commissioner of DMV, §8.01-308.
Secretary of Commonwealth.
Service on generally, §8.01-329.
State corporation commission.
Service on clerk generally, §12.1-19.1.
Time for nonresident to respond for process from statutory agent, §8.01-312.
Unincorporated associations or orders or unincorporated common carriers.
Principal office outside state and transacting business in state, §8.01-306.
Stock insurers conversion to mutual insurer.
Compelling completion of mutualization, §38.2-1014.
Substitute service, §8.01-296.
Aircraft accidents.
Nonresident operator or owner of aircraft, §§8.01-307 to 8.01-313. See within this heading, "Secretary of the Commonwealth."
Motor vehicle accidents.
Nonresident motor vehicle operators, §§8.01-307 to 8.01-313. See within this heading, "Commissioner of motor vehicles."
Notice on statutory agent, §8.01-326.1.
Service by publication.
See SERVICE BY PUBLICATION.
Summons.
Civil actions.
Circuit courts, VA SCt Rule 3:5.
Sunday prohibition, §8.01-289.
Supreme court.
Generally, VA SCt Rule 5:1.
Prescription of forms of writs, §8.01-286.
Surface mining.
Notice of noncompliance served on operator, §45.1-186.1.
Surplus lines insurance.
Insurers subject to unlicensed insurers process act, §38.2-4812.
Licensing of brokers.
Agent for service, §38.2-1857.2.
Tax commissioner and department of taxation.
Writs, notices, etc., §58.1-216.
Form of writs, processes and orders, §58.1-217.

SERVICE OF NOTICE, PROCESS AND OTHER PAPERS —Cont'd
Taxes or assessments for local improvements.
How notice given, §15.2-2409.
Telephone cooperatives.
Registered office or agent, §56-490.
Termination of residual parental rights, §16.1-283.
Timeliness of service, §§8.01-275.1, 8.01-288.
Tobacco product manufacturers' responsibilities.
Enforcement of requirements.
Agent for service, §3.2-4208.
Tobacco products distributors, §58.1-1021.04:1.
Town charter annulled.
Copy of notice and ordinance, §15.2-3703.
Town seeking city status.
Notice of petition to circuit court for grant of city status, §15.2-3803.
Trademarks and service marks.
Out-of-state registrants, §59.1-92.14.
Trailer dealer license plate violations.
Service of summons, §46.2-1992.54.
Transition of city to town.
Citizen petition, §15.2-4102.
Petition by governing body, §15.2-4101.
Transition of counties to cities.
Notice of petition alleging eligibility, §15.2-3903.
Trustees.
Execution of bond that designates clerk as attorney for service, §64.2-1419.
Adjudication of due diligence, §64.2-1421.
Duties of clerk, §64.2-1420.
Nonresidents, §64.2-1426.
Trusts.
Methods of giving notice, §64.2-707.
Unemployment compensation.
Claims adjudication.
Judicial review of commission decisions, §§60.2-625, 60.2-631.
Employer taxation.
Judicial review, §60.2-500.
Unincorporated associations or orders.
How process served, §§8.01-305, 8.01-306.
Unincorporated common carriers.
How process served, §§8.01-305, 8.01-306.
Uninsured or underinsured motor vehicle.
Institution of action against owner or operator, §38.2-2206.
Unknown defendants or parties.
Service by publication.
Limitation on rehearing to correct injustice, §8.01-322.
Notice of subsequent proceedings, §8.01-318.
Unlawful detainer.
Substitute service mailing requirements.
Actions in district courts, §8.01-296.
Unlicensed insurers, §§38.2-800 to 38.2-807.
Unlicensed nonresident insurance brokers and agents, §§38.2-808 to 38.2-811.
Unlicensed public adjusters process, §§38.2-812 to 38.2-815.
Valid service, §8.01-288.
Viatical settlement brokers.
Clerk of commission.
Agent for service, appointment, §38.2-1865.1.
Waiver of service of process, §8.01-286.1.
Warrants, district court civil actions brought on, §16.1-80.
Watercraft sales and use tax.
Dealers certificate of registration.
Notice of suspension or revocation, §58.1-1406.

SERVICE OF NOTICE, PROCESS AND OTHER PAPERS —Cont'd
When service timely, §8.01-275.1.
Who may serve process, §8.01-293.
Witnesses.
How summons served, §8.01-296.
Additional method of serving, §8.01-298.

SESQUICENTENNIAL OF AMERICAN CIVIL WAR.
Virginia sesquicentennial of the American Civil War commission and fund, §§30-266 to 30-274.

SESSIONS OF GENERAL ASSEMBLY, VA Const Art IV §6.

SET ASIDES.
Procurement by public bodies, §2.2-4310.
Transportation improvement program set-aside fund, §58.1-816.1.

SETBACK LINES.
Ordinances of localities regulating, §15.2-2279.

SETOFF.
Assignee claims of plaintiff, §8.01-423.
Bank deposits and collections.
Collection of items by payor banks.
Items subject to setoff, §8.4-303.
Civil procedure, §§8.01-421 to 8.01-423.
Collection of accounts receivable by the Commonwealth.
Treasury offset programs of United States.
Participation, §§2.2-4806, 2.2-4809.
Funds transfers.
Beneficiary's bank, §8.4A-502.
Insurance companies, rehabilitation and liquidation.
Mutual debts or credits, §38.2-1515.
Landlord and tenant.
Residential landlords and tenants.
Defenses to landlord actions for possession or rent, §55-248.25.
Motor vehicle insurance or uninsured motorist coverage.
Medical benefit offset against prohibited, §38.2-2216.
Pleading equitable defenses, §8.01-422.
Railroads.
Injuries to railroad employees.
Set-off of insurance, §8.01-60.
Secured transactions.
Banks.
Security interests in deposit accounts, §8.9A-340.
State lottery.
Setoff of debts to Commonwealth from prizes, §58.1-4026.
Transferee claims of plaintiff, §8.01-423.

SETOFF DEBT COLLECTION, INCOME TAX, §§58.1-520 to 58.1-535.
Accounting to claimant agency, §58.1-532.
Action by department of taxation upon notification by claimant agency, §58.1-524.
Administrative costs.
Exceeding amount of delinquent debt.
Participation in program not permitted, §58.1-522.
Administrative costs recovery, §58.1-520.1.
Appeals from hearings, §58.1-527.
Application of funds on deposit, §58.1-535.

SETOFF DEBT COLLECTION, INCOME TAX —Cont'd
Assistance in collection.
Sums due claimant agency, §58.1-523.
Certification of debt by claimant agencies, §58.1-528.
Confidentiality, §§58.1-532, 58.1-533.
Costs of administration of article.
Annual statement by department of taxation, §58.1-531.
Credit to debtor's obligation, §58.1-532.
Definitions, §58.1-520.
Delinquent local taxes.
Scope of hearing, §58.1-526.
Disposition of proceeds collected, §58.1-531.
Errors in setoff program, §58.1-531.1.
Finalization of setoff, §58.1-528.
Notice of final setoff, §58.1-529.
Hearing on setoff, §58.1-526.
Appeals, §58.1-527.
Right to hearing, §58.1-525.
Identifying information, §58.1-521.
Interest on error in setoff program, §58.1-531.1.
Mandatory usage, §58.1-521.
Multiple claims.
Priorities, §58.1-530.
Notification of department of taxation by claimant agency, §§58.1-524, 58.1-525.
Participation in setoff program not permitted where debt below certain levels, §58.1-522.
Petition for judicial review, §58.1-527.
Priorities in claims to be setoff, §58.1-530.
Remedy in addition to other remedies, §58.1-521.
Rules and regulations, §58.1-534.
Service of notice of intention to setoff, §58.1-525.
Use of information obtained, §58.1-533.

SETOFF DEBT COLLECTION, LOTTERY PRIZES, §58.1-4026.

SETTING ASIDE DEFAULT JUDGMENT, §8.01-428.

SETTING ASIDE PATERNITY DETERMINATION.
Genetic test establishing individual not father, §20-49.10.

SETTLEMENT AGENTS.
Consumer real estate settlement protection act.
See CONSUMER REAL ESTATE SETTLEMENT PROTECTION ACT.
Real estate settlement agents.
Generally, §§55-525.16 to 55-525.32.
See REAL ESTATE SETTLEMENTS.

SETTLEMENTS, §§8.01-424, 8.01-425.
Alternative dispute resolution proceedings.
Generally.
See ALTERNATIVE DISPUTE RESOLUTION.
Assault and battery.
Dismissal of misdemeanor charges in lieu of settlement, §19.2-151.
Assignments of income for the benefit of creditors.
Trustee powers, §55-162.
Assignments of property for the benefit of creditors, §55-159.
Attorney general, authority, §2.2-514.
Attorneys at law.
Insurance claims, notice of settlement payments, §38.2-236.

SETTLEMENTS —Cont'd
Bank deposits and collections.
Collection of items by depositary and collecting banks.
Settlement of items.
Medium and time of settlement, §8.4-211.1.
Provisional status, §8.4-201.
When provisional credits become final, §8.4-213.
Children's settlements.
Court approval, §8.01-424.
Guardian ad litem, §8.01-9.
Payment of small amounts through court without intervention of fiduciary, §8.01-606.
Claims against the state.
Tort claims act, §8.01-195.5.
Collection of money payable to state.
Comptroller's power to adjust old claims, §8.01-216.
Commissioners in chancery.
Settlement of accounts of special receivers and special commissioners, §§8.01-617 to 8.01-619.
Confidentiality agreements.
Attorney general, authority, §2.2-514.
Consumer real estate settlement protection act.
See CONSUMER REAL ESTATE SETTLEMENT PROTECTION ACT.
Contribution among joint contractors and co-obligors not affected, §11-13.
Co-obligors, §§11-10, 11-11.
Crediting contract, §11-11.
Counties, cities or towns.
Voluntary settlement of annexation, transition or immunity issues, §§15.2-3400, 15.2-3401.
Court of appeals.
Pending appeal, VA SCt Rule 5A:36.
Settlement conference, VA SCt Rule 5A:37.
Credit counseling.
Debt settlement.
Defined, §6.2-2000.
Creditor compounding or compromising with joint contractor or co-obligor, §§11-10, 11-11.
Crediting contract, §11-11.
Death taxes.
Interstate compromise and arbitration of death taxes, §§58.1-920 to 58.1-930.
See ESTATE TAX.
Derivative proceeding by stockholder, §13.1-672.1.
Dispute resolution proceedings.
Generally, §§8.01-576.4 to 8.01-576.12.
Eminent domain proceedings.
Pretrial conferences, §25.1-219.
Title transfer by certificate.
Agreement on amount of compensation, §25.1-317.
Fidelity and surety insurers.
Expense of securing bond allowed in settlement of account, §38.2-2410.
Fiduciaries.
How fiduciary may compromise claim, §8.01-425.
Inventories and accounts, §§64.2-1206, 64.2-1305, 64.2-1308.
Chancery causes, §64.2-1315.
Commissioners in chancery, §64.2-1316.
Failure to make, §64.2-1216.
Forfeiture of remuneration by fiduciaries, §64.2-1217.

SETTLEMENTS —Cont'd
Fiduciaries —Cont'd
Inventories and accounts —Cont'd
Generally, §§64.2-1300 to 64.2-1317.
See FIDUCIARIES.
When required, §§64.2-1301, 64.2-1302.
Years to be included, §64.2-1207.
Highways and roads.
Construction contracts.
Adjustment of claims, §33.1-386.
Husband and wife.
Notice of claim for expenses arising out of injury to wife, §55-36.
Insurance claims.
Notice of settlement payments, §38.2-236.
Unfair practices, §38.2-510.
Replacement and repair, §38.2-517.
Joint contractors, §11-10.
Crediting contract, §11-11.
Life insurance policies.
Individual life policies, §38.2-3312.
Industrial life insurance, §38.2-3350.
Viatical settlements generally, §§38.2-6000 to 38.2-6016.
See VIATICAL SETTLEMENTS.
Local taxes.
Offers of compromise, §58.1-3994.
Local treasurers.
Accounts, §58.1-3137.
Medical services lien.
Death claims settled by compromise or suit, §8.01-66.10.
Necessity for settlement or judgment, §8.01-66.11.
Minors settlement.
Court approval, §8.01-424.
Guardian ad litem, §8.01-9.
Payment of small amounts through court without intervention of fiduciary, §8.01-606.
Motor carriers, passengers.
Self-insurers.
Applicability of unfair claims settlement practices, §46.2-2056.
Motor carriers, property.
Self-insurers.
Applicability of unfair claims settlement practices, §46.2-2146.
Motor vehicle insurance.
Notice of settlement of claim, §38.2-2226.1.
Notice.
Insurance claims, notice of settlement payments, §38.2-236.
Part performance extinguishing obligation, §11-12.
Personal injuries.
Husband and wife.
Notice of claim for expenses arising out of injury to wife, §55-36.
Persons with disability.
Court approval, §8.01-424.
Power of attorney.
Authority of agent as to claims and litigation, §64.2-1633.
Property rights of married women.
Notice of claim for expenses arising out of injury to wife, §55-36.
Public school funds.
Proceedings to compel settlement of accounts, §22.1-121.
Settlement by treasurer, §22.1-120.
Real property.
Consumer real estate settlement protection act.
See CONSUMER REAL ESTATE SETTLEMENT PROTECTION ACT.

SETTLEMENTS —Cont'd
Real property —Cont'd
Real estate settlements, generally, §§55-525.8 to 55-525.32.
See REAL ESTATE SETTLEMENTS.
Residential real property transactions, generally.
See RESIDENTIAL REAL PROPERTY TRANSACTIONS.
Wet settlement act.
See MORTGAGES AND DEEDS OF TRUST.
Release of liability as condition of settlement.
Rescission in personal injury action or claim, §8.01-425.1.
State corporation commission.
Powers, §12.1-15.
Structured settlements, §§59.1-475 to 59.1-477.1.
Construction of provisions, §59.1-477.1.
Definitions, §59.1-475.
Disclosures to payee.
Required disclosures, §59.1-475.1.
Secured transactions.
Third parties.
Assignments.
Restrictions on assignments, §8.9A-406.
Transfer of payment rights.
Agreement, §59.1-477.1.
Approval, §59.1-476.
Procedure, §59.1-477.
Effect, §59.1-476.1.
Waiver of provisions by payee prohibited, §59.1-477.1.
Supreme court.
Settlement of pending appeal, VA SCt Rule 5:38.
Tax claims, prosecutions or penalties, §58.1-105.
Timber cutting encroachment, §55-335.
Tobacco manufacturers' master settlement agreement, §§3.2-4200 to 3.2-4219.
Assignment and contribution of escrow funds to Commonwealth, §§3.2-4202, 3.2-4203.
Trespass.
Timber cutting encroachment, §55-335.
Trusts.
Nonjudicial settlement agreements involving trusts, §64.2-709.
Unemployment compensation.
Employer taxation.
Collections, §60.2-521.
Viatical settlements generally, §§38.2-6000 to 38.2-6016.
See VIATICAL SETTLEMENTS.
Virginia property and casualty insurance guaranty association.
Binding effect on receiver or liquidator, §38.2-1609.
Waste management.
Expedited settlements, §10.1-1406.
Weights and measures.
Civil penalties, §3.2-5646.
Workers' compensation.
Memorandums of agreement.
Construction of provisions, §65.2-701.
Subrogation actions, §65.2-309.
Expenses, §65.2-311.
Settlements of third-party actions, §8.01-424.1.
Subrogation rights construed, §65.2-812.
Wrongful death actions.
Approval of court required, §8.01-55.
Compromise bars action, §8.01-51.

SETTLING BOUNDARIES BETWEEN LOCALITIES.
Commissioners establishing lines, §§15.2-3100 to 15.2-3105.
Relocation or change by agreement, court ordered adjustment, §§15.2-3106 to 15.2-3109.

SEVENTY-SEVEN.
Wireless telephone state police access number, §56-484.18.

SEVERANCE BENEFITS.
Public officers and employees.
Severance benefits announced prior to departure.
Agency heads, §2.2-106.
Governor's secretaries, §2.2-200.
Signed statement from appointees, §2.2-109.01.
State officers and employees.
Payment to, §2.2-2831.
Transitional severance benefits.
Eligibility for, §2.2-3202.

SEVERANCE OF CHARGES.
District courts.
Criminal and traffic cases, VA SCt Rule 7C:4.
Right to separate trials, VA SCt Rule 3A:10.

SEVERANCE OF PARTIES.
Codefendants' right to separate trials, VA SCt Rule 3A:10.
District courts.
Criminal and traffic cases, VA SCt Rule 7C:4.
Joint trial of defendants prejudicial, §19.2-262.1.
Multiple claimant litigation, §8.01-267.5.

SEVERANCE TAX ON COAL, GAS OR OIL.
Delinquent taxes.
Exoneration from lien, etc., §58.1-3959.
Local coal severance license taxes, §§58.1-3740 to 58.1-3745.
Authority to levy tax, §58.1-3741.
Definitions, §58.1-3740.
Lien on real and personal property of businesses severing coal, §58.1-3745.
Local coal road improvement severance license tax, §58.1-3741.
Distribution, §58.1-3742.
Paid to locality in which coal is severed, §58.1-3743.
Rate, §58.1-3741.
Uniform ordinance provisions, applicability, §58.1-3744.
Local license tax on persons engaging in business of severing, §§58.1-3712 to 58.1-3713.4.
Additional one percent tax on gas, §58.1-3713.4.
Coal and gas road improvement tax, §58.1-3713.
Water projects, §58.1-3713.01.
Coal and gas severance tax, §58.1-3712.
Oil severance tax, §58.1-3712.1.
Validation of coal and gas severance tax ordinances, §58.1-3713.3.
Real property tax assessment of mineral lands.
Alternative to procedure for specially and separately assessing, §58.1-3286.

SEWAGE DISPOSAL, §§15.2-2122 to 15.2-2133, 32.1-163 to 32.1-166.
Acceptance of gifts and grants, §15.2-2122.
Acquisition from sanitary district, §15.2-2116.
Acquisition of real estate or rights or easements, §15.2-2122.

SEWAGE DISPOSAL —Cont'd
Agreements.
Federal agencies, §32.1-166.
Alternative discharging sewage systems, §32.1-164.
Approval of systems by counties, §§15.2-2126 to 15.2-2133.
Disapproval of sewage system or extension by governing body, §15.2-2127.
Enjoining violation, §15.2-2133.
Extension of service in excess of number of connections for which approval given, §15.2-2130.
Hotel corporations, inapplicability of provision, §15.2-2131.
Master plan for sewage adopted by governing body.
Denial of application for sewage system, §15.2-2128.
Noncompliance with provisions, §§15.2-2132, 15.2-2133.
Notice in writing to governing body of county.
Establishment of system in county, §15.2-2126.
Further information in notice, §15.2-2129.
Borrowing money for purposes of establishing, constructing, etc., §15.2-2122.
Building permits.
Considerations, §32.1-165.
Capacity requirements, sewage treatment plant, §15.2-2123.
Chamber and bundled expanded polystyrene effluent distribution systems, §32.1-164.9.
Charging and collecting fees or other charges, §15.2-2122.
Civil penalty.
Sewer use standards violations, imposition, procedure, §15.2-2122.
Connections.
Mandatory connection in certain counties, §15.2-2110.
Construction of new, expanded or upgraded treatment plant.
Capability to treat sewage.
Requirements, §15.2-2123.
Septage treatment capability.
Notification to DEQ prior to issuance of certificate of construction, §15.2-2123.
Contracts between localities to prevent pollution, §§15.2-2124, 15.2-2125.
Contracts by localities with sewerage purification company, §15.2-2117.
Defined terms, §32.1-163.
Discharges into waters of the state.
Approval of systems and works, §62.1-44.19.
Hearings, §§62.1-44.25 to 62.1-44.30.
Certification, §62.1-44.15.
Joint supervision, §62.1-44.18.
Ohio river valley water sanitation commission.
Jurisdiction, §62.1-74.
Permits.
Applications.
When application considered complete, §62.1-44.15:3.
Public hearings and permit procedures before the board, §62.1-44.15:02.
Prohibitions, §62.1-44.18:2.
Violations, §§62.1-44.31, 62.1-44.32.
Discounted fees and charges for low-income and disabled customers, §15.2-2119.
Eminent domain by county, city or town.
Condemnation of existing system, §15.2-1906.

SEWAGE DISPOSAL —Cont'd
Exclusive service areas.
Joint agreements by political subdivisions, §15.2-2112.
Fees and charges for sewer services, §§15.2-2119, 15.2-5139.
Gathering places.
Regulations, §32.1-200.
Inspection of system upon installation, §32.1-164.1.
Joint agreements by political subdivisions, §15.2-2112.
Lien for charges.
Certain counties, §15.2-2118.
Enforcement, §15.2-2120.
Loans.
Betterment loans to repair or replace failing onsite systems, §32.1-164.1:2.
Long range plan for onsite sewage, §32.1-163.2.
Mandatory connection in certain counties, §15.2-2110.
Marinas, §32.1-246.
Methane or other combustible gas.
Building or facility to collect and use for electric energy.
Loans to local governments, §§15.2-2430 to 15.2-2440.
See VIRGINIA INFRASTRUCTURE PROJECT LOAN FUND.
Multistate entities operating certain sewage treatment facilities.
Governing board, §56-264.2.
Onsite operation and maintenance fund, §32.1-164.8.
Onsite sewage disposal systems.
See SEPTIC TANKS.
Onsite sewage indemnification fund, §32.1-164.1:01.
Onsite sewage system professionals.
Regulation generally, §§54.1-2300 to 54.1-2302.
See WATERWORKS OPERATORS.
Onsite soil evaluators.
Personal liability, §32.1-163.1.
Permit application backlogs, §32.1-163.4.
Permits.
Land application, marketing and distribution of sewage sludge, §62.1-44.19:3.
Certification of sewage sludge land applicators, §62.1-44.19:3.1.
Local enforcement of sewage sludge regulations, §62.1-44.19:3.
Notification to local governing bodies of application, §62.1-44.19:3.4.
Septage disposal, §62.1-44.19:3.3.
Letters in lieu of, §32.1-164.
Police powers over lands lying beyond localities boundaries, §15.2-1725.
Pollution prevention.
Contracts between localities, §§15.2-2124, 15.2-2125.
Polystyrene effluent distribution systems, §32.1-164.9.
Power and authority to establish, construct, etc., §15.2-2122.
Pretreatment requirements.
Standards for use and services, §15.2-2122.
Privately-owned sewerage facilities.
Cessation of operations.
Closure plan required, §62.1-44.18:3.
Permit requirements, §62.1-44.18:3.

SEWAGE DISPOSAL —Cont'd
Public utilities.
Generally, §§56-232 to 56-265.
See PUBLIC UTILITIES.
Regulation of sewage disposal by locality generally, §15.2-2111.
Repair or replacement of system.
Betterment loans to repair or replace failing onsite systems, §32.1-164.1:2.
Reporting parties.
Identity confidentiality, §32.1-163.3.
Residential property transfer disclosure.
Wastewater system located on property.
Owner makes no representations, §55-519.
Resources authority generally, §§62.1-197 to 62.1-223.
See RESOURCES AUTHORITY.
Retail sales and use tax.
Machinery, tools and equipment brought into Virginia for use in constructing sewer systems, §§58.1-604.1 to 58.1-604.3.
Sanitarians.
Personal liability defined, §32.1-163.1.
Sanitary districts.
Bond issues, §§21-122 to 21-140.3.
See SANITARY DISTRICTS BONDS.
General provisions, §§21-112.22 to 21-140.3.
See SANITARY DISTRICTS.
Sanitation districts law of 1938.
General provisions, §§21-141 to 21-223.
See SANITATION DISTRICTS LAW OF 1938.
Sanitation districts law of 1946.
General provisions, §§21-224 to 21-290.
See SANITATION DISTRICTS LAW OF 1946.
Septage.
Capability of sewage treatment plant to accept.
Authority of locality to limit, §15.2-2123.
Notification to DEQ.
Required prior to issuance of certificate of construction, §15.2-2123.
Septic tank permits.
Appeals from denials, §32.1-164.1.
Validity, §32.1-164.1:1.
Voluntary system upgrades for systems that are not failing, §32.1-164.1:3.
Septic tanks generally.
See SEPTIC TANKS.
Service districts, §§15.2-2400 to 15.2-2403.3.
Sewage and sewerage facilities.
Approval of systems and works, §62.1-44.19.
Certificates for discharge, §62.1-44.15.
Land application, marketing and distribution of sewage sludge, §62.1-44.19:3.
Certification of sewage sludge land applicators, §62.1-44.19:3.1.
Local enforcement of sewage sludge regulations, §62.1-44.19:3.2.
Notification to local governing bodies of application, §62.1-44.19:3.4.
Septage disposal, §62.1-44.19:3.3.
Sewerage systems not regulated as public utilities, §§56-265.10 to 56-265.13.
Application of chapter, §56-265.13.
Customer complaints, §56-265.11.
Defined terms, §56-265.10.
Hampton Roads area refuse collection and disposal system authority, §15.2-5102.1.
Hampton Roads sanitation district, §21-291.2.
Notice to energy utilities that such system includes a sewage treatment plant, §56-265.11:1.

SEWAGE DISPOSAL —Cont'd
Sewerage systems not regulated as public utilities —Cont'd
Opinion of commission, §56-265.12.
Public ground use without consent or compensation, §56-14.
Sewer use standards, §15.2-2122.
Soil evaluators, §32.1-164.
Personal liability, §32.1-163.1.
Standards for use and services, §15.2-2122.
Surveys, borings, soundings, etc.
Entry on lands, §15.2-2122.
Underground utility line damage prevention.
Private sewer laterals, sewer system laterals, §56-265.19:1.
Uniform schedule of civil penalties.
Adoption, violations of sewer use standards, §15.2-2122.
Violations.
Sewer use standards, civil penalty, imposition, procedure, §15.2-2122.
Water facilities revolving fund, §§62.1-224 to 62.1-232.
See WATER FACILITIES REVOLVING FUND.

SEWAGE DISPOSAL AUTHORITIES.
Generally, §§15.2-5100 to 15.2-5159.
See WATER AND WASTE AUTHORITIES.

SEWAGE DISPOSAL BONDS.
Sewage and sewerage facilities.
Damage or trespass to, §18.2-162.
Diverting service, §18.2-163.
Metering devices, tampering with, §18.2-163.
Water control board.
Limitations on power to require construction of, §62.1-44.15:1.

SEWAGE DISPOSAL SYSTEMS, §§15.2-2122 to 15.2-2133.

SEWAGE HANDLING AND DISPOSAL APPEAL REVIEW BOARD.
Agreements with federal agencies, §32.1-166.
Alternative discharging sewage systems.
Fees for installation and monitoring inspections, §32.1-164.
Appeals fees, §32.1-166.10.
Civil penalties, schedule of, §32.1-164.
Duties, §§32.1-164, 32.1-166.6.
Interpretation of application of regulations, §32.1-166.9.
Meetings, §32.1-166.4.
Members, §32.1-166.1.
Oath, §32.1-166.3.
Officers, §32.1-166.2.
Offices, §32.1-166.5.
Onsite sewage disposal systems.
Application fee, §32.1-164.
Powers, §32.1-164.
Recommendation for modifications of regulations, §32.1-166.9.
Record of decisions, §32.1-166.8.
Regulations, §32.1-164.
Secretary, §32.1-166.2.
Septic tanks.
Permits, §32.1-164.1.
Subpoenas, §32.1-166.7.
Witnesses, §32.1-166.7.

SEWAGE TREATMENT, §§15.2-2122 to 15.2-2133, 32.1-163 to 32.1-166.
See SEWAGE DISPOSAL.

SEWERAGE COMPANIES, §§56-261 to 56-265.
Alley use without consent or compensation, §56-14.
Certificates of public convenience and necessity, §§56-265.1 to 56-265.9.
Charges, §56-264.1.
Contracts by localities with, §15.2-2117.
Duties, §§56-261, 56-261.1.
Failure to perform, §56-262.
Commission investigations, §56-263.
Quo warranto, §56-264.
Powers of commission not limited, §56-265.
Public ground use without consent or compensation, §56-14.
Public service companies generally.
See PUBLIC SERVICE COMPANIES.
Public utilities generally, §§56-232 to 56-265.
See PUBLIC UTILITIES.
Small sewer utilities, §§56-265.13:1 to 56-265.13:7.
Cooperative associations.
Organization as, §13.1-301.
Street use without consent or compensation, §56-14.
Systems not regulated as public utilities, §§56-265.10 to 56-265.13.

SEWER AUTHORITIES.
Generally, §§15.2-5100 to 15.2-5159.
See WATER AND WASTE AUTHORITIES.

SEWERS.
Combined sewer overflow matching fund, §§62.1-241.11, 62.1-241.12.
Damage or trespass to, §18.2-162.
Diverting service, §§8.01-44.7, 18.2-163.
Limitation of actions.
Assessments for sewers, §8.01-240.
Metering devices, tampering with, §§8.01-44.7, 18.2-163.
Public service companies.
Generally, §§56-1 to 56-46.3.
See PUBLIC SERVICE COMPANIES.
Statute of limitations.
Assessments for sewers, §8.01-240.
Stormwater management, §§62.1-44.15:24 to 62.1-44.15:50.
See STORMWATER MANAGEMENT.
Underground utility line damage prevention.
Private sewer laterals, sewer system laterals, §56-265.19:1.
Urban county executive form of government.
Maintenance of sewer lines, §15.2-816.

SEX CHANGES.
Amendments to vital records, §32.1-269.

SEX DISCRIMINATION, VA Const Art I §11.
Discrimination generally.
See DISCRIMINATION.
Equal credit opportunities, §§6.2-500 to 6.2-513.
See EQUAL CREDIT OPPORTUNITIES.
Equal pay, §40.1-28.6.
Fair employment contracting act, §§2.2-4200, 2.2-4201.
Fair housing law, §§36-96.1 to 36-96.23.
See FAIR HOUSING.
Fire insurance policies, §§38.2-2114, 38.2-2115.
Health insurance.
Abortion coverage restriction, §38.2-3451.
Health maintenance organizations, §38.2-4312.
Human rights act, §§2.2-3900 to 2.2-3903.
Life insurance, §38.2-508.2.

SEX DISCRIMINATION —Cont'd
Motor vehicle insurance.
Issuance, §38.2-2213.
Refusal to renew, §38.2-2212.
Procurement by public bodies, §2.2-4310.
Employment discrimination by contractors, §2.2-4311.

SEX EDUCATION.
Family life education generally, §§22.1-207.1, 22.1-207.2.

SEX OFFENDER AND CRIMES AGAINST MINORS REGISTRY.
Generally, §§9.1-900 to 9.1-922.

SEX OFFENDER REGISTRATION AND NOTIFICATION, §§9.1-900 to 9.1-922.
Access to registry, §9.1-912.
Dissemination of information via Internet site, §9.1-913.
Applicability.
Offenses requiring registration, §9.1-902.
People required to register, §9.1-901.
Change of address.
Reregistration, §9.1-903.
Child-care services and facilities.
Automatic notification of registration to certain entities, §9.1-914.
Colleges and universities.
Enrollment data reported to state police for comparison against registry, §23-2.2:1.
Enrollment or employment at institutions of higher learning.
Information required, §9.1-906.
Commercial drivers' licenses.
Cancellation of endorsement for conviction of offense requiring registration, §46.2-341.18:3.
Instruction permit to drive school bus.
Non-eligibility while registration required, §46.2-341.10.
Non-eligibility for license while registration required, §46.2-341.9.
Committed residents under jurisdiction of department of behavioral health and developmental services required to register.
Duty upon release or discharge, §37.2-921.
Construction and interpretation, §9.1-920.
Corrections department, duties on receipt of prisoners, §53.1-23.2.
Criminal offenses.
Misuse of registry information, §9.1-918.
Notice of penalty on forms and documents, §9.1-919.
Day care centers.
Automatic notification of registration to certain entities, §9.1-914.
Designation of location where offender has no legal residence, §9.1-903.
Dissemination of information, §9.1-912.
Automatic notification of registration to certain entities, §9.1-914.
Internet site, §9.1-913.
Limitations on liability, §9.1-917.
Misuse of registry information, §9.1-918.
Requests for registry data, §9.1-916.
Drivers' licenses.
Application to include notice of duty, §46.2-323.
Information in application.
Compared with information in national sex offender registry, §46.2-323.

SEX OFFENDER REGISTRATION AND NOTIFICATION —Cont'd
Expungement of records.
Petition for removal from registry, §9.1-910.
Failure to register or reregister, §§9.1-907, 18.2-472.1.
False information, §18.2-472.1.
FOI act, records excluded from chapter, §2.2-3706.
Foster care.
Automatic notification of registration to certain entities, §9.1-914.
Goals, §9.1-900.
Harassment.
Misuse of registry information, §9.1-918.
Notice of penalty on forms and documents, §9.1-919.
Information included, §9.1-903.
Maintenance, §9.1-911.
Information technologies agency.
Exemption of information systems from provisions related to, §9.1-921.
Internet site.
Dissemination of information, §9.1-913.
Intimidation.
Misuse of registry information, §9.1-918.
Notice of penalty on forms and documents, §9.1-919.
Investigations.
Failure to register or reregister, §9.1-907.
Juvenile justice department.
Release or discharge of person for whom registration required.
Notice of registration requirements, §16.1-278.7:02.
Limitations on liability.
Dissemination of information, §9.1-917.
Maintenance, §§9.1-911, 19.2-390.1.
Mentally incapacitated victims.
Determinations by court and defendant's advice of rights, §9.1-902.
Minor victims.
Determinations by court and defendant's advice of rights, §9.1-902.
Misuse of registry information, §9.1-918.
Notice of penalty on forms and documents, §9.1-919.
Motor vehicles department.
Electronic transfer of information.
Change of address notification, §46.2-324.
DMV identification cards, §46.2-345.
Driver education program, §46.2-323.
Expiration of drivers' license, §46.2-330.
Nonresident offenders.
Registration, when required, §9.1-905.
Notice.
Automatic notification of registration to certain entities, §9.1-914.
Electronic notification to requesting persons, §9.1-914.
Misuse of registry information.
Notice of penalty on forms and documents, §9.1-919.
Objections.
Failure to register or reregister.
Objection to affidavit of state police in lieu of testimony, §18.2-472.1.
Petition for relief from registration requirement, §9.1-909.
Petition for removal from registry, §9.1-910.

SEX OFFENDER REGISTRATION AND NOTIFICATION —Cont'd
Physically helpless victims.
Determinations by court and defendant's advice of rights, §9.1-902.
Postrelease supervisions for conviction of registration violations.
Felons sentenced for offenses committed on or after July 1, 2006, §19.2-295.2:1.
Prima facie evidence.
Failure to register or reregister.
Affidavit of state police prima facie evidence of failure to register, §18.2-472.1.
Procedures for registration, §9.1-903.
Proof of residence, §9.1-903.
Purpose, §9.1-900.
Registration.
Colleges and universities.
Enrollment or employment at institutions of higher learning.
Information required, §9.1-906.
Duration of registration requirements, §9.1-908.
Failure to register or reregister, §§9.1-907, 18.2-472.1.
Jail prisoner escape or release notice, §53.1-116.1.
New residents, §9.1-905.
Nonresident offenders, when required, §9.1-905.
Offenses requiring registration, §9.1-902.
People required to register, §9.1-901.
Petition for relief from requirement, §9.1-909.
Prisoner intake notice, §53.1-116.1:01.
Procedures, §9.1-903.
Release of certain prisoners, §53.1-116.1.
Reregistration, §9.1-904.
Duration of registration requirements, §9.1-908.
Failure to register or reregister, §§9.1-907, 18.2-472.1.
Petition for relief from requirement, §9.1-909.
Release of certain prisoners.
Duty to register, §53.1-116.1.
Reports by law-enforcement officers, etc., §19.2-390.
Requests for registry data.
Virginia criminal sentencing commission, §9.1-916.
Required registration.
Offenses requiring registration, §9.1-902.
People required to register, §9.1-901.
Reregistration, §9.1-904.
Duration of registration requirements, §9.1-908.
Failure to register or reregister, §§9.1-907, 18.2-472.1.
Petition for relief from requirement, §9.1-909.
Rules and regulations, §9.1-915.
School bus drivers.
Commercial driver's licenses.
Cancellation of endorsement for conviction of offense requiring registration, §46.2-341.18:3.
Instruction permit to drive school bus.
Non-eligibility while registration required, §46.2-341.10.
Prohibition from driving school bus while registration required, §46.2-339.
Schools.
Automatic notification of registration to certain entities, §9.1-914.
Registration of school to receive notice of offender registration, §22.1-79.
Secure facilities.
Receipt of person for whom registration required.
Information to be forwarded to state police, §16.1-249.1.

SEX OFFENDER REGISTRATION AND NOTIFICATION —Cont'd
Sentencing commission.
Requests for registry data, §9.1-916.
Severability of provisions, §9.1-920.
Sexually violent offenses.
Offense for which registration is required, §9.1-902.
State police department.
Dissemination of information, §9.1-912.
Rules and regulations, §9.1-915.
Sentencing commission.
Requests for registry data, §9.1-916.
Statewide automated victim notification (SAVIN) system.
Use of registry data by, §9.1-922.
Superintendent of state police.
Duties, §19.2-390.1.
Time for registration, §9.1-903.
Duration of registration requirements, §9.1-908.
Time for reregistration, §9.1-904.
Duration of registration requirements, §9.1-908.
Venue.
Failure to register, providing false registration information, §18.2-472.1.
Victim of offense is minor, physically helpless or mentally incapacitated.
Determination by court and defendant's advice of rights, §9.1-902.
Virginia criminal sentencing commission.
Requests for registry data, §9.1-916.
Virginia information technologies agency.
Exemption of information systems from provisions related to, §9.1-921.

SEX OFFENDER TREATMENT PROVIDERS.
Certified practices advisory committee, §54.1-3611.

SEX OFFENSES PROHIBITING PROXIMITY TO CHILDREN, §18.2-370.2.
Punishment authorized for felony, §18.2-10.
Punishment authorized for misdemeanor offense, §18.2-11.

SEX OFFENSES PROHIBITING RESIDING IN PROXIMITY TO CHILDREN, §18.2-370.3.

SEXUAL ABUSE.
Child sexual abuse.
See CHILD SEXUAL ABUSE.
Defined, §18.2-67.10.
Landlord and tenant.
Termination of tenancies.
Early termination by victims of family abuse, sexual abuse or criminal sexual assault, §§55-225.16, 55-248.21.
Persons with disability.
Limitation of actions.
When cause of action deemed to accrue, §8.01-249.
Schools, sexual abuse of student by teacher or school board employee.
Policies of school board to address complaints, §22.1-253.13:7.
Sexual abuse defined, §18.2-67.10.
Sexual battery, §18.2-67.4.
Aggravated sexual battery, §18.2-67.3.
Bail.
Presumption against admission to bail, §19.2-120.
Jail prisoner escape or release notice, §53.1-116.1.

SEXUAL ABUSE —Cont'd
Sexual battery —Cont'd
Aggravated sexual battery —Cont'd
Prisoner intake notice, §53.1-116.1:01.
Punishment upon conviction of certain subsequent felony sexual assault, §18.2-67.5:2.
Bail.
Presumption against admission to bail, §19.2-120.
Punishment upon conviction of third misdemeanor offense, §18.2-67.5:1.
Statute of limitations.
Persons with disability.
When cause of action deemed to accrue, §8.01-249.
Victim's identity.
Nondisclosure of information revealing, §19.2-11.2.

SEXUAL ASSAULT, §§18.2-61 to 18.2-67.10.
Abduction with intent to defile, §18.2-48.
Seizure and forfeiture of property used in connection with abduction, §19.2-386.32.
Suspension of sentence, placing on probation, §19.2-303.
Suspended sentence in addition to active sentence, §18.2-48.
Threatening, attempting or assisting, §18.2-49.
Aggravated sexual battery, §18.2-67.3.
Jail prisoner escape or release notice, §53.1-116.1.
Prisoner intake notice, §53.1-116.1:01.
Attempts, §18.2-67.5.
Jail prisoner escape or release notice, §53.1-116.1.
Prisoner intake notice, §53.1-116.1:01.
Bail.
Presumption against admission to bail, §19.2-120.
Carnal knowledge of child between thirteen and fifteen, §18.2-63.
Convict escape or release notice, §53.1-160.1.
Jail prisoner escape or release notice, §53.1-116.1.
Prisoner intake notice, §53.1-116.1:01.
Carnal knowledge of juvenile detained in jail, detention facility or committed to juvenile justice department, §18.2-64.1.
Jail prisoner escape or release notice, §53.1-116.1.
Prisoner intake notice, §53.1-116.1:01.
Child victims' testimony.
Use of two-way closed-circuit television, §18.2-67.9.
Civil commitment of sexually violent predators, §§37.2-900 to 37.2-920.
See SEXUALLY VIOLENT PREDATORS, CIVIL COMMITMENT.
Confidentiality of records.
Persons receiving domestic or sexual violence services, §63.2-104.1.
Convict escape or release notice, §53.1-160.1.
Correctional employee carnal knowledge of defendant or convicted person, §18.2-64.2.
Database of prisoners incarcerated for sexually violent offenses.
Director's duties, §§37.2-903, 37.2-905.1.
Death of victim, §18.2-63.1.
Definitions, §18.2-67.10.
Depositions of complaining witnesses, §18.2-67.
Discretionary felony sentencing guidelines, §17.1-805.
Evidence.
Admissibility, §18.2-67.7.
False accusations.
Impeachment of witnesses, prior false accusations in sexual assault cases, VA SCt Rule 2:608.

SEXUAL ASSAULT —Cont'd
Evidence —Cont'd
Hearsay exceptions.
Recent complaints, VA SCt Rule 2:803.
Prior sexual conduct, VA SCt Rule 2:412.
Fabrication of charge against accused, admissibility of evidence showing, §18.2-67.7.
False accusations.
Impeachment of witnesses, prior false accusations in sexual assault cases, VA SCt Rule 2:608.
Forcible sodomy, §18.2-67.1.
Jail prisoner escape or release notice, §53.1-116.1.
Prisoner intake notice, §53.1-116.1:01.
Freedom of information act.
Exclusions from chapter.
Rape crisis center records, §2.2-3705.2.
Hearsay exceptions.
Recent complaint exception, §19.2-268.2.
Hepatitis B or C.
Testing person charged, §18.2-62.
HIV testing of persons charged, §18.2-62.
Husband and wife.
Compelling spousal testimony, §19.2-271.2.
Inanimate or animate sexual penetration.
Firearm used or displayed, §18.2-53.1.
Murder of the first degree, §18.2-32.
Object sexual penetration, §18.2-67.2.
Jail prisoner escape or release notice, §53.1-116.1.
Prisoner intake notice, §53.1-116.1:01.
Interception of wire, electronic or oral communication.
Order authorizing.
When attorney general may apply, §19.2-66.
Juvenile serious or habitual offender comprehensive action program, §§16.1-330.1, 16.1-330.2.
Landlord and tenant.
Termination of tenancies.
Early termination by victims of family abuse, sexual abuse or criminal sexual assault, §§55-225.16, 55-248.21.
Law enforcement agencies.
Policies and procedures for response, §9.1-1301.
Medical personnel performing physical evidence recovery kit.
Sexual assault victims incapable of making informed decision, §54.1-2970.1.
Mob crimes, §18.2-42.1.
Object sexual penetration, §18.2-67.2.
Inanimate or animate sexual penetration.
Firearm used or displayed, §18.2-53.1.
Murder of the first degree, §18.2-32.
Jail prisoner escape or release notice, §53.1-116.1.
Prisoner intake notice, §53.1-116.1:01.
Personal identifying information.
Confidentiality.
Records of persons receiving domestic or sexual violence services, §63.2-104.1.
Person transported through or across Commonwealth.
Venue, §18.2-359.
Physical resistance, proof not required, §18.2-67.6.
Polygraph examinations.
Victim not to be required to submit to as condition of proceeding with investigation, §19.2-9.1.
Preliminary hearings closed, §18.2-67.8.
Prior sexual conduct.
Evidence, VA SCt Rule 2:412.

SEXUAL ASSAULT —Cont'd
Rape.
See RAPE.
Reputation or opinion evidence of complaining witness.
Admissibility, §18.2-67.7.
Resistance physically, proof not required, §18.2-67.6.
Schools and education.
Sexual assault avoidance, treatment, and counseling.
Family life education, §§22.1-207.1, 22.1-207.1:1.
Sentence of person twice previously convicted of certain violent felonies, §19.2-297.1.
Sexual conduct between complaining witness and accused.
Admissibility, §18.2-67.7.
Sexually violent predators.
Civil commitment, §§37.2-900 to 37.2-920.
See SEXUALLY VIOLENT PREDATORS, CIVIL COMMITMENT.
Office of sexually violent predator services.
Establishment, §37.2-900.1.
Subsequent felony sexual assaults punishment upon conviction, §18.2-67.5:2.
Suspension of sentence, placing on probation, §19.2-303.
Television testimony of child victim, §18.2-67.9.
Treatment program for prisoners convicted of, §37.2-903.
Unchaste character or prior sexual conduct of complaining witness.
Admissibility, §18.2-67.7.
Venue.
Person transported through or across Commonwealth, §18.2-359.
Victim under 18 years of age, §18.2-359.
Victim's death, §18.2-63.1.
Victim's identity.
Nondisclosure of information revealing, §19.2-11.2.
Violent felony sexual assault.
Punishment upon conviction of subsequent assault, §18.2-67.5:3.
Witnesses.
Impeachment, prior false accusations in sexual assault cases, VA SCt Rule 2:608.
Workers' compensation.
Coverage of victims, §65.2-301.

SEXUAL BATTERY, §18.2-67.4.
Aggravated sexual battery, §18.2-67.3.
Bail.
Presumption against admission to bail, §19.2-120.
Jail prisoner escape or release notice, §53.1-116.1.
Payment of medical fees in gathering evidence, §19.2-165.1.
Prisoner intake notice, §53.1-116.1:01.
Punishment upon conviction of certain subsequent felony sexual assault, §18.2-67.5:2.
Suspension of sentence, placing on probation, §19.2-303.
Attempts, §§18.2-67.4, 18.2-67.5.
Aggravated sexual battery, §18.2-67.3.
Jail prisoner escape or release notice, §53.1-116.1.
Prisoner intake notice, §53.1-116.1:01.
Punishment upon conviction of third misdemeanor offense, §18.2-67.5:1.
Carrying of concealed weapon by person convicted of.
Disqualification for concealed weapons permit, §18.2-308.09.

SEXUAL BATTERY —Cont'd
Child victims' testimony.
Using two-way closed-circuit television, §18.2-67.9.
Death of victim, §18.2-63.1.
Deposition of complaining witness, §18.2-67.
Discretionary felony sentencing guidelines, §17.1-805.
Hepatitis B or C.
Testing person charged, §18.2-62.
HIV testing of persons charged, §18.2-62.
Infected sexual battery, §18.2-67.4:1.
Medical fees in gathering evidence, §19.2-165.1.
Mob crimes, §18.2-42.1.
Physical resistance, proof not required, §18.2-67.6.
Preliminary hearings, closing, §18.2-67.8.
Punishment upon conviction of third misdemeanor offense, §18.2-67.5:1.
Rape shield law, §18.2-67.7.
Recent complaint hearsay exception, §19.2-268.2.
Sentence of person twice previously convicted of certain violent felonies, §19.2-297.1.
Unchaste character or prior sexual conduct of complaining witness, §18.2-67.7.
Venue, person transported through or across Commonwealth, §18.2-359.
Victim's identity.
Nondisclosure of information revealing, §19.2-11.2.

SEXUALLY TRANSMITTED DISEASES, §§32.1-55 to 32.1-60.

SEXUALLY VIOLENT OFFENSES.
Sex offender and crimes against minors registry.
Generally, §§9.1-900 to 9.1-922.
See SEX OFFENDER REGISTRATION AND NOTIFICATION.
Offense for which registration is required, §9.1-902.

SEXUALLY VIOLENT PREDATORS, CIVIL COMMITMENT, §§37.2-900 to 37.2-920.
Advisory board.
Appointment by commissioner, powers, duties, immunity, §37.2-916.
Alternatives to full commitment.
Report by commissioner, §37.2-908.
Appointment of counsel for person subject to commitment, §37.2-915.
Assessment of prisoner for possible commitment, §§37.2-904, 37.2-905.1.
Attorney general to represent Commonwealth, §37.2-915.
Burden of proof.
Review of continuation of secure inpatient treatment.
Hearing, §37.2-910.
Challenges to validity of prior convictions or sentences.
Prisoner or defendant prohibited from raising, §37.2-901.
Civil proceedings, proceedings deemed, §37.2-908.
Clear and convincing proof.
Standard of proof at trial, §37.2-908.
Commission of new criminal offense.
Person committed to department of behavioral health and developmental services, §37.2-919.

SEXUALLY VIOLENT PREDATORS, CIVIL COMMITMENT —Cont'd
Commitment review committee, §37.2-902.
Freedom of information act.
Exclusions from chapter, §2.2-3703.
Conditional release, placing committed person on, §37.2-912.
Emergency custody of person placed on, revocation, §37.2-913.
Leaving Commonwealth without court permission, §37.2-918.
Modification or removal of conditions, §37.2-914.
Petition for, §37.2-911.
Criminal history information, health records, presentence and postsentence reports, victim impact statements.
Access to records, §37.2-905.2.
Department of behavioral health and developmental services provided, §37.2-909.
Database of prisoners incarcerated for sexually violent offenses.
Access to records, §37.2-905.2.
Director's duties, §§37.2-903, 37.2-905.1.
Definitions, §37.2-900.
Determining whether to file commitment petition.
Review of prisoner or defendant by attorney generally, §37.2-905.
Discovery, §37.2-908.
Emergency custody order.
Person placed on conditional release, §37.2-913.
Escape of committed person, §37.2-917.
Experts.
Right of prisoner or defendant to assistance of, §37.2-907.
Finding that person not sexually violent predator.
Actions by court, §37.2-908.
Hearings.
Probable cause hearing, §37.2-906.
Review of continuation of inpatient treatment hearing, §37.2-910.
Less restrictive alternatives to involuntary commitment, §37.2-908.
Mental health examination.
Assessment of prisoner for possible commitment, §§37.2-904, 37.2-905.1.
Court referral of mentally incompetent defendant to attorney general for review, §37.2-905.
Refusal by defendant or prisoner to cooperate, §37.2-906.
Mistrial, §37.2-908.
Modification or removal of conditions of release, §37.2-914.
Office of sexually violent predator services.
Establishment, §37.2-900.1.
Petition for civil commitment.
Mailing copy to prisoner or defendant, §37.2-906.
Petition for release, §37.2-911.
Placement of committed persons, §37.2-909.
Probable cause hearing, §37.2-906.
Recommendations following assessment of prisoner, §37.2-904.
Refusal by defendant or prisoner to cooperate with mental health examination, §37.2-906.
Review of continuation of secure inpatient treatment.
Hearing, procedure, reports, disposition, §37.2-910.
Review of prisoner or defendant by attorney generally, §37.2-905.

SEXUALLY VIOLENT PREDATORS, CIVIL COMMITMENT —Cont'd
Rights of prisoners and defendants, §37.2-901.
Secure facility for control, care and treatment of committed persons.
Placement of committed persons, §37.2-909.
Review of continuation of inpatient treatment hearing, §37.2-910.
Sex offender and crimes against minors registry.
Receipt of person required to register.
Information to be forwarded to state police, §16.1-249.1.
Siting new facility, designating existing facility.
Notice to elected officials of jurisdiction, advisory committee, §37.2-909.
Standard of proof at trial.
Clear and convincing proof, §37.2-908.
Treatment program for prisoners convicted of rape or sexual assault, §37.2-903.
Trial, time for holding, jury trial, right to, §37.2-908.
Unconditional release.
Petition, §37.2-911.

SHAD.
Taking methods, restrictions, §29.1-531.

SHAKEN BABY SYNDROME.
State department of social services.
Information related to, §63.2-214.2.

SHAKESPEARE FESTIVAL.
Virginia Shakespeare Festival, Williamsburg, designated as official Shakespeare festival of the Commonwealth, §1-510.

SHARECROPPERS.
Advances secured by fraudulent promise to perform agricultural labor, §18.2-201.
Distress.
Rent payments not in money.
Remedy, §55-238.
Failure to perform promise to deliver crop, §18.2-200.
Removal of crop by tenant before rents and advances satisfied, §18.2-100.

SHARED RIDE TAXI SYSTEM, §15.2-949.

SHARED-USE PATHS.
Roller skates, skateboards, etc., §46.2-904.

SHARE INSURANCE.
Credit unions, §§6.2-1331 to 6.2-1343.

SHARES.
Stock generally.
See STOCK AND STOCKHOLDERS.

SHARING OF LOCAL CONSTITUTIONAL OFFICERS, §§15.2-1602, 15.2-1637.

SHEEP.
Destruction of sheep.
Shooting enclosures, §§3.2-6035 to 3.2-6042.
False pedigree, §18.2-205.
Larceny, §18.2-97.
Livestock.
Diseases.
See LIVESTOCK AND ANIMAL DISEASES.
Generally.
See LIVESTOCK.

SHEEP INDUSTRY BOARD, §§3.2-2100 to 3.2-2114.
Assessments.
Collection of, §3.2-2112.

SHEEP INDUSTRY BOARD —Cont'd
Assessments —Cont'd
Delinquent assessments, §3.2-2114.
Disposition of, §3.2-2112.
Referendum, §3.2-2112.
Definitions, §3.2-2100.
Duties and responsibilities, §3.2-2101.
Education.
Referendum, §3.2-2104.
Established, §3.2-2101.
Governor.
Action on referendum results, §3.2-2109.
Market development.
Referendum, §3.2-2104.
Membership, §3.2-2103.
Misdemeanors, §3.2-2114.
Predator control.
Referendum, §3.2-2104.
Promotion of sheep industry.
Referendum, §3.2-2104.
Prosecution, §3.2-2114.
Purposes, §3.2-2101.
Quorum, §3.2-2103.
Records, §3.2-2113.
Referendum, §3.2-2104.
Action of governor, §3.2-2109.
Assessments, §3.2-2104.
Collection and distribution of, §3.2-2112.
Delinquent assessments, §3.2-2114.
Ballot rules, §3.2-112.
Distribution of ballots, §3.2-2106.
Canvass of results, §§3.2-112, 3.2-2106.
Certification of results, §3.2-2106.
Conduct of, §3.2-112.
Management of, §3.2-2106.
Notice, §3.2-2106.
Persons eligible to vote, §3.2-2108.
Question printed on ballots, §3.2-2107.
Reports to tax commissioner, §3.2-2112.
Research.
Referendum, §3.2-2104.
Sheep industry promotion and development fund.
Created, §3.2-2111.
Dedicated revenues, diversion, §3.2-1100.
Subsequent referendum, §3.2-2105.

SHELL BUILDING INITIATIVE.
Locality or other political subdivision participating in programs, §15.2-941.

SHELLEY'S CASE.
Abolishment of rule, §55-14.

SHELLFISH.
Clams generally, §§28.2-500 to 28.2-562.
See OYSTERS AND CLAMS.
Crabs, §§28.2-700 to 28.2-713.
See CRABS.
Eels.
Pots.
Channel restrictions, §28.2-710.
Identification, §28.2-712.
Health and sanitation provisions.
Generally, §§28.2-800 to 28.2-826.
See FISHING, TIDAL WATERS.
Oyster planting grounds, §§28.2-600 to 28.2-650.
See OYSTER PLANTING GROUNDS.
Oysters generally, §§28.2-500 to 28.2-562.
See OYSTERS AND CLAMS.

SHELTER CARE FOR CHILDREN.
Juvenile detention and other care facilities generally, §§16.1-315 to 16.1-322.7.
See JUVENILE DETENTION AND OTHER CARE FACILITIES.

SHELTERS.
Animal shelters.
See ANIMAL SHELTERS.
Emergencies or disasters.
Immunity of person owning or controlling real estate or other premises.
Voluntarily and without compensation granting use of premises, §44-146.23.
Motor vehicle sales and use tax exemption for vehicles, §58.1-2403.
School buses.
Shelters on bus routes, §22.1-185.

SHENANDOAH.
Cemeteries.
Location restrictions, §57-26.
Towns generally.
See TOWNS.

SHENANDOAH COUNTY.
Automobile graveyards, screening ordinance, §15.2-903.
Confederate cemeteries and graves.
Disbursement of funds appropriated for upkeep, §10.1-2211.
Local and regional libraries.
Boards not mandatory, §42.1-36.
Mines and minerals.
Presumed to exist in certain lands, §55-154.
Suits to extinguish claim or right, §55-155.
Port of Virginia economic and infrastructure development zone grant fund, §62.1-132.3:2.
Public defenders office.
Established, §19.2-163.04.
Revolutionary war cemeteries and graves.
Disbursement of funds appropriated for upkeep, §10.1-2211.1.
School board.
Salary of members, §22.1-32.
Winchester regional airport authority, 1987 ch 687, 1995 ch 258, 1995 ch 338.

SHENANDOAH NATIONAL PARK.
Jurisdiction.
Commonwealth and United States, §1-402.

SHENANDOAH RIVER.
Scenic river, §10.1-417.

SHENANDOAH VALLEY REGIONAL AIRPORT COMMISSION, 1956 ch 628, 1958 ch 396, 1978 ch 18, 1988 ch 209, 1994 ch 773.

SHERBETS.
Generally, §§3.2-5212 to 3.2-5217.
See MILK AND MILK PRODUCTS.

SHERIFFS, VA Const Art VII §4.
Abduction, disclosure of information and assistance to, §18.2-50.
Abolition of constitutional offices.
Referendum election, §24.2-685.
Change in form of government having effect of abolishing office, §24.2-686.
Absence without leave from National Guard.
Taking person into custody, §44-41.1.
Account of receipts and disbursements, §15.2-1615.

SHERIFFS —Cont'd
Allowances to injured sheriffs or deputy sheriffs and dependents.
Authorization of governing body of locality to make, §15.2-1511.
Animals used or trained by law enforcement agencies.
Killing or injuring, §18.2-144.1.
Appeal of compensation board decisions, §15.2-1636.9.
Appropriation of funds for operation of office, §15.2-1613.
Arrest records.
Records kept by sheriff, §15.2-1722.
Arrest without warrant, §19.2-81.
Family abuse or violence, §19.2-81.3.
Stalking, §19.2-81.3.
Assault and battery against, §18.2-57.
Assistance to officer in execution of office, refusal, §18.2-463.
Attendance of court as officer, §17.1-112.
Attorneys' fees and expenses when prosecuted for act arising out of performance of duties, §15.2-1607.
Audit of books, papers, etc., §15.2-1615.
Auxiliary police forces in localities, §§15.2-1731 to 15.2-1736.
See POLICE.
Barricades, lines and perimeters established.
Crossing, §18.2-414.2.
Bicycles.
Disposition of unclaimed bicycles in possession, §15.2-1720.
Bill for boarding or lodging juries.
Presentation to governing body, §15.2-1614.1.
Board and lodging of juries.
Presentation of bill to governing body, §15.2-1614.1.
Boating safety.
Enforcement of provisions, §29.1-745.
Bonds.
Local officers generally, §§15.2-1527 to 15.2-1533.
See LOCAL OFFICERS AND EMPLOYEES.
Penalty of bond, §15.2-1528.
Bribery of public officers generally, §§18.2-438 to 18.2-450.
See PUBLIC OFFICERS AND EMPLOYEES.
Capital murder, killing law enforcement officer, §18.2-31.
Carnal knowledge of defendant or convicted person, §18.2-64.2.
Carrying concealed weapons.
Inapplicability of provisions, §18.2-308.
Central criminal records exchange, reports to, §19.2-390.
Virginia crime code references, required use, §19.2-390.01.
Chief deputy.
Authority of death of sheriff, §15.2-1617.
Child abuse or neglect reports.
Reason to suspect, required reports, fine for failure, §63.2-1509.
Circuit courts.
Attendance of court, §17.1-112.
City status granted town.
Appointment by circuit court, §15.2-3826.
Elections, §15.2-3820.
Qualification for office, §15.2-3821.
Sharing offices, §15.2-3822.
Terms of office, §15.2-3820.

SHERIFFS —Cont'd
City status granted town —Cont'd
Town sergeant to continue in office and be sheriff, §15.2-3818.
Transfer of jurisdiction, §15.2-3822.
Vacancy, §15.2-3821.
Civil commitment of mentally ill persons.
Persons with intellectual disability.
Jail confinement with criminals, prohibited, §37.2-832.
Transportation of admitted persons.
Detention in jail after order of admission, §37.2-831.
Clerical assistance expenses.
Recordkeeping, §15.2-1609.4.
Closed circuit television system.
Allowance of expense by compensation board, §15.2-1615.1.
Collection of delinquent local taxes other than real estate, §58.1-3934.
Collection of money payable to state.
Writ of venditioni exponas, §§8.01-211 to 8.01-213.
Communicable disease reports, §32.1-116.3.
Communications system.
Joint state and local communication systems, §§52-16 to 52-19.
Compelling attendance of witnesses.
Inmates as witnesses.
Confinement overnight in municipal correctional facilities, §8.01-410.
Confidentiality of records concerning child, §16.1-301.
Conservation police officers.
Ex officio wardens, §29.1-202.
County board form of government, §15.2-408.
County executive form of government.
Compensation and expense allowances paid by compensation board to county adopting form of government, §15.2-1609.8.
Powers and duties, §15.2-530.
Selection, terms and vacancies, §15.2-536.
County manager form of government.
Compensation and expense allowances paid by compensation board to county adopting form of government, §15.2-1609.8.
Selection, term and vacancies, §15.2-635.
Course of instruction to be completed by deputy sheriff.
Completion required, §15.2-1612.1.
Courthouse security, §§53.1-119, 53.1-120.
Courts-martial.
Processes and sentences, execution, §44-50.
Naval militia, §44-71.
Criminal fines and penalties.
Collection and disposition of fines, §19.2-350.
Criminal history background.
Appointment of deputies, §15.2-1603.
Crop liens for advances to tenants and laborers.
Verified statements of advances, §43-29.
Dead bodies.
Disposition, §32.1-288.
Death of sheriff during term of office, §15.2-1617.
Allowances by governing body of locality, §15.2-1511.
Decibel level of sound.
Proper equipment to determine.
Standards established by division of purchases and supply, §2.2-1112.

SHERIFFS —Cont'd
Default or misconduct in office by deputy or other officer, §§15.2-1623 to 15.2-1625.
Delinquent local taxes other than real estate, collection, §58.1-3934.
Deposit of funds, §15.2-1615.
Deputies.
Acting in place of sheriff, §15.2-1616.
Allowances to injured deputy sheriffs and dependents.
Authorization of governing body of locality to make, §15.2-1511.
Health insurance continued, §15.2-1511.01.
Use of accrued vacation, compensatory or sick leave to supplement allowance, §15.2-1511.01.
Appointment, powers, removal, §15.2-1603.
Auxiliary, reserve or special deputies.
Vehicles used by.
Personal property tax classification, §58.1-3506.
Certification through training required, §15.2-1706.
Chief deputy.
Authority on death of sheriff, §15.2-1617.
Collection of fees and payment into treasury of county or city, §15.2-1609.3.
Compensable injury suffered by deputy.
Allowance authorized, §15.2-1511.
Health insurance continued, §15.2-1511.01.
Use of accrued vacation, compensatory or sick leave to supplement, §15.2-1511.01.
Completion by full-time deputy of course of instruction, §15.2-1612.1.
Counties where no police department has been established.
Authority and immunity of sheriff and deputies, §15.2-1730.1.
Courtroom security officers, correctional officers or law-enforcement officers.
Salaries, §15.2-1609.2.
Death of sheriff during term of office, §15.2-1617.
Decertification, §15.2-1707.
Default or misconduct in office, §§15.2-1623 to 15.2-1625.
Employment by county or city of greater number of law enforcement deputies than fixed by compensation board.
Payment of compensation by county or city, §15.2-1609.1.
Employment of off-duty officers, §15.2-1712.
Expenses incurred, recordkeeping, §15.2-1609.4.
Health insurance.
Continuation.
Compensable injury suffered by deputy, §15.2-1511.01.
Jury service.
Automatic exemption, §8.01-341.
Law-enforcement deputies, county without police force.
Number employed, §15.2-1609.1.
Legal fees and expenses for prosecution of act committed in discharge of duties, §15.2-1711.
Local vehicle licenses.
Issuance free of charge for vehicles owned by deputies, §46.2-752.
Mileage allowances, §15.2-1609.3.
Minimum qualifications for office, §15.2-1705.
Number, §15.2-1609.1.
Part-time.
Compensation, §15.2-1609.9.

SHERIFFS —Cont'd
Deputies —Cont'd
Part-time —Cont'd
Services performed by, record and reports, §15.2-1609.9.
Premises liability.
Duty of care owed to law enforcement officers, §8.01-226.
Record of expenses incurred, §15.2-1609.4.
Reserve deputies.
Vehicles used by.
Personal property tax classification, §58.1-3506.
Salaries, §15.2-1609.2.
Payment by Commonwealth, §15.2-1609.7.
Serving as town sergeant of town located in county, §15.2-1534.
Special deputies.
Vehicles used by.
Personal property tax classification, §58.1-3506.
Supervisors or investigators.
Salary, §15.2-1609.2.
Virginia retirement system.
County or city participating.
Benefits provided deputies, §51.1-138.
Detoxification centers.
Transporting public inebriates to, §18.2-388.
Direction of traffic.
Authority to deputize persons, §46.2-1310.
Hand signals, §46.2-1310.
Disability in performance of duty.
Compensating sheriff or deputy, §15.2-1618.
Distress.
Landlord and tenant, §55-230.
Entry by force to levy or attach, §55-235.
Rent payments not in money, §55-238.
Return of execution, §55-237.
Storage and sale of personal property removed from premises, §55-237.1.
Residential premises, §55-248.38:2.
Local taxes, collection by distress generally, §§58.1-3940 to 58.1-3961.
See TAX COLLECTION.
District court judges, dual officeholding prohibited, §16.1-69.19.
Drivers' licenses.
Service of notice of suspension or revocation of license, §46.2-416.
Fee for service, §46.2-370.
Driving while intoxicated.
Preliminary analysis of breath.
Duties and responsibilities, §18.2-267.
Dual office holding, §15.2-1534, VA Const Art VII §6.
Duties, §15.2-1609.
Ejectment.
Authority to store and sell personal property removed from premises, §8.01-156.
Election, §§15.2-1609, 24.2-217, VA Const Art VII §4.
Economic interest statement as requirement of candidate, §24.2-502.
Primary schedule for year 2001 and each tenth year thereafter, §24.2-515.1.
Vacancies, special election, §24.2-226.
Electronic surveillance generally.
See ELECTRONIC SURVEILLANCE.
Eminent domain.
Removal of forcible resistance to right of entry, §25.1-246.

SHERIFFS —Cont'd
Escape of prisoner convicted of or charged with felony.
Voluntarily allowing, §18.2-475.
Escape of prisoner not convicted of or charged with felony.
Willfully and deliberately permitting, §18.2-476.
Escheats.
Inquests.
Jury of inquests, §55-173.
Expense allowances paid by Commonwealth, §15.2-1609.7.
Expense allowances paid by compensation board.
Counties adopting certain optional forms of government, §15.2-1609.8.
Expense of office request filed with compensation board, §15.2-1636.7.
Expenses by locality to provide uniforms and personal equipment, §15.2-1613.
Expenses, record, §15.2-1609.4.
Explosives.
Notice of theft to, §59.1-139.
Facsimile service of process on corporations, §13.1-637.
False alarms, §18.2-461.
False impersonations, §18.2-174.
False reports to police officers, §18.2-461.
Family abuse or violence.
Emergency protective orders.
When authorized, §16.1-253.4.
Fees.
Collection and payment into treasury of county or city, §15.2-1609.3.
Distraining or levying on tangible property officer neither sells nor receives payment, §15.2-1609.3.
Effort to serve order, notice, etc., when person not found, §17.1-268.
Fieri facias.
Sale of property subject to prior security interest, §8.01-480.
Firearm or object similar in appearance, pointed, held or brandished.
Immunity from civil liability for making arrest under provision, §18.2-282.
Firearms disposal.
Disposal of unclaimed firearms in possession of sheriff, §15.2-1721.
Firearm shows.
Notice, §54.1-4201.1.
Fleeing or eluding law-enforcement officers, §46.2-817.
Fraudulent transactions discovered, reporting to auditor of, §30-138.
Funeral processions under sheriff's escort.
Fine schedule, VA SCt Rule 3B:2.
Impeding or disrupting, §46.2-828.1.
Prepayment of fine, §16.1-69.40:1.
Yielding right-of-way, §46.2-828.
Furloughed prisoners.
Notice of to sheriffs, §53.1-37.
Furniture and equipment purchases.
Payment for items, §15.2-1615.1.
General provisions as to local constitutional officers, §§15.2-1600 to 15.2-1607.
See LOCAL CONSTITUTIONAL OFFICERS.
Guards summoned or employed by jailer on order of court.
Payment of salaries and expenses, §19.2-328.

SHERIFFS —Cont'd
Gunshot wounds.
Reports on wounds by health care professionals, §54.1-2967.
Handgun purchases by, §59.1-148.3.
Hand signals for direction of traffic, §46.2-1309.
Hepatitis C test, positive results.
Convicted prostitutes or injection drug users tested.
Limited disclosure to, §18.2-346.1.
Hepatitis testing, §32.1-45.2.
Highway construction and maintenance by prisoners.
Notice to local law enforcement, §53.1-56.
HIV testing, §32.1-45.2.
Hostage or barricaded person situation.
Emergency control of telephone service, §18.2-50.2.
Hunting incident reports.
Duty of law-enforcement agency or emergency medical service provider to report, §29.1-530.4.
Hunting while under influence of intoxicant or narcotic drug.
Enforcement authority, §18.2-285.
Hypertension or heart disease.
Presumed to be suffered in line of duty, §15.2-1511.
Immunity from liability for acceptance of dead body for disposition, §32.1-288.
Immunity from liability for disclosure of information about former deputies, §15.2-1709.
Immunity of sheriffs and deputies in counties where no police department has been established, §15.2-1730.1.
Impersonating, §18.2-174.
Improper release of prisoners, §53.1-116.3.
Incident records.
Records kept by sheriff, §15.2-1722.
Injury or illness as result of performance of duty.
Compensation of sheriff or deputy, §15.2-1618.
Inmate needed as witness in civil action.
Confinement by sheriff in convenient city or county correctional institution, §8.01-410.
In person and photo lineups.
Written policies and procedures for conducting.
Establishment, required, §19.2-390.02.
Training standards and model policy, §9.1-102.
Inspection of books, papers and receipt books and statements.
Auditor of public accounts or other certified public accountant, §15.2-1615.
Interjurisdictional law-enforcement authority and agreements, §§15.2-1724 to 15.2-1730.
Investigative records.
Records kept by sheriff, §15.2-1722.
Jail duties, §§15.2-1609, 53.1-116 to 53.1-127.1.
Courthouse security, §§53.1-119, 53.1-120.
Failure to comply with requirements of board, §53.1-125.
Fee for costs of keeping prisoner, §53.1-131.3.
Contract for collection of fees owed, §53.1-127.5.
Installment or deferred payment agreements, §53.1-127.3.
Fines imposed upon prisoners, §53.1-116.
Fines imposed upon sheriffs, §53.1-118.
Good conduct credits, §53.1-116.
Home/electronic incarceration program, §53.1-131.2.

SHERIFFS —Cont'd
Jail duties —Cont'd
Improper release of prisoners, §53.1-116.3.
Industry programs, §§53.1-133.1 to 53.1-133.9.
Jail governance.
Participation, §53.1-106.
Keeper of jails, §53.1-116.2.
Prisoner provisions, §53.1-126.
Recordation, §§53.1-116, 53.1-123.
Daily prisoner tally, §53.1-122.
Rules violations, §53.1-117.
Reports, §53.1-121.
Court requested, §53.1-124.
Stores, §53.1-127.1.
Telephone services.
Fees considered public funds, §53.1-127.1.
Temporary guards, §53.1-93.
Transfers, §53.1-79.1.
Court adopted jails, §53.1-75.
Prisoner to be included in jailor account, §53.1-76.
Visitors, §53.1-127.
Fees for electronic visitation or messaging, §53.1-127.2.
Work release, §53.1-131.
Jail prisoner work on local government property, §53.1-129.
Jail prisoner work on property of sheriff, §53.1-130.
Job performance information disclosed to prospective employer of former deputy.
Immunity of sheriff for disclosure, §15.2-1709.
Judgment against officer for money due by officer, §15.2-1622.
Jurors.
Automatic exemption, §8.01-341.
Summoning to act impartially, §18.2-465.
Juvenile proceedings.
Service of summons, §16.1-264.
Juvenile records confidentiality, §16.1-301.
Killed in line of duty.
Allowances to dependents by governing body of locality, §15.2-1511.
Landlord and tenant.
Distress, §55-230.
Entry by force to levy or attach, §55-235.
Rent payments not in money, §55-238.
Return of execution, §55-237.
Storage and sale of personal property removed from premises, §55-237.1.
Residential premises, §55-248.38:2.
Notice service, §55-248.31:1.
Law enforcement expenditures.
State assistance to local government, §§9.1-165 to 9.1-172.
Law enforcement officers generally.
See LAW ENFORCEMENT OFFICERS.
Lease of real estate for collection of local taxes, §§58.1-3947, 58.1-3948.
Line of duty act, §§9.1-400 to 9.1-408.
Lineups.
In person and photo lineups.
Written policies and procedures for conducting.
Establishment, required, §19.2-390.02.
Training standards and model policy, §9.1-102.
Livestock liens for advances to tenants and laborers.
Verified statements of advances, §43-29.
Local constitutional officers generally, §§15.2-1600 to 15.2-1607.
See LOCAL CONSTITUTIONAL OFFICERS.

SHERIFFS —Cont'd
Lottery director to have powers of, §58.1-4006.
Machine gun manufacturer's and dealer's stock.
Inspection upon demand, §18.2-294.
Mailing order, warrant or process, §15.2-1620.
Mailing process, §15.2-1620.
Malicious bodily injury to law enforcement officers, §18.2-51.1.
Firearm used or displayed, §18.2-53.1.
Mechanics' and materialmen's liens.
Service of notices, §43-14.1.
Medical and rehabilitation of employees.
Appointment as deputies, §15.2-1603.
Mileage allowance, §15.2-1609.3.
Report as to mileage, §15.2-1609.4.
Militia duty exemption, §44-5.
Missing child reports.
Duty to immediately enter identifying and descriptive data, §15.2-1718.
Missing law enforcement officers.
Blue Alert program, §§52-34.7 to 52-34.9.
Missing senior adult reports.
Duties on receipt of, §15.2-1718.1.
Money received by officer.
Judgment against officer for money due, §15.2-1622.
Mopeds.
Disposition of unclaimed mopeds in possession, §15.2-1720.
Motor vehicles.
Auxiliary lights, §46.2-1029.
Auxiliary, reserve, or special deputies.
Vehicles used by.
Personal property tax classification, §58.1-3506.
Flashing blue or red and blue warning lights, §46.2-1022.
Flashing of headlights, §46.2-1029.1.
Markings, §15.2-1610.
Warnings, sirens and whistles, §46.2-1061.
Noise levels.
Proper equipment to determine decibel level of sound.
Standards established by division of purchases and supply, §2.2-1112.
Obligation of or for person in custody.
Limited by law, §15.2-1619.
Obstructing justice by threats, force or false statements, §18.2-460.
Office expenses.
Recordkeeping, §15.2-1609.4.
Parole of prisoners.
Notice prior to release, §53.1-160.
Partial or total disability in performance of duty, §15.2-1618.
Part-time deputies.
Compensation, §15.2-1609.9.
Services performed by, record and reports, §15.2-1609.9.
Pawnbrokers.
Records, §54.1-4011.
Reports, §54.1-4010.
Payment for certain items in budget, §15.2-1615.1.
Payment for services only as allowed by statute, §17.1-266.
Payment of salaries and expense allowances.
Commonwealth to pay, §15.2-1609.7.
Payments to sheriff, receipts for, §15.2-1621.

SHERIFFS —Cont'd
Personnel records.
Records kept by sheriff, §15.2-1722.
Police generally.
See POLICE.
Postage, payment, §15.2-1615.1.
Powers, §15.2-1609.
Counties where no police department has been established, §15.2-1730.1.
Precious metals dealers.
Exemptions from provisions, §54.1-4109.
Permits, §54.1-4108.
Record requirements, §§54.1-4101, 54.1-4101.1.
Premises liability.
Duty of care owed to law enforcement officers, §8.01-226.
Presumption as to injury or illness as result of performance of duty, §15.2-1618.
Prisoner construction and maintenance of highways, §53.1-56.
Prisoner estates.
Commitment to, §53.1-226.
Disposal of unclaimed personal property, §53.1-228.
Prisoner furloughs, §53.1-37.
Prisoner work for localities, state agencies or nonprofit organizations, §53.1-59.
Processing fee for admission to regional jail, §15.2-1613.1.
Protective orders.
Emergency protective orders.
Family abuse, §19.2-81.3.
When authorized, §16.1-253.4.
Public inebriates.
Transporting to detoxification centers, §18.2-388.
Purchase of office furniture, office equipment, stationery, etc.
Payment of items, §15.2-1615.1.
Radio signal, message or transmission.
Use during commission of crime, §18.2-462.1.
Receipt books, §15.2-1614.
Receipt for payments made to officers, §15.2-1621.
Judgment against officer for failing to make return, §15.2-1622.
Record of expenses incurred, §15.2-1609.4.
Record of services performed by part-time deputy, §15.2-1609.9.
Records, §15.2-1722.
Confidentiality of records concerning children, §16.1-301.
Referendum election for abolition of constitutional offices, §24.2-685.
Change in form of government having effect of abolishing office, §24.2-686.
Refusal to aid officer, §18.2-463.
Refusing to receive prisoners, §18.2-476.
Regional jails.
Processing fee, §15.2-1613.1.
Removal of public officers from office generally, §§24.2-230 to 24.2-238.
Repair costs of automobile police radio equipment.
Recordkeeping, §15.2-1609.4.
Reports.
Central criminal records exchange, §19.2-390.
Expenses, §15.2-1609.4.
Services performed by part-time deputies, §15.2-1609.9.
Travel expenses statement, §15.2-1609.5.

SHERIFFS —Cont'd
Resignation.
Date resignation becomes not revocable, §§24.2-226, 24.2-228.1.
Retention of books, checks, receipt books and statements, §15.2-1614.
Retention of unclaimed property in possession, §15.2-1719.
Retired officers.
Carrying concealed weapon, §18.2-308.
Reward offers.
Apprehension of escaped inmates, §19.2-7.
Riot or unlawful assembly.
Dispersal, duty, §18.2-411.
Immunity of officers quelling, §18.2-412.
Salaries, §15.2-1609.2.
Payment by Commonwealth, §15.2-1609.7.
Payment by compensation board.
Counties adopting certain optional forms of government, §15.2-1609.8.
Supplementation by county or city, §15.2-1605.1.
Sale of firearms by law-enforcement agencies, §59.1-148.4.
Sale of unclaimed property in possession of sheriff, §15.2-1719.
Sales.
Fee after distraining or levying on tangible personal property officer neither sells nor receives payment, §15.2-1609.3.
Settlement between parties to claim or suit.
Recovery of fees and expenses for levy and return and advertisement of sale, §15.2-1609.3.
Search warrants, execution, §19.2-56.
Secondhand article sales.
Building fixtures.
Inspections by sheriffs, §59.1-122.
Permits.
Issuance and revocation, §59.1-118.
Reports, §59.1-121.
Security for courthouse, §§53.1-119, 53.1-120.
Service of notice, process and other papers.
Clerk of circuit court to deliver or send process to sheriff, §17.1-214.
Corporations.
Facsimile service, §13.1-637.
Daily receipt of process from clerk's office, §8.01-294.
Deputy acting in place of sheriff, §15.2-1616.
Driver's license suspension or revocation notice, §46.2-416.
Fee for service, §46.2-370.
Fees.
Effort to serve order, notice, etc., when person not found, §17.1-268.
Fee transmitted by circuit court clerk to sheriff, §17.1-216.
Persons who may serve process, §8.01-293.
Process appearing to be duly served, §8.01-295.
Process sent by mail, §15.2-1620.
Return, §8.01-294.
State corporation commission writs, processes and orders, §12.1-29.
Tax commissioner, writs, processes and orders from, §58.1-217.
Territorial limits, §8.01-295.
Sexual battery of defendant or convicted person, §18.2-67.4.
Sexually violent predators, civil commitment.
Database of prisoners incarcerated for sexually violent offenses.
Access to records, §37.2-905.2.

SHERIFFS —Cont'd
Special police in localities, §§15.2-1737 to 15.2-1746.
See POLICE.
Standard uniforms, §15.2-1610.
State corporation commission.
Execution of writs, processes and orders, §12.1-29.
Statement as to travel expenses, §15.2-1609.5.
Stationery.
Payment for purchase, §15.2-1615.1.
Strip search policy, development, §19.2-59.1.
Supplies.
Payment for purchases, §15.2-1615.1.
Record of expenses, §15.2-1609.4.
Telephone equipment purchases.
Payment for items, §15.2-1615.1.
Telephone expenses.
Recordkeeping, §15.2-1609.4.
Terms, §§15.2-1609, 24.2-217, VA Const Art VII §4.
City status granted to town, §15.2-3820.
Tire puncturing device use authorized, §33.1-345.
Total disability retirement benefits, §15.2-1618.
Town granted city status.
Appointment by circuit court, §15.2-3826.
Elections, §15.2-3820.
Qualification for office, §15.2-3821.
Sharing of office, §15.2-3822.
Terms of office, §15.2-3820.
Town sergeant to continue in office and be sheriff, §15.2-3818.
Transfer of jurisdiction, §15.2-3822.
Vacancy, §15.2-3821.
Town law enforcement.
Tripartite contract with governing body, §15.2-1726.
Training.
Criminal justice training academies, §§15.2-1747 to 15.2-1753.
See CRIMINAL JUSTICE TRAINING ACADEMIES.
Travel expenses.
Agreement with county or city regarding, §15.2-1609.6.
Recordkeeping, §15.2-1609.4.
Submission of statement, §15.2-1609.5.
Trespass by hunters, fishers or trappers.
Enforcement of provisions, §18.2-136.1.
Unclaimed property in possession of sheriff.
Disposal, §15.2-1719.
Bicycles or mopeds, §15.2-1720.
Firearms or other weapons, §15.2-1721.
Uniforms, §15.2-1610.
Alternate clothing, §15.2-1611.
Expenses by locality to provide, §15.2-1613.
Unlawful wearing of officer's uniform, §§15.2-1612, 18.2-175.
Urban county executive form of government.
Compensation and expense allowances paid by compensation board to county adopting form of government, §15.2-1609.8.
Department of law enforcement, §15.2-836.
Vacancies in office.
City status granted town, §15.2-3821.
County board form of government, §15.2-408.
Interim appointment by court, §24.2-227.
Special election to fill, §24.2-226.
Time to qualify and give bond if required, §24.2-229.
Victims of crime.
Notification requirement, §53.1-133.02.
Immunity, §8.01-226.11.

SHERIFFS —Cont'd
Volunteer citizen support units.
Local vehicle licenses.
Issuance free of charge, §46.2-752.
Weapons.
Disposal of unclaimed firearms or other weapons in possession of sheriff, §15.2-1721.
Workers' compensation.
Coverage.
Off-duty, §65.2-102.
Employee defined, §65.2-101.
Heart disease.
Presumptions as to death or disability from, §65.2-402.
Hypertension.
Presumptions as to death or disability from, §65.2-402.
Injury where weather constitutes particular risk of employment of public safety officer, §65.2-301.1.
Service of commission subpoenas, §65.2-202.
Wounds caused by concealable weapons.
Reports by health care providers, §54.1-2967.
Writ of venditioni exponas.
Collection of money payable to state, §§8.01-211 to 8.01-213.

SHERIFFS' SALES.
Decedents' estates.
Disposition of property when no person entitled thereto, §64.2-611.
Distraining or levying on tangible property officer neither sells nor receives payment.
Fees to be collected, §15.2-1609.3.
Distress, §55-230.
Keeper liens.
Enforcement, §43-34.
Settlement between parties to claim or suit and sale not permitted.
Recovery of fees and expenses for levy and return and advertisement of sale, §15.2-1609.3.
Timber brands.
Unbranded timber, §59.1-115.

SHIELDS.
Underground coal mines.
Employees inside or outside to wear, §45.1-161.175.

SHIP MANUFACTURING AND SHIP REPAIR COMPANIES.
Community colleges.
Apprenticeship program for employees, §23-220.01.

SHIPPING SOLID WASTE OR MEDICAL WASTE UPON NAVIGABLE WATERS, §10.1-1454.1.

SHIPS.
ABC licenses.
Mixed beverages carrier licenses.
Common carriers of passengers, §4.1-210.
Attachment of ship of more than twenty tons, §8.01-538.
Ballast water discharge, §§28.2-109 to 28.2-111.
Boat common or contract carriers.
Generally.
See MOTOR LAUNCH CARRIERS.
Boat dealers, §§29.1-800 to 29.1-827.
Boating safety, §§29.1-734 to 29.1-746.
Boating under the influence, §19.2-81.
Boat registration and identification, §§29.1-700 to 29.1-711.

SHIPS —Cont'd
Boats and other watercraft.
See BOATS AND OTHER WATERCRAFT.
Boat titling certificates, §§29.1-712 to 29.1-733.1.
Uniform certificate of title for watercraft, §§29.1-733.2 to 29.1-733.29.
Branch pilots.
Generally, §§54.1-900 to 54.1-927.
See BRANCH PILOTS.
Sight-seeing carriers by boat.
See SIGHT-SEEING CARRIERS.
Watercraft sales and use tax, §§58.1-1400 to 58.1-1410.
See WATERCRAFT SALES AND USE TAX.

SHIPWRECKS.
Underwater historic property, §10.1-2214.

SHIPYARDS.
Criminal history record information.
Dissemination to, §19.2-389.

SHOCAP COMMITTEES, §16.1-330.1.
Immunity, §16.1-330.2.

SHOES.
Underground coal mines.
Protective footwear, §45.1-161.175.
X rays, fluoroscopes, etc., in fitting of footwear, §18.2-321.

SHOOTING AT CARS, TRAINS, VESSELS, ETC., §18.2-154.

SHOOTING AT MARKED VEHICLES, §18.2-154.

SHOOTING IN COMMITTING OR ATTEMPTING FELONY, §18.2-53.

SHOOTING PRESERVES, §§29.1-600 to 29.1-612.
Bobwhite quail.
Sales, §29.1-544.
Defined terms, §29.1-100.
Licensing, §29.1-600.
Nonresident hunting, §29.1-304.
Ownership or leasing prerequisite, §29.1-601.
Revocation, §29.1-609.
Nonmigratory game birds.
Hunting, §29.1-514.
Pen-raised game birds.
Hunting, §29.1-514.
Provision violations, §29.1-554.
Rules and regulations, §29.1-600.1.
Trespass upon licensed preserve, §18.2-131.

SHOOTING RANGES.
Applicability of local noise ordinance, §15.2-917.

SHOOTING WITH INTENT TO MAIM, KILL, ETC., §18.2-51.
Aggravated malicious wounding, §18.2-51.2.
Discretionary felony sentencing guidelines, §17.1-805.
Lesser offenses, conviction under certain indictments, §18.2-54.
Sentence of person twice previously convicted of certain violent felonies, §19.2-297.1.

SHOPLIFTING, §§18.2-23, 18.2-103.
Agents of merchant.
Defined, §18.2-106.
Arrest of suspects.
Child arrest, §16.1-246.
Immunity.
Exemption from civil liability, §8.01-226.9.
Civil action for damages, §8.01-44.4.

SHOPLIFTING —Cont'd
Civil liability to owner upon conviction, §18.2-104.1.
Detention of suspect, §18.2-105.1.
Child detention, §16.1-246.
Electronic detection devices to shield against.
Manufacture, sale, etc., §18.2-105.2.
Evidence.
Use of photographs as evidence, §19.2-270.1.
Immunity.
Detention of suspects.
Exemption from civil liability, §8.01-226.9.
Photographs.
Use of photographs as evidence, §19.2-270.1.
Prima facie evidence.
Willful concealment of goods and merchandise while still on premises, §18.2-23.
Proof of ownership to property, §19.2-284.
Punishment for conviction, §18.2-104.
Warrantless arrests.
Arrest without warrant authorized, §19.2-81.
Willful concealment of goods and merchandise while still on premises, §18.2-23.

SHOPPERS.
Private security services businesses.
Exceptions, §9.1-140.

SHOPPING CARTS.
Removal from store premises, §18.2-102.1.

SHOPPING CENTERS.
Drug transactions on premises.
Closure of nuisance premises, §§48-16, 48-17.
Common nuisance, §§18.2-258, 18.2-258.01.
Energy allocation equipment, §§56-245.2, 56-245.3.
Fire alarms.
Maliciously activating, §18.2-212.
Lists of tenants.
Owners or operators to file with commissioner of revenue, §58.1-3901.
Peeping or spying, §18.2-130.
Removal of carts from store premises, §18.2-102.1.
Smoke bombs.
Setting off in public buildings, §18.2-87.1.
Submetering, §§56-245.2, 56-245.3.

SHOPS.
Maintaining fortified drug houses, §18.2-258.02.

SHORE EROSION CONTROL, §§10.1-700 to 10.1-704.
Advisory service, §10.1-702.
Conservation and recreation department.
Duties, §10.1-701.
Dredged material.
Use for beach nourishment, §10.1-704.
Living shorelines.
Marine resources commission.
General permit, use for stabilizing tidal shorelines, §28.2-104.1.
Marine science institute.
Cooperation and coordination with, §10.1-703.
Shore erosion.
Defined, §10.1-700.

SHORELINES.
Comprehensive plan.
Coastal resource management guidance, §15.2-2223.2.
Living shorelines.
Marine resources commission.
General permit, use for stabilizing tidal shorelines, §28.2-104.1.

SHORELINES —Cont'd
Ungranted shores of the sea, marshes and meadowlands, §§28.2-1500 to 28.2-1514.
See UNGRANTED SHORES OF THE SEA.

SHORT-TERM DISABILITY.
Sickness and disability program for state employees.
Generally, §§51.1-1100 to 51.1-1140.
See SICKNESS AND DISABILITY PROGRAM.
State police with work-related injury, §9.1-401.1.

SHORT-TERM RENTALS.
Taxation.
Merchants' capital tax, §§58.1-3509, 58.1-3510.
Short-term rental personal property tax, §§58.1-3510.4 to 58.1-3510.7.

SHOTGUNS.
Carrying loaded firearms in public areas, §18.2-287.4.
Children or minors, possession or transportation of certain shotguns, §18.2-308.7.
Criminal history background check, firearms transfers, §18.2-308.2:2.
Hunting restrictions, §§29.1-519, 29.1-528.
Sawed-off shotguns generally, §§18.2-299 to 18.2-307.
Semi-automatic folding stock shotguns.
Delinquent children.
Driving privilege loss for possession, §16.1-278.9.
Serial number or other identification.
Removing, altering, etc., §18.2-311.1.
Streetsweepers.
Delinquent children.
Driving privilege loss for possession, §16.1-278.9.
Importation, sale, etc., §18.2-308.8.
Striker 12's.
Importation, sale, etc., §18.2-308.8.
Transportation of loaded rifle or shotgun.
Ordinances regulating, §15.2-915.2.
Use in commission of crime.
Forfeiture, §19.2-386.29.
Use or display in committing felony, §18.2-53.1.
Weapons generally.
See WEAPONS.
Weapons offenses generally.
See WEAPONS OFFENSES.

SHOW CAUSE ORDERS.
Attorney discipline.
District committees proceedings, VA SCt Rule Pt 6 §IV Par 13-16.
Driving while intoxicated.
Revocation of probation, education and rehabilitation of person convicted, §18.2-271.1.
Insurance companies, rehabilitation and liquidation.
Application for receiver by state corporation commission, §38.2-1505.
Juvenile disposition orders, §16.1-292.
Local treasurer securing final discharge from liability, §58.1-3146.
Nonlawyer not allowed to issue rule, §16.1-88.03.
Obscene books, proceeding against, §18.2-384.
Removal of public officers from office, §24.2-235.

SHOW CAUSE ORDERS —Cont'd
Service of notice, process and other papers.
Persons who may serve criminal show cause orders, §8.01-293.

SHRIMP.
Defined as crustacea, §28.2-800.

SHRINERS.
Special license plates for members, §46.2-746.7.

SHRINK WRAP LICENSES.
Uniform computer information transactions act, §§59.1-501.1 to 59.1-509.2.

SHRUBS.
Sales on highways.
Counties prohibiting, §15.2-1219.

SHURIKEN.
See MARTIAL ARTS WEAPONS.

SHUTTERS.
Roads, streets or public rights-of-way.
Localities permitting owners or occupants of property abutting, §15.2-2010.

SIBLINGS.
Assault and battery against family or household member, §§18.2-57.2, 18.2-57.3.
Foster care.
Placement and visitation for siblings, §63.2-900.2.
Visitation rights generally, §63.2-912.

SICK LEAVE.
County manager form of government.
Establishing times and conditions of employment, §15.2-640.
Local constitutional officers.
Employees of officer, §15.2-1605.
Sickness and disability program for state employees.
Generally, §§51.1-1100 to 51.1-1140.
See SICKNESS AND DISABILITY PROGRAM.
Nonparticipating employees, §51.1-1106.
Participating employees, §§51.1-1104, 51.1-1105.
Urban county executive form of government.
Establishing time and conditions of employment, §15.2-849.
Virginia retirement system.
Service credit for accumulated sick leave, §51.1-142.2.

SICKLE CELL DISEASES.
Discovery reports, §32.1-66.
Testing of infants, §32.1-65.
Failure to test, §32.1-73.
Treatment duties of board, §32.1-67.
Voluntary program for control, §§32.1-68, 32.1-69.

SICKNESS AND DISABILITY PROGRAM, §§51.1-1100 to 51.1-1140.
Accounting to board.
Policies to provide for, §51.1-1139.
Advance premium deposit reserve, §51.1-1139.
Board.
Defined, §51.1-1100.
Duties, §51.1-1101.
Powers, §51.1-1102.
Definitions, §51.1-1100.
Disability benefits.
Appeal of case decisions related to payment of, §51.1-1135.1.
Catastrophic disability.
Supplemental benefits for, §51.1-1131.

SICKNESS AND DISABILITY PROGRAM —Cont'd
Disability benefits —Cont'd
Employer contributions during disability absence, §51.1-1131.1.
Exclusions and limitations, §51.1-1135.
Felonies.
Benefits not payable to participating employee convicted of, §51.1-1135.
Health insurance coverage during disability absences, §51.1-1132.
Life and accident insurance coverage disability absences, §51.1-1133.
Nonwork related disability benefits, §§51.1-1109 to 51.1-1118.
Optional insurance during disability absences, §51.1-1134.
Work-related disability benefits, §§51.1-1119 to 51.1-1130.
Disability insurance trust fund, §51.1-1140.
Eligible employees.
Defined, §51.1-1100.
Participation in program, §51.1-1103.
Employer contributions during disability absence, §51.1-1131.1.
Exemption of benefits from process, §51.1-1138.
Family and personal leave, §§51.1-1107, 51.1-1108.
Funding of program, §51.1-1140.
Hybrid retirement program.
Disability program for participants, §§51.1-1150 to 51.1-1183.
See HYBRID RETIREMENT PROGRAM.
Limitation on coverage, §51.1-1136.
Long-term care insurance and benefits, §51.1-1135.2.
Nonwork related disability benefits, §§51.1-1109 to 51.1-1118.
Adjustments to disability benefits, §51.1-1114.
Applicability of provisions, §51.1-1109.
Cessation of disability benefits, §51.1-1116.
Elective surgery or other procedures, §51.1-1110.
Long-term disability benefit, §§51.1-1112, 51.1-1113.
Offsets not allowed, §51.1-1114.
Overpayment, §51.1-1114.
Rehabilitation incentive, §51.1-1115.
Service retirement of participating employees receiving, §51.1-1117.
Short-term disability benefit, §§51.1-1110, 51.1-1111.
Survivor benefits, §51.1-1118.
Participating employees.
Sick leave benefit, §§51.1-1104, 51.1-1105.
Participation in program, §51.1-1103.
Records.
Employers, §51.1-1137.
Rehabilitation incentive.
Nonwork related disability benefits, §51.1-1115.
Work-related disability benefits, §51.1-1126.
Sick leave.
Nonparticipating employees, §51.1-1106.
Participating employees, §51.1-1104.
Use by, §51.1-1105.
Survivor benefits.
Nonwork related disability benefits, §51.1-1118.
Work-related disability benefits, §51.1-1129.
Work-related disability benefits, §§51.1-1119 to 51.1-1130.
Adjustments in supplemental disability benefits, §51.1-1125.

SICKNESS AND DISABILITY PROGRAM —Cont'd
Work-related disability benefits —Cont'd
Applicability of provisions, §51.1-1119.
Cessation of supplemental disability benefits, §51.1-1127.
Coordination of benefits, §51.1-1130.
Initial benefit period, §51.1-1120.
Long-term disability benefits.
Supplemental long-term disability benefit, §§51.1-1123, 51.1-1124.
Offset by military disability, prohibition, §51.1-1125.
Rehabilitation incentive, §51.1-1126.
Service retirement of participating full-time employees receiving supplemental disability benefits, §51.1-1128.
Short-term disability benefits.
Supplemental short-term disability benefit, §§51.1-1121, 51.1-1122.
Survivor benefits, §51.1-1129.

SIDEWALKS.
Converting to bicycle paths, §15.2-2001.
Disabled persons.
Rights of persons with disabilities, §51.5-44.
Discrimination against persons with disabilities, §51.5-44.
Driving on sidewalks, §46.2-903.
Electric power-assisted bicycles.
Operating on sidewalks, §46.2-904.
Firearms.
Semi-automatic rifles or pistols and shotguns.
Carrying loaded firearms in public areas, §18.2-287.4.
Foot-scooters.
Operating on sidewalks, §46.2-904.
Limitation of actions.
Lien for assessments for sidewalks, §8.01-240.
Mechanics' and materialmen's liens.
Structures permanently annexed to freehold.
Classification, §43-2.
Picketing.
Illegal picketing, §40.1-53.
Powers of localities, §15.2-2001.
Retail sales and use tax.
Machinery, tools and equipment brought into state for use in constructing, §§58.1-604.1 to 58.1-604.3.
Rights of persons with disabilities, §51.5-44.
Roller skating, skateboarding or bicycle riding.
Locality by ordinance prohibiting, §46.2-904.
Scooters.
Operating on sidewalks, §46.2-904.
Service districts, §§15.2-2400 to 15.2-2403.3.
Snow and ice removal.
City or town powers, §15.2-1115.
Northern Virginia Planning District 8, §15.2-2025.
Spitting in public places, §18.2-322.
Statute of limitations.
Lien for assessments for sidewalks, §8.01-240.
Taxes or assessments for local improvements, §§15.2-2404 to 15.2-2413.

SIDE YARDS.
Ordinances regulating, §15.2-2279.

SIDS.
Autopsies, §32.1-285.1.
Investigations of death.
Child fatality review team, §§32.1-283.1, 32.1-283.2.

SIGHT-SEEING CARRIERS.
Boats, sight-seeing carriers by.
Defined, §46.2-2000.
Exemptions from provisions, §46.2-2099.21.
Insurance coverage, §46.2-2099.30.
Certificate of public convenience and necessity.
Requirement of certificate, §46.2-2099.4.
Employee liens, §§43-24 to 43-26.
Not required to incorporate as public service companies, §13.1-620.
Public service companies generally, §§56-1 to 56-87.
See PUBLIC SERVICE COMPANIES.
Refusal of service, §46.2-2099.11.
Routes.
Specific routes authorized, §46.2-2099.5.
Supplier liens, §§43-24 to 43-26.
Tickets, §46.2-2099.5.
Transportation companies generally, §§56-99.2 to 56-140.
See TRANSPORTATION COMPANIES.

SIGNALS BY DRIVERS, §§46.2-848 to 46.2-851.
See TRAFFIC INFRACTIONS.

SIGNATURES.
Bonds issued by locality, §15.2-2613.
Business trusts.
False documents, §13.1-1205.
Circuit courts.
Electronic filing of documents.
Digital signatures and seals, §17.1-258.4.
Drainage projects.
Withdrawal of persons signing petition, §21-303.
Drivers' licenses.
Applicant's signature, §46.2-323.
E-commerce.
Uniform electronic transactions act, §§59.1-479 to 59.1-497.
Environmental covenants, §10.1-1240.
Equal credit opportunities.
Signatures of all parties not discriminatory, §6.2-504.
Facsimile signatures.
Counsel or pro se litigants, VA SCt Rule 1:4.
Law firm pleadings, VA SCt Rule 1:5.
Signing of pleadings, §8.01-271.1.
False pretenses, obtaining by, §18.2-178.
Fire insurance.
Exclusion of liability for vicious animals, §38.2-2128.
Forgery.
Obtaining by false pretense or token on writing, §18.2-172.
Signature of another, maliciously affixing to writing, §18.2-172.2.
General assembly.
Prefiled bills, §30-19.3.
Investment securities.
Effect, §§8.8A-205, 8.8A-208, 8.8A-306.
Judicial notice.
Judicial or official documents, §8.01-387.
Letters of credit, §8.5A-104.
Maliciously affixing signature of another to writing, §18.2-172.2.
Mechanics' and materialmen's liens.
Waivers.
Forgeries, §43-13.1.
Motions.
Pleadings, §8.01-271.1.

SIGNATURES —Cont'd
Nurse practitioners.
Prescriptions.
Acceptance of signature, §54.1-2957.02.
Physician assistants.
When signature accepted, §54.1-2952.2.
Pleadings.
Counsel of record.
Defined, VA SCt Rule 1:5.
Pleadings, motions and other papers, §8.01-271.1.
Power of attorney.
Execution of power, §64.2-1603.
Putative father registry.
Signature of registrant required on form, §63.2-1250.
Referendum petitions, §24.2-684.1.
Adopting or changing form of county government, §15.2-301.
Sanitation districts law of 1938.
Signatures on petition for creation, §21-148.
Sanitation districts law of 1946.
Signatures on petition for creation, §21-231.
Schools and education.
Electronic records and electronic signatures from parents.
Boards to adopt policies regarding, §22.1-79.3.
Share certificates, bonds, notes or debentures issued by corporations, §13.1-647.
Small business financing authority.
Bond issues, §2.2-2303.
Transportation board.
Federal transportation grant anticipation revenue notes.
Signatures required, §33.1-23.18.
Voter registration.
Signature of voter, duties of registrars, §24.2-404.
Wills.
Execution procedure, §§64.2-403, 64.2-404.
Presumption of formal execution by military personnel, §64.2-408.
Revocation, §64.2-410.

SIGNS.
Agritourism activity liability.
Limited liability, warning required, §3.2-6402.
Air pollution control.
Qualified fumigation facilities, §10.1-1308.1.
Alcoholic beverages.
Compliance with transportation department integrated directional sign program and outdoor advertising provisions, §4.1-113.1.
Limitations on placement locations, §4.1-112.2.
Notice of violation, penalty for failure to take corrective action, §4.1-320.
Regulation of outdoor advertising by ABC board, §4.1-111.
Amusement device rider safety.
Owner or operator to post, §59.1-522.
Bridges.
Loitering on bridges or highway rights-of-way, §46.2-930.
Buses.
Hampton.
Transit buses used to transport school children, advisory signs, §46.2-1090.
Coal mine safety.
Underground coal mines.
Electricity.
Danger signs posted at transformer stations, §45.1-161.184.

SIGNS —Cont'd
Coal mine safety —Cont'd
Underground coal mines —Cont'd
Openings, §45.1-161.166.
Travel ways, §45.1-161.166.
No smoking, §45.1-161.179.
Worked-out areas, §45.1-161.228.
Elections.
Political campaign signs, regulation by localities, §15.2-109.
Polling places.
Accessible to elderly, disabled or handicapped voters.
Signs for special entrances, §24.2-604.1.
Electric power lines.
Overhead high voltage line safety.
Warning signs, §59.1-409.
Fishing.
Marine tourism activity liability.
Warning required, §28.2-1107.
Trespass by hunters, trappers or fishers on posted property.
Destruction of signs and posting land of another, §18.2-135.
Highway signs.
Children at play, §33.1-210.2.
Damaging or removing, §46.2-832.
Displacement, removal or destruction, §33.1-345.
Eminent domain and damages.
Billboard signs, adjustment or relocation, §33.1-95.2.
Fine schedule, VA SCt Rule 3B:2.
Injury to barriers, signs, etc., §33.1-193.
Integrated directional sign program.
Participation fees, §33.1-12.01.
Loitering on bridges or highway rights-of-way, §46.2-930.
Metric system.
Signs bearing metric units of measurement, §33.1-190.2.
Motor vehicle and traffic regulation, localities, §§46.2-1300, 46.2-1312.
Obeying highway signs, §§46.2-830, 46.2-830.1.
Pedestrians.
Signs at marked crosswalks, §46.2-924.
Scenic highway signs, §33.1-65.
Secondary system of state highways.
Installation and maintenance of signs, §33.1-69.01.
Signs, lights and markings generally, §§46.2-830 to 46.2-836.
State highway system.
Character of signs, etc., §33.1-36.
Traffic infractions.
Demerit points, §46.2-492.
Uniform traffic control devices on highways, §46.2-830.
Universities and colleges.
Directional signs, §33.1-223.2:3.
Virginia byways signs, §33.1-65.
Hospitals.
Charity care policies, posting, §32.1-137.01.
Hunting.
Trespass by hunters, trappers or fishers on posted property.
Destruction of signs and posting land of another, §18.2-135.
Marinas.
Dump stations, §32.1-246.1.
Marine tourism activity liability.
Warning required, §28.2-1107.

SIGNS —Cont'd
Motorcycle dealers, §46.2-1993.28.
Motor vehicle dealers.
Improvements to facilities or installment of signs.
Coercion as to, prohibited, §46.2-1569.
Visible permanent sign, §46.2-1534.
Motor vehicle equipment.
Windshields and windows.
Signs, decals and stickers on windshields, etc., §46.2-1052.
Motor vehicle size and weight.
Crossing bridge or culvert, §46.2-1130.
No trespass.
Posting on property of another, §18.2-119.1.
Outdoor advertising.
Alcoholic beverages.
Compliance with transportation department integrated directional sign program and outdoor advertising provisions, §4.1-113.1.
Limitations on placement locations, §4.1-112.2.
Notice of violation, penalty for failure to take corrective action, §4.1-320.
Regulation of outdoor advertising by ABC board, §4.1-111.
Exempt signs and advertising structures, §33.1-355.
False and misleading signs, §§33.1-379 to 33.1-381.
Pruning of vegetation that obstructs motorist view of signs.
Selective pruning permits, §33.1-371.1.
Overhead high voltage line safety.
Warning signs, §59.1-409.
Parking.
No-parking signs.
County authority to erect, §46.2-1225.
County ordinance regulations, §46.2-1224.
Pedestrians.
Signs at marked crosswalks, §46.2-924.
Property owners' associations.
Pesticide application in common areas.
Notice consisting of conspicuous signs, §55-510.3.
Railroad crossings.
Crossbucks or signal boards.
Similar signs prohibited, §56-408.
Railroad signs.
Failure to give.
Comparative negligence, §56-416.
Real estate cooperatives.
Advertising signs on common elements, §55-451.
School buses.
Authority of local school board to install signs or devices to indicate bus stops, §33.1-223.2:18.
Signs and markings on buses using alternative fuels, §46.2-1089.1.
T&M vehicle dealers.
Required, §46.2-1935.
Tanning facilities.
Warning signs, §59.1-310.4.
Time-shares.
Warning signs.
Project activities.
Inherent risks, liability limited, §55-376.4.
Traffic control devices on highways, §§46.2-830 to 46.2-836.
Traffic infractions.
Evasion of traffic control devices, §46.2-833.1.
Hauling hazardous cargo through tunnels in violation of posted signs, §46.2-815.

SIGNS —Cont'd
Traffic infractions —Cont'd
Highway signs.
Demerit points, §46.2-492.
Fine schedule, VA SCt Rule 3B:2.
Lane-use control signals, §46.2-805.
Left turn on steady red light after stopping, §46.2-836.
Maximum fine for violating Title 46.2, §46.2-113.
Municipal erection of signs and markers, §§46.2-1300, 46.2-1312.
Obeying highway signs, §§46.2-830, 46.2-830.1.
Obeying traffic lights, §46.2-833.
Prepayment of fine, §16.1-69.40:1.
Right turn on steady red light after stopping, §46.2-835.
School or school crossing speed limit signs, §46.2-873.
Signals by law-enforcement officers, crossing guards and flaggers, §46.2-834.
Signs, lights and markings generally, §§46.2-830 to 46.2-836.
Speeding.
Signs measuring speed by radar, §46.2-883.
Speeding conviction prohibited unless markers installed, §46.2-879.
Unofficial traffic control devices, §46.2-831.
Trailer dealers, §46.2-1992.27.
Trapping.
Trespass by hunters, trappers or fishers on posted property.
Destruction of signs and posting land of another, §18.2-135.
Trespass.
No trespass.
Posting on property of another, §18.2-119.1.
Posted property.
Trespass by hunters, trappers or fishers.
Destruction of signs and posting land of another, §18.2-135.
Underground utility line damage prevention.
Installation not involving excavation, exemption, §56-265.15:1.
Whistleblowing.
Fraud and abuse whistleblower protection act.
Notice of protection to employees, §2.2-3013.
Winter sports safety act.
Warnings required on tickets, passes and contracts, §8.01-227.12.
Zoning.
Abandoned nonconforming signs.
Removal, §15.2-2307.
Removal of nonconforming signs, §15.2-2307.

SIMPLE ASSAULT, §18.2-57.

SIMULATED ELECTIONS.
Minors entering polling place to vote in, §24.2-604.

SIMULCAST HORSE RACING.
Defined, §59.1-365.
Percentage retained, §59.1 392.
Regulations and conditions promulgated by racing commission, §59.1-369.

SIMULTANEOUS DEATH, §§64.2-2200 to 64.2-2208.
Bona fide purchasers.
Protection, §64.2-2206.
Citation, §64.2-2207.
Co-owners with right of survivorship.
Requirement of survival by 120 hours, §64.2-2203.

SIMULTANEOUS DEATH —Cont'd
Donative disposition in governing instruments.
Requirement of survival by 120 hours, §64.2-2202.
Effective date of provisions, §64.2-2208.
Evidence of death or status, §64.2-2204.
Exceptions, §64.2-2205.
Murderers barred from claiming property rights of decedent.
Application of act, §64.2-2511.
Payors.
Protection, §64.2-2206.
Personal liability of recipient, §64.2-2206.
Presumptions.
Survival by 120 hours, §64.2-2201.
Donative dispositions in governing instruments, §64.2-2202.
Survival by 120 hours, §64.2-2201.
Donative dispositions in governing instruments, §64.2-2202.
Exceptions, §64.2-2205.
Third parties.
Protection, §64.2-2206.
Uniformity of application and construction, §64.2-2207.

SINGLE ACT RULE.
Long-arm statute, §8.01-328.1.

SINGLE-BEAM HEADLIGHTS, §46.2-1031.

SINGLE-EMPLOYEE ENTERPRISES.
Jury service.
Voluntary exemption, §8.01-341.1.

SINGLE-TRIP TEMPORARY REGISTRATION OR PERMIT.
Oversize or overweight vehicles, §46.2-652.
Fee, §46.2-652.1.
Transportation of manufactured homes exceeding size permitted, §46.2-653.

SIRENS.
Emergency vehicles, §46.2-1061.
Motor vehicle equipment generally, §§46.2-1059 to 46.2-1062.

SITUS FOR TAXATION.
Food and beverage taxes.
Counties, cities or towns, §58.1-3841.
License tax, §§58.1-3708, 58.1-3709.
Motor vehicle taxes and license fees imposed by localities, §46.2-752.
Personal property taxes, §§58.1-3511 to 58.1-3514.

SITUS OF REAL PROPERTY IN VIRGINIA.
Long-arm statute, §8.01-328.1.

SIX-PACK RINGS.
Plastic holding devices.
Beverage sales, §10.1-1415.2.

SIX-YEAR EDUCATIONAL TECHNOLOGY PLAN FOR VIRGINIA.
Cooperation of council of higher education and state board of education, §23-9.8.

SKATEBOARD FACILITIES.
City or town powers to provide and operate.
Liability of county, city or town in operating.
Agreements with landowners, §29.1-509.

SKATEBOARDS.
Attaching to vehicle on highway, §46.2-932.
Locality prohibiting skateboarding on sidewalks or crosswalks, §46.2-904.

SKATEBOARDS —Cont'd
Motorized skateboards.
Crosswalks, operating in, §46.2-908.1.
Defined, §46.2-100.
Highways.
Operating on, restrictions, §46.2-908.1.
Persons less than 14 years old.
Operating, supervision required, §46.2-908.1.
Overtaking and passing vehicles, §46.2-907.
Tailgating vehicles by pedestrians, §46.2-932.

SKEET SHOOTING.
Local noise control ordinances.
Applicability to sport shooting ranges, §15.2-917.

SKIING.
Water skiing.
See WATER SKIING.
Winter sports safety act, §§8.01-227.11 to 8.01-227.23.
See WINTER SPORTS SAFETY ACT.

SKILLED TRADES.
Apprenticeship, §§40.1-117 to 40.1-126.
See APPRENTICESHIP.
Industrial hygiene and safety profession.
Protection of job title, §§40.1-139 to 40.1-142.

SKIN COLOR.
Discrimination.
Fair employment contracting act, §§2.2-4200, 2.2-4201.
Human rights act, §§2.2-3900 to 2.2-3903.
Procurement by public bodies, §2.2-4310.
Employment discrimination by contractors, §2.2-4311.

SKIN DIVING.
Boating safety, §29.1-734.1.
Spearfishing.
Engaging in while intoxicated, §§29.1-738 to 29.1-738.6.

SKIP TRACING.
Collection of accounts receivable by Commonwealth, §2.2-4807.

SKYDIVING.
Duty of care and liability for damages of land owners, §29.1-509.

SKYROCKETS.
Fireworks.
See FIREWORKS.

SLANDER.
Attorneys.
Liability for words used in professional conduct proceedings, §54.1-3908.
Audiovisual recording of motion picture in commercial theater.
Unlawful, arrest or detention by theater owner.
No civil liability for slander, §18.2-187.2.
Banks, derogatory statements affecting, §6.2-940.
Congress, speech or debate privilege, US Const Art I §6.
Criminal offense, §18.2-417.
Damages.
Mitigation of damages, §8.01-46.
Newspaper or print media, §8.01-48.
Radio and television broadcast, §8.01-49.
Employment-related information disclosure.
Prospective or current employer disclosing.
Immunity, good faith presumption, §8.01-46.1.
False publications, §18.2-209.

SLANDER —Cont'd
General assembly members, speech or debate privilege, VA Const Art IV §9.
Insulting word, §8.01-45.
Insurance business, defamation with respect to, §38.2-504.
Internet defamatory material.
Liability of provider or user, §8.01-49.1.
Justification, §8.01-46.
Limitation of actions, §8.01-247.1.
Newspapers or print media.
Mitigation of damages, §8.01-48.
Radio and television broadcast.
Defamatory statements on air, §8.01-49.
Savings institutions.
Defamation of institutions and certain federal agencies prohibited, §6.2-1107.
School personnel reporting bomb threats, alcohol or drug use, etc.
Immunity for reporting, §8.01-47.
Shoplifting suspect's arrest or detention.
Exemption from civil liability of merchant, agent or employee, §8.01-226.9.
Statute of limitations, §8.01-247.1.
Trust companies, derogatory statements affecting, §§6.2-940, 6.2-1042.

SLAUGHTERHOUSES.
Sanitary requirements for food establishments, §§3.2-5105 to 3.2-5119.

SLAVERY, US Const Amds 13 to US US 15.

SLAYER'S ACT, §§64.2-2500 to 64.2-2511.
Acquisition of property as result of slaying.
Prohibition, §64.2-2501.
Appointment powers, §64.2-2507.
Burden of proving decedent slain, §64.2-2500.
Common law rights and remedies, §64.2-2511.
Construction of chapter, §64.2-2511.
Defined terms, §64.2-2500.
Designation of slayer as predeceasing decedent, §64.2-2502.
Federal law preempting chapter.
Return of payment, property or benefit received by person not entitled except for preemption, §64.2-2511.
Future interests, §§64.2-2504, 64.2-2506.
Insurance proceeds, §64.2-2508.
Interests dependent on survivorship or continuance of life, §64.2-2505.
Kinship to decedent.
Established through kinship to slayer, §64.2-2502.
Persons acquiring from slayers, §64.2-2509.
Property held in concurrent ownership without survivorship.
Severance of interest of decedent effected, §64.2-2503.
Property held in concurrent ownership with right of survivorship.
Vesting of slayer's interest effected, §64.2-2503.
Receipt of benefit as result of slaying.
Prohibition, §64.2-2501.
Record of judicial proceedings, §64.2-2510.
Remainders, §§64.2-2504, 64.2-2506.
Reversions, §64.2-2504.
Simultaneous death act applicability, §64.2-2511.
Statute preventing lapse of legacy or devises.
Applicability, §64.2-2502.

SLAYERS' PROPERTY RIGHTS, §§64.2-2500 to 64.2-2511.
See SLAYER'S ACT.

SLEDDING.
Winter sports safety act, §§8.01-227.11 to 8.01-227.23.
See WINTER SPORTS SAFETY ACT.

SLEEP DISORDERS.
Polysomnographic technologists, §§54.1-2957.14, 54.1-2957.15.

SLEEPING BAGS.
Bedding and upholstered furniture generally, §§32.1-212 to 32.1-226.
See BEDDING AND UPHOLSTERED FURNITURE.

SLEEPING ON SHOULDER OF HIGHWAY.
Drivers, §46.2-830.1.

SLINGSHOTS.
Carrying concealed weapons, §18.2-308.
Convicted felons, possession, transportation or concealing, §18.2-308.2.
Courthouses, carrying weapon into, §18.2-283.1.
School property, possession on, §18.2-308.1.
Use in commission of crime.
Forfeiture, §19.2-386.29.

SLOW MOVING VEHICLES.
Designation of lanes for, §46.2-804.
Impeding traffic, §46.2-877.
Fine schedule, VA SCt Rule 3B:2.
Maximum fine for violating Title 46.2, §46.2-113.
Slow moving traffic to keep to right, §46.2-804.
Fine schedule, VA SCt Rule 3B:2.
Maximum fine for violating Title 46.2, §46.2-113.
Vehicle emblems, §46.2-1081.

SLUGS.
Manufacturing, selling, etc., for unlawful uses, §18.2-180.
Unlawful operation of telephones, parking meters, vending machines, etc., §18.2-179.

SLUICEWAYS.
Waters of the state.
Cooperation with federal agencies, §62.1-132.14.
Items of cooperation, §62.1-149.

SLUM CLEARANCE.
Housing revitalization zones, §§36-157 to 36-170.
See HOUSING REVITALIZATION ZONES.
Redevelopment of blighted areas, §§36-48 to 36-55.
Tax increment financing, §§58.1-3245 to 58.1-3245.5.

SMALL BUSINESS AND SUPPLIER DIVERSITY DEPARTMENT, §§2.2-1603 to 2.2-1617.
Capital access fund for disadvantaged businesses.
Management, §2.2-1605.
Colleges and universities.
Vendors.
Procurement by public institutions, §2.2-1609.
Contracts.
Performance agreements.
Extension of performance period, §11-7.1.
Cooperation among state departments and agencies.
Interdepartmental board, §2.2-1608.
Creation, §2.2-1603.
Data collection process, §2.2-1610.
Definitions, §2.2-1604.
Director.
Appointment, §2.2-1603.

SMALL BUSINESS AND SUPPLIER DIVERSITY DEPARTMENT —Cont'd
Director —Cont'd
Powers, §2.2-1606.
Duties, §2.2-1605.
Freedom of information act, exclusions from chapter, §2.2-3705.6.
Interdepartmental board, §2.2-1608.
Nonstock corporation to assist small businesses, §2.2-1607.
Offices, §2.2-1603.
One-stop small business permitting program, §2.2-1617.
Powers, §2.2-1605.
Director, §2.2-1606.
Procurement by public bodies.
Businesses from department's list, participation, §2.2-4310.
Vendors, use by public institutions of higher education, §2.2-1609.
Recommendations, submission, §2.2-1610.
Recycling duties, §10.1-1425.7.
Reports, §2.2-1610.
Secretary of commerce and trade.
Agency responsibility, §2.2-204.
Small business investment grant fund, §2.2-1616.
Small business jobs grant fund program, §2.2-1615.
Small business new jobs and retraining programs, §2.2-1614.
Vendors.
Colleges and universities.
Procurement by public institutions, §2.2-1609.
Virginia jobs investment program, §2.2-1611.
Virginia new jobs program, §2.2-1612.
Workforce retraining program, §2.2-1613.

SMALL BUSINESS ASSISTANCE.
Nonprofit corporation to assist.
Certified development company (eff until 1/1/2014), §2.2-903.
Department of business assistance may establish (eff until 1/1/2014), §2.2-903.

SMALL BUSINESS COMMISSION.
Compensation and expenses, §30-182.
Creation, §30-182.
Duties, §30-183.
Legislative services division.
Staff assistance, §30-182.
Membership, terms, §30-182.
Powers, §30-183.
Purpose, §30-182.
Recommendations.
Voting on, §30-182.

SMALL BUSINESS CORPORATIONS (S CORPORATIONS).
See S CORPORATIONS.

SMALL BUSINESS ENVIRONMENTAL COMPLIANCE ASSISTANCE FUND, §§10.1-1197.1 to 10.1-1197.4.

SMALL BUSINESSES.
Administrative agency appeals.
Small businesses impacted by agency decisions or actions, considerations, VA SCt Rule 2A:6.
Clean air act compliance, §§10.1-1323 to 10.1-1326.
Colleges and universities.
Procurement of goods and services from certain vendors (eff until 1/1/2014), §2.2-1404.1.

SMALL BUSINESSES —Cont'd
Commission, §§30-182, 30-183.
Deception in obtaining certificate, §18.2-213.1.
Home-based businesses.
Property owners' associations.
Allowed, reasonable restrictions, §55-513.2.
Local ordinances supporting, §15.2-965.1.
Mortgage lender and broker act.
Exemption of investment companies from act, §6.2-1602.
One-stop small business permitting program, §2.2-1617.
One-stop small business permitting program (eff until 1/1/2014), §2.2-904.1.
Procurement by public bodies.
Participation, §2.2-4310.
Property owners' associations.
Home-based businesses allowed, reasonable restrictions, §55-513.2.
Service disabled veteran status of owner, §2.2-2001.
Small business investment grant fund, §§2.2-904.03, 2.2-1616.
Small business jobs grant fund program, §§2.2-904.02, 2.2-1615.
Small business new jobs and retraining programs, §2.2-1614.
Small business new jobs and retraining programs (eff until 1/1/2014), §2.2-904.01.
Technical and environmental compliance assistance program, §§10.1-1323 to 10.1-1326.

SMALL BUSINESS FINANCING AUTHORITY, §§2.2-2279 to 2.2-2314.
Accounts and accounting.
Funds of authority, §2.2-2304.
Administrative process act.
Exemption from applicability, §2.2-2314.
Exemptions, §2.2-4002.
Assets of authority.
Pledges, §2.2-2300.
Audits, §2.2-2312.
Board of directors, §2.2-2282.
Meetings, §2.2-2283.
Bond issues.
Authority to issue, §2.2-2285.
Authorization by resolution, §2.2-2298.
Contents of resolution, §2.2-2299.
Contracts with bondholders, §2.2-2305.
Interest, §2.2-2298.
Investment of public funds.
Bonds as legal investments and securities, §2.2-2307.
Liability of Commonwealth, §2.2-2297.
Limitations, §2.2-2299.
Maturity, §2.2-2298.
Modification of rates or terms, §2.2-2285.
Payment, §2.2-2296.
Pledges of authority, §2.2-2300.
Powers and duties, §2.2-2287.
Private activity bond financing.
Form for request, §2.2-2292.
Protection of bondholders, §2.2-2306.
Redemption of bonds, §2.2-2301.
Refunding bonds, §2.2-2301.
Rights of bondholders, §2.2-2306.
Security for bonds, §§2.2-2291, 2.2-2296.
Security for deposits, §2.2-2305.
Signatures, §2.2-2303.
Tax exemptions.
Limitations, §2.2-2291.

SMALL BUSINESS FINANCING AUTHORITY —Cont'd
Bond issues —Cont'd
Tax exemptions —Cont'd
Public hearings, §2.2-2292.
Trust indenture, bond secured by, §2.2-2302.
Umbrella bonds.
Authority to issue, §2.2-2289.
Use of proceeds to purchase ninety percent guaranteed portion of loans, §2.2-2288.
Capital access fund for disadvantaged businesses, §2.2-2311.
Chairman and vice-chairman, §2.2-2282.
Condemnation of property.
Power to condemn, §2.2-2286.
Construction and interpretation of article, §2.2-2281.
Contracts.
Authority to enter into, §2.2-2285.
Bondholders, §2.2-2305.
Creation, §2.2-2280.
Defined terms, §2.2-2279.
Eminent domain.
Power to condemn property, §2.2-2286.
Executive director, §2.2-2284.
Expenses, §2.2-2308.
Fees, §2.2-2291.
Funds of authority.
Accounts and accounting, §2.2-2304.
Expenses, §2.2-2308.
Indemnification.
Bond issues.
Liability of Commonwealth, §2.2-2297.
Industrial development authorities.
Technical assistance.
Duty to render, §2.2-2285.
Insurance.
Authority to obtain, §2.2-2285.
Insurance and guarantee fund, §2.2-2290.
Investment of public funds.
Bond issues.
Bonds as legal investments and securities, §2.2-2307.
Loans.
Authority to obtain, §2.2-2285.
Investment in, purchase or assignment, §2.2-2294.
Loans to lenders, §2.2-2293.
Powers and duties, §2.2-2287.
Meetings.
Board of directors, §2.2-2283.
Members, §2.2-2282.
Notice.
Public hearings.
Tax exemptions on bond issues, §2.2-2292.
Officers, §2.2-2282.
Offices.
Powers and duties of authority, §2.2-2285.
Pledges by authority, §2.2-2300.
Powers and duties.
Authority, §2.2-2285.
Bond issues, §2.2-2287.
Umbrella bonds.
Authority to issue, §2.2-2289.
Use of proceeds to purchase ninety percent guaranteed portion of loans, §2.2-2288.
Condemnation of property, §2.2-2286.
Executive director, §2.2-2284.
Loans, §2.2-2287.
Preferred lenders.
Agreements authorizing loan decisioning, processing functions and responsibilities, §2.2-2279.
Credit authority, provided, allocation, §2.2-2279.

SMALL BUSINESS FINANCING AUTHORITY —Cont'd
Preferred lenders —Cont'd
Defined, §2.2-2279.
Private activity bond financing.
Form for request, §2.2-2292.
Private activity bonds.
Establishment of guidelines, §15.2-5003.
Public hearings.
Tax exemptions on bond issues, §2.2-2292.
Purpose, §2.2-2280.
Records.
Executive director.
Powers and duties, §2.2-2284.
Reports.
Annual report, §2.2-2312.
Rules and regulations, §2.2-2295.
Seals and sealed instruments.
Powers and duties of authority, §2.2-2285.
Short title, §2.2-2279.
Signatures.
Bond issues, §2.2-2303.
Staff, §2.2-2282.
Authority to employ, §2.2-2285.
Tax exemptions, §2.2-2313.
Limitations, §2.2-2291.
Technical assistance.
Duty to render, §2.2-2285.
Trusts.
Bond issues.
Trust indenture, bond secured by, §2.2-2302.
Umbrella bonds.
Authority to issue, §2.2-2289.
Virginia export fund.
Creation and management, §2.2-2309.
Virginia small business growth fund, §2.2-2310.

SMALL BUSINESS INVESTMENT ACT.
Certified development company under act.
Nonprofit corporation established to assist small business (eff until 1/1/2014), §2.2-903.

SMALL BUSINESS INVESTMENT GRANT FUND, §§2.2-904.03, 2.2-1616.

SMALL BUSINESS JOBS GRANT FUND PROGRAM, §2.2-904.02.

SMALL BUSINESS NEW JOBS AND RETRAINING PROGRAMS, §2.2-1614.

SMALL BUSINESS NEW JOBS AND RETRAINING PROGRAMS (EFF UNTIL 1/1/2014), §2.2-904.01.

SMALL CLAIMS COURTS, §§16.1-122.1 to 16.1-122.7.
Appeals, §16.1-122.7.
Commencement of actions, §16.1-122.3.
Continuances, §16.1-122.3.
Establishment by counties or cities, §16.1-122.1.
Evidence rule suspended, §16.1-122.5.
Fee taxed as costs, §16.1-122.3.
Informal hearings, §16.1-122.5.
Judgment and collection, §16.1-122.6.
Jurisdiction, §16.1-122.2.
Notice of process, service, §16.1-122.3.
Pleadings allowed, §16.1-122.3.
Removal, §16.1-122.4.
Representation, §16.1-122.4.

SMALL EMPLOYER HEALTH INSURANCE POOLING, §§38.2-3551 to 38.2-3555.
Definitions, §38.2-3551.

SMALL EMPLOYER HEALTH INSURANCE POOLING —Cont'd
Health insurance issuers.
Defined, §38.2-3551.
Requirements, §38.2-3554.
Public policy to support, §2.2-302.1.
Rulemaking by commission, §38.2-3555.
Small employer health group cooperatives, §38.2-3552.
Defined, §38.2-3551.
Membership in, §38.2-3553.

SMALL ESTATES, §§64.2-600 to 64.2-605.
Construction of provisions, §64.2-605.
Defined terms, §64.2-600.
Discharge and release of payor, §64.2-603.
Funeral expenses, §64.2-604.
Small assets.
Payment or delivery by affidavit, §64.2-601.
Payment or delivery without affidavit, §64.2-602.

SMALL GRAINS, §§3.2-2200 to 3.2-2214.
Assessment for market development, education and promotion.
Delinquent assessment.
Collection, §3.2-1102.
Expenditure of moneys collected, §3.2-2211.
Handlers.
Criminal penalties for certain acts, §3.2-2214.
Deduction of assessment from payment to farmer, §3.2-2212.
Records, §3.2-2213.
Criminal penalties for falsification or failure to preserve, §3.2-2214.
Report and payment by, §3.2-2212.
Criminal penalties for false reports, §3.2-2214.
Interest, §3.2-2212.
Referendum on question, §§3.2-2205 to 3.2-2209.
Virginia small grains fund, §3.2-2211.
Dedicated revenues, diversion, §3.2-1100.
Definitions, §3.2-2200.
Elections.
Assessment for market development, education and promotion.
Referendum on question, §§3.2-2205 to 3.2-2209.
Production area designations, §3.2-2210.
Referendum.
Assessment for market development, education and promotion, §§3.2-2205 to 3.2-2209.
Virginia small grains board, §§3.2-2200 to 3.2-2214.
Appointment of members, §3.2-2201.
Compensation, §3.2-2203.
Composition, §3.2-2201.
Duties, §3.2-2204.
Officers, §3.2-2203.
Powers, §3.2-2204.
Production area designations, §3.2-2210.
Terms of members, §3.2-2202.
Vacancies, §3.2-2202.

SMALL INVESTOR-OWNED UTILITIES, §§56-531 to 56-534.
Commission regulation, §56-533.
Conflict of laws, §56-534.
Defined terms, §56-531.
Public service companies generally, §§56-1 to 56-87.
See PUBLIC SERVICE COMPANIES.
Public utilities generally, §§56-232 to 56-265.
See PUBLIC UTILITIES.

SMALL INVESTOR-OWNED UTILITIES —Cont'd
Rates, §56-532.

SMALL INVESTOR-OWNED UTILITY ACT, §§56-531 to 56-534.

SMALL LOAN ACT.
General provisions.
See CONSUMER FINANCE.

SMALL RENEWABLE ENERGY PROJECTS, §§10.1-1197.5 to 10.1-1197.11.

SMALL WATER OR SEWER UTILITIES, §§56-265.13:1 to 56-265.13:7.
Applicability of chapter, §56-265.13:3.
Chapter citation, §56-265.13:1.
Defined terms, §56-265.13:2.
Public ground use without consent or compensation, §56-14.
Public service companies generally.
See PUBLIC SERVICE COMPANIES.
Public utilities generally.
See PUBLIC UTILITIES.
Rates, §56-265.13:4.
Changes, §56-265.13:5.
Hearings, §56-265.13:6.
Receivership appointment, §56-265.13:6.1.
Civil penalties against utility, §56-265.13:6.1.
Regulation by commission, §56-265.13:7.
Services, §56-265.13:4.

SMART CARDS.
Unlawful electronic communication devices, §§18.2-190.1 to 18.2-190.8.

SMITH COUNTY.
Director of emergency management, §44-146.19.

SMITHFIELD.
Tidewater airport commission, 1962 ch 606, 1964 ch 45.

SMITHFIELD HAMS, §§3.2-5419 to 3.2-5421.
Advertising or labeling as such.
Criminal penalties for violations, §3.2-5421.
Only genuine Smithfield hams, §3.2-5420.
Defined, §3.2-5419.

SMITHFIELD PLANTATION HOUSE.
Association for the preservation of Virginia antiquities.
Appropriations for maintenance, §10.1-2212.

SMITH ISLAND BRIDGE AUTHORITY, 1960 ch 506, 1962 ch 500.

SMOKE BOMBS.
Setting off in certain public buildings, §18.2-87.1.

SMOKE DETECTORS.
Adult day care centers, §36-99.5:1.
Assisted living facilities, §36-99.5:1.
Colleges and universities, §36-99.3.
Deaf and hearing-impaired, §36-99.5.
Dormitory buildings, §§36-99.3, 36-99.5.
Hotels or motels.
Deaf and hearing-impaired, §36-99.5.
Juvenile care facilities, §36-99.4.
Landlord and tenant.
Residential landlords and tenants.
Installation o f fire detection devices by tenant, §55-248.18.
Tenant removing or tampering with, §§55-225.4, 55-248.16.

SMOKE DETECTORS —Cont'd
Locality required in certain buildings, §15.2-922.
Multiple-family dwelling units.
Deaf and hearing-impaired, §36-99.5.
Nursing homes and facilities, §36-99.5:1.
One-family dwelling units.
Deaf and hearing-impaired, §36-99.5.
Two-family dwelling units.
Deaf and hearing-impaired, §36-99.5.

SMOKE EMISSION.
City or town powers to regulate, §15.2-1116.
County regulations, §15.2-1217.

SMOKELESS TOBACCO.
Tobacco generally.
See TOBACCO.
Tobacco products tax, §§58.1-1021.01 to 58.1-1021.05.
See TOBACCO PRODUCTS TAX.

SMOKE MANAGEMENT PLANS.
Prescribed burn prescription, §10.1-1150.4.

SMOKE PROJECTORS MOUNTED ON VEHICLES, §§46.2-109, 46.2-1086, 46.2-1087.

SMOKE SCREEN EMISSION DEVICES, §§46.2-1086, 46.2-1087.

SMOKING.
Cigarettes.
Fire-safe cigarettes, §§59.1-293.1 to 59.1-293.9.
See FIRE-SAFE CIGARETTES.
Generally.
See CIGARETTES.
Food-producing establishments.
Workrooms of food-producing establishments, §3.2-5114.
Gas pumps, proximity to, §46.2-819.4.
Health care facilities.
Smoking near medical oxygen sources, §18.2-511.1.
Indoor clean air act, §§15.2-2820 to 15.2-2833.
See SMOKING IN PUBLIC PLACES.
Local government personnel.
Use of tobacco products on job, §15.2-1504.
Underground coal mines, §§45.1-161.177 to 45.1-161.180.
See SMOKING IN UNDERGROUND COAL MINES.

SMOKING IN PUBLIC PLACES, §§15.2-2820 to 15.2-2833.
Applicability of act, §15.2-2821.
Catering.
Exception to restaurant smoking ban.
Preparation or storage of food for catering services, §15.2-2825.
Child day centers.
Prohibition on smoking, §15.2-2824.
Definitions, §15.2-2820.
Department of corrections.
No-smoking areas.
Inapplicability to office, work, or other areas, §15.2-2823.
Designated smoking areas.
Building requirements, §15.2-2827.
Requiring physical modifications or alterations to structure, §15.2-2827.
Responsibility of building proprietors and managers, §15.2-2827.
Restaurants, §15.2-2825.

SMOKING IN PUBLIC PLACES —Cont'd
Designated smoking areas —Cont'd
Ventilation systems and existing physical barriers, §15.2-2827.
Elevators.
Prohibition on smoking, §15.2-2824.
Entertainment and cultural facilities.
Local regulation of smoking, §15.2-2830.
Fines.
Enforcement of ordinances, §15.2-2833.
Violation of statewide smoking ban, §§15.2-2824 to 15.2-2826.
Health care facilities.
Local regulation of smoking, §15.2-2830.
Health department facilities.
Local regulation of smoking, §15.2-2830.
Prohibition on smoking, §15.2-2824.
Hospital emergency rooms.
Prohibition on smoking, §15.2-2824.
Hot-dog stands.
Exception to restaurant smoking ban, §15.2-2825.
Hotel lobby areas.
Local regulation of smoking, §15.2-2831.
Indoor recreational facilities.
Local regulation of smoking, §15.2-2830.
Indoor service lines and cashier lines.
Prohibition on smoking, §15.2-2824.
Law enforcement officers.
Enforcement of act by summons, §15.2-2822.
Local regulation of smoking, §§15.2-2828 to 15.2-2833.
Common areas in an educational facilities, §15.2-2829.
Employee smoking in private workplaces.
Designation of smoking and no-smoking areas, §15.2-2828.
Mandatory provisions of ordinance, §15.2-2829.
Nonconformity with state provisions, §15.2-2828.
No state preemption, §15.2-2828.
Optional provisions of ordinances, §15.2-2830.
Ordinances not authorized, §15.2-2831.
Posting of signs, §15.2-2832.
Private work places, §15.2-2831.
Public places, §15.2-2830.
Smoking permitted signs, §15.2-2832.
"No-smoking areas" designation of, §15.2-2825.
Educational facilities, §15.2-2826.
Recreational facilities, §15.2-2826.
Restaurants, §15.2-2825.
Retail stores, §15.2-2826.
No-smoking signs.
Enforcement of ordinances, §15.2-2833.
Local regulation of smoking, §15.2-2832.
Restaurants, §15.2-2825.
Polling rooms.
Prohibition on smoking, §15.2-2824.
Private clubs.
Exception to restaurant smoking ban, §15.2-2825.
Private conference or meeting rooms.
Local regulation of smoking, §15.2-2831.
Public building and facilities.
No-smoking areas, §15.2-2823.
Public elementary, intermediate and high schools.
Prohibition on smoking, §15.2-2824.
Pushcart operations.
Exception to restaurant smoking ban, §15.2-2825.
Restaurants.
Affirmative defense of proprietor, §15.2-2825.
Defined, §15.2-2820.
Designation of No-smoking areas, §15.2-2825.

SMOKING IN PUBLIC PLACES —Cont'd
Restaurants —Cont'd
Exceptions to restaurant smoking ban, §15.2-2825.
Outdoor area of a restaurant, §15.2-2825.
Responsibility of building proprietors and managers, §15.2-2827.
Statewide smoking ban, §15.2-2825.
Where smoking permitted, §15.2-2825.
Retail and service establishments.
Local regulation of smoking, §15.2-2830.
Retail tobacco stores.
Inapplicability of act, §15.2-2821.
School buses and public conveyances.
Local regulation of smoking, §15.2-2829.
Prohibition on smoking, §15.2-2824.
Shopping centers or malls.
Local regulation of smoking, §15.2-2831.
Statewide smoking ban, §§15.2-2824 to 15.2-2827.
Designation of No-smoking areas, §§15.2-2825, 15.2-2826.
Penalty for violation, §§15.2-2824 to 15.2-2826.
Prohibition on smoking generally, §15.2-2824.
Public building and facilities, §15.2-2823.
Responsibility of building proprietors and managers, §15.2-2827.
Restaurants, §15.2-2825.
Smoking permitted signs, §15.2-2825.
Tobacco manufacturing facilities.
Inapplicability of act, §15.2-2821.
Tobacco warehouses.
Inapplicability of act, §15.2-2821.
Wait or bus staff in restaurants.
Consent of employee to work in smoking area, §15.2-2825.

SMOKING IN UNDERGROUND COAL MINES, §§45.1-161.177 to 45.1-161.180.
Allowing persons to work in mine with smoker's articles or while smoking, §45.1-161.178.
Entry as consent to search for smoking materials, §45.1-161.177.
Magazines for storage of explosive materials.
Smoking in or carrying smoker's articles, §45.1-161.180.
Matches, lighters, etc., prohibited, §45.1-161.177.
Oil houses, tipples, etc.
Smoking in or carrying articles, §45.1-161.180.
Posting of notice, §45.1-161.179.
Prohibited, §45.1-161.177.
Smoker's search program.
Operators to institute, §45.1-161.177.

SMOKING RELATED COSTS INCURRED BY STATE.
Tobacco manufacturers' responsibilities, §§3.2-4200 to 3.2-4219.
Assignment and contribution of escrow funds to Commonwealth, §§3.2-4202, 3.2-4203.
Virginia foundation for healthy youth, §§32.1-354 to 32.1-367.
See VIRGINIA FOUNDATION FOR HEALTHY YOUTH.

SMYTH COUNTY.
Confederate cemeteries and graves.
Disbursement of funds appropriated for upkeep, §10.1-2211.
School board.
Salary of members, §22.1-32.

SMYTH-MARION AUTHORITY.
Generally.
See ECONOMIC DEVELOPMENT AUTHORITIES.

SNAKEHEAD FISH.
Introducing into waters of Commonwealth, §18.2-313.2.
Nonindigenous aquatic nuisance species act, §§29.1-571 to 29.1-577.
See NONINDIGENOUS AQUATIC NUISANCE SPECIES ACT.

SNAKES.
Handling or using so as to endanger human life or health, §18.2-313.
Keeping of reptiles, §29.1-569.

SNOWMOBILES.
Defined, §46.2-100.
Lights and reflectors, §46.2-1016.
Motor vehicle registration.
Exemption from registration, §46.2-679.
Winter sports safety act, §§8.01-227.11 to 8.01-227.23.
See WINTER SPORTS SAFETY ACT.

SNOW REMOVAL.
City or town powers, §15.2-1115.
Northern Virginia Planning District 8.
Public sidewalks, §15.2-2025.
Private entities.
Removal of snow and ice from public highways, §33.1-200.2.
Service districts, §§15.2-2400 to 15.2-2403.3.
Volunteer fire departments and rescue squads.
Removal of snow from driveways, §33.1-200.1.

SNUFF.
Tobacco products tax, §§58.1-1021.01 to 58.1-1021.05.
See TOBACCO PRODUCTS TAX.

SOAPS.
Phosphorus use in cleaning agents, §§62.1-193.1 to 62.1-193.3.

SOCIAL SECURITY DISABILITY PAYMENTS.
Behavioral health and developmental services.
Commissioner authorized to receive and expend for individuals receiving services in state facilities, §37.2-704.
Golden passport card.
Free entry and parking in state parks for persons receiving, §10.1-202.1.

SOCIAL SECURITY FOR STATE AND LOCAL EMPLOYEES, §§51.1-700 to 51.1-707.
See PUBLIC OFFICERS AND EMPLOYEES.

SOCIAL SECURITY NUMBERS.
Access prohibited, §§2.2-3815, 2.2-3816.
Breach of personal information, notice requirement, §18.2-186.6.
Circuit court clerks.
Secure remote access to land records, §§17.1-279, 17.1-292 to 17.1-295.
Commercial drivers' licenses.
Proof.
Applicants may be required to present, §46.2-341.12.
Compulsory school attendance.
Students to present social security numbers, §22.1-260.
Computers.
Using computer to gather identifying information, §18.2-152.5:1.

SOCIAL SECURITY NUMBERS —Cont'd
Deed books.
Recordation of documents in, §17.1-227.
Drivers' licenses.
Proof of social security number or non-work status.
Applicants may be required to present, §46.2-323.
Commercial drivers' licenses, §46.2-341.12.
Duplicate or reissued licenses, §46.2-343.
Renewal, applicant required to appear in person before DMV, §46.2-330.
Elections.
Name of voter erroneously omitted from pollbook.
Information to be provided by voter, §24.2-652.
Government data collection and dissemination practices act.
Access prohibited, §§2.2-3815, 2.2-3816.
Disclosure unlawful, §2.2-3806.
Identification cards not to display, §2.2-3808.
License certificates not to display, §2.2-3808.
Mail not to display or reveal, §2.2-3808.
Requirement to disclose unlawful, §2.2-3808.
Health insurance.
Public officers and employees.
Plan to provide identification number other than social security number, §2.2-2818.
Health professions department.
Subpoena power, §54.1-2506.
Identification cards.
Government data collection and dissemination practices act.
Identification cards not to display, §2.2-3808.
Proof required of applicant, §46.2-345.
Identity theft, §§18.2-186.3, 18.2-186.3:1, 18.2-186.5.
Government data collection and dissemination practices act.
Mail not to display or reveal, §2.2-3808.
Independent candidates petition for candidacy.
Voters signing petition to provide, §24.2-506.
Judgments provided via remote access.
Social security number display, §8.01-449.
Licensing.
Generally, §54.1-116.
License certificates not to display.
Government data collection and dissemination practices act, §2.2-3808.
Local taxes.
Disclosure of account numbers for administrative purposes, §58.1-3017.
Marriage records.
Blocking access to, §32.1-267.
Parents to report number at time of child's birth, §32.1-257.1.
Personal information privacy.
Notice of breach of personal information, §18.2-186.6.
Restricted use, §59.1-443.2.
Personalty identified with number proceeded by letters VA, §18.2-96.1.
Possession with removed, altered, etc., mark, §18.2-96.1.
Removal, alternation, etc., of mark, §18.2-96.1.
Protection, §§2.2-3815, 2.2-3816.
Public officers and employees.
Health insurance.
Plan to provide identification number other than social security number, §2.2-2818.

SOCIAL SECURITY NUMBERS —Cont'd
Recordation of documents.
Deed books.
Documents recorded in, §17.1-227.
Renewal of business, trade, profession, occupation or driver's license, certificate, registration or authorization.
Applicant to provide, §63.2-1937.
Secure remote access to land records, §§17.1-279, 17.1-292 to 17.1-295.
State corporation commission.
Documents filed with commission containing.
Deletion, removal, refusal to accept documents, §12.1-19.
Taxpayers', disclosure by department of taxation, §58.1-209.
Tax returns.
Income tax withholding.
Employer's returns, §58.1-478.1.
Unemployment compensation.
Disclosure of number, §60.2-101.
Use of person's identity with intent to coerce, intimidate or harass, §18.2-186.4.
Virginia retirement system.
Disclosure of number, §51.1-124.5.
Voter or voter registration lists.
Furnished to others, not to contain numbers, §24.2-406.
Mail registration applications, §24.2-416.5.
Unlawful disclosure, §§24.2-407.1, 24.2-1002.1.
Motor vehicles department employees, §24.2-411.1.
State-designated voter registration agencies, §24.2-411.2.
Voter petitions calling for referendum, §24.2-684.1.
Voters to provide officer of election prior to voting, §24.2-643.

SOCIAL SECURITY PAYMENTS.
Power of attorney.
Authority of agent.
Benefits from governmental programs or civil or military service, §64.2-1635.

SOCIAL SERVICES, §§63.2-100 to 63.2-2204.
Adoption.
Generally, §§63.2-1200 to 63.2-1248.
See ADOPTION.
Special needs children.
Adoption assistance payments, §§63.2-1300 to 63.2-1304.
Medical assistance, uniform act, §§63.2-1400 to 63.2-1405.
Adult protective services, §§63.2-1603 to 63.2-1610.
Adult abuse.
Defined, §63.2-100.
Adult protective services unit.
Established within state department, duties, §63.2-1604.
Definitions, §63.2-1603.
Emergency order for protective services, §63.2-1609.
Emergency defined, §63.2-1603.
Involuntary protective services, §63.2-1608.
Report of suspected abuse, neglect or exploitation, §63.2-1606.
Services provided by local departments, §63.2-1605.

SOCIAL SERVICES —Cont'd
Adult protective services —Cont'd
Suspected abuse, neglect or exploitation.
Photographs, x-rays or medical imaging of incapacitated person.
Taking without consent as part of medical evaluation, §63.2-1606.1.
Report, §63.2-1606.
Voluntary protective services, §63.2-1610.
Adult services.
Adult protective services.
Protection of aged or incapacitated adults, §§63.2-1603 to 63.2-1610.
Appeals to commissioner.
Home-based and adult foster care services, §63.2-1602.1.
Domestic violence prevention services, §§63.2-1611 to 63.2-1615.
Foster care services, §63.2-1601.
Agency approved providers of services to adults, §63.2-1601.1.
Home-based services, §63.2-1600.
Other services, §63.2-1602.
Appeals.
Adult services.
Home-based and adult foster care services.
Appeals to commissioner, §63.2-1602.1.
Appropriations by counties and cities, §63.2-400.
Auditor of public accounts.
Expenses incurred in rendering services.
Administrative expenses of state department, §63.2-404.
Board for the blind and vision impaired.
Generally.
See BLIND AND VISION IMPAIRED, BOARD FOR.
Caregivers grant program, §§63.2-2200 to 63.2-2204.
Child abuse or neglect, §§63.2-1500 to 63.2-1527.
See CHILD ABUSE AND NEGLECT.
Child support enforcement.
Generally, §§63.2-1900 to 63.2-1960.
See CHILD SUPPORT ENFORCEMENT BY DEPARTMENT OF SOCIAL SERVICES.
Child welfare agencies.
Generally.
See CHILD WELFARE AGENCIES.
Comptroller.
Expenses incurred in rendering services.
Administrative expenses of state department, §63.2-404.
Confidentiality of records of department and local boards, §§63.2-102 to 63.2-105.
County manager form of government.
Responsibility of county manager, §15.2-615.
Definitions, §63.2-100.
Department for the blind and vision impaired.
Generally.
See BLIND AND VISION IMPAIRED, DEPARTMENT FOR.
Disclosure of confidential department or local board information.
Criminal penalty, §§63.2-102, 63.2-104.
District homes for aged, indigent, infirmed and incapacitated persons act.
Uncodified, §63.2-1700.
Domestic violence prevention services, §§63.2-1611 to 63.2-1615.
Local departments of social services.
Responsibilities, §63.2-1613.

SOCIAL SERVICES —Cont'd
Domestic violence prevention services —Cont'd
Policy of Commonwealth, §63.2-1611.
State department of social services.
Agency to coordinate state services, §63.2-1611.
Functions and services funded by department, §63.2-1615.
Grants funds, receipt, §63.2-1614.
Responsibilities, §63.2-1612.
Eligibility for medical assistance, medical care and social services.
Determination by commissioner, §63.2-405.
Failure of county or city to provide.
Deductions, withholding payments, §63.2-408.
Faith-based and community initiatives, §63.2-703.
Family and children's trust fund, §§63.2-2100 to 63.2-2103.
Foster care, §§63.2-900 to 63.2-915.
See FOSTER CARE.
Funding of marriage and family programs.
State department of social services, §63.2-214.1.
Funding of public assistance and social services, §§63.2-400 to 63.2-412.
Appropriations by counties and cities, §63.2-400.
Children's residential facilities.
Construction and operation by local boards, §63.2-411.
Expenditures by state department.
Purposes, §63.2-403.
Expenses of auditor of public accounts, comptroller and state treasurer, §63.2-404.
Failure of county or city to provide.
Deductions, withholding payments, §63.2-408.
Foster care.
Appropriations by counties and cities, §63.2-400.
Reimbursement of counties and cities, §63.2-401.
Lien on property of applicant or recipient.
No lien to attach, §63.2-409.
Medical assistance, medical care and social services eligibility.
Determination by commissioner, §63.2-405.
Needy persons engaged in work or training programs.
Assistance to, costs of administration, §63.2-412.
Other necessary or incidental public assistance or socials services.
County or city providing, §63.2-407.
Payment for by counties and cities.
Appropriations, §63.2-400.
Reimbursement, §63.2-401.
Pool of funds under comprehensive services act, §63.2-410.
Reimbursement of counties and cities, §63.2-401.
Reimbursement to Commonwealth.
Local boards, §63.2-402.
Social security act or regulations of department of health and human services amendments.
Authority of state board to adopt standards, requirements or procedures, §63.2-406.
Work or training programs.
Assistance to needy persons engaged in, cost of administration, §63.2-412.
Human services information and referral program, §§63.2-222 to 63.2-227.
See HUMAN SERVICES INFORMATION AND REFERRAL PROGRAM.
Human trafficking.
State department of social services.
Information related to, §63.2-214.3.

SOCIAL SERVICES —Cont'd
Interstate compact for the placement of children, §63.2-1000.
Implementation, §§63.2-1100 to 63.2-1105.
Licensing and regulation.
Adult day care center.
Generally, §§63.2-1700 to 63.2-1819.
See ADULT DAY CARE CENTERS.
Assisted living facilities.
Generally, §§63.2-1700 to 63.2-1819.
See ASSISTED LIVING FACILITIES.
Child welfare agencies.
Generally, §§63.2-1700 to 63.2-1819.
See CHILD WELFARE AGENCIES.
Lien on property of applicant or recipient.
No lien to attach, §63.2-409.
Local boards of social services, §§63.2-300 to 63.2-323.
Abandoned children.
Authority to take custody and place, §63.2-910.1.
Acceptance or expenditure of funds received as pension, insurance or other benefit.
Child placed by or entrusted to board, §63.2-320.
Administration of law, responsibility, §63.2-313.
Adoption.
Agency or local board placement generally, §§63.2-1221 to 63.2-1229.
Authority of boards to consent to and place for, §§63.2-900, 63.2-903.
Entrustment agreements, §§63.2-1221 to 63.2-1223.
Generally, §§63.2-1200 to 63.2-1248.
See ADOPTION.
Advisory boards.
Localities in which government official constitutes board, §63.2-305.
Appointment, §63.2-301.
Arrest, indictment or prosecution of department employee.
Payment of legal fees and expenses, §63.2-318.
Baccalaureate degree.
Required of personnel directing client services, §63.2-219.
Board in single county.
How established, §63.2-302.
Budget request.
Commission to review, §63.2-205.
Submission of budget to governing body, §63.2-316.
Chairman and vice-chairman, §63.2-312.
Chief of administrative officers of composing board.
District boards, §63.2-307.
Child placed by or entrusted to board.
Acceptance or expenditure of funds received as pension, insurance or other benefit, §63.2-320.
Child protective services records and information.
Confidentiality, discretionary release, §63.2-105.
Children's residential facilities.
Construction and operation by local boards, reimbursement, §63.2-411.
Child welfare and other services, §63.2-319.
City boards, how constituted, §63.2-304.
City council members.
Appointment to city board, §63.2-304.
Combination of counties and cities.
Establishment of one board, §§63.2-300, 63.2-306.

SOCIAL SERVICES —Cont'd
Local boards of social services —Cont'd
Combination of counties and cities —Cont'd
Fiscal officer for district board, §63.2-311.
Compensation and expenses, §63.2-310.
Fiscal officer for district board, §63.2-311.
Confidentiality of records, information and statistical registries, §§63.2-102 to 63.2-105.
Cooperation with juvenile and domestic relations court, §63.2-321.
Counsel to give advice or represent board and employees, §63.2-317.
Arrest, indictment or prosecution of department employee.
Payment of legal fees and expenses, §63.2-318.
Deposit of funds received, §63.2-314.
Destruction or disposal of records.
Adoption of regulations by state board, §63.2-217.
District boards.
Chief of administrative officers of subdivisions composing board, §63.2-307.
Local board for York county and City of Poquoson district, §63.2-307.
Two or more political subdivision establishing, §§63.2-300, 63.2-306.
Fiscal officer, compensation, §63.2-311.
Eligibility for continued receipt of public assistance.
Information to applicant regarding rights and responsibilities, §63.2-501.
Emergency payments issued to local boards, §63.2-323.
Employee education, professional and training requirements and performance standards.
Commissioner to enforce, §63.2-208.
State board to establish, §63.2-219.
Entrustment agreements.
Parent or guardian entrusting child to board for placement, §§63.2-900, 63.2-903.
Established by county of city.
Board in single county, §63.2-302.
City boards, §63.2-304.
Requirement, §63.2-300.
Special forms of county government, §63.2-303.
Fee schedules, establishment, §63.2-314.
Fees for court order services, §63.2-314.
Fiscal officer.
District boards, §63.2-311.
Foster care generally, §§63.2-900 to 63.2-915.
See FOSTER CARE.
Governing bodies authorized to make grant, §63.2-314.
Government official designated as board, §§63.2-302, 63.2-304.
Advisory board established, §63.2-305.
Grants, gifts, contributions, bequest or legacies.
Authorize to receive and disburse funds, §63.2-314.
Grievance procedures, §63.2-219.
Hearings, conducting, §63.2-322.
Interest in public assistance social services persons served by local department.
Duty of board, §63.2-321.
Local directors.
Board to direct activities, §63.2-321.
Meetings, §63.2-312.
Oaths, administering, §63.2-322.
Public assistance generally, §§63.2-500 to 63.2-805.
See PUBLIC AID AND ASSISTANCE.

SOCIAL SERVICES —Cont'd
Local boards of social services —Cont'd
Quorum, §63.2-309.
Regulations, establishment, §63.2-314.
Reports.
Commissioner may require, §63.2-205.
Furnishing commissioner and governing bodies, §63.2-315.
Schools.
Discipline of students.
Interagency agreement, child abuse and neglect investigations, §63.2-1511.
Secretary.
Local director to act as, §63.2-312.
Services provided, §63.2-319.
Special forms of county government.
Provision for establishing, §63.2-303.
Subpoenas issued by board, §63.2-322.
Criminal penalty for failure to obey, §63.2-106.
Suspension or removal of members, §63.2-308.
Temporary assistance for needy families, §§63.2-600 to 63.2-621.
See TEMPORARY ASSISTANCE FOR NEEDY FAMILIES (TANF).
Temporary custody of minor.
Right to accept, §63.2-900.
Terms, term limitation, §63.2-301.
Training of personnel.
Commissioner to direct, §63.2-204.
Two or more political subdivision establishing, §§63.2-300, 63.2-306.
Local departments of social services, §§63.2-324 to 63.2-336.
Arrest, indictment or prosecution of department employee.
Payment of legal fees and expenses, §63.2-318.
Child abuse and neglect, §§63.2-1500 to 63.2-1527.
See CHILD ABUSE AND NEGLECT.
Child-protective services units, §63.2-1503.
Combination departments.
Two or governments establishing, §63.2-324.
Cooperation with public and private agencies, §63.2-334.
Counsel to give advise or represent board and employees, §63.2-317.
Arrest, indictment or prosecution of department employee.
Payment of legal fees and expenses, §63.2-318.
Counties having special form of government, §63.2-331.
County manager form of government, §15.2-626.
Criminal background investigations.
Record information, dissemination, §19.2-389.
Criminal history and central registry checks.
Placement of children, §63.2-901.1.
Director.
Agent of commissioner in implementing laws, §63.2-333.
Appointment, §63.2-325.
Bond, §63.2-328.
Compensation, §63.2-330.
Local board to direct, §63.2-321.
Powers and duties, §63.2-332.
Removal by commissioner, §63.2-327.
Secretary of local board, §§63.2-312, 63.2-332.
Service at pleasure of board, §63.2-326.
Employees, §§63.2-325, 63.2-326.
Bond for certain employees, §63.2-329.
Compensation, §63.2-330.

SOCIAL SERVICES —Cont'd
Local departments of social services —Cont'd
Foster care generally, §§63.2-900 to 63.2-915.
See FOSTER CARE.
Independent living services for juvenile on release from commitment, §16.1-293.
Public assistance generally, §§63.2-500 to 63.2-805.
See PUBLIC AID AND ASSISTANCE.
Records of cases handled and business transacted, §63.2-335.
Report on work and proceedings, §63.2-336.
Required for cities and counties, §63.2-324.
Temporary assistance for needy families, §§63.2-600 to 63.2-621.
See TEMPORARY ASSISTANCE FOR NEEDY FAMILIES (TANF).
Urban county executive form of government, §15.2-835.
Local superintendents of public welfare.
Generally.
See SUPERINTENDENTS OF PUBLIC WELFARE.
Other necessary or incidental public assistance or social services.
County or city providing, §63.2-407.
Payment by counties and cities.
Appropriations, §63.2-400.
Reimbursement, §63.2-401.
Public assistance.
Generally, §§63.2-500 to 63.2-805.
See PUBLIC AID AND ASSISTANCE.
Reimbursement to Commonwealth.
Local boards, §63.2-402.
Shaken baby syndrome.
State department of social services.
Information related to, §63.2-214.2.
Social security act or regulations of department of health and human services amendments.
Authority of state board to adopt standards, requirements or procedures, §63.2-406.
Spending limitations.
State department of social services.
Marriage and family programs, §63.2-214.1.
State board of social services.
Advisory to commissioner, §63.2-216.
Chairman, vice-chairman and secretary, §63.2-215.
Destruction or disposal of records by local boards.
Adoption of regulations, §63.2-217.
Education, professional and training requirements and performance standards.
Board to establish, §63.2-219.
Fiscal impact of regulation.
Board to examine before adopting, §63.2-217.
Hearings, conducting, §§63.2-220, 63.2-221.
Human research.
Adoption of regulations, §63.2-218.
Investigations.
Administration of oaths, conducting hearings and issuing subpoenas, §§63.2-220, 63.2-221.
At direction of governor, §63.2-221.
Power to conduct, §63.2-216.
Main office, location, §63.2-215.
Meetings, quorum, §63.2-215.
Number of members, §63.2-215.
Oaths, administering, §§63.2-220, 63.2-221.
Persons ineligible for appointment, §63.2-215.
Powers and duties generally, §63.2-216.

SOCIAL SERVICES —Cont'd
State board of social services —Cont'd
Public assistance generally, §§63.2-500 to 63.2-805.
See PUBLIC AID AND ASSISTANCE.
Qualifications and experience, §63.2-215.
Regulations.
Adoption, §63.2-217.
Human research, §63.2-218.
Enforcement by commissioner, §63.2-203.
Social security act or regulations of department of health and human services amendments.
Authority of state board to adopt standards, requirements or procedures, §63.2-406.
Subpoenas issued by board, §§63.2-220, 63.2-221.
Criminal penalty for failure to obey, §63.2-106.
Temporary assistance for needy families, §§63.2-600 to 63.2-621.
See TEMPORARY ASSISTANCE FOR NEEDY FAMILIES (TANF).
Terms and term limitation, §63.2-215.
State department of social services.
Agents and employees.
Bond, §63.2-214.
Employment, §63.2-212.
Powers, duties, titles, salaries and remuneration, §63.2-213.
Baccalaureate degree.
Required of personnel directing client services, §63.2-219.
Child abuse or neglect, §§63.2-1500 to 63.2-1527.
See CHILD ABUSE AND NEGLECT.
Child-protective services differential response system, §63.2-1504.
Child-protective services units, §63.2-1502.
Commissioner.
Access to information of department and local boards, §63.2-102.
Appeals by public assistance applicants or recipient, §§63.2-517 to 63.2-519.
Appointment, §63.2-201.
Budget request by local boards.
Review, §63.2-205.
Collection and publication of statistics, §63.2-204.
Conferences to further cooperation, conducting, §63.2-204.
Cooperation with federal agencies, §63.2-206.
Cooperation with local authorities, §63.2-204.
Education, professional and training requirements and performance standards for personnel.
Enforcement, §63.2-208.
Eligibility for medical assistance, medical care and social services.
Determination, §63.2-405.
Forms required to administer chapter, prescribing, §63.2-205.
Grants-in-aid, funds and gifts.
Authority to receive, §63.2-207.
Powers and duties, §63.2-203.
Regulations adopted by state board.
Enforcement, §63.2-203.
Reports by local boards, requiring, §63.2-205.
Supervision and control of department, §63.2-200.
Term, §63.2-202.
Training of local board personnel, §63.2-204.
Vacancies, filling, §63.2-202.
Confidentiality of records, information and statistical registries, §§63.2-102 to 63.2-105.

SOCIAL SERVICES —Cont'd
State department of social services —Cont'd
Counsel to represent local boards and department.
Approval, reimbursement of local boards, §63.2-317.
Created, §63.2-200.
Division heads.
Appointment by commissioner, §63.2-210.
Powers and duties, §63.2-211.
Divisions, §63.2-209.
Eligibility for medical assistance, medical care and social services.
Determination by commissioner, §63.2-405.
Employee education, professional and training requirements and performance standards.
Commissioner to enforce, §63.2-208.
State board to establish, §63.2-219.
Expenditures of appropriated funds.
Purposes, §63.2-403.
Funding for marriage and family programs, §63.2-214.1.
Human services information and referral program.
Duties of department, §63.2-226.
Public assistance generally, §§63.2-500 to 63.2-805.
See PUBLIC AID AND ASSISTANCE.
Records and information from other agencies.
Receipt by, use, §63.2-101.
Regional offices, establishment by commissioner, §63.2-209.
Shaken baby syndrome.
Information related to, §63.2-214.2.
Spending on marriage and family programs, §63.2-214.1.
Temporary assistance for needy families, §§63.2-600 to 63.2-621.
See TEMPORARY ASSISTANCE FOR NEEDY FAMILIES (TANF).
Work or training programs.
Assistance to needy persons engage in, cost of administration, §63.2-412.
State treasurer.
Expenses incurred in rendering services.
Administrative expenses of state department, §63.2-404.
Support of dependent children and custodians.
Collection of support generally.
See CHILD SUPPORT.
TANF, §§63.2-600 to 63.2-621.
See TEMPORARY ASSISTANCE FOR NEEDY FAMILIES (TANF).
Temporary assistance for needy families, §§63.2-600 to 63.2-621.
See TEMPORARY ASSISTANCE FOR NEEDY FAMILIES (TANF).
Unemployment compensation, §§60.2-100 to 60.2-637.
See UNEMPLOYMENT COMPENSATION.
VIEW.
Virginia initiative for employment not welfare, §§63.2-608 to 63.2-613.
Virginia caregivers grant program, §§63.2-2200 to 63.2-2204.
Virginia initiative for employment not welfare, §§63.2-608 to 63.2-613.
Welfare.
Generally, §§63.2-500 to 63.2-805.
See PUBLIC AID AND ASSISTANCE.
Work or training programs.
Assistance to needy persons engage in, cost of administration, §63.2-412.

SOCIAL SERVICES BOARD.
County manager form of government, §15.2-626.
Legal representation of employees, §15.2-1519.
Liability insurance for employees, §15.2-1519.
Local welfare boards.
General provisions.
See WELFARE BOARDS, LOCAL.
Urban county executive form of government, §15.2-835.

SOCIAL SERVICES BOARDS, LOCAL.
Generally.
See WELFARE BOARDS, LOCAL.

SOCIAL SERVICES BOARD, STATE.
Civil actions against members or employees.
Attorney general or assistant representing, §2.2-507.

SOCIAL SERVICES DEPARTMENT.
Behavioral health and developmental services department.
Collaboration, §51.5-120.
Child support collection.
Admissibility and identification of support payment records, §20-60.2.
Contents of support orders, §20-60.3.
Delivery of notice to party at last known address, §20-60.6.
Electronic data transmission of information to department, §20-60.4.
Support payment provisions transferred to department, §20-60.5.
Civil actions against members or employees.
Attorney general or assistant representing, §2.2-507.
Criminal background investigations.
Record information, dissemination, §19.2-389.
Desertion and nonsupport.
Immediate income deduction of initial support order, §20-79.2.
Freedom of information act.
Excluded records, §2.2-3705.5.
Home energy assistance program.
See HOME ENERGY ASSISTANCE PROGRAM.
Liens.
Child support collection. See within this heading, "Child support collection."
Prisoner work release earnings.
Use, §§53.1-60, 53.1-61.
Prisons.
Ineligibility of prisoner for public assistance benefits due to incarceration.
Notice by department to social services department, §53.1-31.3.
Putative father registry.
Established in department, §63.2-1249.
Generally, §§63.2-1249 to 63.2-1253.
Secretary of health and human resources.
Agency responsibility, §2.2-212.
Sexually violent predators, civil commitment.
Database of prisoners incarcerated for sexually violent offenses.
Access to records, §37.2-905.2.
Spousal support.
Admissibility and identification of support payment records, §20-60.2.
Contents of support orders, §20-60.3.
Electronic data transmission of information into department, §20-60.4.

SOCIAL SERVICES DEPARTMENT —Cont'd
Spousal support —Cont'd
Subsequent enforcement proceedings.
Delivery of notice to party at last known address, §20-60.6.
Support payment provisions transferred to department, §20-60.5.
Tax information.
Disseminating client information to Department of Taxation, §2.2-3803.
Tax commissioner authorized to divulge, §58.1-3.

SOCIAL SERVICES, LOCAL DEPARTMENTS.
Adoption.
Agency adoption.
See ADOPTION.
General provisions.
See ADOPTION.
County executive form of government, §§15.2-518, 15.2-527.
County manager form of government, §15.2-626.
Defined, §63.2-100.
Legal representation of employees, §15.2-1519.
Liability insurance for employees, §15.2-1519.
Notice.
Initial notice by certified mail, subsequent notices by regular mail, §63.2-100.1.
Urban county executive form of government, §15.2-835.

SOCIAL WORKER-CLIENT PRIVILEGE, §8.01-400.2, VA SCt Rule 2:506.

SOCIAL WORKERS, §§54.1-3700 to 54.1-3709.
Adult abuse, neglect or exploitation.
Report to local department of social services, §63.2-1606.
Authenticity and reasonableness of medical bills, §8.01-413.01.
Bills for medical services.
Presumption of authenticity and reasonableness, §8.01-413.01.
Board of social work, §§54.1-3703 to 54.1-3705.
Child abuse or neglect reports.
Reason to suspect, required reports, fine for failure, §63.2-1509.
Continuing education, §54.1-3708.
Defined terms, §54.1-3700.
Designation as, §54.1-3709.
Disasters, state or local emergency.
Immunity.
Abandonment of person owed duty in response to disaster, §8.01-225.01.
Unable to provide required care because of lack of resources, §8.01-225.02.
Donation of services.
Tax credit, §58.1-439.22.
Drug administration or prescription, §54.1-3702.
Duty to protect third parties.
Violent behavior or serious harm by client, §54.1-2400.1.
Educational requirements for licensure, §54.1-3707.1.
Exemptions from licensing, §54.1-3701.
Free clinics.
Immunity for services provided, §54.1-106.
Health benefit programs.
Provider willing to meet terms and conditions not to be excluded, §38.2-3407.

SOCIAL WORKERS —Cont'd
Health services plans.
Coverage of clinical social workers services, §38.2-4221.
Immunity.
Disasters, state or local emergency.
Abandonment of person owed duty in response to disaster, §8.01-225.01.
Unable to provide required care because of lack of resources, §8.01-225.02.
License requirements, §54.1-3706.
Exemptions, §54.1-3701.
Licenses continued, §54.1-3707.
Medical bills.
Presumption of authenticity and reasonableness, §8.01-413.01.
Privileged communications, §8.01-400.2, VA SCt Rule 2:506.
Professional corporations generally, §§13.1-542.1 to 13.1-556.
See PROFESSIONAL CORPORATIONS.
Professional limited liability companies.
Generally, §§13.1-1100 to 13.1-1123.
See PROFESSIONAL LIMITED LIABILITY COMPANIES.
Professions and occupations regulation generally.
See HEALTH PROFESSIONS DEPARTMENT.
Prohibited acts by licensees generally, §54.1-2409.1.
Records or papers of patients.
Admissibility of copies, §8.01-413.
Right of patient, attorney or authorized insurer to copies, §8.01-413.
Subpoenas, §8.01-413.
Standardized HCFA-1500 health insurance claims forms for services.
Acceptance by insurers required, §38.2-322.
Tax credit.
Donation of services, §58.1-439.22.
Title restrictions.
Applicability, §54.1-3513.
Sex offender treatment provider, §54.1-3611.
Unlawful designation as, §54.1-3709.
Unlawful procurement of licensure, §54.1-102.
Unlawful use of licensure, §54.1-111.

SOCIETIES.
Burial societies, §§38.2-4000 to 38.2-4022.
Cooperative associations generally, §§13.1-301 to 13.1-311.1.
See COOPERATIVE ASSOCIATIONS.
Credit unions, §§6.2-1300 to 6.2-1380.
See CREDIT UNIONS.
Fraternal benefit societies, §§38.2-4100 to 38.2-4137.
See FRATERNAL BENEFIT SOCIETIES.
Industrial loan associations, §§6.2-1400 to 6.2-1421.
See INDUSTRIAL LOAN ASSOCIATIONS.
Insignia, button or emblem.
Illegal use of registered insignia, §18.2-177.
Unauthorized wearing or displaying on motor vehicles of certain associations or societies, §18.2-176.

SOCIETIES FOR THE PREVENTION OF CRUELTY TO ANIMALS.
Property tax exemptions, §58.1-3613.

SOCIETY OF CERTIFIED PUBLIC ACCOUNTANTS.
Special license plates for members, §46.2-746.8.

SOCIETY OF THE 173RD AIRBORNE BRIGADE.
Special license plates, §46.2-746.2:2.

SOD.
Structures, materials, etc., deemed permanently annexed to freehold, §43-2.

SODA WATER.
Marks on containers, §§59.1-93 to 59.1-102.
See MARKS ON CERTAIN CONTAINERS.

SODOMY.
Abduction with intent to defile, §18.2-48.
Punishment upon conviction of certain subsequent violent felony sexual assault, §18.2-67.5:3.
Seizure and forfeiture of property used in connection with abduction, §19.2-386.32.
Threatening, attempting or assisting, §18.2-49.
Childhood sexual abuse, §8.01-249.
Civil commitment of sexually violent predators.
See SEXUALLY VIOLENT PREDATORS, CIVIL COMMITMENT.
Crimes against nature, §18.2-361.
Punishment upon conviction of certain subsequent felony sexual assault, §18.2-67.5:2.
Venereal disease testing, §32.1-58.
Discretionary felony sentencing guidelines, §17.1-805.
Divorce.
Effect of cohabitation after knowledge of sodomy, §20-94.
Grounds for divorce from bond of matrimony, §20-91.
Forcible sodomy, §18.2-67.1.
Attempts, §18.2-67.5.
Jail prisoner escape or release notice, §53.1-116.1.
Prisoner intake notice, §53.1-116.1:01.
Capital murder, killing in commission of, §18.2-31.
Child victims' testimony.
Using two-way closed-circuit television, §18.2-67.9.
Death of victim, §18.2-63.1.
Deferral of proceedings, defendant placed on probation.
Counseling or therapy, completion.
Violation against spouse, §18.2-67.1.
Deposition of complaining witness, §18.2-67.
Firearm used or displayed, §18.2-53.1.
HIV or hepatitis B or C.
Testing of persons charged, §18.2-62.
Jail prisoner escape or release notice, §53.1-116.1.
Mandatory minimum term of confinement.
Complaining witness less than 13.
Offender more than 3 years older than victim, §18.2-67.1.
Murder of the first degree, killing in commission of, §18.2-32.
Payment of medical fees in gathering evidence, §19.2-165.1.
Physical resistance, proof not required, §18.2-67.6.
Preliminary hearings, §§18.2-67.8, 19.2-218.1, 19.2-218.2.
Prisoner intake notice, §53.1-116.1:01.
Probation, conditions, §19.2-303.
Punishment upon conviction of certain subsequent violent felony sexual assault, §18.2-67.5:3.
Sentence of person twice previously convicted of certain violent felonies, §19.2-297.1.

SODOMY —Cont'd
Forcible sodomy —Cont'd
Suspension of sentence, §19.2-303.
Complaining witness less than 13.
Offender more than 3 years older than victim, §18.2-67.1.
Counseling or therapy, completion.
Violation against spouse, §18.2-67.1.
Unchaste character or prior sexual conduct of complaining witness, §18.2-67.7.
Venue, person transported through or across Commonwealth, §18.2-359.
Medical fees in gathering of evidence, §19.2-165.1.
Preliminary hearings.
Forcible sodomy, §§18.2-67.8, 19.2-218.1, 19.2-218.2.
Sexually violent predators.
Civil commitment generally.
See SEXUALLY VIOLENT PREDATORS, CIVIL COMMITMENT.
Taking indecent liberties with children, §18.2-370.
Custodians or persons in supervisory relationship, §18.2-370.1.
Jail prisoner escape or release notice, §53.1-116.1.
Prisoner intake notice, §53.1-116.1:01.
Punishment upon conviction of certain subsequent felony sexual assault, §18.2-67.5:2.

SOFAS.
Bedding and upholstered furniture generally, §§32.1-212 to 32.1-226.
See BEDDING AND UPHOLSTERED FURNITURE.

SOFT DRINK EXCISE TAX, §§58.1-1700 to 58.1-1705.

SOFT DRINKS.
Litter tax imposed on manufacturers, wholesalers, etc., §58.1-1708.

SOFTWARE.
Computer crimes, §§18.2-152.1 to 18.2-152.15.
See COMPUTER CRIMES.
Intangible personal property tax, §§58.1-1100 to 58.1-1118.
See PERSONAL PROPERTY TAXES.
Open source initiative.
Public officers and employees.
Ownership of copyrights developed by state employees, §2.2-2822.
Property capable of embezzlement, §18.2-152.8.
Retail sales and use tax.
Commercial and industrial exemptions, §58.1-609.3.
Unlawful electronic communication devices, §§18.2-190.1 to 18.2-190.8.

SOIL AND WATER CONSERVATION, §§10.1-500 to 10.1-559.
Agricultural stewardship, §§3.2-400 to 3.2-410.
See AGRICULTURAL STEWARDSHIP.
Attorney general.
Defense of claims, §10.1-501.1.
Duties, §10.1-501.
Board, §§10.1-500 to 10.1-505.
See SOIL AND WATER CONSERVATION BOARD.
City.
Defined, §10.1-500.
County.
Defined, §10.1-500.

SOIL AND WATER CONSERVATION —Cont'd
Database of critical data attributes.
Nutrients and sediments entering state waters.
Onsite best management practices implemented by state to limit, §2.2-220.3.
Defense of claims, §10.1-501.1.
District director.
Defined, §10.1-500.
Districts, §§10.1-506 to 10.1-559.
See SOIL AND WATER CONSERVATION DISTRICTS.
Due notice.
Defined, §10.1-500.
Erosion and sediment control, §§62.1-44.15:51 to 62.1-44.15:66.
Governing body of a city or county.
Defined, §10.1-500.
Government or governmental.
Defined, §10.1-500.
Land occupier.
Defined, §10.1-500.
Locality.
Defined, §10.1-500.
Nutrients and sediments entering state waters.
Database of critical data attributes.
Onsite best management practices implemented by state to limit, §2.2-220.3.
Occupier of land.
Defined, §10.1-500.
Soil and water conservation district.
Defined, §10.1-500.

SOIL AND WATER CONSERVATION BOARD, §§10.1-500 to 10.1-505.
Administrative officer, §10.1-503.
Chairman, §10.1-504.
Composition, §10.1-502.
Continuation, §10.1-502.
Defined, §10.1-500.
Duties, §10.1-505.
Employees, §10.1-503.
Executive committee, §10.1-503.
Mail notice.
Initial notice by certified mail, subsequent notices by regular mail, §10.1-500.1.
Nutrient management plans.
Nitrogen application rates, regulations regarding, §10.1-104.2:1.
Regulations for, §§10.1-104.2, 10.1-505.
Quorum, §10.1-504.
Resource management plans, §§10.1-104.7 to 10.1-104.9.
Supplemental environmental projects.
Requiring persons to undertake, §10.1-104.6.

SOIL AND WATER CONSERVATION DISTRICTS, §§10.1-506 to 10.1-559.
Accounts, §10.1-535.
Action on application and statement, §10.1-518.
Actions.
Certificate of secretary of Commonwealth, §10.1-522.
Agents.
District acts as agent for the United States, §10.1-547.
Agricultural best management practices cost-share assistance program, §10.1-546.1.
Annexation or consolidation.
Determination of boundaries, §10.1-521.
Benefits extension, §10.1-551.
Board.
Duty of directors after certification, §10.1-557.

SOIL AND WATER CONSERVATION DISTRICTS —Cont'd
Board —Cont'd
Information furnished by directors, §10.1-534.
Bonds, surety.
Officers and employees, §10.1-535.
Boundaries.
Determination of status of district boundaries, §10.1-521.
Certificate of dissolution.
Certified copies to state board of elections, §10.1-518.1.
Effect of issuance, §10.1-558.
Civil actions against members or employees.
Legal representation of district, §2.2-507.
Composition of district.
Change.
Certified copies to state board of elections, §10.1-518.1.
Composition of governing body, §10.1-515.
Contracts, §10.1-548.
Evidence.
Certificate of secretary of Commonwealth, §10.1-522.
Remaining in force, §10.1-520.
Control measures, §10.1-541.
Cooperation between districts, §10.1-549.
Cooperation with state agencies, §10.1-550.
Creation of new districts, §10.1-506.
Application and statement to secretary of Commonwealth, §10.1-517.
Certified copies to state board of elections, §10.1-518.1.
Petitions, §10.1-507.
Demonstrational project, §10.1-540.
Directors.
Advice and consultation from representatives of governing bodies, §10.1-537.
Agents, officers and employees, §10.1-532.
Bonds, surety.
Officers and employees, §10.1-535.
Chairman, §10.1-530.
Delegation of powers, §10.1-533.
Duties, §10.1-529.1.
Elections.
Independent candidates' petitions.
Number of signatures required, §24.2-506.
Governing body, §10.1-529.
Information furnished board, §10.1-534.
Notice of election, §10.1-523.
Quorum, §10.1-531.
Removal from office, §10.1-536.
Status.
Transfer, merger or division of districts, §10.1-516.
Terms of office, §10.1-530.
Vacancies, §10.1-530.
District defined, §10.1-500.
Division, transfer or merger of districts.
Contracts to remain in force, §10.1-520.
Status of directors, §10.1-516.
Education.
Virginia Envirothon, §10.1-549.1.
Elections.
Ballots, §10.1-524.
Canvassing returns, §10.1-525.
Certification of, §24.2-680.
Certification of returns, §10.1-525.
Determination of candidates elected, §10.1-527.
Expenses and publication of results, §10.1-528.

SOIL AND WATER CONSERVATION DISTRICTS —Cont'd
Elections —Cont'd
Names of nominees furnished to electoral board, §10.1-524.
Notice of election for district directors, §10.1-523.
Persons eligible to vote, §10.1-526.
Petitions of independent candidates for director.
Number of signatures required, §24.2-506.
Termination of district.
Referendum, §10.1-555.
Equipment and material.
Making available to land occupiers, §10.1-544.
Evidence.
Certificate of secretary of Commonwealth, §10.1-522.
Expenses of directors, §10.1-531.
Feasibility of operation, §10.1-514.
Financial aid, §10.1-542.
Freedom of information, §10.1-539.
Hearings.
Adjournment.
Desirable appearance of additional territory, §10.1-511.
Income tax.
Credit for purchase of advanced technology pesticide and fertilizer application equipment, §58.1-337.
Corporate tax credit, §58.1-436.
Interpretation of provisions.
District as political subdivision, §10.1-538.
Landowner petitions.
Termination of district, §10.1-553.
Material and equipment.
Making available, §10.1-554.
Renting machinery and equipment, §10.1-552.
Modification of districts.
Petitions, §10.1-507.
Name of district.
Change of name, §10.1-518.
Certified copies to state board of elections, §10.1-518.1.
Need for districts.
Determination, §10.1-512.
Determination district not needed, §10.1-513.
New districts.
Creation, §10.1-506.
Certified copies to state board of elections, §10.1-518.1.
Petitions, §10.1-507.
Approval, §10.1-510.
Contents, §10.1-508.
Disapproval, §10.1-509.
Nominating petitions, §10.1-523.
Renewal after disapproval or denial, §10.1-519.
Termination of district, §10.1-553.
Once in five years, §10.1-559.
Preventative measures, §10.1-541.
Program and plan development, §10.1-546.
Project acquisition and administration, §10.1-547.
Real property.
Acquisition, improvement and disposition, §10.1-543.
Structures.
Construction, maintenance and operation, §10.1-545.
Records, §10.1-535.
Removal of directors, §10.1-536.
Renting machinery and equipment, §10.1-552.

SOIL AND WATER CONSERVATION DISTRICTS —Cont'd
Risk management plan for public liability, §2.2-1837.
Rules and regulations, §10.1-548.
Surveys, §10.1-539.
Termination of district.
Certificate of dissolution.
Certified copies to state board of elections, §10.1-518.1.
Effect of issuance, §10.1-558.
Determination of board, §10.1-556.
Hearings, §10.1-554.
Petition by landowners, §10.1-553.
Petitions limited to once in five years, §10.1-559.
Referendum, §10.1-555.
Virginia Envirothon, §10.1-549.1.
Watershed improvements districts.
Powers, §§10.1-632, 10.1-633.

SOIL SCIENTISTS, WETLAND PROFESSIONALS AND GEOLOGISTS, §§54.1-2200 to 54.1-2208.4.
Board, §§54.1-2200.1, 54.1-2200.2.
Certification requirements, §§54.1-2203 to 54.1-2205.
Examination waiver, §54.1-2206.
Geologists, §54.1-2208.3.
Exceptions, §§54.1-2201, 54.1-2208.1.
Minimum qualifications for geologists, §54.1-2208.2.
Professional wetland delineators, §§54.1-2206.1, 54.1-2206.2.
Conduct, professional, §54.1-2207.
Geologist certification, §54.1-2208.4.
Criminal offenses.
Misrepresentation, §54.1-2208.
Defined terms, §54.1-2200.
Geologist certification.
Examination waiver, §54.1-2208.3.
Minimum qualifications, §54.1-2208.2.
Professional ethics and conduct, §54.1-2208.4.
Voluntary, §54.1-2208.1.
Professional conduct, §54.1-2207.
Unlawful procurement of licensure, §54.1-102.
Unlawful representation, §54.1-2208.
Unlawful use of licensure, §54.1-111.

SOLAR EASEMENTS, §§55-352 to 55-354.

SOLAR ENERGY.
Community association covenants restricting collection devices.
Prohibition, exception, §§67-700, 67-701.
Green job creation tax credit, §58.1-439.12:05.
Green roofing.
Incentives and regulatory flexibility, §58.1-3852.
Personal property taxes.
Classification of property for manufacturing renewable energy products, §58.1-3506.
Photovoltaic, solar and wind energy utilization grant program, §§67-1000 to 67-1003.
Property exempt from taxation.
Certified equipment, facilities or devices, §58.1-3661.
Real property taxes.
Classification of improvements to property used for design and manufacture of renewable energy products, §58.1-3221.4.
Renewable energy portfolio standard program.
Investor-owned incumbent electric utility.
Sale of electricity from renewable sources through, §56-585.2.

SOLAR ENERGY —Cont'd
Residential property transfer disclosures.
Right to install solar energy collection devices, §55-519.
Solar energy center.
Center purposes, §45.1-391.
Solar photovoltaic manufacturing incentive grant program, §45.1-392.
Voluntary solar resource development fund, §§67-1300 to 67-1305.
Administration, §67-1302.
Definitions, §67-1300.
Electric utilities.
Defined, §67-1300.
Duties, §67-1301.
Establishment, §67-1302.
Reports, §67-1304.
Revolving loan program, §67-1303.
Scope of program, §67-1304.
Solar energy projects, eligible, §67-1303.
Uses of money, permitted, §§67-1302, 67-1303.

SOLE CUSTODY.
Court may order, §20-124.2.
Defined, §20-124.1.

SOLE PROPRIETORSHIPS.
Jury service.
Voluntary exemption, §8.01-341.1.

SOLICITATION.
ABC offenses.
Solicitation by persons interested in manufacture, etc., of alcoholic beverages, §4.1-330.
Attorneys.
Professional employment by attorneys, §§54.1-3939 to 54.1-3944.
See ATTORNEYS AT LAW.
Boat dealers.
Prohibitions, §29.1-827.
Bribery.
Games, contests or sports participants, manager, coaches or trainers, §18.2-443.
General assembly members soliciting money or other thing of value for services, §30-103.
Public servants or party officials, §§18.2-447, 18.2-449.
Cemetery operators, perpetual care trust funds and preneed burial contracts.
Prohibited acts, §54.1-2327.
Child labor, §40.1-112.
Motor vehicle dealers.
Prohibited solicitation and compensation, §46.2-1537.
T&M vehicle dealers.
Prohibited solicitations and compensation, §46.2-1938.

SOLICITATION OF CHARITABLE OR CIVIC CONTRIBUTIONS, §§57-48 to 57-69.
Attorney general.
Civil investigative demands, §57-59.
Charge uses, §57-65.
Charitable gifts generally.
See CHARITABLE GIFTS.
Civil investigative demands.
Attorney general, §57-59.
Commercial co-ventures.
Defined, §57-48.
Registration of charitable organizations, §57-61.2.
Conflict of laws, §§57-62, 57-69.
Contracts with professional fundraisers, §57-54.
Filing to become public record, §57-56.

SOLICITATION OF CHARITABLE OR CIVIC CONTRIBUTIONS —Cont'd
Defined terms, §57-48.
Deposits by professional fundraisers, §57-61.
Disclosures, §57-55.2.
Financial statements, §57-55.3.
For-profit organizations, §57-55.2:1.
Effective date of provisions, §57-69.
Exemptions from provisions, §57-60.
Federated fund-raising organizations.
Withholding from donations designated for member agencies, disclosure, §57-58.
Fees, §57-65.
Financial exploitation of mentally incapacitated persons, §18.2-178.1.
Hearing.
Time notice, §57-61.1.
Information filed to become public record, §57-56.
Judicial review, §57-67.
Local ordinances, §57-63.
Model ordinance promulgation, §57-66.
Online filing.
Annual registration statements, §57-50.
Out-of-state enforcement proceedings, §57-64.
Professional fundraisers.
Solicitation notices, §57-61.
Prohibited acts, §57-57.
Out-of-state enforcement proceedings, §57-64.
Penalties for violations, §57-59.
Reciprocal agreements, §57-50.
Filing to become public record, §57-56.
Records of professional fundraisers, §57-61.
Registering exemption from provisions.
Application, fee, §57-60.
Registration of charitable organizations, §57-49.
Commercial co-ventures, §57-61.2.
Effective date, §57-61.1.
Exploitation of, §57-57.
Federated fund-raising organizations.
Withholding from donations designated for member agencies, disclosure, §57-58.
Filing to become public record, §57-56.
Online filing, §57-50.
Ratio of fund-raising expenses to contributions to be included, §57-58.
Suspension, §57-61.1.
Registration of nonresidents, §57-51.
Effective date, §57-61.1.
Exploitation of, §57-57.
Filing to become public record, §57-56.
Online filing, §57-50.
Ratio of fundraising expenses to contributions to be included, §57-58.
Suspension, §57-61.1.
Registration of professional fundraisers, §57-61.
Disclosures, §57-55.2:1.
Effective date, §57-61.
Filings to become public record, §57-56.
Ratio of fundraising expenses to contributions to be included, §57-58.
Suspension, §57-61.1.
Rules and regulations, §57-66.
Solicitation notices.
Professional fund-raisers, §57-61.
Terrorism, prohibition against support of, §§57-49, 57-57.
Seizure of property connected with terrorism, §57-59.

SOLICITATION OF CHARITABLE OR CIVIC CONTRIBUTIONS —Cont'd
Warnings, publication of, §§57-52, 57-52.1.

SOLICITATION OF PROFESSIONAL EMPLOYMENT BY ATTORNEYS, §§54.1-3939 to 54.1-3944.

SOLICITATION OF PROSTITUTION, §18.2-346.
Venereal disease testing, §32.1-58.

SOLICITATION TO COMMIT FELONY, §18.2-29.

SOLID RUBBER TIRES.
Restrictions, §46.2-1041.
Fine schedule, VA SCt Rule 3B:2.
Maximum fine for violating Title 46.2, §46.2-113.
Pretrial payment of fine, §16.1-69.40:1.

SOLID WASTE DISPOSAL ACT.
Community service.
Recycling duties for probationers.
Civil immunity, §8.01-226.8.
State programs to implement, §§2.2-617, 2.2-618.

SOLID WASTE MANAGEMENT, §§10.1-1408.1 to 10.1-1414, 15.2-901, 15.2-927 to 15.2-939.
Abandoned facilities.
Financial responsibility, §10.1-1410.
Burn pits.
Operating at closed landfills, §10.1-1410.3.
Casting into waters, §§62.1-194, 62.1-194.2.
Big Sandy river, §62.1-194.3.
Categories of facilities, §10.1-1408.1.
Certification of operators, §10.1-1408.2.
Charging and collecting compensation, §15.2-928.
Closure of landfills.
Burn pits.
Operating at closed landfills, §10.1-1410.3.
Postclosure monitoring, maintenance and plans, §10.1-1410.2.
Prioritization and procedure, §10.1-1413.2.
Coal combustion byproducts in designated flood plains.
Use, reuse or reclamation not exempted from definition of solid waste, §10.1-1402.02.
Collection and disposal of garbage generally, §15.2-927.
Community service.
Recycling duties for probationers.
Civil immunity, §8.01-226.8.
Contracting for services, §§10.1-1412, 15.2-930.
Authorization to enter into contract, §15.2-932.
Requiring delivery to certain facilities, §15.2-931.
With other localities or Commonwealth to provide or supply services, §15.2-928.
Environmental restoration sites.
Property tax classification and exemption, §58.1-3664.
Expansion of facilities.
Notice on limitations, §10.1-1408.1.
Facility operators, §§54.1-2209 to 54.1-2212.
Certification and on-site presence, §10.1-1408.2.
Fee by certain counties, §15.2-2159.
Fee exemption, §15.2-936.
Household hazardous waste.
Storage, §10.1-1408.1.
Landfill closure.
Requirements, §10.1-1413.2.
Leaves or grass clippings in landfill, §15.2-935.
Local and regional plans, §10.1-1411.

SOLID WASTE MANAGEMENT —Cont'd
Methane or other combustible gas.
Building or facility to collect or use for electric energy.
Loans to local governments, §§15.2-2430 to 15.2-2440.
See VIRGINIA INFRASTRUCTURE PROJECT LOAN FUND.
Motor carriers, property.
Exemptions from provisions, §46.2-2101.
Motor vehicles.
Local regulation of vehicle construction, parking, etc., §46.2-1304.1.
Overweight permits for solid waste haulers, §46.2-1144.
Notice.
Closing sanitary landfills, §10.1-1410.1.
Open dumps, §10.1-1408.1.
Operators, §§54.1-2209 to 54.1-2212.
Certification and on-site presence, §10.1-1408.2.
Penalties.
Financial responsibility for abandoned facilities, §10.1-1410.
Unauthorized disposal or refusal to use facilities, §15.2-928.
Permits.
Closure of landfill.
Postclosure monitoring, maintenance and plans, §10.1-1410.2.
Landfill siting review, §10.1-1408.4.
Requirement, §10.1-1408.1.
Revocation or amendment, §10.1-1409.
Wetlands.
Special provisions regarding, §10.1-1408.5.
Private companies, displacement, §15.2-934.
Prohibiting disposal in unauthorized area, §15.2-928.
Rechargeable battery disposal and recycling, §10.1-1425.39.
Recycling and waste disposal powers generally, §15.2-928.
Recycling survey reports, §10.1-1411.
Refuse collection and disposal authorities, §§15.2-5100 to 15.2-5159.
See WATER AND WASTE AUTHORITIES.
Regional and local plans, §10.1-1411.
Regulating generally, §15.2-930.
Requiring delivery to certain facilities, §§15.2-931, 15.2-933.
Requiring property owners to remove from property, §15.2-901.
Sanitary landfills.
Final closing plans, §10.1-1410.1.
Separation of solid waste generally, §15.2-937.
Service districts, §§15.2-2400 to 15.2-2403.3.
Ships, barges or other vessels transporting nonhazardous solid waste on navigable waters, §10.1-1454.1.
Siting approval for facility.
Locality enacting ordinance regulating, §15.2-929.
Siting of landfills.
Review, §10.1-1408.4.
Solid waste management facilities.
Providing and operating, §15.2-928.
Siting approval, §15.2-929.
State aid, §10.1-1413.
Treatment facilities.
Resources authority generally, §§62.1-197 to 62.1-223.
See RESOURCES AUTHORITY.

SOLID WASTE MANAGEMENT —Cont'd
Urban county executive form of government.
Regulation of garbage, trash and refuge pickup and disposal services, §15.2-815.
Contracting for services, §15.2-815.
Waste information and assessment program, §10.1-1413.1.
Wetlands.
Permits.
Special provisions regarding wetlands, §10.1-1408.5.

SOLID WASTE OR RECYCLING REVOLVING FUND, §§62.1-241.1 to 62.1-241.10.
Audits, §62.1-241.4.
Collection of money, §62.1-241.5.
Conflict of laws, §62.1-241.10.
Construction of provisions, §62.1-241.10.
Creation, §62.1-241.2.
Defined terms, §62.1-241.1.
Deposit of money, §62.1-241.3.
Grants to local governments, §62.1-241.7.
Preferences, §62.1-241.8.
Loans to local governments, §62.1-241.6.
Preferences, §62.1-241.8.
Sale of loans, §62.1-241.9:1.
Management, §62.1-241.2.
Powers of authority, §62.1-241.9:2.

SOLS.
Standards of learning for public schools, §22.1-253.13:1.

SONG OF THE COMMONWEALTH.
Song emeritus, §1-510.

SON OF SAM LAW, §§19.2-368.19 to 19.2-368.22.

SONS OF CONFEDERATE VETERANS.
Armories, use for meetings, §44-133.
Pelham Chapel leasing, §57-5.
Special license plates, §46.2-746.22.

SONS OF TEMPERANCE.
Benevolent associations generally.
See BENEVOLENT ASSOCIATIONS OR ORGANIZATIONS.
Land conveyances to sons, §§57-19, 57-20.

SORING HORSES, §§3.2-6570, 18.2-403.2.

SORORITIES.
Hazing, §18.2-56.
Initiation or induction.
Rules and regulations, §23-9.2:3.
Special license plates.
College fraternities and sororities, §46.2-746.7.

SOUND RECORDING.
Truth in music advertising act, §§59.1-466.1 to 59.1-466.4.

SOUTHAMPTON COUNTY.
Confederate cemeteries and graves.
Disbursement of funds appropriated for upkeep, §10.1-2211.
Port of Virginia economic and infrastructure development zone grant fund, §62.1-132.3:2.
Public defenders office.
Established, §19.2-163.04.
Retail sales and use tax.
Additional sales tax for Northern Virginia and Hampton Roads, §58.1-603.1.
Additional use tax for Northern Virginia and Hampton Roads, §58.1-604.01.

SOUTHAMPTON COUNTY —Cont'd
School board.
Salary of members, §22.1-32.
Tidewater airport commission, 1962 ch 606, 1964 ch 45.

SOUTH BOSTON.
Halifax economic development authority, §15.2-4903.
Industrial development authority.
Board of supervisors.
Appointment of members to board of authority, §15.2-4904.
School board.
Salary of members, §22.1-32.

SOUTHEASTERN INTERSTATE FOREST FIRE PROTECTION COMPACT.
Forest wardens and fires, §10.1-1149.

SOUTHEASTERN PUBLIC SERVICE AUTHORITY OF VIRGINIA, 1977 ch 544, 2000 ch 580, 2000 ch 596.

SOUTHEAST INTERSTATE LOW-LEVEL RADIOACTIVE WASTE MANAGEMENT COMPACT, §§10.1-1500 to 10.1-1504.
Alternates.
Commissioners, §10.1-1501.
Expenses, §10.1-1502.
Commissioners, §10.1-1501.
Expenses, §10.1-1502.
Cooperation of state and local agencies, §10.1-1503.
Enactment, §10.1-1500.
Enforcement, §10.1-1504.
Penalties, §10.1-1504.

SOUTHERN CROSS OF HONOR.
Wearing when not entitled, §18.2-176.

SOUTHERN DAIRY COMPACT, §§3.2-3300 to 3.2-3303.
Commission, §3.2-3300.
Members, §3.2-3301.
Cooperation by departments, agencies and officers of Commonwealth, §3.2-3302.
Enactment, §3.2-3300.
Milk commission.
Powers preserved, §3.2-3303.
Text, §3.2-3300.

SOUTHERN GROWTH POLICIES AGREEMENT, §§2.2-5700 to 2.2-5702.
Enactment, §2.2-5700.
Southern growth policies board, §2.2-5700.1.
Text of agreement, §2.2-5700.

SOUTHERN REGIONAL EDUCATION BOARD MINORITY DOCTORAL PROGRAM.
Stephen J. Wright scholars program established, §23-38.53:11.

SOUTHERN REGIONAL EDUCATION COMPACT, §§22.1-358, 22.1-359.
Board of control for southern regional education, §22.1-358.
Defaulting states, §22.1-358.
Effective date, §22.1-358.
Entry into compact, §22.1-358.
Funding, §22.1-358.
Purpose, §22.1-358.
Southern regional education board, §22.1-358.
Virginia's representatives, §22.1-359.
Termination, §22.1-358.
Withdrawal, §22.1-358.

SOUTHERN STATES ENERGY BOARD, §§2.2-5600, 2.2-5601.

SOUTHERN STATES ENERGY COMPACT, §§2.2-5600 to 2.2-5603.
Enactment, §2.2-5600.
Text of compact, §2.2-5600.

SOUTHERN VIRGINIA HIGHER EDUCATION CENTER, §§23-231.24 to 23-231.29.
Contracts for educational services, §23-231.26.
Cooperation of other agencies, §23-231.29.
Created, §23-231.24.
Duties, §23-231.24.
Employees.
Personnel administration system.
Exemptions, §2.2-2905.
Executive director, §23-231.27.
Gifts and grants, §23-231.28.
Governing board, §§23-231.25, 23-231.26.
Staff, §23-231.27.

SOUTH HILL.
Mecklenburg-Brunswick airport commission, 1975 ch 211, 1982 ch 42.

SOUTH MAYO RIVER.
Scenic river, §10.1-418.5.

SOUTHSIDE REGIONAL AIRPORT AUTHORITY AT BLACKSTONE, 1992 ch 371.

SOUTHSIDE VIRGINIA TOURISM DEVELOPMENT AUTHORITY, §§15.2-5509 to 15.2-5515.
Created, §15.2-5510.
Definitions, §15.2-5509.
Directors, §15.2-5511.
Executive director, §15.2-5513.
Executive director, §15.2-5513.
Gifts and grants, §15.2-5514.
Officers, §15.2-5511.
Powers, §15.2-5512.
Severability of chapter, §15.2-5515.
Terms of office, §15.2-5511.

SOUTHWEST REGIONAL RECREATION AUTHORITY, §§15.2-6016 to 15.2-6024.
Acquire or lease property.
Power, §15.2-6020.
Board of directors.
Appointment, §15.2-6018.
Authority governed by, §15.2-6018.
Bylaws and rules.
Power, §15.2-6019.
Executive director.
Appointment, §15.2-6019.
Meetings, §15.2-6019.
Quorum, §15.2-6019.
Terms, §15.2-6018.
Vacancies, §15.2-6018.
Bonds and revenue refunding bonds.
Not debt of Commonwealth, §15.2-6022.
Power to issue, §15.2-6020.
Civil penalty.
Localities within recreation area.
Allocation to authority, §15.2-6023.1.
Violation of rules, §15.2-6023.
Contract power, §15.2-6020.
Costs incidental to administration.
Payment, §15.2-6019.
Definitions, §15.2-6017.
Eminent domain.
Property not acquired through exercise of power, §15.2-6020.

SOUTHWEST REGIONAL RECREATION AUTHORITY —Cont'd
Established, §15.2-6016.
Executive director.
Appointment, §15.2-6019.
Expenses incurred in carrying out chapter.
Payment, §15.2-6019.
Insurance against losses.
Power to purchase, §15.2-6020.
Kentucky, Tennessee and West Virginia.
Cooperation, §15.2-6020.
Landowners and other with property interest.
Contracts to hold harmless, §15.2-6020.
Limiting liability, §15.2-6024.
Off-road recreational vehicles.
Operation in localities embraced by authority, §46.2-800.2.
Ordinance violations.
Civil penalty.
Localities within recreation area, allocation to authority, §15.2-6023.1.
Powers, §15.2-6020.
Public corporation, §15.2-6020.
Rangers.
Southwest regional recreation area.
Appointment, powers, salary, uniforms, shield, ID, §15.2-6021.
Recreational purposes.
Defined, §15.2-6017.
Southwest regional recreation area.
Defined, §15.2-6017.
Establishing and maintaining, §15.2-6016.
Rangers.
Appointment, powers, salary, uniforms, shield, ID, §15.2-6021.
Violation of rules.
Civil penalty, §15.2-6023.
Violations of ordinances.
Civil penalty.
Localities within recreation area, allocation to authority, §15.2-6023.1.

SOUTHWEST VIRGINIA CULTURAL HERITAGE FOUNDATION, §§2.2-2734 to 2.2-2737.
Administration, §2.2-2735.
Board of trustees, §2.2-2735.
Duties, §2.2-2736.
Established, §2.2-2734.
Officers and members, §2.2-2735.
Powers, §2.2-2736.
Purpose, §2.2-2734.
Staff, §2.2-2737.

SOUTHWEST VIRGINIA HEALTH FACILITIES AUTHORITY, §§15.2-5368 to 15.2-5386.
Applicability of provisions.
Limitations, §15.2-5386.
Appropriations by participating localities, §15.2-5375.
Board of directors.
Compensation of members, §15.2-5372.
Meetings, §15.2-5371.
Members, §15.2-5370.
Compensation, §15.2-5372.
Officers, §15.2-5370.
Quorum, §15.2-5371.
Vacancies, §15.2-5370.
Bond issues.
Issuance of bonds, §15.2-5377.
Legal investments, §15.2-5379.

SOUTHWEST VIRGINIA HEALTH FACILITIES AUTHORITY —Cont'd
Bond issues —Cont'd
Other laws.
Applicability, §15.2-5385.
Participating localities, §15.2-5376.
Powers of authority, §15.2-5374.
Revenues of hospital or health center.
Payable from, §15.2-5380.
Sale of bonds, §15.2-5377.
Security for payment, §15.2-5378.
Receivers, §15.2-5382.
Creation, §15.2-5368.
Definitions, §15.2-5369.
Eminent domain, §15.2-5383.
Established, §15.2-5368.
Executive director, §15.2-5373.
Exemption of property from foreclosure or execution sale and judgment lien, §15.2-5381.
Investments of entities owned or controlled by authority.
Law governing, §15.2-5374.
Limitations on, §15.2-5386.
Powers, §15.2-5374.
Eminent domain, §15.2-5383.
Receivers, §15.2-5382.
Records, §15.2-5384.
Reports, §15.2-5384.
Staff, §15.2-5373.
Supplemental nature of provisions, §15.2-5385.

SOUTHWEST VIRGINIA HIGHER EDUCATION CENTER, §§23-231.2 to 23-231.7.
Constituent institutions, §23-231.3.
Contracts for educational services, §23-231.4.
Cooperation with other agencies, §23-231.7.
Creation, §23-231.2.
Donations.
Application for and acceptance of gifts and grants, §23-231.6.
Duties, §23-231.2.
Executive director, §23-231.5.
Gifts and grants.
Application for and acceptance, §23-231.6.
Interagency cooperation, §23-231.7.
Membership of governing board, §23-231.3.
Officers, §23-231.3.
Powers of board, §23-231.4.
Southwest Virginia cultural heritage foundation.
Board of trustees, §2.2-2735.
Staff, §23-231.5.

SOUTHWEST VIRGINIA PUBLIC EDUCATION CONSORTIUM, §§22.1-350 to 22.1-354.
Cooperation with other agencies, §22.1-354.
Creation, §22.1-350.
Donations.
Application for and acceptance, §22.1-353.
Executive director, §22.1-352.
Functions and duties, §22.1-351.
Gifts and grants.
Application for and acceptance, §22.1-353.
Governing board, §22.1-350.
Interagency cooperation, §22.1-354.
Location of offices, §22.1-352.
Region defined, §22.1-350.
Staff support, §22.1-352.
Technical assistance to local school boards, §22.1-351.

SOVEREIGN IMMUNITY.
Authorities to develop former federal areas, §15.2-6322.
BVU authority, §15.2-7221.
Claims against the state.
Fraudulent claims, waiver of sovereign immunity, §8.01-216.8.
Colleges and universities.
Restructured financial and administrative operations, §23-38.88.
Contractors.
Governmental immunity defense.
Actions for damages from blasting, etc., §8.01-224.
County, city and town operation of recreational facilities.
Agreements with landowners, §29.1-509.
Emergency management assistance compact, §44-146.28:1.
Fort Monroe authority, §2.2-2350.
Governmental immunity defense.
Contractors.
Actions for damages from blasting, etc., §8.01-224.
Health, §32.1-4.
Highway corporations, §56-545.
Law-enforcement employees, firefighters and emergency medical technicians.
Overtime compensation, §9.1-706.
Lottery of state, prize distribution, §58.1-4013.
Northern Neck Chesapeake Bay public access authority.
Participating political subdivisions, §15.2-6629.
Port authority, §62.1-145.
Public-private education facilities and infrastructure act, §56-575.15.
Public-private transportation act, §56-571.
Commonwealth, §56-571.
Local governments, §56-571.
Recreational facilities operated by county, city or town.
Agreements with landowners, §29.1-509.
State treasurer.
Risk management division.
Sovereign immunity not waived, §2.2-1842.
Tort claims act.
General provisions, §§8.01-195.1 to 8.01-195.9.
See CLAIMS AGAINST THE STATE.
Tourism authority, §2.2-2326.
Underground utility line damage prevention, §56-265.28.

SOYBEANS, §§3.2-2300 to 3.2-2314.
Assessment.
Delinquent assessments.
Collection, §3.2-1102.
Expenditure of moneys collected, §3.2-2311.
Handlers.
Criminal penalties for certain acts, §3.2-2314.
Deduction of assessment from payment to farmer, §3.2-2312.
Records, §3.2-2313.
Report and payment, §3.2-2312.
Interest, §3.2-1102.
Referendum on question, §§3.2-2305 to 3.2-2309.
Virginia soybean fund, §3.2-2311.
Dedicated revenues, diversion, §3.2-1100.
Definitions, §3.2-2300.
Elections.
Referendum on question of assessment, §§3.2-2305 to 3.2-2309.

SOYBEANS —Cont'd
Referendum.
Question of assessment for research, promotion, etc., §§3.2-2305 to 3.2-2309.
Virginia soybean board, §§3.2-2300 to 3.2-2314.
Appointment of members, §3.2-2301.
Compensation, §3.2-2303.
Composition, §3.2-2301.
Duties, §3.2-2304.
Officers, §3.2-2303.
Powers, §3.2-2304.
Terms of members, §3.2-2302.
Vacancies, §3.2-2302.

SPACE FLIGHT ACTIVITIES.
Aerospace advisory council, §§2.2-2699.1, 2.2-2699.2.
Commercial space flight authority.
Generally, §§2.2-2201 to 2.2-2217.
See COMMERCIAL SPACE FLIGHT AUTHORITY.
Income tax revenue generated by commercial space flight entities.
Transfer of revenue to, §58.1-423.
Liability and immunity, §§8.01-227.8 to 8.01-227.10.
Definitions, §8.01-227.8.
Immunity of space flight entity, §8.01-227.9.
Signed written warning required, §8.01-227.10.

SPACEPORT ACTIVITIES.
Retail sales and use tax exemption, §58.1-609.3.

SPAM.
Civil damages, §18.2-152.12.
Defined, §18.2-152.2.
Falsification or forged communications, §18.2-152.4.
Transmission of unsolicited commercial electronic mail, §18.2-152.3:1.

SPANISH WAR VETERANS.
Benevolent associations generally.
See BENEVOLENT ASSOCIATIONS OR ORGANIZATIONS.
Land conveyances to association, §§57-19, 57-20.

SPARK ARRESTORS.
Cleaning and maintaining locomotives designed with, §56-413.01.

SPAYING DOGS AND CATS, §§3.2-6574 to 3.2-6580.

SPCA.
Property tax exemptions, §58.1-3613.

SPEARFISHING.
Engaging in while under the influence, §§29.1-738 to 29.1-738.6.

SPECIAL ASSESSMENT FOR LAND PRESERVATION, §§58.1-3229 to 58.1-3244.
See REAL PROPERTY TAXES.

SPECIAL COMMISSIONERS.
Collection of money and failing to account, §18.2-114.1.
Commissioners in chancery generally, §§8.01-607 to 8.01-619.
See COMMISSIONERS IN CHANCERY.
Judicial sales generally, §§8.01-96 to 8.01-113.
See JUDICIAL SALES.
Sale of delinquent tax lands.
Appointment to sell property and execute deeds, §58.1-3969.

SPECIAL CONSERVATORS OF THE PEACE, §§9.1-150.1 to 9.1-150.4, 19.2-13 to 19.2-15.
Criminal justice services board.
Duties, §9.1-150.2.
Criminal justice services department.
Powers, §9.1-150.3.
Defined, §9.1-150.1.
Fees.
Criminal justice services department, powers, §9.1-150.3.
Park authorities.
Appointment, §15.2-5706.
Qualifications.
Duty to establish, §9.1-150.2.
Training regulations.
Board, duties, §9.1-150.2.
Unlawful conduct, §9.1-150.4.

SPECIAL CONSTRUCTION AND FORESTRY EQUIPMENT.
Defined, §46.2-100.
Registration and titling of vehicles in state not required, §46.2-600.
Security interests in, perfecting, §46.2-636.1.

SPECIAL COUNSEL.
Employment by governor, state department, agency, official, etc., §§2.2-510, 2.2-510.1.
Illegal practice of law cases.
Employment by attorney general to prosecute, §2.2-512.

SPECIAL COUNTY, DISTRICT, CITY OR TOWN TAX.
School purposes, §§22.1-102 to 22.1-106.

SPECIAL COURTS.
Annexation, consolidation of localities, incorporation of towns, transition of localities, etc., §§15.2-3000 to 15.2-3004.
Annexation generally, §§15.2-3200 to 15.2-3235.
See ANNEXATION.
Appointment by supreme court, §15.2-3000.
Boundary relocation or change by agreement.
Localities unable to agree, request to convene special court, §15.2-3109.
City no longer qualifying for city status.
Judicial determination generally, §§15.2-4000 to 15.2-4005.
See REVERSION OF CITIES TO TOWNS.
Composition of court, §15.2-3000.
Consolidation of localities generally, §§15.2-3500 to 15.2-3550.
See CONSOLIDATION OF LOCALITIES.
Contraction of corporate limits of cities or towns.
Appointment of special courts, §15.2-3237.
Powers of court, §15.2-3238.
Towns located in two more counties, §§15.2-3241 to 15.2-3243.
Designation of judges to compose panel of judges, §15.2-3002.
Incorporation of town by judicial proceedings, §§15.2-3600 to 15.2-3605.
Priority of proceedings, §15.2-3001.
Service on special court, §15.2-3003.
Sitting without jury, §15.2-3000.
Transition of counties to cities.
Generally, §§15.2-3900 to 15.2-3919.
See TRANSITION OF COUNTIES TO CITIES.
Transition of towns to cities generally, §§15.2-3800 to 15.2-3834.
See TRANSITION OF TOWNS TO CITIES.

SPECIAL COURTS —Cont'd
Annexation, consolidation of localities, incorporation of towns, transition of localities, etc. —Cont'd
Vacancies on court occurring during trial, §15.2-3004.
Voluntary settlement of annexation, transition or immunity issues.
Appointment of special court, §15.2-3400.
Dams or impoundment of water.
Disputes between jurisdiction, §§15.2-2135 to 15.2-2141.

SPECIAL COURTS-MARTIAL, §§44-42 to 44-54.

SPECIAL DAMAGES.
Real estate cooperatives, §55-436.

SPECIAL DAYS AND OBSERVANCES.
See HOLIDAYS.

SPECIAL EDUCATION, §§22.1-213 to 22.1-221.
Child-day programs.
Children below compulsory school attendance, §22.1-216.
Children with disabilities.
Dispute resolution for placement of handicapped children, §§22.1-214, 22.1-214.1.
Residing within its jurisdiction.
Defined, §22.1-215.
Contract facilities.
Use of public or private facilities and personnel, §22.1-216.
Cost of education provided to children, §22.1-215.
Cost of transporting children with disabilities attending programs, §22.1-221.
Court of appeals.
Appellate jurisdiction as to hearing officer decisions, §17.1-405.
Curriculum guidelines, §22.1-214.3.
Deaf or hearing impaired.
Individualized education programs, §22.1-217.02.
Information on educational and other services, §22.1-217.01.
Definitions, §22.1-213.
Children with disabilities, residing within its jurisdiction, §22.1-215.
Parent, §22.1-213.1.
Supervise, §22.1-214.2.
Visually impaired children, §22.1-217.
Development and approval, §22.1-214.3.
Emotionally disturbed children.
Dispute resolution for placement of handicapped children, §§22.1-214, 22.1-214.1.
Programs for innovative methods of teaching emotionally children, §22.1-217.1.
Federal funds.
Use not restricted, §22.1-219.
Handicapped children.
Defined, §22.1-213.
Dispute resolution, §22.1-214.
Hearing officers, §§22.1-214, 22.1-214.1.
Power of local governments to appropriate and expend funds, §22.1-220.
Supervision of education programs, §§22.1-214, 22.1-214.2.
Individualized education programs.
Deaf or hearing impaired students, §22.1-217.02.
Information regarding procedures and rights relating to placement and withdrawal, §22.1-215.1.

SPECIAL EDUCATION —Cont'd
Intellectual disability.
Dispute resolution for placement of handicapped children, §§22.1-214, 22.1-214.1.
Programs for innovative methods of teaching mentally retarded children, §22.1-217.1.
Interstate compact on the placement of children.
Duty to process placements through compact, §22.1-218.1.
Local funds.
Programs for innovative methods of teaching mentally ill children, §22.1-217.1.
Use not restricted, §22.1-219.
Mediation.
Dispute resolution for placement of handicapped children, §22.1-214.
Medical assistance services department.
Special education health services.
Interagency agreement, §32.1-326.3.
Memorandum of agreement relating to special education health services, §22.1-274.02.
Mentally ill children.
Dispute resolution for placement of handicapped children, §§22.1-214, 22.1-214.1.
Placement.
Information regarding procedures and rights relating to placement and withdrawal, §22.1-215.1.
Preschool special education program for children with disabilities.
Reimbursement to school board, §22.1-218.
Private nonsectarian school, agency or institution.
Reimbursement for child placed in, §22.1-218.
Reimbursement for placement in private school, agency or institution, §22.1-218.
Related services.
Defined, §22.1-213.
Research programs for development of innovative teaching methods, §22.1-217.1.
Residential placement in state institutions.
Submission of plan to state board for public school program, §22.1-215.
Rules promulgation.
Public school placement of children in state facilities, §22.1-215.
School divisions to provide, §22.1-215.
Specific learning disability.
Defined, §22.1-213.
State funds.
Use not restricted, §22.1-219.
Traineeships for special education personnel, §23-38.10:1.
Transportation of children with disabilities attending public or private program, §22.1-221.
Visually impaired children.
Braille instruction, §22.1-217.
Dispute resolution for placement of handicapped children, §§22.1-214, 22.1-214.1.
Information on educational and other services, §22.1-217.01.
Visually impaired, defined, §22.1-217.
Withdrawal.
Information regarding procedures and rights relating to placement and withdrawal, §22.1-215.1.

SPECIAL ELECTIONS.
Abolition of constitutional offices.
Request for, §24.2-685.
Change of government having effect of abolishing office, §24.2-686.
Closing registration records before elections, §24.2-416.
Constitutional and local office vacancies, §24.2-226.
Request for special election, §24.2-685.
Day special elections to be held, §24.2-682.
Defined, §24.2-101.
General election laws, applicability, §24.2-681.
How superintended and determined, §24.2-681.
Implementation of changes to election law.
When effective for special elections, §24.2-101.1.
Pari-mutuel wagering on horses.
Local referendum, §59.1-391.
Persons eighteen years of age at next general election.
Advanced registration and voting in intervening special election, §24.2-403.
Petitions.
Vacancies in elected constitutional and local offices, §24.2-226.
Political party nominations by other than primary.
Deadline for nominating, §24.2-510.
Referendum elections.
Calling, ascertaining results and certifying, §24.2-684.
Explanation of each referendum question, §24.2-687.
Voter petition requirements, §24.2-684.1.
Removal of county courthouse, §15.2-1645.
Time for special elections, §24.2-682.
Urban county executive form of government.
Board of supervisors.
Additional supervisors or vacancy on board, §15.2-802.
Vacancies in office.
Commencement and expiration of term of officer elected to fill, §24.2-201.
Constitutional and local offices, §24.2-226.
Writ for special election to fill, §24.2-683.
Voter registration records closed before election, §24.2-416.
Writ for special election to fill vacancy, §24.2-683.

SPECIAL FORCES ASSOCIATION.
Motor vehicle license plates, §46.2-746.2:4.

SPECIAL FUND ACCOUNT OF TRANSPORTATION DISTRICTS.
Motor vehicle fuel sales tax.
Disposition of revenues, §58.1-1724.

SPECIAL GRAND JURIES, §§19.2-206 to 19.2-215.
See GRAND JURIES.

SPECIAL IMPROVEMENTS TAX.
Taxes or assessments for local improvements, §§15.2-2404 to 15.2-2413.
See TAXES OR ASSESSMENTS FOR LOCAL IMPROVEMENTS.
Transportation districts.
District within city of Charlottesville and county of Albemarle.
Levy, rate, collection, use, §33.1-453.

SPECIAL INDORSEMENT.
Negotiable instruments, §8.3A-205.

SPECIALIZED BIOTECHNOLOGY RESEARCH PERFORMANCE GRANT PROGRAM, §59.1-284.24.

SPECIALIZED TRANSPORTATION INCENTIVE FUND, §15.2-4217.1.

SPECIAL JURIES.
Civil cases, §8.01-362.

SPECIAL JUSTICES.
Canons of judicial conduct.
Compliance with code, VA SCt Rule Pt 6 §III Canon 6.
Civil commitment of mentally ill persons.
Appointment by chief judge, §37.2-803.
Completion of training program, §37.2-803.
Fees and expenses, §§37.2-803, 37.2-804.
Involuntary temporary detention.
Seven days, twenty-four hours availability, §37.2-809.

SPECIAL LAWS.
General assembly not to enact, VA Const Art IV §14.

SPECIAL LICENSE PLATES, §§46.2-711 to 46.2-749.130.
See MOTOR VEHICLE LICENSE PLATES.

SPECIAL MASTERS.
Sale of delinquent tax lands.
Appointment, §58.1-3970.1.
Order of reference to, §58.1-3969.

SPECIAL NEEDS CHILDREN.
Adoption.
Assistance payments, §§63.2-1300 to 63.2-1304.
Assistance, subsidy payments.
Medical assistance, uniform act, §§63.2-1400 to 63.2-1405.
Assistance for adoption of.
See ADOPTION.

SPECIAL OR CHARTER PARTY CARRIERS.
Employee liens, §§43-24 to 43-26.
Incorporation as public service company, §13.1-620.
Public service companies generally, §§56-1 to 56-87.
See PUBLIC SERVICE COMPANIES.
Supplier liens, §§43-24 to 43-26.
Transportation companies generally, §§56-99.2 to 56-140.
See TRANSPORTATION COMPANIES.

SPECIAL ORDERS.
Assisted living facilities, adult day care centers and child welfare agencies.
License or regulatory violations, §63.2-1709.

SPECIAL POLICE.
Generally, §§15.2-1737 to 15.2-1746.
See POLICE.

SPECIAL RECEIVERS, §§8.01-591 to 8.01-599.
See RECEIVERS.

SPECIAL SESSIONS OF GENERAL ASSEMBLY, VA Const Art IV §6.

SPECIAL SESSIONS OF SUPREME COURT, §§17.1-306, 17.1-308.

SPECIAL TERMS OF CIRCUIT COURT, §§17.1-518 to 17.1-522.

SPECIAL TOWN SCHOOL DISTRICTS.
Continuation, §22.1-33.

SPECIAL UNEMPLOYMENT COMPENSATION ADMINISTRATION FUND, §§60.2-314 to 60.2-317.
See UNEMPLOYMENT COMPENSATION FUND.

SPECIFIC PERFORMANCE.
Leases, UCC.
Lessors default, §8.2A-521.
Letters of credit.
Wrongful dishonor or repudiation, §8.5A-111.
Members of congress, US Const Art I §6.
Sales, UCC.
Right of buyers, §8.2-716.
Uniform computer information transactions act.
Remedies, §59.1-508.11.
Voting agreements.
Corporations, §13.1-671.1.
Writ of possession on judgment, §8.01-470.

SPEECH AND LANGUAGE THERAPY.
Health insurance coverage.
Family access to medical insurance security plan, §§32.1-351 to 32.1-353.
Schools and education.
Employment of speech therapists by school board, §22.1-274.

SPEECH-IMPAIRED PERSONS.
Assistive technology device warranties, §§59.1-470 to 59.1-474.
Interpreters.
Civil cases, §8.01-384.1.
Privilege, evidence, VA SCt Rule 2:507.
Local school boards.
Transfer of assistive technology devices to school division, §22.1-129.1.
Special education, §§22.1-213 to 22.1-221.
See SPECIAL EDUCATION.

SPEECH-LANGUAGE THERAPISTS.
Health insurance.
Public officers and employees.
Required coverage, §2.2-2818.

SPEECH OR DEBATE PRIVILEGE.
General assembly members, VA Const Art IV §9.

SPEECH PATHOLOGISTS, §§54.1-2600 to 54.1-2604.
Board of audiology and speech-language pathology, §54.1-2602.
Defined terms, §54.1-2600.
Exemptions from licensing, §54.1-2601.
Free clinics.
Immunity for services provided, §54.1-106.
Health benefit programs.
Provider willing to meet terms and conditions not to be excluded, §38.2-3407.
Health services plans, coverage of services, §38.2-4221.
Professional corporations generally, §§13.1-542.1 to 13.1-556.
See PROFESSIONAL CORPORATIONS.
Professions and occupations regulation generally.
See HEALTH PROFESSIONS DEPARTMENT.
Prohibited acts, §54.1-2409.1.
Provisional license, §54.1-2604.
Unlawful procurement of licensure, §54.1-102.
Unlawful use of licensure, §54.1-111.

SPEED AND STOPPING DISTANCE TABLES, §46.2-880.

SPEEDING.
Authority to change speed limits, §46.2-878.
Bridges and tunnels, §46.2-881.
Conviction requires installation of markers, §46.2-870.
Demerit points, §46.2-492.
Dirt and gravel roads.
Maximum speed limit on, §46.2-873.1.
Drag racing, §§46.2-865 to 46.2-867.
Electrical or microcomputer devices, §46.2-882.
Electric power-assisted bicycles.
Maximum speed, §46.2-908.1.
Fines schedule, VA SCt Rule 3B:2.
Maximum fine for violating Title 46.2, §46.2-113.
Generally, §46.2-870.
Impeding traffic by slow speed, §46.2-877.
Maximum fine for violating Title 46.2, §46.2-113.
Maximum safe speed, §46.2-861.
Maximum speed limits, §46.2-870.
Highways in cities and towns, §§46.2-874, 46.2-875.
Nonsurface treated highways, §46.2-873.1.
Passenger vehicles towing certain trailers, §46.2-876.
Rural rustic roads, §46.2-873.2.
School buses, §46.2-871.
School crossings, §46.2-873.
Vehicles operating under special permit, §46.2-872.
Minimum speed limits, §46.2-877.
Mopeds.
Speed restrictions, §46.2-914.
Nonsurface treated highways.
Maximum speed limit on, §46.2-873.1.
Operating vehicle at 15 miles per hour or more over applicable speed.
Certain city ordinance prohibiting, §46.2-874.1.
Operating vehicle at 20 miles per hour or more over applicable speed.
Certain town ordinance prohibiting, §46.2-874.1.
Permits set by commissioner of highways, §46.2-878.
Prepayment of fine, §§16.1-69.40:1, 46.2-878.3.
Radar.
Law enforcement officers.
Compulsory minimum training standards, §9.1-102.
Radar devices, §46.2-882.
Reckless driving, §§46.2-861, 46.2-862.
Drag racing, §§46.2-865 to 46.2-867.
Residence districts, §46.2-878.2.
Rural rustic roads.
Maximum speed limit on, §46.2-873.2.
School crossings.
Maximum speed limits, §46.2-873.
Signs measuring speed by radar, §46.2-883.
Tables of speeding and stopping distance, §46.2-880.
Vehicles operating under special permits, §46.2-872.
Work zones, §46.2-878.1.

SPEEDING TO ELUDE POLICE, §46.2-817.

SPEEDOMETERS.
Good working order requirement, §46.2-1080.
Radar calibration tests, §§46.2-882, 46.2-942.

SPEEDWAYS.
License tax, §58.1-3728.

SPEEDY TRIAL, §19.2-243, VA Const Art I §8, US Const Amd 6.
Appeals by Commonwealth.
Dismissal because of speedy trial violation, §19.2-398.
Defense objections.
Written pretrial motion, §19.2-266.2.

SPELEOGENS.
Cave protection.
General provisions, §§10.1-1000 to 10.1-1008.
See CAVE PROTECTION.

SPELEOTHEMS.
Cave protection.
General provisions, §§10.1-1000 to 10.1-1008.
See CAVE PROTECTION.

SPENDTHRIFT TRUSTS.
Commutation of certain life estates, §55-277.
Creditor's claims against settlor.
Rules, §64.2-747.
Self-settled spendthrift trusts, §64.2-745.1.
Life insurance policies creating, §38.2-3118.
Limitation to proportionate part of proceeds, §38.2-3119.
Segregation of proceeds not required, §38.2-3121.
Qualified trustees, §64.2-745.2.
Unenforceable against state statute so providing, §64.2-744.
Validity, §64.2-743.

SPERM DONORS, HIV TESTS, §32.1-45.3.

SPICE.
Synthetic cannabinoids.
See SYNTHETIC CANNABINOIDS.

SPILL RESPONSE COUNCIL, §§62.1-44.34:24 to 62.1-44.34:28.
Cooperation of agencies and institutions, §62.1-44.34:27.
Coordination of activities with emergency response council, §62.1-44.34:26.
Creation, §62.1-44.34:25.
Defined terms, §62.1-44.34:24.
Members, §62.1-44.34:25.
Purpose, §62.1-44.34:25.
Reports, §62.1-44.34:28.
Responsibilities, §62.1-44.34:26.

SPILLS OF DANGEROUS OR UNHEALTHY SUBSTANCES.
Counties, cities or towns.
General power to abate or remove, §15.2-900.
Oil spills.
Discharges into waters of the state, §§62.1-44.34:14 to 62.1-44.34:23.
See OIL DISCHARGES INTO WATERS OF STATE.
Spill response council, §§62.1-44.34:24 to 62.1-44.34:28.
See SPILL RESPONSE COUNCIL.

SPINAL CORD INJURIES.
Birth-related neurological injury compensation, §§38.2-5000 to 38.2-5021.
See BIRTH-RELATED NEUROLOGICAL INJURY COMPENSATION.

SPIRITUAL HEALING.
Abuse and neglect of children.
Treatment solely by spiritual means through prayer, §18.2-371.1.

SPIRIT VINEGAR.
Generally, §§3.2-5500 to 3.2-5507.
See VINEGAR.

SPITTING IN PUBLIC PLACES, §18.2-322.
Uniform fine schedule, VA SCt Rules 3C:1, 3C:2.

SPLIT-INTEREST TRUSTS.
Applicability, §64.2-739.
Internal revenue code references, interpretation, §64.2-740.
Modification of trust, §64.2-736.
Powers of courts, §64.2-741.
Prohibitions, §64.2-738.
Severability of provisions, §64.2-741.

SPOKESPERSONS.
State departments, agencies, boards or commissions.
List, publication, duties, §30-34.14.

SPORTS.
Admission tax to sporting events, §§58.1-3817, 58.1-3818.
Surcharge on admissions, §58.1-3840.
Anabolic steroids.
Public high school students.
Use during athletic training period.
Ineligibility to compete in athletic competitions, §22.1-276.3.
Artificial turf or other athletic surfaces.
Purchases by public bodies.
Cooperative procurement, §2.2-4304.
Bribery of participants, managers, coaches or trainers, §18.2-442.
Solicitation or acceptance, §18.2-443.
Concession stands at youth athletic activities.
Exemption from regulations applicable to restaurants, §35.1-25.
Gambling.
Exceptions to article, certain sporting events, §18.2-333.
Leaves of absence for state employees, §2.2-124.
Public high school students.
Anabolic steroids used by student during athletic training period.
Ineligibility to compete in athletic competitions, §22.1-276.3.
Team physicians.
Immunity from liability, §8.01-225.1.
Ticket scalping, ordinances prohibiting, §15.2-969.
Unemployment compensation.
Eligibility for benefits, §60.2-616.

SPORTS AUTHORITY OF HAMPTON ROADS, VIRGINIA, 1986 ch 426.

SPORTS BRIBERY.
Participants, managers, coaches or trainers, §18.2-442.
Solicitation or acceptance, §18.2-443.

SPORTS HALL OF FAME.
Official sports hall of fame of Commonwealth, §1-511.

SPORT SHOOTING RANGES.
Applicability of local noise ordinances, §15.2-917.

SPORTS OFFICIALS.
Workers' compensation.
Employee not to include, §65.2-101.

SPOT BLIGHT ABATEMENT, §36-49.1:1.

SPOTLIGHTS.
Deer hunting, §§29.1-523, 29.1-525.

SPOTLIGHTS —Cont'd
Employment of spotlight under certain circumstances, §18.2-509.
Motor vehicle equipment, §46.2-1019.
Fine schedule, VA SCt Rule 3B:2.
Maximum fine for violating Title 46.2, §46.2-113.
Trespass by spotlight on agricultural land, §18.2-121.2.

SPOTSYLVANIA COUNTY.
Coastal primary sand dunes and beaches.
Zoning ordinances, §28.2-1403.
Confederate cemeteries and graves.
Disbursement of funds appropriated for upkeep, §10.1-2211.
Cutting grass or lawn area of residential real property.
Requiring owner of occupied property, §15.2-1215.
Fingerprinting school employees, §22.1-296.2.
Public defenders office.
Established, §19.2-163.04.
School board.
Fingerprinting applicants for employment, §22.1-296.2.
Salary of members, §22.1-32.
Tax map reference number.
Circuit court clerk indexing by, §17.1-252.
Transient occupancy tax.
Disposition of revenues, §58.1-3819.
Water and sewage systems.
Lien for charges and taxes imposed, §15.2-2118.
Water supplies.
Test results, §32.1-175.1.

SPOUSAL ABUSE.
Abuse of accused by victim.
Admissibility in criminal trial, §19.2-270.6.
Assault and battery against family or household member, §§18.2-57.2, 18.2-57.3.
Armed forces members found guilty.
Reporting findings to military family advocacy representative, §18.2-57.4.
Criminal jurisdiction, §16.1-278.14.
Discretionary felony sentencing guidelines, §17.1-805.
Domestic violence.
Generally.
See DOMESTIC VIOLENCE.
Evidence.
Medical evidence in juvenile and domestic relations district court, §16.1-245.1.
Forcible sodomy, §18.2-67.1.
Jail prisoner escape or release notice, §53.1-116.1.
Prisoner intake notice, §53.1-116.1:01.
Punishment upon conviction of certain subsequent violent felony sexual assault, §18.2-67.5:3.
Hospital records.
Evidence in juvenile and domestic relations district courts, §16.1-245.1.
Medical records.
Evidence in juvenile and domestic relations district courts, §16.1-245.1.
Object sexual penetration, §18.2-67.2.
Jail prisoner escape or release notice, §53.1-116.1.
Prisoner intake notice, §53.1-116.1:01.
Punishment upon conviction of certain subsequent violent felony sexual assault, §18.2-67.5:3.
Pandering, §18.2-368.
Preliminary hearings, §§19.2-218.1, 19.2-218.2.
Prostitution.
Placing or leaving wife for, §18.2-368.

SPOUSAL ABUSE —Cont'd
Rape of spouse, §18.2-61.
Convict escape or release notice, §53.1-160.1.
Punishment upon conviction of certain subsequent violent felony sexual assault, §18.2-67.5:3.
Sodomy, §18.2-67.1.
Jail prisoner escape or release notice, §53.1-116.1.
Prisoner intake notice, §53.1-116.1:01.
Punishment upon conviction of certain subsequent violent felony sexual assault, §18.2-67.5:3.
Venue.
Juvenile and domestic relations district court proceedings, §16.1-243.

SPOUSAL PRIVILEGE, §8.01-398, VA SCt Rule 2:504.
Child abuse or neglect.
Inapplicability of privilege in legal proceeding, §63.2-1519.
Confidential communications between spouses during marriage.
Privilege to refuse to disclose and to prevent disclosure, §19.2-271.2.

SPOUSAL SUPPORT, §§20-60.1 to 20-60.6.
Abstracts of judgments.
Money judgments for arrearages, §16.1-278.18.
Annulment of marriage.
Court authority to decree, §20-107.1.
Appeals.
Court of appeals.
Finality of decisions, §17.1-410.
Jurisdiction, §17.1-405.
Applicability of chapter, §20-60.1.
Arrearages.
Interest, §20-78.2.
Money judgments, §16.1-278.18.
Cessation upon cohabitation, remarriage or death, §20-109.
Changes in circumstances.
Reopening of proceedings, §20-112.
Chart for determining, §§20-108.1, 20-108.2.
Cohabitation, cessation upon, §20-109.
Commitment for failure to comply with obligation, §16.1-278.16.
Contempt.
Sentencing to jail, workhouse, etc., §16.1-292.
Contents of support orders.
Mandatory requirements, §20-60.3.
Court of appeals.
Appellate jurisdiction, §17.1-405.
Finality of decision of court, §17.1-410.
Death.
Cessation upon death, §20-109.
Desertion and nonsupport generally, §§20-61 to 20-88.02:1.
See DESERTION AND NONSUPPORT.
Disposition in juvenile proceedings, §16.1-278.15.
Failure to comply with support obligation, §16.1-278.16.
Pendente lite support, §16.1-278.17.
Formula for determination, §16.1-278.17:1.
Divorce.
Court authority to decree, §20-107.1.
Duration.
Modification for defined duration, §20-109.
Evidence, §20-108.1.
Admissibility and identification of support payment records, §20-60.2.
Expert witnesses in hearings, §8.01-375.
Factors for consideration, §20-107.1.

SPOUSAL SUPPORT —Cont'd
Factors for determining, §20-108.1.
Failure to comply with support obligation, §16.1-278.16.
Sentencing, §16.1-292.
Garnishment.
Entry of support order, §§8.01-514, 20-78.1.
Guidelines for determining, §20-108.1.
Income withholding.
Garnishment.
Time limit for return of summons, §20-78.1.
Interest on arrearage, §20-78.2.
Interstate family support, §§20-88.32 to 20-88.82.
See INTERSTATE FAMILY SUPPORT ACT.
Jail inmate work release earnings, §53.1-131.
Judgment created by operation of law.
Lien against real estate, §16.1-278.15.
Judgments and decrees.
Decree as lien on real estate, §8.01-460.
Judgments for money, arrearages, §16.1-278.18.
Juvenile and domestic relations district court jurisdiction, §16.1-241.
Legal separation.
Court authority to decree, §20-107.1.
Lien against real estate.
Judgment created by operation of law, §16.1-278.15.
Mandatory contents of support orders, §20-60.3.
Modification of support, §20-109.
Necessaries doctrine, §55-37.
Order for support.
Recognizance for compliance with order or decree, §20-114.
Respondent failure to perform order, §20-113.
Retroactive modification, §20-112.
Payroll deductions.
Failure to comply with support obligation, §16.1-278.16.
Pendente lite support, §16.1-278.17.
Formula for determination, §16.1-278.17:1.
Petitions.
Contents, VA SCt Rule 8:3.
Premarital agreements.
Parties may contract with respect to, §20-150.
Prisoner estates.
Use, §53.1-224.
Prisoner work release earnings.
Use, §53.1-60.
Recognizance for compliance with support obligation, §16.1-278.16.
Remarriage.
Cessation of spousal support, §§20-109, 20-110.
Sentencing.
Failure to comply with obligation, §§16.1-278.16, 16.1-292.
Recognizance for compliance with order or decree.
Confinement for noncompliance, §20-115.
Separation from spouse.
Cases involving after separation, §16.1-278.15.
Social services department.
Admissibility and identification of support payment records, §20-60.2.
Contents of support orders, §20-60.3.
Electronic data transmission of information into department, §20-60.4.
Subsequent enforcement proceedings.
Delivery of notice to party at last known address, §20-60.6.
Support payment provisions transferred to department, §20-60.5.

SPOUSAL SUPPORT —Cont'd
Stipulations.
Effect of stipulations, §20-109.
Support orders.
Abstracts of orders, etc., §20-60.4.
Mandatory contents, §20-60.3.
Transmittal of information to social services department, §20-60.4.
Support payment provisions.
Payment options, §20-60.5.
Transfer of functions to social services department, §20-60.5.
Support payment records.
Social services department.
Admissibility and identification, §20-60.2.
Temporary support, §20-103.
Time for filing.
Garnishment.
Child support orders.
Time limit for return of summons, §20-78.1.
Transfer of venue.
Juvenile and domestic relations district court proceedings, §16.1-243.
Venue.
Juvenile and domestic relations district court proceedings, §16.1-243.
Virginia retirement system assets.
Amenability to process, §51.1-124.4.
Vocational evaluation.
Proceedings for determining support, §20-108.1.
Waiver of spousal support, §20-109.
Workers' compensation.
Availability to be claimed, §65.2-531.
Work release earnings of jail inmates, §53.1-131.

SPOUSES.
Abuse of spouse.
See SPOUSAL ABUSE.
Compelling testimony in criminal case, §19.2-271.2.
Competency to testify in criminal case, §19.2-271.1.
Curtesy, §64.2-301.
Debts of husband.
Liability of wife, §55-35.
Descent and distribution.
Community property rights at death, §§64.2-315 to 64.2-324.
Elective share of surviving spouse, §§64.2-300 to 64.2-308.
Exempt property and allowances, §§64.2-309 to 64.2-314.
Rights of married persons, §§64.2-300 to 64.2-324.
Simultaneous death, §§64.2-2200 to 64.2-2208.
Dower, §64.2-301.
Forcible sodomy, §18.2-67.1.
Punishment upon conviction of certain subsequent violent felony sexual assault, §18.2-67.5:3.
Group life insurance coverages, §38.2-3323.
Health insurance.
Group accident and sickness coverages.
Spouses, dependent children or others, §38.2-3525.
Income tax.
Estimated tax.
Declarations, §58.1-490.
Divorce following filing of joint return.
Refund, §58.1-499.
Generally, §§58.1-490 to 58.1-499.

SPOUSES —Cont'd
Income tax —Cont'd
Individual income tax, §58.1-324.
One spouse nonresident, §58.1-326.
Returns, §58.1-341.
Life insurance.
Group life insurance coverages of spouses, §38.2-3323.
Marital object sexual penetration, §18.2-67.2.
Punishment upon conviction of certain subsequent violent felony sexual assault, §18.2-67.5:3.
Property rights of married women, §§55-35 to 55-47.1.
See MARRIED WOMEN'S PROPERTY RIGHTS.
Rape, §18.2-61.
Punishment upon conviction of certain subsequent violent felony sexual assault, §18.2-67.5:3.
Recordation tax, state.
Deeds to which husband and wife only parties.
Deeds not taxable, §58.1-810.
Surviving spouse.
See SURVIVING SPOUSES AND DEPENDENTS.

SPRING GUNS.
Setting, §18.2-281.

SPRING STICKS.
Concealed weapons and concealed handgun permits, §§18.2-307.1 to 18.2-308.015.
Carrying concealed weapons, §18.2-308.
Convicted felons, possession, transportation or concealing, §18.2-308.2.
Courthouses.
Carrying weapon into, §18.2-283.1.
Defined, §18.2-308.
School property, possession on, §18.2-308.1.

SPRINKLER SYSTEMS.
Fire suppression systems standards for hospitals, §§32.1-126.3, 36-99.9:1.
Prisoner crimes, §53.1-203.

SQUARE DANCING.
Official folk dance of Commonwealth, §1-510.

SQUATTERS' RIGHTS.
See ADVERSE POSSESSION.

SQUIRRELS.
Hunting, §29.1-516.
Sale of game, §29.1-536.
Trapping seasons, §29.1-530.

STABBING IN COMMITTING OR ATTEMPTING FELONY, §18.2-53.

STABBING WITH INTENT TO MAIM, KILL, ETC., §18.2-51.
Aggravated malicious wounding, §18.2-51.2.
Lesser offenses, conviction under certain indictments, §18.2-54.

STABLES.
Counties regulating horse riding schools, §15.2-1223.

STADIUM AUTHORITY FINANCING FUND, §15.2-5811.

STADIUMS.
Baseball stadium authority, §§15.2-5800 to 15.2-5819.
Counties, cities or towns providing and operating, §15.2-1808.
Encouraging use of facilities in certain cities, §15.2-1129.

STADIUMS —Cont'd
Excise tax for events at major league baseball stadiums, §58.1-3840.
Hampton Roads sports facility authority, §§15.2-5900 to 15.2-5916.
Public-private education facilities and infrastructure act, §§56-575.1 to 56-575.18.
See PUBLIC BUILDINGS.
Virginia Beach arena, §§15.2-5921 to 15.2-5927.
See VIRGINIA BEACH ARENA.

STAFF OFFICERS, NATIONAL GUARD.
Qualifications, §44-28.

STAFFORD COUNTY.
Admission tax, §58.1-3818.02.
Coastal primary sand dunes and beaches.
Zoning ordinances, §28.2-1403.
Former officers and employees.
Restrictions on activities, §15.2-1408.
Parking ordinances.
Regulation or prohibition of parking of certain vehicles, §46.2-1222.1.
Public defenders office.
Established, §19.2-163.04.
School board.
Fingerprinting applicants for employment, §22.1-296.2.
Salary of members, §22.1-32.
Taxes and assessments on electricity customer.
Construction of electric transmission line, §15.2-2404.
Transient occupancy tax.
Disposition of revenues, §58.1-3819.
Water and sewage systems.
Lien for charges and taxes imposed, §15.2-2118.
Well abandonment ordinance.
Duty of owner to cap or close well.
Locality adopting ordinance, §32.1-176.5.
Well construction.
Testing requirements, §32.1-176.5.

STAGNANT WATER.
Draining of grounds covered by.
City or town powers, §15.2-1115.

STAIRWELLS.
Spitting in public places, §18.2-322.

STALACTITE.
Cave protection.
General provisions, §§10.1-1000 to 10.1-1008.
See CAVE PROTECTION.

STALAGMITE.
Cave protection.
General provisions, §§10.1-1000 to 10.1-1008.
See CAVE PROTECTION.

STALE CHECKS, §8.4-404.

STALKING, §18.2-60.3.
Arrest.
Warrantless arrest, §19.2-81.3.
Carrying concealed weapon by person convicted of, ineligible persons.
Disqualification for concealed weapons permit, §18.2-308.09.
Civil actions against an individual, §8.01-42.3.
Confidentiality of records.
Persons receiving domestic or sexual violence services, §63.2-104.1.
Damages.
Compensatory and punitive damages.
Civil actions against an individual, §8.01-42.3.

STALKING —Cont'd
Discretionary felony sentencing guidelines, §17.1-805.
Personal identifying information.
Confidentiality.
Records of persons receiving domestic or sexual violence services, §63.2-104.1.
Protective orders, §19.2-152.10.
Assault and battery of person protected by protective order, §18.2-60.4.
Emergency orders authorized, §19.2-152.8.
Entry of order in addition to sentence imposed for violation, §18.2-60.4.
Law enforcement officers, prohibition on orders against, §19.2-152.8.
Preliminary orders, §19.2-152.9.
Registry, §19.2-387.1.
State police department, duties, §52-45.
Venue, §19.2-152.11.
Violation of orders, §18.2-60.4.
Voter registration application.
Post office box address, §24.2-418.
Voter registration lists.
Post office box address, §§24.2-405, 24.2-406.
Warrantless arrests, §19.2-81.3.

STALLIONS.
Lien on offspring, §43-41.
Recordation of lien, §43-42.

STAMPS.
Batteries, storage, §59.1-189.
Rebuilt batteries, §59.1-190.
Cigarette excise tax generally, §§58.1-1000 to 58.1-1022.
See CIGARETTE TAX.
Damage stamp program, §§29.1-352 to 29.1-358.
National forest stamps, §§29.1-408 to 29.1-411.
Virginia migratory waterfowl conservation stamp, §29.1-339.2.

STANDARDIZED ADA FORMS.
Acceptance by insurers required, §38.2-322.

STANDARDIZED HCFA-1500 HEALTH INSURANCE CLAIMS FORMS.
Acceptance by insurers required, §38.2-322.

STANDARDIZED UB-82 CLAIMS FORMS.
Acceptance by health insurer, §38.2-322.

STANDARD NONFORFEITURE PROVISIONS.
Fraternal benefit societies.
Nonforfeiture benefit, §38.2-4120.
Life insurance generally, §§38.2-3200 to 38.2-3229.
See LIFE INSURANCE.

STANDARDS OF LEARNING.
Schools and education, §22.1-253.13:1.

STANDARDS OF LEARNING END-OF-COURSE ASSESSMENTS.
Grades 3, 5, and 8, §22.1-253.13:1.

STANDARDS OF QUALITY FOR PUBLIC SCHOOLS, §§22.1-253.13:1 to 22.1-253.13:9.

STANDBY GUARDIANSHIPS FOR INCAPACITATED CHILDREN, §§16.1-349 to 16.1-355.

STANDING.
Appeal of agency order or decision, §45.1-361.9.
Condominiums.
Non-compliance with condominium instruments, §55-79.53.

STANDING —Cont'd
Condominiums —Cont'd
Special declarant rights.
Transfers, §55-79.74:3.
Conservation easements, §10.1-1013.
Derivative action by stockholder, §13.1-672.1.
Easements.
Conservation easements, §10.1-1013.
Gas and oil exploration.
Appeal of agency's decisions, §45.1-361.23.
Citizen suits, §45.1-361.25.
Limited liability companies.
Derivative actions, conditions precedent, §13.1-1042.
Petroleum products franchises.
Provision violation actions, §59.1-21.12.
Third parties.
Custodial trusts, §64.2-911.
Estates in land, §55-22.

STANDING ARMIES IN TIME OF PEACE, VA Const Art I §13.

STARLINGS.
Nuisance bird law, §§3.2-900, 3.2-901.

STARVING.
Murder of the first degree, §18.2-32.

STATE.
Boundaries, §§1-300 to 1-313.
See BOUNDARIES OF COMMONWEALTH.
Collection of money payable to state, §§8.01-196 to 8.01-216.
Adjustment of old claims, §8.01-216.
Commencement of proceedings, §8.01-196.
Against whom action instituted, §8.01-198.
Correction of mistakes against state, §8.01-200.
Executions, §§8.01-201, 8.01-202.
Institution of proceedings, §8.01-196.
Against whom action instituted, §8.01-198.
Judgment against deceased obligors, §8.01-210.
Limitation of actions, §8.01-251.
Name in which action brought, §8.01-197.
Nature of judgment, §8.01-199.
No abatement of action, §8.01-197.
Purchase money.
When to collect and make deed, §8.01-207.
Sale of real estate.
Disposition of proceeds of sale, §8.01-207.
How sale made, §8.01-205.
Notice, §8.01-204.
Purchase money, §§8.01-207, 8.01-209.
Return where sale not made because of prior encumbrance, §8.01-215.
Terms of sale, §8.01-206.
When sale to be made, §8.01-204.
When successor of officer to make deed, §8.01-208.
Where to be sold, §8.01-214.
Writ of fieri facias, §8.01-201.
Writ of fieri facias.
Goods and chattel liable before real estate, §8.01-203.
Sale of real estate authorized, §8.01-201.
Writ of venditioni exponas.
Contents, §8.01-211.
Delivery of goods and chattels levied to sheriff, §8.01-212.
Issuance to sheriff of adjacent county, §8.01-211.
Sale of levied goods and chattels, §8.01-213.
Contracting with health maintenance organizations, authority, §38.2-4320.

STATE —Cont'd
Criminal appeals by Commonwealth.
Pretrial appeals, §§19.2-398 to 19.2-409.
See APPEALS.
Descent and distribution.
Personalty, §64.2-201.
Discovery.
Criminal cases, VA SCt Rule 3A:11.
Emblems.
Official emblems and designations of Commonwealth, §1-510.
English language.
Official language of Commonwealth, §1-511.
Escheat, §§55-168 to 55-201.1.
See ESCHEAT.
Flag of the Commonwealth.
See FLAG OF THE COMMONWEALTH.
Fraudulent claims against the state, §§8.01-216.1 to 8.01-216.19.
See FRAUDULENT CLAIMS AGAINST THE STATE.
Health maintenance organizations.
Authority of Commonwealth to contract with, §38.2-4320.
Insect.
Special license plates, §46.2-728.3.
Insurance policies, §38.2-316.
Judgment for costs against Commonwealth prohibited except when otherwise provided, §17.1-629.
Judgment or decree for costs on behalf of Commonwealth, §17.1-628.
Judgments and decrees.
Collection of money payable to state.
Force of judgment of bond for purchase money, §8.01-209.
Nature of judgment, §8.01-199.
Correction of mistakes against state, §8.01-200.
Deceased obligors, §8.01-210.
Keys to buildings of Commonwealth.
Possession or duplication, §18.2-503.
Language.
English as official language, §1-511.
Lending of credit, VA Const Art X §10.
Limitation of actions.
Collection of money payable to state.
Proceedings to enforce judgment, §8.01-251.
Commonwealth not within statute of limitations, §8.01-231.
Medical malpractice, §§38.2-2800 to 38.2-2814.
Mortgage lender and broker act.
Agencies of exempt from chapter, §6.2-1602.
Motor carriers, passengers.
Government vehicles.
Exclusions, §46.2-2000.1.
Motor carriers, property.
Government vehicles.
Exemptions from provisions, §46.2-2101.
Northwest territory.
Cession of territory northwest of Ohio river, §1-303.
Officers and employees generally.
See PUBLIC OFFICERS AND EMPLOYEES.
Official emblems and designations of Commonwealth, §1-510.
Poet laureate, §1-512.
Property tax exemptions, §58.1-3606, VA Const Art X §6.
Veterans, VA Const Art X §6-A.
Real property tax credit when land acquired by Commonwealth.
Credit on current year's taxes, §§58.1-3360 to 58.1-3363.

STATE —Cont'd
Real property tax credit when land acquired by Commonwealth —Cont'd
Service charge levied on real property owned by Commonwealth, §58.1-3403.
Notice to governor, §58.1-3404.
Retirement system, §§51.1-124.1 to 51.1-169.
See VIRGINIA RETIREMENT SYSTEM.
Sale of real estate.
Collection of money payable to state. See within this heading, "Collection of money payable to state."
Satisfaction of judgments.
Marking satisfied judgments in favor of state, §8.01-457.
Seals of the Commonwealth, §§1-500 to 1-505.
Setoff debt collection, income tax, §§58.1-520 to 58.1-535.
See SETOFF DEBT COLLECTION, INCOME TAX.
Statute of limitations.
Collection of money payable to state.
Proceedings to enforce judgment, §8.01-251.
Commonwealth not within statute of limitations, §8.01-231.
Stock subscriptions, VA Const Art X §10.
Tax exempt property, VA Const Art X §6.
Veterans, VA Const Art X §6-A.
Toll bridges.
Conveyance and purchase by state, §§33.1-264, 33.1-265.
United States acquired lands.
Jurisdiction over lands acquired by United States, §§1-400 to 1-408.

STATE ABC STORES, §§4.1-119 to 4.1-122.

STATE AGENCIES.
See STATE DEPARTMENTS AND AGENCIES.

STATE AID.
Budget of state.
Estimates by nonstate agencies for annual budget, §2.2-1505.
Planning and budget department.
Estimates by nonstate agencies for annual budget, §2.2-1505.
Planning district commissions, §15.2-4216.
Locality to inform commission of applications, §15.2-4213.

STATE ARCHAEOLOGIST, §§10.1-2300, 10.1-2301.

STATE ARCHIVISTS.
Librarian of Virginia to name, §42.1-79.

STATE AUDITOR, §§30-130 to 30-142.

STATE BAR.
See VIRGINIA STATE BAR.

STATE BAR FUND, §54.1-3913.

STATE BIRD.
Special license plates incorporating the official bird, §46.2-728.1.

STATE BOARD FOR COMMUNITY COLLEGES, §§23-214 to 23-231.1:1.
See COMMUNITY COLLEGES.

STATE BOARD OF CAREER AND TECHNICAL EDUCATION.
Board of education.
Designated as state agency, §22.1-227.

STATE BOARD OF CAREER AND TECHNICAL EDUCATION —Cont'd
Board of education —Cont'd
General provisions.
See BOARD OF EDUCATION.

STATE BOARD OF CORRECTIONS, §§53.1-2 to 53.1-6.
See CORRECTIONS BOARD.

STATE BOARD OF EDUCATION.
Generally, §§22.1-8 to 22.1-20.
See BOARD OF EDUCATION.

STATE BOARD OF ELECTIONS.
Generally, §§24.2-102 to 24.2-105.
See ELECTIONS.

STATE BOARD OF HEALTH, §§32.1-5 to 32.1-15.
See HEALTH, STATE BOARD.

STATE BOARD OF JUVENILE JUSTICE, §§66-4 to 66-10.

STATE BOARD OF SOCIAL SERVICES.
Generally, §§63.2-215 to 63.2-221.
See SOCIAL SERVICES.

STATE BUILDINGS AND PROPERTY.
Blind persons.
Business and enterprises for generally.
See BLIND AND VISUALLY IMPAIRED.
Building code.
Appeals from decision of building official, §36-98.2.
Applicability of code to state buildings, §36-98.1.
Credit unions, leasing space, §2.2-1151.
Division of engineering and buildings, §§2.2-1129 to 2.2-1167.
See ENGINEERING AND BUILDINGS DIVISION.
Fire prevention code.
Applicability, §27-99.
Fire protection review of plans and inspections of state buildings, §27-5.5.
High performance buildings.
Definitions, §2.2-1182.
Energy conservation and environmental standards compliance for new buildings, §2.2-1183.
Exemption from design and construction standards, §2.2-1183.
Title of act, §2.2-1182.
Inspections.
Asbestos abatement in state-owned and public school buildings, §2.2-1163.
Standards for inspections, §2.2-1164.
Fire protection, §27-5.5.
Risk management division.
Inspection for insurance purposes, §2.2-1834.
Insurance.
Risk management division.
Inspection for insurance purposes, §2.2-1834.
Insurance plan for state buildings and property, §2.2-1836.
List and replacement value, §2.2-1833.
Risk management plan for public liability, §2.2-1837.
State insurance reserve trust fund, §2.2-1835.
Inventory of real property.
General services department, §2.2-1136.
Persons with physical disabilities.
Access to, §§2.2-1159 to 2.2-1161.
Plans.
Fire protection review, §27-5.5.
Public buildings generally.
See PUBLIC BUILDINGS.

STATE BUILDINGS AND PROPERTY —Cont'd
Risk management division.
Inspection for insurance purposes, §2.2-1834.
Insurance plan for state buildings and property, §2.2-1836.
List and replacement value, §2.2-1833.
Risk management plan for public liability, §2.2-1837.
State insurance reserve trust fund, §2.2-1835.
State-owned buildings and properties.
List and replacement value, §2.2-1833.

STATE CAPITOL.
Capitol district.
Seat of government, §2.2-620.
Capitol Square.
See CAPITOL SQUARE.
Damage to trees, fences or herbage on, §18.2-139.
Damaging, §18.2-138.
Flag of the Commonwealth.
When flag to be suspended over, §1-509.

STATE CASE REGISTRY.
Child support enforcement by department of social services.
Establishment, contents, §63.2-1905.

STATE CERTIFIED SEED BOARD, §§3.2-4021 to 3.2-4027.
See SEED BOARD.

STATE CHILD FATALITY REVIEW TEAM, §32.1-283.1.

STATE COMPTROLLER.
See COMPTROLLER.

STATE CONSOLIDATED OFFICE BUILDINGS.
Location, construction or lease.
Responsibility of division of engineering and buildings, §2.2-1137.

STATE COORDINATOR OF EMERGENCY MANAGEMENT.
Appointment by governor, §§44-146.17, 44-146.18.
Authority in undeclared emergency, §44-146.18:2.
Emergency management and disasters generally, §§44-146.13 to 44-146.28.
See EMERGENCY MANAGEMENT.
Hazardous materials emergency response, §§44-146.34 to 44-146.40.
Register of shippers of hazardous radioactive material, §44-146.30.

STATE CORPORATION COMMISSION, §§12.1-1 to 12.1-43, VA Const Art IX §1.
Acquisition of control of insurers, §§38.2-1323 to 38.2-1328.
Administering laws for regulation and control of corporations.
Powers and duties of commission, VA Const Art IX §2.
Advance sheets to Virginia reports.
Distribution to, §17.1-316.
Affiliated interests.
Public service companies. See within this heading, "Public service companies."
Agricultural cooperative association, §§13.1-313 to 13.1-345.
See AGRICULTURAL COOPERATIVE ASSOCIATIONS.

STATE CORPORATION COMMISSION —Cont'd
Air carriers.
See AIR CARRIERS.
Annual report to governor, §12.1-4.
Annuities.
Generally.
See ANNUITIES.
Appeal bond, §12.1-39.
Appeals, §12.1-39, VA Const Art IX §4.
Method of taking and prosecuting, §12.1-40.
Record on appeal.
Fees charged by clerk.
Making up, certifying, transmitting, §12.1-21.2.
Security for appeal, §8.01-676.1.
Assessment for administration of insurance laws, §§38.2-400 to 38.2-415.
Assignments of risks.
Workers' compensation insurance and self-insurance. See within this heading, "Workers' compensation insurance and self-insurance."
Attorneys.
Power to employ counsel for employee, §12.1-15.1.
Authority, §56-265.30.
Bailiff.
Appointment by commission, §12.1-18.
Deputy bailiff, §12.1-23.
Powers and duties, §12.1-23.
Service of writs, processes and orders, §12.1-29.
Banks generally.
See BANKS.
Blanket bond covering members of staff, §12.1-24.
Bonds of members of staff, §12.1-24.
Branch pilot fees and charges, §§54.1-918 to 54.1-923.
Breach of personal information, notice requirement.
Enforcement actions, §18.2-186.6.
Broker-dealers, investment advisors, investment advisor representatives and agents.
Registration with commission, §§13.1-504 to 13.1-506.
Building and loan associations.
See SAVINGS INSTITUTIONS.
Bureau of insurance.
See INSURANCE BUREAU.
Businesses operating under assumed name.
Filing of copy, §59.1-70.
Cease and desist orders.
Insurance title violations, §38.2-219.
Censure.
Conflicts of interest violations, §12.1-10.
Certificates of public convenience.
Public utilities. See within this heading, "Public utilities."
Certification of facts by clerk upon request, §12.1-20.
Chairman, §12.1-7, VA Const Art IX §1.
Annual elections, §12.1-7.
Term, §12.1-7.
Charging off delinquent taxes and registration fees, power, §12.1-15.
Civil actions against agents or investigators.
Attorney general or assistant representing, §2.2-507.
Clandestine organizations.
Information to be filed by, §18.2-421.

STATE CORPORATION COMMISSION —Cont'd
Clerk.
Agent for service.
Foreign nonprofit corporations, §§13.1-928, 13.1-929.
Appointment by commission, §12.1-18.
Attestation of writs, processes and orders, §12.1-29.
Certification of facts, §12.1-20.
Copies of records, duties, §12.1-19.
Documents or information filed with commission.
Personal identifiable information contained in documents, §12.1-19.
Duties, §12.1-19.
Fees to be charged, §12.1-21.1.
Foreign corporations, agent for service.
Failure to appoint or maintain registered agent in Commonwealth, §13.1-766.
Withdrawn corporations, §13.1-767.
Insurance agents, nonresidents.
Agent for service of process, §38.2-1836.
Nonprofit corporations, agent for service.
Failure to maintain registered agent in Commonwealth, §13.1-836.
Nonresident registered broker-dealers, investment advisors, investment advisor representatives or agents.
Appointment of clerk as agent for service of process, §13.1-517.
Nonresident retail franchisor.
Appointment of clerk as agent for service of process, §13.1-566.
Personal identifiable information contained in documents filed.
Authority of clerk, immunity.
Deletion or removal of information, refusal to accept document, §12.1-19.
Reciprocal insurers.
Appointment as agent for service, §38.2-1216.
Records, duties, §12.1-19.
Service of process on statutory agent, §12.1-19.1.
Corporations, clerk as agent for service.
Failure to maintain registered agent or agent not found at registered office, §13.1-637.
Nonresident retail franchisor.
Appointment as agent for service, §13.1-566.
Unlicensed insurers' agent for service, §38.2-801.
Commissioner of financial institutions.
Employee or agent placed by commission to administer banking laws, §12.1-16.
Violations of commissioner's orders, civil penalties, §6.2-946.
Commissioner of insurance.
Employee or agent placed by commission to administer insurance laws, §12.1-16.
Commonwealth to be complainant, §12.1-27.
Communications between parties or staff, §12.1-30.1.
Compressed natural gas service regulations, §56-232.2.
Compromise.
Power to settle claims, §12.1-15.
Concurrent jurisdiction of commission and court, §12.1-38.
Confidential information.
Investigations of securities violations, §13.1-518.
Conflicts of interest, §12.1-10.
Constables.
Execution of writs, processes and orders, §12.1-29.
Consumer finance companies.
See CONSUMER FINANCE COMPANIES.

STATE CORPORATION COMMISSION —Cont'd
Consumer finance generally.
See CONSUMER FINANCE.
Consumers' interests, representing.
Division of consumer counsel, §2.2-517.
Contempt.
Power to punish for, §§12.1-13, 12.1-34, VA Const Art IX §3.
Continuing education of insurance agents, §§38.2-1866 to 38.2-1874.
Control acquisition of insurers, §§38.2-1323 to 38.2-1328.
Cooperative associations generally, §§12.1-1 to 12.1-43.
See COOPERATIVE ASSOCIATIONS.
Cooperative nonprofit life benefit companies, §§38.2-3800 to 38.2-3818.
Copies.
Charges for, §12.1-21.2.
Copies of rules of practice and procedure furnished, §12.1-25.
Corporations generally, §§13.1-601 to 13.1-779.
See CORPORATIONS.
Correction of taxes assessed by, §§58.1-2030 to 58.1-2035.
Correspondence mailed by commission deemed delivered, §12.1-43.
Costs, fees and expenses.
Authority of commission same as courts of record, §12.1-32.
Courts of record powers, commission to have, §12.1-13.
Creation, §12.1-2.
Credit life insurance and credit health insurance, §§38.2-3717 to 38.2-3738.
See CREDIT INSURANCE.
Credit unions, §§6.2-1300 to 6.2-1380.
See CREDIT UNIONS.
Definitions, §12.1-1.
Delegation of powers and duties with respect to insurance and banking, §12.1-16.
Delinquency proceedings, rehabilitation and liquidation of insurers, §§38.2-1500 to 38.2-1522.
Delinquent taxes and registration fees, power to charge off, §12.1-15.
Dental services plans, §§38.2-4500 to 38.2-4523.
See DENTAL SERVICES PLANS.
Deposit of funds received, §12.1-17.
Devices on certain containers.
Description filing and publication, §59.1-94.
Fee, §§59.1-95, 59.1-95.1.
Disclosure statement by members.
Filing, time, form, §§2.2-3114, 2.2-3117.
Dishonor, refusal or charge back of payment.
Charge to person owing payment plus penalty, §12.1-17.
Disobedience of commission orders, fines, §12.1-33.
District court criminal jurisdiction.
Exception when jurisdiction in commission, §16.1-128.
Division of securities counsel created in office of attorney general.
Technical assistance provided by commission, §13.1-527.3.
Docketing judgments, §12.1-37.
Documents filed with commission.
Personal identifiable information contained in documents.
Deletion, removal, refusal to accept document, §12.1-19.

STATE CORPORATION COMMISSION —Cont'd
Duties, §12.1-2, VA Const Art IX §2.
Elected by general assembly, §12.1-6, VA Const Art IX §1.
Electric authorities.
Articles of dissolution, filing with, §15.2-5428.
Articles of incorporation, filing with, §15.2-5405.
Electric utilities.
Facility construction consideration factors, §56-46.1.
Electric utility restructuring.
Advancement of competition, §56-596.
Consumer education program, §§56-592, 56-592.1.
Net energy metering.
Regulations of commission, §56-594.
Nondiscriminatory access to transmission and distribution system.
Powers and duties of commission as to, §56-578.
Powers and duties of commission.
Consumer education and protection, §56-592.
Default service, §56-585.
Divestiture, functional separation and other corporate relationships, §56-590.
Nondiscriminatory access to transmission and distribution system, §56-578.
Regional transmission entity, §56-579.
Transmission and distribution of electric energy, §56-580.
Rates.
Regulation of rates subject to commission's jurisdiction, §56-581.
Regional transmission entities.
Duties of commission as to, §56-579.
Reports.
Advancement of competition, §56-596.
Work group discussion convened by SCC.
Commission on electric utility restructuring members participating in, §30-202.
Electric vehicle charging services.
Regulation of rates, charges and fees, §56-232.2:1.
Eligibility to serve as member, §12.1-9.
Environmental impact of construction of electrical utility facilities, §56-46.1.
Equal credit opportunities.
Investigations, §6.2-510.
Public to be informed of rights, §6.2-509.
Regulations, §6.2-506.
Acts committed under prior regulations, limitation on liability, §6.2-507.
Evidence.
Rules of evidence to be as in courts of record, §12.1-30.
Examination of insurance companies, §§38.2-1317 to 38.2-1321.1.
Execution of writs, processes and orders, §12.1-29.
Expedited or special handling, filings, provision of services.
Request, fee charged, §12.1-21.2.
Failure to qualify, §12.1-11.
Farm and forest land protection.
Plan to implement policies.
Preparation, requirement, §3.2-206.
Federal lien registrations, §§55-142.1 to 55-142.9.
Federal railroad administration track safety and inspection program.
Participation in, §56-129.1.
Fees.
Authority of commission with respect to same as courts of record, §12.1-32.
Charged by clerk, §12.1-21.1.

STATE CORPORATION COMMISSION —Cont'd
Fees —Cont'd
Court fee and expenses, §12.1-32.
Devices on certain containers, §§59.1-95, 59.1-95.1.
Facts certified by clerk upon request, §12.1-20.
Miscellaneous charges, §12.1-21.2.
Recording of agricultural cooperative association marketing contracts, §13.1-330.
Fidelity and surety insurance.
Generally, §§38.2-2400 to 38.2-2420.
Fieri facias.
Notice.
Sale of property subject to prior security interest, §8.01-480.
Financial institution holding companies.
Acquisition of interests in financial institutions, §§6.2-700 to 6.2-715.
Generally.
See FINANCIAL INSTITUTION HOLDING COMPANIES.
Findings by hearing examiners, report to commission, §12.1-31.
Fines.
Contempt, punishment for, §12.1-34.
Disobedience of commission orders, §12.1-33.
Power to impose and collect, limit on amount, §12.1-13.
Governor.
Annual report to, §12.1-4.
Appointment of members, §12.1-6.
Hazardous liquid pipeline safety.
Implementation of federal act, §56-555.
Heads of divisions and bureaus, appointment by commission, §12.1-18.
Health insurance generally, §§38.2-3400 to 38.2-3571.
See HEALTH INSURANCE.
Hearing examiners, §12.1-31.
Hearings, §12.1-28.
Public sessions, §12.1-26.
Highway corporations.
Certificates of authority, §56-539.
Applications, §56-540.
Termination, §56-551.
Default, §56-549.
Improvement fund, §56-552.
Powers of commission, §56-542.
Roadway operator powers and duties, §56-543.
Utility crossings, §56-547.
Home protection companies.
Generally, §§38.2-2600 to 38.2-2616.
Hydroelectric power, §62.1-83.
Eminent domain.
Reservation, §62.1-94.
Employment of experts, §62.1-100.
License approval.
Duration, §62.1-94.
Intangible water-power value, §62.1-95.
Navigation provisions, §62.1-91.
Prevention of unreasonable obstructions, §62.1-91.
Terms, §§62.1-91, 62.1-95.
Time limits, §62.1-93.
Transfers of license, §62.1-96.
Value of license, §62.1-95.
Licenses application to construct or reconstruct, §62.1-85.
Granting, §62.1-89.
Hearing notice, §62.1-86.
Investigations, §62.1-88.

STATE CORPORATION COMMISSION —Cont'd
Hydroelectric power —Cont'd
Licenses application to construct or reconstruct —Cont'd
Modification of plans, §62.1-90.
Priority of location or appropriation, §62.1-92.
Rejection, §62.1-90.
Provision violations, §62.1-97.
Regulation, §62.1-82.
Reports, §62.1-100.
Rules, §62.1-100.
Immunity on insurance companies examinations, §38.2-1321.1.
Impeachment, VA Const Art IV §17, Art IX §1.
Imposition of penalties not to relieve from other penalties, §12.1-14.
Indemnification.
Power to indemnify employee, §12.1-15.1.
Industrial loan associations, §§6.2-1400 to 6.2-1421.
See INDUSTRIAL LOAN ASSOCIATIONS.
Injunctions.
Insurance violations, §38.2-220.
Power to issue temporary and permanent injunctions, §12.1-13.
Insurance agents.
Generally, §§38.2-1800 to 38.2-1874.
See INSURANCE AGENTS.
Insurance antitrust provisions, §§38.2-700 to 38.2-705.
Insurance companies.
Generally.
See INSURANCE COMPANIES.
Insurance holding companies, §§38.2-1322 to 38.2-1334.
Insurance information and privacy protection.
Generally, §§38.2-600 to 38.2-620.
See INSURANCE INFORMATION AND PRIVACY PROTECTION.
Hearings and procedures before commission, §38.2-615.
Powers of commission, §38.2-614.
Insurance, powers relative to, §38.2-200.
Delegation of functions, §38.2-1836.1.
Exclusive agency contract subject to approval by commission, §38.2-203.
Recommendations to general assembly, §38.2-201.
Rules and regulations regarding voting equity securities of domestic stock insurers, §38.2-202.
Insurance rates generally, §§38.2-1900 to 38.2-1928.
See INSURANCE RATES.
Insurance unfair trade practices.
Powers of commission, §38.2-515.
Interest.
Judgments, §12.1-36.
Investigations.
Insurance or reinsurance transactions.
Immunity of commission members or employees, §38.2-229.
Retail franchises, §13.1-567.
Securities violations, §13.1-518.
Joint underwriting association, basic property insurance, §§38.2-2700 to 38.2-2713.
Judgments in favor of Commonwealth, §12.1-35.
Docketing, §12.1-37.
Interest, §12.1-36.
Lien of judgment, §12.1-37.
Time judgment takes effect, §12.1-36.

STATE CORPORATION COMMISSION —Cont'd
Jurisdiction.
Concurrent jurisdiction of commission and court, §12.1-38.
Powers and duties generally, §12.1-12.
Jury service.
Automatic exemption, §8.01-341.
Liability insurance.
Generally, §§38.2-2200 to 38.2-2234.
Licensing of insurers, §§38.2-1024 to 38.2-1039.1.
Refusal, suspension or revocation, §§38.2-1040 to 38.2-1044.
Liens.
Judgments of commission, §12.1-37.
Life insurance.
Generally, §§38.2-3100 to 38.2-3354.
See LIFE INSURANCE.
Limitation of actions.
Appeals, §12.1-39.
Supersedeas, petitions for writs of, §12.1-41.
Limited liability companies generally, §§13.1-1000 to 13.1-1080.
See LIMITED LIABILITY COMPANIES.
Local government group self-insurance pools.
Approval required, §15.2-2706.
Filing financial statement and deficit correction financial plan with, §15.2-2707.
Long-term care insurance, §§38.2-5200 to 38.2-5210.
Mail.
Service of process by commission, §12.1-19.1.
Tax assessments, report forms and correspondence mailed by commission deemed delivered, §12.1-43.
Majority of commission to constitute quorum, §12.1-8.
Managed care health insurance plans.
Certificate of quality.
Certificates of quality assurance generally, §§32.1-137.1 to 32.1-137.6.
See MANAGED CARE HEALTH INSURANCE PLANS.
Mandamus.
Issuance of writ to commission.
Supreme court jurisdiction, §§12.1-39, 17.1-309.
Mandatory retirement, VA Const Art IX §1.
Market analyses concerning insurance companies or insurance transactions.
Confidentiality, §38.2-1317.2.
Marks on certain containers.
Description filing and publication, §59.1-94.
Fee, §§59.1-95, 59.1-95.1.
Medical malpractice claims reported to.
Duty of insurers of health care providers, §38.2-2228.2.
Medicare supplement policies, §§38.2-3600 to 38.2-3609.
Meetings and communications between commissioners and parties or staff, §12.1-30.1.
Methods of making payments to, §12.1-17.
Motor carriers.
Railroad corporations. See within this heading, "Railroad corporations."
Motor vehicle accidents.
Duty of insurance carrier after notice of accident, §46.2-424.
Motor vehicle insurance.
Assignment of insurance risks, §§46.2-464 to 46.2-471.
See MOTOR VEHICLE INSURANCE.

STATE CORPORATION COMMISSION —Cont'd
Motor vehicle title loans.
Acquisition of corporation, §6.2-2208.
Cease and desist orders, §6.2-2220.
Investigations, §6.2-2212.
Notice.
Change of location or additional location, §6.2-2207.
Suspension or revocation of licenses.
Notice of proposed suspension or revocation, §6.2-2221.
Multistate trust institutions, generally, §§6.2-803, 6.2-1065 to 6.2-1073.
See TRUST COMPANIES.
Mutual assessment property and casualty insurers, §§38.2-2500 to 38.2-2529.
Names on certain containers.
Description publication and filing.
Fee, §§59.1-94, 59.1-95, 59.1-95.1.
Natural gas pipeline companies.
Regulation of service, §56-232.1.
Service to federal, state and local governmental facilities, §56-232.3.
Nonprofit corporations generally, §§13.1-801 to 13.1-945.
See NONPROFIT CORPORATIONS.
Notice.
Fieri facias.
Sale of property subject to prior security interest, §8.01-480.
Orders, rules and regulations promulgated by commission, §12.1-28.
Returnable to location of commission, §12.1-5.
Notice of opportunity to introduce evidence and be heard.
Required before entering finding, order or judgment, VA Const Art IX §3.
Notice of proposed rule or regulation contents, VA Const Art IX §3.
Number of members, §12.1-6, VA Const Art IX §1.
Oath of office, §12.1-11.
Power to administer, §12.1-13, VA Const Art IX §3.
Offices of commission.
Location, §12.1-5.
Optometric services plans, §§38.2-4500 to 38.2-4523.
See OPTOMETRIC SERVICES PLANS.
Parties.
Commonwealth to be complainant and party against whom complaint preferred defendant, §12.1-27.
Meetings and communications between commissioners and parties, §12.1-30.1.
Penalties imposition power not to relieve from other penalties, §12.1-14.
Penalty for dishonor, refusal or charge back of payment, §12.1-17.
Permanent commission, §12.1-2.
Personal identifiable information contained in filed documents.
Deletion, removal, refusal to accept document.
Authority, immunity, §12.1-19.
Personal information protection.
Notice of breach of personal information.
Enforcement actions, §18.2-186.6.
Petitions.
Writs of supersedeas, §12.1-41.
Petroleum storage tank discharges.
Insurance pool establishment, §62.1-44.34:12.

STATE CORPORATION COMMISSION —Cont'd
Pilotage rates and charges, §§54.1-918 to 54.1-923.
Port authority.
Powers not affected, §62.1-138.
Powers, §12.1-2, VA Const Art IX §2.
Compromise and settlement, §12.1-15.
Courts of record powers, commission to have, §12.1-13.
Premium finance companies, §§38.2-4700 to 38.2-4712.
See INSURANCE PREMIUM FINANCE COMPANIES.
Presumptions.
Tax assessments, report forms and correspondence mailed by commission deemed delivered, §12.1-43.
Procedures of commission, VA Const Art IX §3.
Production of documents and records.
Power to compel, §12.1-13, VA Const Art IX §3.
Professional corporations generally, §§13.1-542.1 to 13.1-556.
See PROFESSIONAL CORPORATIONS.
Prohibition.
Issuance of writ to commission.
Supreme court jurisdiction, §§12.1-39, 17.1-309.
Protection of public interest, §56-46.3.
Publication.
Orders, rules and regulations promulgated by commission, §12.1-28.
Public-private education facilities and infrastructure act, §§56-575.1 to 56-575.18.
See PUBLIC BUILDINGS.
Public-private transportation act, §§56-556 to 56-574.
See TRANSPORTATION.
Public service companies.
Adjustment of claims and settlement of controversies, §56-38.
Affiliated interests.
Appeals of decisions, §56-86.
Contract approval, §56-77.
Dividend payments to.
Orders prohibiting, §56-83.
Obligation assumption approval, §56-82.
Payment accounts.
Exclusions from, §56-78.
Payments as operating expenses or capital expenditures.
Orders prohibiting treatment of, §56-81.
Payments to.
Proof of costs, §56-79.
Procedure, §56-84.
Provision violations, §56-85.
Rules to carry out chapter, §56-87.
Supervision by commission, §56-80.
Capitalization of permits, franchises or contracts for consolidation.
Commission power, §56-66.
Complaint.
Examination of, §56-43.
Compressed natural gas service regulations, §56-232.2.
Designation by commission, §56-1.1.
Duties as to, §56-36.
Electrical utility facility considerations, §56-46.1.
Electric line construction complaints, §56-46.2.
Inspection of company books, §56-36.
Natural gas pipelines.
Regulation of service, §56-232.1.

STATE CORPORATION COMMISSION —Cont'd
Public service companies —Cont'd
Public utilities. See within this heading, "Public utilities."
Railroad corporations. See within this heading, "Railroad corporations."
Rates.
Appeals, §56-8.2.
Notice when rates are reduced, §56-40.
Utility pole use, §56-41.1.
Regulation of, §56-35.
Regulation of electric vehicle charging services, §56-232.2:1.
Remedies of persons aggrieved by corporation's violation of law, §56-6.
Reports to commission by, §56-36.
Right of one to cross the works of another.
Contests by companies whose works are crossed, §56-19.
Work to proceed, §56-21.
Submission of plans, §56-18.
Securities, issuance.
Application, §56-60.
Action of commission, §56-61.
Void if order not obtained, §56-67.
Commonwealth liability, §56-74.
Joint actions with commission of another state, §56-62.
Order required before acting as surety, §56-59.
Proceeds.
Accounting for disposition of, §56-70.
Provision violations, §56-71.
Sewerage companies.
Commission powers not limited, §56-265.
Failure to perform duties.
Quo warranto, §56-264.
Small investor-owned telephone utilities, §§56-532, 56-533.
Telephone cooperatives. See within this heading, "Telephone cooperatives."
Transportation companies. See within this heading, "Transportation companies."
Utility lines.
Crossing railroads, §56-16.1.
Municipalities, §56-16.2.
Utility pole rates, §56-41.1.
Utility transfers.
Asset changes, §56-89.
Procedure, §56-90.
Sales, §56-90.1.
Control changes, §56-88.1.
Provision violations, §56-91.
Security changes, §56-89.
Procedure, §56-90.
Water supply companies.
Commission powers not limited, §56-265.
Failure to perform duties, §56-262.
Quo warranto, §56-264.
Public service corporations.
Sewerage companies.
Failure to perform duties, §56-262.
Public service corporation taxation generally, §§58.1-2600 to 58.1-2690.
See PUBLIC SERVICE CORPORATION TAXATION.
Public sessions, §12.1-26.
Public sessions held other than location of commission, §12.1-5.
Public utilities.
Acts substitution, §56-247.
Capital resource conservation, §56-235.1.

STATE CORPORATION COMMISSION —Cont'd
Public utilities —Cont'd
Certificates of public convenience and necessity.
Allotment of territories, §56-265.3.
Appeals from orders, §56-265.7.
Application of provisions, §56-265.8.
Electric utility services of state or local governments, §56-265.4:1.
Gas service, §56-265.4:5.
Non-utility gas service, §56-265.4:6.
Issuance, §56-265.2.
Operation as a telephone utility, §56-265.4:4.
Operation in territory of another certificate holder, §56-265.4.
Provision violations, §56-265.6.
Water and sewer service, §56-265.3:1.
Charges.
Churches, §56-236.1.
Schedules, §56-236.
Conservation of energy, §56-235.1.
Construction project review, §56-234.3.
Curtailment of service in times of emergency or shortage, §56-250.
Energy allocation equipment, §§56-245.2, 56-245.3.
Extension of service, §56-255.
Fuel cost recovery, §56-249.6.
Fuel price and purchase monitoring, §56-248.1.
Gas pipeline construction, §56-265.2:1.
Investigation of operations, §56-234.4.
Jurisdiction of commission over electric utility.
Federal governmental facility ceasing to be customer, §56-235.7.
Natural gas pipeline safety, §56-257.2.
New generation facilities.
Review and approval, §56-234.3.
Performance-based ratemaking.
Gas and electric utilities, §56-235.6.
Pipelines.
Rights-of-way, §56-259.
Procedures, §56-247.1.
Projected operation programs of electric utilities, §56-234.3.
Purchasing practices, §56-233.1.
Rates.
Alternative forms of telephone regulation, §56-235.5.
Alternative price regulations, §56-235.2.
Applications for changes.
Investigation procedures, §56-235.3.
Changes, §56-237.
Effective if not suspended, §56-240.
Hearings, §56-237.2.
Notice, §56-237.1.
Suspension of proposed rates, §56-238.
Appeals, §56-239.
Churches, §56-236.1.
Electric utility restructuring.
Generally, §§56-576 to 56-596.
See ELECTRIC UTILITY RESTRUCTURING.
Fixing by commission, §56-235.
Income tax costs for investor-owned utility.
Determining.
Utility part of publicly-traded, consolidated group, §56-235.2.
Increases, temporary, §56-245.
Jurisdiction, §56-234.
Just and reasonable determinations, §56-235.2.
Multiple rate increases within any twelve-month period, §56-235.4.

STATE CORPORATION COMMISSION —Cont'd
Public utilities —Cont'd
Rates —Cont'd
Performance-based ratemaking.
Gas and electric utilities, §56-235.6.
Reductions, temporary, §56-242.
Duration, §56-243.
Increases to make up for losses due to excessive temporary reduction, §56-244.
Review, §56-234.2.
Schedules, §56-236.
Special charges or incentives, §56-235.2.
Stand-by electric service at renewable cogeneration facilities.
Regulations requiring rates for, §56-235.1:1.
Records, §56-249.2.
Regulation of compressed natural gas service, §56-232.2.
Regulation of natural gas pipeline companies, §56-232.1.
Reports, §56-249.
Fuel transactions of electric utilities, §56-249.3.
Filing, §56-249.4.
Sewerage companies.
Commission powers not limited, §56-265.
Duty failures, §§56-262 to 56-264.
Failure to perform duties.
Investigations, §56-263.
Small investor-owned telephone utilities, §§56-532, 56-533.
Standard commercial units.
Prescription, §56-248.
State operation.
Revenue collection and disposition.
Disputes, §56-520.
Submetering, §§56-245.2, 56-245.3.
Suspension of enforcement of proposed rates.
Pending investigation, §56-238.
Telegraph and telephone companies. See within this heading, "Telegraph or telephone companies."
Telephone cooperatives. See within this heading, "Telephone cooperatives."
Tests and equipment therefor, §56-246.
Transfer of operations, §56-249.1.
Underground utility line damage prevention.
Advisory committee established, §56-265.31.
Civil penalties for violations, §56-265.32.
Notification centers.
Certification, §56-265.16:1.
Water supply companies.
Commission powers not limited, §56-265.
Duty failures, §§56-262 to 56-264.
Failure to perform duties.
Investigations, §56-263.
Punishment for contempt, §12.1-34.
Qualifications prescribed for judges of courts of record.
At least one member to have, §12.1-9.
Quorum, §12.1-8.
Railroad corporations.
Crossings.
Bridges.
Proceedings to remodel or replace existing bridges or crossings, §56-366.3.
Clearance inspections, §56-417.1.
Protective devices.
Installation of automatically operated devices, §56-406.1.
Maintenance cost of automatically operated devices, §56-406.2.

STATE CORPORATION COMMISSION —Cont'd
Railroad corporations —Cont'd
Crossings —Cont'd
State roads.
Elimination of crossings by construction of replacement of public highways, §56-369.
Elimination of grade crossings by change of alignment of roads, §56-369.
Failures to remove causes of complaint, §56-440.
Information to be furnished to commission, §56-446.
Safety.
Clearance inspections, §56-417.1.
Unused track assessments, §56-451.1.
Real estate settlement agents.
Confidentiality of information obtained by commission, §55-525.32.
Generally, §§55-525.16 to 55-525.32.
See REAL ESTATE SETTLEMENTS.
Licensing authority, §55-525.16.
Orders, rules, regulations, summonses, subpoenas.
Issuance by licensing authority, §55-525.28.
Receipts for currency received for payments, §12.1-17.
Records.
Clerk's duties, §12.1-19.
Rehabilitation and liquidation of insurers, §§38.2-1500 to 38.2-1522.
Removal, §12.1-10, VA Const Art IX §1.
Reports.
Annual report to governor, §12.1-4.
Hearing examiners, findings, §12.1-31.
Residual market facility, basic property insurance, §§38.2-2700 to 38.2-2713.
Responses to hearing examiners' report, §12.1-31.
Retail supply choice for natural gas customers.
Powers and duties as to, §56-235.8.
Retirement, VA Const Art IX §1.
Appearance as counsel prohibitions, §51.1-309.
Censure or removal of members, VA Const Art VI §10.
Early retirement, §51.1-305.
Mandatory retirement.
Generally, specific provisions applicable to member, §51.1-305.
Normal retirement, §51.1-305.
Notice, §51.1-305.
Recall to service, payment, §17.1-327.
Retirement system generally, §§51.1-300 to 51.1-309.
See JUDICIAL RETIREMENT SYSTEM.
Temporary recall, §12.1-11.1.
Risk retention groups and purchasing groups, §§38.2-5100 to 38.2-5115.
Road tax on motor carriers, §§58.1-2700 to 58.1-2712.2.
See ROAD TAX ON MOTOR CARRIERS.
Rulemaking power, §12.1-13, VA Const Art IX §3.
Savings banks, §6.2-1192.
Rules of evidence to be as in courts of record, §12.1-30.
Rules of practice and procedure.
Admissibility of evidence.
Exhibits and testimony, 5 VAC 5-20-240.
Admissions.
Discovery in adjudicatory proceedings, 5 VAC 5-20-280.
Affidavits.
Subpoenas, 5 VAC 5-20-250.

STATE CORPORATION COMMISSION —Cont'd
Rules of practice and procedure —Cont'd
Agents.
Interrogatories, answer, 5 VAC 5-20-260.
Requests for production of documents, answer, 5 VAC 5-20-260.
Applicability of rules, 5 VAC 5-20-10.
Applications, 5 VAC 5-20-80.
Copies and format, 5 VAC 5-20-150.
Exhibits and testimony, 5 VAC 5-20-240.
Memorandum of completeness, 5 VAC 5-20-160.
Attorneys at law.
Authorized to appear, 5 VAC 5-20-30.
Consumer counsel, 5 VAC 5-20-30.
Briefs.
Written briefs, 5 VAC 5-20-200.
Broadcasting of proceedings, 5 VAC 5-20-40.
Burden of proof.
Adjudicatory proceedings, 5 VAC 5-20-90.
Calendars.
Extension of time, 5 VAC 5-20-230.
Holidays and weekends.
Filing of pleadings, 5 VAC 5-20-140.
Commission staff.
Commission and hearing examiners may confer with, 5 VAC 5-20-60.
Ex parte proceedings, 5 VAC 5-20-40, 5 VAC 5-20-60.
Participation in proceedings, 5 VAC 5-20-80, 5 VAC 5-20-100.
Subpoenas, 5 VAC 5-20-250.
Workpapers, 5 VAC 5-20-260.
Requests to examine workpapers, 5 VAC 5-20-270.
Confidential information, 5 VAC 5-20-170.
Continuances, 5 VAC 5-20-230.
Declaratory judgments, 5 VAC 5-20-100.
Discovery.
Adjudicatory proceedings, 5 VAC 5-20-280.
Electronic media, 5 VAC 5-20-40.
Electronic pleadings, 5 VAC 5-20-20.
Briefs, 5 VAC 5-20-200.
Exhibits, 5 VAC 5-20-240.
Extension of time, 5 VAC 5-20-230.
Facsimile pleadings, 5 VAC 5-20-140.
Hearing examiners.
Proceedings before hearing examiners, 5 VAC 5-20-120.
Transcripts, 5 VAC 5-20-180.
Informal complaints, 5 VAC 5-20-70.
Memorandum of completeness, 5 VAC 5-20-160.
Motions.
Adjudicatory proceedings, initiation of, 5 VAC 5-20-90.
Discovery in adjudicatory proceedings.
Material in possession of commission staff, 5 VAC 5-20-280.
Extension of time, 5 VAC 5-20-230.
Generally, 5 VAC 5-20-110.
Interrogatories, objection to, 5 VAC 5-20-260.
Oral motions, 5 VAC 5-20-20.
Request for production of documents, objection to, 5 VAC 5-20-260.
Subpoenas for other regulatory agencies, 5 VAC 5-20-250.
Notice and publication.
Promulgation of general orders, rules or regulations, 5 VAC 5-20-100.
Notice of participation as a respondent.
Regulatory proceedings, 5 VAC 5-20-80.

STATE CORPORATION COMMISSION —Cont'd
Rules of practice and procedure —Cont'd
Oral argument, 5 VAC 5-20-210.
Petitions for rehearing or reconsideration, 5 VAC 5-20-220.
Petitions.
Copies and format, 5 VAC 5-20-150.
Non-adjudicatory proceedings, 5 VAC 5-20-100.
Rehearing or reconsideration, 5 VAC 5-20-220.
Extension of time, 5 VAC 5-20-230.
Pleadings.
Amendments, 5 VAC 5-20-130.
Copies and format, 5 VAC 5-20-150.
Electronic pleadings, 5 VAC 5-20-20, 5 VAC 5-20-140.
Exhibits and testimony, 5 VAC 5-20-240.
Extension of time, 5 VAC 5-20-230.
Filing, 5 VAC 5-20-140.
Signatures required, 5 VAC 5-20-20.
Promulgation of general orders, rules or regulations, 5 VAC 5-20-100.
Pro se representation.
Hearings, 5 VAC 5-20-30.
Rules of evidence, 5 VAC 5-20-190.
Rule to show cause.
Initiation of proceedings, 5 VAC 5-20-90.
Service of notice, process and other papers.
Petitions, 5 VAC 5-20-100.
Pleadings, 5 VAC 5-20-140.
Signatures.
Pleadings, 5 VAC 5-20-20.
Subpoenas.
Generally, 5 VAC 5-20-250.
Other regulatory agency subpoenas, 5 VAC 5-20-250.
Witnesses, 5 VAC 5-20-280.
Transcripts, 5 VAC 5-20-180.
Venue.
Depositions.
Discovery in adjudicatory proceedings, 5 VAC 5-20-280.
Waiver or modification of rules, 5 VAC 5-20-10.
Witnesses.
Public witnesses, 5 VAC 5-20-80.
Requests to examine workpapers supporting witnesses' testimony, 5 VAC 5-20-270.
Subpoena of witnesses, 5 VAC 5-20-250.
Discovery in adjudicatory proceedings, 5 VAC 5-20-280.
Rules of practice and procedure to be prescribed by commission, §12.1-25, VA Const Art IX §3.
Savings and loan associations.
See SAVINGS INSTITUTIONS.
Savings banks.
See SAVINGS BANKS.
Savings institutions.
See SAVINGS INSTITUTIONS.
Seal, §12.1-3.
Certification of facts by clerk to be sealed, §12.1-20.
Fee for affixing seal of commission, §12.1-21.1.
Securities.
Regulatory authority of commission, §13.1-523.1.
Securities regulation generally, §§13.1-501 to 13.1-527.3.
See SECURITIES.
Service marks.
Virginia trademark and service mark act (1998).
Generally, §§59.1-92.1 to 59.1-92.22.
See TRADEMARKS AND SERVICE MARKS.

STATE CORPORATION COMMISSION —Cont'd
Service of notice, process and other papers.
Clerk appointed as agent for service.
Corporations.
Failure to maintain registered agent or agent not found at registered office, §13.1-637.
Foreign corporations, failure to maintain registered office in Commonwealth, §13.1-766.
Foreign stock corporation, withdrawn corporation, §13.1-767.
Nonprofit corporations.
Failure to maintain registered agent in Commonwealth, §13.1-836.
Foreign corporations, failure to maintain agent in Commonwealth, §13.1-928.
Foreign corporations, withdrawal, §13.1-929.
Nonresident broker-dealers, investment advisors, investment advisor representatives or agents, §13.1-517.
Nonresident insurance agents, §38.2-1836.
Nonresident issuers of securities, §13.1-517.
Reciprocal insurers, §38.2-1216.
Trademark and service mark registration.
Service on out-of-state registrants, §59.1-92.14.
Unlicensed insurers, §38.2-801.
Clerk as statutory agent, §12.1-19.1.
Execution of writs, processes and orders, §12.1-29.
Method of service by commission, §12.1-19.1.
Nonresident retail franchisors.
Appointment of clerk as agent, §13.1-566.
Parties entitled to, §12.1-27.
Returnable to location of commission, §12.1-5.
Sessions.
Public sessions, §12.1-26.
Public sessions other than location of commission, §12.1-5.
Settlements.
Powers, §12.1-15.
Sewerage companies.
Cooperative associations.
Organization of, §13.1-301.
Small sewer companies.
Rates.
Changes, §56-265.13:6.
Receivership appointments, §56-265.13:6.1.
Regulation by commission, §56-265.13:7.
Systems not regulated as public utilities.
Complaints, §56-265.11.
Opinion of commission, §56-265.12.
Sheriffs.
Execution of writs, processes and orders, §12.1-29.
Signature of clerk on certification of facts, §12.1-20.
Small investor-owned telephone utilities.
Rates, §56-532.
Regulation of by commission, §56-533.
Small renewable energy projects.
Limitation of commission jurisdiction, §10.1-1197.8.
Statute of limitations.
Appeals, §12.1-39.
Supersedeas, petition for writs of, §12.1-41.
Stock corporations generally.
See CORPORATIONS.
Stop orders.
Security registration statements, denying or revoking effectiveness, §13.1-513.
Supersedeas.
Petitions for writs of, §12.1-41.

STATE CORPORATION COMMISSION —Cont'd
Supreme court.
Appeals from actions of commission, §12.1-39, VA Const Art IX §4.
Special rules applicable to appeals to supreme court, VA SCt Rule 5:21.
Surplus lines insurance law, §§38.2-4805.1 to 38.2-4816.
See SURPLUS LINES INSURANCE.
Taxation of public service corporations generally, §§58.1-2600 to 58.1-2690.
See PUBLIC SERVICE CORPORATION TAXATION.
Taxes assessment, correction, §§58.1-2030 to 58.1-2035.
Appeal, §58.1-2033.
Clerical error, §58.1-2035.
Determination, §58.1-2032.
Hearing, §58.1-2031.
Notice, §58.1-2031.
Other erroneous assessment, §58.1-2034.
Petition, §58.1-2030.
Tax information.
Tax commissioner authorized to divulge, §58.1-3.
Telegraph or telephone companies.
Agreements between companies.
Submission to commission, §56-482.
Certificates of public convenience and necessity, §56-265.4:4.
Cooperatives, telephones. See within this heading, "Telephone cooperatives."
Duty to inform, §56-479.
Extension of service upon poll, §56-484.2.
Foreign companies.
Licensing, §56-484.
Inspections by commission, §56-479.
Interexchange telephone companies.
Rates, §56-482.1.
Reports, §56-482.1.
Long distance service, change of carriers, §56-479.1.
Obstructing commission in discharge of duties, §56-483.
Offering of communications services, §56-484.7:1.
Approval, §56-484.7:2.
Revocation, §56-484.7:4.
Pay telephone registration, §§56-508.15, 56-508.16.
Powers not restricted, §56-484.3.
Public utilities generally. See within this heading, "Public utilities."
Questions as to reasonableness, justice or validity of rates, rules and regulations, §56-480.
Rates.
Commission powers, §56-241.
Impermissible basis, §56-241.1.
Interexchange telephone service, §56-481.1.
Local services provided by new entrants, §56-481.2.
Resales of telephone services, §56-241.2.
Time limit on institution, §56-480.1.
Reduction of service upon poll, §56-484.2.
Rules and regulations, §§56-479, 56-484.3.
Small investor-owned telephone utilities, §§56-532, 56-533.
Underground utility line damage prevention.
Notification centers.
Certification, §56-265.16:1.
Telephone cooperatives.
Certificates of adoption, §56-507.
Regulation of, §56-502.

STATE CORPORATION COMMISSION —Cont'd
Telephone cooperatives —Cont'd
Rural service extensions, §56-508.
Temporary recall of member, §12.1-11.1.
Terms, §12.1-6, VA Const Art IX §1.
Title insurance, §§38.2-4600 to 38.2-4616.
See TITLE INSURANCE.
Trademarks and service marks generally, §§59.1-92.1 to 59.1-92.22.
See TRADEMARKS AND SERVICE MARKS.
Transportation companies.
Accident investigations, §56-131.
Additions.
Penalties for failure to make, §56-130.
Examinations of works and equipment, §56-128.
Federal railroad administration track safety and inspection program.
Participation by commission, §56-129.1.
Improvements.
Penalties for failure to make, §56-130.
Provision violations.
Penalties, §56-140.
Railroad corporations. See within this heading, "Railroad corporations."
Rates and charges.
Commission authority over, §56-99.2.
Repairs.
Penalties for failure to make, §56-130.
Trust companies.
Violations of commissioner's orders, civil penalties, §6.2-1046.
Trust subsidiaries.
Violations of commissioner's orders, civil penalties, §6.2-1064.
Uninsured motorists fund.
Supervision and control, §38.2-3000.
Utility aggregation cooperatives.
Regulation by commission, §56-231.50.
Rules and regulations, §56-231.50:1.
Utility consumer services cooperatives.
Regulation by commission, §56-231.34.
Rules and regulations, §56-231.34:1.
Utility lines.
Crossing of railroads, §56-16.1.
Municipalities, §56-16.2.
Utility transfers.
Asset changes, §56-89.
Procedure, §56-90.
Sales, §56-90.1.
Control changes, §56-88.1.
Provisions violations, §56-91.
Security changes, §56-89.
Procedure, §56-90.
Vacancy on commission, §§12.1-6, 12.1-11, VA Const Art IX §1.
Virginia energy plan.
Development.
Division of energy to consult with SCC, §67-201.
Waiver of penalty or interest upon tax, power, §12.1-15.
Water and waste authorities.
Filing articles of dissolution with, §15.2-5109.
Issuance of certificate of incorporation or charter, §15.2-5108.
Water supply companies.
Small water utilities.
Rate changes, §56-265.13:6.
Receivership appointments, §56-265.13:6.1.
Regulation by commission, §56-265.13:7.
Systems not regulated as public utilities.
Complaints, §56-265.11.

STATE CORPORATION COMMISSION —Cont'd
Water supply companies —Cont'd
Systems not regulated as public utilities —Cont'd
Opinion of commission, §56-265.12.
Witnesses.
Power to compel attendance, §12.1-13, VA Const Art IX §3.
Workers' compensation insurance and self-insurance.
Administrative fund.
Access to returns, §65.2-1001.
Assessment of tax, §65.2-1003.
Self-insurers.
Access to payroll reports, §65.2-1006.
Assignments of risks.
Applications, §65.2-820.
Action upon, §65.2-822.
Confidentiality of information, §65.2-823.
Disclosures not required, §65.2-824.
Rates, §65.2-821.
Rules and regulations, §65.2-821.
Group self-insurance associations, §65.2-802.
Information on statutory requirements.
Distribution, §65.2-800.
Rate information, §65.2-817.
Provision violations, §65.2-819.
Service standards, §65.2-818.
Provision violations, §65.2-819.

STATE CORRECTIONAL FACILITIES.
Prisons generally, §§53.1-18 to 53.1-67.1.
See PRISONS.

STATE COUNCIL OF HIGHER EDUCATION.
Generally, §§23-9.3 to 23-9.14:2.
See COUNCIL OF HIGHER EDUCATION.
Secretary of education.
Agency responsibility, §2.2-208.

STATE DEBT, VA Const Art X §9.

STATE DEFENSE FORCE, §§44-54.4 to 44-54.12.
Acknowledgments, §§55-113 to 55-115.
Who may perform notarial acts, §55-118.1.
Actions or suits, power to maintain, §44-99.
Active duty.
Defined, §44-54.4.
Infractions of military discipline, punishment, §44-54.10.
Mission of force, §44-54.4.
Regulations.
Generally, §§44-75.1 to 44-84.
Adjutant general to prescribe regulations, §§44-54.5, 44-54.7.
Age requirement, §44-54.6.
Appropriations, allowances made to organizations, §44-114.
Arms, §44-54.12.
Exemption form levy and sale, §44-96.
Arrest, exemption from, §44-97.
Attorneys, employment of special counsel to defend member sued civilly or criminally prosecuted, §44-100.
Care of military property, §§44-103 to 44-111.
Commissioned officers.
Administration of oaths, §44-54.8.
Commission not to vacate civil office, §44-102.
Composition of units, §44-54.5.
Defense of member sued civilly or criminally prosecuted, §44-100.
Definitions, §44-54.4.
Discharge, §44-54.11.

STATE DEFENSE FORCE —Cont'd
Discipline, §44-54.10.
Subject to military discipline, §44-115.
Dishonorable discharge, §44-54.11.
Dismissal from service, §44-54.11.
Employment of members, interference with, §44-98.
Enlisted members, §44-54.6.
Equipment, §44-54.12.
Exemption from levy and sale, §44-96.
Facilities, §44-54.12.
Force structure, §44-54.5.
Grade structure, §44-54.9.
Immunity for acts done while in discharge of military duty, §44-100.
Insignia, §44-54.9.
Leaves of absence for state employees, §44-204.
License plates.
Special plates, §46.2-743.
Line of duty act, §§9.1-400 to 9.1-408.
Members, §44-54.6.
Mission of force when called to state active duty, §44-54.4.
Motor vehicle registration.
City or county decals.
Vehicles owned or leased by members, §46.2-752.
Oaths, administration of, §44-54.8.
Officers, appointment by governor, §44-54.6.
Organization, §44-54.4.
Public safety medal of valor, §§9.1-800, 9.1-801.
Qualifications, §44-54.6.
Regulations, §44-54.7.
Right to own and keep real and personal property, §44-99.
State appropriations, allowances made to organizations, §44-114.
Training duty, §44-75.2.
Defined, §44-54.4.
Uniforms, §44-54.9.
Exemption from levy and sale, §44-96.
United States military service, §44-54.4.
Unorganized militia.
Incorporation into, §44-88.
Volunteers, force to consist of, §44-54.6.
Workers' compensation.
Average weekly wage of member, §65.2-101.
Coverage, §65.2-103.

STATE DEPARTMENTS AND AGENCIES, §§2.2-600 to 2.2-614.3.
Abandonment of property presumption.
Intangible personalty held for owner by public agency, §55-210.9.
Accounting system.
Fiscal year, §2.2-805.
Funds received, report to comptroller, §2.2-807.
Uniform financial accounting and control, §2.2-803.
Acquisitions, conveyances and transfers of property, §§2.2-1147 to 2.2-1156.
Approval of department of general services required.
Acquisition of property for capital improvements by agencies, §2.2-1154.
Approval of department of general services to governor.
Required to transfer property, §§2.2-1150, 2.2-1151.
Boy Scouts of America.
Equal access to state-owned or controlled property, §2.2-1147.2.

STATE DEPARTMENTS AND AGENCIES —Cont'd
Acquisitions, conveyances and transfers of property —Cont'd
Breast-feeding.
Right to breast-feed at locations owned, leased or controlled by Commonwealth, §2.2-1147.1.
Cable TV companies, utility companies, public service corporations and political subdivision.
Conveyance of right-of-way easements over state property, §2.2-1151.
Capital improvements, acquisition for.
Approval of department of general services required, §2.2-1154.
Communications towers, antennas or radio distribution devices.
Conveyance of state property, §2.2-1151.
Wireless broadband services in unserved area.
Lease or conveyance of interest in state-owned communication towers, §2.2-1150.2.
Credit unions.
Leasing space to in-state owned office buildings, §2.2-1151.
Definitions, §2.2-1147.
Department of transportation.
Conveyances to by state institutions or public corporations, §2.2-1152.
Exceptions to approval requirements, §2.2-1149.
Girls Scouts of the USA.
Equal access to state-owned or controlled property, §2.2-1147.2.
Governor or attorney general.
Actions to be taken or approvals by designees, §2.2-1148.
Prior approval of governor required, §2.2-1149.
Transfer of agency property, prior approval required, §§2.2-1150 to 2.2-1152.
Guidelines adopted by department of general services.
Following required, §2.2-1149.
Highway purposes.
Conveyance to department of transportation, §2.2-1152.
In name of Commonwealth, §2.2-1148.
Interest property of Commonwealth, §2.2-1148.
Lease to university related foundations.
Colleges or universities, §2.2-1155.
Review by department of general services, §2.2-1149.
Sale lease or conveyance of state property, §2.2-1150.
Sale or lease of surplus property by department of general services, §2.2-1156.
State police communication tower or site.
Lease or conveyance of interest in, §2.2-1150.1.
Temporary transfers between state agencies, §2.2-1155.
Transfer to another department, agency or institution, §2.2-1150.
Acting officer.
Appointment in case of temporary disability, §2.2-605.
Address confidentiality program.
Victims of domestic violence.
State or local agencies, use of designated address, §2.2-515.2.
Administrative organization prescribed by law, VA Const Art V §9.

STATE DEPARTMENTS AND AGENCIES —Cont'd
Administrative process act, §§2.2-4000 to 2.2-4031.
Agency heads.
Appointments, confirmation process, §2.2-106.
Severance benefits provided departing agency heads.
Publicly announced, §2.2-106.
Alternative work schedules.
Establishment, reporting requirements, §2.2-2817.1.
Annual reports to governor and general assembly.
Consolidated reports, §2.2-608.
Governor may require any agency to submit, §2.2-608.
Posting on agency or department website, §2.2-608.
Time for submitting, agencies required by law to submit, §2.2-608.
Appointing authorities.
Heads of agencies, duties, assignment of duties, §2.2-602.
Appointment and removal of administrative officers by governor, VA Const Art V §10.
Appointment of agency heads, §2.2-106.
Asbestos contractors and workers.
Interdepartmental implementation plan, §54.1-502.
Asbestos projects.
Contract award requirements, §54.1-514.
Assessment of mandates imposed on localities, §2.2-613.
Assignment of tasks to officer or employees, §2.2-604.
Assistant to the Governor for intergovernmental affairs, office of, §§2.2-300 to 2.2-303.
Assisting armed forces in unlawful detention of United States citizens, §2.2-614.2:1.
Attorney general.
Legal services provided in civil matters, §2.2-507.
Attorneys at law.
Conflicts of interest.
Successive government and private employment, VA SCt Rule Pt 6 §II Rule 1.11.
Auditor of public accounts, §§30-130 to 30-142.
See AUDITOR OF PUBLIC ACCOUNTS.
Authorities.
See AUTHORITIES.
Behavioral health and developmental services department.
Generally.
See BEHAVIORAL HEALTH AND DEVELOPMENTAL SERVICES DEPARTMENT.
Review of agency applications for funds or services used in substance abuse programs, §37.2-311.
Boards.
See BOARDS.
Bonds, surety.
State and court officers generally, §§49-12 to 49-21.
See BONDS, SURETY.
Budget of state.
Six-year capital outlay plan.
Agency submission of information, §2.2-1517.

STATE DEPARTMENTS AND AGENCIES —Cont'd
Charities.
Limitations on government actions, §2.2-614.3.
Checks.
Acceptance of revenue by commercially acceptable means, §2.2-614.1.
Child abduction prevention in state buildings.
Code Adam alert programs, §2.2-1161.1.
Code Adam alert programs.
Child abduction prevention in state buildings, §2.2-1161.1.
Collection and dissemination of information by state agencies.
Personal information, privacy protection.
Government data collection and dissemination practices act, §§2.2-3800 to 2.2-3809.
See GOVERNMENT DATA COLLECTION AND DISSEMINATION PRACTICES ACT.
Social security numbers, protection, §§2.2-3815, 2.2-3816.
Commissions.
See COMMISSIONS.
Committees.
See COMMITTEES, STATE GOVERNMENT.
Communication towers owned by state in unserved areas.
Wireless broadband services.
Lease or conveyance of license to provider by department, agency, institution responsible for tower, §2.2-1150.2.
Competitive government act, §§2.2-5512, 2.2-5513.
Computers.
Information technologies agency, §§2.2-2005 to 2.2-2031.
See INFORMATION TECHNOLOGIES AGENCY.
Information technology plans.
Submission to CIO, §2.2-2014.
Purchasing information technology, §2.2-2012.
Confidential data maintained by state agencies.
Standards for protection.
Development by information technologies agency, §2.2-2009.
Conflicts of interest, disclosure of economic interests.
Confirmation of agency head appointments, §2.2-106.
Consumers' interests, representing.
Division of consumer counsel, §2.2-517.
Contracts and agreements.
General power to make and enter into, §2.2-601.
Copies of documents.
Furnishing without costs to law enforcement, §2.2-610.
Copies of records.
Vital records, §32.1-272.
Corrections department, §§53.1-8 to 53.1-17.
See CORRECTIONS DEPARTMENT.
Councils.
See COUNCILS.
Court costs and fees.
Compensation for services not otherwise compensable, §19.2-332.
Credit cards.
Acceptance of revenue by commercially acceptable means, §2.2-614.1.

STATE DEPARTMENTS AND AGENCIES —Cont'd
Criminal background checks.
Sensitive positions in state agencies, §2.2-1201.1.
Criminal justice information system.
Participation, §9.1-129.
Security and accuracy, §9.1-130.
Debit cards.
Acceptance of revenue by commercially acceptable means, §2.2-614.1.
Debt collection act.
Collection of accounts receivable by Commonwealth, §§2.2-4800 to 2.2-4809.
See COLLECTION OF ACCOUNTS RECEIVABLE BY COMMONWEALTH.
Definitions, §2.2-600.
Delegation of tasks to officer or employees, §2.2-604.
Department and commissioner of social services.
Generally, §§63.2-200 to 63.2-214.3.
See SOCIAL SERVICES.
Department for the aging and rehabilitative services.
Generally, §§51.5-116 to 51.5-181.
See AGING AND REHABILITATIVE SERVICES, DEPARTMENT FOR.
Department for the blind and vision impaired.
Generally.
See BLIND AND VISION IMPAIRED, DEPARTMENT FOR.
Department for the deaf and hard-of-hearing.
Generally.
See DEAF OR HEARING IMPAIRED.
Department of accounts.
Claims against the state, §§2.2-814 to 2.2-816.
Generally, §§2.2-800 to 2.2-813.2.
See COMPTROLLER.
Department of agriculture and consumer services.
Charitable gaming generally, §§18.2-340.15 to 18.2-340.37.
See CHARITABLE GAMING.
Department of behavioral health and developmental services.
See BEHAVIORAL HEALTH AND DEVELOPMENTAL SERVICES DEPARTMENT.
Department of business assistance (eff until 1/1/2014), §§2.2-900 to 2.2-904.1.
Department of conservation and recreation, §§10.1-100 to 10.1-114.
See CONSERVATION AND RECREATION DEPARTMENT.
Department of corrections, §§53.1-8 to 53.1-17.
See CORRECTIONS DEPARTMENT.
Department of criminal justice services.
Center for school safety, §9.1-184.
Comprehensive community-corrections act for local responsible offenders, §§9.1-173 to 9.1-183.
See COMMUNITY CORRECTIONS.
Court-appointed special advocate program, §§9.1-151 to 9.1-157.
Criminal justice information system, §§9.1-126 to 9.1-137.
See CRIMINAL JUSTICE INFORMATION SYSTEM.
Generally, §§9.1-100 to 9.1-116.
See CRIMINAL JUSTICE SERVICES DEPARTMENT.

STATE DEPARTMENTS AND AGENCIES —Cont'd
Department of criminal justice services —Cont'd
Law enforcement expenditures, §§9.1-165 to 9.1-172.
Private security services businesses.
Licensing, certifying, registering and regulation, §§9.1-138 to 9.1-150.
See PRIVATE SECURITY SERVICES BUSINESSES.
Department of emergency management.
See EMERGENCY MANAGEMENT DEPARTMENT.
Department of environmental quality, §§10.1-1182 to 10.1-1187.7.
See ENVIRONMENTAL QUALITY DEPARTMENT.
Department of fire programs, §§9.1-200 to 9.1-208.
Department of forensic science, §§9.1-1100 to 9.1-1113.
See FORENSIC SCIENCE DEPARTMENT.
Department of general services.
Asbestos abatement.
State-owned and public school buildings, §§2.2-1162 to 2.2-1167.
See ASBESTOS ABATEMENT.
Division of consolidated laboratory services, §§2.2-1103 to 2.2-1108.
See GENERAL SERVICES DEPARTMENT.
Division of engineering and buildings, §§2.2-1129 to 2.2-1161.1.
See ENGINEERING AND BUILDINGS DIVISION.
Division of purchases and supply, §§2.2-1109 to 2.2-1128.
See PURCHASES AND SUPPLY DIVISION.
Division of support services, §§2.2-1168 to 2.2-1172.
Generally, §§2.2-1100 to 2.2-1102.
Department of health, §§32.1-16 to 32.1-23.
See HEALTH COMMISSIONER AND DEPARTMENT OF HEALTH.
Department of health professions, §§54.1-2500 to 54.1-2510.
See HEALTH PROFESSIONS DEPARTMENT.
Department of historic resources, §§10.1-2200 to 10.1-2214.
See HISTORIC RESOURCES DEPARTMENT.
Department of housing and community development, §§36-131 to 36-139.7.
See HOUSING AND COMMUNITY DEVELOPMENT DEPARTMENT.
Department of human resources management, §§2.2-1200 to 2.2-1208.
See HUMAN RESOURCES MANAGEMENT DEPARTMENT.
Department of labor and industry.
Generally, §§40.1-1 to 40.1-11.3.
See LABOR AND INDUSTRY DEPARTMENT.
Department of law.
Division of consumer council, §2.2-517.
Division of debt collection, §2.2-518.
Generally, §§2.2-500 to 2.2-516.
See ATTORNEY GENERAL.
Department of medical assistance services, §§32.1-323 to 32.1-330.3.
See MEDICAL ASSISTANCE SERVICES DEPARTMENT.

STATE DEPARTMENTS AND AGENCIES —Cont'd
Department of military affairs, §§44-8 to 44-24.1.
See MILITARY AFFAIRS DEPARTMENT.
Department of mines, minerals and energy.
Energy division, §45.1-390.
Generally.
See MINES, MINERALS AND ENERGY DEPARTMENT.
Geology and mineral resources division, §§45.1-383 to 45.1-389.
Department of minority business enterprise (eff until 1/1/2014), §§2.2-1400 to 2.2-1405.
See MINORITY BUSINESS ENTERPRISE DEPARTMENT (EFF UNTIL 1/1/2014).
Department of motor vehicles.
See MOTOR VEHICLES DEPARTMENT.
Department of planning and budget, §§2.2-1500 to 2.2-1514.
See PLANNING AND BUDGET DEPARTMENT.
Department of professional and occupational regulation.
See PROFESSIONAL AND OCCUPATIONAL REGULATION DEPARTMENT.
Department of rail and public transportation, §§33.1-391.2 to 33.1-391.5.
See RAIL AND PUBLIC TRANSPORTATION DEPARTMENT.
Department of small business and supplier diversity, §§2.2-1603 to 2.2-1617.
See SMALL BUSINESS AND SUPPLIER DIVERSITY DEPARTMENT.
Department of social services.
See SOCIAL SERVICES DEPARTMENT.
Department of state police, §§52-1 to 52-11.5.
See STATE POLICE DEPARTMENT.
Department of taxation.
Generally, §§58.1-200 to 58.1-220.
See TAX COMMISSIONER AND DEPARTMENT OF TAXATION.
Department of treasury.
Disbursement from state treasury, §§2.2-1819 to 2.2-1827.
Division of risk management, §§2.2-1832 to 2.2-1843.
Generally, §§2.2-1800 to 2.2-1812.
See STATE TREASURER.
Revenue stabilization fund, §§2.2-1828 to 2.2-1831.
State depositories.
Deposit of money paid into state treasury, §§2.2-1813 to 2.2-1818.
Department of veterans services, §§2.2-2000 to 2.2-2004.
See VETERANS SERVICES DEPARTMENT.
Designation according to standard nomenclature system, §2.2-600.
Directors.
Authority generally, §2.2-603.
Disabilities, persons with.
Agency designation of officials to review effect of decisions on, §2.2-604.1.
Discrimination.
Human rights act, §§2.2-3900 to 2.2-3903.
Dispute resolution.
Virginia administrative dispute resolution act, §§2.2-4115 to 2.2-4119.
Division of purchases and supply, §§2.2-1109 to 2.2-1128.
See PURCHASES AND SUPPLY DIVISION.

STATE DEPARTMENTS AND AGENCIES —Cont'd
Domestic violence victims.
Address confidentiality program.
State or local agencies, use of designated address, §2.2-515.2.
Duties of agencies and appointing authorities, §2.2-602.
Electronic funds transfers.
Acceptance of revenue by commercially acceptable means, §2.2-614.1.
Employees discussing function and policies of agencies, §2.2-603.
Employment and training department.
See GOVERNOR'S EMPLOYMENT AND TRAINING DEPARTMENT.
Environmental impact reports, §§10.1-1188 to 10.1-1192.
E-Verify program for new hires.
State agencies to participate, §40.1-11.2.
Executive reorganization, §§2.2-127 to 2.2-133.
Fair employment contracting act, §§2.2-4200, 2.2-4201.
Family formation, stability and autonomy.
Considered in developing policies and regulations, §2.2-606.
Farm and forest land protection.
Capital projects.
Environment impact statements, §3.2-205.
Review of impact on farm forest lands, §3.2-204.
Conversion of farm and forest lands.
Impact of agency actions.
Plan, report, §3.2-206.
Federal contracts.
Reporting, §2.2-603.
Federal grants.
Acceptance of grants and funds from federal government, §2.2-611.
General power to accept, §2.2-601.
Reporting, §2.2-603.
Federal REAL ID act.
Participation limited, §2.2-614.2.
Fiscal year, §2.2-805.
Foreign trade zones.
Public corporations, §§62.1-159, 62.1-160, 62.1-162.
Foundations.
See FOUNDATIONS.
Fraudulent transactions discovered, reporting to auditor of, §30-138.
Freedom of information act, §§2.2-3700 to 2.2-3714.
See FREEDOM OF INFORMATION.
Game and inland fisheries department, §§29.1-109 to 29.1-113.
General powers, §2.2-601.
Governmental fraud, §§18.2-498.1 to 18.2-498.5.
Government performance and results act, §§2.2-5510, 2.2-5511.
Governor's secretaries, §§2.2-200 to 2.2-229.
Heads of state agencies.
Acting officer.
Appointment, temporary disability, §2.2-605.
Appointing authorities, §2.2-602.
Directors, authority, §2.2-603.
Home based employees, satellite offices.
Report on status and efficiency, §2.2-2817.1.
Human rights act, §§2.2-3900 to 2.2-3903.
Implementation of federal mandates act, §§2.2-615 to 2.2-619.

STATE DEPARTMENTS AND AGENCIES —Cont'd
Imprest funds.
State treasury, allowable funds, §2.2-1824.
Indoor clean air act, §§15.2-2820 to 15.2-2833.
See SMOKING IN PUBLIC PLACES.
Information from administrative officers required by governor, VA Const Art V §8.
Information officer, appointment, duties, §2.2-603.
Information officers.
List, publication, duties, §30-34.14.
Information supplied to governor, §2.2-602.
Information technologies agency, §§2.2-2005 to 2.2-2031.
See INFORMATION TECHNOLOGIES AGENCY.
Information technology access for blind or visually impaired.
State agencies, institutions of higher education and political subdivision to provide, §§2.2-3500 to 2.2-3504.
Information technology plans.
Submission to CIO, §2.2-2014.
Information technology purchases, §2.2-2012.
Inspector general, state.
Cooperation of state agencies and officers, §2.2-310.
Interpreters for deaf in state agency proceedings, §§2.2-3400 to 2.2-3402.
Investment of public funds, §§2.2-4500 to 2.2-4519.
See INVESTMENT OF PUBLIC FUNDS.
Jail industry program goods and services.
Purchases, §53.1-133.8.
Joint legislative audit and review commission.
Analysis of state agency budget submissions, §30-58.4.
Cooperation, §§30-59, 30-59.1.
Judicial inquiry and review commission.
Assistance and information, §17.1-917.
Latino advisory board, §§2.2-2459 to 2.2-2461.
Legislative program review and evaluation.
Access to information, §30-69.
Livestock raised by state institutions and agencies.
Selling instead of slaughtering, §2.2-614.
Lobbying by officers and employees of state agencies.
Registration requirements, §2.2-421.
Lobbyists, employment prohibited, §2.2-434.
Lottery department.
Generally, §§58.1-4000 to 58.1-4027.
See LOTTERY, STATE.
Mail handing.
Division of support services, general services department, §2.2-1169.
Mandates imposed on localities, assessment, §2.2-613.
Medical services lien.
Lien in favor of departments on claim for personal injuries, §8.01-66.9.
Messenger services.
Division of support services, general services department, duties, §2.2-1169.
Motor vehicle license plates.
Special plates for appointed officials, §46.2-736.2.
Motto or slogan, registration, §2.2-416.
Use, §2.2-417.
Notice.
Initial notice by certified mail, subsequent notices by regular mail, §2.2-601.1.

STATE DEPARTMENTS AND AGENCIES —Cont'd
Nutrient management plans.
Required for state lands, §10.1-104.4.
Oath of office.
Form of general oath required of officers, §49-1.
Office furniture and equipment.
Acquisition and maintenance.
Division of support services, general services department, §2.2-1170.
Office hours, §2.2-3322.
Ohio river valley water sanitation commission.
Cooperation duties, §62.1-74.
Parcel services.
Division of support services, general services department, §2.2-1169.
Payroll funds.
State treasury, allowable funds, §2.2-1824.
Performance of duties assigned to agency, §2.2-604.
Petty cash.
State treasury, allowable funds, §2.2-1824.
Policy development, considerations, §2.2-606.
Printing and copying services.
Division of support services, general services department, §2.2-1171.
Prison made goods and services, purchases of, §§53.1-47 to 53.1-55.
Procurement generally.
By agencies and departments, §§2.2-4300 to 2.2-4377.
See PUBLIC PROCUREMENT.
Promotion and employment lists.
Agencies to establish and maintain, §2.2-602.
Prompt payment of bills, §§2.2-4347 to 2.2-4356.
Publications.
State publications depository program, §2.2-609.
Public procurement act, §§2.2-4300 to 2.2-4377.
See PUBLIC PROCUREMENT.
Public safety medal of valor, §§9.1-800, 9.1-801.
Purchases of equipment, supplies, printing and nonprofessional services.
Division of purchases and supply generally, §§2.2-1109 to 2.2-1128.
See PURCHASES AND SUPPLY DIVISION.
Purchases of prison made goods, §§53.1-47 to 53.1-55.
REAL ID act.
Participation limited, §2.2-614.2.
Receipt of public funds.
Report to comptroller, §2.2-807.
Records to be kept, §2.2-609.
Recycling duties, §§10.1-1425.6 to 10.1-1425.9.
Agency purchasing programs, §2.2-4323.
Reduction or discontinuance of service to locality.
Notification, §2.2-612.
Reporting transfers of employees, §2.2-607.
Reports required to governor or general assembly.
Consolidated reports, §2.2-608.
Governor may require any agency to submit, §2.2-608.
Posting on agency or department website, §2.2-608.
Time for submitting, report required by law, §2.2-608.
Rights of Virginians with disabilities.
See DISABILITY OR HANDICAP.
Risk management plan for public liability, §2.2-1837.

STATE DEPARTMENTS AND AGENCIES —Cont'd
Roanoke river basin bi-state commission.
Cooperation by state agencies, §62.1-69.41.
Rosters of employees.
Agencies to establish and maintain, §2.2-602.
Security audit.
Information technologies agency, §2.2-2009.
Security for public deposits, §§2.2-4400 to 2.2-4411.
See SECURITY FOR PUBLIC DEPOSITS.
Senior citizens, designation of officials to review effect of decisions on, §2.2-604.1.
Sensitive positions.
Criminal background checks for positions designated as sensitive, §2.2-1201.1.
Service of notice, process and other papers.
Initial notice by certified mail, subsequent notices by regular mail, §2.2-601.1.
Setoff debt collection, income tax, §§58.1-520 to 58.1-535.
See SETOFF DEBT COLLECTION, INCOME TAX.
Severance benefits for departing agency head.
Public announcement prior to departure, §2.2-106.
Sickness or temporary disability of officer.
Acting officer, appointment, §2.2-605.
Small business and supplier diversity department, §§2.2-1603 to 2.2-1617.
Smoking in public places.
Indoor clean air act, §§15.2-2820 to 15.2-2833.
See SMOKING IN PUBLIC PLACES.
Social security numbers, protection, §§2.2-3815, 2.2-3816.
Special counsel, employment, §§2.2-510, 2.2-510.1.
Special license plates for appointed officials, §46.2-736.2.
Spokespersons.
List, publication, duties, §30-34.14.
Standard nomenclature system, designation, §2.2-600.
State holidays and other special days, §§2.2-3300 to 2.2-3322.
See HOLIDAYS.
State inspector general, office of.
Cooperation of state agencies and officers, §2.2-310.
State officers and employees.
Conflict of interests.
State and local government generally, §§2.2-3100 to 2.2-3127.
See PUBLIC OFFICERS AND EMPLOYEES.
Fraud and abuse whistleblower protection act, §§2.2-3009 to 2.2-3014.
See WHISTLEBLOWING.
Generally, §§2.2-2800 to 2.2-2831.
See PUBLIC OFFICERS AND EMPLOYEES.
Grievance procedure, §§2.2-3000 to 2.2-3008.
See PUBLIC OFFICERS AND EMPLOYEES.
Termination or layoffs from employment with Commonwealth.
Workforce transition act of 1995, §§2.2-3200 to 2.2-3206.
See PUBLIC OFFICERS AND EMPLOYEES.
Virginia personnel act.
Personnel administration system generally, §§2.2-2900 to 2.2-2905.
See PUBLIC OFFICERS AND EMPLOYEES.
State records management, §§42.1-76 to 42.1-90.1.
See STATE RECORDS MANAGEMENT.

STATE DEPARTMENTS AND AGENCIES —Cont'd
Strategic plans.
Development and maintenance, §2.2-5510.
Review, §2.2-5511.
Substance abuse services council, §§2.2-2696, 2.2-2697.
Surface coal mining.
Applicability of act, §45.1-259.
Surplus property.
Control of agency until final disposition, §2.2-1153.
Disposition, §2.2-1124.
Proceeds from disposition, §2.2-1125.
Notification to division of engineering and buildings.
Property not used or required, §2.2-1153.
Sale or lease by department of general services, §2.2-1156.
Technology resource.
Designation by each state agency, §2.2-2014.
Telecommunications.
Information technologies agency, §§2.2-2005 to 2.2-2031.
See INFORMATION TECHNOLOGIES AGENCY.
Information technology plans.
Submission to CIO, §2.2-2014.
Purchasing information technology, §2.2-2012.
Telecommuting.
Duties of heads of agencies, §2.2-2817.1.
Terminated employees.
Annual report, §2.2-1201.
Severance benefits announced prior to departure.
Agency heads, §2.2-106.
Governor's secretaries, §2.2-200.
Transfer of employee reports, §2.2-607.
Transportation accountability commission.
Information to be furnished from state agencies, §30-285.
Unclaimed property, disposition of.
Intangible personalty held for owner by public agency, §55-210.9.
Uniform financial accounting and control, §2.2-803.
Victims of domestic violence.
Address confidentiality program.
State or local agencies, use of designated address, §2.2-515.2.
Virginia administrative dispute resolution act, §§2.2-4115 to 2.2-4119.
Virginia commission on higher education board appointments, §§2.2-2518 to 2.2-2522.
Virginia register act.
Generally, §§2.2-4100 to 2.2-4104.
See ADMINISTRATIVE CODE AND REGISTER OF REGULATIONS.
Virginia Wallops research park leadership council, §15.2-2403.2.
Volunteers in state service.
State government volunteers act, §§2.2-3600 to 2.2-3605.
Water control board cooperation, §62.1-44.42.
Watershed protection.
Coordination task force.
Cooperation with state agencies, §10.1-1197.

STATE EMERGENCY MEDICAL SERVICES ADVISORY BOARD, §32.1-111.10.
Regulations of department concerning, §32.1-111.4.

STATE EMPLOYEES.
Bonds of state and county officers generally.
See BONDS, SURETY.
Cash match plan for employees of Commonwealth, §§51.1-607 to 51.1-613.
Deferred compensation plan, §§51.1-600 to 51.1-605.
Expenses of public officials.
Generally.
See EXPENSES OF PUBLIC OFFICIALS.
Mileage.
See MILEAGE.
Travel.
See TRAVEL EXPENSES.
Family and personal leave.
Sickness and disability program.
Generally, §§51.1-1100 to 51.1-1140.
See SICKNESS AND DISABILITY PROGRAM.
Group insurance, §§51.1-500 to 51.1-514.
See PUBLIC OFFICERS AND EMPLOYEES.
Long-term disability.
Sickness and disability program.
Generally, §§51.1-1100 to 51.1-1140.
See SICKNESS AND DISABILITY PROGRAM.
Mileage.
See MILEAGE.
Public employees generally.
See PUBLIC OFFICERS AND EMPLOYEES.
Removal from office, §§24.2-230 to 24.2-238.
Retirement system of Virginia, §§51.1-124.1 to 51.1-169.
See VIRGINIA RETIREMENT SYSTEM.
Sickness and disability program.
Generally, §§51.1-1100 to 51.1-1140.
See SICKNESS AND DISABILITY PROGRAM.
Tobacco indemnification and community revitalization commission, §3.2-3106.

STATE EXECUTIVE COUNCIL FOR COMPREHENSIVE SERVICES FOR AT-RISK YOUTH AND FAMILIES, §§2.2-2648, 2.2-2649.

STATE FIRE MARSHALS.
Fire marshals generally.
See FIRE MARSHALS.
Fire prevention code.
Employment by fire programs director.
Enforcement of safety standards, §9.1-207.
Inspection of certain state facilities, §9.1-207.
Powers and duties generally, §9.1-206.
Qualifications, §9.1-206.
Enforcement, §27-98.
Injunctions, §27-101.

STATE FISH.
Brook trout.
Freshwater fish, §1-510.
Striped bass.
Saltwater fish, §1-510.

STATE FLAG.
Sale by division of purchases and supply, §2.2-1128.

STATE FORESTER, §§10.1-1104 to 10.1-1119.
Accounts, §10.1-1118.
Appointment, §10.1-1100.
Cost of fighting forest fires.
Recovery, §10.1-1141.
Damaging land or timber, §10.1-1111.

STATE FORESTER —Cont'd
Equipment rentals, §10.1-1117.
Establishment of nurseries, §10.1-1114.
Estimate of revenue collected from forest products tax.
Submission to governor, §58.1-1605.
Evidence.
Conservation of forest supply, §10.1-1119.
Failure to leave seed trees uncut.
Inspection or planting by state forester, §10.1-1168.
Fees.
Specialized services or rentals of equipment, §10.1-1117.
Fire.
Kindling fires, §10.1-1111.
Notices relating to forest fires, §10.1-1112.
Forest protection for cities and counties.
Agreements with federal agencies, §10.1-1126.
Contracts with cities, §10.1-1125.
Furnishing seedlings and technical assistance, §10.1-1130.
Forestry services for landowners.
Administration by state forester, §10.1-1132.
Authority of state forester, §10.1-1131.
Funds.
Forest reserves, §10.1-1106.
Reforestation operations fund, §10.1-1116.
Gifts, §10.1-1107.
Insect infestation and diseases of forest trees.
Investigations, §10.1-1179.
Inspections.
Seedlings, §10.1-1114.
Kindling fires, §10.1-1111.
Notice.
Forest fires and trespasses, §10.1-1112.
Notices, §10.1-1166.
Nurseries, §10.1-1114.
Permits.
Special use permits, duties, §10.1-1152.
Funds credited to department, §10.1-1156.
Powers and duties, §§10.1-1104, 10.1-1105.
Prescribed burning and certified prescribed burn managers.
Development and administration of certification process and training course, §10.1-1150.2.
Revocation of certification, §10.1-1150.6.
Publications, §10.1-1119.
Purchase of lands, §10.1-1107.
Real estate tax special assessment for land preservation.
Reforestation of area, §10.1-1169.
Uniform standards for determining real estate use, §58.1-3240.
Reforestation operations fund, §10.1-1116.
Reforesting, §10.1-1106.
Reports to general assembly, §10.1-1119.
Sale of trees, §10.1-1115.
Seeds and seedlings, §10.1-1114.
Seedling plant beds, fumigation, §10.1-1114.
Silvicultural practices, §10.1-1126.1.
Water pollution.
Issuance of special orders, §10.1-1181.2.
Notice by owner or operator of commercial harvesting of timber, §10.1-1181.2.
Specialized services, §10.1-1117.
State land evaluation advisory council.
Member of, §58.1-3239.
Timber.
Cutting and removing, §10.1-1111.
Preservation, §10.1-1106.

STATE FORESTER —Cont'd
Timber —Cont'd
Sale of trees, §10.1-1115.
Seeds and seedlings, §10.1-1114.
Timber preservation, §10.1-1106.
Trespass, §§10.1-1112, 10.1-1113.
Violation of provisions, §10.1-1110.
Waste and unappropriated lands, §10.1-1108.
Water pollution.
Silvicultural activities.
Issuance of special orders, §10.1-1181.2.

STATE FORESTS.
Damaging land or timber, §10.1-1111.
Defined, §10.1-1107.
Forest fires.
Kindling of fires, §10.1-1111.
Notice requirements, §10.1-1112.
Hunting and trapping, §§10.1-1151 to 10.1-1157.
Kindling fires, §10.1-1111.
Purchase of land, §10.1-1107.
Warrant, survey or patent, §10.1-1109.
Waste and unappropriated lands, §10.1-1108.

STATE FUTURE FARMERS OF AMERICA.
Property exempt from taxation, §58.1-3619.

STATE GEOLOGIST.
Appointment, §45.1-383.
Confidentiality of information gathered, §45.1-385.
General powers and duties, §45.1-384.
Immunity from trespass prosecution, §45.1-389.
Uranium ore exploration.
Confidentiality of logs, surveys and reports, §45.1-285.

STATE GOVERNMENT.
Acquisitions, conveyances and transfers of property.
State departments and agencies generally, §§2.2-1147 to 2.2-1156.
See STATE DEPARTMENTS AND AGENCIES.
Administrative process act, §§2.2-4000 to 2.2-4031.
Agencies related to general operation of state government.
General provisions, §§2.2-600 to 2.2-614.3.
Assistant to the Governor for intergovernmental affairs, office of, §§2.2-300 to 2.2-303.
Authorities.
See AUTHORITIES.
Boards.
See BOARDS.
Bonds, notes or other obligations issued by Commonwealth, §§2.2-4900 to 2.2-4906.
Interest on obligations, §§2.2-5000 to 2.2-5003.
Collection and dissemination of information by state agencies.
Personal information, privacy protection.
Government data collection and dissemination practices act, §§2.2-3800 to 2.2-3809.
See GOVERNMENT DATA COLLECTION AND DISSEMINATION PRACTICES ACT.
Social security numbers, protection, §§2.2-3815, 2.2-3816.
Commissions.
See COMMISSIONS.
Committees.
See COMMITTEES, STATE GOVERNMENT.

STATE GOVERNMENT —Cont'd
Competitive government act, §§2.2-5512, 2.2-5513.
Councils.
See COUNCILS.
Debt collection act.
Collection of accounts receivable by Commonwealth, §§2.2-4800 to 2.2-4809.
See COLLECTION OF ACCOUNTS RECEIVABLE BY COMMONWEALTH.
Department for the aging and rehabilitative services.
Generally, §§51.5-116 to 51.5-181.
See AGING AND REHABILITATIVE SERVICES, DEPARTMENT FOR.
Department of accounts.
Claims against the state, §§2.2-814 to 2.2-816.
Generally, §§2.2-800 to 2.2-813.2.
See COMPTROLLER.
Department of business assistance (eff until 1/1/2014), §§2.2-900 to 2.2-904.1.
Department of criminal justice services.
Center for school safety, §9.1-184.
Comprehensive community-corrections act for local responsible offenders, §§9.1-173 to 9.1-183.
See COMMUNITY CORRECTIONS.
Court-appointed special advocate program, §§9.1-151 to 9.1-157.
Criminal justice information system, §§9.1-126 to 9.1-137.
See CRIMINAL JUSTICE INFORMATION SYSTEM.
Generally, §§9.1-100 to 9.1-116.
See CRIMINAL JUSTICE SERVICES DEPARTMENT.
Law enforcement expenditures, §§9.1-165 to 9.1-172.
Private security services businesses.
Licensing, certifying, registering and regulation, §§9.1-138 to 9.1-150.
See PRIVATE SECURITY SERVICES BUSINESSES.
Department of fire programs, §§9.1-200 to 9.1-208.
Department of forensic science, §§9.1-1100 to 9.1-1113.
See FORENSIC SCIENCE DEPARTMENT.
Department of general services.
Asbestos abatement.
State-owned and public school buildings, §§2.2-1162 to 2.2-1167.
See ASBESTOS ABATEMENT.
Division of consolidated laboratory services, §§2.2-1103 to 2.2-1108.
See GENERAL SERVICES DEPARTMENT.
Division of engineering and buildings, §§2.2-1129 to 2.2-1161.1.
See ENGINEERING AND BUILDINGS DIVISION.
Division of purchases and supply, §§2.2-1109 to 2.2-1128.
See PURCHASES AND SUPPLY DIVISION.
Division of support services, §§2.2-1168 to 2.2-1172.
Generally, §§2.2-1100 to 2.2-1102.
Department of human resources management, §§2.2-1200 to 2.2-1208.
See HUMAN RESOURCES MANAGEMENT DEPARTMENT.

STATE GOVERNMENT —Cont'd
Department of law.
Division of consumer council, §2.2-517.
Division of debt collection, §2.2-518.
Generally, §§2.2-500 to 2.2-516.
See ATTORNEY GENERAL.
Department of minority business enterprise (eff until 1/1/2014), §§2.2-1400 to 2.2-1405.
See MINORITY BUSINESS ENTERPRISE DEPARTMENT (EFF UNTIL 1/1/2014).
Department of planning and budget, §§2.2-1500 to 2.2-1514.
See PLANNING AND BUDGET DEPARTMENT.
Department of small business and supplier diversity, §§2.2-1603 to 2.2-1617.
See SMALL BUSINESS AND SUPPLIER DIVERSITY DEPARTMENT.
Department of treasury.
Disbursement from state treasury, §§2.2-1819 to 2.2-1827.
Division of risk management, §§2.2-1832 to 2.2-1843.
Generally, §§2.2-1800 to 2.2-1812.
See STATE TREASURER.
Revenue stabilization fund, §§2.2-1828 to 2.2-1831.
State depositories.
Deposit of money paid into state treasury, §§2.2-1813 to 2.2-1818.
Department of veterans services, §§2.2-2000 to 2.2-2004.
See VETERANS SERVICES DEPARTMENT.
Discrimination.
Human rights act, §§2.2-3900 to 2.2-3903.
Employment and training department.
See GOVERNOR'S EMPLOYMENT AND TRAINING DEPARTMENT.
Executive reorganization, §§2.2-127 to 2.2-133.
Fair employment contracting act, §§2.2-4200, 2.2-4201.
Foundations.
See FOUNDATIONS.
Freedom of information act, §§2.2-3700 to 2.2-3714.
See FREEDOM OF INFORMATION.
Government performance and results act, §§2.2-5510, 2.2-5511.
Governor.
Generally, §§2.2-100 to 2.2-135.
See GOVERNOR.
Governor's secretaries, §§2.2-200 to 2.2-229.
Human rights act, §§2.2-3900 to 2.2-3903.
Implementation of federal mandates act, §§2.2-615 to 2.2-619.
Information technologies agency, §§2.2-2005 to 2.2-2031.
See INFORMATION TECHNOLOGIES AGENCY.
Information technology access for blind or visually impaired.
State agencies, institutions of higher education and political subdivision to provide, §§2.2-3500 to 2.2-3504.
Insurance.
Risk management division.
Risk management plan for claims against political subdivisions or constitutional officers, §2.2-1839.
Interpreters for deaf in state agency proceedings, §§2.2-3400 to 2.2-3402.
Investment of public funds, §§2.2-4500 to 2.2-4519.
See INVESTMENT OF PUBLIC FUNDS.

STATE GOVERNMENT —Cont'd
Latino advisory board, §§2.2-2459 to 2.2-2461.
Office hours, §2.2-3322.
Privatization of programs or activities.
Loss of jobs due to.
Report to governor, §2.2-203.2:1.
Public procurement act, §§2.2-4300 to 2.2-4377.
See PUBLIC PROCUREMENT.
Secretary of the Commonwealth.
Generally, §§2.2-400 to 2.2-410.
See SECRETARY OF THE COMMONWEALTH.
Security for public deposits, §§2.2-4400 to 2.2-4411.
See SECURITY FOR PUBLIC DEPOSITS.
Social security numbers, protection, §§2.2-3815, 2.2-3816.
State holidays and other special days, §§2.2-3300 to 2.2-3322.
See HOLIDAYS.
State officers and employees.
Conflicts of interests.
State and local government generally, §§2.2-3100 to 2.2-3127.
See PUBLIC OFFICERS AND EMPLOYEES.
Fraud and abuse whistleblower protection act, §§2.2-3009 to 2.2-3014.
See WHISTLEBLOWING.
Generally, §§2.2-2800 to 2.2-2831.
See PUBLIC OFFICERS AND EMPLOYEES.
Grievance procedure, §§2.2-3000 to 2.2-3008.
See PUBLIC OFFICERS AND EMPLOYEES.
Termination or layoffs from employment with Commonwealth.
Workforce transition act of 1995, §§2.2-3200 to 2.2-3206.
See PUBLIC OFFICERS AND EMPLOYEES.
Virginia personnel act.
Personnel administration system generally, §§2.2-2900 to 2.2-2905.
See PUBLIC OFFICERS AND EMPLOYEES.
Strategic plans.
Development and maintenance, §2.2-5510.
Review, §2.2-5511.
Substance abuse services council, §§2.2-2696, 2.2-2697.
Virginia commission on higher education board appointments, §§2.2-2518 to 2.2-2522.
Virginia register act.
Generally, §§2.2-4100 to 2.2-4104.
See ADMINISTRATIVE CODE AND REGISTER OF REGULATIONS.
Volunteers in state service.
State government volunteers act, §§2.2-3600 to 2.2-3605.
Workforce development coordination, §§2.2-435.6, 2.2-435.7.

STATE GOVERNMENT VOLUNTEERS ACT, §§2.2-3600 to 2.2-3605.

STATE HIGHWAY PLAT BOOK, §17.1-238.

STATE HIGHWAY SYSTEM.
Generally, §§33.1-25 to 33.1-47.1.
See HIGHWAYS AND ROADS.
Prisoner construction and maintenance, §§53.1-56 to 53.1-59.

STATE HOLIDAYS AND OTHER SPECIAL DAYS, §§2.2-3300 to 2.2-3322.
See HOLIDAYS.

STATE INSPECTOR GENERAL.
Appointment, §2.2-308.

STATE INSPECTOR GENERAL —Cont'd
Cooperation of state agencies and officers, §2.2-310.
Definitions, §2.2-307.
Duties, §2.2-309.
Corrections department and board, §2.2-309.3.
Juvenile justice, §2.2-309.4.
Tobacco indemnification and community revitalization commission, §2.2-309.2.
Enforcement of laws, §2.2-311.
Investigators.
Enforcement of laws, §2.2-311.
Office of.
Created, §2.2-308.
Powers, §2.2-309.
Corrections department and board, §2.2-309.3.
Juvenile justice, §2.2-309.4.
Tobacco indemnification and community revitalization commission, §2.2-309.2.
Reports, §2.2-313.
Fraudulent transactions discovered by state agencies, courts, §30-138.
Subpoenas, §2.2-312.

STATE INTERNAL AUDITOR.
Electronic funds transfers.
Payment of amounts due and owing Commonwealth, §2.2-211.
General provisions for state agencies for general operation of government, §§2.2-600 to 2.2-614.3.
See STATE DEPARTMENTS AND AGENCIES.
Secretary of finance.
Agency responsibility, §2.2-211.

STATE LAND EVALUATION ADVISORY COUNCIL, §58.1-3239.

STATE LAW LIBRARY.
Additions to library, §42.1-62.
Books constituting library, §42.1-61.
Computer expenses, §42.1-63.
Managed by supreme court, §42.1-60.
Regulation of library, §42.1-63.
Use of library, persons permitted, §42.1-64.

STATE LIBRARY.
See LIBRARY OF VIRGINIA.

STATE LOTTERY BOARD.
Generally, §§58.1-4000 to 58.1-4027.
See LOTTERY, STATE.

STATE LOTTERY DEPARTMENT.
Employees.
Personnel administration system.
Exemptions, §2.2-2905.
Generally, §§58.1-4000 to 58.1-4027.
See LOTTERY, STATE.

STATE MINERALS MANAGEMENT PLAN.
Exploration activities on state owned uplands, §2.2-1157.

STATE OF EMERGENCY.
Declaration.
Authority of governor and agencies under control, §44-146.28.
Governor's powers, §§44-146.17, 44-146.28.
Masks, hoods or other devices hiding face.
Exception for prohibition on wearing, §18.2-422.
Supreme court.
Convening, §17.1-304.
Terrorism.
Generally.
See TERRORISM.

STATE OFFICERS AND EMPLOYEES.
Administrative process act, §§2.2-4000 to 2.2-4031.
Attorney general.
Generally, §§2.2-500 to 2.2-516.
See ATTORNEY GENERAL.
Collection and dissemination of information by state agencies.
Personal information, privacy protection.
Government data collection and dissemination practices act, §§2.2-3800 to 2.2-3809.
See GOVERNMENT DATA COLLECTION AND DISSEMINATION PRACTICES ACT.
Social security numbers, protection, §§2.2-3815, 2.2-3816.
Competitive government act, §§2.2-5512, 2.2-5513.
Conflicts of interest.
Ethics in public contracting, §§2.2-4367 to 2.2-4377.
State and local government generally, §§2.2-3100 to 2.2-3127.
See PUBLIC OFFICERS AND EMPLOYEES.
Debt collection act.
Collection of accounts receivable by Commonwealth, §§2.2-4800 to 2.2-4809.
See COLLECTION OF ACCOUNTS RECEIVABLE BY COMMONWEALTH.
Discrimination.
Human rights act, §§2.2-3900 to 2.2-3903.
Ethics in public contracting, §§2.2-4367 to 2.2-4377.
Fair employment contracting act, §§2.2-4200, 2.2-4201.
Fraud and abuse whistleblower protection act, §§2.2-3009 to 2.2-3014.
See WHISTLEBLOWING.
Freedom of information act, §§2.2-3700 to 2.2-3714.
See FREEDOM OF INFORMATION.
Generally, §§2.2-2800 to 2.2-2831.
See PUBLIC OFFICERS AND EMPLOYEES.
Governor, §§2.2-100 to 2.2-135.
See GOVERNOR.
Grievance procedure, §§2.2-3000 to 2.2-3008.
See PUBLIC OFFICERS AND EMPLOYEES.
Human rights act, §§2.2-3900 to 2.2-3903.
Information technology access for blind or visually impaired.
State agencies, institutions of higher education and political subdivisions to provide, §§2.2-3500 to 2.2-3504.
Inspector general, state.
Cooperation of state agencies and officers, §2.2-310.
Interpreters for deaf in state agency proceeding, §§2.2-3400 to 2.2-3402.
Investment of public funds, §§2.2-4500 to 2.2-4519.
See INVESTMENT OF PUBLIC FUNDS.
Public contracting, ethics in, §§2.2-4367 to 2.2-4377.
Public procurement act, §§2.2-4300 to 2.2-4377.
See PUBLIC PROCUREMENT.
Purchases of equipment, supplies, printing and nonprofessional services.
Division of purchases and supply generally, §§2.2-1109 to 2.2-1128.
See PURCHASES AND SUPPLY DIVISION.

STATE OFFICERS AND EMPLOYEES —Cont'd
Secretary of administration, §§2.2-200 to 2.2-202, 2.2-203.
Secretary of commerce and trade, §§2.2-200 to 2.2-202, 2.2-204 to 2.2-207.
Secretary of education, §§2.2-200 to 2.2-202, 2.2-208.
Secretary of finance, §§2.2-200 to 2.2-202, 2.2-211.
Secretary of health and human resources, §§2.2-200 to 2.2-202, 2.2-212, 2.2-214.
Secretary of natural resources, §§2.2-200 to 2.2-202, 2.2-215 to 2.2-220.3.
Secretary of public safety, §§2.2-200 to 2.2-202, 2.2-221 to 2.2-224.1.
Secretary of technology, §§2.2-200 to 2.2-202, 2.2-225.
Secretary of the Commonwealth.
Generally, §§2.2-400 to 2.2-410.
See SECRETARY OF THE COMMONWEALTH.
Secretary of transportation, §§2.2-200 to 2.2-202, 2.2-228, 2.2-229.
Secretary of veterans affairs and homeland security, §§2.2-200 to 2.2-202, 2.2-230 to 2.2-233.
Security for public deposits, §§2.2-4400 to 2.2-4411.
See SECURITY FOR PUBLIC DEPOSITS.
Social security numbers, protection, §§2.2-3815, 2.2-3816.
State departments and agencies, generally.
State agencies related to operation of government, §§2.2-600 to 2.2-614.3.
See STATE DEPARTMENTS AND AGENCIES.
State inspector general.
Cooperation of state agencies and officers, §2.2-310.
Termination or layoffs from employment with Commonwealth.
Workforce transition act of 1995, §§2.2-3200 to 2.2-3206.
See PUBLIC OFFICERS AND EMPLOYEES.
Virginia personnel act.
Personnel administration system generally, §§2.2-2900 to 2.2-2905.
See PUBLIC OFFICERS AND EMPLOYEES.

STATE OF THE COMMONWEALTH ADDRESS.
Governor to communicate to general assembly, VA Const Art V §5.

STATE OF THE UNION ADDRESS.
Message to congress, US Const Art II §3.

STATE OPERATION OF PUBLIC UTILITIES, §§56-509 to 56-528.
See PUBLIC UTILITIES, STATE OPERATION.

STATE OWNED MOTOR VEHICLES.
Centralized fleet management, §§2.2-1173 to 2.2-1181.
Alternative fuel vehicle conversion fund, §2.2-1176.1.
Alternative fuel vehicles, replacement of vehicles, §2.2-1176.
Assignments.
Director's duties, §2.2-1175.
Use of vehicles, §2.2-1178.
Commuting.
Use of vehicles, §2.2-1179.
Contract rentals.
Approval, §2.2-1176.
Defined terms, §2.2-1173.

STATE OWNED MOTOR VEHICLES —Cont'd
Centralized fleet management —Cont'd
Director.
Defined, §2.2-1173.
Duties, §2.2-1175.
Exceptions, §2.2-1174.
Finance.
Fleet management internal service fund, §2.2-1181.
Guidance documents, §2.2-1180.
Leases.
Approval, §2.2-1176.
Limits on assignments, §2.2-1178.
Minimum mileage, §2.2-1178.
Purchases.
Approval, §2.2-1176.
Director's duties, §2.2-1175.
Records.
Director's duties, §2.2-1175.
Repairs and maintenance.
Director's duties, §2.2-1175.
Guidance documents, §2.2-1180.
Requests.
Procedure, §2.2-1178.
Storage.
Guidance documents, §2.2-1180.
Surplus vehicles.
Transfer, §2.2-1177.
Transfer of surplus vehicles, §2.2-1177.
Use of vehicles, §2.2-1178.
Commuting, §2.2-1179.
Guidance documents, §2.2-1180.
Vehicles assigned to centralized fleet, §2.2-1174.
Drivers' licenses.
Applicability to persons, §46.2-367.
Applicability to vehicles, §46.2-366.
Governor's powers, §2.2-120.
Approval of purchase of passenger type vehicles, §2.2-121.
Transfer of vehicles among departments, §2.2-121.
Insurance for state motor vehicles.
Risk management division, §2.2-1838.
Motor vehicle license plates, §§46.2-750, 46.2-750.1, 46.2-751.
Display requirements, §46.2-750.
Passenger vehicles, §46.2-751.
Vehicles used for police work, §46.2-750.1.
Vehicles used for security or transportation purposes involving governor or members of general assembly, §46.2-750.
Registration, §§46.2-750, 46.2-751.
Security or transportation vehicles involving governor or members of the general assembly.
Permanent or temporary license plates, §46.2-750.

STATE PARK ACQUISITION AND DEVELOPMENT FUND, §10.1-202.

STATE PARK CONSERVATION RESOURCES FUND, §10.1-202.
Conservation, small watershed flood control and area development fund, §§10.1-636 to 10.1-649.
Proceeds from disposition of state surplus materials.
Deposit into fund, §2.2-1125.

STATE PARK PROJECTS FUND, §10.1-202.

STATE PARKS, §§10.1-200 to 10.1-205.
Acquisition of real property.
Lands of scenic beauty, recreational utility or historical interest, §10.1-201.

STATE PARKS —Cont'd
Acquisition of real property —Cont'd
Master plan, §10.1-200.1.
Admittance to park or facilities, §10.1-200.3.
Appalachian Trail.
Establishment, protection and maintenance, §10.1-203.
Bond issues.
Development revenue bonds. See within this heading, "Development revenue bonds."
Capital improvement projects.
Authority of director of department of conservation and recreation, §10.1-112.
Conservation and recreation department.
Duties related to parks and outdoor recreation, §10.1-200.
Development revenue bonds, §§10.1-300 to 10.1-312.
Bond issues.
Legal and authorized investments, §10.1-312.
Remedies of bondholders, §10.1-309.
Revenue bonds, §10.1-303.
Debts of Commonwealth, §10.1-305.
Sale and proceeds, §10.1-304.
Trust indenture, §10.1-306.
Revenue refunding bonds, §10.1-311.
Camping and recreational facilities.
Defined, §10.1-300.
Charges, §10.1-307.
Cost of camping and recreational facilities.
Defined, §10.1-300.
Payment, §10.1-302.
Director.
General powers, §10.1-301.
Fees, §10.1-307.
Remedies.
Bondholders and trustees, §10.1-309.
Sinking fund, §10.1-308.
Trust funds, §10.1-310.
Disabled veteran's passport, §10.1-202.2.
Establishment and maintenance of Appalachian Trail, §10.1-203.
False Cape.
Management of state park, §10.1-205.
Fees.
Admittance to park or facilities, §10.1-200.3.
Fines.
Littering.
Civil penalties, §10.1-200.2.
Parking illegally.
Civil penalty, §10.1-200.3.
Uniform fine schedule, VA SCt Rule 3C:2.
Free entry and parking.
Golden passport card, §10.1-202.1.
Funds.
State park acquisition and development fund, §10.1-202.
State park conservation resources fund, §10.1-202.
State park projects fund, §10.1-202.
Gifts and funds.
State park acquisition and development fund, §10.1-202.
State park conservation resources fund, §10.1-202.
State park projects fund, §10.1-202.
Golden passport card, §10.1-202.1.
Historical interest land.
Acquisition, §10.1-201.
Improvements to be undertaken.
Development of master plan prior to, §10.1-200.1.
Lands of scenic beauty.
Acquisition, §10.1-201.

STATE PARKS —Cont'd
Littering.
Civil penalties, §10.1-200.2.
Long-range plan for acquisition, maintenance, etc., §10.1-200.
Master planning, §10.1-200.1.
Notice.
Solicitation of public comment on planning, §10.1-200.1.
Outdoor recreation and parks.
Conservation and recreation department duties, §10.1-200.
Parking, §10.1-200.3.
Parks generally.
See PARKS AND RECREATION.
Stages of master plan, §10.1-200.1.
Standard against which public to determine extent to which Commonwealth meeting needs.
Development by department of conservation and recreation, §10.1-200.
Statewide system of trails, §10.1-204.
Trails.
Appalachian Trail, §10.1-203.
Statewide system of trails, §10.1-204.
Uniform fine schedule, VA SCt Rule 3C:2.
Veterans.
Disabled veteran's passport, §10.1-202.2.

STATE POLICE COMMUNICATIONS SYSTEM, §§52-12 to 52-19.
Availability, §52-14.
Control, §52-15.
Establishment, §52-12.
Installation, §52-13.
Joint state and local police communications system, §§52-16 to 52-19.
Contracts with counties, cities and towns, §52-17.
Districts, §52-18.
Establishment of radio and teletype system, §52-16.
Maintenance of radio and teletype system, §52-16.
Rules and regulations, §52-19.
Maintenance, §52-13.
Operation, §52-13.
Use options, §52-14.

STATE POLICE DEPARTMENT, §§52-1 to 52-11.5.
Absence without leave from National Guard.
Power to take person into custody, §44-41.1.
Acknowledgment powers of officers, §52-9.
Acquisition of military property, §52-11.3.
Affidavit powers of officers, §52-9.
Air carriers.
Enforcement, §5.1-145.
Aircraft accidents.
Jurisdiction, §5.1-23.
Amber Alert program.
Activation, §52-34.3.
Definitions, §52-34.1.
Established, §52-34.2.
Animals used or trained by law enforcement agencies.
Killing or injuring, §18.2-144.1.
Applicant fingerprint database, §52-46.
Appointment of special police officers, §52-6.
Appointment of supervisory officers, §52-6.1.
Arrest, §§52-20 to 52-22.
Ordinance violations, §52-22.
Warrantless arrests, §§19.2-81, 52-20, 52-21.
Family abuse or violence, §19.2-81.3.

STATE POLICE DEPARTMENT —Cont'd
Arrest —Cont'd
Warrantless arrests —Cont'd
Stalking, §19.2-81.3.
Arson investigators.
Appointment, §27-56.
Reports of stolen explosives to, §27-97.1.
Assault and battery against, §18.2-57.
Assisted living facilities.
Registration of facility with state police.
Receipt of sex offender registration notices, §63.2-1732.
Badges.
Retention upon retirement, §52-9.1:1.
Bureau of criminal investigation.
Duties, §52-8.1.
Established, §52-1.
Oath power of members, §52-9.
Personalty permanently marked.
Assignment of number to personalty in violation to rightful owner, §18.2-96.1.
Powers, §52-8.1.
Summons, §52-9.
Carrying concealed weapons.
Central criminal records exchange.
Entering information into system, §18.2-308.07.
Inapplicability of provisions to retired officers, §18.2-308.
Central criminal records information.
Authority of superintendent of state police, §19.2-387.
Child pornography image registry, §19.2-390.3.
Civil actions against employees.
Attorney general or assistant representing, §2.2-507.
Clothing, uniforms, §52-9.1.
Colleges and universities.
Reporting campus crime, §23-9.1:1.
Communications system, §§52-12 to 52-19.
See STATE POLICE COMMUNICATIONS SYSTEM.
Communication tower or site.
Lease or conveyance of interest in, §2.2-1150.1.
Copies of documents requested from state agency.
Agency furnishing at no cost, §2.2-610.
Crime in Virginia report.
Gang-related criminal information, §52-28.1.
Crime reporting program generally, §§52-25 to 52-30.
See CRIME REPORTING PROGRAM.
Criminal history record information checks.
Firearms transfers, §18.2-308.2:2.
Criminal investigations by department.
Disclosure of records and reports, §52-8.3.
Criminal street gang membership.
Reporting by entering on criminal gang file of Virginia criminal information network, §52-8.6.
Defense counsel for officers, §52-11.
Defined terms.
Commercial motor vehicle.
Regulation powers and duties, §52-8.4.
Hate crimes.
Reporting, §52-8.5.
Motor carrier.
Regulation powers and duties, §52-8.4.
Safety inspection.
Regulation powers and duties, §52-8.4.
Transport vehicle.
Regulation powers and duties, §52-8.4.

STATE POLICE DEPARTMENT —Cont'd
Department of agriculture and consumer services.
Assistance in conducting investigations, §18.2-340.35.
Division for drug law enforcement and investigation.
Establishment, §52-1.
Powers and duties, §52-8.1:1.
Domestic violence policies and procedures, §9.1-1300.
Drivers' licenses.
Information in application.
Duty to compare with information in criminal information network and national sex offender registry, §46.2-323.
Drug control records.
Reports on inspections, §54.1-3405.
Drug investigation special trust account, §52-4.3.
Duties, §52-4.
Aircraft accident investigations, §52-8.
Criminal law enforcement, §52-8.
Highway accidents.
Causes and prevention, §52-4.2.
Enhanced 911 emergency telephone system.
Wireless telephone access number, §56-484.18.
Establishment, §52-1.
False impersonation, §18.2-174.
Fees.
Acceptance by officers, §52-10.
Fingerprints.
Applicant fingerprint database, §52-46.
Firearms disposal.
Unclaimed firearms and other weapons, §52-11.5.
Firearm shows.
Notification by sponsor, §54.1-4201.1.
Firearms licensing.
Criminal records checks, §52-4.4.
Firearm transfers.
Criminal history record information checks, §18.2-308.2:2.
Fire protection.
Investigations, §27-56.
Criminal prosecutions, §27-59.
Expenses paid by insurance companies, §27-57.
Powers, §27-60.
Right of entry, §27-58.
Records.
Duties, §27-55.
Fleeing or eluding police, §46.2-817.
Fraudulent transactions discovered by state agencies, courts.
Report to superintendent of department, §30-138.
Free tuition and required fees to state supported colleges or universities.
Children or spouses of officers killed in line of duty, §23-7.4:1.
Furnishing information regarding criminal violation.
Immunity, §52-49.
Fusion intelligence center, §52-47.
Confidentiality and immunity from service of process, §52-48.
Gang-related criminal information.
Crime in Virginia report, §52-28.1.
Handgun purchases by, §59.1-148.3.
Hate crimes.
Reporting, §52-8.5.
Heart disease.
Presumption as to death or disability, §65.2-402.

STATE POLICE DEPARTMENT —Cont'd
HEAT fund.
Administered by superintendent of department, §38.2-414.
Hepatitis C test, positive results.
Convicted prostitutes or injection drug users tested.
Limited disclosure to, §18.2-346.1.
Hepatitis, meningitis, tuberculosis and HIV.
Workers' compensation.
Presumption on death or disability from, §65.2-402.1.
Highway patrol, §52-4.
Hostage or barricaded person situation.
Emergency control of telephone service, §18.2-50.2.
Hunting incident reports.
Duty of law-enforcement agency or emergency medical service provider to report, §29.1-530.4.
Hunting while under influence of intoxicant or narcotic drug.
Enforcement of provision, §18.2-285.
Hypertension.
Presumption as to death or disability, §65.2-402.
Immunity.
Furnishing information regarding criminal violation, §52-49.
Impersonating, §18.2-174.
Injury in the line of duty.
Short-term disability benefit, §9.1-401.1.
In person and photo lineups.
Written policies and procedures for conducting.
Establishment, required, §19.2-390.02.
Training standards and model policy, §9.1-102.
Insurance fraud.
Definitions, §52-36.
Duties of department, §52-37.
Duties of insurers, their employees and insurance professionals, §52-40.
Evidence, documentation and related materials.
Access to, §52-38.
Confidentiality, §52-39.
Immunity of agents, §52-39.
Immunity of insurer providing information, §52-41.
Insurance fraud investigation unit, §52-37.
Other law-enforcement authority.
Effect of provisions on, §52-44.
Powers of department, §52-37.
Access to evidence, documentation and related materials, §52-38.
Reports, §52-43.
Reward fund, §52-42.
Investigation of elected officials, §52-8.2.
Jury service.
Automatic exemption, §8.01-341.
Killed in line of duty.
Tuition and required fees for state supported colleges or universities.
Waiver for child or spouse of officer, §23-7.4:1.
Line of duty act, §§9.1-400 to 9.1-408.
Lineups.
In person and photo lineups.
Written policies and procedures for conducting.
Establishment, required, §19.2-390.02.
Training standards and model policy, §9.1-102.
Malicious bodily injury to law enforcement officers, §18.2-51.1.
Firearm used or displayed, §18.2-53.1.

STATE POLICE DEPARTMENT —Cont'd
Metropolitan Washington airports authority rules or regulations.
Powers upon facilities elsewhere in Commonwealth, §5.1-157.
Microcomputer devices use to measure speed.
Limit on number allowed to purchase, §46.2-882.
Military property acquisition, §52-11.3.
Missing children information clearinghouse generally, §§52-31 to 52-34.
See MISSING CHILDREN INFORMATION CLEARINGHOUSE.
Missing senior adult.
Senior alert program, §§52-34.4 to 52-34.6.
Motor carrier regulations, §52-8.4.
Newly acquired territory of cities.
Services of police, §52-11.2.
Oath powers of officers, §52-9.
Powers, §52-8.
Private highways.
Policing of, §56-550.
Protective orders.
Emergency orders, family abuse, §19.2-81.3.
Registry, §19.2-387.1.
Duties, §52-45.
Records.
Child pornography image registry, §19.2-390.3.
Sex offender and crimes against minors registry, §§9.1-900 to 9.1-922.
Regulations, §52-8.4.
Firearm shows, §52-8.4:1.
Traffic infractions, §52-8.4:2.
Report of family abuse, §19.2-81.3.
Retention of badges upon retirement, §52-9.1:1.
Retired officers carrying concealed weapons, §18.2-308.
Sale of firearms by law-enforcement agencies, §59.1-148.4.
Secretary of public safety.
Agency responsibility, §2.2-221.
Senior alert program.
Missing senior adult, §§52-34.4 to 52-34.6.
Sex offender and crimes against minors registry, §§9.1-900 to 9.1-922.
Dissemination of information, §9.1-912.
Sentencing commission.
Requests for registry data, §9.1-916.
Sexual assault policies and procedures, §9.1-1301.
Sexually violent predators, civil commitment.
Database of prisoners incarcerated for sexually violent offenses.
Access to records, §37.2-905.2.
Short-term disability benefit, §9.1-401.1.
Special police officers.
Appointment, §52-6.
State health commissioner.
Assistance duties, §52-11.1.
Subpoenas.
Issuance, §19.2-73.2.
Superintendent.
Appointment, §52-2.
Arrests for violations of ordinances, §52-22.
Bond, §52-3.
Communications system generally, §§52-12 to 52-15.
Crime reporting program generally, §§52-25 to 52-30.
See CRIME REPORTING PROGRAM.
Head of department, §52-1.

STATE POLICE DEPARTMENT —Cont'd
Superintendent —Cont'd
Missing children information clearinghouse.
Establishment, §§52-31, 52-31.1.
Motor carrier regulations, §52-8.4.
Oath, §52-3.
Powers, §52-8.
Salary, §52-3.
Term of office, §52-2.
Supervisory officers.
Appointment, §52-6.1.
Surety bonds of officers, §52-7.
Terrorism.
Furnishing information regarding.
Immunity, §52-49.
Traffic infractions, §52-8.4:2.
Tuition and required fees for state supported colleges and universities.
Waiver for child or spouse of officer killed in line of duty, §23-7.4:1.
Unclaimed property in possession of.
Disposal, §52-11.4.
Firearms and other weapons, §52-11.5.
Uniforms, §52-9.1.
Unlawful wearing of officer's uniform, §18.2-175.
Wearing of same or similar uniforms by non-officers, §52-9.2.
Virginia Amber Alert program.
Activation, §52-34.3.
Definitions, §52-34.1.
Established, §52-34.2.
Warrantless arrests, §§52-20, 52-21.
Wireless telephone access number, §56-484.18.
Wiretapping.
Court-ordered interception of communications.
When authorized, §19.2-66.
Witness protection program, §52-35.
Workers' compensation.
Coverage.
Off-duty, §65.2-102.
Heart disease.
Presumptions as to death or disability from, §65.2-402.
Hepatitis, meningitis, tuberculosis and HIV.
Presumption on death or disability from, §65.2-402.1.
Hypertension.
Presumptions as to death or disability from, §65.2-402.
Injury where weather constitutes particular risk of employment of public safety officer, §65.2-301.1.

STATE POLICE OFFICERS AND INVESTIGATORS, SPECIAL, §§52-23, 52-24.

STATE POLICE RETIREMENT SYSTEM, §§51.1-200 to 51.1-210.
Additional service retirement allowance, §51.1-206.
Administration, §51.1-200.
Allowance for service retirement, §51.1-206.
Beneficiary of service retirement allowance in service as covered employee.
Cessation of retirement allowance while employed, §51.1-206.
Constituency, §51.1-202.
Continuation of previous system, §51.1-200.
Contributions by Commonwealth, §51.1-204.
Coordination of past and present plans.
Benefits continued, §51.1-402.
Creditable service, §51.1-203.

STATE POLICE RETIREMENT SYSTEM —Cont'd
Death before retirement, §51.1-207.
Deferred retirement.
Members terminating service, §51.1-205.
Defined terms, §51.1-201.
Disability benefit, §51.1-210.
Disability resulting from misconduct of another, §51.1-209.
Disclosure requirements, §§51.1-1000 to 51.1-1004.
Financial reports, §51.1-1003.
Scope, §51.1-1000.
Statement of benefits, §51.1-1002.
Summary plan description, §51.1-1001.
Use of electronic media, §51.1-1004.
Early retirement, §51.1-205.
Service retirement allowance, §51.1-206.
Effective date of retirement, §51.1-205.
Health insurance credits, §51.1-1400.
Membership, §51.1-202.
Normal retirement, §51.1-205.
Retirement allowance, §51.1-206.
Pooling of assets for investment, §51.1-124.31.
Post-retirement supplements, §51.1-208.
Service retirement, §51.1-205.
Allowance, §51.1-206.
Creditable service, §51.1-203.
State contributions, §51.1-204.
Supplements after retirement, §51.1-208.

STATE PROPERTY.
See STATE BUILDINGS AND PROPERTY.

STATE PUBLICATIONS DEPOSITORY PROGRAM, §§42.1-92 to 42.1-97.
Catalog of publications produced by state agencies.
Copies, distribution, costs, §42.1-96.
Duty of Librarian of Virginia to prepare and publish, requirements, §42.1-95.
Cooperation with Library of Virginia, §42.1-94.
Definitions, §42.1-93.
Duties of Library of Virginia, §42.1-94.
Establishment and administration.
Duty of Library of Virginia, §42.1-94.
Local or regional agencies, duties, §42.1-94.
Report by librarian, failure of agency, §42.1-97.
Policy and purpose of chapter, §42.1-92.
Report by Librarian of Virginia, filing, time.
Agencies not furnishing or providing information, §42.1-97.
Short title, §42.1-92.
State agencies, duties, §42.1-94.
Report by librarian, failure of agency, §42.1-97.

STATE RACING OPERATIONS FUND, §59.1-370.1.

STATE RECORDATION TAX, §§58.1-800 to 58.1-817.
See RECORDATION TAX, STATE.

STATE RECORDATION TAX EXEMPTIONS, §58.1-811.

STATE RECORDS MANAGEMENT, §§42.1-76 to 42.1-90.1.
Advisory committees to assist in developing regulations.
Library board may establish, §42.1-82.
Agencies with public records.
Audit of management practice.
Authority of Librarian of Virginia, §42.1-90.1.

STATE RECORDS MANAGEMENT —Cont'd
Agencies with public records —Cont'd
Disposition, requirements, duties, §42.1-86.1.
Duties, §42.1-85.
Archival public records.
Care, storage, requirements, §42.1-87.
Audit of agency management practice.
Authority of Librarian of Virginia, §42.1-90.1.
Closed records.
Opening for public access, time, §42.1-78.
Confidentiality of records made confidential by law, §42.1-78.
Conversion or migration of electronic records.
Duty of officials responsible for, force of original, §42.1-85.
Cooperation with Library of Virginia.
Agencies with public records, §42.1-85.
Copy of chapter furnished, time.
Persons elected, reelected, appointed or reappointed to governing body or agency subject to chapter, §42.1-76.1.
Custodian and trustee of public records.
Library of Virginia, §42.1-79.
Custodians to deliver records at expiration of term, §42.1-88.
Definitions, §42.1-77.
Disaster or emergency.
Plan for preservation of records.
Development, Library of Virginia, §42.1-86.
Disposal, destruction or other disposition of public records.
Procedures, regulations.
Library board to issue, §42.1-82.
Requirements, duties of agencies, §42.1-86.1.
Electronic archival records.
Library of Virginia, powers, §42.1-79.
Essential public records.
Program for selection and preservation.
Establishment, maintenance, Library of Virginia, §42.1-86.
Expiration of term of records custodians.
Delivery of all records, §42.1-88.
False entries or destruction by officers, §18.2-472.
Forging, §18.2-168.
Legislative intent, §42.1-76.
Librarian of Virginia.
State archivists.
Librarian of Virginia to name, §42.1-79.
Library board.
Duties, §42.1-82.
Powers, §42.1-82.
Library of Virginia.
Archival and management function.
Vested in, §42.1-79.
Audit of agency management practices.
Librarian, authority, §42.1-90.1.
Duties, §42.1-85.
Essential public records program.
Establishment and maintenance, §42.1-86.
Official custodian and trustee of Commonwealth of public records, §42.1-79.
Powers as official repository of public records, §42.1-79.
Review of proposed legislation affecting public records, §42.1-79.
Open to public access, §42.1-78.
Persons elected, reelected, appointed or reappointed to governing body or agency subject to chapter.
Copy of chapter furnished, time, §42.1-76.1.

STATE RECORDS MANAGEMENT —Cont'd
Petition for return of public records not in authorized possession, §42.1-89.
Proposed legislation affecting public records.
Review by Library of Virginia, §42.1-79.
Records officers.
Designation by state agency or political subdivision, duties, §42.1-85.
Recovery copies of essential public records.
Requirements for making, force of original, §42.1-86.
Seizure of public records not in authorized possession, §42.1-90.
State archivists.
Librarian of Virginia to name, §42.1-79.
Storage of records, §42.1-87.
Theft or destruction, §18.2-107.
Time for opening records to public acccss.
Closed records, §42.1-78.
Training and education.
Requirements and compliance with chapter.
Library of Virginia to develop and make available, §42.1-85.
Unnecessary records for transaction of business.
Transfer, storage, §42.1-87.
Virginia public records act, §42.1-76.
Vital records.
Generally, §§32.1-249 to 32.1-276.
See VITAL RECORDS.

STATE REGISTRAR OF VITAL RECORDS.
Appointments, §32.1-251.
Birth certificates.
Delayed birth certificates.
Filing and registration, §§32.1-259, 32.1-260.
Deaths in Commonwealth.
Persons seventeen years of age or older.
Furnishing monthly report to state board of elections, §24.2-408.
Duties, §32.1-252.
Furnishing information to on demand, §32.1-275.
Matching birth and death certificates, §32.1-275.1.
Missing children birth records.
Duties as to, §32.1-275.2.
Preservation of original documents, §32.1-270.
Registration districts.
Establishment, consolidation of subdivision, §32.1-253.
Supplying information on demand, §32.1-275.
Virginia vital statistics automation fund, §32.1-273.1.
Vital records generally, §§32.1-249 to 32.1-276.
See VITAL RECORDS.

STATE RETIREMENT SYSTEM, §§51.1-124.1 to 51.1-169.
See VIRGINIA RETIREMENT SYSTEM.

STATE REVENUE BOND ACT, §§33.1-267 to 33.1-295.
See TRANSPORTATION REVENUE BONDS.

STATES OTHER THAN VIRGINIA.
Admission of new states, US Const Art IV §3.
Bill of attainder, US Const Art I §10.
Bills of credit, US Const Art I §10.
Commerce, US Const Art I §§8, 9.
Compacts between the states or with foreign powers, US Const Art I §10.

STATES OTHER THAN VIRGINIA —Cont'd
Contracts.
Impairing obligations of contracts, US Const Art I §10.
Controversies between citizens of different states, US Const Art III §2.
Controversies between states, US Const Art III §2.
Duties and imposts, US Const Art I §10.
Equal suffrage in senate, US Const Art V.
Exports, US Const Art I §§9, 10.
Ex post facto laws, US Const Art I §10.
Full faith and credit clause, US Const Art IV §1.
Gold and silver coin tender in payment of debts, US Const Art I §10.
Impairing obligations of contracts, US Const Art I §10.
Imports and exports, US Const Art I §10.
Invasion.
Protection against, US Const Art IV §4.
Legal tender, US Const Art I §10.
Letters of marque or reprisal, US Const Art I §10.
Limitations on powers of the state, US Const Art I §10.
Money.
Coining money, US Const Art I §10.
Motor carriers, passengers.
Government vehicles.
Exclusions, §46.2-2000.1.
Motor carriers, property.
Government vehicles.
Exemptions from provisions, §46.2-2101.
New states, US Const Art IV §3.
Powers, US Const Art I §10.
Reserved to state, US Const Amd 10.
Protection and aid of states, US Const Art IV §4.
Republican form of government guaranteed, US Const Art IV §4.
Reservation of powers to state, US Const Amd 10.
Right to coin money, US Const Art I §10.
Suits against, US Const Amd 11.
Tender in payment of debts, US Const Art I §10.
Tonnage, US Const Art I §10.
Treaties, US Const Art I §10.
Troops or ships of war in time of peace, US Const Art I §10.
War, US Const Art I §10.

STATE TREASURER, §§2.2-1800 to 2.2-1812.
Accounts.
Depositories, §2.2-1810.
Appointment, §2.2-1800.
Appropriations, §2.2-1802.
Bad checks.
Payments into state treasury, §2.2-1804.
Bond issues.
Custody.
Duties of state treasurer, §2.2-1807.
Checks.
Depository accounts, §2.2-1810.
Payments into state treasury.
Means of payment, §2.2-1804.
Reproductions.
Admissibility into evidence, §2.2-1812.
Subpoenas to produce checks or drafts, §2.2-1812.
Unpresented checks.
Duties, §2.2-1811.
Collections.
Disbursements.
Recovery audits of state contracts, §2.2-1822.1.

STATE TREASURER —Cont'd
Custodian.
Federal grants and funds received by state agencies, §2.2-611.
Depository accounts, §2.2-1810.
Deposits into state treasury, §2.2-1802.
Payments into state treasury.
Means of payment, §2.2-1804.
Record of deposits, §2.2-1805.
Regulations for deposit procedures, authority, §2.2-1803.
Disbursements, §§2.2-1819 to 2.2-1827.
Appropriations.
Payments made in accordance with, §2.2-1819.
Collections.
Recovery audits of state contracts, §2.2-1822.1.
Deposits as credits to state treasury, §2.2-1821.
Electronic payment systems.
Warrants for payment of claims, §2.2-1825.
Imprest funds, §2.2-1824.
Lump-sum transfers prohibited, §2.2-1823.
Payments made in accordance with appropriations, §2.2-1819.
Payroll funds, §2.2-1824.
Petty cash funds, §2.2-1824.
Register of warrants for payment of claims, §2.2-1825.
Warrants.
Conditions to issue, §2.2-1822.
Procedure, §2.2-1821.
Warrants for payment of claims.
Issuance, §2.2-1825.
Lost or destroyed warrants, §2.2-1826.
No bond required, §2.2-1827.
Replacement warrants, §2.2-1826.
No bond required, §2.2-1827.
Withdrawals.
Procedure, §2.2-1821.
Drafts.
Payments into state treasury.
Means of payment, §2.2-1804.
Duties of employees, §2.2-1801.
Duties of state treasurer.
Custody of invested funds, accounts, bonds and certificates of indebtedness, §2.2-1807.
Unpresented checks, §2.2-1811.
Warrants on state treasury, §2.2-1809.
Electronic funds transfers.
Record of transfers, §2.2-1805.
Family and children's trust fund.
Management, §63.2-2103.
Federal grants and funds received by state agencies.
Custodian, §2.2-611.
General authority, §2.2-1800.
General provisions regarding state agencies and general operation of government, §§2.2-600 to 2.2-614.3.
See STATE DEPARTMENTS AND AGENCIES.
Investment of excess funds, §2.2-1806.
Custody of treasurer, §2.2-1807.
Payments from state treasury, §§2.2-1819 to 2.2-1827. See within this heading, "Disbursements."
Payments into state treasury, §2.2-1802.
Bad checks, §2.2-1804.
Means of payment, §2.2-1804.
Records.
Payments into state treasury.
Record of payments, §2.2-1805.

STATE TREASURER —Cont'd
Reports.
Revenue stabilization fund.
Auditor of public accounts, §2.2-1829.
Revenue stabilization fund, §§2.2-1828 to 2.2-1831.
Additional amount for deposit in excess of mandatory deposit.
Governor to recommend in budget, §2.2-1829.
Auditor of public accounts.
Reports, §2.2-1829.
Creation, §2.2-1828.
Decline in revised general fund forecast.
Transfers to cover difference, §2.2-1830.
Establishment, §2.2-1828.
Revised general fund forecast.
Decline, transfers to cover difference, §2.2-1830.
Sources or components of general fund revenues, §2.2-1831.
Risk management division, §§2.2-1832 to 2.2-1843.
Bonds, surety.
Courts, funds under control.
Blanket surety bond plan, §2.2-1841.
Insurance for state motor vehicles, §2.2-1838.
Insurance plan for state buildings and property, §2.2-1836.
Local officers and employees.
Bonds, surety.
Blanket surety bond plan, §2.2-1840.
Political subdivisions.
Risk management plan for claims against, §2.2-1839.
Public officers and employees.
Bonds, surety.
Blanket surety bond plan, §2.2-1840.
Risk management plan for claims against, §2.2-1839.
Risk management and loss prevention plans, §2.2-1843.
Risk management plan for public liability, §2.2-1837.
Sovereign immunity not waived, §2.2-1842.
State insurance reserve trust fund, §2.2-1835.
State-owned buildings and properties.
Inspection for insurance purposes, §2.2-1834.
List and replacement value, §2.2-1833.
State owned motor vehicles.
Insurance plan, §2.2-1838.
Transfer to department of the treasury from department of general services, §2.2-1832.
Securities.
Authority to transfer or sell, §2.2-1808.
See TREASURER OF STATE.
Staff.
Appointments, §2.2-1801.
Duties, §2.2-1801.
State board and state department of social services.
Expenses of auditor in rendering services.
Paid as administrative expense of department, §63.2-404.
State depositories, §§2.2-1813 to 2.2-1818.
Amount limits, §2.2-1814.
Bonds, surety, §2.2-1815.
Deposits as credits to state treasury, §2.2-1821.
Designation, §2.2-1813.
Electronic funds transfers, §2.2-1816.
Lost or failed checks, drafts or transfers.
Liability of state, §2.2-1817.
Exclusive, §2.2-1813.

STATE TREASURER —Cont'd
State depositories —Cont'd
Liability for lost or failed checks, drafts or transfers, §2.2-1817.
Limits on amounts and time, §2.2-1814.
Lost or failed checks, drafts or transfers.
Liability of state, §2.2-1817.
Qualified public depositories, §2.2-1815.
Secured, §2.2-1815.
Time limits, §2.2-1814.
Transfers of public funds, §2.2-1816.
Transportation department bonds and securities.
Responsibility of state, §2.2-1818.
Transfers.
Disbursements generally, §§2.2-1819 to 2.2-1827.
See within this heading, "Disbursements."
Invested funds, §2.2-1806.
Lump-sum transfers prohibited, §2.2-1823.
Vicarious liability, §2.2-1801.
Warrants on state treasury.
Duties, §2.2-1809.
List of warrants, §2.2-1809.
Withdrawals.
Invested funds, §2.2-1806.

STATE VETERINARIAN.
Animal shelters.
Power to inspect, §3.2-6502.
Avian influenza control.
Powers, §3.2-6023.
Circuit court judges.
Enforcement of orders of state veterinarian, §3.2-6014.
Contagious and infectious diseases, livestock and poultry.
Appraisement of condemned cattle, §3.2-6020.
Biological residues, abatement, §3.2-6002.
Damages, §3.2-6019.
Duty to protect livestock and poultry, §3.2-6001.
Duty when animals suspected of having disease, §3.2-6003.
Enforcement of orders.
Circuit court judges, §3.2-6014.
Law enforcement officers, §3.2-6013.
Euthanasia or slaughter by owner, §3.2-6009.
Importation, proclamation prohibiting, §3.2-6010.
Violations, §3.2-6011.
Laboratory for diagnosis of diseases, §3.2-5903.
Law enforcement officers.
Authority to execute orders, §3.2-6013.
Prevention and eradication, §3.2-6002.
Regulations, penalty for violations, §3.2-6023.
Quarantine.
Disposition of quarantined animals with potential to impact livestock or poultry, §3.2-6008.
Domestic animals not permitted to enter or leave quarantine, §3.2-6007.
Individuals exposed, §3.2-6006.
Notice of quarantine, §3.2-6005.
Right of entry, §3.2-6000.
Separation and caring for diseased animals.
Regulations, §3.2-6004.
USDA, cooperation with, §3.2-6015.
Vaccine, authority to test, §3.2-6017.
Violations.
Liability for damages, §3.2-6019.
Penalty, §3.2-6018.
Prevention and control measures, §3.2-6023.
Definitions, §3.2-5900.
Designation, §3.2-5901.

STATE VETERINARIAN —Cont'd
Dogs.
Commercial dog breeders.
Right of entry for inspections, §3.2-6507.3.
Domestic animals generally, §§3.2-5900 to 3.2-5905.
Employment, §3.2-5901.
Importation of animals.
Certificate of veterinary inspection, §3.2-5902.
Laboratory for diagnosis of diseases, §3.2-5903.
Law enforcement officers.
Duty to execute orders of state veterinarian, §3.2-6013.
Mistreated animals.
Seizure and impoundment of animals, §3.2-6569.
Powers and duties, §3.2-6001.
Quarantine.
Generally, §§3.2-6003 to 3.2-6008.
Shooting enclosures.
Seizure and disposal of livestock in unlicensed enclosures, §3.2-6036.
Premises where animals are kept.
Power to inspect, §3.2-6502.
Quarantine.
Contagious and infectious diseases, livestock and poultry.
Disposition of quarantined animals with potential to impact livestock or poultry, §3.2-6008.
Domestic animals not permitted to enter or leave quarantine, §3.2-6007.
Individuals exposed, §3.2-6006.
Notice of quarantine, §3.2-6005.
Generally, §§3.2-6003 to 3.2-6008.
Right of entry, §3.2-6000.
Contagious and infectious diseases, livestock and poultry, §3.2-6000.
Seizure and impoundment of animals, §3.2-6569.
Vaccines.
Contagious and infectious diseases, livestock and poultry.
Vaccine, authority to test, §3.2-6017.

STATE WATER COMMISSION, §§30-186, 30-187.

STATE WATER CONTROL BOARD PERMIT PROGRAM FUND, §62.1-44.15:7.

STATEWIDE AGENCIES RADIO SYSTEM (STARS).
Freedom of information act requests.
Excluded records, §2.2-3705.2.

STATEWIDE BUILDING CODE, §§36-97 to 36-119.1.
See BUILDING CODE.

STATEWIDE COMMUNITY-BASED CORRECTIONS SYSTEM FOR STATE-RESPONSIBLE OFFENDERS, §§53.1-67.2 to 53.1-67.6.

STATEWIDE DISCRETIONARY SENTENCING GUIDELINES FOR FELONY CASES, §17.1-805.

STATEWIDE EMERGENCY MEDICAL SERVICES SYSTEM AND SERVICES, §§32.1-111.1 to 32.1-111.16.

STATEWIDE FACILITATOR FOR VICTIMS OF DOMESTIC VIOLENCE, §2.2-515.1.
Address confidentiality program, §2.2-515.2.

STATEWIDE FIRE PREVENTION CODE, §§27-94 to 27-101.
See FIRE PREVENTION CODE.

STATEWIDE HUMAN SERVICES INFORMATION AND REFERRAL PROGRAM, §§63.2-222 to 63.2-227.

STATEWIDE POISON CONTROL SYSTEM, §32.1-111.15.

STATEWIDE PREHOSPITAL AND INTERHOSPITAL TRAUMA TRIAGE PLAN, §32.1-111.3.

STATION AGENTS.
Issuance of summons for boarding without paying, §15.2-4503.

STATIONERY.
Commonwealths' attorneys, treasurers or commissioners of revenue purchasing.
Manner of payment, §15.2-1636.15.
Sheriffs purchasing.
Payment for items, §15.2-1615.1.

STATISTICAL DATA.
Planning and budget department.
Coordination and review, §2.2-1501.

STATUS OFFENDERS, JUVENILES.
Disposition in juvenile proceedings, §16.1-278.6.
Juvenile proceedings generally, §§16.1-246 to 16.1-309.1.
See JUVENILE PROCEEDINGS.
Trespass after having been forbidden to do so, §§18.2-119, 18.2-120.

STATUTE OF FRAUDS.
Bankruptcy, promise to pay debt after.
Writing required, §11-2.01.
Contracts void as to creditors and purchasers unless in writing, §11-1.
Easements.
Solar easements.
Creation, §55-353.
Fences.
Division fences.
Requirements for agreement to bind successors in title, §55-321.
Health spas.
Contracts, §§59.1-297, 59.1-298.
Invention development services.
Contract requirements, §59.1-209.
Investment securities.
Inapplicable, §8.8A-113.
Landlord and tenant.
Recoveries for rent and for use and occupation, §55-227.
Leases, UCC, §8.2A-201.
Limited liability companies.
Contributions by members.
Promises to make contributions, §13.1-1027.
Filing requirements, §13.1-1003.
Resignation of member.
Written notification requirements, §13.1-1032.
Manufactured home lot rental, §55-248.42.
Prudent investor rule.
Waiver of act provisions, §64.2-781.
Real estate.
Contract void as to creditors and purchasers unless in writing, §11-1.
Written evidence required to maintain action, §11-2.

STATUTE OF FRAUDS —Cont'd
Sales, UCC, §8.2-201.
Modification of contract, §8.2-209.
When writing not required, §8.2-201.
Solar easements.
Creation, §55-353.
Solicitation of charitable or civic contributions.
Contracts with professional fund-raisers, §57-54.
Wills, §64.2-404.
Written evidence required to maintain action, §11-2.

STATUTE OF LIMITATIONS.
Abatement, revival and survival.
Suspension or tolling of statute of limitations, §8.01-229.
Abortion.
Attempts, §19.2-8.
Abuse and neglect of children.
When cause of action deemed to accrue, §8.01-249.
Abuse of process.
When cause of action deemed to accrue, §8.01-249.
Abutting landowners taxed or assessed for improvement.
Appeals, §15.2-2410.
Accountants.
Complaints against CPAs or CPA firms, time for filing, §54.1-4425.
Accounts and accounting.
Claims against decedents' estates.
Time within which statute not to run, §64.2-552.
Accrual of right of action, §8.01-230.
Actual innocence.
Petition for writ of actual innocence, VA SCt Rule 5:7B.
Administrators. See within this heading, "Fiduciaries."
Adoption.
Attempts, §19.2-8.
Bill of review, §8.01-623.
Refusal, §8.01-671.
Curators.
Appeal from proceeding before clerk, §64.2-445.
Final order not subject to attack after six months, §63.2-1216.
Rehearing by supreme court, §19.2-325.
Time within which petition must be presented, §8.01-671.
Workers' compensation commission, §65.2-706.
Adverse possession, §8.01-236.
Advertising.
Unsolicited facsimile transmissions.
Tort liability for injury, §8.01-40.2.
Agricultural equipment warranties, §59.1-207.8.
Amended tax returns, §58.1-1823.
Amercement, §19.2-8.
Antitrust laws, §59.1-9.14.
Appeals.
Appraisement of estates.
Appeal from proceeding before clerk, §64.2-445.
Appraisement of estates.
Appeal from proceeding before clerk, §64.2-445.
Asbestos.
Injuries, §8.01-243.
Removal of asbestos, §8.01-250.1.
Rule of actions, §8.01-249.
Assessment of taxes, §58.1-104.
Income tax, §58.1-312.

STATUTE OF LIMITATIONS —Cont'd
Assessment of taxes —Cont'd
Omitted taxes by department of taxation, §58.1-1812.
Taxpayer problem resolution program, §58.1-1818.
Waiver of time limitation, §58.1-101.
Assessment of omitted or additional state taxes, §58.1-220.
Assignments.
Avoidance of assignments without consideration or upon consideration of marriage, §8.01-253.
Attachment and garnishment.
Rehearing when judgment rendered on publication, §8.01-575.
Attempts to commit crime.
Abortion, §19.2-8.
Obtaining public assistance by fraud, §19.2-8.
Attorneys at law.
Licensing.
Practicing without authority, §19.2-8.
Bail and recognizance.
Contracts.
Personal actions based on contracts, §8.01-246.
Bank deposits and collections, §8.4-111.
Unauthorized signature or alteration.
Claims against bank, §8.4-406.
Bank franchise tax.
Criminal prosecutions, §19.2-8.
Banking and finance.
Bankruptcy and insolvency.
Time claims against insolvent bank barred, §6.2-923.
Money on deposit.
Bank or personal corporation doing banking business, §8.01-249.
Bequests.
Enforcement, §8.01-254.
Bill of review, §8.01-623.
Appeals.
Refusal, §8.01-671.
Bills of lading.
Limitations in bill of lading or tariff, §8.7-309.
Birth-related neurological injury compensation claims, §38.2-5013.
Tolling of statutes by filing of claim, §38.2-5005.
Bonds issued by locality.
Contesting validity of proposed issue, §15.2-2627.
Judicial determination of validity, contesting, §15.2-2653.
Bonds, surety.
Fiduciaries, §8.01-245.
Bond validation proceeding appeals, §15.2-2656.
Breach of fiduciary duty, §8.01-245.
Breach of implied warranties on new homes, §55-70.1.
Breast implants, §8.01-249.
Building code violations.
Criminal prosecution, §§19.2-8, 36-106.
Business opportunity sales, §59.1-269.
Campaign finance disclosure, §24.2-953.
Catch-all provision, §8.01-248.
Cemeteries.
Actions for damages, §57-26.
Damage done to adjacent land, §57-26.
Child abuse and neglect.
When cause of action deemed to accrue, §8.01-249.
Childhood sexual abuse.
When cause of action deemed to accrue, §8.01-249.
Children or minors.
Abuse and neglect of children.
When cause of action deemed to accrue, §8.01-249.

STATUTE OF LIMITATIONS —Cont'd
Children or minors —Cont'd
Desertion and nonsupport.
Limitation not applicable to prosecution, §19.2-8.
Disability which tolls statute, §8.01-229.
Parent or guardian action against tortfeasor, §8.01-243.
Wills, suit to impeach or establish, §64.2-448.
Saving in favor of infants, §64.2-448.
Cigarette tax.
Criminal prosecutions, §19.2-8.
Circuit court dockets.
Reinstatement of cases struck from docket, §8.01-335.
Striking of certain cases from docket, §8.01-335.
Circuit courts.
Pleading, VA SCt Rule 3:18.
Civil rights actions, §8.01-243.
Claims against counties.
Appeal from disallowance, §15.2-1246.
Illegal or improper allowance, §15.2-1245.
Claims against decedents' estates.
Time within which statute not to run, §64.2-552.
Claims against dissolved corporations, §13.1-746.1.
Nonprofit corporations, §§13.1-908, 13.1-908.1.
Claims against the state.
Agencies of state incorporated for charitable or educational purposes.
Recovery of money paid into state treasury, §55-200.
Fraudulent claims, §8.01-216.9.
Presenting claim for payment.
Allowance made by court of record, §2.2-815.
Proceedings to enforce judgment, §8.01-251.
Referral to governor.
Claim not presented within time limits, §2.2-816.
State not within statute of limitations, §8.01-231.
Time for representing claim against state, §8.01-255.
Tort claims against the Commonwealth, §§8.01-195.6, 8.01-195.7.
Clerks of court.
Appraisement of estates.
Appeal from proceeding before clerk, §64.2-445.
Curators.
Appeal from proceeding before clerk, §64.2-445.
Clerk's office closed.
Last day of limitation period falling on, §1-210.
Code of Virginia.
Repeal of statute.
Effect of repeal of general acts by code, §1-4.
Collection of local taxes, §58.1-3940.
Waiver of time limitation on assessment, §58.1-3903.1.
Collection of state taxes, §58.1-1802.1.
Assessment of omitted taxes, §58.1-1812.
Conversion of trust taxes prosecutions, §58.1-1816.
Commercial code.
Documents of title.
Limitations in bill of lading or tariff, §8.7-309.
Limitations in warehouse receipt or tariff, §8.7-204.
Leases of personal property.
Default, §8.2A-506.
Sales.
Statute of limitations and contract for sale, §8.2-725.

STATUTE OF LIMITATIONS —Cont'd
Commissioner of accounts.
Time within which statute not to run, §64.2-552.
Computation of period.
Last day falling on Saturday, Sunday, legal holiday, clerk's office closed, §1-210.
Computer crimes.
Civil actions, §8.01-40.1.
Civil relief, §18.2-152.12.
Tort liability for injury to person or property, §8.01-44.5.
Computer information transactions, §59.1-508.5.
Condominiums.
Enforcement of lien for assessment, §55-79.84.
Instruments.
Challenges to validity of amendments, §55-79.71.
Lien for assessments, §55-79.84.
Warranties against structural defects, §55-79.79.
Actions for breach of warranty, §55-79.79.
Conflicts of interest.
General assembly members.
Criminal prosecution, §30-128.
Public officers and employees, §2.2-3125.
Constitution of Virginia.
Effect of revision or amendment of constitution, §1-4.
Consumer credit.
Revolving credit open accounts.
When cause of action deemed to accrue, §8.01-249.
Consumer protection.
Suspension of statute, §59.1-204.1.
Violations of act.
When cause of action deemed to accrue, §8.01-249.
Contracts, §8.01-246.
Accrual of right of action, §8.01-230.
Actions based on contracts, §§8.01-246, 8.01-247.
Gaming contracts, §11-15.
Generally, §8.01-246.
Highway contracts, §§33.1-192, 33.1-192.1.
Executed after June 30, 1976, §33.1-192.1.
New promise in writing, §8.01-229.
Personal actions based on contracts, §8.01-246.
Rescission.
When cause of action deemed to accrue, §8.01-249.
Revolving credit open accounts.
When cause of action deemed to accrue, §8.01-249.
Sale of goods.
Breach of contract, §8.2-725.
Limitations by agreements may be reduced to less than one year, §8.2-725.
Contribution.
When cause of action deemed to accrue, §8.01-249.
Controlled substances.
Damages.
Minors, liability of drug dealers, §8.01-227.7.
Conversion of trust taxes prosecutions, §58.1-1816.
Correction of erroneous local tax assessments.
Appeal by locality of commissioner's correction, §58.1-3982.
Local taxes.
Application to commissioner of revenue, §58.1-3980.
Waiver of time limitation on assessment, §58.1-3903.1.

STATUTE OF LIMITATIONS —Cont'd
Correction of erroneous local tax assessments —Cont'd
Local taxes —Cont'd
Application to court to correct, §58.1-3984.
Refunds of taxes erroneously paid, §58.1-3990.
Correction of erroneous state tax assessments.
Application to circuit court for correction, §58.1-1825.
Filing of amended return, §58.1-1823.
Protective claim for refund, §58.1-1824.
Correction of taxes assessed by state corporation commission, §58.1-2030.
Counterclaims.
Tolling, commencement of plaintiff's action, §8.01-233.
Counties.
Claims against countics.
Appeal from disallowance, §15.2-1246.
Illegal or improper allowance, §15.2-1245.
Credit.
Equal credit opportunity act.
Violations of chapter, §6.2-505.
Credit line deed of trust.
Limitation on enforcement when no date fixed for maturity, §8.01-242.
Creditors' suits.
Debts proved in creditors' suits, §8.01-229.
Credit services businesses, §59.1-335.11.
Criminal cases.
Lapse of time after finding of probable cause.
Limitation on prosecution, §19.2-243.
Limitation of actions for recovery of court costs, §19.2-341.
Murder or manslaughter.
No limitation, §19.2-8.1.
Criminal fines and penalties.
Collection of penalties other than fines, §19.2-341.
Cross-claims.
Tolling, commencement of plaintiff's action, §8.01-233.
Curators.
Appeal from proceeding before clerk, §64.2-445.
Generally. See within this heading, "Fiduciaries."
Custodial trustee.
Actions against trustees, §64.2-915.
Generally. See within this heading, "Fiduciaries."
Damages.
Accrual of right of action, §8.01-230.
Cemeteries.
Damage to adjacent land, §57-26.
Controlled substances.
Minors, liability of drug dealers, §8.01-227.7.
Suspension of limitations during criminal proceedings, §8.01-229.
Death.
Effect of death, §8.01-229.
Debts.
Creditors' suits, §8.01-229.
Decedents.
Filing claims, §64.2-552.
Devise for payment of debts, §8.01-229.
Decedents' estates.
Claims against estate.
Time within which statute not to run, §64.2-552.
Enforcement of bequests and legacies, §8.01-254.
Decrees pro confesso.
Setting aside for fraud, §8.01-428.
Deeds.
After-acquired property, §55-53.

STATUTE OF LIMITATIONS —Cont'd
Deeds —Cont'd
Objections to irregularities in advertising sales made by trustees under deeds of trust, §55-24.
Defamation, §8.01-247.1.
Default judgments.
Setting aside for fraud, §8.01-428.
Defenses.
Bar of expiration of limitation period.
Raised only as affirmative defense in responsive pleading, §8.01-235.
Delinquent tax land sales, §58.1-3940.
Claims for surplus received from sale, §58.1-3967.
Waiver of time limitation on assessment, §58.1-3903.1.
Department of professional regulation.
Complaints.
Time for filing, §54.1-307.1.
Descent and distribution.
Claims of succession by illegitimate children.
Adjudication of parenthood, §64.2-102.
Elective shares.
Claiming, §64.2-302.
Extension of time, §64.2-303.
Refunds of distributions, §64.2-556.
Settlement of accounts and distribution, §64.2-552.
Desertion and nonsupport.
Limitation not applicable to prosecution for desertion or nonsupport of wife or child, §19.2-8.
Detinue.
Actions to recover personal property, §8.01-243.
Devisavit vel non, §64.2-448.
Directors of corporations, unlawful distributions, §13.1-692.
Disabilities.
Effect of disabilities upon right of entry, §8.01-237.
Discrimination against persons with disabilities, §51.5-46.
Dismissal, discontinuance and nonsuit.
Suspension or statute of limitations, §8.01-229.
Dispute resolution proceedings.
Vacating orders and agreements, §8.01-576.12.
Dissolution of stock corporations.
Claims against, §13.1-746.1.
Known claims, §13.1-746.
Distress.
Landlord and tenant, §55-230.
Rents, §55-230.
Time within which rent may be distrained, §55-230.
District court judgments.
Enforcement, §16.1-94.1.
Divorce.
Adultery.
Lapse of five years before instituting suit, §20-94.
Buggery.
Lapse of five years before instituting suit, §20-94.
Documents of title.
Bills of lading.
Limitation in bill or tariff, §8.7-309.
Warehouse receipts.
Limitation in warehouse receipt or tariff, §8.7-204.
Drivers' licenses.
Suspension of licenses for unsatisfied judgments.
Custody and application of cash or securities deposited, §46.2-426.

STATUTE OF LIMITATIONS —Cont'd
Drug dealers liability, §8.01-227.7.
Effective date of chapter.
Rights and remedies existing when chapter takes effect, §8.01-256.
Ejectment.
Landlord and tenant, §§55-240 to 55-242, 55-247, 55-248.
Elective shares.
Claiming, §§64.2-302, 64.2-303.
Extension of time, §64.2-303.
Electric utility restructuring.
Retail customers private right of action, §56-593.
Email service providers.
Spam, civil relief for injury by, §18.2-152.12.
Eminent domain.
Title transfer by certificate.
Commencement of condemnation proceedings, §25.1-313.
Petition for determination of just compensation, §25.1-318.
Emotional distress, §8.01-243.
Enforcement of district court judgments, §16.1-94.1.
Entry on action for land, §8.01-236.
Equal credit opportunities.
Remedies for provision violations, §6.2-505.
Tolling, §6.2-510.
Equity securities of domestic stock insurers.
Restrictions upon purchase and sale, action to recover profits, §38.2-214.
Escheat.
Recovery of money paid into state treasury, §55-200.
Estate tax.
Criminal prosecutions, §19.2-8.
Evictions.
Mortgagee relief from forfeiture, §55-241.
Relief against such forfeiture, §55-240.
Suits against landlord, §55-248.
Tenant relief, §55-247.
Trustee relief from forfeiture, §55-241.
Executions.
Enforcement of judgment, §8.01-251.
Motion within five years, §§8.01-255.2, 8.01-476.
New execution after loss of property sold under indemnity bond, §§8.01-255.2, 8.01-476.
Executors, administrators or officers unable to receive service or defend suit.
Authority excludes defending actions or expiration of duties.
Filing tolls statute of limitations if suit names proper estate of deceased, §8.01-6.2.
Extension of time.
Suspension of statute. See within this heading, "Suspension of statute."
Fair housing.
Civil action by aggrieved person, §36-96.18.
Fee simple determinable.
Action for determination of determinable fee simple estate, §8.01-255.1.
Felony.
Within what time an indictment for felony must be tried or accused be forever discharged, §19.2-243.
Fiduciaries.
Annual settlement not required when statement filed within year in pending suit, §64.2-1217.
Bonds, §8.01-245.
Distribution of estate.
Suit for refund within five years, §64.2-556.

STATUTE OF LIMITATIONS —Cont'd
Fiduciaries —Cont'd
Exhibition of accounts every three years when sum does not exceed $10,000, §64.2-1313.
Inventories.
Filing with commissioners of accounts within four months, §64.2-1300.
Liability for failure to make defense, §64.2-1415.
Personal actions based on contracts, §8.01-246.
Fieri facias.
Judgment liens.
When lien ceases, §8.01-505.
When writ may be destroyed, §8.01-484.
Food and beverage tax.
Criminal prosecutions, §19.2-8.
Foreign countries.
Actions on contracts governed by law of another country barred in Virginia, §8.01-247.
Forest products tax.
Criminal prosecutions, §19.2-8.
Fraud and deceit.
Contract actions, §8.01-248.
Medical malpractice claims, §8.01-243.
Personal actions, §8.01-243.
When cause of action deemed to accrue, §8.01-249.
Frauds, statute of, §11-2.
Fraudulent and voluntary conveyances.
Loans of goods and chattels.
Recordation within five years, §55-87.
Pretend loans and reservations to be recorded, §55-87.
Freedom of information.
District court proceedings to enforce rights and privileges, §16.1-83.
Fuel taxes, §§58.1-2285, 58.1-2286.
Sales tax in certain transportation districts.
Limitations period for imposition of tax, §58.1-2299.16.
Waiver of time limit, §58.1-2299.17.
Fugitives from justice.
Limitation on prosecutions not applicable to fugitives, §19.2-8.
Funds in court registry.
Recovery of unclaimed money paid into state treasury, §8.01-605.
Gambling contracts, §11-15.
Gambling losses, recovery, §11-15.
General assembly.
Conflicts of interest.
Prosecution of violations, §30-128.
Gifts.
Suits to avoid, §8.01-253.
Grants.
Suits to repeal grant, §8.01-238.
Ground rents.
Actions for recovery, §8.01-239.
Groundwater management.
Criminal prosecution, §62.1-270.
Guardian and ward.
Fiduciaries. See within this heading, "Fiduciaries."
Liability for failure to make defense, §64.2-1415.
Health insurance.
Contestability period, §38.2-3528.
Individual policies, §38.2-3503.
Legal actions, §38.2-3540.
Highways.
Suits on contracts for construction, §§33.1-192, 33.1-192.1.
Execution after June 30, 1976, §33.1-192.1.

STATUTE OF LIMITATIONS —Cont'd
Human rights, division of.
Filing of complaint deemed filing with any state agency in terms of compliance with time limits, §2.2-522.
Husband and wife.
Descent and distribution.
Elective share of surviving spouse.
When share may be claimed, §64.2-303.
Limitation not applicable to prosecution for desertion or nonsupport of wife or child, §19.2-8.
Renunciation of will, §64.2-303.
Implied warranties on new homes, breach, §55-70.1.
Income tax.
Assessment of tax imposed, §58.1-312.
Criminal prosecutions, §19.2-8.
Individual taxpayers.
Failure or refusal to file return or making false statement, §58.1-348.
Income tax withholding.
Refunds on overpayments, §58.1-479.
Indemnification.
When cause of action deemed to accrue, §8.01-249.
Injunctions.
Suspension of statute.
Actions stayed by injunctions, §8.01-229.
Insurance.
Birth-related neurological injury compensation.
Time for filing claim, §38.2-5013.
Tolling statute by filing claim, §38.2-5005.
Life insurance.
Group life insurance policies.
Prohibited policy provisions, §38.2-3338.
Industrial life insurance policies.
Prohibited provisions, §38.2-3354.
Prohibited policy provisions, §§38.2-3316, 38.2-3354.
Policies provisions, §38.2-314.
Life insurance policies, §§38.2-3316, 38.2-3338, 38.2-3354.
Insurance information and privacy protection, individual remedies, §38.2-617.
Interest.
Usury, §6.2-305.
Interstate family support.
Arrearages, §20-88.69.
Invasion of privacy.
Unauthorized use of name or picture, §8.01-40.
Judgments and decrees.
Attachment and garnishment.
Rehearing when judgment rendered on publication, §8.01-575.
Defendants served by publication and not appearing.
Petition for rehearing, §8.01-322.
Enforcement, §8.01-251.
Liens.
Fieri facias.
When lien ceases, §8.01-505.
Limitations on enforcement of judgments, §8.01-251.
New action after arrest or reversal of judgment, §8.01-229.
Setting aside default judgments, §8.01-428.
Suit to enforce judgment lien.
When lien of fieri facias ceases, §8.01-505.
Judicial sales.
Disturbance of purchaser's title, §8.01-113.

STATUTE OF LIMITATIONS —Cont'd
Junk fax.
Tort liability for injury, §8.01-40.2.
Juvenile and domestic relations district courts.
Errors.
Time for raising claim of error, §16.1-272.1.
Juvenile proceedings, adjudicatory or transfer hearings, §16.1-277.1.
Labor and employee relations.
Free speech rights under federal labor law, §8.01-243.
Landlord and tenant.
Against person in possession by reentry, §55-248.
Distress, §55-230.
Ejectment, §§55-240 to 55-242, 55-247, 55-248.
Evictions.
Mortgagee relief from forfeiture, §55-241.
Relief against forfeiture, §55-240.
Suits against landlord, §55-248.
Tenant relief, §55-247.
Trustee relief from forfeiture, §55-241.
Reentry upon premises, §§55-240 to 55-242, 55-247, 55-248.
Against person in possession by reentry, §55-248.
Relief from forfeiture for tenant's breach of covenant, §55-241.
Relief of owner, etc., in equity, §55-242.
Time in which tenant restored to possession, §55-247.
When defendant barred of relief, §55-240.
Relief from forfeiture for tenant's breach of covenant, §55-241.
Time in which tenant restored to possession, §55-247.
Time within which rent may be distrained, §55-230.
Larceny.
Petit larceny, §19.2-8.
Law-enforcement employees, firefighters and emergency medical technicians.
Overtime compensation, §9.1-705.
Leases, UCC.
Default, §8.2A-506.
Legacies.
Enforcement of legacies, §8.01-254.
Lemon law, §59.1-207.16.
Letters of credit, §8.5A-115.
Libel, §8.01-247.1.
Liens.
Assessments for water, sewers or sidewalks, §8.01-240.
Condominiums.
Assessment liens, §55-79.84.
Judgment liens.
Fieri facias.
When lien ceases, §8.01-505.
Mechanics' liens, §43-17.
Unpaid purchase money, §8.01-241.
Extension of limitation form, §8.01-241.1.
Water, sewer or sidewalk assessments, §8.01-240.
Life insurance, contestability period, §38.2-3107.
Excluded or restricted coverage, inapplicability, §38.2-3110.
Group life insurance, §38.2-3326.
Policy provisions, §38.2-3338.
Individual life insurance, §38.2-3305.
Industrial life insurance, §38.2-3345.
Policy provisions, §38.2-3354.

STATUTE OF LIMITATIONS —Cont'd
Life insurance, contestability period —Cont'd
Reinstated policy, running of period not affected, §38.2-3109.
Litter tax.
Criminal prosecutions, §19.2-8.
Local tax collection, §58.1-3940.
Malfeasance in office, §19.2-8.
Malicious prosecution.
Accrual of actions, §8.01-249.
Mandamus.
Petition for mandamus, §8.01-644.1.
Manslaughter.
No limitation on prosecutions, §19.2-8.1.
Marriage.
Transfers upon consideration of marriage, §8.01-253.
Mechanics' and materialmen's liens.
Claims in memorandum, §43-4.
Enforcement, §43-17.
Perfection.
General contractors, §43-4.
Suit to enforce lien, §43-17.
Medicaid fraud.
Fraudulently obtaining benefits or payments, §32.1-312.
Unintentionally obtaining excess benefits, §32.1-313.
Medical malpractice, §8.01-243.
Action against health care provider, §§8.01-243, 8.01-243.1.
Minors, §8.01-243.1.
Review panel.
Joinder of additional parties or causes of action, §8.01-581.2:1.
Rendition of opinion, §8.01-581.7:1.
Medical malpractice review panels.
Joinder of additional parties or causes of action, §8.01-581.2:1.
Rendition of panel's opinion, §8.01-581.7:1.
Mentally ill.
Claims against the state.
Suit to impeach or establish will, §64.2-448.
Saving in favor of person of unsound mind, §64.2-448.
Suspension of statute.
Disabilities which toll statute of limitations, §8.01-229.
Military active duty of party or attorney.
Extension of time for filing pleading, §44-97.1.
Minors.
Abuse and neglect of children.
When cause of action deemed to accrue, §8.01-249.
Actions by parent or guardian against tort-feasor, §8.01-243.
Controlled substances.
Liability of drug dealers, §8.01-227.7.
Desertion and nonsupport, §19.2-8.
Disabilities which toll statute of limitations, §8.01-229.
Wills.
Suit to impeach or establish will, §64.2-448.
Saving in favor of infants, §64.2-448.
Misdemeanors.
Generally, §19.2-8.
Money.
Bond deposit.
Bank or personal corporation doing banking business, §8.01-249.

STATUTE OF LIMITATIONS —Cont'd
Money —Cont'd
Escheat.
Recovery of money paid into state treasury, §55-200.
Liens.
Unpaid purchase money, §8.01-241.
Unpaid purchase money.
No maturity date given, §8.01-242.
Monopolies and corporate trusts.
Virginia antitrust act, §59.1-9.14.
Mortgages and deeds of trust.
Limitation of enforcement, §8.01-241.
Extension of limitation form, §8.01-241.1.
No maturity date given, §8.01-242.
Objections to irregularities in advertising sales made by trustees under deeds of trust, §55-24.
Rent.
Relief from forfeiture for nonpayment, §55-241.
Mortgages and deeds of trust and deeds of trust.
Enforcement of lien.
Extension of limitation forms, §8.01-241.1.
Limitation of enforcement, §8.01-241.
No maturity date given, §8.01-242.
Objections to irregularities in advertising sales made by trustees under deeds of trust, §55-24.
Rent.
Relief from forfeiture for nonpayment, §55-241.
Motions.
Executions.
Motion within five years for new execution, §8.01-476.
Motor fuel and special fuel tax.
Criminal prosecutions, §19.2-8.
Motor vehicle warranties.
Enforcement, §59.1-207.16.
Murder.
No limitation on prosecutions, §19.2-8.1.
Museums.
Property loaned to, recovering, §55-210.32.
Mutual assessment life, accident and sickness insurers.
Fraudulent misstatements of defense, §38.2-3911.
Incontestability of policy, §38.2-3912.
Mutual holding companies conversion to stock holding companies, §§38.2-1005.1:1 to 38.2-1005.1:13.
Negotiable instruments, §8.3A-118.
Deposit accounts and certificates of deposit, §8.3A-118.1.
New homes, breach of implied warranties, §55-70.1.
New promise in writing.
Effect, §8.01-229.
Nonfelonious offenses.
Malfeasance in office, §19.2-8.
Nonprofit corporations, claims against dissolved corporations, §§13.1-908, 13.1-908.1.
Nonresidents.
Rehearing.
Parties served by publication and not appearing, §8.01-322.
Suit to impeach or establish will, §64.2-448.
Saving in favor of nonresident, §64.2-448.
Nonsuit.
Suspension or tolling of statute of limitations, §8.01-229.

STATUTE OF LIMITATIONS —Cont'd
Taxes —Cont'd
Correction of erroneous tax assessments —Cont'd
State taxes —Cont'd
Protective claim for refund, §58.1-1824.
Criminal prosecutions, §19.2-8.
Delinquent taxes.
Period of limitations on collection, §58.1-1802.1.
Forest products tax.
Remedy of aggrieved taxpayer.
Limitation, §58.1-1622.
Fraudulent returns.
Commencement of prosecutions, §58.1-452.
Insurance companies.
Estimated taxes.
Refunds, §58.1-2526.
Local improvements.
Appeal by property owner, §15.2-2410.
Local taxes.
Limitation on collection, §58.1-3940.
Waiver of time limitation on assessment, §58.1-3903.1.
Motor fuel and special fuel tax.
Criminal prosecutions, §19.2-8.
Refunds of local taxes erroneously paid, §58.1-3990.
Refunds, protective claim, §58.1-1824.
Release of liens for taxes delinquent twenty years or more, §58.1-3341.
Retail sales and use tax.
Period of limitations, §58.1-634.
Sales and use tax.
Imposition of tax by chapter, §58.1-634.
Tax returns.
Amended return, filing, §58.1-1823.
Tax returns.
Filing amended returns, §58.1-1823.
Third-party claims, §8.01-243.
Time-shares, §55-383.
Tire tax.
Criminal prosecutions, §19.2-8.
Tolling of statutes. See within this heading, "Suspension of statute."
Torts.
Personal injuries, §8.01-243.
Toxic substances.
Discharge, dumping or emission, §19.2-8.
Trade secrets, §59.1-340.
Uniform trade secrets act.
Action for misappropriation, §59.1-340.
Trespass on land, §8.01-243.
Trusts.
Custodial trusts.
Limitation of actions against custodial trustees, §64.2-915.
Revocable trusts.
Contesting validity, §64.2-753.
Trustee, actions against, §64.2-796.
Unauthorized use of name or picture, §8.01-40.
Unclaimed property.
Effect of expiration of action period, §55-210.17.
Enforcement of provisions, §55-210.25.
Judicial review of decisions of state treasurer, §55-210.22.
Unemployment compensation, §60.2-514.
False statements to obtain or increase benefits, §19.2-8.
Taxation.
Proceeding to establish liability for taxes, §60.2-514.

STATUTE OF LIMITATIONS —Cont'd
Ungranted shores of sea, marsh and meadowlands.
Claim to lands designated in inventory, §28.2-1509.
Ungranted shores of the sea.
Claims to designated land, §28.2-1511.
Effect of legal disability, §28.2-1512.
Uniform computer information transactions act, §59.1-508.5.
Uniform statewide building code.
Civil penalty, §36-106.
Criminal prosecutions for violations, §19.2-8.
Unlawful search and seizure, §8.01-243.
Unsolicited facsimile transmissions.
Tort liability for injury, §8.01-40.2.
Usury, §6.2-305.
Warehouse receipts.
Contractual limitation of warehouseman's liability, §8.7-204.
Limitation in receipt or tariff, §8.7-204.
Warranties.
Real estate cooperatives, §§55-490, 55-491.
Warrants for payment of money drawn on local treasurers.
Presentation within two years required, §58.1-3134.
Waste management violations.
Commencing prosecutions, §10.1-1455.
Water and waste authority bonds.
Time for contesting validity, §15.2-5126.
Water companies and waterworks.
Assessment.
Liens for assessments, §8.01-240.
Waters of the state.
Ground water management, §62.1-270.
Pollution control offenses, §§62.1-44.31, 62.1-44.32.
Wills.
Bona fide purchasers of real estate.
Devises without notice, §64.2-456.
Intestacy, §64.2-458.
Later wills, §64.2-457.
Elective shares.
Claiming, §64.2-302.
Extension of time, §64.2-303.
Probate.
Clerk orders.
Appeals, §64.2-445.
Establishment bills, §64.2-448.
Tolling, §64.2-448.
Impeachment bills, §64.2-448.
Tolling, §64.2-448.
Refunds of distributions, §64.2-556.
Settlement of accounts and distributions.
Claims, §64.2-552.
Witness fees.
Claim for allowance for attendance and mileage.
Time limit on presenting claim for payment, §17.1-615.
Workers' compensation, §65.2-601.
Appeal from award, §65.2-706.
Filing time, §§65.2-601, 65.2-602.
Incapacity after permanent loss, §65.2-501.
Occupational diseases claims, §§65.2-405, 65.2-406.
Person under disability, §65.2-528.
Tolling of statute of limitations, §65.2-602.
Occupational disease claims, §65.2-405.
Workers' compensation award found void ab initio.
Tolling of limitations applicable to civil actions on claim, §8.01-229.

STATUTE OF LIMITATIONS —Cont'd
Writing.
New promise in writing, §8.01-229.
Wrongful death, §8.01-244.
Improvements to real property.
Damages arising out of defective or unsafe condition of improvement, §8.01-250.
No action when deceased has compromised claim, §8.01-51.
Wrongful discharge, §8.01-243.
Zoning.
Appeals to board of zoning appeals, §15.2-2311.
Zoning decision by local governing body.
Time for filing contest, §15.2-2285.

STATUTE OF REPOSE, §8.01-250.
Banking.
Objections to debiting of accounts, §8.4A-505.
Mines and minerals, §55-154.

STATUTES.
Code of Virginia generally, §§1-1 to 1-9.
See CODE OF VIRGINIA.
Full faith and credit clause, US Const Art IV §1.
International law.
Power of congress to punish offenses against, US Const Art I §8.
President of the United States.
Approval of laws by president, US Const Art I §7.
Veto, US Const Art I §7.
Retroactive laws.
Ex post facto laws.
Prohibited, US Const Art I §§9, 10.
Rules of statutory construction generally.
See STATUTORY CONSTRUCTION.
Supreme law of the land, US Const Art VI.

STATUTORY AGENT FOR SERVICE OF PROCESS OR NOTICE.
Address for mailing of process, §8.01-312.
Specific addresses, §8.01-313.
Certificate filed with court, §8.01-326.1.
Copy of process sent to defendant, §8.01-326.1.
Defined, §8.01-285.
Duties of agent, §8.01-312.
Effective date of service, §8.01-326.1.
Effect of service on, §8.01-312.
Legal force and validity, §8.01-312.
Motor vehicle weight violation.
Operator of vehicle statutory agent, §46.2-1132.
Nonresident aircraft operator or owner.
Secretary of Commonwealth, §8.01-309.
Nonresident motor vehicle operator.
Address for mailing process, §8.01-313.
Commissioner of DMV, §8.01-308.
Secretary of Commonwealth.
Service on generally, §8.01-329.
State corporation commission.
Service on clerk generally, §12.1-19.1.
Time for nonresident to respond for process from statutory agent, §8.01-312.
Unincorporated associations or orders or unincorporated common carriers.
Principal office outside state and transacting business in state, §8.01-306.

STATUTORY BURGLARY.
Entering dwelling with intent to commit larceny, assault and battery or other felony, §18.2-91.
Entering dwelling with intent to commit murder, rape, arson or robbery, §18.2-90.

STATUTORY BURGLARY —Cont'd
Entering dwelling with intent to commit other misdemeanor, §18.2-92.

STATUTORY CONSTRUCTION.
Absentee and early voting.
Military and overseas voters, §24.2-469.
Age of majority, §1-204.
Boat titling.
Uniform certificate of title for watercraft, §29.1-733.27.
Citations.
Short title citations, §1-244.
Constitutional references, §1-211.
County government.
Optional forms of government.
Change in form.
Effect, §1-229.
Criminal procedure, §§19.2-1 to 19.2-5.
Defined terms.
See DEFINED TERMS.
Deletions.
Stricken language for deletions, §1-246.
Effective dates of laws, §1-214.
Gender.
Masculine includes feminine and neuter, §1-216.
General rules of construction, §1-202.
Headlines of sections, §1-217.
Italics for additions or changes, §1-246.
Magistrates.
Transitional provisions, §§19.2-26 to 19.2-29.
Mail.
Certified mail equivalent to registered mail, §1-206.
Subsequent notices sent by regular mail, §1-206.
Majority authority, §1-222.
Manufacturer, §1-222.1.
Number, §1-227.
Ordinances.
Local ordinance incorporating state law by reference, §1-220.
Supremacy of federal and state law over, §1-248.
Parent and child.
Rights of parents to make decisions concerning upbringing, education and care of child, §1-240.1.
Political subdivisions.
Delegation of duties assigned to, §1-213.
Population of counties, cities, towns and political subdivisions.
Classifications, §1-236.
Defined, §1-235.
Reenactment.
Definition of reenacted, §1-238.
Repeal.
Construction against implied repeal, §1-239.
Revival of former act.
Repeal of repealing act not to effect, §1-240.
Severability, §1-243.
Short title citations, §1-244.
Stricken language for deletions, §1-246.
Summaries of legislation, §1-247.
Supremacy of federal and state law over, §1-248.
Time, computation, §1-210.
Time zone, §1-253.
Weights and measures, §1-256.

STATUTORY EMPLOYER ACT, §65.2-302.

STATUTORY RAPE.
Carnal knowledge of child between thirteen and fifteen years of age, §18.2-63.
Convict escape or release notice, §53.1-160.1.

STATUTORY RAPE —Cont'd
Carnal knowledge of child between thirteen and fifteen years of age —Cont'd
Jail prisoner escape or release notice, §53.1-116.1.
Juvenile detained in jail, detention facility or committed to juvenile justice department, §18.2-64.1.
Jail prisoner escape or release notice, §53.1-116.1.
Prisoner intake notice, §53.1-116.1:01.
Prisoner intake notice, §53.1-116.1:01.
Punishment upon conviction of certain subsequent felony sexual assault, §18.2-67.5:2.
Child sexual abuse generally.
See CHILD SEXUAL ABUSE.
Incest, §18.2-366.
Adult survivor.
When cause of action deemed to accrue, §8.01-249.
Sentence of person twice previously convicted of certain violent felonies, §19.2-297.1.
Sexual assault, §18.2-63.
Commonwealth's attorneys.
Multidisciplinary response to sexual assault, §15.2-1627.4.
Convict escape or release notice, §53.1-160.1.
Suspension of sentence, placing on probation, §19.2-303.

STAUNTON.
Blue Ridge regional tourism council, §§2.2-2609, 2.2-2610.
Circuit court, establishment, §17.1-500.
Confederate cemeteries and graves.
Disbursement of funds appropriated for upkeep, §10.1-2211.
Medical care facilities.
Certificates of public need.
Moratorium exceptions, §32.1-102.3:2.
Public defenders office.
Established, §19.2-163.04.
Revolutionary war cemeteries and graves.
Disbursement of funds appropriated for upkeep, §10.1-2211.1.
Shenandoah Valley regional airport commission, 1956 ch 628, 1958 ch 396, 1978 ch 18, 1988 ch 209, 1994 ch 773.

STAUNTON RIVER.
Scenic river, §10.1-418.

STAYS.
Arbitration.
Proceedings to stay arbitration, §8.01-581.02.
Attorney discipline.
Stays pending appeals.
Appeals from board proceedings, VA SCt Rule Pt 6 §IV Par 13-26.
Bail and recognizance.
Stay of execution to allow for expedited hearing at higher court.
Grant or denial of bail, §19.2-124.
Increase, revocation or ordering new or additional sureties, §19.2-132.
Capital punishment.
Habeas corpus, §53.1-232.1.
Derivative proceedings by stockholders.
Review and evaluation of allegations commenced by corporation, §13.1-672.1.
Executions.
Motion to quash, §8.01-477.

STAYS —Cont'd
Executions —Cont'd
Writ of actual innocence.
Effect on execution dates and stays, §19.2-327.3.
Immunity of county from city-initiated annexation and city incorporation.
Annexation or corporation proceedings commenced prior to filing petition, §15.2-3301.
Insolvent insurers, proceedings to which party.
Defense by Virginia life, accident and sickness insurance guaranty association, §38.2-1714.
Defense by Virginia property and casualty insurance guaranty association, §38.2-1616.
Limited liability companies.
Derivative actions, stay of proceedings, §13.1-1042.
Medical malpractice review panels.
Request for review of malpractice claims, §8.01-581.2.
New trial.
Effect of failure to make motion for a new trial, §8.01-384.
Public contracts, protest of award, §2.2-4362.
Security for appeal, suspension of execution of judgment.
Limitation, dissipation of assets, §8.01-676.1.
State corporation commission.
Petitions for writs of, §12.1-41.
Zoning appeals, §15.2-2311.

STEAM BATHS.
Medicine and other healing arts professions.
Exceptions and exemptions from licensure, §54.1-2901.

STEAMSHIP COMPANIES.
Dead bodies used for scientific study.
Receipts, §32.1-299.
Employee liens, §§43-24 to 43-26.
Nonresident companies.
Liability as common carrier, §56-122.
Public service companies generally, §§56-1 to 56-87.
See PUBLIC SERVICE COMPANIES.
Special regulatory revenue tax, §§58.1-2660 to 58.1-2665.
Tickets acquired in violation of credit card fraud statute.
Discounted ticket obtained from other than agent of company.
Presumption ticket acquired under circumstances constituting violation of provisions, §18.2-198.
Transportation companies generally, §§56-99.2 to 56-140.
See TRANSPORTATION COMPANIES.

STEAM SIGNAL ACT, §56-414.

STEEPLECHASES.
ABC equine event licenses.
Authorized conduct, §4.1-206.
Local license taxes, §4.1-233.
State license fees, §4.1-231.
Equine activity liability act, §§3.2-6200 to 3.2-6203.
Pari-mutual wagering license, §59.1-378.1.

STEERING AND SUSPENSION SYSTEMS, §§46.2-1063 to 46.2-1065.
Fine schedule, VA SCt Rule 3B:2.
Maximum fine for violating Title 46.2, §46.2-113.

STEERS.
Larceny, §18.2-97.
Livestock.
Diseases.
See LIVESTOCK AND ANIMAL DISEASES.
Generally.
See LIVESTOCK.

STEM CELL RESEARCH.
Christopher Reeve stem cell research fund, §§23-286.1, 23-286.2.

STEPCHILDREN.
Assault and battery against family or household member, §§18.2-57.2, 18.2-57.3.

STEPPARENTS.
Assault and battery against family or household member, §§18.2-57.2, 18.2-57.3.
Custody or visitation of child awarded to person with legitimate interest, §§20-124.1, 20-124.2.
Juvenile proceedings to consider custody, visitation, support, etc.
Petitions filed by party with legitimate interest, §§16.1-241, 16.1-278.15, 20-107.2.

STEPS TO ADVANCE VIRGINIA'S ENERGY PLAN (SAVE).
Natural gas utilities.
SAVE plans, §§56-603, 56-604.

STERILIZATION.
Dogs and cats, §§3.2-6574 to 3.2-6580.
Special license plates for supporters of dog and cat sterilization programs, §46.2-749.2:7.
Humans, §§54.1-2974 to 54.1-2980.

STERLING SILVER SALES, §18.2-233.

STEROIDS.
Drug control act.
Generally, §§54.1-3400 to 54.1-3472.
See DRUG CONTROL.
Drug offenses.
Generally, §§18.2-247 to 18.2-264.
See DRUG OFFENSES.
Manufacturing, selling, etc., anabolic steroids with intent to manufacture, sell, etc., §18.2-248.5.
Physical therapists.
Administration of certain topical drugs, §54.1-3408.
Public high school students.
Use of anabolic steroids by student during athletic training period.
Ineligibility to compete in athletic competitions, §22.1-276.3.
Schedule III controlled drug, §54.1-3450.
Teachers.
Anabolic steroids.
Procuring, selling, administering.
Suspension or revocation of license, §22.1-292.2.

STEWARDS.
Appointment by racing commission, §59.1-370.
Summary suspension of pari-mutuel wagering permits, §59.1-390.

STICKER PRICE.
Motorcycle dealers advertising, §46.2-1993.81.
Motor vehicle advertising, §46.2-1581.
T&M vehicle dealer advertising, §46.2-1990.
Trailer dealer advertising, §46.2-1992.84.

STILLBORN BABIES.
Certificate of birth resulting in still birth, §32.1-258.1.

STILLS OR DISTILLING EQUIPMENT.
Articles subject to forfeiture, §4.1-336.
Confiscation proceedings, §4.1-338.
Illegal manufacture and bottling, §§4.1-300, 4.1-301, 4.1-314.

STIPULATIONS.
Depositions.
Audio-visual depositions, §8.01-412.4.
Discovery, VA SCt Rule 4:4.
Dispute resolution proceedings.
Effect of written settlement agreement, §8.01-576.11.
Eminent domain.
Dismissal of proceedings, §25.1-251.
Judge pro tempore of circuit court.
Hearing cases, §17.1-110.
Sizes of type in printed contracts, §11-4.
Spousal support.
Effect of stipulations, §20-109.
Summary jury trial.
Documentary and testimony evidence, §8.01-576.3.

STIRRING UP LITIGATION, §§18.2-451 to 18.2-455.

STOCK AND STOCKHOLDERS.
Abandonment of property presumption, §55-210.6:1.
Agricultural cooperative associations, §13.1-322.
Purchasing businesses of other associations, persons, etc., §13.1-338.
Authorized shares.
Defined, §13.1-603.
Banks.
See BANKS.
Building and loan associations.
See SAVINGS INSTITUTIONS.
Commonwealth or unit of government subscribing to, VA Const Art X §10.
Conversion of mutual holding companies to stock holding companies, §§38.2-1005.1:1 to 38.2-1005.1:13.
Cooperative associations.
Investments in other stock, §13.1-303.
Issuance with nominal or par value required, §13.1-301.
Liens on rotating stock, §13.1-310.
Limitation on individual stockholding, §13.1-302.
Permissible limitation of stock ownership, §13.1-307.
Purchasing other business by issuance of shares, §13.1-304.
Subscribers voting of stockholders prior to full payment, §13.1-305.
Corporations.
Shareholders.
Generally, §§13.1-654 to 13.1-671.1.
See CORPORATIONS.
Shares generally, §§13.1-638 to 13.1-653.
See CORPORATIONS.
Credit unions, §§6.2-1300 to 6.2-1380.
See CREDIT UNIONS.
Derivative proceedings, §§13.1-672.1 to 13.1-672.6.
Determination proceedings, §§13.1-776, 13.1-777.
Equity securities of domestic stock insurers.
Restrictions upon purchase and sale, §38.2-214.

STOCK AND STOCKHOLDERS —Cont'd
Financial institutions.
Reclassification or conversion of banking institution shares, §6.2-105.
Industrial development corporations.
Authority for others to acquire, own and transfer, §13.1-988.
Authority to issue, §13.1-986.
Members to have rights of shareholders, §13.1-995.
Inspection of records, §§13.1-771 to 13.1-773.
Insurance companies.
Investments generally, §§38.2-1400 to 38.2-1447.
Intangible personal property tax, §§58.1-1100 to 58.1-1118.
See PERSONAL PROPERTY TAXES.
Interest.
Stock option financing contracts.
Contract rate more than legal rate, §6.2-321.
Investment of public funds.
Legal investments.
Funds other than sinking funds, §2.2-4501.
Investment securities.
Commercial code, §§8.8A-101 to 8.8A-601.
See INVESTMENT SECURITIES.
Nonprofit corporations.
Prohibited, §13.1-814.
Power of attorney.
Authority of agent, §64.2-1627.
Operation of entity or business, §64.2-1630.
Authority of agent as to retirement plans, §64.2-1636.
Preferred stock.
Insurance companies.
Investment in, §38.2-1423.
Professional corporations generally, §§13.1-542.1 to 13.1-556.
See PROFESSIONAL CORPORATIONS.
Public service companies.
Issuance of stocks, bonds, etc., §§56-55 to 56-75.
See PUBLIC SERVICE COMPANIES.
Savings and loan associations.
See SAVINGS INSTITUTIONS.
Securities generally, §§13.1-501 to 13.1-527.3.
See SECURITIES.
Securities registered in joint names, §§13.1-434 to 13.1-436.
Stock insurers converted to mutual insurers.
Acquisition of shares, §38.2-1010.
Outstanding stock, determination of value, §38.2-1015.
Payment for shares, §38.2-1009.
Taxation of corporate stock, VA Const Art X §5.
Trust companies.
See TRUST COMPANIES.
Trusts.
Power of trustee, §64.2-778.
Voting shares or exercising control.
Duty of trustee to act in best interest of beneficiaries, §64.2-764.
Unclaimed property, disposition of, §55-210.6:1.
Utility consumer services cooperatives.
Power to issue nonassessable nonvoting stock, §56-231.23.

STOCK CAR DRIVERS.
Special license plates.
License plates bearing name, numbers and color schemes used by professional drivers, §46.2-749.69:1.

STOCK CORPORATIONS, §§13.1-601 to 13.1-779.
See CORPORATIONS.

STOCK INSURERS.
Conversion of mutual holding companies to stock holding companies, §§38.2-1005.1:1 to 38.2-1005.1:13.
Conversion to mutual insurers, §§38.2-1006 to 38.2-1018.
Incorporation of domestic insurers, §38.2-1000.
Licensing of insurers.
Fully paid in capital stock requirements, §38.2-1028.
Generally, §§38.2-1024 to 38.2-1039.1.
Refusal, suspension or revocation, §§38.2-1040 to 38.2-1044.
Mergers, §§38.2-1017, 38.2-1018.
Title insurance.
Companies authorized to transact title insurance, §38.2-4603.

STOCK OPTIONS.
Corporations, §13.1-646.

STOCKYARDS.
Commission merchants.
Generally, §§3.2-4709 to 3.2-4737.
See COMMISSION MERCHANTS.

STOKING OF FURNACES AND BOILERS.
City or town powers, §15.2-1116.
County regulations, §15.2-1217.

STOLEN GOODS.
Receipt of stolen property.
See RECEIPT OF STOLEN GOODS.
Sale of stolen property, §18.2-108.01.
Secondhand article sales generally, §§59.1-116.1 to 59.1-136.
See SECONDHAND ARTICLE SALES.

STONES OR MISSILES.
Stoning dwellings, §18.2-279.
Throwing at railroad cars, vessels, motor vehicles, etc., §18.2-154.

STONEWALL JACKSON MEMORIAL, INCORPORATED.
Property exempt from taxation, §58.1-3607.

STOP LIGHTS.
Signs, lights and markings generally, §§46.2-830 to 46.2-836.
See TRAFFIC INFRACTIONS.
Supplemental high mount stop light, §46.2-1014.1.
Fine schedule, VA SCt Rule 3B:2.
Maximum fine for violating Title 46.2, §46.2-113.

STOP ORDERS.
Cease and desist orders generally.
See CEASE AND DESIST ORDERS.
Potato board.
Seed potatoes, stop sale orders, §3.2-1819.
Security registration statements.
State corporation commission.
Denying effectiveness or revoking effectiveness, §13.1-513.

STOPPAGE OF DELIVERY.
Leases, UCC.
Right of lessor, §8.2A-526.

STOPPING DISTANCE AND SPEED TABLES, §46.2-880.

STOPPING ON HIGHWAYS.
Traffic infractions.
Generally, §§46.2-888 to 46.2-893.
See TRAFFIC INFRACTIONS.

STOPPING PAYMENT OF CHECK, §8.4-403.
Bank's right to subrogation on improper payment, §8.4-407.
When items subject to stop order, §8.4-303.

STORAGE.
Agricultural commodities.
Warehouse receipts.
Storage under government bond, §8.7-201.
Alcoholic beverages.
Warehouse receipts.
Storage under government bond, §8.7-201.
Self storage insurance, §§38.2-1881 to 38.2-1886.
Unsanitary food conditions, §3.2-5119.

STORAGE BATTERIES, §§59.1-189 to 59.1-191.
See BATTERIES.

STORAGE TANKS.
Building code inspections, §36-99.6.
Financial responsibility of owners and operators, §62.1-44.34:12.
Petroleum storage tank fund, §§62.1-44.34:10 to 62.1-44.34:13.
Virginia petroleum storage tank fund, §62.1-44.34:11.
Waters of the state.
Board powers and duties, §62.1-44.34:9.
Defined terms, §62.1-44.34:8.
Oil discharges, §§62.1-44.34:14 to 62.1-44.34:23.
See OIL DISCHARGES INTO WATERS OF STATE.

STORED-VALUE CARDS.
Scanning device or re-encoder.
Unlawful use on payment card of another, §18.2-196.1.

STOREHOUSES.
See WAREHOUSES AND WAREHOUSEMEN.

STORES.
Drug transactions taking place on premises.
Premises deemed common nuisance, §§18.2-258, 18.2-258.01, 48-16, 48-17.
Fire alarms.
Maliciously activating, §18.2-212.
Fortified drug houses, §18.2-258.02.
Sales of purchaser information, §§59.1-442 to 59.1-444.

STORM DRAIN SYSTEMS.
Oil discharges generally.
See OIL DISCHARGES INTO WATERS OF STATE.
Stormwater management, §§62.1-44.15:24 to 62.1-44.15:50.
See STORMWATER MANAGEMENT.

STORMWATER MANAGEMENT, §§62.1-44.15:24 to 62.1-44.15:50.
Actions, §62.1-44.15:48.
Actions to ensure compliance, §62.1-44.15:38.
Administrative cost recovery, §62.1-44.15:36.
Appeals, §62.1-44.15:46.
Final appeal to Court of Appeals, §62.1-44.15:47.
Rules and regulations, review of validity, §62.1-44.15:43.
Board.
Promulgation of regulations, §10.1-107.

STORMWATER MANAGEMENT —Cont'd
Bonds, surety.
Security for permit, §62.1-44.15:34.
Certificates of competence.
Education and training programs, §62.1-44.15:30.
Chesapeake Bay preservation act land-disturbing activity.
Coverage under VSMP program, §62.1-44.15:34.
Chesapeake Bay watershed nutrient credit exchange program.
Nutrient credit use by regulated entities, §62.1-44.19:21.
Common interest community ceding responsibility to governmental entity.
Immunity for civil liability, §62.1-44.15:41.
Compliance schedule, §62.1-44.15:38.
Confidential information, §62.1-44.15:40.
Cooperation with federal and state agencies, §62.1-44.15:50.
Corrective action agreements, §62.1-44.15:38.
Costs.
Recovery of administrative costs, §62.1-44.15:36.
Definitions, §62.1-44.15:24.
Department.
Duties, §62.1-44.15:32.
Environmental quality department, generally, §§10.1-1182 to 10.1-1187.7.
See ENVIRONMENTAL QUALITY DEPARTMENT.
Review and evaluation schedule, §62.1-44.15:38.
Right of entry, §62.1-44.15:39.
Education and training programs, §62.1-44.15:30.
Enforcement.
MS4 localities.
Authority, §62.1-44.15:49.
Water control board, §62.1-44.15:25.
Establishment of programs, §62.1-44.15:27.
Federal and state agencies.
Cooperation with, §62.1-44.15:50.
Fees.
Permit fees, §62.1-44.15:28.
Standards and specifications, compliance, §62.1-44.15:31.
Fund, §62.1-44.15:29.
Permit fees, §62.1-44.15:28.
Green roof incentive programs.
Rate incentive program based upon stormwater runoff reduction, §15.2-977.
Hearings.
Conduct, §62.1-44.15:45.
Right to hearings, §62.1-44.15:44.
Information to be furnished, §62.1-44.15:40.
Injunctions, §62.1-44.15:48.
Noncompliance with special orders, §62.1-44.15:42.
Inspections, §62.1-44.15:37.
Standards and specifications, compliance, §62.1-44.15:31.
Water control board, §62.1-44.15:25.
Investigations, §62.1-44.15:37.
Water control board, §62.1-44.15:25.
Local program.
Adopting program by ordinance, §15.2-2114.
Enforcement.
MS4 localities, §62.1-44.15:49.
Establishment of programs, §62.1-44.15:27.
Ordinances, more stringent, §62.1-44.15:33.
Monitoring, §62.1-44.15:37.
Nonpoint nutrient offsets.
Nutrient offset fund, §10.1-2128.2.

STROKE TRIAGE PLAN.
Emergency medical services, §32.1-111.3.

STRONTIUM SULFIDE.
Defective drywall.
Consumer protection act.
Definition, §59.1-198.
Violations, §59.1-200.
Correction and restoration assistance fund, §§36-156.1, 36-156.2.
Real estate brokers, salespersons and rental agents.
Disclosures to owner by property manager, §54.1-2135.
Disclosures to prospective buyers, §54.1-2131.
Disclosures to prospective tenants, §§54.1-2133, 54.1-2134.

STRUCTURAL DEFECTS.
Condominium units.
Warranty against, §55-79.79.
Implied warranties on new homes, §55-70.1.

STRUCTURAL FAILURES.
Securing site of, §44-208.

STRUCTURED SETTLEMENTS, §§59.1-475 to 59.1-477.1.
Constriction of provisions, §59.1-477.1.
Definitions, §59.1-475.
Disclosures to payee.
Required disclosures, §59.1-475.1.
Secured transactions.
Third parties.
Assignments.
Restrictions on assignments, §8.9A-406.
Transfer of payment rights.
Agreement, §59.1-477.1.
Approval, §59.1-476.
Procedure, §59.1-477.
Effect, §59.1-476.1.
Waiver of provisions by payee prohibited, §59.1-477.1.

STUART.
Cemeteries.
Location restrictions, §57-26.
Towns generally.
See TOWNS.

STUDDED TIRES, §§46.2-1044, 46.2-1045.
Fine schedule, VA SCt Rule 3B:2.
Pretrial payment of fine, §16.1-69.40:1.

STUDENT ASSISTANCE AUTHORITIES.
Secretary of education.
Agency responsibility, §2.2-208.
Student loans.
Generally, §§23-38.10:2 to 23-38.10:7.
See STUDENT LOANS.

STUDENT FINANCIAL AID.
Brown v. Board of Education scholarship program and fund, §§30-231.01 to 30-231.10.
College savings plan, §§23-38.75 to 23-38.87:1.
See COLLEGE SAVINGS PLAN.
College savings program, §§23-38.72 to 23-38.74.
Community college incentive scholarship program, §§23-220.2 to 23-220.4.
Graduate and undergraduate assistance program, §§23-38.19:1, 23-38.19:2.
Guaranteed assistance program and fund, §§23-38.53:4 to 23-38.53:6.
Loans generally, §§23-38.10:2 to 23-38.10:7.
See STUDENT LOANS.

STUDENT FINANCIAL AID —Cont'd
Scholarship assistance program, §§23-38.45 to 23-38.52.
Scholarships generally, §§23-31 to 23-38.10:1.
See SCHOLARSHIPS.
Stephen J. Wright scholars program, §23-38.53:11.
Tuition assistance grants, §§23-38.11 to 23-38.19:2.
See COLLEGES AND UNIVERSITIES.
Tuition remission.
Senior citizens, §§23-38.54 to 23-38.60.
Unfunded scholarships, §23-31.

STUDENT INTERNSHIP PROGRAMS.
Identification of programs exempt from federal and state laws, §22.1-17.3.

STUDENT LOANS, §§23-38.10:2 to 23-38.10:7.
Additional student loan funds, §23-38.10:7.
Basis of awards, §23-38.10:3.
Biennial audits, §23-38.10:6.
Collection of loans, §23-38.10:4.
Dentist loan repayment program, §32.1-122.9:1.
Health professions.
Suspension of license for delinquency, §54.1-2400.5.
Health workforce recruitment, §32.1-122.20.
Interest.
Contract rate more than legal rate.
Educational loans by banks or savings institutions, §6.2-323.
Educational loans by private college or university, §6.2-324.
Life insurance provisions for, §38.2-3113.3.
Nursing loans.
State board repayment program, §32.1-122.6:01.
Tuition loan repayment program, §32.1-122.6:04.
Payment of loans, §23-38.10:4.
Plea of infancy.
Disaffirmance of contracts, §8.01-278.
Private grants and loans, VA Const Art VIII §11.
Rate of interest, §23-38.10:3.
Student loan vendors.
Policies addressing, §23-4.3:2.
Tax information.
Tax commissioner authorized to divulge to chief executive officer of guarantor, §58.1-3.

STUDENT RECORDS.
Child custody and visitation arrangements.
Access to by either parent, §20-124.6.
Closed meetings.
Educational institution discussing, §2.2-3711.
Colleges and universities.
Birth certificate required as condition of enrollment.
Retention of copy in student's record, §23-2.1:2.
School and mental health records of student upon attendance at institution of higher education, §23-2.1:3.
Evidence, submission of copies, §8.01-390.1.
Parental access to academic records, §20-124.6.
Public school pupils, §§22.1-287 to 22.1-289.
Access to records, §22.1-287.
Cooperation with local law-enforcement agencies, §22.1-288.1.
Directory information, §22.1-287.1.
Furnishing information to public or private schools, colleges, etc., §22.1-288.
Immunization records, §22.1-271.2.
Limitations on access, §22.1-287.

STUDENT RECORDS —Cont'd
Public school pupils —Cont'd
Missing children notations, §22.1-288.1.
Personal identifying information, disclosure, §22.1-287.
Student criminal records.
Dissemination and maintenance, §22.1-288.2.
Transfer of scholastic records, §22.1-289.

STUDY GROUPS.
Gubernatorial commissions to include, §2.2-134.

STUN WEAPONS.
Airports.
Carrying weapon into air carrier airport terminal, §18.2-287.01.
Convicted felons, possession or transportation or concealing, §18.2-308.2.
Courthouses, carrying weapon into, §18.2-283.1.
Defined, §18.2-308.1.
School property, possession on, §18.2-308.1.
Use in commission of crime.
Forfeiture, §19.2-386.29.

STURGEON.
Taking and sale, §28.2-303.

SUBCONTRACTORS.
Building code, §§36-97 to 36-119.1.
See BUILDING CODE.
Contractors generally.
See CONTRACTORS.
Kickbacks.
Public contracts, §2.2-4372.
Mechanics' and materialmen's liens.
Fund improprieties, §43-13.
Perfection, §43-7.
Affidavits.
Sufficiency, §43-8.
Lien of general contractor to inure to benefit of, §43-18.
Memorandums.
Sufficiency, §43-8.
Notice.
Sufficiency, §43-8.
Personal liability of owners or general contractors, §43-11.
Fund improprieties, §43-13.
Public procurement act, §§2.2-4300 to 2.2-4377.
See PUBLIC PROCUREMENT.
Workers' compensation.
Requirements for public construction projects, §2.2-4332.

SUBDIVIDED LAND SALES, §§55-336 to 55-347.
Blanket encumbrances, §55-342.
Common facilities, §55-344.
Defined terms, §55-337.
Exemptions from provisions, §55-338.
Membership camping.
Application of provisions, §59.1-314.
Penalties for provision violations, §55-347.
Property owners' associations, §55-344.
Restraints on alienation, §55-343.
Short title of chapter, §55-336.

SUBDIVIDED LAND SALES ACT OF 1978, §§55-336 to 55-347.
See SUBDIVIDED LAND SALES.

SUBDIVISIONS, §§15.2-2240 to 15.2-2279.
Accounting for fees for common improvements, §15.2-2256.

SUBDIVISIONS —Cont'd
Administration and enforcement of regulations, §15.2-2255.
Advance payments by developer for off-site improvements.
Reimbursement, optional ordinance provisions, §15.2-2242.
Advisory plans examiner board.
Expedited land development review, §15.2-2263.
Urban county executive form of government, §15.2-851.
Amendments to ordinance, §15.2-2253.
Application of county regulations in area subject to municipal jurisdiction, §15.2-2249.
Application of municipal subdivision regulations beyond corporate limits, §15.2-2248.
Bond, escrow, letter of credit or other performance guarantees.
Escrowed funds.
Authority in certain towns to use for other improvements, §15.2-2242.
Periodic partial and final release, §15.2-2245.
Boundary line relocation, §15.2-2275.
Building of houses, ordinances regulating, §15.2-2279.
Chesapeake Bay preservation areas.
Designation by localities in Tidewater Virginia, §62.1-44.15:74.
Enforcement of provisions, authority of local governments, §62.1-44.15:73.
Outside Tidewater area, adoption of provisions, §62.1-44.15:75.
State agency consistency, §62.1-44.15:78.
Clustering of single-family dwellings.
Provisions of subdivision ordinance, §15.2-2242.
Codification or recodification of ordinances, §15.2-1433.
Commercial real estate.
Approval of plats, site plans and development plans, §15.2-2259.
Common improvements.
Accounting for fees, §15.2-2256.
Comprehensive plan.
Generally, §§15.2-2222.1 to 15.2-2232.
See PLANNING AND DEVELOPMENT.
Consent statement by owners, proprietors and trustees.
Plat or deed of dedication to contain, §15.2-2264.
Conveyance of common or shared easements.
Ordinance to include provisions, §15.2-2241.
Conveyance of subdivided property to other than developer or locality.
Validity of final plat approval, time period, §§15.2-2209.1, 15.2-2261.
Coordination of streets, ordinance to include provisions, §15.2-2241.
Cost of certain facilities.
Payment by subdivider of pro rata share, §15.2-2243.
County regulations applied in area subject to municipal jurisdiction, §15.2-2249.
Covenant modification in certain counties, §15.2-2257.
Dam break inundation zone.
Land of proposed subdivision within.
Fact set forth in plat, §15.2-2258.
Subdivision within.
Contract-ready costs for conducting upgrades to impounding structure.
Study, estimate provided, payment by developer, §15.2-2243.1.

SUBDIVISIONS —Cont'd
Dedication for public use, ordinance to include provisions, §15.2-2241.
Bonding requirements for acceptance of dedication, §15.2-2241.1.
Dedication of rights to develop property.
County manager plan of government.
Authority to accept, §15.2-750.
Defined, §15.2-2201.
Development.
Defined, §15.2-2201.
Disagreement between county and municipal as to regulation, §15.2-2250.
Drainage district.
Part of proposed subdivision within.
Fact noted on plat, §15.2-2258.
Easements transferred on recordation of approved plats, §15.2-2265.
Escrowed funds.
Optional provisions of subdivision ordinance.
Authority in certain towns to use funds for other improvements, §15.2-2242.
Expedited land development review, §15.2-2263.
Urban county executive form of government, §15.2-851.
Family members.
Subdivision of lot for conveyance to, §15.2-2244.
Additional method, §15.2-2244.1.
Subdivision of lot held in trust for a family member, §15.2-2244.2.
Grading or paving, locality not obligated to pay for, §15.2-2268.
Home buyers in planned development unit provided copy of approved plat.
Counties requiring, §15.2-1216.
Hunting within one-half mile, county prohibiting, §15.2-1210.
Indexing plats or maps.
Circuit court clerks, §17.1-251.
Inspection prior to release of performance guarantee, §15.2-2245.
Mandatory provisions of subdivision ordinance, §15.2-2241.
Manufactured homes.
Applicability of subdivision ordinance, §15.2-2247.
Modifying covenants in certain counties, §15.2-2257.
Multiple phase development.
Validity of underlying preliminary plat, time period.
Approval of final plat, §§15.2-2209.1, 15.2-2260.
Municipal subdivision regulations applied beyond corporate limits, §15.2-2248.
Notice of change, amendment, alteration or deletion of ordinances.
Codification or recodification of ordinances, §15.2-1433.
Notice of plans, ordinances or amendments generally, §15.2-2204.
Official map of locality, §§15.2-2233 to 15.2-2238.
Off-site improvements, funding.
Optional ordinance provisions, §15.2-2242.
Open space developments, preservation of.
Provisions of subdivision ordinance, §15.2-2242.
Optional provisions of subdivision ordinance, §15.2-2242.
Ordinance to assure orderly subdivision of land and development.
Adoption by locality, §15.2-2240.

SUBDIVISIONS —Cont'd
Ordinance to assure orderly subdivision of land and development —Cont'd
Amendments, preparation and adoption, §15.2-2253.
Changing, altering, amending, etc., in codification or recodification, §15.2-1433.
Codification or recodification, §15.2-1433.
Filing and recording, §15.2-2252.
Mandatory provisions, §15.2-2241.
Notice and public hearing, §15.2-2251.
Optional provisions of ordinance, §15.2-2242.
Payment by subdivider of pro rata share cost of certain facilities, §15.2-2243.
Periodic partial and final release of performance guarantees, §15.2-2245.
Planning commission to prepare and recommend, §15.2-2251.
Subdivision of lot for conveyance to family member, §15.2-2244.
Additional method, §15.2-2244.1.
Subdivision of lot held in trust for a family member, §15.2-2244.2.
Owner's associations, §§55-508 to 55-516.2.
See PROPERTY OWNERS' ASSOCIATIONS.
Payment by developer of pro rate share for off-site improvements.
Optional ordinance provisions, §15.2-2242.
Payments by subdivider.
Pro rata share of cost of certain facilities, §15.2-2243.
Planned unit development.
Defined, §15.2-2201.
Planning and development generally, §§15.2-2200 to 15.2-2239.
See PLANNING AND DEVELOPMENT.
Planning commissions.
Generally, §§15.2-2210 to 15.2-2222.
See PLANNING COMMISSIONS.
Plans examiner board.
Expedited land development review, §15.2-2263.
Urban county executive form of government, §15.2-851.
Plat of subdivision.
Defined, §15.2-2201.
Preparation requirements, §§15.2-2209.1, 15.2-2262.
Proposed plats, §§15.2-2258, 15.2-2259.
Preliminary subdivision plats, §15.2-2260.
Proposed subdivision plat.
Planning commission action, §15.2-2259.
Submission for approval, §15.2-2258.
Provisions of subdivision ordinance.
Mandatory provisions, §15.2-2241.
Optional provisions, §15.2-2242.
Public hearing on ordinances, plans or amendments, §§15.2-1433, 15.2-2204.
Real property taxes.
Lots and open spaces in certain planned development subdivisions, §58.1-3284.1.
Special assessment for land preservation, §§58.1-3229 to 58.1-3244.
See REAL PROPERTY TAXES.
Subdivided or rezoned lots, §58.1-3285.
Recording plat.
Before January 1, 1953, validation, §15.2-2266.
Effect, §15.2-2265.
Provisions effective after ordinance adopted, §15.2-2254.
Validity, §15.2-2261.
Zoning conflicts, §15.2-2261.1.

SUBDIVISIONS —Cont'd
Release of performance guarantees.
Periodic partial and final release, §15.2-2245.
Relocation of boundary lines, §15.2-2275.
Requisites of plat preparation, §§15.2-2209.1, 15.2-2262.
Restraining violation, §15.2-2208.
Restricting ingress and egress to subdivision.
Petition by subdivision inhabitants, §15.2-2267.
Road impact fees, §§15.2-2317 to 15.2-2329.
See ROAD IMPACT FEES.
Setback lines, ordinances regulating and establishing, §15.2-2279.
Sewage, water and drainage facilities.
Payment by subdivider of pro rata share of cost, §15.2-2243.
Sidewalks, sewers, curves and gutter improvements.
Locality not obligated to pay for, §15.2-2268.
Optional provisions of subdivision ordinance, §15.2-2242.
Site plan.
Defined, §15.2-2201.
Submission for approval, §15.2-2258.
Submission in accordance with zoning ordinance, §15.2-2246.
Validity of recorded plan, §15.2-2261.
Statement of consent to subdivision, §15.2-2264.
Statement that streets do not meet state standards.
Optional ordinance provisions, §15.2-2242.
Statutory provisions effective after ordinance adopted, §15.2-2254.
Streets.
Mandatory ordinance provisions, §15.2-2241.
Surveyors, §54.1-408.
Time for filing plat for recordation.
Ordinance provisions, §15.2-2241.
Transfer of streets, alleys or other public use.
Recordation of approved plats to operate as transfer, §15.2-2265.
Tree planting and replacement during development process, §15.2-961.
Conservation of trees.
Locality within Planning District 8 classified as nonattainment area for air quality standards, §15.2-961.1.
Urban county executive form of government.
Expedited land development review, §15.2-851.
Optional provisions of subdivision ordinance, §15.2-851.1.
Utility fixtures and systems, submission for approval, §15.2-2269.
Vacation of interests granted to locality, §15.2-2270.
Vacation of lot lines, §15.2-2275.
Vacation of plat, §15.2-2278.
After sale of lot, §15.2-2272.
Application processing fee, §15.2-2273.
Before sale of lot, §15.2-2271.
Application processing fee, §15.2-2273.
Effect, §15.2-2274.
Duties of clerks when plat vacated, §15.2-2276.
Fee for processing application, §15.2-2273.
County manager plan of government, §15.2-743.
Validation of plats before January 1, 1953, §15.2-2266.
Validity of recorded plats or final site plans.
Time of validity, §§15.2-2209.1, 15.2-2261.
Water, sewer and other facilities, regulations, §15.2-2121.

SUBDIVISIONS —Cont'd
Zoning conflicts with recorded plat or final site plan, §15.2-2261.1.
Zoning ordinance.
Site plans submitted in accordance with, §15.2-2246.

SUBJECT MATTER JURISDICTION.
Jurisdiction generally.
See JURISDICTION.

SUBLEASES.
Landlord preapproval and rental agreement provisions.
Residential landlords and tenants, §55-248.7.
Leases, UCC, §8.2A-305.
Defined, §8.2A-103.
Prior approval by landlord.
Residential landlords and tenants, §55-248.7.
Unlawful sublease of motor vehicle, §18.2-115.1.

SUBMERGED AQUATIC VEGETATION (SAV).
Permits for use of state-owned bottomlands.
Effect on considered when granting or denying, §28.2-1205.
Joint application and review process.
Coordinated review of water resources projects, §28.2-1205.1.

SUBMERGED LANDS, §§28.2-1200 to 28.2-1213.
Boundaries of abutting owners, §28.2-1202.
Commercial fishing piers.
Construction requirements, §28.2-302.
Commission authority, §28.2-1204.
Commonwealth, conveyance of state-owned bottomlands, §28.2-1200.1.
Defined terms.
Lawful survey, §28.2-1202.
Easements, §28.2-1208.
Irrigation of subaqueous beds, §28.2-1203.
Islands.
Unappropriated islands which rise from common lands, §28.2-1201.
Jurisdiction and ownership of Commonwealth over, §1-302.
Marine habitat and waterways improvement fund, §28.2-1204.2.
Natural oyster beds, rocks or shores.
Issuance of grants, §28.2-1200.
Penalties for violations, §§28.2-1211, 28.2-1213.
Permits.
Cessation of activities, §28.2-1212.
Compliance, §28.2-1212.
Encroachments, §28.2-1207.
Fees, §28.2-1206.
Inspections, §28.2-1212.
Monitoring, §28.2-1212.
Use of state-owned bottom lands, §28.2-1205.
Joint application and review process.
Coordinated review of water resources projects, §28.2-1205.1.
Property obstructions or hazards.
Removal, §28.2-1210.
Renewable energy leases, §28.2-1208.
Restoration, §28.2-1212.
Structures, maintenance or removal, §28.2-1209.
Submerged aquatic vegetation.
Development of guidelines, §28.2-1204.1.
Ungranted beds to remain in common, §28.2-1200.
Unlawful use of subaqueous beds, §28.2-1203.
Injunctions, §28.2-1211.

SUBORDINATION OF COMMERCIAL CODE LEASE.
Priority subject to, §8.2A-311.

SUBPOENA DUCES TECUM ISSUED BY CLERK OF COURT, VA SCt Rule 4:9.
Production by a person not party, VA SCt Rule 4:9A.

SUBPOENAS.
Administrative process act.
Hearings, §2.2-4022.
Antitrust laws.
Investigations by attorney general, §59.1-9.10.
Arbitration.
Attendance of witnesses, §8.01-581.06.
Production of documents and things, §8.01-581.06.
Attorney discipline.
District committees proceedings, VA SCt Rule Pt 6 §IV Par 13-16.
Limited right to discovery, VA SCt Rule Pt 6 §IV Par 13-11.
Attorneys at law.
Authority of board, §54.1-3925.3.
Criminal subpoena directed to member of bar, VA SCt Rule 3A:12.
Discipline or disability proceedings, §54.1-3938.1.
Bail bondsmen.
Criminal justice services department investigations, §9.1-185.3.
Bail enforcement agents.
Criminal justice services department, §9.1-186.3.
Boat dealers.
Hearings.
Director powers, §29.1-803.
Building code technical review board.
Compelling attendance of witnesses, §36-115.
Checks.
State treasurer.
Subpoenas to produce checks or drafts, §2.2-1812.
Child support enforcement.
Power of department social services, §63.2-1903.
Commissioners in chancery.
Compelling attendance of witnesses, §8.01-612.
Commission on human rights.
County manager plan of government, §15.2-725.
Condominiums.
Real estate board.
Investigations of complaints, §55-79.99.
Continuing and community-based care providers.
Investigation and subpoena powers of commission, §38.2-4930.
County board form of government.
Inquiry into official conduct of office or officer, §15.2-403.
County, city or town governing body.
Investigations relating to governmental affairs, §15.2-1409.
County executive form of government.
Inquiry into official conduct of office or officer, §15.2-506.
County manager form of government.
Inquiry into official conduct of office or officer.
Issuance by board of supervisors, §15.2-606.
County manager plan of government.
Commission on human rights, §15.2-725.
Inquiry into official conduct of office or officer, §15.2-709.
Courts-martial, naval militia.
Powers to issue, §44-70.

SUBPOENAS —Cont'd
Credit unions.
Examinations.
Powers of commission, §6.2-1309.
Criminal cases.
Compelling attendance of witnesses.
Form, VA SCt Rules Part 3A Appx Form 8.
Criminal procedure.
Compelling attendance of witnesses, VA SCt Rule 3A:12.
Electronic format.
Response to subpoena for information stored in, §19.2-267.2.
Dairies and dairy products.
Milk commission.
Noncompliance with subpoenas of, §3.2-3218.
Death taxes, interstate compromise and arbitration, §58.1-924.
Department of agriculture and consumer services.
Authority to issue for attendance of witnesses, §18.2-340.18.
Discovery.
Uniform interstate depositions and discovery act.
Applicable laws, §8.01-412.11.
Application to court to enforce, quash or modify subpoena, §8.01-412.13.
Defined, §8.01-412.9.
Generally, §8.01-412.10.
Service, §8.01-412.11.
District court clerk, issuance, §16.1-69.40.
District court judges.
Power to issue, §16.1-69.25.
Election contests for general assembly elections, §24.2-803.
Employment records, §8.01-413.1.
Ethics advisory panels, senate and house of general assembly.
Power to issue, §30-115.
Farm produce sales.
Commission merchants.
Agriculture and consumer services commissioner, §§3.2-4723, 3.2-4726.
Fiduciaries.
Subpoena powers, §64.2-1203.
Fishing, tidal waters.
Hearings.
Commission powers, §28.2-216.
Governing bodies of localities.
Investigations relating to governmental affairs, §15.2-1409.
Governor's power to issue, §2.2-109.
Health professions department director.
Powers, §54.1-2506.
Health records.
Disclosure of patient's records in compliance with, §32.1-127.1:03.
Health spas.
Commissioner investigations, §59.1-308.2.
Hospital records, §8.01-413.
Human rights, division of.
Subpoena duces tecum, issuance, §2.2-521.
Insurance companies examinations.
Powers of state corporation commission, §38.2-1318.
Internet.
Identifying anonymous persons.
Tortious or illegal communications, §8.01-407.1.
Invention development services, §59.1-215.
Juvenile proceedings, §16.1-265.

SUBPOENAS —Cont'd
Law enforcement officers.
Issuance, §19.2-73.2.
Local boards of social services, §63.2-322.
Failure to obey subpoena issued by boards, criminal penalty, §63.2-106.
Meat and poultry products inspection.
Agriculture and consumer services commissioner, §3.2-5416.
Medicaid investigations.
Authority of attorney general, §32.1-320.
Medical assistance services director.
Powers, §32.1-324.1.
Medical malpractice review panels.
Compelling attendance of witnesses, §8.01-581.6, MedMal Rule 6.
Production of documents and things, §8.01-581.6, MedMal Rule 6.
Medical records, §8.01-413.
Records of pro se party or nonparty witness, §32.1-127.1:03.
Membership camping.
Investigations, §59.1-334.
Military judges and presidents of courts-martial.
Powers to issue, §44-47.
Motor vehicle accidents.
Authority of law-enforcement officers to issue subpoena, §46.2-939.
Nonlawyer not allowed to issue, §16.1-88.03.
Parole revocation hearings.
Powers of hearing officers, §53.1-165.
Pay-per-call services.
Investigations by commissioner, §59.1-433.
Prisoner litigation reform, §8.01-695.
Professional and occupational regulation department.
Director authority, §54.1-307.
Public accountants, §54.1-4408.
Racing commission, issuance, §59.1-369.
Real estate appraiser board.
Power, §54.1-2015.
Real estate board.
Condominiums.
Investigations of complaints, §§55-79.99.
Real estate cooperatives.
Board power, §55-503.
Investigative powers of agency, §55-503.
Retail franchise investigations.
Power of state corporation commission to issue, §13.1-567.
Service contracts, extended.
Commissioner investigations, §59.1-439.
Sewage handling and disposal appeal review board, §32.1-166.7.
Social services board.
Failure to obey, §63.2-106.
Local boards, §63.2-322.
State board, §§63.2-220, 63.2-221.
Solicitation of charitable or civic contributions.
Investigations, §57-59.
Special education.
Issuance of subpoenas by hearing officers, §22.1-214.1.
State board of corrections.
Powers, §53.1-6.
State board of social services, §§63.2-220, 63.2-221.
Failure to obey subpoena issued by boards, criminal penalty, §63.2-106.

SUBPOENAS —Cont'd
State inspector general, §2.2-312.
State police department.
Issuance, §19.2-73.2.
State treasurer.
Checks.
Subpoenas to produce checks or drafts, §2.2-1812.
Tax commissioner and department of taxation.
Production of confidential tax returns, reproduction as compliance, §58.1-109.
Telegraph or telephone companies.
Duty to furnish information in response to, §18.2-431.
Travel clubs.
Commissioner investigations, §59.1-451.
Unemployment compensation.
Claims adjudication, §60.2-626.
Urban county executive form of government.
Human rights investigations, §15.2-854.
Inquiry into official conduct of office or officer, §15.2-814.
Wills.
Probate.
Compelling production of will, §64.2-449.
Witnesses.
Compelling attendance of witnesses, §8.01-407.
Workers' compensation commission.
Powers, §65.2-202.

SUBPOENAS DUCES TECUM.
Analysis evidence, §19.2-187.2.
Antitrust laws.
Investigations by attorney general, §59.1-9.10.
Attorneys at law.
Authority of board, §54.1-3925.3.
Furnishing copies to counsel, VA SCt Rule 1:12.
Banking and credit records.
Criminal investigations, §19.2-10.1.
Computers.
Remote computing service.
Administrative subpoena for record from provider, §19.2-10.2.
Condominiums.
Real estate board.
Investigations of complaints, §§55-79.99.
Courts-martial, naval militia.
Powers to issue, §44-70.
Criminal cases, VA SCt Rule 3A:12.
Form, VA SCt Rules Part 3A Appx Form 9.
Criminal procedure.
Banking and credit card records, §19.2-10.1.
Copying documents, VA SCt Rule 3A:12.
District courts.
Civil cases, §16.1-89.
Criminal cases, §16.1-131.
Filing requirements, VA SCt Rule 7A:12.
Power to issue, §16.1-69.25.
Requests for subpoenas duces tecum.
Filing requirements, VA SCt Rule 7A:12.
Furnishing copies to counsel, VA SCt Rule 7A:10.
Service on counsel of record, VA SCt Rule 7A:10.
Electronic communication service.
Administrative subpoena for record from provider, §19.2-10.2.
Electronic storage of documents or information.
Criminal cases, VA SCt Rule 3A:12.
Fees for preparation and issuance, §17.1-275.

SUBPOENAS DUCES TECUM —Cont'd
Fiduciaries.
Subpoena powers, §64.2-1203.
Financial institutions.
Criminal procedure.
Banking and credit card records, §19.2-10.1.
Fishing, tidal waters.
Hearings.
Commission powers, §28.2-216.
Generally.
See PRODUCTION OF DOCUMENTS AND THINGS.
Governmental bodies of localities.
Investigations relating to governmental affairs, §15.2-1409.
Health professions department director.
Power to issue, §54.1-2506.
Health spas.
Commissioner investigations, §59.1-308.2.
Invention development services, §59.1-215.
Juvenile and domestic relations district courts, §16.1-265.
Requests for subpoenas for witnesses and records, VA SCt Rule 8:13.
Medical assistance services director.
Power to issue, §32.1-324.1.
Medical records, §8.01-413.
Form of notice to provider, §32.1-127.1:03.
Membership camping.
Investigations, §59.1-334.
Military judges and presidents of courts-martial.
Powers to issue, §44-47.
Parole revocation hearings.
Powers of hearing officer, §53.1-165.
Pay-per-call services.
Commissioner investigations, §59.1-433.
Public accountants, §54.1-4408.
Real estate board.
Condominiums, §55-79.99.
Real estate cooperatives, §55-503.
Real estate cooperatives.
Investigative powers of agencies, §55-503.
Remote computing service.
Administrative subpoena for record from provider, §19.2-10.2.
Retail franchise investigations by state corporation commission, §13.1-567.
Service contracts, extended.
Commissioner investigations, §59.1-439.
Solicitation of charitable or civic contributions.
Investigations, §57-59.
State board of corrections.
Hearing powers, §53.1-6.
Tax commissioner and department of taxation.
Production of confidential tax returns, reproduction as compliance, §58.1-109.
Travel clubs.
Commissioner investigations, §59.1-451.
Unemployment compensation.
Claims adjudication, §60.2-626.
Wills.
Probate, §§64.2-446, 64.2-448, 64.2-449.
Compelling production of will, §64.2-449.
Establishment bills, §64.2-448.
Impeachment bills, §64.2-448.
Workers' compensation commission.
Power to issue, §65.2-202.

SUBROGATION.
Bank deposits and collections.
Payor bank's right to subrogation on improper payment, §8.4-407.
Boat dealers.
Fraud actions, §29.1-810.
Child support enforcement by department of social services.
Reimbursement from noncustodial parent, §63.2-1908.
Reimbursement of department for foster care expenditures, §63.2-1910.
Crime victim and witness assistance programs.
Claimant's right of action subrogated to Commonwealth, §19.2-368.15.
Fire insurance policies.
Standard provisions, §38.2-2105.
Health insurance.
Hospital, medical, surgical, etc., policies, provisions and limitations upon recovery forbidden, §38.2-3405.
Homes service contract providers.
Reimbursement insurance policies.
Right of insurer to seek against provider, §38.2-2626.
Husband and wife.
Reimbursement for expenses arising out of injury to wife, §55-36.
Insurance companies.
Enforcement of right in name of insured, §38.2-207.
John Doe actions, §38.2-2206.
Landlord and tenant.
Grantee rights, §55-217.
Lessee rights, §55-218.
Letters of credit, §8.5A-117.
Medical services lien.
Death claims settled by compromise or suit, §8.01-66.10.
Municipal or business corporations, §8.01-66.4.
Motorcycle dealers surety, §46.2-1993.20.
Motor vehicle liability medical benefit of insurer.
Right of subrogation not retained, §38.2-2209.
Right of subrogation to recover from third party not retained, §38.2-2209.
Petroleum storage tank discharges, §62.1-44.34:11.
Pleading in alternative, §8.01-281.
Storage tank discharges, §62.1-44.34:11.
Trailer dealers surety, §46.2-1992.20.
Uninsured or underinsured motorist coverage.
Insurers paying claim under endorsement, §38.2-2206.
Waters of the state.
Storage tank discharges, §62.1-44.34:11.
Workers' compensation.
Insurance and self-insurance, §65.2-812.
Subrogation of employer to employees' rights, §65.2-309.
Expenses, §65.2-311.
Settlement of third-party action, §8.01-424.1.
Uninsured employer's fund.
Commission rights, §65.2-1204.

SUBSEQUENT REMEDIAL MEASURES.
Evidence, relevancy, VA SCt Rule 2:407.
Inadmissible to prove negligence, §8.01-418.1.

SUBSIDIARIES.
Banks.
Acquisition of interests in financial institutions.
Cooperative agreements with other regulatory authorities, §6.2-706.

SUBSIDIARIES —Cont'd
Banks —Cont'd
Acquisition of interests in financial institutions —Cont'd
Presumptions regarding control of entities, §6.2-701.
Insurance business of controlled subsidiaries, §6.2-887.
Investment in stock or securities of controlled subsidiary corporations, §6.2-885.
Real estate brokerage business of controlled subsidiaries, §6.2-888.
Regulation by commission, §6.2-886.
Insurance companies, §§38.2-1335 to 38.2-1340.
Investments in stock, §38.2-1427.3.
Merger between constituent corporation of holding company and indirect subsidiary, §13.1-719.1.
Merger between parent corporation and subsidiary or between subsidiaries, §13.1-719.

SUBSTANCE ABUSE.
ABC board.
Substance abuse prevention program, §4.1-103.02.
Accounts and accounting, facilities.
Access to records, accounts and reports, §37.2-703.
Private funds provided for individuals receiving services, §37.2-705.
Social Security and other federal payments.
Commissioner authorized to receive and expend for individuals receiving services in state facilities, §37.2-704.
System of records, accounts and reports to be prescribed, §37.2-703.
Admissions.
Maliciously or knowingly contriving or conspiring to obtain, §37.2-431.
Alcoholic beverages, provision or sale to individuals receiving services, §37.2-430.
Aliens.
District court judges.
Power to commit, §16.1-69.28.
Alternative treatment.
Spiritual means without drugs or material remedy, §37.2-414.
Attorneys at law.
Virginia Bar Association.
Civil immunity when participating in certain activities, §8.01-226.1.
Background check of children's residential facility employees, §37.2-408.1.
Behavioral health authorities.
General provisions, §§37.2-600 to 37.2-615.
See BEHAVIORAL HEALTH AUTHORITIES.
Burning or destroying facilities, §18.2-77.
Certificates of need for medical care facilities, §§32.1-102.1 to 32.1-102.11.
See MEDICAL CARE FACILITIES.
Certified substance abuse counseling assistants.
Practice.
Scope, supervision, etc., §54.1-3507.2.
Title.
Use of title, §54.1-3507.3.
Certified substance abuse counselors.
Grandfathering in certain counselors, §54.1-3509.
Practice.
Scope, supervision, etc., §54.1-3507.1.
Title.
Use of title, §54.1-3507.3.

SUBSTANCE ABUSE —Cont'd
Children or minors.
Background check of residential facility employees, §37.2-408.1.
Children, psychiatric treatment, §§16.1-335 to 16.1-348.
See MENTAL HEALTH.
Newborn children.
Juvenile and domestic relations district courts, proceedings, §16.1-241.3.
Residence of children born in state facilities, §37.2-714.
School-age children in state facilities, §37.2-713.
Treatment centers for.
Juvenile proceedings.
Mental examinations and treatment, §16.1-275.
Civil commitment of mentally ill persons.
General provisions, §§37.2-800 to 37.2-920.
See CIVIL COMMITMENT OF MENTALLY ILL PERSONS.
Commitment for treatment of drug or alcohol abuse, §18.2-254.
Community corrections.
Generally, §§9.1-173 to 9.1-183.
See COMMUNITY CORRECTIONS.
Substance abuse assessment, testing and treatment as mandated, §9.1-176.
Community mental health services boards.
General provisions, §§37.2-500 to 37.2-512.
See COMMUNITY MENTAL HEALTH SERVICES BOARDS.
Confidential information.
Exchange of information about individuals receiving services, §37.2-711.
Religious preferences and affiliations of individuals receiving services, §37.2-712.
Conservators of the peace.
Authority, §37.2-426.
Construction of state facilities.
Razing buildings, §37.2-700.
Council on substance abuse services, §§2.2-2696, 2.2-2697.
Criminal background check of children's residential facility employees, §37.2-408.1.
Criminal offenses.
Drug sales on or near state hospitals, §18.2-255.2.
Crisis intervention teams, §§9.1-187 to 9.1-190.
Critical incidents or deaths of individuals receiving services.
Notice to designated protection and advocacy system director, §37.2-709.
Notice to representative of individual, §37.2-709.1.
Death of person in custody.
Payments to persons standing in loco parentis, §64.2-558.
Defeating drug and alcohol screening tests, §18.2-251.4.
Definitions, §37.2-100.
Judicial authorization of treatment, §37.2-1100.
Department of behavioral health and developmental services.
See BEHAVIORAL HEALTH AND DEVELOPMENTAL SERVICES DEPARTMENT.
Designated class 1 misdemeanors, §19.2-299.2.
Directors of state facilities.
Duties, §37.2-707.
Employment, §37.2-707.
Qualifications, §37.2-707.
Salaries, §37.2-708.

SUBSTANCE ABUSE —Cont'd
Discharge of patients from state institutions.
Alcoholism, reports to motor vehicles department, §46.2-401.
Reports to motor vehicles department, §46.2-401.
Discharge, release, etc.
Reports to motor vehicles department, §46.2-401.
Disorderly conduct on grounds of facility, §37.2-429.
District court judges.
Power to commit insane, drug-addicted and inebriated persons, §16.1-69.28.
Drivers' licenses.
Suspension of license of person not competent because of alcoholism or drug addiction, §46.2-400.
Drug offenders.
Commitment of convicted person for treatment of drug or alcohol abuse, §18.2-254.
Drug sales on or near state hospital property, §18.2-255.2.
Elderly individuals.
Separate state facilities for, §37.2-702.
Employees of state facilities.
Salaries, §37.2-708.
Escape from facility.
Aiding and abetting, §37.2-428.
Examination of condition of facilities, §37.2-701.
Exchange of information about individuals receiving services, §37.2-711.
Expenses of care, treatment or training, and maintenance.
Amount.
Limitations, §37.2-715.
Assessments and contracts by department, §37.2-717.
Collection by department.
When not required, §37.2-720.
Decedents' estates.
Liability of estate of individual receiving services, §37.2-721.
Investigation by department of financial ability to pay, §37.2-717.
Liability for, §37.2-715.
Estate of individual receiving services, §37.2-721.
Statement forms to be completed by person liable for support of individual receiving services, §37.2-719.
Order to compel payment, §37.2-718.
Revenue fund, §37.2-716.
Statement forms to be completed by person liable for support of individual receiving services, §37.2-719.
Fishing licenses.
Issuance to patients in state institutions, §29.1-313.
Freestanding state facilities.
Authorized, §37.2-702.
Health care data reporting.
Generally, §§32.1-276.2 to 32.1-276.11.
See HEALTH CARE DATA REPORTING.
Health insurance.
Coverage for biologically based mental illness, §38.2-3412.1:01.
Mental health and substance abuse services, §38.2-3412.1.
Public officers and employees.
Required coverage, §2.2-2818.

SUBSTANCE ABUSE —Cont'd
Health insurance coverage for services, §38.2-3412.1.
Hospitals.
Protocols, §32.1-127.
Human research.
Board regulations, §37.2-402.
Human rights.
Rights of individuals receiving services, §37.2-400.
Hybrid retirement program.
Disability program for participants.
Noncovered disability, §51.1-1176.
Incompetency.
Conservators.
See CONSERVATORS.
Generally.
See INCOMPETENCY.
Guardian and ward.
See GUARDIAN AND WARD.
Interference with officers and employees, §37.2-429.
Involuntary admission.
Children, psychiatric inpatient treatment, §§16.1-341 to 16.1-346.
Criminal defendants.
Acquittal of defendant by reason of insanity, §19.2-182.3.
Firearms possessed by person involuntarily admitted or ordered.
Disqualification for concealed weapons permit, §18.2-308.09.
Purchase, possession or transportation, §18.2-308.1:3.
Prisoners, §§53.1-40.1 to 53.1-40.10.
Prisoners with mental illness, §53.1-40.2.
Discharge, §53.1-40.7.
Release from custody imminent, civil admission proceeding, §53.1-40.9.
Psychiatric inpatient treatment of minors, §§16.1-341 to 16.1-346.
Judicial authorization of treatment, §§37.2-1100 to 37.2-1109.
Actions not authorized by chapter, §37.2-1102.
Antipsychotic medication, electroconvulsive therapy.
Ordering, time restrictions, §37.2-1102.
Appeals from order, §37.2-1105.
Appointment of attorney to represent interests of person for whom treatment sought, §37.2-1101.
Authority of circuit or district courts, §37.2-1101.
Clear and convincing evidence.
Standard of proof, §37.2-1101.
Costs of detention, testing or treatment, payment, §37.2-1107.
Definitions, §37.2-1100.
Electronic filing of petitions and orders, §37.2-1109.
Emergency custody order, §37.2-1103.
Findings required for authorizing treatment, §37.2-1101.
Incapable of making an informed decision.
Standard of proof required, §37.2-1101.
Lack of capacity to consent to treatment, claim based on.
Health professional or hospital not liable on, §37.2-1106.
Lack of consent to treatment, claim based on.
Health professional or hospital not liable on, §37.2-1106.

SUBSTANCE ABUSE —Cont'd
Judicial authorization of treatment —Cont'd
Law-enforcement officers sent beyond territorial jurisdiction.
Execution of emergency custody order, §37.2-1103.
Order authorizing treatment.
Requirements, §37.2-1101.
Other laws, effect of chapter on, §37.2-1108.
Petition.
Request for authorization of treatment, §37.2-1101.
Request for authorization of treatment, §37.2-1101.
Risks and benefits of treatment.
Investigation by appointed attorney, §37.2-1101.
Standard of proof.
Clear and convincing evidence, §37.2-1101.
Temporary detention in hospital, §37.2-1104.
Training center or hospital.
Admission to, ordering, §37.2-1102.
Juvenile proceedings.
Court-ordered counseling or treatment.
Payment of costs, §16.1-290.1.
Disposition of persons adjudged mentally ill or intellectually disabled, §16.1-278.11.
Juvenile court commitment, §16.1-280.
Legal representatives of individuals receiving services.
Persons prohibited from becoming, §37.2-401.
Licensed substance abuse treatment practitioners, §§54.1-3507, 54.1-3508.
Title.
Use of title, §54.1-3507.3.
Licensing of facilities, §§37.2-403 to 37.2-422.
See LICENSING OF MENTAL HEALTH FACILITIES.
Life-sharing communities, §63.2-1808.1.
Living wills, §§54.1-2981 to 54.1-2993.
See LIVING WILLS.
Mental or physical disorders.
Judicial authorization of treatment, §§37.2-1100 to 37.2-1109.
Mistreatment of individuals receiving services, §37.2-427.
Newborn children.
Juvenile and domestic relations district courts, proceedings, §16.1-241.3.
Opiate addiction treatment providers.
Conditions for initial licensure, §37.2-406.
Prevention program, ABC board, §4.1-103.02.
Prisoners.
Involuntary commitment, §§53.1-40.1 to 53.1-40.10.
Private funds provided for individuals receiving services, §37.2-705.
Probation.
Treatment or education programs as condition of probation, §18.2-258.1.
Probation and parole officer powers, §53.1-145.
Probationer or parolee suspected of abuse of alcohol.
Probation or parole officer's power to order alcohol screening, §53.1-145.
Property transfers of nonresidents, §§64.2-1426 to 64.2-1432.
Provider supervision of persons maintaining or operating services, §37.2-413.
Racing commission.
Alcohol and drug testing of pari-mutuel wagering licensees personnel, §59.1-369.

SUBSTANCE ABUSE —Cont'd
Razing buildings.
Construction of state facilities, §37.2-700.
Records.
Access to, §37.2-703.
Facilities.
Recordkeeping requirements, §32.1-274.
System to be prescribed, §37.2-703.
Religious practices.
Religious preferences and affiliations of individuals receiving services.
Collection and dissemination of information concerning, §37.2-712.
Spiritual means of treatment without drugs or material remedy, §37.2-414.
Reports.
Access to records, accounts and reports, §37.2-703.
Patient-level data and financial data, §37.2-710.
System of records, accounts and reports to be prescribed, §37.2-703.
Representatives of individuals receiving services.
Persons prohibited from becoming legally authorized representative, §37.2-401.
Residence.
Children born in state facilities, §37.2-714.
Individuals in state facilities, §37.2-713.
Retirement and pensions.
Hybrid retirement program.
Disability program for participants, noncovered disability, §51.1-1176.
Rights of individuals receiving services, §37.2-400.
Salaries of state mental health clinic employees.
Supplementing by certain counties and cities, §15.2-1508.4.
Sale, lease, exchange, redemption or other disposition of realty.
Disposition of real estate of persons under disability generally, §§8.01-67 to 8.01-80.
See PERSONS WITH DISABILITY.
Screening and assessment for abuse.
Designated class 1 misdemeanors, §19.2-299.2.
Social Security and other federal payments.
Commissioner authorized to receive and expend for individuals receiving services in state facilities, §37.2-704.
Substance abuse screening and assessment.
Defeating drug and alcohol screening tests, §18.2-251.4.
Drug conviction, §§18.2-252, 18.2-254.
Felony conviction generally, §18.2-251.01.
Supervision of persons maintaining or operating services, §37.2-413.
Surplus property.
Certain property not to be declared surplus, §37.2-701.
Termination of residual parental rights, §16.1-283.
Treatment of mental or physical disorders.
Judicial authorization of treatment, §§37.2-1100 to 37.2-1109.
Trust fund.
Definitions, §37.2-317.
Unclaimed personal property of individuals receiving services.
Disposal, §37.2-706.
Venereal disease testing upon admittance, §32.1-59.

SUBSTANCE ABUSE —Cont'd
Veterans, national guard or military reserve members.
Community corrections.
Special treatment procedures, §9.1-173.1.
Department of veterans services.
Establishment of mental health and rehabilitative services program, §2.2-2001.1.
Violations.
Admission of person without reasonable cause.
Maliciously or knowingly contriving or conspiring to obtain, §37.2-431.
Authority of personnel appointed conservators of the peace, §37.2-426.
Disorderly conduct, §37.2-429.
Escape from facility.
Aiding and abetting, §37.2-428.
Interference with officers and employees, §37.2-429.
Mistreatment of individuals receiving services, §37.2-427.
Provision or sale of alcoholic beverages to individuals receiving services, §37.2-430.
Zoning of group homes for mentally ill, or persons with intellectual or developmental disability, §15.2-2291.

SUBSTANCE ABUSE COUNSELORS.
Health professional civil immunity, §8.01-581.13.

SUBSTANCE ABUSE SCREENING AND ASSESSMENT.
Condition for suspension of sentence.
Drug conviction, §§18.2-252, 18.2-254.
Defeating drug and alcohol screening tests, §18.2-251.4.
Designated class 1 misdemeanors, §19.2-299.2.
Felony conviction, §18.2-251.01.

SUBSTANCE ABUSE SERVICES COUNCIL, §§2.2-2696, 2.2-2697.

SUBSTANCE ABUSE TESTING.
Condition of suspended sentence or probation.
Drug conviction, §§18.2-252, 18.2-254.
Felony conviction generally, §18.2-251.01.
Defeating drug and alcohol screening tests, §18.2-251.4.
Hospices and home health care organizations.
Drug-free workplace policies and drug testing, §32.1-162.9:1.
Mining.
Accidents, testing for intoxicants, §45.1-161.78.
Pre-employment substance abuse screening policy and program, §45.1-161.87.

SUBSTITUTED PERFORMANCE.
Leases, UCC, §8.2A-404.
Sales, UCC, §8.2-614.

SUBSTITUTE JUDGES.
Courts of record.
Designation of judges to hold courts and assist other judges, §§17.1-105 to 17.1-107.

SUBSTITUTE SERVICE, §8.01-296.
Aircraft accidents.
Nonresident operator or owner of aircraft, §§8.01-307 to 8.01-313.
Motor vehicle accidents.
Nonresident motor vehicle operators, §§8.01-307 to 8.01-313.
Notice on statutory agent, §8.01-326.1.

SUBSTITUTE SERVICE —Cont'd
Service by publication.
See SERVICE BY PUBLICATION.

SUBSTITUTE VEHICLE, HIRING.
Cost, recovery.
Person entitled to recover for damages or destruction of vehicle, §8.01-66.
Insurance company to provide.
Person entitled to recover cost of hiring substitute vehicle, §8.01-66.

SUBSTITUTION OF COUNSEL.
District courts, §16.1-69.32:1.

SUBSTITUTION OF PARTIES.
Circuit courts, VA SCt Rule 3:17.
Discontinuance of suit.
When suit discontinued unless revived, §8.01-18.
Presumption of death determination revoked.
Substitution of supposed decedent in pending actions, §64.2-2308.

SUBURBAN BUS LINES.
Motor vehicle sales and use tax.
Exemption.
See MOTOR VEHICLE SALES AND USE TAX.
Special regulatory revenue tax, §§58.1-2660 to 58.1-2665.

SUBVERSIVES.
Emergency management organization employment prohibited, §44-146.25.

SUBWAYS.
Obstructions or encroachments, §15.2-2009.
Roads, streets and public rights-of-way.
Localities generally, §§15.2-2000 to 15.2-2030.
See ROADS, STREETS AND PUBLIC RIGHTS OF WAY.
Use permits for transportation and utilities, §15.2-2015.

SUCCESSION TO OFFICE OF GOVERNOR, VA Const Art V §16.

SUDDEN INFANT DEATH SYNDROME.
Autopsies, §§32.1-285, 32.1-285.1.
Investigations of death.
Child fatality review team, §§32.1-283.1, 32.1-283.2.
Medical examiner, §32.1-283.

SUFFOLK.
Circuit court, establishment, §17.1-500.
Circuit court of county to constitute circuit court of city.
Inapplicability of provision to Suffolk, §17.1-505.
Coastal primary sand dunes and beaches.
Zoning ordinances, §28.2-1403.
Mentally ill, or persons with intellectual or developmental disability.
Zoning of group homes of eight or fewer single-family residences, §15.2-2291.
Personal property tax relief for elderly or handicapped.
Motor vehicles, alternative tax rates.
Ordinance to raise income and financial worth limitations, §58.1-3506.2.
Port of Virginia economic and infrastructure development zone grant fund, §62.1-132.3:2.
Public defenders office.
Established, §19.2-163.04.
Public service corporations, taxation of property.
Restriction of imposition of additional tax, §58.1-2606.

SUFFOLK —Cont'd
Retail sales and use tax.
Additional sales tax for Northern Virginia and Hampton Roads, §58.1-603.1.
Additional use tax for Northern Virginia and Hampton Roads, §58.1-604.01.
School board.
Fingerprinting applicants for employment, §22.1-296.2.
Salary of members, §22.1-32.
Sports authority of Hampton Roads, Virginia, 1986 ch 426.
Subdivision of lot for conveyance to family member, §15.2-2244.
Tidewater airport commission, 1962 ch 606, 1964 ch 45.
Well abandonment ordinance.
Duty of owner to cap or close well.
Locality adopting ordinance, §32.1-176.5.
Well construction.
Standards, §32.1-176.4.
Testing requirements, §32.1-176.5.

SUFFOLK DEVELOPMENT AUTHORITY.
Generally.
See ECONOMIC DEVELOPMENT AUTHORITIES.

SUFFRAGE, US Const Amds 14, 19, 26.

SUGAR VINEGAR, §§3.2-5500 to 3.2-5507.
See VINEGAR.

SUGGESTED RETAIL PRICE.
Motorcycle dealers advertising, §46.2-1993.81.
Motor vehicle advertising, §46.2-1581.
T&M vehicle dealer advertising, §46.2-1990.
Trailer dealer advertising, §46.2-1992.84.

SUICIDE.
Assisted suicide, §8.01-622.1.
Behavioral health and developmental services department.
Lead agency for suicide prevention across lifespan program, §37.2-312.1.
Colleges and universities.
Policies addressing student mental health, §23-9.2:8.
Estates in land.
Effect of suicide on conveyance of estates, §55-4.
Life insurance, grounds of defense, §38.2-3106.
Life prolonging procedures, withholding or withdrawal.
Euthanasia or mercy killing prohibited, §54.1-2990.
Not suicide, §54.1-2991.
Real property.
Effect of suicide on conveyance of property, §55-4.
Residential property transfer disclosures.
Actions for failure to disclose, §55-524.
Schools and education.
Student at imminent risk of suicide.
Duties of administrative or instructional personnel, §22.1-272.1.
Youth suicide prevention, §32.1-73.7.

SUITABLE WORK.
Failure of individual to apply for available, suitable work.
Disqualification for unemployment compensation benefits, §60.2-618.

SUIT FEES.
Generally.
See COURT COSTS AND FEES.

SUITS AND OTHER JUDICIAL PROCEEDINGS TAX, §§58.1-1727 to 58.1-1729.

SULFUR.
Defective drywall.
Consumer protection act.
Definition, §59.1-198.
Violations, §59.1-200.
Correction and restoration assistance fund, §§36-156.1, 36-156.2.
Real estate brokers, salespersons and rental agents.
Disclosures to owner by property manager, §54.1-2135.
Disclosures to prospective buyers, §54.1-2131.
Disclosures to prospective tenants, §§54.1-2133, 54.1-2134.

SUMMARY CASE DECISION.
Administrative process act.
Request, grounds, procedure, §2.2-4020.1.

SUMMARY COURTS-MARTIAL.
National guard, §44-45.
Generally, §§44-42 to 44-54.
Naval militia, §44-67.
Generally, §§44-67 to 44-74.
Powers of punishment, §44-69.

SUMMARY DISPOSITION BY COURT OF APPEALS, VA SCt Rule 5A:27.

SUMMARY JUDGMENTS.
Administrative process act.
Exemptions from case decisions, §2.2-4018.
Circuit courts, VA SCt Rule 3:20.
Depositions.
Motions sustained pursuant to agreement, §8.01-420.
District courts.
Special rule for pleadings, VA SCt Rule 7B:2.
Motion for summary judgment, §8.01-377.1.
Depositions as basis for summary judgment, §8.01-420, VA SCt Rule 4:7.
Responses submitted in support of motion for summary judgment.
Depositions as basis for request for admission, §8.01-420.
Sustaining as to punitive damages claim only, §8.01-420.
Motion to strike the evidence.
Court error in denying motion, VA SCt Rule 1:11.
Prisoners, pro se actions, §8.01-696.
Punitive damages.
Sustaining of motion as to punitive damages claim only, §8.01-420.
Requests for admission.
Responses submitted in support of motion for summary judgment.
Depositions as basis for request for admission, §8.01-420.

SUMMARY JURY TRIAL, §§8.01-576.1 to 8.01-576.3.
Election by parties, §8.01-576.1.
Selection of jury, §8.01-576.2.
Trial procedures, §8.01-576.3.

SUMMARY PUNISHMENT FOR CONTEMPT.
Appeals.
District court judges' sentence for contempt, §18.2-459.
Cases in which courts and judges may punish, §18.2-456.

SUMMARY PUNISHMENT FOR CONTEMPT —Cont'd
District court judges' power to punish, §18.2-458.
Appeal from sentence, §18.2-459.
Fine and imprisonment limited unless jury impaneled, §18.2-457.

SUMMER CAMPS, §§35.1-1 to 35.1-28.
Administrative process.
Applicability of administrative process act, §35.1-4.
Initial notice by certified mail, subsequent notices by regular mail, §35.1-1.1.
Child day care centers.
Dual licenses for certain day care centers, §63.2-1810.
Definitions, §35.1-1.
Disease reporting, §32.1-37.
Enforcement of provisions, §35.1-2.
Health commissioner and department of health.
Board's authority vested in commissioner, §35.1-3.
Enforcement of provisions, §35.1-2.
Right of entry, §35.1-5.
Health, state board.
Commissioner vested with board's authority, §35.1-3.
Enforcement of provisions, §35.1-2.
Orders, §35.1-6.
Rules and regulations, §§35.1-11, 35.1-12, 35.1-16.
Injunctions.
Violations, §35.1-7.
Inspections, §35.1-22.
Right of entry, §35.1-5.
Licensing, §§35.1-18, 35.1-20.
Advice and assistance to applicants, §35.1-24.
Display of license, §35.1-21.
Membership camping generally, §§59.1-311 to 59.1-335.
See MEMBERSHIP CAMPING.
Notice.
Initial notice by certified mail, subsequent notices by regular mail, §35.1-1.1.
Nudist camps for juveniles.
License not to be issued to owner or lessee conducting, §35.1-18.
Ordinances.
Local ordinances superseded, §35.1-9.
Penalties for violations, §35.1-7.
Public school programs, §§22.1-211, 22.1-212.
Rules and regulations, §§35.1-11, 35.1-12, 35.1-16.
Administrative process act.
Applicability, §35.1-4.
Penalties for violations, §35.1-7.

SUMMER SCHOOLS.
At-risk students, §22.1-253.13:1.
Failure of literacy tests, §22.1-253.13:1.
Public school students required to attend, §22.1-254.01.
Remediation program for at-risk students, §22.1-253.13:1.

SUMMONS.
Abandoned motor vehicles.
First-class mail, §46.2-1200.1.
Arrest warrants, issuance of summons in lieu of warrant.
Copy left with accused, §19.2-75.
Execution and return, §19.2-76.

SUMMONS —Cont'd
Arrest warrants, issuance of summons in lieu of warrant —Cont'd
Form of summons, VA SCt Rules Part 3A Appx Form 3.
Issuance and service, §19.2-74.
Mailing, §19.2-76.2.
Failure to appear on return date, §19.2-76.3.
Medical facility, issuance on premises.
Person under suspicion of DWI taken to facility, §19.2-73.
Misdemeanor and certain other cases, §19.2-73.
Notice of issuance, §19.2-73.1.
Quarterly reports on unexecuted summons, §19.2-76.1.
Attachment.
Claim of exemption form, §8.01-546.
Trucks and tractor trucks, civil penalty for certain violations.
Attachment and seizure of vehicle for unpaid fees and penalties, §46.2-613.4.
What attachment to command, §8.01-546.
Attorney discipline.
District committees proceedings, VA SCt Rule Pt 6 §IV Par 13-16.
Limited right to discovery, VA SCt Rule Pt 6 §IV Par 13-11.
Attorney-issued summons, §8.01-407.
Boards of equalization.
Power to summon taxpayers or agents, §58.1-3386.
Failure to obey, §58.1-3387.
Boating accidents.
Investigating officer powers, §29.1-739.
Bonds, surety.
Who may execute bond for writ or order, §8.01-4.2.
Commissioners of revenue power to summon taxpayers and other persons, §58.1-3110.
Commonwealth's attorney issuing summons for witness, §19.2-267.
Conductors, motormen and station and depot agents.
Issuance for failure to pay fare, §15.2-4503.
Conservation police officers.
Power to issue, §29.1-205.
Crop liens for advances to tenants and laborers.
Further showings as to advances, §43-29.
Desertion and nonsupport.
Commencement of proceedings, §20-65.
Detinue.
Commencement of action, §8.01-114.
Hearing to review issuance of order or process, §8.01-119.
Distress warrants.
Title to property levied on, district court proceedings, §16.1-120.
District court civil cases.
Title to property levied on under distress or execution, §16.1-120.
District court judges.
Power to issue, §16.1-69.25.
Drainage projects.
Proceedings on petitions, §21-297.
Driving while intoxicated.
Refusal of chemical test, issuance, §18.2-268.3.
Endangered species.
Enforcement of provisions, §3.2-1010.
Execution.
Title to property levied on, district court proceedings, §16.1-120.

SUMMONS —Cont'd
Extradition of witnesses.
Securing attendance from another state in criminal proceedings, §19.2-277.
Fiduciaries.
Inventories and accounts.
Failure to make return, §64.2-1215.
Fieri facias.
Interrogatories to judgment debtor, §8.01-506.
Failure to appear and answer, §8.01-508.
Proceedings in court of county or city where debtor resides, §8.01-506.2.
Fire marshals, local.
Powers, §§27-32, 27-34.2.
Fishing, tidal waters.
Issuance instead of being taken into custody, §28.2-901.
Garnishment.
See GARNISHMENT.
General assembly.
Attendance of witnesses or production of evidence, §30-10.
Juvenile proceedings, §16.1-263.
Law enforcement officer issuing summons for witness, §19.2-267.1.
Livestock liens for advances to tenants and laborers.
Further showings as to advances, §43-29.
Medicaid benefits.
Fraud or misrepresentations.
Issuance for violations, §32.1-321.4.
Motorcycle dealers.
Service of summons for license plate violations, §46.2-1993.54.
Motor vehicle dealers.
Dealer license plate violations, §46.2-1557.2.
Motor vehicles.
Acknowledgment of future receipt of official notices, §46.2-203.1.
Photo-monitoring systems to enforce traffic light signals.
Execution for violation, §15.2-968.1.
Port authority police.
Powers, §62.1-132.12.
Quo warranto.
How summons directed and served, §8.01-639.
Release on summons and promise to appear, §46.2-936.
Service of notice, process and other papers generally.
See SERVICE OF NOTICE, PROCESS AND OTHER PAPERS.
State board of corrections.
Investigations.
Corrections department director powers, §53.1-15.
Subpoena, defined, §8.01-2.
Tax commissioner and department of taxation.
Compelling attendance of witness and production of books and papers, §58.1-216.
Representation of witness, §58.1-1834.
Production of confidential tax returns, §58.1-109.
Toll roads and bridges.
Failure to pay toll, summons issued, §46.2-819.3:1.
Traffic infractions.
Parking ordinance violation, §46.2-941.
Traffic light signal violation monitoring system.
Execution for violation, §15.2-968.1.
Trailer dealer license plate violations.
Service of summons, §46.2-1992.54.

SUMMONS —Cont'd
Unlawful entry and detainer, §8.01-126.
When summons returnable to circuit court, §8.01-125.
Who may serve process, §8.01-293.
Wills.
Probate.
Appearances of interested parties, §64.2-446.
Witnesses.
Issuance of summons, to whom directed, §8.01-407.
Service of summons, §§8.01-296, 8.01-298.
Zoning.
Civil summon for violation, §15.2-2209.

SUMMONS IN LIEU OF WARRANT.
Misdemeanors and ordinance violations, §19.2-74.

SUMMONS TO ANSWER INTERROGATORIES.
Ascertaining judgment debtors estate, §8.01-506.
Proceedings in court of county or city where debtor resides, §8.01-506.2.

SUNDAY BEER AND WINE SALES.
Referendum, §4.1-123.

SUNDAY CLOSING LAWS.
ABC stores, exceptions, §4.1-120.
Wine and beer sales, referendum, §4.1-123.

SUNDAYS.
ABC stores.
Closed, exceptions, §4.1-120.
Clams.
Restrictions on taking or loading, §28.2-531.
Computation of time.
Last day for performing act falling on, §1-210.
Court proceedings not required to meet on, §1-210.
Distress warrants.
Issuance on, §55-230.
Employee protection and safety.
Choosing as day of rest.
See EMPLOYEE PROTECTION AND SAFETY.
Holidays falling on, §2.2-3300.
Hunting.
Limitations, §29.1-521.
Nonmigratory game birds, §29.1-514.
Oysters and clams.
Dredging or scraping on private ground, §28.2-515.
Restrictions on taking or loading, §28.2-530.
Persons with communicable diseases of public health significance.
Isolation beyond forty-eight hour period, §32.1-48.03.
Isolation hearings, §32.1-48.04.
Service of notice, process and other papers.
Exceptions to Sunday prohibition, §8.01-289.
No civil process on Sunday, §8.01-289.
Return of process, §8.01-294.
Tax returns and payment of taxes.
Filing or payment date falling on, §58.1-8.
Time-shares.
Purchaser cancellation rights, §55-376.
Tobacco warehouses.
Hours, §61.1-38.
Underground utility line damage prevention.
Notice requirements.
Calculation, §56-265.17.
Operator duties, §56-265.19.

SUNDAYS —Cont'd
Wine and beer sales.
Referendum, §4.1-123.

SUNGLASSES.
Sale of nonprescription sunglasses.
Physicians, §54.1-3202.

SUNSHADING OR TINTING FILMS OR APPLICATIONS.
Motor vehicles, §§46.2-1052, 46.2-1053.

SUPERFUND AMENDMENTS AND REAUTHORIZATION ACT.
State programs to implement, §§2.2-617, 2.2-618.

SUPERINTENDENT OF PUBLIC INSTRUCTION, §§22.1-21 to 22.1-24, VA Const Art VIII §6.
Appointment, §22.1-21, VA Const Art VIII §6.
Child abuse or neglect.
Notice to superintendent of public instruction.
Board of education licensee as subject of founded complaint of child abuse or neglect, §63.2-1503.
Duties in general, §22.1-23.
Interstate agreement on qualification of educational personnel.
Superintendent designated state official, §22.1-317.
National school lunch act.
Administration of act, §22.1-24.
Oath of office, §22.1-22.
Public school system.
Administration, §22.1-22.
Qualifications, §22.1-21.
School buildings.
Duty to close buildings unfit for occupancy, §22.1-136.
School buses.
Distribution of funds when superintendent effects insurance, §22.1-197.
Insurance.
When superintendent to obtain insurance, §22.1-191.
Secretary of the board of education, §22.1-23.

SUPERINTENDENTS OF PUBLIC WELFARE.
County board form of government, §15.2-412.

SUPERINTENDENTS OF SCHOOLS, §§22.1-58 to 22.1-70.3.
Appointment, §§22.1-60 to 22.1-62.
Ineligibility to hold office, §22.1-63.
Same person by two or more school divisions, §22.1-62.
Terms of contract, §22.1-60.
When state board to appoint superintendent, §22.1-61.
Compulsory school attendance.
Generally, §§22.1-254 to 22.1-269.1.
See COMPULSORY SCHOOL ATTENDANCE.
Report of children not enrolled after opening of school, §22.1-261.
County board form of government, §15.2-410.
Delinquency disposition disclosures to, §16.1-305.1.
Discipline of division superintendents, §22.1-65.
Duties, §22.1-70.
Evaluation.
By local school board, §22.1-60.1.
Performance objectives, §22.1-253.13:5.
Expenses of superintendents, §22.1-67.

SUPERINTENDENTS OF SCHOOLS —Cont'd
Expiration of contracts, date, §22.1-60.
Free public schools.
Administration, §22.1-2.
Ineligibility to hold office, §22.1-63.
Internet.
Acceptable Internet use policies for public and private schools, §22.1-70.2.
Licensing.
Standards of quality.
Licensing requirements, §22.1-253.13:2.
Meetings of school board.
Attendance requirement, §22.1-69.
Oath of office, §22.1-64.
Part-time superintendent.
Appointment of same person by two or more school divisions.
Approval by state board, §22.1-62.
Position qualifications, §22.1-59.
Powers, §22.1-70.
Professional development programs, §22.1-253.13:5.
Qualifications, §22.1-59.
Recordkeeping requirements, §22.1-68.
Removal from office, §22.1-65.
Renegotiation of contract.
Notice to board members, §22.1-60.
Reporting requirements.
Student ratios reported to local school boards, §22.1-70.1.
Required, §22.1-58.
School buildings.
Approval of plans of buildings by division superintendent, §22.1-140.
Social history reports prepared by intake officers.
Duty to provide information, §22.1-288.2.
Standards of quality.
Licensing requirements, §22.1-253.13:2.
Statutory requirement, §22.1-58.
Suspension from office, §22.1-65.
Teacher shortage areas.
Designation, §22.1-70.3.
Travel and per diem expenses, §22.1-67.
Urban county executive form of government, §15.2-837.
Vacancy in office, §22.1-66.
Appointment after vacancy occurring, §22.1-60.
Violation of education title.
Penalty, §22.1-292.

SUPERINTENDENTS OF SOCIAL SERVICES.
Urban county executive form of government, §15.2-835.

SUPERSEDEAS.
Eminent domain.
Appeal of order confirming just compensation, §25.1-239.
Hospital or health center commission no longer necessary, §15.2-5218.
Stays generally.
See STAYS.
Supreme court.
Jurisdiction, §17.1-310.

SUPERVISION OF ADULT OFFENDERS, INTERSTATE COMPACT FOR, §§53.1-176.1 to 53.1-176.3.
Enactment, §53.1-176.1.
Generally, §53.1-176.2.

SUPERVISION OF ADULT OFFENDERS, INTERSTATE COMPACT FOR —Cont'd
State council for interstate adult offender supervision, §53.1-176.3.
Text, §53.1-176.2.

SUPPLEMENTAL HIGH MOUNT STOP LIGHT.
Motor vehicle equipment, §46.2-1014.1.
Fine schedule, VA SCt Rule 3B:2.
Maximum fine for violating Title 46.2, §46.2-113.

SUPPLIERS AGREEMENTS.
Equipment dealers protection, §§59.1-352.1 to 59.1-352.10.
See FARM EQUIPMENT AND MACHINERY DEALERSHIPS.

SUPPLIES, PURCHASES BY STATE AGENCIES.
Division of purchases and supply generally, §§2.2-1109 to 2.2-1128.
See PURCHASES AND SUPPLY DIVISION.

SUPPLY CONTRACTS.
Leases, UCC.
Lessee under finance lease as beneficiary of, §8.2A-209.

SUPPORT GUIDELINES, §§20-108.1, 20-108.2.

SUPPORT LIENS, §§63.2-1927 to 63.2-1935.

SUPPORT OF CHILD OR SPOUSE, §§20-60.1 to 20-60.6.
Abstracts of judgments.
Money judgments for arrearages, §16.1-278.18.
Appeals.
Court of appeals.
Finality of decisions, §17.1-410.
Jurisdiction, §17.1-405.
Applicability of provisions, §20-60.1.
Arrearages.
Interest, §20-78.2.
Money judgments, §16.1-278.18.
Business, trade or professional licenses.
Notice as revocation or suspension in support order, §20-60.3.
Chart for determining, §§20-108.1, 20-108.2.
Child support.
See CHILD SUPPORT.
Child support enforcement.
Generally, §§63.2-1900 to 63.2-1960.
See CHILD SUPPORT ENFORCEMENT BY DEPARTMENT OF SOCIAL SERVICES.
Collection of support generally.
See CHILD SUPPORT.
Commitment for failure to comply with obligation, §16.1-278.16.
Contempt.
Sentencing to jail, workhouse, etc., §16.1-292.
Contents of support orders, §20-60.3.
Copies of support payment records.
Admissibility and identification, §20-60.2.
Court of appeals.
Appellate jurisdiction, §17.1-405.
Finality of decisions, §17.1-410.
Desertion and nonsupport generally, §§20-61 to 20-88.02:1.
See DESERTION AND NONSUPPORT.
Disposition in juvenile proceedings, §16.1-278.15.
Failure to comply with support obligation, §16.1-278.16.

SUPPORT OF CHILD OR SPOUSE —Cont'd
Disposition in juvenile proceedings —Cont'd
Pendente lite support, §16.1-278.17.
Formula for determination, §16.1-278.17:1.
Evidence, §20-108.1.
Admissibility and identification of support payment records, §20-60.2.
Failure to comply with support obligation, §16.1-278.16.
Sentencing, §16.1-292.
Guidelines, §§20-108.1, 20-108.2.
Health care coverage.
Contests of support order, §20-60.3.
Determining child support, §20-108.1.
Homestead exemption of householder.
Debts to which exemptions not to apply, §34-5.
Interest on arrearage, §20-78.2.
Interstate family support, §§20-88.32 to 20-88.82.
See INTERSTATE FAMILY SUPPORT ACT.
Judgment created by operation of law.
Lien against real estate, §16.1-278.15.
Judgments and decrees.
Decree as lien on real estate, §8.01-460.
Juvenile and domestic relations district court jurisdiction, §16.1-241.
Lien against real estate.
Judgment created by operation of law, §16.1-278.15.
Life insurance.
Maintaining existing policy, designating children beneficiaries, §20-108.1.
Money judgments for arrears, §16.1-278.18.
Notice as to withholding payments.
Contents of support order, §20-60.3.
Payment, §20-60.5.
Payroll deductions.
Failure to comply with support obligation, §16.1-278.16.
Pendente lite support, §16.1-278.17.
Petitions.
Contents, VA SCt Rule 8:3.
Public assistance applicants or recipients.
Failure to support child living in same home, §63.2-510.
Proceedings against person liable to support applicant or recipient, §63.2-511.
Rebuttable presumption of child support, §§20-108.1, 20-108.2.
Recognizance for compliance with support obligation, §16.1-278.16.
Retroactive determination of liability for child support, §20-108.1.
Sentencing for failure to comply with obligation, §§16.1-278.16, 16.1-292.
Spousal support.
See SPOUSAL SUPPORT.
Subsequent enforcement proceedings.
Delivery of notice to party at last known address, §20-60.6.
Transfer of venue.
Juvenile and domestic relations district court proceedings, §16.1-243.
Transmission of data between courts and department of social services, §20-60.4.
Unemployment compensation.
Intercept of benefits, §60.2-608.
Venue.
Juvenile and domestic relations district court proceedings, §16.1-243.
Vocational evaluation.
Proceedings for determining support, §20-108.1.

SUPPORT OF PARENTS BY CHILDREN, §20-88.

SUPPORT SERVICES DIVISION, §§2.2-1168 to 2.2-1172.

SUPPRESSION OF EVIDENCE.
Appeals allowed Commonwealth, §19.2-398, VA Const Art VI §1.
Objections raised before trial, §19.2-266.2.
Search warrants, §19.2-60.
Wiretapping.
Contents of intercepted communication, §19.2-68.
Wiretapping evidence, when excluded, §19.2-65.

SUPREME COURT, §§17.1-300 to 17.1-329.
Acting as counsel in case pending in court or which may be taken to court by appeal.
Clerks, deputy clerks or employees of court, prohibition, §17.1-202.
Adjournment.
Failure to sit on day to which adjourned, §17.1-120.
From day to day, §17.1-120.
Matter not determined at term to stand continued, §17.1-122.
Period not exceeding 30 days, §17.1-119.
Advance sheets of Virginia reports.
Printing and distribution, §17.1-317.
Amicus curiae briefs, VA SCt Rule 5:30.
Color of cover, VA SCt Rule 5:31.
Oral argument, VA SCt Rule 5:33.
Annexation.
Appeals to supreme court, §15.2-3221.
When order entered by supreme court.
Judgment of special court reversed or modified, §15.2-3222.
Appeals.
Death sentence, review, §17.1-313.
Delayed appeal in criminal cases.
Motion for, §19.2-321.2.
Generally, §§8.01-676.1 to 8.01-688.
See APPEALS.
Jurisdiction, §17.1-310.
Where criminal jurisdiction exercised, §17.1-312.
Multi-party cases, appeal from partial final judgment, VA SCt Rule 5:8A.
Non-compliance with rules, sanctions, VA SCt Rule 5:1A.
Appellant.
Defined, §8.01-669.
Appellant's opening brief, VA SCt Rule 5:27.
Color of cover, VA SCt Rule 5:31.
Appellate jurisdiction, VA Const Art VI §1.
Appellee's brief, VA SCt Rule 5:28.
Color of cover, VA SCt Rule 5:31.
Reply brief.
Color of cover, VA SCt Rule 5:31.
Appendices.
Assumptions, VA SCt Rule 5:32.
Color of cover, VA SCt Rule 5:31.
Contents, VA SCt Rule 5:32.
Form, VA SCt Rule 5:6.
Table of contents, VA SCt Rule 5:32.
When required, VA SCt Rule 5:32.
Applicability of rules.
Direct appeal from trial court, VA SCt Rule 5:8.
Fraudulent claims against the state.
Civil investigative demands, §8.01-216.19.
Appointment of clerk and deputies, §§17.1-200, 17.1-201.

SUPREME COURT —Cont'd
Appointment or election by court to fill any office or post.
Votes made in writing and recorded in order or minute book, §17.1-104.
Assessment for administration of insurance laws.
Appeals from assessments, §38.2-405.
Assignment of error, VA SCt Rule 5:25.
Appeals from the state corporation commission, VA SCt Rule 5:21.
Attorneys at law.
Change of address or other contact information, VA SCt Rule 5:1.
Effect of qualification to practice before court, §54.1-3903.
Foreign attorneys.
Admittance to practice without examination, VA SCt Rules 1A:1, 1A:2.
Revocation of license, VA SCt Rule 1A:3.
Non-compliance with rules, sanctions, VA SCt Rule 5:1A.
Rules regarding client accounts, §54.1-3915.1.
State bar governance. See within this heading, "State bar governance."
Audio-visual depositions.
Rulemaking authority, §8.01-412.6.
Audit of books and accounts of clerk, §17.1-204.
Availability of rules of court, §8.01-3.
Bonds issued by localities.
Judicial determination of validity.
Appeals to supreme court, §15.2-2656.
Bonds, surety.
Appeal bond, §8.01-676.1.
Circuit court appeals.
Additional bond required by appellate court, VA SCt Rules Part 5 Appx Form 6.
Appeal of right to court of appeals.
Bond for costs alone, VA SCt Rules Part 5 Appx Form 1.
Bond for costs and suspension, VA SCt Rules Part 5 Appx Form 2.
Bond for costs alone required by appellate court, VA SCt Rules Part 5 Appx Form 3.
Bond for costs and suspension required by appellate court, VA SCt Rules Part 5 Appx Form 5.
Bond for suspension alone required by appellate court, VA SCt Rules Part 5 Appx Form 4.
Form for execution and acknowledgment of bonds, VA SCt Rules Part 5 Appx Form 10.
Irrevocable letters of credit, VA SCt Rules Part 5 Appx Form 11.
State corporation commission appeals.
Appeal of right to supreme court.
Bond for costs alone, VA SCt Rules Part 5 Appx Form 8.
Bond for costs and suspension, VA SCt Rules Part 5 Appx Form 9.
Workers' compensation commission.
Appeals.
Appeal of right to court of appeals.
Bond for costs alone, VA SCt Rules Part 5 Appx Form 7.
Brief in opposition, VA SCt Rule 5:18.
Service by mail.
Computation of time, VA SCt Rule 1:7.
Briefs.
Amicus curiae brief, VA SCt Rule 5:30.
Color of cover, VA SCt Rule 5:31.

SUPREME COURT —Cont'd
Briefs —Cont'd
Appeals from the state corporation commission, VA SCt Rule 5:21.
Arguments made on brief not waived by oral argument, §8.01-679.1.
Brief in opposition, VA SCt Rule 5:18.
Service by mail, VA SCt Rule 1:7.
Brief of appellee, VA SCt Rule 5:28.
Color of cover, VA SCt Rule 5:31.
Copies, VA SCt Rule 5:26.
Extension of time, VA SCt Rule 5:26.
Filing time, VA SCt Rule 5:26.
Form, VA SCt Rule 5:6.
Length, VA SCt Rule 5:26.
Opening brief of appellant, VA SCt Rule 5:27.
Color or cover, VA SCt Rule 5:31.
Reference to parties, VA SCt Rule 5:26.
Reply brief, VA SCt Rule 5:19.
United States supreme court.
Certification of questions of law, VA SCt Rule 5:40.
Censure of judges.
Jurisdiction in matters, VA Const Art VI §1.
Certification for review.
Court of appeals, §17.1-409.
Notice of appeal from court of appeals, VA SCt Rule 5:14.
Record on appeal from court of appeals, VA SCt Rule 5:15.
Certiorari.
Record on appeal.
Certiorari when part of record omitted, §8.01-673.
Change of place or time for holding session, §17.1-116.
Chief justice.
See SUPREME COURT JUSTICES.
Claims against the state.
Fraudulent claims.
Civil investigative demands.
Applicability of rules, §8.01-216.19.
Clerical errors.
Motion in lieu of writ, §8.01-677.
Clerk, §§17.1-200 to 17.1-204.
See SUPREME COURT CLERK.
Collection of revenue cases.
Writ of mandamus, prohibition or other summary process not the issue, §17.1-309.
Complaints for retirement, censure or removal of judge.
Hearings upon, VA Const Art VI §10.
Composition, §17.1-300.
Computation of time.
Brief in opposition.
Service by mail, VA SCt Rule 1:7.
Concurrence of justices for decision to become judgment, §17.1-308, VA Const Art VI §2.
Conflict between divisions or with prior decision of court.
Rehearing, §17.1-308.
Consolidation of counties, cities or towns into single county or city.
Appeals to supreme court, §15.2-3528.
Constitutionality of laws.
Appellate jurisdiction, VA Const Art VI §1.
Contemporaneous objection rule, VA SCt Rule 5:25.
Contempt generally, §§18.2-456 to 18.2-459.
See CONTEMPT.

SUPREME COURT —Cont'd
Continuance of matters not determined at term, §17.1-122.
Convening of court, VA SCt Rule 5:3.
Correction of erroneous local tax assessments.
Appeals by locality or taxpayer aggrieved by action of court of record, §58.1-3992.
Correction of erroneous state tax assessments.
Appeals from final order of court to, §58.1-1828.
Correction of taxes assessed by state corporation commission.
Appeals, §58.1-2033.
Costs, VA SCt Rule 5:35.
Appendix, VA SCt Rule 5:32.
Costs recovered by party substantially prevailing, §17.1-604.
Taxing as part of costs allowed.
Reproducing brief and appendix, §17.1-605.
United States supreme court.
Certification of questions of law, VA SCt Rule 5:40.
Courthouse repairs ordered by circuit judge.
Appeal to supreme court, §15.2-1643.
Court of appeals.
Certification of case for review by supreme court, §17.1-409.
Reversing and remanding case for new trial.
Petition for appeal to supreme court, §17.1-412.
Review of decisions by supreme court, §17.1-411.
Courts of record.
Defined as including, §1-212.
Covers of documents, VA SCt Rule 5:31.
Created, appointment, §17.1-314.
Criminal appeals by Commonwealth.
Pretrial appeals, §§19.2-398 to 19.2-409.
See APPEALS.
Criminal jurisdiction.
Where exercised, §17.1-312.
Damages.
Award of damages to appellee, §8.01-682.
Dams or water impoundment disputes.
Disputes between jurisdictions.
Special court proceedings.
Appeals to supreme court, §15.2-2140.
Chief justice to designate circuit judges as special courts, §15.2-2135.
Death penalty.
Actual innocence.
Petition for writ of actual innocence, VA SCt Rule 5:7B.
Habeas corpus petitions filed by prisoners held under sentence of death.
Exclusive jurisdiction to award writ, §17.1-310.
Intellectual disability claim preserved for court consideration.
Persons sentenced to death prior to April 29, 2003, §8.01-654.2.
Petition for writ in cases where death sentence imposed, VA SCt Rule 5:7A.
Review of death sentence, §17.1-313.
Special rule applicable to cases, VA SCt Rule 5:22.
Decision and order.
Entry of decision in lower court, §8.01-685.
Furnishing copies of opinions to counsel, §8.01-684.
Issuance of execution, §8.01-685.
Notice of, VA SCt Rule 5:34.
Rendering final judgment, §8.01-681.
Transmittal of decisions, §8.01-683.
Declaring law unconstitutional.
Majority must concur, §17.1-308.

SUPREME COURT —Cont'd
Decrees pro confesso.
Correcting clerical errors.
When court may grant relief, §8.01-429.
Setting aside decree.
When court may grant relief, §8.01-429.
Default judgments.
Setting aside default judgments.
Correcting clerical errors, §8.01-429.
When appellate court may grant relief, §8.01-429.
Defined, §1-249.
Rules of practice, VA SCt Rule 5:1.
Delayed appeal in criminal cases.
Motion for, §19.2-321.2.
Denial of appeal, VA SCt Rule 5:20.
Destruction of building.
Changing place or time for holding session, §17.1-116.
Dismissal of appeal.
Increase in penalty of security, §8.01-676.1.
Petition filing fee not received, VA SCt Rule 5:17.
Disposition of record.
Appeal from court of appeals, VA SCt Rule 5:16.
District court rules of practice and procedure.
Formulation by courts, §16.1-69.32.
District courts.
Court system subordinate to court, §16.1-69.30.
Order books, etc., of former district courts in custody of clerk, §8.01-688.
Divisions.
Sitting and rendering final judgment, VA Const Art VI §2.
When in divisions, VA SCt Rule 5:3.
Docketing.
Perfection of appeal, VA SCt Rule 5:23.
Effective date of new rules and amendments, §8.01-3.
Election of successor justice, §17.1-303.
Emergency, state of.
Convening of court, §17.1-304.
En banc.
Setting and rendering final judgment, §17.1-308.
En banc panels.
Sitting and rendering final judgments, VA SCt Rule 5:3, VA Const Art VI §2.
Excess fees paid into state treasury retained by court, §17.1-285.
Executive secretary, §17.1-314.
Administrator of circuit court system, §17.1-502.
Duties, §17.1-315.
Magistrates.
Duty to render judicial administration assistance, §19.2-43.
Virginia reports.
Advance sheets, printing and distribution, §17.1-317.
Custody and distribution of reports of supreme court and court of appeals, §17.1-319.
Printing and binding, §17.1-316.
Extension of time, VA SCt Rule 5:5.
Briefs, VA SCt Rule 5:26.
Failure to sit generally, effect, §17.1-121.
Fees charged by clerk, §17.1-328.
Disposition, §17.1-329.
Filing error.
Appeals filed in wrong appellate court, §8.01-677.1.
Flags, display in courtrooms, §17.1-118.
Forms.
Appeal bonds, VA SCt Rules Part 5A Appx Forms 1 to 12, VA SCt Rules Part 5 Appx Forms 1 to 11.

SUPREME COURT —Cont'd
Forms —Cont'd
Service of notice, process and other papers.
Prescription of forms of writs, §8.01-286.
Forms of writs and process.
Authority to prescribe, §8.01-3.
Habeas corpus.
Appellate review during recess of the supreme court, §8.01-664.
Intellectual disability claim preserved for supreme court consideration.
Persons sentenced to death prior to April 29, 2003, §8.01-654.2.
Jurisdiction, §17.1-310.
Jurisdiction to award writs, VA Const Art VI §1.
Original jurisdiction, VA SCt Rule 5:7.
Petition for writ in cases where death sentence imposed, VA SCt Rule 5:7A.
Harmless errors, §8.01-678.
Hearings upon complaint for retirement, censure or removal of judge, VA Const Art VI §10.
Holding other office by justice, prohibition, §17.1-102.
Hospital authorities, dissolution.
Appeals to court, §15.2-5367.
In divisions.
Setting and rendering final judgment, §17.1-308.
Information and recommendations as to other courts, §17.1-307.
Injunctions.
Appellate review, §8.01-626.
Petition for review of grant or denial of injunctive relief, §8.01-626, VA SCt Rule 5:17A.
Insurance law administration assessments.
Appeals from assessments, §38.2-405.
Interlocutory judgments.
Appeal by permission, §8.01-670.1.
Cases on an equitable claim, §8.01-670.
Time period within which presented, §8.01-671.
Jail utilization, §53.1-78.
Judgments and decrees.
Interlocutory judgments.
Appeal by permission, §8.01-670.1.
Cases on an equitable claim, §8.01-670.
Time period within which presented, §8.01-671.
Issuance of execution, §8.01-685.
Setting aside judgment of trial court.
Criteria, §8.01-680.
Judicial emergency, §§17.1-330, 17.1-331.
Judicial power of Commonwealth vested in, VA Const Art VI §1.
Jurisdiction.
Appeals, writs of error and supersedeas, §17.1-310.
Appellate jurisdiction, VA Const Art VI §1.
Extraordinary writs.
Original jurisdiction, VA SCt Rule 5:7.
Habeas corpus, §17.1-310.
Habeas corpus, appeals, writs of error and supersedeas, etc., VA Const Art VI §1.
Judicial censure, retirement and removal, VA Const Art VI §1.
Judicial inquiry and review commission.
Complaints filed by, §17.1-906.
Jurisdictional amount, §8.01-672.
Mandamus and prohibition, §17.1-309.
Jurisdictional amount, §8.01-672.
Petition for appeal.
Circuit court judgments, §8.01-672.

SUPREME COURT —Cont'd
Justices.
See SUPREME COURT JUSTICES.
Juvenile and domestic relations district court.
Rules of practice and procedure.
Promulgation by supreme court, §16.1-69.32.
Law library of state.
Additions to, §42.1-62.
Management of, §42.1-60.
Regulation and computer expenses, §42.1-63.
Local treasurer securing final discharge from liability, §58.1-3147.
Location of clerk's office, §17.1-203.
Mail filing, VA SCt Rule 5:5.
Majority concurrence in declaring law unconstitutional, §17.1-308.
Mandamus.
Application for writ, §8.01-649.
Caption of writ against judges, VA SCt Rule 5:7.
Jurisdiction of writs, §17.1-309.
Jurisdiction to issue writs, VA Const Art VI §1.
Original jurisdiction, VA SCt Rule 5:7.
Stay of proceedings by justice of supreme court, §8.01-651.
When writ to issue and be tried, §17.1-311.
Mandates, VA SCt Rule 5:36.
Medical malpractice review panels.
Rulemaking authority, §8.01-581.11.
Selection, §8.01-581.3.
Modification or annulment of rules of court.
Authority of generally assembly, §8.01-3.
Motions, VA SCt Rule 5:4.
Form, VA SCt Rule 5:6.
Multi-party cases, appeal from partial final judgment, VA SCt Rule 5:8A.
Notice of appeal.
Appeal from court of appeals, VA SCt Rule 5:14.
Appeals from the state corporation commission, VA SCt Rule 5:21.
Direct appeal from trial court, VA SCt Rule 5:9.
Extension of time, VA SCt Rule 5:5.
Notice of decision and order, VA SCt Rule 5:34.
Number of justices, §17.1-300, VA Const Art VI §2.
Objections.
Contemporaneous objection rule, VA SCt Rule 5:25.
Record on appeal.
Transcript or written statement, VA SCt Rule 5:11.
Obscene books, proceedings against.
Appeals to supreme court, §18.2-384.
Occupational safety and health.
Enforcement of provisions, §40.1-49.5.
Office of executive secretary, §17.1-314.
Administrator of circuit court system, §17.1-502.
Duties, §17.1-315.
Printing and binding Virginia reports, §17.1-316.
Virginia reports.
Advance sheets, printing and distribution, §17.1-317.
Custody and distribution of reports of supreme court and court of appeals, §17.1-319.
Opening brief of appellant, VA SCt Rule 5:27.
Color of cover, VA SCt Rule 5:31.
Opinions of court, VA SCt Rule 5:36, VA Const Art VI §6.
Citing unpublished judicial dispositions, VA SCt Rule 5:1.
Furnishing copies to counsel, §8.01-684.

SUPREME COURT —Cont'd
Opinions of court —Cont'd
United States supreme court.
Certification of questions of law, VA SCt Rule 5:40.
Oral argument.
Length, VA SCt Rule 5:33.
Notice, VA SCt Rule 5:33.
Waiver, VA SCt Rule 5:33.
Orders, VA SCt Rule 5:4.
Perfection of appeal, VA SCt Rule 5:23.
Petition for appeal.
Appeals filed in wrong appellate court, §8.01-677.1.
Appeals from the state corporation commission, VA SCt Rule 5:21.
Cases in which awarded, §8.01-670.
Court of appeals.
Time period within which presented, §8.01-671.
Dismissal, §8.01-675.1.
Increase in penalty of security, §8.01-676.1.
Docketing, VA SCt Rule 5:23.
Endorsement, §8.01-674.
Exception, §8.01-670.
Extension of time, VA SCt Rule 5:5.
Filing requirements, §8.01-674.
Finality of dismissal, §8.01-675.1.
Form and content, VA SCt Rule 5:17.
Grant of petition, VA SCt Rule 5:23.
Interlocutory judgments.
Appeal by permission, §8.01-670.1.
Jurisdictional amount.
Circuit court judgments, §8.01-672.
Mail filing requirements, §8.01-674.
Petitioner, defined, §8.01-669.
Referral to justices, §8.01-674.
Rehearing, §8.01-675.2, VA SCt Rule 5:37.
Reinstatement of dismissal, §8.01-675.1.
Security, §8.01-676.1.
Time for filing, VA SCt Rule 5:17.
Time period within which presented, §8.01-671.
When deemed filed, §8.01-674.
When granted, §8.01-670.
With whom filed, §8.01-674.
Petition for rehearing, §8.01-675.2, VA SCt Rule 5:37.
Color of cover, VA SCt Rule 5:31.
Denial of appeal, VA SCt Rule 5:20.
Extension of time, VA SCt Rule 5:5.
Petition for review.
Trial court grant or denial of injunctive relief, §8.01-626, VA SCt Rule 5:17A.
Place for holding session.
Changing, §17.1-116.
Pleadings, VA SCt Rule 5:6.
Covers of documents, VA SCt Rule 5:31.
Form, VA SCt Rule 5:6.
Responsive pleadings, VA SCt Rule 5:7.
Practice of law by justices, prohibition, §17.1-102.
Presiding justice when chief justice absent, §17.1-301.
Pretrial payment of fines.
Designation of offenses and schedule of fines by rule, §§16.1-69.40:1, 16.1-69.40:2.
Prisoners.
Pro se litigants, VA SCt Rule 5:7.
Pro hac vice fund, §17.1-205.
Prohibition, writ of.
Application for writ, §8.01-649.
Caption for writ against judges, VA SCt Rule 5:7.

SUPREME COURT —Cont'd
Prohibition, writ of —Cont'd
Jurisdiction of writs, §17.1-309.
Jurisdiction to issue writs, VA Const Art VI §1.
Original jurisdiction, VA SCt Rule 5:7.
Stay of proceedings by justice of supreme court, §8.01-651.
When writ to issue and be tried, §17.1-311.
Pro se litigants.
Responsive pleading of prisoners, VA SCt Rule 5:7.
Psychiatric treatment of children.
Preparation of admission forms, §16.1-336.1.
Publication, indexing and annotation of rules, §8.01-3.
Public officers, removal.
Right of appeal to, §24.2-237.
Public service companies.
Rate cases, §56-8.2.
Public service corporation tax assessment review.
Appeals to supreme court, §§58.1-2675, 58.1-2676.
Purchases through division of purchases and supply.
Printing of court records, inapplicability of provisions, §2.2-1119.
Quorum, §17.1-300.
Rate cases, §56-8.2.
Recall to services of retired judges, members of state corporation commission and workers' compensation commission.
Payment for services, §17.1-327.
Recommendations as to other courts, §17.1-307.
Record on appeal.
Appeal from court of appeals, VA SCt Rule 5:15.
Disposition of record, VA SCt Rule 5:16.
Appeals from the state corporation commission, VA SCt Rule 5:21.
Binding of records, §8.01-673.
Certification for review.
Appeal from court of appeals, VA SCt Rule 5:15.
Direct appeal from trial court, VA SCt Rule 5:10.
Authorization of judge to act, VA SCt Rule 5:12.
Preparation and transmission, VA SCt Rule 5:13.
Transcript or written statement, VA SCt Rule 5:11.
Failure of trial court to deliver record to appellate court, §8.01-679.
Inspection of records, §8.01-673.
Omission of part of record, §8.01-673.
Retention of records, §8.01-673.
Return of records, §8.01-673.
Regulations for practice in courts of Commonwealth.
Authority to prescribe, §8.01-3.
Rehearings, §17.1-308.
Petition for appeal, §8.01-675.2, VA SCt Rule 5:37.
Color of cover, VA SCt Rule 5:31.
Denial on appeal, VA SCt Rule 5:20.
Extension of time, VA SCt Rule 5:5.
Removal of deputy clerks, §17.1-201.
Removal of public officers.
Right of appeal to supreme court, §24.2-237.
Reply brief, VA SCt Rule 5:19.
Color of cover, VA SCt Rule 5:31.
Rule compliance, VA SCt Rule 5:29.
Reporter, §17.1-321.
Delivery of opinions by clerk to reporter, §17.1-323.
Duties, §17.1-322.
Salary, §17.1-326.

SUPREME COURT —Cont'd
Reports of supreme court, §§17.1-316 to 17.1-320.
Retired judges, members of state corporation commission and Virginia workers' compensation commission recalled to service.
Payment for services, §17.1-327.
Retirement and removal of judges.
Jurisdiction in matters, VA Const Art VI §1.
Retirement of justice.
Designation as senior justice, §17.1-301.
Richmond.
Sessions held at Richmond, §17.1-304.
Right of appeal to supreme court.
Removal of public officers from office, §24.2-237.
Voter registration objections.
Decisions of circuit courts concerning, §24.2-433.
Road tax on motor carriers.
Appeals by motor carriers, §58.1-2709.
Rules of practice and procedure.
Circuit courts.
Formulation of rules, §17.1-503.
Commonwealth court, authorization to make, VA Const Art VI §5.
District courts, promulgation, §16.1-69.32.
Non-compliance, sanctions, VA SCt Rule 5:1A.
Rules of practice, system of pleading and rules of evidence.
Authority to prepare, effective date, availability, publication, §8.01-3.
Salaries of justices, §17.1-324.
Salary of clerk and deputy clerk, §17.1-325.
Salary of reporter, §17.1-326.
Sanctions.
Appendices.
Noncompliance with rule, VA SCt Rule 5:32.
Scope of rules, VA SCt Rule 5:1.
Security for appeal, §8.01-676.1, VA SCt Rule 5:24.
Time for filing, §8.01-676.1.
Selection of chief justice, VA Const Art VI §3.
Senior justice, designation, §17.1-301.
Sentence of death, review, §17.1-313.
Sentencing commission.
Created as agency of supreme court, §17.1-800.
Service of notice, process and other papers, VA SCt Rule 5:1.
Prescription of forms of writs, §8.01-286.
Sessions, §17.1-304, VA SCt Rule 5:2.
Special sessions, §17.1-305.
Cases heard at special session, effect, §17.1-306.
Setting aside trial court judgments.
Criteria, §8.01-680.
Settlement of pending appeal, VA SCt Rule 5:38.
Sitting and rendering final judgment en banc or in divisions, §17.1-308.
Size of paper.
Briefs and other pleadings, VA SCt Rule 5:6.
Small claims court forms.
Prescribed by supreme court, §16.1-122.3.
Special sessions, §17.1-305.
Cases heard at special session, effect of decision, §17.1-306.
Standards for writings to be docketed, §55-108.
Use of copies admitted to record elsewhere, §55-109.
State bar governance.
Administrative agency of the court.
Designation of bar, §54.1-3910.
Client account rules, §54.1-3915.1.

SUPREME COURT —Cont'd
State bar governance —Cont'd
Exemptions from licensing examination, §54.1-3931.
Fees, §54.1-3912.
Organization of bar, §54.1-3910.
Powers of court, §54.1-3909.
Restrictions, §54.1-3915.
State corporation commission.
Appeals from actions of commission, §12.1-39, VA Const Art IX §4.
Notice of decision and order, VA SCt Rule 5:34.
Special rules applicable to appeals, VA SCt Rule 5:21.
Successor justice.
Election on vacancy occurring or existing, §17.1-303.
Supersedeas.
Jurisdiction, §17.1-310.
Taxes.
Correction of erroneous tax assessments.
Appeals by locality or taxpayer aggrieved by action of court of record, §58.1-3992.
Terms, §17.1-304.
Tie breaker in selection of chief circuit judge and exercise of appointment powers by circuit court judges.
Chief justice of supreme court, §17.1-501.
Time computation.
Service by mail, VA SCt Rule 1:7.
Time for holding session.
Changing, §17.1-116.
Towns incorporated by judicial proceeding.
Appeal to supreme court, §15.2-3605.
Trademarks and service marks, registration and protection.
Appeal of SCC decision, §59.1-92.18.
Transfer of appeal.
Filing error, §8.01-677.1.
Trial court management.
Reporting requirements of chief judges of circuit and district courts, VA SCt Rule 1:15.
Unconstitutionality of laws, declaration by court.
Concurrence of justices required, VA Const Art VI §2.
Majority must concur in declaring, §17.1-308.
United States supreme court.
Certification of questions of law, VA SCt Rule 5:40.
Procedure upon appeal or petition to supreme court, VA SCt Rule 5:39.
Vacancy occurring or existing in office of justice.
Election of successor, §17.1-303.
Variance between rule of court and enactment.
Effect given to enactment, §8.01-3.
Virginia reports.
Advance sheets, printing and distribution, §17.1-317.
Furnishing to law school libraries destroyed by fire, §17.1-320.
Printing and binding reports of supreme court, §17.1-316.
Reporter of courts, §§17.1-321 to 17.1-323.
Voter registration denials.
Appeal of judgments rendered against petitioner, §24.2-422.
Voter registration objections.
Appeal of right from decision of circuit court, §24.2-433.

SUPREME COURT —Cont'd
Writ of error.
Criminal cases generally, §§19.2-317 to 19.2-327. See WRIT OF ERROR.
Jurisdiction, §17.1-310.

SUPREME COURT CLERK, §§17.1-200 to 17.1-204.
Acting as counsel in case pending in supreme court or which may be taken to court by appeal, §17.1-202.
Advance sheets of Virginia reports.
Distribution to, §17.1-317.
Appointment, holding office at pleasure of court, §17.1-200.
Appointment of deputies by court, §17.1-201.
Audit of books and accounts, §17.1-204.
Deputies.
Appointment and removal by court, §17.1-201.
Failure to deliver record to appellate court, §8.01-679.
Fees.
Attorney licensing, entering order, §17.1-328.
Attorneys qualifying to practice in court, administering oath and entering order, §17.1-328.
Authentication of record, document or paper under seal of court, §17.1-328.
Copy of record or document, §17.1-328.
Disposition of fees, §17.1-329.
Law license certificate under seal of court and certification of qualification, §17.1-328.
Other services not specifically mentioned, §17.1-328.
Petition presented in case, §17.1-328.
Verifying and certifying record or document, §17.1-328.
Fidelity and surety insurers.
Notice of revocation of insurer's license furnished to clerk, §38.2-2412.
Location of clerk's office, §17.1-203.
Order books, etc., of former district courts in clerk's custody, §8.01-688.
Performance of duties and services as court may require, §17.1-200.
Pro hac vice fund, §17.1-205.
Removal of deputies by court, §17.1-201.
Richmond.
Location of main office, §17.1-203.
Salary of clerk and deputy clerk, §17.1-326.
Secure remote access to records, §§17.1-292 to 17.1-295.
Transmittal of decisions, §8.01-683.

SUPREME COURT JUSTICES.
Absence of chief justice.
Presiding justice, §17.1-301.
Advance sheets to Virginia reports.
Distribution to, §17.1-316.
Chief justice, §17.1-300.
Absence, presiding justice, §17.1-301.
Administration of judicial system, VA Const Art VI §4.
Assigning of justices to other courts, VA Const Art VI §4.
Declining to serve as or resigning as such, §17.1-300.
District court congestion in work.
Designation of district judge from another district or retired judge to assist, §16.1-69.35.

SUPREME COURT JUSTICES —Cont'd
Chief justice —Cont'd
District court system, administrative supervision, §16.1-69.30.
Election contest of electors for president and vice-president or primaries for United States senate or statewide office.
Appointment of circuit judges to sit with chief judge of circuit, §24.2-805.
Election contest of other primaries and elections.
Appointment of circuit court judges to sit with chief judge of circuit, §24.2-806.
Election recount.
Designation of judges to sit with chief judge of circuit, §24.2-801.
Judicial conference for district courts.
Chairman of executive committee, §16.1-219.
President of conference, §16.1-219.
Medical care facilities.
Certificates of public need.
Enjoining projects undertaken without certificate, §32.1-102.9.
Recounts in elections.
Designation of judges to sit with chief judge of circuit, §24.2-801.
Selection, VA Const Art VI §3.
Tie breaker in selection of chief judge of circuit court or exercise of appointment power by circuit court judges, §17.1-501.
Commissioned by governor, VA Const Art VI §9.
Compelling attendance as witness.
Prior court permission required, §8.01-407.
Compensation of senior justice, §17.1-302.
Disclosure statement.
Filing, time, form, §§2.2-3114, 2.2-3117.
Dual office holding, §17.1-102.
Elective office holding prohibition, §17.1-102.
Failure to timely qualify, §17.1-101.
Holding non-judicial elective office prohibited, VA Const Art VI §11.
Holding other office prohibited, §17.1-102.
Incompatible activities, VA Const Art VI §11.
Jury service.
Automatic exemption, §8.01-341.
Number, §17.1-300, VA Const Art VI §2.
Performance evaluation program, §17.1-100.
Practice of law prohibited, §17.1-102, VA Const Art VI §11.
Presiding justice when chief justice absent, §17.1-301.
Privileged from arrest under civil process, §§8.01-327.1, 8.01-327.2.
Qualifications, VA Const Art VI §7.
Revised constitution not to affect, VA Const Sched §4.
Time for qualifying, §17.1-101.
Quorum, §17.1-300.
Residency requirement, VA Const Art VI §7.
Retired justices.
Designation as senior justice, §17.1-302.
Recalled to service.
Payment for services, §17.1-327.
Salaries, §17.1 324.
Senior justice, §17.1-302.
Selection by general assembly, VA Const Art VI §7.
Senior justice, designation, §17.1-302.
Special counsel, employment, §§2.2-510, 2.2-510.1.
Successor justice.
Election when vacancy in office, §17.1-303.

SUPREME COURT JUSTICES —Cont'd
Terms, VA Const Art VI §7.
Tie breaker in selection of chief judge of circuit court or exercise of power of appointment by circuit judges.
Chief justice of supreme court, §17.1-501.
Time for qualifying, §17.1-101.
Vacancy in office.
Election of successor, §17.1-303.
Vacation of office.
Failure to timely qualify, §17.1-101.

SUPREME COURT OF UNITED STATES.
Appointment, compensation and tenure of justices, US Const Art III §1.
Certification of questions of law.
Certification procedures, VA SCt Rule 5:40.
Chief justice presides in impeachment of president, US Const Art I §3.
Jurisdiction, US Const Art III §2.
President of the United States.
Appointment of justices, US Const Art II §2.
Virginia supreme court.
Procedure upon appeal or petition to United States supreme court, VA SCt Rule 5:39.

SUPREME COURT OF VIRGINIA.
Administrative process act.
Exemptions, §2.2-4002.
Bonds, surety.
Employees.
Blanket surety bond plan.
Risk management division, §2.2-1840.
Budget of state.
Estimates of financial needs, §2.2-1506.
Employees.
Personnel administration system.
Exemptions, §2.2-2905.

SUPREME COURT REPORTER.
Advance sheets, printing and distribution, §17.1-317.
Appointment and salary, §17.1-321.
Custody and distribution, §17.1-319.
Duties, §17.1-322.
Law school libraries destroyed by fire.
Furnishing to, §17.1-320.
Opinions delivered by clerk of supreme court to reporter, §17.1-323.
Printing and binding of volumes, §17.1-316.
Reporter of court, §§17.1-321 to 17.1-323.
Salaries, §17.1-326.

SURETY BAIL BONDSMEN.
Court clerks, furnishing with information.
Revocation of licenses, §38.2-2412.
Criminal justice services department.
Revocation of license of property and casualty insurance agent, notice of, §38.2-2412.1.
Violations by property and casualty insurance agent, notice of, §38.2-2412.2.
Insurance agents generally.
See INSURANCE AGENTS.

SURETY INSURANCE.
Fidelity and surety insurance generally, §§38.2-2400 to 38.2-2420.
See FIDELITY AND SURETY INSURANCE.
Rates generally, §§38.2-1900 to 38.2-1928.
See INSURANCE RATES.

SURETYSHIP.
See BONDS, SURETY.

SURFACE COAL MINING.
Adjacent property owners.
Mining rights.
Generally, §§45.1-161.310, 45.1-161.311.
Applicability of act.
Exemption of certain mining operations, §45.1-253.
Blasters.
Training and certification, §45.1-256.
Certification of blasters, §45.1-256.
Contracts.
Forfeiture of performance bond.
Performance of reclamation operations, §45.1-248.
Corporations.
Applicability of act, §45.1-259.
Designating unsuitable areas for mining, §45.1-252.
Emergency seizure of coal properties by Commonwealth, §§45.1-161.312 to 45.1-161.322.
Acquisition expenses, §45.1-161.321.
Applicability of provisions, §45.1-161.318.
Condemnation proceedings, §45.1-161.320.
Declaration of policy, §45.1-161.313.
Gubernatorial powers of operation, §45.1-161.315.
Leases of property, §45.1-161.319.
Operating expenses, §45.1-161.321.
Proclamation of emergency, §45.1-161.314.
Public uses.
Defined, §45.1-161.313.
Interruption, §45.1-161.314.
Purchases of property, §45.1-161.319.
Restoration of property to owner or operator, §45.1-161.322.
Subjects of seizure, §45.1-161.312.
Virginia fuel commission.
Duties, §45.1-161.316.
Members, §45.1-161.317.
Powers, §45.1-161.316.
Enforcement of act.
Abatement notice, §45.1-245.
Administrative review of notice or order, §45.1-249.
Cease and desist orders, §45.1-245.
Citizen suits, §45.1-246.
Civil and criminal penalties, §45.1-246.
Disciplinary action against permittees, §45.1-245.
Fines, §45.1-246.
Generally, §45.1-245.
Impeding, etc., §45.1-257.
Injunctive relief, §45.1-245.
Exemption of certain mining operations, §45.1-253.
Forfeiture of performance bond, §45.1-247.
Performance of reclamation operations by director, §45.1-248.
Government-financed highway or construction.
Extraction of coal as incidental part of financing.
Exemption from act, §45.1-253.
Hearings.
Conduct of formal hearings, §45.1-250.
Impeding, etc., enforcement of act, §45.1-257.
Inapplicability of act, §45.1-253.
Inspections.
Right of citizens to accompany inspectors, §45.1-246.1.
Mine inspections.
See MINE INSPECTIONS.

SURFACE COAL MINING —Cont'd
Mine licensing.
See MINE LICENSING.
Mine safety requirements, §§45.1-161.253 to 45.1-161.292.
Monitoring, §45.1-244.
National pollutant discharge elimination system permits, §45.1-254.
Noncommercial use.
Extraction of coal by landowner.
Exemption of act, §45.1-253.
Permits.
National pollutant discharge elimination system permits, §45.1-254.
Public participation.
Process of issuing or revising permits, §45.1-239.
Public utilities.
Applicability of act, §45.1-259.
Release of performance bond, §45.1-247.
Replacement of water supply, §45.1-258.
Rulemaking authority.
Forfeiture or release of performance bond, §45.1-247.
Safety requirements, §§45.1-161.253 to 45.1-161.292.
See COAL MINE SAFETY.
State departments and agencies.
Applicability of act, §45.1-259.
Training of blasters, §45.1-256.
Trust for coal interests.
Known owners, §45.1-161.311:8.
Missing owners, §§45.1-161.311:3 to 45.1-161.311:7.
Unsuitable areas for mining.
Designation, §45.1-252.
Water supply replacement, §45.1-258.

SURFACE FOREMAN.
Certification of coal mine workers.
Generally, §§45.1-161.24 to 45.1-161.41.

SURFACE MINING, §§45.1-180 to 45.1-197.18.
Adjacent property owners.
Mineral mines, §§45.1-161.311:1, 45.1-161.311:2.
Mining rights generally, §§45.1-161.310, 45.1-161.311.
Appeal of department decisions, §45.1-194.
Authority of director, §45.1-180.3.
Coal surface mining.
General provisions, §§45.1-226 to 45.1-270.7.
See COAL SURFACE MINING.
Safety generally, §§45.1-161.253 to 45.1-161.292.
See COAL MINE SAFETY.
Collection of debts, §45.1-186.2.
Conflicts of law.
Local waiver of chapter applicability, §45.1-197.
Contracts.
Orphaned lands, §§45.1-197.5, 45.1-197.6.
Cost of reclamation.
Collection of debts, §45.1-186.2.
Definitions, §45.1-180.
Orphaned lands, §45.1-197.3.
Disturbed land.
Additional bond to cover amended estimate of land to be disturbed, §45.1-187.
Defined, §45.1-180.
Eminent domain.
Orphaned lands, §45.1-197.7.
Exemption for restricted mining, §45.1-180.4.
Federal agency assistance, §45.1-192.
Gas and oil exploration, §§45.1-361.1 to 45.1-361.44.
See GAS AND OIL EXPLORATION.

SURFACE MINING —Cont'd
Injunctions.
Enforcement mechanism, §45.1-180.3.
Enjoining mining operation, §45.1-193.1.
Interference with reclamation, §45.1-188.
Lead agency for inspections undertaken pursuant to permit.
Department of mines, minerals and energy, §45.1-161.6.
Legislative findings, §45.1-180.2.
Local agency assistance, §45.1-192.
Local preemption of chapter provisions, §45.1-197.
Local standards and regulations, §45.1-197.
Mine inspections.
See MINE INSPECTIONS.
Mine licensing.
See MINE LICENSING.
Minerals reclamation fund, §§45.1-197.8 to 45.1-197.18.
Collection of debt.
Cost of reclamation exceeds member's forfeited payments, etc., §45.1-197.13.
Construction of article, §45.1-197.17.
Creation, §45.1-197.8.
Decreases in fund size, §45.1-197.14.
Discontinuance of fund, §45.1-197.16.
Membership, §45.1-197.9.
Membership payments, §§45.1-197.9, 45.1-197.11.
Order of return of payments, §45.1-197.15.
Payments required, §45.1-197.9.
Purpose of fund, §45.1-197.17.
Reclamation funding, §45.1-197.18.
Reclamation work, §45.1-197.12.
Funding, §45.1-197.18.
Purpose of fund, §45.1-197.17.
Release of bonds and other securities, §45.1-197.10.
Return of member payments, §§45.1-197.11, 45.1-197.14.
Revocation of permits, §45.1-197.12.
Supervision, §45.1-197.8.
Termination of fund, §45.1-197.16.
Mine safety requirements, §§45.1-161.304 to 45.1-161.309.
Notice of noncompliance.
Service on operator, §45.1-186.1.
Orphaned lands, §§45.1-197.3 to 45.1-197.7.
Acceptance of federal funds, gifts, etc., §45.1-197.7.
Agreements with owners or lessees, §45.1-197.5.
Contracts for reclamation, §45.1-197.6.
Defined, §45.1-197.3.
Priorities for reclamation, §45.1-197.4.
Reclamation by director, §45.1-197.5.
Survey, §45.1-197.4.
Permits.
Additional bonding requirement, §45.1-185.
Application, §§45.1-181 to 45.1-185.
Approval by department, §45.1-181.
Bond of operator, §§45.1-183, 45.1-185.
Furnishing copy of map, etc., to landowner, §45.1-181.
Issuance, §45.1-184.
Names and addresses of adjoining landowners, §45.1-184.1.
Operations plan, §45.1-182.1.
Renewal fee, §45.1-181.
Required, §45.1-181.
Review of operations plan and reclamation provisions, §45.1-184.

SURFACE MINING —Cont'd
Permits —Cont'd
Statement of chief local official, §45.1-184.1.
Powers of director, §45.1-180.3.
Public policy, §45.1-180.2.
Report of reclamation work, §45.1-185.
Restricted mining exemption, §45.1-180.4.
Rulemaking authority, §45.1-180.3.
State agency assistance, §45.1-192.
Uncompleted project.
Succession of one operator by another, §45.1-184.2.
Uranium ore exploration, §§45.1-272 to 45.1-285.10.
See URANIUM ORE EXPLORATION.
Violators of act, §45.1-191.

SURFACE WATER MANAGEMENT AREAS, §§62.1-242 to 62.1-253.
Agreements among persons withdrawing surface water, §62.1-245.
Defined terms, §62.1-242.
Information from persons withdrawing surface water, §62.1-244.
Permits to withdraw surface water, §62.1-248.
Application requirements, §62.1-248.1.
Cancellation, §62.1-251.
Existing ground water withdrawals in existing ground water management areas, §62.1-260.
Not required, §62.1-243.
Riparian rights, §62.1-253.
State agency review, §62.1-250.
Suspension, §62.1-251.
Water-use classifications, §62.1-249.
Proceedings to study surface water management area, §62.1-246.
Provision violations, §62.1-252.
Riparian rights, §62.1-253.
State agency review, §62.1-250.
Use of water in area, §62.1-247.
Water-use classifications, §62.1-249.

SURFACE WATERS.
Drainage projects.
General provisions, §§21-292 to 21-426.
See DRAINAGE PROJECTS.
Impoundment of surface waters.
General provisions, §§62.1-104 to 62.1-115.
See IMPOUNDMENT OF SURFACE WATERS.
Surface water management areas.
General provisions, §§62.1-242 to 62.1-253.
See SURFACE WATER MANAGEMENT AREAS.

SURFBOARDING.
Manipulating surfboards while intoxicated, §§29.1-738 to 29.1-738.6.
Restrictions, §29.1-742.

SURF CLAMS.
Clams generally.
See OYSTERS AND CLAMS.

SURFING.
Juvenile violations of ordinances regulating.
Summons issued by officer.
Juvenile and domestic relations district court may proceed on, §16.1-260.

SURFRIDER FOUNDATION.
Motor vehicle license plates.
Special license plates, §46.2-749.130.

SURGEONS.
Licensing generally, §§54.1-2900 to 54.1-2993.
See MEDICINE AND OTHER HEALING ARTS PROFESSIONS.
Oral or maxillofacial surgeons, §§54.1-2700, 54.1-2709.1 to 54.1-2709.5.
Physicians or surgeons.
See PHYSICIANS OR SURGEONS.

SURPLUS LINES INSURANCE, §§38.2-4805.1 to 38.2-4816.
Adoption of rules and regulations by state corporation commission, §38.2-4813.
Alien insurers, unlicensed.
Required approval for coverage to be placed, §38.2-4811.
Annual maintenance fund assessment, §38.2-4809.1.
Annual statement of policies, §38.2-4807.
Applicability of chapter, §38.2-4805.1.
Applicability of general insurance law, §38.2-4815.
Approval of unlicensed insurers.
Required approval for coverage to be placed, §38.2-4811.
Assessment for administration of insurance laws, §§38.2-400 to 38.2-415.
Bonds, surety.
Licensing of brokers, §38.2-1857.2.
Brokers.
Assessment of surplus lines brokers for administration of insurance laws, §§38.2-400 to 38.2-415.
Licensing, §§38.2-1857.1 to 38.2-1857.9.
Payment to, effect, §38.2-4808.
Coverage placed only with unlicensed insurers approved by state corporation commission, §38.2-4811.
Definitions, §38.2-4805.2.
Delivery of policies, §38.2-4810.
Exchange of information between commission and department of taxation, §38.2-4816.
Fees.
Licensing of brokers, §38.2-1857.3.
Foreign insurer, unlicensed.
Required approval for coverage to be placed, §38.2-4811.
General insurance law, effect of provisions, §38.2-4815.
Insurance agents generally, §§38.2-1800 to 38.2-1813.
See INSURANCE AGENTS.
Issuance of policies, §38.2-4810.
Larceny, report by insurers of acts deemed, §38.2-1810.
License taxes.
Overpayment of assessment or taxes, §38.2-4809.1.
License taxes on insurers, §38.2-4809.
Licensing of brokers, §§38.2-1857.1 to 38.2-1857.9.
Accepting surplus lines business, §38.2-1857.6.
Administrative action taken against broker.
Report to commission, §38.2-1857.5.
Applications, §38.2-1857.2.
Assumed or fictitious name.
Licensee operating under.
Notification to commission, §38.2-1857.5.
Bonds, surety, §38.2-1857.2.
Business entities, §38.2-1857.2.

SURPLUS LINES INSURANCE —Cont'd
Licensing of brokers —Cont'd
Change of name.
Report to commission, §38.2-1857.5.
Change of residence.
Out-of-state move, effect, §38.2-1857.5.
Report to commission, §38.2-1857.5.
Disciplinary actions, §38.2-1857.7.
Hearing, §38.2-1857.8.
Eligibility for licenses, §38.2-1857.1.
Exclusivity, §38.2-1857.6.
Fees, §38.2-1857.3.
Felony conviction.
Report to commission, §38.2-1857.5.
Hearing.
Disciplinary actions, §38.2-1857.8.
Insurance agents, licensing as, §38.2-1857.1.
Nonresidents, §§38.2-1857.2, 38.2-1857.9.
Placing surplus lines business, §38.2-1857.6.
Reciprocal agreements, §38.2-1857.9.
Reciprocity, §38.2-1857.2.
Reports to commission, §38.2-1857.5.
Residence removed from Commonwealth.
Termination of licensing authority, §38.2-1857.5.
Service of notice, process and other papers.
Agent for service, §38.2-1857.2.
Suspension, revocation or refusal to renew, §38.2-1857.7.
Hearing, §38.2-1857.8.
Termination of licensing authority.
Removal from Commonwealth, §38.2-1857.5.
Term of license, §38.2-1857.4.
Nonresidents.
Licensing of brokers, §38.2-1857.9.
Notice to insured.
Policy procured or placed with insurer approved to issue surplus lines insurance but not licensed or regulated by commission, §38.2-4806.
Overpayment of assessment or taxes, §38.2-4809.1.
Payments by insurers to, §38.2-1812.
Payments to brokers, effect, §38.2-4808.
Penalties for violations, §38.2-4814.
Reciprocity.
Licensing of brokers, §38.2-1857.2.
Records, §38.2-4807.
Reporting and accounting for premium, §38.2-1813.
Reports.
Licensing of brokers.
Reports to commission, §38.2-1857.5.
Rules and regulations by commission, §38.2-4813.
Scope of chapter, §38.2-4805.1.
Service of notice, process and other papers.
Insurers subject to unlicensed insurers process act, §38.2-4812.
Licensing of brokers.
Agent for service, §38.2-1857.2.
Sharing commissions, §38.2-1812.
Taxes.
Exchange of information between commission and department of taxation, §38.2-4816.
License taxes on insurers, licensees to pay, §38.2-4809.
Overpayment of assessment or taxes, §38.2-4809.1.
Unlicensed insurer, acting as agent for, §38.2-1802.
Unlicensed insurers process act, insurers subject to, §38.2-4812.

SURPLUS LINES INSURANCE —Cont'd
Violations of chapter, punishment, §38.2-4814.

SURPLUS MOTOR VEHICLES.
State owned motor vehicles.
Transfer, §2.2-1177.

SURPLUS PROPERTY.
Classification.
Criteria established by division of engineering and buildings, §2.2-1153.
Control of property by state agency.
Until final disposition, §2.2-1153.
Definition of surplus materials.
Disposition by state agency or institution, §2.2-1124.
Disposition of surplus materials.
State agencies or institutions, §2.2-1124.
Federal government.
Acquisition of surplus materials from, §2.2-1123.
Notification to division of engineering and buildings.
Property not used or required by state agency, §2.2-1153.
Sale or lease by department of general services, §2.2-1156.
Schools and education.
Real property, §22.1-129.

SURROGACY CONTRACTS, §§20-156 to 20-165.
Clinical management of pregnancy, §20-163.
Conflicts of law.
Virginia law to control, §20-157.
Court-approved contracts.
Determination of parentage, §20-158.
Orders, §20-160.
Permissible, §20-159.
Petition and hearing for court approval, §20-160.
Requirements, §20-160.
Termination, §20-161.
Death of spouse.
Determination of parentage, §20-158.
Definitions, §20-156.
Determination of parentage, §20-158.
Divorce.
Determination of parentage, §20-158.
Donors of sperm or ova.
Parental rights or duties, §32.1-257.
Dual parentage prohibition, §20-164.
Health care providers.
Immunity from liability, §20-163.
Liability of surrogate brokers, §20-165.
Marriage of surrogate, §20-163.
Mentally or physically handicapped child.
Parental responsibility of intended parents, §20-163.
Non-court approved contracts.
Determination of parentage, §20-158.
Requirements, §20-162.
Permissible contracts, §20-159.
Relation of parent and child, §20-164.
Requirements.
Contracts not approved by court, §20-162.
Court-approved contracts, §20-160.
Surrogate brokers prohibition, §20-165.
Termination of court-approved contracts, §20-161.

SURRY COUNTY.
Coastal primary sand dunes and beaches.
Zoning ordinances, §28.2-1403.
Confederate cemeteries and graves.
Disbursement of funds appropriated for upkeep, §10.1-2211.

SURRY COUNTY —Cont'd
Port of Virginia economic and infrastructure development zone grant fund, §62.1-132.3:2.
Retail sales and use tax.
Additional sales tax for Northern Virginia and Hampton Roads, §58.1-603.1.
Additional use tax for Northern Virginia and Hampton Roads, §58.1-604.01.
School board.
Salary of members, §22.1-32.

SURVEILLANCE.
Evidence of electronically recorded conversations, §8.01-420.2.
Interception of wire, electronic or oral communications, §§19.2-61 to 19.2-70.3.
See ELECTRONIC SURVEILLANCE.
Library electronic surveillance devices, §42.1-73.1.

SURVEYORS, §§54.1-400 to 54.1-411.
Board for architects, professional engineers, land surveyors and landscape architects, §§54.1-403 to 54.1-405.
Boundaries of localities established by commissioners.
Appointment to run boundary and make plats, §15.2-3101.
Building plans, §54.1-410.
Business license, requirements for obtaining, §54.1-410.1.
Code of professional practice and conduct.
Regulations of board, §54.1-404.
Continuing education, §54.1-404.2.
Corner monumentation, §54.1-407.
Defined terms, §54.1-400.
Emeritus designation for retirees, §54.1-405.
Examinations, §54.1-405.
Landscape architect license distinguished, §54.1-409.
Monumentation on corners, §54.1-407.
Mortgages and deeds of trust.
Lender may not require particular surveyor, §6.2-410.
Organization for practice, §54.1-411.
Oysters, §28.2-557.
Professional corporations.
Generally, §§13.1-542.1 to 13.1-556.
See PROFESSIONAL CORPORATIONS.
Shareholder qualifications, special provisions, §13.1-549.
Professional limited liability companies.
Generally, §§13.1-1100 to 13.1-1123.
See PROFESSIONAL LIMITED LIABILITY COMPANIES.
Special provisions, §13.1-1111.
Registration, §54.1-411.
Requirement of licensure, §54.1-406.
Exemptions, §§54.1-401 to 54.1-402.1.
Subdivisions, §54.1-408.
Unlawful procurement of licensure, §54.1-102.
Unlawful use of licensure, §54.1-111.
Unlicensed activities.
Cease and desist order, civil penalty, §54.1-402.2.

SURVEYS.
Boundaries.
Lines established by commissioners, §15.2-3101.
Motion for judgment to establish boundaries, §8.01-181.
Coordinate systems of Virginia, §§55-287 to 55-297.

SURVEYS —Cont'd
Drainage projects.
Adoption of surveys already made, §21-332.
Assistance in making survey, §21-326.
Complete survey, §21-325.
Cost of survey, §21-335.
Insurance information.
Marketing and research surveys, §38.2-605.
Mines and mining.
Adjacent property owners.
Right to survey, §45.1-161.311.
Mineral mines, §45.1-161.311:2.
Official map of locality.
Power of local planning commissions, §15.2-2233.
Oysters.
Baylor survey.
Crossings, §28.2-555.
Erosion control devices, §28.2-556.
Reestablishment of lines, §§28.2-552, 28.2-553.
Removal of oysters planted by mistake, §28.2-559.
Sale of charts and plats, §28.2-554.
Conclusive evidence, §28.2-551.
Marker removal, §28.2-561.
Permanent markers, §28.2-558.
Planting grounds, §28.2-625.
General oyster planting grounds.
Assignments, §28.2-607.
Resurveys, §§28.2-614, 28.2-615.
Riparian oyster planting grounds.
Assignments, §28.2-600.
Transfers, §28.2-602.
Resurveys, §28.2-552.
Removal of oysters planted by mistake, §28.2-559.
Railroad corporations.
Powers, §56-346.
Surface mining.
Orphaned lands, §45.1-197.4.
Unified or centralized system for geographic information.
Locality requiring by ordinance, §15.2-962.

SURVEYS OR QUESTIONNAIRES REQUIRING STUDENT PARTICIPATION.
School boards to adopt policies prohibiting during school day, §22.1-79.3.

SURVIVAL OF ACTIONS, §§8.01-25, 8.01-56.
Community associations.
Directors and officers, survival of immunity after discontinuance entity, §13.1-870.2.
Corporations.
Termination of corporate existence, §13.1-755.
Eminent domain.
Highways and roads, §33.1-98.
Nonprofit corporations.
Directors.
Survival of immunity after discontinuance entity, §13.1-870.1.
Termination of corporate existence, §13.1-917.
Tax exempt organizations.
Immunity defense.
Survival of immunity after discontinuance of entity, §8.01-220.1:1.
Wrongful death, §8.01-56.

SURVIVING SPOUSES AND DEPENDENTS.
Accrued and undistributed income elections, §64.2-429.
Black lung disease.
Death benefit payments, §65.2-513.

SURVIVING SPOUSES AND DEPENDENTS —Cont'd
Coal workers' pneumoconiosis.
Death benefit payments, §65.2-513.
Community property rights at death.
Generally, §§64.2-315 to 64.2-324.
See COMMUNITY PROPERTY RIGHTS AT DEATH.
Credit unions.
Membership, §6.2-1327.
Crime victim and witness assistance programs.
Persons eligible for awards, §19.2-368.4.
Descent and distribution.
Administrators.
Appointing preferences, §64.2-502.
Personalty.
Distribution of, §64.2-201.
Realty.
Distribution of, §64.2-200.
Spouses omitted from wills.
Portion to take, §64.2-422.
Elective shares.
Abandonment.
Effect upon, §64.2-308.
Amount, §64.2-306.
Claiming, §64.2-302.
Extension of time, §64.2-303.
Rights upon, §64.2-304.
Desertion.
Effect upon, §64.2-308.
Family residence rights, §64.2-307.
Exempt property, §64.2-310.
Claiming, §64.2-313.
Determination, §64.2-312.
Documentation, §64.2-312.
Source, §64.2-312.
Waiver, §64.2-314.
Family allowances, §64.2-313.
Claiming, §64.2-313.
Determination, §64.2-312.
Documentation, §64.2-312.
Source, §64.2-312.
Waiver, §64.2-314.
Family residence rights, §64.2-307.
Health insurance.
Line of duty act.
Continued coverage, §9.1-401.
Public officers and employees.
Continued coverage purchases through department, §2.2-1205.
Procedure, §2.2-2819.
Qualifications, §2.2-2819.
Termination, §2.2-2819.
Continued coverage purchases through plan sponsor, §2.2-1206.
Homestead allowances, §64.2-311.
Claiming, §64.2-313.
Determination, §64.2-312.
Documentation, §64.2-312.
Source, §64.2-312.
Waiver, §64.2-314.
Law officers' retirement system.
Death before retirement, §51.1-218.
Line of duty act.
Claims for payments, §9.1-403.
Health insurance.
Continued coverage, §9.1-401.
Marital deduction elections.
Powers of executors and administrators, §64.2-107.

SURVIVING SPOUSES AND DEPENDENTS —Cont'd
Marital deduction formula clauses.
Construction, §64.2-430.
Public officers and employees.
Health insurance.
Continued coverage purchases through department, §2.2-1205.
Procedure, §2.2-2819.
Qualifications, §2.2-2819.
Termination, §2.2-2819.
Continued coverage purchases through plan sponsor, §2.2-1206.
Slayer of decedent.
Bar as to property rights or receipt of benefits, §§64.2-2500 to 64.2-2511.
See SLAYER'S ACT.
Utility consumer services cooperatives.
Patronage capital.
Payment to spouse or next of kin of deceased person, §56-231.31.
Wills.
Omitted spouses.
Portion to take, §64.2-422.
Workers' compensation.
Dependency.
Determinations, §§65.2-515, 65.2-516.
Termination, §65.2-517.
Payments.
Receipt by whom, §65.2-525.
Wrongful death.
Classes of beneficiaries, §§8.01-53, 8.01-54.

SURVIVORSHIP.
Custodial trusts, §64.2-905.
Divorce from bond of matrimony.
Extinguishment of right of survivorship, §20-111.
Joint tenancies, §55-20.
Exceptions, §55-21.
Securities registered in joint name to apply to survivorship, §§13.1-434 to 13.1-436.

SUSPENDED SENTENCES, §19.2-303.
Come-back time, §19.2-306.
Defendant sentenced to detention center incarceration program, §19.2-316.2.
Defendant sentenced to diversion center incarceration program, §19.2-316.3.
Fixing period of suspension, §19.2-303.1.
Global positioning system.
Wearing device as condition of suspended sentence, §19.2-303.
Installment payment of criminal fines and penalties, §19.2-356.
Mandatory minimum.
Definition, suspension prohibited, §18.2-12.1.
Revocation or suspension, §19.2-303.
Detention center incarceration program.
Voluntary withdrawal, removal or failure to comply with terms and conditions, §19.2-316.2.
Diversion center incarceration program.
Voluntary withdrawal, removal or failure to comply with terms and conditions, §19.2-316.3.
Substance abuse screening and assessment.
Drug conviction, §18.2-252.
Felony conviction generally, §18.2-251.01.

SUSPENDING BONDS.
Recording in bond book, §17.1-230.

SUSPENSION OF DRIVERS' LICENSES.
See DRIVERS' LICENSES.

SUSPENSION OF EXECUTION OF SENTENCE.
See SENTENCING.

SUSPENSION OF LAWS PROHIBITED, VA Const Art I §7.

SUSPENSION OF PUBLIC OFFICER FROM OFFICE.
Pending hearing and appeal, §24.2-236.

SUSPENSION OR EXPULSION OF PUBLIC SCHOOL PUPILS, §§22.1-277 to 22.1-277.2.
Alternative education programs.
Authority of school boards, §22.1-277.2:1.
Exclusion from admission, §22.1-277.2.
Exclusion from admission, §22.1-277.2.
Expulsion, §§22.1-277, 22.1-277.06 to 22.1-277.08.
Readmission, §22.1-277.06.
Guidelines for school board policies, §22.1-279.6.
Hazing, §18.2-56.
Long-term suspension, §§22.1-277, 22.1-277.05.
Readmission, §§22.1-277.04 to 22.1-277.06.
Short-term suspension, §§22.1-277, 22.1-277.04.

SUSSEX COUNTY.
Port of Virginia economic and infrastructure development zone grant fund, §62.1-132.3:2.
School board.
Salary of members, §22.1-32.

SWANS.
Hunting.
Assisting other hunters after obtaining bag limit.
Calling swans, §29.1-521.

SWASTIKAS.
Placing on certain property, §18.2-423.1.

SWEARING, ABUSIVE LANGUAGE TO ANOTHER, §18.2-416, VA SCt Rule 3C:2.
Action for insulting words, §8.01-45.

SWEARING IN PUBLIC, §18.2-388, VA SCt Rule 3C:2.

SWEARING, TELEPHONE OR CITIZENS BAND RADIO, §18.2-427.

SWIMMING OR BATHING AREA.
Placement of markers designating public area.
Petition requesting, costs, motorboating or water skiing prohibited, §29.1-734.

SWIMMING POOLS.
Counties, cities or towns.
Agreements with landowners, §29.1-509.
City or town powers, §15.2-1110.
Leasing land held or owned by locality for purposes of, §15.2-1810.
Operating within sanitary district, §15.2-1811.
Ordinances requiring fencing, §15.2-921.
Fencing required by ordinance, §15.2-921.
Gate requirements, ordinances setting, §15.2-921.
Mechanics' and materialmen's liens.
Structures permanently annexed to freehold.
Classification, §43-2.
Urban county executive form of government.
Appropriation to nonprofit entity owning, §15.2-820.
Water quality tests, §32.1-248.1.

SWINE.
Estrays, §§55-202 to 55-206.
False pedigree, §18.2-205.
False pretense in obtaining registration, §18.2-205.
Garbage feeding, §§3.2-6031 to 3.2-6034.
Hog cholera.
Virus violations, §3.2-6017.
Larceny, §18.2-97.
Livestock.
Diseases.
See LIVESTOCK AND ANIMAL DISEASES.
Generally.
See LIVESTOCK.
Maiming, killing or poisoning, §18.2-144.
Pork industry board, §§3.2-2000 to 3.2-2009.
See PORK INDUSTRY BOARD.
Shooting enclosures, §§3.2-6035 to 3.2-6042.
Smithfield hams, §§3.2-5419 to 3.2-5421.
See SMITHFIELD HAMS.

SWITCHBLADES.
Carrying concealed weapons, §18.2-308.
Convicted felons, possession, transportation or concealing, §18.2-308.2.
Courthouses, carrying weapon into, §18.2-283.1.
Minors, furnishing to, §18.2-309.
School property, possession on, §18.2-308.1.
Selling or having in possession, §18.2-311.
Use in commission of crime.
Forfeiture, §19.2-386.29.

SWORDS.
Machete or other bladed weapon.
Brandishing with intent to intimidate, §18.2-282.1.

SYNAGOGUES.
Generally.
See CHURCHES AND OTHER PLACES OF WORSHIP.
Rabbi-penitent privilege, §8.01-400, VA SCt Rule 2:503.
Religion generally.
See RELIGION.
Swastika, placing on property, §18.2-423.1.
Trespass upon synagogue property, §18.2-128.

SYNTHETIC CANNABINOIDS, §18.2-248.1:1.
Custody of substances, law-enforcement agencies, §19.2-386.25.
Disposal of seized substances, marijuana and paraphernalia, §19.2-386.23.
Destruction prior to trial, §19.2-386.24.
Drug houses.
Maintaining fortified drug houses, §18.2-258.02.
Firearms, possession, §18.2-308.4.
Forfeiture of property used in connection with or derived from illegal drug transaction, §19.2-386.22.
Juvenile detention and other care facilities.
Delivery to detainees, §18.2-474.1.
Minors.
Distributing instruments for use in administering to, §18.2-255.1.
Selling or distributing to, §18.2-255.
Nuisances.
Premises deemed common nuisance, §18.2-258.
Prisoners.
Crimes by, felonies, §53.1-203.
Delivery to, §18.2-474.1.
Probationer or parolee suspected of illegal use.
Probation or parole officer's power to order testing, §53.1-145.

SYNTHETIC CANNABINOIDS —Cont'd
Probation for first time offenders, §18.2-251.
Removal of public officer from office.
Manufacture, sale, etc., §24.2-233.
Schools and education.
Expulsion of students for certain drug offenses, §22.1-277.08.
Reports of certain acts to school authorities, §22.1-279.3:1.
School property, colleges campuses, libraries, etc.
Sales on or near properties, §18.2-255.2.
Seizure of property used in connection with or derived from illegal drug transaction, §19.2-386.22.
Disposal of seized substances, marijuana and paraphernalia, §19.2-386.23.

SYPHILIS.
Infected sexual battery.
Sex with another with intent to transmit disease, §18.2-67.4:1.
Venereal diseases generally, §§32.1-55 to 32.1-60.

SYRINGES.
Driving while intoxicated.
Chemical tests of blood.
Reuse of single-use-only needles or syringes, §18.2-268.5.
Drug paraphernalia, §§18.2-265.1 to 18.2-265.5.
Retail sales and use tax exemptions, §58.1-609.10.

T

TABLES.
Motor vehicle speed and stopping distances, §46.2-880.

TABLES OF SPEED AND STOPPING DISTANCES, §46.2-880.

TABLET COMPUTERS.
Portable electronics insurance, §§38.2-1875 to 38.2-1880.

TAG ACT.
Tuition assistance grant, §§23-38.11 to 23-38.19:2.
See COLLEGES AND UNIVERSITIES.

TAILGATING, §46.2-816.
Commercial motor vehicles.
Disqualification for multiple serious traffic violations, §46.2-341.20.
Demerit points, §46.2-492.
Fine schedule, VA SCt Rule 3B:2.
Fire apparatus, §46.2-921.
Maximum fine for violating Title 46.2, §46.2-113.
Prepayment of fine, §16.1-69.40:1.

TAIL LIGHTS.
Bicycles, §46.2-1015.
Electric power-assisted bicycles, §46.2-1015.
Fine schedule, VA SCt Rule 3B:2.
Maximum fine for violating Title 46.2, §46.2-113.
Mopeds, §46.2-1015.
Motorcycles, §46.2-1012.
Motor vehicles, §46.2-1013.

TAKEOVERS.
Corporations.
Affiliated transactions, §§13.1-725 to 13.1-727.1.
Control share acquisition, §§13.1-728.1 to 13.1-728.9.

TAKING INDECENT LIBERTIES WITH CHILDREN, §§18.2-370, 18.2-370.01.
Custodians or persons in supervisory relationship, §18.2-370.1.
Jail prisoner escape or release notice, §53.1-116.1.
Prisoner intake notice, §53.1-116.1:01.
Discretionary felony sentencing guidelines, §17.1-805.
HIV or hepatitis B or C.
Testing of persons charged, §18.2-62.
Jail prisoner escape or release notice, §53.1-116.1.
Prisoner intake notice, §53.1-116.1:01.
Punishment upon conviction of certain subsequent felony sexual assault, §18.2-67.5:2.
Recent complaint hearsay exception, §19.2-268.2.
Suspension of sentence, placing on probation, §19.2-303.

TAKING OF PRIVATE PROPERTY, VA Const Art I §11, US Const Amd V.
Eminent domain generally.
See EMINENT DOMAIN.

TALKING SOFTWARE.
Assistive technology device warranties, §§59.1-470 to 59.1-474.

TAMPERING.
Ballot containers, voting or registration equipment, etc., §24.2-1009.
Cable television service, §18.2-165.1.
Fire hydrants, §18.2-162.1.
Jury box, §18.2-467.
Lottery equipment or machinery, §58.1-4018.
Motor vehicle odometer, §46.2-112.
Parking meters, vending machines, pay telephones, etc., §18.2-152.

T&M VEHICLE DEALERS, §§46.2-1900 to 46.2-1991.
Advertising, §46.2-1936.
Enforcement of article, §46.2-1991.
Regulated practices, §46.2-1990.
Audits, §46.2-1928.
Bill of sale.
Completed buyer's order constitutes, §46.2-1930.
Bonds, surety.
Applicants for license, §46.2-1927.
Business hours, §46.2-1934.
Buyer's order.
Contents, §46.2-1930.
Copies, §46.2-1930.
Certificate of dealer registration, §46.2-1908.
Applications, §46.2-1909.
Action on, §46.2-1914.
Change in form of ownership, line-make or name, §46.2-1917.
Denial, suspension or revocation.
Appeals, §46.2-1987.
Court of appeals, §46.2-1988.
Equitable remedies not impaired, §46.2-1989.
Grounds, §46.2-1985.
Notice and hearings, §46.2-1986.
Expiration, §46.2-1921.
Fees, §46.2-1919.
Collection, §46.2-1920.
Issuance, §46.2-1921.
Renewal, §46.2-1921.
Certificate of title, §46.2-1945.

T&M VEHICLE DEALERS —Cont'd
Certificate of vehicle registration and license plates, §46.2-1947.
Certificates of ownership.
Temporary certificates, §46.2-1943.
Certification of qualification.
Dealers, §46.2-1911.
Salespersons, §46.2-1912.
Coercion.
Manufacturers or distributors, §46.2-1976.
Retail installment sales contracts.
Coercion by manufacturer or distributor, §46.2-1975.
Commissioner.
General powers, §46.2-1901.
Powers.
Hearings, §46.2-1904.
Consignment contracts.
Contents, §46.2-1931.
Dealer-arranged financing.
Purchase conditional on, notice required, §46.2-1930.1.
Dealer-operator.
Continued operation on loss of, §46.2-1913.
Definitions, §46.2-1900.
Distributors.
Certain disclosures required by, §46.2-1933.
Electronic filing system.
Fees, §46.2-1930.1.
Examination of licensee, §46.2-1928.
Fees.
License and registration fees, §46.2-1919.
Collection, §46.2-1920.
Manual transaction fee, §46.2-1930.2.
Remote electronic filing system, §46.2-1930.1.
Franchises.
Civil penalties, §46.2-1982.
Discontinuance of distributors, §46.2-1978.
Filing, §46.2-1973.
Hearings, §46.2-1982.
Late model and factory repurchase franchises, §46.2-1983.
Offering constitutes engaging in business in state, §46.2-1908.
Retail franchising act.
Exemption, §46.2-1974.
Right of first refusal.
Manufacturers or distributors, §46.2-1977.
Sale or transfer.
Manufacturer or distributor right of first refusal, §46.2-1977.
Warranty obligations, §46.2-1979.
Hearings.
Powers of commissioner, §46.2-1904.
Injunctions.
Suit to enjoin violations, §46.2-1905.
Inspections.
Required, §46.2-1940.
Exceptions, §46.2-1941.
Insurance.
Coercing purchaser to provide, §46.2-1937.
License plates.
Prerequisites to receiving, §46.2-1948.
License plates.
Cancellation, §46.2-1962.
Dealer's license prerequisite to receiving, §46.2-1948.
Design, §46.2-1949.
Display, §46.2-1949.
Distinguished between various types of dealers, §46.2-1950.

T&M VEHICLE DEALERS —Cont'd
License plates —Cont'd
Foreign dealer's licenses, §46.2-1960.
Franchise or independent dealer's license plates distinguished from factory dealers and T & M dealers, §46.2-1950.
Insurance.
Required, §46.2-1948.
Movement to salesrooms, §46.2-1959.
Newly purchased vehicles, §46.2-1956.
Operation without prohibited, §46.2-1957.
Penalties for violations of article, §46.2-1963.
Promotional plates, §46.2-1951.
Registration of dealers, §46.2-1947.
Removal.
Department investigators, §46.2-1962.
Revocation, §46.2-1948.
Temporary license plates.
Alternative print-on-demand program, §46.2-1964.1.
Application, §46.2-1966.
Current titling and registration, §46.2-1967.
Misstatements and false information, §46.2-1967.
Destruction on expiration, §46.2-1970.
Display, §46.2-1964.
Expiration, §46.2-1971.
Information to be placed on by dealer, §46.2-1968.
Issuance, §46.2-1964.
Suspension of right of dealer to issue, §46.2-1969.
To whom plates shall not be issued, §46.2-1967.
Penalties for violations of provisions, §46.2-1972.
Records, §46.2-1965.
Suspension of right of dealer to issue, §46.2-1969.
Temporary transport plates.
Issuance and use of, §46.2-1954.
Transferable dealer's plates, §46.2-1949.
Transport to place of shipment or delivery, §46.2-1958.
Use, §46.2-1952.
Certain vehicles, §46.2-1953.
Traveling from one establishment to another for having special equipment installed, §46.2-1955.
Use of old plates, §46.2-1944.
Licenses.
Applications, §46.2-1909.
Action on, §46.2-1914.
Bonds, surety, §46.2-1927.
Certificate of qualification.
Issuance, §46.2-1911.
Prerequisite to issuance of license, §46.2-1911.
Changes in form of ownership, line-make or name, §46.2-1917.
Denial, suspension or revocation.
Acts of officers, directors, partners and salespersons, §46.2-1984.
Appeals, §46.2-1987.
Court of appeals, §46.2-1988.
Equitable remedies not impaired, §46.2-1989.
Grounds, §46.2-1985.
Notice and hearings, §46.2-1986.
Display, §46.2-1915.
Established place of business.
Required, §46.2-1910.
Expiration, §46.2-1921.

T&M VEHICLE DEALERS —Cont'd
Licenses —Cont'd
Fees, §46.2-1919.
Collection, §46.2-1920.
Issuance, §46.2-1921.
Multi-year licenses, §46.2-1921.
Nonresidents, §46.2-1908.
Renewal, §46.2-1921.
Required, §46.2-1908.
Salespersons.
Display, §46.2-1918.
Temporary supplemental license, §46.2-1916.
Transferable dealer's license plates, §46.2-1948.
Manual transaction fee, §46.2-1930.2.
Manufacturers.
Certain disclosures required by, §46.2-1933.
Operation of dealership by, §46.2-1980.
Motor vehicle safety inspections.
Inspection of vehicles required, §46.2-1940.
Exceptions, §46.2-1941.
No liability insurance included.
Stamping on bill of sale, §46.2-1930.1.
Nonprofit organizations.
Consigning donated T&M vehicles to dealers.
Certificate authorizing, §46.2-1908.1.
Odometers.
Disclosure, §46.2-1932.
Operation of dealership by manufacturer, §46.2-1980.
Penalties.
Violations of chapter, §46.2-1907.
Place of business.
Business hours, §46.2-1934.
Change of location, §46.2-1915.
Dealers required to have established place, §46.2-1910.
Location to be specified, §46.2-1915.
Supplemental sales locations, §46.2-1916.
Records.
Maintenance, §46.2-1929.
Temporary license plates, §46.2-1965.
Registration.
Use of old number, §46.2-1944.
Remote electronic filing system.
Fees, §46.2-1930.1.
Retail franchising.
Exemption of franchises from act, §46.2-1974.
Retail installment sales contracts.
Coercion by manufacturer or distributor with respect to, §46.2-1975.
Rules and regulations.
Promulgation, §46.2-1906.
Salespersons.
Certificate of qualification, §46.2-1912.
Licenses.
Display, §46.2-1918.
Notice on termination, §46.2-1918.
Selling for other than his employer, §46.2-1939.
Service facilities.
Ownership, §46.2-1981.
Signs.
Required, §46.2-1935.
Solicitations.
Prohibited solicitations and compensation, §46.2-1938.
Supplemental sales locations, §46.2-1916.
Temporary supplemental license, §46.2-1916.
Temporary transport plates.
Issuance and use of, §46.2-1954.
Traveling from one establishment to another for having special equipment installed, §46.2-1955.

T&M VEHICLE DEALERS —Cont'd
Termination of business, §46.2-1946.
Title.
Certificates of title, §46.2-1945.
Transport to place of shipment or delivery.
Movement by manufacturer, §46.2-1958.
Unfair, deceptive and misleading acts or practices.
Advertising, §46.2-1990.
Violations of chapter.
Penalties, §46.2-1907.
Warranties.
Obligations, §46.2-1979.

TANF, §§63.2-600 to 63.2-621.
See TEMPORARY ASSISTANCE FOR NEEDY FAMILIES (TANF).

TANGIBLE PERSONAL PROPERTY.
Segregation for local taxation, VA Const Art X §4.

TANGIER, TOWN OF.
Motor vehicle regulation.
Adoption of local ordinances paralleling motor vehicles title, §46.2-115.

TANK WAGONS.
Defined, §58.1-2201.
Overweight permits, §46.2-1144.1.

TANNING FACILITIES, §§59.1-310.1 to 59.1-310.6.
Application of provisions, §59.1-310.2.
Defined terms, §59.1-310.1.
Medicine and other healing arts professions.
Exceptions and exemptions from licensure, §54.1-2901.
Notice to customers, §59.1-310.3.
Operational requirements, §59.1-310.5.
Peeping or spying, §18.2-130.
Provision violations.
Penalties, §59.1-310.6.
Warning signs, §59.1-310.4.

TAPE RECORDINGS.
District court proceedings, §16.1-69.35:2.
Tapes generally.
See RECORDED DEVICES.

TAPPAHANNOCK-ESSEX COUNTY AIRPORT AUTHORITY, 1988 ch 871.

TARGET SHOOTING ORGANIZATIONS.
Carrying concealed weapons, when provisions not applicable, §18.2-308.

TASERS.
Use in commission of crime.
Forfeiture, §19.2-386.29.

TASK FORCES.
Gubernatorial commissions to include, §2.2-134.

TASTING LICENSES.
Alcoholic beverage samples, selling or giving, §4.1-206.
Government store on premises of licensed distiller.
Charge to consumers to participate in tasting event, §4.1-206.
Limitations, §4.1-221.1.

TASTINGS CONDUCTED BY LICENSEE.
Gourmet shop beer and wine licensees, §4.1-209.
Persons granted retail wine and beer licenses, §4.1-209.

TASTINGS CONDUCTED BY MANUFACTURERS.
Beer, wine or spirits manufacturers, §4.1-201.1.
Permit, §4.1-212.

TATTOOING MINORS, §18.2-371.3.

TATTOO PARLORS.
Barber and cosmetology licensure generally, §§54.1-700 to 54.1-706.
County, city or town regulating, §15.2-912.
Temporary assistance for needy families (TANF).
Prohibited uses of benefits, §63.2-621.

TAXABLE INCOME.
Corporations, §58.1-402.
Allocation and apportionment, §§58.1-406 to 58.1-423.
Modifications to taxable income, §58.1-403.
Transacting or conducting entire business within Commonwealth, §58.1-405.
Estates or trust, §§58.1-361, 58.1-362.
Nonresidents, §58.1-362.
Individual taxpayers, §58.1-322.
Partners, §58.1-391.
Withheld taxes not deductible in computing, §58.1-481.

TAXABLE PROPERTY, VA Const Art X §1.

TAX AMNESTY PROGRAM, §58.1-1840.1.

TAX ASSESSMENTS.
Aircraft sales and use tax, §58.1-1502.
Bank franchise tax.
Assessment of real and leased tangible personal property, §58.1-1203.
Computation of net capital, §58.1-1205.
Net capital measure of tax, §58.1-1202.
Rate of tax, §§58.1-1204, 58.1-1204.1.
Boards of equalization, §§58.1-3370 to 58.1-3389.
See REAL PROPERTY TAXES.
Cigarette use tax.
Failure to make return or incorrect return, §58.1-1020.
Collection of state taxes generally, §§58.1-1800 to 58.1-1818.
See TAX COLLECTION.
Commissioners of revenue to assist subjects of taxation, §58.1-3103.
Correction of erroneous tax assessments.
Local taxes generally, §§58.1-3980 to 58.1-3995.
See CORRECTION OF ERRONEOUS TAX ASSESSMENTS.
State taxes generally, §§58.1-1820 to 58.1-1835.
See CORRECTION OF ERRONEOUS TAX ASSESSMENTS.
Correctness.
Department of taxation assessments prima facie correct, §58.1-205.
Double assessments.
Correction of state tax double assessments, §58.1-1827.
Forest products tax.
Tax rates, §§58.1-1604 to 58.1-1607.
Income tax.
Jeopardy assessments, §§58.1-313, 58.1-314.
Limitations on assessment, §58.1-312.

TAX ASSESSMENTS —Cont'd
Income tax —Cont'd
Memorandum assessments, payment in currency, §58.1-352.
Taxpayer problem resolution program, §58.1-1818.
Injunctions.
Local tax assessments, §58.1-3993.
Intangible personal property tax.
Delinquents, assessment on estimates, §58.1-1113.
Invalidity dependent upon whether rights prejudiced, §58.1-3961.
Jeopardy assessments.
Forest products tax, §58.1-1616.
Income tax, §§58.1-313, 58.1-314.
Income tax withholding, §58.1-473.
Retail sales and use tax, §58.1-631.
Land preservation special assessment.
Real property taxes, §§58.1-3229 to 58.1-3244.
License tax on telegraph, telephone, water, heat, light, power and pipeline companies, §§58.1-2633, 58.1-2634.
Limitation on assessment, §58.1-104.
Waiver of time limitation, §58.1-101.
Assessment of omitted or additional state taxes, §58.1-220.
Omitted taxes.
Agencies other than tax department, §58.1-2025.
Local taxes or levies, §58.1-3903.
Forms for assessment, §58.1-3905.
Personal property taxes.
Intangible personal property tax.
Delinquents, assessment on estimates, §58.1-1113.
Situs for assessment, §§58.1-3511 to 58.1-3514.
Prima facie correctness.
Assessment of tax by department of taxation, §58.1-205.
Problem resolution program, §58.1-1818.
Public service corporation taxation.
Administrative and judicial review of assessments, §§58.1-2670 to 58.1-2676.
Generally, §§58.1-2600 to 58.1-2690.
See PUBLIC SERVICE CORPORATION TAXATION.
Special provisions for assessments in counties having county executive or county manager governments, §§58.1-2680 to 58.1-2683.
Real property taxes.
Assessment generally, §§58.1-3250 to 58.1-3294.
See REAL PROPERTY TAXES.
Special assessment for land preservation, §§58.1-3229 to 58.1-3244.
Tax increment financing, §§58.1-3245 to 58.1-3245.5.
Taxpayer problem resolution program, §58.1-1818.
Rolling stock tax, §§58.1-2655 to 58.1-2657.
Soft drink excise tax, §58.1-1702.
Special regulatory revenue tax on public service corporations, §§58.1-2663, 58.1-2664.
When taxes not to be assessed or assessed only in part, §58.1-2664.
Tax increment financing.
Blighted areas, §§58.1-3245 to 58.1-3245.5.
Watercraft sales and use tax, §§58.1-1402, 58.1-1403.

TAX BILLS.
County board form of government.
Board of supervisors requiring commissioners of revenue to prepare, §15.2-409.

TAX BILLS —Cont'd
Property taxes.
Electronic billing, §58.1-3912.
Mailing bills, §58.1-3912.
Website access, §58.1-3912.

TAX COLLECTION.
Accrued taxes prior to repeal of tax, §58.1-10.
Agencies, taxes administered by.
Additional proceedings.
Jurisdiction and venue, §58.1-2022.
Estates in hands of or debts due third party, §58.1-2020.
Judgment or decree, §58.1-2023.
Enforcement in foreign jurisdiction, §58.1-2024.
Memorandum of lien.
Taxes assessed by state corporation commission, §58.1-2021.
Omitted taxes, §58.1-2025.
Third parties.
Estates in hand of or debts due by, §58.1-2020.
Aircraft sales and use tax, §58.1-1503.
Barratry, inapplicability of article, §18.2-451.
Clerks of courts of record, §§58.1-3173 to 58.1-3177.
Commissioners of revenue.
Generally, §§58.1-3100 to 58.1-3122.2.
See COMMISSIONERS OF REVENUE.
Consumer utility tax.
Discount for collection, §58.1-3816.1.
District courts, plaintiff suing on sworn claim, §16.1-88.
Donations to general fund, §58.1-17.
Erroneous written advice by department.
Abatement of tax, interest or penalty, §58.1-1835.
Forest products tax, §§58.1-1609, 58.1-1610.
General assembly powers, VA Const Art IV §14.
Income tax.
Individual income tax, §58.1-351.
Duty of county and city treasurer, §58.1-353.
Problem resolution program, §58.1-1818.
Installment collection.
State taxes.
Agreements for the payment of taxes, §58.1-1817.
Intangible personal property tax, §58.1-1117.
Local taxes, §§58.1-3910 to 58.1-3961.
Actions to enforce payments, §58.1-3953.
Judgment or decree, §58.1-3955.
Enforcement in foreign jurisdiction, §58.1-3956.
Procedure, §58.1-3954.
Venue, §58.1-3953.
Administrative costs, payment of, §58.1-3958.
Assessment not invalid unless rights prejudiced by error, §58.1-3961.
Attachment.
Collection out of estate in hands of or debts due by third party, §58.1-3952.
Attorney compensation, employment to collect taxes, §58.1-3957.
Bills to taxpayers or obligees on mortgages or deeds of trust.
Treasurers to mail to, §58.1-3912.
Crediting payments, §58.1-3913.
Criminal penalties for failure to file returns or false statements, §58.1-3916.1.
Delinquent taxes.
Administrative costs, §58.1-3958.
Attorneys hired to collect local taxes, §58.1-3934.

TAX COLLECTION —Cont'd
Local taxes —Cont'd
Delinquent taxes —Cont'd
Beneficiary statement prior to delinquency, §58.1-3926.
Card system record and index of delinquent real estate in Norfolk, §58.1-3932.
Collection by distress, suit, lien, etc., §§58.1-3940 to 58.1-3961.
Subsequent collection on subjects other than real estate, §58.1-3933.
Waiver of time limitation on assessment, §58.1-3903.1.
Collection of subjects other than real estate by sheriff or person employed for purpose, §58.1-3934.
Estates in hands of or debts due by third parties, §58.1-3952.
Exoneration from lien, payment of taxes, §58.1-3959.
Liability of treasurers for taxes returned delinquent, §58.1-3935.
Liens of delinquent real estate, recordings, §58.1-3930.
List of uncollectible taxes and delinquents.
List of delinquent town real estate taxes filed with county treasurers in certain towns, §58.1-3938.
Lists to speak as of June 30 of each year, §58.1-3922.
Omission of taxes from list, §58.1-3936.
Publication, §58.1-3924.
Submission to local governing bodies, §58.1-3924.
Time treasurer to make out list, §58.1-3921.
Treasurers to make out, §58.1-3921.
Notice by beneficiary under lien, §58.1-3926.
Omission of taxes from delinquent list, §58.1-3936.
Petition to ascertain, §58.1-3959.
Private collection agents used to collect taxes other than real estate taxes.
Employment by locality, compensation, credit for taxes collected, treasurer given, §58.1-3919.1.
Notice prior to referring to private agent required, §58.1-3919.1.
Town taxes, lists of delinquents filed with county treasurer in certain towns, §58.1-3938.
Treasurers not liable for taxes returned delinquent and not afterwards received, §58.1-3935.
When property taxes delinquent, §58.1-3922.
Delinquent taxes, procedures, §58.1-3934.
Delivery of receipts to taxpayers when taxes collected, §58.1-3914.
Distress.
Credit out of rent, tenant paying taxes or levies, §58.1-3944.
Land lying partly in one county and partly in another, §58.1-3945.
Limitation on collection of local taxes, §58.1-3940.
Waiver of time limitation on assessment, §58.1-3903.1.
Motor vehicles purchased by bona fide purchases for value, §58.1-3942.
Nonresident owners of county, city or town where land lies, §58.1-3946.

TAX COLLECTION —Cont'd
Local taxes —Cont'd
Distress —Cont'd
Notice to secured party prior to sale for distress, §58.1-3942.
Priority of security interest perfected prior to distress, §58.1-3942.
Property distrained, §58.1-3941.
Sale of part of property distrained on, §58.1-3943.
Sales for distress.
Notice to secured party, §58.1-3942.
Security interest not bar to distress, §58.1-3942.
Shares of crops belonging to landlord owning taxes, §58.1-3943.
Taxes or other charges not paid when due, §58.1-3919.
Tenant paying taxes or levies to have credit out of rents, §58.1-3944.
What property distrained, §58.1-3941.
Electronic billing, §58.1-3912.
Estates in hands of or debts due by third parties, §58.1-3952.
Exoneration from lien, payment of taxes, §58.1-3959.
Failure to pay taxes, §58.1-3915.
Fee to cover administrative costs and reasonable attorneys or collection agency fees, §58.1-3958.
Injunctions, §58.1-3993.
Interest on funds in prepayment of taxes, §58.1-3920.1.
Interest on taxes not paid by following day due, §58.1-3918.
Lease of real estate for collection of taxes, §58.1-3947.
Notice to tenant prior to leasing, §58.1-3948.
Lien of delinquent real estate taxes, recording, §58.1-3930.
Liens.
Estate in hands of or debts due by third parties, §58.1-3952.
Limitation on collection, §58.1-3940.
Waiver of time limitation on assessment, §58.1-3903.1.
Local delinquent tax collectors, §58.1-3934.
Mailing bills to taxpayers or obligees on mortgages or deeds of trust, §58.1-3912.
Nonresident owners of county, city or town where land lies.
Treasurers remedies, §58.1-3946.
Notice of taxes due, §58.1-3911.
Offers of compromise, §58.1-3994.
Ordinances providing dates for filing returns, setting penalties, interest, etc., §58.1-3916.
Payment by treasurers of collected taxes into treasuries of political subdivisions, §58.1-3910.
Petition to ascertain delinquent taxes, §58.1-3959.
Prepayment of taxes, §58.1-3920.
Interest on funds received, §58.1-3920.1.
Private collection agents.
Use to collect delinquent taxes other than real estate taxes, §58.1-3919.1.
Public service corporations.
Assessment by state corporation commission in locality requiring installment payments, §58.1-3917.
Receipt of taxes and levies by treasurers without penalty, §58.1-3913.

TAX COLLECTION —Cont'd
Local taxes —Cont'd
Receipts to taxpayers when taxes collected, §58.1-3914.
Reciprocal agreement.
Collection by town treasurer, §58.1-3910.
Tax deeds made under repealed sections, validation, §58.1-3960.
Taxes or other charges not paid by first day following day due, §58.1-3919.
Interest on taxes, §58.1-3918.
Taxpayer problem resolution program, §58.1-1818.
Third parties.
Estates in hands of or debts due by, §58.1-3952.
Town taxes, delinquent taxes.
Filing list with county treasurers in certain towns, §58.1-3938.
Subsequent collection of subjects other than real estate, §58.1-3933.
Town treasurers.
Reciprocal agreements to collect, §58.1-3910.
Treasurer to collect and pay over taxes, §58.1-3910.
Validation of tax deeds under repealed sections, §58.1-3960.
Website access, §58.1-3912.
Local treasurers generally, §§58.1-3123 to 58.1-3172.1.
See TREASURERS, LOCAL.
Motor vehicle sales and use tax, §58.1-2406.
Out-of-state collections, §58.1-14.
Overcollection of taxes administered by DMV, §58.1-16.
Personal property taxes.
Intangible personal property tax, §58.1-1117.
Probate tax, local, §§58.1-3806, 58.1-3807.
Cities having no court for probate of wills or issuance of grants of administration, §58.1-3807.
Probate tax, state.
Undervaluation of estate, additional tax, §58.1-1717.
Real property taxes.
Prince William county senior citizens and disabled persons.
Ordinance prescribing alternative due dates, §58.1-3916.02.
Service charge in lieu of payment, §§58.1-3400 to 58.1-3407.
Taxpayer problem resolution program, §58.1-1818.
Reciprocal agreements with other states.
Governor authorized to enter into, §58.1-2.
Recordation tax, local, §58.1-3803.
Cities having no court for recordation of deeds and other instruments, §58.1-3804.
Recordation tax, state, §58.1-812.
Department of taxation, §58.1-813.
Repeal of tax.
Collection of taxes accruing prior to, §58.1-10.
Retail sales and use tax, §58.1-625.
Dealers, tax collectible from, §§58.1-612 to 58.1-622.
Local sales or use taxes, §§58.1-605, 58.1-606.
Memorandum of lien, delinquent taxes, §58.1-632.
Soft drink excise tax, §58.1-1703.
State taxes, §§58.1-1800 to 58.1-1818, VA Const Art X §7.
Additional proceedings for collection, §58.1-1806.
Appointment of collectors for delinquent state taxes, §58.1-1803.
Assessment of omitted taxes, §58.1-1812.

TAX COLLECTION —Cont'd
State taxes —Cont'd
Charge-off of delinquent state taxes, §58.1-1802.
Collection out of estate in hands of or debts due third party, §58.1-1804.
Collectors of delinquent state taxes.
Appointment by department of taxation, §58.1-1803.
Contract collector fund.
Establishment, §58.1-1803.
Installment agreements for payment, §58.1-1817.
Contract collector fund.
Establishment, §58.1-1803.
Conversion of trust taxes, §58.1-1816.
Corporate officer conversion of trust taxes, §58.1-1816.
Corporate officer liability for failure to collect and account for tax, §58.1-1815.
Corporate officer liability for failure to file returns or keep records, §58.1-1814.
Corporate officer or employee liability for failure to pay, §58.1-1813.
Crediting local treasurers, §58.1-1801.
Criminal liability for failure to file returns or keep records, §58.1-1814.
Debts due third party, §58.1-1804.
Entering padlocked premises of delinquent business enterprise, §58.1-1805.
Failure to collect and account for tax, §58.1-1815.
Failure to file returns or keep records, §58.1-1814.
Failure to pay tax.
Liability of corporate officer or employee of member, manager or employee of partnership or limited liability company, §58.1-1813.
Foreign jurisdiction, collection in, §58.1-1808.
Installment agreements to pay, §58.1-1817.
Judgment or decree for collection of taxes, §58.1-1807.
Enforcement in foreign jurisdiction, §58.1-1808.
Lien on real estate, §58.1-1805.
Jurisdiction over Commonwealth for purposes of determining validity, amount and priority, §58.1-1809.
Limitation of prosecution for conversion of trust taxes, §58.1-1816.
Limitation on assessment of omitted taxes, §58.1-1812.
Limitations on collection, §58.1-1802.1.
Limited liability company member, manager or employee.
Liability for failure to pay, §58.1-1813.
List of delinquent taxes, §58.1-1800.
Transmittal to department of taxation, §58.1-1801.
Memorandum of lien, §58.1-1805.
Notice of intent to file lien, §58.1-1805.
Notification and record of charge-off of delinquent state taxes, §58.1-1802.
Omitted taxes.
Assessment, §58.1-1812.
Padlocking doors of delinquent business enterprise, §58.1-1805.
Partnership member or employee liability for failure to pay, §58.1-1813.
Partnership officer conversion of trust taxes, §58.1-1816.
Partnership officer liability for failure to collect and account for tax, §58.1-1815.

TAX COLLECTION —Cont'd
State taxes —Cont'd
Partnership officer liability for failure to file returns or keep records, §58.1-1814.
Period of limitation on assessment of omitted taxes, §58.1-1812.
Period of limitation on collection, §58.1-1802.1.
Receipt of state taxes by local treasurer, §58.1-1800.
Recordation of memorandum of lien, §58.1-1805.
Suspension of period of limitation on collection, §58.1-1802.1.
Validity, amount and priority of tax liens.
Jurisdiction over Commonwealth for purposes of determining, §58.1-1809.
Venue for filing memorandum of lien, §58.1-1805.
Venue of proceedings for collection of taxes, §58.1-1806.
Tax amnesty program, §58.1-1840.1.
Taxpayer bill of rights, §58.1-1845.
Tire tax, §58.1-642.
Watercraft sales and use tax, §58.1-1403.

TAX COMMISSIONER AND DEPARTMENT OF TAXATION, §§58.1-200 to 58.1-220.
Abatement of tax, interest or penalty.
Erroneous written advice by department, §58.1-1835.
Advice to comptroller of amounts to be charged state collecting officers, §58.1-211.
Advisory aid and assistance.
Equalizing property assessment.
Rendering to localities, §58.1-202.
Affidavit of commissioner as evidence.
Prima facie evidence, §58.1-110.
Aircraft sales and use tax, §§58.1-1500 to 58.1-1510.
See AIRCRAFT SALES AND USE TAX.
Amounts to be charged state collecting officer.
Department advice to comptroller, §58.1-211.
Appointment of commissioner by governor, §58.1-200.
Assistants.
Employment or removal by commissioner, §58.1-213.
Bond of commissioner, §58.1-201.
Charge for sale of publication, §58.1-215.
Cigarette tax.
Excise tax, §§58.1-1000 to 58.1-1022.
See CIGARETTE TAX.
Use tax, §§58.1-1018 to 58.1-1021.
Civil actions against agents, investigators or auditors.
Attorney general or assistant representing, §2.2-507.
Classifications of real property by commissioner, §58.1-208.
Clerks.
Employment or removal by commissioner, §58.1-213.
Collection and publication of property tax data, §58.1 207.
Collection of state taxes generally, §§58.1-1800 to 58.1-1818.
See TAX COLLECTION.
Commissioners of revenue.
Books and forms of commissioners furnished by department, §58.1-3114.
Delivery of copy of tax books to department, §58.1-3118.

TAX COMMISSIONER AND DEPARTMENT OF TAXATION —Cont'd
Commissioners of revenue —Cont'd
Instruction to commissioners provided by tax commissioner, §58.1-3105.
Intangible personal property returns forwarded to department by commissioner, §58.1-3113.
Misconduct or incapacity of commissioners reported by tax commissioner, §58.1-3122.
Separate books for state and local levies prescribed by department, §58.1-3116.
Communications sales and use tax.
Generally, §§58.1-645 to 58.1-662.
See COMMUNICATIONS SALES AND USE TAX.
Compromise of prosecutions, penalties or doubtful or disputed claims, §58.1-105.
Comptroller authorized to collect delinquent taxes.
Referral to commissioner, §2.2-808.
Conduct of sessions and investigations other than location of office, §58.1-212.
Continuing education program for assessing officers and boards of equalization, §58.1-206.
Contracts.
Public private partnership contracts.
Financing agency technology needs, §58.1-202.2.
Correction of erroneous tax assessments.
State taxes generally, §§58.1-1820 to 58.1-1835.
See CORRECTION OF ERRONEOUS TAX ASSESSMENTS.
Criminal fines and penalties.
Collections, §19.2-349.
Defined, §58.1-1.
Department of social services.
Disseminating tax information to department of taxation.
Client information, §2.2-3803.
Destruction of returns, reports and working papers of department, §58.1-107.
Duties of commissioner generally, §58.1-202.
Electronic funds transfers.
Payment of amounts due and owing Commonwealth, §2.2-211.
Payment of taxes by, §58.1-202.1.
Employment or removal of clerks and assistants by commissioner, §58.1-213.
Enforcement of revenue laws.
Institution of proceeding, actions and prosecutions.
Power of commissioner, §58.1-202.
Erroneous written advice by department.
Abatement of tax, interest or penalty, §58.1-1835.
Estate tax generally, §§58.1-900 to 58.1-938.
See ESTATE TAX.
Estimated amount of money locality and school district to receive during fiscal year.
Notice, §15.2-2502.
Estimated tax.
Refusal of taxpayer to file return, §58.1-111.
Evidence.
Affidavit of tax commissioner as prima facie evidence, §58.1-110.
Examination of books and records of taxpayers, §58.1-219.
Federal earned income tax credit.
Taxpayers claiming.
Duty to obtain information from taxpayers, §58.1-202.

TAX COMMISSIONER AND DEPARTMENT OF TAXATION —Cont'd
Fees.
Reproductions.
In compliance with order to produce confidential tax return, §58.1-109.
Fillable forms.
Requirement to ensure, time period, §58.1-202.3.
Forms of books, schedules and blanks used in assessment and collection of state taxes.
Duty of commissioner to prescribe, §58.1-202.
Fillable forms.
Requirement to ensure, time period, §58.1-202.3.
General reassessment procedures manual and guidelines.
Making available annually to localities, §58.1-202.
Hospitals.
Nonprofit hospitals.
Submission of returns and information to department, §58.1-113.
Income tax, §§58.1-300 to 58.1-549.
See INCOME TAX.
Income tax withholding, §§58.1-460 to 58.1-486.3.
See INCOME TAX WITHHOLDING.
Inspection of records and documents by department, §58.1-103.
Insurance companies license tax, §§58.1-2500 to 58.1-2533.
See INSURANCE COMPANIES LICENSE TAX.
Intangible personal property tax, §§58.1-1100 to 58.1-1118.
See PERSONAL PROPERTY TAXES.
Interpretation and enforcement of laws.
Effect of regulations, rulings, etc., §58.1-205.
Issuance of regulations relating to, §58.1-203.
Publication of rulings or other interpretations, §58.1-204.
Intervention in action or proceedings.
Constitutionality, construction or validity of state law in question.
Power of commissioner, §58.1-202.
Investigations.
Unreasonable and unjust assessment and collection of state taxes.
Power of commissioner, §58.1-202.
Judicial notice.
Rulings and administrative interpretations, §58.1-205.
Land book.
Copy delivered to department by commissioners of revenue, §58.1-3310.
Local income tax, §§58.1-540 to 58.1-549.
Local levy rates, publication showing, §58.1-210.
Mail.
Initial notice by certified mail, subsequent notices by regular mail, §58.1-105.1.
Motor fuel sales tax, §§58.1-1718.1 to 58.1-1724.4.
Bracket system, rule promulgation, §§58.1-1719, 58.1-1724.2.
Notice of proposed regulations issued by commissioner, §58.1-203.
Oath of commissioner, §58.1-201.
Office of commissioner, location, §58.1-212.
Powers of commissioner, §58.1-202.
Payment of taxes by electronic funds transfer.
Authority to accept, §58.1-202.1.
Public-private partnership contracts.
Agency technology needs financing, §58.1-202.2.

TAX COMMISSIONER AND DEPARTMENT OF TAXATION —Cont'd
Prima facie evidence.
Affidavit of tax commissioner, §58.1-110.
Production of documents and things.
Writs, notices, etc., compelling production of books and papers, §58.1-216.
Property tax data, collection and publication, §58.1-207.
Property tax exemptions.
Report to department for compilation of information and submission to finance committees, §58.1-3605.1.
Publication.
Property tax data, §58.1-207.
Rates of local levies, §58.1-210.
Rulings, decisions, orders and regulations, §58.1-204.
Public-private partnership contracts.
Financing agency technology needs, §58.1-202.2.
Public private partnership oversight committee.
Review and approval of terms, §58.1-202.2.
Public service corporation taxation generally, §§58.1-2600 to 58.1-2690.
See PUBLIC SERVICE CORPORATION TAXATION.
Qualifications of commissioner, §58.1-200.
Refusal of taxpayer to file return.
Estimation of amount of taxes due, §58.1-111.
Regulations relating to interpretation and enforcement of laws.
Effect of regulations, rulings, etc., §58.1-205.
Issuance by tax commissioner, §58.1-203.
Publications of rulings, decisions, etc., §58.1-204.
Removal or suspension of commissioners of revenue.
Institution of proceedings, powers of commissioner, §58.1-202.
Reports to General Assembly.
Required annual reports, §58.1-202.
Reproduction of tax returns.
Admissibility in evidence, §58.1-108.
Authority of commissioner, §58.1-106.
Compliance with order directing production of confidential tax returns, §58.1-109.
Destruction, §58.1-107.
Retail sales and use tax generally, §§58.1-600 to 58.1-639.
See RETAIL SALES AND USE TAX.
Rulings, decisions, orders, regulations.
Effect, §58.1-205.
Publication, §58.1-204.
Rulings in individual cases, §58.1-203.
Sales of publications, charge for, §58.1-215.
Seals tax, §§58.1-1725, 58.1-1726.
Secretary of finance.
Agency responsibility, §2.2-211.
Service of notice, process and other papers.
Writs, notices, processes and orders, §§58.1-216, 58.1-217.
Setoff debt collection, income tax, §§58.1-520 to 58.1-535.
See SETOFF DEBT COLLECTION, INCOME TAX.
Settlement of doubtful or disputed claims, §58.1-105.
Social security account numbers, disclosure, §58.1-209.
Soft drink excise tax, §§58.1-1700 to 58.1-1705.
State land evaluation advisory council.
Commissioner member of, §58.1-3239.

TAX COMMISSIONER AND DEPARTMENT OF TAXATION —Cont'd
Subpoenas.
Production of confidential tax returns, reproduction as compliance, §58.1-109.
Subpoenas duces tecum.
Production of confidential tax returns, reproduction as compliance, §58.1-109.
Suits and other judicial proceedings, tax on, §§58.1-1727 to 58.1-1729.
Summons.
Compelling attendance of witness and production of books and papers, §58.1-216.
Representation of witness, §58.1-1834.
Production of confidential tax returns.
Reproduction as compliance with, §58.1-109.
Surplus lines insurance.
Exchange of information between commission and department of taxation, §38.2-4816.
Tax forms.
Fillable forms.
Requirement to ensure, time period, §58.1-202.3.
Promulgation and distribution, §58.1-214.
Taxpayer bill of rights, §58.1-1845.
Technology.
Public-private partnership contracts.
Financing agency needs, 58.1-202.2.
Technology partnership fund, §58.1-202.2.
Term of commissioner, §58.1-200.
Tire tax, §§58.1-640 to 58.1-644.
Vacancies in commissioner's office, §58.1-200.
Venue.
Proceeding against witnesses failing or refusing to attend as ordered by summons, §58.1-216.
Waiver of time limitation on assessment of omitted or additional state taxes, §58.1-220.
Watercraft sales and use tax, §§58.1-1400 to 58.1-1410.
See WATERCRAFT SALES AND USE TAX.
Wills and administrations tax, §§58.1-1711 to 58.1-1718.
See PROBATE TAX, STATE.
Withholding by pass-through entities, §§58.1-486.1 to 58.1-486.3.
Witnesses.
Fees and mileage.
Allowance to witnesses summoned, §58.1-218.
Service of writs, notices, etc., compelling attendance, §58.1-216.
Representation of witness, §58.1-1834.
Writs, notices, processes and orders, §§58.1-216, 58.1-217.
Writ taxes, §§58.1-1727 to 58.1-1729.

TAX CREDITS.
Agricultural best management practices, §58.1-339.3.
Aircraft sales and use tax, §58.1-1504.
Bank franchise tax.
Credit against state for amounts paid cities, towns and counties, §58.1-1213.
Clean fuel vehicle and advanced cellulosic biofuels job creation, §58.1-439.1.
Coalfield employment enhancement, §58.1-439.2.
Corporation income tax, §§58.1-432 to 58.1-439.28.
Agricultural best management practices tax credit, §58.1-439.5.

TAX CREDITS —Cont'd
Corporation income tax —Cont'd
Biodiesel and green diesel fuels producers, §58.1-439.12:02.
Cigarettes manufactured and exported, §58.1-439.12:01.
Day-care facility investment tax credit, §58.1-439.4.
Employees with disabilities, §58.1-439.11.
Neighborhood assistance act tax credit, §§58.1-439.18 to 58.1-439.24.
Recyclable materials.
Purchase of machinery and equipment for processing of, §58.1-439.7.
Temporary assistance for needy families.
Certain employers hiring recipients, §58.1-439.9.
Waste motor oil burning equipment.
Purchase of, §58.1-439.10.
Worker retraining tax credit, §58.1-439.6.
Day-care facility investment tax credit, §58.1-439.4.
Education improvement scholarships tax credits, §§58.1-439.25 to 58.1-439.28.
Enterprise zones.
Business tax credit, §59.1-280.
Real property investment tax credits, §59.1-280.1.
Estates or trust income tax, §§58.1-370, 58.1-371.
Historic rehabilitation tax credit, §58.1-339.2.
Income tax.
Individual income tax, §§58.1-332 to 58.1-339.12, 58.1-439.4.
Insurance companies license tax.
Retaliatory cost paid to other states, §58.1-2510.
License taxes.
Contractors.
Town within county imposing similar tax, §58.1-3714.
Water, heat, light or power companies.
Virginia coal employment and production incentive tax credit, §58.1-2626.1.
Livable home tax credit, §58.1-339.7.
Local income tax, §58.1-546.
Low-income housing credit, §§36-55.63, 36-139.5.
Major business facility job tax credit, §58.1-439.
Motor vehicle sales and use tax, §58.1-2424.
Neighborhood assistance act tax credit, §§58.1-439.18 to 58.1-439.24.
Amount of credits, §§58.1-439.20, 58.1-439.21.
Individuals, §58.1-439.24.
Carry over, §58.1-439.21.
Individuals, §58.1-439.24.
Contracting services.
Donation of, §58.1-439.23.
Definitions, §58.1-439.18.
Individual, §58.1-439.24.
Individuals.
Donations by, §58.1-439.24.
Professional services.
Donation of, §58.1-439.22.
Proposals, §58.1-439.20.
Public policy, §58.1-439.19.
Personal property taxes.
Credit in prorating jurisdiction.
Person moving from nonprorating locality to prorating locality, §58.1-3516.
Qualified equity and subordinated debt investments tax credit, §58.1-339.4.
Real property taxes.
Land acquired by United States, Commonwealth, political subdivision or church, §§58.1-3360 to 58.1-3363.

TAX CREDITS —Cont'd
Real property taxes —Cont'd
Rehabilitated, renovated or replacement residential structures, §58.1-3220.01.
Retail sales and use tax.
Bad debts, §58.1-621.
Repossessions of property by dealers, §58.1-620.
Taxes paid to another state, §58.1-611.
Road tax on motor carriers.
Credit for payment of diesel fuel tax, §58.1-2706.
Credit for payment of liquefied gases tax, §58.1-2706.
Credit for payment of motor fuel tax, §58.1-2706.
False statements, §58.1-2710.
Waste motor oil burning equipment tax credit, §58.1-439.7.
Watercraft sales and use tax, §58.1-1409.
Withholding, §58.1-480.

TAX DAY.
Defined, §58.1-1.
Personal property taxes, §58.1-3515.

TAX DEDUCTIONS.
Bank franchise tax.
Deductions from gross capital, §58.1-1206.
Income tax.
Individual income tax.
Virginia taxable income of residents, §58.1-322.
Marital deduction.
Election powers of personal representatives, §64.2-107.
Wills.
Construction of formula clauses, §64.2-430.
Tire tax, §58.1-642.

TAX DELINQUENCIES.
Collection of state taxes generally, §§58.1-1800 to 58.1-1818.
See TAX COLLECTION.
Collectors of delinquent state taxes.
Appointment by department of taxation, §58.1-1803.
Contract collector fund.
Establishment, §58.1-1803.
Forest products tax, §58.1-1615.
Intangible personal property tax.
Assessment on estimates, §58.1-1113.
Local taxes.
Generally, §§58.1-3921 to 58.1-3938.
See TAX COLLECTION.
Sale of delinquent tax lands, §§58.1-3965 to 58.1-3975.
See SALE OF DELINQUENT TAX LANDS.
Personal property taxes.
Intangible personal property tax.
Assessment on estimates, §58.1-1113.
Real property taxes.
Proration of taxes after purchase of part of tract, §58.1-3227.
Release of delinquent lien to facilitate conveyance, §58.1-3228.
Real property tax special assessment for land preservation.
Removal of parcels from, §58.1-3235.
Retail sales and use tax.
Memorandum of lien, §58.1-632.
Sale of delinquent tax lands, §§58.1-3965 to 58.1-3975.
See SALE OF DELINQUENT TAX LANDS.
State corporation commission's power to charge off, §12.1-15.

TAXES, §§58.1-1 to 58.1-3995.
Abatement of tax, interest or penalty.
Erroneous written advice by department, §58.1-1835.
ABC licenses.
Continuation or reissuance, license tax for.
Failure to pay, late payment with penalty in lieu of reapplying for license, §4.1-203.
Excise tax on beer and wine coolers, §§4.1-236 to 4.1-240.
Local license taxes, §4.1-233.
Tax on wine and other alcoholic beverages, §§4.1-234, 4.1-235.
ABC offenses.
Excise tax on beer and wine coolers.
Nonpayment, §4.1-332.
Failure to pay taxes, §§4.1-331, 4.1-332.
Abutting property owners, VA Const Art X §3.
Actions, tax on suits and other judicial proceedings, §§58.1-1727 to 58.1-1729.
Additional state taxes.
Waiver of time limitation on assessment, §58.1-220.
Administrative process act.
Exemptions from case decisions, §2.2-4018.
Admissions tax, §§58.1-3817, 58.1-3818, 58.1-3840.
Excise tax, city or town having general taxing powers, §58.1-3840.
Scott county.
Off-track horse race wagering facilities, §58.1-3818.01.
Stafford county, §58.1-3818.02.
Agricultural cooperative association, §13.1-341.
Air carriers.
Taxes not affected by chapter, §5.1-150.
Aircraft sales and use tax, §§58.1-1500 to 58.1-1510.
See AIRCRAFT SALES AND USE TAX.
Amnesty program, §58.1-1840.1.
Appeals, writ tax.
Time for paying.
Appeals from general district courts in civil cases, §16.1-107.
Apples commercially produced in state.
Excise tax, §§3.2-1208 to 3.2-1217.
Assessment for administration of insurance laws, §§38.2-400 to 38.2-415.
Auctioneer local license taxes, §54.1-605.
Automobile graveyards.
Ordinances taxing and regulating, §15.2-903.
Bad checks.
Income tax payments by, §58.1-486.
Issued in payment of, §18.2-182.1.
Payment by, §58.1-12.
Retail sales and use tax, §58.1-637.
Bank franchise tax, §§58.1-1200 to 58.1-1217.
See BANK FRANCHISE TAX.
Barge and rail usage tax credit.
International trade facilities using port facilities located in Commonwealth, §58.1-439.12:09.
Baseball stadium authority.
Entitlement to tax revenues derived from major league baseball, §15.2-5814.
Bawdy places, buildings and other structures harboring.
Cost of corrective action by locality collected as tax, §15.2-908.1.
Beef industry council, §§3.2-1102, 3.2-1306.
Beer excise tax, §§4.1-236 to 4.1-240.

TAXES —Cont'd
Bills of general assembly creating or renewing tax credits.
Expiration date of not longer than five years from effective date of credit.
Provision required in bill, §30-19.1:11.
Boards of equalization, §§58.1-3370 to 58.1-3389.
See REAL PROPERTY TAXES.
Bonds issued by locality.
Levy and collection of annual taxes, §15.2-2624.
Boxing and wrestling events.
Gross receipts taxes, §54.1-833.
Business, professional and occupational licensing tax, §§58.1-3700 to 58.1-3735.
See LICENSE TAXES.
Business trusts.
Classification, §13.1-1207.
BVU authority.
Exemption, §15.2-7220.
Capitation tax.
Constitutional provisions, US Const Art I §9.
Elections.
Denial or abridgment of the right to vote for failure to pay tax prohibited, US Const Amd 24.
Captive insurers.
Tax on premiums collected, §38.2-1108.
Charitable events.
Municipal corporations.
Tax on admissions, §15.2-1104.1.
Checks.
Bad checks.
Income tax payments by, §58.1-486.
Payment by, §58.1-12.
Retail sales and use tax, §58.1-637.
Churches or ministry.
Tax in support of prohibited, VA Const Art I §16.
Cigarette tax.
Generally, §§58.1-1000 to 58.1-1022.
See CIGARETTE TAX.
Local taxes, §§58.1-3830 to 58.1-3832.
Corporate or partnership officer willful failure to collect and account for, §58.1-3907.
Excise tax, city or town having general taxing powers, §58.1-3840.
Tobacco products tax, §§58.1-1021.01 to 58.1-1021.05.
City or town power generally, §15.2-1104.
Classes and segregation, VA Const Art X §1.
Coal surface mining reclamation fund.
Assessment of reclamation tax revenues, §§45.1-270.4, 45.1-270.4:1.
Collection of reclamation tax, §45.1-270.5.
Nonpayment of reclamation tax, §45.1-270.5.
Special assessment, §45.1-270.4:1.
Collection of taxes.
State taxes generally, §§58.1-1800 to 58.1-1818.
See TAX COLLECTION.
Taxes administered by agencies, §§58.1-2020 to 58.1-2025.
College building authority.
Exemption of bonds from taxes, §23-30.33.
Colleges and universities.
Tax exemption for bond issues, §23-25.
Commercial delivery service.
Filing returns, payment of taxes by, §58.1-9.
Commissioners of revenue.
Generally, §§58.1-3100 to 58.1-3122.2.
See COMMISSIONERS OF REVENUE.
Communications sales and use tax, §§58.1-645 to 58.1-662.
See COMMUNICATIONS SALES AND USE TAX.

TAXES —Cont'd
Compromise of doubtful or disputed claims.
Authority of tax commissioner, §58.1-105.
Condominiums.
Separate taxes, §55-79.42.
Congress.
Powers of congress, US Const Art I §8.
Conservation easements, §10.1-1011.
Consumer utility taxes, §§58.1-3814 to 58.1-3816.2.
Cooperative associations, §13.1-311.
Cooperative nonprofit life benefit companies.
Gross premium receipts, §38.2-3812.
Corn market development, education and promotion assessment, §§3.2-1405 to 3.2-1409.
Corporate stock, VA Const Art X §5.
Corporation income tax, §§58.1-400 to 58.1-455.
See INCOME TAX.
Correction of erroneous tax assessments.
State taxes generally, §§58.1-1820 to 58.1-1835.
See CORRECTION OF ERRONEOUS TAX ASSESSMENTS.
Correction of taxes assessed by state corporation commission, §§58.1-2030 to 58.1-2035.
County, city or town ordinance imposing.
Affirmative vote of majority of governing body required, VA Const Art VII §7.
County discount for early payment, §15.2-1201.2.
Credit unions.
Franchise taxes.
Exemption, §6.2-1304.
Deed of gift.
Recordation tax exemption, §58.1-811.
Definitions, §58.1-1.
Delinquent local taxes.
Generally, §§58.1-3921 to 58.1-3938.
See TAX COLLECTION.
Delinquent tax land sales.
Generally, §§58.1-3965 to 58.1-3975.
See SALE OF DELINQUENT TAX LANDS.
Dental services plans, §38.2-4521.
Disclaimer of property interests.
Tax qualified disclaimer, §64.2-2612.
Disclosure of information by preparers without consent, §58.1-4.
Distress.
Landlord and tenant.
Priority of creditors, §§55-231, 55-233.
Distribution of assets of persons or corporations assessed with.
Liability of recipient of improper corporate distribution, §58.1-7.
Priority of taxes, §58.1-6.
Donations to general fund, §58.1-17.
Double taxation.
Persons engaged in more than one business, §58.1-5.
Drainage projects.
Assessment and collection generally, §§21-367 to 21-392.
See DRAINAGE PROJECTS.
Drivers' licenses.
Willful failure or refusal to pay taxes, §46.2-320.
Drug blight on property.
Locality undertaking corrective action.
Costs and expenses collected as taxes, §15.2-907.

TAXES —Cont'd
Educational facilities authority.
Bond issues exempt from taxes, §23-30.53.
Egg board.
See EGG BOARD.
Elections.
Denial or abridgment of right to vote.
Failure to pay poll or other tax, US Const Amd 24.
Electricity consumption, §§58.1-2900 to 58.1-2903.
Assessment, §58.1-2902.
Collection, §58.1-2901.
Imposition, §58.1-2900.
Rate, §58.1-2900.
Remittance, §58.1-2901.
Special regulatory tax, §§58.1-2902, 58.1-2903.
Use relating to special regulatory tax, §58.1-2903.
Electric suppliers.
Corporations, §58.1-400.2.
Minimum tax, §58.1-400.3.
Electronic funds transfer.
Payment of taxes by, §§58.1-9, 58.1-202.1.
Employer taxation for unemployment compensation, §§60.2-500 to 60.2-538.
See UNEMPLOYMENT COMPENSATION.
E-911 tax, §58.1-1730.
Enterprise zone business tax credit, §59.1-280.
Enterprise zone development.
Local enterprise zone development taxation program, §§58.1-3245.6 to 58.1-3245.12.
Enterprise zone real property investment tax credit, §59.1-280.1.
Erroneous written advice by department.
Abatement of tax, interest or penalty, §58.1-1835.
Escheat generally, §§55-168 to 55-201.1.
See ESCHEAT.
Estate or trust income taxation, §§58.1-360 to 58.1-383.
See INCOME TAX.
Estate tax, §§58.1-900 to 58.1-938.
See ESTATE TAX.
Excise taxes.
Apples commercially produced in state, §§3.2-1208 to 3.2-1217.
Cigarette tax, §§58.1-1000 to 58.1-1022.
See CIGARETTE TAX.
City or town having general taxing powers, §58.1-3840.
Forest products tax, §§58.1-1600 to 58.1-1622.
See FOREST PRODUCTS TAX.
Pork industry board, §§3.2-2006 to 3.2-2009.
Powers of congress, US Const Art I §8.
Soft drink excise tax, §§58.1-1700 to 58.1-1705.
Executors and administrators.
Powers to make election regarding marital deduction, §64.2-107.
Exemption from taxation.
Interstate insurance product regulation compact.
Commission exempt from taxation by compacting states, §38.2-6200.
Exempt property generally, §§58.1-3600 to 58.1-3666.
See PROPERTY EXEMPT FROM TAXATION.
Exports, US Const Art I §§9, 10.
False tax returns, §58.1-11.
Federal lien registration, §§55-142.1 to 55-142.9.
Fiduciaries responsibility, §§58.1-21 to 58.1-24.
Accounts not settled until taxes paid or provided for, §58.1-22.

TAXES —Cont'd
Fiduciaries responsibility —Cont'd
Distribution of funds, securities, money or other property.
Payment of taxes or provision for payment required, §58.1-21.
Inquiries required of fiduciary, §58.1-23.
Reimbursement of fiduciary.
Out of estate, §58.1-24.
Fillable tax forms.
Commissioner required to ensure, time period, §58.1-202.3.
Food and beverage tax, §§58.1-3833, 58.1-3834.
Excise tax on meals.
City or town having general taxing powers, §58.1-3840.
Situs for taxation, §58.1-3841.
Forest products tax, §§58.1-1600 to 58.1-1622.
See FOREST PRODUCTS TAX.
Franchise taxes, VA Const Art X §5.
Bank franchise tax, §§58.1-1200 to 58.1-1217.
Freedom of information act.
Records excluded, §2.2-3705.7.
Fuel taxes, §§58.1-2200 to 58.1-2299.20.
See FUEL TAXES.
General assembly powers, VA Const Art IV §14.
General fund.
State taxes paid into, §58.1-13.
Health services plans.
License taxes in lieu of all other state and local license fees or license taxes and income taxes, §38.2-4226.
Housing development authority.
Exemption from taxes, §36-55.37.
Income tax, §§58.1-300 to 58.1-549, US Const Amd 16.
See INCOME TAX.
Indians.
Constitutional provisions, US Const Amd 14.
Individual income tax, §§58.1-320 to 58.1-355.
See INCOME TAX.
Inspection of records and documents by department of taxation, §58.1-103.
Insurance companies.
License tax, §§58.1-2500 to 58.1-2533.
See INSURANCE COMPANIES LICENSE TAX.
Taxes applicable to insurance companies, §58.1-2508.
Insurance laws administration, assessment for, §§38.2-400 to 38.2-415.
Intangible personal property tax, §§58.1-1100 to 58.1-1118.
See PERSONAL PROPERTY TAXES.
Interest.
Rate of interest on omitted taxes, assessments and refunds, §58.1-15.
International trade facilities using port facilities located in Commonwealth.
Barge and rail usage tax credit, §58.1-439.12:09.
Interstate insurance product regulation compact.
Commission exempt from taxation by compacting states, §38.2-6200.
Jail authorities.
Exemption, §53.1-95.15.
Joint subcommittee to evaluate tax preferences, §§30-336 to 30-338.
Administrative staff support, §30-337.
Compensation and reimbursement, §30-337.
Established, §30-336.
Executive summary, §30-337.

TAXES —Cont'd
Joint subcommittee to evaluate tax preferences —Cont'd
Members and terms, §30-337.
Powers and duties, §30-337.
Quorum, §30-337.
Technical advisory group, §30-337.
Judicial sales.
Ascertainment of delinquent taxes, §8.01-97.
When purchase price insufficient to pay taxes, etc., §8.01-98.
Junkyards.
Ordinances taxing and regulating, §15.2-903.
Land conservation foundation, §10.1-1024.
Landlord and tenant.
Distress.
Priority of creditors, §§55-231, 55-233.
Legal services plans.
Application fees paid by organization in lieu of other taxes, §38.2-4416.
License taxes.
Generally, §§58.1-3700 to 58.1-3735.
See LICENSE TAXES.
Insurance companies, §§58.1-2500 to 58.1-2533.
See INSURANCE COMPANIES LICENSE TAX.
Telegraph, telephone, water, heat, light, power and pipeline companies, §§58.1-2620 to 58.1-2635.
See PUBLIC SERVICE CORPORATION TAXATION.
Liens.
Federal lien registration, §§55-142.1 to 55-142.9.
Life, accident and sickness insurance guaranty association.
Tax write-offs of certificates of contributions, §38.2-1709.
Life tenancies.
Recovery at death of life tenant of taxes paid, §55-25.
Limitation of actions.
Assessment of taxes imposed by department of taxation, §58.1-104.
Waiver of time limitation on assessment of taxes, §58.1-101.
Limitations on powers of states, US Const Art I §10.
Limited liability companies.
Registration fees, §§13.1-1061 to 13.1-1066.
Limit of tax or revenue, VA Const Art X §8.
Literary fund.
Loans for construction of school facilities.
Levy of taxes for purpose of repaying loans, §22.1-159.
Litigation tax, §§58.1-1727 to 58.1-1729.
Litter tax, §§58.1-1706 to 58.1-1710.
Local improvements.
Taxes or assessments generally, §§15.2-2404 to 15.2-2413.
See TAXES OR ASSESSMENTS FOR LOCAL IMPROVEMENTS.
Local income tax, §§58.1-540 to 58.1-549.
Local retirement system assets.
Exemption, §51.1-802.
Local technology zone incentives, §58.1-3850.
Local tourism zones.
Cities, counties, towns.
Establishment, authority, tax incentives, regulatory flexibility, providing, §§58.1-3851, 58.1-3851.1.
Local vehicle taxes and license fees, §46.2-752.
Machinery and tools tax, §§58.1-3507, 58.1-3508.

TAXES —Cont'd
Mail.
Filing of returns or payment of taxes by, §58.1-9.
Initial notice by certified mail, subsequent notices by regular mail, §58.1-105.1.
Marriage license tax, §20-15.
Meals tax.
County food and beverage tax, §§58.1-3833, 58.1-3834.
Excise tax, city or town having general taxing powers, §58.1-3840.
Situs for taxation, §58.1-3841.
Merchants capital tax, §§58.1-3509, 58.1-3510.
Mining taxes.
Subsurface substances proved to exist.
Imposition of tax, §55-155.
Mortgages and deeds of trust.
Title to real estate sold.
Unaffected by nonlisting, §55-64.1.
Mosquito control, §32.1-194.
Motor carriers, passengers.
Provisions of chapter provide no relief from fees, taxes, etc., §46.2-2011.31.
Motor vehicle fuel sales tax, §§58.1-1718.1 to 58.1-1724.4.
Motor vehicle license plate fees.
See MOTOR VEHICLE LICENSE PLATES.
Motor vehicle registration.
Evidence of payment of taxes or exemption from taxes, §46.2-649.
Motor vehicle registration fees.
City or county decals, §§46.2-752 to 46.2-756.
Generally, §§46.2-685 to 46.2-704.
See MOTOR VEHICLE REGISTRATION.
Motor vehicle rentals, §§58.1-1734 to 58.1-1741.
See MOTOR VEHICLE RENTALS.
Motor vehicles.
Revocation of driver's license for failure to pay taxes, §46.2-399.
Motor vehicle sales and use tax, §§58.1-2400 to 58.1-2426.
See MOTOR VEHICLE SALES AND USE TAX.
Motor vehicle title certificate fee, §46.2-627.
Natural area preserves.
Gifts, devises and bequests, §10.1-217.
Natural gas consumption tax, §§58.1-2904 to 58.1-2907.
Collection and remittance, §58.1-2905.
Imposition of tax, §58.1-2904.
Special regulatory tax, §§58.1-2906, 58.1-2907.
Nonprofit corporations, annual registration fees, §§13.1-936.1, 13.1-936.2.
Notice.
Initial notice by certified mail, subsequent notices by regular mail, §58.1-105.1.
Nuisance bawdy places, §15.2-908.1.
Oath or affirmation unnecessary on return, §58.1-11.
Omitted state taxes.
Waiver of time limitation on assessment, §58.1-220.
Omitted taxes.
Local taxes or levies, §58.1-3903.
Forms for assessment, §58.1-3905.
Optometric services plans, §38.2-4521.
Ordinances imposing.
Affirmative vote of majority of governing body required, VA Const Art VII §7.
Outdoors foundation, §10.1-1803.
Out-of-state tax collections, §58.1-14.

TAXES —Cont'd
Overcollection of taxes administered by DMV, §58.1-16.
Overpayment rate.
Interest rate on tax refunds, §58.1-15.
Pari-mutuel wagering on horses.
Admissions tax, §59.1-393.
Percentage retained, §59.1-392.
Parks, recreation facilities and playgrounds.
System of public recreation and playgrounds, annual tax, §15.2-1807.
Tax on property for maintenance and operation, §15.2-1806.
Partnership income tax, §§58.1-390.1 to 58.1-395.
Payment of taxes.
Bad check, §58.1-12.
Commercial delivery service, §58.1-9.
Electronic funds transfer, §58.1-9.
Mail, §58.1-9.
Saturday, Sunday or legal holiday, due day falling on, §58.1-8.
Peanuts.
Excise tax, §§3.2-1905 to 3.2-1910.
See PEANUTS.
Penalty for payment by bad check, §58.1-12.
Personal property taxes.
Exempt property generally, §§58.1-3600 to 58.1-3666.
See PROPERTY EXEMPT FROM TAXATION.
Intangible personal property tax, §§58.1-1100 to 58.1-1118.
See PERSONAL PROPERTY TAXES.
Merchants' capital tax, §§58.1-3509, 58.1-3510.
Tangible personal property, §§58.1-3500 to 58.1-3522.
See PERSONAL PROPERTY TAXES.
Tax relief act of 1998, §§58.1-3523 to 58.1-3535.
See PERSONAL PROPERTY TAX RELIEF ACT OF 1998.
Personal representatives.
Power to make election regarding marital deduction, §64.2-107.
Persons engaged in more than one business, §58.1-5.
Poll tax.
Failure to pay poll or other tax.
Denial or abridgment of right to vote, US Const Amd 24.
Prohibited, US Const Amd 24.
Pork industry board.
Excise tax, §§3.2-2006 to 3.2-2009.
Port authority, §62.1-145.
Power of attorney.
Authority of agent as to taxes, §64.2-1637.
Powers of congress, US Const Art I §8.
Presumption of correction.
Assessment made pursuant to ruling, §58.1-205.
Principal and income.
Adjustments between principal and income because of taxes, §64.2-1029.
Income taxes.
Payment, §64.2-1028.
Special taxes or assessments for improvement representing addition of value to principal, §64.2-1030.
Priority of taxes, levies and fees in distributions, §58.1-6.
Privileged or confidential tax information.
Attorney general's authority to request and share information, §58.1-3.2.

TAXES —Cont'd
Privileged or confidential tax information —Cont'd
Availability of information to audit local tax returns, §58.1-3.1.
Motor carrier road tax.
International fuel tax agreement.
Information exchanges under agreement, §58.1-2712.2.
Motor vehicle fuel sales tax, §58.1-1724.1.
Real property tax.
Assessment cards and sheets, public disclosure, §58.1-3331.
Income-producing property, reports by owners, §58.1-3294.
Retail sales and use tax.
Report of gross misuse of exemption certificates, §58.1-623.1.
Return filed, §58.1-1714.
Road tax for motor carriers.
International fuel tax agreement.
Information exchanges under agreement, §58.1-2712.2.
Secrecy of information generally, §58.1-3.
Setoff debt collection act.
Exemption, use of information, §58.1-533.
Tax commissioner's authority to request and share information, §58.1-3.2.
Taxpayer bill of rights, §58.1-1845.
Tax preparers.
Not to disclose information without consent, §58.1-4.
Town officers provided information by commissioners of revenue, §58.1-3109.
Transfer of credit or other tax attribute.
Deemed consent to disclosure, §58.1-3.3.
Treasurers books and papers pertaining to office, §58.1-3127.
Wills and administration, tax on.
Return filed, §58.1-1714.
Privilege taxes.
Insurance companies license tax, §§58.1-2500 to 58.1-2533.
See INSURANCE COMPANIES LICENSE TAX.
License taxes generally, §§58.1-3700 to 58.1-3735.
See LICENSE TAXES.
Probate tax.
Local tax, §§58.1-3805 to 58.1-3808.
Authorization, §§58.1-1718, 58.1-3805.
State tax, §§58.1-1711 to 58.1-1718.
See PROBATE TAX, STATE.
Professional corporations.
Income and property taxes, §13.1-554.1.
Professional limited liability companies.
Income and property taxes, §13.1-1120.
Property taxes.
Exempt property generally, §§58.1-3600 to 58.1-3666.
See PROPERTY EXEMPT FROM TAXATION.
Intangible personal property tax, §§58.1-1100 to 58.1-1118.
See PERSONAL PROPERTY TAXES.
Machinery and tools tax, §§58.1-3507, 58.1-3508.
Merchants' capital tax, §§58.1-3509, 58.1-3510.
Property subject to state taxation, §58.1-100.
Real property taxes generally, §§58.1-3200 to 58.1-3389.
See REAL PROPERTY TAXES.
Tangible personal property, §§58.1-3500 to 58.1-3522.
See PERSONAL PROPERTY TAXES.

TAXES —Cont'd
Property taxes —Cont'd
Tax relief act of 1998, §§58.1-3523 to 58.1-3535.
See PERSONAL PROPERTY TAX RELIEF ACT OF 1998.
Public school authority.
Bonds exempt from taxation, §22.1-172.
Public school funds.
Duty to levy school tax.
County appropriations for public schools, §22.1-94.
Public service corporations generally, §§58.1-2600 to 58.1-2690.
See PUBLIC SERVICE CORPORATION TAXATION.
Public utilities.
Consumer utility taxes, §§58.1-3814 to 58.1-3816.2.
Railroads.
State taxation, §58.1-2608.
Rate of interest on omitted taxes, assessments and refunds, §58.1-15.
Real estate cooperatives, §55-428.
Real estate tax abatement program.
Derelict buildings.
Authority to remove, demolish or renovate, §15.2-907.1.
Real property taxes.
Exempt property generally, §§58.1-3600 to 58.1-3666.
See PROPERTY EXEMPT FROM TAXATION.
Generally, §§58.1-3200 to 58.1-3389.
See REAL PROPERTY TAXES.
Reciprocal agreements with other states for collection of taxes.
Governor authorized to enter into, §58.1-2.
Recordation tax, local, §§58.1-3800 to 58.1-3804.
Recordation tax, state, §§58.1-800 to 58.1-817.
See RECORDATION TAX, STATE.
Records.
Inspection by department of taxation, §58.1-103.
Retention by taxpayers, §58.1-102.
Registration of federal liens, §§55-142.1 to 55-142.9.
Repeal of tax.
Collection of taxes accrued prior to repeal, §58.1-10.
Reproduction of tax returns.
Admissibility in evidence, §58.1-108.
Authority of commissioner, §58.1-106.
Destruction, §58.1-107.
Resources authority.
Exemption, §62.1-219.
Retail sales and use tax.
Communications sales and use tax, §§58.1-645 to 58.1-662.
See COMMUNICATIONS SALES AND USE TAX.
Generally, §§58.1-600 to 58.1-639.
See RETAIL SALES AND USE TAX.
Retention of records by taxpayers, §58.1-102.
Returns.
See TAX RETURNS.
Revenue bills, US Const Art I §7.
Revenue stabilization fund, VA Const Art X §8.
Road impact fees, §§15.2-2317 to 15.2-2329.
See ROAD IMPACT FEES.
Road tax on motor carriers, §§58.1-2700 to 58.1-2712.2.
See ROAD TAX ON MOTOR CARRIERS.

TAXES —Cont'd
Roll-back taxes.
Real estate tax special assessment for land preservation.
Change in use or zoning of real estate, §58.1-3237.
Rolling stock tax, §§58.1-2652 to 58.1-2659.
See PUBLIC SERVICE CORPORATION TAXATION.
Sale of delinquent tax lands, §§58.1-3965 to 58.1-3975.
See SALE OF DELINQUENT TAX LANDS.
Sales taxes.
Aircraft sales and use tax, §§58.1-1500 to 58.1-1510.
See AIRCRAFT SALES AND USE TAX.
Cigarette excise tax, §§58.1-1000 to 58.1-1022.
See CIGARETTE TAX.
Cigarette tax, localities, §§58.1-3830 to 58.1-3832.
Corporate or partnership officer willful failure to collect and account for, §58.1-3907.
Forest products tax, §§58.1-1600 to 58.1-1622.
See FOREST PRODUCTS TAX.
Motor fuel sales tax, §§58.1-1718.1 to 58.1-1724.4.
Motor fuel sales tax in certain counties, §§58.1-1724.2, 58.1-1724.4.
Motor vehicle sales and use tax, §§58.1-2400 to 58.1-2426.
See MOTOR VEHICLE SALES AND USE TAX.
Retail sales and use tax generally, §§58.1-600 to 58.1-639.
See RETAIL SALES AND USE TAX.
Tire recycling fee, §§58.1-640 to 58.1-644.
Tobacco products tax, §§58.1-1021.01 to 58.1-1021.05.
Watercraft sales and use tax, §§58.1-1400 to 58.1-1410.
See WATERCRAFT SALES AND USE TAX.
Sanitary districts.
Levy and expenditure of taxes, §21-118.3.
Levy of assessments in certain cities and counties, §21-120.
Special taxing districts, §21-119.
Unified water supply and sewerage systems, §21-118.5.
Sanitary districts bonds.
Payment of interest on serial bonds, §§21-137.2, 21-138.
Sinking fund for term bonds, §21-137.1.
Sanitation districts law of 1938.
Exemption of bonds from taxation, §21-156.
Saturday, Sunday or legal holiday.
Filing of returns and payment.
Falling on, §58.1-8.
Savings institutions.
Depositories for federal taxes, §6.2-1170.
Schools and education, special taxes, §§22.1-102 to 22.1-106.
School taxes.
Special county, district, city or town tax, §§22.1-102 to 22.1-106.
Seals tax, §§58.1-1725, 58.1-1726.
Secrecy of tax information, §58.1-3.
Attorney general's authority to request and share information, §58.1-3.2.
Availability for necessary audit of local tax returns, §58.1-3.1.
Motor carrier road tax.
International fuel tax agreement.
Information exchanges under agreement, §58.1-2712.2.

TAXES —Cont'd
Secrecy of tax information —Cont'd
Motor vehicle fuel sales tax, §58.1-1724.1.
Real property tax.
Assessment cards and sheets, public disclosure, §58.1-3331.
Income-producing realty, reports by owners, §58.1-3294.
Retail sales and use tax.
Report of gross misuse of exemption certificates, §58.1-623.1.
Return filed, §58.1-1714.
Road tax for motor carriers.
International fuel tax agreement.
Information exchanges under agreement, §58.1-2712.2.
Setoff debt collection act.
Exemption, use of information, §58.1-533.
Tax commissioner's authority to request and share information, §58.1-3.2.
Taxpayer bill of rights, §58.1-1845.
Tax preparers.
Not to disclose information without consent, §58.1-4.
Town officers provided information by commissioners of revenue, §58.1-3109.
Transfer of credit or other tax attribute.
Deemed consent to disclosure, §58.1-3.3.
Treasurers books and papers pertaining to office, §58.1-3127.
Wills and administration, tax on.
Return filed, §58.1-1714.
Segregation of property for local taxation, VA Const Art X §4.
Service districts.
Power to levy and collect annual tax on property, §15.2-2403.
Setoff debt collection, income tax, §§58.1-520 to 58.1-535.
See SETOFF DEBT COLLECTION, INCOME TAX.
Settlement of doubtful or disputed claims.
Authority of tax commissioner, §58.1-105.
Severance tax on coal, gases or oil.
Local coal severance license taxes, §§58.1-3740 to 58.1-3745.
Local license tax on persons engaging in business of severing coal, gases or oil, §§58.1-3712 to 58.1-3713.4.
Local tax alternative to specially and separately assessing mineral lands, §58.1-3286.
Small business financing authority.
See SMALL BUSINESS FINANCING AUTHORITY.
Small grain market development, education and promotion.
Referendum on question of assessment, §§3.2-2205 to 3.2-2209.
Soft drink excise tax, §§58.1-1700 to 58.1-1705.
Solicitation of charitable or civic contributions.
Misrepresentations as to deductions, §57-57.
Soybean research, promotion, etc.
Referendum on question of assessment, §§3.2-2305 to 3.2-2309.
Special county, district, city or town tax.
School purposes, §§22.1-102 to 22.1-106.
Special improvements tax.
Transportation district within city of Charlottesville and county of Albemarle.
Levy, rate, collection, use, §33.1-453.

TAXES —Cont'd
Special regulatory revenue tax.
Public service corporation, §§58.1-2660 to 58.1-2665.
State corporation commission.
Correction of taxes assessed by, §§58.1-2030 to 58.1-2035.
State taxation, property subject to, §58.1-100.
Statute of limitations.
Assessment of taxes imposed by the department of taxation, §58.1-104.
Waiver of time limitation on assessment of taxes, §58.1-101.
Criminal prosecutions, §19.2-8.
Stock corporation annual registration fees, §13.1-775.1.
Collection of unpaid bills, §13.1-775.2.
Suits and other judicial proceedings, §§58.1-1727 to 58.1-1729.
Surplus lines insurance.
License taxes on insurers, licensees to pay, §38.2-4809.
Tangible personal property.
Generally, §§58.1-3500 to 58.1-3522.
See PERSONAL PROPERTY TAXES.
Tax relief act of 1998, §§58.1-3523 to 58.1-3535.
See PERSONAL PROPERTY TAX RELIEF ACT OF 1998.
Taxable property, VA Const Art X §1.
Tax amnesty program, §58.1-1840.1.
Tax forms.
Fillable forms.
Commissioner required to ensure, time period, §58.1-202.3.
Promulgation and distribution by department of taxation, §58.1-214.
Taxpayer bill of rights, §58.1-1845.
Telecommunications companies.
State taxation, §58.1-2608.
Tennessee Valley Authority.
Apportionment of payments received from authority in lieu of taxes, §58.1-3406.
Tire tax, §§58.1-640 to 58.1-644.
Tobacco board excise tax, §§3.2-2405 to 3.2-2410.
Tobacco products tax, §§58.1-1021.01 to 58.1-1021.05.
Tourism zones.
Cities, counties, towns.
Establishment, authority, tax incentives, regulatory flexibility, providing, §§58.1-3851, 58.1-3851.1.
Town imposing.
Two-third vote of council members, §15.2-1427.
Transient occupancy tax, §§58.1-3819 to 58.1-3826.
Excise tax, city or town having general taxing powers, §58.1-3840.
Imposition, §58.1-3843.
Transportation districts.
Annual special improvements tax, §§33.1-415, 33.1-435.
Payment of proceeds to transportation trust fund, §33.1-436.
Use of revenues, §§33.1-415, 33.1-435.
Transportation infrastructure bank.
Tax exemption, §33.1-23.12.
Trusts.
Modification of trust to achieve settlor's tax objectives, §64.2-734.
Tax savings.
Discretionary powers, exercise, §64.2-776.

TAXES —Cont'd
Underpayment rate.
Interest rate on omitted taxes and assessments, §58.1-15.
Unemployment compensation.
Employer taxation, §§60.2-500 to 60.2-538.
See UNEMPLOYMENT COMPENSATION.
Uniformity of taxes, VA Const Art X §1.
Use taxes.
Aircraft sales and use tax, §§58.1-1500 to 58.1-1510.
See AIRCRAFT SALES AND USE TAX.
Cigarette tax, localities, §§58.1-3822 to 58.1-3832.
Forest products tax, §§58.1-1600 to 58.1-1622.
See FOREST PRODUCTS TAX.
Motor vehicle sales and use tax, §§58.1-2400 to 58.1-2426.
See MOTOR VEHICLE SALES AND USE TAX.
Retail sales and use tax generally, §§58.1-600 to 58.1-639.
See RETAIL SALES AND USE TAX.
Watercraft sales and use tax, §§58.1-1400 to 58.1-1410.
See WATERCRAFT SALES AND USE TAX.
Utilities.
Consumer utility taxes, §§58.1-3814 to 58.1-3816.2.
Venue.
Collection of taxes.
Preferred forum, §8.01-261.
Tax offenses, §19.2-245.2.
Virginia communications sales and use tax act, §§58.1-645 to 58.1-662.
See COMMUNICATIONS SALES AND USE TAX.
Virginia retirement system.
Exemption of assets, §51.1-124.4.
Virginia tax amnesty program, §58.1-1840.1.
Waiver of time limitation on assessment of omitted or additional state taxes, §58.1-220.
Watercraft sales and use tax, §§58.1-1400 to 58.1-1410.
See WATERCRAFT SALES AND USE TAX.
Watershed improvements districts.
Annual taxes, §10.1-631.
Collection of taxes, §10.1-627.
Levy of tax, §10.1-626.
Wills and administrations tax, local, §§58.1-3805 to 58.1-3808.
Wills and administrations tax, state tax, §§58.1-1711 to 58.1-1718.
See PROBATE TAX, STATE.
Workers' compensation commission administrative fund, §65.2-1000.
Carrier withdrawal from business within the Commonwealth, §65.2-1004.
Exclusivity of tax, §65.2-1005.
Payments, §65.2-1002.
Failure to pay, §65.2-1004.
Returns, §65.2-1001.
Filing failures, §65.2-1003.
Self-insurers, §65.2-1006.
Workers' compensation uninsured employer's fund.
Financing, §65.2-1201.

TAXES ADMINISTERED BY AGENCIES OR LOCALITIES.
Admission tax, §§58.1-3817, 58.1-3818.
Scott county.
Off-track horse race wagering facilities, §58.1-3818.01.

TAXES ADMINISTERED BY AGENCIES OR LOCALITIES —Cont'd
Admission tax —Cont'd
Stafford county, §58.1-3818.02.
Cigarette tax.
Local taxes, §§58.1-3830 to 58.1-3832.
Corporate or partnership officer willful failure to collect and account for, §58.1-3907.
Collection of taxes assessed by state corporation commission, §§58.1-2030 to 58.1-2035.
Consumer utility taxes, §§58.1-3814 to 58.1-3816.2.
Food and beverage tax, §§58.1-3833, 58.1-3834.
Fuel taxes, §§58.1-2200 to 58.1-2299.20.
See FUEL TAXES.
Insurance companies license tax, §§58.1-2500 to 58.1-2533.
See INSURANCE COMPANIES LICENSE TAX.
License taxes generally, §§58.1-3700 to 58.1-3735.
See LICENSE TAXES.
Probate tax.
Cities or counties, authorization, §58.1-1718.
Generally, §§58.1-3805 to 58.1-3808.
Public service corporations generally, §§58.1-2600 to 58.1-2690.
See PUBLIC SERVICE CORPORATION TAXATION.
Real property taxes, §§58.1-3200 to 58.1-3389.
See REAL PROPERTY TAXES.
Recordation tax, §§58.1-3800 to 58.1-3804.
Road tax on motor carriers, §§58.1-2700 to 58.1-2712.2.
See ROAD TAX ON MOTOR CARRIERS.
State corporation commission.
Correction of taxes assessed by, §§58.1-2030 to 58.1-2035.
Tangible personal property, machinery and tools and merchants' capital tax, §§58.1-3500 to 58.1-3522.
See PERSONAL PROPERTY TAXES.
Transient occupancy tax, §§58.1-3819 to 58.1-3826.
Wills and administrations tax, §§58.1-3805 to 58.1-3808.
Cities or counties, authorization, §58.1-1718.

TAXES ADMINISTERED BY DEPARTMENT OF TAXATION.
Aircraft sales and use tax, §§58.1-1500 to 58.1-1510.
See AIRCRAFT SALES AND USE TAX.
Bank franchise tax, §§58.1-1200 to 58.1-1217.
See BANK FRANCHISE TAX.
Cigarette tax, §§58.1-1000 to 58.1-1022.
See CIGARETTE TAX.
Collection of state taxes, §§58.1-1800 to 58.1-1818.
See TAX COLLECTION.
Corporation income tax, §§58.1-400 to 58.1-455.
See INCOME TAX.
Correction of erroneous tax assessments, §§58.1-1820 to 58.1-1835.
See CORRECTION OF ERRONEOUS TAX ASSESSMENTS.
Estate or trust income taxation, §§58.1-360 to 58.1-383.
See INCOME TAX.
Estate tax, §§58.1-900 to 58.1-938.
See ESTATE TAX.

TAXES ADMINISTERED BY DEPARTMENT OF TAXATION —Cont'd
Forest products tax, §§58.1-1600 to 58.1-1622.
See FOREST PRODUCTS TAX.
General provisions, §§58.1-100 to 58.1-113.
Income tax, §§58.1-300 to 58.1-549.
See INCOME TAX.
Individual income tax, §§58.1-320 to 58.1-355.
See INCOME TAX.
Intangible personal property tax, §§58.1-1100 to 58.1-1118.
See PERSONAL PROPERTY TAXES.
Litter tax, §§58.1-1706 to 58.1-1710.
Motor vehicle fuel sales tax, §§58.1-1718.1 to 58.1-1724.4.
Partnership income tax, §§58.1-390.1 to 58.1-395.
Probate tax, state, §§58.1-1711 to 58.1-1718.
See PROBATE TAX, STATE.
Recordation tax, §§58.1-800 to 58.1-817.
See RECORDATION TAX, STATE.
Retail sales and use tax, §§58.1-600 to 58.1-639.
See RETAIL SALES AND USE TAX.
Seals, §§58.1-1725, 58.1-1726.
Soft drink excise tax, §§58.1-1700 to 58.1-1705.
Suits and other judicial proceedings, §§58.1-1727 to 58.1-1729.
Tire tax, §§58.1-640 to 58.1-644.
Watercraft sales and use tax, §§58.1-1400 to 58.1-1410.
See WATERCRAFT SALES AND USE TAX.
Wills and administrations tax, §§58.1-1711 to 58.1-1718.
See PROBATE TAX, STATE.
Writ taxes, §§58.1-1727 to 58.1-1729.

TAXES OR ASSESSMENTS FOR LOCAL IMPROVEMENTS, §§15.2-2404 to 15.2-2413.
Agreements between governing body and abutting landowners, §15.2-2405.
Amount assessed reported to collector of taxes, §15.2-2407.
Amount of assessment, notice, §15.2-2408.
How given, objections, §15.2-2409.
Appeals, §15.2-2410.
Procedure, §15.2-2411.
Assessments or apportionment of cost, §15.2-2406.
Authority to impose, §15.2-2404.
Correction of erroneous assessments of local levies by application to court.
Inapplicability of provisions to local improvements, §58.1-3985.
Cost.
How assessed and apportioned, §15.2-2406.
County manager plan of government.
Authority to impose assessment, §15.2-740.
Payment generally, §15.2-727.
Postponement of payment, §15.2-718.
Docketing of abstracts of resolutions or ordinances, §15.2-2412.
Elderly or permanently and totally disabled property owners.
Postponement of payment, §15.2-2407.
How imposed, §15.2-2405.
Installment payments, §15.2-2413.
Lien of judgment of assessment, §15.2-2411.
Notice to abutting landowners, §15.2-2405.
Notice to landowner of amount of assessment, §15.2-2408.
How given, objections, §15.2-2409.

TAXES OR ASSESSMENTS FOR LOCAL IMPROVEMENTS —Cont'd
Objections to assessment, §15.2-2409.
Appeals, §15.2-2410.
Procedure, §15.2-2411.
Petition for imposition, §15.2-2405.
Postponement of payment of assessment, §15.2-2407.
Purposes of imposition, §15.2-2404.
Report of assessments to collector of taxes, §15.2-2407.
Taxes or assessments upon abutting property owners generally, VA Const Art X §3.
Time limitation waiver, §58.1-3903.1.
Time limit for appeals, §15.2-2410.

TAX EVASION.
Tax offenses generally.
See TAX OFFENSES.

TAX EXEMPTIONS.
Aircraft sales and use tax, §58.1-1505.
Arts foundation.
Gifts and bequests to fund, §2.2-2704.
Authorities for development of former federal areas.
Bonds, §15.2-6314.
Baseball stadium authority bonds, §15.2-5810.
Behavioral health authorities, §37.2-609.
Blind or visually impaired.
Vending stands, §51.5-98.
BVU authority, §15.2-7220.
Cigarette excise tax, §58.1-1002.
Cigarette use tax.
Products on which sales tax paid, §58.1-1018.
Commercial or industrial structures.
Rehabilitation, renovation or replacement, §58.1-3221.
Commercial space flight authority.
Bond issues, §2.2-2214.
Communications sales and use tax, §58.1-648.
Consumer utility taxes, §58.1-3816.2.
Criminal justice training academies, §15.2-1751.
Damaged, destroyed or razed buildings by fortuitous happenings.
Abatement of levies, §58.1-3222.
Department of agriculture and consumer services.
Interim certification of tax exempt status.
Authority of commission to issue, §18.2-340.18.
Economic development partnership authority, §2.2-2243.
Elderly or handicapped.
Real property taxes, §§58.1-3210 to 58.1-3217.
Electric authorities, §§15.2-5423, 15.2-5423.1.
Electric utility bonds, §15.2-5422.
Federal transportation grant anticipation revenue notes, §33.1-23.25.
Forest products tax, §58.1-1608.
Fort Monroe authority, §2.2-2347.
Fraternal benefit societies, §38.2-4124.
General assembly powers, VA Const Art IV §14.
Hampton Roads sports facility bonds, §15.2-5910.
Health workforce development authority, §32.1-122.7:2.
Hospital authorities, §15.2-5361.
Hotel and motel structures.
Rehabilitated, renovated or replacement structures, §58.1-3220.1.
Income tax.
Corporations, §58.1-401.

TAX EXEMPTIONS —Cont'd
Income tax —Cont'd
Individual income tax.
Exemptions and exclusions, §58.1-321.
Withholding exemption certificates, §§58.1-461, 58.1-470.
Fraudulent certificates or failure to supply, §58.1-471.
Industrial development authority bonds, §15.2-4912.
Innovation and entrepreneurship investment authority, §2.2-2230.
Insurance companies license tax, §58.1-2502.
Insurers' securities deposited with state treasurer, §38.2-1056.
License taxes, §58.1-3703.
Heat, light and power companies, §58.1-2627.
Limitations imposed on peddlers, itinerant merchants and peddlers at wholesale, §58.1-3719.
Local trusts to fund postemployment benefits other than pensions, §15.2-1546.
Metropolitan Washington airports authority, §5.1-172.
Middle Peninsula Chesapeake Bay public access authority, §15.2-6617.
Military property, §44-131.
Motor vehicle sales and use tax, §58.1-2403.
Northern Neck Chesapeake Bay public access authority, §15.2-6643.
Offshore wind development authority, §67-1211.
On prizes and sales of tickets, §58.1-4025.
Park authorities, §15.2-5708.
Personal property taxes.
Farm animals, grains, agricultural products, etc.
Governing body may exempt, §58.1-3505.
Intangible personal property tax.
Exempt professions and businesses, §58.1-1103.
Planning district commissions, §15.2-4219.
Property exempt from taxation, §§58.1-3600 to 58.1-3666, VA Const Art X §6.
See PROPERTY EXEMPT FROM TAXATION.
Veterans, VA Const Art X §6-A.
Public building authority, §2.2-2278.
Real property taxes.
Elderly or handicapped exemption, §§58.1-3210 to 58.1-3217.
See REAL PROPERTY TAXES.
Service charges in lieu of real property taxation, §§58.1-3400 to 58.1-3407.
Real property transfer on death act.
Transfer on death deeds, exemption from recordation tax, §64.2-628.
Recordation tax, state, §58.1-811.
Recreational facility authority bonds, §15.2-5613.
Rehabilitated commercial or industrial structures, §58.1-3221.
Rehabilitated hotel or motel structures, §58.1-3220.1.
Rehabilitated residential real estate.
Real property taxes, §58.1-3220.
Renovated commercial or industrial structures, §58.1-3221.
Renovated hotel or motel structures, §58.1-3220.1.
Renovated residential structures.
Real property taxes, §58.1-3220.
Replacement commercial or industrial structures, §58.1-3221.

TAX EXEMPTIONS —Cont'd
Replacement hotel or motel structures, §58.1-3220.1.
Replacement residential structures.
Real property taxes, §58.1-3220.
Resources authority, §62.1-219.
Retail sales and use tax.
Agricultural exemptions, §58.1-609.2.
Commercial and industrial exemptions, §58.1-609.3.
Energy star qualified products, §58.1-609.1.
Exceptions, local sales and use taxes, §58.1-609.13.
Gift transactions, §58.1-604.6.
Governmental and commodities exemptions, §58.1-609.1.
Hurricane preparedness equipment, limited exemption, §58.1-611.3.
Media-related exemptions, §58.1-609.6.
Miscellaneous exemptions, §58.1-609.10.
Reports to general assembly on tax exemptions studies, §58.1-609.12.
Modular building manufacturers and retailers, §58.1-610.1.
Motor vehicles, machinery, etc., brought into Virginia for use in performing contracts, use tax on, §58.1-604.3.
Nonprofit entities, §58.1-609.11.
Reports to general assembly on tax exemptions, §58.1-609.12.
Railroad rolling stock.
Commercial and industrial exemptions, §58.1-609.3.
School supplies, limited exemption, §58.1-611.2.
Absorption of tax, advertising, prohibition, inapplicability, §58.1-626.
Collection by dealer during limited period, §58.1-625.
Service exemptions, §58.1-609.5.
Road tax on motor carriers, §58.1-2702.
Small business financing authority, §2.2-2313.
Bond issues.
Limitations, §2.2-2291.
Public hearings, §2.2-2292.
Tax exempt organization.
Defined, §58.1-1.
Tire tax, §58.1-642.
Tobacco indemnification and community revitalization commission, §3.2-3110.
Tourism authority, §2.2-2324.
Transfer on death deeds, exemption from recordation tax, §64.2-628.
Transportation board.
Federal transportation grant anticipation revenue notes, §33.1-23.25.
Transportation districts, §15.2-4532.
Bonds, §15.2-4519.
Transportation infrastructure bank, §33.1-23.12.
Veterans.
Property exempt from taxation, VA Const Art X §6-A.
Veterans services fund.
Gifts and bequests, §2.2-2719.
Virginia arts foundation fund.
Gifts and bequests to fund, §2.2-2704.
Virginia Commonwealth University health system authority, §23-50.16:16.
Virginia foundation for healthy youth.
Tax-exempt status, §32.1-365.

TAX EXEMPTIONS —Cont'd
Virginia health workforce development authority, §32.1-122.7:2.
Virginia life, accident and sickness insurance guaranty association, §38.2-1712.
Virginia offshore wind development authority, §67-1211.
Virginia property and casualty insurance guaranty association, §38.2-1613.
Virginia regional industrial facilities authorities.
Bonds, §15.2-6411.
Water and waste authorities, §15.2-5132.
Watercraft sales and use tax, §58.1-1404.
Wireless service authorities.
Bond issues, §15.2-5431.21.
Woodrow Wilson bridge and tunnel compact, §33.1-320.2.

TAX EXEMPT ORGANIZATIONS.
Defined, §58.1-1.
Immunity of officers, §8.01-220.1:1.
Survival of actions.
Immunity defense.
Survival of immunity after discontinuance of entity, §8.01-220.1:1.

TAX FORMS.
Promulgation and distribution by department of taxation, §58.1-214.

TAXICABS.
ABC offenses.
Limitation on carrying alcoholic beverages, §4.1-312.
Advertising.
Limitations, §46.2-2060.
Common carriers.
Provisions to not make cabs into common carriers, §46.2-2061.
Criminal enforcement of provisions, §46.2-2066.
Drivers' licenses.
Localities may require license for for-hire passenger vehicles, §46.2-310.
Employee liens, §§43-24 to 43-26.
Financial data.
Locality requiring operator to submit, §46.2-2062.
High-occupancy vehicle lanes, use, §33.1-46.2.
Identification of vehicle as cab.
Roof signs and markings, §46.2-2059.1.
Insurance, §46.2-2057.
Licenses.
Locally regulated, §46.2-2063.
License tax.
Exemption from local tax.
Nonprofit transportation service serving elderly and disabled, §15.2-967.1.
Limitation on localities authority, §58.1-3703.
Locally regulated.
Licensing and license taxation, §46.2-2063.
Restrictions on imposition, §46.2-2064.
Number of cabs, §46.2-2067.
Operator qualifications, §46.2-2065.
Rates, regulations, etc., §46.2-2062.
Stand regulation, §46.2-2065.
Motor vehicle license plates.
Issuance of designated plates, §46.2-711.
Motor vehicle registration.
Fees for vehicles used and designed for passenger transportation, §46.2-694.
Motor vehicle titling.
Information required on transfer of title, §46.2-624.

TAXICABS —Cont'd
Not required to incorporate as public service companies, §13.1-620.
Permits.
City or town providing for issuance, §15.2-2015.
Requirement, §46.2-2059.
Personal property taxes.
Classification, §58.1-3503.
Public service companies generally, §§56-1 to 56-87.
See PUBLIC SERVICE COMPANIES.
Rates and charges.
Regulation by locality, §46.2-2062.
Retail sales and use tax.
Parts, tires, etc., sold or leased by operators, §58.1-609.3.
Roof signs and marking identifying vehicle as.
Requirement, §46.2-2059.1.
School transportation.
Insurance coverage for taxicabs providing transportation of students, §22.1-190.
Self-insurers, §46.2-2058.
Shared ride taxi system, §15.2-949.
Supplier liens, §§43-24 to 43-26.
Transportation companies generally, §§56-99.2 to 56-140.
See TRANSPORTATION COMPANIES.
Workers' compensation.
Employee not to mean driver excluded from taxation by federal unemployment tax act, §65.2-101.

TAXIDERMY PERMITS, §29.1-415.
Issuance, §29.1-413.
By whom, §29.1-420.
Required, §29.1-412.
Sale of unclaimed or mounted specimens, §29.1-415.

TAX INCREMENT FINANCING, §§58.1-3245 to 58.1-3245.5.

TAX INFORMATION SECRECY, §58.1-3.
Attorney general's authority to request and share information, §58.1-3.2.
Availability of information to audit local tax returns, §58.1-3.1.
Motor carrier road tax.
International fuel tax agreement.
Information exchanges under agreement, §58.1-2712.2.
Motor vehicle fuel sales tax, §58.1-1724.1.
Real property tax.
Assessment cards and sheets, public disclosure, §58.1-3331.
Income-producing realty, reports by owners, §58.1-3294.
Retail sales and use tax.
Report of gross misuse of exemption certificates, §58.1-623.1.
Return filed, §58.1-1714.
Road tax for motor carriers.
International fuel tax agreement.
Information exchanges under agreement, §58.1-2712.2.
Setoff debt collection act.
Exemption, use of information, §58.1-533.
Tax commissioner's authority to request and share information, §58.1-3.2.
Taxpayer bill of rights, §58.1-1845.
Tax preparers not to disclose information without consent, §58.1-4.

TAX INFORMATION SECRECY —Cont'd
Town officers provided information by commissioners of revenue, §58.1-3109.
Transfer of credit or other tax attribute.
Deemed consent to disclosure, §58.1-3.3.
Treasurers books and papers pertaining to office, §58.1-3127.
Wills and administration, tax on.
Return filed, §58.1-1714.

TAXING COSTS OF LITIGATION.
Law of costs generally, §§17.1-600 to 17.1-629.
See COURT COSTS AND FEES.

TAX LIENS.
Collection of state taxes.
Memorandum of lien, §58.1-1805.
Collection of taxes assessed by state corporation commission.
Memorandum of lien, §58.1-2021.
Delinquent local treasurers, judgment and executions, §58.1-3172.
Delinquent tax lands.
Lien for taxes paid, §58.1-3974.
Estate tax, unpaid taxes, §58.1-908.
Forest products tax, §58.1-1603.
Income tax.
Jeopardy assessment.
Memorandum of lien, §58.1-313.
Memorandum of lien.
Collection of state taxes, §58.1-1805.
Collection of taxes assessed by state corporation commission, §58.1-2021.
Income tax, jeopardy assessment, §58.1-313.
Retail sales and use tax delinquencies, §58.1-632.
Public service corporation taxation, §58.1-2612.
Real property taxes, §§58.1-3340 to 58.1-3345.
Accumulated amounts of tax deferred in interest, §58.1-3219.1.
Deferral programs for elderly or handicapped, §58.1-3216.
Delinquent taxes, recording, §58.1-3930.
Release of delinquent lien to facilitate conveyance, §58.1-3228.
Release on portion of real estate upon payment of taxes, §58.1-3226.1.
Retail sales and use tax delinquencies.
Memorandum of lien, §58.1-632.
Sale of delinquent tax lands.
Nonjudicial sale of properties of minimal size and value, §58.1-3975.
Taxes paid on real estate, §58.1-3974.
State corporation commission.
Collection of taxes.
Assessed by, §58.1-2021.

TAX MAP REFERENCE NUMBER.
Circuit court clerk indexing by, §17.1-252.

TAX OFFENSES.
Aircraft sales and use tax.
Misrepresenting value of aircraft or amount of tax due, §58.1-1503.
Carnivals, circuses or speedways.
Licensed tax violation, §58.1-3728.
Cigarette tax.
Counterfeit stamps, §58.1-1015.
Evading, §58.1-1017.
Failure to file monthly report, §58.1-1008.
Failure to keep adequate records, §§58.1-1003, 58.1-1007.
Failure to preserve records, §58.1-1007.

TAX OFFENSES —Cont'd
Cigarette tax —Cont'd
Interference with enforcement of chapter, §58.1-1006.
Possession with intent to distribute tax-paid cigarettes, §58.1-1017.1.
Refusal to allow audit or inspection of records, §58.1-1007.
Removal, reuse, unauthorized sale, etc., §58.1-1015.
Sale of unstamped cigarettes by wholesale dealers, §58.1-1010.
Stamps not properly affixed, §58.1-1003.
Unlawful sale of stamps, §58.1-1009.
Use tax.
Failure to preserve record, §58.1-1021.
Refusal to allow audit or inspection, §58.1-1021.
Commissioners of revenue.
Failure to deliver personal property book, §58.1-3118.
Improper destruction of return, §58.1-3112.
Refusal to permit access to records or information.
To commissioner, §58.1-3111.
Confidential tax documents.
Disseminating or publishing, §58.1-3.
Corporate income.
Fraudulent return, §58.1-452.
Estimated tax.
Failure or refusal to file declarations, §58.1-496.
False or fraudulent statements and declaration, §58.1-496.
False returns, §58.1-498.
False claim of employment status.
Evading withholding or payment of income tax, §58.1-485.1.
False returns, §58.1-11.
Forest products tax.
Failure to make return, keep records or permit examination, §58.1-1618.
Failure to make transporters report, §58.1-1614.
Income tax.
Failure or refusal to file return, §58.1-348.
False statements on returns, §58.1-348.
Local taxes.
False or fraudulent information on certificate of residency, §58.1-547.
Rental payments to nonresidents.
Supplying false or fraudulent information, §58.1-316.
Sale of real property by nonresidents.
Supplying false or fraudulent information, §58.1-317.
Intangible personal property tax.
False or fraudulent understatement with intent to evade, §58.1-1114.
Local tax officers.
Disclosure of secret information, §58.1-3.
Manufactured homes.
Permits required before moving, §58.1-3520.
Marinas.
Failure to file list of boat owners, §58.1-3902.
Mobile homes.
Permits required before moving violation, §58.1-3520.
Motor carriers road tax.
False statements, §58.1-2710.
Motor vehicles sales and use tax.
Evading tax, §58.1-2402.
Real estate taxes.
Failure to obey board of equalization summons, §58.1-3387.

TAX OFFENSES —Cont'd
Recordation tax, state misrepresentation to clerk, §58.1-812.
Records and documents.
Failure to make available for inspection, §58.1-103.
Retail sales and use tax.
Absorption of tax, §58.1-626.
Dealer's certificate of registration.
Engaging in business without, §58.1-613.
Failure to file return, §58.1-636.
Failure to keep records, §58.1-623.
Failure to pay or collect, §58.1-625.
False or fraudulent returns, §58.1-636.
Misuse of exemption certificate, §58.1-623.1.
Refusal to permit examination of records, §58.1-633.
Tax collection.
Conversion of trust taxes, §58.1-1816.
Failure to collect and account for tax, §58.1-1815.
Failure to file return, §58.1-1815.
Failure to keep record, §58.1-1814.
Padlock businesses entering premises without prior approval, §58.1-1805.
Tax preparers.
Disclosure of information, §58.1-4.
Tenants.
Failure to file list of tenants, §58.1-3901.
Treasurers.
Failure to deliver receipts upon collection of taxes, §58.1-3914.
Failure to mail bills to taxpayers, §58.1-3912.
Omission of taxes from delinquent list, §58.1-3946.
Watercraft sales and use tax.
Misrepresenting value of watercraft or amount of tax due, §58.1-1403.
Withholding income.
Employers failure to make return, withhold tax, pay tax or furnish employee with withholding statements, §58.1-485.
False or fraudulent information on certificate of residency, §58.1-547.
Withholding tax.
Fraudulent withholding exemption certificate or failure to supply information, §58.1-471.

TAX OFFICERS.
Clerks of courts of record, §§58.1-3173 to 58.1-3177.
Commissioners of revenue.
Generally, §§58.1-3100 to 58.1-3122.2.
See COMMISSIONERS OF REVENUE.
Treasurers, local.
Generally, §§58.1-3123 to 58.1-3172.1.
See TREASURERS, LOCAL.

TAXPAYER BILL OF RIGHTS, §58.1-1845.

TAXPAYER PROBLEM RESOLUTION PROGRAM, §58.1-1818.

TAXPAYERS.
Bill of rights for Virginia taxpayers, §58.1-1845.
Defined, §58.1-1.
Examination of books and records by tax commissioner, §58.1-219.
Retention of records, §58.1-102.

TAX PENALTIES.
Aircraft sales and use tax, §58.1-1510.
Bad check, payment of tax by, §58.1-12.
Bank franchise tax.
Failure to comply with chapter, §58.1-1216.

TAX PENALTIES —Cont'd
Compromise of prosecution and compromise in lieu of penalty.
Offers in compromise, authority of department of taxation to accept, §58.1-105.
Estimated license tax on water, heat, light, power or pipeline companies, §58.1-2648.
Forest products tax.
Deficiencies, §58.1-1620.
Delinquent taxpayer, §58.1-1615.
Failure to pay when due, §58.1-1619.
General fund.
Paid into, §58.1-13.
Income tax.
Corporations.
Failure to make report or return, §58.1-450.
Fraudulent returns, §58.1-451.
Nonpayment, §58.1-455.
Underestimated tax payment on extension of time for filing return, §58.1-453.
Estimated tax by nonresidents upon real property sale, failure to file, §58.1-317.
Failure to report on rental payments to nonresident payees, §58.1-316.
False or fraudulent understatement, §58.1-308.
Individual income tax.
Delinquent individuals or fiduciaries, procuring returns from, §58.1-350.
Failure to pay in full, §58.1-351.
Underestimated tax payment by individual extending time for filing return, §58.1-344.
Individual taxpayers.
Failure to file return on time, §58.1-347.
Income tax withholding.
Failure of employer to withhold, §58.1-475.
Insurance companies license tax.
Failure to make report or pay tax, §58.1-2507.
Failure to pay estimated tax, §58.1-2527.
Intangible personal property tax.
Failure to file return, §58.1-1113.
Failure to pay when due, §58.1-1116.
False or fraudulent understatement, §58.1-1114.
Litter tax, §58.1-1709.
Local taxes.
Failure to pay by December 5, §58.1-3915.
Ordinances setting penalties, §58.1-3916.
Omission of state taxes, §58.1-1812.
Omitted taxes.
Local taxes or levies, §58.1-3903.
Taxes administered by agencies other than tax department, §58.1-2025.
Personal property taxes.
Intangible personal property tax.
Failure to pay when due, §58.1-1116.
False or fraudulent understatement, §58.1-1114.
Ordinances setting penalties and interest, §58.1-3916.
Property taxes.
Failure to pay by December 5, §58.1-3915.
Public service corporation taxation.
Failure to file timely reports, §58.1-2610.
Failure to pay tax, §58.1-2611.
Real estate tax special assessment for land preservation.
Failure to report change in use or misstatement in application, §58.1-3238.
Retail sales and use tax.
Failure to file, false returns or fraudulent returns, §58.1-635.
Road tax on motor carriers, §58.1-2709.
Watercraft sales and use tax, §58.1-1408.

TAX PREPARERS.
Disclosure of information without consent, §58.1-4.

TAX REFUNDS.
Amended returns, filing, §58.1-1823.
Correction of erroneous state tax assessments.
Amended returns.
Reassessment and refunding upon filing, §58.1-1823.
Erroneous assessment of local taxes.
Action by court, §58.1-3987.
Correction by commissioner of revenue, §58.1-3981.
Ordinance providing, §58.1-3990.
Erroneous assessment of state taxes, §§58.1-1820 to 58.1-1835.
Interest on overpayments or improper collection, §58.1-1833.
Protective claim for refund, §58.1-1824.
Refunding upon filing of amended return, §58.1-1823.
Erroneous written advice by department.
Abatement of tax, interest or penalty, §58.1-1835.
Filing amended return, §58.1-1823.
Forest products tax, §58.1-1620.
Amount paid by taxpayer in excess of correct amount due, §58.1-1621.
Fuel taxes.
Uses eligible for refund, §58.1-2259.
Income tax.
Individual taxpayers.
Estimated tax overpayments, §58.1-499.
Loans in anticipation of income tax refunds.
Refund anticipation loans, §§6.2-2500 to 6.2-2505.
Local income tax, §58.1-546.
Overpayment, §58.1-309.
Setoff debt collection, §§58.1-520 to 58.1-535.
See SETOFF DEBT COLLECTION, INCOME TAX.
Income tax withholding.
Overpayments, §58.1-479.
Insurance company license tax, §58.1-2526.
Overpayments, §58.1-2507.
Intangible personal property tax, §58.1-1115.
Interest rate, §58.1-15.
License tax on water, heat, light, power or pipeline companies.
Estimated tax, §58.1-2647.
Limitation on filing amended returns, §58.1-1823.
Loans in anticipation of income tax refunds.
Refund anticipation loans, §§6.2-2500 to 6.2-2505.
Local income tax, §58.1-546.
Motor vehicle sales and use tax, §58.1-2423.
Overpayment rate of interest, §58.1-15.
Personal property taxes.
Intangible personal property tax, §58.1-1115.
Tax already paid, §58.1-3516.
Taxes paid city or county by nonresident, §58.1-3511.
Probate tax, state.
Overvaluation of estate, §58.1-1717.
Rate of interest, §58.1-15.
Real property taxes.
Public taking of private real estate, §58.1-3362.
Refund anticipation loans.
Loans in anticipation of income tax refunds, §§6.2-2500 to 6.2-2505.

TAX REFUNDS —Cont'd
Retail sales and use tax.
Certain building materials, §58.1-608.1.
Road tax on motor carriers.
Motor carriers giving bond, §58.1-2707.
False statements, §58.1-2710.
Setoff debt collection, income tax, §§58.1-520 to 58.1-535.
See SETOFF DEBT COLLECTION, INCOME TAX.
Taxpayer bill of rights, §58.1-1845.
Voluntary contribution to certain organizations.
Requirements, §58.1-344.3.

TAX RELIEF ACT OF 1998.
Personal property taxes, §§58.1-3523 to 58.1-3535.
See PERSONAL PROPERTY TAX RELIEF ACT OF 1998.

TAX RETURNS.
Aircraft sales and use tax.
Failure to make or fraudulent return, §58.1-1510.
Amended returns, filing, §58.1-1823.
Amnesty program, §58.1-1840.1.
Bank franchise tax.
Auditing, §58.1-1214.
Banks and liquidation, §58.1-1215.
Filing, §58.1-1207.
Cigarette use tax, §58.1-1019.
Failure to make or incorrect return, assessments, §58.1-1020.
Commercial delivery service.
Filing returns by, §58.1-9.
Commissioners of revenue.
See COMMISSIONERS OF REVENUE.
Communications sales and use tax, §58.1-654.
Confidential tax returns.
Order directing tax commissioner to produce.
Reproductions as compliance, §58.1-109.
Correction of erroneous state tax assessments.
Amended return.
Reassessment and refunding upon filing, §58.1-1823.
Destruction of returns of department of taxation, §58.1-107.
Disclosure of information by preparers without consent, §58.1-4.
Estate tax.
Amended returns, §58.1-906.
Filing returns, §58.1-905.
Generation skipping transfers.
Amended returns, §58.1-938.
Filing, §58.1-937.
Estimated tax.
Individuals, §§58.1-490 to 58.1-499.
Refusal of taxpayer to file state return, §58.1-111.
Return filing frequency.
Waiver of penalty, §58.1-112.
Evidence.
Reproductions, §58.1-108.
False returns, §58.1-11.
Filing.
Commercial delivery service, §58.1-9.
Mail, §58.1-9.
Refusal of taxpayer to file state return.
Estimated tax, §58.1-111.
Saturday, Sunday or legal holiday, due day falling on, §58.1-8.
Fillable tax forms.
Commissioner required to ensure, time period, §58.1-202.3.

TAX RETURNS —Cont'd
Forest products tax.
Absconding taxpayer, §58.1-1616.
Delinquent taxpayers, department to make return, §58.1-1615.
Failure to make return, §58.1-1618.
Filed by manufacturer, §58.1-1612.
Unmanufactured product shipped or sold for shipping out of Commonwealth, §58.1-1613.
Freedom of information act.
Records excluded, §2.2-3705.7.
Hospitals.
Nonprofit hospitals, §58.1-113.
Income tax.
Amended return.
Change in federal taxable income, §58.1-311.
Corporations.
Affiliated corporations, separate, combined or consolidated returns, §58.1-442.
Several liability of affiliated corporations, §58.1-444.
Worldwide consolidation or combination prohibited, §58.1-443.
Estimation of corporate tax, no return filed, §58.1-454.
Execution, §58.1-447.
Extension of time for filing, §58.1-453.
Failure to make, §58.1-450.
Fraudulent returns, §§58.1-451, 58.1-452.
Disposition, §58.1-307.
Estates or trust, §58.1-381.
Extension of time for filing, §58.1-383.
Place of filing, §58.1-382.
Filing of individual, estate or trust returns with department, §58.1-306.
Individual income tax, §58.1-341.
Delinquent individuals or fiduciaries, procuring, §58.1-350.
Extension of time for filing, §58.1-344.
Failure or refusal to file or false statements, §58.1-348.
Prima facie evidence, §58.1-349.
Failure to file in time, §58.1-347.
Nonresident commuters into state daily, §58.1-342.
Place of filing, §58.1-343.
Voter registration application included in packet, §58.1-341.1.
Income tax withholding.
Employer's returns, §58.1-472.
Annual returns filed with tax commissioner, §58.1-478.
Continuation of liability until notice, §58.1-476.
Extensions, §58.1-477.
Social security number, §58.1-478.1.
Willful failure to make returns, §58.1-485.
Intangible personal property tax, §§58.1-1107 to 58.1-1113.
Forwarded to department of taxation by commissioners of revenue, §58.1-3113.
Limitation on filing amended returns, §58.1-1823.
Local taxes.
Ordinances by counties, cities and towns providing dates for filing, §58.1-3916.
Mail, filing by, §58.1-9.
Nonprofit hospitals, §58.1-113.
Oaths or affirmations unnecessary, §58.1-11.
Personal property taxes, §§58.1-3517 to 58.1-3519.
Filing with commissioner of revenue, §58.1-3900.

TAX RETURNS —Cont'd
Personal property taxes —Cont'd
Intangible personal property.
Forwarded to department of taxation by commissioners of revenue, §58.1-3113.
Intangible personal property tax, §§58.1-1107 to 58.1-1113.
Ordinances setting dates for filing tax returns, §58.1-3916.
Preparers not to disclose information without consent, §58.1-4.
Probate tax, state.
Filing, §58.1-1714.
Refusal of taxpayer to file state return.
Estimated tax, §58.1-111.
Reproductions.
Admissibility in evidence, §58.1-108.
Authority of tax commissioner to make, §58.1-106.
Destruction, §58.1-107.
Order directing tax commissioner to produce confidential tax returns, §58.1-109.
Retail sales and use tax.
Dealers returns, §58.1-615.
Estimated tax on failure to file or fraudulent return, §58.1-618.
Extensions, §58.1-617.
Failure to file, false returns or fraudulent returns, §§58.1-635, 58.1-636.
Motor vehicles, machinery, etc., brought into Virginia for use in performing contracts, use tax on, §58.1-604.2.
Saturdays, Sundays or legal holidays.
Day for filing falling on, §58.1-8.
Virginia tax amnesty program, §58.1-1840.1.

TAX SALES.
Bill in equity for sale of delinquent tax lands, §§58.1-3965 to 58.1-3975.
See SALE OF DELINQUENT TAX LANDS.
Condominiums.
Special declarant rights.
Transfers, §55-79.74:3.
Real estate cooperatives.
Special declarant rights, transfers of, §55-461.

TAX SITUS.
Food and beverage taxes.
Counties, cities or towns, §58.1-3841.
License taxes, §§58.1-3708, 58.1-3709.
Personal property taxes, §§58.1-3511 to 58.1-3514.

TAX YEAR.
Defined, §58.1-1.
Income tax, residency for portion of, §58.1-303.
Real property tax assessment, §58.1-3281.

TAZEWELL COUNTY.
All-terrain vehicles.
Use on Pocahontas Trail, §46.2-915.1.
Automobile graveyards, screening ordinance, §15.2-903.
Coal miners' memorial.
Richlands coal miners' memorial.
Official designation, §1-510.
Confederate cemeteries and graves.
Disbursement of funds appropriated for upkeep, §10.1-2211.
Dams.
Restrictions, §29.1-532.
Drug treatment court.
Established, §18.2-254.1.

TAZEWELL COUNTY —Cont'd
Revolutionary war cemeteries and graves.
Disbursement of funds appropriated for upkeep, §10.1-2211.1.
Richlands coal miners' memorial.
Official designation, §1-510.
School board.
Salary of members, §22.1-32.
Transient occupancy tax.
Disposition of revenues, §58.1-3819.
Virginia coalfield economic development authority, §§15.2-6000 to 15.2-6015.

TEACHERS.
Advisory board on teacher education and licensure, §22.1-305.2.
Affordable housing.
Workforce housing alternatives.
School division personnel, §15.2-958.2.
Alcohol or drug use, incidents involving.
Immunity for personnel reporting, §8.01-47.
Algebra readiness intervention services.
Standards of quality, §22.1-253.13:2.
Alternate routes to licensure.
Defined, §22.1-298.1.
Education preparation programs, §22.1-298.2.
Anabolic steroids.
Procuring, selling, administering.
Suspension or revocation of license, §22.1-292.2.
Arrest.
Report of arrest for felony or class 1 misdemeanor, §19.2-83.1.
Assault and battery.
Construction of certain actions taken by teachers, §18.2-57.
Assignment by division superintendent, §22.1-297.
Assistant principals generally.
See PRINCIPALS, PUBLIC SCHOOLS.
Asthma medications, self-administration by student.
Immunity of school board employees supervising, §8.01-226.5:1.
Possession and self-administration of inhaled asthma medications by asthmatic students, §22.1-274.2.
Athletic coaching assignment.
Child abuse or neglect.
Persons required to report, §63.2-1509.
Employment contracts, §22.1-302.
Autism spectrum disorder, training required of personnel, §22.1-298.3.
Auto-injectable epinephrine, self-administration by student.
Immunity of principal supervising, §8.01-226.5:1.
Automated external defibrillators.
Requirements for licensure, §22.1-298.1.
Beginning teacher assistance program.
Immunity from civil liability, §22.1-303.1.
Mentor teacher programs, §22.1-305.1.
Biennial review, §22.1-289.1.
Bomb threats, firebombs or explosives, incidents involving.
Immunity for personnel reporting, §8.01-47.
Cardiopulmonary resuscitation.
Requirements for licensure, §22.1-298.1.
Child abuse or molestation.
Condition of employment.
Complaint search required, §22.1-296.4.
Conviction data required, §22.1-296.1.

TEACHERS —Cont'd
Child abuse or neglect, founded complaint against teacher.
Dismissal of teacher.
Grounds, §22.1-307.
Notification to board of education of dismissal on certain grounds, §22.1-313.
Notice to school board, §63.2-1503.
Child abuse or neglect reports.
Complaints against school personnel, §63.2-1511.
Interagency agreement, child abuse and neglect investigations, §63.2-1511.
Investigation procedures and release of information, §63.2-1516.1.
Standard for determining if report unfounded, §63.2-1511.
Reason to suspect, required reports, fine for failure, §63.2-1509.
Posting notice of employee obligations, §22.1-291.3.
Child abuse recognition and intervention education, §22.1-298.1.
Clinical faculty programs, §22.1-290.1.
Compacts.
Interstate agreement on qualification of educational personnel, §§22.1-316 to 22.1-318.
Compensation, §§22.1-289.1, 22.1-296.
Student teacher programs.
Compensation of cooperating teachers, §23-8.2:1.
Compulsory school attendance.
Daily maintenance of attendance records, §22.1-259.
General provisions, §§22.1-254 to 22.1-269.1.
See COMPULSORY SCHOOL ATTENDANCE.
Confidentiality of personnel files and performance indicators, §22.1-295.1.
Conflicts of interest.
Teacher awards.
Exclusion from scope of provisions, §2.2-3104.1.
Contact or other actions designed to maintain order and control.
Not construed as simple assault or assault and battery, §18.2-57.
Continuing contract status.
Effect of not achieving, §22.1-304.
Probationary period of employment completed, §22.1-304.
Continuing education.
Income tax deductions of tuition, §58.1-322.
Corporal punishment against student.
Restriction on using, §63.2-1511.
Corporal punishment prohibited, §22.1-279.1.
Criminal records checks, §§22.1-296.1, 22.1-296.2.
Data coordinator/instructional resource teachers.
Standards of quality, §22.1-253.13:2.
Definitions.
Clinical faculty programs, §22.1-290.1.
Grievance procedures, §22.1-306.
Education preparation programs, §22.1-298.2.
Employee personnel files, §22.1-295.1.
Employment contracts.
Athletic coaching assignment, §22.1-302.
Effect of continuing contract status, §22.1-304.
Execution, §22.1-302.
Extracurricular activity sponsorship, §22.1-302.
Licensure required, §22.1-299.
Nonrenewal of contract of probationary teacher, §22.1-305.

TEACHERS —Cont'd
Employment contracts —Cont'd
Nonrenewal of contract of teacher not achieving continuing contract status, §22.1-304.
Probationary terms of service, §22.1-303.
Temporarily employed teachers.
Qualifications, §22.1-302.
Virginia school for the deaf and blind, §22.1-349.
Written contract required, §22.1-302.
Employment of teachers, §22.1-295.
English language learner teachers.
Standards of quality, §22.1-253.13:2.
Epinephrine, self-administration by student.
Immunity of principal supervising, §8.01-226.5:1.
Evaluations.
Confidentiality of personnel files and performance indicators, §22.1-295.1.
Performance objectives, §22.1-253.13:5.
When evaluations to be given, §22.1-295.
Extracurricular activity sponsorship.
Employment contracts, §22.1-302.
Fingerprinting applicants for employment, §22.1-296.2.
First aid.
Requirements for licensure, §22.1-298.1.
Force used to quell disturbance or remove student.
Not construed as simple assault or assault and battery, §18.2-57.
Full-time equivalent instructional positions, §22.1-253.13:1.
Grants.
Strategic compensation grant initiative, §§22.1-318.1, 22.1-318.2.
Grievance procedure for school board employees.
School board to establish, §22.1-79.
Grievance procedures.
Civil actions against hearing panel members.
Attorney general or assistant representing, §2.2-507.
Definitions, §22.1-306.
Dismissal, etc.
Consideration of merits during notice, §22.1-309.
Grounds, §22.1-307.
Notification to board of education of dismissal or resignation on certain grounds, §22.1-313.
Reasons for recommendation upon request, §22.1-309.
Recommendation of dismissal or placement on probation, §22.1-309.
Grounds and procedure for suspension, §22.1-315.
Guidelines for rulemaking, §22.1-308.
Hearing before school board or hearing officer, §§22.1-311 to 22.1-314.
Appellate review, §22.1-314.
Decision generally, §§22.1-313, 22.1-314.
Dismissal, recommendation for, §22.1-311.
Hearing officer appointment, qualifications and duties, §22.1-311.
Issue of grievability, §22.1-314.
Judicial review, §22.1-314.
Private unless teacher requests public one, §22.1-311.
Record of hearing, §22.1-311.
Right to cross-examination of witnesses, §22.1-311.
Right to representation, §22.1-311.
Witnesses who are employees of school board, release time to attend hearing, §22.1-311.

TEACHERS —Cont'd
Grievance procedures —Cont'd
Rulemaking authority, §22.1-308.
Suspension, §22.1-315.
Grounds and procedure for suspension, §22.1-315.
Grounds for dismissal, §22.1-307.
Health insurance credits.
Retirement systems, §51.1-1401.
Health insurance for local employees, officers, teachers.
Participation, §2.2-1204.
Health-related services.
Instructional employee refusing to perform nonemergency management, §22.1-274.
Hepatitis B or C exposure incident.
School board employee exposed to or exposing another.
Consent to testing and release of information, §32.1-45.1.
HIV exposure incident.
School board employee exposed to or exposing another.
Consent to testing and release of information, §32.1-45.1.
Human trafficking, awareness and training materials, §22.1-16.5.
Immunity.
Beginning teacher assistance program, §22.1-303.1.
Good faith actions in scope of employment, §8.01-220.1:2.
Peer review, §22.1-303.1.
Student conduct involving explosive or drugs and alcohol.
Immunity for investigating or reporting, §8.01-47.
Incentive payments.
Strategic compensation grant initiative, §§22.1-318.1, 22.1-318.2.
Inhaled asthma medications, student's self-administration.
Immunity of school board employees supervising, §8.01-226.5:1.
Possession and self-administration of inhaled asthma medications by asthmatic students, §22.1-274.2.
Institutes for training teachers.
Guidelines to be developed by state council of higher education, §23-9.13:1.
Interstate agreement on qualification of educational personnel, §§22.1-316 to 22.1-318.
Juvenile justice department.
Education division, employment of teachers, §66-13.1.
Licensure.
Advisory board on teacher education and licensure, §22.1-305.2.
Anabolic steroids.
Procuring, selling, administering, suspension or revocation, §22.1-292.2.
Certification or training in emergency first aid, cardiopulmonary resuscitation and use of automated external defibrillators, §22.1-298.1.
Denial, suspension, revocation.
Board of education investigations.
Freedom of information act exclusion, §2.2-3705.3.
Closed meetings, §2.2-3711.
Education preparation programs, §22.1-298.2.

TEACHERS —Cont'd
Licensure —Cont'd
Online courses only, teachers of, §22.1-298.1.
Reciprocity, §22.1-298.1.
Regulations governing, §22.1-298.1.
Required, §22.1-299.
Standards of quality, §22.1-253.13:2.
Teach for America provisional license, §22.1-299.4.
Test security procedures.
Revocation of license for violation, §22.1-292.1.
Lie detector test, refusal to submit.
Teacher not to be dismissed or placed on probation, §22.1-307.
Loans.
Teaching scholarship loans.
State board authorized to award, §22.1-290.
Long-term care insurance.
Program for employees of local governments, local officers and teachers, §2.2-1207.
Assumption of responsibility.
Board of trustees, Virginia Retirement System, §51.1-513.3.
Trust fund, §51.1-513.4.
Program for persons within Virginia retirement system, §2.2-1208.
Mathematics intervention services.
Standards of quality, §22.1-253.13:2.
Medical examinations and records.
Employee payment of costs, §22.1-301.
Tuberculosis certificate, §22.1-300.
Mentor teacher programs, §22.1-305.1.
Middle school teacher corps.
Incentives to teachers, §22.1-199.1.
Military service.
Active duty service.
Compensation of public school employees called to active duty, §22.1-289.2.
National teacher certification incentive program and fund, §22.1-299.2.
Nonemergency health-related services.
Instructional personnel refusing to perform, §22.1-274.
Online courses only, teachers of.
Licenses, §22.1-298.1.
Opportunity educational institution.
Teachers of schools under supervision, §22.1-27.4.
Payment of salary, §22.1-296.
Peer review.
Immunity from civil liability, §22.1-303.1.
Performance indicators.
Confidentiality, §22.1-295.1.
Planning time for elementary school teachers, §22.1-291.1.
Polygraph examinations, refusal to submit.
Teacher not to be dismissed or placed on probation, §22.1-307.
Principals generally.
See PRINCIPALS, PUBLIC SCHOOLS.
Probationary terms of service, §22.1-303.
Entitlement to continuing contract after completion, §22.1-304.
Nonrenewal of contract, §22.1-305.
Probation, grounds for placing on, §22.1-307.
Professional development programs, §22.1-253.13:5.
Psychotropic drugs, schools prohibited from recommending for students, §22.1-274.3.
Ratio of students to teachers.
Standards of quality, §22.1-253.13:2.
Reading specialists.
Standards of quality, §22.1-253.13:2.

TEACHERS —Cont'd
Reassignment of principals or supervisors to teaching position, §22.1-294.
Reduction in workforce.
Factors to be considered, §22.1-304.
Reemployment.
Continuing contract status not achieved, §22.1-304.
Removal of student from class for disruptive behavior, §22.1-276.2.
Resignation of teacher, §22.1-304.
Retirement systems.
Health insurance credits, §51.1-1401.
Locality establishing, §15.2-1510.
Public school teacher supplemental retirement, §§51.1-617, 51.1-618.
RIF, §22.1-304.
Scholarship loans.
Teaching scholarship loans.
State board authorized to award, §22.1-290.
School personnel generally.
See SCHOOL PERSONNEL.
Self-defense or defense of others.
Not construed as simple assault or assault and battery, §18.2-57.
Shortages.
Designation of teacher shortage areas, §22.1-70.3.
Middle school teacher corps.
Incentives to teachers, §22.1-199.1.
Reporting, §22.1-79.
Simple assault.
Construction of certain actions taken by teachers, §18.2-57.
Standards of quality.
Compliance with standards, §22.1-253.13:8.
Strategic compensation grant initiative, §§22.1-318.1, 22.1-318.2.
Student teachers.
Defined, §22.1-290.1.
Supervisors.
Child abuse or molestation.
Conviction data required as condition of employment, §22.1-296.1.
Generally.
See PRINCIPALS, PUBLIC SCHOOLS.
Suspension.
Grounds and procedure for suspension, §22.1-315.
Teach for America provisional license, §22.1-299.4.
Temporarily employed teachers.
Qualifications, §22.1-302.
Terms of service, §22.1-303.
Test security procedures.
Revocation of license for violation, §22.1-292.1.
Training and professional development.
Autism spectrum disorder, §22.1-298.3.
Clinical faculty programs, §22.1-290.1.
Tuberculosis certificate, §22.1-300.
Violations of education title.
Penalty, §22.1-292.
Virginia retirement system.
Employees of institutes of higher education, §51.1-126.
Virginia school for the deaf and blind.
Terms of employment of teachers, §22.1-349.
Virginia teaching scholarship loan program, §22.1-290.01.
Collaboration between council of higher education and state board of education, §23-38.10:1.
Weapons, force used to obtain possession of.
Not construed as simple assault or assault and battery, §18.2-57.

TEAM PHYSICIANS.
Athletic events.
Immunity from liability, §8.01-225.1.

TEAR GAS.
Illegal use, §18.2-312.

TECHNICAL DIPLOMAS.
Schools and education.
Requirements, §22.1-253.13:4.

TECHNICAL EDUCATION FOR PRISONERS, §§53.1-32.1, 53.1-41.
Boot camp participants, §53.1-67.1.
Good time credits, §53.1-197.
Juvenile detention and other care facilities, §66-25.1:2.
Youthful offenders, §§53.1-63, 53.1-64.

TECHNICAL SPECIALISTS IN MINE SPECIALTIES.
Appointment by director of department of mines, minerals and energy, §45.1-161.23.

TECHNOLOGY.
Agriculture and consumer services department.
Emerging crops and technologies, program to support, §3.2-102.
Disability or handicap.
Assistive technology loan fund authority, §§51.5-53 to 51.5-59.
Educational technology foundation.
Establishment by local school board, §22.1-212.2:2.
Educational technology grants.
Public school educational technology grants program, §§22.1-175.6 to 22.1-175.9.
Local technology zones, §58.1-3850.
Public school educational technology grants program, §§22.1-175.6 to 22.1-175.9.
Radiological technology advisory board, §§54.1-2956.8, 54.1-2956.8:2.
Radiological technology practitioners.
Licensing generally, §§54.1-2950.1 to 54.1-2957.01.
See MEDICINE AND OTHER HEALING ARTS PROFESSIONS.
Six year educational technology plan for Virginia.
Cooperation with council of higher education, §23-9.8.
Small business technical and environmental compliance assistance program, §§10.1-1323 to 10.1-1326.
See AIR POLLUTION.
Wafer technology.
Semiconductor memory or logic wafer manufacturing performance grant programs, §§59.1-284.14, 59.1-284.15.
Weights and measures.
National Institute of Standard and Technology.
See WEIGHTS AND MEASURES.

TECHNOLOGY AND SCIENCE COMMISSION, §§30-85 to 30-88.

TECHNOLOGY INFRASTRUCTURE FUND, §§2.2-2022 to 2.2-2024.
Contributions, §2.2-2023.
Created, §2.2-2023.
Definitions, §2.2-2022.
Major projects, funding, §2.2-2023.
Plan identifying, §2.2-2024.

TECHNOLOGY INFRASTRUCTURE FUND —Cont'd
Purpose, §2.2-2022.
Uses, §2.2-2023.
Plan identifying, §2.2-2024.

TECHNOLOGY RESOURCE.
Designation by each state agency, §2.2-2014.

TECHNOLOGY, SECRETARY OF, §§2.2-200 to 2.2-202, 2.2-225.
Office of telework promotion and broadband assistance, §2.2-225.1.

TECHNOLOGY SERVICES COUNCIL.
Alternative work schedules.
Establishment of policy, §2.2-203.1.
Flex time.
Establishment of policy on telecommuting and alternative work schedules, §2.2-203.1.
Telecommuting.
Establishment of policy, §2.2-203.1.

TECHNOLOGY TRUST FUND.
Fees, §17.1-279.

TEENAGE SMOKING.
Virginia foundation for healthy youth, §§32.1-354 to 32.1-367.
See VIRGINIA FOUNDATION FOR HEALTHY YOUTH.

TEETH.
Workers' compensation.
Medical attention furnished upon loss of natural teeth, §65.2-603.

TELECOMMUNICATIONS.
Automatic dialing-announcing devices, §§59.1-518.1 to 59.1-518.4.
BVU authority, §§15.2-7200 to 15.2-7226.
See BVU AUTHORITY.
Cellular telephones.
See CELLULAR TELEPHONES.
Circuit courts.
Electronic video and audio communication systems.
Use to conduct hearings, §17.1-513.2.
Colleges and universities.
First warning and emergency notification systems, §23-9.2:11.
Communications sales and use tax, §§58.1-645 to 58.1-662.
See COMMUNICATIONS SALES AND USE TAX.
Consumer utility taxes.
Generally, §§58.1-3814 to 58.1-3816.2.
Corporations, notice communicated by telephone, telegraph, etc., §13.1-610.
Dark fiber.
Defined, §15.2-1500.
District courts.
Civil cases.
Use of electronic video and audio communication systems to conduct hearings, §16.1-93.1.
E-911 tax, §58.1-1730.
Election polling places.
Wireless communication between voting machines or with outside equipment while polls open, §24.2-625.2.
Fraudulent sale or receipt of telephone records, §18.2-152.17.
Freedom of information act exclusions, §§2.2-3705.2, 2.2-3705.6.

TELECOMMUNICATIONS —Cont'd
Income tax on telecommunication companies, §§58.1-401, 58.1-403, 58.1-434, 58.1-2608.
Juvenile proceedings.
Electronic video and audio communication systems.
Use to conduct hearings, §16.1-276.3.
Local emergency telecommunications requirements, §56-484.16.
Localities providing telecommunications services, §15.2-2160.
Multiline telephone systems (MLTS).
Emergency calls, §§56-484.19 to 56-484.25.
See EMERGENCY TELEPHONE CALLS.
Obtaining telegraph or telephone services without payment, §18.2-187.1.
Open meetings.
Freedom of information act.
Electronic communication meetings, §2.2-3708.
Exceptions to prohibition, §2.2-3708.1.
General assembly, electronic mode prohibited, §2.2-3707.01.
Minutes, §2.2-3707.
Procurement by public bodies.
Approval requirement, §§2.2-4303, 2.2-4304.
Public-private education facilities and infrastructure act, §§56-575.1 to 56-575.18.
See PUBLIC BUILDINGS.
Public service corporation taxation, §§58.1-2620 to 58.1-2635.
See PUBLIC SERVICE CORPORATION TAXATION.
Public utilities generally, §§56-232 to 56-265.
See PUBLIC UTILITIES.
Sales and use tax.
Communications sales and use tax, §§58.1-645 to 58.1-662.
See COMMUNICATIONS SALES AND USE TAX.
Search warrants.
Obtaining records concerning electronic communication service or remote computing service, §19.2-70.3.
State government.
Information technologies agency, §§2.2-2005 to 2.2-2031.
See INFORMATION TECHNOLOGIES AGENCY.
Telegraph or telephone companies, §§56-458 to 56-484.3.
See TELEGRAPH OR TELEPHONE COMPANIES.
Telegraph or telephone messages.
See TELEGRAPH OR TELEPHONE MESSAGES.
Telephone carrier identification, §§59.1-424 to 59.1-427.
Telephone company license tax, §§58.1-2620 to 58.1-2635.
See PUBLIC SERVICE CORPORATION TAXATION.
Telephone offenses generally, §§18.2-426 to 18.2-431.
Telephone records.
Fraudulent sale or receipt, §18.2-152.17.
Telephone solicitation sales, §§59.1-21.1 to 59.1-21.7:1.
Underground utility line damage prevention, §§56-265.14 to 56-265.32.
See UNDERGROUND UTILITY LINE DAMAGE PREVENTION.

TELECOMMUNICATIONS —Cont'd
Unlawful electronic communications devices, §§18.2-190.1 to 18.2-190.8.

TELECOMMUNICATIONS COMPANIES.
Income tax.
Corporate income tax.
Modifications to taxable income, §58.1-403.
Minimum tax on, §58.1-400.1.
State taxation, §58.1-2608.
Tax credit, §58.1-434.
Telegraph or telephone companies generally.
See TELEGRAPH OR TELEPHONE COMPANIES.

TELECOMMUTING.
Local government employees, §15.2-1512.3.
Secretary of administration.
Establishment of policy, §2.2-203.1.
State agencies.
Duties of heads of agencies, §2.2-2817.1.

TELECONFERENCES.
Audio-visual depositions, §§8.01-412.2 to 8.01-412.7.
Open meetings.
Freedom of information act.
Electronic communication meetings, §2.2-3708.
Exceptions to prohibition, §2.2-3708.1.
General assembly, electronic mode prohibited, §2.2-3707.01.
Minutes, §2.2-3707.

TELEGRAPH COMPANY LICENSE TAX, §§58.1-2620 to 58.1-2635.
See PUBLIC SERVICE CORPORATION TAXATION.

TELEGRAPH OR TELEPHONE COMPANIES, §§56-458 to 56-484.3.
Actually competitive determinations.
Anti-competitive acts, §56-479.2.
Continuation, §56-235.5.
Agreements between companies, §56-482.
Articles of incorporation.
Statement of kinds of business and brief description, §13.1-620.
Billing agents.
Defined, §56-479.3.
Products, goods, services.
Charging to customer's bill, §56-479.3.
Billing products, goods, services to customer's bill.
Customer's authorization and verification required, §56-479.3.
BVU authority.
Generally, §§15.2-7200 to 15.2-7226.
See BVU AUTHORITY.
Carrier identification, §§59.1-424 to 59.1-427.
Citation of chapter, §59.1-424.
Consumer protection, prohibited practices, §59.1-200.
Defined terms, §59.1-425.
Enforcement of provisions, §59.1-427.
Notice, §59.1-426.
Provision violations, §59.1-427.
Cellular telephones.
See CELLULAR TELEPHONES.
Certificate to operate as telephone utility, §56-265.4:4.
Commission powers, §56-484.3.
Communications sales and use tax, §§58.1-645 to 58.1-662.
See COMMUNICATIONS SALES AND USE TAX.

TELEGRAPH OR TELEPHONE COMPANIES —Cont'd

Competition.
Anti-competitive acts, §56-479.2.
Competitive determinations, §56-235.5.
Local exchange services, §56-235.5:1.
Consent to use city or town property required, §15.2-2017, VA Const Art VII §8.
Consumer utility tax.
Generally, §§58.1-3814 to 58.1-3816.2.
Cooperatives, telephones, §§56-485 to 56-508.
See TELEPHONE COOPERATIVES.
Corporations, notice communicated by telegraphs, §13.1-610.
Criminal offenses committed by telephone.
Duty of telephone company, §18.2-431.
Customers of telephone company.
Disclosing or inducing disclosure of information concerning, §18.2-166.
Damage or trespass to, §18.2-162.
Anti-competitive acts, §56-479.2.
Triple damages, §56-5.
Definitions, §§56-235.5, 56-484.1.
Pole attachments for cable television systems or telecommunications services providers, §56-466.1.
Designation as public service corporation, §56-1.1.
Disclosing or inducing disclosure of information concerning, §18.2-166.
Diverting service, §§8.01-44.7, 18.2-163.
E-911 tax, §58.1-1730.
Eminent domain.
Lines, relocation of, §56-458.1.
Construction of provisions, §56-459.
Right of, §56-464.
Enhanced 911 emergency telephone systems.
E-911 tax, §58.1-1730.
Enhanced public safety telephone services act, §§56-484.12 to 56-484.17:1.
Extension and reduction of telephone service, §§56-484.1 to 56-484.3.
Extension of service upon poll, §56-484.2.
Foreign companies.
Licensing, §56-484.
Franchise to occupy parks, streets, etc., §56-462.
Fraudulent sale or receipt of telephone records, §18.2-152.17.
Hostage or barricaded person situation.
Emergency control of telephone service, §18.2-50.2.
Immunity.
Hostage or barricaded person situation.
Good faith reliance on order of law enforcement officer to interrupt, reroute, etc., communications, §18.2-50.2.
Income tax on corporations.
Telephone companies exclusively local mutual associations.
Exemptions, §58.1-401.
Income tax on telecommunications companies.
Credit, §58.1-434.
Minimum tax, §58.1-400.1.
Modifications to taxable income, §58.1-403.
Injunctions.
Anti-competitive acts, §56-479.2.
Inspections by commission, §56-479.
Intercepting or monitoring customer calls, §18.2-167.1.
Uniform fine schedule, VA SCt Rules 3C:1, 3C:2.

TELEGRAPH OR TELEPHONE COMPANIES —Cont'd

Interexchange telephone companies.
Rates, §56-482.1.
Reports, §§56-482.1, 56-482.2.
Joint ventures with other telephone companies.
Power to enter into, §13.1-627.
License tax.
Generally, §§58.1-2620 to 58.1-2635.
See PUBLIC SERVICE CORPORATION TAXATION.
Local license taxes, §§58.1-2690, 58.1-3731.
Lines.
Crossing railroads, §56-16.1.
Duties where wires cross other works, §56-33.
Endangering life or limb by stringing wires across other works, §56-468.
Erection, §56-458.
Consent of appropriate authorities, §56-460.
Cost to state, §56-461.
Franchises to occupy public ground, §56-462.
Restoring condition of ground, §56-467.
Rights-of-way, §56-463.
Height of, §56-466.
Location, §56-466.
Overhead high voltage line safety, §§59.1-406 to 59.1-414.
Application of provisions, §59.1-413.
Permits to place, §56-15.
Pole use rates, §56-41.1.
Private highways.
Crossings, §56-547.
Relocation, §56-458.1.
Construction of provisions, §56-459.
Restoring condition of ground, §56-467.
Rights-of-way, §56-463.
Submerged lands.
Structures, maintenance or removal, §28.2-1209.
Underground utility line damage prevention, §§56-265.14 to 56-265.32.
See UNDERGROUND UTILITY LINE DAMAGE PREVENTION.
Local exchange services.
Carrier common line charge, §56-235.5:1.
Competition, §56-235.5:1.
Local mutual associations.
Retail sales and use tax exemption, §58.1-609.3.
Long distance service or change of carriers, §56-479.1.
Metering devices, tampering with, §§8.01-44.7, 18.2-163.
Modification of provisions, §56-465.
Multiline telephone systems (MLTS).
Emergency calls, §§56-484.19 to 56-484.25.
See EMERGENCY TELEPHONE CALLS.
900 numbers, §§59.1-429 to 59.1-434.
Obstructing commission in discharge of duties, §56-483.
Obtaining services without payment, §18.2-187.1.
Offering of communications services, §56-484.7:1.
Approval, §56-484.7:2.
Revocation, §56-484.7:4.
Operator assistance at pay stations, §56-480.2.
Partnership agreements with other telephone companies.
Power to enter into, §13.1-627.
Pay-per-call services, §§59.1-429 to 59.1-434.

TELEGRAPH OR TELEPHONE COMPANIES —Cont'd
Pay stations.
Operator assistance at, §56-480.2.
Pay telephone registration, §§56-508.15, 56-508.16.
Pay telephones.
Slugs, manufacturing, selling, etc., for unlawful uses, §18.2-180.
Stealing from or tampering with, §18.2-152.
Unlawful operation, §18.2-179.
Penalties for provision violations, §56-483.
Pipelines, §§56-257 to 56-260.1.
Pole attachments.
Cable television systems and telecommunication services providers, §56-466.1.
Products, goods, services.
Charging to customer's bill.
Customer's authorization and verification required, §56-479.3.
Provisions subject to change, §56-465.
Public ground use without consent or compensation, §56-14.
Public service companies.
Generally, §§56-1 to 56-46.3.
See PUBLIC SERVICE COMPANIES.
Public utilities generally, §§56-232 to 56-265.
See PUBLIC UTILITIES.
Railroad corporations, §56-383.
Railroad tracks.
Construction, maintenance or operation of lines along and parallel to, §56-458.
Rates.
Alternative forms of regulation, §56-235.5.
Commission powers, §56-241.
Impermissible basis, §56-241.1.
Interexchange telephone service, §56-481.1.
Local exchange services provided by new entrants, §56-481.2.
Multiple rate increases within any twelve-month period, §56-235.4.
Operator assistance at pay stations, §56-480.2.
Questions as to reasonableness, justice or validity, §56-480.
Resales of telephone services, §56-241.2.
Time limit on institution of, §56-480.1.
Reduction of service upon poll, §56-484.2.
Reporting failures, §§56-482, 56-483.
Restoring condition of ground, §56-467.
Retail sales and use tax.
Commercial and industrial exemptions.
Telephone company chartered as local mutual association, §58.1-609.3.
Rights of way.
Public rights-of-way use fee, §56-468.1.
Reimbursement for relocation costs, §56-468.2.
Roads, streets, etc.
Right of occupation, §56-458.
Rules.
Questions as to reasonableness, justice or validity, §56-480.
Sales and use tax.
Communications sales and use tax, §§58.1-645 to 58.1-662.
See COMMUNICATIONS SALES AND USE TAX.
Secondhand article sales.
Company equipment, §§59.1-125 to 59.1-130.
Small investor-owned telephone utilities, §§56-531 to 56-534.

TELEGRAPH OR TELEPHONE COMPANIES —Cont'd
Special regulatory revenue tax, §§58.1-2660 to 58.1-2665.
Subpoenas.
Duty to furnish information in response to, §18.2-431.
Taxes.
Local license tax, §58.1-2690.
Special regulatory revenue tax, §§58.1-2660 to 58.1-2665.
Telecommunications relay service.
Responsibilities of department, §51.5-115.
Telephone directories.
Notice of criminal offenses, §18.2-431.
Telephone records.
Fraudulent sale or receipt of telephone records, §18.2-152.17.
Text telephones.
Responsibilities of department, §51.5-115.
Trespass, §18.2-162.
Unlawful use of or injury to, §18.2-164.
Use of city or town property, consent required, VA Const Art VII §8.
Wireless service authorities, §§15.2-5431.1 to 15.2-5431.37.
See WIRELESS SERVICE AUTHORITIES.

TELEGRAPH OR TELEPHONE MESSAGES.
Copying or obstructing, §18.2-164.

TELEGRAPHS.
Public service companies.
Generally, §§56-1 to 56-87.
See PUBLIC SERVICE COMPANIES.
Public utilities.
Generally, §§56-232 to 56-265.
See PUBLIC UTILITIES.
Telegraph companies.
Generally, §§56-458 to 56-484.3.
See TELEGRAPH OR TELEPHONE COMPANIES.
Telegraph company license tax, §§58.1-2620 to 58.1-2635.
See PUBLIC SERVICE CORPORATION TAXATION.

TELEMARKETERS.
Automatic dialing-announcing devices, §§59.1-518.1 to 59.1-518.4.
Telephone solicitation sales, §§59.1-21.1 to 59.1-21.7:1.

TELEMEDICINE.
Health insurance coverage, §38.2-3418.16.
Office of telework promotion and broadband assistance.
Duties, §2.2-225.1.

TELEPHONE CARRIER IDENTIFICATION, §§59.1-424 to 59.1-427.

TELEPHONE COMMUNICATION DEVICES FOR THE DEAF.
Assistive technology device warranties, §§59.1-470 to 59.1-474.

TELEPHONE COMPANY LICENSE TAX, §§58.1-2620 to 58.1-2635.
See PUBLIC SERVICE CORPORATION TAXATION.

TELEPHONE COOPERATIVES, §§56-485 to 56-508.
Board of directors, §§56-491, 56-492.
Powers, §56-492.

TELEPHONE COOPERATIVES —Cont'd
Bylaws, §56-492.
Disposition of revenues and receipts, §56-493.
Carrier identification, §§59.1-424 to 59.1-427.
Citation of chapter, §59.1-424.
Defined terms, §59.1-425.
Enforcement of provisions, §59.1-427.
Notice, §59.1-426.
Provision violations, §59.1-427.
Certificates of adoption, §56-507.
Certificates of incorporation, §56-488.
Amendments, §§56-504, 56-505.
Fees, §56-505.
Filing, §56-490.
Certificates of membership, §56-493.
Certificate to operate as a telephone utility, §56-265.4:4.
Citation of chapter, §56-485.
Commission regulation, §56-502.
Conflict of laws, §56-506.
Consolidation, §56-500.
Fees, §56-505.
Construction of chapter, §56-506.
Covenants, §56-498.
Defined terms, §56-487.
Designation as public service corporation, §56-1.1.
Dissolution, §56-503.
Fees, §56-505.
Eminent domain, §56-495.
Fees, §56-505.
Formation, §56-486.
Lines.
Duties where wires cross other works, §56-33.
Overhead high voltage line safety, §§59.1-406 to 59.1-414.
Application of provisions, §59.1-413.
Permits to place, §56-15.
Pole use rates, §56-41.1.
Private highways.
Crossings, §56-547.
Railroad crossings, §56-16.1.
Submerged lands.
Structures, maintenance or removal, §28.2-1209.
Underground utility line damage prevention, §§56-265.14 to 56-265.32.
See UNDERGROUND UTILITY LINE DAMAGE PREVENTION.
Members, §§56-493, 56-494.
Service to, §56-494.
Mergers, §§56-500, 56-505.
Fees, §56-505.
900 numbers, §§59.1-429 to 59.1-434.
Nonprofit corporation provisions.
Application, §56-490.
Obligations.
Issuance of, §56-497.
Purchase of own obligations, §56-499.
Officers, §56-491.
Pay-per-call services, §§59.1-429 to 59.1-434.
Pay telephone registration, §§56-508.15, 56-508.16.
Pipelines, §§56-257 to 56-260.1.
Powers, §56-495.
Property.
Disposition of, §56-496.
Provisions adoption, §56-507.
Public ground use without consent or compensation, §56-14.

TELEPHONE COOPERATIVES —Cont'd
Public service companies generally, §§56-1 to 56-87.
See PUBLIC SERVICE COMPANIES.
Public utilities generally, §§56-232 to 56-265.
See PUBLIC UTILITIES.
Purpose, §56-486.
Rates.
Alternative forms of regulation, §56-235.5.
Commission powers, §56-241.
Impermissible basis, §56-241.1.
Multiple rate increases within any twelve-month period, §56-235.4.
Resales of telephone services, §56-241.2.
Rural service extensions, §56-508.
Secondhand article sales.
Company equipment, §§59.1-125 to 59.1-130.
Service of notice, process and other papers.
Registered office or agent, §56-490.
Service to members and nonmembers, §56-494.
Extension of service to territory not being served, §56-508.
Small investor-owned telephone utilities, §§56-531 to 56-534.
Stock corporation provisions.
Application, §56-490.
Term limitations, §56-489.
Title of chapter, §56-485.
Voting by members, §56-493.
Word limitations, §56-489.

TELEPHONE COOPERATIVES ACT, §§56-485 to 56-508.
See TELEPHONE COOPERATIVES.

TELEPHONE CREDIT CARDS.
Excepted from chapter on credit card sales, §6.2-431.

TELEPHONE DIRECTORIES.
Notice of criminal offenses, §18.2-431.

TELEPHONE NUMBER OF PUBLIC OFFICIAL.
Internet publication of personal information of public officials, §18.2-186.4:1.

TELEPHONE NUMBER OF VICTIM OF CRIME.
Nondisclosure, §19.2-11.2.

TELEPHONE OFFENSES, §§18.2-426 to 18.2-431.
Annoying calls.
Causing telephone to ring with intent to annoy, §18.2-429.
Cellular telephones.
Prisoners.
Illegal conveyance to or possession by, §18.2-431.1.
Duties of telephone companies, §18.2-431.
Emergencies, relinquishing line.
Emergency call defined, §18.2-426.
False information to another by telephone, §18.2-428.
Fraudulent sale or receipt of telephone records, §18.2-152.17.
Intercepting or monitoring customer calls.
Uniform fine schedule, §18.2-167.1, VA SCt Rules 3C:1, 3C:2.
Pay telephones.
Slugs manufactured, sold, etc., for unlawful uses, §18.2-180.
Stealing from or tampering with, §18.2-152.
Unlawful operation, §18.2-179.

TELEPHONE OFFENSES —Cont'd
Profane, threatening or indecent language, §18.2-427.
Subpoenas issued by circuit court.
Duties of telephone company, §18.2-431.
Telephone directory to contain notice explaining offenses, §18.2-431.
Telephonic instruments, obtaining long distance service without payment.
Selling or transferring, §18.2-167.
Venue for offenses under article, §18.2-430.

TELEPHONE ORDERS.
Cigarette delivery sales, §§18.2-246.6 to 18.2-246.15.
See CIGARETTES.

TELEPHONE PRIVACY PROTECTION, §§59.1-510 to 59.1-518.
Abandoned solicitation calls, §59.1-513.1.
Automatic dialing-announcing devices, §§59.1-518.1 to 59.1-518.4.
Blocking of caller identification services.
Prohibited, §59.1-513.
Caller identification services.
Blocking prohibited, §59.1-513.
Transmitting name and number of person on whose behalf call is being made, §59.1-513.
Calling time restrictions, §59.1-511.
Civil penalties, §59.1-517.
Damages.
Action in name of Commonwealth, §59.1-517.
Individual action for damages, §59.1-515.
Definitions, §59.1-510.
Do not call registry.
Unwanted calls to numbers listed, prohibited, §59.1-514.
Enforcement of provisions, §59.1-517.
Identification of telephone solicitor.
Required, §59.1-512.
Injunctions.
Action in name of Commonwealth, §59.1-517.
Investigations.
Commissioner of agriculture and consumer services department, §59.1-516.
Live person not able to speak to person answering.
Prerecorded identification message, §59.1-513.1.
Name and number of person on whose behalf call is being made.
Transmitting on caller identification instead of solicitor information, §59.1-513.
Name of telephone solicitor.
Identification required, §59.1-512.
National do not call registry.
Unwanted calls to numbers listed, prohibited, §59.1-514.
Other provisions not limited, §59.1-518.
Request not to receive telephone solicitation calls, §59.1-514.
Time of calling.
Restrictions, §59.1-511.
Unwanted telephone solicitation calls.
Prohibited, §59.1-514.

TELEPHONE RECORDS.
Fraudulent sale or receipt, §18.2-152.17.

TELEPHONES.
Automatic dialing-announcing devices, §§59.1-518.1 to 59.1-518.4.
Cellular telephones.
Prisoners.
Illegal conveyance to or possession by, §18.2-431.1.

TELEPHONES —Cont'd
Cellular telephones —Cont'd
School buses.
Use of wireless telecommunications devices by persons driving, §46.2-919.1.
Circuit courts.
Telephonic communication systems.
Use to conduct hearings, §17.1-513.2.
Credit cards.
Telephone credit cards exempted from credit card sales chapter, §6.2-431.
Criminal offenses, §§18.2-426 to 18.2-431.
See TELEPHONE OFFENSES.
District courts.
Civil cases.
Use of telephonic communication systems to conduct hearings, §16.1-93.1.
Hostage or barricaded person situation.
Emergency control of telephone service, §18.2-50.2.
Juvenile detention and other care facilities.
Cellular telephones.
Illegal conveyance to or possession by, §18.2-431.1.
Juvenile proceedings.
Telephonic communication systems.
Use to conduct hearings, §16.1-276.3.
Mine safety.
Underground coal mines.
Telephone service or equivalent two-way communication, §45.1-161.191.
Multiline telephone systems (MLTS).
Emergency calls, §§56-484.19 to 56-484.25.
See EMERGENCY TELEPHONE CALLS.
Pay telephones.
Criminal conduct, §§18.2-152, 18.2-179, 18.2-180.
Prisoners.
Cellular telephones.
Illegal conveyance to or possession by, §18.2-431.1.
Public school funds, §22.1-89.3.
Public service companies.
Generally, §§56-1 to 56-87.
See PUBLIC SERVICE COMPANIES.
Public utilities.
Generally, §§56-232 to 56-265.
See PUBLIC UTILITIES.
Solicitation sales, §§59.1-21.1 to 59.1-21.7:1.
See TELEPHONE SOLICITATION SALES.
Telephone companies.
Generally, §§56-458 to 56-484.3.
See TELEGRAPH OR TELEPHONE COMPANIES.
Telephone company license tax, §§58.1-2620 to 58.1-2635.
See PUBLIC SERVICE CORPORATION TAXATION.
Underground utility line damage prevention, §§56-265.14 to 56-265.32.
See UNDERGROUND UTILITY LINE DAMAGE PREVENTION.
Virginia telephone privacy protection act, §§59.1-510 to 59.1-518.

TELEPHONE SOLICITATION SALES, §§59.1-21.1 to 59.1-21.7:1.
Actions.
Personal suits, §§59.1-68.3, 59.1-68.5.
Suits by attorneys for the Commonwealth and city and county attorneys, §59.1-68.4.
Authority of attorney general, §59.1-68.2.

TELEPHONE SOLICITATION SALES —Cont'd
Automatic dialing-announcing devices, §§59.1-518.1 to 59.1-518.4.
Definitions, §59.1-518.1.
Disconnect requirement, §59.1-518.3.
Violations of act, §59.1-518.4.
When devices prohibited, §§59.1-518.2, 59.1-518.3.
Cancellation of sale, §59.1-21.3.
Seller misrepresentation of nature or purpose of transaction, §59.1-21.7.
Citation of chapter, §59.1-21.1.
Consumer protection, prohibited practices, §59.1-200.
Definitions, §59.1-21.2.
Automatic dialing-announcing devices, §59.1-518.1.
Enforcement of provisions, §59.1-21.7:1.
Goods, tender of, §59.1-21.6.
Lease-purchase agreements.
Application of provisions, §59.1-207.19.
Membership camping.
Application of provisions, §59.1-322.
Payments, tender of, §59.1-21.5.
Penalties for provision violations, §59.1-21.7:1.
Promotional prizes and gifts.
Representation of being specially selected, §59.1-418.
Representation of eligibility to win, §59.1-417.
Representations of having won, §59.1-416.
Receipts, §59.1-21.4.
Suits by attorneys for the Commonwealth and city and county, §59.1-68.4.
Telephone privacy protection, §§59.1-510 to 59.1-518.
Virginia telephone privacy protection act, §§59.1-510 to 59.1-518.
Written agreements, §59.1-21.5.

TELEPHONIC CONVERSATIONS.
Limitation on use as evidence, §8.01-420.2.

TELETYPES.
Corporations, notice communicated by, §13.1-610.

TELEVISION.
Advertising.
Consumer protection.
Application of provisions, §59.1-199.
Board of education.
Public broadcasting stations, powers and duties related to, §22.1-20.1.
Cable television.
See CABLE TELEVISION AND SERVICE.
Campaign disclosures.
Advertisements.
See CAMPAIGN FINANCE DISCLOSURE.
Cathode ray tube recycling, §10.1-1425.26.
Child's testimony by closed circuit television.
Child abuse or neglect, §63.2-1521.
Criminal proceeding, §18.2-67.9.
Counties equipping and maintaining television transmission and relay facilities, §15.2-1224.
Criminal trials.
Child victims.
Testimony using two-way closed-circuit television, §18.2-67.9.
Judicial discretion to permit broadcasting, §19.2-266.
Defamation.
Defamatory statements in broadcasts, §8.01-49.

TELEVISION —Cont'd
Educational television stations.
Locality establishing and operating, §15.2-966.
Election polling places.
News media visiting, photographing or filming inside, interviews, §24.2-604.
False publications.
Stated, delivered or transmitted to television station, §18.2-209.
Income tax.
Motion picture production tax credit, §58.1-439.12:03.
Intangible personal property tax, §§58.1-1100 to 58.1-1118.
See PERSONAL PROPERTY TAXES.
Machinery and tools tax, §§58.1-3507, 58.1-3508.
Manufactured home lot rental.
Fee prohibitions, §55-248.45.
Motor vehicles equipped with television, §46.2-1077.
Display of obscene materials which can be seen from outside of the vehicle, §46.2-1077.01.
Viewing motion pictures or similar displays while driving, §46.2-1077.
Personal property taxes.
Classification of television instruments and equipment, §58.1-3504.
Public television stations.
Board of education, powers and duties related to, §22.1-20.1.
Surplus state materials.
Sale to public television stations, §2.2-1124.
Recorded device piracy.
Application of provisions, §59.1-41.2.
Remote broadcasts by television station.
Amber warning lights on vehicles used for broadcast, §46.2-1025.
Residential landlord obligations, §55-248.13:2.
Retail sales and use tax.
Media-related exemptions, §58.1-609.6.
Telegraph or telephone companies.
Pole attachments.
Cable television systems, §56-466.1.
Trial publicity.
Attorneys at law.
Professional responsibility, VA SCt Rule Pt 6 §II Rule 3.5.

TELEVISION-EQUIPPED VEHICLES, §46.2-1077.
Display of obscene materials which can be seen from outside of the vehicle, §46.2-1077.01.
Viewing motion pictures or similar displays while driving, §46.2-1077.

TELEVISION REPORTERS.
Police lines or barricades.
Exemption from provisions, §15.2-1714.

TELEWORK EXPENSES TAX CREDIT, §58.1-439.12:07.

TELEWORK PROMOTION AND BROADBAND ASSISTANCE.
Office of, §2.2-225.1.

TELLER'S CHECKS.
Defined as negotiable instrument, §8.3A-104.
Effect of obligation for which taken, §8.3A-310.
Lost, destroyed or stolen, §8.3A-312.
Negotiable instruments generally, §§8.3A-101 to 8.3A-605.
See NEGOTIABLE INSTRUMENTS.

TELLER'S CHECKS —Cont'd
Refusal to pay, §8.3A-411.

TEMPORARILY CLOSING RIGHTS-OF-WAY, §§15.2-2013, 15.2-2014.

TEMPORARY ASSISTANCE FOR NEEDY FAMILIES (TANF), §§63.2-600 to 63.2-621.
Administered by state department, §63.2-600.
Appeal of boards decisions, §63.2-618.
Application, §63.2-602.
Assignment to Commonwealth any rights of support, §63.2-602.
Benefits not being used for children.
Appointment of personal representatives for recipients, §63.2-507.
Cash assistance, §63.2-617.
Change in residence of recipient, §63.2-521.
Child care services, §63.2-620.
Children born to TANF recipients.
Financial benefits paid to family, §63.2-604.
Child support enforcement by department of social services.
Generally, §§63.2-1900 to 63.2-1960.
See CHILD SUPPORT ENFORCEMENT BY DEPARTMENT OF SOCIAL SERVICES.
Compulsory school attendance laws, compliance, §63.2-606.
Cooperation in locating parent, §63.2-602.
Creation of program, §63.2-600.
Diversionary cash assistance, §63.2-617.
Drug tests.
Parolees or probationers failing, §63.2-605.
Eligibility, §63.2-602.
Childhood immunizations, §63.2-603.
Children born to TANF recipients, §63.2-604.
Compulsory school attendance laws, compliance, §63.2-606.
Financial eligibility, §63.2-614.
Parolees or probationers failing drug tests, §63.2-605.
Residence of unemancipated minor custodial parent, §63.2-607.
Virginia initiative for employment not welfare (VIEW), §§63.2-608 to 63.2-610.
Evaluation to measure achievements, §63.2-619.
Financial eligibility, §63.2-614.
Freedom of information act.
Exclusions from chapter, §2.2-3705.5.
Full employment program (FEP).
Replacement of TANF and food stamp benefits, §63.2-608.
Fund, §63.2-601.1.
Goals, §63.2-601.
Identification of parents, §63.2-602.
Immunization of eligible child, required, §63.2-603.
Income disregards, §63.2-614.
Income tax.
Corporations.
Credit for certain employers hiring recipients, §58.1-439.9.
Limitations on TANF assistance.
Providing assistance and social services for recipients subject to limitations, §63.2-616.
Misidentification of another as parent.
Criminal penalty, §63.2-602.
Motor vehicle resale to recipients.
Surplus state motor vehicles sold to social services departments, §2.2-1124.
Parentage determination, §63.2-602.

TEMPORARY ASSISTANCE FOR NEEDY FAMILIES (TANF) —Cont'd
Parolees or probationers failing drug tests, §63.2-605.
Personal representatives for recipients.
Benefits not being used for children, §63.2-507.
Prohibited uses of benefits, §63.2-621.
Report by commissioner.
Annual report, §63.2-619.
Residence of unemancipated minor custodial parent, §63.2-607.
Savings accounts for educational expenses.
Established by individuals receiving assistance under certain programs, §63.2-505.
School attendance.
Compulsory school attendance laws, compliance, §63.2-606.
Skill development training.
Tuition and other expenses of recipients, §63.2-615.
Statewide TANF program funding pool program, §63.2-601.2.
Time limit for receipt of financial assistance.
VIEW participants, §63.2-613.
Transitional food stamps benefits following termination of TANF assistance, §63.2-505.1.
Tuition and other expenses.
Recipient enrolled in skill development training, §63.2-615.
Two-parent families and single-parent families treated same, §63.2-602.
Unemancipated minor custodial parent, residence, §63.2-607.
Virginia initiative for employment not welfare (VIEW), §63.2-608.
Case management, §63.2-611.
Child care, transportation, counseling and medical assistance.
Services provided to families, §63.2-611.
Coordinated services, §63.2-610.
Exemptions, §63.2-609.
Hardship exceptions to time limit for receipt of assistance, §63.2-613.
Income disregards, §63.2-614.
Motor vehicle sales to participants, §63.2-611.
Services to families, §63.2-611.
Statewide intensive case management ratio, §63.2-611.
Termination of financial assistance.
Services provided, §63.2-611.
Time limit on receipt of financial assistance, §63.2-612.
Hardship exceptions, §63.2-613.
Workers' compensation.
Ineligibility for certain benefits, §§65.2-500, 65.2-502, 65.2-512.
Voter registration agencies designated by state, §24.2-411.2.
Persons authorized to receive applications, §24.2-415.1.

TEMPORARY CERTIFICATES OF OWNERSHIP.
Trailer dealer unable to deliver certificate of title or certificate of origin at time of sale, §46.2-1992.35.

TEMPORARY DRIVER'S PERMIT, §46.2-344.
Certification of Virginia residency, §46.2-323.1.
Issuance to license holder from out of state, §46.2-335.2.

TEMPORARY FAMILY HEALTH CARE STRUCTURES.
Defined, §15.2-2292.1.
Zoning ordinances, §15.2-2292.1.

TEMPORARY INJUNCTIONS.
Affidavit requirement, §8.01-628.
Duration to be fixed therein, §8.01-624.
Injunctions generally, §§8.01-620 to 8.01-634.
See INJUNCTIONS.

TEMPORARY INSURANCE CONTRACTS, §38.2-304.

TEMPORARY LICENSE PLATES.
Motorcycle dealers issuing, §§46.2-1993.55 to 46.2-1993.63.
See MOTORCYCLE DEALERS.
Trailer dealers issuing, §§46.2-1992.56 to 46.2-1992.65.
See TRAILER DEALERS.

TEMPORARY RESTRAINING ORDERS.
Cease and desist orders.
See CEASE AND DESIST ORDERS.
Injunctions generally, §§8.01-620 to 8.01-634.
See INJUNCTIONS.
Protective orders.
See PROTECTIVE ORDERS.

TENANCIES AT WILL.
Waste, §55-215.

TENANCIES FOR LIFE.
See LIFE ESTATES.

TENANCIES FROM MONTH TO MONTH.
Abandoned unit rentals, §55-248.33.
Condominium conversion.
Notice requirements, §55-79.94.
Failure of tenant to vacate at expiration, §55-223.
Manufactured home lot rental.
Secured parties taking possession of abandoned homes.
Conversion and termination of rental agreement, §55-248.44:1.
Notice to terminate, §55-222.
Presumption as to tenancy period, §55-248.7.
Termination notice, §55-248.37.
Time-share conversion projects.
Termination of tenancies, §55-374.

TENANCIES FROM WEEK TO WEEK.
Abandoned unit rentals, §55-248.33.
Termination notice, §55-248.37.

TENANCIES FROM YEAR TO YEAR.
Failure of tenant to vacate at expiration of term, §55-223.
Notice to terminate, §55-222.
Waste, §55-215.
Works on watercourses.
Forfeiture by tenant of works damaged or destroyed, §62.1-126.

TENANCIES IN COMMON.
Accounting in equity, §8.01-31.
Condominiums.
Termination of condominium.
Vesting of title, §55-79.72:1.
Ejectment.
General provisions, §§8.01-131 to 8.01-165.
See EJECTMENT.
Joinder as parties, §8.01-10.

TENANCIES IN COMMON —Cont'd
Partition of land.
General provisions, §§8.01-81 to 8.01-93.
See PARTITION OF LAND.
Partnerships.
Determining whether partnership established, §50-73.88.
Real property tax lien on real estate jointly owned, §58.1-3343.
Shares of corporations, voting entitlement, §13.1-662.
TOD security registration.
Multiple owners of security registered in beneficiary form, §64.2-613.
Waste, §55-212.

TENANCY BY THE ENTIRETIES.
Corporate securities registered in joint tenants with right of survivorship, §§13.1-434 to 13.1-436.
Divorce from bond of matrimony.
Extinguishment of tenancy, §20-111.
Husband and wife.
Joint ownership of property, §55-20.1.
Real or personal property, §55-20.2.
Murderers barred from claiming property rights of decedent, §64.2-2503.
Partnerships.
Determining whether partnership established, §50-73.88.
Principal family residence, §55-20.1.
Trusts, §§55-20.1, 55-20.2.
Property rights of married women, §55-37.
Responsibility for spouse's obligations, §55-37.
Shares of corporations, voting entitlement, §13.1-662.
TOD security registration.
Multiple owners of security registered in beneficiary form, §64.2-613.

TENANT RELOCATION PAYMENTS.
County manager plan of government.
Rehabilitation of buildings, §15.2-737.

TENANTS.
Landlord and tenant generally, §§55-217 to 55-248.
See LANDLORD AND TENANT.

TEN-DAY RIGHT TO EXAMINE POLICY.
Individual life insurance, §38.2-3301.
Industrial life insurance, §38.2-3342.

TENDER.
Legal tender, US Const Art I §10.

TENNESSEE.
Boundary with, §1-306.

TENNESSEE-BIG SANDY RIVER BASIN.
Preparation of plans and programs for management, §62.1-44.38.

TENNESSEE VALLEY AUTHORITY.
Apportionment of payments received from authority in lieu of taxes, §58.1-3406.

TENNIS COURTS.
Urban county executive form of government.
Appropriation to nonprofit entity owning, §15.2-820.

TENT SHOWS OR PERFORMANCES.
License tax on traveling shows or performances, §58.1-3728.

TERM DAY, VA SCt Rule 1:15 Sched.

TERMINAL ILLNESS.
Anatomical gifts.
Advance health care directive, effect of gift, §32.1-291.21.
Health insurance.
Coverage for hospice care, §38.2-3418.11.
Living wills, §§54.1-2981 to 54.1-2993.
See LIVING WILLS.

TERMINATION OF CORPORATE EXISTENCE.
Corporations, §§13.1-750 to 13.1-755.
Nonprofit corporations, §§13.1-912 to 13.1-917.
Articles of termination, §13.1-816.

TERMINATION OF INSURANCE COVERAGE.
Adverse underwriting decisions generally, §§38.2-610 to 38.2-612.
Individual health insurance coverage, §38.2-3430.7.

TERMINATION OF PARENTAL RIGHTS.
Adoption.
Birth father not married to mother of child.
Consent to prior to birth, §63.2-1202.
Entrustment agreements.
Agency or local board placement, §§63.2-1221 to 63.2-1223.
Generally.
See ADOPTION.
Notice of consent.
Not required by person whose rights terminated, §63.2-1202.
Restoration of parental rights where pre-adoptive parents not identified, §16.1-283.2.
Appointment of counsel for child, §§16.1-266 to 16.1-268.
Disposition of abused, neglected or abandoned children or children without parental care, §16.1-278.2.
Emancipation of minor.
Effect of order of emancipation as to parent's guardianship, §16.1-334.
Generally, §§16.1-331 to 16.1-334.1.
Evidence.
Putative father registry certificate of search, §63.2-1252.
Juvenile and domestic relations district court jurisdiction, §16.1-241.
Parental care and custody of child.
Trespass after having been forbidden to do so, §§18.2-119, 18.2-120.
Putative father registry, §§63.2-1249 to 63.2-1253.
See PUTATIVE FATHER REGISTRY.
Residual rights, §16.1-283.
Termination of right of parent to inherit from or through child, §64.2-102.

TERMINATION OF PREGNANCY.
Abortion generally, §§18.2-71 to 18.2-76.1.
See ABORTION.

TERM LIMITS.
Governor, VA Const Art V §1.
Public school authority.
Chairman, §22.1-164.

TERM PAPERS.
Preparation, selling, etc., for profit, §18.2-505.
Injunction, §18.2-507.
Person and prepared defined, §18.2-506.
Punishment, §18.2-508.

TERMS OF ELECTED OFFICERS.
Attorney general, §24.2-210, VA Const Art V §15.

TERMS OF ELECTED OFFICERS —Cont'd
Circuit court clerks, §24.2-217.
City councils, §24.2-222.
Commissioners of revenue, §24.2-217.
Commonwealth's attorneys, §24.2-217.
County supervisors, §24.2-218.
Governor, §24.2-210, VA Const Art V §1.
House of delegates, general assembly, §24.2-215.
House of representatives, United States, §24.2-208.
Lieutenant governor, §24.2-210, VA Const Art V §13.
Mayors, §24.2-222.
School boards, §24.2-223.
Senators, general assembly, §24.2-214.
Senators, United States, §24.2-206.
Sheriffs, §24.2-217.
Treasurers, §24.2-217.
Vacancies in office, §24.2-200.
When term begins and expires, §24.2-201.

TERRITORIES.
Constitution of the United States, US Const Art IV §3.
Territory of Virginia.
See STATE.

TERRORISM.
Accessory before the fact or principal in second degree, how punished, §18.2-18.
Aiding and abetting, §18.2-46.5.
Bioterrorism.
Agricultural crops or animals.
Penalties, §18.2-46.7.
Capital murder, killing in commission of, §18.2-31.
Charitable or civic solicitation.
Prohibition against support of terrorism, §§57-49, 57-57.
Seizure of property connected with terrorism, §57-59.
Committing act of terrorism.
Penalties, §18.2-46.5.
Conspiracy, §18.2-46.5.
Definitions, §18.2-46.4.
Drugs or devices.
Administering or dispensing during disaster or emergency caused by.
Commissioner of health may authorize persons not authorized to administer or dispense, §32.1-42.1.
Emergency management and disaster law generally, §§44-146.13 to 44-146.28.
See EMERGENCY MANAGEMENT.
Emergency preparedness programs, §44-146.18.
Fire insurance.
Coverage of losses due to terrorism, §38.2-2102.
Freedom of information act.
Exclusions from chapter.
Engineering and construction drawings and plans, §2.2-3705.2.
Furnishing information concerning.
Immunity, §52-49.
Fusion intelligence center, §52-47.
Confidentiality and immunity from service of process, §52-48.
Highway and rod construction.
Emergency preparedness.
Waiver of statutory regulations to expedite construction, §33.1-223.2:5.

TERRORISM —Cont'd
Hoax, reimbursement of expenses in responding to, §15.2-1716.1.
Immunity.
Architects and engineers.
Rescue or relief assistance, §8.01-226.2.
Furnishing information concerning, §52-49.
Infectious biological substances or radiological agents.
Possessing, destroying or damaging facility manufacturing or storing or causing bodily injury, §18.2-52.1.
Interception of wire, electronic or oral communication.
Order authorizing.
When attorney general may apply, §19.2-66.
Man-made disasters.
Architects.
Rescue or relief assistance.
Civil immunity for licensed professional architects, §8.01-226.2.
Emergency management and disaster law generally, §§44-146.13 to 44-146.28.
See EMERGENCY MANAGEMENT.
Engineers.
Rescue or relief assistance.
Civil immunity for licensed professional engineers, §8.01-226.2.
Marine police responsibilities, §28.2-106.
Motor vehicle license plates.
Fight terrorism, §46.2-749.62.
Presumption of death.
Terrorist attacks on September 11, 2001, §64.2-2300 (note).
Removal of public officers, §24.2-233.
Seizure and forfeiture.
Property used in connection with or derived from, §19.2-386.15.
Separate and distinct offenses, §18.2-46.10.
Solicitation of charitable or civic contributions.
Prohibition against support of terrorism, §§57-49, 57-57.
Seizure of property connected with terrorism, §57-59.
State emergency preparedness programs, §44-146.18.
Terrorism risk insurance act.
Coverage of losses due to terrorism, exclusions, §38.2-2102.
Threats.
Death or bodily injury to family members, §18.2-60.
Venue, §18.2-46.8.
Violations as separate and distinct offenses, §18.2-46.10.
Weapons.
Possession, manufacture, distribution, etc.
Penalties, §18.2-46.6.

TERRORISM RISK INSURANCE ACT.
Coverage of losses due to terrorism, exclusions, §38.2-2102.

TESTIMONIALS.
Fee for issuance by secretary of the Commonwealth, §2.2-409.

TESTING FOR SUBSTANCE ABUSE.
Defeating drug and alcohol screening tests, §18.2-251.4.

TESTING FOR SUBSTANCE ABUSE —Cont'd
Substance abuse screening and assessment.
Drug conviction, §§18.2-252, 18.2-254.
Felony conviction generally, §18.2-251.01.

TESTING KITS.
Consumer home medical testing kits.
Warning required, §18.2-502.2.

TESTOSTERONE.
Schedule III controlled drug, §54.1-3450.

TESTS FOR DRUGS.
Driving while intoxicated.
Chemical testing to determine alcohol or drug content of blood, §§18.2-268.1 to 18.2-268.12.
See DRIVING WHILE INTOXICATED.
Probation for first time drug offenders.
Condition of probation, §18.2-251.

TESTS OF BLOOD.
Boats and other watercraft.
Operating while under the influence, §§29.1-738.2, 29.1-738.3.
Descent and distribution.
Evidence of paternity, §64.2-103.
Driving while intoxicated.
Chemical testing to determine alcohol or drug content, §§18.2-268.1 to 18.2-268.12.
See DRIVING WHILE INTOXICATED.
HIV test.
Notification of insurance-required test results, §38.2-613.01.
Paternity, §§20-49.3, 20-49.4.
Descent and distribution.
Evidence of paternity, §64.2-103.
Spearfishing.
Engaging in while under the influence, §§29.1-738.2, 29.1-738.3.
Surfboarding.
Manipulating surfboard while under the influence, §§29.1-738.2, 29.1-738.3.
Waterskiing.
Manipulating skis while under the influence, §§29.1-738.2, 29.1-738.3.

TESTS OF BREATH.
Boats and other watercraft.
Operating while under the influence, §§29.1-738.1 to 29.1-738.3.
Driving while intoxicated.
Chemical testing to determine alcohol or drug content of blood, §§18.2-268.1 to 18.2-268.12.
See DRIVING WHILE INTOXICATED.
Preliminary analysis of breath, §18.2-267.
Spearfishing.
Engaging in while under the influence, §§29.1-738.1 to 29.1-738.3.
Surfboarding.
Manipulating while under the influence, §§29.1-738.1 to 29.1-738.3.
Waterskiing.
Manipulating skis while under the influence, §§29.1-738.1 to 29.1-738.3.

TEST-TUBE BABIES.
Status of children of assisted conception.
Generally, §§20-156 to 20-165.

TETANUS.
Colleges and universities.
Required immunization of students, §23-7.5.
Immunizations.
Required immunizations of children, §32.1-46.

TETANUS —Cont'd
Immunizations —Cont'd
Virginia immunization information system (VIIS), §32.1-46.01.

TEXTBOOKS, §§22.1-238 to 22.1-243.
Approval of textbooks, §22.1-238.
Basal textbooks, §22.1-239.
Colleges and universities.
Policies addressing textbook sales and bookstores, §23-4.3:1.
Contracts with publishers, §22.1-241.
Damage, fees, §22.1-243.
Distribution of textbooks and consumable materials, §22.1-243.
Free textbooks, VA Const Art VIII §3.
Regulations, §22.1-242.
Retail sales and use tax exemption, §58.1-609.10.

TEXTING WHILE DRIVING.
Use of handheld communications devices in motor vehicles, §46.2-1078.1.
Commercial drivers' licenses, disqualifications, §§46.2-341.20, 46.2-341.20:5.
Holders of provisional drivers' licenses, §46.2-334.01.
Reckless driving, mandatory fine, §46.2-868.

TEXT MESSAGING.
Colleges and universities.
First warning and emergency notification systems, §23-9.2:11.

TEXT TELEPHONES.
Responsibilities of department, §51.5-115.

THANKSGIVING.
ABC stores.
Closed, §4.1-120.
Legal holidays, §2.2-3300.

THEATERS.
Child labor, §40.1-101.
Issuance of theatrical permit, §40.1-102.
Drive-in theaters.
County regulating certain motion pictures shown at, §15.2-1222.
Drug houses.
Maintaining fortified drug houses, §18.2-258.02.
Drug transactions on premises.
Closure of nuisance premises, §§48-16, 48-17.
Common nuisance, §§18.2-258, 18.2-258.01.
Encouraging use of facilities in certain cities, §15.2-1129.
Exits.
Fire protection, §27-51.
Inspections, §27-52.
Local safety provisions, §27-54.
Penalties for violations, §27-53.
Fire alarms.
Maliciously activating, §18.2-212.
Fire exits, §§27-51 to 27-54.
Retail sales and use tax.
Media-related exemptions, §58.1-609.6.
Smoke bombs.
Setting off in public buildings, §18.2-87.1.

THE CROOKED ROAD.
Southwest Virginia cultural heritage foundation, §§2.2-2734 to 2.2-2737.

THEFT.
Ballot containers, voting or registration equipment, etc., §24.2-1009.

THEFT —Cont'd
Cargo theft, §18.2-147.1.
Clams, §§28.2-527, 28.2-528.
Revocation of licenses, §28.2-528.
Computer services, §18.2-152.6.
Credit cards or card numbers, §18.2-192.
Documents of title.
Stolen documents, §8.7-601.
Drivers' licenses.
Unlawful procurement of license or permit, §46.2-105.1.
Employee theft.
Civil action for damages, §8.01-44.4.
Explosives.
Notice of, §59.1-139.
Reports of stolen explosives, §27-97.1.
Larceny generally, §§18.2-95 to 18.2-109.
See LARCENY.
Motor vehicle registration.
Unlawful procurement of certificate, §46.2-105.1.
Oysters, §§28.2-527, 28.2-528.
Revocation of licenses, §28.2-528.
Proof of ownership to property, §19.2-284.
Public records, §18.2-107.
Shoplifting.
Civil action for damages, §8.01-44.4.
Timber, larceny of, §55-334.1.

THERAPEUTICALLY EQUIVALENT DRUG PRODUCTS, §54.1-3408.03.

THERAPEUTIC PHARMACEUTICAL AGENTS, §§54.1-3222 to 54.1-3224.
Certification for healing arts practice, §54.1-3222.
Disciplinary actions, §54.1-3224.
Qualifications for certification, §54.1-3223.
Summary suspension of certification, §54.1-3224.

THERAPISTS, OCCUPATIONAL.
Licensing generally, §§54.1-2950.1 to 54.1-2957.01.
See MEDICINE AND OTHER HEALING ARTS PROFESSIONS.

THERAPISTS, PHYSICAL.
Licensing generally, §§54.1-2900 to 54.1-2993.
See MEDICINE AND OTHER HEALING ARTS PROFESSIONS.

THERAPISTS, RESPIRATORY.
Licensing generally, §§54.1-2950.1 to 54.1-2957.01.
See MEDICINE AND OTHER HEALING ARTS PROFESSIONS.

THERMAL IMAGING.
Fire programs department.
Thermal imaging camera grant fund, §9.1-205.

THERMOSTATS.
Mercury thermostat recycling, §10.1-1425.26.

THESIS.
Preparation or selling for profit, §18.2-508.
Injunction, §18.2-507.
Person and prepared defined, §18.2-506.
Punishment, §18.2-508.

THE UNIVERSITY.
University of Virginia.
General provisions, §§23-62 to 23-91.23:1.
See UNIVERSITY OF VIRGINIA.

3RD INFANTRY REGIMENT (OLD GUARD).
Special license plates, §46.2-746.2:3.

THIRD PARTIES.
Duty to mental health service provider to protect.
Violent behavior or serious harm by client, §54.1-2400.1.
Local taxes.
Payment on behalf of taxpayer, §58.1-3018.
Secured transactions.
Rights of third parties, §§8.9A-401 to 8.9A-409.
See SECURED TRANSACTIONS.

THIRD-PARTY CLAIMS.
Amendments, VA SCt Rule 1:8.
Asbestos-related injuries.
Consolidation or bifurcation of issues or claims, §8.01-374.1.
Attachments.
How and when claims tried, §8.01-573.
Circuit courts, VA SCt Rule 3:13.
Custodial trusts, §§64.2-910, 64.2-911.
District courts, VA SCt Rule 7B:10.
General rules as to pleadings, VA SCt Rule 1:4.
Limitation third-party beneficiary doctrine, §55-22.
Limited partnerships.
Liability of limited partners to third parties, §50-73.24.
Nonsuit.
Consent of adverse party filing third-party claim required, §8.01-380.
Petroleum storage tank discharges, §62.1-44.34:12.
Pleading in alternative, §8.01-281.
Products liability.
Consolidation or bifurcation of issues or claims, §8.01-374.1.
Satisfaction of judgments.
Payment by third parties releasing recognizances, §8.01-457.
Settlements.
Workers' compensation.
Subrogation of employer to employee's rights.
Settlement of third-party action, §8.01-424.1.
Size of paper, VA SCt Rule 1:16.
Standing.
Estates in land, §55-22.
Statute of limitations, §8.01-243.
Transfers to minors, §64.2-1915.
Workers' compensation.
Subrogation of employer to employee's rights.
Settlement of third-party action, §8.01-424.1.

THIRD-PARTY STANDING.
Estates in land, §55-22.

THIRD-PARTY TAX PAYMENT AGREEMENTS.
Local taxes, §58.1-3018.

THIRD YEAR STUDENT PRACTICE RULE, VA SCt Rule Pt 6 §IV Par 15.

THISTLE.
Musk thistle, curled thistle.
Counties, cities, towns.
Authority to control, §15.2-902.

THOMAS JEFFERSON MEMORIAL FOUNDATION.
Property exempt from taxation, §58.1-3607.

THREAT ASSESSMENT TEAMS.
Public institutions of higher education.
Freedom of information act requests.
Excluded records, §2.2-3705.4.

THREATENING LETTERS.
Extortion of money by, §18.2-59.

THREATS.
Abduction, §18.2-49.
Bomb threats, §18.2-83.
Causing, inciting, etc., commission of act, §18.2-84.
False information, §18.2-83.
Clandestine organizations, §§18.2-420, 18.2-421.
Criminal street gangs.
Used to encourage individual to join or remain with gang, commit felony, §18.2-46.3.
Death or bodily injury to person or family member, §18.2-60.
Discretionary felony sentencing guidelines, §17.1-805.
Extortion, §18.2-59.
Governor or immediate family, §§18.2-60.1, 18.2-60.2.
Marriage.
Taking or detaining person with intent to compel, §18.2-355.
Motor vehicle dealers.
Waiver of dealer rights.
Threats, etc., by manufacturer, etc., to obtain, §46.2-1572.3.
Obstructing justice by threats or force, §18.2-460.
Bail, presumption against admitting to bail for certain offense, §19.2-120.
Prostitution.
Placing or leaving wife for, §18.2-368.
Protective orders, §19.2-152.10.
Preliminary protective orders, §19.2-152.9.
Venue, §19.2-152.11.
Recognizance to keep the peace, §§19.2-19 to 19.2-25.
Security of government information.
Chief information officer (CIO), duties, §2.2-2009.
Stalking, §18.2-60.3.
Assault and battery of person protected by protective order, §18.2-60.4.
Violation of protective orders, §18.2-60.4.
State databases and data communications.
Information officers for state agencies, duty to report threats, §2.2-603.
Telephones or citizens band radios.
Use of threatening language, §18.2-427.
Voter influencing, §24.2-1005.
Voter registration interference, §24.2-1002.

THREE STRIKES LAW.
Assault and battery against family or household member.
Felony, third or subsequent conviction, §18.2-57.2.
Carrying concealed weapons.
Third or subsequent violation, §18.2-308.
Drivers' licenses, §46.2-316.
Driving while intoxicated.
Mandatory minimum sentences, §18.2-270.
Subsequent offenses, sentencing, §18.2-270.
Motor vehicle equipment, §46.2-112.
Motor vehicle habitual offenders, §§46.2-356 to 46.2-363.
Parole, §53.1-151.
Stalking.
Felony for third conviction, §18.2-60.3.
Trespassing on railroad tracks, §18.2-159.
Violent felonies, §19.2-297.1.
Voluntary manslaughter, §19.2-297.1.
Weapons offenses, §19.2-297.1.

THREE STRIKES LAW —Cont'd
Wounding with intent to maim, kill, etc., §19.2-297.1.

THROAT CANCER.
Presumption as to death or disability.
Firefighters, §65.2-402.

THROUGH TRAFFIC.
Limited access street, §15.2-2026.

THROWING MISSILES, ETC., AT CARS, TRAINS, ETC., §18.2-154.

THROWING OBJECTS FROM PLACES HIGHER THAN ONE STORY.
Reckless endangerment, §18.2-51.3.

THROWING STARS.
See MARTIAL ARTS WEAPONS.

TICKETS.
Credit card fraud used to obtain from transportation companies.
Discounted ticket obtained from other than agent of company.
Presumption ticket acquired under circumstances constituting violation, §18.2-198.
Resale of tickets to certain public events.
Ordinances prohibiting, §15.2-969.
Right to work, §40.1-66.
Scalping.
Ordinances prohibiting, §15.2-969.
State lottery.
Alteration or forgery, §58.1-4017.
Cash or debit cards.
Only method of payment, §58.1-4014.1.
Ineligible persons to purchase, §58.1-4019.
Instant ticket license, §58.1-4019.1.
Internet sales, prohibition, §58.1-4007.2.
Presentation of counterfeited or altered ticket, §58.1-4017.
Price, §58.1-4014.
Sale to persons under eighteen prohibited, §58.1-4015.
Tax exemption on sales, §58.1-4025.
Who may sell, §58.1-4014.
Transportation district trains.
Boarding without lawful payment of fare or with fraudulent or counterfeit ticket, §18.2-160.1.

TICKET SCALPING.
Ordinances prohibiting, §15.2-969.

TICKS.
Healing arts professionals.
Lyme disease testing, disclosures required, §54.1-2963.2.

TIDAL EROSION.
Localities constructing dams, levees, seawalls, etc., §15.2-970.

TIDAL WATER FISHING, §§28.2-200 to 28.2-907.
See FISHING, TIDAL WATERS.

TIDAL WATERS.
Clams generally, §§28.2-500 to 28.2-562.
See OYSTERS AND CLAMS.
Coastal primary sand dunes and beaches, §§28.2-1400 to 28.2-1420.
See COASTAL PRIMARY SAND DUNES AND BEACHES.
Crabs, §§28.2-700 to 28.2-713.
See CRABS.

TIDAL WATERS —Cont'd
Eels.
Pots.
Channel restrictions, §28.2-710.
Identification, §28.2-712.
Fishing in generally.
See FISHING, TIDAL WATERS.
Oyster planting grounds generally, §§28.2-600 to 28.2-650.
See OYSTER PLANTING GROUNDS.
Oysters generally, §§28.2-500 to 28.2-562.
See OYSTERS AND CLAMS.
Pots.
Channel restrictions, §28.2-710.
Sanitation districts law of 1938, §§21-141 to 21-223.
See SANITATION DISTRICTS LAW OF 1938.
Submerged lands, §§28.2-1200 to 28.2-1213.
See SUBMERGED LANDS.
Ungranted shores of the sea, marshes and meadowlands, §§28.2-1500 to 28.2-1514.
See UNGRANTED SHORES OF THE SEA.
Wetlands, §§28.2-1300 to 28.2-1320.
See WETLANDS.

TIDEWATER AIRPORT COMMISSION, 1962 ch 606, 1964 ch 45.

TIDEWATER, OIL OR GAS DRILLING, §62.1-195.1.

TIDEWATER RECREATION AND STADIUM AUTHORITY, 1968 ch 288.
Amended in 1970, 1970 ch 304.
Repeal of chapter 288, 1968 acts, 1987 ch 39.

TIDEWATER TRANSPORTATION DISTRICT.
Commission members, §15.2-4507.
Transportation districts generally, §§15.2-4500 to 15.2-4534.

TIDEWATER VIRGINIA.
Chesapeake Bay preservation areas.
Designation by counties, cities and towns, §62.1-44.15:74.
Enforcement of provisions, authority of local governments, §62.1-44.15:73.

TIE BREAKER.
Circuit courts.
Exercise of powers of appointment.
Chief justice of supreme court, §17.1-501.
Selection of chief judge.
Chief justice of supreme court, §17.1-501.
Counties designating, §§15.2-1420, 15.2-1421.
Determination by lot, §24.2-674.
Selection, §§22.1-40, 22.1-53.
School divisions composed of single county.
Alternative methods, §22.1-44.
School boards.
County board form of government, §15.2-410.
County executive form of government, §15.2-531.
County manager form of government, §15.2-627.
Urban county executive form of government, §15.2-837.
Transportation board, §33.1-1.

TIER-CITIES.
Defined, §1-252.
Towns generally.
See TOWNS.

TIGER SWALLOWTAIL BUTTERFLY.
Special license plates, §46.2-728.3.

TIMBER.
Agricultural and forestal districts, §§15.2-4300 to 15.2-4407.
Big Sandy river.
Obstructing or dumping solid waste into, §62.1-194.3.
Casting into waters, §§62.1-194, 62.1-194.2.
Cutting timber, §§55-331 to 55-335.
Division of engineering and buildings controlled lands.
Management, harvesting and sale, §2.2-1158.
Drift property generally, §§55-202 to 55-210.
Forest management of state-owned lands fund, §§10.1-1120 to 10.1-1123.
Forest products tax, §§58.1-1600 to 58.1-1622.
See FOREST PRODUCTS TAX.
Game and inland fisheries department.
Director powers, §29.1-111.
Larceny of things fixed to freehold, §18.2-99.
Motor vehicle registration.
Registration of logging vehicles, §46.2-648.
Open-space land.
Acquisition of title subject to timber rights, §10.1-1703.
Principal and income.
Allocations to principal and income, §64.2-1020.
Real property tax assessment.
Apportionment of value of standing timber between owner of soil and owner of standing timber, §58.1-3309.
Real estate tax lien on timber in certain counties, §58.1-3345.
Reduction in value, §58.1-3293.
Standing timber, §58.1-3284.
Reforestation of timberlands, §§10.1-1170 to 10.1-1176.
See REFORESTATION OF TIMBERLANDS.
Sales.
Payments to localities, §29.1-111.
Sales, UCC.
Applicability of chapter, §8.2-107.
Special construction and forestry equipment.
Defined, §46.2-100.
Security interests in.
Perfecting, §46.2-636.1.
Titling or registration in state.
Not required, §46.2-600.
State forester.
Distribution of seeds and seedlings, §10.1-1114.
Preservation of timber, §10.1-1106.
Sale of trees, §10.1-1115.
Trees generally.
See TREES.

TIMBER BRANDS, §§59.1-103 to 59.1-115.
Adoption by persons engaged in lumbering or rafting on certain waters, §59.1-103.
Branded timber.
Unlawful cutting down, possessing or converting, §59.1-114.
Branding iron misuse, §59.1-111.
Certificates.
Evidence of right to use, §59.1-105.
Conversion of timber, §59.1-107.
Defacement, §59.1-107.
Defined terms.
Timber dealers, §59.1-108.
Effect of branding, §59.1-113.
Fraudulently impressing brand on timber, §59.1-112.
Fraudulent use, §59.1-107.

TIMBER BRANDS —Cont'd
Obliteration, willful, §59.1-107.
Sale of unclaimed timber, §59.1-106.
Timber dealers.
Adoption of brands or trademark, §59.1-109.
Branding irons, §59.1-111.
Defined, §59.1-108.
Unbranded timber.
Sheriffs' sales, §59.1-115.
Use without authority, §59.1-110.

TIMBER CUTTING, §§55-331 to 55-335.
Personal property taxes.
Classification of equipment used for harvesting and other silvicultural activities, §58.1-3506.
Separate classification for machinery used in certain businesses, §58.1-3508.2.
Silvicultural activities affecting water quality, §§10.1-1181.1 to 10.1-1181.7.

TIME, COMPUTATION, §1-210.
Computation of time.
Electronic filing and service, VA SCt Rule 1:17.
Effective date of statutes.
See EFFECTIVE DATE OF STATUTES.

TIME FOR COMMENCING CIRCUIT COURT TERMS, VA SCt Rule 1:15 Sched.

TIME FOR FILING.
Appeals.
Administrative agency appeals.
Notice of appeal, VA SCt Rule 2A:2.
Petition for appeal, VA SCt Rule 2A:4.
Courts not of record, §16.1-106.
Denial of appeal.
Petition for rehearing, VA SCt Rule 5:20.
Juvenile and domestic relations district court.
Appeal from conviction, VA SCt Rule 3A:19.
Notice of appeal.
Administrative agency appeal, VA SCt Rule 2A:2.
Court of appeals, §17.1-408, VA SCt Rule 5A:6.
Appeal from workers' compensation commission, VA SCt Rule 5A:11.
Supreme court.
Appeal from court of appeals, VA SCt Rule 5:14.
Appeal from state corporation commission, VA SCt Rule 5:21.
Appeal from trial court, VA SCt Rule 5:9.
Petition for appeal to supreme court, VA SCt Rule 5:17.
Right of appeal, §16.1-132.
Transcript of proceedings appealed.
Court of appeals, VA SCt Rule 5A:8.
Supreme court, VA SCt Rule 5:11.
United States supreme court.
Deferred mandate from Virginia supreme court, VA SCt Rule 5:39.
Withdrawal of appeal, §16.1-133.
Briefs.
Court of appeals, VA SCt Rule 5A:19.
Brief in opposition to granting appeal, VA SCt Rule 5A:13.
Reply brief, VA SCt Rule 5A:14.
Supreme court.
Brief in opposition, VA SCt Rule 5:18.
Reply brief, VA SCt Rule 5:19.
Computation of time, §1-210.
Criminal cases.
Defenses and objections, VA SCt Rule 3A:9.

TIME FOR FILING —Cont'd
Criminal cases —Cont'd
Discovery requests.
Felony cases, VA SCt Rule 3A:11.
Reopening of case after conviction, §16.1-133.1.
Right of appeal, §16.1-132.
Withdrawal of appeal, §16.1-133.
Date pleading filed noted on papers, §17.1-129.
Disclosure statements.
General assembly members, §30-110.
State officers and employees, §2.2-3114.
Discovery requests.
Felony cases, VA SCt Rule 3A:11.
Misdemeanors, VA SCt Rule 7C:5.
Preliminary hearings for felony, VA SCt Rule 7C:5.
District courts.
Notice of hearing in civil cases, §16.1-83.
Filing date and time noted on pleading papers, §17.1-129.
Garnishment.
Child support orders.
Time limit for return of summons, §8.01-514.
Motions.
Reply.
Court of appeals, VA SCt Rule 5A:2.
Supreme court, VA SCt Rule 5:4.
New trial, §16.1-97.1.
Notice of appeal. See within this heading, "Appeals."
Notice of hearing.
District courts, §16.1-83.
Public assistance.
Appeals to commissioner of board's decision, §63.2-517.
Release of deed of trust or other lien.
Certificate of satisfaction or partial satisfaction by lien creditor, §55-66.3.
Replies.
Motions.
Court of appeals, VA SCt Rule 5A:2.
Supreme court, VA SCt Rule 5:4.
Reports by state agencies.
Law requiring reports to governor or general assembly, §2.2-608.
Sentence of person twice previously convicted for certain violent felonies.
Notice of intention to seek punishment pursuant section, §19.2-297.1.
Service of notice, process and other papers, when timely, §8.01-275.1.
Subpoena requests, VA SCt Rule 7A:12.
Supreme court of United States.
Appeals to.
Deferred mandate by Virginia supreme court, VA SCt Rule 5:39.
Third-party claims, VA SCt Rule 7B:10.
Trusts.
Resignation of trustee.
Notice, §64.2-758.
Transfer of principal place of business.
Notice, §64.2-706.
Verification of pleadings.
Objections to motion to strike, VA SCt Rule 1:10.

TIME FOR JUDGE TO QUALIFY FOR OFFICE.
Judges of courts of record, §17.1-101.

TIMEKEEPERS AT SPORTING EVENTS.
Workers' compensation.
Employee not to include sports official, §65.2-101.

TIME LIMITS FOR COMMENCING ACTIONS OR OTHER PROCEEDINGS.
See STATUTE OF LIMITATIONS.

TIME SERVED.
Credit for time spent in confinement while awaiting trial, §53.1-187.

TIME-SHARES, §§55-360 to 55-400.
Administration of chapter.
Common interest community board, §55-362.1.
Administrative process act.
Hearings in accordance with, §55-399.1.
Advertising.
Practice regulations, §55-374.1.
Application of chapter, §55-361.1.
Assessment against time-share estate.
Levy by association, authority, lien, §55-370.
Bond, letter of credit or cash.
Filing with board.
Protection of escrow deposits, §55-375.
Books and records of association, §55-370.01.
Building code applicability, §55-364.
Buyer's acknowledgment, §55-376.5.
Cancellation rights of purchasers, §55-376.
Cash deposits, §55-375.
Cease and desist orders, §55-396.
Cancellation, §55-397.
Class actions, §55-384.
Closed sessions.
Meetings of board of directors, §55-370.01.
Common interest community board.
Administration of chapter, §55-362.1.
General powers and duties, §55-396.
Compliance determination.
Board requested to make, §55-396.
Condominium units.
Sale time-share estate in unit prior to substantial completion.
Bond to insure completion filed, §55-79.58.
Contracts.
Buyer's acknowledgment, §55-376.5.
Conversion time-share projects.
Defined, §55-362.
Public offering statements, §55-374.
Right of first refusal, §55-374.
Criminal penalty for violations, §55-400.
Damages sought.
Actual damages sustained.
Award limited to, §55-383.
Deeds.
Recording and delivery, §55-376.2.
Defined terms, §55-362.
Time-share estate occupancy expenses, §55-369.
Year, §55-374.2.
Deposits.
Escrow of, §55-375.
Action alleging failure to comply.
Compliance determination prior to filing, §55-382.
Developer control period, §55-369.
Electronic communications and filings.
Authorized, §55-370.01.
E-mail.
Electronic communications between board of directors and members, §55-370.01.
Enjoining violations, §55-396.
Escrow of deposits.
Action alleging failure to comply.
Compliance determination prior to filing, §55-382.

TIME-SHARES —Cont'd
Exchange companies offering exchange programs, §55-374.2.
Exchange program defined, §55-362.
Fees.
Registration fees, §55-392.1.
Fee simple interest to common elements.
Transfer to estate owners' association, §55-369.
Financial records, §55-385.
Financing, §§55-387 to 55-389.
Gift or prize included in offering, §55-374.1.
Hearing officer.
Hearings conducted by, §55-399.1.
Horizontal property regimes generally, §§55-79.1 to 55-79.38.
See HORIZONTAL PROPERTY REGIMES.
Improvements promised by developer.
Obligation to complete, §55-386.
Action alleging noncompliance.
Compliance determination prior to filing, §55-382.
Inspection of books and records.
Right of member, withheld from inspection, §55-370.01.
Instruments, §55-367.
Severability, §55-365.1.
Investigations by board, §55-399.
Liens, §55-381.
Unpaid and past due assessment levied against estate, §55-370.
List of names and addresses of current members.
Association to maintain, §55-370.01.
Local ordinance applicability, §55-364.
Location of books and records.
Association to provide members with, §55-370.01.
Loss of time-share estate.
Possibility of reverter, §55-376.1.
Mails to members by association, §55-370.01.
Maintenance fee.
Collection from estate owners.
Developer control period, §55-369.
Management of estate, §55-368.
Developer control period, §55-369.
Owners' association control, §55-370.
Management of use, §55-371.
Mechanics' and materialmen's liens.
Perfection.
Subcontractors, §43-7.
Meetings of board of directors, §55-370.01.
Membership camping.
Application of provisions, §§59.1-314, 59.1-321.
Generally, §§59.1-311 to 59.1-335.
See MEMBERSHIP CAMPING.
Monetary penalty for violations, §55-400.
Nonmaterial error or omission.
Insufficient to permit cancellation of contract, §55-383.
Owners' association annual report, §55-370.1.
Owners' association control, §55-370.
Partitions, §55-372.
Permitted, §55-366.
Possibility of reverter.
Conditions generally, §55-376.1.
Public offering statement, §55-374.
Validity, §55-376.1.
Project activities provided by project professionals.
Injury to or death of participant.
Immunity from liability of project professional, §55-376.3.

TIME-SHARES —Cont'd
Project activities provided by project professionals —Cont'd
Injury to or death of participant —Cont'd
Warning signs required, §55-376.3.
Project activity defined, §55-362.
Project professional defined, §55-362.
Property owners' associations generally.
Applicability of provisions, §55-508.
Provision violations.
Penalties, §55-400.
Rights of the injured, §55-382.
Statute of limitations, §55-383.
Public offering statements, §55-374.
Amendments to reflect material changes, §§55-374, 55-398.
Board regulation, §55-398.
Statute of limitations, §55-383.
Purchases.
Buyer's acknowledgment, §55-376.5.
Real estate cooperatives.
Public offering statements.
Required information, §55-480.
Records.
Books and records of association, §55-370.01.
Keeping financial records, §55-385.
Resellers, §55-394.4.
Registration, §§55-390 to 55-394.4.
Amendment, §55-394.1.
Fees, §55-392.1.
Report, developer, §55-394.1.
Resellers, §55-394.3.
Revocation by board, §55-396.
Cancellation, §55-397.
Termination, §55-394.2.
Removal of director of association from office, §55-370.01.
Resale, §55-380.
Buyer's acknowledgment, §55-376.5.
Disclosures, required, §55-380.1.
Registration of resellers, §55-394.3.
Rescission of contract, §55-383.
Resellers.
Prohibited practices, §55-394.3.
Recordkeeping, §55-394.4.
Rules and regulations.
Power of board, §55-396.
Sales.
Buyer's acknowledgment, §55-376.5.
Status, §55-363.
Statute of limitations, §55-383.
Swimming, spas, sports or cultural and historical activities.
Death of or injury to participant resulting from inherent risks.
Immunity of professionals providing activities, §§55-376.3, 55-376.4.
Temporary cease and desist orders, §55-396.
Terminations, §55-373.
Title of chapter, §55-360.
Travel clubs.
Application of provisions, §59.1-453.
Use management, §55-371.
Use of terms, §55-364.1.
Venue of proceedings before board, §55-399.1.
Zoning applicability, §55-364.

TIME ZONE.
Statutory construction, §1-253.

TINTED WINDOWS AND WINDSHIELDS.
Motor vehicles, §46.2-1052.

TIRE PILE FIRES.
Liability, §10.1-1418.3.

TIRE RECYCLING FEE, §§58.1-640 to 58.1-644.
Collection, §58.1-642.
Deductions, §58.1-642.
Definitions, §58.1-640.
Exemptions, §58.1-642.
Rate, §58.1-641.
Retail sales and use tax chapter.
Applicability of provisions, §58.1-644.
Statute of limitations.
Criminal prosecutions, §19.2-8.

TIRES.
Burning.
Liability for large waste tire pile fires, §10.1-1418.3.
Chains, §46.2-1044.
Cleats, etc., on tires, §§46.2-1044, 46.2-1045.
Devices for puncturing motor vehicle tires.
Manufacturing, distributing or possessing, §18.2-147.2.
Police use authorized, §33.1-345.
Improper disposal of tires, §10.1-1418.2.
Improper or inadequate tires, §§46.2-1041, 46.2-1043, 46.2-1044.
Fine schedule, VA SCt Rule 3B:2.
Maximum fine for violating Title 46.2, §46.2-113.
Pretrial payment of fine, §16.1-69.40:1.
Loading of tires, §46.2-1043.1.
Military and emergency laws.
Laws continued in effect, motor vehicle tires, §44-207.
Motor vehicle size and weight.
Tire loading, §46.2-1043.1.
Regrooved or recut tires, §46.2-1042.
Removal of waste tire piles, §10.1-1418.4.
Lien for removal, §10.1-1418.5.
Right of entry.
Removal of waste tire piles, §10.1-1418.4.
Solid rubber tire restrictions, §46.2-1041.
Studded tires, §§46.2-1044, 46.2-1045.
Tire tread depth, §46.2-1043.
Fine schedule, VA SCt Rule 3B:2.
Pretrial payment of fine, §16.1-69.40:1.
Tractor engines and tractors, §46.2-1046.

TIRE TAX, §§58.1-640 to 58.1-644.

TIRE TREAD DEPTH, §46.2-1043.
Fine schedule, VA SCt Rule 3B:2.
Pretrial payment of fine, §16.1-69.40:1.

TISSUE BANKS.
Anatomical gifts generally, §§32.1-291.1 to 32.1-291.25.
See ANATOMICAL GIFTS.

TITLE.
Abandoned vessels.
Acquiring, §29.1-733.1.
Actions.
Suit by beneficial owner when legal title in another, §8.01-12.
Adverse possession.
Limitation of actions, §8.01-236.
After-acquired property.
Validity of deed, §55-52.
Boats and other watercraft.
Certificates of title, §§29.1-712 to 29.1-733.1.
Uniform certificate of title for watercraft, §§29.1-733.2 to 29.1-733.29.

TITLE —Cont'd
Bona fide purchasers.
Devises of real estate without notice, §64.2-456.
Intestacy, §64.2-458.
Later wills, §64.2-457.
Business trusts.
Property title records.
Organizational changes, §13.1-1285.
Cemeteries.
Condemned land, §57-25.
Civil aircraft of the United States.
Recordation of instruments affecting, §55-100.
Clouds on title, §§55-153 to 55-155.
Preferred venue for removal, §8.01-261.
Condominiums.
Termination of condominium, §55-79.72:1.
Conservation and development department.
Division of ports.
Transfer of title, §62.1-131.
Cooperatives, §55-440.
Special declarant rights, transfers of, §55-461.
Corporations.
Property title records.
Corporate changes, §13.1-781.
Correctional institutions, §53.1-19.
Custodial trust property, §64.2-901.
Decedents' estates.
Community property rights at death.
Perfection.
Devisees, §64.2-319.
Heirs, §64.2-319.
Personal representatives, §64.2-319.
Surviving spouse, §64.2-318.
Foreign executor conveyances, §64.2-524.
Deeds, §§55-48 to 55-79.
See DEEDS.
Delinquent tax lands sales.
Title acquired, §58.1-3967.
Distress warrants.
Property levied on, district court proceedings, §§16.1-119 to 16.1-122.
Doctrine of worthier title.
Abolished, §55-14.1.
Documents of title.
General provisions, §§8.7-101 to 8.7-603.
See DOCUMENTS OF TITLE.
Drift property, §55-207.
Ejectment.
Conveyance of legal title to vendee, etc., §8.01-146.
Eminent domain.
Effort to purchase, prerequisites, §25.1-204.
Highways and roads.
Recordation of certificates, §33.1-122.
Taking possession and title to property before or during condemnation, §33.1-119.
Title transfer by certificate, §§25.1-300 to 25.1-318.
See EMINENT DOMAIN.
Equal credit opportunities.
Signature requirement not discriminatory, §6.2-504.
Exchange accommodation titleholder.
Exchange facilitators act, §§55-525.1 to 55-525.7.
Execution.
Property levied on, district court proceedings, §§16.1-119 to 16.1-122.
Fraudulent conversion of property subject to title in another, §18.2-115.
Fraudulent conveyances.
Purchasers unaffected by record of deed or contract, §55-100.

TITLE —Cont'd
Fraudulent conveyances —Cont'd
United States civil aircraft.
Recordation of instruments affecting, §55-100.
Void, §55-80.
Hampton Roads port commission.
Transfer of title, §62.1-131.
Highways and roads.
Eminent domain.
Recordation of certificates, §33.1-122.
Taking possession and title to property before or during condemnation, §33.1-119.
Horizontal property regimes generally, §§55-79.1 to 55-79.38.
See HORIZONTAL PROPERTY REGIMES.
Judicial sales.
Setting aside sale, §8.01-113.
Leases, UCC, §8.2A-302.
Limitation of actions.
Adverse possession, §8.01-236.
Manufactured homes.
Cancellation of title, §46.2-653.
Mortgages and deeds of trust generally, §§6.2-406 to 6.2-423, 55-58 to 55-66.6.
See MORTGAGES AND DEEDS OF TRUST.
Motor vehicles, §§46.2-616 to 46.2-644.
See MOTOR VEHICLE TITLING.
Museums.
Property loaned to museums, §§55-210.34, 55-210.37.
Nonprofit corporations.
Property title records.
Corporate changes, §13.1-945.
Partition of land.
Decree of partition to vest legal title, §8.01-88.
Purchasers unaffected by record of deed or contract, §55-100.
Quieting title, §§55-153 to 55-155.
Real estate cooperatives, §55-440.
Special declarant rights, transfers of, §55-461.
Recordation.
Decrees affecting title to land, §55-138.
Documents generally, §§55-106 to 55-112.
Sale of delinquent tax lands.
Title acquired, §58.1-3967.
Sales, UCC.
Passing of title, §8.2-401.
Power to transfer title, §8.2-403.
Reservation for securities, §8.2-401.
Warranty of title, §8.2-312.
School property.
Property of joint and regional schools, §22.1-26.
Title to property vested in school board, §22.1-125.
Title to school board real estate, §22.1-128.
Secondhand article sales.
Watches, §59.1-133.
Securities.
Unclaimed securities, disposition of.
Transfer of record of ownership, §55-210.18:1.
State port authority of Virginia.
Transfer, §62.1-131.
Statute of limitations.
Adverse possession, §8.01-236.
Subdivided land sales.
Blanket encumbrances, §55-342.
Timber brands.
Effect of branding, §59.1-113.
Unlawfully cutting down, possessing or converting branded timber, §59.1-114.
Time-shares.
Transfer time, §55-369.

TITLE —Cont'd
Torrens system.
Acts establishing continued in force, §55-112.
Unclaimed property.
Sale to pass title, §55-210.18.
Ungranted shores of sea, marsh and meadowlands.
Claim to lands designated in inventory, §28.2-1509.
United States civil aircraft.
Recordation of instruments affecting, §55-100.
Vessels, abandoned.
Acquiring, §29.1-733.1.
Watches, secondhand article sales, §59.1-133.
Worthier title.
Doctrine abolished, §55-14.1.

TITLE INSURANCE, §§38.2-4600 to 38.2-4616.
Agency or agent defined, §38.2-4601.1.
Applicability of chapter, §38.2-4600.
Applicable laws, §38.2-4602.
Availability of owner's title insurance, notification to buyer, §38.2-4616.
Binders or other temporary insurance, §38.2-4605.
Claim reserve, §38.2-4609.
Class of insurance and companies to which chapter applies, §38.2-4600.
Commissions and other payments, prohibition, §38.2-4614.
Companies which may transact title insurance, §38.2-4603.
Company defined, §38.2-4601.
County manager plan of government.
Purchase of real estate, §15.2-728.
Defined, §38.2-123.
Exchange of information, §38.2-4615.
Filing of forms with state corporation commission, §38.2-4606.
Foreign title insurance companies.
Unearned premium reserve, §38.2-4610.1:1.
Forms to be filed with state corporation commission, §38.2-4606.
Grouping policies into classes, §38.2-4608.
Information exchange, §38.2-4615.
Interim binders, §38.2-4605.
Investigation by commission, §38.2-4615.
Investment in plant and equipment, §38.2-4604.
Kickbacks, §38.2-4614.
Laws applicable, §38.2-4602.
Loss and loss adjustment expense reserve, §38.2-4609.
Total recorded loss reserves, §38.2-4610.2.
Maximum risk, §38.2-4607.
Notification to buyers of availability of owner's title insurance, §38.2-4616.
Plant and equipment, investment in, §38.2-4604.
Rates, §38.2-4608.
Real estate settlements.
Availability of owner's insurance.
Notification to purchaser by settlement agent, §55-525.11.
Settlement agents.
Accounting by insurers acting as agents, §55-525.29.
Generally, §§55-525.16 to 55-525.32.
See REAL ESTATE SETTLEMENTS.
Persons who may act as, §55-525.19.
Title insurance premiums payable to insurer or agent.
Held in agent's settlement escrow account, §55-525.24.

TITLE INSURANCE —Cont'd
Rebates, §38.2-4614.
Release from unearned premium reserve, §38.2-4610.1.
Residential real property transactions.
Notification to buyers of availability of owner's title insurance, §38.2-4616.
Security for policyholders, unearned premium reserve, §38.2-4613.
Single risk, maximum risk assumed, §38.2-4607.
Stock insurers.
Companies which may transact title insurance, §38.2-4603.
Total recorded loss reserves, §38.2-4610.2.
Unearned premium reserve, §§38.2-4610.1, 38.2-4613.
Foreign title insurance companies, §38.2-4610.1:1.

TITLE INSURANCE AGENTS.
Continuing education, §§38.2-1866 to 38.2-1874.
Larcenous acts, report to commission, §38.2-1810.
Licensing of insurance agents generally, §§38.2-1822 to 38.2-1836.1.
Examination required, §38.2-1814.1.
License required, §38.2-1814.1.
Pre-licensing education course, §38.2-1814.1.

TITLES OF NOBILITY, US Const Art I §§9, 10.

TITLING OF MOTOR VEHICLES, §§46.2-616 to 46.2-644.
See MOTOR VEHICLE TITLING.

TJ21.
Virginia higher education opportunity act of 2011, §§23-38.87:10 to 23-38.87:21.
See COLLEGES AND UNIVERSITIES.

TOBACCO.
ABC board.
Tobacco sales records.
Access and inspection, §4.1-103.01.
Attorney general, enforcement of provisions.
Powers of investigators with office of attorney general, §2.2-509.1.
Board of national tobacco trust entity.
Attorney general, service on board, §2.2-515.
Governor may serve on board, §2.2-116.
Burley tobacco.
Fees for sale, §§61.1-55, 61.1-56.
Handling and sale, §61.1-59.
Commingling, §61.1-58.
Enforcement of provisions, §61.1-57.
Information to be accurate and substantiated, §61.1-60.
Moving after weighing, §61.1-58.
Provision violations, §61.1-61.
Cigarette delivery sales, §§18.2-6 to 18.2-15.
See CIGARETTES.
Cigarettes.
Fire-safe cigarettes, §§59.1-293.1 to 59.1-293.9.
See FIRE-SAFE CIGARETTES.
Commission.
Indemnification and community revitalization commission, §§3.2-3100 to 3.2-3111.
Definitions.
Tobacco board, §3.2-2400.
Warehouseman, §61.1-53.
Distributors.
Inspections, access to premises for, §58.1-1021.04:2.
License required, §58.1-1021.04:1.

TOBACCO —Cont'd
Distributors —Cont'd
Purchase of tobacco products for resale, §58.1-1021.04:4.
Recordkeeping requirements, §58.1-1021.04:2.
Rules promulgation, §58.1-1021.04:5.
Unlicensed importation, transportation or possession, §58.1-1021.04:3.
Escrow fund.
Manufacturers' responsibilities.
Assignment and contribution of escrow funds to Commonwealth, §§3.2-4202, 3.2-4203.
Manufactures' responsibilities, §§3.2-4200, 3.2-4201.
Federal tobacco litigation.
Virginia foundation for healthy youth, §§32.1-354 to 32.1-367.
See VIRGINIA FOUNDATION FOR HEALTHY YOUTH.
Fire-safe cigarettes, §§59.1-293.1 to 59.1-293.9.
See FIRE-SAFE CIGARETTES.
Gas pumps.
Smoking in proximity, §46.2-819.4.
Indemnification and community revitalization commission, §§3.2-3100 to 3.2-3111.
Indoor clean air act, §§15.2-2820 to 15.2-2833.
See SMOKING IN PUBLIC PLACES.
Leaf tobacco.
Prevention of frauds in sale, §§61.1-47 to 61.1-54.
Information required where tobacco delivered by person other than grower or landlord, §61.1-48.
Person delivering must impart true name of owner, §61.1-47.
Placing of tickets or cards, §61.1-49.
Inspection of tickets or cards, §61.1-50.
Provision violations, §61.1-51.
Penalties, §61.1-52.
Warehouseman defined, §61.1-53.
Warehouse accounts to be kept, §61.1-40.
Penalty for failure to report sales, §61.1-43.
Lighters.
Sales to minors of novelty lighters prohibited, §18.2-371.4.
Local government personnel.
Use on job, §15.2-1504.
Manufactured tobacco.
False branding, §61.1-44.
Prevention of frauds in sale.
Purpose, §61.1-54.
Master settlement agreement.
Manufacturers' responsibilities, §§3.2-4200 to 3.2-4219.
Assignment and contribution of escrow funds to Commonwealth, §§3.2-4202, 3.2-4203.
Oxygen sources, health care facilities.
Smoking, §18.2-511.1.
Paraphernalia.
Novelty lighters, sales to minors prohibited, §18.2-371.4.
Public assistance.
Temporary assistance for needy families (TANF).
Prohibited uses of benefits, §63.2-621.
Public officers and employees.
Use of tobacco products by state employees, §2.2-2902.
Qualified escrow fund.
Manufacturers' responsibilities, §§3.2-4200, 3.2-4201.
Assignment and contribution of escrow funds to Commonwealth, §§3.2-4202, 3.2-4203.

TOBACCO —Cont'd
Sales to minors, §18.2-371.2.
Novelty lighters, sales to minors prohibited, §18.2-371.4.
Uniform fine schedule, VA SCt Rules 3C:1, 3C:2.
Smoking in proximity to gas pumps, §46.2-819.4.
Smoking in proximity to oxygen sources, health care facilities, §18.2-511.1.
Smoking in public places.
Virginia indoor clean air act, §§15.2-2820 to 15.2-2833.
See SMOKING IN PUBLIC PLACES.
Special license plates celebrating Virginia's tobacco heritage, §46.2-749.5.
Taxation.
Technology industries in tobacco-dependent localities, §§58.1-439.13 to 58.1-439.17.
Tobacco board excise tax, §§3.2-2405 to 3.2-2410.
Tobacco products tax, §§58.1-1021.01 to 58.1-1021.05.
Temporary assistance for needy families (TANF).
Prohibited uses of benefits, §63.2-621.
Tobacco indemnification and community revitalization commission, §§3.2-3100 to 3.2-3111.
Virginia's tobacco heritage.
Special license plates celebrating, §46.2-749.5.
Visually handicapped persons operating newsstands in courthouse.
Locality authorizing operation, §15.2-1805.
Warehouses, §§61.1-38 to 61.1-46.1.
See TOBACCO WAREHOUSES.

TOBACCO BOARD, §§3.2-2400 to 3.2-2411.
Appointment of members, §3.2-2401.
Chairman, §3.2-2404.
Composition, §3.2-2401.
Cooperation with other agricultural organizations, §3.2-2405.
Definitions, §3.2-2400.
Employees, §3.2-2405.
Enforcement of provisions.
Assistance by state and county officers, §3.2-1103.
Excise tax.
Administration of funds, §3.2-2405.
Bright flue-cured tobacco promotion fund, §3.2-2407.
Collection and disposition, §3.2-2408.
Dark-fired tobacco promotion fund, §3.2-2407.1.
Dedicated revenues, diversion, §3.2-1100.
Expenditure of moneys collected, §3.2-2407.
Levy, §3.2-2406.
Payment, §3.2-2408.
Records of tax collected, §3.2-2409.
Unpaid tax collection and interest, §3.2-2410.
Handlers.
Records of tax collected, §3.2-2409.
Maximum charges for tobacco auction warehouse services, §61.1-46.1.
Members, §§3.2-2401 to 3.2-2404.
Production areas of flue-cured tobacco, designation, §3.2-2402.
Terms of office, §3.2-2403.
Vacancies, §3.2-2403.
Violations of provisions, §3.2-2411.
Warehouses.
Records of tax collected, §3.2-2409.

TOBACCO HOGSHEADS.
Vehicles hauling.
Fastening load, §46.2-1155.
Fine for failure to fasten, VA SCt Rule 3B:2.

TOBACCO INDEMNIFICATION AND COMMUNITY REVITALIZATION COMMISSION, §§3.2-3100 to 3.2-3111.
Accounts and accounting.
Form of accounts, §3.2-3109.
Administrative duties, §3.2-3106.
Audits.
Accounts, §3.2-3109.
Chairman, §3.2-3102.
Executive summary, §3.2-3102.
Compensation, §3.2-3102.
Composition, §3.2-3102.
Contracts.
Performance agreements.
Extension of performance period, §11-7.1.
Counsel, §3.2-3105.
Creation, §3.2-3101.
Declaration of public purpose, §3.2-3110.
Defined terms, §3.2-3100.
Endowment fund, §§3.2-3104, 3.2-3106.
Duties, §3.2-3103.
Employees, §3.2-3106.
Executive director.
Appointment, §3.2-3106.
False statements or false claims, §3.2-3107.
Freedom of information act requests.
Grant application to commission.
Excluded records, §2.2-3705.6.
Fund, §3.2-3106.
Distributions from fund, §3.2-3108.
Endowment fund, §§3.2-3104, 3.2-3106.
Limitations on claims, §3.2-3107.
Payments from fund, §3.2-3107.
Grant application to commission.
Freedom of information act requests.
Excluded records, §2.2-3705.6.
Limitations on claims from fund, §3.2-3107.
Meetings.
Closed meetings permitted.
Discussions of records excluded from freedom of information act, §2.2-3711.
Powers, §3.2-3103.
Purpose, §3.2-3101.
Declaration of public purpose, §3.2-3110.
Records of grant applications submitted to commission.
Freedom of information act requests.
Excluded records, §2.2-3705.6.
Research, §3.2-3103.
Secretary of commerce and trade.
Agency responsibility, §2.2-204.
State inspector general.
Powers and duties, §2.2-309.2.
Tax exemption, §3.2-3110.
Technical experts.
Employment, §3.2-3106.
Terms, §3.2-3102.
Vacancies, §3.2-3102.

TOBACCO INDEMNIFICATION AND COMMUNITY REVITALIZATION FUND, §3.2-3106.
Distributions from fund, §3.2-3108.
Endowment fund.
Tobacco indemnification and community revitalization commission, §§3.2-3104, 3.2-3106.
Limitations on claims, §3.2-3107.
Payments from fund, §3.2-3107.

TOBACCO MANUFACTURING FACILITIES.
Litter tax imposed on manufacturers, wholesalers, etc., §58.1-1708.

TOBACCO MANUFACTURING FACILITIES —Cont'd
Minors.
Purchasing or possessing or sales to, §18.2-371.2.
Uniform fine schedule, VA SCt Rules 3C:1, 3C:2.

TOBACCO PRODUCTS MANUFACTURERS' RESPONSIBILITIES, §§3.2-4200 to 3.2-4219.
Certification of compliance with escrow requirement, §3.2-4201.
Civil action for failure to place funds into escrow, §3.2-4201.
Civil penalty for failure to comply, §3.2-4201.
Confidentiality of information filed with attorney general, violation, criminal penalty, §58.1-3.
Definitions, §3.2-4200.
Enforcement of requirements, §3.2-4204.
Directory of cigarettes approved for stamping and sale, §3.2-4206.
Bonds, surety.
Newly-qualified and elevated-risk nonparticipating manufacturers, §3.2-4206.1.
Enforcement of requirements, §§3.2-4204 to 3.2-4219.
Attorney General.
Audits and investigations, authority to conduct, §3.2-4215.1.
Injunctions, power to seek, §3.2-4212.
Recovery of costs and fees, §3.2-4216.
Review of determination to not list or remove from directory, §3.2-4213.
Attorney general.
Injunctions, power to seek, §3.2-4212.
Recovery of costs and fees, §3.2-4216.
Review of determination to not list or remove from directory, §3.2-4213.
Bonds, surety.
Newly-qualified and elevated-risk nonparticipating manufacturers, §3.2-4206.1.
Certifications by manufacturers, §3.2-4205.
Civil penalties, §3.2-4212.
Confiscation and forfeiture of contraband cigarettes, §3.2-4212.
Conflict of laws, §3.2-4218.
Costs and fees.
Recovery by attorney general, §3.2-4216.
Definitions, §3.2-4204.
Directory of cigarettes approved for stamping and sale, §3.2-4206.
Bonds, surety.
Newly-qualified and elevated-risk nonparticipating manufacturers, §3.2-4206.1.
Prohibition against stamping or sale or import of cigarettes not in, §3.2-4207.
Removal of listing, §3.2-4207.
Review of determination to not list or remove from directory, §3.2-4213.
Disgorgement of profits for violations, §3.2-4217.
English language.
Pleadings in English sufficient, §3.2-4215.
False statements.
Materially false statements, §3.2-4219.
Importation of cigarettes.
Prohibition against certain imports, §3.2-4207.
Information to be submitted, §§3.2-4209, 3.2-4210.
Additional information required, §3.2-4209.1.
Injunctions, §3.2-4212.

TOBACCO PRODUCTS MANUFACTURERS' RESPONSIBILITIES —Cont'd
Enforcement of requirements —Cont'd
Investigators with office of attorney general, §2.2-509.1.
Jurisdiction.
Submission to jurisdiction of Commonwealth, §3.2-4215.
Materially false statements, §3.2-4219.
Misdemeanors, §3.2-4212.
Nonparticipating manufacturers.
Agent for service of process, §3.2-4208.
Certifications by, §3.2-4205.
Defined, §3.2-4204.
Joint and several liability, §3.2-4208.1.
Penalties, §3.2-4212.
Presumptions, §3.2-4217.1.
Qualified escrow fund.
Information to be provided, §3.2-4210.
Regulations, §3.2-4214.
Remedies, §3.2-4212.
Disgorgement of profits for violations, §3.2-4217.
Revocation or suspension of privilege to purchase stamps at discounted rate, §3.2-4212.
Service of notice, process and other papers.
Agent for service, §3.2-4208.
Stamping agents.
Information to be submitted by, §3.2-4209.
Additional information required, §3.2-4209.1.
Freedom of information act.
Investigations by attorney general.
Records excluded from act's application, §2.2-3705.3.
Investigations by attorney general.
Freedom of information act.
Records excluded from act's application, §2.2-3705.3.
Joint and several liability.
Nonparticipating manufacturers, §3.2-4208.1.
Master settlement agreement.
Defined, §3.2-4200.
Required to become participating manufacturer, §3.2-4201.
Prohibition from selling cigarettes to consumers.
Second violation, §3.2-4201.
Qualified escrow fund, §3.2-4200.
Assignment and contribution of escrow funds to Commonwealth, §§3.2-4202, 3.2-4203.
Enforcement of requirements.
Information to be provided, §3.2-4210.
Required to placed funds into, §3.2-4201.
Release of funds from escrow, §3.2-4201.
Requirements generally, §3.2-4201.

TOBACCO PRODUCTS TAX, §§58.1-1021.01 to 58.1-1021.05.
Defined terms, §58.1-1021.01.
Distributors.
Inspections, access to premises for, §58.1-1021.04:2.
License required, §58.1-1021.04:1.
Purchase of tobacco products for resale, §58.1-1021.04:4.
Recordkeeping requirements, §58.1-1021.04:2.
Rules promulgation, §58.1-1021.04:5.
Unlicensed importation, transportation or possession, §58.1-1021.04:3.
Imposition, §58.1-1021.02.
Manufacturers' reports, §58.1-1021.02:1.

TOBACCO PRODUCTS TAX —Cont'd
Payment, §58.1-1021.03.
Overpayment, §58.1-1021.04.
Use of revenues, §58.1-1021.05.
Rate, §58.1-1021.02.
Returns, §58.1-1021.03.
Failure to file, §58.1-1021.04.
Fraudulent returns, §58.1-1021.04.
Rules promulgation, §58.1-1021.04:5.

TOBACCO QUOTA HOLDERS OR PRODUCERS OF QUOTA TOBACCO.
Income tax deduction.
Contract payments to under American Jobs Creation Act, §§58.1-322, 58.1-402.

TOBACCO SETTLEMENT.
Master settlement, §§3.2-4200 to 3.2-4219.
Assignment and contribution of escrow funds to Commonwealth, §§3.2-4202, 3.2-4203.
Virginia foundation for healthy youth, §§32.1-354 to 32.1-367.
See VIRGINIA FOUNDATION FOR HEALTHY YOUTH.

TOBACCO WAREHOUSES, §§61.1-38 to 61.1-46.1.
Agricultural cooperative association marketing contract.
Warehouse soliciting or permitting member of association to breach, §13.1-329.
Burley tobacco.
Fees for sale, §§61.1-55, 61.1-56.
Handling and sale.
Commingling, §61.1-58.
Information to be accurate and substantiated, §61.1-60.
Moving after weighing, §61.1-58.
Provision violations.
Penalty, §61.1-61.
Sales, §61.1-59.
Discontinuance, §61.1-38.
Establishment, §61.1-38.
False branding of manufactured tobacco, §61.1-44.
Flue-cured tobacco.
Charges in sale and handling, §61.1-46.1.
Insurance.
Publication, §61.1-46.
Itemized list of charges, §61.1-39.
Leaf tobacco.
Placing of tickets or cards, §61.1-49.
Inspections, §61.1-50.
Provision violations, §§61.1-51, 61.1-52.
Leaf tobacco accounts, §61.1-40.
Penalty for failure to report sales, §61.1-43.
Marketing contract executed by agricultural cooperative association members.
Warehouse soliciting or permitting member to breach, §13.1-329.
Nesting, §61.1-45.
Receipts of warehouses generally, §§61.1-2 to 61.1-6.
See WAREHOUSE RECEIPTS.
Records, §61.1-42.
Leaf tobacco.
Information required where tobacco delivered by person other than grower or landlord, §61.1-48.
Record of purchase or delivery, §61.1-47.
Reports, §61.1-41.

TOBOGGANING.
Winter sports safety act, §§8.01-227.11 to 8.01-227.23.
See WINTER SPORTS SAFETY ACT.

TOD SECURITY REGISTRATION.
Acceptance of request for registration in beneficiary form, §64.2-617.
Applicable laws on registering beneficiary form, §64.2-613.
Cancellation of registration in beneficiary form, §64.2-615.
Change of registration in beneficiary form, §64.2-615.
Conditions for registration, §64.2-619.
Creditors' rights against beneficiaries and other transferees, §64.2-618.
Discharge of registering entity from claim to security, §64.2-617.
Disclaimer of property interests.
Disclaimer of beneficiary designation, §64.2-2610.
Effect of registering in beneficiary form, §64.2-615.
Examples, §64.2-619.
Form of registration in beneficiary form, §64.2-615.
Joint tenancy ownership, registration in beneficiary form, §64.2-613.
LDPS.
Substituting name to beneficiary's decedents, §64.2-619.
Lineal descendants per stirpes.
Substituting named beneficiary's decedents, §64.2-619.
Nontestamentary transfer on death, §64.2-618.
Origination of registration in beneficiary form, §64.2-614.
Ownership on death of owner, §64.2-616.
Protection of registering entity, §64.2-617.
Sole ownership, registration in beneficiary form, §64.2-613.
Substituting named beneficiary's decedents, §64.2-619.
Survivorship.
Ownership on death of owner, §64.2-616.
Terms for registration, §64.2-619.
When security registered in beneficiary form, §64.2-614.
Words indicating registration in beneficiary form, §64.2-615.

TOILET FACILITIES IN PUBLIC GATHERING PLACES, §§32.1-198 to 32.1-202.

TOLL BRIDGES, §§33.1-255 to 33.1-266.
Applicability of chapter, §33.1-266.
Approval of plans by board, §33.1-262.
Ascertainment of right to demand tolls, §33.1-257.
Automatic vehicle identification system, §§46.2-819.1, 46.2-819.3.
Video-monitoring systems.
Installed in conjunction with, §46.2-819.3:1.
Cessation of privilege, §33.1-255.
Construction of chapter, §33.1-266.
Costs of construction, §33.1-262.
Failure to pay toll, §46.2-819.
Administrative fee.
Recovery of expenses for collecting unpaid toll, §46.2-819.3.
Civil penalty, §46.2-819.3.
Invoice for failure to pay, §§46.2-819.6, 46.2-819.7.
Proof by use of photo-monitoring system, §§46.2-819.1, 46.2-819.3.
Proof by use of video-monitoring system, §46.2-819.3:1.

TOLL BRIDGES —Cont'd
Fish.
Bridge not to obstruct fish, §33.1-256.
Fixing or changing rates.
Determining, §33.1-257.
Free use of toll bridges, etc.
State officers and employees, §33.1-252.
Information derived from automatic electronic toll collection system.
Disclosure of information as to individually identified motor vehicle.
Prohibition, exception, injunction or mandamus by aggrieved person, §33.1-252.2.
Inspection, §33.1-262.
Navigable waters.
Bridge not to obstruct navigation, §33.1-256.
Permission required to erect or maintain over navigable water, §33.1-261.
Obstruction of navigation or fish, §33.1-256.
Photo-monitoring system, §§46.2-819.1, 46.2-819.3.
Special police.
Appointment, §33.1-258.
Qualifications, §33.1-259.
Salary and fees, §33.1-260.
State purchase of toll bridges, §§33.1-264, 33.1-265.
Transportation infrastructure bank, §§33.1-23.6 to 33.1-23.13.
Video-monitoring system, §46.2-819.3:1.
Woodrow Wilson bridge and tunnel compact, §33.1-320.2.

TOLL FACILITIES REVOLVING ACCOUNT.
Allocation of highway funds, §33.1-23.03:4.

TOLL FACILITY OPERATORS.
Vehicle owner data.
Commissioner of DMV.
Supplying operator upon request, §46.2-208.

TOLL-FREE TELEPHONE NUMBERS.
Charitable gaming organizations.
Gamblers anonymous toll-free number to be posted, §18.2-340.19.
Commissioner of social services.
Complaints against adult or child care agencies, §63.2-1728.
Consumer counsel, division of.
Programs to facilitate resolution of complaints, §2.2-517.
Department of health.
Services provided by department for the aging, §32.1-23.1.
Firearm licensing.
Criminal record checks, §52-4.4.
Human trafficking hotline.
Employers who must post notice regarding, §40.1-11.3.
Ignition interlock system manufacturers or distributors, §18.2-270.2.
Insurance bureau.
Content requirements of policies, §38.2-305.
Lottery tickets.
Gamblers anonymous or other compulsive gambler organization, §58.1-4007.1.
Pari-mutuel wagering licensees.
Posting number of gamblers anonymous or other compulsive gambler organizations, §59.1-369.

TOLL ROAD AUTHORITIES.
Chesterfield county toll road authority, 1980 ch 619.

TOLL ROAD CORPORATION OF VIRGINIA.
Virginia highway corporation act of 1988, §§56-535 to 56-552.
See HIGHWAY CORPORATIONS.

TOLL ROADS.
Applicability of motor vehicles title, §46.2-101.
Automatic vehicle identification system, §§46.2-819.1, 46.2-819.3.
Dulles access highway, §46.2-819.5.
Video-monitoring system installed in conjunction with, §46.2-819.3:1.
Dulles access highway.
Photo-monitoring system or automatic vehicle identification system.
Enforcement through use of, §46.2-819.5.
Failure to pay toll, §46.2-819.
Administrative fee.
Recovery of expenses for collecting unpaid toll, §46.2-819.3.
Civil penalty, §46.2-819.3.
Invoice for failure to pay, §§46.2-819.6, 46.2-819.7.
Proof by use of photo-monitoring system, §§46.2-819.1, 46.2-819.3.
Dulles access highway, §46.2-819.5.
Proof by use of video-monitoring system, §46.2-819.3:1.
Summons issued, §46.2-819.3:1.
Vehicle owner data.
Commissioner of DMV supplying facility operator, §46.2-208.
High-occupancy toll lanes, §§33.1-56.1 to 33.1-56.5.
Highway corporations, §§56-535 to 56-552.
HOT lanes.
High-occupancy toll lanes, §§33.1-56.1 to 33.1-56.5.
Information derived from automatic electronic toll collection system.
Disclosure of information as to individually identified motor vehicle.
Prohibition, exception, injunction or mandamus by aggrieved person, §33.1-252.2.
Interstate highway system.
Tolls for use of interstate highway system components, §33.1-23.03:10.
Leasing or rental companies.
Notice of failure to pay toll.
Proof by use of video-monitoring system, §46.2-819.3:1.
Owner contesting invoice on grounds that another was operating vehicle, §46.2-819.3:1.
Payment after receiving invoice for failure to pay.
Proof by video-monitoring system, §46.2-819.3:1.
Photo-monitoring system, §§46.2-819.1, 46.2-819.3.
Dulles access highway, §46.2-819.5.
Public-private transportation act, §§56-556 to 56-574.
Route 81, prior approval for imposition or collection of tolls, §33.1-23.03:10.
School buses.
Exemption from payment of tolls, §22.1-187.
Tolls may vary to encourage off-peak hours travel, §33.1-223.2:12.
Transportation infrastructure bank, §§33.1-23.6 to 33.1-23.13.
Video-monitoring system, §46.2-819.3:1.

TOMBS.
Vandalism, §18.2-127.
Civil action to recover damages, §8.01-44.6.

TOOLS.
Machinery and tools tax, §§58.1-3507, 58.1-3508.

TOP JOBS ACT.
Virginia higher education opportunity act of 2011, §§23-38.87:10 to 23-38.87:21.
See COLLEGES AND UNIVERSITIES.

TOPLESS ENTERTAINMENT.
Human trafficking hotline.
Employers who must post notice regarding, §40.1-11.3.

TOP PERSON.
Coal mines.
Certification, §§45.1-161.24 to 45.1-161.41.
Employment and duties, §45.1-161.250.

TORNADOES.
Emergency management and disaster law generally, §§44-146.13 to 44-146.28.
See EMERGENCY MANAGEMENT.
Schools and education, drills in, §22.1-137.1.

TORRENS SYSTEM.
Acts establishing continued in force, §55-112.

TORT CLAIMS ACT.
Baseball stadium authority.
Applicability of provisions, §15.2-5818.
Claims evaluation program, §8.01-195.9.
Definitions, §8.01-195.2.
Effective date of act, §8.01-195.3.
Jurisdiction of claims under act, §8.01-195.4.
Notice of claim, §8.01-195.6.
Recovery of claims against the state, §§8.01-192 to 8.01-195.
Release of claims, §8.01-195.8.
Right to jury trial, §8.01-195.4.
Service of notice, process and other papers, §8.01-195.4.
Settlement of claims, §8.01-195.5.
Short title, §8.01-195.1.
Statute of limitations, §§8.01-195.6, 8.01-195.7.
Transportation districts.
Liability of districts, §15.2-4533.
Venue.
Preferred venue, §8.01-261.

TORTS.
Advertising.
Unsolicited facsimile transmissions, §8.01-40.2.
Attorneys.
Loss of debts or money, §64.2-1415.
Attorneys' fees.
Lien for fees, §54.1-3932.
Baseball stadium authority liability, §15.2-5817.
Birth-related neurological injury compensation, §§38.2-5000 to 38.2-5021.
See BIRTH-RELATED NEUROLOGICAL INJURY COMPENSATION.
Cities.
Tort claims for damages.
Notice to be given counties, cities and towns, §15.2-209.
Claims against the state.
Sovereign immunity.
See SOVEREIGN IMMUNITY.
Tort claims act, §§8.01-195.1 to 8.01-195.9.
See TORT CLAIMS ACT.

TORTS —Cont'd
Claims against the state —Cont'd
Wrongful incarceration for a felony conviction, compensation, §§8.01-195.10 to 8.01-195.12.
Claims against the United States.
Medical services provided by the federal government, §8.01-37.1.
Collection of money payable to the state.
Generally, §§8.01-196 to 8.01-216.
See STATE.
Comparative negligence.
Bank deposits and collections.
Unauthorized signature or alteration, §8.4-406.
Negotiable instruments.
Forged or altered instrument, §§8.3A-405, 8.4-406.
Railroad signs.
Failure to give, §56-416.
Computer crimes.
Action for injury to person or property, §8.01-44.5.
Condominiums, §55-79.80:1.
Confidential communications.
Qualified interpreters and communications assistants.
Divulgence of communications, §8.01-44.3.
Contractors.
Independent contractors.
Completion or acceptance of work not bar to tort action against, §8.01-39.
Contribution among tortfeasors.
When enforced, §8.01-34.
Contributory negligence.
See CONTRIBUTORY NEGLIGENCE.
Conversion.
Drift property, §55-209.
Estrays, §55-209.
Counties.
Tort claims for damages.
Notice to be given counties, cities and towns, §15.2-209.
Custodial trusts.
Liability of trustee, §64.2-911.
Damages.
Generally.
See DAMAGES.
Limitation on recovery of punitive damages, §8.01-38.1.
Loss of income not diminished by reimbursement, §8.01-35.
Defamation.
See DEFAMATION.
Dram shop liability not Virginia law, §4.1-304.
Drift property.
Conversion, §55-209.
Trover, §55-209.
Driving intoxicated.
Exemplary damages for persons injured by, §8.01-44.5.
Dry cleaners.
Loss or injury to clothing, §8.01-42.
Dyeing clothing.
Loss or injury in process, §8.01-42.
Electric authorities.
Tort claims against certain authorities, §15.2-5406.2.
Emancipated minors.
Recovery of lost wages, §8.01-37.
Employee theft, §8.01-44.4.
Estrays.
Conversion, §55-209.
Trover, §55-209.

TORTS —Cont'd
Ethnic intimidation, §8.01-42.1.
Fiduciaries.
Loss of debts or money, §64.2-1415.
Fishing, inland waters.
Landowners' duty of care, §29.1-509.
Fraud and deceit.
See FRAUD.
Governmental tort immunity.
Tort claims act.
General provisions, §§8.01-195.1 to 8.01-195.9.
See TORT CLAIMS ACT.
Guardians.
Transfers to minors.
Custodians.
Liability to third persons, §64.2-1916.
Ward liability, §64.2-1916.
Hate crimes, §8.01-42.1.
HIV.
Confidentiality of tests, §32.1-36.1.
Hospitals.
Charitable or tax exempt institutions, liability, §8.01-38.
Tort liability.
Immunity from civil liability, §8.01-44.1.
Hotels.
Liability of guests for hotel damage, §8.01-42.2.
Loss or injury to clothing in dry cleaning or laundering, §8.01-42.
Hunting.
Deer.
Blaze orange clothing requirement, §29.1-530.1.
Landowners' duty of care, §29.1-509.
Husband and wife.
Actions by and against married women, §§55-36, 55-37.
Infant, personal injury to.
Joinder of action of tort to infant.
Action for recovery of expenses incurred, §8.01-36.
Lien for expenses in attempt to cure infant of injuries, §8.01-36.
Limitation of time for commencing action, §8.01-243.
Interspousal tort immunity.
Defense abolished, §8.01-220.1.
Intoxicated drivers.
Exemplary damages for persons injured by, §8.01-44.5.
Invasion of privacy.
Unauthorized use of name or picture, §8.01-40.
John Doe actions.
Owner or operator of vehicle causing injury or damage unknown, §38.2-2206.
Joinder of action of tort to infant.
Action for recovery of expenses, §8.01-36.
Junk fax.
Unsolicited facsimile transmissions, §8.01-40.2.
Laundries.
Loss or injury to clothing, §8.01-42.
Limitation of actions, §8.01-243.
Accrual of personal actions, §8.01-249.
Accrual of right of action, §8.01-230.
Actions for which no limitation specified, §8.01-248.
Limited liability companies.
Third-party liability of members.
No personal liability, §13.1-1019.
Loss wages.
Recovery in action for injuries to emancipated infant, §8.01-37.

TORTS —Cont'd
Malpractice.
Human sterilization, §54.1-2979.
Medical malpractice.
Birth-related neurological injury compensation, §§38.2-5000 to 38.2-5021.
General provisions, §§8.01-581.1 to 8.01-581.20.
See MEDICAL MALPRACTICE.
Medical services.
Claims for medical services provided by United States, §8.01-37.1.
Metering devices of public services or utilities.
Tampering with, §8.01-44.7.
Metropolitan Washington airports authority.
Liability, §5.1-173.
Minors.
Emancipated minors.
Recovery of lost wages, §8.01-37.
Joinder of action of tort to infant.
Action for recovery of expenses incurred, §8.01-36.
Transfers to minors.
Liability to third persons, §64.2-1916.
Negligence.
See NEGLIGENCE.
Oil discharges, §62.1-44.34:20.
Good Samaritan liability for assistance in containment and cleanup, §62.1-44.34:18.
Partnerships.
Liability of partnership for partner's actionable conduct, §50-73.95.
Personal injuries.
Accrual of right of action, §8.01-230.
Pleading.
Tort and contract claims, §8.01-272.
Products liability.
See PRODUCTS LIABILITY.
Punitive damages.
See PUNITIVE DAMAGES.
Racial intimidation, §8.01-42.1.
Railroad corporations.
Employee injuries.
Liability for, §56-441.
Enclosed tracks.
Liability for injury on, §56-431.
Liability for damage from fires set by engines or trains, §56-428.
Non-enclosed tracks.
Liability for injuries, §56-432.
Real estate cooperatives.
Liability, §55-468.
Recreational activities.
Landowners' duty of care, §29.1-509.
Religious intimidation, §8.01-42.1.
Rescission of release of liability in personal injury action or claim.
Release executed as condition of settlement, §8.01-425.1.
Right of action.
Violation of statutory duty, §8.01-221.
Secured transactions.
Secured party not obligated in tort, §8.9A-402.
Shoplifting and employee theft, §8.01-44.4.
Snow removal from public highways by private entities.
Liability, §33.1-200.2.
Sovereign immunity.
See SOVEREIGN IMMUNITY.
Statute of limitations, §8.01-243.
Accrual of actions, §8.01-249.
Accrual of right of action, §8.01-230.

TORTS —Cont'd
Statute of limitations —Cont'd
Actions for which no limitation specified, §8.01-248.
Third party standing.
Custodial trusts, §64.2-911.
Tort claims act.
Claims against the state, §§8.01-195.1 to 8.01-195.9.
See TORT CLAIMS ACT.
Towns.
Tort claims for damages.
Notice to be given counties, cities and towns, §15.2-209.
Trade secrets.
Conflict of laws, §59.1-341.
Transfers to minors.
Custodians.
Liability to third persons, §64.2-1916.
Transportation districts, §§33.1-421, 33.1-442.
Liability of Commonwealth, counties or cities, §15.2-4526.
Liability of districts, §15.2-4533.
Trapping.
Landowners' duty of care, §29.1-509.
Trespass generally.
See TRESPASS.
Trover.
Drift property, §55-209.
Estrays, §55-209.
Unauthorized use of name or picture, §8.01-40.
Universities and colleges.
Immunity from civil liability, §8.01-44.1.
Unsolicited facsimile transmissions, §8.01-40.2.
Vaccine-related injury or death, §8.01-44.2.
Wages.
Recovery of lost wages.
Action for injuries to emancipated infant, §8.01-37.
Watercraft, personal.
Operation restriction violations, §29.1-748.
Workers' compensation, §§65.2-100 to 65.2-1310.
See WORKERS' COMPENSATION.
Workers' compensation insurance.
Required.
Effect, §65.2-800.
Wrongful death.
General provisions, §§8.01-50 to 8.01-56.
See WRONGFUL DEATH.
Wrongful distraint or attachment, §8.01-41.

TOTAL DISABILITY.
Sickness and disability program for state employees.
Generally, §§51.1-1100 to 51.1-1140.
See SICKNESS AND DISABILITY PROGRAM.

TOUR BUSES.
Sight-seeing carriers.
Certificate of public convenience and necessity.
Requirement of certificate, §46.2-2099.4.
Defined, §46.2-2000.
Refusal of service, §46.2-2099.11.
Routes.
Specific routes authorized, §46.2-2099.5.
Tickets, §46.2-2099.5.

TOUR GUIDES.
Locality regulating, §15.2-946.

TOURISM.
Agritourism activity liability, §§3.2-6400 to 3.2-6402.

TOURISM —Cont'd
Blue Ridge regional tourism council, §§2.2-2609, 2.2-2610.
Excursion trains, §§46.2-2099.41 to 46.2-2099.44.
Assignment of liability, §46.2-2099.42.
Notice on tickets, §46.2-2099.43.
Certification, §46.2-2099.41.
Defined, §46.2-2000.
Liability of operator, §46.2-2099.42.
Notice on tickets, §46.2-2099.43.
Railroad companies.
Use of company facilities, §46.2-2099.42.
Tickets.
Notice on tickets, §46.2-2099.43.
Fishing, tidal waters.
Marine tourism activity liability, §§28.2-1105 to 28.2-1107.
License plates.
Special license plates promoting tourism on Virginia's Eastern Shore, §46.2-749.7:3.
Localities promoting resources and advantages, §15.2-940.
Local tourism zones.
Establishment, tax incentives, regulatory flexibility.
City, county, town authority, §58.1-3851.
Tax revenues, entitlement, §58.1-3851.1.
Power to designate, §15.2-982.
Marine tourism activity liability, §§28.2-1105 to 28.2-1107.
Defined terms, §28.2-1105.
Limitations on liability, §28.2-1106.
Warning required, §28.2-1107.
Residential property transfer disclosures.
Permissive disclosure, tourism activity zone, §55-519.3.
Sight-seeing carriers.
Generally.
See SIGHT-SEEING CARRIERS.
Southwest Virginia cultural heritage foundation, §§2.2-2734 to 2.2-2737.
Tourism financing development authority, §§15.2-5516 to 15.2-5522.

TOURISM AUTHORITY, §§2.2-2315 to 2.2-2327.
Accounts and accounting.
Funds of authority, §2.2-2323.
Advertising, §2.2-2318.
Audits.
Accounts and accounting, §2.2-2323.
Board of directors, §2.2-2316.
Contracts.
Performance agreements.
Extension of performance period, §11-7.1.
Powers and duties, §2.2-2318.
Cooperative marketing fund.
Administration and management, §2.2-2319.
Cooperative tourism advertising fund.
Administration and management, §2.2-2318.
Creation, §2.2-2315.
Executive director, §§2.2-2316, 2.2-2317.
Experts.
Authority to employ, §2.2-2318.
Film industry.
Duty to encourage, stimulate and support, §2.2-2318.
Funds of authority.
Accounts and accounting, §2.2-2323.
Authorized investments, §2.2-2322.
Secured deposits, §2.2-2322.

TOURISM AUTHORITY —Cont'd
Governor's motion picture opportunity fund.
Administration and management, §2.2-2318.
Creation and purposes, §2.2-2320.
Grants.
Authority to receive, §§2.2-2318, 2.2-2321.
Insurance.
Authority to obtain, §2.2-2318.
Liberal construction of provisions, §2.2-2327.
Members, §2.2-2316.
Officers, §2.2-2316.
Periodicals.
Authority to issue and carry and charge for advertising, §2.2-2318.
Personnel administration system.
Exemption from act, §2.2-2325.
Powers and duties.
Authority, §2.2-2318.
Executive director, §2.2-2317.
Public procurement.
Exemption from act, §2.2-2325.
Purpose, §2.2-2315.
Records.
Executive director.
Powers and duties, §2.2-2317.
Reports.
Annual report, §2.2-2323.
Seals and sealed instruments.
Powers and duties, §2.2-2318.
Secretary of commerce and trade.
Agency responsibility, §2.2-204.
Short title, §2.2-2315.
Sovereign immunity, §2.2-2326.
Tax exemptions, §2.2-2324.

TOURISM CORPORATION.
Southwest Virginia cultural heritage foundation.
Board of trustees, §2.2-2735.

TOURISM DEVELOPMENT AUTHORITY.
Buchanan county tourist train development authority, §§15.2-6700 to 15.2-6704.
LENOWISCO and Cumberland plateau planning district commissions, §§15.2-5500 to 15.2-5508.
Southside Virginia, §§15.2-5509 to 15.2-5515.

TOURISM FINANCING DEVELOPMENT AUTHORITY, §§15.2-5516 to 15.2-5522.
Board of directors, §15.2-5518.
Dissolution of authority.
Resolution, §15.2-5521.
Citation of act, §15.2-5516.
Conflict of laws.
Provisions controlling, §15.2-5522.
Creation, §15.2-5517.
Dissolution, §15.2-5521.
Expenses.
Liability for payment, §15.2-5520.
Liability, §15.2-5520.
Powers, §15.2-5519.
Records.
Board of directors, §15.2-5518.
Severability of provisions, §15.2-5522.
Status, §15.2-5517.
Title of act, §15.2-5516.

TOURISM ZONES.
Establishment, tax incentives, regulatory flexibility.
City, county, town authority, §58.1-3851.
Tax revenues, entitlement, §58.1-3851.1.

TOURISM ZONES —Cont'd
Power to designate, §15.2-982.

TOURIST CAMPS.
Retail sales and use tax.
Service exemptions, §58.1-609.5.
Water quality tests at recreational facilities, §32.1-248.1.

TOURIST GUIDES.
Locality regulating, §15.2-946.

TOUTING, §59.1-398.

TOW DOLLY.
Not considered vehicle, §46.2-1119.
Optional registration, §46.2-648.1.

TOWERS.
Sale or lease of state property for communications towers, §2.2-1151.
State police communication tower or site.
Lease or conveyance of interest in, §2.2-1150.1.
Wireless broadband services in unserved areas.
Lease or conveyance of license to providers of interest in state owned communications to towers.
State department, agency, institution responsible for tower, §2.2-1150.2.

TOWING VEHICLES.
Accident or emergency scene.
Tow trucks en route to or from.
Exemption from certain traffic regulations, §46.2-920.1.
Brakes on trailers, §46.2-1070.
Bridge or culvert.
Crossing by vehicle weighing more than weight limit, §46.2-1130.
Combination vehicles being towed in emergencies.
Permissible lengths, §46.2-1153.
Complaints against tow truck drivers, §46.2-119.
Connection between vehicles.
Requirements, §46.2-1118.
Consumer counsel, division of.
Consumer complaints regarding towing of vehicles, §2.2-517.
County manager plan of government.
Removal or immobilization of trespassing vehicles, §15.2-719.
Criminal justice services department.
Tow truck operators, registration, §§9.1-102, 46.2-116.
Prohibited acts, §46.2-118.
Revocation or suspension of registration, §46.2-117.
Escape of vehicle contents.
Failure to prevent, §§46.2-1155, 46.2-1156.
Fine schedule, VA SCt Rule 3B:2.
Maximum fine for violating Title 46.2, §46.2-113.
Flag or light at end of load, §46.2-1121.
Flashing amber warning lights, §46.2-1025.
Flashing high-intensity amber warning lights, §46.2-1026.
Flashing of headlights, §46.2-1029.1.
House trailer or camping trailer.
Occupancy prohibited, §46.2-813.
Immunity from liability, §46.2-1231.1.
Improper towing, §§46.2-1116, 46.2-1118.
Inoperable motor vehicles on residential or commercial property.
Ordinances restricting keeping of vehicles.
Removal by localities, §§15.2-904, 15.2-905.

TOWING VEHICLES —Cont'd
Length of vehicles.
Combination vehicles being towed in emergencies, §46.2-1153.
Exceptions in case of breakdown, §46.2-1154.
Load extending too far beyond front, §46.2-1120.
Load extending too far beyond side, §46.2-1111.
Motor vehicle equipment.
Lettering on tow trucks, §46.2-1076.
Motor vehicle registration, §46.2-649.1.
Municipal powers.
Motor vehicle and traffic regulation generally, §§46.2-1300 to 46.2-1314.
See LOCAL GOVERNMENT.
Municipal regulation of towing fees, §§46.2-1233 to 46.2-1233.2.
Advisory board, §46.2-1233.2.
Authority to regulate, §46.2-1233.
Limitation on charges for certain vehicles, §46.2-1233.1.
Ordinances.
Authority of localities to regulate certain towing, §46.2-1217.
Parking.
Disabled or handicapped, §46.2-1246.
Ordinances prohibiting or limiting, §46.2-1224.
Removal or immobilization of vehicles for outstanding parking violations, §46.2-1216.
Parking lot owners or operators, §46.2-1231.
Passenger vehicles towing certain trailers.
Fine schedule, VA SCt Rule 3B:2.
Maximum fine for violating Title 46.2, §46.2-113.
Maximum speed limit, §46.2-876.
Prepayment of fine, §16.1-69.40:1.
Police-requested towing, §46.2-1217.
Pretrial payment of fine, §16.1-69.40:1.
Prohibited acts, §46.2-118.
Registration of tow truck operators.
Complaints against, §46.2-119.
Criminal justice services department, §§9.1-102, 46.2-116.
Prohibited acts, §46.2-118.
Revocation or suspension of registration, §46.2-117.
Tow truck defined, §46.2-1118.
Unlicensed or uninspected vehicles, §46.2-1150.
Vehicle exceeding weight limitations, §§46.2-1123 to 46.2-1127.
Fine schedule, VA SCt Rule 3B:2.
Gross weight, §46.2-1126.
Interstate highways, §46.2-1127.
Maximum fine for violating Title 46.2, §46.2-113.
Pretrial payment of fine, §16.1-69.40:1.
Single axle weight, §46.2-1124.
Tandem axle weight, §46.2-1125.
Vehicles designed for towing disabled vehicles, §46.2-1151.
Weighing certain tow trucks, §46.2-1152.
Weight of vehicles and loads, §46.2-1123.
Weight per inch of tire width, §46.2-1124.
Vehicles owned and controlled by towing and recovery business but not tow trucks.
Flashing amber warning lights, §46.2-1025.
Wheel lift apparatus.
Tow trucks towing vehicles by, §46.2-1118.

TOWN ADMINISTRATORS.
Chief administrative officer.
Appointment and duties, §§15.2-1540, 15.2-1541.

TOWN AIRPORTS.
Generally, §§5.1-31 to 5.1-47.
See AIRPORTS.

TOWN ATTORNEYS.
Authorized, appointment, salary and duties, §15.2-1542.
Defense of localities and political subdivisions, governing bodies, officers or employees, §15.2-1520.
Manufactured home lot rental.
Injunctive relief powers, §55-248.52.

TOWN BONDS.
Debt limitation, VA Const Art VII §10.
Tax increment financing.
Blighted areas, §§58.1-3245 to 58.1-3245.5.

TOWN CLERKS.
Appointing or designating, §§15.2-1536, 15.2-1538.
General duties, §15.2-1539.

TOWN COUNCILS.
Clerk for governing body.
Appointment, §15.2-1538.
Duties, §15.2-1539.
Required officers, §15.2-1536.
Election, §24.2-222.
Alternative election by ordinance, §24.2-222.1.
Economic interest statement as requirement of candidate, §24.2-502.
Governing bodies generally, VA Const Art VII §5.
Independent candidates' petition of candidacy.
Number of signatures required, §24.2-506.
Primary candidates' petition of candidacy.
Number of signatures required, §24.2-521.
Governing bodies of localities generally, §§15.2-1400 to 15.2-1433.
See LOCALITIES.
Mayor.
Alternative election by ordinance, §24.2-222.1.
Meetings of governmental bodies generally, §§15.2-1415 to 15.2-1421.
See LOCALITIES.
Militia duty exemption, §44-5.
Ordinance appropriating money, borrowing money or imposing tax.
Affirmative vote of majority of governing body required, VA Const Art VII §7.
Public officers from office generally, §§24.2-230 to 24.2-238.
Ordinances and other actions by local governing bodies.
Generally, §§15.2-1425 to 15.2-1433.
See ORDINANCES.
Salaries, §15.2-1414.7.
Special license plates, §46.2-736.2.
Taxes.
Council to make, §58.1-3005.
Special levies to pay interest and retire bonds, §58.1-3006.
Two-third vote required, §15.2-1427.
Term, §24.2-222.
Interim appointment, §24.2-228.
Special election to fill, §24.2-226.
Time to qualify and give bond if required, §24.2-229.

TOWN ELECTIONS.
Annexation.
Elections in town following annexation, §15.2-3226.

TOWN ELECTIONS —Cont'd
Annulment of charter, §§15.2-3704, 15.2-3705.
Bonds issued by locality, §§15.2-2610, 15.2-2611.
Change of city to town.
City no longer qualifying for city status.
Town council and other elected officers, §15.2-4005.
Town council and other elected officers, §15.2-4115.
Charters, §15.2-201.
Consolidation of counties, cities or towns into single county or city, §§15.2-3538 to 15.2-3540.
Consolidation of like units of local government.
Conduct of election, §15.2-3506.
Election of town officers after consolidation approved, §15.2-3509.
Order for election, §15.2-3505.
Result of election, §15.2-3507.
Constitutional and local officers generally, §§24.2-217 to 24.2-224.
Contest of elections generally, §§24.2-803 to 24.2-814.
Control of election process.
Electoral board and general registrar of county within which town situated, §24.2-601.
Costs paid by town, §24.2-600.
Governing bodies generally, VA Const Art VII §5.
Incorporation of towns by judicial proceedings.
First elections, §15.2-3604.
Local electoral boards generally, §§24.2-106 to 24.2-109.
See ELECTIONS.
Precinct requirements, §24.2-308.
Reapportionment.
Governing body elected by district, decennial reapportionment, VA Const Art VII §5.
Referendum elections.
Calling, ascertaining results and certifying generally, §24.2-684.
Reversion of city to town.
City no longer qualifying for city status.
Town council and other elected officers, §15.2-4005.
Town council and other elected officers, §15.2-4115.
Town granted city status, §15.2-3801.
Vacancies in elected constitutional and local offices generally, §§24.2-225 to 24.2-229.1.

TOWN EXECUTIVES.
Chief administrative officer.
Appointment and duties, §§15.2-1540, 15.2-1541.

TOWN FIRE MARSHALS.
Generally, §§27-30 to 27-37.1.
See FIRE MARSHALS.

TOWN GRANTED CITY STATUS, §§15.2-3800 to 15.2-3834.
See TRANSITION OF TOWNS TO CITIES.

TOWN HALL.
Damaging public buildings, §18.2-138.

TOWNHOUSES.
Burning or destroying meeting houses, §18.2-79.

TOWN MANAGERS.
Chief administrative officer.
Appointment and duties, §§15.2-1540, 15.2-1541.

TOWN OFFICERS AND EMPLOYEES.
Bonds of officers generally, §§15.2-1527 to 15.2-1533.
See LOCAL OFFICERS AND EMPLOYEES.
Bribery of public officers generally, §§18.2-438 to 18.2-450.
See PUBLIC OFFICERS AND EMPLOYEES.
Cash match plan for employees of Commonwealth, §§51.1-607 to 51.1-613.
Chief administrative officer.
Appointment and duties, §§15.2-1540, 15.2-1541.
City status granted to town.
Generally, §§15.2-3800 to 15.2-3834.
See TRANSITION OF TOWNS TO CITIES.
Conflicts of interest.
Ethics in public contracting, §§2.2-4367 to 2.2-4377.
Constitutional officers, §§15.2-1600 to 15.2-1637.
See LOCAL CONSTITUTIONAL OFFICERS.
Defacement of buildings, walls, fences, other structures.
Removal or repair by employees.
Immunity, §15.2-908.
Deferred compensation plan, §§51.1-600 to 51.1-605.
See PUBLIC OFFICERS AND EMPLOYEES.
Dual office holding, §§15.2-1534, 15.2-1535, VA Const Art VII §6.
Election of certain officers.
Constitutional and local officers.
Generally, §§24.2-217 to 24.2-224.
Vacancies in elected constitutional and local offices, §§24.2-225 to 24.2-229.1.
Qualification to hold, VA Const Art II §5.
Election of governing bodies, VA Const Art II §5.
Embezzlement, §18.2-112.
Misuse of public assets, §18.2-112.1.
Ethics in public contracting, §§2.2-4367 to 2.2-4377.
Fire marshals generally, §§27-30 to 27-37.1.
See FIRE MARSHALS.
Governing bodies of localities generally, §§15.2-1400 to 15.2-1433.
See LOCALITIES.
Grievance procedure.
Local government personnel generally, §§15.2-1506 to 15.2-1507.1.
Group insurance program, §§51.1-500 to 51.1-514.
See PUBLIC OFFICERS AND EMPLOYEES.
Hazardous materials coordinator, §44-146.38.
Health insurance program.
Participation, §2.2-1204.
Immunity of members of local governmental entities, §15.2-1405.
Defacement of buildings, walls, fences, other structures.
Removal or repair by employees, §15.2-908.
Joint officers and employees, §§15.2-1513 to 15.2-1516.
Leaves of absence.
Military duty, §44-93.
Discrimination in hiring prohibited, §44-93.4.
Penalty for employer failure to comply, §44-93.5.
Reemployment, §44-93.3.
Supplement of military pay and additional life insurance benefits, §44-93.1.
State defense force or national defense executive reserve training, §44-204.

TOWN OFFICERS AND EMPLOYEES —Cont'd
Local government personnel generally, qualifications for office, etc., §§15.2-1500 to 15.2-1543.
See LOCAL OFFICERS AND EMPLOYEES.
Long-term care insurance.
Program for employees of local government, local officers, teachers.
Board of trustees, Virginia Retirement system.
Assumption of responsibility, §51.1-513.3.
Establishment by department of human resource management, §2.2-1207.
Trust fund, §51.1-513.4.
Military duty leaves of absence, §44-93.
Discrimination in hiring prohibited, §44-93.4.
Penalty for employer failure to comply, §44-93.5.
Reemployment, §44-93.3.
Supplement of military pay and additional life insurance benefits, §44-93.1.
Misuse of public assets, §18.2-112.1.
National defense executive reserve training.
Leave of absence, §44-204.
Public contracting, ethics in, §§2.2-4367 to 2.2-4377.
Removal of officers from office, §§24.2-230 to 24.2-238.
Residency, §§15.2-1505, 15.2-1525.
Removal of residence from jurisdiction officer required to reside, §15.2-1526.
Retirement generally, §§51.1-800 to 51.1-823.
See LOCAL RETIREMENT SYSTEMS.
Sergeants.
See SERGEANTS.
Social security coverage, §§51.1-700 to 51.1-707.
See PUBLIC OFFICERS AND EMPLOYEES.
State defense force training.
Leave of absence, §44-204.
Telecommuting, §15.2-1512.3.
Travel expenses to person on business of locality, §§15.2-1508.1 to 15.2-1508.4.
Vacancies.
Elected constitutional and local offices, §§24.2-224 to 24.2-229.1.

TOWN PARKS.
Liability in operating.
Agreements with landowners, §29.1-509.
Sale, VA Const Art VII §9.

TOWN POLICE.
Disciplinary actions, §54.1-3224.
Jury service.
Automatic exemption, §8.01-341.

TOWNS.
Abandoned graveyards.
Eminent domain, §57-36.
Abandoned motor vehicles.
Ordinances for removal and disposition of unattended or immobilized vehicles, §§46.2-1213, 46.2-1215.
Abandonment of territory.
Contraction of corporate limits of cities or towns, §§15.2-3236 to 15.2-3245.
See BOUNDARIES.
Abatement of nuisances, §15.2-1115.
Acquiring real property outside boundaries, §15.2-1800.
Acquisition of real property for public use, §15.2-1800.
Approval of deeds, acceptance by locality, §15.2-1803.

TOWNS —Cont'd
Acquisition of real property for public use —Cont'd
Development of business or industry, §15.2-1802.
Near parks or other public property, §15.2-1801.
Action by or against in own name, §15.2-1404.
Admissions tax.
Excise tax, town having general taxing powers, §58.1-3840.
Advertisement and enactment of certain fees and levies, §15.2-107.
Affordable housing.
Building permit fees.
Wavier for permit fees, §15.2-958.4.
Community reinvestment in contracts for investment of funds.
Consideration of affordable housing, §2.2-4327.
Agricultural and forestal districts, §§15.2-4300 to 15.2-4314.
Airports.
Generally, §§5.1-31 to 5.1-47, 15.2-1123.
See AIRPORTS.
Air raid precautions, §§44-147 to 44-151.
Alcoholic beverage sales at licensed establishment.
Temporary injunction.
Meeting place for persons committing serious criminal violations, §48-17.1.
Alleys.
Public service company use without consent or compensation, §56-14.
Alteration or vacation of public rights of way, §§15.2-2006 to 15.2-2008.
Alternative discharging sewage systems.
Actions, §32.1-164.
Amateur radio antennas.
Height restrictions, §15.2-2293.1.
Animal ordinances, §3.2-6543.
Dangerous dogs, controlling, §3.2-6540.
Dog and cat licensing, §§3.2-6521 to 3.2-6536.
Dogs running at large.
Prohibiting, §3.2-6538.
Keeping of animals and fowl, §3.2-6544.
Permits for pet shops and dealers in companion animals, §3.2-6537.
Rabid animals, §3.2-6522.
Rabies control, §3.2-6525.
Regulation of keeping animals and fowl, §3.2-6544.
Shelters.
Sales of animals from, §3.2-6545.
Vicious dogs, controlling, §3.2-6540.1.
Annexation.
Agreements between towns and counties defining town's annexation rights, §§15.2-3231 to 15.2-3235.
See ANNEXATION.
Generally, §§15.2-3200 to 15.2-3235.
See ANNEXATION.
Voluntary settlement, §§15.2-3400, 15.2-3401.
Annual audit, §15.2-2511.
Annual statement of revenues, expenditures and fund balances.
Audited financial report.
Filing with auditor of public accounts, §15.2-2510.
Annulment of charters, §§15.2-3700 to 15.2-3712.
Appropriations to towns by counties, §15.2-1202.
Arbitration of disputes, §15.2-1404.

TOWNS —Cont'd
Armories.
Conveyances of public grounds for armory building purposes, §44-130.
Joint use of public buildings for, §44-129.
Manufactured home lot rentals.
Injunctive relief powers, §55-248.52.
Assessment power, §15.2-1104.
Assessments for local improvements, §§15.2-2404 to 15.2-2413.
See TAXES OR ASSESSMENTS FOR LOCAL IMPROVEMENTS.
Assistance by officers or employees beyond jurisdictional limits, §15.2-1724.
Associations of political subdivisions, §§15.2-1303 to 15.2-1305.
Auctions, §15.2-1114.
Audit of accounts and records, §15.2-2511.
Auditors.
Duties of local government auditors, §15.2-2511.2.
Bad checks to localities.
Ordinances providing fee for passing, §15.2-106.
Bequests.
Power to accept or refuse, §15.2-1108.
Beverages.
Powers generally, §15.2-1109.
Bicycles.
Licensing, §15.2-1720.
Prohibiting on sidewalks or crosswalks, §46.2-904.
Unclaimed property disposition, §15.2-1720.
Blighted areas.
Tax increment financing, §§58.1-3245 to 58.1-3245.5.
Boards of equalization, §§58.1-3370 to 58.1-3389.
See REAL PROPERTY TAXES.
Boating safety regulation, §§29.1-744 to 29.1-746.
Body politic of Commonwealth, §15.2-1402.
Bond from licensee or permittee, requiring, §15.2-1125.
Bond not required to be posted to exercise right, §15.2-1126.
Bonds.
Debt limitation, VA Const Art VII §10.
Bonds of officers generally, §§15.2-1527 to 15.2-1533.
See LOCAL OFFICERS AND EMPLOYEES.
Bookkeeping and accounting system for use by local government.
Auditor of public accounts to devise, §15.2-2509.
Borrowing money, §15.2-1105.
Boundaries.
Agreements between towns and counties defining town's annexation rights, §§15.2-3231 to 15.2-3235.
See ANNEXATION.
Annexation.
Generally, §§15.2-3200 to 15.2-3235.
See ANNEXATION.
Voluntary settlement, §§15.2-3400, 15.2-3401.
Charters.
Incorporation by reference, §15.2-207.
Consolidation.
Counties, cities or towns consolidating into single county or city, §§15.2-3520 to 15.2-3550.
See CONSOLIDATION OF LOCALITIES.
Like units of local government, §§15.2-3500 to 15.2-3519.
See CONSOLIDATION OF LOCALITIES.
Contraction of corporate limits of cities or towns, §§15.2-3236 to 15.2-3245.
See BOUNDARIES.

TOWNS —Cont'd
Boundaries —Cont'd
Establishment of boundary lines by commissioners, §§15.2-3100 to 15.2-3105.
See BOUNDARIES.
Relocation or change by agreement, §§15.2-3106 to 15.2-3109.
See BOUNDARIES.
Branch pilot licenses, §54.1-908.
Budgets.
Amendment, §15.2-2507.
Approved budget.
Publication, §15.2-2503.
Contents, §15.2-2504.
Discretionary funds to be included in itemized expenditures, §15.2-2503.
Establishment of funds for accounting and budgeting, §15.2-2501.
Estimated amount of money needed for ensuing fiscal year.
Submission by officers and heads of agencies, time, §15.2-2503.
Estimated amount of state money to be received during fiscal year.
Notification by compensation board and department of taxation, §15.2-2502.
Information furnished by department, offices, divisions, etc., §15.2-2508.
Preparation and approval for informative and fiscal planning, §15.2-2503.
Publication and notice, §15.2-2506.
Public hearing, §15.2-2506.
Reserve for contingencies and capital improvements, §15.2-2505.
Special budget provisions, §15.2-2513.
Tax rate for budget year.
Fixing, time, §15.2-2503.
Time for preparation, §15.2-2503.
Building code.
Statewide code generally, §§36-97 to 36-119.1.
See BUILDING CODE.
Buildings.
Persons with physical disabilities.
Access to public buildings, §§2.2-1159 to 2.2-1161.
Burial, §15.2-1111.
Cemeteries on private property.
Official local register of places of burial, §15.2-978.
Property exempt belonging to memorial or monumental association, §15.2-978.
Business and industrial development, acquiring land, §15.2-1802.
Capital construction projects by state.
Availability of preliminary plans to locality upon request, §15.2-2202.
Capital improvement programs, §15.2-2239.
Local government facilities private capital lending, §§15.2-1815 to 15.2-1817.
Cat licensing, §§3.2-6521 to 3.2-6536.
Cemeteries, §§15.2-1111, 15.2-1121.
Conveyance of land to governing body for cemetery use, §57-22.
Costs of suits, removal and reinterment, §57-37.
Eminent domain, §57-25.
Abandoned graveyards, §57-36.
Land conveyances, §57-22.
Location restrictions, §57-26.
Proceedings for removal of remains and sale of land vacated, §57-39.

TOWNS —Cont'd
Cemeteries —Cont'd
Trustees.
Appointment, §57-23.
Removal, §57-23.
Change of city to town.
City no longer qualifying for city status, §§15.2-4000 to 15.2-4005.
See REVERSION OF CITIES TO TOWNS.
Transition of city to town status generally, §§15.2-4100 to 15.2-4120.
See REVERSION OF CITIES TO TOWNS.
Charter powers not affected by title, §15.2-100.
Charters, §§15.2-200 to 15.2-209.
Abolition of local constitutional office.
Special elections, §15.2-206.
Use of charter provisions not authorized, §15.2-205.
Annulment, §§15.2-3700 to 15.2-3712.
Agreement with board of supervisors of county, §15.2-3701.
Annulment of surrendered charter, §15.2-3706.
Authorization, §15.2-3700.
Effect, §15.2-3707.
Election.
Order, conduct of election, §15.2-3704.
Results, §15.2-3705.
Ordinance required, §15.2-3702.
Pending suits, effect, §15.2-3711.
Publication of copy of notice and ordinance, §15.2-3703.
Records and documents of former town to pass to county or counties, §15.2-3710.
Repeal of charter, §15.2-3712.
Service of notice, §15.2-3702.
Special debt district, §15.2-3709.
Transfer of property and indebtedness, §15.2-3708.
Bill not introduced or failing to pass in general assembly, §§15.2-201, 15.2-202.
Boundaries incorporated by reference, §15.2-207.
Elections, §15.2-201.
Evidence of compliance, §15.2-203.
Procedure, §15.2-200.
Public hearing, §15.2-202.
Reversion of city to town.
Resulting town charters, §15.2-4112.
Uniform charter powers, §15.2-204.
Chesapeake Bay preservation areas.
Designation by towns in Tidewater Virginia, §62.1-44.15:74.
Enforcement of provisions, authority of local governments, §62.1-44.15:73.
Outside Tidewater area, adoption of provisions, §62.1-44.15:75.
Water quality protection requirements, §62.1-44.15:76.
Chief administrative officer.
Appointment and duties, §§15.2-1540, 15.2-1541.
Churches and other places of worship.
Land held in adverse possession limitations, §57-17.
Local fees, restrictions on charging, §15.2-108.1.
Cigarette tax, §§58.1-3830 to 58.1-3832.
Corporate or partnership officer.
Willful failure to collect and account for, §58.1-3907.
Excise tax, town having general taxing powers, §58.1-3840.
City status, granting, §§15.2-3800 to 15.2-3834.
See TRANSITION OF TOWNS TO CITIES.

TOWNS —Cont'd
Closing temporarily public rights of way, §§15.2-2013, 15.2-2014.
Coastal primary sand dunes and beaches.
Zoning, §28.2-1403.
Boards, §§28.2-1404, 28.2-1405.
Review of decisions, §§28.2-1410 to 28.2-1415.
Collection of state funds locally by financial officer, disposition, §15.2-1537.1.
Commission on local government, §§15.2-2900 to 15.2-2908.
See COMMISSION ON LOCAL GOVERNMENT.
Community correctional facilities, §§53.1-177 to 53.1-179.
Community development authorities.
Water and waste authorities generally, §§15.2-5152 to 15.2-5158.
Comprehensive plan, §§15.2-2222.1 to 15.2-2232.
Condemnation.
Eminent domain generally, §§15.2-1901 to 15.2-1906.
See LOCALITIES.
Conditional zoning, §§15.2-2296 to 15.2-2303.
Condominiums.
Conversion condominiums.
Enactment, authority, §55-79.94.
Conduit entities.
Local government facilities private capital lending, §§15.2-1815 to 15.2-1817.
Consent of town to use public property, VA Const Art VII §8.
Consent to use streets, roads, alleys, etc., §§15.2-2015 to 15.2-2018.
Consolidation.
Counties, cities or towns consolidating into single county or city, §§15.2-3520 to 15.2-3550.
See CONSOLIDATION OF LOCALITIES.
Like units of local government, §§15.2-3500 to 15.2-3519.
See CONSOLIDATION OF LOCALITIES.
Constitutional officers.
Abolition of office.
Charter enactment or amendment, §§15.2-205, 15.2-206.
Generally, §§15.2-1600 to 15.2-1637.
See LOCAL CONSTITUTIONAL OFFICERS.
Consumer utility taxes, §§58.1-3814 to 58.1-3816.2.
See BOUNDARIES.
Contraction of corporate limits of cities or towns, §§15.2-3236 to 15.2-3245.
See BOUNDARIES.
Contractor licensing, §54.1-1117.
Contracts.
Solid waste management, §10.1-1412.
Contracts containing provision to arbitrate disputes, §15.2-1404.
Coordinator of emergency management, §44-146.19.
Corporation or company, terms not to include municipal corporations, VA Const Art IX §7.
Correctional facilities, local.
Generally, §§53.1-68 to 53.1-133.9.
See JAILS.
Council.
Generally.
See TOWN COUNCILS.
Governing bodies of localities generally, §§15.2-1400 to 15.2-1433.
See LOCALITIES.

TOWNS —Cont'd
Council —Cont'd
Meetings of governmental bodies generally, §§15.2-1415 to 15.2-1421.
See LOCALITIES.
Ordinances and other actions by local governing bodies.
Generally, §§15.2-1425 to 15.2-1433.
See ORDINANCES.
Salaries, §15.2-1414.7.
Court costs and fees.
Collection of cost of transporting prisoners, §19.2-338.
Courthouses.
Generally, §§15.2-1638 to 15.2-1655.
See COURTHOUSES.
Removal of county courthouse.
Donation of land and money by town, §15.2-1648.
Bonds issued to finance, §§15.2-1649, 15.2-1650.
Crimestoppers information, confidentiality of information, §15.2-1713.1.
Crosswalks.
Prohibiting bicycles, roller skates or skateboards, §46.2-904.
Curb ramps, specifications, §15.2-2021.
Dams.
Construction for purpose of providing public water supply, §§15.2-2134, 15.2-2142.
Disputes between jurisdictions.
Special court proceedings, §§15.2-2135 to 15.2-2141.
Dance halls.
Regulation by localities, §15.2-912.3.
Dangerous, offensive or unhealthy business, trade or employment, §15.2-1113.
Deannexation.
Contraction of corporate limits of cities or towns, §§15.2-3236 to 15.2-3245.
See BOUNDARIES.
Debt limitation, VA Const Art VII §10.
Deeds conveying real estate, approval and acceptance, §15.2-1803.
Defense production zones.
Authority to establish, grant incentives, regulatory flexibility, enterprise zone taxation, §58.1-3853.
Defined, §§1-254, 15.2-102, 27-40.3, VA Const Art VII §1.
Derelict structures, removal or rehabilitation.
Grants, §36-155.
Detention, correctional and penal institutions, §15.2-1120.
Development of business and industry, acquiring land, §15.2-1802.
Directional signs.
Integrated directional sign program.
Participation fees, §33.1-12.01.
Disabled or handicapped persons.
Access to public buildings, §§2.2-1159 to 2.2-1161.
Access to public transportation, §51.5-44.
Disasters, fires, floods, etc.
Sending officers, agents or employees beyond jurisdictional limits to assist, §15.2-1724.
Discharge of firearms, §15.2-1113.
Discontinuance of service by state agency to locality.
Notification, §2.2-612.
Discount for early payment of tax or assessment, §15.2-1104.

TOWNS —Cont'd
Disorderly conduct in public places.
Authority to adopt ordinance prohibiting, §18.2-415.
Dog ordinances, §3.2-6543.
Dangerous dogs, §3.2-6540.
Licensing, §§3.2-6521 to 3.2-6536.
Rabid animal, §3.2-6522.
Rabies control, §3.2-6525.
Running at large, §3.2-6538.
Vicious dogs, §3.2-6540.1.
Donations.
Power to accept or refuse, §15.2-1108.
Donations to vestries for charitable purposes.
Exercise of powers, §57-4.
Draining or razing of ground subject to be covered by stagnant water, §15.2-1115.
Driving under the influence reimbursement.
Emergency response expenses, §15.2-1716.
Driving while intoxicated.
Chemical testing to determine alcohol or drug content of blood.
Ordinances paralleling provisions authorized, §18.2-268.12.
Dual office holding, §§15.2-1534, 15.2-1535.
Ejectment proceeding against owner of property encroaching or obstructing right of way, §15.2-2009.
Elections.
Annexation.
Elections following annexation, §15.2-3226.
Annulment of charter, §§15.2-3704, 15.2-3705.
Bonds issued by locality, §§15.2-2610, 15.2-2611.
Change of city to town.
City no longer qualifying for city status.
Town council and other elected officers, §15.2-4005.
Town council and other elected officers, §15.2-4115.
Charters, §15.2-201.
Consolidation of counties, cities or towns into single county or city, §§15.2-3538 to 15.2-3540.
Consolidation of like units of local government.
Conduct of election, §15.2-3506.
Election of town officers after consolidation approved, §15.2-3509.
Order for election, §15.2-3505.
Result of election, §15.2-3507.
Constitutional and local officers generally, §§24.2-217 to 24.2-224.
Contest of election generally, §§24.2-803 to 24.2-814.
Control of electoral process, §24.2-601.
Costs, §24.2-600.
Governing bodies generally, VA Const Art VII §5.
Incorporation of towns by judicial proceedings.
First elections, §15.2-3604.
Local electoral boards generally, §§24.2-106 to 24.2-109.
Paper ballots in lieu of voting machines, §24.2-308.
Reapportionment, VA Const Art VII §5.
Action challenging boundaries of election district.
Attorney general, legal services, §2.2-508.
Referendum elections.
Calling, ascertaining results and certifying, §24.2-684.
Reversion of city to town.
City no longer qualifying for city status.
Town council and other elected officers, §15.2-4005.

TOWNS —Cont'd
Elections —Cont'd
Reversion of city to town —Cont'd
Town council and other elected officers, §15.2-4115.
Seeking city status, §15.2-3801.
Vacancies in elected constitutional and local officers generally, §§24.2-225 to 24.2-229.1.
Electrical energy requirements.
Aggregating for purposes of negotiating purchase of electricity, §56-589.
Electrical utility facility construction, §56-46.1.
Electric authorities, §§15.2-5400 to 15.2-5431.
See ELECTRIC AUTHORITIES.
Electric personal assistive mobility devices.
Licensing and disposition of unclaimed property, §15.2-1720.
Electric power and energy.
Purchase of, §15.2-1133.
Electric power-assisted bicycles.
Licensing and disposition of unclaimed property, §15.2-1720.
Emergency management and disasters.
Declaration of local emergency, §44-146.21.
Generally, §§44-146.13 to 44-146.28.
See EMERGENCY MANAGEMENT.
Immunity from liability, §44-146.23.
Joint action by political subdivisions, §44-146.20.
Powers and duties of political subdivisions generally, §44-146.19.
Emergency medical services.
Fire/EMS departments.
Ordinances relating to powers and duties of fire/EMS departments, §27-14.
Governing bodies of towns.
Powers, §32.1-111.14.
Mutual aid, §§27-2 to 27-4.
Eminent domain.
Cemeteries, §57-25.
Abandoned graveyards, §57-36.
Federal water resources development projects, §62.1-150.
Generally, §§15.2-1901 to 15.2-1906.
See LOCALITIES.
Oyster planting grounds, §28.2-628.
Spot blight abatement procedure, §36-49.1:1.
Water supplies and water lines, §15.2-1907.
Wetlands.
Condemnation for compensatory mitigation of wetlands, §15.2-1907.1.
Encroachment or obstruction of rights of way, §15.2-2009.
Energy conservation and costs savings.
Facilities owned by state and local governments.
Energy and operational efficiency performance-based contracting act, §§11-34.1 to 11-34.4.
Enterprise zone development.
General provisions, §§62.1-44.15:51 to 62.1-44.15:66.
Local enterprise zone development taxation program, §§58.1-3245.6 to 58.1-3245.12.
Enumeration of population, §15.2-1414.
Environmental impact report for major state project.
Duty of department of environmental quality to submit to locality, §15.2-2202.
Estimated amount of state money to be received during fiscal year and other information.
Notification by compensation board and department of taxation, §15.2-2502.

TOWNS —Cont'd
Excise taxes, town having general taxing powers, §58.1-3840.
Explosive or inflammable substances, powers generally, §59.1-140.
Explosives or inflammable substances, §15.2-1113.
Farmer major drought, flood and hurricane disaster assistance.
Grant programs for emergency financial assistance, authority, §3.2-505.
Farmers markets.
Establishing local retail markets, §3.2-3502.
Farmlands, designation of important farmlands, §3.2-205.
Fences.
Lawful fences, §55-299.
Financial report.
Filing audited report with auditor of public accounts, §15.2-2510.
Firearms, discharging, §15.2-1113.
Firearms, unclaimed property disposition, §15.2-1721.
Fire companies.
Contracts, §27-23.6.
Defined, §27-8.1.
Dissolution, §27-10.
Duty of members upon alarm, §27-11.
Entry, right of, §27-17.
Equipment, §27-15.2.
Purchase of service-issued boots or helmet by certain firefighters, §27-15.3.
Formation, §27-8.
Joint operations.
Ordinances to effectuate, §27-23.10.
Supervision and control, §27-23.9.
Limit on number of persons in, §27-8.
Officers.
Appointment, §27-13.
Authority when answering alarm or operating at an emergency incident, §27-15.1.
Penalty for disobeying, §27-19.
Property seizure and preservation, §27-34.1.
Ordinances.
Powers and duties relating to fire/EMS departments, §27-14.
Organization, §27-9.
Property destruction to prevent spread of fire, §27-20.
Owner recovery of damages, §27-21.
Property which would have been destroyed by fire, §27-22.
Relief for firefighters and dependents, §27-39.
Remaining on premises after fire extinguished, §27-17.1.
Remedying inflammable or unsafe conditions, §27-61.
Penalties for neglect of duties by local officers, §27-62.
Fire departments.
Bylaws, §27-7.
Check stubs, §27-7.
Chiefs, §27-6.1.
Authority when answering alarm or operating at an emergency incident, §27-15.1.
Penalty for disobeying, §27-19.
Compensation, §27-7.
Property seizure and preservation, §27-34.1.
Contracts to furnish fire protection, §§27-2, 27-2.1, 27-3.1, 27-4.

TOWNS —Cont'd
Fire departments —Cont'd
Employees, §27-6.1.
Compensation, §27-7.
Entry, right of, §27-17.
Equipment, §27-15.2.
Purchase of service-issued boots or helmet by certain firefighters, §27-15.3.
Establishment, §27-6.1.
Joint operations.
Ordinances to effectuate, §27-23.10.
Supervision and control, §27-23.9.
Ordinances.
Powers and duties relating to fire/EMS departments, §27-14.
Pay records, §27-7.
Property destruction to prevent spread of fire, §27-20.
Owner recovery of damages, §27-21.
Property which would have been destroyed by fire, §27-22.
Relief for firefighters and dependents, §§27-39 to 27-40.4.
Remaining on premises after fire extinguished, §27-17.1.
Remedying inflammable or unsafe conditions, §27-61.
Penalties for neglect of duties by local officers, §27-62.
Time cards, §27-7.
Firefighters, financial relief for.
Authorization to provide, §27-39.
Fire marshals generally, §§27-30 to 27-37.1.
See FIRE MARSHALS.
Fire prevention.
Building exits.
Local safety provisions, §27-54.
Enforcement of code, §27-98.
Statewide standards, §27-96.
Fire programs fund, allocation to, §38.2-401.
Fires.
Regulating or prohibiting making of fires, §15.2-922.1.
Fire suppression system connection to local water utility, §15.2-2113.
Fireworks.
Use and exhibition, §15.2-1113.
Firing and stoking furnaces and boilers, §15.2-1116.
Fiscal year.
Uniform fiscal year for all localities, §15.2-2500.
Food and food products.
Powers generally, §15.2-1109.
Foot-scooters.
Prohibiting on sidewalks or crosswalks, §46.2-904.
Former federal areas, authorities for development, §§15.2-6300 to 15.2-6322.
Franchise, privilege, lease or right of use of public property, §§15.2-2100 to 15.2-2108.1:1.
Amending and extending franchise, §15.2-2105.
Awarding franchise, §15.2-2102.
No satisfactory bid, §15.2-2103.
Bids, §15.2-2102.
No satisfactory bid, §15.2-2103.
Bond of person awarded, §15.2-2104.
Enforcement of obedience, §15.2-2106.
Freedom of information act.
Excluded records, §2.2-3705.6.
Granting, §15.2-2100.
Mandamus, §15.2-2106.
Number of years, §15.2-2100.

TOWNS —Cont'd
Franchise, privilege, lease or right of use of public property —Cont'd
Publication of notice of ordinance proposing, §15.2-2101.
Telegraph or telephone corporation to occupy parks, streets, etc., §56-462.
Use of property without consent, §15.2-2107.
Fraud and deceit in sales, §15.2-1114.
Fuel-burning equipment, §15.2-1116.
Funds established for accounting and budgeting, §15.2-2501.
Gambling devices, illegal possession.
Failure to enforce, enforcement by governor and attorney general, §18.2-338.
Garbage removal and disposal.
General powers of locality as to waste and recycling, §§15.2-901, 15.2-927 to 15.2-939.
Garnishment.
Wages and salaries of officials, clerks and employees, §§8.01-524, 8.01-525.
General grant of powers, §15.2-1102.
General powers of local government, §§15.2-900 to 15.2-982.
See LOCALITIES.
Gifts.
Power to accept or refuse, §15.2-1108.
Going out of business special sale permits.
Issuance, inspections, etc., §18.2-224.
Golf carts and utility vehicles.
Designation of public highways for operation, §46.2-916.2.
Governing bodies.
Dual office holding, VA Const Art VII §6.
Election generally, VA Const Art VII §5.
Generally, §§15.2-1400 to 15.2-1433.
See LOCALITIES.
Ordinance appropriating money, borrowing money or imposing tax.
Affirmative vote of majority of governing body required, VA Const Art VII §7.
Town councils generally.
See TOWN COUNCILS.
Governmental fraud, §§18.2-498.1 to 18.2-498.5.
Grants.
Power to accept or refuse, §15.2-1108.
Grievance procedure.
Local government personnel generally, §§15.2-1506 to 15.2-1507.1.
Group insurance.
Local government group self-insurance pools, §§15.2-2700 to 15.2-2709.
See LOCAL GOVERNMENT GROUP SELF-INSURANCE POOLS.
Hazardous materials emergency response.
Coordinator of emergency management to enter into agreements with, §44-146.36.
Hazardous materials coordinator, appointment, §44-146.38.
Health insurance program.
Long-term care insurance.
Board of trustees, Virginia Retirement system.
Assumption of responsibility, §51.1-513.3.
Establishment by department of human resource management, §2.2-1207.
Trust fund, §51.1-513.4.
Participation, §2.2-1204.
Hearings.
Public hearings generally.
See PUBLIC HEARINGS.

TOWNS —Cont'd
Height restrictions on amateur radio antennas, §15.2-2293.1.
Helicopter landings.
Zoning ordinances, §15.2-2293.2.
Highway design, right-of-way acquisition and construction.
Assumption of responsibility.
Agreement with Commonwealth transportation board, §33.1-12.1.
Historic areas, landmarks, buildings or structures.
Acquiring and preserving, §15.2-2306.
Holding more than one office, §§15.2-1534, 15.2-1535.
Hospital or health center commissions, §§15.2-5200 to 15.2-5219.
See HOSPITAL OR HEALTH CENTER COMMISSIONS.
Hospitals, sanatoria, homes, clinics, etc., §15.2-1119.
Housing revitalization zones, §§36-157 to 36-170.
See HOUSING REVITALIZATION ZONES.
Human transporters.
Licensing and disposition of unclaimed property, §15.2-1720.
Hunting.
Park restrictions, §29.1-527.
School restrictions, §29.1-527.
Immunity of members of local governmental entities, §15.2-1405.
Immunity when operating park, recreational facility or playground, §15.2-1809.
Impoundment of water.
Disputes between jurisdictions.
Special court proceedings, §§15.2-2135 to 15.2-2141.
Providing public water supply, §15.2-2134.
Improvements.
Taxes or assessments, §§15.2-2404 to 15.2-2413.
See TAXES OR ASSESSMENTS FOR LOCAL IMPROVEMENTS.
Income earned during disability retirement, §27-40.4.
Income tax, §§58.1-540 to 58.1-549.
Incorporated communities.
Defined as including, §1-224.
Incorporation by judicial proceeding, §§15.2-3600 to 15.2-3605.
Appeals, §15.2-3605.
Appointment of special court, §15.2-3600.
Charter request, §15.2-3603.
Commission on local government, §§15.2-2900 to 15.2-2908.
See COMMISSION ON LOCAL GOVERNMENT.
Election.
How first election ordered and held, §15.2-3604.
Filing petition with circuit court, §15.2-3600.
Governing body may become party, §15.2-3600.
Hearing before commission on local government, §15.2-3601.
Order for incorporations, §15.2-3602.
Petition for incorporation of community, §15.2-3600.
Plat attached to petition, §15.2-3600.
Proof required for incorporation, §15.2-3602.
Proof to accompany petition, §15.2-3600.
Request to general assembly for charter, §15.2-3603.

TOWNS —Cont'd
Incorporation by judicial proceeding —Cont'd
Special courts to hear cases, §§15.2-3000 to 15.2-3004.
Indoor clean air act, §§15.2-2820 to 15.2-2833.
See SMOKING IN PUBLIC PLACES.
Industrial development authorities.
General provisions, §§15.2-4900 to 15.2-4920.
See INDUSTRIAL DEVELOPMENT AUTHORITIES.
Virginia regional industrial facilities authorities, §§15.2-6400 to 15.2-6416.
See VIRGINIA REGIONAL INDUSTRIAL FACILITIES AUTHORITIES.
Inhabitants.
Defined.
See LOCAL GOVERNMENT GROUP SELF-INSURANCE POOLS.
Inoperable motor vehicles, keeping on residential property.
Ordinances permitted in certain counties, §15.2-905.
Insurance.
Local government group self-insurance pools, §§15.2-2700 to 15.2-2709.
See LOCAL GOVERNMENT GROUP SELF-INSURANCE POOLS.
Insurance by licensee or permittee, requiring, §15.2-1125.
Interference with students attending or boarding at schools.
Ordinances preventing, §15.2-1717.
Internet.
Legal notices, publication.
Website may be used as well as newspaper, §15.2-107.1.
Internet use by library employees and patrons.
Acceptable Internet use policies, establishment.
Local governments without library boards, §42.1-36.1.
Investigations by local governing bodies, §15.2-1409.
Jails.
Generally, §§53.1-68 to 53.1-133.9.
See JAILS.
Power to provide and operate detentive, correctional and penal institutions, §15.2-1120.
Joint activities.
Regional competitiveness act, §§15.2-1306 to 15.2-1310.
Joint aid agreements by localities, §15.2-1300.1.
Joint exercise of powers, §§15.2-1300 to 15.2-1302, VA Const Art VIII §3.
Joint officers and employees, §§15.2-1513 to 15.2-1516.
Jurisdiction over lands, buildings and structures.
Police jurisdiction, §15.2-1124.
Juvenile detention and other care facilities.
Operating and maintaining.
Generally, §§16.1-315 to 16.1-322.7.
See JUVENILE DETENTION AND OTHER CARE FACILITIES.
Keys to buildings of political subdivision.
Possession or duplication, §18.2-503.
Lakes or other natural or artificial water, §15.2-1110.
Landlord and tenant.
Lock requirements of town.
Residential landlords and tenants, §55-248.13:1.

TOWNS —Cont'd
Landlord and tenant —Cont'd
Peephole requirements of town.
Residential landlords and tenants, §55-248.13:1.
Land preservation special assessment.
Real property taxes, §§58.1-3229 to 58.1-3244.
See REAL PROPERTY TAXES.
Laser speed detection devices.
Use by town to measure speed of automobile prohibited, §46.2-882.
Law library assessment as part of cost in civil actions, §42.1-70.
Lease, franchise, privilege or right of use of public property, §§15.2-2100 to 15.2-2108.1:1.
Legal enumeration of population, §15.2-1414.
Legal notices, publication.
Mail, alternative method for notice, §15.2-107.2.
Website may be used as well as newspaper, §15.2-107.1.
Lending of credit, VA Const Art X §10.
Level between lot and street constitute danger to life and limb, §15.2-1115.
Libraries.
Generally, §§58.1-3700 to 58.1-3735.
See LICENSE TAXES.
Local and regional, §§42.1-33 to 42.1-45.
Municipal library, §42.1-49.
License fees and taxes on motor vehicles, trailers and semitrailers, §46.2-752.
Licenses.
Requiring issuance in connection with enforcement of ordinance or regulation, §15.2-1125.
Liens against real estate, §15.2-104.
Light, ventilation, sanitation and use and occupancy of buildings, §15.2-1117.
Limitations on amount of outstanding bonds, §§15.2-2634, 15.2-2635.
Limited access streets, §15.2-2026.
Loans for repair of failed septic systems, §15.2-958.6.
Lobbying by local government employees.
Registration and reporting requirements, §2.2-422.
Local correctional facilities generally, §§53.1-68 to 53.1-133.9.
See JAILS.
Local government facilities private capital lending, §§15.2-1815 to 15.2-1817.
Defined terms, §15.2-1815.
Financing agreements, power to enter into, §15.2-1816.
Real estate taxes, §15.2-1817.
Localities generally.
See LOCALITIES.
Locality defined as including, §1-221.
Location of town in two or more counties.
Contraction of corporate limits of town, §§15.2-3241 to 15.2-3243.
Long-term care insurance.
Program for employees of local government, local officers, teachers.
Board of trustees, Virginia Retirement System.
Assumption of responsibility, §51.1-513.3.
Establishment by department of human resource management, §2.2-1207.
Trust fund, §51.1-513.4.
Machinery and tools tax, §§58.1-3507, 58.1-3508.
Semiconductor manufacturing or food processing.
Separate classifications, §58.1-3508.1.

TOWNS —Cont'd
Magistrate's office located in county serving municipality.
Jurisdiction over offenses, §15.2-1124.
Mandates of state.
Assessment and catalog by commission on local government, §15.2-2903.
Assessment by state agencies, §2.2-613.
Manufactured home lot rental.
Powers, §55-248.49.
Maps.
Official map, §§15.2-2233 to 15.2-2238.
Master plan of state agency affecting locality's comprehensive plan.
Duty of state agency to furnish on request, §15.2-2202.
Mayors.
Acknowledgments.
Validating certain acts, §55-126.
Salaries, §15.2-1414.7.
Transition of towns to cities.
Mayor of town to continue in office, §15.2-3814.
Meals tax.
Excise tax, town having general taxing powers, §58.1-3840.
Situs for taxation of food and beverages, §58.1-3841.
Medical services in emergencies, mutual aid, §§27-2 to 27-4.
Meetings of governmental bodies generally, §§15.2-1415 to 15.2-1421.
See LOCALITIES.
Merchants' capital tax, §§58.1-3509, 58.1-3510.
Methamphetamine lab cleanup costs.
Liability of offender in separate civil action, §15.2-1716.2.
Methane or other combustible gas.
Building or facility to collect and use for electric power.
Loans to local governments, §§15.2-2430 to 15.2-2440.
See VIRGINIA INFRASTRUCTURE PROJECT LOAN FUND.
Military units, aiding, §15.2-1112.
Militia, requests for assistance by localities, §§44-78.1, 44-113.
Milk and milk products.
Powers generally, §15.2-1109.
Mopeds, licensing, §15.2-1720.
Mopeds, unclaimed property disposition, §15.2-1720.
Mosquito control districts.
Creation, §32.1-187.
Special tax, §32.1-194.
Motor carriers, passengers.
Common carriers.
Terminals.
Local licensing, §46.2-2095.
Government vehicles.
Exclusions, §46.2-2000.1.
Taxicabs.
Licensing and license taxation, §46.2-2063.
Restrictions on imposition, §46.2-2064.
Number of cabs, §46.2-2067.
Operator qualifications, §46.2-2065.
Regulation by localities, §46.2-2062.
Stand regulation, §46.2-2065.
Motor carriers, property.
Government vehicles.
Exemptions from provisions, §46.2-2101.

TOWNS —Cont'd
Motorcycles, use of transportation facilities or projects.
Discrimination as to use of facilities or projects prohibited.
State or federal funds used by locality, §33.1-13.1.
Motor fuels.
Local ordinances, §59.1-167.
Motor vehicle license plates.
Commemorative license plates for counties, cities and towns, §46.2-749.4:4.
Special license plates bearing seal, symbol or emblem, §46.2-749.4.
Motor vehicles.
Solid waste management.
Local regulation of vehicle construction, parking, etc., §46.2-1304.1.
Motor vehicle sales and use tax.
Local tax prohibited, §58.1-2418.
Sales and use tax revenue disposition, §58.1-2425.
Motor vehicles and traffic regulation.
Applicability of county ordinances, §46.2-1310.
During state of war, §44-205.
Generally, §§46.2-1300 to 46.2-1314.
See LOCALITIES.
Photo-monitoring systems to enforce traffic light signals, §15.2-968.1.
Powers generally, §15.2-2028.
Motor vehicle size and weight.
Excessive size and weight permits, §46.2-1140.
Town ordinances fixing weight limits, §46.2-1138.2.
Mount Vernon named reserved, §15.2-103.
Municipality or municipal corporation.
Defined as including, §1-224.
Mutual aid in fire or medical service emergencies, §§27-2 to 27-4.
Naming roads, streets and alleys, §15.2-2019.
Noise ordinances.
Civil penalties for noise ordinance violations.
Adoption of uniform schedule, §15.2-980.
Nuisances, §15.2-1115.
Numbers displayed on buildings fronting public right of way, §15.2-2024.
Obscenity.
Adoption of ordinances prohibiting, §15.2-926.2.
Officers and employees.
Bonds of officers generally, §§15.2-1527 to 15.2-1533.
See LOCAL OFFICERS AND EMPLOYEES.
Cash match plan for employees of Commonwealth, §§51.1-607 to 51.1-613.
Chief administrative officer.
Appointment and duties, §§15.2-1540, 15.2-1541.
City status granted to town generally, §§15.2-3800 to 15.2-3834.
See TRANSITION OF TOWNS TO CITIES.
Constitutional officers.
Generally, §§15.2-1600 to 15.2-1637.
See LOCAL CONSTITUTIONAL OFFICERS.
Deferred compensation plan, §§51.1-600 to 51.1-605.
Dual office holding, §§15.2-1534, 15.2-1535.
Fire marshals generally, §§27-30 to 27-37.1.
See FIRE MARSHALS.
Governing bodies of localities generally, §§15.2-1400 to 15.2-1433.
See LOCALITIES.

TOWNS —Cont'd
Officers and employees —Cont'd
Grievance procedure.
Local government personnel generally, §§15.2-1506 to 15.2-1507.1.
Group insurance program, §§51.1-500 to 51.1-514.
See PUBLIC OFFICERS AND EMPLOYEES.
Immunity of members of local governmental entities, §15.2-1405.
Joint officers and employees, §§15.2-1513 to 15.2-1516.
Local government personnel generally, §§15.2-1500 to 15.2-1543.
See LOCAL OFFICERS AND EMPLOYEES.
Local trusts to fund postemployment benefits other than pensions, §§15.2-1544 to 15.2-1549.
Meetings of governmental bodies generally, §§15.2-1415 to 15.2-1421.
See LOCALITIES.
Police officers.
Civil papers, service, §15.2-1704.
Generally, §§15.2-1700 to 15.2-1753.
See POLICE.
Removal of public officers generally, §§24.2-230 to 24.2-238.
See REMOVAL OF PUBLIC OFFICERS FROM OFFICE.
Residence of officers.
Removal of residence from jurisdiction officer required to reside, §15.2-1526.
Residency, §§15.2-1505, 15.2-1525.
Retirement generally, §§51.1-800 to 51.1-823.
See LOCAL RETIREMENT SYSTEMS.
Social security coverage generally, §§51.1-700 to 51.1-707.
Telecommuting, §15.2-1512.3.
Travel expenses to person on business of locality, §§15.2-1508.1 to 15.2-1508.4.
Official map, §§15.2-2233 to 15.2-2238.
Oils, lubricating.
Local ordinances, §59.1-167.
Ordinances and other actions by local governing body, §§15.2-1425 to 15.2-1433.
See ORDINANCES.
Ordinance violations.
State police arrests, §52-22.
Oysters.
Planting grounds.
Condemnation, §28.2-628.
Park authorities, §§15.2-5700 to 15.2-5714.
See PARK AUTHORITIES.
Parking or storage of vehicles.
Providing and operating places for, §15.2-1122.
Parks, recreational facilities and playgrounds, §§15.2-1806 to 15.2-1811.
See LOCALITIES.
Parole officers.
Compensation, §§53.1-146, 53.1-147.
Powers, §53.1-146.
Pawnbrokers.
Licensing generally, §§54.1-4000 to 54.1-4014.
See PAWNBROKERS.
Pawnshops, §15.2-1114.
Peddlers, §15.2-1114.
Penalty and interest for failure to pay accounts when due, §15.2-105.
Permits.
Requiring issuance in connection with enforcement of ordinance or regulation, §15.2-1125.

TOWNS —Cont'd
Personal property taxes.
Exempt property generally, §§58.1-3600 to 58.1-3666.
See PROPERTY EXEMPT FROM TAXATION.
Generally, §§58.1-3500 to 58.1-3522.
See PERSONAL PROPERTY TAXES.
Machinery and tools tax, §§58.1-3507, 58.1-3508.
Semiconductor manufacturing or food processing.
Separate classifications, §58.1-3508.1.
Merchants' capital tax, §§58.1-3509, 58.1-3510.
Tax relief act of 1998, §§58.1-3523 to 58.1-3535.
See PERSONAL PROPERTY TAX RELIEF ACT OF 1998.
Personnel generally, qualifications for office, bond, §§15.2-1500 to 15.2-1543.
See LOCAL OFFICERS AND EMPLOYEES.
Persons with physical disabilities.
Access to public buildings, §§2.2-1159 to 2.2-1161.
Photo-monitoring systems to enforce traffic light signals, §15.2-968.1.
Physical examinations, §27-40.1:1.
Planning and development.
Generally, §§15.2-2200 to 15.2-2239.
See PLANNING AND DEVELOPMENT.
Subdivisions, §§15.2-2240 to 15.2-2279.
See SUBDIVISIONS.
Zoning, §§15.2-2280 to 15.2-2316.2.
See ZONING.
Planning commissions, §§15.2-2210 to 15.2-2222.
Planning district commissions, §§15.2-4200 to 15.2-4222.
See PLANNING DISTRICT COMMISSIONS.
Playgrounds.
Jury service.
Automatic exemption, §8.01-341.
Police officers.
Civil papers, service, §15.2-1704.
Generally, §§15.2-1700 to 15.2-1753.
See POLICE.
Political campaign signs, regulation of, §15.2-109.
Polluted, adulterated, etc., water, §15.2-1110.
Population.
Classifications, §1-236.
Defined, §1-235.
Enumeration, §15.2-1414.
Ports.
Locality subordinate to port authority, §62.1-132.
Management, §62.1-163.
Powers, §§15.2-1100 to 15.2-1133.
Auditoriums, civic centers, coliseums, etc.
Encouraging use of facilities, §15.2-1129.
Joint exercise, §§15.2-1300 to 15.2-1302.
Local government generally, §§15.2-900 to 15.2-982.
See LOCALITIES.
Personnel systems, §15.2-1131.
Uniform charter powers, §§15.2-1100 to 15.2-1126.
Abatement or removal of nuisances, §15.2-1115.
Airports and facilities, §15.2-1123.
Assessment power, §15.2-1104.
Auctions, §15.2-1114.
Bond not prerequisite to exercise of right, §15.2-1126.
Books, records, accounts and systems of accounting, §15.2-1106.
Borrowing money and issuing in evidences of indebtedness, §15.2-1105.
Cemeteries and burials, §§15.2-1111, 15.2-1121.

TOWNS —Cont'd
Powers —Cont'd
Uniform charter powers —Cont'd
Charter of provisions not affected by grant, §15.2-1103.
Conflicts between provisions and charter, §15.2-1102.
Control and management of affairs, §15.2-1106.
Dangerous, offenses or unhealthful business, trade or employment, §15.2-1113.
Detentive, correctional and penal institutions, §15.2-1120.
Establishing, consolidating, abolishing or changing departments, offices, etc., §15.2-1107.
Exercise of powers by governing body, §15.2-1100.
Exercise of powers regardless whether set out or incorporated in charger, §15.2-1100.
Explosives or inflammable substances, §15.2-1113.
Firearms discharge, §15.2-1113.
Fireworks exhibitions, §15.2-1113.
Firing and stoking furnaces and boilers, §15.2-1116.
Food and food products, §15.2-1109.
Fraud and deceit in sales, §15.2-1114.
Fuel-burning equipment, §15.2-1116.
General grant of power, §15.2-1102.
Gifts, donations, bequests or grants, §15.2-1108.
Hospitals, sanatoria, homes, etc., §15.2-1119.
Lakes and other waters, §15.2-1110.
Licenses and permits, §15.2-1125.
Light, ventilation, sanitation and use and occupancy of building, §15.2-1117.
Military units, aiding, §15.2-1112.
Milk and milk products, §15.2-1109.
Nuisances, §15.2-1115.
Organizing departments, offices, boards, etc., §15.2-1107.
Outside boundaries, exercise of powers, §15.2-1101.
Parking or storage of vehicles, §15.2-1122.
Pawnshops, §15.2-1114.
Peddlers, §15.2-1114.
Police jurisdiction over land, buildings and structures, §15.2-1124.
Private pools and lakes, §15.2-1110.
Renumeration of powers not exclusive, §15.2-1102.
Safety devices on storage equipment, §15.2-1113.
Secondhand dealers, §15.2-1114.
Smoke emissions, §15.2-1116.
Swimming pools, §15.2-1110.
Taxing power, §15.2-1104.
Unsafe, dangerous or unsanitary public or private buildings, walls or structures, §15.2-1115.
Weights and measures, §15.2-1114.
Vacant building registration, §15.2-1127.
Precious metals dealers.
Licensing generally, §§54.1-4100 to 54.1-4111.
See PRECIOUS METALS DEALERS.
Presumptions, §§27-40.1, 27-40.2.
Prison made goods and services, purchases of, §§53.1-47 to 53.1-55.
Private pools and lakes operated by clubs and associations, §15.2-1110.
Private roads.
Residential developments.
Designation as highways for law enforcement purposes, §46.2-1307.

TOWNS —Cont'd
Private streets.
Approvals, §56-546.
Grade crossings, §56-548.
Probation officers.
Compensation, §§53.1-146, 53.1-147.
Powers, §53.1-146.
Procurement of goods and services.
Adoption of alternative policies and procedures.
Exemption from general law, §2.2-4343.
Procurement by public bodies, generally, §§2.2-4300 to 2.2-4377.
See PUBLIC PROCUREMENT.
Tie bids.
Preference for local products and firms, §2.2-4328.
Prompt payment of bills, §§2.2-4352, 2.2-4354.
Property taxes.
Exempt property generally, §§58.1-3600 to 58.1-3666.
See PROPERTY EXEMPT FROM TAXATION.
Machinery and tools tax, §§58.1-3507, 58.1-3508.
Semiconductor manufacturing or food processing.
Separate classifications, §58.1-3508.1.
Merchants' capital tax, §§58.1-3509, 58.1-3510.
Real property taxes generally, §§58.1-3200 to 58.1-3389.
See REAL PROPERTY TAXES.
Tangible personal property, §§58.1-3500 to 58.1-3522.
See PERSONAL PROPERTY TAXES.
Tax rate for budget year.
Fixing, time, §15.2-2503.
Tax relief act of 1998, §§58.1-3523 to 58.1-3535.
See PERSONAL PROPERTY TAX RELIEF ACT OF 1998.
Publication of legal notices.
Mail, alternative method for notice, §15.2-107.2.
Website may be used as well as newspaper, §15.2-107.1.
Publications.
State publications depository program.
Generally, §§42.1-92 to 42.1-97.
See STATE PUBLICATIONS DEPOSITORY PROGRAM.
Public gathering places.
Application of provisions, §32.1-202.
Public service company use without consent or compensation, §56-14.
Public hearings.
Generally.
See PUBLIC HEARINGS.
Public procurement.
Contracts for investment of funds.
Consideration of affordable housing, §2.2-4327.
Public property, restrictions on selling, §15.2-2100.
Public property use, consent of town required, VA Const Art VII §8.
Public school special tax, §§22.1-102 to 22.1-106.
Public service companies.
Regulatory powers, §56-37.
Public service corporations, local taxation of property, §§58.1-2606, 58.1-2607.
Review of property assessments by governing body, §58.1-2602.
Public transportation.
Persons with disabilities.
Access to, §51.5-44.

TOWNS —Cont'd
Public utilities.
Electric authorities, §§15.2-5400 to 15.2-5431.
See ELECTRIC AUTHORITIES.
Generally, §§15.2-2109 to 15.2-2121.
See LOCALITIES.
Radar.
Use by town to measure speed of automobile, §46.2-882.
Railroad crossings.
Bells to be sounded, §56-414.
Failures to signal, §§56-415, 56-416.
Cars obstructing streets or tracks, §§56-412.1, 56-412.2.
Crossbucks, §§56-405.2, 56-408.
Similar signs prohibited, §56-408.
Horns to be sounded, §56-414.
Failure to signal, §§56-415, 56-416.
Maintenance, §56-405.
Protective devices, §§56-406.1 to 56-408.
Signal boards, §§56-405.2, 56-408.
Similar signs prohibited, §56-408.
Whistles.
Failure to signal, §§56-415, 56-416.
Whistles to be sounded, §56-414.
Railroads.
Failure to remove causes of complaint, §56-440.
Local taxation of property, §58.1-2607.
Track removal, §56-451.1.
Real estate cooperatives.
Applicability of local ordinances, §55-429.
Conversion buildings, §55-487.
Real property.
Acquiring for development of business or industry, §15.2-1802.
Acquiring near parks or other public property, §15.2-1801.
Acquiring outside boundaries, §15.2-1800.
Acquisition or transfer generally, §15.2-1800.
Approval and acceptance of deeds conveying, §15.2-1802.
Condemnation generally, §§15.2-1901 to 15.2-1906.
See EMINENT DOMAIN.
School construction or improvement.
Tenancy in common with school board, §15.2-1800.1.
Real property taxes.
Exempt property generally, §§58.1-3600 to 58.1-3666.
See PROPERTY EXEMPT FROM TAXATION.
Generally, §§58.1-3200 to 58.1-3389.
See REAL PROPERTY TAXES.
Reapportionment of districts or wards, VA Const Art VIII §5.
Reciprocal insurance contracts, power to enter into, §38.2-1204.
Recordation tax, state.
Agreements with landowners, §29.1-509.
Exemption, §58.1-811.
Recreational facilities authorities, §§15.2-5600 to 15.2-5616.
See RECREATIONAL FACILITIES AUTHORITY.
Redistricting of election districts.
Action challenging boundaries of election district.
Attorney general, legal services, §2.2-508.
Reduction of corporate limits of cities or towns, §§15.2-3236 to 15.2-3245.
See BOUNDARIES.
Reduction of service by state agency to locality.
Notification, §2.2-612.

TOWNS —Cont'd
Refunding bonds, §§15.2-2643 to 15.2-2649.
Refuse collection and disposal authorities, §§15.2-5100 to 15.2-5159.
See WATER AND WASTE AUTHORITIES.
Refuse removal and disposal.
General powers of locality as to waste and recycling, §§15.2-901, 15.2-927 to 15.2-939.
Regional cooperation act, §§15.2-4200 to 15.2-4222.
See PLANNING DISTRICT COMMISSIONS.
Regional partnerships.
Regional competitiveness act, §§15.2-1306 to 15.2-1310.
Religious organizations.
Land held in adverse possession limitations, §57-17.
Removal of county courthouse.
Donation of land and money, §15.2-1648.
Funds issued to finance, §§15.2-1649, 15.2-1650.
Removal of nuisances, §15.2-1115.
Removal of public officers from office, §§24.2-230 to 24.2-238.
See REMOVAL OF PUBLIC OFFICERS FROM OFFICE.
Removal or rehabilitation of derelict structures.
Grants, §36-155.
Rental inspections of units located in rental inspection district.
Residential rental dwelling units.
Building code compliance, §36-105.1:1.
Residence of officers and employees, §§15.2-1505, 15.2-1525.
Removal of residence from jurisdiction officer required to reside, §15.2-1526.
Residential developments.
Private roads.
Designation as highways for law enforcement purposes, §46.2-1307.
Resolutions.
Ordinances and other actions generally, §§15.2-1425 to 15.2-1433.
See ORDINANCES.
Resources authority.
Grants to local governments, §62.1-218.
Issuing and selling local obligations to authority, §62.1-216.
Nonpayment by localities, investigations, withholding state funds, §62.1-216.1.
Water facilities revolving fund, §62.1-229.
Restaurants.
Fairs, exemption from provisions by ordinance, §35.1-26.
Retirement system of Virginia.
Generally, §§51.1-124.1 to 51.1-169.
See VIRGINIA RETIREMENT SYSTEM.
Revenues, expenditures and fund balances statement.
Filing with auditor of public accounts, §15.2-2510.
Rewards in felony and misdemeanor cases.
Authorization offer and pay, §15.2-1713.
Crimestoppers information, confidentiality of information, §15.2-1713.1.
Road construction and maintenance by prisoners, §53.1-59.
Road impact fees, §§15.2-2317 to 15.2-2329.
See ROAD IMPACT FEES.
Roller skates.
Prohibiting on sidewalks or crosswalks, §46.2-904.

TOWNS —Cont'd
Rolling stock tax distribution, §§58.1-2658, 58.1-2658.1.
Safety devices on storage equipment, §15.2-1113.
Salary of council members and mayors, §15.2-1414.7.
Sale of property, VA Const Art VII §9.
Scooters.
Prohibiting on sidewalks or crosswalks, §46.2-904.
Seal, §15.2-1402.
Secondhand dealers, §15.2-1114.
Self insurance.
Local government group self-insurance pools, §§15.2-2700 to 15.2-2709.
See LOCAL GOVERNMENT GROUP SELF-INSURANCE POOLS.
Selling certain property, restrictions, §15.2-2100.
Septic system repair loan program, §15.2-958.6.
Sergeants.
Generally.
See SERGEANTS.
Service districts, §§15.2-2400 to 15.2-2403.3.
Service stations.
Local regulation of sanitary conditions.
Application of public gathering place provisions, §32.1-202.
Setback lines and side yards.
Ordinances regulating, §15.2-2279.
Setoff debt collection, income tax, §§58.1-520 to 58.1-535.
See SETOFF DEBT COLLECTION, INCOME TAX.
Severance tax on coal, gas or oil.
License tax on persons engaging in business of severing, §§58.1-3712 to 58.1-3713.4.
Local coal severance license taxes, §§58.1-3740 to 58.1-3745.
Sewage disposal authorities, §§15.2-5100 to 15.2-5159.
See WATER AND WASTE AUTHORITIES.
Sewage disposal systems.
Generally, §§15.2-2122 to 15.2-2133.
See SEWAGE DISPOSAL SYSTEMS.
Sewer authorities, §§15.2-5100 to 15.2-5159.
See WATER AND WASTE AUTHORITIES.
Sheriff as law enforcement officer.
Tripartite contract with governing body, §15.2-1726.
Sidewalks.
Electric power-assisted bicycles.
Operating on sidewalks, §46.2-904.
Prohibiting roller skates, skateboards or bicycles, §46.2-904.
Sight-seeing carriers.
Application of provisions.
See SMOKING.
Skateboards.
Prohibiting on sidewalks or crosswalks, §46.2-904.
Smoke emissions, §15.2-1116.
Smoking in public places.
Virginia indoor clean air act, §§15.2-2820 to 15.2-2833.
See SMOKING IN PUBLIC PLACES.
Snow removal from sidewalks, §15.2-1115.
Solicitation of charitable or civic contributions.
Local ordinances, §57-63.
Solid waste management.
General powers of locality as to waste and recycling, §§15.2-901, 15.2-927 to 15.2-939.

TOWNS —Cont'd
Solid waste or recycling revolving fund.
Grants, §62.1-241.7.
Preferences, §62.1-241.8.
Loans, §62.1-241.6.
Preferences, §62.1-241.8.
Sale of loans, §62.1-241.9:1.
Speed limits.
Highways in cities and towns.
Authority of municipality to increase or decrease speed limits, §46.2-875.
Spot blight abatement, §36-49.1:1.
Stadiums or arenas, providing and operating, §15.2-1808.
State funds collected locally by financial officer, disposition, §15.2-1537.1.
Stock subscriptions, VA Const Art X §10.
Stormwater management program, adopting by ordinance, §15.2-2114.
Stormwater service districts, towns within.
Allocation of revenues, §15.2-2403.3.
Streets and alleys.
Construction and maintenance by prisoners, §53.1-59.
Construction or improvement of streets, roads, etc., outside of town, §15.2-2004.
Generally, §§15.2-2000 to 15.2-2030.
See ROADS, STREETS AND PUBLIC RIGHTS OF WAY.
Jurisdiction over public rights of way within boundaries of incorporated town, §15.2-2000.
Local authority over highways, §§33.1-224 to 33.1-246.
See LOCAL ROAD AUTHORITIES.
Private streets.
Approvals, §56-546.
Grade crossings, §56-548.
Public service company use without consent or compensation, §56-14.
Railroad crossings.
Bells to be sounded, §56-414.
Failure to signal, §§56-415, 56-416.
Cars obstructing thoroughfares or tracks, §§56-412.1, 56-412.2.
Crossbucks, §§56-405.2, 56-408.
Similar signs prohibited, §56-408.
Horns to be sounded, §56-414.
Failure to signal, §§56-415, 56-416.
Maintenance, §56-405.
Protective devices, §§56-406.1 to 56-408.
Signal boards, §56-405.2.
Similar signs prohibited, §56-408.
Whistles to be sounded, §56-414.
Failure to signal, §§56-415, 56-416.
Telegraph or telephone lines.
Erection, §§56-458, 56-460.
Cost to state, §56-461.
Restoring condition of ground, §56-467.
Subdivisions generally, §§15.2-2240 to 15.2-2279.
See SUBDIVISIONS.
Support of dependent children, §27-40.
Surface water management areas.
Study proceedings, §62.1-246.
Swimming pools, §15.2-1110.
Leasing land to person, firm or corporation, §15.2-1810.
Taxes.
Admission tax, §58.1-3840.
Bank franchise tax, §§58.1-1200 to 58.1-1217.
Boards of equalization, §§58.1-3370 to 58.1-3389.
See REAL PROPERTY TAXES.

TOWNS —Cont'd
Taxes —Cont'd
Charitable events.
Admissions to, §15.2-1104.1.
Cigarette tax, §§58.1-3830 to 58.1-3832, 58.1-3840.
Collection of local taxes generally, §§58.1-3910 to 58.1-3961.
See TAX COLLECTION.
Consumer utility taxes, §§58.1-3814 to 58.1-3816.2.
Correction of erroneous tax assessments, §§58.1-3980 to 58.1-3995.
See CORRECTION OF ERRONEOUS TAX ASSESSMENTS.
Delinquent taxes.
Collection of local taxes generally.
See TAX COLLECTION.
Interest and penalty, §58.1-3916.
Sale of delinquent tax lands, §§58.1-3965 to 58.1-3975.
See SALE OF DELINQUENT TAX LANDS.
Discount for early payment, §15.2-1104.
Distress.
Collection of local taxes by distress, §§58.1-3940 to 58.1-3961.
See TAX COLLECTION.
Excise tax, §58.1-3840.
Exempt property, §§58.1-3600 to 58.1-3666.
See PROPERTY EXEMPT FROM TAXATION.
Generally, §§58.1-3700 to 58.1-3735.
See LOCAL TAXES.
Income tax, §§58.1-540 to 58.1-549.
Local improvements, §§15.2-2404 to 15.2-2413.
See TAXES OR ASSESSMENTS FOR LOCAL IMPROVEMENTS.
Machinery and tools tax, §§58.1-3507, 58.1-3508.
Meals tax, §58.1-3840.
Merchants' capital tax, §§58.1-3509, 58.1-3510.
Ordinance imposing, two-third vote of council members, §15.2-1427.
Personal property taxes generally, §§58.1-3500 to 58.1-3522.
See PERSONAL PROPERTY TAXES.
Personal property tax relief act of 1998, §§58.1-3523 to 58.1-3535.
See PERSONAL PROPERTY TAX RELIEF ACT OF 1998.
Power generally, §15.2-1104.
Prepayment, §§58.1-3920, 58.1-3920.1.
Real property taxes generally, §§58.1-3200 to 58.1-3389.
See REAL PROPERTY TAXES.
Schools and education special tax, §§22.1-102 to 22.1-106.
Tax increment financing, §§58.1-3245 to 58.1-3245.5.
Tax increment financing.
Blighted areas, §§58.1-3245 to 58.1-3245.5.
Telecommunications services.
Providing, §15.2-2160.
Telegraph or telephone companies.
Certificate to town to operate as a telephone utility, §56-265.4:4.
Offering of communications services, §56-484.7:1.
Approval, §56-484.7:2.
Revocation, §56-484.7:4.
Restoring condition of ground, §56-467.
Wireless service authorities, §§15.2-5431.1 to 15.2-5431.37.
See WIRELESS SERVICE AUTHORITIES.

TOWNS —Cont'd
Telegraph or telephone lines.
Erection, §§56-458, 56-460.
Cost to state, §56-461.
Franchises to occupy public ground, §56-462.
Temporary closing public rights of way, §§15.2-2013, 15.2-2014.
Terrorism hoax.
Reimbursement of expenses in responding to, §15.2-1716.1.
Tort claims for damages.
Notice to be given counties, cities and towns, §15.2-209.
Tourism zones.
Establishment, tax incentives, regulatory flexibility.
Authority, §58.1-3851.
Tax revenues, entitlement, §58.1-3851.1.
Power to designate, §15.2-982.
Town attorney.
Authorized, appointment, salary and duties, §15.2-1542.
Defense of localities and political subdivisions, governing bodies, officers or employees, §15.2-1520.
Town clerks.
Appointing or designating, §§15.2-1536, 15.2-1538.
General duties, §15.2-1539.
Town sergeant.
Allowances to injured sergeants or deputies and dependents.
Authorization of governing body of locality to make, §15.2-1511.
Chief law enforcement officer, §15.2-1701.
City status granted town.
Continuance in office, sheriffs, §15.2-3818.
Death or injury of sergeant or deputy.
Allowances by governing body of locality, §15.2-1511.
Killed in line of duty.
Allowances to dependents by governing body of locality, §15.2-1511.
Town treasurer.
City status granted to town.
Continuance in office, appointment when no treasurer, §15.2-3816.
Elections, §15.2-3820.
Qualification for office, §15.2-3821.
Terms, §15.2-3820.
Vacancies, §15.2-3821.
Deputies.
Appointment, powers, removal, §15.2-1603.
Dual office holding, §15.2-1534.
Generally.
See TREASURERS, LOCAL.
Traffic lights.
Photo-monitoring systems to enforce traffic light signals, §15.2-968.1.
Transient room rentals tax.
Excise tax, town having general taxing powers, §58.1-3840.
Imposition, §58.1-3843.
Transition of city to town status.
City no longer qualifying for city status, §§15.2-4000 to 15.2-4005.
See REVERSION OF CITIES TO TOWNS.
Transition of city to town status generally, §§15.2-4100 to 15.2-4120.
See REVERSION OF CITIES TO TOWNS.

TOWNS —Cont'd
Transition of towns to cities.
Commission on local government, §§15.2-2900 to 15.2-2908.
See COMMISSION ON LOCAL GOVERNMENT.
Generally, §§15.2-3800 to 15.2-3834.
See TRANSITION OF TOWNS TO CITIES.
Special courts to hear cases, §§15.2-3000 to 15.2-3004.
Transportation board or department disposing of surplus realty.
Notice to local governing body, §33.1-223.2:2.
Transportation of offensive substances, §15.2-1113.
Trash removal and disposal.
General powers of locality as to waste and recycling, §§15.2-901, 15.2-927 to 15.2-939.
Travel expenses to persons on business of locality, §§15.2-1508.1 to 15.2-1508.4.
Unclaimed property in possession of sheriff or police.
Disposition, §15.2-1719.
Bicycles or mopeds, §15.2-1720.
Firearms or other weapons, §15.2-1721.
Uniform charter powers, §§15.2-1100 to 15.2-1126.
Unsafe, dangerous or unsanitary public or private buildings, §15.2-1115.
Use of streets, roads, alleys, etc., §§15.2-2015 to 15.2-2018.
Vacant building registration, §15.2-1127.
Vacation or alteration of public rights of way, §§15.2-2006 to 15.2-2008.
Vehicle license fees and taxes, §46.2-752.
Veteran's preference for employment, §15.2-1509.
Virginia Commonwealth University health system authority.
Authority to lend or donate money or other property, §23-50.16:11.
Virginia infrastructure project loan fund, §§15.2-2430 to 15.2-2440.
See VIRGINIA INFRASTRUCTURE PROJECT LOAN FUND.
Virginia retirement system generally, §§51.1-124.1 to 51.1-169.
See VIRGINIA RETIREMENT SYSTEM.
Voluntary settlement of annexation, transition or immunity issues, §§15.2-3400, 15.2-3401.
Volunteer firefighters.
Construction of provisions, §27-49.
Defined terms, §27-42.
Disputed questions of fact, §27-48.
Levy for funds, §27-47.
Payments for hospital and medical services, §27-46.
Payments for partial disability, §27-45.
Payments for total and permanent disability, §27-44.
Payments on death, §27-43.
Provisions effective upon adoption, §27-50.
Provisions for relief, §27-41.
Record of names, §27-42.
Volunteer firefighting or emergency medical services companies.
Contracts, §27-23.6.
Waste and recycling.
General powers of locality, §§15.2-901, 15.2-927 to 15.2-939.

TOWNS —Cont'd
Water authorities, §§15.2-5100 to 15.2-5159.
See WATER AND WASTE AUTHORITIES.
Water facilities revolving fund.
Grants, §§62.1-230, 62.1-230.1.
Preference, §62.1-230.1.
Loans, §§62.1-229, 62.1-230.1.
Preference, §62.1-230.1.
Waterfront, wharf property, public landings, etc.
Restrictions on selling, §15.2-2100.
Waters of the state.
Extraordinary hardship program, §62.1-44.15:2.
Federal development projects.
Acquisition of lands, §62.1-150.
Cooperation, §§62.1-148, 62.1-149.
Items of cooperation, §62.1-149.
Flood control measures, §62.1-148.1.
Liberal construction, §62.1-152.
Ratification of former resolutions and ordinances, §62.1-151.
Policy of state.
Construction of provisions, §62.1-13.
Provision violations.
Notification, §62.1-44.15:4.
Water control board duties.
Localities particularly affected, §62.1-44.15:01.
Water supply.
Notice of violations, §32.1-175.1.
Water supply revolving fund.
Grants, §§62.1-239, 62.1-239.1.
Preferences, §62.1-239.1.
Loans, §§62.1-238, 62.1-239.1.
Preferences, §62.1-239.1.
Water supply systems.
Generally, §§15.2-2134 to 15.2-2156.
See WATER SUPPLY SYSTEMS.
Weapons, unclaimed property disposition, §15.2-1721.
Weed removal, §15.2-1115.
Weights and measures, §15.2-1114.
Well covers.
Authority to require and regulate, §18.2-318.
Wetlands.
Condemnation for compensatory mitigation of wetlands, §15.2-1907.1.
Wetlands zoning, §28.2-1302.
Boards, §§28.2-1303 to 28.2-1305.
Permits, §§28.2-1306 to 28.2-1308.
Administrative review, §§28.2-1310 to 28.2-1313.
Judicial review, §28.2-1315.
Wireless service authorities, §§15.2-5431.1 to 15.2-5431.37.
See WIRELESS SERVICE AUTHORITIES.
Writ of error in criminal case, §19.2-317.
Zoning.
Coastal primary sand dunes and beaches, §28.2-1403.
Boards, §§28.2-1404, 28.2-1405.
Review of decisions, §§28.2-1410 to 28.2-1415.
Generally, §§15.2-2280 to 15.2-2316.2.
See ZONING.
Wetlands, §28.2-1302.
Boards, §§28.2-1303 to 28.2-1305.
Permits, §§28.2-1306 to 28.2-1308.
Review, §§28.2-1310 to 28.2-1313.
Judicial review, §28.2-1315.

TOWN SCHOOL BOARDS.
Generally, §§22.1-28 to 22.1-57.5.
See LOCAL SCHOOL BOARDS.

TOWN SCHOOL DISTRICTS.
Continuation of special town school districts, §22.1-33.

TOWN SCHOOL DIVISION FUNDS, §§22.1-113, 22.1-114.

TOWN SERGEANTS.
Allowances to injured sergeants or deputies and dependents.
Authorization of governing body of locality to make, §15.2-1511.
Chief law enforcement officer, §15.2-1701.
City status granted town.
Continuance in office, sheriffs, §15.2-3818.
Deputy sheriff serving as for town located in county, §15.2-1534.
Generally.
See SERGEANTS.
Killed in line of duty.
Allowances to dependents by governing body of locality, §15.2-1511.
Workers' compensation.
Employee defined, §65.2-101.

TOWNSHIPS.
Transition of county to city.
Towns located within county becoming city automatically continued as townships, §15.2-3916.

TOWN STREETS.
Local authority over highways, §§33.1-224 to 33.1-246.
See LOCAL ROAD AUTHORITIES.

TOWN TAXES.
Additional tax to pay interest and retire bonds, §58.1-3006.
Admissions tax.
Excise tax, town having general taxing powers, §58.1-3840.
Bank franchise tax.
Branch banks, §58.1-1211.
Record of deposits through branches, §58.1-1212.
Credit against state tax, §58.1-1213.
Generally, §§58.1-1200 to 58.1-1217.
Imposition, §58.1-1208.
Boards of equalization, §§58.1-3370 to 58.1-3389.
See REAL PROPERTY TAXES.
Bonded indebtedness.
Additional tax to pay interest and retire bonds, §58.1-3006.
Change to fiscal tax year, §58.1-3010.
Changing rate of tax during calendar year, §58.1-3012.
Cigarette tax, §§58.1-3830 to 58.1-3832.
Charitable events.
Admissions to, §15.2-1104.1.
Cigarette tax, §§58.1-3830 to 58.1-3832.
Corporate or partnership officer.
Willful failure to collect and account for, §58.1-3907.
Excise tax, town having general taxing powers, §58.1-3840.
Collection of local taxes generally, §§58.1-3910 to 58.1-3961.
See TAX COLLECTION.
Consumer utility taxes, §§58.1-3814 to 58.1-3816.2.

TOWN TAXES —Cont'd
Corporate officer or partnership officer liability for failure to pay certain taxes, §58.1-3906.
Willful failure to collect and account for, §58.1-3907.
Correction of erroneous tax assessments, §§58.1-3980 to 58.1-3995.
See CORRECTION OF ERRONEOUS TAX ASSESSMENTS.
Council of town to make levies, §58.1-3005.
Delinquent taxes.
Collection of local taxes generally.
See TAX COLLECTION.
Interest and penalty, §58.1-3916.
Sale of delinquent tax lands generally, §§58.1-3965 to 58.1-3975.
See SALE OF DELINQUENT TAX LANDS.
Different rates of levy on different classes of property, §58.1-3008.
Disasters.
Relief from taxes, §58.1-3014.
Distress.
Collection of local taxes by distress generally, §§58.1-3940 to 58.1-3961.
See TAX COLLECTION.
Enterprise zones.
Excise tax, town having general taxing powers, §58.1-3840.
Local enterprise zone development taxation program, §§58.1-3245.6 to 58.1-3245.12.
Excise tax, town having general taxing powers, §58.1-3840.
Exempt property, §§58.1-3600 to 58.1-3666.
See PROPERTY EXEMPT FROM TAXATION.
Funds not available, allocated, etc., until appropriated, §58.1-3005.
Generally, §§58.1-3700 to 58.1-3735.
See LICENSE TAXES.
Income tax, §§58.1-540 to 58.1-549.
Increase of local tax levy.
Notice and hearing prior to, §58.1-3007.
Injunctions against assessment or collection of taxes, §58.1-3993.
Interest for failure to pay tax, §58.1-3916.
Local improvements, §§15.2-2404 to 15.2-2413.
See TAXES OR ASSESSMENTS FOR LOCAL IMPROVEMENTS.
Local taxes generally, §§58.1-3000 to 58.1-3018.
See LOCAL TAXES.
Machinery and tools tax, §§58.1-3507, 58.1-3508.
Semiconductor manufacturing or food processing.
Separate classifications, §58.1-3508.1.
Meals tax.
Excise tax, town having general taxing powers, §58.1-3840.
Situs for taxation of sale of food and beverages, §58.1-3841.
Merchants' capital tax, §§58.1-3509, 58.1-3510.
Mosquito control districts, §32.1-194.
Motor vehicle sales and use tax.
Local tax prohibited, §58.1-2418.
Occupations, tax on prohibited, §58.1-3009.
Omitted local taxes or levies, §58.1-3903.
Forms for assessment, §58.1-3905.
Omitted lands, §58.1-3904.
Ordinance imposing, affirmative vote of majority of governing body required, VA Const Art VII §7.
Two-third vote of council members, §15.2-1427.

TOWN TAXES —Cont'd
Ordinances providing criminal penalties for failure to file returns or false statements, §58.1-3916.1.
Ordinances providing dates for filing returns, setting penalties, interest, etc., §58.1-3916.
Payment of taxes, §58.1-3916.
Payrolls, tax on prohibited, §58.1-3009.
Penalty for failure to pay tax, §58.1-3916.
Personal property tax relief act of 1998, §§58.1-3523 to 58.1-3535.
See PERSONAL PROPERTY TAX RELIEF ACT OF 1998.
Power generally, §15.2-1104.
Prepayment, §§58.1-3920, 58.1-3920.1.
Public school special tax, §§22.1-102 to 22.1-106.
Real property taxes generally, §§58.1-3200 to 58.1-3389.
See REAL PROPERTY TAXES.
Returns.
Due date for filing, §58.1-3916.
Sale of delinquent tax lands, §§58.1-3965 to 58.1-3975.
See SALE OF DELINQUENT TAX LANDS.
Service district assessment upon governmental subdivision.
Severance tax on coal, gas or oil.
License tax on persons engaging in business of severing, §§58.1-3712 to 58.1-3713.4.
Local coal severance license taxes, §§58.1-3740 to 58.1-3745.
Severance tax on coal, gas or oil.
License tax on persons engaging in business of severing, §§58.1-3712 to 58.1-3713.4.
Local coal severance license taxes, §§58.1-3740 to 58.1-3745.
Social security account numbers.
Disclosure for administrative purposes, §58.1-3017.
Special levy to pay interest and retire bonds, §58.1-3006.
Special tax school purposes, §§22.1-102 to 22.1-106.
Subjects of local taxation, §58.1-3000.
Tangible personal property generally, §§58.1-3500 to 58.1-3522.
See PERSONAL PROPERTY TAXES.
Tax increment financing, §§58.1-3245 to 58.1-3245.5.
Telephone or telegraph companies, local tax, §58.1-2690.
To whom property generally taxed and by whom listed, §58.1-3015.
Retention of property for payment of taxes.
Listed by and taxed to person other than owner, §58.1-3016.
Transient room rentals tax.
Excise tax, town having general taxing powers, §58.1-3840.
Imposition, §58.1-3843.
Travel campgrounds.
Excise tax, town having general taxing powers, §58.1-3840.
Use of July 1 as effective date of assessment, §58.1-3011.

TOWN TREASURERS.
Bonds of local officers generally, §§15.2-1527 to 15.2-1533.
See LOCAL OFFICERS AND EMPLOYEES.

TOWN TREASURERS —Cont'd
City status granted to town.
Continuance in office, appointment when no treasurer, §15.2-3816.
Elections, §15.2-3820.
Qualification for office, §15.2-3821.
Terms, §15.2-3820.
Vacancies, §15.2-3821.
Deputies.
Appointment, powers, removal, §15.2-1603.
Dual office holding, §15.2-1534.
Generally.
See TREASURERS, LOCAL.

TOW TRUCK OPERATORS.
Criminal justice services department.
Registration, §9.1-102.
Registration.
Criminal justice services department, §9.1-102.
Towing vehicles generally.
See TOWING VEHICLES.

TOXIC RELEASE INVENTORY.
Environmental quality department, §10.1-1186.1.

TOXIC SUBSTANCES.
Fish consumption advisories, §32.1-248.01.
Hazardous materials emergency response, §§44-146.34 to 44-146.40.
Inspection warrants, §§19.2-393 to 19.2-397.
Conduct of inspection, testing or collection of samples, §19.2-396.
Definitions, §19.2-393.
Duration of warrant, §19.2-395.
Issuance of warrant, §19.2-394.
Refusing to permit authorized inspection, §19.2-397.
Special procedure for drilling, §19.2-396.
Less toxic goods and products.
Procurement by public bodies, §2.2-4314.
Statute of limitations.
Criminal prosecution for discharge, dumping or emission, §19.2-8.
Waters of the state.
Closing of waters, §32.1-248.
Fish consumption advisories, §32.1-248.01.

TOXIC SUBSTANCES INFORMATION, §§32.1-239 to 32.1-245.
Advice of board, §32.1-245.
Defined terms, §32.1-239.
Designation of state information agency, §32.1-240.
Diagnosis of employee injuries and illnesses, §32.1-244.
Duties of board, §32.1-241.
Inter-agency cooperation, §32.1-243.
Operators' duties to report knowledge of toxicities, §32.1-244.
Powers of board, §32.1-241.
Reports of board, §32.1-245.

TOXIC WATERS.
Discharge reduction, §§62.1-44.17:2, 62.1-44.17:3.
Instream toxics removal or remediation technologies.
Evaluation and review, §62.1-44.17:4.
Water quality monitoring, information and restoration, §§62.1-44.19:4 to 62.1-44.19:10.

TOY FIREARMS.
Selling or giving firearm discharging blank or ball charges, §18.2-284.

TOY VEHICLES.
Defined, §46.2-100.
Electrically powered toy vehicles.
Spill-proof, sealed or gelled electrolyte batteries.
Required to operate, §46.2-908.1.
Use on highways, restrictions, §46.2-932.

TRACKING DEVICES.
Bail and recognizance.
Conditions of bail, §19.2-123.
Home/electronic incarceration.
Community-based corrections system for state-responsible offenders.
Program included, §§53.1-67.2 to 53.1-67.6.
Community corrections.
Generally, §§9.1-173 to 9.1-183.
See COMMUNITY CORRECTIONS.
Mandated services, §9.1-176.
Criminal fines and penalties.
Installment payments as condition to program, §19.2-354.
Fee by participant towards cost of program, §53.1-150.
Offenders sentenced to confinement in jails, §53.1-131.2.
Release of accused or juvenile on unsecured bond or promise to appear, §19.2-123.
Hunting, use of GPS to manage dogs, §29.1-516.
Probation.
Wearing device as condition of probation, §19.2-303.
Search warrant to permit use of tracking device, §19.2-56.2.
Suspended sentences.
Wearing device as condition of suspended sentence, §19.2-303.

TRACTORS.
Farm tractors.
Defined, §46.2-100.
Motor vehicle registration exemption, §46.2-667.
Insurance coverage for exempted vehicles, §46.2-684.1.
Traction engines and tractors.
Issuance of special permits for operation on highway, §46.2-1046.
Transportation board.
General powers and duties of board.
Inapplicability of provisions to certain engines and tractors, §33.1-23.

TRACTOR TRAILERS.
Brakes on trailers, §46.2-1070.
Braking distances, §46.2-1067.
Parking, ordinances prohibiting or limiting, §46.2-1224.

TRADE AND COMMERCE.
Agricultural equipment warranties, §§59.1-207.7, 59.1-207.8.
Antitrust laws, §§59.1-9.1 to 59.1-9.17.
See ANTITRUST.
Batteries, storage, §§59.1-189 to 59.1-191.
See BATTERIES.
Brands on timber, §§59.1-103 to 59.1-115.
See TIMBER BRANDS.
Business opportunity sales, §§59.1-262 to 59.1-269.
See BUSINESS OPPORTUNITY SALES.
Comparison price advertising, §§59.1-207.40 to 59.1-207.44.
See COMPARISON PRICE ADVERTISING.

TRADE AND COMMERCE —Cont'd
Conspiracies to rig government bids, §§59.1-68.6 to 59.1-68.8.
Consumer protection, §§59.1-196 to 59.1-207.
See CONSUMER PROTECTION.
Credit services businesses, §§59.1-335.1 to 59.1-335.12.
See CREDIT SERVICES BUSINESSES.
Devices on certain containers, §§59.1-93 to 59.1-102.
See DEVICES ON CERTAIN CONTAINERS.
Emergency petroleum products supplies, §§59.1-21.18:2 to 59.1-21.18:4.
Enterprise zones, §§59.1-279 to 59.1-284.01, 59.1-538 to 59.1-549.
See ENTERPRISE ZONES.
Equal credit opportunities, §§6.2-500 to 6.2-513.
See EQUAL CREDIT OPPORTUNITIES.
Explosives generally, §§59.1-137 to 59.1-141.
See EXPLOSIVES.
Extended service contracts, §§59.1-435 to 59.1-441.
See SERVICE CONTRACTS, EXTENDED.
Farm machinery dealerships.
See FARM EQUIPMENT AND MACHINERY DEALERSHIPS.
Firearms generally, §§59.1-148.3, 59.1-148.4.
See FIREARMS.
Foreign trade zones, §§62.1-159 to 62.1-162.
General assembly power to regulate trade, VA Const Art IV §14.
Gift certificate disclosures, §§59.1-530 to 59.1-532.
Gifts, promotional, §§59.1-415 to 59.1-423.
See PROMOTIONAL PRIZES AND GIFTS.
Health clubs.
See HEALTH CLUBS.
Health spas, §§59.1-294 to 59.1-310.
Heavy equipment dealers, §§59.1-353 to 59.1-363.
See HEAVY EQUIPMENT DEALERS.
Home solicitation sales, §§59.1-21.1 to 59.1-21.7:1.
See HOME SOLICITATION SALES.
Independent sales representatives, §§59.1-455 to 59.1-459.
See SALES REPRESENTATIVES, INDEPENDENT.
Influenza vaccine price gouging, §§59.1-533 to 59.1-537.
Insurance, unfair trade practices, §§38.2-500 to 38.2-518.
See INSURANCE, UNFAIR TRADE PRACTICES.
Invention development services, §§59.1-208 to 59.1-215.
See INVENTION DEVELOPMENT SERVICES.
Lease-purchase agreements, §§59.1-207.17 to 59.1-207.27.
See LEASE-PURCHASE AGREEMENTS.
Livestock purchases from unknown persons, §§59.1-192 to 59.1-195.
See LIVESTOCK.
Lubricating oils, §§59.1-149 to 59.1-167.3.
See LUBRICATING OILS.
Marks on certain containers, §§59.1-93 to 59.1-102.
See MARKS ON CERTAIN CONTAINERS.
Membership camping, §§59.1-311 to 59.1-335.
See MEMBERSHIP CAMPING.
Motion picture fair competition, §§59.1-255 to 59.1-260.
See MOTION PICTURES.

TRADE AND COMMERCE —Cont'd
Motor fuels, §§59.1-149 to 59.1-167.3.
See MOTOR FUELS.
Motor vehicle manufacturers' warranty adjustment, §§59.1-207.34 to 59.1-207.39.
See MOTOR VEHICLE WARRANTIES.
Motor vehicle rentals.
Collision damage waiver, §§59.1-207.28 to 59.1-207.33.
See MOTOR VEHICLE RENTALS.
Motor vehicle repair facilities, §§59.1-207.1 to 59.1-207.6.
See MOTOR VEHICLE REPAIR FACILITIES.
Motor vehicle warranty enforcement, §§59.1-207.9 to 59.1-207.16:1.
See MOTOR VEHICLE WARRANTIES.
Names on certain containers, §§59.1-93 to 59.1-102.
See NAMES ON CERTAIN CONTAINERS.
Oils, lubricating, §§59.1-149 to 59.1-167.3.
See LUBRICATING OILS.
Overhead high voltage line safety, §§59.1-406 to 59.1-414.
See OVERHEAD HIGH VOLTAGE LINE SAFETY.
Pari-mutuel wagering on horses, §§59.1-364 to 59.1-405.
See PARI-MUTUEL WAGERING.
Pay-per-call services, §§59.1-429 to 59.1-434.
See PAY-PER-CALL SERVICES.
Personal information privacy, §§59.1-442 to 59.1-444.
Petroleum products franchises, §§59.1-21.8 to 59.1-21.18:1.
See PETROLEUM PRODUCTS FRANCHISES.
Prizes, promotional, §§59.1-415 to 59.1-423.
See PROMOTIONAL PRIZES AND GIFTS.
Recorded devices, §§59.1-41.1 to 59.1-41.6.
See RECORDED DEVICES.
Rent-to-own agreements, §§59.1-207.17 to 59.1-207.27.
See LEASE-PURCHASE AGREEMENTS.
Secondhand article sales, §§59.1-116.1 to 59.1-136.
See SECONDHAND ARTICLE SALES.
Septic system inspectors, §§59.1-310.7 to 59.1-310.10.
Storage batteries, §§59.1-189 to 59.1-191.
See BATTERIES.
Tanning facilities, §§59.1-310.1 to 59.1-310.6.
See TANNING FACILITIES.
Telephone carrier identification, §§59.1-424 to 59.1-427.
Telephone solicitation sales, §§59.1-21.1 to 59.1-21.7:1.
See TELEPHONE SOLICITATION SALES.
Timber brands, §§59.1-103 to 59.1-115.
See TIMBER BRANDS.
Trade secrets, §§59.1-336 to 59.1-343.
See TRADE SECRETS.
Transacting business under assumed name, §§59.1-69 to 59.1-76.
See TRANSACTING BUSINESS UNDER ASSUMED NAME.
Travel clubs, §§59.1-445 to 59.1-454.
See TRAVEL CLUBS.
Workers' compensation, §§65.2-100 to 65.2-1310.
See WORKERS' COMPENSATION.

TRADE ASSOCIATIONS.
Solicitation of charitable or civic contributions.
Exemption from provisions, §57-60.

TRADE ASSOCIATIONS —Cont'd
Suits by and against unincorporated associations or orders, §8.01-15.

TRADEMARKS AND SERVICE MARKS.
Abandonment of mark.
Cancellation of registration, §59.1-92.10.
Actions.
Infringement, §59.1-92.12.
Remedies generally, §59.1-92.13.
Appeals from final action of commission, §59.1-92.18.
Assignment of mark, §59.1-92.8.
Attorneys' fees.
Infringement actions, §59.1-92.13.
Acts committed with knowledge, requirements for recovering, §59.1-92.12.
Business opportunity sales.
Prohibited acts, §59.1-266.
Cancellation of registration, §59.1-92.10.
Change of name of applicant for registration, §59.1-92.8.
Changing or removing with intent to defraud, §18.2-214.
Classification of goods and services.
Commission by regulation may establish, §59.1-92.11.
Clerical error in granting registration.
Cancellation of registration, §59.1-92.10.
Common law rights not adversely affected, §59.1-92.15.
Confusion with mark or trade name previously used.
Cancellation of registration, §59.1-92.10.
Criminal penalties for knowing and intentional infringement, §59.1-92.13.
Dairy milk cases or milk crates.
Defacing, obliterating, etc., §18.2-102.2.
Damages.
Infringement actions, §59.1-92.13.
Acts committed with knowledge, requirement for recovering, §59.1-92.12.
Definitions, §59.1-92.2.
Destruction of infringing materials.
Criminal proceedings, §59.1-92.13.
Distinctive nature of mark.
Prima facie evidence, §59.1-92.3.
Evidence in proceedings before commission.
Final judgments of court of record, §59.1-92.17.
Expenses of regulation, fees to be used for, §59.1-92.20.
Fees prescribed by commission, §59.1-92.16.
Fees to recover expense of regulation, §59.1-92.20.
Final judgments of courts of record offered in evidence in proceedings before commission, §59.1-92.17.
Forms.
Commission's powers, §59.1-92.19.
Fraudulently obtained registration, cancellation, §59.1-92.10.
Generic name for goods or services.
Cancellation of registration upon mark becoming, §59.1-92.10.
Infringement, §59.1-92.12.
Remedies generally, §59.1-92.13.
Injunctions.
Infringement, §59.1-92.13.
Motor vehicle equipment.
Unapproved equipment for sale, §46.2-1004.

TRADEMARKS AND SERVICE MARKS —Cont'd
Name change of applicant for registration, §59.1-92.8.
Nonresident registrants.
Service on, §59.1-92.14.
Olympic symbols, prohibition on use, §59.1-92.21.
Partial cancellation of registration, §59.1-92.10.
Profits recovered in infringement actions.
Acts committed with knowledge, requirements, §59.1-92.12.
Record of marks registered or renewed.
Commission to keep for public examination, §59.1-92.9.
Registration.
Amendment to application, §59.1-92.5.
Application, §59.1-92.4.
Assignment of mark.
New certificate issued, §59.1-92.8.
Cancellation, §59.1-92.10.
Certificate, §59.1-92.6.
Change of name of applicant, §59.1-92.8.
Classification of goods and services, §59.1-92.11.
Disclaimer of unregistrable component, commission may require, §59.1-92.5.
Drawing or specimen to accompany application, commission may require, §59.1-92.4.
Fees to be prescribed by commission, §59.1-92.16.
Filing of application, §59.1-92.5.
Ineligibility for registration, §59.1-92.3.
Infringement, §59.1-92.12.
Issuance of certificate, §59.1-92.6.
New certificate upon assignment of mark, §59.1-92.8.
Notice of nonentitlement to registration, §59.1-92.5.
Partial cancellation, §59.1-92.10.
Record of marks registered, §59.1-92.9.
Renewal, §59.1-92.7.
Single application falling within multiple classes, §59.1-92.11.
Term, §59.1-92.7.
Remedies for infringement, §59.1-92.13.
Rulemaking by commission, §59.1-92.19.
Sales, UCC.
Buyer's obligation against infringement, §8.2-312.
Notice of claim or litigation to person answerable over, §8.2-607.
Warranty against infringement, §8.2-312.
Service of notice, process and other papers.
Out-of-state registrants, §59.1-92.14.
Supreme court appeals from final action of commission, §59.1-92.18.
Timber brands generally, §§59.1-103 to 59.1-115.
See TIMBER BRANDS.
Virginia trademark and service mark act (1998).
Chapter known as, §59.1-92.1.
Water and waste authorities.
Powers, §15.2-5114.

TRADE NAMES.
Amending pleading to reflect correct name.
Confusion in similar names, §8.01-6.2.
Dentists.
Practicing under, §54.1-2718.
Liquid fuels, lubricating oils and similar product sales.
Assisting in violation, §18.2-230.
False trade name, §18.2-229.
Imitating indicia of trade name, §18.2-228.

TRADE NAMES —Cont'd
Liquid fuels, lubricating oils and similar product sales —Cont'd
Labeling requirement for lubricating oil, §18.2-231.
Misdemeanor for violating provision, §18.2-232.
Sale from pump indicating other trade name, §18.2-227.
Motor vehicle equipment.
Unapproved equipment for sale, §46.2-1004.
Secured transactions.
Name of debtor and secured party, §8.9A-503.
Solicitation of charitable or civic contributions.
Prohibited acts, §57-57.

TRADE SECRETS, §§59.1-336 to 59.1-343.
Air pollution control.
Protection of confidential information, §10.1-1314.1.
Asbestos NESHAP, §40.1-51.33.
Attorneys' fees, §59.1-338.1.
Citation of chapter, §59.1-336.
Code commission.
Contracting with publishers, §30-147.
Conflict of laws, §59.1-341.
Damages, §59.1-338.
Defined terms, §59.1-336.
Effective date of provisions, §59.1-343.
Freedom of information act.
Exclusions from chapter.
Information provided to the environmental quality department, §2.2-3705.6.
Proprietary information gathered during licensing process, §2.2-3705.6.
Vendor proprietary information software, §2.2-3705.1.
Injunctions, §59.1-337.
Insurance rate filings not open to public inspection.
Burden of proving information constitutes trade secret, §38.2-1907.
Mine inspections.
Confidentiality of trade secrets, §45.1-161.84.
Mineral mine safety.
Protection of confidential trade secrets during inspections, §45.1-161.292:57.
Occupational safety and health, §40.1-51.4:1.
Pesticide control.
Protection of trade secrets, §3.2-3908.
Pollution prevention program.
Protection of trade secrets, §10.1-1425.16.
Preservation of, §59.1-339.
Procurement by public bodies.
Trade secrets not subject to public disclosure, §2.2-4342.
Small employer health insurance.
Health insurance provider disclosures, §38.2-3434.
Statute of limitations, §59.1-340.
Waste management.
Plans and specifications to be provided to department.
Exemption from freedom of information act for trade secrets, §10.1-1458.
Workforce council.
Confidentiality, §2.2-2673.

TRADES, LICENSE TAXES.
Generally, §§58.1-3700 to 58.1-3735.
See LICENSE TAXES.

TRADESMAN LICENSURE, §§54.1-1128 to 54.1-1135.
Applications, §54.1-1130.

TRADESMAN LICENSURE —Cont'd
Building official reports, §54.1-1134.
Continuing education, §54.1-1133.
Defined terms, §54.1-1128.
Denial grounds, §54.1-1134.
Examinations, §54.1-1130.
Exemptions, §54.1-1131.
Expiration, §54.1-1132.
Necessity, §54.1-1129.
Prohibited acts, §54.1-1134.
Renewal, §54.1-1132.
Revocation grounds, §54.1-1134.

TRADE UNIONS.
Apprenticeship, §§40.1-117 to 40.1-126.
See APPRENTICESHIP.
Labor.
See LABOR.
Labor disputes, §§40.1-70 to 40.1-75.
Labor unions.
Generally, §§40.1-52 to 40.1-54.3.
See LABOR UNIONS.
Mediation and conciliation of labor disputes, §§40.1-70 to 40.1-75.
Occupational safety and health, §§40.1-44.1 to 40.1-51.4:5.
See OCCUPATIONAL SAFETY AND HEALTH.
Registration of name or insignia.
Illegal use of registered insignia, §18.2-177.
Right to work, §§40.1-58 to 40.1-69.
See RIGHT TO WORK.
Strikes by government employees, §§40.1-55 to 40.1-57.1.
Unauthorized wearing or displaying on motor vehicles of button, insignia or emblem of, §18.2-176.

TRAFFIC ACCIDENTS, §§46.2-894 to 46.2-902.
See MOTOR VEHICLE ACCIDENTS.

TRAFFIC CIRCLES.
Circular intersection defined, §46.2-100.
Circular intersections, path of travel, §46.2-807.
Driver approaching or entering, §46.2-822.
Rotary traffic islands, §46.2-807.
Fine schedule, VA SCt Rule 3B:2.
Maximum fine for violating Title 46.2, §46.2-113.

TRAFFIC CONTROL DEVICES.
Bicycles.
Proceeding through intersection at red light, §46.2-833.
County, city or town authority.
Devices erected by towns on primary roads maintained by VDOT, §33.1-47.
Damaging or removing, §46.2-832.
Defined, §46.2-100.
Demerit points, §46.2-492.
Detention for violations on basis of radio message, §46.2-833.
Evasion of traffic control device, §46.2-833.1.
Fine schedule, VA SCt Rule 3B:2.
Maximum fine for violating title, §46.2-113.
Prepayment of fine, §16.1-69.40:1.
Generally, §§46.2-830 to 46.2-836.
Lane-use control signals, §46.2-805.
Defined, §46.2-100.
Law-enforcement officers, crossing guards and flaggers, signals by, §46.2-834.
Left turn on steady red light after stopping, §46.2-836.

TRAFFIC CONTROL DEVICES —Cont'd
Mopeds and motorcycles.
Proceeding through intersection at red light, §46.2-833.
Municipal erection of signs and signals, §§46.2-1300, 46.2-1312.
Obeying highway signs, §§46.2-830, 46.2-830.1.
Obeying traffic lights, §46.2-833.
Photo-monitoring systems to enforce traffic light signals.
Local powers, §15.2-968.1.
Vehicle owner data.
Supplying system operator, §46.2-208.
Powers of local government, §§46.2-1300, 46.2-1312.
Residential areas, installation of traffic control measures, §33.1-223.2:19.
Private financing, §33.1-223.2:20.
Right turn on steady red light after stopping, §46.2-835.
Signs, lights and markings generally, §§46.2-830 to 46.2-836.
See TRAFFIC INFRACTIONS.
Size, design or color, §46.2-1312.
Speeding conviction prohibited unless markers installed, §46.2-879.
Unofficial traffic control devices, §46.2-831.

TRAFFIC INFRACTIONS.
Accidents.
Generally, §§46.2-894 to 46.2-902.
See MOTOR VEHICLE ACCIDENTS.
All-terrain vehicles.
Generally.
See ALL-TERRAIN VEHICLES.
Animals.
Riding animals on highway.
After sunset, §46.2-800.1.
Controlled access highways, §46.2-808.
Appeal to circuit court.
Jury trial and measure of proof, §19.2-258.1.
Appearances.
Written appearance and waiver of hearing, §19.2-254.1.
Applicability of traffic regulations to drivers of all vehicles, §§46.2-800, 46.2-801.
Arrest warrants.
Exception to notice rule, §19.2-75.
Failure to appear on return date of mailed summons, §19.2-76.3.
Mailing of summons, §19.2-76.2.
Assessment of fees.
Fees not allowed law-enforcement officers, §46.2-218.
Bench trial.
Measure of proof, §19.2-258.1.
Bicycles.
General provisions, §§46.2-903 to 46.2-908.
See BICYCLES.
Bifurcated trial.
Prior traffic record considered prior to sentencing, §46.2-943.
Blocking access to premises, §46.2-818.
Breakdown on highway.
Emergency flashing lights and moving of vehicles, §46.2-888.
Cell phones or other wireless telecommunications devices.
Using while operating vehicle.
Holders of provisional drivers' licenses, §46.2-334.01.

TRAFFIC INFRACTIONS —Cont'd
Child charged with traffic infractions, disposition, §16.1-278.10.
Circular intersections.
Path of travel, §46.2-807.
Yielding right-of-way, §46.2-822.
Coasting in neutral, §46.2-811.
Fine schedule, VA SCt Rule 3B:2.
Prepayment of fine, §16.1-69.40:1.
Commercial drivers' licenses.
Change of address, failure to notify department, §46.2-341.11.
Disqualification for multiple serious traffic violations, §46.2-341.20.
Commercial vehicle operator.
Damaging or threatening, §46.2-818.
Limitation to use of certain lanes of interstate highways, §46.2-803.1.
Controlled access highways.
Crossovers posted for authorized vehicles.
Use by driver of unauthorized vehicle, §46.2-808.1.
Prohibited vehicle uses, §46.2-808.
Court of appeals.
Petition for appeal, VA SCt Rule 5A:12.
Criminal fines and penalties.
Failure of provision for payment, §46.2-395.
Failure or refusal to pay.
Suspension of driver's license, §46.2-395.
General penalty for violations, §46.2-113.
Installment payment authorized, §19.2-354.
Pretrial payment of fines, §16.1-69.40:1.
Criminal procedure, §§46.2-936 to 46.2-947.
Admissibility of speedometer tests, §46.2-942.
Arraignment, §46.2-940.
Arrest of nonresidents, §§46.2-944 to 46.2-947.
Bifurcated trial.
Prior traffic record considered prior to sentencing, §46.2-943.
Driving while privilege to drive suspended or revoked.
Impoundment of vehicle, §46.2-301.
DWI or habitual offender offenses, §46.2-301.1.
Issuance of warrant, §46.2-301.
Highway safety corridors, violations committed within, §46.2-947.
Issuance of subpoenas.
Motor vehicle accidents, §46.2-939.
Issuance of summons.
Parking ordinance violation, §46.2-941.
Issuance of warrant.
Failure to comply with summons, §46.2-938.
Misdemeanor arrest, §§46.2-936, 46.2-937.
Nonresidents' arrest, §§46.2-944 to 46.2-947.
Release on summons and promise to appear, §46.2-936.
Sentencing, §46.2-943.
Written appearance and waiver of hearing, §19.2-254.1.
Crossing solid or double solid line, §46.2-804.
Fine schedule, VA SCt Rule 3B:2.
Prepayment of fine, §16.1-69.40:1.
Crossovers on controlled access highways.
Use by unauthorized vehicles, §46.2-808.1.
Cruising ordinances.
No-cruising areas, §46.2-1219.1.
Damaging traffic control devices, §46.2-832.
Defined, §§18.2-8, 46.2-100.

TRAFFIC INFRACTIONS —Cont'd
Disabled vehicle in highway.
Failure to use proper warning device, VA SCt Rule 3B:2.
Maximum fine for violating Title 46.2, §46.2-113.
Discharging cargo or passengers.
Stopping on highways, §46.2-893.
Disposition of fines in traffic cases, §46.2-1308.
Disregarding signal by law-enforcement officer to stop, §§46.2-817, 46.2-834.
District courts.
Fees in certain criminal cases, §16.1-69.48:1.
Jurisdiction, §16.1-123.1.
Driver sleeping on shoulder of highway, §46.2-830.1.
Drivers of public passenger-carrying vehicles.
Age limits for drivers, §46.2-810.
Driving in center lane of three-lane highway, §46.2-804.
Fine schedule, VA SCt Rule 3B:2.
Prepayment of fine, §16.1-69.40:1.
Driving more than 13 hours in a 24-hour period, §46.2-812.
Fine schedule, VA SCt Rule 3B:2.
Prepayment of fine, §16.1-69.40:1.
Driving on right side of highway, §46.2-802.
Fine schedule, VA SCt Rule 3B:2.
Prepayment of fine, §16.1-69.40:1.
Driving through safety zone, §46.2-814.
Fine schedule, VA SCt Rule 3B:2.
Maximum fine for violating Title 46.2, §46.2-113.
Prepayment of fine, §16.1-69.40:1.
Driving too fast for highway and traffic conditions, §46.2-861.
Emergency stopping on highways.
Moving, emergency flashing lights, §46.2-888.
Emergency vehicles.
Generally, §§46.2-920 to 46.2-922.
Escort vehicles.
Impeding or disrupting vehicles operating under valid highway hauling permit, §46.2-828.2.
Evasion of traffic control devices, §46.2-833.1.
Excessive size and weight permits.
Impeding or disrupting vehicles operating under valid highway hauling permit, §46.2-828.2.
Expungement of court records.
Juvenile records, §16.1-306.
Failure to appear.
Waiver of hearing, §19.2-258.1.
Fines.
Failure or refusal to pay fines or costs.
Suspension of driver's license, §46.2-395.
General penalty, §46.2-113.
Installment payment authorized, §19.2-354.
Maximum penalty, §46.2-113.
Prepayment, §16.1-69.40:1.
Pretrial payment of fine, §16.1-69.40:1.
Schedule, VA SCt Rule 3B:2.
Speeding in certain residence districts, §46.2-878.2.
Fire or emergency.
Stopping in vicinity of fire or emergency, §46.2-890.
Fleeing or eluding police, §46.2-817.
Following too closely, §46.2-816.
Demerit points, §46.2-492.
Fine schedule, VA SCt Rule 3B:2.
Fire apparatus, §46.2-921.
Maximum fine for violating Title 46.2, §46.2-113.
Prepayment of fine, §16.1-69.40:1.

TRAFFIC INFRACTIONS —Cont'd
Forfeiture of vehicles.
Vehicle equipped with smoke projectors, etc., §46.2-1087.
For-hire vehicles.
Displaying not-for-hire license plates, §46.2-724.
Funeral processions.
Impeding or disrupting, §46.2-828.1.
Improper joining of or passing through, §46.2-828.
General penalty, §46.2-113.
Green lane-use control signal, §46.2-805.
Guaranteed arrest bond certificates, automobile clubs and associations.
Acceptance in lieu of cash bail in event of motor vehicle law violations, §38.2-2408.
Hauling.
Hazardous cargo through tunnels in violation of posted signs, §46.2-815.
High-occupancy toll lanes.
Entering without paying toll, §33.1-56.3.
Highway hauling permits.
Escort vehicles.
Impeding or disrupting vehicles operating under valid highway hauling permit, §46.2-828.2.
Highway safety corridors, violations committed within, §46.2-947.
Highway signs, §§46.2-830, 46.2-830.1.
Demerit points, §46.2-492.
Fine schedule, VA SCt Rule 3B:2.
Prepayment of fine, §16.1-69.40:1.
Uniform traffic control devices on highways, §46.2-830.
Highway work zones.
Decreased maximum speed limits, §46.2-878.1.
Hitchhiking, §46.2-929.
Horn signal when overtaking vehicle.
Fine schedule, VA SCt Rule 3B:2.
Maximum fine for violating Title 46.2, §46.2-113.
Prepayment of fine, §16.1-69.40:1.
Horse-driven vehicles.
Prohibited on controlled access highways, §46.2-808.
HOT lanes.
Fine schedule, VA SCt Rules 3B:2, 3C:2.
High-occupancy toll lanes.
Entering without paying toll, §33.1-56.3.
HOV lane restrictions, §33.1-46.2.
Fine schedule, VA SCt Rule 3B:2.
Improper driving.
Lesser offense of reckless driving, §46.2-869.
Improperly stopped or parked on highway, §46.2-888.
Improper passing, §§46.2-837 to 46.2-844.
Indictable offenses.
Pretrial payment of fine, §16.1-69.40:1.
Injuring traffic control devices, §46.2-832.
Interstate highways.
Commercial vehicles limited to use of certain lanes, §46.2-803.1.
Jaywalking, §46.2-923.
Jury trial on appeal to circuit court, §19.2-258.1.
Measure of proof, §19.2-258.1.
Juvenile and domestic relations district court jurisdiction, §16.1-241.
Keeping to right in crossing intersections or railroads, §46.2-803.
Fine schedule, VA SCt Rule 3B:2.
Prepayment of fine, §16.1-69.40:1.

TRAFFIC INFRACTIONS —Cont'd
Lane changing without first ascertaining safety of move, §46.2-804.
Fine schedule, VA SCt Rule 3B:2.
Prepayment of fine, §16.1-69.40:1.
Lane-use control signals, §46.2-805.
License plates.
Vehicles operated for-hire displaying not-for-hire plates, §46.2-724.
Local government powers, §§46.2-1300 to 46.2-1314.
See LOCALITIES.
Loitering on bridges or highway rights-of-way, §46.2-930.
Fine schedule, VA SCt Rule 3B:2.
Maximum fine, §46.2-113.
Maximum safe speed, §46.2-861.
Maximum speed limits.
Generally, §46.2-870.
Highways in cities and towns, §§46.2-874, 46.2-875.
Nonsurface treated highways, §46.2-873.1.
Passenger vehicles towing certain trailers, §46.2-876.
Prepayment of fines, §46.2-878.3.
Residence districts.
Operation of vehicle at 15 miles per hour or more over applicable speed.
Certain city ordinance prohibiting, §46.2-874.1.
Operation of vehicle at 20 miles per hour or more over applicable speed.
Certain town ordinance prohibiting, §46.2-874.1.
School buses, §46.2-871.
School crossings, §46.2-873.
Vehicles operating under special permits, §46.2-872.
Measure of proof, §19.2-258.
Appeal to circuit courts, §19.2-258.1.
Mechanical breakdown on highway.
Emergency flashing lights and moving of vehicle, §46.2-888.
Minimum speed limits, §46.2-877.
Misdemeanor for arrest purposes, §46.2-937.
Mobile infrared transmitters.
Unlawful possession, §46.2-1077.1.
Mopeds.
Generally.
See MOPEDS.
Motion picture equipment.
Viewing motion pictures or similar displays while driving, §46.2-1077.1.
Motor carrier regulations of state police, §52-8.4.
Motorcycles.
Generally.
See MOTORCYCLES.
Rider safety, §§46.2-1188 to 46.2-1192.
See MOTORCYCLE RIDER SAFETY.
Motor fuel retail sales establishments.
Driving motor vehicles from without payment for fuel, §46.2-819.2.
Motor vehicle equipment.
General provisions, §§46.2-1000 to 46.2-1088.
See MOTOR VEHICLE EQUIPMENT.
Move over law violation, §46.2-921.1.
Negligence per se.
Occupying trailer being towed on highway, §46.2-813.

TRAFFIC INFRACTIONS —Cont'd
Negligence per se —Cont'd
Riding animals on highways after sunset, §46.2-800.1.
Nitrous oxide devices connected to engines, §46.2-1088.4.
No-cruising ordinances, §46.2-1219.1.
Occupying trailer being towed on highway, §46.2-813.
Fine schedule, VA SCt Rule 3B:2.
Prepayment of fine, §16.1-69.40:1.
Offenses involving motor vehicles generally.
See MOTOR VEHICLE AND TRAFFIC OFFENSES.
One-way streets and roads, §46.2-806.
Fine schedule, VA SCt Rule 3B:2.
Left turn on steady red light after stopping, §46.2-836.
Demerit points, §46.2-492.
Prepayment of fine, §16.1-69.40:1.
Overtaking, §§46.2-837 to 46.2-844.
Parking.
Commuter parking lots owned by DOT.
Parking not in conformance with signs and pavement markings, §46.2-1219.2.
Conditions precedent to issuance of summons for violation, §46.2-941.
Dimming headlights on parked vehicles, §46.2-1035.
Emergency or parking brakes, §46.2-1068.
Fine schedule, VA SCt Rule 3B:2.
Generally, §§46.2-1216 to 46.2-1239.
See PARKING.
Handicapped persons.
Holders of special license plates and decals, §46.2-731.
Improper use of handicap parking space, §46.2-731.
Fine schedule, VA SCt Rule 3B:2.
Pretrial payment of fine, §16.1-69.40:1.
Lights on parked vehicles, §46.2-1037.
Location of parked vehicles, §46.2-889.
Maximum fine for violating Title 46.2, §46.2-113.
Near fire apparatus, §46.2-921.
Requirements for parking, §46.2-1071.
Setting hand brake and turning wheels to curb on parked vehicle, §46.2-1071.
Passing, §§46.2-837 to 46.2-844.
Bicycles, moped, animal or animal-drawn vehicle, §46.2-839.
Driving too closely to vehicle being overtaken in same direction, §46.2-838.
Fine schedule, VA SCt Rule 3B:2.
Maximum fine for violating Title 46.2, §46.2-113.
Giving way to overtaking vehicle when driving abreast on divided highway, §46.2-842.1.
Giving way to the right to overtaking vehicle, §46.2-842.
Increasing speed when passed by overtaking vehicle, §46.2-842.
Left passing when lane is not clearly visible, §46.2-843.
Left passing when oncoming traffic is too near to permit it safely, §46.2-843.
Passing to the right of vehicle proceeding in same direction, §46.2-841.
Prepayment of fine, §16.1-69.40:1.
Reckless driving, §§46.2-854, 46.2-856, 46.2-858, 46.2-859.

TRAFFIC INFRACTIONS —Cont'd
Passing —Cont'd
Remaining on right side of highway when meeting vehicle proceeding in opposite direction, §46.2-837.
Returning to right side of highway before safely clear of overtaken vehicle, §46.2-838.
Stopped school buses, §46.2-844.
Truck or tractor trailer impeding passage of following traffic by another passing truck or tractor trailer on upgrade, §46.2-843.
Pedestrians.
General provisions, §§46.2-923 to 46.2-935.
See PEDESTRIANS.
Photo-monitoring systems to enforce traffic light signals.
Monetary penalty for violation, §15.2-968.1.
Playing on highways, §46.2-932.
Pleas or forfeitures admissible in civil actions, §8.01-418.
Presumption of innocence, §19.2-258.1.
Pretrial payment of fine, §16.1-69.40:1.
Failure of provision for payment, §46.2-395.
Failure or refusal to pay.
Suspension of driver's license, §46.2-395.
Installment payments authorized, §19.2-354.
Traffic infractions and uniform fine schedule, VA SCt Rule 3B:2.
Written appearance and waiver of hearing, §19.2-254.1.
Prior traffic record.
Consideration in sentencing, §46.2-943.
Private roads.
Yielding right-of-way before entering public highway or sidewalk, §46.2-826.
Fine schedule, VA SCt Rule 3B:2.
Maximum fine for violating Title 46.2, §46.2-113.
Prepayment of fine, §16.1-69.40:1.
Provisional drivers' licenses, violations, §46.2-334.01.
Public passenger-carrying vehicles.
Prohibited operation by minors, §46.2-810.
Railroad crossings, §§46.2-884 to 46.2-887.
Crossing tracks without shifting gears, §46.2-886.
Disobeying warning signals, §46.2-884.
Drivers to stop, look and listen at railroad crossings, §46.2-886.
Failure to stop vehicle at railroad crossing, §46.2-885.
Fine schedule, VA SCt Rule 3B:2.
Maximum fine for violating Title 46.2, §46.2-113.
Moving crawler-type tractors, steam shovels, etc., over railroad grade crossings, §46.2-887.
Passing at a railroad grade crossing, §46.2-858.
Prepayment of fine, §16.1-69.40:1.
Reckless driving.
General provisions, §§46.2-852 to 46.2-868.
See RECKLESS DRIVING.
Red lane-use control signal, §46.2-805.
Registration of vehicle.
Driving on expired registration, §46.2-613.
Failure to obtain registration, §46.2-600.
Fine schedule, VA SCt Rule 3B:2.
Pretrial payment of fine, §16.1-69.40:1.
Removing traffic control devices, §46.2-832.
Revocation of drivers' licenses.
See DRIVERS' LICENSES.
Riding animals on highway after sunset, §46.2-800.1.
Fine schedule, VA SCt Rule 3B:2.

TRAFFIC INFRACTIONS —Cont'd
Riding animals on highway after sunset —Cont'd
Prepayment of fine, §16.1-69.40:1.
Right-of-way, §§46.2-820 to 46.2-829.
Demerit points, §46.2-492.
Designation of stop and yield right-of-way intersections, §46.2-1301.
Driver approaching or entering circular intersection, §46.2-822.
Driver approaching or entering traffic circle, §46.2-822.
Driver on left to yield to driver on right entering intersection at same time, §46.2-820.
Driver turning left to yield to oncoming vehicle, §46.2-825.
Driving over fire hose, §46.2-922.
Fine schedule, VA SCt Rule 3B:2.
Following too near fire apparatus, §46.2-921.
Maximum fine for violating Title 46.2, §46.2-113.
Obeying yield right-of-way sign at intersection, §46.2-821.
Pedestrian, §46.2-924.
Prepayment of fine, §16.1-69.40:1.
Reckless driving, §46.2-863.
Stopping and yielding when approaching intersection of highway controlled by stop sign, §46.2-821.
Stopping and yielding when entering public highway or sidewalk from private road, etc., §46.2-826.
Uncontrolled T intersections, §46.2-824.
Yielding or stopping when approaching intersection controlled by yield right-of-way sign, §46.2-821.
Yielding right-of-way to emergency vehicle, §46.2-829.
Yielding to funeral procession under police escort, §46.2-828.
Yielding to left turning vehicle given right-of-way automatic signal device, §46.2-825.
Yielding to pedestrian boarding or alighting from a bus, §46.2-927.
Yielding to U.S. armed services, national guard, etc., vehicles, §46.2-827.
Right turn on red light, §46.2-835.
Rotary traffic islands, §46.2-807.
Fine schedule, VA SCt Rule 3B:2.
Prepayment of fine, §16.1-69.40:1.
Running a red light, §46.2-805.
Fine schedule, VA SCt Rule 3B:2.
Prepayment of fine, §16.1-69.40:1.
Schedule of fines, VA SCt Rule 3B:2.
Failure or refusal to pay fines or costs.
Suspension of driver's license, §46.2-395.
Installment payment authorized, §19.2-354.
Pretrial payment of fines, §16.1-69.40:1.
School buses.
Generally, §§46.2-917 to 46.2-919.
See SCHOOL BUSES.
Passing a stopped school bus, §§46.2-844, 46.2-859.
School crossings.
Maximum speed limits, §46.2-873.
Self-propelled machinery or equipment.
Prohibited on controlled access highways, §46.2-808.
Serious traffic violation.
Additional fine for vehicles of certain gross weight, §46.2-113.

TRAFFIC INFRACTIONS —Cont'd
Sidewalks.
Driving on sidewalks, §46.2-903.
Signals by drivers, §§46.2-848 to 46.2-851.
Backing, stopping or turning without giving required signal, §46.2-848.
Change of course after giving signal, §46.2-850.
Fine schedule, VA SCt Rule 3B:2.
How signals given, §46.2-849.
Improper signals, §46.2-849.
Maximum fine for violating Title 46.2, §46.2-113.
Prepayment of fine, §16.1-69.40:1.
Reckless driving, §46.2-860.
Signals prior to moving standing vehicle into traffic, §46.2-851.
Signs, lights and markings, §§46.2-830 to 46.2-836.
Bicycles, mopeds and motorcycles.
Red light, proceeding through intersection at, §46.2-833.
Comprehensive highway access management standards, §33.1-198.1.
Damaging or removing signs, §46.2-832.
Demerit points, §46.2-492.
Evasion of traffic control devices, §46.2-833.1.
Fine schedule, VA SCt Rule 3B:2.
Maximum fine for violating Title 46.2, §46.2-113.
Lane-use control signals, §46.2-805.
Left turn on steady red light after stopping, §46.2-836.
Maximum fine for violating Title 46.2, §46.2-113.
Municipal erection of signs and markers, §§46.2-1300, 46.2-1312.
Obeying highway sign, §§46.2-830, 46.2-830.1.
Drivers sleeping or resting on shoulder, §46.2-830.1.
Obeying traffic lights, §46.2-833.
Powers of local governments, §§46.2-1300, 46.2-1312.
Prepayment of fine, §16.1-69.40:1.
Right turn on steady red light after stopping, §46.2-835.
School or school crossing speed limit signs, §46.2-873.
Signals by law-enforcement officers, crossing guards and flaggers, §46.2-834.
Speeding conviction prohibited unless markers installed, §46.2-879.
Uniform traffic control devices on highways, §46.2-830.
Unofficial traffic control devices, §46.2-831.
Size, weight and length limitations.
Fine schedule, VA SCt Rule 3B:2.
Height limitations, §46.2-1110.
Length limitations, §46.2-1112.
Pretrial payment of fine, §16.1-69.40:1.
Vehicles exceeding weight limitations, §§46.2-1123 to 46.2-1127.
Width limitations, §46.2-1105.
Slow moving traffic to keep right, §46.2-804.
Fine schedule, VA SCt Rule 3B:2.
Prepayment of fine, §16.1-69.40:1.
Slow moving vehicles.
Impeding traffic, §46.2-877.
Speeding.
Authority to change speed limits, §46.2-878.
Bridges and tunnels, §46.2-881.
Conviction requires installation of markers, §46.2-879.
Demerit points, §46.2-492.

TRAFFIC INFRACTIONS —Cont'd
Speeding —Cont'd
Drag racing, §§46.2-865 to 46.2-867.
Electrical or microcomputer devices, §46.2-882.
Exceeding speed limits set by commissioner of highways, §46.2-878.
Fine schedule, VA SCt Rule 3B:2.
Maximum fine for violating Title 46.2, §46.2-113.
Forfeiture of right-of-way, §46.2-823.
Generally, §46.2-870.
Highways in cities and towns, §§46.2-874, 46.2-875.
Highway work zones, §46.2-878.1.
Impeding traffic by slow speed, §46.2-877.
Maximum fine for violating Title 46.2, §46.2-113.
Maximum safe speed, §46.2-861.
Minimum speed limits, §46.2-877.
Nonsurface treated highways.
Maximum speed limit on, §46.2-873.1.
Passenger vehicles towing certain trailers, §46.2-876.
Prepayment of fines, §§16.1-69.40:1, 46.2-878.3.
Radar devices, §46.2-882.
Reckless driving.
Drag racing, §§46.2-865 to 46.2-867.
Exceeding speed limit, §§46.2-861, 46.2-862.
Residence districts, §46.2-878.2.
Operation of vehicle at 15 miles per hour or more over applicable speed.
Certain city ordinance prohibiting, §46.2-874.1.
Operation of vehicle at 20 miles per hour or more over applicable speed.
Certain town ordinance prohibiting, §46.2-874.1.
School buses, §46.2-871.
School crossings, §46.2-873.
Signs measuring speed by radar, §46.2-883.
Slow moving traffic designated lane, §46.2-804.
Tables of speeding and stopping distances, §46.2-880.
Vehicles operating under special permits, §46.2-872.
State police department infractions, §52-8.4:2.
State police motor carrier regulations, §52-8.4.
Stopped at or near fire or accident so as to interfere with emergency operations, §46.2-890.
Stopping.
Blind pedestrians guided by dog or cane, §46.2-933.
Demerit points, §46.2-492.
Disabled vehicle in highway.
Failure to use proper warning device, VA SCt Rule 3B:2.
Discharging cargo or passengers, §46.2-893.
Disregarding signal by law-enforcement officer to stop, §§46.2-817, 46.2-829.
Failure to use flashing signals when stopped on highway, §46.2-1040.
Fine schedule, VA SCt Rule 3B:2.
General rule, §46.2-888.
Hand signal by law-enforcement officer.
Disregarding signal to stop, §46.2-817.
Highway construction and maintenance vehicles, §46.2-891.
Improperly stopping or parking on highway, §§46.2-888, 46.2-890.
Left turn onto one-way street or road or steady red light after stopping, §46.2-836.

TRAFFIC INFRACTIONS —Cont'd
Stopping —Cont'd
Location of parked vehicles, §46.2-889.
Maximum fine for violating Title 46.2, §46.2-113.
Passing stopped school bus, §46.2-844.
Prepayment of fine, §16.1-69.40:1.
Right turn on red light, §46.2-835.
Rural mail carriers, §46.2-892.
School buses, §46.2-893.
Signals prior to moving standing vehicle into traffic, §46.2-851.
Signals required on stopping, §46.2-848.
Tables of speed and stopping distances, §46.2-880.
Vehicle of another to impede its progress, §46.2-818.
Vehicles entering certain highways, §46.2-821.
Vehicles entering public highway or sidewalk from private road, etc., §46.2-826.
Vicinity of fire or emergency, §46.2-890.
Yielding right of way generally, §§46.2-820 to 46.2-829.
Stopping signal by law-enforcement officer.
Disregarding signal to stop, §46.2-817.
Stopping vehicle of another.
Purpose to impede its progress, §46.2-818.
Summons and process.
Acknowledgment of future receipt of official notices, §46.2-203.1.
Suspension of drivers' licenses.
See DRIVERS' LICENSES.
Tables of speed and stopping distances, §46.2-880.
Television equipment.
Viewing motion pictures or similar displays while driving, §46.2-1077.1.
Toll roads or toll bridges.
Automatic vehicle identification system, §§46.2-819.1, 46.2-819.3.
Dulles access highway, §46.2-819.5.
Video-monitoring system installed in conjunction with, §46.2-819.3:1.
Dulles access highway.
Photo-monitoring system or automatic vehicle identification system.
Enforcement through use of, §46.2-819.5.
Failure to pay toll, §46.2-819.
Invoice for failure to pay, §§46.2-819.6, 46.2-819.7.
Proof by use of photo-monitoring system, §§46.2-819.1, 46.2-819.3.
Dulles access highway, §46.2-819.5.
Proof by use of video-monitoring system, §46.2-819.3:1.
Photo-monitoring system, §§46.2-819.1, 46.2-819.3.
Dulles access highway, §46.2-819.5.
Video-monitoring system, §46.2-819.3:1.
Towing vehicles.
Generally, §§46.2-1150 to 46.2-1154.
See TOWING VEHICLES.
Toy vehicles.
Use on highways, restrictions, §46.2-932.
Traffic circles.
Yielding right-of-way, §46.2-822.
Fine schedule, VA SCt Rule 3B:2.
Prepayment of fine, §16.1-69.40:1.
Traffic control devices.
Damaging or removing traffic control devices, §46.2-832.
Signs, lights and markings generally, §§46.2-830 to 46.2-836.

TRAFFIC INFRACTIONS —Cont'd
Traffic lights, §46.2-833.
Bicycles, mopeds and motorcycles.
Red light, proceeding through intersection at, §46.2-833.
Detention for violations on basis of radio message, §46.2-833.
Evading traffic control device, §46.2-833.1.
Fine schedule, VA SCt Rule 3B:2.
Maximum fine for violating Title 46.2, §46.2-113.
Prepayment of fine, §16.1-69.40:1.
Traffic light signal violation monitoring system.
Monetary penalty for violation, §15.2-968.1.
Trial, §19.2-258.
Turning, §§46.2-845 to 46.2-847.
Fine schedule, VA SCt Rule 3B:2.
Improper position or method of turning at intersection, §46.2-846.
Improper U-turn, §46.2-845.
Left turns by bicycles and mopeds, §46.2-847.
Maximum fine for violating Title 46.2, §46.2-113.
Prepayment of fine, §16.1-69.40:1.
Uncontrolled T intersections.
Yielding right-of-way, §46.2-824.
Fine schedule, VA SCt Rule 3B:2.
Maximum fine for violating Title 46.2, §46.2-113.
Prepayment of fine, §16.1-69.40:1.
Uniform fine schedule, VA SCt Rule 3B:2.
Failure or refusal to pay fines or costs.
Suspension of driver's license, §46.2-395.
Installment payment authorized, §19.2-354.
Pretrial payment of fine, §16.1-69.40:1.
Uniformity with general laws of Commonwealth, §15.2-1201.
U-turns improperly executed, §46.2-845.
Fine schedule, VA SCt Rule 3B:2.
Maximum fine for violating Title 46.2, §46.2-113.
Prepayment of fine, §16.1-69.40:1.
Viewing motion pictures or similar displays while driving, §46.2-1077.1.
Violations of motor vehicles title, §46.2-113.
Waiver of court appearance.
Child charged with traffic infractions, §16.1-302.
War, traffic regulations during, §44-205.
Written appearance and waiver of hearing, §19.2-254.1.

TRAFFICKING IN DRUGS.
Intensified drug enforcement jurisdictions, §15.2-1715.
Police going or being sent beyond territorial limits of locality to enforce drug laws, §15.2-1724.

TRAFFIC LIGHT PHOTO-MONITORING SYSTEMS.
Defined, §15.2-968.1.
Discipline of local government employees for violations, §15.2-968.1.
Enforcement of traffic light signals.
Local powers, §15.2-968.1.
Engineering safety analysis before installing, §15.2-968.1.
Evaluation of systems by locality, §15.2-968.1.
Information collected, use, restrictions, §15.2-968.1.
Inspection of photographs at proceeding adjudicate violation, §15.2-968.1.

TRAFFIC LIGHT PHOTO-MONITORING SYSTEMS —Cont'd
Installing as intersections.
Localities, requirements, factors considered, §15.2-968.1.
Local power to use, §15.2-968.1.
Monetary penalty imposed for violation.
Not deemed conviction, not part of operating record, §15.2-968.1.
Operator liable for, §15.2-968.1.
Owner defined, §15.2-968.1.
Private entities providing systems and support.
Agreement to be compensated, §15.2-968.1.
Proof of violation, §15.2-968.1.
Public awareness program conducted by locality, §15.2-968.1.
Rebuttable presumption.
Defendant owner, lessee, renter of vehicle at time of violation, §15.2-968.1.
Signs placed before intersection where system in use, §15.2-968.1.
Summons for violation, execution, §15.2-968.1.
Vehicle owner data.
Commissioner of DMV.
Supplying traffic light photo-monitoring system operator, §46.2-208.

TRAFFIC LIGHTS.
Signs, lights and markings generally, §§46.2-830 to 46.2-836.
See TRAFFIC INFRACTIONS.

TRAFFIC REGULATIONS.
Accidents generally, §§46.2-894 to 46.2-902.
See MOTOR VEHICLE ACCIDENTS.
Aggressive driving, §46.2-868.1.
Restricted permit to operate, §46.2-392.
Suspension of driver's license, §46.2-392.
Applicability to drivers of all vehicles, §§46.2-800, 46.2-801.
Bicycles.
Generally, §§46.2-903 to 46.2-908.
See BICYCLES.
Cell phones or other wireless telecommunications devices.
Using while operating vehicle.
Emailing or texting while driving, §46.2-1078.1.
Commercial drivers' licenses, disqualifications, §§46.2-341.20, 46.2-341.20:5.
Reckless driving, mandatory fine, §46.2-868.
Holders of provisional drivers' licenses, §46.2-334.01.
Child charged with traffic infractions, disposition, §16.1-278.10.
Colleges and universities.
Rulemaking authority, §23-9.2:3.
Distracted driving.
Using handheld communications device, §46.2-1078.1.
Commercial drivers' licenses, disqualifications, §§46.2-341.20, 46.2-341.20:5.
Holders of provisional drivers' licenses, §46.2-334.01.
Reckless driving, mandatory fine, §46.2-868.
District court jurisdiction, traffic infractions, §16.1-123.1.
Driving two abreast in single land, §46.2-857.
Emailing while driving.
Using handheld communications device, §46.2-1078.1.
Commercial drivers' licenses, disqualifications, §§46.2-341.20, 46.2-341.20:5.

TRAFFIC REGULATIONS —Cont'd
Emailing while driving —Cont'd
Using handheld communications device —Cont'd
Holders of provisional drivers' licenses, §46.2-334.01.
Reckless driving, mandatory fine, §46.2-868.
Emergency vehicles.
Generally, §§46.2-920 to 46.2-922.
Escort duties.
Law enforcement vehicles conducting.
Exemption from certain regulations, §46.2-920.
Fines for traffic infractions.
Failure of provision for payment, §46.2-395.
Failure or refusal to pay.
Suspension of driver's license, §46.2-395.
Installment payment authorized, §19.2-354.
Maximum fine for violating Title 46.2, §46.2-113.
Pretrial waiver of appearance, plea of guilty and fine payment, §16.1-69.40:1.
Golf carts and utility vehicles.
Operation upon highways, §§46.2-916.1 to 46.2-916.3.
Interstate highway system.
Trucks and combination vehicles required to keep to right.
Signs requiring under certain circumstances.
DOT to post, §46.2-804.
Juvenile and domestic relations district court.
Jurisdiction, traffic infractions, §16.1-241.
Local government powers, §§46.2-1300 to 46.2-1314.
See LOCALITIES.
Motor vehicle equipment.
General provisions, §§46.2-1000 to 46.2-1088.
See MOTOR VEHICLE EQUIPMENT.
Move over law.
Drivers approaching stationary emergency vehicles, §46.2-921.1.
Parking.
Generally, §§46.2-1216 to 46.2-1239.
See PARKING.
Pedestrians.
Generally, §§46.2-923 to 46.2-935.
See PEDESTRIANS.
Playing on highways, §46.2-932.
Railroad crossings.
Generally, §§46.2-884 to 46.2-887.
See RAILROAD CROSSINGS.
Reckless driving.
Generally, §§46.2-852 to 46.2-868.
See RECKLESS DRIVING.
School buses.
Generally, §§46.2-917 to 46.2-919.
See SCHOOL BUSES.
Slow moving traffic vehicles.
Designation of lanes for.
Commonwealth transportation board or local authorities, §46.2-804.
Texting while driving.
Using handheld communications device, §46.2-1078.1.
Commercial drivers' licenses, disqualifications, §§46.2-341.20, 46.2-341.20:5.
Holders of provisional drivers' licenses, §46.2-334.01.
Reckless driving, mandatory fine, §46.2-868.
Towing vehicles.
Generally, §§46.2-1150 to 46.2-1154.
See TOWING VEHICLES.
Toy vehicles.
Use on highways, restrictions, §46.2-932.

TRAFFIC REGULATIONS —Cont'd
Traffic infractions.
Generally, §§46.2-894 to 46.2-947.
See TRAFFIC INFRACTIONS.
Wildlife Center of Virginia.
Vehicles owned or controlled by.
Exemption from certain traffic regulations, §46.2-920.2.

TRAFFIC SCHOOLS.
Driver training schools, §§46.2-1700 to 46.2-1707.
See DRIVER TRAINING SCHOOLS.

TRAFFIC SIGNS.
Generally, §§46.2-830 to 46.2-836.
See TRAFFIC INFRACTIONS.

TRAIL BIKES.
All-terrain vehicle traffic regulation, §46.2-915.1.
Certificates of title, §§46.2-644.1 to 46.2-644.3.
Exhaust system, §46.2-1051.
Helmet law, all-terrain vehicles, §46.2-915.1.
Lights, §46.2-1016.
Local government restrictions, §46.2-1051.

TRAILER DEALERS, §§46.2-1992 to 46.2-1992.85.
Advertising, §46.2-1992.28.
Civil penalty for violation, §46.2-1992.85.
False advertising.
Denial, suspension or revocation of dealers license, §46.2-1992.79.
Regulated practices, §46.2-1992.84.
Regulations for enforcement of article, §46.2-1992.85.
At cost, below cost or dollars off cost.
Not to be used in advertising, §46.2-1992.84.
Auctions, trailers sold at.
Inspection requirements not applicable, §46.2-1992.33.
Auctions, vehicle being transported to or from.
Use of dealer's plates, §46.2-1992.45.
Audits.
Examination of licensees' records, §46.2-1992.21.
Bait advertising, §46.2-1992.84.
Bill of sale.
Completed buyer's order, §46.2-1992.23.
Bonds, surety.
Applicants for license, §46.2-1992.20.
Business hours, §46.2-1992.26.
Buyer's order, §46.2-1992.23.
Certificate of dealer registration.
Application, §46.2-1992.7.
Denial.
Heaving, §46.2-1992.12.
Fees, §46.2-1992.17.
Collection, §46.2-1992.18.
Renewal, §46.2-1992.19.
Term of registration, §46.2-1992.19.
Time for commissioner to act, §46.2-1992.12.
Certificate of ownership.
Temporary certificate of ownership.
Dealer unable to deliver to purchaser certificate of title or certificate of origin at time of sale, §46.2-1992.35.
Certificate of qualification for dealer-operator.
Continued operation on loss of certificate, §46.2-1992.11.
Required for issuance of license, §46.2-1992.9.
Certificate of title.
Dealer to obtain on purchase of trailer, §46.2-1992.37.

TRAILER DEALERS —Cont'd
Certificates of qualification for salesperson.
Required for issuance of license, §46.2-1992.10.
Change in name of dealer, §46.2-1992.15.
Change of location of place of business, §46.2-1992.13.
Civil penalty for violation, §46.2-1992.5.
Coercing purchaser to provide insurance coverage, §46.2-1992.29.
Coercion of dealers by manufacturers or distributors, §§46.2-1992.68, 46.2-1992.69.
Commission or compensation paid to person in connection with sale, §46.2-1992.30.
Consignments, §46.2-1992.24.
Continued operation on loss of dealer-operator certificate of qualifications, §46.2-1992.11.
Contracts.
Consignment contracts, §46.2-1992.24.
Copy of buyer's order made available to buyer, §46.2-1992.23.
Court of appeals.
Appealing denial, suspension or revocation of licenses, §46.2-1992.82.
Dealer arranged financing.
Notice on buyer's order, §46.2-1992.23.
Dealer-operator certificate of qualification.
Required for issuance of license, §46.2-1992.9.
Dealer-operator to hold certificate of qualification.
Continued operation on loss of certificate, §46.2-1992.11.
Dealer rebates, advertising, §46.2-1992.84.
Definitions, §46.2-1992.
Depositions.
Commissioner of motor vehicles powers with respect to hearings, §46.2-1992.2.
Disclosure of place of assembly or manufacturer, §46.2-1992.25.
Distributor.
License and registration fee, §46.2-1992.17.
Distributor branch.
License and registration fee, §46.2-1992.17.
Distributor representative.
License and registration fee, §46.2-1992.17.
Enjoining violations, §46.2-1992.3.
Established place of business required for issuing, §46.2-1992.8.
Examination of business, §46.2-1992.21.
Factory branch.
License and registration fee, §46.2-1992.17.
Factory representative.
License and registration fee, §46.2-1992.17.
False advertising.
Denial, suspension or revocation of license, §46.2-1992.79.
Fees.
License and registration, §46.2-1992.17.
Manual transaction fee, §46.2-1992.23:2.
On-line systems filing fee, §46.2-1992.23:1.
Finance charges or interest rates, advertising, §46.2-1992.84.
Foreign dealer's license, operation of trailer under, §46.2-1992.52.
Franchises, §§46.2-1992.56 to 46.2-1992.77.
Additional franchises granted in relevant market area, §46.2-1992.69.
Civil penalties, §46.2-1992.75.
Coercion of dealers, §§46.2-1992.68, 46.2-1992.69.
Designation of family member successor, §46.2-1992.69.
Discontinuance of distributors, §46.2-1992.71.

TRAILER DEALERS —Cont'd
Franchises —Cont'd
Distributor discontinued, §46.2-1992.71.
Exemption from retail franchising act, §46.2-1992.67.
Filing new, amended, modified, etc., franchise with commissioner, §46.2-1992.66.
First refusal of manufacturer or distributor to acquire, §46.2-1992.70.
Hearings and notice, §46.2-1992.75.
Late model and factory and repurchase franchises, §46.2-1992.76.
License plates.
Distinction between factory trailer dealers, §46.2-1992.42.
Manufacturer, factory branch, etc., owning or operating, §46.2-1992.73.
Manufacturer or distributors right of first refusal on sale or transfer, §46.2-1992.70.
Ownership, operation or control in manufacture, factory branch, etc., §46.2-1992.73.
Replacing franchise dealer, §46.2-1992.69.
Retail franchising act, exemption from, §46.2-1992.67.
Retail installment sales contracts, prohibited coercion by manufacturer or distributor, §46.2-1992.68.
Sale or transfer of ownership of dealership, §46.2-1992.69.
First refusal by manufacturer or distributor, §46.2-1992.70.
Service facility ownership, §46.2-1992.74.
Termination, cancellation or expiration, §46.2-1992.69.
Two-year period for replacing franchised dealer, §46.2-1992.66.
Warranty obligations, §46.2-1992.72.
Watercraft trailers and watercraft trailer dealers, applicability, §46.2-1992.76.
Free or at no cost.
Use of words in advertising, §46.2-1992.84.
Hearings.
Denial of license or certificate of dealer registration, §46.2-1992.12.
Powers of commissioner of motor vehicles, §46.2-1992.2.
Hours of business, §46.2-1992.26.
Identification of business by permanent sign, §46.2-1992.27.
Independent dealers.
License plates.
Distinguish between factory trailer dealers, §46.2-1992.42.
Inspection of trailers prior to sale, §§46.2-1992.32, 46.2-1992.34.
Itemization of deficiencies made available to purchaser, §46.2-1992.34.
Not required of certain sellers, §46.2-1992.33.
Insurance.
Coercing purchaser to provide coverage, §46.2-1992.29.
Invoice price or dollars over invoice used in advertising, §46.2-1992.84.
Late model and factory repurchase franchises, §46.2-1992.76.
License, §§46.2-1992.6 to 46.2-1992.19.
Addition or deletion of partner, §46.2-1992.15.
Application, §46.2-1992.7.
Bond of applicant, §46.2-1992.20.
Change in form of ownership, §46.2-1992.15.

TRAILER DEALERS —Cont'd
License —Cont'd
Dealer-operator certificate of qualification.
Required for issuance of license, §46.2-1992.9.
Denial, suspension and revocation, §§46.2-1992.78 to 46.2-1992.83.
Appeals, §§46.2-1992.81, 46.2-1992.82.
Corporations officers or directors.
Committing acts, §46.2-1992.78.
Equitable relief not impaired, §46.2-1992.83.
Grounds, §46.2-1992.79.
Hearings, §§46.2-1992.12, 46.2-1992.80.
Notice, §46.2-1992.80.
Partnerships officers, directors or trustees committing acts, §46.2-1992.78.
Salespersons.
Committing acts, responsibility of licensee, §46.2-1992.78.
Display, §46.2-1992.13.
Established place of business required for issuing, §46.2-1992.8.
Fees, §46.2-1992.17.
Collection, §46.2-1992.18.
Multi-year licenses, §46.2-1992.19.
Renewal, §46.2-1992.19.
Required, §46.2-1992.6.
Salesperson to carry when engaged in business, §46.2-1992.16.
Salesperson to hold certificate of qualification for issuance, §46.2-1992.10.
Supplemental sales locations, §46.2-1992.14.
Termination of business upon suspension, revocation or cancellation, §46.2-1992.38.
Term of license, §46.2-1992.17.
Time for commissioner to act, §46.2-1992.12.
Unlawful to engage in business without license, §46.2-1992.6.
License plates, §§46.2-1992.39 to 46.2-1992.65.
Cancellation by department of motor vehicles investigators, §46.2-1992.53.
Certificate of vehicle registration and license plates, §46.2-1992.39.
Design, §46.2-1992.41.
Distinction between dealers, §46.2-1992.42.
Foreign dealers, operation under, §46.2-1992.52.
Franchised or independent dealers to be issued appropriate plates, §46.2-1992.42.
License of dealer required for issuance of dealer plates, §46.2-1992.40.
Manufacturer moving trailers to place of shipment or delivery, §46.2-1992.50.
Movement by dealers to salesrooms, §46.2-1992.51.
Multi-year plate, §46.2-1992.41.
Newly purchased trailers, use, §46.2-1992.48.
Operation of trailer without plates.
Dealer not to permit, §46.2-1992.49.
Promotional license plates, §46.2-1992.43.
Reissuance after removal, §46.2-1992.53.
Removal for violations, §46.2-1992.53.
Revocation by commission of motor vehicles, §46.2-1992.40.
Service of summons on dealers for violations, §46.2-1992.54.
Temporary license plates issued by dealers, §§46.2-1992.56 to 46.2-1992.65.
Alternative print-on-demand program, §46.2-1992.56:1.
Application by dealers, §§46.2-1992.56, 46.2-1992.58.

TRAILER DEALERS —Cont'd
License plates —Cont'd
Temporary license plates issued by dealers —Cont'd
Application for current titling and registration, §46.2-1992.59.
Bona fide purchasers or owners of trailers, persons to whom issued, §46.2-1992.59.
Criminal penalty, §46.2-1992.64.
Department of motor vehicles authorized to issue, §46.2-1992.56.
Destruction of plates on expiration, §46.2-1992.62.
Display, §46.2-1992.56.
Expiration, §46.2-1992.63.
Identification number of trailer, §46.2-1992.60.
Insertion of dealer name, date of issuance and expiration, §46.2-1992.60.
Inspection of records kept by dealers, §46.2-1992.57.
Misstatement of fact or false information, §46.2-1992.59.
Records to be kept by dealers, §46.2-1992.57.
Suspension of right to issue, §46.2-1992.61.
To whom plates not to be issued, §46.2-1992.59.
Watercraft trailers and watercraft trailer dealers, applicability, §46.2-1992.65.
Term of plates, §46.2-1992.41.
Transferable plates, §46.2-1992.41.
Transport plates, §46.2-1992.45.
Temporary transport plates, §§46.2-1992.46, 46.2-1992.47.
Unlawful uses, §46.2-1992.44.
Use generally, §46.2-1992.44.
Use on certain vehicles, §46.2-1992.45.
Use on newly purchased trailer, §46.2-1992.48.
Use on vehicles traveling from one establishment to another for purposes of having special equipment installed, §46.2-1992.47.
Violations, §46.2-1992.54.
Watercraft trailer dealers, applicability, §46.2-1992.55.
List of salespersons employed, §46.2-1992.16.
List price, sticker price or suggested retail price.
Advertising, §46.2-1992.84.
Location of place of business occupied by licensee to be specified, §46.2-1992.13.
Manual transaction fee, §46.2-1992.23:2.
Manufacturer.
License and registration fee, §46.2-1992.17.
Movement of trailers to salesrooms, §46.2-1992.51.
Name change of dealer, §46.2-1992.15.
Newly purchased trailers.
Use of dealer's plates, §46.2-1992.48.
New trailers, advertising as, §46.2-1992.84.
Nonprofit organizations.
Consigning donated trailers to dealers.
Certificate authorizing, §46.2-1992.6:1.
Fees, §46.2-1992.17.
Nonresidence.
Fee for registration of dealers licensed in other state, §46.2-1992.17.
Oaths.
Administration of oaths by commissioner of motor vehicles, §46.2-1992.2.
On-line systems filing fee, §46.2-1992.23:1.
Operation of trailer without dealer license plates.
Dealer not to permit, §46.2-1992.49.

TRAILER DEALERS —Cont'd
Penalties for violation, §46.2-1992.5.
Permanent supplemental license, §46.2-1992.14.
Place of assembly or manufacture, disclosure, §46.2-1992.25.
Powers of commissioner of motor vehicles, §46.2-1992.1.
Enjoining violations, §46.2-1992.3.
Hearings under chapter, §46.2-1992.2.
Promulgation of regulations, §46.2-1992.4.
Promotional license plates, §46.2-1992.43.
Rebuilder salesperson.
License and registration fee, §46.2-1992.17.
Records, §46.2-1992.22.
Registration of trailer.
Certificate of vehicle registration and license plate, §46.2-1992.39.
Regulations promulgated by commissioner of motor vehicles, §46.2-1992.4.
Retail installment contracts.
Notice on buyer's order, §46.2-1992.23.
Prohibited coercion of dealer by manufacturer or distributor, §46.2-1992.68.
Salesperson employed by more than one dealer, §46.2-1992.16.
Salesperson list, §46.2-1992.16.
Salesperson selling for other than employer, §46.2-1992.31.
Salesperson to carry license when engaged in business, §46.2-1992.16.
Salesperson to hold certification of qualification for issuance of license, §46.2-1992.10.
Service facility ownership, §46.2-1992.74.
Signs, §46.2-1992.27.
Solicitation of sale through person with pecuniary interest, §46.2-1992.30.
Special equipment installed in trailer.
Use of dealer plates or temporary transport plates, §46.2-1992.47.
Special orders placed by dealer with manufacturer outside state on behalf of nonresident customer.
Inspection requirements not applicable, §46.2-1992.33.
Subpoenas.
Commissioner of motor vehicles powers with respect to hearings, §46.2-1992.2.
Summons issued on dealer for license plates violations, §46.2-1992.54.
Temporary certificate of ownership.
Dealer unable to deliver to purchaser certificate of title or origin at time of sale, §46.2-1992.35.
Temporary license plates issued by dealers, §§46.2-1992.56 to 46.2-1992.65.
Alternative print-on-demand program, §46.2-1992.56:1.
Application by dealers, §§46.2-1992.56, 46.2-1992.58.
Authorization of department of motor vehicles to issues, §46.2-1992.56.
Bona fide purchasers or owners, issuance to, §46.2-1992.59.
Criminal penalties for violations, §46.2-1992.64.
Destruction of plates upon expiration, §46.2-1992.62.
Expiration, §46.2-1992.63.
Forwarding by dealer of application for current titling and registration, §46.2-1992.59.
Identification number of trailers, §46.2-1992.60.
Inspection of dealer's records, §46.2-1992.57.

TRAILER DEALERS —Cont'd
Temporary license plates issued by dealers —Cont'd
Misstatements and false information, §46.2-1992.59.
Name of dealer, date of issuance and expiration inserted on plates, §46.2-1992.60.
Persons to whom temporary plates not to be issued, §46.2-1992.59.
Records to be kept by dealer, §46.2-1992.57.
Refunds or credit fees not to be issued, §46.2-1992.63.
Suspension of right of dealer to issue, §46.2-1992.61.
Watercraft trailers and watercraft trailer dealers, applicability of provisions, §46.2-1992.65.
Temporary supplemental license, §46.2-1992.13.
Termination of business, §46.2-1992.38.
Transport plates.
Temporary transport plates, §46.2-1992.46.
Use on vehicles having special equipment installed, §46.2-1992.47.
Use on certain trailers, §46.2-1992.45.
Unlawful to engage in business without license, §46.2-1992.6.
Used trailers.
Inspection requirements not applicable, §46.2-1992.33.
Use of license plates generally, §46.2-1992.44.
VA DLR.
Abbreviation to be included in advertisement, §46.2-1992.28.
Warranty obligations of manufacturers, factory branches, distributors or distributor branches, §46.2-1992.72.
Watercraft trailer dealer.
License and registration fee, §46.2-1992.17.
Witnesses.
Commissioner of motor vehicles powers with respect to hearings, §46.2-1992.2.

TRAILER PARKS.
Lists of tenants.
Owners or operators to file with commissioner of revenue, §58.1-3901.
Manufactured home lot rental, §§55-248.41 to 55-248.52.
See MANUFACTURED HOME LOT RENTAL.
Mobile homes, §§36-85.2 to 36-85.36.
See MOBILE HOMES.

TRAILERS.
Antique trailers.
Special license plates, §46.2-730.
Dealers, §§46.2-1992 to 46.2-1992.85.
Defined, §46.2-100.
Disabled vehicle in highway.
Failure to use proper warning device, §46.2-111, VA SCt Rule 3B:2.
Garage keeper's lien.
Towing, recovering and storage costs, §46.2-644.01.
License plates.
Antique trailers.
Special license plates, §46.2-730.
Temporary license plates.
Issued by dealers, §§46.2-1992.56 to 46.2-1992.65.
Trailer dealers, §§46.2-1992.39 to 46.2-1992.65.
Transfer of license plates by owners selling or transferring registered trailers, §46.2-1992.36.
Watercraft trailers, §46.2-1992.55.

TRAILERS —Cont'd
Manufacturer moving trailers to placement of shipment or delivery.
Permits issued by local law authorities in lieu of license plates, §46.2-1992.50.
Mobile homes.
Generally, §§36-85.2 to 36-85.36.
See MOBILE HOMES.
Motor vehicle registration.
Evidence of tax payments required, §46.2-649.
Parking, ordinances prohibiting or limiting, §46.2-1224.
Personal property taxes.
Alternative method for filing, §58.1-3518.1.
Reflectors and reflectorized material.
Rear end of certain trailers, §46.2-1088.5.
Registration card.
Operator required to carry, exhibition to law enforcement, failure to carry, penalty, §46.2-104.
Retail sales and use tax exemption, §58.1-609.1.
T&M vehicle dealers, §§46.2-1900 to 46.2-1991.
See T&M VEHICLE DEALERS.
Towing trailer on highway.
Occupancy prohibited, §46.2-813.
Warranty obligations of trailer manufacturers, factory branch, distributor or distributor branch, §46.2-1992.72.

TRAINEES.
Workers' compensation.
Employee defined, §65.2-101.

TRAINERS.
Athletic trainers, §§54.1-2957.4 to 54.1-2957.6.

TRAINING LAW ENFORCEMENT AND CORRECTIONAL OFFICERS.
Criminal justice training academies, §§15.2-1747 to 15.2-1753.
See CRIMINAL JUSTICE TRAINING ACADEMIES.

TRAINS.
Railroad locomotives, cars or rolling stock.
See RAILROADS.

TRAMWAYS.
Appeal of agency decisions, §33.1-212.
Condemnation of private property prohibited, §33.1-213.
Construction along or across public highways, §33.1-211.
Occupational safety and health.
Rules and regulations, §40.1-44.1.

TRANSACTING BUSINESS UNDER ASSUMED NAME, §§59.1-69 to 59.1-76.
Certificate.
Failure to file.
Effect on right of action, §59.1-76.
Filing.
Duties of clerk, §59.1-74.
Filing of copy with commission, §59.1-70.
Required, §59.1-69.
Insurance agents.
Conducting business under, §38.2-1822.
Insurance agents, corporations acting as, §38.2-1822.
Limited partnerships, §50-73.21.
Penalties for violations, §59.1-75.
Service of notice, process and other papers.
Fees charged by circuit court clerk, §17.1-275.

TRANSACTING BUSINESS UNDER ASSUMED NAME —Cont'd
Surplus lines brokers.
Licensee operating under.
Notification to commission, §38.2-1857.5.

TRANSACTION RECOVERY ACT, VIRGINIA CONTRACTORS, §§54.1-1118 to 54.1-1127.

TRANSACTION RECOVERY ACT, VIRGINIA REAL ESTATE.
Real estate brokers, salespersons and rental agents, §§54.1-2112 to 54.1-2120.

TRANSACTION RECOVERY FUND.
Motor vehicle dealers, §§46.2-1527.1 to 46.2-1527.11.
See MOTOR VEHICLE DEALERS.

TRANSCRIPTS.
Altering diplomas or transcripts, §18.2-172.1.
Appeals by Commonwealth in criminal cases, §19.2-405.
College transcripts.
Falsifying or altering and fraudulently using, §18.2-172.1.
Commercial drivers' licenses.
Disqualification.
Arresting officer to request transcripts of driver's conviction record, §46.2-384.
Correct statement of evidence and incidents of civil trial in circuit court.
Transcripts certified by reporter or other designated individual deemed prima facie correct, §17.1-128.
Court of appeals.
Record on appeal.
Objections, VA SCt Rule 5A:8.
Transcript or written statement of appeals from trial court, VA SCt Rule 5A:8.
Court reporters.
Furnishing copy of transcript, §8.01-420.3.
District court clerks.
Power to make out and attest, §16.1-69.42.
District court judges.
Power to certify, §16.1-69.27.
Drivers' licenses.
Driving while privilege to drive suspended or revoked.
Arresting officer to request transcripts of driver's conviction record, §46.2-384.
Driving while intoxicated.
Motor vehicle accidents.
Arresting officer to request transcripts of driver's conviction records, §46.2-384.
Falsifying diplomas or transcripts, §18.2-172.1.
Felony trial transcripts.
Certified transcript deemed prima facie correct, §19.2-165.
Grand juries.
Multi-jurisdiction grand juries.
Safeguarding of transcripts, notes, etc., §19.2-215.9.
Juvenile and domestic relations district courts.
Reporters and transcripts of proceedings, VA SCt Rule 8:11.
Motor vehicle accidents.
Driving while intoxicated.
Arresting officer to request transcripts of driver's conviction records, §46.2-384.
Reckless driving.
Arresting officer to request transcripts of driver's conviction records, §46.2-384.

TRANSCRIPTS —Cont'd
Objections.
Appellate courts.
Record on appeal, VA SCt Rule 5A:8.
Prima facie correct statement of evidence and incidents of trial.
Transcript certified by reporter or other individual designated, §17.1-128.
Reckless driving.
Motor vehicle accidents.
Arresting officer to request transcripts of driver's conviction records, §46.2-384.
Recording evidences and incidents of civil trial in circuit court.
Judge ordering, §17.1-128.
Stenographic transcripts.
Evidentiary effect, §8.01-420.3.
Supreme court.
Record on appeal.
Objections, VA SCt Rule 5:11.
Transcript or written statement, VA SCt Rule 5:11.
Unemployment compensation.
Claims adjudication, §60.2-623.1.

TRANSFERABLE SHARES.
Securities generally, §§13.1-501 to 13.1-527.3.
See SECURITIES.

TRANSFER AGENTS.
Securities registered in joint names, §§13.1-434 to 13.1-436.

TRANSFER OF DOMICILE.
Redomestication of insurers, §§38.2-1019 to 38.2-1023.

TRANSFER OF JUVENILE CASE TO CIRCUIT COURT, §16.1-269.1.
Appeals by juvenile, §16.1-269.4.
Offenses committed while incarcerated in state correctional facility, §16.1-271.
Placement of juvenile, §16.1-269.5.
Power of circuit court over juvenile offenders, §16.1-272.
Retention by juvenile court, §16.1-269.3.
Waiver of jurisdiction and transfer, §16.1-270.

TRANSFER OF VENUE ACT, §8.01-265.

TRANSFER ON DEATH DEEDS.
Real property transfer on death act, §§64.2-621 to 64.2-638.
See REAL PROPERTY TRANSFER ON DEATH ACT.

TRANSFER ON DEATH SECURITY REGISTRATION.
Generally.
See TOD SECURITY REGISTRATION.

TRANSFERS TO MINORS, §§64.2-1900 to 64.2-1922.
Accounting, §64.2-1918.
Application of provisions, §64.2-1920.
Citation of provisions, §64.2-1922.
Conflict of laws, §64.2-1921.
Conservators, transfers by, §64.2-1905.
Construction of provisions, §64.2-1922.
Custodial property.
Care, §64.2-1911.
Control, §64.2-1908.
Creation, manner of, §64.2-1908.
Designation of initial custodian, §64.2-1908.
Effecting transfer, §64.2-1908.

TRANSFERS TO MINORS —Cont'd
Custodial property —Cont'd
Receipts for, §64.2-1907.
Use of, §64.2-1913.
Custodians.
Care of property, §64.2-1911.
Compensation, §64.2-1914.
Death, §64.2-1917.
Designation of successor custodian, §64.2-1917.
Duties, §64.2-1911.
Expenses, §64.2-1914.
Liability to third persons, §64.2-1916.
Nomination, §64.2-1902.
Powers, §64.2-1912.
Removal, §64.2-1917.
Renunciations, §64.2-1917.
Resignations, §64.2-1917.
Surety bonds, §64.2-1914.
Use of property, §64.2-1913.
Defined terms, §64.2-1900.
Minors, §64.2-1908.
Effect of transfers, §64.2-1910.
Gifts, transfers by, §64.2-1903.
Joint custodianship, §64.2-1909.
Obligors, transfers by, §64.2-1906.
Personal representatives, transfers by, §§64.2-1904, 64.2-1905.
Powers of appointment, transfer by exercise of, §64.2-1903.
Qualified minor's trust.
Defined, §64.2-1900.
Transfer of property to, §64.2-1913.
Scope of provisions, §64.2-1901.
Single custodianship, §64.2-1909.
Termination of custodianship, §64.2-1919.
Third party liability, §64.2-1915.
Trustees, transfers by, §§64.2-1904, 64.2-1905.
Trusts, transfers by, §64.2-1904.
Validity of transfers, §64.2-1910.
Ward liability, §64.2-1916.
Wills, transfers by, §64.2-1904.

TRANSIENT LODGING PLACES.
See HOTELS.

TRANSIENT OCCUPANCY TAX, §§58.1-3819 to 58.1-3826.
Additional transient occupant tax, §§58.1-3822 to 58.1-3825.2.
City or town having general taxing powers.
Excise tax, §58.1-3840.
Imposition, §58.1-3843.
Combined transient occupancy and food and beverage tax.
Certain counties, §58.1-3842.
Corporate officer or partnership officer liability for failure to pay, §58.1-3906.
Willful failure to collect and account for, §58.1-3907.
Limitation on county tax within boundary of town, §§58.1-3823 to 58.1-3826.
Northern Virginia regional transient occupancy tax, §58.1-1742.
Scope of tax, §58.1-3826.

TRANSIT AUTHORITIES.
Charlottesville-Albemarle regional transit authority, §§15.2-7022 to 15.2-7035.
See CHARLOTTESVILLE-ALBEMARLE REGIONAL TRANSIT AUTHORITY.
Richmond metropolitan authority, §§15.2-7000 to 15.2-7021.
See RICHMOND METROPOLITAN AUTHORITY.

TRANSIT AUTHORITIES —Cont'd
Washington metropolitan area transit authority.
See WASHINGTON METROPOLITAN AREA TRANSIT AUTHORITY.

TRANSIT DISTRICTS.
Generally, §§15.2-4500 to 15.2-4534.
See TRANSPORTATION DISTRICTS.

TRANSITION OF CITIES TO TOWN STATUS.
City no longer qualifying for city status, §§15.2-4000 to 15.2-4005.
See REVERSION OF CITIES TO TOWNS.
Transition of cities to town status generally, §§15.2-4100 to 15.2-4120.
See REVERSION OF CITIES TO TOWNS.

TRANSITION OF COUNTIES TO CITIES, §§15.2-3900 to 15.2-3919.
Annexation.
Moratorium on suits pending transition to city, §15.2-3902.
Appeals, §15.2-3909.
Appointment of special court, §15.2-3901.
Assistance of state agencies in gathering and presenting evidence, §15.2-3908.
Authorized, §15.2-3900.
Charter commission.
Appointment upon entry of order, compensation, §15.2-3910.
Charter provisions, §15.2-3911.
Optional provisions, §15.2-3912.
Public hearing, §15.2-3913.
Rejection or adoption at election, §15.2-3914.
Cities declared cities prior to July 1, 1978.
Provisions not affect organization, government, etc., §15.2-3917.
Congressional, senatorial and legislative districts, §15.2-3919.
Department of transportation services, continuance, §15.2-3918.
Election on question of rejecting or adopting charter, §15.2-3914.
Election to determine if voters of county desire city status, §15.2-3907.
Hearing and decision by court, §15.2-3907.
Intervention.
Time limit for intervenors, §15.2-3905.
Moratorium on annexation suits, §15.2-3902.
Notice of public hearing on charter, §15.2-3913.
Ordinance petitioning court to declare eligibility, §15.2-3901.
Parties, §15.2-3904.
Petition to circuit court alleging eligibility, §15.2-3901.
Pretrial conferences.
Matters considered, §15.2-3906.
Publication of notice and ordinance, §15.2-3903.
Publication of notice of public hearing on charter, §15.2-3913.
Publication of order limiting time for intervenors, §15.2-3905.
Public hearing on charter, §15.2-3913.
Service of notice of petition for order declaring county eligibility, §15.2-3903.
Streets, optional status, §15.2-3918.
Town council.
No action required on transition of county to city, §15.2-3915.

TRANSITION OF COUNTIES TO CITIES —Cont'd
Townships right to obtain city status, §15.2-3916.
Towns to continue as townships within city, §15.2-3916.

TRANSITION OF TOWNS TO CITIES, §§15.2-3800 to 15.2-3834.
Agreement between town and county concerning proposed city, §15.2-3802.
Appeals, §15.2-3809.
Appointment of special court, §15.2-3800.
Assets of town, §15.2-3813.
Assistance of state agencies in gathering and presenting evidence, §15.2-3808.
Assumption and reimbursement of debt by city, §15.2-3829.
Circuit court.
Appointment of electoral board, sheriff, attorney for Commonwealth circuit court clerk, §15.2-3826.
Costs and expenses apportioned between county and city, §15.2-3830.
Jurisdiction of circuit for county wherein city situated, §15.2-3825.
Commissioner of revenue appointed where town has no commissioner, §15.2-3817.
Commissioner of revenue or assessor of town to continue in office, §15.2-3817.
Congressional, senatorial and legislative districts not to change, §15.2-3834.
Constitutional officers.
County officers whose homesite becomes part of city.
Tenure and reelection, §15.2-3823.
Election and terms, §15.2-3820.
Qualification of officers, §15.2-3821.
Sharing of offices, §15.2-3822.
Transfer of jurisdiction, §15.2-3822.
Vacancies, §15.2-3821.
Contracting debts, borrowing money and authorizing issuance of bonds, §15.2-2632.
Costs and expenses of circuit court apportioned between city and county, §15.2-3830.
Council of town to continue in office, §15.2-3815.
Election of additional members, §15.2-3815.
County sales and use tax becomes city sales and use tax, §15.2-3828.
Declining to accept city status on terms and conditions imposed by court, §15.2-3810.
Effect when town becomes city, §15.2-3812.
Election of additional members to council, §15.2-3815.
Election of local constitutional officers after town becomes city, §15.2-3820.
Elections of mayor and councilman after town becomes city, §15.2-3819.
Eminent domain power, §15.2-3832.
Equitable adjustments of debt assumed by city, §15.2-3829.
Hearing and decision by court, §15.2-3807.
Inapplicability of provisions to cities already existing, §15.2-3833.
Intervenors, time limit, §15.2-3805.
Liabilities of town, §15.2-3813.
Mayor of town to continue in office, §15.2-3814.
Officers of town to be officers of city.
Election of successors, §15.2-3812.

TRANSITION OF TOWNS TO CITIES —Cont'd
Officers of town to be officers of city —Cont'd
Expiration of term, §15.2-3824.
Order granting city status to town, §15.2-3807.
Ordinance declining to accept city on terms and conditions imposed by court, §15.2-3810.
Ordinance petitioning court for city status, §15.2-3800.
Parties, §15.2-3804.
Petition filed for circuit court, §15.2-3800.
Pretrial conference.
Matters considered, §15.2-3806.
Proceeding final for three years, §15.2-3811.
Property taxes accruing before transition, §15.2-3828.
Publication of copy of notice and ordinance seeking city status, §15.2-3803.
Publication of order of time limit for intervenors, §15.2-3805.
Referendum on question of seeking city status, §15.2-3801.
Registrars, duties, §15.2-3831.
Registration of voters, §15.2-3831.
Sergeant to continue in office, §15.2-3818.
Service of notice of petition for grant of city status, §15.2-3803.
Terms of office mayor and councilman after town becomes city, §15.2-3819.
Three year finality limitations, §15.2-3811.
Transfer of assessments to city books, §15.2-3827.
Treasurer appointed when town has not treasurer, §15.2-3816.
Treasurer to continue in office, §15.2-3816.
Water, light, power and fuel.
Authority of city to provide, §15.2-3832.

TRANSPLANT COUNCIL.
Established, membership, duties, §32.1-297.1.

TRANSPLANTS.
Anatomical gifts generally, §§32.1-291.1 to 32.1-291.25.
See ANATOMICAL GIFTS.
Liver, heart and lung transplants.
Medical assistance service plans, §32.1-325.
Virginia donor registry, §§32.1-291.20, 32.1-292.2.
Virginia transplant council, §32.1-297.1.

TRANSPORTATION.
Animals.
Requirements, §3.2-6508.
Violation of requirements, §18.2-403.1.
Charlottesville-Albemarle regional transit authority, §§15.2-7022 to 15.2-7035.
See CHARLOTTESVILLE-ALBEMARLE REGIONAL TRANSIT AUTHORITY.
Community service landscaping program, §33.1-12.2.
Counties, cities or towns.
Comprehensive plans.
Coordination of state and local transportation, §15.2-2222.1.
Designation of source of revenue for mass transit, §15.2-948.
Shared ride taxi system, §15.2-949.
System of public transportation for localities not members of transportation district, §15.2-947.
Federal transportation grant anticipation revenue notes, §§33.1-23.14 to 33.1-23.26.

TRANSPORTATION —Cont'd
Financing transportation projects.
Transportation infrastructure bank, §§33.1-23.6 to 33.1-23.13.
Food.
Unsanitary conditions, §3.2-5119.
Hazardous radioactive materials, §44-146.30.
Joint commission on transportation accountability, §§30-282 to 30-286.
Local income tax.
Revenues to be applied and expended for, §58.1-548.
Mine safety.
Underground coal mines, §§45.1-161.133 to 45.1-161.152.
See COAL MINE SAFETY.
Northern Virginia transportation authority, §§15.2-4829 to 15.2-4840.
Public-private transportation act, §§56-556 to 56-574.
Affected jurisdictions.
Notice to, comments by, §56-563.
Approval of plan, §56-560.
Audit of cost estimates, §56-560.
Certificate termination, §56-572.
Dedication of assets, §56-572.
Citation of act, §56-556.
Comprehensive agreements, §56-566.
Conceptual proposal.
Posting, public comment, §56-573.1:1.
Condemnation, §56-569.
Contributions to governor, governor's PAC, governor's secretaries.
Prohibited during approval process, violation, civil penalty, §§2.2-3104.01, 56-573.3.
Cost of processing, reviewing and evaluating requests.
Fee charged by responsible public entity authorized, §56-560.
Dedication of public property, §56-564.
Default, remedies, §56-568.
Definitions, §56-557.
Eminent domain, §56-569.
Federal, state and local assistance, §56-567.
Financing facility, §56-567.1.
Freedom of information act.
Excluded records, §2.2-3705.6.
Gifts to governor, governor's PAC, governor's secretaries.
Prohibited during approval process, violation, civil penalty, §§2.2-3104.01, 56-573.3.
Guidelines, adoption by responsible public entity, §56-575.3:1.
Interim agreement with private entity, §§56-566.1, 56-575.9:1.
Interim or comprehensive agreement, §56-560.
Local license tax on transportation facility owned directly or indirectly by government.
Prohibition, §58.1-3703.
Local public entities.
Conceptual proposal.
Posting, public comment, §56-573.1:1.
Material and information.
Required for approval, §56-560.
Material default, remedies, §56-568.
Multiple public entities.
Approval by required, §56-566.2.
Police powers within facility, §56-571.
Powers and duties of private entity, §56-565.
Comprehensive agreement to incorporate duties, §56-566.

TRANSPORTATION —Cont'd
Public-private transportation act —Cont'd
Prerequisite for operation, §56-559.
Procurement records.
Public inspection, making available.
Interim or comprehensive agreement entered into, §56-573.1:1.
Project considerations enumerated, §56-560.
Property exempt from taxation.
Property indirectly owned by government, §58.1-3606.1.
Property taxes.
Leasehold interest or concession of government agency's tax exempt property.
Assessment for local property tax purposes prohibited, §58.1-3203.
Public comment.
Conceptual proposal.
Providing opportunity, §56-573.1:1.
Public inspection.
Conceptual proposal.
Making available for, §56-573.1:1.
Public procurement act not applicable, §56-573.1.
Public property.
Dedication, §56-564.
Purpose of act, §56-558.
Qualifying transportation facility.
Approval or development or operation as, §56-560.
Federal, state and local assistance, §56-567.
Financing, §56-567.1.
Material default, remedies, §56-568.
Powers and duties of private entity, §56-565.
Taking over, public entity, §56-568.
Recordation tax exemption.
Document recorded in connection with concession under act, §58.1-811.
Requirement of operation, §56-559.
Responsible public entity.
Approval by, §56-560.
Service contracts, §56-561.
Sovereign immunity.
Commonwealth, §56-573.
Local public entities, §56-573.
State agencies, departments and institutions.
Conceptual proposal.
Posting, public comment, §56-573.1:1.
Taking over facility.
Public entity, §56-568.
Title of act, §56-556.
Tolls or user fees.
Comprehensive agreement to provide for user fees, §56-566.
Imposition by private entity, §56-565.
Utility crossings, §56-570.
Cost to be borne by operator, §56-570.
Violations of law within facility, §56-571.
Virginia highway corporation act.
Applicability of chapter, §56-574.
Preservation, §56-574.
Public procurement.
Public-private transportation act.
Nonapplicability of procurement act, §56-573.1.
Public-transportation act.
Legislative findings, §56-558.
Recordation tax, state.
Distributions to cities and counties for, §58.1-816.
Richmond metropolitan authority, §§15.2-7000 to 15.2-7021.
See RICHMOND METROPOLITAN AUTHORITY.

TRANSPORTATION —Cont'd
School bus stops.
Installation of signs or devices to indicate bus stops, §33.1-223.2:18.
School students.
Generally, §§22.1-176 to 22.1-198.
See SCHOOL BUSES.
Secretary of transportation, §§2.2-200 to 2.2-202, 2.2-228, 2.2-229.
Service districts, §§15.2-2400 to 15.2-2403.3.
Shared ride taxi systems, §15.2-949.
Solid waste or medical waste transported by ship, barge or vessel upon navigable waters, §10.1-1454.1.
Traffic control measures.
Installation in residential areas, §33.1-223.2:19.
Private financing, §33.1-223.2:20.
Transportation districts.
Generally, §§15.2-4500 to 15.2-4534.
See TRANSPORTATION DISTRICTS.
Waste kitchen grease, §§3.2-5508 to 3.2-5516.

TRANSPORTATION ACCIDENTS.
Securing site of, §44-208.

TRANSPORTATION ACCOUNTABILITY COMMISSION, §§30-282 to 30-286.
Administrative staff support, §30-283.
Establishment and purpose, §30-282.
Expense reimbursement, §30-286.
Information to be furnished from state agencies, §30-285.
Members, §30-282.
Powers and duties, §30-284.

TRANSPORTATION AND UNDERGROUND COAL MINES, §§45.1-161.133 to 45.1-161.152.
See COAL MINE SAFETY.

TRANSPORTATION BOARD, §§33.1-1 to 33.1-23.
Accident reports filed by law enforcement officers.
Copies supplied board for speed reduction purposes, §46.2-373.
Acquisition or establishment of ferries, §33.1-254.
Acquisitions, conveyances and transfers of property.
Highways, rights-of-ways and landings.
Request to board for transfer to authority, §33.1-223.2:17.
Actions for violations of rules or regulations, §33.1-19.
Administrative process act.
Rules and regulations developed in accordance with, §33.1-19.
Airports.
Cooperation with United States agencies as to flight strips, airfields and roads, §5.1-50.
At-large members, §33.1-2.
Biodiesel and other alternative fuels.
Use in public transportation vehicles encouraged, §§67-500, 67-501.
Bonds of members, §33.1-9.
Bookkeeping system, §33.1-14.
Chairman.
Secretary of transportation, §§33.1-1, 33.1-3.
Cities and towns.
Assumption by city or town of responsibility for design, acquisition and construction of urban system highways.
Agreements between board and cities and towns, §33.1-12.1.

TRANSPORTATION BOARD —Cont'd
Cities and towns —Cont'd
Directional signs.
Integrated directional sign program, participation fees, §33.1-12.01.
Civil actions against employees.
Attorney general or assistant representing, §2.2-507.
Commissioner of highways, §33.1-3.
Compliance with federal acts.
Board powers, §33.1-12.
Concession payment account.
Terms and conditions of allocations, §33.1-23.03:9.
Construction contracts.
Board powers, §33.1-12.
Construction of chapter, §33.1-23.
Coordination of planning and financing of transportation needs, §33.1-12.
Criminal penalty.
Violation of rules or regulations, §33.1-19.
Damages caused by violation of rules or regulations.
Civil liability, §33.1-19.
Defense of employees, §33.1-11.
Department of rail and public transportation actions.
Monitoring and approving, §33.1-12.
Depositions.
Preservation of testimony in civil proceedings, §33.1-4.
Design-build contracts.
Authority to award, §33.1-12.
Disclosure statement by members.
Filing, time, form, §§2.2-3114, 2.2-3117.
Employees.
Defense of employees, §33.1-11.
Personnel hiring, §33.1-8.
Engineers.
Authority to employ, §33.1-8.
Bonds, surety.
Responsibility of state, §2.2-1818.
Evidence.
Board's rules and regulations as evidence, §33.1-22.
Expenses.
Federal transportation grant anticipation revenue notes, §33.1-23.20.
Farm machinery.
Inapplicability of board powers, §33.1-23.
Federal transportation grant anticipation revenue notes, §§33.1-23.14 to 33.1-23.26.
Additional funding, §33.1-23.22.
Approvals.
Authority to obtain, §33.1-23.19.
Authorization of notes, §33.1-23.15.
Bond issues, issuance, §33.1-23.15.
Citation of act, §33.1-23.14.
Costs.
Additional funding, §33.1-23.22.
Definitions, §33.1-23.14.
Deposit of proceeds, §33.1-23.21.
Details of notes, §33.1-23.17.
Eligible securities, notes as, §33.1-23.26.
Execution.
Form and manner, §33.1-23.18.
Expenses, §33.1-23.20.
GARVEE approval.
Authority to obtain, §33.1-23.19.
Investment of proceeds, §33.1-23.24.
Proceeds from notes.
Deposit, §33.1-23.21.

TRANSPORTATION BOARD —Cont'd
Federal transportation grant anticipation revenue notes —Cont'd
Proceeds from notes —Cont'd
Investment, §33.1-23.24.
Use, §33.1-23.16.
Project-specific reimbursements, application, §33.1-23.23.
Reimbursements.
Project-specific reimbursements, application, §33.1-23.23.
Sale, §33.1-23.17.
Securities.
Notes as eligible securities, §33.1-23.26.
Short title, §33.1-23.14.
Signatures required, §33.1-23.18.
Tax exemption, §33.1-23.25.
Terms of notes, §33.1-23.17.
Uses of proceeds, authorized, §33.1-23.16.
Financial and investment advisors.
Board powers to engage, §33.1-12.
Financial plans for transportation construction projects, review, §33.1-23.5:3.
Fixed-price contracts for construction projects.
Board powers, §33.1-12.
Force and effect of law.
Rules and regulations, §33.1-19.
Formally known as state highway and transportation board, §33.1-1.
General powers and duties of board, §§33.1-12, 33.1-13.
Commissioner's powers, §33.1-13.
Inapplicability of provisions to certain engines and tractors, §33.1-23.
Highway corporations.
Improvement fund, §56-552.
Prerequisites to construction and operation, §56-544.
Highways, commissioner of, §33.1-3.
Highway user fees.
Criteria for establishment, §33.1-12.
Improvement fund, §56-552.
Interagency cooperation, §33.1-12.
Interstate compacts.
Board powers, §33.1-12.
Investments.
Liability exemption of officers and employees, §33.1-23.03:7.
Land use planning, integration of transportation planning and programming, §33.1-12.
Limited access highways, §§33.1-57 to 33.1-61.
See HIGHWAYS AND ROADS.
Local transportation districts.
Generally, §§33.1-409 to 33.1-425, 33.1-430 to 33.1-446.
See TRANSPORTATION DISTRICTS.
Location of main office, §33.1-7.
Location of routes.
Board powers, §33.1-12.
Establishment, §33.1-18.
Mail.
Initial notice by certified mail, subsequent notices by regular mail, §33.1-13.04.
Main office, §33.1-7.
Meetings and minutes, §33.1-6.
Naming of highways.
Board powers, §33.1-12.
Notice.
Initial notice by certified mail, subsequent notices by regular mail, §33.1-13.04.

TRANSPORTATION BOARD —Cont'd
Number of members, §33.1-1.
Oaths of members, §33.1-9.
Offices, §33.1-7.
Official maps of localities.
Consultation with board, copy sent to board, §15.2-2237.
Ore tenus.
Hearings, §33.1-4.
Policies and operation of departments, review and approval, §33.1-12.
Populations with limited mobility.
Goals for addressing transportation needs of populations.
Establishment of specific mobility goals, §33.1-23.03:002.
Preservation of testimony.
How testimony of members taken in civil proceedings, §33.1-4.
Prisoner construction and maintenance of highways, §§53.1-56 to 53.1-59.
Private highways.
Approval, §56-544.
Public access authorities.
Highways, rights-of-ways and landings.
Request to board for transfer to authority, §33.1-223.2:17.
Purchases through division of purchases and supply.
Provisions not mandatory to, exceptions, §2.2-1119.
Quorum, §33.1-6.
References to commission or board, §33.1-1.
Removal of members, §33.1-1.
Renewable energy co-location of distribution facilities.
Rights-of-way as part of state highway system, §67-1105.
Residency requirements, §33.1-2.
Richmond metropolitan authority.
General powers, §15.2-7014.
Limited access toll highway.
Approval required by board, §15.2-7018.
State highway maintenance and constructions funds.
Use for authority facilities, §15.2-7005.
Right-of-way transactions.
Furnishing information, §33.1-16.
Roads over dams.
Generally, §§33.1-176 to 33.1-181.
See HIGHWAYS AND ROADS.
Rulemaking authority, §33.1-19.
Salaries and expenses.
How paid, §33.1-10.
Scenic highways and Virginia byways, §§33.1-62 to 33.1-66.
See HIGHWAYS AND ROADS.
School board in Virginia Beach.
Sale of property to commissioner of highways, §22.1-129.
Secondary system of state highways generally, §§33.1-67 to 33.1-88.
See HIGHWAYS AND ROADS.
Signatures.
Federal transportation grant anticipation revenue notes, signatures required, §33.1-23.18.
State highway system generally, §§33.1-25 to 33.1-47.1.
See HIGHWAYS AND ROADS.
State revenue bond act, §§33.1-267 to 33.1-295.
See TRANSPORTATION REVENUE BONDS.

TRANSPORTATION BOARD —Cont'd
Statewide interest, §33.1-2.
Statewide transportation plan.
Board to develop and update, §33.1-23.03.
Statistics and information.
Gathering and reporting, §33.1-13.05.
Term of members, §33.1-1.
Tie breaker, §33.1-1.
Traffic regulations.
Board powers, §33.1-12.
Transfer of interest in and control over highways, §33.1-223.2:17.
Transportation districts.
Commission member, §15.2-4507.
Planning process and procedure, §§15.2-4527, 15.2-4528.
Transportation infrastructure bank, §§33.1-23.6 to 33.1-23.13.
Tree trimming.
Policies to be developed, §33.1-84.1.
Vacancies, §33.1-1.
Voting privileges of chairman, §33.1-1.

TRANSPORTATION COMMISSIONS.
Criminal background investigations.
Record information, dissemination, §19.2-389.
Investment of public funds, §2.2-4513.

TRANSPORTATION COMPANIES, §§56-99.2 to 56-140.
Accident investigations, §56-131.
Additions.
Penalties for failure to make, §56-130.
Boat carriers.
See SIGHT-SEEING CARRIERS.
Charter party carriers generally.
See SPECIAL OR CHARTER PARTY CARRIERS.
Dead bodies used for scientific study.
Receipts, §32.1-299.
Employee liens, §§43-24 to 43-26.
Examinations of works and equipment, §56-128.
Executive sedans generally.
See LIMOUSINES AND EXECUTIVE SEDAN CARRIERS.
Federal railroad administration track safety and inspection program.
Participation by commission, §56-129.1.
Fish.
Requirements to carry and ship, §29.1-540.
Freight arrival.
Notification, §56-117.
Freight bills, §56-118.
Game.
Requirements to carry and ship, §29.1-540.
Household goods carriers.
See HOUSEHOLD GOODS CARRIERS.
Improvements.
Penalties for failure to make, §56-130.
Liability as common carrier.
Adjustment of claims against carriers, §56-123.
Limitations upon, §56-119.
Nonresident common carriers, §56-122.
Procedure and action on claims, §56-124.
Suits against unincorporated carriers, §56-125.
Limousines and executive sedan carriers.
See LIMOUSINES AND EXECUTIVE SEDAN CARRIERS.
Motor launch carriers.
See MOTOR LAUNCH CARRIERS.
Moving companies.
See HOUSEHOLD GOODS CARRIERS.

TRANSPORTATION COMPANIES —Cont'd
Personal property taxes.
Apportioned assessment, §58.1-3511.
Petroleum tank truck carriers.
Employee liens, §§43-24 to 43-26.
Not required to incorporate as public service companies, §13.1-620.
Public service companies generally, §§56-1 to 56-87.
See PUBLIC SERVICE COMPANIES.
Supplier liens, §§43-24 to 43-26.
Provision violations.
Penalties, §56-140.
Public service companies.
Generally, §§56-1 to 56-46.3.
See PUBLIC SERVICE COMPANIES.
Railroads.
See RAILROADS.
Rates and charges, §§56-99.2, 56-102.
Car service charges.
Adjustment of claims, §56-123.
Charging other than published tariff, §56-102.
Commission authority, §56-99.2.
Demurrage.
Payment of claims, §56-123.
Storage.
Adjustment of claims, §56-123.
Repairs.
Penalties for failure to make, §56-130.
Retail sales and use tax.
Examination of books, records and other documents of, §58.1-633.
Rolling stock tax, §§58.1-2652 to 58.1-2659.
See PUBLIC SERVICE CORPORATION TAXATION.
Seafood.
Bill of lading requirement, §28.2-824.
Removal from condemned areas, §§28.2-810 to 28.2-815.
Shellfish.
Bill of lading requirement, §28.2-824.
Removal from condemned areas.
Sealing of motor vehicles used in transporting, §28.2-812.
Shooting at or throwing missiles at cars, §18.2-154.
Sight-seeing carriers.
Boat carriers.
See SIGHT-SEEING CARRIERS.
Generally.
See SIGHT-SEEING CARRIERS.
Special or charter party carriers.
See SPECIAL OR CHARTER PARTY CARRIERS.
Special regulatory revenue tax, §§58.1-2660 to 58.1-2665.
Supplier liens, §§43-24 to 43-26.
Taxation of public service corporations generally, §§58.1-2600 to 58.1-2690.
See PUBLIC SERVICE CORPORATION TAXATION.
Taxicabs.
See TAXICABS.
Unlawful to charge other than published tariff, §56-102.

TRANSPORTATION DEPARTMENT.
Accident or emergency scene.
Department vehicles en route to or from.
Exemption from certain traffic regulations, §46.2-920.1.

TRANSPORTATION DEPARTMENT —Cont'd
Airports.
Construction of roads to airports and landing fields and cooperation with aviation department on other facility improvements, §5.1-49.
Bid acceptance, §2.2-4322.
Bonds, surety.
Responsibility of state, §2.2-1818.
City status granted to counties.
Continuation of services of department, §15.2-3918.
Civil actions against employees.
Attorney general or assistant representing, §2.2-507.
Colleges and universities.
Safety- or congestion management-related highway projects requested by colleges or universities, public hearings prior to undertaking, §33.1-223.2:28.
Commissioner of highways.
Authority to change speed limits, §46.2-878.
Liaison duties with other organizations, §33.1-190.4.
Commonwealth of Virginia federal transportation grant anticipation revenue notes, §§33.1-23.14 to 33.1-23.26.
Community service landscaping program, §33.1-12.2.
Comprehensive roadside management program, §33.1-223.2:9.
Consolidation of counties, cities or towns into single county or city.
Continuation of services of Department of Transportation after consolidation, §15.2-3530.
Conveyance of property held by state institution or public corporation to department, §2.2-1152.
Defense of employees, §33.1-11.
Disposition of surplus real property.
Notice to governing body or mayor of locality, §33.1-223.2:2.
Eminent domain.
Oysters.
Planting grounds, §28.2-628.
Employees as prison guards, §53.1-58.
Engineers.
Bonds, surety.
Responsibility of state, §2.2-1818.
Farm and forest land protection.
Plan for implementation of policies.
Preparation, requirement, §3.2-206.
Federal transportation grant anticipation revenue notes, §§33.1-23.14 to 33.1-23.26.
Freedom of information act.
Excluded records, §2.2-3705.6.
Exclusions from chapter.
Cost estimates prepared from confidential use of department, §2.2-3705.7.
Free passage over bridges and ferries.
Unlawful for department to permit, §33.1-251.
Grass mowing.
Maintenance of property acquired for transportation project.
Duty of department, §33.1-223.2:10.
Handbills, leaflets, bulletins, literature, advertisements.
Distribution on highways, public roadways and medians.
Prohibition or regulation, §46.2-931.

TRANSPORTATION DEPARTMENT —Cont'd
Highway construction or improvement projects.
Contractor performance bonds.
Locally administered transportation improvement projects, §33.1-223.2:22.
Noise abatement practices and technologies, §33.1-223.2:21.
Northern Virginia transportation district.
Analysis of transportation projects, §33.1-13.03:1.
Highway corporations.
Default, §56-549.
Inspection agreements, §56-544.
Highway safety corridors.
Established, §33.1-223.2:8.
Intermodal office of secretary of transportation, §2.2-229.
Investments.
Liability exemption of officers and employees, §33.1-23.03:7.
Landfill gas pipelines.
Department permission to place within highway right-of-way.
Notice to counties through which pipeline passes, §33.1-223.2:11.
Land use permits.
Issuance to company other than public service company, §2.2-1151.1.
Performance sureties.
Claims against company resolved before release, §2.2-1151.1.
Lighting systems.
Design requirements, §2.2-1111.
Limited access highways, §§33.1-57 to 33.1-61.
Mail.
Initial notice by certified mail, subsequent notices by regular mail, §33.1-13.04.
Main office location, §33.1-7.
Maintenance of property acquired for transportation project.
Duty of department, §33.1-223.2:10.
Maps.
Preparation at request and expense of local governing bodies or other groups, §33.1-222.
Northern Virginia transportation district.
Analysis of transportation projects, §33.1-13.03:1.
Notice.
Initial notice by certified mail, subsequent notices by regular mail, §33.1-13.04.
Oysters.
Planting grounds.
Condemnation, §28.2-628.
Plats.
Preparation at request and expense of local governing bodies or other groups, §33.1-222.
Prisons.
Employment and training of prisoners.
Highway construction and maintenance.
Payments by transportation department, §53.1-57.
Private highways.
Inspections, §56-544.
Recycling duties, §10.1-1425.8.
Reports.
Annual report, §33.1-13.03.
Right-of-way usage.
Land use permits to other than public service companies, §2.2-1151.1.
Route 29 bypass, construction, §33.1-223.2:9.

TRANSPORTATION DEPARTMENT —Cont'd
Safety service patrol program.
Exemption from certain traffic regulations, §46.2-920.1.
Sale of merchandise on highways, public roadways or medians.
Prohibition or regulation, §46.2-931.
School board in Virginia Beach.
Sale of property to department, §22.1-129.
School bus stops.
Installation of signs or devices to indicate bus stops, §33.1-223.2:18.
Secretary of transportation.
Agency responsibility, §2.2-228.
Intermodal office of, §2.2-229.
Secondary system of state highways.
Periodic examination of maintenance project approval process, §33.1-223.2:26.
Solicitation of contributions on highways, public roadways, medians.
Prohibition or regulation, §46.2-931.
State highway plat book.
Installation in circuit court clerk's office by department, §17.1-238.
Subdivision plats.
Review of preliminary subdivision plats, §15.2-2260.
Surplus real property, disposition.
Notice to local governing body or mayor, §33.1-223.2:2.
Traffic control measures.
Installation in residential areas, §33.1-223.2:19.
Private financing, §33.1-223.2:20.
Training of local government employees.
Administration of local maintenance and construction projects, §33.1-223.2:27.
Transition of county to city.
Continuation of services of department, §15.2-3918.
Transportation infrastructure bank, §§33.1-23.6 to 33.1-23.13.
Weed removal.
Maintenance of property acquired for transportation project.
Duty of department, §33.1-223.2:10.

TRANSPORTATION DISTRICT ACT OF 1964, §§15.2-4500 to 15.2-4534.

TRANSPORTATION DISTRICTS, §§15.2-4500 to 15.2-4534, 33.1-409 to 33.1-425, 33.1-430 to 33.1-446.
Abolition of local districts, §§33.1-424, 33.1-445.
Advisory boards, §§33.1-412, 33.1-413, 33.1-434.
Appointment of members, §§33.1-413, 33.1-434.
Creation, §§33.1-412, 33.1-434.
Defined, §§33.1-409, 33.1-430.
Albemarle county.
District within the city of Charlottesville and county of Albemarle, §§33.1-447 to 33.1-463.
Allocation of funds to districts, §§33.1-418, 33.1-439.
Reimbursement for advances to district, §§33.1-419, 33.1-440.
Annual special improvements tax, §§33.1-415, 33.1-435.
Payment of proceeds to transportation trust fund, §33.1-436.
Appropriations, §15.2-4524.
Boarding without lawful payment of fare or with fraudulent or counterfeit ticket, §18.2-160.1.

TRANSPORTATION DISTRICTS —Cont'd
Body corporate and politic, §15.2-4505.
Bonds or other interest bearing obligations, §15.2-4519.
Debt on Commonwealth or court or city not created, §15.2-4526.
Issuance to finance contract by county or city with commission, §15.2-4521.
Judicial determination of validity, §15.2-4520.
Charlottesville.
District within the city of Charlottesville and county of Albemarle, §§33.1-447 to 33.1-463.
Commissions.
Accounts and records, §15.2-4514.
Bond of members, §15.2-4509.
Chairman, §§33.1-411, 33.1-432.
Compensation and expenses, §15.2-4510.
Composition, §§33.1-411, 33.1-432.
Creation, §15.2-4506.
Criminal history record information on commission employees, §15.2-4517.1.
Defined, §§33.1-409, 33.1-430.
Meetings, §15.2-4511.
Members, §15.2-4507.
Money collected, received, etc., §15.2-4513.
Officers, §15.2-4508.
Powers and duties, §§33.1-411, 33.1-414, 33.1-433.
Powers and functions, §§15.2-4515, 15.2-4518.
Fares, schedules, franchising and routes, §15.2-4516.
Quorum, §§33.1-411, 33.1-432.
Quorum and action, §15.2-4512.
Two or more commissions with at least one jurisdiction located within D.C. metro area operating a commuter railway, §15.2-4507.
Conductors, motormen and station and depot agents.
Authorization to issue summons, §15.2-4503.
Construction of chapter, §§33.1-425, 33.1-446.
Contracts, §15.2-4521.
Agreements with transportation board, §§33.1-416, 33.1-436.
Enforcement, venue, §15.2-4522.
Preferred venue, §8.01-261.
Creation, §§33.1-410, 33.1-431.
By ordinance, §15.2-4504.
Criminal history record information.
Commission employees and contractors of commission, §15.2-4517.1.
Declaration of policy, §15.2-4501.
Definitions, §§15.2-4502, 33.1-409, 33.1-430.
District within the city of Charlottesville and county of Albemarle, §§33.1-447 to 33.1-463.
Abolition, §33.1-462.
Acceptance of highway into appropriate highway system.
Completion of construction or improvement, §33.1-460.
Advancement of funds or provision of matching funds to district.
Money not otherwise specifically allocated or obligated, §33.1-456.
Reimbursement of advanced funds, §33.1-457.
Advisory board.
Creation, §33.1-450.
Members, appointment, terms, vacancy, meetings, report, §33.1-451.
Approval of transportation board.
Construction or improvement of transportation improvement, §33.1-460.

TRANSPORTATION DISTRICTS —Cont'd
District within the city of Charlottesville and county of Albemarle —Cont'd
Commission.
Members, chairman, quorum, §33.1-449.
Powers and duties, §33.1-452.
Powers of district exercised by, §33.1-449.
Complete authority for acts authorized, §33.1-463.
Contract with transportation board.
Performance of district purposes, §33.1-454.
Cooperation with other political subdivisions, §33.1-458.
Creation, §33.1-448.
Definitions, §33.1-447.
Enlargement of district, §33.1-461.
Expiration of district, §33.1-448.
Liberal construction of chapter, §33.1-463.
Notice of hearing.
Creation of district, §33.1-448.
Petition to abolish district, §33.1-462.
Petition to create district, §33.1-448.
Petition to enlarge district, §33.1-461.
Powers, jurisdiction and duties of localities and officers not affected, §33.1-455.
Publication of notice.
Hearing on creation of district, §33.1-448.
Resolution of governing bodies.
Abolition of district, §33.1-462.
Creation of district, §33.1-448.
Enlargement of district, §33.1-461.
Special improvements tax.
Levy, rate, collection, use, §33.1-453.
Payment to transportation board, agreement, §33.1-454.
Tort liability not imposed on locality or landowner, §33.1-459.
Eminent domain, §15.2-4518.
Employees of public transportation systems.
Protection, §15.2-4517.
Enlargement of district, §§15.2-4504, 33.1-423, 33.1-444.
Procedure, §15.2-4529.
Establishment, §§33.1-410, 33.1-431.
Exemption form taxation, §15.2-4532.
Fares, schedules, franchising and routes.
Regulation by commission, §15.2-4516.
Hearing on question of creating.
District in county with population of more than 500,000, §33.1-431.
Indemnity and liability insurance, §15.2-4518.
Intergovernmental cooperation, §§33.1-420, 33.1-441.
Jurisdiction of localities and officers, etc., not affected, §§33.1-417, 33.1-438.
Liability not imposed on Commonwealth or county or city, §15.2-4526.
Liberal construction of provisions, §15.2-4534.
Local government group self-insurance pools, §§15.2-2700 to 15.2-2709.
See LOCAL GOVERNMENT GROUP SELF-INSURANCE POOLS.
Median strips in interstate highways.
Acquisition, §15.2-4523.
Member of local governing body placed on commission, §15.2-1535.
Metropolitan districts, 1970 ch 697.
Motor carriers, passengers.
Exclusions, §46.2-2000.1.
Motor fuel sales tax, §§58.1-1718.1 to 58.1-1724.4.
Multicounty transportation improvement districts.
Abolition of district, §15.2-4516.

TRANSPORTATION DISTRICTS —Cont'd
Multicounty transportation improvement districts —Cont'd
Advisory boards, §15.2-4505.
Agreements with Commonwealth transportation board, §15.2-4508.
Allocation of funds, §15.2-4510.
Commission, §15.2-4504.
Powers and duties, §15.2-4506.
Construction of chapter provisions, §15.2-4517.
Cooperation between district and other political subdivisions, §15.2-4512.
Definitions, §15.2-4502.
Enlargement of district, §15.2-4515.
Hearing on creating district, §15.2-4503.
Jurisdiction of counties and officers not affected, §15.2-4509.
Petition by property owners for creating, §15.2-4503.
Purposes, §15.2-4501.
Reimbursement to county for advances to district, §15.2-4511.
Resolution creating district, §15.2-4503.
Short title, §15.2-4500.
Special improvements tax, §15.2-4507.
Tort liability of Commonwealth, county or landowner, §15.2-4513.
Validation of districts, §15.2-4518.
Name, §15.2-4505.
Northern Virginia transportation district, 1964 ch 630, 1968 ch 449, 1974 ch 251, 1980 ch 144, 1981 ch 227.
Established pursuant to state code, §15.2-4503.1.
Notice of hearing on creating district.
Counties with population of more than 500,000, §33.1-431.
Ordinance creating, §15.2-4504.
Ordinance enlarging district, §15.2-4504.
Petition to governing body to create.
District in counties with population of more than 500,000, §33.1-431.
Powers granted in addition to other powers, §15.2-4525.
Powers of commissions, §§15.2-4515, 15.2-4518.
Powers of localities and officers, etc., not affected, §§33.1-417, 33.1-438.
Protection of employees of public transportation systems, §15.2-4517.
Reciprocal insurance contracts.
Power to commission to enter into, §38.2-1204.
Reimbursement for advances to district, §§33.1-419, 33.1-440.
Resolution by governing body.
Creating district in counties with population of 500,000 or more, §33.1-431.
Single jurisdictional district.
Ordinance creating district, §15.2-4504.
Summons issued by conductor, motormen, etc., §15.2-4503.
Taxes.
Annual special improvements tax, §§33.1-415, 33.1-435.
Payment of proceeds to transportation trust fund, §33.1-436.
Use of revenues, §§33.1-415, 33.1-435.
Termination of local districts, §§33.1-424, 33.1-445.
Territorial jurisdiction.
Enlargement of local districts, §§33.1-423, 33.1-444.
Tort liability, §§15.2-4533, 33.1-421, 33.1-442.

TRANSPORTATION DISTRICTS —Cont'd
Transportation district act of 1964.
Short title, §15.2-4500.
Transportation improvements.
Approval required, §33.1-422.
Defined, §§33.1-409, 33.1-430.
Transportation plan.
Preparation by commission, §15.2-4515.
Procedure, §15.2-4528.
Process, §15.2-4527.
Venue for actions to enforce contracts.
Contracts between commission and component government, §15.2-4522.
Withdrawal from district, §15.2-4530.
Financial obligations, §15.2-4531.
Zoning.
Payments for certain changes in zoning classifications or use, §33.1-437.

TRANSPORTATION ENHANCEMENT GRANTS.
Highways and roads.
Construction projects, use, §33.1-223.2:15.

TRANSPORTATION EQUIPMENT TRUST CERTIFICATES.
Insurance companies investments, §38.2-1420.

TRANSPORTATION IMPROVEMENT PROGRAM SET-ASIDE FUND, §58.1-816.1.

TRANSPORTATION INFRASTRUCTURE BANK, §§33.1-23.6 to 33.1-23.13.
Creation, §33.1-23.8.
Deferral of payments, §33.1-23.8.
Definitions, §33.1-23.7.
Disbursements from bank, §33.1-23.8.
Eligibility for funds, §33.1-23.9.
Funding.
Grants to the bank, §33.1-23.10.
Grants to the bank, §33.1-23.10.
Legislative findings, §33.1-23.6.
Loan fund, §33.1-23.8.
Loans from.
Conditions, §33.1-23.11.
Management, §33.1-23.8.
Project obligations, §33.1-23.11.
Project selection, §33.1-23.9.
Property exempt from taxation, §33.1-23.12.
Purposes, §33.1-23.6.
Reports, §33.1-23.13.
Tax exemption, §33.1-23.12.
Terms of loans and grants from the bank, §33.1-23.11.
Use of funds, §33.1-23.8.

TRANSPORTATION OF HAZARDOUS RADIOACTIVE MATERIALS.
See HAZARDOUS MATERIALS TRANSPORTATION.

TRANSPORTATION OF PUPILS.
School buses, §§22.1-176 to 22.1-198.
See SCHOOL BUSES.

TRANSPORTATION PARTNERSHIP OPPORTUNITY FUND, §33.1-221.1:8.

TRANSPORTATION REVENUE BONDS, §§33.1-267 to 33.1-295.
Acquisition of projects, §§33.1-270, 33.1-271.
Improvement of acquired projects, §33.1-273.
Allocation of funds, §33.1-23.4:01.
Alternative methods.
Supplemental additional powers conferred by article, §33.1-294.

TRANSPORTATION REVENUE BONDS —Cont'd
Appropriations, §33.1-285.1.
Approvals for bonds, §33.1-279.1.
Cessation of tolls, §33.1-287.
Citation of act, §33.1-267.
Commonwealth of Virginia contract revenue bonds.
Not debt of Commonwealth or pledge of faith and credit of Commonwealth, §33.1-277.
Commonwealth of Virginia credit assistance revenue bonds.
Not debt of Commonwealth or pledge of faith and credit of Commonwealth, §33.1-277.
Power of board to issue, §33.1-269.
Commonwealth of Virginia federal highway reimbursement anticipation notes.
Not debt of Commonwealth or pledge of faith and credit of Commonwealth, §33.1-277.
Commonwealth of Virginia toll revenue bonds.
Not debt of Commonwealth or pledge of faith and credit of Commonwealth, §33.1-277.
Commonwealth of Virginia transportation program revenue bonds.
Not debt of Commonwealth or pledge of faith and credit of Commonwealth, §33.1-277.
Competing bridges, ferries and tunnels, §33.1-291.
Condemnation of projects and property, §33.1-272.
Construction of article, §§33.1-294, 33.1-295.
Construction of projects, §§33.1-270, 33.1-274.
Contributions, §33.1-289.
Credit of state not pledged, §33.1-277.
Definitions, §33.1-268.
Financing multiple projects, §33.1-282.
Form of bonds, §33.1-278.
General powers of board, §33.1-269.
Highway connections, §33.1-275.
Improvement of projects acquired, §33.1-273.
Incidental powers of board, §33.1-292.
Issuance of bonds, §33.1-279.
Liberal construction of article, §33.1-295.
Limitation for bonds, §33.1-279.1.
Multiple projects.
Financing projects together, §33.1-282.
Powers of board, §§33.1-269, 33.1-292.
Purchase of projects, §33.1-271.
Refunding bonds, §33.1-293.
Remedies of bondholders and trustee, §33.1-290.
Reserve funds and appropriations, §33.1-285.1.
Resolution for bonds, §33.1-276.
Revenue refunding bonds, §33.1-293.
Revenues, §33.1-285.
Board use of certain funds, §33.1-288.
Sale of bonds.
Bonds as legal investments, §33.1-280.
Sales and paying agent, §33.1-279.1.
Use of proceeds, §33.1-281.
Sales and paying agent, §33.1-279.1.
Security for bonds, §33.1-277.
Short title, §33.1-267.
Sinking fund, §33.1-286.
Terms of bonds, §33.1-278.
Title of act, §33.1-267.
Toll revenues, §33.1-285.
Trust funds.
Proceeds as trust funds, §33.1-283.
Trust indenture, §33.1-284.

TRANSPORTATION, SECRETARY OF, §§2.2-200 to 2.2-202, 2.2-228, 2.2-229.
Secondary system of state highways.
Periodic examination of maintenance project approval process, §33.1-223.2:26.

TRANSPORTATION TRUST FUND.
Allocation of highway funds, §§33.1-23.03:1, 33.1-23.03:5.
Interstate highway system.
Tolls for use of components of system, §33.1-23.03:10.
Annual special improvements tax.
Disposition of proceeds, §§33.1-416, 33.1-436.
Budget bill.
Amounts diverted from fund included in bill, §2.2-1509.2.
Concession payment account.
Deposit of payments, §§33.1-23.03:1, 33.1-23.03:9.
Interstate highway system.
Tolls for use of components of system, §33.1-23.03:10.
Motor vehicle dealers, civil penalty for violations.
Deposit into fund, §46.2-1993.5.
Motor vehicle rental tax.
Disposition of revenue, §58.1-1741.
Motor vehicle sales and use tax revenue disposition, §58.1-2425.
Northern Virginia transportation district fund, §58.1-815.1.
Retail sales and use tax revenue disposition, §58.1-638.
Transportation improvement program set-aside fund, §58.1-816.1.
U.S. route 58 corridor development fund, §58.1-815.

TRANSPORTING CONTROLLED SUBSTANCE INTO COMMONWEALTH, §18.2-248.01.

TRANSPORTING SOLID WASTE OR MEDICAL WASTE UPON NAVIGABLE WATERS, §10.1-1454.1.

TRANSPORT PLATES.
Motorcycle dealers, §§46.2-1993.45, 46.2-1993.46.
Trailer dealers, §§46.2-1992.45 to 46.2-1992.47.

TRAP AND TRACE DEVICES.
Application for and issuance of order, §19.2-70.2.
Defined, §19.2-61.
General prohibition on use, §19.2-70.1.

TRAPPING.
Bag limits, §29.1-530.
Exceeding, §29.1-550.
Restitution, §29.1-551.
Penalties, §§29.1-550, 29.1-551.
Prescribing, §§29.1-506, 29.1-508.
Baiting.
Prohibited acts, §29.1-521.1.
Bears.
Big game defined, §29.1-510.
Big game.
Defined, §29.1-510.
Birds.
Closed season, §29.1-512.
Conservation police officers.
Generally, §§29.1-200 to 29.1-218.
See CONSERVATION POLICE OFFICERS.
Cruelty to animals provisions not to prevent, §3.2-6570.

TRAPPING —Cont'd
Damage liability of trapper, §29.1-530.
Deer.
Big game defined, §29.1-510.
Defined terms, §29.1-100.
Big game, §29.1-510.
Fee, §29.1-509.
Land, §29.1-509.
Landowner, §29.1-509.
Premises, §29.1-509.
Small game, §29.1-510.
Trap, §29.1-526.
Wild animals, §29.1-540.
Wild birds, §29.1-540.
Endangered species, §§29.1-563 to 29.1-570.
Falcons.
Permits to take, hold and transport, §29.1-419.
Issuance, §29.1-413.
Required, §29.1-412.
Fines, uniform schedule, VA SCt Rules 3C:1, 3C:2.
Fur-bearing animals, §§29.1-517, 29.1-530.
Fur dealer permits, §§29.1-400 to 29.1-407.
Game and inland fisheries generally.
See GAME AND INLAND FISHERIES.
Game protection fund, §29.1-101.
Hawks.
Permits to take, hold and transport, §29.1-419.
Issuance, §29.1-413.
Required, §29.1-412.
Highways.
Restrictions near, §29.1-526.
Identification, §29.1-521.
Impeding lawful trapping, §29.1-521.1.
Juvenile violations.
Summons issued by officer.
Juvenile and domestic relations district court may proceed on, §16.1-260.
Landowners' duty of care, §29.1-509.
Licensing.
Altering, §29.1-337.1.
Borrowing or lending, §29.1-337.1.
Carrying licenses, §29.1-336.
Destroyed licenses, §29.1-334.
Disabled persons and disabled veterans.
Lifetime license, §29.1-309.1.
Displaying licenses, §29.1-337.
Exemptions, §29.1-301.
False statements, §29.1-337.1.
Fees, §29.1-309.
Issuance.
Accounting, §29.1-332.
Agents for sale, §29.1-327.
By whom, §29.1-323.
Delivery and return of licenses, §29.1-330.
Evidence of entitlement, §29.1-325.
Procedure, §29.1-331.
Reports, §29.1-333.
Telephone and online sales, §29.1-327.
Lost licenses, §29.1-334.
Minors.
State junior resident trapping license, §29.1-309.3.
Multiple-year licenses, §29.1-328.
Persons entitled to resident licenses, §29.1-319.
Required, §§29.1-300, 29.1-335.
Nonresidents, §29.1-321.
Revocation, §29.1-338.
Reckless handling of firearm, §18.2-56.1.
Senior citizens.
Special lifetime license, §29.1-309.2.

TRAPPING —Cont'd
Licensing —Cont'd
Terms, §29.1-328.
Lifetime hunting and fishing endowment fund, §29.1-101.1.
Limitations, §29.1-521.
Methods of taking.
Prescribing, §29.1-508.
Minors.
State junior resident trapping license, §29.1-309.3.
National forest permits, §§29.1-408 to 29.1-411.
Nuisance fur-bearing animals, §29.1-517.
Nuisance species.
Open season, §§29.1-511, 29.1-530.
Owls.
Permits to take, hold and transport, §29.1-419.
Issuance, §29.1-413.
Required, §29.1-412.
Possession of game, §29.1-537.
Forfeiture, §29.1-557.
Posted property.
Destruction of posted signs or posting land of another, §18.2-135.
Method of posting land, §18.2-134.1.
Trespass on, §18.2-134.
Preserves.
Violations, §29.1-554.
Provision violations.
Conspiracies, §29.1-505.1.
Deer.
Killing deer illegally, §29.1-548.
Restitution, §29.1-551.
Migratory game birds, §29.1-547.
Penalties, §29.1-546.
Self-incrimination, §29.1-561.
Taking game during closed season or exceeding bag limit, §29.1-550.
Restitution, §29.1-551.
Violation of sanctuaries, refuges and preserves, §29.1-554.
Reckless handling of firearms, §18.2-56.1.
Refuges.
Violations, §29.1-554.
Regulations, §§29.1-501 to 29.1-505.
Residents of counties bordering on streams, §29.1-322.
Sale of game, §29.1-536.
Penalties for provision violations, §29.1-553.
Salt, putting out for wildlife in location used by hunters.
Prohibited acts, §29.1-521.1.
Sanctuaries.
Violations, §29.1-554.
Search without warrant to enforce game laws, §19.2-59.
Seasons, §29.1-530.
Birds, §29.1-512.
Closing, §29.1-507.
Fur-bearing animals, §29.1-530.
Nuisance species, §29.1-511.
Prescribing, §§29.1-506, 29.1-508.
Shortening, §29.1-507.
Taking game during closed season.
Penalties, §§29.1-550, 29.1-551.
Restitution, §29.1-551.
Wild animals, §§29.1-511, 29.1-512.
Senior citizens.
Special lifetime license, §29.1-309.2.
Small game.
Defined, §29.1-510.

TRAPPING —Cont'd
State forests, §§10.1-1151 to 10.1-1157.
See HUNTING AND TRAPPING IN STATE FORESTS.
Storage of game, §29.1-541.
Taking methods, restrictions.
Unlawful devices to be destroyed, §29.1-556.
Transportation of game, §29.1-540.
Trespass by trappers, §18.2-132.
Enforcement of provisions, §18.2-136.1.
Posted property, §18.2-134.
Destruction of posted signs or posting land of another, §18.2-135.
Method of posting, §18.2-134.1.
Refusal of person on land, etc., of another to identify himself, §18.2-133.
Uniform fine schedule, VA SCt Rules 3C:1, 3C:2.
Visits to traps, §29.1-521.
Wild animals.
Seasons, §§29.1-511, 29.1-512.

TRAP SHOOTING.
Local noise control ordinances.
Applicability to sport shooting ranges, §15.2-917.

TRASH.
Counties, cities or towns, §§15.2-901, 15.2-927 to 15.2-939.
Charging and collecting compensation, §15.2-928.
Collection and disposal generally, §15.2-927.
Contracting for services, §15.2-930.
Authorization to enter into contract, §15.2-932.
Requiring delivery to certain facilities, §15.2-931.
Contracting with other localities to provide or supply services, §15.2-928.
Fee exemption, §15.2-936.
Fee for solid waste disposal by certain counties, §15.2-2159.
Leaves or grass clippings in landfill, §15.2-935.
Penalties for unauthorized disposal or failure to use facility, §15.2-928.
Private waste companies, displacement, §15.2-934.
Prohibiting disposal in unauthorized places, §15.2-928.
Recycling and waste disposal powers generally, §15.2-928.
Regulation generally, §15.2-930.
Requiring delivery to certain facilities, §15.2-933.
Requiring property owners to remove from property, §15.2-901.
Separation of solid waste generally, §15.2-937.
Service districts, §§15.2-2400 to 15.2-2403.3.
Solid waste management facilities.
Providing and operating, §15.2-928.
Siting approval, §15.2-929.
Urban county executive form of government.
Regulation of pickup and disposal services, contracting for services, §15.2-815.
Recycling generally.
See RECYCLING.
Refuse collection vehicles.
Flashing amber warning lights, §46.2-1025.
Parking, ordinances prohibiting or limiting, §46.2-1224.
Safety inspections, §46.2-1175.1.
Solid waste management generally, §§10.1-1408.1 to 10.1-1414.
See SOLID WASTE MANAGEMENT.

TRAUMA CENTER FUND.
Created, purpose, §18.2-270.01.

TRAUMA CENTER FUND —Cont'd
Driving while intoxicated offenders.
Payment to fund by multiple offenders, §18.2-270.01.

TRAUMA REGISTRY.
Emergency medical services patient care information system, §32.1-116.1.

TRAUMATIC BRAIN INJURY.
Commonwealth neurotrauma initiative.
Aging and rehabilitative services, department for, §§51.5-178 to 51.5-181.

TRAUMA TRIAGE PLAN, §32.1-111.3.

TRAVEL ACCIDENT INSURANCE AGENTS.
Licensing of agents generally, §§38.2-1822 to 38.2-1836.1.

TRAVEL AGENCIES.
Travel insurance, §§38.2-1887 to 38.2-1890.

TRAVEL BAGGAGE INSURANCE AGENTS.
Licensing without examination, §38.2-1814.

TRAVEL CAMPGROUNDS.
Excise tax, city or town having general taxing powers, §58.1-3840.
Transient occupancy tax, §§58.1-3819 to 58.1-3826.

TRAVEL CLUBS, §§59.1-445 to 59.1-454.
Agreements, §59.1-448.
Consumer protection, prohibited practices, §59.1-200.
Defined terms, §59.1-445.
Deposits.
Escrow, §59.1-447.1.
Escrow of deposits, §59.1-447.1.
Exemption from provisions, §59.1-453.
Investigations, §59.1-451.
Letters of credit, §59.1-447.
Prohibited practices, §59.1-449.
Provision violations.
Penalties, §59.1-454.
Public offering statement.
Contents, §59.1-448.1.
Required, §59.1-448.1.
Records, production of, §59.1-452.
Registration, §59.1-446.
Regulations, §59.1-450.
Surety bonds, §59.1-447.

TRAVELERS' CHECKS.
Negotiable instruments, defined as, §8.3A-104.
Unclaimed property, disposition of, §55-210.3:02.

TRAVEL EXPENSES.
Attorney general, deputies, assistants and employees, §2.2-504.
County police officers transporting violator to jail.
Jail of another county or city adopted as jail of county, §15.2-1609.6.
Ethics advisory panels, senate and house of general assembly, §30-112.
General assembly members, §30-19.13.
Ascertaining distance from place other than courthouse, §30-19.18.
Attending legislative committees during recess of assembly, §30-19.15.
Judicial council, §17.1-704.
Jurors allowances, §§17.1-618 to 17.1-623.

TRAVEL EXPENSES —Cont'd
Mental health clinics located in certain counties.
Supplementation by counties and cities, §15.2-1508.4.
Persons traveling on business of locality, §15.2-1508.1.
Commonwealth required to bear portion of expenses, §15.2-1508.2.
Rate of reimbursement per mile, §15.2-1508.1.
Supplementation of expenses by certain counties and cities, §§15.2-1508.3, 15.2-1508.4.
Public officers and employees.
See PUBLIC OFFICERS AND EMPLOYEES.
Sheriffs and deputies.
Agreement with county or city regarding, §15.2-1609.6.
Mileage allowances, §15.2-1609.3.
Report by sheriff as to mileage, §15.2-1609.4.
Statement of expenses, §15.2-1609.5.
State department of health.
Supplementation by certain counties, §15.2-1508.3.
Witnesses' allowances, §§17.1-611 to 17.1-617.

TRAVELING SALESPERSONS.
License tax on peddlers, §58.1-3717.
Limitations on taxes imposed, §58.1-3719.
Peddlers at wholesale, §58.1-3718.

TRAVEL INSURANCE, §§38.2-1887 to 38.2-1890.
Applicability of title, §38.2-1890.
Definitions, §38.2-1887.
Information provided to customers, §38.2-1888.
Licenses.
Suspension, revocation or termination, §38.2-1889.
Rulemaking authority, §38.2-1890.
Sale of insurance, requirements for, §38.2-1888.
Suspension, revocation or termination of licenses, §38.2-1889.
Travel accident insurance agents.
Licensing of agents generally, §§38.2-1822 to 38.2-1836.1.
Travel retailers.
Sale of insurance, requirements for, §38.2-1888.

TRAVEL TRAILERS.
Excessive size and weight permits.
Towing motor homes or travel trailers, §46.2-1139.
Impeding or disrupting vehicles operating under valid highway hauling permit, §46.2-828.2.
T&M vehicle dealers, §§46.2-1900 to 46.2-1991.
See T&M VEHICLE DEALERS.

TRAWLING IN TIDAL WATERS, §§28.2-314 to 28.2-319.
Construction of provisions, §28.2-318.
Drag nets, §28.2-314.
Forfeiture of property, §28.2-319.
Prima facie evidence of violation, §28.2-317.
Trawl nets, §28.2-314.
Limited permissibility, §28.2-315.
Vessel restrictions, §28.2-316.

TREASON AND RELATED OFFENSES, §§18.2-481 to 18.2-485, US Const Art I §6.
Approvers.
Admittance in any case barred, §19.2-256.
Arrest report to central criminal records exchange, §19.2-390.
Defined, §18.2-481.
Extradition.
Fugitives from justice, §19.2-86.

TREASON AND RELATED OFFENSES —Cont'd
Misprision of treason, §18.2-482.
Overthrow of government.
Advocating change by force, violence, etc., §18.2-484.
Punishment, §18.2-481.
Race insurrection against another race.
Conspiring to incite, §18.2-485.
Usurped government, attempting or instigating others to establish, §18.2-483.
War.
Levying against United States, US Const Art III §3.

TREASURER OF STATE.
Depositories of state, §6.2-915.
Deposits.
State depositories, §6.2-915.
Deposits by insurers with, §§38.2-1045 to 38.2-1058.
Escheats.
Publication of certification of escheated lands, §55-183.
Rules and regulations, §55-200.1.
Sale of escheated lands, §§55-184.1 to 55-191.
Felony to dispose of insurers' securities illegally, §38.2-1058.
Insurers' deposits.
Enforcement of policyholder's or general creditor's lien on deposit.
Party to bill, §38.2-1046.
Generally, §§38.2-1045 to 38.2-1058.
Investment of funds in state treasury.
Selection of investment management services, §2.2-4343.
Literary fund.
Accountant for fund, §22.1-143.
General provisions, §§22.1-142 to 22.1-161.
See LITERARY FUND.
Mandamus.
Writ to secure construction of act directing payment out of state treasury, §8.01-653.
Motor vehicle proof of financial responsibility.
Assessment for expenses of holding deposits, §46.2-455.
Deposit of moneys or securities.
Certification of value, §46.2-454.
Notice.
Unclaimed property, §55-210.13.
Primary candidates to pay fees to, §24.2-524.
Receivers.
Moneys deposited in court.
Accounting requirements, §8.01-604.
Recover of money paid into state treasury, §8.01-605.
State depositories, §6.2-915.
Temporary assistance for needy families fund, §63.2-601.1.
Tobacco indemnification and community revitalization commission.
Endowment fund custodian, §§3.2-3104, 3.2-3106.
Unclaimed property.
Declining receipt of, §55-210.23.
Disposition of funds record, §55-210.19.
Enforcement of provisions, §55-210.25.
Penalties for violation, §55-210.26:1.
Examination of records, §55-210.24.
Foreign actions, §55-210.15.
Interest, §55-210.26:1.
Interstate agreements and cooperation, §55-210.11:01.

TREASURER OF STATE —Cont'd
Unclaimed property —Cont'd
Notice, §55-210.13.
Rules and regulations, §55-210.27.
Safe deposit box property.
Reimbursement of costs to holder, §55-210.15.
Sales, §55-210.18.
Claims to property of proceeds of sale, §§55-210.20 to 55-210.22.
Disposition of funds record, §55-210.19.
Securities.
Transfer of record of ownership, §55-210.18:1.
Voluntary solar resource development fund, §67-1302.
Workers' compensation.
Custodian of securities, §65.2-801.

TREASURERS, LOCAL, §§58.1-3123 to 58.1-3172.1, VA Const Art VII §4.
Abolition of constitutional offices.
Referendum elections, §24.2-685.
Change in form of government having effect of abolishing office, §24.2-686.
Account of receipts and expenditures and statement, §§58.1-3127, 58.1-3135.
Annual settlement, §58.1-3137.
Appeal from discharge from liability, §58.1-3147.
Appeal of compensation board decisions, §15.2-1636.9.
Appointment of county treasurer as treasurer of town located in county, §15.2-1534.
Attachment of estate in hands of or debts due by third parties.
Collection of delinquent taxes, §58.1-3952.
Attorney general to proceed against delinquent treasurers, §58.1-3171.
Lien of judgment and execution in proceeding, §58.1-3172.
Audit upon termination of office, §58.1-3136.
Bond of deputies, §58.1-3126.
Bond of local officers generally, §§15.2-1527 to 15.2-1533.
See LOCAL OFFICERS AND EMPLOYEES.
Bond of treasurer.
Amount, §§15.2-1529, 15.2-1530.
Appointment as finance officer for jointly owned schools.
No additional bond required, §15.2-1531.
Destruction of bonds and bond coupons, §58.1-3130.
Examination by commissioner of accounts, §58.1-3125.
Liability for violations of article, §58.1-3144.
Local officers generally, §§15.2-1527 to 15.2-1533.
See LOCAL OFFICERS AND EMPLOYEES.
New bond, insufficiency of old bonds, §58.1-3125.
Pledge of securities by depository, §58.1-3158.
Books open for inspection, §58.1-3127.
Checks signed by county treasurer.
Disbursement of money deposited, §58.1-3162.
Circuit court clerks.
Delivery of books, tax tickets, etc., to upon vacancy of office, §58.1-3138.
City charters not affected by provisions, §58.1-3148.
City treasurers.
Collection of state license fees, §15.2-1636.4.
Salary, §15.2-1608.1.
Collection and payment over taxes and levies, §§58.1-3127, 58.1-3127.1.

TREASURERS, LOCAL —Cont'd
Collection of corporations unpaid bills for registration fees and franchise taxes, §58.1-2814.
Collection of local taxes generally by treasurers, §§58.1-3921 to 58.1-3938.
See TAX COLLECTION.
Conflicts between city charters and special provisions.
Charters not affected by provisions, §58.1-3148.
Corporation registration fees and franchise taxes.
Collection of unpaid bills for, §58.1-2814.
County board form of government, §15.2-408.
County executive form of government.
Director of finance to exercise powers, §15.2-522.
County finance board.
Abolishment by ordinance, §58.1-3151.
Compensation to citizen member, §58.1-3153.
Investment directions, §58.1-3156.
Membership, §58.1-3151.
Organization, §58.1-3152.
Procedure, §58.1-3152.
Report of treasurer to, §58.1-3160.
County manager form of government.
Director of finance to exercise powers, §15.2-620.
County manager plan of government, §§15.2-711 to 15.2-713.
County seats.
Office of county treasurer maintained at, §58.1-3124.
County treasurer.
Collection and payment of license fees and other fees of county commissioners of revenue, §15.2-1636.3.
Salary, §15.2-1608.2.
Dealing in warrants.
Prohibited, §58.1-3139.
Deduction of taxes due from party in whose favor warrant drawn, §58.1-3133.
Delinquent taxes.
Collection generally, §§58.1-3921 to 58.1-3938.
See TAX COLLECTION.
Delinquent treasurers.
Attorney general to proceed against, §58.1-3171.
Lien of judgment and execution in proceeding, §58.1-3172.
Deposit of money received, §58.1-3149.
Approval, §58.1-3154.
Banking institutions outside of Commonwealth, §58.1-3155.
Bond or pledge of securities by depository, §58.1-3158.
Disbursement, §58.1-3162.
Duties of depository officers, §58.1-3150.
Duties of treasurer, §58.1-3158.
Excess deposits not permitted by depository officers, §58.1-3150.
Interest on deposits, payment, §58.1-3161.
Local funds deposited in banking institutions outside of Commonwealth, §58.1-3155.
Loss of funds deposited, liability for, §58.1-3163.
No liability for loss of funds deposited in accordance with article, §58.1-3163.
Selection, §58.1-3154.
State revenue into state treasury, §58.1-3168.
Deposit of state money received, §2.2-806.
Deputies.
Appointment, powers, removal, §15.2-1603.
Bond.
In liability on bond, §58.1-3126.

TREASURERS, LOCAL —Cont'd
Destruction of records after audit, §58.1-3129.
Directors of finance.
Included in term treasurer.
Directors performing duties of treasurers, §58.1-3123.
Disbursement of money deposited, §58.1-3162.
Discharge from liability, §58.1-3145.
Appeal, §58.1-3147.
Rule to show cause, §58.1-3146.
Distress, collection of local taxes by generally, §§58.1-3940 to 58.1-3961.
See TAX COLLECTION.
District court judges, dual officeholding prohibited, §16.1-69.19.
Dual office holding, §15.2-1534, VA Const Art VII §6.
Election, §24.2-217, VA Const Art VII §4.
Economic interest statement as requirement of candidates, §24.2-502.
Primary schedule.
In year 2001 and each tenth year thereafter, §24.2-515.1.
Vacancy, special election, §24.2-226.
Electronic billing of taxpayers, §58.1-3912.
Embezzlement.
Use of public money except as provided by law, §58.1-3141.
Escheat reports, §55-171.
Estates in hands of or debts due by third parties.
Collection by application to third party, §58.1-3952.
Expense of office request filed with compensation board, §15.2-1636.7.
Failure to pay over revenue.
Interest chargeable against treasurer, §58.1-3169.
Failure to pay warrant, remedy, §58.1-3140.
Federal grants, gifts or forfeitures.
Collection of amounts to be received, §58.1-3127.1.
Final settlement, §58.1-3137.
Fraudulent transactions discovered, reporting to auditor of, §30-138.
General provisions as to local constitutional officers, §§15.2-1600 to 15.2-1607.
See LOCAL CONSTITUTIONAL OFFICERS.
Hearing on discharge from final liability, §58.1-3146.
Income tax collection duties, §58.1-353.
Income tax payments received.
Deposit, record-keeping, reports, §2.2-806.
Insurers conversion to stock corporation.
Treatment of money received, §15.2-1608.1.
Intangible personal property tax.
Collection, §58.1-1117.
List of delinquent taxes, treasurer to make, §§58.1-1800, 58.1-1801.
Receipt of state taxes, §58.1-1800.
Interest chargeable against treasurer for failure to pay over revenue, §58.1-3169.
Interest on deposits, §58.1-3161.
Interest on fund belongs to fund, §58.1-3142.
Interpretation of term treasurer, §58.1-3123.
Investment directions to treasurer, §58.1-3156.
Investment of public funds.
Liability, §2.2-4516.
Land book.
Copies delivered by commissioners of revenue to, §58.1-3310.
Book not to be altered after delivery to treasurer, §58.1-3311.

TREASURERS, LOCAL —Cont'd
Lease of real estate for collection of taxes, §§58.1-3947, 58.1-3948.
Lien of judgment and execution in proceeding against delinquent treasurers, §58.1-3172.
Mailing bills to taxpayers, §58.1-3912.
Manufactured home permits.
Moving home to place where to be used as place of residence.
Issuance by local treasurers, §58.1-3520.
Mobile home permits.
Moving mobile home to place where to be used as place of residence.
Issuance by local treasurer, §58.1-3520.
Money received to be deposited, §58.1-3149.
Disbursement, §58.1-3162.
Duties of depository officers, §58.1-3150.
Duties of treasurers, §58.1-3158.
Excess deposits not permitted by depository officers, §58.1-3150.
Interest, §58.1-3161.
No liability for loss of funds deposited in accordance with article, §58.1-3163.
Motor vehicle license plates.
Special license plates, §46.2-737.
Notice.
Final discharge, §58.1-3145.
Proceedings against delinquent treasurers, recordation, §58.1-3171.
Real estate tax exemption or deferral for elderly or handicapped program, §58.1-3213.1.
Show-cause rule on discharge of liability, §58.1-3146.
Taxes due, §58.1-3911.
Office furniture, equipment and appliances.
Manner of paying for purchases, §15.2-1636.15.
Office of county treasurer.
Where maintained, §58.1-3124.
Ouster proceedings, institution by governor, §58.1-3164.
Substitute, appointment of, §58.1-3165.
Continuation in office upon removal of predecessor, §58.1-3166.
Suspension of officer proceeded against, §58.1-3165.
Paid tax tickets.
Destruction, §58.1-3129.
Payment of state revenue into state treasury, §58.1-3168.
Personal property books.
Alteration after delivery by commissioner of revenue to treasurer, §58.1-3119.
Copy delivered to treasurer by commissioner of revenue, §58.1-3118.
Petition for destruction of bonds and bond coupons, §58.1-3130.
Primary elections.
Payment of costs of primaries, §24.2-518.
Publication of notice of final discharge, §58.1-3145.
Publication of notice to show cause on discharge of liability, §58.1-3146.
Public money not to be used except as provided by law, §58.1-3141.
Rabies certificate.
Veterinarian to forward information to, §3.2-6529.
Real property tax apportionment.
Notice of motion, §58.1-3226.
Real property tax liens.
Release of lien on portion of real estate upon payment of taxes, §58.1-3226.1.

TREASURERS, LOCAL —Cont'd
Receipt of public funds.
Report to comptroller, §2.2-807.
Recordation of liens of delinquent real estate taxes.
In office of, §58.1-3930.
Recordation of notice of proceedings against delinquent treasurers, §58.1-3171.
Records destruction after audit, §58.1-3129.
Referendum election for abolition of constitutional offices, §24.2-685.
Change in form of government having effect of abolishing office, §24.2-686.
Refusal to answer questions touching tax liability, §58.1-3128.
Remote access to nonconfidential public records maintained by, §58.1-3172.1.
Removal from office.
Public officers from office generally, §§24.2-230 to 24.2-238.
Violations of article, §58.1-3144.
Report of treasurer to county finance board, §58.1-3160.
Retail sales and use tax.
Authority to require production of information, §58.1-3128.1.
Salaries.
City treasurer, §15.2-1608.1.
Supplementation by county or city, §15.2-1605.1.
Salaries of local constitutional officers generally, §§15.2-1636.1 to 15.2-1636.20.
See CONSTITUTIONAL LOCAL OFFICERS.
Salaries, proportion borne by Commonwealth and locality, §15.2-1636.14.
Salary based on population bracket of county and city.
Population determined by preceding census, §15.2-1636.11.
Settlement.
Annual settlement, §58.1-3137.
Final settlement, §58.1-3137.
Special license plates, §46.2-737.
Statement of accounts, §58.1-3135.
State revenue deposited into state treasury, §58.1-3168.
Stationery.
Manner of paying for purchases, §15.2-1636.15.
Substitute, appointment on institution of ouster proceedings, §58.1-3165.
Continuation in office upon removal of predecessor, §58.1-3166.
Successors.
Delivery of books, tax tickets, etc., to, §58.1-3138.
Summoning taxpayers and other persons, §58.1-3128.
Supplementation of salaries by county or city, §15.2-1605.1.
Supplies.
Manner of paying for purchases, §15.2-1636.15.
Supreme court appeal on discharge from liability, §58.1-3147.
Tax increment financing ordinance.
Transmission of copy of ordinance to, §58.1-3245.3.
Tax tickets.
Destruction, §58.1-3129.
Telephone service or repairs.
Manner of paying for purchases, §15.2-1636.15.
Term, §§15.2-1608, 24.2-217, VA Const Art VII §4.
Termination of office, §58.1-3136.
Final settlements, §58.1-3137.

TREASURERS, LOCAL —Cont'd
Urban county executive form of government.
Director of finance to exercise powers, §15.2-829.
Vacancies in office.
Delivery of books, tax tickets, etc., to successor or court clerk, §58.1-3138.
Interim appointment by courts, §24.2-227.
Special election to fill, §24.2-226.
Time to qualify and give bond if required, §24.2-229.
Violations of article, penalty generally, §58.1-3144.
Warrants for payment of money.
Deduction of taxes due from party in whose favor warrant drawn, §58.1-3133.
How warrants paid, §58.1-3132.
Limitation on payment.
Presentment within two years required, §58.1-3134.
Paid in order presented, §58.1-3131.
Presentation within two years, §58.1-3134.
Release of information.
Prohibited, exceptions, §58.1-3131.
Remedy for failure to pay, §58.1-3140.
Treasurer not to deal in, §58.1-3139.
Warrant book, §58.1-3131.
Website access to property tax bills, §58.1-3912.
Workers' compensation.
Employees defined, §65.2-101.

TREASURERS OF POLITICAL CAMPAIGNS.
Campaign finance disclosure generally.
See CAMPAIGN FINANCE DISCLOSURE.

TREASURY BOARD, §§2.2-2415 to 2.2-2420.
Bond issues.
Bond anticipation notes, use, §2.2-2418.
Combination sales prohibited, §2.2-2420.
Refunding bonds, §2.2-2419.
Bonds received by comptroller in settlement of claims.
Cancellation, §2.2-811.
Colleges and universities.
Bond issues.
Issuing agent, §23-19.
Composition, §2.2-2415.
Contracts.
Review and approval of financial terms, §2.2-2417.
Duties, §2.2-2416.
Energy efficiency projects, §2.2-2417.
Establishment, §2.2-2415.
Government non-arbitrage investment.
Powers, §2.2-4702.
Investment of public funds.
Government non-arbitrage investment.
Authorization to provide certain assistance, §2.2-4700.
Powers of issuers, §2.2-4703.
Powers.
Government non-arbitrage investment, §2.2-4702.
Local government investment pool, §2.2-4605.
Securities lending, §2.2-4506.
Local government investment pool.
Powers, §2.2-4605.
Meetings, §2.2-2415.
Powers, §2.2-2416.
Contracts.
Review and approval of financial terms, §2.2-2417.
Investment of public funds.
Government non-arbitrage investment, §2.2-4702.

TREASURY BOARD —Cont'd
Public procurement.
Financial services, §2.2-2417.
Security for public deposits.
Powers, §2.2-4405.
Subrogation to depositor's rights, §2.2-4406.
Tobacco indemnification and community revitalization commission.
Endowment fund trustee, §§3.2-3104, 3.2-3106.

TREASURY BONDS.
Investment of public funds, §2.2-4505.

TREASURY DEPARTMENT.
Creation, §2.2-1800.
Debt capacity advisory committee, §§2.2-2712 to 2.2-2714.
Disbursement from state treasury, §§2.2-1819 to 2.2-1827.
Division of risk management, §§2.2-1832 to 2.2-1843.
Drug investigation special trust account, §52-4.3.
Electronic funds transfers.
Payment of amounts due and owing Commonwealth, §2.2-211.
Generally, §§2.2-1800 to 2.2-1812.
See STATE TREASURER.
General provisions regarding state agencies and general operation of government, §§2.2-600 to 2.2-614.3.
See STATE DEPARTMENTS AND AGENCIES.
Revenue stabilization fund, §§2.2-1828 to 2.2-1831.
Risk management division, §§2.2-1832 to 2.2-1843.
Secretary of finance.
Agency responsibility, §2.2-211.
State depositories.
Deposit of money paid into state treasury, §§2.2-1813 to 2.2-1818.
Treasurer of state generally.
See TREASURER OF STATE.

TREASURY OF STATE.
Colleges and universities.
Disposition of proceeds and revenues, §§23-21, 23-28.
Public funds generally.
See PUBLIC FUNDS.
Public utilities, state operation.
Payments, §56-518.
State treasurer generally.
See TREASURER OF STATE.

TREASURY STOCK.
Securities generally, §§13.1-501 to 13.1-527.3.
See SECURITIES.

TREATIES.
Documents of title.
Relation of article to treaties, §8.7-103.
Relationship of article to United States treaty, §8.7-103.
President of the United States, US Const Art II §2.
Real property taxes.
Service charge in lieu of payment.
International or treaty exempted property, §58.1-3405.
Service charge on owners of real estate exempted by international law or treaty, §58.1-3405.
States other than Virginia, US Const Art I §10.

TREATIES —Cont'd
Supreme law of the land, US Const Art VI.

TREATISES.
Hearsay exception, §8.01-401.1.

TREBLE DAMAGES.
Antitrust actions.
Instituted on behalf of Commonwealth or localities, §59.1-9.15.
Personal actions, §59.1-9.12.
Bad checks, §8.01-27.2.
Combinations to injure others in reputation, trade, etc., §18.2-500.
Electronic communication devices.
Unlawful devices.
Electronic communication service provider, civil relief, §18.2-190.8.
Fraudulent claims against the state, §8.01-216.3.
Lemon law, §59.1-207.15.
Motor vehicle warranties, §59.1-207.15.
Oil discharges, §62.1-44.34:20.
Petroleum products franchise agreements, §59.1-21.11.
Public service companies.
Liability for damages to company property, §56-5.
Timber cutting encroachment, §55-332.
Waters of the state.
Oil discharges, §62.1-44.34:20.

TREE CANOPY OR TREE COVER.
Conservation of trees during development process.
Locality located in Planning District 8 classified as nonattainment area for air quality standards, §15.2-961.1.
Replacement of trees during development process, §15.2-961.

TREE FARMING.
Zoning ordinances.
Special use permit not required for certain agricultural activities, §15.2-2288.

TREES.
Agricultural and forestal districts, §§15.2-4300 to 15.2-4407.
Capitol grounds.
Injuries to trees growing on, §18.2-139.
Carrying axe while hunting for purposes of cutting trees without permission of landowner, §18.2-141.
Christmas trees, commercially grown.
Hunter damage.
Damage stamp program, §§29.1-352 to 29.1-358.
Conservation and recreation department.
Sale of trees, §10.1-113.
Counties, cities or towns.
Conservation of trees during development process.
Locality within Planning District 8 classified as nonattainment area for air quality standards, §15.2-961.1.
Planting and replacement of trees during development process, §15.2-961.
Planting of trees destroyed during construction process, §15.2-960.
Sales on highways.
Counties prohibiting, §15.2-1219.
Dam safety.
Prohibited vegetation, §10.1-609.2.
Destruction of trees on private property, public parks, refuges or sanctuaries, §18.2-140.

TREES —Cont'd
Forest management of state-owned lands fund, §§10.1-1120 to 10.1-1123.
Forest products tax, §§58.1-1600 to 58.1-1622.
See FOREST PRODUCTS TAX.
Fruit trees.
Bears.
Killing bears damaging fruit trees, §29.1-529.
Deer.
Killing deer damaging fruit trees, §29.1-529.
Elk.
Killing elk damaging fruit trees, §29.1-529.
Hunter damages.
Damage stamp program, §§29.1-352 to 29.1-358.
Rabbits and squirrels.
Killing for damaging fruit trees, §29.1-516.
Log transportation permits, §46.2-1149.2.
Outdoor recreation.
Making property available for timber uses, §10.1-208.
Public squares.
Injuries to trees growing on, §18.2-139.
Real estate tax lien on timber in certain counties, §58.1-3345.
Real property tax assessment.
Apportionment of value of standing timber between owner of soil and owner of standing timber, §58.1-3309.
Reduction in value of timberland, §58.1-3293.
Standing timber trees, §58.1-3284.
Reforestation of timberlands, §§10.1-1170 to 10.1-1176.
See REFORESTATION OF TIMBERLANDS.
Roadside trees.
Trimming and pruning.
Policies to be developed, §33.1-84.1.
Subdivisions and development.
Conservation of trees during development process.
Locality within Planning District 8 classified as nonattainment area for air quality standards, §15.2-961.1.
Planting and replacement of trees during development process, §15.2-961.
Timber.
See TIMBER.

TRESPASS, §§18.2-119 to 18.2-136.1.
After having been forbidden to do so, §18.2-119.
Instigating trespass, §18.2-120.
Animals running at large, §55-330.
Permitting, §18.2-121.1.
Unincorporated communities and villages, §§55-323 to 55-330.
See ANIMALS RUNNING AT LARGE.
Burial grounds.
Injuries to, §18.2-127.
Violation of sepulture, §18.2-126.
Capitol Square.
Jurisdiction over offenses committed, §18.2-124.
Uniform fine schedule, VA SCt Rules 3C:1, 3C:2.
Cemeteries.
Disinterment or displacement of dead human body, §18.2-126.
Injuries to, §18.2-127.
Nighttime trespassing upon, §18.2-125.
Uniform fine schedule, VA SCt Rules 3C:1, 3C:2.
Churches, §18.2-128.
Injuries to churches and church property, §18.2-127.
Uniform fine schedule, VA SCt Rules 3C:1, 3C:2.

TRESPASS —Cont'd
Computer trespass, §18.2-152.4.
Personal trespass by computer, §18.2-152.7.
Viruses, §18.2-152.14.
Conspiracy to trespass after having been forbidden to do so, §18.2-23.
Counties preventing, §15.2-1218.
Crossing lawful fence, §§55-306 to 55-309.
Disinterment or displacement of dead human body, §18.2-126.
Distress.
Landlord and tenant.
Irregularities not to void, §55-236.
Drift property, §§55-202 to 55-210.
Entering property of another for purposes of damaging, §18.2-121.
Estrays, §§55-202 to 55-206.
Family abuse.
Protective orders.
Trespass after having been forbidden to do so, §§18.2-119, 18.2-120.
Fences.
Crossing lawful fences, §§55-306 to 55-309.
Fishers, §18.2-132.
Destruction of posted signs, §18.2-135.
Enforcement of provisions, §18.2-136.1.
Posted property, §18.2-134.
Refusal of person on land of another to identify himself, §18.2-133.
Fish hatcheries, §29.1-554.
Graveyards.
Injuries to, §18.2-127.
Violation of sepulture, §18.2-126.
Housing authorities.
No trespass policy.
Authorities to adopt, §36-22.1.
Hunters, §18.2-132.
Destruction of posted signs, §18.2-135.
Enforcement of provisions, §18.2-136.1.
Posted property, §18.2-134.
Refusal of person on land of another to identify himself, §18.2-133.
Right to go on lands of another to retrieve dogs, falcons, hawks or owls, §18.2-136.
Trespass upon licensed shooting preserve, §18.2-131.
Jamestown-Yorktown foundation.
Violation of regulations.
Request of person to leave property, failure to leave, §23-289.
Landlord and tenant.
Distress.
Irregularities not to void, §55-236.
Liability of possessor of real property for harm to trespasser, §8.01-219.1.
Livestock.
Running at large, §55-330.
Localities.
Designation of local law-enforcement agency to enforce trespass violations, §15.2-1717.1.
Method of posting, §18.2-134.1.
Motor vehicles.
Immobilization of trespassing vehicles, regulation by localities, §46.2-1232.
Parking.
Immobilization of trespassing vehicles, regulation by localities, §46.2-1232.
Peeping or spying into structure occupied as dwelling, §18.2-130.
Third misdemeanor offense, punishment, §18.2-67.5:1.

TRESPASS —Cont'd
Police.
Local law-enforcement agency.
Designation to enforce trespass violations, §15.2-1717.1.
Posted property, §18.2-134.
Destruction of posted signs, §18.2-135.
Posting no trespassing signs on property of another, §18.2-119.1.
Preventing service to persons not forbidden to trespass, §18.2-120.
Protective orders.
Trespass after having been forbidden to do so, §§18.2-119, 18.2-120.
Public transportation, §18.2-160.2.
Railroad corporations.
Powers, §56-346.
Railroad tracks, §18.2-159.
Running at large, §55-330.
Permitting animals, §18.2-121.1.
School property, §18.2-128.
Schools and education.
Model policies for codes of student conduct, §22.1-279.6.
Sepulture, violation of, §18.2-126.
Shooting preserve, §18.2-131.
Spotlights on agricultural lands, §18.2-121.2.
State forester.
Liability in performance of duties, §10.1-1113.
Notices relating to trespasses, §10.1-1112.
State geologist.
Immunity from prosecution, §45.1-389.
Statute of limitations.
Trespass to land, §8.01-243.
Submerged lands.
Unlawful use of subaqueous beds, §28.2-1203.
Injunctions, §28.2-1211.
Timber cutting, §§55-331 to 55-335.
Trappers, §18.2-132.
Destruction of posted signs, §18.2-135.
Enforcement of provisions, §18.2-136.1.
Posted property, §18.2-134.
Refusal of person on land of another to identify himself, §18.2-133.
Unlawful entry and detainer.
General provisions, §§8.01-124 to 8.01-130.
See UNLAWFUL ENTRY AND DETAINER.
Judgment not to bar action for trespass, §8.01-130.
Waterfowl blinds.
Stationary blind direction, §29.1-349.
Winter sports safety act.
Trespasser liability, §8.01-227.20.

TRESPASSING VEHICLES.
County manager plan of government.
Removal or immobilization, §15.2-719.

TRIAL.
Bench trial.
See BENCH TRIAL.
Jury trial.
See JURY TRIAL.
Pretrial scheduling order, VA SCt Rule 1:18.
Uniform pretrial scheduling order, VA SCt Rule Pt 1 Appx Form 3.
Scheduling civil cases for trial, VA SCt Rule 1:20.
Separate trials.
Civil cases, §§8.01-272, 8.01-281.
Criminal cases, VA SCt Rules 3A:10, 7C:4.

TRIAL BY JURY.
Criminal cases, §§19.2-260 to 19.2-264.1.
See JURY TRIAL.
Generally.
See JURY TRIAL.

TRIAL DE NOVO.
Appeals from general district courts in civil cases, §16.1-113.
District court criminal case appeals, §16.1-136.
Driving while intoxicated.
Commercial motor vehicles, §46.2-341.26:4.
Remand by appellate court, §8.01-681.
Waiver of jury trial, §19.2-262.

TRIAL LAWYERS ASSOCIATION.
Judicial conference for district courts.
Honorary members, president and secretary, §16.1-218.

TRIAL PUBLICITY.
Attorneys at law.
Professional responsibility, VA SCt Rule Pt 6 §II Rule 3.5.

TRICHLOROETHYLENE.
Litter control and recycling.
Products containing trichloroethylene prohibited, §10.1-1424.2.

TRIGGERMAN RULE.
Homicide, §§18.2-18, 18.2-31.

TRIGON BLUE CROSS/BLUE SHIELD.
Conversion from mutual insurance company to stock corporation.
Commonwealth health research fund as depository for conversion funds, §23-284.
Disposition of property received by locality on conversion, §15.2-1512.1.
Localities treatment of money received as result of conversion, §15.2-1608.1.

TRIP INSURANCE.
Travel insurance, §§38.2-1887 to 38.2-1890.

TROUT.
Brook trout as official freshwater state fish, §1-510.
Farming.
Permit fee, §29.1-417.
Fishing, inland waters.
Generally.
See FISHING, INLAND WATERS.
Lifetime trout fishing license, §29.1-302.4.
Special permits for groups of handicapped persons.
Issuance to fish designated stocked waters, §29.1-314.
Propagation and sale, §29.1-531.

TROVER.
Detinue.
General provisions, §§8.01-114 to 8.01-123.
See DETINUE.
Drift property, §55-209.
Effect of judgment, §8.01-219.
Estrays, §55-209.

TRUANCY.
Complaint to court for parents failure to comply with law, §22.1-262.
Juvenile offenses, intake and petitions, §16.1-260.
Misdemeanor offense, §22.1-263.
Proceedings against child, §22.1-267.

TRUANCY —Cont'd
Suspension of student's driver's license.
Ten or more consecutive unexcused absences, §46.2-334.001.

TRUANT OFFICERS.
Appointment, §22.1-258.
Complaint or noncompliance with compulsory school requirements, §22.1-262.
Delivery of child to school, §22.1-266.
Duties, §22.1-261.
Immunity, §22.1-258.

TRUCK AND ORNAMENTALS RESEARCH STATION, §§23-155.01 to 23-155.04.

TRUCK CARGO OR LOADS.
Fastening loads, §46.2-1155.
Fine and costs, VA SCt Rule 3B:2.
Load covers, §46.2-1156.
Fine and costs, VA SCt Rule 3B:2.
Loading vehicle to prevent escape of contents, §§10.1-1424, 46.2-1156.
Clean up of escaped objects, §10.1-1424.
Fine and costs, VA SCt Rule 3B:2.

TRUCKS.
Defined, §46.2-100.
Garage keeper's lien.
Towing, recovering and storage costs.
Liability for costs of trailers or semitrailers, §46.2-644.01.
Motor vehicles.
Generally.
See MOTOR VEHICLES.
Pickup trucks.
Motor vehicle license plates.
Exemption from displaying for-hire license plates, §46.2-711.
Motor vehicle registration.
Additional fee, §46.2-694.
Tobacco heritage special license plates.
Issuance for display on trucks, restrictions, §46.2-749.5.
Truck stops.
Human trafficking hotline.
Employers who must post notice regarding, §40.1-11.3.
Weigh stations.
Civil penalty for certain violations by trucks and tractor trucks, §46.2-613.1.
Attachment and seizure of vehicle for unpaid fees and penalties, §46.2-613.4.
Service of process.
Operator as agent for, §46.2-613.2.
Procedures for issuance and service, §46.2-613.5.
Special processing of penalties, §46.2-613.3.

TRUCK STOPS.
Human trafficking hotline.
Employers who must post notice regarding, §40.1-11.3.

TRUST ACCOUNTS.
Attorneys at law.
IOLTA accounts generally, VA SCt Rule Pt 6 §IV Par 20.
Maintenance of trust accounts generally, VA SCt Rule Pt 6 §IV Par 20.
Virginia State Bar approved financial institution agreement, VA SCt Rule Pt 6 §IV Appx A.
Insurance adjusters.
Escrow or trust accounts, §38.2-1845.16.

TRUST ACCOUNTS —Cont'd
Multiple-party accounts.
Generally, §§6.2-604 to 6.2-620.
See MULTIPLE-PARTY ACCOUNTS.
Prisons.
Inmate trust accounts, §53.1-43.1.

TRUST COMPANIES, §§6.2-1000 to 6.2-1099.
Abandonment of property presumption.
Intangible interest in business associations, §55-210.6:1.
Property of dissolved associations, §55-210.7.
Refunds, §55-210.6:2.
Affiliated trust companies.
Defined, §6.2-1013.
Prohibited transactions, §6.2-1020.
Transactions prohibited, §6.2-1020.
Appeals.
Removal of directors and officers, §6.2-1026.
Articles of incorporation.
Statement of kind of business, §13.1-620.
Audits, §6.2-1035.
Bad check law generally, §§18.2-181 to 18.2-185.
Bank franchise tax, §§58.1-1200 to 58.1-1217.
See BANK FRANCHISE TAX.
Board of directors, §6.2-1029.
Bonds, surety, §6.2-1016.
Branch offices, §6.2-1028.
Capital.
Minimum capital, §6.2-1018.
Private trust companies, §6.2-1075.
Cease and desist orders.
Commissioner of financial institution, §6.2-1036.
Certificates of authority.
Application, §6.2-1015.
Bonds, surety, §6.2-1016.
Fees.
Application fee, §6.2-1015.
Issuance, §6.2-1017.
Refusal to issue.
Commissions, fees, etc., for sale of stock, §6.2-1021.
Minimum capital, §6.2-1018.
Required, §§6.2-1014, 6.2-1017.
Revocation.
Continuation of provisions, §6.2-1037.
Failure to maintain bonds, §6.2-1016.
State of incorporation, §6.2-1018.
Surrender of certificate.
Continuation of provisions, §6.2-1037.
Commissioner's orders.
Violations, civil penalties, §6.2-1046.
Common trust funds, §6.2-1009.
Conservation of assets.
Powers of state corporation commission, §6.2-1036.
Control.
Defined, §6.2-1013.
Restriction on control, §6.2-1024.
Voting shares, acquisition, §6.2-1023.
Control shares.
Acquisition of control, §6.2-1023.
Restriction on control, §6.2-1024.
Corporations generally, §§13.1-601 to 13.1-779.
See CORPORATIONS.
Dealing with self or affiliates.
Doing a trust business, §6.2-1008.
Deeds and trusts.
Powers as trustees, §§6.2-820, 6.2-1002.
Definitions, §§6.2-1000, 6.2-1013.
Control person, §6.2-1024.

TRUST COMPANIES —Cont'd
Definitions —Cont'd
Private trust companies, §6.2-1074.
Departments.
Banking department separate from trust department, §6.2-821.
Depository or receiving or collection agency for county.
Urban county executive form of government, §15.2-829.
Deposits.
Insolvency.
Receiving when insolvent, §6.2-945.
Derogatory statements affecting trust company, §§6.2-940, 6.2-1042.
Directors, §6.2-1029.
Bonds, surety, §§6.2-868, 6.2-1027.
Civil liability, §§6.2-944, 6.2-1045.
Embezzlement, §§6.2-943, 6.2-1044.
Private trust companies, §6.2-1079.
Removal, §6.2-1026.
Trust officers.
Appointment, §6.2-821.
Violations.
Generally, §§6.2-944, 6.2-1045.
Dividends.
Declaration of dividend, §6.2-1022.
Private trust companies.
Restrictions, §6.2-1077.
Doing business without authority, §6.2-1039.
Embezzlement.
Directors, officers or employees, §§6.2-943, 6.2-1044.
Emergencies.
Suspension of business during emergency, §6.2-1002.
Entities authorized to engage in trust business, §6.2-1001.
Examinations.
Deceiving examining officer, §§6.2-943, 6.2-1044.
Suspected person, §6.2-1039.
Executors and administrators.
Oaths.
Who may take oath for corporate fiduciary, §6.2-1004.
Powers as trustees, §§6.2-820, 6.2-1002.
Security not required, §6.2-1003.
Federal securities and obligations.
May be held for account without physical possession, §6.2-1006.
Securities to be kept separate, §6.2-1006.
Fees.
Annual fee, §6.2-1033.
Certificates of authority.
Application fee, §6.2-1015.
Investigation of application, §6.2-1033.
Fiduciaries.
Appointment of cofiduciary, §6.2-1011.
Company and fiduciary capacity, §6.2-1006.
Holding stock or other securities as fiduciaries in name of nominee, §6.2-1010.
Oaths.
Who may take oath for corporate fiduciary, §6.2-1004.
Security not required, §6.2-1003.
Voting of bank shares as fiduciary, §6.2-1011.
Fines.
Violations of commissioner's orders, civil penalties, §6.2-1046.
Fraudulent acts.
Directors, officers or employees, §§6.2-943, 6.2-1044.

TRUST COMPANIES —Cont'd
Guardians.
Bond without security upon appointment, §6.2-1003.
Oaths.
Who may take oath for corporate fiduciary, §6.2-1004.
Husband and wife.
Powers of trust companies, §§6.2-820, 6.2-1002.
Incapacitated persons.
Powers as fiduciary, §§6.2-820, 6.2-1002.
Insurance companies investments in stocks or obligations, §38.2-1425.
Insurance premium finance companies.
Not subject to restrictions and obligations imposed by chapter, §38.2-4700.
Investigations.
Fees, §6.2-1033.
State corporation commission, §6.2-1032.
Investments.
Common trust funds, §6.2-1009.
How funds invested, §6.2-1007.
Separately held for each trust, §6.2-1006.
Landlord and tenant.
Powers, §§6.2-820, 6.2-1002.
Libel and slander.
Derogatory statements affecting trust company, §§6.2-940, 6.2-1042.
License tax.
Limitation on localities authority, §58.1-3703.
Logo or symbol.
Use in prohibited manner, §59.1-92.22.
Marketing materials or solicitation.
Use of trust company's name, logo or symbol, §§6.2-941, 6.2-1043.
Married women.
Separate property of spouse.
Powers, §§6.2-820, 6.2-1002.
Minors.
Powers as trustee, §§6.2-820, 6.2-1002.
Multistate trust institutions, §§6.2-1065 to 6.2-1073.
Application to establish foreign trust office, §6.2-1066.
Conditions for approval, §6.2-1070.
Fees, §6.2-1073.
Foreign applications to be filed with state, §6.2-1069.
Authority to operate in state, §§6.2-803, 6.2-1067.
Closing notice to be filed with state, §6.2-1068.
Definitions, §6.2-1065.
Enforcement, §6.2-1072.
Examination of in-state and foreign offices, §6.2-1071.
Fees.
Application fee, §6.2-1073.
Supervisory services of state, §6.2-1071.
Merger notice to be filed with state, §6.2-1068.
Office or branch in state required, §6.2-1067.
Acquiring an office in state, §6.2-1068.
Additional offices in state, §6.2-1068.
Establishing new office in state, §6.2-1068.
Regulations, §6.2-1073.
Reports on periodic basis, §6.2-1071.
Municipal corporations.
Fiscal or transfer agents, §§6.2-820, 6.2-1002.
Name.
Unlawful use of terms, §6.2-1040.
Use of name in prohibited manner, §59.1-92.22.
Name, logo or symbol.
Use in marketing materials or solicitation, §§6.2-941, 6.2-1043.

TRUST COMPANIES —Cont'd
National emergency laws.
Suspension of business during actual or threatened enemy attack or other emergency, §6.2-1002.
Oaths.
Who may take oath for corporate fiduciary, §6.2-1004.
Officers and employees.
Bonds, surety, §§6.2-868, 6.2-1027.
Civil liability, §§6.2-944, 6.2-1045.
Embezzlement, §§6.2-943, 6.2-1044.
False statements, §§6.2-901, 6.2-907, 6.2-1041.
Removal of officers.
Appeal from order, §6.2-1026.
Unlawful to act after removal, §6.2-1026.
Violations.
Generally, §§6.2-944, 6.2-1045.
Offices, §6.2-1028.
Private trust companies, §6.2-1078.
Operating plans.
Defined, §6.2-1013.
Private trust companies.
Defined, §6.2-1074.
Required, §6.2-1076.
Powers.
Generally, §§6.2-820, 6.2-1002.
Private trust companies, §6.2-1076.
Limitations on, §6.2-1080.
Private trust companies, §§6.2-1074 to 6.2-1080.
Capital.
Minimum capital, §6.2-1075.
Control, §6.2-1075.
Definitions, §6.2-1074.
Directors or managers, §6.2-1079.
Dividends.
Restrictions, §6.2-1077.
Offices, §6.2-1078.
Operating plan.
Defined, §6.2-1074.
Required, §6.2-1076.
Organization, §6.2-1075.
Powers, §6.2-1076.
Limitations on, §6.2-1080.
Reacquisition of shares or interests.
Restrictions, §6.2-1077.
Prohibited acts by entities engaging in trust business, §6.2-1001.
Receivers.
Appointment.
Protection of creditors, §6.2-1038.
Conservation of assets.
Powers of state corporation commission, §6.2-1036.
Powers, §§6.2-820, 6.2-1002, 6.2-1036.
Reports, §6.2-1031.
Riots.
Suspension of business during riots, §6.2-1002.
Rules and regulations.
State corporation commission, §6.2-1034.
Securities.
Nominee for fiduciary holding, §6.2-1010.
Separation of banking and trust functions, §6.2-821.
State corporation commission.
Accounts, etc., of suspected person.
Examinations, §6.2-1039.
Certificates of authority generally. See within this heading, "Certificates of authority."
Investigations and examinations, §6.2-1032.
Fees, §6.2-1033.

TRUST COMPANIES —Cont'd
State corporation commission —Cont'd
Receivers, §6.2-1038.
Remedial powers, §6.2-1036.
Removal of directors and officers, §6.2-1026.
Reports to commission, §6.2-1031.
Rules and regulations, §6.2-1034.
Violations of commissioner's orders, civil penalties, §6.2-1046.
Statement of kind of business in articles of incorporation, §13.1-620.
Stock.
Acquisition of stock of trust company, §6.2-1023.
Dividends, §6.2-1022.
No-par stock prohibited, §6.2-1019.
Option plans, §6.2-1019.
Payment of shares, §6.2-1019.
Reacquisition of shares, §6.2-1022.
Sale of stock.
Commissions, fees, etc., not permitted, §6.2-1021.
Suspension.
Violation of trust investment, §6.2-1012.
Suspension of operation of bank.
During actual or threatened enemy attack or other emergency, §6.2-1002.
Trust business.
Certificate of authority required, §6.2-1014.
Trust funds.
Collateral security delivered by banking department to trust department, §6.2-1005.
Common trust funds, §6.2-1009.
Custody, §6.2-1006.
Deposit or other use in banking department, §6.2-1005.
Investments.
How invested, §6.2-1007.
Prompt investment and distribution, §6.2-1007.
Separately held for each trust, §6.2-1006.
Liens on securities set apart for trust fund, §6.2-1005.
Trust subsidiaries.
General provisions, §§6.2-1047 to 6.2-1064.
See TRUST SUBSIDIARIES.
Unclaimed property, disposition of, §§55-210.24 to 55-210.24:2.
Intangible interest in business associations, §55-210.6:1.
Property of dissolved associations, §55-210.7.
Records, §§55-210.24 to 55-210.24:2.
Refunds, §55-210.6:2.
Unlawful use of name, §6.2-1040.
War.
Suspension of business during actual or threatened enemy attacks, §6.2-1002.
Wills.
Lodging for safekeeping, §64.2-409.

TRUSTEES.
Advertising goods, wares or merchandise as.
False advertising, §18.2-216.
Agricultural cooperative associations, voluntary dissolution.
Appointment for winding up affairs, §13.1-332.
Ancillary proceedings.
Property transfers to nonresident fiduciary, §§64.2-1426 to 64.2-1432.
Appointment, §64.2-1412.
Bank qualification as committee or guardian, §64.2-1414.

TRUSTEES —Cont'd
Benevolent associations.
Holding personal property, §57-21.
Bond.
Nonresidents, §64.2-1426.
Bonds, surety, §64.2-1400.
Recording in bond book, §17.1-230.
Cemeteries.
Appointment, §57-23.
Actions, appointment for, §57-24.1.
Disposition of property for maintenance and care.
Holding of such property, §57-32.
Duties, §57-24.
Jointly owned cemeteries, §57-29.
Land conveyances to, §57-22.
Powers, §57-24.
Removal, §57-23.
Church property.
Appointment of trustees to effectuate purposes of conveyances, §57-8.
Holding personal property, §57-10.
Suits by and against, §§57-11, 57-13.
Suits by trustees to have land sold or mortgaged, §§57-14, 57-15.
Conservation easements.
Power to donate conservation easements, §64.2-108.
Corporate trustees.
Substitute trustee, appointment, §64.2-1405.
Corporations.
Limitation on qualifying as, §64.2-1400.
Service of notice, process and other papers.
On whom process served, §8.01-303.
Corporations, single shareholder.
Trustee of single trust, §13.1-611.
Court orders for payments due from, §64.2-1418.
Defined terms.
Deed or other writing, §64.2-1403.
Disclaimer of property interests.
Disclaimer of interest by trustee, §64.2-2606.
Disqualifications, §64.2-1423.
Ejectment.
When trustee not to recover, §8.01-147.
Environmental liability, §64.2-1422.
Evictions.
Relief from forfeiture, §55-241.
Execution of trust until new trustee appointed, §64.2-1407.
Fees for appointing and qualifying, §17.1-275.
Fiduciaries generally.
See FIDUCIARIES.
Fuel taxes.
Duties of suppliers as trustee, §58.1-2237.
Alternative fuels, §58.1-2257.
Guardian and ward generally, §§64.2-1700 to 64.2-1922.
See GUARDIAN AND WARD.
Improvements to land.
Exception as to trustees, §8.01-174.
Incompetency.
Conservators.
See CONSERVATORS.
Generally.
See INCOMPETENCY.
Guardian and ward.
See GUARDIAN AND WARD.
Inventories and accounts.
Deadlines, §64.2-1305.
Generally, §§64.2-1300 to 64.2-1317.
See FIDUCIARIES.

TRUSTEES —Cont'd
Inventories and accounts —Cont'd
Statements, §64.2-1305.
Testamentary trustees.
Filing of accounts, §64.2-1306.
Exemption by consent of beneficiaries where will does not require inventory or accounts, §64.2-1307.
Trustees under a will waiving accounts, §64.2-1307.
Statements, §64.2-1306.
Investments.
Asset placement in financial institutions, §64.2-1413.
Prudent investor rule, §§64.2-780 to 64.2-791.
See PRUDENT INVESTOR RULE.
Investment securities.
Authenticating trustee.
Registration of securities.
Duties, §8.8A-407.
Signature.
Effect, §8.8A-208.
Juvenile proceedings.
Education and maintenance of committed child.
Estate in hands of trustee, §16.1-290.
Landlord and tenant.
Evictions.
Relief from forfeiture, §55-241.
Law corporations may qualify as, §13.1-546.1.
Life insurance.
Designation of testamentary trustee as beneficiary, §38.2-3112.
Nonresidents, §64.2-1426.
Property transfers to nonresident fiduciary, §§64.2-1426 to 64.2-1432.
Petitions for appointment.
Retention of petitions by circuit court clerk, time, destruction, §17.1-213.
Powers.
Conservation easements.
Power to donate, §64.2-108.
Incorporation by reference into trust instrument, §§64.2-105, 64.2-106.
Releases, §§64.2-2700 to 64.2-2704.
Principal and income.
Uniform principal and income act, §§64.2-1000 to 64.2-1032.
See PRINCIPAL AND INCOME.
Professional law corporations may qualify as, §13.1-546.1.
Property transfers to foreign trustees, §§64.2-1426 to 64.2-1432.
Prudent investor rule, §§64.2-780 to 64.2-791.
See PRUDENT INVESTOR RULE.
Qualifications, §§64.2-1400, 64.2-1403, 64.2-1423.
Information to be provided to clerk, §64.2-1409.
Real estate cooperatives.
Associations.
Proper exercise assumed without inquiries, §55-475.
Organization of associations, §55-458.
Recordation tax, state.
Exemptions, §58.1-811.
Recording bond taken in bond book, §17.1-230.
Religious organizations.
Appointment of trustees to effectuate purposes of conveyances, §57-8.
Holding personal property, §57-10.
Suits by and against, §57-11.
Suits by members against trustees, §57-13.

TRUSTEES —Cont'd
Religious organizations —Cont'd
Suits by trustees to have land sold or mortgaged, §57-15.
Removal, §64.2-1412.
Service of notice, process and other papers.
Corporations.
On whom process served, §8.01-303.
Execution of bond that designates clerk as attorney for service, §64.2-1419.
Adjudication of due diligence, §64.2-1421.
Duties of clerk, §64.2-1420.
Nonresidents, §64.2-1426.
Shareholder in stock corporation.
Single shareholder, §13.1-611.
Transferee of purchaser from corporation of owned shares, not personally liable, §13.1-644.
Voting entitlement, §13.1-662.
Shares of corporations, voting entitlement.
Bankruptcy trustee, §13.1-662.
Substituted trustees.
Appointment, §64.2-1405.
Execution of trust until new trustee appointed, §64.2-1407.
Equity court powers, §64.2-1408.
Notice, §64.2-1406.
Security transfers, §64.2-1425.
Surety bonds, §§64.2-1400, 64.2-1412.
Qualifications, §64.2-1403.
Qualifying without security, §64.2-1411.
Tax matters.
Fiduciary responsibility generally, §§58.1-21 to 58.1-24.
Testamentary trustees.
Death of trustee before filing and settlement of fiduciary's account.
Obligation of trustee's personal representatives, §64.2-1312.
Filing of accounts, §64.2-1306.
Trustees under a will waiving accounts, §64.2-1307.
Life insurance, designation as beneficiary, §38.2-3112.
Qualification, §64.2-1400.
Jurisdiction, §§64.2-1401, 64.2-1402.
Statements, §64.2-1306.
Substituted testamentary trustees.
Appointment, §64.2-1405.
Surety bonds, §64.2-1401.
Tobacco indemnification and community revitalization commission.
Endowment fund, §§3.2-3104, 3.2-3106.
Transfers to minors, §§64.2-1904, 64.2-1905.
Uniform prudent investor act, §§64.2-780 to 64.2-791.
See PRUDENT INVESTOR RULE.
Veterans.
Trustees for incapacitated ex-service persons and their beneficiaries, §64.2-2016.
Payments from U.S. department of veterans' affairs, §64.2-2017.
Wills.
Trust devises or bequests, §64.2-426.
Workers' compensation.
Exercise of rights, §65.2-527.
Payments.
Lump sum payments.
Appointment of trustees, §65.2-523.
Time limitations upon persons under a disability, §65.2-528.

TRUST FUND ORDER BOOK, §17.1-125.

TRUST INCOME TAXATION, §§58.1-360 to 58.1-363.
Accounting, returns, procedures, §§58.1-380 to 58.1-383.
Credits, §§58.1-370, 58.1-371.
Accumulated distributions, trust beneficiary receiving, §58.1-370.
Historic rehabilitation tax credit, §58.1-339.2.
Taxes paid other states, §58.1-371.
Estimated tax.
Failure to pay, §58.1-492.
Imposition, §58.1-360.
Low-income housing credit, §58.1-435.
Returns, §58.1-381.
Extension of time for filing, §58.1-383.
Place of filing, §58.1-382.
Share of nonresident income from Virginia sources, §58.1-363.
Taxable income, §58.1-361.
Nonresidents, §58.1-362.

TRUSTS, §§64.2-700 to 64.2-808.
Accepting trusteeship, §64.2-754.
Accrued and undistributed income elections, §64.2-429.
Additional compensation to trustee, §64.2-761.
Additional trustee.
Appointment by court, grounds, §64.2-757.
Administration of trust.
Conflict between trustee's fiduciary and personal interest, §64.2-764.
Cost of administration.
Duty to incur only reasonable costs, §64.2-767.
Duties of trustee, §64.2-763.
Cost of administration, §64.2-767.
Inform and report, §64.2-775.
Loyalty, §64.2-764.
Prudent administration, §64.2-766.
Records, §64.2-772.
Expenses.
Reimbursement of trustee, §64.2-762.
Impairment.
Modification or termination of trust, §64.2-730.
Inability to administer.
Modification or termination of trust, §64.2-730.
Interests of beneficiaries.
Duty of trustee, §64.2-764.
Keeping beneficiaries informed.
Duty of trustee, §64.2-775.
Place for administration, §64.2-706.
Prudent administration.
Duty of trustee, §64.2-766.
Records.
Duty of trustee to keep, §64.2-772.
Request for information by beneficiary.
Duty of trustee to respond, §64.2-775.
Role of court, §64.2-710.
Value insufficient to justify cost.
Modification or termination, §64.2-732.
Advancement for protection of trust.
Lien to secure reimbursement, §64.2-762.
Amendment.
Revocable trusts, §64.2-751.
Capacity required, §64.2-750.
Animals.
Care of animal alive during settlor's lifetime, §64.2-726.
Antitrust laws, §§59.1-9.1 to 59.1-9.17.
See ANTITRUST.
Applicability of uniform trust code, §64.2-700.

TRUSTS —Cont'd
Appointment of trustee.
Additional trustee or special fiduciary.
Court appointment, grounds, §64.2-757.
Different trustee.
Value insufficient to justify cost of administration, §64.2-732.
Judicial proceedings involving trusts.
Proceedings to appoint or remove trustees, §64.2-712.
Successor.
Vacancy in trusteeship, §64.2-757.
Approval or disapproval.
Termination, modification, combination or division trust.
Proceeding, §64.2-728.
Assignee of beneficiary.
Attachment of distributions for beneficiary's benefit, §64.2-742.
Mandatory distribution overdue, §64.2-748.
Spendthrift provisions, §§64.2-743, 64.2-744.
Assignment of income for the benefit of creditors, §§55-161 to 55-167.
Assignment of property for the benefit of creditors, §§55-156 to 55-160.
At-risk youth and families.
State trust fund, §2.2-5213.
Attachment of distributions to or for benefit of beneficiary.
Claimant against whom spendthrift provision not enforceable, §64.2-744.
Attorneys' fees and costs.
Liability of trustees and rights of persons dealing with trustees, §64.2-795.
Banks.
Deposit by fiduciary or agent to personal credit.
Items drawn by or payable to him as a fiduciary or agent, §6.2-897.
Trust powers, §§6.2-819 to 6.2-821.
See BANKS.
Banks and financial institutions.
Exception to trustee's bond requirement, §64.2-755.
Beneficiaries not ascertainable.
Noncharitable trust without ascertainable beneficiary, §64.2-727.
Beneficiaries not specified.
Real estate trusts, §55-17.1.
Best interest of beneficiaries.
Duty of trustee to act in, §64.2-764.
Bonds, surety.
Trustee's bond, §64.2-755.
Borrowing money.
Power of trustee, §64.2-778.
Breach of trust.
Compelling former trust to redress.
Duty of trustee, §64.2-774.
Cotrustees.
Duty to prevent and redress, §64.2-756.
Damages, §64.2-793.
Limitations, absence of breach, §64.2-794.
Exculpation of trustee, §64.2-799.
Remedies, §64.2-792.
Removal of trustee, §64.2-759.
Business or enterprise.
Power of trustee, §64.2-778.
Business trusts, §§13.1-1200 to 13.1-1285.
See BUSINESS TRUSTS.
Capacity of settlor.
Requirement for creating trust, §64.2-720.
Revocable trust, §64.2-750.

TRUSTS —Cont'd
Cemeteries.
Disposition of property for maintenance and care, §57-35.
Certification of trust, §64.2-804.
Changing character of trust property.
Power of trustee, §64.2-778.
Charitable gifts.
Validity, §55-26.1.
Charitable trusts.
Attorney general.
Qualified beneficiaries.
Treated as, §64.2-708.
Cy pres.
Modification or termination, §64.2-731.
Disposition or distribution of trust property, §64.2-737.
Enforcement of trust by settlor, §64.2-723.
Modification.
Cy pres, §64.2-731.
Settlor may maintain proceeding, §64.2-728.
Modification of trust, §64.2-736.
Purposes for which created, §64.2-723.
Qualified beneficiaries.
Charitable organization and attorney general treated as, §64.2-708.
Defined, §64.2-701.
Selection of charitable purpose by court.
Failure of terms to indicate charitable purpose, §64.2-723.
Termination.
Cy pres, §64.2-731.
Vacancy in trusteeship.
Filling, §64.2-757.
Circumstances not anticipated.
Modification or termination of trust, §64.2-730.
Claims against trust.
Defense.
Duty of trustee, §64.2-773.
Claims of trust.
Enforcement.
Duty of trustee, §64.2-773.
Coal interests.
Known owners, §45.1-161.311:8.
Missing owners, §§45.1-161.311:3 to 45.1-161.311:7.
Collection of trust property.
Duty of trustee, §64.2-774.
Power of trustee, §64.2-778.
College building authority.
Trust under trust indenture.
Enforcement of rights and duties, §23-30.32.
Combination of trusts, §64.2-735.
Approval or disapproval.
Proceeding, §64.2-728.
Commercial space flight authority.
Bond issues.
See COMMERCIAL SPACE FLIGHT AUTHORITY.
Trust for postemployment benefits, §2.2-2203.4.
Common law of trusts.
Supplementary to uniform code provisions, §64.2-704.
Common trust funds.
General provisions, §6.2-1009.
Community land trusts.
Defined, §55-221.1.
Not considered landlords, §55-221.1.
Compensation of trustee, §64.2-761.
Compromise and settlement.
Nonjudicial settlement agreements involving trusts, §64.2-709.

TRUSTS —Cont'd
Condominiums.
Lien for assessments.
Appointment of trustee to conduct sale, §55-79.84.
Termination of condominium.
Sale proceeds, §55-79.72:1.
Conflict between trustee's fiduciary and personal interest.
Transactions involving investment and management of trust property.
Voidable by beneficiary, §64.2-764.
Consent of beneficiaries.
Liability of trustees, §64.2-800.
Noncharitable irrevocable trust.
Termination or modification, §64.2-729.
Conservatorship of estate of incapacitated persons.
Powers of conservator.
Transfer of assets into irrevocable trust, §64.2-2023.
Construction and interpretation.
Existing relationships.
Applicability of uniform trust code, §64.2-808.
Reference to former section or provision of code, §64.2-108.2.
Severability clause, §64.2-807.
Terms of trust.
Construed to prevail over uniform code provisions, exceptions, §64.2-703.
Governing law, §64.2-705.
Principal place of business designated by terms.
Validity, §64.2-706.
Uniformity.
Uniform trust code construed to promote, §64.2-805.
Constructive trusts.
Cemeteries.
Costs of suits, removal and reinterment.
Residue, §57-37.
Murderers barred from claiming property rights of decedent.
Persons acquiring from slayer protected, §64.2-2509.
Real estate cooperatives.
Termination sale proceeds, §55-454.
Continuation of trust wasteful or impracticable.
Modification or termination of trust, §64.2-730.
Continuing judicial supervision, §64.2-710.
Control of trust property.
Trustee to take, §64.2-771.
Conveyance or transfer of property to trust instead of trustee.
Deemed conveyance or transfer to trustee, §64.2-772.
Corporations, single shareholder, §13.1-611.
Cotrustees.
Breach of trust.
Duty to prevent and redress, §64.2-756.
Delegation of performance of function.
Restriction, §64.2-756.
Dissenting trustee joining in action.
Not liable, exception, §64.2-756.
Failure to join in action.
Trustee not liable, §64.2-756.
Majority decision, actions by, §64.2-756.
Participation in performance of functions.
Requirement, exception, §64.2-756.
Reasonable care, duty to exercise, §64.2-756.
Vacancy, §64.2-756.

TRUSTS —Cont'd
Creating trusts.
Animal care, §64.2-726.
Foreign jurisdictions, §64.2-721.
Fraud, duress or undue influence.
Creation induced by, §64.2-724.
Methods, §64.2-719.
Noncharitable trust without ascertainable beneficiary, §64.2-727.
Notice that trust established.
Duty of trustee, §64.2-775.
Oral trusts.
Establishing by clear and convincing evidence, §64.2-725.
Purposes lawful, not against public policy and possible to achieve, §64.2-722.
Requirements, §64.2-720.
Creditors.
Beneficiaries' creditors.
Attachment of distributions for beneficiary's benefit, §64.2-742.
Discretionary trusts, §64.2-746.
Mandatory distribution overdue, §64.2-748.
Spendthrift provisions, §§64.2-743, 64.2-744.
Public assistance, claims for reimbursement, §64.2-745.
Settlors, claims against.
Trust containing spendthrift provision.
Rules, §64.2-747.
Self-settled spendthrift trusts, §64.2-745.1.
Custodial trusts, §§64.2-900 to 64.2-918.
See CUSTODIAL TRUSTS.
Cy pres.
Termination or modification.
Charitable trusts, §64.2-731.
Damages.
Breach of trust, §64.2-793.
Limitations, absence of breach, §64.2-794.
Death.
Life events affecting administration or distribution of trust, trustees' liability, §64.2-798.
Decanting principal or income to second trust.
Powers of trustee to appoint to a second trust, §64.2-778.1.
Declaration by owner of property.
Method of creating trust, §64.2-719.
Declining trusteeship, §64.2-754.
Defense of claims.
Duty of trustee, §64.2-773.
Definite beneficiaries.
Defined, §64.2-720.
Noncharitable trust without ascertainable beneficiary, §64.2-727.
Requirement for creating trust, §64.2-720.
Definitions, §64.2-701.
Definite beneficiaries, §64.2-720.
Mandatory distributions, §64.2-748.
Noncharitable irrevocable trust, §64.2-729.
Delegation of powers and duties by trustee, §64.2-769.
Delivery of property to settlor.
Revocable trusts.
Revocation of trust by delivery, §64.2-751.
Delivery to last known address.
Permissible method of notice or sending documents, §64.2-707.
Designation of trust property.
Duty of trustee, §64.2-772.
Directing actions.
Power to direct, §64.2-770.

TRUSTS —Cont'd
Disclaimer of property interests.
Disclaimer of beneficiary designation, §64.2-2610.
Disclaimer of interest by trustee, §64.2-2606.
Discretionary powers.
Exercise by trustee, duty, §64.2-776.
Discretionary trusts.
Creditor prohibited from compelling distribution, §64.2-746.
Disposition or distribution of trust property.
Charitable trusts, §64.2-737.
Delivery of property to settlor.
Revocation of trust, §64.2-751.
Discretionary distributions.
Exercise of power, §64.2-776.
Discretionary trusts.
Creditor prohibited from compelling distribution, §64.2-746.
Mandatory distribution overdue.
Assignee or creditor of beneficiary reaching mandatory distribution, §64.2-748.
Overdue distribution.
Assignee or creditor of beneficiary reaching mandatory distribution, §64.2-748.
Powers of trustee, §64.2-778.
Proposal for distribution.
Distribution upon termination, §64.2-779.
Return of distribution received.
Beneficiary determined invalid, §64.2-753.
Revocable trusts.
Distribution of trust property as revocation, §64.2-753.
Termination of trust.
Distribution upon, §64.2-779.
Unanticipated circumstances or inability to administer.
Modification or termination of trust, §64.2-730.
Value insufficient to justify cost of administration.
Termination of trust, §64.2-732.
Division of trust, §64.2-735.
Approval or disapproval.
Proceeding, §64.2-728.
Divorce.
Life events affecting administration or distribution of trust.
Trustees' liability, §64.2-798.
Duties of trustee.
Administration of trust, §64.2-763.
Collection of trust property, §64.2-774.
Control and protection of trust property, §64.2-771.
Delegation, §64.2-769.
Discretionary powers.
Exercising, §64.2-776.
Enforcement and defense of claims, §64.2-773.
Following directions, §64.2-770.
Impartiality, §64.2-765.
Inform and report, §64.2-775.
Loyalty, §64.2-764.
Prudent administration, §64.2-766.
Recordkeeping and identification of trust property, §64.2-772.
Revocable trusts.
Owed exclusively to settlor, §64.2-752.
Special skills and expertise in trustee, §64.2-768.
Uniform code governs, §64.2-703.
Educational facilities authority.
Money received deemed trust funds, §23-30.51.
Educational gifts.
Validity, §55-26.1.

TRUSTS —Cont'd
Educational requirements, completion.
Life events affecting administration or distribution of trust.
Trustees' liability, §64.2-798.
Electronic filing of documents.
Instruments for which electronic medium not acceptable, §17.1-258.6.
Electronic records and signatures, §64.2-806.
E-mail or other electronic message.
Permissible method of notice or sending documents, §64.2-707.
Employee benefit trusts.
Unclaimed funds, distribution of, §55-210.10:1.
Employee trusts.
Restraints on the power of alienation of property construed, §55-13.1.
Enforcement of claims.
Duty of trustee, §64.2-773.
Environmental law.
Defined, §64.2-701.
Powers with respect to possible liability for violation, §64.2-778.
Escheat of estates, §55-193.
Evidence.
Oral trusts.
Establishing by clear and convincing evidence, §64.2-725.
Exchange facilitators.
Qualified escrow or qualified trust.
Deposit of exchange funds, §55-525.3.
Exculpation of trustee.
Breach of trust, §64.2-799.
Existing relationships.
Application of uniform trust code, §64.2-808.
Expenses incurred in administration of trust.
Duty of trustee to incur only reasonable costs, §64.2-767.
Reimbursement of trustee, §64.2-762.
Following directions.
Duty of trustee, §64.2-770.
Foreign corporations.
Engaging in trust business in Virginia, §6.2-803.
Former trustee.
Delivery of property to successor, §64.2-760.
Fraud, duress or undue influence.
Creation induced by, §64.2-724.
Funds.
Common trust funds, §6.2-1009.
General assembly.
Member or immediate family beneficiaries or have proportional interest.
Treating trust's assets for purposes of disclosure statements, §30-111.
General powers of trustee, §64.2-777.
Generic terms.
Construction, §64.2-101.
Good faith.
Liability of trustees and rights of persons dealing with trustees.
Protection of persons dealing with trustee, §64.2-803.
Guardian ad litem.
Appointment in judicial proceedings, §64.2-713.
Historic resources.
Tax credits, §58.1-339.2.
Housing authorities.
Bonds, trust indentures and mortgages, §§36-29 to 36-35.
See HOUSING AUTHORITIES.

TRUSTS —Cont'd
Identification of trust property.
Duty of trustee, §64.2-772.
Impairment of trust administration.
Modification or termination of trust, §64.2-730.
Impartiality between beneficiaries.
Duty of trustee, §64.2-765.
Impracticable to continue trust.
Modification or termination of trust, §64.2-730.
Inability to administer trust.
Modification or termination of trust, §64.2-730.
Income trust conversion to total return unitrust, §64.2-1003.
Incorporation by reference.
Original documents incorporated into trust instrument, §64.2-104.
Specific powers of trustee, §64.2-778.
Indefinite class.
Selection of beneficiary from.
Power in trustee, §64.2-720.
Innovation and entrepreneurship investment authority.
Bond issues.
Funds received deemed trust funds, §2.2-2224.
Proceedings to enforce rights, bondholders or trustees, §2.2-2225.
Trust agreement securing, §2.2-2223.
Inspection of trust property.
Actions without accepting trusteeship, §64.2-754.
Intention to create trust.
Requirement for creating trust, §64.2-720.
Interests of beneficiaries.
Uniform code governs, §64.2-703.
Internal revenue code references, interpretation.
Split-interest trusts, §64.2-740.
Invading principal.
Powers of trustee, §64.2-778.
Inventories and accounts.
Generally, §§64.2-1300 to 64.2-1317.
See FIDUCIARIES.
Investigation of trust property.
Actions without accepting trusteeship, §64.2-754.
Investment of public funds.
Trustee of public funds, §2.2-4514.
Investment of trust funds.
Conflict between trustee's fiduciary and personal interest, §64.2-764.
Whole property of 2 or more trusts.
Records maintained clearly indicating respective interests, §64.2-772.
Investments.
Prompt investment of funds, §6.2-1007.
Real estate investment trusts.
See REAL ESTATE INVESTMENT TRUSTS.
Jail authorities.
Bond issuance, §53.1-95.11.
Judicial proceedings involving trusts.
Administration of trust, §64.2-710.
Compensation of trustee.
Additional compensation allowed by court, §64.2-761.
Enforcement and defense of claims.
Duty of trustee, §64.2-773.
Powers of trustee, §64.2-778.
Jurisdiction over trust and trustee, §64.2-711.
Pleadings, parties, orders, notice, §64.2-713.
Proceedings to appoint or remove trustees, §64.2-712.
Removal of trustee, §64.2-759.

TRUSTS —Cont'd
Judicial proceedings involving trusts —Cont'd
Supervision.
Judicial supervision, §64.2-710.
Judicial supervision, §64.2-710.
Jurisdiction.
Personal jurisdiction over trust and trustee, §64.2-711.
Knowledge of fact, §64.2-702.
Land trusts.
Domestic insurer investing in real property.
Ownership through land trusts, §38.2-1441.
Successor trustees, §55-17.1.
Trust not to fail for lack of specifics, §55-17.1.
Deemed personal property of beneficiary, §55-17.1.
Judgment lien, §55-17.1.
Power of trustee to sell, lease, etc., §55-17.1.
Leases.
Power of trustee, §64.2-778.
Liability of trustees and rights of persons dealing with trustees, §§64.2-792 to 64.2-804.
Attorneys' fees and costs, §64.2-795.
Beneficiary's consent, release, or ratification, §64.2-800.
Breach of trust.
Damages, §64.2-793.
Exculpation of trustee, §64.2-799.
Limitations, absence of breach, §64.2-794.
Remedies, §64.2-792.
Certification of trust, §64.2-804.
Exculpation of trustee, §64.2-799.
Good faith.
Protection of persons dealing with trustee, §64.2-803.
Life events affecting administration or distribution, §64.2-798.
Limitation of actions against trustee, §64.2-796.
Limitation on personal liability, §64.2-801.
Partnerships, interest as a general partner, §64.2-802.
Protection of persons dealing with trustee, §64.2-803.
Reliance on trust instrument, §64.2-797.
Liens.
Trust funds.
Held by bank or trust companies.
Security set apart, §6.2-1005.
Lien to secure reimbursement.
Advancement for protection of trust, §64.2-762.
Limitation of actions.
Revocable trusts.
Contesting validity of trust, §64.2-753.
Trustee, actions against, §64.2-796.
Literary gifts.
Validity, §55-26.1.
Loans of trust property.
Power of trustee, §64.2-778.
Local trusts to fund postemployment benefits other than pensions, §§15.2-1544 to 15.2-1549.
Loyalty.
Duty of trustee, §64.2-764.
Mail.
First-class mail.
Permissible method of notice or sending documents, §64.2-707.
Marriage.
Life events affecting administration or distribution of trust.
Trustees' liability, §64.2-798.

TRUSTS —Cont'd
Methods of giving notice, §64.2-707.
Mistake of fact or law.
Reformation, §64.2-733.
Modification of trust.
Approval or disapproval of proposed modification.
Proceeding, §64.2-728.
Charitable trusts, §64.2-736.
Combination and division, §64.2-735.
Cy pres, §64.2-731.
Judicial proceedings.
Pleading, parties, orders, notice, §64.2-713.
Noncharitable irrevocable trust.
Consent of all beneficiaries or court approval, §64.2-729.
Tax objectives.
Achieving settlor's objectives, §64.2-734.
Unanticipated circumstances or inability to administer, §64.2-730.
Uneconomic trust, §64.2-732.
Mortgages and deeds of trust, §§6.2-406 to 6.2-423, 55-58 to 55-66.6.
See MORTGAGES AND DEEDS OF TRUST.
Multistate trust institutions, §§6.2-1065 to 6.2-1073.
Application to establish foreign trust office, §6.2-1066.
Conditions for approval, §6.2-1070.
Fees, §6.2-1073.
Foreign applications to be filed with state, §6.2-1069.
Authority to operate in state, §§6.2-803, 6.2-1067.
Closing notice to be filed with state, §6.2-1068.
Definitions, §6.2-1065.
Enforcement, §6.2-1072.
Examination of in-state and foreign offices, §6.2-1071.
Fees.
Application fee, §6.2-1073.
Supervisory services of state, §6.2-1071.
Merger notice to be filed with state, §6.2-1068.
Office or branch in state required, §6.2-1067.
Acquiring an office in state, §6.2-1068.
Additional offices in state, §6.2-1068.
Establishing new office in state, §6.2-1068.
Regulations, §6.2-1073.
Reports on periodic basis, §6.2-1071.
Noncharitable irrevocable trust.
Termination or modification.
Consent of all beneficiaries or court approval, §64.2-729.
Noncharitable trust without ascertainable beneficiary, §64.2-727.
Notice.
Establishment of trust.
Duty of trustee, §64.2-775.
Judicial proceedings involving trusts, §64.2-713.
Knowledge of fact, §64.2-702.
Methods and waiver, §64.2-707.
Resignation of trustee, §64.2-758.
Transfer of principal place of business, §64.2-706.
Options.
Power of trustee, §64.2-778.
Oral trusts.
Establishing by clear and convincing evidence, §64.2-725.
Orders of court.
Judicial proceedings involving trusts, §64.2-713.
Organization conducting activities through employees.
Notice or knowledge of fact, §64.2-702.

TRUSTS —Cont'd
Overdue distribution.
Assignee or creditor of beneficiary reaching.
Mandatory distributions, §64.2-748.
Parent and child relationship, establishing.
Determining rights in and to property pursuant to trust, §64.2-102.
Parties.
Judicial proceedings involving trusts, §64.2-713.
Partnerships.
Liability of trustees and rights of persons dealing with trustees.
Interest as a general partner, §64.2-802.
Perpetual care for pet cemeteries, §§57-39.22, 57-39.25.
Perpetual care trust funds.
Generally, §§54.1-2310 to 54.1-2342.
Personal delivery.
Permissible method of notice or sending documents, §64.2-707.
Personal jurisdiction over trustee and beneficiaries, §64.2-711.
Personal liability of trustee, limitations, §64.2-801.
Pets.
Trust created for care of animal or animals, §64.2-726.
Pleadings.
Judicial proceedings involving trusts, §64.2-713.
Port authority.
Proceeds of bonds and revenues, §62.1-143.
Remedies of trustees, §62.1-144.
Power of attorney.
Agent authorized to create trust on settlor's behalf.
Method of creating trust, §64.2-719.
Authority of agent.
Estates, trusts and other beneficial interests, §64.2-1632.
Revocable trusts.
Agent under power exercising settlor's powers, §64.2-751.
Powers of appointment.
Exercise in favor of trustee.
Method of creating trust, §64.2-719.
Revocable trusts.
Holder of power of withdrawal.
Power of withdrawal defined, §64.2-701.
Rights of settlor, §64.2-752.
Powers of trustee.
Delegation, §64.2-769.
Discretionary powers.
Duty when exercising, §64.2-776.
Distribution of trust property upon termination, §64.2-779.
General powers, §64.2-777.
Power to direct actions, §64.2-770.
Special power to appoint to a second trust, §64.2-778.1.
Specific powers of trustee, §64.2-778.
Uniform code governs, §64.2-703.
Preneed funeral contracts, §54.1-2824.
Irrevocable trust, §54.1-2820.
Preservation of trust property.
Actions without accepting trusteeship, §64.2-754.
Presumptions.
Conflict between trustee's fiduciary and personal interest.
Transaction affected by, §64.2-764.
Holder of power to direct fiduciary.
Person other than beneficiary holding power, §64.2-770.

TRUSTS —Cont'd
Principal and income.
Uniform principal and income act, §§64.2-1000 to 64.2-1032.
See PRINCIPAL AND INCOME.
Principal place of business.
Trustees, §64.2-706.
Principles of equity.
Supplementary to uniform code provisions, §64.2-704.
Property taxed held in trust for benefit of another.
Listed and taxed to trustee, §58.1-3015.
Proposal for distribution.
Distribution upon termination, §64.2-779.
Prosecuting or defending claim.
Powers of trustee, §64.2-778.
Protection of trust property.
Duty of trustee, §64.2-771.
Provisions, void, §55-19.5.
Prudent administration.
Delegation of duties and powers by trustee, §64.2-769.
Duty of trustee, §64.2-766.
Prudent investor rule.
Conflict between trustee's fiduciary and personal interest.
Presumption against conflict, §64.2-764.
Public building authority.
Bond issues.
Trust agreement securing, §2.2-2265.
Funds received deemed trust funds, §2.2-2267.
Public school authority.
Trust indenture as security for payment and bonds, §22.1-168.
Public school funds.
Trust funds, §22.1-111.
Purposes of trust.
Permissible purposes, §64.2-722.
Qualified trustees.
Successor trustees, §64.2-745.2.
Ratification of beneficiaries.
Trustees' liability, §64.2-800.
Real estate cooperatives.
Organization of associations, §55-458.
Real estate investment trusts.
Recordation of deeds, §55-106.4.
Real property.
Domestic insurer investing in real property.
Ownership through land trusts, §38.2-1441.
Employee trusts.
Restraints on the power of alienation of property construed, §55-13.1.
Failure for lack of specifics, §55-17.1.
Deemed personal property of beneficiary, §55-17.1.
Judgment liens, §55-17.1.
Power of trustee to sell, lease, etc., §55-17.1.
Power of trustee, §64.2-778.
Real property taxes.
Land conservation incentives, §58.1-513.
Reasonable care, skill and caution.
Delegation of duties and powers by trustee, §64.2-769.
Duty of trustee to exercise, §64.2-766.
Reasonable costs.
Duty of trustee to incur, §64.2-767.
Records.
Administration, records of.
Duty of trustee to keep, §64.2-772.

TRUSTS —Cont'd
Reference to former section or provision of code.
Construction and interpretation, §64.2-108.2.
Reformation of trust.
Mistake of fact or law, §64.2-733.
Rejection of trusteeship, §64.2-754.
Relations among trustees.
Uniform code governs, §64.2-703.
Release of beneficiaries.
Trustees' liability, §64.2-800.
Reliance on trust instrument, §64.2-797.
Removal of trustee, §64.2-758.
Delivery of property to successor, §64.2-760.
Judicial proceedings involving trusts.
Proceedings to appoint or remove trustees, §64.2-712.
Value insufficient to justify cost of administration, §64.2-732.
Reports.
Duty of trustee, §64.2-775.
Representation in judicial proceedings.
Persons with disability, unborn or incapacitated persons, §64.2-713.
Representing and binding others, §§64.2-714 to 64.2-718.
Agents, §64.2-716.
Appointment of representative, §64.2-718.
Consent of person who may represent and bind another.
Effect, §64.2-714.
Conservators, §64.2-716.
Fiduciaries and parents, §64.2-716.
Guardians, §64.2-716.
Holder of general testamentary power of appointment.
Representation by, §64.2-715.
Identity or location of person unknown.
Substantially identical interest.
Representation by person having, §64.2-717.
Matters representative may act on, §64.2-718.
Minor, incapacitated or unborn individual.
Substantially identical interest.
Representation by person having, §64.2-717.
Notice to person who may represent and bind another.
Effect, §64.2-714.
Parents, §64.2-716.
Personal representatives, §64.2-716.
Persons designated by settlor or beneficiaries, §64.2-716.
Several persons or interests.
Appointment of representative for, §64.2-718.
Substantially identical interest.
Representation by person having, §64.2-717.
Trustees, §64.2-716.
Request for information by beneficiary.
Duty of trustee to respond, §64.2-775.
Resignation of trustee, §64.2-758.
Delivery of property to successor, §64.2-760.
Return of distributed property.
Revocable trusts.
Trust determined invalid.
Duty of beneficiary, §64.2-753.
Revocable trusts.
Amendment, §64.2-751.
Capacity required, §64.2-750.
Capacity of settlor to create, amend, revoke or add property, §64.2-750.
Conservator or guardian of settlor.
Exercising settlor's powers, §64.2-751.

TRUSTS —Cont'd
Revocable trusts —Cont'd
Contesting validity of trust.
Limitation of action, §64.2-753.
Delivery of property to settlor.
Revocation of trust, §64.2-751.
Distribution of trust property, §64.2-753.
Duties of trustee.
Owed exclusively to settlor, §64.2-752.
Holder of power of withdrawal.
Rights of settlor, §64.2-752.
Liability of trustee.
Distribution pending contest of validity, §64.2-753.
Trustee without knowledge trust amended or revoked, §64.2-751.
Limitation of action.
Contesting validity of trust, §64.2-753.
Power of attorney.
Agent under power exercising settlor's powers, §64.2-751.
Return of distributed property.
Trust determined invalid.
Duty of beneficiary, §64.2-753.
Revocation, §64.2-751.
Capacity required, §64.2-750.
Rights of beneficiaries.
Subject to settlor's control, §64.2-752.
Validity, contesting.
Limitation of action, distribution of trust property, §64.2-753.
Richmond metropolitan authority.
Bond issues.
Trust agreements, §§15.2-7007, 15.2-7008.
Rule against perpetuities, §§55-12.1 to 55-12.6.
Determination of lives in being, §55-13.2.
Employee trusts, §55-13.1.
Sale, encumbrance or other transaction.
Conflict between trustee's fiduciary and personal interest, §64.2-764.
Power of trustee, §64.2-778.
Savings and loan associations.
Exception to trustee's bond requirement, §64.2-755.
Trust powers, §§6.2-1081 to 6.2-1099.
Savings banks.
Trust powers, §6.2-1099.
Savings institutions.
Accounts of fiduciaries, §6.2-1176.
Beneficiaries.
Savings accounts held by various trustees for same beneficiary, §6.2-1178.
Trust powers, §§6.2-1081 to 6.2-1099.
Scope of uniform trust code, §64.2-700.
Second trust.
Powers of trustee to appoint to a second trust, §64.2-778.1.
Secured transactions.
Name of debtor and secured party, §8.9A-503.
Securities registered in joint names, §§13.1-434 to 13.1-436.
Selection of beneficiary from indefinite class.
Power in trustee, §64.2-720.
Validity of power in trustee, §64.2-720.
Self-settled spendthrift trusts, §64.2-745.1.
Service of notice, process and other papers.
Methods of giving notice, §64.2-707.
Severability clause, §64.2-807.
Shareholder in stock corporation.
Single shareholder, §13.1-611.

TRUSTS —Cont'd
Small business financing authority.
Bond issues.
Trust indenture, bond secured by, §2.2-2302.
Special fiduciary.
Appointment by court, grounds, §64.2-757.
Decision on whether transaction conflicts with trustee's fiduciary and personal interest, §64.2-764.
Special powers of appointment.
Exercise, §55-25.1.
Special skills and expertise in trustee.
Duty to use, §64.2-768.
Specific powers of trustee, §64.2-778.
Spendthrift trusts.
Commutation of certain life estates, §55-277.
Creditor's claims against settlor.
Rules, §64.2-747.
Self-settled spendthrift trusts, §64.2-745.1.
Life insurance policies creating, §38.2-3118.
Limitation to proportionate part of proceeds, §38.2-3119.
Segregation of proceeds not required, §38.2-3121.
Qualified trustees, §64.2-745.2.
Validity, requirement, sufficiency to restrain transfer of beneficiary's interest, §64.2-743.
Unenforceable against state statute so providing, §64.2-744.
Split-interest trusts.
Applicability, §64.2-739.
Internal revenue code references.
Interpretation, §64.2-740.
Modification of trust, §64.2-736.
Powers of courts, §64.2-741.
Prohibitions, §64.2-738.
Severability of provisions, §64.2-741.
Stock and stockholders.
Power of trustee, §64.2-778.
Voting shares or exercising control.
Duty of trustee to act in best interest of beneficiaries, §64.2-764.
Successor trustees.
Acts or omissions of prior trustee.
Liability, §64.2-774.
Delivery of property to, §64.2-760.
Duty to take steps to compel, §64.2-774.
Land trusts, §55-17.1.
Qualified trustees, §64.2-745.2.
Vacancy in trusteeship.
Appointment, §64.2-757.
Taxation.
Objectives related to taxes.
Modification of trust to achieve settlor's objectives, §64.2-734.
Saving taxes.
Discretionary powers, exercise, §64.2-776.
Taxed property held in trust for benefit of another.
Listed and taxed to trustee, §58.1-3015.
Termination of trust, §64.2-728.
Approval or disapproval of proposed termination.
Proceeding, §64.2-728.
Cy pres, §64.2-731.
Distribution of trust property, §64.2-779.
Judicial proceedings.
Pleading, parties, orders, notice, §64.2-713.
Noncharitable irrevocable trust.
Consent of all beneficiaries or court approval, §64.2-729.
Powers of trustee on termination, §64.2-778.

TRUSTS —Cont'd
Termination of trust —Cont'd
Unanticipated circumstances or inability to administer, §64.2-730.
Uneconomic trust, §64.2-732.
Terms of trust.
Construed to prevail over provisions of uniform code, exceptions, §64.2-703.
Meaning and effect.
Governing law, §64.2-705.
Principal place of business designated by terms.
Validity, §64.2-706.
Testamentary additions to trusts, §64.2-427.
Testamentary trusts.
Disclaimer of property interests.
Disclaimer of beneficiary designation, §64.2-2610.
Time.
Resignation of trustee.
Notice, §64.2-758.
Transfer of principal place of business.
Notice, §64.2-706.
Tobacco indemnification and community revitalization commission.
Endowment fund, §§3.2-3104, 3.2-3106.
Total return unitrust, §64.2-1003.
Transfer of principal place of business, §64.2-706.
Transfer of property to persons as trustee.
Method of creating trust, §64.2-719.
Transfers in trust of pecuniary amounts, §64.2-428.
Transfers on death.
Nonprobate, §64.2-620.
Transfers to minors, §64.2-1904.
Trust companies.
Banks.
Trust powers, §§6.2-819 to 6.2-821.
See BANKS.
Exception to trustee's bond requirement, §64.2-755.
Trust director.
Fiduciary status and immunity from liability, §64.2-770.
Trustees.
Duties not specified.
Real estate trusts, §55-17.1.
Unanticipated circumstances.
Modification or termination of trust, §64.2-730.
Uneconomic trust.
Termination or modification, §64.2-732.
Uniformity of application and construction, §64.2-805.
Uniform trust code, §§64.2-700 to 64.2-808.
Vacancy in trusteeship, §64.2-757.
Cotrustees, §64.2-756.
Successor.
Appointment, §64.2-757.
Validity of trust created in other jurisdiction, §64.2-721.
Value insufficient to justify cost of administration.
Modification or termination, §64.2-732.
Voidable transactions.
Conflict between trustee's fiduciary and personal interest, §64.2-764.
Void provisions, §55-19.5.
Void trusts.
Fraud, duress or undue influence.
Creation induced by, §64.2-724.

TRUSTS —Cont'd
Voting trusts.
Corporations, §13.1-670.
Waiver of notice requirement, §64.2-707.
Waste to continue trust.
Modification or termination of trust, §64.2-730.
Wills.
Trust devises or bequests, §64.2-426.
Testamentary additions to trusts, §64.2-427.
Wireless service authorities.
Bond issues.
Trust agreement securing, §15.2-5431.22.
Trust funds, §15.2-5431.28.
Workers' compensation.
Payments.
Lump sum payments, §65.2-523.

TRUST SUBSIDIARIES, §§6.2-1047 to 6.2-1064.
Appeals.
Removal of directors and officers, §6.2-1052.
Appointment to or acceptance of any office or trust security.
When not required, §6.2-1056.
Branches, §6.2-1055.
Certificate of authority.
Required, §6.2-1054.
Common trust funds, §6.2-1009.
Dealing with self or affiliates.
Doing a trust business, §6.2-1008.
Definitions, §6.2-1047.
Deposits.
Funds held or received by trust subsidiaries.
Deposits with affiliate banks, §6.2-1057.
Insolvency.
Receiving when insolvent, §6.2-945.
Directors.
Bonds, surety, §§6.2-868, 6.2-1027, 6.2-1053.
Civil liability, §§6.2-944, 6.2-1063.
Election.
Report to state corporation commission, §6.2-1051.
Embezzlement, §§6.2-943, 6.2-1062.
Management, §6.2-1050.
Qualification, §6.2-1050.
Removal, §6.2-1052.
Violations generally, §§6.2-944, 6.2-1063.
Embezzlement.
Directors, officers or employees, §§6.2-943, 6.2-1062.
Engaging in trust business, §6.2-1049.
Federal securities and obligations.
May be held for account without physical possession, §6.2-1006.
Securities to be kept separate, §6.2-1006.
Fiduciaries.
Appointment of cofiduciary, §6.2-1011.
Federal securities and obligations.
Subsidiary and fiduciary capacity, §6.2-1006.
Holding stock or other securities as fiduciaries in name of nominee, §6.2-1010.
Security.
When security not required, §6.2-1056.
Substitution of subsidiary bank under common ownership as fiduciary, §6.2-1059.
Substitution of trust subsidiary as fiduciary, §6.2-1058.
Voting of bank shares as fiduciary, §6.2-1011.
Fines.
Violations of commissioner's orders, civil penalties, §6.2-1064.

TRUST SUBSIDIARIES —Cont'd
Funds.
Common trust funds, §6.2-1009.
Investments.
Common trust funds, §6.2-1009.
Officers or employees.
Bonds, surety, §§6.2-868, 6.2-1027, 6.2-1053.
Civil liability, §§6.2-944, 6.2-1063.
Directors generally, §6.2-1052.
Embezzlement, §§6.2-943, 6.2-1062.
False statements, §§6.2-901, 6.2-907, 6.2-1041, 6.2-1061.
Removal of officers, §6.2-1052.
Violations generally, §§6.2-944, 6.2-1063.
Offices.
Location, §6.2-1055.
Organization, §6.2-1048.
Permissible business, §6.2-1049.
Powers.
Same powers and restrictions as bank trust departments, §6.2-1060.
Restrictions.
Same restrictions as bank trust departments, §6.2-1060.
Securities.
Federal securities and obligations, §6.2-1006.
Nominee for fiduciary holding, §6.2-1010.
When not required of trust subsidiaries, §6.2-1056.
State corporation commission.
Directors.
Report to commission of election of directors, §6.2-1051.
Removal of directors and officers, §6.2-1052.
Violations of commissioner's orders, civil penalties, §6.2-1064.
Subsidiary banks.
Substitution under common ownership as fiduciaries, §6.2-1059.
Substitution.
Subsidiary bank under common ownership, substitution as fiduciary, §6.2-1059.
Trust subsidiary as fiduciary, §6.2-1058.
Suspension.
Violation of trust investment, §6.2-1012.
Trust funds.
Common trust funds, §6.2-1009.
Investments, §6.2-1007.

TRUTHFULNESS.
Impeachment of witnesses.
Reputation for truthtelling, VA SCt Rule 2:608.

TRUTH-IN-LENDING.
Consumer finance companies.
Making and payment of loans.
Compliance with federal truth-in-lending regulation Z, §6.2-1524.

TRUTH IN MUSIC ADVERTISING ACT, §§59.1-466.1 to 59.1-466.4.
Civil penalties, §59.1-466.3.
Definitions, §59.1-466.1.
Injunctions.
Restraining prohibited acts, §59.1-466.3.
Prohibited acts, §59.1-466.2.
Civil penalties, §59.1-466.3.
Restraining, §59.1-466.3.

TRUTH IN SENTENCING LAW, §19.2-295.1.

TUBERCULIN PURIFIED PROTEIN DERIVATIVE.
Nurses possessing and administering.
Polices and guidelines, adoption, §32.1-50.2.

TUBERCULOSIS, §§32.1-49 to 32.1-54.
Cattle.
Slaughter, §3.2-6021.
Tag or brand identifying animal as affected with.
Altering, substituting, etc., §3.2-6016.
Examination.
Persons suspected of having active tuberculosis, §32.1-50.
Health care provider reports, §32.1-116.3.
Nurse obtaining specimens for.
Exemption from licensing requirement, §54.1-2901.
Public school employees.
Certificate as condition of employment, §22.1-300.
Reports of active tuberculosis, §32.1-50.
Treatment planning, §32.1-50.1.
Workers' compensations.
Presumption on death or disability, §65.2-402.1.

TUITION ASSISTANCE GRANTS, §§23-38.11 to 23-38.19:2.
See COLLEGES AND UNIVERSITIES.

TUITION CHARGES, COLLEGES AND UNIVERSITIES.
Credit hour threshold, §23-7.4.
In-state tuition, eligibility, §§23-7.4, 23-7.4:2.
Determinations, §23-7.4:3.
Military personnel on active duty stationed in Virginia.
Domicile for in-state tuition of dependents, §23-7.4.
National Guard.
Tuition grants for members, §23-7.4:2.
Reduction in tuition and fees charged.
Eligibility of students not domiciled in Virginia, §23-7.4:2.
Waiver for spouses and children of certain military and public safety personnel, §23-7.4:1.

TUITION REMISSION.
Senior citizens, §§23-38.54 to 23-38.60.
Unfunded scholarships, §23-31.

TUNNELS.
Chesapeake Bay bridge and tunnel district, §33.1-253.
Construction contracts.
Competitive sealed bidding.
Public-private transportation act, §56-573.1.
Noise abatement measures.
Local matching funds not required in connection with certain facilities, §33.1-252.1.
Transportation revenue bonds.
Competing tunnels, §33.1-291.
Woodrow Wilson bridge and tunnel compact, §33.1-320.2.

TUNNEL TOLLS.
Woodrow Wilson bridge and tunnel compact, §33.1-320.2.

TURKEYS.
Birds generally.
See BIRDS.
Generally.
See POULTRY.
Hunting, §29.1-514.
Assisting other hunters after obtaining bag limit.
Calling turkeys, §29.1-521.
Licensing, §29.1-305.
Limitations.
Application of provisions, §29.1-521.

TURKEYS —Cont'd
Taking during closed season, §29.1-552.
Restitution, §29.1-551.

TURNING, MOTOR VEHICLES, §§46.2-845 to 46.2-847.
Fine schedule for violations, VA SCt Rule 3B:2.
Improper position or method of turning at intersection, §46.2-846.
Improper U-turn, §46.2-845.
Left turns by bicycles and mopeds, §46.2-847.
Maximum fine for traffic infraction, §46.2-113.
Prepayment of fines, §16.1-69.40:1.
Right turn on red, §46.2-835.

TURNPIKES.
Public service companies generally, §§56-1 to 56-46.3.
See PUBLIC SERVICE COMPANIES.

TURN SIGNALS.
Motor vehicle lights and turn signals generally, §§46.2-1010 to 46.2-1040.
See MOTOR VEHICLE EQUIPMENT.
Signals by drivers generally, §§46.2-848 to 46.2-851.
See TRAFFIC INFRACTIONS.

TUTORIAL INSTRUCTION.
Disabilities, schools for students with.
Exemption of home-based tutorial instruction from provisions, §22.1-320.

TWELVE-MONTH EMPLOYEES.
Schools and education.
Criminal records checks, §§22.1-296.1, 22.1-296.2.
Employee personnel files, §22.1-295.1.
Fingerprinting required, §22.1-296.2.
Payment of wages, §22.1-296.
Tuberculosis certificate, §22.1-300.

TWIN COUNTY AIRPORT COMMISSION, 1964 ch 379.

TWISTING INSURANCE CONTRACTS.
Insurance agents, §38.2-1831.
Insurance consultants.
Refusal or revocation of license, §38.2-1843.

TWO-WAY ELECTRONIC VIDEO AND AUDIO COMMUNICATIONS.
Appearance of accused in criminal case, §19.2-3.1.
Juvenile appearance at detention hearing, §16.1-250.
Juvenile appearance at review hearing on confinement, §16.1-284.1.
Juvenile appearance before intake officers, §16.1-260.
Preliminary hearings, testimony regarding certificates of analysis, §19.2-187.01.
Sexually violent predators, civil commitment.
Probable cause hearing, §37.2-906.

TWO-WAY RADIO COMMUNICATIONS.
Interference with emergency communications, §18.2-165.2.

TWO-YEAR COLLEGE TRANSFER GRANT PROGRAM, §§23-38.10:8 to 23-38.10:13.

TYPEWRITERS.
Identification or serial numbers.
Failure to report removal or alteration, §18.2-214.1.

U

UCC, §§8.1A-101 to 8.11-108.
See COMMERCIAL CODE.

UCITA.
Uniform computer information transactions act, §§59.1-501.1 to 59.1-509.2.

ULTIMATE FACT IN ISSUE RULE, §8.01-401.2.

ULTRASOUND.
Abortion.
Fetal transabdominal ultrasound to determine gestational age, §18.2-76.

ULTRAVIOLET LAMPS.
Medicine and other healing arts professions.
Exceptions and exemptions from licensure, §54.1-2901.

ULTRA VIRES.
Corporations, §13.1-629.
Nonprofit corporations, §13.1-828.

UMBILICAL CORD BLOOD BANK INITIATIVE.
Established, §32.1-69.3.
Practitioners to provide pregnant women with certain information, §54.1-2403.02.
Publication of information, §32.1-69.4.

UMPIRES.
Fire insurance.
Citizenship of Virginia required, §38.2-2122.
Court appointed umpires, §38.2-2121.
Oath, §38.2-2122.

UMPIRES AT SPORTING CONTESTS.
Workers' compensation.
Employee not to include sports official, §65.2-101.

UNATTENDED MOTOR VEHICLES, §§46.2-1209 to 46.2-1217.
See ABANDONED MOTOR VEHICLES.

UNAUTHORIZED PRACTICE OF LAW.
Generally, VA SCt Rule Pt 6 §IV.
See ATTORNEYS AT LAW.
Opinions.
Incorporation into code, §54.1-3910.
Text of opinions.
See Volume Containing Legal Ethics and Unauthorized Practice Opinions.
Practice of law limitation generally.
See PRACTICE OF LAW LIMITATION.
Real estate settlement agents.
Guidelines to avoid or and prevent.
Complaints concerning noncompliance, Virginia state bar to receive, §55-525.30.
Regulations adopted by Virginia state bar, §55-525.30.
Injunctions, §55-525.31.
Special counsel to prosecute.
Employment by attorney general, §2.2-512.

UNAUTHORIZED USE OF AIRCRAFT, §18.2-102.

UNAUTHORIZED USE OF ANIMAL, §18.2-102.

UNAUTHORIZED USE OF AUTOMOBILE, §18.2-102.

UNAUTHORIZED USE OF BOAT OR VESSEL, §18.2-102.

UNAUTHORIZED USE OF NAME OR PICTURE, §8.01-40.

UNAUTHORIZED USE OF VEHICLE, §18.2-102.

UNBORN CHILD.
Administering drug or thing, etc., with intent to destroy unborn child, §18.2-71.

UNCHASTE CHARACTER.
Rape shield law, §18.2-67.7.
Slander and libel, §18.2-417.

UNCLAIMED LOTTERY PRIZES, §58.1-4020.

UNCLAIMED PROPERTY, §§55-210.1 to 55-210.30.
Abandoned or assumed abandoned property.
Escheat, §§55-168 to 55-201.1.
See ESCHEAT.
Agreements to locate, §55-210.27:1.
Applicability of provisions, §55-210.28:1.
Bicycles in possession of sheriff or police, §15.2-1720.
Business association dissolutions, §55-210.7.
Business association interests, §55-210.6:1.
Business association refunds, §55-210.6:2.
Checks, drafts and similar instruments, §55-210.3:02.
Money orders, §55-210.3:02.
Travelers' checks, §55-210.3:02.
Church property, §57-11.
Proceedings by trustees or members to settle, §57-15.
Citation of chapter, §55-210.1.
Colleges and universities.
Disposition of unclaimed property, §23-4.2.
Construction of chapter, §55-210.29.
Court held property, §§55-210.9:1, 55-210.9:2.
Credit balances, §55-210.8:1.
Declining receipt of, §55-210.23.
Defined terms, §55-210.2.
Property, §55-210.3:01.
Disposition of funds received, §55-210.19.
Dividends, §55-210.6:1.
Crediting owners account, §55-210.16:1.
Drift property, §§55-202 to 55-210.
Due diligence to locate owner, §55-210.12.
Penalty for violation, §55-210.26:1.
Electric personal assistive mobility devices.
Licensing and disposition of unclaimed property, §15.2-1720.
Employee benefit trust distributions, §55-210.10:1.
Enforcement of provisions, §55-210.25.
Penalties for violations, §55-210.26:1.
Escheat, §§55-168 to 55-201.1.
See ESCHEAT.
Estrays, §§55-202 to 55-206.
Examination of records, §55-210.24.
Exemptions from act.
State police.
Disposal of unclaimed property in possession of, §52-11.4.
Expiration of action period, §55-210.17.
Financial institution deposits and funds, §55-210.3:01.
Firearms in possession of sheriff or police, §15.2-1721.
Foreign owners or actions, §§55-210.11, 55-210.11:01.
Freedom of information act.
Excluded records, §2.2-3705.7.
Gift certificates, §55-210.8:1.
Holders relieved of liability, §55-210.15.

UNCLAIMED PROPERTY —Cont'd
Intangible personalty held by fiduciary, §55-210.8.
Intangible personalty held by public agency, §55-210.9.
Intangible property, rules for taking custody of, §55-210.2:2.
Interest, §55-210.26:1.
Credited to owner, §55-210.16:1.
Life insurance funds, §55-210.4:01.
Demutualization proceeds, §55-210.4:2.
Lottery prizes, §58.1-4020.
Mental health facilities.
Disposal of unclaimed personal property of individuals receiving services, §37.2-706.
Mobile infrared transmitters, §46.2-1077.1.
Money orders, §55-210.3:02.
Mopeds in possession of sheriff or police, §15.2-1720.
Motor vehicles.
Reporting requirements of garages, parking lots, etc., §46.2-1218.
Museums.
Property loaned to museums, §§55-210.31 to 55-210.38.
See MUSEUMS.
Notice, §55-210.13.
Oysters.
General oyster planting grounds.
Leases becoming vacant, §28.2-619.
Presumption of abandonment, §55-210.2:1.
Exceptions, §55-210.11.
Foreign laws, §55-210.28.
Records, §§55-210.24 to 55-210.24:2.
Religious organizations, §57-11.
Proceedings by trustees or members to settle, §57-15.
Remittances by holder, §55-210.12.
Reports by holders of property, §§55-210.10:2, 55-210.12.
Declining receipt, §55-210.23.
Verified reports, §55-210.24.
Rules for taking custody of intangible property, §55-210.2:2.
Rules promulgation, §55-210.27.
Safe deposit boxes, §55-210.3:3.
Reimbursement of costs to holder, §55-210.15.
Sales, §55-210.18.
Claims to property of proceeds sold, §§55-210.20 to 55-210.22.
Disposition of funds, §55-210.19.
Securities.
Sales, §55-210.18.
Transfer of record of ownership, §55-210.18:1.
Severability of provisions, §55-210.30.
Sheriff or police possessing.
Disposal, §15.2-1719.
Bicycles and mopeds, §15.2-1720.
Firearms or other weapons, §15.2-1721.
State police.
Disposal of unclaimed property in possession of, §52-11.4.
Firearms and other weapons, §52-11.5.
Statute of limitations, §55-210.17.
Judicial review of decisions of state treasurer, §55-210.22.
Stocks.
Distributions, §55-210.6:1.
Timber.
Sale, §§59.1-106, 59.1-115.
Sheriffs' sales, §59.1-115.

UNCLAIMED PROPERTY —Cont'd
Travelers' checks, §55-210.3:02.
Utility deposits, §55-210.5.
Wages, §55-210.8:2.
Weapons in possession of sheriff or police, §15.2-1721.

UNCONSCIONABILITY.
Leases, UCC, §8.2A-108.
Real estate cooperatives.
Contract terms or agreements, §55-434.
Sales, UCC, §8.2-302.
Uniform computer information transactions act.
Enforceability of contracts, §59.1-501.11.

UNCONSTITUTIONALITY OF STATE LAW.
Appeals by Commonwealth.
Dismissal because statute ruled unconstitutional, §19.2-398.
Declared by supreme court.
Majority to concur in declaring, §17.1-308.
Defense objections raised before trial, §19.2-266.2.

UNCONTROLLED T INTERSECTIONS.
Yielding right-of-way, §46.2-824.

UNDERAGE CONSUMPTION, PURCHASE OR POSSESSION OF ALCOHOL, §4.1-305.

UNDERAGE MARRIAGE WITH CONSENT OF PARENT, §§20-48, 20-49.

UNDERAGE SMOKING.
Novelty lighters.
Sales to minors prohibited, §18.2-371.4.
Tobacco sales to minors, §18.2-371.2.
Uniform fine schedule, VA SCt Rule 3C:1.
Virginia foundation for healthy youth, §§32.1-354 to 32.1-367.

UNDERCOVER OPERATIONS BY LAW ENFORCEMENT.
Freedom of information act.
Criminal records not disclosed, §2.2-3706.

UNDERGROUND COAL MINES.
Adjacent property owners.
Mining rights generally, §§45.1-161.310, 45.1-161.311.
Emergency seizure of coal properties by Commonwealth, §§45.1-161.312 to 45.1-161.322.
Acquisition expenses, §45.1-161.321.
Applicability of provisions, §45.1-161.318.
Condemnation proceedings, §45.1-161.320.
Declaration of policy, §45.1-161.313.
Gubernatorial powers of operation, §45.1-161.315.
Leases of properties, §45.1-161.319.
Operating expenses, §45.1-161.321.
Proclamation of emergency, §45.1-161.314.
Public uses.
Defined, §45.1-161.313.
Interruption, §45.1-161.314.
Purchase of properties, §45.1-161.319.
Restoration of property to owner or operator, §45.1-161.322.
Subjects of seizure, §45.1-161.312.
Virginia fuel commission.
Duties, §45.1-161.316.
Members, §45.1-161.317.
Powers, §45.1-161.316.
Mine inspections.
See MINE INSPECTIONS.

UNDERGROUND COAL MINES —Cont'd
Mine licensing.
See MINE LICENSING.
Safety requirements applicable to, §§45.1-161.105 to 45.1-161.252.
See COAL MINE SAFETY.
Smoking in, §§45.1-161.177 to 45.1-161.180.
Trust for coal interests.
Known owners, §45.1-161.311:8.
Missing owners, §§45.1-161.311:3 to 45.1-161.311:7.

UNDERGROUND MINERAL MINES.
Adjacent property owners.
Mining rights, §§45.1-161.311 to 45.1-161.311:2.
Explosions.
Procedure, §45.1-161.292:50.
Mine inspections.
See MINE INSPECTIONS.
Mine licensing.
See MINE LICENSING.
Mineral mine safety act, §§45.1-161.292:1 to 45.1-161.292:73.
See MINERAL MINE SAFETY.
Mine safety requirements, §§45.1-161.293 to 45.1-161.303.

UNDERGROUND STORAGE TANKS.
Building code inspections, §36-99.6.
Discharges into waters of the state, §§62.1-44.34:8, 62.1-44.34:9.
Oil.
Exemption from provisions, §62.1-44.34:23.
Petroleum storage tank fund, §§62.1-44.34:10 to 62.1-44.34:13.
Financial responsibility of owners and operators, §62.1-44.34:12.
Petroleum storage tank fund.
Disbursements in taking corrective action for release of petroleum, §62.1-44.34:11.

UNDERGROUND UTILITY LINE DAMAGE PREVENTION, §§56-265.14 to 56-265.32.
Abandoned lines, §§56-265.19, 56-265.24.
Advisory committee to state corporation commission.
Establishment, §56-265.31.
Agricultural purposes.
Tilling soil, exemption, §56-265.15:1.
Calculation of time periods, §56-265.15.
Citation of chapter, §56-265.14.
Civil penalties for violations, §56-265.32.
Color code, §56-265.21.
Conflict of laws, §56-265.29.
Defined terms, §56-265.15.
Depth requirements for utility lines, §56-265.26:1.
Designers.
Defined, §56-265.15.
Notice to notification centers, §56-265.17:1.
Operators' responses, §56-265.17:3.
Emergencies, excavation during.
Exemption, §56-265.15:1.
Enforcement by state corporation commission, §56-265.30.
Excavator duties, §56-265.24.
Meetings between excavators and operators, §56-265.22:1.
Excavator liability, §56-265.25.
Exemptions from chapter, §56-265.15:1.
Hand digging.
Defined, §56-265.15.

UNDERGROUND UTILITY LINE DAMAGE PREVENTION —Cont'd
Hand digging —Cont'd
Exemption, §56-265.15:1.
Highways, roads, street repairs.
Exemption of certain repairs, §56-265.15:1.
Line depth requirements, §56-265.26:1.
Locators, §56-265.19.
Nonmetallic lines, §56-265.20:1.
Marking by color, §56-265.21.
Operator duties, §56-265.19.
Meetings between excavators and operators, §56-265.22:1.
Mining excavations.
Exemption, §56-265.15:1.
Nonmetallic lines, §56-265.20:1.
Notice prior to excavation or demolition, §56-265.17.
Contract locator acting on behalf of operator.
Failure to perform duties, §56-265.19.
Designers notice to notification centers, §56-265.17:1.
Operators' responses, §56-265.17:3.
Duty of operator upon, §56-265.19.
Exceptions, §56-265.23.
Meetings between excavators and operators, §56-265.22:1.
Notification centers, §56-265.16:1.
Recordation of by telephone, §56-265.22.
Required information, §56-265.18.
Notification centers.
Designers, §56-265.17:1.
Operators' responses, §56-265.17:3.
Meetings between excavators and operators, §56-265.22:1.
Operators to join, §56-265.16:1.
Record of notification, §56-265.22.
Special project notice, §56-265.17.
Operator liability, §56-265.25.
Responses to designer notices, §56-265.17:3.
Prohibition exemptions, §56-265.15:1.
Project owners, §56-265.17:2.
Railroads.
Excavation on railroad owned land, exemption, §56-265.15:1.
Recurring noncompliance by localities, other political subdivisions.
Response, demand, §56-265.32.
Routine maintenance, §56-265.15:1.
Exception, §56-265.23.
Sewer system laterals, private sewer laterals, §56-265.19:1.
Defined, §56-265.15.
Sign installation not involving excavation.
Exemption, §56-265.15:1.
Sovereign immunity, §56-265.28.
Special fund establishment, §56-265.32.
Special project notice.
Defined, §56-265.15.
Excavation or demolition, §56-265.17.
Time periods, calculation, §56-265.15.
Violations.
Civil penalties, §56-265.32.

UNDERINSURED MOTOR VEHICLES.
Action instituted against vehicle owner or operator, §38.2-2206.
Arbitration under uninsured motorist endorsement, §38.2-2206.
Certificate of self-insurance.
Exemption from chapter, §46.2-361.

UNDERINSURED MOTOR VEHICLES —Cont'd
Costs of defending vehicle owner or operator.
Relief from liability for insurer, §38.2-2206.
Insurance coverage, §38.2-2206.
Certificate of self-insurance.
Exemption from chapter, §46.2-368.
Required notice of optional coverage available, §38.2-2202.
Registration of uninsured motor vehicles, §§46.2-705 to 46.2-710.
Registration of vehicles.
Additional fee, §46.2-705.
Certificates required of applicants for registration, §46.2-706.
Confidentiality of insurance information, §46.2-706.1.
Definitions, §46.2-705.
Disposition of collected fees, §46.2-710.
False evidence of insurance, §46.2-707.
Furnishing certificate of insurance, §46.2-707.
Hearing prior to suspension, §46.2-708.
Insurance and surety companies to verify insurance information, §46.2-706.1.
Operating vehicle without payment of fee, §46.2-707.
Proof of financial responsibility, §46.2-709.
Reportable accidents.
Suspension of driver's license and registration, §46.2-708.
Return of suspended driver's license and indicia of titling and registration, §46.2-709.
Suspension of driver's license and indicia of titling and registration, §§46.2-706, 46.2-708.
Verification of certificates, §46.2-706.
Workers' compensation.
Automobiles, home protection, etc., rates, §§38.2-2000 to 38.2-2027.
See INSURANCE RATES.

UNDERPASSES.
Obstructions or encroachments, §15.2-2009.
Roads, streets and public rights-of-way.
Localities generally, §§15.2-2000 to 15.2-2030.
See ROADS, STREETS AND PUBLIC RIGHTS OF WAY.
Use permits for transportation and utilities, §15.2-2015.

UNDERSERVED AREAS.
Clinical nurse specialists.
Pilot programs for obstetrical and pediatric care in underserved areas, §32.1-11.5.
Free health care to underserved populations.
Optometrists rendering, §54.1-3202.
Pharmacists providing, §54.1-3301.
Practice nursing by nurses rendering, §54.1-3001.
Practitioners of healing arts providing, §54.1-2901.
Veterinarians providing, §54.1-3801.
Health workforce recruitment, §32.1-122.20.
Medically underserved areas, §§32.1-122.5 to 32.1-122.8.
Pilot programs for obstetrical and pediatric care in underserved areas, §32.1-11.5.
Natural gas distribution service within any underserved area or county, §15.2-2109.3.
Veterinarians.
Free care in underserved areas, §54.1-3801.

UNDERTAKERS.
Burial society contracts forbidden, §38.2-4022.

UNDERTAKERS —Cont'd
Licensing generally, §§54.1-2800 to 54.1-2825.
See FUNERAL SERVICES.

UNDERWRITING ASSOCIATIONS.
Joint associations, §38.2-1915.
Basic property insurance, §§38.2-2700 to 38.2-2713.
Commercial liability insurance, §§38.2-2900 to 38.2-2913.
Examination of, §38.2-1925.
Medical malpractice, §§38.2-2800 to 38.2-2814.
Workers' compensation, automobiles, home protection, etc., rates, §38.2-2002.

UNDUE INFLUENCE.
Trusts.
Creation induced by, §64.2-724.

UNEARNED PREMIUM RESERVES.
Insurance companies, §38.2-1312.
Title insurers, §38.2-4610.1.
Foreign insurers, §38.2-4610.1:1.

UNEMPLOYMENT.
Economic crisis strike force, §2.2-205.1.
Governor's development opportunity fund.
New jobs, requirements, §2.2-115.
High unemployment areas.
Economic development partnership authority.
Marketing plan, §2.2-2238.
Veterans services department.
Programs to reduce unemployment among veterans, §2.2-2001.2.

UNEMPLOYMENT COMPENSATION, §§60.2-100 to 60.2-637.
Actions, §60.2-118.
Collection of taxes, §60.2-521.
Limitations, §60.2-514.
Reimbursement of expenses of attorney general, §60.2-120.
Administration, §§60.2-108 to 60.2-121.
Appointment of commissioners, §60.2-108.
Bonds of commissioners, §60.2-109.
Collections in financing administrative expenditures, §60.2-117.
Compensation of commissioners, §60.2-108.
Duties of commission, §60.2-111.
Employment stabilization, §60.2-113.
Employment stabilization, §60.2-113.
Income withholding orders, §60.2-114.1.
Powers of commission, §60.2-111.
Reciprocal agreements, §60.2-116.
Records, §60.2-114.
Reports, §60.2-114.
State-federal cooperation, §60.2-115.
State job service division, §60.2-400.
Creation, §60.2-110.
Unemployment compensation administration fund.
General expenditures, §60.2-308.
Unemployment insurance services division.
Creation, §60.2-110.
Administrative process act.
Exemptions from case decisions, §2.2-4018.
Application of provisions.
Contingencies, §60.2-103.
Attorney representation.
Individual or employing unit appearing before officer of commission, §60.2-123.
Attorney representatives.
Fee for representing individual or employing unit.
Amount approved by commission, §60.2-123.

UNEMPLOYMENT COMPENSATION —Cont'd
Benefits, §§60.2-600 to 60.2-637.
Assignments, §60.2-600.
Based on benefit year, §60.2-605.
Child support intercept of benefits, §60.2-608.
Claims adjudication, §§60.2-619 to 60.2-631.
Computation, §§60.2-601 to 60.2-609.
Deprivation for convictions, §60.2-635.
Disqualification for benefits, §60.2-618.
Eligibility, §§60.2-612 to 60.2-618.
Aliens, §60.2-617.
Conditions, §60.2-612.
Disqualification for benefits, §60.2-618.
Educational institution employees, §60.2-615.
Individuals in training, §60.2-613.
Public officers and employees, §60.2-615.
Service required during immediately preceding benefit year, §60.2-614.
Services connected with sports or athletic events, §60.2-616.
Extended benefits.
Defined terms, §60.2-610.
Maximum total amount, §60.2-607.
Receipt of, §60.2-611.
Falsely attempting to obtain or increase benefits, §60.2-632.
False or misleading statements.
Notice of penalties, §60.2-637.
Fraudulent claims, penalty, §60.2-636.
Irregular wages, §60.2-606.
Limitations on payment, §60.2-102.
Maintenance of benefit accounts, §60.2-300.
Maximum total amount, §60.2-607.
Non-fixed period payment wages, §60.2-606.
Nonprofit organizations.
Employees.
Financing of benefits to, §60.2-501.
Payments, §60.2-601.
Receipt of back pay.
Repayment of benefits, §60.2-634.
Receiving benefits to which not entitled, §60.2-633.
Reciprocal agreements, §60.2-609.
Table.
Maximum total amount, §60.2-607.
Weekly benefit amount, §60.2-602.
Reductions, §§60.2-603, 60.2-604.
Bills of general assembly.
Unemployment compensation bills affecting net revenues of Commonwealth, §30-19.03:1.2.
Child support enforcement by department of social services.
Attachment of benefits through employment commission, §63.2-1941.
Citation of title, §60.2-100.
Claims adjudication, §§60.2-619 to 60.2-631.
Appeals, §60.2-619.
Commission review, §§60.2-622, 60.2-630.
Judicial review, §60.2-625.
Powers, §60.2-626.
Set-asides, §60.2-630.
Superseded by board of review, §60.2-631.
Vacating determinations and decisions, §60.2-630.
Hearings and decisions, §60.2-620.
Redetermination of claims, §60.2-629.
Tribunals, §60.2-621.
Board of review, §60.2-631.
Deputy determination and decisions, §60.2-619.
Redetermination of claims, §60.2-629.

UNEMPLOYMENT COMPENSATION —Cont'd
Claims adjudication —Cont'd
Deputy determination and decisions —Cont'd
Set-asides or vacating determinations, §60.2-630.
Fees.
Limitation on, §60.2-122.
Orders to compel, §60.2-627.
Procedure, §60.2-623.
Recordation of hearings, §§60.2-623, 60.2-623.1.
Representation by counsel, §60.2-123.
Self-incrimination, §60.2-628.
Witness expenses, §60.2-624.
Commission defined, §60.2-208.
Commission on unemployment compensation, §§30-218 to 30-224.
Chairman and vice-chairman, §30-219.
Compensation and expenses, §30-221.
Established, §30-218.
Executive summary of activities and work.
Submission by chairman, §30-224.
Meetings, quorum, §30-220.
Membership, terms, vacancies, §30-219.
Powers and duties, §30-222.
Purpose, §30-218.
Recommendations.
Voting on, §30-220.
Report.
Annual report to general assembly and governor, §30-222.
Staffing, §30-223.
Contingencies affecting operation of title, §60.2-103.
Criminal cases, §60.2-119.
Reimbursement of expenses of attorney general, §60.2-120.
Defined terms, §§60.2-200 to 60.2-229.
Agricultural labor, §60.2-201.
American aircraft, §60.2-228.
American vessel, §60.2-228.
Annual payroll, §60.2-202.
Average annual payroll, §60.2-203.
Base period, §60.2-204.
Benefit ratio, §60.2-530.
Benefits, §60.2-205.
Benefit year, §60.2-206.
Calendar quarter, §60.2-207.
Certain federal acts and statutes, §60.2-231.
Child support obligations, §60.2-608.
Commission, §60.2-208.
Eligibility period, §60.2-610.
Employer, §60.2-210.
Employing unit, §60.2-211.
Employment, §60.2-212.
Agricultural employment, §60.2-214.
Charitable organizations, §60.2-213.
Commonwealth, within and without, §60.2-217.
Domestic employment, §60.2-215.
Higher education, §60.2-213.
Hospitals, §60.2-213.
Obtaining a determination or opinion, §60.2-212.2.
Outside of the United States, §60.2-216.
Religious organizations, §60.2-213.
Services, §60.2-219.
Determination whether services constitute employment, §60.2-500.
Special exclusion, §60.2-212.1.
State, §60.2-213.
Subdivisions, §60.2-213.
Taxed by federal law, §60.2-218.

UNEMPLOYMENT COMPENSATION —Cont'd
Defined terms —Cont'd
Employment office, §60.2-222.
Exhaustee, §60.2-610.
Extended benefit period, §60.2-610.
Extended benefits, §60.2-610.
Foreign contractor, §60.2-527.
Fund, §60.2-223.
Hospital, §60.2-221.
Institution of higher education, §60.2-220.
Insured work, §60.2-224.
Payroll, §60.2-530.
Rate of insured unemployment, §60.2-610.
Regular benefits, §60.2-610.
State, §60.2-225.
State law, §60.2-610.
State off indicator, §60.2-610.
State on indicator, §60.2-610.
State or local child support enforcement agency, §60.2-608.
Suitable employment, §60.2-613.
Taxes, §60.2-209.
Tax rate, §60.2-534.
Transfers for purpose of obtaining lower tax rate, §60.2-536.5.
Unemployment, §60.2-226.
Unemployment compensation, §60.2-608.
Unemployment compensation administration fund, §60.2-227.
Wages, §60.2-229.
Week, §60.2-230.
Digital recordings.
Claims adjudication.
Electronic or digital recording of proceedings in lieu of transcripts, §60.2-623.
Directory of new hires.
Commission furnishing information for use, §60.2-114.
Discharge for misconduct connected with work.
Disqualification for benefits, §60.2-618.
Disclosure of income withholding orders, §60.2-114.1.
Disputed claims, procedure, §60.2-623.
Disqualification for benefits, §60.2-618.
Distribution of relevant material, §60.2-105.
Divisions created, §60.2-110.
State job service division, §60.2-400.
Drug testing of employees.
Disqualification for benefits upon confirmed positive test, §60.2-618.
Employer posting duties, §60.2-106.
Employer taxation, §§60.2-500 to 60.2-538.
Agreements by employees to pay, §§60.2-107, 60.2-516.
Allocation of benefit costs, §60.2-504.
Amount of taxes, §60.2-515.
Benefit charges of employers, §60.2-529.
Benefit charges of individuals.
Computation, §60.2-528.
Benefit costs allocation, §60.2-504.
Benefit ratio, §60.2-530.
Collection of taxes, §§60.2-519 to 60.2-524.
Amount of taxes.
Pool cost charges, §60.2-532.
Bad check charges, §60.2-519.1.
Civil actions, §60.2-521.
Delinquent employers.
Adjustment of rate, §60.2-538.
Increase of rate.
Pool cost charges, §60.2-532.

UNEMPLOYMENT COMPENSATION —Cont'd
Employer taxation —Cont'd
Collection of taxes —Cont'd
Injunctions, §60.2-522.
Interest, §60.2-519.
Taxes accrued while employer was in armed forces, §60.2-520.
Priorities under legal dissolutions or distributions, §60.2-523.
Refunds, §60.2-524.
Service charge for payment of taxes by certain means, §60.2-519.2.
Computation of tax rate, §§60.2-525 to 60.2-538.
Acquisition of one employing unit by another, §60.2-535.
Review of decision, §60.2-536.
Benefit ratio, §60.2-530.
Delinquent employers, §60.2-538.
Pool cost charges, §60.2-532.
Employer, §60.2-529.
Experience rating tax rate, §60.2-531.
Acquisition of one employing unit by another, §60.2-535.
Pool cost charges, §60.2-532.
Review of decision, §60.2-536.
Failure to respond to requests for information, §60.2-528.1.
Foreign contractors, §60.2-527.
Pool cost charges, §60.2-532.
Fractional percents, §60.2-517.
Fund balance factor, §60.2-533.
Generally, §60.2-526.
Pool cost charges, §60.2-532.
Individuals, §60.2-528.
Notice to employer, §60.2-526.
Overpayments, failure to respond in a timely manner to request for information, §60.2-528.1.
Pool cost charges, §60.2-532.
Reduced tax rate permissible under federal amendment, §60.2-537.
State of employer's benefit charges and taxes, §60.2-525.
Table, §60.2-531.
Tax rate defined, §60.2-534.
Coverage election, §60.2-510.
Coverage period, §60.2-508.
Coverage termination, §60.2-509.
Criminal offense, penalty.
Transfer of trade or business for purpose of obtaining lower rate, §18.2-204.3.
Deduction from employee wages, §60.2-516.
Election as to coverage, §60.2-510.
Employees of Indian tribes or tribal units.
Financing of benefits to, §60.2-507.1.
Evaluation of employing unit as employer, §60.2-500.
Fractional percents, §60.2-517.
Fund balance factor, §60.2-533.
Group accounts, §60.2-505.
How taxes payable, §60.2-511.
Increase of rate, §60.2-515.
Limitation on proceedings to establish liability, §60.2-514.
Lower rate.
Transfer of trade or business for purpose of obtaining.
Criminal offense, penalty, §18.2-204.3.
Nonprofit organizations.
Bonding, §60.2-502.

UNEMPLOYMENT COMPENSATION —Cont'd
Employer taxation —Cont'd
Nonprofit organizations —Cont'd
Employees.
Financing of benefits to, §60.2-501.
Authority to terminate elections, §60.2-503.
Period of coverage, §60.2-508.
Provision violations.
Penalties, §60.2-518.
Public officers and employees.
Financing of benefits to, §§60.2-506, 60.2-507.
Refunds, §60.2-524.
Reporting requirements, §§60.2-511 to 60.2-518.
Failure to file, §60.2-513.
How taxes payable, §60.2-511.
Payroll and tax reports, §60.2-512.
When taxes payable, §60.2-511.
Termination of coverage, §60.2-509.
Transfer of trade or business for purpose of obtaining lower rate.
Criminal offense, penalty, §18.2-204.3.
When taxes payable, §§60.2-511, 60.2-512.
Employment commission.
Commission on unemployment compensation.
Defined to mean Virginia Employment Commission, §§30-218 to 30-224.
Generally, §§30-218 to 30-224.
Employment defined, §60.2-212.
Agricultural employment, §60.2-214.
Charitable organizations, §60.2-213.
Commonwealth, within and without, §60.2-217.
Domestic employment, §60.2-215.
Higher education, §60.2-213.
Hospitals, §60.2-213.
Obtaining a determination or opinion, §60.2-212.2.
Outside of the United States, §60.2-216.
Religious organizations, §60.2-213.
Services, §60.2-219.
Determination whether services constitute employment, §60.2-500.
Special exclusion, §60.2-212.1.
State, §60.2-213.
Subdivisions, §60.2-213.
Taxed by federal law, §60.2-218.
Erroneous payments.
Employer failure to respond to requests for information, §60.2-528.1.
Failure to respond to requests for information.
Employer taxation.
Computation of tax rate, §60.2-528.1.
Failure without good cause to apply for available, suitable work.
Disqualification for benefits, §60.2-618.
False or misleading statements.
Benefits.
Notice of penalties, §60.2-637.
Fees.
Limitation on, §60.2-122.
Fines, penalties and costs owed to Commonwealth or political subdivision.
Commission furnishing information to political subdivision or Commonwealth, §60.2-114.
Food stamp overissuance.
Withholding benefits, §60.2-608.2.
Fraudulent claims.
Benefits, penalty, §60.2-636.
Fund, §§60.2-300 to 60.2-317.
See UNEMPLOYMENT COMPENSATION FUND.
Income tax.
Deduction and withholding of federal income tax, §60.2-608.1.

UNEMPLOYMENT COMPENSATION —Cont'd
Income withholding orders, §60.2-114.1.
Indians.
Employees of Indian tribes or tribal units.
Financing of benefits to, §60.2-507.1.
Job service.
Special employment service account.
Purpose, §60.2-309.
Liability of Commonwealth and commission, §60.2-102.
Licenses.
Loss of or failure to renew license required as a condition of employment.
Disqualification for benefits, §60.2-618.
Limitation of actions, §60.2-514.
Overpayments.
Employer taxation.
Failure of employer to respond in a timely manner to request for information, §60.2-528.1.
Posters, employer duties, §60.2-106.
Publication of relevant material, §60.2-105.
Records, §60.2-114.
Reports, §60.2-114.
Failure to file, §60.2-513.
Payroll and tax reports, §60.2-512.
Representation by counsel, §60.2-123.
Reservation of right to amend or appeal, §60.2-104.
Rights, waiver of, §60.2-107.
Social security numbers.
Disclosure of, §60.2-101.
State job service division, §60.2-400.
Creation, §60.2-110.
Statute of limitations, §60.2-514.
Criminal prosecution for fraudulently obtained benefits, §19.2-8.
Taxation.
Federal income tax.
Deduction and withholding, §60.2-608.1.
Transfers for purpose of obtaining lower tax rate, §60.2-536.1.
Advisory opinion by commission, §60.2-536.2.
Definitions, §60.2-536.5.
Determination whether business transfer illegal, §60.2-500.
Interpretation of provisions, §60.2-536.4.
Penalties for violations, §60.2-536.3.
Unemployment compensation administration fund.
Defined, §60.2-227.
Unemployment insurance services division.
Creation, §60.2-110.
Veterans skills database, §60.2-113.1.
Violation of provisions.
Deprivation of benefits for convictions, §60.2-635.
Employer taxation, §60.2-518.
Falsely attempting to obtain or increase benefits, §60.2-632.
Penalties, §§60.2-121, 60.2-518.
Receiving benefits to which not entitled, §60.2-633.
Virginia new hire reporting center.
Employing unit to report, §60.2-114.
Voluntarily leaving work without good cause.
Disqualification for benefits, §60.2-618.
Waiver of rights, §60.2-107.
Weekly benefit amount, §60.2-602.
Deductions, §§60.2-603, 60.2-604.
Work records.
Employing unit to keep, §60.2-114.

UNEMPLOYMENT COMPENSATION ADMINISTRATION FUND, §§60.2-306 to 60.2-313.
Auditor expenses.
Payments, §60.2-313.
Comptroller expenses.
Payments, §60.2-313.
Continued, §60.2-306.
Defined, §60.2-227.
Disbursements upon warrant, §60.2-312.
Expenditures, §60.2-308.
Financing, §60.2-310.
Payments upon warrant, §60.2-312.
Replacing funds lost or expended for unnecessary purposes, §60.2-311.
Sources, §60.2-307.
Special employment service account, §60.2-309.
Financing, §60.2-310.
State treasurer expenses.
Payments, §60.2-313.

UNEMPLOYMENT COMPENSATION FUND, §§60.2-300 to 60.2-305.
Accounts, separate, §60.2-300.
Appropriation of moneys, §60.2-303.
Benefit account.
Credits to, §60.2-302.
Unclaimed money, §60.2-302.
Clearing account.
Credits to, §60.2-301.
Maintenance, §60.2-300.
Payment to credit federal unemployment trust fund, §60.2-301.
Refund payment, §60.2-301.
Continuation, §60.2-300.
Disbursements upon warrant, §60.2-304.
Payments upon warrant, §60.2-304.
Special fund, §§60.2-314 to 60.2-317.
Bad check charges, §60.2-519.1.
Continued, §60.2-314.
Continuously available to commission, §60.2-317.
Disbursements upon warrant, §60.2-316.
Interest.
Past-due taxes.
Collection and deposit, §60.2-519.
Payments into, §60.2-301.
Payments into, §60.2-314.
Payments upon warrant, §60.2-316.
Use, §60.2-315.
Use of money credited to Commonwealth in unemployment trust fund, §§60.2-302, 60.2-305.

UNEMPLOYMENT INSURANCE.
Credit involuntary unemployment insurance.
Defined, §38.2-122.1.
Disclosure and readability, §38.2-233.
Unemployment compensation generally, §§60.2-100 to 60.2-637.
See UNEMPLOYMENT COMPENSATION.

UNEXCUSED ABSENCE FROM SCHOOL.
Suspension of student's driver's license.
Ten or more consecutive unexcused absences, §46.2-334.001.

UNFAIR AND DECEPTIVE TRADE PRACTICES.
Boat dealers.
Board powers, §29.1-802.
Consumer counsel, division of.
Programs to facilitate resolution of complaints, §2.2-517.

UNFAIR AND DECEPTIVE TRADE PRACTICES —Cont'd
Fraternal benefit societies.
Unfair competition and unfair and deceptive acts and practices, §38.2-4133.
Highway contractors' association.
Effect of engaging in certain activities, §33.1-341.
Home protection companies, §38.2-2612.
Insurance generally, §§38.2-500 to 38.2-518.
See INSURANCE, UNFAIR TRADE PRACTICES.
Motor vehicle dealers.
Advertising, §46.2-1581.
Price-gouging.
Post-disaster anti-price gouging act, §§59.1-525 to 59.1-529.1.
T&M vehicle dealers.
Advertising, §46.2-1990.
Viatical settlements, §38.2-6013.

UNFAIR TRADE PRACTICES ACT, §§38.2-500 to 38.2-518.
See INSURANCE, UNFAIR TRADE PRACTICES.

UNGRANTED SHORES OF THE SEA, §§28.2-1500 to 28.2-1514.
Amended or supplemental inventories.
Claims to lands and supplemental inventories, §28.2-1511.
Authorized uses, §28.2-1502.
Claims to inventoried land, §28.2-1509.
Amended or supplemental inventories, §28.2-1510.
Claims to lands and supplemental inventories, §28.2-1511.
Historical evidence of claims, §28.2-1514.
Definitions, §28.2-1500.
Evidence.
Historical evidence of claims, §28.2-1514.
Initial inventories.
Defined, §28.2-1500.
Effect, §28.2-1508.
Filing, §28.2-1506.
Notice of filing, §28.2-1507.
Limitation of actions.
Claims to designated land, §28.2-1511.
Effect of legal disability, §28.2-1512.
Lis pendens.
Filing of notice, §28.2-1513.
Management of lands, §28.2-1503.
Management plan preparation, §28.2-1504.
Marine resources commission.
Management of lands, §28.2-1503.
Powers and duties, §28.2-1501.
Preparation of management plan, §28.2-1504.
Notice.
Filing notice of lis pendens, §28.2-1513.
Ownership, §28.2-1502.
Persons with disability.
Effect of disability, §28.2-1512.
Powers and duties of commission, §28.2-1501.
Statute of limitations.
Claims to designated land, §28.2-1511.
Effect of legal disability, §28.2-1512.
Virginia coastal land management advisory council.
Establishment, §28.2-1505.

UNIFORM ACT FOR OUT OF STATE PAROLEE SUPERVISION, §§53.1-166, 53.1-167.
See ESTATE TAX.

UNIFORM ACT ON ADOPTION AND MEDICAL ASSISTANCE.
See ADOPTION.

UNIFORM ACT ON INTERSTATE COMPROMISE AND ARBITRATION OF DEATH TAXES, §§58.1-920 to 58.1-930.

UNIFORM ACT TO SECURE ATTENDANCE OF WITNESSES FROM WITHOUT STATE IN CRIMINAL PROCEEDINGS, §§19.2-272 to 19.2-282.
See WITNESSES.

UNIFORM ADULT GUARDIANSHIP AND PROTECTIVE PROCEEDINGS JURISDICTION ACT, §§64.2-2100 to 64.2-2120.
See GUARDIAN AND WARD.

UNIFORM ANATOMICAL GIFT ACT, REVISED, §§32.1-291.1 to 32.1-291.25.
See ANATOMICAL GIFTS.

UNIFORM ARBITRATION ACT, §§8.01-581.01 to 8.01-581.016.
See ARBITRATION.

UNIFORM AUDIO-VISUAL DEPOSITION ACT, §8.01-412.2.

UNIFORM CERTIFICATE OF TITLE FOR WATERCRAFT ACT, §§29.1-733.2 to 29.1-733.29.

UNIFORM CHILD CUSTODY JURISDICTION AND ENFORCEMENT ACT, §§20-146.1 to 20-146.38.
See CHILD CUSTODY.

UNIFORM CODE OF MILITARY JUSTICE.
Incorporated as part of military laws of Virginia, §44-40.

UNIFORM COMMERCIAL CODE, §§8.1A-101 to 8.11-108.
See COMMERCIAL CODE.

UNIFORM COMPUTER INFORMATION TRANSACTIONS ACT, §§59.1-501.1 to 59.1-509.2.
Acceptance, §59.1-502.3.
Conditional offer or acceptance, §59.1-502.5.
Copies, §59.1-506.9.
Electronic agents, §59.1-502.6.
Varying terms, §59.1-502.4.
Access contracts, §59.1-506.11.
Access restrictions.
Automatic restraints in information, §59.1-506.5.
Accuracy of informational content.
Implied warranties, §59.1-504.4.
Acknowledgments.
Electronic acknowledgment of receipt of electronic message.
Effect, §59.1-502.15.
Adoption of terms of record as terms of contract, §59.1-502.8.
Alteration of terms by agreement.
Modification and rescission, §59.1-503.3.
Anticipatory repudiation.
Breach of contract, §59.1-507.9.
Retraction, §59.1-507.10.
Applicability of chapter, §59.1-501.3.
Assent to terms.
Manifesting assent, §59.1-501.12.
Attribution.
Determination, §59.1-502.13.
Efficacy and commercial reasonableness of procedures, §59.1-502.12.

UNIFORM COMPUTER INFORMATION TRANSACTIONS ACT —Cont'd
Authentications.
Effect, §59.1-501.8.
Legal effect and enforceability, §59.1-501.7.
Proof, §59.1-501.8.
Automatic restraints in information, §59.1-506.5.
Battle of forms.
Terms of contract formed by conduct, §59.1-502.10.
Breach of contract, §§59.1-507.1 to 59.1-507.10.
Anticipatory repudiation, §59.1-507.9.
Retraction, §59.1-507.10.
Assurance of performance, §59.1-507.8.
Copies.
Previous vested grant of rights, §59.1-507.5.
Refusal of defective tender, §59.1-507.4.
Duties upon rightful refusal, §59.1-507.6.
Revocation of acceptance, §59.1-507.7.
Cure of breach, §59.1-507.3.
Determination, §59.1-507.1.
Material breach, §59.1-507.1.
Cure of breach, effect, §59.1-507.3.
Refusal of defective tender.
Copies, §59.1-507.4.
Waiver of remedies, §59.1-507.2.
Cancellation.
Remedies, §59.1-508.2.
Choice of forum, §59.1-501.10.
Choice of law, §59.1-501.9.
Citation of chapter, §59.1-501.1.
Click-on licenses.
Mass-market licenses, §59.1-502.9.
Conditional offer or acceptance, §59.1-502.5.
Excuse by failure of presupposed condition, §59.1-506.15.
Conduct.
Contracts.
Terms of contract formed by conduct, §59.1-502.10.
Conflict of laws, §59.1-501.5.
Construction and interpretation of chapter, §59.1-501.6.
Construction and interpretation of contract, §§59.1-503.1 to 59.1-503.10.
Future performances.
Continuing contractual terms, §59.1-503.4.
License grants.
Rights included and excluded, §59.1-503.7.
Modification and rescission, §59.1-503.3.
Nonprofit libraries, archives or educational institutions.
Licenses to, §59.1-503.10.
Open terms.
Performance in reasonable time and manner, §59.1-503.6.
Terms to be specified, §59.1-503.5.
Parol or extrinsic evidence, §59.1-503.1.
Practical construction, §59.1-503.2.
Satisfactory performance, §59.1-503.9.
Successive performances.
Continuing contractual terms, §59.1-503.4.
Construction and interpretation of warranties.
Multiple warranties, §59.1-504.8.
Consumer defenses.
Electronic error, §59.1-502.14.
Consumer protection law governs, §59.1-501.4:1.
Continuing use.
Remedies, §59.1-508.13.

UNIFORM COMPUTER INFORMATION TRANSACTIONS ACT —Cont'd
Contract formation, §59.1-502.2.
Releases, §59.1-502.7.
Contracts.
Legal consequence, determination of, §59.1-501.17.
Copies.
Acceptance of copies, §59.1-506.9.
Effect of acceptance, §59.1-506.10.
Revocation of acceptance, §59.1-507.7.
Breach of contract.
Previous vested grant of rights, §59.1-507.5.
Refusal of defective tender, §59.1-507.4.
Duties upon rightful refusal, §59.1-507.6.
Revocation of acceptance, §59.1-507.7.
Delivery of copies, §59.1-506.6.
Payment, §59.1-506.7.
Performance related delivery, §59.1-506.7.
Inspection of copies, §59.1-506.8.
Loss of copies.
Risk of loss, assessment, §59.1-506.14.
Refusal of defective tender.
Breach of contract, §59.1-507.4.
Duties upon rightful refusal, §59.1-507.6.
Revocation of acceptance, §59.1-507.7.
Risk of loss, assessment, §59.1-506.14.
Course of dealing.
Parol or extrinsic evidence, §59.1-503.1.
Practical construction, §59.1-503.2.
Course of performance.
Parol or extrinsic evidence, §59.1-503.1.
Practical construction, §59.1-503.2.
Damages.
Licensee's damages, §59.1-508.9.
Licensor's damages, §59.1-508.8.
Liquidated damages.
Remedies, §59.1-508.4.
Measurement of damages, §59.1-508.7.
Dealers.
Contracts involving publishers, dealers and end-users, §59.1-506.13.
Defined terms, §§59.1-501.2, 59.1-501.3.
Delegates.
Performance by, §59.1-505.5.
Digital signatures.
Attribution.
Determination, §59.1-502.13.
Efficacy and commercial reasonableness of procedures, §59.1-502.12.
Disclosures.
Pretransaction disclosures.
Internet type transactions, §59.1-501.14:1.
Discontinuing use.
Remedies, §59.1-508.14.
Downloads.
Pretransaction disclosures.
Internet type transactions, §59.1-501.14:1.
Duration of releases, §59.1-502.7.
Effective date of act.
Previous rights and transactions, §59.1-509.2.
Electronic agents.
Offer and acceptance, §59.1-502.6.
Review of record or term, §59.1-501.13:1.
Electronic error, §59.1-502.14.
Electronic messages.
When receipt effective, §59.1-502.15.
Enable use.
Licensor's obligation to enable use, §59.1-506.2.
Enforceability, §59.1-501.5.
Formal requirements, §59.1-502.1.
Unconscionable contracts, §59.1-501.11.

UNIFORM COMPUTER INFORMATION TRANSACTIONS ACT —Cont'd
Error, electronic.
Contracts, §59.1-502.14.
Evidence.
Extrinsic evidence, §59.1-503.1.
Parol evidence, §59.1-503.1.
Exclusions from chapter, §59.1-501.3.
Federal law.
Effect of preemption, §59.1-501.5.
Financing.
Finance licenses, §59.1-505.8.
Financier not a licensee, §59.1-505.7.
Licensor's rights, effect, §59.1-505.11.
Obligations irrevocable and independent, §59.1-505.9.
Remedies and enforcement, §59.1-505.10.
Formal requirements, §59.1-502.1.
Formation and terms, §§59.1-502.1 to 59.1-502.16.
Fraud.
Remedies, §59.1-508.6.
Future performances.
Continuing contractual terms, §59.1-503.4.
General provisions, §§59.1-501.1 to 59.1-501.17.
Ideas for creation, development or enhancement of computer information.
No formal contract, §59.1-502.16.
Immediate performance, §59.1-506.4.
Indeterminate terms, §59.1-502.2.
Inspection of copies, §59.1-506.8.
Invalidity of provisions.
Severability, §59.1-509.1.
Jurisdiction.
Choice of forum, §59.1-501.10.
Knowledge, defined, §59.1-501.17.
License grants.
Dealers.
Contracts involving publishers, dealers and end-users, §59.1-506.13.
Electronic self-help, limitations, §59.1-508.16.
Finance licenses, §59.1-505.8.
Financing.
Licensor's rights, effect, §59.1-505.11.
Licensee's damages, §59.1-508.9.
Licensor's damages, §59.1-508.8.
Licensor's obligation to enable use, §59.1-506.2.
Possession and prevention of use.
Right of licensor, §59.1-508.15.
Rights included and excluded, §59.1-503.7.
Transfer of licensee's interest, §59.1-505.6.
Limitation of actions.
Remedies, §59.1-508.5.
Liquidated damages.
Remedies, §59.1-508.4.
Manifesting assent, §59.1-501.12.
Manner of formation, §59.1-502.2.
Mass-market licenses, §59.1-502.9.
Material misrepresentation.
Remedies, §59.1-508.6.
Measurement of damages, §59.1-508.7.
Merchantability.
Warranties, §59.1-504.3.
Modification and rescission, §59.1-503.3.
Modification of computer program.
Effect on warranty, §59.1-504.7.
Notice.
Termination of obligations, §59.1-506.17.
Offer and acceptance, §59.1-502.3.
Acceptance that varies terms, §59.1-502.4.
Conditional offer or acceptance, §59.1-502.5.
Electronic agents, §59.1-502.6.

UNIFORM COMPUTER INFORMATION TRANSACTIONS ACT —Cont'd
Online services.
Access contracts, §59.1-506.11.
Open terms.
Performance in reasonable time and manner, §59.1-503.6.
Terms to be specified, §59.1-503.5.
Opportunity to review record or term, §59.1-501.13:1.
Ownership of informational rights, §59.1-505.1.
Parol or extrinsic evidence, §59.1-503.1.
Performance, §§59.1-506.1 to 59.1-506.18.
Access contracts, §59.1-506.11.
Automatic restraints in information, §59.1-506.5.
Breach of contract.
Adequate assurance of performance, §59.1-507.8.
Completing performance.
Remedies, §59.1-508.12.
Conditional contracts.
Excuse by failure of presupposed condition, §59.1-506.15.
Copy acceptance, §59.1-506.9.
Effect of acceptance, §59.1-506.10.
Copy delivery, §59.1-506.6.
Payment, §59.1-506.7.
Performance related delivery, §59.1-506.7.
Copy inspection.
Right to inspect, §59.1-506.8.
Copy loss.
Risk of loss, assessment, §59.1-506.14.
Dealers.
Contracts involving publishers, dealers and end-users, §59.1-506.13.
Electronic regulation, §59.1-506.5.
Generally, §59.1-506.1.
Immediate performance, §59.1-506.4.
Licensor's obligation to enable use, §59.1-506.2.
Satisfactory performance.
Submissions of information, §59.1-506.3.
Service agreements, §59.1-506.12.
Specific performance.
Remedies, §59.1-508.11.
Support contracts, §59.1-506.12.
Surviving rights.
Rights surviving termination, §59.1-506.16.
Termination of obligations, §59.1-506.16.
Delivery, §59.1-506.18.
Enforcement, §59.1-506.18.
Notice of termination, §59.1-506.17.
Possession and prevention of use.
Remedies.
Right of licensor, §59.1-508.15.
Practical construction, §59.1-503.2.
Pretransaction disclosures.
Internet type transactions, §59.1-501.14:1.
Previous rights and transactions, §59.1-509.2.
Principles of law and equity supplementing provisions, §59.1-501.16.
Purposes.
Construction and interpretation, §59.1-501.6.
Questions to be determined by court, §59.1-501.17.
Quitclaim grants, §59.1-504.1.
Records.
Adoption of terms of record as terms of contract, §59.1-502.8.
Legal effect and enforceability, §59.1-501.7.
Manifesting assent, §59.1-501.12.

UNIFORM COMPUTER INFORMATION TRANSACTIONS ACT —Cont'd
Recoupment.
Remedies, §59.1-508.10.
Releases, §59.1-502.7.
Remedies, §§59.1-508.1 to 59.1-508.16.
Cancellation, §59.1-508.2.
Completing performance, §59.1-508.12.
Continuing use, §59.1-508.13.
Contractual modification of remedies, §59.1-508.3.
Cumulative effect, §59.1-508.1.
Discontinuing use, §59.1-508.14.
Electronic self-help, limitations, §59.1-508.16.
Fraud, §59.1-508.6.
Generally, §59.1-508.1.
Licensee's damages, §59.1-508.9.
Licensor's damages, §59.1-508.8.
Licensor's rights.
Electronic self-help, limitations, §59.1-508.16.
Possession and prevention of use, §59.1-508.15.
Limitation of actions, §59.1-508.5.
Limitations imposed by contract, §59.1-508.3.
Liquidated damages, §59.1-508.4.
Material misrepresentation, §59.1-508.6.
Measurement of damages, §59.1-508.7.
Possession and prevention of use.
Right of licensor, §59.1-508.15.
Recoupment, §59.1-508.10.
Specific performance, §59.1-508.11.
Substitute transactions.
Licensor's damages, §59.1-508.8.
Repudiation.
Anticipatory repudiation.
Breach of contract, §59.1-507.9.
Retraction, §59.1-507.10.
Rescission of agreement, §59.1-503.3.
Review of record or term, §59.1-501.13:1.
Satisfactory performance, §59.1-503.9.
Submissions of information, §59.1-506.3.
Scope of chapter, §59.1-501.3.
Self-destruct commands.
Automatic restraints in information, §59.1-506.5.
Service agreements, §59.1-506.12.
Severability of provisions, §59.1-509.1.
Shrink wrap licenses.
Mass-market licenses, §59.1-502.9.
Specific performance.
Remedies, §59.1-508.11.
Statute of limitations, §59.1-508.5.
Subcontracts, §59.1-505.5.
Substitute transactions.
Remedies.
Licensor's damages, §59.1-508.8.
Successive performances.
Continuing contractual terms, §59.1-503.4.
Supplemental principles, §59.1-501.16.
Support contracts, §59.1-506.12.
Surviving rights.
Rights surviving termination, §59.1-506.16.
Termination of obligations.
Performance, §59.1-506.16.
Delivery, §59.1-506.18.
Enforcement, §59.1-506.18.
Notice of termination, §59.1-506.17.
Third party beneficiaries.
Warranties, §59.1-504.9.
Time for taking action, how determined, §59.1-501.17.
Title of provisions, §59.1-501.1.
Title to copy, §59.1-505.2.

UNIFORM COMPUTER INFORMATION TRANSACTIONS ACT —Cont'd
Transfer of contractual interest, §59.1-505.3.
Effect, §59.1-505.4.
Subcontracts, §59.1-505.5.
Transfer of information and rights, §§59.1-505.1 to 59.1-505.11.
Contractual interest, §59.1-505.3.
Effect, §59.1-505.4.
Delegates.
Performance by, §59.1-505.5.
Financing.
Finance licenses, §59.1-505.8.
Financier not a licensee, §59.1-505.7.
Licensor's rights, effect, §59.1-505.11.
Obligations irrevocable and independent, §59.1-505.9.
Remedies and enforcement, §59.1-505.10.
Licensee's interest, §59.1-505.6.
Ownership of informational rights, §59.1-505.1.
Subcontracts, §59.1-505.5.
Title to copy, §59.1-505.2.
Unconscionable contracts, §59.1-501.11.
Unsolicited submissions.
No formal contract, §59.1-502.16.
Usage of trade.
Parol or extrinsic evidence, §59.1-503.1.
Practical construction, §59.1-503.2.
Variation of provisions by agreement, §59.1-501.15.
Waiver of remedies.
Breach of contract, §59.1-507.2.
Warranties, §§59.1-504.1 to 59.1-504.10.
Accuracy of informational content, §59.1-504.4.
Conflict of warranties, §59.1-504.8.
Cumulation of warranties, §59.1-504.8.
Disclaimer of warranty, §59.1-504.6.
Express warranties, §59.1-504.2.
Fitness for particular purpose, §59.1-504.5.
Free software, §59.1-504.10.
Implied warranties, §§59.1-504.3 to 59.1-504.5.
Free software, §59.1-504.10.
Merchantability, §59.1-504.3.
Modification of computer program.
Effect on warranty, §59.1-504.7.
Modification of warranty, §59.1-504.6.
Multiple warranties.
Construction and interpretation, §59.1-504.8.
Noninfringement, §59.1-504.1.
Noninterference, §59.1-504.1.
Quitclaim grants, §59.1-504.1.
Third party beneficiaries, §59.1-504.9.

UNIFORM CRIME REPORTING PROGRAM, §§52-25 to 52-30.
See CRIME REPORTING PROGRAM.

UNIFORM CRIMINAL EXTRADITION ACT.
Generally, §§19.2-84 to 19.2-118.
See EXTRADITION.

UNIFORM CUSTODIAL TRUSTS ACT, §§64.2-900 to 64.2-918.
See CUSTODIAL TRUSTS.

UNIFORM DISCLAIMER OF PROPERTY INTERESTS ACT, §§64.2-2600 to 64.2-2614.
See DISCLAIMER OF PROPERTY INTERESTS.

UNIFORM DISPOSITION OF COMMUNITY PROPERTY RIGHTS AT DEATH, §§64.2-315 to 64.2-324.
See COMMUNITY PROPERTY RIGHTS AT DEATH.

UNIFORM DISPOSITION OF UNCLAIMED PROPERTY ACT, §§55-210.1 to 55-210.30.
See UNCLAIMED PROPERTY.

UNIFORM ELECTRONIC TRANSACTIONS ACT, §§59.1-479 to 59.1-497.
Acceptance of electronic records by public bodies, §59.1-496.
Acknowledgment of documents, §59.1-489.
Applicability of chapter, §59.1-481.
Effective date, §59.1-482.
Change or error in record, §59.1-488.
Citation of chapter, §59.1-479.
Consent of parties, §59.1-483.
Construction and application, §59.1-484.
Contracts.
Automated transactions generally, §59.1-492.
Formation, §59.1-492.
Conversion of public records to electronic format, §59.1-495.
Defined terms, §59.1-480.
Effective date, §59.1-482.
Electronic signatures.
Attribution, §59.1-487.
Effect, §59.1-487.
Evidence, admissibility, §59.1-491.
Legal effect or enforceability, §59.1-485.
Use not required, §59.1-483.
Error in record, §59.1-488.
Evidence.
Admissibility of electronic records or signatures, §59.1-491.
Legal effect or enforceability of electronic records, signatures and contracts, §59.1-485.
Mail requirements.
Electronic information delivery, §59.1-486.
Negotiable instruments.
Transferable records, §59.1-494.
Notarization of documents, §59.1-489.
Notes.
Transferable records, §59.1-494.
Promissory notes.
Transferable records, §59.1-494.
Public bodies.
Acceptance of electronic records, §59.1-496.
Filing of electronic records, §59.1-496.
Purpose, §59.1-484.
Records.
Electronic display as satisfying requirements, §59.1-486.
Evidence, admissibility, §59.1-491.
Interoperability with other systems, §59.1-497.
Legal effect or enforceability, §59.1-485.
Public bodies.
Conversion of records to electronic format, §59.1-495.
Retention, §59.1-490.
Sending and receiving, §59.1-493.
Standardization, §59.1-497.
Transferable records, §59.1-494.
Scope of chapter, §59.1-481.
Securities.
Transferable records, §59.1-494.
Standardization of formats, §59.1-497.
Title, §59.1-479.
Writing requirement.
Information delivered in writing, requirement satisfied, §59.1-486.
Legal effect or enforceability of electronic records, signatures and contracts, §59.1-485.

UNIFORM ENFORCEMENT OF FOREIGN JUDGMENTS ACT.
Domesticating foreign judgments generally, §§8.01-465.1 to 8.01-465.5.

UNIFORM ENVIRONMENTAL COVENANTS ACT, §§10.1-1238 to 10.1-1250.
See ENVIRONMENTAL COVENANTS.

UNIFORM FEDERAL LIEN REGISTRATION ACT, §§55-142.1 to 55-142.9.

UNIFORM FINE SCHEDULES.
Nontraffic prepayable offenses, VA SCt Rule 3C:2.
Traffic infractions, VA SCt Rule 3B:2.

UNIFORM FLAG ACT, §§18.2-486 to 18.2-492.

UNIFORM FOREIGN COUNTRY MONEY-JUDGMENTS RECOGNITION ACT, §§8.01-465.6 to 8.01-465.13.
See FOREIGN JUDGMENTS.

UNIFORM FOREIGN DEPOSITIONS ACT.
See DEPOSITIONS.

UNIFORM FOREIGN-MONEY CLAIMS ACT, §§8.01-465.14 to 8.01-465.25.
See FOREIGN JUDGMENTS.

UNIFORM GIFTS TO MINORS ACT.
Uniform transfers to minors act, §§64.2-1900 to 64.2-1922.
See TRANSFERS TO MINORS.

UNIFORM INTERNATIONAL WILLS ACT, §§64.2-433 to 64.2-442.
See WILLS.

UNIFORM INTERSTATE DEPOSITIONS AND DISCOVERY ACT, §§8.01-412.8 to 8.01-412.15.
See DISCOVERY.

UNIFORM INTERSTATE FAMILY SUPPORT ACT, §§20-88.32 to 20-88.82.
See INTERSTATE FAMILY SUPPORT ACT.

UNIFORMITY OF GOVERNMENT, VA Const Art I §14.

UNIFORMITY OF TAXES, VA Const Art X §1.

UNIFORM MACHINE GUN ACT, §§18.2-288 to 18.2-298.
See MACHINE GUNS.

UNIFORM MILITARY AND OVERSEAS VOTERS ACT, §§24.2-451 to 24.2-470.
See ABSENTEE AND EARLY VOTING.

UNIFORM PARTNERSHIP ACT, §§50-73.79 to 50-73.149.
See PARTNERSHIPS.

UNIFORM POWER OF ATTORNEY ACT, §§64.2-1600 to 64.2-1642.
See POWER OF ATTORNEY.

UNIFORM PRETRIAL SCHEDULING ORDER, VA SCt Rule Pt 1 Appx Form 3.

UNIFORM PRINCIPAL AND INCOME ACT, §§64.2-1000 to 64.2-1032.
See PRINCIPAL AND INCOME.

UNIFORM PRUDENT INVESTOR ACT, §§64.2-780 to 64.2-791.
See PRUDENT INVESTOR RULE.

UNIFORM PRUDENT MANAGEMENT OF INSTITUTIONAL FUNDS ACT, §§64.2-1100 to 64.2-1108.
See MANAGEMENT OF INSTITUTIONAL FUNDS.

UNIFORM REAL PROPERTY ACQUISITION POLICY ACT OF 1972.
See EMINENT DOMAIN.

UNIFORM REAL PROPERTY ELECTRONIC RECORDING ACT, §§55-142.10 to 55-142.15.

UNIFORM REAL PROPERTY TRANSFER ON DEATH ACT, §§64.2-621 to 64.2-638.
See REAL PROPERTY TRANSFER ON DEATH ACT.

UNIFORM RECOGNITION OF ACKNOWLEDGMENTS ACT, §§55-118.1 to 55-118.9.
See ACKNOWLEDGMENTS.

UNIFORM RELOCATION ASSISTANCE POLICY ACT OF 1972.
See EMINENT DOMAIN.

UNIFORMS.
Bail bondsmen, §9.1-185.12.
Bail enforcement agents.
Uniform and identification, §9.1-186.10.
Military property, care of, §§44-103 to 44-111.
National Guard, §44-39.
Uniforms exempt from levy and sale, §44-96.
Protection of uniforms of the armed forces of the United States, §44-120.
Schools and education.
Board of education guidelines, §22.1-79.2.
Sheriffs.
Alternate clothing, §15.2-1611.
Expenses by locality to provide, §15.2-1613.
Standard uniforms, §15.2-1610.
Wearing by unauthorized person, §15.2-1612.
State defense force, §44-54.9.
Unlawful wearing of officer's uniform, §18.2-175.

UNIFORM SIMULTANEOUS DEATH ACT, §§64.2-2200 to 64.2-2208.

UNIFORM STATEWIDE BUILDING CODE, §§36-97 to 36-119.1.
See BUILDING CODE.

UNIFORM STATUTORY RULE AGAINST PERPETUITIES, §§55-12.1 to 55-12.6.
Applicability, §§55-12.5, 55-12.6.
Construction and interpretation, §55-12.6.
Effective date, §55-12.5.
Exclusions, §55-12.4.
General rule, §55-12.1.
Nonvested property interest or power of appointment.
Time of creation, §55-12.2.
Reformation, §55-12.3.
Remedies.
Reformation, §55-12.3.
Time of creation of nonvested property interest or power of appointment, §55-12.2.

UNIFORM SYSTEM OF FINANCIAL ACCOUNTING.
State departments and agencies, §2.2-803.

UNIFORM SYSTEM OF MARKING AND SIGNING HIGHWAYS, §46.2-830.

UNIFORM TRADE SECRETS ACT, §§59.1-336 to 59.1-343.
See TRADE SECRETS.

UNIFORM TRAFFIC CONTROL DEVICES ON HIGHWAYS, §46.2-830.

UNIFORM TRANSFERS ON DEATH (TOD) SECURITIES REGISTRATION ACT, §§64.2-612 to 64.2-619.
See TOD SECURITY REGISTRATION.

UNIFORM TRANSFERS TO MINORS ACT, §§64.2-1900 to 64.2-1922.
See TRANSFERS TO MINORS.

UNIFORM TRUST CODE, §§64.2-700 to 64.2-808.
See TRUSTS.

UNINCORPORATED ASSOCIATIONS.
Actions by and against entities, §8.01-15.
Limited liability companies generally, §§13.1-1000 to 13.1-1080.
See LIMITED LIABILITY COMPANIES.
Pleadings.
Ownership, §8.01-279.
Reciprocal insurance, §§38.2-1200 to 38.2-1231.
Service of notice, process and other papers.
How process served, §§8.01-305, 8.01-306.

UNINCORPORATED COMMON CARRIERS.
Service of notice, process and other papers.
How process served, §§8.01-305, 8.01-306.

UNINSURED EMPLOYER'S FUND, §§65.2-1200 to 65.2-1206.

UNINSURED MEDICAL CATASTROPHE FUND, §32.1-324.3.

UNINSURED MOTORISTS FUND, §§38.2-3000, 38.2-3001.

UNINSURED MOTOR VEHICLES.
Accidents.
Suspension of driver's license and registration for involvement in a reportable accident, §46.2-708.
Arbitration under uninsured motorist endorsement, §38.2-2206.
Certificate of self-insurance.
Exemption from chapter, §46.2-368.
Insurance coverage, §38.2-2206.
Certificate of self-insurance.
Exemption from chapter, §46.2-368.
Medical benefit offset against coverage prohibited, §38.2-2216.
Required notice of optional coverage available, §38.2-2202.
Registration of vehicles, §§46.2-705 to 46.2-710.
Additional fee, §46.2-706.
Certificates required of applicants for registration, §46.2-706.
Confidentiality of insurance information, §46.2-706.1.
Definitions, §46.2-705.
Disposition of collected fees, §46.2-710.
False evidence of insurance, §46.2-707.
Furnishing certificate of insurance, §46.2-707.
Hearing prior to suspension, §46.2-708.
Insurance and surety companies to verify insurance information, §46.2-706.1.
Operating vehicle without payment of fee, §46.2-707.
Proof of financial responsibility, §46.2-709.
Reportable accidents.
Suspension of driver's license and registration, §46.2-708.
Return of suspended driver's license and indicia of titling and registration, §46.2-709.
Suspension of driver's license and indicia of titling and registration for certain violations, §§46.2-706, 46.2-708.

UNINSURED MOTOR VEHICLES —Cont'd
Registration of vehicles —Cont'd
Verification of certificates, §46.2-706.
Workers' compensation.
Automobiles, home protection, etc., rates, §§38.2-2000 to 38.2-2027.
See INSURANCE RATES.

UNIONS.
Labor unions.
General provisions, §§40.1-52 to 40.1-54.3.
See LABOR UNIONS.

UNITED DAUGHTERS OF THE CONFEDERACY.
Property tax exemption, §58.1-3607.
State recordation tax exemption, §58.1-811.

UNITED STATES.
Acknowledgments by military personnel, §§55-114.1, 55-115.
Acknowledgments outside of the United States, §55-114.
Acknowledgment within the United States, §55-113.
Acquisition of lands.
Jurisdiction over lands acquired by United States, §§1-400 to 1-408.
Aircraft.
Article not applicable to public aircraft owned by, §5.1-11.
Federally certificated airlines and interstate service.
Applicability of provisions, §5.1-12.
Recordation of instruments affecting, §55-100.
Airports.
Acquisition of airport previously operated by, §5.1-2.22.
Appropriations, US Const Art I §9.
Assistant to the Governor for intergovernmental affairs, office of, §§2.2-300 to 2.2-303.
Balloons.
Release prohibitions, §29.1-556.1.
Banks.
Federal areas, facilities in, §6.2-835.
Federal reserve system, generally, §§6.2-811, 6.2-892.
Government deposits.
Pledging assets to secure, §6.2-890.
Civil aircraft.
Recordation of instruments affecting, §55-100.
Civilian employees or contractors serving outside United States.
Extension of driver's license expiration, §46.2-221.2.
Corps of engineers.
Port authority cooperation, §62.1-132.14.
Customs.
Congress.
Power to lay and collect, US Const Art I §8.
Duty of tonnage, US Const Art I §10.
Importation of persons, US Const Art I §9.
Tonnage, US Const Art I §10.
Dams for hydroelectric power.
Jurisdiction, §62.1-103.
Decedents' estates.
Duties of executors and administrators with respect to certain obligations of, §64.2-516.
Defined, §1-255.
Diplomatic service of the United States.
Drivers' licenses.
Extension of licenses for armed services or foreign service personnel, §46.2-221.2.

UNITED STATES —Cont'd
Documents of title.
Treaty or statute.
Relation of article, §8.7-103.
Federal associations.
Savings and loan associations.
See SAVINGS INSTITUTIONS.
Federal Bureau of Investigation.
Crime reporting program.
State police reporting duties, §52-30.
Federal deposit insurance corporation.
Savings institutions.
Appointment as receiver for, §6.2-1199.
Membership in, §6.2-1108.
Federal home loan banks.
Membership in savings institutions, §6.2-1108.
Federal reserve system.
Generally, §§6.2-811, 6.2-892.
Garnishment.
Service upon federal government, §8.01-523.
Gifts.
Foreign presents to United States officials, US Const Art I §9.
Hazardous materials transportation.
Regulations of United States, §10.1-1454.
Health insurance mandate.
Mandated coverage for individuals, prohibition, §38.2-3430.1:1.
Hydroelectric power dams.
Jurisdiction, §62.1-103.
Immigration and naturalization service.
Commitment of aliens to correctional facilities.
Notification, §53.1-218.
Insurance companies investments, §§38.2-1415, 38.2-1432.
Jails for prisoners, §53.1-79.
Judges.
United States courts, US Const Art III §1.
Jurisdiction over lands acquired by United States, §§1-400 to 1-408.
Letters of marque and reprisal, US Const Art I §§8, 10.
Lien registrations, §§55-142.1 to 55-142.9.
Locality, sanitary district or other political subdivision acquiring property from, §15.2-952.
Medical services.
Proof of claims by affidavit, §8.01-37.1.
Military affairs.
Legal services.
Licensing requirements, §54.1-3900.
Military personnel.
Acknowledgments, §§55-114.1, 55-115.
Who may perform notarial acts, §55-118.1.
Mortgage lender and broker act.
Agencies of exempt from chapter, §6.2-1602.
Motor carriers, passengers.
Government vehicles.
Exclusions, §46.2-2000.1.
Motor carriers, property.
Government vehicles.
Exemptions from provisions, §46.2-2101.
National forest permits, §§29.1-408 to 29.1-411.
Obligations.
Issuing agents for sale of obligations during emergency proclaimed by president or war, §44-206.
Parties.
Actions to which United States a party, US Const Art III §2.

UNITED STATES —Cont'd
Port authority.
Cooperation, §62.1-132.13.
Corps of engineers, §62.1-132.14.
Grants and loans, §62.1-132.15.
Post office.
Constitutional provisions, US Const Art I §8.
Prisoners of the United States in local correctional facilities.
Payment to localities, §53.1-90.
Property and fiscal officer.
Appointment, designation or detailing by governor, §44-24.
Recordation of judgments, §§55-140 to 55-142.01.
Recordation tax exemptions, §58.1-811.
Registration of federal liens, §§55-142.1 to 55-142.9.
Retirement system.
Virginia retirement system membership, §51.1-127.
Securities.
Security registration exemption, §13.1-514.
Social security for state and local employees, §§51.1-700 to 51.1-707.
See PUBLIC OFFICERS AND EMPLOYEES.
Soil and water conservation districts.
Acting as agent for, §10.1-547.
Statutes.
Approval of laws by president, US Const Art I §7.
Ex post facto laws, US Const Art I §§9, 10.
Full faith and credit, US Const Art IV §1.
Limitations on legislation, US Const Art I §9.
Proof, US Const Art IV §1.
Revenue bills, US Const Art I §7.
Supreme law of land, US Const Art VI.
Veto, US Const Art I §7.
Streams.
Improvement of navigability.
City assurances, §62.1-156.
Powers of cities to bind themselves, §62.1-157.
City cooperation, §62.1-155.
Suits against, US Const Art III §2.
Titles of nobility.
Prohibited, US Const Art I §§9, 10.
Unemployment compensation.
Reciprocal agreements, §60.2-116.
State-federal cooperation, §60.2-115.
Water resources development projects, §§62.1-148 to 62.1-152.
Weights and measures.
Constitutional provisions, US Const Art I §8.

UNITED STATES ACQUIRED LANDS.
Alcoholic beverages.
Sale.
Mixed alcoholic beverages.
Licensing sale on lands ceded to or owned by United States, §1-404.
Shenandoah national park.
Sale.
Jurisdiction of United States, §1-402.
Taxation.
Jurisdiction of Commonwealth, §1-402.
Consent to acquisition of lands.
Conditional consent given, §1-400.
Jurisdiction.
Additional jurisdiction ceded, §1-401.
Concurrent jurisdiction ceded, §1-400.
Political subdivisions.
Concurrent jurisdiction over certain lands leased to, §1-407.

UNITED STATES ACQUIRED LANDS —Cont'd
Jurisdiction —Cont'd
Political subdivisions.
Concurrent jurisdiction over certain lands leased to, §1-407.
Recorded title.
Prerequisite to vesting of jurisdiction, §1-405.
Relinquishment by United States, §1-408.
Shenandoah national park, §1-402.
Marshlands.
Conveyance of certain lands to United States, §1-403.
Political subdivisions.
Concurrent jurisdiction over certain lands leased to, §1-407.
Conveyance of lands ceded to and no longer used by United States to, §1-406.
Real property tax credit on current year's taxes, §§58.1-3360 to 58.1-3363.
Relinquishment by United States of jurisdiction, §1-408.
Reversion to Commonwealth, §1-405.
Shenandoah national park, §1-402.
Waste and unappropriated lands.
Conveyance of certain lands to United States, §1-403.

UNITED STATES ATTORNEYS.
Federal employees prohibited, exception, §2.2-2801.

UNITED STATES DISTRICT ATTORNEYS.
Militia duty exemption, §44-5.

UNITED STATES DISTRICT COURTS.
Drivers' licenses.
Authority of judges to revoke or suspend driver's license, §46.2-415.
Suspension for failure to comply with federal traffic citations, §46.2-416.1.

UNITED STATES FLAG.
Condominiums.
Display, restrictions, affirmative defense, action by unit owners' association, §55-79.75:2.
Public offering statements.
Limitation or prohibition on display required, §55-79.90.
Defacing, mutilating, etc.
Uniform flag act, §§18.2-486 to 18.2-492.
Display in courtrooms of courts of record, §17.1-118.
Pledge of allegiance in public schools.
Guidelines on constitutional rights and restrictions relating to recitation, §22.1-202.
Administrative rulemaking exemptions, §2.2-4006.
Public school instruction in history and principles, §22.1-202.

UNITED STATES GOVERNMENT MILITARY INSTALLATIONS.
Authorities for development of former federal areas, §§15.2-6300 to 15.2-6322.

UNITED STATES HOUSING ACT OF 1937.
Counties, cities or towns.
Participation in certain leasing programs, §15.2-957.

UNITED STATES HOUSING AND COMMUNITY DEVELOPMENT ACT.
Counties, cities or towns.
Participation in federal development programs, §15.2-956.

UNITED STATES MAGISTRATES.
Drivers' licenses.
Authority to revoke or suspend driver's license, §46.2-415.

UNITED STATES OLYMPIC COMMITTEE EMBLEM.
Prohibition on use to induce sale of goods or services or to promote performance or competition, §59.1-92.21.

UNITED STATES PARK POLICE.
Agreements to enforce state and county laws on federal property, §15.2-1729.

UNITED STATES POSTAL SERVICE.
Militia duty exemption, §44-5.
National change of address systems.
DMV.
Contract with postal service to use, §§46.2-324, 46.2-342, 46.2-416, 46.2-606.

UNITED STATES SECRETARY OF DEFENSE.
Adjutant general to make returns and reports to, §44-15.

UNITED WE STAND.
Special license plates, §46.2-749.78.

UNIVERSITIES AND COLLEGES.
Brown v. Board of Education scholarship program and fund, §§30-231.01 to 30-231.10.
Christopher Newport University, §§23-49.23 to 23-49.33.
See CHRISTOPHER NEWPORT UNIVERSITY.
College building authority, §§23-30.23 to 23-30.38.
See COLLEGE BUILDING AUTHORITY.
College of William and Mary and Richard Bland College generally, §§23-39 to 23-49.1:1.
See COLLEGE OF WILLIAM AND MARY.
College savings plan, §§23-38.75 to 23-38.87:1.
See COLLEGE SAVINGS PLAN.
College savings program, §§23-38.72 to 23-38.74.
Community colleges.
Generally, §§23-214 to 23-231.1:1.
See COMMUNITY COLLEGES.
Council of higher education.
Generally, §§23-9.3 to 23-9.14:2.
See COUNCIL OF HIGHER EDUCATION.
Educational facilities authority.
Generally, §§23-30.39 to 23-30.58.
See EDUCATIONAL FACILITIES AUTHORITY.
Generally, §§23-1.01 to 23-9.2:8.
See COLLEGES AND UNIVERSITIES.
George Mason University, §§23-91.24 to 23-91.33.
See GEORGE MASON UNIVERSITY.
Gifts for educational, literary or charitable purposes.
Generally.
See CHARITABLE GIFTS.
Guaranteed assistance program and fund, §§23-38.53:4 to 23-38.53:6.
Institutional funds.
Uniform prudent management of institutional funds act, §§64.2-1100 to 64.2-1108.
See MANAGEMENT OF INSTITUTIONAL FUNDS.
James Madison University, §§23-164.1 to 23-164.10.
See JAMES MADISON UNIVERSITY.
Loans to students, §§23-38.10:2 to 23-38.10:7.
Longwood University, §§23-182 to 23-191.
See LONGWOOD UNIVERSITY.

UNIVERSITIES AND COLLEGES —Cont'd
New College Institute, §§23-231.30 to 23-231.36.
Norfolk State University, §§23-174.1 to 23-174.7.
See NORFOLK STATE UNIVERSITY.
Nuclear energy consortium, §§67-1400 to 67-1406.
See NUCLEAR ENERGY.
Old Dominion University, §§23-49.11 to 23-49.22:4.
See OLD DOMINION UNIVERSITY.
Police departments.
Generally, §§23-232 to 23-238.
See CAMPUS POLICE.
Procurement by public bodies, §§2.2-4300 to 2.2-4377.
See PUBLIC PROCUREMENT.
Purchases and supply division.
Direct purchases by agency, charitable corporation or institutions of higher education, §2.2-1120.
Radford University, §§23-155.1 to 23-155.10.
See RADFORD UNIVERSITY.
Recycling duties, §§10.1-1425.6 to 10.1-1425.9.
Restructured financial and administrative operations.
Generally, §§23-38.88 to 23-38.121.
See COLLEGES AND UNIVERSITIES.
Savings program, §§23-38.72 to 23-38.74.
Scholarship assistance program, §§23-38.45 to 23-38.52.
See SCHOLARSHIPS.
Scholarships generally, §§23-31 to 23-38.10:1.
See SCHOLARSHIPS.
Senior citizens' higher education, §§23-38.54 to 23-38.60.
Sexually violent predators, civil commitment.
Database of prisoners incarcerated for sexually violent offenses.
Access to records, §37.2-905.2.
Smoke detectors, §§36-99.3, 36-99.5.
Southern Virginia higher education center, §§23-231.24 to 23-231.29.
Southwest Virginia higher education center, §§23-231.2 to 23-231.7.
Tuition assistance grants, §§23-38.11 to 23-38.19:2.
See COLLEGES AND UNIVERSITIES.
University of Mary Washington, §§23-91.34 to 23-91.44.
See UNIVERSITY OF MARY WASHINGTON.
University of Virginia, §§23-62 to 23-91.23:1.
See UNIVERSITY OF VIRGINIA.
Virginia Commonwealth University, §§23-50.4 to 23-50.16.
See VIRGINIA COMMONWEALTH UNIVERSITY.
Virginia Military Institute, §§23-92 to 23-113.
See VIRGINIA MILITARY INSTITUTE.
Virginia Polytechnic Institute and State University, §§23-114 to 23-155.05.
See VIRGINIA POLYTECHNIC INSTITUTE AND STATE UNIVERSITY.
Virginia State University, §§23-165.1 to 23-174.
See VIRGINIA STATE UNIVERSITY.

UNIVERSITY OF MARY WASHINGTON, §§23-91.34 to 23-91.44.
Board of visitors, §§23-91.34 to 23-91.40.
Campus police departments, §§23-232 to 23-238.
Reporting campus crime, §23-9.1:1.
Colleges generally, §§23-1.01 to 23-9.2:8.
See COLLEGES AND UNIVERSITIES.

UNIVERSITY OF MARY WASHINGTON —Cont'd
Conferring of degrees, §23-91.42.
Curriculum, §23-91.43.
License plates.
Special license plates, §46.2-749.
Sale, etc., of real estate, §23-91.44.
Transfer of property, §23-91.35.
Tuition, fees and other charges, §23-91.41.

UNIVERSITY OF VIRGINIA, §§23-62 to 23-91.23:1.
Board of visitors, §§23-69 to 23-79.
Closed meetings, §2.2-3711.
Prohibition on federal employees, exception, §2.2-2801.
Campus police departments.
General provisions, §§23-232 to 23-238.
See CAMPUS POLICE.
Reporting campus crime, §23-9.1:1.
Capital projects.
Medical center, §23-77.4.
Chief medical examiner.
Teaching duties, §32.1-279.
Clinch Valley College, §§23-91.20 to 23-91.23.
Donations, §§23-81 to 23-85.
Freedom of information act.
Excluded records.
Security or ownership interest in entity not traded on securities exchange, §2.2-3705.7.
General provisions, §§23-62 to 23-68.
Graduate marine science consortium.
Fishery resource grant program, §§28.2-245 to 28.2-247.
Insurance.
Medical center employees.
Group life, accidental death and dismemberment, and disability policies, §2.2-2817.2.
Leases by medical center, §23-77.4.
Life insurance.
Medical center employees.
Group life, accidental death and dismemberment, and disability policies, §2.2-2817.2.
Nursing scholarships, §23-36.2.
Payroll and other transactions.
Processing, §2.2-803.1.
Public procurement.
Exemptions from chapter, §2.2-4343.
Qatar branch campus, §23-91.23:1.
School of medicine and hospital.
Birth-related neurological injury compensation.
Plan for review of claims, §38.2-5008.
Grants for students, §32.1-122.6.
Retirement plans, §51.1-126.3.
Security or ownership interest in entity not traded on securities exchange.
Freedom of information act.
Excluded records, §2.2-3705.7.
Special license plates, §46.2-749.
Student financial aid.
Nursing scholarships, §23-36.2.
Universities generally, §§23-1.01 to 23-9.2:8.
See COLLEGES AND UNIVERSITIES.

UNIVERSITY OF VIRGINIA MEDICAL CENTER.
Employees.
Personnel administration system.
Exemptions, §2.2-2905.
Management generally, §§23-77.3, 23-77.4.

UNIVERSITY OF VIRGINIA'S COLLEGE AT WISE.
Tuition charges.
Kentucky and Tennessee residents.
Reduced tuition charges under certain circumstances, §23-7.4:2.

UNIVERSITY RELATED FOUNDATIONS.
Lease of property institutions of higher learning, §2.2-1155.

UNKNOWN PARTIES.
Service by publication, §8.01-316.

UNLAWFUL ASSEMBLY.
Crimes by mobs, §§18.2-38 to 18.2-46.
Riot or unlawful assembly generally, §§18.2-404 to 18.2-414.2.
See RIOT OR UNLAWFUL ASSEMBLY.

UNLAWFUL DETENTION OF CITIZENS.
Assisting armed forces in unlawful detention of United States citizens, §2.2-614.2:1.

UNLAWFUL EMPLOYMENT PRACTICES.
Local constitutional officers, §15.2-1604.

UNLAWFUL ENTRY AND DETAINER, §§8.01-124 to 8.01-130.
Appeal as to possession is appeal of entire case, §8.01-128.
Appeal from judgment of general district court, §8.01-129.
Breaking and entering to execute writ of possession, §8.01-470.
Circuit courts.
Motion for judgment, §8.01-124.
Continuances.
Establishment of final rent and damages after issuance of writ of possession, §8.01-128.
Corporations preparing summons without attorney intervention.
District court civil cases, §16.1-88.03.
Damages, §8.01-128.
Default of defendant.
Entry of judgment from statement presented by plaintiff setting forth amount due, §8.01-126.
Descent and distribution.
Family residence rights, §64.2-307.
Detinue.
General provisions, §§8.01-114 to 8.01-123.
See DETINUE.
District courts.
Appeal from judgment of general district court, §8.01-129.
Civil jurisdiction, §16.1-77.
Corporations or partnerships preparing summons without attorney intervention, §16.1-88.03.
Issuance of summons, §8.01-126.
Landlord proceeding against tenants for unlawful detainer.
Plaintiff suing on sworn claim, §16.1-88.
Evictions.
Forfeiture prevention, §55-243.
Evidence, use of photocopy or printout of original document, §8.01-126.
Failure of defendant to appear.
Entry of judgment from statement presented by plaintiff setting forth amount due, §8.01-126.
Fees for services of district court judges, clerks and magistrates, §16.1-69.48:2.
Judgments and decrees.
Action for trespass or ejectment not barred, §8.01-130.

UNLAWFUL ENTRY AND DETAINER —Cont'd
Judgments and decrees —Cont'd
Damages, §8.01-128.
Writs of possession.
Continuances to establish final rent and damages, §8.01-128.
Notice of intent to execute, §8.01-470.
Landlord and tenant.
Abuse of access, §55-248.10:1.
Plaintiff suing on sworn claim in district court, §16.1-88.
Residential landlords and tenants.
Post-termination remedies of landlord, §55-248.35.
Magistrates.
Issuance of summons, §8.01-126.
Motion for judgment, §8.01-124.
Notice.
Writs of possession.
Intent to execute, §8.01-470.
Partnerships preparing summons without attorney intervention.
District court civil cases, §16.1-88.03.
Redemption tender.
Defined, §§55-243, 55-248.34:1.
Forfeiture prevention in nonpayment of rent cases, §§55-243, 55-248.34:1.
Service of notice, process and other papers.
Substitute service mailing requirements.
Actions in district courts, §8.01-296.
Summons and process, §8.01-126.
When summons returnable to circuit court, §8.01-125.
Termination of tenancy under residential landlord and tenant act.
Initial hearing on summons issued, time for, §8.01-126.
Trial by jury, §8.01-125.
Venue.
Preferred forum, §8.01-261.
Verdict.
Damages, §8.01-128.
Writ of possession.
Continuances to establish final rent and damages, §8.01-128.
Execution, premises locked, breaking and entry, §8.01-470.
Notice.
Intent to execute, §8.01-470.
Rent payments accepted by landlord, writ not to issue, §8.01-471.
Returnable writs, §§8.01-470, 8.01-471.
Time for issuing writ, §8.01-471.

UNLICENSED DRIVING.
See DRIVING WHILE LICENSE SUSPENDED OR REVOKED.

UNLICENSED INSURERS PROCESS, §§38.2-800 to 38.2-807.

UNLICENSED NONRESIDENT BROKERS AND AGENTS PROCESS, §§38.2-808 to 38.2-811.

UNLICENSED PRACTICE OR UNLAWFUL USE OF PROFESSIONAL LICENSE, §54.1-111.
Real estate settlement agents.
Unlicensed practice, penalties, §55-525.31.
Time limitation on prosecution, §19.2-8.

UNLICENSED PUBLIC ADJUSTERS PROCESS, §§38.2-812 to 38.2-815.

UNNATURAL PERSONS.
Felonies, punishment, §18.2-10.

UNORGANIZED MILITIA, §§44-85 to 44-90.
Active duty.
Regulations.
Generally, §§44-75.1 to 44-84.
Composition, §44-4.
Discipline.
Subject to military discipline, §44-115.
Draft, §44-89.
Failure to appear, punishment for, §44-90.
Governor to designate persons in county and city to make draft, §44-89.
Incorporation into Virginia state defense force, §44-88.
Manner of ordering out for service, §44-87.
Ordering out for service, §44-86.
Manner of ordering, §44-87.
Penalties, §44-85.
Regulation, §44-85.
State defense force.
Incorporation into, §44-88.
When ordered out for service, §44-86.

UNPAID PURCHASE MONEY LIENS.
Limitation of enforcement, §8.01-241.
No maturity date given, §8.01-242.

UNPAVED SECONDARY ROAD FUND.
Allocation of highway funds, §33.1-23.1:1.

UNSAFE BUILDINGS.
City or town powers, §15.2-1115.

UNSAFE VEHICLES.
Removal from highway, §46.2-1001.

UNSATISFIED JUDGMENTS.
Driver's license, suspension, §46.2-417.

UNSOLICITED CREDIT CARDS, §§6.2-425 to 6.2-427.
Card holder liability in absence of request for, consent to issuance or use, §6.2-425.
Costs and attorneys' fees in suit, §6.2-427.
Evidence of request or consent, §6.2-427.
When request, consent or use not condition precedent, §6.2-426.

UNSOLICITED FACSIMILE TRANSMISSIONS, §8.01-40.2.
Consumer protection violations, §59.1-200.

UNSOLICITED GOODS.
Deemed gift to recipient, §11-2.2.

UNTESTED EVIDENCE.
Writ of actual innocence, §§19.2-327.2 to 19.2-327.6, VA SCt Rule 5:7B.
Nonbiological evidence, writ based on, §§19.2-327.10 to 19.2-327.14.

UPHOLSTERED FURNITURE, §§32.1-212 to 32.1-226.
See BEDDING AND UPHOLSTERED FURNITURE.

URANIUM ORE EXPLORATION, §§45.1-272 to 45.1-285.10.
Abandoned exploration holes, §45.1-276.
Affidavits.
Abandoning exploration holes, §45.1-276.
Applicability of administrative process act, §45.1-281.
Confidentiality.
Logs, surveys and reports, §45.1-285.

URANIUM ORE EXPLORATION —Cont'd
Definitions, §45.1-273.
Defined as mining, §§45.1-280, 45.1-283.
Exploration holes.
Abandonment, §45.1-275.
Developing as water wells, §45.1-278.
Plugging, §45.1-277.
Fines, §45.1-282.
Hearings.
Applicability of administrative procedure act, §45.1-281.
Injunctions.
Enjoining regulatory violations, §45.1-282.
Inspections.
Right of inspection by chief, §45.1-280.
Legislative findings, §45.1-272.
Local authority, §45.1-284.
Maps or plats.
Proposed exploration activity area, §45.1-275.
Mining permits, §§45.1-274, 45.1-283.
Permit requirements, §§45.1-274, 45.1-283.
Plugging of exploration holes, §45.1-277.
Powers of director, §45.1-279.
Proposed exploration activity area.
Maps or plats of area, §45.1-275.
Public policy, §45.1-272.
Right of inspection by chief, §45.1-280.
Rulemaking authority, §45.1-279.
State authority, §45.1-284.

URBAN AREAS.
Issues.
Report by secretary of commerce and trade, §2.2-206.
Transportation districts.
Generally, §§15.2-4500 to 15.2-4534.
See TRANSPORTATION DISTRICTS.

URBAN BUS LINES.
Motor vehicle sales and use tax exemption, §58.1-2403.
Special regulatory revenue tax, §§58.1-2660 to 58.1-2665.

URBAN COUNTY EXECUTIVE FORM OF GOVERNMENT, §§15.2-800 to 15.2-858.
Absence or disability of officer, §15.2-808.
Accounts and records of county affairs, §15.2-830.
Accounts kept for each item of appropriation, §15.2-827.
Administrative head of county.
County executive, §15.2-811.
Adoption of urban county executive form, §15.2-801.
Advisory plans examiner board.
Expedited land development review procedures, §15.2-851.
Affordable housing.
Zoning ordinances for affordable dwelling units, §15.2-2304.
Agricultural agent, §15.2-841.
Applicability of provisions, §15.2-800.
Appointment of county officers and employees, §15.2-807.
Appointment of members of certain boards, authorities and commissions, §15.2-824.
Appropriations for county treasury, §15.2-827.
Appropriations to recreational facilities, §15.2-820.
Assessment of real estate, §15.2-828.
Board of equalization of real estate assessment, §15.2-840.

URBAN COUNTY EXECUTIVE FORM OF GOVERNMENT —Cont'd
Attack dogs.
Authority to prohibit training on residential property, §3.2-6541.
Attorney for the Commonwealth.
Powers and duties, §15.2-836.
Selection, terms and vacancies, §15.2-807.
Audit of books of officer handling public fund, §15.2-844.
Audit of claims against county for goods and services, §15.2-830.
Bills for property taxes.
Electronic billing of taxpayers, §58.1-3912.
Mailing, §58.1-3912.
Website access, §58.1-3912.
Board of equalization of real estate assessment, §15.2-840.
Board of health, §15.2-839.
Board of social services, §15.2-835.
Board of supervisors.
Administrative staff, §15.2-846.
Allowances, §15.2-846.
Appointment of county executive, §15.2-804.
Appointment of county officers and employees, §15.2-807.
Budget, §15.2-847.
Compensation of officers and employees, §15.2-809.
County clerk, §15.2-838.
Elections, §15.2-802.
General powers, §15.2-803.
Increase of number of districts prior to general election.
Special election for additional supervisors, §15.2-802.
Inquiry into official conduct of office or officer, §15.2-814.
Membership, §15.2-802.
Powers of county vested in, §15.2-802.
Providing for and setting up department, §15.2-821.
Quorum, §15.2-802.
Removal of county executives, §15.2-805.
Removal of department heads or persons assigned to county executive office, §15.2-821.
Salaries and expenses, §§15.2-846, 15.2-847.
Terms, §15.2-802.
Vacancies, §15.2-802.
Vice-chairman, §15.2-802.
Zoning procedures.
Disclosures and land use proceedings, §15.2-852.
Board of zoning appeals.
Disclosures by members in land use proceedings, §15.2-852.
Bonds of officers, §15.2-850.
Budget, §15.2-847.
County executive.
Submission of proposed budget board, §15.2-811.
Buildings, storerooms and warehouses.
Powers of director of public works, §15.2-834.
Business or financial interest in land use proceedings.
Disclosures by board of supervisors, planning commissioner or board of zoning appeals, §15.2-852.
Chairman.
County chairman to be chairman, §15.2-802.
Child-care services and facilities.
Regulation generally, §15.2-914.

URBAN COUNTY EXECUTIVE FORM OF GOVERNMENT —Cont'd
City petitioning to become part of county, §15.2-818.
Claims against county, §15.2-830.
Responsibility of director of finance, §15.2-830.
Clerk of circuit court.
County clerk to act as, §15.2-838.
Commissioner of revenue.
Director of finance exercising powers, §15.2-828.
Commission on human rights, §15.2-853.
Investigations, §15.2-854.
Committee for audit and review of county agencies and county-funded functions, §15.2-825.
Compensation of officers and employees, §§15.2-809, 15.2-848.
Board to establish schedule of compensation, §15.2-845.
Conditional zoning, §15.2-2303.
Conditions of employment, establishing, §15.2-849.
Counties that may adopt urban county executive form, §15.2-801.
County attorneys.
Department of law enforcement may include, §15.2-836.
County chairman.
Chairman of board of supervisors, §15.2-802.
County clerk.
Clerk of board, §15.2-838.
Department of records, §15.2-838.
Selection, terms and vacancies, §15.2-807.
County electoral boards.
Officers not affected by adoption of plan, §15.2-813.
County executive.
Absence or disability, §15.2-806.
Acting as director or head of department, §15.2-812.
Appointment, qualifications and compensation, §15.2-804.
Bonds, §15.2-850.
Devotion of full time to work, §15.2-804.
Powers and duties, §15.2-811.
Recommendations as to appointment of county officers and employees, §15.2-807.
Removal, §15.2-805.
Right to take part in discussions and present views before board, §15.2-807.
County treasurer.
Director of finance exercising powers, §15.2-829.
Death, resignation, removal, etc., of officer.
Audit and investigation of officer's accounts, §15.2-844.
Department of assessments, §15.2-840.
Department of education, §15.2-837.
Department of farm and home demonstration, §15.2-841.
Department of finance, director.
Accounts and records, §15.2-830.
Assessment of real estate, §15.2-828.
Obligations of chief assessing officer, §15.2-833.
Assistants, §15.2-832.
Bond of director, §15.2-850.
Claims against county, §15.2-830.
Death, resignation, removal, etc., of director.
Audit and investigation of accounts, §15.2-844.
Deposit of money, §15.2-829.
Exercise of powers of commissioners of revenue, §15.2-828.

URBAN COUNTY EXECUTIVE FORM OF GOVERNMENT —Cont'd
Department of finance, director —Cont'd
Exercise of powers of county treasurer, §15.2-829.
Expenditures and accounts, §15.2-827.
General duties, §15.2-826.
Powers of commissioner of revenue, §15.2-828.
Powers of county treasurer, §15.2-829.
Purchasing agent, §15.2-831.
Department of health, §15.2-839.
Department of law enforcement, §15.2-836.
Department of public safety, §15.2-842.
Department of public utilities, §15.2-843.
Department of public works, §15.2-834.
Department of records, §15.2-838.
Department of social services, §15.2-835.
Departments and commissions generally, §15.2-823.
Deposit of county money, §15.2-829.
Depository or receiving and collection agency for county funds.
Designating bank or trust company, §15.2-829.
Designation of form of government, §15.2-800.
Designation of officer or employee to exercise power or perform duty, §15.2-822.
Development and housing authority.
Appointment of commissioner, §15.2-824.
Disbursement or payment of county money, §15.2-829.
Disclosures in land use proceedings, §15.2-852.
Discrimination.
Commission on human rights, human rights ordinance, §15.2-853.
Investigations, §15.2-854.
Drains and other public works.
Power of director of public works, §15.2-834.
Election districts.
Change in district boundaries, §15.2-856.
Judicial review, mandamus, §15.2-857.
Division of county into districts, §15.2-855.
Function, §15.2-855.
Increasing or diminishing number.
Judicial review, mandamus, §15.2-857.
Reapportionment of representation, §15.2-856.
Judicial review, mandamus, §15.2-857.
Elections.
Board of supervisors, §15.2-802.
Enumeration of departments and commissions, §15.2-823.
Expedited land development review procedures, §15.2-851.
Expenditures and accounts, §15.2-827.
Federal employment not to disqualify officer or employee, §15.2-807.
Fee system abolished, §15.2-848.
Firearms.
Semi-automatic firearms and shotguns.
Carrying loaded firearms in public areas, §18.2-287.4.
Fire protection.
Department of public safety, §15.2-842.
Former officers and employees, restrictions on activities, §15.2-810.
Garbage, trash and refuge pickup and disposal services.
Ordinances regulating, contracting for services in certain counties, §15.2-815.
General provisions as to adopting and changing forms of government, §§15.2-300 to 15.2-307.
See COUNTIES.

URBAN COUNTY EXECUTIVE FORM OF GOVERNMENT —Cont'd
Goods and services, claims against county, §15.2-830.
Health officer, §15.2-839.
Hearing on removal of county executive, §15.2-805.
Historic structures, demolition, §15.2-819.
Holidays, vacation and sick leave.
Establishing times and conditions of employment, §15.2-849.
Home demonstration agent, §15.2-841.
Human rights ordinance, §15.2-853.
Information provided prospective buyers in planned development unit, §15.2-1216.
Inquiry into official conduct of office or officer, §15.2-814.
Interest on money deposited with bank or trust company, §15.2-829.
Jails, sheriff's duties, §15.2-836.
Judges and clerks of elections.
Officers not affected by adoption of plan, §15.2-813.
Jury commissioners.
Officers not affected by adoption of plan, §15.2-813.
Land use proceeding disclosure, §15.2-852.
Lobbying by former officers and employees.
Restrictions, §15.2-810.
Magistrates.
Officers not affected by adoption of plan, §15.2-813.
Officers not affected by adoption of plan, §15.2-813.
Park authority.
Appointment of members, §15.2-824.
Parks and playgrounds.
Supervision and control by department of education, §15.2-837.
Payments to county for compensation and expense allowances for constitutional officers.
County not having certain officers, §15.2-1636.17.
Performance reviews of county agencies or county funded programs, §15.2-825.
Personnel management, §15.2-849.
Planning commission.
Appointee from each election district, §15.2-855.
Appointment of members, §15.2-824.
Disclosures by members in land use proceedings, §15.2-852.
Plans examiner board.
Expedited land development review, §15.2-851.
Police, §15.2-836.
Department of public safety, §15.2-842.
Providing for and setting up department, §15.2-821.
Public hearing on salary and allowances to supervisors, §15.2-846.
Public meeting on removal of county executive, §15.2-805.
Public utilities owned, operated and controlled by county.
Powers of department of public utilities, §15.2-843.
Purchases, §15.2-831.
Purchasing agent.
Director of finance, §15.2-831.
Real estate assessments, §15.2-828.
Board of equalization of real estate assessment, §15.2-840.

URBAN COUNTY EXECUTIVE FORM OF GOVERNMENT —Cont'd
Reapportionment of representation in governing body, §15.2-856.
Judicial review, mandamus, §15.2-857.
Reassessment of real estate, §15.2-828.
Recreational facilities.
Donations to legal entities owning, §15.2-820.
Registrars.
Officers not affected by adoption of plan, §15.2-813.
Removal of county executive, §15.2-805.
Removal of department heads or persons assigned to county executive office, §15.2-821.
Restrictions on activities of former officers and employees, §15.2-810.
Salary and allowances of employees.
Established by supervisors, §15.2-847.
Salary and allowances of supervisors, §15.2-846.
Sanitary districts, §15.2-858.
Powers of department of public utilities, §15.2-843.
Schedule of compensation, §15.2-845.
School board, §15.2-837.
Appointee from each election district, §15.2-855.
Appointment of members, §15.2-824.
Number of members, terms, tie breaker, §15.2-837.
Sewer lines.
Maintenance, §15.2-816.
Sheriff.
Compensation and expense allowances paid by compensation board to county adopting form of government, §15.2-1609.8.
Powers and duties, §15.2-836.
Selection, terms and vacancies, §15.2-807.
Special elections.
Board of supervisors.
Additional supervisors or vacancies, §15.2-802.
Subdivision and site plans and other development plans.
Expedited land development review procedures, §15.2-851.
Optional provisions of subdivision ordinance, §15.2-851.1.
Superintendent of schools, §15.2-837.
Superintendent of social services, §15.2-835.
Supplies, materials and equipment.
Purchase, transfer and sale, §15.2-831.
Suspension or removal of officers and employees, §15.2-808.
Tie breaker.
School board, §15.2-837.
Times and conditions of employment, establishing, §15.2-849.
Undersized sewer lines, §15.2-816.
Unincorporated areas not to be incorporated after adoption of form of government, §§15.2-814, 15.2-817.
Volunteer rescue squads and fire-fighting companies.
Sale of supplies, materials and equipment to at cost, §15.2-831.
Water and sewer authority.
Appointment of members, §15.2-824.
Work day and hours of employment.
Establishing times and conditions of employment, §15.2-849.

URBAN COUNTY EXECUTIVE FORM OF GOVERNMENT —Cont'd
Zoning.
Affordable dwelling unit ordinances, §15.2-2304.
Amendments to zoning ordinance.
Use of plans, profiles, elevations and other demonstrative materials, §15.2-2285.
Conditional zoning, §15.2-2303.
Disclosures and land use proceedings, §15.2-852.

URBAN COUNTY EXECUTIVES.
Generally, §§15.2-804 to 15.2-814.
See URBAN COUNTY EXECUTIVE FORM OF GOVERNMENT.

URBAN DEVELOPMENT AREAS.
Comprehensive plans by localities, §15.2-2223.1.

URBAN LEAGUE OF HAMPTON ROADS.
Motor vehicle license plates, §46.2-749.86.

URBANNA, TOWN OF.
Golf carts or utility vehicles.
Designating public highways for operation, authority, §46.2-916.2.

URBAN PUBLIC-PRIVATE PARTNERSHIP REDEVELOPMENT FUND.
Annual audit, §15.2-2416.
Creation and management, §15.2-2415.
Definitions, §15.2-2414.
Grants and loans, §15.2-2417.
Reports, §15.2-2418.

URBAN RENEWAL.
Housing revitalization zones, §§36-157 to 36-170.
See HOUSING REVITALIZATION ZONES.
Redevelopment projects, §§36-48 to 36-55.
See REDEVELOPMENT PROJECTS.

URBAN TRANSPORTATION SERVICE DISTRICTS, §15.2-2403.1.
Impact fees, §§15.2-2328, 15.2-2329.

URINARY ACCESSORIES.
Retail sales and use tax exemption, §58.1-609.10.

URINE TESTS.
Bail, use of results at hearing, §19.2-123.

USAGE OF TRADE.
Commercial code.
General provisions, §8.1A-303.
Sales, UCC.
Implied warranties, §8.2-314.

USED GOODS SALES, §§59.1-116.1 to 59.1-136.
See SECONDHAND ARTICLE SALES.

USED MOTOR OIL.
Management and recycling program, §10.1-1422.6.
Surplus state materials, disposition.
Recycling encouraged, §2.2-1124.

USED MOTOR VEHICLES.
Advertising, §18.2-221.
Motor vehicle dealers, §46.2-1581.
Prohibited acts, §46.2-1508.2.
T&M vehicle dealers, §46.2-1990.
Prohibited acts.
Display, parking, selling or advertising sale of certain used vehicles, §46.2-1508.2.

USE OF CONSTITUTIONAL PROTECTION IN CIVIL ACTION, §8.01-223.1.

USE PERMITS.
Roads, streets and public rights-of way.
Transportation and utilities, §15.2-2015.

USE TAXES.
Aircraft, §§58.1-1500 to 58.1-1510.
See AIRCRAFT SALES AND USE TAX.
Cigarette tax, localities, §§58.1-3830 to 58.1-3832.
Corporate or partnership officer, willful failure to collect and account for, §58.1-3907.
Cigarette tax, state, §§58.1-1018 to 58.1-1021.
Communications sales and use tax, §§58.1-645 to 58.1-662.
See COMMUNICATIONS SALES AND USE TAX.
Forest products tax, §§58.1-1600 to 58.1-1622.
See FOREST PRODUCTS TAX.
Interstate agreement for simplification and uniformity of taxation.
Virginia delegation to multistate tax administration discussions.
See RETAIL SALES AND USE TAX.
Local use taxes, §58.1-606.
Motor vehicles, §§58.1-2400 to 58.1-2426.
See MOTOR VEHICLE SALES AND USE TAX.
Retail sales and use tax generally, §§58.1-600 to 58.1-639.
See RETAIL SALES AND USE TAX.
Watercraft, §§58.1-1400 to 58.1-1410.
See WATERCRAFT SALES AND USE TAX.

U.S. ROUTE 58 CORRIDOR DEVELOPMENT FUND, §58.1-815.

U.S. ROUTE 58 CORRIDOR DEVELOPMENT PROGRAM, §33.1-221.1:2.

USS COLE ATTACK VICTIMS.
Motor vehicle license plates, §46.2-749.66.

USUAL AND REGULAR COURSE OF BUSINESS.
Agricultural cooperative association disposition of assets, §13.1-340.

USURPED GOVERNMENT.
Attempting or instigating others to establish, §18.2-483.

USURY, §§6.2-304 to 6.2-308.
Assignment of contract.
Assertion of defenses, §6.2-307.
Consumer finance companies.
Excess of charges permitted by law, §6.2-1523.
Maximum rate of charge, §6.2-1520.
Contracts.
Brokers-dealers.
Extensions of credit under securities and exchange act of 1934.
Exceptions to contract rate of interest, §6.2-322.
Credit unions.
Exceptions to contract rate of interest, §6.2-1302.
Corporations.
Prohibited from pleading, §6.2-308.
Credit unions.
Exceptions to contract rate of interest, §6.2-1302.
Damages.
Recovery of twice total usurious interest paid, §6.2-305.
Defenses.
Borrowers, §6.2-307.
Corporations, partnerships, real estate investment trusts and certain joint ventures.
Prohibited from pleading, §6.2-308.
Inapplicable to certain loans, §6.2-308.
Error in computation or similar mistake, §6.2-305.

USURY —Cont'd
Injunctions.
Sale of property pending action.
Preventing, §6.2-305.
Joint ventures.
Prohibited from pleading, §6.2-308.
Judgments and decrees, §6.2-304.
Lease-purchase agreements generally, §§59.1-207.17 to 59.1-207.27.
See LEASE-PURCHASE AGREEMENTS.
Limitation of actions, §6.2-305.
Limited liability companies.
Prohibited from pleading usury, §6.2-308.
Partnerships.
Prohibited from pleading, §6.2-308.
Pleading, §6.2-304.
Who may plead, §6.2-308.
Real estate investment trust.
Prohibited from pleading, §6.2-308.
Recovery of twice total usurious interest paid, §6.2-305.
Waiver of rights prohibited, §6.2-306.

UTILITIES.
Acquisition, disposition or sale of assets or securities, §§56-88 to 56-92.
Affiliated interests, regulation of relations, §§56-76 to 56-87.
See PUBLIC SERVICE COMPANIES.
Certificates of public convenience and necessity, §§56-265.1 to 56-265.9.
See PUBLIC UTILITIES.
Consent of city or town required to use public property, VA Const Art VII §8.
Consumer utility taxes, §§58.1-3814 to 58.1-3816.2.
Corporations generally, §§13.1-601 to 13.1-779.
See CORPORATIONS.
Estimated tax.
Water, heat, light, power and pipeline companies, §§58.1-2640 to 58.1-2651.
See PUBLIC SERVICE CORPORATION TAXATION.
Home energy assistance program.
See HOME ENERGY ASSISTANCE PROGRAM.
License tax by counties, cities or towns, §58.1-3731.
License tax on telegraph, telephone, water, heat, light, power and pipeline companies, §§58.1-2620 to 58.1-2635.
See PUBLIC SERVICE CORPORATION TAXATION.
Manufactured home lot rental.
Charge prohibitions, §55-248.45:1.
Public service companies.
Generally, §§56-1 to 56-46.3.
See PUBLIC SERVICE COMPANIES.
Public utilities.
Generally, §§56-232 to 56-265.
See PUBLIC UTILITIES.
Small water or sewer public utilities, §§56-265.13:1 to 56-265.13:7.
Special regulatory revenue tax, §§58.1-2660 to 58.1-2665.
State corporation commission generally, §§12.1-1 to 12.1-43.
See STATE CORPORATION COMMISSION.
State operation of public utilities, §§56-509 to 56-528.
See PUBLIC UTILITIES, STATE OPERATION.

UTILITIES —Cont'd
Taxation of public service corporations generally, §§58.1-2600 to 58.1-2690.
See PUBLIC SERVICE CORPORATION TAXATION.
Transfer of assets or securities, §§56-88 to 56-92.
Underground utility line damage prevention, §§56-265.14 to 56-265.32.
See UNDERGROUND UTILITY LINE DAMAGE PREVENTION.
Use of city or town public property, consent required, VA Const Art VII §8.

UTILITY AGGREGATION COOPERATIVES, §§56-231.38 to 56-231.52.
Actions.
Violation of rules or regulations.
Right of action, §56-231.50:2.
Adoption of provisions.
Certificate of adoption, §56-231.47.
Articles of incorporation, §56-231.41.
Attorneys' fees.
Actions for violation of rules or regulations, §56-231.50:2.
Right of action, §56-231.50:2.
Board of directors, §56-231.44.
Officers.
Election, §56-231.45.
Bylaws, §56-231.42.
Certificate of adoption.
Adoption of provisions, §56-231.47.
Citation of act, §56-231.52.
Conflict of laws, §56-231.51.
Applicability of other laws, §56-231.48.
Construction of provisions, §56-231.51.
Damages.
Violation of rules or regulations.
Right of action, §56-231.50:2.
Definitions, §56-231.38.
Formation.
Authorized, §56-231.39.
Injunctions.
Violation of rules or regulations.
Right of action, §56-231.50:2.
Members, §56-231.46.
Defined, §56-231.38.
Names, §56-231.40.
Articles of incorporation to contain, §56-231.41.
Obligations.
Defined, §56-231.38.
Powers as to, §56-231.43.
Officers, §56-231.45.
Patronage capital.
Defined, §56-231.38.
Powers, §56-231.43.
Property.
Powers as to property, §56-231.43.
Purposes, §56-231.39.
Rates and charges.
Restructuring costs, §56-231.49.
Restructuring costs, §56-231.49.
Rules and regulations.
State corporation commission, §56-231.50:1.
Violation of rules or regulations.
Right of action, §56-231.50:2.
Separation of regulated and unregulated businesses, §56-231.50:1.
Short title of act, §56-231.52.
State corporation commission.
Regulation by commission, §56-231.50.
Rules and regulations, §56-231.50:1.

UTILITY CONSUMER SERVICES COOPERATIVES, §§56-231.15 to 56-231.37.
Actions.
Violation of rules or regulations.
Right of action, §56-231.34:2.
Adequate service, §56-231.33.
Articles of incorporation, §56-231.17.
Amendment, §56-231.22.
Filing, §56-231.19.
Attorneys' fees.
Actions for violation of rules or regulations, §56-231.34:2.
Board of directors, §56-231.28.
Powers, §56-231.29.
Change of name.
Amendments to articles of incorporation, §56-231.22.
Citation of act, §56-231.37.
Classes of members, §56-231.30.
Conflict of laws, §56-231.36.
Construction of provisions, §56-231.36.
Covenants in connection with obligations, §56-231.26.
Damages.
Violation of rules or regulations.
Right of action, §56-231.34:2.
Definitions, §56-231.15.
Dissolution, §56-231.21.
Fees.
Applicable provisions, §56-231.35.
Formation authorized, §56-231.16.
Injunctions.
Violation of rules or regulations.
Right of action, §56-231.34:2.
Members.
Defined, §56-231.15.
Rights and liabilities, §56-231.30.
Service to, §56-231.32.
Adequate service, §56-231.33.
Name change.
Amendments to articles of incorporation, §56-231.22.
Names.
Articles of incorporation to contain, §56-231.17.
Change of name.
Amendment to articles of incorporation, §56-231.22.
Other corporations names not to include certain terms, §56-231.18.
Obligations.
Covenants in connection with, §56-231.26.
Defined, §56-231.15.
Power to issue, §56-231.25.
Power to purchase own obligations, §56-231.27.
Patronage capital.
Defined, §56-231.15.
Spouse or next of kin of deceased person.
Payment to, §56-231.31.
Powers, §56-231.23.
Obligations.
Issuance, §56-231.25.
Purchase of own obligations, §56-231.27.
Property, §§56-231.23, 56-231.24.
Property.
Powers as to property, §§56-231.23, 56-231.24.
Purposes, §56-231.16.
Rate, §56-231.33.
Rules and regulations, §56-231.34:1.
Violations.
Right of action, §56-231.34:2.

UTILITY CONSUMER SERVICES COOPERATIVES —Cont'd
Separation of regulated and unregulated businesses, §56-231.34:1.
Short title of act, §56-231.37.
State corporation commission.
Regulation by commission, §56-231.34.
Rules and regulations, §56-231.34:1.
Stock and stockholders.
Power to issue nonassessable nonvoting stock, §56-231.23.
Termination, §56-231.21.

UTILITY FACILITIES.
Relocation or removal of facilities within secondary highway construction projects, §33.1-69.2.

UTILITY FACILITIES ACT.
Certificates of public convenience and necessity.
Generally, §§56-265.1 to 56-265.9.
See PUBLIC UTILITIES.

UTILITY LINES.
Construction, §56-46.2.
Environmental, economic and service reliability factors, §56-46.1.
Crossing of railroads, §56-16.1.
Municipalities, §56-16.2.
Duty where wires cross other works, §56-33.
Overhead high voltage line safety, §§59.1-406 to 59.1-414.
Application of provisions, §59.1-414.
Defined terms, §59.1-407.
Enforcement of provisions, §59.1-412.
Exemption from provisions, §59.1-413.
Prohibited conduct, §59.1-408.
Scope of provisions, §59.1-406.
Temporary safety arrangements, §59.1-410.
Notice requirements, §59.1-411.
Warning signs, §59.1-409.
Permits, §56-15.
Pole use rates, §56-41.1.
Private highways.
Crossings, §56-547.
Secondhand article sales.
Company equipment, §§59.1-125 to 59.1-130.
Submerged lands.
Structures, maintenance or removal, §28.2-1209.
Underground utility line damage prevention, §§56-265.14 to 56-265.32.
See UNDERGROUND UTILITY LINE DAMAGE PREVENTION.

UTILITY METERS.
Defined terms, §56-245.2.
Good working condition requirements, §56-245.1.
Standards, §56-245.3.

UTILITY TRANSFERS ACT, §§56-88 to 56-92.

UTILITY VEHICLES.
Defined, §46.2-100.
Fort Monroe authority.
Responsibility for vehicles within area of operation, §2.2-2341.1.
Motor vehicle registration.
Exemption, §46.2-676.
Insurance coverage for exempted vehicles, §46.2-684.1.
Operation upon highways, §§46.2-676, 46.2-916.1 to 46.2-916.3.
Designation of public highways for operation, §46.2-916.2.

UTILITY VEHICLES —Cont'd
Operation upon highways —Cont'd
Possession of valid driver's license, §46.2-916.3.
Restriction operation, §46.2-916.3.
Slow-moving vehicle emblem, §46.2-916.3.
Sunrise and sunset unless equipped with lights, §§46.2-676, 46.2-916.3.

UTILIZATION REVIEW OF HEALTH CARE SERVICES.
Definitions.
Private review agents, §32.1-138.6.
Health insurance plans.
See HEALTH INSURANCE.
Independent exterior review of adverse utilization review decisions, §§38.2-5900 to 38.2-5905.
Assessment of insurers to fund appeals, §38.2-5903.
Bureau of insurance.
Review by, §38.2-5901.
Definitions applicable, §38.2-5900.
Impartial health entity.
Contracts with for purpose of performing review, §38.2-5902.
Managed care ombudsman.
Office of the managed care ombudsman, §38.2-5904.
Office of the managed care ombudsman, §38.2-5904.
Regulations, §38.2-5905.
Internal appeal process and external review, §§38.2-3556 to 38.2-3571.
See HEALTH INSURANCE.
Private review agents, §§32.1-138.6 to 32.1-138.15.
Actions.
No private right of action created, §32.1-138.14.
Certificates of registration.
Defined, §32.1-138.6.
Denial, §32.1-138.11.
Expiration, §32.1-138.10.
Issuance, §32.1-138.7.
Renewal, §32.1-138.10.
Required, §32.1-138.7.
Revocation, §32.1-138.11.
Transfer.
Not transferable, §32.1-138.7.
Confidentiality of patient-specific medical records and information, §32.1-138.13.
Definitions, §32.1-138.6.
Health regulatory boards.
Consultation with, §32.1-138.8.
Patient-specific medical records and information.
Access and confidentiality, §32.1-138.13.
Regulations, §§32.1-138.7, 32.1-138.15.
Standards for approval, §32.1-138.9.
Waiver of requirements of provisions, §32.1-138.12.

UTTERING.
Bad check law generally, §§18.2-181 to 18.2-185.
Forged coins or bank notes, §18.2-170.
Having in possession, §18.2-173.
Forged public records, §18.2-168.
Other writings, §18.2-172.

U-TURNS.
Improper U-turns, §46.2-845.
Fine schedule, VA SCt Rule 3B:2.
Maximum fine for violating Title 46.2, §46.2-113.

UVA.
Generally, §§23-62 to 23-91.23:1.
See UNIVERSITY OF VIRGINIA.

V

VACANCIES IN ELECTED OFFICE.
Attorney general, §24.2-213.
Constitutional and local offices, §§24.2-225 to 24.2-229.1.
Applicability of provisions, §24.2-225.
Elections, §24.2-226.
Filling vacancy in constitutional office, §24.2-228.1.
Interim appointment.
Court appointment of officers other than local governing body, §24.2-227.
Local governing bodies, §24.2-228.
Legitimacy of votes by appointees, §24.2-229.1.
Mayors.
Interim appointments, §24.2-228.
Time to qualify and give bond, §24.2-229.
General assembly, §24.2-216.
Writs of election issued, VA Const Art IV §7.
Governor, §24.2-211.
House of representatives, United States, §24.2-209.
Lieutenant governor, §24.2-212.
President.
Appointments during senate recess, US Const Art II §2.
Senators, United States, §24.2-207.
When term of officer elected to fill commences and expires, §24.2-201.

VACANT BUILDINGS.
City or town power to require registration, §15.2-1127.
Derelict buildings.
Authority to remove, demolish or renovate, §§15.2-906, 15.2-907.1.
Locality appointed as receiver to repair derelict and blighted buildings, §15.2-907.2.

VACANT PROPERTY.
Counties, cities or towns.
Requiring owners to cut grass, weeds or other foreign growth, §15.2-901.

VACATION LEAVE.
Accumulated vacation time.
Local constitutional officers and employees.
Computing Commonwealth's financial obligations, §15.2-1605.
County manager form of government.
Establishing times and conditions of employment, §15.2-640.
Local constitutional officers.
Employees of officer, §15.2-1605.
Urban county executive form of government.
Establishing times and conditions of employment, §15.2-849.

VACATION OF PUBLIC RIGHTS-OF-WAY, §§15.2-2006 to 15.2-2008.

VACATION OF SUBDIVISION PLATS, §15.2-2278.
After sale of lot, §15.2-2272.
Before sale of lot, §15.2-2271.
Duty of clerk when plat vacated, §15.2-2276.
Effect, §15.2-2274.

VACATION OF SUBDIVISION PLATS —Cont'd
Fee for processing application, §15.2-2273.
County manager plan of government, §15.2-743.

VACATION SCHOOLS.
Public school programs, §§22.1-211, 22.1-212.

VACATION TIME-SHARES, §§55-360 to 55-400.
Administration of chapter.
Common interest community board, §55-362.1.
Administrative process act.
Hearings in accordance with, §55-399.1.
Advertising.
Practice regulations, §55-374.1.
Application of chapter, §55-361.1.
Assessment against time-share estate.
Levy by association, authority, lien, §55-370.
Bond, letter of credit or cash.
Filing with board.
Protection of escrow deposits, §55-375.
Books and records of association, §55-370.01.
Building code applicability, §55-364.
Buyer's acknowledgment, §55-376.5.
Cancellation rights of purchasers, §55-376.
Cash deposits, §55-375.
Cease and desist orders, §55-396.
Cancellation, §55-397.
Class actions, §55-384.
Closed sessions.
Meetings of board of directors, §55-370.01.
Common interest community board.
Administration of chapter, §55-362.1.
Contracts.
Buyer's acknowledgment, §55-376.5.
Conversion time-share projects.
Defined, §55-362.
Public offering statements, §55-374.
Right of first refusal, §55-374.
Criminal penalties for violations, §55-400.
Damages sought.
Actual damages sustained.
Award limited to, §55-383.
Deeds.
Recording and delivery, §55-376.2.
Defined terms, §55-362.
Time-share estate occupancy expenses, §55-369.
Year, §55-374.2.
Deposits.
Escrow of, §55-375.
Action alleging noncompliance.
Compliance determination prior to filing, §55-382.
Developer control period, §55-369.
Electronic communications and filings.
Authorized, §55-370.01.
E-mail.
Electronic communications between board of directors and members, §55-370.01.
Exchange companies offering exchange programs, §55-374.2.
Exchange program defined, §55-362.
Fee simple interest to common elements.
Transfer to estate owners' association, §55-369.
Financial records, §55-385.
Financing, §§55-387 to 55-389.
Gift or prize included in offering, §55-374.1.
Hearing officer.
Hearings conducted by, §55-399.1.
Horizontal property regimes generally, §§55-79.1 to 55-79.38.
See HORIZONTAL PROPERTY REGIMES.

VACATION TIME-SHARES —Cont'd
Improvements promised by developer.
Obligation to complete, §55-386.
Action alleging noncompliance.
Compliance determination prior to filing, §55-382.
Inspection of books and records.
Right of member, withheld from inspection, §55-370.01.
Instruments, §55-367.
Severability, §55-365.1.
Investigations by board, §55-399.
Liens, §55-381.
Unpaid and past due assessment levied against estate, §55-370.
List of names and addresses of current members.
Association to maintain, §55-370.01.
Local ordinance applicability, §55-364.
Location of books and records.
Association to provide members with, §55-370.01.
Mails to members by association, §55-370.01.
Maintenance fee.
Collection from estate owners.
Developer control period, §55-369.
Management of estate, §55-368.
Developer control period, §55-369.
Owners' association control, §55-370.
Management of use, §55-371.
Mechanics' and materialmen's liens.
Perfection.
Subcontractors, §43-7.
Meetings of board of directors, §55-370.01.
Membership camping.
Application of provisions, §§59.1-314, 59.1-321.
Generally, §§59.1-311 to 59.1-335.
See MEMBERSHIP CAMPING.
Monetary penalty for violations, §55-400.
Nonmaterial error or omission.
Insufficient to permit cancellation of contract, §55-383.
Owners' association annual report, §55-370.1.
Owners' association control, §55-370.
Partitions, §55-372.
Permitted, §55-366.
Project activities provided by project professionals.
Injury to or death of participant.
Immunity from liability of project professional, §55-376.3.
Warning signs, §55-376.3.
Project activity defined, §55-362.
Project professional defined, §55-362.
Property owners' associations generally.
Applicability of provisions, §55-508.
Provision violations.
Penalties, §55-400.
Rights of the injured, §55-382.
Statute of limitations, §55-383.
Public offering statements, §55-374.
Amendments to reflect material changes, §§55-374, 55-398.
Board regulation, §55-398.
Statute of limitations, §55-383.
Purchases.
Buyer's acknowledgment, §55-376.5.
Real estate cooperatives.
Public offering statements.
Required information, §55-480.
Records.
Books and records of association, §55-370.01.

VACATION TIME-SHARES —Cont'd
Records —Cont'd
Keeping financial records, §55-385.
Resellers, §55-394.4.
Registration, §§55-390 to 55-394.4.
Amendment, §55-394.1.
Resellers, §55-394.3.
Revocation and reinstatement, §55-397.
Revocation by board, §55-396.
Cancellation, §55-397.
Termination, §55-394.2.
Removal of director of association from office, §55-370.01.
Resale, §55-380.
Buyer's acknowledgment, §55-376.5.
Disclosures, required, §55-380.1.
Records of resellers, §55-394.4.
Registration of resellers, §55-394.3.
Rescission of contract, §55-383.
Resellers.
Prohibited practices, §55-394.3.
Sales.
Buyer's acknowledgment, §55-376.5.
Status, §55-363.
Statute of limitations, §55-383.
Swimming, spas, sports or cultural and historical activities.
Death of or injury to participant resulting from inherent risks.
Immunity of professionals providing activities, §§55-376.3, 55-376.4.
Terminations, §55-373.
Title of chapter, §55-360.
Travel clubs.
Application of provisions, §59.1-453.
Use management, §55-371.
Use of terms, §55-364.1.
Venue of proceedings before board, §55-399.1.
Zoning applicability, §55-364.

VACCINATIONS.
Children.
Influenza vaccine, administration to minors by pharmacists or nurses, §§32.1-46.02, 54.1-3408.
Required immunizations, duty of parent or guardian, §32.1-46.
College and university students, §23-7.5.
Commissioner authority to require, §32.1-43.
Dogs.
Rabies control, §32.1-48.2.
Epidemics.
Powers of commissioners, §32.1-48.
Exclusion from school of children not immunized, §32.1-47.
Health insurance.
Preventive services, coverages required.
Federal market reforms, §38.2-3442.
HPV.
Required immunizations of children, §32.1-46.
Influenza or pneumococcal vaccinations.
Hospitals.
Administration under standing order or protocol, §32.1-126.4.
Pharmacists or nurses, administration to minors, §§32.1-46.02, 54.1-3408.
Price gouging, §§59.1-533 to 59.1-537.
Local health department immunization certificates, §32.1-46.
Public assistance.
Temporary assistance for needy families.
Required of eligible child, §63.2-603.

VACCINATIONS —Cont'd
Public health emergency involving vaccine-preventable disease, §32.1-47.1.
Public school students, §22.1-271.2.
Exclusion from school of children not immunized, §32.1-47.
State veterinarian.
Contagious and infectious diseases, livestock and poultry.
Vaccine, authority to test, §3.2-6017.
Temporary assistance for needy families.
Required of eligible child, §63.2-603.
Vaccine-related injury or death.
Action for gross negligence, §8.01-44.2.
Virginia immunization information system (VIIS), §32.1-46.01.

VACCINE-RELATED INJURY OR DEATH.
Tort action for gross negligence, §8.01-44.2.

VA DLR.
Motor vehicle dealers.
Denoting of abbreviation in advertising, §46.2-1535.

VALENTINE MUSEUM AT RICHMOND.
Schools and education.
Appropriations for providing exhibits to the public schools, §10.1-2212.

VALIDATING STATUTES.
Effect of repeal by provisions of 1950 code, §1-6.

VALIDATION OF MARRIAGE.
Affirmation of marriage generally.
See AFFIRMATION OF MARRIAGE.
Carrying certain defects on belief of parties in lawful marriage, §20-31.
Licenses issued by clerk of county court, §20-37.
Remedial marriage statute, §20-118.

VALUATION OF DECEDENT'S PROPERTY.
Time property valued, §64.2-305.

VALUATION OF INSURERS ASSETS, §§38.2-1306.2, 38.2-1306.3.

VALUE ENGINEERING.
Capital projects by Commonwealth, §2.2-1133.
Localities using for capital projects, §15.2-2239.

VANDALISM, §§18.2-137 to 18.2-152.
Church property, cemeteries, burial grounds, etc., §18.2-127.
Civil action to recover damages, §8.01-44.6.
Entering property of another for purposes of damaging, §18.2-121.
Ethnic motivated vandalism.
Tort liability, §8.01-42.1.
Fences or gates.
Pulling down fences or leaving open gates, §18.2-143.
Hate crimes.
Entering property for purposes of damaging, §18.2-121.
Tort liability for injury to person or property, §8.01-42.1.
Localities.
Willful and malicious damage to or defacement of public or private facilities.
Authority to enact ordinance making unlawful, §15.2-1812.2.
Clean-up, beautification, landscaping.
Community service may include, §15.2-1812.2.

VANDALISM —Cont'd
Localities —Cont'd
Willful and malicious damage to or defacement of public or private facilities —Cont'd
Criminal penalty, mandatory minimum fine, §15.2-1812.2.
Deferring proceedings, placing defendant on probation, community service, §15.2-1812.2.
Locality cleaning or covering defacement at owner's expense, §15.2-1812.2.
Restitution, required for probation or suspension of sentence, §15.2-1812.2.
Private property, §18.2-137.
Authority of locality to remove or repair defacement, §15.2-908.
Public buildings, §18.2-138.
Religious motivated vandalism.
Tort liability, §8.01-42.1.
Schools and education.
Model policies for codes of student conduct, §22.1-279.6.
Trees or shrubs, §18.2-140.
Vehicles, aircraft or boats.
Breaking or preventing operation, §18.2-146.

VANITY LICENSE PLATES, §§46.2-711 to 46.2-749.130.
See MOTOR VEHICLE LICENSE PLATES.

VANPOOLING, §§46.2-1400 to 46.2-1407.
Inapplicability of laws.
Motor carriers, §46.2-1401.
Overtime compensation and minimum wage, §46.2-1406.
Workers' compensation, §46.2-1402.
Liability insurance coverage, §38.2-2217.1.
Liability of employer, §§46.2-1402, 46.2-1403.
Municipal licenses and taxes, §46.2-1405.
Payment, §46.2-1404.
Reduced transit fares, §46.2-1404.
Ridesharing arrangement, defined, §46.2-1400.
Special license plates, §46.2-749.10.
Vehicles deemed not commercial vehicles or buses, §46.2-1407.

VARIABLE ANNUITIES.
Authority to issue, §38.2-3113.
Defined, §38.2-107.
Group variable annuities.
Certificates issued pursuant to, §38.2-3114.
Investments of insurers allocated to separate accounts, §38.2-1443.
Separate accounts established by insurers, §38.2-3113.
Special rights and procedures for owners, §38.2-3113.
Statements required in contracts, §38.2-3114.

VARIABLE LIFE INSURANCE.
Authority to issue, §38.2-3113.
Defined, §38.2-105.
Group variable life insurance.
Certificates issued pursuant to, §38.2-3114.
Investments of insurers allocated to separate accounts, §38.2-1443.
Special accounts established by insurers, §38.2-3113.
Special voting rights and procedures for owners, §38.2-3113.
Statements required in contracts, §38.2-3114.

VARIANCE BETWEEN EVIDENCE AND ALLEGATIONS, §8.01-377.

VARIANCES.
Emergency medical services.
Applications for variances, §32.1-111.9.
Zoning.
Applications for, §15.2-2310.
Defined, §15.2-2201.
Permitted provisions in ordinances, §15.2-2286.
Powers and duties of board of zoning appeal, §15.2-2309.

VARICELLA VACCINE.
Required immunizations of children, §32.1-46.

VASAP.
Boating and related activities.
Under the influence, §29.1-738.5.
Commission, §18.2-271.2.
Driver improvement programs, §§46.2-489 to 46.2-506.
See DRIVER IMPROVEMENT PROGRAMS.
Driving while intoxicated.
Education and rehabilitation of persons charged or convicted, §18.2-271.1.
Driving while privilege suspended or revoked.
Second conviction, intervention, VASAP compliance, §46.2-355.1.
Ignition interlock system.
Certification by commission on VASAP, §18.2-270.2.
Supervision by VASAP required, §18.2-270.1.
Oath of office of case managers and employees, §18.2-271.4.
Restoration of license to person found habitual offender.
Evaluation prior to restoration, §46.2-360.

VASECTOMIES.
Sterilization.
Doctor's liability for performing, §54.1-2979.
Informed consent, §§54.1-2974 to 54.1-2976.

VCU, §§23-50.4 to 23-50.16.
See VIRGINIA COMMONWEALTH UNIVERSITY.

VEGETABLES.
Agricultural and forestal districts, §§15.2-4300 to 15.2-4407.
Crops.
See CROPS.
Purchases through division of purchases and supply.
Provisions not mandatory, §2.2-1119.

VEHICLE IDENTIFICATION NUMBERS (VIN).
Abandoned motor vehicles.
Altered, missing or tampered with, procedure, §46.2-1206.
Removal or alteration, §§46.2-1074, 46.2-1075.
Salvage vehicles.
Alteration, removal, or missing, duties of licensees, §46.2-1603.1.

VEHICLE SAFETY INSPECTIONS.
Law enforcement officers certified to perform.
Removal of unsafe vehicles from highway, §46.2-1001.

VEHICLES FOR HIRE.
Permits for using streets, highways, roads, etc.
City or town providing for issuance, §15.2-2015.

VENDING MACHINES.
Airtrip insurance, sales by, §38.2-1807.
Connecting or returning planes coverage, §38.2-3515.

VENDING MACHINES —Cont'd
County tax on food and beverages.
Tax not levied on food and beverages sold through, §58.1-3833.
Litter tax.
Persons selling goods, wares, merchandise through.
Generally, §§58.1-1707 to 58.1-1710.
Levy, §58.1-1707.
Retail sales and use tax.
Tax collectible from dealers, §58.1-614.
Slugs manufactured, sold, etc., for unlawful uses, §18.2-180.
Stealing from or tampering with, §18.2-152.
Tobacco product sales, §18.2-371.2.
Fire-safe cigarettes, §§59.1-293.1 to 59.1-293.9.
See FIRE-SAFE CIGARETTES.
Unlawful operation, §18.2-179.

VENDING STANDS.
Blind and visually impaired.
Compliance with provisions, §51.5-93.
Suspension for noncompliance, §51.5-94.
Contracts for equipment and merchandise, §51.5-80.
Contracts to furnish services, §51.5-81.
Duties of department generally, §51.5-86.
Funds set aside for equipment and services, §51.5-97.
Installation and supervision on federal property, §51.5-82.
Licensure of adult blind residents as operators, §51.5-84.
Ownership of stands and equipment, §51.5-91.
Performance of duties by department staff, §51.5-96.
Provision of stand and merchandise, §51.5-90.
Regulations for administration of article, §51.5-95.
Reporting requirements, §51.5-92.
Rest areas on interstate highways, §51.5-100.
Revocation of privilege to operate, §51.5-87.
Selection of location and operator, §51.5-85.
Approval of custodian, §51.5-88.
Capitol, stand near, §51.5-89.
Placement of persons in department vacancies, §51.5-89.
Surveys of business opportunities, §51.5-83.
Tax exemptions, §51.5-98.
Business enterprises for the blind.
Generally.
See BLIND AND VISUALLY IMPAIRED.

VENDITIONI EXPONAS, WRIT OF.
Collection of money payable to state, §§8.01-211 to 8.01-213.
Contents, §8.01-211.
Delivery of goods and chattels levied to sheriff, §8.01-212.
Issuance to sheriff of adjacent county, §8.01-211.
Sale of goods and chattels levied, §8.01-213.
Death of officer taking property before sale, §8.01-486.
Issuance and proceedings thereon, §8.01-485.
Landlord distress actions, §55-237.
Landlord distress actions, §55-237.

VENDORS.
Comptroller.
Vendor accounting information, standard, §2.2-1115.1.
Deeds.
Notation of lien, §55-48.

VENDORS —Cont'd
Door-to-door.
Ordinances regulating, §15.2-913.
Electronic voting systems.
Recommended security practices, §24.2-629.
Information technologies agency.
Vendor accounting information, standard, §2.2-1115.1.
Liens.
Equitable liens, §55-53.
Mortgages and deeds of trust.
Generally, §§6.2-406 to 6.2-423, 55-58 to 55-66.6.
See MORTGAGES AND DEEDS OF TRUST.
Manufactured home lot rental.
Restrictions on choice of vendors, §55-248.45.
Purchases and supply division.
Vendor accounting information, standard, §2.2-1115.1.

VENDOR'S LIENS.
Double indexing by circuit court clerk.
Deed of conveyance of real estate with vendor's lien reserved, §17.1-249.
Protection of assignee or transferee of debts secured by real estate, §55-66.01.
Release, §55-66.3.

VENEER LOG SUPPLIERS.
Intangible personal property tax.
Generally, §§58.1-1100 to 58.1-1118.
See PERSONAL PROPERTY TAXES.
Suppliers subject to tax, §58.1-1105.

VENEREAL DISEASES, §§32.1-55 to 32.1-60.
AIDS generally.
See AIDS AND HIV.
Defined terms, §32.1-55.
Educational information distribution, §32.1-56.
Local health department immunizations, §32.1-57.
Minor deemed adult for purposes of consent.
Determining presence of disease or treating, §54.1-2969.
Reports, §32.1-36.
Testing and treatment, §32.1-57.
Persons convicted of certain crimes, §32.1-58.
Persons in certain state institutions, §32.1-59.
Prenatal testing, §32.1-60.
Failure to comply, §32.1-73.

VENIRE FACIAS.
Summoning grand jury, §19.2-194.
Irregularities not to violate indictment or finding, §19.2-203.

VENTILATION.
City or town powers as to buildings, §15.2-1117.
Coal mines.
Underground coal mines, §§45.1-161.208 to 45.1-161.235.
See COAL MINE SAFETY.
New, privately owned residential dwellings.
Promulgation of regulations for HVAC facilities, §36-99.6:3.

VENUE.
Administrative process act, §2.2-4003.
Court review, §2.2-4026.
Adoption.
Filing petition, §63.2-1201.
Inapplicability of chapter, §8.01-259.
Annexation.
City or town filing petition with circuit court, §15.2-3202.

VENUE —Cont'd
Antitrust actions, §59.1-9.9.
Investigations by attorney general, §59.1-9.10.
Applicability of chapter, §8.01-259.
Appraisal rights, corporations.
Fair value determinations, §13.1-740.
Arbitration, §8.01-581.015.
Construction contracts, §8.01-262.1.
Attachment, §§8.01-261, 8.01-537.
Attorneys' fees.
Transfer of venue, §8.01-266.
Automatic vehicle identification systems.
Toll roads and toll bridges, §§46.2-819.1, 46.2-819.3.
Autopsies, §32.1-285.
Benevolent associations.
Trustee holding personal property, §57-21.
Bigamy violation, §18.2-362.
Big Sandy river.
Obstructing or dumping refuse into, §62.1-194.3.
Biotechnology research act, §2.2-5507.
Birth certificates.
Delayed birth certificate registration, §32.1-260.
Boundaries.
Clearing watercourses between counties of obstructions, §62.1-6.
Criminal offenses committed on boundary of two counties, or county and city, etc., §19.2-249.
Bulkheads, §§62.1-164, 62.1-165.
Category A venue.
Forums enumerated, §8.01-261.
Category B venue.
Forums enumerated, §8.01-262.
Cemeteries.
Disposition of property for maintenance and care.
Trusteeship for administering funds, §57-35.
Eminent domain, §57-25.
Improvement of abandoned and neglected cemeteries, §57-39.1.
Proceedings for removal of remains and sale of land vacated, §57-39.
Removal of remains from abandoned family graveyard, §§57-38.1, 57-38.2.
Trustees.
Administration of care and maintenance funds, §57-35.
Appointment, §§57-23, 57-24.1.
Removal, §57-23.
Change of name, §8.01-217.
Change of venue.
By court, §8.01-265.
Conservatorship of estate of incapacitated persons, §64.2-2001.
Criminal cases, §§19.2-251 to 19.2-253.
Discretion of judge, §8.01-267.
General assembly power to provide, VA Const Art IV §14.
Guardianship of incapacitated persons, §64.2-2001.
Check cashing or acceptance.
Credit card number required as condition.
Violation actions, §6.2-428.
Child custody.
Juvenile and domestic relations district court proceedings, §16.1-243.
Child pornography.
Possession, reproduction, distribution, and facilitation of child pornography, §18.2-374.1:1.
Production, publication, etc., with intent to distribute, financing, etc., §18.2-374.1.

VENUE —Cont'd
Child support.
Juvenile and domestic relations district court proceedings, §16.1-243.
Child visitation.
Juvenile and domestic relations district court proceedings, §16.1-243.
Church property.
Abandoned property actions, §57-11.
Appointment of trustees to effectuate purposes of conveyances, §57-8.
Determination of rights on division of church, §57-9.
Land held in adverse possession, §57-17.
Suits by members to have land sold or mortgaged, §§57-14, 57-15.
Suits by trustees to have land sold or mortgaged, §57-15.
Cigarette sales or stamping.
Prosecution of offenses involving reports or statements concerning, §19.2-245.01.
Civil commitment of mentally ill persons.
Appeal of involuntary admission, mandatory outpatient treatment or certification order.
Transfer of case on finding of inconvenient forum, §37.2-821.
Coal.
Port authority.
Expediting shipments, §62.1-134.1.
Coal property seizures by Commonwealth.
Condemnation proceedings, §45.1-161.320.
Restoration of property to owner or operator, §45.1-161.322.
Coastal primary sand dunes and beaches.
Fines, §28.2-1420.
Injunctions, §28.2-1419.
Collection of state taxes.
Agencies other than tax department, §58.1-2022.
Filing of memorandum of lien, §58.1-1805.
State corporation commission assessments, §58.1-2021.
Proceedings for, §58.1-1806.
Communicable diseases of public health significance.
Isolation of persons, §§32.1-48.03, 32.1-48.04.
Compensation board decision appeals, §15.2-1636.9.
Concept not jurisdictional, §8.01-258.
Condominiums.
Real estate board.
Investigations of complaints, §§55-79.98, 55-79.99.
Conflicts of interest.
General assembly members.
Prosecutions for violations, §30-129.
Public officers and employees, §2.2-3127.
Conservators of property of absentees.
Appointment, §64.2-2400.
Constitution of the United States, US Const Art III §2.
Construction contracts.
Bringing action under, §8.01-262.1.
Consumer protection.
Investigative orders, §59.1-201.
Cooperative nonprofit life benefit companies, suits against company, §38.2-3813.
Corporations.
Annual registration fees.
Collection of unpaid bills, §13.1-775.2.
Appraisal rights.
Fair value determinations, §13.1-740.

VENUE —Cont'd
Corporations —Cont'd
Dissolution, §13.1-747.
Elections and other matters.
Judicial review, §13.1-669.1.
Records.
Court-ordered inspection by shareholders, §13.1-773.
Registration fees.
Collection of unpaid bills, §13.1-775.2.
Correction of erroneous state tax assessments.
Application to circuit court for correction, §58.1-1825.
Costs on transfer or retention, §8.01-266.
Criminal cases, §§19.2-244 to 19.2-253.
Accessories before or after fact, where indicted or tried, §18.2-21.
Bigamy, §18.2-262.
Bomb threat prosecutions, §18.2-83.
Capital cases for multiple murders, §19.2-247.
Change of venue, §19.2-251.
Admittance of accused to bail and recognizance, §19.2-252.
Motion for change of venue, §19.2-244.
Procedure upon and after change of venue, §19.2-253.
When and how venue may be changed, §19.2-251.
Cigarette sales or stamping.
Offenses involving reports or statements concerning, §19.2-245.01.
Computer crime prosecutions.
County or city violation considered to have been committed in, §19.2-249.2.
Conflicts of interest.
General assembly, §30-129.
Conspiracy to commit felony, §18.2-22.
Conspiracy to trespass after having been forbidden to do so, §18.2-23.
County or city in which offense committed, §19.2-244.
Credit card offense prosecutions, §18.2-198.1.
Crimes against nature.
Person transported through or across Commonwealth, §18.2-359.
Driving while intoxicated.
Trial of warrant summons, §18.2-268.4.
Embezzlement or larceny committed within Commonwealth, §19.2-245.
False pretense.
Obtaining money, gift certificate or other property by, §18.2-178.
False statements to obtain money or credit, §18.2-186.
Forgery, §19.2-245.1.
Fraudulent conversion of leased personal property, §18.2-118.
Fraudulent conversion of property subject to lien or title in another, §18.2-115.
Homicide committed but venue of offense unknown, §19.2-247.
Homicide, death occurring without Commonwealth, §18.2-37.
Identity theft.
Locality committed in, §18.2-186.3.
Indecent liberties with children.
Person transported through or across Commonwealth, §18.2-359.
Injury inflicted by person within Commonwealth upon one outside Commonwealth, §19.2-246.
Jurisdiction of corporate authorities, §19.2-250.

VENUE —Cont'd
Criminal cases —Cont'd
Larceny.
Conspiracy to commit, §18.2-23.
Lynching, jurisdiction of actions and prosecutions, §18.2-46.
Mobs, crimes by.
Jurisdiction of actions and prosecutions, §18.2-46.
Mortal wound, etc., inflicted in one county and death ensues in another, §19.2-248.
Objection to venue, VA SCt Rule 1:2.
Offenses committed on boundary of two counties, or city and county, etc., §19.2-249.
Offenses committed within town situated in two or more counties, §19.2-249.1.
Offenses committed without and made punishable within Commonwealth, §19.2-245.
Prostitution.
Person transported through or across Commonwealth, §18.2-359.
Public assistance fraud prosecutions, §63.2-522.
Unauthorized uses of food stamps, electronic transfer cards and energy assistance, §63.2-523.
Question raised before verdict or finding of guilt, §19.2-244.
Racketeering offenses, §18.2-517.
Remand of accused not admitted to bail, §19.2-252.
Removal of state criminal cases to federal courts.
State prosecution, §19.2-9.
Sex offender registration.
Failure to register, providing false registration information, §18.2-472.1.
Sexual assault.
Person transported through or across Commonwealth, §18.2-359.
Person under 18 years of age, §18.2-359.
State lottery offenses.
Larceny of ticket, fraudulent notification of prizes, §58.1-4018.1.
Tax offenses, §19.2-245.2.
Telephone offenses, §18.2-430.
Fraudulent sale or receipt of telephone records, §18.2-152.17.
Threats of death of bodily injury to person or family member, §18.2-60.
Unlawful sexual intercourse.
Person transported through or across Commonwealth, §18.2-359.
Violent felonies.
Person transported through or across Commonwealth, §18.2-359.
When questions raised, VA SCt Rule 3A:2.1.
Damage stamp program.
Claim filing and adjudication, §29.1-356.
Dams.
Applications for leave to build or rebuild, §62.1-116.
Hydroelectric power, §62.1-97.
Orders for construction or destruction, §29.1-532.
Declaratory judgments, §8.01-185.
Delinquent tax lands sales, §58.1-3967.
Delivery of goods.
Permissible venue, §8.01-262.
Desertion and nonsupport.
Effect of divorce proceedings, §20-79.
Venue of offense, §20-83.
Directors of nonprofit corporations, judicial review of elections, §13.1-861.

VENUE —Cont'd
Disease prevention and control.
Public safety employee testing, §32.1-45.2.
Dissolution.
Corporations, §13.1-747.
Judicial dissolution, §13.1-747.
Nonprofit corporations, §13.1-909.
District courts.
Civil cases, §16.1-76, VA SCt Rule 7B:11.
Criminal and traffic cases, VA SCt Rule 7C:2.
Motion to transfer, VA SCt Rule 7B:11.
Docks, §§62.1-164, 62.1-165.
Driving while intoxicated.
Trial of warrant summons, §18.2-268.4.
Election contests.
Electors for president or vice-president or primaries for United States senate or state office, §24.2-805.
Other primaries and elections, §24.2-806.
Recounts.
Filing petitions, §24.2-801.
Election law offenses.
Filing of complaints and allegations concerning, §24.2-1019.
Embezzlement, §19.2-245.
Emergency protective orders, §19.2-152.11.
Escheats.
Duty failures by escheators, §§55-189, 55-190.
Exhumations, §32.1-286.
Expungement of police and court records, §19.2-392.2.
Farm produce sales.
Commission merchants.
Civil suits and criminal prosecutions, §3.2-4735.
Fidelity and surety insurers, civil proceedings against, §38.2-2415.
Fiduciaries.
Conservators of property of absentees.
Appointment, §64.2-2400.
Property transfers to foreign fiduciaries, §64.2-1427.
Resignation, §64.2-1424.
Financial exploitation of mentally incapacitated persons, §18.2-178.1.
Firefighters.
Volunteer firefighters.
Disputed questions of fact, §27-48.
Fire insurance, court appointment of umpire, §38.2-2121.
Fire investigations.
Issuance of warrants, §27-32.2.
Restitution for property seizure, §27-34.1.
Fire marshals, local.
Entry to investigate releases of hazardous or regulated substances, §27-37.1.
Fishing, tidal waters.
Provision violations, §28.2-907.
Fishways.
Orders for construction or destruction, §29.1-532.
Forfeitures.
Criminal forfeitures, §19.2-386.1.
Surety bonds, §32.1-174.1.
Forgery, §19.2-245.1.
Forum convenient to parties and witnesses, §8.01-257.
Forum non conveniens.
Child custody proceeding.
Uniform child custody jurisdiction and enforcement act, §20-146.18.
District courts, VA SCt Rule 7B:11.

VENUE —Cont'd
Forum non conveniens —Cont'd
Juvenile and domestic relations district courts, VA SCt Rule 8:10.
Freedom of information act.
Enforcement, §2.2-3713.
Open meetings.
Denial of rights or privileges, §2.2-3712.
Gas and oil exploration.
Appeal of agency order or decision, §45.1-361.9.
General rule, §8.01-257.
Guardians.
Appointment, §64.2-1702.
Habeas corpus.
Inapplicability of chapter, §8.01-259.
Health care professional referrals.
Failure to disclose interest in referral facilities, §54.1-2964.
Health code violations, §§32.1-27, 32.1-27.1.
Heavy equipment dealers.
Provision violations, §59.1-358.
High-occupancy toll lanes.
Prosecution of offenses, §33.1-56.3.
Home care organizations.
Injunctions to cease providing services, §32.1-162.13.
Homicide.
Crime committed but venue of offense unknown, §19.2-247.
Death occurring outside the Commonwealth, §18.2-37.
Hospitals.
Clinical privileges for podiatrists or midwives, §32.1-134.4.
Financial interest in out-patient service providers.
Disclosure violations, §32.1-125.2.
Staff membership or privileges.
Physician denial, expulsion or curtailment, §32.1-134.1.
Hydroelectric power dams, §62.1-97.
Identity theft.
Locality committed in, §18.2-186.3.
Impoundment of surface waters.
Riparian owner rights.
Application for leave to store floodwaters, §62.1-107.
Improper message transmission.
Permissible venue, §8.01-262.
Improper venue, §8.01-264.
Collateral attack.
Solely on ground of improper venue, §8.01-258.
Motion challenging venue, §8.01-276.
Income tax return preparer, action to enjoin, §58.1-348.2.
Income tax setoff debt collection.
Appeals from hearings, §58.1-527.
Indictments, presentments or informations.
Effect of defects in indictments, §19.2-226.
Industrial hygiene and safety profession.
Protection of use of job titles.
Enforcement, §40.1-141.
Injunctions, §8.01-627.
Inmate litigation, §8.01-693.
Inspection of records by nonprofit corporation members.
Court-ordered inspections, §13.1-935.
Inspection of records by shareholders.
Court-ordered inspection, §13.1-773.
Insurance companies.
Rehabilitation and liquidation, §38.2-1502.
Application for receiver by state corporation commission, §38.2-1505.

VENUE —Cont'd
Insurance companies —Cont'd
Rehabilitation and liquidation —Cont'd
Injunction proceedings, §38.2-1507.
Interstate family support.
Inappropriate tribunal, §20-88.49.
Jail facilities, substandard.
Prisoner confinement limitations and transfers, §§53.1-69, 53.1-70.
Juvenile and domestic relations district courts.
Motion to transfer venue, VA SCt Rule 8:10.
Original venue, §16.1-243.
Transfer of venue, §16.1-243.
Juvenile proceedings, §16.1-243.
Keeper liens.
Enforcement, §43-34.
Landings, §§62.1-164, 62.1-165.
Landlord and tenant.
Retaliatory actions, §55-248.40.
Larceny, §19.2-245.
Conspiracy to commit, §18.2-23.
Letters of credit, §8.5A-116.
Local taxes, proceedings for collection, §58.1-3953.
Local treasurer securing final discharge from liability, §58.1-3145.
Lost shareholders.
Proceeding for determination, §13.1-777.
Lynching, §18.2-46.
Mechanics' and materialmen's liens.
Enforcement, §43-22.
Perfection.
Hearings on validity, §43-17.1.
Medicaid benefits.
Fraudulently obtaining, §§32.1-312, 32.1-321.3, 32.1-321.4.
Investigations, §32.1-320.
Medical assistance services director.
Subpoena applications, §32.1-324.1.
Medical care facilities.
Certificates of public need.
Enjoining projects, §32.1-102.8.
Meetings.
Court-ordered meetings of members of nonprofit corporations, §13.1-840.
Membership camping.
Investigations, §59.1-334.
Memorandum of lien.
Collection of state taxes, §58.1-1805.
Collection of taxes assessed by state corporation commission, §58.1-2021.
Midwives.
Hospital privileges, §32.1-134.4.
Mills.
Applications for leave to build or rebuild, §62.1-116.
Mine closure orders.
Review of decisions, §45.1-161.91.
Misdelivery of message.
Permissible venue, §8.01-262.
Mob violence.
Jurisdiction of actions and prosecutions, §18.2-46.
Mortal wound, etc.
Inflicted in one county and death ensues in another, §19.2-248.
Injury inflicted by person within Commonwealth upon one outside Commonwealth, §19.2-246.
Motion challenging venue.
Extension of time, §8.01-264, VA SCt Rule 1:9.

VENUE —Cont'd
Motor vehicle sales and use tax appeals, §58.1-2426.
Multiple murders, §19.2-247.
Multiple parties, §8.01-263.
Nonprofit corporations.
Court-ordered inspection, §13.1-935.
Inspection of members' list, §13.1-845.
Court-ordered meetings, §13.1-840.
Directors.
Judicial review of elections, §13.1-861.
Dissolution, §13.1-909.
Meetings.
Court-ordered, §13.1-840.
Records.
Court-ordered inspection for members, §13.1-935.
Nonresident defendants.
Permissible venue, §8.01-262.
Nursing homes.
Provision violations.
Penalties, §32.1-27.1.
Objections.
Award of court costs to inconvenient party, §8.01-266.
Venue improperly laid, §8.01-264.
Open meetings.
Freedom of information act.
Denial of rights or privileges, §2.2-3712.
Overhead high voltage line safety.
Enforcement of provisions, §59.1-412.
Oysters and clams.
Improvement of navigability of streams.
Claims for damages to oyster and clamming grounds, §62.1-158.
Pari-mutuel wagering on horses.
Racing commission.
Appeals of decisions, §59.1-373.
Pay-per-call services.
Orders to compel, §59.1-433.
Permissible venue, §§8.01-260, 8.01-262.
Forums enumerated, §8.01-262.
Personal information privacy.
Provision violations, §59.1-444.
Personal representative, petition for appointment.
For public assistance recipients, §63.2-507.
Petition to ascertain delinquent real estate tax, §58.1-3959.
Petroleum products franchises.
Provision violation actions, §59.1-21.12.
Physicians.
Hospital staff membership or privileges.
Denial, curtailment or expulsion, §32.1-134.1.
Piers, §§62.1-164, 62.1-165.
Podiatrists.
Hospital privileges, §32.1-134.4.
Port authority.
Coal.
Expediting shipments, §62.1-134.1.
Port of Reedville.
Appointment of agent, §62.1-163.
Power of attorney.
Petition to court for construction of power, §64.2-1614.
Preferred venue, §§8.01-260, 8.01-261.
Forums enumerated, §8.01-261.
Prisoner litigation, §8.01-693.
Professions and occupations licensure.
Enforcement of provisions, §54.1-111.

VENUE —Cont'd
Property owners' associations.
Compliance by lot owners with provisions.
Arbitration or alternative dispute resolutions, §55-515.
Proper venue, §8.01-260.
Protective orders, §19.2-152.11.
Public assistance fraud prosecutions, §63.2-522.
Unauthorized uses of food stamps, electronic transfer cards and energy assistance, §63.2-523.
Public assistance recipients.
Personal representative, petition for appointment, §63.2-507.
Public officers and employees.
Conflicts of interest, §2.2-3127.
Public service companies.
Wagonway construction, §56-16.
Public service corporation tax assessments.
Applications to circuit courts for review, §58.1-2670.1.
Public utilities, state operation.
Compensation to utilities, §56-522.
Injunctions against violation of provisions, §56-525.
Restoration of possession to utility, §56-521.
Quo warranto.
Duty failures by water and sewerage companies, §56-264.
Racing commission.
Pari-mutuel wagering on horses.
Appeals of decisions, §59.1-373.
Railroad corporations.
Cattle guards.
Appeals of decisions, §56-435.
Enclosed lands, §56-433.
Real estate cooperatives.
Site of alternative dispute resolutions or arbitrations, §55-492.
Real property tax apportionment of city taxes.
Apportionment when part of real estate becomes separately owned, §58.1-3224.
Real property tax proration of delinquent tax petitions.
Purchase of part of tract, §58.1-3227.
Reciprocal insurers, suits against, §38.2-1217.
Records.
Court-ordered inspection by shareholders, §13.1-773.
Court-ordered inspections.
Nonprofit corporation members, §13.1-935.
Stock corporation shareholders, §13.1-773.
Recounts in elections.
Filing of petition, §24.2-801.
Reedville port.
Appointment of agent, §62.1-163.
Referendum election petitions.
Request for abolition of constitutional offices, §24.2-685.
Registration fees.
Collection of stock corporation unpaid bills, §13.1-775.2.
Domestic and foreign corporations.
Collection of unpaid bills, §13.1-775.2.
Release of liens, §43-68.
Religious organizations.
Abandoned property actions, §57-11.
Appointment of trustees to effectuate purposes of conveyances, §57-8.
Determination of property rights on division of church or society, §57-9.

VENUE —Cont'd
Religious organizations —Cont'd
Land held in adverse possession, §57-17.
Suits by members to have land sold or mortgaged, §§57-14, 57-15.
Richmond circuit court.
Antitrust actions.
Investigations by attorney general, §59.1-9.10.
Condominiums.
Investigations by board of complaints.
Orders to compel, §55-79.99.
Dams for hydraulic power.
Provision violation, §62.1-97.
Escheats.
Duty failures by escheators, §§55-189, 55-190.
Health spa investigations, §59.1-308.2.
Hydroelectric power dam violations, §62.1-97.
Insurance companies, rehabilitation and liquidation.
Application for receiver by state corporation commission, §38.2-1505.
Filing of delinquency proceedings, §38.2-1502.
Insurers deposits with state treasurer.
Bill to enforce policyholder or general creditors lien, §38.2-1046.
Jurisdiction over offenses committed over Capitol Square, §18.2-124.
Medical assistance services director.
Subpoena application, §32.1-324.1.
Membership camping investigation, §59.1-334.
Motor vehicle sales and use tax appeal, §58.1-2426.
Pari-mutuel wagering on horses.
Appeals of racing commission decision, §59.1-373.
Pay-per-call services.
Orders to compel, §59.1-433.
Public service corporation tax assessment review, §58.1-2670.1.
Public utilities, state operation.
Injunctions against violation of provisions, §56-525.
Real estate board investigations of complaints.
Orders to compel, §55-79.99.
Release of lien, §43-68.
Service contracts, extended.
Orders to compel, §59.1-439.
Solicitation of charitable or civic contributions.
Obstruction of investigation, §57-59.
Unemployment compensation.
Employer taxation, §§60.2-500, 60.2-522.
Vital records.
Amendment petition, §32.1-269.
Disclosure petition, §32.1-271.
Wills.
Probate jurisdiction, §64.2-443.
Sale of delinquent tax lands, §58.1-3967.
Sales of purchaser information.
Provision violations, §59.1-444.
Service contracts, extended.
Orders to compel, §59.1-439.
Setoff debt collection, income tax.
Appeals from hearings, §58.1-527.
Sewerage companies.
Failure to perform duties.
Quo warranto, §56-264.
Sexual sterilization, §§54.1-2975 to 54.1-2977.
Shareholder determination proceedings, §13.1-777.
Shareholder meetings, court-ordered, §13.1-656.

VENUE —Cont'd
Solicitation of charitable or civic contributions.
Local license appeals, §57-63.
Obstruction of investigations, §57-59.
Spousal abuse.
Juvenile and domestic relations district court proceedings, §16.1-243.
Spousal support.
Juvenile and domestic relations district court proceedings, §16.1-243.
Stalking.
Protective orders, §19.2-152.11.
State lottery actions.
Collection of debt owed licensed agent, §58.1-4021.
Stock insurers conversion to mutual insurers.
Proceedings to compel completion of mutualization, §38.2-1013.
Streams.
Improvement of navigability.
Claims for damages to oyster and clamming grounds, §62.1-158.
Submerged lands.
Injunctions, §28.2-1211.
Support of spouse or child.
Juvenile and domestic relations district court proceedings, §16.1-243.
Taxation.
Criminal offenses, §19.2-245.2.
Erroneous assessment correction.
Application to court, §58.1-1825.
Inapplicability of chapter, §8.01-259.
Income tax return preparer, action to enjoin, §58.1-348.2.
Motor vehicle sales and use tax appeals, §58.1-2426.
Public service corporation tax assessments.
Applications to circuit courts for review, §58.1-2670.1.
Real property taxes.
Apportionment of city taxes.
Part of real estate becomes separately owned, §58.1-3224.
Petition to ascertain delinquent tax, §58.1-3959.
Unemployment compensation tax.
Evaluation of employing unit as employer, §60.2-500.
Tax collection.
Local taxes, §58.1-3953.
Real property tax.
Petition when part of delinquent tract purchased, §58.1-3227.
Sale of land for delinquent taxes, §58.1-3967.
State corporation commission, taxes assessed by.
Filing memorandum of lien, §58.1-2021.
State taxes.
Agencies other than tax department, §58.1-2022.
Income tax setoff debt collection.
Appeals from hearings, §58.1-527.
Memorandum of lien, §58.1-1805.
State corporation commission assessments, §58.1-2021.
Proceedings for collection, §58.1-1806.
State corporation commission assessments.
Memorandum of lien, §58.1-2021.
Unemployment compensation tax.
Collection by injunctive relief, §60.2-522.
Witnesses.
Proceeding against witnesses disobeying summons, §58.1-216.

VENUE —Cont'd
Terrorist acts, §18.2-46.8.
Time-shares.
Board proceedings, §55-399.1.
Tobacco warehouses.
Establishment, §61.1-38.
Toll bridge photo-monitoring system.
Actions under, §§46.2-819.1, 46.2-819.3.
Transfer of venue.
Juvenile and domestic relations district courts, §16.1-243.
Transportation district contract enforcement, §15.2-4522.
Travel clubs.
Orders to compel, §59.1-451.
Trustees.
Appointment, §64.2-1412.
Removal, §64.2-1412.
Substitute trustees, §64.2-1405.
Surety bonds, §64.2-1412.
Unclaimed property, disposition of.
Claims to property of proceeds of sale, §55-210.22.
Unemployment compensation.
Civil actions, §60.2-118.
Claims adjudication, §60.2-625.
Appellate review of board of review, §60.2-631.
Criminal cases, §60.2-119.
Employer taxation.
Collection of taxes by injunctive relief, §60.2-522.
Evaluation of employing unit as employer, §60.2-500.
Unknown defendants.
Permissible venue, §8.01-262.
Venereal diseases.
Compelling examinations, testing or treatment, §32.1-57.
Violent offenses resulting in serious bodily injury.
Protective orders, §19.2-152.11.
Visitation of child.
Juvenile and domestic relations district court proceedings, §16.1-243.
Vital records.
Amendment petitions, §32.1-269.
Disclosure petitions, §32.1-271.
Voter registration.
Appeal of cancellation, §24.2-430.
Appeal of denial, §24.2-422.
Wagonway construction, §56-16.
Waters of the state.
Big Sandy river.
Obstructing or dumping refuse into, §62.1-194.3.
Bulkheads, §§62.1-164, 62.1-165.
Clearing watercourses between counties of obstructions, §62.1-6.
Contaminating state waters, §62.1-194.1.
Docks, §§62.1-164, 62.1-165.
Improvement of navigability.
Claims for damages to oyster and clamming grounds, §62.1-158.
Landings, §§62.1-164, 62.1-165.
Obstructing state waters, §62.1-194.1.
Big Sandy river, §62.1-194.3.
Piers, §§62.1-164, 62.1-165.
Surface water rights.
Application for leave to store floodwaters, §62.1-107.
Wharves, §§62.1-164, 62.1-165.

VENUE —Cont'd
Waters of the state —Cont'd
Works on watercourses.
Applications for leave to build or rebuild, §62.1-116.
Water supply companies.
Quo warranto action, §56-264.
Wetlands.
Permits, §28.2-1315.
Provision violations.
Fines, §28.2-1320.
Wharves, §§62.1-164, 62.1-165.
Where cause of action arose.
Permissible forum, §8.01-262.
Wills.
Grant of powers to personal representatives or trustees, §64.2-106.
Probate, §64.2-443.
Establishment bills, §64.2-448.
Impeachment bills, §64.2-448.
Recording, §64.2-455.
Workers' compensation.
Compliance filing violations, §65.2-806.
Disagreements as to compensation, §65.2-702.
False statements or representations, §65.2-312.
Lump sum payments.
Appointment of trustees, §65.2-523.

VERDICT.
Acquittal by reason of insanity.
Statement of fact within verdict, §19.2-182.2.
Asbestos-related injuries.
Consolidation or bifurcation of issues or claims.
Special interrogatories to jury, §8.01-374.1.
Claims against the state.
Recovery of claims, §8.01-194.
Criminal cases.
Acquittal by reason of insanity.
Statement of fact within verdict, §19.2-182.2.
Alternative forms of verdicts, VA SCt Rule 3A:16.
Bifurcated jury trials, VA SCt Rule 3A:17.1.
Content of judgment order, §19.2-307, VA SCt Rules Part 3A Appx Form 10.
Substantial compliance with form required, VA SCt Rule 3A:22.
Conviction of attempt or as accessory on felony indictment.
Effect of general verdict of not guilty, §19.2-286.
Conviction of lesser offense, VA SCt Rule 3A:17.
Faulty counts.
Effect of general verdict of guilty, §19.2-291.
General verdict of not guilty of felony.
Bar to prosecution for attempt or being an accessory, §19.2-286.
Indictment for murder.
Accused found guilty of punishable homicide, §19.2-288.
Multiple defendants, §19.2-287, VA SCt Rule 3A:17.
Petit larceny.
Faulty counts in indictment, §19.2-291.
Grand larceny prosecution, §19.2-289.
Value of stolen object greater than $200, §19.2-290.
Poll of jury, VA SCt Rule 3A:17.
Return of verdict, VA SCt Rule 3A:17.
Sentencing orders, VA SCt Rule 3A:22, VA SCt Rule Part 3A Appx Form 10.
Separate verdicts, VA SCt Rule 3A:16.
Setting aside verdict.
Accused guilty of part of offense charged, §19.2-285.

VERDICT —Cont'd
Damages reduced and accepted under protest, §8.01-383.1.
Death by wrongful act.
Distribution of recovery when verdict fails to designate beneficiaries, §8.01-54.
Interrogatories submitted to jury with general verdict form, §8.01-379.3.
Detinue.
No verdict as to omission of price or value of items, §8.01-120.
Estates in land.
Action against several defendants, §8.01-142.
Effect of cessation of plaintiff's rights, §8.01-150.
How verdict to specify estate of plaintiff, §8.01-153.
How verdict to specify premises recovered, §8.01-151.
How verdict to specify undivided interest or share, §8.01-152.
Jury finds for plaintiffs, §8.01-149.
Improvements to land.
Balance after offsetting damages against improvements, §§8.01-171, 8.01-172.
Interest.
Date at which interest begins, §8.01-382.
Interrogatories upon issues of fact, §8.01-379.3.
Medical malpractice.
Limitation on recovery of damages, §8.01-581.15.
Motion to set aside verdict, VA SCt Rule 3A:15.
Prejudgment interest, §8.01-382.
Products liability.
Consolidation or bifurcation of issues or claims.
Special interrogatories to jury, §8.01-374.1.
Quo warranto, §8.01-643.
Sentencing orders, VA SCt Rule 3A:22, VA SCt Rule Part 3A Appx Form 10.
Setting aside jury verdict.
When final judgment may be entered, §8.01-430.
Summary jury trial.
When verdict binding, §8.01-576.3.
Unlawful entry and detainer.
Damages, §8.01-128.
Wrongful death.
Distribution of recovery when verdict fails to do so, §8.01-54.
Interrogatories submitted to jury with general verdict form, §8.01-379.3.

VERIFICATION OF PLEADINGS, VA SCt Rule 1:10.
Electronic filing and service, VA SCt Rule 1:17.

VERMIN.
Pesticide control act, §3.2-3900.

VESSELS.
Abandoned vessels.
Acquiring title, §29.1-733.1.
Removal of vessels constituting obstruction or hazardous use of waters, §15.2-909.
ABC licenses.
Mixed beverages carrier licenses.
Common carriers of passengers, §4.1-210.
Admiralty, US Const Art I §8.
Drift property, §§55-202 to 55-210.
Jurisdiction of courts, US Const Art III §2.
Attachments of vessels of more than twenty tons, §8.01-538.
Bailee's failure to return, §18.2-117.
Ballast water discharge, §§28.2-109 to 28.2-111.

VESSELS —Cont'd
Beacons.
Lien for cost of repairing or replacing, §62.1-188.
Offenses relating to, §62.1-187.
Boating safety, §§29.1-734 to 29.1-746.
Boat storage places.
Lien of keepers, §§43-32 to 43-36.
Lists of boat owners.
Filing requirements, §58.1-3902.
Branch pilots generally, §§54.1-900 to 54.1-927.
See BRANCH PILOTS.
Buoys.
Lien for cost of repairing or replacing, §62.1-188.
Offenses relating to, §62.1-187.
Burning boat, etc., used for lodging, §18.2-77.
Charter boats.
Saltwater recreational fishing license, §28.2-302.8.
Closing waters found toxic, §32.1-248.
Concealed weapons, §18.2-308.
Constitution of the United States.
Bound to and from one state not to be obliged to clear, etc., in another, US Const Art I §9.
Crabs.
Dredging.
Restrictions, §28.2-707.
Harvesting restrictions, §28.2-705.
Scraping.
Restrictions, §28.2-706.
Taking limitations, §28.2-713.
Day marks.
Lien for cost of repairing or replacing, §62.1-188.
Offenses relating to, §62.1-187.
Dealers generally, §§29.1-800 to 29.1-827.
See BOAT DEALERS.
Decedents' estates.
Transfers, §64.2-606.
Defrauding keepers, §18.2-189.
Destruction with intent to defraud, §18.2-150.
Disappearance of persons from.
Presumption of death, §64.2-2300.
Discharges into waters of the state, §62.1-44.33.
No-discharge zones, §62.1-44.33.
Oil discharges generally, §§62.1-44.34:14 to 62.1-44.34:23.
See OIL DISCHARGES INTO WATERS OF STATE.
Sanitation districts law, §21-222.
Discrimination against persons with disabilities, §51.5-44.
Drift property, §§55-202 to 55-210.
Drug transaction on, §§18.2-258, 18.2-258.01, 48-16, 48-17.
Entering.
Criminal intent, §18.2-147.
Dwelling, §§18.2-90, 18.2-91.
Fishing, tidal waters.
Menhaden taken with purse net restrictions, §28.2-411.
Oysters.
Dredging equipment, §28.2-516.
Seizures.
Provision violations, §§28.2-900 to 28.2-902.
Trawling.
License restrictions, §28.2-316.
Prima facie evidence of violation, §28.2-317.
Fraud in procuring, §18.2-206.
Head boats.
Saltwater recreational fishing license, §28.2-302.8.
Identification generally, §§29.1-700 to 29.1-711.
Illegal drug transactions.
Closure of nuisance premises, §§48-16, 48-17.

VESSELS —Cont'd
Insurance coverage, liability, §§38.2-2200 to 38.2-2234.
Insurance fraud, §18.2-150.
Joyriding, §18.2-102.
Repossession, §18.2-148.
Liens of keepers, §43-32.
Appeals, §43-36.
Enforcement, §43-34.
Validity, §43-35.
Liens, self-service storage, §§55-418, 55-419.
Marinas.
Dump stations.
Signs or notices, §32.1-246.1.
List of boat owners, §58.1-3902.
Sewage facilities, §32.1-246.
Menhaden taken with purse nets.
Restrictions, §28.2-411.
No-discharge zones, §62.1-44.33.
Obstruction or hazard to use of waters.
Removal of vessels, §§15.2-909, 28.2-1210.
Personal property taxes.
Classification, §§58.1-3503, 58.1-3506.
Proration, §58.1-3516.
Situs, §§58.1-3511, 58.1-3512.
Personal watercraft, §§29.1-748 to 29.1-750.
Presumption of death.
Disappearance of persons on board ship or vessel underway on high seas, §64.2-2300.
Range lights.
Anchoring on range of, §62.1-189.
Recreational fishing boats.
Saltwater recreational fishing license, §28.2-302.7.
Reissuance, §28.2-302.7:1.
Registration generally, §§29.1-700 to 29.1-711.
Removal of obstructions or hazards from waters, §§15.2-909, 28.2-1210.
Rental boats.
Injury to, §18.2-149.
Safety requirements, §29.1-736.
Saltwater recreational fishing license, §28.2-302.8.
Repossession, §18.2-148.
Rights of persons with disabilities, §51.5-44.
Safety, §§29.1-734 to 29.1-746.
Saltwater recreational fishing license, §§28.2-302.1 to 28.2-302.10:1.
Sanitation districts law.
Discharges of marine sewerage, §21-222.
Self-incrimination, §29.1-561.
Self-service storage liens, §§55-418, 55-419.
Shooting at, §18.2-154.
Sight-seeing carriers.
See SIGHT-SEEING CARRIERS.
Stolen boats.
Receiving or transferring possession, §18.2-109.
Titling certificates.
Generally, §§29.1-712 to 29.1-733.1.
Uniform certificate of title for watercraft, §§29.1-733.2 to 29.1-733.29.
Trawling.
License restrictions, §28.2-316.
Prima facie evidence of violation, §28.2-317.
Unauthorized use, §§18.2-102, 18.2-148.
Vandalism, §18.2-146.
Watercraft sales and use tax, §§58.1-1400 to 58.1-1410.
See WATERCRAFT SALES AND USE TAX.

VETERANS.
Agent Orange.
See AGENT ORANGE.
VETERANS —Cont'd
Burial vaults supplied at costs by department.
Eligible veterans and family members.
Burial at state operated veterans cemeteries, §2.2-2001.
Civil commitment of mentally ill persons.
Veterans admitted or transferred.
Veterans affairs hospital, center or other facility, §§37.2-841, 37.2-842.
Colleges and universities.
Course credit for military experience, §23-9.2:3.7.
In-state tuition charges, eligibility, §23-7.4:2.
Restructured financial and administrative operations.
Employment, §23-38.118.
Community corrections.
Special treatment procedures, §9.1-173.1.
Confederate veterans.
Cemeteries and graves, §10.1-2211.
Cremation.
Identification of unclaimed remains of veterans, §54.1-2808.2.
Disabled veterans.
College tuition and fees.
Waiver for spouses and children of certain military personnel, §23-7.4:1.
Fishing licenses for inland waters, §29.1-302.
Hunting licenses, §29.1-302.
Partially disabled veterans, §29.1-302.02.
Pittsylvania county.
Exemption from solid waste disposal fee, §15.2-2159.
Real property tax exemption, §§58.1-3219.5 to 58.1-3219.8.
Special license plates, §46.2-739.
State parks.
Disabled veteran's passport, §10.1-202.2.
Tax credits, §§58.1-3360 to 58.1-3363.
Discharges and names of persons serving during war, recording.
Circuit court clerks, §§17.1-261 to 17.1-265.
DMV identification cards.
Veterans identification cards, §46.2-345.1.
Fishing, inland waters.
Licensing.
Disabled veterans, §29.1-302.
Special permits for veterans, §29.1-312.
High school diplomas.
Korean War veteran honorary diploma, §22.1-17.4.
Vietnam war veteran honorary high school diploma, §§2.2-3310, 22.1-17.4.
World War II veteran honorary high school diploma, §22.1-17.4.
Homestead exemption of householder.
Additional exemption for certain veterans, §34-4.1.
Honorably discharged veterans.
Special license plates, §46.2-743.
Housing projects.
Fair housing law, §§36-96.1 to 36-96.23.
See FAIR HOUSING.
Hunting licenses.
Disabled veterans, §29.1-302.
Partially disabled veterans, §29.1-302.02.
Special permits for veterans, §29.1-312.
Identification cards, §46.2-345.1.
Incompetency.
Conservators.
See CONSERVATORS.
Generally.
See INCOMPETENCY.

VETERANS —Cont'd
Incompetency —Cont'd
Guardian and ward.
See GUARDIAN AND WARD.
Korean War.
High school diplomas, §22.1-17.4.
Special license plates for veterans, §46.2-743.
Veterans appreciation week, §2.2-3309.1.
Local government employment.
Preference, §15.2-1509.
Mental health and rehabilitation services support program.
Community corrections, special treatment procedures, §9.1-173.1.
Establishment by department of veterans services, §2.2-2001.1.
Operation Desert Shield.
Special license plates for veterans, §46.2-743.
Operation Desert Storm.
Special license plates for veterans, §46.2-743.
Operation Iraqi Freedom.
Special license plates for veterans, §46.2-743.
Personal property taxes.
Classification of veterans motor vehicles, §58.1-3506.
Power of attorney.
Authority of agent.
Benefits from governmental programs or civil or military service, §64.2-1635.
POW/MIA flag.
Display, §2.2-3310.1.
Preference in employment.
Local government employment, §15.2-1509.
Property tax exemptions, VA Const Art X §6-A.
Public officers and employees.
Personnel administration system.
Preferences for veterans, surviving spouses and children, §2.2-2903.
Real property taxes.
Disabled veterans.
Exemption, §§58.1-3219.5 to 58.1-3219.8.
Tax credits, §§58.1-3360 to 58.1-3363.
Exemption, VA Const Art X §6-A.
Recordation of names, discharges, etc., of men serving during war.
Circuit court clerks, §§17.1-261 to 17.1-265.
Small business owner holding service disabled status.
Certification by department, §2.2-2001.
State parks.
Disabled veteran's passport, §10.1-202.2.
Surviving spouses of honorably discharged veterans.
Special license plates, §46.2-743.
Trustees for incapacitated ex-service persons and their beneficiaries, §64.2-2016.
Payments from U.S. department of veterans' affairs, §64.2-2017.
Unemployment compensation.
Veterans services department, programs to reduce unemployment among veterans, §2.2-2001.2.
Veterans skills database, §60.2-113.1.
Veterans of foreign wars.
Special license plates, §46.2-746.4.
Vietnam veterans.
Agent Orange exposure.
See AGENT ORANGE.
Special license plates, §46.2-743.
Vietnam war.
High school diplomas, §§2.2-3310, 22.1-17.4.

VETERANS —Cont'd
Virginia Korean War veterans appreciation week, §2.2-3309.1.
World War II.
Honorary high school diplomas, §22.1-17.4.
Special license plates, §46.2-743.
Veterans appreciation week, §2.2-3309.1.

VETERANS ADMINISTRATION.
Loans insured or guaranteed by.
Interest rate more than legal rate, §6.2-329.

VETERANS AFFAIRS AND HOMELAND SECURITY, SECRETARY OF, §§2.2-200 to 2.2-202, 2.2-230 to 2.2-233.

VETERANS' CEMETERIES.
Burial vaults supplied at costs by department.
Eligible veterans and family members.
Burial at state operated veterans cemeteries, §2.2-2001.
Confederate cemeteries and graves, §10.1-2211.

VETERANS DAY.
Legal holidays, §2.2-3300.

VETERANS MEMORIAL.
County, city or town, §15.2-1812.
Damage to memorials, actions, §15.2-1812.1.

VETERANS OF FOREIGN WARS OF THE UNITED STATES.
Armories, use for meetings, §44-133.
Benevolent associations generally.
See BENEVOLENT ASSOCIATIONS OR ORGANIZATIONS.
Land conveyances to, §§57-19, 57-20.
Land quantity limitations, §57-20.
Property exempt from taxation, §58.1-3607.
Special license plates, §46.2-746.2:6.

VETERANS OF IWO JIMA.
Special license plates, §46.2-746.4.

VETERANS OF WORLD WAR I AUXILIARIES.
Property tax exemptions, §58.1-3612.

VETERANS' ORGANIZATIONS.
Armories, use for meetings, §44-133.
Charitable gaming.
General provisions, §§18.2-340.15 to 18.2-340.37.
See CHARITABLE GAMING.
Names or insignia, registration, alteration, cancellation, §§2.2-411 to 2.2-417.
See REGISTRATION OF NAMES OR INSIGNIA OF ORGANIZATIONS.
Registration of name or insignia.
Illegal use of insignia, §18.2-177.
Solicitation of charitable or civic contributions.
Exemption from provisions.
Veterans' posts or organization grant tax exempt status, §57-60.
Unauthorized wearing or displaying on motor vehicles of button, insignia or emblem of, §§18.2-176, 18.2-177.

VETERANS PREFERENCE.
Local government employment, §15.2-1509.
Public officers and employees.
Personnel administration system.
Preferences, §2.2-2903.

VETERANS SERVICE ORGANIZATIONS, JOINT LEADERSHIP COUNCIL, §§2.2-2681, 2.2-2682.
Composition, §2.2-2681.

VETERANS SERVICE ORGANIZATIONS, JOINT LEADERSHIP COUNCIL —Cont'd
Duties, §2.2-2682.
Established, §2.2-2681.
Meetings, §2.2-2681.
Powers, §2.2-2682.
Recommendations, §2.2-2682.
Reports.
Annual executive summary of interim activity, §2.2-2682.

VETERANS SERVICES BOARD, §§2.2-2452 to 2.2-2454.
Appointment of members, §2.2-2452.
Chairman, §2.2-2452.
Compensation of members, §2.2-2453.
Composition, §2.2-2452.
Duties, §2.2-2454.
Established, §2.2-2452.
Investigations.
Powers and duties, §2.2-2454.
Members, §2.2-2452.
Compensation, §2.2-2453.
Reimbursement for expenses, §2.2-2453.
Officers, §2.2-2452.
Policies and procedures.
Powers and duties, §2.2-2454.
Powers, §2.2-2454.
Recommendations.
Powers and duties, §2.2-2454.
Reimbursement for expenses, §2.2-2453.
Secretary, §2.2-2452.
Staffing, §2.2-2452.
Standing committees, §2.2-2452.
Vacancies, §2.2-2452.
Vice chairman, §2.2-2452.

VETERANS SERVICES DEPARTMENT, §§2.2-2000 to 2.2-2004.
Administrative process act.
Exemptions, §2.2-4002.
Administrative responsibilities, §2.2-2001.
Board of veterans services, §§2.2-2452 to 2.2-2454.
Burial vaults.
Supplied at costs to eligible veterans and family members.
Burial at state operated veterans cemeteries, §2.2-2001.
Commissioner.
Appointed by governor, §2.2-2000.
Head of department, §2.2-2000.
Personnel, responsibilities regarding, §2.2-2002.1.
Powers and duties, §§2.2-2000, 2.2-2003, 2.2-2004.
Term, §2.2-2000.
Veteran, qualification requirement, §2.2-2000.
Coordinator.
Commissioner to appoint, §2.2-2004.
Created, §2.2-2000.
Electronic preparation of disability claims, §2.2-2001.
General provisions regarding state agencies and general operation of government, §§2.2-600 to 2.2-614.3.
See STATE DEPARTMENTS AND AGENCIES.
Guidelines for eligibility to participate in programs.
Establishment, §2.2-2001.
Joint leadership council on veterans service organizations, §§2.2-2681, 2.2-2682.
Mental health and rehabilitation services support program.
Establishment, §2.2-2001.1.

VETERANS SERVICES DEPARTMENT —Cont'd
Offices, §2.2-2002.
Personnel, §2.2-2002.1.
Secretary of public safety.
Agency responsibility, §2.2-221.
Secretary of veterans affairs and homeland security.
Agencies for which responsible, §2.2-230.
Service offices, maintaining, personnel, §2.2-2002.
Small business owner holding service disabled status.
Certification, §2.2-2001.
Unemployment.
Programs to reduce unemployment among veterans, §2.2-2001.2.
Veterans care centers.
Certificates of public need for medical care facilities, §§32.1-102.1 to 32.1-102.11.
Veterans service organizations, joint leadership council, §§2.2-2681, 2.2-2682.
Veterans services foundation, §§2.2-2715 to 2.2-2719.
Virginia War Memorial.
Administrative process act.
Exemptions, §2.2-4002.
Division within department, §§2.2-2001, 2.2-2001.3.

VETERANS SERVICES FOUNDATION, §§2.2-2715 to 2.2-2719.
Administrative and other services.
Agency designated to provide, §2.2-2715.
Audits, §2.2-2717.
Authority, §2.2-2716.
Bonds, surety.
Persons handling funds, §2.2-2715.
Bylaws.
Authority to adopt, §2.2-2715.
Closed meetings, §2.2-3711.
Composition, §2.2-2715.
Established, §2.2-2715.
Gifts and bequests, §2.2-2719.
Meetings.
Closed meetings, §2.2-3711.
Members, §2.2-2715.
Powers, §2.2-2716.
Purpose, §2.2-2715.
Records, §2.2-2717.
Reports.
Quarterly report on funding levels and services, §2.2-2715.
Secretary of public safety.
Agency responsibility, §2.2-221.
Secretary of veterans affairs and homeland security.
Agencies for which responsible, §2.2-230.
Tax exemption.
Gifts and bequests to the veterans services fund, §2.2-2719.
Veterans services fund, §2.2-2718.
Administration, §2.2-2716.
Bonds, surety.
Persons handling funds, §2.2-2715.
Gifts and bequests.
Tax exemption, §2.2-2719.

VETERANS SERVICES FUND, §2.2-2718.
Administration, §2.2-2716.
Bonds, surety.
Persons handling funds, §2.2-2715.

VETERANS SERVICES FUND —Cont'd
Gifts and bequests.
Tax exemption, §2.2-2719.

VETERINARIANS, §§54.1-3800 to 54.1-3813.
Aqueous solutions.
Sales to veterinarians, §54.1-3418.
Boarding establishments for animals.
Veterinary care requirements, §§3.2-6518, 3.2-6519.
Misdemeanor for violating, §18.2-403.1.
Board of veterinary medicine, §§54.1-3802 to 54.1-3804.
Continuing education, §54.1-3805.2.
Controlled substances.
Restrictions on dispensing, §§54.1-3302 to 54.1-3304.1.
Criminal offenses as to animals.
Exceptions regarding veterinarians, §3.2-6506.
Cruelty to animals, immunity for reporting, §54.1-3812.1.
Disclosure forms, §54.1-3806.1.
Drugs.
Dispensation restrictions, §54.1-3409.
Emergency care for animals, immunity, §8.01-225.2.
Equine dental technicians.
Defined, §54.1-3813.
Registration, §54.1-3813.
Refusal to grant or renew, revocation or suspension, §54.1-3807.
Unlawful performance of duties, §54.1-3813.
Equine dentistry.
Performance of tasks under veterinarian's supervision, §54.1-3813.
Exceptions from licensing, §54.1-3801.
Free care in underserved areas, §54.1-3801.
Good Samaritan veterinarians, §§8.01-225.2, 54.1-3811.
Good faith actions as to injured or sick animals, §3.2-6507.
Groomers.
Veterinary care requirements, §3.2-6518.
Immunity.
Emergency care, §8.01-225.2.
Good faith actions as to injured or sick animals, §3.2-6507.
Good Samaritan veterinarians, §§8.01-225.2, 54.1-3811.
Reporting cruelty to animals, §54.1-3812.1.
Impoundment of animals by licensed veterinarians, §3.2-6565.
Injured or sick animal.
Action by veterinarian, §3.2-6507.
Good Samaritan veterinarians, §3.2-6518.
License requirements, §54.1-3805.
Exceptions, §54.1-3801.
Temporary licenses, §54.1-3805.1.
Medical malpractice.
Health professional civil immunity, §8.01-581.13.
Oleaginous solutions.
Sales to veterinarians, §54.1-3418.
Practice of veterinary medicine, §54.1-3800.
Prescriptions, §54.1-3409.
Professional corporations, §§13.1-542.1 to 13.1-556.
See PROFESSIONAL CORPORATIONS.
Professional limited liability companies.
Generally, §§13.1-1100 to 13.1-1123.
See PROFESSIONAL LIMITED LIABILITY COMPANIES.

VETERINARIANS —Cont'd
Professions and occupations regulation generally.
See HEALTH PROFESSIONS DEPARTMENT.
Prohibited acts by licensees generally, §54.1-2409.1.
Provision violations.
Conviction reports, §54.1-3810.
Penalties, §54.1-3809.
Rabies certificates.
Copy to owner, information forwarded to treasurer of locality, §3.2-6529.
Refusal to grant or renew, revocation or suspension.
License or registration to practice, §54.1-3807.
Release of records, §54.1-3812.
Sale of dogs and cats by dealers.
Certification by veterinarian.
Generally, §§3.2-6512 to 3.2-6517.
State veterinarian.
See STATE VETERINARIAN.
Temporary licenses, §54.1-3805.1.
Unclaimed animal left with veterinarian.
Sale after notice, §3.2-6520.
Unlawful procurement of licensure, §54.1-102.
Unlawful use of licensure, §54.1-111.
Veterinary technicians, §54.1-3806.
Equine teeth, planing, §54.1-3813.

VETO POWER OF GOVERNOR, VA Const Art V §6.

VETO POWER OF THE PRESIDENT, US Const Art I §7.

VFW.
Armories, use for meetings, §44-133.

VIADUCT COMPANIES.
Public ground use without consent or compensation, §56-14.

VIADUCTS.
Obstructions or encroachments, §15.2-2009.
Roads, streets and public rights-of-way.
Localities generally, §§15.2-2000 to 15.2-2030.
See ROADS, STREETS AND PUBLIC RIGHTS OF WAY.
Use permits for transportation and utilities, §15.2-2015.

VIATICAL SETTLEMENTS, §§38.2-6000 to 38.2-6016.
Advertising, §38.2-6010.
Authority of commission, §38.2-6014.
Broker licensing, §§38.2-1865.1 to 38.2-1865.5.
Agents of settlement providers.
Presumption, §38.2-1865.1.
Application, §38.2-1865.1.
Business entity acting as, §38.2-1865.1.
Clerk of commission.
Agent for service, appointment, §38.2-1865.1.
License processing fee, §38.2-1865.1.
License required, §38.2-1865.1.
Life and annuities insurance agents, §38.2-1865.1.
Nonresidents, §38.2-1865.4.
Presumption.
Agents of settlement providers, §38.2-1865.1.
Reciprocal agreements, §38.2-1865.4.
Refusal, revocation or suspension.
Due process rights, §38.2-1865.3.
Grounds, §38.2-1865.2.
Renewal of license, §38.2-1865.1.
Reports, §38.2-1865.5.

VIATICAL SETTLEMENTS —Cont'd
Broker licensing —Cont'd
Service of notice, process and other papers.
Clerk of commission.
Agent for service, appointment, §38.2-1865.1.
Term of license, §38.2-1865.1.
Written agreement with viator.
Required to seek or obtain compensation, §38.2-1865.1.
Brokers, §38.2-6001.
Civil remedies, §38.2-6012.
Confidential information, §38.2-6005.
Consent requirements, §38.2-6008.
Contract approval, §38.2-6003.
Definitions, §38.2-6000.
Disclosure statements, §38.2-6007.
Examination of licensees, §38.2-6006.
Fraud, §38.2-6011.
Immunity from liability, §38.2-6015.
Investigation of licensees, §38.2-6006.
Licenses.
Brokers, §38.2-6001.
Providers, §38.2-6002.
Prerequisites to contracting, §38.2-6008.
Privacy policy, §38.2-6005.
Prohibited practices, §38.2-6009.
Providers, §38.2-6002.
Records retention, §38.2-6006.
Reports of licensees, §38.2-6004.
Rescission of contract, §38.2-6007.
Right to rescind, §38.2-6008.
Revocation or suspension of license.
Providers, §38.2-6002.
Securities laws, applicability, §38.2-6016.
Two-year limitations period, §38.2-6009.
Unfair trade practices, §38.2-6013.

VICARIOUS LIABILITY.
Husband and wife.
Responsibility for other spouse's obligations, §55-37.
Parental liability for minor child.
Minor operating vehicle, §§8.01-64, 8.01-65.
Private property damage, §8.01-44.
Public property damage, §8.01-43.

VICE-PRESIDENT OF THE UNITED STATES.
Age, US Const Amd 12.
Bribery, US Const Art II §4.
Compelling attendance as witness.
Prior court permission required, §8.01-407.
Electors.
Majority vote is necessary to elect president or vice-president, US Const Art II §1, Amd 12.
Failure to qualify, US Const Amd 20.
Impeachment, US Const Art II §4.
Jury service.
Automatic exemption, §8.01-341.
Oaths, US Const Art VI, Amd 14.
President of the Senate, US Const Art I §3.
Qualifications, US Const Amd 12.
Removal, US Const Art II §4.
Succession to office of president, US Const Art II §1, Amds 20, 25.
Upon death, resignation or removal of president, US Const Amd 25 §1.
Treason, US Const Art II §4.
Vacancy in office, US Const Art II §1, Amd 20.
Nomination by president, US Const Amd 25 §2.
Confirmation by majority vote of both houses of congress, US Const Amd 25 §2.

VICIOUS DOGS, §3.2-6540.1.

VICTIM AND WITNESS PROTECTION, §19.2-11.01.

VICTIM IMPACT STATEMENTS, §19.2-11.01.
Admission of victim's testimony upon finding that defendant guilty, §19.2-295.3.
Death penalty post-sentence reports, §19.2-264.5.
Juvenile cases, §16.1-273.
Presentence reports and investigations by probation officers, §19.2-299.
When required, §19.2-299.1.

VICTIMS OF CRIME.
Acquittal by reason of insanity.
Confinement of acquittee.
Notice of unescorted community visit by acquittee, §19.2-182.4.
Address confidentiality program.
Domestic violence, §2.2-515.2.
Addresses or telephone numbers.
Nondisclosure, §§19.2-11.2, 19.2-269.2.
Assistance programs.
Criminal justice services department.
Establishment, §9.1-104.
Attorney general.
Notice of filing and disposition of appeal or habeas corpus proceeding, §2.2-510.
Child pornography.
Mandatory restitution to victims as condition of sentencing, §19.2-305.1.
Compensating victims, §§19.2-368.1 to 19.2-368.18.
Crime victim and witness assistance, §§19.2-368.1 to 19.2-368.18.
See CRIME VICTIM AND WITNESS ASSISTANCE.
Death penalty.
Victim impact statements, §19.2-264.5.
Discharge of prisoner.
Notice to victim, §53.1-133.02.
Domestic violence.
Address confidentiality program, §2.2-515.2.
Statewide facilitator for victims of domestic violence, §2.2-515.1.
Address confidentiality program, §2.2-515.2.
Employment.
Leave given to crime victims to attend criminal proceedings, §40.1-28.7:2.
Escape of prisoner.
Notice to victim, §53.1-133.02.
Exclusion from criminal trials, §19.2-265.01, VA SCt Rule 2:615.
Inapplicability to victim unless exclusion otherwise required, §19.2-265.1.
Freedom of information act requests.
Criminal records not disclosed.
Identifying information, §2.2-3706.
Hate crimes.
Tort liability, §8.01-42.1.
Identity of victim.
Nondisclosure of information revealing, §19.2-11.2.
Identity theft.
Victim assistance, §18.2-186.3.
Juvenile proceedings.
Delinquency.
Right of victim to be present at proceedings, §16.1-302.1.
Victim impact statements, §16.1-273.

VICTIMS OF CRIME —Cont'd
Labor.
Leave given to crime victims to attend criminal proceedings, §40.1-28.7:2.
Landlord and tenant.
Family abuse, tenant victim.
Termination of lease due solely to act of abuse against tenant prohibited, §55-248.31.
Termination of tenancies.
Early termination by victims of family abuse, sexual abuse or criminal sexual assault, §§55-225.16, 55-248.21.
Name change by prisoner.
Notice to victim, §53.1-133.02.
Nondisclosure of addresses or telephone numbers of crime victims, §§19.2-11.2, 19.2-269.2.
Notification program, immunity for those involved, §8.01-226.11.
Prisoners, victim seeking to visit with.
Department policy to assist victims, §53.1-30.
Protection, generally, §19.2-11.01.
Public school students.
Transfer to school within division, §22.1-3.3.
Restitution.
Compensating victims of crime, §§19.2-368.1 to 19.2-368.18.
See CRIME VICTIM AND WITNESS ASSISTANCE.
Rights of victims, VA Const Art I §8-A.
Security freezes.
Consumer credit reports, §§59.1-444.1, 59.1-444.2.
Sentencing.
Victim impact statements.
Admission of victim impact testimony, §19.2-295.3.
When required, §19.2-299.1.
Serious youth offender release and review hearing notice, §16.1-285.2.
Sex offender registration and notification.
Victim of offense is minor, physically helpless or mentally incapacitated.
Determination by court and defendant's advice of rights, §9.1-902.
Sexual and domestic violence victim fund, §9.1-116.1.
Sexual assault nurse examiners.
Administration of preventive medication to victims, §54.1-3408.
Sexual assault victims incapable of making informed decision.
Medical personnel performing physical evidence recovery kit, §54.1-2970.1.
Stalking victims.
Notice of discharge of prisoner, §18.2-60.3.
Protective orders, §§19.2-152.8 to 19.2-152.11.
Assault and battery of person protected by protective order, §18.2-60.4.
Violation of orders, §18.2-60.4.
Students at public schools.
Transfer to other school within division, §22.1-3.3.
Transfer of prisoner.
Notice to victim, §53.1-133.02.
Victim impact statements.
Death penalty, §19.2-264.5.
Juvenile proceedings, §16.1-273.
Presentence reports and investigations by probation officers, §19.2-299.
When required, §19.2-299.1.
Violent offenses.
Offenses resulting in serious bodily injury.
Protective orders, §§19.2-152.8 to 19.2-152.11.

VICTIMS OF CRIME —Cont'd
Virginia sexual and domestic violence victim fund, §9.1-116.1.
Work release.
Notice to victim, §53.1-133.02.

VIDEO AND AUDIO APPEARANCE OF ACCUSED, §19.2-3.1.

VIDEO AND AUDIO APPEARANCE OF CHILD.
At detention hearing, §16.1-250.
At review hearing on confinement, §16.1-284.1.
Before intake officers, §16.1-260.
Sexually violent predators, civil commitment.
Probable cause hearing, §37.2-906.

VIDEOCONFERENCES.
Audio-visual depositions, §§8.01-412.2 to 8.01-412.7.
Open meetings.
Freedom of information act.
Electronic communication meetings, §2.2-3708.
Exceptions to prohibition, §2.2-3708.1.
General assembly, electronic mode prohibited, §2.2-3707.01.
Minutes, §2.2-3707.

VIDEO GAMES.
License tax on amusement machines and amusement operators, §§58.1-3720 to 58.1-3723.
Sexually explicit material.
Selling, renting or loaning to minors prohibited, §18.2-391.

VIDEO-MONITORING SYSTEMS.
Toll facilities.
Installation by localities within, §46.2-819.3:1.

VIDEOTAPED STATEMENTS AS EVIDENCE.
Child abuse or neglect, §63.2-1523.

VIDEOTAPES.
Agent Orange.
Cancer registry.
Information to be provided to, §32.1-70.
Congenital anomalies reporting and education system.
Report information, §32.1-69.1.
Generally.
See RECORDED DEVICES.
Obscene videotapes generally, §§18.2-372 to 18.2-388.
See OBSCENITY AND RELATED OFFENSES.

VIDEOTAPING ANOTHER UNLAWFULLY, §18.2-386.1.

VIENNA PARKING AUTHORITY, TOWN OF, 1991 ch 446.

VIETNAMESE-AMERICAN HERITAGE FLAG.
Recognition by Commonwealth, §2.2-3310.2.

VIETNAMESE COMMUNITIES.
Vietnamese-American heritage flag.
Recognition by Commonwealth, §2.2-3310.2.
Vietnam human rights day, §2.2-3310.3.

VIETNAM VETERANS.
Agent Orange exposure.
See AGENT ORANGE.
Honorary high school diplomas, §§2.2-3310, 22.1-17.4.
Special license plates, §46.2-743.
Vietnam War Memorial dedication and veterans' recognition week, §2.2-3310.

VIEW.
Virginia initiative for employment not welfare, §§63.2-608 to 63.2-613.
Workers' compensation.
Ineligibility for certain benefits, §§65.2-500, 65.2-502, 65.2-512.

VIEW BY JURIES.
Civil cases, §8.01-376.
Criminal cases, §19.2-264.1.

VIEWING OF PROPERTY.
Eminent domain.
Just compensation, §25.1-231.
Vacation and alteration of public right-of-way, §§15.2-2006 to 15.2-2008.

VILLAGES.
Animals running at large.
Unincorporated communities and villages, §§55-323 to 55-330.
See ANIMALS RUNNING AT LARGE.

VINEGAR, §§3.2-5500 to 3.2-5507.
Adulteration.
Sale prohibited, §3.2-5506.
When deemed adulterated, §3.2-5502.
Containers.
Marking, §3.2-5505.
Contents, §3.2-5501.
Criminal penalties, §3.2-5507.
Definitions, §3.2-5500.
Pyroligneous or acetic acid.
Not to be sold as vinegar, §3.2-5503.
Sales.
Prohibited sales, §§3.2-5503, 3.2-5504, 3.2-5506.

VINTON.
Confederate cemeteries and graves.
Disbursement of funds appropriated for upkeep, §10.1-2211.

VIOLATION OF STATUTORY DUTY.
Right to recover damages, §8.01-221.

VIOLENT FELONS.
Adoption.
Violent sex offenders prohibited from adopting, §63.2-1205.1.
Arrest.
DNA analysis.
Saliva or tissue samples, §§19.2-310.2:1, 19.2-310.3:1.
Midpoint of sentencing range, §17.1-805.
Mob crimes, §18.2-42.1.
Offenses resulting in serious bodily injury.
Protective orders, §19.2-152.10.
Emergency orders, §19.2-152.8.
Law enforcement officers, prohibition on orders against, §19.2-152.8.
Preliminary protective orders, §19.2-152.9.
Venue, §19.2-152.11.
Persons previously convicted of violent felonies, §19.2-297.1.
Person transported through or across Commonwealth.
Venue of prosecution, §18.2-359.
Sexually violent offenders.
Adoption.
Prohibition, §63.2-1205.1.
Sex offender and crimes against minors registry.
Generally, §§9.1-900 to 9.1-922.
See SEX OFFENDER REGISTRATION AND NOTIFICATION.

VIOLENT FELONS —Cont'd
Three time loser law, §19.2-297.1.

VIOLENT OVERTHROW OF GOVERNMENT.
Advocating change by force, violence, etc., §18.2-484.

VIRGINIA ADMINISTRATIVE CODE AND REGISTER OF REGULATIONS.
Code commission.
Powers and duties generally, §§30-145 to 30-155.
See CODE COMMISSION.
Generally, §§2.2-4100 to 2.2-4104.
See ADMINISTRATIVE CODE AND REGISTER OF REGULATIONS.

VIRGINIA ADMINISTRATIVE DISPUTE RESOLUTION ACT, §§2.2-4115 to 2.2-4119.

VIRGINIA AGRICULTURAL COUNCIL, §§3.2-2900 to 3.2-2905.
Appointment of members, §3.2-2901.
Compensation, §3.2-2903.
Composition, §3.2-2901.
Definitions, §3.2-2900.
Duties, §3.2-2904.
Officers, §3.2-2903.
Powers, §3.2-2904.
Reports.
Annual report, §3.2-2904.
Terms of members, §3.2-2902.
Vacancies, §3.2-2902.

VIRGINIA AIRCRAFT SALES AND USE TAX ACT, §§58.1-1500 to 58.1-1510.
See AIRCRAFT SALES AND USE TAX.

VIRGINIA AIRPORTS REVOLVING FUND, §§5.1-30.1 to 5.1-30.10.
Collection of money due, §5.1-30.4.
Construction of chapter, §5.1-30.10.
Creation of fund, §5.1-30.2.
Definitions, §5.1-30.1.
Deposit of money, §5.1-30.3.
Expenditures, §5.1-30.3.
Investments, §5.1-30.3.
Loans to local government, §5.1-30.5.
Annual report on loans, §5.1-30.9.
Pledging loans to secure bonds, §5.1-30.6.
Sale of loans, §5.1-30.7.
Management of fund, §5.1-30.2.
Resources authority powers, §5.1-30.8.

VIRGINIA ALCOHOL SAFETY ACTION PROGRAM.
Advisory board, §18.2-271.2.
Boating and related activities.
Under the influence, §29.1-738.5.
Commission, §18.2-271.2.
Driver improvement programs, §§46.2-489 to 46.2-506.
See DRIVER IMPROVEMENT PROGRAMS.
Driving while intoxicated.
Education and rehabilitation of persons charged or convicted, §18.2-271.1.
Driving while privilege suspended or revoked.
Second conviction, intervention, VASAP compliance, §46.2-355.1.
Ignition interlock system.
Certification by commission on VASAP, §18.2-270.2.
Supervision by VASAP required, §18.2-270.1.
Oath of office of case managers and employees, §18.2-271.4.

VIRGINIA ALCOHOL SAFETY ACTION PROGRAM —Cont'd
Restoration of license to person found habitual offender.
Evaluation prior to restoration, §46.2-360.

VIRGINIA ALTERNATIVE FUELS REVOLVING FUND, §§33.1-223.3 to 33.1-223.9.

VIRGINIA AMBER ALERT PROGRAM.
Activation, §52-34.3.
Definitions, §52-34.1.
Established, §52-34.2.

VIRGINIA ANTIQUITIES ACT, §§10.1-2300 to 10.1-2306.

VIRGINIA ANTITRUST ACT, §§59.1-9.1 to 59.1-9.17.

VIRGINIA ARTS FOUNDATION, §§2.2-2700 to 2.2-2704.

VIRGINIA ASBESTOS NESHAP ACT, §§40.1-51.23 to 40.1-51.41.

VIRGINIA-ASIAN ADVISORY BOARD, §§2.2-2448 to 2.2-2451.
Chairman, §2.2-2449.
Cooperation from state agencies, §2.2-2451.
Duties, §2.2-2450.
Established, §2.2-2448.
Members, §2.2-2449.
Powers, §2.2-2450.
Purpose, §2.2-2448.
Staff, §2.2-2451.

VIRGINIA ASSISTIVE TECHNOLOGY DEVICE WARRANTIES ACT, §§59.1-470 to 59.1-474.

VIRGINIA ASSOCIATION FOR COMMUNITY CONFLICT RESOLUTION.
Motor vehicle license plates.
Special license plates, §46.2-749.119.

VIRGINIA ASSOCIATION OF BROADCASTERS.
Freedom of information advisory council.
Recommendation list, citizen members of council, §30-178.

VIRGINIA ASSOCIATION OF COUNTIES.
Farmland preservation office.
Cooperative development with, §3.2-201.
Freedom of information advisory council.
Recommendation list, local government representative to, §30-178.

VIRGINIA ASSOCIATION OF INDEPENDENT SCHOOLS.
Charitable or civic contributions solicitation.
Exemptions from provisions.
Educational institutions accredited by, §57-60.

VIRGINIA AUCTIONEERS' LICENSE ACT, §§54.1-600 to 54.1-607.

VIRGINIA AUTO INSURANCE PLAN.
Assignment of risk generally, §§46.2-464 to 46.2-471.
See MOTOR VEHICLE INSURANCE.
Insurance rates.
Workers' compensation, automobiles, home protection, etc., §§38.2-2000 to 38.2-2027.
See INSURANCE RATES.

VIRGINIA BANK FRANCHISE TAX ACT, §§58.1-1200 to 58.1-1217.
See BANK FRANCHISE TAX.

VIRGINIA BASEBALL STADIUM AUTHORITY, §§15.2-5800 to 15.2-5819.

VIRGINIA BASEBALL STADIUM FINANCING FUND, §15.2-5811.

VIRGINIA BEACH.
Arena, §§15.2-5921 to 15.2-5927.
See VIRGINIA BEACH ARENA.
Behavioral health authorities.
Authorized to establish, §37.2-601.
Generally, §§37.2-600 to 37.2-615.
See BEHAVIORAL HEALTH AUTHORITIES.
Boundaries.
Territorial limits of city, concurrent jurisdiction with the Commonwealth, §15.2-1725.1.
Circuit court, establishment, §17.1-500.
Coastal primary sand dunes and beaches.
Permits and standards of use.
Sandbridge Beach subdivision, exemption, §28.2-1408.2.
Zoning ordinances, §28.2-1403.
Debt limitation, applicability, §58.1-3245.4:1.
Former officers and employees.
Restrictions on activities, §15.2-1408.
Improvements.
Taxes or assessments for local improvements.
Authority to impose, §15.2-2404.
How cost assessed or apportioned, §15.2-2406.
Medical care facilities.
Certificates of public need.
Moratorium exceptions, §32.1-102.3:2.
Metropolitan transportation district, 1970 ch 697.
Outdoor performing arts amphitheater, area or similar facility.
Mixed beverages license, §4.1-210.
Retail on-premises wine and beer license, §4.1-209.
Parking violations.
Removal or immobilization of vehicles.
Outstanding parking violations, §46.2-1216.
Personal property tax relief for elderly or handicapped.
Motor vehicles, alternative tax rates.
Ordinance to raise income and financial worth limitations, §58.1-3506.2.
Personal watercraft.
Instruction by rental agents, §29.1-749.2.
Minimum distance from shoreline.
City ordinance regulating, penalty for violation, §29.1-748.1.
Port authority.
Board of commissioners, §62.1-129.
Port of Virginia economic and infrastructure development zone grant fund, §62.1-132.3:2.
Public defenders office.
Established, §19.2-163.04.
Public service corporations, taxation of property.
Restriction of imposition of additional tax, §58.1-2606.
Railroads.
Norfolk light rail system, extension to Virginia Beach, §33.1-221.1:8 (note).
Referendum elections.
Specific charter authorization required, §24.2-684.
Retail sales and use tax.
Additional sales tax for Northern Virginia and Hampton Roads, §58.1-603.1.
Additional use tax for Northern Virginia and Hampton Roads, §58.1-604.01.

VIRGINIA BEACH —Cont'd
Sandbridge Beach subdivision.
Coastal primary sand dunes and beaches.
Permits and standards of use, exemption, §28.2-1408.2.
Sand dunes on Atlantic shoreline.
Emergency sand and grading activities, §28.2-1409.
School board.
Fingerprinting applicants for employment, §22.1-296.2.
Salary of members, §22.1-32.
Sale of property to by school board to Department of transportation or commissioner of highways, §22.1-129.
School zones.
Establishing authorized, marking, §46.2-873.
Semi-automatic firearms and shotguns.
Carrying loaded firearms in public areas, §18.2-287.4.
Sewage dumping stations, regulation, §§62.1-44.19:1, 62.1-44.19:2.
Sports authority of Hampton Roads, Virginia, 1986 ch 426.
Streets and alleys.
Alteration and vacation.
Viewers, §15.2-2007.1.
Summons and process.
Who may serve process, §8.01-293.
Tax map reference number.
Circuit court clerk indexing by, §17.1-252.
Territorial limits of city, concurrent jurisdiction with the Commonwealth, §15.2-1725.1.
Tidewater airport commission, 1962 ch 606, 1964 ch 45.
Voluntary property maintenance and zoning inspectors, §15.2-1132.
Wall construction testing requirements, §32.1-176.5.
Well abandonment ordinance.
Duty of owner to cap or close well.
Locality adopting ordinance, §32.1-176.5.
Zoning ordinances.
Coastal primary sand dunes and beaches, §28.2-1403.

VIRGINIA BEACH ARENA, §§15.2-5921 to 15.2-5927.
Acquisition or lease involving facility site.
Report and plan regarding funding, §15.2-5923.
Arena financing fund, §15.2-5925.
Bond issues.
Generally, §15.2-5924.
Review by state treasurer in advance of bond issues, §15.2-5923.
Charges and fees for facility, §15.2-5926.
Construction contracts involving facility site.
Report and plan regarding funding, §15.2-5923.
Definitions, §15.2-5921.
Pledge of state or locality not created, §15.2-5927.
Powers of city, §15.2-5922.
Review by state treasurer in advance of bond issues, §15.2-5923.
Tax revenues from operation of facility.
City entitled to, §15.2-5926.

VIRGINIA BEACH DEVELOPMENT AUTHORITY.
Generally.
See ECONOMIC DEVELOPMENT AUTHORITIES.

VIRGINIA BEEF INDUSTRY COUNCIL, §§3.2-1300 to 3.2-1308.
See BEEF INDUSTRY COUNCIL.

VIRGINIA BICENTENNIAL OF THE AMERICAN WAR OF 1812 COMMISSION, §§30-293 to 30-300.
Acceptance of donations and gifts, §30-296.
Administrative staff support, §30-299.
Compensation of members, §30-296.
Established, §30-293.
Fund, §30-297.
Meetings, §30-295.
Members, §30-294.
Officers, §30-294.
Powers and duties, §30-298.
Purpose, §30-293.
Quorum, §30-295.
Staffing, §30-299.
Sunset provision, §30-300.
Termination, §30-300.
Terms of office, §30-294.

VIRGINIA BIOTECHNOLOGY RESEARCH ACT, §§2.2-5500 to 2.2-5509.

VIRGINIA BIOTECHNOLOGY RESEARCH PARK AUTHORITY, 1993 ch 946, 2000 ch 731.

VIRGINIA BIRTH-RELATED NEUROLOGICAL INJURY COMPENSATION ACT, §§38.2-5000 to 38.2-5021.
See BIRTH-RELATED NEUROLOGICAL INJURY COMPENSATION.
Motion to refer to workers' compensation commission.
Determining whether action satisfies act, §8.01-273.1.

VIRGINIA BLUE ALERT PROGRAM.
Missing law enforcement officers, §§52-34.7 to 52-34.9.

VIRGINIA BOARD FOR PEOPLE WITH DISABILITIES, §§51.5-31 to 51.5-35.1.
See DISABILITY OR HANDICAP.

VIRGINIA BOWLER.
Special license plates, §46.2-749.9.

VIRGINIA BREEDERS FUND, §59.1-372.

VIRGINIA BROADBAND INFRASTRUCTURE LOAN FUND, §§15.2-2419 to 15.2-2429.
Audits and auditors.
Auditor of public accounts, §15.2-2422.
Authority.
Annual audit, §15.2-2422.
Collection of money due fund, §15.2-2423.
Defined, §15.2-2419.
Management of fund, §§15.2-2420, 15.2-2421.
Pledge of loans to secure bonds, §15.2-2426.
Powers of the Authority, §15.2-2428.
Bond issues.
Pledge of loans to secure bonds of authority, §15.2-2426.
Construction of act, §15.2-2428.
Contracts.
Refinancing agreements, §15.2-2424.
Creation, §15.2-2420.
Definitions, §15.2-2419.
Deposit of money, §§15.2-2421, 15.2-2427.
Insurance.
Loans to local governments, §15.2-2424.
Investments, §§15.2-2420, 15.2-2421, 15.2-2426.

VIRGINIA BROADBAND INFRASTRUCTURE LOAN FUND —Cont'd
Loans.
Local governments, §15.2-2424.
Pledge of loans to secure bonds of Authority, §15.2-2426.
Prioritization of loans, §15.2-2425.
Sale of loans, §15.2-2427.
Management of fund, §§15.2-2420, 15.2-2421.

VIRGINIA BUSINESS-EDUCATION PARTNERSHIP PROGRAM, §2.2-208.

VIRGINIA BYWAYS, §§33.1-62 to 33.1-66.
See HIGHWAYS AND ROADS.

VIRGINIA CAREER READINESS CERTIFICATION PROGRAM, §2.2-2674.01.

VIRGINIA CAREGIVERS GRANT FUND, §63.2-2202.

VIRGINIA CAREGIVERS GRANT PROGRAM, §§63.2-2200 to 63.2-2204.

VIRGINIA CENTER FOR COAL AND ENERGY RESEARCH, §§23-135.7:1 to 23-135.7:7.
Virginia energy plan.
Development.
Division of energy to consult center, §67-201.

VIRGINIA CENTER FOR SCHOOL SAFETY, §9.1-184.
School safety audits, duties, §22.1-279.8.

VIRGINIA CENTRAL CRIMINAL RECORDS EXCHANGE.
Generally, §§19.2-387 to 19.2-392.
See CENTRAL CRIMINAL RECORDS EXCHANGE.
Sex offender and crimes against minors registry, §§9.1-900 to 9.1-922.
See SEX OFFENDER REGISTRATION AND NOTIFICATION.
State police communications system, §§52-12 to 52-19.
See STATE POLICE COMMUNICATIONS SYSTEM.

VIRGINIA CHILD PROTECTION ACCOUNTABILITY SYSTEM.
Child abuse and neglect, §63.2-1530.

VIRGINIA COAL.
Preference for use in state facilities, §2.2-4325.

VIRGINIA COAL EMPLOYMENT AND PRODUCTION INCENTIVE TAX CREDIT.
License tax on water, heat, light or power companies, §58.1-2626.1.

VIRGINIA COALFIELD COALITION AUTHORITY, §§33.1-426 to 33.1-429.
Board of commissioners, §33.1-427.
Creation, §33.1-426.
General powers, §33.1-429.
Limited power of authority, §33.1-428.

VIRGINIA COALFIELD ECONOMIC DEVELOPMENT AUTHORITY, §§15.2-6000 to 15.2-6015.

VIRGINIA COALITION FOR OPEN GOVERNMENT.
Freedom of information advisory council.
Recommendation list, citizen members of council, §30-178.

VIRGINIA COAL MINE SAFETY BOARD, §§45.1-161.98 to 45.1-161.100.

VIRGINIA COAL RESEARCH AND DEVELOPMENT ADVISORY BOARD, §23-135.7:7.

VIRGINIA COAL SURFACE MINING CONTROL AND RECLAMATION ACT OF 1979, §§45.1-226 to 45.1-270.7.
See COAL SURFACE MINING.

VIRGINIA COASTAL ENERGY RESEARCH CONSORTIUM, §§67-600 to 67-604.

VIRGINIA COASTAL LAND MANAGEMENT ADVISORY COUNCIL, §28.2-1505.

VIRGINIA CODE.
Electronic access, §30-34.10:2.
General provisions, §§1-1 to 1-9.
See CODE OF VIRGINIA.

VIRGINIA CODE COMMISSION, §§30-145 to 30-155.
See CODE COMMISSION.

VIRGINIA COLLEGE BUILDING AUTHORITY ACT OF 1966, §§23-30.23 to 23-30.38.

VIRGINIA COMMERCIAL FEED ACT, §§3.2-4800 to 3.2-4817.
See FEED.

VIRGINIA COMMISSION FOR THE ARTS, §§2.2-2508 to 2.2-2510.

VIRGINIA COMMISSION ON HIGHER EDUCATION BOARD APPOINTMENTS, §§2.2-2518 to 2.2-2522.

VIRGINIA COMMISSION ON THE CENTENNIAL OF THE WOODROW WILSON PRESIDENCY, §§30-319 to 30-325.

VIRGINIA COMMONWEALTH UNIVERSITY, §§23-50.4 to 23-50.16.
Board of visitors, §§23-50.6 to 23-50.10:01.
Health systems authority.
Appointment of board of visitors to authority board of directors, §23-50.16:5.
Tuition fees and other charges, fixing, §23-50.11.
Campus police departments.
General provisions, §§23-232 to 23-238.
See CAMPUS POLICE.
Reporting campus crime, §23-9.1:1.
Virginia Commonwealth University health system authority.
Enforcement of rules and regulation of authority, §23-50.16:10.
Chief medical examiner.
Teaching duties, §32.1-279.
Conferring of degrees, §23-50.12.
Conveyance of real property, §23-50.13.
Corporate name, §23-50.4.
Health system authority.
Campus police departments.
Enforcement of rules and regulation of authority, §23-50.16:10.
General provisions, §§23-50.16:1 to 23-50.16:35.
See VIRGINIA COMMONWEALTH UNIVERSITY HEALTH SYSTEM AUTHORITY.
Medical center operations, §23-50.16.
Medical College of Virginia.
Grants for students, §32.1-122.6.
Dental students, §32.1-122.9.
Northern Virginia division, §23-50.16:01.
Nursing scholarships, §23-36.2.

VIRGINIA COMMONWEALTH UNIVERSITY —Cont'd
Public procurement.
Exemptions from chapter, §2.2-4343.
Qatar branch campus, §23-50.16:36.
Registered agent for process or notice, §23-50.14.
Special license plates, §46.2-749.
Transfer of property, rights, duties, etc., of former institutions, §23-50.5.
Tuition, fees and other charges, §23-50.11.
Universities generally, §§23-1.01 to 23-9.2:8.
See COLLEGES AND UNIVERSITIES.
Virginia center on aging, §23-50.15.

VIRGINIA COMMONWEALTH UNIVERSITY HEALTH SYSTEM AUTHORITY, §§23-50.16:1 to 23-50.16:35.
Acquisition and disposition of property, §23-50.16:11.
Acquisition and disposition of shares or obligations of other entities, §23-50.16:14.
Administrative process act exemption, §23-50.16:34.
Agent for Virginia Commonwealth University in operating hospital facility, §23-50.16:23.
Assignment of rights and obligations under contracts by university to authority, §23-50.16:21.
Audit of accounts, §23-50.16:8.
Auditor of public accounts, annual audit of authority, §23-50.16:8.
Board of directors.
Appointment, terms, removal, etc., §23-50.16:5.
Approval of capital project, §23-50.16:18.
Closed meetings, §2.2-3711.
Grievance rights for employees, developing and adopting, §23-50.16:24.
Meetings, §23-50.16:5.
Not considered meetings of board of visitors of university, §23-50.16:32.
Telephonic or video meetings, §23-50.16:32.
Bond issues.
Exemption from taxation, §23-50.16:16.
Existing bonds, assumption or making payments on, §23-50.16:31.
Legal investments, §23-50.16:30.
Liability on bond, §23-50.16:26.
Mortgages and deeds of trust, mortgages, trust indentures, securing bond, §23-50.16:28.
Not debt of Commonwealth or political subdivisions, §23-50.16:26.
Power of authority, §§23-50.16:6, 23-50.16:25.
Remedies of obligees of authority, §23-50.16:29.
Security for bond, §23-50.16:28.
Terms, conditions, maturity, form, §23-50.16:27.
Campus police department of Virginia Commonwealth University.
Enforcement of property laws of Commonwealth and rules and regulations of authority, §23-50.16:10.
Capital projects, §23-50.16:18.
Certificate of public need.
Not required on transfer of hospital facilities, §23-50.16:22.
Certified public accountant, audit of authority, §23-50.16:8.
Chapter liberally construed, §23-50.16:33.
Citation of act, §23-50.16:1.
Cities.
Authority to lend or donate money or property, §23-50.16:11.

VIRGINIA COMMONWEALTH UNIVERSITY HEALTH SYSTEM AUTHORITY —Cont'd
Collection of rates, rentals, fees and other charges, §23-50.16:13.
Counties.
Authority to lend or donate money or other property, §23-50.16:11.
Created, §23-50.16:3.
Declaration of necessity, §23-50.16:2.
Definitions, §23-50.16:4.
Deposit of money of authority, §23-50.16:14.
Director.
Appointment, salary and power, §23-50.16:7.
Disposal of project, §23-50.16:11.
Dissolution of authority.
Reversion to Virginia Commonwealth University, §23-50.16:35.
Election of employee not to become employed by authority, §23-50.16:24.
Eminent domain, §23-50.16:12.
Employees, §23-50.16:24.
Insurance, §23-50.16:24.2.
Personnel administration system.
Exemptions, §2.2-2905.
Retirement, §23-50.16:24.1.
Employment discrimination.
Prohibited, §23-50.16:24.
Enforcement of rules and regulations governing access to, conduct in and use of property and facilities, §23-50.16:10.
Exemption from taxation, §23-50.16:16.
Fees, rates, rentals and other charges, §23-50.16:13.
Findings of general assembly, §23-50.16:2.
Freedom of information act.
Excluded records, §2.2-3705.7.
Funds held by or for university, transfer to authority, §23-50.16:17.
Governor.
Appointment of members of board of directors, §23-50.16:5.
Grants.
Acceptance by authority, §23-50.16:11.
Grievance rights of employees.
Board of directors to develop and adopt procedure, §23-50.16:24.
Health insurance.
Continued coverage of employees, §23-50.16:24.
Hospital facilities, operation, §23-50.16:20.
Injunctions.
Remedies of obligees of authority, §23-50.16:29.
Insurance.
Employees, §23-50.16:24.2.
Investment of operating fund, §23-50.16:14.
Investments in bonds issued by authority, §23-50.16:30.
Joint ventures.
Participation in, §23-50.16:14.
Lease, conveyance or transfer of assets and liabilities by Virginia Commonwealth University, §23-50.16:17.
Lease of hospital facilities or other parts from university to authorities, §23-50.16:17.
Leases of real property by authority, §23-50.16:19.
Liberal construction of chapter, §23-50.16:33.
Licenses, permits, certificates of public need or other authorization.
Transferred to authority, §23-50.16:22.
Loans.
Acceptance by authority, §23-50.16:11.

VIRGINIA COMMONWEALTH UNIVERSITY HEALTH SYSTEM AUTHORITY —Cont'd
Mandamus.
Remedies of obligees of authority, §23-50.16:29.
Meetings of board of directors, §23-50.16:5.
Meetings not considered meetings of board of visitors of Virginia Commonwealth University, §23-50.16:32.
Telephonic or video meetings, §23-50.16:32.
Mission of Medical College of Virginia hospitals, §23-50.16:2.
Nonprofit entities, creation by authority, §23-50.16:14.
Operation of hospital facilities, §23-50.16:20.
Authority as agent for Virginia Commonwealth University, §23-50.16:23.
Operation of project, §23-50.16:9.
Personnel act exemption, §23-50.16:34.
Police officers and auxiliary forces, authority to employ, §23-232.
Police powers, §23-50.16:10.
Powers generally, §23-50.16:6.
Powers to operate project, §23-50.16:9.
Private individuals, assets or earnings not to inure to benefit of, §23-50.16:15.
Projects.
Capital projects, §23-50.16:18.
Defined, §23-50.16:4.
Disposal, §23-50.16:11.
Operation, §23-50.16:9.
Prompt payment of bills, §23-50.16:6.
Public instrumentality, §23-50.16:3.
Public procurement act exemption, §23-50.16:34.
Public purpose, exercise of powers of authority, §23-50.16:15.
Purpose, §23-50.16:3.
Remedies of obligees of authority, §23-50.16:29.
Removal of members of board of directors, §23-50.16:5.
Retirement of employees.
Benefits, §23-50.16:24.1.
Reversion to Virginia Commonwealth University on dissolution of authority, §23-50.16:35.
State and local government conflicts of interest act.
Applicability to members of board, §23-50.16:5.
Substitution of authority for university as party to agreement, §23-50.16:21.
Tax exemptions, §23-50.16:16.
Title of act, §23-50.16:1.
Towns.
Authority to lend or donate money or other property, §23-50.16:11.
Transfer of employment to authority, §23-50.16:24.
Transfer of facilities to authority, §23-50.16:17.
Virginia retirement system.
Continued membership of employees transferred to authority, §23-50.16:24.
Workforce transition act exemption, §23-50.16:34.

VIRGINIA COMMUNICATIONS SALES AND USE TAX ACT, §§58.1-645 to 58.1-662.
See COMMUNICATIONS SALES AND USE TAX.

VIRGINIA COMMUNITY COLLEGE SYSTEM.
State board for community colleges.
Generally, §§23-214 to 23-231.1:1.
See COMMUNITY COLLEGES.

VIRGINIA COMPREHENSIVE MONEY LAUNDERING ACT, §§18.2-246.1 to 18.2-246.5.
See MONEY LAUNDERING.

VIRGINIA COMPUTER CRIMES ACT, §§18.2-152.1 to 18.2-152.15.
See COMPUTER CRIMES.

VIRGINIA CONGENITAL ABNORMALITIES REPORTING AND EDUCATION SYSTEM, §§32.1-69.1, 32.1-69.2.

VIRGINIA CONSUMER FINANCE ACT.
See CONSUMER FINANCE.

VIRGINIA CONSUMER PROTECTION ACT, §§59.1-196 to 59.1-207.

VIRGINIA CONTRACTOR TRANSACTION RECOVERY ACT, §§54.1-1118 to 54.1-1127.

VIRGINIA COOPERATIVE EXTENSION AND AGRICULTURAL EXPERIMENT STATION DIVISION, §§23-132.1 to 23-132.12.
See COOPERATIVE EXTENSION AND AGRICULTURAL EXPERIMENT STATION DIVISION.

VIRGINIA COORDINATE SYSTEM, §§55-287 to 55-297.

VIRGINIA CORD BLOOD BANK INITIATIVE.
Established, §32.1-69.3.
Practitioners to provide pregnant women with certain information, §54.1-2403.02.
Publication of information, §32.1-69.4.

VIRGINIA CORRECTIONAL ENTERPRISES.
Jails.
County and city jail farms, §§53.1-96 to 53.1-115.2.
See COUNTY AND CITY JAIL FARMS.
Jails generally, §§53.1-68 to 53.1-133.9.
See JAILS.
Prisons.
See PRISONS.

VIRGINIA CREDIT UNION ACT, §§6.2-1300 to 6.2-1380.

VIRGINIA CREDIT UNION SHARE INSURANCE ACT, §§6.2-1331 to 6.2-1343.

VIRGINIA CRIMINAL INFORMATION NETWORK.
Central criminal records exchange, §§19.2-387 to 19.2-392.
See CENTRAL CRIMINAL RECORDS EXCHANGE.
Criminal justice information system, §§9.1-126 to 9.1-137.
See CRIMINAL JUSTICE INFORMATION SYSTEM.
Sex offender and crimes against minors registry, §§9.1-900 to 9.1-922.
See SEX OFFENDER REGISTRATION AND NOTIFICATION.
State police communications system, §§52-12 to 52-19.
See STATE POLICE COMMUNICATIONS SYSTEM.
Virginia central criminal records exchange, §§19.2-387 to 19.2-392.
See CENTRAL CRIMINAL RECORDS EXCHANGE.

VIRGINIA CRIMINAL SENTENCING COMMISSION, §§17.1-800 to 17.1-806.

VIRGINIA DEFECTIVE DRYWALL CORRECTION AND RESTORATION ASSISTANCE FUND, §§36-156.1, 36-156.2.

VIRGINIA DISABILITY COMMISSION, §§30-232 to 30-238.

VIRGINIA DISASTER RESPONSE FUNDS.
Disbursement, §44-146.18:1.
Hazardous materials emergency response program disbursement, §44-146.37.

VIRGINIA DISTRIBUTION CENTER.
Availability to public broadcasting stations and public bodies, §2.2-1122.

VIRGINIA DIVISION OF UNITED DAUGHTERS OF CONFEDERACY.
State recordation tax exemption, §58.1-811.

VIRGINIA DONOR REGISTRY, §§32.1-291.20, 32.1-292.2.

VIRGINIA DRUG FREE DAY, §2.2-3313.

VIRGINIA ECONOMIC DEVELOPMENT PARTNERSHIP AUTHORITY, §§2.2-2234 to 2.2-2246.
See ECONOMIC DEVELOPMENT PARTNERSHIP AUTHORITY.

VIRGINIA EGG BOARD, §§3.2-1600 to 3.2-1610.
See EGG BOARD.

VIRGINIA ELECTRIC UTILITY RESTRUCTURING ACT, §§56-576 to 56-596.
See ELECTRIC UTILITY RESTRUCTURING.

VIRGINIA EMERGENCY RESPONSE COUNCIL, §44-146.40.

VIRGINIA EMERGENCY SERVICES AND DISASTER LAW OF 1973, §§44-146.13 to 44-146.28.
See EMERGENCY MANAGEMENT.

VIRGINIA ENERGY PLAN.
Generally, §§67-100 to 67-1003.
See ENERGY.

VIRGINIA ENVIRONMENTAL EXCELLENCE PROGRAM, §§10.1-1187.1 to 10.1-1187.7.
See ENVIRONMENTAL EXCELLENCE PROGRAM.

VIRGINIA ENVIROTHON.
Soil and water conservation districts, §10.1-549.1.

VIRGINIA ESTATE TAX ACT, §§58.1-900 to 58.1-938.
See ESTATE TAX.

VIRGINIA ESTUARINE AND COASTAL RESEARCH RESERVE SYSTEM, §§28.2-1103, 28.2-1104.
Establishment, §28.2-1103.
Intergovernmental coordination, §28.2-1104.
Public policy, §28.2-1103.

VIRGINIA EXPORT FUND.
Creation and management, §2.2-2309.

VIRGINIA FAIR HOUSING LAW, §§36-96.1 to 36-96.23.
See FAIR HOUSING.

VIRGINIA FARM BUREAU FEDERATION.
Cooperative development with office of farmland preservation, §3.2-201.

VIRGINIA FARMER DROUGHT, FLOOD AND HURRICANE DISASTER ACT.
See FARMER MAJOR DROUGHT, FLOOD AND HURRICANE DISASTER ASSISTANCE.

VIRGINIA FARM LINK PROGRAM.
Administered by farmland preservation office, §3.2-201.
Created, §3.2-202.

VIRGINIA FERTILIZER ACT.
See FERTILIZER.

VIRGINIA FIRMS.
Procurement by public bodies.
Preferences, §2.2-4324.

VIRGINIA FLAG.
Defacing, mutilating, etc., §§18.2-486 to 18.2-492.

VIRGINIA FOUNDATION FOR HEALTHY YOUTH, §§32.1-354 to 32.1-367.
Accounts and accounting, §§32.1-362, 32.1-363.
Board of trustees.
Appointment, §32.1-357.
Composition, §32.1-357.
Duties, §32.1-359.
Endowment, management, §32.1-361.1.
Corporate powers, §§32.1-356, 32.1-365.
Public purpose, §32.1-365.
Creation, §32.1-355.
Definitions, §32.1-354.
Director.
Appointment, §32.1-358.
Defined, §32.1-354.
Endowment, §32.1-361.1.
Fund.
Audits and accounts, §§32.1-362, 32.1-363.
Creation, §32.1-360.
Defined, §32.1-354.
Deposit of funds, §32.1-360.
Endowment, §32.1-361.1.
Use of disbursements, §32.1-361.
Health care fund, §§32.1-366, 32.1-367.
Established, §32.1-366.
Uses, §32.1-367.
Legal counsel, §32.1-359.
Legislative purpose, §32.1-355.
Obesity.
Virginia youth obesity prevention.
Division of foundation, §32.1-355.
Personnel hiring, §§32.1-356, 32.1-358.
Powers, §§32.1-356, 32.1-365.
Public purpose, §32.1-365.
Public policy, §32.1-355.
Reporting requirements, §32.1-364.
Rulemaking authority, §32.1-356.
Tax-exempt status, §32.1-365.
Teenage smoking.
Entities and programs to prevent.
Use of distributed funds, §32.1-361.
Virginia health care fund, §§32.1-366, 32.1-367.
Established, §32.1-366.
Uses, §32.1-367.
Virginia tobacco settlement foundation.
Division of VFHY, §32.1-355.

VIRGINIA FRAUD AGAINST TAXPAYERS ACT.
Fraudulent claims against the state, §§8.01-216.1 to 8.01-216.19.
Fraudulent clams against the state.
See FRAUDULENT CLAIMS AGAINST THE STATE.

VIRGINIA FUEL COMMISSION.
Emergency coal property seizures, §§45.1-161.316, 45.1-161.317.

VIRGINIA FUEL CONVERSION AUTHORITY, 1980 ch 223.
Amended in 1981, 1981 ch 211.
Repeal of chapter 223, 1980 acts, 1988 ch 239.

VIRGINIA FUELS TAX ACT.
Fuel taxes, §§58.1-2200 to 58.1-2299.20.
See FUEL TAXES.

VIRGINIA FUSION INTELLIGENCE CENTER, §52-47.
Confidentiality.
Information relative to criminal intelligence or terrorism investigation, §52-48.
Immunity from service of process, §52-48.
Review of information contained in database, §52-48.
Unauthorized release or dissemination of information, §52-48.

VIRGINIA GAS AND OIL ACT, §§45.1-361.1 to 45.1-361.44.
See GAS AND OIL EXPLORATION.

VIRGINIA GAS AND OIL BOARD, §§45.1-361.13 to 45.1-361.15.

VIRGINIA GENERAL CONDEMNATION ACT.
See EMINENT DOMAIN.

VIRGINIA GEOGRAPHIC INFORMATION NETWORK, §§2.2-2025 to 2.2-2030.
See INFORMATION TECHNOLOGIES AGENCY.

VIRGINIA GEOGRAPHIC INFORMATION NETWORK ADVISORY BOARD, §2.2-2423.

VIRGINIA GEOTHERMAL RESOURCE CONSERVATION ACT, §§45.1-179.1 to 45.1-179.11.

VIRGINIA GOVERNMENTAL FRAUDS ACT, §§18.2-498.1 to 18.2-498.5.

VIRGINIA GUARANTEED ASSISTANCE PROGRAM AND FUND, §§23-38.53:4 to 23-38.53:6.

VIRGINIA HAZARDOUS MATERIALS EMERGENCY RESPONSE PROGRAM, §§44-146.34 to 44-146.40.

VIRGINIA HEALTH CARE FUND, §§32.1-366, 32.1-367.

VIRGINIA HEALTH SAVINGS ACCOUNT PLAN, §38.2-5601.
Exemption from creditors' claims, §38.2-5604.
High deductible health plans, §38.2-5602.1.

VIRGINIA HEALTH SPA ACT, §59.1-295.

VIRGINIA HEALTH WORKFORCE DEVELOPMENT AUTHORITY, §§32.1-122.7 to 32.1-122.7:2.

VIRGINIA HEARING IMPAIRMENT IDENTIFICATION AND MONITORING SYSTEM, §§32.1-64.1, 32.1-64.2.
Virginia immunization information system (VIIS).
Linkages to other databases containing certain health records, §32.1-46.01.

VIRGINIA HIGHER EDUCATION OPPORTUNITY ACT OF 2011, §§23-38.87:10 to 23-38.87:21.
Assessment and certification of institutions by council, §23-38.87:21.
Basic operations and instruction funding need, §23-38.87:13.
Definitions, §23-38.87:11.
Economic and innovation incentives, §23-38.87:16.
Fixing of fees and tuition rates, §23-38.87:18.
Funding policy, §23-38.87:12.
Higher education advisory committee, §23-38.87:20.
Legislative purpose, §23-38.87:10.
Need-based financial aid, §23-38.87:15.
Per student enrollment-based funding, §23-38.87:14.
Six-year plan for each institution, §23-38.87:17.
STEM public-private partnership, §23-38.87:19.
Title of act, §23-38.87:10.

VIRGINIA HIGHER EDUCATION TUITION TRUST FUND, §§23-38.75 to 23-38.87:1.
See COLLEGE SAVINGS PLAN.

VIRGINIA HIGHLANDS COMMUNITY COLLEGE.
Southwest Virginia cultural heritage foundation.
Board of trustees, §2.2-2735.

VIRGINIA HIGHWAY CORPORATION ACT OF 1988, §§56-535 to 56-552.
See HIGHWAY CORPORATIONS.

VIRGINIA HISTORICAL SOCIETY.
Battle Abbey at Richmond.
Appropriations for maintenance, §10.1-2212.
Property exempt from taxation, §58.1-3607.

VIRGINIA HISTORY MONTH, §2.2-3318.

VIRGINIA HOME.
Property tax exemption, §58.1-3607.

VIRGINIA HOME PROTECTION COMPANY ACT, §§38.2-2600 to 38.2-2616.

VIRGINIA HOME SOLICITATION SALES ACT, §§59.1-21.1 to 59.1-21.7:1.

VIRGINIA HOUSING COMMISSION, §§30-257 to 30-262.
Compensation and expenses, §30-260.
Meetings, §30-259.
Members, §30-258.
Powers and duties, §30-261.
Purpose of commission, §30-257.
Staffing, §30-262.

VIRGINIA HOUSING DEVELOPMENT AUTHORITY ACT, §§36-55.24 to 36-55.52.
See HOUSING DEVELOPMENT AUTHORITY.

VIRGINIA HUNTERS WHO CARE, INC.
Voluntary contributions.
Hunting permit or license to include language permitting, §29.1-330.
Deposit of contribution into feed the hungry fund, §29.1-332.

VIRGINIA INDEPENDENT SCHOOLS ASSOCIATION.
Charitable or civic contributions solicitation.
Exemptions from provisions.
Educational institutions accredited by association, §57-60.

VIRGINIA INDIGENT HEALTH CARE TRUST FUND.
Counties, cities or towns.
Power to make appropriations of public funds, personal property or real estate to, §15.2-953.

VIRGINIA INDOOR CLEAN AIR ACT.
Smoking in public places, §§15.2-2820 to 15.2-2833.
See SMOKING IN PUBLIC PLACES.

VIRGINIA INDUSTRIAL DEVELOPMENT CORPORATION ACT, §§13.1-981 to 13.1-998.

VIRGINIA INDUSTRIALIZED BUILDING SAFETY LAW, §§36-70 to 36-85.1.

VIRGINIA INFORMATION TECHNOLOGIES AGENCY, §§2.2-2005 to 2.2-2031.
See INFORMATION TECHNOLOGIES AGENCY.

VIRGINIA INFRASTRUCTURE PROJECT LOAN FUND, §§15.2-2430 to 15.2-2440.
Administration and management.
Virginia resources authority, §15.2-2431.
Ad valorem taxes.
Levy and collect by local government.
Terms and conditions of loan, §15.2-2435.
Audit of fund annually, §15.2-2433.
Bonds of resources authority.
Pledge of loans to secure, §15.2-2437.
Bonds or notes of local government.
Loans evidenced by, §15.2-2435.
Chapter liberally construed, §15.2-2440.
Collection of money due fund, §15.2-2434.
Creation, §15.2-2431.
Definitions, §15.2-2430.
Deposit of money belonging to fund, §15.2-2432.
Distribution of loans from fund.
Guidelines, §15.2-2431.
Interest rates and repayment rates.
Establishment, §15.2-2431.
Investment of money in fund, §15.2-2432.
Loans to local governments, §15.2-2435.
Pledge of authority's bonds to secure, §15.2-2437.
Prioritization of loans, §15.2-2436.
Sale of loans, §15.2-2438.
Local government defined, §15.2-2430.
Methane or other combustible gas.
Building or facility to collect or use for electric power.
Project defined, §15.2-2430.
Powers of resources authority, §15.2-2439.
Prioritization of loans, §15.2-2436.
Project defined, §15.2-2430.
Recovery of amounts due fund.
Proceedings, §15.2-2434.
Revenue sufficient to pay project costs and indebtedness incurred.
Duty of local government to product.
Terms and conditions of loan, §15.2-2435.
Sale of loans to local governments, §15.2-2438.
Special funds.
Duty of local government to establish, §15.2-2435.
Terms and conditions of loans to local governments, §15.2-2435.

VIRGINIA INITIATIVE FOR EMPLOYMENT NOT WELFARE, §§63.2-608 to 63.2-613.
Workers' compensation.
Ineligibility for certain benefits, §§65.2-500, 65.2-502, 65.2-512.

VIRGINIA INSTITUTE OF MARINE SCIENCE, §§28.2-1100 to 28.2-1102.
Catching hard-shell clams.
Use of hydraulic dredges, §28.2-520.
Continued, §28.2-1100.
Duties, §28.2-1100.
Funds, §28.2-1101.
Marine organisms, taking, §28.2-1101.
Property violations, §28.2-1102.
Services of other agencies, §28.2-1101.
Virginia estuarine and coastal research reserve system, §§28.2-1103, 28.2-1104.

VIRGINIA INTERAGENCY COORDINATING COUNCIL, §2.2-2664.

VIRGINIA INVESTMENT PARTNERSHIP ACT, §§2.2-5100 to 2.2-5104.

VIRGINIA-ISRAEL ADVISORY BOARD, §§2.2-2424, 2.2-2425.
Duties, §2.2-2425.
Establishment, §2.2-2424.
Powers, §2.2-2425.
Purpose, §2.2-2424.
Reports.
Annual executive summary, §2.2-2424.

VIRGINIA JOBS INVESTMENT PROGRAM, §2.2-1611.

VIRGINIA JOBS INVESTMENT PROGRAM (EFF UNTIL 1/1/2014), §2.2-903.1.

VIRGINIA JUVENILE COMMUNITY CRIME CONTROL ACT, §§16.1-309.2 to 16.1-309.10.
See JUVENILE COMMUNITY CRIME CONTROL.

VIRGINIA KOREAN WAR VETERANS APPRECIATION WEEK, §2.2-3309.1.

VIRGINIA LAND CONSERVATION BOARD OF TRUSTEES, §10.1-1018.

VIRGINIA LAND CONSERVATION FOUNDATION, §§10.1-1017 to 10.1-1026.
Cooperative development with office of farmland preservation, §3.2-201.
See LAND CONSERVATION FOUNDATION.

VIRGINIA LAND CONSERVATION INCENTIVES.
Real property taxes, §§58.1-510 to 58.1-513.

VIRGINIA LAND EVALUATION AND SITE ASSESSMENT SYSTEM.
Agricultural and forestal districts.
Evaluating land for inclusion in district, §15.2-4306.
Withdrawal of land from district, §15.2-4314.

VIRGINIA LAW OFFICERS' RETIREMENT SYSTEM, §§51.1-211 to 51.1-221.
See LAW OFFICERS' RETIREMENT SYSTEM.

VIRGINIA LEASE-PURCHASE AGREEMENT ACT, §§59.1-207.17 to 59.1-207.27.

VIRGINIA LIFE, ACCIDENT AND SICKNESS INSURANCE GUARANTY ASSOCIATION, §§38.2-1700 to 38.2-1721.
See LIFE, ACCIDENT AND SICKNESS INSURANCE GUARANTY ASSOCIATION.

VIRGINIA LITTER TAX ACT, §§58.1-1706 to 58.1-1710.

VIRGINIA MANUFACTURED HOUSING CONSTRUCTION AND SAFETY STANDARDS ACT, §§36-85.2 to 36-85.15.
See MANUFACTURED HOUSING.

VIRGINIA MANUFACTURED HOUSING TRANSACTION RECOVERY FUND, §§36-85.31 to 36-85.36.
See MANUFACTURED HOUSING.

VIRGINIA MARITIME ASSOCIATION.
Ballast water discharge.
Adoption of forms, §28.2-111.
Services, §28.2-110.

VIRGINIA MEDICAID PRIOR AUTHORIZATION ADVISORY COMMITTEE.
Administrative process act.
Exemptions, §2.2-4002.

VIRGINIA MEMBERSHIP CAMPING ACT, §§59.1-311 to 59.1-335.

VIRGINIA MILITARY ADVISORY COUNCIL, §§2.2-2666.1 to 2.2-2666.3.
Secretary of veterans affairs and homeland security.
Agencies for which responsible, §2.2-230.
Virginia freedom of information act.
Records excluded from application of act, §2.2-3705.2.

VIRGINIA MILITARY CODE, §§44-1 to 44-122.

VIRGINIA MILITARY FAMILY RELIEF FUND, §44-102.2.
Tax refunds, voluntary contributions to, §58.1-344.3.

VIRGINIA MILITARY INSTITUTE, §§23-92 to 23-113.
Admission of cadets, §§23-104 to 23-107.2.
Board of visitors, §§23-93 to 23-103.
Prohibition on federal employees, exception, §2.2-2801.
Cadets, §§23-104 to 23-109.
Campus police departments.
General provisions, §§23-232 to 23-238.
See CAMPUS POLICE.
Reporting campus crime, §23-9.1:1.
Colleges and universities generally, §§23-1.01 to 23-9.2:8.
See COLLEGES AND UNIVERSITIES.
Commissioned officers as students, §23-108.
Conferring of degrees, §23-110.
Corporate name, §23-92.
Criteria for admission, §23-105.
Financial assistance with tuition and board, §23-106.
Military scholarship cadets, §§23-107.1, 23-107.2.
Musicians, §23-112.
National guard service.
Required for military scholarship cadets, §23-107.2.
Officers to be officers of militia, §44-117.
Payroll and other transactions.
Processing, §2.2-803.1.
Service requirements.
Cadets received on state account, §23-107.
Special license plates, §46.2-749.
State cadets.
Admission, §23-105.

VIRGINIA MILITARY INSTITUTE —Cont'd
State cadets —Cont'd
Financial assistance with tuition and board, §23-106.
Military scholarship cadets, §§23-107.1, 23-107.2.
Service requirements for cadets received on state account, §23-107.
Water supply, §23-113.

VIRGINIA MILITARY PARENTS EQUAL PROTECTION ACT, §§20-124.7 to 20-124.10.

VIRGINIA MILITARY SURVIVORS AND DEPENDENTS EDUCATION PROGRAM, §23-7.4:1.

VIRGINIA MINIMUM WAGE ACT, §§40.1-28.8 to 40.1-28.12.

VIRGINIA MODEL INTERSTATE PAROLE AND PROBATION HEARINGS ACT, §§53.1-168 to 53.1-176.

VIRGINIA MOTION PICTURE FAIR COMPETITION ACT, §§59.1-255 to 59.1-260.

VIRGINIA MOTOR SPORTS INITIATIVE.
Special license plates, §46.2-749.69:1.

VIRGINIA MOTOR VEHICLE RENTAL TAX, §§58.1-1734 to 58.1-1741.
See MOTOR VEHICLE RENTALS.

VIRGINIA MOTOR VEHICLE SALES AND USE TAX ACT, §§58.1-2400 to 58.1-2426.
See MOTOR VEHICLE SALES AND USE TAX.

VIRGINIA MOTOR VEHICLE WARRANTY ENFORCEMENT ACT, §§59.1-207.9 to 59.1-207.16:1.

VIRGINIA MUNICIPAL LEAGUE.
Freedom of information advisory council.
Recommendation list, local government representative to, §30-178.

VIRGINIA MUSEUM OF FINE ARTS, §§23-253.1 to 23-253.7.
Arts commission.
Construction and interpretation, §2.2-2509.
Employees.
Personnel administration system.
Exemptions, §2.2-2905.

VIRGINIA MUSEUM OF NATURAL HISTORY.
Employees.
Personnel administration system.
Exemptions, §2.2-2905.

VIRGINIA MUSHROOM FESTIVAL, §2.2-3321.

VIRGINIA NATIONAL GUARD.
General provisions, §§44-25 to 44-54.3.
See NATIONAL GUARD.
Militia generally, §§44-1 to 44-122.
See MILITIA.
Naval militia, §§44-55 to 44-74.
See NAVAL MILITIA.
State defense force, §§44-54.4 to 44-54.12.
See STATE DEFENSE FORCE.

VIRGINIA NAVAL MUSEUM AUTHORITY, 1975 ch 488, 1980 ch 334.

VIRGINIA NEW JOBS PROGRAM, §2.2-1612.

VIRGINIA NEW JOBS PROGRAM (EFF UNTIL 1/1/2014), §2.2-903.2.

VIRGINIA NONSTOCK CORPORATION ACT, §§13.1-801 to 13.1-945.
See NONPROFIT CORPORATIONS.

VIRGINIA NOTARY ACT, §§47.1-1 to 47.1-30.
See NOTARIES.

VIRGINIANS WITH DISABILITIES ACT.
Generally, §§51.5-1 to 51.5-46.
See DISABILITY OR HANDICAP.

VIRGINIA NUCLEAR ENERGY CONSORTIUM, §§67-1400 to 67-1406.
See NUCLEAR ENERGY.

VIRGINIA OFFICE FOR PROTECTION AND ADVOCACY.
Disability or handicap.
Conversion of office into nonprofit entity for protection, advocacy, etc, services, §51.5-39.13.
Protection and advocacy system generally, §§51.5-39.1 to 51.5-39.13.
See DISABILITY OR HANDICAP.

VIRGINIA OFFSHORE WIND DEVELOPMENT AUTHORITY, §§67-1200 to 67-1211.
See OFFSHORE WIND DEVELOPMENT AUTHORITY.

VIRGINIA OUTDOORS FOUNDATION.
See OUTDOORS FOUNDATION.

VIRGINIA PERSONNEL ACT.
Personnel administration system generally, §§2.2-2900 to 2.2-2905.
See PUBLIC OFFICERS AND EMPLOYEES.

VIRGINIA PETROLEUM PRODUCTS FRANCHISE ACT, §§59.1-21.8 to 59.1-21.18:1.

VIRGINIA PETROLEUM STORAGE TANK FUND, §62.1-44.34:11.

VIRGINIA POLYTECHNIC INSTITUTE AND STATE UNIVERSITY, §§23-114 to 23-155.05.
Advanced research institute.
Coastal energy research consortium, §§67-600 to 67-604.
Agriculture education unit, §3.2-101.
Board of visitors, §§23-114 to 23-122.1.
Campus police departments.
General provisions, §§23-232 to 23-238.
See CAMPUS POLICE.
Reporting campus crime, §23-9.1:1.
Clifton Forge-Covington branch, §§23-135.12 to 23-135.16.
Cooperative extension and agricultural experiment station division, §§23-132.1 to 23-132.12.
See COOPERATIVE EXTENSION AND AGRICULTURAL EXPERIMENT STATION DIVISION.
Coordinate system duties, §55-297.
Curriculum, §23-130.
Donations.
Governmental aid and individual donations, §§23-136 to 23-141.
Electric power and energy purchase contracts, §23-155.05.
Faculty.
Appointment of professors, §§23-124 to 23-128.
Farmer major drought, flood and hurricane disaster assistance.
Extension division, §3.2-503.
Governmental aid and individual donations, §§23-136 to 23-141.
Nautical school, §§23-142 to 23-146.
Officers to be officers of militia, §44-117.
Payroll and other transactions.
Processing, §2.2-803.1.

VIRGINIA POLYTECHNIC INSTITUTE AND STATE UNIVERSITY —Cont'd
Public procurement.
Exemptions from chapter, §2.2-4343.
Roanoke technical institute, §§23-135.8 to 23-135.11.
School of mines continued, §23-131.
Soil scientist scholarships, §§23-38.3 to 23-38.10.
See SCHOLARSHIPS.
Special license plates, §46.2-749.
State land evaluation advisory council.
Dean of college of agriculture member of, §58.1-3239.
Student financial aid.
Soil scientist scholarships, §§23-38.3 to 23-38.10.
See SCHOLARSHIPS.
Truck and ornamentals research station, §§23-155.01 to 23-155.04.
Universities generally, §§23-1.01 to 23-9.2:8.
See COLLEGES AND UNIVERSITIES.
Wytheville branch, §§23-135.17 to 23-135.21.

VIRGINIA PORK INDUSTRY BOARD, §§3.2-2000 to 3.2-2009.
See PORK INDUSTRY BOARD.

VIRGINIA PORT AUTHORITY ACT, §§62.1-128 to 62.1-147.2.

VIRGINIA PORT VOLUME INCREASE TAX CREDIT, §58.1-439.12:10.

VIRGINIA POST-DISASTER ANTI-PRICE GOUGING ACT, §§59.1-525 to 59.1-529.1.

VIRGINIA PRESS ASSOCIATION.
Freedom of information advisory council.
Recommendation list, citizen members of council, §30-178.

VIRGINIA PRISONER LITIGATION REFORM ACT, §§8.01-689 to 8.01-697.

VIRGINIA PRIVATE WELL CONSTRUCTION ACT, §§32.1-176.1 to 32.1-176.7.

VIRGINIA PRODUCTS WITH RECYCLED CONTENT.
Procurement by public bodies.
Preferences, §2.2-4324.

VIRGINIA PROPERTY AND CASUALTY INSURANCE GUARANTY ASSOCIATION, §§38.2-1600 to 38.2-1623.

VIRGINIA PROPERTY INSURANCE ASSOCIATION.
Rates.
Workers' compensation, automobiles, home protection, etc., §§38.2-2000 to 38.2-2027.
See INSURANCE RATES.

VIRGINIA PUBLIC BUILDING AUTHORITY, §§2.2-2260 to 2.2-2278.
See PUBLIC BUILDING AUTHORITY.

VIRGINIA PUBLIC GUARDIAN AND CONSERVATOR PROGRAM.
Aging and rehabilitative services, department for, §§51.5-149 to 51.5-151.

VIRGINIA PUBLIC PROCUREMENT ACT, §§2.2-4300 to 2.2-4377.
See PUBLIC PROCUREMENT.

VIRGINIA PUBLIC RECORDS ACT, §§42.1-76 to 42.1-90.1.
See STATE RECORDS MANAGEMENT.

VIRGINIA PUBLIC SCHOOL AUTHORITY.
Generally, §§22.1-162 to 22.1-175.
See PUBLIC SCHOOL AUTHORITY.

VIRGINIA PUBLIC SCHOOL CONSTRUCTION GRANTS PROGRAM, §§22.1-175.1 to 22.1-175.5.

VIRGINIA PUBLIC SCHOOL EDUCATIONAL TECHNOLOGY GRANTS PROGRAM, §§22.1-175.6 to 22.1-175.9.

VIRGINIA QUALITY LABEL.
Agricultural grades, marks and brands, §§3.2-4312 to 3.2-4321.
See AGRICULTURAL GRADES, MARKS AND BRANDS.

VIRGINIA RACKETEER INFLUENCED AND CORRUPT ORGANIZATION (RICO) ACT, §§18.2-512 to 18.2-517.
See RACKETEERING.

VIRGINIA READING THE LAW PROGRAM, §54.1-3926.

VIRGINIA REAL ESTATE COOPERATIVE ACT, §§55-424 to 55-506.

VIRGINIA REAL ESTATE TIME-SHARE ACT, §§55-360 to 55-400.
See TIME-SHARES.

VIRGINIA REAL ESTATE TRANSACTION RECOVERY ACT.
Real estate brokers, salespersons and rental agents, §§54.1-2112 to 54.1-2120.

VIRGINIA RECORDATION TAX ACT, §§58.1-800 to 58.1-817.
See RECORDATION TAX, STATE.

VIRGINIA REGIONAL INDUSTRIAL FACILITIES AUTHORITIES.
Audits, §15.2-6413.
Board, §15.2-6403.
Bonds.
Investments in, §15.2-6410.
Issues, §15.2-6409.
Pledging faith and credit of Commonwealth or other political subdivisions, §15.2-6412.
Tax exemption, §15.2-6411.
Creation of authorities, procedure, §15.2-6402.
Definitions, §15.2-6400.
Dissolution of authority, §15.2-6415.
Donations, §15.2-6406.
Land use regulations, applicability, §15.2-6408.
Liberally construed, §15.2-6416.
Office of authority, §15.2-6404.
Powers, §15.2-6405.
Purpose and findings, §15.2-6401.
Records and accounts, §15.2-6413.
Revenue sharing, §15.2-6407.
Tax revenue remittance, §15.2-6406.
Title to property, §15.2-6404.
Tort liability, §15.2-6414.

VIRGINIA REMOVAL OR REHABILITATION OF DERELICT STRUCTURES FUND, §§36-152 to 36-156.

VIRGINIA REPORTS, §§17.1-316 to 17.1-320.
Advance sheets, printing and distribution, §17.1-317.
Custody and distribution, §17.1-319.
Law school libraries destroyed by fire.
Furnishing to, §17.1-320.

VIRGINIA REPORTS —Cont'd
Printing and binding volumes, §17.1-316.
Reporter of court, §§17.1-321 to 17.1-323.

VIRGINIA RESIDENTIAL LANDLORD AND TENANT ACT, §§55-248.2 to 55-248.40.
See LANDLORD AND TENANT.

VIRGINIA RESIDENTIAL PROPERTY DISCLOSURE ACT, §§55-517 to 55-525.
See RESIDENTIAL PROPERTY TRANSFER DISCLOSURES.

VIRGINIA RESOURCES AUTHORITY, §§62.1-197 to 62.1-223.
Administrative process act.
Exemptions, §2.2-4002.
Virginia infrastructure project loan fund, §§15.2-2430 to 15.2-2440.
See VIRGINIA INFRASTRUCTURE PROJECT LOAN FUND.

VIRGINIA RETAIL SALES AND USE TAX ACT, §§58.1-600 to 58.1-639.
See RETAIL SALES AND USE TAX.

VIRGINIA RETIREMENT SYSTEM, §§51.1-124.1 to 51.1-169.
Acknowledgment by spouse, §51.1-165.1.
Actuarial investigation, §51.1-124.22.
Actuary.
Employment as technical advisor to board, §51.1-124.22.
Additional service retirement allowance, §51.1-155.
Administration by board, §51.1-124.22.
Hybrid retirement program, §51.1-169.
Administrative fees.
Board, charging and collecting, §51.1-124.22.
Advisory committee to the board of trustees, §§51.1-124.25, 51.1-124.26.
Allowance for disability retirement, §51.1-157.
Assets, §§51.1-147 to 51.1-150.
Account of retirement allowances, §51.1-148.
Custodians, §51.1-149.
Deposits, §51.1-150.
Distribution upon repeal of system, §51.1-124.7.
Exemption from process, §51.1-124.4.
Members' contribution account, §51.1-147.
Payments, §51.1-149.
Pooling for investment, §51.1-124.31.
Repeal of system.
Distribution upon, §51.1-124.7.
Retirement allowance account, §51.1-148.
Tax exemption, §51.1-124.4.
Automatic rollover of mandatory cash-out.
Board selection of retirement plan provider and investment product.
Loss from, board not liable, §51.1-124.30.
Benefit restoration plan, §§51.1-1300 to 51.1-1304.
Benefits, §§51.1-152 to 51.1-169.
Acknowledgment by spouse of member, §51.1-165.1.
Additional service retirement allowance, §51.1-155.
Administration, §51.1-1301.
Allowance for disability retirement, §§51.1-156, 51.1-157.
Cessation, §51.1-160.
Allowance for service retirement, §51.1-155.
Allowance reduction, §51.1-167.
Application of provisions, §51.1-1304.

VIRGINIA RETIREMENT SYSTEM —Cont'd
Benefits —Cont'd
Changes due to legislation, §51.1-124.8.
Contribution withdrawals before retirement, §51.1-161.
Convicted felons, loss of benefits, §51.1-124.13.
Creditable compensation defined, §51.1-124.3.
Death after retirement, §51.1-163.
Death before retirement, §51.1-162.
Definitions, §51.1-1300.
Disability retirement, §§51.1-156, 51.1-157.
Cessation of allowance, §51.1-160.
Medical examinations, §51.1-159.
Supplemental benefits, effect of disability, §51.1-138.
Election of benefit options, revocation, §51.1-165.
Final compensation, limitations on average, §51.1-152.
Hybrid retirement program, §51.1-169.
Increases in post-retirement supplements, §51.1-166.
Involuntary separation, §§51.1-155.1, 51.1-155.2.
Joint and last survivor option, §51.1-165.
Legislation which effects a change in the amount of a benefit, §51.1-124.8.
Level income option, §51.1-165.
Limits on creditable compensation.
Computing benefits, §51.1-168.
Local plans, §51.1-1302.
Lump-sum distributions, §51.1-165.01.
Lump-sum payments for workers' compensation settlements, §51.1-158.
Mandatory payment of allowance, §51.1-168.
Maximum benefits, §51.1-168.
Medical examinations for disability retirement, §51.1-159.
Monthly payments, §51.1-124.6.
Optional benefits, §51.1-165.
Partial lump-sum option, §51.1-165.01.
Past and present plans coordinated.
Continuation of benefits, §51.1-402.
Political subdivision participation, §51.1-138.
Post-retirement supplements, §51.1-166.
Reduction in allowance, §51.1-167.
Disability retirement allowance, §51.1-157.
Restoration plan, §§51.1-1300 to 51.1-1304.
Service retirement, §§51.1-153, 51.1-155.
Special retirement allowance guarantee.
Disability retirement allowance, §51.1-157.
Standards, §51.1-1303.
Straight life option, §51.1-165.
Withdrawal of contributions before retirement, §51.1-161.
Workers' compensation guarantee.
Disability retirement allowance, §51.1-157.
Workers' compensation settlements.
Acceptance of lump-sum payments, §51.1-158.
Bills of general assembly.
Impact statements, §30-19.1:7.
Board of trustees.
Advisory committees, §§51.1-124.25, 51.1-124.26.
Chief investment officer, §51.1-124.24.
Closed meetings, §2.2-3711.
Compensation and expense reimbursement, §51.1-124.20.
Conflicts of interest, §51.1-124.21.
Disclosure statement by members.
Filing, time, form, §§2.2-3114, 2.2-3117.
Duties, §51.1-124.22.
Fees collected, §51.1-124.22.

VIRGINIA RETIREMENT SYSTEM —Cont'd
Board of trustees —Cont'd
Fund responsibilities, §51.1-124.30.
Commonwealth health research fund, §51.1-124.36.
Group insurance program generally, §§51.1-500 to 51.1-514.
Judicial retirement system.
Administration, §51.1-300.
Long-term care insurance.
Program for local government employees, officers, teachers, §2.2-1207.
Assumption of responsibility, §51.1-513.3.
Program for state employees and persons with 5 or years creditable service retirement plan, §2.2-1208.
Assumption of responsibility, §51.1-513.2.
Trust fund for long term care programs, §51.1-513.4.
Medical board, §51.1-124.23.
Membership, §51.1-124.20.
Powers, §51.1-124.22.
State police officers' retirement system.
Administration, §51.1-200.
Bona fide occupational qualification.
Age.
Compulsory service retirement, §51.1-154.
Chief investment officer, §51.1-124.24.
City reverting to town status or losing status as city.
Withdrawal of city system.
Employee or retiree retention of benefits, §51.1-124.12.
Compulsory service retirement, §51.1-154.
Conflicts of interest, state and local government employees, §51.1-124.21.
Continuation of supplemental retirement system, §51.1-124.2.
Contributions, §§51.1-144 to 51.1-146.
Accumulated contributions under abolished system, §51.1-401.
Deduction from employee's compensation, §51.1-144.
Defined contribution plan for eligible members, §51.1-126.5.
Public school division employees, §51.1-126.6.
Employer contributions, §51.1-145.
Failure to make, §51.1-146.
Employer payment of member contributions, §51.1-144.
Equivalent amount in lieu of all members contributions, §51.1-144.
Hybrid retirement program, §51.1-169.
Member contributions, §51.1-144.
Transfer of member contributions paid by employer, §51.1-144.
Convicted felons, loss of benefits, §51.1-124.13.
Creditable service.
Equivalents to service, §51.1-141.
Hybrid retirement program, §51.1-169.
Involuntary separation, §§51.1-155.1, 51.1-155.2.
Portability of service credit, §51.1-143.1.
Prior service or membership credits, §51.1-142.2.
Portability of service credit, §51.1-143.1.
School division superintendents, §51.1-142.3.
Service equivalents, §51.1-141.
Death before retirement.
Payment of accumulated contributions, §51.1-162.
Deferred compensation plan, §§51.1-600 to 51.1-605.
See PUBLIC OFFICERS AND EMPLOYEES.

VIRGINIA RETIREMENT SYSTEM —Cont'd
Defined contribution plan for eligible members, §51.1-126.5.
Immunity from losses suffered.
Board of trustees, retirement system employees and retirement system advisory committee, §51.1-124.22.
Public school division employees, §51.1-126.6.
Defined contribution plan for local public school boards, §§51.1-617, 51.1-618.
Defined terms, §§51.1-124.3, 51.1-124.12, 51.1-126.5.
Past and present plans coordinated, §51.1-400.
Director.
Appointment by board, §51.1-124.22.
Disability retirement allowance, §51.1-157.
Disability retirement of past and present plans coordinated, §51.1-404.
Disclosure requirements, §§51.1-1000 to 51.1-1004.
Financial reports, §51.1-1003.
Scope, §51.1-1000.
Statement of benefits, §51.1-1002.
Summary plan description, §51.1-1001.
Use of electronic media, §51.1-1004.
Discretion exercised by employee over accounts.
Board not liable, §51.1-124.30.
Early retirement.
Involuntary separation, §§51.1-155.1, 51.1-155.2.
Service retirement allowance, §51.1-155.
Service retirement requirements, §51.1-153.
Eligible rollover distribution, §51.1-124.4.
Employee exemption from personnel acts, §51.1-124.27.
Employer contributions, §§51.1-145, 51.1-146.
Hybrid retirement program, §51.1-169.
Employer reporting failures, §51.1-146.
Errors in payment, §51.1-124.9.
Evaluation and overseeing, §§30-78 to 30-84.
Federal employees prohibited, exception.
Federal retirees, §2.2-2801.
Felony convictions, loss of benefits, §51.1-124.13.
Freedom of information act.
Exclusions from chapter.
Records of the retirement system, §2.2-3705.7.
General assembly members.
Creditable compensation defined, §51.1-124.3.
Government data collection and dissemination practices act.
Excluded systems, §2.2-3803.
Group insurance program, §§51.1-500 to 51.1-514.
See PUBLIC OFFICERS AND EMPLOYEES.
Health insurance credits.
Constitutional officers, §51.1-1403.
Coverage for retired employees, §2.2-2818.
Definitions, §51.1-1405.
General registrars, §51.1-1403.
Local government employees, §51.1-1402.
Participation, §51.1-1405.
Retired state employees, §51.1-1400.
Retired teachers, §51.1-1401.
Social service employees, §51.1-1403.
Hybrid retirement program, §51.1-169.
Disability program for participants, §§51.1-1150 to 51.1-1183.
See HYBRID RETIREMENT PROGRAM.
Judges participating, §51.1-302.

VIRGINIA RETIREMENT SYSTEM —Cont'd
Impact statements.
Bills of the general assembly, §30-19.1:7.
Implied consent.
Deduction of contribution from employee's compensation, §51.1-144.
Insurance premiums.
Failure to report or pay, §51.1-146.
Investments, §§51.1-124.30 to 51.1-124.36.
Board as trustee of funds, §51.1-124.30.
Chief investment officer, §51.1-124.24.
Commonwealth health research fund, §51.1-124.36.
Deposits distinguished, §51.1-124.33.
Exclusivity of provisions, §51.1-124.35.
Hybrid retirement program, §51.1-169.
Liability for losses, §51.1-124.30.
Pooling of assets, §51.1-124.31.
Public procurement act exemption, §51.1-124.32.
Retention of investments that become ineligible, §51.1-124.34.
Standard of care, §51.1-124.30.
Involuntary separation, §2.2-3204.
Joint legislative audit and review commission.
Evaluation of retirement system, §§30-78 to 30-84.
Judicial retirement system, §§51.1-300 to 51.1-309.
See JUDICIAL RETIREMENT SYSTEM.
Law officers' retirement system, §§51.1-211 to 51.1-221.
See LAW OFFICERS' RETIREMENT SYSTEM.
Limits on creditable compensation.
Computing benefits, §51.1-168.
Local government employees.
Health insurance credits, §51.1-1402.
Involuntary separation, §51.1-155.2.
Local health departments and directors, §32.1-31.
Local retirement systems, §§51.1-800 to 51.1-823.
See LOCAL RETIREMENT SYSTEMS.
Local school boards.
Borrowing from Virginia retirement system, §§22.1-161.1 to 22.1-161.8.
See LOCAL SCHOOL BOARDS.
Long-term care insurance.
Program for local government employees, officers, teachers, §2.2-1207.
Assumption of responsibility by board, §51.1-513.3.
Program for persons within Virginia retirement system, §2.2-1208.
Program for state employees and persons with 5 or years creditable service retirement plan, §2.2-1208.
Assumption of responsibility by board, §51.1-513.2.
Trust fund for long-term care programs, §51.1-513.4.
Lump-sum distribution.
Partial lump-sum, §51.1-165.01.
Mandatory cash-out, distribution to rollover plan, §51.1-124.4.
Medical board, §51.1-124.23.
Membership, §§51.1-125 to 51.1-129.
Cessation of, §51.1-128.
Composition of membership, §51.1-125.
Employees of institutions of higher education, §51.1-126.
Employees of teaching hospitals, §51.1-126.1.
Federal employees' retirement system, §51.1-127.
Holding more than one position, §51.1-125.

VIRGINIA RETIREMENT SYSTEM —Cont'd
Membership —Cont'd
Hybrid retirement program, §51.1-169.
Limitation on, §51.1-129.
Political subdivision participation, §§51.1-133 to 51.1-135.
Public school divisions.
Certain employees of, §51.1-126.6.
Virginia port authority, §51.1-126.4.
Withdrawal, §51.1-128.
Military service credit.
Service rendered on active duty on leave from covered position, §51.1-142.2.
Monthly benefit payments, §51.1-124.6.
Normal retirement.
Retirement allowance, §51.1-155.
Optional benefits, §51.1-165.
Optional plans.
Coordination of limits, §51.1-126.8.
Employees of institutions of higher education, §51.1-126.
Maximum contributions, §51.1-126.8.
Outdoors foundation, §51.1-126.7.
Employee retirement, §51.1-126.7.
Overpayments by employer, recovery, §51.1-124.9.
Oversight commission, §§30-78 to 30-84.
Activity funding, §30-84.
Agency cooperation, §30-83.
Citation of provisions, §30-78.
Consultants, §30-82.
Cooperative of other agencies, §30-83.
Duties, §30-80.
Employees, §30-82.
Funding, §30-84.
Joint legislative audit and review commission, §30-79.
Powers, §30-80.
Purpose of provisions, §30-79.
Reports, §30-81.
Title of chapter, §30-78.
Past and present plans coordinated.
Accumulated contributions under abolished system, §51.1-401.
Continuation of benefits, §51.1-402.
Defined terms, §51.1-400.
Disability retirement, §51.1-404.
Life insurance amount, §51.1-402.
Service retirement, §51.1-403.
Special retirement guarantees, §51.1-405.
Payment errors, §51.1-124.9.
Personnel act exemption for system employees, §51.1-124.27.
Political subdivision participation, §§51.1-130 to 51.1-139.
Additional retirement allowance resolution, §51.1-130.
Annual actuarial evaluation provided to participating localities.
Locally-specific data on which evaluation based provided, §51.1-137.1.
Benefits of membership, §51.1-138.
Chief fiscal officer duties, §51.1-136.
Compulsory membership, §51.1-135.
Contributions by employers, §51.1-137.
Department head duties, §51.1-136.
Deputy sheriffs.
Benefit coverage provided, §51.1-138.
Eligible employees, §51.1-132.
Employer contributions, §51.1-137.
Employers in default, §51.1-139.

VIRGINIA RETIREMENT SYSTEM —Cont'd
Political subdivision participation —Cont'd
Group insurance program, §51.1-504.
Involuntary separation of certain employees, §51.1-155.2.
Limitation on membership, §51.1-133.
Local pension system membership, §51.1-131.
Membership of local pension systems, §51.1-131.
Membership options, §51.1-134.
Membership requests of governing bodies, §51.1-130.
Optional membership, §51.1-134.
Resolution requesting membership, §51.1-130.
Social security act benefits.
Plan of agreement to extend required, §51.1-130.
Portability of service credit, §51.1-143.1.
Post-retirement supplements, §51.1-138.
Public institution of higher education employees.
Creditable compensation defined, §51.1-124.3.
Optional retirement plan, §51.1-126.
Public procurement act exemption for investments, §51.1-124.32.
Purchases of equipment, supplies, printing and nonprofessional services, §2.2-1110.
Record falsification, §51.1-124.10.
Recovery of payments procured by fraud, false statement, etc., §51.1-124.11.
Recovery of payments procured by fraud, false statement, etc., §51.1-124.11.
Reduction of allowance.
Disability retirement allowance, §51.1-157.
Refund of contributions before retirement, §51.1-161.
Replacement employer when employer required to withdraw, §51.1-124.12.
Retirement allowance, §51.1-155.
Disability retirement allowance, §51.1-157.
Rollover distribution, §51.1-124.4.
School boards.
Borrowing from Virginia retirement system, §§22.1-161.1 to 22.1-161.8.
See LOCAL SCHOOL BOARDS.
Involuntary separation, §51.1-155.1.
School division superintendents.
Prior service or membership credits, §51.1-142.3.
Schools and education.
Borrowing by school boards from Virginia retirement system, §§22.1-161.1 to 22.1-161.8.
See LOCAL SCHOOL BOARDS.
Certain employees of public school divisions, §51.1-126.6.
Security or ownership interest in entity not traded on securities exchange.
Freedom of information act.
Excluded records, §2.2-3705.7.
Service retirement allowance, §51.1-155.
Coordination of past and present plans, §51.1-403.
Sick leave.
Service credit for accumulated sick leave, §51.1-142.2.
Social security for state and local employees, §§51.1-700 to 51.1-707.
See PUBLIC OFFICERS AND EMPLOYEES.
Social security number disclosure, §51.1-124.5.
Special retirement allowance guarantee.
Coordination of past and present plans, §51.1-405.
Disability retirement allowance, §51.1-157.
State employee defined, §51.1-124.3.

VIRGINIA RETIREMENT SYSTEM —Cont'd
State police retirement system, §§51.1-200 to 51.1-210.
See STATE POLICE RETIREMENT SYSTEM.
Supplemental benefits after retirement, §51.1-166.
Supplemental retirement system continued, §51.1-124.2.
Terminated employees.
Involuntary separation, §2.2-3204.
Tobacco indemnification and community revitalization commission.
Employees, §3.2-3106.
Town losing status as town.
Withdrawal of town from system.
Employee or retiree retention of benefits, §51.1-124.12.
Virginia Commonwealth University health system authority.
Continued membership of employees transferred to authority, §23-50.16:24.
Virginia outdoors foundation.
Employee retirement, §51.1-126.7.
Virginia port authority.
Group insurance, §51.1-502.3.
Withdrawal of funds.
Procedure when employer required to withdraw, §51.1-124.12.
Workers' compensation guarantee.
Disability retirement allowance, §51.1-157.

VIRGINIA RETIREMENT SYSTEM OVERSIGHT, §§30-78 to 30-84.
See VIRGINIA RETIREMENT SYSTEM.

VIRGINIA REVENUE STAMPS.
Cigarette excise tax generally, §§58.1-1000 to 58.1-1022.
See CIGARETTE TAX.

VIRGINIA ROANOKE RIVER BASIN ADVISORY COMMITTEE, §§62.1-69.34 to 62.1-69.35:2.
Compensation, §62.1-69.35.
Composition, §62.1-69.34.
Established, §62.1-69.34.
Expenses, reimbursement, §62.1-69.35.
Meetings, §62.1-69.34.
Members, §62.1-69.34.
Purpose, §62.1-69.34.
Reimbursement for expenses, §62.1-69.35.
Reports.
Annual executive summary of interim activity, §62.1-69.35:2.
Staffing, §62.1-69.35:1.

VIRGINIA ROUTE 44.
HOV designation within certain cities prohibited, §33.1-46.2.

VIRGINIA RURAL REHABILITATION CORPORATION.
See RURAL REHABILITATION CORPORATION.

VIRGINIA SAVINGS AND LOAN TRUST POWERS ACT, §§6.2-1081 to 6.2-1099.

VIRGINIA SCHOOL FOR THE DEAF AND BLIND.
Admissions procedures, §22.1-348.
Board of visitors.
Establishment, §22.1-346.2.
Secretary of education, powers and duties, §2.2-208.

VIRGINIA SCHOOL FOR THE DEAF AND BLIND —Cont'd
Educational programs, §22.1-348.
Employment of teachers.
Terms of employment, §22.1-349.
Exclusion of children not immunized, §32.1-47.
General provisions, §§22.1-346 to 22.1-349.
Persons eligible, §22.1-348.
Teachers.
Terms of employment of teachers, §22.1-349.

VIRGINIA SECURITIES ACT, §§13.1-501 to 13.1-527.3.

VIRGINIA SECURITY FOR PUBLIC DEPOSITS ACT, §§2.2-4400 to 2.2-4411.
See SECURITY FOR PUBLIC DEPOSITS.

VIRGINIA SELF-SERVICE STORAGE ACT, §§55-416 to 55-423.

VIRGINIA SENIOR ALERT PROGRAM, §§52-34.4 to 52-34.6.

VIRGINIA SESQUICENTENNIAL OF AMERICAN CIVIL WAR COMMISSION AND FUND, §§30-266 to 30-274.
Advisory council.
Appointment, §30-267.
Chairman and vice-chairman, §30-267.
Established in the legislative branch, §30-266.
Fund established, §30-270.
Gifts, grants, donation.
Authority to solicit, accept, use and dispose of, §30-271.
Librarian of Virginia.
Advisory council member, §30-267.
Meetings, quorum, voting on recommendations, §30-269.
Membership, §30-267.
Compensation and expenses, §30-271.
Powers and duties of commission, §30-272.
Purpose, §30-266.
Report, submission to general assembly, §30-272.
Staffing by legislative services division, §30-273.
Sunset, expiration of chapter, §30-274.

VIRGINIA SEXUAL AND DOMESTIC VIOLENCE VICTIM FUND, §9.1-116.1.

VIRGINIA'S FUTURE, COUNCIL ON, §§2.2-2683 to 2.2-2689.
Advisory committees.
Authority to establish, §2.2-2687.
Balanced accountability scorecard.
Publication, §2.2-2686.
Chairman.
Governor to serve as, §2.2-2685.
Composition, §2.2-2685.
Conflicts of interest.
Disclosure requirements.
Advisory committees, applicability, §2.2-2687.
Cooperation of government entities, §2.2-2688.
Defined terms, §2.2-2683.
Duties, §2.2-2686.
Established, §2.2-2684.
Executive director.
Authority to hire or appoint, §2.2-2688.
Meetings, §2.2-2685.
Members, §2.2-2685.
Performance management system.
Defined, §2.2-2683.

VIRGINIA'S FUTURE, COUNCIL ON —Cont'd
Performance management system —Cont'd
Duties regarding, §2.2-2686.
Strategic plans.
Development and maintenance, §2.2-5510.
Review, §2.2-5511.
Purpose, §2.2-2684.
Quorum, §2.2-2685.
Reports.
Annual executive summary of interim activity, §2.2-2689.
Balanced accountability scorecard.
Publication, §2.2-2686.
Roadmap for Virginia's future.
Defined, §2.2-2683.
Duties regarding, §2.2-2686.
Staff, §2.2-2688.
Strategic plans.
Development and maintenance, §2.2-5510.
Review, §2.2-5511.
Terms, §2.2-2685.
Vacancies, §2.2-2685.
Vice-chairman, §2.2-2685.

VIRGINIA SHAKESPEARE FESTIVAL, WILLIAMSBURG.
Designated as official Shakespeare festival of the Commonwealth, §1-510.

VIRGINIA SHEEP INDUSTRY BOARD, §§3.2-2100 to 3.2-2114.

VIRGINIA SHELL BUILDING INITIATIVE.
Locality or other political subdivision participating in programs, §15.2-941.

VIRGINIA SHERIFFS' INSTITUTE.
Special license plates, §46.2-749.110.

VIRGINIA SMALL BUSINESS FINANCING AUTHORITY, §§2.2-2279 to 2.2-2314.
See SMALL BUSINESS FINANCING AUTHORITY.

VIRGINIA SMALL BUSINESS GROWTH FUND, §2.2-2310.

VIRGINIA SMALL ESTATE ACT, §§64.2-600 to 64.2-605.

VIRGINIA SOFT DRINK EXCISE TAX ACT, §§58.1-1700 to 58.1-1705.

VIRGINIA SOLAR EASEMENT ACT, §§55-352 to 55-354.

VIRGINIA STATE APPLE BOARD, §§3.2-1201 to 3.2-1217.

VIRGINIA STATE BAR.
Advance sheets to Virginia reports.
Distribution to secretary, §17.1-316.
Annual meetings, VA SCt Rule Pt 6 §IV Par 8.
Appeals from disciplinary board or circuit court determination, VA SCt Rule 5:21.
Classes of membership, VA SCt Rule Pt 6 §IV Par 3.
Client protection fund rules.
Amendments to rules, VSB CPF Rule IX.
Amount of loss.
Determination, VSB CPF Rule III.
Application for reimbursement, VSB CPF Rule II.
Board.
Amendments to rules, VSB CPF Rule IX.
Construction and interpretation of rules, VSB CPF Rule VII.
Defined, VSB CPF Rule I.
Meetings, VSB CPF Rule VI.

VIRGINIA STATE BAR —Cont'd
Client protection fund rules —Cont'd
Claimant.
Defined, VSB CPF Rule I.
Construction and interpretation of rules, VSB CPF Rule VII.
Definitions, VSB CPF Rule I.
Dishonest conduct.
Defined, VSB CPF Rule I.
Fund.
Authorized investments, VSB CPF Rule VIII.
Defined, VSB CPF Rule I.
Payments from fund.
Assignment of claim, VSB CPF Rule IV.
Receivership costs, VSB CPF Rule V.
Investigations.
Processing petitions, VSB CPF Rule III.
Lawyer.
Defined, VSB CPF Rule I.
Meetings of board, VSB CPF Rule VI.
Payments from fund.
Assignment of claim, VSB CPF Rule IV.
Petitioner.
Defined, VSB CPF Rule I.
Petitions.
Application for reimbursement, VSB CPF Rule II.
Processing petitions, VSB CPF Rule III.
Receivership.
Payment of costs, VSB CPF Rule V.
Reimbursable losses.
Defined, VSB CPF Rule I.
Right to reimbursement, VSB CPF Rule III.
Reimbursement.
Application for reimbursement, VSB CPF Rule II.
Reimbursable losses.
Defined, VSB CPF Rule I.
Right to reimbursement, VSB CPF Rule III.
Reports.
Processing petitions, VSB CPF Rule III.
Computerized legal research.
Virginia state bar ordered to contract to provide, VA SCt Rule Pt 6 §IV Par 21.
Continuing legal education rule, VA SCt Rule Pt 6 §IV Par 17.
Legal ethics course, VA SCt Rule Pt 6 §IV Par 13.1.
Suspension for failure to complete course, VA SCt Rule Pt 6 §IV Par 13.2.
Council, VA SCt Rule Pt 6 §IV Par 5.
Election, VA SCt Rule Pt 6 §IV Par 6.
Meetings, VA SCt Rule Pt 6 §IV Par 7.
Powers, VA SCt Rule Pt 6 §IV Par 9.
Disbarment of attorneys.
Procedure for disbarring, VA SCt Rule Pt 6 §IV Par 13.
Disbursements, VA SCt Rule Pt 6 §IV Par 12.
Client protection fund rules.
Payments from fund, VSB CPF Rule IV.
Disciplinary rules.
Procedure for disciplining, VA SCt Rule Pt 6 §IV Par 13.
Dues, VA SCt Rule Pt 6 §IV Par 17.
Education.
Continuing legal education requirements, VA SCt Rule Pt 6 §IV Par 17.
Legal ethics course, VA SCt Rule Pt 6 §IV Par 13.1.
Suspension for failure to complete, VA SCt Rule Pt 6 §IV Par 13.2.

VIRGINIA STATE BAR —Cont'd
Election of council, VA SCt Rule Pt 6 §IV Par 6.
Fiduciary, attorney acting as.
Failure to make return as to settlement.
Report to state bar, §§64.2-1215, 64.2-1309.
Financial responsibility.
Required of members, VA SCt Rule Pt 6 §IV Par 18.
Insurance policies, §54.1-3917.1.
Judicial conference for district courts.
Honorary members, president and secretary, §16.1-218.
Judicial inquiry and review commission.
Transmission of certain information to general assembly, §17.1-918.
Law corporations, VA SCt Rule Pt 6 §IV Par 14.
Practice of law by attorneys, VA SCt Rule Pt 6 §IV Par 14.
Legal aid services fund.
Additional fees collected by clerks of court, §17.1-278.
Legal ethics.
Opinions.
Incorporation into code, §54.1-3910.
Text of opinions.
See Volume Containing Legal Ethics and Unauthorized Practice Opinions.
Promulgation of legal ethics opinions, VA SCt Rule Pt 6 §IV Par 10.
Suspension for failure to complete legal ethics course, VA SCt Rule Pt 6 §IV Par 13.1.
Legal services plans, sponsor of plan, §38.2-4403.
License revocation procedure, §54.1-3935.
Professional corporations or limited liability companies, §54.1-3937.
Meetings of the council, VA SCt Rule Pt 6 §IV Par 7.
Membership, VA SCt Rule Pt 6 §IV Par 2.
Classes of membership, VA SCt Rule Pt 6 §IV Par 3.
Name, VA SCt Rule Pt 6 §IV Par 1.
Officers, VA SCt Rule Pt 6 §IV Par 4.
Online legal research.
Virginia state bar ordered to contract to provide, VA SCt Rule Pt 6 §IV Par 21.
Organization and government, §§54.1-3909 to 54.1-3918.
Out-of-state attorneys.
Application to appear pro hoc vice before a Virginia tribunal, VA SCt Rules Part 1A Appx Form 1.
When allowed by comity to participate in trial of case, VA SCt Rule 1A:4.
Powers of the council, VA SCt Rule Pt 6 §IV Par 9.
Proceedings pending disciplinary actions, §54.1-3936.
Real estate settlement agents.
Unauthorized practice of law, guidelines to avoid or prevent.
Complaints concerning noncompliance, receipt, §55-525.30.
Regulations establishing, §55-525.30.
Registration, VA SCt Rule Pt 6 §IV Par 2.
Resignation of attorneys.
Procedure, VA SCt Rule Pt 6 §IV Par 13.
Rules of court.
Promulgation, VA SCt Rule Pt 6 §IV Par 10.
Settlements of estates.
Attorneys as fiduciaries.
Failure to make settlements, §64.2-1216.

VIRGINIA STATE BAR —Cont'd
Suspending attorneys.
Procedure, VA SCt Rule Pt 6 §IV Par 13.
Administrative suspension, VA SCt Rule Pt 6 §IV Par 19.
Third year student practice rule, VA SCt Rule Pt 6 §IV Par 15.
Unauthorized practice of law.
Legal ethics opinions.
Incorporation into code, §54.1-3910.
Text of opinions.
See Volume Containing Legal Ethics and Unauthorized Practice Opinions.
Promulgation of unauthorized practice of law opinions, VA SCt Rule Pt 6 §IV Par 10.
Real estate settlement agents, guidelines to avoid or prevent.
Complaints concerning noncompliance, receipt, §55-525.30.
Regulations establishing, §55-525.30.
Rules of the supreme court, VA SCt Rule Pt 6 §I.
See ATTORNEYS AT LAW.

VIRGINIA STATE CRIME COMMISSION, §§30-156 to 30-164.
Freedom of information act.
Exclusions from chapter, §2.2-3703.

VIRGINIA STATE DEFENSE FORCE.
Generally, §§44-54.4 to 44-54.12.
See STATE DEFENSE FORCE.
Line of duty act, §§9.1-400 to 9.1-408.

VIRGINIA STATE LIBRARY AND ARCHIVES.
See LIBRARY OF VIRGINIA.

VIRGINIA STATE UNIVERSITY, §§23-165.1 to 23-174.
Bequests and gifts, §23-170.
Board of visitors, §§23-165.1 to 23-165.6, 23-166 to 23-170.
Campus police departments.
General provisions, §§23-232 to 23-238.
See CAMPUS POLICE.
Reporting campus crime, §23-9.1:1.
Conferring of degrees, §23-165.8.
Controlled by general assembly, §23-174.
Cooperative extension and agricultural experiment station division, §§23-132.1 to 23-132.12.
See COOPERATIVE EXTENSION AND AGRICULTURAL EXPERIMENT STATION DIVISION.
Cooperative extension service program.
Funding authority and unified plan, §23-165.11.
Recognition, §23-165.11.
Reports, §23-165.11.
Corporate name, §23-165.2.
Curriculum, §23-165.9.
Governmental aid, §23-170.
School of agriculture continued, §23-165.10.
Special license plates, §46.2-749.
Tuition, fees and other charges, §23-165.7.
Universities generally, §§23-1.01 to 23-9.2:8.
See COLLEGES AND UNIVERSITIES.

VIRGINIA STATEWIDE FIRE PREVENTION CODE ACT, §§27-94 to 27-101.

VIRGINIA'S TOBACCO HERITAGE.
Special license plates celebrating, §46.2-749.5.

VIRGINIA STOCK CORPORATION ACT, §§13.1-601 to 13.1-779.
See CORPORATIONS.

VIRGINIA STORMWATER MANAGEMENT PROGRAM, §§62.1-44.15:24 to 62.1-44.15:50.
See STORMWATER MANAGEMENT.

VIRGINIA STUDENT ASSISTANCE AUTHORITIES, 1980 ch 229, 1992 ch 630.

VIRGINIA TAXABLE INCOME.
Residents, §58.1-322.

VIRGINIA TAX AMNESTY PROGRAM, §58.1-1840.1.

VIRGINIA TAX ON WILLS AND ADMINISTRATIONS ACT, §§58.1-1711 to 58.1-1718.
See PROBATE TAX, STATE.

VIRGINIA TAXPAYER BILL OF RIGHTS, §58.1-1845.

VIRGINIA TEACHING SCHOLARSHIP LOAN PROGRAM, §22.1-290.01.
Collaboration between council of higher education and state board of education, §23-38.10:1.

VIRGINIA TECH.
Generally.
See VIRGINIA POLYTECHNIC INSTITUTE AND STATE UNIVERSITY.
Universities generally, §§23-1.01 to 23-9.2:8.
See COLLEGES AND UNIVERSITIES.

VIRGINIA TECHNOLOGY INFRASTRUCTURE FUND, §§2.2-2022 to 2.2-2024.

VIRGINIA TELEPHONE PRIVACY PROTECTION ACT, §§59.1-510 to 59.1-518.

VIRGINIA TOBACCO INDEMNIFICATION AND COMMUNITY REVITALIZATION COMMISSION, §§3.2-3100 to 3.2-3111.

VIRGINIA TOBACCO SETTLEMENT FOUNDATION.
Division of Virginia foundation for healthy youth, §32.1-355.
Virginia foundation for healthy youth, §§32.1-354 to 32.1-367.
See VIRGINIA FOUNDATION FOR HEALTHY YOUTH.

VIRGINIA TOBACCO SETTLEMENT FUND, §§32.1-360 to 32.1-363.

VIRGINIA TORT CLAIMS ACT, §§8.01-195.1 to 8.01-195.9.
See TORT CLAIMS ACT.

VIRGINIA TOURISM AUTHORITY, §§2.2-2315 to 2.2-2327.
See TOURISM AUTHORITY.

VIRGINIA TRADEMARK AND SERVICE MARK ACT (1998), §§59.1-92.1 to 59.1-92.22.
See TRADEMARKS AND SERVICE MARKS.

VIRGINIA TRANSPLANT COUNCIL.
Established, membership, duties, §32.1-297.1.

VIRGINIA TRANSPORTATION SERVICE DISTRICT ACT.
See TRANSPORTATION DISTRICTS.

VIRGINIA TRUCK AND ORNAMENTALS RESEARCH STATION, §§23-155.01 to 23-155.04.

VIRGINIA UNEMPLOYMENT COMPENSATION ACT, §§60.2-100 to 60.2-637.

VIRGINIA UNIFORM PARTNERSHIP ACT, §§50-73.79 to 50-73.149.
See PARTNERSHIPS.

VIRGINIA UNIFORM TRANSFERS TO MINORS ACT, §§64.2-1900 to 64.2-1922.
See TRANSFERS TO MINORS.

VIRGINIA VOTER REGISTRATION SYSTEM.
Voter registration generally, §§24.2-400 to 24.2-447.
See VOTER REGISTRATION.

VIRGINIA WALLOPS RESEARCH PARK LEADERSHIP COUNCIL, §15.2-2403.2.

VIRGINIA WAR MEMORIAL.
Administrative process act.
Exemptions, §2.2-4002.
Board.
Bylaws, §2.2-2465.
Compensation and expenses, §2.2-2465.
Duties, §2.2-2466.
Established, §2.2-2465.
Members, §2.2-2465.
Powers, §2.2-2466.
Terms of office, §2.2-2465.
Veterans services department.
Division, §§2.2-2001, 2.2-2001.3.

VIRGINIA WAR MEMORIAL CARILLON.
City of Richmond.
Agreement for use, proceeds, §2.2-1130.
Division of engineering and buildings.
Custody, control and supervision, §2.2-1129.

VIRGINIA WASTE MANAGEMENT ACT, §§10.1-1400 to 10.1-1458.

VIRGINIA WATERCRAFT SALES AND USE TAX ACT, §§58.1-1400 to 58.1-1410.
See WATERCRAFT SALES AND USE TAX.

VIRGINIA WATER RESOURCES AND WETLANDS PROTECTION PROGRAM, §§62.1-44.15:20 to 62.1-44.15:23.1.

VIRGINIA WOMEN'S INSTITUTE FOR LEADERSHIP AT MARY BALDWIN COLLEGE.
Officers to be officers of militia, §44-117.

VIRGINIA WORKERS' COMPENSATION INSURANCE PLAN.
Insurers writing insurance required to participate, §38.2-2015.
Rates.
Workers' compensation, automobiles, home protection, etc., §§38.2-2000 to 38.2-2027.
See INSURANCE RATES.

VIRGINIA WORKFORCE COUNCIL, §§2.2-2669 to 2.2-2674.1.

VIRGINIA WORLD WAR II VETERANS APPRECIATION WEEK, §2.2-3309.1.

VIRTUAL SCHOOLS, §§22.1-212.23 to 22.1-212.27.
Accreditation standards, §22.1-253.13:3.
Annual report, §22.1-212.25.
Definitions, §22.1-212.23.
Innovation technical advisory group, §22.1-212.8:1.
Multidivision online providers.
Approval, §22.1-212.24.
Contracts with local school boards, §22.1-212.24.
Defined, §22.1-212.23.

VIRTUAL SCHOOLS —Cont'd
Policies and procedures.
Development by superintendent, §22.1-212.25.
Students.
Eligibility, §22.1-212.27.
Tuition, §22.1-212.27.
Teachers and administrators.
Requirements, §22.1-212.26.
Website providing information, §22.1-212.25.

VIRTUAL VIRGINIA PROGRAM.
Schools and education, §22.1-212.2.

VIRUSES AFFECTING COMPUTERS.
Computer trespass, §18.2-152.14.

VIRUSES AFFECTING HUMANS.
Biotechnology research act, §§2.2-5500 to 2.2-5509.
Genetically engineered organisms.
Biotechnology research act, §§2.2-5500 to 2.2-5509.
Infectious biological substance crimes, §18.2-52.1.

VISAS.
Colleges and universities.
Reporting of student's failure to enroll or visa violations, §23-2.2.
Criminal history record information, dissemination, §19.2-389.
Fictitious, facsimile or simulated visas.
Manufacture, sale, possession, etc., §18.2-204.2.
In-state tuition to state supported colleges or universities.
Alien or political refugee establishing eligibility, §23-7.4.

VISITATION OF CHILD.
Abduction by parent, §18.2-49.1.
Abduction punishable as contempt in pending proceeding, §18.2-47.
Seizure and forfeiture of property used in connection with abduction, §19.2-386.32.
Advance notice of relocation or change of address, §20-124.5.
Best interest of child considered, §16.1-278.15.
Injunctions, filing of petition.
Petitioner convicted of certain crimes, §20-124.2.
Change of address, notice, §20-124.5.
Child abuse or neglect.
Preliminary protective orders.
Allowance of visitation, §16.1-253.
Removal orders.
Allowance of reasonable visitation, §16.1-252.
Concurrent jurisdiction, §16.1-244.
Disposition in juvenile court proceedings, §16.1-278.15.
Factors for consideration, §20-107.2.
Foster care.
Natural parents, siblings and grandparents, §63.2-912.
Grandparent visitation.
Foster care, §63.2-912.
Injunctions, filing of petition.
Best interest of child, petitioner convicted of certain crimes, §20-124.2.
Juvenile and domestic relations district court jurisdiction, §16.1-241.
Mediation.
Fees for mediation services, §16.1-274.

VISITATION OF CHILD —Cont'd
Military personnel called to active duty.
Adjudication based on changed circumstances because of.
Petition expedited on docket, §20-108.
Delegation of visitation to family member, §20-124.8.
Military parents equal protection act, §§20-124.7 to 20-124.10.
Notice of relocation or change of address, §20-124.5.
Parental abduction, §18.2-49.1.
Abduction punishable as contempt in pending proceeding, §18.2-47.
Seizure and forfeiture of property used in connection with abduction, §19.2-386.32.
Persons with legitimate interests.
Awarding custody or visitation to, §20-124.2.
Defined, §20-124.1.
Petition by party with legitimate interest, §16.1-278.15.
Relocation, notice, §20-124.5.
Separate maintenance decree.
Authority of court to make further decree, §20-107.2.
Transfer of venue.
Juvenile and domestic relations district court proceedings, §16.1-243.
Trespass after having been forbidden to do so, §§18.2-119, 18.2-120.
Uniform child custody jurisdiction and enforcement act.
Temporary orders enforcing provisions made by court of another state.
Authority of courts of Commonwealth to issue, §20-146.25.
Venue.
Juvenile and domestic relations district court proceedings, §16.1-243.

VISUAL AND AUDIBLE SIGNAL SYSTEM.
Assistive technology device warranties, §§59.1-470 to 59.1-474.

VISUALLY IMPAIRED.
Advisory board for Virginia industries for the blind, §51.5-72.1.
Board for the blind and vision impaired, §§51.5-61 to 51.5-63.
Business enterprises for the blind.
Vending stands, §§51.5-80 to 51.5-100.
See BLIND AND VISUALLY IMPAIRED.
Courthouses.
Operating stands for sale of newspapers, periodicals, etc.
Localities authorizing, §15.2-1805.
Definitions, §51.5-60.
Department for the blind and vision impaired, §§51.5-60 to 51.5-99.
Disability or handicap generally.
See DISABILITY OR HANDICAP.
Library services, §51.5-74.
Manufacturing and service industrial training, §51.5-72.
Financial reporting of schools, §51.5-75.
Register of the blind, §51.5-68.
Confidentiality, §51.5-69.
Rehabilitation center, §51.5-73.
Rehabilitation council, §51.5-71.
Sale and distribution of goods made by the blind, §§51.5-101 to 51.5-105.

VISUALLY IMPAIRED —Cont'd
Schools for manufacturing and service industrial training, §51.5-72.
Financial reporting, §51.5-75.
Vending stands, §§51.5-80 to 51.5-100.
Virginia school for the deaf and blind, §§22.1-346 to 22.1-349.

VITA.
Virginia information technologies agency, §§2.2-2005 to 2.2-2031.
See INFORMATION TECHNOLOGIES AGENCY.

VITAL RECORDS, §§32.1-249 to 32.1-276.
Adoption records, §32.1-262.
Racial designations.
Issued without, §32.1-262.
Amendments, §32.1-269.
Statements of racial designation, §32.1-272.
Annulment reports, §§32.1-268, 32.1-268.1.
Birth certificates, §§32.1-257 to 32.1-261.
Accuracy, verification by parent, §32.1-257.
Adopted child.
Corrected date of birth for foreign-born child, establishment by court, §63.2-1220.01.
Securing for, §63.2-1220.
Adoption.
New certificate.
Established on proof of adoption, §32.1-261.
Alcoholic beverages.
Establishing false identification or false age to consume, purchase or possess, §4.1-305.
Amendments, §32.1-269.
Assisted conception, child resulting from.
Full information on father, §32.1-257.
Birth occurring in institution or en route.
Responsibility for preparing, §32.1-257.
Birth occurring on moving conveyance.
Child first removed from conveyance in Commonwealth, §32.1-257.
Birth occurring outside institution.
Responsibility for preparing, §32.1-257.
Child welfare agencies.
Required on enrollment in regulated child day program, §63.2-1809.
Colleges and universities.
Birth certificate required as condition of enrollment.
Retention of copy in student's record, §23-2.1:2.
Delayed birth certificates, §32.1-259.
Registration by court order, §32.1-260.
Filing with state registrar, §32.1-257.
Fraudulent use, §18.2-204.1.
Manufacturing fictitious birth certificate, §18.2-204.1.
Marriage prohibited by law, deemed null or void or dissolved by court.
Child born of legitimate, full information on father, §32.1-257.
Matching birth and death certificates, §32.1-275.1.
Mother not married to natural father.
Entering name of father, sworn acknowledgment of paternity, §32.1-257.
Notation of missing children, §32.1-275.2.
Paternity judgment.
Person desiring to have father's name entered based on, §32.1-257.
Paternity proceedings.
New birth record, §20-49.8.
Registered by state registrar, §32.1-257.

VITAL RECORDS —Cont'd
Birth certificates —Cont'd
Social security number.
Parent to report at time of birth, §32.1-257.1.
Stillbirth, requirements, §32.1-258.1.
Change of name.
Transmittal of certified copy, §8.01-217.
Transmittal of order to state registrar of vital records, §8.01-217.
City registrars, §§32.1-254, 32.1-255.
Confidentiality of information, §32.1-271.
Copies, certified.
Fees, §32.1-273.
Issuance, §32.1-272.
County registrars, §§32.1-254, 32.1-255.
Death certificates, §32.1-263.
Date of death unknown.
Determination, §32.1-263.
Death occurring in moving conveyance.
Body first removed in Commonwealth, §32.1-263.
Funeral director or first person assuming custody of body.
Duty to file, §32.1-263.
Matching birth and death certificates, §32.1-275.1.
Medical certification, §32.1-263.
Place of death unknown, §32.1-263.
Time extensions, §32.1-266.
Deaths in Commonwealth of persons seventeen years of age or older.
Monthly report furnished to state board of elections, §24.2-408.
Defined terms, §32.1-249.
Divorce reports, §§32.1-268, 32.1-268.1.
Duties of board, §32.1-250.
Evidence.
Hearsay exceptions, VA SCt Rule 2:803.
Fetal death reports, §32.1-264.
Filing time extensions, §32.1-266.
Genealogical research database company.
Online vital records index, §32.1-271.
Hearsay exceptions, VA SCt Rule 2:803.
Institution authorities.
Duties to keep, §32.1-274.
Local health department duties, §§32.1-254, 32.1-255.
Marriage records, §32.1-267.
Name change.
Transmittal of order to state registrar of vital records, §8.01-217.
Online vital records index, §32.1-271.
Paternity proceedings.
Birth certificates.
New birth record, §20-49.8.
Transmission of birth record to state registrar, §20-49.8.
Preservation of original documents, §32.1-270.
Provision violations.
Penalties, §32.1-276.
Racial designation statements.
Certified copies, §32.1-272.
Registration districts.
Establishment, consolidation of subdivision, §32.1-253.
Searches of files.
Fees, §32.1-273.
Special registrars.
Appointment recommendations, §32.1-254.
Fees, §32.1-256.
State records management.
General provisions, §§42.1-76 to 42.1-90.1.
See STATE RECORDS MANAGEMENT.

VITAL RECORDS —Cont'd
State registrar.
Appointments, §32.1-251.
Birth certificates.
Delayed birth certificates.
Filing and registration, §§32.1-259, 32.1-260.
Deaths in Commonwealth of persons seventeen years of age or older.
Report furnished monthly to state board of elections, §24.2-408.
Duties, §32.1-252.
Furnishing information to on demand, §32.1-275.
Matching birth and death certificates, §32.1-275.1.
Missing children birth records.
Duties as to, §32.1-275.2.
Preservation of original documents, §32.1-270.
Registration districts.
Establishment, consolidation of subdivision, §32.1-253.
Supplying information on demand, §32.1-275.
Virginia vital statistics automation fund, §32.1-273.1.

VITAMINS.
Folic acid.
Birth defects.
Distribution of information on prevention, §32.1-69.1:1.
Sales.
Healing arts restrictions, §54.1-2963.
Taxation.
Exemption where used in farm feeds, §58.1-609.2.

VMI, §§23-92 to 23-113.
See VIRGINIA MILITARY INSTITUTE.

VOCATIONAL EDUCATION.
Career and technical education generally.
See CAREER AND TECHNICAL EDUCATION.
Community colleges.
See COMMUNITY COLLEGES.

VOCATIONAL REHABILITATION FOR DISABLED PERSONS.
See DISABILITY OR HANDICAP.

VOCATIONAL REHABILITATION SERVICES.
Workers' compensation, §65.2-603.

VOICE-OVER-INTERNET PROTOCOL SERVICE.
Defined, §56-1.
E-911 access.
Notice to subscribers of lack of, §56-484.12:1.
Plan for, §56-484.12:2.
Regulation of, §56-1.3.

VOICE-SYNTHESIZED COMPUTER MODULES.
Assistive technology device warranties, §§59.1-470 to 59.1-474.

VOIDABLE RETAIL FRANCHISES, §13.1-565.

VOIDABLE TRANSFERS.
Insurance companies, rehabilitation and liquidation, §38.2-1513.

VOID CONTRACTS.
Creditors and purchasers oral contracts, §11-1.
Gaming contracts, §11-14.
Indemnification provisions in construction contracts, §§11-4.1, 11-4.4.
Indemnification provisions in motor carrier transportation contracts, §11-4.5.

VOID CONTRACTS —Cont'd
Public construction contracts.
Unreasonable delays in performance.
Provisions barring damages void, §2.2-4335.

VOID MARRIAGES, §20-45.1.
Bigamous marriage, §§20-38.1, 20-43.
Consanguineous marriages, §20-38.1.
Effect of premarital agreements, §20-151.
Homosexual marriages, §20-45.2.
Incestuous marriages, §20-38.1.
Legitimation of children, §20-31.1.
Underage marriage without parental consent, §20-48.

VOLUNTARILY LEAVING WORK WITHOUT GOOD CAUSE.
Disqualification for unemployment compensation benefits, §60.2-618.

VOLUNTARY ADMISSION TO MENTAL HEALTH FACILITIES.
See MENTAL HEALTH.

VOLUNTARY APPRENTICESHIP, §§40.1-117 to 40.1-126.

VOLUNTARY COORDINATED HOUSING PRESERVATION AND DEVELOPMENT DISTRICTS.
County manager plan of government, §15.2-735.

VOLUNTARY DISSOLUTION OF CORPORATIONS, §13.1-742.

VOLUNTARY DISSOLUTION OF NONPROFIT CORPORATIONS, §§13.1-902, 13.1-903.

VOLUNTARY ENVIRONMENTAL ASSESSMENT, §§10.1-1193, 10.1-1194.
Burden of proof, §10.1-1198.
Disclosure of violation.
Immunity, §10.1-1199.
Evidence.
Consent required for admissibility, §10.1-1198.
Immunity.
Disclosure of violation, §10.1-1199.
Privileges, §10.1-1198.

VOLUNTARY MANSLAUGHTER.
Declared felony, §18.2-30.
Discretionary felony sentencing guidelines, §17.1-805.
Drivers' licenses.
One year revocation upon suspension, §46.2-389.
Persons convicted not to be licensed, §46.2-316.
Mob crimes, §18.2-42.1.
Murder indictment.
Verdict when accused found guilty of punishable homicide, §19.2-288.
Punishment, §18.2-35.
Sentence of person twice previously convicted, §19.2-297.1.
Three time loser law, §19.2-297.1.

VOLUNTARY PRO BONO PUBLIC SERVICE, VA SCt Rule Pt 6 §II Rule 6.1.

VOLUNTARY REMEDIATION.
Hazardous waste cleanups.
See HAZARDOUS WASTE CLEANUPS.

VOLUNTARY SMOKE MANAGEMENT GUIDELINES FOR VIRGINIA.
Prescribed burn prescription.
Inclusion of smoke management plan, §10.1-1150.4.

VOLUNTEER EMERGENCY FAMILIES FOR CHILDREN.
Criminal history record information free of charge to applicant, §19.2-389.

VOLUNTEER FIRE COMPANIES AND FIREFIGHTERS, §§27-6.1 to 27-23.1.
Approval by local governing body for establishing, §15.2-955.
Assault and battery against, §18.2-57.
Billing of property owners on behalf of volunteer fire departments, §38.2-2130.
Ordinances allowing for, §27-14.
Boat registration, exemption, §29.1-702.
Boat title certificates.
Fee exemption, §29.1-718.
Charitable gaming, §§18.2-340.15 to 18.2-340.37.
See CHARITABLE GAMING.
Child labor law exemption, §40.1-79.1.
Criminal history record information free of charge to applicant, §19.2-389.
Donations or gifts to volunteer and nonprofit organizations, §15.2-953.
Driver information.
Commissioner of DMV.
Supplying member or applicant for membership, §46.2-208.
Fire insurance.
Coverage for volunteer fire department costs, §38.2-2130.
Health insurance program of locality.
Participation, §15.2-1517.
Hepatitis, meningitis, tuberculosis and HIV.
Workers' compensation.
Presumption on death or disability from, §65.2-402.1.
Loans to volunteer firefighting organizations, §15.2-954.
Local vehicle licenses.
Issuance free of charge, §46.2-752.
Motor vehicle sales and use tax exemption, §58.1-2403.
Pension fund, §§51.1-1200 to 51.1-1211.
See VOLUNTEER FIREFIGHTERS' AND RESCUE SQUAD WORKERS' SERVICE AWARD FUND.
Registering vehicles, license plates, §46.2-649.1:1.
Relief for firefighters and dependents, §§27-41 to 27-50.
See FIREFIGHTERS.
Snow removal from driveways, §33.1-200.1.
State employees.
Leave for.
Volunteer fire and rescue services, §2.2-2821.2.
Surplus state materials.
Sale to volunteer fire departments, §2.2-1124.
Tuition reimbursement for personnel, §15.2-954.1.
Workers' compensation.
Hepatitis, meningitis, tuberculosis and HIV.
Presumption on death or disability from, §65.2-402.1.

VOLUNTEER FIREFIGHTERS' AND RESCUE SQUAD WORKERS' SERVICE AWARD FUND, §§51.1-1200 to 51.1-1211.
Administration and management, §51.1-1200.
Application for membership, §51.1-1204.
Board, §§51.1-1200, 51.1-1201.
Distributions by board, §51.1-1206.
Powers and duties, §51.1-1202.

VOLUNTEER FIREFIGHTERS' AND RESCUE SQUAD WORKERS' SERVICE AWARD FUND —Cont'd
Creation, §51.1-1200.
Creditable service.
More than one department or squad.
Length of service not affected by serving in, §51.1-1208.
Prior creditable service.
Determination, §51.1-1207.
Definitions, §51.1-1203.
Equivalent benefits, §51.1-1205.
Failure of member to maintain eligibility.
Effect, §51.1-1209.
Falsification of records.
Criminal penalty, §51.1-1211.
Fees.
Administrative fee for rejoining fund, §51.1-1210.
Payments by members, §51.1-1204.
Delinquency.
Effect of being six months delinquent, §51.1-1209.
Prior creditable service.
Determination, §51.1-1207.
Transfer from one department or squad to another.
Effect, §51.1-1208.

VOLUNTEER FIREFIGHTING ORGANIZATIONS, §§27-6.1 to 27-23.1.
See VOLUNTEER FIRE COMPANIES AND FIREFIGHTERS.

VOLUNTEER NEUTRALS.
Dispute resolution proceedings, §8.01-576.7.

VOLUNTEER RESCUE SQUADS.
Counties, cities or towns.
Approval by local governing body for establishing, §15.2-955.
Gifts or donations to volunteer and nonprofit organizations, §15.2-953.
Loans to volunteer rescue organizations, §15.2-954.
Tuition reimbursement for personnel, §15.2-954.1.
Driving under the influence reimbursement, §15.2-1716.
Generally.
See RESCUE SQUADS.
Health insurance program of locality.
Participation by volunteer firefighters, §15.2-1517.
State employees.
Leave for.
Volunteer fire and rescue services, §2.2-2821.2.
Terrorism hoax.
Reimbursement of expenses in responding to, §15.2-1716.1.

VOLUNTEERS.
Attorneys at law.
Voluntary pro bono public service, VA SCt Rule Pt 6 §II Rule 6.1.
Dispute resolution proceedings.
Volunteer neutrals, §8.01-576.7.
Emergency families for children.
Criminal history record information free of charge to applicant, §19.2-389.
Hospice programs.
Civil immunity, §8.01-226.4.
Liability insurance.
Localities and political subdivisions, §15.2-1518.
State service, §§2.2-3600 to 2.2-3605.

VOLUNTEERS —Cont'd
Volunteer fire companies and firefighters, §§27-6.1 to 27-23.1.
See VOLUNTEER FIRE COMPANIES AND FIREFIGHTERS.
Volunteer rescue squads.
See VOLUNTEER RESCUE SQUADS.

VOLUNTEERS IN STATE SERVICE, §§2.2-3600 to 2.2-3605.
Aid.
Solicitation of aid from community, §2.2-3604.
Attorneys at law.
Voluntary pro bono public service, VA SCt Rule Pt 6 §II Rule 6.1.
Benefits, §2.2-3605.
Declaration of legislative intent, §2.2-3600.
Defined terms, §2.2-3601.
Departmental responsibilities, §2.2-3603.
Emergency services personnel, §2.2-3602.
Insurance.
Liability insurance, §2.2-3605.
Lodging, §2.2-3605.
Meals, §2.2-3605.
Recognition.
Departmental responsibilities, §2.2-3603.
Reimbursement of expenses, §2.2-3602.
Transportation, §2.2-3605.
Scope of chapter, §2.2-3602.
Short title, §2.2-3600.
Solicitation of aid from community, §2.2-3604.
Status of volunteers, §2.2-3602.
Supervision.
Departmental responsibilities, §2.2-3603.

VOTE INFLUENCING.
Bribery, intimidation, etc., of person receiving ballot, §24.2-1005.
Soliciting or accepting bribe, §24.2-1007.

VOTER PARTICIPATION AND REGISTRATION LISTS.
Persons who may obtain, §24.2-405.
Statement for persons receiving, §24.2-407.

VOTER QUALIFICATIONS, §24.2-643, VA Const Art II §1.
Persons eighteen years of age, US Const Amd 26.
Advanced registration and voting in intervening primary or special election, §24.2-403.
Persons entitled to register and vote, §24.2-400.
Persons moving from Commonwealth fewer than thirty days from presidential election, §24.2-402.
Persons moving from precinct, §24.2-401.
Qualified voter defined, §24.2-101.
Qualified voter in a town defined, §24.2-101.
Qualified voters permitted to vote, §24.2-643.
Unqualified persons voting, §24.2-1004.

VOTER REGISTRATION, §§24.2-400 to 24.2-447, VA Const Art II §2.
Absentee ballots for military and overseas voters.
Methods of registration, §24.2-457.
Absentee registration for federal elections.
Temporary registration.
Absentee application, §24.2-419.
Application, §24.2-419.
Address change to another county or city.
Inactive status assignment, §§24.2-428, 24.2-428.1.
Return to active status, §24.2-428.2.

VOTER REGISTRATION —Cont'd
Address change to another county or city —Cont'd
Notice, §24.2-424.
Timely receipt of application, §24.2-114.
Voter list maintenance program, §24.2-428.
Address of voter.
Individuals permitted to provide post office box address, §24.2-418.
Advance notice.
Other times and locations for registration, §24.2-415.
Agreement to mail or deliver application of another.
Destruction of or failure to mail or deliver, §24.2-1002.01.
American conservation and youth service corps.
Presumptions as to residence of participants, §24.2-417.1.
Annexation by city or town, §15.2-3226.
Appeals.
Cancellation for improper registration, §24.2-430.
Denial, §24.2-422.
Objecting to registration, §24.2-433.
Application, §24.2-418, VA Const Art II §2.
Absentee application, §24.2-419.
Destruction of or failure to mail or deliver, §24.2-1002.01.
Electronic application, §24.2-416.7.
Falsification, §24.2-1002.01.
Mail application.
Failure to mail, §24.2-1002.01.
Included in individual income tax return packets, §58.1-341.1.
Registrar to indicate, §24.2-114.
New application sent to voter denied registration, §24.2-422.
Post office box address, individuals permitted to provide, §24.2-418.
Receipt for voter registration applicants, §24.2-418.1.
Transfer or change of address.
Timely receipt, §24.2-114.
Armed forces members.
Absentee applications, §24.2-419.
Extended time for registration, §24.2-420.1.
Campaigning at registration locations, §24.2-1003.
Cancellation.
Appeal from decision, §24.2-430.
Deceased or disqualified voters, §24.2-427.
Hearing on alleged improper registration, §24.2-429.
Improper registration, §24.2-429.
Motor vehicles department.
Driver license compact, §24.2-427.
Notice of cancellation for improper registration, §24.2-429.
Objections to registration, §§24.2-431 to 24.2-434.
Records to be retained for four years, §24.2-435.
Voluntary cancellation, §24.2-427.
Central criminal records exchange.
Monthly list of felony convictions to state board, §24.2-409.
Federal convictions, §24.2-409.1.
Central record-keeping system.
Duties of state board of elections, §24.2-404.
Challenging registration, §24.2-429.
Appeal, §24.2-430.
Objections to registration, §§24.2-431 to 24.2-434.

VOTER REGISTRATION —Cont'd
Change of address to another county or city.
Inactive status assignment, §§24.2-428, 24.2-428.1.
Return to active status, §24.2-428.2.
Notice, §§24.2-423, 24.2-424.
Notice to registrar by electronic means, §24.2-416.7.
Timely receipt of application, §24.2-114.
Voter list maintenance program, §24.2-428.
Children eighteen years of age at next general election.
Advanced registration and voting in intervening primary or special election, §24.2-403.
Citizenship status.
Department of motor vehicles to furnish lists of noncitizens, §24.2-410.1.
City status granted town, §15.2-3831.
Civil right to be eligible to register to vote.
Restoration, persons convicted of felony, §53.1-231.2.
Clerks of circuit courts.
List of incompetent determinations furnished state board, §24.2-410.
Closing records before elections, §24.2-416.
Conflicts as to registration.
Records controlling, §24.2-445.
Consolidation of like units of local government, §15.2-3516.
Content requirements of applications, §24.2-418.
Continuance of registration.
Persons registered prior to title, §24.2-447.
Contraction of corporate limits of city or town.
Transfer of registration records of voters residing in territory transferred, §15.2-3240.
Days and hours for registration.
Final registration day, §24.2-414.
Notice, §24.2-415.
Office of general registrar, §24.2-411.
Other times for voter registration, §24.2-412.
Time for closing of registrar's office on final day, §24.2-414.1.
Deceased voters.
Cancellation of registration, §24.2-427.
Deaths in Commonwealth of persons seventeen years of age or older.
State registrar of vital records to furnish monthly report, §24.2-408.
Denial.
Appeal, §24.2-422.
New application sent to voter denied registration, §24.2-422.
Notice in writing, §24.2-114.
Destruction of or failure to mail or deliver application, §24.2-1002.01.
Destruction of records.
Records reconstruction, §24.2-446.
Disabled or handicapped voters.
Accessibility of registration location, §24.2-413.
Discrimination prohibited, §51.5-43.
Disqualified voters.
Cancellation of registration, §24.2-427.
Disturbing registration process.
Excluding person from place of registration, §24.2-114.
DMV transfer of information in records.
Electronic transfer, §46.2-208.1.
Duplicate registrations, preventing.
Exchange of registered voter lists with other states, §24.2-404.4.

VOTER REGISTRATION —Cont'd
Duties of state board, §24.2-404.
Exchange of registered voter lists with other states, §24.2-404.4.
Secretary as state coordinator for national voter registration act, §24.2-404.1.
Verification of registered voter lists, §24.2-404.3.
Elderly voters.
Accessible registration locations, §24.2-413.
Election offenses generally, §§24.2-1000 to 24.2-1019.
See ELECTION OFFENSES.
Electronic application for registration, §24.2-416.7.
Electronic notice.
Change of address within Commonwealth, §24.2-424.
Change of voter's name, pilot program, §24.2-423.
Entitlement to register and vote, §24.2-400.
Persons eighteen years of age at next general election.
Advance registration and voting in intervening primary or special elections, §24.2-403.
Persons moving from Commonwealth fewer than thirty days before presidential election, §24.2-402.
Persons moving from precincts, place of voting, §24.2-401.
Persons to be registered, §24.2-417.
Exchange of registered voter lists with other states, §24.2-404.4.
Excluding person from place of registration.
Disturbing registration process, §24.2-114.
Extended time for registration, §24.2-420.1.
Felonies.
Illegal registrations, §24.2-1004.
Felony conviction disqualifying voter.
Cancellation of registration, §24.2-427.
Felony convictions list.
Federal convictions, §24.2-409.1.
Transmission to state board, §24.2-409.
Restoration of right to register to vote, §53.1-231.2.
Final registration day, §24.2-414.
Time for closing of registrar's office on final day, §24.2-414.1.
Handicapped or disabled voters.
Accessibility of registration location, §24.2-413.
Discrimination prohibited, §51.5-43.
Hearing on cancellation for improper registration, §24.2-429.
Illegal registrations, §24.2-1004.
Improper registration, §24.2-429.
Appeal from decision cancelling registration, §24.2-430.
Inactive status.
Procedures for assigning registered voters to, §§24.2-428, 24.2-428.1.
Return to active status, §24.2-428.2.
Incapacity determination.
Cancellation of registration, §24.2-427.
Income tax return packets.
Mail application included in individual income tax return packet, §58.1-341.1.
Information required to be furnished by applicants, §24.2-418, VA Const Art II §2.
Inspection of records by registered voters, §24.2-444.
Instructions for voter registration drives, §24.2-416.6.
Interference with, §24.2-1002.

VOTER REGISTRATION —Cont'd
Lists of felony convictions.
Federal convictions, §24.2-409.1.
Transmission to state board, §24.2-409.
Lists of incompetents.
Clerks of circuit courts to furnish monthly to state board, §24.2-410.
Lists of registered voters and persons voting at elections.
Persons who may obtain, §§24.2-405, 24.2-407.
Statement for persons receiving, §24.2-407.
Social security number protection. See within this heading, "Social security numbers."
Locations for registration.
Accessibility, §24.2-413.
Department of motor vehicles, §24.2-411.1.
Notice, §24.2-415.
Office of general registrar, §24.2-411.
Other locations, §24.2-412.
Persons authorized to receive applications, §24.2-415.1.
State-designated voter registration agencies, §24.2-411.2.
Mail registration, §§24.2-416.1 to 24.2-416.6.
Any person may register by mail, §24.2-416.1.
Applicability of sections, §24.2-416.1.
Applications.
Forms, §24.2-416.2.
Distribution, §24.2-416.3.
Included in individual income tax return packets, §58.1-341.1.
Registrar to indicate, §24.2-114.
Timeliness, §24.2-416.4.
Date of return, §24.2-416.4.
In person voting required, exceptions, §24.2-416.1.
Social security number disclosure, §24.2-416.5.
Mental incompetent determination.
Clerks of circuit courts to furnish list to state board, §24.2-410.
Merchant marine.
Absentee applications, §24.2-419.
Extended for members to register, §24.2-420.1.
Military personnel.
Absentee applications, §24.2-419.
Methods of registration, §24.2-457.
Extended time for registration, §24.2-420.1.
Minors eighteen years of age at next general election.
Advanced registration and voting in intervening primary or special election, §24.2-403.
Motor vehicles department.
Citizenship status.
Department of motor vehicles to furnish lists of noncitizens, §24.2-410.1.
Notice submitted to department.
Cancellation of registration, §24.2-427.
Registration at offices of, §24.2-411.1.
Moving from Commonwealth fewer than thirty days before presidential election.
Place of voting of persons moving, §24.2-402.
Moving from precinct.
Place of voting of persons moving, §24.2-401.
Multi-family residential buildings.
Locations for registration, §24.2-412.
Multiple voter registrations.
Soliciting from any one person, §24.2-1002.01.
Name change.
Notice, §24.2-423.
National voter registration act.
Commissioner of elections, duties, §24.2-404.1.

VOTER REGISTRATION —Cont'd
National voter registration act —Cont'd
Secretary of state board of elections, duties, §24.2-404.1.
Notification requirements.
Advance notice.
Other times and locations, §24.2-415.
Cancellation for improper registration, §24.2-429.
Change of address within Commonwealth, §24.2-424.
Change of name, §24.2-423.
Date, hours and location, §24.2-415.
Denial of registration, §24.2-114.
Electronic notice.
Change of address within Commonwealth, §24.2-424.
Change of voter's name, pilot program, §24.2-423.
Internet postings required, §24.2-415.
Other times and locations.
Advance notice, §24.2-415.
Person objected to, §24.2-432.
Reconstruction of records, §24.2-446.
When notice not required, §24.2-415.
Oaths.
Information on application provided under oath, VA Const Art II §2.
Objecting to registration, §§24.2-431 to 24.2-434.
Appeal from decision of court, §24.2-433.
Notice to person objecting to decision of court, §24.2-432.
Petition to court, §24.2-431.
Presumption if petition not brought within six months of registration, §24.2-434.
Office of general registrar.
Location and time for registration, §24.2-411.
Order at place of registration.
Registrar to preserve, §24.2-114.
Overseas voters.
Absentee registration, §24.2-419.
Persons eighteen years of age at next general election.
Advanced registration and voting in intervening primary or special election, §24.2-403.
Persons entitled to register, §24.2-400.
Persons moving from precinct.
Place of voting, §24.2-401.
Persons to be registered, §24.2-417.
Petition objecting to registration, §24.2-431.
Petitions to appeal denial, §24.2-422.
Photograph of voter.
Department of motor vehicles to provide assistance in providing voter registration cards with, §24.2-411.1.
Duties of registrars, §24.2-404.
Place of voting.
Persons moving from Commonwealth fewer than thirty days before presidential elections, §24.2-402.
Persons moving from precinct, §24.2-401.
Power of attorney.
Prohibition on use of power of attorney, §24.2-123.
Presidential elections.
Persons moving from Commonwealth fewer than thirty days before, §24.2-402.
Temporary registration.
Absentee application, §24.2-419.
Application, §24.2-419.
Presumption if petition objecting to registration not brought within six months of registration, §24.2-434.

VOTER REGISTRATION —Cont'd
Primaries, §24.2-403.
Prior registration.
Continuance of registration, §24.2-447.
Publication.
Advance notice.
Other times and locations for registration, §24.2-415.
Public inspection of records, §24.2-444.
Qualifications of voters.
Generally.
See VOTER QUALIFICATIONS.
Registration required, VA Const Art II §1.
Receipt for voter registration applicants, §24.2-418.1.
Records.
Closed before elections, §24.2-416.
Controlling in event of conflict, §24.2-445.
Defined, §24.2-101.
Duties of registrars and state board to maintain, §24.2-444.
Freedom of information act.
Exclusions from chapter, §2.2-3703.
Public inspections, §24.2-444.
Reconstruction.
Destruction of records, §24.2-446.
Retention.
Cancellation records, §24.2-435.
Registered voter defined, §24.2-101.
Registrar of vital records.
Monthly report as to deaths in the Commonwealth, §24.2-408.
Registrars, §§24.2-110 to 24.2-114, VA Const Art II §8.
Absentee voting.
Duties generally, §§24.2-706, 24.2-710.
Persons entitled to vote absentee, §24.2-700.
Appointment by electoral boards, §§24.2-109, 24.2-110.
Assistant to general registrar, §24.2-112.
Special assistant, §24.2-113.
Carrying concealed weapons.
Permit required, §18.2-308.
Compensation, §24.2-111.
Contiguous jurisdiction.
Registering voters in, §24.2-114.
Deemed employees of county or city, §24.2-122.
Defense in civil actions, §24.2-121.
Department of motor vehicles, §24.2-411.1.
Duties, §24.2-114.
Employees, §24.2-112.
Expenses, §24.2-111.
Interference with duties, §24.2-1002.
Locality to pay expenses, §24.2-111.
Mail registration, indicating on application, §24.2-114.
Mileage expenses, payment, §24.2-111.
Multijurisdictional staffing, §24.2-114.
Nepotism in appointment of general registrar, §24.2-110.
Oath of office, §24.2-120.
Office of general registrar, §24.2-411.
Order at place of registration.
Preserving, §24.2-114.
Pollbooks, duties, §24.2-114.
Powers, §24.2-114.
Prohibition as to officeholding, §§24.2-110, 24.2-119.
Prohibitions as to political activity, §24.2-110.
Qualification, §24.2-110.

VOTER REGISTRATION —Cont'd
Registrars —Cont'd
Records, duties of registrars and state board to maintain, §24.2-444.
Removal, §24.2-109.
Signatures on petitions by registered voters.
Determining, §24.2-114.
Soliciting application for registration or ballot.
Prohibition, §24.2-114.
Special assistant registrars, §24.2-113.
State-designated agencies, §24.2-411.2.
Telephone number of office to be listed in telephone directory, §24.2-411.
Term, §24.2-110.
Training program, §24.2-114.
Vacancies, §24.2-110.
Registration of groups conducting voter registration drives, §24.2-416.6.
Report as to deaths of persons in Commonwealth seventeen years of age or older.
State registrar of vital records to furnish, §24.2-408.
Residence change to another county or city, §24.2-424.
Inactive status assignment, §§24.2-428, 24.2-428.1.
Return to active status, §24.2-428.2.
Voter list maintenance program, §24.2-428.
Restoration of civil right to be eligible to register to vote, §53.1-231.2.
Signature of voter.
Duties of registrars, §24.2-404.
Social security numbers.
Lists furnished to others not to contain, §24.2-406.
Mail registration applications, §24.2-416.5.
Unlawful disclosure, §§24.2-407.1, 24.2-1002.1.
Motor vehicles department employees, §24.2-411.1.
State-designated voter registration agencies, §24.2-411.2.
Special elections, §24.2-403.
Special officers.
Appointing to preserve order, §24.2-114.
State board of elections.
Duties, §24.2-404.
Secretary as coordinator for administration of national voter registration act, §24.2-404.1.
Records, duties of registrars and state board to maintain, §24.2-444.
State-designated voter registration agencies.
Persons authorized to receive applications, §24.2-415.1.
Registrars, §24.2-411.2.
Stealing or tampering with equipment, §24.2-1009.
Temporary absentee registration for federal elections.
Absentee application, §24.2-419.
Application, §24.2-419.
Temporary residents outside United States.
Absentee applications, §24.2-419.
Time for registration.
Extended time for certain persons, §24.2-420.1.
Final registration day, §24.2-414.
Time for closing of registrar's office on final day, §24.2-414.1.
Notice, §24.2-415.
Office of general registrar, §24.2-411.
Other times for voter registration, §24.2-412.
Town granted city status, §15.2-3831.

VOTER REGISTRATION —Cont'd
Training for groups conducting voter registration drives, §24.2-416.6.
Transfer of registration to another county or city.
Inactive status assignment, §§24.2-428, 24.2-428.1.
Return to active status, §24.2-428.2.
Timely receipt of application, §24.2-114.
Voter list maintenance program, §24.2-428.
Venue.
Appeal by person denied registration, §24.2-422.
Appeals on cancellation for improper registration, §24.2-430.
Voluntary cancellation, §24.2-427.
Voter list maintenance program, §24.2-428.
Return of voter to active status, §24.2-428.2.
Voter qualifications.
Generally.
See VOTER QUALIFICATIONS.
Registration required, VA Const Art II §1.
Voter registration system defined, §24.2-101.

VOTING AT ELECTIONS.
Absentee voting.
Generally, §§24.2-700 to 24.2-713.
See ABSENTEE AND EARLY VOTING.
Military and overseas voters act, §§24.2-451 to 24.2-470.
See ABSENTEE AND EARLY VOTING.
Advice or assistance in casting ballot, §24.2-649.
Violation of law, §24.2-1006.
Age requirement, US Const Amd 26.
Arrest under civil process.
Privileged from civil arrest, §§8.01-327.1, 8.01-327.2.
Bribery, intimidation, etc., of person receiving ballot, §24.2-1005.
Challenged voters, §24.2-651.
Convicted felons.
Restoration of voting rights, §53.1-231.1.
Defaced paper ballots, §24.2-645.
Discrimination against disabled persons, §51.5-43.
Felonies.
Multiple voting, §24.2-1004.
Folding paper ballot and handing to officer who deposits in unopened box, §24.2-646.
Identification required by voter, §24.2-643.
Mandatory voter identification at polling place.
Pilot project requiring, §24.2-643.
Method of voting, VA Const Art II §3.
Military and overseas voters act, §§24.2-451 to 24.2-470.
See ABSENTEE AND EARLY VOTING.
Multiple voting, §24.2-1004.
Voting by person shown as having already voted, §24.2-651.1.
Name of voter erroneously omitted from pollbook, §24.2-652.
Name of voter not appearing on pollbook, §24.2-653.
Not having same choice of candidates.
Conduct of elections, §24.2-309.
Order of voting.
Officers to decide, §24.2-608.
Paper ballots, §24.2-644.
Handling, §24.2-646.
Permitted use, §24.2-646.1.

VOTING AT ELECTIONS —Cont'd
Paper ballots —Cont'd
Provisional ballots, absentee ballots not received, §24.2-653.1.
Presidential electors, §24.2-644.
Privileges of voters during election, VA Const Art II §9.
Procedure, §24.2-643.
Provisional voting.
Absentee ballots lost or not received, §24.2-653.1.
Name of voter not appearing on pollbook, §24.2-653.
Proof of identity not presented, §24.2-643.
Voting by person shown as having already voted, §24.2-651.1.
Qualified voters permitted to vote, §24.2-643.
Persons eighteen years of age at next general election.
Advanced registration and voting in intervening primary or special election, §24.2-403.
Persons entitled to register and vote, §24.2-400.
Qualified voter defined, §24.2-101.
Qualified voter in a town defined, §24.2-101.
Unqualified persons voting, §24.2-1004.
Voter qualifications, §24.2-643, VA Const Art II §1.
Persons eighteen years of age, US Const Amd 26.
Persons entitled to register and vote, §24.2-400.
Persons moving from Commonwealth fewer than thirty days from presidential election, §24.2-402.
Persons moving from precinct, §24.2-401.
Registered voter defined, §24.2-101.
Registration.
See VOTER REGISTRATION.
Restoration of civil right to be eligible to register to vote, §53.1-231.2.
Secrecy in casting votes, VA Const Art II §3.
Soliciting or accepting bribe to influence or procure vote, §24.2-1007.
Suffrage, US Const Amds 14, 15, 19, 26.
Unintentionally or accidentally defacing ballot, §24.2-645.
Unqualified persons voting, §24.2-1004.
Voter qualifications, §24.2-643.
Persons eighteen years of age, US Const Amd 26.
Persons eighteen years of age at next general election.
Advanced registration and voting in intervening primary or special election, §24.2-403.
Persons entitled to register and vote, §24.2-400.
Persons moving from Commonwealth fewer than thirty days from presidential election, §24.2-402.
Persons moving from precinct, §24.2-401.
Qualified voter defined, §24.2-101.
Qualified voter in a town defined, §24.2-101.
Qualified voters permitted to vote, §24.2-643.
Unqualified persons voting, §24.2-1004.
Voter shown as having already voted, §24.2-651.1.
Voting ballot other than ballot received from officers, §24.2-1011.
Voting order.
Officers to decide, §24.2-608.
Woman suffrage, US Const Amd 19.
Write-in votes, §24.2-644, VA Const Art II §3.
Abstract of votes.
No person elected by write-in, §24.2-671.
Federal write-in absentee ballots, §24.2-702.1.
Intent of voter discernible, §24.2-467.

VOTING AT ELECTIONS —Cont'd
Write-in votes —Cont'd
Federal write-in absentee ballots —Cont'd
Methods of registration, §24.2-457.
Military and overseas voters.
Authorized, §24.2-461.
Publication of information, §24.2-465.
Time to register by mail, §24.2-419.
No person elected by write-in, §24.2-671.
Presidential elections, §24.2-644.
Voting equipment, §24.2-648.

VOTING BOOTHS.
Requirements at polling places, §24.2-609.

VOTING BY UNQUALIFIED PERSONS, §24.2-1004.

VOTING EQUIPMENT, ELECTRONIC VOTING OR COUNTING SYSTEMS, §§24.2-625 to 24.2-642.
Absentee ballots.
Casting on voting equipment, §24.2-707.
Experimental use of voting systems and ballots prior to approval of system, §24.2-631.
Accessible voting devices for individuals with disabilities, §24.2-626.1.
Accuracy of device to register and count votes.
Report on capacity, §§24.2-628, 24.2-629.
Acquisition by governing bodies, §24.2-626.
Actual voting.
Officers and others not permitted to see, §24.2-638.
Applicability of elections title, §24.2-625.
Authorized use, §§24.2-628, 24.2-629.
Ballots, §24.2-640.
Sample ballots, §24.2-641.
Custodians of voting equipment, §24.2-632.
Absentee voting.
Persons entitled to vote absentee, §24.2-700.
Oath of office, §24.2-120.
Demonstration of equipment, §24.2-635.
On election day, §24.2-647.
Determination of vote on voting equipment, §24.2-657.
Devices with printed return sheets, §24.2-658.
Keys to voting equipment.
Delivery to circuit court clerk after election, §24.2-659.
Locking voting and counting devices after election, §24.2-659.
Printed return sheets, §24.2-658.
Evidence in recount proceedings, §24.2-659.
Recount occurring in precincts using.
Printed return sheets as evidence, §24.2-659.
Direct recording electronic machines, use of, §24.2-626.
Disabled or other voters needing assistance, §24.2-649.
Accessible voting devices, §24.2-626.1.
Duties of officers of election, §24.2-639.
Election day demonstrations of equipment, §24.2-647.
Electronic systems and ballots.
Authorized use, §24.2-629.
Experimental use of approved systems, §24.2-630.
Experimental use prior to approval of system, §24.2-631.
Security of ballots or voting or counting equipment, §24.2-625.1.
Errors, opportunity to correct, §24.2-629.

VOTING EQUIPMENT, ELECTRONIC VOTING OR COUNTING SYSTEMS —Cont'd
Examination and approval of mechanical voting devices, §24.2-628.
Examination of electronic systems and ballots, §24.2-629.
Examination of equipment as to proper condition, §24.2-633.
Exhibition of equipment containing sample ballots, §24.2-635.
Experimental use of approved systems, §24.2-630.
Experimental use of voting systems and ballots prior to approval of system, §24.2-631.
Furniture and equipment to be at polling places, §24.2-637.
Governing bodies to acquire, §24.2-626.
Inoperative equipment, §24.2-642.
Inspection of face of voting device after voter casts vote, §24.2-638.
Instructions as to use, §24.2-636.
Keys to voting equipment.
Delivery prior to opening of polls to officers of election, §24.2-639.
Delivery to circuit court clerk after election, §24.2-659.
Retained in custody of electoral board, §24.2-634.
Unauthorized possession, §24.2-1010.
Locking after preparation, §24.2-634.
Locking voting and counting devices after polls closed, §§24.2-654, 24.2-659.
Mechanical voting devices.
Authorized use and requirements, §24.2-628.
Modification of equipment to conform to federal or state requirements.
Pre-authorization by board of elections, §24.2-626.
Notice of inoperative equipment, §24.2-642.
Notice of preparation of equipment, §24.2-633.
Number of voting devices, §24.2-627.
Officers of election.
Duties, §24.2-639.
Instructions as to use, §24.2-636.
Overvotes.
Reporting of ballots with, §24.2-629.
Plain view of voting equipment, §24.2-638.
Polling places.
Demonstration of voting equipment on election day, §24.2-647.
Furniture and equipment to be at, §24.2-637.
Precincts, number of voting devices provided for, §24.2-627.
Preparation of equipment notice, §24.2-633.
Protection against tampering or damage, §24.2-634.
Removal from plain view of officers, §24.2-638.
Inoperative devices, §24.2-642.
Reporting of ballots with under-votes or over-votes, §24.2-629.
Report on capacity of device accuracy, §§24.2-628, 24.2-629.
Requirements for approval of mechanical voting devices, §24.2-628.
Requirements for use of electronic systems and ballots, §24.2-629.
Sample ballots, §24.2-641.
Sealing equipment, §24.2-633.
After ascertaining vote, §24.2-654.
Securing after preparation, §24.2-634.
Security of ballots or voting or counting equipment, §24.2-625.1.
Stealing or tampering with, §24.2-1009.

VOTING EQUIPMENT, ELECTRONIC VOTING OR COUNTING SYSTEMS —Cont'd
Substitution of device in good order for inoperative device, §24.2-642.
Testing of equipment prior to election.
Presence of electoral board member or representative, §24.2-632.
Undervotes.
Reporting of ballots with, §24.2-629.
Unlocking counter compartment of equipment, §24.2-638.
Vendors of electronic systems.
Recommended security practices, §24.2-629.
Wireless communication between voting machines or with outside equipment while polls open, §24.2-625.2.
Write-in votes on voting equipment, §24.2-648.
Written plans and procedures to ensure security of electronic systems, §24.2-625.1.
Zero, counter not registering, §24.2-639.

VOTING GROUPS.
Articles of amendment, §13.1-888.
Corporations.
Actions by single and multiple groups, §13.1-667.
Quorum and voting requirements, §13.1-666.
Record date for, §13.1-660.
Removal of director, §13.1-680.
Vacancy on board of directors, filling, §13.1-682.
Voting on amendments to articles of incorporation, §13.1-708.
Nonprofit corporations.
Action by single or multiple groups, §13.1-850.
Record date, §13.1-844.
Voting on amendments to articles of incorporation, §13.1-887.
Voting requirements, §13.1-849.
Change in, §13.1-851.

VOTING-TRUST CERTIFICATES.
Securities generally, §§13.1-501 to 13.1-527.3.
See SECURITIES.

VPI.
Universities generally, §§23-1.01 to 23-9.2:8.
See COLLEGES AND UNIVERSITIES.
Virginia Polytechnic Institute and State University.
See VIRGINIA POLYTECHNIC INSTITUTE AND STATE UNIVERSITY.

VSU.
Universities generally, §§23-1.01 to 23-9.2:8.
See COLLEGES AND UNIVERSITIES.
Virginia state university, §§23-165.1 to 23-174.
See VIRGINIA STATE UNIVERSITY.

VTIC FUND.
Fire programs department.
Thermal imaging camera grant fund, §9.1-205.

W

WACHAPREAGUE, TOWN OF.
Golf carts or utility vehicles.
Designating public highways for operation, authority, §46.2-916.2.

WAFER TECHNOLOGY.
Semiconductor memory of logic wafer manufacturing performance grant programs, §§59.1-284.14, 59.1-284.15.

WAGE ASSIGNMENTS.
Certain assignments not affected, §40.1-33.
Forfeiture of wages, §40.1-29.
Garnishment.
General provisions, §§8.01-466 to 8.01-525.
See GARNISHMENT.
Income withholding.
See INCOME WITHHOLDING.
Nonresident employers.
Registration, §40.1-30.
Partial assignments invalid, §40.1-32.
Registration of nonresident employers, §40.1-30.
Requirements, §40.1-31.
Statement of earnings, §40.1-29.
Time and medium of payment, §40.1-29.
Violations of provisions, §40.1-29.
Withholding wages, §40.1-29.

WAGE EXEMPTIONS.
Garnishment, §§34-29 to 34-34.
Injunction restraining garnishment of wages, §34-2.
Maximum portion of disposable earnings subject to garnishment, §34-29.
Minors' wages, §34-33.
Out-of-Commonwealth garnishment of exempt wages.
Prohibited, §34-32.
Plain language interpretation on reverse side of garnishment summons, §8.01-512.3.
Retirement benefits, §34-34.
Revocation of exemption, §34-31.

WAGE PURCHASES, §6.2-1525.

WAGERING.
Boxing or wrestling events.
Prohibition, §§54.1-834, 54.1-835.
Charitable gaming, §§18.2-340.15 to 18.2-340.37.
See CHARITABLE GAMING.
Gambling generally, §§18.2-325 to 18.2-340.
See GAMBLING.
Gaming contracts, §§11-14 to 11-16.
Prize money for pari-mutuel wagering not deemed to be part of, §59.1-364.

WAGES.
Assignments, §§40.1-29 to 40.1-33.
See WAGE ASSIGNMENTS.
Bad checks issued on behalf of business firm or corporation in payment of, §18.2-182.
Consumer finance companies.
Amount collectible under assignment, §6.2-1526.
Validity and payment of assignment, §6.2-1526.
Consumer finance law.
Wage purchases, §6.2-1525.
Criminal penalty for pay violations, §40.1-29.
Exemption from execution, attachment, garnishment and distress.
Assignment of wages, §§6.2-1526, 6.2-1528.
Failure to make payment.
Civil penalty, §40.1-29.
Garnishment.
General provisions, §§8.01-511 to 8.01-525.
See GARNISHMENT.
Gross wages earned during pay period.
Statement furnished employee upon request, §40.1-29.
Income tax withholding, §§58.1-460 to 58.1-486.3.
See INCOME TAX WITHHOLDING.
Insurance companies, rehabilitation and liquidation.
Priority of claims for wages, §38.2-1514.

WAGES —Cont'd
Medium of payment, §40.1-29.
Minimum wage act, §§40.1-28.8 to 40.1-28.12.
See MINIMUM WAGE ACT.
Notice.
Failure of employer to make payment, §40.1-29.
Payday loan act, §§6.2-1800 to 6.2-1829.
See PAYDAY LOANS.
Pay periods.
Employers to establish, §40.1-29.
Rates of pay.
Employers to establish, §40.1-29.
Sales representatives, independent.
Payment, §59.1-457.
Support of child or spouse.
Withholding of wages.
Failure to comply with support obligation, §16.1-278.16.
Unemployment compensation, §60.2-114.1.
Termination of employment.
Payment of wages due, §40.1-29.
Time of payment, §40.1-29.
Unclaimed wages.
Disposition, §55-210.8:2.
Withholding income tax, §§58.1-460 to 58.1-486.3.
See INCOME TAX WITHHOLDING.

WAGONWAYS.
Public service company duties, §56-16.

WAHOOS.
University of Virginia.
General provisions, §§23-62 to 23-91.23:1.
See UNIVERSITY OF VIRGINIA.

WAIVER OF JURY TRIAL.
Circuit courts, VA SCt Rule 3A:13.
Criminal cases, §19.2-262.
De novo trials, §19.2-262.

WAKE JUMPING.
Reckless operation of personal watercraft, §29.1-738.03.

WALLS.
Defacement of walls on private property.
Authority of locality to remove or repair, §15.2-908.
Endangerment to public health or safety.
Locality requiring removal, repair or securing, §15.2-906.

WAR.
Air raid precautions, §§44-147 to 44-151.
Articles of war, US Const Art I §8.
Banks.
Suspension of business during actual or threatened enemy attack, §6.2-815.
Congress.
Articles of war, US Const Art I §8.
Declaration of war, US Const Art I §8.
Continuity of local government in case of enemy attack or other disaster, §15.2-1413.
Declaration by congress, US Const Art I §8.
Emergency management and disaster law generally, §§44-146.13 to 44-146.28.
See EMERGENCY MANAGEMENT.
Firefighters, mobilization, §§44-152 to 44-159.
General assembly quorum, proclamation by governor, VA Const Art IV §8.
Grand jury.
Presentment as dispensable in certain cases, US Const Amd 5.

WAR —Cont'd
Issuing agents for sale of obligations of United States, §44-206.
Landlord and tenant.
Rent relief, §55-226.
Power of attorney to execute deeds and writings.
Validity when power defective, §55-56.
Quartering soldiers in homes, US Const Amd 3.
States.
May not make without consent of congress, US Const Art I §10.
Traffic regulations during state of war, §44-205.
Treason.
In levying against the United States, US Const Art III §3.
Trust companies.
Suspension of business during actual or threatened enemy attack, §6.2-1002.

WAREHOUSEMAN'S LIEN.
Documents of title, §§8.7-209, 8.7-210.

WAREHOUSE RECEIPTS, §§61.1-2 to 61.1-6.
Delivery with goods without obtaining, §61.1-5.
Documents of title.
General provisions, §§8.7-101 to 8.7-603.
See DOCUMENTS OF TITLE.
Failure to state warehouseman's interest in goods, §61.1-4.
Fraudulent negotiation from mortgaged goods, §61.1-6.
Issuance for goods not received, §61.1-1.
Issuance of duplicate receipts not so marked, §61.1-3.
Issued containing false statements, §61.1-2.

WAREHOUSES AND WAREHOUSEMEN.
ABC law.
Bailment system of warehousing.
Prohibited fees and charges, §4.1-133.
Importation of beverages not under customs or IRS bonds.
Storage in approved warehouses, §4.1-130.
Importation of beverages under customs bonds.
Storage in warehouses, §4.1-131.
Transportation into or within Commonwealth under IRS bonds.
Storage in warehouses, §4.1-132.
Wine stored in bonded warehouses.
Bond to secure tax liability, §4.1-238.
Apples and peaches.
Controlled atmosphere storage, §§3.2-4600 to 3.2-4613.
Controlled atmosphere storage.
Apples and peaches, §§3.2-4600 to 3.2-4613.
Cotton warehouses.
Licensure and regulation generally, §§3.2-4764 to 3.2-4775.
See COTTON HANDLERS.
County purchasing agents duties.
County board form of government, §15.2-414.
Documents of title.
General provisions, §§8.7-101 to 8.7-603.
See DOCUMENTS OF TITLE.
Drug houses.
Maintaining fortified drug houses, §18.2-258.02.
Drug transactions on premises.
Closure of nuisance premises, §§48-16, 48-17.
Common nuisance, §§18.2-258, 18.2-258.01.
Entering with intent to commit larceny, assault and battery or other felony, §18.2-91.

WAREHOUSES AND WAREHOUSEMEN —Cont'd
Farm winery.
Bonded warehouses on or off premises.
Storing wine, §4.1-207.
Liens.
Warehouseman's lien, §8.7-209.
Enforcement, §8.7-210.
Prescription drugs.
Warehousers' permits, §54.1-3435.4.
Safe-deposit or storage business.
Conducted by safe-deposit company from banks and trust companies, §§6.2-2300 to 6.2-2314.
See SAFE-DEPOSIT OR STORAGE BUSINESSES.
Self storage insurance, §§38.2-1881 to 38.2-1886.
Tobacco.
Fraud and deceit.
Violations constituting misdemeanor, §61.1-51.
General provisions, §§61.1-38 to 61.1-46.1.
See TOBACCO WAREHOUSES.
Wineries.
Farm winery.
Bonded warehouses on or off premises.
Storing wine, §4.1-207.

WARNING LIGHTS.
Amber, purple or green flashing warning lights, §§46.2-1025, 46.2-1026.
Blue or red and blue flashing warning lights, §46.2-1022.
Emergency vehicle exemption from traffic regulations.
When exemption applicable, §46.2-920.
Red or red and white flashing warning lights, §§46.2-1023, 46.2-1024.
Emergency vehicle exemption from traffic regulations.
When exemption applicable, §46.2-920.
School buses, §46.2-1090.1.

WARNING SIGNS.
Agritourism activity liability.
Limited liability, warning required, §3.2-6402.
Time-shares.
Project activities.
Inherent risks, liability limited, §55-376.4.

WARNING TO DISPERSE.
Riot or unlawful assembly, remaining at place after warning, §18.2-407.

WAR OF 1812.
Bicentennial of the American War of 1812 commission, §§30-293 to 30-300.
See VIRGINIA BICENTENNIAL OF THE AMERICAN WAR OF 1812 COMMISSION.

WARRANT BOOK.
Local treasurers.
Duties, §58.1-3131.

WARRANTIES.
Agricultural equipment, §§59.1-207.7, 59.1-207.8.
Alcoholic beverages.
Implied warranty of merchantability, §8.2-314.
Anatomical gifts.
Transfers of blood or human tissue, §32.1-297.
Assistive technology device warranties, §§59.1-470 to 59.1-474.
Bank deposits and collections.
Depositary and collecting banks.
Documents of title, §8.7-508.
Encoding and retention warranties, §8.4-207.3.

WARRANTIES —Cont'd
Bank deposits and collections —Cont'd
Depositary and collecting banks —Cont'd
Presentment warranties, §8.4-207.2.
Transfer warranties, §8.4-207.1.
Beverages.
Implied warranty of merchantability, §8.2-314.
Bills of lading.
Collecting banks.
Warranties of collecting bank as to bills, §8.7-508.
Warranties on negotiation or transfer, §8.7-507.
Blood, §32.1-297.
Boats and other watercraft.
Compensation for warranty work, §§29.1-828, 29.1-829.
Career and technical education.
Corporate projects.
Issuance of warranties by school board, §22.1-233.
Computer information transactions, §§59.1-504.1 to 59.1-504.10.
Condominiums.
Special declarant rights.
Transferor liability, §55-79.74:3.
Structural defects, §55-79.79.
Deeds.
Covenant of general warranty.
Effect, §55-68.
With general warranty..
Construed, §55-70.
Implied warranties on new homes, §55-70.1.
Special warranties, §55-69.
With special warranty construed, §55-70.
Documents of title.
Negotiation and transfer, §8.7-507.
Collecting bank's warranties as to documents, §8.7-508.
Escheated lands.
Grants without warranty, §55-186.1.
Farm machinery dealerships.
Suppliers, payment of dealer's claims, §59.1-352.8.
Food and food establishments.
Implied warranty and merchantability, §8.2-314.
Home warranties.
Implied warranties on new homes, §55-70.1.
Real estate cooperatives, §§55-488 to 55-491.
Human tissue, §32.1-297.
Husband and wife.
Conveyances from husband and wife construed, §55-41.
Implied warranties.
Assistive technology device warranties, §§59.1-470 to 59.1-474.
Beverages, §8.2-314.
Blood or human tissue transfers, §32.1-297.
Food and food establishments, §8.2-314.
Homes.
New homes, §55-70.1.
Leases, §§8.2A-211 to 8.2A-214.
Real estate cooperatives, §§55-489, 55-490.
Sales, UCC, §§8.2-312, 8.2-314 to 8.2-317.
Insurance applicants' statements, declarations and descriptions not deemed, §38.2-309.
Investment securities.
Direct holding, §8.8A-108.
Indirect holding, §8.8A-109.
Signatures.
Authenticating trustee, registrar or transfer agent signatures, §8.8A-208.

WARRANTIES —Cont'd
Investment securities —Cont'd
Signatures —Cont'd
Guaranteeing signatures.
Effect, §8.8A-306.
Indorsement or instructions.
Effect of guaranteeing, §8.8A-306.
Leases, UCC.
Cumulative nature, §8.2A-215.
Exclusion or modification, §8.2A-214.
Express warranties, §8.2A-210.
Third-party beneficiaries, §8.2A-216.
Fitness for particular purpose.
Implied warranty, §8.2A-213.
Exclusion or modification, §8.2A-214.
Implied warranty.
Exclusion or modification, §8.2A-214.
Fitness for particular purpose, §8.2A-213.
Interference or infringement, §8.2A-211.
Merchantability, §8.2A-212.
Instruction of warranties, §8.2A-215.
Interference or infringement, §8.2A-211.
Exclusion or modification, §8.2A-214.
Merchantability.
Implied warranty, §8.2A-213.
Exclusion or modification, §8.2A-214.
Modification, §8.2A-214.
Third-party beneficiaries, §8.2A-216.
Letters of credit, §8.5A-110.
Manufactured housing.
Dealer alterations, §36-85.26.
Limitation on damages, §36-85.28.
Presenting claims for warranties and defects, §36-85.24.
Warranty requirements for manufacturer, dealer and supplier, §36-85.23.
Warranty service, §36-85.25.
Married women's property rights.
Conveyances from husband and wife construed, §55-41.
Motorcycle manufacturer, factory branch, distributor or distributor branch, §46.2-1993.70.
Motor vehicle dealers.
Obligations as to warranties, §46.2-1571.
Motor vehicle manufacturers' warranty adjustment, §§59.1-207.34 to 59.1-207.39.
See MOTOR VEHICLE WARRANTIES.
Motor vehicle warranty enforcement, §§59.1-207.9 to 59.1-207.16:1.
See MOTOR VEHICLE WARRANTIES.
Negotiable instruments.
Presentment warranties, §8.3A-417.
Transfer warranties, §8.3A-416.
New home warranties, §55-70.1.
Organ donation.
Transfers of blood or human tissue, §32.1-297.
Property rights of married women.
Conveyances from husband and wife construed, §55-41.
Real estate cooperatives.
Express warranties, §55-488.
Implied warranties, §55-489.
Exclusion, §55-490.
Modification, §55-490.
Special declarant rights, transfers of, §55-461.
Residential property transfer disclosures.
Exemptions, §55-518.
Sales, UCC.
Course of dealing or usage of trade, §8.2-314.
Damages for breach, §8.2-714.

WARRANTIES —Cont'd
Sales, UCC —Cont'd
Express warranties, §8.2-313.
Cumulation and conflict, §8.2-317.
Exclusion and modification, §8.2-316.
Fitness for particular purpose.
Implied warranty, §8.2-315.
Exclusion or modification, §8.2-316.
Implied warranties.
Course of dealing or usage of trade, §8.2-314.
Cumulation and conflict, §8.2-317.
Exclusion or modification, §8.2-316.
Fitness for particular purpose, §8.2-315.
Infringement of enjoyment of goods, §8.2-312.
Merchantability, §8.2-314.
Infringement of enjoyment of goods, §8.2-312.
Merchantability.
Implied warranty, §8.2-314.
Exclusion or modification, §8.2-316.
Registration card, conditioning warranty upon return by purchaser, §8.2-317.1.
Title, §8.2-312.
Seeds.
Disclaimers, nonwarranties and limited warranties, §3.2-4017.
T&M vehicle dealers.
Obligations, §46.2-1979.
Third party beneficiaries, §8.2-318.
Uniform computer information transactions act, §59.1-504.9.
Trailer manufacturers, factory branches, distributors or distributor branches, §46.2-1992.72.
Uniform computer information transactions act, §§59.1-504.1 to 59.1-504.10.
Warehouse receipts.
Collecting banks.
Warranties of collecting bank as to receipts, §8.7-508.
Warranties on negotiation or transfer, §8.7-507.

WARRANTLESS ARRESTS.
Aliens.
Enforcement of immigration laws, §19.2-81.6.
Issuance of warrant, §19.2-82.
Assault and battery, §19.2-81.
Domestic violence, §19.2-81.3.
Automobile accidents, §19.2-81.
Boating under the influence, §19.2-81.
Bringing person arrested before appropriate court without unnecessary delay, §19.2-80.
Close pursuit doctrine, §19.2-77.
Comity.
Arrest by officers of other states, §19.2-79.
Conservation police officers.
Powers, §19.2-81.
Conservators of the peace.
Powers generally, §19.2-18.
Correctional officers, §19.2-81.1.
Power to detain, §19.2-81.2.
Domestic violence, §19.2-81.3.
Driving under the influence, §19.2-81.
Duty of arresting officer, §19.2-80.
Escape, flight and pursuit.
Arrest anywhere in Commonwealth, §19.2-77.
Inmate escape, §19.2-81.1.
Exceeding posted speed limit, §46.2-882.
Extradition of criminals.
Procedure upon arrest without warrant, §19.2-100.
Family abuse, §19.2-81.3.

WARRANTLESS ARRESTS —Cont'd
Fishing, tidal waters.
Provision violations, §28.2-900.
Illegal aliens, §19.2-81.6.
Issuance of warrant, §19.2-82.
Law-enforcement officials.
Policies and procedures, §19.2-82.
Magistrates.
Personal appearance before magistrate, §19.2-82.
Malicious mischief, §19.2-81.
Monuments and memorials.
Malicious mischief, §19.2-81.
Offenses.
Committed in presence of law enforcement officer, §19.2-81.
Officers of other states making arrest, §19.2-79.
Parolees, §53.1-162.
Personal appearance before magistrate, §19.2-82.
Persons charged with crimes in another jurisdiction.
Outstanding arrest warrants, §19.2-81.
Policies and procedures, §19.2-82.
Prisoners.
Arrest without warrant by correctional officers, §19.2-81.1.
Power of correctional officers to detain, §19.2-81.2.
Probable cause requirement, §19.2-81.
Judicial determination, §19.2-82.
Probation officers, §53.1-149.
Procedure upon arrest without warrant, §19.2-82.
Recognizance to keep the peace, §19.2-22.
Schools and education.
Carrying weapon on school property, §19.2-81.
Sentencing.
Willing or knowing failure to submit to custody of sheriff, §19.2-298.
Shoplifting, §19.2-81.
Speeding traffic infraction, §46.2-882.
Stalking, §19.2-81.3.
State police arrests, §52-20.
Procedure after, §52-21.
Summons in lieu of warrant authorized, §19.2-81.
Uniform of officer making arrest, §19.2-78.
Watercraft accidents, §19.2-81.
Weapons.
Carrying weapon on school property, §19.2-81.
Within three hours of occurrence.
Arrest for DWI, §19.2-81.

WARRANTLESS SEARCHES.
Conservation police officers, §29.1-208.
Enforcement of game laws.
Exception to prohibition, §19.2-56.
Firearm dealers.
Records, §54.1-4201.
Inspection warrants.
Toxic substances, §§19.2-393 to 19.2-397.
Motor vehicles department.
Authority of law-enforcement officers, §46.2-217.
Officers of the law.
Effect of unlawful searches, §19.2-59.
Pawnbroker records and shops, §54.1-4011.
Precious metals dealers.
Records and articles of dealers, §54.1-4101.1.
Suppression of evidence.
Unreasonable search and seizure.
Written pretrial motion requirement, §19.2-266.2.

WARRANTLESS SEARCHES —Cont'd
Unlawful.
Penalties, §19.2-59.
Unreasonable search and seizure.
Suppression of evidence.
Written pretrial motion requirement, §19.2-266.2.
Written pretrial motion.
Suppression of evidence.
Unreasonable search and seizure, §19.2-266.2.

WARRANTS.
Amendment of warrant.
District court criminal cases.
Procedure on appeal when warrant defective, §16.1-137.
Tried on amended warrant, §16.1-129.2.
Animals.
Crossing lawful fences.
Duty to issue warrant when animal impounded, §55-309.
Arrest warrants, §§19.2-71 to 19.2-83.2, VA SCt Rule 3A:4, VA SCt Rule Part 3A Appx Form 3.
See ARREST WARRANTS.
Building code.
Inspection warrants, §36-105.
Conservation police officers.
Searches and seizures, §29.1-208.
Defective warrants.
District court criminal cases tried on, §16.1-129.2.
Desertion and nonsupport.
Commencement of proceedings, §20-66.
No warrant of arrest to issue, §20-70.
Distress warrants.
See DISTRESS WARRANTS.
District court civil cases.
Action brought on warrant, §16.1-79.
When action deemed brought, §16.1-86.
District court clerks, power to issue, §16.1-69.40.
District court criminal cases.
Offenses tried on, §16.1-69.40.
Defective warrants, procedure on appeal, §16.1-137.
Procedure when warrant defective, §16.1-129.2.
District court judges.
Power to issue, §16.1-69.25.
Driving while intoxicated.
Refusal of chemical test, issuance, §18.2-268.3.
Endangered species, §29.1-567.
Estrays, §§55-202 to 55-206.
Extradition of criminals.
Issuance and recital of warrant of arrest, §19.2-92.
Manner and place of execution of warrant of arrest, §19.2-93.
Fences.
Animals crossing lawful fences.
Duty to issue warrant when animal impounded, §55-309.
Fire marshals, local.
Powers, §27-34.2.
Fire prevention code.
Duration, §27-98.3.
Issuance, §27-98.2.
Fishing, tidal waters.
Arrests, §28.2-900.
Governor.
Returns, §2.2-112.
Health commissioner.
Entry to inspect, §32.1-25.

WARRANTS —Cont'd
Inspection warrants.
Toxic substances, §§19.2-393 to 19.2-397.
Zoning ordinance may provide for issuance, §15.2-2286.
Landlord and tenant.
Distress, §§55-230 to 55-232.2.
When distress made, §55-230.
Magistrates powers, §19.2-45.
Medicaid benefits.
Fraud or misrepresentations.
Issuance for violations, §32.1-321.4.
New warrants.
District court criminal cases.
Original warrant defective, §16.1-129.2.
Procedure on appeal when warrant defective, §16.1-137.
Occupational safety and health, §§40.1-49.10 to 40.1-49.12.
See OCCUPATIONAL SAFETY AND HEALTH.
Public school funds.
Payment of claims, §§22.1-122, 22.1-124.
Recognizance to keep the peace, §19.2-20.
Search warrants.
Generally, §§19.2-52 to 19.2-60.
See SEARCH WARRANTS.
Statement of witness for arrest warrant, VA SCt Rules Part 3A Appx Form 2.
Service of notice, process and other papers generally.
See SERVICE OF NOTICE, PROCESS AND OTHER PAPERS.
Simulation of warrants, §18.2-213.
Small claims courts.
Civil warrant to commence actions, §16.1-122.3.
Toxic substances.
Inspection warrants, §§19.2-393 to 19.2-397.

WARRANTS FOR ARREST, §§19.2-71 to 19.2-83.2, VA SCt Rule 3A:4, VA SCt Rule Part 3A Appx Form 3.
See ARREST WARRANTS.

WARRANTS FOR SETTLEMENT OF CLAIMS AGAINST COUNTIES, §§15.2-1243, 15.2-1244.

WARRANTS FOR THE PAYMENT OF MONEY.
Local treasurers.
Dealing in warrants prohibited, §58.1-3139.
Deduction of taxes due from party in whose favor warrant drawn, §58.1-3133.
Failure to pay, remedy, §58.1-3140.
How paid, §58.1-3132.
Payable in order received, §58.1-3131.
Presentation within two years required, §58.1-3134.
Release of information.
Prohibited, exceptions, §58.1-3131.
Warrant book, §58.1-3131.

WARRANTS IN DEBT.
Corporations preparing without attorney intervention.
District court civil cases, §16.1-88.03.
Interpleader in district courts.
Initial pleading, §16.1-77.
Partnerships preparing without attorney intervention.
District court civil cases, §16.1-88.03.

WARRANTS OF DISTRESS.
See DISTRESS WARRANTS.

WARRANTS ON STATE TREASURY.
Disbursement warrants.
Conditions to issuance, §2.2-1822.

WARRANTS ON STATE TREASURY —Cont'd
Disbursement warrants —Cont'd
Procedure, §2.2-1821.
Lost or destroyed warrants.
Replacement warrants.
Payment of claims, §2.2-1826.
No bond required, §2.2-1827.
Payment of claims.
Issuance, §2.2-1825.
Replacement warrants, §2.2-1826.
No bond required, §2.2-1827.
Replacement warrants.
Payment of claims, §2.2-1826.
No bond required, §2.2-1827.
State treasurer.
List of warrants, §2.2-1809.

WARREN COUNTY.
Automobile graveyards, screening ordinance, §15.2-903.
Confederate cemeteries and graves.
Disbursement of funds appropriated for upkeep, §10.1-2211.
Highways and roads.
Dirt and gravel roads.
Maximum speed limits on nonsurface treated highways, §46.2-873.1.
Private roads, designation as highways for law-enforcement purposes, §46.2-1307.1.
Port of Virginia economic and infrastructure development zone grant fund, §62.1-132.3:2.
Public defenders office.
Established, §19.2-163.04.
School board.
Salary of members, §22.1-32.
Well abandonment ordinance.
Duty of owner to cap or close well.
Locality adopting ordinance, §32.1-176.5.
Well construction.
Testing requirements, §32.1-176.5.
Winchester regional airport authority, 1987 ch 687, 1995 ch 258, 1995 ch 338.

WASHINGTON COUNTY.
Confederate cemeteries and graves.
Disbursement of funds appropriated for upkeep, §10.1-2211.
Cutting grass or lawn area of residential real property.
Requiring owner of occupied property, §15.2-1215.
Excursion passenger train operated in county.
Certification, §46.2-2099.41.
Revolutionary war cemeteries and graves.
Disbursement of funds appropriated for upkeep, §10.1-2211.1.
School board.
Salary of members, §22.1-32.
Southwest Virginia cultural heritage foundation.
Board of trustees, §2.2-2735.
Transient occupancy tax.
Disposition of revenues, §58.1-3819.

WASHINGTON COUNTY DEVELOPMENT AUTHORITY.
Generally.
See ECONOMIC DEVELOPMENT AUTHORITIES.

WASHINGTON DULLES INTERNATIONAL AIRPORT.
Metropolitan Washington airports authority.
Acquisition from United States, authorization, §5.1-154.

WASHINGTON DULLES INTERNATIONAL AIRPORT —Cont'd
Metropolitan Washington airports authority —Cont'd
Generally, §§5.1-152 to 5.1-177.
See METROPOLITAN WASHINGTON AIRPORTS AUTHORITY.

WASHINGTON, GEORGE.
George Washington day.
Legal holidays, §2.2-3300.

WASHINGTON METROPOLITAN AREA TRANSIT AUTHORITY.
Created, 1958 ch 627.
Amended in 1962, 1962 ch 67.
Amended in 1964, 1964 ch 626.
Amended in 1966, 1966 ch 2.
Amended in 1969, 1969 Ex Sess ch 21.
Amended in 1970, 1970 ch 590.
Amended in 1971, 1971 ch 171.
Amended in 1972, 1972 ch 571.
Amended in 1973, 1973 ch 508.
Amended in 1974, 1974 ch 576.
Amended in 1977, 1977 ch 592.
Amended in 1981, 1981 ch 378.
Amended in 1984, 1984 ch 610.
Amended in 1987, 1987 ch 112.
Amended in 1988, 1988 ch 890.
Amended in 1995, 1995 ch 150.
Amended in 1997, 1997 ch 736.

WASHINGTON METROPOLITAN TRANSPORTATION DISTRICT.
Commission members, §15.2-4507.
Transportation districts generally, §§15.2-4500 to 15.2-4534.

WASHINGTON REDSKINS.
Motor vehicle license plates for supporters, §46.2-749.73.

WASTE, §§55-211 to 55-216.
Conservators, §55-213.
Curators.
Duties, §64.2-451.
Decedents' estates.
Actions by executors or administrators, §64.2-520.
Escheats.
Prevention by escheators, §55-180.
Executors and administrators.
Powers prior to qualification, §64.2-511.
Suits against executors and administrators, §64.2-546.
Procedure, §64.2-548.
Guardians, §55-213.
Mortgages and deeds of trust.
Duty of parties, §55-59.
Zoning ordinances.
Special use permit not required for agricultural activities, §15.2-2288.

WASTE KITCHEN GREASE.
Transportation, §§3.2-5508 to 3.2-5516.
Appeals, §3.2-5516.
Definitions, §3.2-5508.
Individual use, §3.2-5510.
Penalties for violations, §3.2-5515.
Appeals from civil penalties, §3.2-5516.
Records.
Registrants, §3.2-5511.
Registration.
Applications, §3.2-5509.

WASTE KITCHEN GREASE —Cont'd
Transportation —Cont'd
Registration —Cont'd
Certificate.
Issuance, §3.2-5509.
Possession, §3.2-5512.
Exemption.
Individual use, §3.2-5510.
Fees, §3.2-5509.
Motor vehicles.
Information on, §3.2-5512.
Revocation, §3.2-5513.
Appeals, §3.2-5516.
Suspension, §3.2-5513.
Appeals, §3.2-5516.
Term, §3.2-5509.
Waste kitchen grease fund, §3.2-5514.

WASTELANDS.
Sale of unappropriated land, §§41.1-16 to 41.1-20.
See LAND OFFICE.

WASTE MANAGEMENT, §§10.1-1400 to 10.1-1407.1.
Abandoned waste sites.
Access, §10.1-1406.1.
Advisory committees, §10.1-1403.
Applicant defined, §10.1-1400.
Board.
Continuation, §10.1-1401.
Defined, §10.1-1400.
Further duties, §10.1-1402.01.
Initial notice by certified mail, subsequent notices by regular mail, §10.1-1400.1.
Powers and duties, §10.1-1402.
Coal combustion byproducts in designated flood plains.
Use, reuse or reclamation not exempted from definition of solid waste, §10.1-1402.02.
Coal mines.
Conditional exemption for coal mining overburden or solid waste, §10.1-1406.2.
Composting defined, §10.1-1400.
Continuation of board, §10.1-1401.
Continuation of department, §10.1-1404.
Definitions, §10.1-1400.
Department defined, §10.1-1400.
Director.
Defined, §10.1-1400.
Initial notice by certified mail, subsequent notices by regular mail, §10.1-1400.1.
Powers and duties, §10.1-1405.
Disclosure statement defined, §10.1-1400.
Disposal defined, §10.1-1400.
Enforcement of provisions, §10.1-1455.
Environmental laboratory certification program.
Division of consolidated laboratory services to establish, §2.2-1105.
Equity defined, §10.1-1400.
Exemptions from liability, §10.1-1406.
Coal and mineral mining overburden or solid waste.
Conditional exemption for, §10.1-1406.2.
Federal acts defined, §10.1-1400.
Fees.
Conformance with federal requirements, §10.1-1402.3.
Nonhazardous solid waste management facilities, §10.1-1402.1:1.
Permit fee regulations, §10.1-1402.1.

WASTE MANAGEMENT —Cont'd
Funds.
Permit program fund established, §10.1-1402.2.
Hazardous material.
Defined, §10.1-1400.
Hazardous materials transportation, §§10.1-1450 to 10.1-1454.
See HAZARDOUS MATERIALS TRANSPORTATION.
Hazardous substance.
Defined, §10.1-1400.
Hazardous waste.
Defined, §10.1-1400.
Hazardous waste facilities siting, §§10.1-1433 to 10.1-1449.
See HAZARDOUS WASTE FACILITIES SITING.
Hazardous waste generation.
Defined, §10.1-1400.
Hazardous waste management, §§10.1-1426 to 10.1-1429.
See HAZARDOUS WASTE MANAGEMENT.
High-level radioactive waste.
Defined, §10.1-1400.
Information to be provided to department by persons dealing with waste, §10.1-1458.
Inspections, §10.1-1456.
Judicial review, §10.1-1457.
Key personnel.
Defined, §10.1-1400.
Lead acid batteries, §§10.1-1425.1 to 10.1-1425.5.
See LEAD ACID BATTERIES.
Localities particularly affected by board regulations, §10.1-1402.01.
Low-level radioactive waste.
Defined, §10.1-1400.
Mail notice.
Initial notice by certified mail, subsequent notices by regular mail, §10.1-1400.1.
Manifest.
Defined, §10.1-1400.
Mineral mines.
Conditional exemption for mineral mining overburden or solid waste, §10.1-1406.2.
Mixed radioactive waste.
Defined, §10.1-1400.
Notice.
Initial notice by certified mail, subsequent notices by regular mail, §10.1-1400.1.
Local government notification of violations, §10.1-1407.1.
Nuclear waste.
Defined, §10.1-1400.
Open dump.
Defined, §10.1-1400.
Penalties, §10.1-1455.
Permits.
Fee regulations, §10.1-1402.1.
Program fund established, §10.1-1402.2.
Person.
Defined, §10.1-1400.
Plans and specifications to be provided to department, §10.1-1458.
Pollution prevention program, §§10.1-1425.10 to 10.1-1425.19.
See POLLUTION PREVENTION PROGRAM.
Powers and duties of board, §10.1-1402.
Radioactive waste, §§10.1-1430 to 10.1-1432.
See RADIOACTIVE WASTE.
Recycling.
See RECYCLING.

WASTE MANAGEMENT —Cont'd
Resource conservation.
Defined, §10.1-1400.
Resource recovery.
Defined, §10.1-1400.
Resource recovery system.
Defined, §10.1-1400.
Right of entry, §10.1-1456.
Sanitary landfill.
Defined, §10.1-1400.
Settlements.
Expedited settlements, §10.1-1406.
Sludge.
Defined, §10.1-1400.
Solid waste.
Defined, §10.1-1400.
Solid waste management, §§10.1-1408.1 to 10.1-1413.2.
See SOLID WASTE MANAGEMENT.
Solid waste management facility.
Defined, §10.1-1400.
Special orders issued for violations, §10.1-1455.
State agency duties, §§10.1-1425.6 to 10.1-1425.9.
Transport or transportation.
Defined, §10.1-1400.
Treatment.
Defined, §10.1-1400.
Universities' duties, §§10.1-1425.6 to 10.1-1425.9.
Upgrade to treatment works, reimbursements to localities for, §10.1-1186.01.
Vegetative waste.
Defined, §10.1-1400.
Violation of provisions.
Notification of local governments, §10.1-1407.1.
Waste.
Defined, §10.1-1400.
Waste management.
Defined, §10.1-1400.
Waters of the state.
See WATERS OF THE STATE.
Water transportation of solid waste, §10.1-1454.1.
Yard waste.
Defined, §10.1-1400.

WASTE MANAGEMENT BOARD.
Brownfields restoration and land renewal.
Voluntary remediation program, §10.1-1232.
Enforcement of provisions.
Intervention in federal Environmental Protection Agency cases, §10.1-1186.4.
Environmental quality department.
Continuation of board, §10.1-1184.
Dispute resolution powers, §10.1-1186.3.
Freedom of information act.
Excluded records.
Federal environmental enforcement actions, §2.2-3705.7.
Solid waste or recycling revolving fund.
Grants to local governments, §§62.1-241.7, 62.1-241.8.

WASTE MANAGEMENT FACILITY OPERATORS, §§54.1-2209 to 54.1-2212.
Unlawful procurement of licensure, §54.1-102.
Unlawful use of licensure, §54.1-111.

WASTE MOTOR OIL BURNING EQUIPMENT TAX CREDIT, §58.1-439.7.

WASTE TIRES.
Disposal, §10.1-1422.1.
Partial reimbursement for, §10.1-1422.4.

WASTE TIRES —Cont'd
Trust fund established, §10.1-1422.3.

WASTEWATER SYSTEMS LOCATED ON RESIDENTIAL PROPERTY.
Residential real estate property transfers.
No representations by owner with respect to, §55-519.

WASTEWATER TREATMENT FACILITIES.
Certificates for discharge, §62.1-44.15.
County employees.
Background checks, §15.2-634.1.
Damage or trespass to, §18.2-162.
Discharges into waters of the state, §§62.1-44.18 to 62.1-44.19:3.4.
Certification, §62.1-44.15.
Ohio river valley water sanitation commission.
Jurisdiction, §62.1-74.
Violations, §§62.1-44.31, 62.1-44.32.
Diverting service, §§8.01-44.7, 18.2-162.1, 18.2-163.
Extraordinary hardship program, §62.1-44.15:2.
Metering devices, tampering with, §§8.01-44.7, 18.2-163.
Resources authority generally, §§62.1-197 to 62.1-223.
See RESOURCES AUTHORITY.
Water control board.
Limitations on power to require construction of, §62.1-44.15:1.
Water facilities revolving fund, §§62.1-224 to 62.1-232.
See WATER FACILITIES REVOLVING FUND.

WASTEWATER WORKS OPERATORS.
Generally, §§54.1-2300 to 54.1-2302.
See WATERWORKS OPERATORS.

WATCHES, SECONDHAND ARTICLE SALES, §§59.1-131 to 59.1-136.

WATCH RESALES, §§59.1-131 to 59.1-136.
See SECONDHAND ARTICLE SALES.

WATER AND WASTE AUTHORITIES, §§15.2-5100 to 15.2-5159.
Annexation.
Annexation by municipality not member of authority, §15.2-5116.
Appomattox River water authority, 1962 ch 88.
Articles of incorporation, §15.2-5103.
Amendment, §15.2-5110.
Filing, §15.2-5107.
Audits, §15.2-5145.
Billing agents, water utility as, §15.2-5151.
Blacksburg-Christiansburg-V.P.I. water authority, 1956 ch 148.
Board, §15.2-5113.
Bond issues, §§15.2-5125 to 15.2-5134.
Bondholder's remedies, §15.2-5141.
Community development authorities.
Validation of proceedings, §15.2-5159.
Exemption from taxation, §15.2-5132.
Interim receipts and temporary bonds, §15.2-5128.
Investments, §15.2-5144.
Issuance, §15.2-5125.
Limitations upon issuance of additional bonds, §15.2-5130.
Mutilated, lost or destroyed bonds, §15.2-5128.
Not debts of Commonwealth or participating political subdivision, §15.2-5131.
Presumption of validity, §15.2-5126.
Proceeds, §15.2-5127.

WATER AND WASTE AUTHORITIES —Cont'd
Bond issues —Cont'd
Provisions only requirements for issuance, §15.2-5129.
Refunding bonds, §15.2-5142.
Purchase on open market or otherwise, §15.2-5143.
Time for contesting validity, §15.2-5126.
Trust agreement, §15.2-5133.
Unclaimed funds due on matured bonds or coupons, §15.2-5134.
Bonds, surety.
Employees.
Blanket surety bond plan.
Risk management division, §2.2-1840.
Budget, §15.2-5145.
Certificates of incorporation.
Issuance, §15.2-5108.
Charter.
Issuance, §15.2-5108.
Chesapeake water authority, 1970 ch 743.
Chief administrative or executive officers, §15.2-5113.
Community development authorities, §§15.2-5152 to 15.2-5158.
Connections, §15.2-5137.
Contracts.
Interest rate, cashflow or other bases, §15.2-5135.
Power of authority of locality, §15.2-5147.
Use of system, §15.2-5115.
Conveyance to authority, powers of locality.
Generally, §§15.2-5147, 15.2-5148.
Creation.
More than one authority, §15.2-5150.
Ordinance, resolution or agreement, §15.2-5102.
Public hearings, §15.2-5105.
Voters petition requesting agreement and referendum, §15.2-5106.
Definitions, §15.2-5101.
Delinquent payment of rates and charges, §15.2-5124.
Dissolution of authority, §15.2-5109.
Electric energy systems, providing and operating, §15.2-5119.
Eminent domain, §15.2-5114.
Employees.
Bonds, surety.
Blanket surety bond plan.
Risk management division, §2.2-1840.
Exemption from taxation, §15.2-5132.
Financial reports, §15.2-5145.
Grants to authority, powers of locality, §15.2-5147.
Hampton Roads area refuse collection and disposal system authority, §15.2-5102.1.
Insurance for employees, §15.2-5117.
Intellectual property rights.
Powers, §15.2-5114.
Joinder of another locality or authority, §15.2-5112.
Joining more than one authority, §15.2-5150.
Money received held as trust fund, §15.2-5140.
Notice.
Ordinance, agreement or resolution and notice of hearing, §15.2-5104.
Ordinance, resolution or agreement creating, §15.2-5102.
Advertisement and notice of public hearing, §15.2-5104.
Articles of incorporation included, §15.2-5103.
Public hearing, referendum, §15.2-5105.

WATER AND WASTE AUTHORITIES —Cont'd
Petition by voters requesting agreement and referendum, §15.2-5106.
Planning district 1 or Planning District 2.
Enforcement charges, §15.2-5138.1.
Powers, §15.2-5114.
Certain counties and cities, §15.2-5120.
Publication.
Ordinance, agreement or resolution and notice of hearing, §15.2-5104.
Public hearings, §15.2-5105.
Notice, §15.2-5104.
Railroad structures, interference with, §15.2-5149.
Rates and charges, §15.2-5136.
Delinquent payment, §15.2-5124.
Discounted fees and charges for low-income and disabled customers, §15.2-2119.
Enforcement, §15.2-5138.
Authority operating in Planning district 1 or Planning District 2, §15.2-5138.1.
Liens, §§15.2-2119, 15.2-5139.
Referendum on adopting ordinance, resolution or agreement creating, §15.2-5105.
Referendum on creating, voters petition requesting, §15.2-5106.
Refuse collection systems.
Operation, displacement of private companies, §15.2-5121.
Sewage treatment plants to include capacity standards, §15.2-5123.
Southeastern public service authority of Virginia, 1977 ch 544, 2000 ch 580, 2000 ch 596.
Specification of projects, §15.2-5111.
State corporation commission.
Filing articles of dissolution with, §15.2-5109.
Issuance of certificate of incorporation or charter, §15.2-5108.
State land, use, §15.2-5146.
Street lights in King George county, §15.2-5118.
Termination of authority, §15.2-5109.
Virginia water and waste authorities act.
Title of chapter, §15.2-5100.
Water and sewer connections, §15.2-5137.
Water supply impoundment facilities.
Approval, §15.2-5122.
Withdrawal from authority, §15.2-5112.

WATER, ATTEMPT TO POISON, §18.2-54.1.

WATER COMMISSION.
Compensation, §30-186.
Functions, §30-187.
Legislative services, division of.
Staff to commission, §30-186.
Membership, §30-186.
Staff, §30-186.
Voting on recommendations, §30-186.

WATER COMPANIES.
Articles of incorporation.
Conducting business as public service company, statement required, §13.1-620.
City or town water works, sale of, VA Const Art VII §9.
Consumer utility taxes generally, §§58.1-3814 to 58.1-3816.2.
Cooperative associations.
Organization as, §13.1-301.
Damage or trespass to, §18.2-162.

WATER COMPANIES —Cont'd
Designation as public utility and service corporation or company, §56-1.2.
Estimated tax, §§58.1-2640 to 58.1-2651.
See PUBLIC SERVICE CORPORATION TAXATION.
License tax.
County, city or town, §58.1-3731.
Generally, §§58.1-2620 to 58.1-2635.
See PUBLIC SERVICE CORPORATION TAXATION.
Limitation of actions.
Liens for assessments, §8.01-240.
Meters.
Good working condition requirements, §56-245.1.
Pipelines, §§56-257 to 56-260.1.
Public utilities.
Generally, §§56-232 to 56-265.
See PUBLIC UTILITIES.
Special regulatory revenue tax, §§58.1-2660 to 58.1-2665.
Statute of limitations.
Liens for assessments, §8.01-240.

WATER COMPANY LICENSE TAX.
Estimated tax, §§58.1-2640 to 58.1-2651.
See PUBLIC SERVICE CORPORATION TAXATION.
License tax, §§58.1-2620 to 58.1-2635.
See PUBLIC SERVICE CORPORATION TAXATION.

WATER CONSERVATION.
Ordinances requiring installation of devices, §15.2-923.
State building maintenance and utilization standards, §2.2-1131.

WATER CONTROL BOARD, §§62.1-44.7 to 62.1-44.15:5.2.
Aboveground oil storage tank registration, §62.1-44.34:19.1.
Approval of sewerage systems and works, §62.1-44.19.
Hearings, §§62.1-44.25 to 62.1-44.30.
Authority to speak and act for Commonwealth, §62.1-44.41.
Certificates for discharge, §62.1-44.15.
Chairman, §62.1-44.14.
Civil penalties.
Power to order, §62.1-44.15.
Confined animal feeding operations.
Chesapeake Bay watershed nutrient credit exchange program, §62.1-44.19:21.
General permits, §62.1-44.17:1.
Construction of provisions, §62.1-44.44.
Continued, §62.1-44.7.
Cooperation with other agencies, §62.1-44.42.
Dams for hydroelectric power.
Applications, §62.1-85.
Defined terms.
Ceases operation, §62.1-44.15:1.1.
Locality particularly affected, §62.1-44.15:01.
Duties, §62.1-44.15.
Ground water management, §62.1-256.
Localities particularly affected, §62.1-44.15:01.
Planning for the development, conservation and utilization of water resources, §62.1-44.36.
Potomac river basin commission.
Construction of provisions, §62.1-69.
Enforcement of provisions.
Intervention in federal Environmental Protection Agency cases, §10.1-1186.4.

WATER CONTROL BOARD —Cont'd
Enforcement remedies, §62.1-44.23.
Environmental quality department.
Continuation of board, §10.1-1184.
Dispute resolution powers, §10.1-1186.3.
Executive director, §62.1-44.14.
Extraordinary hardship program, §62.1-44.15:2.
Federal aid.
Applications for, §62.1-44.43.
Filing of standards, policies, rules or regulations, §62.1-44.12.
Freedom of information act.
Excluded records.
Federal environmental enforcement actions, §2.2-3705.7.
Gifts.
Authority to accept, §62.1-44.43.
Grants.
Authority to accept, §62.1-44.43.
Ground water management.
Duties, §62.1-256.
Initiation of ground water management areas study, §62.1-257.
Permits to withdraw.
Issuance of special orders, §62.1-268.
Provision violations.
Penalties, §§62.1-269, 62.1-270.
Withdrawal permits, §§62.1-262, 62.1-266.
Existing ground water withdrawals in existing ground water management areas, §62.1-260.
Existing ground water withdrawals in newly established ground water management areas, §62.1-261.
Issuance criteria, §62.1-263.
Issuance of special exceptions, §62.1-267.
Public water supplies, §62.1-264.
Drought relief wells, §62.1-265.
Hearings, §62.1-44.26.
Appeals, §62.1-44.30.
Decisions, §62.1-44.28.
Judicial review, §62.1-44.29.
Planned use conflicts, §62.1-44.37.
Right to, §62.1-44.25.
Rules of evidence, §62.1-44.27.
Hydroelectric power dams.
Applications, §62.1-85.
Impoundment of surface waters.
Riparian owner rights.
Application for leave to store floodwaters, §62.1-107.
Examination of petitions reports to court, §62.1-109.
Information to be furnished to, §§62.1-44.21, 62.1-44.39.
Inspections, §§62.1-44.13, 62.1-44.15.
Instream toxics removal or remediation technologies.
Evaluation and review, §62.1-44.17:4.
Intervention in actions involving surface water withdrawals, §62.1-44.23:1.
Investigations, §§62.1-44.13, 62.1-44.15.
Judicial review of final decisions, §62.1-44.29.
Limitation on authority.
Erosion and sediment control, §62.1-44.15:66.
Mail notice.
Initial notice by certified mail, subsequent notices by regular mail, §62.1-44.3:1.
Meetings, §62.1-44.11.
Members.
Appointment, §62.1-44.8.

WATER CONTROL BOARD —Cont'd
Members —Cont'd
Number, §62.1-44.8.
Qualifications, §62.1-44.9.
Terms, §62.1-44.8.
No-discharge zones, §62.1-44.33.
Oil discharges.
Aboveground storage tank registration, §62.1-44.34:19.1.
Aboveground storage tank regulation, §62.1-44.34:15.1.
Administrative fees, §62.1-44.34:21.
Contingency plans, §62.1-44.34:15.
Enforcement of provisions, §62.1-44.34:20.
Financial responsibility, §62.1-44.34:16.
Permit program fund, §62.1-44.15:7.
Permits.
Stormwater management.
Terms, §62.1-44.15:26.
Persons aggrieved by final decisions.
Judicial review, §62.1-44.29.
Planned use conflicts.
Resolution, §62.1-44.37.
Plans and programs for the management of water resources, §62.1-44.38.
Comprehensive water supply planning process, §62.1-44.38:1.
Water supply plans, §62.1-44.38:1.
Advisory committee, §62.1-44.38:2.
Polluted water samples.
Analysis, §29.1-214.
Pollution control offenses, §§62.1-44.31, 62.1-44.32.
Potomac river basin commission.
Application of provisions, §62.1-69.
Potomac river riparian rights.
Dispute resolution, §62.1-44.116.
Review of uses, §62.1-44.115.
Poultry waste management program, §62.1-44.17:1.1.
Powers, §62.1-44.15.
Additional powers, §62.1-44.43.
Authorized to speak and act for Commonwealth, §62.1-44.41.
Limitations, §62.1-44.15:1.
Protection permits.
Coordinated review of water resources projects, §62.1-44.15:5.01.
General permit for water quality improvement activities, §62.1-44.15:5.1.
Potomac river.
Low-flow protections, §62.1-44.15:5.02.
Public hearings and permit procedures before the board, §62.1-44.15:02.
Provision violations.
Notification of local governments and property owners, §62.1-44.15:4.
Public funds.
Administration of funds, §62.1-44.43.
Ready-mixed concrete plants.
General permits for discharge of stormwater and process wastewater, §62.1-44.15:5.2.
Public hearings and permit procedures before the board, §62.1-44.15:02.
Records of proceedings, §62.1-44.12.
Regulations.
Testing of validity, §62.1-44.24.
Reports on planning and status, §62.1-44.40.
Right of entry, §62.1-44.20.
Riparian rights, existing.
Construction of provisions, §62.1-44.44.

WATER CONTROL BOARD —Cont'd
Rules and regulations, §62.1-44.33.
Sewage discharges.
Joint supervision, §62.1-44.18.
Prohibitions, §62.1-44.18:2.
Sewerage systems.
Limitations on powers, §62.1-44.15:1.
Solid waste transportation by water.
Regulation, §10.1-1454.1.
Special orders, §62.1-44.15:1.1.
Failure to comply with, §§62.1-44.31, 62.1-44.32.
Hearings.
Decision requirements, §62.1-44.28.
Oil discharges, §62.1-44.34:20.
Statement of water resource policy, §62.1-44.36.
Storage tanks.
Petroleum storage tank fund.
Administration, §62.1-44.34:11.
Powers and duties, §§62.1-44.34:9, 62.1-44.34:11.
Stormwater management.
Powers and duties, §62.1-44.15:25.
Rules and regulations.
Development, §62.1-44.15:28.
Surface water management areas.
Agreements among persons withdrawing surface water, §62.1-245.
Information from persons withdrawing surface water, §62.1-244.
Provision violations.
Penalties, §62.1-252.
State agency review, §62.1-250.
Study proceedings, §62.1-246.
Use of water in area, §62.1-247.
Water-use classifications, §62.1-249.
Withdrawal permits, §62.1-248.
Cancellation, §62.1-251.
State agency review, §62.1-250.
Suspension, §62.1-251.
Technical advice to be made available, §62.1-44.39.
Waste, industrial.
Discharge prohibitions, §62.1-44.18:2.
Regulation, §62.1-44.16.
Waste, non-industrial non-sewage.
Discharge prohibitions, §62.1-44.18:2.
Regulations, §62.1-44.17.
Waste treatment works, limitations on powers, §62.1-44.15:1.
Watercraft discharges, §62.1-44.33.
Oil.
Contingency plans, §62.1-44.34:15.
Financial responsibility, §62.1-44.34:16.
Water facilities revolving fund.
Grants to local governments, §62.1-230.
Preference, §62.1-230.1.
Loans to local governments.
Preference, §62.1-230.1.
Sale of loans, §62.1-231.1.
Water pollution.
Nonpoint source pollution.
Lead agency for nonpoint source pollution program, §62.1 44.15.
Water supply emergency ordinances.
Application of owner supply system serving locality for assistance from board, §15.2-924.
Water supply plan advisory committee, §62.1-44.38:2.
Water supply plans, §62.1-44.38:1.
Well construction.
Inter-agency cooperation, §32.1-176.7.

WATERCOURSES.
Eminent domain.
Highways and roads.
Taking road materials from streams, rivers, etc., §33.1-117.
Highways and roads.
Eminent domain.
Taking road materials from streams, rivers, etc., §33.1-117.
Fish ponds or water storage areas.
Use of streams and lowlands obstructed by newly constructed highways, §33.1-208.
Statutes declaring streams and rivers to be highways, §33.1-183.
Rights of improving navigation preserved, §62.1-7.

WATERCRAFT.
Ballast water discharge, §§28.2-109 to 28.2-111.
Boating safety generally, §§29.1-734 to 29.1-746.
Boats generally.
See BOATS AND OTHER WATERCRAFT.
Branch pilots, §§54.1-900 to 54.1-927.
Dealers generally, §§29.1-800 to 29.1-827.
See BOAT DEALERS.
Liability insurance.
Private pleasure watercraft.
Optional coverage, §38.2-2232.
Personal watercraft, §§29.1-748 to 29.1-750.
Registration and identification of boats, §§29.1-700 to 29.1-711.
Sales and use tax, §§58.1-1400 to 58.1-1410.
See WATERCRAFT SALES AND USE TAX.
Salesmen and demonstrators.
Licensing, §§29.1-808 to 29.1-825.
Titling certificates, §§29.1-712 to 29.1-733.1.
Uniform certificate of title for watercraft, §§29.1-733.2 to 29.1-733.29.

WATERCRAFT SALES AND USE TAX, §§58.1-1400 to 58.1-1410.
Amount of tax, determination, §58.1-1402.
Basis of tax, §58.1-1403.
Civil penalties and interest, §58.1-1408.
Credit against tax, §58.1-1409.
Dealer certificate of registration, §58.1-1406.
Definitions, §58.1-1401.
Disposition of funds, §58.1-1410.
Estimate of tax, §58.1-1403.
Exemption, §58.1-1404.
Game protection fund.
Transfer to fund of collections, §58.1-1410.
General fund, payment of funds collected into, §58.1-1410.
Imposition, §58.1-1402.
Misrepresentation, §58.1-1403.
Motor deemed watercraft.
Circumstances under which, §58.1-1401.1.
Payment, time for, §58.1-1405.
Rate against sale price, market value or gross receipts, §58.1-1402.
Records.
Retention of documents, §58.1-1407.
Registration certificate of dealer, §58.1-1406.
Retention of documents, §58.1-1407.
Time for payment, §58.1-1405.
Title of chapter, §58.1-1400.
Virginia watercraft sales and use tax act, §58.1-1400.

WATERCRAFT TRAILER DEALERS.
Defined, §46.2-1992.

WATERCRAFT TRAILER DEALERS —Cont'd
Trailer dealers generally, §§46.2-1992 to 46.2-1992.85.
See TRAILER DEALERS.

WATERCRAFT TRAILERS.
License plates, §46.2-1992.55.
Temporary license plates issued by dealers, §§46.2-1992.56 to 46.2-1992.65.

WATER DAMAGE INSURANCE.
Defined, §38.2-112.

WATER EMERGENCIES.
Ordinances restricting nonessential use of ground water, §§15.2-923, 15.2-924.

WATER FACILITIES REVOLVING FUND, §§62.1-224 to 62.1-232.
Audits, §62.1-227.
Brownfields restoration and land renewal.
Remediation of contaminated properties, §62.1-229.2.
Collection of money, §62.1-228.
Conflict of laws, §62.1-232.
Construction of provisions, §62.1-232.
Creation, §62.1-225.
Defined terms, §62.1-224.
Deposit of money, §62.1-226.
Grants to local governments, §§62.1-230, 62.1-230.1.
Loans to local governments, §§62.1-229, 62.1-230.1.
Sale of loans, §62.1-231.1.
Loans to secure bonds of authority, §62.1-231.
Management, §62.1-225.
Open-space land.
Loans for land conservation, §62.1-229.3.
Remediation of contaminated properties.
Loans for, §62.1-229.2.
Stormwater runoff control best management practices, loans for, §62.1-229.4.

WATER FIXTURES.
Secondhand fixtures.
Company equipment, §§59.1-125 to 59.1-130.
Fixtures, buying or receiving with intent to defraud, §18.2-237.
Sales, §§59.1-116.1 to 59.1-124.

WATERFOWL.
Birds generally.
See BIRDS.
Blinds.
Application of provisions, §29.1-350.
Floating blinds, §29.1-342.
Distance from stationary blinds, §29.1-346.
Issuance time, §29.1-346.
License plates, §29.1-346.
Hunting from unlicensed blinds, §29.1-340.
Licenses.
Applications, §29.1-348.
Fees, §29.1-343.
Renewal, §29.1-347.
Provision violations.
Penalty, §29.1-351.1.
Regulations, §29.1-351.
Riparian rights, §29.1-344.
Forfeiture, §29.1-345.
Stationary blinds, §29.1-344.1.
Time for obtaining, §29.1-344.2.
Stationary blinds, §§29.1-341, 29.1-341.1.
Distance requirements, §29.1-349.
Floating blind to keep distance, §29.1-346.

WATERFOWL —Cont'd
Blinds —Cont'd
Stationary blinds —Cont'd
Nonriparian owners, §29.1-345.
Time for obtaining license, §29.1-345.1.
Defined terms.
Public waters, §29.1-340.
Feeding.
Localities may prohibit feeding, §29.1-527.1.
Hunting.
Application of provisions, §29.1-350.
Blaze orange clothing requirement, §29.1-530.1.
Computer-assisted remote hunting, §29.1-530.3.
Distance requirements, §29.1-349.
Provision violations.
Penalty, §29.1-351.1.
Unlicensed blinds, hunting from, §29.1-340.
Virginia migratory waterfowl conservation stamp, §29.1-339.2.

WATERFRONT PROPERTY.
Franchise, privilege, lease or right to use city or town property, §§15.2-2100 to 15.2-2108.1:1.
Sale of city or town property, §15.2-2100, VA Const Art VII §9.

WATER ICES.
Generally, §§3.2-5212 to 3.2-5217.
See MILK AND MILK PRODUCTS.

WATER INUNDATED PROPERTY.
Property exempt from taxation, §58.1-3620.
Perpetual easements permitting, VA Const Art X §6.

WATER MANAGEMENT, GROUND, §§62.1-254 to 62.1-270.
See GROUNDWATER MANAGEMENT.

WATER PIPES.
Drug paraphernalia, §§18.2-265.1 to 18.2-265.5.
Secondhand pipes.
Buying or receiving with intent to defraud, §18.2-237.

WATER POLLUTION.
Agricultural landowners.
Resource management plans, §§10.1-104.7 to 10.1-104.9.
Casting solid waste into waters, §§62.1-194 to 62.1-194.3.
Certified pollution control equipment and facilities.
Property exempt from taxation, §58.1-3660.
Chesapeake Bay watershed nutrient credit exchange program, §§62.1-44.19:12 to 62.1-44.19:23.
Citizen water quality monitoring program, §62.1-44.19:11.
City or town powers, §15.2-1110.
Clams.
Dredging clams in polluted areas for replanting, §28.2-650.
Cleaning agents, §§62.1-193.1 to 62.1-193.3.
Clean water farm award program, §10.1-104.3.
Confined animal feeding operations, §62.1-44.17:1.
Chesapeake Bay watershed nutrient credit exchange program, §62.1-44.19:21.
Conservation police officers.
Samples, §§29.1-213, 29.1-214.
Counties general powers, §15.2-1200.

WATER POLLUTION —Cont'd
Database of critical data attributes.
Nutrients and sediments entering state waters.
Onsite best management practices implemented by state to limit, §2.2-220.3.
Fishing, tidal waters.
Condemnation.
Periods, §28.2-808.
Procedure, §28.2-807.
Emergency closings, §28.2-809.
Notice, §28.2-804.
Cessation of activities, §28.2-805.
Removal of shellfish from, §28.2-810.
Identification, §28.2-817.
Loading and unloading restrictions, §28.2-819.
Permits, §§28.2-811, 28.2-815.
Provision violations, §§28.2-821, 28.2-822.
Records, §28.2-813.
Reports, §28.2-814.
Sealing of motor vehicles, §28.2-812.
Seed-stock shellfish, §28.2-820.
Supervision, §28.2-816.
Standards, §28.2-806.
Ground water management, §§62.1-254 to 62.1-270.
Industrial discharges, §§62.1-44.16, 62.1-44.17.
Judicial review of final decisions of water control board, §62.1-44.29.
Lead agency for nonpoint source pollution program, §10.1-104.1.
Limitation of actions.
Criminal prosecutions for discharge of toxic substances, §19.2-8.
Nonpoint source pollution.
Lead agency for nonpoint source pollution program, §§10.1-104.1, 62.1-44.15.
Water quality assessment, §10.1-2127.
Nutrients and sediments entering state waters.
Onsite best management practices implement by state to limit.
Database of critical data attributes, §2.2-220.3.
Oil discharges, §§62.1-44.34:14 to 62.1-44.34:23.
See WATERS OF THE STATE.
Permit fees, §§62.1-44.15:7, 62.1-44.15:8.
Persons aggrieved by decisions of water control board.
Judicial review, §62.1-44.29.
Policy of state, VA Const Art XI §1.
Property exempt from taxation.
Equipment, facilities, etc., used for abating, VA Const Art X §6.
Rappahannock river basin commission, §§62.1-69.25 to 62.1-69.33:2.
Ready-mixed concrete plant discharges.
General permits for discharge of stormwater and process wastewater, §62.1-44.15:5.2.
Public hearings and permit procedures before the board, §62.1-44.15:02.
Resource management plans, §§10.1-104.7 to 10.1-104.9.
Secretary of natural resources.
Water quality information provided citizens of Commonwealth.
Lead secretary to ensure, §2.2-216.
Sewage discharges, §§62.1-44.18 to 62.1-44.19:3.4.
Distribution of sewage sludge without permit, §62.1-44.19:3.
Sewers, pumping stations, ventilation stations, etc.
Contracts between localities to operate to prevent pollution, §15.2-2124.

WATER POLLUTION —Cont'd
Shipping or transporting solid waste or medical waste upon navigable waters, §10.1-1454.1.
Silvicultural activities affecting water quality, §§10.1-1181.1 to 10.1-1181.7.
Conduct of activities, §10.1-1181.2.
Defined, §10.1-1181.1.
Enforcement of provisions.
Injunctions, §10.1-1181.6.
Final decisions, §10.1-1181.4.
Funds.
Virginia forest water quality fund, §10.1-1181.7.
Injunctions, §10.1-1181.6.
Judicial review, §10.1-1181.5.
Notice of commercial harvesting of timber, §10.1-1181.2.
Operator.
Defined, §10.1-1181.1.
Owner.
Defined, §10.1-1181.1.
Penalties, §10.1-1181.3.
Pollution.
Defined, §10.1-1181.1.
Silvicultural activity.
Defined, §10.1-1181.1.
Special orders.
Defined, §10.1-1181.1.
Issuance, §10.1-1181.2.
State forester.
Issuance of special orders, §10.1-1181.2.
Solid waste or medical waste.
Discharge into water, §§62.1-194 to 62.1-194.3.
Transported by ship, barge or other vessel upon navigable waters, §10.1-1454.1.
Spill response council, §§62.1-44.34:24 to 62.1-44.34:28.
State policy as to waters, §§62.1-10 to 62.1-13.
Statute of limitations.
Criminal prosecutions for discharge of toxic substance, §19.2-8.
Storage tank discharges, §§62.1-44.34:8, 62.1-44.34:9.
Petroleum storage tank fund, §§62.1-44.34:10 to 62.1-44.34:13.
Water quality improvement act, §§10.1-2117 to 10.1-2134.
Board.
Powers and duties, §10.1-2125.
Cooperative programs.
Establishment, §10.1-2118.
Nonpoint source pollution program, §§10.1-2123, 10.1-2124.
Point source pollution program, §§10.1-2120 to 10.1-2122.
Definitions, §10.1-2117.
Director.
Powers and duties, §10.1-2126.
Effect of provisions on other authority, §10.1-2119.
Natural resources commitment fund, §10.1-2128.1.
Nonpoint source pollution funding, §10.1-2132.
Nonpoint source pollution water quality assessment, §10.1-2127.
Nutrient offset fund, §10.1-2128.2.
Point source pollution funding, §10.1-2131.
Reports.
Directors of department of environmental quality and conservation and recreation, §10.1-2134.
State comptroller, §10.1-2133.

WATER POLLUTION —Cont'd
Water quality improvement act —Cont'd
Virginia natural resources commitment fund, §10.1-2128.1.
Water quality improvement fund, §§10.1-2128 to 10.1-2130.
Watershed coordination program, §10.1-2124.
Water quality information provided citizens of Commonwealth.
Secretary of natural resources.
Lead secretary to ensure, §2.2-216.
Waters of the state generally.
See WATERS OF THE STATE.

WATER POLLUTION CONTROL ACT.
State programs to implement, §§2.2-617, 2.2-618.

WATER-POWER DEVELOPMENT.
Generally, §§62.1-80 to 62.1-103.

WATER PURIFICATION COMPANIES.
Contracts by localities with, §15.2-2117.

WATER QUALITY AT RECREATIONAL FACILITIES.
Control board, §§62.1-44.15, 62.1-44.36.
Tests for, §32.1-248.1.

WATER RESOURCES AND WETLANDS PROTECTION PROGRAM, §§62.1-44.15:20 to 62.1-44.15:23.1.

WATER RIGHTS.
Waters of the state.
Surface water rights.
Application for leave to store floodwaters, venue, §62.1-107.

WATERSHED IMPROVEMENT DISTRICTS, §§10.1-614 to 10.1-635.
Agents, §10.1-624.
Audits, §10.1-624.
Ballots.
Referendum, §10.1-618.
Bond issues.
Governing body, §§10.1-629, 10.1-630.
Type of bonds issued, §10.1-630.
Bonds, surety, §10.1-624.
Debts, §10.1-633.
Eminent domain, §10.1-635.
Employees, §10.1-624.
Establishment, §10.1-614.
Petitions, §10.1-615.
Situated in more than one soil and water conservation district, §10.1-621.
Feasibility of proposed district, §10.1-617.
Fiscal powers of governing body, §10.1-628.
Incur debts and accept gifts, §10.1-633.
Type of indebtedness incurred or bonds issued, §10.1-630.
Nature of powers granted, §10.1-632.
Gifts, §10.1-633.
Governing body, §10.1-623.
Fiscal powers, §10.1-628.
Order to incur indebtedness or issue bonds, §10.1-629.
Type of indebtedness incurred or bonds issued, §10.1-630.
Powers granted.
Nature of powers, §§10.1-632, 10.1-633.
Power to incur debts and accept gifts, §10.1-633.
Hearings.
Petitions, §10.1-616.
Inclusion of additional territory, §10.1-622.

WATERSHED IMPROVEMENT DISTRICTS —Cont'd
Officers, agents and employees, §10.1-624.
Organization of district.
Declaration of organization, §10.1-620.
Petitions.
Establishment, §10.1-615.
Notice and hearings, §10.1-616.
Questions submitted to qualified voters.
Referendum, §10.1-634.
Referendum.
Ballots, §10.1-618.
Consideration of results, §10.1-619.
Creation of district, §10.1-617.
Procedure, §10.1-634.1.
Questions submitted to qualified voters, §10.1-634.
Service charges, §10.1-626.
Collection, §10.1-627.
Taxation.
Annual taxes, §10.1-631.
Collection of tax or service charge, §10.1-627.
Levy of tax or service charge, §10.1-626.
Status and general powers of district, §10.1-625.

WATERSHED PLANNING AND PERMITTING COORDINATION TASK FORCE, §§10.1-1193 to 10.1-1197.

WATERSHED PROTECTION.
Advisory panels.
Coordination task force, §10.1-1195.
Coordination task force, §10.1-1194.
Advisory panels, §10.1-1195.
Cooperation of state agencies, §10.1-1197.
Guiding principles, §10.1-1196.
Guiding principles, §10.1-1196.
Permitting, §10.1-1193.
Planning, §10.1-1193.
Police powers over lands lying beyond localities boundaries, §15.2-1725.
Reports.
Environmental quality department, §10.1-1193.
Stormwater management, §§62.1-44.15:24 to 62.1-44.15:50.
See STORMWATER MANAGEMENT.
Water quality improvement act.
Watershed coordination program, §10.1-2124.
Watershed planning.
Defined, §10.1-1196.

WATER SHORTAGES.
Ordinances restricting nonessential use of ground water, §§15.2-923, 15.2-924.

WATER SKIING.
Manipulating water skis while intoxicated, §§29.1-738 to 29.1-738.6.
Placement of markers designating public area.
Water skiing prohibited, §29.1-734.
Restrictions, §29.1-742.

WATERS OF THE STATE.
Altering water properties to make them detrimental, §62.1-44.5.
Bathing grounds.
Assignments, §28.2-633.
Beach assignments, §28.2-633.
Beach conservation and development, §§10.1-705 to 10.1-711.
See BEACH CONSERVATION AND DEVELOPMENT.
Beacons.
Offenses relating to.
Punishment of, §62.1-187.

WATERS OF THE STATE —Cont'd
Big Sandy river.
Tributaries, obstructing or dumping solid waste into, §62.1-194.3.
Boating safety, §§29.1-734 to 29.1-746.
Boat races.
Watercraft, personal.
Application of provisions, §29.1-750.
Boundaries.
Lawful fences constituted by streams or canals, §§55-299 to 55-303.
Branch pilots.
Licensing generally, §§54.1-900 to 54.1-927.
See BRANCH PILOTS.
Buffers.
Forest buffers.
Riparian forest buffer protection for waterways tax credit, §58.1-339.10.
Bulkheads, §§62.1-164, 62.1-165.
Buoys.
Offenses relating to.
Punishment of, §62.1-187.
Burials at sea.
Prerequisites to allowing, §32.1-284.
Canals generally.
See CANALS.
Casting solid waste into waters, §62.1-194.2.
Certificates for discharge, §62.1-44.15.
Private rights not affected, §62.1-44.22.
Violations, §§62.1-44.31, 62.1-44.32.
Chesapeake Bay.
Drilling for oil or gas, §62.1-195.1.
Chesapeake Bay and Virginia waters clean-up and oversight act, §§62.1-44.117, 62.1-44.118.
Chesapeake Bay preservation, §§62.1-44.15:67 to 62.1-44.15:79.
Chesapeake Bay watershed nutrient credit exchange program, §§62.1-44.19:12 to 62.1-44.19:20.
Citation of chapter, §62.1-44.2.
Clams generally, §§28.2-500 to 28.2-562.
See OYSTERS AND CLAMS.
Cleaning agents.
Enforcement of provisions, §62.1-193.3.
Prohibitions, §62.1-193.1.
Exceptions, §62.1-193.2.
Provision violations.
Penalty, §62.1-193.3.
Clearing watercourses between counties of obstructions, §62.1-6.
Closing upon finding of toxic substances, §32.1-248.
Coastal primary sand dunes and beaches, §§28.2-1400 to 28.2-1420.
See COASTAL PRIMARY SAND DUNES AND BEACHES.
Combined sewer overflow matching fund, §§62.1-241.11, 62.1-241.12.
Confined animal feeding operations, §62.1-44.17:1.
Chesapeake Bay watershed nutrient credit exchange program, §62.1-44.19:21.
Conflict of laws, §62.1-44.6.
Rights of localities not affected, §62.1-13.
Conservation police officers.
Daylight hours patrol of lakes from Memorial Day through Labor Day, §29.1-739.2.
Contaminating, §62.1-194.1.
Control board, §§62.1-44.7 to 62.1-44.15:5.2.
See WATER CONTROL BOARD.

WATERS OF THE STATE —Cont'd
Court powers to erect obstructions limited, §§62.1-8, 62.1-9.
Crabs, §§28.2-700 to 28.2-713.
See CRABS.
Crimes.
Big Sandy river tributaries.
Obstructing or dumping solid waste into, §62.1-194.3.
Casting solid waste into waters, §§62.1-194, 62.1-194.2.
Chesapeake Bay.
Drilling for oil or gas, §62.1-195.1.
Contaminating state waters, §62.1-194.1.
Notification of local governments and property owners, §62.1-44.15:4.
Obstructing state waters, §§62.1-194.1, 62.1-194.2.
Pollution control offenses, §§62.1-44.31, 62.1-44.32.
Crossings by public service companies.
Limitations on crossing rights if altering, closing or obstructing stream involved, §56-32.
Dams generally.
See DAMS.
Day marks.
Offenses relating to.
Punishment of, §62.1-187.
Deer.
Killing a deer in, §29.1-516.
Definitions.
Beneficial use, §62.1-10.
Ceases operation, §62.1-44.15:1.1.
Discharge of oil, §62.1-44.34:14.
Locality particularly affected, §62.1-44.15:01.
Owner, §62.1-44.31.
Petroleum storage tank fund, §62.1-44.34:10.
State water control law, §62.1-44.3.
Storage tanks, §62.1-44.34:8.
Stormwater management, §62.1-44.15:24.
Water, §62.1-10.
District court judges.
Jurisdiction over, §16.1-69.29.
Docks, §§62.1-164, 62.1-165.
Domestic use without certification or permit, §62.1-44.5.
Dredging sand and gravel.
Beach replenishment projects.
Expedited review of proposal and permit process, §28.2-1205.2.
Damages, §62.1-192.
Injunctions, §62.1-192.
Prohibited, §62.1-190.
Exemptions, §62.1-193.
Penalties for violation, §62.1-191.
Drift property, §§55-202 to 55-210.
Environmental laboratory certification program.
Division of consolidated laboratory services to establish, §2.2-1105.
Exhibitions.
Personal watercraft.
Application of provisions, §29.1-750.
Federal development projects, §§62.1-148 to 62.1-152.
Acquisition of lands, §62.1-150.
Liberal construction, §62.1-152.
Local cooperation, §62.1-148.
Flood control measures, §62.1-148.1.
Items of cooperation, §62.1-149.
Ratification of former resolutions and ordinances, §62.1-151.

WATERS OF THE STATE —Cont'd
Fences.
Lawful fences constituted by streams or canals, §§55-299 to 55-303.
Fish consumption advisories, §32.1-248.01.
Fish hatcheries.
Water integrity violations, §29.1-554.
Fishing, tidal waters, §§28.2-200 to 28.2-907.
See FISHING, TIDAL WATERS.
Foreign trade zones on ports, §§62.1-159 to 62.1-162.
See PORTS.
Forest buffers.
Riparian forest buffer protection for waterways tax credit, §58.1-339.10.
Groundwater management, §§62.1-254 to 62.1-270.
See GROUNDWATER MANAGEMENT.
Highway corporations.
Roadway operator powers, §56-543.
Hydroelectric power, §§62.1-80 to 62.1-103.
See HYDROELECTRIC POWER.
Impoundment of surface waters, §§62.1-104 to 62.1-115.
See IMPOUNDMENT OF SURFACE WATERS.
Industrial consumption without certification or permit, §62.1-44.5.
Industrial establishment regulation.
Discharge prohibitions, §62.1-44.5.
Landings, §§62.1-164, 62.1-165.
Mail notice.
Initial notice by certified mail, subsequent notices by regular mail, §62.1-44.3:1.
Marine parades.
Personal watercraft.
Application of provisions, §29.1-750.
Mills generally.
See MILLS.
Motorboat races.
Watercraft, personal.
Application of provisions, §29.1-750.
Navigability of streams, improvement, §§62.1-155 to 62.1-158.
See STREAMS.
Navigation aids.
Protection of, §§62.1-187 to 62.1-189.
No-discharge zones, §62.1-44.33.
Obstructing, §§62.1-194.1, 62.1-194.2.
Offshore waters.
Jurisdiction and ownership of Commonwealth over, §1-302.
Ohio river basin commission, §§62.1-79.1, 62.1-79.2.
Ohio river valley water sanitation commission, §§62.1-70 to 62.1-79.
See OHIO RIVER VALLEY WATER SANITATION COMMISSION.
Oil discharges, §§62.1-44.34:14 to 62.1-44.34:23.
Aboveground storage tanks.
Registration, §62.1-44.34:19.1.
Regulations for, §62.1-44.34:15.1.
Exemptions from, §62.1-44.34:17.
Access to records and facilities, §62.1-44.34:19.2.
Applicability of administrative process act, §62.1-44.34:22.
Contingency plans, §62.1-44.34:15.
Defined terms, §62.1-44.34:14.
Discharge prohibitions and liability, §62.1-44.34:18.
Discharge reporting, §62.1-44.34:19.
Enforcement of provisions, §62.1-44.34:20.

WATERS OF THE STATE —Cont'd
Oil discharges —Cont'd
Exception from provisions, §62.1-44.34:23.
Fees, §62.1-44.34:21.
Financial responsibility for vessels and facilities, §62.1-44.34:16.
Exemptions, §62.1-44.34:17.
Ohio river valley water sanitation commission.
Jurisdiction, §62.1-74.
Provision violations.
Penalties, §62.1-44.34:20.
Records, §62.1-44.34:19.2.
Spill response council, §§62.1-44.34:24 to 62.1-44.34:28.
Storage tanks, §§62.1-44.34:8, 62.1-44.34:9.
Petroleum storage tank fund, §§62.1-44.34:10 to 62.1-44.34:13.
Oysters generally, §§28.2-500 to 28.2-562.
See OYSTERS AND CLAMS.
Permits.
Confined animal feeding operations, §62.1-44.17:1.
Chesapeake Bay watershed nutrient credit exchange program, §62.1-44.19:21.
Conformance with federal requirements, §62.1-44.15:8.
Discharge of sewage, industrial waste or other wastes.
Applications.
When application considered complete, §62.1-44.15:3.
Fees, §§62.1-44.15:7, 62.1-44.15:8.
Industrial waste discharges, §62.1-44.18:2.
Permit program fund, §62.1-44.15:7.
Public hearings and permit procedures before the board, §62.1-44.15:02.
Ready-mixed concrete plant discharges, general permits, §62.1-44.15:5.2.
Sewage discharges, §62.1-44.18:2.
Sewage disposal.
Privately-owned sewerage facilities, §62.1-44.18:3.
Violations, §§62.1-44.31, 62.1-44.32.
Virginia water protection permits, §62.1-44.15:20.
Coordinated review of water resources projects, §62.1-44.15:5.01.
Instream flow, preservation of, §62.1-44.15:22.
Potomac river.
Low-flow protections, §62.1-44.15:5.02.
Public hearings and permit procedures before the board, §62.1-44.15:02.
Water withdrawals, §62.1-44.15:22.
Wetland and stream mitigation banks, §62.1-44.15:23.
Wetlands, impacts to, §62.1-44.15:21.
Waste, non-industrial non-sewage, §62.1-44.18:2.
Personal watercraft.
Operation restrictions, §§29.1-748, 29.1-750.
Petroleum storage tank fund.
Defined terms, §62.1-44.34:10.
Established, §62.1-44.34:11.
Financial responsibility, §62.1-44.34:12.
Levy of fee for maintenance, §62.1-44.34:13.
Phosphorus use in cleaning agents, §§62.1-193.1 to 62.1-193.3.
Piers, §§62.1-164, 62.1-165.
Planning responsibility for the development, conservation and utilization of state water resources, §§62.1-44.36, 62.1-44.38.
Comprehensive water supply planning process, §62.1-44.38:1.

WATERS OF THE STATE —Cont'd
Planning responsibility for the development, conservation and utilization of state water resources —Cont'd
State water supply plan advisory committee, §62.1-44.38:2.
Water supply plans, §62.1-44.38:1.
Policy of state, §§62.1-10 to 62.1-13.
Construction of provisions, §§62.1-12, 62.1-13.
Defined terms, §62.1-10.
Flow restrictions, §62.1-11.
Right to use, limitations upon, §62.1-11.
State regulation and conservation, §62.1-11.
Waters declared natural resource, §62.1-11.
Pollution control enforcement.
Hearings, §62.1-44.26.
Board decisions, §62.1-44.28.
Judicial review, §62.1-44.29.
Right to, §62.1-44.25.
Rules of evidence, §62.1-44.27.
Information to be furnished to board, §62.1-44.21.
Intervention of Commonwealth, §62.1-44.23:1.
Private rights, §62.1-44.22.
Regulation validity, §62.1-44.24.
Remedies, §62.1-44.23.
Right of entry, §62.1-44.20.
Pollution control offenses, §§62.1-44.31, 62.1-44.32.
Port authority, §§62.1-128 to 62.1-147.2.
See PORT AUTHORITY.
Potomac river basin commission, §§62.1-64 to 62.1-69.
See POTOMAC RIVER BASIN COMMISSION.
Poultry waste management program, §62.1-44.17:1.1.
Protection of watersheds.
See WATERSHED PROTECTION.
Provisions supplementary to existing laws, §62.1-44.6.
Purpose of provisions, §62.1-44.2.
Quality control by Commonwealth, §62.1-44.4.
Quality monitoring, information and restoration, §§62.1-44.19:4 to 62.1-44.19:10.
Assessment of sources of toxic contamination, §62.1-44.19:10.
Citizen right-to-know provisions, §62.1-44.19:6.
Control of discharges to toxic-impaired water, §62.1-44.19:8.
Definitions, §62.1-44.19:4.
Discharge control, §62.1-44.19:8.
Fish advisory information, transmission, §62.1-44.19:9.
Hot-line.
Citizen right-to-know provisions, §62.1-44.19:6.
Impaired waters, §§62.1-44.19:7, 62.1-44.19:8.
Defined, §62.1-44.19:4.
Monitoring generally, §62.1-44.19:5.
Plans to address impaired waters, §62.1-44.19:7.
Reports, §62.1-44.19:5.
Toxics information, transmission, §62.1-44.19:9.
Transmission of toxics information, §62.1-44.19:9.
Railroad crossings, §56-362.
Rappahannock river basin commission, §§62.1-69.25 to 62.1-69.33:2.
Recreational use without certification or permit, §62.1-44.5.
Regattas.
Watercraft, personal.
Application of provisions, §29.1-750.
Resolution of use conflicts, §62.1-44.37.

WATERS OF THE STATE —Cont'd
Resources authority, §§62.1-197 to 62.1-223.
See RESOURCES AUTHORITY.
Rights of improving navigation preserved.
Construction, §62.1-9.
Riparian rights, existing.
Construction of provisions, §62.1-44.44.
Sewage discharges, §§62.1-44.18 to 62.1-44.19:3.4.
Approval of systems and works, §62.1-44.19.
Hearings, §§62.1-44.25 to 62.1-44.30.
Certificate or permit required, §62.1-44.5.
Certification, §62.1-44.15.
Joint supervision, §62.1-44.18.
Notice, §62.1-44.5.
Ohio river valley water sanitation commission.
Jurisdiction, §62.1-74.
Permits.
Applications.
When application considered complete, §62.1-44.15:3.
Public hearings and permit procedures before the board, §62.1-44.15:02.
Privately-owned sewerage facilities, §62.1-44.18:3.
Prohibitions, §62.1-44.18:2.
Violations, §§62.1-44.31, 62.1-44.32.
Shore erosion control, §§10.1-700 to 10.1-704.
See SHORE EROSION CONTROL.
Solid waste discharge into waters, §62.1-194.2.
Solid waste or recycling revolving fund, §§62.1-241.1 to 62.1-241.10.
See SOLID WASTE OR RECYCLING REVOLVING FUND.
Spill response council, §§62.1-44.34:24 to 62.1-44.34:28.
See SPILL RESPONSE COUNCIL.
Standards of quality, §62.1-44.4.
Storage tanks.
Board powers and duties, §62.1-44.34:9.
Definitions, §62.1-44.34:8.
Petroleum storage tank fund, §§62.1-44.34:10 to 62.1-44.34:13.
Stormwater management, §§62.1-44.15:24 to 62.1-44.15:50.
See STORMWATER MANAGEMENT.
Streams, improvement of navigability, §§62.1-155 to 62.1-158.
See STREAMS.
Submerged lands, §§28.2-1200 to 28.2-1213.
Surface water impoundment, §§62.1-104 to 62.1-115.
See IMPOUNDMENT OF SURFACE WATERS.
Surface water management areas, §§62.1-242 to 62.1-253.
See SURFACE WATER MANAGEMENT AREAS.
Timber.
Persons engaged in lumbering or rafting on certain waters.
Adoption of mark of designation, §59.1-103.
Sale of unclaimed timber found adrift, §59.1-106.
Timber brands.
Adoption by persons engaged in lumbering or rafting on certain waters, §59.1-103.
Toll bridges.
Bridge not to obstruct navigation or fish, §33.1-256.
Permission required to erect or maintain toll bridges over navigable water, §33.1-261.
Tournaments.
Personal watercraft.
Application of provisions, §29.1-750.

WATERS OF THE STATE —Cont'd
Toxics discharge reduction.
Definitions, §62.1-44.17:2.
Quality monitoring, information and restoration generally, §§62.1-44.19:4 to 62.1-44.19:10.
Reports, §62.1-44.17:3.
Toxic substances.
Closing of waters upon finding, §32.1-248.
Fish consumption advisories, §32.1-248.01.
Prohibition of waste discharges, §62.1-44.5.
Underwater historic property, §10.1-2214.
Ungranted shores of the sea, marshes and meadowlands, §§28.2-1500 to 28.2-1514.
See UNGRANTED SHORES OF THE SEA.
Valid uses not affected, §62.1-12.
Virginia water resources and wetlands protection program, §§62.1-44.15:20 to 62.1-44.15:23.1.
Waste, industrial.
Discharge prohibitions, §62.1-44.18:2.
Notice of unauthorized discharge, §62.1-44.5.
Hearings, §§62.1-44.25 to 62.1-44.30.
Regulations, §62.1-44.16.
Violations, §§62.1-44.31, 62.1-44.32.
Waste, non-industrial and non-sewage.
Discharge prohibitions, §62.1-44.18:2.
Hearings, §§62.1-44.25 to 62.1-44.30.
Regulations, §62.1-44.17.
Violations, §§62.1-44.31, 62.1-44.32.
Watercraft discharges, §62.1-44.33.
Oil discharges generally, §§62.1-44.34:14 to 62.1-44.34:23.
See OIL DISCHARGES INTO WATERS OF STATE.
Watercraft, personal.
Operation restrictions, §29.1-748.
Water facilities revolving fund, §§62.1-224 to 62.1-232.
See WATER FACILITIES REVOLVING FUND.
Waterfowl blinds.
Application of provisions, §29.1-350.
Blaze orange clothing requirement, §29.1-530.1.
Floating blinds, §§29.1-342, 29.1-346.
Hunting waterfowl from unlicensed blinds, §29.1-340.
Nonriparian owners, §29.1-345.
Time for obtaining license, §29.1-345.1.
Provision violations, §29.1-351.1.
Riparian rights, §§29.1-344 to 29.1-345.1.
Stationary blinds, §§29.1-341, 29.1-341.1, 29.1-349.
Water quality improvement act, §§10.1-2117 to 10.1-2134.
See WATER POLLUTION.
Water quality information provided citizens of Commonwealth.
Secretary of natural resources, §2.2-216.
Water supply plans, §62.1-44.38:1.
Advisory committee, §62.1-44.38:2.
Water supply revolving fund, §§62.1-233 to 62.1-241.
See WATER SUPPLY REVOLVING FUND.
Wetland and stream replacement fund, §62.1-44.15:23.1.
Wetlands, §§28.2-1300 to 28.2-1320.
See WETLANDS.
Wharves, §§62.1-164, 62.1-165.
Works on watercourses generally, §§62.1-116 to 62.1-127.
See WORKS ON WATERCOURSES.

WATER SUPPLY, §§32.1-167 to 32.1-176.
Analyses of samples by division of consolidated laboratory services.
No fee for required analyses, §2.2-1104.
Chronically noncompliant waterworks.
Identification and elimination, §32.1-174.4.
Citizen water quality monitoring program, §62.1-44.19:11.
Defined terms, §32.1-167.
Diverting or wasting, §18.2-162.1.
Electric utility duties, §32.1-174.2.
Emergency orders, §32.1-175.
Emergency ordinances, §15.2-924.
Exemption from provisions, §32.1-168.
Federal safe drinking water act.
Matching fund, §32.1-171.2.
Gathering places.
Regulations, §32.1-200.
Gray water.
Guidelines regarding reuse of, §32.1-248.2.
Operational fee, §32.1-171.1.
Permits, §32.1-172.
Additional or amended permits, §32.1-173.
Revocation, §32.1-174.
Poisoning, §18.2-54.1.
Police powers over lands lying beyond localities boundaries, §15.2-1725.
Private waterworks.
Receivers for.
Appointment, grounds, petition, §32.1-174.3.
Property taxation of water system owned by political subdivision.
Partial taxation by one political subdivision of utility property owned by another, §58.1-3663.
Rainwater.
Guidelines regarding use of, §32.1-248.2.
Rates.
Increased finance required changes, §32.1-173.1.
Receivers for private waterworks.
Appointment, grounds, petition, §32.1-174.3.
Regulations, §32.1-170.
Retail sales and use tax.
Machinery, tools and equipment brought into state for use in constructing water systems, §§58.1-604.1 to 58.1-604.3.
Sale of city or town facilities, VA Const Art VII §9.
Supervision, §32.1-169.
Surety bond requirements of permit holders, §32.1-174.1.
Technical assistance as to sources and purity, §32.1-171.
Violation of provisions.
Notice to local governments, §32.1-175.1.
Penalties, §32.1-176.
Water quality information provided citizens of Commonwealth.
Secretary of natural resources, §2.2-216.
Watershed protection.
See WATERSHED PROTECTION.

WATER SUPPLY ASSISTANCE GRANT FUND, §32.1-171.2.

WATER SUPPLY COMPANIES, §§56-261 to 56-265.
Alley use without consent or compensation, §56-14.
Certificates of public convenience and necessity, §§56-265.1 to 56-265.9.
Charges, §56-264.1.
Damage or trespass to, §18.2-162.

WATER SUPPLY COMPANIES —Cont'd
Designation as public utility and service corporation or company, §56-1.2.
Diverting service, §§8.01-44.7, 18.2-163.
Duties, §§56-261, 56-261.1.
Failure to perform, §56-262.
Commission investigations, §56-263.
Quo warranto, §56-264.
Fire protection, §56-261.2.
Hydrants, §56-261.2.
Metering devices, tampering with, §§8.01-44.7, 18.2-163.
Political subdivision owning water system.
Property taxation by one political subdivision of utility property owned by another.
Partial taxation, §58.1-3663.
Powers of commission not limited, §56-265.
Property taxation.
Partial taxation by one political subdivision of utility property owned by another, §58.1-3663.
Public ground use without consent or compensation, §56-14.
Public service companies.
Generally, §§56-1 to 56-46.3.
See PUBLIC SERVICE COMPANIES.
Public utilities.
Generally, §§56-232 to 56-265.
See PUBLIC UTILITIES.
Small water utilities, §§56-265.13:1 to 56-265.13:7.
Street use without consent or compensation, §56-14.
Systems not regulated as public utilities, §§56-265.10 to 56-265.13.

WATER SUPPLY REVOLVING FUND, §§62.1-233 to 62.1-241.
Audits, §62.1-236.
Collection of money, §62.1-237.
Conflict of laws, §62.1-241.
Construction of provisions, §62.1-241.
Creation, §62.1-234.
Defined terms, §62.1-233.
Deposit of money, §62.1-235.
Grants to local governments, §62.1-237.
Preferences, §62.1-239.1.
Loans, §62.1-238.
Preferences, §62.1-239.1.
Management, §62.1-234.

WATER SUPPLY SYSTEMS, §§15.2-2134 to 15.2-2156.
Acquisition by eminent domain.
Local governments, §§15.2-1908 to 15.2-1916.
See EMINENT DOMAIN.
Acquisition from sanitary district, §15.2-2116.
Acquisition of waterworks systems, §15.2-2146.
Approval of system by counties, §§15.2-2149 to 15.2-2156.
Disapproval of system by governing body, §15.2-2151.
Enjoining violation, §15.2-2156.
Extension of service in excess of number of connections originally given, §15.2-2153.
Hotel corporations, inapplicability of provisions, §15.2-2154.
Noncompliance with provisions, §§15.2-2155, 15.2-2156.
Notice to county of intention to establish or extend existing system, §§15.2-2149 to 15.2-2152.

WATER SUPPLY SYSTEMS —Cont'd
Approval of system by counties —Cont'd
State board of health, when approval not required, §15.2-2150.
City acquiring plant within one mile of another city, §15.2-2147.
Connections.
Fire suppression systems, §15.2-2113.
Mandatory connection in certain counties, §15.2-2110.
Contracting with another locality for acquisition of water supply, §15.2-2148.
Contracts by localities with water purification company, §15.2-2117.
Cooperative associations.
Organization of, §13.1-301.
Dams.
Construction for purposes of providing public water supply, §15.2-2134.
Construction across navigable stream, §15.2-2142.
Disputes between jurisdictions.
Special courts, §§15.2-2135 to 15.2-2141.
Eminent domain.
Existing systems, §15.2-1906.
Powers of localities to acquire water work system, §15.2-2146.
Water supplies and water lines, §15.2-1907.
Exclusive service areas.
Joint agreements by political subdivisions, §15.2-2112.
Fire suppression system connections.
Locality requiring by ordinance, §15.2-2113.
Impoundment of water.
Disputes between jurisdictions.
Special court proceedings, §§15.2-2135 to 15.2-2141.
Inspection of public and private water supply, §15.2-2144.
Joint agreements by political subdivisions, §15.2-2112.
Lien for charges.
Certain counties, §15.2-2118.
Enforcement, §15.2-2120.
Mandatory connection in certain counties, §15.2-2110.
Poisoning, §18.2-54.1.
Power of locality to provide and operate, §15.2-2143.
Regulation of water service by locality generally, §15.2-2111.
Service districts, §§15.2-2400 to 15.2-2403.3.
Use of streets by one city in another to sell water, §15.2-2145.

WATER SYSTEMS NOT REGULATED AS PUBLIC UTILITIES, §§56-265.10 to 56-265.13.
Application of chapter, §56-265.13.
Customer complaints, §56-265.11.
Defined terms, §56-265.10.
Opinion of commission, §56-265.12.
Public ground use without consent or compensation, §56-14.

WATER TRANSPORTATION.
Transportation districts.
Generally, §§15.2-4500 to 15.2-4534.
See TRANSPORTATION DISTRICTS.

WATER WELLS.
Abandoned wells, duty of person causing to fill, §18.2-316.

WATER WELLS —Cont'd
Abandonment, closing and capping.
Duty of property owner, ordinance adopted by certain localities, §32.1-176.5.
Attempts to poison, §18.2-54.1.
Construction, §§32.1-176.1 to 32.1-176.7.
See WELL CONSTRUCTION.
Covers, §18.2-317.
Authority of counties, cities and towns to require and regulate, §18.2-318.
Drillers, §54.1-1103.
Gas and oil exploration.
Developing a gas or oil well as a water well, §45.1-361.39.
Gas wells.
Operator's right to sample water and quality, §45.1-361.43.
Replacement of water supply by operator, §45.1-361.44.
Mechanics' and materialmen's liens.
Structures permanently annexed to freehold.
Classification, §43-2.
Uranium ore exploration.
Developing exploration hole as water well, §45.1-278.
Water well systems providers.
Certification, §§54.1-1128 to 54.1-1130.
Well construction, §§32.1-176.1 to 32.1-176.7.
See WELL CONSTRUCTION.

WATER WELL SYSTEMS PROVIDERS.
Certification, §§54.1-1128 to 54.1-1130.
Application, examination, issuance, §54.1-1130.
Continuing education, §54.1-1129.1.
Definitions, §54.1-1128.
Levels, §54.1-1129.1.
Renewal and reinstatement, §54.1-1129.1.
Required, §54.1-1129.

WATERWORKS OPERATORS, §§54.1-2300 to 54.1-2302.
Board for waterworks and wastewater works operators and onsite sewage system professionals, §54.1-2301.
Defined terms, §54.1-2300.
License requirements, §54.1-2302.
Unlawful procurement of licensure, §54.1-102.
Unlawful use of licensure, §54.1-111.

WATERWORKS SYSTEMS.
Acquisition by eminent domain.
Local governments, §§15.2-1908 to 15.2-1916.
See EMINENT DOMAIN.
Poisoning, §18.2-54.1.
Water supply systems generally.
See WATER SUPPLY SYSTEMS.

WATERWORKS TECHNICAL ASSISTANCE FUND, §32.1-171.1.

WAX TECHNICIANS.
Barber and cosmetology licensure generally, §§54.1-700 to 54.1-706.
Waiver of examination, §54.1-703.1.

WAYNESBORO.
Blue Ridge regional tourism council, §§2.2-2609, 2.2-2610.
Circuit court, establishment, §17.1-500.
Flood control barriers.
Taxes or assessments for local improvements, §15.2-2404.
Public defenders office.
Established, §19.2-163.04.

WAYNESBORO —Cont'd
School board.
Fingerprinting applicants for employment, §22.1-296.2.
Salary of members, §22.1-32.
Shenandoah valley regional airport commission, 1988 ch 209.

WEAPONS, §§18.2-279 to 18.2-287.4, 18.2-308 to 18.2-311.1.
ABC offenses.
Violations by armed person, §4.1-318.
Confiscation proceedings, §4.1-338.
Acquittal by reason of insanity.
Possession or transportation of firearms by persons so acquitted, §18.2-308.1:1.
Aggravated malicious wounding, §18.2-51.2.
Airports.
Carrying weapon in air carrier airport terminal, §18.2-287.01.
Alcoholic beverages.
Carrying concealed handgun while under the influence, §18.2-308.12.
Aliens.
Permit to carry concealed weapon.
Disqualification for concealed weapons permit, §18.2-308.09.
Possession or transportation of assault weapons, §18.2-308.2:01.
Unlawful possession, transportation or carrying concealed.
Persons not lawfully in country, §18.2-308.2:01.
Appeals.
Carrying concealed weapons.
Appeal of denial of permit, §18.2-308.08.
Assault firearms, possession or transportation by aliens, §18.2-308.2:01.
Bail bondsmen.
Firearms training and usage, §9.1-185.11.
Bail enforcement agents.
Training and usage, §9.1-186.9.
Blackjacks, brass knucks, switchblades, etc.
Selling or having in possession, §18.2-311.
Body armor, wearing while committing violent crime in possession of firearm or knife, §18.2-287.2.
Bows and arrows.
Locality prohibiting shooting of arrow from bow and landing on the property of another, §15.2-916.
Capitol police.
Firearms or weapons in possession of division.
Destruction of unclaimed weapons, §30-34.2:2.
Carjacking, §18.2-58.1.
Carrying concealed weapons, §18.2-308.
Appeal of denial of permit, §18.2-308.08.
Application for permit, §18.2-308.02.
Processing, §18.2-308.04.
Supreme Court website, inclusion on application, §18.2-308.015.
Carrying concealed handgun with permit, §18.2-308.01.
Central criminal records exchange.
Entering information into system, §18.2-308.07.
Convicted felons, §18.2-308.2.
Criminal history record checks, §18.2-308.04.
Fees, §18.2-308.03.
Denial of permit, §18.2-308.08.
Fees, §18.2-308.03.
Forfeiture of firearms, §19.2-386.27.
Issuance of de facto permit, §18.2-308.05.

WEAPONS —Cont'd
Carrying concealed weapons —Cont'd
Issuance of permit, §18.2-308.04.
Nonresident concealed handgun permits, §18.2-308.06.
Persons not lawfully in country, §18.2-308.2:01.
Petition to court of appeals from final decision of circuit court as to permits, §17.1-406.
Probation and parole officers, §53.1-145.
Reciprocity, §18.2-308.014.
Renewal of permit, §18.2-308.010.
Replacement permits, §18.2-308.011.
Suspension or revocation of permit, §18.2-308.013.
Child-care services and facilities.
Possession or storage of firearms and ammunition at facilities.
Ordinances regulating, certain localities, §15.2-914.
Children or minors.
Access to loaded firearms, §18.2-56.2.
Child using firearm, §18.2-56.2.
Delinquent children.
Unlawful use or possession of handgun or streetsweeper.
Driving privilege loss, §16.1-278.9.
Furnishing weapons to minors, §18.2-309.
Loaded firearm recklessly left so as to endanger child's life, §18.2-56.2.
Possession or transportation of firearms, §18.2-308.7.
Handgun or streetsweeper possessed or used by delinquent child.
Loss of driving privileges, §16.1-278.9.
Churches or other places of worship.
Carrying dangerous weapons to, §18.2-283.
Concealed weapons, §§18.2-307.1 to 18.2-308.015.
Appeal of denial of permit, §18.2-308.08.
Application for permit, §18.2-308.02.
Processing, §18.2-308.04.
Supreme Court website, inclusion on application, §18.2-308.015.
Carrying concealed handgun with permit, §18.2-308.01.
Central criminal records exchange.
Entering information into system, §18.2-308.07.
Criminal history record checks, §18.2-308.04.
Fees, §18.2-308.03.
Definitions, §18.2-307.1.
Denial of permit, §18.2-308.08.
Fees, §18.2-308.03.
Issuance of de facto permit, §18.2-308.05.
Issuance of permit, §18.2-308.04.
Nonresident concealed handgun permits, §18.2-308.06.
Private security services businesses.
Armed security officers, §9.1-146.
Employee of electronic security business, authority to carry, §9.1-141.
Reciprocity, §18.2-308.014.
Renewal of permit, §18.2-308.010.
Replacement permits, §18.2-308.011.
Suspension or revocation of permit, §18.2-308.013.
Conservators of the peace.
Special conservators, carrying, §19.2-13.
Controlled substances.
Possessing firearm while possessing controlled substance, §18.2-308.4.
Convicted felons, possession or transportation, §18.2-308.2.
Petition to possess, transport, etc., §18.2-308.2.

WEAPONS —Cont'd
County regulation.
Hunting prohibited in certain areas, §15.2-1210.
Outdoor shooting of firearms and bows.
Authority to prohibit in certain areas, exemption, shooting deer, §15.2-1209.
Permits to sell or purchase pistols or revolvers.
Certain counties requiring, §15.2-1208.
Sellers of pistols and revolvers.
Reports of sales.
Power repealed, destruction of records, §15.2-1207.
Courthouses, carrying weapon into, §18.2-283.1.
Criminal history record information check.
Concealed weapons permits, §18.2-308.04.
Fees, §18.2-308.03.
Firearms transfers, §18.2-308.2:2.
Requesting under false pretenses or disseminating, §18.2-308.2:2.
Dealers in firearms.
Licensing, §§54.1-4200 to 54.1-4202.
Delinquency disposition disclosure.
Unlawful purchase, possession or use of weapon, §16.1-305.1.
Delinquent children.
Unlawful use or possession of handgun or streetsweeper.
Driving privilege loss, §16.1-278.9.
Disability or handicap.
Hunting from stationary vehicle, §29.1-521.3.
Disarming a law-enforcement or correctional officer, §18.2-57.02.
Discharging firearm in public place, §18.2-280.
Disqualification for concealed weapons permit, §18.2-308.09.
Discharging firearm or missile within or at building or dwelling, §§18.2-279, 18.2-280.
Discretionary felony sentencing guidelines, §17.1-805.
Disposition of firearms surrendered to locality, §15.2-915.5.
Drug offenders.
Purchase or possession of firearm by persons convicted of certain misdemeanor drug offenses, §18.2-308.1:5.
Drugs.
Carrying concealed handgun while under the influence, §18.2-308.12.
Emergency services and disaster law.
Chapter not to interfere with right to keep and bear arms, §44-146.15.
Employee storing at workplace in locked private motor vehicle, §15.2-915.
Explosives generally, §§59.1-137 to 59.1-141.
See EXPLOSIVES.
Firearm dealers.
Licensing, §§54.1-4200 to 54.1-4202.
Firearms.
See FIREARMS.
Fireworks generally.
See FIREWORKS.
Forfeiture of firearms.
Carrying concealed weapons violations, §19.2-386.27.
Controlled substances or drug offenses.
Possession of firearms while in possession of controlled substance or committing drug offense, §18.2-308.4.
Semi-automatic firearms and shotguns.
Carrying loaded in public areas, §18.2-287.4.

WEAPONS —Cont'd
Forfeiture of firearms —Cont'd
Unlawful concealment, possession, transportation or carrying, §19.2-386.28.
Forfeiture of weapons used in commission of crime, §19.2-386.29.
Hunting.
Permissible weapons, §29.1-519.
Reckless handling of firearm, §18.2-56.1.
Restrictions, §§29.1-519, 29.1-521.
Under the influence of intoxicant or narcotic drug, §18.2-285.
Jails.
Regional jails.
Officers.
Authority to carry weapons, §53.1-109.01.
Juvenile detention and other care facilities.
Delivery to detainees, §18.2-474.1.
Larceny of firearm, §18.2-95.
Loaded firearm recklessly left as to endanger child's life, §18.2-56.2.
Machine guns, §§18.2-288 to 18.2-298.
Motor vehicles.
Employee storing firearm or ammunition at workplace in locked private motor vehicle, §15.2-915.
Shooting from, §§18.2-286, 18.2-286.1, 29.1-521.2.
Disqualification for concealed weapons permit, §18.2-308.09.
Muzzleloaders.
Hunting.
Licenses, §29.1-307.
Restrictions, §29.1-517.
Offenses, generally, §§18.2-279 to 18.2-287.4, 18.2-308 to 18.2-311.1.
Ordinances governing purchase, possession, etc., of firearms, ammunition or components, §15.2-915.
Ordinances governing transportation of loaded rifle or shotgun, §15.2-915.2.
Paramilitary activity prohibited, §18.2-433.2.
Parole officers.
Authority to carry, §53.1-145.
Permits.
Carrying concealed weapons.
Appeal of denial of permit, §18.2-308.08.
Application for permit, §18.2-308.02.
Processing, §18.2-308.04.
Supreme Court website, inclusion on application, §18.2-308.015.
Central criminal records exchange.
Entering information into system, §18.2-308.07.
Denial of permit, §18.2-308.08.
Fees, §18.2-308.03.
Issuance of de facto permit, §18.2-308.05.
Issuance of permit, §18.2-308.04.
Nonresident concealed handgun permits, §18.2-308.06.
Reciprocity, §18.2-308.014.
Renewal of permit, §18.2-308.010.
Replacement permits, §18.2-308.011.
Required, §18.2-308.
Suspension or revocation of permit, §18.2-308.013.
Sell or purchase pistols or revolvers.
Certain counties requiring, §15.2-1208.
Plastic firearms, manufacture, import, etc., §18.2-308.5.
Pointing, holding or brandishing firearm, air or gas operated weapon or object similar in appearance, §18.2-282.

WEAPONS —Cont'd
Prisoner crimes, §53.1-203.
Delivery to prisoners, §18.2-474.1.
Juvenile corrections facilities, §18.2-477.2.
Prison officers and employees.
Authority to carry, §53.1-29.
Private security services businesses.
Concealed weapons.
Armed security officers, §9.1-146.
Employee of electronic security business, authority to carry, §9.1-141.
Probation officers.
Authority to carry, §53.1-145.
Public areas, carrying loaded firearm in, §18.2-287.4.
Receipt of stolen firearms, §18.2-108.1.
Reckless handling of firearms, §18.2-56.1.
Loaded firearm left so as to endanger child's life, §18.2-56.2.
Recklessly leaving loaded firearm as to endanger child's life, §18.2-56.2.
Records of permits to sell, destruction of, §15.2-1208.
Restricted ammunition.
Use or attempted use in commission or attempted commission of crime, §18.2-308.3.
Right to bear arms, VA Const Art I §13, US Const Amd 2.
Riots.
Deadly or dangerous weapon carried at time of riot, §18.2-405.
Robbery, §18.2-58.
Sale, disposition of firearms surrendered to locality, §15.2-915.5.
Sawed-off shotguns and sawed-off rifles, §§18.2-299 to 18.2-307.
School or school property.
Arrest for carrying on school property, §16.1-246.
Discharging, §18.2-280.
Disqualification for concealed weapons permit, §18.2-308.09.
Pointing, holding or brandishing firearm, air or gas operated weapon or object similar in appearance, §18.2-282.
Possession on school property, §18.2-308.1.
Selling or furnishing firearms to persons prohibited from possessing or transporting, §18.2-308.2:1.
Semi-automatic firearms and shotguns.
Carrying loaded in public areas, §18.2-287.4.
Sentence of persons twice previously convicted of certain violent felonies, §19.2-297.1.
Serial number or identification on firearm.
Removing, altering, etc., §18.2-311.1.
Shooting from vehicles so as to endanger persons, §§18.2-286, 18.2-286.1, 29.1-521.2.
Disqualification for concealed weapons permit, §18.2-308.09.
Shooting, stabbing, etc.
Commission of or attempting felony, §18.2-53.
Intent to maim, kill, etc., §18.2-51.
Special conservators of the peace.
Carrying of weapons, §19.2-13.
Spring guns, setting, §18.2-281.
State police.
Unclaimed firearms or other weapons in possession of.
Disposal, §52-11.5.

WEAPONS —Cont'd
Streetsweepers or striker 12's, importation, sale, etc., §18.2-308.8.
Streetsweeper possession or use by delinquent child.
Loss of driving privileges, §16.1-278.9.
Surrender of firearms to locality.
Disposition by locality, §15.2-915.5.
Terrorism.
Possession, manufacture, distribution, etc.
Penalties, §18.2-46.6.
Three time loser law, §19.2-297.1.
Toy firearms.
Discharging blank or ball charges.
Selling or giving, §18.2-284.
Transportation of loaded rifle or shotgun.
Ordinances regulating, §15.2-915.2.
Unclaimed firearms or other weapons in possession of sheriff or police.
Capitol police.
Destruction of unclaimed weapons, §30-34.2:2.
Disposal, §§15.2-1719, 15.2-1721.
Use or display of firearm in committing a felony, §18.2-53.1.
Forfeiture of weapon used in commission of crime, §19.2-386.29.
Warrantless arrests.
Carrying weapon on school property, §19.2-81.

WEAPONS COLLECTING ORGANIZATION.
Carrying concealed weapons, when provisions not applicable, §18.2-308.

WEAPONS OFFENSES, §§18.2-279 to 18.2-287.4, 18.2-308 to 18.2-311.1.
Acquittal by reason of insanity.
Possession or transportation of firearms by persons so acquitted, §18.2-308.1:1.
Aggravated malicious wounding, §18.2-51.2.
Airports.
Carrying weapon in air carrier airport terminal, §18.2-287.01.
Alcoholic beverages.
Carrying concealed handgun while under the influence, §18.2-308.12.
Aliens, possession or transportation of assault weapons, §18.2-308.2:01.
Assault firearms, possession or transportation by aliens, §18.2-308.2:01.
Blackjacks, brass knucks, switchblades, etc.
Selling or having in possession, §18.2-311.
Body armor, wearing while committing violent crime in possession of firearm or knife, §18.2-287.2.
Carjacking, §18.2-58.1.
Carrying concealed weapons, §18.2-308.
Convicted felons, §18.2-308.2.
Children or minors.
Access to loaded firearms, §18.2-56.2.
Furnishing weapons to minors, §18.2-309.
Possession or transportation of firearms, §18.2-308.7.
Handgun or streetsweeper possessed or used by delinquent child.
Loss of driving privileges, §16.1-278.9.
Churches or other places of worship.
Carrying dangerous weapons to, §18.2-283.
Concealed weapons and concealed handgun permits, §§18.2-307.1 to 18.2-308.015.
Controlled substances.
Possessing firearm while possessing controlled substance, §18.2-308.4.

WEAPONS OFFENSES —Cont'd
Convicted felons, possession or transportation, §18.2-308.2.
Courthouses, carrying weapon into, §18.2-283.1.
Criminal history background check, firearm transfers.
Requesting under false pretenses or disseminating, §18.2-308.2:2.
Disability or handicap.
Hunting from stationary vehicle, §29.1-521.3.
Discharging firearm in public place, §18.2-280.
Disqualification for concealed weapons permit, §18.2-308.09.
Discharging firearm or missile within or at building or dwelling, §§18.2-279, 18.2-280.
Discretionary felony sentencing guidelines, §17.1-805.
Drug offenders.
Purchase or possession of firearm by persons convicted of certain misdemeanor drug offenses, §18.2-308.1:5.
Drugs.
Carrying concealed handgun while under the influence, §18.2-308.12.
Hunting.
Reckless handling of firearm, §18.2-56.1.
Under the influence of intoxicant or narcotic drug, §18.2-285.
Larceny of firearm, §18.2-95.
Machine guns, §§18.2-288 to 18.2-298.
Motor vehicles.
Shooting from, §§18.2-286, 18.2-286.1, 29.1-521.2.
Disqualification for concealed weapons permit, §18.2-308.09.
Paramilitary activity prohibited, §18.2-433.2.
Plastic firearms, manufacture, import, etc., §18.2-308.5.
Pointing, holding or brandishing firearm, air or gas operated weapon or object similar in appearance, §18.2-282.
Prisoners, delivery to, §18.2-474.1.
Public areas, carrying loaded firearm in, §18.2-287.4.
Receipt of stolen firearms, §18.2-108.1.
Reckless handling of firearms, §18.2-56.1.
Loaded firearm left so as to endanger child's life, §18.2-56.2.
Restricted ammunition.
Use or attempted use in commission or attempted commission of crime, §18.2-308.3.
Riots.
Deadly or dangerous weapon carried at time of riot, §18.2-405.
Robbery, §18.2-58.
Sawed-off shotguns and sawed-off rifles, §§18.2-299 to 18.2-307.
School or school property.
Arrest for carrying on school property, §16.1-246.
Discharging, §18.2-280.
Disqualification for concealed weapons permit, §18.2-308.09.
Pointing, holding or brandishing firearm, air or gas operated weapon or object similar in appearance, §18.2-282.
Possession on school property, §18.2-308.1.
Selling or furnishing firearms to persons prohibited from possessing or transporting, §18.2-308.2:1.
Semi-automatic firearms and shotguns.
Carrying loaded in public areas, §18.2-287.4.

WEAPONS OFFENSES —Cont'd
Sentence of persons twice previously convicted of certain violent felonies, §19.2-297.1.
Serial number or identification on firearm.
Removing, altering, etc., §18.2-311.1.
Shooting from vehicles so as to endanger persons, §§18.2-286, 18.2-286.1, 29.1-521.2.
Disqualification for concealed weapons permit, §18.2-308.09.
Shooting, stabbing, etc.
Commission of or attempting felony, §18.2-53.
Intent to maim, kill, etc., §18.2-51.
Spring guns, setting, §18.2-281.
Streetsweepers or striker 12's, importation, sale, etc., §18.2-308.8.
Streetsweeper possession or use by delinquent child.
Loss of driving privileges, §16.1-278.9.
Three time loser law, §19.2-297.1.
Toy firearms.
Discharging blank or ball charges.
Selling or giving, §18.2-284.
Use or display of firearm in committing a felony, §18.2-53.1.
Forfeiture of weapon used in commission of crime, §19.2-386.29.

WEARING APPAREL.
Domestic dog or cat hide, fur or pelt.
Selling garments containing prohibited, §3.2-6589.
Hunting.
Blaze orange clothing requirement, §29.1-530.1.
Mine safety.
Underground coal mines.
Protective clothing, §45.1-161.175.
Personal property taxes.
Classification, §58.1-3504.

WEATHER CLOSINGS.
Public school funds.
Reduction for short school term.
Exception for severe weather conditions or other emergencies, §22.1-98.

WEB.
Internet generally.
See INTERNET.

WEBER CITY SANITATION COMMISSION.
Name changed to Moccasin Gap sanitation commission, 1971 ch 178.

WEEDS.
Counties, cities or towns.
Cutting of weeds on vacant property, §15.2-901.
Noxious weed control, §15.2-902.
Removal, §15.2-1115.
Department of transportation.
Removal from property acquired for transportation project, §33.1-223.2:10.
Invasive species.
Development of strategies to eradicate and prevent, §2.2-220.2.
Noxious weeds.
Counties, cities or towns.
Authority to control, §15.2-902.
Generally, §§3.2-800 to 3.2-809.

WEIGHING MACHINES.
License tax on coin machine operators.
Exemption of operators of weighing machines, §58.1-3721.

WEIGHMASTERS, PUBLIC, §§3.2-5800 to 3.2-5820.
Agriculture and consumer services commissioner.
Powers, §3.2-5801.
Criminal penalties, §3.2-5820.
Definitions, §3.2-5800.
Fees.
Licenses, §3.2-5805.
Licenses.
Application, §3.2-5803.
Record of applications and licenses, §3.2-5804.
Renewal, §3.2-5807.
Expiration, §3.2-5807.
Fees, §3.2-5805.
Granting, §3.2-5804.
Issuance, §§3.2-5805, 3.2-5806.
Limited licenses, §3.2-5806.
Oath and seal, §3.2-5808.
Prohibited conduct of unlicensed weighmasters, §3.2-5816.
Qualifications, §§3.2-5802, 3.2-5804.
Record of applications and licenses, §3.2-5804.
Renewal applications, §3.2-5807.
Renewal fees, §3.2-5805.
Revocation, §3.2-5817.
Seal, §3.2-5808.
Suspension, §3.2-5817.
Unlicensed weighmasters, §§3.2-5815, 3.2-5816.
Motor vehicles.
Determining weight of vehicle or combination of vehicles, §3.2-5812.
Oaths, §3.2-5808.
Unlicensed weighmasters, §§3.2-5815, 3.2-5816.
Violations of provisions.
Criminal penalties, §3.2-5820.
Prohibited acts, §§3.2-5818, 3.2-5819.
Certain acts by persons not licensed, §3.2-5816.
Suspension or revocation of license, §3.2-5817.
Weighing devices.
Capacity of scales not to be exceeded, §3.2-5812.
Requirements, §3.2-5811.
Weight certificates, §§3.2-5809, 3.2-5810.
Copies to be retained and kept open for inspection, §3.2-5813.
Prohibited acts as to, §§3.2-5818, 3.2-5819.
Weighmasters in other states.
Certificates issued by, §3.2-5814.

WEIGHT LOSS CENTERS.
Disclosure requirements, §18.2-502.1.
Health clubs generally.
See HEALTH CLUBS.
Health spas generally, §§59.1-294 to 59.1-310.

WEIGHTS AND MEASURES, §§3.2-5600 to 3.2-5648.
Actions.
Civil penalties or injunctions, §3.2-5646.
Advertising.
Commodities in package form, §3.2-5626.
Discounts.
Failure to pay advertised cash discount, §3.2-5632.
Price, §3.2-5631.
Agriculture and consumer services board.
Rules and regulations, §3.2-5607.
Agriculture and consumer services commissioner.
Condemnation of incorrect weights and measures, §3.2-5613.
Impersonating commissioner, §3.2-5644.

WEIGHTS AND MEASURES —Cont'd
Agriculture and consumer services commissioner —Cont'd
Local sealers.
Concurrent authority with, §3.2-5619.
Obstructing commissioner, §3.2-5643.
Powers and duties generally, §3.2-5601.
Police power, §3.2-5614.
Sealing or marking of weights and measures, §3.2-5613.
Searches and seizures, §3.2-5612.
Stage II vapor recovery programs.
Enforcement authority for, §3.2-5633.
Stop-sale, stop-use and stop-removal orders, §3.2-5612.
Warning instead of report of violation, §3.2-5647.
Calibration of equipment.
Commissioner establishment of schedules for, §3.2-5701.1.
City or town powers, §15.2-1114.
Civil penalties, §3.2-5646.
Service agencies and technicians, §3.2-5714.
Condemnation of incorrect weights and measures, §3.2-5613.
Disposition of rejected weights and measures, §3.2-5621.
Conflict of laws.
Local ordinances in conflict with provisions, §3.2-5619.
Congress, US Const Art I §8.
Consumer protection, prohibited practices, §59.1-200.
County powers, §15.2-1232.1.
Criminal penalties, §3.2-5645.
Impersonating commissioner or sealer, §3.2-5644.
Obstructing commissioner and sealers, §3.2-5643.
Service agencies and technicians, §3.2-5713.
Stop-sale, stop-use and stop-removal orders, §3.2-5612.
Customary system in use in United States.
Recognized, §3.2-5603.
Definitions, §3.2-5600.
Service agencies and technicians, §3.2-5700.
Fees, §3.2-5629.
Local sealers, §3.2-5616.
Service agencies and technicians.
Certification of service technicians, §3.2-5708.
Registration of service agencies, §§3.2-5704, 3.2-5705.
Forest products.
Board feet.
Determining number in tree or log, §3.2-5642.
Cord.
Use of word in connection with purchase or sale, §3.2-5641.
Fund, §3.2-5628.
Groceries.
Certain merchants to provide scales for use of customers, §3.2-5640.
Injunctions.
Violations of provisions, §3.2-5646.
Investigations.
Agriculture and consumer services commissioner, §3.2-5610.
Livestock.
Sale of livestock.
Day and hour of livestock sale.
Announcement, §3.2-5639.
Determination of weight of livestock on date of sale, §3.2-5638.

WEIGHTS AND MEASURES —Cont'd
Livestock —Cont'd
Scale house in establishment where livestock bought from producers, §3.2-5636.
Type registering weighbeams or automatic weight recorders.
Required, §3.2-5637.
Local sealers, §§3.2-5615 to 3.2-5619.
Impersonating sealer, §3.2-5644.
Obstructing sealer, §3.2-5643.
Meat, §3.2-5634.
Metric system.
Recognized, §3.2-5603.
Statutory construction.
Weights and measures deemed to include metric equivalents, §1-256.
Motor carriers, property.
See MOTOR CARRIERS, PROPERTY.
National Institute of Standards and Technology.
Advice and recommendations, §3.2-5606.
Definitions, table, etc., of institute to govern, §3.2-5603.
Specifications and tolerances for weighing and measuring devices, §3.2-5620.
Oysters, §28.2-526.
Point-of-sale systems.
Inspection and accuracy testing, §3.2-5602.
Poultry, §3.2-5634.
Presumptions.
Use of weight, measure or weighing or measuring device.
Presumptive proof, §3.2-5648.
Pricing of retail merchandise, §§3.2-5627, 3.2-5630.
Repair, §3.2-5709.
Rules and regulations.
Board of agriculture and consumer services, §3.2-5607.
Sales.
Bulk sale and delivery of commodities, §3.2-5635.
How certain commodities to be sold, §3.2-5622.
Information to be shown on packages, §§3.2-5623, 3.2-5624.
Livestock.
Day and hour of livestock sale.
Announcement, §3.2-5639.
Determination of weight of livestock on date of sale, §3.2-5638.
Misleading containers prohibited, §3.2-5625.
Seafood, §3.2-5634.
Oysters, §28.2-526.
Sealing or marking, §3.2-5613.
Searches and seizures.
Agriculture and consumer services commissioner, §3.2-5612.
Service agencies and technicians, §§3.2-5700 to 3.2-5714.
Authorized services, §3.2-5709.
Board of agriculture and consumer services.
Delegation of authority, §3.2-5702.
Powers, §3.2-5701.
Certificate of conformance, §3.2-5710.
Certification of service technicians, §3.2-5707.
Denial, suspension or revocation, §3.2-5712.
Fee, §3.2-5708.
Civil penalties, §3.2-5714.
Criminal penalties, §3.2-5713.
Definitions, §3.2-5700.
Registration of service agencies, §3.2-5703.
Denial, suspension or revocation, §3.2-5712.

WEIGHTS AND MEASURES —Cont'd
Service agencies and technicians —Cont'd
Registration of service agencies —Cont'd
Fees, §§3.2-5704, 3.2-5705.
Service report, §3.2-5711.
Standards and calibrating equipment.
Examination and verification, §3.2-5706.
Settlement.
Civil penalties, §3.2-5646.
Standards, §3.2-5604.
Cities and counties.
Testing and inspection of standards procured by, §3.2-5608.
Field standards, §3.2-5605.
Office standards, §3.2-5605.
Statutory construction, §1-256.
Testing and inspection.
Point-of-sale systems, §3.2-5602.
Standards procured by cities and counties, §3.2-5608.
Weights and measures offered for sale or commercial use, §3.2-5609.
United States.
Constitutional provisions, US Const Art I §8.
Verification and calibration of equipment.
Commissioner establishment of schedules for, §3.2-5701.1.

WELDING.
Underground coal mines.
Surface areas, §45.1-161.242.

WELFARE, §§63.2-100 to 63.2-2204.
Adoption.
Special needs children.
Adoption assistance payments, §§63.2-1300 to 63.2-1304.
Assistance, subsidy payments.
Medical assistance, uniform act, §§63.2-1400 to 63.2-1405.
Board for the blind and vision impaired.
See BLIND AND VISION IMPAIRED, BOARD FOR.
Board of social services.
Generally.
See SOCIAL SERVICES BOARD.
Child support enforcement, §§63.2-1900 to 63.2-1960.
See CHILD SUPPORT ENFORCEMENT BY DEPARTMENT OF SOCIAL SERVICES.
Child welfare agencies.
Generally.
See CHILD WELFARE AGENCIES.
Commissioner of social services.
Generally.
See COMMISSIONER OF SOCIAL SERVICES.
Confidentiality of department or local board records, §§63.2-102 to 63.2-105.
Congress.
Power of congress to provide for general welfare, US Const Art I §8.
Definitions relating to social services, §63.2-100.
Department for the blind and vision impaired.
Generally.
See BLIND AND VISION IMPAIRED, DEPARTMENT FOR.
Department of social services.
Generally.
See SOCIAL SERVICES DEPARTMENT.
Social services generally, §§63.2-200 to 63.2-214.3.
See SOCIAL SERVICES.

WELFARE —Cont'd
Desertion and nonsupport.
Spousal support.
Limitations on orders resulting in eligibility for medical assistance, §20-88.02:1.
Transfer of assets to qualify for assistance, §20-88.02.
Funding of public assistance and social services.
Generally, §§63.2-400 to 63.2-412.
See SOCIAL SERVICES.
Generally, §§63.2-500 to 63.2-805.
See PUBLIC AID AND ASSISTANCE.
Human services information and referral program, §§63.2-222 to 63.2-227.
See HUMAN SERVICES INFORMATION AND REFERRAL PROGRAM.
Local boards of public welfare.
Generally.
See WELFARE BOARDS, LOCAL.
Local boards of social services.
Generally, §§63.2-300 to 63.2-323.
See SOCIAL SERVICES.
Local departments and directors of social services.
Generally, §§63.2-324 to 63.2-336.
See SOCIAL SERVICES.
Local superintendents of public welfare.
Generally.
See SUPERINTENDENTS OF PUBLIC WELFARE.
Prisoner work release earnings.
Use, §§53.1-60, 53.1-61.
Prisons.
Ineligibility of prisoner for benefits due to incarceration.
Notice by department to social services department, §53.1-31.3.
Public aid and assistance generally.
See PUBLIC AID AND ASSISTANCE.
Support of dependent children and caretakers.
Collection of support generally.
See CHILD SUPPORT.
Temporary assistance for needy families, §§63.2-600 to 63.2-621.
See TEMPORARY ASSISTANCE FOR NEEDY FAMILIES (TANF).
VIEW.
Virginia initiative for employment not welfare, §§63.2-608 to 63.2-613.
Virginia initiative for employment not welfare, §§63.2-608 to 63.2-613.

WELFARE BOARDS, LOCAL.
Abused, neglected or abandoned children or children without parental care.
Placement, §16.1-278.2.
Accounting system for county boards.
Centralized system of accounting for counties, §15.2-1541.1.
Adoption.
Agency adoption.
See ADOPTION.
General provisions.
See ADOPTION.
Centralized purchasing by chief administrative officer, §15.2-1231.
Centralized system for accounting for counties, §15.2-1541.1.
Child placement.
Abused, neglected or abandoned children or children without parental care, §16.1-278.2.

WELFARE BOARDS, LOCAL —Cont'd
Child placement —Cont'd
Children in need of services.
Disposition for supervision, care and rehabilitation, §16.1-278.4.
Delinquent children, disposition, §16.1-278.8.
Juvenile proceedings.
Entrustment agreements.
Approval, §16.1-277.01.
Children in need of services.
Disposition for supervision, care and rehabilitation, §16.1-278.4.
Delinquent children disposition, §16.1-278.8.
Family violence.
General provisions.
See CHILD ABUSE AND NEGLECT.
Foster care plans, §§16.1-281, 16.1-282.
Review of foster care placement, §16.1-282.
Legal representation, §15.2-1519.
Liability insurance for employees, §15.2-1519.
Sexually violent predators, civil commitment.
Database of prisoners incarcerated for sexually violent offenses.
Access to records, §37.2-905.2.
Superintendents of public welfare, local.
See SUPERINTENDENTS OF PUBLIC WELFARE.

WELFARE DEPARTMENTS.
Department of social services, generally.
See SOCIAL SERVICES DEPARTMENT.
Legal representation of employees, §15.2-1519.
Liability insurance for employees, §15.2-1519.
Local departments and directors of social services.
Generally, §§63.2-324 to 63.2-336.
See SOCIAL SERVICES.
Social services generally, §§63.2-200 to 63.2-214.3.
See SOCIAL SERVICES.
Welfare generally, §§63.2-500 to 63.2-805.
See PUBLIC AID AND ASSISTANCE.

WELFARE FRAUD, §63.2-522.
Assistant attorney for Commonwealth prosecution fraud cases.
Payment for legal services by department, §63.2-525.
Denial of benefits, §63.2-524.
Fraud prevention and investigation units, §63.2-526.
Fraud recovery special fund, §63.2-526.
Statewide fraud control program, §63.2-526.
Unauthorized uses of food stamps, electronic transfer cards and energy assistance, §63.2-523.

WELL CONSTRUCTION, §§32.1-176.1 to 32.1-176.7.
Agricultural property, construction adjacent, §32.1-176.5:2.
Citation of article, §32.1-176.1.
Defined terms, §32.1-176.3.
Express geothermal permits, §32.1-176.4.
Inspections, §32.1-176.6.
Inter-agency cooperation, §32.1-176.7.
Issuance of special orders, §32.1-175.01.
Laboratories.
Testing for oil contamination.
Department to maintain list of private laboratories, §32.1-176.5:1.
Legislative findings, §32.1-176.2.

WELL CONSTRUCTION —Cont'd
Permits, §32.1-176.5.
Applications.
Fees, §32.1-176.4.
Express geothermal permits, §32.1-176.4.
Policy of Commonwealth, §32.1-176.2.
Private well construction, restrictions, §32.1-176.5:2.
Special orders.
Issuance, §32.1-175.01.
Testing for oil contamination, §32.1-176.5:1.

WELLNESS PROGRAMS.
Health insurance, §38.2-3454.

WELLS.
Attempt to poison, §18.2-54.1.
Construction of private water wells, §§32.1-176.1 to 32.1-176.7.
See WELL CONSTRUCTION.
Water wells generally.
See WATER WELLS.

WESTERN VIRGINIA PUBLIC EDUCATION CONSORTIUM, §§22.1-354.1 to 22.1-354.5.
Cooperation of other agencies, §22.1-354.5.
Creation, §22.1-354.1.
Definition of Western Virginia, §22.1-354.1.
Duties, §22.1-354.2.
Cooperation of other agencies in performance of, §22.1-354.5.
Executive director, §22.1-354.3.
Functions, §22.1-354.2.
Gifts and grants.
Acceptance, §22.1-354.4.
Governing board, §22.1-354.1.
Location of office, §22.1-354.3.
Staff support, §22.1-354.3.

WESTMORELAND COUNTY.
Coastal primary sand dunes and beaches.
Zoning ordinances, §28.2-1403.
Northern Neck Chesapeake Bay public access authority, §§15.2-6626 to 15.2-6651.
See NORTHERN NECK CHESAPEAKE BAY PUBLIC ACCESS AUTHORITY.
Northern Neck-Middle Peninsula public education consortium.
Inclusion in region, §22.1-354.6.
School board.
Fingerprinting applicants for employment, §22.1-296.2.
Salary of members, §22.1-32.

WEST POINT, TOWN OF.
Middle Peninsula regional airport authority, 1997 ch 871.

WEST VIRGINIA.
Boundaries of Commonwealth.
Loudoun county, Virginia.
Boundary with Jefferson county, West Virginia, §1-313.

WETLAND PROFESSIONALS, §§54.1-2200 to 54.1-2208.4.
See SOIL SCIENTISTS, WETLAND PROFESSIONALS AND GEOLOGISTS.

WETLANDS, §§28.2-1300 to 28.2-1320.
Boards.
Jurisdiction, §28.2-1303.
Meetings, §28.2-1304.
Space to be supplied by local governing body, §28.2-1305.

WETLANDS —Cont'd
Boards —Cont'd
Members, §28.2-1303.
Officers, §28.2-1304.
Records, §28.2-1304.
Reports, §28.2-1304.
Review of decisions, §§28.2-1310 to 28.2-1313.
Rules, §28.2-1304.
Services.
Local governing body to supply, §28.2-1305.
Commission powers and duties, §28.2-1301.
Compensatory mitigation for adverse impacts to, §33.1-223.2:1.
Condemnation for compensatory mitigation of wetlands, §25.1-109.
Defined terms, §§28.2-1300, 28.2-1302.
Eminent domain.
Condemnation for compensatory mitigation of wetlands, §25.1-109.
Inspections, §28.2-1317.
Investigations, §28.2-1316.
Localities.
Condemnation for compensatory mitigation of wetlands, §15.2-1907.1.
Mitigation banking.
Compensatory mitigation for adverse impacts, §33.1-223.2:1.
Permits for use and development of wetlands conditioned on compensatory mitigation.
Purchase of credits from bank, §28.2-1308.
Monitoring, §28.2-1317.
Permits.
Expedited permits, §28.2-1307.
Issuance, §28.2-1306.
Time for, §28.2-1314.
Modification of board decision, §28.2-1313.
Procedures, administrative, §28.2-1307.
Remand of board decision, §28.2-1313.
Required, §28.2-1306.
Reversal of board decision, §28.2-1313.
Reviews, §§28.2-1310, 28.2-1311.
Judicial review, §28.2-1315.
Procedure, §28.2-1312.
Standards for use and development of wetlands, §28.2-1308.
Utilization of guidelines, §28.2-1308.
Property taxes, §58.1-3666.
Provision violations.
Penalties, §§28.2-1318, 28.2-1320.
Injunctions, §28.2-1319.
Prosecutions, §28.2-1316.
Real property taxes.
Assessment of residential property containing wetlands, §58.1-3284.3.
Restoration, §28.2-1317.
Solid waste management.
Permits.
Special provisions regarding wetlands, §10.1-1408.5.
Standards for use and development, §28.2-1308.
Virginia water resources and wetlands protection program, §§62.1-44.15:20 to 62.1-44.15:23.1.
Waters of the state generally.
See WATERS OF THE STATE.
Wetland and stream replacement fund, §62.1-44.15:23.1.
Zoning, §28.2-1302.

WHARVES, §§62.1-164, 62.1-165.
Boundaries of localities to embrace.
Localities bordering Chesapeake Bay or Atlantic Ocean, §15.2-3105.

WHARVES —Cont'd
Clam planting grounds.
Riparian owner rights to build bulkheads or wharves, §28.2-630.
Franchise, privilege, lease or right to use city or town property, §§15.2-2100 to 15.2-2108.1:1.
Obstruction or hazard to lawful use of waters.
Removal, repair, etc., §§15.2-909, 28.2-1210.
Oyster planting grounds.
Riparian oyster planting grounds, §28.2-602.
Police powers over lands lying beyond localities boundaries, §15.2-1725.
Riparian owner rights.
Notice to oyster ground holder or lessee, §28.2-630.
Sale of city or town property, §15.2-2100, VA Const Art VII §9.

WHEAT.
Generally, §§3.2-2200 to 3.2-2214.
See SMALL GRAINS.

WHEELCHAIRS.
Assistive technology device warranties, §§59.1-470 to 59.1-474.
Defined, §46.2-100.
Lifts.
Accessibility mechanics, certification, §§54.1-1140 to 54.1-1143.
Retail sales and use tax exemption, §58.1-609.10.
Motor vehicle registration exemption, §46.2-677.
Statewide system of trails, §10.1-204.
Workers' compensation.
Medical attention to be furnished, §65.2-603.

WHISTLEBLOWING.
Complaints against adult or child care agencies.
Discrimination or retaliation against complainant prohibited, §63.2-1730.
Fraud and abuse whistleblower protection act, §§2.2-3009 to 2.2-3014.
Defined terms, §2.2-3010.
Discrimination against whistleblowers prohibited, §2.2-3011.
Freedom of information act.
Exclusions from chapter, §2.2-3705.3.
Good faith requirement, §2.2-3011.
Grievance procedure.
Applicability, §2.2-3012.
Notice of protection to employees, §2.2-3013.
Policy of state, §2.2-3009.
Retaliation against whistleblowers prohibited, §2.2-3011.
Reward fund, §2.2-3014.
Fraudulent claims against the state.
Certain actions barred, §8.01-216.8.
Employment discrimination relief, §8.01-216.8.
Whistleblowing awards for private plaintiffs, §8.01-216.7.
Hospitals.
Discrimination or retaliation against complainant or person cooperating with government agency, §32.1-125.4.
Nursing homes, §§32.1-138.4, 32.1-138.5.
Occupational safety and health, §§40.1-51.2 to 40.1-51.2:2.

WHISTLES.
Motor vehicle equipment generally, §§46.2-1059 to 46.2-1062.
See MOTOR VEHICLE EQUIPMENT.

WHISTLES —Cont'd
Railroad crossings.
Failure to whistle, §§56-414, 56-416.
Whistle to be sounded, §56-414.

WHITE CANE LAW.
Effect of failure to use cane or guide dog, §46.2-934.
Liability for injuries to blind pedestrians, §46.2-932.1.
Unlawful for person not blind to carry, §18.2-212.1.
Vehicles to stop for pedestrians guided by dog or carrying recognized cane, §46.2-933.

WHITE CANE SAFETY DAY, §2.2-3315.1.

WHITE SLAVE ACT, §18.2-355.

WHOLESALE.
Use of word in advertising or offer for sale, §18.2-220.

WHOLESALE BEER OR WINE LICENSES.
Authorized conduct, §§4.1-207, 4.1-208.
Restricted wholesale wine licenses, §4.1-207.1.
Grounds for refusal to grant, §4.1-223.
Local license taxes, §4.1-233.
State license fees, §§4.1-231, 4.1-232.

WHOLESALE DISTRIBUTORS OF PRESCRIPTION DRUGS.
Licensing, §§54.1-3435, 54.1-3435.1.

WHOLESALE MERCHANTS.
License taxes, §58.1-3716.

WHOLESALERS.
Cigarette excise tax.
Generally, §§58.1-1000 to 58.1-1022.
See CIGARETTE TAX.
Cigarettes.
Illegal sale or distribution.
Enforcement of illegal sale or distribution of cigarettes, §§58.1-1031 to 58.1-1037.
See CIGARETTES.
License tax for privilege of selling to persons for resale.
Localities limitation on levying, §58.1-3703.
Use of word in advertising or offer for sale, §18.2-220.

WHOOPING COUGH.
Immunization.
Required immunizations of children, §32.1-46.
Virginia immunization information system (VIIS), §32.1-46.01.

WIDE-LOAD ESCORT.
Law enforcement vehicles.
Exemption from certain traffic regulations, §46.2-920.

WIDOWS.
Accrued and undistributed income elections, §64.2-429.
Black lung disease.
Death benefit payments, §65.2-513.
Coal workers' pneumoconiosis.
Death benefit payments, §65.2-513.
Community property rights at death.
Generally, §§64.2-315 to 64.2-324.
See COMMUNITY PROPERTY RIGHTS AT DEATH.
Credit unions.
Membership, §6.2-1327.

WIDOWS —Cont'd
Crime victim and witness assistance programs.
Eligibility for award, §19.2-368.4.
Descent and distribution.
Administrators.
Appointing preferences, §64.2-502.
Personalty.
Distribution of, §64.2-502.
Realty.
Distribution of, §64.2-200.
Spouses omitted from wills.
Portion to take, §64.2-422.
Elective shares.
Abandonment.
Effect upon, §64.2-308.
Amount, §64.2-306.
Claiming, §64.2-302.
Extension of time, §64.2-303.
Rights upon, §64.2-304.
Desertion.
Effect upon, §64.2-308.
Family residence rights, §64.2-307.
Exempt property, §64.2-310.
Claiming, §64.2-313.
Determination, §64.2-312.
Documentation, §64.2-312.
Source, §64.2-312.
Waiver, §64.2-314.
Family allowances, §64.2-309.
Claiming, §64.2-313.
Determination, §64.2-312.
Documentation, §64.2-312.
Source, §64.2-312.
Waiver, §64.2-314.
Family residence rights, §64.2-307.
Homestead allowances, §64.2-311.
Claiming, §64.2-313.
Determination, §64.2-312.
Documentation, §64.2-312.
Source, §64.2-312.
Waiver, §64.2-314.
Marital deduction elections.
Powers of executors and administrators, §64.2-107.
Marital deduction formula clauses.
Construction, §64.2-430.
Right of entry.
Property rights of married women, §55-38.
Servicemen's readjustment act of 1944, eligibility for guaranty of credit.
Qualification to contract for and purchase real or personal property, §11-8.
Wills.
Omitted spouses.
Portion to take, §64.2-422.
Workers' compensation.
Dependency.
Determinations, §§65.2-515, 65.2-516.
Termination, §65.2-517.
Payments.
Receipt by whom, §65.2-525.
Wrongful death.
Classes of beneficiaries, §§8.01-53, 8.01-54.

WIFE AND HUSBAND.
See HUSBAND AND WIFE.

WILDLIFE CENTER OF VIRGINIA.
Vehicles owned or controlled by.
Exemption from certain traffic regulations, §46.2-920.2.

WILDLIFE CONSERVATION.
Special license plates, §46.2-749.1.

WILDLIFE DISEASES.
Control, eradication, regulations.
Board of game and inland fisheries.
Authority, §29.1-103.1.

WILDLIFE HABITAT, REFUGE OR SANCTUARY.
Destruction of trees, shrubs, etc., in, §18.2-140.
Provision violations, §29.1-554.
Shooting preserves generally, §§29.1-600 to 29.1-612.
See SHOOTING PRESERVES.

WILDLIFE MANAGEMENT.
Prescribed burning and certified prescribed burn managers, §§10.1-1150.1 to 10.1-1150.6.
Wildlife violator compact, §29.1-530.5.
Regulations, promulgation, §29.1-103.

WILDLIFE VIOLATOR COMPACT, §29.1-530.5.
Regulations, promulgation, §29.1-103.

WILD SPANISH MUSTANGS FUND, §10.1-1027.

WILL BOOK.
Documents recorded in, §17.1-231.
General index and daily index, §17.1-249.
List of heirs recorded in, §64.2-509.
Numbering, §17.1-249.

WILLIAM AND MARY COLLEGE, §§23-39 to 23-49.1:1.
See COLLEGE OF WILLIAM AND MARY.

WILLIAMSBURG.
Buses.
Restricting nonscheduled buses over designated streets, §46.2-1304.
Circuit court.
Keeping of docket books, §8.01-446.
Circuit court, establishment of, §17.1-500.
Coastal primary sand dunes and beaches.
Zoning ordinances, §28.2-1403.
Confederate cemeteries and graves.
Disbursement of funds appropriated for upkeep, §10.1-2211.
Grand jury.
Selection of jurors from James City County and city.
Service on county grand jury, §19.2-194.
Grass, weeds, other foreign growth on occupied or vacant property.
Cutting by property owners, ordinance prescribing, §15.2-901.
Joint court system with James City county.
Removal, approval of electorate required.
Inapplicability of provisions, §15.2-1646.
Port of Virginia economic and infrastructure development zone grant fund, §62.1-132.3:2.
Public service corporations, taxation of property.
Restriction of imposition of additional tax, §58.1-2606.
Retail sales and use tax.
Additional sales tax for Northern Virginia and Hampton Roads, §58.1-603.1.
Additional use tax for Northern Virginia and Hampton Roads, §58.1-604.01.
Revolutionary war cemeteries and graves.
Disbursement of funds appropriated for upkeep, §10.1-2211.1.

WILLIAMSBURG —Cont'd
School board.
Salary of members, §22.1-32.
Underground relocation of electric, telephone and cable TV distribution lines.
Taxes and assessments on abutting property owners, §15.2-2404.
Virginia Shakespeare Festival, Williamsburg, designated as official Shakespeare festival of the Commonwealth, §1-510.

WILLIAMSBURG AREA DESTINATION MARKETING COMMITTEE, §58.1-3823.

WILLIAMSBURG AREA TRANSIT AUTHORITY, §§15.2-6800 to 15.2-6809.
Advisory committees, §15.2-6808.
Chairman and vice-chairman, §15.2-6803.
Citation of act, §15.2-6800.
Compensation of members, §15.2-6807.
Counties and cities embraced by, §15.2-6802.
Allocation of certain expenses among, §15.2-6806.
Creation, §15.2-6801.
Duties and responsibilities, §§15.2-6801, 15.2-6809.
Executive director, §15.2-6804.
Expenses.
Allocation of certain expenses among component members, §15.2-6806.
Members, §15.2-6803.
Compensation, §15.2-6807.
Powers, §15.2-6801.
Quorum, §15.2-6805.
Staff, §15.2-6804.
Title of act, §15.2-6800.

WILLS, §§64.2-400 to 64.2-458.
Acts subsequent to execution.
Effect, §64.2-413.
Advancements.
Hotchpot, bringing into, §64.2-206.
Satisfaction of devise or bequest, §64.2-417.
Advertising.
Drawing of wills, §64.2-402.
Anatomical gifts.
Amendment or revocation of gift prior to donor's death, §32.1-291.6.
Invalidation of will after donor's death, effect, §32.1-291.5.
Method of making gift prior to donor's death, §32.1-291.5.
Refusal of gift, §32.1-291.7.
Annuity purchases.
Construction, §64.2-424.
Attestation.
Execution procedure, §§64.2-403, 64.2-404.
Augmented estates, §64.2-305.
Banks.
Reference to converted national bank in will, §6.2-824.
Bequests that fail pass to residuary, §64.2-416.
Burning, §64.2-410.
Cemeteries.
Disposition of property for maintenance and care.
Limitation on amount, §57-34.
Charitable gifts.
Generally.
See CHARITABLE GIFTS.
Chattel.
Conveyance requirements, §55-3.
Clerk's duty of safekeeping, §64.2-409.
Concealing, §18.2-504.

WILLS —Cont'd
Construction, §§64.2-414 to 64.2-432.
Accrued and undistributed income elections, §64.2-429.
Advancements.
Satisfaction of devise or bequest, §64.2-417.
Annuity purchases, §64.2-424.
Bequests that fail pass to residuary, §64.2-416.
Condemnation awards, §64.2-415.
Descendants of devisee or legatees.
When take, §64.2-418.
Devises that fail pass to residuary, §64.2-416.
Effect as if executed immediately before death, §64.2-414.
Federal estate and generation-skipping transfer tax laws.
Certain formula clauses construed to refer to, §64.2-432.
Federal gift tax exclusions, §64.2-431.
Freehold estates to include leasehold, §64.2-415.
Generic terms, §64.2-101.
Insurance proceeds, §64.2-415.
Interest on pecuniary legacies, §64.2-425.
Legacies that fail pass to residuary, §64.2-416.
Marital deduction formula clauses, §64.2-430.
Pecuniary amount of specific property, §64.2-415.
Pecuniary requests, satisfaction by fiduciaries, §64.2-428.
Powers of appointment in residuary clauses, §64.2-423.
Pretermitted children, §§64.2-419, 64.2-420.
Reference to former section or provision of code, §64.2-108.2.
Security bequests, §64.2-415.
Separate writings, §64.2-400.
Spouse's survivorship.
Construction of certain conditions, §64.2-421.
Time at which will speaks, §64.2-414.
Transfers in trust of pecuniary amount, §64.2-428.
Trust devises or bequests, §64.2-426.
Conveyances subsequent to execution.
Effect, §64.2-413.
Curators, §§64.2-443, 64.2-451.
Decedents' estates.
Generally.
See DECEDENTS' ESTATES.
Defined terms, §64.2-100.
Augmented estates, §64.2-300.
Environmental law, §64.2-105.
Estate, §64.2-300.
Fiduciary, §64.2-105.
Generic terms, §64.2-101.
Property, §64.2-300.
Descendants of devisees or legatees.
When to take estate, §64.2-418.
Destroying, §18.2-504.
Devisavit vel non, §§64.2-448, 64.2-449.
Establishment bills.
Filing, §64.2-448.
Impeachment bills.
Filing, §64.2-448.
Devises that fail pass to residuary, §64.2-416.
Disclaimer of property interests.
Disclaimer of beneficiary designation, §64.2-2610.
Generally, §§64.2-2600 to 64.2-2614.
See DISCLAIMER OF PROPERTY INTERESTS.
Drafter's name to appear on first page of recorded documents, §17.1-223.
Educational gifts.
Generally.
See CHARITABLE GIFTS.

WILLS —Cont'd
Elective shares.
Abandonment.
Effect upon, §64.2-308.
Amount, §64.2-306.
Claiming, §64.2-302.
Extension of time, §64.2-303.
Rights upon, §64.2-304.
Desertion.
Effect upon, §64.2-308.
Electronic filing of documents.
Instruments for which electronic medium not acceptable, §17.1-258.6.
Electronic format.
Certified copy, §64.2-455.
Emancipated minors.
Execution of wills, effects of order of emancipation, §16.1-334.
Estates in land.
Will necessary to convey, §55-2.
Estate which may be disposed of, §64.2-401.
Execution procedure, §§64.2-403, 64.2-404.
Exceptions, §§64.2-407, 64.2-408.
Presumption of formal execution by military personnel, §64.2-408.
Executors and administrators, §§64.2-500 to 64.2-620.
See EXECUTORS AND ADMINISTRATORS.
Exempt property rights.
Additional nature, §64.2-310.
Family allowances.
Additional nature, §64.2-313.
Federal estate and generation-skipping transfer tax laws.
Certain formula clauses construed to refer to, §64.2-432.
Federal gift tax exclusions.
Construction of powers of appointment, §64.2-431.
Fiduciaries.
Executors and administrators, §§64.2-500 to 64.2-620.
See EXECUTORS AND ADMINISTRATORS.
Incorporation by reference of powers, §§64.2-105, 64.2-106.
Personal representatives generally, §§64.2-500 to 64.2-620.
See EXECUTORS AND ADMINISTRATORS.
Satisfaction of pecuniary bequests or transfers in trust of pecuniary amount, §64.2-428.
Wrongful payments.
Liability, §64.2-101.
Fraudulent conveyances.
Pretend loans and reservations.
Recordation, §55-87.
Gifts.
Charitable gifts.
See CHARITABLE GIFTS.
Goods.
Conveyance requirements, §55-3.
Guardians.
Appointment, §64.2-1701.
Void appointments, §64.2-1701.
Termination of guardianship, §64.2-1803.
Holographic wills, §64.2-404.
Homestead allowances, §64.2-311.
Homicide.
Slayers barred from property rights of decedent, §§64.2-2500 to 64.2-2511.
See SLAYER'S ACT.
Incorporation by reference.
Letters and memoranda, §64.2-104.

WILLS —Cont'd
Interest on pecuniary legacies.
Construction, §64.2-425.
International wills, §§64.2-433 to 64.2-442.
Certificate, §64.2-437.
Effect, §64.2-438.
Construction, §64.2-440.
Definitions, §64.2-433.
Information registration, §64.2-442.
Persons authorized to act, §64.2-441.
Eligibility, §64.2-441.
Requirement, §§64.2-435, 64.2-436.
Revocation, §64.2-439.
Source of law, §64.2-440.
Validity, §64.2-434.
Landlord and tenant.
Passing of powers to devisees without express statements, §55-220.
Rent.
Who liable for, §55-229.
Who may recover, §55-228.
Leasehold estates.
Devises construed, §64.2-415.
Legacies that fail pass to residuary, §64.2-416.
Lists.
Separate writings, §64.2-400.
Literary gifts generally.
See CHARITABLE GIFTS.
Living wills, §§54.1-2981 to 54.1-2993.
See LIVING WILLS.
Lodging for safekeeping, §64.2-409.
Marital deductions.
Construction of formula clauses, §64.2-430.
Election powers of executors and administrators, §64.2-107.
Married persons, rights, §§64.2-300 to 64.2-324.
Community property rights at death, §§64.2-315 to 64.2-324.
Elective share of surviving spouse, §§64.2-300 to 64.2-308.
Exempt property and allowances, §§64.2-309 to 64.2-314.
Simultaneous death, §§64.2-2200 to 64.2-2208.
Microfilm copies, §64.2-455.
Military personnel.
Personalty dispositions, §64.2-408.
Presumption of formal execution, §64.2-408.
Murder.
Slayers barred from property rights of decedent, §§64.2-2500 to 64.2-2511.
See SLAYER'S ACT.
Nonresidents.
Personalty, disposition of, §64.2-407.
Notice to interested parties, §64.2-508.
Obliterating, §64.2-410.
Omitted spouses.
Portion of estate to receive, §64.2-422.
Parent and child relationship, establishing.
Determining rights in and to property pursuant to will, §64.2-102.
Pecuniary amount of specific property.
Construction of bequests or devises, §64.2-415.
Personal representatives generally, §§64.2-500 to 64.2-620.
See EXECUTORS AND ADMINISTRATORS.
Persons who may execute, §64.2-401.
Power of appointment.
Exceptions, §§64.2-407, 64.2-408.
Murderers barred from claiming property rights of decedent, §64.2-2507.
Residuary clauses construed, §64.2-423.

WILLS —Cont'd
Power of appointment —Cont'd
Rule against perpetuities, §§55-12.1 to 55-12.6.
Validity, §64.2-406.
Preparer's name to appear on first page of recorded documents, §17.1-223.
Presumptions.
Death presumption, §§64.2-2300 to 64.2-2309.
See DEATH PRESUMPTION.
Formal execution by military personnel, §64.2-408.
Pretermitted children, §§64.2-419, 64.2-420.
Prisoners.
Capacity to make, §53.1-221.
Probate, §§64.2-443 to 64.2-454.
Clerk orders.
Appeals, §64.2-445.
Clerk powers and duties, §64.2-444.
Clerk restrictions.
Death presumptions, §64.2-2303.
Compelling production of will, §64.2-449.
Curators, §§64.2-443, 64.2-451.
Devisavit vel non, §§64.2-448, 64.2-449.
Eldercare facilities.
Residency determination, §64.2-443.
Establishment bills, §64.2-448.
Tolling, §64.2-448.
Evidence.
What may be admitted, §64.2-449.
Ex parte proceedings, §64.2-446.
Final decrees or orders, §§64.2-446, 64.2-448.
Foreign proved wills.
Admittance, §64.2-450.
Hearing of motions, §64.2-446.
Impeachment bills, §64.2-448.
Tolling, §64.2-448.
Interested parties, §64.2-449.
Appearances, §64.2-446.
Circuit court powers, §64.2-446.
Hearing of motions, §64.2-446.
Jurisdiction, §64.2-443.
Proving of wills.
Deposition of witnesses, §64.2-447.
Foreign proved wills, §64.2-450.
Self-proving, §64.2-452.
Alternate methods, §64.2-453.
Requirements for recording instruments generally, §17.1-223.
Self-proving, §64.2-452.
Alternate methods, §64.2-453.
Testamentary papers, §64.2-446.
Probate tax.
Local tax, §§58.1-3805 to 58.1-3808.
State tax, §§58.1-1711 to 58.1-1718.
See PROBATE TAX, STATE.
Real property.
Creation of estates in land, §55-6.
Heir limitations construed, §55-13.
Heirs of his body or words of like import, §55-14.
Real property tax assessment on death of owner, §58.1-3342.
Recordation, §§64.2-455 to 64.2-458.
Bona fide purchasers of real estate without notice, §64.2-456.
Intestacy, §64.2-458.
Later wills, §64.2-457.
Certificate not signed by clerk, §§55-137.1, 55-137.2.
Documents recorded in will book, §17.1-231.
Effect, §64.2-455.

WILLS —Cont'd
Recordation —Cont'd
Location, §64.2-455.
Requirements for filing or recording documents generally, §17.1-223.
Reference to former section or provision of code.
Construction, §64.2-108.2.
Religious organizations.
Transfers of property to, §57-7.1.
Requisites and execution, §§64.2-400 to 64.2-409.
Residuary clauses.
Passing of devises, bequests and legacies that fail, §64.2-416.
Powers of appointment, §64.2-423.
Revivals, §64.2-411.
Designation of when made, §64.2-414.
Remarriages to former spouse, §64.2-412.
Revocation, §§64.2-410 to 64.2-413.
Annulments, §64.2-412.
Divorce, §64.2-412.
No revocation by other change, §64.2-412.
Revivals, §64.2-411.
Designation of when made, §64.2-414.
Remarriages to former spouse, §64.2-412.
Rights of married persons, §§64.2-300 to 64.2-324.
Community property rights at death, §§64.2-315 to 64.2-324.
Elective share of surviving spouse, §§64.2-300 to 64.2-308.
Exempt property and allowances, §§64.2-309 to 64.2-314.
Simultaneous death, §§64.2-2200 to 64.2-2208.
Rule against perpetuities, §§55-12.1 to 55-12.6.
Safe deposits or storage.
Death of sole lessee.
Limited access to safe deposit box, §6.2-2302.
Safekeeping, clerks duties, §64.2-409.
Samuel Miller's will.
Trust funds.
Construction of will, §22.1-111.
Scrivener's act, §17.1-223.
Seamen.
Personalty, disposition of, §64.2-408.
Securities.
Construction of bequests, §64.2-415.
Filings by executors.
Continuation of powers, §64.2-607.
Transfers.
Nonresident decedents, §64.2-608.
Self-proving, §64.2-452.
Alternate methods, §64.2-453.
Separate writings.
Validity, §64.2-400.
Signature requirement, §§64.2-403, 64.2-404.
Simultaneous death, §§64.2-2200 to 64.2-2208.
Murderers barred from claiming property rights of decedent.
Application of act, §64.2-2511.
Slayers barred from property rights of decedent, §§64.2-2500 to 64.2-2511.
See SLAYER'S ACT.
Soldiers.
Personalty, disposition of, §64.2-408.
Spouse's survivorship.
Construction of certain conditions, §64.2-421.
Tearing, §64.2-410.
Term construed, §64.2-100.
Testamentary additions to trusts, §64.2-427.
Transfers to minors, §64.2-1904.

WILLS —Cont'd
Trust devises or bequests, §64.2-426.
Testamentary additions to trusts, §64.2-427.
Trusts.
Incorporation by reference.
Specific powers of trustee, §64.2-778.
Venue.
Actions to impeach or establish a will, §8.01-261.
Recording, §64.2-455.
Witnesses.
Execution procedure, §§64.2-403, 64.2-404.
Interested persons as competent witnesses, §64.2-405.
Presumption of formal execution by military personnel, §64.2-408.
Writing requirement, §§64.2-403, 64.2-404.

WILLS AND ADMINISTRATIONS TAX.
Local tax, §§58.1-3805 to 58.1-3808.
Authorization, §58.1-1718.
State probate tax, §§58.1-1711 to 58.1-1718.
See PROBATE TAX, STATE.

WINCHESTER.
Arts and cultural district.
Creation, tax incentives, regulatory flexibility, powers, §15.2-1129.1.
Assistant attorney for the Commonwealth.
Dual office holding, §15.2-1534.
Circuit court, establishment, §17.1-500.
Confederate cemeteries and graves.
Disbursement of funds appropriated for upkeep, §10.1-2211.
Grass, weeds, other foreign growth on occupied or vacant property.
Cutting by property owners, ordinance prescribing, §15.2-901.
Personal property tax proration.
Payment of prorated taxes, §58.1-3516.1.
Port of Virginia economic and infrastructure development zone grant fund, §62.1-132.3:2.
Public defenders office.
Established, §19.2-163.04.
Revolutionary war cemeteries and graves.
Disbursement of funds appropriated for upkeep, §10.1-2211.1.
School board.
Fingerprinting applicants for employment, §22.1-296.2.

WINCHESTER PARKING AUTHORITY, 1964 ch 221, 1966 ch 515.

WINCHESTER REGIONAL AIRPORT AUTHORITY, 1987 ch 687, 1995 ch 258, 1995 ch 338.

WIND ENERGY.
Clean energy manufacturing incentive grant program, §§59.1-284.25 to 59.1-284.27.
Green job creation tax credit, §58.1-439.12:05.
Offshore wind energy.
Virginia offshore wind development authority, §§67-1200 to 67-1211.
See OFFSHORE WIND DEVELOPMENT AUTHORITY.
Personal property taxes.
Classification of property for manufacturing renewable energy products, §58.1-3506.
Photovoltaic, solar and wind energy utilization grant program, §§67-1000 to 67-1003.
Real property taxes.
Classification of improvements to property used for design and manufacture of renewable energy products, §58.1-3221.4.

WIND ENERGY —Cont'd
Renewable electricity production program.
Grants, §§67-900 to 67-903.
Renewable energy portfolio standard program.
Investor-owned incumbent electric utility.
Sale of electricity from renewable sources through, §56-585.2.
Virginia offshore wind development authority, §§67-1200 to 67-1211.
See OFFSHORE WIND DEVELOPMENT AUTHORITY.

WINDING UP BUSINESS TRUST, §13.1-1236.

WINDING UP LIMITED PARTNERSHIPS, §50-73.51.
Certificate of cancellation, §50-73.52:4.

WINDSHIELDS AND WINDOWS, §§46.2-1052 to 46.2-1058.
Absence of windshield, §46.2-1057.
Bullet-proof glass.
Reporting vehicles equipped with glass, §46.2-109.
Defroster or defogger, §46.2-1055.1.
Fine schedule for violations, VA SCt Rule 3B:2.
Garages.
Bullet-proof glass.
Reporting vehicles equipped with glass, §46.2-109.
Sale or installation of motor vehicle glass, §59.1-207.5:1.
Handicapped parking placards.
See PARKING FOR DISABLED OR HANDICAPPED.
Maximum fine for violating Title 46.2, §46.2-113.
Missing windshield, §46.2-1057.
Motor vehicle repair facilities.
Sale or installation of motor vehicle glass, §59.1-207.5:1.
Pretrial payment of fines for violations, §16.1-69.40:1.
Replacement of glass in vehicle, §46.2-1058.
Safety glass, absence, §46.2-1056.
Sale or installation of motor vehicle glass, §59.1-207.5:1.
Signs on windshields, §46.2-1052.
Sunshading or tinting films or applications, §§46.2-1052, 46.2-1053.
View of driver obstructed, §46.2-1054.

WINDSHIELD WIPERS.
Inadequate wipers, §46.2-1055.
Fine schedule, VA SCt Rule 3B:2.
Maximum fine for violating Title 46.2, §46.2-113.
Required display of headlights, §46.2-1030.

WIND TURBINES.
Local property taxation of public service corporations.
Rate of tax on electric suppliers utilizing turbines, §58.1-2606.

WINE.
ABC act.
Generally, §§4.1-100 to 4.1-354.
See ALCOHOLIC BEVERAGES.
Administration of licenses.
Generally, §§4.1-200 to 4.1-240.
Advertising, §4.1-209.
Point-of-sale advertising materials, §4.1-216.1.
Agritourism activity liability, §§3.2-6400 to 3.2-6402.
Authorized conduct by licensees, §4.1-207.

WINE —Cont'd
Banquet licenses.
Authorized conduct, §4.1-209.
Falsifying applications, §4.1-325.1.
Local license taxes, §4.1-233.
Manufacturers, bottlers and wholesalers.
Limitations on issuance to, §4.1-215.
State license fees, §§4.1-231, 4.1-232.
Board, §§3.2-3000 to 3.2-3006.
Advertising, §3.2-3006.
Chairman, §3.2-3003.
Duties of board, §3.2-3004.
Expense reimbursement, §3.2-3003.
Meetings, §3.2-3001.
Members, §3.2-3001.
Terms of office, §3.2-3002.
Officers, §3.2-3003.
Powers of board, §3.2-3004.
Purpose of board, §3.2-3001.
Revenue-producing activities, §3.2-3006.
Terms of office, §3.2-3002.
Wine promotion fund, §3.2-3005.
Dedicated revenues, diversion, §3.2-1100.
Common carriers.
Direct shipment of beer and wine.
Annual fee on shipper's license, §4.1-231.
Records of licensees, §4.1-204.
Contract winemaking facility.
Authority to operate, §4.1-207.
Convenience grocery store licenses.
Authorized conduct, §4.1-209.
Local license taxes, §4.1-233.
State license fees, §§4.1-231, 4.1-232.
Definitions, §4.1-100.
Delivery permits, §4.1-212.1.
State license fees, §4.1-231.
Direct shipment of beer and wine.
Annual fee on shipper's license, §4.1-231.
Records of licensees, §4.1-204.
Farm wineries.
Bonded warehouses on or off premises.
Storing wine, §4.1-207.
Class A licensees.
Out-of-state products, use.
Limitation, §4.1-219.
Class B licensees.
Out-of-state products, use.
Limitation, §4.1-219.
Defined, §4.1-100.
Delivery or shipping wine.
License authority, §4.1-207.
Licenses.
Authorized conduct, §4.1-207.
State license fees, §§4.1-231, 4.1-232.
Limitation on licensees, §4.1-219.
Local license taxes, §4.1-233.
Manufacture of wine.
License authority, §4.1-207.
Nonstock corporation established and operated to assist distribution of wines.
Agriculture and consumer services commissioner, §3.2-102.
Out-of-state products.
Use, limitation on licensees, §4.1-219.
Persons outside the Commonwealth.
Shipping wine to, accepting shipments from, §4.1-207.
Sales to other winery or farm winery in closed containers for use in manufacture of wine, §4.1-201.

WINE —Cont'd
Farm wineries —Cont'd
Sunday retail sales.
In county restricting Sunday beer and wine sales, §4.1-123.
Zoning, licensed farm wineries, §15.2-2288.3.
Fees.
State license fees, §§4.1-231, 4.1-232.
Flight of wines and beers.
Retail on-premises licensees.
Selling, §4.1-201.
Franchises.
Generally, §§4.1-400 to 4.1-418.
See WINE FRANCHISES.
Fulfillment warehouse licenses.
Authorized conduct, §4.1-209.
Shipper's licenses, §4.1-209.1.
State license fees, §4.1-231.
Gift shop licenses.
Authorized conduct, §4.1-209.
Limitation on license, §4.1-220.
Local license taxes, §4.1-233.
State license fees, §§4.1-231, 4.1-232.
Gourmet shop licenses.
Authorized conduct, §4.1-209.
Local license taxes, §4.1-233.
State license fees, §§4.1-231, 4.1-232.
Internet wine retailer.
Defined, §4.1-100.
Licenses, granting, §4.1-207.
Kegs.
Permit to sell in, §4.1-212.
Licenses.
See ALCOHOLIC BEVERAGE LICENSES.
Liter tax on wine, §§4.1-234, 4.1-235, 58.1-1708.
Local license taxes, §4.1-233.
Marketing portal licenses.
Authorized conduct, §4.1-209.
Shipper's licenses, §4.1-209.1.
State license fees, §4.1-231.
Mixed beverages licenses.
Authorized licenses for on-premises consumption, §4.1-210.
Ordinances regulating time of sale, §4.1-129.
Outdoor performing arts.
Amphitheaters licenses.
Retail on-premises wine and beer licenses, §4.1-209.
Prohibiting transfer of wine by licensees, §4.1-327.
Referendum.
Sunday wine sales, §4.1-123.
Regulation of licenses.
Generally, §§4.1-200 to 4.1-240.
Resort complex.
Retail on-premises wine and beer license.
Sale of wine and beer in hotel classified as, §4.1-208.
Restricted wholesale wine licenses.
Authorized conduct, §4.1-207.1.
Retail off-premises wine and beer licenses.
Authorized conduct, §4.1-209.
Local license taxes, §4.1-233.
Prohibited acts by employees, §4.1-325.2.
State license fees, §§4.1-231, 4.1-232.
Retail off-premises winery licenses.
Authorized conduct, §4.1-207.
Local license taxes, §4.1-233.
State license fees, §§4.1-231, 4.1-232.
Retail on-and-off premises wine and beer licenses.
Authorized conduct, §4.1-209.

WINE —Cont'd
Retail on-and-off premises wine and beer licenses —Cont'd
Local license taxes, §4.1-233.
Prohibited acts by employees, §4.1-325.2.
State license fees, §§4.1-231, 4.1-232.
Retail on-premises wine and beer licenses.
Authorized conduct, §4.1-209.
Flight of wines and beers.
Selling, §4.1-201.
Local license taxes, §4.1-233.
Prohibited acts by employees, §4.1-325.2.
Samples, providing, §4.1-201.
State license fees, §§4.1-231, 4.1-232.
Salesmen representing out-of-state wholesalers.
Permits, §4.1-212.
Samples.
Gourmet shop licensees.
Authority to give, §4.1-209.
Retail-on premises licensee providing, §4.1-201.
Shipper's licenses.
Annual fee on shipper's license, §4.1-231.
Authorized conduct, §4.1-209.1.
Local license taxes, §4.1-233.
Records of licensees, §4.1-204.
State license fees, §§4.1-231, 4.1-232.
Sunday wine sales.
Referendum, §4.1-123.
Tasting licenses.
Authorized conduct, §4.1-206.
Tastings conducted by licensee.
Gourmet shop licensees, §4.1-209.
Persons granted retail on-premises or retail on-and-off premises licenses, §4.1-209.
Tastings conducted by manufacturers, §4.1-201.1.
Permit, §4.1-212.
Taxation.
Liter tax on wine, §§4.1-234, 4.1-235, 58.1-1708.
Local license taxes, §4.1-233.
Temporary licenses, §4.1-211.
Time of sale.
Local ordinances regulating, §4.1-129.
Unlicensed person.
Sale of or purchase for resale of wine, §4.1-326.
Virginia wine promotion fund, §3.2-3005.
Dedicated revenues, diversion, §3.2-1100.
Warehouses.
Wine stored in bonded warehouses.
Bond to secure tax liability, §4.1-238.
Wholesale wine licenses.
Authorized conduct, §4.1-207.
Grounds for refusal to grant, §4.1-223.
Local license taxes, §4.1-233.
Restricted wholesale wine licenses.
Authorized conduct, §4.1-207.1.
State license fees, §§4.1-231, 4.1-232.
Wine importers' licenses.
Authorized conduct, §4.1-207.
Limitation on license, §4.1-218.
Local license taxes, §4.1-233.
State license fees, §§4.1-231, 4.1-232.
Winery licenses.
Authorized conduct, §§4.1-207, 4.1-207.1.
Local license taxes, §4.1-233.
Manufacture and sale of cider, §4.1-213.
Sales to other winery or farm winery in closed containers for use in manufacture of wine, §4.1-201.
State license fees, §§4.1-231, 4.1-232.

WINE —Cont'd
Winery licenses —Cont'd
Tasting licenses.
Authorized conduct, §4.1-206.

WINE COOLERS.
ABC act.
Generally, §§4.1-100 to 4.1-354.
See ALCOHOLIC BEVERAGES.
Commissions.
Excise tax on wine coolers, §4.1-239.
Definitions, §4.1-100.
Excise taxes on beer and wine coolers, §§4.1-236 to 4.1-240.
Bond required to secure excise tax liability, §4.1-238.
Credit or debit card payment, §4.1-240.
Monthly reports.
Filing by nonresident manufacturer, §4.1-239.
Nonpayment, §4.1-332.
Payment of tax, §4.1-236.
Monthly reports, §4.1-239.
Refund and adjustments, §4.1-237.
Transportation regulations, §4.1-112.
Wine franchises.
Generally, §§4.1-100 to 4.1-418.
See WINE FRANCHISES.

WINE COOLERS EXCISE TAX, §§4.1-236 to 4.1-240.
Nonpayment, §4.1-332.

WINE FRANCHISES, §§4.1-400 to 4.1-418.
ABC act.
Generally, §§4.1-100 to 4.1-354.
See ALCOHOLIC BEVERAGES.
Amendment of agreement.
Agreement, defined, §4.1-401.
Good cause criteria, §4.1-406.
Notice of intent, §4.1-407.
Remedies, §4.1-409.
Transfer of business, §4.1-408.
Appellate review of board proceedings, §4.1-410.
Applicability of act, §4.1-402.
Cancellation of agreement.
Agreement, defined, §4.1-401.
Good cause criteria, §4.1-406.
Notice of intent, §4.1-407.
Remedies, §4.1-409.
Transfer of business, §4.1-408.
Change in management of winery, §4.1-414.
Coercion prohibition, §4.1-403.
Conflicts of laws, §4.1-416.
Construction of act, §§4.1-400, 4.1-402.
Definitions, §4.1-401.
Designated sales territories, §4.1-404.
Discrimination prohibition, §4.1-415.
Dual distributorships.
Defined, §4.1-401.
Sale of winery, §4.1-405.
Fixing of prices, §4.1-411.
Good faith obligation of agreement, §4.1-418.
Increase of prices, §4.1-412.
Inducement prohibition, §4.1-403.
Judicial review of board proceedings, §4.1-410.
Management of winery, §4.1-414.
Nonrenewal of agreement.
Agreement, defined, §4.1-401.
Notice of intent, §4.1-407.
Remedies, §4.1-409.
Transfer of business, §4.1-408.

WINE FRANCHISES —Cont'd
Price of product, §4.1-411.
Increase of prices, §4.1-412.
Primary area of responsibility, §4.1-404.
Purpose of act, §4.1-400.
Reasonableness.
Requirement of agreement, §4.1-418.
Refusal to renew agreement.
Good cause criteria, §4.1-406.
Resignation from agreement.
Agreement, defined, §4.1-401.
Good cause criteria, §4.1-406.
Notice of intent, §4.1-407.
Remedies, §4.1-409.
Transfer of business, §4.1-408.
Retaliatory action, §4.1-413.
Right of free association, §4.1-417.
Sale of winery, §4.1-405.
Termination of agreement.
Agreement, defined, §4.1-401.
Good cause criteria, §4.1-406.
Notice of intent, §4.1-407.
Remedies, §4.1-409.
Transfer of business, §4.1-408.
Unabridged right of free association, §4.1-417.
Waiver of compliance with act, §4.1-416.
Wholesaler's unilateral resignation from agreement.
Agreement, defined, §4.1-401.
Good cause criteria, §4.1-406.
Notice of intent, §4.1-406.
Transfer of business, §4.1-408.

WINE IMPORTERS.
Licenses.
Authorized conduct, §4.1-207.
Limitation on license, §4.1-218.
Local license taxes, §4.1-233.
State license fees, §§4.1-231, 4.1-232.

WINERIES.
Agriculture and consumer services commissioner.
Nonstock corporation established and operated to assist distribution of wines, §3.2-102.
Agritourism activity liability, §§3.2-6400 to 3.2-6402.
Authorized conduct by licensees, §4.1-207.
Contract winemaking facility.
Authority to operate, §4.1-207.
Delivery permits, §4.1-212.1.
State license fees, §4.1-231.
Farm wineries.
Bonded warehouses on or off premises.
Storing wine, §4.1-207.
Capital expenditures for new wineries and capital improvements to existing wineries.
Farm wineries and vineyards tax credit, §58.1-339.12.
Cider.
Manufacture and sale, §4.1-213.
Class A licensees.
Out-of-state products, use.
Limitation, §4.1-219.
Class B licensees.
Out-of-state products.
Limitation, §4.1-219.
Delivery or shipping wine.
License authority, §4.1-207.
Income tax credit, §58.1-339.12.
Licenses.
Authorized conduct, §4.1-207.

WINERIES —Cont'd
Farm wineries —Cont'd
Licenses —Cont'd
Limitation on license, §4.1-219.
State license fees, §§4.1-231, 4.1-232.
Limitation on licensees, §4.1-219.
Local license taxes, §4.1-233.
Manufacture of wine.
License authority, §4.1-207.
Nonstock corporation established and operated to assist distribution of wines.
Agriculture and consumer services commissioner, §3.2-102.
Out-of-state products.
Use, limitation on licensees, §4.1-219.
Persons outside the Commonwealth.
Shipping wine to, accepting shipments from, §4.1-207.
Sales to other winery or farm winery in closed containers for use in manufacture of wine, §4.1-201.
Sunday retail sales.
In county restricting Sunday beer and wine sales, §4.1-123.
Zoning, licensed farm wineries, §15.2-2288.3.
Fulfillment warehouse licenses, §4.1-209.
Shipper's licenses, §4.1-209.1.
State license fees, §4.1-231.
Income tax credit.
Farm wineries and vineyards tax credit, §58.1-339.12.
Internet wine retailer.
Licenses, granting, §4.1-207.
Licenses.
Authorized conduct, §§4.1-207, 4.1-207.1.
Cider, manufacture and sale, §4.1-213.
Delivery permits, §4.1-212.1.
State license fees, §4.1-231.
Fulfillment warehouse licenses, §4.1-209.
Shipper's licenses, §4.1-209.1.
State license fees, §4.1-231.
Local license taxes, §4.1-233.
Marketing portal licenses, §4.1-209.
Shipper's licenses, §4.1-209.1.
State license fees, §4.1-231.
Sales to other winery or farm winery in closed containers for use in manufacture of wine, §4.1-201.
Shipper's licenses.
Authorized conduct, §4.1-209.1.
State license fees, §§4.1-231, 4.1-232.
Tasting licenses.
Authorized conduct, §4.1-206.
Local license taxes, §4.1-233.
Marketing portal licenses, §4.1-209.
Shipper's licenses, §4.1-209.1.
State license fees, §4.1-231.
Restricted wholesale wine licenses.
Authorized conduct, §4.1-207.1.
Retail off-premises winery licenses.
Authorized conduct, §4.1-207.
Shipper's licenses.
Authorized conduct, §4.1-209.1.
State license fees, §§4.1-231, 4.1-232.
Storage of wine in bonded warehouses.
Permit, §4.1-212.
Tasting licenses.
Authorized conduct, §4.1-206.
Tours.
Agritourism activity liability, §§3.2-6400 to 3.2-6402.

WINERIES —Cont'd
Wholesale wine licenses.
Authorized conduct, §4.1-207.
Restricted wholesale wine licenses.
Authorized conduct, §4.1-207.1.
Wine importers' licenses.
Authorized conduct, §4.1-207.
Zoning.
Licensed farm wineries, §15.2-2288.3.

WINE VINEGAR.
Vinegar generally, §§3.2-5500 to 3.2-5507.
See VINEGAR.

WINTER SPORTS SAFETY ACT, §§8.01-227.11 to 8.01-227.23.
Accidents.
Duties of participants, §8.01-227.17.
Applicability of article, §8.01-227.23.
Assumption of risks, §8.01-227.19.
Children and minors.
Common law regarding capacity and standard of measuring conduct not abrogated, §8.01-227.21.
Definitions, §8.01-227.11.
Duties of participants, §8.01-227.17.
Assumption of risks, §8.01-227.19.
Helmets, §8.01-227.18.
Freestyle terrain.
Barricade, §8.01-227.14.
Opportunity to view in advance, §8.01-227.12.
Grooming or snowmaking operations.
Signs indicating operation of, §8.01-227.12.
Helmets, §8.01-227.18.
Inspection of tramways, §8.01-227.16.
Instruction on use of tramways, §8.01-227.16.
Liability of operator, §8.01-227.20.
Applicability of article, §8.01-227.23.
Failure to fulfill duty not negligence per se, §8.01-227.22.
Maps, §8.01-227.13.
Minors.
Common law regarding capacity and standard of measuring conduct not abrogated, §8.01-227.21.
Nighttime activities.
Lighting standards, §8.01-227.12.
Notices required on tickets, passes and contracts, §8.01-227.12.
Operator liability, §8.01-227.20.
Applicability of article, §8.01-227.23.
Failure to fulfill duty not negligence per se, §8.01-227.22.
Participants, duties and responsibilities, §8.01-227.17.
Assumption of risks, §8.01-227.19.
Helmets, §8.01-227.18.
Passenger tramways, §8.01-227.16.
Duties of participants, §8.01-227.17.
Liability of operator, §8.01-227.20.
Presumption of knowledge of inherent risks, §8.01-227.19.
Applicability of article, §8.01-227.23.
Ski patrol and first aid, §8.01-227.12.
Ski trails.
Signs indicating level of difficulty, §8.01-227.12.
Trail maps, §8.01-227.13.
Trespasser liability, §8.01-227.20.
Vehicles.
Lights required, §8.01-227.15.
Red or orange flag, §8.01-227.15.

WINTER SPORTS SAFETY ACT —Cont'd
Warnings required on tickets, passes and contracts, §8.01-227.12.

WIRE COMMUNICATIONS INTERCEPTION, §§19.2-61 to 19.2-70.3.
See ELECTRONIC SURVEILLANCE.

WIRELESS BROADBAND SERVICES.
Communication towers owned by state in unserved areas.
Lease or conveyance of license to provider by state department, agency, institution responsible for tower, §2.2-1150.2.
Virginia broadband infrastructure loan fund, §§15.2-2419 to 15.2-2429.

WIRELESS E-911 COST RECOVERY SUBCOMMITTEE, §56-484.15.

WIRELESS E-911 FUND, §56-484.17.

WIRELESS E-911 SERVICES BOARD.
Annual report, §56-484.14.
Composition, §56-484.13.
Developments in enhanced 9-1-1 service and multiline telephone systems.
Monitoring, report, §56-484.14.
Plan for implementing statewide enhanced wireless emergency services.
Development, duty, §56-484.14.
Powers and duties, §56-484.14.
Secretary of technology.
Agency responsibility, §2.2-225.
Statewide electronic addressing database.
Development, duty, §56-484.14.

WIRELESS E-911 SURCHARGE.
Collection by CMRS providers, §56-484.17.

WIRELESS PHONES.
See CELLULAR TELEPHONES.

WIRELESS SERVICE AUTHORITIES, §§15.2-5431.1 to 15.2-5431.37.
Approval of referendum, §15.2-5431.6.
Articles of incorporation, §15.2-5431.4.
Filing, §15.2-5431.7.
Audits, §15.2-5431.33.
Board, §15.2-5431.10.
Bond issues.
Contest of validity, §15.2-5431.15.
Faith and credit of government not pledged, §15.2-5431.20.
Further approval not required, §15.2-5431.18.
Interest rate swap agreements, §15.2-5431.24.
Interim receipts, §15.2-5431.17.
Legal investments, §15.2-5431.32.
Limitations contained in agreement, §15.2-5431.19.
Lost or mutilated bond, §15.2-5431.17.
Powers generally, §15.2-5431.11.
Proceeds, §15.2-5431.16.
Refunding bonds, §15.2-5431.30.
Purchase in open market, §15.2-5431.31.
Remedies of bondholder, §15.2-5431.29.
Tax exemption, §15.2-5431.21.
Temporary bonds, §15.2-5431.17.
Terms and conditions, §15.2-5431.14.
Trust agreement securing, §15.2-5431.22.
Trust funds, §15.2-5431.28.
Unclaimed funds due, §15.2-5431.23.
Certificate of incorporation, §15.2-5431.8.
Charter, §15.2-5431.8.
Closed meetings, §2.2-3711.

WIRELESS SERVICE AUTHORITIES —Cont'd
Connection fees, §15.2-5431.25.
Construction of chapter, §15.2-5431.1.
Cumulative, §15.2-5431.37.
Contracts by, §15.2-5431.12.
Interest rate swap agreements, §15.2-5431.24.
Termination of service, §15.2-5431.35.
Conveyance of property, §15.2-5431.35.
Creation, §15.2-5431.3.
Definitions, §15.2-5431.2.
Dissolution, §15.2-5431.9.
Financial statement, §15.2-5431.33.
Hearing on resolution, §15.2-5431.6.
Immunity of members, §15.2-5431.36.
Insurance for employees, §15.2-5431.13.
Lease of property, §15.2-5431.35.
Members of board, §15.2-5431.10.
Powers, §15.2-5431.11.
Public hearing.
Creation of authority, §15.2-5431.3.
Rates and charges, §15.2-5431.25.
Enforcement of payment, §15.2-5431.26.
Lien, §15.2-5431.27.
Resolution creating, §15.2-5431.3.
Advertisement, §15.2-5431.5.
Articles of incorporation, §15.2-5431.4.
Resolution to dissolve, §15.2-5431.9.
Supplemental nature of provisions, §15.2-5431.37.
Suspension of services.
Enforcement of payment, §15.2-5431.26.
Title of chapter, §15.2-5431.1.
Trust funds, §15.2-5431.28.
Use of state land, §15.2-5431.34.

WIRELESS TELEPHONE STATE POLICE ACCESS NUMBER, §56-484.18.

WIRETAPPING.
Interception of wire, electronic or oral communications, §§19.2-61 to 19.2-70.3.
See ELECTRONIC SURVEILLANCE.

WIRING OF FUNDS.
Banks, §6.2-832.

WISE COUNTY.
Coal severance tax.
Local coal severance license taxes.
Local coal road improvement severance license tax.
Distribution, §58.1-3742.
Confederate cemeteries and graves.
Disbursement of funds appropriated for upkeep, §10.1-2211.
Cumberlands airport commission, 1958 ch 439.
Cutting grass or lawn area of residential real property.
Requiring owner of occupied property, §15.2-1215.
Electric utility restructuring.
Transmission and distribution of electric energy.
Applicability of provisions suspended, §56-580.
Local licensing of motor vehicles, trailers or semitrailers.
Evidence of payment of all fees due county or solid waste authority.
Required prior to issuing license, §46.2-752.
School board.
Salary of members, §22.1-32.
Solid waste disposal fee, §15.2-2159.
Tax map reference number.
Circuit court clerk indexing by, §17.1-252.

WISE COUNTY —Cont'd
Transient occupancy tax.
Disposition of revenues, §58.1-3819.
Virginia coalfield economic development authority, §§15.2-6000 to 15.2-6015.

WITHHOLDING AND DELIVERY OF PROPERTY OF DEBTOR.
Child support enforcement by department of social services.
Orders for, §§63.2-1929 to 63.2-1935.

WITHHOLDING EXEMPTION CERTIFICATES, §§58.1-461, 58.1-470.
Fraudulent certificates or failure to supply information, §58.1-471.

WITHHOLDING INCOME TAX, §§58.1-460 to 58.1-486.3.
See INCOME TAX WITHHOLDING.

WITHHOLDING OF INCOME.
See INCOME WITHHOLDING.

WITNESS AND CRIME VICTIM ASSISTANCE PROGRAM, §§19.2-368.1 to 19.2-368.18.
See CRIME VICTIM AND WITNESS ASSISTANCE.

WITNESSES, VA SCt Rules 2:601 to 2:615.
ABC board.
Allowances to witnesses, §4.1-109.
Requiring forensic scientist to appear, §4.1-352.
Self-incrimination, §4.1-350.
Addresses or telephone numbers of witnesses in criminal proceedings.
Nondisclosure, §§19.2-11.2, 19.2-269.2.
Adverse interests.
Impeachment, VA SCt Rule 2:607.
Adverse parties.
Effect of refusal to testify, §8.01-401.
Adverse witnesses.
Impeachment, §8.01-403.
Affirmation, VA SCt Rule 2:603.
Allowances to witnesses generally, §§17.1-611 to 17.1-617. See within this heading, "Fees and travel expenses."
Anatomical gifts.
Amendment or revocation of gift prior to donor's death, §32.1-291.6.
Method of making gift prior to donor's death, §32.1-291.5.
Refusal to make gift, §32.1-291.7.
Antitrust laws, §59.1-9.10.
Arbitration.
Compelling attendance of witnesses, §8.01-581.06.
Cross-examination, §8.01-581.04.
Arrest.
Securing witness from or for another state, §19.2-275.
Assistance programs.
Crime victims and witnesses.
See CRIME VICTIM AND WITNESS ASSISTANCE.
Criminal justice services department.
Establishment, §9.1-104.
Attorney discipline.
District committees proceedings, VA SCt Rule Pt 6 §IV Par 13-16.
Reinstatement.
Character witnesses, VA SCt Rule Pt 6 §IV Par 13-25.
Attorneys at law.
Rules of professional conduct.
Lawyer as witness, VA SCt Rule Pt 6 §II Rule 3.7.

WITNESSES —Cont'd
Auditor of public accounts.
Powers as to, §30-136.
Bail.
Conditions of release of material witness, §19.2-127.
Bias, VA SCt Rule 2:610.
Boat dealers.
Witness fees, hearings, §29.1-803.
Bribery, §18.2-441.1.
Immunity of witnesses, §18.2-445.
Building code technical review board.
Compelling attendance of witnesses, §36-115.
Calling by court, VA SCt Rule 2:614.
Child abuse or neglect.
Physicians-patient privilege and husband-wife privilege.
Inapplicability, §63.2-1519.
Two way closed circuit television.
Testimony of child, §63.2-1521.
Videotaped recording of complaining witness, §63.2-1523.
Child custody and visitation.
Uniform child custody jurisdiction and enforcement act.
Taking testimony in another state, §20-146.10.
Children, psychiatric treatment.
Hearing on involuntary commitment, §16.1-344.
Child victims.
Competency to testify, §§8.01-396.1, 19.2-267.
Two-way closed-circuit television, §18.2-67.9.
Cleric-penitent privilege, §8.01-400, VA SCt Rule 2:503.
Commissioners in chancery.
Compelling attendance of witnesses, §8.01-612.
Compelling attendance of witnesses.
Arrest.
Securing witness from or for another state, §19.2-275.
Attendance before commissioner of another state, §8.01-407.
Commissioners in chancery, §8.01-612.
Convict witnesses.
Criminal cases, §19.2-271.1.
Execution of process in another locality, §8.01-409.
Inmate witnesses.
Civil cases, §8.01-410.
Issuance of summons, §8.01-407.
Prior permission requirement, §8.01-407.
Recognizance taken upon continuance of case, §8.01-408.
Compensation.
Criminal cases.
Misdemeanor cases, §19.2-331.
Out-of-state witnesses, §19.2-330.
State officers and employees, §19.2-332.
Fees and travel expenses. See within this heading, "Fees and travel expenses."
Competency.
Certain judicial officers in criminal cases, §19.2-271, VA SCt Rule 2:605.
Child witnesses, §8.01-396.1.
Criminal cases, §19.2-267.
Clerks of court, VA SCt Rule 2:605.
Convicts as witnesses.
Court issuance of release order to director, §19.2-269.1.
Generally, §19.2-269.
Court personnel, VA SCt Rule 2:605.
General rule, VA SCt Rule 2:601.

WITNESSES —Cont'd
Competency —Cont'd
Husband and wife, §8.01-398.
Child abuse or neglect.
Inapplicability of privilege in legal proceeding, §63.2-1519.
Inmates as witnesses, §§8.01-410, 19.2-267.
Judges, §19.2-271, VA SCt Rule 2:605.
Jurors, VA SCt Rule 2:606.
Presumption, §8.01-396.
Prostitution, procuring prosecutions, §18.2-360.
Rulings, incompetency, VA SCt Rule 2:601.
Wills.
Execution procedure, §§64.2-403, 64.2-404.
Interested persons, §64.2-405.
Compulsory process, US Const Amd 6.
Confrontation clause, VA Const Art I §8, US Const Amd 6.
Contradiction.
Prior inconsistent statements, §§8.01-403, 8.01-404, VA SCt Rule 2:613.
Corroboration.
Incapacity of one party to testify, §8.01-397.
Court personnel.
Competency, VA SCt Rule 2:605.
Credibility.
Hearsay exceptions.
Attacking and supporting credibility of hearsay declarant, VA SCt Rule 2:806.
Preliminary determinations, VA SCt Rule 2:104.
Credit unions.
Examinations.
Powers of commission as to witnesses, §6.2-1309.
Crime victim and witness assistance program, §§19.2-11.01 to 19.2-11.4.
See CRIME VICTIM AND WITNESS ASSISTANCE.
Criminal cases.
Administration of oath to witness, §§8.01-405, 19.2-267.
Allowances to.
Generally, §§17.1-611 to 17.1-617.
Maximum number of witnesses to be paid, §17.1-617.
Change of venue.
Recognition of witnesses, §19.2-252.
Child victims' testimony, §19.2-267.
Using two-way closed-circuit television, §18.2-67.9.
Compelling attendance of witnesses, §§8.01-407, 19.2-267, VA SCt Rule 3A:12.
Inmate witnesses, §19.2-267.
Compensation.
Allowances, §19.2-328.
Generally, §§17.1-611 to 17.1-617.
Maximum number to be paid, §17.1-617.
Misdemeanor cases, §19.2-331.
Out-of-state witnesses, §19.2-330.
State officers and employees, §19.2-332.
Competency.
Prostitution, procuring prosecutions, §18.2-360.
Confrontation, VA Const Art I §8, US Const Amd 6.
Contempt, procedure, §19.2-11.
Convict witnesses.
Competency to testify, §19.2-269.
Court issuance of release order to director, §19.2-269.1.
Department of motor vehicles' crash investigation team, §§8.01-402, 19.2-267.

WITNESSES —Cont'd
Criminal cases —Cont'd
Failure to appear.
Authority of law-enforcement officer to issue summons, §19.2-267.1.
Former testimony.
When statement by accused as witness not received as evidence, §19.2-270.
Gambling prosecutions.
Immunity, §18.2-337.
Husband and wife.
Compelling testimony, §19.2-271.2.
Competency to testify, §19.2-271.1.
Immunity.
Bribery prosecutions, §§18.2-445, 18.2-450.
Combinations to injure others in reputation, trade, business or profession.
Protection of persons testifying or producing evidence, §18.2-501.
Drug offense prosecutions, §18.2-262.
Former trial testimony of accused as witness, §19.2-270.
Gambling prosecutions, §18.2-337.
Investigation of elected officials, §52-8.2.
Perjury prosecutions, §18.2-437.
Inmate witnesses, §19.2-267.
Interpreters in criminal cases, §§19.2-164, 19.2-164.1.
Judicial officers.
Competency to testify, §19.2-271, VA SCt Rule 2:605.
Nondisclosure of addresses or telephone numbers of witnesses, §§19.2-11.2, 19.2-269.2.
Polygraph requested of complaining witness.
Written notice, §19.2-9.1.
Prior inconsistent statements reduced to writing, §19.2-268.1, VA SCt Rule 2:613.
Right of accused to testify, §19.2-268.
Securing attendance from another state.
Compensation to out-of-state witnesses, §19.2-330.
General provisions, §§19.2-272 to 19.2-282.
See EXTRADITION OF WITNESSES.
Summons issued by Commonwealth's attorney, §19.2-267.
Summons issued by law enforcement officer, §19.2-267.1.
Witness assistance program.
General provisions, §§19.2-368.1 to 19.2-368.18.
See CRIME VICTIM AND WITNESS ASSISTANCE.
Cross-examination.
Prior inconsistent statements, §8.01-404.
Scope, VA SCt Rule 2:611.
Deaf and hearing impaired persons.
Interpreters in criminal cases, §19.2-164.1.
Privileged communications by interpreters, §§8.01-400.1, 19.2-164.
Recording testimony of deaf witness, §8.01-406.
Death by wrongful act.
Health care providers, actions against.
Certification of expert witness opinion, §8.01-50.1.
Death taxes, interstate compromise and arbitration, §58.1-924.
Department of agriculture and consumer services.
Compelling attendance of witnesses, §18.2-340.18.
Depositions.
Exclusion of deposition for failure to testify ore tenus, §8.01-396.

WITNESSES —Cont'd
Desertion and nonsupport.
Competency of spouses as witnesses, §20-82.
District courts.
Compelling attendance of witnesses, VA SCt Rule 7A:12.
Recognizance upon continuance of case.
Criminal cases, §16.1-131.
Drug offenses.
Self-incrimination, witness not excused from testifying, §18.2-262.
Election law offense prosecutions.
Immunity, §24.2-1018.
Escheats.
Inquests, §55-173.
Ethics advisory panels, senate and house of general assembly.
Power to compel attendance by subpoena, §30-115.
Evidence rules, VA SCt Rules 2:601 to 2:615.
Exclusion of witnesses, VA SCt Rule 2:615.
Civil cases, §8.01-375.
Criminal cases, §19.2-265.1.
Complaining witness.
Misdemeanor cases prosecuted without attorney, §19.2-265.5.
Victims and family members, §19.2-265.01.
Expert witnesses, §8.01-401.1, VA SCt Rules 2:701 to 2:706.
Basis of expert testimony, VA SCt Rule 2:703.
Chiropractor as expert witness, §8.01-401.2.
Exclusion, VA SCt Rule 2:615.
Exclusion of witnesses in civil cases, §8.01-375.
Facts or data used in testimony, VA SCt Rule 2:705.
Fees for attendance and mileage for witness compelled to attend and testify, §17.1-612.
Credit counseling.
Private right of action to enforce provisions, §6.2-2023.
Nonsuit.
Determination of reasonableness of expenses, §8.01-380.
Hearsay exceptions, §8.01-401.1.
Learned treatises, VA SCt Rule 2:706.
Hearsay exceptions, VA SCt Rule 2:803.
Medical malpractice.
Certification of expert witness opinion, §8.01-20.1.
Number each party may call, §8.01-581.20.
Treating health care provider witnesses, number not limited, §8.01-581.20.
Opinion testimony, VA SCt Rule 2:702.
Lay witnesses, VA SCt Rule 2:701.
Ultimate issue, VA SCt Rule 2:704.
Podiatrist as expert witness, §8.01-401.2:1.
Use of experts generally, VA SCt Rule 2:702.
Wrongful death.
Health care providers, actions against.
Certification of expert witness opinion, §8.01-50.1.
Fair housing.
Witness fees, §36-96.19.
Fees and travel expenses, §§17.1-611 to 17.1-617.
Allowances to witnesses generally, §17.1-612.
Allowances to witnesses summoned for Commonwealth, §17.1-611.
Boat dealers.
Hearings, §29.1-803.
Certificate of payment, §17.1-613.
Certification of list of entries made on behalf of witnesses, §17.1-614.

WITNESSES —Cont'd
Fees and travel expenses —Cont'd
Claim for payment, time limitation, §17.1-615.
Criminal cases.
Misdemeanor cases, §19.2-331.
Number of witnesses paid, §17.1-617.
Out-of-state witnesses, §19.2-330.
State officers and employees, §19.2-332.
Entering and certifying attendance, proceedings to compel payment for attendance.
Charged to party for whom witness attended, §17.1-269.
Expert witnesses compelled to attend and testify, §17.1-612.
Credit counseling.
Private right of action to enforce provisions, §6.2-2023.
Fair housing, §36-96.19.
Juvenile proceedings, §16.1-276.
List of entries made on behalf of witnesses, §17.1-614.
Nonallowance of entry for witness, §17.1-616.
Nonresident witnesses, allowances, §17.1-612.
Nonsuit.
Determination of reasonableness of expenses, §8.01-380.
Number of witnesses paid in criminal cases, §17.1-617.
Payment by treasurer of county or city, §17.1-611.
Payment of allowances generally, §17.1-612.
Payment out of state treasury, §17.1-613.
Time limitation for presenting claim, §17.1-615.
Prisoners' health care.
Involuntary admission and treatment, §53.1-40.8.
Restrictions on costs, §17.1-616.
State board of corrections investigations, §53.1-115.
Summoning, fee for, §17.1-272.
Tax commissioner, allowance for witnesses summoned by, §58.1-218.
Time limitation for presenting claim, §17.1-615.
Unemployment compensation.
Claims adjudication, §60.2-624.
When entry for witnesses not allowed, §17.1-616.
Workers' compensation commission.
Hearings, §65.2-202.
Fire investigations.
State police powers, §27-60.
Fire marshals, local.
Powers to compel, §27-32.
Forensic science department.
Professionals qualified to testify, §9.1-1102.
General assembly.
Administration of oaths, §30-11.
Attendance of witnesses, §30-10.
Privilege of members, clerks and assistants, §30-6.
Grand juries.
Multi-jurisdiction grand juries.
Counsel for witness, §19.2-215.5.
Examination of witnesses, §19.2-215.8.
Warnings given to witnesses, §19.2-215.7.
When witness in contempt, §19.2-215.7.
Special grand juries.
Presence of counsel for a witness, §19.2-209.
Health regulatory boards.
Interview of fact witnesses by investigative staff, §54.1-2400.2.
Hearsay exceptions.
Credibility.
Attacking and supporting credibility of hearsay declarant, VA SCt Rule 2:806.

WITNESSES —Cont'd
Hearsay exceptions —Cont'd
Dead man rule, VA SCt Rule 2:805.
Identification, statement by witness, VA SCt Rule 2:803.
Homicide.
Capital murder, §18.2-31.
Husband and wife in criminal cases.
Compelling testimony, §19.2-271.2.
Competency to testify, §19.2-271.1.
Identification, statement by witness.
Hearsay exceptions, VA SCt Rule 2:803.
Immunity.
Bribery prosecutions, §§18.2-445, 18.2-450.
Combinations to injure others in reputation, trade, business or profession.
Protection of persons testifying or producing evidence, §18.2-501.
Drug offense prosecutions, §18.2-262.
Election law offense prosecutions, §24.2-1018.
Former testimony by accused, §19.2-270.
Gambling prosecutions, §18.2-337.
Houses of prostitution.
Abating public nuisances, §48-15.
Investigation of elected officials, §52-8.2.
Multi-jurisdiction grand jury testimony, §19.2-215.7.
Perjury prosecutions, §18.2-437.
Special grand jury proceedings.
Compelling witness to testify or produce evidence.
Invocation of right to incriminate bona fide, §19.2-208.
Impeachment, VA SCt Rule 2:607.
Adverse interests, VA SCt Rule 2:607.
Character witness, cross-examination, VA SCt Rule 2:608.
Conviction of crime, VA SCt Rule 2:609.
Grounds, VA SCt Rule 2:607.
Juvenile case transferred to circuit court.
Transfer hearing statements by child, §16.1-269.2.
Perjury, unadjudicated, VA SCt Rule 2:608.
Prior false accusations, sexual assault cases, VA SCt Rule 2:608.
Prior inconsistent statement, §8.01-403, VA SCt Rule 2:613.
Reduction to writing, §19.2-268.1.
Reputation for truthtelling, VA SCt Rule 2:608.
Specific instances of conduct, VA SCt Rule 2:608.
Inmate as witness, §§8.01-410, 19.2-269, 19.2-269.1.
Insurance companies.
Annual actuarial opinions, §38.2-1315.1.
Examinations.
Power of state corporation commission, §38.2-1318.
Insurance rate investigations by attorney general, §38.2-1916.1.
Interest of witness.
Presumption of competency to testify, §8.01-396.
Internet.
Identifying anonymous persons.
Tortious or illegal communications.
Procedure for identifying, §8.01-407.1.
Interpreters, VA SCt Rule 2:604.
Non-English speaking persons in civil cases, §8.01-384.1:1.
Non-English speaking persons in criminal cases, §19.2-164.

WITNESSES —Cont'd
Interpreters —Cont'd
Privileged communications.
Interpreters for the deaf, §§8.01-400.1, 19.2-164.
Interrogation.
By court, VA SCt Rule 2:614.
Mode and order of interrogation and presentation, VA SCt Rule 2:611.
Judicial inquiry and review commission.
Fees and mileage, §17.1-915.
Order compelling attendance and testimony, §17.1-909.
Powers as to, §§17.1-903, 17.1-907.
Jurors as witnesses.
Competency, VA SCt Rule 2:606.
Juvenile and domestic relations district courts.
Compelling attendance of witnesses, VA SCt Rule 8:13.
Juvenile proceedings.
Prisoners.
Transportation orders, §16.1-276.2.
Summons requiring attendance in testimony, §16.1-265.
Lack of personal knowledge, VA SCt Rule 2:602.
Lay witness opinion.
Ultimate fact in issue, §8.01-401.3.
Leading questions, VA SCt Rule 2:611.
Learned treatises.
Expert witnesses, VA SCt Rule 2:706.
Living will requirements, §54.1-2983.
Material witnesses.
Conditions of release, §19.2-127.
Meat and poultry products inspection.
Agriculture and consumer services commissioner, §3.2-5416.
Medical malpractice.
Expert witnesses.
Certification of expert witness opinion, §8.01-20.1.
Certification of expert witness opinion at time of service of process, §16.1-83.1.
Number each party may call, §8.01-581.20.
Treating health care provider witnesses, number not limited, §8.01-581.20.
Medical malpractice review panels.
Appearance of panel members as witnesses, §8.01-581.8.
Attorney-issued summons, §8.01-407.
Compelling attendance of witnesses, §8.01-581.6, MedMal Rule 6.
Expert testimony, §8.01-581.6, MedMal Rule 7.
Medicine and health care professions.
Medical reports or records as evidence in district court proceedings.
Testimony of health care providers, §16.1-88.2.
Mental health.
Children, psychiatric treatment.
Hearing on involuntary commitment, §16.1-344.
Mode and order of interrogation and presentation, VA SCt Rule 2:611.
Motor vehicle dealers.
Power of board to summon witnesses, §46.2-1504.
Motor vehicles department.
Summoning witnesses and taking testimony, §46.2-369.
Non-English speaking persons.
Interpreters in civil cases, §8.01-384.1:1.
Interpreters in criminal cases, §19.2-164.
Oaths, VA SCt Rule 2:603.
Who may administer, §8.01-405.

WITNESSES —Cont'd
Obstructing justice by threats or force, §18.2-460.
Bail, presumption against admitting to bail for certain offense, §19.2-120.
Opinion testimony.
Expert witnesses, §8.01-401.1, VA SCt Rule 2:702.
Hearsay exception, §8.01-401.1.
Ultimate issue, VA SCt Rule 2:704.
Lay witnesses, VA SCt Rule 2:701.
Ultimate fact in issue, §8.01-401.3, VA SCt Rule 2:704.
Order of interrogation and presentation, VA SCt Rule 2:611.
Parties.
Presumption of competency to testify, §8.01-396.
Perjury, §§18.2-434 to 18.2-437.
Perpetuation of testimony.
Abolition of common-law proceeding, §8.01-420.1.
Personal knowledge or experience.
Lack of, VA SCt Rule 2:602.
Opinion testimony by lay witnesses, VA SCt Rule 2:701.
Physician-patient privilege, §8.01-399, VA SCt Rule 2:505.
Child abuse or neglect.
Inapplicability in legal proceedings, §63.2-1519.
Police officers.
Witness fees for attendance as witness, §15.2-1710.
Polygraph examination.
Inadmissible in any proceeding, §8.01-418.2.
Prejudice, VA SCt Rule 2:610.
Preliminary hearings.
Examination of witnesses, §19.2-183.
Sequestration of witnesses, §19.2-184.
Presentation of evidence.
Mode and order of interrogation and presentation, VA SCt Rule 2:611.
Priest-penitent privilege, §8.01-400, VA SCt Rule 2:503.
Prior inconsistent statements.
Criminal cases, §19.2-268.1.
Cross-examination, §8.01-404.
Impeaching witness proving adverse, §8.01-403, VA SCt Rule 2:613.
Prior sexual conduct.
Evidence, VA SCt Rule 2:412.
Prisoners' health care.
Involuntary admission and treatment.
Witness fees, §53.1-40.8.
Privileged from arrest under civil process.
Grand jury witnesses, §§8.01-327.1, 8.01-327.2.
Professional counselor-client privilege, §8.01-400.2, VA SCt Rule 2:506.
Prostitution.
Houses of prostitution.
Immunity to witnesses, §48-15.
Protection of witness to crime, §19.2-11.01.
Psychiatric treatment of children.
Hearing on involuntary commitment, §16.1-344.
Psychologist-client privilege, §8.01-400.2, VA SCt Rule 2:506.
Clinical psychologist, §8.01-399, VA SCt Rule 2:505.
Public accountants.
Hearings, §54.1-4416.
Qualifications.
Preliminary determinations, VA SCt Rule 2:104.
Rabbi-penitent privilege, §8.01-400, VA SCt Rule 2:503.

WITNESSES —Cont'd
Recognizances.
Conditions, §19.2-135.
Continuance of criminal case in district court, §16.1-131.
Recordation of testimony.
Deaf witnesses, §8.01-406.
Refreshing memory, use of writings, VA SCt Rule 2:612.
Rule on witnesses, VA SCt Rule 2:615.
Civil trials, §8.01-375.
Criminal trials, §§19.2-265.01, 19.2-265.1, 19.2-265.5.
Preliminary hearings, §19.2-184.
Securing attendance from another state in criminal proceedings, §§19.2-272 to 19.2-282.
See EXTRADITION OF WITNESSES.
Self-incrimination.
Constitutional provisions, US Const Amd 5.
Sequestration, VA SCt Rule 2:615.
Civil trials, §8.01-375.
Criminal trials, §§19.2-265.01, 19.2-265.1, 19.2-265.5.
Preliminary hearings, §19.2-184.
Service of notice, process and other papers.
Additional method of serving summons, §8.01-298.
Sewage handling and disposal appeal review board, §32.1-166.7.
Sex offender and crimes against minors registry.
Failure to register or provision of false information.
Calling custodian of records as adverse witness, §18.2-472.1.
Sexual assault.
Recent complaint hearsay exception, §19.2-268.2.
Social worker-client privilege, §8.01-400.2, VA SCt Rule 2:506.
Spousal immunity.
Spouse right of action exception, §8.01-398.
Spousal privilege.
Child abuse or neglect.
Inapplicability of privilege in legal proceeding, §63.2-1519.
State board of corrections investigations.
Witness fees, §53.1-15.
State corporation commission.
Power to compel attendance, §12.1-13, VA Const Art IX §3.
Summary jury trial.
Testimony of non-party witnesses, §8.01-576.3.
Summons and process.
Fee for summoning, §17.1-272.
Service of summons, §§8.01-296, 8.01-298.
Tax commissioner and department of taxation.
Fees and mileage.
Allowance to witnesses summoned, §58.1-218.
Service of writs, notices, etc., compelling attendance, §58.1-216.
Representation of witness, §58.1-1834.
Treason.
Two witnesses required, US Const Art III §3.
Ultimate fact in issue rule, §8.01-401.3.
Unemployment compensation.
Claims adjudication.
Fees, §60.2-624.
Victim and witness assistance.
See CRIME VICTIM AND WITNESS ASSISTANCE.
Voters during election, privilege from attendance at court, VA Const Art II §9.

WITNESSES —Cont'd
Wills.
Execution procedure, §§64.2-403, 64.2-404.
Interested persons as competent witnesses, §64.2-405.
Presumption of formal execution by military personnel, §64.2-408.
Probate.
Evidence.
What may be admitted, §64.2-449.
Proving of wills.
Depositions, §64.2-447.
Self-proving, §§64.2-452, 64.2-453.
Witness assistance.
See CRIME VICTIM AND WITNESS ASSISTANCE.
Witness protection program, §52-35.
Workers' compensation commission.
Witness fees, §65.2-202.
Writing used to refresh memory, VA SCt Rule 2:612.
Wrongful death.
Health care providers, actions against.
Certification of expert witness opinion, §8.01-50.1.

WITNESS FEES.
Crime victim and witness assistance.
See CRIME VICTIM AND WITNESS ASSISTANCE.
Generally.
See WITNESSES.

WITNESS PROTECTION, §§19.2-11.01, 52-35.

WOLVES.
Hybrid canines, §§3.2-6581 to 3.2-6584.
Importation, §29.1-542.

WOMAN SUFFRAGE, US Const Amd 19.

WOMEN, COUNCIL ON, §§2.2-2630, 2.2-2631.
Budget of state.
Review and comment prior to submission, §2.2-2631.
Composition, §2.2-2630.
Creation, §2.2-2630.
Powers and duties, §2.2-2631.
Purpose, §2.2-2630.
Research.
Powers and duties, §2.2-2631.
Scholarships.
Establishment, §2.2-2631.

WOMEN, INFANTS AND CHILDREN SPECIAL SUPPLEMENTAL FOOD PROGRAM.
Voter registration agencies designated by state, §24.2-411.2.
Persons authorized to receive applications, §24.2-415.1.

WOMEN-OWNED BUSINESSES.
Colleges and universities.
Procurement of goods and services from (eff until 1/1/2014), §2.2-1404.1.
Deception in obtaining certificate, §18.2-213.1.
Local ordinances supporting, §15.2-965.1.
Procurement by public bodies.
Participation, §2.2-4310.

WOMEN'S ATTORNEYS ASSOCIATION.
Judicial conference for district courts.
Honorary members, president and secretary, §16.1-218.

WOOD.
Agricultural and forestal districts.
Wood products, §§15.2-4300 to 15.2-4407.
Forest management of state-owned lands fund, §§10.1-1120 to 10.1-1123.
Forest products tax, §§58.1-1600 to 58.1-1622.
See FOREST PRODUCTS TAX.
Reforestation of timberlands, §§10.1-1170 to 10.1-1176.
See REFORESTATION OF TIMBERLANDS.
Timber.
See TIMBER.
Timber brands, §§59.1-103 to 59.1-115.
See TIMBER BRANDS.
Trees.
See TREES.

WOODLAWN PLANTATION.
Appropriations for maintenance, §10.1-2212.

WOODROW WILSON BIRTHPLACE FOUNDATION, INCORPORATED.
Woodrow Wilson home at Staunton.
Appropriations for maintenance, §10.1-2212.

WOODROW WILSON BRIDGE AND TUNNEL COMPACT, §33.1-320.2.

WOODROW WILSON PRESIDENCY CENTENNIAL COMMISSION, §§30-319 to 30-325.
Advisory council, §30-323.
Chair and vice-chair, §30-320.
Compensation of members, §30-322.
Duties, §30-323.
Established, §30-319.
Expenses of members, §30-322.
Expiration of chapter, §30-325.
Fund established, §30-321.
Meetings, §30-320.
Members, §30-320.
Powers, §30-323.
Purpose, §30-319.
Reporting, §30-323.
Staff support, §30-324.
Sunset provision, §30-325.
Terms of office, §30-320.

WOODROW WILSON REHABILITATION CENTER.
Special education.
Child's individualized education program calls for placement in.
Reimbursement to school board, §22.1-218.
State police officers' disability retirement.
Entitlement to maintenance and services, §51.1-209.

WOODS.
Setting fire to, §18.2-86.
Carelessly damaging property by fire, §18.2-88.
Intentionally setting fire whereby another damaged or jeopardized, §18.2-87.

WOOD WASTES.
Boilers and heating equipment using.
Division of engineering and buildings to maintain information on, §2.2-1135.
Renewable electricity production program.
Grants, §§67-900 to 67-903.

WOODY SHRUB ROSA MULTIFLORA.
Noxious weed control.
Counties, cities or towns, §15.2-902.

WORK DAY.
County manager form of government.
Establishing times and conditions of employment, §15.2-640.
Urban county executive form of government.
Establishing time and conditions of employment, §15.2-849.

WORKED-OUT AREAS OF COAL MINES.
Posting danger signs, sealing or ventilating, §45.1-161.228.

WORKER RETRAINING TAX CREDIT.
Income tax on corporations, §58.1-439.6.

WORKERS' COMPENSATION, §§65.2-100 to 65.2-1310.
Acceptance of provisions, presumption, §65.2-300.
Actions on awards found void ab initio.
Tolling of limitation period, §8.01-229.
Administrative process act.
Exemptions from case decisions, §2.2-4018.
Agreements as to compensation, §65.2-701.
Disagreements, §65.2-702.
Enforcement, §65.2-710.
AmeriCorps members.
Ineligibility to receive certain benefits, §§65.2-500, 65.2-502, 65.2-512.
Assignments.
Compensation, §65.2-531.
Attempt by employee to injure another.
Compensation not allowed, §65.2-306.
Attorneys' fees, §§65.2-713, 65.2-714.
Average weekly wage.
Compensation to dependents of employee killed, §65.2-512.
Deduction of voluntary payments by employer, §65.2-520.
Defined, §65.2-101.
Partial disability.
Compensation for, §65.2-502.
Post-injury average weekly wage.
Partial disability, compensation for, §65.2-502.
Awards, §65.2-704.
Conclusiveness, §65.2-706.
Interest on appealed awards, §65.2-707.
Cost of living adjustments, §65.2-709.
Enforcement, §65.2-710.
Procurement by fraud, misrepresentation or unreported changes in condition, §65.2-712.
Recordation, §65.2-710.
Reviews, §65.2-705.
Changes in conditions, §65.2-708.
Interest on appealed awards, §65.2-707.
Satisfying, §65.2-710.
Black lung disease.
Compensation calculations, §65.2-504.
Special provisions for, §65.2-514.
Death benefits, §65.2-513.
Special provisions, §65.2-514.
Breach of rule or regulation.
Compensation not allowed, §65.2-306.
Burden of proof.
Defenses to allowance of compensation, §65.2-306.
Cancer.
Presumption as to death or disability from cancer, §65.2-402.
Children or minors.
Compensation upon death from other causes, §65.2-511.

WORKERS' COMPENSATION —Cont'd
Children or minors —Cont'd
Death benefits, §65.2-512.
Chronic occupational lung diseases, §65.2-513.
Special provisions, §65.2-514.
Who may receive payment, §65.2-525.
Determination of dependency, §§65.2-515, 65.2-516.
Termination of dependency, §65.2-517.
Child support enforcement by department of social services.
Attachment of benefits through workers' compensation commission, §63.2-1941.
Claims.
Appliances.
Supplying, §65.2-603.
Artificial limbs, §65.2-603.
Chiropractic treatment, §65.2-603.
Effect of filing claims, §65.2-601.1.
Filing time, §§65.2-601, 65.2-602.
Independent medical examination, §65.2-606.
Medical examinations ordered by employer or commission, §65.2-607.
Medical treatment.
Duty to furnish, §65.2-603.
Panel of physicians.
Supplying, §65.2-603.
Prescription drugs, use of therapeutically equivalent instead of brand name, §65.2-603.1.
Presumption that injuries arose out of and were in course of employment, §65.2-105.
Stay of debt collection activities by health care providers, §65.2-601.1.
Vocational rehabilitation.
Duty to furnish, §65.2-603.
Coal workers' pneumoconiosis.
Compensation calculations.
Special provisions, §65.2-514.
Death benefits, §65.2-513.
Special provisions, §65.2-514.
Commission.
Initial notice by certified mail, subsequent notices by regular mail, §65.2-101.1.
Personnel administration system, exemptions, §2.2-2905.
Compensation not allowed, grounds, §65.2-306.
Conservatorship.
Receipt of payment, §65.2-525.
Contractors.
Coverage, §65.2-302.
Indemnity of principal from subcontractors, §65.2-304.
Proceedings against contractors, §65.2-303.
Recovery from subcontractors, §65.2-303.
Controlled substance, use by employee.
Compensation not allowed, §65.2-306.
Copies of notices, opinions, etc., furnished employee, employer and compensation carrier, §65.2-715.
Cost of living adjustments, §65.2-709.
Coverage exclusivity, §65.2-307.
Creditor claims.
Exemption from, §65.2-531.
Criminal justice training academy trainees.
Employment and coverage status, §65.2-106.
Criminal offenses.
Payroll reports.
Withholding or providing false or misleading information, §65.2-1006.

WORKERS' COMPENSATION —Cont'd
Death benefits, §65.2-512.
Chronic occupational lung diseases, §65.2-513.
Special provisions, §65.2-514.
Compensation upon death from other causes, §65.2-511.
Who may receive payment and receipt, §65.2-525.
Deductions from amount to be paid as compensation.
Voluntary payments by employer, §65.2-520.
Defenses to allowance of compensation, §65.2-306.
Defined terms, §65.2-101.
Child, §65.2-515.
Disability, §65.2-1102.
Health systems area, §65.2-1300.
Hospital, §65.2-1300.
Injurious exposure, §65.2-404.
Medical attention, §65.2-603.
Medical care, §65.2-603.
Medical report, §65.2-603.
Medical service, §65.2-603.
Occupational disease, §65.2-400.
Other party, §65.2-800.
Parent, §65.2-515.
Peer review.
Medical costs, §65.2-1300.
Physician.
Peer review of medical costs, §65.2-1300.
Utilization review.
Peer review of medical costs, §65.2-1300.
Dependents.
Death benefits, §65.2-512.
Chronic occupational lung diseases, §65.2-513.
Special provisions, §65.2-514.
Compensation upon death from other causes, §65.2-511.
Determination of dependency, §§65.2-515, 65.2-516.
Termination of dependency, §65.2-517.
Who may receive payment, §65.2-525.
Disagreements as to compensation, §65.2-702.
Disallowance grounds, §65.2-306.
Disclosures.
Duty of employee or dependent receiving payments, §65.2-712.
Earning change reports, §65.2-712.
Emergency management activities, §44-146.23.
Employee.
Defined, §65.2-101.
Criminal justice training academy trainees, employment and coverage status, §65.2-106.
Employer.
Defined, §65.2-101.
Employer protection when employee sues third party, §§65.2-310, 65.2-311.
Determination of employer's offset, §65.2-313.
Employment change reports, §65.2-712.
Employment status determination by commission.
Estoppel effect, §65.2-706.1.
Exclusivity of coverage, §65.2-307.
Executive officers.
Rejecting coverage, §65.2-300.
False statements or representations.
Awards, §65.2-312.
Firefighters.
Extraterritorial action.
Coverage, §27-1.
Injury where weather constitutes particular risk of employment of public safety officer, §65.2-301.1.

WORKERS' COMPENSATION —Cont'd
Firefighters —Cont'd
Off-duty.
Coverage, §65.2-102.
First responders off duty during state of emergency.
Coverage, §65.2-104.
Food stamp employment and training program participants.
Ineligibility to receive certain benefits, §§65.2-500, 65.2-502, 65.2-512.
Foreign injuries, §65.2-508.
Fraud, procuring payments by.
Recovery by commission, §65.2-712.
Generic prescription drugs.
Use of therapeutically equivalent instead of brand name, §65.2-603.1.
Guardians.
Receipt of payment, §65.2-525.
Hazardous substance discharges.
Preventing, cleaning up, treating, etc., §44-146.23.
Hearings, §65.2-704.
Commission member absent, appointment of deputy to participate, §65.2-705.
Costs, §65.2-713.
Depositions, §65.2-703.
Disagreements as to compensation, §65.2-702.
Interrogatories, §65.2-703.
Rehearings, §65.2-705.
Heart disease.
Presumptions as to death or disability from, §65.2-402.
Hepatitis, meningococcal meningitis, tuberculosis or HIV.
Presumptions, death or disability, §65.2-402.1.
Hospital charges for services, §65.2-714.
Hypertension.
Presumptions as to death or disability from, §65.2-402.
IME, §65.2-606.
Imprisonment.
Reports, §65.2-712.
Suspension of benefits, §65.2-510.1.
Incapacitated persons.
Payments.
Receipt by whom, §65.2-525.
Independent medical examinations, §65.2-606.
Infectious disease.
Death or disability from.
Presumptions, §65.2-402.1.
Information provided employee, employer and compensation carrier, §65.2-715.
Injured employee not eligible for lawful employment.
Not entitled to partial disability compensation, §65.2-502.
Injury defined, §65.2-101.
Insurance and self-insurance.
Deductibles on policies, §65.2-813.1.
Drug-free workplace programs.
Premium discounts, §65.2-813.2.
Generally, §§65.2-800 to 65.2-824.
See WORKERS' COMPENSATION INSURANCE AND SELF-INSURANCE.
Intoxication of employee.
Compensation not allowed, §65.2-306.
Joint employer liability, §65.2-529.
Judicial retirement system.
Workers' compensation guarantee.
Disability retirement allowance, §51.1-308.

WORKERS' COMPENSATION —Cont'd
Jurisdiction.
Employee status.
Confirming jurisdiction.
Res judicata effect of judicial determination, §8.01-420.5.
Law enforcement officers.
Injury where weather constitutes particular risk of employment of public safety officer, §65.2-301.1.
Off-duty coverage, §65.2-102.
License taxes.
Contractors.
Requirements, §58.1-3714.
Liens.
Third party suit.
Settlement proceeds or verdict in, §65.2-309.
Uninsured or underinsured motorist benefits.
Lien of employer, §65.2-309.1.
Limitation of action.
Actions on awards found void ab initio.
Tolling of limitation period, §8.01-229.
Limitations upon persons under disability, §65.2-528.
Marriage.
Report of remarriage, §65.2-712.
Medical attention duties of employer, §65.2-603.
Medical examinations ordered by employer or commission, §65.2-607.
Medical records.
Furnishing copies of, §65.2-604.
Referral to another health care provider, §65.2-604.
Medical service liability of employer, §65.2-605.
Memorandum of agreements, §65.2-701.
Disagreements, §65.2-702.
Enforcement, §65.2-710.
Mineral mine safety.
Mine rescue crews, §§45.1-161.71, 45.1-161.292:44.
Mine rescue teams, §45.1-161.292:49.
Misconduct by employee.
Compensation not allowed for willful misconduct, §65.2-306.
Misdemeanors.
Payroll reports, withholding or providing false or misleading information, §65.2-1006.
Misrepresentation, procuring payments by.
Recovery by commission, §65.2-712.
Motor carriers, property.
Noncompliance with workers' compensation provisions, §46.2-2133.
Motor vehicle insurance.
Liability covered by workers' compensation law, §46.2-476.
Subrogation of employees' rights.
Uninsured or underinsured motorists benefits, §65.2-309.1.
Uninsured or underinsured motorist benefits.
Lien of employer, §65.2-309.1.
National guard coverage, §65.2-103.
Notice.
Accidents, §65.2-600.
Rejection of coverage by executive officer, §65.2-300.
Tolling of statute of limitations, §65.2-602.
Occupational diseases, §§65.2-400 to 65.2-407.
Accident provisions applicable, §65.2-403.
Carrier liability, §65.2-404.
Defined terms, §65.2-400.
Employer liability, §65.2-404.

WORKERS' COMPENSATION —Cont'd
Occupational diseases —Cont'd
Heart disease.
Presumptions as to death or disability from, §65.2-402.
Hypertension.
Presumptions as to death or disability from, §65.2-402.
Notice, §65.2-405.
Ordinary diseases of life coverage, §65.2-401.
Respiratory disease.
Presumptions as to death or disability from, §65.2-402.
Statute of limitations, §65.2-406.
Tolling, §65.2-405.
Waiver of rights, §65.2-407.
Panel of physicians.
Employer liability for medical services ordered by commission, §65.2-605.
Supplying, §65.2-603.
Partial disability.
AmeriCorps members.
Ineligibility to receive partial incapacity benefits, §65.2-502.
Black lung compensation calculations, §65.2-504.
Commencement of compensation, §65.2-509.
Compensation after second injury in same employment, §65.2-506.
Compensation for disability, §65.2-502.
Cost of living adjustments, §65.2-709.
Food stamp employment and training program participants.
Ineligibility to receive partial incapacity benefits, §65.2-502.
Foreign injuries, §65.2-508.
Limitations upon total compensation, §§65.2-518, 65.2-519.
Permanent partial disability.
Compensation for, §65.2-503.
Compensation to employees' distributees upon death, §65.2-511.
Incapacity after permanent loss, §65.2-501.
Successive permanent injuries in same employment.
Compensation for, §65.2-507.
Pneumoconiosis disability compensation calculations, §65.2-504.
Post-injury average weekly wage.
Rules for calculating, §65.2-502.
Successive injuries in different employments, §65.2-505.
Suspension of benefits.
Compensation for partial incapacity, §65.2-510.
Imprisonment, §65.2-510.1.
Refusal of employment, §65.2-510.
Payments.
Distributees to receive upon death, §65.2-511.
Failure to make within two weeks, §65.2-524.
Junior dependents made in good faith, §65.2-526.
Lump sums, §§65.2-522, 65.2-523.
Receipt by whom, §65.2-525.
Time of payments, §65.2-521.
Voluntary payments by employer, §65.2-520.
Peer review of medical costs, §§65.2-1300 to 65.2-1310.
Corrective actions, §65.2-1306.
Defined terms, §65.2-1300.
Regional peer review committees, §§65.2-1302, 65.2-1303.
Statewide coordinating committee, §§65.2-1301, 65.2-1302.
Contracts, §65.2-1309.

WORKERS' COMPENSATION —Cont'd
Peer review of medical costs —Cont'd
Statewide coordinating committee —Cont'd
Immunity of members, §65.2-1307.
Peer review program, §65.2-1305.
Funding, §65.2-1310.
Privileged communications, §65.2-1308.
Regional peer review committee, §65.2-1303.
Rules and regulations, §65.2-1309.
Staff, §65.2-1309.
Utilization review program, §65.2-1304.
Funding, §65.2-1310.
Physician charges for services, §65.2-714.
Pneumoconiosis disability compensation calculations, §65.2-504.
Prescription drugs.
Use of therapeutically equivalent instead of brand name, §65.2-603.1.
Presumptions.
Acceptance of provisions, §65.2-300.
Cancer.
Death or disability from, §65.2-402.
Dependency.
Wholly dependent, §65.2-515.
Heart disease.
Death or disability from, §65.2-402.
Hepatitis, meningococcal meningitis, tuberculosis or HIV.
Death or disability, §65.2-402.1.
Hypertension.
Death or disability from, §65.2-402.
Infectious disease, death or disability from, §65.2-402.1.
Injuries arose out of and were in course of employment.
Employee physically or mentally unable to testify, §65.2-105.
Pneumoconiosis over silicosis, §65.2-504.
Respiratory disease.
Death or disability from, §65.2-402.
Priority against assets of employer, §65.2-530.
Procurement of construction services by public bodies.
Requirements for contractors and subcontractors, §2.2-4332.
Professional employer organizations.
Defined, §65.2-101.
Registration with commission, requirements before offering services, service agreements, §65.2-803.1.
Civil penalty for noncompliance, §65.2-805.
Public officers and employees, §2.2-2821.
Public safety officers.
Injury where weather constitutes particular risk of employment, §65.2-301.1.
Qualifying as self-insurer, effect of, §65.2-305.
Receipt of payment, §65.2-525.
Records.
Accidents, §65.2-900.
Confidentiality, §65.2-903.
Refusal of employee to accept treatment, §65.2-603.
Refusal of employment, §65.2-510.
Compensation for partial incapacity, §65.2-510.
Rejection of coverage by executive officer, §65.2-300.
Remarriage, disclosure by employee or dependent, §65.2-712.
Remedies, exclusivity, §65.2-307.
Reports.
Accidents, §65.2-900.

WORKERS' COMPENSATION —Cont'd
Reports —Cont'd
Days of operation of business, §65.2-901.
Employee numbers and hours of labor, §65.2-901.
Failure to make, §65.2-902.
Payroll reports of self-insurers, §65.2-1006.
Respiratory disease.
Presumptions as to death or disability from, §65.2-402.
Retaliatory discharges, §65.2-308.
Ridesharing.
Inapplicability of workers' compensation law, §46.2-1402.
Rights exercised by guardians, trustees or conservators, §65.2-527.
Safety appliance, failure to use.
Compensation not allowed, §65.2-306.
Second injury fund, §§65.2-1100 to 65.2-1106.
Self-inflicted injury.
Compensation not allowed for intentional self-inflicted injury, §65.2-306.
Sexual assault victims, §65.2-301.
State defense force coverage, §65.2-103.
Statute of limitations.
Actions on awards found void ab initio.
Tolling of limitation period, §8.01-229.
Statutory employers.
Coverage, §65.2-302.
Indemnity of principal from subcontractors, §65.2-304.
Proceedings against owners or contractors, §65.2-303.
Recovery from subcontractors, §65.2-303.
Student status, change in.
Reporting, §65.2-712.
Subcontracting.
Coverage, §65.2-302.
Indemnity of principal from subcontractors, §65.2-304.
Proceedings against owners or contractors, §65.2-303.
Recovery from subcontractors, §65.2-303.
Subrogation of employer to employees' rights, §65.2-309.
Expenses, §65.2-311.
Settlement of third-party action, §8.01-424.1.
Termination of employer's offset, §65.2-313.
Uninsured or underinsured motorists benefits, §65.2-309.1.
Successive injuries in different employments, §65.2-505.
Successive permanent injuries in same employment, §65.2-507.
Surviving spouse or parent.
Payment of compensation, §65.2-525.
Suspension of benefits.
Imprisonment, §65.2-510.1.
Medical examinations ordered by employers or commission.
Refusals to submit, §65.2-607.
Refusal of employment, §65.2-510.
Compensation for partial incapacity, §65.2-510.
Taking out insurance, effect of, §65.2-305.
Temporary assistance for needy families (TANF).
Virginia initiative for employment not welfare (VIEW).
Ineligibility for certain benefits, §§65.2-500, 65.2-502, 65.2-512.
Third party suit.
Lien against settlement proceeds or verdict in, §65.2-309.

WORKERS' COMPENSATION —Cont'd
Title of provisions, §65.2-100.
Total disability.
AmeriCorps members.
Ineligibility to receive benefits, §65.2-500.
Black lung compensation calculations, §65.2-504.
Commencement of compensation, §65.2-509.
Compensation after second injury in same employment, §65.2-506.
Compensation for disability, §65.2-500.
Cost of living adjustments, §65.2-709.
Food stamp employment and training program participants.
Ineligibility to receive benefits, §65.2-500.
Foreign injuries, §65.2-508.
Limitations upon total compensation, §§65.2-518, 65.2-519.
Permanent total disability.
Compensation for, §65.2-503.
Compensation to employees' distributees upon death, §65.2-511.
Incapacity after permanent loss, §65.2-501.
Successive permanent injuries in same employment.
Compensation for, §65.2-507.
Pneumoconiosis disability compensation calculations, §65.2-504.
Subsequent accidental injury after leaving employment, §65.2-505.
Successive injuries in different employments, §65.2-505.
Suspension of benefits.
Imprisonment, §65.2-510.1.
Refusal of employment, §65.2-510.
Uninsured employer's fund, §§65.2-1200 to 65.2-1206.
Victim impact statements.
Commission utilization in determining claims, §19.2-299.1.
Virginia initiative for employment not welfare (VIEW).
Ineligibility for certain benefits, §§65.2-500, 65.2-502, 65.2-512.
Virginia retirement system.
Disability retirement allowance.
Workers' compensation guarantee, §51.1-157.
Vocational rehabilitation duties of employer, §65.2-603.
Voluntary payments by employer, §65.2-520.
Voluntary subjection to provisions, §65.2-305.
Weather.
Injury where weather constitutes particular risk of employment of public safety officer, §65.2-301.1.

WORKERS' COMPENSATION COMMISSION, §§65.2-200 to 65.2-204.
Address changes by employees, §65.2-711.
Administrative fund, §§65.2-1000 to 65.2-1008.
Appeals.
Commission orders, from.
Notice of appeal, VA SCt Rule 5A:11.
Court of appeals.
Finality of decisions, §17.1-410.
Jurisdiction of court of appeals, §17.1-405.
Security for appeal, §8.01-676.1.
Attorney-issued summons, §8.01-407.
Bailiffs.
Powers and duties, §65.2-203.
Birth-related neurological injury compensation.
Authorized to hear and determine claim, §38.2-5003.

WORKERS' COMPENSATION COMMISSION —Cont'd
Birth-related neurological injury compensation —Cont'd
Motion to refer to commission.
Determining whether action satisfies, §8.01-273.1.
Cancellation notices, §65.2-804.
Provision violations, §§65.2-805, 65.2-806.
Certificate of self-insurance, §65.2-808.
Compliance filings, §65.2-804.
Provision violations, §§65.2-805, 65.2-806.
Continuation of commission, §65.2-200.
Costs of insurance.
Deduction from wages.
Imposition of fines and refunds, §65.2-807.
Court of appeals.
Appellate jurisdiction as to final decisions of, §17.1-405.
Finality of decisions, §17.1-410.
Special rule applicable to appeals, VA SCt Rule 5A:11.
Deputy commissioners.
Powers and duties, §65.2-203.
Disclosure statement by members.
Filing, time, form, §§2.2-3114, 2.2-3117.
Duties, §65.2-201.
Employment status.
Determination by commission.
Estoppel effect, §65.2-706.1.
Expenses, §65.2-204.
Hearings, §65.2-704.
Costs, §§65.2-713, 65.2-807.
Depositions, §65.2-703.
Disagreements as to compensation, §65.2-702.
Interrogatories, §65.2-703.
Rehearings, §65.2-705.
Information on statutory requirements.
Preparation and distribution, §65.2-800.
Insurance and self-insurance.
Approval of forms, §65.2-813.
Certification, §65.2-801.
Rate information, §65.2-817.
Provision violations, §65.2-819.
Service standards, §65.2-818.
Provision violations, §65.2-819.
Jurisdiction, §65.2-700.
Jury service.
Automatic exemption, §8.01-341.
Meetings, §65.2-204.
Members, §65.2-200.
Offices, §65.2-204.
Orders.
Recordation, enforcement and satisfaction, §65.2-710.
Powers, §65.2-201.
Subpoenas, §65.2-202.
Professional employer organizations.
Registration with commission, requirements before offering services, service agreements, §65.2-803.1.
Civil penalty for noncompliance, §65.2-805.
Quorum for exercise of functions, §65.2-201.
Rejection of coverage.
Filing, §65.2-300.
Reports, §65.2-712.
Representative of employees.
Not more than one member classified as, §65.2-200.
Representative of employers.
Not more than one member classified as, §65.2-200.

WORKERS' COMPENSATION COMMISSION —Cont'd
Retired members.
Appearance as counsel prohibitions, §51.1-309.
Payment for services, §17.1-327.
Salaries, §65.2-204.
Second injury fund.
Awards, §§65.2-1103, 65.2-1104.
Disbursements, §65.2-1100.
Restitution, §65.2-1105.
Summons.
Attorney-issued summons, §8.01-407.
Suspension of benefits.
Address changes by employees.
Failure to report, §65.2-711.
Uninsured employer's fund.
Administration, §65.2-1200.
Awards, §65.2-1203.
Recoupments, §65.2-1204.
Subrogation, §65.2-1204.
Vacancies, filling, §65.2-200.

WORKERS' COMPENSATION INSURANCE AND SELF-INSURANCE, §§65.2-800 to 65.2-824.
Agent for receipt of cancellation of policy notices, §65.2-804.
Agents conducting business for carrier who has been suspended.
Penalties, §65.2-819.
Agreements of insurers, §65.2-811.
Applicability of provisions to policies, §65.2-813.
Losses from explosions of boilers or fly wheels, §65.2-816.
Assignments of risks.
Applications, §65.2-820.
Action upon, §65.2-822.
Confidentiality of information, §65.2-823.
Disclosures not required, §65.2-824.
Rates, §65.2-821.
Rules and regulations, §65.2-821.
Boiler explosions.
Applicability of provisions to policies against, §65.2-816.
Cancellation of policy.
Cancellation notices, §§65.2-804 to 65.2-806.
Notice to commission by carrier or association, §65.2-804.
Certificate of self-insurance, §65.2-808.
Compliance filings, §65.2-804.
Provision violations, §§65.2-805, 65.2-806.
Construction contracts by public bodies.
Owner-controlled insurance program.
Purchase by public body in connection with, §2.2-4308.1.
Costs.
Deduction from wages, §65.2-807.
Criminal offenses.
Payroll reports.
Withholding or providing false or misleading information, §65.2-1006.
Deductibles on insurance policies, §65.2-813.1.
Defined terms, §38.2-119.
Corporation, §65.2-803.
Firm, §65.2-803.
Other party, §65.2-800.
Those conducting his business, §65.2-800.
Drug-free workplace programs.
Premium discounts, §65.2-813.2.

WORKERS' COMPENSATION INSURANCE AND SELF-INSURANCE —Cont'd
False or fraudulent statements as to business or condition of carriers, §65.2-819.
Fly wheel catastrophes.
Applicability of provisions to policies against, §65.2-816.
Group self-insurance associations, §65.2-802.
Administrative prohibitions, §65.2-803.
Cancellation notices, §65.2-804.
Provision violations, §§65.2-805, 65.2-806.
Service company affiliation prohibitions, §65.2-803.
Written evidence of membership, §65.2-815.
Insurance.
General laws not to amend or repeal provisions, §38.2-900.
License tax on insurance companies.
Exemptions and exclusions, §58.1-2502.
Methods of securing, §65.2-801.
Misdemeanors.
Payroll reports, withholding or providing false or misleading information, §65.2-1006.
Notice.
Cancellation notices, §§65.2-804 to 65.2-806.
Renewal notices, §§65.2-804 to 65.2-806.
Service requirements, §65.2-810.
Payroll reports, §65.2-1006.
Policy clause requirements, §65.2-809.
Promises of insurer, §65.2-811.
Rates.
Information, §65.2-817.
Provision violations, §65.2-819.
Workers' compensation, automobiles, home protection, etc., §§38.2-2000 to 38.2-2027.
See INSURANCE RATES.
Renewal notices, §§65.2-804 to 65.2-806.
Required, §65.2-800.
Service standards, §§65.2-818, 65.2-819.
Provision violations, §65.2-819.
Subrogation, §65.2-812.
Virginia property and casualty insurance guaranty association, §§38.2-1600 to 38.2-1623.
Virginia workers' compensation insurance plan.
Insurers writing workers' compensation insurance required to participate, §38.2-2015.
Written evidence of coverage, §65.2-814.

WORK FARMS.
County and city jail farms, §§53.1-96 to 53.1-115.2.
See COUNTY AND CITY JAIL FARMS.

WORKFORCE COUNCIL, §§2.2-2669 to 2.2-2674.1.
Community colleges.
Facility use or equipment fees, §2.2-2672.
Regional workforce training centers, §2.2-2671.
Compensation of members, §2.2-2669.
Composition, §2.2-2669.
Defined terms, §2.2-2674.1.
Duties, §2.2-2670.
Establishment, §2.2-2669.
Facility use or equipment fees, §2.2-2672.
Fees.
Facility use or equipment fees, §2.2-2672.
Local workforce investment boards.
Defined, §2.2-2674.1.
Duties regarding, §2.2-2670.
Powers, §2.2-2670.

WORKFORCE COUNCIL —Cont'd
Purpose, §2.2-2669.
Regional workforce centers.
Powers and duties, §2.2-2670.
Regional workforce training centers, §2.2-2671.
Staff, §2.2-2669.
Trade secrets.
Confidentiality, §2.2-2673.
Training courses and programs, §2.2-2670.
Workforce development training fund.
Duties regarding, §2.2-2670.
Workforce network.
Duties regarding, §2.2-2670.
Workforce training access fund, §2.2-2674.
Workforce training access program, §2.2-2674.

WORKFORCE DEVELOPMENT AND TRAINING PROGRAMS.
Chief workforce development officer.
Duty of governor as, §2.2-435.7.
Workforce program evaluations.
Sharing of information by specified agencies, §2.2-435.8.

WORKFORCE DEVELOPMENT COORDINATION.
Chief workforce development officer, §2.2-435.6.

WORKFORCE DEVELOPMENT TRAINING FUND.
Workforce council, duties regarding, §2.2-2670.

WORKFORCE INVESTMENT BOARDS.
Evaluation of effectiveness of loca boards.
Chief workforce development officer.
Duty of governor as, §2.2-435.7.

WORKFORCE NETWORK.
Workforce council.
Duties regarding, §2.2-2670.

WORKFORCE PROGRAM EVALUATIONS.
Sharing of information by specified agencies, §2.2-435.8.

WORKFORCE RETRAINING PROGRAM.
Department of business assistance to develop (eff until 1/1/2014), §2.2-904.
Small business and supplier diversity department to develop, §2.2-1613.

WORKFORCE TRAINING.
Access fund, §2.2-2674.
Access program, §2.2-2674.
Chief workforce development officer, §2.2-435.6.
Retraining program.
Department of business assistance to develop, §2.2-904.
Virginia jobs investment program, §2.2-1611.
Virginia jobs investment program (eff until 1/1/2014), §2.2-903.1.
Workforce council, §§2.2-2669 to 2.2-2674.1.
See WORKFORCE COUNCIL.
Workforce network.
Workforce council, duties regarding, §2.2-2670.
Workforce transition act of 1995.
Termination or layoffs from employment with Commonwealth, §§2.2-3200 to 2.2-3206.
See PUBLIC OFFICERS AND EMPLOYEES.

WORKFORCE TRAINING ACCESS FUND, §2.2-2674.

WORKFORCE TRAINING ACCESS PROGRAM, §2.2-2674.

WORKFORCE TRANSITION ACT OF 1995.
Termination or layoffs from employment with Commonwealth, §§2.2-3200 to 2.2-3206.
See PUBLIC OFFICERS AND EMPLOYEES.

WORKMANLIKE CONSTRUCTION.
Implied warranties on new homes, §55-70.1.

WORK-OUT CLUBS, §§59.1-294 to 59.1-310.
See HEALTH CLUBS.

WORK PERMITS FOR CHILD.
Judicial consent to apply for, §§16.1-241, 16.1-278.13.

WORK-PRODUCT.
Discovery of trial preparation materials, VA SCt Rule 4:1.
Limitations on waiver of attorney-client privilege and work product protection, §8.01-420.7.

WORK RELEASE PROGRAMS.
Community-based corrections system for state-responsible offenders.
Program included, §53.1-67.6.
Community corrections.
Generally, §§9.1-173 to 9.1-183.
See COMMUNITY CORRECTIONS.
Optional programs, §9.1-176.
Criminal fines and penalties.
Installment payments as condition to program, §19.2-354.
Establishment, §53.1-60.
Fee towards cost of participation in program, §53.1-150.
Furloughs, §53.1-132.
Ineligibility, §53.1-62.
Jail prisoners, §53.1-131.
Notice to crime victims, §53.1-133.02.
Notice to law enforcement, §53.1-160.
Opportunities, §53.1-41.
Use of earnings, §53.1-61.

WORKS OF ART, LOCALITIES.
Locality acquiring and housing, §15.2-945.

WORKS ON WATERCOURSES, §§62.1-116 to 62.1-127.
Applications for leave to build or rebuild, §62.1-116.
Commission.
Appointment, §62.1-118.
New commissioners, §62.1-121.
Duties, §62.1-119.
Meetings, §62.1-118.
Oath, §62.1-119.
Reports, §62.1-119.
Granting of leave, §62.1-122.
Damage payments, §62.1-123.
Damages, unforeseen, §62.1-127.
Forfeiture of works damaged or destroyed, §62.1-126.
Time limitations, §62.1-125.
Vested rights unaffected, §62.1-124.
Notice, §62.1-117.
Further notice, §62.1-120.
Refusal to grant, §62.1-122.
Hydroelectric power generally, §§62.1-80 to 62.1-103.
See HYDROELECTRIC POWER.
Impoundment of surface waters.
Application of provisions, §62.1-114.
Surface water management areas generally, §§62.1-242 to 62.1-253.
See SURFACE WATER MANAGEMENT AREAS.

WORK STOPPAGES.
Right to work, §40.1-66.

WORLD WAR I.
Memorial record maintained by circuit court clerk, §17.1-263.
Recordation of discharges of those serving, §17.1-262.
Recordation of names of men serving during, §17.1-261.

WORLD WAR I MEMORIAL RECORD.
Circuit court clerk to maintain, §17.1-263.

WORLD WAR II.
Discharges of men serving during.
Recording information, §17.1-264.
Historical material relating to, §§42.1-30, 42.1-31.
Pearl Harbor remembrance day, §2.2-3309.
Veterans honorary high school diplomas, §22.1-17.4.
Veterans' special license plate, §46.2-743.
Virginia World War II veterans appreciation week, §2.2-3309.1.

WORLD WAR II VETERANS APPRECIATION WEEK, §2.2-3309.1.

WORLD WAR II VETERANS HONORARY HIGH SCHOOL DIPLOMA, §22.1-17.4.

WORLD WIDE WEB.
Cigarette delivery sales, §§18.2-246.6 to 18.2-246.15.
See CIGARETTES.
Generally.
See INTERNET.
Information technologies agency, §§2.2-2005 to 2.2-2031.
See INFORMATION TECHNOLOGIES AGENCY.

WORTHIER TITLE.
Doctrine abolished, §55-14.1.

WORTHLESS CHECKS.
Bad check law generally, §§18.2-181 to 18.2-185.
Civil actions for bad checks, recovery of costs, §17.1-626.1.

WOUNDING IN COMMITTING OR ATTEMPTING FELONY, §18.2-53.

WOUNDING WITH INTENT TO MAIM, KILL, ETC., §18.2-51.
Aggravated malicious wounding, §18.2-51.2.
Discretionary felony sentencing guidelines, §17.1-805.
Lesser offenses, conviction under certain indictments, §18.2-54.
Sentence of person twice previously convicted of certain violent felonies, §19.2-297.1.
Three time loser law, §19.2-297.1.

WOUNDS INFLICTED BY WEAPONS, REPORTS, §54.1-2967.

WRAP-AROUND MORTGAGES.
Insurance companies investments, §38.2-1435.

WRECKS.
Motor vehicle accidents generally, §§46.2-894 to 46.2-902.
See MOTOR VEHICLE ACCIDENTS.

WRESTLING.
Generally, §§54.1-828 to 54.1-835.
See BOXING, MARTIAL ARTS AND WRESTLING EVENTS.

WRESTLING —Cont'd
Unlawful procurement of licensure, §54.1-102.
Unlawful use of licensure, §54.1-111.

WRITE-IN VOTES, §24.2-644.
Federal write-in absentee ballots, §24.2-702.1.
Intent of voter discernible, §24.2-467.
Methods of registration, §24.2-457.
Military and overseas voters.
Authorized, §24.2-461.
Publication of information, §24.2-465.
Time to register by mail, §24.2-419.
Presidential elections, §24.2-644.
Provision to be made for casting votes for persons other than listed candidates, VA Const Art II §3.
Voting equipment, §24.2-648.

WRITERS.
Intellectual property.
Colleges and universities, §§23-4.3, 23-4.4.
Protection of rights, US Const Art I §8.

WRITINGS NOT PURPORTING TO BE SEALED, §11-3.

WRITINGS PARTIALLY PROVED BOOK.
Documents recorded in, §17.1-234.

WRITINGS USED TO REFRESH MEMORY.
Witnesses, VA SCt Rule 2:612.

WRIT OF ACTUAL INNOCENCE, §§19.2-327.2 to 19.2-327.6, VA SCt Rule 5:7B.
Actions against the Commonwealth, §19.2-327.6.
Nonbiological evidence, writ based on, §19.2-327.14.
Allegations.
Unknown or untested human biological evidence, §19.2-327.3.
Burden of proof, §19.2-327.5.
Nonbiological evidence, writ based on, §19.2-327.13.
Claims of relief, §19.2-327.6.
Nonbiological evidence, writ based on, §19.2-327.14.
Contents of petition, §19.2-327.3.
Nonbiological evidence, writ based on, §19.2-327.11.
Effect on other actions, §19.2-327.6.
Nonbiological evidence, writ based on, §19.2-327.14.
Execution dates and stays.
Effect, §19.2-327.3.
Nonbiological evidence, writ based on, §19.2-327.11.
Findings of fact.
Determination that findings required, §19.2-327.4.
Nonbiological evidence, writ based on, §19.2-327.12.
Form, VA SCt Rules Part 5A Appx Form 12.
Hearings in circuit court.
Findings of fact.
Determination that findings required, §19.2-327.4.
Nonbiological evidence, writ based on, §19.2-327.12.
Issuance, §19.2-327.2.
Nonbiological evidence, writ based on, §19.2-327.10.
Nonbiological evidence, writ based on, §§19.2-327.10 to 19.2-327.14.
Actions against the Commonwealth, §19.2-327.14.
Authority to issue, §19.2-327.10.

WRIT OF ACTUAL INNOCENCE —Cont'd
Nonbiological evidence, writ based on —Cont'd
Burden of proof, §19.2-327.13.
Claims of relief, §19.2-327.14.
Contents of petition, §19.2-327.11.
Effect on other actions, §19.2-327.14.
Execution dates and stays, effect, §19.2-327.11.
Findings of fact.
Determination that findings required, §19.2-327.12.
Issuance, §19.2-327.10.
Relief, §19.2-327.13.
Return of service, §19.2-327.11.
Right to counsel, §19.2-327.11.
Standard of proof, §19.2-327.13.
Petition for writ of actual innocence, VA SCt Rule Pt 5A Appx Form 12, VA SCt Rule Pt 5 Appx Form 12.
Petition from Supreme Court of Virginia, §19.2-327.2, VA SCt Rule 5:7B.
Contents, §19.2-327.3, VA SCt Rule 5:7B.
Qualifications, §19.2-327.2.
Relief, §19.2-327.5.
Alternative avenues, §19.2-327.6.
Nonbiological evidence, writ based on, §19.2-327.14.
Claims of relief, §19.2-327.6.
Nonbiological evidence, writ based on, §19.2-327.14.
Nonbiological evidence, writ based on, §19.2-327.13.
Return of service, §19.2-327.3.
Nonbiological evidence, writ based on, §19.2-327.11.
Right to counsel, §19.2-327.3.
Nonbiological evidence, writ based on, §19.2-327.11.
Standard of proof, §19.2-327.5.
Nonbiological evidence, writ based on, §19.2-327.13.
Unknown or untested human biological evidence.
Allegations, §19.2-327.3.

WRIT OF ASSISTANCE.
Judgments on specific property.
Delivery by sheriff to plaintiff, §8.01-470.

WRIT OF CAPIAS AD SATISFACIENDUM.
Abolishment, §8.01-467.

WRIT OF DISTRINGAS.
Abolishment, §8.01-467.

WRIT OF ELEGIT.
Abolishment, §8.01-467.

WRIT OF ENTRY.
Abolished, §8.01-165.
Ejectment.
General provisions, §§8.01-131 to 8.01-165.
See EJECTMENT.

WRIT OF ERROR.
Bonds, surety.
How bonds made payable, §49-20.
Criminal cases, §§19.2-317 to 19.2-327.
Accused, §19.2-317.
Appeal from denial, §19.2-319.
Appeal on judgment for contempt, §19.2-318.
Certification of judgment of appellate court, §19.2-327.
Commonwealth, §19.2-317.
Compliance with rules of court, §19.2-320.

WRIT OF ERROR —Cont'd
Criminal cases —Cont'd
County, city or town, §19.2-317.
Decision of appellate court, §19.2-324.
Denial by judge or justice no bar to allowance by court, §19.2-323.
Entry of judgment of appellate court, §19.2-327.
Filing petition for writ, §19.2-321.
Indigent defendants, §19.2-326.
Payment of expenses of indigent defendants, §19.2-326.
Petitioner to comply with court rules, §19.2-320.
Plaintiff unable to pay printing costs, §19.2-325.
Previous denial no bar to allowance by court, §19.2-323.
Remedy when plaintiff in error unable to pay printing costs, §19.2-325.
Suspension of execution of sentence, §19.2-319.
Appellate review of judgment, §19.2-322.1.
With whom petition filed, §19.2-321.
Criminal forfeiture, §19.2-386.13.
Motion for new trial.
Effect of failure to make motion, §8.01-384.
Supreme court.
Jurisdiction, §17.1-310.

WRIT OF EXTENDI FACIAS.
Abolishment, §8.01-467.

WRIT OF FIERI FACIAS.
See FIERI FACIAS.

WRIT OF FORMEDON.
Abolished, §8.01-165.
Ejectment.
General provisions, §§8.01-131 to 8.01-165.
See EJECTMENT.

WRIT OF LEVARI FACIAS.
Abolishment, §8.01-467.

WRIT OF POSSESSION.
Breaking and entering to execute, §8.01-470.
Corporation preparing without intervention of lawyer, §16.1-88.03.
District court civil cases.
Corporation or partnership preparing without attorney intervention, §16.1-88.03.
Issuance after papers returned to circuit court, §16.1-116.
Return, §16.1-99.
Failure to make or improper return, §16.1-101.
Liability for money collected after return day, §16.1-102.
District court clerk, issuance, §16.1-69.40.
Failure to make return of writ issued by general district court.
Proceedings against officers, §16.1-101.
Fee for serving, §17.1-272.
Improper return of writ issued by general district court.
Proceedings against officers, §16.1-101.
Issuance.
Circuit court, issuance after paper returned, §16.1 116.
General district court, issuance upon judgment rendered, §16.1-98.
Judgments.
General district court, issuance on, §16.1-98.
Personal property, §§8.01-470, 8.01-472.
Specific property, §8.01-470.
Partnership preparing without intervention of lawyer, §16.1-88.03.

WRIT OF POSSESSION —Cont'd
Return.
Writ issued from general district court, §16.1-99.
Failure to make return or improper return, §16.1-101.
Liability for money collected after return day, §16.1-102.
Service.
Persons who may execute writs, §8.01-293.
Sheriffs.
Who may serve, §8.01-293.
Unlawful entry and detainer.
Persons who may execute writs, §8.01-293.
Rent payments accepted by landlord, writ not to issue, §8.01-471.
Returnable writs, §§8.01-470, 8.01-471.
Time for issuing writ, §8.01-471.

WRIT OF RIGHT.
Abolished, §8.01-165.
Ejectment.
General provisions, §§8.01-131 to 8.01-165.
See EJECTMENT.

WRIT OF SCIRE FACIAS.
Abolished, §8.01-24.

WRIT OF VENIRE FACIAS.
Summoning grand jury, §19.2-194.
Irregularities not to violate indictment or finding, §19.2-203.

WRITS FOR SPECIAL ELECTIONS.
Filling vacancies, §24.2-683.

WRIT TAXES, §§58.1-1727 to 58.1-1729.
Prisoners' health care.
Involuntary admission and treatment.
Appeal of order authorizing, §53.1-40.4.
Time for paying.
Appeals from general district courts in civil cases, §16.1-107.

WRITTEN APPEARANCE AND WAIVER OF HEARING.
Nontraffic offenses for which prepayment authorized, §19.2-254.2.
Traffic infractions, §19.2-254.1.

WRONGFUL DEATH, §§8.01-50 to 8.01-56.
Abatement or dismissal of action.
Limitations period for bringing another action, §8.01-244.
Actions against estates of deceased residents and nonresidents.
Appointment of administrator, §64.2-454.
Asbestos-related injuries.
Consolidation or bifurcation of issues or claims, §8.01-374.1.
Certification of expert witness opinion.
Actions against health care providers, §8.01-50.1.
Classification of beneficiaries.
Failure of verdict to specify beneficiaries, §8.01-54.
When determined, §8.01-53.
Commencement of action, §8.01-50.
Compromise of claims.
Action barred, §8.01-51.
Approval of court required, §8.01-55.
Persons with disability, §8.01-424.
Creditor process exemptions.
Actions for wrongful death, §34-28.1.
Damages.
Amount of damages, §8.01-52.

WRONGFUL DEATH —Cont'd
Department of medical assistance services.
Notice to department of action against nursing home.
Department having paid for services to decedent, §8.01-66.5.
Determination of beneficiary classification, §8.01-53.
Discovery.
Protective orders, §8.01-420.01.
Exemptions from creditor process.
Wrongful death actions exempt, §34-28.1.
Health care providers, actions against.
Certification of expert witness opinion, §8.01-50.1.
Sympathy, admissibility of expressions of, §8.01-52.1.
How action brought, §8.01-50.
Improvements to real property.
Limitation of actions.
Damages arising out of defective or unsafe condition of improvement, §8.01-250.
In camera review of expert witness opinion.
Actions against health care providers, §8.01-50.1.
Independent contractors.
Completion or acceptance of work not bar to action against contractor, §8.01-39.
Life expectancy tables, §8.01-419.
Limitation of actions, §8.01-244.
Improvements to real property.
Damages arising out of defective or unsafe condition of improvement, §8.01-250.
Lynching, civil liability, §18.2-44.
Persons suffering death from mob attempting to lynch another, §18.2-45.
Medical evidence.
Authenticity and reasonableness of medical bills, §8.01-413.01.
Minor as decedent, §8.01-50.
Mortality tables, §8.01-419.
Nursing homes, actions against.
Notice to department of medical assistance services.
Department having paid for services to decedent, §8.01-66.5.
Oil discharges.
Good Samaritan liability for assistance in containment and cleanup, §62.1-44.34:18.
Personal representatives.
Suits upon judgment and contracts of decedent, §64.2-519.
Persons with disability.
Settlement of claims, §8.01-424.
Products liability.
Consolidation or bifurcation of issues or claims, §8.01-374.1.
Protective orders.
Discovery, §8.01-420.01.
Railroad corporations.
Liability for death of employees, §56-441.
Renunciation of interest by beneficiary, §8.01-53.
Settlement of claims.
Persons with disability, §8.01-424.
Statute of limitations, §8.01-244.
Improvements to real property.
Damages arising out of defective or unsafe condition of improvement, §8.01-250.
Survival of action.
Death or change of defendant party, §8.01-56.
Verdict.
Distribution of recovery when verdict fails to do so, §8.01-54.

WRONGFUL DEATH —Cont'd
Verdict —Cont'd
Interrogatories submitted to jury with general verdict form, §8.01-379.3.

WRONGFUL DISCHARGE.
Statute of limitations, §8.01-243.
Work-related injuries, §40.1-27.1.

WRONGFUL INCARCERATION FOR A FELONY CONVICTION.
Compensation, §§8.01-195.10 to 8.01-195.12.
Amount of compensation, §8.01-195.11.
Assistance grant, §8.01-195.11.
Continued compensation, conditions, §8.01-195.12.
Defined terms, §8.01-195.10.
Purpose of article, §8.01-195.10.
Release from liability as condition, §8.01-195.12.
Subsequent convictions, effect, §8.01-195.12.

WYTHE COUNTY.
Assistant attorney for the Commonwealth.
Dual office holding, §15.2-1534.
Blue Ridge regional tourism council, §§2.2-2609, 2.2-2610.
Confederate cemeteries and graves.
Disbursement of funds appropriated for upkeep, §10.1-2211.
Dams.
Restrictions, §29.1-532.
Dirt and gravel roads.
Maximum speed limits on nonsurface treated highways, §46.2-873.1.
Public defenders office.
Established, §19.2-163.04.
Revolutionary war cemeteries and graves.
Disbursement of funds appropriated for upkeep, §10.1-2211.1.
School board.
Salary of members, §22.1-32.
Transient occupancy tax.
Disposition of revenues, §58.1-3819.
Water and sewage systems.
Mandatory connection, §15.2-2110.
Western Virginia public education consortium.
Inclusion in Western Virginia, §22.1-354.1.

WYTHE DEVELOPMENT AUTHORITY.
Generally.
See ECONOMIC DEVELOPMENT AUTHORITIES.

WYTHEVILLE.
Pulaski and Wytheville parking authority, 1968 ch 682.
Virginia Polytechnic Institute and State University.
Wytheville branch, §§23-135.17 to 23-135.21.

X

X-RAY MACHINES.
Exemption from provisions, §32.1-228.
Radiation control.
Inspections, §§32.1-229.1, 32.1-229.2.
Registration, inspection and certification.
Therapeutic X-ray machines, §32.1-229.

X-RAYS.
Adult abuse, neglect or exploitation.
Photographs, x-rays or medical imaging of incapacitated person.
Taking without consent as part of medical evaluation, §63.2-1606.1.
Child abuse or neglect.
Photographs and X-rays of child, evidence, §63.2-1520.
Use in fitting of footwear, §18.2-321.
Workers' compensation.
Limitation of actions, §65.2-406.
Waiver of rights, §65.2-407.

Y

YEARBOOKS.
School board authorized contracts providing.
Competitive negotiation, §2.2-4346.

YELLOW DOG CONTRACTS.
Labor unions, §40.1-61.

YIELDING RIGHT-OF-WAY.
Traffic regulations generally, §§46.2-820 to 46.2-829.
See TRAFFIC INFRACTIONS.

YMCA.
Counties, cities or towns.
Appropriations to charitable institutions and associations, §15.2-953.
Property tax exemptions, §58.1-3606.

YORK COUNTY.
Automobile graveyards, screening ordinance, §15.2-903.
Coastal primary sand dunes and beaches.
Zoning ordinances, §28.2-1403.
Confederate cemeteries and graves.
Disbursement of funds appropriated for upkeep, §10.1-2211.
Cutting grass or lawn area of residential real property.
Requiring owner of occupied property, §15.2-1215.
Director of emergency management, §44-146.19.
Joint court system with city of Poquoson.
Removal, approval of electorate required.
Inapplicability of provisions, §15.2-1646.
Mentally ill, or persons with intellectual or developmental disability.
Zoning of group homes of eight or fewer single-family residences, §15.2-2291.
Parking on secondary highways, §46.2-1222.
Poles or subsurface structures.
Placing under or along road or street not in state highway system.
Permit from county engineer.
Ordinance requiring, authority to adopt, §56-15.
Poquoson river.
Oysters.
Planting grounds.
Public oyster rocks, beds, and shoals declared, §28.2-647.
Port of Virginia economic and infrastructure development zone grant fund, §62.1-132.3:2.
Public service corporations, taxation of property.
Restriction of imposition of additional tax, §58.1-2606.
Retail sales and use tax.
Additional sales tax for Northern Virginia and Hampton Roads, §58.1-603.1.
Additional use tax for Northern Virginia and Hampton Roads, §58.1-604.01.

YORK COUNTY —Cont'd
School board.
Salary of members, §22.1-32.
Social services.
District board of social services.
Local director serving as board, §63.2-307.
Transient occupancy tax.
Additional tax, rate, revenues, disposition, §58.1-3823.
Disposition of revenues, §58.1-3819.
Water and sewage systems.
Lien for charges and taxes imposed, §15.2-2118.
Well abandonment ordinance.
Duty of owner to cap or close well.
Locality adopting ordinance, §32.1-176.5.
Well construction.
Testing requirements, §32.1-176.5.

YORK RIVER BASIN.
Preparation of plans and programs for management, §62.1-44.38.

YORKTOWN DAY, §2.2-3302.

YORKTOWN VICTORY CENTER.
Jamestown-Yorktown foundation operation, §§23-287 to 23-290.

YORKTOWN VICTORY DAY.
Legal holidays, §2.2-3300.

YOUNG MEN'S CHRISTIAN ASSOCIATIONS.
Counties, cities or towns.
Appropriations to charitable institutions and associations, §15.2-953.
Property tax exemptions, §58.1-3606.

YOUNG WOMEN'S CHRISTIAN ASSOCIATIONS.
Counties, cities or towns.
Appropriations to charitable institutions and associations, §15.2-953.

YOUTH AND FAMILY SERVICES DEPARTMENT.
See JUVENILE JUSTICE DEPARTMENT.

YOUTH, COMMISSION ON, §§30-174 to 30-177.

YOUTHFUL OFFENDER FACILITIES AND PROGRAMS, §§53.1-63 to 53.1-67.
See PRISONS.

YOUTH HEALTH RISK BEHAVIOR SURVEY, §32.1-73.8.

YOUTH SERVICES CITIZEN BOARDS, §§66-34, 66-35.

YOUTH SUICIDE PREVENTION, §32.1-73.7.

YWCA.
Counties, cities or towns.
Appropriations to charitable institutions and associations, §15.2-953.

Z

ZEBRA MUSSEL.
Introducing into waters of Commonwealth, §18.2-313.2.
Nonindigenous aquatic nuisance species act, §§29.1-571 to 29.1-577.
See NONINDIGENOUS AQUATIC NUISANCE SPECIES ACT.

ZERO TOLERANCE LAW, §18.2-266.1.
Watercraft operated by person under drinking age after consuming alcohol, §29.1-738.02.

ZONING, §§15.2-2280 to 15.2-2316.2.
Abate or remedy violation.
Order on admission or finding of liability, §15.2-2209.
Action to enforce zoning violation.
Memorandum, filing, requirement, contents, §8.01-268.
Recording, expiration, §15.2-2208.
Adjoining locality, when notice required to be given, §15.2-2204.
Administrator.
Applications for special exceptions and variances, §15.2-2310.
Appointment or designation, ordinance providing for, §15.2-2286.
Affordable dwelling unit ordinance, §§15.2-2304, 15.2-2305.
Affordable housing.
Creation and preservation.
Purpose of ordinances, §15.2-2283.
Agricultural activities.
Special use permit not required for certain activities, §15.2-2288.
Agricultural and forestall lands.
Preservation.
Purpose of ordinances, §15.2-2283.
Aircraft noise attenuation features.
Buildings and structures within airport noise zones, §15.2-2295.
Airport safety zoning, §15.2-2294.
Airspace, §15.2-2293.
Amateur radio antennas.
Height restrictions, §15.2-2293.1.
Amending or reenacting ordinance, §15.2-2285.
Change in zoning map classification, notice, §15.2-2204.
Amendment, supplement or change of regulations, districts, etc., §15.2-2286.
Animal shelters, §3.2-6548.
Appeals to board of zoning appeals, §15.2-2311.
Certiorari to review decision of board, §15.2-2314.
Procedure on appeal, §15.2-2312.
Assisted living facilities of eight or fewer residents, §15.2-2291.
Barratry, inapplicability of article, §18.2-451.
Binding development agreements in New Kent county, §15.2-2303.1.
Biomass.
Small-scale conversion of biomass to alternative fuel.
Special exception or special use permit not required, §15.2-2288.01.
Board of zoning appeals.
Alternates, appointment, §15.2-2308.
Appeals to board, §15.2-2311.
Procedure on appeal, §15.2-2312.
Certiorari to review decision of board, §15.2-2314.
Continuation of existing boards, §15.2-2203.
Creation, membership, organization, etc., §15.2-2308.
Joint boards, §15.2-2308.
Meetings, §15.2-2309.
Powers and duties, §15.2-2309.
Buildings in violation of zoning ordinance.
Nonconforming but not illegal.
Building constructed in accordance with building permit, §15.2-2307.
Suit to prevent construction, §15.2-2313.
Burden of proof.
Trial of scheduled violations, §15.2-2209.

ZONING —Cont'd
Business or financial relationship.
Land use proceedings in Loudoun county.
Disclosures required, §15.2-2287.1.
Career and technical education.
Corporate projects.
Applicability of zoning laws, §22.1-233.
Cash proffers, collected or accepted, §15.2-2303.1:1.
Cemeteries, §57-26.
Approved uses, §15.2-2288.5.
Certiorari to review decision of board, §15.2-2314.
Change in zoning map classification.
Amendment of ordinance involving, notice, §15.2-2204.
Change, modification or reversal of written order, requirement, etc., §15.2-1433.
Time limit, §15.2-2311.
Chesapeake Bay preservation areas.
Designation by localities in Tidewater Virginia, §62.1-44.15:74.
Enforcement of provisions, authority of local governments, §62.1-44.15:73.
Outside Tidewater area, adoption of provisions, §62.1-44.15:75.
State agency consistency, §62.1-44.15:78.
Civil penalties for violations, §15.2-2209.
Civil summons for violations, §15.2-2209.
Classification of territory by locality, §15.2-2280.
Clustering of single-family dwellings to preserve open space, §§15.2-2286, 15.2-2286.1.
Coastal primary sand dunes and beaches.
Cities, §28.2-1403.
Boards, §§28.2-1404, 28.2-1405.
Review of decisions, §§28.2-1410 to 28.2-1415.
Codification or recodification of ordinances, §15.2-1433.
Commercial fishermen and seafood buyers operating from waterfront residences.
Protection of businesses from zoning ordinances, §15.2-2307.1.
Comprehensive plan, §§15.2-2222.1 to 15.2-2232.
See PLANNING AND DEVELOPMENT.
Conditional zoning, §§15.2-2296 to 15.2-2303.
Administration and enforcement, §15.2-2299.
Amendment or variation of condition, §15.2-2302.
Certain localities, §15.2-2303.
Conditional zoning index, §15.2-2300.
Conditions as part of rezoning or amendment to rezoning map, §15.2-2297.
High-growth localities, §15.2-2298.
Dam break inundation zones.
Development area within, §15.2-2295.2.
Declaration of legislative policy and findings, §15.2-2296.
Defined, §15.2-2201.
Discrimination in housing prohibited, §15.2-2296.
High-growth localities, §15.2-2298.
Map to show existence of conditions attaching to zoning, §15.2-2300.
Notice by landlord of intention to implement, §§15.2-2297, 15.2-2298.
Petition for review of decision of zoning administrator, §15.2-2301.
Condominiums, §55-79.43.
County and municipal airports.
Authority to zone property not limited, §5.1-38.

ZONING —Cont'd
Conflicts with statutes, local ordinances or regulations, §15.2-2315.
Construction on mountain ridges, regulation, §15.2-2295.1.
Contest of decision of local governing body.
Time for filing, §15.2-2285.
County manager plan of government.
Dedication of rights to develop property.
Acceptance, authority to include provision for, §15.2-750.
Zoning ordinances regulating storage of junked and repair of motor vehicles.
Civil penalties for violations, §15.2-730.
Dam break inundation zones.
Modification, application, conditional use permit or special exception for proposed development within.
Modification, ordinance requiring, §15.2-2295.2.
Defined, §15.2-2201.
Delinquent real estate taxes.
Satisfactory evidence that taxes paid, §15.2-2286.
Development agreements in New Kent county, §15.2-2303.1.
Development rights, transfer of.
Definitions, §15.2-2316.1.
Localities may provide for, §15.2-2316.2.
Disasters.
Repairing, rebuilding or replacing buildings damaged by.
Restoring in nonconforming condition, §15.2-2307.
Disclosure of equitable ownership of real estate, §15.2-2289.
Districts, classification of territory into, §15.2-2280.
Downzoning of undeveloped or underdeveloped property.
Tax credit, §15.2-2286.
Enforcement of zoning ordinance violation.
Action.
Memorandum, filing, requirement, contents, §8.01-268.
Recording, expiration, §15.2-2208.
Environmental site assessment.
Ordinance provisions requiring, §15.2-2286.
Fair housing.
Civil action by attorney general.
Legality of local zoning or land use ordinance, §36-96.17.
Family day care homes.
Single-family residence, §15.2-2292.
Family health care structures.
Temporary structures, §15.2-2292.1.
Farm wineries.
Licensed farm wineries, §15.2-2288.3.
Fines.
Penalties for violating ordinance, §15.2-2286.
Schedule, ordinance adopting, §15.2-2209.
Group homes for mentally ill, or persons with intellectual or developmental disability.
Single-family residences, §15.2-2291.
Height restrictions on amateur radio antennas, §15.2-2293.1.
Helicopter landings, §15.2-2293.2.
Historic areas.
Protection against destruction or encroachment.
Purpose of ordinances, §15.2-2283.
Historic sites and architectural areas, §15.2-2306.

ZONING —Cont'd
Horizontal property regimes.
Supplemental rules and regulations by planning and zoning commissions, §55-79.33.
Hospital authorities.
Compliance with laws, §15.2-5317.
Housing crisis.
Extension of approvals to address housing crisis, §15.2-2209.1.
Impairment of vested rights prohibited, §15.2-2307.
Incentive zoning.
Defined, §15.2-2201.
Ordinance may provide for administration, §15.2-2286.
Incorporated area of municipality.
Jurisdiction of governing body, §15.2-2281.
Inspection warrants.
Ordinance may provide for issuance, §15.2-2286.
Junked vehicle storage and repair of motor vehicles.
County manager plan of government.
Ordinances regulating, §15.2-730.
Jurisdiction of localities, §15.2-2281.
Local technology zones, §58.1-3850.
Loudoun county.
Business or financial relationship.
Disclosure in land use proceedings, §15.2-2287.1.
Manufactured housing.
Uniform regulations for, §15.2-2290.
Map.
Official map of locality, §§15.2-2233 to 15.2-2238.
Preparation by planning commission, §15.2-2285.
Memorandum of lis pendens.
Action to enforce ordinance violation.
Recording, expiration, §15.2-2208.
Requirement, filing, contents, §8.01-268.
Mentally ill, or persons with intellectual or developmental disability.
Group homes of eight or fewer single-family residences, §15.2-2291.
Military bases, installations and airports.
Encroachment upon, protection against.
Purpose of zoning ordinance, §15.2-2283.
Misdemeanors, ordinance violations, §15.2-2286.
Mixed use development, §15.2-2201.
Modification from ordinance provisions.
Dam break inundation zones.
Development area within, §15.2-2295.2.
Granting, §15.2-2286.
Mountain ridges.
Regulation of construction, §15.2-2295.1.
Nonconforming uses, §15.2-2307.
Notice.
By applicants, when locality may require, §15.2-2206.
Changes, alterations, amendments, etc., of ordinances in codification, §15.2-1433.
Direct mail or other means in planning or zoning matter, §15.2-2205.
Plans, ordinances or amendments generally, §15.2-2204.
Change in zoning map classification, §15.2-2204.
Oath regarding property interests of local officers, §15.2-2287.
Occupancy limitations in residential dwelling units.
Punishment for violation, §15.2-2286.

ZONING —Cont'd
Occupancy limitations in residential dwelling units —Cont'd
Violations, obtaining information.
Subpoena, §15.2-2286.
Open space.
Preservation of open space by clustering of single-family dwellings, §§15.2-2286, 15.2-2286.1.
Ordinances, §15.2-2280.
Amending or reenacting, §15.2-2285.
Changes, amendments, alterations, etc., in codification of ordinances, §15.2-1433.
Coastal primary sand dunes and beaches, §28.2-1403.
Codification or recodification, §15.2-1433.
Generally, §15.2-2280.
Matters considered in drawing and applying, §15.2-2284.
Penalties for violating, §15.2-2286.
Permitted provisions, §15.2-2286.
Preparation and adoption, §15.2-2285.
Purposes, §15.2-2283.
Overcrowding of land.
Protection against.
Purpose of ordinances, §15.2-2283.
Penalties for violating ordinance, §15.2-2286.
Planned unit development.
Defined, §15.2-2201.
Planning and development generally, §§15.2-2200 to 15.2-2239.
See PLANNING AND DEVELOPMENT.
Planning commissions.
Generally, §§15.2-2210 to 15.2-2222.
See PLANNING COMMISSIONS.
Preparation of ordinance, §15.2-2285.
Proffered cash payments and expenditures.
Alternative improvements.
Utilization of proffered cash payments for, §15.2-2303.2.
Amount of proffered cash payments received during fiscal year.
Inclusion in capital improvement program, §15.2-2303.2.
Cash payments not accepted during fiscal year.
Notification to commission on local government, §15.2-2303.2.
Collecting or accepting after final inspection, §15.2-2303.1:1.
Commission on local government, report by, §15.2-2303.2.
Conditional zoning, §15.2-2303.
Forfeiture by locality of cash payments.
Failure to timely begin work on improvements for which cash payments proffered, §15.2-2303.2.
Reports to commission on local government, §15.2-2303.2.
Voluntary agreement to earlier payment date, §15.2-2303.3.
Waiver of future rights as part of proffer, severable and void, §15.2-2303.3.
When locality may require payment, §15.2-2303.3.
Proffered conditions.
Conditional zoning, §15.2-2303.
Proposed ordinance, §15.2-2285.
Public hearing.
Changes, amendments, etc., to ordinances in codification, §15.2-1433.
Plans, ordinances or amendments, §15.2-2204.
Purposes of ordinances, §15.2-2283.

ZONING —Cont'd
Real estate cooperatives.
Applicability of land use ordinances, §§55-424, 55-429.
Subdivided or rezoned lots, §58.1-3285.
Regulations to be uniform, §15.2-2282.
Residential uses.
Localities may not require special use permit for certain residential uses, §15.2-2288.1.
Sexual offender treatment office.
Prohibited in residentially zoned subdivision, §15.2-2283.1.
Restraining violation, §15.2-2208.
Schedule of civil penalties for violations of specific provisions of zoning ordinance.
Adoption of ordinance establishing, §15.2-2209.
Setback lines and side yards.
Ordinances regulating, §15.2-2279.
Sexual offender treatment office.
Prohibited in residentially zoned subdivision, §15.2-2283.1.
Signs.
Abandoned nonconforming signs.
Removal, §15.2-2307.
Special exceptions.
Applications, §15.2-2310.
Dam break inundation zones.
Development area within, §15.2-2295.2.
Defined, §15.2-2201.
Permitted provisions in zoning ordinance, §15.2-2286.
Power of board of zoning appeals, §15.2-2309.
Special use permits.
Additional extensions of expiration or schedule, §15.2-2288.4.
Agricultural activities, not required, §15.2-2288.
Certain residential uses, not required, §15.2-2288.1.
Extension of expiration dates, §15.2-2288.4.
Licensed farm wineries, not required, §15.2-2288.3.
Temporary structures, not required, §15.2-2288.2.
Subdivisions and developments.
Generally, §§15.2-2240 to 15.2-2279.
See SUBDIVISIONS.
Site plan submitted in accordance with zoning ordinance, §15.2-2246.
Summons.
Civil summon for violation, §15.2-2209.
Temporary structures.
Family health care structures, §15.2-2292.1.
Special use permit not required for certain temporary structures, §15.2-2288.2.
Time limits.
Appeals, §15.2-2311.
Changing, modifying or reversing written order, requirement, etc., §15.2-2311.

ZONING —Cont'd
Time limits —Cont'd
Contest of decision of local governing body, filing, §15.2-2285.
Proceeding to prevent construction in violation of ordinance, §15.2-2313.
Time-shares.
Applicability, §55-364.
Use of terms by developer, §55-364.1.
Transfer of development rights.
Definitions, §15.2-2316.1.
Localities may provide for, §15.2-2316.2.
Transportation districts.
Payments for certain changes in zoning classifications or use, §33.1-437.
Tree conservation during development process.
Locality within Planning District 8 classified and nonattainment area for air quality standards, §15.2-961.1.
Tree planting and replacement during development process, §15.2-961.
Trial in district court of violations, §15.2-2209.
Uniformity of regulations, §15.2-2282.
Uniform schedule of civil penalties for violations of specific provisions of zoning ordinance.
Adoption of ordinance establishing, §15.2-2209.
Unincorporated territory in county.
Jurisdiction of governing body, §15.2-2281.
Urban county executive form of government.
Business or financial relationship disclosures in land use proceedings.
Board of supervisors, planning commission and board of zoning appeals, §15.2-852.
Validation of ordinances prior to January 1, 1971, §15.2-2316.
Variances.
Applications, §15.2-2310.
Defined, §15.2-2201.
Permitted provisions in ordinance, §15.2-2286.
Powers and duties of board of zoning appeal, §15.2-2309.
Vested rights not impaired, §15.2-2307.
Waiver of trial, admission of liability and payment of penalty, §15.2-2209.
Wetlands, §28.2-1302.
Cities, §28.2-1302.
Boards, §§28.2-1303 to 28.2-1305.
Permits, §§28.2-1306 to 28.2-1308.
Review, §§28.2-1310 to 28.2-1315.
Wineries.
Licensed farm wineries, §15.2-2288.3.

ZOOS.
Admission tax, §§58.1-3817, 58.1-3818.

ZYGOTE INTRAFALLOPIAN TUBE TRANSFERS.
Donor HIV tests, §32.1-45.3.